Third Finance Act 2010 – read on

Don't miss out on the Coalition Government's next major piece of legislation. Tolley will be publishing supplements to the Yellow and Orange books to update you on the changes in the Autumn Finance Act.

Supplements will contain the Act and the relevant sections of the books which have changed due to the third Finance Act.

These will publish when the Act has Royal Assent, estimated to be November 2010.

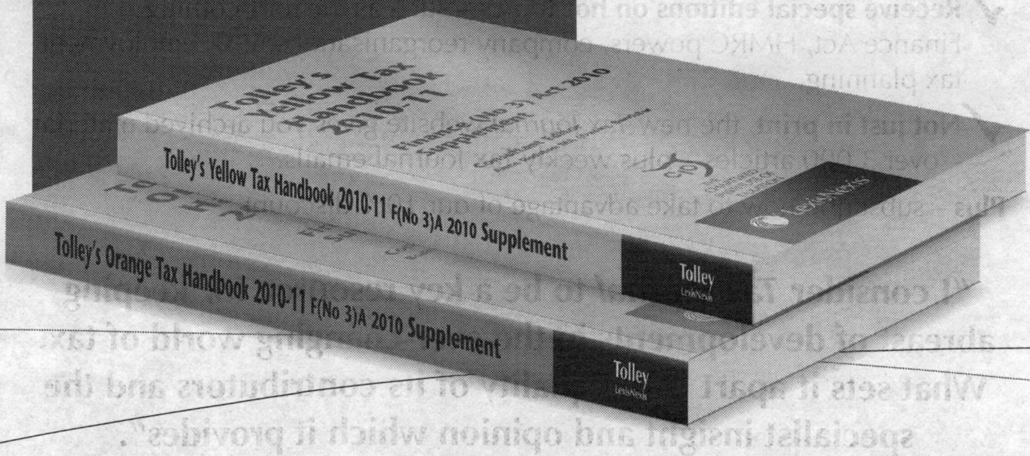

Make sure you get your supplements as soon as they publish – order today!

Email orders@lexisnexis.co.uk or visit **www.lexisnexis.co.uk/tax** quoting **AD11196**

www.lexisnexis.co.uk/tax

SOLUTIONS FOR KNOWLEDGE-DRIVEN PROFESSIONALS

Client Development | Research & Knowledge Solutions | Practice & Productivity Management | Risk & Compliance

Tolley's Orange Tax Handbook 2010–11

37th Edition

Part 2:

STAMP TAXES

INSURANCE PREMIUM TAX

LANDFILL TAX

AGGREGATES LEVY

CLIMATE CHANGE LEVY

Consultant Editor

Roderick Cordara QC SC(NSW) MA(Cantab) FIIT

Barrister
Essex Court Chambers

LexisNexis®

Members of the LexisNexis Group worldwide

United Kingdom	LexisNexis Butterworths, a Division of Reed Elsevier (UK) Ltd, Halsbury House, 35 Chancery Lane, London, WC2A 1EL, and London House, 20–22 East London Street, Edinburgh EH7 4BQ
Australia	LexisNexis Butterworths, Chatswood, New South Wales
Austria	LexisNexis Verlag ARD Orac GmbH & Co KG, Vienna
Canada	LexisNexis Butterworths, Markham, Ontario
Czech Republic	Nakladatelství Orac sro, Prague
France	LexisNexis SA, Paris
Germany	LexisNexis Deutschland GmbH, Frankfurt and Munster
Hong Kong	LexisNexis Butterworths, Hong Kong
Hungary	HVG-Orac, Budapest
India	LexisNexis Butterworths, New Delhi
Italy	Giuffrè Editore, Milan
Malaysia	Malayan Law Journal Sdn Bhd, Kuala Lumpur
New Zealand	LexisNexis Butterworths, Wellington
Poland	Wydawnictwo Prawnicze LexisNexis, Warsaw
Singapore	LexisNexis Butterworths, Singapore
South Africa	LexisNexis Butterworths, Durban
Switzerland	Stämpfli Verlag AG, Berne
USA	LexisNexis, Dayton, Ohio

First published in 1976

Published by LexisNexis Butterworths

A CIP Catalogue record for this book is available from the British Library.

ISBN 9781405751483 (set); 9781405755429 (Part 2)

Printed in the UK by CPI William Clowes Ltd, Beccles, NR34 7TL

Visit LexisNexis Butterworths at www.lexisnexis.co.uk or email the editorial department on: yellowandorange@lexisnexis.co.uk

Publishers' Note

Finance Acts 2010—key dates

Budget Day	24 March 2010
Finance Act 2010 passed	8 April 2010
Emergency Budget	22 June 2010
Finance (No 2) Act 2010 passed	27 July 2010
Finance (No 3) Act 2010	Expected Autumn 2010

Tax legislation

Tolley's Yellow and Orange Tax Handbooks are indispensable to the practitioner who needs to refer to the tax legislation as currently in force. Each year the legislation is augmented and amended by one or more Finance Acts and lesser amendments are made from time to time by a variety of other statutes. An increasing amount of the detailed regulation of taxes is contained in statutory instruments—orders or regulations—which are also amended frequently. The Handbooks are normally published annually. They contain the text of the relevant statutes and statutory instruments as amended together with current texts of extra-statutory concessions, statements of practice, published official interpretations and decisions and selected press releases.

The Orange Tax Handbook covers value added tax, stamp taxes, insurance premium tax, landfill tax, aggregates levy and climate change levy. Its companion volume, the Yellow Tax Handbook, covers income tax, corporation tax, capital gains tax, inheritance tax, National Insurance contributions, tax credits and petroleum revenue tax.

This edition of the Orange Tax Handbook contains texts as they applied at July 2010. It does not take account of changes made after that date.

Organisation

The contents of this Handbook are arranged in separate sections for each of the taxes covered. The start of each section is marked with a grey tab on the front edge of the book. The texts in each section are arranged in the following order—UK statutes, statutory instruments, EC legislation for VAT, extra-statutory concessions, statements of practice, VAT Notices with the force of law, press releases (published by HMRC, and extracts from Hansard). Within each of those categories, items are printed in chronological order. To enable individual items to be located quickly, an item reference is printed in bold type in the outside top corner of each page.

Provisions relating to National Insurance contributions which were formerly in this Handbook have been moved into the Yellow Tax Handbook. This is due to the transfer of functions from the DSS to HMRC in relation to National Insurance contributions matters. It also reflects practitioners' needs, particularly those dealing with PAYE who want to see income tax and NICs together. Inheritance Tax and Petroleum Revenue Tax are located in the Yellow Tax Handbook as they are direct taxes and therefore more appropriately positioned there.

Amendments and modifications

Amendments to existing legislation which take effect during the calendar year are made in the text of the amended legislation. An **Amendment** note under the amended text indicates the authority for the amendment and, where appropriate, the timing of its commencement. All relevant provisions of the current Finance Act are reproduced in full but otherwise the text of provisions which merely amend other Acts is generally omitted and replaced by a note indicating the legislation amended.

Sometimes the effect of a provision is modified by a later Act or statutory instrument but the scope of the modification is limited in some way so that the original provision remains generally unaffected. In this case, the original provision is printed without modification but a **Cross reference** to the later Act or statutory instrument is provided, see below.

Prospective amendments

The Handbook sets out the text of the legislation as it applies for the current tax year. Amendments which are stated to come into effect on a specified date after the end of that year are therefore strictly outside the scope of the current edition and are not made in the text of the Act affected. However, a **Prospective amendment** note is provided to indicate the existence of the amendment and the provision making the prospective amendment is retained in full in successive editions of the Handbook until the amendment becomes effective.

Retrospective amendments

For the tax legislation as it applied in an earlier year, reference should be made to the appropriate earlier edition of the Orange Tax Handbook. Care must be taken, however, to ensure that amendments made retrospectively are not overlooked. A list of provisions affected by amendments made retrospectively by this year's Finance Act is provided at the front of this edition. Similar lists are provided for amendments made by each year's Finance Act(s) in the corresponding earlier editions.

Repealed legislation

Generally, repealed legislation is omitted. Exceptionally, where it may be necessary to refer to the repealed text in dealing with tax liabilities for the current year, the text is retained and is printed in italics.

Defined terms

Where a word or phrase used in the main Acts has been defined elsewhere, a cross-reference to the definition is provided in a **Definitions** note below the text.

Cross references

The notes under each section or Schedule paragraph include references to commentary and to relevant statutory provisions, statutory instruments, published HMRC practice and other published or unpublished official and professional bodies' views. These are presented under the following headings—

Commentary—refers to paragraph numbers for commentary relating to the provision in *De Voil Indirect Tax Service* or *Simon's Taxes*.

Concession; Statement of Practice; HMRC Interpretations—refer to published official practice separately reproduced in the same section of this Handbook.

Press releases etc—refer to published or unpublished official and professional bodies' views reproduced in this Handbook or BDO Stoy Hayward's Orange Tax Guide.

Cross reference—refers to provisions in the same or another Act or statutory instrument.

Simon's Tax Cases—provides references to the most significant cases reported in *Simon's Tax Cases* and *Simon's Tax Cases Special Commissioners' Decisions*. Cases decided on the previous corresponding statutory provision are marked by an asterisk.

Note—introduces other references not within any of the above categories.

July 2010

Contents

CLIMATE CHANGE LEVY

Detailed contents lists are provided at the beginning of each subject group.

List of abbreviations

art	article
CA 1985	Companies Act 1985
CAA 2001	Capital Allowances Act 2001
CCL	Climate change levy
CED(GR)A 1979	Customs & Excise Duties (General Relief) Act 1979
CEMA 1979	Customs & Excise Management Act 1979
CGTA 1979	Capital Gains Tax Act 1979
Ch	Chapter(s) of statute
col	column(s)
Comrs	Commissioners
CPA 1947	Crown Proceedings Act 1947
CTA 2009/2010	Corporation Tax Act 2009/2010
CTA 2010	Corporation Tax Act 2010
DLT	Development land tax
edn	edition
EEC	European Economic Community
ESC	Extra-statutory concession
FA	Finance Act
F(No 2)A	Finance (No 2) Act
Gp	Group (VAT legislation)
HA 1980	Highways Act 1980
HM	Her Majesty
HMRC	Her Majesty's Revenue & Customs
HMSO	Her Majesty's Stationery Office
IA	Interpretation Act
ICAEW	Institute of Chartered Accountants in England & Wales
IOM	Isle of Man
IoT	Institute of Taxation
IPT	Insurance Premium Tax
IR	Inland Revenue
LIFFE	London International Financial Futures and Options Exchange
LPA 1925	Law of Property Act 1925
NB	(nota bene) note well

NHA 1980	National Heritage Act 1980
OJ	Official Journal of the European Communities
para	paragraph(s)
PAYE	Pay as you earn
PCTA 1968	Provisional Collection of Taxes Act 1968
PEP	Personal equity plan
PET	Potentially exempt transfer
PR	Press releases
Pt	Part(s)
r	rule(s)
RA 1898	Revenue Act 1898
reg	regulations
RD	Revenue decisions
Regulations	EC Regulations
RI	Revenue interpretation
s	section(s)
SA 1891	Stamp Act 1891
Sch	Schedule
SDMA 1891	Stamp Duties Management Act 1891
SDLT	Stamp duty land tax
SDRT	Stamp duty reserve tax
SD(TP)A 1992	Stamp Duty (Temporary Provisions) Act 1992
SI	Statutory Instrument
SP	Statement of Practice
STC	Simon's Tax Cases
STI	Simon's Tax Intelligence
sub-para	sub-paragraph(s)
sub-s	sub-section(s)
TA	Income and Corporation Taxes Act
Taxes Act 1970	Income and Corporation Taxes Act 1970
Taxes Act 1988	Income and Corporation Taxes Act 1988
TMA 1970	Taxes Management Act 1970
VAT	Value added tax
VATA 1994	Value Added Tax Act 1994
vol	volume(s)

Retrospective legislation

Subscribers are advised to retain Handbooks for earlier years to use when dealing with tax for those years. Each Handbook shows the legislation operative for the corresponding year so far as it was known at the time of the passing of the Finance Act of that year. In view of the increasing practice of passing tax legislation with retrospective effect, it is necessary when dealing with past years to consider whether the provisions have been affected or amended by subsequent legislation.

Stamp Taxes

Contents

Stamp Taxes Statutes

Contents

STAMP DUTIES MANAGEMENT ACT 1891

ARRANGEMENT OF SECTIONS

An Act to consolidate the Law relating to the Management of Stamp Duties.

[21st July 1891]

Application of Act

1 Act to apply to all stamp duties

All duties for the time being chargeable by law as stamp duties shall be under the care and management of the Commissioners, and this Act shall apply to all such duties and to all fees which are for the time being directed to be collected or received by means of stamps.

Mode of recovering Money received for Duty

2 Moneys received for duty and not appropriated to be recoverable in High Court

(1) Every person who, having received any sum of money as or for any duty, or any fee collected by means of a stamp, does not apply the money to the due payment of the duty or fee, and improperly withholds or detains the same, shall be accountable for the amount of the duty or fee, and the same shall be a debt from him to Her Majesty, and recoverable as such accordingly.

(2), (3) . . . [1]

Amendments—[1] Sub-ss (2), (3) repealed by FA 1999 s 115, Sch 18 para 6, Sch 20 Pt V(4) with effect from 1 October 1999.

Sale of Stamps

3–8

. . .

Amendments—These sections repealed by FA 1999 s 115, Sch 18 para 6, Sch 20 Pt V(4) with effect from 1 October 1999.

Allowance for Spoiled Stamps

9 Procedure for obtaining allowance

Subject to such regulations as the Commissioners may think proper to make, and to the production of such evidence by statutory declaration or otherwise as the Commissioners may require, allowance is to be made by the Commissioners for stamps spoiled in the cases hereinafter mentioned; (that is to say,):

(1) The stamp on any material inadvertently and undesignedly spoiled, obliterated, or by any means rendered unfit for the purpose intended, before the material bears the signature of any person or any instrument written thereon is executed by any party:

(2), (3) . . . [4]

(4) The stamp on any bill of exchange signed by or on behalf of the drawer which has not been accepted or made use of in any manner whatever or delivered out of his hands for any purpose other than by way of tender for acceptance:

(5) The stamp on any promissory note signed by or on behalf of the maker which has not been made use of in any manner whatever or delivered out of his hands:

(6) The stamp on any bill of exchange or promissory note which from any omission or error has been spoiled or rendered useless, although the same, being a bill of exchange, may have been accepted or indorsed, or, being a promissory note, may have been delivered to the payee, provided that another completed and duly stamped bill of exchange or promissory note is produced identical in every particular, except in the correction of the error or omission, with the spoiled bill or note:

(7) The stamp used for any of the following instruments; that is to say,

- (*a*) An instrument executed by any party thereto, but afterwards found to be absolutely void from the beginning:
- (*b*) An instrument executed by any party thereto, but afterwards found unfit, by reason of any error or mistake therein, for the purpose originally intended:
- (*c*) An instrument executed by any party thereto which has not been made use of for any purpose whatever, and which by reason of the inability or refusal of some necessary party to sign the same or to complete the transaction according to the instrument, is incomplete and insufficient for the purpose for which it was intended:
- (*d*) An instrument executed by any party thereto, which by reason of the refusal of any person to act under the same, or for want of enrolment or registration within the time required by law, fails of the intended purpose or becomes void:
- (*e*) An instrument executed by any party thereto . . . [3] which becomes useless in consequence of the transaction intended to be thereby effected being effected by some other instrument duly stamped:

Provided as follows:—

- (*a*) That the application for relief is made within [two years][1] after the stamp has been spoiled or become useless or in the case of an executed instrument after the date of the instrument, or, if it is not dated, within [two years][1] after the execution thereof by the person by whom it was first or alone executed or within such further time as the Commissioners may prescribe in the case of any instrument sent abroad for execution or when from unavoidable circumstances any instrument for which another has been substituted cannot be produced within the said period;
- (*b*) That in the case of an executed instrument no legal proceeding has been commenced in which the instrument could or would have been given or offered in evidence, and that the instrument is given up to be cancelled;
- (*c*) . . . [2]

Amendments—[1] Words in sub-s (7), proviso (*a*) in both places, substituted by the Revenue Act 1898 s 13.

[2] Sub-s (7)(*c*) repealed by the Statute Law (Repeals) Act 1993 s 1(1), Sch 1 Pt IX.

[3] Words omitted from sub-s (7) repealed by FA 1996 Sch 39 Pt III para 10(1), (2), (4), (5), Sch 41 Pt VIII(4), with effect from 29 April 1996, except in relation to an instrument which has been accidentally spoiled if an application for allowance under this section was made before that date.

[4] Sub-ss (2) and (3) repealed by FA 1999 s 115, Sch 18 para 6, Sch 20 Pt V(4) with effect from 1 October 1999.

10 Allowance for misused stamps

When any person has inadvertently used for an instrument liable to duty a stamp of greater value than was necessary, or has inadvertently used a stamp for an instrument not liable to any duty, the Commissioners may, on application made within [two years][1] after the date of the instrument, or, if it is not dated, within [two years][1] after the execution thereof by the person by whom it was first or alone executed, and upon the instrument, if liable to duty, being stamped with the proper duty, cancel and allow as spoiled the stamp so misused.

Amendments—[1] Words, in both places, substituted by the Revenue Act 1898 s 13.

Stamp Taxes

11 Allowance how to be made

In any case in which allowance is made for spoiled or misused stamps the Commissioners may give in lieu thereof other stamps of the same denomination and value, or if required, and they think proper, stamps of any other denomination to the same amount in value, or in their discretion, the same value in money, [. . .][1].

Amendments—[1] Words repealed by FA 1999 s 115, Sch 18 para 6, Sch 20 Pt V(4) with effect from 1 October 1999.

12 Stamps not wanted may be repurchased by the Commissioners

Amendments—This section repealed by FA 1999 s 115, Sch 18 para 6, Sch 20 Pt V(4) with effect from 1 October 1999.

[Allowance for Lost or Spoiled Instruments][1]

[12A Lost or spoiled instruments

(1) This section applies where the Commissioners are satisfied that:

(*a*) an instrument which was executed and duly stamped ("the original instrument") has been accidentally lost or spoiled; and

(*b*) in place of the original instrument, another instrument made between the same persons and for the same purpose ("the replacement instrument") has been executed; and

(*c*) an application for relief under this section is made to the Commissioners; and either

(*d*) where the original instrument has been lost, the applicant undertakes to deliver it up to the Commissioners to be cancelled if it is subsequently found; or

(*e*) where the original instrument has been spoiled:

(i) the application is made within two years after the date of the original instrument, or if it is not dated, within two years after the time when it was executed, or within such further time as the Commissioners may allow; and

(ii) no legal proceeding has been commenced in which the original instrument has been or could or would have been given or offered in evidence; and

(iii) the original instrument is delivered up to the Commissioners to be cancelled.

(2) Where this section applies:

(*a*) the replacement instrument shall not be chargeable with any duty, but shall be stamped with the duty with which it would otherwise have been chargeable in accordance with the law in force at the time when it was executed, and shall be deemed for all purposes to be duly stamped; and

(*b*) if any duty, interest [or penalty][2] was paid in respect of the replacement instrument before the application was made, the Commissioners shall pay to such person as they consider appropriate an amount equal to the duty, interest [or penalty][2] so paid.

(3) For the purposes of this section the Commissioners may require the applicant to produce such evidence by statutory declaration or otherwise as they think fit.][1]

Amendments—[1] This section and preceding cross heading inserted by FA 1996 Sch 39 Pt III para 10(1), (3), (4), (5), with effect from 29 April 1996, except in relation to an instrument which has been accidentally spoiled if an application for allowance under s 9 of this Act was made before that date.

[2] Words in sub-s (2)(*b*) substituted by FA 1999 s 114, Sch 17 para 2 with effect in relation to penalties in respect of things done or omitted after 30 September 1999.

Offences relating to Stamps

13 [Offences in relation to dies and stamps][2]

[(1)] [3] [A person commits an offence who][3] does, or causes or procures to be done, or knowingly aids, abets, or assists in doing, any of the acts following; that is to say,

(1), (2) . . . [1]

(3) Fraudulently prints or makes an impression upon any material from a genuine die;

(4) Fraudulently cuts, tears, or in any way removes from any material any stamp, with intent that any use should be made of such stamp or of any part thereof;

(5) Fraudulently mutilates any stamp, with intent that any use should be made of any part of such stamp;

(6) Fraudulently fixes or places upon any material or upon any stamp, any stamp or part of a stamp which, whether fraudulently or not, has been cut, torn, or in any way removed from any other material, or out of or from any other stamp;

(7) Fraudulently erases or otherwise either really or apparently removes from any stamped material any name, sum, date, or other matter or thing whatsoever thereon written, with the intent that any use should be made of the stamp upon such material;

(8) Knowingly sells or exposes for sale or utters or uses . . . [1] any stamp which has been fraudulently printed or impressed from a genuine die;

(9) Knowingly, and without lawful excuse (the proof whereof shall lie on the person accused) has in his possession . . . [1] any stamp which has been fraudulently printed or impressed from a genuine die, or any stamp or part of a stamp which has been fraudulently cut, torn, or otherwise removed from any material, or any stamp which has been fraudulently mutilated, or any stamped material out of which any name, sum, date, or other matter or thing has been fraudulently erased or otherwise either really or apparently removed, . . . [4]

[(2) A person guilty of an offence under this section is liable—

(*a*) on summary conviction, to imprisonment for a term not exceeding six months or a fine not exceeding the statutory maximum, or both;

(*b*) on conviction on indictment, to imprisonment for a term not exceeding ten years or a fine, or both.][5]

Cross references—See the Criminal Justice Act 1948 s 1 (references to penal servitude or to imprisonment with hard labour are to be construed as sentence to imprisonment only);
Criminal Law Act 1967 s 1 (abolition of distinction between felony and misdemeanour);
Magistrates' Courts Act 1980 s 17, Sch 1 para 12 (offences under this section triable on indictment or triable summarily).

Amendments—[1] Sub-paras (1), (2) and words in sub-paras (8), (9) repealed by the Forgery Act 1913 s 20 and Schedule.
[2] Words in heading substituted by FA 1999 s 115, Sch 18 para 5(1), (2) with effect in relation to things done or omitted after 30 September 1999.
[3] Sub-s (1) numbered as such and words therein substituted by FA 1999 s 115, Sch 18 para 5(1), (3), with effect in relation to things done or omitted after 30 September 1999.
[4] Words in sub-para (9) repealed by FA 1999 s 115, Sch 18 para 5(1), (4) Sch 20 Pt V(3) with effect in relation to things done or omitted after 30 September 1999.
[5] Sub-s (2) inserted by FA 1999 s 115, Sch 18 para 5 with effect in relation to things done or omitted after 30 September 1999.

16 Proceedings for detection of forged dies, etc

On information given before a justice upon oath that there is just cause to suspect any person of being guilty of any of the offences aforesaid, such justice may, by a warrant under his hand, cause every house, room, shop, building, or place belonging to or occupied by the suspected person, or where he is suspected of being or having been in any way engaged or concerned in the commission of any such offence, or of secreting any machinery, implements, or utensils applicable to the commission of any such offence, to be searched, and if upon such search any of the said several matters and things are found, the same may be seized and carried away, and shall afterwards be delivered over to the Commissioners.

Cross references—See Revenue Act 1898, s 12 (application of this section to the manufacture of paper used for excise licences).

17–20

. . .

Amendments—Sections 17–20 repealed by FA 1999 s 115, Sch 18 para 6, Sch 20 Pt V(4) with effect from 1 October 1999.

21 Penalty for frauds in relation to duties

Any person who practices or is concerned in any fraudulent act, contrivance, or device, not specially provided for by law, with intent to defraud Her Majesty of any duty shall incur [a penalty not exceeding £3,000][1].

Amendments—[1] Words substituted by FA 1999 s 114, Sch 17 para 2 with effect in relation to penalties in respect of things done or omitted after 30 September 1999.

Miscellaneous

22 As to discontinuance of dies

Whenever the Commissioners determine to discontinue the use of any die, and provide a new die to be used in lieu thereof, and give public notice thereof in the [London, Edinburgh and Belfast Gazettes][1], then from and after any day to be stated in the notice (such day not being within one month after the same is so published) the new die shall be the only lawful die for denoting the duty chargeable in any case in which the discontinued die would have been used; and every instrument first executed by any person, or bearing date after the day so stated, and stamped with the discontinued die, shall be deemed to be not duly stamped:

Provided as follows:

(*a*) If any instrument stamped as last aforesaid, and first executed after the day so stated at any place out of the United Kingdom, is brought to the Commissioners within fourteen days after it has been received in the United Kingdom, then upon proof of the facts to the satisfaction of the Commissioners the stamp thereon shall be cancelled, and the instrument shall be stamped with the same amount of duty by means of the lawful die, without the payment of any penalty:

(*b*) All persons having in their possession any material stamped with the discontinued die, and which by reason of the providing of such new die has been rendered useless, may at any time within six months after the day stated in the notice send the same to the chief office or one of the head offices, and the Commissioners may thereupon cause the stamp on such material to be cancelled, and the same material, or, if the Commissioners think fit, any other material, to be stamped with the new die, in lieu of and to an equal amount with the stamp so cancelled.

Cross references—See Revenue Act 1898 s 10 (application of this section to notices issued under that section).

Amendments—[1] Words substituted by FA 1998 s 150 with effect from 31 July 1998.

23 Application of Act to excise labels

The provisions of this Act in reference to offences relating to stamps shall apply to any label now or hereafter provided by the Commissioners for denoting any [duty of excise other than a duty of excise chargeable on goods imported into the United Kingdom][1], and any label so provided shall be deemed to be included in the term "stamp" as defined by this Act.

Amendments—[1] Words substituted by the Customs and Excise Management Act 1979 Sch 4 para 12, Table, Pt I, with effect from 1 April 1979.

24 Declarations, how to be made

Any statutory declaration to be made in pursuance of or for the purposes of this or any other Act for the time being in force relating to duties may be made before any of the Commissioners, or any officer or person authorised by them in that behalf, or before any commissioner for oaths or any justice or notary public in any part of the United Kingdom, or at any place out of the United Kingdom, before any person duly authorised to administer oaths there.

Cross references—See Revenue Act 1898 s 7 (6) (application of this section to affidavits and oaths).

25 Mode of granting licences

Amendments—This section repealed by FA 1999 s 115, Sch 18 para 6, Sch 20 Pt V(4) with effect from 1 October 1999.

26 Recovery of fines

Amendments—This section repealed by FA 1999 Sch 20 Pt V(3) with effect in relation to things done or omitted from 1 October 1999.

27 Definitions

In this Act, unless the context otherwise requires—

The expression "Commissioners" means Commissioners of Inland Revenue:

The expression "officer" means officer of Inland Revenue:

The expression "chief office" means chief office of Inland Revenue:

The expression "head offices" means the head office of Inland Revenue in Edinburgh and Dublin:

The expression "duty" means any stamp duty for the time being chargeable by law:

The expression "material" includes every sort of material upon which words or figures can be expressed:

The expression "instrument" includes every written document:

The expression "die" includes any plate, type, tool, or implement whatever used under the direction of the Commissioners for expressing or denoting any duty, or rate of duty, or the fact that any duty or rate of duty or penalty has been paid, or that an instrument is duly stamped, or is not chargeable with any duty or for denoting any fee, and also any part of any such plate, type, tool, or implement:

The expressions "forge" and "forged" include counterfeit and counterfeited:

The expression "stamp" means as well a stamp impressed by means of a die as an adhesive stamp for denoting any duty or fee:

The expression "stamped" is applicable as well to instruments and material impressed with stamps by means of a die as to instruments and material having adhesive stamps affixed thereto:

The expressions "executed" and "execution" [have the same meaning as in the Stamp Act 1891][1]:

The expression "justice" means justice of the peace.

Amendments—[1] Words in the definition of "executed" and "execution" substituted by FA 1994 s 239(2), (3).

Short Title

30 Short title

This Act may be cited as the Stamp Duties Management Act, 1891.

STAMP ACT 1891

(54 & 55 Vict. Chapter 39)

ARRANGEMENT OF SECTIONS

PART I

REGULATIONS APPLICABLE TO INSTRUMENTS GENERALLY

Charge of duty upon Instruments

An Act to consolidate the Enactments granting and relating to the Stamp Duties upon Instruments and certain other enactments relating to Stamp Duties.

[21st July 1891]

Construction—FA 1899, Pt II to be construed together with this Act; see FA 1899, s 14;
FA 1907 Pt II to be construed together with this Act; see FA 1907 s 30(2);
RA 1909 Pt II to be construed together with this Act; see RA 1909 s 12(1);
FA 1930 Pt IV to be construed together with this Act; see FA 1930 s 53(4);
FA 1946 Pt VII to be construed together with this Act; see FA 1946 s 67(7);
FA 1947 Pt VI to be construed together with this Act; see FA 1947 s 74(7);
FA 1948 Pt VII to be construed together with this Act; see FA 1948 s 82(6);
FA 1949 Pt IV to be construed together with this Act; see FA 1949 s 52(5);
FA 1952 s 74 to be construed as one with this Act; see FA 1952 s 74(5);
FA 1953 s 31 to be construed as one with this Act; see FA 1953 s 31(3);
FA 1959 Pt IV to be construed as one with this Act; see FA 1959 s 37(2);
FA 1960 s 74 to be construed as one with this Act; see FA 1960 s 74(9);
FA 1963 Pt IV to be construed as one with this Act; see FA 1963 s 73(4);
FA 1964 s 23 to be construed as one with this Act; see FA 1964 s 23(3);
FA 1965 s 90 to be construed as one with this Act; see FA 1965 s 90(6);
FA 1966 Pt VIII, so far as it relates to stamp duties, to be construed as one with this Act; see FA 1966 s 53(2);
FA 1967 Pt V to be construed as one with this Act; see FA 1967 s 45(3);
FA 1970 Pt III, so far as it relates to stamp duties, to be construed as one with this Act; see FA 1970 s 36(5);
FA 1973 Pt V to be construed as one with this Act; see FA 1973 s 59(3);
FA 1974 Sch 11 to be construed as one with this Act; see FA 1974 s 57(3);
FA 1976 s 127 to be construed as one with this Act; see FA 1976 s 127(5);
FA 1985 Pt III to be construed as one with this Act; see FA 1985 s 98(4);
FA 1986 Pt III to be construed as one with this Act; see FA 1986 s 114(4);
FA 1987 Pt III, except s 56 and Sch 7 (stamp duty reserve tax), to be construed as one with this Act; see FA 1987 s 72(4);
FA 1988 ss 140, 141, 143 to be construed as one with this Act; see FA 1988 ss 140(5), 141(5), 143(8);
FA 1990 ss 107–109 to be construed as one with this Act; see FA 1990 s 111(2);
FA 1994 Pt VI to be construed as one with this Act; see FA 1994 s 257(3).
FA 1995 Pt V to be construed as one with this Act; see FA 1995 s 161(3).
FA 1996 s 186 to be construed as one with this Act; see FA 1996 s 186(4).
FA 1999 Pt VI, so far as it relates to stamp duties, to be construed as one with this Act; see FA 1999 s 123(1)(*a*).
FA 2000 ss 118–122, 128, 129, 131, Schs 33 and 34 to be construed as one with this Act; see FA 2000 ss 118(9), 119(10), 120(9), 121(9), 122(7), 128(9), 129(4), 131(7), Sch 33, para 9(2).
FA 2001 s 92 and Sch 30 to be construed as one with this Act; see FA 2001 s 92(7).
FA 2002 ss 111, 113, 115, 116 and Schs 34–37 to be construed as one with this Act; see FA 2002 s 116(3), Sch 34, para 11, Sch 35 para 12, and Sch 36 para 10.
FA 2003 s 125 to be construed as one with this Act; see FA 2003 s 125(3).
FA 2003 s 128 to be construed as one with this Act; see FA 2003 s 128(6).
FA 2003 s 129 to be construed as one with this Act; see FA 2003 s 129(7).
FA 2003 Sch 15 para 33 to be construed as one with this Act; see FA 2003 Sch 15 para 33(9).

PART I

REGULATIONS APPLICABLE TO INSTRUMENTS GENERALLY

Charge of Duty upon Instruments

1 Charge of duties in schedule

Statement of Practice SP 11/91—Interaction of stamp duty and VAT: stamp duty to be calculated on VAT-inclusive consideration.

Amendments—This section repealed by FA 1999 Sch 20 Pt V(2) with effect in relation to instruments executed, or bearer instruments issued, from 1 October 1999, subject to the provisions in FA 1999 Sch 20 Pt V(2) Note 2. Previously the text read—

"From and after the commencement of this Act the stamp duties to be charged for the use of Her Majesty upon the several instruments specified in the First Schedule to this Act shall be the several duties in the said schedule specified, which duties shall be in substitution for the duties theretofore chargeable under the enactments repealed by this Act, and shall be subject to the exemptions contained in this Act and in any other Act for the time being in force."

2 All duties to be paid according to regulations of Act

All stamp duties for the time being chargeable by law upon any instruments are to be paid and denoted according to the regulations in this Act contained, and except where express provision is made to the contrary are to be denoted by impressed stamps only.

3 How instruments are to be written and stamped

(1) Every instrument written upon stamped material is to be written in such manner, and every instrument partly or wholly written before being stamped is to be so stamped, that the stamp may appear on the face of the instrument, and cannot be used for or applied to any other instrument written upon the same piece of material.

(2) If more than one instrument be written upon the same piece of material, every one of the instruments is to be separately and distinctly stamped with the duty with which it is chargeable.

Cross references—See FA 1988 s 143(7) (UK company shares paired with foreign company shares; this section not to apply in relation to a bearer instrument issued after 8 December 1987 representing shares in the UK or foreign companies or a right to an allotment of or to subscribe for such shares).

4 Instruments to be separately charged with duty in certain cases

Except where express provision to the contrary is made by this or any other Act—

(*a*) An instrument containing or relating to several distinct matters is to be separately and distinctly charged, as if it were a separate instrument, with duty in respect of each of the matters;

(*b*) An instrument made for any consideration in respect whereof it is chargeable with *ad valorem* duty, and also for any further or other valuable consideration or considerations, is to be separately and distinctly charged, as if it were a separate instrument, with duty in respect of each of the considerations.

Cross references—See FA 1989 s 173(2) (insurance: abolition of certain duties).

5 Facts and circumstances affecting duty to be set forth in instruments

All the facts and circumstances affecting the liability of any instrument to duty, or the amount of the duty with which any instrument is chargeable, are to be fully and truly set forth in the instrument; and every person who, with intent to defraud Her Majesty,

(*a*) executes any instrument in which all the said facts and circumstances are not fully and truly set forth; or

(*b*) being employed or concerned in or about the preparation of any instrument, neglects or omits fully and truly to set forth therein all the said facts and circumstances;

shall incur [a penalty not exceeding £3,000][1].

Simon's Tax Cases—*Re Brown Root McDermott Fabricators Ltd's and anor's application* [1996] STC 483; *Parinv (Hatfield) Ltd v IRC* [1998] STC 305.

Amendments—[1] Words substituted by FA 1999 s 114, Sch 17 para 3 with effect in relation to penalties in respect of things done or omitted after 30 September 1999.

6 Mode of calculating ad valorem duty in certain cases

(1) Where an instrument is chargeable with *ad valorem* duty in respect of—

(*a*) any money in any foreign or colonial currency, or

(*b*) any stock or marketable security,

the duty shall be calculated on the value, on the day of the date of the instrument, of the money in British currency according to the current rate of exchange, or of the stock or security according to the average price thereof.

(2) Where an instrument contains a statement of current rate of exchange, or average price, as the case may require, and is stamped in accordance with that statement, it is, so far as regards the subject matter of the statement, to be deemed duly stamped, unless or until it is shown that the statement is untrue, and that the instrument is in fact insufficiently stamped.

Cross references—See FA 1985 s 88 (this section to apply instead of FA 1899, s 12 to instruments executed after 31 July 1985).

Use of Adhesive Stamps

9 Penalty for frauds in relation to adhesive stamps

(1) If any person—

(*a*) fraudulently removes or causes to be removed from any instrument any adhesive stamp, or affixes to any other instrument or uses for any postal purposes any adhesive stamp which has been so removed, with intent that the stamp may be used again; or

(*b*) sells or offers for sale, or utters, any adhesive stamp which has been so removed or utters any instrument, having thereon any adhesive stamp which has to his knowledge been so removed as aforesaid;

[he is liable to a penalty not exceeding £3,000][2].

(2) . . . [1]

Cross references—See the Revenue Act 1898, s 7 ("instrument" includes any postal packet within the meaning of the Post Office Protection Act 1884; fines incurred under this section may be recovered summarily).

Amendments—[1] Sub-s (2) repealed by the Revenue Act 1898, s 7 (4).

[2] Words in sub-s (1) substituted by FA 1999 s 114, Sch 17 para 3 with effect in relation to penalties in respect of things done or omitted after 30 September 1999.

Appropriated Stamps and Denoting Stamps

11 Denoting stamps

Where the duty with which an instrument is chargeable depends in any manner upon the duty paid upon another instrument, the payment of the last-mentioned duty shall, upon application to the Commissioners and production of both the instruments, be denoted upon the first-mentioned instrument in such manner as the Commissioners think fit.

Cross references—See FA 1984 s 111(2) (application of this section where an agreement for a lease for a term exceeding 35 years is duly stamped and a conveyance, transfer, etc is subject to the agreement).

Adjudication Stamps

[12 Adjudication by Commissioners][1]

[(1) Subject to such regulations as the Commissioners may think fit to make, the Commissioners may be required by any person to adjudicate with reference to any executed instrument upon the questions—

(*a*) whether it is chargeable with duty;

(*b*) with what amount of duty it is chargeable;

(*c*) whether any penalty is payable under section 15B (penalty on late stamping);

(*d*) what penalty is in their opinion correct and appropriate.

(2) The Commissioners may require to be furnished with an abstract of the instrument and with such evidence as they may require as to the facts and circumstances relevant to those questions.

(3) The Commissioners shall give notice of their decision upon those questions to the person by whom the adjudication was required.

(4) If the Commissioners decide that the instrument is not chargeable with any duty, it may be stamped with a particular stamp denoting that it has been the subject of adjudication and is not chargeable with any duty.

(5) If the Commissioners decide that the instrument is chargeable with duty and assess the amount of duty chargeable, the instrument when stamped in accordance with their decision may be stamped with a particular stamp denoting that it has been the subject of adjudication and is duly stamped.

(6) Every instrument stamped in accordance with subsection (4) or (5) shall be admissible in evidence and available for all purposes notwithstanding any objection relating to duty.][1]

Press releases etc—Principal Registry, Family Division 28-2-78 (application for grant of representation: production of deed or instrument to Probate Registry: presentation to Controller of Stamps for preliminary adjudication).

Simon's Tax Cases—s 12(1), *Marx v Estates and General Investments Ltd* [1975] STC 671.

s 12(2), *Parinv (Hatfield) Ltd v IRC* [1998] STC 305.

Cross references—See FA 2000 Sch 32 para 4(2) (instruments ceasing to be stamped even if instrument has been stamped in accordance with sub-s (5) above).

FA 2000 Sch 32 para 4(3) (sub-s (6) above does not apply to an instrument ceasing to be stamped at any time when it is not duly stamped).

FA 2000 Sch 32 para 7 (application of this section in relation to any additional duty chargeable on an instrument to which FA 2000 Sch 32 applies).

Amendments—[1] This section substituted by FA 1999 s 109(3), Sch 12 para 1 with effect for instruments executed after 30 September 1999. This does not apply to transfers or other instruments relating to units under a unit trust scheme by virtue of FA 1999 s 122. Previously the text read—.

"12 Assessment of duty by Commissioners

(1) Subject to such regulations as the Commissioners may think fit to make, the Commissioners may be required by any person to express their opinion with reference to any executed instrument upon the following questions:

(*a*) whether it is chargeable with any duty;

(*b*) with what amount of duty it is chargeable.

(2) The Commissioners may require to be furnished with an abstract of the instrument, and also with such evidence as they may deem necessary, in order to show to their satisfaction whether all the facts and circumstances affecting the liability of the instrument to duty, or the amount of the duty chargeable thereon, are fully and truly set forth therein.

(3) If the Commissioners are of opinion that the instrument is not chargeable with any duty, it may be stamped with a particular stamp denoting that it is not chargeable with any duty.

(4) If the Commissioners are of opinion that the instrument is chargeable with duty, they shall assess the duty with which it is in their opinion chargeable, and when the instrument is stamped in accordance with the assessment it may be stamped with a particular stamp denoting that it is duly stamped.

(5) Every instrument stamped with the particular stamp denoting either that it is not chargeable with any duty, or is duly stamped, shall be admissible in evidence, and available for all purposes notwithstanding any objection relating to duty.

(6) Provided as follows:

(*a*) An instrument upon which the duty has been assessed by the Commissioners shall not, if it is unstamped or insufficiently stamped, be stamped otherwise than in accordance with the assessment;

(*b*) Nothing in this section . . . shall authorise the stamping after the execution thereof of any instrument which by law cannot be stamped after execution;

(*c*) A statutory declaration made for the purpose of this section shall not be used against any person making the same in any proceeding whatever, except in an inquiry as to the duty with which the instrument to which it relates is chargeable; and every person by whom any such declaration is made shall, on payment of the duty chargeable upon the instrument to which it relates, be relieved from any fine or disability to which he may be liable by reason of the omission to state truly in the instrument any fact or circumstances required by this Act as stated therein."

[12A Adjudication: supplementary provisions][1]

[(1) An instrument which has been the subject of adjudication by the Commissioners under section 12 shall not, if it is unstamped or insufficiently stamped, be stamped otherwise than in accordance with the Commissioners' decision on the adjudication.

(2) If without reasonable excuse any such instrument is not duly stamped within 30 days after the date on which the Commissioners gave notice of their decision, or such longer period as the Commissioners may allow, the person by whom the adjudication was required is liable to a penalty not exceeding £300.

(3) A statutory declaration made for the purposes of section 12 shall not be used against the person making it in any proceedings whatever, except in an inquiry as to the duty with which the instrument to which it relates is chargeable or as to the penalty payable on stamping that instrument.

(4) Every person by whom any such declaration is made shall, on payment of the duty chargeable upon the instrument to which it relates, and any interest or penalty payable on stamping, be relieved from any penalty to which he may be liable by reason of the omission to state truly in the instrument any fact or circumstance required by this Act to be so stated.][1]

Cross references—See FA 2000 Sch 32 para 5 (sub-s (1) above does not prevent an instrument to which FA 2000 Sch 32 applies which is stamped with less than the appropriate amount of duty from being stamped with additional duty).

FA 2000 Sch 32 para 7 (application of this section in relation to any additional duty chargeable on an instrument to which FA 2000 Sch 32 applies).

Amendments—[1] This section inserted by FA 1999 s 109(3), Sch 12 para 1 with effect in relation to instruments executed after 30 September 1999. This does not apply to transfers or other instruments relating to units under a unit trust scheme by virtue of FA 1999 s 122.

[13 Appeal against Commissioners' decision on adjudication][1]

[(1) A person who is dissatisfied with a decision of the Commissioners on an adjudication under section 12 may appeal against it.

(2) The appeal must be brought within 30 days of notice of the decision on the adjudication being given under section 12(3).

(3) An appeal may only be brought on payment of—

(*a*) duty and any penalty in conformity with the Commissioners' decision, and

(*b*) any interest that in conformity with that decision would be payable on stamping the instrument on the day on which the appeal is brought.

(4) An appeal which relates only to the penalty payable on late stamping may be brought to the [First-tier Tribunal][2] in accordance with section 13A below.

(5) Any other appeal may be brought in accordance with section 13B below to the High Court of the part of the United Kingdom in which the case has arisen.][1]

Press releases etc—Law Society 18-7-90 (if no appeal received and no duty paid within 28 days, one reminder is issued; after further 14 days document is returned unstamped).

Cross references—See FA 1965 s 91 (courts may order repayment of sums with such interests as the courts may determine).

Stamp Taxes

FA 2000 Sch 32 para 7 (application of this section in relation to any additional duty chargeable on an instrument to which FA 2000 Sch 32 applies).

Amendments—[1] This section substituted by FA 1999 s 109(3), Sch 12 para 2 with effect in relation to instruments executed after 30 September 1999. This does not apply to transfers or other instruments relating to units under a unit trust scheme by virtue of FA 1999 s 122. Previously the text read:

"13 Persons dissatisfied may appeal

(1) Any person who is dissatisfied with the assessment of the Commissioners may, within twenty-one days after the date of the assessment, and on payment of duty in conformity therewith, appeal against the assessment to the High Court of the part of the United Kingdom in which the case has arisen, and may for that purpose require the Commissioners to state and sign a case, setting forth the question upon which their opinion was required, and the assessment made by them.

(2) The Commissioners shall thereupon state and sign a case and deliver the same to the person by whom it is required, and the case may, within seven days thereafter, be set down by him for hearing.

(3) Upon the hearing of the case the court shall determine the question submitted, and, if the instrument in question is in the opinion of the court chargeable with any duty, shall assess the duty with which it is chargeable.

(4) If it is decided by the court that the assessment of the Commissioners is erroneous, any excess of duty which may have been paid in conformity with the erroneous assessment, together with any fine or penalty which may have been paid in consequence thereof, shall be ordered by the court to be repaid to the appellant . . .

(5) . . ."

[2] Words in sub-s (4) substituted for words "Special Commissioners" by the Transfer of Tribunal Functions and Revenue and Customs Appeals Order, SI 2009/56 art 3, Sch 1 paras 1, 2 with effect from 1 April 2009.

[13A Appeal to the [First-tier Tribunal][2]][1]

[(1) The following provisions apply in relation to an appeal under section 13(4).

(2) Notice of appeal must be given in writing to the Commissioners, specifying the grounds of appeal.

(3), (4) . . . [2]

(5) On the appeal the [First-tier Tribunal][2] may—

(*a*) if it appears . . . [2] that no penalty should be paid, set the decision aside;

(*b*) if the amount determined appears . . . [2] to be appropriate, confirm the decision;

(*c*) if the amount determined appears . . . [2] to be excessive, reduce it to such other amount (including nil) as [the tribunal considers][2] appropriate;

(*d*) if the amount determined appears . . . [2] to be insufficient, increase it to such amount as [the tribunal considers][2] appropriate.

(6) . . . [2]

[(7) In addition to any right of appeal on a point of law under section 11(2) of the Tribunals, Courts and Enforcement Act 2007, the person liable to the penalty may appeal to the Upper Tribunal against the amount of the penalty which has been determined under subsection (5), but not against any decision which falls under section 11(5)(*d*) or (*e*) of that Act and was made in connection with the determination of the amount of the penalty.

(7A) Section 11(3) and (4) of the Tribunals, Courts and Enforcement Act 2007 applies to the right of appeal under subsection (7) as it applies to the right of appeal under section 11(2) of that Act.][2]

(8) On an appeal under subsection (7) the [Upper Tribunal][2] has the same powers as are conferred on the [First-tier Tribunal][2] by subsection (5) above.][1]

Cross references—FA 2000 Sch 32 para 7 (application of this section in relation to any additional duty chargeable on an instrument to which FA 2000 Sch 32 applies).

Amendments—[1] This section inserted by FA 1999 s 109(3), Sch 12 para 2 with effect in relation to instruments executed after 30 September 1999. This does not apply to transfers or other instruments relating to units under a unit trust scheme by virtue of FA 1999 s 122.

[2] Words in heading substituted for words "Special Commissioners", sub-ss (3), (4), (6) repealed, in sub-s (5) words substituted and repealed, sub-ss (7), (7A) substituted for previous sub-s (7), and words in sub-s (8) substituted, by the Transfer of Tribunal Functions and Revenue and Customs Appeals Order, SI 2009/56 art 3, Sch 1 paras 1, 3 with effect from 1 April 2009. This section previously read as follows—

"(1) The following provisions apply in relation to an appeal under section 13(4).

(2) Notice of appeal must be given in writing to the Commissioners, specifying the grounds of appeal.

(3) On the hearing of the appeal the Special Commissioners may allow the appellant to put forward a ground not specified in the notice of appeal, and take it into consideration, if satisfied that the omission was not wilful or unreasonable.

(4) The powers conferred by sections 46A(1)(*c*) and (2) to (4) and sections 56B to 56D of the Taxes Management Act 1970 (power of Lord Chancellor to make regulations as to jurisdiction, practice and procedure in relation to appeals) are exercisable in relation to appeals to which this section applies.

(5) On the appeal the Special Commissioners may—

(*a*) if it appears to them that no penalty should be paid, set the decision aside;

(*b*) if the amount determined appears to them to be appropriate, confirm the decision;

(*c*) if the amount determined appears to them to be excessive, reduce it to such other amount (including nil) as they consider appropriate;

(*d*) if the amount determined appears to them to be insufficient, increase it to such amount as they consider appropriate.

(6) Section 56A of the Taxes Management Act 1970 (general right of appeal on point of law) applies in relation to a decision of the Special Commissioners under this section.

(7) Without prejudice to that right of appeal, an appeal lies against the amount of a penalty determined by the Special Commissioners under this section, at the instance of the person liable to the penalty, to the High Court.

(8) On an appeal under subsection (7) the court has the same powers as are conferred on the Special Commissioners by subsection (5) above.".

[13B Appeal to the High Court][1]

[(1) The following provisions apply in relation to an appeal under section 13(5).

(2) The appellant may for the purposes of the appeal require the Commissioners to state and sign a case setting out the questions upon which they were required to adjudicate and their decision upon them.

(3) The Commissioners shall thereupon state and sign a case and deliver the same to the person by whom it is required, and the case may, within 30 days thereafter, be set down by him for hearing.

(4) On the appeal the court shall determine the questions submitted and may give such directions as it thinks fit with respect to the repayment of any duty or penalty paid in conformity with the Commissioners' decision.][1]

Cross references—FA 2000 Sch 32 para 7 (application of this section in relation to any additional duty chargeable on an instrument to which FA 2000 Sch 32 applies).

Amendments—[1] This section inserted by FA 1999 s 109(3), Sch 12 para 2 with effect in relation to instruments executed after 30 September 1999. This does not apply to transfers or other instruments relating to units under a unit trust scheme by virtue of FA 1999 s 122.

Production of Instruments in Evidence

14 Terms upon which instruments not duly stamped may be received in evidence

(1) Upon the production of an instrument chargeable with any duty as evidence in any court of civil judicature in any part of the United Kingdom, or before any arbitrator or referee, notice shall be taken by the judge arbitrator, or referee of any omission or insufficiency of the stamp thereon, and [the instrument may][1], on payment to the officer of the court whose duty it is to read the instrument, or to the arbitrator or referee, of the amount of the unpaid duty, and [any interest or penalty][1] payable on stamping the same, and of a further sum of one pound, be received in evidence, saving all just exceptions on other grounds.

(2) The officer, or arbitrator, or referee receiving [the duty and any interest or penalty][1] shall give a receipt for the same, and make an entry in a book kept for that purpose of the payment and of the amount thereof, and shall communicate to the Commissioners the name or title of the proceeding in which, and of the party from whom, he received [the duty and any interest or penalty][1], and the date and description of the instrument, and shall pay over to such person as the Commissioners may appoint the money received by him for [the duty and any interest or penalty][1].

(3) On production to the Commissioners of any instrument in respect of which [any duty, interest or penalty][1] has been paid, together with the receipt, the payment of [the duty, interest and penalty][1] shall be denoted on the instrument.

(4) Save as aforesaid, an instrument executed in any part of the United Kingdom, or relating, wheresoever executed, to any property situate, or to any matter or thing done or to be done, in any part of the United Kingdom, shall not, except in criminal proceedings, be given in evidence, or be available for any purpose whatever, unless it is duly stamped in accordance with the law in force at the time when it was [executed][1].

Simon's Tax Cases—s 14(4), *Terrapin International Ltd v IRC* [1976] STC 197; *Re Brown Root McDermott Fabricators Ltd's and anor's application* [1996] STC 483; *Parinv (Hatfield) Ltd v IRC* [1998] STC 305.

HMRC Interpretation RI 174—*(Parinv (Hatfield) Ltd v IRC* [1996] STC 933—off-shore declaration of trust ineffective to avoid ad valorem duty on subsequent transfers).

Cross references—See FA 1984 s 109(3), (4) (reduction of stamp duty on conveyances and transfers with effect from 20 March 1984; how sub-s (4) of this section applies to instruments executed after 12 March 1984 but stamped after 19 March 1984);

FA 1984 s 110(4) (extension of stamp duty relief on sales at discount with effect from 20 March 1984; how sub-s (4) of this section applies to instruments executed after 12 March 1984 but stamped after 19 March 1984);

FA 1985 s 82(7) (abolition of stamp duty in respect of gifts inter vivos from 26 March 1985; instruments executed after 18 March 1985 which are stamped after 25 March 1985; modification of sub-s (4) above);

FA 1985 s 85(4) (abolition of certain fixed duties from 26 March 1985; modification of sub-s (4) above);

FA 1988 s 140(3) (abolition of unit trust instrument duty; modification of sub-s (4) above where a trust instrument executed after 15 March 1988 is not stamped before 22 March 1988 and where a trust instrument in respect of a property becoming trust property after 15 March 1988 is not stamped before 22 March 1988);

FA 1988 s 141(3) (abolition of duty on documents relating to transactions of capital companies; modification of sub-s (4) above where the relevant document in respect of a transaction occurring after 15 March 1988 is not stamped before 22 March 1988);

FA 1988 s 141(3) (abolition of duty on documents relating to transactions of capital companies; modification of sub-s (4) above where an exempt transaction occurs before 16 March 1988 in respect of which a relevant event occurs after 15 March 1988 and the relevant duty is not paid before 22 March 1988);

FA 1993 s 201(3) (increase in stamp duty threshold from 16 March 1993 in respect of conveyance or transfer on sale; applicable law for the purposes of sub-s (4) above);

FA 1993 s 204(3) (method of denoting stamp duty to be prescribed by Treasury regulations; for the purposes of sub-s (4) above the method is to be that in force when an instrument was first executed);

FA 1994 ss 244(5), 245(8) (with effect from an appointed day, instruments on transfer of land in Northern Ireland are required to be produced to the Commissioners and no instrument will be deemed for the purposes of this section to be duly stamped unless it is so produced).

FA 2000 Sch 32 para 4(3) (sub-s (1) above does not apply to an instrument if it cease to be stamped, at any time when it is not duly stamped, unless the unpaid duty and any interest or penalty is paid in accordance with sub-s (1)).

FA 2000 Sch 32 para 6 (application of sub-s (4) in relation to any instrument to which FA 2000 Sch 32 applies).

FA 2002 s 115(5)(*a*) (where an instrument is chargeable with duty under FA 2002 s 115, sub-s (4) above does not apply in relation to it until after the period specified in FA 2002 s 115(2)).

FA 2008 ss 98(6), 99(3), 100(4) (for the purposes of sub-s (4) the law in force at the time of execution of an instrument executed on or after 13 March 2008 but before 19 March 2008, and not stamped before 19 March 2008, is deemed to be the law as varied in accordance with FA 2008 ss 98, 99, 100, Sch 32).

Amendments—[1] Words in sub-ss (1)–(4) substituted by FA 1999 s 109(3), Sch 12 para 3 with effect in relation to instruments executed after 30 September 1999. This does not apply to transfers or other instruments relating to units under a unit trust scheme by virtue of FA 1999 s 122.

Stamping of Instruments after Execution

[15 Stamping after execution][1]

[(1) An unstamped or insufficiently stamped instrument may be stamped after being executed on payment of the unpaid duty and any interest or penalty payable.

(2) Any interest or penalty payable on stamping shall be denoted on the instrument by a particular stamp.][1]

Cross references—See FA 1986 ss 69(5), 72(3) (instruments transferring relevant securities of UK companies to specified persons; extension of sub-s (2) above to such instruments and persons);

FA 1994 s 240 (where an agreement for a lease and the lease giving effect to the agreement are presented together for stamping, the agreement is treated, for penalty, if any, under this section, as executed on the date on which the lease was first executed).

FA 2000 Sch 32 para 7 (application of this section in relation to any additional duty chargeable on an instrument to which FA 2000 Sch 32 applies).

Amendments—[1] This section substituted by FA 1999 s 109(1) with effect in relation to instruments executed after 30 September 1999. This does not apply to transfers or other instruments relating to units under a unit trust scheme by virtue of FA 1999 s 122. Previously the text read:

"15 Penalty upon stamping instruments after execution

(1) Save where other express provision is in this Act made, any unstamped or insufficiently stamped instrument may be stamped after the execution thereof, on payment of the unpaid duty and penalty of ten pounds, and also by way of further penalty, where the unpaid duty exceeds ten pounds, of interest on such duty, at the rate of five pounds per centum per annum, from the day upon which the instrument was first executed up to the time when the amount of interest is equal to the unpaid duty.

(2) In the case of such instruments hereinafter mentioned as are chargeable with *ad valorem* duty, the following provisions shall have effect:

(*a*) The instrument, unless it is written upon duly stamped material, shall be duly stamped with the proper *ad valorem* duty before the expiration of thirty days after it is first executed, or after it has been first received in the United Kingdom in case it is first executed at any place out of the United Kingdom, unless the opinion of the Commissioners with respect to the amount of duty with which the instrument is chargeable, has, before such expiration, been required under the provisions of this Act:

(*b*) If the opinion of the Commissioners with respect to any such instrument has been required, the instrument shall be stamped in accordance with the assessment of the Commissioners within fourteen days after notice of the assessment:

(*c*) If any such instrument executed after the sixteenth day of May one thousand eight hundred and eighty-eight has not been or is not duly stamped in conformity with the foregoing provisions of this subsection, the person in that behalf herein-after specified shall incur a fine of ten pounds, and in addition to the penalty payable on stamping the instrument there shall be paid a further penalty equivalent to the stamp duty thereon, unless a reasonable excuse for the delay in stamping, or the omission to stamp, or the insufficiency of stamp, be afforded to the satisfaction of the Commissioners, or of the court, judge, arbitrator, or referee before whom it is produced:

(*d*) The instruments and persons to which the provisions of this subsection are to apply are as follows—

Title of Instrument as described in the First Schedule to this Act	*Person liable to Penalty*
Bond, covenant, or instrument of any kind whatsoever.	The obligee, covenantee, or other person taking the security.
Conveyance on sale.	The vendee or transferee.
Lease or tack.	The lessee.
[Agreement for lease or tack chargeable under section 75.]	[The person contracting for the lease or tack to be granted to him or another.]
. . .	. . .
[*Unit Trust Instrument.*][2]	[*The trustees.*]

(3) Provided that save where other express provision is made by this Act in relation to any particular instrument:

(*a*) Any unstamped or insufficiently stamped instrument which has been first executed at any place out of the United Kingdom, may be stamped, at any time within thirty days after it has been first received in the United Kingdom, on payment of the unpaid duty only: and

(*b*) The Commissioners may, if they think fit, . . . mitigate or remit any penalty payable on stamping.

(4) The payment of any penalty payable on stamping is to be denoted on the instrument by a particular stamp."

[15A Late stamping: interest][1]

[(1) Interest is payable on the stamping of an instrument which—

(*a*) is chargeable with *ad valorem* duty, and

(*b*) is not duly stamped within 30 days after the day on which the instrument was executed (whether in the United Kingdom or elsewhere).

(2) Interest is payable on the amount of the unpaid duty from the end of the period of 30 days mentioned in subsection (1)(*b*) until the duty is paid.

If an amount is lodged with the Commissioners in respect of the duty, the amount on which interest is payable is reduced by that amount.

(3) Interest shall be calculated at the rate applicable under section 178 of the Finance Act 1989 (power of Treasury to prescribe rates of interest).

(4) The amount of interest shall be rounded down (if necessary) to the nearest multiple of £5.

No interest is payable if that amount is less than £25.

(5) Interest under this section shall be paid without any deduction of income tax and shall not be taken into account in computing income or profits for any tax purposes.][1]

Cross references—FA 2000 Sch 32 para 7 (application of this section in relation to any additional duty chargeable on an instrument to which FA 2000 Sch 32 applies).

FA 2002 s 115(5)(*b*) (where an instrument is chargeable with duty under FA 2002 s 115, this section applies in relation to it as if it had been executed at the end of the period specified in FA 2002 s 115(2)).

Amendments—[1] This section inserted by FA 1999 s 109(1) with effect in relation to instruments executed after 30 September 1999. This does not apply to transfers or other instruments relating to units under a unit trust scheme by virtue of FA 1999 s 122.

[15B Late stamping: penalties][1]

[(1) A penalty is payable on the stamping of an instrument which is not presented for stamping within 30 days after—

(*a*) if the instrument is executed in the United Kingdom [or relates to land in the United Kingdom][2], the day on which it is so executed;

(*b*) if the instrument is executed outside the United Kingdom [and does not relate to land in the United Kingdom][2], the day on which it is first received in the United Kingdom.

[(1A) For the purposes of subsection (1) every instrument that (whether or not it also relates to any other transaction) relates to a transaction which to any extent involves land in the United Kingdom is an instrument relating to land in the United Kingdom.][2]

(2) If the instrument is presented for stamping within one year after the end of the 30-day period mentioned in subsection (1), the maximum penalty is £300 or the amount of the unpaid duty, whichever is less.

(3) If the instrument is not presented for stamping until after the end of the one-year period mentioned in subsection (2), the maximum penalty is £300 or the amount of the unpaid duty, whichever is greater.

(4) The Commissioners may, if they think fit, mitigate or remit any penalty payable on stamping.

(5) No penalty is payable if there is a reasonable excuse for the delay in presenting the instrument for stamping.][1]

Cross references—FA 2000 Sch 32 para 7 (application of this section in relation to any additional duty chargeable on an instrument to which FA 2000 Sch 32 applies).

FA 2002 s 115(5)(*b*) (where an instrument is chargeable with duty under FA 2002 s 115, this section applies in relation to it as if it had been executed at the end of the period specified in FA 2002 s 115(2)).

Amendments—[1] This section inserted by FA 1999 s 109(1) with effect in relation to instruments executed after 30 September 1999. This does not apply to transfers or other instruments relating to units under a unit trust scheme by virtue of FA 1999 s 122.

[2] Words in sub-s (1) inserted, and sub-s (1A) inserted, by FA 2002 s 114 with effect for instruments executed after 23 July 2002.

Entries upon Rolls, Books, etc

16 Rolls, books etc, to be open to inspection

Every public officer having in his custody any rolls, books, records, papers, documents, or proceedings, the inspection whereof may tend to secure any duty, or to prove or lead to the discovery of any fraud or omission in relation to any duty, shall at all reasonable times permit any person thereto authorised by the Commissioners to inspect the rolls, books, records, papers, documents, and proceedings, and to take such notes and extracts as he may deem necessary, without fee or reward, and in case of refusal shall for every offence incur [a penalty not exceeding £300][1].

Cross references—See FA 1946 s 56 ("public officers" includes the trustees and managers of a unit trust scheme, and their agents, officers or servants).

Amendments—[1] Words substituted by FA 1999 s 114, Sch 17 para 3 with effect in relation to penalties in respect of things done or omitted after 30 September 1999.

17 Penalty for enrolling, etc, instrument not duly stamped

If any person whose office it is to enrol, register, or enter in or upon any rolls, books, or records any instrument chargeable with duty, enrols, registers, or enters any such instrument not being duly stamped, he shall incur [a penalty not exceeding £300][1].

Amendments—[1] Words in sub-s (1) substituted by FA 1999 s 114, Sch 17 para 3 with effect in relation to penalties in respect of things done or omitted after 30 September 1999.

PART II
REGULATIONS APPLICABLE TO PARTICULAR INSTRUMENTS

Instruments of Apprenticeship

25 Meaning of instrument of apprenticeship

Every writing relating to the service or tuition of any apprentice, clerk, or servant placed with any master to learn any profession, trade, or employment (except articles of clerkship to a solicitor or law agent or writer to the signet) is to be deemed an instrument of apprenticeship.

Amendments—This section repealed by the Statute Law (Repeals) Act 2008 s 1, Sch 1 Part 8 with effect from 21 July 2008.

Bills of Sale

41 Bills of sale

A bill of sale is not to be registered under any Act for the time being in force relating to the registration of bills of sale unless the original, duly stamped, is produced to the proper officer.

Charter-parties

49 Provisions as to duty on charter-party

(1) For the purposes of this Act the expression "charter-party" includes any agreement or contract for the charter of any ship or vessel or any memorandum, letter, or other writing between the captain, master, or owner of any ship or vessel, and any other person for or relating to the freight or conveyance of any money, goods, or effects on board of the ship or vessel.

(2) . . . [1, 2]

Amendments—[1] Sub-s (2) repealed by FA 1949 s 52(10), Sch 11 Pt V and FA (Northern Ireland) 1949 s 16, Sch 4 Pt II.
[2] This section repealed by the Statute Law (Repeals) Act 2008 s 1, Sch 1 Part 8 with effect from 21 July 2008.

Conveyances on Sale

54 Meaning of "conveyance on sale"

Amendments—This section repealed by FA 1999 Sch 20 Pt V(2) with effect in relation to instruments executed, or bearer instruments issued, from 1 October 1999, subject to the provisions in FA 1999 Sch 20 Pt V(2) Note 2. Previously the text read:

> "For the purposes of this Act the expression "conveyance on sale" includes every instrument, and every decree or order of any court or of any commissioners, whereby any property, or any estate or interest in any property, upon the sale thereof is transferred to or vested in a purchaser, or any other person on his behalf or by his direction.".

55 How ad valorem duty to be calculated in respect of stock and securities

(1) Where the consideration, or any part of the consideration, for a conveyance on sale consists of any stock or marketable security, the conveyance is to be charged with *ad valorem* duty in respect of the value of the stock or security.

[(1A) For the purposes of subsection (1), it is immaterial—

(*a*) whether, at the time of the execution of the conveyance on sale, the stock or marketable security is or has been issued or is to be issued; and

(*b*) in a case where the stock or marketable security is to be issued, when it is to be, or is, issued and whether the issue is certain or contingent.][1]

(2) Where the consideration, or any part of the consideration, for a conveyance on sale consists of any security not being a marketable security, the conveyance is to be charged with *ad valorem* duty in respect of the amount due on the day of the date thereof for principal and interest upon the security.

Amendments—[1] Sub-s (1A) inserted by FA 2000 s 126(1), (2), with effect for instruments executed after 27 July 2000.

56 How consideration consisting of periodical payments to be charged

(1) Where the consideration, or any part of the consideration, for a conveyance on sale consists of money payable periodically for a definite period not exceeding twenty years, so that the total amount to be paid can be previously ascertained, the conveyance is to be charged in respect of that consideration with *ad valorem* duty on such total amount.

(2) Where the consideration, or any part of the consideration, for a conveyance on sale consists of money payable periodically for a definite period exceeding twenty years or in perpetuity, or for any indefinite period not terminable with life, the conveyance is to be charged in respect of that consideration with *ad valorem* duty on the total amount which will or may, according to the terms of sale, be payable during the period of twenty years next after the day of the date of the instrument.

(3) Where the consideration, or any part of the consideration, for a conveyance on sale consists of money payable periodically during any life or lives, the conveyance is to be charged in respect of that consideration with *ad valorem* duty on the amount which will or may, according to the terms of sale, be payable during the period of twelve years next after the day of the date of the instrument.

(4) . . . [1]

Statement of Practice SP 11/91—Interaction of stamp duty and VAT; stamp duty to be calculated on the VAT-inclusive consideration.

Simon's Tax Cases—s 56(2), *Quietlece v IRC* [1983] STC 17; *Blendett Ltd v IRC* [1984] STC 95.

Amendments—[1] Sub-s (4) repealed by FA 1971 s 69, Sch 14 Pt VI, and FA (Northern Ireland) 1971 s 9, Sch 3 Pt I.

57 How conveyance in consideration of a debt, etc, to be charged

Where any property is conveyed to any person in consideration, wholly or in part, of any debt due to him, or subject either certainly or contingently to the payment or transfer of any money or stock, whether being or constituting a charge or incumbrance upon the property or not, the debt, money, or stock is to be deemed the whole or part, as the case may be, of the consideration in respect whereof the conveyance is chargeable with *ad valorem* duty.

Regulations—See the Stamp Duty (Exempt Instruments) Regulations, SI 1987/516.

SP 6/90—Conveyances and transfers of property subject to a debt.

Cross references—See FA 1980 s 102 (reduction in consideration where the debt exceeds the value of the property transferred in payment thereof);

FA 1981 s 107(1), (4) (sale of houses at discount by local authorities; notwithstanding this section, the discount not chargeable with stamp duty in respect of instruments executed after 22 March 1981);

F(No 2)A 1983 s 15(1) (this section not to apply in relation to conveyances or transfers by which disposal of land is effected by constituency associations of political parties on reorganisation of constituencies).

58 Direction as to duty in certain cases

(1) Where property contracted to be sold for one consideration for the whole is conveyed to the purchaser in separate parts or parcels by different instruments, the consideration is to be apportioned in such manner as the parties think fit, so that a distinct consideration for each separate part or parcel is set forth in the conveyance relating thereto, and such conveyance is to be charged with *ad valorem* duty in respect of such distinct consideration.

(2) Where property contracted to be purchased for one consideration for the whole by two or more persons jointly, or by any person for himself and others, or wholly for others, is conveyed in parts or parcels by separate instruments to the persons by or for whom the same was purchased for distinct parts of the consideration, the conveyance of each separate part or parcel is to be charged with *ad valorem* duty in respect of the distinct part of the consideration therein specified.

(3) Where there are several instruments of conveyance for completing the purchaser's title to property sold, the principal instrument of conveyance only is to be charged with *ad valorem* duty, and the other instruments are to be respectively charged with such other duty as they may be liable to, but the last-mentioned duty shall not exceed the *ad valorem* duty payable in respect of the principal instrument.

(4) Where a person having contracted for the purchase of any property, but not having obtained a conveyance thereof, contracts to sell the same to any other person, and the property is in consequence conveyed immediately to the sub-purchaser [then, except where—

(*a*) the chargeable consideration moving from the sub-purchaser is less than the value of the property immediately before the contract of sale to him, and

(*b*) the conveyance is not one to which section 107 of the Finance Act 1981 (sales of houses at discount by local authorities etc) applies][1],

the conveyance is to be charged with ad valorem duty in respect only of the consideration moving from the sub-purchaser.

(5) Where a person having contracted for the purchase of any property but not having obtained a conveyance contracts to sell the whole, or any part or parts thereof, to any other person or persons, and the property is in consequence conveyed by the original seller to different persons in parts or parcels [then, except where the aggregate of the chargeable consideration for the sale of all such parts or parcels is less than the value of the whole of the property immediately before the contract for their sale or, as the case may be, the first contract for the sale of any of them][1], the conveyance of each part or parcel is to be charged with *ad valorem* duty in respect only of the consideration moving from the sub-purchaser thereof, without regard to the amount or value of the original consideration.

(6) Where a sub-purchaser takes an actual conveyance of the interest of the person immediately selling to him, which is chargeable with *ad valorem* duty in respect of the consideration moving from him, and is duly stamped accordingly, any conveyance to be afterwards made to him of the same property by the original seller shall be chargeable only with such other duty as it may be liable to, but the last-mentioned duty shall not exceed the *ad valorem* duty.

[(7) Any reference in subsection (4) or subsection (5) of this section to chargeable consideration is a reference to consideration which falls to be brought into account in determining the duty (if any) chargeable on the conveyance to the sub-purchaser or, as the case may be, on the conveyance of each of the parts or parcels in question; and in any case where it is necessary for the purposes of either of those subsections to determine [the value at any time of any property, that value shall be taken to be the price which the property might reasonably be expected to fetch on a sale at that time in the open market][3].][2]

Cross references—See FA 1963 s 67(5) (application of this section to "purchaser" and "sale" in that section);

Simon's Tax Cases—s 58(1), *Re Brown Root McDermott Fabricators Ltd's and anor's application* [1996] STC 483.

Modifications—FA 1991 s 112 (modification of this section, with effect from an appointed day, where property mentioned in sub-ss (1), (2) above includes exempt property as defined).

FA 2000 Sch 34 para 3 (modification of this section where part of the property referred to in sub-ss (1), (2) above consists of intellectual property).

FA 2001 Sch 30 para 2(1) (modification of this section where any part or parcel of the property referred to in sub-s (1) above consists of an estate or interest in land situated wholly or partly in a disadvantaged area).

FA 2001 Sch 30 para 2(2) (modification of this section where any part or parcel of the property referred to in sub-s (2) above consists of an estate or interest in land situated wholly or partly in a disadvantaged area, and both or (as the case may be) all the relevant persons are connected with one another).

FA 2003 Sch 20 para 2 (modification of sub-s (1) above where part of the property referred to therein consists of stock and marketable securities).

FA 2003 Sch 20 para 2 (modification of sub-s (2) above where part of the property referred to therein consists of stock and marketable securities and both (or, as the case may be, all) of the relevant persons are connected with one another).

Amendments—[1] Words in sub-ss (4), (5) inserted by FA 1984 s 112(1), (2), (4) where the contract for the sub-sale or the first contract for the sub-sale of a part is entered into after 19 March 1984.

[2] Sub-s (7) inserted by FA 1984 s 112(3), (4).

[3] Words in sub-s (7) substituted by FA 1985 s 82(2), (8) with effect from 26 March 1985.

59 Certain contracts to be chargeable as conveyances on sale

Cross references—See FA 1958 s 34 (instruments chargeable by reference to this heading disregarded for the purposes of that section);

Electricity Act 1989 s 103 (electricity treated as goods for the purposes of this section);

Electricity (Northern Ireland Consequential Amendments) Order, SI 1992/232 (electricity in Northern Ireland treated as goods for the purposes of this section).

Amendments—This section repealed by FA 1999 Sch 20 Pt V(2) with effect in relation to instruments executed, or bearer instruments issued, from 1 October 1999, subject to the provisions in FA 1999 Sch 20 Pt V(2) Note 2. Previously the text read:

"(1) Any contract or agreement . . . for the sale of any equitable estate or interest in any property whatsoever, or for the sale of any estate or interest in any property except lands, tenements, hereditaments, or heritages, or property locally situate out of the United Kingdom, or goods, wares or merchandise, or stock, or marketable securities, or any ship or vessel, or part interest, share, or property of or in any ship or vessel, shall be charged with the same *ad valorem* duty, to be paid by the purchaser, as if it were an actual conveyance on sale of the estate, interest, or property contracted or agreed to be sold.

(2) Where the purchaser has paid the said *ad valorem* duty and before having obtained a conveyance or transfer of the property, enters into a contract or agreement for the sale of the same, the contract or agreement shall be charged, if the consideration for that sale is in excess of the consideration for the original sale, with the *ad valorem* duty payable in respect of such excess consideration, [but shall not otherwise be chargeable . . .].

(3) Where duty has been duly paid in conformity with the foregoing provisions, the conveyance or transfer made to the purchaser or sub-purchaser, or any other person on his behalf or by his direction, shall not be chargeable with any duty, and the Commissioners, upon application, either shall denote the payment of the *ad valorem* duty upon the conveyance or transfer, or shall transfer the *ad valorem* duty thereto upon production of the contract or agreement, or contracts or agreements, duly stamped.

(4) . . .

(5) [Provided that where any such contract or agreement . . . would, apart from this section, not be chargeable with any duty], and a conveyance or transfer made in conformity with the contract or agreement is presented to the Commissioners for stamping with the *ad valorem* duty chargeable thereon within the period of six months after the first execution of the contract or agreement, or within such longer period as the Commissioners may think reasonable in the circumstances of the case, the conveyance or transfer shall be stamped accordingly, and the same, and the said contract or agreement, shall be deemed to be duly stamped. Nothing in this proviso shall alter or affect the provisions as to the stamping of a conveyance or transfer after the execution thereof.

(6) Provided also, that the *ad valorem* duty paid upon any such contract or agreement shall be returned by the Commissioners in case the contract or agreement be afterwards rescinded or annulled, or for any other reason be not substantially performed or carried into effect, so as to operate as or be followed by a conveyance or transfer."

60 As to sale of an annuity or right not before in existence

Where upon the sale of any annuity or other right not before in existence such annuity or other right is not created by actual grant or conveyance, but is only secured by bond, warrant of attorney, covenant, contract, or otherwise, the bond or other instrument, or some one of such instruments, if there be more than one, is to be charged with the same duty as an actual grant or conveyance, and is for the purposes of this Act to be deemed an instrument of conveyance on sale.

61 Principal instrument, how to be ascertained

(1) In the cases hereinafter specified the principal instrument is to be ascertained in the following manner:

(*a*), (*b*) . . . [1]

(*c*) Where in Scotland there is a disposition or assignation executed by the seller, and any other instrument is executed for completing the title, the disposition or assignation is to be deemed the principal instrument.

(2) In any other case the parties may determine for themselves which of several instruments is to be deemed the principal instrument, and may pay the *ad valorem* duty thereon accordingly.

Simon's Tax Cases—s 61(2), *Parinv (Hatfield) Ltd v IRC* [1998] STC 305.

Amendments—[1] Sub-s (1)(*a*), (*b*) repealed by FA 1949 s 52, Sch 11 Pt V, and FA (Northern Ireland) 1949 s 16, Sch 4 Pt II.

Conveyances on any Occasion except Sale or Mortgage

62 What is to be deemed a conveyance on any occasion, not being a sale or mortgage

Concession G5—Transfer of stock from persons to themselves operating as executors' assent.

Statement of Practice SP 11/91—Interaction of stamp duty and VAT: stamp duty to be calculated on the VAT-inclusive consideration.

Cross references—See FA 1902 s 9 (extension of proviso to the retirement of a trustee).

Amendments—This section repealed by FA 1999 Sch 20 Pt V(2) with effect in relation to instruments executed, or bearer instruments issued, from 1 October 1999, subject to the provisions in FA 1999 Sch 20 Pt V(2) Note 2. Previously the text read:

> "Every instrument, and every decree or order of any court or of any commissioners, whereby any property on any occasion, except a sale or mortgage, is transferred to or vested in any person, is to be charged with duty as a conveyance or transfer of property.
>
> Provided that a conveyance or transfer made for effectuating the appointment of a new trustee is not to be charged with any higher duty than [50p]."

Duplicates and Counterparts

72 Provision as to duplicates and counterparts

Cross-references—See SDMA 1891 s 12A (Stamping of replicas of documents which have been spoilt or lost).

Amendments—This section repealed by FA 1999 Sch 20 Pt V(2) with effect in relation to instruments executed, or bearer instruments issued, from 1 October 1999, subject to the provisions in FA 1999 Sch 20 Pt V(2) Note 2. Previously the text read:

> "The duplicate or counterpart of an instrument chargeable with duty (except the counterpart of an instrument chargeable as a lease, such counterpart not being executed by or on behalf of any lessor or grantor), is not to be deemed duly stamped unless it is stamped as an original instrument, or unless it appears by some stamp impressed thereon that the full and proper duty has been paid upon the original instrument of which it is the duplicate or counterpart."

Exchange and Partition or Division

73 As to exchange, etc

Cross references—See FA 1994 s 241(3), (6) (this section ceases to apply to exchange of property and accordingly in relation to instruments giving effect to the exchange executed after 7 December 1993 in pursuance of contracts made on or after 30 November 1993). See consequential *Amendments* below.

Amendments—This section repealed by FA 1999 Sch 20 Pt V(2) with effect in relation to instruments executed, or bearer instruments issued, from 1 October 1999, subject to the provisions in FA 1999 Sch 20 Pt V(2) Note 2. Previously the text read:

> "Where . . . upon the partition or division of any [estate or interest in land] any consideration exceeding in amount or value one hundred pounds is paid or given, or agreed to be paid or given, for equality, the principal or only instrument whereby the . . . partition or division is effected is to be charged with the same *ad valorem* duty as a conveyance on sale for the consideration, and with that duty only; and where in any such case there are several instruments for completing the title of either party, the principal instrument is to be ascertained, and the other instruments are to be charged with duty in the manner hereinbefore provided in the case of several instruments of conveyance."

Leases

75 Agreements for not more than thirty-five years to be charged as leases

Statement of Practice SP 11/91—Interaction of stamp duty and VAT: stamp duty to be calculated on the VAT-inclusive consideration.

Amendments—This section repealed by FA 1999 Sch 20 Pt V(2) with effect in relation to instruments executed, or bearer instruments issued, from 1 October 1999, subject to the provisions in FA 1999 Sch 20 Pt V(2) Note 2. Previously the text read:

> "(1) An agreement for a lease or tack, or with respect to the letting of any lands, tenements, or heritable subjects for any term . . . , or for any indefinite term, is to be charged with the same duty as if it were an actual lease or tack made for the term and consideration mentioned in the agreement.
>
> [(2) Where duty has been duly paid on an agreement for a lease or tack and, subsequent to that agreement, a lease or tack is granted which either—
>
> (*a*) is in conformity with the agreement, or
>
> (*b*) relates to substantially the same property and term as the agreement,
>
> then the duty which would otherwise be charged on the lease or tack shall be reduced (or, as the case may be, extinguished) by the deduction therefrom of the duty paid on the agreement.]"

Stamp Taxes

77 Directions as to duty in certain cases

(1) A [lease][3], or agreement for a [lease][3], or with respect to any letting, is not to be charged with any duty in respect of any penal rent, or increased rent in the nature of a penal rent, thereby reserved or agreed to be reserved or made payable, or by reason of being made in consideration of the surrender or abandonment of any existing lease, tack, or agreement of or relating to the same subject matter.

(2) A lease made for any consideration in respect whereof it is chargeable with *ad valorem* duty, and in further consideration either of a covenant by the lessee to make, or of his having previously made, any substantial improvement of or addition to the property demised to him, or of any covenant relating to the matter of the lease, is not to be charged with any duty in respect of such further consideration.

(3), (4) . . . [1]

(5) . . . [2]

Statement of Practice SP 11/91—Interaction of stamp duty and VAT: stamp duty to be calculated on the VAT-inclusive consideration.

Revenue and other press releases—IR Tax Bulletin August 1995 paras 13–15 (Stamp Office will not seek to refuse exemption under this section merely on the grounds of *de minimis* changes in the property subject to the lease).

Cross references—See the Revenue Act 1909 s 8 (non-application of this section as respects any further consideration in the lease).

Amendments—[1] Sub-ss (3), (4) repealed by FA 1963 ss 56(4), 73(8)(*b*), Sch 14 Pt IV, and FA (Northern Ireland) 1963 ss 5(4), 21, Sch 3 Pt II.

[2] Sub-s (5) repealed by FA 1999 Sch 20 Pt V(2) with effect in relation to instruments executed, or bearer instruments issued, from 1 October 1999, subject to the provisions in FA 1999 Sch 20 Pt V(2) Note 2. Previously the text read:

> "(5) An instrument whereby the rent reserved by any other instrument chargeable with duty and duly stamped as a lease or tack is increased is not to be charged with duty otherwise than as a lease or tack in consideration of the additional rent thereby made payable."

[3] "Lease" substituted for the words "lease or tack" by FA 1999 s 112(4), Sch 14 para 2 with effect in relation to instruments executed after 30 September 1999. This does not apply to transfers or other instruments relating to units under a unit trust scheme by virtue of FA 1999 s 122.

Marketable Securities . . .

83 Penalty on issuing, etc, foreign, etc, security not duly stamped

Every person who in the United Kingdom . . . [2] assigns, transfers, negotiates, . . . [2] any foreign security or [Commonwealth][1] government security not being duly stamped, shall incur [a penalty not exceeding £300][3].

Cross references—See FA 1990 ss 109(1), 111(1) (this section not to apply from an appointed day).

Note—This section was to be repealed by FA 1990 Sch 19 Pt VI with effect from an appointed day in accordance with FA 1990 ss 107–111. The Treasury order specifying the appointed day for the purposes of FA 1990 ss 107–110 was to coincide with the start of paperless trading under the Stock Exchange's planned TAURUS system (IR press release, 20-3-90). However, on 11-3-93 the London Stock Exchange News Release 6/93 announced that TAURUS had been abandoned.

Amendments—[1] Word substituted by FA 1963 s 62(4), and FA (Northern Ireland) 1963 s 11(3).

[2] Words repealed by FA 1973 s 59(7), Sch 22 Pt V.

[3] Words substituted by FA 1999 s 114, Sch 17 para 3 with effect in relation to penalties in respect of things done or omitted after 30 September 1999.

Stock Certificates to Bearer

109 Penalty for issuing stock certificate unstamped

(1) Where the holder of a stock certificate to bearer has been entered on the register of the local authority as the owner of the share of stock described in the certificate, the certificate shall be forthwith cancelled so as to be incapable of being re-issued to any person.

(2) . . . [1]

Cross references—See FA 1899 s 5(2) (application of this section to any instrument chargeable with stamp duty as a stock certificate to bearer, and as if "company or body of persons" were mentioned as well as "local authority");

FA 1990 ss 109(2)(*a*), 111(1) (this section not to apply from an appointed day).

Note—Sub-s (1) was to be repealed by FA 1990 Sch 19 Pt VI with effect from an appointed day in accordance with FA 1990 ss 107–111. The Treasury order specifying the appointed day for the purposes of FA 1990 ss 107–110 was to coincide with the start of paperless trading under the Stock Exchange's planned TAURUS system (IR press release, 20-3-90). However, on 11-3-93 the London Stock Exchange News Release 6/93 announced that TAURUS had been abandoned.

Amendments—[1] Sub-s (2) repealed by FA 1963 s 73(8)(*b*), Sch 14 Pt IV, and FA (Northern Ireland) 1963 s 21, Sch 3 Pt II.

Warrants for Goods

111 Provisions as to warrants for goods

(1) For the purposes of this Act the expression "warrant for goods" means any document or writing, being evidence of the title of any person therein named, or his assigns, or the holder thereof, to the property in any goods, wares, or merchandise lying in any warehouse or dock, or upon any wharf, and signed or certified by or on behalf of the person having the custody of the goods, wares, or merchandise.

(2), (3) . . . [1, 2]

Amendments—[1] Sub-ss (2), (3) repealed by FA 1949 s 52(10), Sch 11 Pt V, and FA (Northern Ireland) 1949 s 16, Sch 4 Pt II.
[2] This section repealed by the Statute Law (Repeals) Act 2008 s 1, Sch 1 Part 8 with effect from 21 July 2008.

PART III
SUPPLEMENTAL

Miscellaneous

117 Conditions and agreements as to stamp duty void

Every condition of sale framed with the view of precluding objection or requisition upon the ground of absence or insufficiency of stamp upon any instrument executed after the sixteenth day of May one thousand eight hundred and eighty-eight, and every contract, arrangement, or undertaking for assuming the liability on account of absence or insufficiency of stamp upon any such instrument or indemnifying against such liability, absence, or insufficiency, shall be void.

119 Instruments relating to Crown property

Except where express provision to the contrary is made by this or any other Act, an instrument relating to property belonging to the Crown, or being the private property of the sovereign, is to be charged with the same duty as an instrument of the same kind relating to property belonging to a subject.

121 Recovery of penalties

Cross references—See FA 1986 ss 68(6), 71(6) (extension of this section to fines imposed for failure to inform the Commissioners of certain facts in relation to depository receipts and clearance services).

Note—The functions of the Lord Advocate are hereby transferred to the Advocate General for Scotland by virtue of the Transfer of Functions (Lord Advocate and Advocate General for Scotland) Order, SI 1999/679.

Amendments—This section repealed by FA 1999 Sch 20 Pt V(3) with effect in relation to things done or omitted from 1 October 1999.

122 Definitions

(1) In this Act, unless the context otherwise requires,—

The expression "Commissioners" means Commissioners of Inland Revenue:

The expression "material" includes every sort of material upon which words or figures can be expressed:

The expression "instrument" includes every written document:

The expression "stamp" means as well a stamp impressed by means of a die as an adhesive stamp:

The expression "stamped", with reference to instruments and material, applies as well to instruments and material impressed with stamps by means of a die as to instruments and material having adhesive stamps affixed thereto:

The expressions "executed" and "execution", with reference to instruments not under seal, mean signed and signature [(but subject to subsection (1A) of this section)][3]:

The expression "money" includes all sums expressed in British or in any foreign or colonial currency:

The expression "stock" includes any share in any stocks or funds transferable [by the Registrar of Government Stock][6] . . . [5], [any strip (within the meaning of section 47 of the Finance Act 1942) of any such stocks or funds,][4] . . . [1], and any share in the stocks or funds of any foreign or colonial state or government, or in the capital stock or funded debt of any county council, corporation, company, or society in the United Kingdom, or of any foreign or colonial corporation, company, or society:

The expression "marketable security" means a security of such a description as to be capable of being sold in any stock market in the United Kingdom:

The expression "steward" of a manor includes deputy steward.[7]

[The expression "tribunal" means the First-tier Tribunal or, where determined by or under Tribunal Procedure Rules, the Upper Tribunal][8]

[(1A) For the purposes of this Act a deed (or, in Scotland, a deed for which delivery is required) shall be treated as executed when it is delivered or, if it is delivered subject to conditions, when the conditions are fulfilled.][2]

(2) In the application of this Act to Scotland expressions referring to the High Court shall be construed as referring to the Court of Session sitting as the Court of Exchequer.

Cross references—See FA 1946 s 54(1) ("stock" includes units under a unit trust scheme);

FA 1986 s 81(2) (transactions transferring stock carried out by a market maker in the ordinary course of his business; modification of the definition of "stamp" in sub-s (1) above in respect of stamp denoting exemption from stamp duty).

Amendments—[1] Words in the definition "stock" repealed by the Statute Law (Repeals) Act 1993 s 1(1), Sch 1 Pt IX.
[2] Sub-s (1A) inserted by FA 1994 s 239(1), (3) in relation to any instrument except one which, on or before 7 December 1993, has been executed for the purposes of this Act as it has effect before this amendment.
[3] Words in the definition of "executed" and "execution" in sub-s (1) added by FA 1994 s 239(1), (3) in relation to any instrument except one which, on or before 7 December 1993, has been executed for the purposes of this Act as it has effect before this amendment.
[4] Words in the definition "stock" inserted by FA 1996 Sch 40 para 1.

5 Words in the definition of "stock" repealed by the Irish Registers of Government Stock (Closure and Transfer) Order, SI 2002/2521 art 10(2), Sch 2, Pt I with effect from 28 October 2002.

6 Words in the definition of "stock" substituted by Government Stock (Consequential and Transitional Provision) (No 2) Order, SI 2004/1662, art 1, Schedule para 6 with effect from 1 July 2004.

7 Words repealed by the Statute Law (Repeals) Act 2008 s 1, Sch 1 Pt 8 with effect from 21 July 2008.

8 Definition of the expression "tribunal" inserted by the Transfer of Tribunal Functions and Revenue and Customs Appeals Order, SI 2009/56 art 3, Sch 1 paras 1, 4 with effect from 1 April 2009.

Repeal; Commencement; Short title

124 Commencement

This Act shall come into operation on the first day of January one thousand eight hundred and ninety-two.

125 Short title

This Act may be cited as the Stamp Act, 1891.

SCHEDULES

FIRST SCHEDULE

STAMP DUTIES ON INSTRUMENTS

Section 1

Statement of Practice SP 11/91—Interaction of stamp duty and VAT: stamp duty to be calculated on the VAT-inclusive consideration.

Simon's Tax Cases—*Marx v Estates and General Investments Ltd* [1975] STC 671; *Coventry City Council v IRC* [1978] STC 151; *Cummins Engine Co Ltd v IRC* [1981] STC 604; *L M Tenancies 1 plc v IRC* [1998] STC 326.

Notes—This schedule repealed by FA 1999 Sch 20 Pt V(2) with effect in relation to instruments executed, or bearer instruments issued, from 1 October 1999, subject to the provisions in FA 1999 Sch 20 Pt V(2)

For instruments executed, or bearer instruments issued before 1 October 1999, see the text below.

Any reference (express or implied) in any enactment, instrument or other document to any of the headings in Schedule 1 to the Stamp Act 1891 (other than the heading "Bearer Instrument") shall be construed, so far as is required for continuing its effect, as being or, as the case may require, including a reference to the corresponding provision of FA 1999 Sch 13.

Any reference (express or implied) in any enactment, instrument or other document to the heading "Bearer Instrument" in Schedule 1 to the Stamp Act 1891 shall be construed, so far as is required for continuing its effect, as being or, as the case may require, including a reference to FA 1999 Sch 15.

AGREEMENT for a lease or tack, or for any letting.

See Lease or Tack, and section 75.

AGREEMENT for sale of property.

See Conveyance on Sale, and section 59.

ANNUITY, conveyance in consideration of:

See Conveyance on Sale, and section 56.

purchase of:

See Conveyance on Sale, and section 60.

instruments relating to, upon any other occasion:

See Bond, Covenant, etc.

ASSIGNMENT or ASSIGNATION.

Upon a sale, or otherwise.

See Conveyance.

[BEARER INSTRUMENT

(1) Inland bearer instrument (other than deposit certificate for overseas stock).	*Duty of an amount equal to three times the transfer duty.*
(2) Overseas bearer instrument (other than deposit certificate for overseas stock or bearer instrument by usage).	*Duty of an amount equal to three times the transfer duty.*
(3) Instrument excepted from paragraph (1) or (2) of this heading.	*Duty of 10p for every £50 or part of £50] of the market value.*
(4) Inland or overseas bearer instrument given in substitution for a like instrument duly stamped ad valorem (whether under this heading or not).	*Duty of 10p.*

EXEMPTIONS

1. Instrument constituting, or used for transferring, stock which is exempt from all stamp duties on transfer by virtue of General Exemption (1) in this Schedule or of any other enactment.

2 . . .

3. Renounceable letter of allotment, letter of rights or other similar instrument where the rights under the letter or instrument are renounceable not later than six months after the issue of the letter or instrument.

BILL OF SALE—

Absolute. See Conveyance on Sale.

And see section 41.

BOND in relation to any annuity upon the original creation and sale thereof.

See Conveyance on Sale, and section 60.

BOND, COVENANT, or INSTRUMENT of any kind whatsoever:

(1) Being the only or principal or primary security for any annuity (except upon the original creation thereof by way of sale or security, and except a superannuation annuity), or for any sum or sums of money at stated periods, not being interest for any principal sum secured by a duly stamped instrument, nor rent reserved by a lease or tack:

For a definite and certain period, so that the total amount to be ultimately payable can be ascertained.	*The same* ad valorem *duty as a bond or covenant for such total amount.*
For the term of life or any other indefinite period: For every £5, and also for any fractional part of £5, of the annuity or sum periodically payable	*10p*

(2) Being a collateral or auxiliary or additional or substituted security for any of the above mentioned purposes where the principal or primary instrument is duly stamped:

Where the total amount to be ultimately payable can be ascertained	{ *The same* ad valorem *duty as a bond or covenant of the same kind for such total amount.*

In any other case:

For every £10 and also for any fractional part of £10 of the annuity or sum periodically payable	*5p*

(3) . . .

BOND given pursuant to the directions of any Act, or of the Commissioners or the Commissioners of Customs, or any of their officers, for or in respect of any of the duties of excise or customs, or for preventing frauds or evasions thereof, or for any other matter or thing relating thereto:

Note—Instruments under this heading are exempt from all stamp duties and the words and figures were repealed by FA 1949 ss 35, 52(10), Sch 8 Pt I, Sch 11 Pt V and FA (Northern Ireland) 1949 ss 8, 16, Sch 2 Pts I, II.

BOND on obtaining letters of administration in . . . Ireland, or a confirmation of testament in Scotland . . .

CONVEYANCE or TRANSFER on sale—

Of any property . . . :

. . . And see sections 54, 55, 56, 57, 58, 59, 60 and 61.

CONVEYANCE or TRANSFER of any kind not hereinbefore described *50p*

And see section 62.

COUNTERPART.

See duplicate.

COVENANT in relation to any annuity upon the original creation and sale thereof.

See Conveyance On Sale, and section 60.

COVENANT in relation to any annuity (except upon the original creation and sale thereof) or to other periodical payments.

See Bond, Covenant, & c.

DECLARATION of any use or trust of or concerning any property by any writing, not being a will, or an instrument chargeable with ad valorem duty as a unit trust instrument	*50p*

DISPOSITION of heritable property in Scotland to singular successors or purchasers.

See Conveyance On Sale.

DISPOSITION of heritable property in Scotland to a purchaser, containing a clause declaring all or any part of the purchase money a real burden upon, or affecting, the heritable property thereby disposed, or any part thereof.

See Conveyance On Sale . . .

DISPOSITION in Scotland, containing constitution of feu or ground annual right.

See Conveyance On Sale, and section 56.

DISPOSITION in Scotland of any property or of any right or interest therein not described in this schedule	*50p*

DUPLICATE or COUNTERPART of any instrument chargeable with any duty:

Where such duty does not amount to 50p	*The same duty as the original instrument.*
In any other case	*50p*

And see section 72.

FEU CONTRACT in Scotland.

See Conveyance On Sale, and section 56.

LEASE or TACK—

(1) . . .

(2) For any definite term less than a year:

(a) Of any furnished dwelling-house or apartments where the rent for such term exceeds £500	*£1*
(b) Of any lands, tenements, or heritable subjects except or otherwise than as aforesaid.	*The same duty as a lease for a year at the rent reserved for the definite term.*

(3) For any other definite term or for any indefinite term:

Of any lands, tenements, or heritable subjects—

Where the consideration, or any part of the consideration, moving either to the lessor or to any other person, consists of any money, stock, security or other property:	
In respect of such consideration	*The same duty as a conveyance on a sale for the same consideration.*
Where the consideration or any part of the consideration is any rent:	
In respect of such consideration:	
If the rent, whether reserved as a yearly rent or otherwise, is at a rate or average rate:	

	[If the term does not exceed 7 years or is indefinite	*If the term exceeds 7 years but does not exceed 35 years*	*If the term exceeds 35 years but does not exceed 100 years*	*If the term exceeds 100 years*
	£p	*£p*	*£p*	*£p*
Not exceeding £5 per annum.	*Nil*	*0.10*	*0.60*	*1.20*
Exceeding £5 and not exceeding £10.	*Nil*	*0.20*	*1.20*	*2.40*
Exceeding £10 and not exceeding £15.	*Nil*	*0.30*	*1.80*	*3.60*
Exceeding £15 and not exceeding £20.	*Nil*	*0.40*	*2.40*	*4.80*
Exceeding £20 and not exceeding £25.	*Nil*	*0.50*	*3.00*	*6.00*
Exceeding £25 and not exceeding £50.	*Nil*	*1.00*	*6.00*	*12.00*
Exceeding £50 and not exceeding £75.	*Nil*	*1.50*	*9.00*	*18.00*
Exceeding £75 and not exceeding £100.	*Nil*	*2.00*	*12.00*	*24.00*
Exceeding £100 and not exceeding £150.	*Nil*	*3.00*	*18.00*	*36.00*
Exceeding £150 and not exceeding £200.	*Nil*	*4.00*	*24.00*	*48.00*
Exceeding £200 and not exceeding £250.	*Nil*	*5.00*	*30.00*	*60.00*
Exceeding £250 and not exceeding £300.	*Nil*	*6.00*	*36.00*	*72.00*
Exceeding £300 and not exceeding £350.	*Nil*	*7.00*	*42.00*	*84.00*
Exceeding £350 and not exceeding £400.	*Nil*	*8.00*	*48.00*	*96.00*
Exceeding £400 and not exceeding £450.	*Nil*	*9.00*	*54.00*	*108.00*
Exceeding £450 and not exceeding £500.	*Nil*	*10.00*	*60.00*	*120.00*
Exceeding £500: for any full sum of £50 and also for any fractional part thereof.	*0.50*	*1.00*	*6.00*	*12.00]*

(4) Of any other kind whatsoever not hereinbefore described *2.00*

And see sections 75, . . . 77 . . .

MORTGAGE, BOND, DEBENTURE, COVENANT (except a marketable security otherwise specially charged with duty), and WARRANT OF ATTORNEY to confess and enter up judgment.

(1) Being the only or principal or primary security (other than an equitable mortgage) for the payment or repayment of money—

Not exceeding £300	*5p for every £50 or part of £50 of the amount secured.*
Exceeding £300	*10p for every £100 or part of £100 of the amount secured*

(2) Being a collateral, or auxiliary, or additional, or substituted security (other than an equitable mortgage), or by way of further assurance for the above-mentioned purpose where principal or primary security is duly stamped:

For every £200 and also for any fractional part of £200 of the amount secured — *5p*

(3) Being an equitable mortgage:

For every £100, and any fractional part of £100, of the amount secured — *5p*

(4) Transfer Assignment, Disposition or Assignation of any mortgage, bond, debenture, or covenant (except a marketable security), or of any money or stock secured by any such instrument, or by any warrant of attorney to enter up judgment, or by any judgment within the meaning of the Judgments Enforcement (Northern Ireland) Order 1981:

For every £200 and also for any fractional part of £200, of the amount transferred, assigned, or disposed, exclusive of interest which is not in arrear — *5p*

And also where any further money is added to the money already secured — *The same duty as a principal security for such further money.*

(5) Reconveyance, Release, Discharge, Surrender, Resurrender, Warrant To Vacate, or Renunciation [in whole or in part] of any such security as aforesaid, or of the money thereby secured:

For every £200 and also for any fractional part of £200 of the total amount or value of the money at any time secured — *5p*

Note—FA 1971 s 64 abolished stamp duties under this heading.

PARTITION or DIVISION—Instruments effecting:

In the case specified in section 73, see that section.

In any other case — *50p*

RELEASE or RENUNCIATION of any property, or of any right or interest in any property—

Upon a sale.

See Conveyance On Sale.

. . .

In any other case — *50p*

RENUNCIATION.

See . . . Release.

SUPERANNUATION ANNUITY.

See Bond, Covenant, &c.

SURRENDER—

. . .

Of any . . . kind whatsoever not chargeable with duty as a conveyance on sale . . . — *50p*

TACK of lands, &c, in Scotland.

See Lease Or Tack.

TRANSFER.

See Conveyance Or Transfer.

General exemptions from all stamp duties

(1) Transfer of shares in the Government or Parliamentary stocks or funds or strips (within the meaning of section 47 of the Finance Act 1942) of such stocks or funds.

(2) Instruments for the sale, transfer, or other disposition either absolutely . . . or otherwise, of any ship or vessel, or any part, interest, share, or property of or in any ship or vessel.

(3) . . .

(4) Testaments, testamentary instruments, and disposition mortis causa in Scotland.

(5) . . .

(6) Instruments made by, to, or with the Commissioners of Works for any of the purposes of the Act 15 & 16 Vict., c 28.

Act 15 & 16 Vict c 28—ie Commissioners of Works Act 1852.

Notes—This schedule repealed by FA 1999 Sch 20 Pt V(2) with effect in relation to instruments executed, or bearer instruments issued, from 1 October 1999, subject to the provisions in FA 1999 Sch 20 Pt V(2)

For instruments executed, or bearer instruments issued before 1 October 1999, see the text above.

The word "transfer" substituted for the words "conveyance or transfer" in enactments relating to stamp duty: FA 2003 Sch 20 para 3.

FINANCE ACT 1895

(58 & 59 Vict. Chapter 16)

PART II

STAMPS

12 Collection of stamp duty in cases of property vested by Act or purchased under statutory power

Where after the passing of this Act, by virtue of any Act, whether passed before or after this Act, either—

(*a*) any [stock or marketable securities are][1] vested by way of sale in any person; or

(*b*) any person is authorised to purchase [stock or marketable securities][1];

such person shall within three months after the passing of the Act, or the date of vesting, whichever is later, or after the completion of the purchase, as the case may be, produce to the Commissioners of Inland Revenue a copy of the Act printed by the Queen's printer of Acts of Parliament or some instrument relating to the vesting in the first case, and an instrument of [transfer][1] of the property in the other case, duly stamped with the ad valorem duty payable upon a [transfer][1] on sale of the property; and in default of such production, the duty with interest thereon at the rate of five per cent. per annum from the passing of the Act, date of vesting, or completion of the purchase, as the case may be, shall be a debt to Her Majesty from such person.

Cross references—See FA 1991 s 114 (modification of FA 1949 s 36 where the Act mentioned in this section and by virtue of which property is vested or a person is authorised to purchase property is passed on or after an appointed day).

FA 2000 Sch 34 para 5 (where property consists wholly of intellectual property no instrument of conveyance need be produced to the Commissioners under this section).

FA 2003 s 125(2) (this section does not apply to property other than stock or marketable securities).

Amendments—[1] Words substituted by FA 2003 s 125(4), Sch 20 para 4 with effect—

(a) in relation to instruments effecting land transactions that—

(i) are SDLT transactions within the meaning of FA 2003 Sch 19 or

(ii) would be such transactions but for an exemption or relief from stamp duty land tax;

(b) in relation to other instruments, if they are executed on or after the implementation date for the purposes of stamp duty land tax.

The implementation date is 1 December 2003 (by virtue of SI 2003/2899).

FA 2003 s 125 and Sch 20 have effect subject to FA 2003 Sch 15 para 13(2), (3).

FINANCE ACT 1898

(61 & 62 Vict. Chapter 10)

PART II

STAMPS

6 Removal of doubt as to 54 & 55 Vict c 39, ss 54, 57, so far as regards foreclosure decrees

For the removal of doubts with reference to the effect of sections fifty-four and fifty-seven of the Stamp Act 1891, it is hereby declared that the definition of "conveyance on sale" in the said section fifty-four includes a decree or order for, or having the effect of an order for, foreclosure. Provided that—

(*a*) the *ad valorem* stamp duty upon any such decree or order shall not exceed the duty on a sum equal to the value of the property to which the decree or order relates, and where the decree or order states the value that statement shall be conclusive for the purpose of determining the amount of the duty; and

(*b*) where *ad valorem* stamp duty is paid upon such decree or order, any conveyance following upon such decree or order shall be exempt from the *ad valorem* stamp duty.

REVENUE ACT 1898

(61 & 62 Vict. Chapter 46)

PART II

STAMPS

7 Amendments of 54 & 55 Vict c 39

(1) . . . [2]

(2) Any document referring to any Act or enactment repealed by the Stamp Act 1891, shall unless the context otherwise requires be construed to refer to that Act or the corresponding enactment in that Act.

(3) . . . [1]

(4) The expression "instrument" in section nine of the Stamp Act 1891, includes any postal packet within the meaning of the [Postal Services Act 2000][4], and subsection two of the said section is hereby repealed.

(5) . . . [3]

(6) Section twenty-four of the Stamp Duties Management Act 1891, is hereby declared to apply to affidavits and oaths as well as to statutory declarations.

Amendments—[1] Sub-s (3) repealed by the Statute Law Revision Act 1908.

[2] Sub-s (1) repealed by F(1909–10)A 1910, s 96, Sch 6.

[3] Sub-s (5) repealed by FA 1999 Sch 20 Pt V(3) with effect in relation to things done or omitted from 1 October 1999.

[4] Words in sub-s (4) substituted by the Postal Services Act 2000 (Consequential Modifications No 1) Order, SI 2001/1149 art 3(1), Sch 1 para 6 with effect from 26 March 2001.

10 Amendment of 54 & 55 Vict c 38, s 22

(1) Whenever the Commissioners of Inland Revenue give public notice in the London, Edinburgh, Belfast and Dublin Gazettes that the use of any die, as defined by the Stamp Duties Management Act 1891, has been discontinued, then, whether a new die has been provided or not, from and after any day to be stated in the notice (that day not being within one month after the notice is so published), that die shall not be a lawful die for denoting the payment of duty, and every instrument first executed by any person, or bearing date, after the day stated in the notice, and stamped with duty denoted by the discontinued die, shall be deemed to be not duly stamped.

(2) The provisos to section twenty-two of the Stamp Duties Management Act 1891, shall apply, subject to the necessary modifications, where a notice is published under this section in the same manner as they apply where a notice is published under that section.

(3) . . . [1]

Amendments—[1] Sub-s (3) repealed by the Post Office Act 1969 s 141, Sch 11 Pt II.

12 Extension of certain sections of 54 & 55 Vict c 38, to paper used for excise licences

Sections fourteen, fifteen, and sixteen of the Stamp Duties Management Act 1891 (which relate to frauds in connection with the manufacture of paper), shall extend to paper used for excise licences, in like manner as if it were paper provided by the Commissioners of Inland Revenue for receiving the impression of a die.

FINANCE ACT 1899

(62 & 63 Vict. Chapter 9)

PART II

STAMPS

5 Extension of stamp duty on share warrants and stock certificates to bearer

(1) . . . [1]

(2) . . . [2] section one hundred and nine of the Stamp Act 1891 (which relates to the penalty for issuing stock certificates unstamped), shall apply to any instrument chargeable with stamp duty . . . [2] as a stock certificate to bearer in the same manner as it applies to the stock certificates to bearer named in that section, and as if "company or body of persons" were mentioned in subsection one of that section as well as "local authority".

Cross references—See FA 1990 ss 109(2)(*b*), 111(1) (sub-s (2) not to apply with effect from an appointed day).

Note—Sub-s (2) was to be repealed by FA 1990 Sch 19 Pt VI with effect from an appointed day in accordance with FA 1990 ss 107–111. The Treasury order specifying the appointed day for the purposes of FA 1990 ss 107–110 was to coincide with the start of paperless trading under the Stock Exchange's planned TAURUS system (IR press release, 20-3-90). However, on 11-3-93 the London Stock Exchange News Release 6/93 announced that TAURUS had been abandoned.

Amendments—[1] Sub-s (1) repealed by FA 1963 ss 59(1), (3), 73(8)(*b*), Sch 14 Pt IV, and FA (Northern Ireland) 1963 ss 8(1), 21, Sch 3 Pt II.

[2] Words in sub-s (2), in both places, repealed by FA 1963 ss 59(1), (3), 73(8)(*b*), Sch 14 Pt IV, and FA (Northern Ireland) 1963 s 21, Sch 3 Pt II.

14 Construction of Part of Act

This Part of this Act shall be construed together with the Stamp Act 1891.

FINANCE ACT 1900

(63 & 64 Vict. Chapter 7)

PART II

STAMPS

10 Conveyances on sale

A conveyance on sale made for any consideration in respect whereof it is chargeable with *ad valorem* duty, and in further consideration of a covenant by the purchaser to make, or of his having previously made, any substantial improvement of or addition to the property conveyed to him, or of any covenant relating to the subject matter of the conveyance, is not chargeable, and shall be deemed not to have been chargeable, with any duty in respect of such further consideration.

FINANCE ACT 1902

(2 Edw. 7 Chapter 7)

PART II

STAMPS

9 Amendment of 54 & 55 Vict c 39, s 62

Amendments—This section repealed by FA 1999 Sch 20 Pt V(2) with effect in relation to instruments executed, or bearer instruments issued, from 1 October 1999, subject to the provisions in FA 1999 Sch 20 Pt V(2) Note 2. Previously the text read:

> "The provision of section sixty-two of the Stamp Act 1891, limiting to [50p] the duty on conveyances or transfers made for effectuating the appointment of a new trustee, shall apply to any conveyance or transfer for effectuating the retirement of a trustee, although no new trustee is appointed."

This Act repealed in full by the Statute Law (Repeals) Act 2008 s 1, Sch 1 Pt 8 with effect from 21 July 2008.

REVENUE ACT 1903

(3 Edw. 7 Chapter 46)

PART II

STAMPS

7 Reduction of stamp duty in the case of substituted securities

Amendments—This section repealed by FA 1999 Sch 20 Pt V(2) with effect in relation to instruments executed, or bearer instruments issued, from 1 October 1999, subject to the provisions in FA 1999 Sch 20 Pt V(2) Note 2. Previously the text read:

> "The whole amount of duty payable under or by reference to paragraph two of the heading "Mortgage, Bond, Debenture, Covenant, and Warrant of Attorney", in the First Schedule to the Stamp Act 1891, on any instrument being a collateral or auxiliary or additional or substituted security, or by way of further assurance, shall not exceed [50p]."

FINANCE ACT 1907

(7 Edw. 7 Chapter 13)

PART II

STAMPS

7 Stamping of hire-purchase agreement

Any agreement for or relating to the supply of goods on hire, whereby the goods in consideration of periodical payments will or may become the property of the person to whom they are supplied [shall not be charged with any stamp duty][1].

Amendments—[1] Words substituted by FA 1985 s 85(2), (3) in respect of instruments executed after 25 March 1985 and instruments executed after 18 March 1985 which are not stamped before 26 March 1985.

PART VII

GENERAL

30 Construction, and short title

(1) . . . [1]

(2) . . . [2]

Part II of this Act shall be construed together with the Stamp Act 1891.

. . . [2]

(3) This Act may be cited as the Finance Act 1907.

Amendments—[1] Sub-s (1) repealed by the Statute Law Revision Act 1927.

[2] Words in sub-s (2) repealed by the Statute Law Revision Act 1927, the Customs and Excise Act 1952 s 320, Sch 12 Pt I and FA 1975 ss 52(2), 59(5), Sch 13 Pt I.

REVENUE ACT 1909

(9 Edw. 7 Chapter 43)

PART II

STAMPS

8 Amendment of section 77 of the Stamp Act 1891

The provisions of subsection (2) of section seventy-seven of the Stamp Act 1891 (which exempt a lease from stamp duty in respect of certain further considerations) shall not apply as respects any further consideration in the lease consisting of a covenant which if it were contained in a separate deed would be chargeable with *ad valorem* stamp duty, and accordingly the lease shall in any such case be charged with duty in respect of any such further consideration under section four of the said Act.

PART III

MISCELLANEOUS

12 Construction, and short title

(1) . . . [2] Part II of this Act shall be construed together with the Stamp Act 1891, and the Acts amending that Act.

(2) . . . [1]

(3) This Act may be cited as the Revenue Act 1909.

Amendments—[1] Sub-s (2) repealed by the Statute Law Revision Act 1927.

[2] Words in sub-s (1) repealed by the Customs and Excise Act 1952 s 320, Sch 12 Pt I.

FINANCE ACT 1928

(18 & 19 Geo. 5 Chapter 17)

PART III

MISCELLANEOUS

30 Exemptions from income tax, estate duty and stamp duties in case of trust funds and gifts for reduction of National Debt

(1) . . . [1]

(2)–(3) . . . [2]

(4) Any instrument by which any property is transferred to trustees to be held upon trust in accordance with directions which are valid and effective under the said section nine or by which any property is conveyed by way of absolute gift to the National Debt Commissioners to be applied by them in reduction of the National Debt shall be exempt from stamp duty.

Amendments—[1] Sub-s (1) repealed by ICTA 1952 s 527, Sch 25 Pt I.

[2] Sub-ss (2), (3) repealed by FA 1975 ss 52(2), 59(5), Sch 13 Pt I.

35 Construction, short title, application and repeal

(1) . . . [3]

(2) . . . [2]

(3) Any reference in this Act to any enactment shall be construed as a reference to that enactment as amended by any subsequent enactment, including this Act.

(4) This Act may be cited as the Finance Act 1928.

(5) Such provisions of this Act as relate to matters with respect to which the Parliament of Northern Ireland has power to make laws shall not extend to Northern Ireland.

(6) . . . [1]

Amendments—[1] Sub-s (6) repealed by the Statute Law Revision Act 1950.

[2] Sub-s (2) repealed by the Statute Law Revision Act 1953.

[3] Sub-s (1) repealed by the Statute Law (Repeals) Act 1986.

FINANCE ACT 1930

(20 & 21 Geo. 5 Chapter 28)

PART IV

STAMPS

42 Relief from transfer stamp duty in case of transfer of property as between associated companies

(1) Stamp duty under [Part I of Schedule 13 to the Finance Act 1999 ([transfer][9] on sale)][6], shall not be chargeable on an instrument to which this section applies:

Provided that no such instrument shall be deemed to be duly stamped unless either it is stamped with the duty to which it would but for this section be liable, or it has in accordance with the provisions of section twelve of the said Act been stamped with a particular stamp denoting either that it is not chargeable with any duty or that it is duly stamped.

[(2) This section applies to any instrument as respects which it is shown to the satisfaction of the Commissioners [that—

(*a*) the effect of the instrument is to convey or transfer a beneficial interest in property from one body corporate [("the transferor") to another ("the transferee")][8], and

(*b*) the bodies in question are associated at the time the instrument is executed][2]][1]

[unless at the time the instrument is executed arrangements are in existence by virtue of which at that or some later time any person has or could obtain, or any persons together have or could obtain, control of the transferee but not of the transferor.][7]

[(2A) For the purposes of this section bodies corporate are associated at a particular time if at that time one is the parent of the other or another body corporate is the parent of each.][2]

[(2B) For the purposes of this section one body corporate is the parent of another at a particular time if at that time the first body—

[(*a*)] [7] is beneficial owner of not less than 75 per cent of the ordinary share capital of the second body][3];

[(*b*) is beneficially entitled to not less than 75 per cent of any profits available for distribution to equity holders of the second body; and

(*c*) would be beneficially entitled to not less than 75 per cent of any assets of the second body available for distribution to its equity holders on a winding-up.][7]

[(3) The ownership referred to in [paragraph (*a*) of][7] subsection [(2B)][4] is ownership either directly or through another body corporate or other bodies corporate, or partly directly and partly through another body corporate or other bodies corporate, and Part I of Schedule 4 to the Finance Act 1938 (determination of amount of capital held through other bodies corporate) shall apply for the purposes of [that paragraph][8] . . . [4]][1]

[(4) In this section "ordinary share capital", in relation to a body corporate, means all the issued share capital (by whatever name called) of the body corporate, other than capital the holders of which have a right to a dividend at a fixed rate but have no other right to share in the profits of the body corporate.][5]

[(5) [Chapter 6 of Part 5 of the Corporation Tax Act 2010][10] shall apply for the purposes of paragraphs (*b*) and (*c*) of subsection (2B) as it applies for the purposes of [section 151(4)(*a*) and (*b*)][10] of that Act; but this is subject to subsection (6).

(6) In determining for the purposes of this section whether a body corporate is the parent of the transferor, [sections 171(1)(*b*) and (3), 173, 174 and 176 to 178 of the Corporation Tax Act 2010][10] shall not apply for the purposes of paragraph (*b*) or (*c*) of subsection (2B).

(7) In this section, "control" shall be construed in accordance with [section 1124 of the Corporation Tax Act 2010][10].][7]

Cross references—See FA 1967 s 27(3) (this section shall not apply to any instrument executed on or after 1 August 1967 unless it is shown to the satisfaction of the Commissioners that the instrument was not executed in pursuance of or in connection with an arrangement specified under that section).

See Stamp Duty and Stamp Duty Reserve Tax (Open-ended Investment Companies) Regulations, SI 1997/1156 reg 11 (disapplication of s 42 as regards any beneficial interest in property transferred to or from an open-ended investment company).

Statement of Practice SP 3/98—Stamp duty—group relief.

Amendments—[1] Sub-ss (2), (3) substituted by FA 1967 s 27(2).

[2] Words in sub-s (2) substituted by FA 1995 s 149(2), (7), in relation to instruments executed after 30 April 1995.

[3] Sub-ss (2A), (2B) inserted by FA 1995 s 149(3), (7) in relation to instruments executed after 30 April 1995.

[4] Word in sub-s (3) substituted and words omitted repealed by FA 1995 s 149(4), (7), Sch 29, Pt X, in relation to instruments executed after 30 April 1995.

[5] Sub-s (4) inserted by FA 1995 s 149(5), (7) in relation to instruments executed after 30 April 1995.

[6] Words in sub-s (1) substituted by FA 1999 s 112(4), Sch 14 para 3 with effect in relation to instruments executed after 30 September 1999. This does not apply to transfers or other instruments relating to units under a unit trust scheme by virtue of FA 1999 s 122. Previously the text read "the heading 'Conveyance or Transfer on Sale' in the First Schedule to the Stamp Act 1891".

[7] Words in sub-s (2) after para (*b*), in sub-s (2B) reference to "(*a*)" and whole of paras (*b*), (*c*), and words in sub-s (3) inserted, and sub-ss (5), (6), (7) inserted by FA 2000 s 123(3), (4), (5)(*a*), (6), with effect for instruments executed after 27 July 2000.

[8] Words in sub-s (2) substituted for "to another", words in sub-s (3) substituted for "this section" by FA 2000 s 123(2), (5)(*b*), with effect for instruments executed after 28 July 2000.

[9] The word "transfer" substituted for the words "conveyance or transfer" in enactments relating to stamp duty by FA 2003 Sch 20 para 3.

[10] In sub-s (5) words substituted for words "Schedule 18 to the Income and Corporation Taxes Act 1988" and "paragraphs (*a*) and (*b*) of section 413(7)", in sub-s (6) words substituted for words "paragraphs 5(3) and 5B to 5E of Schedule 18 to the Income and Corporation Taxes Act 1988", in sub-s (7) words substituted for words "section 840 of the Income and Corporation Taxes Act 1988", by CTA 2010 s 1177, Sch 1 para 150. CTA 2010 has effect for corporation tax purposes for accounting periods ending on or after 1 April 2010, and for income and capital gains tax purposes for the tax year 2010–11 and subsequent tax years.

PART VI

MISCELLANEOUS AND GENERAL

53 Construction, short title, application and repeal

(1) . . . [3]

(2) . . . [2]

(3) . . . [4]

(4) Part IV of this Act shall be construed as one with the Stamp Act 1891.

(5) Any reference in this Act to any enactment shall be construed as a reference to that enactment as amended by any subsequent enactment, including this Act.

(6) This Act may be cited as the Finance Act 1930.

(7) Such of the provisions of this Act as relate to matters with respect to which the Parliament of Northern Ireland has power to make laws shall not extend to Northern Ireland.

(8) . . . [1]

Amendments—[1] Sub-s (8) repealed by the Statute Law Revision Act 1950.

[2] Sub-s (2) repealed by the Statute Law Revision Act 1953.

[3] Sub-s (1) repealed by FA 1964 s 26(7), Sch 9.

[4] Sub-s (3) repealed by FA 1975 ss 52(2), 59(5), Sch 13 Pt I.

FINANCE ACT 1931

(21 & 22 Geo. 5 Chapter 28)

PART III

LAND VALUE TAX

28 Production to Commissioners of instruments transferring land

(1) On the occasion of—

(*a*) any transfer on sale of the fee simple of land;

(*b*) the grant of any lease of land for a term of seven or more years;

(*c*) any transfer on sale of any such lease;

it shall be the duty of the transferee, lessee, or proposed lessee to produce to the Commissioners the instrument by means of which the transfer is effected, or the lease granted or agreed to be granted, as the case may be, and to comply with the requirements of the Second Schedule to this Act, and if he fails so to produce any such instrument within thirty days after the execution thereof or, in the case of an instrument first executed at any place out of Great Britain after the instrument is first received in Great Britain, or fails to comply with the requirements of the said Schedule, he shall be liable on summary conviction to a fine not exceeding [level 3 on the standard scale][1]

(2) Where in accordance with the provisions of the last foregoing subsection any agreement for any lease of land for a term of seven or more years has been produced to the Commissioners, and the requirements of the said Second Schedule with respect thereto are complied with, it shall not be necessary under this section to produce to the Commissioners the instrument granting the lease in pursuance of the agreement or to comply with the requirements of the said Schedule with respect thereto, unless that instrument is inconsistent with the agreement, but the Commissioners shall, if any such instrument is produced to them and application is made for that purpose, denote on the instrument that the instrument has been so produced.

(3) This section shall not apply with respect to any instrument which relates[

(*a*)][4] solely to incorporeal hereditaments or to a grave or right of burial . . . [2][; or

(*b*) to an SDLT transaction within the meaning of paragraph 1(2) of Schedule 19 to the Finance Act 2003.][4]

(4) Notwithstanding anything in section twelve of the Stamp Act 1891, no instrument required by this section to be produced to the Commissioners shall be deemed, for the purposes of section fourteen of that Act, to be duly stamped unless it is stamped with a stamp denoting that the instrument has been so produced.

(5) This section shall come into operation on the first day of September, nineteen hundred and thirty-one.

[(6) . . .][3]

Press releases etc—IR Tax Bulletin August 1995 para 28 (an agreement for lease presented with the lease giving effect to it within 30 days of execution of the lease will satisfy the requirements of s 28 above).

Cross references—See FA 1985 s 89(1) (this section not to apply in relation to instruments prescribed by regulations made by statutory instruments).

Amendments—[1] Words substituted by virtue of the Criminal Justice Act 1982 ss 38, 46 (replacing previous increase in fine by Land Commission Act 1967 s 87(1), Sch 14, to £50).

[2] Words in sub-s (3) repealed by the Land Commission Act 1967 s 101, Sch 17.

[3] Sub-s (6) inserted by the Land Commission Act 1967 s 87(1), Sch 14, and repealed by the Statute Law (Repeals) Act 1998 Sch 1 Pt IV Group 2 with effect from 19 November 1998.

[4] Sub-s (3)(*a*) numbered as such, and sub-s (3)(*b*) inserted by the Stamp Duty Land Tax (Consequential Amendment of Enactments) Regulations, SI 2003/2867, reg 2, Schedule para 4 with effect from 1 December 2003.

34 Provisions as to expenses

Any expenses incurred by the Commissioners . . . [1] for the purposes of this Part of this Act . . . [1] shall be paid out of moneys provided by Parliament.

Amendments—[1] Words repealed by FA 1934 ss 27, 30, Sch 4.

44 Construction, short title, application and repeal

(1) . . . [3]

(2) . . . [2]

(3) Any reference in this Act to any enactment shall be construed as a reference to that enactment as amended by any subsequent enactment, including this Act.

(4) This Act may be cited as the Finance Act 1931.

(5) Such of the provisions of this Act as relate to matters with respect to which the Parliament of Northern Ireland has power to make laws shall not extend to Northern Ireland.

(6) . . . [1]

Amendments—[1] Sub-s (6) repealed by the Statute Law Revision Act 1950.

[2] Sub-s (2) repealed by the Statute Law Revision Act 1953.

[3] Sub-s (1) repealed by the Statute Law (Repeals) Act 1971.

SCHEDULES

[SCHEDULE 2

REQUIREMENTS IN CONNECTION WITH PRODUCTION OF INSTRUMENTS OF TRANSFER

1 Any person required by section 28 of this Act to produce any instrument to the Commissioners shall furnish to the Commissioners with the instrument a document (signed by the transferee or lessee or by some person on his behalf and showing his address) giving particulars—

(*a*) of the description of the instrument;

(*b*) of the date of the instrument;

(*c*) of the names and addresses of the transferor and transferee or lessor and lessee;

(*d*) of the situation of the land to which the transaction relates, including any dimensions stated in the instrument and, if necessary for the identification of the land, a description of the boundaries of the land, or a plan;

(*e*) of the estate or interest transferred, including, where the transaction is the assignment or grant of a lease or the transfer of a fee simple subject to a lease, the term of the lease, the date of the commencement of the term and the rent reserved;

(*f*) of the consideration, if any, other than the rent shown under sub-paragraph (*e*), showing separately any capital payment, any debt released, any debt covenanted to be paid or to which the transaction is made subject, any periodical payment (including any charge) covenanted to be paid, any terms surrendered, any land exchanged and any other thing representing money or money's worth comprised in the consideration for the transaction;

(*g*) of any minerals, mineral rights, sporting rights, timber or easements reserved, and of any restrictions, covenants or conditions affecting the value of the estate or interest transferred or granted; and

(*h*) of the information given to the transferee or lessee by any relevant authority when requested, in connection with the transaction, to state what entries (if any) relating to the land to which the transaction relates were shown in any relevant register.

2 In paragraph 1(*h*)—

(*a*) in relation to land in England or Wales—

"relevant authority" means a local planning authority within the meaning of the Town and Country Planning Act 1990, and

"relevant register" means a register kept by the authority under section 69(1) of that Act;

(*b*) in relation to land in Scotland—

"relevant authority" means a local authority within the meaning of the Town and Country Planning (Scotland) Act 1997, and

"relevant register" means a register kept by the authority under section 36(1) of that Act.][1]

Cross references—See FA 1985 s 89(2) (exemption from s 28 of this Act in relation to prescribed instruments; powers to obtain particulars mentioned in this Schedule in respect of such exempt instruments).

Amendments—[1] Sch 2 substituted by the Statute Law (Repeals) Act 1998 Sch 2 para 10 with effect from 19 November 1998.

FINANCE ACT 1938

(1 & 2 Geo. 6 Chapter 46)

PART V
NATIONAL DEFENCE CONTRIBUTION

42 Further provisions as to subsidiary companies

(1) For the purposes of this section and section twenty-two of the Finance Act 1937 (which provides for the amalgamation for the purposes of the national defence contribution of the profits or losses of bodies corporate with the profits or losses of their subsidiaries), a body corporate shall be deemed to be a subsidiary of another body corporate if and so long as not less than three-quarters of its ordinary share capital is owned by that other body corporate, whether directly or through another body corporate or other bodies corporate, or partly directly and partly through another body corporate or other bodies corporate.

(2) The amount of ordinary share capital of one body corporate owned by a second body corporate through another body corporate or other bodies corporate, or partly directly and partly through another body corporate or other bodies corporate, shall be determined in accordance with the provisions of Part I of the Fourth Schedule to this Act.

(3) In this section and Part I of the said Schedule references to ownership shall be construed as references to beneficial ownership, and the expression "ordinary share capital", in relation to a body corporate, means all the issued share capital (by whatever name called) of the body corporate, other than capital the holders whereof have a right to a dividend at a fixed rate or a rate fluctuating in accordance with the standard rate of income tax, but have no other right to share in the profits of the body corporate.

PART VII
MISCELLANEOUS AND GENERAL

55 Short title, construction, extent and repeals

(1) This Act may be cited as the Finance Act 1938.

(2) . . . [3]

(3) . . . [2]

(4) . . . [4]

(5) Any reference in this Act to any other enactment shall be construed as a reference to that enactment as amended by any subsequent enactment, (unless the context otherwise requires) this Act.

(6) Such of the provisions of this Act as relate to matters with respect to which the Parliament of Northern Ireland has power to make laws shall not extend to Northern Ireland.

(7) . . . [1]

Amendments—[1] Sub-s (7) repealed by the Statute Law Revision Act 1950.

[2] Sub-s (3) repealed by the Statute Law Revision Act 1953.

[3] Sub-s (2) repealed by F(No 2)A 1964 s 10(4), Sch 4.

[4] Sub-s (4) repealed by FA 1975 ss 52(2), 59(5), Sch 13 Pt I.

SCHEDULES

FOURTH SCHEDULE

PROVISIONS RELATING TO SUBSIDIARY COMPANIES FOR PURPOSE OF NATIONAL DEFENCE CONTRIBUTION

Section 42

PART I
PROVISIONS FOR DETERMINING AMOUNT OF CAPITAL HELD THROUGH OTHER BODIES CORPORATE

(1) Where, in the case of a number of bodies corporate, the first directly owns ordinary share capital of the second and the second directly owns ordinary share capital of the third, then, for the purposes of this Schedule, the first shall be deemed to own ordinary share capital of the third through the

second, and, if the third directly owns ordinary share capital of a fourth, the first shall be deemed to own ordinary share capital of the fourth through the second and third, and the second shall be deemed to own ordinary share capital of the fourth through the third, and so on.

(2) In this Part of this Schedule—

(*a*) any number of bodies corporate of which the first directly owns ordinary share capital of the next and the next directly owns ordinary share capital of the next but one and so on, and, if they are more than three, any three or more of them, are referred to as "a series";

(*b*) in any series—

(i) that body corporate which owns ordinary share capital of another through the remainder is referred to as "the first owner";

(ii) that other body corporate the ordinary share capital of which is so owned is referred to as "the last owned body corporate";

(iii) the remainder, if one only, is referred to as an "intermediary" and, if more than one, referred to as "a chain of intermediaries";

(*c*) a body corporate in a series which directly owns ordinary share capital of another body corporate in the series is referred to as an "owner";

(*d*) any two bodies corporate in a series of which one owns ordinary share capital of the other directly, and not through one or more of the other bodies corporate in the series, are referred to as being directly related to one another.

(3) Where every owner in a series owns the whole of the ordinary share capital of the body corporate to which it is directly related, the first owner shall be deemed to own through the intermediary or chain of intermediaries the whole of the ordinary share capital of the last owned body corporate.

(4) Where one of the owners in a series owns a fraction of the ordinary share capital of the body corporate to which it is directly related, and every other owner in the series owns the whole of the ordinary share capital of the body corporate to which it is directly related, the first owner shall be deemed to own that fraction of the ordinary share capital of the last owned body corporate through the intermediary or chain of intermediaries.

(5) Where—

(*a*) each of two or more of the owners in a series owns a fraction, and every other owner in the series owns the whole, of the ordinary share capital of the body corporate to which it is directly related; or

(*b*) every owner in a series owns a fraction of the ordinary share capital of the body corporate to which it is directly related;

the first owner shall be deemed to own through the intermediary or chain of intermediaries such fraction of the ordinary share capital of the last owned body corporate as results from the multiplication of those fractions.

(6) Where the first owner in any series owns a fraction of the ordinary share capital of the last owned body corporate in that series through the intermediary or chain of intermediaries in that series, and also owns another fraction or other fractions of the ordinary share capital of the last owned body corporate, either—

(*a*) directly; or

(*b*) through an intermediary or intermediaries which is not a member or are not members of that series; or

(*c*) through a chain or chains of intermediaries of which one or some or all are not members of that series; or

(*d*) in a case where the series consists of more than three bodies corporate, through an intermediary or intermediaries which is a member or are members of the series, or through a chain or chains of intermediaries consisting of some but not all of the bodies corporate of which the chain of intermediaries in the series consists;

then, for the purpose of ascertaining the amount of the ordinary share capital of the last owned body corporate owned by the first owner, all those fractions shall be aggregated and the first owner shall be deemed to own the sum of those fractions.

FINANCE ACT 1944

(7 & 8 Geo. 6 Chapter 23)

PART VII

MISCELLANEOUS

45 Exemption of certain assignments by seamen from stamp duty

Stamp duty shall not be charged, and shall be deemed never to have been chargeable, on any assignment rendered valid by Regulation forty-seven D of the Defence (General) Regulations 1939 (which relates to assignments of wages in payment of contributions to certain bodies representing the interests of or providing benefits for seamen).

49 Short title, construction, extent and repeals

(1) This Act may be cited as the Finance Act 1944.

(2) . . . [5]

(3) . . . [4]

(4) . . . [3]

(5) . . . [1]

(6) . . . [6]

(7) Any reference in this Act to any other enactment shall, except so far as the context otherwise requires, be constructed as a reference to that enactment as amended by or under any other enactment, including this Act.

(8) The provisions of the Fourth Schedule to this Act shall, if provision in that behalf is made by an Act of the Parliament of Northern Ireland, apply with any necessary modifications to death duties payable in Northern Ireland as they apply to death duties payable in England, but save as aforesaid such of the provisions of this Act as relate to matters with respect to which the Parliament of Northern Ireland has power to make laws shall not extend to Northern Ireland.

(9) . . . [2]

Amendments—[1] Sub-s (5) is spent (and *repealed* by the Statute Law (Repeals) Act 2008 s 1, Sch 1 Pt 8 with effect from 21 July 2008).

[2] Sub-s (9) repealed by the Statute Law Revision Act 1950.

[3] Sub-s (4) repealed by the Statute Law Revision Act 1953.

[4] Sub-s (3) repealed by the Purchase Tax Act 1963 s 41 (1), Sch 4 Pt I.

[5] Sub-s (2) repealed by the Statute Law (Repeals) Act 1971.

[6] Sub-s (6) repealed by FA 1975 ss 52(2), (3), 59(5), Sch 13 Pt I.

FINANCE ACT 1946

(9 & 10 Geo. 6 Chapter 64)

PART VII

STAMP DUTY

Cross references—See FA 1963 s 65 (references to a unit trust scheme shall be deemed not to include references to (*a*) any common investment scheme or common deposit scheme under the Charities Act 1960 ss 22, 22A, or under Charities Act 1993 ss 24, 25(*b*) any unit trust scheme the units in which are, under the trust instrument, required to be held only by bodies of persons established for charitable purposes only, or trustees of trusts so established);

FA 1981 s 110 (references in this Part to unit trust schemes not to include pooled pension funds of exempt occupational pension schemes);

Stamp Duty and Stamp Duty Reserve Tax (Definition of Unit Trust Scheme) Regulations, SI 1992/197 (exemption from stamp duty in relation to transfer of units of a scheme made under the Administration of Justice Act 1982 s 42(1)).

Stamp Duty and Stamp Duty Reserve Tax (Pension Funds Pooling Schemes) Regulations, SI 1996/1584 (exemption from stamp duty in relation to transfers of units of a pension fund pooling scheme).

52 Exemption from stamp duty of documents connected with nationalisation schemes

Where, by any Act passed after the beginning of the present Session which embodies any scheme for the carrying on of any industry or part of an industry, or of any undertaking, under national ownership or control, provision is made for the transfer of any property, as part of the initial putting into force of the scheme, to the Crown or to a body corporate constituted for the purposes of that scheme or any previous scheme for such national ownership or control as aforesaid—

(*a*) in considering whether any and if so what duty is payable under section twelve of the Finance Act 1895 (which requires Acts to be stamped as conveyances on sale in certain cases) the consideration for the transfer shall be left out of account;

(*b*) . . . [1]

(*c*) stamp duty shall not be payable on any conveyance, agreement or assignment made or instrument executed solely for the purpose of giving effect to the transfer.

Amendments—[1] Para (*b*) repealed by FA 1973 s 59(7), Sch 22 Pt V.

54 Units under unit trust schemes to be treated as stock

Amendments—This section repealed by FA 1999 s 139, Sch 20 Pt V(5) with effect in relation to instruments executed from 6 February 2000.

56 Supplemental provisions

Amendments—This section repealed by FA 1999 s 139, Sch 20 Pt V(5) with effect in relation to instruments executed from 6 February 2000

57 Interpretation of Part VII

Regulations—See the Stamp Duty and Stamp Duty Reserve Tax (Definitions of Unit Trust Scheme) Regulations, SI 1988/268; Stamp Duty and Stamp Duty Reserve Tax (Definition of Unit Trust Scheme) Regulations, SI 1992/197.

Cross references—See Stamp Duty and Stamp Duty Reserve Tax (Open-ended Investment Companies) Regulations, SI 1997/1156 reg 3 (sub-ss (1A) and (1B) above have effect in relation to open-ended investment companies as for unit trust schemes).

Amendments—This section repealed by FA 1999 s 139, Sch 20 Pt V(5) with effect in relation to instruments executed from 6 February 2000. The repeals of sub-ss (1A) and (1B) have effect subject to FA 1999 Sch 19 para 17(4). This section was replaced by FA 1999, Sch 19 para 17(3).

67 Short title, construction, extent and repeals

(1) This Act may be cited as the Finance Act 1946.

(2) . . . [5]

(3) . . . [4]

(4) . . . [3]

(5) . . . [1]

(6) . . . [6]

(7) Part VII of this Act shall be construed as one with the Stamp Act 1891.

(8) Any reference in this Act to any other enactment shall, except so far as the context otherwise requires, be construed as a reference to that enactment as amended by or under any other enactment, including this Act.

(9) Save as otherwise expressly provided, such of the provisions of this Act as relate to matters with respect to which the Parliament of Northern Ireland has power to make laws shall not extend to Northern Ireland.

(10), (11) . . . [2]

Amendments—[1] Sub-s (5) is spent.

[2] Sub-s (10), (11) repealed by the Statute Law Revision Act 1950.

[3] Sub-s (4) repealed by the Statute Law Revision Act 1953.

[4] Sub-s (3) repealed by the Purchase Tax Act 1963 s 41(1), Sch 4 Pt I.

[5] Sub-s (2) repealed by the Statute Law (Repeals) Act 1971.

[6] Sub-s (6) repealed by FA 1975 ss 52(2), 59(5), Sch 13 Pt I.

FINANCE ACT 1947

(10 & 11 Geo. 6 Chapter 35)

PART VI

STAMP DUTIES

57 Exemption of transfers of stock guaranteed by Treasury

(1) Where the payment of principal and interest on any stock to which this section applies is guaranteed by the Treasury, transfers of the stock shall be exempt from all stamp duties.

(2) This section applies to . . . [2]

. . . [1]

. . . [2]

. . . [1]

. . . [2] any . . . [2] stock to which it may be applied by direction of the Treasury, being stock issued by a body corporate constituted for the purposes of any scheme for the carrying on of any industry or part of an industry, or of any undertaking, under national ownership or control which may be embodied in any Act passed after the beginning of the present Session.

Notes—Transfers of the following stocks are exempt from stamp duty under this provision by reason of directions given by the Treasury:—

British Electricity 3 per cent Guaranteed Stock 1968–1973.

British Electricity 3 per cent Guaranteed Stock 1974–1977.

British Electricity 3 per cent Guaranteed Stock 1976–1979.

British Electricity 4 per cent Guaranteed Stock 1974–1979.

British Gas 3 per cent Guaranteed Stock 1990–1995.

British Gas 4 per cent Guaranteed Stock 1969–1972.

Various British Transport Stocks were also exempted by direction of the Treasury but these have been renamed by the Transport Act 1962 s 36 and now fall within General Exemption (1) Stamp Act 1891.

This section was to be repealed by FA 1990 Sch 19 Pt VI with effect from an appointed day in accordance with FA 1990 ss 107–111. The Treasury order specifying the appointed day for the purposes of FA 1990 ss 107–110 was to coincide with the start of paperless trading under the Stock Exchange's planned TAURUS system (IR press release, 20-3-90). However, on 11-3-93 the London Stock Exchange News Release 6/93 announced that TAURUS had been abandoned.

Amendments—[1] Words in sub-s (2) repealed by the Air Corporations Act 1949 s 41, Sch 3.

[2] Words in sub-s (2) repealed by the Electricity Act 1989 s 112(4), Sch 18.

PART VII

MISCELLANEOUS

74 Short title, construction, extent and repeals

(1) This Act may be cited as the Finance Act 1947.

(2) . . . [3]

(3) . . . [2]

(4), (5) . . . [1]

(6) . . . [4]

(7) Part VI of this Act shall be construed as one with the Stamp Act 1891.

(8) . . . [1]

(9) Any reference in this Act to any other enactment shall, except so far as the context otherwise requires, be construed as a reference to that enactment as amended by or under any other enactment, including this Act.

(10) Such of the provisions of this Act as relate to matters with respect to which the Parliament of Northern Ireland has power to make laws shall not extend to Northern Ireland.

(11) . . . [1]

Amendments—[1] Sub-ss (4), (5), (8), (11) are spent (and sub-s (8) *repealed* by the Statute Law (Repeals) Act 2008 s 1, Sch 1 Pt 8 with effect from 21 July 2008)).

[2] Sub-s (3) repealed by the Purchase Tax Act 1963 s 41(1), Sch 4 Pt I.

[3] Sub-s (2) repealed by FA 1964 s 26(7), Sch 9.

[4] Sub-s (6) repealed by FA 1975 ss 52(2), 59(5), Sch 13 Pt I.

FINANCE ACT 1949

(12, 13 & 14 Geo. 6 Chapter 47)

PART IV

STAMP DUTIES

35 Abolition of and exemptions from other duties

Amendments—This section repealed by FA 1999 Sch 20 Pt V(2) with effect in relation to instruments executed, or bearer instruments issued, from 1 October 1999, subject to the provisions in FA 1999 Sch 20 Pt V(2) Note 2. Previously the text read:

"(1) In relation to instruments made or executed on or after the date of the passing of this Act, the Stamp Act 1891, shall have effect as if it had been enacted

(*a*) without the headings or parts of headings in the First Schedule thereto which are mentioned in Part I of the Eighth Schedule to this Act (and are not so mentioned only in an exemption); but

(*b*) with the exemptions provided for by the said Part I.

(2) The composition mentioned in Part II of the said Eighth Schedule shall no longer be payable, and the duties so mentioned are abolished.

(3) . . .".

36 Amendments as to conveyances on sale

(1) . . . [1]

(2) . . . [1]

(3) . . . [1]

(4) Section twelve of the Finance Act 1895 (which relates to duty on property vested by Act or purchased under statutory powers), shall not require any person who is authorised after the coming into force of this section to purchase any property as mentioned in the said section twelve to include in the instrument of conveyance required by that section to be produced to the Commissioners any goods, wares or merchandise forming part of the property nor, if the property consists wholly of goods, wares or merchandise, to produce any instrument of conveyance thereof to the Commissioners.[2]

Cross references—See FA 1991 s 114 (modification of sub-s (4) above, with effect from an appointed day, where exempt property, as defined, is acquired under FA 1895, s 12).

Amendments—[1] Sub-ss (1), (2), (3) repealed by FA 1956 s 44(9), Sch 5 Pt II.

[2] Sub-s (4) is to be amended and sub-s (5) added by FA 1991, s 110(7) with effect from a day to be appointed, where exempt property, as defined, is acquired under FA 1895, s 12.

PART VII

MISCELLANEOUS

52 Short title, construction, extent and repeals

(1) This Act may be cited as the Finance Act 1949.

(2) . . . [1]

(3) . . . [2]
(4) . . . [3]
(5) Part IV of this Act shall be construed as one with the Stamp Act 1891.
(6) . . . [4]
(7) . . . [1]
(8) Any reference in this Act to any other enactment shall, except so far as the context otherwise requires, be construed as a reference to that enactment as amended by or under any other enactment, including this Act.
(9) Save as otherwise expressly provided, such of the provisions of this Act as relate to matters with respect to which the Parliament of Northern Ireland has power to make laws shall not extend to Northern Ireland.
(10) . . . [1]
(11) . . .

Note—Sub-s (11) is not relevant to this work.
Amendments—[1] Sub-ss (2), (7), (10) are spent.
[2] Sub-s (3) is repealed by the Statute Law Revision Act 1953.
[3] Sub-s (4) repealed by FA 1975 ss 52(2), 59(5), Sch 13 Pt I.
[4] Sub-s (6) repealed by the Statute Law (Repeals) Act 1989.

FINANCE ACT 1951

(14 & 15 Geo. 6 Chapter 43)

PART V
MISCELLANEOUS

42 Exemption from stamp duties of transfers of International Bank stock

(1) Transfers of any stock of the International Bank for Reconstruction and Development shall be exempt from all stamp duties.
(2) This section shall have effect as from the twenty-sixth day of April, nineteen hundred and fifty-one.

Note—This section was to be repealed by FA 1990 Sch 19 Pt VI with effect from an appointed day in accordance with FA 1990 ss 107–111. The Treasury order specifying the appointed day for the purposes of FA 1990 ss 107–110 was to coincide with the start of paperless trading under the Stock Exchange's planned TAURUS system (IR press release, 20-3-90). However, on 11-3-93 the London Stock Exchange News Release 6/93 announced that TAURUS had been abandoned.

44 Short title, construction, extent and repeals

(1) This Act may be cited as the Finance Act 1951.
(2) . . . [1]
(3) . . . [2]
(4) . . . [1]
(5) . . . [5]
(6) . . . [3]
(7) . . .
(8) Such of the provisions of this Act as relate to matters with respect to which the Parliament of Northern Ireland has power to make laws shall not extend to Northern Ireland.
(9) . . . [4]

Note—Sub-s (7) is not relevant to this work.
Amendments—[1] Sub-ss (2), (4) are spent.
[2] Sub-s (3) repealed by the Statute Law Revision Act 1953.
[3] Sub-s (6) repealed by the Statute Law (Repeals) Act 1971.
[4] Sub-s (9) repealed by the Statute Law (Repeals) Act 1974.
[5] Sub-s (5) repealed by FA 1975 ss 52(2), 59(5), Sch 13 Pt I.

FINANCE ACT 1952

(15 & 16 Geo. 6 & 1 Eliz. 2 Chapter 33)

PART VI
MISCELLANEOUS AND GENERAL

74 Stamp duties (exemption for certain transfers to joint boards or joint committees of local authorities)

(1) Where provision is made either—
(*a*) . . . [3]
(*b*) by an order under the Public Health Act 1936 or the Local Government (Scotland) Act 1947 for the transfer of any property to a joint board constituted under section six of the said Act

of 1936 or to a joint board or joint committee constituted under section one hundred and nineteen or one hundred and twenty of the said Act of 1947, as the case may be, [from another local authority][1];

then, in considering whether any and if so what duty is payable under section twelve of the Finance Act 1895, (which relates to the stamp duty payable in connection with certain statutory conveyances), the consideration for the transfer shall be left out of account.

(2) . . . [3]

(3) No stamp duty shall be payable on any conveyance, agreement or assignment made, or instrument executed, solely for the purpose of giving effect to a transfer of property to a joint board or joint committee constituted under section one hundred and nineteen or one hundred and twenty of the Local Government (Scotland) Act 1947 [from another local authority][1].

(4) In this section ["local authority" has the meaning assigned to it by section [842A][4] of the Income and Corporation Taxes Act 1988][2].

(5) This section shall be construed as one with the Stamp Act 1891.

Amendments—[1] Words in sub-ss (1)(*b*), (3) substituted by FA 1974 s 52, Sch 12 para 6.
[2] Words in sub-s (4) substituted by TA 1988 Sch 29 para 32 Table.
[3] Sub-ss (1)(*a*), (2) repealed by the Water Act 1989 Sch 27 Pt I with effect from 1 September 1989 by virtue of SI 1989/1530.
[4] Section number in sub-s (4) substituted by FA 1990 s 127(3), (4), Sch 18 para 1 with effect from 1 April 1990.

76 Short title, construction, extent and repeals

(1) This Act may be cited as the Finance Act 1952.

(2) . . . [1]

(3) . . . [2]

(4) . . . [3]

(5) . . . [1]

(6) Any reference in this Act to any other enactment shall, except so far as the context otherwise requires, be construed as a reference to that enactment as amended or applied by or under any other enactment, including this Act.

(7) Such of the provisions of Parts I and VI of this Act as relate to matters with respect to which the Parliament of Northern Ireland has power to make laws shall not extend to Northern Ireland.

(8) The enactments specified in the Fourteenth Schedule to this Act are hereby repealed to the extent mentioned in the third column of that Schedule, but this repeal has effect—

(*a*)–(*b*) . . . [4]

(*c*)–(*d*) . . . [4]

Note—Sub-s (8)(*c*) is not relevant to this work.

Amendments—[1] Sub-s (2), (5), are spent (and *repealed* by the Statute Law (Repeals) Act 2008 s 1, Sch 1 Pt 8 with effect from 21 July 2008).
[2] Sub-s (3) repealed by the Purchase Tax Act 1963 s 41(1), Sch 4 Pt I.
[3] Sub-s (4) repealed by the Income and Corporation Taxes Act 1970 s 538(1), Sch 16.
[4] Sub-s (8)(*a*), (*b*), (*d*) repealed by the Statute Law (Repeals) Act 1974.

FINANCE ACT 1953

(1 & 2 Eliz. 2 Chapter 34)

PART IV

MISCELLANEOUS AND GENERAL

31 Stamp duties

(1) There shall be exempt from all stamp duties instruments of the following descriptions, being instruments made or executed for the purposes of any savings committee, savings group or other similar body affiliated to the National Savings Committee or the Scottish Savings Committee, that is to say—

(*a*) . . . [2]

(*b*) . . . [2] any agreement . . . [3] whereby a person so acting makes himself responsible for money, stamps or other things supplied for the purposes of the body he acts for.

(2) . . . [1]

(3) This section shall be construed as one with the Stamp Act 1891.

Amendments—[1] Sub-s (2) repealed by FA 1958 s 40, Sch 9 Pt III, and FA 1963 s 73(8), Sch 14 Pt IV.
[2] Sub-s (1)(*a*) and words in sub-s (1)(*b*) repealed by FA 1970 s 36(8), Sch 8 Pt V.
[3] Words in sub-s (1)(*b*) repealed by FA 1971 s 69, Sch 14 Pt VI.

35 Short title, construction, extent and repeals

(1) This Act may be cited as the Finance Act 1953.

(2) . . . [4]

(3) . . . [1]

(4) . . . [2]

(5) Any reference in this Act to any other enactment shall, except so far as the context otherwise requires, be construed as a reference to that enactment as amended or applied by or under any other enactment, including this Act.
(6) Such of the provisions of this Act as relate to matters in respect of which the Parliament of Northern Ireland has power to make laws shall not extend to Northern Ireland, but nothing in this subsection shall affect the application to Northern Ireland of section thirty-three of this Act.
(7) . . . [3]

Amendments—[1] Sub-s (3) repealed by the Purchase Tax Act 1963 s 41(1), Sch 4 Pt I.
[2] Sub-s (4)(*a*), (*b*) repealed by the Income and Corporation Taxes Act 1970 s 538(1), Sch 16, and sub-s (4)(*c*) is spent (sub-s (4) *repealed* by the Statute Law (Repeals) Act 2008 s 1, Sch 1 Pt 8 with effect from 21 July 2008).
[3] Sub-s (7) repealed by the Statute Law (Repeals) Act 1974.
[4] Sub-s (2) repealed by the Customs and Excise Management Act 1979 s 177(3), Sch 6 Pt I.

FINANCE ACT 1958

(6 & 7 Eliz. 2 Chapter 56)

PART VI
STAMP DUTIES

34 Conveyances on sale, etc

(1)–(3) . . . [1]
(4) . . . [3]
(5)–(7) . . . [1]
(8) . . . [2]
(9), (10) . . . [1]

Cross references—See FA 1963 s 55 (certificate in respect of certain conveyances or transfers on sale to be in the form described in sub-s (4) above).

Amendments—[1] Sub-ss (1)–(3), (5)–(7), (9) and (10) repealed by FA 1963 s 73(8), Sch 14 Pt IV.
[2] Sub-s (8) repealed by FA 1970 s 36(8), Sch 8 Pt V.
[3] Sub-s (4) repealed by FA 1999 Sch 20 Pt V(2) with effect in relation to instruments executed, or bearer instruments issued, from 1 October 1999, subject to the provisions in FA 1999 Sch 20 Pt V(2) Note 2. Previously the text read:

"(4) References in this section to an instrument being certified at a particular amount mean that it contains a statement certifying that the transaction effected by the instrument does not form part of a larger transaction or series of transactions in respect of which the amount or value, or aggregate amount or value, of the consideration exceeds that amount; and for this purpose—
(a) any sale or contract or agreement for the sale of goods, wares or merchandise shall be disregarded in the case either—
(i) of an instrument chargeable under the said heading "Conveyance or Transfer on sale", other than an actual conveyance or transfer of the goods, wares or merchandise (with or without other property); or
(ii) of an instrument chargeable by reference to that heading under section fifty-nine of the Stamp Act 1891 (which makes a contract or agreement for sale of certain property chargeable with duty as if it were an actual conveyance on sale); and
(*b*) any such statement as aforesaid shall be construed as leaving out of account any matter which in accordance with paragraph (*a*) of this subsection is to be disregarded.".

FINANCE ACT 1959

(7 & 8 Eliz. 2 Chapter 58)

PART IV
STAMP DUTIES

30 Stamp duty on policies of insurance

(1)–(3) . . . [1]
(4) . . . [5]
(*a*)–(*b*) . . . [3]
(*c*) . . . [1]
. . . [3] . . . [5]
(5) . . . [4]
(6) Notwithstanding the repeal of section ninety-three of the Stamp Act 1891, a contract for such insurance as is mentioned in section five hundred and six of the Merchant Shipping Act 1894, shall continue to be admissible in evidence although not embodied in a marine policy as required by section twenty-two of the Marine Insurance Act 1906.
(7) This section shall apply in relation to instruments made or executed after the beginning of August, nineteen hundred and fifty-nine.

Amendments—[1] Sub-ss (1)–(3) and (4) (*c*) repealed by FA 1970 s 36(8), Sch 8 Pt IV.
[3] Sub-s (4)(*a*), (*b*), and the words omitted from sub-s (4) repealed by the Statute Law (Repeals) Act 1976 Sch 1, Pt XVIII.
[4] Sub-s (5) repealed by the Statute Law (Repeals) Act 1976 Sch 1, Pt XVIII.
[5] Words in sub-s (4) repealed by FA 1989 Sch 17 Pt IX.

PART V
MISCELLANEOUS

37 Short title, construction, extent and repeal

(1) This Act may be cited as the Finance Act 1959.

(2) Parts I to IV of this Act shall be construed as one with the enactments mentioned in this subsection respectively, that is to say—

(*a*) . . . [3]

(*b*) . . . [1]

(*c*) . . . [2]

(*d*) Part IV with the Stamp Act 1891.

(3) Any reference in this Act to any other enactment shall, except so far as the context otherwise requires, be construed as a reference to that enactment as amended or applied by or under any other enactment including this Act.

(4) Such of the provisions of this Act as relate to matters in respect of which the Parliament of Northern Ireland has power to make laws shall not extend to Northern Ireland.

(5) The enactments specified in the Eighth Schedule to this Act are hereby repealed to the extent mentioned in the third column of that Schedule, and, except as otherwise provided in that column, the said repeals shall have effect—

(*a*) . . .

(*b*) in the case of the enactments specified in Part II thereof, in relation to instruments made or executed after the beginning of August, nineteen hundred and fifty-nine;

(*c*) in the case of the enactments specified in Part III thereof, in relation to any yearly period beginning after the fifth day of April, nineteen hundred and fifty-nine; and

(*d*) . . .

Note—Sub-s (5)(*a*), (*d*) are not relevant to this work.

Amendments—[1] Sub-s (2)(*b*) repealed by the Purchase Tax Act 1963 s 41(1), Sch 4 Pt I.
[2] Sub-s (2)(*c*) repealed by TA 1970 s 538(1), Sch 16.
[3] Sub-s (2)(*a*) repealed by CEMA 1979 s 177(3), Sch 6 Pt I.

FINANCE ACT 1960

(8 & 9 Eliz. 2 Chapter 44)

PART V
MISCELLANEOUS

74 Visiting forces and allied headquarters (stamp duty exemptions)

(1) Subsections (2) to (4) of this section shall have effect with a view to conferring exemptions from stamp duty (corresponding to exemptions applicable in the case of Her Majesty's forces) in relation to any visiting force of a designated country, and in those subsections "a force" means any such visiting force as aforesaid.

(2) There shall be exempted from all stamp duties any contract, conveyance or other document made with a view to building or enlarging barracks or camps for a force, or to facilitating the training in the United Kingdom of a force, or to promoting the health or efficiency of a force.

(3), (4) . . . [1]

(5) Subsections (2) to (4) of this section shall have effect in relation to any designated allied headquarters as if—

(*a*) the headquarters were a visiting force of a designated country;

(*b*) the members of that force consisted of such of the persons serving at or attached to the headquarters as are members of the armed forces of a designated country;

(*c*) the references to the country to which a force belongs included both any designated allied headquarters and, in relation to any such person as aforesaid, the country of whose armed forces he is a member.

(6) For the purposes of this section—

(*a*) "allied headquarters" means any international military headquarters established or to be established under the North Atlantic Treaty;

(*b*) "designated" means designated for the purpose in question by or under any Order in Council;

(*c*) "visiting force" means any body, contingent or detachment of a country's forces which is for the time being or is to be present in the United Kingdom on the invitation of Her Majesty's Government in the United Kingdom.

(7) Any Order in Council under this section may be varied or revoked by a subsequent Order in Council.

(8) . . . [2]

(9) This section shall be construed as one with the Stamp Act 1891.

Cross references—See the Visiting Forces and Allied Headquarters (Stamp Duties) (Designation) Order, SI 1961/581 (visiting forces and headquarters);

The Visiting Forces (Stamp Duties) (Designation) Order, SI 1964/925 (visiting forces).

Amendments—[1] Sub-ss (3), (4) repealed by FA 1970 s 36(8), Sch 8 Pt V.

[2] Sub-s (8) repealed by the Northern Ireland Constitution Act 1973 s 41(1), Sch 6 Pt I.

[74A Visiting forces and allied headquarters (stamp duty land tax exemptions)

(1) This section has effect with a view to conferring exemptions from stamp duty land tax corresponding to exemptions applicable in the case of Her Majesty's forces in relation to any visiting force of a designated country.

In this section "a force" means any such visiting force.

(2) A land transaction entered into with a view to building or enlarging barracks or camps for a force, or to facilitating the training in the United Kingdom of a force, or to promoting the health or efficiency of a force, is exempt from charge for the purposes of stamp duty land tax.

(3) Relief under this section must be claimed in a land transaction return or an amendment of such a return.

(4) Subsection (2) of this section has effect in relation to any designated allied headquarters as if—

(*a*) the headquarters were a visiting force of a designated country;

(*b*) the members of that force consisted of such of the persons serving at or attached to the headquarters as are members of the armed forces of a designated country;

(*c*) the references to the country to which a force belongs included both any designated allied headquarters and, in relation to any such person as is mentioned in paragraph (*b*), the country of whose armed forces he is a member.

(5) For the purposes of this section—

(*a*) "allied headquarters" means any international military headquarters established or to be established under the North Atlantic Treaty;

(*b*) "designated" means designated for the purpose in question by or under any Order in Council;

(*c*) "visiting force" means any body, contingent or detachment of country's forces which is for the time being or is to be present in the United Kingdom on the invitation of Her Majesty's Government in the United Kingdom;

(*d*) "land transaction" has the meaning given by section 43(1) of the Finance Act 2003;

(*e*) "land transaction return" has the meaning given by section 76(1) of that Act.][1]

Amendments—[1] Section 74A inserted by the Stamp Duty Land Tax (Consequential Amendment of Enactments) Regulations, SI 2003/2867, reg 2, Schedule, para 6 with effect from 1 December 2003.

STOCK TRANSFER ACT 1963

(1963 Chapter 18)

1 Simplified transfer of securities

(1) Registered securities to which this section applies may be transferred by means of an instrument under hand in the form set out in Schedule 1 to this Act (in this Act referred to as a stock transfer), executed by the transferor only and specifying (in addition to the particulars of the consideration, of the description and number or amount of the securities, and of the person by whom the transfer is made) the full name and address of the transferee.

(2) The execution of a stock transfer need not be attested; and where such a transfer has been executed for the purpose of a stock exchange transaction, the particulars of the consideration and of the transferee may either be inserted in that transfer or, as the case may require, supplied by means of separate instruments in the form set out in Schedule 2 to this Act (in this Act referred to as brokers transfers), identifying the stock transfer and specifying the securities to which each instrument relates and the consideration paid for those securities.

(3) Nothing in this section shall be construed as affecting the validity of any instrument which would be effective to transfer securities apart from this section; and any instrument purporting to be made in any form which was common or usual before the commencement of this Act, or any other form authorised or required for that purpose apart from this section, shall be sufficient, whether or not it is completed in accordance with the form, if it complies with the requirements as to execution and contents which apply to a stock transfer.

(4) This section applies to fully paid up registered securities of any description, being—

(*a*) securities issued by any company [as defined in section 1(1) of the Companies Act 2006][8] except a company limited by guarantee or an unlimited company;

(*b*) securities issued by any body (other than a company [as so defined][8]) incorporated in Great Britain by or under any enactment or by Royal Charter except a building society within the meaning of the Building Societies Act [1986][4] or a society registered under the Industrial and Provident Societies Act 1893;

(*c*) securities issued by the Government of the United Kingdom, except stock or bonds in [the National Savings Stock Register][2] . . . [1], and except national savings certificates;

(*d*) securities issued by any local authority;

[(*e*) units of an authorised unit trust scheme or a recognised scheme within the meaning of [Part 17 of the Financial Services and Markets Act 2000][7]][5].

[(*f*) shares issued by an open-ended investment company within the meaning of the open-ended Investment Companies Regulations 2001.][6]

Amendments—[1] Words in sub-s 4 (*c*) repealed by FA 1964 ss 24, 26(7), Sch 8 para 10, Sch 9.

[2] Words in sub-s (4)(*c*) substituted by the Post Office Act 1969 s 108(1) (*f*).

[4] Figures in sub-s (4) (*b*) substituted by the Building Societies Act 1986 s 120(1), Sch 18 Pt I para 5.

[5] Sub-s (4)(*e*) substituted by the Financial Services Act 1986 s 212(2), Sch 16 para 4(*a*).

[6] Sub-s (4)(*f*) substituted by the open-ended Investment Companies Regulations, SI 2001/1228 reg 84, Sch 7 para 2 with effect from 1 December 2001 (by virtue of SI 2001/3538).

[7] Words in sub-s (4)(*e*) substituted by the Financial Services and Markets Act 2000 (Consequential Amendments and Repeals) Order, SI 2001/3649 art 270 with effect from 1 December 2001.

[8] In sub-s (4)(*a*), words substituted for words "within the meaning of the Companies Act 1985", and in sub-s (4)(*b*), words substituted for words "within the meaning of the said Act", by the Companies Act 2006 (Consequential Amendments, Transitional Provisions and Savings) Order, SI 2009/1941 art 2(1), Sch 1 para 10 with effect from 1 October 2009.

2 Supplementary provisions as to simplified transfer

(1) Section 1 of this Act shall have effect in relation to the transfer of any securities to which that section applies notwithstanding anything to the contrary in any enactment or instrument relating to the transfer of those securities; but nothing in that section affects—

(*a*) any right to refuse to register a person as the holder of any securities on any ground other than the form in which those securities purport to be transferred to him; or

(*b*) any enactment or rule of law regulating the execution of documents by companies or other bodies corporate, or any articles of association or other instrument regulating the execution of documents by any particular company or body corporate.

(2) Subject to the provisions of this section, any enactment or instrument relating to the transfer of securities to which section 1 of this Act applies shall, with any necessary modifications, apply in relation to an instrument of transfer to which it applies apart from this subsection; and without prejudice to the generality of the foregoing provision, [the references to an instrument of transfer in section 775 of the Companies Act 2006 (certification of instrument of transfer)][5] shall be construed as including a reference to a broker's transfer.

(3) In relation to the transfer of securities by means of a stock transfer and a brokers transfer—

(*a*) any reference in any enactment or instrument (including in particular [section 770(1)(*a*) of the Companies Act 2006 (registration of transfer)][5] . . . [3]) to the delivery or lodging of an instrument (or proper instrument) of transfer shall be construed as a reference to the delivery or lodging of the stock transfer and the brokers transfer;

(*b*) any such reference to the date on which an instrument of transfer is delivered or lodged shall be construed as a reference to the date by which the later of those transfers to be delivered or lodged has been delivered or lodged; and

(*c*) subject to the foregoing provisions of this subsection, the brokers transfer (and not the stock transfer) shall be deemed to be the [transfer][4] for the purposes of the enactments relating to stamp duty[2].

(4) . . . [1]

Amendments—[1] Sub-s (4) repealed by the Requirements of Writing (Scotland) Act 1995 s 14(2), Sch 5.

[2] Sub-s (3)(*c*) and preceding word "and" repealed by FA 1990, Sch 19, Part VI with effect from a day to be appointed.

[3] Words in sub-s (3)(*a*) repealed by FA 1999 Sch 20 Pt V(5) with effect in relation to instruments executed from 6 February 2000.

[4] The word "transfer" substituted for the words "conveyance or transfer" in enactments relating to stamp duty by FA 2003 Sch 20 para 3.

[5] Words in sub-ss (2), (3)(*a*) substituted by the Companies Act 2006 (Consequential Amendments etc) Order, SI 2008/948 art 3(1), Sch 1 para 37 with effect from 6 April 2008.

3 Additional provisions as to transfer forms

(1) References in this Act to the forms set out in Schedule 1 and Schedule 2 include reference to forms substantially corresponding to those forms respectively.

(2) The Treasury may by order amend the said Schedules either by altering the forms set out therein or by substituting different forms for those forms or by the addition of forms for use as alternatives to those forms; and references in this Act to the forms set out in those Schedules (including references in this section) shall be construed accordingly.

(3) Any order under subsection (2) of this section which substitutes a different form for a form set out in Schedule 1 to this Act may direct that subsection (3) of section 1 of this Act shall apply, with any necessary modifications, in relation to the form for which that form is substituted as it applies to any form which was common or usual before the commencement of this Act.

(4) Any order of the Treasury under this section shall be made by statutory instrument, and may be varied or revoked by a subsequent order; and any statutory instrument made by virtue of this section shall be subject to annulment in pursuance of a resolution of either House of Parliament.

[(5) An order under subsection (2) of this section may—

(*a*) provide for forms on which some of the particulars mentioned in subsection (1) of section 1 of this Act are not required to be specified;

(*b*) provide for that section to have effect, in relation to such forms as are mentioned in the preceding paragraph or other forms specified in the order, subject to such amendments as are so specified (which may include an amendment of the reference in subsection (1) of that section to an instrument under hand);

(*c*) provide for all or any of the provisions of the order to have effect in such cases only as are specified in the order.][1]

Amendments—[1] Sub-s (5) inserted by the Stock Exchange (Completion of Bargains) Act 1976 ss 6, 7(4), and extends to Northern Ireland in accordance with the provisions of s 5(1), (2) of this Act. It came into effect on 12 February 1979 by virtue of SI 1979/55.

4 Interpretation

(1) In this Act the following expressions have the meanings hereby respectively assigned to them, that is to say—

"local authority" means, in relation to England and Wales,

[[(*a*) a billing authority or a precepting authority, as defined in section 69 of the Local Government Finance Act 1992;

[(*aa*) a fire and rescue authority in Wales constituted by a scheme under section 2 of the Fire and Rescue Services Act 2004 or a scheme to which section 4 of that Act applies;][3]][2]

(*b*) a levying body within the meaning of section 74 of [the Local Government Finance Act 1988][3]; and

(*c*) a body as regards which section 75 of that Act applies,][1]

and, in relation to Scotland, a county council, a town council and any statutory authority, commissioners or trustees to whom section 270 of the Local Government (Scotland) Act 1947 applies;

"registered securities" means transferable securities the holders of which are entered in a register (whether maintained in Great Britain or not);

"securities" means shares, stock, debentures, debenture stock, loan stock, bonds, units of a [collective investment scheme within the meaning of the [Financial Services and Markets Act 2000][3], and other securities of any description;

"stock exchange transaction" means a sale and purchase of securities in which each of the parties is a member of a stock exchange acting in the ordinary course of his business as such or is acting through the agency of such a member;

"stock exchange" means the Stock Exchange, London, and any other stock exchange (whether in Great Britain or not) which is declared by order of the Treasury to be a recognised stock exchange for the purposes of this Act.

(2) Any order of the Treasury under this section shall be made by statutory instrument, and may be varied or revoked by a subsequent order.

Amendments—[1] Paras (*a*)–(*c*) in the definition of "local authority" substituted by the Local Government Finance (Repeals, Savings and Consequential Amendments) Order, SI 1990/776 art 8, Sch 3 para 8.

[2] Para (*a*) in the definition of "local authority" substituted for para (*a*) by the Local Government Finance Act 1992 s 117(1), Sch 13 para 12.

[3] Para (*aa*) in the definition of "local authority" and words in para (*b*) substituted by the Fire and Rescue Services Act 2004 s 53, Sch 1 para 18 with effect from 1 October 2004 (by virtue of SI 2004/2304). In Wales, the Fire and Rescue Services Act, in so far as it was not already in force, came into force on 10 November 2004 (by virtue of SI 2004/2917).

[4] Words in the definition of "securities" substituted by the Financial Services and Markets Act 2000 (Consequential Amendments and Repeals) Order, SI 2001/3649 art 271 with effect from 1 December 2001.

5 Application to Northern Ireland

(1) This Act, so far as it applies to things done outside Great Britain, extends to Northern Ireland.

(2) Without prejudice to subsection (1) of this section, the provisions of this Act affecting securities issued by the Government of the United Kingdom shall apply to any such securities entered in a register maintained in Northern Ireland.

(3) . . . [1]

(4) Except as provided by this section, this Act shall not extend to Northern Ireland.

Amendments—[1] Sub-s (3) repealed by the Northern Ireland Constitution Act 1973 s 41(1), Sch 6 Pt I.

FINANCE ACT 1963

(1963 Chapter 25)

An Act to grant certain duties, to alter other duties, and to amend the law relating to the National Debt and the Public Revenue, and to make further provision in connection with Finance

[31st July 1963]

PART IV
STAMP DUTIES

Reduction of duties

55 Reduced duty on conveyance or transfer on sale

Amendments—This section repealed by FA 1999 Sch 20 Pt V(2) with effect in relation to instruments executed, or bearer instruments issued, from 1 October 1999, subject to the provisions in FA 1999 Sch 20 Pt V(2) Note 2. Previously the text read:

"(1) Subject to subsections (1A) to (3) below and to the following provisions of this Part of this Act, the stamp duty chargeable under the heading "Conveyance or Transfer on sale" in Schedule 1 to the Stamp Act 1891 shall be charged by reference to the amount or value of the consideration for the sale at the following rates, that is to say—

(*a*) where the amount or value of the consideration is £60,000 or under and the instrument is certified, as described in section 34(4) of the Finance Act 1958 at £60,000, nil;

(*b*) where paragraph (*a*) above does not apply and—

(i) the amount or value of the consideration does not exceed £500, and

(ii) the instrument is certified as described in section 34(4) of the Finance Act 1958 at £250,000, the rate of 50p for every £50 or part of £50 of the consideration;

(*c*) where paragraph (*a*) above does not apply and—

(i) the amount or value of the consideration exceeds £500 but does not exceed £250,000, and

(ii) the instrument is certified as described in section 34(4) of the Finance Act 1958 at £250,000, the rate of £1 for every £100 or part of £100 of the consideration;

(*d*) where paragraphs (*a*) to (*c*) above do not apply and—

(i) the amount or value of the consideration does not exceed £500,000, and

(ii) the instrument is certified as described in section 34(4) of the Finance Act 1958 at £500,000, the rate of [£2.50p] for every £100 or part of £100 of the consideration; and

(*e*) in any other case the rate of [£3.50p] for every £100 or part of £100 of the consideration;]

and any duty chargeable by reference to that heading shall be charged accordingly.

(1A) In relation to duty chargeable under or by reference to the heading mentioned in subsection (1) above as it applies to a conveyance or transfer of stock or marketable securities, that subsection shall have effect as if for the words from "following rates" to the end of paragraph (*e*) there were substituted the words "rate of 50p for every £100 or part of £100 of the consideration".

(2) In relation to duty chargeable by reference to the heading mentioned in subsection (1) above by virtue of the heading "Lease or Tack" in the said Schedule 1 in a case where part of the consideration consists of rent and that rent exceeds £600 a year, subsection (1) above shall have effect as if

(*a*) paragraph (*a*) and, in paragraphs (*b*) and (*c*), the words "paragraph (*a*) above does not apply and" were omitted and

(*b*) in paragraph (*d*) for the words "paragraphs (*a*) to (*c*)" there were substituted the words "paragraphs (*b*) and (*c*)".

(3) Nothing in this section shall affect any enactment imposing an upper limit on the amount of duty chargeable *ad valorem*.

(4) . . ."

56 Reduced duty on leases

Amendments—This section repealed by FA 1999 Sch 20 Pt V(2) with effect in relation to instruments executed, or bearer instruments issued, from 1 October 1999, subject to the provisions in FA 1999 Sch 20 Pt V(2) Note 2. Previously the text read:

"(1), (2) . . .

(3) For the purposes of the said heading a lease granted for a fixed term and thereafter until determined shall be treated as a lease for a definite term equal to the fixed term together with such further period as must elapse before the earliest date at which the lease can be determined; and section 75 of the said Act of 1891 (agreements for leases) shall be construed accordingly.

(4) Section 76, subsections (3) and (4) of section 77 and section 78 of the said Act of 1891 shall cease to have effect."

57 Miscellaneous reductions

Amendments—This section repealed by FA 1999 Sch 20 Pt V(2) with effect in relation to instruments executed, or bearer instruments issued from 1 October 1999, subject to the provisions in FA 1999 Sch 20 Pt V(2) Note 2. Previously the text read:

"(1) The rates of stamp duty chargeable under or by reference to the following headings or parts of headings in Schedule 1 to the Stamp Act 1891, that is to say—

Bond, Covenant or Instrument of any kind whatsoever

. . .

Mortgage, Bond, Debenture, Covenant and Warrant of Attorney,

. . .

shall be those at which the duty would be chargeable if section 52 of the Finance Act 1947 (which doubled the rates) had not been enacted.

(2) . . ."

Bearer Instruments

59 Stamp duty on bearer instruments

Amendments—This section repealed by FA 1999 Sch 20 Pt V(2) with effect in relation to instruments executed, or bearer instruments issued, from 1 October 1999, subject to the provisions in FA 1999 Sch 20 Pt V(2) Note 2. Previously the text read:

"(1) . . .

(2) For the purposes of the heading set out in subsection (1) above—

(*a*) "inland bearer instrument" means any of the following instruments issued by or on behalf of any company or body of persons corporate or unincorporate formed or established in the United Kingdom, that is to say—

(i) any marketable security transferable by delivery;

(ii) any share warrant or stock certificate to bearer and any instrument to bearer (by whatever name called) having the like effect as such a warrant or certificate;

(iii) any deposit certificate to bearer;

(iv) any other instrument to bearer by means of which any stock can be transferred;

(*b*) "overseas bearer instrument" means an instrument issued otherwise than by or on behalf of any such company or body of persons as is mentioned in paragraph (*a*) above, being an instrument described in sub-paragraphs (i) to (iv) of that paragraph or a bearer instrument by usage;

(*c*) "deposit certificate" means an instrument acknowledging the deposit of stock and entitling the bearer to rights (whether expressed as units or otherwise) in or in relation to the stock deposited or equivalent stock; and "deposit certificate for overseas stock" means a deposit certificate in respect of stock of any one company or body of persons not being such a company or body as is mentioned in paragraphs (*a*) above;

(*d*) "bearer instrument by usage" means an instrument not described in the said sub-paragraphs (i) to (iv) which is used for the purpose of transferring the right to any stock, being an instrument delivery of which is treated by usage as sufficient for the purpose of a sale on the market, whether that delivery constitutes a legal transfer or not;

. . .

(3) For the purposes of the said heading "the transfer duty" means the duty which would be chargeable under the heading "Conveyance or Transfer on sale" in the said Schedule 1 in respect of an instrument in writing transferring the stock constituted by or transferable by means of the inland or overseas bearer instrument in question for a consideration equal to the market value of that stock; and the instrument so postulated shall be taken to transfer the stock on the day of issue or transfer (depending on whether section 60(1) or (2) of this Act applies) and to be executed in pursuance of a contract made on that day.

(4) For the purposes of this section and the two next following sections, "stock" includes securities, and references to stock include references to any interest in, or in any fraction of, stock or in any dividends or other rights arising out of stock and any right to an allotment of or to subscribe for stock; "transfer" includes negotiation and "transferable", "transferred" and "transferring" shall be construed accordingly; and a bearer instrument by usage used for the purpose of transferring the right to any stock shall be treated as transferring that stock on delivery of the instrument, and as issued by the person by whom or on whose behalf it was first issued, whether or not it was then capable of being used for transferring the right to the stock without execution by the holder.

(5) . . .".

60 Payment of duty

Amendments—This section repealed by FA 1999 Sch 20 Pt V(2) with effect in relation to instruments executed, or bearer instruments issued, from 1 October 1999, subject to the provisions in FA 1999 Sch 20 Pt V(2) Note 2. Previously the text read:

"(1) Duty under the heading set out in subsection (1) of section 59 of this Act shall be chargeable on issue in the case of the following instruments that is to say—

(*a*) any instrument issued in Great Britain; and

(*b*) any instrument issued by or on behalf of a company or body of persons corporate or unincorporate formed or established in Great Britain, not being a foreign loan security:

and for the purposes of this subsection "foreign loan security" means a security issued outside the United Kingdom in respect of a loan which is expressed in a currency other than sterling and is neither offered for subscription in the United Kingdom nor offered for subscription with a view to an offer for sale in the United Kingdom of securities in respect of the loan.

(2) Duty under the said heading in respect of any instrument not chargeable under subsection (1) above shall be chargeable on transfer in Great Britain of the stock constituted by or transferable by means of the instrument: Provided that the duty chargeable by virtue of this subsection on the transfer of stock shall be chargeable only where duty would be chargeable under or by reference to the heading "Conveyance or Transfer on sale" in Schedule 1 to the Stamp Act 1891 if the transfer were effected by an instrument not being a bearer instrument.

(3) Any instrument which is chargeable under the said heading on issue shall, before being issued, be produced to the Commissioners (together with such particulars in writing of the instrument as the Commissioners may require) and shall be deemed to be duly stamped if, and only if, it is stamped with a particular stamp denoting that it has been produced to the Commissioners: and within six weeks of the date on which any such instrument is issued, or such longer time as the Commissioners may allow, a statement in writing containing the date of issue and such

further particulars as the Commissioners may require in respect of that instrument shall be delivered to the Commissioners, and the duty chargeable in respect of that instrument shall be paid to the Commissioners on delivery of that statement or within such longer time as the Commissioners may allow.

(4) If default is made in complying with subsection (3) above in respect of any instrument, the person by whom or on whose behalf the instrument is issued, and any person who acts as the agent of that person for the purposes of the issue, shall be liable to a fine not exceeding the aggregate of £50 and an amount equal to the stamp duty chargeable in respect of that instrument, and shall also be liable to pay to Her Majesty the duty chargeable in respect of that instrument and interest on the duty at the rate of five per cent per annum from the date of the default.

(5) Where any instrument which is chargeable under the said heading on transfer of the stock constituted by or transferable by means of the instrument is presented to the Commissioners for stamping, the person presenting it, and the owner of the instrument, shall furnish to the Commissioners such particulars in writing as they may require for determining the amount of duty chargeable on that instrument.

(6) Any person who in Great Britain transfers, or is concerned as broker or agent in transferring, any stock by or by means of any such instrument as is mentioned in subsection (5) above shall, if the instrument is not duly stamped, be liable to a fine not exceeding the aggregate of £50 and an amount equal to the stamp duty chargeable in respect of that instrument, and shall also be liable to pay to Her Majesty the duty chargeable in respect of that instrument and interest on the duty at the rate of five per cent per annum from the date of the transfer in question.

(7) If any person, in furnishing particulars under this section in respect of any instrument, wilfully or negligently furnishes any particulars which are false in any material respect, he shall be liable to a fine not exceeding the aggregate of £50 and an amount equal to twice the amount by which the stamp duty which ought to be charged in respect of that instrument exceeds the stamp duty paid in respect thereof.

(8) Where any such instrument as is mentioned in subsection (5) above has been stamped *ad valorem* or with a stamp indicating that it is chargeable under paragraph (4) of the said heading and with the duty specified in that paragraph, that instrument shall be deemed for all purposes other than subsection (7) above to have been duly stamped.

(9) Any instrument which is deemed to be duly stamped by virtue of subsection (3) or (8) of this section shall be deemed to be duly stamped in Northern Ireland, and any instrument which is deemed to be duly stamped by virtue of the corresponding provisions in force in Northern Ireland shall be deemed to be duly stamped in Great Britain."

61 Ascertainment of market value

Amendments—This section repealed by FA 1999 Sch 20 Pt V(2) with effect in relation to instruments executed, or bearer instruments issued, from 1 October 1999, subject to the provisions in FA 1999 Sch 20 Pt V(2) Note 2. Previously the text read:

"(1) In relation to an instrument which is chargeable on issue, the market value of the stock constituted by or transferable by means of that instrument shall be taken for the purposes of section 59 of this Act to be—

(*a*) where the stock was offered for public subscription (whether in registered or in bearer form) within twelve months before the issue of the instrument, the amount subscribed for the stock;

(*b*) in any other case, the value of the stock on the first day within one month after the issue of the instrument on which stock of that description is dealt in on a stock exchange in the United Kingdom or, if stock of that description is not so dealt in, the value of the stock immediately after the issue of the instrument.

(2) In relation to an instrument which is chargeable on transfer of the stock constituted by or transferable by means of that instrument, the market value of that stock shall be taken for the purposes of the said section 59 to be the value of that stock—

(*a*) in the case of a transfer pursuant to a contract of sale, on the date when the contract is made;

(*b*) in any other case, on the day preceding that on which the instrument is presented to the Commissioners for stamping, or, if it is not so presented, on the date of the transfer."

Miscellaneous

62 Commonwealth stock

Amendments—This section repealed by FA 1999 Sch 20 Pt V(2) with effect in relation to instruments executed, or bearer instruments issued, from 1 October 1999, subject to the provisions in FA 1999 Sch 20 Pt V(2) Note 2. Previously the text read:

"(1) In Schedule 1 to the Stamp Act 1891, the heading "Conveyance or Transfer whether on sale or otherwise" (which relates to Canadian and colonial stock) shall be omitted, and any transfer of stock to which that heading applied shall be chargeable with stamp duty under the heading appropriate to a like transfer of other stock.

(2)–(6) . . ."

63 Securities for annual and other payments

Amendments—This section repealed by FA 1999 Sch 20 Pt V(2) with effect in relation to instruments executed, or bearer instruments issued, from 1 October 1999, subject to the provisions in FA 1999 Sch 20 Pt V(2) Note 2. Previously the text read:

"In determining whether an instrument is—

(*a*) the only principal or primary security for any annuity or for any sum or sums of money within the meaning of paragraph (1) of the heading "Bond, Covenant or Instrument of any kind whatsoever" in Schedule I to the Stamp Act 1891; or

(b) the only, principal or primary security for the payment or repayment of money within the meaning of paragraph (1) of the heading "Mortgage, Bond, Debenture, Covenant and Warrant of Attorney" in that Schedule, no account shall be taken of any other instrument which is a security for the same annuity, sum or sums, or for the same payment or repayment, as the case may be, or for any part thereof, unless that other instrument is chargeable with stamp duty under either of the said paragraphs and is duly stamped."

65 Miscellaneous exemptions

(1) . . .[1]

(2) . . .[2]

(3) No stamp duty shall be chargeable in respect of any form of application for legal aid under the Legal Aid and Advice Acts 1949 and 1960 or the Legal Aid (Scotland) Acts, 1949 and 1960, or in respect of any form relating to the offer and acceptance of a certificate pursuant to an application for legal aid under those Acts.[3]

Cross references—See FA 1985 s 81 (renunciation of rights to company shares; sub-s (1) above not to apply to instruments if the rights are renounced under them after 31 July 1985 except where an offer for the rights became unconditional before 28 June 1985).

Amendments—[1] Sub-s (1) repealed by FA 1999 Sch 20 Pt V(2) with effect in relation to instruments executed, or bearer instruments issued, from 1 October 1999, subject to the provisions in FA 1999 Sch 20 Pt V(2) Note 2. Previously the text read:

'(1) Any instrument which is exempt from duty under the heading set out in section 59(1) of this Act by virtue of exemption 3 in that heading or would be so exempt if it were otherwise chargeable under that heading shall be exempt from stamp duty under or by reference to the heading "Conveyance or Transfer on sale" in Schedule 1 to the Stamp Act 1891.'

[2] Sub-s (2) repealed by FA 1999 Sch 20 Pt V(5) with effect in relation to instruments executed from 6 February 2000.

[3] Sub-s (3) repealed by the Statute Law (Repeals) Act 2008 s 1, Sch 1 Pt 8 with effect from 21 July 2008.

67 Prohibition of circulation of blank transfers

(1) Where a transfer in blank relating to registered stock of any description has been delivered, pursuant to a sale of that stock, to or to the order of the purchaser or any person acting on his behalf, any person who in Great Britain parts with possession of that transfer, or who removes it or causes or permits it to be removed from Great Britain, before it has been duly completed shall be liable to a [penalty][3] not exceeding the aggregate of [£300][3] and an amount equal to twice the stamp duty chargeable in respect of that transfer.

(2) For the purposes of this section "transfer in blank" means a transfer in which the name of the transferee has not been inserted, and a transfer shall be treated as duly completed if, and only if, the name of the transferee is inserted therein, being the name of—

(*a*) the purchaser of the stock under the sale;

(*b*) a person entitled to a charge upon the stock for money lent to that purchaser;

(*c*) a nominee holding as a bare trustee for that purchaser or for any such person as is mentioned in paragraph (*b*) above; or

(*d*) a person acting as the agent of that purchaser for the purposes of the sale.

(3) . . .[1]

[(4) In this section—

(*a*) "stock" includes securities;

(*b*) references to stock include any interest in, or in any fraction of, stock or in any dividends or other rights arising out of stock and any right to an allotment of or to subscribe for stock; and

(*c*) "transfer" includes any instrument used for transferring stock.

(4A) Nothing in this section applies to—

(*a*) an instrument which is chargeable with duty at the rate specified in paragraph 5 of Schedule 15 to the Finance Act 1999 (certain bearer instruments issued by or on behalf of non-UK companies) and is duly stamped, or

(*b*) renounceable letters of allotment, letters of rights or other similar instruments where the rights under the letter or other instrument are renounceable not later than six months after its issue.][2]

(5) References in this section to the purchaser . . .[1] of any stock include references to any person to whom the rights of the purchaser . . .[1] are transmitted by operation of law; and in relation to a transfer chargeable with duty in accordance with section 58(4) or (5) of the Stamp Act 1891 (transfers to sub-purchasers) references in this section to the purchaser and a sale shall be construed as references to the sub-purchaser and a sub-sale.

(6) This section shall come into force on such date as the Treasury may by order made by statutory instrument direct.

Note—This section came into force on 26 October 1963 by virtue of the Registered Securities (Completion of Blank Transfers) Order, SI 1963/1743.

This section was to be repealed by FA 1990 Sch 19 Pt VI with effect from an appointed day in accordance with FA 1990 ss 107–111. The Treasury order specifying the appointed day for the purposes of FA 1990 ss 107–110 was to coincide with the start of paperless trading under the Stock Exchange's planned TAURUS system (IR press release, 20-3-90). However, on 11-3-93 the London Stock Exchange News Release 6/93 announced that TAURUS had been abandoned.

Cross references—See FA 1990 ss 109(3), 111(1) (this section not to apply with effect from an appointed day).

Amendments—[1] Sub-s (3) and words in sub-s (5) repealed by FA 1985 s 98(6), Sch 27 Pt IX(1).

2 Sub-s (4) substituted by sub-ss (4) and (4A) by FA 1999 s 113(3), Sch 16 para 2 with effect in relation to bearer instruments issued after 30 September 1999. For prospective repeal of FA 1999 s 113, Sch 16 para 2 see FA 1999 s 123(3). Previously the text read:

'(4) In this section references to stock shall be construed in accordance with subsection (4) of section 59 of this Act, and "transfer" includes any instrument used for transferring stock; but nothing in this section applies—

(*a*) to any instrument which is chargeable with duty under paragraph (3) of the heading "Bearer Instrument" set out in subsection (1) of that section and is duly stamped or

(*b*) to any instrument which is exempt from duty by virtue of exemption 3 in that heading, or would be so exempt if it were otherwise chargeable under that heading.'

3 Words and figures in sub-s (1) substituted by FA 1999 s 114, Sch 17 para 6 with effect in relation to penalties in respect of things done or omitted after 30 September 1999. For prospective repeal of FA 1999 Sch 17 para 6 see FA 1999 s 123(3). Previously the text read 'fine' and '£50'.

PART V

MISCELLANEOUS

73 Short title, commencement, construction, extent, amendments and repeals

(1) This Act may be cited as the Finance Act 1963.

(2) Part IV of this Act (except section 67) shall come into force on the 1st August 1963.

(3) . . . [2]

(4) . . . [1] Part IV shall be construed as one with the Stamp Act 1891.

(5) Any reference in this Act to any other enactment shall, except so far as the context otherwise requires, be construed as a reference to that enactment as amended or applied by or under any other enactment, including this Act.

(6) Such of the provisions of this Act as relate to matters in respect of which the Parliament of Northern Ireland has power to make laws shall not extend to Northern Ireland.

(7) . . .

(8) The enactments mentioned in Schedule 14 to this Act—

(*a*) so far as they are mentioned in Part I of that Schedule are hereby repealed to the extent mentioned in the second column of that Part as from the date specified in relation thereto in the third column of that Part;

(*b*) so far as they are mentioned in any other Part of that Schedule are hereby repealed to the extent mentioned in the third column of that Part,

but subject as regards the repeals contained in any Part of that Schedule to any provision in relation thereto made at the end of that Part.

(9) The provisions of Schedules 13 and 14 to this Act as to the operation or effect of repeals contained in those Schedules are without prejudice to the provisions of section 38(2) of the Interpretation Act 1889.

Note—Sub-s (7) is not relevant to this work.

Amendments—[1] Words repealed by TA 1970 ss 538(1), 539(1), Sch 16, FA 1975 ss 50, 52(2), (3), 59, Sch 13 Pt I and CEMA 1979 s 177(3), Sch 6 Pt I.

2 Sub-s (3) repealed by CEMA 1979 s 177(3), Sch 6 Pt I.

FINANCE ACT 1965

(1965 Chapter 25)

PART V

MISCELLANEOUS AND GENERAL

90 Stamp duty: conveyances and transfers

(1) Subject to the provisions of this section, any instrument whereby property is conveyed or transferred to any person in contemplation of a sale of that property shall be treated for the purposes of the Stamp Act 1891 as a [transfer][3] on sale of that property for a consideration equal to the value of that property.

(2) If on a claim made to the Commissioners not later than two years after the making or execution of an instrument chargeable with duty in accordance with subsection (1) of this section, it is shown to their satisfaction—

(*a*) that the sale in contemplation of which the instrument was made or executed has not taken place and the property has been reconveyed or re-transferred to the person from whom it was conveyed or transferred or to a person to whom his rights have been transmitted on death or bankruptcy; or

(*b*) that the sale has taken place for a consideration which is less than the value in respect of which duty was paid on the instrument by virtue of this section,

the Commissioners shall repay the duty paid by virtue of this section, in a case falling under paragraph (a) of this subsection, so far as it exceeds the stamp duty which would have been payable apart from this section and, in a case falling under paragraph (b) of this subsection, so far as it exceeds the stamp duty which would have been payable if the instrument had been stamped in accordance with subsection (1) of this section in respect of a value equal to the consideration in question:

. . . [1]

(3) No instrument chargeable with duty in accordance with subsection (1) of this section shall be deemed to be duly stamped unless the Commissioners have been required to express their opinion thereon under section 12 of the said Act of 1891 and have expressed their opinion thereon in accordance with that section.

(4) The foregoing provisions of this section shall apply whether or not an instrument conveys or transfers other property in addition to the property in contemplation of the sale of which it is made or executed, but those provisions shall not affect the stamp duty chargeable on the instrument in respect of that other property.

(5) For the purposes . . . [1] of subsection (1) of this section, the value of property conveyed or transferred by an instrument chargeable with duty in accordance with [that subsection][2] shall be determined without regard to—

(*a*) any power (whether or not contained in the instrument) on the exercise of which the property, or any part of or any interest in, the property, may be re-vested in the person from whom it was conveyed or transferred or in any person on his behalf;

(*b*) any annuity reserved out of the property or any part of it, or any life or other interest so reserved, being an interest which is subject to forfeiture;

but if on a claim made to the Commissioners not later than two years after the making or execution of the instrument it is shown to their satisfaction that any such power as is mentioned in paragraph (a) of this subsection has been exercised in relation to the property and the property or any property representing it has been re-conveyed or re-transferred in the whole or in part in consequence of that exercise the Commissioners shall repay the stamp duty paid by virtue of this subsection, in a case where the whole of such property has been so re-conveyed or re-transferred, so far as it exceeds the stamp duty which would have been payable apart from this subsection and, in any other case, so far as it exceeds the stamp duty which would have been payable if the instrument had operated to convey or transfer only such property as is not so re-conveyed or re-transferred.

(6) This section shall be construed as one with the said Act of 1891.

(7) This section shall come into force on 1st August 1965.

Amendments—[1] Words in sub-ss (2), (5) repealed by FA 1985 s 98(6), Sch 27 Pt IX(1).

[2] Words in sub-s (5) substituted by FA 1985 s 82(3).

[3] The word "transfer" substituted for the words "conveyance or transfer" in enactments relating to stamp duty by FA 2003 Sch 20 para 3.

91 Interest where stamp duty repaid under judgment

Amendments—This section repealed by FA 1999 Sch 20 Pt V(1) with effect from 1 October 1999, subject to the provisions in FA 1999 Sch 20 Pt V(1) Note 2. Previously the text read:

> 'Where under section 13(4) of the Stamp Act 1891 (appeals against assessment of stamp duty) a court orders any sum to be repaid by the Commissioners of Inland Revenue, the court may order it to be repaid with such interest as the court may determine.'

97 Short title, construction, extent and repeal

(1) This Act may be cited as the Finance Act 1965.

(2) . . . [1]

(3) Any reference in this Act to any other enactment shall, except so far as the context otherwise requires, be construed as a reference to that enactment as amended or applied by or under any enactment, including this Act.

(4) Save as otherwise expressly provided, such of the provisions of this Act as relate to matters in respect of which the Parliament of Northern Ireland has power to make laws shall not extend to Northern Ireland.

(5) . . .

Note—Sub-s (5) is not relevant to this work.

Amendments—[1] Sub-s (2) repealed by TA 1970 s 538(1), Sch 16.

FINANCE ACT 1966

(1966 Chapter 18)

PART VII

MISCELLANEOUS

45 Harbour reorganisation schemes: corporation tax and stamp duty

(1)–(4) . . . [1]

(5) Where a certified harbour reorganisation scheme contains provision for the transfer of an undertaking, or of any other description of property, to a harbour authority, then, in considering whether any and if so what duty is payable under section 12 of the Finance Act 1895 (which relates to the stamp duty payable in connection with certain statutory conveyances), the consideration for the transfer shall be left out of account; and no stamp duty shall be payable on any contract or agreement for any such transfer if the contract or agreement is conditional on the making and certification of a harbour reorganisation scheme.

(6) In this section—

"harbour authority" has the same meaning as in the Harbours Act 1964;

"harbour reorganisation scheme" means any statutory provision providing for the management by a harbour authority of any harbour or group of harbours in the United Kingdom, and "certified", in relation to any harbour reorganisation scheme, means certified by a Minister of the Crown or Government department as so providing with a view to securing, in the public interest, the efficient and economical development of the harbour or harbours in question; [1]

and in this section and in Schedule 12 to this Act "transferor", in relation to any trade, means the body from whom the trade is transferred, whether or not the transfer is effected by that body.

(7) . . . [1]

Amendments—[1] Sub-ss (1)–(4), (7) and words omitted from sub-s (6) repealed by TA 1970 s 538(1), Sch 16.

53 Short title, construction, extent and repeals

(1) This Act may be cited as the Finance Act 1966.

(2) In this Act . . . [1] so much of Part VII as relates to stamp duties shall be construed as one with the Stamp Act 1891.

(3) Any reference in this Act to any other enactment shall, except so far as the context otherwise requires, be construed as a reference to that enactment as amended or applied by or under any other enactment, including this Act.

(4) Except as otherwise expressly provided, such of the provisions of this Act as relate to matters in respect of which the Parliament of Northern Ireland has power to make laws shall not extend to Northern Ireland.

(5) . . . [3]

(6) . . . [2]

(7) . . .

Note—Words omitted from sub-s (2) are not relevant to this work.
Sub-s (7) is not relevant to this work.

Amendments—[1] Words in sub-s (2) repealed in part by TA 1970 s 538(1), Sch 16 and FA 1975 ss 52(2), (3), 59(5), Sch 13 Pt I.

[2] Sub-s (6) repealed by the Statute Law (Repeals) Act 1978.

[3] Sub-s (5) repealed by the Statute Law (Repeals) Act 1989.

FINANCE ACT 1967

(1967 Chapter 54)

PART V
STAMP DUTIES

27 Conveyances and transfers on sale: reduction of duty, and amendment of provisions for exemption

(1) . . . [1]

(2) . . .

(3) The said section 42 shall not apply to any instrument executed on or after the said 1st August unless it is also shown to the satisfaction of the Commissioners that the instrument was not executed in pursuance of or in connection with an arrangement whereunder—

(*a*) the consideration, or any part of the consideration, for the [transfer][3] was to be provided or received, directly or indirectly, by a person other than a body corporate which at the time of the execution of the instrument was associated within the meaning of the said section 42 with either the transferor or the transferee (meaning, respectively, the body from whom and the body to whom the beneficial interest was conveyed or transferred), or

(*b*) the said interest was previously conveyed or transferred, directly or indirectly, by such a person, or

(*c*) the transferor and the transferee were to cease to be associated within the meaning of the said section 42 by reason of [the transferor or a third body corporate ceasing to be the transferee's parent (within the meaning of the said section 42)][2];

and, without prejudice to the generality of paragraph (a) above, an arrangement shall be treated as within that paragraph if it is one whereunder the transferor or the transferee or a body corporate associated with either as there mentioned, was to be enabled to provide any of the consideration, or was to part with any of it, by or in consequence of the carrying out of a transaction or transactions involving, or any of them involving, a payment or other disposition by a person other than a body corporate so associated.

This subsection shall, as respects instruments executed on or after the said 1st August, have effect in substitution for section 50 of the Finance Act 1938.

Note:—Sub-s (2) substitutes FA 1930, s 42(2), (3) for s 42(2).

Statement of Practice SP 3/98—Stamp duty—group relief.

Amendments—[1] Sub-s (1) repealed by FA 1972 s 134, Sch 28 Pt XI.

[2] Words in sub-s (3)(*c*) substituted by FA 1995 s 149(6), (7) in relation to instruments executed after 30 April 1995.

[3] The word "transfer" substituted for the words "conveyance or transfer" in enactments relating to stamp duty by FA 2003 Sch 20 para 3.

30 Exemption for bearer instruments relating to stock in foreign currencies

Amendments—This section repealed by FA 1999 Sch 20 Pt V(2) with effect in relation to instruments executed, or bearer instruments issued, from 1 October 1999, subject to the provisions in FA 1999 Sch 20 Pt V(2) Note 2. Previously the text read:

'(1) Subject to subsection (2) below, no duty shall be chargeable under the heading "Bearer Instrument" in Schedule 1 to the Stamp Act 1891 on the issue on or after 1st August 1967 of any instrument which relates to stock expressed in any currency other than sterling or in any units of account defined by reference to more than one currency (whether or not including sterling), or on the transfer on or after that date of the stock constituted by, or transferable by means of, any such instrument.

(2) Where the stock to which any instrument relates consists of a loan for the repayment of which there is an option between sterling and one or more other currencies, that subsection shall apply to the instrument if the option is exercisable only by the holder of the stock, and shall not apply to it in any other case.

(3) Where the capital stock of any company or body of persons is not expressed in terms of any currency, it shall be treated for the purposes of subsection (1) above as expressed in the currency of the territory under the law of which the company or body is formed or established; and a unit under a unit trust scheme, or a share in a foreign mutual fund, shall be treated for the purposes of this section as capital stock of a company or body formed or established in the territory by the law of which the scheme or fund is governed.

(4) . . .

(5) In this section—

"foreign mutual fund" means a fund administered under arrangements governed by the law of a territory outside the United Kingdom whereby subscribers to the fund are entitled to participate in, or receive payments by reference to, profits or income arising to the fund from the acquisition, holding, management or disposal of investments, and "share", in relation to a foreign mutual fund, means the right of a subscriber, or of another in his right, to participate in, or receive payments by reference to, profits or income so arising;

. . .

"stock", except in the expression "capital stock", shall be construed in accordance with section 59(4) of the Finance Act 1963; and

"unit trust scheme", and "unit" in relation to a unit trust scheme have the meanings given to them by section 57 of the Finance Act 1946.'

PART VI
MISCELLANEOUS

45 Citation, interpretation, construction, extent and repeals

(1) This Act may be cited as the Finance Act 1967.

(2) . . .

(3) In this Act—

(*a*), (*b*) . . .

(*c*) . . .

(*d*)–(*f*) . . .

(*g*) Part V shall be construed as one with the Stamp Act 1891.

(*h*) . . .

(4), (5) . . .

(6) Any reference in this Act to any other enactment shall, except so far as the context otherwise requires, be construed as a reference to that enactment as amended or applied by or under any other enactment, including this Act.

(7) Except as otherwise expressly provided, such of the provisions of this Act as relate to matters in respect of which the Parliament of Northern Ireland has power to make laws shall not extend to Northern Ireland.

(8) The enactments mentioned in Schedule 16 to this Act are hereby repealed to the extent mentioned in the third column of that Schedule, but subject to any provision in relation thereto made at the end of any Part of that Schedule.

Note—Sub-s (2), (3)(*a*), (*b*), (*c*), (*d*), (*e*), (*f*), (*h*), (4), (5) are either repealed or not relevant to stamp duty. Sub-s (2) is spent.

PROVISIONAL COLLECTION OF TAXES ACT 1968

(1968 Chapter 2)

1 Temporary statutory effect of House of Commons resolutions affecting . . . , stamp duty reserve tax,[2] . . .

(1) This section applies only to . . . , [stamp duty reserve tax,][3] [stamp duty land tax,][9] . . .

(1A) . . . [4]

(2) Subject to that, and to the provisions of subsections (4) to (8) below, where the House of Commons passes a resolution which—

(*a*) provides for the renewal for a further period of any tax in force or imposed during the previous financial year (whether at the same or a different rate, and whether with or without modifications) or for the variation or abolition of any existing tax, and

(*b*) contains a declaration that it is expedient in the public interest that the resolution should have statutory effect under the provisions of this Act,

the resolution shall, for the period specified in the next following subsection, have statutory effect as if contained in an Act of Parliament and, where the resolution provides for the renewal of a tax, all enactments which were in force with reference to that tax as last imposed by Act of Parliament shall during that period have full force and effect with respect to the tax as renewed by the resolution. In this section references to the renewal of a tax include references to its reimposition, and references to the abolition of a tax include references to its repeal.

(3) The said period is—

(*a*) in the case of a resolution passed in [November or December][5] in any year, one expiring with [5th May in the next calendar year][6];

[(*aa*) in the case of a resolution passed in February or March in any year, one expiring with 5th August in the same calendar year; and][8]

(*b*) in the case of any other resolution, one expiring at the end of four months after the date on which it is expressed to take effect or, if no such date is expressed, after the date on which it is passed.

(4) A resolution shall cease to have statutory effect under this section unless within the next [thirty][7] days on which the House of Commons sits after the day on which the resolution is passed—

(*a*) a Bill renewing, varying or, as the case may be, abolishing the tax is read a second time by the House, or

(*b*) a Bill is amended by the House [in Committee or on Report, or by any [Public Bill Committee][10] of the House][1] so as to include provision for the renewal, variation or, as the case may be, abolition of the tax.

(5) a resolution shall also cease to have statutory effect under this section if—

(*a*) the provisions giving effect to it are rejected during the passage of the Bill containing them through the House, or

(*b*) an Act comes into operation renewing, varying or, as the case may be, abolishing the tax, or

(*c*) Parliament is dissolved or prorogued.

(6) Where, in the case of a resolution providing for the renewal or variation of a tax, the resolution ceases to have statutory effect by virtue of subsection (4) or (5) above, or the period specified in subsection (3) above terminates, before an Act comes into operation renewing or varying the tax, any money paid in pursuance of the resolution shall be repaid or made good, and any deduction made in pursuance of the resolution shall be deemed to be an unauthorised deduction.

(7) Where any tax as renewed or varied by a resolution is modified by the Act renewing or varying the tax, any money paid in pursuance of the resolution which would not have been payable under the new conditions affecting the tax shall be repaid or made good, and any deduction made in pursuance of the resolution shall, so far as it would not have been authorised under the new conditions affecting the tax, be deemed to be an unauthorised deduction.

(8) When during any session a resolution has had statutory effect under this section, statutory effect shall not be again given under this section in the same session to the same resolution or to a resolution having the same effect.

Note—Words omitted from the heading and sub-s (1) are not relevant for the purposes of stamp duty.
Sub-s (1A) is not relevant for the purposes of stamp duty.

Amendments—[1] Words in sub-s (4)(*b*) added by FA 1968 s 60.

[2] Words in the heading inserted by virtue of FA 1986 s 86(3).

[3] Words in sub-s (1) inserted by FA 1986 s 86(3).

[4] Sub-s (1A) repealed by FA 1993 ss 205(3), 213, Sch 23 Pt VI in relation to resolutions passed after 27 July 1993.

[5] Words in sub-s (3)(*a*) substituted for the words "March or April" by FA 1993 s 205 (4), (7) in relation to resolutions passed after 27 July 1993.

[6] Words in sub-s (3)(*a*) substituted for the words "5th August in the same calendar year" by FA 1993 s 205 (4), (7) in relation to resolutions passed after 27 July 1993.

[7] Word in sub-s (4) substituted for the word "twenty-five" by FA 1993 s 205(5), (7) in relation to resolutions passed after 27 July 1993.

[8] Words in sub-s (3) inserted by F(No2)A 1997 s 50 in relation to resolutions passed after 31 July 1997.

[9] Words inserted by FA 2003 s 123(1), Sch 18 para 1 with effect in accordance with FA 2003 s 124, Sch 19.
[10] Words in sub-s (4)(*b*) substituted by FA 2007 s 112(1) with effect from 19 July 2007.

TAXES MANAGEMENT ACT 1970

(1970 Chapter 9)

Note—For the relevant text of this Act as applicable to stamp duty reserve tax, see the Stamp Duty Reserve Tax Regulations, SI 1986/1711 reg 20 and Schedule.

FINANCE ACT 1970

(1970 Chapter 24)

PART III

MISCELLANEOUS

Stamp Duties

32 Abolition of certain stamp duties, and amendments as to rates and other matters

Amendments—This section repealed by FA 1999 Sch 20 Pt V(2) with effect in relation to instruments executed, or bearer instruments issued, from 1 October 1999, subject to the provisions in FA 1999 Sch 20 Pt V(2) Note 2. Previously the text read:

"The provisions of Schedule 7 to this Act shall have effect, being—

(*a*) in the case of those in Part I of that Schedule, provisions abolishing, or consequential on the abolition of, certain stamp duties,

(*b*) in the case of those in Part II of that Schedule, provisions making general amendments of or in connection with the enactments relating to stamp duties, and

(*c*) in the case of those in Part III of that Schedule, special provisions required for the purposes of those enactments in connection with the introduction of the new currency provided for by the Decimal Currency Act, 1967."

33 Composition by stock exchanges in respect of transfer duty

(1) The Commissioners may enter into an agreement with, or with persons acting on behalf of, [any recognised investment exchange or recognised clearing house][4] for the composition, in accordance with the provisions of this section, of the stamp duty chargeable under or by reference to [Part I or paragraph 16 of Schedule 13 to the Finance Act 1999 ([transfer][5] on sale or otherwise)][1] on such instruments as may be specified in the agreement, . . . [2] . . . [4]

(2) An agreement under this section shall provide—

(*a*) for every instrument to which the agreement relates to bear on its face an indication of the amount of stamp duty chargeable thereon,

(*b*) for the issue in respect of every such instrument by or on behalf of the [recognised investment exchange or recognised clearing house][4], of a certificate (which may relate to more than one such instrument) to the effect that stamp duty to the amount so indicated has been, or will be, accounted for to the Commissioners,

(*c*) for the delivery to the Commissioners, by or on behalf of the [recognised investment exchange or recognised clearing house][4], of periodical accounts in respect of instruments to which the agreement relates, giving such particulars with respect thereto as may be specified in the agreement, and

(*d*) for the payment to the Commissioners, by or on behalf of the [recognised investment exchange or recognised clearing house][4], and on the delivery of any such account, of the aggregate amount of the stamp duty chargeable as mentioned in subsection (1) above on instruments to which the agreement relates during the period to which the account relates;

and any such agreement may contain such other terms and conditions as the Commissioners think proper.

(3) . . . [3]

(4) An instrument to which an agreement under this section relates and in respect of which a certificate to the effect mentioned in subsection (2) (*b*) above has been issued by or on behalf of the [recognised investment exchange or recognised clearing house][4], in question shall be treated for the purposes of the Stamp Act 1891 as stamped with the amount of duty indicated on the face of the instrument.

(5) A [recognised investment exchange or recognised clearing house][4], or person making default in delivering any account required by an agreement under this section, or in paying any amount in accordance with such an agreement, shall be liable to a fine not exceeding £50 for any day during which the default continues; and, in addition, every amount payable under such an agreement shall bear interest at the rate of 5 per cent. per annum, recoverable by Her Majesty, from the due date for delivery of the account by reference to which it is payable until the actual date of payment.

(6) Except in so far as the context otherwise requires, any reference to a stamp in section 9 or 10 of the Stamp Duties Management Act, 1891 (allowances for spoiled stamps) shall include a reference to any indication of an amount of stamp duty on the face of any instrument to which an agreement under this section relates.

[(7) In this section "recognised investment exchange" and "recognised clearing house" have the meanings given by section 285(1) of the Financial Services and Markets Act 2000.][4]

Cross references—See FA 1976 s 127(7) (extension of this section to Northern Ireland);

FA 1986 s 84(3), (6) (stamp duty exemption with effect from an appointed date on an instrument effecting a transfer of stock if an agreement under this section is in force at the time of the transfer).

Notes—This section was to be repealed by FA 1990 Sch 19 Pt VI with effect from an appointed day in accordance with FA 1990 ss 107–111. The Treasury order specifying the appointed day for the purposes of FA 1990 ss 107–110 was to coincide with the start of paperless trading under the Stock Exchange's planned TAURUS system (IR press release, 20-3-90). However, on 11-3-93 the London Stock Exchange News Release 6/93 announced that TAURUS had been abandoned.

Amendments—[1] Words in sub-s (1) substituted by FA 1999 s 112(4), Sch 14 para 5 with effect in relation to instruments executed after 30 September 1999. This does not apply to transfers or other instruments relating to units under a unit trust scheme by virtue of FA 1999 s 122. For prospective repeal of FA 1999 Sch 14 para 5 see FA 1999 s 123(3). Previously the text read 'the heading "Conveyance or Transfer on Sale" [or "Conveyance or Transfer of any kind not hereinbefore described"] in Schedule 1 to the Stamp Act 1891'.

[2] Words in sub-s (1) repealed by FA 1976 s 132(5), Sch 15 Pt VI.

[3] Sub-s (3) repealed by FA 1976 ss 127(4), 132(5), Sch 15 Pt VI.

[4] Words in sub-ss (1), (2)(*b*)–(*d*), (4), (5) substituted; and sub-s (7) added; by the Financial Services and Markets Act 2000 (Consequential Amendments) (Taxes) Order, SI 2001/3629 art 4 with effect from 1 December 2001 (immediately after the coming into force of the Financial Services and Markets Act 2000 ss 411, 432(1), Sch 20).

[5] 5 The word "transfer" substituted for the words "conveyance or transfer" in enactments relating to stamp duty by FA 2003 Sch 20 para 3.

36 Citation, interpretation, construction, extent and repeals

(1) This Act may be cited as the Finance Act, 1970.

(2) In this Act—

(*a*) except where the context otherwise requires, "the Board" means the Commissioners of Inland Revenue,

(*b*), (*c*) . . .

(3) . . . [1]

(4) . . .

(5) Part III of this Act, so far as it relates to stamp duties, shall be construed as one with the Stamp Act 1891.

(6) Any reference in this Act to any other enactment shall, except so far as the context otherwise requires, be construed as a reference to that enactment as amended or applied by or under any other enactment, including this Act.

(7) Except as otherwise expressly provided such of the provisions of this Act as relate to matters in respect of which the Parliament of Northern Ireland has power to make laws shall not extend to Northern Ireland.

(8) The enactments mentioned in Schedule 8 to this Act (which include enactments which are spent or otherwise unnecessary) are hereby repealed to the extent mentioned in the third column of that Schedule, but subject to any provision in relation thereto made at the end of any Part of that Schedule.

Note—Sub-ss (2)(*b*), (*c*) and (4) are not relevant to this work.

Amendments—[1] Sub-s (3) repealed by CEMA 1979 s 177(3), Sch 6 Pt I.

SCHEDULES

SCHEDULE 7

STAMP DUTIES

Section 32

Note—This Schedule repealed by FA 1999 Sch 20 Pt V(2) with effect in relation to instruments executed, or bearer instruments issued, from 1 October 1999, subject to the provisions in FA 1999 Sch 20 Pt V(2) Note 2. For instruments executed, or bearer instruments issued before 1 October 1999, the text should read:

PART I
ABOLITION OF CERTAIN DUTIES

Duties abolished as from 1st August 1970

1—*(1) This paragraph has effect as from 1st August 1970.*

(2) The following stamp duties are hereby abolished—

(a) the duty of 6d. specified in Schedule 1 to the Stamp Act 1891 under the heading beginning "Agreement or any Memorandum of an Agreement" (the provisions consequential on this abolition being those contained in sub-paragraph (3) below);

(b) the duty of 6d. specified in that Schedule under the heading "Policy of Insurance other than Life Insurance" inserted by section 30(1) of the Finance Act 1959 (and so that a policy of insurance other than life insurance shall be exempt from all stamp duties);

(c) the duty of £10 or £6 imposed on a certificate of registration for an alkali or other works by section 9(6) of the Alkali, &c Works Regulation Act 1906 as amended by section 47 of the Finance Act 1922; and

(d) the duty of 10s. imposed on the memorandum and on the articles of association of a company by virtue of section 3 and section 9 (c) respectively of the Companies Act 1948 (which provide that each of those documents is to be stamped as if it were a deed).

(3) In consequence of sub-paragraph (2) (a) above—

(a) . . .

(b) . . .

(c) . . .

Duties abolished as from 1st February 1971

2—*(1) This paragraph has effect as from 1st February 1971.*

(2) The following stamp duties are hereby abolished—

(a) the duty of 2d. specified in Schedule 1 to the Stamp Act 1891 under the heading beginning "Bill of Exchanges or Promissory Note" inserted by Section 33 (1) of the Finance Act 1961 and

(b) the duty of 2d. specified in that Schedule under the heading beginning "Receipt".

(3) No application for relief in respect of the duty referred to in sub-paragraph (2) (a) above may be made under any of sections 9 to 12 of the Stamp Duties Management Act 1891 (spoiled, misused and unwanted stamps); and no repayment shall be made under any agreement entered into under section 39 of the Finance Act 1956 (composition for the said duty by bankers) in respect of any form supplied by a banker to a customer and returned to the banker unused or spoiled on or after the said 1st February.

PART II
GENERAL AMENDMENTS

3 *This Part of this Schedule, except paragraph 5, has effect as from 1st August 1970.*

Bearer Instruments

6—*(1)–(3)* . . .

(4) Where an overseas bearer instrument in respect of a loan expressed in sterling has been stamped ad valorem, or with the denoting stamp referred to in section 60(3) of the Finance Act 1963 or with duty under paragraph (4) of the said heading, duty shall not be charged under that heading by reason only that the instrument is amended on its face pursuant to an agreement for the variation of any of its original terms or conditions.

Conveyance or transfer on sale

13—*(1) Section 114 of the Stamp Act 1891 (composition for stamp duty on transfers of colonial etc, stock) shall cease to have effect, but transfers of any stock in respect of which payments have been made under that section shall continue to be exempt from stamp duty.*

(2) . . .

Mortgages, etc

16—*(1)–(3)* . . .

(4) The duty chargeable under paragraph (4) of the said heading on the transfer, assignment, disposition or assignation to any person of, or of the money or stock secured by, any collateral, auxiliary, additional or substituted security (including any instrument by way of further assurance) shall not exceed 50p. if a transfer, assignment, disposition or assignation to the same person of (or, as the case may be, of the money or stock secured by) the principal or primary security has been duly stamped with the duty chargeable under that paragraph.

(5) . . . *; and the duty chargeable under that paragraph shall not in any case exceed 50p.*

PART III

SPECIAL PROVISIONS CONNECTED WITH THE NEW CURRENCY

Late stamping, etc

19—*(1) Where immediately before 15th February 1971 any instrument chargeable with stamp duty is either not stamped or overstamped or insufficiently stamped, the amount of duty then chargeable, or properly chargeable, on the instrument, or, in the case of an insufficiently stamped instrument, the amount of additional duty then chargeable thereon, shall thereafter become, for all the purposes of the enactments relating to stamp duties—*

(a) the equivalent of that amount in the new currency, reduced where that equivalent is not a multiple of 5p to the nearest such multiple, or

(b) 5p if the said equivalent is less than 10p.

(2) In sub-paragraph (1) above, "the new currency" means the new currency of the United Kingdom provided for by the Decimal Currency Act 1967.

Note—This schedule repealed by FA 1999 Sch 20 Pt V(2) with effect in relation to instruments executed, or bearer instruments issued, from 1 October 1999, subject to the provisions in FA 1999 Sch 20 Pt V(2) Note 2. For instruments executed, or bearer instruments issued before 1 October 1999, see the above text.

FINANCE ACT 1971

(1971 Chapter 68)

PART V

MISCELLANEOUS

64 Stamp duty—abolition of duty on bonds, mortgages etc

Amendments—This section repealed by FA 1999 Sch 20 Pt V(2) with effect in relation to instruments executed, or bearer instruments issued, from 1 October 1999, subject to the provisions in FA 1999 Sch 20 Pt V(2) Note 2. Previously the text read:

'(1) The following stamp duties are hereby abolished—

(*a*) except as respects any instrument increasing the rent reserved by another instrument, the duties chargeable by virtue of paragraph (1) and paragraph (2) (securities for annuities other than superannuation annuities and for certain other periodic sums) of the heading in Schedule 1 to the Stamp Act 1891 "Bond, Covenant, or Instrument of any kind whatsoever",

(*b*) the duties chargeable by virtue of the heading in that Schedule "Bond of any kind whatsoever not specifically charged with any duty", and

(*c*) the duties chargeable by virtue of the heading in that Schedule beginning "Mortgage, Bond, Debenture, Covenant".

(2) Subject to section 4 of the said Act of 1891 (separate charges on instruments containing or relating to several distinct matters) . . . , any instrument which, but for subsection (1) above, would be chargeable with duty under a heading mentioned in that subsection shall not be chargeable with duty under any other heading in the said Schedule 1.

(3) For the avoidance of doubt it is hereby declared that paragraph (*c*) of subsection (1) above does not affect the amount of any duty chargeable under the said Schedule 1 by reference to the heading mentioned in that paragraph.

(4) This section has effect as from 1st August 1971.'

69 Citation, interpretation, construction, extent and repeals

(1) This Act may be cited as the Finance Act 1971.

(2), (3) . . .

(4) Except so far as the context otherwise requires, any reference in this Act to any enactment shall be construed as a reference to that enactment as amended, and as including a reference to that enactment as applied, by or under any other enactment, including this Act.

(5), (6) . . .

(7) The enactments mentioned in Schedule 14 to this Act (Part VI of which includes certain obsolete enactments) are hereby repealed to the extent mentioned in the third column of that Schedule, but subject to any provision at the end of any Part of that Schedule.

Note—Sub-ss (2), (3), (5), (6) are not relevant to this work.

FINANCE ACT 1972

(1972 Chapter 41)

PART VII

MISCELLANEOUS

126 Abolition of stamp duty on bank notes and of bankers' licences

Amendments—This section repealed by FA 1999 Sch 20 Pt V(2) with effect in relation to instruments executed, or bearer instruments issued, from 1 October 1999, subject to the provisions in FA 1999 Sch 20 Pt V(2) Note 2. Previously the text read:

'(1) The following are hereby abolished—

(*a*) the stamp duty chargeable by virtue of the heading "BANK NOTE" in Schedule 1 to the Stamp Act 1891;

(*b*) the licences required to be taken out under section 24 of the Stamp Act 1815 (licences for bankers etc issuing certain promissory notes).

(2) This section takes effect on 25th June 1972; and if on or after that date and before the passing of this Act a person pays any duty in respect of a licence of the kind mentioned in subsection (1)(*b*) above which would not have been payable if this Act had then been in force the Commissioners of Inland Revenue shall, on application made to them within two years after the date of payment, repay the duty.'

FINANCE ACT 1973

(1973 Chapter 51)

PART V

STAMP DUTY

47 Stamp duty on documents relating to chargeable transactions of capital companies

(1) If at the time, or as a result, of the occurrence after 31st July 1973 of any of the transactions relating to a capital company which are specified in Part I of Schedule 19 to this Act (in this section referred to as "chargeable transactions")

(a) the place of effective management of the capital company is in Great Britain, or

(b) the registered office of the capital company is in Great Britain but the place of its effective management is outside the member States,

then, subject to subsection (2) below, there shall be delivered to the Commissioners, within one month of the transaction, a statement in such form and containing such particulars with respect to the transaction as the Commissioners may prescribe.

(2) The obligation to deliver a statement to the Commissioners under subsection (1) above shall not apply in relation to a chargeable transaction falling within sub-paragraph (a) or sub-paragraph (b) of paragraph 1 of Schedule 19 to this Act if the transaction consists of or includes—

(a) the formation of a company which is to be incorporated with limited liability under the [Companies Act 1985][1] and is to have a share capital, or

(b) an allotment of shares in respect of which there is a duty under section 52 (1) of that Act to deliver a return to the registrar of companies, or

(c) the registration of a limited partnership (which is effected by sending or delivering a statement under section 8 of the Limited Partnerships Act 1907 to the registrar of companies), or

(d) such a change in the contribution or liability of a member of a limited partnership as gives rise to a duty under section 9 of the Limited Partnerships Act 1907 to send or deliver a statement thereof to the registrar of companies.

(3) In any case where, by virtue of subsection (2) (a) above, there is no obligation to deliver to the Commissioners a statement under subsection (1) above with respect to a chargeable transaction, a statement with respect thereto shall be delivered to the registrar of companies, in addition to the memorandum and articles to be delivered under [section 10 (1) of the Companies Act 1985][1], and

(a) that statement shall be registered by the registrar of companies upon the stamp duty chargeable in accordance with subsection (5) below being paid, and

(b) unless that statement is so registered, the registrar of companies shall not register the memorandum and articles under [section 12 of the Companies Act 1985][1].

(4) If, by virtue of subsection (2) above, there is no obligation to deliver to the Commissioners a statement under subsection (1) above with respect to a chargeable transaction, then

(a) the return or statement required to be delivered or sent to the registrar of companies as mentioned in subsection (2) above, or

(b) the statement required to be delivered to the registrar of companies under subsection (3) above,

shall contain the like particulars with respect to the transaction as would be required to be contained in a statement under subsection (1) above if the obligation under that subsection did apply.

(5) Subject to subsection (6) below, where a chargeable transaction occurs, the relevant document shall be charged with ad valorem stamp duty of £1 for every £100 or part of £100 of the amount determined in relation to that document under Part II of Schedule 19 to this Act.

(6) If the relevant document relates to a chargeable transaction which, by virtue of Part III of Schedule 19 to this Act, is an exempt transaction for the purposes of this section then, except as provided in that Part, stamp duty shall not be chargeable on the document under subsection (5) above, but the document shall not be treated as duly stamped unless it is stamped, in accordance with section 12 of the Stamp Act 1891, with a particular stamp denoting either that it is not chargeable with any duty or that it is duly stamped.

(7) If a chargeable transaction occurs and the stamp duty (if any) chargeable in accordance with this section on the relevant document is not paid within one month from the date of the transaction,—

(a) the duty, if any, which is so chargeable shall be a debt due to Her Majesty from the capital company to which the transaction relates, or, if that capital company is not a body corporate, shall be a debt due to Her Majesty for which each of the members of the capital company shall be jointly and severally liable; and

(b) the capital company or, if it is not a body corporate, each of its members jointly and severally shall incur a fine equal to 5 per cent of the duty chargeable and a similar fine for every month from the date of the transaction, other than the first, during which the duty remains unpaid.

(8) The supplementary provisions in Part IV of Schedule 19 to this Act shall have effect in relation to chargeable transactions and, in consequence of the provisions of this section, the amendments in Part V of that Schedule shall have effect.

(9) In this section and in Schedule 19 to this Act —

"registered office", in relation to a limited partnership formed in accordance with the Limited Partnerships Act 1907 means the principal place of business of the partnership;

"the relevant document", in relation to a chargeable transaction, means the statement required to be delivered under subsection (1) above or, if subsection (2) above applies,—

(a) the return or statement required to be delivered or sent to the registrar of companies as mentioned in subsection (2) above, or

(b) the statement required to be delivered to the registrar of companies under subsection (3) above.[2]

Simon's Tax Cases—*Cambridge Petroleum Royalties Ltd v IRC* [1982] STC 325; *Swithland Investments Ltd and anor v IRC* [1990] STC 448.

Amendments—[1] Words in sub-s (2) (*a*), (3) substituted by the Companies Consolidation (Consequential Provisions) Act 1985 Sch 2 with effect from 1 July 1985.

[2] This section repealed by FA 1988 Sch 14 Pt XI with effect from 22 March 1988, but is reproduced here for the purposes of FA 1988 s 141(4).

50 Temporary statutory effect of House of Commons resolution affecting stamp duties

(1) Where the House of Commons passes a resolution which—

(*a*) provides for the variation or abolition of an existing stamp duty . . . [1]; and

(*b*) is expressed to have effect for a period stated in the resolution in accordance with the following provisions of this section; and

(*c*) contains a declaration that it is expedient in the public interest that the resolution should have statutory effect under the provisions of this section;

then, subject to subsection (3) of this section, the resolution shall for the period so stated have statutory effect as if contained in an Act of Parliament.

(2) The period to be stated in a resolution is a period expressed as beginning on a date so stated and ending on, or thirty-one days or such less number of days as may be so stated after, the earliest of the dates mentioned in this subsection; and those dates are—

(*a*) the [thirtieth][2] day on which, after the day the resolution is passed, the House of Commons sits without a Bill containing provisions to the same effect as the resolution being read a second time and without a Bill being amended (whether by the House or a Committee of the House or a [Public Bill Committee][4] so as to include such provisions;

(*b*) the rejection of such provisions during the passage through the House of a Bill containing them;

(*c*) the dissolution or prorogation of Parliament; and

(*d*) the expiration of the period of [six][3] months beginning with the day on which the resolution takes effect.

(3) A resolution shall cease to have statutory effect under this section if an Act comes into operation varying or abolishing the duty.

(4) The ending of the period for which a resolution has statutory effect under the provisions of this section shall not affect the validity of anything done during that period.

Cross references—See F(No 2)A 1975 s 72 (extension of this section to Northern Ireland).

Amendments—[1] Words in sub-s (1)(*a*) repealed by FA 1975 Sch 13 Pt I, with effect from 13 March 1975.

[2] Word in sub-s (2)(*a*) substituted by FA 1993 s 207 in relation to resolutions passed after 27 July 1993.

[3] Word in sub-s (2)(*d*) substituted by FA 1993 s 207 in relation to resolutions passed after 27 July 1993.

[4] Words in sub-s (2)(*a*) substituted by FA 2007 s 112(1) with effect from 19 July 2007.

PART VI

MISCELLANEOUS AND GENERAL

54 Amendments consequential on establishment of The Stock Exchange

(1) In the enactments relating to . . . stamp duty—

(*a*) references to the Stock Exchange, London or the London Stock Exchange, a stock exchange in the United Kingdom or a recognised stock exchange in the United Kingdom shall be construed as references to The Stock Exchange;

(*b*) references to quotation on a stock exchange in the United Kingdom or a recognised stock exchange in the United Kingdom shall be construed as references to listing in the Official List of The Stock Exchange; and

(*c*) references to a member of a stock exchange in the United Kingdom shall be construed as references to a member of The Stock Exchange;

and those enactments shall have effect subject to the amendments specified in Schedule 21 to this Act.

(2) This section shall be deemed to have come into operation on 25th March 1973 but shall not affect the operation of any enactment in relation to anything done before that day.

Amendments—Words omitted from sub-s (1) repealed by TA 1988 s 844(4), Sch 31.

59 Citation, interpretation, construction, extent and repeals

(1) This Act may be cited as the Finance Act 1973.

(2) . . .

(3) In this Act—

(*a*) . . . [2]

(*b*) . . . [3]

(*c*) . . .

(*d*) . . . [1]

(*e*) Part V shall be construed as one with the Stamp Act 1891.

(4) Except so far as the context otherwise requires, any reference in this Act to any enactment shall be construed as a reference to that enactment as amended, and as including a reference to that enactment as applied, by or under any other enactment, including this Act.

(5) Except as otherwise expressly provided, such of the provisions of this Act as relate to matters in respect of which the Parliament of Northern Ireland has power to make laws do not extend to Northern Ireland.

(6) If the Parliament of Northern Ireland passes provisions amending or replacing any enactment of that Parliament referred to in this Act the reference shall be construed as a reference to the enactment as so amended or, as the case may be, as a reference to those provisions.

(7) The enactments mentioned in Schedule 22 to this Act (which include certain enactments which had ceased to have effect before the commencement of this Act) are hereby repealed to the extent specified in the third column of that Schedule, but subject to any provision at the end of any Part of that Schedule.

Note—Sub-ss (2), (3) (*c*) are not relevant to this work.

Amendments—[1] Sub-s (3) (*d*) repealed by FA 1975 ss 57(2), 59(5), Sch 13 Pt I.

[2] Sub-s (3)(*a*) repealed by CEMA 1979 s 177(3), Sch 6 Pt I.

[3] Sub-s (3)(*b*) repealed by VATA 1983 s 50(2), Sch 11.

SCHEDULES

SCHEDULE 19

STAMP DUTY ON DOCUMENTS RELATING TO CHARGEABLE TRANSACTIONS OF CAPITAL COMPANIES

Section 47

PART III

EXEMPT TRANSACTIONS

10—*(1) A chargeable transaction shall be an exempt transaction for the purposes of section 47 of this Act if it is shown to the satisfaction of the Commissioners—*

(a) that, by virtue of the transaction, a capital company which is in the process of being formed or which is already in existence

(i) has acquired share capital of another capital company to the extent that, after the transaction, not less than 75 per cent of the issued share capital of that other company is beneficially owned by the first company, or

(ii) has acquired the whole or any part of the undertaking of another capital company, and

(b) that the conditions specified in sub-paragraph (2) below are fulfilled in relation to the transaction;

and in this paragraph the first company mentioned in paragraph (a) above is referred to as "the acquiring company" and the other company mentioned in sub-paragraph (i) or (ii) of that paragraph is referred to as "the acquired company".

(2) The conditions referred to in sub-paragraph (1) above are

(a) that the place of effective management or the registered office of the acquired company is in a member State; and

(b) that so much, if any, of the consideration (taking no account of such part thereof as consists of the assumption or discharge by the acquiring company of liabilities of the acquired company) for the acquisition referred to in that sub-paragraph as does not consist

(i) where shares are to be acquired, of the issue of shares in the acquiring company to the holders of shares in the acquired company in exchange for the shares held by them in the acquired company,

(ii) where the whole or any part of the undertaking is to be acquired, of the issue of shares in the acquiring company to the acquired company or to holders of shares in the acquired company,

consists wholly of a payment in cash which does not exceed 10 per cent of the nominal value of the shares which make up the balance of the consideration.

(3) If, at any time within the period of five years beginning with the occurrence of a chargeable transaction which is an exempt transaction falling within paragraph (a) (i) of sub-paragraph (1) above, the acquiring company

(a) ceases to retain at least 75 per cent of the issued share capital of the acquired company, or

(b) disposes of any of the shares in the acquired company which it held immediately after the occurrence of the chargeable transaction,

duty shall then become chargeable, and shall be payable in accordance with sub-paragraph (4) below; but for the purpose of determining whether paragraph (a) or paragraph (b) above applies, any disposal of shares shall be disregarded if it is effected

(i) by a transfer forming part of a chargeable transaction which is itself an exempt transaction by virtue of any provision of sub-paragraph (1) above, or

(ii) in the course of the winding-up of the acquiring company.

(4) If sub-paragraph (3) above applies, then, within one month of the date on which the holding of share capital referred to in paragraph (a) of that sub-paragraph first falls below 75 per cent or, as the case may be, the date of the first disposal of any of the shares referred to in paragraph (b) of that sub-paragraph (in this paragraph referred to as "the date of charge"), there shall be paid to the Commissioners duty corresponding to the stamp duty which would have been charged under subsection (5) of section 47 of this Act on the relevant document if the chargeable transaction had not been an exempt transaction.

(5) If sub-paragraph (4) above applies, subsection (7) of section 47 of this Act shall apply

(a) as if the chargeable transaction had never been an exempt transaction; and

(b) as if for the reference in that subsection to the date of the transaction there were substituted a reference to the date of charge;

and, in addition, interest on the duty payable under that sub-paragraph at the rate of 5 per cent per annum from the date when the chargeable transaction occurred to the date of charge shall be a debt due to Her Majesty from the acquiring company.

[(6) This paragraph applies also where the acquired company is a corporation or body of persons which is not a capital company for the purposes of this Schedule but which is treated as such in another member State; and paragraph 3 (1) above shall apply for the interpretation of this sub-paragraph as it applies for the interpretation of paragraph 1 above.][1]

Amendments—[1] Sub-para (6) added by FA 1976 s 128.
This Schedule repealed by FA 1988 Sch 14 Pt XI with effect from 22 March 1988.
This paragraph is reproduced here for the purposes of FA 1988 s 141(4).

FINANCE ACT 1974

(1974 Chapter 30)

PART IV

MISCELLANEOUS AND GENERAL

49 Increase of certain stamp duties

Amendments—This section repealed by FA 1999 Sch 20 Pt V(2) with effect in relation to instruments executed, or bearer instruments issued, from 1 October 1999, subject to the provisions in FA 1999 Sch 20 Pt V(2) Note 2. Previously the text read:

"(1) The provisions of Schedule 11 to this Act shall have effect, being provisions increasing, or connected with the increase of, certain stamp duties.

(2)–(3) . . . "

57 Citation, interpretation, construction and repeals

(1) This Act may be cited as the Finance Act 1974.

(2) . . .

(3) In this Act—

(*a*)–(*d*) . . . [1, 2, 3]

(4) Except so far as the context otherwise requires, any reference in this Act to any enactment shall be construed as a reference to that enactment as amended, and as including a reference to that enactment as applied, by or under any other enactment, including this Act.

(5) If the Northern Ireland Assembly passes provisions amending or replacing any enactment of the Parliament of Northern Ireland, or any Order in Council made under section 1(3) of the Northern Ireland (Temporary Provisions) Act 1972 referred to in this Act, the reference shall be construed as a reference to the enactment or order as so amended or, as the case may be, as a reference to those provisions.

(6) The enactments mentioned in Schedule 14 to this Act (which include certain enactments which had ceased to have effect before the commencement of this Act) are hereby repealed to the extent specified in the third column of that Schedule, but subject to any provision at the end of any Part of that Schedule.

Note—Sub-ss (2), (3)(*b*) are not relevant to this work.

Amendments—[1] Sub-s (3)(*a*) repealed in part by CEMA 1979 s 177(3), Sch 6 Pt I and VATA 1983 s 50(2), Sch 11; remainder of that subsection is spent.

[2] Sub-s (3)(*c*) repealed by FA 1985 s 98(6), Sch 27 Pt X.

[3] Sub-s (3)(*d*) repealed by FA 1999 Sch 20 Pt V(2) with effect in relation to instruments executed, or bearer instruments issued, from 1 October 1999, subject to the provisions in FA 1999 Sch 20 Pt V(2) Note 2. Previously the text read:

"(*d*) Schedule 11 shall be construed as one with the Stamp Act 1891.".

SCHEDULE 11

INCREASE OF CERTAIN STAMP DUTIES

Section 49

Note—This schedule repealed by FA 1999 Sch 20 Pt V(2) with effect in relation to instruments executed, or bearer instruments issued, from 1 October 1999, subject to the provisions in FA 1999 Sch 20 Pt V(2) Note 2. For instruments executed, or bearer instruments issued before 1 October 1999, the text should read:

PART I
PROVISIONS HAVING EFFECT IN GREAT BRITAIN

1—*(1) This Part of this Schedule, except paragraphs 6 and 7, shall be deemed to have had effect as from 1st May 1974; and paragraphs 6 (1) and 7 shall have effect as from 1st August, 1974.*

(2) This Part of this Schedule shall not extend to Northern Ireland.

(3) The Commissioners may make such arrangements operating for such period as they may think proper for the charge of duty on any instrument giving effect to a stock exchange transaction (as defined in section 4 of the Stock Transfer Act 1963) in respect of which settlement was due before 1st May 1974 to be the same as if this Act had not been passed, and any instrument stamped in accordance with such arrangements shall be deemed to be duly stamped for all purposes.

PART II
PROVISIONS HAVING EFFECT IN NORTHERN IRELAND

11—*(1) This Part of this Schedule shall have effect as from 1st August 1974.*

(2) This Part of this Schedule shall not extend to Great Britain.

(3) The Commissioners may make such arrangements operating for such period as they may think proper for the charge of duty on any instrument giving effect to a stock exchange transaction (as defined in section 4 of the Stock Transfer Act (Northern Ireland) 1963) in respect of which settlement was due before 1st August 1974 to be the same as if this Act had not been passed, and any instrument stamped in accordance with such arrangements shall be deemed to be duly stamped for all purposes.

Note—This schedule repealed by FA 1999 Sch 20 Pt V(2) with effect in relation to instruments executed, or bearer instruments issued, from 1 October 1999, subject to the provisions in FA 1999 Sch 20 Pt V(2) Note 2. For instruments executed, or bearer instruments issued before 1 October 1999, see the above text.

FINANCE (NO 2) ACT 1975

(1975 Chapter 45)

PART IV

MISCELLANEOUS AND GENERAL

72 Extension of Finance Act 1973 s 50 to stamp duties in Northern Ireland

Section 50 of the Finance Act 1973 (temporary statutory effect of House of Commons resolution affecting stamp duties) shall extend to Northern Ireland and apply to stamp duties having effect there as well as to stamp duties having effect in Great Britain.

FINANCE ACT 1976

(1976 Chapter 40)

PART V

MISCELLANEOUS AND SUPPLEMENTARY

127 Stamp duty: stock exchange transfers

(1) Stamp duty shall not be chargeable on any transfer to a stock exchange nominee . . . [1]

(2) . . . [2]

(3) . . . [3]

(4) . . .

(5) This section shall be construed as one with the Stamp Act 1891 and in this section—

. . . [3]

"stock exchange nominee" means any person designated for the purposes of this section as a nominee of The Stock Exchange by an order made by the Secretary of State;

. . . [3]

(6) The power to make an order under subsection (5) above shall be exercisable by statutory instrument and includes power to vary or revoke a previous order.

(7) Section 33 of the Finance Act 1970 shall extend to Northern Ireland; and in the application of that section . . . [3] to Northern Ireland for any reference to the Stock Transfer Act 1963 there shall be substituted a reference to the Stock Transfer Act (Northern Ireland) 1963.

Note—Sub-ss (1), (4)–(7) were to be repealed by FA 1990 Sch 19 Pt VI with effect from an appointed day in accordance with FA 1990 ss 107–111. The Treasury order specifying the appointed day for the purposes of FA 1990 ss 107–110 was to coincide with the start of paperless trading under the Stock Exchange's planned TAURUS system (IR press release, 20-3-90). However, on 11-3-93 the London Stock Exchange News Release 6/93 announced that TAURUS had been abandoned.

Sub-s (4) amends FA 1970 s 33(1),

SEPON Limited have been designated as a nominee of The Stock Exchange under sub-s (5), by The Stock Exchange (Designation of Nominees) (Stamp Duty) Order, SI 1979/370 which came into operation on 30 March 1979.

Cross references—See FA 1986 s 88(1)(*a*) (stamp duty reserve tax on instruments relating to agreements to transfer chargeable securities for consideration),

FA 1986 s 97(2)(*a*) (stamp duty reserve tax exemption on instruments relating to arrangements to provide clearance services),

FA 1989 s 175 (stamp duty and stamp duty reserve tax exemptions in certain circumstances involving stock exchange nominees),

FA 1989 s 176 (relief from double stamp duty reserve tax and stamp duty reserve tax exemption in certain circumstances involving stock exchange nominees).

Amendments—[1] Words in sub-s (1) repealed by FA 1986 s 84(1), (4), Sch 23, Pt IX(4) in relation to any transfer giving effect to a transaction carried out on or after 27 October 1986 (ie the day on which The Stock Exchange rule prohibiting a person from carrying on business as both a broker and a jobber is abolished).

[2] Sub-s (2) repealed by FA 1986 s 85(4), Sch 23, Pt IX(4) in relation to any transfer giving effect to a transaction carried out on or after 27 October 1986.

[3] Sub-s (3), the definitions of "jobber" and "stock exchange transaction" in sub-s (5) and the words "and this section" in sub-s (7) repealed by FA 1986 s 114(6), Sch 23 Pt IX(4) with effect from 20 March 1989 by virtue of FA 1986 (Stamp Duty Repeals) Order, SI 1989/291.

131 Inter-American Development Bank

(1) The following provisions of this section shall have effect on the United Kingdom's becoming a member of the Inter-American Development Bank ("the Bank").

(2) . . .

(3) No stamp duty shall be chargeable [Schedule 15 to the Finance Act 1999 (bearer instruments)][1] on the issue of any instrument by the Bank or on the transfer of the stock constituted by, or transferable by means of, any instrument issued by the Bank.

Notes—Sub-s (2) is not relevant to this work.

Sub-s (3) was to be repealed by FA 1990 Sch 19 Pt VI with effect from an appointed day in accordance with FA 1990 ss 107–111. The Treasury order specifying the appointed day for the purposes of FA 1990 ss 107–110 was to coincide with the start of paperless trading under the Stock Exchange's planned TAURUS system (IR press release, 20-3-90). However, on 11-3-93 the London Stock Exchange News Release 6/93 announced that TAURUS had been abandoned.

Amendments—[1] Words in sub-s (3) substituted by FA 1999 s 113(3), Sch 16 para 3 with effect in relation to bearer instruments issued after 30 September 1999. For prospective repeal of FA 1999 s 113, Sch 16 para 3 see FA 1999 s 123(3). Previously the text read 'under the heading "Bearer Instrument" in Schedule 1 to the Stamp Act 1891'.

INTERPRETATION ACT 1978

(1978 Chapter 30)

Note—See under VAT Statutes, *ante*.

FINANCE ACT 1980

(1980 Chapter 48)

PART V

STAMP DUTY

97 Shared ownership transactions

(1) A lease to which this section applies shall, instead of being chargeable with stamp duty under [Part II of Schedule 13 to the Finance Act 1999 (lease)][9], be chargeable with stamp duty under [Part I of that Schedule ([transfer][10] on sale)][9] as if it were a conveyance for a consideration equal to the value [or sum][1] stated in the lease in accordance with subsection (2)(*d*) below; and where stamp duty has been paid on a lease in accordance with this section stamp duty shall not be chargeable under that Act on any instrument executed in pursuance of the lease whereby the reversion is transferred to the lessee.

(2) This section applies to any lease granted by a body mentioned in subsection (3) below, being a lease which—

(*a*) is of a dwelling for the exclusive use of the lessee or, if there are joint lessees, of those lessees;

[(*b*) is granted partly in consideration of a premium calculated by reference to—

(i) the market value of the dwelling, or

(ii) a sum calculated by reference to that value, and partly in consideration of rent][2];

(*c*) provides for the lessee to acquire the reversion; and

(*d*) contains a statement of the market value referred to in [paragraph (*b*) (i) above or, as the case may be, the sum referred to in paragraph (*b*) (ii) above][2] and a statement to the effect that the parties intend duty to be charged in accordance with this section by reference to that value [or as the case may be, to that sum][3].

(3) The bodies referred to in subsection (2) above are—

[(*a*) a local housing authority within the meaning of the Housing Act 1985;

(*b*) a housing association [within the meaning of][6] the Housing Associations Act 1985 or [Part VII][6] of the Housing (Northern Ireland) Order 1981;][4]

(*c*) a development corporation established by an order made, or having effect as if made, under the New Towns Act 1965;

[(*cc*) a housing action trust established under Part III of the Housing Act 1988;][7]

(*d*) the Commission for the New Towns;

(*e*) . . . [8]

(*f*) the Northern Ireland Housing Executive;

(*g*) . . . [5]

(4) For the purposes of subsection (1) above an instrument transferring a reversion shall not be regarded as executed in pursuance of a lease in respect of which duty has been paid in accordance with this section unless it contains a statement to the effect that it has been so executed.

Cross references—See FA 1981 s 108(5), (6), (7) (stamp duty on a lease of a house granted by a body referred to in sub-s (3) above in consideration of rent and premium, lease instrument being executed after 22 March 1981);

FA 1987 s 54(2), (3), (4) (extension of the application of this section to leases granted by and to certain persons after 31 July 1987 under shared ownership schemes of local authorities and housing associations).

Amendments—[1] Words in sub-s (1) inserted by FA 1981 s 108(2), (7), with effect from 23 March 1981.

[2] Sub-s (2)(*b*) and words in sub-s (2)(*d*) substituted by FA 1981 s 108(3), (4), (7), in relation to lease instruments executed after 22 March 1981.

[3] Words in sub-s (2)(*d*) added by FA 1981 s 108(3)(*b*), (7), with effect from 23 March 1981.

[4] Sub-s (3)(*a*), (*b*) substituted by the Housing (Consequential Provisions) Act 1985 s 6(2), Sch 2 para 43, with effect from 1 April 1986.

[5] Sub-s (3)(*g*) repealed by the Housing (Consequential Provisions) Act 1985 s 6(2), Sch 1 Pt I, with effect from 1 April 1986.

[6] Words in sub-s (3)(*b*) substituted by FA 1987 s 54(1).

[7] Sub-s (3)(*cc*) inserted by FA 1988 s 142(1).

[8] Sub-s (3)(*e*) repealed by the Government of Wales Act 1998 Sch 18 Pt IV, with effect from 1 October 1998 by virtue of The Government of Wales Act 1998 (Commencement No 1) Order, SI 1998/2244.

[9] Words in sub-s (1) substituted by FA 1999 s 112(4), Sch 14 para 6 with effect in relation to instruments executed after 30 September 1999. This does not apply to transfers or other instruments relating to units under a unit trust scheme by virtue of FA 1999 s 122. Previously the text read 'the heading "Lease or Tack" in Schedule 1 to the Stamp Act 1891' and 'the heading "Conveyance or Transfer on Sale" in that Schedule' respectively.

[10] The word "transfer" substituted for the words "conveyance or transfer" in enactments relating to stamp duty by FA 2003 Sch 20 para 3.

98 Maintenance funds for historic buildings

(1) No stamp duty shall be chargeable on any instrument whereby property ceases to be comprised in a settlement if as a result of the property or part of it becoming comprised in another settlement (otherwise than by virtue of the instrument itself) there is by virtue of [paragraph 9 (1) or 17 (1) of Schedule 4 to the Capital Transfer Tax Act 1984 there is no charge to capital transfer tax in respect of the property ceasing to be comprised in the settlement or a reduced charge to that tax by virtue of paragraph 9 (4) or 17 (4) of that Schedule][1]; but where only part of the property becomes comprised in the other settlement this subsection shall not affect the stamp duty chargeable on the instrument by reference to the other part.

(2) An instrument in respect of which stamp duty is not chargeable by virtue only of this section or in respect of which the duty chargeable is reduced by virtue of this section shall not be treated as duly stamped unless it is stamped in accordance with section 12 of the Stamp Act 1891 with a stamp denoting that it is not chargeable with any duty or that it is duly stamped.

Cross references—See FA 1986 s 100 (CTT to be known as inheritance tax and CTTA 1984 as Inheritance Tax Act 1984 with effect from 25 July 1986 and references in this section to CTT to be construed accordingly).

Amendments—[1] Words in sub-s (1) substituted by IHTA 1984 Sch 8 para 19 with effect from 1 January 1985.

101 Unit trusts

Amendments—This section repealed by FA 1999 Sch 20 Pt V(5) with effect in relation to instruments executed from 6 February 2000.

102 Conveyance in consideration of debt

(1) Where—

(*a*) any property is conveyed to any person wholly or in part in consideration of a debt due to him; and

(*b*) apart from this section the consideration in respect of which the conveyance would be chargeable with *ad valorem* duty by virtue of section 57 of the Stamp Act 1891 (which deems the debt to be the consideration) would exceed the value of the property conveyed,

that consideration shall be treated as reduced to that value.

(2) Where subsection (1) above applies in relation to any conveyance, it shall not be treated as duly stamped unless it is stamped in accordance with section 12 of the said Act of 1891 with a stamp denoting that it is not chargeable with any duty or that it is duly stamped.

FINANCE ACT 1981

(1981 Chapter 35)

PART VI

STAMP DUTY

107 Sale of houses at discount by local authorities etc

(1) Where a [transfer][18] to which this section applies is subject contingently to the payment of any money (whether by virtue of that [transfer][18] or otherwise), then, notwithstanding section 57 of the Stamp Act 1891 that money shall not be deemed to be part of the consideration in respect of which the [transfer][18] is chargeable with *ad valorem* duty.

(2) . . .[3]

(3) This section applies to any [transfer][18] on sale of a dwelling-house (including the grant of a lease) at a discount by—

(*a*) any Minister of the Crown or Northern Ireland department;

(*b*) a [local housing authority within the meaning of the Housing Act 1985][4], a county council, a district council within the meaning of the Local Government Act (Northern Ireland) 1972 or in Scotland a [council constituted under section 2 of the Local Government etc (Scotland) Act 1994][10], the common good of such a council or any trust under its control;

(*c*) the Housing Corporation;

[(*ca*) . . . ;][8]

(*d*) *[Scottish Homes]*[9];

(*e*) the Northern Ireland Housing Executive;

[(*ea*) a registered social landlord within the meaning of Part 1 of the Housing Act 1996;][12]

(*f*) a housing association registered[—;

(i) in Scotland under the Housing Association Act 1985, or

(ii) in Northern Ireland, under Part II of the Housing (Northern Ireland) Order 1992][13]

[(*ff*) a housing action trust established under Part III of the Housing Act 1988;][7]

(*g*) a development corporation established by an order made or having effect as if made under the New Towns Act 1965 or the New Towns (Scotland) Act 1968 or an urban development corporation established by an order made under section 135 of the Local Government, Planning and Land Act 1980;

(*h*) the Commission for the New Towns or a new town commission established under section 7 of the New Towns Act (Northern Ireland) 1965;

(*i*) . . .[15];

(*j*) the Council of the Isles of Scilly;

(*k*) a police authority within the meaning of [section 101(1) of the Police Act 1996][11] or section 2(1) or 19(9)(*b*) of the Police (Scotland) Act 1967 or [the Northern Ireland Policing Board][16];

(*ka*) . . .[17]

(*l*) an Education and Libraries Board established under the Education and Libraries (Northern Ireland) Order 1972;

(*m*) any person mentioned in paragraph (*e*), (i), (*j*) or (*l*) of section 1(10) of the Tenants' Rights, Etc. (Scotland) Act 1980;

[(*n*) the United Kingdom Atomic Energy Authority;][1]

[(*o*) such other body as the Treasury may, by order made by statutory instrument, prescribe for the purposes of this section.][2]

[(3A) This section also applies to any [transfer][18] on sale of a dwelling house where the [transfer][18] is made pursuant to a sub-sale made at a discount by a body falling within [subsection (3) (*ea*) or (*f*)][14] above.][1]

[(3B) This section also applies to a [transfer][18] on sale (including the grant of a lease) by a person against whom the right to buy under Part V of the Housing Act 1985 exercisable by virtue of section 171A of that Act (preservation of right to buy on disposal to private sector landlord) to a person who is the qualifying person for the purposes of the preserved right to buy and in relation to whom that dwelling-house is the qualifying dwelling-house.][6]

[(3C) A grant under section 20 or 21 of the Housing Act 1996 (purchase grants in respect of disposals at a discount by registered social landlords) shall not be treated as part of the consideration for a [transfer][18] to which this section applies made by a body falling within subsection (3)(*ea*) above.][12]

(4) This section applies to instruments executed on or after 23rd March 1981 and shall be deemed to have come into force on that date.

Cross references—See Stamp Act 1891, s 58 (4) (conveyances or transfers to which this section applies resulting from sub-sales).

Amendments—[1] Sub-s (3)(*n*) and sub-s (3A) added by FA 1984 s 110(1)–(4) with respect to instruments executed after 19 March 1984 or executed after 12 March 1984 and stamped after 19 March 1984.

[2] Sub-s (3)(*o*) added by FA 1984 s 110(1), (5) with respect to instruments executed after 26 July 1984.

[3] Sub-s (2) repealed by FA 1985 Sch 27, Pt IX(1).

[4] Words in sub-s (3)(*b*) substituted by the Housing (Consequential Provisions) Act 1985 s 6(2), Sch 2 para 48, with effect from 1 April 1986.

[6] Sub-s (3B) inserted by the Housing and Planning Act 1986 Sch 5 para 18 with effect from 17 August 1992.

[7] Sub-s (3) (*ff*) inserted by FA 1988 s 142(2).

[8] Sub-s (3)(*ca*) inserted by the Housing Act 1988 Sch 17 para 105, and repealed by the Government of Wales Act 1998 Sch 18 Pt VI with effect from 1 November 1998 by virtue of the Government of Wales Act 1998 (Commencement No 1) Order, SI 1998/2244.

[9] Words in sub-s (3) (*d*) substituted by the Housing (Scotland) Act 1988 s 3(3), Sch 2 para 1.

[10] Words in sub-s (3)(*b*) substituted for the words "regional, district or islands council" by the Local Government etc (Scotland) Act 1994 s 180(1), Sch 13 para 123, as from a day to be appointed.

[11] Words in sub-s (3)(*k*) substituted by the Police Act 1996 s 103(1), Sch 7 Pt II para 33.

[12] Sub-s (3)(*ea*) and (3C) inserted by the Housing Act 1996 s 55(1), Sch 3 para 1 with effect from 1 October 1996.

[13] Words in sub-s (3)(*f*) substituted for the words "under the Housing Associations Act 1985 or Article 124 of the Housing (Northern Ireland) Order 1981" by the Housing Act 1996 s 55(1), Sch 3 para 1 with effect from 1 October 1996.

[14] Words in sub-s (3A) substituted for the words "subsection (3)(*f*)" by the Housing Act 1996 s 55(1), Sch 3 para 1 with effect from 1 October 1996.

[15] Sub-s (3)(*i*) repealed by the Government of Wales Act 1998 Sch 18 Pt IV with effect from 1 October 1998 by virtue of the Government of Wales Act 1998 (Commencement No 1) Order, SI 1998/2244.

[16] Words in sub-s (3)(*k*) substituted by the Police (Northern Ireland) Act 2000 s 78(1), Sch 6 para 7 with effect from 4 November 2001 (by virtue of SR 2001/396).

[17] Sub-s (3)(*ka*) repealed by the Criminal Justice and Police Act 2001 ss 128(1), 138(2), Sch 6 para 64, Sch 7 para 5 with effect from 1 April 2002 (by virtue of SI 2002/344).

[18] The word "transfer" substituted for the words "conveyance or transfer" in enactments relating to stamp duty by FA 2003 Sch 20 para 3.

Prospective amendments—Sub-s (3)(*d*) to be repealed by the Housing (Scotland) Act 2001 s 112, Sch 10 para 8 with effect from a date to be appointed.

108 Shared ownership transactions

(1) Section 97 of the Finance Act 1980 (shared ownership transactions) shall have effect with the amendments specified in subsections (2) to (4) below.

(2)–(4) . . .

(5) Where a lease is granted by a body mentioned in subsection (3) of the said section 97 which—

(*a*) is of a dwelling for the exclusive use of the lessee or, if there are joint lessees, of those lessees;

(*b*) provides that the lessee may on payment of a sum require the terms of the lease to be altered so that the rent payable under it is reduced;

(*c*) is granted partly in consideration of rent and partly in consideration of a premium calculated by reference to—

(i) the premium obtainable on the open market for the grant of a lease containing the same terms as the lease but with the substitution for the rent payable under the lease of the minimum rent, or

(ii) a sum calculated by reference to that premium; and

(*d*) contains a statement of the minimum rent and the premium referred to in paragraph (*c*) (i) above or, as the case may be, the sum referred to in paragraph (*c*) (ii) above and a statement to the effect that the parties intend duty to be charged in accordance with this section by reference to that rent and that premium or, as the case may be, that sum,

the lease shall be chargeable to stamp duty as if the premium paid by the lessee were equal to the premium or, as the case may be, the sum, stated in the lease in accordance with paragraph (d) above and the rent payable were as so stated.

(6) In subsection (5) above "minimum rent" in relation to any lease means the lowest rent which could become payable under the lease if it were altered as mentioned in paragraph (*b*) of that subsection at the date when the lease is granted.

(7) This section applies to instruments executed on or after 23rd March 1981 and shall be deemed to have come into force on that date.

Cross references—See FA 1987 s 54(2), (3), (4) (extension of the application of sub-ss (5), (6) above to leases granted by and to certain persons after 31 July 1987 under shared ownership schemes of local authorities and housing associations).

110 Pooled pension funds

Amendments—This section repealed by FA 1999 s 139, Sch 20 Pt V(5) with effect for instruments executed from 6 February 2000.

FINANCE ACT 1982

(1982 Chapter 39)

PART V

STAMP DUTY

129 Exemption from duty on grants, transfers to charities, etc

(1) Where any conveyance, transfer or lease is made or agreed to be made to a body of persons established for charitable purposes only or to the trustees of a trust so established or to the Trustees of the National Heritage Memorial Fund [or to the National Endowment for Science, Technology and the Arts][2], no stamp duty shall be chargeable [under Part I or II, *or paragraph 16,*[3] of Schedule 13 to the Finance Act 1999][1] on the instrument by which the conveyance, transfer or lease, or the agreement for it, is effected.

(2) An instrument in respect of which stamp duty is not chargeable by virtue only of subsection (1) above shall not be treated as duly stamped unless it is stamped in accordance with section 12 of the Stamp Act 1891 with a stamp denoting that it is not chargeable with any duty.

(3) This section applies to instruments executed on or after 22nd March 1982 and shall be deemed to have come into force on that date.

Cross references—See FA 1983 s 46(3)(*c*) (stamp duty exemption under this section for Historic Buildings and Monuments Commission for England).

Amendments—[1] Words in sub-s (1) substituted by FA 1999 s 112(4), Sch 14 para 7 with effect in relation to instruments executed after 30 September 1999. This does not apply to transfers or other instruments relating to units under a unit trust scheme by virtue of FA 1999 s 122. Previously the text read 'by virtue of any of the following headings in Schedule 1 to the Stamp Act 1891, namely, "Conveyance or Transfer on Sale", "Conveyance or Transfer of any kind not hereinbefore described" and "Lease or Tack",'.

[2] Words in sub-s (1) inserted by the National Lottery Act 1998 s 24 with effect from 2 July 1998.

[3] Words in sub-s (1) repealed by FA 2008 s 99, Sch 32 para 12 with effect in relation to instruments executed on or after 13 March 2008 and not stamped before 19 March 2008.

This amendment does not have effect in relation to an instrument effecting a land transaction or a duplicate or counterpart of such an instrument. "Land transaction" has the same meaning as in FA 2003 Pt 4, except that it does not include a transfer of an interest in a property-investment partnership (within the meaning of FA 2003 Sch 15) (FA 2008 s 99, Sch 32 para 22).

FINANCE ACT 1983

(1983 Chapter 28)

PART IV

MISCELLANEOUS AND SUPPLEMENTARY

Miscellaneous

46 Historic Buildings and Monuments Commission for England

(1)–(2) . . . [3]

(3) For the purposes of the enactments set out below, the [Historic Buildings and Monuments Commission][4] shall be treated as a body of persons established for charitable purposes only—

(*a*) . . . [3]

(*b*) . . . [3]

(*c*) . . . [2] section 129 of the Finance Act 1982 (reliefs from stamp duty).

(4) . . . [2]

(5) . . . [1]

Amendments—[1] Sub-s (5) repealed by IHTA 1984 s 277, Sch 9.

[2] Words in sub-s (3)(*c*) and sub-s (4) repealed by FA 1985 s 98(6), Sch 27 Pt IX(2).

[3] Sub-s (1), (2), (3)(*a*), (*b*) repealed by TA 1988 s 844(4), Sch 31.

[4] Words in sub-s (3) substituted by TA 1988 Sch 29 para 32 Table.

FINANCE (NO 2) ACT 1983

(1983 Chapter 49)

PART III

MISCELLANEOUS AND SUPPLEMENTARY

15 Relief from stamp duty for local constituency associations of political parties on reorganisation of constituencies

(1) In a case falling within paragraph (*a*) or paragraph (*b*) of subsection (4) of section [7 above, section 57 of the Stamp Act 1891 shall not apply in relation to a [transfer][3] by which the disposal or, in the case of paragraph (*b*), either of the disposals referred to in that paragraph is effected.][1]

(2) . . . [2]

Notes—Relevant provisions of s 7 referred to in sub-s (1) above are—

"7 Relief for local constituency associations of political parties on reorganisation of constituencies

(1) In this section "relevant date" means the date of coming into operation of an Order in Council under section 3 of the House of Commons (Redistribution of Seats) Act 1949 (orders specifying new parliamentary constituencies) and, in relation to any relevant date,—

(*a*) "former parliamentary constituency" means an area which, for the purposes of parliamentary elections, was a constituency immediately before that date but is no longer such a constituency after that date; and

(*b*) "new parliamentary constituency" means an area which, for the purposes of parliamentary elections, is a constituency immediately after that date but was not such a constituency before that date.

(2) In this section "local constituency association" means an unincorporated association (whether described as an association, a branch or otherwise) whose primary purpose is to further the aims of a political party in an area which at any time is or was the same or substantially the same as the area of a parliamentary constituency or two or more parliamentary constituencies and, in relation to any relevant date,—

(*a*) "existing association" means a local constituency association whose area was the same, or substantially the same, as the area of a former parliamentary constituency or two or more such constituencies; and

(*b*) "new association" means a local constituency association whose area is the same, or substantially the same, as the area of a new parliamentary constituency or two or more such constituencies.

(3) For the purposes of this section, a new association is a successor to an existing association if any part of the existing association's area is comprised in the new association's area.

(4) In any case where, before, on or after a relevant date,—

(*a*) an existing association disposes of land to a new association which is a successor to the existing association, or

(*b*) an existing association disposes of land to a body (whether corporate or unincorporated) which is an organ of the political party concerned and, as soon as practicable thereafter, that body disposes of the land to a new association which is a successor to the existing association,

the parties to the disposal or, where paragraph (*b*) above applies, to each of the disposals, shall be treated for the purposes of corporation tax in respect of chargeable gains or, as the case may require, capital gains tax as if the land disposed of were acquired from the existing association or the body making the disposal for a consideration of such an amount as would secure that on the disposal neither a gain nor a loss accrued to that association or body."

Amendments—[1] Words in sub-s (1) substituted by FA 1985 s 82(4) in relation to instruments executed after 25 March 1985 and instruments executed after 18 March 1985 which are stamped after 25 March 1985.

2 Sub-s (2) repealed by FA 1985 s 98(6), Sch 27 Pt IX(1).
3 The word "transfer" substituted for the words "conveyance or transfer" in enactments relating to stamp duty by FA 2003 Sch 20 para 3.

FINANCE ACT 1984

(1984 Chapter 43)

PART IV
STAMP DUTY

109 Reduction of stamp duty on conveyances and transfers

Amendments—This section repealed by FA 1999 Sch 20 Pt V(2) with effect in relation to instruments executed, or bearer instruments issued, from 1 October 1999, subject to the provisions in FA 1999 Sch 20 Pt V(2) Note 2. Previously the text read:

"(1) (*amends* FA 1963 s 55(1), (2) and FA (Northern Ireland) 1963 s 4(1), (2)).
(2) (*repeals* FA 1974 Sch 11 Pt III).
(3) Subject to subsection (4) below, subsections (1) and (2) above apply—
(*a*) to instruments executed on or after 20th March 1984; and
(*b*) to instruments executed on or after 13th March 1984 which are stamped on or after 20th March 1984;
and, for the purposes of section 14(4) of the Stamp Act 1891 (instruments not to be given in evidence etc unless stamped in accordance with the law in force at the time of first execution), the law in force at the time of execution of an instrument falling within paragraph (*b*) above shall be deemed to be that as varied in accordance with subsections (1) and (2) above.
(4) In the case of an instrument giving effect to a stock exchange transaction, as defined in section 4 of the Stock Transfer Act 1963 subsections (1) to (3) above do not apply unless the transaction takes place on or after 12th March 1984 and is one in respect of which settlement is due on or after 13th March 1984.
(5) This section shall be deemed to have come into force on 20th March 1984."

110 Extension of stamp duty relief on sales at discount

(1)–(3) (*amend* FA 1981 s 107(3) and *insert* s 107(3A)).

(4) Subsections (2) and (3) above have effect with respect to instruments—

(*a*) executed on or after 20th March 1984, or

(*b*) executed on or after 13th March 1984 and stamped on or after 20th March 1984,

and, for the purposes of section 14(4) of the Stamp Act 1891 (instruments not to be given in evidence etc unless stamped in accordance with the law in force at the time of first execution), the law in force at the time of execution of an instrument falling within paragraph (b) above shall be deemed to be that as varied in accordance with subsections (2) and (3) above.

(5) (*amends* FA 1981 s 107(3)).

111 Agreements for leases

(1) . . . [2]

(2) In any case where—

(*a*) an interest in land is conveyed or transferred subject to an agreement for a [lease][3] for a term exceeding 35 years, or

(*b*) a [lease][3] is granted subject to an agreement for a [lease][3] for a term exceeding 35 years,

then, whether or not the conveyance, transfer, [lease][3] is expressed to be so subject, it shall not be taken to be duly stamped unless there is denoted upon the conveyance, transfer, [lease][3] the duty paid on the agreement; and section 11 of the Stamp Act 1891 shall have effect for this purpose as if the duty chargeable on the conveyance, transfer, [lease][3] depended on the duty paid on the agreement.

(3) For the purposes of subsection (2) above, an interest conveyed or transferred or, as the case may be, a [lease][3] granted is not to be regarded as subject to an agreement for a [lease][3] if that agreement is directly enforceable against another interest in the land in relation to which the interest conveyed or transferred or, as the case may be, the [lease][3] granted is a superior interest.

(4) . . . [1]

(5) This section applies to any agreement for a [lease][3] entered into on or after 20th March 1984 and shall be deemed to have come into force on that date.

Amendments—[1] Sub-s (4) repealed by FA 1999 Sch 20 Pt V(1) with effect from 1 October 1999, subject to the provisions in FA 1999 Sch 20 Pt V(1) Note 2. Previously the text amended the Stamp Act 1891 s 15(2).
2 Sub-s (1) repealed by FA 1999 Sch 20 Pt V(2) with effect in relation to instruments executed, or bearer instruments issued, from 1 October 1999, subject to the provisions in FA 1999 Sch 20 Pt V(2) Note 2. Previously the text amended the Stamp Act 1891 s 75(1) and substituted s 75(2)).
3 "Lease" substituted for the words "lease or tack" throughout the section by FA 1999 s 112(4), Sch 14 para 2 with effect in relation to instruments executed after 30 September 1999. This does not apply to transfers or other instruments relating to units under a unit trust scheme by virtue of FA 1999 s 122.

PART VI
MISCELLANEOUS AND SUPPLEMENTARY

Miscellaneous

126 Tax exemptions in relation to designated international organisations

(1) Where—

(*a*) the United Kingdom or any of the Communities is a member of an international organisation; and

(*b*) the agreement under which it became a member provides for exemption from tax, in relation to the organisation, of the kind for which provision is made by this section;

the Treasury may, by order made by statutory instrument, designate that organisation for the purposes of this section.

(2) Where an organisation has been so designated, the provisions mentioned in subsection (3) below shall, with the exception of any which may be excluded by the designation order, apply in relation to that organisation.

(3) The provisions are—

(*a*) . . . [2]

(*b*) . . .

(*c*) no stamp duty shall be chargeable under [Schedule 15 to the Finance Act 1999 (bearer instruments)][5] on the issue of any instrument by the organisation or on the transfer of the stock constituted by, or transferable by means of, any instrument issued by the organisation;

[(*d*) no stamp duty reserve tax shall be chargeable under section 93 (depositary receipts) or 96 (clearance services) of the Finance Act 1986 in respect of the issue of securities by the organisation.][3]

[(4) The Treasury may, by order made by statutory instrument, designate any of the Communities or the European Investment Bank for the purposes of this section, and references in subsections (2) and (3) above to an organisation designated for the purposes of this section include references to a body so designated by virtue of this subsection.][1]

[(5) Subsection (3) above, as it applies by virtue of subsection (4) above, shall be read as if the words "under [Schedule 15 to the Finance Act 1999 (bearer instruments)][5]" were omitted.][4]

Note—Words omitted from sub-s (3) are not relevant to stamp duty.

Cross references—See FA 1985 s 96(2) (revocation or variation of the provisions giving stamp duty exemption in respect of issues and transfers of loan stock of European Communities and Investment Bank);

FA 1986 ss 78(4), 79(3) (stamp duty exemption on an instrument transferring loan capital issued or raised by an organisation which is designated under this section at the time of transfer).

Amendments—[1] Sub-s (4) inserted by FA 1985 s 96(1).

[2] Sub-s (3)(*a*) repealed by TA 1988 s 844(4), Sch 31.

[3] Sub-s (3)(*d*) inserted by FA 1990 s 114(1) and applies in relation to the issue of securities by a designated organisation or body according to FA 1990 s 114(2), (3).

[4] Sub-s (5) inserted by FA 1985 s 96(1).

[5] Words in sub-ss (3)(*c*) and (5) substituted by FA 1999 s 113(3), Sch 16 para 4 with effect in relation to bearer instruments issued after 30 September 1999. For prospective repeal of FA 1999 s 113, Sch 16 para 4 see FA 1999 s 123(3). Previously the text read 'the heading "Bearer Instrument" in Schedule 1 to the Stamp Act 1891'.

FINANCE ACT 1985

(1985 Chapter 54)

An Act to grant certain duties, to alter other duties, and to amend the law relating to the National Debt and the Public Revenue, and to make further provision in connection with Finance

[25th July 1985]

PART III
STAMP DUTY

81 Renounceable letters of allotment etc

(1) Subsection (2) below applies where there is an arrangement whereby—

(*a*) rights under an instrument are renounced in favour of a person (A),

(*b*) the rights are rights to shares in a company (company B), and

(*c*) A, or a person connected with A, or A and such a person together, has or have control of company B or will have such control in consequence of the arrangement.

[(2) The instrument shall not be exempt by virtue of paragraph 24(*d*) of Schedule 13 to the Finance Act 1999 (renounceable letters of allotment, etc) from stamp duty under or by reference to Part I of that Schedule ([transfer][3] on sale).][2]

(3) References in this section to shares in company B include references to its loan capital to which [section 79(4) of the Finance Act 1986 does not apply by virtue of section 79(5) or (6)][2] (convertible loan capital and excessive return capital).

(4) In this section "shares" includes stock.

(5) For the purposes of this section a person has control of company B if he has power to control company B's affairs by virtue of holding shares in, or possessing voting power in relation to, company B or any other body corporate.

(6) For the purposes of this section one person is connected with another if he would be so connected for the purposes of the [Taxation of Chargeable Gains Tax Act 1992][1].

(7) This section applies to instruments if rights are renounced under them on or after 1st August 1985, except where the arrangement concerned includes an offer for the rights and on or before 27th June 1985 the offer became unconditional as to acceptances.

Cross references—See FA 1986 s 78(10) (in construing sub-s (3) above, the effect of FA 1986 s 78 (loan capital) to be ignored).

Notes—This section was to be repealed by FA 1990 Sch 19 Pt VI with effect from an appointed day in accordance with FA 1990 ss 107–111. The Treasury order specifying the appointed day for the purposes of FA 1990 ss 107–110 was to coincide with the start of paperless trading under the Stock Exchange's planned TAURUS system (IR press release, 20-3-90). However, on 11-3-93 the London Stock Exchange News Release 6/93 announced that TAURUS had been abandoned.

Amendments—[1] Words in sub-s (6) substituted by TCGA 1992 s 290(1), Sch 10 para 9.

[2] Sub-s (2) and words in sub-s (3) substituted by FA 1999 s 112(4), Sch 14 para 8 with effect in relation to instruments executed after 30 September 1999. This does not apply to transfers or other instruments relating to units under a unit trust scheme by virtue of FA 1999 s 122. For prospective repeal of FA 1999 Sch 14 para 8 see FA 1999 s 123(3). Previously the text read:

"(2) The instrument shall not be exempt by virtue of section 65 (1) of the Finance Act 1963 (renounceable letters of allotment etc) or section 14(1) of the Finance Act (Northern Ireland) 1963 (corresponding provision for Northern Ireland) from stamp duty under or by reference to the heading "Conveyance or Transfer on Sale" in Schedule 1 to the Stamp Act 1891.' and

'section 126(1) of the Finance Act 1976 does not apply by virtue of section 126(2) or (3)' respectively.".

[3] The word "transfer" substituted for the words "conveyance or transfer" in enactments relating to stamp duty by FA 2003 Sch 20 para 3.

82 Gifts inter vivos

(1) The stamp duty chargeable by virtue of section 74 of the Finance (1909–10) Act 1910 (gifts inter vivos) is abolished.

(2) (*amends* Stamp Act 1891, s 58 (7)).

(3) (*amends* FA 1965 s 90(5) and FA (Northern Ireland) 1965, s 4(5)).

(4) (*amends* F(No 2)A 1983 s 15(1)).

(5) *An instrument—*

(a) in respect of which stamp duty would be chargeable by virtue of section 74 of the 1910 Act apart from this section, and

(b) on which stamp duty is not chargeable under [Part I of Schedule 13 to the Finance Act 1999 ([transfer][2] on sale)][1],

shall not be deemed to be duly stamped unless it has, in accordance with section 12 of the 1891 Act, been stamped with a particular stamp denoting that it is duly stamped or that it is not chargeable with any duty.[3]

(6) This section applies to—

(*a*) instruments executed on or after 26th March 1985, and

(*b*) instruments executed on or after 19th March 1985 which are stamped on or after 26th March 1985.

(7) For the purposes of section 14 (4) of the Stamp Act 1891 (instruments not to be given in evidence etc unless stamped in accordance with the law in force at the time of first execution), the law in force at the time of execution of an instrument falling within subsection (6) (*b*) above shall be deemed to be that as varied in accordance with this section.

(8) The preceding provisions of this section shall be deemed to have come into operation on 26th March 1985.

(9) *Subsection (5) above does not apply to an instrument which is required by regulations under section 87 (1) or (2) below to be certified.*[3]

Cross references—See the Stamp Duty (Exempt Instruments) Regulations, SI 1987/516 for certain instruments executed after 30 April 1987 to which sub-s (5) above does not apply.

Amendments—[1] Words in sub-s (5) substituted by FA 1999 s 112(4), Sch 14 para 9 with effect in relation to instruments executed after 30 September 1999. This does not apply to transfers or other instruments relating to units under a unit trust scheme by virtue of FA 1999 s 122. Previously the text read 'the heading "Conveyance or Transfer on Sale" in Schedule 1 to the Stamp Act 1891'.

[2] The word "transfer" substituted for the words "conveyance or transfer" in enactments relating to stamp duty by FA 2003 Sch 20 para 3.

[3] Sub-ss (5), (9) repealed by FA 2008 s 100(1) with effect in relation to instruments executed on or after 13 March 2008, other than instruments effecting a land transaction (within the meaning of FA 2008 Sch 32 para 22).

83 Transfers in connection with divorce[, dissolution of civil partnership,][4] etc

(1) Stamp duty under [Part I of Schedule 13 to the Finance Act 1999 ([transfer][3] on sale)][2] shall not be chargeable on an instrument by which property is conveyed or transferred from one party to a marriage to the other if the instrument—

(*a*) is executed in pursuance of an order of a court made on granting in respect of the parties a decree of divorce, nullity of marriage or judicial separation, or

(*b*) is executed in pursuance of an order of a court which is made in connection with the dissolution or annulment of the marriage or the parties' judicial separation and which is made at any time after the granting of such a decree, or

[(*bb*) is executed in pursuance of an order of a court which is made at any time under section 22A, 23A or 24A of the Matrimonial Causes Act 1973, or][1]

(*c*) is executed at any time in pursuance of an agreement of the parties made in contemplation of or otherwise in connection with the dissolution or annulment of the marriage[, their judicial separation or the making of a separation order in respect of them][1].

[(1A) Stamp duty under Part 1 of Schedule 13 to the Finance Act 1999 shall not be chargeable on an instrument by which property is conveyed or transferred from one party to a civil partnership to the other if the instrument—

(*a*) is executed in pursuance of an order of a court made on granting in respect of the parties an order or decree for the dissolution or annulment of the civil partnership or their judicial separation;

(*b*) is executed in pursuance of an order of a court which is made in connection with the dissolution or annulment of the civil partnership or the parties' judicial separation and which is made at any time after the granting of such an order or decree for dissolution, annulment or judicial separation as mentioned in paragraph (*a*);

(*c*) is executed in pursuance of an order of a court which is made at any time under any provision of Schedule 5 to the Civil Partnership Act 2004 that corresponds to section 22A, 23A or 24A of the Matrimonial Causes Act 1973; or

(*d*) is executed at any time in pursuance of an agreement of the parties made in contemplation of or otherwise in connection with the dissolution or annulment of the civil partnership, their judicial separation or the making of a separation order in respect of them.][4]

(2) *An instrument in respect of which stamp duty is not chargeable under the heading mentioned in subsection (1) [or (1A)][4] above by virtue only of that subsection shall be chargeable under this subsection with stamp duty of [£5][2].*[5]

(3) This section applies to instruments executed on or after 26th March 1985 and shall be deemed to have come into operation on that date.

Cross references—See the Stamp Duty (Exempt Instruments) Regulations, SI 1987/516 for stamp duty exemption in respect of certain instruments executed after 30 April 1987 otherwise chargeable under this section.

Amendments—[1] Sub-s (1)(*bb*) inserted and words in sub-s (1)(*c*) substituted (for "or their judicial separation") by the Family Law Act 1996 s 66(1), Sch 8 Pt I para 33, subject to a saving in s 66(2), Sch 9 para 5.

[2] Words in sub-s (1) and figures in sub-s (2) substituted by FA 1999 s 112(4), Sch 14 para 10 with effect in relation to instruments executed after 30 September 1999. This does not apply to transfers or other instruments relating to units under a unit trust scheme by virtue of FA 1999 s 122. Previously the text read 'the heading "Conveyance or Transfer on Sale" in Schedule 1 to the Stamp Act 1891' and '50p'.

[3] The word "transfer" substituted for the words "conveyance or transfer" in enactments relating to stamp duty by FA 2003 Sch 20 para 3.

[4] Sub-s (1A), words in sub-s (2) and words in heading, inserted by Tax and Civil Partnership Regulations, SI 2005/3229 regs 40, 41 with effect from 5 December 2005 (reg 1(1)).

[5] Sub-s (2) repealed by FA 2008 s 99, Sch 32 paras 1, 2 with effect in relation to instruments executed on or after 13 March 2008 and not stamped before 19 March 2008.

This amendment does not have effect in relation to an instrument effecting a land transaction or a duplicate or counterpart of such an instrument. "Land transaction" has the same meaning as in FA 2003 Pt 4, except that it does not include a transfer of an interest in a property-investment partnership (within the meaning of FA 2003 Sch 15) (FA 2008 s 99, Sch 32 para 22).

84 Death: varying dispositions, and appropriations

(1) Where, within the period of two years after a person's death, any of the dispositions (whether effected by will, under the law relating to intestacy or otherwise) of the property of which he was competent to dispose are varied by an instrument executed by the persons or any of the persons who benefit or would benefit under the dispositions, stamp duty under [Part I of Schedule 13 to the Finance Act 1999 ([transfer][2] on sale)][1] shall not be chargeable on the instrument.

(2) Subsection (1) above does not apply where the variation is made for any consideration in money or money's worth other than consideration consisting of the making of a variation in respect of another of the dispositions.

(3) Subsection (1) above applies whether or not the administration of the estate is complete or the property has been distributed in accordance with the original dispositions.

(4) Where property is appropriated by a personal representative in or towards satisfaction of a general legacy of money, stamp duty under the heading mentioned in subsection (1) above shall not be chargeable on an instrument giving effect to the appropriation.

(5) Where on an intestacy property is appropriated by a personal representative in or towards satisfaction of any interest of a surviving [spouse or civil partner][3] in the intestate's estate, stamp duty under the heading mentioned in subsection (1) above shall not be chargeable on an instrument giving effect to the appropriation.

(6) The reference in subsection (5) above to an interest in the intestate's estate—

(*a*) includes a reference to the capital value of a life interest which the surviving [spouse or civil partner][3] has under the Intestates' Estates Act 1952 elected to have redeemed, and

(*b*) in Scotland, includes a reference to prior rights (within the meaning of the Succession (Scotland) Act 1964) but, without prejudice to subsection (7) below, not to such rights as are mentioned in that subsection.

(7) Where in Scotland, on an intestacy or otherwise, property is appropriated by a personal representative in or towards satisfaction of the right of a husband to *jus relicti*, of a wife to *jus* [*relictae*, of issue to *legitim* or rights under section 131 of the Civil Partnership Act 2004, or of a civil partner to rights under section 131 of that Act][3], stamp duty under the heading mentioned in subsection (1) above shall not be chargeable on an instrument giving effect to the appropriation.

(8), (9) . . . [4]

(10) Subject to subsection (11) below, this section applies to instruments executed on or after 26th March 1985 and shall be deemed to have come into operation on that date.

(11) Subsections (5) to (7) above . . . [4] apply to instruments executed on or after 1st August 1985.

Cross references—See the Stamp Duty (Exempt Instruments) Regulations, SI 1987/516 for stamp duty exemption in respect of certain instruments executed after 30 April 1987 otherwise chargeable under this section.

Amendments—[1] Words in sub-s (1) and figures in sub-s (8) substituted by FA 1999 s 112(4), Sch 14 para 11 with effect in relation to instruments executed after 30 September 1999. This does not apply to transfers or other instruments relating to units under a unit trust scheme by virtue of FA 1999 s 122. Previously the text read 'the heading "Conveyance or Transfer on Sale" in Schedule 1 to the Stamp Act 1891' and '50p'.

[2] The word "transfer" substituted for the words "conveyance or transfer" in enactments relating to stamp duty by FA 2003 Sch 20 para 3.

[3] Words in sub-ss (5), (6)(*a*) inserted, and words in sub-s (7) substituted by Tax and Civil Partnership Regulations, SI 2005/3229, regs 40, 42, with effect from 5 December 2005 (reg 1(1)).

[4] Sub-ss (8), (9), and words "and, so far as it relates to subsection (5) or (7), subsection (8) above" in sub-s (11), repealed by FA 2008 s 99, Sch 32 paras 1, 3 with effect in relation to instruments executed on or after 13 March 2008 and not stamped before 19 March 2008. Sub-ss (8), (9) previously read as follows—

"(8) An instrument in respect of which stamp duty is not chargeable under the heading mentioned in subsection (1) above by virtue only of subsection (1), (4), (5) or (7) above shall be chargeable under this subsection with stamp duty of [£5].

(9) But an instrument which is chargeable under subsection (8) above shall not be treated as duly stamped unless it has, in accordance with section 12 of the Stamp Act 1891, been stamped with a particular stamp denoting that it is duly stamped.".

This amendment does not have effect in relation to an instrument effecting a land transaction or a duplicate or counterpart of such an instrument. "Land transaction" has the same meaning as in FA 2003 Part 4, except that it does not include a transfer of an interest in a property-investment partnership (within the meaning of FA 2003 Sch 15) (FA 2008 s 99, Sch 32 para 22).

85 Repeal of certain fixed duties

(1) (*repeals certain headings in* Stamp Act 1891 Sch 1).

(2) (*amends* FA 1907 s 7).

(3) This section and that Schedule apply to—

(*a*) instruments executed on or after 26th March 1985, and

(*b*) instruments executed on or after 19th March 1985 which are not stamped before 26th March 1985.

(4) For the purposes of section 14(4) of the Stamp Act 1891 (instruments not to be given in evidence etc unless stamped in accordance with the law in force at the time of first execution), the law in force at the time of execution of an instrument falling within subsection (3)(*b*) above shall be deemed to be that as varied in accordance with this section.

(5) This section and that Schedule shall be deemed to have come into operation on 26th March 1985.

86 Abolition of duty on contract notes

(*repeals* F(1909–10)A 1910, s 77 (1), (2)).

87 Certificates

(1) The Commissioners may make regulations providing that an instrument which is of a kind specified in them—

(*a*) shall be certified to be an instrument of that kind, and

(*b*) shall not be treated as duly stamped if it is not so certified.

(2) The Treasury may make regulations providing that an instrument which is of a kind specified in them, and which would apart from this subsection be chargeable with stamp duty of a fixed amount under any provision so specified, shall not be charged with such duty under that provision if it is certified to be an instrument of that kind.

(3) Certification under this section shall be by such method as the regulations may specify, and in particular they may provide for a certificate to be borne by or attached to or otherwise associated with an instrument in such manner as they may specify.

(4) A certificate under this section shall be in such form and signed by such person as the regulations may specify.

(5) Regulations under this section may contain such incidental or consequential provisions as the Commissioners or Treasury (as the case may be) think fit.
(6) Regulations under this section may make different provision for different cases or descriptions of case.
(7) The power to make regulations under this section shall be exercisable by statutory instrument subject to annulment in pursuance of a resolution of the House of Commons.

88 Exchange rates

Section 12 of the Finance Act 1899 (fixed exchange rate for foreign currency) shall not apply to instruments executed on or after 1st August 1985, and section 6 of the Stamp Act 1891 (exchange rate at date of instrument) shall apply to instruments to which section 12 of the 1899 Act would apply if this Act had not been passed.

89 Exemption from section 28 of Finance Act 1931

(1) Section 28 of the Finance Act 1931 (production to Commissioners of instruments transferring land and furnishing of particulars) shall not apply in relation to any instrument (an "exempt instrument") which falls within any class prescribed for the purposes of this section by regulations made by the Commissioners.
(2) Regulations under this section may—
 (*a*) provide that the particulars mentioned in Schedule 2 to the 1931 Act shall be furnished to the Commissioners, in accordance with the requirements of the regulations, in respect of exempt instruments or such descriptions of exempt instruments as may be prescribed by the regulations;
 (*b*) make different provision in relation to different cases or kinds of case and in respect of different parts of Great Britain.
(3) Any person who fails to comply with any requirement imposed by regulations made under this section shall be liable on summary conviction to a fine not exceeding level 3 on the standard scale [1]. . .
(4) The power to make regulations under this section shall be exercisable by statutory instrument; and a statutory instrument containing regulations under this section shall be subject to annulment in pursuance of a resolution of the House of Commons.
(5) Section 35 (*x*) of the 1931 Act (which gives power by regulations to exempt certain instruments in Scotland where particulars are obtained through the General Register of Sasines and which is superseded by the power given by this section) shall cease to have effect.
(6) Regulations made under section 35 (*x*) shall have effect after the commencement of this section as if they were made under this section and as if they imposed on the Keeper of the Registers of Scotland the duty mentioned in section 35 (*x*).

Regulations—See The Stamp Duty (Exempt Instruments) Regulations, SI 1985/1688.
Amendments—[1] Words in sub-s (3) repealed by the Statute Law (Repeals) Act 1993 s 1(1), Sch 1 Pt XIV.

PART V
MISCELLANEOUS AND SUPPLEMENTARY

96 European Communities and Investment Bank: exemptions

(1) (*inserts* FA 1984 s 126(4), (5)).
(2) An order made by virtue of subsection (4) of section 126 of the Finance Act 1984 may revoke or vary the European Communities (Loan Stock) (Stamp Duties) Order 1972 (which provides for exemption from stamp duty in respect of issues and transfers of loan stock of the bodies referred to in that subsection, other than the Economic Community).

98 Short title, interpretation, construction and repeals

(1) This Act may be cited as the Finance Act 1985.
(2)–(3) (*not relevant to stamp duty*).
(4) Part III of this Act shall be construed as one with the Stamp Act 1891.
(5) (*not relevant to stamp duty*).
(6) The enactments specified in Schedule 27 to this Act are hereby repealed to the extent specified in the third column of that Schedule, but subject to any provision at the end of any Part of that Schedule.

FINANCE ACT 1986

(1986 Chapter 41)

ARRANGEMENT OF SECTIONS

An Act to grant certain duties, to alter other duties, and to amend the law relating to the National Debt and the Public Revenue, and to make further provision in connection with Finance

[25th July 1986]

PART III
STAMP DUTY

Securities

64 Stock or marketable securities: reduction of rate

Amendments—This section repealed by FA 1999 Sch 20 Pt V(2) with effect in relation to instruments executed, or bearer instruments issued, from 1 October 1999, subject to the provisions in FA 1999 Sch 20 Pt V(2) Note 2. Previously the text amended FA 1963 s 55 *and FA (Northern Ireland) 1963 s 4.*

65 Bearers: consequential provisions etc

Amendments—This section repealed by FA 1999 Sch 20 Pt V(2) with effect in relation to instruments executed, or bearer instruments issued, from 1 October 1999, subject to the provisions in FA 1999 Sch 20 Pt V(2) Note 2. Previously the text amended SA 1891, Sch 1 heading "Bearer Instrument", FA 1963 s 59(3) and FA (Northern Ireland) 1963, s 8.

66 Company's purchase of own shares

(1) This section applies where a company purchases its own shares under section [690][3] of the Companies Act [2006][3] . . . [3].

(2) [Any return which relates to any of the shares][1] purchased and is delivered to the registrar of companies under section [707][3]][1] of that Act . . . [3] shall be charged with stamp duty, and treated for all purposes of the Stamp Act 1891, as if it were an instrument transferring the shares [to which it relates][1] on sale to the company in pursuance of the contract (or contracts) of purchase concerned.

(2A) . . . [2]

(3) Subject to subsection (4) below, this section applies to any [such return][3] which is delivered to the registrar of companies on or after the day of The Stock Exchange reforms.

(4) This section does not apply to any return to the extent that the shares to which it relates were purchased under a contract entered into before the day of The Stock Exchange reforms.

(5) In this section "the day of The Stock Exchange reforms" means the day on which the rule of The Stock Exchange that prohibits a person from carrying on business as both a broker and a jobber is abolished.

Note—This section was to be repealed by FA 1990 Sch 19 Pt VI with effect from an appointed day in accordance with FA 1990 ss 107–111. The Treasury order specifying the appointed day for the purposes of FA 1990 ss 107–110 was to coincide with the start of paperless trading under the Stock Exchange's planned TAURUS system (IR press release, 20-3-90). However, on 11-3-93 the London Stock Exchange News Release 6/93 announced that TAURUS had been abandoned.

Amendments—[1] Words in sub-s (2) substituted and inserted; and reference in sub-ss (2), (3) inserted by FA 2003 s 195, Sch 40 para 2 with effect for any acquisition of shares by a company on or after 1 December 2003 (by virtue of SI 2003/3077).

[2] Sub-s (2A) repealed by FA 2008 s 99, Sch 32 paras 4, 5 with effect in relation to instruments executed on or after 13 March 2008 and not stamped before 19 March 2008. Sub-s (2A) previously read as follows—

"(2A) Any return which relates to the cancellation of any of the shares purchased and is delivered to the registrar of companies under section 169A of the Companies Act 1985 shall be chargeable under this subsection with stamp duty of £5.".

[3] In sub-s (1), figures substituted for figures "162" and "1985", and words "or Article 47 of the Companies (Northern Ireland) Order 1982" repealed, in sub-s (2), reference substituted for reference "169(1) or (1B)", and words " or, as the case may be, Article 53 of that Order" repealed, and in sub-s (3), words substituted for words "return under section 169[(1) or (1B] of the Companies Act 1985 or Article 53 of the Companies (Northern Ireland) Order 1982,", by the Companies Act 2006 (Consequential Amendments) (Taxes and National Insurance) Order, SI 2009/1890 art 7(*a*)–(*c*) with effect from 1 October 2009.

Depositary receipts

67 Depositary receipts

(1) Subject to subsection (9) below, subsection (2) or (3) below (as the case may be) applies where an instrument [(other than a bearer instrument)][6] transfers relevant securities of a company incorporated in the United Kingdom to a person who at the time of the transfer falls within subsection (6), (7) or (8) below.

[(2) If stamp duty is chargeable on the instrument under Part I of Schedule 13 to the Finance Act 1999 ([transfer][4] on sale), the rate at which that duty is chargeable is 1.5% of the amount or value of the consideration for the sale to which the instrument gives effect.

(3) [In any other case—

(*a*) stamp duty is chargeable on the instrument under this subsection, and

(*b*)][7] subject to subsection (5), the rate at which that duty is chargeable is 1.5% of the value of the securities at the date the instrument is executed.][2]

(4) . . . [1]

(5) In a case where—

(*a*) securities are issued, or securities sold are transferred, and (in either case) they are to be paid for in instalments,

(*b*) the person to whom they are issued or transferred holds them and transfers them to another person when the last instalment is paid,

(*c*) the transfer to the other person is effected by an instrument in the case of which subsection (3) above applies,

(*d*) before the execution of the instrument mentioned in paragraph (*c*) above an instrument is received by a person falling (at the time of the receipt) within subsection (6), (7) or (8) below,

(*e*) the instrument so received evidences all the rights which (by virtue of the terms under which the securities are issued or sold as mentioned in paragraph (*a*) above) subsist in respect of them at the time of the receipt, and

(*f*) the instrument mentioned in paragraph (*c*) above contains a statement that paragraphs (*a*), (*b*) and (*e*) above are fulfilled,

subsection (3) above shall have effect as if the reference to the value there mentioned were to an amount (if any) equal to the total of the instalments payable, less those paid before the transfer to the other person is effected.

(6) A person falls within this subsection if his business is exclusively that of holding relevant securities—

(*a*) as nominee or agent for a person whose business is or includes issuing depositary receipts for relevant securities, and

(*b*) for the purposes of such part of the business mentioned in paragraph (*a*) above as consists of issuing such depositary receipts (in a case where the business does not consist exclusively of that).

(7) A person falls within this subsection if—

(*a*) he is specified for the purposes of this subsection by the Treasury by order made by statutory instrument, and

(*b*) his business is or includes issuing depositary receipts for relevant securities.

(8) A person falls within this subsection if—

(*a*) he is specified for the purposes of this subsection by the Treasury by order made by statutory instrument,

(*b*) he does not fall within subsection (6) above but his business includes holding relevant securities as nominee or agent for a person who falls within subsection (7)(*b*) above at the time of the transfer, and

(*c*) he holds relevant securities as nominee or agent for such a person, for the purposes of such part of that person's business as consists of issuing depositary receipts for relevant securities (in a case where that business does not consist exclusively of that).

(9) Where an instrument transfers relevant securities of a company incorporated in the United Kingdom—

(*a*) to a company which at the time of the transfer falls within subsection (6) above *and is resident in the United Kingdom*[3], and

(*b*) from a company which at that time falls within that subsection *and is so resident*[3],

subsections (2) to (5) above shall not apply and [stamp duty is not chargeable on the instrument][5].

[(9A) In this section "bearer instrument" has the meaning given in paragraph 3 of Schedule 15 to the Finance Act 1999.][6]

(10) This section applies to any instrument executed on or after the day on which the rule of The Stock Exchange that prohibits a person from carrying on business as both a broker and a jobber is abolished.

Cross references—See FA 1988 s 143(6) (UK company shares paired with foreign company shares; in relation to certain instruments transferring paired shares and executed after 29 July 1988, the foreign company to be treated for the purposes of this section as incorporated in the UK);

FA 1990 ss 108(8), 111(1) (abolition of stamp duty with effect from an appointed day on transfer of securities).

Note—This section was to be repealed by FA 1990 Sch 19 Pt VI with effect from an appointed day in accordance with FA 1990 ss 107–111. The Treasury order specifying the appointed day for the purposes of FA 1990 ss 107–110 was to coincide with the start of paperless trading under the Stock Exchange's planned TAURUS system (IR press release, 20-3-90). However, on 11-3-93 the London Stock Exchange News Release 6/93 announced that TAURUS had been abandoned.

Amendments—[1] Sub-s (4) repealed by FA 1997 s 99(1), Sch 18 Pt VII with effect for any instrument executed on or after 20 October 1997 (the date appointed under FA 1997 s 97 by virtue of SI 1997/2428) except an instrument which transfers relevant securities which were acquired by the transferor before that date. Previously the text read:

"(4) Subsection (3) above shall have effect as if "£1.50" read "£1" in a case where—

(*a*) at the time of the transfer the transferor is a qualified dealer in securities of the kind concerned or a nominee of such a qualified dealer,

(*b*) the transfer is made for the purposes of the dealer's business,

(*c*) at the time of the transfer the dealer is not a market maker in securities of the kind concerned, and

(*d*) the instrument contains a statement that paragraphs (*a*) to (*c*) above are fulfilled."

[2] Sub-ss (2) and (3) substituted by FA 1999 s 112(4), Sch 14 para 12 with effect in relation to instruments executed after 30 September 1999. This does not apply to transfers or other instruments relating to units under a unit trust scheme by virtue of FA 1999 s 122. For prospective repeal of FA 1999 Sch 14 para 12 see FA 1999 s 123(3). Previously the text read:

"(2) If stamp duty is chargeable on the instrument under the heading "Conveyance or Transfer on Sale" in Schedule 1 to the Stamp Act 1891, the rate at which the duty is charged under that heading shall be the rate of £1.50 for every £100 or part of £100 of the amount or value of the consideration for the sale to which the instrument gives effect.

(3) If stamp duty is chargeable on the instrument under the heading "Conveyance or Transfer of any kind not hereinbefore described" in Schedule 1 to the Stamp Act 1891, the rate at which the duty is charged under that heading shall (subject to [subsection] (5) below) be the rate of £1.50 for every £100 or part of £100 of the value of the securities at the date the instrument is executed."

[3] Words in sub-s (9) repealed by FA 2000 s 134(3), (5), Sch 40 Pt III with effect for stamp duty purposes for instruments executed after 28 July 2000 and for stamp duty reserve tax purposes for securities transferred after 28 July 2000.

[4] The word "transfer" substituted for the words "conveyance or transfer" in enactments relating to stamp duty by FA 2003 Sch 20 para 3.

[5] In sub-s (9), words "the stamp duty chargeable on the instrument is £5" substituted by FA 2008 s 99, Sch 32 paras 4, 6 with effect in relation to instruments executed on or after 13 March 2008 and not stamped before 19 March 2008.

[6] Words in sub-s (1) and whole of sub-s (9A) inserted, and words in sub-s (3) substituted by FA 2008 s 99, Sch 32 paras 13, 14 with effect in relation to instruments executed on or after 13 March 2008 and not stamped before 19 March 2008. If a day is appointed under FA 1990 s 111 (abolition day), FA 2008 Sch 32 paras 14, 15 cease to have effect in accordance with FA 1990 s 108 (FA 2008 s 99, Sch 32 para 23).

Sub-s (3) previously read as follows—

"(3) If stamp duty is chargeable on the instrument under paragraph 16 of Schedule 13 to the Finance Act 1999 (transfer otherwise than on sale), then, subject to subsection (5), the rate at which that duty is chargeable is 1.5% of the value of the securities at the date the instrument is executed.".

68 Depositary receipts: notification

(1) A person whose business is or includes issuing depositary receipts for relevant securities of a company incorporated in the United Kingdom shall notify the Commissioners of that fact before the end of the period of one month beginning with the date on which he first issues such depositary receipts.

(2) A person whose business includes (but does not exclusively consist of) holding relevant securities (being securities of a company incorporated in the United Kingdom)—

(*a*) as nominee or agent for a person whose business is or includes issuing depositary receipts for relevant securities, and

(*b*) for the purposes of such part of the business mentioned in paragraph (*a*) above as consists of issuing such depositary receipts (in a case where the business does not consist exclusively of that),

shall notify the Commissioners of that fact before the end of the period of one month beginning with the date on which he first holds such relevant securities as such a nominee or agent and for such purposes.

(3) A company which is incorporated in the United Kingdom and becomes aware that any shares in the company are held by a person such as is mentioned in subsection (1) or (2) above shall notify the Commissioners of that fact before the end of the period of one month beginning with the date on which the company first becomes aware of that fact.

(4) A person who fails to comply with subsection (1) or (2) above shall be liable to a [penalty][1] not exceeding £1,000.

(5) A company which fails to comply with subsection (3) above shall be liable to a [penalty][1] not exceeding £100.

(6) . . . [2]

Cross references—See FA 1988 s 143(6) (UK company shares paired with foreign company shares; in relation to certain instruments transferring paired shares and executed after 29 July 1988, the foreign company to be treated for the purposes of this section as incorporated in the UK);

FA 1990 ss 109(4), (5), 111(1) (abolition of the requirement of notification under sub-ss (1), (2), (3) with effect from an appointed day).

Note—This section was to be repealed by FA 1990 Sch 19 Pt VI with effect from an appointed day in accordance with FA 1990 ss 107–111. The Treasury order specifying the appointed day for the purposes of FA 1990 ss 107–110 was to coincide with the start of paperless trading under the Stock Exchange's planned TAURUS system (IR press release, 20-3-90). However, on 11-3-93 the London Stock Exchange News Release 6/93 announced that TAURUS had been abandoned.

Amendments—[1] Words in sub-ss (4) and (5) substituted by FA 1999 s 114, Sch 17 para 8 with effect in relation to penalties in respect of things done or omitted after 30 September 1999. For prospective repeal of FA 1999 Sch 17 para 8 see FA 1999 s 123(3). Previously the text read 'fine'.

[2] Sub-s (6) repealed by FA 1999 Sch 20 Pt V(3) with effect in relation to things done or omitted from 1 October 1999.

69 Depositary receipts: supplementary

(1) For the purposes of sections 67 and 68 above a depositary receipt for relevant securities is an instrument acknowledging—

(*a*) that a person holds relevant securities or evidence of the right to receive them, and

(*b*) that another person is entitled to rights, whether expressed as units or otherwise, in or in relation to relevant securities of the same kind, including the right to receive such securities (or evidence of the right to receive them) from the person mentioned in paragraph (*a*) above,

except that for those purposes a depositary receipt for relevant securities does not include an instrument acknowledging rights in or in relation to securities if they are issued or sold under terms providing for payment in instalments and for the issue of the instrument as evidence that an instalment has been paid.

(2) The Treasury may by regulations provide that for subsection (1) above (as it has effect for the time being) there shall be substituted a subsection containing a different definition of a depositary receipt for the purposes of sections 67 and 68 above.

(3) References in this section and sections 67 and 68 above to relevant securities, or to relevant securities of a company, are to shares in or stock or marketable securities of any company (which, unless otherwise stated, need not be incorporated in the United Kingdom).

(4) For the purposes of section 67 (3) above the value of securities at the date the instrument is executed shall be taken to be the price they might reasonably be expected to fetch on a sale at that time in the open market.

(5) . . . [2]

(6)–(8) . . . [1]

(9) The power to make regulations or an order under this section shall be exercisable by statutory instrument subject to annulment in pursuance of a resolution of the House of Commons.

Note—This section was to be repealed by FA 1990 Sch 19 Pt VI with effect from an appointed day in accordance with FA 1990 ss 107–111. The Treasury order specifying the appointed day for the purposes of FA 1990 ss 107–110 was to coincide with the start of paperless trading under the Stock Exchange's planned TAURUS system (IR press release, 20-3-90). However, on 11-3-93 the London Stock Exchange News Release 6/93 announced that TAURUS had been abandoned.

Amendments—[1] Sub-ss (6) to (8) repealed by FA 1997 s 99(2), Sch 18 Pt VII with effect for any instrument executed on or after 20 October 1997 (the date appointed under FA 1997 s 97 by virtue of SI 1997/2428) except an instrument which transfers relevant securities which were acquired by the transferor before that date. Previously the text read:

"(6) For the purposes of section 67 (4) above a person is a qualified dealer in securities of a particular kind if he deals in securities of that kind and—

(*a*) is a member of a recognised stock exchange (within the meaning given by section 841 of the Taxes Act 1988, or

(*b*) is designated a qualified dealer by order made by the Treasury.

(7) For the purposes of section 67 (4) above a person is a market maker in securities of a particular kind if he—

(*a*) holds himself out at all normal times in compliance with the rules of The Stock Exchange as willing to buy and sell securities of that kind at a price specified by him, and

(*b*) is recognised as doing so by the Council of The Stock Exchange.

(8) The Treasury may by regulations provide that for subsection (7) above (as it has effect for the time being) there shall be substituted a subsection containing a different definition of a market maker for the purposes of section 67 (4) above."

[2] Sub-s (5) repealed by FA 1999 Sch 20 Pt V(1) with effect from 1 October 1999, subject to the provisions in FA 1999 Sch 20 Pt V(1) Note 2. Previously the text read:

"(5) Where section 67 (3) above applies, section 15 (2) of the Stamp Act 1891 (stamping of instruments after execution) shall have effect as if the instrument were specified in the first column of the table in paragraph (*d*) and the transferee were specified (opposite the instrument) in the second."

Clearance services

70 Clearance services

(1) Subject to subsection (9) [and section 97A][2] below, subsection (2) or (3) below (as the case may be) applies where an instrument [(other than a bearer instrument)][8] transfers relevant securities of a company incorporated in the United Kingdom to a person who at the time of the transfer falls within subsection (6), (7) or (8) below.

[(2) If stamp duty is chargeable on the instrument under Part I of Schedule 13 to the Finance Act 1999 ([transfer][6] on sale), the rate at which that duty is chargeable is 1.5% of the amount or value of the consideration for the sale to which the instrument gives effect.

(3) [In any other case—

(*a*) stamp duty is chargeable on the instrument under this subsection, and

(*b*)][8] subject to subsection (5), the rate at which that duty is chargeable is 1.5% of the value of the securities at the date the instrument is executed.][4]

(4) . . . [3]

(5) In a case where—

(*a*) securities are issued, or securities sold are transferred, and (in either case) they are to be paid for in instalments,

(*b*) the person to whom they are issued or transferred holds them and transfers them to another person when the last instalment is paid,

(*c*) the transfer to the other person is effected by an instrument in the case of which subsection (3) above applies,

(*d*) before the execution of the instrument mentioned in paragraph (*c*) above an instrument is received by a person falling (at the time of the receipt) within subsection (6), (7) or (8) below,

(*e*) the instrument so received evidences all the rights which (by virtue of the terms under which the securities are issued or sold as mentioned in paragraph (*a*) above) subsist in respect of them at the time of the receipt, and

(*f*) the instrument mentioned in paragraph (*c*) above contains a statement that paragraphs (*a*), (*b*) and (*e*) above are fulfilled,

subsection (3) above shall have effect as if the reference to the value there mentioned were to an amount (if any) equal to the total of the instalments payable, less those paid before the transfer to the other person is effected.

(6) A person falls within this subsection if his business is exclusively that of holding [shares, stock or other marketable][1] securities—

(*a*) as nominee or agent for a person whose business is or includes the provision of clearance services for the purchase and sale of relevant securities, and

(*b*) for the purposes of such part of the business mentioned in paragraph (*a*) above as consists of the provision of such clearance services (in a case where the business does not consist exclusively of that).

(7) A person falls within this subsection if—

(*a*) he is specified for the purposes of this subsection by the Treasury by order made by statutory instrument, and

(*b*) his business is or includes the provision of clearance services for the purchase and sale of relevant securities.

(8) A person falls within this subsection if—

(*a*) he is specified for the purposes of this subsection by the Treasury by order made by statutory instrument,

(*b*) he does not fall within subsection (6) above but his business includes holding relevant securities as nominee or agent for a person who falls within subsection (7) (*b*) above at the time of the transfer, and

(*c*) he holds relevant securities as nominee or agent for such a person, for the purposes of such part of that person's business as consists of the provision of clearance services for the purchase and sale of relevant securities (in a case where that business does not consist exclusively of that).

(9) Where an instrument transfers relevant securities of a company incorporated in the United Kingdom—

(*a*) to a company which at the time of the transfer falls within subsection (6) above . . . [5], and

(*b*) from a company which at that time falls within that subsection . . . [5],

subsections (2) to (5) above shall not apply and [stamp duty is not chargeable on the instrument][7].

[(9A) In this section "bearer instrument" has the meaning given in paragraph 3 of Schedule 15 to the Finance Act 1999.][8]

(10) This section applies to any instrument executed on or after the day on which the rule of The Stock Exchange that prohibits a person from carrying on business as both a broker and a jobber is abolished.

Cross references—See FA 1986 s 97A (disapplication of this section in relation to clearance services where an election is made under s 97A(1)).

FA 1988 s 143(6) (UK company shares paired with foreign company shares; in relation to certain instruments transferring paired shares and executed after 29 July 1988, the foreign company to be treated for the purposes of this section as incorporated in the UK);

FA 1990 ss 108(8), 111(1) (abolition of stamp duty with effect from an appointed day on transfer of securities).

Note—This section was to be repealed by FA 1990 Sch 19 Pt VI with effect from an appointed day in accordance with FA 1990 ss 107–111. The Treasury order specifying the appointed day for the purposes of FA 1990 ss 107–110 was to coincide with the start of paperless trading under the Stock Exchange's planned TAURUS system (IR press release, 20-3-90). However, on 11-3-93 the London Stock Exchange News Release 6/93 announced that TAURUS had been abandoned.

Amendments—[1] Words in sub-s (6) substituted by FA 1987 s 52 in relation to instruments executed after 31 July 1987.

[2] Words in sub-s (1) inserted by FA 1996 s 182(1), (6), with effect from 1 July 1996.

[3] Sub-s (4) repealed by FA 1997 s 99 (3), Sch 18 Pt VII with effect for any instrument executed on or after 20 October 1997 (the date appointed under FA 1997 s 97 by virtue of SI 1997/2428) except an instrument which transfers relevant securities which were acquired by the transferor before that date. Previously the text read:

"(4) Subsection (3) above shall have effect as if "£1.50" read "£1" in a case where—

(*a*) at the time of the transfer the transferor is a qualified dealer in securities of the kind concerned or a nominee of such a qualified dealer,

(*b*) the transfer is made for the purposes of the dealer's business,

(*c*) at the time of the transfer the dealer is not a market maker in securities of the kind concerned, and

(*d*) the instrument contains a statement that paragraphs (*a*) to (*c*) above are fulfilled."

[4] Sub-ss (2) and (3) substituted by FA 1999 s 112(4), Sch 14 para 13 with effect in relation to instruments executed after 30 September 1999. This does not apply to transfers or other instruments relating to units under a unit trust scheme by virtue of FA 1999 s 122. For prospective repeal of FA 1999 Sch 14 para 13 see FA 1999 s 123(3). Previously the text read:

"(2) If stamp duty is chargeable on the instrument under the heading "Conveyance or Transfer on Sale" in Schedule 1 to the Stamp Act 1891, the rate at which the duty is charged under that heading shall be the rate of £1.50 for every £100 or part of £100 of the amount or value of the consideration for the sale to which the instrument gives effect.

(3) If stamp duty is chargeable on the instrument under the heading "Conveyance or Transfer of any kind not hereinbefore described" in Schedule 1 to the Stamp Act 1891, the rate at which the duty is charged under that heading shall (subject to [subsection] (5) below) be the rate of £1.50 for every £100 or part of £100 of the value of the securities at the date the instrument is executed."

[5] Words in sub-s (9) repealed by FA 2000 s 134(3), (5), Sch 40 Pt III with effect for stamp duty purposes for instruments executed after 28 July 2000 and for stamp duty reserve tax purposes for securities transferred after 28 July 2000.

[6] The word "transfer" substituted for the words "conveyance or transfer" in enactments relating to stamp duty by FA 2003 Sch 20 para 3.

[7] In sub-s (9), words "the stamp duty chargeable on the instrument is £5" substituted by FA 2008 s 99, Sch 32 paras 4, 7 with effect in relation to instruments executed on or after 13 March 2008 and not stamped before 19 March 2008.

[8] Words in sub-s (1) and whole of sub-s (9A) inserted, and words in sub-s (3) substituted by FA 2008 s 99, Sch 32 paras 13, 15 with effect in relation to instruments executed on or after 13 March 2008 and not stamped before 19 March 2008.

If a day is appointed under FA 1990 s 111 (abolition day), FA 2008 Sch 32 paras 14, 15 cease to have effect in accordance with FA 1990 s 108 (FA 2008 s 99, Sch 32 para 23).

Sub-s (3) previously read as follows—

"(3) If stamp duty is chargeable on the instrument under paragraph 16 of Schedule 13 to the Finance Act 1999 (transfer otherwise than on sale), then, subject to subsection (5), the rate at which that duty is chargeable is 1.5% of the value of the securities at the date the instrument is executed."

71 Clearance services: notification

(1) A person whose business is or includes the provision of clearance services for the purchase and sale of relevant securities of a company incorporated in the United Kingdom shall notify the Commissioners of that fact before the end of the period of one month beginning with the date on which he first provides such clearance services.

(2) A person whose business includes (but does not exclusively consist of) holding relevant securities (being securities of a company incorporated in the United Kingdom)—

(*a*) as nominee or agent for a person whose business is or includes the provision of clearance services for the purchase and sale of relevant securities, and

(*b*) for the purposes of such part of the business mentioned in paragraph (*a*) above as consists of the provision of such clearance services (in a case where the business does not consist exclusively of that),

shall notify the Commissioners of that fact before the end of the period of one month beginning with the date on which he first holds such relevant securities as such a nominee or agent and for such purposes.

(3) A company which is incorporated in the United Kingdom and becomes aware that any shares in the company are held by a person such as is mentioned in subsection (1) or (2) above shall notify the Commissioners of that fact before the end of the period of one month beginning with the date on which the company first becomes aware of that fact.

(4) A person who fails to comply with subsection (1) or (2) above shall be liable to a [penalty][1] not exceeding £1,000.

(5) A company which fails to comply with subsection (3) above shall be liable to a [penalty][1] not exceeding £100.

(6) . . .[2]

Cross references—See FA 1988 s 143(6) (UK company shares paired with foreign company shares; in relation to certain instruments transferring paired shares and executed after 29 July 1988, the foreign company to be treated for the purposes of this section as incorporated in the UK);

FA 1990 ss 109(4), (5), 111(1) (abolition of the requirement of notification under sub-ss (1), (2), (3) with effect from an appointed day).

Note—This section was to be repealed by FA 1990 Sch 19 Pt VI with effect from an appointed day in accordance with FA 1990 ss 107–111. The Treasury order specifying the appointed day for the purposes of FA 1990 ss 107–110 was to coincide with the start of paperless trading under the Stock Exchange's planned TAURUS system (IR press release, 20-3-90). However, on 11-3-93 the London Stock Exchange News Release 6/93 announced that TAURUS had been abandoned.

Amendments—[1] Words in sub-ss (4) and (5) substituted by FA 1999 s 114, Sch 17 para 8 with effect in relation to penalties in respect of things done or omitted after 30 September 1999.

[2] Sub-s (6) repealed by FA 1999 Sch 20 Pt V(3) with effect in relation to things done or omitted from 1 October 1999.

72 Clearance services: supplementary

(1) References in sections 70 and 71 above to relevant securities, or to relevant securities of a company, are to shares in or stock or marketable securities of any company (which, unless otherwise stated, need not be incorporated in the United Kingdom).

(2) For the purposes of section 70(3) above the value of securities at the date the instrument is executed shall be taken to be the price they might reasonably be expected to fetch on a sale at that time in the open market.

(3) . . .[2]

(4) . . .[1]

Note—This section was to be repealed by FA 1990 Sch 19 Pt VI with effect from an appointed day in accordance with FA 1990 ss 107–111. The Treasury order specifying the appointed day for the purposes of FA 1990 ss 107–110 was to coincide with the start of paperless trading under the Stock Exchange's planned TAURUS system (IR press release, 20-3-90). However, on 11-3-93 the London Stock Exchange News Release 6/93 announced that TAURUS had been abandoned.

Amendments—[1] Sub-s (4) repealed by FA 1997 s 99 (4), Sch 18 Pt VII with effect for any instrument executed on or after 20 October 1997 (the date appointed under FA 1997 s 97 by virtue of SI 1997/2428) except an instrument which transfers relevant securities which were acquired by the transferor before that date. Previously the text read:

"(4) For the purposes of section 70(4) above 'qualified dealer' and 'market maker' have at any particular time the same meanings as they have at that time for the purposes of section 67 (4) above."

[2] Sub-s (3) repealed by FA 1999 Sch 20 Pt V(1) with effect from 1 October 1999, subject to the provisions in FA 1999 Sch 20 Pt V(1) Note 2. Previously the text read:

"(3) Where section 70(3) above applies, section 15 (2) of the Stamp Act 1891 (stamping of instruments after execution) shall have effect as if the instrument were specified in the first column of the table in paragraph (*d*) and the transferee were specified (opposite the instrument) in the second."

[Transfers between depositary receipt system and clearance system

72A Transfers between depositary receipt system and clearance system

(1) Where an instrument transfers relevant securities of a company incorporated in the United Kingdom between a depositary receipt system and a clearance system—

(*a*) the provisions of section 67(2) to (5) or, as the case may be, section 70(2) to (5) above shall not apply, and

[(*b*) stamp duty is not chargeable on the instrument.][2]

(2) A transfer between a depositary receipt system and a clearance system means a transfer—

(*a*) from (or to) a company that at the time of the transfer falls within section 67(6) above, and

(*b*) to (or from) a company that at that time falls within section 70(6) above.

(3) This section does not apply to a transfer from a clearance system (that is, from such a company as is mentioned in subsection (2)(*b*) above) if at the time of the transfer an election is in force under section 97A below in relation to the clearance services for the purposes of which the securities are held immediately before the transfer.][1]

Amendments—[1] This section inserted by FA 2000 s 134(1), (5) with effect for stamp duty purposes for instruments executed after 28 July 2000.

[2] Sub-s (1)(*b*) substituted by FA 2008 s 99, Sch 32 paras 4, 8 with effect in relation to instruments executed on or after 13 March 2008 and not stamped before 19 March 2008. Sub-s (1)(*b*) previously read as follows—

"(*b*) the stamp duty chargeable on the instrument is £5.".

Reconstructions and acquisitions

73 Reconstructions etc: amendments

Amendments—This section repealed by s 114(6) of, and Sch 23, Pt IX(1) to, this Act (this section amended FA 1927 s 55; FA 1980 Sch 18 para 12; FA 1985 ss 78, 79).

74 Reconstructions etc: repeals

(*repeals* FA 1927 s 55; FA (Northern Ireland) 1928, s 4; FA 1980 Sch 18, para 12(1), (1A); FA 1985 ss 78, 79, 80 *and amends* FA 1980 Sch 18 para 12(3)).

75 Acquisitions: reliefs

(1) This section applies where a company (the acquiring company) acquires the whole or part of an undertaking of another company (the target company) in pursuance of a scheme for the reconstruction of the target company.

(2) If the first and second conditions (as defined below) are fulfilled, stamp duty under [Part I of Schedule 13 to the Finance Act 1999 ([transfer][3] on sale)][1] shall not be chargeable on an instrument executed for the purposes of or in connection with the transfer of the undertaking or part.

(3) An instrument on which stamp duty is not chargeable by virtue only of subsection (2) above shall not be taken to be duly stamped unless it is stamped with the duty to which it would be liable but for that subsection or it has, in accordance with section 12 of the Stamp Act 1891, been stamped with a particular stamp denoting that it is not chargeable with any duty.

(4) The first condition is . . . [4] that the consideration for the acquisition—

(*a*) consists of or includes the issue of [non-redeemable][2] shares in the acquiring company to all the shareholders of the target company;

(*b*) includes nothing else (if anything) but the assumption or discharge by the acquiring company of liabilities of the target company.

[In paragraph (*a*) above, "non-redeemable shares" means shares which are not redeemable shares.][2]

(5) The second condition is that—

(*a*) the acquisition is effected for bona fide commercial reasons and does not form part of a scheme or arrangement of which the main purpose, or one of the main purposes, is avoidance of liability to stamp duty, income tax, corporation tax or capital gains tax,

(*b*) after the acquisition has been made, each shareholder of each of the companies is a shareholder of the other, and

(*c*) after the acquisition has been made, the proportion of shares of one of the companies held by any shareholder is the same[, or as nearly as may be the same,][4] as the proportion of shares of the other company held by that shareholder.

[(5A) If immediately before the acquisition the target company or the acquiring company holds any of its own shares, the shares are to be treated for the purposes of subsections (4) and (5) as having been cancelled before the acquisition (and, accordingly, the company is to be treated as if it were not a shareholder of itself).][5]

(6) This section applies to any instrument which is executed after 24th March 1986 unless it is executed in pursuance of an unconditional contract made on or before 18th March 1986.

(7) This section shall be deemed to have come into force on 25th March 1986.

Press releases etc—ICAEW TR631 August 1986 (relief not available on company partition).

Cross references—See Stamp Duty and Stamp Duty Reserve Tax (Open-ended Investment Companies) Regulations, SI 1997/1156 , Reg 12 (this section not to apply as regards open-ended investment companies).

Amendments—[1] Words in sub-s (2) substituted by FA 1999 s 112(4), Sch 14 para 14 with effect in relation to instruments executed after 30 September 1999. This does not apply to transfers or other instruments relating to units under a unit trust scheme by virtue of FA 1999 s 122. Previously the text read 'the heading "Conveyance or Transfer on Sale" in Schedule 1 to the Stamp Act 1891'.

[2] Words in sub-s (4) inserted by FA 2000 s 127(1)–(3), with effect for instruments executed after 28 July 2000.

[3] The word "transfer" substituted for the words "conveyance or transfer" in enactments relating to stamp duty by FA 2003 Sch 20 para 3.

[4] Words "that the registered office of the acquiring company is in the United Kingdom and" in sub-s (4) repealed, words in sub-s (5)(*c*) inserted by FA 2006 s 169(2), s 178, Sch 26 Pt 7(5) with effect in relation to instruments executed after 19 July 2006.

[5] Sub-s (5A) inserted by FA 2007 s 74(1), (4) with effect in relation to any instrument executed on or after the day on which FA 2007 is passed (19 July 2007).

76 Acquisitions: further provisions about reliefs

(1) This section applies where a company (the acquiring company) acquires the whole or part of an undertaking of another company (the target company).

(2) If [the first and second conditions (as defined below)][3] is fulfilled, and stamp duty under [Part I of Schedule 13 to the Finance Act 1999 ([transfer][4] on sale)][1] is chargeable on an instrument executed for the purposes of or in connection with—

(*a*) the transfer of the undertaking or part, or

(*b*) the assignment to the acquiring company by a creditor of the target company of any relevant debts (secured or unsecured) owed by the target company,

the rate at which the duty is charged under that heading shall not exceed that mentioned in subsection (4) below.

(3) [The first condition][3] is . . . [5] that the consideration for the acquisition—

(*a*) consists of or includes the issue of [non-redeemable shares (within the meaning of section 75(4)(*a*) above)][2] in the acquiring company to the target company or to all or any of its shareholders;

(*b*) includes nothing else (if anything) but cash not exceeding 10 per cent of the nominal value of those shares, or the assumption or discharge by the acquiring company of liabilities of the target company, or both.

[(3A) The second condition applies only in relation to an instrument transferring land in the United Kingdom and is that the acquiring company is not associated with another company that is a party to arrangements with the target company relating to shares of the acquiring company issued in connection with the transfer of the undertaking or part.][3]
[(3B) Where an instrument transfers land in the United Kingdom together with other property, the provisions of this section apply as if there were two separate instruments, one relating to land in the United Kingdom and the other relating to other property.][3]
(4) The rate is [0.5%][1] of the amount or value of the consideration for the sale to which the instrument gives effect.
(5) An instrument on which, by virtue only of [this section][3], the rate at which stamp duty is charged is not to exceed that mentioned in subsection (4) above shall not be taken to be duly stamped unless it is stamped with the duty to which it would be liable but for [this section][3] or it has, in accordance with section 12 of the Stamp Act 1891, been stamped with a particular stamp denoting that it is duly stamped.
(6) In subsection (2)(*b*) above "relevant debts" means—
 (*a*) any debt in the case of which the assignor is a bank or trade creditor, and
 (*b*) any other debt incurred not less than two years before the date on which the instrument is executed.
[(6A) For the purposes of subsection (3A) above—
 (*a*) companies are associated if one has control of the other or both are controlled by the same person or persons, and
 (*b*) "arrangements" includes any scheme, agreement or understanding, whether or not legally enforceable.
The references in paragraph (*a*) above to control shall be construed in accordance with [sections 450 and 451 of the Corporation Tax Act 2010][6].][3]
(7) This section applies to any instrument executed on or after the day on which the rule of The Stock Exchange that prohibits a person from carrying on business as both a broker and a jobber is abolished.

Cross references—See FA 2002 s 113, Sch 25 (withdrawal of the relief for company acquisitions where the claim to the relief on an instrument includes a transfer of land to an acquiring company, and control of the acquiring company changes within two years of the execution of that instrument).
Stamp Duty and Stamp Duty Reserve Tax (Open-ended Investment Companies) Regulations, SI 1997/1156 , Reg 12 (this section not to apply as regards open-ended investment companies).

Amendments—[1] Words in sub-ss (2) and (4) substituted by FA 1999 s 112(4), Sch 14 para 15 with effect in relation to instruments executed after 30 September 1999. This does not apply to transfers or other instruments relating to units under a unit trust scheme by virtue of FA 1999 s 122. Previously the text read 'the heading "Conveyance or Transfer on Sale" in Schedule 1 to the Stamp Act 1891' and 'the rate of 50p for every £100 or part of £100' respectively.
[2] Words in sub-s (3)(*a*) substituted for "shares" by FA 2000 s 127(4), with effect for instruments executed after 28 July 2000.
[3] Words in sub-ss (2), (3), (5) substituted, and sub-ss (3A), (3B), (6A) inserted, by FA 2002 s 112 with effect for instruments executed after 23 April 2002. These amendments are deemed to have come into force on 24 April 2002. They do not apply to an instrument giving effect to a contract made before 18 April 2002, unless—
 (*a*) the instrument is made in consequence of the exercise after that date of any option, right of pre-emption or similar right, or
 (*b*) the instrument transfers the property in question to, or vests it in, a person other than the purchaser under the contract because of an assignment (or, in Scotland, assignation) or further contract made after that date.
[4] The word "transfer" substituted for the words "conveyance or transfer" in enactments relating to stamp duty by FA 2003 Sch 20 para 3.
[5] Words "that the registered office of the acquiring company is in the United Kingdom and" in sub-s (3) repealed by FA 2006 s 169(3), s 178, Sch 26 Pt 7(5) with effect in relation to instruments executed after 19 July 2006.
[6] In sub-s (6A) words substituted for words "section 416 of the Taxes Act 1988" by CTA 2010 s 1177, Sch 1 para 196. CTA 2010 has effect for corporation tax purposes for accounting periods ending on or after 1 April 2010, and for income and capital gains tax purposes for the tax year 2010–11 and subsequent tax years.

77 Acquisition of target company's share capital

(1) Stamp duty under [Part I of Schedule 13 to the Finance Act 1999 ([transfer][2] on sale)][1] shall not be chargeable on an instrument transferring shares in one company (the target company) to another company (the acquiring company) if the conditions mentioned in subsection (3) below are fulfilled.
(2) An instrument on which stamp duty is not chargeable by virtue only of subsection (1) above shall not be taken to be duly stamped unless it is stamped with the duty to which it would be liable but for that subsection or it has, in accordance with section 12 of the Stamp Act 1891, been stamped with a particular stamp denoting that it is not chargeable with any duty.
(3) The conditions are that—
 (*a*) . . . [3]
 (*b*) the transfer forms part of an arrangement by which the acquiring company acquires the whole of the issued share capital of the target company,

(*c*) the acquisition is effected for bona fide commercial reasons and does not form part of a scheme or arrangement of which the main purpose, or one of the main purposes, is avoidance of liability to stamp duty, stamp duty reserve tax, income tax, corporation tax or capital gains tax,

(*d*) the consideration for the acquisition consists only of the issue of shares in the acquiring company to the shareholders of the target company,

(*e*) after the acquisition has been made, each person who immediately before it was made was a shareholder of the target company is a shareholder of the acquiring company,

(*f*) after the acquisition has been made, the shares in the acquiring company are of the same classes as were the shares in the target company immediately before the acquisition was made,

(*g*) after the acquisition has been made, the number of shares of any particular class in the acquiring company bears to all the shares in that company the same proportion[, or as nearly as may be the same proportion,][3] as the number of shares of that class in the target company bore to all the shares in that company immediately before the acquisition was made, and

(*h*) after the acquisition has been made, the proportion of shares of any particular class in the acquiring company held by any particular shareholder is the same[, or as nearly as may be the same,][3] as the proportion of shares of that class in the target company held by him immediately before the acquisition was made.

[(3A) If immediately before the acquisition the target company or the acquiring company holds any of its own shares, the shares are to be treated for the purposes of subsection (3) as having been cancelled before the acquisition (and, accordingly, the company is to be treated as if it were not a shareholder of itself).][4]

(4) In this section references to shares and to share capital include references to stock.

(5) This section applies to any instrument executed on or after 1st August 1986.[1]

Cross references—See Stamp Duty and Stamp Duty Reserve Tax (Open-ended Investment Companies) Regulations, SI 1997/1156 reg 12 (this section not to apply as regards open-ended investment companies).

Notes—This section was to be repealed by FA 1990 Sch 19 Pt VI with effect from an appointed day in accordance with FA 1990 ss 107–111. The Treasury order specifying the appointed day for the purposes of FA 1990 ss 107–110 was to coincide with the start of paperless trading under the Stock Exchange's planned TAURUS system (IR press release, 20-3-90). However, on 11-3-93 the London Stock Exchange News Release 6/93 announced that TAURUS had been abandoned.

Amendments—[1] Words in sub-s (1) substituted by FA 1999 s 112(4), Sch 14 para 16 with effect in relation to instruments executed after 30 September 1999. This does not apply to transfers or other instruments relating to units under a unit trust scheme by virtue of FA 1999 s 122. For prospective repeal of FA 1999 Sch 14 para 16 see FA 1999 s 123(3). Previously the text read 'the heading "Conveyance or Transfer on Sale" in Schedule 1 to the Stamp Act 1891'.

[2] The word "transfer" substituted for the words "conveyance or transfer" in enactments relating to stamp duty by FA 2003 Sch 20 para 3.

[3] In sub-s (3), para (*a*) repealed, words in paras (*g*), (*h*) inserted by FA 2006 s 169(4), s 178, Sch 26 Pt 7(5) with effect in relation to instruments executed after 19 July 2006. Sub-s (3)(*a*) previously read as follows—

"the registered office of the acquiring company is in the United Kingdom,".

[4] Sub-s (3A) inserted by FA 2007 s 74(2), (4) with effect in relation to any instrument executed on or after the day on which FA 2007 is passed (19 July 2007).

Loan capital, letters of allotment, etc

78 Loan capital

(1)–(6) . . . [2]

(7) In this section "loan capital" means—

(*a*) any debenture stock, corporation stock or funded debt, by whatever name known, issued by a body corporate or other body of persons (which here includes a local authority and any body whether formed or established in the United Kingdom or elsewhere);

(*b*) any capital raised by such a body if the capital is borrowed or has the character of borrowed money, and whether it is in the form of stock or any other form;

(*c*) stock or marketable securities issued by the government of any country or territory outside the United Kingdom.

[(*d*) any capital raised under arrangements which fall within section 48A of the Finance Act 2005 [or section 507 of the Corporation Tax Act 2009][4] (alternative finance investment bonds).][3]

(8) . . . [2]

(9) In this section "designated international organisation" means an international organisation designated for the purposes of section [324 of the Taxes Act 1988][1] by an order made under subsection (1) of that section.

(10)–(14) . . . [2]

Cross references—See FA 1986 s 79 (references to this section in sub-ss (7), (9), (10) and (14) above include a reference to s 79).

Amendments—[1] Words in sub-s (9) substituted by TA 1988 Sch 29 para 32 Table.

[2] Sub-ss (1)–(6), (8) and (10)–(14) repealed by FA 1999 Sch 20 Pt V(2) with effect in relation to instruments executed, or bearer instruments issued, from 1 October 1999, subject to the provisions in FA 1999 Sch 20 Pt V(2) Note 2. Previously the text read:

"(1) This section (which reproduces the effect of a resolution having statutory effect under section 50 of the Finance Act 1973 for the period beginning on 25th March 1986 and ending on 6th July 1986) shall be deemed to have had effect during, and only during, that period.

(2) The following provisions shall not apply.

(*a*) in section 62 of the Finance Act 1963 subsections (2) and (6) (commonwealth stock);

(*b*) in section 11 of the Finance Act (Northern Ireland) 1963, subsections (2) and (5) (commonwealth stock);

(*c*) section 29 of the Finance Act 1967 (local authority capital);

(*d*) section 6 of the Finance Act (Northern Ireland) 1967 (local authority capital);

(*e*) section 126 of the Finance Act 1976 (loan capital).

(3) Stamp duty under the heading "Bearer Instrument" in Schedule 1 to the Stamp Act 1891 shall not be chargeable on the issue of an instrument which relates to loan capital or on the transfer of the loan capital constituted by, or transferable by means of, such an instrument.

(4) Stamp duty shall not be chargeable on an instrument which transfers loan capital issued or raised by—

(*a*) the financial support fund of the Organisation for Economic Co-operation and Development,

(*b*) the Inter-American Development Bank, or

(*c*) an organisation which was a designated international organisation at the time of the transfer (whether or not it was such an organisation at the time the loan capital was issued or raised).

(5) Stamp duty shall not be chargeable on an instrument which transfers short-term loan capital.

(6) Where stamp duty under the heading "Conveyance or Transfer on Sale" in Schedule 1 to the Stamp Act 1891 is chargeable on an instrument which transfers loan capital, the rate at which the duty is charged under that heading shall be the rate of 50p for every £100 or part of £100 of the amount or value of the consideration for the sale to which the instrument gives effect.

(8) In this section "short-term loan capital" means loan capital the date (or latest date) for the repayment of which is not more than 5 years after the date on which it is issued or raised.

(10) In construing sections 80(3) and 81 (3) of the Finance Act 1985 (definitions by reference to section 126 of the Finance Act 1976) the effect of this section shall be ignored.

(11) This section applies to any instrument which falls within section 60(1) of the Finance Act 1963 and is issued after 24th March 1986 and before 7th July 1986.

(12) This section applies to any instrument which falls within section 60(2) of that Act if the loan capital constituted by or transferable by means of it is transferred after 24th March 1986 and before 7th July 1986.

(13) This section applies, in the case of instruments not falling within section 60(1) or (2) of that Act, to any instrument which is executed after 24th March 1986 and before 7th July 1986, unless it is executed in pursuance of a contract made on or before 18th March 1986.

(14) In this section references to section 60(1) of the Finance Act 1963 include references to section 9(1)(*a*) of the Finance Act (Northern Ireland) 1963 and references to section 60(2) of the former Act include references to section 9(1)(*b*) of the latter.".

3 Sub-s (7)(*d*) inserted by FA 2008 s 154(1), (2) with effect in relation to instruments executed on or after 21 July 2008 (and for this purpose it does not matter when the arrangements falling within FA 2005 s 48A are made).

4 In sub-s (7)(*d*), words inserted by CTA 2009 s 1322, Sch 1 paras 322, 323. CTA 2009 applies for corporation tax purposes for accounting periods ending on or after 1 April 2009 and for income tax and capital gains tax purposes for the tax year 2009–10 and subsequent tax years.

79 Loan capital: new provisions

(1) . . . [3]

(2) Stamp duty under [Schedule 15 to the Finance Act 1999 (bearer instruments)][2] shall not be chargeable on the issue of an instrument which relates to loan capital or on the transfer of the loan capital constituted by, or transferable by means of, such an instrument.

(3) Stamp duty shall not be chargeable on an instrument which transfers loan capital issued or raised by—

(*a*) the financial support fund of the Organisation for Economic Co-operation and Development,

(*b*) the Inter-American Development Bank, or

(*c*) an organisation which was a designated international organisation at the time of the transfer (whether or not it was such an organisation at the time the loan capital was issued or raised).

(4) Subject to subsections (5) and (6) below, stamp duty shall not be chargeable on an instrument which transfers any other loan capital.

(5) Subsection (4) above does not apply to an instrument transferring loan capital which, at the time the instrument is executed, carries a right (exercisable then or later) of conversion into shares or other securities, or to the acquisition of shares or other securities, including loan capital of the same description.

(6) Subject to [subsections (7) to (7B)][7] below, subsection (4) above does not apply to an instrument transferring loan capital which, at the time the instrument is executed or any earlier time, carries or has carried—

(*a*) a right to interest the amount of which exceeds a reasonable commercial return on the nominal amount of the capital,

(*b*) a right to interest the amount of which falls or has fallen to be determined to any extent by reference to the results of, or of any part of, a business or to the value of any property, or

(*c*) a right on repayment to an amount which exceeds the nominal amount of the capital and is not reasonably comparable with what is generally repayable (in respect of a similar nominal amount of capital) under the terms of issue of loan capital listed in the Official List of The Stock Exchange.

(7) Subsection (4) above shall not be prevented from applying to an instrument by virtue of subsection (6) (*a*) or (*c*) above by reason only that the loan capital concerned carries a right to interest, or (as the case may be) to an amount payable on repayment, determined to any extent by reference to an index showing changes in the general level of prices payable in the United Kingdom over a period substantially corresponding to the period between the issue or raising of the loan capital and its repayment.

[(7A) Subsection (4) above shall not be prevented from applying to an instrument by virtue of subsection (6)(*b*) above by reason only that the loan capital concerned carries a right to interest which—

(*a*) reduces in the event of the results of a business or part of a business improving, or the value of any property increasing, or

(*b*) increases in the event of the results of a business or part of a business deteriorating, or the value of any property diminishing.][5]

[(7B) Subsection (4) shall not be prevented from applying to a capital market instrument by virtue of subsection (6)(*b*) by reason only that the capital market investment concerned carries or has carried a right to interest which ceases or reduces if, or to the extent that, the issuer, after meeting or providing for other obligations specified in the capital market arrangement concerned, has insufficient funds available from that capital market arrangement to pay all or part of the interest otherwise due.][7]

[(8) Where stamp duty is chargeable under Part I of Schedule 13 of the Finance Act 1999 ([transfer][6] on sale) on an instrument which transfers loan capital, the rate at which duty is charged under that Part shall be 0.5% of the amount or value of the consideration for the sale to which the instrument gives effect.][1]

[(8A) In the application of this section to loan capital that falls within paragraph (*d*) of section 78(7) (alternative finance investment bonds)—

(*a*) subsection (6) has effect as if—

(i) paragraph (*a*) were omitted, and

(ii) for paragraph (*c*) there were substituted—

"(*c*) a right at the end of the bond term (within the meaning of section 48A(1) of the Finance Act 2005 [or section 507(1) of the Corporation Tax Act 2009][9]) to a payment of an amount that exceeds the aggregate of—

(i) the amount paid for the issue of the bond, and

(ii) the notional payment amount;

and for this purpose the "notional payment amount" means the amount of the payments that would represent a reasonable commercial return (within the meaning of section 48A(1) of the Finance Act 2005 [or section 507(1) of the Corporation Tax Act 2009][9]) on the bond over the bond term, less the amount of the payments actually made.",

(*b*) subsections (6)(*b*), (7), (7A), (7B) and (13) have effect as if references to interest were references to additional payments ("additional payments" having the same meaning as in section 48A of the Finance Act 2005 [or section 507 of the Corporation Tax Act 2009][9]), and

(*c*) subsections (7B) and (13) also have effect as if—

(i) references to a capital market investment were references to the loan capital falling within paragraph (*d*) of section 78(7), and

(ii) references to a capital market arrangement were to the arrangements under which that loan capital is raised.][8]

(9)–(11) . . . [3]

(12) Subsections (7), (9), . . . [4] of section 78 above shall apply as if references to that section included references to this.

[(13) In this section—

"capital market instrument" means an instrument transferring a capital market investment issued as part of a capital market arrangement, and

"capital market investment" and "capital market arrangement" have the same meaning as in section 72B of the Insolvency Act 1986 (see paragraphs 1 to 3 of Schedule 2A to that Act).][7]

Statement of Practice SP 3/84—FA 1976 s 126(2) (precursor of sub-s (5) above) did not exclude from exemption loan capital carrying an unexpired right to conversion into or acquisition of loan capital which itself is within the exemption.

Cross references—See FA 1987 s 50(3)(*b*), (*c*) (further exemption under other headings in Stamp Act 1891, Sch 1 for instruments falling under this section).

Notes—Sub-ss (2)–(8) and words in sub-s (12) were to be repealed by FA 1990 Sch 19 Pt VI with effect from an appointed day in accordance with FA 1990 ss 107–111. The Treasury order specifying the appointed day for the purposes of FA 1990 ss 107–110 was to coincide with the start of paperless trading under the Stock Exchange's planned TAURUS system (IR press release, 20-3-90). However, on 11-3-93 the London Stock Exchange News Release 6/93 announced that TAURUS had been abandoned.

Amendments—[1] Sub-s (8) substituted by FA 1999 s 112(4), Sch 14 para 17 with effect in relation to instruments executed after 30 September 1999. This does not apply to transfers or other instruments relating to units under a unit trust scheme by virtue of FA 1999 s 122. For prospective repeal of FA 1999 Sch 14 para 17 see FA 1999 s 123(3). Previously the text read:

"(8) Where stamp duty under the heading "Conveyance or Transfer on Sale" in Schedule 1 to the Stamp Act 1891 is chargeable on an instrument which transfers loan capital, the rate at which the duty is charged under that heading shall be the rate of 50p for every £100 or part of £100 of the amount or value of the consideration for the sale to which the instrument gives effect."

[2] Words in sub-s (2) substituted by FA 1999 s 113(3), Sch 16 para 5 with effect in relation to bearer instruments issued after 30 September 1999. For prospective repeal of FA 1999 s 113, Sch 16 para 5 see FA 1999 s 123(3). Previously the text read 'the heading "Bearer Instrument" in Schedule 1 to the Stamp Act 1891'.

[3] Sub-ss (1), (9)–(11) repealed by FA 1999 Sch 20 Pt V(2) with effect in relation to instruments executed, or bearer instruments issued, from 1 October 1999, subject to the provisions in FA 1999 Sch 20 Pt V(2) Note 2. Previously the text read:

"(1) The following provisions shall cease to have effect—

(*a*) in section 62 of the Finance Act 1963 subsections (2) and (6) (commonwealth stock);

(*b*) in section 11 of the Finance Act (Northern Ireland) 1963, subsections (2) and (5) (commonwealth stock);

(*c*) section 29 of the Finance Act 1967 (local authority capital);

(*d*) section 6 of the Finance Act (Northern Ireland) 1967 (local authority capital);

(*e*) section 126 of the Finance Act 1976 (loan capital).

(9) This section applies to any instrument which falls within section 60(1) of the Finance Act 1963 and is issued after 31st July 1986.

(10) This section applies to any instrument which falls within section 60(2) of that Act if the loan capital constituted by or transferable by means of it is transferred after 31st July 1986.

(11) This section applies, in the case of instruments not falling within section 60(1) or (2) of that Act, to any instrument which is executed after 31st July 1986."

[4] Words in sub-s (12) repealed by FA 1999 Sch 20 Pt V(2) with effect in relation to instruments executed, or bearer instruments issued, from 1 October 1999, subject to the provisions in FA 1999 Sch 20 Pt V(2) Note 2. Previously the text read '(10) and (14)'.

[5] Sub-s (7A) inserted by FA 2000 s 133(1). For the purposes of stamp duty, this amendment has effect for instruments executed after 20 March 2000. For the purposes of stamp duty reserve tax, this amendment has effect in accordance with the commencement provisions set out in FA 2000 s 133(3) (broadly with effect after 20 March 2000).

[6] The word "transfer" substituted for the words "conveyance or transfer" in enactments relating to stamp duty by FA 2003 Sch 20 para 3.

[7] Words in sub-s (6) substituted for words "subsection (7)", and sub-ss (7B), (13) inserted, by FA 2008 s 101 with effect in relation to any instrument executed on or after 21 July 2008.

[8] Sub-s (8A) inserted by FA 2008 s 154(1), (4) with effect in relation to any instrument executed on or after 21 July 2008 (and for this purpose it does not matter when the arrangements falling within FA 2005 s 48A are made).

[9] In sub-s (8A)(*a*)(ii), in substituted sub-s (6)(*c*), words inserted in both places, and in sub-s (8A)(*b*), words inserted, by CTA 2009 s 1322, Sch 1 paras 322, 324. CTA 2009 applies for corporation tax purposes for accounting periods ending on or after 1 April 2009 and for income tax and capital gains tax purposes for the tax year 2009–10 and subsequent tax years.

80 Bearer letters of allotment etc

Amendments—This section repealed by FA 1999 Sch 20 Pt V(2) with effect in relation to instruments executed, or bearer instruments issued, from 1 October 1999, subject to the provisions in FA 1999 Sch 20 Pt V(2) Note 2. Previously the text read:

"(1) In Schedule 1 to the Stamp Act 1891, in the heading "Bearer Instrument", paragraph 2 of the exemptions (bearer letter of allotment etc required to be surrendered not later than six months after issue) shall be omitted.

(2) This section applies to any instrument which falls within section 60(1) of the Finance Act 1963 and is issued after 24th March 1986, unless it is issued by a company in pursuance of a general offer for its shares and the offer became unconditional as to acceptances on or before 18th March 1986.

(3) This section applies to any instrument which falls within section 60(2) of that Act if the stock constituted by or transferable by means of it is transferred after 24th March 1986.

(4) In this section the reference to section 60(1) of the Finance Act 1963 includes a reference to section 9(1)(*a*) of the Finance Act (Northern Ireland) 1963 and the reference to section 60(2) of the former Act includes a reference to section 9(1) (*b*) of the latter.

(5) This section shall be deemed to have come into force on 25th March 1986.'"

Changes in financial institutions

[80A Sales to intermediaries

[(1) Stamp duty shall not be chargeable on an instrument transferring stock of a particular kind on sale to a person or the person's nominee if—

(*a*) the person is a member of a regulated market on which stock of that kind is regularly traded; and

(*b*) the person is an intermediary and is recognised as such by the market in accordance with arrangements approved by the Commissioners.][2]

[(1A) Stamp duty shall not be chargeable on an instrument transferring stock of a particular kind on sale to a person or the person's nominee if—

(*a*) the person is a member of a multilateral trading facility, or a recognised foreign exchange, on which stock of that kind is regularly traded;

(*b*) the person is an intermediary and is recognised as such by the facility or exchange in accordance with arrangements approved by the Commissioners; and

(*c*) the sale is effected on the facility or exchange.][2]

[(1B) Stamp duty shall not be chargeable on an instrument transferring stock of a particular kind on sale to a person or the person's nominee if—

(*a*) the person is an intermediary who is approved for the purposes of this section by the Commissioners; and
(*b*) stock of that kind is regularly traded on a regulated market.][2]

[(1C) Stamp duty shall not be chargeable on an instrument transferring stock of a particular kind on sale to a person or the person's nominee if—
(*a*) the person is an intermediary who is approved for the purposes of this section by the Commissioners;
(*b*) stock of that kind is regularly traded on a multilateral trading facility or a recognised foreign exchange; and
(*c*) the sale is effected on the facility or exchange.][2]

[(2) Stamp duty shall not be chargeable on an instrument transferring stock of a particular kind on sale to a person or the person's nominee if—
(*a*) the person is a member of a regulated market, a multilateral trading facility or a recognised foreign options exchange;
(*b*) options to buy or sell stock of that kind are regularly traded on, and are listed by or quoted on, that market, facility or exchange;
(*c*) the person is an options intermediary and is recognised as such by that market, facility or exchange in accordance with arrangements approved by the Commissioners; and
(*d*) stock of that kind is regularly traded on a regulated market.][2]

[(2A) Stamp duty shall not be chargeable on an instrument transferring stock of a particular kind on sale to a person or the person's nominee if—
(*a*) the person is a member of a regulated market, a multilateral trading facility or a recognised foreign options exchange;
(*b*) options to buy or sell stock of that kind are regularly traded on, and are listed by or quoted on, that market, facility or exchange;
(*c*) the person is an options intermediary and is recognised as such by that market, facility or exchange in accordance with arrangements approved by the Commissioners; and
(*d*) the sale is effected on a relevant qualifying exchange on which stock of that kind is regularly traded or is effected on a relevant qualifying exchange pursuant to the exercise of a relevant option and options to buy or sell stock of that kind are regularly traded on, and are listed by or quoted on, that exchange;

and in paragraph (d) "relevant qualifying exchange" means a multilateral trading facility, a recognised foreign options exchange or a recognised foreign exchange.][2]

[(2B) Stamp duty shall not be chargeable on an instrument transferring stock of a particular kind on sale to a person or the person's nominee if—
(*a*) the person is an options intermediary who is approved for the purposes of this section by the Commissioners;
(*b*) options to buy or sell stock of that kind are regularly traded on, and are listed by or quoted on, a regulated market, a multilateral trading facility or a recognised foreign options exchange; and
(*c*) stock of that kind is regularly traded on a regulated market.][2]

[(2C) Stamp duty shall not be chargeable on an instrument transferring stock of a particular kind on sale to a person or the person's nominee if—
(*a*) the person is an options intermediary who is approved for the purposes of this section by the Commissioners;
(*b*) options to buy or sell stock of that kind are regularly traded on, and are listed by or quoted on, a regulated market, a multilateral trading facility or a recognised foreign options exchange; and
(*c*) the sale is effected on a relevant qualifying exchange on which stock of that kind is regularly traded or is effected on a relevant qualifying exchange pursuant to the exercise of a relevant option and options to buy or sell stock of that kind are regularly traded on, and are listed by or quoted on, that exchange;

and in paragraph (c) "relevant qualifying exchange" means a multilateral trading facility, a recognised foreign options exchange or a recognised foreign exchange.][2]

(4) For the purposes of this section—
(*a*) an intermediary is a person who carries on a bona fide business of dealing in stock and does not carry on an excluded business; and
(*b*) an options intermediary is a person who carries on a bona fide business of dealing in quoted or listed options to buy or sell stock and does not carry on an excluded business.

(5) The excluded businesses are the following—
(*a*) any business which consists wholly or mainly in the making or managing of investments;
(*b*) any business which consists wholly or mainly in, or is carried on wholly or mainly for the purpose of, providing services to persons who are connected with the person carrying on the business;
(*c*) any business which consists in insurance business;

(*d*) any business which consists in managing or acting as trustee in relation to a pension scheme or which is carried on by the manager or trustee of such a scheme in connection with or for the purposes of the scheme;

(*e*) any business which consists in operating or acting as trustee in relation to a collective investment scheme or is carried on by the operator or trustee of such a scheme in connection with or for the purposes of the scheme.

(6) A sale is effected on [a facility or][2] an exchange for the purposes of [this section][2] if (and only if)—

(*a*) it is subject to the rules of [the facility or exchange][2]; and

(*b*) it is reported to [the facility or exchange][2] in accordance with the rules of [the facility or exchange][2].

[(6A) The Commissioners may approve a person for the purposes of this section only if the person is authorised under the law of an EEA State to provide any of the investment services or activities listed in Section A 2 or 3 of Annex I to the Directive (execution of orders on behalf of clients and dealing on own account), whether or not the person is authorised under the Directive.][2]

(7) An instrument on which stamp duty is not chargeable by virtue only of this section shall not be deemed to be duly stamped unless it has been stamped with a stamp denoting that it is not chargeable with any duty; and notwithstanding anything in section 122(1) of the Stamp Act 1891, the stamp may be a stamp of such kind as the Commissioners may prescribe.][1]

Cross references—See FA 2002 s 117 (the Treasury may by regulations extend the application of this section to any market that is not a recognised exchange but is prescribed by order under the Financial Services and Markets Act 2000 s 118(3)).

Stamp Duty and Stamp Duty Reserve Tax (Extension of Exceptions relating to Recognised Exchanges) Regulations, SI 2002/1975 (with effect from 26 July 2002, the application of the provision specified in FA 2002 s 117(2) (which includes this section) is extended to the market known as OFEX).

F(No 2)A 2005 s 50 (power of the Treasury to extend the application of this section to any market which is not a recognised exchange, but is a multilateral trading facility or (assuming compliance with the provisions of Title II of the European Parliament and Council Directive 2004/39/EC) would be such a facility).

Modifications—Stamp Duty and Stamp Duty Reserve Tax (Extension of Exceptions relating to Recognised Exchanges) Regulations, SI 2005/1990 regs 3, 4 (modification of this section in its application to prescibed multilateral trading facilities. For definition of "prescribed multilateral trading facility" see SI 2005/1990 reg 2).

Amendments—[1] This section inserted by FA 1997, s 97(1) with effect from 20 October 1997 as appointed by SI 1997/2428, and repealed by FA 1997 Sch 18 Pt VII with effect from the day appointed under FA 1990 s 111.

[2] Sub-ss (1)–(2C) substituted for sub-ss (1)–(3); in sub-s (6), words inserted, and words substituted for the words "subsection (1) or (2) above", and "the exchange" (wherever occurring); and sub-s (6A) inserted, by FA 2007 s 73, Sch 21 para 1 with effect in relation to any instrument executed on or after 1 November 2007: FA 2007 Sch 21 para 1(5).

Sub-ss (1)–(3) previously read as follows—

"(1) Stamp duty shall not be chargeable on an instrument transferring stock of a particular kind on sale to a person or his nominee if—

(*a*) the person is a member of an EEA exchange, or a recognised foreign exchange, on which stock of that kind is regularly traded;

(*b*) the person is an intermediary and is recognised as an intermediary by the exchange in accordance with arrangements approved by the Commissioners; and

(*c*) the sale is effected on the exchange.

(2) Stamp duty shall not be chargeable on an instrument transferring stock of a particular kind on sale to a person or his nominee if—

(*a*) the person is a member of an EEA exchange or a recognised foreign options exchange;

(*b*) options to buy or sell stock of that kind are regularly traded on that exchange and are listed by or quoted on that exchange;

(*c*) the person is an options intermediary and is recognised as an options intermediary by that exchange in accordance with arrangements approved by the Commissioners; and

(*d*) the sale is effected on an EEA exchange, or a recognised foreign exchange, on which stock of that kind is regularly traded or subsection (3) below applies.

(3) This subsection applies if—

(*a*) the sale is effected on an EEA exchange, or a recognised foreign options exchange, pursuant to the exercise of a relevant option; and

(*b*) options to buy or sell stock of the kind concerned are regularly traded on that exchange and are listed by or quoted on that exchange.".

[80B Intermediaries: supplementary

(1) For the purposes of section 80A above the question whether a person is connected with another shall be determined in accordance with the provisions of [section 1122 of the Corporation Tax Act 2010][5].

(2) In section 80A above and this section—

"collective investment scheme" has the meaning given in section [235 of the Financial Services and Markets Act 2000][3];

["the Directive" means Directive 2004/39/EC of the European Parliament and of the Council of 21 April 2004 on markets in financial instruments, as amended from time to time;][4]

. . . [4]

"EEA State"[, in relation to any time, means a State which at that time is a member State or any other State which at that time][4] is a contracting party to the agreement on the European Economic Area signed at Oporto on the 2nd May 1992 as adjusted by the Protocol signed at Brussels on the 17th March 1993 [(as modified or supplemented from time to time)][4];

["insurance business" means business which consists of the effecting or carrying out of contracts of insurance and, for the purposes of this definition, "contract of insurance" has the meaning given in Article 3(1) of the Financial Services and Markets Act 2000 (Regulated Activities) Order 2001;

"the operator", in relation to a collective investment scheme, shall be construed in accordance with section 237(2) of the Financial Services and Markets Act 2000;][3]

"quoted or listed options" means options which are quoted on or listed by an EEA exchange or a recognised foreign options exchange;

"stock" includes any marketable security;

["trustee", in relation to a collective investment scheme, means a trustee or a depositary within the meaning given in section 237(2) of the Financial Services and Markets Act 2000.][3]

[(2A) Each of the following expressions—

"multilateral trading facility", and

"regulated market",

has the same meaning in section 80A above as it has for the purposes of the Directive.][4]

(3) In section 80A above "recognised foreign exchange" means a market which—

(*a*) is not in an EEA State; and

(*b*) is specified in regulations made by the Treasury under this subsection.

(4) In section 80A above and this section "recognised foreign options exchange" means a market which—

(*a*) is not in an EEA State; and

(*b*) is specified in regulations made by the Treasury under this subsection.

(5) In section 80A above "the exercise of a relevant option" means—

(*a*) the exercise by the options intermediary concerned of an option to buy stock; or

(*b*) the exercise of an option binding the options intermediary concerned to buy stock.

[(5A) The Treasury may by regulations amend section 80A above and this section (as they have effect for the time being) in order to extend the exemption from duty under that section][4]

(6) The Treasury may by regulations provide that section 80A above shall not have effect in relation to instruments executed in pursuance of kinds of agreement specified in the regulations.

(7) The Treasury may by regulations provide that if—

(*a*) an instrument falls within [any of subsections (1) to (2C)][4] of section 80A above, and

(*b*) stamp duty would be chargeable on the instrument apart from that section,

stamp duty shall be chargeable on the instrument at a rate, specified in the regulations, which shall not exceed [0.1%][2] of the consideration for the sale.

(8) The Treasury may by regulations change the meaning of "intermediary" or "options intermediary" for the purposes of section 80A above by amending subsection (4) or (5) of that section (as it has effect for the time being).

(9) The power to make regulations under subsections (3) to (8) above shall be exercisable by statutory instrument subject to annulment in pursuance of a resolution of the House of Commons.][1]

Amendments—[1] This section inserted by FA 1997, s 97(1) with effect from 20 October 1997 as appointed by SI 1997/2428, and repealed by FA 1997 Sch 18 Pt VII with effect from the day appointed under FA 1990 s 111.

[2] Words in sub-s (7) substituted by FA 1999 s 112(4), Sch 14 para 18 with effect in relation to instruments executed after 30 September 1999. This does not apply to transfers or other instruments relating to units under a unit trust scheme by virtue of FA 1999 s 122. For prospective repeal of FA 1999 Sch 14 para 18 see FA 1999 s 123(3). Previously the text read '10p for every £100 or part of £100'.

[3] Words in definition of "collective investment scheme" substituted, and definition of "insurance business", "trustee" and "the operator" substituted by the Financial Services and Markets Act 2000 (Consequential Amendments) (Taxes) Order, SI 2001/3629 arts 6, 7 with effect for any instrument executed after 30 November 2001.

[4] In sub-s (2), definition inserted, definition of "EEA exchange" repealed, and words "means a State which" in definition of "EEA State" substituted, and words inserted; sub-ss (2A), (5A) inserted; and in sub-s (7), words substituted for the words "subsection (1) or (2)" by FA 2007 ss 73, 114, Sch 21 para 2, Sch 27 Pt 4(2) with effect in relation to any instrument executed on or after 1 November 2007: FA 2007 Sch 21 para 1(5).

Definition of "EEA exchange" previously read as follows—

" 'EEA exchange' means a market which appears on the list drawn up by an EEA State pursuant to Article 16 of European Communities Council Directive No 93/22/EEC on investment services in the securities field;".

[5] In sub-s (1) words substituted for words "section 839 of the Income and Corporation Taxes Act 1988" by CTA 2010 s 1177, Sch 1 para 197. CTA 2010 has effect for corporation tax purposes for accounting periods ending on or after 1 April 2010, and for income and capital gains tax purposes for the tax year 2010–11 and subsequent tax years.

[80C Repurchases and stock lending

(1) This section applies where a person (A) has entered into an arrangement with another person (B) under which—

(*a*) B is to transfer stock of a particular kind to A or his nominee, and (*b*) stock of the same kind and amount is to be transferred by A or his nominee to B or his nominee,

and the conditions set out in subsection [(2A) or][3] (3) below are fulfilled.

(2) Stamp duty shall not be chargeable on an instrument transferring stock to B or his nominee or A or his nominee in accordance with the arrangement.

[(2A) The conditions in this subsection are—

(*a*) that A or B is authorised under the law of an EEA State to provide any of the investment services or activities listed in Section A 2 or 3 of Annex I to the Directive (execution of orders on behalf of clients and dealing on own account) in relation to stock of the kind concerned, whether or not A or B is authorised under the Directive; and

(*b*) that stock of the kind concerned is regularly traded on a regulated market.][3]

(3) The conditions [in this subsection][3] are—

(*a*) that the arrangement is effected on [a regulated market, a multilateral trading facility][3] or a recognised foreign exchange; and

(*b*) that stock of the kind concerned is regularly traded on that [market, facility or][3] exchange.

(4) An arrangement does not fall within subsection (1) above if—

(*a*) the arrangement is not such as would be entered into by persons dealing with each other at arm's length; or

(*b*) under the arrangement any of the benefits or risks arising from fluctuations, before the transfer to B or his nominee takes place, in the market value of the stock accrues to, or falls on, A.

(5) An instrument on which stamp duty is not chargeable by virtue only of subsection (2) above shall not be deemed to be duly stamped unless it has been stamped with a stamp denoting that it is not chargeable with any duty; and notwithstanding anything in section 122(1) of the Stamp Act 1891, the stamp may be a stamp of such kind as the Commissioners may prescribe.

(6) An arrangement is effected on [a market, a facility or][3] an exchange for the purposes of subsection (3) above if (and only if)

(*a*) it is subject to the rules of [the market, facility or exchange][3]; and

(*b*) it is reported to [the market, facility or exchange][3] in accordance with the rules of [the market, facility or exchange][3].

(7) In this section—

["the Directive" has the meaning given in section 80B(2) above;

"EEA State" has the meaning given in section 80B(2) above;][3]

. . . [3]

"recognised foreign exchange" has the meaning given in section 80B(3) above.

[(7A) Each of the following expressions—

"multilateral trading facility", and

"regulated market",

has the same meaning in this section as it has for the purposes of the Directive.][3]

(8) The Treasury may by regulations provide that if stamp duty would be chargeable on an instrument but for subsection (2) above, stamp duty shall be chargeable on the instrument at a rate, specified in the regulations, which shall not exceed [0.1%][2] of the consideration for the transfer.

(9) The Treasury may by regulations amend this section (as it has effect for the time being) in order—

(*a*) to change the conditions for exemption from duty under this section; or

(*b*) to provide that this section does not apply in relation to kinds of arrangement specified in the regulations.

(10) The power to make regulations under subsection (8) or (9) above shall be exercisable by statutory instrument subject to annulment in pursuance of a resolution of the House of Commons.][1]

Cross references—See FA 2002 s 117 (the Treasury may by regulations extend the application of this section to any market that is not a recognised exchange but is prescribed by order under the Financial Services and Markets Act 2000 s 118(3)).

European Single Currency (Taxes) Regulations, SI 1998/3177 regs 25, 27 and 29 for details on replacement of stock in a euroconversion.

Stamp Duty and Stamp Duty Reserve Tax (Extension of Exceptions relating to Recognised Exchanges) Regulations, SI 2002/1975 (with effect from 26 July 2002, the application of the provision specified in FA 2002 s 117(2) (which includes this section) is extended to the market known as OFEX).

F(No 2)A 2005 s 50 (power of the Treasury to extend the application of this section to any market which is not a recognised exchange, but is a multilateral trading facility or (assuming compliance with the provisions of Title II of the European Parliament and Council Directive 2004/39/EC) would be such a facility).

Modifications—Stamp Duty and Stamp Duty Reserve Tax (Extension of Exceptions relating to Recognised Exchanges) Regulations, SI 2005/1990 regs 3, 5 (modification of this section in its application to prescibed multilateral trading facilities. For definition of "prescribed multilateral trading facility" see SI 2005/1990 reg 2).

Amendments—[1] This section inserted by FA 1997, s 98(1) in relation to instruments executed on or after 20 October 1997 as appointed by SI 1997/2428, and repealed by FA 1997 Sch 18 Pt VII with effect from the day appointed under FA 1990 s 111.

2 Words in sub-s (8) substituted by FA 1999 s 112(4), Sch 14 para 19 with effect in relation to instruments executed after 30 September 1999. This does not apply to transfers or other instruments relating to units under a unit trust scheme by virtue of FA 1999 s 122. For prospective repeal of FA 1999 Sch 14 para 19 see FA 1999 s 123(3). Previously the text read '10p for every £100 or part of £100'.

3 Words in sub-ss (1), (3), (6), (7) inserted; sub-ss (2A), (7A) inserted; in sub-s (3), words substituted for the words "an EEA exchange"; in sub-s (6), words substituted for the words "the exchange" wherever occurring; in sub-s (7), definition of "EEA exchange" and following word "and" repealed, by FA 2007 ss 73, 114, Sch 21 para 5, Sch 27 Pt 4(2) with effect in relation to any instrument executed on or after 1 November 2007.
Definition of "EEA exchange" previously read as follows—

" 'EEA exchange' has the meaning given in section 80B(2) above;".

[80D Repurchases and stock lending: replacement stock on insolvency

(1) This section applies where—

(*a*) A and B have entered into an arrangement falling within section 80C(1),

(*b*) the conditions in subsection (2A) or (3) of that section are met,

(*c*) stock is transferred to A or A's nominee, and

(*d*) the conditions in subsection (2) below are met.

(2) The conditions in this subsection are that—

(*a*) A and B are not connected persons within the meaning of [section 1122 of the Corporation Tax Act 2010][2],

(*b*) after B has transferred stock under the arrangement, A or B becomes insolvent,

(*c*) it becomes apparent (whether before or after the insolvency occurs) that, as a result of the insolvency, stock will not be transferred to B or B's nominee in accordance with the arrangement,

(*d*) the party who does not become insolvent ("the solvent party") or the solvent party's nominee acquires replacement stock, and

(*e*) the replacement stock is acquired before the end of the period of 30 days beginning with the day on which the insolvency occurs ("the insolvency date").

(3) Where collateral is provided under the arrangement (or under arrangements of which that arrangement forms part), stamp duty is not chargeable on any instrument transferring to the solvent party or the solvent party's nominee—

(*a*) replacement stock acquired using the collateral (whether directly or indirectly), or

(*b*) where the solvent party uses the whole of the value of the collateral to acquire replacement stock, any further replacement stock.

(4) Where no collateral is provided as mentioned in subsection (3), stamp duty is not chargeable on any instrument transferring replacement stock to the solvent party or the solvent party's nominee.

(5) Subsections (3) and (4) may apply as regards more than one instrument (and where those subsections apply as regards more than one instrument, the instruments may be executed by different persons).

(6) But those subsections apply only as regards replacement stock up to the amount of stock which will not be transferred as a result of the insolvency.

(7) An instrument on which stamp duty is not chargeable by virtue only of subsection (3) or (4) is not to be deemed to be duly stamped unless it has been stamped with a stamp denoting that it is not chargeable with any duty.

(8) Despite section 122(1) of the Stamp Act 1891, the stamp mentioned in subsection (7) may be a stamp of such kind as the Commissioners for Her Majesty's Revenue and Customs may prescribe.

(9) For the purposes of this section, a person becomes insolvent—

(*a*) if a company voluntary arrangement takes effect under Part 1 of the Insolvency Act 1986,

(*b*) if an administration application (within the meaning of Schedule B1 to that Act) is made or a receiver or manager, or an administrative receiver, is appointed,

(*c*) on the commencement of a creditor's voluntary winding up (within the meaning of Part 4 of that Act) or a winding up by the court under Chapter 6 of that Part,

(*d*) if an individual voluntary arrangement takes effect under Part 8 of that Act,

(*e*) on the presentation of a bankruptcy petition (within the meaning of Part 9 of that Act),

(*f*) if a compromise or arrangement takes effect under Part 26 of the Companies Act 2006,

(*g*) if a bank insolvency order takes effect under Part 2 of the Banking Act 2009,

(*h*) if a bank administration order takes effect under Part 3 of that Act, or

(*i*) on the occurrence of any corresponding event which has effect under or as a result of the law of Scotland or Northern Ireland or a country or territory outside the United Kingdom.

(10) In this section—

"collateral" means an amount of money or other property which is payable to, or made available for the benefit of, a party to an arrangement or that party's nominee for the purpose of securing the discharge of the requirement to transfer stock to that party or the nominee;

"replacement stock", in the event of a party to an arrangement becoming insolvent, is stock of the same kind as the stock which will not be transferred to the other party or that party's nominee as a result of the insolvency.][1]

Amendments—[1] Section 80D inserted by FA 2009 s 83, Sch 37 paras 1, 2 with effect where the insolvency in question occurs on or after 1 September 2008. FA 2009 s 83(3). FA 2009 s 83 and FA 2009 Sch 37 cease to have effect—

(a) in relation to the amendments made to Part 3 of FA 1986, when the repeal of sections 80 to 85 of that Act (by Part 6 of Schedule 19 to, and in accordance with sections 107 to 109 of, FA 1990) comes into force, and

(b) in relation to the amendments made to Part 4 of FA 1986, when the repeal of that Part (by Part 7 of Schedule 19 to, and in accordance with section 110 of, FA 1990) comes into force.

[2] In sub-s (2)(*a*) words substituted for words "section 839 of the Taxes Act 1988" by CTA 2010 s 1177, Sch 1 para 198. CTA 2010 has effect for corporation tax purposes for accounting periods ending on or after 1 April 2010, and for income and capital gains tax purposes for the tax year 2010–11 and subsequent tax years.

81 Sales to market makers

Amendments—This section repealed by FA 1997 s 97(2), Sch 18 Pt VII with effect from 20 October 1997 as appointed by SI 1997/2428. Previously this section was repealed by FA 1990 Sch 19 Pt VI with effect from an appointed day in accordance with FA 1990 ss 107–111. The Treasury order specifying the appointed day for the purposes of FA 1990 ss 107–110 was to coincide with the start of paperless trading under the Stock Exchange's planned TAURUS system (IR press release, 20-3-90). However, on 11-3-93 the London Stock Exchange News Release 6/93 announced that TAURUS had been abandoned.

82 Borrowing of stock by market makers

Amendments—This section repealed by FA 1997 s 98(2), Sch 18 Pt VII with effect from 20 October 1997 as appointed by SI 1997/2428. This section previously repealed by FA 1990 Sch 19 Pt VI with effect from an appointed day in accordance with FA 1990 ss 107–111. The Treasury order specifying the appointed day for the purposes of FA 1990 ss 107–110 was to coincide with the start of paperless trading under the Stock Exchange's planned TAURUS system (IR press release, 20-3-90). However, on 11-3-93 the London Stock Exchange News Release 6/93 announced that TAURUS had been abandoned.

83 Composition agreements

(*amended* FA 1970 s 33 *and is repealed by the* Financial Services and Markets Act 2000 (Consequential Amendments) (Taxes) Order, SI 2001/3629 art 109, Schedule *with effect from 1 December 2001*).

84 Miscellaneous exemptions

(1) (*amends* FA 1976 s 127(1)).

(2) Stamp duty shall not be chargeable on an instrument effecting a transfer of stock if—

(*a*) the transferee is a recognised investment exchange or a nominee of a recognised investment exchange, and

(*b*) an agreement which relates to the stamp duty which would (apart from this subsection) be chargeable on the instrument, and was made between the Commissioners and the investment exchange under section 33 of the Finance Act 1970 is in force at the time of the transfer.

(3) Stamp duty shall not be chargeable on an instrument effecting a transfer of stock if—

(*a*) the transferee is a recognised clearing house or a nominee of a recognised clearing house, and

(*b*) an agreement which relates to the stamp duty which would (apart from this subsection) be chargeable on the instrument, and was made between the Commissioners and the clearing house under section 33 of the Finance Act 1970 is in force at the time of the transfer.

(4) (*amends* FA 1976 s 127(1)).

(5) Subsection (2) above applies to any instrument giving effect to a transaction carried out on or after such day as the Commissioners may appoint by order made by statutory instrument.

(6) Subsection (3) above applies to any instrument giving effect to a transaction carried out on or after such day as the Commissioners may appoint by order made by statutory instrument.

Note—This section was to be repealed by FA 1990 Sch 19 Pt VI with effect from an appointed day in accordance with FA 1990 ss 107–111. The Treasury order specifying the appointed day for the purposes of FA 1990 ss 107–110 was to coincide with the start of paperless trading under the Stock Exchange's planned TAURUS system (IR press release, 20-3-90). However, on 11-3-93 the London Stock Exchange News Release 6/93 announced that TAURUS had been abandoned.

85 Supplementary

(1) (*amend* FA 1920 s 42(1)).

(2)–(4) (*spent*).

(5) In sections 81, 82 and 84 above and this section—

(*a*) "the day of The Stock Exchange reforms" means the day on which the rule of The Stock Exchange that prohibits a person from carrying on business as both a broker and a jobber is abolished,

(*b*) references to a recognised investment exchange are to a recognised investment exchange within the meaning [given by section 285(1)(*a*) of the Financial Services and Markets Act 2000][1], and

(*c*) references to a recognised clearing house are to a recognised clearing house within the meaning [given by section 285(1)(*b*) of the Financial Services and Markets Act 2000][1], and

(*d*) "stock" includes marketable security.

Notes—The day of The Stock Exchange reforms was 27 October 1986.

This section was to be repealed by FA 1990 Sch 19 Pt VI with effect from an appointed day in accordance with FA 1990 ss 107–111. The Treasury order specifying the appointed day for the purposes of FA 1990 ss 107–110 was to coincide with the start of paperless trading under the Stock Exchange's planned TAURUS system (IR press release, 20-3-90). However, on 11-3-93 the London Stock Exchange News Release 6/93 announced that TAURUS had been abandoned.

Amendments—[1] Words in sub-s (5)(*b*), (*c*) substituted by the Financial Services and Markets Act 2000 (Consequential Amendments) (Taxes) Order, SI 2001/3629 arts 6, 8 with effect for any instrument executed after 30 November 2001.

PART IV
STAMP DUTY RESERVE TAX

Construction—FA 1999 Pt VI, so far as it relates to stamp duty reserve tax, to be construed as one with Pt IV of this Act; see FA 1999 s 123(1)(*a*).

Cross references—See FA 1989 ss 175, 176 (stock exchange nominees exempt from stamp duty reserve tax in prescribed circumstances);
FA 1990 ss 110, 111(1) (abolition of stamp duty reserve tax with effect from an appointed day).

Note—This Part was to be repealed by FA 1990 Sch 19 Pt VI with effect from an appointed day in accordance with FA 1990 ss 107–111. The Treasury order specifying the appointed day for the purposes of FA 1990 ss 107–110 was to coincide with the start of paperless trading under the Stock Exchange's planned TAURUS system (IR press release, 20-3-90). However, on 11-3-93 the London Stock Exchange News Release 6/93 announced that TAURUS had been abandoned.

Introduction

86 The tax: introduction

(1) A tax, to be known as stamp duty reserve tax, shall be charged in accordance with this Part of this Act.

(2) The tax shall be under the care and management of the Board.

(3) Section 1 of the Provisional Collection of Taxes Act 1968 shall apply to the tax; and accordingly in subsection (1) of that section after the words "petroleum revenue tax" there shall be inserted the words "stamp duty reserve tax".

[(4) Stamp duty reserve tax shall be chargeable in accordance with the provisions of this Part of this Act—

(*a*) whether the agreement, transfer, issue or appropriation in question is made or effected in the United Kingdom or elsewhere, and

(*b*) whether or not any party is resident or situate in any part of the United Kingdom.][1]

Cross references—See FA 1990 ss 110, 111(1) (abolition of stamp duty reserve tax with effect from an appointed day).

Amendments—[1] Sub-s (4) added by FA 1996 s 187(1), with effect (i) in relation to an agreement, if the agreement is conditional and the condition is satisfied on or after 1 July 1996 or the agreement is not conditional and is made on or after that date, and (ii) in relation to a transfer, issue or appropriation made or effected on or after 1 July 1996.

The principal charge

87 The principal charge

(1) This section applies where a person (A) agrees with another person (B) to transfer chargeable securities (whether or not to B) for consideration in money or money's worth.

(2) There shall be a charge to stamp duty reserve tax under this section on . . . [1, 2] the relevant day, . . . [1].

(3) In subsection (2) above "the relevant day" means—

(*a*) in a case where the agreement is conditional, the day on which the condition is satisfied, and

(*b*) in any other case, the day on which the agreement is made.

(4) . . . [1]

(5) . . . [1]

(6) Tax under this section shall be charged at the rate of [0.5 per cent][2] of the amount or value of the consideration mentioned in subsection (1) above.

(7) For the purposes of subsection (6) above the value of any consideration not consisting of money shall be taken to be the price it might reasonably be expected to fetch on a sale in the open market at the time the agreement mentioned in subsection (1) above is made.

[(7A) Where—

(*a*) there would be no charge to tax under this section, or

(*b*) there would, under section 92 below, be a repayment or cancellation of tax,

in relation to some of the chargeable securities to which the agreement between A and B relates if separate agreements had been made between them for the transfer of those securities and for the transfer of the remainder, this section and sections 88(5) and 92 below shall have effect as if such separate agreements had been made.][3]

(7B) . . . [3]

(8) . . . [3]

(9) This section applies where the agreement to transfer is made on or after the day on which the rule of The Stock Exchange that prohibits a person from carrying on business as both a broker and a jobber is abolished.

(10) This section has effect subject to sections 88 to 90 below.

Simon's Tax Cases—s 87(1) *Save & Prosper Securities Ltd v IRC* [2000] STC (SCD) 408.

Cross references—See FA 1990 ss 110(1), (2), 111(1) (abolition of stamp duty reserve tax with effect from an appointed day);
FA 1997 s 100 (mergers of authorised unit trusts);
FA1997 s 101 (direction to hold trust property on other trusts);
Stamp Duty and Stamp Duty Reserve Tax (Definition of Unit Trust Scheme) Regulations, SI 1992/197 (units of a scheme made under the Administration of Justice Act 1982 s 42(1) are not chargeable securities).

Stamp Duty and Stamp Duty Reserve Tax (Open-ended Investment Companies) Regulations, SI 1997/1156 regs 8 and 10 (exemption from stamp duty on conversion of an authorised unit trust to an open-ended investment company and exemption from stamp duty reserve tax on the amalgamation of an authorised unit trust with an open-ended investment company).
FA 2009 Sch 56 (penalty for failure to make payments on time).

Amendments—[1] In sub-s (2), the words omitted and the whole of sub-ss (4), (5), (8) repealed by FA 1996 ss 188(1), (5), 192(1), (6), Sch 41 Pt VII, with effect in relation to an agreement to transfer securities if the agreement is conditional and the condition is satisfied on or after 1 July 1996 or the agreement is not conditional and is made on or after that date.

[2] Words in sub-s (6) substituted by FA 1996 s 194(1), (7)(*a*), with effect where the agreement to transfer is conditional and the condition is satisfied on or after 1 July 1996 or the agreement is not conditional and is made on or after that date.

[3] Sub-s (7A) substituted and sub-s (7B) repealed by FA 1997 s 106(2), (3), Sch 18 Part VII in relation to an agreement to transfer securities if the agreement is conditional and the condition is satisfied on or after 4 January 1997 or the agreement is not conditional and is made on or after that date.

88 [Special cases][13]

(1) An instrument on which stamp duty is not chargeable by virtue of—

[(*aa*) paragraph 24(*d*) of Schedule 13 to the Finance Act 1999 (renounceable letters of allotment etc.),][1]

(*a*) section 127(1) of the Finance Act 1976 (transfer to stock exchange nominee), or

(*b*) section 84(2) or (3) above [, or

(*c*) Part I of Schedule 19 to the Finance Act 1999 (transfers etc of units in unit trusts),][16]

shall be disregarded in construing [section 92(1A) and (1B) below][6].

[(1A) An instrument on which stamp duty is not chargeable by virtue of section 186 of the Finance Act 1996 (transfers of securities to members of electronic transfer systems etc) shall be disregarded in construing [section 92(1A) and (1B) below][6] unless—

(*a*) the transfer is made by a stock exchange nominee; and

(*b*) the maximum stamp duty chargeable on the instrument, apart from section 186 of the Finance Act 1996, would be [£5][15];

and in this subsection "stock exchange nominee" means a person designated for the purposes of section 127 of the Finance Act 1976 as a nominee of The Stock Exchange by an order made by the Secretary of State under subsection (5) of that section.][2]

[(1B) An instrument on which stamp duty is not chargeable by virtue of section 42 of the Finance Act 1930 or section 11 of the Finance Act (Northern Ireland) 1954 (transfer between associated bodies corporate) shall be disregarded in construing [section 92(1A) and (1B) below][6] in any case where—

(*a*) the property mentioned in section 42(2)(*a*) of the Finance Act 1930 or, as the case may be, section 11(2)(*a*) of the Finance Act (Northern Ireland) 1954 consists of [or includes][10] chargeable securities of any particular kind acquired in the period of two years ending with the day on which the instrument was executed; and

(*b*) the body corporate from which the [transfer][17] there mentioned is effected acquired [any of those chargeable securities][11]—

(i) in a transaction which was given effect by an instrument of transfer on which stamp duty was not chargeable by virtue of section [80A][7] above;

(ii) in pursuance of an agreement to transfer securities as regards which section 87 above did not apply by virtue of section [88A][8] above; . . . [11]

[(ii*a*) in pursuance of an agreement to transfer securities which was made for the purpose of performing the obligation to transfer chargeable securities described in [section 89AA(1)(*a*) below and as regards which section 87 above did not apply by virtue of section 89AA(2) below];[14] or][11]

(iii) in circumstances with regard to which the charge to stamp duty or stamp duty reserve tax was treated as not arising by virtue of regulations under section 116 or 117 of the Finance Act 1991.][3]

[(1C) Where—

(*a*) there is an arrangement falling within subsection (1) of section 80C above (stamp duty relief for transfers in accordance with certain arrangements for B to transfer stock to A or his nominee and for A or his nominee to transfer stock of the same kind and amount back to B or his nominee), and

(*b*) under the arrangement stock is transferred to A or his nominee by an instrument on which stamp duty is not chargeable by virtue only of section 80C(2) above, but

(*c*) it becomes apparent that stock of the same kind or amount will not be transferred to B or his nominee by A or his nominee in accordance with the arrangement,

[then, if section 80D does not apply,][18] the instrument shall be disregarded in construing section 92(1A) and (1B) below.][9]

[(1D) Where—

(*a*) an instrument transferring stock in accordance with an arrangement is stamped under section 80C(5) above, but (*b*) the instrument should not have been so stamped because the arrangement fell within section 80C(4)(*a*) or (*b*) above, and

(*c*) apart from section 80C above stamp duty would have been chargeable on the instrument,

the instrument shall be deemed to be duly stamped under section 80C(5) above, but shall be disregarded in construing section 92(1A) and (1B) below.][9]

(2)–(3) . . .[4]

[(4) If chargeable securities cannot (apart from this subsection) be identified for the purposes of subsection (1B) above, securities shall be taken as follows, that is to say, securities of the same kind acquired later in the period of two years there mentioned (and not taken for the purposes of that subsection in relation to an earlier instrument) shall be taken before securities acquired earlier in that period.][12]

[(5) If, in the case of an agreement (or of two or more agreements between the same parties) to transfer chargeable securities—

(*a*) the conditions in section 92(1A) and (1B) below are not satisfied by virtue only of the application of subsection (1B) above in relation to the instrument (or any one or more of the two or more instruments) in question, but

(*b*) not all of the chargeable securities falling to be regarded for the purposes of that subsection as transferred by the instrument (or by the two or more instruments between them) were acquired as mentioned in paragraphs (*a*) and (*b*) of that subsection,

stamp duty reserve tax shall be repaid or cancelled under section 92 below in accordance with subsection (5A) below.][12]

[(5A) Any repayment or cancellation of tax falling to be made by virtue of subsection (5) above shall be determined as if (without prejudice to section 87(7A) above) there had instead of the agreement (or the two or more agreements) in question been—

(*a*) a separate agreement (or two or more separate agreements) relating to such of the securities as were acquired as mentioned in paragraphs (*a*) and (*b*) of subsection (1B) above, and

(*b*) a single separate agreement relating to such of the securities as do not fall within those paragraphs,

and as if the instrument in question (or the two or more instruments in question between them) had related only to such of the securities as do not fall within those paragraphs.][12]

[(6) Where a person enters into an agreement for securities to be transferred to him or his nominee, the securities shall be treated for the purposes of subsections (1B)(*a*) and (4) above as acquired by that person at the time when he enters into the agreement, unless the agreement is conditional, in which case they shall be taken to be acquired by him when the condition is satisfied.][5]

Cross references—See FA 1990 ss 110, 111(1) (abolition of stamp duty reserve tax with effect from an appointed day).

Amendments—[1] Sub-s (1)(*aa*), (*ab*) substituted by FA 1999 s 112(4), Sch 14 para 20 with effect in relation to instruments executed after 30 September 1999. This does not apply to transfers or other instruments relating to units under a unit trust scheme by virtue of FA 1999 s 122. For prospective repeal of FA 1999 Sch 14 para 20 see FA 1999 s 123(3). Previously the text read:

"[(*aa*)section 65(1) of the Finance Act 1963 (renounceable letters of allotment etc),]

[(*ab*) section 14(1) of the Finance Act (Northern Ireland) 1963 (renounceable letters of allotment etc),]"

[2] Sub-s (1A) inserted by FA 1996 s 189, with effect in relation to an agreement to transfer securities if an instrument is executed after 30 June 1996 in pursuance of the agreement.

[3] Sub-s (1B) inserted by FA 1996 s 190(1), (3), with effect where the instrument on which stamp duty is not chargeable by virtue of FA 1930 s 42, or FA(NI) 1954 s 11, is executed on or after 4 January 1996 in pursuance of an agreement to transfer securities made on or after that date.

[4] Sub-ss (2), (3) repealed by FA 1996 s 188(3), (5), Sch 41 Pt VII, with effect in relation to an agreement to transfer securities if the agreement is conditional and the condition is satisfied on or after 1 July 1996 or the agreement is not conditional and is made on or after that date.

[5] Sub-ss (4)–(6) added by FA 1996 s 190(2), (3), with effect where the instrument on which stamp duty is not chargeable by virtue of FA 1930 s 42, or FA(NI) 1954 s 11, is executed on or after 4 January 1996 in pursuance of an agreement to transfer securities made on or after that date.

[6] Words in sub-ss (1), (1A), (1B) substituted by FA 1996 s 192(2), (6), with effect in relation to an agreement to transfer securities if the agreement is conditional and the condition is satisfied on or after 1 July 1996 or the agreement is not conditional and is made on or after that date.

[7] Section number in sub-s (1B)(*b*)(i) substituted for "81" by FA 1997 s 97(3) in relation to an agreement to transfer chargeable securities if the securities were acquired in a transaction with effect from 20 October 1997 as appointed by SI 1997/2428.

[8] Section number in sub-s (1B)(*b*)(ii) substituted for "89" by FA 1997 s 102(3) in relation to property consisting of chargeable securities if the securities were acquired in pursuance of an agreement to transfer securities (*a*) in the case of an agreement which is not conditional, if the agreement is made on or after 20 October 1997 as appointed by SI 1997/2428; and (*b*) in the case of a conditional agreement, if the condition is satisfied on or after that day.

[9] Sub-ss (1C) and (1D) inserted by FA 1997 s 103 (4) in relation to instruments executed on or after 20 October 1997 as appointed by SI 1997/2428.

[10] Words in sub-s (1B)(*a*) inserted by FA 1997 s 106(5) where the instrument is executed on or after 4 January 1997 in pursuance of an agreement to transfer securities made on or after that date.

[11] Words in sub-s (1B)(*b*) substituted, in sub-s (1B)(ii) deleted, and sub-s (1B)(iia) inserted by FA 1997 s 106(5) where the instrument is executed on or after 4 January 1997 in pursuance of an agreement to transfer securities made on or after that date.

12 Sub-ss (4), (5) and (5A) substituted for sub-ss (4) and (5) by FA 1997 s 106(6) where the instrument is executed on or after 4 January 1997 in pursuance of an agreement to transfer securities on or after that date.

13 Heading substituted by FA 1997 s 106(7).

14 Words in sub-s (1B)(iia) substituted for the words "paragraph (*a*) of subsection (1) of section 89B below as regards which section 87 above did not apply by virtue of that subsection" by FA 1997 s 103(3) in relation to property consisting of chargeable securities if the securities were acquired in pursuance of (*a*) an agreement to transfer securities which is not conditional if the agreement is made on or after 20 October 1997 as appointed by SI 1997/2428; and (*b*) a conditional agreement if the condition is satisfied on or after that date.

15 Figures in sub-s (1A) substituted by FA 1999 s 112(4), Sch 14 para 20 with effect in relation to instruments executed after 30 September 1999. This does not apply to transfers or other instruments relating to units under a unit trust scheme by virtue of FA 1999 s 122. For prospective repeal of FA 1999 Sch 14 para 20 see FA 1999 s 123(3). Previously the text read '50p'.

16 Word in sub-s (1)(*b*) and sub-s (1)(*c*) inserted by FA 1999 Sch 19 para 10 with effect from 6 February 2000.

17 The word "transfer" substituted for the words "conveyance or transfer" in enactments relating to stamp duty by FA 2003 Sch 20 para 3.

18 In sub-s (1C), words inserted by FA 2009 s 83, Sch 37 paras 1, 3 with effect where the insolvency in question occurs on or after 1 September 2008. FA 2009 s 83(3). FA 2009 s 83 and Sch 37 cease to have effect—

(a) in relation to the amendments made to Part 3 of FA 1986, when the repeal of sections 80 to 85 of that Act (by Part 6 of Schedule 19 to, and in accordance with sections 107 to 109 of, FA 1990) comes into force, and

(b) in relation to the amendments made to Part 4 of FA 1986, when the repeal of that Part (by Part 7 of Schedule 19 to, and in accordance with section 110 of, FA 1990) comes into force.

[88A Section 87: exceptions for intermediaries

[(1) Section 87 above shall not apply as regards an agreement to transfer securities of a particular kind to B or B's nominee if—

(*a*) B is a member of a regulated market on which securities of that kind are regularly traded; and

(*b*) B is an intermediary and is recognised as such by the market in accordance with arrangements approved by the Commissioners for Her Majesty's Revenue and Customs ("the Commissioners").][2]

[(1A) Section 87 above shall not apply as regards an agreement to transfer securities of a particular kind to B or B's nominee if—

(*a*) B is a member of a multilateral trading facility, or a recognised foreign exchange, on which securities of that kind are regularly traded;

(*b*) B is an intermediary and is recognised as such by the facility or exchange in accordance with arrangements approved by the Commissioners; and

(*c*) the agreement is effected on the facility or exchange.][2]

[(1B) Section 87 above shall not apply as regards an agreement to transfer securities of a particular kind to B or B's nominee if—

(*a*) B is an intermediary who is approved for the purposes of this section by the Commissioners; and

(*b*) securities of that kind are regularly traded on a regulated market.][2]

[(1C) Section 87 above shall not apply as regards an agreement to transfer securities of a particular kind to B or B's nominee if—

(*a*) B is an intermediary who is approved for the purposes of this section by the Commissioners;

(*b*) securities of that kind are regularly traded on a multilateral trading facility or a recognised foreign exchange; and

(*c*) the agreement is effected on the facility or exchange.][2]

[(2) Section 87 above shall not apply as regards an agreement to transfer securities of a particular kind to B or B's nominee if—

(*a*) B is a member of a regulated market, a multilateral trading facility or a recognised foreign options exchange;

(*b*) options to buy or sell securities of that kind are regularly traded on, and are listed by or quoted on, that market, facility or exchange;

(*c*) B is an options intermediary and is recognised as such by that market, facility or exchange in accordance with arrangements approved by the Commissioners; and

(*d*) securities of that kind are regularly traded on a regulated market.][2]

[(2A) Section 87 above shall not apply as regards an agreement to transfer securities of a particular kind to B or B's nominee if—

(*a*) B is a member of a regulated market, a multilateral trading facility or a recognised foreign options exchange;

(*b*) options to buy or sell securities of that kind are regularly traded on, and are listed by or quoted on, that market, facility or exchange;

(*c*) B is an options intermediary and is recognised as such by that market, facility or exchange in accordance with arrangements approved by the Commissioners; and

(*d*) the agreement is effected on a relevant qualifying exchange on which securities of that kind are regularly traded or is effected on a relevant qualifying exchange pursuant to the exercise of a relevant option and options to buy or sell securities of that kind are regularly traded on, and are listed by or quoted on, that exchange;

and in paragraph (d) "relevant qualifying exchange" means a multilateral trading facility, a recognised foreign options exchange or a recognised foreign exchange.][2]

[(2B) Section 87 above shall not apply as regards an agreement to transfer securities of a particular kind to B or B's nominee if—

(*a*) B is an options intermediary who is approved for the purposes of this section by the Commissioners;

(*b*) options to buy or sell securities of that kind are regularly traded on, and are listed by or quoted on, a regulated market, a multilateral trading facility or a recognised foreign options exchange; and

(*c*) securities of that kind are regularly traded on a regulated market.][2]

[(2C) Section 87 above shall not apply as regards an agreement to transfer securities of a particular kind to B or B's nominee if—

(*a*) B is an options intermediary who is approved for the purposes of this section by the Commissioners;

(*b*) options to buy or sell securities of that kind are regularly traded on, and are listed by or quoted on, a regulated market, a multilateral trading facility or a recognised foreign options exchange; and

(*c*) the agreement is effected on a relevant qualifying exchange on which securities of that kind are regularly traded or is effected on a relevant qualifying exchange pursuant to the exercise of a relevant option and options to buy or sell securities of that kind are regularly traded on, and are listed by or quoted on, that exchange;

and in paragraph (c) "relevant qualifying exchange" means a multilateral trading facility, a recognised foreign options exchange or a recognised foreign exchange.][2]

(4) For the purposes of this section—

(*a*) an intermediary is a person who carries on a bona fide business of dealing in chargeable securities and does not carry on an excluded business; and

(*b*) an options intermediary is a person who carries on a bona fide business of dealing in quoted or listed options to buy or sell chargeable securities and does not carry on an excluded business.

(5) The excluded businesses are the following—

(*a*) any business which consists wholly or mainly in the making or managing of investments;

(*b*) any business which consists wholly or mainly in, or is carried on wholly or mainly for the purpose of, providing services to persons who are connected with the person carrying on the business;

(*c*) any business which consists in insurance business;

(*d*) any business which consists in managing or acting as trustee in relation to a pension scheme or which is carried on by the manager or trustee of such a scheme in connection with or for the purposes of the scheme;

(*e*) any business which consists in operating or acting as trustee in relation to a collective investment scheme or is carried on by the operator or trustee of such a scheme in connection with or for the purposes of the scheme.

(6) An agreement is effected on [a facility or][2] an exchange for the purposes of [this section][2] if (and only if)—

(*a*) it is subject to the rules of [the facility or exchange][2]; and

(*b*) it is reported to [the facility or exchange][2] in accordance with the rules of [the facility or exchange][2].][1]

[(6A) The Commissioners may approve a person for the purposes of this section only if the person is authorised under the law of an EEA State to provide any of the investment services or activities listed in Section A 2 or 3 of Annex I to the Directive (execution of orders on behalf of clients and dealing on own account), whether or not the person is authorised under the Directive.][2]

Cross references—See FA 2002 s 117 (the Treasury may by regulations extend the application of this section to any market that is not a recognised exchange but is prescribed by order under the Financial Services and Markets Act 2000 s 118(3)).

Stamp Duty and Stamp Duty Reserve Tax (Extension of Exceptions relating to Recognised Exchanges) Regulations, SI 2002/1975 (with effect from 26 July 2002, the application of the provision specified in FA 2002 s 117(2) (which includes this section) is extended to the market known as OFEX).

F(No 2)A 2005 s 50 (power of the Treasury to extend the application of this section to any market which is not a recognised exchange, but is a multilateral trading facility or (assuming compliance with the provisions of Title II of the European Parliament and Council Directive 2004/39/EC) would be such a facility).

Modifications—Stamp Duty and Stamp Duty Reserve Tax (Extension of Exceptions relating to Recognised Exchanges) Regulations, SI 2005/1990 regs 3, 6 (modification of this section in its application to prescibed multilateral trading facilities. For definition of "prescribed multilateral trading facility" see SI 2005/1990 reg 2).

Amendments—[1] This section inserted by FA 1997 s 102(1) in relation to an agreement to transfer securities (*a*) in the case of an agreement which is not conditional, if the agreement is made on or after 20 October 1997 as appointed by SI 1997/2428; and (*b*) in the case of a conditional agreement, if the condition is satisfied on or after that date and repealed by FA 1997 Sch 18 Part VII with effect from the day appointed under FA 1990 s 111.

2 Sub-ss (1)–(2C) substituted for sub-ss (1)–(3); in sub-s (6), words inserted, and words substituted for the words "subsection (1) or (2) above", and "the exchange" (wherever occurring); and sub-s (6A) inserted, by FA 2007 s 73, Sch 21 para 3 with effect in relation to any agreement to transfer securities—

(a) in a case where the agreement is conditional, if the condition is satisfied on or after 1 November 2007, and

(b) in any other case, if the agreement is made on or after that date.: FA 2007 Sch 21 para 3(5).

Sub-ss (1)–(3) previously read as follows—

"(1) Section 87 above shall not apply as regards an agreement to transfer securities of a particular kind to B or his nominee if—

(*a*) B is a member of an EEA exchange, or a recognised foreign exchange, on which securities of that kind are regularly traded;

(*b*) B is an intermediary and is recognised as an intermediary by the exchange in accordance with arrangements approved by the Board; and

(*c*) the agreement is effected on the exchange.

(2) Section 87 above shall not apply as regards an agreement to transfer securities of a particular kind to B or his nominee if—

(*a*) B is a member of an EEA exchange or a recognised foreign options exchange;

(*b*) options to buy or sell securities of that kind are regularly traded on that exchange and are listed by or quoted on that exchange;

(*c*) B is an options intermediary and is recognised as an options intermediary by that exchange in accordance with arrangements approved by the Board; and

(*d*) the agreement is effected on an EEA exchange, or a recognised foreign exchange, on which securities of that kind are regularly traded or subsection (3) below applies.

(3) This subsection applies if—

(*a*) the agreement is effected on an EEA exchange, or a recognised foreign options exchange, pursuant to the exercise of a relevant option; and

(*b*) options to buy or sell securities of the kind concerned are regularly traded on that exchange and are listed by or quoted on that exchange.".

[88B Intermediaries: supplementary

(1) For the purposes of section 88A above the question whether a person is connected with another shall be determined in accordance with the provisions of [section 1122 of the Corporation Tax Act 2010][4].

(2) In section 88A above and this section—

"collective investment scheme" has the meaning given in section [235 of the Financial Services and Markets Act 2000][2];

["the Directive" means Directive 2004/39/EC of the European Parliament and of the Council of 21 April 2004 on markets in financial instruments, as amended from time to time;][3]

. . . [3]

"EEA State"[, in relation to any time, means a State which at that time is a member State or any other State which at that time][3] is a contracting party to the agreement on the European Economic Area signed at Oporto on the 2nd May 1992 as adjusted by the Protocol signed at Brussels on the 17th March 1993 [(as modified or supplemented from time to time)][3];

["insurance business" means business which consists of the effecting or carrying out of contracts of insurance and, for the purposes of this definition, "contract of insurance" has the meaning given by Article 3(1) of the Financial Services and Markets Act 2000 (Regulated Activities) Order 2001;

"the operator", in relation to a collective investment scheme, shall be construed in accordance with section 237(2) of the Financial Services and Markets Act 2000;][2]

"quoted or listed options" means options which are quoted on or listed by an EEA exchange or a recognised foreign options exchange;

"recognised foreign exchange" and "recognised foreign options exchange" have the meanings given, respectively, by subsections (3) and (4) of section 80B above;

["trustee", in relation to a collective investment scheme, means a trustee or a depositary within the meaning given in section 237(2) of the Financial Services and Markets Act 2000.][2]

[(2A) Each of the following expressions—

"multilateral trading facility", and

"regulated market",

has the same meaning in section 88A above as it has for the purposes of the Directive.][3]

(3) In section 88A above "the exercise of a relevant option" means—

(*a*) the exercise by B of an option to buy securities; or

(*b*) the exercise of an option binding B to buy securities.

[(3A) The Treasury may by regulations amend section 88A above and this section (as they have effect for the time being) in order to extend the exemption from tax under that section.][3]

(4) The Treasury may by regulations provide that section 88A above shall not have effect in relation to kinds of agreement specified in the regulations.

(5) The Treasury may by regulations provide that if—

(*a*) an agreement falls within [any of subsections (1) to (2C)][3] of section 88A above, and (*b*) section 87 above would, apart from section 88A, apply to the agreement,

section 87 shall apply to the agreement but with the substitution of a rate of tax not exceeding 0.1 per cent for the rate specified in subsection (6) of that section.

(6) The Treasury may by regulations change the meaning of "intermediary" or "options intermediary" for the purposes of section 88A above by amending subsection (3) or (5) of that section (as it has effect for the time being).

(7) The power to make regulations under subsections [(3A)][3] to (6) above shall be exercisable by statutory instrument subject to annulment in pursuance of a resolution of the House of Commons.][1]

Amendments—[1] This section inserted by FA 1997 s 100(1) in relation to an agreement to transfer securities (*a*) in the case of an agreement which is not conditional, if the agreement is made on or after 20 October 1997 as appointed by SI 1997/2428; and (*b*) in the case of a conditional agreement, if the condition is satisfied on or after that date and repealed by FA 1997 Sch 18 Part VII with effect from the day appointed under FA 1990 s 111.

[2] Words in definition of "collective investment scheme", and definitions of "insurance business", and "the trustee" and "the operator", substituted by the Financial Services and Markets Act 2000 (Consequential Amendments) (Taxes) Order, SI 2001/3629 arts 6, 9. SI 2001/3629 art 9 has effect in relation to—

(*a*) an agreement to transfer chargeable securities which is not conditional, if the agreement is made after 30 November 2001;

(*b*) a conditional agreement to transfer such securities, if the condition is satisfied after that date.

[3] In sub-s (2), definition inserted, definition of "EEA exchange" repealed, and words "means a State which" in definition of "EEA State" substituted, and words inserted; sub-ss (2A), (3A) inserted; and in sub-s (5), words substituted for the words "subsection (1) or (2)"; and in sub-s (7), figure substituted for "(4)", by FA 2007 ss 73, 114, Sch 21 para 4, Sch 27 Pt 4(2) with effect in relation to any agreement to transfer securities—

(*a*) in a case where the agreement is conditional, if the condition is satisfied on or after 1 November 2007, and

(*b*) in any other case, if the agreement is made on or after that date.

Definition of "EEA exchange" previously read as follows—

" 'EEA exchange' means a market which appears on the list drawn up by an EEA State pursuant to Article 16 of European Communities Council Directive No 93/22/EEC on investment services in the securities field;".

[4] In sub-s (1) words substituted for words "section 839 of the Income and Corporation Taxes Act 1988" by CTA 2010 s 1177, Sch 1 para 199. CTA 2010 has effect for corporation tax purposes for accounting periods ending on or after 1 April 2010, and for income and capital gains tax purposes for the tax year 2010–11 and subsequent tax years.

89 Section 87: exceptions for market makers etc

Cross references—See FA 1990 ss 110, 111(1) (abolition of stamp duty reserve tax with effect from an appointed day).

Amendments—This section repealed by FA 1997 s 102(2), Sch 18 Part VII in relation to an agreement to transfer securities (*a*) in the case of an agreement which is not conditional, if the agreement is made on or after 20 October 1997 as appointed by SI 1997/2428; and (*b*) in the case of a conditional agreement, if the condition is satisfied on or after that date.

[89A Section 87: exceptions for public issues

(1) Section 87 above shall not apply as regards an agreement to transfer securities other than units under a unit trust scheme to B or B's nominee if—

(*a*) the agreement is part of an arrangement, entered into by B in the ordinary course of B's business as an issuing house, under which B (as principal) is to offer the securities for sale to the public,

(*b*) the agreement is conditional upon the admission of the securities to the Official List of The Stock Exchange,

(*c*) the consideration under the agreement for each security is the same as the price at which B is to offer the security for sale, and

(*d*) B sells the securities in accordance with the arrangement referred to in paragraph (*a*) above.

(2) Section 87 above shall not apply as regards an agreement if the securities to which the agreement relates are newly subscribed securities other than units under a unit trust scheme and—

(*a*) the agreement is made in pursuance of an offer to the public made by A (as principal) under an arrangement entered into in the ordinary course of A's business as an issuing house,

(*b*) a right of allotment in respect of, or to subscribe for, the securities has been acquired by A under an agreement which is part of the arrangement,

(*c*) both those agreements are conditional upon the admission of the securities to the Official List of The Stock Exchange, and

(*d*) the consideration for each security is the same under both agreements;

and for the purposes of this subsection, "newly subscribed securities" are securities which, in pursuance of the arrangement referred to in paragraph (a) above, are issued wholly for new consideration.

(3) Section 87 above shall not apply as regards an agreement if the securities to which the agreement relates are registered securities other than units under a unit trust scheme and—

(*a*) the agreement is made in pursuance of an offer to the public made by A,

(*b*) the agreement is conditional upon the admission of the securities to the Official List of The Stock Exchange, and (*c*) under the agreement A issues to B or his nominee a renounceable letter of acceptance, or similar instrument, in respect of the securities.

(4) The Treasury may by regulations amend paragraph (*b*) of subsection (1) above, paragraph (*c*) of subsection (2) above, and paragraph (*b*) of subsection (3) above (as they have effect for the time being); and the power to make regulations under this section shall be exercisable by statutory instrument subject to annulment in pursuance of a resolution of the House of Commons.][1]

Cross references—See FA 1990 ss 110, 111(1) (abolition of stamp duty reserve tax with effect from an appointed day).

Amendments—[1] This section inserted by F (No 2) A 1987, s 100 (1) in relation to agreements to transfer securities made after 7 May 1987.

[89AA Section 87: exception for repurchases and stock lending

(1) This section applies where a person (P) has entered into an arrangement with another person (Q) under which—

(*a*) Q is to transfer chargeable securities of a particular kind to P or his nominee, and

(*b*) chargeable securities of the same kind and amount are to be transferred by P or his nominee to Q or his nominee,

and the conditions set out in subsection [(2A) or][2] (3) below are fulfilled.

(2) Section 87 above shall not apply as regards an agreement to transfer chargeable securities to P or his nominee or Q or his nominee in accordance with the arrangement.

[(2A) The conditions in this subsection are—

(*a*) that P or Q is authorised under the law of an EEA State to provide any of the investment services or activities listed in Section A 2 or 3 of Annex I to the Directive (execution of orders on behalf of clients and dealing on own account) in relation to securities of the kind concerned, whether or not P or Q is authorised under the Directive; . . . [3]

(*b*) that securities of the kind concerned are regularly traded on a regulated market[; and

(*c*) that chargeable securities are transferred to P or his nominee and Q or his nominee in pursuance of the arrangement.][3]][2]

(3) The conditions [in this subsection][2] are—

(*a*) that the agreement is effected on [a regulated market, a multilateral trading facility][2] or a recognised foreign exchange;

(*b*) that securities of the kind concerned are regularly traded on that [market, facility or][2] exchange; and

(*c*) that chargeable securities are transferred to P or his nominee and Q or his nominee in pursuance of the arrangement.

(4) An arrangement does not fall within subsection (1) above if—

(*a*) the arrangement is not such as would be entered into by persons dealing with each other at arm's length; or

(*b*) under the arrangement any of the benefits or risks arising from fluctuations, before the transfer to Q or his nominee takes place, in the market value of the chargeable securities accrues to, or falls on, P.

(5) An agreement is effected on [a market, a facility or][2] an exchange for the purposes of subsection (3) above if (and only if)—

(*a*) it is subject to the rules of [the market, facility or exchange][2]; and

(*b*) it is reported to [the market, facility or exchange][2] in accordance with the rules of [the market, facility or exchange][2].

(6) In this section—

["the Directive" has the meaning given in section 88B(2) above;

"EEA State" has the meaning given in section 88B(2) above;][2]

. . . [2]

"recognised foreign exchange" has the meaning given in section 80B(3) above.

[(6A) Each of the following expressions—

"multilateral trading facility", and

"regulated market",

has the same meaning in this section as it has for the purposes of the Directive.][2]

(7) The Treasury may by regulations provide that if section 87 would apply as regards an agreement but for subsection (2) above, section 87 shall apply as regards the agreement but with the substitution of a rate of tax not exceeding 0.1 per cent. for the rate specified in subsection (6) of that section.

(8) The Treasury may by regulations amend this section (as it has effect for the time being) in order—

(*a*) to change the conditions for exemption from tax under this section; or

(*b*) to provide that this section does not apply in relation to kinds of arrangement specified in the regulations.

(9) The power to make regulations under subsection (7) or (8) above shall be exercisable by statutory instrument subject to annulment in pursuance of a resolution of the House of Commons.][1]

Cross references—See FA 2002 s 117 (the Treasury may by regulations extend the application of this section to any market that is not a recognised exchange but is prescribed by order under the Financial Services and Markets Act 2000 s 118(3)).

European Single Currency (Taxes) Regulations, SI 1998/3177 regs 26 and 28 for details on replacement of chargeable securities in a euroconversion.

Stamp Duty and Stamp Duty Reserve Tax (Extension of Exceptions relating to Recognised Exchanges) Regulations, SI 2002/1975 (with effect from 26 July 2002, the application of the provision specified in FA 2002 s 117(2) (which includes this section) is extended to the market known as OFEX).

F(No 2)A 2005 s 50 (power of the Treasury to extend the application of this section to any market which is not a recognised exchange, but is a multilateral trading facility or (assuming compliance with the provisions of Title II of the European Parliament and Council Directive 2004/39/EC), would be such a facility).

Modifications—Stamp Duty and Stamp Duty Reserve Tax (Extension of Exceptions relating to Recognised Exchanges) Regulations, SI 2005/1990 regs 3, 7 (modification of this section in its application to prescibed multilateral trading facilities. For definition of "prescribed multilateral trading facility" see SI 2005/1990 reg 2).

Amendments—[1] This section inserted by FA 1997 s 103(1), in relation to an agreement to transfer securities (*a*) in the case of an agreement which is not conditional, if the agreement is made on or after 20 October 1997 as appointed by SI 1997/2428; and (*b*) in the case of a conditional agreement, if the condition is satisfied on or after that date and repealed by FA 1997 Sch 18 Part VII with effect from the day appointed under FA 1990 s 111.

[2] Words in sub-ss (1), (3), (5), (6) inserted; sub-ss (2A), (6A) inserted; in sub-s (3), words substituted for the words "an EEA exchange"; in sub-s (5), words substituted for the words "the exchange" wherever occurring; and in sub-s (6), definition of "EEA exchange" repealed, by FA 2007 ss 73, 114, Sch 21 para 6, Sch 27 Pt 4(2) with effect in relation to any agreement to transfer securities—

(a) in a case where the agreement is conditional, if the condition is satisfied on or after 1 November 2007, and

(b) in any other case, if the agreement is made on or after that date.

Definition of "EEA exchange" previously read as follows—

" 'EEA exchange' has the meaning given in section 88B(2) above;".

[3] In sub-s (2A) word "and" at end of para (*a*) repealed, and para (*c*) and preceding word "and" inserted, by the Stamp Duty Reserve Tax (Amendment of section 89AA of the Finance Act 1986) Regulations, SI 2008/3236 reg 2 with effect in a case where the agreement is conditional, if the condition is satisfied on or after 18 December 2008, and in any other case, if the agreement is made on or after that date.

[89AB Section 87: exception for repurchases and stock lending in case of insolvency

(1) This section applies where—

(*a*) P and Q have entered into an arrangement falling within section 89AA(1),

(*b*) the only reason that the conditions in subsection (2A) or (3) of that section are not met is that chargeable securities of the same kind and amount as those transferred to P or P's nominee are not transferred to Q or Q's nominee, and

(*c*) the conditions in subsection (2) below are met.

(2) The conditions in this subsection are that—

(*a*) P and Q are not connected persons within the meaning of [section 1122 of the Corporation Tax Act 2010][2],

(*b*) after Q has transferred securities under the arrangement, either P or Q becomes insolvent,

(*c*) it becomes apparent (whether before or after the insolvency occurs) that, as a result of the insolvency, securities will not be transferred to Q or Q's nominee in accordance with the arrangement.

(3) Section 87 does not apply as regards an agreement to transfer chargeable securities to P or P's nominee, or Q or Q's nominee, in accordance with the arrangement.

(4) Subsections (5) and (6) apply if—

(*a*) the party who does not become insolvent ("the solvent party") or the solvent party's nominee acquires replacement securities, and

(*b*) the replacement securities are acquired before the end of the period of 30 days beginning with the day on which the insolvency occurs ("the insolvency date").

(5) Where collateral is provided under the arrangement (or under arrangements of which that arrangement forms part), section 87 does not apply as regards any agreement to transfer to the solvent party or the solvent party's nominee—

(*a*) replacement securities acquired using the collateral (whether directly or indirectly), or

(*b*) where the solvent party uses the whole of the value of the collateral to acquire replacement securities, any further replacement securities.

(6) Where no collateral is provided as mentioned in subsection (5), section 87 does not apply as regards any agreement to transfer replacement securities to the solvent party or the solvent party's nominee.

(7) Subsections (5) and (6) may apply as regards more than one agreement (and where those subsections apply as regards more than one agreement, the agreements may be with different persons).

(8) But those subsections apply only as regards replacement securities up to the amount of securities which will not be transferred as a result of the insolvency.

(9) For the purposes of this section, a person becomes insolvent—

(*a*) if a company voluntary arrangement takes effect under Part 1 of the Insolvency Act 1986,

(*b*) if an administration application (within the meaning of Schedule B1 to that Act) is made or a receiver or manager, or an administrative receiver, is appointed,

(*c*) on the commencement of a creditor's voluntary winding up (within the meaning of Part 4 of that Act) or a winding up by the court under Chapter 6 of that Part,
(*d*) if an individual voluntary arrangement takes effect under Part 8 of that Act,
(*e*) on the presentation of a bankruptcy petition (within the meaning of Part 9 of that Act),
(*f*) if a compromise or arrangement takes effect under Part 26 of the Companies Act 2006,
(*g*) if a bank insolvency order takes effect under Part 2 of the Banking Act 2009,
(*h*) if a bank administration order takes effect under Part 3 of that Act, or
(*i*) on the occurrence of any corresponding event which has effect under or as a result of the law of Scotland or Northern Ireland or a country or territory outside the United Kingdom.

(10) In this section—

"collateral" means an amount of money or other property which is payable to, or made available for the benefit of, a party to an arrangement or that party's nominee for the purpose of securing the discharge of the requirement to transfer securities to that party or the nominee;

"replacement securities", in the event of a party to an arrangement becoming insolvent, are chargeable securities of the same kind as the securities which will not be transferred to the other party or that party's nominee as a result of the insolvency.][1]

Amendments—[1] Section 89AB inserted by FA 2009 s 83, Sch 37 paras 4, 5 with effect where the insolvency in question occurs on or after 1 September 2008. FA 2009 s 83(3). FA 2009 s 83 and FA 2009 Sch 37 cease to have effect—

(a) in relation to the amendments made to Part 3 of FA 1986, when the repeal of sections 80 to 85 of that Act (by Part 6 of Schedule 19 to, and in accordance with sections 107 to 109 of, FA 1990) comes into force, and

(b) in relation to the amendments made to Part 4 of FA 1986, when the repeal of that Part (by Part 7 of Schedule 19 to, and in accordance with section 110 of, FA 1990) comes into force.

[2] In sub-s (2)(*a*) words substituted for words "section 839 of the Taxes Act 1988" by CTA 2010 s 1177, Sch 1 para 200. CTA 2010 has effect for corporation tax purposes for accounting periods ending on or after 1 April 2010, and for income and capital gains tax purposes for the tax year 2010–11 and subsequent tax years.

[89B Section 87: exceptions for stock lending and collateral security arrangements]

Cross references—See FA 1990 ss 110, 111(1) (abolition of stamp duty reserve tax with effect from an appointed day).

Amendments—This section inserted by FA 1996 s 191, with effect in relation to agreements to transfer chargeable securities in pursuance of an arrangement entered into after 30 June 1996 and repealed by FA 1997 s 103(2), Sch 18 Pt VII in relation to an agreement to transfer securities (*a*) in the case of an agreement which is not conditional, if the agreement is made on or after 20 October 1997 as appointed by SI 1997/2428; and (*b*) in the case of a conditional agreement, if the condition is satisfied on or after that date.

90 Section 87: other exceptions

(1) Section 87 above shall not apply as regards an agreement to transfer a unit under a unit trust scheme [to or from the managers][12] under the scheme.

[(1A) Section 87 above shall not apply as regards an agreement to transfer a unit under a unit trust scheme if an instrument executed at the same time as the agreement and giving effect to the agreement would be exempt from stamp duty (if stamp duty were otherwise chargeable) by virtue of—

(*a*) section 42 of the Finance Act 1930 or section 11 of the Finance Act (Northern Ireland) 1954 (transfers between associated companies), or
(*b*) regulations under section 87(2) of the Finance Act 1985 (power to exempt instruments from stamp duty of fixed amount).][12][, or
(*c*) section 96 of the Finance Act 1997 (demutualisation of insurance companies).][16]

[(1B) Section 87 above shall not apply as regards an agreement to transfer trust property to the unit holder on the surrender to the managers of a unit under a unit trust scheme.

The reference here to the surrender of a unit has the same meaning as in Part II of Schedule 19 to the Finance Act 1999.][13]

(2) . . .[14]

(3) Section 87 above shall not apply as regards an agreement to transfer securities constituted by or transferable by means of—

[(*a*) a non-UK bearer instrument;][6]
(*b*) . . .[2]

[(3A) Section 87 above shall not apply as regards an agreement to transfer chargeable securities constituted by or transferable by means of [a UK bearer instrument][7] unless subsection (3B), (3C) or (3E) below applies to the instrument.][3]

[(3B) This subsection applies to any instrument which falls within [the exemption conferred by paragraph 16 of Schedule 15 to the Finance Act 1999 (renounceable letters of allotment etc.)][7] (renounceable letter of allotment etc where rights are renounceable not later than six months after issue).][3]

[(3C) This subsection applies to an instrument if—

(*a*) the instrument was issued by a body corporate incorporated in the United Kingdom [(other than an SE which has its registered office outside the United Kingdom following a transfer in accordance with Article 8 of Council Regulation (EC) 2157/2001 on the Statute for a European Company (Societas Europaea))][17];

[(*b*) stamp duty under Schedule 15 to the Finance Act 1999 was not chargeable on the issue of the instrument by virtue only of the exemption conferred by paragraph 17 of that Schedule (non-sterling bearer instruments); and][8]

(*c*) the instrument is not exempt.][3]

[(3D) An instrument is exempt for the purposes of subsection (3C) above if—

(*a*) the chargeable securities in question are, or a depositary receipt for them is, listed on a recognised stock exchange; and

(*b*) the agreement to transfer those securities is not made in contemplation of, or as part of an arrangement for, a takeover of the body corporate which issued such instrument.][3]

[(3E) This subsection applies to an instrument if—

(*a*) the instrument was issued by a body corporate incorporated in the United Kingdom [(other than an SE which has its registered office outside the United Kingdom following a transfer in accordance with Article 8 of Council Regulation (EC) 2157/2001 on the Statute for a European Company (Societas Europaea))][17]:

[(*b*) stamp duty under Schedule 15 to the Finance Act 1999 was not chargeable on the issue of the instrument—

(i) by virtue only of the exemption conferred by section 79(2) above (bearer instruments relating to loan capital), or

(ii) by virtue only of that provision and paragraph 17 of that Schedule (non-sterling bearer instruments);][9]

(*c*) by virtue of section 79(5) (convertible loan capital) or 79(6) (loan capital carrying special rights) above, stamp duty would be chargeable on an instrument transferring the loan capital to which the instrument relates; and

(*d*) the instrument is not exempt.][3]

[(3F) An instrument is exempt for the purposes of subsection (3E) above if—

(*a*) the chargeable securities in question are, or a depositary receipt for them is, listed on a recognised stock exchange;

(*b*) the agreement to transfer those securities is not made in contemplation of, or as part of an arrangement for, a takeover of the body corporate which issued the instrument; and

(*c*) those securities do not carry any right of the kind described in section 79(5) above (right of conversion into, or acquisition of, shares or other securities) by the exercise of which [chargeable securities which are not listed][10] on a recognised stock exchange may be obtained.][3]

(4) Section 87 above shall not apply as regards an agreement which forms part of an arrangement falling within section 93 (1) or 96 (1) below.

[(5) Section 87 above shall not apply as regards an agreement to transfer securities which the Board are satisfied are held, when the agreement is made, [for the purposes of a business][11] within subsection (6) below.][1]

[(6) [A business is within this subsection if, or so far as, it consists of][11] that of holding shares, stock or other marketable securities—

(*a*) as nominee or agent for a person whose business is or includes the provision of clearance services for the purchase and sale of shares, stock or other marketable securities, and

(*b*) for the purpose of such part of the business mentioned in paragraph (*a*) above as consists of the provision of such clearance services (in a case where the business does not consist exclusively of that);

and in this subsection, "marketable securities" shall be construed in accordance with section 122(1) of the Stamp Act 1891.][1]

[(7) Section 87 above shall not apply as regards an agreement to transfer securities to—

(*a*) a body of persons established for charitable purposes only, or

(*b*) the trustees of a trust so established, or

(*c*) the Trustees of the National Heritage Memorial Fund, or

(*d*) the Historic Buildings and Monuments Commission for England.][1]

[or

(e) the National Endowment for Science, Technology and the Arts.][5]

[(7A) Section 87 above does not apply as regards an agreement to transfer any shares in a company which are held by the company (whether in accordance with section [724][19] of the Companies Act [2006][19] (treasury shares) or otherwise).][15]

[(8) for the purposes of subsections (3D) and (3F) above—

(*a*) references to a depositary receipt for chargeable securities shall be construed in accordance with section 94(1) below;

[(*b*) references to anything listed on a recognised stock exchange shall be construed in accordance with section 1005 of the Income Tax Act 2007;][18]

(*c*) there is a takeover of a body corporate if a person, on his own or together with connected persons, loses or acquires control of it.][4]

[(9) For the purposes of subsection (8) above—

(*a*) any question whether a person is connected with another shall be determined in accordance with section 286 of the Taxation of Chargeable Gains Act 1992;

(*b*) "control" shall be construed in accordance with [sections 450 and 451 of the Corporation Tax Act 2010][20].][4]

Cross references—See FA 1986 s 97A(3), (4) (exclusion from charge to stamp duty reserve tax under sub-ss (4), (5) above does not apply to agreements connected with clearance services where an election is made under s 97A(1)).

FA 1990 ss 110, 111(1) (abolition of stamp duty reserve tax with effect from an appointed day).

Amendments—[1] Sub-ss (5), (6), (7) substituted and added by FA 1987 Sch 7 paras 1, 5, 6 and deemed always to have had effect.

[2] Sub-s (3)(*b*) repealed by FA 1997 s 105(1), (4), Sch 18 Pt VII with effect in relation to an agreement if the inland bearer instrument in question was issued on or after 26 November 1996 and (*a*) in the case of an agreement which is not conditional, the agreement is made on or after that date, or (*b*) in the case of a conditional agreement, the condition is satisfied on or after that date.

[3] Sub-ss (3A)–(3F) inserted by FA 1997 s 105(2), (4) with effect as in note 2 above.

[4] Sub-ss (8),(9) added by FA 1997 s 105(3), (4) with effect as in note 2 above.

[5] Sub-s (7)(*e*) inserted by the National Lottery Act 1998 s 24 with effect from 2 July 1998.

[6] Sub-s (3)(*a*) substituted by FA 1999 s 113(3), Sch 16 para 6 with effect in relation to bearer instruments issued after 30 September 1999. For prospective repeal of FA 1999 s 113, Sch 16 para 6 see FA 1999 s 123(3). Previously the text read:

"(*a*) an overseas bearer instrument, within the meaning of the heading "Bearer Instrument" in Schedule 1 to the Stamp Act 1891;"

[7] Words in sub-ss (3A) and (3B) substituted by FA 1999 s 113(3), Sch 16 para 6 with effect in relation to bearer instruments issued after 30 September 1999. For prospective repeal of FA 1999 s 113, Sch 16 para 6 see FA 1999 s 123(3). Previously the text read 'the heading "Bearer Instrument" in Schedule 1 to the Stamp Act 1891' and 'exemption 3 in the heading "Bearer Instrument" in Schedule 1 to the Stamp Act 1891' respectively.

[8] Sub-s (3C)(*b*) substituted by FA 1999 s 113(3), Sch 16 para 6 with effect in relation to bearer instruments issued after 30 September 1999. For prospective repeal of FA 1999 s 113, Sch 16 para 6 see FA 1999 s 123(3). Previously the text read:

"(*b*) stamp duty under the heading "Bearer Instrument" in Schedule 1 to the Stamp Act 1891 was not chargeable on the issue of the instrument by virtue only of—

(i) section 30 of the Finance Act 1967 (exemption for bearer instruments relating to stock in foreign currencies); or

(ii) section 7 of the Finance Act (Northern Ireland) 1967 (which makes similar provision for Northern Ireland); and".

[9] Sub-s (3E)(*b*) substituted by FA 1999 s 113(3), Sch 16 para 6 with effect in relation to bearer instruments issued after 30 September 1999. For prospective repeal of FA 1999 s 113, Sch 16 para 6 see FA 1999 s 123(3). Previously the text read:

"(*b*) stamp duty under the heading "Bearer Instrument" in Schedule 1 to the Stamp Act 1891 was not chargeable on the issue of the instrument—

(i) by virtue only of subsection (2) of section 79 above (exemption for bearer instruments relating to loan capital); or

(ii) by virtue only of that subsection and one or other of the provisions mentioned in subsection (3C)(b)(i) and (ii) above;".

[10] Words in sub-s (3F)(*c*) substituted by FA 1999 s 120(2) with effect in relation to instruments issued from 9 March 1999. For prospective repeal of FA 1999 s 120 see FA 1999 s 123(3).

[11] Words in sub-ss (5) and (6) substituted by FA 1999 s 120(3) with effect in relation to agreements to transfer securities made from 9 March 1999. For prospective repeal of FA 1999 s 120 see FA 1999 s 123(3).

[12] Words "to the managers" in sub-s (1) substituted and sub-s (1A) inserted by FA 1999 Sch 19 para 11 with effect from 6 February 2000, where this is the relevant day for the purposes of FA 1986 s 87.

[13] Sub-s (1B) inserted by FA 1999 Sch 19 para 11 with effect from 6 February 2000, where the surrender is within the meaning of FA 1999 Sch 19 Pt II.

[14] Sub-s (2) repealed by FA 1999 Sch 20 Pt V(5) with effect in relation to instruments executed from 6 February 2000.

[15] Sub-s (7A) inserted by FA 2003 s 195, Sch 40 para 3 with effect for any acquisition of shares by a company on or after 1 December 2003 (by virtue of SI 2003/3077).

[16] In sub-s (1A), para (*c*) and preceding word ", or" inserted by FA 2005 s 97(2), (5) with effect where the relevant day for the purposes of FA 1986 s 87 falls on or after 7 April 2005.

[17] Words in sub-ss (3C)(*a*), (3E)(*a*) inserted by F(No 2)A 2005 s 58(1), (2) with effect for the purposes of determining whether or not stamp duty or stamp duty reserve tax is chargeable in respect of anything done on or after 1 April 2005: F(No 2)A 2005 s 58(4).

[18] Sub-s (8)(*b*) substituted by FA 2007 s 109, Sch 26 para 6 with effect from 19 July 2007.

[19] In sub-s (7A), figures substituted for figures "162A" and "1985", by the Companies Act 2006 (Consequential Amendments) (Taxes and National Insurance) Order, SI 2009/1890 art 7(*d*) with effect from 1 October 2009.

[20] In sub-s (9)(*b*) words substituted for words "section 416 of the Income and Corporation Taxes Act 1988" by CTA 2010 s 1177, Sch 1 para 201. CTA 2010 has effect for corporation tax purposes for accounting periods ending on or after 1 April 2010, and for income and capital gains tax purposes for the tax year 2010–11 and subsequent tax years.

91 Liability to tax

(1) Where tax is charged under section 87 above as regards an agreement, B shall be liable for the tax.

(2) . . . [1]

Cross references—See FA 1990 ss 110, 111(1) (abolition of stamp duty reserve tax with effect from an appointed day).

Amendments—[1] Sub-s (2) repealed by F (No 2) A 1987, s 100 (2), Sch 9, Pt IV, and the repeal is deemed always to have had effect.

92 Repayment or cancellation of tax

(1) If, as regards an agreement to transfer securities to B or his nominee, tax is charged under section 87 above and it is proved to the Board's satisfaction that at a time [on or after the relevant day (as defined in section 87(3))][5] but before the expiry of the period of six years [beginning with that day][5] the conditions mentioned in [subsections (1A) and (1B) below][6] have been fulfilled, [subsections (2) to (4A) of this section shall apply].[6]

[(1A) The first condition is that an instrument is (or instruments are) executed in pursuance of the agreement and the instrument transfers (or the instruments between them transfer) to B or, as the case may be, to his nominee all the chargeable securities to which the agreement relates.][7]

[(1B) The second condition is that the instrument (or each instrument) transferring the chargeable securities to which the agreement relates—

(*a*) so far as those securities are stock or marketable securities within the meaning of section 125 of the Finance Act 2003 (abolition of stamp duty except on instruments relating to stock or marketable securities)—

(i) is duly stamped in accordance with the enactments relating to stamp duty, or

(ii) is not chargeable with stamp duty or otherwise required to be stamped under those enactments; or

(*b*) so far as those securities are not stock or marketable securities within the meaning of that section, is an instrument that, disregarding that section, would not be chargeable with any *ad valorem* stamp duty under those enactments.][9]

[(1C) If, as regards an agreement to transfer shares in a company to that company ("the own-shares agreement")—

(*a*) tax is charged under section 87 above, and

(*b*) it is proved to the Board's satisfaction that at a time in the period of six years beginning on the relevant day (as defined in section 87(3)) the conditions mentioned in subsection (1D) have been fulfilled in respect of those shares,

subsections (2) to (4A) apply.][10]

[(1D) The conditions referred to in subsection (1C) are—

(*a*) that, in relation to the transfer made in pursuance of the own-shares agreement, a return has been made in respect of each of those shares in accordance with section [707][11] of the Companies Act [2006][11] (disclosure by company of purchase of own shares), and

(*b*) that any such return has been duly stamped in accordance with section 66.][10]

(2) If any of the tax charged has been paid, and a claim for repayment is made within the period of six years mentioned in subsection (1) [or, as the case may be, (1C)][10] above, the tax paid shall be repaid; and where the tax paid is not less than £25 it shall be repaid with interest on it at the [rate applicable under section 178 of the Finance Act 1989][2] from [the date on which the payment was made until the order for repayment is issued][3].

(3) To the extent that the tax charged has not been paid, the charge shall be cancelled by virtue of this subsection.

(4) . . . [4]

[(4A) Interest paid under subsection (2) above shall not constitute income for any tax purposes.][1]

(5) . . . [4]

[(6) In this section "the enactments relating to stamp duty" means the Stamp Act 1891 and any enactment which amends or is required to be construed together with that Act.][7]

[(7) This section shall have effect in relation to a person to whom the chargeable securities are transferred by way of security for a loan to B as it has effect in relation to a nominee of B.][8]

Note—For the rate applicable under FA 1989 s 178, see SI 1989/1297 *post.*

Cross references—See FA 1986 s 88(1), (1A), (1B) (certain instruments to be disregarded in construing sub-ss (1A), (1B) above). FA 1990 ss 110, 111(1) (abolition of stamp duty reserve tax with effect from an appointed day).

Amendments—[1] Sub-s (4A) inserted by FA 1987 Sch 7 paras 1, 7 and deemed always to have had effect.

[2] Words in sub-s (2) substituted by FA 1989 s 179(1) (*f*).

[3] Words in sub-s (2) substituted by FA 1989 s 180(5), (7) and deemed always to have had effect.

[4] Sub-ss (4), (5) repealed by FA 1989 Sch 17 Pt X with effect from 18 August 1989 by virtue of FA 1989 s 178(1) (Appointed Day No 1) Order, SI 1989/1298.

[5] Words in sub-s (1) substituted by FA 1996 s 188(4), (5), with effect in relation to an agreement to transfer securities if the agreement is conditional and the condition is satisfied on or after 1 July 1996 or the agreement is not conditional and is made on or after that date.

[6] Words in sub-s (1) substituted by FA 1996 s 192(3), (6), with effect in relation to an agreement to transfer securities if the agreement is conditional and the condition is satisfied on or after 1 July 1996 or the agreement is not conditional and is made on or after that date.

[7] Sub-ss (1A), (1B) inserted (but see fn 9 below) and sub-s (6) added by FA 1996 s 192(4), (5), (6), with effect in relation to an agreement to transfer securities if the agreement is conditional and the condition is satisfied on or after 1 July 1996 or the agreement is not conditional and is made on or after that date.

[8] Sub-s (7) inserted by FA 1997 s 106(8), (9) in relation to an agreement to transfer securities if the agreement is conditional and the conditions satisfied on or after 4 January 1997 or the agreement is not conditional and is made on or after that date.

[9] Sub-s (1B) substituted by the Stamp Duty and Stamp Duty Land Tax (Consequential Amendment of Enactments) Regulations, SI 2003/2868, regs 3, 4 with effect from 1 December 2003. Sub-s (1B) (as inserted by FA 1996) previously read as follows?

"(1B) The second condition is that the instrument (or each instrument) transferring the chargeable securities to which the agreement relates is duly stamped in accordance with the enactments relating to stamp duty if it is an instrument which, under those enactments, is chargeable with stamp duty or otherwise required to be stamped.".

10 Sub-ss (1C), (1D) inserted, and words in sub-s (2) inserted, by FA 2003 s 195, Sch 40 para 4 with effect for any acquisition of shares by a company on or after 1 December 2003 (by virtue of SI 2003/3077).

11 In sub-s (1D)(*a*), references substituted for references "169(1) or (1B)" and "1985", by the Companies Act 2006 (Consequential Amendments) (Taxes and National Insurance) Order, SI 2009/1890 art 7(*e*) with effect from 1 October 2009.

Other charges

93 Depositary receipts

(1) Subject to subsection (7) below and section 95 below, there shall be a charge to stamp duty reserve tax under this section where in pursuance of an arrangement—

(*a*) a person falling within subsection (2) below has issued or is to issue a depositary receipt for chargeable securities, and

(*b*) chargeable securities of the same kind and amount are transferred or issued to [the person mentioned in paragraph (*a*) above or][1] a person falling within subsection (3) below, or are appropriated by [the person mentioned in paragraph (*a*) above or a person falling within subsection (3) below][2] towards the eventual satisfaction of the entitlement of the receipt's holder to receive chargeable securities.

(2) A person falls within this subsection if his business is or includes issuing depositary receipts for chargeable securities.

(3) A person falls within this subsection if his business is or includes holding chargeable securities as nominee or agent for the person who has issued or is to issue the depositary receipt.

(4) Subject to subsections [(6) and][6](7) below, tax under this section shall be charged at the rate of [1.5 per cent][3] of the following—

(*a*) in a case where the securities are issued, their price when issued;

(*b*) in a case where the securities are transferred for consideration in money or money's worth, the amount or value of the consideration;

(*c*) in any other case, the value of the securities.

(5) . . .[5]

(6) In a case where—

(*a*) securities are issued, or securities sold are transferred, and (in either case) they are to be paid for in instalments,

(*b*) the person to whom they are issued or transferred holds them and transfers them to another person when the last instalment is paid,

(*c*) subsection (4) (*c*) above applies in the case of the transfer to the other person,

(*d*) before the making of the transfer to the other person an instrument is received by a person falling within [subsection (2) or (3)][2] above,

(*e*) the instrument so received evidences all the rights which (by virtue of the terms under which the securities are issued or sold as mentioned in paragraph (*a*) above) subsist in respect of them at the time of the receipt, and

(*f*) the transfer to the other person is effected by an instrument containing a statement that paragraphs (*a*), (*b*) and (*e*) above are fulfilled,

subsection (4)(c) above shall have effect as if the reference to the value there mentioned were to an amount (if any) equal to the total of the instalments payable, less those paid before the transfer to the other person is effected.

(7) Where tax is (or would apart from this subsection be) charged under this section in respect of a transfer of securities, and *ad valorem* stamp duty is chargeable on any instrument effecting the transfer, then—

(*a*) if the amount of the duty is less than the amount of tax found by virtue of [subsections (4) and][7] (6) above, the tax charged under this section shall be the amount so found less the amount of the duty;

(*b*) in any other case, there shall be no charge to tax under this section in respect of the transfer.

(8) Where tax is charged under the preceding provisions of this section, the person liable for the tax shall (subject to subsection (9) below) be the person who has issued or is to issue the depositary receipt.

(9) Where tax is charged under the preceding provisions of this section in a case where securities are transferred, and at the time of the transfer the person who has issued or is to issue the depositary receipt is not resident in the United Kingdom and has no branch or agency in the United Kingdom, the person liable for the tax shall be the person to whom the securities are transferred.

(10) Where chargeable securities are issued or transferred on sale under terms providing for payment in instalments and for an issue of other chargeable securities, and (apart from this subsection) tax would be charged under this section in respect of that issue, tax shall not be so charged but—

(*a*) if any of the instalments becomes payable by a person falling within subsection (2) or (3) above, there shall be a charge to stamp duty reserve tax under this section when the instalment becomes payable;

(*b*) the charge shall be at the rate of [1.5 per cent of the amount][4] of the instalment payable;
(*c*) the person liable to pay the instalment shall be liable for the tax.

(11) Subject to subsection (12) below, this section applies where securities are transferred, issued or appropriated after 18th March 1986 (whenever the arrangement was made).

(12) This section does not apply, in the case of securities which are transferred, if the Board are satisfied that they were acquired or appropriated by the transferor on or before 18th March 1986 for or towards the eventual satisfaction of the entitlement of a person to receive securities of the same kind under a depositary receipt (whether issued on or before that date or to be issued after that date).

Cross references—See FA 1984 s 126(3)(*d*) (no stamp duty reserve tax chargeable under this section in respect of issue of securities by designated international organisations);

FA 1990 ss 110(1), (3), (5), 111(1) (abolition of stamp duty reserve tax with effect from an appointed day),

FA 1990 ss 110(7), 111(1) (abolition of stamp duty reserve tax not to have effect where before the appointed day securities are issued or transferred on sale under terms mentioned in sub-s (10) above).

FA 2009 Sch 56 (penalty for failure to make payments on time).

Amendments—[1] Words in sub-s (1)(*b*) inserted by FA 1996 s 193(1), (2)(*a*), (4), with effect (i) in relation to the charge to tax under sub-s (1) of this section, where securities are transferred, issued or appropriated after 30 June 1996 (whenever the arrangement was made), and (ii) in relation to the charge to tax under sub-s (10) of this section, in relation to instalments payable after 30 June 1996.

[2] Words in sub-ss (1)(*b*) and (6) substituted by FA 1996 s 193(1), (2)(*b*), (3), (4), with effect (i) in relation to the charge to tax under sub-s (1) of this section, where securities are transferred, issued or appropriated after 30 June 1996 (whenever the arrangement was made), and (ii) in relation to the charge to tax under sub-s (10) of this section, in relation to instalments payable after 30 June 1996.

[3] Words in sub-ss (4) and (5) substituted by FA 1996 s 194(2)(*a*), (*b*), (7)(*b*), with effect, in relation to the charge to tax under sub-s (1) of this section, where securities are transferred, issued or appropriated after 30 June 1996 (whenever the arrangement was made).

[4] Words in sub-s (10) substituted by FA 1996 s 194(2)(*c*), (7)(*c*), with effect, in relation to the charge to tax under sub-s (10) of this section, in relation to instalments payable after 30 June 1996.

[5] Sub-s (5) repealed by FA 1997 s 104(1), Sch 18 Pt VII where securities are transferred on or after 20 October 1997 (the day appointed for the purposes of FA 1997 s 102 by virtue of SI 1997/2428) unless the securities were acquired by the transferor before that date. Previously the text read:

"(5) In a case where the securities are transferred and—
(*a*) the transfer is effected by an instrument on which stamp duty under the heading 'Conveyance or Transfer of any kind not hereinbefore described' in Schedule 1 to the Stamp Act 1891 is chargeable,
(*b*) at the time of the transfer the transferor is a qualified dealer in securities of the kind concerned or a nominee of such a qualified dealer,
(*c*) the transfer is made for the purposes of the dealer's business,
(*d*) at the time of the transfer the dealer is not a market maker in securities of the kind concerned, and
(*e*) the instrument contains a statement that paragraphs (*b*) to (*d*) above are fulfilled,
subsection (4) above shall have effect [as if '1.5 per cent' read '1 per cent'."

[6] Words in sub-s(4) substituted for "(5) to" by FA 1997 s 104(2) with effect as in note 5 above.

[7] Words in sub-s (7) substituted for "subsections (4) to" by FA 1997 s 104(2) with effect as in note 5 above.

94 Depositary receipts: supplementary

(1) For the purposes of section 93 above a depositary receipt for chargeable securities is an instrument acknowledging—
(*a*) that a person holds chargeable securities or evidence of the right to receive them, and
(*b*) that another person is entitled to rights, whether expressed as units or otherwise, in or in relation to chargeable securities of the same kind, including the right to receive such securities (or evidence of the right to receive them) from the person mentioned in paragraph (*a*) above,

except that for those purposes a depositary receipt for chargeable securities does not include an instrument acknowledging rights in or in relation to securities if they are issued or sold under terms providing for payment in instalments and for the issue of the instrument as evidence that an instalment has been paid.

(2) The Treasury may by regulations provide that for subsection (1) above (as it has effect for the time being) there shall be substituted a subsection containing a different definition of a depositary receipt for the purposes of section 93 above.

(3) For the purposes of section 93(4) (*b*) above the value of any consideration not consisting of money shall be taken to be the price it might reasonably be expected to fetch on a sale in the open market at the time the securities are transferred.

(4) For the purposes of section 93(4) (*c*) above the value of the securities shall be taken to be the price they might reasonably be expected to fetch on a sale in the open market at the time they are transferred or appropriated (as the case may be).

(5)–(7) . . .[2]

(8) . . .[1]

(9) The power to make regulations or an order under this section shall be exercisable by statutory instrument subject to annulment in pursuance of a resolution of the House of Commons.

Cross references—See FA 1990 ss 110, 111(1) (abolition of stamp duty reserve tax with effect from an appointed day).

Amendments—[1] Sub-s (8) repealed by FA 1996 s 194(3), (7)(*b*), Sch 41 Pt VII, with effect, in relation to the charge to tax under s 93(1) of this Act, where securities are transferred, issued or appropriated after 30 June 1996 (whenever the arrangement was made).

[2] Sub-ss (5)–(7) repealed by FA 1997 s 104(2), Sch 18 Pt VII where securities are transferred on or after 20 October 1997 (the day appointed for the purposes of FA 1997 s 102 by virtue of SI 1997/2428) unless the securities were acquired by the transferor before that date. Previously the text read:

"(5) For the purposes of section 93(5) above a person is a qualified dealer in securities of a particular kind if he deals in securities of that kind and—

(*a*) is a member of a recognised stock exchange (within the meaning given by section 841 of the Taxes Act 1988), or

(*b*) is designated a qualified dealer by order made by the Treasury.

(6) For the purposes of section 93(5) above a person is a market maker in securities of a particular kind if he—

(a) holds himself out at all normal times in compliance with the rules of The Stock Exchange as willing to buy and sell securities of that kind at a price specified by him, and

(b) is recognised as doing so by the Council of The Stock Exchange.

(7) The Treasury may by regulations provide that for subsection (6) above (as it has effect for the time being) there shall be substituted a subsection containing a different definition of a market maker for the purposes of section 93 (5) above."

95 Depositary receipts: exceptions

(1) Where securities are transferred—

(*a*) to a company which at the time of the transfer falls within subsection (6) of section 67 above *and is resident in the United Kingdom*[5], and

(*b*) from a company which at that time falls within that subsection *and is so resident*[5],

[subject to section 97C,][6] there shall be no charge to tax under section 93 above in respect of the transfer.

[(2) There shall be no charge to tax under section 93 above in respect of a transfer, issue or appropriation of a UK bearer instrument, except in the case of—

(*a*) an instrument within the exemption conferred by paragraph 16 of Schedule 15 to the Finance Act 1999 (renounceable letters of allotment etc where rights are renounceable not later than six months after issue), or

(*b*) an instrument within the exemption conferred by paragraph 17 of that Schedule (non-sterling instruments) which—

(i) does not raise new capital, and

(ii) is not issued in exchange for an instrument raising new capital.][2]

[(2A) For the purpose of subsection (2)(*b*)—

(*a*) an instrument is regarded as raising new capital only if the condition in subsection (2B) is met, and

(*b*) an instrument is regarded as issued in exchange for an instrument raising new capital only if the conditions in subsection (2C) are met.

(2B) The condition mentioned in subsection (2A)(*a*) is that the instrument—

(*a*) is issued in conjunction with—

(i) the issue of relevant securities for which only cash is subscribed, or

(ii) the granting of rights to subscribe for relevant securities which are granted for a cash consideration only and exercisable only by means of a cash subscription; or

(*b*) is issued to give effect to the exercise of such rights as are mentioned in paragraph (*a*)(ii).

(2C) The conditions mentioned in subsection (2A)(*b*) are that—

(*a*) the instrument is issued in conjunction with the issue of relevant securities by a company in exchange for relevant securities issued by another company, and

(*b*) immediately before the exchange an instrument relating to those other securities—

(i) was regarded for the purposes of subsection (2)(*b*) as raising new capital or as issued in exchange for an instrument raising new capital, or

(ii) would have been so regarded if the amendments made to this section by section 117 of the Finance Act 1999 had been in force at the time of its issue,

and accordingly was or would have been within the exception conferred by subsection (2).

(2D) For the purposes of subsections (2B) and (2C) 'relevant securities' means chargeable securities which are either—

(*a*) shares the holders of which have a right to a dividend at a fixed rate but have no other right to share in the profits of the company, or

(*b*) loan capital within the meaning of section 78 above,

and which, in either case, do not carry any rights (of conversion or otherwise) by the exercise of which chargeable securities other than relevant securities may be obtained.][3]

(3) There shall be no charge to tax under section 93 above in respect of an issue by a company (company X) of securities in exchange for shares in another company (company Y) where company X—

(*a*) has control of company Y, or

(*b*) will have such control in consequence of the exchange or of an offer as a result of which the exchange is made

[and the shares in company Y are held under a depositary receipt scheme][1].

(4) For the purposes of subsection (3) above company X has control of company Y if company X has power to control company Y's affairs by virtue of holding shares in, or possessing voting power in relation to, company Y or any other body corporate.

[(5) For the purposes of subsection (3) above, the cases where shares are held under a depositary receipt scheme are those cases where, in pursuance of an arrangement,—

(*a*) a depositary receipt for chargeable securities has been, or is to be, issued by a person falling within section 93(2) above in respect of the shares in question or shares of the same kind and amount; and

(*b*) the shares in question are held by that person, or by a person whose business is or includes holding chargeable securities as nominee or agent for that person, towards the eventual satisfaction of the entitlement of the receipt's holder to receive chargeable securities.

[(6) Where an arrangement is entered into under which—

(*a*) a company issues securities to persons in respect of their holdings of securities issued by another company, and

(*b*) the securities issued by the other company are cancelled,

the issue shall be treated for the purposes of this section as an issue of securities in exchange for securities issued by the other company.][4]

(7) In this section "depositary receipt for chargeable securities" has the same meaning as in section 93 above (see section 94 above).][1]

Cross references—See FA 1990 ss 110, 111(1) (abolition of stamp duty reserve tax with effect from an appointed day).

Amendments—[1] Words in sub-s (3), and sub-ss (5), (6) and (7) inserted by FA 1998 s 151 with effect where the issue by company X referred to in FA 1986 ss 95(3), (6), 97(4) or (7) is an issue on or after 1 May 1998.

[2] Sub-s (2) substituted by FA 1999 s 113(3), Sch 16 para 7 with effect in relation to bearer instruments issued after 30 September 1999. For prospective repeal of FA 1999 s 113, Sch 16 para 7, ss 116 and 117 see FA 1999 s 123(3). FA 1999 s 116 provides transitional arrangements for bearer instruments issued between 30 January 1999 and 8 March 1999; the text of sub-s (2) should read:

"(2) There shall be no charge to tax under section 93 above in respect of a transfer, issue or appropriation of an inland bearer instrument, within the meaning of the heading 'Bearer Instrument' in Schedule 1 to the Stamp Act 1891, except in the case of—

(*a*) an instrument within exemption 3 in that heading (renounceable letters of allotment etc where rights are renounceable not later than six months after issue); or

(*b*) an instrument within the stamp duty exemption for non-sterling instruments which is issued in connection with a company merger or takeover (whether or not involving the company issuing the instrument).

In paragraph (*b*) 'the stamp duty exemption for non-sterling instruments' means the exemption from stamp duty provided for by section 30 of the Finance Act 1967 or section 7 of the Finance Act (Northern Ireland) 1967."

FA 1999 s 117 provides transitional arrangements for bearer instruments issued between 9 March 1999 and 30 September 1999; the text of sub-s (2) should read:

"(2) There shall be no charge to tax under section 93 above in respect of a transfer, issue or appropriation of an inland bearer instrument, within the meaning of the heading 'Bearer Instrument' in Schedule 1 to the Stamp Act 1891, except in the case of—

(*a*) an instrument within exemption 3 in that heading (renounceable letters of allotment etc where rights are renounceable not later than six months after issue); or

(*b*) an instrument within the stamp duty exemption for non-sterling instruments which—

(i) does not raise new capital, and

(ii) is not issued in exchange for an instrument raising new capital.

In paragraph (*b*) 'the stamp duty exemption for non-sterling instruments' means the exemption from stamp duty provided for by section 30 of the Finance Act 1967 or section 7 of the Finance Act (Northern Ireland) 1967."

[3] Sub-ss (2A), (2B), (2C), (2D) inserted by FA 1999 s 117(2) with effect in relation to any bearer instrument issued after 8 March 1999, except one giving effect to an agreement for a company merger or takeover entered into in writing by the companies involved before 30 January 1999.

[4] Sub-s (6) substituted by FA 1999 s 117(3) with effect in relation to any bearer instrument issued after 8 March 1999, except one giving effect to an agreement for a company merger or takeover entered into in writing by the companies involved before 30 January 1999.

[5] Words in sub-s (1) repealed by FA 2000 s 134(3), (5), Sch 40 Pt III with effect for stamp duty purposes for instruments executed after 28 July 2000 and for stamp duty reserve tax purposes for securities transferred after 28 July 2000.

[6] In sub-s (1), words inserted by FA 2010 s 54(1), (2) with effect in relation to transfers of chargeable securities on or after 1 October 2009 (FA 2010 s 54(6)).

[95A Depositary receipts: exception for replacement securities][1]

[(1) There shall be no charge to tax under section 93 above in respect of the transfer, issue or appropriation of chargeable securities ("the new securities") issued by a company in place of existing securities of the same company ("the old securities") if the following conditions are met.

(2) The first condition is that the old securities are held under a depositary receipt scheme.

(3) The second condition is that—

(*a*) there was a charge to tax under section 93 above in respect of the transfer, issue or appropriation—

(i) of the old securities, or

(ii) of earlier securities in relation to which on a previous application of this section those securities were the new securities,

or there would have been such a charge if that section had been in force; or

(*b*) there would have been such a charge but for section 95(2) or (3) above.

(4) The third condition is that there is an arrangement under which—

(*a*) the new securities are transferred, issued or appropriated as mentioned in section 93(1)(*b*), and

(*b*) the old securities are cancelled.

(5) For the purposes of subsection (2) above the cases in which securities are held under a depositary receipt scheme are those specified (in relation to shares) in section 95(5) above.

(6) The exception provided by this section applies only to the extent that the value of the new securities immediately after their issue does not exceed the value of the old securities immediately before the issue of the new securities.][1]

Amendments—[1] This section inserted by FA 1999 s 118(1) with effect in relation to securities issued from 1 May 1998. For prospective repeal of FA 1999 s 118 see FA 1999 s 123(3).

96 Clearance services

(1) Subject to subsection (5) below and [sections 97 and 97A][1] below, there shall be a charge to stamp duty reserve tax under this section where—

(*a*) a person (A) whose business is or includes the provision of clearance services for the purchase and sale of chargeable securities has entered into an arrangement to provide such clearance services for another person, and

(*b*) in pursuance of the arrangement, chargeable securities are transferred or issued to A or to a person whose business is or includes holding chargeable securities as nominee for A.

(2) Subject to subsections [(4) and][6] (5) below, tax under this section shall be charged at the rate of [1.5 per cent][2] of the following—

(*a*) in a case where the securities are issued, their price when issued;

(*b*) in a case where the securities are transferred for consideration in money or money's worth, the amount or value of the consideration;

(*c*) in any other case, the value of the securities.

(3) . . . [5]

(4) In a case where—

(*a*) securities are issued, or securities sold are transferred, and (in either case) they are to be paid for in instalments,

(*b*) the person to whom they are issued or transferred holds them and transfers them to another person when the last instalment is paid,

(*c*) subsection (2) (*c*) above applies in the case of the transfer to the other person,

(*d*) before the making of the transfer to the other person an instrument is received by A or a person whose business is or includes holding chargeable securities as nominee for A,

(*e*) the instrument so received evidences all the rights which (by virtue of the terms under which the securities are issued or sold as mentioned in paragraph (*a*) above) subsist in respect of them at the time of the receipt, and

(*f*) the transfer to the other person is effected by an instrument containing a statement that paragraphs (*a*), (*b*) and (*e*) above are fulfilled,

subsection (2) (c) above shall have effect as if the reference to the value there mentioned were to an amount (if any) equal to the total of the instalments payable, less those paid before the transfer to the other person is effected.

(5) Where tax is (or would apart from this subsection be) charged under this section in respect of a transfer of securities and *ad valorem* stamp duty is chargeable on any instrument effecting the transfer, then—

(*a*) if the amount of the duty is less than the amount of tax found by virtue of [subsections (2) and][7] (4) above, the tax charged under this section shall be the amount so found less the amount of the duty;

(*b*) in any other case, there shall be no charge to tax under this section in respect of the transfer.

(6) Where tax is charged under the preceding provisions of this section, the person liable for the tax shall (subject to subsection (7) below) be A.

(7) Where tax is charged under the preceding provisions of this section in a case where securities are transferred to a person other than A, and at the time of the transfer A is not resident in the United Kingdom and has no branch or agency in the United Kingdom, the person liable for the tax shall be the person to whom the securities are transferred.

(8) Where chargeable securities are issued or transferred on sale under terms providing for payment in instalments and for an issue of other chargeable securities, and (apart from this subsection) tax would be charged under this section in respect of that issue, tax shall not be so charged but—

(*a*) if any of the instalments becomes payable by A or by a person whose business is or includes holding chargeable securities as nominee for A, there shall be a charge to stamp duty reserve tax under this section when the instalment becomes payable;

(*b*) the charge shall be at the rate of [1.5 per cent of the amount][3] of the instalment payable;

(*c*) the person liable to pay the instalment shall be liable for the tax.

(9) For the purposes of subsection (2) (*b*) above the value of any consideration not consisting of money shall be taken to be the price it might reasonably be expected to fetch on a sale in the open market at the time the securities are transferred.

(10) For the purposes of subsection (2) (*c*) above the value of securities shall be taken to be the price they might reasonably be expected to fetch on a sale in the open market at the time they are transferred.

(11) . . . [5]

(12) . . . [4]

(13) Subject to subsection (14) below, this section applies where securities are transferred or issued after 18th March 1986 (whenever the arrangement was made).

(14) This section does not apply, in the case of securities which are transferred, if the Board are satisfied—

(*a*) that on or before 18th March 1986 the transferor (or, where the transferor transfers as agent, the principal) agreed to sell securities of the same kind and amount to the person (other than A) referred to in subsection (1) (*a*) above, and

(*b*) that the transfer is effected in pursuance of that agreement.

Cross references—See FA 1984 s 126(3)(*d*) (no stamp duty reserve tax chargeable under this section in respect of issue of securities by designated international organisations);

FA 1986 s 97A(3), (4) (disapplication of this section where an election is made under s 97A(1)).

FA 1986 s 97A(11) (deemed transfer of securities within sub-s (1) above where an election for an alternative system of charge in respect of clearance services is terminated).

FA 1990 ss 110(1), (4), (6), 111(1) (abolition of stamp duty reserve tax with effect from an appointed day),

FA 1990 ss 110(8), 111(1) (abolition of stamp duty reserve tax not to have effect where before the appointed day securities are issued or transferred on sale under terms mentioned in sub-s (8) above).

FA 2009 Sch 56 (penalty for failure to make payments on time).

Simon's Tax Cases—*HSBC Holdings plc and another v R&C Comrs* [2010] STC 58.

Amendments—[1] Words in sub-s (1) substituted by FA 1996 s 196(2), (6), with effect from 1 July 1996.

[2] Words in sub-ss (2), (3) substituted by FA 1996 s 194(4)(*a*), (*b*), (7)(*d*), with effect, in relation to the charge to tax under sub-s (1) of this section, where securities are transferred or issued after 30 June 1996 (whenever the arrangement was made).

[3] Words in sub-s (8) substituted by FA 1996 s 194(4)(*c*), (7)(*e*), with effect, in relation to the charge of tax under sub-s (8) of this section, in relation to instalments payable after 30 June 1996.

[4] Sub-s (12) repealed by FA 1996 ss 194(5), (7)(*d*), Sch 41 Pt VII, with effect, in relation to the charge to tax under sub-s (1) of this section, where securities are transferred or issued after 30 June 1996 (whenever the arrangement was made).

[5] Sub-ss (3) and (11) repealed by FA 1997 s 104(3)(4), Sch 18 Pt VII where securities are transferred on or after 20 October 1997 (the day appointed for the purposes of FA 1997 s 102 by virtue of SI 1997/2428) unless the securities were acquired by the transferor before that date. Previously the text read as follows—

"(3) In a case where the securities are transferred and—

(*a*) the transfer is effected by an instrument on which stamp duty under the heading 'Conveyance or Transfer of any kind not hereinbefore described' in Schedule 1 to the Stamp Act 1891 is chargeable,

(*b*) at the time of the transfer the transferor is a qualified dealer in securities of the kind concerned or a nominee of such a qualified dealer,

(*c*) the transfer is made for the purposes of the dealer's business,

(*d*) at the time of the transfer the dealer is not a market maker in securities of the kind concerned, and

(*e*) the instrument contains a statement that paragraphs (*b*) to (*d*) above are fulfilled,

subsection (2) above shall have effect [as if '1.5 per cent' read '1 per cent'."

"(11) For the purposes of subsection (3) above 'qualified dealer' and 'market maker' have at any particular time the same meanings as they have at that time for the purposes of section 93(5) above."

[6] Words in sub-s (2) substituted for the words "(3) to" by FA 1997, s 104(4) with effect as in note 5 above.

[7] Words in sub-s (5)(*a*) substituted for the words "subsections (2) to" by FA 1997, s 104(4) with effect as in note 5 above.

97 Clearance services: exceptions

(1) Where securities are transferred—

(*a*) to a company which at the time of the transfer falls within subsection (6) of section 70 above *and is resident in the United Kingdom*[6], and

(*b*) from a company which at that time falls within that subsection *and is so resident*[6],

[subject to section 97C,][7] there shall be no charge to tax under section 96 above in respect of the transfer.

(2) . . . [1]

[(3) There shall be no charge to tax under section 96 above in respect of a transfer or issue of a UK bearer instrument, except in the case of—

(*a*) an instrument within the exemption conferred by paragraph 16 of Schedule 15 to the Finance Act 1999 (renounceable letters of allotment etc. where rights are renounceable not later than six months after issue), or

(*b*) an instrument within the exemption conferred by paragraph 17 of that Schedule (non-sterling instruments) which—

(i) does not raise new capital, and

(ii) is not issued in exchange for an instrument raising new capital.][3]

[(3A) For the purpose of subsection (3)(*b*)—

(*a*) an instrument is regarded as raising new capital only if the condition in subsection (3B) is met, and

(*b*) an instrument is regarded as issued in exchange for an instrument raising new capital only if the conditions in subsection (3C) are met.

(3B) The condition mentioned in subsection (3A)(*a*) is that the instrument—

(*a*) is issued in conjunction with—

(i) the issue of relevant securities for which only cash is subscribed, or

(ii) the granting of rights to subscribe for relevant securities which are granted for a cash consideration only and exercisable only by means of a cash subscription; or

(*b*) is issued to give effect to the exercise of such rights as are mentioned in paragraph (*a*)(ii).

(3C) The conditions mentioned in subsection (3A)(*b*) are that—

(*a*) the instrument is issued in conjunction with the issue of relevant securities by a company in exchange for relevant securities issued by another company, and

(*b*) immediately before the exchange an instrument relating to those other securities—

(i) was regarded for the purposes of subsection (3)(*b*) as raising new capital or as issued in exchange for an instrument raising new capital, or

(ii) would have been so regarded if the amendments made to this section by section 117 of the Finance Act 1999 had been in force at the time of its issue,

and accordingly was or would have been within the exception conferred by subsection (3).

(3D) For the purposes of subsections (3B) and (3C) 'relevant securities' means chargeable securities which are either—

(*a*) shares the holders of which have a right to a dividend at a fixed rate but have no other right to share in the profits of the company, or

(*b*) loan capital within the meaning of section 78 above,

and which, in either case, do not carry any rights (of conversion or otherwise) by the exercise of which chargeable securities other than relevant securities may be obtained.][4]

(4) There shall be no charge to tax under section 96 above in respect of an issue by a company (company X) of securities in exchange for shares in another company (company Y) where company X—

(*a*) has control of company Y, or

(*b*) will have such control in consequence of the exchange or of an offer as a result of which the exchange is made

[and the shares in company Y are held under a clearance services scheme.][2]

(5) For the purposes of subsection (4) above company X has control of company Y if company X has power to control company Y's affairs by virtue of holding shares in, or possessing voting power in relation to, company Y or any other body corporate.

[(6) For the purposes of subsection (4) above, the cases where shares are held under a clearance services scheme are those cases where—

(*a*) an arrangement falling within paragraph (*a*) of subsection (1) of section 96 above has been entered into; and

(*b*) in pursuance of that arrangement, the shares are held by the person referred to in that paragraph as A or by a person whose business is or includes holding chargeable securities as nominee for that person.][2]

[(7) Where an arrangement is entered into under which—

(*a*) a company issues securities to persons in respect of their holdings of securities issued by another company, and

(*b*) the securities issued by the other company are cancelled,

the issue shall be treated for the purposes of this section as an issue of securities in exchange for securities issued by the other company.][5]

Cross references—See FA 1990 ss 110, 111(1) (abolition of stamp duty reserve tax with effect from an appointed day).

Amendments—[1] Sub-s (2) repealed by FA 1996 s 196(4), Sch 41 Pt VII, with effect in relation to any transfer effected after 30 June 1996.

[2] Words in sub-s (4), and sub-s (6) inserted by FA 1998 s 151 with effect where the issue by company X referred to in FA 1986 ss 95(3), (6), 97(4) or (7) is an issue on or after 1 May 1998.

3 Sub-s (3) substituted by FA 1999 s 113(3), Sch 16 para 8 with effect in relation to bearer instruments issued after 30 September 1999. For prospective repeal of FA 1999 s 113, Sch 16 para 8, ss 105 and 106 see FA 1999 s 123(3). FA 1999 s 116 provides transitional arrangements for bearer instruments issued between 30 January 1999 and 8 March 1999; the text of sub-s (3) should read:

"(3) There shall be no charge to tax under section 96 above in respect of a transfer or issue of an inland bearer instrument, within the meaning of the heading "Bearer Instrument" in Schedule 1 to the Stamp Act 1891, except in the case of—

(*a*) an instrument within exemption 3 in that heading (renounceable letters of allotment etc where rights are renounceable not later than six months after issue); or

(*b*) an instrument within the stamp duty exemption for non-sterling instruments which is issued in connection with a company merger or takeover (whether or not involving the company issuing the instrument).

In paragraph (*b*) 'the stamp duty exemption for non-sterling instruments' means the exemption from stamp duty provided for by section 30 of the Finance Act 1967 or section 7 of the Finance Act (Northern Ireland) 1967."

FA 1999 s 117 provides transitional arrangements for bearer instruments issued between 9 March 1999 and 30 September 1999; the text of sub-s (3) should read:

"(3) There shall be no charge to tax under section 96 above in respect of a transfer or issue of an inland bearer instrument, within the meaning of the heading "Bearer Instrument" in Schedule 1 to the Stamp Act 1891, except in the case of—

(*a*) an instrument within exemption 3 in that heading (renounceable letters of allotment etc. where rights are renounceable not later than six months after issue); or

(*b*) an instrument within the stamp duty exemption for non-sterling instruments which —

(i) does not raise new capital, and

(ii) is not issued in exchange for an instrument raising new capital.

In paragraph (*b*) 'the stamp duty exemption for non-sterling instruments' means the exemption from stamp duty provided for by section 30 of the Finance Act 1967 or section 7 of the Finance Act (Northern Ireland) 1967."

4 Sub-ss (3A), (3B), (3C), (3D) inserted by FA 1999 s 117(5) with effect in relation to any bearer instrument issued after 8 March 1999, except one giving effect to an agreement for a company merger or takeover entered into in writing by the companies involved before 30 January 1999.

5 Sub-s (7) substituted by FA 1999 s 117(6) with effect in relation to any bearer instrument issued after 8 March 1999, except one giving effect to an agreement for a company merger or takeover entered into in writing by the companies involved before 30 January 1999.

6 Words in sub-s (1) repealed by FA 2000 s 134(3), (5), Sch 40 Pt III with effect for stamp duty purposes for instruments executed after 28 July 2000 and for stamp duty reserve tax purposes for securities transferred after 28 July 2000.

7 In sub-s (1), words inserted by FA 2010 s 54(1), (3) with effect in relation to transfers of chargeable securities on or after 1 October 2009 (FA 2010 s 54(6)).

[97AA Clearance services: further exception][1]

[(1) There shall be no charge to tax under section 96 above in respect of the transfer or issue of chargeable securities ("the new securities") issued by a company in place of existing securities of the same company ("the old securities") if the following conditions are met.

(2) The first condition is that the old securities are held under a clearance services scheme.

(3) The second condition is that—

(*a*) there was a charge to tax under section 96 above in respect of the transfer or issue—

(i) of the old securities, or

(ii) of earlier securities in relation to which on a previous application of this section those securities were the new securities,

or there would have been such a charge if that section had been in force; or

(*b*) there would have been such a charge but for section 97(3) or (4) above.

(4) The third condition is that there is an arrangement under which—

(*a*) the new securities are transferred or issued as mentioned in section 96(1)(*b*), and

(*b*) the old securities are cancelled.

(5) For the purposes of subsection (2) above the cases in which securities are held under a clearance services scheme are those specified (in relation to shares) in section 97(6) above.

(6) The exception provided by this section applies only to the extent that the value of the new securities immediately after their issue does not exceed the value of the old securities immediately before the issue of the new securities.][1]

Amendments—[1] This section inserted by FA 1999 s 118(3) with effect in relation to securities issued from 1 May 1998. For prospective repeal of FA 1999 s 118 see FA 1999 s 123(3).

[97A Clearance services: election for alternative system of charge

(1) A person whose business is or includes the provision of clearance services for the purchase and sale of chargeable securities or relevant securities (an "operator") may, with the approval of the Board, elect that stamp duty and stamp duty reserve tax shall be chargeable in accordance with this section in connection with those clearance services.

(2) An election under subsection (1) above—

(*a*) shall come into force on such date as may be notified to the operator by the Board in giving their approval; and (*b*) shall continue in force unless and until it is terminated in accordance with the following provisions of this section.

(3) If and so long as an election under subsection (1) above is in force, stamp duty or stamp duty reserve tax (as the case may require) shall, in connection with the clearance services to which the election relates, be chargeable in relation to—

(*a*) a transfer or issue falling within section 70(1) or 96(1) above,

(*b*) an agreement falling within section 90(4) above by virtue of section 96(1) above, or

(*c*) an agreement falling within section 90(5) above,

as it would be chargeable apart from sections 70, 90(4) and (5) and 96 above.

(4) Where stamp duty or stamp duty reserve tax is chargeable by virtue of subsection (3) above in relation to a transfer, issue or agreement, sections 70, 90(4) and (5) and 96 above shall not have effect in relation to that transfer, issue or agreement.

(5) Nothing in subsection (3) or (4) above affects the application of section 70 or 96 above in relation to a transfer falling within section 70(1) or 96(1) above by the operator or his nominee to, or to a nominee of, another operator in relation to whom no election under subsection (1) above is for the time being in force.

(6) The Board may require the operator, as a condition of the approval of his election under subsection (1) above, to make and maintain such arrangements as they may consider satisfactory—

(*a*) for the collection of stamp duty reserve tax chargeable in accordance with this section, and

(*b*) for complying, or securing compliance, with the provisions of this Part and of regulations under section 98 below, so far as relating to such tax.

(7) Where the operator is not resident in the United Kingdom and has no branch or agency in the United Kingdom, the Board may require him, as a condition of the approval of his election under subsection (1) above, to appoint and, so long as the election remains in force, maintain a tax representative.

(8) A person shall not be an operator's tax representative under this section unless that person—

(*a*) has a business establishment in the United Kingdom, and

(*b*) is approved by the Board.

(9) A person who is at any time an operator's tax representative under this section—

(*a*) shall be entitled to act on the operator's behalf for the purposes of stamp duty and stamp duty reserve tax in connection with the clearance services to which the operator's election under subsection (1) above relates,

(*b*) shall secure (where appropriate by acting on the operator's behalf) the operator's compliance with and discharge of the obligations and liabilities to which the operator is subject, in connection with the clearance services to which the operator's election under subsection (1) above relates, by virtue of legislation relating to stamp duty or stamp duty reserve tax (including obligations and liabilities arising before he became the operator's tax representative), and

(*c*) shall be personally liable in respect of any failure to secure the operator's compliance with or discharge of any such obligation or liability, and in respect of anything done for purposes connected with acting on the operator's behalf,

as if the obligations and liabilities imposed on the operator were imposed jointly and severally on the tax representative and the operator.

(10) An election under subsection (1) above may be terminated—

(*a*) by not less than thirty days' notice given by the operator to the Board or by the Board to the operator; or

(*b*) if there is or has been a breach of a condition of the approval of the election imposed by virtue of subsection (6) or (7) above, by a notice—

(i) given by the Board to the operator,

(ii) taking effect on the giving of the notice or at such later time as may be specified in the notice, and

(iii) stating that it is given by reason of the breach of condition.

(11) Where an election under subsection (1) above is terminated, section 96 above shall have effect as if chargeable securities of the same amounts and kinds as are, immediately before the termination, held by the operator or his nominee in connection with the provision of the clearance services, had, immediately after the termination, been transferred to the operator or, as the case may be, to the nominee by a transfer falling within subsection (1) of that section.

(12) In this section "relevant securities" has the same meaning as in section 70 above.][1]

[(13) Nothing in section 70(9) or 97(1) above has effect to prevent a charge to stamp duty or stamp duty reserve tax arising—

(*a*) on a transfer to which subsection (5) above applies, or

(*b*) on a deemed transfer under subsection (11) above.][2]

Cross references—See FA 1990 ss 108, 110, 111(1) (abolition of stamp duty and stamp duty reserve tax with effect from an appointed day).

Amendments—[1] This section inserted by FA 1996 s 196(3), (6), with effect from 1 July 1996.

2 Sub-s (13) inserted by FA 2000 s 134(4), (5) with effect for stamp duty purposes for instruments executed after 28 July 2000 and for stamp duty reserve tax purposes for securities transferred after 28 July 2000.

[97B Transfer between depositary receipt system and clearance system

(1) There shall be no charge to tax under section 93 or 96 above where securities are transferred between a depositary receipt system and a clearance system.

[(1A) Subsection (1) is subject to section 97C.][2]

(2) A transfer between a depositary receipt system and a clearance system means a transfer—

(*a*) from (or to) a company which at the time of the transfer falls within section 67(6) above, and

(*b*) to (or from) a company which at that time falls within section 70(6) above.

(3) This section does not apply to a transfer from a clearance system (that is, from such a company as is mentioned in subsection (2)(*b*) above) if at the time of the transfer an election is in force under section 97A above in relation to the clearance services for the purposes of which the securities are held immediately before the transfer.][1]

Amendments—[1] This section inserted by FA 2000 s 134(2), (5) with effect for stamp duty reserve tax purposes for securities transferred after 28 July 2000.

2 Sub-s (1A) inserted by FA 2010 s 54(1), (4) with effect in relation to transfers of chargeable securities on or after 1 October 2009 (FA 2010 s 54(6)).

[97C Transfers to non-EU depositary receipt and clearance services systems

(1) This section applies where arrangements are made in accordance with which chargeable securities are—

(*a*) issued to an EU system, and

(*b*) subsequently transferred from an EU system to a non-EU system.

(2) Nothing in section 95(1), 97(1) or 97B(1) disapplies a charge to tax under section 93 or 96 in respect of that transfer if—

(*a*) the chargeable securities have not previously been transferred, or

(*b*) where they have previously been transferred, the transfer (or, if more than one, each of them) was an exempt transfer.

(3) For the purposes of subsection (1)(*a*) chargeable securities are issued to an EU system if—

(*a*) pursuant to an arrangement of the kind mentioned in section 93(1), they are issued to a nominee in respect of an EU depositary receipt issuer, or

(*b*) pursuant to an arrangement of the kind mentioned in section 96(1), they are issued to a nominee in respect of an EU clearance service operator.

(4) For the purposes of subsection (1)(*b*)—

(*a*) a transfer is from an EU system if it is from a company which is incorporated under the law of a member State and at the time of the transfer falls within section 67(6) or 70(6), and

(*b*) a transfer is to a non-EU system if it is to a company which is not incorporated under the law of a member State and at the time of the transfer falls within section 67(6) or 70(6).

(5) In this section—

"arrangements" includes any agreement, understanding, scheme, transaction or series of transactions (whether or not legally enforceable);

"EU clearance service operator" means a person—

(*a*) whose business is or includes the provision of clearance services for the purchase and sale of chargeable securities, and

(*b*) who—

(i) if it is a company, is incorporated under the law of a member State, and

(ii) in any other case, is resident in a member State;

"EU depositary receipt issuer" means a person—

(*a*) whose business is or includes issuing depositary receipts for chargeable securities, and

(*b*) who—

(i) if it is a company, is incorporated under the law of a member State, and

(ii) in any other case, is resident in a member State;

"exempt transfer" means a transfer in respect of which, by reason of section 90(5), 95(1), 97(1) or 97B(1), no charge to stamp duty reserve tax arises;

"nominee"—

(*a*) in respect of an EU clearance service operator, means a person whose business is or includes holding chargeable securities as nominee for the EU clearance service operator, and

(*b*) in respect of an EU depositary receipt issuer, means a person whose business is or includes holding chargeable securities as nominee or agent for the EU depositary receipt issuer.][1]

Amendments—[1] This section inserted by FA 2010 s 54(1), (5) with effect in relation to transfers of chargeable securities on or after 1 October 2009 (FA 2010 s 54(6)).

General

98 Administration etc

(1) The Treasury may make regulations—

(*a*) providing that provisions of the Taxes Management Act 1970 specified in the regulations shall apply in relation to stamp duty reserve tax as they apply in relation to a tax within the meaning of that Act, with such modifications (specified in the regulations) as they think fit;

(*b*) making with regard to stamp duty reserve tax such further provision as they think fit in relation to administration, assessment, collection and recovery.

[(1A) The power conferred on the Treasury by subsection (1) above includes power to make provision conferring or imposing on the Board functions which involve the exercise of a discretion.][1]

(2) The power to make regulations under subsection (1) above shall be exercisable by statutory instrument subject to annulment in pursuance of a resolution of the House of Commons.

Regulations—See the Stamp Duty Reserve Tax Regulations, SI 1986/1711; the Stamp Duty and Stamp Duty Reserve Tax (Definition of Unit Trust Scheme and Open-ended Investment Company) Regulations, SI 2001/964.

Cross references—See FA 1989 s 177 (prescribed form for the manner in which notice and information are to be given with regard to stamp duty reserve tax);

FA 1990 ss 110, 111(1) (abolition of stamp duty reserve tax with effect from an appointed day).

FA 2004 s 313(4)(*d*) (disclosure of tax avoidance schemes: no liability to a penalty under this section by reason of any failure to include in any return or account any reference number or information required by virtue of FA 2004 s 313(3)(*a*).

FA 2009 Sch 55 (penalty for failure to make returns etc).

FA 2009 Sch 56 (penalty for failure to make payments on time).

Amendments—[1] Sub-s (1A) inserted by FA 1996 s 195.

99 Interpretation

(1) This section applies for the purposes of this Part of this Act.

[(1A) "Bearer instrument" has the same meaning as in Schedule 15 to the Finance Act 1999.

An instrument is a "UK bearer instrument" or "non-UK bearer instrument" according to whether it is issued by or on behalf of a UK company or a non-UK company within the meaning of that Schedule.][10]

(2) "The Board" means the Commissioners of Inland Revenue.

[(3) Subject to the following provisions of this section, "chargeable securities" means—

(*a*) stocks, shares or loan capital,

(*b*) interests in, or in dividends or other rights arising out of, stocks, shares or loan capital,

(*c*) rights to allotments of or to subscribe for, or options to acquire, stocks, shares or loan capital, and

(*d*) units under a unit trust scheme.][1]

[(4) "Chargeable securities" does not include securities falling within paragraph (*a*), (*b*) or (*c*) of subsection (3) above which are issued or raised by a body corporate not incorporated in the United Kingdom unless—

(*a*) they are registered in a register kept in the United Kingdom by or on behalf of the body corporate by which they are issued or raised, or

(*b*) in the case of shares, they are paired with shares issued by a body corporate incorporated in the United Kingdom, or

(*c*) in the case of securities falling within paragraph (*b*) or (*c*) of subsection (3) above, paragraph (*a*) or (*b*) above applies to the stocks, shares or loan capital to which they relate][1][, or

(*d*) they are issued or raised by an SE (whether or not in the course of its formation in accordance with Article 2 of Council Regulation (EC) 2157/2001 on the Statute for a European Company (Societas Europaea)) and, at the time when it falls to be determined whether the securities are chargeable securities, the SE has its registered office in the United Kingdom.][15]

[(4A) "Chargeable securities" does not include securities falling within paragraph (*a*), (*b*) or (*c*) of subsection (3) above if—

(*a*) they are securities issued or raised by an SE (whether or not in the course of its formation in accordance with Article 2 of Council Regulation (EC) 2157/2001 on the Statute for a European Company (Societas Europaea)), and

(*b*) at the time when it falls to be determined whether the securities are chargeable securities, the SE has its registered office outside the United Kingdom;][15]

[(5) "Chargeable securities" does not include securities falling within paragraph (*a*), (*b*) or (*c*) of subsection (3) above if—

(*a*) in the case of stock or marketable securities within the meaning of section 125 of the Finance Act 2003 (abolition of stamp duty except on instruments relating to stock or marketable securities), they are securities the transfer of which is exempt from all stamp duties;

(*b*) in any other case, they are securities the transfer of which, disregarding that section, would be exempt from all stamp duties.][14]

[(5ZA) "Chargeable securities" does not include securities falling within paragraph (*b*) or (*c*) of subsection (3) above if the stocks, shares or loan capital to which the securities relate—

(*a*) are stock or marketable securities within the meaning of section 125 of the Finance Act 2003 (abolition of stamp duty except on instruments relating to stock or marketable securities) the transfer of which is exempt from all stamp duties, or

(*b*) are securities the transfer of which, disregarding that section, would be exempt from all stamp duties.][14]

[(5A) "Chargeable securities" does not include a unit under a unit trust scheme if—

(*a*) all the trustees under the scheme are resident outside the United Kingdom and the unit is not registered in a register kept in the United Kingdom by or on behalf of the trustees under the scheme; or

(*b*) under the terms of the scheme the trust property can only be invested in exempt investments.

(5B) For the purposes of subsection (5A)(*b*)—

(*a*) an investment other than an interest under a collective investment scheme is an exempt investment if, and only if—

(i) it is not an investment on the transfer of which *ad valorem* stamp duty would be chargeable, . . . [14]

[(ia) it is not an investment on the acquisition of which stamp duty land tax would be chargeable under Part 4 of the Finance Act 2003, and][14]

(ii) it is not a chargeable security;

(*b*) an interest under a collective investment scheme is an exempt investment if, and only if, the scheme is an authorised unit trust scheme or an open-ended investment company and under the terms of the scheme the property subject to the scheme—

(i) cannot be invested in such a way that income can arise to the trustees or the company that will be chargeable to tax in their hands otherwise than under Case III of Schedule D, and

(ii) can only be invested in exempt investments;

(*c*) a derivative is an exempt investment if, and only if, it relates wholly to one or more exempt investments; and

(*d*) funds held for the purposes of the day to day management of the unit trust scheme are not regarded as investments.

[In this subsection "an authorised unit trust scheme", "collective investment scheme" and "an open-ended investment company" have the same meanings as in Part 17 of the Financial Services and Markets Act 2000.][13]][12]

[(6) "Chargeable securities" does not include interests in depositary receipts for stocks or shares.][1]

[(6A) For the purposes of subsection (4) above, shares issued by a body corporate which is not incorporated in the United Kingdom ("the foreign company") are paired with shares issued by a body corporate which is so incorporated ("the UK company") where—

(*a*) the articles of association of the UK company and the equivalent instruments governing the foreign company each provide that no share in the company to which they relate may be transferred otherwise than as part of a unit comprising one share in that company and one share in the other, and

(*b*) such units have been offered for sale to the public in the United Kingdom and, at the same time, [other][7] such units have been offered for sale to the public at a broadly equivalent price in the country in which the foreign company is incorporated.][1]

[(6B) For the purposes of subsection (4) above, shares issued by a body corporate which is not incorporated in the United Kingdom ("the foreign company") are paired with shares issued by a body corporate which is so incorporated ("the UK company") where—

(*a*) the articles of association of the UK company and the equivalent instruments governing the foreign company each provide that no share in the company to which they relate may be transferred otherwise than as part of a unit comprising one share in that company and one share in the other, and

(*b*) the shares issued by the foreign company, and the shares issued by the UK company, are issued to give effect to an allotment of the shares (as part of such units) as fully or partly paid bonus shares.][8]

(7) A depositary receipt for stocks or shares is an instrument acknowledging—

(*a*) that a person holds stocks or shares or evidence of the right to receive them, and

(*b*) that another person is entitled to rights, whether expressed as units or otherwise, in or in relation to stocks or shares of the same kind, including the right to receive such stocks or shares (or evidence of the right to receive them) from the person mentioned in paragraph (*a*) above,

except that a depositary receipt for stocks or shares does not include an instrument acknowledging rights in or in relation to stocks or shares if they are issued or sold under terms providing for payment in instalments and for the issue of the instrument as evidence that an instalment has been paid.

(8) The Treasury may by regulations provide that for subsection (7) above (as it has effect for the time being) there shall be substituted a subsection containing a different definition of a depositary receipt; and the power to make regulations under this subsection shall be exercisable by statutory instrument subject to annulment in pursuance of a resolution of the House of Commons.
[(9) "Unit trust scheme" and related expressions have the meanings given by Part IV of Schedule 19 to the Finance Act 1999.][2]
[(9A) But "unit trust scheme" does not include arrangements falling within section 48A of the Finance Act 2005 [or section 507 of the Corporation Tax Act 2009][17] (alternative finance investment bonds).][16]
(10) In interpreting "chargeable securities" in sections 93, 94, [95,][9] [95A,][11] [96, [97][9][,97AA][11] and 97A][5] above—

[(*a*) paragraph (*a*) of subsection (4) above and the reference to that paragraph in paragraph (*c*) of that subsection shall be ignored, and][3]
(*b*) the effect of [section 133(3) of the Companies Act 2006 (transactions in shares registered in overseas branch register)][18] shall be ignored for the purposes of subsection (5) above.

[(11) In interpreting "chargeable securities" in section 93 or 96 above in a case where—

(*a*) newly subscribed shares, or
(*b*) securities falling within paragraph (*b*) or (*c*) of subsection (3) above which relate to newly subscribed shares,

are issued in pursuance of an arrangement such as is mentioned in that section (or an arrangement which would be such an arrangement if the securities issued were chargeable securities), paragraph (b) of subsection (4) above and the reference to that paragraph in paragraph (c) of that subsection shall be ignored.][4]
[(12) In subsection (11) above, "newly subscribed shares" means shares issued wholly for new consideration in pursuance of an offer for sale to the public.][4]
[(13) Where the calculation of any tax in accordance with the provisions of this Part results in an amount which is not a multiple of one penny, the amount so calculated shall be rounded to the nearest penny, taking any 1/2p as nearest to the next whole penny above.][6]

Cross references—See FA 1990 ss 110, 111(1) (abolition of stamp duty reserve tax with effect from an appointed day); FA 1990 s 113 (modifications of sub-ss (6A), (9) and insertion of sub-s (6B) in specified circumstances).
FA 1999 Sch 15 (bearer instruments).

Modification—Sub-ss (5), (5A) modified and sub-s (5C) inserted, in relation to open-ended investment companies, by the Stamp Duty and Stamp Duty Reserve Tax (Open-ended Investment Companies) Regulations, SI 1997/1156, regs 4, 4B, as amended by the Stamp Duty and Stamp Duty Reserve Tax (Open-ended Investment Companies) (Amendment No 2) Regulations, SI 1999/3261, reg 5, and the Stamp Duty and Stamp Duty Reserve Tax (Definition of Unit Trust Scheme and Open-ended Investment Company) Regulations, SI 2001/964 with effect for sub-ss (5), (5A) from 6 February 2000, and for sub-s (5C) from 6 April 2001.

Amendments—[1] Sub-ss (3)–(6A) substituted for sub-ss (3)–(6) by FA 1988 s 144(2), (6) in relation to—

(a) agreements to transfer chargeable securities made after 8 December 1987; and
(b) transfer, issue or appropriation of chargeable securities after 8 December 1987 in pursuance of an arrangement whenever made.

[2] Sub-s (9) substituted by FA 1999 Sch 19 para 12 with effect from 6 February 2000.
[3] Sub-s (10)(*a*) substituted by FA 1988 s 144(4), (6).
[4] Sub-ss (11), (12) added by FA 1988 s 144(5), (6) with effect as described in [1] above.
[5] Words in sub-s (10) substituted for the words "and 96" by FA 1996 s 196(5), (6), with effect from 1 July 1996.
[6] Sub-s (13) inserted by FA 1996 s 180(6).
[7] Words in sub-ss (6A) inserted and amended by FA 1990 s 113 with effect from 26 July 1990.
[8] Sub-s (6B) inserted by FA 1990 s 113 with effect from 26 July 1990.
[9] Words in sub-s (10) inserted by FA 1998 s 151 with effect where the issue by company X referred to in FA 1986 ss 95(3), (6), 97(4) or (7) is an issue on or after 1 May 1998.
[10] Sub-s (1A) inserted by FA 1999 s 113(3), Sch 16 para 9 with effect in relation to bearer instruments issued after 30 September 1999. For prospective repeal of FA 1999 s 113, Sch 16 para 9 see FA 1999 s 123(3).
[11] Words in sub-s (10) inserted by FA 1999 s 118(2), (4) with effect in relation to securities issued from 1 May 1998. For prospective repeal of FA 1999 s 118 see FA 1999 s 123(3).
[12] Words in sub-s (5), and sub-ss (5A) and (5B) inserted by FA 1999 Sch 19 para 12 with effect from 6 February 2000.
[13] Words in sub-s (5B) substituted by the Financial Services and Markets Act 2000 (Consequential Amendments) (Taxes) Order, SI 2001/3629 arts 6, 10. SI 2001/3629 art 19 has effect in relation to—

(a) an agreement to transfer chargeable securities which is not conditional, if the agreement is made after 30 November 2001;
(b) a conditional agreement to transfer such securities, if the condition is satisfied after that date.

[14] Sub-ss (5), (5ZA) substituted for sub-s (5), and in sub-s (5B), para (*a*)(ia) inserted, by the Stamp Duty and Stamp Duty Land Tax (Consequential Amendment of Enactments) Regulations, SI 2003/2868 regs 3, 5 with effect from 1 December 2003.
[15] Sub-ss (4)(*d*), (4A) inserted by F(No 2)A 2005 s 57 with effect for the purpose of determining, in relation to anything occurring on or after 1 April 2005, whether securities (whenever issued or raised) are chargeable securities for the purposes of FA 1986 Pt IV.
[16] Sub-s (9A) inserted by FA 2008 s 154(1), (5) with effect in relation to:

(a) agreements to transfer chargeable securities made on or after 21 July 2008, and
(b) the transfer, issue or appropriation of chargeable securities after that day in pursuance of an agreement made after that day;

16 (and for this purpose it does not matter when the arrangements falling within FA 2005 s 48A are made).

17 In sub-s (9A), words inserted by CTA 2009 s 1322, Sch 1 paras 322, 325. CTA 2009 applies for corporation tax purposes for accounting periods ending on or after 1 April 2009 and for income tax and capital gains tax purposes for the tax year 2009–10 and subsequent tax years.

18 In sub-s (10)(*b*), words substituted for words "paragraph 8 of Schedule 14 to the Companies Act 1985 (share registered overseas) and of section 118 of the Companies Act (Northern Ireland) 1960 and paragraph 7 of Schedule 14 to the Companies (Northern Ireland) Order 1986 (equivalent provision for Northern Ireland)", by the Companies Act 2006 (Consequential Amendments) (Taxes and National Insurance) Order, SI 2009/1890 art 7(*f*) with effect from 1 October 2009.

PART VII

MISCELLANEOUS AND SUPPLEMENTARY

114 Short title, interpretation, construction and repeals

(1) This Act may be cited as the Finance Act 1986.

(2), (3) . . .

(4) Part III of this Act shall be construed as one with the Stamp Act 1891.

(5) . . .

(6) The enactments and Orders specified in Schedule 23 to this Act are hereby repealed to the extent specified in the third column of that Schedule, but subject to any provision at the end of any Part of that Schedule.

Note—Sub-ss (2), (3), (5) are not relevant to stamp duty.

BUILDING SOCIETIES ACT 1986

(1986 Chapter 53)

An Act to make fresh provision with respect to building societies and further provision with respect to conveyancing services

[25th July 1986]

PART XI

MISCELLANEOUS AND SUPPLEMENTARY AND CONVEYANCING SERVICES

Miscellaneous and supplementary

109 Exemption from stamp duty

[(1)] [1] The following instruments shall be exempted from all such stamp duties (if any) as apart from this section would be chargeable on them, that is to say—

(*a*) any copy of the rules of a building society;

(*b*) any transfer of a share in a building society;

(*c*) any bond or other security to be given to, or on account of, a building society or by an officer of a building society;

(*d*) any instrument appointing an agent of a building society or revoking such an appointment; and

(*e*) any other instrument whatsoever which is required or authorised to be given, issued, signed, made or produced in pursuance of this Act or of the rules of a building society.

[(2) No transfer effected by subsection (6) or (7) of section 97 shall give rise to any liability to stamp duty.][1]

Amendments—[1] Sub-s (1) numbered as such, and sub-s (2) inserted, by FA 1988 s 145, Sch 12 para 8.

FINANCE ACT 1987

(1987 Chapter 16)

An Act to grant certain duties, to alter other duties, and to amend the law relating to the National Debt and the Public Revenue, and to make further provision in connection with Finance

[15th May 1987]

PART III

STAMP DUTY AND STAMP DUTY RESERVE TAX

Stamp duty

48 Unit trusts

(*amends* FA 1946 s 57).

49 Contract notes

Amendments—This section repealed by FA 1999 Sch 20 Pt V(2) with effect in relation to instruments executed, or bearer instruments issued, from 1 October 1999, subject to the provisions in FA 1999 Sch 20 Pt V(2) Note 2. Previously the text repealed F(1909–10)A 1910, ss 78, 79 so far as unrepealed.

50 Warrants to purchase Government stock, etc

(1) Where an interest in, a right to an allotment of or to subscribe for, or an option to acquire [or to dispose of][1], exempt securities is transferred to or vested in any person by any instrument, no stamp duty shall be chargeable on the instrument by virtue of [Part I, *or paragraph 16*[6] of Schedule 13 to the Finance Act 1999 ([transfer][5] on sale or otherwise)].[3]

(2) No stamp duty under [Schedule 15 to the Finance Act 1999 (bearer instruments)][2] shall be chargeable—

(*a*) on the issue of an instrument which relates to such an interest, right or option as is mentioned in subsection (1) above, or

(*b*) on the transfer of the interest, right or option constituted by, or transferable by means of, such an instrument.

(3) For the purposes of this section, "exempt securities" means—

(*a*) securities the transfer of which is exempt from all stamp duties,

(*b*) securities constituted by or transferable by means of an instrument the issue of which is [exempt from stamp duty under paragraph 1 of Schedule 15 to the Finance Act 1999 (issue of bearer instrument) by virtue of paragraph 17 of that Schedule (certain non-sterling instruments)][2], or

(*c*) securities the transfer of which is [exempt from stamp duty under that Schedule by virtue of paragraph 17 of that Schedule or section 79(2) of the Finance Act 1986][2];

and "securities" means stock or marketable securities and includes loan capital as defined in section 78(7) of the Finance Act 1986.

(4), (5) . . . [4]

Note—This section was to be repealed by FA 1990 Sch 19 Pt VI with effect from an appointed day in accordance with FA 1990 ss 107–111. The Treasury order specifying the appointed day for the purposes of FA 1990 ss 107–110 was to coincide with the start of paperless trading under the Stock Exchange's planned TAURUS system (IR press release, 20-3-90). However, on 11-3-93 the London Stock Exchange News Release 6/93 announced that TAURUS had been abandoned.

Amendments—[1] Words in sub-s (1) inserted by F (No 2) A 1987, s 99 (1).

[2] Words in sub-ss (2), (3)(*b*)(*c*) substituted by FA 1999 s 113(3), Sch 16 para 10 with effect in relation to bearer instruments issued after 30 September 1999. For prospective repeal of FA 1999 s 113, Sch 16 para 10 see FA 1999 s 123(3). Previously the text read 'the heading "Bearer Instrument" in Schedule 1 to the Stamp Act 1891', 'by virtue of section 30 of the Finance Act 1967 or section 7 of the Finance Act (Northern Ireland) 1967 [or section 79(2) of the Finance Act 1986] exempt from stamp duty under the heading "Bearer Instrument" in Schedule 1 to the Stamp Act 1891' and 'by virtue of section 30 of the Finance Act 1967 or section 7 of the Finance Act (Northern Ireland) 1967 [or section 79(2) of the Finance Act 1986] from stamp duty under that heading' respectively.

[3] Words in sub-s (1) substituted by FA 1999 s 112(4), Sch 14 para 21 with effect in relation to instruments executed after 30 September 1999. This does not apply to transfers or other instruments relating to units under a unit trust scheme by virtue of FA 1999 s 122. For prospective repeal of FA 1999 Sch 14 para 21 see FA 1999 s 123(3). Previously the text read:

"either of the following headings in Schedule 1 to the Stamp Act 1891—

(*a*) "Conveyance or Transfer on Sale";

(*b*) "Conveyance or Transfer of any kind not hereinbefore described"."

[4] Sub-ss (4) and (5) repealed by FA 1999 Sch 20 Pt V(2) with effect in relation to instruments executed, or bearer instruments issued, from 1 October 1999, subject to the provisions in FA 1999 Sch 20 Pt V(2) Note 2. Previously the text read:

"(4) Subsection (1) above applies to any instrument executed on or after 1st August 1987.

(5) Subsection (2) above applies—

(*a*) to any instrument which falls within section 60(1) of the Finance Act 1963 or section 9(1) (*a*) of the Finance Act (Northern Ireland) 1963, and is issued on or after 1st August 1987, and

(*b*) to any instrument which falls within section 60(2) of the Finance Act 1963 or section 9(1)(*b*) of the Finance Act (Northern Ireland) 1963, if the interest, right or option constituted by or transferable by means of it is transferred on or after 1st August 1987."

[5] The word "transfer" substituted for the words "conveyance or transfer" in enactments relating to stamp duty by FA 2003 Sch 20 para 3.

[6] Words in sub-s (1) repealed by FA 2008 s 99, Sch 32 paras 16, 17 with effect in relation to instruments executed on or after 13 March 2008 and not stamped before 19 March 2008.

51 Bearer instruments relating to stock in foreign currencies

Amendments—This section repealed by FA 1999 Sch 20 Pt V(2) with effect in relation to instruments executed, or bearer instruments issued, from 1 October 1999, subject to the provisions in FA 1999 Sch 20 Pt V(2) Note 2. Previously the text amended FA 1967 s 30 and FA (Northern Ireland) 1967 s 7.

52 Clearance services

(*amended* FA 1986 s 70(6) *and is repealed by* FA 1990 Sch 19 Pt VI *with effect from an appointed day*).

53 Borrowing of stock by market makers

(*amended* FA 1986 s 82(6) *and is repealed by* FA 1990 Sch 19 Pt VI *with effect from an appointed day and by* FA 1997, Sch 18 Pt VII *with effect from a day appointed under* FA 1977 s 98(4)).

54 Shared ownership transactions

(1) (*amends* FA 1980 s 97(3)(*b*)).

(2) Section 97 of the Finance Act 1980 and section 108(5) and (6) of the Finance Act 1981 shall apply to a lease within subsection (3) below as they apply to a lease granted by a body mentioned in section 97(3) of the Finance Act 1980.

(3) A lease is within this subsection if it is granted—

(*a*) by a person against whom the right to buy under Part V of the Housing Act 1985 is exercisable by virtue of section 171A of that Act (preservation of right to buy on disposal to private sector landlord), and

(*b*) to a person who is the qualifying person for the purposes of the preserved right to buy and in relation to whom that dwelling-house is the qualifying dwelling-house.

(4) This section applies to leases granted on or after 1st August 1987.

55 Crown exemption

(1) Where any conveyance, transfer or lease is made or agreed to be made—

[(*a*)] [3] to a Minister of the Crown or

[(*b*)] [3] to the Solicitor for the affairs of Her Majesty's Treasury, [or

[(*c*)] [3] to the Welsh Ministers, the First Minister for Wales, the Counsel General to the Welsh Assembly Government or the National Assembly for Wales Commission][5],][1] [or

(*d*) to the Northern Ireland Assembly Commission,][4]

no stamp duty shall be chargeable [under Part I or II, or paragraph 16[6] of Schedule 13 to the Finance Act 1999][2] on the instrument by which the conveyance, transfer or lease, or the agreement for it, is effected.

(2) In this section "Minister of the Crown" has the same meaning as in the Ministers of the Crown Act 1975.

(3) Article 3 (6) of the Secretary of State for the Environment Order 1970 and Article 4 (5) of the Secretary of State for Transport Order 1976 (which exempt transfers by, to or with those Ministers) shall cease to have effect.

(4) This section applies to instruments executed on or after 1st August 1987.

Note—In this section references to a Minister of the Crown shall be read as including the Scottish Ministers, the Lord Advocate and the Parliamentary corporation by virtue of the Scotland Act 1998 with effect from a date to be appointed by Statutory Instrument.

Amendments—[1] Words in sub-s (1) inserted by the Government of Wales Act 1998 Sch 12 para 25 with effect from 1 April 1999 by virtue of the Government of Wales Act 1998 (Commencement No 4) Order, SI 1999/782.

[2] Words in sub-s (1) substituted by FA 1999 s 112(4), Sch 14 para 22 with effect in relation to instruments executed after 30 September 1999. This does not apply to transfers or other instruments relating to units under a unit trust scheme by virtue of FA 1999 s 122. Previously the text read

'by virtue of any of the following headings in Schedule 1 to the Stamp Act 1891—

(*a*) "Conveyance or Transfer on Sale",

(*b*) "Conveyance or Transfer of any kind not herein before described",

(*c*) "Lease or Tack",'

[3] References to "(*a*)", "(*b*)" and "(*c*)" in sub-s (1) inserted by FA 2000 s 132(1), (2) with effect from 28 March 2000.

[4] Sub-s (1)(*d*) and word "or" preceding it inserted by FA 2000 s 132(1), (3), with effect for instruments executed after 27 March 2000.

[5] Words in sub-s (1)(*c*) substituted by the Government of Wales Act 2006 s 160(1), Sch 10 para 20 with effect from 25 May 2007, being the date on which the initial period ended (following the appointment of the First Minister) (Government of Wales Act 2006 ss 46, 161(4), (5)).

[6] Words in sub-s (1) repealed by FA 2008 s 99, Sch 32 paras 16, 18 with effect in relation to instruments executed on or after 13 March 2008 and not stamped before 19 March 2008.
This amendment does not have effect in relation to an instrument effecting a land transaction or a duplicate or counterpart of such an instrument. "Land transaction" has the same meaning as in FA 2003 Part 4, except that it does not include a transfer of an interest in a property-investment partnership (within the meaning of FA 2003 Sch 15) (FA 2008 s 99, Sch 32 para 22).

Stamp duty reserve tax

56 Stamp duty reserve tax

Schedule 7 to this Act (which contains miscellaneous amendments of Part IV of the Finance Act 1986) shall have effect.[1]

Amendments—[1] This section repealed by FA 1990 Sch 19 Pt VII with effect from an appointed day.

PART VI
MISCELLANEOUS AND SUPPLEMENTARY

72 Short title, interpretation, construction and repeals

(1) This Act may be cited as the Finance Act 1987.

(2), (3) (*not relevant to stamp duty*).

(4) Part III of this Act, except section 56 and Schedule 7, shall be construed as one with the Stamp Act 1891.

(5), (6) (*not relevant to stamp duty*).

(7) The enactments specified in Schedule 16 to this Act (which include enactments which are spent or otherwise unnecessary) are hereby repealed to the extent specified in the third column of that Schedule, but subject to any provision at the end of any Part of that Schedule.

SCHEDULE 7
STAMP DUTY RESERVE TAX
Section 56

Note—This Schedule amended FA 1986 ss 87, 88, 89, 90, 92 and is repealed by FA 1990 Sch 19 Pt VII with effect from an appointed day. Sch 7 para (4) is also repealed by FA 1997 Sch 18 Pt VII in relation to an agreement to transfer securities (*a*) in the case of an agreement which is not conditional, if the agreement is made on or after 20 October 1997 (as appointed by SI 1997/2428 under FA 1997 s 102(6)); and (*b*) in the case of a conditional agreement, if the condition is satisfied on or after that date.

FINANCE ACT 1988
(1988 Chapter 39)

An Act to grant certain duties, to alter other duties, and to amend the law relating to the National Debt and the Public Revenue, and to make further provision in connection with Finance.

[29th July 1988]

PART IV
MISCELLANEOUS AND GENERAL

Stamp duty and stamp duty reserve tax

140 Abolition of stamp duty under the heading "Unit Trust Instrument"

Amendments—This section repealed by FA 1999 Sch 20 Pt V(2) with effect in relation to instruments executed, or bearer instruments issued, from 1 October 1999, subject to the provisions in FA 1999 Sch 20 Pt V(2) Note 2. Previously the text read:

"(1) The stamp duty chargeable by virtue of the heading in Schedule 1 to the Stamp Act 1891 "Unit Trust Instrument" is abolished; and accordingly that heading and the following enactments, namely—

(*a*) section 53 of the Finance Act 1946;

(*b*) section 24 of the Finance (No 2) Act (Northern Ireland) 1946;

(*c*) section 30 of the Finance Act 1962; and

(*d*) section 3 of the Finance Act (Northern Ireland) 1962,

shall cease to have effect.

(2) Subsection (1) above shall have effect in relation to—

(*a*) any trust instrument executed on or after 22nd March 1988;

(*b*) any trust instrument executed on or after 16th March 1988 which is not stamped before 22nd March 1988;

(*c*) any property becoming trust property on or after 22nd March 1988; and

(*d*) any property becoming trust property on or after 16th March 1988 in respect of which the trust instrument is not stamped before 22nd March 1988.

(3) For the purposes of section 14 (4) of the Stamp Act 1891 (instruments not to be given in evidence etc unless stamped in accordance with the law in force at the time of execution), the law in force—

(*a*) at the time of execution of a trust instrument falling within subsection (2)(b) above; or

(*b*) on the day on which property falling within subsection (2)(d) above becomes trust property,

shall be deemed to be that as varied in accordance with this section.

(4) In this section "trust instrument" and "trust property" have the meanings given by section 57 of the Finance Act 1946 or section 28 of the Finance (No 2) Act (Northern Ireland) 1946.

(5) This section shall be construed as one with the Stamp Act 1891.

(6) This section shall be deemed to have come into force on 22nd March 1988."

141 Abolition of stamp duty on documents relating to transactions of capital companies

Amendments—This section repealed by FA 1999 Sch 20 Pt V(2) with effect in relation to instruments executed, or bearer instruments issued, from 1 October 1999, subject to the provisions in FA 1999 Sch 20 Pt V(2) Note 2. Previously the text read:

"(1) The stamp duties chargeable by virtue of section 47 of the Finance Act 1973 and Article 8 of the Finance (Miscellaneous Provisions) (Northern Ireland) Order 1973 (stamp duties on documents relating to chargeable transactions of capital companies) are abolished; and accordingly—

(*a*) that section, section 48 of that Act and Schedule 19 to that Act; and

(*b*) that Article, Article 9 of that Order and Schedule 2 to that Order,

shall cease to have effect.

(2) Subsection (1) above shall have effect in relation to—

(*a*) any transaction occurring on or after 22nd March 1988;

(*b*) any transaction occurring on or after 16th March 1988 in respect of which the relevant document is not stamped before 22nd March 1988;

(*c*) any exempt transaction occurring before 22nd March 1988 in respect of which a relevant event occurs on or after 22nd March 1988; and (*d*) any exempt transaction occurring before 16th March 1988 in respect of which a relevant event occurs on or after 16th March 1988 and the relevant duty is not paid before 22nd March 1988.

(3) For the purposes of section 14(4) of the Stamp Act 1891 (instruments not to be given in evidence etc unless stamped in accordance with the law in force at the time of execution), the law in force—

(*a*) in a case falling within subsection (2)(*b*) above, at the time of execution of the relevant document; or

(*b*) in a case falling within subsection (2)(*d*) above, on the day on which the relevant event occurs,

shall be deemed to be that as varied in accordance with this section.

(4) In this section—

"exempt transaction" means a transaction which is exempt by virtue of paragraph 10(1) of Schedule 19 to the Finance Act 1973;

"relevant document" has the meaning given by section 47 of that Act;

"relevant duty" means the duty payable under paragraph 10(4) of Schedule 19 to that Act;

"relevant event" means such an event as is mentioned in paragraph 10(3) (*a*) or (*b*) of Schedule 19 to that Act,

and any reference in this subsection to section 47 of or Schedule 19 to that Act includes a reference to Article 8 of or Schedule 2 to the Finance (Miscellaneous Provisions) (Northern Ireland) Order 1973.

(5) This section shall be construed as one with the Stamp Act 1891.

(6) This section shall be deemed to have come into force on 22nd March 1988."

142 Stamp duty: housing action trusts

(*amends* FA 1980 s 97; FA 1981 s 107).

143 Stamp duty: paired shares

(1) This section applies where—

(*a*) the articles of association of a company incorporated in the United Kingdom ("the UK company") and the equivalent instruments governing a company which is not so incorporated ("the foreign company") each provide that no share in the company to which they relate may be transferred otherwise than as part of a unit comprising one share in that company and one share in the other; and

(*b*) such units are to be or have been offered for sale to the public in the United Kingdom and, at the same time, [other][1] such units are to be or, as the case may be, have been offered for sale to the public at a broadly equivalent price in the country in which the foreign company is incorporated ("the foreign country").

[(2) In relation to an instrument to which this subsection applies, no duty is chargeable under paragraph 1 of Schedule 15 to the Finance Act 1999 (bearer instruments: charge on issue); but this does not affect the other requirements of that Schedule.][2]

(3) [Subsection (2) above applies][3] to any bearer instrument issued on or after 1st November 1987 which represents shares in the UK company, or a right to an allotment of or to subscribe for such shares, if the purpose of the issue is—

(*a*) to make such shares available for sale (as part of such units as are referred to in subsection (1) above) in pursuance of either of the offers referred to in subsection (1)(*b*) above or of any other offer for sale of such units to the public made at the same time and at a broadly equivalent price in a country other than the United Kingdom or the foreign country; or

(*b*) to give effect to an allotment of such shares (as part of such units) as fully or partly paid bonus shares.

[(4) In relation to an instrument to which this subsection applies—

(*a*) the foreign company shall be treated for the purposes of Schedule 15 to the Finance Act 1999 (stamp duty on bearer instruments) as a UK company, and

(*b*) paragraph 17 of that Schedule (exemption for non-sterling instruments) shall not apply.][4]

(5) [Subsection (4) above applies][3] to any bearer instrument issued on or after 9th December 1987 which represents shares in the foreign company, or a right to an allotment of or to subscribe for such shares, and is not issued for the purpose—

(*a*) of making shares in the foreign company available for sale (as part of such units as are referred to in subsection (1) above) in pursuance of either of the offers referred to in subsection (1)(*b*) above or of any other offer such as is mentioned in subsection (3)(*a*) above; or

(*b*) of giving effect to an allotment of such shares (as part of such units) as fully or partly paid bonus shares.

(6) In relation to any instrument which transfers such units as are referred to in subsection (1) above and is executed on or after the date of the passing of this Act, the foreign company shall be treated for the purposes of sections 67 and 68 (depositary receipts) and 70 and 71 (clearance services) of the Finance Act 1986 as a company incorporated in the United Kingdom.

(7) Section 3 of the Stamp Act 1891 (which requires every instrument written upon the same piece of material as another instrument to be separately stamped) shall not apply in relation to any bearer instrument issued on or after 9th December 1987 which represents shares in the UK company or the foreign company, or a right to an allotment of or to subscribe for such shares.

(8) This section shall be construed as one with the Stamp Act 1891.

(9) Subsections (2) and (3) above, together with subsection (1) above so far as relating to them, shall be deemed to have come into force on 1st November 1987, and subsections (4), (5) and (7) above, together with subsection (1) above so far as relating to them, shall be deemed to have come into force on 9th December 1987.

Cross references—See FA 1990 s 112 (modification of sub-s(1)(*b*) by the substitution of the word "other" for the words "an equal number of" in specified circumstances).

Note—This section was to be repealed by FA 1990 Sch 19 Pt VI with effect from an appointed day in accordance with FA 1990 ss 107–111. The Treasury order specifying the appointed day for the purposes of FA 1990 ss 107–110 was to coincide with the start of paperless trading under the Stock Exchange's planned TAURUS system (IR press release, 20-3-90). However, on 11-3-93 the London Stock Exchange News Release 6/93 announced that TAURUS had been abandoned.

Amendments—[1] Sub-s (1)(*b*) amended by FA 1990 s 112 with effect from 26 July 1990.

[2] Sub-s (2) substituted by FA 1999 s 113(3), Sch 16 para 11 with effect in relation to bearer instruments issued after 30 September 1999. For prospective repeal of FA 1999 s 113, Sch 16 para 11 see FA 1999 s 123(3). Previously the text read:

"(2) In relation to an instrument to which subsection (3) below applies, any duty chargeable on issue under the heading "Bearer Instrument" in Schedule 1 to the Stamp Act 1891 (which, apart from this subsection, would be payable by virtue of section 60 of the Finance Act 1963 or section 9 of the Finance Act (Northern Ireland) 1963) shall not be so payable; but nothing in this subsection shall be taken as affecting the other requirements of that section."

[3] Words in sub-ss (3) and (5) substituted by FA 1999 s 113(3), Sch 16 para 11 with effect in relation to bearer instruments issued after 30 September 1999. For prospective repeal of FA 1999 s 113, Sch 16 para 11 see FA 1999 s 123(3). Previously the text read 'This subsection applies'.

[4] Sub-s (4) substituted by FA 1999 s 113(3), Sch 16 para 11 with effect in relation to bearer instruments issued after 30 September 1999. For prospective repeal of FA 1999 s 113, Sch 16 para 11 see FA 1999 s 123(3). Previously the text read:

"(4) In relation to an instrument to which subsection (5) below applies—

(*a*) the foreign company shall be treated—

(i) for the purposes of sections 59 and 60 of the Finance Act 1963 (which make provision in respect of stamp duty under the heading "Bearer Instrument" in Schedule 1 to the Stamp Act 1891) as a company formed or established in Great Britain; and

(ii) for the purposes of sections 8 and 9 of the Finance Act (Northern Ireland) 1963 (which make corresponding provision for Northern Ireland) as a company formed or established in Northern Ireland; and

(*b*) section 30 of the Finance Act 1967 and section 7 of the Finance Act (Northern Ireland) 1967 (exemption for bearer instruments relating to stock in foreign currencies) shall not apply."

144 Stamp duty reserve tax: paired shares etc

(*amended* FA 1986 s 99 *and sub-s (3) repealed by* FA 1999 Sch 20 Pt V(5) *with effect in relation to instruments executed from 6 February 2000*).

Miscellaneous

147 Interpretation etc

(1) In this Act "the Taxes Act 1970" means the Income and Corporation Taxes Act 1970 and "the Taxes Act 1988" means the Income and Corporation Taxes Act 1988.

(2)–(3) (*not relevant to stamp duty*).

FINANCE ACT 1989

(1989 Chapter 26)

ARRANGEMENT OF SECTIONS

PART III

MISCELLANEOUS AND GENERAL

An Act to grant certain duties, to alter other duties, and to amend the law relating to the National Debt and the Public Revenue, and to make further provision in connection with Finance.

[27th July 1989]

PART III

MISCELLANEOUS AND GENERAL

Stamp duty etc

173 Insurance: abolition of certain duties

Amendments—This section repealed by FA 1999 Sch 20 Pt V(2) with effect in relation to instruments executed, or bearer instruments issued, from 1 October 1999, subject to the provisions in FA 1999 Sch 20 Pt V(2) Note 2. Previously the text read:

"(1) Stamp duty shall not be chargeable under—

(*a*) the heading "Policy of Life Insurance" in Schedule 1 to the Stamp Act 1891, or

(*b*) paragraph (3) of the heading "Bond, Covenant, or Instrument of any kind whatsoever" in that Schedule (superannuation annuities).

(2) Subject to section 4 of the Stamp Act 1891 (separate charges on instruments containing or relating to several distinct matters) an instrument which, but for subsection (1) above, would be chargeable with stamp duty under paragraph (3) of the heading mentioned in paragraph (*b*) of that subsection shall not be chargeable with stamp duty under any other provision of the Stamp Act 1891.

(3) (*repeals* SA 1891 s 100).

(4) (*repeals* SA 1891, s 118).

(5) (*repeals* FA 1966 s 47(3); FA (Northern Ireland) 1966 s 5(3)).

(6) Subsections (1) and (2) above apply to instruments made after 31st December 1989.

(7) So far as it relates to section 100(1) of the 1891 Act, subsection (3) above applies where a person receives, or takes credit for, a premium or consideration for insurance after 30th November 1989.

(8) So far as it relates to section 100 (2) of the 1891 Act, subsection (3) above applies where the policy is made after 31st December 1989.

(9) Subsection (4) above applies to instruments of assignment made after 31st December 1989.

(10) Subsection (5) above applies where the policy is varied after 31st December 1989 (whenever it was made)."

174 Unit trusts

Amendments—This section repealed by FA 1999 Sch 20 Pt V(5) with effect in relation to instruments executed from 6 February 2000.

175 Stamp duty: stock exchange nominees

(1) The Treasury may by regulations provide that where—

(*a*) circumstances would (apart from the regulations) give rise to a charge to stamp duty under [Part I of Schedule 13 to the Finance Act 1999 ([transfer][2] on sale)][1] and to a charge to stamp duty reserve tax,

(*b*) the circumstances involve a stock exchange nominee, and

(*c*) the circumstances are such as are prescribed,

the charge to stamp duty shall be treated as not arising.

(2) The power to make regulations under this section shall be exercisable by statutory instrument subject to annulment in pursuance of a resolution of the House of Commons.

(3) In this section—

(*a*) "prescribed" means prescribed by the regulations, and

(*b*) "stock exchange nominee" means a person designated for the purposes of section 127 of the Finance Act 1976 as a nominee of The Stock Exchange by an order made by the Secretary of State under subsection (5) of that section.

Notes—This section was to be repealed by FA 1990 Sch 19 Pt VI with effect from an appointed day in accordance with FA 1990 ss 107–111. The Treasury order specifying the appointed day for the purposes of FA 1990 ss 107–110 was to coincide with the start of paperless trading under the Stock Exchange's planned TAURUS system (IR press release, 20-3-90). However, on 11-3-93 the London Stock Exchange News Release 6/93 announced that TAURUS had been abandoned.

Amendments—[1] Words in sub-s (1)(*a*) substituted by FA 1999 s 112(4), Sch 14 para 23 with effect in relation to instruments executed after 30 September 1999. This does not apply to transfers or other instruments relating to units under a unit trust scheme by virtue of FA 1999 s 122. For prospective repeal of FA 1999 Sch 14 para 23 see FA 1999 s 123(3). Previously the text read 'the heading "Conveyance or Transfer on Sale" in Schedule 1 to the Stamp Act 1891'.

[2] The word "transfer" substituted for the words "conveyance or transfer" in enactments relating to stamp duty by FA 2003 Sch 20 para 3.

176 Stamp duty reserve tax: stock exchange nominees

(1) The Treasury may by regulations provide that where—

(*a*) circumstances would (apart from the regulations) give rise to two charges to stamp duty reserve tax, (*b*) the circumstances involve a stock exchange nominee, and

(*c*) the circumstances are such as are prescribed,

such one of the charges as may be prescribed shall be treated as not arising.

(2) The Treasury may by regulations provide that where—

(*a*) circumstances would (apart from the regulations) give rise to a charge to stamp duty reserve tax and a charge to stamp duty,

(*b*) the circumstances involve a stock exchange nominee, and

(*c*) the circumstances are such as are prescribed,

the charge to stamp duty reserve tax shall be treated as not arising.

(3) The Treasury may by regulations provide that a provision of an Act by virtue of which there is no charge to stamp duty reserve tax shall also apply in circumstances which involve a stock exchange nominee and are such as are prescribed.

(4) The Treasury may by regulations provide that a provision of an Act by virtue of which the rate at which stamp duty reserve tax is charged is less than it would be apart from the provision shall also apply in circumstances which involve a stock exchange nominee and are such as are prescribed.

(5) The power to make regulations under this section shall be exercisable by statutory instrument subject to annulment in pursuance of a resolution of the House of Commons.

(6) In this section—

(*a*) "prescribed" means prescribed by the regulations, and

(*b*) "stock exchange nominee" means a person designated for the purposes of section 127 of the Finance Act 1976 as a nominee of The Stock Exchange by an order made by the Secretary of State under subsection (5) of the section.[1]

Amendments—[1] This section repealed by FA 1990 Sch 19 Pt VII with effect from an appointed day.

177 Stamp duty reserve tax: information

Regulations under section 98(1) of the Finance Act 1986 (administration etc of stamp duty reserve tax) may include—

(*a*) provision that notice which the regulations require to be given to the Commissioners of Inland Revenue shall be given in a manner or form specified by the Commissioners;

(*b*) provision that information which the regulations require to be supplied to the Commissioners shall be supplied in a manner or form specified by the Commissioners.[1]

Amendments—[1] This section repealed by FA 1990 Sch 19 Pt VII with effect from an appointed day.

Interest etc

178 Setting of rates of interest

(1) The rate of interest applicable for the purposes of an enactment to which this section applies shall be the rate which for the purposes of that enactment is provided for by regulations made by the Treasury under this section.

(2) This section applies to—

[(*aa*) section 15A of the Stamp Act 1891;][2]

(*a*)–(*e*)

(*f*) sections [86, . . .][1] of the Taxes Management Act 1970,

(*g*)–(*k*) . . .

(*l*) section 92 of the Finance Act 1986 and

(*m*)–(*o*) . . . [, and

(*p*) section 110 of the Finance Act 1999.][3]

[(*q*) . . .

[(*r*) sections 87, 88 and 89 of the Finance Act 2003.][4]

. . .

(3) Regulations under this section may—

(*a*) make different provision for different enactments or for different purposes of the same enactment,

(*b*) either themselves specify a rate of interest for the purposes of an enactment or make provision for any such rate to be determined by reference to such rate or the average of such rates as may be referred to in the regulations,

(*c*) provide for rates to be reduced below, or increased above, what they otherwise would be by specified amounts or by reference to specified formulae,

(*d*) provide for rates arrived at by reference to averages to be rounded up or down,

(*e*) provide for circumstances in which alteration of a rate of interest is or is not to take place, and

(*f*) provide that alterations of rates are to have effect for periods beginning on or after a day determined in accordance with the regulations in relation to interest running from before that day as well as from or from after that day.

(4) The power to make regulations under this section shall be exercisable by statutory instrument which shall be subject to annulment in pursuance of a resolution of the House of Commons.

(5) . . .[5]

(6) . . .

(7) Subsection (1) shall have effect for periods beginning on or after such day as the Treasury may by order made by statutory instrument appoint and shall have effect in relation to interest running from before that day as well as from or from after that day; and different days may be appointed for different enactments.

Note—For the application of TMA 1970 s 86 (as modified) to stamp duty reserve tax, see Stamp Duty Reserve Tax Regulations, SI 1986/1711 reg 20, Sch Pt II.

Provisions omitted from this section are not relevant to stamp duty.

Cross references—See the Taxes (Interest Rate) Regulations, SI 1989/1297.

Amendments—[1] Sub-s (2)(*f*) amended by FA 1994 ss 196, 199(2), (3), Sch 19 Pt III para 44 (words omitted are not relevant to stamp duty).

[2] Sub-s (2)(*aa*) inserted by FA 1999 s 109(2) with effect in relation to instruments executed after 30 September 1999. This does not apply to transfers or other instruments relating to units under a unit trust scheme by virtue of FA 1999 s 122.

[3] Sub-s (2)(*p*) inserted by FA 1999 s 110(9) with effect in relation to instruments executed after 30 September 1999. This does not apply to transfers or other instruments relating to units under a unit trust scheme by virtue of FA 1999 s 122.

[4] Sub-s (2)(*r*) inserted by FA 2003 s 123(1), Sch 18 para 4 with effect in accordance with FA 2003 s 124, Sch 19.

[5] Sub-s (5) repealed by FA 1999 s 105(6)(*a*) with effect from 21 July 2009.

179 Provisions consequential on section 178

(1)–(3) . . .

(4) Any amendment made by subsection (1) . . . above shall have effect in relation to any period for which section 178(1) above has effect for the purposes of the enactment concerned.

(5) . . .

Note—Sub-s (1)(*f*) amended FA 1986 s 92 with effect from 18 August 1989. The rest of sub-s (1) and sub-ss (2), (3), (5) not relevant to stamp duty.

180 Repayment interest: period of accrual

(1)–(4) . . .

(5) (*amends* FA 1986 s 92).

(6) . . .

(7) The amendments made by this section shall be deemed always to have had effect.

Note—Sub-ss (1)–(4), (6) not relevant to stamp duty.

Miscellaneous

182 Disclosure of information

(1) A person who discloses any information which he holds or has held in the exercise of tax functions[, tax credit functions][4][, child trust fund functions][8] [or social security functions][3] is guilty of an offence if it is information about any matter relevant, for the purposes of [any of those functions—

(*a*) to tax or duty in the case of any identifiable person,

[(*aa*) to a tax credit in respect of any identifiable person,][4]

[(*ab*) to a child trust fund of any identifiable person,][8]

(*b*) to contributions payable by or in respect of any identifiable person, or

(*c*) to statutory sick pay[, statutory maternity pay, [ordinary statutory paternity pay, additional statutory paternity pay][13] or statutory adoption pay][5] in respect of any identifiable person.][3]

(2) In this section "tax functions" means functions relating to tax or duty—

(*a*) of . . . , the Board and their officers,

(*b*) of any person carrying out the administrative work of any tribunal mentioned in subsection (3) below, and

(*c*) of any other person providing, or employed in the provision of, services to any person mentioned in paragraph (*a*) or (*b*) above.

[(2ZA) In this section "tax credit functions" means the functions relating to tax credits—

(*a*) of the Board,

(*b*) of any person carrying out the administrative work of the General Commissioners or the Special Commissioners, and

(*c*) of any other person providing, or employed in the provision of, services to the Board or to any person mentioned in paragraph (*b*) above.][4]

[(2ZB) In this section "child trust fund functions" means the functions relating to child trust funds—

(*a*) of the Board and their officers,

(*b*) of any person carrying out the administrative work of the [First-tier Tribunal or an appeal tribunal constituted under Chapter 1 of Part 2 of the Social Security (Northern Ireland) Order 1998][12], or

(*c*) of any person providing, or employed in the provision of, services to the Board or any person mentioned in paragraph (*b*) above.][8]

[(2A) In this section "social security functions" means—

(*a*) the functions relating to contributions, [child benefit, guardian's allowance,][6] statutory sick pay[, statutory maternity pay, [ordinary statutory paternity pay, additional statutory paternity pay][13] or statutory adoption pay][5]—

(i) of the Board and their officers,

(ii) of any person carrying out the administrative work of [the First-tier Tribunal or Upper Tribunal][12], and

(iii) of any other person providing, or employed in the provision of, services to any person mentioned in sub-paragraph (i) or (ii) above, and

(*b*) the functions under Part III of the Pension Schemes Act 1993 or Part III of the Pension Schemes (Northern Ireland) Act 1993 of the Board and their officers and any other person providing, or employed in the provision of, services to the Board or their officers.][3]

(3) The tribunals referred to in subsection (2)(*b*) above are—

(*a*) . . . the Special Commissioners,

(*b*) . . .[1]

(*c*) . . .

(*d*) . . .

(4) A person who discloses any information which—

(*a*) he holds or has held in the exercise of functions—

(i) of the Comptroller and Auditor General and any member of the staff of the National Audit Office, . . . [2]

(ii) of the Parliamentary Commissioner for Administration and his officers,

[(iii) of the Auditor General for Wales and any member of his staff, . . .[9]

[(iv) of the Public Services Ombudsman for Wales and any member of his staff, or][11]

(v) of the Scottish Public Services Ombudsman and any member of his staff,][9]

(*b*) is, or is derived from, information which was held by any person in the exercise of tax functions[, tax credit functions][4][, child trust fund functions][8] [or social security functions][3], and

(*c*) is information about any matter relevant, for the purposes of [tax functions[, tax credit functions][4][, child trust fund functions][8] or social security functions—

(i) to tax or duty in the case of any identifiable person,

[(ia) to a tax credit in respect of any identifiable person,][4]

[(ib) to a child trust fund of any identifiable person,][8]

(ii) to contributions payable by or in respect of any identifiable person, or

(iii) to [child benefit, guardian's allowance,][6] statutory sick pay [, statutory maternity pay, [ordinary statutory paternity pay, additional statutory paternity pay][13] or statutory adoption pay][5] in respect of any identifiable person.][3]

is guilty of an offence.

(5) Subsections (1) and (4) above do not apply to any disclosure of information—

(*a*) with lawful authority,

(*b*) with the consent of any person in whose case the information is about a matter relevant to tax or duty[, to a tax credit or to a child trust fund][8] [or to contributions, statutory sick pay[, statutory maternity pay, [ordinary statutory paternity pay, additional statutory paternity pay][3] or statutory adoption pay][5]][3], or

(*c*) which has been lawfully made available to the public before the disclosure is made.

(6) For the purposes of this section a disclosure of any information is made with lawful authority if, and only if, it is made—

(*a*) by a Crown servant in accordance with his official duty,

(*b*) by any other person for the purposes of the function in the exercise of which he holds the information and without contravening any restriction duly imposed by the person responsible,

(*c*) to, or in accordance with an authorisation duly given by, the person responsible,

(*d*) in pursuance of any enactment or of any order of a court, or

(*e*) in connection with the institution of or otherwise for the purposes of any proceedings relating to any matter within the general responsibility of . . . the Board,

and in this subsection "the person responsible" means . . . , the Board, the Comptroller[, the Parliamentary Commissioner, the Auditor General for Wales[, [the Public Services Ombudsman for Wales][11] or the Scottish Public Services Ombudsman][9],][2] as the case requires.

(7) It is a defence for a person charged with an offence under this section to prove that at the time of the alleged offence—

(*a*) he believed that he had lawful authority to make the disclosure in question and had no reasonable cause to believe otherwise, or

(*b*) he believed that the information in question had been lawfully made available to the public before the disclosure was made and had no reasonable cause to believe otherwise.

(8) A person guilty of an offence under this section is liable—

(*a*) on conviction on indictment, to imprisonment for a term not exceeding two years or a fine or both, and

(*b*) on summary conviction, to imprisonment for a term not exceeding six months or a fine not exceeding the statutory maximum or both.

(9) No prosecution for an offence under this section shall be instituted in England and Wales or in Northern Ireland except—

(*a*) by . . . the Board, . . . , or

(*b*) by or with the consent of the Director of Public Prosecutions or, in Northern Ireland, the Director of Public Prosecutions for Northern Ireland.

(10) In this section—

"the Board" means the Commissioners of Inland Revenue,

["child trust fund" has the same meaning as in the Child Trust Funds Act 2004,][8]

. . .

["contributions" means contributions under Part I of the Social Security Contributions and Benefits Act 1992 or Part I of the Social Security Contributions and Benefits (Northern Ireland) Act 1992;][3]

"Crown servant" has the same meaning as in the Official Secrets Act 1989 and

["tax credit" means a tax credit under the Tax Credits Act 2002,][4] and

"tax or duty" means any tax or duty within the general responsibility of . . . the Board.

[(10A) In this section, in relation to disclosure of information "identifiable person" means a person whose identity is specified in the disclosure or can be deduced from it.][7]

(11) In this section—

(*a*) references to the Comptroller and Auditor General include the Comptroller and Auditor General for Northern Ireland,

(*b*) references to the National Audit Office include the Northern Ireland Audit Office, and

(*c*) references to the Parliamentary Commissioner for Administration include the Health Service Commissioner for England . . . [11], . . . [9] the [Assembly, Ombudsman for Northern Ireland][10] and the Northern Ireland Commissioner for Complaints.

[(11A) In this section, references to [ordinary statutory paternity pay, additional statutory paternity pay][13] or statutory adoption pay include statutory pay under Northern Ireland legislation corresponding to Part 12ZA or Part 12ZB of the Social Security Contributions and Benefits Act 1992 (c 4).][5]

(12) This section shall come into force on the repeal of section 2 of the Official Secrets Act 1911.

Amendments—[1] Sub-s (3)(*c*) repealed by Statute Law (Repeals) Act 2004 Sch 1 Part 5 Group 18, with effect from 22 July 2004.

[2] Sub-s (4)(*a*)(iii) inserted and words in sub-s (6) substituted by the Government of Wales Act 1998 Sch 12 para 31 with effect from 1 February 1999 by virtue of the Government of Wales Act 1998 (Commencement No 3) Order, SI 1999.118. Words in sub-s (6) previously read 'or the Parliamentary Commissioner,'.

[3] Words in sub-ss (1), (4)(*b*), (*c*), (5)(*b*) amended, and sub-s (2A) and definition in sub-s (10) inserted, by the Social Security Contributions (Transfer of Functions, etc) Act 1999 s 6, Sch 6 para 9 with effect from 1 April 1999 by virtue of Social Security Contributions (Transfer of Functions, etc) Act 1999 (Commencement No 1 and Transitional Provisions) Order, SI 1999/527.

[4] Words in sub-ss (1), (4), inserted, sub-ss (1)(*aa*), (4)(*c*)(ia) substituted, sub-s (2ZA) substituted for sub-s (2AA), and in sub-s (10), definition of "tax credit" inserted, by TCA 2002 s 59, Sch 5 para 11(1), (2) with effect from 1 August 2002 (by virtue of SI 2002/1727).

[5] Words in sub-ss (1)(*c*), (2A)(*a*) substituted, and sub-s (11A) inserted, by the Employment Act 2002 s 53, Sch 7 para 1 with effect from 8 December 2002 (by virtue of SI 2002/2866).

[6] Words in sub-ss (2A)(*a*), (4)(*c*)(iii) inserted by TCA 2002 s 59, Sch 5 para 11(1), (4) with effect for the purpose of making subordinate legislation, from 26 February 2003, and for remaining purposes, from 1 April 2003 (by virtue of SI 2003/392).

[7] Sub-s (10A) inserted by Commissioners for Revenue and Customs Act 2005 s 50, Sch 4 para 39 with effect from 18 April 2005 by virtue of the Commissioners for Revenue and Customs Act (Commencement) Order, SI 2005/1126, art 2(2).

[8] Words in sub-ss (1), (4)(*b*), (*c*), (10), sub-ss (1)(*ab*), (2ZB), (4)(*c*)(ib) inserted, words in sub-s (5)(*b*) substituted by Child Trust Funds Act 2004 s 18 with effect from 1 January 2005 (by virtue of Child Trust Funds Act 2004 (Commencement No 1) Order, SI 2004/2422, art 2).

[9] Word in sub-s (4)(*a*)(iii), (11)(*c*) repealed, sub-s (4)(*a*)(v) inserted, words in sub-s (6) substituted by Scottish Public Services Ombudsman Act 2002 (Consequential Provisions and Modifications) Order, SI 2004/1823, art 10 with effect from 14 July 2004.

[10] Words substituted by Ombudsman (Northern Ireland) Order, SI 1996/1298 (NI 8) art 21(1), Sch 5.

[11] Sub-s (4)(*a*)(iv) substituted, words in sub-s (6) substituted, and words in sub-s (11)(*c*) repealed, by the Public Services Ombudsman (Wales) Act 2005, s 39(1), Sch 6, para 22 with effect from 1 April 2006, by virtue of the Public Services Ombudsman (Wales) Act 2005 (Commencement No 1 and Transitional Provisions and Savings) Order, SI 2005/2800. For further effect in relation to complaints made or referred to the Ombudsman about a matter relating to events that occurred before or after 1 April 2006, and in relation to estimates for income and expenses in relation to the financial year ending 31 March 2007, see arts 6, 7 thereof.

[12] In sub-s (2ZB)(*b*), words substituted for words "General Commissioners or the Special Commissioners", in sub-s (2A)(*a*)(ii), words substituted for words "the General Commissioners or the Special Commissioners", and sub-s (3) repealed, by the Transfer of Tribunal Functions and Revenue and Customs Appeals Order, SI 2009/56 art 3(1), Sch 1 paras 166, 167 with effect from 1 April 2009.

[13] In sub-ss (1)(c), (2A)(*a*), (4)(*c*)(iii), (5)(*b*), (11A), words substituted for words "statutory paternity pay", by the Work and Families Act 2006 s 11(1), Sch 1 para 2(*a*) with effect from 6 April 2010 (by virtue of SI 2010/495 art 4(*a*), (*d*)).

General

186 Interpretation etc

(1) In this Act "the Taxes Act 1970" means the Income and Corporation Taxes Act 1970 and "the Taxes Act 1988" means the Income and Corporation Taxes Act 1988.

(2), (3) (*not relevant to stamp duty*).

187 Repeals

(1) The enactments specified in Schedule 17 to this Act (which include unnecessary enactments) are hereby repealed to the extent specified in the third column of that Schedule, but subject to any provision at the end of any Part of that Schedule.

(2) (*not relevant to stamp duty*).

188 Short title

This Act may be cited as the Finance Act 1989.

FINANCE ACT 1990

(1990 Chapter 29)

ARRANGEMENT OF SECTIONS

PART III

STAMP DUTY AND STAMP DUTY RESERVE TAX

Repeals

An Act to grant certain duties, to alter other duties, and to amend the law relating to the National Debt and the Public Revenue, and to make further provision in connection with Finance.

[26th July 1990]

PART III

STAMP DUTY AND STAMP DUTY RESERVE TAX

Repeals

[107 Stamp duty to be abolished on bearer instruments][1]

[(1) Stamp duty shall not be chargeable under Schedule 15 to the Finance Act 1999 (bearer instruments).

(2) Subsection (1) above applies in relation to the charge under paragraph 1 of that Schedule (charge on issue) where the instrument is issued on or after the abolition day.

(3) Subsection (1) above applies in relation to the charge under paragraph 2 of that Schedule (charge on transfer of stock) where the stock constituted by or transferable by means of the instrument is transferred on or after the abolition day.][1]

Amendments—[1] This section substituted by FA 1999 s 113(3), Sch 16 para 12 with effect in relation to bearer instruments issued after 30 September 1999.

108 Transfer of securities: abolition of stamp duty

[(1) Stamp duty shall not be chargeable under Schedule 13 to the Finance Act 1999 (transfer of securities) [or section 67(3) or 70(3) of the Finance Act 1986 (stamp duty on certain transfers to depositary receipt systems and clearance systems)][2].][1]

(7) Subject to subsection (8) below, this section applies if the instrument is executed in pursuance of a contract made on or after the abolition day.

(8) In the case of an instrument—

(*a*) which falls within section 67(1) or (9) of the Finance Act 1986 (depositary receipts) or section 70(1) or (9) of that Act (clearance services), or

(*b*) which does not fall within section 67(1) or (9) or section 70(1) or (9) of that Act and is not executed in pursuance of a contract,

this section applies if the instrument is executed on or after the abolition day.

Amendments—[1] Sub-s (1) substituted for sub-ss (1)–(6) by FA 2003 s 125(4), Sch 20 para 5 with effect—

(*a*) in relation to instruments effecting land transactions that—

(i) are SDLT transactions within the meaning of Schedule 19 (stamp duty land tax: commencement and transitional provisions), or

(ii) would be such transactions but for an exemption or relief from stamp duty land tax;

(*b*) in relation to other instruments, if they are executed on or after the implementation date for the purposes of stamp duty land tax.

The implementation date is 1 December 2003 (by virtue of SI 2003/2899).

FA 2003 s 125 and Sch 20 have effect subject to FA 2003 Sch 15 para 13(2), (3).

[2] Words inserted in sub-s (1) by FA 2008 s 99, Sch 32 para 19 with effect in relation to instruments executed on or after 13 March 2008 and not stamped before 19 March 2008.

109 Stamp duty: other repeals

(1) Section 83 of the Stamp Act 1891 (fine for certain acts relating to securities) shall not apply where an instrument of assignment or transfer is executed, or a transfer or negotiation of the stock constituted by or transferable by means of a bearer instrument takes place, on or after the abolition day.

(2) The following provisions (which relate to the cancellation of certain instruments) shall not apply where the stock certificate or other instrument is entered on or after the abolition day—

(*a*) section 109(1) of the Stamp Act 1891,

(*b*) section 5(2) of the Finance Act 1899,

(*c*), (*d*) . . . [1]

(3) Section 67 of the Finance Act 1963 (prohibition of circulation of blank transfers) shall not apply where the sale is made on or after the abolition day; and section 16 of the Finance Act (Northern Ireland) 1963 (equivalent provision for Northern Ireland) shall not apply where the sale is made on or after the abolition day.

(4) No person shall be required to notify the Commissioners under section 68(1) or (2) or 71(1) or (2) of the Finance Act 1986 (depositary receipts and clearance services) if he first issues the receipts, provides the services or holds the securities as there mentioned on or after the abolition day.

(5) No company shall be required to notify the Commissioners under section 68(3) or 71(3) of that Act if it first becomes aware as there mentioned on or after the abolition day.

(6) The following provisions shall cease to have effect—

(*a*), (*b*) . . . [1]

(*c*) section 33 of the Finance Act 1970 (composition by financial institutions in respect of stamp duty),

(*d*) section 127(7) of the Finance Act 1976 (extension of composition provisions to Northern Ireland), and

(*e*) section 85 of the Finance Act 1986 (provisions about stock, marketable securities, etc).

(7) The provisions mentioned in subsection (6) above shall cease to have effect as provided by the Treasury by order.

(8) An order under subsection (7) above—

(*a*) shall be made by statutory instrument;

(*b*) may make different provision for different provisions or different purposes;

(*c*) may include such supplementary, incidental, consequential or transitional provisions as appear to the Treasury to be necessary or expedient.

(9) . . . [1]

Amendments—[1] Sub-ss (2)(*c*)(*d*), (6)(*a*)(*b*) and (9) repealed by FA 1999 Sch 20 Pt V(5) with effect for instruments executed from 6 February 2000.

110 Stamp duty reserve tax: abolition

(1) Stamp duty reserve tax shall cease to be chargeable.

(2) In relation to the charge to tax under section 87 of the Finance Act 1986 subsection (1) above applies where—

(*a*) the agreement to transfer is conditional and the condition is satisfied on or after the abolition day, or (*b*) the agreement is not conditional and is made on or after the abolition day.

(3) In relation to the charge to tax under section 93(1) of that Act subsection (1) above applies where securities are transferred, issued or appropriated on or after the abolition day (whenever the arrangement was made).

(4) In relation to the charge to tax under section 96(1) of that Act subsection (1) above applies where securities are transferred or issued on or after the abolition day (whenever the arrangement was made).

(5) In relation to the charge to tax under section 93(10) of that Act subsection (1) above applies where securities are issued or transferred on sale, under terms there mentioned, on or after the abolition day.

(6) In relation to the charge to tax under section 96(8) of that Act subsection (1) above applies where securities are issued or transferred on sale, under terms there mentioned, on or after the abolition day.

(7) Where before the abolition day securities are issued or transferred on sale under terms mentioned in section 93(10) of that Act, in construing section 93(10) the effect of subsections (1) and (3) above shall be ignored.

(8) Where before the abolition day securities are issued or transferred on sale under terms mentioned in section 96(8) of that Act, in construing section 96(8) the effect of subsections (1) and (4) above shall be ignored.

111 General

(1) In sections 107 to 110 above "the abolition day" means such day as may be appointed by the Treasury by order made by statutory instrument.

(2) Sections 107 to 109 above shall be construed as one with the Stamp Act 1891.

Paired shares

112 Stamp duty

(1) (*amends* FA 1988 s 143(1)(*b*)).

(2) Subsection (1) above applies where—

(*a*) the offers referred to in section 143(1) are made, or are to be made, on or after the day on which this Act is passed, and

(*b*) before the offers are made, or are to be made, units comprising shares in the two companies concerned were offered (whether before or on or after the day on which this Act is passed) in circumstances where section 143 applied without the amendment made by subsection (1) above.

113 Stamp duty reserve tax

(1) Section 99 of the Finance Act 1986 (stamp duty reserve tax: interpretation) shall be amended as follows.

(2), (3) (*amend* FA 1986 s 99(6A) and *insert* FA 1986 s 99(6B)).

(4) (*amends* FA 1986 s 99(9) *and is repealed by* FA 1999 Sch 20 Pt V(5) *with effect in relation to instruments executed from 6 February 2000*).

(5) Subsection (2) above applies where—

(*a*) the offers referred to in section 99(6A) are made on or after the day on which this Act is passed, and

(*b*) before the offers are made, units comprising shares in the two companies concerned were offered (whether before or on or after the day on which this Act is passed) in circumstances where section 99(6A) applied without the amendment made by subsection (2) above.

(6) Subsections (3) and (4) above apply where—

(*a*) the shares referred to in section 99(6B) are issued on or after the day on which this Act is passed, and

(*b*) before they are issued, units comprising shares in the two companies concerned were offered (whether before or on or after the day on which this Act is passed) in circumstances where section 99(6A) applied without the amendment made by subsection (2) above.

International organisations

114 International organisations

(1) (*inserts* FA 1984 s 126(3)(*d*)).

(2) Where an organisation or body is designated under section 126(1) or (4) before the day on which this Act is passed, subsection (1) above applies in relation to the issue of securities by the organisation or body on or after that day.

(3) Where an organisation or body is designated under section 126(1) or (4) on or after the day on which this Act is passed, subsection (1) above applies in relation to the issue of securities by the organisation or body after the designation.

PART IV
MISCELLANEOUS AND GENERAL

132 Repeals

The enactments specified in Schedule 19 to this Act (which include spent or unnecessary enactments) are hereby repealed to the extent specified in the third column of that Schedule, but subject to any provision at the end of any Part of that Schedule.

133 Short title

This Act may be cited as the Finance Act 1990.

SCHEDULE 19

REPEALS

Section 132

PART VI
STAMP DUTY

Chapter	Short title	Extent of repeal
1891 c 39.	The Stamp Act 1891.	In section 59(1), the words "or stock, or marketable securities,".
		Section 83.
		Section 109(1).
		In Schedule 1, the whole of the heading beginning "Bearer Instrument", and paragraph (1) of the general exemptions at the end of the Schedule.
1899 c 9.	The Finance Act 1899.	Section 5(2).
1946 c 64.	The Finance Act 1946.	Section 54(3) and (4).
		Section 56.
		Section 57(2) to (4).
1946 c 17 (NI).	The Finance (No 2) Act (Northern Ireland) 1946.	Section 25(3) and (4). Section 27.
		Section 28(2) to (4).
1947 c 35.	The Finance Act 1947.	Section 57.
1948 c 49.	The Finance Act 1948.	Section 74.
1950 c 32 (NI).	The Finance (No 2) Act (Northern Ireland) 1950.	Section 3(1).
1951 c 43.	The Finance Act 1951.	Section 42.
1963 c 18.	The Stock Transfer Act 1963.	In section 2(3), in paragraph (*a*) the words "and section 56(4) of the Finance Act 1946", and paragraph (*c*) and the word "and" immediately preceding it.
1963 c 25.	The Finance Act 1963.	Section 55(1A).
		In section 59, subsections (1) to (4).
		Section 60.
		Section 61.
		In section 62, in subsection (1) the words from "and any" to the end, and subsection (4).
		Section 65(1).
		Section 67.
1963 c 22 (NI).	The Finance Act (Northern Ireland) 1963.	Section 4(1A). In section 8, subsections (1) to (4).
		Section 9.
		Section 10.
		In section 11, in subsection (1) the words from "and any" to the end, and subsection (3).

Chapter	Short title	Extent of repeal
		Section 14(1).
		Section 16.
1963 c 24 (NI).	The Stock Transfer Act (Northern Ireland) 1963.	In section 2(3), in paragraph (*a*) the words "and section 27(4) of the Finance (No 2) Act (Northern Ireland) 1946", and paragraph (*c*) and the word "and" immediately preceding it.
1967 c 54.	The Finance Act 1967.	Section 30.
1967 c 20 (NI).	The Finance Act (Northern Ireland) 1967.	Section 7.
1970 c 24.	The Finance Act 1970.	Section 33.
		In Schedule 7, paragraph 6.
1970 c 21 (NI).	The Finance Act (Northern Ireland) 1970.	In Schedule 2, paragraph 6.
1974 c 30.	The Finance Act 1974.	In Schedule 11, paragraphs 2 and 12.
1975 c 80.	The OECD Support Fund Act 1975.	Section 4(2).
1976 c 40.	The Finance Act 1976.	In section 127, subsections (1) and (4) to (7).
		Section 131(3).
1980 c 48.	The Finance Act 1980.	Section 101.
1984 c 43.	The Finance Act 1984.	Section 126(3)(*c*) and (5).
1985 c 6.	The Companies Act 1985.	In Schedule 14, in paragraph 8 the words from "and, unless" to the end.
1985 c 54.	The Finance Act 1985.	Section 81.
1986 c 41.	The Finance Act 1986.	Section 64(1).
		Sections 65 to 72.
		Section 77.
		In section 79, subsections (2) to (8), and in subsection (12) the words "(7), (9),".
		Sections 80 to 85.
SI 1986/1032 (N16).	The Companies (Northern Ireland) Order 1986.	In Schedule 14, in paragraph 7 the words from "and unless" to the end.
1987 c 16.	The Finance Act 1987.	Sections 50 to 53.
1987 c 51.	The Finance (No 2) Act 1987.	Section 99.
1988 c 39.	The Finance Act 1988.	Section 143.
		In Schedule 13, paragraph 19.
1989 c 26.	The Finance Act 1989.	Sections 174 and 175.

1. So far as these repeals relate to bearer instruments, they have effect in accordance with section 107 of this Act.

2. So far as these repeals relate to instruments other than bearer instruments, they have effect in accordance with section 108 of this Act.

3. So far as these repeals relate to—

(*a*) any provision mentioned in subsection (1), (2), (3), (4) or (5) of section 109 of this Act, or

(*b*) any other provision to the extent that it is ancillary to or dependent on any provision so mentioned,

the repeals have effect in accordance with the subsection concerned.

4. So far as these repeals relate to—

(*a*) any provision mentioned in section 109(6) of this Act, or

(*b*) any other provision to the extent that it is ancillary to or dependent on any provision so mentioned,

the repeals have effect in accordance with any order under section 109(7) of this Act.

5. Paragraphs 1 and 2 above have effect subject to paragraphs 3 and 4 above.

PART VII
STAMP DUTY RESERVE TAX

Chapter	Short title	Extent of repeal
1986 c 41.	The Finance Act 1986.	Part IV.
1987 c 16.	The Finance Act 1987.	Section 56.
		Schedule 7.
1987 c 51.	The Finance (No 2) Act 1987.	Section 100.
1988 c 39.	The Finance Act 1988.	Section 144.
		In Schedule 13, paragraph 23.
1989 c 26.	The Finance Act 1989.	Sections 176 and 177.

These repeals have effect in accordance with section 110 of this Act.

FINANCE ACT 1991

(1991 Chapter 31)

An Act to grant certain duties, to alter other duties, and to amend the law relating to the National Debt and the Public Revenue, and to make further provision in connection with Finance.

[25th July 1991]

PART IV

STAMP DUTY

110 Stamp duty abolished in certain cases

[(1) Where apart from this section stamp duty under any of the provisions of Schedule 13 to the Finance Act 1999 would be chargeable on an instrument, stamp duty shall not be so chargeable if the property consists entirely of exempt property.][2]

(2)–(4) . . . [2]

(5) For the purposes of this section exempt property is property other than—

(*a*) land,

(*b*) . . . [1]

(*c*) a licence to occupy land.

(6) This section applies to—

(*a*) an instrument executed in pursuance of a contract made on or after the abolition day;

(*b*) an instrument which is not executed in pursuance of a contract and is executed on or after the abolition day.

(7) For the purposes of this section the abolition day is such day as may be appointed under section 111(1) of the Finance Act 1990 (abolition of stamp duty for securities etc).

Amendments—[1] Sub-s (5)(*b*) repealed by the Trusts of Land and Appointment of Trustees Act 1996 s 25(2), Sch 4 with effect from 1 January 1997 (by virtue of SI 1996/2974), subject to savings in s 25(4), (5).

[2] Sub-ss (1)–(4) substituted by sub-s (1) by FA 1999 s 112(4), Sch 14 para 25 with effect in relation to instruments executed after 30 September 1999. This does not apply to transfers or other instruments relating to units under a unit trust scheme by virtue of FA 1999 s 122. Previously the text read:

"(1) This section applies where—

(*a*) apart from this section stamp duty under any of the headings mentioned in subsection (3) below would be chargeable on an instrument to which this section applies, and

(*b*) the condition mentioned in subsection (4) below is fulfilled.

(2) In such a case stamp duty under the heading concerned shall not be chargeable on the instrument.

(3) The headings are the following headings in Schedule 1 to the Stamp Act 1891—

(*a*) the heading "conveyance or transfer on sale";

(*b*) the heading "conveyance or transfer of any kind not hereinbefore described";

(*c*) the heading beginning "declaration of any use or trust";

(*d*) the heading beginning "disposition in Scotland of any property";

(*e*) . . . ;

(*f*) the heading "partition or division";

(*g*) the heading "release or renunciation of any property, or of any right or interest in any property";

(*h*) the heading "surrender".

(4) The condition is that the property concerned consists entirely of exempt property; . . ."

111 Stamp duty reduced in certain cases

(1) This section applies where—

(*a*) stamp duty under [Part I of Schedule 13 to the Finance Act 1999 ([transfer][2] on sale)][1] is chargeable on an instrument to which this section applies, and

(*b*) part of the property concerned consists of exempt property.

(2) In such a case—

(*a*) the consideration in respect of which duty would be charged (apart from this section) shall be apportioned, on such basis as is just and reasonable, as between the part of the property which consists of exempt property and the part which does not, and

(*b*) the instrument shall be charged only in respect of the consideration attributed to such of the property as is not exempt property.

(3) In this section "exempt property" has the same meaning as in section 110 above.

(4) This section applies to—

(*a*) an instrument executed in pursuance of a contract made on or after the abolition day;

(*b*) an instrument which is not executed in pursuance of a contract and is executed on or after the abolition day.

(5) In this section "the abolition day" has the same meaning as in section 110 above.

Amendments—[1] Words in sub-s (1) substituted by FA 1999 s 112(4), Sch 14 para 26 with effect in relation to instruments executed after 30 September 1999. This does not apply to transfers or other instruments relating to units under a unit trust scheme by virtue of FA 1999 s 122. Previously the text read 'the heading "conveyance or transfer on sale" in Schedule 1 to the Stamp Act 1891'.

2 The word "transfer" substituted for the words "conveyance or transfer" in enactments relating to stamp duty by FA 2003 Sch 20 para 3.

112 Apportionment of consideration for stamp duty purposes

(1) Subsection (2) below applies where part of the property referred to in section 58(1) of the Stamp Act 1891 (consideration to be apportioned between different instruments as parties think fit) consists of exempt property.

(2) Section 58 (1) shall have effect as if "the parties think fit" read "is just and reasonable".

(3) Subsection (4) below applies where—

(*a*) part of the property referred to in section 58(2) of the Stamp Act 1891 (property contracted to be purchased by two or more persons etc) consists of exempt property, and

(*b*) both or (as the case may be) all the relevant persons are connected with one another.

(4) Section 58(2) shall have effect as if the words from "for distinct parts of the consideration" to the end of the subsection read ", the consideration is to be apportioned in such manner as is just and reasonable, so that a distinct consideration for each separate part or parcel is set forth in the conveyance relating thereto, and such conveyance is to be charged with *ad valorem* duty in respect of such distinct consideration".

(5) In a case where subsection (2) or (4) above applies and the consideration is apportioned in a manner that is not just and reasonable, the enactments relating to stamp duty shall have effect as if—

(*a*) the consideration had been apportioned in a manner that is just and reasonable, and

(*b*) the amount of any distinct consideration set forth in any conveyance relating to a separate part or parcel of property were such amount as is found by a just and reasonable apportionment (and not the amount actually set forth).

(6) In this section "exempt property" has the same meaning as in section 110 above.

(7) For the purposes of subsection (3) above—

(*a*) a person is a relevant person if he is a person by or for whom the property is contracted to be purchased;

(*b*) the question whether persons are connected with one another shall be determined in accordance with [section 1122 of the Corporation Tax Act 2010][1].

(8) This section applies where the contract concerned is made on or after the abolition day.

(9) In this section "the abolition day" has the same meaning as in section 110 above.

Amendments—[1] In sub-s (7)(*b*) words substituted for words "section 839 of the Taxes Act 1988" by CTA 2010 s 1177, Sch 1 para 224. CTA 2010 has effect for corporation tax purposes for accounting periods ending on or after 1 April 2010, and for income and capital gains tax purposes for the tax year 2010–11 and subsequent tax years.

113 Certification of instruments for stamp duty purposes

[(1) For the purposes of paragraph 6(1) of Schedule 13 to the Finance Act 1999 (meaning of instrument being certified at an amount)—

(*a*) a sale or contract or agreement for the sale of exempt property within the meaning of section 110 above shall be disregarded; and

(*b*) any statement as mentioned in that provision shall be construed as leaving out of account any matter which is to be so disregarded.][1]

(2), (3) . . .[1]

(4) This section applies to—

(*a*) an instrument executed in pursuance of a contract made on or after the abolition day;

(*b*) an instrument which is not executed in pursuance of a contract and is executed on or after the abolition day.

(5) In this section "the abolition day" has the same meaning as in section 110 above.

Amendments—[1] Sub-ss (1)–(3) substituted by sub-s (1) by FA 1999 s 112(4), Sch 14 para 27 with effect in relation to instruments executed after 30 September 1999. This does not apply to transfers or other instruments relating to units under a unit trust scheme by virtue of FA 1999 s 122. Previously the text read:

"(1) Section 34 of the Finance Act 1958 and section 7 of the Finance Act (Northern Ireland) 1958 shall be amended as mentioned in subsections (2) and (3) below.

(2) In subsection (4) of each of those sections (certification of instrument at a particular amount) the following paragraph shall be substituted for paragraph (a)—

"(*a*) any sale or contract or agreement for the sale of exempt property shall be disregarded; and".

(3) In each of those sections the following subsection shall be inserted after subsection (4)—

'(4A) In subsection (4) above "exempt property" has the same meaning as in section 110 of the Finance Act 1991.'"

114 Acquisition under statute: exempt property

(1)–(3) . . .

(4) This section applies where the Act mentioned in section 12 of the Finance Act 1895, and by virtue of which property is vested or a person is authorised to purchase property, is passed on or after the abolition day.

(5) In this section "the abolition day" has the same meaning as in section 110 above.

Note—Sub-ss (1)–(3) amend FA 1949 s 36 and FA(NI)1949 s 9.

115 Northern Ireland bank notes: duty abolished

Amendments—This section repealed by FA 1999 Sch 20 Pt V(2) with effect in relation to instruments executed, or bearer instruments issued, from 1 October 1999, subject to the provisions in FA 1999 Sch 20 Pt V(2) Note 2. Previously the text read:

"(1) In its application to Northern Ireland, the Stamp Act 1891 shall have effect with the omission from Schedule 1 of the heading "bank note".

(2) The licences required to be taken out under the Bankers' Composition (Ireland) Act 1828 (licences for bankers in Northern Ireland issuing certain promissory notes) are hereby abolished.

(3) This section takes effect on 1st January 1992."

116 Investment exchanges and clearing houses: stamp duty

(1) The Treasury may make regulations providing as mentioned in this section with regard to any circumstances which—

(*a*) would (apart from the regulations) give rise to a charge to stamp duty,

(*b*) involve a prescribed recognised investment exchange or a prescribed recognised clearing house, or a member or nominee (or member or nominee of a prescribed description) of such an exchange [or clearing house, or a nominee (or nominee of a prescribed description) of a member of such an exchange or clearing house, and][3]

(*c*) are such as are prescribed.

(2) The regulations may provide that the charge to stamp duty shall be treated as not arising or (depending on the terms of the regulations) as reduced.

(3) Regulations under this section—

(*a*) shall be made by statutory instrument subject to annulment in pursuance of a resolution of the House of Commons;

(*b*) may include such supplementary, incidental, consequential or transitional provisions as appear to the Treasury to be necessary or expedient;

(*c*) may make different provision for different circumstances;

(*d*) may make any provision in such way as the Treasury think fit (whether by amending enactments or otherwise).

(4) In this section—

[(*aa*) "the Directive" means Directive 2004/39/EC of the European Parliament and of the Council of 21 April 2004 on markets in financial instruments, as amended from time to time,][2]

(*a*) "prescribed" means prescribed by the regulations,

(*b*) "recognised investment exchange" means a recognised investment exchange within the meaning of the [Financial Services and Markets Act 2000][1][, a regulated market within the meaning of the Directive or a multilateral trading facility within the meaning of the Directive][2] and

(*c*) "recognised clearing house" means a recognised clearing house within the meaning of that Act.

Regulations—See Stamp Duty and Stamp Duty Reserve Tax (Investment Exchanges and Clearing Houses) Regulations, SI 1997/2429 and SI 1999/3263.

Stamp Duty and Stamp Duty Reserve Tax (Investment Exchanges and Clearing Houses) (Jiway Limited) Regulations, SI 2000/2995.

Stamp Duty Reserve Tax (Investment Exchanges and Clearing Houses) (The London Stock Exchange) Regulations, SI 2001/255.

Stamp Duty and Stamp Duty Reserve Tax (Investment Exchanges and Clearing Houses) Regulations, SI 2004/3218.

Stamp Duty and Stamp Duty Reserve Tax (Investment Exchanges and Clearing Houses) (Eurex Clearing AG) Regulations, SI 2007/1097.

Stamp Duty and Stamp Duty Reserve Tax (Investment Exchanges and Clearing Houses) (European Central Counterparty Limited and the Turquoise Multilateral Trading Facility) Regulations, SI 2008/1814.

Stamp Duty and Stamp Duty Reserve Tax (Investment Exchanges and Clearing Houses) Regulations, SI 2008/2777.

Stamp Duty and Stamp Duty Reserve Tax (Investment Exchanges and Clearing Houses) Regulations (No 2), SI 2008/3235.

Stamp Duty and Stamp Duty Reserve Tax (Investment Exchanges and Clearing Houses) Regulations, SI 2009/35.

Stamp Duty and Stamp Duty Reserve Tax (Investment Exchanges and Clearing Houses) Regulations (No 2), SI 2009/194.

Stamp Duty and Stamp Duty Reserve Tax (Investment Exchanges and Clearing Houses) Regulations (No 3), SI 2009/397.

Stamp Duty and Stamp Duty Reserve Tax (Investment Exchanges and Clearing Houses) Regulations (No 4), SI 2009/1115.

Stamp Duty and Stamp Duty Reserve Tax (Investment Exchanges and Clearing Houses) Regulations (No 5), SI 2009/1344.

Stamp Duty and Stamp Duty Reserve Tax (Investment Exchanges and Clearing Houses) Regulations (No 9), SI 2009/1828.

Stamp Duty and Stamp Duty Reserve Tax (Investment Exchanges and Clearing Houses) Regulations (No 10), SI 2009/1831.

Stamp Duty and Stamp Duty Reserve Tax (Investment Exchanges and Clearing Houses) Regulations (No 11), SI 2009/1832.

Stamp Duty and Stamp Duty Reserve Tax (Investment Exchanges and Clearing Houses) (Over the Counter) Regulations, SI 2009/3088.

Stamp Duty and Stamp Duty Reserve Tax (Investment Exchanges and Clearing Houses) Regulations, SI 2010/1818.

Stamp Duty and Stamp Duty Reserve Tax (Investment Exchanges and Clearing Houses) Regulations (No 2), SI 2010/1819.

Stamp Duty and Stamp Duty Reserve Tax (Investment Exchanges and Clearing Houses) (Over the Counter) Regulations, SI 2010/1824.

Stamp Duty and Stamp Duty Reserve Tax (Investment Exchanges and Clearing Houses) Regulations (No 3), SI 2010/1877.

Stamp Duty and Stamp Duty Reserve Tax (Investment Exchanges and Clearing Houses) Regulations (No 4), SI 2010/1897 .

Amendments—[1] Words substituted by the Financial Services and Markets Act 2000 s 432(1), Sch 20 para 5 with effect from 1 December 2001 (by virtue of SI 2001/3538).

2 In sub-s (4), para (*aa*) inserted, and words in para (*b*) inserted, by FA 2007 s 73, Sch 21 para 7 with effect from 19 July 2007.

3 In sub-s (1)(*b*), words substituted for words ", or a nominee (or nominee of a prescribed description) of such a clearing house, or a nominee (or nominee of a prescribed description) of a member of such an exchange, and", by FA 2010 s 65. This amendment is treated as always having had effect (FA 2010 s 65(2)).

117 Investment exchanges and clearing houses: SDRT

(1) The Treasury may make regulations providing as mentioned in this section with regard to any circumstances which—

(*a*) would (apart from the regulations) give rise to a charge to stamp duty reserve tax,

(*b*) involve a prescribed recognised investment exchange or a prescribed recognised clearing house, or a member or nominee (or member of nominee of a prescribed description) of such an exchange [or clearing house, or a nominee (or nominee of a prescribed description) of a member of such an exchange or clearing house, and][1]

(*c*) are such as are prescribed.

(2) The regulations may provide that the charge to stamp duty reserve tax shall be treated as not arising or (depending on the terms of the regulations) as reduced.

(3) Subsections (3) and (4) of section 116 above shall apply for the purposes of this section as they apply for the purposes of that.

Regulations—See Stamp Duty and Stamp Duty Reserve Tax (Investment Exchanges and Clearing Houses) Regulations, SI 1997/2429 and SI 1999/3263.

Stamp Duty Reserve Tax (virt-x Exchange Ltd) Regulations, SI 1995/2051.

Stamp Duty and Stamp Duty Reserve Tax (Investment Exchanges and Clearing Houses) (Jiway Limited) Regulations, SI 2000/2995.

Stamp Duty Reserve Tax (Investment Exchanges and Clearing Houses) (The London Stock Exchange) Regulations, SI 2001/255.

Stamp Duty and Stamp Duty Reserve Tax (Investment Exchanges and Clearing Houses) Regulations, SI 2004/3218.

Stamp Duty and Stamp Duty Reserve Tax (Investment Exchanges and Clearing Houses) (Eurex Clearing AG) Regulations, SI 2007/1097.

Stamp Duty and Stamp Duty Reserve Tax (Investment Exchanges and Clearing Houses) (European Central Counterparty Limited and the Turquoise Multilateral Trading Facility) Regulations, SI 2008/1814.

Stamp Duty and Stamp Duty Reserve Tax (Investment Exchanges and Clearing Houses) Regulations, SI 2008/2777.

Stamp Duty and Stamp Duty Reserve Tax (Investment Exchanges and Clearing Houses) Regulations, SI 2009/35.

Stamp Duty and Stamp Duty Reserve Tax (Investment Exchanges and Clearing Houses) Regulations (No 2), SI 2009/194.

Stamp Duty and Stamp Duty Reserve Tax (Investment Exchanges and Clearing Houses) Regulations (No 3), SI 2009/397.

Stamp Duty and Stamp Duty Reserve Tax (Investment Exchanges and Clearing Houses) Regulations (No 4), SI 2009/1115.

Stamp Duty and Stamp Duty Reserve Tax (Investment Exchanges and Clearing Houses) Regulations (No 5), SI 2009/1344.

Stamp Duty and Stamp Duty Reserve Tax (Investment Exchanges and Clearing Houses) Regulations (No 9), SI 2009/1828.

Stamp Duty and Stamp Duty Reserve Tax (Investment Exchanges and Clearing Houses) Regulations (No 10), SI 2009/1831.

Stamp Duty and Stamp Duty Reserve Tax (Investment Exchanges and Clearing Houses) Regulations (No 11), SI 2009/1832.

Stamp Duty and Stamp Duty Reserve Tax (Investment Exchanges and Clearing Houses) (Over the Counter) Regulations, SI 2009/3088.

Stamp Duty and Stamp Duty Reserve Tax (Investment Exchanges and Clearing Houses) Regulations, SI 2010/1818.

Stamp Duty and Stamp Duty Reserve Tax (Investment Exchanges and Clearing Houses) Regulations (No 2), SI 2010/1819.

Stamp Duty and Stamp Duty Reserve Tax (Investment Exchanges and Clearing Houses) (Over the Counter) Regulations, SI 2010/1824.

Stamp Duty and Stamp Duty Reserve Tax (Investment Exchanges and Clearing Houses) Regulations (No 3), SI 2010/1877.

Stamp Duty and Stamp Duty Reserve Tax (Investment Exchanges and Clearing Houses) Regulations (No 4), SI 2010/1897.

Amendments—[1] In sub-s (1)(*b*), words substituted for words ", or a nominee (or nominee of a prescribed description) of such a clearing house, or a nominee (or nominee of a prescribed description) of a member of such an exchange, and", by FA 2010 s 65. This amendment is treated as always having had effect (FA 2010 s 65(2)).

FINANCE (NO 2) ACT 1992

(1992 Chapter 48)

Note—This Act received Royal Assent on 16 July 1992.

SCHEDULE 17

NORTHERN IRELAND ELECTRICITY

Section 77

Interpretation

1—(1) In this Schedule—

"the final accounting period" means the last complete accounting period of NIE ending before the transfer date;

"NIE" means Northern Ireland Electricity;

"the Order" means the Electricity (Northern Ireland) Order 1992;

"successor company" means a company nominated under Article 69(2) of the Order for the purposes of Article 69(1) of the Order;

"transfer date" means the day appointed under Article 69(3) of the Order for the purposes of Article 69(4) of the Order;

"transfer scheme" means a scheme under Article 69(1) of the Order.

(2) This Schedule, so far as it relates to corporation tax on chargeable gains, shall be construed as one with the Capital Gains Tax Act 1979 or, where appropriate, the Taxation of Chargeable Gains Act 1992.

(3) For the purposes of this Schedule a transfer or agreement shall be regarded as made in pursuance of Schedule 10 to the Order if the making of that transfer or agreement is required or authorised by or under paragraph 3 or 5 of that Schedule (allocation of assets and liabilities and variation of transfers by agreement).

Stamp duty reserve tax

9—(1) No agreement made for the purposes of or for purposes connected with the transfer scheme shall give rise to a charge to stamp duty reserve tax.

(2) No agreement which is made in pursuance of Schedule 10 to the Order shall give rise to a charge to stamp duty reserve tax.

(3) This paragraph shall be deemed to have come into force on 1st April 1992.

FINANCE ACT 1993

(1993 Chapter 34)

Note—This Act received Royal Assent on 27 July 1993.

PART V
STAMP DUTY

201 Increase in stamp duty threshold

Amendments—This section repealed by FA 1999 Sch 20 Pt V(2) with effect in relation to instruments executed, or bearer instruments issued, from 1 October 1999, subject to the provisions in FA 1999 Sch 20 Pt V(2) Note 2. Previously the text read:

"(1) (*amends* FA 1963 s 55(1), (2) and FA (Northern Ireland) 1963, s 4(1), (2)).

(2) This section applies to—

(*a*) instruments executed on or after 16th March 1993 and before 23rd March 1993 and not stamped before 23rd March 1993;

(*b*) instruments executed on or after 23rd March 1993.

(3) For the purposes of section 14(4) of the Stamp Act 1891 (instruments not to be given in evidence etc unless stamped in accordance with the law in force at the time of first execution) the law in force at the time of execution of an instrument falling within subsection (2)(*a*) above shall be deemed to be that as varied in accordance with subsection (1) above.

(4) This section shall be deemed to have come into force on 23rd March 1993."

202 Rent to mortgage: England and Wales

(1) Subsection (2) below applies where—

(*a*) a person exercises the right to acquire on rent to mortgage terms under Part V of the Housing Act 1985 and

(*b*) in pursuance of the exercise of that right a conveyance of the freehold is executed in his favour as regards the dwelling-house concerned.

(2) For the purposes of the enactments relating to stamp duty chargeable under [Part I of Schedule 13 to the Finance Act 1999 ([transfer][2] on sale)][1], the consideration for the sale shall be taken to be equal to the price which, by virtue of section 126 of the Housing Act 1985 would be payable for the dwelling-house on a conveyance if the person were exercising the right to buy under Part V of that Act.

(3) Subsection (4) below applies where—

(*a*) a person exercises the right to acquire on rent to mortgage terms under Part V of the Housing Act 1985 and

(*b*) in pursuance of the exercise of that right a lease is executed in his favour as regards the dwelling-house concerned.

(4) In such a case—

(*a*) the lease shall not be chargeable with stamp duty under [Part II of Schedule 13 to the Finance Act 1999 (lease)][2] but shall be chargeable with stamp duty under [Part I of that Schedule ([transfer][3] on sale)][2] as if it were a conveyance on sale;

(*b*) for the purposes of the enactments relating to stamp duty chargeable under [Part I of that Schedule][2] the consideration for the sale mentioned in paragraph (*a*) above shall be taken to be equal to the price which, by virtue of section 126 of the Housing Act 1985 would be payable for the dwelling-house on a grant if the person were exercising the right to buy under Part V of that Act.

(5) This section shall apply where the conveyance or lease is executed after the day on which this Act is passed.

Amendments—[1] Words in sub-s (2) substituted by FA 1999 s 112(4), Sch 14 para 28 with effect in relation to instruments executed after 30 September 1999. This does not apply to transfers or other instruments relating to units under a unit trust scheme by virtue of FA 1999 s 122. Previously the text read 'the heading "Conveyance or Transfer on Sale" in Schedule 1 to the Stamp Act 1891'.

[2] Words in sub-s (4) substituted by FA 1999 s 112(4), Sch 14 para 28 with effect in relation to instruments executed after 30 September 1999. This does not apply to transfers or other instruments relating to units under a unit trust scheme by virtue of FA 1999 s 122. Previously the text read 'the heading "Lease or Tack" in Schedule 1 to the Stamp Act 1891', 'the heading "Conveyance or Transfer on Sale" in that Schedule' and 'the heading "Conveyance or Transfer on Sale" ' respectively.

[3] The word "transfer" substituted for the words "conveyance or transfer" in enactments relating to stamp duty by FA 2003 Sch 20 para 3.

203 Rent to loan: Scotland

(1) Subsection (2) below applies where—

(*a*) a person exercises the right to purchase a house by way of the rent to loan scheme under Part III of the Housing (Scotland) Act 1987 and

(*b*) in pursuance of the exercise of that right a heritable disposition of the house is executed in favour of him.

(2) For the purposes of the enactments relating to stamp duty chargeable under [Part I of Schedule 13 to the Finance Act 1999 ([transfer][2] on sale)][1], the consideration for the sale shall be taken to be equal to the price which, by virtue of section 62 of the Housing (Scotland) Act 1987 would be payable for the house if the person were exercising the right to purchase under section 61 of that Act.

(3) This section shall apply where the disposition is executed after the day on which this Act is passed.

Amendments—[1] Words in sub-s (2) substituted by FA 1999 s 112(4), Sch 14 para 29 with effect in relation to instruments executed after 30 September 1999. This does not apply to transfers or other instruments relating to units under a unit trust scheme by virtue of FA 1999 s 122. Previously the text read 'the heading "Conveyance or Transfer on Sale" in Schedule 1 to the Stamp Act 1891'.

[2] The word "transfer" substituted for the words "conveyance or transfer" in enactments relating to stamp duty by FA 2003 Sch 20 para 3.

204 Method of denoting stamp duty

(1) The Treasury may make regulations as to the method by which stamp duty is to be denoted.

(2) In particular, regulations under this section may—

(*a*) provide for duty to be denoted by impressed stamps or adhesive stamps or by a record printed or made by a machine or implement or by such other method as may be prescribed;

(*b*) provide for one method only to be used, whether generally or in prescribed cases;

(*c*) provide for alternative methods to be available, whether generally or in prescribed cases;

(*d*) make different provision for different cases;

and cases may be designated by reference to the type of instrument concerned, the geographical area involved, or such other factors as the Treasury think fit.

(3) Regulations under this section may provide that where stamp duty is denoted by a method which (in the case of the instrument concerned) is required or permitted by the law in force at the time it is stamped, for the purposes of section 14(4) of the Stamp Act 1891 (instruments not to be given in evidence etc unless stamped in accordance with the law in force at the time of *first*[1] execution) the method shall be treated as being in accordance with the law in force at the time when the instrument was *first*[1] executed.

(4) Regulations under this section may include such supplementary, incidental, consequential or transitional provisions as appear to the Treasury to be necessary or expedient.

(5) Regulations under this section may make provision in such way as the Treasury think fit, and in particular may amend or repeal or modify the effect of any provision of any Act.

(6) In this section "prescribed" means prescribed by regulations under this section.

(7) The power to make regulations under this section shall be exercisable by statutory instrument subject to annulment in pursuance of a resolution of the House of Commons.

Amendments—[1] Words in sub-s (3) repealed by FA 2000 s 156, Sch 40 Pt III with effect from 28 July 2000.

PART VI
MISCELLANEOUS AND GENERAL

Statutory effect of resolutions etc

205 The 1968 Act

(1) The Provisional Collection of Taxes Act 1968 shall be amended as follows.

(2)–(3) (*not relevant to stamp duty*).

(4)–(5) (*amend* PCTA 1968 s 1).

(6) (*not relevant to stamp duty*).

(7) This section shall apply in relation to resolutions passed after the day on which this Act is passed.

207 Stamp duty

(1) (*amends* FA 1973 s 50(2)).

(2) This section shall apply in relation to resolutions passed after the day on which this Act is passed.

FINANCE ACT 1994

(1994 Chapter 9)

An Act to grant certain duties, to alter other duties, and to amend the law relating to the National Debt and the Public Revenue, and to make further provision in connection with Finance.

[3rd May 1994]

PART VI
[STAMP DUTY]

Amendments—Part Heading substituted by F(No 2)A 2005 s 48(3), (5) with effect from 30 July 2009 (by virtue of SI 2009/2094 art 2). Heading previously read "Stamp duty and stamp duty land tax".

239 Execution of deeds

(1) (*amends* SA 1891, s 122).

(2) (*amends* SDMA 1891, s 27).

(3) This section shall apply to any instrument except one which, on or before 7th December 1993, has been executed for the purposes of the Stamp Act 1891 as that Act has effect before amendment by this section.

[240 Time for presenting agreement for lease][1]

[(1) This section applies if there are presented for stamping at the same time in pursuance of Schedule 13 to the Finance Act 1999—

(*a*) an agreement for a lease, and

(*b*) the lease which gives effect to the agreement,

and the duty (if any) chargeable on the agreement is paid.

(2) Section 15A of that Act (interest payable on late stamping) applies in relation to the agreement as if the reference to the day on which the instrument was executed were to the day on which the lease was executed.

(3) For the purposes of section 15B of that Act (penalty on late stamping) the agreement is treated—

(*a*) as if it had been executed at the same time and place as the lease, and

(*b*) where the lease was executed outside the United Kingdom, as if it had been first received in the United Kingdom at the same time as the lease.

(4) For the purposes of this section a lease gives effect to an agreement if the lease is granted subsequent to the agreement and either is in conformity with the agreement or relates to substantially the same property and term as the agreement.

(5) References in this section to an agreement for a lease include missives of let in Scotland.][1]

Amendments—[1] This section substituted by FA 1999 s 109(3), Sch 12 para 4 with effect in relation to instruments executed after 30 September 1999. This does not apply to transfers or other instruments relating to units under a unit trust scheme by virtue of FA 1999 s 122. Previously the text read:

"240 Time for presenting agreements for leases

(1) If there are presented for stamping at the same time in pursuance of the Stamp Act 1891—

(*a*) an agreement for a lease or tack, and

(*b*) the lease or tack which gives effect to the agreement,

and the duty (if any) chargeable on the agreement is paid, the agreement shall be treated for the purposes of section 15 of that Act (penalty upon stamping instruments after execution) as if it had been first executed when the lease or tack which gives effect to the agreement was first executed.

(2) No lease or tack shall be treated as duly stamped unless—

(*a*) it contains a certificate that there is no agreement to which it gives effect, or

(*b*) it is stamped with a stamp denoting—

(i) that there is an agreement to which it gives effect which is not chargeable with duty, or

(ii) the duty paid on the agreement to which it gives effect.

(3) For the purposes of this section a lease or tack gives effect to an agreement if the lease or tack is granted subsequent to the agreement and either is in conformity with the agreement or relates to substantially the same property and term as the agreement.

(4) Subsection (1) above shall apply to agreements executed on or after 6th May 1994; and subsection (2) above shall apply to any lease or tack executed on or after that day."

[240A Requirements before lease treated as duly stamped][1]

[(1) A lease shall not be treated as duly stamped unless—

(*a*) it contains a certificate that there is no agreement to which it gives effect, or

(*b*) it is stamped with a stamp denoting—

(i) that there is an agreement to which it gives effect which is not chargeable with duty, or

(ii) the duty paid on the agreement to which it gives effect.

(2) For the purposes of this section a lease gives effect to an agreement if the lease is granted subsequent to the agreement and either is in conformity with the agreement or relates to substantially the same property and term as the agreement.

(3) References in this section to a lease do not include, and references in this section to an agreement do include, missives of let in Scotland.][1]

Amendments—[1] This section inserted by FA 1999 s 109(3), Sch 12 para 4 with effect in relation to instruments executed after 30 September 1999. This does not apply to transfers or other instruments relating to units under a unit trust scheme by virtue of FA 1999 s 122.

241 Exchange, partition, etc

(1) Where—

(*a*) the consideration for the transfer or vesting of any estate or interest in land or the grant of any [lease][1] consists of or includes any property, and

(*b*) for the purposes of stamp duty chargeable under or by reference to [Part I of Schedule 13 to the Finance Act 1999 ([transfer][3] on sale)][1] no amount or value is, apart from this section, attributed to that property on that transfer, vesting or grant,

then, for those purposes, the consideration or, as the case may be, the consideration so far as relating to that property shall be taken to be the market value of the property immediately before the instrument in question is executed and accordingly the instrument shall be charged with ad valorem duty under that heading.

(2) For the purposes of this section the market value of property at any time is the price which that property might reasonably be expected to fetch on a sale at that time in the open market.

(3)–(5) . . . [2]

(6) This section shall apply to instruments executed after 7th December 1993, not being instruments executed in pursuance of a contract made before 30th November 1993.

Press releases etc—IR Tax Bulletin August 1995 (general guidance on stamp duty on exchanges of interests in land and buildings).

Amendments—[1] Words in sub-s (1) substituted by FA 1999 s 112(4), Sch 14 para 30 with effect in relation to instruments executed after 30 September 1999. This does not apply to transfers or other instruments relating to units under a unit trust scheme by virtue of FA 1999 s 122. Previously the text read 'lease or tack' and 'the heading "Conveyance or Transfer on Sale" in Schedule 1 to the Stamp Act 1891' respectively.

[2] Sub-ss (3)–(5) repealed by FA 1999 Sch 20 Pt V(2) with effect in relation to instruments executed, or bearer instruments issued, from 1 October 1999, subject to the provisions in FA 1999 Sch 20 Pt V(2) Note 2. Previously the text read:

"(3) Stamp duty shall not be chargeable under the heading "Exchange or Excambion" in Schedule 1 to the Stamp Act 1891, and section 73 of that Act (exchange and partition or division) shall cease to apply to the exchange of property; . . .

(4), (5) . . .".

[3] The word "transfer" substituted for the words "conveyance or transfer" in enactments relating to stamp duty by FA 2003 Sch 20 para 3.

242 Where consideration not ascertainable from conveyance or lease

(1) Where, for the purposes of stamp duty chargeable under or by reference to [Part I of Schedule 13 to the Finance Act 1999 ([transfer][3] on sale)][2], the consideration, or any part of the consideration, for—

(*a*) the transfer or vesting of any estate or interest in land, or

(*b*) the grant of any [lease][1],

cannot, apart from this subsection, be ascertained at the time the instrument in question is executed, the consideration for the transfer, vesting or grant shall for those purposes be taken to be the market value immediately before the instrument is executed of the estate or interest transferred or vested or, as the case may be, the [lease][1] granted.

(2) Where, for the purposes of stamp duty chargeable under [paragraph 12 of Schedule 13 to the Finance Act 1999][2], the rent, or any part of the rent, payable under any [lease][1] cannot, apart from this subsection, be ascertained at the time it is executed, the rent shall for those purposes be taken to be the market rent at that time.

(3) For the purposes of this section—

(*a*) the cases where consideration or rent cannot be ascertained at any time do not include cases where the consideration or rent could be ascertained on the assumption that any future event mentioned in the instrument in question were or were not to occur, and

(*b*) the market rent of a [lease][1] at any time is the rent which the [lease][1] might reasonably be expected to fetch at that time in the open market,

and in this section "market value" has the same meaning as in section 241 above.

(4) This section shall apply to instruments executed after 7th December 1993.

Press releases etc—IR Tax Bulletin August 1995 (general guidance on stamp duty where the consideration is unascertainable).

Amendments—[1] "Lease" substituted for the words "lease or tack" throughout the section by FA 1999 s 112(4), Sch 14 para 31 with effect in relation to instruments executed after 30 September 1999. This does not apply to transfers or other instruments relating to units under a unit trust scheme by virtue of FA 1999 s 122.

2 Words in sub-ss (1) and (2) substituted by FA 1999 s 112(4), Sch 14 para 31 with effect in relation to instruments executed after 30 September 1999. This does not apply to transfers or other instruments relating to units under a unit trust scheme by virtue of FA 1999 s 122. Previously the text read 'the heading "Conveyance or Transfer on Sale" in Schedule 1 to the Stamp Act 1891' and 'paragraph (3) of the heading "Lease or Tack" in Schedule 1 to that Act' respectively.

3 The word "transfer" substituted for the words "conveyance or transfer" in enactments relating to stamp duty by FA 2003 Sch 20 para 3.

243 Agreements to surrender leases

(1) Where, in pursuance of any agreement, any lease is surrendered (or, in Scotland, renounced) at any time otherwise than by deed, the agreement shall be treated for the purposes of [stamp duty][1] as if it were a deed executed at that time effecting the surrender (or, as the case may be, renunciation).
(2) This section shall apply to any agreement made after 7th December 1993.

Press releases etc—IR Tax Bulletin August 1995 paras 25, 26 (documents which merely record an agreement to surrender may be stampable).

Amendments—[1] Words in sub-s (1) substituted by FA 1999 s 112(4), Sch 14 para 32 with effect in relation to instruments executed after 30 September 1999. This does not apply to transfers or other instruments relating to units under a unit trust scheme by virtue of FA 1999 s 122. Previously the text read 'any duty chargeable under the Stamp Act 1891'.

244 Production of documents on transfer of land in Northern Ireland

(1) Subject to section 245 below, on the occasion of—
(*a*) any transfer on sale of any freehold interest in land in Northern Ireland, or
(*b*) the grant, or any transfer on sale, of any lease of such land,

the transferee, lessee or proposed lessee shall produce to the Commissioners the instrument by means of which the transfer is effected or the lease granted or agreed to be granted, as the case may be.
(2) Any transferee, lessee or proposed lessee required to produce any instrument under subsection (1) above shall produce with it a document (signed by him or by some person on his behalf and showing his address) giving such particulars as may be prescribed.
(3) Any person who, within thirty days—
(*a*) after the execution of an instrument which he is required under subsection (1) above to produce, or
(*b*) in the case of such an instrument executed at a place outside Northern Ireland, after it is first received in Northern Ireland,

fails to comply with that subsection or subsection (2) above shall be liable on summary conviction to a fine not exceeding level 1 on the standard scale.
(4) Where any agreement for any lease of land in Northern Ireland is produced to the Commissioners together with a document (signed as mentioned in subsection (2) above) giving such particulars as may be prescribed—
(*a*) it shall not be necessary to produce to them the instrument granting the lease, or any further such document as is referred to in that subsection, unless that instrument is inconsistent with the agreement, but
(*b*) the Commissioners shall, if any such instrument is produced to them and application is made for that purpose, denote on the instrument that it has been produced to them.

(5) Notwithstanding anything in section 12 of the Stamp Act 1891, no instrument required by this section to be produced to the Commissioners shall be deemed, for the purposes of section 14 of that Act, to be duly stamped unless it is stamped with a stamp denoting that the instrument has been so produced.

Notes—This section came into force on 4 November 1996 by virtue of Finance Act 1994, sections 244 and 245, (Commencement) Order, SI 1996/2316.

Cross references—See Stamp Duty (Production of Documents) (Northern Ireland) Regulations, SI 1996/2348, Reg 3, Sch (particulars to be given in a document produced pursuant to sub-s (2) above).

245 Production of documents: supplementary

(1) Section 244 above shall not apply to any instrument (an "exempt instrument") falling within any prescribed class; but regulations may, in respect of exempt instruments or such descriptions of exempt instruments as may be prescribed, require such a document as is mentioned in subsection (2) of that section to be furnished in accordance with the regulations to the Commissioner of Valuation for Northern Ireland.
[(2) The information contained in any document produced to the Commissioners under section 244(2) above shall be available for use by the Commissioner of Valuation for Northern Ireland.][2]
(3) Any person who fails to comply with any requirement imposed by virtue of subsection (1) above shall be liable on summary conviction to a fine not exceeding level 3 on the standard scale.
(4) Section 244 above shall also not apply to any instrument which relates solely to—
(*a*) incorporeal hereditaments or to a grave or right of burial, . . .[1]
(*b*) land subject to land purchase annuities which are registered in the Land Registry in Northern Ireland[, or
(*c*) an SDLT transaction within the meaning of paragraph 1(2) of Schedule 19 to the Finance Act 2003.][1]

(5) In this section and section 244 above—

"lease"—

(*a*) includes an underlease or other tenancy and an agreement for a lease, underlease or tenancy, but

(*b*) does not include a mortgage, charge or lien on any property for securing money or money's worth,

and "lessee" and "grant" shall be construed accordingly,

"prescribed" means prescribed by regulations, and

"regulations" means regulations made by the Commissioners under this section.

(6) The power to make regulations under this section shall be exercisable by statutory instrument which shall be subject to annulment in pursuance of a resolution of the House of Commons.

(7) Regulations under this section may make different provision for different cases.

(8) This section and section 244 above shall come into force on such day as the Treasury may by order made by statutory instrument appoint.

Notes—This section came into force on 4 November 1996 by virtue of Finance Act 1994, sections 244 and 245, (Commencement) Order, SI 1996/2316.

Cross references—See Stamp Duty (Production of Documents) (Northern Ireland) Regulations, SI 1996/2348, Reg 4–6, (classes of instruments which are exempt instruments for the purposes of sub-s (1) above and certain documents to be produced to the Registrar of Titles or the Registrar of Deeds and then furnished by the registrar to the Commissioner of Valuation for Northern Ireland under sub-s (2) above).

Amendments—[1] In sub-s (4), word in para (*a*) repealed, word in para (*b*) inserted, and para (*c*) inserted by the Stamp Duty Land Tax (Consequential Amendment of Enactments) Regulations, SI 2003/2867, reg 2, Schedule, para 22 with effect from 1 December 2003.

[2] Sub-s (2) substituted by F(No 2)A 2005 s 48(2), (5) with effect from 30 July 2009 (by virtue of SI 2009/2094 art 2). Sub-s (2) previously read as follows—

"(2) The information contained in—

(*a*) any document produced to the Commissioners under section 244(2) above, or]

(*b*) any return delivered to the Commissioners under Part 4 of the Finance Act 2003 (stamp duty land tax),

shall be available for use by the Commissioner of Valuation for Northern Ireland.".

PART VIII
MISCELLANEOUS AND GENERAL

General

257 Interpretation and construction

(1), (2) (*not relevant to stamp duty*).

(3) Part VI of this Act shall be construed as one with the Stamp Act 1891.

FINANCE ACT 1995

(1995 Chapter 4)

An Act to grant certain duties, to alter other duties, and to amend the law relating to the National Debt and the Public Revenue, and to make further provision in connection with Finance.

[1st May 1995]

PART V
STAMP DUTY

149 Transfer: associated bodies

(1)–(5) (*amend* FA 1930 s 42).

(6) (*amends* FA 1967 s 27).

(7) This section shall apply in relation to instruments executed on or after the day on which this Act is passed.

151 [Lease][2]: associated bodies

(1) Stamp duty under [Part II of Schedule 13 to the Finance Act 1999 (lease)][1] shall not be chargeable on an instrument which is—

(*a*) a [lease][2],

(*b*) an agreement for a [lease][2], or

(*c*) an agreement with respect to a letting,

as respects which the condition in subsection (2) below is satisfied.

[This subsection is subject to subsection (4A) below.][3]

(2) The condition is that it is shown to the satisfaction of the Commissioners of Inland Revenue that—

(*a*) the lessor is a body corporate and the lessee is another body corporate,

(*b*) those bodies are associated at the time the instrument is executed, (*c*) in the case of an agreement, the agreement is for the [lease][2] or letting to be granted to the lessee or to a body corporate which is associated with the lessee at the time the instrument is executed, and

(*d*) the instrument is not executed in pursuance of or in connection with an arrangement falling within subsection (3) below.

(3) An arrangement falls within this subsection if it is one under which—

(*a*) the consideration, or any part of the consideration, for the [lease][2] or agreement was to be provided or received (directly or indirectly) by a person other than a body corporate which at the relevant time was associated with either the lessor or the lessee, or

(*b*) the lessor and the lessee were to cease to be associated by reason of the lessor or a third body corporate ceasing to be the lessee's parent;

and the relevant time is the time of the execution of the instrument.

(4) Without prejudice to the generality of paragraph (*a*) of subsection (3) above, an arrangement shall be treated as within that paragraph if it is one under which the lessor or the lessee or a body corporate associated with either at the relevant time was to be enabled to provide any of the consideration, or was to part with any of it, by or in consequence of the carrying out of a transaction which involved (or transactions any of which involved) a payment or other disposition by a person other than a body corporate associated with the lessor or the lessee at the relevant time.

[(4A) An instrument shall not be exempt from stamp duty by virtue of subsection (1) above if at the time the instrument is executed arrangements are in existence by virtue of which at that or some later time any person has or could obtain, or any persons together have or could obtain, control of the lessee but not of the lessor.][3]

(5) An instrument mentioned in subsection (1) above shall not be treated as duly stamped unless—

(*a*) it is duly stamped in accordance with the law that would apply but for that subsection, or

(*b*) it has, in accordance with section 12 of the Stamp Act 1891, been stamped with a particular stamp denoting either that it is not chargeable with any duty or that it is duly stamped.

(6) In this section—

(*a*) references to the lessor are to the person granting the [lease][2] or (in the case of an agreement) agreeing to grant the [lease][2] or letting;

(*b*) references to the lessee are to the person being granted the [lease][2] or (in the case of an agreement) agreeing for the [lease][2] or letting to be granted to him or another.

(7) For the purposes of this section bodies corporate are associated at a particular time if at that time one is the parent of the other or another body corporate is the parent of each.

(8) For the purposes of this section one body corporate is the parent of another at a particular time if at that time the first body—

[(*a*)] [3] is beneficial owner of not less than 75 per cent of the ordinary share capital of the second body;

[(*b*) is beneficially entitled to not less than 75 per cent of any profits available for distribution to equity holders of the second body; and

(*c*) would be beneficially entitled to not less than 75 per cent of any assets of the second body available for distribution to its equity holders on a winding-up.][3]

(9) In subsection (8) above "ordinary share capital", in relation to a body corporate, means all the issued share capital (by whatever name called) of the body corporate, other than capital the holders of which have a right to a dividend at a fixed rate but have no other right to share in the profits of the body corporate.

(10) The ownership referred to in [paragraph (*a*) of][3] subsection (8) above is ownership either directly or through another body corporate or other bodies corporate, or partly directly and partly through another body corporate or other bodies corporate; and Part I of Schedule 4 to the Finance Act 1938 (determination of amount of capital held through other bodies corporate) shall apply for the purposes of [that paragraph][4].

[(10A) [Chapter 6 of Part 5 of the Corporation Tax Act 2010][5] shall apply for the purposes of paragraphs (*b*) and (*c*) of subsection (8) as it applies for the purposes of [section 151(4)(*a*) and (*b*)][5] of that Act; but this is subject to subsection (10B).

(10B) In determining for the purposes of this section whether a body corporate is the parent of the lessor, [sections 171(1)(*b*) and (3), 173, 174 and 176 to 178 of the Corporation Tax Act 2010][5] shall not apply for the purposes of paragraph (*b*) or (*c*) of subsection (8) above.

(10C) In this section, "control" shall be construed in accordance with [section 1124 of the Corporation Tax Act 2010][5].][3]

(11) This section shall apply in relation to instruments executed on or after the day on which this Act is passed.

Statement of Practice SP 3/98—Stamp duty—group relief.

Amendments—[1] Words in sub-s (1) substituted by FA 1999 s 112(4), Sch 14 para 33 with effect in relation to instruments executed after 30 September 1999. This does not apply to transfers or other instruments relating to units under a unit trust scheme by virtue of FA 1999 s 122. Previously the text read 'the heading "Lease or Tack" in Schedule 1 to the Stamp Act 1891'.

[2] "Lease" substituted for the words "lease or tack" throughout the section by FA 1999 s 112(4), Sch 14 para 33 with effect in relation to instruments executed after 30 September 1999. This does not apply to transfers or other instruments relating to units under a unit trust scheme by virtue of FA 1999 s 122.

[3] Words in sub-s (1), whole of sub-s (4A), in sub-s (8) reference to "(*a*)" and whole of paras (*b*), (*c*), sub-ss (10A)–(10C) and words in sub-s (10) inserted by FA 2000 s 125(1)–(4), (5)(*a*), (6) with effect for instruments executed after 28 July 2000.

[4] Words in sub-s (10) substituted for "this section" by FA 2000 s 125(5)(*b*), with effect for instruments executed after 28 July 2000.

[5] The following amendments made by CTA 2010 s 1177, Sch 1 para 287—

- in sub-s (10A) words substituted for words "Schedule 18 to the Income and Corporation Taxes Act 1988" and "paragraphs (*a*) and (*b*) of section 413(7)";
- in sub-s (10B) words substituted for words "paragraphs 5(3) and 5B to 5E of Schedule 18 to the Income and Corporation Taxes Act 1988"; and
- in sub-s (10C) words substituted for words "section 840 of the Income and Corporation Taxes Act 1988";

CTA 2010 has effect for corporation tax purposes for accounting periods ending on or after 1 April 2010, and for income and capital gains tax purposes for the tax year 2010–11 and subsequent tax years.

PART VI
MISCELLANEOUS AND GENERAL

Miscellaneous

152 Open-ended investment companies

(1) The Treasury may, by regulations, make such provision as they consider appropriate for securing that the enactments specified in subsection (2) below have effect in relation to—

(*a*) open-ended investment companies of any such description as may be specified in the regulations,

(*b*) holdings in, and the assets of, such companies, and

(*c*) transactions involving such companies,

in a manner corresponding, subject to such modifications as the Treasury consider appropriate, to the manner in which they have effect in relation to unit trusts, to rights under, and the assets subject to, such trusts and to transactions for purposes connected with such trusts.

(2) The enactments referred to in subsection (1) above are—

(*a*) the Tax Acts and the Taxation of Chargeable Gains Act 1992; and

(*b*) the enactments relating to stamp duty and [stamp duty reserve tax][1].

(3) The power of the Treasury to make regulations under this section in relation to any such enactments shall include power to make provision which does any one or more of the following, that is to say—

(*a*) identifies the payments which are or are not to be treated, for the purposes of any prescribed enactment, as the distributions of open-ended investment companies;

(*b*) modifies the operation [in relation to open-ended investment companies, or in relation to payments falling to be treated as the distributions of such companies, of any of the following provisions of Part 23 of the Corporation Tax Act 2010—

(i) any provision of Chapter 2, except section 1000(2),

(ii) sections 1030 to 1048,

(iii) section 1049(1) and (3),

(iv) sections 1059 to 1063, and

(v) Chapter 5.][2]

(*c*) applies and adapts any of the provisions of [the enactments relating to stamp duty or stamp duty reserve tax][1] for the purpose of making in relation to transactions involving open-ended investment companies any provision corresponding (with or without modifications) to that which applies under [those enactments][1] in the case of equivalent transactions involving unit trusts;

(*d*) provides for any or all of the provisions of sections 75 to 77 of the Finance Act 1986 to have effect or not to have effect in relation to open-ended investment companies or the undertakings of, or any shares in, such companies;

(*e*) so modifies the operation of any prescribed enactment in relation to any such companies as to secure that arrangements for treating the assets of an open-ended investment company as assets comprised in separate pools are given an effect corresponding, in prescribed respects, to that of equivalent arrangements constituting the separate parts of an umbrella scheme;

(*f*) requires prescribed enactments to have effect in relation to an open-ended investment company as if it were, or were not, a member of the same group of companies as one or more other companies;

(*g*) identifies the holdings in open-ended investment companies which are, or are not, to be treated for the purposes of any prescribed enactment as comprised in the same class of holdings;

(*h*) preserves a continuity of tax treatment where, in connection with any scheme of re-organisation, assets of one or more unit trusts become assets of one or more open-ended investment companies, or vice versa;

(*i*) treats the separate parts of the undertaking of an open-ended investment company in relation to which provision is made by virtue of paragraph (*e*) above as distinct companies for the purposes of any regulations under this section;

(*j*) amends, adapts or applies the provisions of any subordinate legislation made under or by reference to any enactment modified by the regulations.

(4) The power to make regulations under this section shall be exercisable by statutory instrument and shall include power—

(*a*) to make different provision for different cases; and

(*b*) to make such incidental, supplemental, consequential and transitional provision as the Treasury may think fit.

(5) A statutory instrument containing regulations under this section shall be subject to annulment in pursuance of a resolution of the House of Commons.

(6) In this section—

"the enactments relating to stamp duty" means the Stamp Act 1891, and any enactment (including any Northern Ireland legislation) which amends or is required to be construed together with that Act;

["the enactments relating to stamp duty reserve tax" means Part IV of the Finance Act 1986 and any enactment which amends or is required to be construed as one with that Part;][1]

"Northern Ireland legislation" shall have the meaning given by section 24(5) of the Interpretation Act 1978;

"open-ended investment company" has the same meaning as in the Financial Services Act 1986;

"prescribed" means prescribed by regulations under this section;

"subordinate legislation" means any subordinate legislation within the meaning of the Interpretation Act 1978 or any order or regulations made by statutory instrument under Northern Ireland legislation; and

"umbrella scheme" shall have the meaning given by [section 619 of the Corporation Tax Act 2010][2];

and references in this section to the enactments relating to stamp duty, or to any of them, or to Part IV of the Finance Act 1986 shall have effect as including references to enactments repealed by sections 107 to 110 of the Finance Act 1990.

(7) Any reference in this section to unit trusts has effect—

(*a*) for the purposes of so much of this section as confers power in relation to the enactments specified in paragraph (*a*) of subsection (2) above, as a reference to authorised unit trusts (within the meaning of [sections 616 and 619(3) of the Corporation Tax Act 2010)][2]), and

(*b*) for the purposes of so much of this section as confers power in relation to the enactments specified in paragraph (*b*) of that subsection, as a reference to any unit trust scheme (within the meaning given by section 57 of the Finance Act 1946).

(8) For the purposes of this section the enactments which shall be taken to make provision in relation to companies that are members of the same group of companies shall include any enactments which make provision in relation to a case—

(*a*) where one company has, or in relation to another company is, a subsidiary, or a subsidiary of a particular description, or

(*b*) where one company controls another or two or more companies are under the same control.

Regulations—See the Stamp Duty and Stamp Duty Reserve Tax (Definition of Unit Trust Scheme and Open-ended Investment Company) Regulations, SI 2001/964.

Amendments—[1] Words in sub-ss (2)(*b*), (3)(*c*) substituted and in sub-s (6) definition of "the enactments relating to stamp duty reserve tax" inserted by the Finance Act 1999, s 122(4), Sch 19, para 13 with effect from 6 February 2000.

[2] The following amendments made by CTA 2010 s 1177, Sch 1 para 288—

- in sub-s (3)(*b*) words substituted for words "of Chapters II, III and VA of Part VI of the Taxes Act 1988 in relation to open-ended investment companies or in relation to payments falling to be treated as the distributions of such companies;";
- in sub-s (6) in the definition of "umbrella scheme", words substituted for words "section 468 of the Taxes Act 1988"; and
- in sub-s (7)(*a*) words substituted for words "section 468 of the Taxes Act 1988)";

CTA 2010 has effect for corporation tax purposes for accounting periods ending on or after 1 April 2010, and for income and capital gains tax purposes for the tax year 2010–11 and subsequent tax years.

FINANCE ACT 1996

(1996 Chapter 8)

ARRANGEMENT OF SECTIONS

PART VI

STAMP DUTY AND STAMP DUTY RESERVE TAX

An Act to grant certain duties, to alter other duties, and to amend the law relating to the National Debt and the Public Revenue, and to make further provision in connection with Finance.

[29th April 1996]

PART VI

STAMP DUTY AND STAMP DUTY RESERVE TAX

Stamp duty

186 Transfers of securities to members of electronic transfer systems etc

(1) Stamp duty shall not be chargeable on an instrument effecting a transfer of securities if the transferee is a member of an electronic transfer system and the instrument is in a form which will, in accordance with the rules of the system, ensure that the securities are changed from being held in certificated form to being held in uncertificated form so that title to them may become transferable by means of the system.

(2) In this section—

"certificated form" has the same meaning as in the relevant regulations;

"electronic transfer system" means a system and procedures which, in accordance with the relevant regulations, enable title to securities to be evidenced and transferred without a written instrument;

"member", in relation to an electronic transfer system, means a person who is permitted by the operator of the system to transfer by means of the system title to securities held by him in uncertificated form;

"operator" means a person approved by the Treasury under the relevant regulations as operator of an electronic transfer system;

"the relevant regulations" means regulations under section [785][1] of the Companies Act [2006][1] (transfer without written instrument);

"securities" means stock or marketable securities;

"uncertificated form" has the same meaning as it has in the relevant regulations.

(3) This section applies in relation to instruments executed on or after 1st July 1996.

(4) This section shall be construed as one with the Stamp Act 1891.

Amendments—This section repealed by Sch 41 Pt VII with effect from an appointed day in accordance with FA 1990 s 108.

Amendments—[1] In sub-s (2), figures substituted for figures "207" and "1989", by the Companies Act 2006 (Consequential Amendments) (Taxes and National Insurance) Order, SI 2009/1890 art 10 with effect from 1 October 2009.

Stamp duty reserve tax

187 Territorial scope of the tax

(1) (*inserts* FA 1986 s 86(4)).

(2) The amendment made by subsection (1) above shall have effect—

(*a*) in relation to an agreement, if—

(i) the agreement is conditional and the condition is satisfied on or after 1st July 1996; or

(ii) the agreement is not conditional and is made on or after that date; and

(*b*) in relation to a transfer, issue or appropriation made or effected on or after that date.

Amendments—This section repealed by FA 1996 Sch 41 Pt VII with effect from an appointed day in accordance with FA 1990 s 110.

188 Removal of the two month period

(1) (*amends* FA 1986 s 87(2)).

(2) . . . [2]

(3) (*repeals* FA 1986 s 88 (2), (3)).

(4) (*amends* FA 1986 s 92(1)).

(5) The amendments made by this section shall have effect in relation to an agreement to transfer securities if—

(a) the agreement is conditional and the condition is satisfied on or after 1st July 1996; or

(b) the agreement is not conditional and is made on or after that date.[1]

Amendments—[1] This section repealed by Sch 41 Pt VII with effect from an appointed day in accordance with FA 1990 s 110.

[2] Sub-s (2) repealed by FA 1999 Sch 20 Pt V(2) with effect in relation to instruments executed, or bearer instruments issued, from 1 October 1999, subject to the provisions in FA 1999 Sch 20 Pt V(2) Note 2. Previously the text inserted FA 1986 s 88 (1)(*aa*),(*ab*).

189 Transfers to members of electronic transfer systems etc

(1) (*inserts* FA 1986 s 88(1A)).

(2) This section has effect in relation to an agreement to transfer securities if an instrument is executed on or after 1st July 1996 in pursuance of the agreement.

Amendments—This section repealed by Sch 41 Pt VII with effect from an appointed day.

190 Transfers between associated bodies

(1) (*inserts* FA 1986 s 88(1B)).

(2) (*adds* FA 1986 s 88(4)–(6)).

(3) This section has effect where the instrument on which stamp duty is not chargeable by virtue of section 42 of the Finance Act 1930 or section 11 of the Finance Act (Northern Ireland) 1954 is executed on or after 4th January 1996 in pursuance of an agreement to transfer securities made on or after that date.

Amendments—This section repealed by Sch 41 Pt VII with effect from an appointed day in accordance with FA 1990 s 110

191 Stock lending and collateral security arrangements

(1) (*inserts* FA 1986 s 89B).

(2) This section applies in relation to agreements to transfer chargeable securities in pursuance of an arrangement entered into on or after 1st July 1996.

Amendments—This section repealed by Sch 41 Pt VII with effect from an appointed day in accordance with FA 1990 s 110.

192 Repayment or cancellation of tax

(1)–(5) (*repeal* FA 1986 s 87(4), (5), (8), *amend* ss 88(1), (1A), (1B), 92(1), *insert* FA 1986 s 92 (1A), (1B) and *add* s 92(6)).

(6) The amendments made by this section shall have effect in relation to an agreement to transfer securities if—

(*a*) the agreement is conditional and the condition is satisfied on or after 1st July 1996; or

(*b*) the agreement is not conditional and is made on or after that date.

Amendments—This section repealed by Sch 41 Pt VII with effect from an appointed day in accordance with FA 1990 s 110.

193 Depositary receipts

(1)–(3) (*amend* FA 1986 s 93(1), (6)).

(4) This section has effect—

(*a*) so far as relating to the charge to tax under section 93(1) of the Finance Act 1986, where securities are transferred, issued or appropriated on or after 1st July 1996 (whenever the arrangement was made);

(*b*) so far as relating to the charge to tax under section 93(10) of that Act, in relation to instalments payable on or after 1st July 1996.

Amendments—This section repealed by Sch 41 Pt VII with effect from an appointed day in accordance with FA 1990 s 110.

194 Rates of charge expressed as percentages

(1)–(6) (*amend* FA 1986 ss 87(6), 93(4), (5), (10), 96(2), (3), (8), *repeal* ss 94(8), 96(12) and *add* s 99(13)).

(7) Subsections (1) to (5) above have effect in accordance with the following provisions of this subsection, that is to say—

(*a*) in relation to the charge to tax under section 87 of the Finance Act 1986, subsection (1) above applies where—

(i) the agreement to transfer is conditional and the condition is satisfied on or after 1st July 1996; or

(ii) the agreement is not conditional and is made on or after 1st July 1996;

(*b*) in relation to the charge to tax under section 93(1) of that Act, paragraphs (*a*) and (*b*) of subsection (2) above apply where securities are transferred, issued or appropriated on or after 1st July 1996 (whenever the arrangement was made) and subsection (3) above has effect accordingly;

(*c*) in relation to the charge to tax under section 93(10) of that Act, paragraph (*c*) of subsection (2) above applies in relation to instalments payable on or after 1st July 1996;

(*d*) in relation to the charge to tax under section 96(1) of that Act, paragraphs (*a*) and (*b*) of subsection (4) above apply where securities are transferred or issued on or after 1st July 1996 (whenever the arrangement was made) and subsection (5) above has effect accordingly;

(*e*) in relation to the charge to tax under section 96(8) of that Act, paragraph (*c*) of subsection (4) above applies in relation to instalments payable on or after 1st July 1996.

Amendments—This section repealed by Sch 41 Pt VII with effect from an appointed day in accordance with FA 1990 s 110.

195 Regulations concerning administration: sub-delegation to the Board

(*inserted* FA 1986 s 98(1A)).

Amendments—This section repealed by Sch 41 Pt VII with effect from an appointed day in accordance with FA 1990 s 110.

Clearance services

196 Election by operator for alternative system of charge

(*amended* FA 1986 ss 70(1), 96(1), 99(10), *inserted* s 97A *and repealed* s 97(2)).

Amendments—This section repealed by Sch 41 Pt VII with effect from an appointed day in accordance with FA 1990 s 110.

PART VII

MISCELLANEOUS AND SUPPLEMENTAL

Miscellaneous: direct taxation

201 Enactment of Inland Revenue concessions

Schedule 39 to this Act has effect for the purpose of enacting certain extra-statutory concessions relating to income tax, corporation tax, capital gains tax, and stamp duty.

Miscellaneous: other matters

202 Gilt stripping

(1)–(4) (*not relevant to stamp duty or SDRT*).

(5) The Treasury may by regulations make provision for securing that enactments and subordinate legislation which—

(*a*) apply in relation to government securities or to any description of such securities, or

(*b*) for any other purpose refer (in whatever terms) to such securities or to any description of them,

have effect with such modifications as the Treasury may think appropriate in consequence of the making of any provision or arrangements for, or in connection with, the issue or transfer of strips of government securities or the consolidation of such strips into other securities.

(6) Regulations under subsection (5) above may—

(*a*) impose a charge to income tax, corporation tax, capital gains tax, inheritance tax, stamp duty or stamp duty reserve tax;

(*b*) include provision applying generally to, or to any description of, enactments or subordinate legislation;

(*c*) make different provision for different cases; and

(*d*) contain such incidental, supplemental, consequential and transitional provision as the Treasury think appropriate.

(7) The power to make regulations under subsection (5) above shall be exercisable by statutory instrument subject to annulment in pursuance of a resolution of the House of Commons.

(8) Schedule 40 to this Act (which makes provision in relation to strips for taxation purposes) shall have effect.

(9) The enactments that may be modified by regulations under this section shall include section 95 above and the enactments contained in Schedule 40 to this Act.

(10) In this section—

"government securities" means any securities included in Part I of Schedule 11 to the Finance Act 1942;

"modifications" includes amendments, additions and omissions; and

"subordinate legislation" has the same meaning as in the Interpretation Act 1978;

and expressions used in this section and in section 47 of the Finance Act 1942 have the same meanings in this section as in that section.

Supplemental

205 Repeals

(1) The enactments mentioned in Schedule 41 to this Act (which include spent provisions) are hereby repealed to the extent specified in the third column of that Schedule.

(2) The repeals specified in that Schedule have effect subject to the commencement provisions and savings contained in, or referred to, in the notes set out in that Schedule.

206 Short title

This Act may be cited as the Finance Act 1996.

SCHEDULES

SCHEDULE 39

ENACTMENT OF CERTAIN INLAND REVENUE EXTRA-STATUTORY CONCESSIONS

Section 201

PART III

STAMP DUTY

Lost or spoiled instruments

10—(1) The Stamp Duties Management Act 1891 ("the Management Act") shall be amended as follows.

(2) (*amends* SDMA 1891 s 9(7)(*e*)).

(3) (*inserts* SDMA 1891 s 12A).

(4) Subject to subparagraph (5) below, the amendments made by this paragraph shall have effect from the day on which this Act is passed.

(5) The amendments made by this paragraph shall not apply in relation to an instrument which has been accidentally spoiled if an application for allowance under section 9 of the Management Act was made before the day on which this Act is passed.

SCHEDULE 40

GILT STRIPPING: TAXATION PROVISIONS

Section 202

The Stamp Act 1891 (c 39)

1 (amends SA 1891 s 122(1)).

2 . . . [1]

Amendments—[1] Para 2 repealed by FA 1999 Sch 20 Pt V(2) with effect in relation to instruments executed, or bearer instruments issued, from 1 October 1999, subject to the provisions in FA 1999 Sch 20 Pt V(2) Note 2. Previously the text read:

"2—(1)(*amends* SA 1891 Sch 1).

(2) Where any day is appointed as the abolition day for the purposes of sections 107 to 110 of the Finance Act 1990, sub-paragraph (1) above shall cease to have effect in accordance with the provisions of that Act for the coming into force of the repeal of the paragraph mentioned in that sub-paragraph."

SCHEDULE 41

REPEALS

Section 205

PART VII

STAMP DUTY AND STAMP DUTY RESERVE TAX

Chapter	Short title	Extent of repeal
. . .	. . .	. . .
1996 c 8.	The Finance Act 1996.	Sections 186 to 196.

1–3 . . .

4 The repeals in the Finance Act 1996 have effect—

(*a*) so far as relating to stamp duty, in accordance with section 108 of the Finance Act 1990; and

(*b*) so far as relating to stamp duty reserve tax, in accordance with section 110 of the Finance Act 1990.

Note—Details of repeals already in force have not been reproduced.

FINANCE ACT 1997

(1997 Chapter 16)

ARRANGEMENT OF SECTIONS

PART VII

STAMP DUTY AND STAMP DUTY RESERVE TAX

Stamp duty

Stamp duty reserve tax

PART VIII

MISCELLANEOUS AND SUPPLEMENTAL

Supplemental

An Act to grant certain duties, to alter other duties, and to amend the law relating to the National Debt and the Public Revenue, and to make further provision in connection with Finance.

[19th March 1997]

PART VII
STAMP DUTY AND STAMP DUTY RESERVE TAX

Stamp duty

95 Mergers of authorised unit trusts

(1) Stamp duty shall not be chargeable on an instrument transferring any property which is subject to the trusts of an authorised unit trust ("the target trust") to the trustees of another authorised unit trust ("the acquiring trust") if the conditions set out in subsection (2) below are fulfilled.

(2) Those conditions are that—

(*a*) the transfer forms part of an arrangement under which the whole of the available property of the target trust is transferred to the trustees of the acquiring trust;

(*b*) under the arrangement all the units in the target trust are extinguished;

(*c*) the consideration under the arrangement consists of or includes the issue of units ("the consideration units") in the acquiring trust to the persons who held the extinguished units;

(*d*) the consideration units are issued to those persons in proportion to their holdings of the extinguished units; and

(*e*) the consideration under the arrangement does not include anything else, other than the assumption or discharge by the trustees of the acquiring trust of liabilities of the trustees of the target trust.

(3) An instrument on which stamp duty is not chargeable by virtue only of this section shall not be taken to be duly stamped unless it is stamped with the duty to which it would be liable but for this section or it has, in accordance with section 12 of the Stamp Act 1891, been stamped with a particular stamp denoting that it is not chargeable with any duty.

(4) In this section—

"authorised unit trust" means a unit trust scheme in the case of which an order under section [243 of the Financial Services and Markets Act 2000][1] is in force;

"the whole of the available property of the target trust" means the whole of the property subject to the trusts of the target trust, other than any property which is retained for the purpose of discharging liabilities of the trustees of the target trust;

"unit" and "unit trust scheme" have the same meanings as in Part VII of the Finance Act 1946.

(5) Each of the parts of an umbrella scheme (and not the scheme as a whole) shall be regarded for the purposes of this section as an authorised unit trust; and in this section "umbrella scheme" has the same meaning as in section 468 of the Taxes Act 1988 and references to parts of an umbrella scheme shall be construed in accordance with that section.

(6) This section applies to any instrument which is executed—

(*a*) on or after the day on which this Act is passed; but

(*b*) before 1st July 1999.

Amendments—[1] In sub-s (4), words in the definition of "authorised unit trust" substituted by the Financial Services and Markets Act 2000 (Consequential Amendments) (Taxes) Order, SI 2001/3629 arts 97, 99 with effect for any instrument executed after 30 November 2001.

96 Demutualisation of insurance companies

(1) This section applies where there is a relevant transfer, under a scheme, of the whole or any part of the business carried on by a mutual insurance company ("the mutual") to a company which has share capital ("the acquiring company").

(2) Stamp duty shall not be chargeable on an instrument executed for the purposes of or in connection with the transfer if the requirements of subsections (3) and (4) below are satisfied in relation to the shares of a company ("the issuing company") which is either—

(*a*) the acquiring company; or

(*b*) a company of which the acquiring company is a wholly-owned subsidiary.

(3) Shares in the issuing company must be offered, under the scheme, to at least 90 per cent of the persons who immediately before the transfer are members of the mutual.

(4) Under the scheme, all the shares in the issuing company which will be in issue immediately after the transfer has been made, other than shares which are to be or have been issued pursuant to an offer to the public, must be offered to the persons who (at the time of the offer) are—

(*a*) members of the mutual;

(*b*) persons who are entitled to become members of the mutual; or

(*c*) employees, former employees or pensioners of the mutual or of a company which is a wholly-owned subsidiary of the mutual.

(5) An instrument on which stamp duty is not chargeable by virtue only of subsection (2) above shall not be taken to be duly stamped unless it is stamped with the duty to which it would be liable but for that subsection or it has, in accordance with section 12 of the Stamp Act 1891, been stamped with a particular stamp denoting that it is not chargeable with any duty.

(6) For the purposes of this section, a company is a wholly-owned subsidiary of another person ("the parent") if it has no members except the parent and the parent's wholly-owned subsidiaries or persons acting on behalf of the parent or its wholly-owned subsidiaries.

(7) In this section "relevant transfer" means—

[(*a*) a transfer from a company to another person of business consisting of the effecting or carrying out of contracts of insurance which is effected under an insurance business transfer scheme; or

(*b*) a transfer of the whole or any part of the business of a general insurance company carried on through a branch or agency in the United Kingdom which takes place in accordance with any authorisation granted outside the United Kingdom for the purposes of—

[(i) Article 14 of the life assurance consolidation directive, or][2]

(ii) Article 12 of the third non-life insurance directive.][1]

(8) In this section—

["the life assurance consolidation directive" means Directive 2002/83/EC of the European Parliament and of the Council of 5th November 2002 concerning life assurance;][2]

["contract of insurance" has the meaning given by Article 3(1) of the Financial Services and Markets Act 2000 (Regulated Activities) Order 2001;][1]

"employee", in relation to a mutual insurance company or its wholly-owned subsidiary, includes any officer or director of the company or subsidiary and any other person taking part in the management of the affairs of the company or subsidiary;

["general insurance company" means a company which has permission under Part 4 of the Financial Services and Markets Act 2000 or under paragraph 15 of Schedule 3 to that Act (as a result of qualifying for authorisation under paragraph 12(1) of that Schedule) to effect or carry out contracts of insurance;

"insurance business transfer scheme" has the same meaning as in Part 7 of the Financial Services and Markets Act 2000;

"insurance company" means a company which carries on the business of effecting or carrying out contracts of insurance;][1]

"mutual insurance company" means an insurance company carrying on business without having any share capital;

[. . . [2]

"the third non-life insurance directive" means the Council Directive of 18th June 1992 on the co-ordination of laws, regulations and administrative provisions relating to direct insurance other than life assurance and amending Directives 73/239/EEC and 88/357/EEC (No 92/49/EEC);][1]

"pensioner", in relation to a mutual insurance company or its wholly-owned subsidiary, means a person entitled (whether presently or prospectively) to a pension, lump sum, gratuity or other like benefit referable to the service of any person as an employee of the company or subsidiary.

(9) The Treasury may by regulations amend subsection (3) above by substituting a lower percentage for the percentage there mentioned.

(10) The Treasury may by regulations provide that any or all of the references in subsections (3) and (4) above to members shall be construed as references to members of a class specified in the regulations; and different provision may be made for different cases.

(11) The power to make regulations under this section shall be exercisable by statutory instrument subject to annulment in pursuance of a resolution of the House of Commons.

(12) This section applies in relation to instruments executed on or after the day on which this Act is passed.

Cross references—See FA 1986 s 90(1A)(*c*) (exemption from charge under FA 1986 s 87 for agreement to transfer unit under unit trust scheme).

FA 1999 Sch 19 para 6(5)(*c*) (exclusion, in certain cases of change of ownership, of charge to SDRT on surrender of unit to managers).

Amendments—[1] In sub-s (7), paras (*a*), (*b*) substituted; in sub-s (8), definition of "contract of insurance" inserted, definitions of "general insurance company", "insurance business transfer scheme" and "insurance company" substituted for that of "insurance company"; and definitions of "the third life insurance directive" and "the third non-life insurance directive" inserted by the Financial Services and Markets Act 2000 (Consequential Amendments) (Taxes) Order, SI 2001/3629 arts 97, 100 with effect from 1 December 2001 (immediately after the coming into force of the Financial Services and Markets Act 2000 ss 411, 432(1), Sch 20). SI 2001/3629 art 100 has effect for any instrument executed after 30 November 2001 which effects a transfer—

(a) under a scheme falling within the Financial Services and Markets Act 2000 s 105, including an excluded scheme falling within Case 2, 3 or 4 of the Financial Services and Markets Act 2000 s 105(3); or

(b) in relation to which the Financial Services and Markets Act 2000 s 116 applies.

[2] Sub-s (7)(*b*)(i) substituted; words in sub-s (8) inserted; and words in sub-s (8) repealed by the Life Assurance Consolidation Directive (Consequential Amendments) Regulations, SI 2004/3379 reg 5 with effect from 11 January 2005.

97 Relief for intermediaries

(1)–(3) (*insert* FA 1986 s 80A, 80B, *repeal* s 81 and *amend* s 88(1B)(*b*)(i)).

(4) Subsections (1) and (2) above apply to instruments executed on or after the commencement day.

(5) Subsection (3) above applies in relation to an agreement to transfer chargeable securities if the securities were acquired in a transaction which was given effect to by an instrument of transfer executed on or after the commencement day.

(6) For the purposes of this section the commencement day is such day as the Treasury may by order made by statutory instrument appoint.

Note—This section given an effective date of 20 October 1997 by virtue of the Finance Act 1997 (Stamp Duty and Stamp Duty Reserve Tax) (Appointed Day) Order, SI 1997/2428.

98 Repurchases and stock lending

(1), (2) (*insert* FA 1986 s 80C and *repeal* s 82).

(3) This section applies to instruments executed on or after the commencement day.

(4) For the purposes of this section the commencement day is such day as the Treasury may by order made by statutory instrument appoint.

Note—This section given an effective date of 20 October 1997 by virtue of the Finance Act 1997 (Stamp Duty and Stamp Duty Reserve Tax) (Appointed Day) Order, SI 1997/2428.

99 Depositary receipts and clearance services

(1)–(4) (*repeal* FA 1986 ss 67 (4), 69(6)–(8), 70(4), 72(4) and *amend* ss 67(3), 70(3)).

(5) This section applies to any instrument executed on or after the day which is the commencement day for the purposes of section 97 above, except an instrument which transfers relevant securities which were acquired by the transferor before that date.

Stamp duty reserve tax

100 Mergers of authorised unit trusts

(1) Section 87 of the Finance Act 1986 shall not apply as regards an agreement to transfer securities which constitute property which is subject to the trusts of an authorised unit trust ("the target trust") to the trustees of another authorised unit trust ("the acquiring trust") if the conditions set out in subsection (2) below are fulfilled.

(2) Those conditions are that—

(*a*) the agreement forms part of an arrangement under which the whole of the available property of the target trust is transferred to the trustees of the acquiring trust;

(*b*) under the arrangement all the units in the target trust are extinguished;

(*c*) the consideration under the arrangement consists of or includes the issue of units ("the consideration units") in the acquiring trust to the persons who held the extinguished units;

(*d*) the consideration units are issued to those persons in proportion to their holdings of the extinguished units; and

(*e*) the consideration under the arrangement does not include anything else, other than the assumption or discharge by the trustees of the acquiring trust of liabilities of the trustees of the target trust.

(3) Where—

(*a*) stamp duty is not chargeable on an instrument by virtue of section 95(1) above, or

(*b*) section 87 of the Finance Act 1986 does not apply as regards an agreement by virtue of subsection (1) above,

section 87 of the Finance Act 1986 shall not apply as regards an agreement, or a deemed agreement, to transfer a unit to the managers of the target trust which is made in order that the unit may be extinguished under the arrangement mentioned in section 95(2)(a) or, as the case may be, subsection (2)(a) above.

(4) In this section—

"authorised unit trust" means a unit trust scheme in the case of which an order under section [243 of the Financial Services and Markets Act 2000][1] is in force;

"the whole of the available property of the target trust" means the whole of the property subject to the trusts of the target trust, other than any property which is retained for the purpose of discharging liabilities of the trustees of the target trust;

"unit" and "unit trust scheme" have the same meanings as in Part VII of the Finance Act 1946.

(5) Each of the parts of an umbrella scheme (and not the scheme as a whole) shall be regarded for the purposes of this section as an authorised unit trust; and in this section "umbrella scheme" has the same meaning as in section 468 of the Taxes Act 1988 and references to parts of an umbrella scheme shall be construed in accordance with that section.

(6) This section applies—

(*a*) to an agreement which is not conditional, if the agreement is made on or after the day on which this Act is passed but before 1st July 1999; and

(*b*) to a conditional agreement, if the condition is satisfied on or after the day on which this Act is passed but before 1st July 1999.

Amendments—[1] In sub-s (4), words in definition of "authorised unit trust" substituted by the Financial Services and Markets Act 2000 (Consequential Amendments) (Taxes) Order, SI 2001/3629 arts 97, 101 with effect for—

(a) an agreement to transfer chargeable securities which is not conditional, if the agreement is made after 30 November 2001;

(b) a conditional agreement to transfer such securities, if the condition is satisfied after that date.

101 Direction to hold trust property on other trusts

(1) Where an agreement to transfer securities constituting property subject to the trusts of an authorised unit trust ("the absorbed trust") is made by means of a direction by the holders of units in the absorbed trust ("the sellers") to the trustees of another trust ("the continuing trust") to hold the whole of the available property of the absorbed trust on the trusts of the continuing trust, section 87 of the Finance Act 1986 shall not apply as regards the agreement if the conditions set out in subsection (2) below are fulfilled.

(2) Those conditions are that—

(*a*) the trustees of the absorbed trust are the same persons as the trustees of the continuing trust;

(*b*) the agreement forms part of an arrangement under which all the units in the absorbed trust are extinguished;

(*c*) the consideration for the direction by the sellers consists of or includes the issue of units ("the consideration units") in the continuing trust to the sellers;

(*d*) the consideration units are issued to the sellers in proportion to their holdings of the extinguished units; and

(*e*) the consideration for the direction by the sellers does not include anything else, other than the assumption or discharge by the trustees of the continuing trust of liabilities of the trustees of the absorbed trust.

(3) Where section 87 of the Finance Act 1986 does not apply as regards an agreement by virtue of subsection (1) above, that section shall not apply as regards an agreement, or a deemed agreement, to transfer a unit to the managers of the absorbed trust which is made in order that the unit may be extinguished under the arrangement mentioned in subsection (2)(*b*) above.

(4) In this section—

"authorised unit trust" and "unit" have the same meanings as in section 100 above (and section 100(5) applies for the purposes of this section as it applies for the purposes of section 100);

"the whole of the available property of the absorbed trust" means the whole of the property subject to the trusts of the absorbed trust, other than any property which is retained for the purpose of discharging liabilities of the trustees of the absorbed trust.

(5) This section applies—

(*a*) to an agreement which is not conditional, if the agreement is made on or after the day on which this Act is passed but before 1st July 1999; and

(*b*) to a conditional agreement, if the condition is satisfied on or after the day on which this Act is passed but before 1st July 1999.

102 Relief for intermediaries

(1)–(3) (*insert* FA 1986 s 88A, 88B, *repeal* s 89 and *amend* s 88(1B)(*b*)(ii)).

(4) Subsections (1) and (2) above apply to an agreement to transfer securities—

(*a*) in the case of an agreement which is not conditional, if the agreement is made on or after the commencement day; and

(*b*) in the case of a conditional agreement, if the condition is satisfied on or after the commencement day.

(5) Subsection (3) above applies in relation to property consisting of chargeable securities if the securities were acquired in pursuance of an agreement to which subsections (1) and (2) above apply (by virtue of subsection (4) above).

(6) For the purposes of this section the commencement day is such day as the Treasury may by order made by statutory instrument appoint.

Note—This section given an effective date of 20 October 1997 by virtue of the Finance Act 1997 (Stamp Duty and Stamp Duty Reserve Tax) (Appointed Day) Order, SI 1997/2428.

103 Repurchases and stock lending

(1)–(4) (*insert* FA 1986 ss 88(1C), (1D), 89AA, *repeal* s 89B and *amend* s 88(1B)(*b*)(iia)).

(5) Subsections (1) and (2) above apply to an agreement to transfer securities—

(*a*) in the case of an agreement which is not conditional, if the agreement is made on or after the commencement day; and

(*b*) in the case of a conditional agreement, if the condition is satisfied on or after the commencement day.

(6) Subsection (3) above applies in relation to property consisting of chargeable securities if the securities were acquired in pursuance of an agreement to which subsections (1) and (2) above apply (by virtue of subsection (5) above).

(7) Subsection (4) above applies to instruments executed on or after the commencement day.

(8) For the purposes of this section the commencement day is such day as the Treasury may by order made by statutory instrument appoint.

Note—This section given an effective date of 20 October 1997 by virtue of the Finance Act 1997 (Stamp Duty and Stamp Duty Reserve Tax) (Appointed Day) Order, SI 1997/2428.

104 Depositary receipts and clearance services

(1)–(4) (*repeal* FA 1986 ss 93(5), 94(5)–(7), 96(3), (11) and *amend* ss 93(4), (7)(*a*), 96(2), (5)(*a*)).

(5) This section applies where securities are transferred on or after the day which is the commencement day for the purposes of section 102 above, unless the securities were acquired by the transferor before that day.

105 Inland bearer instruments

(1)–(3) (*repeal* FA 1986 s 90(3)(*b*) and *insert* ss 90(3A)–(3F), (8), (9)).

(4) This section applies to an agreement if the inland bearer instrument in question was issued on or after 26th November 1996 and—

(*a*) in the case of an agreement which is not conditional, the agreement is made on or after 26th November 1996; or

(*b*) in the case of a conditional agreement, the condition is satisfied on or after 26th November 1996.

106 Repayment or cancellation of tax

(1) Section 87 of the Finance Act 1986 (the principal charge) shall be amended in accordance with subsections (2) and (3) below.

(2), (3) (*substitutes* FA 1986 s 87(7A) and *repeal* s 87(7B)).

(4) Section 88 of the Finance Act 1986 (special cases) shall be amended in accordance with subsections (5) to (7) below.

(5) (*amends* FA 1986 s 88(1B)(*a*) and (*b*), *and inserts* s 88(1B)(*b*)(iia)).

(6) (*substitutes* FA 1986 s 88(4) and (5)).

(7) (*substitutes heading in* FA 1986 s 88).

(8) (*inserts* FA 1986 s 92(7)).

(9) The amendments made by subsections (2), (3) and (8) above have effect in relation to an agreement to transfer securities if—

(*a*) the agreement is conditional and the condition is satisfied on or after 4th January 1997; or

(*b*) the agreement is not conditional and is made on or after that date.

(10) The amendments made by subsections (5) and (6) above have effect where the instrument on which stamp duty is not chargeable by virtue of section 42 of the Finance Act 1930 or section 11 of the Finance Act (Northern Ireland) 1954 is executed on or after 4th January 1997 in pursuance of an agreement to transfer securities made on or after that date.

PART VIII
MISCELLANEOUS AND SUPPLEMENTAL

Supplemental

112 Interpretation

In this Act "the Taxes Act 1988" means the Income and Corporation Taxes Act 1988.

113 Repeals

(1) The enactments mentioned in Schedule 18 to this Act (which include spent provisions) are hereby repealed to the extent specified in the third column of that Schedule.

(2) The repeals specified in that Schedule have effect subject to the commencement provisions and savings contained or referred to in the notes set out in that Schedule.

114 Short title

This Act may be cited as the Finance Act 1997.

SCHEDULES

SCHEDULE 18

REPEALS

Section 113

PART VII
STAMP DUTY AND STAMP DUTY RESERVE TAX

Chapter	Short title	Extent of repeal
1986 c 41.	The Finance Act 1986	Section 67(4). Section 69(6) to (8). Section 70(4). Section 72(4). Sections 80A to 80C.

Chapter	Short title	Extent of repeal
		Sections 81 and 82.
		Section 87(7B).
		In section 88(1B)(*b*), the word "or" at the end of sub-paragraph (ii).
		Sections 88A and 88B.
		Section 89.
		Section 89AA.
		Section 89B.
		Section 90(3)(*b*).
		Section 93(5).
		Section 94(5) to (7).
		In section 96(3) and (11).
1987 c 16.	The Finance Act 1987	Section 53.
		In Schedule 7, paragraph 4.
1988 c 39.	The Finance Act 1988	In Schedule 13, paragraph 23.
1996 c 8.	The Finance Act 1996	Section 191.
		Section 194(2)(*b*) and (4)(*b*).
1997 c 16.	The Finance Act 1997	Sections 97 to 106.

1 The repeals in sections 80A to 80C of the Finance Act 1986 and sections 97 to 99 and of this Act have effect in accordance with section 108 of the Finance Act 1990.

2 The repeals in sections 67, 69, 70 and 72 of the Finance Act 1986 have effect in accordance with section 99 of this Act.

3 The repeal of section 81 of the Finance Act 1986 has effect in accordance with section 97 of this Act.

4 The repeals of section 82 of the Finance Act 1986 and section 53 of the Finance Act 1987 have effect in accordance with section 98 of this Act.

5 The repeals in sections 87 and 88 of the Finance Act 1986 have effect in accordance with section 106 of this Act.

6 The repeals of sections 88A, 88B and 89AA of the Finance Act 1986 and sections 100 to 106 of this Act have effect in accordance with section 110 of the Finance Act 1990.

7 The repeal of section 89 of the Finance Act 1986 and the repeal in Schedule 7 to the Finance Act 1987 have effect in accordance with section 102 of this Act.

8 The repeals of section 89B of the Finance Act 1986 and section 191 of the Finance Act 1996 have effect in accordance with section 103 of this Act.

9 The repeal of section 90(3)(*b*) of the Finance Act 1986 has effect in accordance with section 105 of this Act.

10 The repeals in sections 93, 94 and 96 of the Finance Act 1986, in Schedule 13 to the Finance Act 1988 and in section 194 of the Finance Act 1996 have effect in accordance with section 104 of this Act.

FINANCE (NO 2) ACT 1997

(1997 Chapter 58)

PART IV
MISCELLANEOUS AND SUPPLEMENTARY

Stamp duty

49 Stamp duty on conveyance or transfer on sale

Simon's Tax Cases—*Swallow Hotels Ltd v IRC* [2000] STC 45.

Amendments—This section repealed by FA 1999 Sch 20 Pt V(2) with effect in relation to instruments executed, or bearer instruments issued, from 1 October 1999, subject to the provisions in FA 1999 Sch 20 Pt V(2) Note 2. Previously the text read:

"(1) Section 55 of the Finance Act 1963 and section 4 of the Finance Act (Northern Ireland) 1963 (both of which provide for rates of stamp duty on conveyance and transfer on sale) shall each be amended in accordance with the provisions of subsections (2) to (4) below.
(2) (*substitutes* FA 1963 s 55(1)(*b*)(*c*) and FA (Northern Ireland) 1963 s 4(1)(*b*)(*c*)).
(3) (*amends* FA 1963 s 55(1A)).
(4) (*amends* FA 1963 s 55(2)).
(5) (*amends* FA (Northern Ireland) 1963 s 4).
(6) This section shall apply to instruments executed on or after 8th July 1997, except where the instrument in question is executed in pursuance of a contract made on or before 2nd July 1997.
(7) This section shall be deemed to have come into force on 8th July 1997."

FINANCE ACT 1998

(1998 Chapter 36)

An Act to grant certain duties, to alter other duties, and to amend the law relating to the National Debt and the Public Revenue, and to make further provision in connection with Finance.

[31 July 1998]

PART V
OTHER TAXES

Stamp duty

149 Stamp duty on conveyance or transfer on sale.

Amendments—This section repealed by FA 1999 Sch 20 Pt V(2) with effect in relation to instruments executed, or bearer instruments issued, from 1 October 1999, subject to the provisions in FA 1999 Sch 20 Pt V(2) Note 2. Previously the text read:

"(1) Section 55 of the Finance Act 1963 and section 4 of the Finance Act (Northern Ireland) 1963 (both of which provide for rates of stamp duty on conveyance or transfer on sale) shall each be amended as follows.
(2) In subsection (1)(*d*) (rate of £1.50p for every £100 etc where consideration does not exceed £500,000 and the instrument is certified at that amount) for "£1.50p" there shall be substituted "£2".
(3) In subsection (1)(*e*) (rate of £2 for every £100 etc) for "£2" there shall be substituted "£3".
(4) This section shall apply to instruments executed on or after 24th March 1998, except where the instrument in question is executed in pursuance of a contract made on or before 17th March 1998.
(5) This section shall be deemed to have come into force on 24th March 1998."

150 Relief from double stamp duties etc.

(1) Where an instrument which is chargeable with stamp duty in Great Britain and in Northern Ireland has been stamped in either of those parts of the United Kingdom—
(*a*) the instrument shall, to the extent of the duty it bears, be deemed to be stamped in the other part of the United Kingdom, but
(*b*) if the stamp duty chargeable on the instrument in that other part of the United Kingdom exceeds the stamp duty chargeable on the instrument in the part of the United Kingdom in which it has been stamped, the instrument shall not be deemed to have been duly stamped in that other part of the United Kingdom unless and until stamped in accordance with the law which has effect in that part of the United Kingdom with a stamp denoting an amount equal to the excess.

(2) An instrument which, by virtue of paragraph (*b*) of subsection (1) above, is not deemed to have been duly stamped in a part of the United Kingdom unless and until stamped with a stamp denoting an amount equal to the excess mentioned in that paragraph may, notwithstanding anything in section 15 of the Stamp Act 1891, be stamped with such a stamp without payment of any penalty at any time within 30 days after it has first been received in that part of the United Kingdom.
(3) (*amends* SDMA 1891 s 22).
(4) (*repeals* the Government of Ireland Act 1920 s 29).
(5) The saving in Part I of Schedule 6 to the Northern Ireland Constitution Act 1973 (repeals) for orders made under section 69 of the Government of Ireland Act 1920 shall cease to have effect in relation to Part IV of the Government of Ireland (Adaptation of the S.R. & O. 1922/80.Taxing Acts) Order 1922 (the provisions of which are either spent or re-enacted with modifications in subsections (2) and (3) above).

Stamp duty reserve tax

151 Depositary receipts and clearance services: exchanges of shares.

(1)–(5) (*amend* FA 1986 ss 95(3), 97(4), 99(10) and *insert* ss 95(5)–(7), 97(6), (7)).
(6) This section applies where the issue by company X referred to in section 95(3) or (6) or 97(4) or (7) of the Finance Act 1986 is an issue on or after 1st May 1998.

HUMAN RIGHTS ACT 1998

(1998 Chapter 42)

An Act to give further effect to rights and freedoms guaranteed under the European Convention on Human Rights; to make provision with respect to holders of certain judicial offices who become judges of the European Court of Human Rights; and for connected purposes.

[9th November 1998]

Note—Please see VAT Statutes *ante* for the text of this Act.

FINANCE ACT 1999

(1999 Chapter 16)

ARRANGEMENT OF SECTIONS

Schedule 18—Stamp duty: minor amendments and repeal of obsolete provisions.
Part I—Minor amendments.
Part II—Obsolete provisions.
Schedule 19—Stamp duty and stamp duty reserve tax: unit trusts.
Part I—Abolition of stamp duty on transfers etc of units in unit trusts.
Part II—Stamp duty reserve tax on dealings with units in unit trusts.
Part III—Minor and consequential amendments.
Part IV—General definitions.

An Act to grant certain duties, to alter other duties, and to amend the law relating to the National Debt and the Public Revenue, and to make further provision in connection with Finance.

[27 July 1999]

PART VI
STAMP DUTY AND STAMP DUTY RESERVE TAX

Stamp duty

109 Interest and penalties on late stamping

(1) (*substitutes* the Stamp Act 1891 ss 15, 15A, 15B (for original s 15)).
(2) (*amends* FA 1989 s 178(2)).
(3) The consequential amendments in Schedule 12 to this Act have effect.
(4) This section applies to instruments executed on or after 1st October 1999.

110 Interest on repayment of duty overpaid etc

(1) A payment by the Commissioners to which this section applies shall be paid with interest at the rate applicable under section 178 of the Finance Act 1989 for the period between the relevant time (as defined below) and the date on which the order for the payment is issued.
(2) This section applies to any repayment by the Commissioners of duty, or any penalty on late stamping, under the enactments relating to stamp duty.
In that case the relevant time is 30 days after the day on which the instrument in question was executed or, if later, the date on which the payment of duty or penalty was made.
(3) This section applies to a repayment by the Commissioners of an amount lodged with them in respect of the duty payable on stamping an instrument if—
(*a*) the instrument is presented for stamping,
(*b*) the instrument is duly stamped, and
(*c*) the repayment is of an amount then repayable.
In that case the relevant time is 30 days after the day on which the instrument was executed or, if later, the date on which the amount was lodged with the Commissioners.
(4) This section also applies to a money payment made by the Commissioners under section 11 of the Stamp Duties Management Act 1891 (allowances for spoiled or misused stamps).
In that case the relevant time is the date on which the duty was paid for the stamp in respect of which the allowance is made.
(5) A payment by the Commissioners under section 12A(2)(*b*) of that Act (allowances for lost or spoiled instruments) is treated for the purposes of this section as a repayment of the duty or penalty by reference to which it is made.
In that case the relevant time is the date on which the payment of duty or penalty was made.
(6) No interest is payable under this section if the amount of the payment to which this section applies is less than £25.
(7) No interest is payable under this section in respect of a payment made in consequence of an order or judgment of a court having power to allow interest on the payment.
(8) Interest paid to any person under this section is not income of that person for any tax purposes.
(9) (*amends* FA 1989 s 178(2)).
(10) This section applies in relation to instruments executed on or after 1st October 1999.

Cross references—See FA 2000 Sch 33 para 5 (application of this section to repayments of any amount paid by way of stamp duty or penalty on late stamping under FA 2000 Sch 33 para 5).

111 Stamp duty on [transfer][1] on sale

(1)–(3) (*amend* FA 1963 s 55)).
(4) This section applies to instruments executed on or after 16th March 1999, except where the instrument in question is executed in pursuance of a contract made on or before 9th March 1999.
(5) This section shall be deemed to have come into force on 16th March 1999.

Amendments—[1] The word "transfer" substituted for the words "conveyance or transfer" in enactments relating to stamp duty by FA 2003 Sch 20 para 3.

112 General amendment of charging provisions

(1) The amount of any stamp duty chargeable *ad valorem*—
(*a*) shall be a percentage of the amount specified in the relevant charging provision, and
(*b*) shall be rounded up (if necessary) to the nearest multiple of £5.

(2) The amount of every fixed stamp duty shall be £5.

(3) The provisions of Schedule 13 to this Act have effect in place of Schedule 1 to the Stamp Act 1891, and certain related enactments, so far as they relate to the instruments (other than bearer instruments) chargeable to duty and the method of calculation and rates of duty.

(4) The consequential amendments in Schedule 14 to this Act have effect.

(5) The percentage rates specified in Schedule 13 and the enactments amended by Schedule 14 correspond to the rates of duty generally in force at the passing of this Act.

In the case of an instrument in relation to which there was then in force transitional provision in connection with an earlier change in the rate of duty having the effect that a different rate applied, the new or amended provisions have effect as if a reference to a percentage corresponding to that different rate were substituted.

(6) This section has effect in relation to instruments executed on or after 1st October 1999.

113 Bearer instruments

(1) The provisions of Schedule 15 to this Act have effect in place of the heading "Bearer Instruments" in Schedule 1 to the Stamp Act 1891, and certain related enactments, and incorporate amendments in relation to bearer instruments corresponding to those made by—

section 109 (interest and penalties on late stamping),

section 112 (general amendment of charging provisions), and

Part I of Schedule 17 to this Act (amendments of penalties other than on late stamping).

(2) The percentage rates specified in Schedule 15 correspond to the rates of duty generally in force at the passing of this Act.

In the case of an instrument in relation to which there was then in force transitional provision in connection with an earlier change in the rate of duty having the effect that a different rate applied, the new provisions have effect as if a reference to a percentage corresponding to that different rate were substituted.

(3) The consequential amendments specified in Schedule 16 to this Act have effect.

(4) This section applies in relation to bearer instruments issued on or after 1st October 1999.

Prospective amendment—This section to be repealed by FA 1999 s 123(3), Sch 20 Pt V(6) with effect on the abolition day appointed by virtue of FA 1990 ss 107–111.

114 Penalties other than on late stamping

(1) The provisions of Schedule 17 to this Act (stamp duty: penalties other than on late stamping) have effect.

(2) The provisions of that Schedule have effect in relation to penalties in respect of things done or omitted on or after 1st October 1999.

115 Minor amendments and repeal of obsolete provisions

Schedule 18 to this Act (stamp duty: minor amendments and repeal of obsolete provisions) has effect.

Stamp duty reserve tax

116 Non-sterling bearer instruments issued in connection with merger or takeover

(1), (2) (*amend* FA 1986 ss 95, 97)).

(3) This section applies to any instrument issued on or after 30th January 1999, except one giving effect to an agreement for a company merger or takeover entered into in writing by the companies involved before that date.

Prospective amendment—This section to be repealed by FA 1999 s 123(3), Sch 20 Pt V(6) with effect on the appointed day by virtue of FA 1990 s 111(1).

117 Scope of exceptions for certain bearer instruments

(1)–(6) (*amend* FA 1986 ss 95(2), 97(3), *insert* ss 95(2A)–(2D), 97(3A)–(3D) and *substitute* ss 95(6), 97(7)).

(7) Subsections (1) to (6) above apply in relation to any instrument issued on or after 9th March 1999, except one giving effect to an agreement for a company merger or takeover entered into in writing by the companies involved before 30th January 1999.

Prospective amendment—This section to be repealed by FA 1999 s 123(3), Sch 20 Pt V(6) with effect on the appointed day by virtue of FA 1990 s 111(1).

118 Relief in case of certain replacement securities

(1)–(4) (*insert* FA 1996 ss 95A, 97AA and *amend* s 99(10)).

(5) This section applies in relation to securities issued on or after 1st May 1998.

119 Power to exempt UK depositary interests in foreign securities

(1) The Treasury may by regulations make provision excluding from the definition of "chargeable securities" in Part IV of the Finance Act 1986 such rights in or in relation to securities as, in accordance with the regulations, are to be treated as exempt UK depositary interests in foreign securities.

(2) Subject to subsection (3), the regulations may—

(*a*) define "depositary interest", "UK depositary interest" and "foreign securities" for this purpose; and

(*b*) exempt such descriptions of UK depositary interests in foreign securities (as so defined) as may from time to time be specified in the regulations.

(3) The regulations shall not make provision for the exemption of a depositary interest unless the terms of issue of the interest are such that it can only be transferred in accordance with regulations under section [785][1] of the Companies Act [2006][1] (transfer of securities without written instrument) or by means of a transfer within section 186(1) of the Finance Act 1996 (transfer of securities to member of electronic transfer system).

(4) The regulations may contain such incidental, supplementary, consequential and transitional provision as appears to the Treasury to be appropriate.

This may include provision modifying the enactments relating to stamp duty reserve tax for the purpose of giving effect to the exemption conferred by regulations under this section (or, where earlier regulations are varied or revoked, withdrawing an exemption formerly conferred).

(5) Regulations under this section may make different provision for different cases.

(6) Regulations under this section shall be made by statutory instrument which shall be subject to annulment in pursuance of a resolution of the House of Commons.

Amendments—[1] In sub-s (3), figures substituted for figures "207" and "1989", by the Companies Act 2006 (Consequential Amendments) (Taxes and National Insurance) Order, SI 2009/1890 art 11(*a*) with effect from 1 October 2009.

Prospective amendment—This section to be repealed by FA 1999 s 123(3), Sch 20 Pt V(6) with effect on the appointed day by virtue of FA 1990 s 111(1).

120 Minor amendments of exceptions to general charge

(1) Section 90 of the Finance Act 1986 (exceptions from the general charge to stamp duty reserve tax) is amended as follows.

(2) (*amend* FA 1986 s 90(3F)(*c*)).

(3) (*amend* FA 1986 s 90(5), (6)).

(4) Subsection (2) above applies to instruments issued on or after 9th March 1999.

(5) Subsection (3) above applies to agreements to transfer securities made on or after 9th March 1999.

Prospective amendment—This section to be repealed by FA 1999 s 123(3), Sch 20 Pt V(6) with effect on the appointed day by virtue of FA 1990 s 111(1).

121 Power to make regulations with respect to administration, etc

(1) The following provisions have effect with respect to the power conferred on the Treasury by section 98(1) of the Finance Act 1986 (stamp duty reserve tax: regulations with respect to administration, etc).

(2) That power includes power to make provision—

(*a*) applying the provisions of the Taxes Management Act 1970 relating to penalties and the payment of interest on overdue tax, and

(*b*) requiring information to be provided, or books, documents or other records to be made available for inspection, and imposing a penalty for failure to do so.

(3) That power includes, and shall be deemed always to have included, power to make provision requiring specified descriptions of persons to account for and pay tax, and any interest on it, on behalf of the person liable to pay it.

Regulations—See the Stamp Duty and Stamp Duty Reserve Tax (Definition of Unit Trust Scheme and Open-ended Investment Company) Regulations, SI 2001/964.

Prospective amendment—This section to be repealed by FA 1999 s 123(3), Sch 20 Pt V(6) with effect on the appointed day by virtue of FA 1990 s 111(1).

Units in unit trusts

122 Stamp duty and stamp duty reserve tax: unit trusts

(1) The following provisions of this Act (which apply generally to instruments executed on or after 1st October 1999)—

(*a*) section 109 and Schedule 12 (interest and penalties on late stamping),

(*b*) section 110 (interest on duty overpaid, etc), and

(*c*) section 112 and Schedules 13 and 14 (general amendment of charging provisions),

do not apply to transfers or other instruments relating to units under a unit trust scheme.

(2) Subsection (1) does not affect the operation of those provisions in relation to stamp duty—

(*a*) on a [transfer][1] on sale of property other than units under a unit trust scheme in relation to which such units form the whole or part of the consideration, or

(*b*) under Schedule 15 to this Act (bearer instruments).

(3) In subsections (1) and (2) "unit" and "unit trust scheme" have the same meaning as in Part VII of the Finance Act 1946 or Part III of the Finance (No 2) Act (Northern Ireland) 1946.

(4) Schedule 19 to this Act (stamp duty and stamp duty reserve tax: unit trusts) has effect.

This subsection and that Schedule come into force on 6th February 2000.

Amendments—[1] The word "transfer" substituted for the words "conveyance or transfer" in enactments relating to stamp duty by FA 2003 Sch 20 para 3.

Supplementary provisions

123 Construction of this Part and other supplementary provisions

(1) This Part—

(*a*) so far as it relates to stamp duty shall be construed as one with the Stamp Act 1891, and

(*b*) so far as it relates to stamp duty reserve tax shall be construed as one with Part IV of the Finance Act 1986.

(2) In this Part—

(*a*) "the enactments relating to stamp duty" means the Stamp Act 1891 and any enactment amending or which is to be construed as one with that Act; and

(*b*) "the enactments relating to stamp duty reserve tax" means Part IV of the Finance Act 1986 and any enactment amending or which is to be construed as one with that Part.

(3) The following provisions of this Part shall cease to have effect on the day appointed under section 111(1) of the Finance Act 1990 (abolition of stamp duty for securities etc):

section 113;
sections 116 to 121;
subsections (1)(*b*) and (2)(*b*) of this section;
in Schedule 13—
paragraph 3,
in paragraph 4 the words "in the case of any other [transfer][1] on sale",
paragraph 7(1)(*b*)(ii) to (iv),
paragraph 24(*a*), (*b*) and (*d*);
in Schedule 14, paragraphs 5, 8, 12, 13, 16 to 21 and 23;
Schedule 15;
in Schedule 16, paragraphs 2 to 11;
in Schedule 17, paragraphs 6 to 8;
Parts I to III of Schedule 19;
in Part IV of that Schedule, the words "and the enactments relating to stamp duty reserve tax" in paragraphs 14(1), 15, 16, 17(1) and 18(1).

(4) The amendment by this Part, or the repeal in consequence of this Part, of any enactment relating to stamp duty does not affect that enactment as applied for any purpose other than stamp duty.

Amendments—[1] The word "transfer substituted for the words "conveyance or transfer" in enactments relating to stamp duty by FA 2003 Sch 20 para 3.

Prospective amendment—Sub-ss (1)(*b*) and (2)(*b*), and the word "and" immediately preceding it, to be repealed by FA 1999 s 123(3), Sch 20 Pt V(6) with effect on the appointed day by virtue of FA 1990 s 111(1).

PART VIII
MISCELLANEOUS AND SUPPLEMENTAL

Supplemental

139 Repeals

(1) The enactments mentioned in Schedule 20 to this Act (which include provisions that are spent or of no practical utility) are hereby repealed to the extent specified in the third column of that Schedule.

(2) The repeals specified in that Schedule have effect subject to the commencement provisions and savings contained or referred to in the notes set out in that Schedule.

140 Short title

This Act may be cited as the Finance Act 1999.

SCHEDULES

SCHEDULE 12

STAMP DUTY: INTEREST AND PENALTIES ON LATE STAMPING

Section 109(3)

Stamp Act 1891 (c 39)

1 (*substitutes* SA 1891 ss 12, 12A for original s 12).

2 (*substitutes* SA 1891 ss 13, 13A, 13B for original s 13).

3 (*amends* SA 1891 s 14).

Finance Act 1994 (c 9)

4 (*substitutes* FA 1994 ss 240, 240A for original s 240).

SCHEDULE 13

STAMP DUTY: INSTRUMENTS CHARGEABLE AND RATES OF DUTY

Section 112(3)

PART I

[TRANSFER][1] ON SALE

Amendments—[1] The word "transfer" substituted for the words "conveyance or transfer" in enactments relating to stamp duty by FA 2003 Sch 20 para 3.

Cross references—See FA 2000 s 118(2), (4) (for the purposes of this Part, in relation to land transferred for consideration of other property, the instrument transferring or vesting the estate or interest shall be taken to be a transfer on sale of the estate or interest).

FA 2000 s 119(2) (for the purposes of this Part, in relation to where an estate or interest in land is transferred to or vested in a company, the instrument transferring or vesting the estate or interest shall be taken to be a transfer on sale of the estate or interest).

FA 2000 s 121(2) (for the purposes of stamp duty chargeable under Part II of this Schedule, in reference to this Part, where a lease is granted to a connected company, the amount or value of consideration for the grant of the lease shall be taken to be the market value, immediately before the instrument granting the lease is executed, of the lease granted, but reduced by the value of so much of any actual consideration as does not consist of property).

FA 2000 s 122(2) (for the purposes of this Part, in relation to where marketable securities are transferred for exempt property, the instrument transferring the marketable securities shall be taken to be a transfer on sale of those securities).

FA 2000 s 130(1) (no stamp duty chargeable under this Part on a conveyance or transfer of an estate or interest in land, or on a lease of land, to registered social landlords etc).

FA 2000 Sch 34 para 2 (stamp duty reduced where part of the property concerned consists of intellectual property).

FA 2001 s 92(1) (no stamp duty chargeable under this Part on a conveyance of land or transfer of an estate or interest in land, or a lease of land, if the land is situated in a disadvantaged area).

FA 2001 Sch 30 para 1(1) (where any land is situated partly in a disadvantaged area and partly outside such an area, liability to stamp duty under this Part I on a conveyance or transfer of an estate or interest in the land, or a lease of the land, shall be determined in accordance with FA 2000 Sch 30 para 1(2))

FA 2003 s 125(1) (stamp duty is chargeable under this Schedule only on instruments relating to stock or marketable securities).

FA 2003 Sch 20 para 1 (application of that paragraph where stamp duty is chargeable under this Part on an instrument that relates partly to stock or marketable securities and partly to property other than stock or marketable securities).

Charge

1—(1) Stamp duty is chargeable on a [transfer][3] on sale.

(2) For this purpose "[transfer on sale]"[2] includes every instrument, and every decree or order of a court or commissioners, by which any property, or any estate or interest in property, is, on being sold, transferred to or vested in the purchaser or another person on behalf of or at the direction of the purchaser.

[(3) Sub-paragraph (1) is subject to sub-paragraphs [(3A)][4] to (6).][1]

[(3A) Stamp duty is not chargeable under sub-paragraph (1) on a transfer of stock or marketable securities where—

(*a*) the amount or value of the consideration for the sale is £1,000 or under, and

(*b*) the instrument is certified at £1,000.][4]

[(4) Where a company acquires any shares in itself by virtue of section [690][6] of the Companies Act [2006][6] (power of company to purchase own shares) or otherwise, sub-paragraph (1) does not apply to any instrument by which the shares are transferred to the company.][1]

[(5) Where a company holds any shares in itself by virtue of section [724][6] of that Act (treasury shares) or otherwise, [sub-paragraph (1) does not apply to any instrument to which sub-paragraph (6) applies.][5]][1]

[(6) This sub-paragraph applies to any instrument for the sale or transfer of any of the shares by the company, other than an instrument which, in the absence of sub-paragraph (5), would be an instrument in relation to which—

(*a*) section 67(2) of the Finance Act 1986 (transfer to person whose business is issuing depositary receipts etc), or

(*b*) section 70(2) of that Act (transfer to person who provides clearance services etc),

applied.][1]

Amendments—[1] Sub-paras (3)–(6) inserted by FA 2003 s 195, Sch 40 para 5 with effect for any acquisition of shares by a company on or after 1 December 2003 (by virtue of SI 2003/3077).

[2] In sub-para (2), words "transfer on sale" substituted for the words "conveyance on sale" by FA 2003 s 125(4), Sch 20 para 6 with effect—

(a) in relation to instruments effecting land transactions that—

(i) are SDLT transactions within the meaning of FA 2003 Sch 19, or

(ii) would be such transactions but for an exemption or relief from stamp duty land tax;

(b) in relation to other instruments, if they are executed on or after the implementation date for the purposes of stamp duty land tax.

The implementation date is 1 December 2003 (by virtue of SI 2003/2899).

FA 2003 s 125 and Sch 20 have effect subject to FA 2003 Sch 15 para 13(2), (3).

3 The word "transfer" substituted for the words "conveyance or transfer" in enactments relating to stamp duty by FA 2003 Sch 20 para 3.

4 In sub-para (3), reference substituted for reference "(4)", and sub-para (3A) inserted, by FA 2008 s 98(1)–(3), with effect in relation to instruments executed on or after 13 March 2008 and not stamped before 19 March 2008.

5 Words in sub-para (5) substituted, by FA 2008 s 99, Sch 32 para 10(1), (2) with effect in relation to instruments executed on or after 13 March 2008 and not stamped before 19 March 2008.
This amendment does not have effect in relation to an instrument effecting a land transaction or a duplicate or counterpart of such an instrument. "Land transaction" has the same meaning as in FA 2003 Part 4, except that it does not include a transfer of an interest in a property-investment partnership (within the meaning of FA 2003 Sch 15) (FA 2008 s 99, Sch 32 para 22).
Sub-para (5) previously read as follows—

"(5) Where a company holds any shares in itself by virtue of section 162A of that Act (treasury shares) or otherwise, any instrument to which sub-paragraph (6) applies is to be treated for the purposes of this Schedule as a conveyance otherwise than on sale, and paragraph 16 applies accordingly."

6 In sub-para (4), figures substituted for figures "162" and "1985", and in sub-para (5), figure substituted for figure "162A", by the Companies Act 2006 (Consequential Amendments) (Taxes and National Insurance) Order, SI 2009/1890 art 11(*b*), (*c*) with effect from 1 October 2009.

Rates of duty

2 Duty under this Part is chargeable by reference to the amount or value of the consideration for the sale.

3 In the case of a conveyance or transfer of stock or marketable securities the rate is 0.5%.

Notes—The word "transfer" substituted for the words "conveyance or transfer" in enactments relating to stamp duty: FA 2003 Sch 20 para 3.

Prospective amendment—Para 3 to be repealed by FA 1999 s 123(3), Sch 20 Pt V(6) with effect on the appointed day by virtue of FA 1990 s 111(1).

4 In the case of any other [transfer][2] on sale the rates of duty are as follows—

1.	Where the amount or value of the consideration is [£125,000][3] or under and the instrument is certified at [£125,000][3]	Nil
2.	Where the amount or value of the consideration is £250,000 or under and the instrument is certified at £250,000	1%
3.	Where the amount or value of the consideration is £500,000 or under and the instrument is certified at £500,000	[3%][1]
4.	Any other case	[4%][1]

Cross references—See FA 2000 Sch 33 para 3 (power to vary stamp duties not to be used to vary any threshold specified in this paragraph).

Amendments—1 Figures in table substituted by FA 2000 s 114(1) with effect for instruments executed after 27 March 2000, except in relation to an instrument giving effect to a contract made before 22 March 2000, unless—

(a) the instrument is made in consequence of the exercise after that date of any option, right of pre-emption or similar right; or

(b) the instrument transfers the property in question to, or vests it in, a person other than the purchaser under the contract, because of an assignment (or, in Scotland, assignation) or further contract made after that date.

Previously the figures read "2.5%" and "3.5%" respectively.

2 The word "transfer" substituted for the words "conveyance or transfer" in enactments relating to stamp duty by FA 2003 Sch 20 para 3.

3 "£125,000" substituted for "£120,000" by FA 2006 s 162(3), with effect in relation to instruments executed after 22 March 2006. Previous figure of "£120,000" substituted for "£60,000" by FA 2005 s 95(3), (5) with effect for instruments executed after 16 March 2005.

Prospective amendment—Words "in the case of any other conveyance or transfer on sale" in para 4 to be repealed by FA 1999 s 123(3), Sch 20 Pt V(6) with effect on the appointed day by virtue of FA 1990 s 111(1).

5 The above provisions are subject to any enactment setting a different rate or setting an upper limit on the amount of duty chargeable.

Meaning of instrument being certified at an amount

6— (1) The references in [paragraphs 1(3A) and][2] 4 above to an instrument being certified at a particular amount mean that it contains a statement that the transaction effected by the instrument does not form part of a larger transaction or series of transactions in respect of which the amount or value, or aggregate amount or value, of the consideration exceeds that amount.

(2) For this purpose a sale or contract or agreement for the sale of goods, wares or merchandise shall be disregarded—

(*a*) in the case of an instrument which is not an actual [transfer][1] of the goods, wares or merchandise (with or without other property);

(*b*) in the case of an instrument treated as such a [transfer][1] only by virtue of paragraph 7 (contracts or agreements chargeable as conveyances on sale);

and any statement as mentioned in sub-paragraph (1) shall be construed as leaving out of account any matter which is to be so disregarded.

Cross references—FA 2000 Sch 34 para 6 (intellectual property to be disregarded for the purposes of this paragraph).

FA 2001 Sch 30 para 3 (a transaction which relates (or the extent to which a transaction relates) to an estate or interest in land which is situated in a disadvantaged area to be disregarded for the purposes of this paragraph).

Amendments—[1] The word "transfer" substituted for the words "conveyance or transfer" in enactments relating to stamp duty by FA 2003 Sch 20 para 3.

[2] In sub-para (1), words substituted for word "paragraph" by FA 2008 s 98(4) with effect in relation to instruments executed on or after 13 March 2008 and not stamped before 19 March 2008.

Contracts or agreements chargeable as conveyances on sale

7—(1) A contract or agreement for the sale of—

(*a*) any equitable estate or interest in property, or

(*b*) any estate or interest in property except—

(i) land,

(ii) goods, wares or merchandise,

(iii) stock or marketable securities,

(iv) any ship or vessel, or a part interest, share or property of or in any ship or vessel, or

(v) property of any description situated outside the United Kingdom,

is chargeable with the same ad valorem duty, to be paid by the purchaser, as if it were an actual conveyance on sale of the estate, interest or property contracted or agreed to be sold.

(2) Where the purchaser has paid *ad valorem* duty and before having obtained a [transfer][1] of the property enters into a contract or agreement for the sale of the same, the contract or agreement is chargeable, if the consideration for that sale is in excess of the consideration for the original sale, with the *ad valorem* duty payable in respect of the excess consideration but is not otherwise chargeable.

(3) Where duty has been paid in conformity with sub-paragraphs (1) and (2), the [transfer][1] to the purchaser or sub-purchaser, or any other person on his behalf or by his direction, is not chargeable with any duty.

(4) In that case, upon application and upon production of the contract or agreement (or contracts or agreements) duly stamped, the Commissioners shall either—

(*a*) denote the payment of the *ad valorem* duty upon the [transfer][1], or

(*b*) transfer the *ad valorem* duty to the [transfer][1].

Cross references—FA 2003 Sch 19 para 6(1) (where in the case of a contract that, apart from this paragraph, would not be chargeable with stamp duty—

(a) a conveyance made in conformity with the contract is effected after the implementation date, and

(b) stamp duty land tax is duly paid in respect of that transaction or no tax is chargeable because of an exemption or relief,

the contract shall be deemed to be duly stamped).

Prospective amendment—Sub-paras (1)(*b*)(i)–(iv) to be repealed by FA 1999 s 123(3), Sch 20 Pt V(6) with effect on the appointed day by virtue of FA 1990 s 111(1).

Amendments—[1] The word "transfer" substituted for the words "conveyance or transfer" in enactments relating to stamp duty by FA 2003 Sch 20 para 3.

8—(1) Where a contract or agreement would apart from paragraph 7 not be chargeable with any duty and a [transfer][1] made in conformity with the contract or agreement is presented to the Commissioners for stamping with the *ad valorem* duty chargeable on it—

(*a*) within the period of six months after the execution of the contract or agreement, or

(*b*) within such longer period as the Commissioners may think reasonable in the circumstances of the case,

the [transfer][1] shall be stamped accordingly, and both it and the contract or agreement shall be deemed to be duly stamped.

(2) Nothing in this paragraph affects the provisions as to the stamping of a conveyance or transfer after execution.

Amendments—[1] The word "transfer" substituted for the words "conveyance or transfer" in enactments relating to stamp duty: FA 2003 Sch 20 para 3.

9 The *ad valorem* duty paid upon a contract or agreement by virtue of paragraph 7 shall be repaid by the Commissioners if the contract or agreement is afterwards rescinded or annulled or is for any other reason not substantially performed or carried into effect so as to operate as or be followed by a [transfer][1].

Amendments—[1] The word "transfer" substituted for the words "conveyance or transfer" in enactments relating to stamp duty: FA 2003 Sch 20 para 3.

PART II
LEASE

Cross references—See FA 2000 s 121(2) (for the purposes of stamp duty chargeable under this Part, in reference to Part I of the Schedule, where a lease is granted to a connected company, the amount or value of consideration for the grant of the lease shall be taken to be the market value, immediately before the instrument granting the lease is executed, of the lease granted, but reduced by the value of so much of any actual consideration as does not consist of property).

FA 2000 s 130(1) (no stamp duty chargeable under this Part on a conveyance or transfer of an estate or interest in land, or on a lease of land, to registered social landlords etc).

FA 2001 s 92(1) (no stamp duty chargeable under this Part on a conveyance of land or transfer of an estate or interest in land, or a lease of land, if the land is situated in a disadvantaged area).

FA 2001 Sch 30 para 1(1) (where any land is situated partly in a disadvantaged area and partly outside such an area, liability to stamp duty under this Part I on a conveyance or transfer of an estate or interest in the land, or a lease of the land, shall be determined in accordance with FA 2000 Sch 30 para 1(2)).

FA 2003 s 128(1) (no stamp duty is chargeable under this Part on a lease of a dwelling granted by a registered social landlord to one or more individuals in accordance with arrangements to which FA 2003 s 128 applies if the lease is for an indefinite term or is terminable by notice of a month or less).

Charge

10 Stamp duty is chargeable on a lease.

Rates of duty

11 In the case of a lease for a definite term less than a year the duty is as follows—

1.	Lease of furnished dwelling-house or apartments where the rent for the term exceeds [£5,000][1]	£5
2.	Any other lease of land	The same duty as for a lease for a year at the rent reserved for the definite term

Cross references—See FA 2000 Sch 33 para 3 (power to vary stamp duties not to be used to vary any threshold specified in this paragraph in respect of rent or the term of a lease).

Amendments—[1] Sum in table substituted by FA 2000 s 115(1)(*a*) with effect for instruments executed after 27 March 2000.

12— (1) In the case of a lease of land for any other definite term, or for an indefinite term, the duty is determined as follows.

(2) If the consideration or part of the consideration moving to the lessor or to any other person consists of any money, stock, security or other property, the duty in respect of that consideration is the same as that on a conveyance on a sale for the same consideration.

But if—

(*a*) part of the consideration is rent, and

(*b*) that rent exceeds £600 a year,

the duty is calculated as if paragraph 1 of the Table in paragraph 4 of this Schedule were omitted.

(3) If the consideration or part of the consideration is rent, the duty in respect of that consideration is determined by reference to the rate or average rate of the rent (whether reserved as a yearly rent or not), as follows.

1.	Term [not more than 7 years][1] or indefinite—	
	(*a*) if the rent is [£5,000][2] or less	Nil
	(*b*) if the rent is more than [£5,000][2]	1%
2.	Term more than 7 years but not more than 35 years	2%
3.	Term more than 35 years but not more than 100 years	12%
4.	Term more than 100 years	24%

Cross references—See FA 2000 Sch 33 para 3 (power to vary stamp duties not to be used to vary any threshold specified in this paragraph in respect of rent or the term of a lease).

Amendments—[1] Words in table substituted by FA 2000 s 116(1) with effect for instruments executed after 30 September 1999, subject to transitional provisions for instruments executed after 30 September 1999 but before 28 March 2000: see FA 2000 Sch 32 below.

[2] Sums in table substituted by FA 2000 s 115(1)(*b*) with effect for instruments executed after 27 March 2000.

13 Stamp duty of £5 is chargeable on a lease not within paragraph 11 or 12 above.

Agreement for a lease charged as a lease

14—(1) An agreement for a lease is chargeable with the same duty as if it were an actual lease made for the term and consideration mentioned in the agreement.
(2) Where duty has been duly paid on an agreement for a lease and subsequent to that agreement a lease is granted which either—

(*a*) is in conformity with the agreement, or

(*b*) relates to substantially the same property and term as the agreement,

the duty which would otherwise be charged on the lease is reduced by the amount of the duty paid on the agreement.
(3) Sub-paragraph (1) does not apply to missives of let in Scotland that constitute an actual lease. Subject to that, references in this paragraph to an agreement for a lease include missives of let in Scotland.

Lease for fixed term and then until determined

15—(1) For the purposes of this Part a lease granted for a fixed term and thereafter until determined is treated as a lease for a definite term equal to the fixed term together with such further period as must elapse before the earliest date at which the lease can be determined.
(2) Paragraph 14 (agreement for a lease charged as a lease) shall be construed accordingly.

PART III
OTHER INSTRUMENTS

[Transfer][1] otherwise than on sale[2]

16—*(1) Stamp duty of £5 is chargeable on a [transfer]*[1] *of property otherwise than on sale.*
(2) In sub-paragraph (1) "[transfer][1]*" includes every instrument, and every decree or order of a court or commissioners, by which any property is transferred to or vested in any person.*[2]

Cross references—See FA 2000 s 130(1) (no stamp duty chargeable under this paragraph on a conveyance or transfer of an estate or interest in land, or on a lease of land, to registered social landlords etc).
FA 2001 s 92(1) (no stamp duty chargeable under this paragraph on a conveyance of land or transfer of an estate or interest in land, or a lease of land, if the land is situated in a disadvantaged area).
FA 2001 Sch 30 para 1(1) (where any land is situated partly in a disadvantaged area and partly outside such an area, liability to stamp duty under this paragraph on a conveyance or transfer of an estate or interest in the land, or a lease of the land, shall be determined in accordance with FA 2001 Sch 30 para 1(2)).

Amendments—[1] The word "transfer" substituted for the words "conveyance or transfer" in enactments relating to stamp duty by FA 2003 Sch 20 para 3.
[2] This para and preceding heading repealed by FA 2008 s 99, Sch 32 paras 9, 10(1), (3) with effect in relation to instruments executed on or after 13 March 2008 and not stamped before 19 March 2008.
This amendment does not have effect in relation to an instrument effecting a land transaction or a duplicate or counterpart of such an instrument. "Land transaction" has the same meaning as in FA 2003 Pt 4, except that it does not include a transfer of an interest in a property-investment partnership (within the meaning of FA 2003 Sch 15) (FA 2008 s 99, Sch 32 para 22).

Declaration of use or trust[2]

17—*(1) Stamp duty of £5 is chargeable on a declaration of any use or trust of or concerning property unless the instrument constitutes a [transfer]*[1] *on sale.*
(2) This does not apply to a will.[2]

Amendments—[1] The word "transfer" substituted for the words "conveyance or transfer" in enactments relating to stamp duty by FA 2003 Sch 20 para 3.
[2] This para and preceding heading repealed by FA 2008 s 99, Sch 32 paras 9, 10(1), (3) with effect in relation to instruments executed on or after 13 March 2008 and not stamped before 19 March 2008.
This amendment does not have effect in relation to an instrument effecting a land transaction or a duplicate or counterpart of such an instrument. "Land transaction" has the same meaning as in FA 2003 Part 4, except that it does not include a transfer of an interest in a property-investment partnership (within the meaning of FA 2003 Sch 15) (FA 2008 s 99, Sch 32 para 22).

Dispositions in Scotland

18—(1) The following are chargeable with duty as a conveyance on sale—

(*a*) a disposition of heritable property in Scotland to singular successors or purchasers;

(*b*) a disposition of heritable property in Scotland to a purchaser containing a clause declaring all or any part of the purchase money a real burden upon, or affecting, the heritable property thereby disponed, or any part of it;

(*c*) . . . [1]

(2) *A disposition in Scotland of any property, or any right or interest in property, that is not so chargeable is chargeable with stamp duty of £5.*[2]

Amendment—[1] Sub-para (1)(*c*) repealed by the Abolition of Feudal Tenure etc (Scotland) Act 2000 s 76(1), (2), Sch 12 Pt I para 61, Sch 13 Pt 1 with effect from 28 November 2004 (by virtue of SI 2003/456).

2 Sub-para (2) repealed by FA 2008 s 99, Sch 32 paras 9, 10(1), (3) with effect in relation to instruments executed on or after 13 March 2008 and not stamped before 19 March 2008.
This amendment does not have effect in relation to an instrument effecting a land transaction or a duplicate or counterpart of such an instrument. "Land transaction" has the same meaning as in FA 2003 Pt 4, except that it does not include a transfer of an interest in a property-investment partnership (within the meaning of FA 2003 Sch 15) (FA 2008 s 99, Sch 32 para 22).

Duplicate or counterpart

19—*(1) A duplicate or counterpart of an instrument chargeable with duty is chargeable with duty of £5.*[1]

(2) The duplicate or counterpart of an instrument chargeable with duty is not duly stamped unless—

(*a*) it is stamped as an original instrument, or

(*b*) it appears by some stamp impressed on it that the full and proper duty has been paid on the original instrument of which it is the duplicate or counterpart.

(3) Sub-paragraph (2) does not apply to the counterpart of an instrument chargeable as a lease, if that counterpart is not executed by or on behalf of any lessor or grantor.

Amendments—[1] Sub-para (1) repealed by FA 2008 s 99, Sch 32 paras 9, 10(1), (3) with effect in relation to instruments executed on or after 13 March 2008 and not stamped before 19 March 2008.
This amendment does not have effect in relation to an instrument effecting a land transaction or a duplicate or counterpart of such an instrument. "Land transaction" has the same meaning as in FA 2003 Pt 4, except that it does not include a transfer of an interest in a property-investment partnership (within the meaning of FA 2003 Sch 15) (FA 2008 s 99, Sch 32 para 22).

Instrument increasing rent

20—(1) An instrument (not itself a lease)—

(*a*) by which it is agreed that the rent reserved by a lease should be increased, or

(*b*) which confirms or records any such agreement made otherwise than in writing,

is chargeable with the same duty as if it were a lease in consideration of the additional rent made payable by it.

(2) Sub-paragraph (1) does not apply to an instrument giving effect to provision in the lease for periodic review of the rent reserved by it.

Partition or division

21—(1) Where on the partition or division of an estate or interest in land consideration exceeding £100 in amount or value is paid or given, or agreed to be paid or given, for equality, the principal or only instrument by which the partition or division is effected is chargeable with the same *ad valorem* duty as a conveyance on sale for the consideration, and with that duty only.

(2) Where there are several instruments for completing the title of either party, the principal instrument is to be ascertained, and the other instruments shall be charged with duty, as provided by sections 58(3) and 61 of the Stamp Act 1891 in the case of several instruments of conveyance.

(3) Stamp duty of £5 is chargeable on an instrument effecting a partition or division to which the above provisions do not apply.[1]

Release or renunciation[2]

22 *Stamp duty of £5 is chargeable on a release or renunciation of property unless the instrument constitutes a [transfer]*[1] *on sale.*[2]

Amendments—[1] The word "transfer" substituted for the words "conveyance or transfer" in enactments relating to stamp duty by FA 2003 Sch 20 para 3.

2 This para and preceding heading repealed by FA 2008 s 99, Sch 32 paras 9, 10(1), (3) with effect in relation to instruments executed on or after 13 March 2008 and not stamped before 19 March 2008.
This amendment does not have effect in relation to an instrument effecting a land transaction or a duplicate or counterpart of such an instrument. "Land transaction" has the same meaning as in FA 2003 Pt 4, except that it does not include a transfer of an interest in a property-investment partnership (within the meaning of FA 2003 Sch 15) (FA 2008 s 99, Sch 32 para 22).

Surrender[2]

23 *Stamp duty of £5 is chargeable on a surrender of property unless the instrument constitutes a [transfer]*[1] *on sale.*[2]

Amendments—[1] The word "transfer" substituted for the words "conveyance or transfer" in enactments relating to stamp duty by FA 2003 Sch 20 para 3.

2 This para and preceding heading repealed by FA 2008 s 99, Sch 32 paras 9, 10(1), (3) with effect in relation to instruments executed on or after 13 March 2008 and not stamped before 19 March 2008.
This amendment does not have effect in relation to an instrument effecting a land transaction or a duplicate or counterpart of such an instrument. "Land transaction" has the same meaning as in FA 2003 Pt 4, except that it does not include a transfer of an interest in a property-investment partnership (within the meaning of FA 2003 Sch 15) (FA 2008 s 99, Sch 32 para 22).

PART IV
GENERAL EXEMPTIONS

24 The following are exempt from stamp duty under this Schedule—

(*a*) transfers of shares in the government or parliamentary stocks or funds or strips (within the meaning of section 47 of the Finance Act 1942) of such stocks or funds;

(*b*) instruments for the sale, transfer, or other disposition (absolutely or otherwise) of any ship or vessel, or any part, interest, share or property of or in a ship or vessel;

(*c*) testaments, testamentary instruments and dispositions *mortis causa* in Scotland;

(*d*) renounceable letters of allotment, letters of rights or other similar instruments where the rights under the letter or other instrument are renounceable not later than six months after its issue.

Prospective amendment—Sub-paras (*a*), (*b*) and (*d*) to be repealed by FA 1999 s 123(3), Sch 20 Pt V(6) with effect on the appointed day by virtue of FA 1990 s 111(1).

25 Stamp duty is not chargeable under this Schedule on any description of instrument in respect of which duty was abolished by—

(*a*) section 64 of the Finance Act 1971 or section 5 of the Finance Act (Northern Ireland) 1971 (abolition of duty on mortgages, bonds, debentures etc), or

(*b*) section 173 of the Finance Act 1989 (life insurance policies and superannuation annuities).

26 Nothing in this Schedule affects any other enactment conferring exemption or relief from stamp duty.

SCHEDULE 14
STAMP DUTY: AMENDMENTS CONSEQUENTIAL ON SECTION 112
Section 112(4)

General amendments

1—(1) Any reference (express or implied) in any enactment, instrument or other document to any of the headings in Schedule 1 to the Stamp Act 1891 (other than the heading "Bearer Instrument") shall be construed, so far as is required for continuing its effect, as being or, as the case may require, including a reference to the corresponding provision of Schedule 13 to this Act.

(2) Sub-paragraph (1)—

(*a*) has effect subject to any express amendment made by this Act, and

(*b*) is without prejudice to the general application of section 17(2) of the Interpretation Act 1978 (general effect of repeal and re-enactment).

2 In the enactments relating to stamp duty for "lease or tack", wherever occurring, substitute "lease".

Finance Act 1930 (c 28)

3 (*amends* FA 1930 s 42(1)).

Finance Act (Northern Ireland) 1954 (c 23 (NI))

4 (*amends* FA(NI) 1954 s 11(1)).

Finance Act 1970 (c 24)

5 (*amends* FA 1970 s 33(1)).

Prospective amendment—This paragraph to be repealed by FA 1999 s 123(3), Sch 20 Pt V(6) with effect on the appointed day by virtue of FA 1990 s 111(1).

Finance Act 1980 (c 48)

6 (*amends* FA 1980 s 97(1)).

Finance Act 1982 (c 39)

7 (*amends* FA 1982 s 129(1)).

Finance Act 1985 (c 54)

8 (*amends* FA 1985 s 81).

Prospective amendment—This paragraph to be repealed by FA 1999 s 123(3), Sch 20 Pt V(6) with effect on the appointed day by virtue of FA 1990 s 111(1).

9 (*amends* FA 1985 s 82(5): *repealed* by FA 2008 s 100(2) in relation to instruments executed on or after 13 March 2008, other than instruments effecting a land transaction (within the meaning of FA 2008 Sch 32 para 22)).

10 (*amended* FA 1985 s 83: sub-para (*b*) *repealed* by FA 2008 s 99, Sch 32 para 20 with effect in relation to instruments executed on or after 13 March 2008 and not stamped before 19 March 2008. This amendment does not have effect in relation to an instrument effecting a land transaction or a duplicate or counterpart of such an instrument. "Land transaction" has the same meaning as in FA 2003 Pt 4, except that it does not include a transfer of an interest in a property-investment partnership (within the meaning of FA 2003 Sch 15) (FA 2008 s 99, Sch 32 para 22)).

11 (*amends* FA 1985 s 84: sub-para (*b*) *repealed* by FA 2008 s 99, Sch 32 para 20 with effect in relation to instruments executed on or after 13 March 2008 and not stamped before 19 March 2008. This amendment does not have effect in relation to an instrument effecting a land transaction or a duplicate or counterpart of such an instrument. "Land transaction" has the same meaning as in FA 2003 Pt 4, except that it does not include a transfer of an interest in a property-investment partnership (within the meaning of FA 2003 Sch 15) (FA 2008 s 99, Sch 32 para 22)).

Finance Act 1986 (c 41)

12 (*amends* FA 1986 s 67: sub-para (3) *repealed* by FA 2008 s 99, Sch 32 para 20 with effect in relation to instruments executed on or after 13 March 2008 and not stamped before 19 March 2008).

Prospective amendment—This paragraph to be repealed by FA 1999 s 123(3), Sch 20 Pt V(6) with effect on the appointed day by virtue of FA 1990 s 111(1).

13 (*amends* FA 1986 s 70:sub-para (3) *repealed* by FA 2008 s 99, Sch 32 para 20 with effect in relation to instruments executed on or after 13 March 2008 and not stamped before 19 March 2008).

Prospective amendment—This paragraph to be repealed by FA 1999 s 123(3), Sch 20 Pt V(6) with effect on the appointed day by virtue of FA 1990 s 111(1).

14 (*amends* FA 1986 s 75(2)).

15 (*amends* FA 1986 s 76).

16 (*amends* FA 1986 s 77(1)).

Prospective amendment—This paragraph to be repealed by FA 1999 s 123(3), Sch 20 Pt V(6) with effect on the appointed day by virtue of FA 1990 s 111(1).

17 (*amends* FA 1986 s 79).

Prospective amendment—This paragraph to be repealed by FA 1999 s 123(3), Sch 20 Pt V(6) with effect on the appointed day by virtue of FA 1990 s 111(1).

18 (*amends* FA 1986 s 80B(7)).

Prospective amendment—This paragraph to be repealed by FA 1999 s 123(3), Sch 20 Pt V(6) with effect on the appointed day by virtue of FA 1990 s 111(1).

19 (*amends* FA 1986 s 80C(8)).

Prospective amendment—This paragraph to be repealed by FA 1999 s 123(3), Sch 20 Pt V(6) with effect on the appointed day by virtue of FA 1990 s 111(1).

20 (*amends* FA 1986 s 88).

Prospective amendment—This paragraph to be repealed by FA 1999 s 123(3), Sch 20 Pt V(6) with effect on the appointed day by virtue of FA 1990 s 111(1).

Finance Act 1987 (c 16)

21 (*amends* FA 1987 s 50(1)).

Prospective amendment—This paragraph to be repealed by FA 1999 s 123(3), Sch 20 Pt V(6) with effect on the appointed day by virtue of FA 1990 s 111(1).

22 (*amends* FA 1987 s 55(1)).

Finance Act 1989 (c 26)

23 (*amends* FA 1989 s 175(1)).

Prospective amendment—This paragraph to be repealed by FA 1999 s 123(3), Sch 20 Pt V(6) with effect on the appointed day by virtue of FA 1990 s 111(1).

National Health Service and Community Care Act 1990 (c 19)

24 (*amends* the National Health Service and Community Care Act 1990 s 61(3)).

Finance Act 1991 (c 31)

25 (*amends* FA 1991 s 110).

26 (*amends* FA 1991 s 111(1)).

27 (*substitutes* FA 1991 s 113(1) (for original sub-ss (1)–(3)).

Finance Act 1993 (c 34)

28 (*amends* FA 1993 s 202).

29 (*amends* FA 1993 s 203(2)).

Finance Act 1994 (c 9)

30 (*amends* FA 1994 s 241(1)).

31 (*amends* FA 1994 s 242).

32 (*amends* FA 1994 s 243).

Finance Act 1995 (c 4)

33 (*amends* FA 1995 s 151).

SCHEDULE 15

STAMP DUTY: BEARER INSTRUMENTS

Section 113(1)

Prospective amendment—This Schedule to be repealed by FA 1999 s 123(3), Sch 20 Pt V(6) with effect on the appointed day by virtue of FA 1990 s 111(1).

PART I
CHARGING PROVISIONS

Charge on issue of instrument

1—(1) Stamp duty is chargeable—

(*a*) on the issue of a bearer instrument in the United Kingdom, and

(*b*) on the issue of a bearer instrument outside the United Kingdom by or on behalf of a UK company.

(2) This is subject to the exemptions in Part II of this Schedule.

Charge on transfer of stock by means of instrument

2 Stamp duty is chargeable on the transfer in the United Kingdom of the stock constituted by or transferable by means of a bearer instrument if duty was not chargeable under paragraph 1 on the issue of the instrument and—

(*a*) duty would be chargeable under Part I of Schedule 13 ([transfer][1] on sale) if the transfer were effected by an instrument other than a bearer instrument, or

(*b*) the stock constituted by or transferable by means of a bearer instrument consists of units under a unit trust scheme.

Amendments—[1] The word "transfer" substituted for the words "conveyance or transfer" in enactments relating to stamp duty by FA 2003 Sch 20 para 3.

Meaning of "bearer instrument"

3 In this Schedule "bearer instrument" means—

(*a*) a marketable security transferable by delivery;

(*b*) a share warrant or stock certificate to bearer or instrument to bearer (by whatever name called) having the like effect as such a warrant or certificate;

(*c*) a deposit certificate to bearer;

(*d*) any other instrument to bearer by means of which stock can be transferred; or

(*e*) an instrument issued by a non-UK company that is a bearer instrument by usage.

Rates of duty

4 The duty chargeable under this Schedule is 1.5% of the market value of the stock constituted by or transferable by means of the instrument, unless paragraph 5 or 6 applies.

5 In the case of—

(*a*) a deposit certificate in respect of stock of a single non-UK company, or

(*b*) an instrument issued by a non-UK company that is a bearer instrument by usage (and is not otherwise within the definition of "bearer instrument" in paragraph 3),

the duty is 0.2% of the market value of the stock constituted by or transferable by means of the instrument.

6 *In the case of an instrument given in substitution for a like instrument stamped ad valorem (whether under this Schedule or not) the duty is £5.*[1]

Amendments—[1] This para repealed by FA 2008 s 99, Sch 32 paras 9, 11(1), (2) with effect in relation to instruments executed on or after 13 March 2008 and not stamped before 19 March 2008.

Ascertainment of market value

7—(1) For the purposes of duty under paragraph 1 (charge on issue of instrument) the market value of the stock constituted by or transferable by means of the instrument is ascertained as follows.

(2) If the stock was offered for public subscription (whether in registered or in bearer form) within twelve months before the issue of the instrument, the market value shall be taken to be the amount subscribed for the stock.

(3) In any other case the market value shall be taken to be—

(*a*) the value of the stock on the first day within one month after the issue of the instrument on which stock of that description is dealt in on a stock exchange in the United Kingdom, or

(*b*) if stock of that description is not so dealt in, the value of the stock immediately after the issue of the instrument.

8—(1) For the purposes of duty under paragraph 2 (charge on transfer of stock by means of instrument) the market value of the stock constituted by or transferable by means of the instrument is ascertained as follows.

(2) In the case of a transfer pursuant to a contract of sale, the market value shall be taken to be the value of the stock on the date when the contract is made.

(3) In any other case, the market value shall be taken to be the value of the stock on the day preceding that on which the instrument is presented to the Commissioners for stamping, or, if it is not so presented, on the date of the transfer.

Meaning of "deposit certificate"

9 In this Schedule a "deposit certificate" means an instrument acknowledging the deposit of stock and entitling the bearer to rights (whether expressed as units or otherwise) in or in relation to the stock deposited or equivalent stock.

Bearer instruments by usage

10—(1) In this Schedule a "bearer instrument by usage" means an instrument—

(*a*) which is used for the purpose of transferring the right to stock, and

(*b*) delivery of which is treated by usage as sufficient for the purposes of a sale on the market, whether that delivery constitutes a legal transfer or not.

(2) A bearer instrument by usage is treated—

(*a*) as transferring the stock on delivery of the instrument, and

(*b*) as issued by the person by whom or on whose behalf it was first issued, whether or not it was then capable of being used for transferring the right to the stock without execution by the holder.

Meaning of "company", "UK company" and "non-UK company"

11 In this Schedule—

"company" includes any body of persons, corporate or unincorporate;

["UK company" means—

(*a*) a company that is formed or established in the United Kingdom (other than an SE which has its registered office outside the United Kingdom following a transfer in accordance with Article 8 of Council Regulation (EC) 2157/2001 on the Statute for a European Company (Societas Europaea)), or

(*b*) an SE which has its registered office in the United Kingdom following a transfer in accordance with Article 8 of that Regulation;][1] and

"non-UK company" means a company that is not a UK company.

Amendments—[1] Definition of "UK company" substituted by F(No 2)A 2005 s 58(3), (4) with effect for the purposes of determining whether or not stamp duty or stamp duty reserve tax is chargeable in respect of anything done on or after 1 April 2005.

[1] That definition previously read as follows—

" 'UK company' means a company that is formed or established in the United Kingdom;".

Meaning of "stock" and "transfer"

12—(1) In this Schedule "stock" includes securities.

(2) References in this Schedule to stock include any interest in, or in any fraction of, stock or in any dividends or other rights arising out of stock and any right to an allotment of or to subscribe for stock.

(3) In this Schedule "transfer" includes negotiation, and "transferable", "transferred" and "transferring" shall be construed accordingly.

PART II

EXEMPTIONS

[Substitute instruments

12A—(1) Stamp duty is not chargeable on a substitute instrument.

(2) A substitute instrument is a bearer instrument given in substitution for a like instrument stamped *ad valorem* (whether under this Schedule or otherwise) ("the original instrument").

(3) The substitute instrument shall not be treated as duly stamped unless it appears by some stamp impressed on it that the full and proper duty has been paid on the original instrument.][1]

Amendments—[1] This para and preceding heading inserted by FA 2008 s 99, Sch 32 paras 9, 11(1), (3) with effect in relation to instruments executed on or after 13 March 2008 and not stamped before 19 March 2008.

Foreign loan securities

13 Stamp duty is not chargeable on a bearer instrument issued outside the United Kingdom in respect of a loan which is expressed in a currency other than sterling and which is not—

(*a*) offered for subscription in the United Kingdom, or

(*b*) offered for subscription with a view to an offer for sale in the United Kingdom of securities in respect of the loan.

Stock exempt from duty on transfer

14 Stamp duty is not chargeable under this Schedule on an instrument constituting, or used for transferring, stock (other than units in a unit trust) that is exempt from all stamp duties on transfer.

Instruments in respect of which duty previously abolished

15 Stamp duty is not chargeable under this Schedule on any description of instrument in respect of which duty was abolished by—

(*a*) section 64 of the Finance Act 1971 or section 5 of the Finance Act (Northern Ireland) 1971 (abolition of duty on mortgages, bonds, debentures etc), or

(*b*) section 173 of the Finance Act 1989 (life insurance policies and superannuation annuities).

Renounceable letters of allotment

16 Stamp duty is not chargeable under this Schedule on renounceable letters of allotment, letters of rights or other similar instruments where the rights under the letter or other instrument are renounceable not later than six months after its issue.

Instruments relating to non-sterling stock

17—(1) Stamp duty is not chargeable under this Schedule on the issue of an instrument which relates to stock expressed—

(*a*) in a currency other than sterling, or

(*b*) in units of account defined by reference to more than one currency (whether or not including sterling),

or on the transfer of the stock constituted by or transferable by means of any such instrument.

(2) Where the stock to which the instrument relates consists of a loan for the repayment of which there is an option between sterling and one or more other currencies, sub-paragraph (1) applies if the option is exercisable only by the holder of the stock and does not apply in any other case.

18 Where the capital stock of a company is not expressed in terms of any currency, it shall be treated for the purposes of paragraph 17 as expressed in the currency of the territory under the law of which the company is formed or established.

19—(1) A unit under a unit trust scheme or a share in a foreign mutual fund shall be treated for the purposes of paragraph 17 as capital stock of a company formed or established in the territory by the law of which the scheme or fund is governed.
(2) A "foreign mutual fund" means a fund administered under arrangements governed by the law of a territory outside the United Kingdom under which subscribers to the fund are entitled to participate in, or receive payments by reference to, profits or income arising to the fund from the acquisition, holding, management or disposal of investments.
(3) In relation to a foreign mutual fund "share" means the right of a subscriber, or of another in his right, to participate in or receive payments by reference to profits or income so arising.

Variation of original terms or conditions

20 Where a bearer instrument issued by or on behalf of a non-UK company in respect of a loan expressed in sterling—

(*a*) has been stamped *ad valorem*, or

[(*b*) has been stamped in accordance with paragraph 12A, or][1]

(*c*) has been stamped with the denoting stamp referred to in paragraph 21(2)(*b*) below,

duty is not chargeable under this Schedule by reason only that the instrument is amended on its face pursuant to an agreement for the variation of any of its original terms or conditions.

Amendments—[1] Para (*b*) substituted by FA 2008 s 99, Sch 32 paras 9, 11(1), (4) with effect in relation to instruments executed on or after 13 March 2008 and not stamped before 19 March 2008. Para (*b*) previously read as follows—

"(*b*) has been stamped with duty under paragraph 6 above (fixed duty on instrument given in substitution for another instrument stamped *ad valorem*), or".

PART III
SUPPLEMENTARY PROVISIONS

Duty chargeable on issue of instrument

21—(1) This paragraph applies where duty is chargeable under paragraph 1 of this Schedule.
(2) The instrument—

(*a*) shall before being issued be produced to the Commissioners, together with such particulars in writing of the instrument as the Commissioners may require, and

(*b*) shall be deemed to be duly stamped if and only if it is stamped with a particular stamp denoting that it has been produced to the Commissioners.

(3) Within six weeks of the date on which the instrument is issued, or such longer time as the Commissioners may allow, a statement in writing containing the date of the issue and such further particulars as the Commissioners may require in respect of the instrument shall be delivered to the Commissioners.
(4) The duty chargeable in respect of the instrument shall be paid to the Commissioners on delivery of that statement or within such longer time as the Commissioners may allow.

22—(1) If default is made in complying with paragraph 21—

(*a*) the person by whom or on whose behalf the instrument is issued, and

(*b*) any person who acts as the agent of that person for the purposes of the issue,

are each liable to a penalty not exceeding the aggregate of £300 and the duty chargeable.
(2) Those persons are also jointly and severally liable to pay to Her Majesty—

(*a*) the duty chargeable, and

(*b*) interest on the unpaid duty from the date of the default until the duty is paid.

Duty chargeable on transfer of stock by means of instrument

23—(1) This paragraph applies where duty is chargeable under paragraph 2 of this Schedule.
(2) Where the instrument is presented to the Commissioners for stamping—

(*a*) the person presenting it, and

(*b*) the owner of the instrument,

shall furnish to the Commissioners such particulars in writing as the Commissioners may require for determining the amount of duty chargeable.
(3) If the instrument is not duly stamped each person who in the United Kingdom—

(*a*) transfers any stock by or by means of the instrument, or

(*b*) is concerned as broker or agent in any such transfer,

is liable to a penalty not exceeding the aggregate of £300 and the amount of duty chargeable.
(4) Those persons are also jointly and severally liable to pay to Her Majesty—

(*a*) the duty chargeable, and

(*b*) interest on the unpaid duty from the date of the transfer in question until the duty is paid.

Supplementary provisions as to interest

24—(1) The following provisions apply to interest under paragraph 22(2) or 23(4).
(2) If an amount is lodged with the Commissioners in respect of the duty, the amount on which interest is payable is reduced by that amount.
(3) Interest is payable at the rate prescribed under section 178 of the Finance Act 1989 for the purposes of section 15A of the Stamp Act 1891 (interest on late stamping).
(4) The amount of interest shall be rounded down (if necessary) to the nearest multiple of £5.
No interest is payable if the amount is less than £25.
(5) The interest shall be paid without any deduction of income tax and shall not be taken into account in computing income or profits for any tax purposes.

Penalty for false statement

25 A person who in furnishing particulars under this Part of this Schedule wilfully or negligently furnishes particulars that are false in any material respect is liable to a penalty not exceeding the aggregate of £300 and twice the amount by which the stamp duty chargeable exceeds that paid.

26 An instrument in respect of which duty is chargeable under paragraph 2 of this Schedule which—

(*a*) has been stamped *ad valorem*, . . . [1]
(*b*) . . . [1]

shall be treated as duly stamped for all purposes other than paragraph 25.

Amendments—[1] Para (*b*) and the "or" before it repealed by FA 2008 s 99, Sch 32 paras 9, 11(1), (5) with effect in relation to instruments executed on or after 13 March 2008 and not stamped before 19 March 2008. Para (*b*) previously read as follows—

"(*b*) has been stamped with a stamp indicating that it is chargeable with a fixed duty under paragraph 6 (instrument in substitution for one stamped *ad valorem*) and has been stamped under that paragraph,".

SCHEDULE 16

STAMP DUTY: AMENDMENTS CONSEQUENTIAL ON SECTION 113

Section 113(3)

General amendment

1—(1) Any reference (express or implied) in any enactment, instrument or other document to the heading "Bearer Instrument" in Schedule 1 to the Stamp Act 1891 shall be construed, so far as is required for continuing its effect, as being or, as the case may require, including a reference to Schedule 15 to this Act.
(2) Sub-paragraph (1)—

(*a*) has effect subject to any express amendment made by this Act, and
(*b*) is without prejudice to the general application of section 17(2) of the Interpretation Act 1978 (general effect of repeal and re-enactment).

Finance Act 1963 (c 25)

2 (*substitutes* FA 1963 s 67(4)).

Prospective amendment—This paragraph to be repealed by FA 1999 s 123(3), Sch 20 Pt V(6) with effect on the appointed day by virtue of FA 1990 s 111(1).

Finance Act 1976 (c 40)

3 (*amends* FA 1976 s 131(3)).

Prospective amendment—This paragraph to be repealed by FA 1999 s 123(3), Sch 20 Pt V(6) with effect on the appointed day by virtue of FA 1990 s 111(1).

Finance Act 1984 (c 43)

4 (*amends* FA 1984 s 126(3)(*c*), (5)).

Prospective amendment—This paragraph to be repealed by FA 1999 s 123(3), Sch 20 Pt V(6) with effect on the appointed day by virtue of FA 1990 s 111(1).

Finance Act 1986 (c 41)

5 (*amends* FA 1986 s 79(2)).

Prospective amendment—This paragraph to be repealed by FA 1999 s 123(3), Sch 20 Pt V(6) with effect on the appointed day by virtue of FA 1990 s 111(1).

6 (*amends* FA 1986 s 90).

Prospective amendment—This paragraph to be repealed by FA 1999 s 123(3), Sch 20 Pt V(6) with effect on the appointed day by virtue of FA 1990 s 111(1).

7—(1) (*substitutes* FA 1986 s 95(2)).

(2) There shall be no charge to tax under section 93 of that Act by virtue of paragraph (*b*) of subsection (2) of section 95 as substituted by sub-paragraph (1) above in the case of an instrument which gives effect to an agreement for a company merger or takeover entered into in writing by the companies involved before 30th January 1999.

Prospective amendment—This paragraph to be repealed by FA 1999 s 123(3), Sch 20 Pt V(6) with effect on the appointed day by virtue of FA 1990 s 111(1).

8—(1) (*substitutes* FA 1986 s 97(3)).

(2) There shall be no charge to tax under section 96 of that Act by virtue of paragraph (*b*) of subsection (3) of section 97 as substituted by sub-paragraph (1) above in the case of an instrument which gives effect to an agreement for a company merger or takeover entered into in writing by the companies involved before 30th January 1999.

Prospective amendment—This paragraph to be repealed by FA 1999 s 123(3), Sch 20 Pt V(6) with effect on the appointed day by virtue of FA 1990 s 111(1).

9 In section 99 of the Finance Act 1986 (interpretation of Part IV), after subsection (1) insert—

"(1A) 'Bearer instrument' has the same meaning as in Schedule 15 to the Finance Act 1999. An instrument is a 'UK bearer instrument' or 'non-UK bearer instrument' according to whether it is issued by or on behalf of a UK company or a non-UK company within the meaning of that Schedule.".

Prospective amendment—This paragraph to be repealed by FA 1999 s 123(3), Sch 20 Pt V(6) with effect on the appointed day by virtue of FA 1990 s 111(1).

Finance Act 1987 (c 16)

10 (*amends* FA 1987 s 50).

Prospective amendment—This paragraph to be repealed by FA 1999 s 123(3), Sch 20 Pt V(6) with effect on the appointed day by virtue of FA 1990 s 111(1).

Finance Act 1988 (c 39)

11 (*amends* FA 1987 s 143).

Prospective amendment—This paragraph to be repealed by FA 1999 s 123(3), Sch 20 Pt V(6) with effect on the appointed day by virtue of FA 1990 s 111(1).

Finance Act 1990 (c 29)

12 (*substitutes* FA 1990 s 107).

SCHEDULE 17
STAMP DUTY: PENALTIES OTHER THAN ON LATE STAMPING

Section 114

PART I
AMENDMENTS OF PENALTIES

Introduction

1 The amendments in this Part of this Schedule—

(*a*) replace administrative fines by penalties;

(*b*) amend provisions imposing a fine or penalty of a specified amount so as to impose a penalty not exceeding a specified amount;

(*c*) increase or modernise in certain cases the maximum penalty.

Stamp Duties Management Act 1891 (c 38)

2 (*amends* SDMA 1891 ss 12A, 21).

Stamp Act 1891 (c 39)

3 (*amends* SA 1891 ss 5, 9(1), 16, 17, 83).

Finance Act 1946 (c 64)

4 (*amends* FA 1946 s 56(3)).

Finance (No 2) Act (Northern Ireland) 1946 (c 17 (NI))

5 (*amends* F(No 2)A (NI) 1946 s 27(3)).

Finance Act 1963 (c 25)

6 (*amends* FA 1963 s 67(1)).

Prospective amendment—This paragraph to be repealed by FA 1999 s 123(3), Sch 20 Pt V(6) with effect on the appointed day by virtue of FA 1990 s 111(1).

Finance Act (Northern Ireland) 1963 (c 22 (NI))

7 (*amends* FA(NI) 1963 s 16(1)).

Prospective amendment—This paragraph to be repealed by FA 1999 s 123(3), Sch 20 Pt V(6) with effect on the appointed day by virtue of FA 1990 s 111(1).

Finance Act 1986 (c 41)

8 (*amends* FA 1986 ss 68(4), (5), 71(4), (5)).

Prospective amendment—This paragraph to be repealed by FA 1999 s 123(3), Sch 20 Pt V(6) with effect on the appointed day by virtue of FA 1990 s 111(1).

PART II
[DETERMINATION OF PENALTY, REVIEWS AND APPEALS][1]

Amendment—[1] Heading substituted by the Transfer of Tribunal Functions and Revenue and Customs Appeals Order, SI 2009/56 art 3, Sch 1 para 279 with effect from 1 April 2009. Text previously read as follows—
"Determination of penalty and appeals"

Introduction

9—(1) This Part of this Schedule applies to penalties under the enactments relating to stamp duty, other than penalties under section 15B of the Stamp Act 1891 (penalty on late stamping).
(2) Nothing in this Part of this Schedule affects criminal proceedings for an offence.
[(3) For the purposes of this Part "tribunal" means the First-tier Tribunal or, where determined by or under Tribunal Procedure Rules, the Upper Tribunal.][1]

Amendment—[1] Sub-para (3) inserted by the Transfer of Tribunal Functions and Revenue and Customs Appeals Order, SI 2009/56 art 3, Sch 1 para 280 with effect from 1 April 2009.

Determination of penalty by officer of Commissioners

10—(1) An officer of the Commissioners authorised by the Commissioners for the purposes of this paragraph may make a determination—
(*a*) imposing the penalty, and
(*b*) setting it at such amount as in the officer's opinion is correct or appropriate.
(2) Notice of the determination must be served on the person liable to the penalty.
The notice must also state—
(*a*) the date on which the notice is issued, and
(*b*) the time within which an appeal against the determination may be made.
(3) After notice of the determination has been served, the determination cannot be altered except—
(*a*) in accordance with sub-paragraph (4),
(*b*) by agreement in writing, or
(*c*) on appeal.
(4) If it is discovered by an officer of the Commissioners authorised by the Commissioners for the purposes of this paragraph that the amount of a penalty determined under this paragraph is or has become insufficient, the officer may make a determination in a further amount so that the penalty is set at the amount which in the officer's opinion is correct or appropriate.
(5) If a person liable to a penalty has died—
(*a*) any determination which could have been made in relation to that person may be made in relation to his personal representatives, and
(*b*) any penalty imposed on them is a debt due from and payable out of the person's estate.
(6) A penalty determined under this paragraph is due and payable at the end of the period of 30 days beginning with the date of the issue of the notice of determination.

11—(1) An appeal [may be made][1] against a determination under paragraph 10.
(2) Notice of appeal must be given in writing to the officer of the Commissioners by whom the determination was made within 30 days of the date of the notice of the determination.
(3) . . . [1]

[(4) The notice of appeal must specify the grounds of appeal.
[(4A) Sections 49A to 49I of the Taxes Management Act 1970 shall apply to appeals under this paragraph, subject to the modifications in sub-paragraphs (4B) to (4E).
(4B) In the application of section 49C(4) for "contained in an agreement in writing under section 54(1) for the settlement of the matter" there is to be substituted "a written agreement under paragraph 10(3)(b) of Schedule 17 to the Finance Act 1999".
(4C) Section 49C(5) and (6) are not to apply.
(4D) In the application of section 49F(2) for "an agreement in writing under section 54(1) for the settlement of the matter in question" there is to be substituted "a written agreement under paragraph 10(3)(b) of Schedule 17 to the Finance Act 1999",
(4E) Sections 49F(3) and (4) are not to apply.
(4F) References to "the tribunal" are to be taken to be references to the "First-tier Tribunal.][1]
(5) . . . [1]
(6) On an appeal under this paragraph the [First-tier Tribunal][1] may—

(*a*) if it appears to them that no penalty has been incurred, set the determination aside;
(*b*) if the amount determined appears . . . [1] to be appropriate, confirm the determination;
(*c*) if the amount determined appears . . . [1] to be excessive, reduce it to such other amount (including nil) as [the First-tier Tribunal considers][1] appropriate;
(*d*) if the amount determined appears to them to be insufficient, increase it to such amount not exceeding the permitted maximum as [the First-tier Tribunal considers][1] appropriate.

Amendments—[1] In sub-para (1) words substituted for the words "lies to the Special Commissioners"; sub-paras (3), (5) repealed; sub-para (4) substituted; sub-paras (4A)–(4F) inserted; in sub-para (6) words at the beginning substituted for the words "Special Commissioners"; in sub para (6)(*b*), (*c*) words "to them" repealed in both places; in sub-para (6)(*c*), (*d*) words substituted for the words "they consider" in both places by the Transfer of Tribunal Functions and Revenue and Customs Appeals Order, SI 2009/56 art 3, Sch 1 para 281 with effect from 1 April 2009. Sub-paras (3), (4), (5) previously read as follows—

"(3) An appeal may be brought out of time with the consent of the Commissioners or the Special Commissioners. The Commissioners—

(*a*) shall give that consent if satisfied, on an application for that purpose, that there was a reasonable excuse for not bringing the appeal within the time limit, and
(*b*) if not so satisfied, shall refer the matter for determination by the Special Commissioners.

(4) The notice of appeal must specify the grounds of appeal, but on the hearing of the appeal the Special Commissioners may allow the appellant to put forward a ground not specified in the notice of appeal, and take it into consideration, if satisfied that the omission was not wilful or unreasonable.
(5) The powers conferred by section 46A(1)(*c*) and (2) to (4) and sections 56B to 56D of the Taxes Management Act 1970 (power of Lord Chancellor to make regulations as to jurisdiction, practice and procedure in relation to appeals to Special Commissioners) apply in relation to appeals under this paragraph."

[11A—(1) This paragraph applies in a case where—

(*a*) notice of appeal may be given to HMRC, but
(*b*) no notice is given before the relevant time limit.

(2) Notice may be given after the relevant time limit if—

(*a*) HMRC agree, or
(*b*) where HMRC do not agree, the tribunal gives permission.

(3) If the following conditions are met, HMRC shall agree to notice being given after the relevant time limit.
(4) Condition A is that the appellant has made a request in writing to HMRC to agree to the notice being given.
(5) Condition B is that HMRC are satisfied that there was reasonable excuse for not giving the notice before the relevant time limit.
(6) Condition C is that HMRC are satisfied that the request under sub-paragraph (4) was made without unreasonable delay after the reasonable excuse ceased.
(7) If a request of the kind referred to in sub-paragraph (4) is made, HMRC must notify the appellant whether or not HMRC agree to the appellant giving notice of appeal after the relevant time limit.
(8) In this paragraph "relevant time limit", in relation to notice of appeal, means the time before which the notice is to be given (but for this paragraph).][1]

Amendment—[1] Paragraph 11A inserted by the Transfer of Tribunal Functions and Revenue and Customs Appeals Order, SI 2009/56 art 3, Sch 1 para 282 with effect from 1 April 2009.

12—(1) . . . [1]
[(2) In addition to any right of appeal on a point of law under section 11(2) of the Tribunals, Courts and Enforcement Act 2007, the person liable to the penalty may appeal to the Upper Tribunal against the amount of the penalty which had been determined under paragraph 11(6) above, but not against any decision which falls under section 11(5)(*d*) or (*e*) of that Act and was made in connection with the determination of the amount of the penalty.

(2A) Section 11(3) and (4) of the Tribunals, Courts and Enforcement Act 2007 applies to the right of appeal under sub-paragraph (2) as it applies to the right of appeal under section 11(2) of that Act.
(3) On an appeal under sub-paragraph (2) the [Upper Tribunal][1] has the same powers as are conferred on the [First-tier Tribunal][1] by paragraph 11(6) above.

Amendment—[1] Sub-para (1) repealed; sub-paras (2), (2A) substituted for former sub-para (2); in sub-para (3) words substituted in the first place for the word "court" and in the second place for the words "Special Commissioners" by the Transfer of Tribunal Functions and Revenue and Customs Appeals Order, SI 2009/56 art 3, Sch 1 para 283 with effect from 1 April 2009. Sub-paras (1), (2) previously read as follows—

"(1) Section 56A of the Taxes Management Act 1970 (general right of appeal on point of law) applies in relation to a decision of the Special Commissioners under paragraph 11.

(2) Without prejudice to that right of appeal, an appeal lies against the amount of a penalty determined by the Special Commissioners under paragraph 11, at the instance of the person liable to the penalty—

(*a*) to the High Court, or

(*b*) in Scotland, to the Court of Session sitting as the Court of Exchequer."

Penalty proceedings before the court

13—(1) Where in the opinion of the Commissioners the liability of a person for a penalty arises by reason of his fraud or the fraud of another person, proceedings for the penalty may be brought—

(*a*) in the High Court, or

(*b*) in Scotland, in the Court of Session sitting as the Court of Exchequer.

(2) Proceedings under this paragraph in England and Wales shall be brought—

(*a*) by and in the name of the Commissioners as an authorised department for the purposes of the Crown Proceedings Act 1947, or

(*b*) in the name of the Attorney General.

Any such proceedings shall be deemed to be civil proceedings by the Crown within the meaning of Part II of the Crown Proceedings Act 1947.
(3) Proceedings under this paragraph in Scotland shall be brought in the name of the Advocate General for Scotland.
(4) Proceedings under this paragraph in Northern Ireland shall be brought—

(*a*) by and in the name of the Commissioners as an authorised department for the purposes of the Crown Proceedings Act 1947 as for the time being in force in Northern Ireland, or

(*b*) in the name of the Attorney General for Northern Ireland.

Any such proceedings shall be deemed to be civil proceedings within the meaning of Part II of the Crown Proceedings Act 1947 as for the time being in force in Northern Ireland.
(5) If in proceedings under this paragraph the court does not find that fraud is proved but considers that the person concerned is nevertheless liable to a penalty, the court may determine a penalty notwithstanding that, but for the opinion of the Commissioners as to fraud, the penalty would not have been a matter for the court.
(6) Paragraph 10 above (determination of penalty by officer of Commissioners) does not apply where proceedings are brought under this paragraph.

Supplementary provisions

14—(1) The Commissioners may in their discretion mitigate any penalty, or stay or compound any proceedings for the recovery of a penalty.
(2) They may also, after judgment, further mitigate or entirely remit the penalty.

15 A penalty may be determined under paragraph 10, or proceedings for a penalty brought under paragraph 13, at any time within six years after the date on which the penalty was incurred.

PART III
POWER TO APPLY PROVISIONS AS TO COLLECTION AND RECOVERY ETC

16—(1) The Treasury may make regulations applying in relation to penalties to which Part II of this Schedule applies such provisions of the Taxes Management Act 1970 as they think fit.
(2) The regulations may apply the provisions of that Act with such modifications as the Treasury think fit.
(3) Regulations under this paragraph shall be made by statutory instrument which shall be subject to annulment in pursuance of a resolution of the House of Commons.

17 Without prejudice to the generality of the power conferred by paragraph 16, regulations under that paragraph may apply—

(*a*) any of the provisions of Part VI of the Taxes Management Act 1970 (collection and recovery), and

(*b*) such of the provisions of Part XI of that Act (miscellaneous and supplemental provisions) as appear to the Treasury to be appropriate.

18 Sections 21, 22 and 35 of the Inland Revenue Regulation Act 1890 (proceedings for fines, etc) do not apply in relation to penalties to which Part II of this Schedule applies.

SCHEDULE 18

STAMP DUTY: MINOR AMENDMENTS AND REPEAL OF OBSOLETE PROVISIONS

Section 115

PART I

MINOR AMENDMENTS

Introduction

1 The provisions of this Part of this Schedule have effect for the purposes of the enactments relating to stamp duty.

Payment by cheque

2—(1) Where—

(*a*) any payment to the Commissioners is made by cheque, and

(*b*) the cheque is paid on its first presentation to the banker on whom it is drawn,

the payment is treated as made on the day on which the cheque was first received by the Commissioners.

(2) Sub-paragraph (1) applies where the cheque was first received by the Commissioners on or after 1st October 1999.

[Admissibility of evidence not affected by offer of settlement etc][1]

3—(1) Statements made or documents produced by or on behalf of a person are not inadmissible in any such proceedings as are mentioned in sub-paragraph (2) by reason only that it has been drawn to that person's attention—

[(*a*) that where serious stamp duty fraud has been committed the Board may accept a money settlement and that the Board will accept such a settlement, and will not pursue a criminal prosecution, if he makes a full confession of all stamp duty irregularities, or][1]

[(*b*) that the extent to which he is helpful and volunteers information is a factor that will be taken into account in determining the amount of any penalty,][1]

and that he was or may have been induced thereby to make the statements or produce the documents.

(2) The proceedings mentioned in sub-paragraph (1) are—

(*a*) any criminal proceedings against the person in question for any form of fraudulent conduct in connection with or in relation to stamp duty, and

(*b*) any proceedings against that person for the recovery of any stamp duty or interest on unpaid stamp duty due from him, and

(*c*) any proceedings for a penalty, or on appeal against the determination of a penalty, in connection with or in relation to stamp duty.

Amendments—[1] Sub-para (1)(*a*), (*b*) substituted, and Heading substituted, by FA 2003 s 206(3)–(5) with effect for statements made, or documents produced, after the passing of FA 2003. The Act received Royal Assent on 10 July 2003.

The Heading previously read as follows—

"Evidence in cases of fraudulent conduct, etc".

Sub-para (1)(*a*), (*b*) previously read as follows—

"(*a*) that pecuniary settlements may be accepted instead of a penalty being determined, or proceedings being instituted, or

(*b*) that, though no undertaking can be given as to whether or not the Commissioners will accept such a settlement in the case of any particular person, it is the practice of the Commissioners to be influenced by the fact that a person has made a full confession of any fraudulent conduct to which he had been a party and has given full facilities for investigation,".

References to duration of lease

4 In relation to Scotland, the expression "term", where referring to the duration of a lease, means "period".

PART II

OBSOLETE PROVISIONS

5—(1)–(5) (*amend* SDMA 1891 s 13).

(6) This paragraph has effect in relation to things done or omitted on or after 1st October 1999.

6—(1) (*repeals* SDMA 1891 ss 2–6, 8, 9(2), (3), 12, 17–20, 25 and *amends* s 11).
(2) This paragraph comes into force on 1st October 1999.

SCHEDULE 19
STAMP DUTY AND STAMP DUTY RESERVE TAX: UNIT TRUSTS

Section 122(4)

Prospective amendment—Parts I–III, and the words "and the enactments relating to stamp duty reserve tax" in paras 14(1), 15, 16, 17(1) and 18(1) of Part IV of this Schedule to be repealed by FA 1999 s 123(3), Sch 20 Pt V(6) with effect on the appointed day by virtue of FA 1990 s 111(1).

PART I
ABOLITION OF STAMP DUTY ON TRANSFERS ETC OF UNITS IN UNIT TRUSTS

1—(1) No stamp duty is chargeable on a transfer or other instrument relating to a unit under a unit trust scheme.
(2) Sub-paragraph (1) does not affect any charge to stamp duty—
(*a*) on a [transfer][1] on sale of property other than units under a unit trust scheme in relation to which such units form the whole or part of the consideration, or
(*b*) under Schedule 15 to this Act (bearer instruments).
(3) This paragraph has effect in relation to instruments executed on or after 6th February 2000.

Prospective amendment—This Part to be repealed by FA 1999 s 123(3), Sch 20 Pt V(6) with effect on the appointed day by virtue of FA 1990 s 111(1).

Amendments—[1] The word "transfer" substituted for the words "conveyance or transfer" in enactments relating to stamp duty by FA 2003 Sch 20 para 3.

PART II
STAMP DUTY RESERVE TAX ON DEALINGS WITH UNITS IN UNIT TRUSTS

Cross reference—See FA 2001 s 94(1) (where there are two or more classes of shares in an open-ended investment company and the company's instrument of incorporation—

(a) provides that shares of one or more of those classes ("the IPA classes") may only be held within an individual pension account, and
(b) does not make such provision in relation to shares of at least one other class,

there is no charge to SDRT under this Part on the surrender of a share of any of the IPA classes with effect for surrenders made or effected after 5 April 2001).

Prospective amendment—This Part to be repealed by FA 1999 s 123(3), Sch 20 Pt V(6) with effect on the appointed day by virtue of FA 1990 s 111(1).

Charge to tax

2—(1) There is a charge to stamp duty reserve tax where—
(*a*) a person authorises or requires the trustees or managers under a unit trust scheme to treat him as no longer interested in a unit under the scheme, or
(*b*) a unit under a unit trust scheme is transferred to the managers of the scheme,
and the unit is a chargeable security.
Those events are referred to in this Part of this Schedule as a "surrender" of the unit to the managers.
(2) The tax is chargeable—
(*a*) whether the surrender is made or effected in the United Kingdom or elsewhere, and
(*b*) whether or not any party is resident or situate in any part of the United Kingdom.
(3) The persons liable for the tax are the trustees of the unit trust.
(4) This paragraph is subject to the exclusions provided for in paragraphs 6[, 6A][1] and 7.

Amendment—[1] Word in sub-para (4) inserted by FA 2001 s 93(2), (6) with effect for surrenders made or effected after 5 April 2001.

Rate of tax

3—(1) Tax under this Part of this Schedule is chargeable at the rate of 0.5% of the market value of the unit.
This is subject to any reduction under paragraph 4 or 5.
(2) The market value of a unit means whichever is higher of—
(*a*) the price the unit might reasonably be expected to fetch on a sale in the open market at the time of surrender, and
(*b*) its cancellation price, or if it is redeemed its redemption price, at that time, calculated in accordance with the trust instrument.

Proportionate reduction of tax by reference to units issued

4—(1) The amount of tax chargeable shall be proportionately reduced if the number of units of the same class as the unit in question that are surrendered to the managers in the relevant two-week period exceeds the number of units of that class issued by the managers in that period.
(2) The "relevant two-week period" in relation to a surrender is the period from the beginning of the week in which the surrender occurs to the end of the following week.
For this purpose a week means a period of seven days beginning with a Sunday.
(3) The reduction is made by applying the following fraction to the amount otherwise chargeable—

$$\frac{I}{S}$$

Where:

I is the number of units of the class issued by the managers in the relevant two-week period, and

S Is the number of units of the class surrendered to the managers in that period.

(4) If a consolidation or sub-division of units affects the comparison of the number of units surrendered and the number of units issued, the numbers shall be determined as if the consolidation or sub-division had not taken place.
"Consolidation or sub-division" includes any alteration of the number of units of the class in question otherwise than in consequence of an increase or reduction in the trust property.
(5) This paragraph does not apply if on the surrender of the unit the unit holder receives anything other than money; and for the purposes of this paragraph no account shall be taken of a surrender or issue that is not entirely for money.
[(6) If a certificate is given in accordance with paragraph 6A(1)(*c*) in respect of a period which includes the relevant two-week period in the case of the unit in question in sub-paragraph (1), there shall be left out of account in applying this paragraph in relation to that unit—
(*a*) any issue of a unit which is to be held within an individual pension account, and
(*b*) any surrender of a unit which, immediately before the surrender, was held within an individual pension account.][1]
[(7) "Individual pension account" has the same meaning in sub-paragraph (6) as it has in paragraph 6A.][1]

Modification—This section is modified, in relation to open-ended investment companies, by the Stamp Duty and Stamp Duty Reserve Tax (Open-ended Investment Companies) Regulations, SI 1997/1156, regs 4, 4A(1), (2), as amended by the Stamp Duty and Stamp Duty Reserve Tax (Open-ended Investment Companies) (Amendment No 2) Regulations, SI 1999/3261, reg 5, with effect from 6 February 2000.

Amendments—[1] Sub-paras (6), (7) inserted by FA 2001 s 93(3), (5) with effect where the relevant two-week period mentioned in FA 1999 Sch 19 para 4(1) ends after 6 April 2001.

Proportionate reduction of tax by reference to assets held

5—(1) The amount of tax chargeable after any reduction under paragraph 4 shall be further reduced if in the relevant two-week period the trust property is invested in both exempt and non-exempt investments.
(2) The reduction is made by applying the following fraction to that amount—

$$\frac{N}{N+E}$$

Where—

N is the average market value of the non-exempt investments over the relevant two-week period, and

E is the average market value of the exempt investments over that period.

(3) In this paragraph "exempt investment" has the same meaning as in section 99(5A)(*b*) of the Finance Act 1986; and "non-exempt investment" means any investment that is not an exempt investment.

Exclusion of charge in certain cases of change of ownership

6—(1) This paragraph applies where in pursuance of arrangements between the person entitled to a unit and another person ("the new owner")—
(*a*) the unit is surrendered to the managers, and

(*b*) the person surrendering the unit authorises or requires the managers or trustees to treat the new owner as entitled to it.

(2) There is no charge to tax under this Part of this Schedule if no consideration in money or money's worth is given in connection with the surrender of the unit or the new owner's becoming entitled to it.

(3) There is no charge to tax under this Part of this Schedule if the new owner is—

(*a*) a body of persons established for charitable purposes only, or

(*b*) the trustees of a trust established for those purposes only, or

(*c*) the Trustees of the National Heritage Memorial Fund, or

(*d*) the Historic Buildings and Monuments Commission for England.

(4) There is no charge to tax under this Part of this Schedule if an instrument executed at the time of the surrender—

(*a*) in pursuance of arrangements between the person entitled to the unit and the new owner, and

(*b*) transferring the unit from the one to the other,

would be exempt from stamp duty (if stamp duty were otherwise chargeable) by virtue of any of the provisions mentioned in sub-paragraph (5).

(5) The provisions referred to in sub-paragraph (4) are—

(*a*) section 42 of the Finance Act 1930 or section 11 of the Finance Act (Northern Ireland) 1954 (transfers between associated companies); and

(*b*) regulations under section 87(2) of the Finance Act 1985 (power to exempt instruments from stamp duty of fixed amount)[; and

(*c*) section 96 of the Finance Act 1997 (demutualisation of insurance companies).][2]

(6) Where by virtue of sub-paragraph (2), (3) or (4) there is no charge to tax, both the surrender and the related issue shall be left out of account for the purposes of paragraph 4.

[Exclusion of charge in case of individual pension accounts

6A—(1) There is no charge to tax under this Part of this Schedule on the surrender of the unit if—

(*a*) immediately before the surrender, the unit is held within an individual pension account,

(*b*) not all the units under the unit trust scheme are so held at that time, and

(*c*) a certificate pursuant to sub-paragraph (2) is contained in, or provided with, the relevant monthly tax return.

(2) The certificate must be given by the persons making the relevant monthly tax return and must state—

(*a*) that at all times in the period to which the return relates the trustees or managers were able to identify which of the units under the scheme were held within individual pension accounts, and

(*b*) that at no time in that period have the trustees or managers imposed any charge on, or recovered any amount from, an IPA unit holder which included an amount directly or indirectly attributable to tax payable by the trustees under this Part of this Schedule.

(3) In sub-paragraph (2), "IPA unit holder" means—

(*a*) a person acquiring, or who has acquired, a unit under the unit trust scheme, where the unit is to be held within an individual pension account,

(*b*) a person holding a unit under the scheme, where the unit is held within an individual pension account, or

(*c*) a person surrendering, or who has surrendered, a unit under the scheme, where immediately before the surrender the unit is or was held within an individual pension account.

(4) In this paragraph—

["individual pension account" has the meaning given by regulations made by the Commissioners of Inland Revenue;][3]

"the relevant monthly tax return", in the case of any surrender, means the notice required by regulations under section 98 of the Finance Act 1986 to be given by the managers (or, failing that, the trustees) under the unit trust scheme to the Commissioners of Inland Revenue containing among other things details of all surrenders in the relevant two-week period;

"the relevant two-week period" has the meaning given by paragraph 4(2).][1]

[(5) Regulations under sub-paragraph (4) shall be made by statutory instrument which shall be subject to annulment in pursuance of a resolution of the House of Commons.][3]

Amendment—[1] This paragraph inserted by FA 2001 s 93(4), (6) with effect for surrenders made or effected after 5 April 2001.

[2] Sub-para (5)(*c*) and preceding word "; and" inserted by FA 2005 s 97(4), (6) with effect for surrenders (within the meaning of FA 1999 Sch 19 Pt 2) occurring on or after 7 April 2005.

[3] Definition of "individual pension account" in sub-para (3) substituted, and sub-para (5) inserted, by FA 2004 s 281, Sch 35 para 46, with effect from 6 April 2006, subject to transitional provisions and savings in FA 2004 Sch 36.

Exclusion of charge in case of in specie redemption

7 There is no charge to tax under this Part of this Schedule if on the surrender of the unit the unit holder receives only such part of each description of asset in the trust property as is proportionate to, or as nearly as practicable proportionate to, the unit holder's share.

Interpretation

8—(1) For the purposes of this Part of this Schedule "issue" in the context of the issue of a unit by the managers under a unit trust scheme includes their transferring an existing unit or authorising or requiring the trustees to treat a person as entitled to a unit under the scheme.
(2) References in this Part of this Schedule to the surrender or issue of a unit under a unit trust scheme do not include a surrender or issue effected by means of, or consisting of the issue of, a certificate to bearer.

Transitional provision

9 This Part of this Schedule applies where the surrender of the unit to the managers occurs on or after 6th February 2000.

Prospective amendment—This paragraph to be repealed by FA 1999 s 123(3), Sch 20 Pt V(6) with effect on the appointed day by virtue of FA 1990 s 111(1).

PART III
MINOR AND CONSEQUENTIAL AMENDMENTS

Prospective amendment—This Part to be repealed by FA 1999 s 123(3), Sch 20 Pt V(6) with effect on the appointed day by virtue of FA 1990 s 111(1).

Finance Act 1986 (c 41)

10 (*amend* FA 1986 s 88(1)).

11—(1) Section 90 of the Finance Act 1986 (exceptions from general charge to stamp duty reserve tax) is amended as follows.
(2) (*amend* FA 1986 s 90(1)).
(3) (*insert* FA 1986 s 90(1A)).
(4) (*insert* FA 1986 s 90(1B)).
(5) The amendments in sub-paragraphs (2) and (3) apply where the relevant day for the purposes of section 87 of the Finance Act 1986 falls on or after 6th February 2000.
(6) The amendment in sub-paragraph (4) applies where the surrender (within the meaning of Part II of Schedule 19 to the Finance Act 1999) occurs on or after 6th February 2000.

12 (*amend* FA 1986 s 99).

Finance Act 1995 (c 4)

13 (*amend* FA 1995 s 152).

Prospective amendment—This paragraph to be repealed by FA 1999 s 123(3), Sch 20 Pt V(6) with effect on the appointed day by virtue of FA 1990 s 111(1).

PART IV
GENERAL DEFINITIONS

Meaning of "unit trust scheme" and related expressions

14—(1) The following definitions apply for the purposes of the enactments relating to stamp duty and the enactments relating to stamp duty reserve tax.
(2) "Unit trust scheme" has [the meaning given by section 237(1) of the Financial Services and Markets Act 2000][1], subject to paragraphs 15 to 18.
(3) In relation to a unit trust scheme—

"trust instrument" means the trust deed or other instrument (whether under seal or not) creating or recording the trusts on which the property in question is held;

"trust property" means the property subject to the trusts of the trust instrument;

"unit" means a right or interest (whether described as a unit, as a sub-unit or otherwise) of a beneficiary under the trust instrument;

"unit holder" means a person entitled to a share of the trust property; and

"certificate to bearer", in relation to a unit, means a document by the delivery of which the unit can be transferred.

Modification—This para is modified, in relation to open-ended investment companies, by the Stamp Duty and Stamp Duty Reserve Tax (Open-ended Investment Companies) Regulations, SI 1997/1156, regs 4, 4A(1), (3), as amended by the Stamp Duty and Stamp Duty Reserve Tax (Open-ended Investment Companies) (Amendment No 2) Regulations, SI 1999/3261, reg 5, with effect from 6 February 2000.

Prospective amendment—The words "and the enactments relating to stamp duty reserve tax" in sub-para (1) to be repealed by FA 1999 s 123(3), Sch 20 Pt V(6) with effect on the appointed day by virtue of FA 1990 s 111(1).

Amendments—[1] Words in sub-para (2) substituted by the Financial Services and Markets Act 2000 (Consequential Amendments) (Taxes) Order, SI 2001/3629 art 104 with effect—

(a) for the purposes of stamp duty, in relation to any instrument executed after 30 November 2001;

(b) for the purposes of stamp duty reserve tax, in relation to—

(i) an agreement to transfer chargeable securities which is not conditional, if the agreement is made after 30 November 2001;

(ii) a conditional agreement to transfer such securities, if the condition is satisfied after that date;

(iii) a surrender (as referred to in FA 1999 Sch 19 Pt 2) which occurs after that date.

Schemes not treated as unit trust schemes

15 References in the enactments relating to stamp duty and the enactments relating to stamp duty reserve tax to a unit trust scheme do not include—

(*a*) a common investment scheme under section 22 of the Charities Act 1960, section 25 of the Charities Act (Northern Ireland) 1964, or section 24 of the Charities Act 1993,

(*b*) a common deposit scheme under section 22A of the Charities Act 1960 or section 25 of the Charities Act 1993, or

(*c*) a unit trust scheme the units in which are under the terms of the trust instrument required to be held only by bodies of persons established for charitable purposes only or trustees of trusts so established.

Prospective amendment—Words "and the enactments relating to stamp duty reserve tax" to be repealed by FA 1999 s 123(3), Sch 20 Pt V(6) with effect on the appointed day by virtue of FA 1990 s 111(1).

16 References in the enactments relating to stamp duty and the enactments relating to stamp duty reserve tax to a unit trust scheme do not include common investment arrangements made by trustees of exempt approved schemes (within the meaning of section 592(1) of the Taxes Act 1988) solely for the purposes of the schemes.

Prospective amendment—The words "and the enactments relating to stamp duty reserve tax" to be repealed by FA 1999 s 123(3), Sch 20 Pt V(6) with effect on the appointed day by virtue of FA 1990 s 111(1).

17—(1) The Treasury may by regulations provide that any scheme of a description specified in the regulations shall be treated as not being a unit trust scheme for the purposes of the enactments relating to stamp duty and the enactments relating to stamp duty reserve tax.

(2) Regulations under this paragraph—

(*a*) may contain such supplementary and transitional provisions as appear to the Treasury to be necessary or expedient, and

(*b*) shall be made by statutory instrument which shall be subject to annulment in pursuance of a resolution of the House of Commons.

(3) This paragraph replaces section 57(1A) and (1B) of the Finance Act 1946 and section 28(1A) and (1B) of the Finance (No2) Act (Northern Ireland) 1946.

(4) Any regulations having effect under those provisions for the purposes of Part VII of the Finance Act 1946 or Part III of the Finance (No2) Act (Northern Ireland) 1946 which are in force immediately before the commencement of this Schedule shall have effect as if made under this paragraph.

Regulations—See the Stamp Duty and Stamp Duty Reserve Tax (Definition of Unit Trust Scheme and Open-ended Investment Company) Regulations, SI 2001/964.

Modification—Sub-para (4) is revoked, in relation to open-ended investment companies, by the Stamp Duty and Stamp Duty Reserve Tax (Open-ended Investment Companies) Regulations, SI 1997/1156, regs 4, 4A(1), (3), as amended by the Stamp Duty and Stamp Duty Reserve Tax (Open-ended Investment Companies) (Amendment No 2) Regulations, SI 1999/3261, reg 5, with effect from 6 February 2000.

Prospective amendment—The words "and the enactments relating to stamp duty reserve tax" in sub-para (1) to be repealed by FA 1999 s 123(3), Sch 20 Pt V(6) with effect on the appointed day by virtue of FA 1990 s 111(1).

Treatment of umbrella schemes

18—(1) For the purposes of the enactments relating to stamp duty and the enactments relating to stamp duty reserve tax each of the parts of an umbrella scheme is regarded as a unit trust scheme and the scheme as a whole is not so regarded.

(2) An "umbrella scheme" means a unit trust scheme—

(*a*) which provides arrangements for separate pooling of the contributions of participants and of the profits or income out of which payments are to be made to them, and

(*b*) under which the participants are entitled to exchange rights in one pool for rights in another;

and a "part of an umbrella scheme" means such of the arrangements as relate to a separate pool.

(3) In relation to a part of an umbrella scheme—

(*a*) any reference to the trust property has effect as a reference to such of the trust property as under the arrangements forms part of the separate pool to which the part of the umbrella scheme relates, and

(*b*) any reference to a unit holder has effect as a reference to a person for the time being having rights in that separate pool.

Prospective amendment—The words "and the enactments relating to stamp duty reserve tax" in sub-para (1) to be repealed by FA 1999 s 123(3), Sch 20 Pt V(6) with effect on the appointed day by virtue of FA 1990 s 111(1).

References to stock in stamp duty enactments include units under unit trust scheme

19 In the enactments relating to stamp duty—

(*a*) any reference to stock includes a unit under a unit trust scheme, and

(*b*) any reference to a stock certificate to bearer includes a certificate to bearer in relation to a unit under a unit trust scheme.

Prospective amendment—The words "and the enactments relating to stamp duty reserve tax" in paras 14(1), 15, 16, 17(1) and 18(1) of Part IV of this Schedule to be repealed by FA 1999 s 123(3), Sch 20 Pt V(6) with effect on the appointed day by virtue of FA 1990 s 111(1).

FINANCIAL SERVICES AND MARKETS ACT 2000

(2000 Chapter 8)

ARRANGEMENT OF SECTIONS

PART XVII

COLLECTIVE INVESTMENT SCHEMES

CHAPTER I

INTERPRETATION

CHAPTER III

AUTHORISED UNIT TRUST SCHEMES

Applications for authorisation

Certificates

PART XVIII

RECOGNISED INVESTMENT EXCHANGES AND CLEARING HOUSES

CHAPTER I

EXEMPTION

General

An Act to make provision about the regulation of financial services and markets; to provide for the transfer of certain statutory functions relating to building societies, friendly societies, industrial and provident societies and certain other mutual societies; and for connected purposes.

[14th June 2000]

PART XVII
COLLECTIVE INVESTMENT SCHEMES

CHAPTER I
INTERPRETATION

235 Collective investment schemes

(1) In this Part "collective investment scheme" means any arrangements with respect to property of any description, including money, the purpose or effect of which is to enable persons taking part in the arrangements (whether by becoming owners of the property or any part of it or otherwise) to participate in or receive profits or income arising from the acquisition, holding, management or disposal of the property or sums paid out of such profits or income.

(2) The arrangements must be such that the persons who are to participate ("participants") do not have day-to-day control over the management of the property, whether or not they have the right to be consulted or to give directions.

(3) The arrangements must also have either or both of the following characteristics—

(*a*) the contributions of the participants and the profits or income out of which payments are to be made to them are pooled;

(*b*) the property is managed as a whole by or on behalf of the operator of the scheme.

(4) If arrangements provide for such pooling as is mentioned in subsection (3)(*a*) in relation to separate parts of the property, the arrangements are not to be regarded as constituting a single collective investment scheme unless the participants are entitled to exchange rights in one part for rights in another.

(5) The Treasury may by order provide that arrangements do not amount to a collective investment scheme—

(*a*) in specified circumstances; or

(*b*) if the arrangements fall within a specified category of arrangement.

236 Open-ended investment companies

(1) In this Part "an open-ended investment company" means a collective investment scheme which satisfies both the property condition and the investment condition.

(2) The property condition is that the property belongs beneficially to, and is managed by or on behalf of, a body corporate ("BC") having as its purpose the investment of its funds with the aim of—

(*a*) spreading investment risk; and

(*b*) giving its members the benefit of the results of the management of those funds by or on behalf of that body.

(3) The investment condition is that, in relation to BC, a reasonable investor would, if he were to participate in the scheme—

(*a*) expect that he would be able to realize, within a period appearing to him to be reasonable, his investment in the scheme (represented, at any given time, by the value of shares in, or securities of, BC held by him as a participant in the scheme); and

(*b*) be satisfied that his investment would be realized on a basis calculated wholly or mainly by reference to the value of property in respect of which the scheme makes arrangements.

(4) In determining whether the investment condition is satisfied, no account is to be taken of any actual or potential redemption or repurchase of shares or securities under—

[*a*) Chapters 3 to 7 of Part 18 of the Companies Act 2006;][1]

(*b*) . . .;[1]

(*c*) corresponding provisions in force in another EEA State; or

(*d*) provisions in force in a country or territory other than an EEA state which the Treasury have, by order, designated as corresponding provisions.

(5) The Treasury may by order amend the definition of "an open-ended investment company" for the purposes of this Part.

1 Sub-s (4)(a) substituted for previous sub-s (4)(a), (b) by the Companies Act 2006 (Consequential Amendments, Transitional Provisions and Savings) Order, SI 2009/1941 art 2(1), Sch 1 para 181 with effect from 1 October 2009.

237 Other definitions

(1) In this Part "unit trust scheme" means a collective investment scheme under which the property is held on trust for the participants.

(2) In this Part—

"trustee", in relation to a unit trust scheme, means the person holding the property in question on trust for the participants;

"depositary", in relation to—

(*a*) a collective investment scheme which is constituted by a body incorporated by virtue of regulations under section 262, or

(*b*) any other collective investment scheme which is not a unit trust scheme,

means any person to whom the property subject to the scheme is entrusted for safekeeping;

"the operator", in relation to a unit trust scheme with a separate trustee, means the manager and in relation to an open-ended investment company, means that company;

"units" means the rights or interests (however described) of the participants in a collective investment scheme.

(3) In this Part—

"an authorised unit trust scheme" means a unit trust scheme which is authorised for the purposes of this Act by an authorisation order in force under section 243;

"an authorised open-ended investment company" means a body incorporated by virtue of regulations under section 262 in respect of which an authorisation order is in force under any provision made in such regulations by virtue of subsection (2)(*l*) of that section;

"a recognised scheme" means a scheme recognised under section 264, 270 or 272.

CHAPTER III
AUTHORISED UNIT TRUST SCHEMES

Applications for authorisation

243 Authorisation orders

(1) If, on an application under section 242 in respect of a unit trust scheme, the Authority—

(*a*) is satisfied that the scheme complies with the requirements set out in this section,

(*b*) is satisfied that the scheme complies with the requirements of the trust scheme rules, and

(*c*) has been provided with a copy of the trust deed and a certificate signed by a solicitor to the effect that it complies with such of the requirements of this section or those rules as relate to its contents,

the Authority may make an order declaring the scheme to be an authorised unit trust scheme.

(2) If the Authority makes an order under subsection (1), it must give written notice of the order to the applicant.

(3) In this Chapter "authorisation order" means an order under subsection (1).

(4) The manager and the trustee must be persons who are independent of each other.

(5) The manager and the trustee must each—

(*a*) be a body corporate incorporated in the United Kingdom or another EEA State, and

(*b*) have a place of business in the United Kingdom,

and the affairs of each must be administered in the country in which it is incorporated.

(6) If the manager is incorporated in another EEA State, the scheme must not be one which satisfies the requirements prescribed for the purposes of section 264.

(7) The manager and the trustee must each be an authorised person and the manager must have permission to act as manager and the trustee must have permission to act as trustee.

(8) The name of the scheme must not be undesirable or misleading.

(9) The purposes of the scheme must be reasonably capable of being successfully carried into effect.

(10) The participants must be entitled to have their units redeemed in accordance with the scheme at a price—

(*a*) related to the net value of the property to which the units relate; and

(*b*) determined in accordance with the scheme.

(11) But a scheme is to be treated as complying with subsection (10) if it requires the manager to ensure that a participant is able to sell his units on an investment exchange at a price not significantly different from that mentioned in that subsection.

Certificates

246 Certificates

(1) If the manager or trustee of a unit trust scheme which complies with the conditions necessary for it to enjoy the rights conferred by any relevant Community instrument so requests, the Authority may issue a certificate to the effect that the scheme complies with those conditions.

(2) Such a certificate may be issued on the making of an authorisation order in respect of the scheme or at any subsequent time.

PART XVIII
RECOGNISED INVESTMENT EXCHANGES AND CLEARING HOUSES

CHAPTER I
EXEMPTION

General

285 Exemption for recognised investment exchanges and clearing houses

(1) In this Act—

(*a*) "recognised investment exchange" means an investment exchange in relation to which a recognition order is in force; and

(*b*) "recognised clearing house" means a clearing house in relation to which a recognition order is in force.

(2) A recognised investment exchange is exempt from the general prohibition as respects any regulated activity—

(*a*) which is carried on as a part of the exchange's business as an investment exchange; or

(*b*) which is carried on for the purposes of, or in connection with, the provision of clearing services by the exchange.

(3) A recognised clearing house is exempt from the general prohibition as respects any regulated activity which is carried on for the purposes of, or in connection with, the provision of clearing services by the clearing house.

286 Qualification for recognition

(1) The Treasury may make regulations setting out the requirements—

(*a*) which must be satisfied by an investment exchange or clearing house if it is to qualify as a body in respect of which the Authority may make a recognition order under this Part; and

(*b*) which, if a recognition order is made, it must continue to satisfy if it is to remain a recognised body.

(2) But if regulations contain provision as to the default rules of an investment exchange or clearing house, or as to proceedings taken under such rules by such a body, they require the approval of the Secretary of State.

(3) "Default rules" means rules of an investment exchange or clearing house which provide for the taking of action in the event of a person's appearing to be unable, or likely to become unable, to meet his obligations in respect of one or more market contracts connected with the exchange or clearing house.

(4) "Market contract" means—

(*a*) a contract to which Part VII of the Companies Act 1989 applies as a result of section 155 of that Act or a contract to which Part V of the Companies (No 2)(Northern Ireland) Order 1990 applies as a result of Article 80 of that Order; and

(*b*) such other kind of contract as may be prescribed.

[(4A) If regulations under subsection (1) require an investment exchange to make information available to the public in accordance with—

(*a*) Article 29.1 of the markets in financial instruments directive and the Commission Regulation, or

(*b*) Article 44.1 of that directive and that Regulation, the regulations may authorise the Authority to waive the requirement in the circumstances specified in the relevant provisions.

(4B) The "relevant provisions" for the purposes of subsection (4A) are—

(*a*) in a case falling within paragraph (a) of that subsection, Article 29.2 of the markets in financial instruments directive and the Commission Regulation, and

(*b*) in a case falling within paragraph (b) of that subsection, Article 44.2 of that directive and that Regulation.

(4C) If regulations under subsection (1) require an investment exchange to make information available to the public in accordance with—

(*a*) Article 30.1 of the markets in financial instruments directive and the Commission Regulation, or

(*b*) Article 45.1 of that directive and that Regulation, the regulations may authorise the Authority to defer the requirement in the circumstances specified, and subject to the requirements contained, in the relevant provisions.

(4D) The "relevant provisions" for the purposes of subsection (4C) are—

(*a*) in a case falling within paragraph (a) of that subsection, Article 30.2 of the markets in financial instruments directive and the Commission Regulation, and

(*b*) in a case falling within paragraph (b) of that subsection, Article 45.2 of that directive and that Regulation.

(4E) "The Commission Regulation" means Commission Regulation 1287/2006 of 10 August 2006.][1]

(5) Requirements resulting from this section are referred to in this Part as "recognition requirements".

[(6) In the case of an investment exchange, requirements resulting from this section are in addition to requirements which must be satisfied by the exchange as a result of section 290(1A) before the Authority may make a recognition order declaring the exchange to be a recognised investment exchange.][2]

Amendments—[1] Sub-ss (4A)–(4E) inserted by the Financial Services and Markets Act 2000 (Markets in Financial Instruments) (Modification of Powers) Regulations, SI 2006/2975 regs 2, 8 with effect from 6 December 2006.

[2] Sub-s (6) inserted by the Financial Services and Markets Act 2000 (Markets in Financial Instruments) Regulations, SI 2007/126 reg 3(2), Sch 2 paras 1, 2 with effect for certain purposes from 1 April 2007, and for remaining purposes from 1 November 2007.

LIMITED LIABILITY PARTNERSHIPS ACT 2000

(2000 Chapter 12)

An Act to make provision for limited liability partnerships

[20th July 2000]

12 Stamp duty

(1) Stamp duty shall not be chargeable on an instrument by which property is conveyed or transferred by a person to a limited liability partnership in connection with its incorporation within the period of one year beginning with the date of incorporation if the following two conditions are satisfied.

(2) The first condition is that at the relevant time the person—

(*a*) is a partner in a partnership comprised of all the persons who are or are to be members of the limited liability partnership (and no-one else), or

(*b*) holds the property conveyed or transferred as nominee or bare trustee for one or more of the partners in such a partnership.

(3) The second condition is that—

(*a*) the proportions of the property conveyed or transferred to which the persons mentioned in subsection (2)(*a*) are entitled immediately after the [transfer][1] are the same as those to which they were entitled at the relevant time, or

(*b*) none of the differences in those proportions has arisen as part of a scheme or arrangement of which the main purpose, or one of the main purposes, is avoidance of liability to any duty or tax.

(4) For the purposes of subsection (2) a person holds property as bare trustee for a partner if the partner has the exclusive right (subject only to satisfying any outstanding charge, lien or other right of the trustee to resort to the property for payment of duty, taxes, costs or other outgoings) to direct how the property shall be dealt with.

(5) In this section "the relevant time" means—

(*a*) if the person who conveyed or transferred the property to the limited liability partnership acquired the property after its incorporation, immediately after he acquired the property, and

(*b*) in any other case, immediately before its incorporation.

(6) An instrument in respect of which stamp duty is not chargeable by virtue of subsection (1) shall not be taken to be duly stamped unless—

(*a*) it has, in accordance with section 12 of the Stamp Act 1891, been stamped with a particular stamp denoting that it is not chargeable with any duty or that it is duly stamped, or

(*b*) it is stamped with the duty to which it would be liable apart from that subsection.

Note—This section comes into force on 6 April 2001 (by virtue of SI 2000/3316 art 2).

Amendments—[1] The word "transfer" substituted for the words "conveyance or transfer" in enactments relating to stamp duty by FA 2003 Sch 20 para 3.

FINANCE ACT 2000

(2000 Chapter 17)

ARRANGEMENT OF SECTIONS

PART IV

STAMP DUTY

Stamp duty

An act to grant certain duties, to alter other duties, and to amend the law relating to the National Debt and the Public Revenue, and to make further provision in connection with finance.

[28 July 2000]

PART IV

STAMP DUTY AND STAMP DUTY RESERVE TAX

Stamp duty

114 Rates: [transfer][1] on sale

(1) (*amends* FA 1999 Sch 13 para 4).

(2) This section applies to instruments executed on or after 28th March 2000.

(3) But this section does not apply to an instrument giving effect to a contract made on or before 21st March 2000, unless—

(*a*) the instrument is made in consequence of the exercise after that date of any option, right of pre-emption or similar right; or

(*b*) the instrument transfers the property in question to, or vests it in, a person other than the purchaser under the contract, because of an assignment (or, in Scotland, assignation) or further contract made after that date.

(4) This section shall be deemed to have come into force on 28th March 2000.

Amendments—[1] The word "transfer" substituted for the words "conveyance or transfer" in enactments relating to stamp duty by FA 2003 Sch 20 para 3.

115 Rates: duty on lease chargeable by reference to rent

(1) (*amends* FA 1999 Sch 13 paras 11, 12(3)).

(2) This section has effect in relation to instruments executed on or after 28th March 2000.

(3) This section shall be deemed to have come into force on 28th March 2000.

116 Rate of duty on seven year leases

(1) (*amends* FA 1999 Sch 13 para 12(3)).

(2) This section applies to instruments executed on or after 1st October 1999, subject to Schedule 32 to this Act (which makes transitional provision for instruments executed on or after 1st October 1999 but before 28th March 2000).

(3) This section shall be deemed to have come into force on 28th March 2000.

117 Power to vary stamp duties

Schedule 33 to this Act (power to vary stamp duties) has effect.

118 Land transferred etc for other property

(1) Subsection (2) applies where—

(*a*) an instrument transferring or vesting an estate or interest in land would not, apart from this section, be or fall to be treated as a [transfer][1] on sale for the purposes of stamp duty; but

(*b*) the transfer or vesting of the estate or interest is for consideration; and

(*c*) the consideration is or includes any property ("the other property").

(2) For the purposes of Part I of Schedule 13 to the Finance Act 1999 (stamp duty on [transfer][1] on sale) the instrument transferring or vesting the estate or interest shall be taken to be a transfer on sale of the estate or interest.

(3) If—

(*a*) the other property is or includes one or more estates or interests in land, and

(*b*) *ad valorem* duty is chargeable on the [transfer][1] of all or any of those estates or interests,

the amount of duty that would (apart from this subsection) be chargeable in consequence of subsection (2) on the transfer on sale there mentioned shall be reduced (but not below nil) by the total of the ad valorem duty chargeable as mentioned in paragraph (b).

(4) If, for the purposes of Part I of Schedule 13 to the Finance Act 1999, the amount or value of the consideration for the transfer on sale mentioned in subsection (2) would (apart from this subsection) exceed the market value of the estate or interest immediately before the execution of the instrument transferring or vesting it, the amount or value of the consideration shall be taken for those purposes to be equal to that market value.

(5) For the purposes of this section, the market value of property at any time is the price which that property might reasonably be expected to fetch on a sale at that time in the open market.

(6) Subsection (2) has effect even though—

(*a*) the transfer or vesting of the estate or interest is the whole or part of the consideration for a sale of the other property; or

(*b*) the transaction is by way of exchange.

(7) Subsection (2) does not affect any charge to stamp duty in respect of the same or any other instrument so far as it relates to the transfer of the other property.

(8) This section is subject to subsection (5) of section 119.

(9) This section shall be construed as one with the Stamp Act 1891.

(10) This section applies to instruments executed on or after 28th March 2000.

(11) But this section does not apply to an instrument giving effect to a contract made on or before 21st March 2000, unless—

(*a*) the instrument is made in consequence of the exercise after that date of any option, right of pre-emption or similar right; or

(*b*) the instrument transfers the property in question to, or vests it in, a person other than the purchaser under the contract, because of an assignment (or, in Scotland, assignation) or further contract made after that date.

(12) This section shall be deemed to have come into force on 28th March 2000.

Amendments—[1] The word "transfer" substituted for the words "conveyance or transfer" in enactments relating to stamp duty by FA 2003 Sch 20 para 3.

119 Transfer of land to connected company

(1) This section applies where an estate or interest in land is transferred to or vested in a company ("A") and—

(*a*) the person transferring or vesting the estate or interest ("B") is connected with A; or

(*b*) some or all of the consideration for the transfer or vesting consists of the issue or transfer of shares in a company with which B is connected.

(2) For the purposes of Part I of Schedule 13 to the Finance Act 1999 (stamp duty on [transfer][1] on sale) an instrument transferring or vesting the estate or interest shall be taken to be a transfer on sale of the estate or interest.

(3) If for those purposes the amount or value of the consideration for the transfer on sale of the estate or interest would, apart from this subsection, be less than the value determined under subsection (4), the consideration shall be taken for those purposes to be the value determined under subsection (4).

(4) That value is—

(*a*) the market value of the estate or interest immediately before the execution of the instrument transferring or vesting it; but

(*b*) reduced by the value of so much of any actual consideration as does not consist of property.

(5) Where—

(*a*) apart from this section, an instrument would be chargeable to stamp duty in accordance with section 118, and (*b*) apart from that section, the instrument would be chargeable to stamp duty in accordance with this section,

the stamp duty chargeable on the instrument shall be determined in accordance with this section (instead of that section).

(6) This section applies only if, in consequence of its application, the instrument transferring or vesting the estate or interest is chargeable with a greater amount of stamp duty than it would be apart from this section and section 118.

(7) For the purposes of this section, the market value of property at any time is the price which that property might reasonably be expected to fetch on a sale at that time in the open market.

(8) In this section—

"company" means any body corporate;

"shares" includes stock and the reference to shares in a company includes a reference to securities issued by a company.

(9) For the purposes of this section, the question whether any person is connected with another shall be determined in accordance with the provisions of [section 1122 of the Corporation Tax Act 2010][2].

(10) This section shall be construed as one with the Stamp Act 1891.

(11) This section applies to instruments executed on or after 28th March 2000.

(12) But this section does not apply to an instrument giving effect to a contract made on or before 21st March 2000, unless—

(*a*) the instrument is made in consequence of the exercise after that date of any option, right of pre-emption or similar right; or

(*b*) the instrument transfers the property in question to, or vests it in, a person other than the purchaser under the contract, because of an assignment (or, in Scotland, assignation) or further contract made after that date.

(13) This section shall be deemed to have come into force on 28th March 2000.

Amendments—[1] The word "transfer" substituted for the words "conveyance or transfer" in enactments relating to stamp duty by FA 2003 Sch 20 para 3.

[2] In sub-s (9) words substituted for words "section 839 of the Taxes Act 1988" by CTA 2010 s 1177, Sch 1 para 311. CTA 2010 has effect for corporation tax purposes for accounting periods ending on or after 1 April 2010, and for income and capital gains tax purposes for the tax year 2010–11 and subsequent tax years.

120 Exceptions from section 119

(1) Section 119 does not apply by virtue of paragraph (*a*) of subsection (1) of that section in any of the following cases (any reference in this section to A or B being taken as a reference to the person referred to as A or B, as the case may be, in that subsection).

(2) Case 1 is where B holds the estate or interest as nominee or bare trustee for A.

(3) Case 2 is where A is to hold the estate or interest as nominee or bare trustee for B.

(4) Case 3 is where B holds the estate or interest as nominee or bare trustee for some other person and A is to hold it as nominee or bare trustee for that other person.

(5) Case 4 is where (in a case not falling within subsection (2) or (4) above)—

(*a*) the transfer or vesting is a [transfer][1] out of a settlement in or towards satisfaction of a beneficiary's interest;

(*b*) the beneficiary's interest is not an interest acquired for money or money's worth; and

(*c*) the [transfer][1] is a distribution of property in accordance with the provisions of the settlement.

(6) Case 5 is where (in a case not falling within subsection (3) above) A—

(*a*) is a person carrying on a business which consists of or includes the management of trusts; and

(*b*) is to hold the estate or interest as trustee acting in the course of that business.

(7) Case 6 is where (in a case not falling within subsection (3) above) A is to hold the estate or interest as trustee and, apart from [section 1122(6) of the Corporation Tax Act 2010][2] (trustees as connected persons), would not be connected with B.

(8) Case 7 is where—

(*a*) B is a company;

(*b*) the transfer or vesting is, or is part of, a distribution of assets (whether or not in connection with the winding up of the company); and

(*c*) the estate or interest was acquired by B by virtue of an instrument which is duly stamped.

(9) This section shall be construed as one with the Stamp Act 1891.

(10) This section applies to instruments executed after the day on which this Act is passed.

Amendments—[1] The word "transfer" substituted for the words "conveyance or transfer" in enactments relating to stamp duty by FA 2003 Sch 20 para 3.

[2] In sub-s (7) words substituted for words "section 839(3) of the Taxes Act 1988" by CTA 2010 s 1177, Sch 1 para 312. CTA 2010 has effect for corporation tax purposes for accounting periods ending on or after 1 April 2010, and for income and capital gains tax purposes for the tax year 2010–11 and subsequent tax years.

121 Grant of lease to connected company

(1) This section applies where a lease is granted to a company ("A") and—

(*a*) the person granting the lease ("B") is connected with A; or (*b*) some or all of the consideration for the grant of the lease consists of the issue or transfer of shares in a company with which B is connected.

(2) Subsection (3) has effect for the purposes of stamp duty chargeable under Part II of Schedule 13 to the Finance Act 1999 (stamp duty on a lease) by reference to Part I of that Schedule ([transfer][1] on sale).

(3) If, apart from this subsection, the amount or value of the consideration for the grant would be less than the value determined under subsection (4), the consideration shall be taken to be the value determined under subsection (4).

(4) That value is—

(*a*) the market value, immediately before the instrument granting the lease is executed, of the lease granted; but

(*b*) reduced by the value of so much of any actual consideration as does not consist of property.

(5) This section applies only if, in consequence of its application, the lease is chargeable with a greater amount of stamp duty than it would be apart from this section.

(6) For the purposes of this section, the market value of property at any time is the price which that property might reasonably be expected to fetch on a sale at that time in the open market.

(7) In this section—

"company" means any body corporate;

"shares" includes stock and the reference to shares in a company includes a reference to securities issued by a company.

(8) For the purposes of this section, the question whether any person is connected with another shall be determined in accordance with the provisions of [section 1122 of the Corporation Tax Act 2010][2].

(9) This section shall be construed as one with the Stamp Act 1891.

(10) This section applies to instruments executed on or after 28th March 2000.

(11) But this section does not apply to an instrument giving effect to a contract made on or before 21st March 2000, unless—

(*a*) the instrument is made in consequence of the exercise after that date of any option, right of pre-emption or similar right; or

(*b*) the instrument transfers the property in question to, or vests it in, a person other than the purchaser under the contract, because of an assignment (or, in Scotland, assignation) or further contract made after that date.

(12) This section shall be deemed to have come into force on 28th March 2000.

Amendments—[1] The word "transfer" substituted for the words "conveyance or transfer" in enactments relating to stamp duty by FA 2003 Sch 20 para 3.

[2] In sub-s (8) words substituted for words "section 839 of the Taxes Act 1988" by CTA 2010 s 1177, Sch 1 para 313. CTA 2010 has effect for corporation tax purposes for accounting periods ending on or after 1 April 2010, and for income and capital gains tax purposes for the tax year 2010–11 and subsequent tax years.

122 Marketable securities transferred etc for exempt property

(1) Subsection (2) applies where—

(*a*) an instrument transferring marketable securities would not, apart from this section, be or fall to be treated as a transfer on sale for the purposes of stamp duty; but

(*b*) the transfer of the marketable securities is for consideration; and

(*c*) the consideration is or includes any qualifying property ("the other property").

(2) For the purposes of Part I of Schedule 13 to the Finance Act 1999 (stamp duty on [transfer][1] on sale) the instrument transferring the marketable securities shall be taken to be a transfer on sale of those securities.

(3) If the amount or value of the consideration for that transfer on sale would (apart from this subsection) exceed the market value of the marketable securities immediately before the execution of the instrument transferring them, the amount or value of the consideration shall be taken to be equal to that market value.

For this purpose the market value of property at any time is the price which that property might reasonably be expected to fetch on a sale at that time in the open market.

(4) Subsection (2) has effect even though—

(*a*) the transfer of the marketable securities is the whole or part of the consideration for a sale of the other property; or

(*b*) the transaction is by way of exchange.

(5) Subsection (2) does not affect any charge to stamp duty in respect of the same or any other instrument so far as it relates to the transfer of the other property.

(6) In this section "qualifying property" means any debt due, stock or securities, to the extent that the debt, stock or securities are not chargeable securities, within the meaning of Part IV of the Finance Act 1986 (stamp duty reserve tax).

(7) This section shall be construed as one with the Stamp Act 1891.

(8) This section applies to instruments executed on or after 28th March 2000.

(9) But this section does not apply to an instrument giving effect to a contract made on or before 21st March 2000, unless—

(*a*) the instrument is made in consequence of the exercise after that date of any option, right of pre-emption or similar right; or

(*b*) the instrument transfers the property in question to, or vests it in, a person other than the purchaser under the contract, because of an assignment (or, in Scotland, assignation) or further contract made after that date.

(10) This section shall be deemed to have come into force on 28th March 2000.

Amendments—[1] The word "transfer" substituted for the words "conveyance or transfer" in enactments relating to stamp duty by FA 2003 Sch 20 para 3.

123 Transfer of property between associated companies: Great Britain

(1) Amend section 42 of the Finance Act 1930 as follows.

(2), (3) (*amend* FA 1930 s 42(2)).

(4) (*amends* FA 1930 s 42(2B)).

(5) (*amends* FA 1930 s 42(3)).

(6) (*adds* FA 1930 s 42(5)–(7)).

(7) This section has effect in relation to instruments executed after the day on which this Act is passed.

124 Transfer of property between associated companies: Northern Ireland

(1) Amend section 11 of the Finance Act (Northern Ireland) 1954 as follows.

(2) After subsection (2) (instruments on which stamp duty not chargeable) insert—

"(2A) But this section does not apply to an instrument by virtue of subsection (2)(*a*) if, at the time the instrument is executed, arrangements are in existence by virtue of which at that or some later time any person has or could obtain, or any persons together have or could obtain, control of the transferee but not of the transferor.".

(3) In subsection (3AA) (body to be parent of another if beneficial owner of 75% of ordinary share capital) after "if at that time the first body" insert "(*a*)" and at the end of the subsection add—

"(*b*) is beneficially entitled to not less than 75 per cent of any profits available for distribution to equity holders of the second body; and

(*c*) would be beneficially entitled to not less than 75 per cent of any assets of the second body available for distribution to its equity holders on a winding-up.".

(4) In subsection (3A)—

(*a*) after "The ownership referred to in" insert "paragraph (*a*) of"; and

(*b*) for "this section" substitute "that paragraph".

(5) At the end of the section add—

"(6) Schedule 18 to the Income and Corporation Taxes Act 1988 shall apply for the purposes of paragraphs (*b*) and (*c*) of subsection (3AA) as it applies for the purposes of paragraphs (*a*) and (*b*) of section 413(7) of that Act; but this is subject to subsection (7).

(7) In determining for the purposes of this section whether a body corporate is the parent of the transferor, paragraphs 5(3) and 5B to 5E of Schedule 18 to the Income and Corporation Taxes Act 1988 shall not apply for the purposes of paragraph (*b*) or (*c*) of subsection (3AA).

(8) In subsection (3AAA), "control" shall be construed in accordance with section 840 of the Income and Corporation Taxes Act 1988.".

(6) This section has effect in relation to instruments executed after the day on which this Act is passed.

125 Grant of leases etc between associated companies

(1) Amend section 151 of the Finance Act 1995 as follows.

(2) (*amends* FA 1995 s 151(1)).

(3) (*inserts* FA 1995 s 151(4A)).

(4) (*amends* FA 1995 s 151(8)).

(5) (*amends* FA 1995 s 151(10)).

(6) (*inserts* FA 1995 s 151(10A)–(10C)).

(7) This section has effect in relation to instruments executed after the day on which this Act is passed.

126 Future issues of stock

(1) Amend section 55 of the Stamp Act 1891 (calculation of ad valorem duty in respect of stock and securities) as follows.

(2) (*inserts* SA 1891 s 55(1A)).

(3) This section has effect in relation to instruments executed on or after the day on which this Act is passed.

127 Company acquisition reliefs: redeemable shares

(1) Amend section 75 of the Finance Act 1986 (acquisitions: reliefs) in accordance with subsections (2) and (3).

(2), (3) (*amend* FA 1986 s 75(4)).

(4) (*amends* FA 1986 s 76(3)(a)).

(5) This section has effect in relation to instruments executed after the day on which this Act is passed.

128 Surrender of leases

(1) Where a lease is or has been surrendered or, in Scotland, renounced at any time, a document evidencing the surrender or renunciation shall be treated for the purposes of stamp duty as if it were a deed executed at that time effecting the surrender or renunciation.

(2) Stamp duty shall be chargeable by virtue of subsection (1) on a document containing a statutory declaration, notwithstanding anything in [land registration rules under the Land Registration Act 2002][1].

(3) Stamp duty shall not be chargeable by virtue of subsection (1) on any lease or agreement for a lease or with respect to any letting if the lease or agreement—

(*a*) is made in consideration of the surrender or renunciation; and

(*b*) relates to the same subject matter as the lease surrendered or renounced.

(4) Stamp duty shall not be chargeable by virtue of subsection (1) on any document if a document falling within subsection (5) has been duly stamped.

(5) The documents that fall within this subsection are—

(*a*) a deed effecting the surrender or renunciation;

(*b*) an agreement which falls to be treated for the purposes of stamp duty as if it were such a deed;

(*c*) any document which falls to be so treated by virtue of subsection (1); and

(*d*) any lease or agreement falling within subsection (3).

(6) A land registrar shall regard a document which by virtue of subsection (4) is not chargeable to stamp duty by virtue of subsection (1) as not duly stamped unless—

(*a*) it is stamped as if it were a deed effecting the surrender or renunciation; or

(*b*) it appears by some stamp impressed on it that the full and proper duty chargeable on such a deed has been paid on another document; or

(*c*) it appears by some stamp impressed on it that a lease or agreement falling within subsection (3) has been duly stamped; or

(*d*) the land registrar is aware of a document falling within subsection (5) which has been duly stamped.

(7) The documents which evidence the surrender or renunciation of a lease shall be taken to include an application, in consequence of the surrender or renunciation of the lease, for—

(*a*) the making in a land register, or

(*b*) the removal from a land register,

of an entry relating to the lease.

(8) In this section—

"land register"—

(*a*) in relation to England and Wales, means the register kept under section 1 of the [Land Registration Act 2002][1];

(*b*) in relation to Scotland, means the Land Register of Scotland or the General Register of Sasines;

(*c*) in relation to Northern Ireland, means the register maintained under section 10 of the Land Registration Act (Northern Ireland) 1970;

"land registrar"—

(*a*) in relation to England and Wales, means the Chief Land Registrar or any other officer of Her Majesty's Land Registry exercising functions of the Chief Land Registrar;

(*b*) in relation to Scotland, means the Keeper of the Registers of Scotland;

(*c*) in relation to Northern Ireland, means the Registrar of Titles or any other official of the Land Registry exercising functions of the Registrar of Titles.

(9) This section shall be construed as one with the Stamp Act 1891.

(10) This section applies to documents relating to the surrender or renunciation of a lease on or after the day on which this Act is passed.

Amendments—[1] Words in sub-ss (2), (8) substituted by the Land Registration Act 2002 ss 133, 136(2), Sch 11 para 39 with effect from 13 October 2003 (by virtue of SI 2003/1725).

129 Abolition of duty on instruments relating to intellectual property

(1) No stamp duty is chargeable on an instrument for the sale, transfer or other disposition of intellectual property.

(2) In subsection (1) "intellectual property" means—

(*a*) any patent, trade mark, registered design, copyright or design right,

(*b*) any plant breeders' rights and rights under section 7 of the Plant Varieties Act 1997,

(*c*) any licence or other right in respect of anything within paragraph (*a*) or (*b*), and

(*d*) any rights under the law of a country or territory outside the United Kingdom that correspond or are similar to those within paragraph (*a*), (*b*) or (*c*).

(3) Schedule 34 to this Act (which contains provisions supplementing this section) has effect.
(4) This section and Schedule 34 shall be construed as one with the Stamp Act 1891.
(5) This section applies to instruments executed on or after 28th March 2000.
(6) This section shall be deemed to have come into force on that date.

130 Transfers to registered social landlords etc

(1) No stamp duty shall be chargeable under Part I or II, or paragraph 16 of Part III, of Schedule 13 to the Finance Act 1999 on a [transfer][1] of an estate or interest in land, or on a lease of land,—

(*a*) to a qualifying landlord controlled by its tenants;
(*b*) to a qualifying landlord by a qualifying transferor; or
(*c*) to a qualifying landlord purchasing the estate or interest, or the grant of the lease, with the assistance of a public subsidy.

(2) For the purposes of this section the cases where a qualifying landlord is controlled by its tenants are those cases where the majority of the board members of the qualifying landlord are tenants occupying properties owned or managed by the qualifying landlord.

(3) For the purposes of subsection (2) a "board member" means—

(*a*) in relation to a qualifying landlord which is a company, a director of the company;
(*b*) in relation to a qualifying landlord which is a body corporate whose affairs are managed by its members, a member;
(*c*) in relation to a qualifying landlord which is a body of trustees, a member of that body of trustees;
(*d*) in relation to a qualifying landlord not falling within any of paragraphs (*a*) to (*c*), a member of the committee of management or other body to which is entrusted the direction of the affairs of the qualifying landlord.

(4) In subsection (3), "company" has the same meaning as in the Companies Act [2006][3] (see section [1][3] of that Act).

(5) In this section "qualifying landlord" means—

(*a*) in relation to England and Wales, any body registered as a social landlord in a register maintained under section 1(1) of the Housing Act 1996;
(*b*) in relation to Scotland—
  (i) any housing association registered in the register maintained under section 3(1) of the Housing Associations Act 1985 by Scottish Homes; or
  (ii) any body corporate whose objects correspond to those of a housing association and which, pursuant to a contract with Scottish Homes, is registered in a register kept for the purpose by Scottish Homes;
(*c*) in relation to Northern Ireland, any housing association registered in the register maintained under Article 14 of the Housing (Northern Ireland) Order 1992.

(6) In this section "qualifying transferor" means any of the following—

(*a*) a qualifying landlord;
(*b*) a housing action trust established under Part III of the Housing Act 1988;
(*c*) a principal council, within the meaning of the Local Government Act 1972;
(*d*) the Common Council of the City of London;
(*e*) a council constituted under section 2 of the Local Government etc (Scotland) Act 1994;
(*f*) Scottish Homes;
(*g*) the Department for Social Development in Northern Ireland;
(*h*) the Northern Ireland Housing Executive.

(7) In this section "public subsidy" means any grant or other financial assistance—

(*a*) made or given by way of a distribution pursuant to section 25 of the National Lottery etc Act 1993 (application of money by distributing bodies);
(*b*) under section 18 of the Housing Act 1996 (social housing grants);
(*c*) under section 126 of the Housing Grants, Construction and Regeneration Act 1996 (financial assistance for regeneration and development);
(*d*) under section 2 of the Housing (Scotland) Act 1988 (general functions of Scottish Homes); or
(*e*) under Article 33 [or 33A][2] of the Housing (Northern Ireland) Order 1992 (housing association grants).

(8) Where stamp duty would be chargeable on an instrument but for paragraph (*c*) of subsection (1), that subsection shall only have effect in relation to the instrument if the instrument is certified to the Board by the qualifying landlord concerned as being an instrument on which stamp duty is by virtue of that paragraph not chargeable.

(9) An instrument on which stamp duty is not chargeable by virtue only of this section shall not be taken to be duly stamped unless—

(*a*) it is stamped with the duty to which it would be liable but for this section; or
(*b*) it has, in accordance with section 12 of the Stamp Act 1891, been stamped with a particular stamp denoting that it is not chargeable with any duty.

(10) This section applies to instruments executed after the day on which this Act is passed.

Amendments—[1] The word "transfer" substituted for the words "conveyance or transfer" in enactments relating to stamp duty by FA 2003 Sch 20 para 3.
[2] Words in sub-s (7)(*e*) inserted by the Housing (Amendment) (Northern Ireland) Order, SI 2006/3337 art 3, Schedule, para 7 with effect from 1 April 2007 (by virtue of SR 2007/37 art 2).
[3] In sub-s (4), words substituted for words "1985" and "735(1)", by the Companies Act 2006 (Consequential Amendments) (Taxes and National Insurance) Order, SI 2009/1890 art 3(4) with effect from 1 October 2009.

131 Relief for certain instruments executed before this Act has effect

(1) This section applies to an instrument of any of the following descriptions executed in the period beginning with 22nd March 2000 and ending with the day on which this Act is passed—

(*a*) an instrument transferring or vesting an estate or interest in land in such circumstances as are mentioned in section 119 (transfer of land to connected company), in a case specified in section 120 (excepted cases);

(*b*) a [transfer][1] of an estate or interest in land, or a lease of land, to a qualifying landlord within the meaning of section 130 (transfers to registered social landlords, etc) from a qualifying transferor within subsection (6)(*c*), (*d*), (*e*), (*f*) or (*h*) of that section.

(2) If the instrument is not stamped until after the day on which this Act is passed, the law in force at the time of its execution shall be deemed for stamp duty purposes to be that which would have applied if it had been executed after that day.

(3) If the Commissioners are satisfied that—

(*a*) the instrument was stamped on or before the day on which this Act is passed,

(*b*) stamp duty was chargeable in respect of it, and

(*c*) had it been stamped after that day no stamp duty, or less stamp duty, would have been chargeable,

they shall pay to such person as they consider appropriate an amount equal to the duty (and any interest or penalty) that would not have been payable if the law in force at the time of execution of the instrument had been that which would have applied had it been executed after that day.

(4) Any such payment must be claimed before 1st April 2001.

(5) Entitlement to a payment is subject to compliance with such conditions as the Commissioners may determine with respect to the production of the instrument, to its being stamped so as to indicate that it has been produced under this section or to other matters.

(6) For the purposes of section 10 of the Exchequer and Audit Departments Act 1866 (Commissioners to deduct repayments from gross revenues) any amount paid under this section shall be treated as a repayment.

(7) This section shall be construed as one with the Stamp Act 1891.

Amendments—[1] The word "transfer" substituted for the words "conveyance or transfer" in enactments relating to stamp duty by FA 2003 Sch 20 para 3.

132 The Northern Ireland Assembly Commission

(1) Amend section 55 of the Finance Act 1987 (Crown exemption from stamp duty) as follows.

(2), (3) (*amend* FA 1987 s 55(1)).

(4) Subsection (3) has effect in relation to instruments executed on or after 28th March 2000.

(5) This section shall be deemed to have come into force on 28th March 2000.

Stamp duty and Stamp duty reserve tax

133 Loan capital where return bears inverse relationship to results

(1) (*Inserts* FA 1986 s 79(7A)).

(2) For the purposes of stamp duty, subsection (1) above has effect where the instrument is executed on or after 21st March 2000.

(3) For the purposes of stamp duty reserve tax, subsection (1) above has effect—

(*a*) in relation to the charge to tax under section 87 of the Finance Act 1986, where—

(i) the agreement to transfer is conditional and the condition is satisfied on or after 21st March 2000, or

(ii) the agreement is not conditional and is made on or after that date;

(*b*) in relation to the charge to tax under section 93(1) of that Act, where securities are transferred, issued or appropriated on or after 21st March 2000 (whenever the arrangement was made);

(*c*) in relation to the charge to tax under section 96(1) of that Act, where securities are transferred or issued on or after 21st March 2000 (whenever the arrangement was made);

(*d*) in relation to the charge to tax under section 93(10) of that Act, where securities are issued or transferred on sale, under terms there mentioned, on or after 21st March 2000;

(*e*) in relation to the charge to tax under section 96(8) of that Act, where securities are issued or transferred on sale, under terms there mentioned, on or after 21st March 2000.

Amendments—This section repealed by FA 2000 s 156, Sch 40 Pt III with effect—

- for stamp duty on bearer instruments in accordance with FA 1990 s 107;
- for stamp duty purposes on instruments other than bearer instruments in accordance with FA 1990 s 108; and
- for stamp duty reserve tax purposes in accordance with FA 1990 s 110.

134 Transfers between depositary receipt systems and clearance systems

(1) (*inserts* FA 1986 s 72A).
(2) (*inserts* FA 1986 s 97B).
(3) (*amends* FA 1986 ss 67(9), 70(9), 95(1) and 97(1)).
(4) (*adds* FA 1986 s 97A(13)).
(5) The amendments in this section have effect as follows—
(*a*) subsection (1), and subsections (3) and (4) as they apply for stamp duty purposes, apply in relation to instruments executed after the day on which this Act is passed;
(*b*) subsection (2), and subsections (3) and (4) as they apply for the purposes of stamp duty reserve tax, apply where the securities are transferred after that day.

Amendments—This section repealed by FA 2000 s 156, Sch 40 Pt III with effect—

– for stamp duty on bearer instruments in accordance with FA 1990 s 107;
– for stamp duty purposes on instruments other than bearer instruments in accordance with FA 1990 s 108; and
– for stamp duty reserve tax purposes in accordance with FA 1990 s 110.

PART VI
MISCELLANEOUS AND SUPPLEMENTARY PROVISIONS

Supplementary provisions

155 Interpretation

In this Act "the Taxes Act 1988" means the Income and Corporation Taxes Act 1988.

156 Repeals

(1) The enactments mentioned in Schedule 40 to this Act (which include provisions that are spent or of no practical utility) are repealed to the extent specified in the third column of that Schedule.
(2) The repeals specified in that Schedule have effect subject to the commencement provisions and savings contained or referred to in the notes set out in that Schedule.

157 Short title

This Act may be cited as the Finance Act 2000

SCHEDULES

SCHEDULE 8
EMPLOYEE SHARE OWNERSHIP PLANS

Section 47

[Exemptions from stamp duty and stamp duty reserve tax

116A Where, under an approved employee share ownership plan, partnership shares or dividend shares are transferred by the trustees to an employee—
(*a*) no *ad valorem* stamp duty is chargeable on any instrument by which the transfer is made, and
(*b*) no stamp duty reserve tax is chargeable on any agreement by the trustees to make the transfer.][1]

Amendment—[1] This paragraph inserted by FA 2001 s 95 with effect for instruments executed (within the meaning of SA 1891) after 11 May 2001, and agreements to transfer shares made after 11 May 2001. But see ITEPA 2003 s 722, Sch 6, para 257 which substitutes FA 2001 s 95, by virtue of which this paragraph is inserted.

SCHEDULE 32
STAMP DUTY ON SEVEN YEAR LEASES: TRANSITIONAL PROVISIONS

Section 116(2)

Introductory

1 In this Schedule—
"additional duty", in relation to an instrument, means additional stamp duty chargeable on the instrument as a result of section 116;
"the appropriate amount of duty", in relation to an instrument, means the stamp duty that would have been chargeable on the instrument if section 116 had been in force when it was executed; and
"the commencement date" means 28th March 2000.

Instruments to which this Schedule applies

2 The instruments to which this Schedule applies are—
(*a*) leases of land for a term of seven years, and

(*b*) agreements for leases of land for a term of seven years,

executed on or after 1st October 1999 and before the commencement date.

Instruments which remain duly stamped

3 An instrument to which this Schedule applies which is stamped with the appropriate amount of duty is duly stamped, whenever it was executed.

Instruments which cease to be duly stamped

4—(1) An instrument to which this Schedule applies which—

(*a*) immediately before the commencement date was duly stamped, but

(*b*) was stamped with less than the appropriate amount of duty,

ceases to be duly stamped on the commencement date.

(2) Sub-paragraph (1) applies even if the instrument has been stamped in accordance with section 12(5) of the Stamp Act 1891 with a stamp denoting that it is duly stamped.

(3) If an instrument ceases to be duly stamped on the commencement date as a result of sub-paragraph (1)—

(*a*) section 12(6) of the Stamp Act 1891 (adjudicated instruments admissible in evidence) does not apply to it at any time when it is not duly stamped, and

(*b*) section 14(1) of that Act (receipt in evidence of insufficiently stamped instruments if unpaid duty paid to court) does not apply to it at any time when it is not duly stamped, unless the unpaid duty and any interest or penalty is paid in accordance with that subsection.

Stamping following earlier adjudication

5 Section 12A(1) of the Stamp Act 1891 (adjudicated instruments not to be stamped other than in accordance with adjudication decision) does not prevent an instrument to which this Schedule applies which is stamped with less than the appropriate amount of duty from being stamped with additional duty.

Use of instruments in evidence, etc

6 Section 14(4) of the Stamp Act 1891 (instruments not to be used unless duly stamped in accordance with law in force when executed) applies in relation to an instrument to which this Schedule applies as if, as respects any time on or after the commencement date, the reference to the law in force at the time when it was executed were to the law in force on the commencement date.

Adjudication, interest and penalties

7—(1) This paragraph applies for the purpose of applying sections 12 to 13B and 15 to 15B of the Stamp Act 1891 (adjudication by Commissioners and interest and penalties on late stamping) in relation to any additional duty chargeable on an instrument to which this Schedule applies.

(2) Those sections continue to apply without modification as respects any other stamp duty chargeable on the instrument.

(3) Those sections have effect as respects the additional duty as if—

(*a*) the additional duty were the only stamp duty chargeable on the instrument;

(*b*) the instrument had been executed on the commencement date; and

(*c*) in the case of an instrument executed outside the United Kingdom and first received in the United Kingdom before the commencement date, the instrument had been first received in the United Kingdom on the commencement date.

(4) Accordingly, those sections apply as respects additional duty as if—

(*a*) references to duty were to additional duty;

(*b*) references to stamping were to stamping with additional duty;

(*c*) references to an instrument's being stamped were to its being stamped with additional duty;

(*d*) references to an instrument's being duly stamped were to its being stamped with all the additional duty chargeable on it;

(*e*) references to an instrument's being unstamped were to its not being stamped with any additional duty;

(*f*) references to an instrument's being insufficiently stamped were to its being stamped with insufficient additional duty;

(*g*) references to adjudication, or an appeal, under any of those sections were to adjudication or an appeal under the section in question as it has effect as respects additional duty; and

(*h*) references to the maximum penalty were to the maximum penalty as respects additional duty.

SCHEDULE 33

POWER TO VARY STAMP DUTIES

Section 117

Power of Treasury to make provision by regulations

1—(1) The Treasury may if they consider it expedient in the public interest make provision by regulations for the variation of an existing stamp duty.

(2) The power conferred by this paragraph includes, in particular, power to alter the descriptions of document in respect of which an existing stamp duty, or an existing rate or amount of duty, is chargeable.

(3) The power to make regulations under this paragraph is exercisable by statutory instrument.

Regulations—Variation of Stamp Duties Regulations, SI 2001/3746.

Power only to be used for cases involving land or shares etc

2—(1) The power conferred by paragraph 1 does not include power—

(*a*) to vary the amount chargeable by way of stamp duty on an excepted instrument, or

(*b*) to cause stamp duty to become chargeable on an excepted instrument.

(2) For the purposes of this paragraph—

(*a*) an "excepted instrument" is any document that is not a relevant property instrument, and

(*b*) a "relevant property instrument" is a document that (whether or not it also relates to any other transaction) relates to a transaction that to any extent involves—

(i) land, stock or marketable securities, or

(ii) any estate or interest in land, stock or marketable securities.

Power not to be used to vary rates or thresholds

3 The power conferred by paragraph 1 does not, except as mentioned in paragraph 1(2), include power to vary—

(*a*) the rate, or rates, of an existing *ad valorem* stamp duty,

(*b*) the amount of an existing fixed stamp duty,

(*c*) any threshold specified in paragraph 4 of Schedule 13 to the Finance Act 1999 (rate bands for [transfer][1] on sale), or

(*d*) any threshold specified in paragraph 11 or 12 of that Schedule (duty on leases) in respect of rent or the term of a lease.

Amendments—[1] The word "transfer" substituted for the words "conveyance or transfer" in enactments relating to stamp duty by FA 2003 Sch 20 para 3.

Approval of regulations by House of Commons

4—(1) An instrument containing regulations under paragraph 1 shall be laid before the House of Commons after being made.

(2) If the regulations are not approved by the House of Commons before the end of the period of 28 days beginning with the day on which they are made, they shall cease to have effect at the end of that period if they have not already ceased to have effect under sub-paragraph (3).

(3) If on any day during that period of 28 days the House of Commons, in proceedings on a motion that (or to the effect that) the regulations be approved, comes to a decision rejecting the regulations, they shall cease to have effect at the end of that day.

(4) Where regulations cease to have effect under sub-paragraph (2) or (3), their ceasing to have effect is without prejudice to anything done in reliance on them.

(5) In reckoning any such period of 28 days take no account of any time during which—

(*a*) Parliament is prorogued or dissolved, or

(*b*) the House of Commons is adjourned for more than four days.

Claim for repayment if regulations not approved

5—(1) Where regulations cease to have effect under paragraph 4(2) or (3), any amount paid by way of stamp duty, or interest or penalty on late stamping, that would not have been payable but for the regulations shall, on a claim, be repaid by the Commissioners.

(2) Section 110 of the Finance Act 1999 (interest on repayment of duty overpaid etc) applies to a repayment under this paragraph of any amount paid by way of stamp duty or penalty on late stamping.

In the case of a repayment under this paragraph, the relevant time for the purposes of that section is 30 days after the day on which the instrument in question was executed or, if later, the date on which the payment of duty or penalty was made.

(3) A claim for repayment must be made within two years after the date of the instrument in question or, if it is not dated, within two years after its execution.
(4) No repayment shall be made on a claim until the instrument in question has been produced to the Commissioners for such cancelling of stamps, and such stamping to denote the making of the repayment or the producing of the instrument under this paragraph, as the Commissioners consider appropriate.
(5) Any repayment shall, subject to any regulations under sub-paragraph (6)(*d*), be made to such person as the Commissioners consider appropriate.
(6) The Commissioners may make provision by regulations—

(*a*) for varying the time limit having effect under sub-paragraph (3);

(*b*) for varying or repealing the condition having effect under sub-paragraph (4);

(*c*) as to any other conditions that must be met before repayment is made;

(*d*) as to the person to whom repayment is to be made.

(7) Regulations under this paragraph shall be made by statutory instrument which shall be subject to annulment in pursuance of a resolution of the House of Commons.

Use in evidence, etc of instruments affected by regulations ceasing to have effect

6—(1) Where regulations cease to have effect under paragraph 4(2) or (3), the following provisions apply to an instrument that—

(*a*) was executed at a time when the regulations were in force, and

(*b*) was at that time chargeable with any amount of stamp duty with which it would not have been chargeable apart from the regulations.

(2) If the instrument was stamped while the regulations were in force, nothing done in pursuance of paragraph 5 (repayment of duty etc) prevents it being treated for any purpose as duly stamped in accordance with the law in force at the time when it was executed.
(3) If the instrument was not stamped while the regulations were in force, the law in force at the time when it was executed shall be deemed to have been what the law would have been apart from the regulations.

Temporary effect of regulations

7—(1) Regulations under paragraph 1 shall not apply in relation to instruments executed after the end of—

(*a*) the period of 18 months beginning with the day on which the regulations were made, or

(*b*) such shorter period as may be specified in the regulations.

(2) This does not affect the power to make further provision by regulations under paragraph 1 to the same or similar effect.

Power to make transitional etc provision

8 Any power to make regulations under this Schedule includes power to make such transitional, supplementary and incidental provision as appears to the authority making the regulations to be necessary or expedient.

Interpretation

9—(1) In relation to a bearer instrument (as defined in paragraph 3 of Schedule 15 to the Finance Act 1999), references in this Schedule to the execution of the instrument shall be read as references to its issue.[1]
(2) This Schedule shall be construed as one with the Stamp Act 1891.

Amendments—[1] Para 9(1) repealed by FA 2000 s 156, Sch 40 Pt III with effect in accordance with FA 1990 s 107.

SCHEDULE 34

ABOLITION OF STAMP DUTY ON INSTRUMENTS RELATING TO INTELLECTUAL PROPERTY: SUPPLEMENTARY PROVISIONS

Section 129

Introduction

1 In this Schedule "intellectual property" has the same meaning as in section 129(1).

Stamp duty reduced in certain other cases

2—(1) This paragraph applies where—

(*a*) stamp duty under Part I of Schedule 13 to the Finance Act 1999 ([transfer][1] on sale) is chargeable on an instrument, and (*b*) part of the property concerned consists of intellectual property.

(2) In such a case—

(*a*) the consideration in respect of which duty would otherwise be charged shall be apportioned, on such basis as is just and reasonable, as between the part of the property which consists of intellectual property and the part which does not, and

(*b*) the instrument shall be charged only in respect of the consideration attributed to such of the property as is not intellectual property.

(3) This paragraph applies to instruments executed on or after 28th March 2000.

Amendments—[1] The word "transfer" substituted for the words "conveyance or transfer" in enactments relating to stamp duty by FA 2003 Sch 20 para 3.

Apportionment of consideration for stamp duty purposes

3—(1) Where part of the property referred to in section 58(1) of the Stamp Act 1891 (consideration to be apportioned between different instruments as parties think fit) consists of intellectual property, that provision shall have effect as if "the parties think fit" read "is just and reasonable".

(2) Where—

(*a*) part of the property referred to in section 58(2) of the Stamp Act 1891 (property contracted to be purchased by two or more persons etc) consists of intellectual property, and

(*b*) both or (as the case may be) all the relevant persons are connected with one another,

that provision shall have effect as if the words from "for distinct parts of the consideration" to the end of the subsection read ", the consideration is to be apportioned in such manner as is just and reasonable, so that a distinct consideration for each separate part or parcel is set forth in the conveyance relating thereto, and such conveyance is to be charged with ad valorem duty in respect of such distinct consideration.".

(3) In a case where sub-paragraph (1) or (2) applies and the consideration is apportioned in a manner that is not just and reasonable, the enactments relating to stamp duty shall have effect as if—

(*a*) the consideration had been apportioned in a manner that is just and reasonable, and

(*b*) the amount of any distinct consideration set forth in any conveyance relating to a separate part or parcel of property were such amount as is found by a just and reasonable apportionment (and not the amount actually set forth).

(4) For the purposes of sub-paragraph (2)—

(*a*) a person is a relevant person if he is a person by or for whom the property is contracted to be purchased;

(*b*) the question whether persons are connected with one another shall be determined in accordance with [section 1122 of the Corporation Tax Act 2010][1].

(5) In sub-paragraph (3) "the enactments relating to stamp duty" means the Stamp Act 1891 and any enactment amending or which is to be construed as one with that Act.

(6) This paragraph applies to instruments executed on or after 28th March 2000.

Amendments—[1] In sub-para (4)(*b*) words substituted for words "section 839 of the Taxes Act 1988" by CTA 2010 s 1177, Sch 1 para 318. CTA 2010 has effect for corporation tax purposes for accounting periods ending on or after 1 April 2010, and for income and capital gains tax purposes for the tax year 2010–11 and subsequent tax years.

Certification of instruments for stamp duty purposes

4—(1) Intellectual property shall be disregarded for the purposes of paragraph 6 of Schedule 13 to the Finance Act 1999 (certification of instrument as not forming part of transaction or series of transactions exceeding specified amount).

(2) Any statement as mentioned in paragraph 6(1) of that Schedule shall be construed as leaving out of account any matter which is to be so disregarded.

(3) This paragraph applies to instruments executed on or after 28th March 2000.

Acquisition under statute

5—(1) Section 12 of the Finance Act 1895 (property vested by Act or purchased under statutory powers) does not require any person who is authorised to purchase any property as mentioned in that section on or after 28th March 2000 to include any intellectual property in the instrument of conveyance required by that section to be produced to the Commissioners.

(2) If the property consists wholly of intellectual property no instrument of conveyance need be produced to the Commissioners under that section.

(3) This paragraph applies where the Act mentioned in that section, and by virtue of which property is vested or a person is authorised to purchase property, is passed on or after 28th March 2000.

SCHEDULE 40

REPEALS

Section 156

Note—All repeals relevant to stamp duty are already in effect and have therefore been omitted.

FINANCE ACT 2001

(2001 Chapter 9)

An Act to grant certain duties, to alter other duties, and to amend the law relating to the National Debt and the Public Revenue, and to make further provision in connection with Finance.

[11 May 2001]

PART 4

OTHER TAXES

Stamp duty and stamp duty reserve tax

92 Stamp duty: exemption for land in disadvantaged areas

(1) [No *ad valorem* stamp duty shall be chargeable on—][1]

(*a*) a [transfer][2] of an estate or interest in land, or

(*b*) a lease of land,

if the land is situated in a disadvantaged area.

(2) Where stamp duty would be chargeable on an instrument but for subsection (1), that subsection shall have effect in relation to the instrument only if the instrument is certified to the Commissioners as being an instrument on which stamp duty is by virtue of that subsection not chargeable.

(3) No instrument which is certified as mentioned in subsection (2) shall be taken to be duly stamped unless—

(*a*) it is stamped in accordance with section 12 of the Stamp Act 1891 with a particular stamp denoting that it is not chargeable with any duty or that it is duly stamped, or

(*b*) it is stamped with the duty to which it would have been liable but for this section.

(4) For the purposes of this section and Schedule 30 to this Act, a disadvantaged area is an area designated as such by regulations made by the Treasury; and any such regulations may—

(*a*) designate specified areas as disadvantaged areas, or

(*b*) provide for areas of a description specified in the regulations to be designated as disadvantaged areas.

(5) If regulations under subsection (4) so provide, the designation of an area as a disadvantaged area shall have effect for such period as may be specified by or determined in accordance with the regulations.

(6) Schedule 30 to this Act (which makes further provision about land in disadvantaged areas) shall have effect.

[(6A) This section and Schedule 30 to this Act have effect subject to section 92A.][1]

(7) This section and Schedule 30 to this Act shall be construed as one with the Stamp Act 1891.

(8) The provisions of this section and Schedule 30 to this Act shall have effect in relation to instruments executed on or after such date as may be specified by order made by the Treasury.

(9) Regulations under subsection (4)—

(*a*) may make different provision for different cases, and

(*b*) may contain such incidental, supplementary, consequential or transitional provision as appears to the Treasury to be necessary or expedient.

(10) The power to make regulations under subsection (4) shall be exercisable by statutory instrument subject to annulment in pursuance of a resolution of the House of Commons.

(11) The power to make an order under subsection (8) shall be exercisable by statutory instrument.

Regulations—Stamp Duty (Disadvantaged Areas) Regulations, SI 2001/3747.

Finance Act 2001, Section 92(8), (Specified Day) Order, SI 2001/3748 (the day specified for the purposes of sub-s (8) above is 30 November 2001).

Statement of Practice SP 1/03—(Disadvantaged areas relief, Stamp Office approach to borderline cases).

Amendments—[1] Words in sub-s (1) substituted, and sub-s (6A) inserted, by FA 2002 s 110(1), (2) with effect from 24 July 2002.

[2] The word "transfer" substituted for the words "conveyance or transfer" in enactments relating to stamp duty by FA 2003 Sch 20 para 3.

[92A Restriction of exemption in the case of residential property etc

(1) Regulations may provide for an exemption conferred by section 92 or by Schedule 30 to this Act not to apply in cases specified by reference to either or both of the following—

(*a*) whether the land in question is residential property;

(*b*) the amount or value of the consideration.

(2) Regulations may contain provision corresponding to or modifying that made by Schedule 30 to this Act in the case of—

(*a*) a building or land only part of which falls within subsection (1)(*a*) or (*b*) of section 92B (meaning of "residential property"), or

(*b*) an interest in or right over land that subsists only partly as mentioned in subsection (1)(*c*) of that section.

(3) Where by virtue of regulations under this section the availability of an exemption depends on the land in question not being, or not being entirely, residential property, the certification under section 92(2) must include a statement that the land is not residential property or, as the case may be, that it is not residential property to the extent stated.

(4) Where by virtue of regulations under this section the availability of an exemption depends on the amount or value of the consideration not exceeding a specified amount, the instrument in question must be certified at that amount (or at a lower amount).

The reference here to an instrument being certified at an amount shall be construed in accordance with paragraph 6 of Schedule 13 to the Finance Act 1999 (c 16) (as if the reference were contained in paragraph 4 of that Schedule).

(5) The power to make regulations under this section is exercisable by the Treasury.

(6) Regulations under this section—

(*a*) may make different provision for different cases, and

(*b*) may contain such incidental, supplementary, consequential or transitional provision as appears to the Treasury to be necessary or expedient.

(7) Regulations under this section must be made by statutory instrument, which shall be subject to annulment in pursuance of a resolution of the House of Commons.][1]

Definitions—"Residential property", s 92B(1).

Cross reference—FA 2002 s 110(6) (regulations under this section may contain provisions revoking the Variation of Stamp Duties Regulations, SI 2001/3746).

Regulations—Stamp Duty (Disadvantaged Areas) (Application of Exemptions) Regulations, SI 2003/1056.

Statement of Practice SP 1/03—(Disadvantaged areas relief, Stamp Office approach to borderline cases).

Amendments—[1] This section inserted by FA 2002 s 110(3) with effect from 24 July 2002.

[92B Meaning of "residential property"

(1) In section 92A "residential property" means—

(*a*) a building that is used or suitable for use as a dwelling, or is in the process of being constructed or adapted for such use,

(*b*) land that is or forms part of the garden or grounds of a building within paragraph (*a*) (including any building or structure on such land);

(*c*) an interest in or right over land that subsists for the benefit of a building within paragraph (*a*) or of land within paragraph (*b*).

(2) For the purposes of subsection (1) use of a building as—

(*a*) residential accommodation for school pupils,

(*b*) residential accommodation for students, other than accommodation falling within subsection (3)(*b*),

(*c*) residential accommodation for members of any of the armed forces, or

(*d*) an institution that is the sole or main residence of at least 90% of its residents and does not fall within any of paragraphs (*a*) to (*f*) of subsection (3),

is use of a building as a dwelling.

(3) For the purposes of subsection (1) use of a building as—

(*a*) a home or other institution providing residential accommodation for children,

(*b*) a hall of residence for students in further or higher education,

(*c*) a home or other institution providing residential accommodation with personal care for persons in need of personal care by reason of old age, disablement, past or present dependence on alcohol or drugs or past or present mental disorder,

(*d*) a hospital or hospice,

(*e*) a prison or similar establishment, or

(*f*) a hotel or inn or similar establishment,

is not use of a building as a dwelling.

(4) Where a building is used in a manner specified in subsection (3), no account shall be taken for the purposes of subsection (1)(*a*) of its suitability for any other use.

(5) Where a building that is not in use is suitable for at least one of the uses specified in subsection (2) and at least one of those specified in subsection (3)—

(*a*) if there is one such use for which it is most suitable, or if the uses for which it is most suitable are all specified in the same subsection, no account shall be taken for the purposes of subsection (1)(*a*) of its suitability for any other use,

(*b*) otherwise, the building shall be treated for those purposes as suitable for use as a dwelling.

(6) Regulations under section 92A may provide that, where there is a single contract for the conveyance, transfer or lease of land comprising or including six or more separate dwellings, none of that land counts as residential property for the purposes of the regulations.
(7) The Treasury may by order amend this section so as to change or clarify the cases where use of a building is, or is not, use of a building as a dwelling for the purposes of subsection (1).
(8) An order under subsection (7) may contain such incidental, supplementary, consequential or transitional provision as appears to the Treasury to be necessary or expedient.
(9) An order under subsection (7) must be made by statutory instrument, which shall be subject to annulment in pursuance of a resolution of the House of Commons.
(10) In this section "building" includes part of a building.][1]

Regulations—Stamp Duty (Disadvantaged Areas) (Application of Exemptions) Regulations, SI 2003/1056.
Statement of Practice SP 1/03—(Disadvantaged areas relief, Stamp Office approach to borderline cases).
Amendments—[1] This section inserted by FA 2002 s 110(3) with effect from 24 July 2002.

93 SDRT: unit trust schemes and individual pension accounts

(1) Schedule 19 to the Finance Act 1999 (which abolishes charges to stamp duty, and introduces a charge to stamp duty reserve tax, in relation to units under a unit trust scheme) is amended as follows.
(2) (*amends* FA 1999 Sch 19 para 2(4)).
(3) (*inserts* FA 1999 Sch 19 para 4(6), (7)).
(4) (*inserts* FA 1999 Sch 19 para 6A).
(5) The amendment made by subsection (3) has effect where the relevant two-week period mentioned in paragraph 4(1) of Schedule 19 to the Finance Act 1999 ends after 6th April 2001.
(6) The other amendments made by this section have effect in relation to surrenders made or effected on or after 6th April 2001.

94 SDRT: open-ended investment companies and individual pension accounts

(1) Where there are two or more classes of shares in an open-ended investment company and the company's instrument of incorporation—

(*a*) provides that shares of one or more of those classes ("the IPA classes") may only be held within an individual pension account, and

(*b*) does not make such provision in relation to shares of at least one other class,

there is no charge to stamp duty reserve tax under Part II of Schedule 19 to the Finance Act 1999 on the surrender of a share of any of the IPA classes.
(2) References in this section to provisions of Schedule 19 to the Finance Act 1999 are references to those provisions as they have effect in relation to open-ended investment companies by virtue of regulations from time to time in force under section 152 of the Finance Act 1995 (as at 6th April 2001, see regulations 3 to 4B of the 1997 Regulations as amended by regulations 4 and 5 of the 1999 (No 2) Regulations).
(3) In this section—

"individual pension account" has the same meaning as it has in regulations from time to time in force under section 638A of the Taxes Act 1988 (as at 6th April 2001, see regulation 4 of the 2001 Regulations);

"open-ended investment company" has the meaning given by paragraph 14(2) of Schedule 19 to the Finance Act 1999;

"surrender", in relation to a share in an open-ended investment company, has the same meaning as it has in Part II of Schedule 19 to the Finance Act 1999.

(4) For the purposes of subsections (2) and (3)—

"the 1997 Regulations" are the Stamp Duty and Stamp Duty Reserve Tax (Open-ended Investment Companies) Regulations 1997;

"the 1999 (No 2) Regulations" are the Stamp Duty and Stamp Duty Reserve Tax (Open-ended Investment Companies) (Amendment No 2) Regulations 1999;

"the 2001 Regulations" are the Personal Pension Schemes (Restriction on Discretion to Approve) (Permitted Investments) Regulations 2001.

(5) This section has effect in relation to surrenders made or effected on or after 6th April 2001.

[95 Exemptions in relation to approved share incentive plans

(1) This section forms part of the SIP code (see section 488 of the Income Tax (Earnings and Pensions) Act 2003 (approved share incentive plans)).
(2) Accordingly, expressions used in this section and contained in the index at the end of Schedule 2 to that Act (approved share incentive plans) have the meaning indicated by that index.
(3) Where, under an approved share incentive plan, partnership shares or dividend shares are transferred by the trustees to an employee—

(*a*) no ad valorem stamp duty is chargeable on any instrument by which the transfer is made, and

(*b*) no stamp duty reserve tax is chargeable on any agreement by the trustees to make the transfer.

(4) But subsection (3) does not apply to—

(*a*) any instrument executed (within the meaning of the Stamp Act 1891) before 6th April 2003, or

(*b*) any agreement to transfer shares made before that date.][1]

Amendments—[1] This section substituted by ITEPA 2003 s 722, Sch 6 para 257 with effect, for income tax purposes, from 2003–04; and for corporation tax purposes, for accounting periods ending after 5 April 2003. For transitional provisions and savings see ITEPA 2003 s 723, Sch 7.

This section previously read as follows—

"95 Exemptions in relation to employee share ownership plans

(1) Schedule 8 to the Finance Act 2000 (employee share ownership plans) is amended as follows.

(2) After paragraph 116 insert—

"Exemptions from stamp duty and stamp duty reserve tax

116A Where, under an approved employee share ownership plan, partnership shares or dividend shares are transferred by the trustees to an employee—

(*a*) no ad valorem stamp duty is chargeable on any instrument by which the transfer is made, and

(*b*) no stamp duty reserve tax is chargeable on any agreement by the trustees to make the transfer.".

(3) This section has effect in relation to—

(*a*) instruments executed (within the meaning of the Stamp Act 1891) after the day on which this Act is passed, and

(*b*) agreements to transfer shares made after the day on which this Act is passed.".

SCHEDULES

SCHEDULE 30

STAMP DUTY: LAND IN DISADVANTAGED AREAS

Section 92

Regulations—Stamp Duty (Disadvantaged Areas) (Application of Exemptions) Regulations, SI 2003/1056.

Stamp duty reduced for land partly in a disadvantaged area

1—(1) Where any land is situated partly in a disadvantaged area and partly outside such an area, liability to [*ad valorem* stamp duty][1] on—

(*a*) a [transfer][2] of an estate or interest in the land, or

(*b*) a lease of the land,

shall be determined in accordance with sub-paragraph (2).

(2) Where liability to stamp duty falls to be determined in accordance with this sub-paragraph—

(*a*) the consideration in respect of which duty would be chargeable, but for the provisions of this paragraph, shall be apportioned, on such basis as is just and reasonable, as between the part of the land which is situated in a disadvantaged area and the part which is not so situated, and

(*b*) the instrument shall be chargeable only in respect of the consideration attributed to such part of the land as is not situated in a disadvantaged area.

(3) Where stamp duty, or a greater amount of stamp duty, would be chargeable on an instrument but for sub-paragraphs (1) and (2), those sub-paragraphs shall have effect in relation to the instrument only if the instrument is certified to the Commissioners as being an instrument in relation to which those sub-paragraphs have effect.

(4) No instrument which is certified as mentioned in sub-paragraph (3) shall be taken to be duly stamped unless—

(*a*) it is stamped in accordance with section 12 of the Stamp Act 1891 with a particular stamp denoting that it is not chargeable with any duty or that it is duly stamped, or

(*b*) it is stamped with the duty to which it would have been liable but for this paragraph.

Amendments—[1] Words in para (1) substituted by FA 2002 s 110(4) with effect from 24 July 2002.

[2] The word "transfer" substituted for the words "conveyance or transfer" in enactments relating to stamp duty by FA 2003 Sch 20 para 3.

Apportionment of consideration for stamp duty purposes

2—(1) Where any part or parcel of the property referred to in section 58(1) of the Stamp Act 1891 (consideration to be apportioned between separate parts or parcels as parties think fit) consists of an estate or interest in land situated wholly or partly in a disadvantaged area, that provision shall have effect—

(*a*) as if "the parties think fit" read "is just and reasonable", and

(*b*) as if "such conveyance is" read "such conveyance is (subject to section 92 of, and Schedule 30 to, the Finance Act 2001)".

(2) Where—

(*a*) any part or parcel of the property referred to in section 58(2) of the Stamp Act 1891 (property contracted to be purchased by two or more persons etc) consists of an estate or interest in land situated wholly or partly in a disadvantaged area, and

(*b*) both or (as the case may be) all the relevant persons are connected with one another,

that provision shall have effect in accordance with sub-paragraph (3).

(3) In a case falling within sub-paragraph (2), section 58(2) of that Act shall have effect as if the words from "for distinct parts of the consideration" to the end of the subsection read ", the consideration is to be apportioned in such manner as is just and reasonable, so that a distinct consideration for each separate part or parcel is set forth in the conveyance relating thereto, and such conveyance is (subject to section 92 of, and Schedule 30 to, the Finance Act 2001) to be charged with *ad valorem* duty in respect of such distinct consideration.".

(4) In a case where sub-paragraph (1) or (3) applies and the consideration is apportioned in a manner that is not just and reasonable, the enactments relating to stamp duty shall have effect as if—

(*a*) the consideration had been apportioned in a manner that is just and reasonable, and

(*b*) the amount of any distinct consideration set forth in any conveyance relating to a separate part or parcel of property were such amount as is found by a just and reasonable apportionment (and not the amount actually set forth).

(5) For the purposes of sub-paragraph (2)—

(*a*) a person is a relevant person if he is a person by or for whom the property is contracted to be purchased; and

(*b*) the question whether persons are connected with one another shall be determined in accordance with [section 1122 of the Corporation Tax Act 2010][1].

(6) In sub-paragraph (4) "the enactments relating to stamp duty" means the Stamp Act 1891 and any enactment amending, or which is to be construed as one with, that Act.

Amendments—[1] In para (5)(*b*) words substituted for words "section 839 of the Taxes Act 1988" CTA 2010 s 1177, Sch 1 para 366. CTA 2010 has effect for corporation tax purposes for accounting periods ending on or after 1 April 2010, and for income and capital gains tax purposes for the tax year 2010–11 and subsequent tax years.

Certification of instruments for stamp duty purposes

3—(1) If or to the extent that [a conveyance, transfer or lease is exempted from stamp duty by section 92(1) or paragraph 1 above (read with section 92A) the transaction in question shall be disregarded][1] for the purposes of paragraph 6 of Schedule 13 to the Finance Act 1999 (certification of instrument as not forming part of transaction or series of transactions exceeding specified amount). [This is without prejudice to section 92A(4) (instrument must be certified where exemption depends on amount or value of consideration).][1]

(2) Any statement as mentioned in paragraph 6(1) of that Schedule shall be construed as leaving out of account any matter which is to be disregarded in accordance with sub-paragraph (1) above.

Amendments—[1] Words in para (1) substituted, and words added, by FA 2002 s 110(5) with effect from 24 July 2002.

FINANCE ACT 2002

(2002 Chapter 23)

An Act to grant certain duties, to alter other duties, and to amend the law relating to the National Debt and the Public Revenue, and to make further provision in connection with finance.

[24 July 2002]

PART 4

STAMP DUTY AND STAMP DUTY RESERVE TAX

Stamp duty

110 Land in disadvantaged areas

(1) (*amends* FA 2001 s 92(1)).

(2) (*inserts* FA 2001 s 92(6A)).

(3) (*inserts* FA 2001 ss 92A, 92B).

(4) (*amends* FA 2001 Sch 30 para 1(1)).

(5) (*amends* FA 2001 Sch 30 para 1(3)).

(6) Regulations under section 92A of the Finance Act 2001 (inserted by subsection (1) above) may contain provision revoking the Variation of Stamp Duties Regulations 2001 (SI 2001/3746) (which provide for section 92(1) of, and paragraph 1 of Schedule 30 to, that Act not to apply in cases where the consideration for the conveyance etc exceeds £150,000).

Regulations—Stamp Duty (Disadvantaged Areas) (Application of Exemptions) Regulations, SI 2003/1056.

111 Withdrawal of group relief

(1) This section applies where—

(*a*) an instrument ("the relevant instrument") transferring land in the United Kingdom from one company ("the transferor company") to another ("the transferee company") has been stamped on the basis that group relief applies,

(*b*) before the end of the period of [three years][1] beginning with the date on which the instrument was executed the transferee company ceases to be a member of the same group as the transferor company, and

(*c*) at the time when [the transferee company ceases][1] to be a member of the same group as the transferor company [it or a relevant associated company holds][1] an estate or interest in land—

(i) that was transferred [to the transferee company][1] by the relevant instrument, or

(ii) that is derived from an estate or interest that was so transferred,

[and that has not subsequently been transferred at market value by a duly stamped instrument on which ad valorem duty was paid and in respect of which group relief was not claimed.][1]

(2) In those circumstances—

(*a*) group relief in relation to the relevant instrument, or an appropriate proportion of it, is withdrawn, and

(*b*) the stamp duty that would have been payable on stamping the relevant instrument but for group relief if the estate or interest in land transferred by that instrument had been transferred at market value, or an appropriate proportion of the duty that would have been so paid, is payable by the transferee company within 30 days after that company ceases to be a member of the same group as the transferor company.

(3) In subsection (2)(*a*) and (*b*) "an appropriate proportion" means an appropriate proportion having regard to what was transferred [to the transferee company][1] by the relevant instrument and [what is held by that company or, as the case may be, that company and any relevant associated companies, at the time it or they cease to be members][1] of the same group as the transferor company.

(4) In this section "group relief" means relief under any of the following provisions—

(*a*) section 42 of the Finance Act 1930 (c 28) or section 11 of the Finance Act (Northern Ireland) 1954 (c 23 (NI)) (transfer of property between associated bodies corporate);

(*b*) section 151 of the Finance Act 1995 (c 4) (leases etc between associated bodies corporate.)

[(4A) In this section "relevant associated company", in relation to the transferee company, means a company that—

(*a*) is a member of the same group as the transferee company immediately before that company ceases to be a member of the same group as the transferor company, and

(*b*) ceases to be a member of the same group as the transferor company in consequence of the transferee company so ceasing.][1]

(5) In this section—

(*a*) references to the transfer of land include the grant or surrender of an estate or interest in or over land;

(*b*) "company" includes any body corporate; and

(*c*) references to a company being in the same group as another company are to the companies being associated bodies corporate within the meaning of the relevant group relief provision.

(6) Schedule 34 to this Act contains provisions supplementing this section.

(7) Where the relevant instrument transfers land in the United Kingdom together with other property, the provisions of this section and of Schedule 34 apply as if there were two separate instruments, one relating to land in the United Kingdom and the other relating to other property.

(8) This section applies where the relevant instrument is executed after 23rd April 2002.

(9) But this section does not apply to an instrument giving effect to a contract made on or before 17th April 2002, unless—

(*a*) the instrument is made in consequence of the exercise after that date of any option, right of pre-emption or similar right, or

(*b*) the instrument transfers the property in question to, or vests it in, a person other than the purchaser under the contract because of an assignment (or, in Scotland, assignation) or further contract made after that date.

(10) This section shall be deemed to have come into force on 24th April 2002.

Cross references—FA 2003 Sch 19 para 6(2) (the references in sub-s (1)(*c*) above to a transfer at market value by a duly stamped instrument on which ad valorem duty was paid and in respect of which group relief was not claimed shall be read, on or after the implementation date, as including a reference to a transfer at market value by a chargeable transaction in respect of which relief under FA 2003 Sch 7 Pt 1 was available but was not claimed. For the implementation date, see FA 2003 Sch 19 para 2).

Amendments—[1] In sub-s (1)(*b*), words substituted for the words "two years", in sub-s (1)(*c*), words substituted for the words "it ceases", "it holds", "to it", and "and that was not subsequently transferred to it by a duly stamped instrument for which group relief was not claimed."; in sub-s (3), words inserted, and words substituted for the words "what the transferee company holds at the time it ceases to be a member"; and sub-s (4A) inserted; by FA 2003 s 126(1)–(5), (9)–(11) with effect for instruments executed after 14 April 2003. FA 2003 s 126 is deemed to have come into force on 15 April 2003.

FA 2003 s 126 does not apply to an instrument giving effect to a contract made on or before 9th April 2003, unless—

(a) the instrument is made in consequence of the exercise after that date of any option, right of pre-emption or similar right, or

(b) the instrument transfers the property in question to, or vests it in, a person other than the purchaser under the contract because of an assignment (or, in Scotland, assignation) or further contract made after that date: FA 2003 s 126(10).

112 Restriction of relief for company acquisitions

(1) Section 76 of the Finance Act 1986 (c 41) (relief where company acquires the whole or part of the undertaking of another company) is amended as follows.
(2) (*amends* FA 1986 s 76(2)).
(3) (*amends* FA 1986 s 76(3)).
(4) (*inserts* FA 1986 s 76(3A), (3B).
(5) (*amends* FA 1986 s 76(5)).
(6) (*inserts* FA 1986 s 76(6A)).
(7) This section applies to instruments executed after 23rd April 2002.
(8) But this section does not apply to an instrument giving effect to a contract made on or before 17th April 2002, unless—

(*a*) the instrument is made in consequence of the exercise after that date of any option, right of pre-emption or similar right, or

(*b*) the instrument transfers the property in question to, or vests it in, a person other than the purchaser under the contract because of an assignment (or, in Scotland, assignation) or further contract made after that date.

(9) This section shall be deemed to have come into force on 24th April 2002.

113 Withdrawal of relief for company acquisitions

(1) This section applies where—

(*a*) an instrument ("the relevant instrument") transferring land in the United Kingdom from one company to another company ("the acquiring company") has been stamped on the basis that relief under section 76 of the Finance Act 1986 (c 41) ("section 76 relief") applies,

(*b*) before the end of the period of [three years][1] beginning with the date on which the instrument was executed control of the acquiring company changes, and

(*c*) at the time control of that company changes the acquiring company [or a relevant associated company][1] holds an estate or interest in land—

(i) that was transferred [to the acquiring company][1] by the relevant instrument, or

(ii) that is derived from an estate or interest so transferred,

[and that has not subsequently been transferred at market value by a duly stamped instrument on which ad valorem duty was paid and in respect of which section 76 relief was not claimed][1].

(2) In those circumstances—

(*a*) section 76 relief in relation to the relevant instrument, or an appropriate proportion of it, is withdrawn, and

(*b*) the additional stamp duty that would have been payable on stamping the relevant instrument but for section 76 relief if the estate or interest in land transferred by that instrument had been transferred at market value, or an appropriate proportion of that additional duty, is payable by the acquiring company within 30 days after control of that company changes.

(3) In subsection (2)(*a*) and (*b*) "an appropriate proportion" means an appropriate proportion having regard to what was transferred by the relevant instrument and [what is held by that company or, as the case may be, by that company and any relevant associated companies][1] at the time control of it changes.

[(3A) In this section "relevant associated company", in relation to the acquiring company, means a company—

(*a*) that is controlled by the acquiring company immediately before the control of that company changes, and

(*b*) of which control changes in consequence of the change of control of that company.][1]

(4) In this section—

(*a*) references to the transfer of land include the grant or surrender of an estate or interest in or over land;

(*b*) "control" shall be construed in accordance with [sections 450 and 451 of the Corporation Tax Act 2010][2]; and

(*c*) references to control of a company changing are to the company becoming controlled—

(i) by a different person,

(ii) by a different number of persons, or

(iii) by two or more persons at least one of whom is not the person, or one of the persons, by whom the company was previously controlled.

(5) Schedule 35 to this Act contains provisions supplementing this section.
(6) Where the relevant instrument transfers land in the United Kingdom together with other property, the provisions of this section and of Schedule 35 apply as if there were two separate instruments, one relating to land in the United Kingdom and the other relating to other property.

(7) This section applies where the relevant instrument is executed after 23rd April 2002.

(8) But this section does not apply to an instrument giving effect to a contract made on or before 17th April 2002, unless—

(*a*) the instrument is made in consequence of the exercise after that date of any option, right of pre-emption or similar right, or

(*b*) the instrument transfers the property in question to, or vests it in, a person other than the purchaser under the contract because of an assignment (or, in Scotland, assignation) or further contract made after that date.

(9) This section shall be deemed to have come into force on 24th April 2002.

Cross references—FA 2003 Sch 19 para 6(3) (the references in sub-s (1)(*c*) above to a transfer at market value by a duly stamped instrument on which ad valorem duty was paid and in respect of which section 76 relief was not claimed shall be read, on or after the implementation date, as including a reference to a transfer at market value by a chargeable transaction on which stamp duty land tax was chargeable and in respect of which relief under FA 2003 Sch 7 Pt 2 was available but was not claimed).

Amendments—[1] In sub-s (1)(*b*), words substituted for the words "two years", "to it", and "and that was not subsequently transferred to it by a duly stamped instrument on which *ad valorem* duty was paid and in relation to which section 76 relief was not claimed", and words inserted; in sub-s (3), words substituted for the words "what the acquiring company holds"; and sub-s (3A) inserted, by FA 2003 s 127(1)–(5) with effect for instruments executed after 14 April 2003.

FA 2003 s 127 shall be deemed to have come into force on 15 April 2003.

FA 2003 s 127 does not apply to an instrument giving effect to a contract made on or before 9 April 2003, unless—

(a) the instrument is made in consequence of the exercise after that date of any option, right of pre-emption or similar right, or

(b) the instrument transfers the property in question to, or vests it in, a person other than the purchaser under the contract because of an assignment (or, in Scotland, assignation) or further contract made after that date: FA 2003 s 127(8).

[2] In sub-s (4)(*b*) words substituted for words "section 416 of the Taxes Act 1988" by CTA 2010 s 1177, Sch 1 paras 368, 372. CTA 2010 has effect for corporation tax purposes for accounting periods ending on or after 1 April 2010, and for income and capital gains tax purposes for the tax year 2010–11 and subsequent tax years.

114 Penalties for late stamping

(1) Section 15B of the Stamp Act 1891 (c 39) (late stamping: penalties) is amended as follows.

(2) (*amends* SA 1891 s 15B(1)).

(3) (*inserts* SA 1891 s 15B(1A)).

(4) This section applies in relation to instruments executed on or after the day on which this Act is passed.

115 Contracts for the sale of an estate or interest in land chargeable as conveyances

(1) This section applies to a contract or agreement for the sale of an estate or interest in land in the United Kingdom where—

(*a*) the amount or value of the consideration exceeds £10 million, or

(*b*) the instrument forms part of a larger transaction or series of transactions in respect of which the amount or value, or aggregate amount or value, of the consideration exceeds £10 million.

(2) If, in the case of such a contract or agreement that is not otherwise chargeable to stamp duty, a [transfer][1] made in conformity with the contract or agreement is not presented to the Commissioners for stamping with the *ad valorem* duty chargeable on it—

(*a*) within the period of 90 days after the execution of the contract or agreement, or

(*b*) within such longer period as the Commissioners may think reasonable in the circumstances of the case,

the contract or agreement shall be chargeable with the same ad valorem duty, to be paid by the purchaser, as if it were an actual conveyance on sale of the estate or interest contracted or agreed to be sold.

(3) The Commissioners—

(*a*) may refuse to allow a longer period unless they are provided with a copy of the contract or agreement and such other evidence as they may reasonably require as to the facts and circumstances relevant to their decision,

(*b*) may allow a longer period subject to compliance with such conditions as they think fit, and

(*c*) shall not allow any longer period if it appears to them that the whole, or substantially the whole, of the intended consideration has been paid or transferred.

(4) Where an instrument to which this section applies is presented for stamping before the end of the period mentioned in subsection (2)—

(*a*) any adjudication to the effect that stamp duty is not chargeable does not affect the operation of this section, and

(*b*) the fact that duty may be chargeable under this section may be denoted on the instrument in such manner as the Commissioners think fit.

(5) Where an instrument is chargeable with duty under this section—

(*a*) section 14(4) of the Stamp Act 1891 (c 39) (inadmissibility of unstamped instruments) does not apply in relation to it until after the end of the period mentioned in subsection (2) above, and (*b*) sections 15A and 15B of that Act (late stamping: interest and penalties), apply in relation to it as if it had been executed at the end of that period.

(6) The *ad valorem* duty paid upon a contract or agreement under this section shall be repaid by the Commissioners if the contract or agreement is afterwards rescinded or annulled or is for any other reason not substantially performed or carried into effect.

(7) Schedule 36 contains provisions supplementing this section.

(8) This section and that Schedule apply to contracts or agreements executed after the day on which this Act is passed.

Amendments—[1] The word "transfer" substituted for the words "conveyance or transfer" in enactments relating to stamp duty by FA 2003 Sch 20 para 3.

116 Abolition of duty on instruments relating to goodwill

(1) No stamp duty is chargeable on an instrument for the sale, transfer or other disposition of goodwill.

(2) Schedule 37 to this Act contains provisions supplementing this section.

(3) This section and that Schedule shall be construed as one with the Stamp Act 1891 (c 39).

(4) This section applies to instruments executed on or after 23rd April 2002.

(5) This section shall be deemed to have come into force on that date.

Stamp duty and stamp duty reserve tax

117 Power to extend exceptions relating to recognised exchanges

(1) The Treasury may by regulations extend the application of the provisions mentioned in subsection (2) to any market (specified by name or by description) that is not a recognised exchange but is prescribed by order under section 118(3) of the Financial Services and Markets Act 2000 (c 8).

(2) The provisions referred to in subsection (1) are—

sections 80A and 80C of the Finance Act 1986 (c 41) (stamp duty: exceptions for sales to intermediaries and for repurchases and stock lending); and

sections 88A and 89AA of that Act (stamp duty reserve tax: exceptions for intermediaries and for repurchases and stock lending).

(3) In subsection (1) "recognised exchange" means an EEA exchange, a recognised foreign exchange or recognised foreign options exchange within the meaning of the provisions mentioned in subsection (2).

(4) Regulations under this section may provide for the application of the provisions mentioned in subsection (2) subject to any adaptations appearing to the Treasury to be necessary or expedient.

(5) Regulations under this section shall be made by statutory instrument which shall be subject to annulment in pursuance of a resolution of the House of Commons.[1]

Cross reference—Stamp Duty and Stamp Duty Reserve Tax (Extension of Exceptions relating to Recognised Exchanges) Regulations SI 2002/1975 (extension of the provisions in sub-s (2) above to the market known as OFEX).

Stamp Duty and Stamp Duty Reserve Tax (Extension of Exceptions relating to Recognised Exchanges) Regulations 2004/2421 (extension of the provisions in sub-s (2) above to the market known as the Alternative Investment Market established under the rules of the London Stock Exchange plc).

Amendments—[1] This section repealed by F(No 2)A 2005 ss 50(6), 70, Sch 11 Pt 3(2) with effect from 11 August 2005 (by virtue of SI 2005/2007).

PART 6

MISCELLANEOUS AND SUPPLEMENTARY PROVISIONS

Supplementary

143 Short title

This Act may be cited as the Finance Act 2002.

SCHEDULES

SCHEDULE 34

STAMP DUTY: WITHDRAWAL OF GROUP RELIEF: SUPPLEMENTARY PROVISIONS

Section 111

Introduction

1—(1) The provisions of this Schedule supplement section 111 (withdrawal of group relief).

(2) Expressions used in this Schedule that are defined for the purposes of that section have the same meaning in this Schedule.

Relief not withdrawn if transferor company leaves group

2—(1) Section 111 does not apply if the transferee company ceases to be a member of the same group as the transferor company by reason of the latter company leaving the group.

(2) The transferor company is regarded as leaving the group if the companies cease to be members of the same group by reason of a transaction relating to shares in—

(*a*) the transferor company, or

(*b*) another company that as a result of the transaction ceases to be a member of the same group as the transferee company.

Relief not withdrawn in case of winding-up

3—(1) Section 111 does not apply if the transferee company ceases to be a member of the same group as the transferor company by reason of anything done for the purposes of, or in the course of, winding up the transferor company or another company that is above the transferor company in the group structure.

(2) For the purposes of this paragraph a company is "above" the transferor company in the group structure if it is the parent (within the meaning of the relevant group relief provision)—

(*a*) of the transferor company, or

(*b*) of another company that is above the transferor company in the group structure.

Relief not withdrawn in case of exempt acquisition

4—(1) Section 111 does not apply if—

(*a*) the transferee company ceases to be a member of the same group as the transferor company as a result of an acquisition of shares by another company ("the parent company") in relation to which acquisition relief applies, and

(*b*) the transferee company is immediately after that acquisition a member of the same group as the parent company ("the new group").

(2) For this purpose—

(*a*) "acquisition relief" means relief under section 75 of the Finance Act 1986 (c 41); and

(*b*) references to an acquisition in relation to which such relief applies are to an acquisition such that an instrument effecting the transfer of the shares is exempt from stamp duty by virtue of that provision.

(3) But if before the end of the period of two years beginning with the date on which the relevant instrument was executed—

(*a*) the transferee company ceases to be a member of the new group, and

(*b*) at the time when [the transferee company ceases][1] to be a member of the new group [it or a relevant associated company (as defined in sub-paragraph (4) below) holds][1] an estate or interest in land that—

(i) was transferred [to the transferee company][1] by the relevant instrument, or

(ii) is derived from an estate or interest that was so transferred,

[and that has not subsequently been transferred at market value by a duly stamped instrument on which ad valorem duty was paid and in respect of which group relief was not claimed,][1]

section 11 and the provisions of this Schedule apply [as if the transferee had then ceased to be a member of the same group as the transferor company and had then held the estate or interest referred to in paragraph (b).][1].

[(4) In sub-paragraph (3)(*b*) "relevant associated company", in relation to the transferee company, means a company that is in the same group as the transferee company immediately before the transferee company ceases to be a member of the new group and which ceases to be a member of the new group in consequence of the transferee company so ceasing.][1]

Cross references—FA 2003 Sch 19 para 6(2) (the references in sub-para (3) above to a transfer at market value by a duly stamped instrument on which ad valorem duty was paid and in respect of which group relief was not claimed shall be read, on or after the implementation date, as including a reference to a transfer at market value by a chargeable transaction in respect of which relief under FA 2003 Sch 7 Pt 1 was available but was not claimed. For the implementation date, see FA 2003 Sch 19 para 2).

Amendments—[1] In sub-para (3)(*b*), words substituted for the words "it ceases", "it holds", "to it", "and that was not subsequently transferred to it by a duly stamped instrument for which group relief was not claimed,", and "as if the company had then ceased to be a member of the same group as the transferor company."; and sub-para (4) inserted, by FA 2003 s 126(6)–(11) with effect for instruments executed after 14 April 2003.

FA 2003 s 126 shall be deemed to have come into force on 15 April 2003.

FA 2003 s 126 does not apply to an instrument giving effect to a contract made on or before 9th April 2003, unless—

(a) the instrument is made in consequence of the exercise after that date of any option, right of pre-emption or similar right, or

(b) the instrument transfers the property in question to, or vests it in, a person other than the purchaser under the contract because of an assignment (or, in Scotland, assignation) or further contract made after that date.

Interest

5—(1) If any duty payable under section 111 is not paid within the period of 30 days within which payment is to be made, interest is payable on the amount remaining unpaid.

(2) The provisions of section 15A(3) to (5) of the Stamp Act 1891 (c 39) (rate of interest on unpaid duty, etc) apply in relation to interest under sub-paragraph (1).

Duty of transferee company to notify particulars

6—(1) The transferee company shall, within the period of 30 days mentioned in section 111(2)(*b*) within which payment is to be made, notify the Commissioners of—

(*a*) the date on which it ceased to be a member of the same group as the transferor company,

(*b*) the relevant land held by it at that time,

(*c*) the nature of the relevant instrument, the date on which it was executed, the parties to the instrument and the date on which the instrument was stamped,

(*d*) the market value of the land transferred to it by the relevant instrument at the date on which that instrument was executed, and

(*e*) the amount of duty and interest payable by it under section 111 or this Schedule.

(2) In sub-paragraph (1)(*b*) the "relevant land" held by the transferee company means every estate or interest to in relation to which section 111(1)(*c*) applies.

(3) In section 98(5) of the Taxes Management Act 1970 (c 9) (penalty for failure to provide information), in the second column of the Table, at the appropriate place insert "paragraph 6 of Schedule 34 to the Finance Act 2002".

Determination, collection and recovery of duty and interest

7 The provisions of regulations under section 98 of the Finance Act 1986 (c 41) (stamp duty reserve tax: administration etc), and the provisions of the Taxes Management Act 1970 applied by those regulations, have effect with the necessary modifications in relation to—

(*a*) the determination by the Commissioners of the duty payable under section 111 or the interest payable thereon,

(*b*) appeals against any such determination, and

(*c*) the collection and recovery of any such duty or interest,

as if it were an amount of stamp duty reserve tax.

Recovery of group relief from another group company or controlling director

8—(1) This paragraph applies where—

(*a*) an amount is payable under section 111 or this Schedule by the transferee company,

(*b*) a notice of determination of the amount payable has been issued by the Commissioners, and

(*c*) the whole or part of that amount is unpaid six months after the date on which it became payable.

(2) The following persons may, by notice under paragraph 8, be required to pay the unpaid amount—

(*a*) the transferor company;

(*b*) any company that, at any relevant time, was a member of the same group as the transferee company and was above it in the group structure;

(*c*) any person who at any relevant time was a controlling director of the transferee company or of a company having control of the transferee company.

(3) For the purposes of this paragraph—

(*a*) a "relevant time" means any time between the execution of the relevant instrument and the transferee company ceasing to be a member of the same group as the transferor company

(*b*) a company is "above" another company in a group structure if it is the parent (within the meaning of the relevant group relief provision)—

(i) of that company, or

(ii) of another company that is above that company in the group structure.

(4) In this paragraph—

["director", in relation to a company, has the meaning given by section 67(1) and (2) of the Income Tax (Earnings and Pensions) Act 2003 and includes any person falling within section 452(1) of the Corporation Tax Act 2010;][1] and

"controlling director", in relation to a company, means a director of the company who has control of it (construing control in accordance with [sections 450 and 451 of the Corporation Tax Act 2010][1]).

Amendment—[1] Definition of "director" substituted and in the definition of "controlling director" words substituted for words "section 416 of the Taxes Act 1988" by CTA 2010.s 1177, Sch 1 paras 368, 375. CTA 2010 has effect for corporation tax purposes for accounting periods ending on or after 1 April 2010, and for income and capital gains tax purposes for the tax year 2010–11 and subsequent tax years. Definition of "director" previously read as follows—

""director", in relation to a company, has the meaning given by section 168(8) of the Taxes Act 1988 (read with subsection (9) of that section) and includes any person falling within section 417(5) of that Act (read with subsection (6) of that section);"

Recovery of group relief from another group company or controlling director: procedure and time limit

9—(1) The Commissioners may serve a notice on a person within paragraph 8(2) requiring him, within 30 days of the service of the notice, to pay the amount that remains unpaid.

(2) Any notice under this paragraph must be served before the end of the period of three years beginning with the date on which the notice of determination mentioned in paragraph 8(1)(*b*) is issued.

(3) The notice must state the amount required to be paid by the person on whom the notice is served.

(4) The notice has effect—

(*a*) for the purposes of the recovery from that person of the amount required to be paid and of interest on that amount, and

(*b*) for the purposes of appeals,

as if it were a notice of determination and that amount were an amount of stamp duty reserve tax due from that person.

(5) A person who has paid an amount in pursuance of a notice under this paragraph may recover that amount from the transferee company.

(6) A payment in pursuance of a notice under this paragraph is not allowed as a deduction in computing any income, profits or losses for any tax purposes.

Power to require information

10—(1) The Commissioners may by notice require any person to furnish them within such time, not being less than 30 days, as may be specified in the notice with such information (including documents or records) as the Commissioners may reasonably require for the purposes of section 111 or this Schedule.

(2) [A relevant lawyer][1] shall not be obliged in pursuance of a notice under this paragraph to disclose, without his client's consent, any information with respect to which a claim to professional privilege could be maintained.

[(2A) "Relevant lawyer" means a barrister, advocate, solicitor or other legal representative communications with whom may be the subject of a claim to professional privilege.][1]

(3) In section 98(5) of the Taxes Management Act 1970 (c 9) (penalty for failure to comply with notice to provide information), in the first column of the Table, at the appropriate place insert "paragraph 10 of Schedule 34 to the Finance Act 2002".

Amendments—[1] In sub-para (2), words substituted for words "A barrister or solicitor", and sub-para (2A) inserted, by the Legal Services Act 2007 s 208, Sch 21 paras 134, 135 with effect from 1 January 2010 (by virtue of SI SI 2009/3250, art 2(*h*)).

Supplementary

11 Section 111 and this Schedule shall be construed as one with the Stamp Act 1891 (c 39).

SCHEDULE 35

STAMP DUTY: WITHDRAWAL OF RELIEF FOR COMPANY ACQUISITIONS: SUPPLEMENTARY PROVISIONS

Section 113

Introduction

1—(1) The provisions of this Schedule supplement section 113 (withdrawal of relief under section 76 of the Finance Act 1986 (c 41)).

(2) Expressions used in this Schedule that are defined for the purposes of that section have the same meaning in this Schedule.

Change of control due to exempt transfer

2 Section 113 does not apply by reason of control of the acquiring company changing as a result of any of the transactions listed in the Schedule to the Stamp Duty (Exempt Instruments) Regulations 1987 (SI 1987/516).

Change of control due to intra-group transfer

3—(1) Section 113 does not apply by reason of control of the acquiring company changing as a result of a transfer of shares ("the intra-group transfer") in relation to which group relief applies.

(2) In this paragraph—

(*a*) "group relief" means relief under section 42 of the Finance Act 1930 (c 28) or section 11 of the Finance Act (Northern Ireland) 1954 (c 23 (NI)) (transfer of property between associated bodies corporate); and (*b*) references to a transfer in relation to which group relief applies are to a transfer such that an instrument effecting the transfer is exempt from stamp duty by virtue of either of the group relief provisions.

(3) But if before the end of the period of two years beginning with the date on which the relevant instrument was executed—

(*a*) a company ("company B") holding shares in the acquiring company to which the intra-group share transfer related, or that are derived from shares to which that instrument related, ceases to be a member of the same group as the company referred to in section 76 as the target company ("company C"), and

(*b*) the acquiring company [or a relevant associated company][1], at that time, holds an estate or interest in land—

(i) that was transferred [to the acquiring company][1] by the relevant instrument, or

(ii) that is derived from an estate or interest so transferred,

[and that has not subsequently been transferred at market value by a duly stamped instrument on which ad valorem duty was paid and in respect of which section 76 relief was not claimed,][1]

the following provisions apply.

(4) In those circumstances—

(*a*) section 76 relief in relation to the relevant instrument (or an appropriate proportion of that relief) is withdrawn, and

(*b*) the additional stamp duty that would have been paid on stamping the relevant instrument but for that relief if the land in question had been transferred by that instrument at market value, or an appropriate proportion of that amount, is payable by the acquiring company within 30 days after company B ceases to be a member of the same group as company C.

(5) In this paragraph—

(*a*) "company" includes any body corporate; and

(*b*) references to a company being in the same group as another company are to the companies being associated bodies corporate within the meaning of the relevant group relief provision.

Cross references—FA 2003 Sch 19 para 6(3) (the references in sub-para (3) above to a transfer at market value by a duly stamped instrument on which ad valorem duty was paid and in respect of which section 76 relief was not claimed shall be read, on or after the implementation date, as including a reference to a transfer at market value by a chargeable transaction on which stamp duty land tax was chargeable and in respect of which relief under FA 2003 Sch 7 Pt 2 was available but was not claimed).

Amendments—[1] In sub-para (3)(*b*), words inserted, and words substituted for the words "to it" and "and that was not subsequently transferred to it by a duly stamped instrument on which *ad valorem* duty was paid and in relation to which section 76 relief was not claimed,", by FA 2003 s 127(6)–(9) with effect for instruments executed after 14 April 2003.

FA 2003 s 127 shall be deemed to have come into force on 15 April 2003.

FA 2003 s 127 does not apply to an instrument giving effect to a contract made on or before 9 April 2003, unless—

(a) the instrument is made in consequence of the exercise after that date of any option, right of pre-emption or similar right, or

(b) the instrument transfers the property in question to, or vests it in, a person other than the purchaser under the contract because of an assignment (or, in Scotland, assignation) or further contract made after that date: FA 2003 s 127(8).

Change of control due to exempt share acquisition

4—(1) Section 113 does not apply by reason of control of the acquiring company changing as a result of a transfer of shares ("the exempt transfer") to another company ("the parent company") in relation to which share acquisition relief applies.

(2) For this purpose—

(*a*) "share acquisition relief" means relief under section 77 of the Finance Act 1986 (c 41); and

(*b*) references to a transfer in relation to which such relief applies are to a transfer such that an instrument effecting the transfer is exempt from stamp duty by virtue of that provision.

(3) But if before the end of the period of two years beginning with the date on which the relevant instrument was executed—

(*a*) control of the parent company changes at a time when that company holds any shares transferred to it by the exempt transfer, or any shares derived from shares so transferred, and

(*b*) the acquiring company [or a relevant associated company][1], at that time, holds an estate or interest in land—

(i) that was transferred [to the acquiring company][1] by the relevant instrument, or

(ii) that is derived from an estate or interest so transferred,

[and that has not subsequently been transferred at market value by a duly stamped instrument on which ad valorem duty was paid and in respect of which section 76 relief was not claimed,][1]

the following provisions apply.

(4) In those circumstances—

(*a*) section 76 relief in relation to the relevant instrument (or an appropriate proportion of that relief) is withdrawn, and

(*b*) the additional stamp duty that would have been paid on stamping the relevant instrument but for that relief if the land in question had been transferred by that instrument at market value, or an appropriate proportion of that additional duty, is payable by the acquiring company within 30 days after control of the parent company changed.

Cross references—FA 2003 Sch 19 para 6(3) (the references in sub-para (3) above to a transfer at market value by a duly stamped instrument on which ad valorem duty was paid and in respect of which section 76 relief was not claimed shall be read, on or after the implementation date, as including a reference to a transfer at market value by a chargeable transaction on which stamp duty land tax was chargeable and in respect of which relief under FA 2003 Sch 7 Pt 2 was available but was not claimed).

Amendments—[1] In sub-para (3)(*b*), words inserted, and words substituted for the words "to it" and "and that was not subsequently transferred to it by a duly stamped instrument on which *ad valorem* duty was paid and in relation to which section 76 relief was not claimed,", by FA 2003 s 127(6)–(9) with effect for instruments executed after 14 April 2003.

FA 2003 s 127 shall be deemed to have come into force on 15 April 2003.

FA 2003 s 127 does not apply to an instrument giving effect to a contract made on or before 9 April 2003, unless—

(a) the instrument is made in consequence of the exercise after that date of any option, right of pre-emption or similar right, or

(b) the instrument transfers the property in question to, or vests it in, a person other than the purchaser under the contract because of an assignment (or, in Scotland, assignation) or further contract made after that date: FA 2003 s 127(8).

Change of control due to interest of loan creditor

5—(1) Section 113 does not apply by reason of control of the acquiring company changing as a result of a loan creditor becoming, or ceasing to be, treated as having control of the company if the other persons who were previously treated as controlling the company continue to be so treated.

(2) In sub-paragraph (1) "loan creditor" has the meaning given by [section 453 of the Corporation Tax Act 2010][1].

Amendments—[1] In sub-para (2), words substituted for words "section 417(7) to (9) of the Taxes Act 1988" by CTA 2010 s 1177, Sch 1 paras 368, 376(a). CTA 2010 has effect for corporation tax purposes for accounting periods ending on or after 1 April 2010, and for income and capital gains tax purposes for the tax year 2010–11 and subsequent tax years

Interest

6—(1) If any duty payable under section 113 or this Schedule is not paid within the period of 30 days within which payment is to be made, interest is payable on the amount remaining unpaid.

(2) The provisions of section 15A(3) to (5) of the Stamp Act 1891 (c 39) (rate of interest on unpaid duty, etc) apply in relation to interest under this paragraph.

Duty of acquiring company to notify particulars

7—(1) The acquiring company shall, within the period of 30 days within which payment is to be made, notify the Commissioners of—

(*a*) the date on which the event occurred by reason of which it is liable to make a payment of duty under section 113 or this Schedule,

(*b*) the relevant land held by it at that time,

(*c*) the nature of the relevant instrument, the date on which it was executed, the parties to the instrument and the date on which the instrument was stamped,

(*d*) the market value of the land transferred to it by the relevant instrument at the date it was executed, and

(*e*) the amount of duty and interest payable by it.

(2) In sub-paragraph (1)(*b*) the "relevant land" held by the acquiring company means every estate or interest to in relation to which section 113(1)(*c*) applies.

(3) In section 98(5) of the Taxes Management Act 1970 (penalty for failure to provide information), in the second column of the Table, at the appropriate place insert "paragraph 6 of Schedule 35 to the Finance Act 2002".

Determination, collection and recovery of duty and interest

8 The provisions of regulations under section 98 of the Finance Act 1986 (c 41) (stamp duty reserve tax: administration etc), and the provisions of the Taxes Management Act 1970 (c 9) applied by those regulations, have effect with the necessary modifications in relation to—

(*a*) the determination by the Commissioners of the duty payable under section 113 or this Schedule, or of the interest payable thereon,

(*b*) appeals against any such determination, and

(*c*) the collection and recovery of any such duty or interest,

as if it were an amount of stamp duty reserve tax.

Recovery of section 76 relief from another group company or controlling director

9—(1) This paragraph applies where—

(*a*) an amount is payable under section 113 or this Schedule by the acquiring company,

(*b*) a notice of determination of the amount payable has been issued by the Inland Revenue, and

(*c*) the whole or part of that amount is unpaid six months after the date on which it became payable.

(2) The following persons may, by notice under paragraph 9, be required to pay the unpaid amount—

(*a*) any company that at any relevant time was a member of the same group as the acquiring company and was above it in the group structure, and

(*b*) any person who at any relevant time was a controlling director of the acquiring company or of a company having control of the acquiring company.

(3) For this purpose a "relevant time" means any time between the execution of the relevant instrument and the change of control by virtue of which the liability to pay the amount arises.

(4) In this paragraph—

(*a*) references to companies being in the same group are to one company having control of the other or both companies being under the control of the same person or persons;

(*b*) a company is "above" another company in a group structure if it controls—

(i) that company, or

(ii) another company that is above that company in the group structure;

(*c*) ["director", in relation to a company, has the meaning given by section 67(1) and (2) of the Income Tax (Earnings and Pensions) Act 2003 and includes any person falling within section 452(1) of the Corporation Tax Act 2010;][1] and

(*d*) "controlling director", in relation to a company, means a director of the company who has control of it.

Amendments—[1] In sub-para (4)(*c*) definition of "director" substituted by CTA 2010 s 1177, Sch 1 paras 368, 376(b). CTA 2010 has effect for corporation tax purposes for accounting periods ending on or after 1 April 2010, and for income and capital gains tax purposes for the tax year 2010–11 and subsequent tax years. Definition of "director" previously read as follows—

""director", in relation to a company, has the meaning given by section 168(8) of the Taxes Act 1988 (read with subsection (9) of that section) and includes any person falling within section 417(5) of that Act (read with subsection (6) of that section);"

Recovery of section 76 relief from another group company or controlling director: procedure and time limit

10—(1) The Commissioners may serve a notice on a person within paragraph 9(2) requiring him, within 30 days of the service of the notice, to pay the amount that remains unpaid.

(2) A notice under this paragraph must be served before the end of the period of three years beginning with the date on the notice of determination mentioned in paragraph 9(1)(*b*) is issued.

(3) The notice must state the amount required to be paid by the person on whom the notice is served.

(4) The notice has effect—

(*a*) for the purposes of the recovery from that person of the amount required to be paid and of interest on that amount, and

(*b*) for the purposes of appeals,

as if it were a notice of determination and that amount were an amount of stamp duty reserve tax due from that person.

(5) A person who has paid an amount in pursuance of a notice under this paragraph may recover that amount from the acquiring company.

(6) A payment in pursuance of a notice under this paragraph is not allowed as a deduction in computing any income, profits or losses for any tax purposes.

Power to require information

11—(1) The Commissioners may by notice require any person to furnish them within such time, not being less than 30 days, as may be specified in the notice with such information (including documents or records) as the Commissioners may reasonably require for the purposes of section 113 or this Schedule.

(2) [A relevant lawyer][1] shall not be obliged in pursuance of a notice under this paragraph to disclose, without his client's consent, any information with respect to which a claim to professional privilege could be maintained.

[(2A) "Relevant lawyer" means a barrister, advocate, solicitor or other legal representative communications with whom may be the subject of a claim to professional privilege.][1]

(3) In section 98(5) of the Taxes Management Act 1970 (c 9) (penalty for failure to comply with notice to provide information), in the first column of the Table, at the appropriate place insert "paragraph 11 of Schedule 35 to the Finance Act 2002".

Amendments—[1] In sub-para (2), words substituted for words "A barrister or solicitor", and sub-para (2A) inserted, by the Legal Services Act 2007 s 208, Sch 21 paras 134, 136 with effect from 1 January 2010 (by virtue of SI 2009/3250, art 2(*h*)).

Supplementary

12 Section 113 and this Schedule shall be construed as one with the Stamp Act 1891 (c 39).

SCHEDULE 36

STAMP DUTY: CONTRACTS CHARGEABLE AS CONVEYANCES: SUPPLEMENTARY PROVISIONS

Section 115(7)

PART 1
SUBSALES

Introduction

1 This Part of this Schedule has effect for affording relief from duty under section 115 (contracts chargeable as conveyances) on a subsale.

Meaning of "subsale"

2 For the purposes of this Schedule there is a subsale—

(*a*) where the purchaser under a contract or agreement for the sale of an estate or interest in land in the United Kingdom ("the original sale"), without having obtained a conveyance of the property contracted to be sold, contracts to sell the whole or part of the property to another person, or

(*b*) where the sub-purchaser under a subsale of an estate or interest in land in the United Kingdom, without having obtained a conveyance of the property contracted to be sold, contracts to sell to another person the whole or part of the property contracted to be sold by the original sale,

so as to entitle that person to call for a conveyance from the original seller.

Relief where duty paid on original sale or earlier subsale

3—(1) Where duty under section 115 has been paid—

(*a*) on the original sale, or

(*b*) on an intervening subsale,

duty under that section on a subsale, or subsequent subsale, is chargeable only in respect of the amount (if any) by which the chargeable consideration on that transaction exceeds the chargeable consideration on the earlier transaction.

(2) If there is more than one such earlier transaction on which duty has been paid, the reference in sub-paragraph (1) to the chargeable consideration on the earlier transaction shall be read as a reference to the higher or highest amount of chargeable consideration on which duty has been paid.

(3) If the subsale does not relate to the whole of the property to which the earlier transaction related, the references in sub-paragraphs (1) and (2) to the chargeable consideration on an earlier transaction shall be read as references to an appropriate proportion of that consideration.

(4) What is an appropriate proportion shall be determined on a just and reasonable basis having regard to the subject matter of the subsale and of the earlier transaction.

(5) For the purposes of this paragraph the chargeable consideration on a transaction is the consideration that falls to be brought into account in determining the duty chargeable on it.

(6) Where under this paragraph duty on a subsale is chargeable in respect of part only of the consideration for the subsale, it is chargeable at the rate that would be applicable if the whole of the chargeable consideration on the subsale were taken into account

PART 2
SUBSEQUENT [TRANSFER][1]

Amendments—[1] The word "transfer" substituted for the words "conveyance or transfer" in enactments relating to stamp duty by FA 2003 Sch 20 para 3.

Introduction

4—(1) This Part of this Schedule has effect for affording relief where *ad valorem* duty is chargeable both—

(*a*) under section 115 on a contract or agreement ("the original sale"), and

(*b*) on a subsequent [transfer][1] by the original seller to the purchaser, or a sub-purchaser, in conformity with that contract or agreement.

(2) References in this Part to the purchaser under the original sale, or a sub-purchaser under a subsale, include a person by whom the rights of the purchaser, or a sub-purchaser, are exercisable by virtue of any assignment (in Scotland, assignation) or agreement (other than a subsale).

Amendments—[1] The word "transfer" substituted for the words "conveyance or transfer" in enactments relating to stamp duty by FA 2003 Sch 20 para 3.

[Transfer][1] of property contracted to be sold

5—(1) Where the original seller conveys the whole of the property contracted to be sold—

(*a*) to the purchaser, or

(*b*) to a sub-purchaser in circumstances in which section 58(4) of the Stamp Act 1891 (c 39) applies (conveyance chargeable only on consideration moving from sub-purchaser),

the [transfer][1] is chargeable with duty only to the extent (if any) that the ad valorem duty chargeable on it (apart from this sub-paragraph) exceeds the duty paid under section 115 on the original sale together with the amount of any such duty paid on an intervening subsale.

(2) Where—

(*a*) the original seller conveys the property contracted to be sold to different sub-purchasers in parts or parcels, and

(*b*) section 58(5) of the Stamp Act 1891 applies (conveyance chargeable only on consideration moving from sub-purchaser),

the [transfer][1] of each part or parcel is chargeable with duty only to the extent (if any) that the ad valorem duty chargeable on it (apart from this sub-paragraph) exceeds an appropriate proportion of the ad valorem duty paid on the original sale together with an appropriate proportion of any such duty paid on an intervening subsale.

(3) What is an appropriate proportion shall be determined on a just and reasonable basis having regard to the subject matter of the [transfer][1] and of the earlier transaction.

(4) Where sub-paragraph (1) or (2) applies to reduce or extinguish the duty payable on a [transfer][1], the Commissioners shall, upon application and upon production of the earlier instrument or instruments, duly stamped, either—

(*a*) denote the payment of the whole of the *ad valorem* duty upon the [transfer][1], or

(*b*) transfer to the [transfer][1] the *ad valorem* duty paid on the earlier instrument or instruments.

Amendments—[1] The word "transfer" substituted for the words "conveyance or transfer" in enactments relating to stamp duty by FA 2003 Sch 20 para 3.

Repayment of duty in certain cases

6—(1) Where—

(*a*) duty is paid under section 115 on the original sale,

(*b*) one or more conveyances or transfers are executed in conformity with that contract or agreement so that the whole of the property contracted to be sold is duly conveyed to a purchaser or to one or more sub-purchasers,

(*c*) those conveyances or transfers are all duly stamped, and

(*d*) the aggregate amount of the duty that would have been paid on those conveyances or transfers but for duty having been previously paid on the original sale is less that the duty paid on the original sale,

the Commissioners shall repay the difference to the person by whom the duty was paid on the original sale.

(2) If duty has been paid under section 115 on one or more intervening subsales, sub-paragraph (1) has effect with the following modifications—

(*a*) the reference to duty having been paid on the original sale shall be read as a reference to duty having been paid either on the original sale or on an intervening subsale;

(*b*) the reference to the amount of duty paid on the original sale shall be read as a reference to the aggregate of the amounts paid on the original sale and any intervening subsales, and

(*c*) any repayment shall be apportioned among the persons by whom those amounts were paid.

(3) The apportionment mentioned in sub-paragraph (2)(*c*) shall be made on a just and reasonable basis having regard to the subject matter of the original sale and of the subsale or subsales in question.

PART 3
GENERAL SUPPLEMENTARY PROVISIONS

Construction of references to duty on transactions

7 Any reference in section 115 or this Schedule to duty chargeable or paid on a transaction is to duty chargeable or paid on the stamping of the instrument by which the transaction is effected.

Transactions relating to land in the UK and to other property

8—(1) Where a transaction relates both to land in the United Kingdom and to other property, section 115 and this Schedule apply as if there were separate transactions.
(2) Similarly, the reference in section 115(1)(*b*) to a series of transactions is to a series of transactions so far as relating to land in the United Kingdom.
(3) If, in a case where a transaction or series of transactions relates partly to land in the United Kingdom and partly to other property, the consideration is not apportioned in a manner that is just and reasonable, section 115 and this Schedule shall have effect as if the consideration had been apportioned in such a manner.

Person claiming relief to establish entitlement

9 It is for a person claiming any relief under this Schedule to prove to the satisfaction of the Commissioners that he is entitled to relief and in what amount.

Construction as one

10 Section 115 and this Schedule shall be construed as one with the Stamp Act 1891 (c 39).

SCHEDULE 37
STAMP DUTY: ABOLITION OF DUTY ON INSTRUMENTS RELATING TO GOODWILL: SUPPLEMENTARY PROVISIONS

Section 116(2)

Reduction of stamp duty where instrument partly relating to goodwill

1—(1) This paragraph applies where stamp duty under Part 1 of Schedule 13 to the Finance Act 1999 (c 16) ([transfer][1] on sale) is chargeable on an instrument that relates partly to goodwill and partly to property other than goodwill.
(2) In such a case—
(*a*) the consideration in respect of which duty would otherwise be charged shall be apportioned, on a just and reasonable basis, as between the goodwill and the other property, and
(*b*) the instrument shall be charged only in respect of the consideration attributed to the other property.
(3) This paragraph applies to instruments executed on or after 23rd April 2002.

Amendments—[1] The word "transfer" substituted for the words "conveyance or transfer" in enactments relating to stamp duty by FA 2003 Sch 20 para 3.

Apportionment of consideration for stamp duty purposes

2—(1) Where part of the property referred to in section 58(1) of the Stamp Act 1891 (c 39) (consideration to be apportioned between different instruments as parties think fit) consists of goodwill, that provision shall have effect as if "the parties think fit" read "is just and reasonable".
(2) Where—
(*a*) part of the property referred to in section 58(2) of the Stamp Act 1891 (property contracted to be purchased by two or more persons etc) consists of goodwill, and
(*b*) both or (as the case may be) all the relevant persons are connected with one another,
that provision shall have effect as if the words from "for distinct parts of the consideration" to the end of the subsection read ", the consideration shall be apportioned in such manner as is just and reasonable, so that a distinct consideration for each separate part or parcel is set forth in the conveyance relating thereto, and such conveyance is to be charged with ad valorem duty in respect of such distinct consideration.".
(3) In a case where sub-paragraph (1) or (2) applies and the consideration is apportioned in a manner that is not just and reasonable, the enactments relating to stamp duty shall have effect as if—
(*a*) the consideration had been apportioned in a manner that is just and reasonable, and
(*b*) the amount of any distinct consideration set forth in any conveyance relating to a separate part or parcel of property were such amount as is found by a just and reasonable apportionment (and not the amount actually set forth).
(4) For the purposes of sub-paragraph (2)—
(*a*) a person is a relevant person if he is a person by or for whom the property is contracted to be purchased;
(*b*) the question whether persons are connected with one another shall be determined in accordance with [section 1122 of the Corporation Tax Act 2010][1].
(5) This paragraph applies to instruments executed on or after 23rd April 2002.

Amendments—[1] In sub-para (4)(*b*) words substituted for words "section 839 of the Taxes Act 1988" by CTA 2010 s 1177, Sch 1 paras 368, 377. CTA 2010 has effect for corporation tax purposes for accounting periods ending on or after 1 April 2010, and for income and capital gains tax purposes for the tax year 2010–11 and subsequent tax years.

Certification of instruments for stamp duty purposes

3—(1) Goodwill shall be disregarded for the purposes of paragraph 6 of Schedule 13 to the Finance Act 1999 (c 19) (certification of instrument as not forming part of transaction or series of transactions exceeding specified amount).

(2) Any statement as mentioned in paragraph 6(1) of that Schedule shall be construed as leaving out of account any matter which is to be so disregarded.

(3) This paragraph applies to instruments executed on or after 23rd April 2002.

Acquisition under statute

4—(1) Section 12 of the Finance Act 1895 (c 16) (property vested by Act or purchased under statutory powers) does not require any person who is authorised to purchase any property as mentioned in that section after 23rd April 2002 to include any goodwill in the instrument of conveyance required by that section to be produced to the Commissioners.

(2) If the property consists wholly of goodwill no instrument of conveyance need be produced to the Commissioners under that section.

(3) This paragraph applies where the Act mentioned in that section, and by virtue of which property is vested or a person is authorised to purchase property, is passed after 23rd April 2002.

Interpretation

5 In this Schedule "the enactments relating to stamp duty" means the Stamp Act 1891 (c 39) and any enactment amending that Act or that is to be construed as one with that Act.

FINANCE ACT 2003

(2003 Chapter 14)

ARRANGEMENT OF SECTIONS

PART 4

STAMP DUTY LAND TAX

An Act to grant certain duties, to alter other duties, and to amend the law relating to the National Debt and the Public Revenue, and to make further provision in connection with finance.

[10 July 2003]

PART 4
STAMP DUTY LAND TAX

Introduction

42 The tax

(1) A tax (to be known as "stamp duty land tax") shall be charged in accordance with this Part on land transactions.

(2) The tax is chargeable—

(*a*) whether or not there is any instrument effecting the transaction,

(*b*) if there is such an instrument, whether or not it is executed in the United Kingdom, and

(*c*) whether or not any party to the transaction is present, or resident, in the United Kingdom.

(3) The tax is under the care and management of the Commissioners of Inland Revenue (referred to in this Part as "the Board").

Land transactions

43 Land transactions

(1) In this Part a "land transaction" means any acquisition of a chargeable interest.

As to the meaning of "chargeable interest" see section 48.

(2) Except as otherwise provided, this Part applies however the acquisition is effected, whether by act of the parties, by order of a court or other authority, by or under any statutory provision or by operation of law.

(3) For the purposes of this Part—

(*a*) the creation of a chargeable interest is—

(i) an acquisition by the person becoming entitled to the interest created, and

(ii) a disposal by the person whose interest or right is subject to the interest created;

(*b*) the surrender or release of a chargeable interest is—

(i) an acquisition of that interest by any person whose interest or right is benefitted or enlarged by the transaction, and

(ii) a disposal by the person ceasing to be entitled to that interest; . . . [2]

(*c*) the variation of a chargeable interest [(other than a lease)][1] is—

(i) an acquisition of a chargeable interest by the person benefitting from the variation, and

(ii) a disposal of a chargeable interest by the person whose interest is subject to or limited by the variation.

[(*d*) the variation of a lease is an acquisition and disposal of a chargeable interest only where—

[(i) it takes effect, or is treated for the purposes of this Part, as the grant of a new lease[, or

(ii) paragraph 15A of Schedule 17A (reduction of rent or term) applies][3].][1]

(4) References in this Part to the "purchaser" and "vendor", in relation to a land transaction, are to the person acquiring and the person disposing of the subject-matter of the transaction.

These expressions apply even if there is no consideration given for the transaction.

(5) A person is not treated as a purchaser unless he has given consideration for, or is a party to, the transaction.

(6) References in this Part to the subject-matter of a land transaction are to the chargeable interest acquired (the "main subject-matter"), together with any interest or right appurtenant or pertaining to it that is acquired with it.

HMRC Manuals—Stamp Duty Land Tax Manual SDLTM00260 (definition of "land transaction")
SDLTM00270 (definition of "acquisition")

SDLTM00280 (definition of "chargeable interest")
SDLTM00290 (meaning of "main subject matter")
SDLTM00300 (method of acquisition of chargeable interest in unimportant)
SDLTM07100 (identity of the purchaser – with examples)
SDLTM07200 ("purchaser" includes a tenant where the interest in land is the grant of a lease)

Amendments—[1] In sub-s (3), words in para (c) inserted, and para (d) inserted, by FA 2004 s 296, Sch 39 paras 1, 2 with effect for any transaction of which the effective date is after 17 March 2004: FA 2004 Sch 39 para 13(3).

[2] Word "and" preceding sub-s (3)(c) repealed by FA 2004 s 326, Sch 42 Pt 4(2) with effect in accordance with FA 2004 Sch 39 para 13.

[3] Words in sub-s (3)(d) inserted by FA 2004 s 297(1), (2), (9) with effect for any transaction of which the effective date is on or after 22 July 2004.

44 Contract and conveyance

(1) This section applies where a contract for a land transaction is entered into under which the transaction is to be completed by a conveyance.

(2) A person is not regarded as entering into a land transaction by reason of entering into the contract, but the following provisions have effect.

(3) If the transaction is completed without previously having been substantially performed, the contract and the transaction effected on completion are treated as parts of a single land transaction. In this case the effective date of the transaction is the date of completion.

(4) If the contract is substantially performed without having been completed, the contract is treated as if it were itself the transaction provided for in the contract.

In this case the effective date of the transaction is when the contract is substantially performed.

(5) A contract is "substantially performed" when—

(*a*) the purchaser[, or a person connected with the purchaser,][1] takes possession of the whole, or substantially the whole, of the subject-matter of the contract, or

(*b*) a substantial amount of the consideration is paid or provided.

(6) For the purposes of subsection (5)(*a*)—

[(*a*) possession includes receipt of rents and profits or the right to receive them, and][1]

(*b*) it is immaterial whether [possession is taken][1] under the contract or under a licence or lease of a temporary character.

(7) For the purposes of subsection (5)(*b*) a substantial amount of the consideration is paid or provided—

(*a*) if none of the consideration is rent, where the whole or substantially the whole of the consideration is paid or provided;

(*b*) if the only consideration is rent, when the first payment of rent is made;

(*c*) if the consideration includes both rent and other consideration, when—

(i) the whole or substantially the whole of the consideration other than rent is paid or provided, or

(ii) the first payment of rent is made.

(8) Where subsection (4) applies and the contract is subsequently completed by a conveyance—

(*a*) both the contract and the transaction effected on completion are notifiable transactions, and

(*b*) tax is chargeable on the latter transaction to the extent (if any) that the amount of tax chargeable on it is greater than the amount of tax chargeable on the contract.

(9) Where subsection (4) applies and the contract is (to any extent) afterwards rescinded or annulled, or is for any other reason not carried into effect, the tax paid by virtue of that subsection shall (to that extent) be repaid by the Inland Revenue.

Repayment must be claimed by amendment of the land transaction return made in respect of the contract.

[(9A) Where—

(*a*) paragraph 12A of Schedule 17A applies (agreement for lease), or

(*b*) paragraph 19(3) to (6) of Schedule 17A applies (missives of let etc in Scotland),

it applies in place of subsections (4), (8) and (9).][2]

(10) In this section—

(*a*) references to completion are to completion of the land transaction proposed, between the same parties, in substantial conformity with the contract; and

(*b*) "contract" includes any agreement and "conveyance" includes any instrument.

[(11) [Section 1122 of the Corporation Tax Act 2010][3] (connected persons) has effect for the purposes of this section.][1]

HMRC Manuals—Stamp Duty Land Tax Manual, SDLTM07700 (contracts, completion and substantial performance)
SDLTM01080 (transfer of rights does not affect operation of s 44 in relation to the original contract)
SDLTM01090a (substantial performance of original contract – examples)
SDLTM07900, 07900a (contract substantially performed when purchaser takes possession – with examples)
SDLTM07950 ("substantially the whole" is usually an amount equal to or greater than 90% of the total consideration due under the contract)

Amendments—[1] Words in sub-s (5)(a) inserted, sub-s (6)(a) substituted, words in sub-s (6)(b) substituted, and sub-s (11) inserted, by FA 2004 s 296, Sch 39 para 15 with effect for any transaction of which the effective date (within the meaning of FA 2003 Pt 4) is on or after 22 July 2004: FA 2004 Sch 39 para 26. These amendments were previously made by the Stamp

Duty and Stamp Duty Land Tax (Variation of the Finance Act 2003) (No 2) Regulations, SI 2003/2816 regs 1, 2, Schedule para 1 with effect from 1 December 2003. Those regulations are revoked by FA 2004 Sch 39 para 14(2).

2 Sub-s (9A) inserted by FA 2004 s 296, Sch 39 paras 1, 3 with effect for any transaction of which the effective date is after 17 March 2004: FA 2004 Sch 39 para 13(3).

3 In sub-s (11) words "Section 839 of the Taxes Act 1988" substituted by CTA 2010 s 1177, Sch 1 paras 400, 401. CTA 2010 has effect for corporation tax purposes for accounting periods ending on or after 1 April 2010, and for income and capital gains tax purposes for the tax year 2010–11 and subsequent tax years.

[44A Contract providing for conveyance to third party

(1) This section applies where a contract is entered into under which a chargeable interest is to be conveyed by one party to the contract (A) at the direction or request of the other (B)—

(*a*) to a person (C) who is not a party to the contract, or

(*b*) either to such a person or to B.

(2) B is not regarded as entering into a land transaction by reason of entering into the contract, but the following provisions have effect.

(3) If the contract is substantially performed B is treated for the purposes of this Part as acquiring a chargeable interest, and accordingly as entering into a land transaction.

The effective date of the transaction is when the contract is substantially performed.

(4) Where the contract is (to any extent) afterwards rescinded or annulled, or is for any other reason not carried into effect, the tax paid by virtue of subsection (3) shall (to that extent) be repaid by the Inland Revenue.

Repayment must be claimed by amendment of the land transaction return made in respect of the contract.

(5) Subject to subsection (6), section 44 (contract and conveyance) does not apply (except so far as it defines "substantial performance") in relation to the contract.

(6) Where—

(*a*) this section applies by virtue of subsection (1)(*b*), and

(*b*) by reason of B's direction or request, A becomes obliged to convey a chargeable interest to B,

section 44 applies to that obligation as it applies to a contract for a land transaction that is to be completed by a conveyance.

(7) Section 44 applies in relation to any contract between B and C, in respect of the chargeable interest referred to in subsection (1) above, that is to be completed by a conveyance.

References to completion in that section, as it so applies, include references to conveyance by A to C of the subject matter of the contract between B and C.

(8) In this section "contract" includes any agreement and "conveyance" includes any instrument.][1]

Amendments—[1] This section inserted by FA 2004 s 296, Sch 39 paras 1, 4(1) with effect for any contract entered into after 17 March 2004: FA 2004 Sch 39 para 13(1).

45 Contract and conveyance: effect of transfer of rights

(1) This section applies where—

(*a*) a contract for a land transaction ("the original contract") is entered into under which the transaction is to be completed by a conveyance, . . . [2]

(*b*) there is an assignment, subsale or other transaction (relating to the whole or part of the subject-matter of the original contract) as a result of which a person other than the original purchaser becomes entitled to call for a conveyance to him[, and

(*c*) paragraph 12B of Schedule 17A (assignment of agreement for lease) does not apply.][1]

References in the following provisions of this section to a transfer of rights are to any such assignment, subsale or other transaction[, and references to the transferor and the transferee shall be read accordingly][1].

(2) The transferee is not regarded as entering into a land transaction by reason of the transfer of rights, but section 44 (contract and conveyance) has effect in accordance with the following provisions of this section.

(3) That section applies as if there were a contract for a land transaction (a "secondary contract") under which—

(*a*) the transferee is the purchaser, and

(*b*) the consideration for the transaction is—

(i) so much of the consideration under the original contract as is referable to the subject-matter of the transfer of rights and is to be given (directly or indirectly) by the transferee or a person connected with him, and

(ii) the consideration given for the transfer of rights.

The substantial performance or completion of the original contract at the same time as, and in connection with, the substantial performance or completion of the secondary contract shall be disregarded [except in a case where the secondary contract gives rise to a transaction that is exempt from charge by virtue of subsection (3) of section 73 (alternative property finance: land sold to financial institution and re-sold to individual)][3].

(4) Where there are successive transfers of rights, subsection (3) has effect in relation to each of them.

The substantial performance or completion of the secondary contract arising from an earlier transfer of rights at the same time as, and in connection with, the substantial performance or completion of the secondary contract arising from a subsequent transfer of rights shall be disregarded.

[(5) Where a transfer of rights relates to part only of the subject-matter of the original contract ("the relevant part")—

(*a*) subsection (8)(*b*) of section 44 (restriction of charge to tax on subsequent conveyance) has effect as if the reference to the amount of tax chargeable on that contract were a reference to an appropriate proportion of that amount, and

(*b*) a reference in the second sentence of subsection (3) above to the original contract, or a reference in subsection (4) above to the secondary contract arising from an earlier transfer of rights, is to that contract so far as relating to the relevant part (and that contract so far as not relating to the relevant part shall be treated as a separate contract).][1]

[(5A) In relation to a land transaction treated as taking place by virtue of subsection (3)—

(*a*) references in Schedule 7 (group relief) to the vendor shall be read as references to the vendor under the original contract;

(*b*) other references in this Part to the vendor shall be read, where the context permits, as referring to either the vendor under the original contract or the transferor.][1]

(6) [Section 1122 of the Corporation Tax Act 2010][4] (connected persons) applies for the purposes of subsection (3)(*b*)(i).

(7) In this section "contract" includes any agreement and "conveyance" includes any instrument.

HMRC Manuals—Stamp Duty Land Tax Manual, SDLTM01060 (transfer of rights to third party by sub-sale, assignment or other transaction)

SDLTM01060a (assignment or sub-sale – with examples)

SDLTM01090a (substantial performance of original contract – examples)

SDLTM01100a (series of transfers – example)

SDLTM01110 (transfer of part only – apportionment of original price)

SDLTM01110a (transfer of part only – example)

Amendments—[1] Sub-s (1)(c) inserted, and words in sub-s (1) inserted; sub-s (5) substituted; and sub-s (5A) inserted; by FA 2004 s 296, Sch 39 para 5(1)–(4) with effect for any transfer of rights occurring after 17 March 2004: FA 2004 Sch 39 para 13(2).

[2] Word "and" preceding sub-s (1)(b) repealed by FA 2004 s 326, Sch 42 Pt 4(2) with effect in accordance with FA 2004 Sch 39 para 13.

[3] Words in sub-s (3) inserted by F(No 2)A 2005 s 49, Sch 10 paras 1, 2 with effect in relation to any transaction of which the effective date is after 19 May 2005.

However, this amendment does not have effect—

(a) in relation to any transaction which is effected in pursuance of a contract entered into and substantially performed on or before the specified date (ie 16 March 2005), or

(b) subject to what follows below, in relation to any other transaction which is effected in pursuance of a contract entered into on or before the specified date (ie 16 March 2005).

The exclusion by para (*b*) above of transactions effected in pursuance of contracts entered into on or before the specified date does not apply—

(a) if there is any variation of the contract or assignment of rights under the contract after that date,

(b) if the transaction is effected in consequence of the exercise after that date of any option, right of pre-emption or similar right, or

(c) if after that date there is an assignment, subsale or other transaction (relating to the whole or part of the subject-matter of the contract) as a result of which a person other than the purchaser under the contract becomes entitled to call for a conveyance to him: F(No 2)A 2005 Sch 10 para 16(5)–(8).

[4] In sub-s (6) words "Section 839 of the Taxes Act 1988" substituted by CTA 2010 s 1177, Sch 1 paras 400, 402. CTA 2010 has effect for corporation tax purposes for accounting periods ending on or after 1 April 2010, and for income and capital gains tax purposes for the tax year 2010–11 and subsequent tax years.

[45A Contract providing for conveyance to third party: effect of transfer of rights

(1) This section applies where—

(*a*) a contract ("the original contract") is entered into under which a chargeable interest is to be conveyed by one party to the contract (A) at the direction or request of the other (B)—

(i) to a person (C) who is not a party to the contract, or

(ii) either to such a person or to B,

and

(*b*) there is an assignment or other transaction (relating to the whole or part of the subject-matter of the original contract) as a result of which a person (D) becomes entitled to exercise any of B's rights under the original contract in place of B.

References in the following provisions of this section to a transfer of rights are to any such assignment or other transaction.

(2) D is not regarded as entering into a land transaction by reason of the transfer of rights, but section 44A (contract providing for conveyance to third party) has effect in accordance with the following provisions of this section.

(3) That section applies as if—

(*a*) D had entered into a contract (a "secondary contract") in the same terms as the original contract except with D as a party instead of B, and

(b) the consideration due from D under the secondary contract were—
(i) so much of the consideration under the original contract as is referable to the subject-matter of the transfer of rights and is to be given (directly or indirectly) by D or a person connected with him, and
(ii) the consideration given for the transfer of rights.

(4) The substantial performance of the original contract shall be disregarded if—
(a) it occurs at the same time as, and in connection with, the substantial performance of the secondary contract, or
(b) it occurs after the transfer of rights.

(5) Where there are successive transfers of rights, subsection (3) has effect in relation to each of them.

(6) The substantial performance of the secondary contract arising from an earlier transfer of rights shall be disregarded if—
(a) it occurs at the same time as, and in connection with, the substantial performance of the secondary contract arising from a subsequent transfer of rights, or
(b) it occurs after that subsequent transfer.

(7) Where a transfer of rights relates to only part of the subject matter of the original contract, or to only some of the rights under that contract—
(a) a reference in subsection (3)(a) or (4) to the original contract, or a reference in subsection (6) to the secondary contract arising from an earlier transfer, is to that contract so far as relating to that part or those rights, and
(b) that contract so far as not relating to that part or those rights shall be treated as a separate contract.

(8) The effective date of a land transaction treated as entered into by virtue of subsection (3) is not earlier than the date of the transfer of rights.

(9) In relation to a such a transaction—
(a) references in Schedule 7 (group relief) to the vendor shall be read as references to A;
(b) other references in this Part to the vendor shall be read, where the context permits, as referring to either A or B.

(10) [Section 1122 of the Corporation Tax Act 2010][2] (connected persons) applies for the purposes of subsection (3)(b).

(11) In this section "contract" includes any agreement.][1]

Amendments—[1] This section inserted by FA 2004 s 296, Sch 39 para 5(1), (5) with effect for any transfer of rights occurring after 17 March 2004: FA 2004 Sch 39 para 13(2).

[2] In sub-s (10) words "Section 839 of the Taxes Act 1988" substituted by CTA 2010 s 1177, Sch 1 paras 400, 403. CTA 2010 has effect for corporation tax purposes for accounting periods ending on or after 1 April 2010, and for income and capital gains tax purposes for the tax year 2010–11 and subsequent tax years.

46 Options and rights of pre-emption

(1) The acquisition of—
(a) an option binding the grantor to enter into a land transaction, or
(b) a right of pre-emption preventing the grantor from entering into, or restricting the right of the grantor to enter into, a land transaction,

is a land transaction distinct from any land transaction resulting from the exercise of the option or right.

They may be "linked transactions" (see section 108).

(2) The reference in subsection (1)(a) to an option binding the grantor to enter into a land transaction includes an option requiring the grantor either to enter into a land transaction or to discharge his obligations under the option in some other way.

(3) The effective date of the transaction in the case of the acquisition of an option or right such as is mentioned in subsection (1) is when the option or right is acquired (as opposed to when it becomes exercisable).

(4) Nothing in this section applies to so much of an option or right of pre-emption as constitutes or forms part of a land transaction apart from this section.

HMRC Manuals—Stamp Duty Land Tax Manual, SDLTM01300 (charge to SDLT arises on acquisition of an option or right of pre-emption)
SDLTM01300a (options and rights of pre-emption – example)

47 Exchanges

(1) Where a land transaction is entered into by the purchaser (alone or jointly) wholly or partly in consideration of another land transaction being entered into by him (alone or jointly) as vendor, this Part applies in relation to each transaction as if each were distinct and separate from the other [(and they are not linked transactions within the meaning of section 108)][3].

(2) A transaction is treated for the purposes of this Part as entered into by the purchaser wholly or partly in consideration of another land transaction being entered into by him as vendor in any case where an obligation to give consideration for a land transaction that a person enters into as purchaser is met wholly or partly by way of that person entering into another transaction as vendor.

(3) As to the amount of the chargeable consideration in the case of exchanges and similar transactions, see—

paragraphs 5 and 6 of Schedule 4 (exchanges, partition etc) ...[1]

[paragraph 17 of that Schedule (arrangements involving public or educational bodies), *and*][2]

Amendments—[1] Words ", and section 58 (relief for certain exchanges of residential property)" repealed by FA 2004 s 326, Sch 42 Pt 4(2) with effect in accordance with FA 2004 Sch 39 para 26. This repeal was previously made by the Stamp Duty and Stamp Duty Land Tax (Variation of the Finance Act 2003) (No 2) Regulations, SI 2003/2816 regs 1, 2, Schedule para 3(5) with effect from 1 December 2003. Those regulations have been revoked by FA 2004 Sch 39 para 14(2).

[2] Words inserted by the SDLT (Amendment of Part 4 of the Finance Act 2003) Regulations, SI 2004/1069 regs 2, 3 with effect from 7 April 2004.

[3] Words in sub-s (1) inserted by FA 2007 s 76(1), (3) with effect in relation to a set of land transactions if the effective date of any of them is on or after 19 July 2007.

Chargeable interests, chargeable transactions and chargeable consideration

48 Chargeable interests

(1) In this Part "chargeable interest" means—

(*a*) an estate, interest, right or power in or over land in the United Kingdom, or

(*b*) the benefit of an obligation, restriction or condition affecting the value of any such estate, interest, right or power,

other than an exempt interest.

(2) The following are exempt interests—

(*a*) any security interest;

(*b*) a licence to use or occupy land;

(*c*) in England and Wales or Northern Ireland—

(i) a tenancy at will;

(ii) an advowson, franchise or manor.

(3) In subsection (2)—

(*a*) "security interest" means an interest or right (other than a rentcharge) held for the purpose of securing the payment of money or the performance of any other obligation; and

(*b*) "franchise" means a grant from the Crown such as the right to hold a market or fair, or the right to take tolls.

[(3A) Section 73B makes additional provision about exempt interests in relation to alternative finance arrangements.][3]

(4) In the application of this Part in Scotland the reference in subsection (3)(*a*) to a rentcharge shall be read as a reference to a feu duty or a payment mentioned in section 56(1) of the Abolition of Feudal Tenure etc (Scotland) Act 2000 (asp 5).

(5) The Treasury may by regulations provide that any other description of interest or right in relation to land in the United Kingdom is an exempt interest.

(6) The regulations may contain such supplementary, incidental and transitional provision as appears to the Treasury to be appropriate.

[(7) This section has effect subject to subsection (3) of section 44A (contract and conveyance to third party) [and to paragraph 15A of Schedule 17A (reduction of rent or term of lease)][2].][1]

HMRC Manuals—Stamp Duty Land Tax Manual, SDLTM00280 (definition of "chargeable interest")
SDLTM00320 (certain exempt interests in land)

Amendments—[1] Sub-s (7) inserted by FA 2004 s 296, Sch 39 paras 1, 4(2) with effect for any contract entered into after 17 March 2004: FA 2004 Sch 39 para 13(1).

[2] Words in sub-s (7) inserted by FA 2004 s 297(1), (3), (9) with effect for any transaction of which the effective date is on or after 22 July 2004.

[3] Sub-s (3A) inserted by FA 2007 s 75(2), (4). This amendment—

(a) has effect in relation to anything that would, but for the exemption provided by this section, be a land transaction with an effective date on or after 22 March 2007, and

(b) applies, in accordance with paragraph (*a*), to interests irrespective of the date of their creation.

49 Chargeable transactions

(1) A land transaction is a chargeable transaction if it is not a transaction that is exempt from charge.

(2) Schedule 3 provides for certain transactions to be exempt from charge.

Other transactions are exempt from charge under other provisions of this Part.

HMRC Manuals—Stamp Duty Land Tax Manual, SDLTM00520 (specific transactions that are exempt from SDLT)

50 Chargeable consideration

(1) Schedule 4 makes provision as to the chargeable consideration for a transaction.

(2) The Treasury may by regulations amend or repeal the provisions of this Part relating to chargeable consideration and make such other provision as appears to them appropriate with respect to—

(*a*) what is to count as chargeable consideration, or

(*b*) the determination of the amount of chargeable consideration.

(3) The regulations may make different provision in relation to different descriptions of transaction or consideration and different circumstances.

HMRC Manuals—Stamp Duty Land Tax Manual, SDLTM03700 (general meaning of chargeable consideration for SDLT purposes)

51 Contingent, uncertain or unascertained consideration

(1) Where the whole or part of the chargeable consideration for a transaction is contingent, the amount or value of the consideration shall be determined for the purposes of this Part on the assumption that the outcome of the contingency will be such that the consideration is payable or, as the case may be, does not cease to be payable.

(2) Where the whole or part of the chargeable consideration for a transaction is uncertain or unascertained, its amount or value shall be determined for the purposes of this Part on the basis of a reasonable estimate.

(3) In this Part—

"contingent", in relation to consideration, means—

(*a*) that it is to be paid or provided only if some uncertain future event occurs, or

(*b*) that it is to cease to be paid or provided if some uncertain future event occurs; and

"uncertain", in relation to consideration, means that its amount or value depends on uncertain future events.

(4) This section has effect subject to—

section 80 (adjustment where contingency ceases or consideration is ascertained), and

section 90 (application to defer payment in case of contingent or uncertain consideration).

[(5) This section applies in relation to chargeable consideration consisting of rent only to the extent that it is applied by paragraph 7 of Schedule 17A.][1]

HMRC Manuals—Stamp Duty Land Tax Manual, SDLTM05010a (contingent consideration calculation – example)

Amendments—[1] Sub-s (5) inserted by FA 2004 s 296, Sch 39 para 22(3) with effect for any transaction of which the effective date (within the meaning of FA 2003 Pt 4) is on or after 22 July 2004: FA 2004 Sch 39 para 26. These amendments were previously made by the Stamp Duty and Stamp Duty Land Tax (Variation of the Finance Act 2003) (No 2) Regulations, SI 2003/2816 regs 1, 2, Schedule para 8(3) with effect from 1 December 2003. Those regulations are revoked by FA 2004 Sch 39 para 14(2).

52 Annuities etc: chargeable consideration limited to twelve years' payments

(1) This section applies to so much of the chargeable consideration for a land transaction as consists of an annuity payable—

(*a*) for life, or

(*b*) in perpetuity, or

(*c*) for an indefinite period, or

(*d*) for a definite period exceeding twelve years.

(2) For the purposes of this Part the consideration to be taken into account is limited to twelve years' annual payments.

(3) Where the amount payable varies, or may vary, from year to year, the twelve highest annual payments shall be taken.

No account shall be taken for the purposes of this Schedule of any provision for adjustment of the amount payable in line with the retail price index.

(4) References in this section to annual payments are to payments in respect of each successive period of twelve months beginning with the effective date of the transaction.

(5) For the purposes of this section the amount or value of any payment shall be determined (if necessary) in accordance with section 51 (contingent, uncertain or unascertained consideration).

(6) References in this section to an annuity include any consideration (other than rent) that falls to be paid or provided periodically.

References to payment shall be read accordingly.

(7) Where this section applies—

(*a*) section 80 (adjustment where contingency ceases or consideration is ascertained) does not apply, and

(*b*) no application may be made under section 90 (application to defer payment in case of contingent or uncertain consideration).

HMRC Manuals—Stamp Duty Land Tax Manual, SDLTM06040 (no deferral or adjustment where chargeable consideration is in the form of an annuity)

53 Deemed market value where transaction involves connected company

[(1) This section applies where the purchaser is a company and—

(*a*) the vendor is connected with the purchaser, or

(*b*) some or all of the consideration for the transaction consists of the issue or transfer of shares in a company with which the vendor is connected.][1]

[(1A) The chargeable consideration for the transaction shall be taken to be not less than—

(*a*) the market value of the subject-matter of the transaction as at the effective date of the transaction, and

(*b*) if the acquisition is the grant of a lease at a rent, that rent.][1]

(2) [Section 1122 of the Corporation Tax Act 2010][2] (connected persons) has effect for the purposes of this section.

(3) In this section—

"company" means any body corporate;

"shares" includes stock and the reference to shares in a company includes a reference to securities issued by a company.

(4) Where this section applies paragraph 1 of Schedule 3 (exemption of transactions for which there is no chargeable consideration) does not apply.

But this section has effect subject to any other provision affording exemption or relief from stamp duty land tax.

(5) This section is subject to the exceptions provided for in section 54.

Amendments—[1] Sub-ss (1), (1A) substituted for sub-s (1) by FA 2004 s 297(1), (4), (9) with effect for any transaction of which the effective date is on or after 22 July 2004.

[2] In sub-s (2) words "Section 839 of the Taxes Act 1988" substituted by CTA 2010 s 1177, Sch 1 paras 400, 404. CTA 2010 has effect for corporation tax purposes for accounting periods ending on or after 1 April 2010, and for income and capital gains tax purposes for the tax year 2010–11 and subsequent tax years.

54 Exceptions from deemed market value rule

(1) Section 53 (chargeable consideration: transaction with connected company) does not apply in the following cases.

In the following provisions "the company" means the company that is the purchaser in relation to the transaction in question.

(2) Case 1 is where immediately after the transaction the company holds the property as trustee in the course of a business carried on by it that consists of or includes the management of trusts.

(3) Case 2 is where—

(*a*) immediately after the transaction the company holds the property as trustee, and

(*b*) the vendor is connected with the company only because of [section 1122(6) of the Corporation Tax Act 2010][1].

(4) Case 3 is where—

(*a*) the vendor is a company and the transaction is, or is part of, a distribution of the assets of that company (whether or not in connection with its winding up), and

(*b*) it is not the case that—

(i) the subject-matter of the transaction, or

(ii) an interest from which that interest is derived,

has, within the period of three years immediately preceding the effective date of the transaction, been the subject of a transaction in respect of which group relief was claimed by the vendor.

Cross references—FA 2003 Sch 19 para 7(3) (the reference in sub-s (4)(*b*) above to group relief having been claimed in respect of a transaction shall be read in relation to a transaction carried out before the implementation date as a reference to relief having been claimed under FA 1930 s 42, Finance Act (Northern Ireland) 1954 s 11, or FA 1995 s 151 in respect of stamp duty on the instrument by which the transaction was effected. For implementation date, see FA 2003 Sch 19 para 2).

Amendments—[1] In sub-s (3)(*b*) words "section 839(3) of the Taxes Act 1988" substituted by CTA 2010 s 1177, Sch 1 paras 400, 405. CTA 2010 has effect for corporation tax purposes for accounting periods ending on or after 1 April 2010, and for income and capital gains tax purposes for the tax year 2010–11 and subsequent tax years.

Amount of tax chargeable

55 Amount of tax chargeable: general

(1) The amount of tax chargeable in respect of a chargeable transaction is a percentage of the chargeable consideration for the transaction.

(2) That percentage is determined by reference to whether the relevant land—

(*a*) consists entirely of residential property (in which case Table A below applies), or

(*b*) consists of or includes land that is not residential property (in which case Table B below applies),

and, in either case, by reference to the amount of the relevant consideration.

Table A: Residential

Relevant consideration	*Percentage*
Not more than [£125,000][1]	0%
More than [£125,000][1] but not more than £250,000	1%
More than £250,000 but not more than £500,000	3%
More than £500,000	4%

Table B: Non-residential or mixed

Relevant consideration	*Percentage*
Not more than £150,000	0%

More than £150,000 but not more than £250,000	1%
More than £250,000 but not more than £500,000	3%
More than £500,000	4%

(3) For the purposes of subsection (2)—

(*a*) the relevant land is the land an interest in which is the main subject-matter of the transaction, and

(*b*) the relevant consideration is the chargeable consideration for the transaction, subject as follows.

(4) If the transaction in question is one of a number of linked transactions—

(*a*) the relevant land is any land an interest in which is the main subject-matter of any of those transactions, and

(*b*) the relevant consideration is the total of the chargeable consideration for all those transactions.

(5) This section has effect subject to—

section 74 ([exercise of collective rights by tenants of flats][2]), and

section 75 (crofting community right to buy),

(which provide for the rate of tax to be determined by reference to a fraction of the relevant consideration).

(6) In the case of a transaction for which the whole or part of the chargeable consideration is rent this section has effect subject to section 56 and Schedule 5 (amount of tax chargeable: rent).

(7) References in this Part to the "rate of tax" are to the percentage determined under this section.

Modification—Stamp Duty Land Tax (Zero-Carbon Homes Relief) Regulations, SI 2007/3437 reg 9 (disapplication of sub-s (4) in relation to the first acquisition of one or more zero-carbon homes where that acquisition is one of a number of linked transactions for the purposes of SI 2007/3437).

Regulations—The Stamp Duty Land Tax (Exemption of Certain Acquisitions of Residential Property) Regulations, SI 2008/2339 (exemption from stamp duty land tax for relevant acquisitions of land for chargeable consideration of not more than £175,000, with effect in relation to acquisitions made on or after 3 September 2008 but before 3 September 2009).

Amendments—[1] £125,000" substituted for "£120,000" by FA 2006 s 162(1), with effect in relation to any transaction of which the effective date (within the meaning of Part 4 of FA 2003) is after 22 March 2006. The figure of "£175,000" is substituted for "£125,000" (in both places) in Table A in relation to transactions with an effective date on or after 22 April 2009 but before 1 January 2010; FA 2009 s 10(1)(*a*).

[2] In sub-s (5), words substituted for words "collective enfranchisement by leaseholders" by FA 2009 s 80(1), (6) with effect in relation to transactions with an effective date on or after 22 April 2009.

Prospective amendments—In sub-s (2), in Table A, the following entry to be substituted for the final entry (cases where relevant consideration is more than £500,000 to be chargeable at 4%) by FA 2010 s 7 with effect in relation to any land transaction of which the effective date is on or after 6 April 2011—

"More than £500,000 but not more than £1,000,000	4%
More than £1,000,000	5%"

Note that this amendment does not have effect in relation to any transaction effected in pursuance of a contract entered into and substantially performed before 25 March 2010, or effected in pursuance of a contract entered into before that date and not excluded by FA 2010 s 7(4) (see FA 2010 s 7(3), (4)).

56 Amount of tax chargeable: rent

Schedule 5 provides for the calculation of the tax chargeable where the chargeable consideration for a transaction consists of or includes rent.

Reliefs

57 Disadvantaged areas relief

(1) Schedule 6 provides for relief in the case of transactions relating to land in a disadvantaged area.

(2) In that Schedule—

Part 1 defines "disadvantaged area",

Part 2 relates to transactions where the land to which the transaction relates is wholly situated in a disadvantaged area,

Part 3 relates to transactions where the land to which the transaction relates is partly situated in a disadvantaged area, and

Part 4 contains supplementary provisions.

HMRC Manuals—Stamp Duty Land Tax Manual, SDLTM00700 (claims for relief – cases where a land transaction return is required).

SDLTM20050–20100 (general explanation of relief).

Statement of Practice SP 1/04—(Disadvantaged areas relief, Stamp Office approach to borderline cases).

[57A Sale and leaseback arrangements

(1) The leaseback element of a sale and leaseback arrangement is exempt from charge if the qualifying conditions specified below are met.

(2) A "sale and leaseback" arrangement means an arrangement under which—

(*a*) A transfers or grants to B a major interest in land (the "sale"), and
(*b*) out of that interest B grants a lease to A (the "leaseback").

(3) The qualifying conditions are—
(*a*) that the sale transaction is entered into wholly or partly in consideration of the leaseback transaction being entered into,
(*b*) that the only other consideration (if any) for the sale is the payment of money or the assumption, satisfaction or release of a debt (or both),
(*c*) that the sale is not a transfer of rights within the meaning of section 45 (contract and conveyance: effect of transfer of rights) or 45A (contract providing for conveyance to third party: effect of transfer of rights), and
(*d*) where A and B are both bodies corporate at the effective date of the leaseback transaction, that they are not members of the same group for the purposes of group relief (see paragraph 1 of Schedule 7) at that date.

(4) In this section—
"debt" means an obligation, whether certain or contingent, to pay a sum of money either immediately or at a future date; and
"money" means money in sterling or another currency.][1]

HMRC Manuals—Stamp Duty Land Tax Manual, SDLTM00700 (claims for relief – cases where a land transaction return is required)

Amendments—[1] This section inserted by FA 2004 s 296, Sch 39 para 16 with effect for any transaction of which the effective date (within the meaning of FA 2003 Pt 4) is on or after 22 July 2004: FA 2004 Sch 39 para 26. This insertion was previously made by the Stamp Duty and Stamp Duty Land Tax (Variation of the Finance Act 2003) (No 2) Regulations, SI 2003/2816, regs 1, 2, Sch para 2 with effect from 1 December 2003. Those regulations are revoked by FA 2004 Sch 39 para 14(2) with effect for any transaction of which the effective date is on or after 22 July 2004.
FA 2004 Sch 39 para 6 amended the old version of this section (ie that inserted by SI 2003/2816) as follows: in sub-s (3), paras (*aa*), (*b*) are substituted for para (*b*), and paras (*c*), (*d*) are inserted; and sub-s (4) is repealed. These amendments have effect for any transaction of which the effective date is after 17 March 2004 and before 22 July 2004: FA 2004 Sch 39 para 13(3), (5).

[57AA First-time buyers

(1) A land transaction is exempt from charge under section 55 if—
(*a*) it is a relevant acquisition of a major interest in land,
(*b*) the land consists entirely of residential property,
(*c*) the relevant consideration (see section 55) for the transaction (other than any consisting of rent) is more than £125,000 but not more than £250,000,
(*d*) the purchaser, or (if more than one) each of the purchasers, is a first-time buyer who intends to occupy the residential property as the purchaser's only or main residence, and
(*e*) (subject to subsection (4)) the transaction is not one of a number of linked transactions.

(2) In this section "first-time buyer" means a person who—
(*a*) has not previously been a purchaser in relation to a relevant acquisition of a major interest in land which consisted of or included residential property,
(*b*) has not previously acquired an equivalent interest in such land under the law of a territory outside the United Kingdom,
(*c*) has not previously been, or been one of the persons who was, "the person" for the purposes of section 71A, 72, 72A or 73 in a case where the first transaction within the meaning of the section concerned was a relevant acquisition of a major interest in land which consisted of or included residential property, and
(*d*) would not have been such a person for those purposes in such a case if the provisions mentioned in paragraph (*c*) had been in force, and had had effect in the territory concerned, at all material times (subject, where required, to appropriate modifications).

(3) In this section "relevant acquisition of a major interest in land" means an acquisition of a major interest in land other than—
(*a*) the grant of a lease for a term of less than 21 years, or
(*b*) the assignment of a lease which has less than 21 years to run.

(4) Subsection (1)(*e*) does not prevent a transaction being exempt from charge under section 55 if each of the linked transactions is one the subject-matter of which is land, or an interest in or right over land, which falls within section 116(1)(*a*), (*b*) or (*c*) by reason of its connection with the same building.][1]

Amendments—[1] This section inserted by FA 2010 s 6(1), (2) with effect in relation to any land transaction of which the effective date is on or after 25 March 2010 but before 25 March 2012 (FA 2010 s 6(6)).

[58A Relief for certain acquisitions of residential property

Schedule 6A provides for relief in the case of certain acquisitions of residential property.][1]

HMRC Manuals—Stamp Duty Land Tax Manual SDLTM00700 (claims for relief – cases where a land transaction return is required).
SDLTM21000–21070 (explanation of scope of this relief).

Amendments—[1] This section substituted for sections 58, 59, by FA 2004 s 296, Sch 39 para 17(1) with effect for any transaction of which the effective date (within the meaning of FA 2003 Pt 4) is on or after 22 July 2004: FA 2004 Sch 39 para 26. The substitution was previously made by the Stamp Duty and Stamp Duty Land Tax (Variation of the Finance Act 2003) (No 2) Regulations, SI 2003/2816 regs 1, 2, Schedule para 3(1) with effect from 1 December 2003. Those regulations are revoked by FA 2004 Sch 39 para 14(2).

[58B Relief for new zero-carbon homes

(1) The Treasury may make regulations granting relief on the first acquisition of a dwelling which is a "zero-carbon home".

[(2) For the purposes of this section—

(*a*) a building, or a part of a building, is a dwelling if it is constructed for use as a single dwelling, and

(*b*) "first acquisition", in relation to a dwelling, means its acquisition when it has not previously been occupied.][2]

(3) For the purpose of subsection (2) land occupied or enjoyed with a dwelling as a garden or grounds is part of the dwelling.

(4) The regulations shall define "zero-carbon home" by reference to specified aspects of the energy efficiency of a building; for which purpose "energy efficiency" includes—

(*a*) consumption of energy,

(*b*) conservation of energy, and

(*c*) generation of energy.

(5) The relief may take the form of—

(*a*) exemption from charge, or

(*b*) a reduction in the amount of tax chargeable.

(6) Regulations under this section shall not have effect in relation to acquisitions on or after 1st October 2012.

(7) The Treasury may by order—

(*a*) substitute a later date for the date in subsection (6);

(*b*) make transitional provision, or provide savings, in connection with the effect of subsection (6).][1]

Regulations—Stamp Duty Land Tax (Zero-Carbon Homes Relief) Regulations, SI 2007/3437.

Amendments—[1] Sections 58B, 58C inserted by FA 2007 s 19(1) with effect from 19 July 2007.

[2] Sub-s (2) substituted by FA 2008 s 93(1), (2); this amendment is treated as always having had effect; and provision included in regulations by virtue of this amendment may be made so as to have effect in relation to acquisitions on or after 1 October 2007.

[58C Relief for new zero-carbon homes: supplemental

(1) Regulations under section 58B—

(*a*) shall include provision about the method of claiming relief (including documents or information to be provided), and

(*b*) in particular, shall include provision about the evidence to be adduced to show that a [dwelling][2] satisfies the definition of "zero-carbon home".

(2) Regulations made by virtue of subsection (1)(*b*) may, in particular—

(*a*) refer to a scheme or process established by or for the purposes of an enactment about building;

(*b*) establish or provide for the establishment of a scheme or process of certification;

(*c*) specify, or provide for the approval of, one or more schemes or processes for certifying energy efficiency.

[(*d*) provide for the charging of fees of a reasonable amount in respect of services provided as part of a scheme or process of certification.][3]

(3) In defining "zero-carbon home" regulations under section 58B may include requirements which may be satisfied in relation to [a dwelling][2] either—

(*a*) by features of the [building which, or part of which, constitutes the dwelling][2], or

(*b*) by other installations or utilities.

(4) Regulations under section 58B may modify the effect of section 108, or another provision of this Part about linked transactions, in relation to a set of transactions of which at least one is the first acquisition of a dwelling which is a zero-carbon home.

(5) In determining whether section 116(7) applies, and in the application of section 116(7), a transaction shall be disregarded if or in so far as it involves the first acquisition of a dwelling which is a zero-carbon home.

(6) Regulations under section 58B—

(*a*) may provide for relief to be wholly or partly withdrawn if a dwelling ceases to be a zero-carbon home, and

(*b*) may provide for the reduction or withholding of relief where a person acquires more than one zero-carbon home within a specified period.

(7) Regulations under section 58B may include provision for relief to be granted in respect of acquisitions occurring during a specified period before the regulations come into force.][1]

Regulations—Stamp Duty Land Tax (Zero-Carbon Homes Relief) Regulations, SI 2007/3437.

Amendments—[1] Sections 58B, 58C inserted by FA 2007 s 19(1) with effect from 19 July 2007.

[2] Words in sub-ss (1), (3) substituted by FA 2008 s 93(3), (4), (6); these amendments are treated as always having had effect; and provision included in regulations by virtue of these amendments may be made so as to have effect in relation to acquisitions on or after 1 October 2007.

[3] Sub-s (2)(d) inserted by FA 2008 s 93(3), (5) with effect from 21 July 2008.

60 Compulsory purchase facilitating development

(1) A compulsory purchase facilitating development is exempt from charge.

(2) In this section "compulsory purchase facilitating development" means—

(*a*) in relation to England and Wales or Scotland, the acquisition by a person of a chargeable interest in respect of which that person has made a compulsory purchase order for the purpose of facilitating development by another person;

(*b*) in relation to Northern Ireland, the acquisition by a person of a chargeable interest by means of a vesting order made for the purpose of facilitating development by a person other than the person who acquires the interest.

(3) For the purposes of subsection (2)(*a*) it does not matter how the acquisition is effected (so that provision applies where the acquisition is effected by agreement).

(4) In subsection (2)(*b*) a "vesting order" means an order made under any statutory provision to authorise the acquisition of land otherwise than by agreement.

(5) In this section "development"—

(*a*) in relation to England and Wales, has the same meaning as in the Town and Country Planning Act 1990 (c 8) (see section 55 of that Act);

(*b*) in relation to Scotland, has the same meaning as in the Town and Country Planning (Scotland) Act 1997 (c 8) (see section 26 of that Act); and

(*c*) in relation to Northern Ireland, has the same meaning as in the Planning (Northern Ireland) Order 1991 (1991/1220 (NI 11)) (see Article 11 of that Order).

HMRC Manuals—Stamp Duty Land Tax Manual, SDLTM00700 (claims for relief – cases where a land transaction return is required).

SDLTM22000–22020 (explanation of this relief).

61 Compliance with planning obligations

(1) A land transaction that is entered into in order to comply with a planning obligation or a modification of a planning obligation is exempt from charge if—

(*a*) the planning obligation or modification is enforceable against the vendor,

(*b*) the purchaser is a public authority, and

(*c*) the transaction takes place within the period of five years beginning with the date on which the planning obligation was entered into or modified.

(2) In this section—

(*a*) in relation to England and Wales—

"planning obligation" means either of the following—

(*a*) a planning obligation within the meaning of section 106 of the Town and Country Planning Act 1990 that is entered into in accordance with subsection (9) of that section, or

(*b*) a planning obligation within the meaning of section 299A of that Act that is entered into in accordance with subsection (2) of that section; and

"modification" of a planning obligation means modification as mentioned in section 106A(1) of that Act;

(*b*) in relation to Scotland, "planning obligation" means an agreement made under section 75 or section 246 of the Town and Country Planning (Scotland) Act 1997;

(*c*) in relation to Northern Ireland—

"planning obligation" means a planning agreement within the meaning of Article 40 of the Planning (Northern Ireland) Order 1991 (1991/1220 (NI 11)) that is entered into accordance with paragraph (10) of that Article, and

"modification" of a planning obligation means modification as mentioned in Article 40A(1) of that Order.

(3) The following are public authorities for the purposes of subsection (1)(*b*)—

Government

A Minister of the Crown or government department

The Scottish Ministers

A Northern Ireland department

[The Welsh Ministers, the First Minister for Wales and the Counsel General to the Welsh Assembly Government][2]

Local government: England

A county or district council constituted under section 2 of the Local Government Act 1972 (c 70)

The council of a London borough

The Common Council of the City of London

The Greater London Authority

Transport for London

The Council of the Isles of Scilly

Local government: Wales

A county or county borough council constituted under section 21 of the Local Government Act 1972

Local government: Scotland

A council constituted under section 2 of the Local Government etc (Scotland) Act 1994 (c 39)

Local government: Northern Ireland

A district council within the meaning of the Local Government Act (Northern Ireland) 1972 (c 9 (NI))

Health: England and Wales

A Strategic Health Authority [established under section 13 of the National Health Service Act 2006][1]

A Special Health Authority established under [section 28 of that Act or section 22 of the National Health Service (Wales) Act 2006][1]

A Primary Care Trust established under [section 18 of the National Health Service Act 2006][1]

A Local Health Board established under [section 11 of the National Health Service (Wales) Act 2006][1]

A National Health Service Trust established under [section 25 of the National Health Service Act 2006 or section 18 of the National Health Service (Wales) Act 2006][1]

Health: Scotland

The Common Services Agency established under section 10(1) of the National Health Service (Scotland) Act 1978 (c 29)

A Health Board established under section 2(1)(a) of that Act

A National Health Service Trust established under section 12A(1) of that Act

A Special Health Board established under section 2(1)(b) of that Act

Health: Northern Ireland

A Health and Social Services Board established under Article 16 of the Health and Personal Social Services (Northern Ireland) Order 1972 (SI 1972/1265 (NI 14))

A Health and Social Services Trust established under Article 10 of the Health and Personal Social Services (Northern Ireland) Order 1991 (SI 1991/194 (NI 1))

Other planning authorities

Any other authority that—

(*a*) is a local planning authority within the meaning of the Town and Country Planning Act 1990 (c 8), or

(*b*) is the planning authority for any of the purposes of the planning Acts within the meaning of the Town and Country Planning (Scotland) Act 1997 (c 8).

Prescribed persons

A person prescribed for the purposes of this section by Treasury order

HMRC Manuals—Stamp Duty Land Tax Manual, SDLTM00700 (claims for relief – cases where a land transaction return is required).

SDLTM22500–22550 (explanation of this relief).

Amendments—[1] In sub-s (3), in entries beginning "A Strategic Health Authority", "A Special Health Authority", "A Primary Care Trust", "A Local Health Board" and "A National Health Service Trust", words substituted by the National Health Service (Consequential Provisions) Act 2006 s 2, Sch 1 paras 232, 233(a)–(e) with effect from 1 March 2007 (National Health Service (Consequential Provisions) Act 2006 s 8(2)).

[2] In subs-s (3), entry "The Welsh Ministers, the First Minister for Wales and the Counsel General to the Welsh Assembly Government" substituted by the Government of Wales Act 2006 s 160(1), Sch 10 paras 62, 63 with effect from 25 May 2007, being the date on which the initial period ended (following the appointment of the First Minister) (Government of Wales Act 2006 ss 46, 161(4), (5))

62 Group relief and reconstruction or acquisition relief

(1) Schedule 7 provides for relief from stamp duty land tax.

(2) In that Schedule—

Part 1 makes provision for group relief,

Part 2 makes provision for reconstruction and acquisition reliefs.

(3) Any relief under that Schedule must be claimed in a land transaction return or an amendment of such a return.

HMRC Manuals—Stamp Duty Land Tax Manual SDLTM00700 (claims for relief – cases where a land transaction return is required).
SDLTM23000–23280 (explanation of group, reconstruction or acquisition relief).

63 Demutualisation of insurance company

(1) A land transaction is exempt from charge if it is entered into for the purposes of or in connection with a qualifying transfer of the whole or part of the business of a mutual insurance company ("the mutual") to a company that has share capital ("the acquiring company").

(2) A transfer is a qualifying transfer if—

(*a*) it is a transfer of business consisting of the effecting or carrying out of contracts of insurance and takes place under an insurance business transfer scheme, or

(*b*) it is a transfer of business of a general insurance company carried on through a permanent establishment in the United Kingdom and takes place in accordance with authorisation granted outside the United Kingdom for the purposes of—

(i) Article 14 of the life assurance Directive, or

(ii) Article 12 of the 3rd non-life insurance Directive,

and, in either case, the requirements of subsections (3) and (4) are met in relation to the shares of a company ("the issuing company") which is either the acquiring company or a company of which the acquiring company is a wholly-owned subsidiary.

(3) Shares in the issuing company must be offered, under the scheme, to at least 90% of the persons who are members of the mutual immediately before the transfer.

(4) Under the scheme all of the shares in the issuing company that will be in issue immediately after the transfer has been made, other than shares that are to be or have been issued pursuant to an offer to the public, must be offered to the persons who (at the time of the offer) are—

(*a*) members of the mutual,

(*b*) persons who are entitled to become members of the mutual, or

(*c*) employees, former employees or pensioners of—

(i) the mutual, or

(ii) a wholly-owned subsidiary of the mutual.

(5) The Treasury may by regulations—

(*a*) amend subsection (3) by substituting a lower percentage for the percentage mentioned there;

(*b*) provide that any or all of the references in subsections (3) and (4) to members shall be construed as references to members of a class specified in the regulations.

Regulations under paragraph (*b*) may make different provision for different cases.

(6) For the purposes of this section a company is the wholly-owned subsidiary of another company ("the parent") if the company has no members except the parent and the parent's wholly-owned subsidiaries or persons acting on behalf of the parent or the parent's wholly-owned subsidiaries.

(7) In this section—

"contract of insurance" has the meaning given by Article 3(1) of the Financial Services and Markets Act 2000 (Regulated Activities) Order 2001 (SI 2001/544);

"employee", in relation to a mutual insurance company or its wholly-owned subsidiary, includes any officer or director of the company or subsidiary and any other person taking part in the management of the affairs of the company or subsidiary;

"general insurance company" means a company that has permission under Part 4 of the Financial Services and Markets Act 2000 (c 8), or paragraph 15 of Schedule 3 to that Act (as a result of qualifying for authorisation under paragraph 12(1) of that Schedule), to effect or carry out contracts of insurance;

"insurance company" means a company that carries on the business of effecting or carrying out contracts of insurance;

"insurance business transfer scheme" has the same meaning as in Part 7 of the Financial Services and Markets Act 2000;

"the life assurance Directive" means the Council Directive of 5th November 2002 concerning life assurance (No 2002/83/EC);

"mutual insurance company" means an insurance company carrying on business without having any share capital;

"the 3rd non-life insurance Directive" means the Council Directive of 18th June 1992 on the co-ordination of laws, regulations and administrative provisions relating to direct insurance other than life insurance and amending Directives 73/239/EEC and 88/357/EEC (No 92/49/EEC);

"pensioner", in relation to a mutual insurance company or its wholly-owned subsidiary, means a person entitled (whether presently or prospectively) to a pension, lump sum, gratuity or other like benefit referable to the service of any person as an employee of the company or subsidiary.

HMRC Manuals—Stamp Duty Land Tax Manual, SDLTM00700 (claims for relief – cases where a land transaction return is required).
SDLTM23500–23520 (explanation of this relief).

64 Demutualisation of building society

A land transaction effected by section 97(6) or (7) of the Building Societies Act 1986 (c 53) (transfer of building society's business to a commercial company) is exempt from charge.

HMRC Manuals—Stamp Duty Land Tax Manual, SDLTM00700 (claims for relief – cases where a land transaction return is required).
SDLTM24000 (explanation of this relief).

64A Initial transfer of assets to trustees of unit trust scheme

. . . [1]

Amendments—[1] Section 64A repealed by FA 2006 s 166(2), s 178, Sch 26 Pt 7(3) with effect in relation to any land transaction of which the effective date is, or is after, 22 March 2006, subject to FA 2006 s 166(5), (6).

65 Incorporation of limited liability partnership

(1) A transaction by which a chargeable interest is transferred by a person ("the transferor") to a limited liability partnership in connection with its incorporation is exempt from charge if the following three conditions are met.

(2) The first condition is that the effective date of the transaction is not more than one year after the date of incorporation of the limited liability partnership.

(3) The second condition is that at the relevant time the transferor—

(*a*) is a partner in a partnership comprised of all the persons who are or are to be members of the limited liability partnership (and no-one else), or

(*b*) holds the interest transferred as nominee or bare trustee for one or more of the partners in such a partnership.

(4) The third condition is that—

(*a*) the proportions of the interest transferred to which the persons mentioned in subsection (3)(*a*) are entitled immediately after the transfer are the same as those to which they were entitled at the relevant time, or

(*b*) none of the differences in those proportions has arisen as part of a scheme or arrangement of which the main purpose, or one of the main purposes, is avoidance of liability to any duty or tax.

(5) In this section "the relevant time" means—

(*a*) where the transferor acquired the interest after the incorporation of the limited liability partnership, immediately after he acquired it, and

(*b*) in any other case, immediately before its incorporation.

(6) In this section "limited liability partnership" means a limited liability partnership formed under the Limited Liability Partnerships Act 2000 (c 12) or the Limited Liability Partnerships Act (Northern Ireland) 2002 (c 12 (NI)).

HMRC Manuals—Stamp Duty Land Tax Manual, SDLTM00700 (claims for relief – cases where a land transaction return is required).
SDLTM24500 (explanation of this relief).

66 Transfers involving public bodies

(1) A land transaction entered into on, or in consequence of, or in connection with, a reorganisation effected by or under a statutory provision is exempt from charge if the purchaser and vendor are both public bodies.

(2) The Treasury may by order provide that a land transaction that is not entered into as mentioned in subsection (1) is exempt from charge if—

(*a*) the transaction is effected by or under a prescribed statutory provision, and

(*b*) either the purchaser or the vendor is a public body.

In this subsection "prescribed" means prescribed in an order made under this subsection.

(3) A "reorganisation" means changes involving—

(*a*) the establishment, reform or abolition of one or more public bodies,

(*b*) the creation, alteration or abolition of functions to be discharged or discharged by one or more public bodies, or

(*c*) the transfer of functions from one public body to another.

(4) The following are public bodies for the purposes of this section—

Government, Parliament etc

A Minister of the Crown

The Scottish Ministers

A Northern Ireland department

[The Welsh Ministers, the First Minister for Wales and the Counsel General to the Welsh Assembly Government][2]

The Corporate Officer of the House of Lords

The Corporate Officer of the House of Commons

The Scottish Parliamentary Corporate Body

The Northern Ireland Assembly Commission

[The National Assembly for Wales Commission][2]

Local government: England

A county or district council constituted under section 2 of the Local Government Act 1972 (c 70)

The council of a London borough

The Greater London Authority

The Common Council of the City of London

The Council of the Isles of Scilly

Local government: Wales

A county or county borough council constituted under section 21 of the Local Government Act 1972

Local government: Scotland

A council constituted under section 2 of the Local Government etc (Scotland) Act 1994 (c 39)

Local government: Northern Ireland

A district council within the meaning of the Local Government Act (Northern Ireland) 1972 (c 9 (NI))

Health: England and Wales

A Strategic Health Authority [established under section 13 of the National Health Service Act 2006][3]

A Special Health Authority established under [section 28 of that Act or section 22 of the National Health Service (Wales) Act 2006][3]

A Primary Care Trust established under [section 18 of the National Health Service Act 2006][3]

A Local Health Board established under [section 11 of the National Health Service (Wales) Act 2006][3]

A National Health Service Trust established under [section 25 of the National Health Service Act 2006 or section 18 of the National Health Service (Wales) Act 2006][3]

Health: Scotland

The Common Services Agency established under section 10(1) of the National Health Service (Scotland) Act 1978 (c 29)

A Health Board established under section 2(1)(*a*) of that Act

A National Health Service Trust established under section 12A(1) of that Act

A Special Health Board established under section 2(1)(*b*) of that Act

Health: Northern Ireland

A Health and Social Services Board established under Article 16 of the Health and Personal Social Services (Northern Ireland) Order 1972 (SI 1972/1265 (NI 14))

A Health and Social Services Trust established under Article 10 of the Health and Personal Social Services (Northern Ireland) Order 1991 (SI 1991/194 (NI 1))

Other planning authorities

Any other authority that—

(*a*) is a local planning authority within the meaning of the Town and Country Planning Act 1990 (c 8), or

(*b*) is the planning authority for any of the purposes of the planning Acts within the meaning of the Town and Country Planning (Scotland) Act 1997 (c 8)

Statutory bodies

A body (other than a company) that is established by or under a statutory provision for the purpose of carrying out functions conferred on it by or under a statutory provision

Prescribed persons

A person prescribed for the purposes of this section by Treasury order

(5) In this section references to a public body include—

(*a*) a company in which all the shares are owned by such a body, and

(*b*) a wholly-owned subsidiary of such a company.

[(6) In this section "company" means a company as defined by section [1][4] of the Companies Act [2006][4].][1]

HMRC Manuals—Stamp Duty Land Tax Manual, SDLTM00700 (claims for relief – cases where a land transaction return is required).

SDLTM25000–25030 (explanation of this relief).

Orders—Finance Act 2003, Section 66 (Prescribed Persons) Order, SI 2005/83; Finance Act 2003, Section 66 (Prescribed Transactions) Order, SI 2005/645; Finance Act 2003, Section 66 (Prescribed Statutory Provisions) Order 2007, SI 2007/1385.

Amendments—[1] Sub-s (6) inserted by F(No 2)A 2005 s 49, Sch 10 paras 17, 18 with effect in relation to any transaction of which the effective date is on or after 20 July 2005: F(No 2)A 2005 Sch 10 para 22(1).

[2] In sub-s (4), entry beginning "The Welsh Ministers," substituted, and entry "The National Assembly for Wales Commission" inserted, by the Government of Wales Act 2006 s 160(1), Sch 10 paras 62, 64 with effect from 25 May 2007 being the date on which the initial period ended (following the appointment of the First Minister) (Government of Wales Act 2006 ss 46, 161(4), (5)).

[3] In sub-s (4), in entries beginning "A Strategic Health Authority", "A Special Health Authority", "A Primary Care Trust", "A Local Health Board" and "A National Health Service Trust", words substituted by the National Health Service (Consequential Provisions) Act 2006 s 2, Sch 1, paras 232, 234 with effect from 1 March 2007.

[4] In sub-s (6), word substituted for words "735(1)" and "1985", and words "or Article 3(1) of the Companies (Northern Ireland) Order 1986" repealed, by the Companies Act 2006 (Consequential Amendments) (Taxes and National Insurance) Order, SI 2009/1890 art 3(5)(a) with effect from 1 October 2009.

67 Transfer in consequence of reorganisation of parliamentary constituencies

(1) Where—

(*a*) an Order in Council is made under the Parliamentary Constituencies Act 1986 (c 56) (orders specifying new parliamentary constituencies), and

(*b*) an existing local constituency association transfers a chargeable interest to—

(i) a new association that is a successor to the existing association, or

(ii) a related body that as soon as practicable transfers the interest or right to a new association that is a successor to the existing association,

the transfer, or where paragraph (b)(ii) applies each of the transfers, is exempt from charge.

(2) In relation to any such order as is mentioned in subsection (1)(*a*)—

(*a*) "the date of the change" means the date on which the order comes into operation;

(*b*) "former parliamentary constituency" means an area that, for the purposes of parliamentary elections, was a constituency immediately before that date but is no longer such a constituency after that date;

(*c*) "new parliamentary constituency" means an area that, for the purposes of parliamentary elections, is such a constituency after that date but was not such a constituency immediately before that date.

(3) In relation to the date of the change—

(*a*) "existing local constituency association" means a local constituency association whose area was the same, or substantially the same, as the area of a former parliamentary constituency or two or more such constituencies, and

(*b*) "new association" means a local constituency association whose area is the same, or substantially the same, as that of a new parliamentary constituency or two or more such constituencies.

(4) In this section—

(*a*) "local constituency association" means an unincorporated association (whether described as an association, a branch or otherwise) whose primary purpose is to further the aims of a political party in an area that at any time is or was the same or substantially the same as the area of a parliamentary constituency or two or more parliamentary constituencies, and

(*b*) "related body", in relation to such an association, means a body (whether corporate or unincorporated) that is an organ of the political party concerned.

(5) For the purposes of this section a new association is a successor to an existing association if any part of the existing association's area is comprised in the new association's area.

HMRC Manuals—Stamp Duty Land Tax Manual, SDLTM00700 (claims for relief – cases where a land transaction return is required).

SDLTM25500–25510 (explanation of this relief).

68 Charities relief

(1) Schedule 8 provides for relief from stamp duty land tax for acquisitions by charities.

(2) Any relief under that Schedule must be claimed in a land transaction return or an amendment of such a return.

HMRC Manuals—Stamp Duty Land Tax Manual, SDLTM00700 (claims for relief – cases where a land transaction return is required).

SDLTM26000–26020 (explanation of this relief).

69 Acquisition by bodies established for national purposes

A land transaction is exempt from charge if the purchaser is any of the following—

(*a*) the Historic Buildings and Monuments Commission for England;

(*b*) the National Endowment for Science, Technology and the Arts;

(*c*) the Trustees of the British Museum;

(*d*) the Trustees of the National Heritage Memorial Fund;

(*e*) the Trustees of the Natural History Museum.

HMRC Manuals—Stamp Duty Land Tax Manual, SDLTM00700 (claims for relief – cases where a land transaction return is required).

SDLTM26500 (explanation of this relief).

70 Right to buy transactions, shared ownership leases etc

Schedule 9 makes provision for relief in the case of right to buy transactions, shared ownership leases and certain related transactions.

HMRC Manuals—Stamp Duty Land Tax Manual, SDLTM00700 (claims for relief – cases where a land transaction return is required).
SDLTM27000–27070 (explanation of this relief).

71 Certain acquisitions by registered social landlord

[(A1) A land transaction under which the purchaser is a profit-making registered provider of social housing is exempt from charge if the transaction is funded with the assistance of a public subsidy.][3]

(1) A land transaction under which the purchaser is a [relevant housing provider][4] is exempt from charge if—

(*a*) the [relevant housing provider][4] is controlled by its tenants,
(*b*) the vendor is a qualifying body, or
(*c*) the transaction is funded with the assistance of a public subsidy.

(2) The reference in subsection (1)(*a*) to a [relevant housing provider][4] "controlled by its tenants" is to a [relevant housing provider][4] the majority of whose board members are tenants occupying properties owned or managed by it.

"Board member", in relation to a [relevant housing provider][4], means—

(*a*) if it is a company, a director of the company,
(*b*) if it is a body corporate whose affairs are managed by its members, a member,
(*c*) if it is body of trustees, a trustee,
(*d*) if it is not within paragraphs (*a*) to (*c*), a member of the committee of management or other body to which is entrusted the direction of the affairs of the [relevant housing provider][4].

(3) In subsection (1)(*b*) "qualifying body" means—

(*a*) a [relevant housing provider][4],
(*b*) a housing action trust established under Part 3 of the Housing Act 1988 (c 50),
(*c*) a principal council within the meaning of the Local Government Act 1972 (c 70),
(*d*) the Common Council of the City of London,
(*e*) the Scottish Ministers,
(*f*) a council constituted under section 2 of the Local Government etc (Scotland) Act 1994 (c 39),
(*g*) Scottish Homes,
(*h*) the Department for Social Development in Northern Ireland, or
(*i*) the Northern Ireland Housing Executive.

(4) In [this section][3] "public subsidy" means any grant or other financial assistance—

(*a*) made or given by way of a distribution pursuant to section 25 of the National Lottery etc Act 1993 (c 39) (application of money by distributing bodies),
(*b*) under section 18 of the Housing Act 1996 (c 52) (social housing grants),
(*c*) under section 126 of the Housing Grants, Construction and Regeneration Act 1996 (c 53) (financial assistance for regeneration and development),
[(*ca*) under section 19 of the Housing and Regeneration Act 2008 (financial assistance by the Homes and Communities Agency),][2]
(*d*) under section 2 of the Housing (Scotland) Act 1988 (c 43) (general functions of the Scottish Ministers), or
(*e*) under Article 33 [or 33A][1] of the Housing (Northern Ireland) Order 1992 (SI 1992/1725 (NI 15)).

HMRC Manuals—Stamp Duty Land Tax Manual, SDLTM00700 (claims for relief – cases where a land transaction return is required).
SDLTM27500 (explanation of this relief).

Amendments—[1] Words in sub-s (4)(*e*) inserted by the Housing (Amendment) (Northern Ireland) Order, SI 2006/3337 art 3, Schedule para 8 with effect from 1 April 2007 (by virtue of SR 2007/37 art 2).

[2] Sub-s (4)(*ca*) inserted by the Housing and Regeneration Act 2008 s 56, Sch 8 para 79 with effect from 1 December 2008 (by virtue of SI 2008/3068, arts 1(2), 2(1)(w), (3)).

[3] Sub-s (A1) inserted and in sub-s (4) words substituted for words "subsection (1)(*c*)" by FA 2009 s 81(1)–(4) with effect in relation to transactions with an effective date on or after 21 July 2009.

[4] In sub-ss (1), (1A), (2), (3)(*a*) words substituted for words "registered social landlord" by the Housing and Regeneration Act 2008 s 277, Sch 9 paras 29, 30(1), (2) with effect from 1 April 2010 (by virtue of SI 2010/862 art 2 (subject to transitional provisions and savings in SI 2010/862 arts 2, 3, Schedule paras 1–4)).

[71A Alternative property finance: land sold to financial institution and leased to [person][2]

(1) This section applies where arrangements are entered into between [a person][2] and a financial institution under which—

(*a*) the institution purchases a major interest in land or an undivided share of a major interest in land ("the first transaction"),
(*b*) where the interest purchased is an undivided share, the major interest is held on trust for the institution and the [person][2] as beneficial tenants in common,

(*c*) the institution (or the person holding the land on trust as mentioned in paragraph (b)) grants to the [person][2] out of the major interest a lease (if the major interest is freehold) or a sub-lease (if the major interest is leasehold) ("the second transaction"), and
(*d*) the institution and the [person][2] enter into an agreement under which the [person][2] has a right to require the institution or its successor in title to transfer to the [person][2] (in one transaction or a series of transactions) the whole interest purchased by the institution under the first transaction.

(2) The first transaction is exempt from charge if the vendor is—
(*a*) the [person][2], or
(*b*) another financial institution by whom the interest was acquired under arrangements of the kind mentioned in subsection (1) entered into between it and the [person][2].

(3) The second transaction is exempt from charge if the provisions of this Part relating to the first transaction are complied with (including the payment of any tax chargeable).

(4) Any transfer to the [person][2] that results from the exercise of the right mentioned in subsection (1)(*d*) ("a further transaction") is exempt from charge if—
(*a*) the provisions of this Part relating to the first and second transactions are complied with, and
(*b*) at all times between the second transaction and the further transaction—
(i) the interest purchased under the first transaction is held by a financial institution so far as not transferred by a previous further transaction, and
(ii) the lease or sub-lease granted under the second transaction is held by the [person][2].

(5) The agreement mentioned in subsection (1)(*d*) is not to be treated—
(*a*) as substantially performed unless and until the whole interest purchased by the institution under the first transaction has been transferred (and accordingly section 44(5) does not apply), or
(*b*) as a distinct land transaction by virtue of section 46 (options and rights of pre-emption).

(6) . . . [2]

(7) A further transaction that is exempt from charge by virtue of subsection (4) is not a notifiable transaction unless the transaction involves the transfer to the [person][2] of the whole interest purchased by the institution under the first transaction, so far as not transferred by a previous further transaction.

(8) [In this section "financial institution" has the meaning given by section 46 of the Finance Act 2005 (alternative finance arrangements).][3]

(9) References in this section to [a person][2] shall be read, in relation to times after the death of the [person][2] concerned, as references to his personal representatives.

(10) This section does not apply in relation to land in Scotland.][1]

Amendments—[1] This section inserted by FA 2005 s 94, Sch 8 para 2 with effect in any case where the effective date (within the meaning of Part 4 of FA 2003) of the first transaction (within the meaning of this section) falls on or after 7 April 2005: FA 2005 Sch 8 para 7(1), (3).

[2] Word "person" substituted for word "individual" and words "a person" substituted for words "an individual" throughout the section, sub-s (6) repealed by FA 2006 s 168(1), (2), s 178, Sch 26 Pt 7(4) with effect in relation to arrangements in which the effective date (within the meaning of FA 2003 s 119(1)) of the first transaction (within the meaning of FA 2003 ss 71A–73) is on or after 19 July 2006.

[3] Sub-s (8) substituted by FA 2007 s 75(3), (4). This amendment—
(a) has effect in relation to anything that would, but for the exemption provided by this section, be a land transaction with an effective date on or after 22 March 2007, and
(b) applies, in accordance with paragraph (*a*), to interests irrespective of the date of their creation.

72 Alternative property finance [in Scotland][1]: land sold to financial institution and leased to [person][2]

(1) This section applies where arrangements are entered into between [a person][2] and a financial institution under which the institution—
(*a*) purchases a major interest in land ("the first transaction"),
(*b*) grants to the [person][2] out of that interest a lease (if the interest acquired is [the interest of the owner][1]) or a sub-lease (if the interest acquired is [the tenant's right over or interest in a property subject to a lease][1]) ("the second transaction"), and
(*c*) enters into an agreement under which the [person][2] has a right to require the institution . . . [1] to transfer the major interest purchased by the institution under the first transaction.

(2) The first transaction is exempt from charge if the vendor is—
(*a*) the [person][2], or
(*b*) another financial institution by whom the interest was acquired under arrangements of the kind mentioned in subsection (1) entered into between it and the [person][2].

(3) The second transaction is exempt from charge if the provisions of this Part relating to the first transaction are complied with (including the payment of any tax chargeable).

(4) A transfer to the [person][2] that results from the exercise of the right mentioned in subsection (1)(*c*) ("the third transaction") is exempt from charge if—
(*a*) the provisions of this Part relating to the first and second transactions are complied with, and
(*b*) at all times between the second and third transactions—

(i) the interest purchased under the first transaction is held by a financial institution, and

(ii) the lease or sub-lease granted under the second transaction is held by the [person][2].

(5) The agreement mentioned in subsection (1)(*c*) is not to be treated—

(*a*) as substantially performed unless and until the third transaction is entered into (and accordingly section 44(5) does not apply), or

(*b*) as a distinct land transaction by virtue of section 46 (options and rights of pre-emption).

(6) . . . [2]

(7) [In this section "financial institution" has the meaning given by section 46 of the Finance Act 2005 (alternative finance arrangements).][3]

(8) . . . [1]

(9) References in this section to [a person][2] shall be read, in relation to times after the death of the [person][2] concerned, as references to his personal representatives.

[(10) This section applies only in relation to land in Scotland.][1]

HMRC Manuals—Stamp Duty Land Tax Manual, SDLTM00700 (claims for relief – cases where a land transaction return is required).

SDLTM28000–28140 (explanation of this relief).

Amendments—[1] In sub-s (1)(b), words substituted; in sub-s (1)(c) words repealed; sub-s (8) repealed; sub-s (10) inserted; and words in heading inserted by FA 2005 ss 94, 104, Sch 8 para 3 and Sch 11 Pt 3(1) with effect in any case where the effective date (within the meaning of Part 4 of FA 2003) of the first transaction (within the meaning of FA 2003 s 71A) falls on or after 7 April 2005: FA 2005 Sch 8 para 7(1), (3).

[2] Word "person" substituted for word "individual" and words "a person" substituted for words "an individual" throughout the section, sub-s (6) repealed by FA 2006 s 168(1), (2), s 178, Sch 26 Pt 7(4) with effect in relation to arrangements in which the effective date (within the meaning of FA 2003 s 119(1)) of the first transaction (within the meaning of FA 2003 ss 71A–73) is on or after 19 July 2006.

[3] Sub-s (7) substituted by FA 2007 s 75(3), (4). This amendment—

(a) has effect in relation to anything that would, but for the exemption provided by this section, be a land transaction with an effective date on or after 22 March 2007, and

(b) applies, in accordance with paragraph (*a*), to interests irrespective of the date of their creation.

[72A Alternative property finance in Scotland: land sold to financial institution and [person][2] in common

(1) This section applies where arrangements are entered into between [a person][2] and a financial institution under which—

(*a*) the institution and the [person][2] purchase a major interest in land as owners in common ("the first transaction"),

(*b*) the institution and the [person][2] enter into an agreement under which the [person][2] has a right to occupy the land exclusively ("the second transaction"), and

(*c*) the institution and the [person][2] enter into an agreement under which the [person][2] has a right to require the institution to transfer to the [person][2] (in one transaction or a series of transactions) the whole interest purchased under the first transaction.

(2) The first transaction is exempt from charge if the vendor is—

(*a*) the [person][2], or

(*b*) another financial institution by whom the interest was acquired under arrangements of the kind mentioned in subsection (1) entered into between it and the [person][2].

(3) The second transaction is exempt from charge if the provisions of this Part relating to the first transaction are complied with (including the payment of any tax chargeable).

(4) Any transfer to the [person][2] that results from the exercise of the right mentioned in subsection (1)(*c*) ("a further transaction") is exempt from charge if—

(*a*) the provisions of this Part relating to the first transaction are complied with, and

(*b*) at all times between the first and the further transaction—

(i) the interest purchased under the first transaction is held by a financial institution and the [person][2] as owners in common, and

(ii) the land is occupied by the [person][2] under the agreement mentioned in subsection (1)(*b*).

(5) The agreement mentioned in subsection (1)(*c*) is not to be treated—

(*a*) as substantially performed unless and until the whole interest purchased by the institution under the first transaction has been transferred (and accordingly section 44(5) does not apply), or

(*b*) as a distinct land transaction by virtue of section 46 (options and rights of pre-emption).

(6) . . . [2]

(7) A further transaction that is exempt from charge by virtue of subsection (4) is not a notifiable transaction unless the transaction involves the transfer to the [person][2] of the whole interest purchased by the institution under the first transaction, so far as not transferred by a previous further transaction.

(8) [In this section "financial institution" has the meaning given by section 46 of the Finance Act 2005 (alternative finance arrangements).][3]

(9) References in this section to [a person][2] shall be read, in relation to times after the death of the [person][2] concerned, as references to his personal representatives.
(10) This section applies only in relation to land in Scotland.][1]

Amendments—[1] This section inserted by FA 2005 s 94, Sch 8 para 4 with effect in any case where the effective date (within the meaning of Part 4 of FA 2003) of the first transaction (within the meaning of this section) falls on or after 7 April 2005: FA 2005 Sch 8 para 7(2), (3).

[2] Word "person" substituted for word "individual" and words "a person" substituted for words "an individual" throughout the section, sub-s (6) repealed by FA 2006 s 168(1), (2) with effect in relation to arrangements in which the effective date (within the meaning of FA 2003 s 119(1)) of the first transaction (within the meaning of FA 2003 ss 71A–73) is on or after 19 July 2006.

[3] Sub-s (8) substituted by FA 2007 s 75(3), (4). This amendment—
(a) has effect in relation to anything that would, but for the exemption provided by this section, be a land transaction with an effective date on or after 22 March 2007, and
(b) applies, in accordance with paragraph (*a*), to interests irrespective of the date of their creation.

73 Alternative property finance: land sold to financial institution and re-sold to [person][2]

(1) This section applies where arrangements are entered into between [a person][2] and a financial institution under which—
(*a*) the institution—
(i) purchases a major interest in land ("the first transaction"), and
(ii) sells that interest to the [person][2] ("the second transaction"), and
(*b*) the [person][2] grants the institution a legal mortgage over that interest.
(2) The first transaction is exempt from charge if the vendor is—
(*a*) the [person][2] concerned, or
(*b*) another financial institution by whom the interest was acquired under other arrangements of the kind mentioned in [section 71A(1), 72(1) or 72A(1)][1] entered into between it and the [person][2].
(3) The second transaction is exempt from charge if the financial institution complies with the provisions of this Part relating to the first transaction (including the payment of any tax chargeable [on a chargeable consideration that is not less than the market value of the interest and, in the case of the grant of a lease at a rent, the rent][2]).
(4) . . . [2]
(5) In this section—
(*a*) [*In this section* "financial institution" has the meaning given by section 46 of the Finance Act 2005 (alternative finance arrangements).][3];
(*b*) "legal mortgage"—
(i) in relation to land in England or Wales, means a legal mortgage as defined in section 205(1)(*xvi*) of the Law of Property Act 1925 (c 20);
(ii) in relation to land in Scotland, means a standard security;
(iii) in relation to land in Northern Ireland, means a mortgage by conveyance of a legal estate or by demise or sub-demise or a charge by way of legal mortgage.
(6) References in this section to [a person][2] shall be read, in relation to times after the death of the [person][2] concerned, as references to his personal representatives.

Note—Words in italics in sub-s (5)(*a*) above represent duplicate text, due to a drafting error in FA 2007 s 75(3), which amended the sub-section.

HMRC Manuals—Stamp Duty Land Tax Manual, SDLTM00700 (claims for relief – cases where a land transaction return is required).
SDLTM28200–28230 (explanation of this relief).

Amendments—[1] Words substituted by FA 2005 s 94, Sch 8 para 5 with effect in any case where the effective date (within the meaning of Part 4 of FA 2003) of the first transaction (within the meaning of FA 2003 s 71A (so far as relating to that section) or s 72A (so far as relating to that section)) falls on or after 7 April 2005: FA 2005 Sch 8 para 7.

[2] Word "person" substituted for word "individual" and words "a person" substituted for words "an individual" throughout the section, words in sub-s (3) inserted, sub-s (4) repealed by FA 2006 s 168(1)–(3) with effect in relation to arrangements in which the effective date (within the meaning of FA 2003 s 119(1)) of the first transaction (within the meaning of FA 2003 ss 71A–73) is on or after 19 July 2006.

[3] Sub-s (5)(a) substituted by FA 2007 s 75(3), (4). This amendment—
(a) has effect in relation to anything that would, but for the exemption provided by this section, be a land transaction with an effective date on or after 22 March 2007, and
(b) applies, in accordance with paragraph (*a*), to interests irrespective of the date of their creation.

[73A [Sections 71A to 73: relationship with Schedule 7][2]

Sections 71A to 73 do not apply to arrangements in which the first transaction is exempt from charge by virtue of Schedule 7.][1]

Amendments—[1] This section inserted by FA 2006 s 168(4) with effect in relation to arrangements in which the effective date (within the meaning of FA 2003 s 119(1)) of the first transaction (within the meaning of FA 2003 ss 71A–73) is on or after 19 July 2006.

[2] Section heading substituted by FA 2008 s 155(1), (2) with effect in relation to alternative finance arrangements entered into on or after 12 March 2008.

[73AB Sections 71A to 72A: arrangements to transfer control of financial institution

(1) Section 71A, 72 or 72A does not apply to alternative finance arrangements if those arrangements, or any connected arrangements, include arrangements for a person to acquire control of the relevant financial institution.

(2) That includes arrangements for a person to acquire control of the relevant financial institution only if one or more conditions are met (such as the happening of an event or doing of an act).

(3) In this section—

"alternative finance arrangements" means the arrangements referred to in section 71A(1), 72(1) or 72A(1);

"arrangements" includes any agreement, understanding, scheme, transaction or series of transactions (whether or not legally enforceable);

"connected arrangements" means any arrangements entered into in connection with the making of the alternative finance arrangements (including arrangements involving one or more persons who are not parties to the alternative finance arrangements);

"relevant financial institution" means the financial institution which enters into the alternative finance arrangements.

(4) [Section 1124 of the Corporation Tax Act 2010][2] applies for the purposes of determining who has control of the relevant financial institution.][1]

Amendments—[1] Section 73AB inserted by FA 2008 s 155(1), (3) with effect in relation to alternative finance arrangements entered into on or after 12 March 2008.

[2] In sub-s (4) words "Section 840 of the Taxes Act 1988" substituted by CTA 2010 s 1177, Sch 1 paras 400, 406. CTA 2010 has effect for corporation tax purposes for accounting periods ending on or after 1 April 2010, and for income and capital gains tax purposes for the tax year 2010–11 and subsequent tax years.

[73B Exempt interests

(1) An interest held by a financial institution as a result of the first transaction within the meaning of section 71A(1)(*a*), 72(1)(*a*) or 72A(1)(*a*) is an exempt interest for the purposes of stamp duty land tax.

(2) That interest ceases to be an exempt interest if—

(*a*) the lease or agreement mentioned in section 71A(1)(*c*), 72(1)(*b*) or 72A(1)(*b*) ceases to have effect, or

(*b*) the right under section 71A(1)(*d*), 72(1)(*c*) or 72A(1)(*c*) ceases to have effect or becomes subject to a restriction.

(3) Subsection (1) does not apply if the first transaction is exempt from charge by virtue of Schedule 7.

(4) Subsection (1) does not make an interest exempt in respect of—

(*a*) the first transaction itself, or

(*b*) a further transaction or third transaction within the meaning of section 71A(4), 72(4) or 72A(4).][1]

Amendments—[1] This section inserted by FA 2007 s 75(1), (4). This amendment—

(a) has effect in relation to anything that would, but for the exemption provided by this section, be a land transaction with an effective date on or after 22 March 2007, and

(b) applies, in accordance with paragraph (*a*), to interests irrespective of the date of their creation.

[73C Alternative finance investment bonds

Schedule 61 to the Finance Act 2009 makes provision for relief from charge in the case of arrangements falling within section 48A of the Finance Act 2005 (alternative finance investment bonds).][1]

Amendments—[1] This section inserted by FA 2009 s 123, Sch 61 paras 24, 25 with effect from 21 July 2009.

[73CA Sections 71A to 73: first-time buyers

(1) Where section 71A, 72, 72A or 73 applies, the first transaction within the meaning of the section concerned is exempt from charge under section 55 if—

(*a*) the transaction is a relevant acquisition of a major interest in land,

(*b*) the land consists entirely of residential property,

(*c*) the relevant consideration (see section 55) for the transaction (other than any consisting of rent) is more than £125,000 but not more than £250,000,

(*d*) the person (within the meaning of the section concerned), or (if more than one) each of them, is a first-time buyer who intends to occupy the residential property as the person's only or main residence, and

(*e*) (subject to subsection (3)) the transaction is not one of a number of linked transactions.

(2) In subsection (1)—

"first-time buyer", and

"relevant acquisition of a major interest in land",

have the same meaning as in section 57AA.

(3) Subsection (4) of section 57AA applies for the purposes of this section.][1]

Amendments—[1] This section inserted by FA 2010 s 6(1), (3) with effect in relation to any land transaction of which the effective date is on or after 25 March 2010 but before 25 March 2012 (FA 2010 s 6(6)).

74 [Exercise of collective rights by tenants of flats][1]

[(1) This section applies where a chargeable transaction is entered into by a person or persons nominated or appointed by qualifying tenants of flats contained in premises in exercise of—

(*a*) a right under Part 1 of the Landlord and Tenant Act 1987 (right of first refusal), or

(*b*) a right under Chapter 1 of Part 1 of the Leasehold Reform, Housing and Urban Development Act 1993 (right to collective enfranchisement).][1]

(2) . . . [1] the rate of tax is determined by reference to the fraction of the relevant consideration produced by dividing the total amount of that consideration by the number of [qualifying flats contained in the premises][1].

(3) The tax chargeable is then determined by applying that rate to the chargeable consideration for the transaction.

[(4) In this section—

"flat" and "qualifying tenant" have the same meaning as in the Chapter or Part of the Act conferring the right being exercised;

"qualifying flat" means a flat that is held by a qualifying tenant who is participating in the exercise of the right.][1]

(5) References in this section to the relevant consideration have the same meaning as in section 55.

HMRC Manuals—Stamp Duty Land Tax Manual, SDLTM00700 (claims for relief – cases where a land transaction return is required).

SDLTM28500–28510 (explanation of this relief).

Simon's Tax Cases—*Elizabeth Court (Bournemouth) Ltd v R&C Comrs* [2009] STC 682.

Amendments—[1] Sub-s (1) substituted, in sub-s (2) words "In that case," repealed and words "flats in respect of which the right of collective enfranchisement is being exercised" substituted, sub-s (4) substituted and the heading substituted by FA 2009 s 80 with effect in relation to transactions with an effective date on or after 22 April 2009. Sub-s (1) previously read as follows—

"(1) This section applies where a chargeable transaction is entered into by an RTE company in pursuance of a right of collective enfranchisement."

Sub-s (4) previously read as follows—

"(4) In this section—

(*a*) "RTE company" has the meaning given by section 4A of the Leasehold Reform, Housing and Urban Development Act 1993 (c 28);

(*b*) "right of collective enfranchisement" means the right exercisable by an RTE company under—

(i) Part 1 of the Landlord and Tenant Act 1987 (c 31), or

(ii) Chapter 1 of Part 1 of the Leasehold Reform, Housing and Urban Development Act 1993 (c 28); and

(*c*) "flat" has the same meaning as in the Act conferring the right of collective enfranchisement."

75 Crofting community right to buy

(1) This section applies where—

(*a*) a chargeable transaction is entered into in pursuance of the crofting community right to buy, and

(*b*) under that transaction two or more crofts are being bought.

(2) In that case, the rate of tax is determined by reference to the fraction of the relevant consideration produced by dividing the total amount of that consideration by the number of crofts being bought.

(3) The tax chargeable is then determined by applying that rate to the amount of the chargeable consideration for the transaction in question.

(4) In this section "crofting community right to buy" means the right exercisable by a crofting community body under Part 3 of the Land Reform (Scotland) Act 2003 (asp 2).

(5) References in this section to the relevant consideration have the same meaning as in section 55.

HMRC Manuals—Stamp Duty Land Tax Manual, SDLTM00700 (claims for relief – cases where a land transaction return is required).

SDLTM29000–29010 (explanation of this relief).

[75A Anti-avoidance

(1) This section applies where—

(*a*) one person (V) disposes of a chargeable interest and another person (P) acquires either it or a chargeable interest deriving from it,

(*b*) a number of transactions (including the disposal and acquisition) are involved in connection with the disposal and acquisition ("the scheme transactions"), and

(*c*) the sum of the amounts of stamp duty land tax payable in respect of the scheme transactions is less than the amount that would be payable on a notional land transaction effecting the acquisition of V's chargeable interest by P on its disposal by V.

(2) In subsection (1) "transaction" includes, in particular—

(*a*) a non-land transaction,

(*b*) an agreement, offer or undertaking not to take specified action,

(*c*) any kind of arrangement whether or not it could otherwise be described as a transaction, and

(*d*) a transaction which takes place after the acquisition by P of the chargeable interest.

(3) The scheme transactions may include, for example—

(*a*) the acquisition by P of a lease deriving from a freehold owned or formerly owned by V;

(*b*) a sub-sale to a third person;

(*c*) the grant of a lease to a third person subject to a right to terminate;

(*d*) the exercise of a right to terminate a lease or to take some other action;

(*e*) an agreement not to exercise a right to terminate a lease or to take some other action;

(*f*) the variation of a right to terminate a lease or to take some other action.

(4) Where this section applies—

(*a*) any of the scheme transactions which is a land transaction shall be disregarded for the purposes of this Part, but

(*b*) there shall be a notional land transaction for the purposes of this Part effecting the acquisition of V's chargeable interest by P on its disposal by V.

(5) The chargeable consideration on the notional transaction mentioned in subsections (1)(*c*) and (4)(*b*) is the largest amount (or aggregate amount)—

(*a*) given by or on behalf of any one person by way of consideration for the scheme transactions, or

(*b*) received by or on behalf of V (or a person connected with V within the meaning of [section 1122 of the Corporation Tax Act 2010][2]) by way of consideration for the scheme transactions.

(6) The effective date of the notional transaction is—

(*a*) the last date of completion for the scheme transactions, or

(*b*) if earlier, the last date on which a contract in respect of the scheme transactions is substantially performed.

(7) This section does not apply where subsection (1)(*c*) is satisfied only by reason of—

(*a*) sections 71A to 73, or

(*b*) a provision of Schedule 9.][1]

Amendments—[1] Sections 75A–75C substituted for section 75A by FA 2007 s 71 with effect in respect of disposals and acquisitions if the disposal mentioned in sub-s (1)(a) above takes place on or after 6 December 2006.

However—

(a) the transitional provisions of the Stamp Duty Land Tax (Variation of the Finance Act 2003) Regulations, SI 2006/3237 Schedule para 1(2)–(5) continue to have effect in relation to FA 2007 s 71 as in relation to that paragraph, and

(b) a provision of FA 2003 s 75C (as inserted by FA 2007 s 71) shall not have effect where the disposal mentioned in sub-s (1)(*a*) above took place before 19 July 2007, if or in so far as the provision would make a person liable for a higher amount of tax than would have been charged in accordance with those regulations.

[2] In sub-s (5)(*b*) words "section 839 of the Taxes Act 1988" substituted by CTA 2010 s 1177, Sch 1 paras 400, 407. CTA 2010 has effect for corporation tax purposes for accounting periods ending on or after 1 April 2010, and for income and capital gains tax purposes for the tax year 2010–11 and subsequent tax years.

[75B Anti-avoidance: incidental transactions

(1) In calculating the chargeable consideration on the notional transaction for the purposes of section 75A(5), consideration for a transaction shall be ignored if or in so far as the transaction is merely incidental to the transfer of the chargeable interest from V to P.

(2) A transaction is not incidental to the transfer of the chargeable interest from V to P—

(*a*) if or in so far as it forms part of a process, or series of transactions, by which the transfer is effected,

(*b*) if the transfer of the chargeable interest is conditional on the completion of the transaction, or

(*c*) if it is of a kind specified in section 75A(3).

(3) A transaction may, in particular, be incidental if or in so far as it is undertaken only for a purpose relating to—

(*a*) the construction of a building on property to which the chargeable interest relates,

(*b*) the sale or supply of anything other than land, or

(*c*) a loan to P secured by a mortgage, or any other provision of finance to enable P, or another person, to pay for part of a process, or series of transactions, by which the chargeable interest transfers from V to P.

(4) In subsection (3)—

(*a*) paragraph (*a*) is subject to subsection (2)(*a*) to (*c*),

(*b*) paragraph (*b*) is subject to subsection (2)(*a*) and (*c*), and

(*c*) paragraph (*c*) is subject to subsection (2)(*a*) to (*c*).

(5) The exclusion required by subsection (1) shall be effected by way of just and reasonable apportionment if necessary.

(6) In this section a reference to the transfer of a chargeable interest from V to P includes a reference to a disposal by V of an interest acquired by P.][1]

Amendments—[1] Sections 75A–75C substituted for section 75A by FA 2007 s 71 with effect in respect of disposals and acquisitions if the disposal mentioned in FA 2003 s 75A(1)(a) takes place on or after 6 December 2006.

However—

(a) the transitional provisions of the Stamp Duty Land Tax (Variation of the Finance Act 2003) Regulations, SI 2006/3237 Schedule para 1(2)–(5) continue to have effect in relation to FA 2007 s 71 as in relation to that paragraph, and

(b) a provision of FA 2003 s 75C (as inserted by FA 2007 s 71) shall not have effect where the disposal mentioned in FA 2003 s 75A(1)(*a*) took place before 19 July 2007, if or in so far as the provision would make a person liable for a higher amount of tax than would have been charged in accordance with those regulations.

[75C Anti-avoidance: supplemental

(1) A transfer of shares or securities shall be ignored for the purposes of section 75A if but for this subsection it would be the first of a series of scheme transactions.

(2) The notional transaction under section 75A attracts any relief under this Part which it would attract if it were an actual transaction (subject to the terms and restrictions of the relief).

(3) The notional transaction under section 75A is a land transaction entered into for the purposes of or in connection with the transfer of an undertaking or part for the purposes of paragraphs 7 and 8 of Schedule 7, if any of the scheme transactions is entered into for the purposes of or in connection with the transfer of the undertaking or part.

(4) In the application of section 75A(5) no account shall be taken of any amount paid by way of consideration in respect of a transaction to which any of sections 60, 61, 63, 64, 65, 66, 67, 69, 71, 74 and 75, or a provision of Schedule 6A or 8, applies.

(5) In the application of section 75A(5) an amount given or received partly in respect of the chargeable interest acquired by P and partly in respect of another chargeable interest shall be subjected to just and reasonable apportionment.

(6) Section 53 applies to the notional transaction under section 75A.

(7) Paragraph 5 of Schedule 4 applies to the notional transaction under section 75A.

(8) For the purposes of section 75A—

(*a*) an interest in a property-investment partnership (within the meaning of paragraph 14 of Schedule 15) is a chargeable interest in so far as it concerns land owned by the partnership,

. . .

(*b*) . . . [2]

[(8A) Nothing in Part 3 of Schedule 15 applies to the notional transaction under section 75A.][2]

(9) For the purposes of section 75A a reference to an amount of consideration includes a reference to the value of consideration given as money's worth.

(10) Stamp duty land tax paid in respect of a land transaction which is to be disregarded by virtue of section 75A(4)(*a*) is taken to have been paid in respect of the notional transaction by virtue of section 75A(4)(*b*).

(11) The Treasury may by order provide for section 75A not to apply in specified circumstances.

(12) An order under subsection (11) may include incidental, consequential or transitional provision and may make provision with retrospective effect.][1]

Amendments—[1] Sections 75A–75C substituted for section 75A by FA 2007 s 71 with effect in respect of disposals and acquisitions if the disposal mentioned in FA 2003 s 75A(1)(a) takes place on or after 6 December 2006.

However—

(a) the transitional provisions of the Stamp Duty Land Tax (Variation of the Finance Act 2003) Regulations, SI 2006/3237 Schedule para 1(2)–(5) continue to have effect in relation to FA 2007 s 71 as in relation to that paragraph, and

(b) a provision of FA 2003 s 75C (as inserted by FA 2007 s 71) shall not have effect where the disposal mentioned in FA 2003 s 75A(1)(*a*) took place before 19 July 2007, if or in so far as the provision would make a person liable for a higher amount of tax than would have been charged in accordance with those regulations.

[2] Sub-s (8)(*b*) and preceding word "and" repealed, and sub-s (8A) inserted, by FA 2010 s 55 in relation to any notional transaction of which the effective date is on or after 24 March 2010. Sub-s (8)(*b*) previously read as follows—

"(*b*) where V or P is a partnership, Part 3 of Schedule 15 applies to the notional transaction as to the transfer of a chargeable interest from or to a partnership.".

Note that these amendments do not have effect in relation to a notional transaction if any scheme transaction is completed before 24 March 2010, effected in pursuance of a contract entered into and substantially performed before that date, or effected in pursuance of a contract entered into before that date and not excluded by FA 2010 s 55(4) (FA 2010 s 55(3), (4)).

Returns and other administrative matters

76 Duty to deliver land transaction return

(1) In the case of every notifiable transaction the purchaser must deliver a return (a "land transaction return") to the Inland Revenue before the end of the period of 30 days after the effective date of the transaction.

(2) The Inland Revenue may by regulations amend subsection (1) so as to require a land transaction return to be delivered before the end of such shorter period after the effective date of the transaction as may be prescribed or, if the regulations so provide, on that date.

(3) A land transaction return in respect of a chargeable transaction must—

(*a*) include an assessment (a "self-assessment") of the tax that, on the basis of the information contained in the return, is chargeable in respect of the transaction, ...[1]

(*b*) ...[1]

HMRC Manuals—Stamp Duty Land Tax Manual SDLTM50100 (details of the required forms).

Cross references—FA 2009 Sch 55 (penalty for failure to make returns etc).

Amendments—[1] Sub-s (3)(*b*) and preceding word "and" repealed by FA 2007 ss 80(1), (2), (9)(*a*), 114, Sch 27 Pt 4(4) with effect in relation to land transactions with an effective date on or after 19 July 2007.

[77 Notifiable transactions

(1) A land transaction is notifiable if it is—

(*a*) an acquisition of a major interest in land that does not fall within one or more of the exceptions in section 77A,

(*b*) an acquisition of a chargeable interest other than a major interest in land where there is chargeable consideration in respect of which tax is chargeable at a rate of 1% or higher or would be so chargeable but for a relief,

(*c*) a land transaction that a person is treated as entering into by virtue of section 44A(3), or

(*d*) a notional land transaction under section 75A.

(2) This section has effect subject to—

(*a*) sections 71A(7) and 72A(7), and

(*b*) paragraph 30 of Schedule 15.

(3) In this section "relief" does not include an exemption from charge under Schedule 3.][1]

HMRC Manuals—Stamp Duty Land Tax Manual, SDLTM00310, 00310a (notifiable transaction – with examples) SDLTM00330, 00330a (whether notification is required – with examples)

Amendments—[1] Sections 77, 77A substituted for s 77 by FA 2008 s 94(1), (2) with effect in relation to transactions with an effective date on or after 12 March 2008.

[77A Exceptions for certain acquisitions of major interests in land

(1) The exceptions referred to in section 77(1)(*a*) are as follows.

1. An acquisition which is exempt from charge under Schedule 3 [other than an acquisition which is exempt by virtue of any regulations made under paragraph 5 of that Schedule][2].

2. An acquisition (other than the grant, assignment or surrender of a lease) where the chargeable consideration for that acquisition, together with the chargeable consideration for any linked transactions, is less than £40,000.

3. The grant of a lease for a term of 7 years or more where—

(*a*) any chargeable consideration other than rent is less than £40,000, and

(*b*) the relevant rent is less than £1,000.

4. The assignment or surrender of a lease where—

(*a*) the lease was originally granted for a term of 7 years or more, and

(*b*) the chargeable consideration for the assignment or surrender is less than £40,000.

5. The grant of a lease for a term of less than 7 years where the chargeable consideration does not exceed the zero rate threshold.

6. The assignment or surrender of a lease where—

(*a*) the lease was originally granted for a term of less than 7 years, and

(*b*) the chargeable consideration for the assignment or surrender does not exceed the zero rate threshold.

(2) Chargeable consideration for an acquisition does not exceed the zero rate threshold if it does not consist of or include—

(*a*) any amount in respect of which tax is chargeable at a rate of 1% or higher, or

(*b*) any amount in respect of which tax would be so chargeable but for a relief.

(3) In this section—

"annual rent" has the meaning given in paragraph 9A of Schedule 5,

"relevant rent" means—

(*a*) the annual rent, or

(*b*) in the case of the grant of a lease to which paragraph 11 or 19 of Schedule 15 applies, the relevant chargeable proportion of the annual rent (as calculated in accordance with that paragraph), and

"relief" does not include an exemption from charge under Schedule 3.][1]

Amendments—[1] Sections 77, 77A substituted for s 77 by FA 2008 s 94(1), (2) with effect in relation to transactions with an effective date on or after 12 March 2008.

[2] Words in sub-s (1), item 1, inserted by the Stamp Duty Land Tax (Variation of Part 4 of the Finance Act 2003) Regulations, SI 2008/2338 reg 2 with effect in relation to transactions with an effective date on or after 3 September 2008, and before 3 September 2009.

78 Returns, enquiries, assessments and related matters

(1) Schedule 10 has effect with respect to land transaction returns, assessments and related matters.

(2) In that Schedule—

Part 1 contains general provisions about returns;

Part 2 imposes a duty to keep and preserve records;

Part 3 makes provision for enquiries into returns;

Part 4 provides for a Revenue determination if no return is delivered;

Part 5 provides for Revenue assessments;

Part 6 provides for relief in case of excessive assessment; and

Part 7 provides for appeals against Revenue decisions on tax.

(3) The Treasury may by regulations make such amendments of that Schedule, and such consequential amendments of any other provisions of this Part, as appear to them to be necessary or expedient from time to time.

[78A Disclosure of information contained in land transaction returns

(1) Relevant information contained in land transaction returns delivered under section 76 (whether before or after the commencement of this section) is to be available for use—

(*a*) by listing officers appointed under section 20 of the Local Government Finance Act 1992, for the purpose of facilitating the compilation and maintenance by them of valuation lists in accordance with Chapter 2 of Part 1 of that Act,

(*b*) as evidence in an appeal by virtue of section 24(6) of that Act to a valuation tribunal . . . [2],

(*c*) by the Commissioner of Valuation for Northern Ireland, for the purpose of maintaining a valuation list prepared, and from time to time altered, by him in accordance with Part 3 of the Rates (Northern Ireland) Order 1977, and

(*d*) by such other persons or for such other purposes as the Treasury may by regulations prescribe.

(2) In this section, "relevant information" means any information of the kind mentioned in paragraph 1(4) of Schedule 10 (information corresponding to particulars required under previous legislation).

(3) The Treasury may by regulations amend the definition of relevant information in subsection (2).

[(4) In this section "valuation tribunal" means—

(*a*) in relation to England: the Valuation Tribunal for England;

(*b*) in relation to Wales: a valuation tribunal established under paragraph 1 of Schedule 11 to the Local Government Finance Act 1988.][2],][1]

Amendments—[1] This section inserted by F(No 2)A 2005 s 48(1), (5) with effect from 30 July 2009 (by virtue of SI 2009/2094 art 2).

[2] In sub-s (1)(*b*), words "established under Schedule 11 to the Local Government Finance Act 1988" repealed, and sub-s (4) inserted, by the Local Government and Public Involvement in Health Act 2007 ss 220, 241, Sch 16 para 9, Sch 18 Pt 17 with effect from 1 October 2009 (by virtue of SI 2008/3110 art 6(*b*), (*d*)(i)).

79 Registration of land transactions etc

(1) A land transaction to which this section applies, or (as the case may be) a document effecting or evidencing a land transaction to which this section applies, shall not be registered, recorded or otherwise reflected in an entry made—

(*a*) in England and Wales, in the register of title maintained by the Chief Land Registrar,

(*b*) in Scotland, in any register maintained by the Keeper of the Registers of Scotland [(other than the Register of Community Interests in Land)][2], or

(*c*) in Northern Ireland, in any register maintained by the Land Registry of Northern Ireland or in the Registry of Deeds for Northern Ireland,

unless there is produced, together with the relevant application, a certificate as to compliance with the requirements of this Part in relation to the transaction [or such information about compliance as the Commissioners for Her Majesty's Revenue and Customs may specify in regulations.][4].

This does not apply where the entry is required to be made without any application or so far as the entry relates to an interest or right other than the chargeable interest acquired by the purchaser under the land transaction that gives rise to the application.

(2) This section applies to every [notifiable][5] land transaction [other than a transaction treated as taking place—

(*a*) under subsection (4) of section 44 (contract and conveyance) or under that section as it applies [by virtue of—

(i) section 45 (contract and conveyance: effect of transfer of rights), or

(ii) paragraph 12B of Schedule 17A (assignment of agreement for lease),][3] or

(*b*) under subsection (3) of section 44A (contract providing for conveyance to third party) or under that section as it applies by virtue of section 45A (contract providing for conveyance to third party: effect of transfer of rights).][1]

[(*c*) under paragraph 12A(2) or 19(3) of Schedule 17A (agreement for lease), or][3]

[(*d*) under paragraph 13 (increase of rent) or 15A (reduction of rent or term) of that Schedule.][3]

In this subsection "contract" includes any agreement and "conveyance" includes any instrument.

[(2A) Subsection (1), so far as relating to the entry of a notice under section 34 of the Land Registration Act 2002 or section 38 of the Land Registration Act (Northern Ireland) 1970 (notice in respect of interest affecting registered land), does not apply where the land transaction in question is the variation of a lease.][3]

(3) The certificate [referred to in subsection (1)][3] must be . . . [5]—

(*a*) a certificate by the Inland Revenue (a "Revenue certificate") that a land transaction return has been delivered in respect of the transaction, . . . [5]

(*b*) . . . [5]

(4) The Inland Revenue may make provision by regulations about Revenue certificates. The regulations may, in particular—

(*a*) make provision as to the conditions to be met before a certificate is issued;

(*b*) prescribe the form and content of the certificate;

(*c*) make provision about the issue of duplicate certificates if the original is lost or destroyed;

(*d*) provide for the issue of multiple certificates where a return is made relating to more than one transaction.

[(5) Part 2 of Schedule 11 imposes a duty to keep and preserve records in respect of transactions that are not notifiable.][5]

(6) The registrar (in Scotland, the Keeper of the Registers of Scotland)—

(*a*) shall allow the Inland Revenue to inspect any certificates . . .[5] produced to him under this section and in his possession, and

(*b*) may enter into arrangements for affording the Inland Revenue other information and facilities for verifying that the requirements of this Part have been complied with.

HMRC Manuals—Stamp Duty Land Tax Manual SDLTM50200 (self-certification required for land transactions which are not notifiable transactions under FA 2003 s 77, eg freehold or leasehold transfers for no chargeable consideration; the grant of a lease for no chargeable consideration or a peppercorn rent; and certain transactions in connection with divorce and death).

Amendments—[1] Words in sub-s (2) substituted by FA 2004 s 296, Sch 39 para 7 with effect in accordance with FA 2004 Sch 39 para 13(1), (2).

[2] Words in sub-s (1)(b) inserted by FA 2004 s 298(1), (3) with effect from 22 July 2004.

[3] Words in sub-s (2)(a) substituted for the words "by virtue of section 45 (contract and conveyance: effect of transfer of rights)," sub-ss (2)(c), (d), (2A) and words in sub-s (3) inserted, by FA 2004 s 297(1), (5)–(7), (10) with effect for any transaction or deemed transaction of which the effective date is after 16 March 2004.

[4] Words in sub-s (1) inserted by F(No 2)A 2005 s 47(2) with effect from 20 July 2005.

[5] Word in sub-s (2) inserted, words in sub-ss (3), (6)(a), and sub-s (3)(b), repealed, and sub-s (5) substituted, by FA 2008 s 94(1), (4), Sch 30 paras 1, 2 with effect in relation to transactions with an effective date on or after 12 March 2008.

80 Adjustment where contingency ceases or consideration is ascertained

(1) Where section 51 (contingent, uncertain or unascertained consideration) applies in relation to a transaction and—

(*a*) in the case of contingent consideration, the contingency occurs or it becomes clear that it will not occur, or

(*b*) in the case of uncertain or unascertained consideration, an amount relevant to the calculation of the consideration, or any instalment of consideration, becomes ascertained,

the following provisions have effect to require or permit reconsideration of how this Part applies to the transaction (and to any transaction in relation to which it is a linked transaction).

(2) If the effect of the new information is that a transaction becomes notifiable ...[1], or that additional tax is payable in respect of a transaction or that tax is payable where none was payable before—

(*a*) the purchaser must make a return to the Inland Revenue within 30 days,

(*b*) the return must contain a self-assessment of the tax chargeable in respect of the transaction on the basis of the information contained in the return,

(*c*) the tax so chargeable is to be calculated by reference to the rates in force at the effective date of the transaction, and

[(*d*) the tax or additional tax payable must be paid not later than the filing date for the return.][5]

(3) The provisions of Schedule 10 (returns, enquiries, assessments and other matters) apply to a return under this section as they apply to a [return under section 76 (general requirement to make land transaction return), subject to the adaptation that references to the effective date of the transaction shall be read as references to the date of the event as a result of which the return is required][2].

(4) If the effect of the new information is that less tax is payable in respect of a transaction than has already been paid,[—

(*a*) the purchaser may, within the period allowed for amendment of the land transaction return, amend the return accordingly;

(*b*) after the end of that period he may (if the land transaction return is not so amended) make a claim to the Inland Revenue for repayment of the amount overpaid][3]

[(4A) Where the transaction ("the relevant transaction") is the grant or assignment of a lease, no claim may be made under subsection (4)—

(*a*) in respect of the repayment (in whole or part) of any loan or deposit that is treated by paragraph 18A of Schedule 17A as being consideration given for the relevant transaction, or

(*b*) in respect of the refund of any of the consideration given for the relevant transaction, in a case where the refund—

(i) is made under arrangements that were made in connection with the relevant transaction, and

(ii) is contingent on the determination or assignment of the lease or on the grant of a chargeable interest out of the lease.][4]

[(5) This section does not apply so far as the consideration consists of rent (see paragraph 8 of Schedule 17A).][2]

HMRC Manuals—Stamp Duty Land Tax Manual, SDLTM05040a (claim for repayment of SDLT after end of period for amendment – example)

Amendments—[1] In sub-s (2), words "or chargeable" repealed by FA 2004 s 326, Sch 42 Pt 4(2) with effect in accordance with FA 2004 Sch 39 para 26. This repeal was previously made by the Stamp Duty and Stamp Duty Land Tax (Variation of the Finance Act 2003) (No 2) Regulations, SI 2003/2816, regs 1, 2, Schedule para 5(2) with effect from 1 December 2003. Those regulations have been revoked by FA 2004 Sch 39 para 14(2).

[2] In sub-s (3), words substituted for the words "land transaction return", and sub-s (5) inserted, by FA 2004 s 296, Sch 39 para 22(4) with effect for any transaction of which the effective date (within the meaning of FA 2003 Pt 4) is on or after 22 July 2004: FA 2004 Sch 39 para 26. These amendments were previously made by the Stamp Duty and Stamp Duty Land Tax (Variation of the Finance Act 2003) (No 2) Regulations, SI 2003/2816 regs 1, 2, Schedule paras 5(3), 8(5) with effect from 1 December 2003. Those regulations are revoked by FA 2004 Sch 39 para 14(2).

[3] In sub-s (4), words substituted for the words "the amount overpaid shall on a claim by the purchaser be repaid together with interest as from the date of payment." by FA 2004 s 299(1), (4) with effect from 22 July 2004.

[4] Sub-s (4A) inserted by F(No 2)A 2005 s 49, Sch 10 paras 1, 15 with effect in relation to any transaction of which the effective date is after 19 May 2005.

However, this amendment does not have effect—

(a) in relation to any transaction which is effected in pursuance of a contract entered into and substantially performed on or before the specified date (ie 16 March 2005), or

(b) subject to what follows below, in relation to any other transaction which is effected in pursuance of a contract entered into on or before the specified date (ie 16 March 2005).

The exclusion by para (*b*) above of transactions effected in pursuance of contracts entered into on or before the specified date does not apply—

(a) if there is any variation of the contract or assignment of rights under the contract after that date,

(b) if the transaction is effected in consequence of the exercise after that date of any option, right of pre-emption or similar right, or

(c) if after that date there is an assignment, subsale or other transaction (relating to the whole or part of the subject-matter of the contract) as a result of which a person other than the purchaser under the contract becomes entitled to call for a conveyance to him: F(No 2)A 2005 Sch 10 para 16(5)–(8).

[5] Sub-s (2)(d) repealed by FA 2007 s 80(1), (3), (9)(b) with effect in relation to returns where the event as a result of which the return is required occurs on or after 19 July 2007.

81 Further return where relief withdrawn

(1) Where relief is withdrawn to any extent under—

[(*za*) paragraph 11 of Schedule 6A (relief for certain acquisitions of residential property),][1]

(*a*) Part 1 of Schedule 7 (group relief),

(*b*) Part 2 of that Schedule (reconstruction or acquisition relief), or

(*c*) Schedule 8 (charities relief),

the purchaser must deliver a further return before the end of the period of 30 days after the date on which the disqualifying event occurred.

(2) The return must—

(*a*) include a self-assessment of the amount of tax chargeable, ...[4]

(*b*) ...[4]

[(2A) Tax payable must be paid not later than the filing date for the return.][4]

(3) The provisions of Schedule 10 (returns, assessments and other matters) apply to a return under this section as they apply to a [return under section 76 (general requirement to deliver land transaction return)][2], with the following adaptations—

(*a*) references to the transaction to which the return relates shall be read as references to the disqualifying event;

(*b*) references to the effective date of the transaction shall be read as references to the date on which the disqualifying event occurs.

(4) In this section "the disqualifying event" means—

[(*za*) in relation to the withdrawal of relief under Schedule 6A, an event mentioned in paragraph (*a*), (*b*) or (*c*) of paragraph 11(2), (3), (4) or (5) of that Schedule;][1]

(*a*) in relation to the withdrawal of group relief, the purchaser ceasing to be a member of the same group as the vendor within the meaning of Part 1 of Schedule 7;

(*b*) in relation to the withdrawal of reconstruction or acquisition relief, the change of control of the acquiring company mentioned in paragraph 9(1)(*a*) of Schedule 7 or, as the case may be, the event mentioned in paragraph 11(1)(*a*) or (2)(*a*) of that Schedule;

(*c*) in relation to the withdrawal of charities relief, a disqualifying event as defined in paragraph 2(3) [or 3(2)][3] of Schedule 8.

Cross references—FA 2009 Sch 55 (penalty for failure to make returns etc).
FA 2009 Sch 56 (penalty for failure to make payments on time).

Amendments—[1] Sub-ss (1)(*za*), (4)(*za*) inserted by FA 2004 s 296, Sch 39 para 17(3) with effect for any transaction of which the effective date (within the meaning of FA 2003 Pt 4) is on or after 22 July 2004: FA 2004 Sch 39 para 26. The insertions were previously made by the Stamp Duty and Stamp Duty Land Tax (Variation of the Finance Act 2003) (No 2) Regulations, SI 2003/2816 regs 1, 2, Schedule para 3(3) with effect from 1 December 2003. Those regulations are revoked by FA 2004 Sch 39 para 14(2).

2 Words in sub-s (3) substituted for "land transaction return" by FA 2004 s 296, Sch 39 para 19(2) with effect for any transaction of which the effective date (within the meaning of FA 2003 Pt 4) is on or after 22 July 2004: FA 2004 Sch 39 para 26. This amendment was previously made by SI 2003/2816 regs 1, 2, Schedule para 5(3) with effect from 1 December 2003. Those regulations are revoked by FA 2004 Sch 39 para 14(2).

3 Words in sub-s (4)(*c*) inserted by FA 2004 s 302(5), (7) with effect for any transaction of which the effective date (within the meaning of FA 2003 Pt 4) is on or after 22 July 2004.

4 Sub-s (2)(*b*) and preceding word "and" repealed, and sub-s (2A) inserted, by FA 2007 ss 80(1), (4), (9)(*c*), 114, Sch 27 Pt 4(4) with effect in relation to returns where the disqualifying event occurs on or after 19 July 2007.

[81A Return or further return in consequence of later linked transaction

(1) Where the effect of a transaction ("the later transaction") that is linked to an earlier transaction is that the earlier transaction becomes notifiable, or that additional tax is payable in respect of the earlier transaction or that tax is payable in respect of the earlier transaction where none was payable before—

(*a*) the purchaser under the earlier transaction must deliver a return or further return in respect of that transaction before the end of the period of 30 days after the effective date of the later transaction,

(*b*) the return must include a self-assessment of the amount of tax chargeable as a result of the later transaction,

(*c*) the tax so chargeable is to be calculated by reference to the rates in force at the effective date of the earlier transaction, and

[(*d*) the tax or additional tax payable must be paid not later than the filing date for the return.][2]

(2) The provisions of Schedule 10 (returns, enquiries, assessments and other matters) apply to a return under this section as they apply to a return under section 76 (general requirement to deliver land transaction return), with the following adaptations—

(*a*) in paragraph 5 (formal notice to deliver return), the requirement in sub-paragraph (2)(*a*) that the notice specify the transaction to which it relates shall be read as requiring both the earlier and later transactions to be specified;

(*b*) references to the effective date of the transaction to which the return relates shall be read as references to the effective date of the later transaction.

(3) This section does not affect any requirement to make a return under section 76 in respect of the later transaction.][1]

Amendments—[1] Inserted by FA 2004 s 296, Sch 39 para 19(1) with effect for any transaction of which the effective date (within the meaning of FA 2003 Pt 4) is on or after 22 July 2004: FA 2004 Sch 39 para 26. This insertion was previously made by the Stamp Duty and Stamp Duty Land Tax (Variation of the Finance Act 2003) (No 2) Regulations, SI 2003/2816 regs 1, 2, Schedule para 5(1) with effect from 1 December 2003. Those regulations are revoked by FA 2004 Sch 39 para 14(2).

2 Sub-s (1)(d) substituted by FA 2007 s 80(1), (5), (9)(d) with effect in relation to returns where the effective date of the later transaction is on or after 19 July 2007.

[81B Declaration by person authorised to act on behalf of individual

(1) This section applies to the declaration mentioned in paragraph 1(1)(*c*) of Schedule 10 . . . [2] (declaration that return . . . [2] is correct and complete).

(2) The requirement that an individual make such a declaration (alone or jointly with others) is treated as met if a declaration to that effect is made by a person authorised to act on behalf of that individual in relation to the matters to which the return or certificate relates.

(3) For the purposes of this section a person is not regarded as authorised to act on behalf of an individual unless he is so authorised by a power of attorney in writing, signed by that individual. In this subsection as it applies in Scotland "power of attorney" includes factory and commission.

(4) Nothing in this section affects the making of a declaration in accordance with—

(*a*) section 100(2) (persons through whom a company acts), or

(*b*) section 106(1) or (2) (person authorised to act on behalf of incapacitated person or minor).][1]

Amendments—[1] Inserted by FA 2004 s 296, Sch 39 para 20 with effect for any transaction of which the effective date (within the meaning of FA 2003 Pt 4) is on or after 22 July 2004: FA 2004 Sch 39 para 26. This insertion was previously made by the Stamp Duty and Stamp Duty Land Tax (Variation of the Finance Act 2003) (No 2) Regulations, SI 2003/2816 regs 1, 2, Schedule para 6 with effect from 1 December 2003. Those regulations are revoked by FA 2004 Sch 39 para 14(2).

2 Words in sub-s (1) repealed by FA 2008 s 94, Sch 30 paras 1, 3 with effect in relation to transactions with an effective date on or after 12 March 2008.

82 Loss or destruction of, or damage to, return etc

(1) This section applies where—

(*a*) a return delivered to the Inland Revenue, or

(*b*) any other document relating to tax made by or provided to the Inland Revenue,

has been lost or destroyed, or been so defaced or damaged as to be illegible or otherwise useless.

(2) The Inland Revenue may treat the return as not having been delivered or the document as not having been made or provided.

(3) Anything done on that basis shall be as valid and effective for all purposes as it would have been if the return had not been made or the document had not been made or provided.

(4) But if as a result a person is charged with tax and he proves to the satisfaction of the [tribunal][1] having jurisdiction in the case that he has already paid tax in respect of the transaction in question, relief shall be given, by reducing the charge or by repayment as the case may require.

Amendments—[1] In sub-s (4) word substituted for the words "General or Special Commissioners" by the Transfer of Tribunal Functions and Revenue and Customs Appeals Order, SI 2009/56 art 3, Sch 1 para 367 with effect from 1 April 2009.

[82A Claims not included in returns

Schedule 11A has effect with respect to claims not included in returns.][1]

Amendments—[1] This section inserted by FA 2004 s 299(1), (2) with effect from 22 July 2004.

83 Formal requirements as to assessments, penalty determinations etc

(1) An assessment, determination, notice or other document required to be used in assessing, charging, collecting and levying tax or determining a penalty under this Part must be in accordance with the forms prescribed from time to time by the Board and a document in the form so prescribed and supplied or approved by the Board is valid and effective.

(2) Any such assessment, determination, notice or other document purporting to be made under this Part is not ineffective—

(*a*) for want of form, or

(*b*) by reason of any mistake, defect or omission in it,

if it is substantially in conformity with this Part and its intended effect is reasonably ascertainable by the person to whom it is directed.

(3) The validity of an assessment or determination is not affected—

(*a*) by any mistake in it as to—

(i) the name of a person liable, or

(ii) the amount of the tax charged, or

(*b*) by reason of any variance between the notice of assessment or determination and the assessment or determination itself.

84 Delivery and service of documents

(1) A notice or other document to be served under this Part on a person may be delivered to him or left at his usual or last known place of abode.

(2) A notice or other document to be given, served or delivered under this Part may be served by post.

(3) For the purposes of section 7 of the Interpretation Act 1978 (c 30) (general provisions as to service by post) any such notice or other document to be given or delivered to, or served on, any person by the Inland Revenue is properly addressed if it is addressed to that person—

(*a*) in the case of an individual, at his usual or last known place of residence or his place of business;

(*b*) in the case of a company—

(i) at its principal place of business,

(ii) if a liquidator has been appointed, at his address for the purposes of the liquidation, or

(iii) at any place prescribed by regulations made by the Inland Revenue.

Liability for and payment of tax

85 Liability for tax

(1) The purchaser is liable to pay the tax in respect of a chargeable transaction.

(2) As to the liability of purchasers acting jointly see—

section 103(2)(*c*) (joint purchasers);
Part 2 of Schedule 15 (partners); and
paragraph 5 of Schedule 16 (trustees).

86 Payment of tax

(1) Tax payable in respect of a land transaction must be paid [not later than the filing date for the land transaction return relating to the transaction.][1]

(2) Tax payable as a result of the withdrawal of relief under—

(*a*) Part 1 of Schedule 7 (group relief),

(*b*) Part 2 of that Schedule (reconstruction or acquisition relief), or

(*c*) Schedule 8 (charities relief),

must be paid [not later than the filing date for the return relating to the withdrawal][1] (see section 81).

(3) Tax payable as a result of the amendment of a return must be paid forthwith or, if the amendment is made before the filing date for the return, not later than that date.

(4) Tax payable in accordance with a determination or assessment by the Inland Revenue must be paid within 30 days after the determination or assessment is issued.

(5) The above provisions are subject to—

(*a*) section 90 (application to defer payment of tax in case of contingent or uncertain consideration), and

(*b*) paragraphs 39 and 40 of Schedule 10 (postponement of payment pending determination of appeal).

[(5A) The above provisions are also subject to paragraph 7 of Schedule 61 to the Finance Act 2009 (payment of tax where land ceases to qualify for relief in respect of alternative finance investment bonds).][2]

(6) This section does not affect the date from which interest is payable (as to which, see section 87).

Cross references—FA 2009 Sch 56 (penalty for failure to make payments on time).

Amendments—[1] Words in sub-ss (1), (2) substituted by FA 2007 s 80(1), (6), (9)(*e*) with effect in relation to land transactions with an effective date on or after 19 July 2007.

[2] Sub-s (5A) inserted by FA 2009 s 123, Sch 61 paras 24, 26 with effect where the effective date of the first transaction (within the meaning given by FA 2009 Sch 61 para 5(2)) is on or after 21 July 2009.

87 Interest on unpaid tax

(1) Interest is payable on the amount of any unpaid tax from the end of the period of 30 days after the relevant date until the tax is paid.

(2) The Inland Revenue may by regulations amend subsection (1) so as to make interest run from the end of such shorter period after the relevant date as may be prescribed or, if the regulations so provide, from that date.

(3) For the purposes of this section "the relevant date" is—

(*a*) in the case of an amount payable because relief is withdrawn under—

[(ia) Schedule 6A (relief for certain acquisitions of residential property),][1]

(i) Part 1 of Schedule 7 (group relief),

(ii) Part 2 of that Schedule (reconstruction or acquisition relief), or

(iii) Schedule 8 (charities relief),

the date of the disqualifying event;

[(*aa*) in the case of an amount payable under section 81A in respect of an earlier transaction because of the effect of a later linked transaction, the effective date of the later transaction;][2]

[(*ab*) in the case of an amount payable under paragraph 3(3) or 4(3) of Schedule 17A (leases that continue after a fixed term and treatment of leases for an indefinite term), the day on which the lease becomes treated as being for a longer fixed term;][3]

(*b*) in the case of a deferred payment under section 90, the date when the deferred payment is due;

(*c*) in any other case, the effective date of the transaction.

(4) In subsection (3)(*a*) "the disqualifying event" means—

[(*za*) in relation to the withdrawal of relief under Schedule 6A an event mentioned in paragraph (*a*), (*b*) or (*c*) of paragraph 11(2), (3), (4) or (5) of that Schedule;][1]

(*a*) in relation to the withdrawal of group relief, the purchaser ceasing to be a member of the same group as the vendor within the meaning of Part 1 of Schedule 7);

(*b*) in relation to the withdrawal of reconstruction or acquisition relief, the change of control of the acquiring company mentioned in paragraph 9(1)(*a*) of that Schedule or, as the case may be, the event mentioned in paragraph 11(1)(*a*) or (2)(*a*) of that Schedule;

(*c*) in relation to the withdrawal of charities relief, a disqualifying event as defined in paragraph 2(3) [or 3(2)][4] of Schedule 8.

(5) Subsection (3)(*c*) applies in a case within section 51 (contingent, uncertain or unascertained consideration) if payment is not deferred under section 90, with the result that interest on any tax payable under section 80 (adjustment where contingency ceases or consideration is ascertained) runs from the effective date of the transaction.

(6) If an amount is lodged with the Inland Revenue in respect of the tax, the amount on which interest is payable is reduced by that amount.

(7) Interest is calculated at the rate applicable under section 178 of the Finance Act 1989 (c 26) (power of Treasury to prescribe rates of interest).

Amendments—[1] In sub-s (3), para (a)(ia) inserted, and sub-s (4)(za) inserted by FA 2004 s 296, Sch 39 para 17(4) with effect for any transaction of which the effective date (within the meaning of FA 2003 Pt 4) is on or after 22 July 2004: FA 2004 Sch 39 para 26. These insertions were previously made by the Stamp Duty and Stamp Duty Land Tax (Variation of the Finance Act 2003) (No 2) Regulations, SI 2003/2816 regs 1, 2, Schedule para 3(4) with effect from 1 December 2003. Those regulations are revoked by FA 2004 Sch 39 para 14(2).

[2] Sub-s (3)(aa) inserted by FA 2004 s 296, Sch 39 para 19(3) with effect for any transaction of which the effective date (within the meaning of FA 2003 Pt 4) is on or after 22 July 2004: FA 2004 Sch 39 para 26. This insertion was previously made by SI 2003/2816 regs 1, 2, Schedule para 5(4) with effect from 1 December 2003. Those regulations are revoked by FA 2004 Sch 39 para 14(2).

[3] Sub-s (3)(ab) inserted by FA 2004 s 296, Sch 39 para 22(5) with effect for any transaction of which the effective date (within the meaning of FA 2003 Pt 4) is on or after 22 July 2004: FA 2004 Sch 39 para 26. This insertion previously made by the Stamp Duty and Stamp Duty Land Tax (Variation of the Finance Act 2003) (No 2) Regulations, SI 2003/2816 regs 1, 2, Schedule para 8(6) with effect from 1 December 2003. Those regulations are revoked by FA 2004 Sch 39 para 14(2).

4 Words in sub-s (4)(c) inserted by FA 2004 s 302(6), (7) with effect for any transaction of which the effective date (within the meaning of FA 2003 Pt 4) is on or after 22 July 2004.

88 Interest on penalties

A penalty under this Part shall carry interest at the rate applicable under section 178 of the Finance Act 1989 from the date it is determined until payment.

89 Interest on repayment of tax overpaid etc

(1) A repayment by the Inland Revenue to which this section applies shall be made with interest at the rate applicable under section 178 of the Finance Act 1989 for the period between the relevant time (as defined below) and the date when the order for repayment is issued.

(2) This section applies to—

(*a*) any repayment of tax, and

(*b*) any repayment of a penalty under this Part.

In that case the relevant time is the date on which the payment of tax or penalty was made.

(3) This section also applies to a repayment by the Inland Revenue of an amount lodged with them in respect of the tax payable in respect of a transaction.

In that case the relevant time is the date on which the amount was lodged with them.

(4) No interest is payable under this section in respect of a payment made in consequence of an order or judgment of a court having power to allow interest on the payment.

(5) Interest paid to any person under this section is not income of that person for any tax purposes.

90 Application to defer payment in case of contingent or uncertain consideration

(1) The purchaser may apply to the Inland Revenue to defer payment of tax in a case where the amount payable depends on the amount or value of chargeable consideration that—

(*a*) at the effective date of the transaction is contingent or uncertain, and

(*b*) falls to be paid or provided on one or more future dates of which at least one falls, or may fall, more than six months after the effective date of the transaction.

(2) The Inland Revenue may make provision by regulations for carrying this section into effect.

(3) The regulations may in particular—

(*a*) specify when an application is to be made;

(*b*) impose requirements as to the form and contents of an application;

(*c*) require the applicant to provide such information as the Inland Revenue may reasonably require for the purposes of determining whether to accept an application;

(*d*) specify the grounds on which an application may be refused;

(*e*) specify the procedure for reaching a decision on an application;

(*f*) make provision for postponing payment of tax when an application has been made;

(*g*) provide for an appeal to the [tribunal][2] against a refusal to accept an application, and make provision in relation to such an appeal corresponding to any provision made in relation to appeals under Part 7 of Schedule 10 (appeals against Revenue decisions on tax);

(*h*) provide for the effect of accepting an application;

(*i*) require the purchaser to make a return or further return, and to make such payments or further payments of tax as may be specified, in such circumstances as may be specified.

(4) The provisions of Schedule 10 (returns, enquiries, assessments and other matters) apply to a return under this section as they apply to a land transaction return.

(5) An application under this section does not affect the purchaser's obligations as regards payment of tax in respect of chargeable consideration that has already been paid or provided or is not contingent and whose amount is ascertained or ascertainable at the time the application is made.

This applies as regards both the time of payment and the calculation of the amount payable.

(6) Regulations under this section may provide that where—

(*a*) a payment is made as mentioned in subsection (5), and

(*b*) an application under this section is accepted in respect of other chargeable consideration taken into account in calculating the amount of that payment,

section 80 (adjustment where contingency ceases or consideration is ascertained) does not apply in relation to the payment and, instead, any necessary adjustment shall be made in accordance with the regulations.

[(7) This section does not apply so far as the consideration consists of rent.][1]

HMRC Manuals—Stamp Duty Land Tax Manual SDLTM50900–52000 (general guidance on making applications under this section, including guidance on pre-transaction and post-transaction rulings).

Amendments—[1] Sub-s (7) inserted by FA 2004 s 296, Sch 39 para 22(6) with effect for any transaction of which the effective date (within the meaning of FA 2003 Pt 4) is on or after 22 July 2004: FA 2004 Sch 39 para 26. This insertion was previously made by the Stamp Duty and Stamp Duty Land Tax (Variation of the Finance Act 2003) (No 2) Regulations, SI 2003/2816 regs 1, 2, Schedule para 8(7) with effect from 1 December 2003. Those regulations are revoked by FA 2004 Sch 39 para 14(2).

2 In sub-s (3)(g) word substituted for the words "General or Special Commissioners" by the Transfer of Tribunal Functions and Revenue and Customs Appeals Order, SI 2009/56 art 3, Sch 1 para 368 with effect from 1 April 2009.

91 Collection and recovery of tax etc

(1) The provisions of Schedule 12 have effect with respect to the collection and recovery of tax.

In that Schedule—

Part 1 contains general provisions, and
Part 2 relates to court proceedings.

(2) The provisions of that Schedule have effect in relation to the collection and recovery of any unpaid amount by way of—

(*a*) penalty under this Part, or

(*b*) interest under this Part (on unpaid tax or penalty),

as if it were an amount of unpaid tax.

92 Payment by cheque

For the purposes of this Part where—

(*a*) payment to the Inland Revenue is made by cheque, and

(*b*) the cheque is paid on its first presentation to the banker on whom it is drawn,

the payment is treated as made on the day on which the cheque was received by the Inland Revenue.

Compliance

93 Information powers

(1) Schedule 13 has effect with respect to the powers of the Inland Revenue to call for documents and information for the purposes of stamp duty land tax.

(2) In that Schedule—

Part 1 confers power on an authorised officer to call for documents or information from the taxpayer;[1]

Part 2 confers power on an authorised officer to call for documents from a third party;[1]

Part 3 confers power on an authorised officer to call for the papers of a tax accountant;

Part 4 imposes restrictions on the powers under [Part 3][1];

Part 5 confers powers on the Board to call for documents or information;[1]

Part 6 provides for an order of a judicial authority for the delivery of documents;

Part 7 provides for entry with a warrant to obtain evidence of an offence;[1]

Part 8 relates to falsification etc of documents.[1]

(3) A person who is required by a notice under Part *1, 2 or*[1] 3 of Schedule 13 to deliver a document or to provide information, or to make a document available for inspection, and who fails to comply with the notice is liable to a penalty not exceeding £300.

(4) If the failure continues after a penalty has been imposed under subsection (3), he is liable to a further penalty or penalties not exceeding £60 for each day on which the failure continues after the day on which the penalty under that subsection was imposed (but excluding any day for which a penalty under this subsection has already been imposed).

(5) No penalty shall be imposed under subsection (3) or (4) in respect of a failure at any time after the failure has been remedied.

(6) A person who is required by a notice under Part *1, 2 or*[1] 3 of Schedule 13 to deliver a document or to provide information, or to make a document available for inspection, and who fraudulently or negligently delivers, provides or makes available any incorrect document or information is liable to a penalty not exceeding £3,000.

Amendments—[1] In sub-s (2), entries repealed and words in entry relating to Part 4 substituted for words "Parts 1 to 3", and in sub-ss (3), (6) words repealed, by the Finance Act 2009, Section 96 and Schedule 48 (Appointed Day, Savings and Consequential Amendments) Order, SI 2009/3054 art 3, Schedule para 11(1), (2) with effect from 1 April 2010. Note that, in relation to a notice given under Part 1 or 2 of Sch 13 before 1 April 2010, s 93(3), (6) apply on and after 1 April 2010 disregarding the amendments made by the Schedule to SI 2009/3054 (SI 2009/3054 art 7(1), (4)

94 Power to inspect premises

(1) If for the purposes of this Part the Board authorise an officer of theirs to inspect any property for the purpose of ascertaining its market value, or any other matter relevant for the purposes of this Part, the person having custody or possession of the property shall permit the officer so authorised to inspect it at such reasonable times as the Board may consider necessary.

(2) A person who wilfully delays or obstructs an officer of the Board acting in pursuance of this section commits an offence and is liable on summary conviction to a fine not exceeding level 1 on the standard scale.[1]

Amendments—[1] This section repealed by the Finance Act 2009, Section 96 and Schedule 48 (Appointed Day, Savings and Consequential Amendments) Order, SI 2009/3054 art 3, Schedule para 11(1), (3) with effect from 1 April 2010. Note that, in relation to an inspection made before 1 April 2010, sub-s (2) continues to have effect on or after that day despite its repeal by SI 2009/3054 (SI 2009/3054 art 7(1), (5)).

95 Offence of fraudulent evasion of tax

(1) A person commits an offence if he is knowingly concerned in the fraudulent evasion of tax by him or any other person.

(2) A person guilty of an offence under this section is liable—

(*a*) on summary conviction to imprisonment for a term not exceeding six months or a fine not exceeding the statutory maximum, or both;

(*b*) on conviction on indictment, to imprisonment for a term not exceeding seven years or a fine, or both.

96 Penalty for assisting in preparation of incorrect return etc

A person who assists in or induces the preparation or delivery of any information, return or other document that—

(*a*) he knows will be, or is likely to be, used for any purpose of tax, and

(*b*) he knows to be incorrect,

is liable to a penalty not exceeding £3,000.

97 Power to allow further time and reasonable excuse for failure

(1) For the purposes of this Part a person shall be deemed not to have failed to do anything required to be done within a limited time if he did it within such further time, if any, as the Inland Revenue may allow.

(2) Where a person had a reasonable excuse for not doing anything required to be done for the purposes of this Part

(*a*) he shall be deemed not to have failed to do it unless the excuse ceased, and

(*b*) after the excuse ceased, he shall be deemed not to have failed to do it if he did it without unreasonable delay after the excuse had ceased.

98 Admissibility of evidence not affected by offer of settlement etc

(1) Statements made or documents produced by or on behalf of a person are not inadmissible in proceedings to which this section applies by reason only that it has been drawn to his attention—

(*a*) that where serious tax fraud has been committed the Board may accept a money settlement and that the Board will accept such a settlement, and will not pursue a criminal prosecution, if he makes a full confession of all tax irregularities, or

(*b*) that the extent to which he is helpful and volunteers information is a factor that will be taken into account in determining the amount of any penalty,

and that he was or may have been induced thereby to make the statements or produce the documents.

(2) The proceedings to which this section applies are—

(*a*) any criminal proceedings against the person in question for any form of fraudulent conduct in connection with or in relation to tax;

(*b*) any proceedings against him for the recovery of any tax due from him;

(*c*) any proceedings for a penalty or on appeal against the determination of a penalty.

99 General provisions about penalties

(1) Schedule 14 has effect with respect to the determination of penalties under this Part and related appeals.

(2) The Board may in their discretion mitigate a penalty under this Part, or stay or compound any proceedings for the recovery of such a penalty.

They may also, after judgment, further mitigate or entirely remit the penalty.

[(2A) Where a person is liable to more than one tax-related penalty in respect of the same land transaction, each penalty after the first shall be reduced so that his liability to such penalties, in total, does not exceed the amount of whichever is (or, but for this subsection, would be) the greatest one.][1]

(3) Nothing in the provisions of this Part relating to penalties affects any criminal proceedings for an offence.

HMRC Manuals—Stamp Duty Land Tax Manual SDLTM86600, 86620 (maximum penalties payable can be reduced or abated by up to 20 per cent (exceptionally 30 per cent where there is spontaneous and complete disclosure and the purchaser has no reason to fear early discovery) for the amount of disclosure by the purchaser; 40 per cent for the amount of co-operation received from the purchaser during the enquiry; 40 per cent for the size and the gravity of the offences).

Amendments—[1] Sub-s (2A) inserted by FA 2004 s 298(1), (4), with effect from 22 July 2004.

Application of provisions

100 Companies

(1) In this Part "company", except as otherwise expressly provided, means any body corporate or unincorporated association, but does not include a partnership.

(2) Everything to be done by a company under this Part shall be done by the company acting through—

(*a*) the proper officer of the company, or

(*b*) another person having for the time being having the express, implied or apparent authority of the company to act on its behalf for the purpose.

Paragraph (*b*) does not apply where a liquidator has been appointed for the company.

(3) Service on a company of any document under or in pursuance of this Part may be effected by serving it on the proper officer.

(4) Tax due from a company that—

(*a*) is not a body corporate, or

(*b*) is incorporated under the law of a country or territory outside the United Kingdom,

may, without prejudice to any other method of recovery, be recovered from the proper officer of the company.

(5) The proper officer may retain out of any money coming into his hands on behalf of the company sufficient sums to pay that tax and, so far as he is not so reimbursed, he is entitled to be indemnified by the company in respect of the liability imposed on him.

(6) For the purposes of this Part—

(*a*) the proper officer of a body corporate is the secretary, or person acting as secretary, of the company, and

(*b*) the proper officer of an unincorporated association, or of a body corporate that does not have a proper officer within paragraph (*a*), is the treasurer, or person acting as treasurer, of the company.

This subsection does not apply if a liquidator or administrator has been appointed for the company.

(7) If a liquidator or administrator has been appointed for the company, then, for the purposes of this Part—

(*a*) the liquidator or, as the case may be, the administrator is the proper officer, and

(*b*) if two or more persons are appointed to act jointly or concurrently as the administrator of the company, the proper officer is—

(i) such one of them as is specified in a notice given to the Inland Revenue by those persons for the purposes of this section, or

(ii) where the Inland Revenue is not so notified, such one or more of those persons as the Inland Revenue may designate as the proper officer for those purposes.

101 Unit trust schemes

(1) This Part (with the exception of the [provision][1] mentioned in subsection (7) below) applies in relation to a unit trust scheme as if—

(*a*) the trustees were a company, and

(*b*) the rights of the unit holders were shares in the company.

(2) Each of the parts of an umbrella scheme is regarded for the purposes of this Part as a separate unit trust scheme and the scheme as a whole is not so regarded.

(3) An "umbrella scheme" means a unit trust scheme—

(*a*) that provides arrangements for separate pooling of the contributions of participants and the profits or income out of which payments are to be made for them, and

(*b*) under which the participants are entitled to exchange rights in one pool for rights in another.

A "part" of an umbrella scheme means such of the arrangements as relate to a separate pool.

(4) In this Part, subject to any regulations under subsection (5)—

"unit trust scheme" has the same meaning as in the Financial Services and Markets Act 2000 (c 8), and

"unit holder" means a person entitled to a share of the investments subject to the trusts of a unit trust scheme.

(5) The Treasury may by regulations provide that a scheme of a description specified in the regulations is to be treated as not being a unit trust scheme for the purposes of this Part. Any such regulations may contain such supplementary and transitional provisions as appear to the Treasury to be necessary or expedient.

(6) [Section 620 of the Corporation Tax Act 2010 (court investment funds treated as authorised unit trusts)][2] applies for the purposes of this Part as it applies for the purposes of that Act, with the substitution for references to an authorised unit trust of references to a unit trust scheme.

(7) An unit trust scheme is not to be treated as a company for the purposes of—

. . . [1]Schedule 7 (group relief, reconstruction relief or acquisition relief).

Amendments—[1] Words in sub-s (1) substituted, words in sub-s (7) repealed by FA 2006 s 166(3), s 178, Sch 26 Pt 7(3) with effect in relation to any land transaction of which the effective date is, or is after, 22 March 2006, subject to FA 2006 s 166(5), (6).

[2] In sub-s (6) words "Section 469A of the Taxes Act 1988 (court common investment funds treated as authorised unit trusts)" substituted by CTA 2010 s 1177, Sch 1 paras 400, 408. CTA 2010 has effect for corporation tax purposes for accounting periods ending on or after 1 April 2010, and for income and capital gains tax purposes for the tax year 2010–11 and subsequent tax years.

102 Open-ended investment companies

(1) The Treasury may by regulations make such provision as they consider appropriate for securing that the provisions of this Part have effect in relation to—

(*a*) open-ended investment companies of such description as may be prescribed in the regulations, and

(*b*) transactions involving such companies,

in a manner corresponding, subject to such modifications as the Treasury consider appropriate, to the manner in which they have effect in relation to unit trust schemes and transactions involving such trusts.

(2) The regulations may, in particular, make provision—

(*a*) modifying the operation of any prescribed provision in relation to open-ended investment companies so as to secure that arrangements for treating the assets of such a company as assets comprised in separate pools are given an effect corresponding to that of equivalent arrangements constituting the separate parts of an umbrella scheme;

(*b*) treating the separate parts of the undertaking of an open-ended investment company in relation to which such provision is made as distinct companies for the purposes of this Part.

(3) Regulations under this section may—

(*a*) make different provision for different cases, and

(*b*) contain such incidental, supplementary, consequential and transitional provision as the Treasury think fit.

(4) In this section—

"open-ended investment company" has the meaning given by section 236 of the Financial Services and Markets Act 2000 (c 8);

"prescribed" means prescribed by regulations under this section; and

"unit trust scheme" and "umbrella scheme" have the same meaning as in section 101.

103 Joint purchasers

(1) This section applies to a land transaction where there are two or more purchasers who are or will be jointly entitled to the interest acquired.

(2) The general rules are that—

(*a*) any obligation of the purchaser under this Part in relation to the transaction is an obligation of the purchasers jointly but may be discharged by any of them,

(*b*) anything required or authorised by this Part to be done in relation to the purchaser must be done by or in relation to all of them, and

(*c*) any liability of the purchaser under this Part in relation to the transaction (in particular, any liability arising by virtue of the failure to fulfil an obligation within paragraph (*a*)), is a joint and several liability of the purchasers.

These rules are subject to the following provisions.

(3) If the transaction is a notifiable transaction, a single land transaction return is required.

(4) The declaration required by paragraph 1(1)(*c*) of Schedule 10 . . . [1] (declaration that return . . . [1] is complete and correct) must be made by all the purchasers.

(5) If the Inland Revenue give notice of an enquiry into the return . . . [1]—

(*a*) the notice must be given to each of the purchasers,

(*b*) the powers of the Inland Revenue as to the production of documents and provision of information for the purposes of the enquiry are exercisable separately (and differently) in relation to each of the purchasers,

(*c*) any of the purchasers may apply for a direction that a closure notice be given (and all of them are entitled to [to be parties to the application][2]), and

(*d*) the closure notice must be given to each of the purchasers.

(6) A Revenue determination or discovery assessment relating to the transaction must be made against all the purchasers and is not effective against any of them unless notice of it is given to each of them whose identity is known to the Inland Revenue.

(7) In the case of an appeal arising from proceedings under this Part relating to the transaction—

(*a*) the appeal may be brought by any of the purchasers,

(*b*) notice of the appeal must be given to any of them by whom it is not brought,

(*c*) the agreement of all the purchasers is required if the appeal is to be settled by agreement,

[(*d*) if it is not settled, and is notified to the tribunal, any of them are entitled to be parties to the appeal, and][2]

[(*e*) the tribunal's decision on the appeal binds all of them.][2]

[(7A) In a case where subsection (7) applies and some (but not all) of the purchasers require HMRC to undertake a review under paragraph 36B or 36C of Schedule 10—

(*a*) notification of the review must be given by HMRC to each of the other purchasers whose identity is known to HMRC,

(*b*) any of the other purchasers may be a party to the review if they notify HMRC in writing,

(*c*) the notice of HMRC's conclusions must be given to each of the other purchasers whose identity is known to HMRC,

(*d*) paragraph 36F of Schedule 10 (effect of conclusions of review) applies in relation to all of the purchasers, and

(*e*) any of the purchasers may notify the appeal to the tribunal under paragraph 36G.][2]

(8) This section has effect subject to—

the provisions of Schedule 15 relating to partnerships, and

the provisions of Schedule 16 relating to trustees.

Amendments—[1] Words in sub-ss (4), (5) repealed by FA 2008 s 94, Sch 30 paras 1, 4 with effect in relation to transactions with an effective date on or after 12 March 2008.

[2] In sub-s (5)(c) words substituted for the words "appear and be heard on the application"; sub-s (7)(d), (e) substituted; sub-s (7A) inserted by the Transfer of Tribunal Functions and Revenue and Customs Appeals Order, SI 2009/56 art 3, Sch 1 para 369 with effect from 1 April 2009. Sub-s (7)(d), (e) previously read as follows—

"(*d*) if it is not settled, any of them are entitled to appear and be heard, and

(*e*) the decision on the appeal binds all of them.".

104 Partnerships

(1) Schedule 15 has effect with respect to the application of this Part in relation to partnerships.

(2) In that Schedule—

Part 1 defines "partnership" and contains other general provisions, and

Part 2 deals with ordinary partnership transactions, and

Part 3 [makes special provision for certain transactions][1].

Amendments—[1] Words in para (2) substituted for the words "excludes certain transactions from stamp duty land tax "by FA 2004 s 304, Sch 41 paras 2(a), 3 with effect for any partnership transaction of which the effective date (within the meaning of FA 2003 Pt 4) is after 22 July 2004. A "partnership transaction" means a transaction mentioned in FA 2003 Sch 15 para 9(1): FA 2004 Sch 41 para 3(2).

105 Trustees

Schedule 16 has effect with respect to the application of this Part in relation to trustees.

106 Persons acting in a representative capacity etc

(1) The person having the direction, management or control of the property of an incapacitated person—

(*a*) is responsible for discharging any obligations under this Part, in relation to a transaction affecting that property, to which the incapacitated person would be subject if he were not incapacitated, and

(*b*) may retain out of money coming into his hands on behalf of the incapacitated person sums sufficient to meet any payment he is liable to make under this Part, and, so far as he is not so reimbursed, is entitled to be indemnified in respect of any such payment.

(2) The parent or guardian of a minor is responsible for discharging any obligations of the minor under this Part that are not discharged by the minor himself.

(3) The personal representatives of a person who is the purchaser under a land transaction—

(*a*) are responsible for discharging the obligations of the purchaser under this Part in relation to the transaction, and

(*b*) may deduct any payment made by them under this Part out of the assets and effects of the deceased person.

(4) A receiver appointed by a court in the United Kingdom having the direction and control of any property is responsible for discharging any obligations under this Part in relation to a transaction affecting that property as if the property were not under the direction and control of the court.

107 Crown application

[(1) This Part binds the Crown, subject to the following provisions of this section.][1]

(2) A land transaction under which the purchaser is any of the following is exempt from charge:

Government

A Minister of the Crown

The Scottish Ministers

A Northern Ireland department

[The Welsh Ministers, the First Minister for Wales and the Counsel General to the Welsh Assembly Government][2]

Parliament etc

The Corporate Officer of the House of Lords

The Corporate Officer of the House of Commons

The Scottish Parliamentary Corporate Body

The Northern Ireland Assembly Commission

[The National Assembly for Wales Commission][2]

The National Assembly for Wales

(3) The powers conferred by Part 7 of Schedule 13 (entry with warrant to obtain information) are not exercisable in relation to premises occupied for the purposes of the Crown.

[(4) Nothing in this section shall be read as making the Crown liable to prosecution for an offence.][1]

Amendments—[1] Sub-s (1) substituted, and sub-s (4) inserted, by FA 2004 s 296, Sch 39 para 21 with effect for any transaction of which the effective date (within the meaning of FA 2003 Pt 4) is on or after 22 July 2004: FA 2004 Sch 39 para 26. These amendments were previously made by the Stamp Duty and Stamp Duty Land Tax (Variation of the Finance Act 2003) (No 2) Regulations, SI 2003/2816 regs 1, 2, Schedule para 7 with effect from 1 December 2003. Those regulations are revoked by FA 2004 Sch 39 para 14(2).

2 In sub-s (2) entry beginning "The Welsh Ministers," inserted and entry "The National Assembly for Wales Commission" substituted, by the Government of Wales Act 2006 s 160(1), Sch 10 paras 62, 65 with effect from 25 May 2007, being the date on which the initial period ended (following the appointment of the First Minister) (Government of Wales Act 2006 ss 46, 161(4), (5)).

Supplementary provisions

108 Linked transactions

(1) Transactions are "linked" for the purposes of this Part if they form part of a single scheme, arrangement or series of transactions between the same vendor and purchaser or, in either case, persons connected with them.

[Section 1122 of the Corporation Tax Act 2010][2] (connected persons) has effect for the purposes of this subsection.

(2) Where there are two or more linked transactions with the same effective date, the purchaser, or all of the purchasers if there is more than one, may make a single land transaction return as if all of those transactions that are notifiable were a single notifiable transaction.

(3) Where two or more purchasers make a single return in respect of linked transactions, section 103 (joint purchasers) applies as if—

(*a*) the transactions in question were a single transaction, and

(*b*) those purchasers were purchasers acting jointly.

[(4) This section is subject to section 47(1).][1]

Amendments—[1] Sub-s (4) inserted by FA 2007 s 76(2), (3) with effect in relation to a set of land transactions if the effective date of any of them is on or after 19 July 2007.

2 In sub-s (1) words "Section 839 of the Taxes Act 1988" substituted by CTA 2010 s 1177, Sch 1 paras 400, 409. CTA 2010 has effect for corporation tax purposes for accounting periods ending on or after 1 April 2010, and for income and capital gains tax purposes for the tax year 2010–11 and subsequent tax years.

109 General power to vary this Part by regulations

(1) The Treasury may if they consider it expedient in the public interest make provision by regulations for the variation of this Part in its application to land transactions of any description.

(2) The power conferred by this section includes, in particular, power to alter—

(*a*) the descriptions of land transaction that are chargeable or notifiable;

(*b*) the descriptions of land transaction in respect of which tax is chargeable at any existing rate or amount.

(3) The power conferred by this section does not, except as mentioned in subsection (2)(*b*), include power to vary any threshold, rate or amount specified in—

(*a*) section 55 (amount of tax chargeable: general), or

(*b*) Schedule 5 (amount of tax chargeable: rent).

(4) This section has effect subject to section 110 (approval of regulations by House of Commons).

(5) Regulations under this section do not apply in relation to any transaction of which the effective date is after the end of—

(*a*) the period of 18 months beginning with the day on which the regulations were made, or

(*b*) such shorter period as may be specified in the regulations.

This does not affect the power to make further provision by regulations under this section to the same or similar effect.

(6) Regulations under this section may include such supplementary, transitional and incidental provision as appears to the Treasury to be necessary or expedient.

(7) The power conferred by this section may be exercised at any time after the passing of this Act.

110 Approval of regulations under general power

(1) An instrument containing regulations under section 109 (general power to vary this Part by regulations) must be laid before the House of Commons after being made.

(2) If the regulations are not approved by the House of Commons before the end of the period of 28 days beginning with the day on which they are made, they shall cease to have effect at the end of that period (if they have not already ceased to have effect under subsection (3)).

(3) If on any day during that period of 28 days the House of Commons, in proceedings on a motion that (or to the effect that) the regulations be approved, comes to a decision rejecting the regulations, they shall cease to have effect at the end of that day.

(4) In reckoning any such period of 28 days take no account of any time during which—

(*a*) Parliament is prorogued or dissolved, or

(*b*) the House of Commons is adjourned for more than four days.

(5) Where regulations cease to have effect under this section, their ceasing to have effect is without prejudice to anything done in reliance on them.

As to claims for repayment, see section 111.

[(6) This section does not apply to regulations containing only provision varying section 57AA or 73CA, or paragraph 15 of Schedule 9, which does not increase any person's liability to tax.][1]

Amendments[1] Subsection (6) inserted by FA 2010 s 6(1), (4) with effect in relation to any land transaction of which the effective date is on or after 25 March 2010 but before 25 March 2012 (FA 2010 s 6(6)).

111 Claim for repayment if regulations under general power not approved

(1) Where regulations cease to have effect under section 110, [a claim may be made to the Inland Revenue for repayment of any tax, interest or penalty that would not have been payable but for the regulations][1].

(2) Section 89 (interest on repayment of tax overpaid etc) applies to a repayment under this section.

(3) A claim for repayment must be made within two years after the effective date of the transaction in question.

(4) The Inland Revenue may make provision by regulations—

(*a*) for varying the time limit for making a claim;

(*b*) as to any other conditions that must be met before repayment is made.

Amendments—[1] In sub-s (1), words substituted for the words "any amount paid by way of tax, or interest or penalty, that would not have been payable but for the regulations shall, on a claim, be repaid by the Inland Revenue" by FA 2004 s 299(1), (5) with effect from 22 July 2004.

112 Power to amend certain provisions before implementation

(1) The Treasury may by regulations amend the following provisions of this Part—

(*a*) Schedule 5 (amount of tax chargeable: rent);

(*b*) subsection (2) of section 55 (amount of tax chargeable: general) so far as relating to the thresholds at which different rates of tax become payable.

(2) The regulations may make such consequential amendments of Schedule 6 (disadvantaged areas relief) as appear to the Treasury to be appropriate.

(3) A statutory instrument containing regulations under this section shall not be made unless a draft of the instrument has been laid before and approved by resolution of the House of Commons.

(4) The power conferred by this section is not exercisable after the implementation date.

113 Functions conferred on "the Inland Revenue"

(1) References in this Part to "the Inland Revenue" are to any officer of the Board, except as otherwise provided.

(2) Any power of the Inland Revenue to make regulations is exercisable only by the Board.

(3) In Schedule 10 (returns, assessments and other administrative matters)—

(*a*) functions of the Inland Revenue under these provisions are exercisable by the Board or an officer of the Board—

(i) paragraph 28 (discovery assessment),

(ii) paragraph 29 (assessment to recover excessive repayment);

(*b*) functions of the Inland Revenue under these provisions are functions of the Board—

(i) paragraph 33 (relief in case of double assessment),

(ii) paragraph 34 (relief in case of mistake in return).

[(3A) The following functions of the Inland Revenue under Schedule 11A (claims not included in returns) are functions of the Board—

(*a*) functions under paragraph 2(1) (form of claims),

(*b*) functions relating to a claim made to the Board.][1]

(4) Nothing in this section affects any provision of this Part that expressly confers functions on the Board, an officer of the Board, a collector or a specific officer of the Board.

Amendments—[1] Sub-s (3A) inserted by FA 2004 s 299(1), (6) with effect from 22 July 2004.

114 Orders and regulations made by the Treasury or the Inland Revenue

(1) Except as otherwise provided, any power of the Treasury or the Inland Revenue to make an order or regulations under this Part, or under any other enactments relating to stamp duty land tax (including enactments passed after this Act), is exercisable by statutory instrument.

(2) Subsection (1) does not apply in relation to the power conferred by—

paragraph 8 of Schedule 5 to this Act (tax chargeable in respect of rent: power to prescribe temporal discount rate),

section 178(5) of the Finance Act 1989 (c 26) (power to prescribe rates of interest).

(3) Except as otherwise provided, a statutory instrument containing any order or regulations made by the Treasury or the Inland Revenue under this Part, or under any other enactments relating to stamp duty land tax (including enactments passed after this Act), shall be subject to annulment in pursuance of a resolution of the House of Commons.

(4) Subsection (3) does not apply to a statutory instrument made under the power conferred by—

section 61(3) (compliance with planning obligations: power to add to list of public authorities);

paragraph 1(3) of Schedule 9 (right to buy transactions: power to add to list of relevant public sector bodies);

paragraph 2(2) of Schedule 19 (commencement and transitional provisions: power to appoint implementation date).

[(5) The first set of regulations under section 58B (new zero-carbon homes) may not be made unless a draft has been laid before and approved by resolution of the House of Commons.][1]

[(6) An order or regulations under this Part—

(*a*) may make provision having effect generally or only in specified cases or circumstances,

(*b*) may make different provision for different cases or circumstances, and
(*c*) may include incidental, consequential or transitional provision or savings.][1]

Cross reference—See F(No 2)A 2005 s 48(6) (disclosure of information contained in land transaction returns: sub-s (3) above does not apply to a Treasury order made under F(No 2)A 2005 s 48(5)).

Amendments—[1] Sub-ss (5), (6) inserted by FA 2007 s 19(2) with effect from 19 July 2007.

[115 General and Special Commissioners, appeals and other proceedings

Schedule 17 makes provision about the General and Special Commissioners, appeals and other proceedings before the Commissioners and related matters.][1]

Amendments—[1] Section 115 repealed by the Transfer of Tribunal Functions and Revenue and Customs Appeals Order, SI 2009/56 art 3, Sch 1 para 370 with effect from 1 April 2009.

Interpretation etc

116 Meaning of "residential property"

(1) In this Part "residential property" means—
(*a*) a building that is used or suitable for use as a dwelling, or is in the process of being constructed or adapted for such use, and
(*b*) land that is or forms part of the garden or grounds of a building within paragraph (*a*) (including any building or structure on such land), or
(*c*) an interest in or right over land that subsists for the benefit of a building within paragraph (*a*) or of land within paragraph (*b*);

and "non-residential property" means any property that is not residential property.

This is subject to the rule in subsection (7) in the case of a transaction involving six or more dwellings.

(2) For the purposes of subsection (1) a building used for any of the following purposes is used as a dwelling—
(*a*) residential accommodation for school pupils;
(*b*) residential accommodation for students, other than accommodation falling with subsection (3)(*b*);
(*c*) residential accommodation for members of the armed forces;
(*d*) an institution that is the sole or main residence of at least 90% of its residents and does not fall within any of paragraphs (*a*) to (*f*) of subsection (3).

(3) For the purposes of subsection (1) a building used for any of the following purposes is not used as a dwelling—
(*a*) a home or other institution providing residential accommodation for children;
(*b*) a hall of residence for students in further or higher education;
(*c*) a home or other institution providing residential accommodation with personal care for persons in need of personal care by reason of old age, disablement, past or present dependence on alcohol or drugs or past or present mental disorder;
(*d*) a hospital or hospice;
(*e*) a prison or similar establishment;
(*f*) a hotel or inn or similar establishment.

(4) Where a building is used for a purpose specified in subsection (3), no account shall be taken for the purposes of subsection (1)(*a*) of its suitability for any other use.

(5) Where a building that is not in use is suitable for use for at least one of the purposes specified in subsection (2) and at least one of those specified in subsection (3)—
(*a*) if there is one such use for which it is most suitable, or if the uses for which it is most suitable are all specified in the same sub-paragraph, no account shall be taken for the purposes of subsection (1)(*a*) of its suitability for any other use,
(*b*) otherwise, the building shall be treated for those purposes as suitable for use as a dwelling.

(6) In this section "building" includes part of a building.

(7) Where six or more separate dwellings are the subject of a single transaction involving the transfer of a major interest in, or the grant of a lease over, them, then, for the purposes of this Part as it applies in relation to that transaction, those dwellings are treated as not being residential property.

(8) The Treasury may by order—
(*a*) amend subsections (2) and (3) so as to change or clarify the cases where use of a building is, or is not to be, use of a building as a dwelling for the purposes of subsection (1);
(*b*) amend or repeal subsection (7) and the reference to that subsection in subsection (1).

Any such order may contain such incidental, supplementary, consequential or transitional provision as appears to the Treasury to be necessary or expedient.

HMRC Manuals—Stamp Duty Land Tax Manual, SDLTM20070 (definition of residential property; HMRC intelligent decision-making tool is available at www.hmrc.gov.uk; non-residential property defined by exclusion from residential property definition)

Statement of Practice SP 1/04—(Disadvantaged areas relief, Stamp Office approach to borderline cases).

117 Meaning of "major interest" in land

(1) References in this Part to a "major interest" in land shall be construed as follows.

(2) In relation to land in England or Wales, the references are to—

(*a*) an estate in fee simple absolute, or
(*b*) a term of years absolute,
whether subsisting at law or in equity.
(3) In relation to land in Scotland, the references are to—
(*a*) the interest of an owner of land, or
(*b*) the tenant's right over or interest in a property subject to a lease.
Until the appointed day for the purposes of the Abolition of Feudal Tenure etc (Scotland) Act 2000 (asp 5), the reference in paragraph (*a*) to the interest of the owner shall be read, in relation to feudal property, as a reference to the estate or interest of the proprietor of the *dominium utile*.
(4) In relation to land in Northern Ireland, the references are to—
(*a*) any freehold estate, or
(*b*) any leasehold estate,
whether subsisting at law or in equity.

118 Meaning of "market value"

For the purposes of this Part "market value" shall be determined as for the purposes of the Taxation of Chargeable Gains Act 1992 (c 12) (see sections 272 to 274 of that Act).

HMRC Manuals—Stamp Duty Land Tax Manual, SDLTM04140 (meaning of market value – consideration by transfer of asset or provision of services)

119 Meaning of "effective date" of a transaction

(1) Except as otherwise provided, the effective date of a land transaction for the purposes of this Part is—
[(*a*) the date of completion, or
(*b*) such alternative date as the Commissioners for Her Majesty's Revenue and Customs may prescribe by regulations.][3].
(2) Other provision as to the effective date of certain descriptions of land transaction is made by—
section 44(4) (contract and conveyance: contract substantially performed without having been completed), . . . [2]
[section 44A(3) (contract providing for conveyance to third party),][1]
[section 45A(8) (contract providing for conveyance to third party: effect of transfer of rights),][1]
section 46(3) (options and rights of pre-emption)
[paragraph 12A(2) of Schedule 17A (agreement for lease followed by substantial performance),][1]
[paragraph 12B(3) of that Schedule (assignment of agreement for lease occurring after agreement substantially performed), and][1]
[paragraph 19(3) of that Schedule (missives of let etc in Scotland followed by substantial performance).][1]

HMRC Manuals—Stamp Duty Land Tax Manual, SDLTM07750–08050 (substantial performance of contract)

Amendments—[1] Words inserted by FA 2004 s 296, Sch 39 para 8 with effect in accordance with FA 2004 Sch 39 para 13(1), (2).
[2] Word "and" repealed by FA 2004 s 326, Sch 42 Pt 4(2) with effect in accordance with FA 2004 Sch 39 para 13.
[3] In sub-s (1), words substituted for the words "the date of completion" by F(No 2)A 2005 s 47(3) with effect from 20 July 2005.

[120 Further provisions relating to leases

Schedule 17A contains further provisions relating to leases.][1]

Amendments—[1] Substituted by FA 2004 s 296, Sch 39 para 22(1) with effect for any transaction of which the effective date (within the meaning of FA 2003 Pt 4) is on or after 22 July 2004: FA 2004 Sch 39 para 26. These amendments were previously made by the Stamp Duty and Stamp Duty Land Tax (Variation of the Finance Act 2003) (No 2) Regulations, SI 2003/2816 regs 1, 2, Schedule para 8(1) with effect from 1 December 2003. Those regulations are revoked by FA 2004 Sch 39 para 14(2).

121 Minor definitions

In this Part—
"assignment", in Scotland, means assignation;
"completion", in Scotland, means—
(*a*) in relation to a lease, when it is executed by the parties (that is to say, by signing) or constituted by any means;
(*b*) in relation to any other transaction, the settlement of the transaction;
"employee" includes an office-holder and related expressions have a corresponding meaning;
["HMRC" means Her Majesty's Revenue and Customs;][1]
"jointly entitled" means—
(*a*) in England and Wales, beneficially entitled as joint tenants or tenants in common,
(*b*) in Scotland, entitled as joint owners or owners in common,
(*c*) in Northern Ireland, beneficially entitled as joint tenants, tenants in common or coparceners;
"land" includes—
(*a*) buildings and structures, and
(*b*) land covered by water;

"registered social landlord" means—

(*a*) in relation to England and Wales, a body registered as a social landlord in a register maintained under section 1(1) of the Housing Act 1996 (c 52);

(*b*) in relation to Scotland, a body registered in the register maintained under section 57 of the Housing (Scotland) Act 2001 (asp 10);

(*c*) in relation to Northern Ireland, a housing association registered in the register maintained under Article 14 of the Housing (Northern Ireland) Order 1992 (SI 1992/1725 (NI 15));

"standard security" has the meaning given by the Conveyancing and Feudal Reform (Scotland) Act 1970 (c 35);

"statutory provision" means any provision made by or under an Act of Parliament, an Act of the Scottish Parliament or any Northern Ireland legislation;

"surrender", in Scotland, means renunciation;

"tax", unless the context otherwise requires, means tax under this Part.

["tribunal" means the First-tier Tribunal or, where determined by or under Tribunal Procedure Rules, the Upper Tribunal.][1]

Amendments—[1] Definitions inserted by the Transfer of Tribunal Functions and Revenue and Customs Appeals Order, SI 2009/56 art 3, Sch 1 para 371 with effect from 1 April 2009.

122 Index of defined expressions

In this Part the expressions listed below are defined or otherwise explained by the provisions indicated—

acquisition relief	Schedule 7, paragraph 8(1)
assignment (in Scotland)	section 121
bare trust	Schedule 16, paragraph 1(2)
the Board (in relation to the Inland Revenue)	section 42(3)
chargeable consideration	section 50 and Schedule 4
chargeable interest	section 48(1)
chargeable transaction	section 49
charities relief	Schedule 8, paragraph 1(1)
closure notice	Schedule 10, paragraph 23(1) (in relation to a land transaction return); . . . [5]
company	section 100 (except as otherwise expressly provided)
completion (in Scotland)	section 121
contingent (in relation to consideration)	section 51(3)
delivery (in relation to a land transaction return)	Schedule 10, paragraph 2(2)
discovery assessment	Schedule 10, paragraph 28(1)
effective date (in relation to a land transaction)	section 119
employee	section 121
exempt interest	section 48(2) to (5)
filing date (in relation to a land transaction return)	Schedule 10, paragraph 2(1)
implementation date	Schedule 19, paragraph 2(2)
the Inland Revenue	section 113
jointly entitled	section 121
land	section 121
land transaction	section 43(1)
land transaction return	section 76(1)
lease (and related expressions)	[Schedule 17A][1]
linked transactions	section 108
main subject-matter (in relation to a land transaction)	section 43(6)
major interest (in relation to land)	section 117
market value	section 118
notice of enquiry	Schedule 10, paragraph 12(1) (in relation to a land transaction return); . . . [5]

notifiable (in relation to a land transaction)	section 77 [(see too sections 71A(7) and 72A(7) [and paragraph 30 of Schedule 15][5])][4]
partnership (and related expressions)	Schedule 15, paragraphs 1 to 4
purchaser	section 43(4)
rate of tax	section 55(7)
reconstruction relief	Schedule 7, paragraph 7(1)
registered social landlord	section 121
residential property	section 116
[Revenue certificate	section 79(3)(*a*)][2]
Revenue determination	Schedule 10, paragraph 25(1)
self-assessment	section 76(3)(*a*)
. . .[5]	. . .[5]
settlement	Schedule 16, paragraph 1(1)
standard security	section 121
statutory provision	section 121
subject-matter (in relation to a land transaction)	section 43(6)
substantial performance (in relation to a contract)	section 44(5) to (7)
surrender (in Scotland)	section 121
tax	section 121
[tribunal	section 121][6]
uncertain (in relation to consideration)	section 51(3)
unit holder	section 101(4)
unit trust scheme	section 101(4)
vendor	section 43(4)[(see too sections 45(5A) and 45A(9))][3]

Amendments—[1] In Column 2 of the entry for "lease and related expressions", words substituted for the words "section 120" by FA 2004 s 296, Sch 39 para 22(7) with effect for any transaction of which the effective date (within the meaning of FA 2003 Pt 4) is on or after 22 July 2004: FA 2004 Sch 39 para 26. This substitution was previously made by the Stamp Duty and Stamp Duty Land Tax (Variation of the Finance Act 2003) (No 2) Regulations, SI 2003/2816 regs 1, 2, Schedule para 8(8) with effect from 1 December 2003. Those regulations are revoked by FA 2004 Sch 39 para 14(2).

[2] Entry inserted by FA 2004 s 296, Sch 39 para 25(4) with effect for any transaction of which the effective date (within the meaning of FA 2003 Pt 4) is on or after 22 July 2004: FA 2004 Sch 39 para 26. This insertion was previously made by the Stamp Duty and Stamp Duty Land Tax (Variation of the Finance Act 2003) (No 2) Regulations, SI 2003/2816 regs 1, 2, Schedule para 11(4) with effect from 1 December 2003. Those regulations are revoked by FA 2004 Sch 39 para 14(2).

[3] Words inserted by FA 2004 s 296, Sch 39 para 5(1), (6) with effect for any transfer of rights occurring after 17 March 2004: FA 2004 Sch 39 para 13(2).

[4] Words inserted by FA 2005 s 94, Sch 8 para 6 with effect in any case where the effective date (within the meaning of Part 4 of FA 2003) of the first transaction (within the meaning of FA 2003 s 71A (so far as relating to that section) or s 72A (so far as relating to that section)) falls on or after 7 April 2005: FA 2005 Sch 8 para 7.

[5] Words in definitions of "closure notice" and "notice of enquiry", and whole of definition of "self-certificate", repealed, and words in definition of "notifiable (in relation to a land transaction)" inserted, by FA 2008 s 94, Sch 30 paras 1, 5 with effect in relation to transactions with an effective date on or after 12 March 2008.

[6] Entry inserted by the Transfer of Tribunal Functions and Revenue and Customs Appeals Order, SI 2009/56 art 3, Sch 1 para 372 with effect from 1 April 2009.

Final provisions

123 Consequential amendments

(1) Schedule 18 contains certain amendments consequential on the provisions of this Part.

(2) The Treasury may by regulations make such other amendments and repeals as appear to them appropriate in consequence of the provisions of this Part.

(3) The regulations may, in particular, make such provision as the Treasury think fit for reproducing in relation to stamp duty land tax the effect of enactments providing for exemption from stamp duty.

124 Commencement and transitional provisions

Schedule 19 makes provision for and in connection with the coming into force of the provisions of this Part.

PART 5
STAMP DUTY

125 Abolition of stamp duty except on instruments relating to stock or marketable securities

(1) Stamp duty is chargeable under Schedule 13 of the Finance Act 1999 (c 16) only on instruments relating to stock or marketable securities.

(2) Section 12 of the Finance Act 1895 (c 16) (collection of stamp duty in cases of property vested by Act or purchased under statutory powers) does not apply to property other than stock or marketable securities.

(3) This section shall be construed as one with the Stamp Act 1891 (c 39).

(4) Part 1 of Schedule 20 to this Act contains provisions supplementing this section and Part 2 of that Schedule provides for consequential amendments and repeals.

(5) This section and that Schedule have effect—

(*a*) in relation to an instrument effecting a land transaction [(or any duplicate or counterpart of such an instrument)][1], if the transaction—

(i) is an SDLT transaction within the meaning of Schedule 19 to this Act (stamp duty land tax: commencement and transitional provisions), or

(ii) would be such a transaction but for an exemption or relief from stamp duty land tax;

(*b*) in relation to an instrument effecting a transaction other than a land transaction [(or any duplicate or counterpart of such an instrument)][1], if the instrument is executed on or after the implementation date for the purposes of stamp duty land tax (see paragraph 2(2) of that Schedule).

For this purpose an instrument effecting both a land transaction and a transaction other than a land transaction [(or any duplicate or counterpart of such an instrument)][1] is treated as if it were two instruments to which paragraph (*a*) and paragraph (*b*) above respectively applied.

(6) Where in the case of an instrument effecting both a land transaction and a transaction other than a land transaction the result of applying subsection (5) is that stamp duty is chargeable on either or both of the deemed instruments, the enactments relating to stamp duty have effect as if—

(*a*) there were two instruments as mentioned in the closing words of that subsection,

(*b*) the consideration had been apportioned between them in a just and reasonable manner, and

(*c*) the amount found on that apportionment to be attributable to the chargeable instrument, or (as the case may be) to each of them, had been set forth distinctly in that instrument.

(7) In subsections (5) and (6) "land transaction" has the same meaning as in Part 4 of this Act.

(8) This section and Schedule 20 have effect subject to [paragraph 31][2] of Schedule 15 to this Act (continued application of stamp duty in relation to certain partnership transactions).

Cross references—See FA 2003 Sch 15 para 31(1) (nothing in this section affects the application of enactments relating to stamp duty in relation to an instrument by which a transfer of an interest in a partnership is effected).

Amendments—[1] Words in sub-s (5) inserted by FA 2004 s 296, Sch 39 para 23 with effect for any transaction of which the effective date (within the meaning of FA 2003 Pt 4) is on or 22 July 2004: FA 2004 Sch 39 para 26. These amendments were previously made by the Stamp Duty and Stamp Duty Land Tax (Variation of the Finance Act 2003) (No 2) Regulations, SI 2003/2816 regs 1, 2, Schedule para 9 with effect from 1 December 2003. Those regulations are revoked by FA 2004 Sch 39 para 14(2).

[2] In sub-s (8), words substituted for the words "paragraph 13(2) and (3)" by FA 2004 s 304, Sch 41 paras 2(b), 3 with effect for any partnership transaction of which the effective date (within the meaning of FA 2003 Pt 4) is after 22 July 2004. A "partnership transaction" means a transaction mentioned in FA 2003 Sch 15 para 9(1): FA 2004 Sch 41 para 3(2).

126 Circumstances in which group relief withdrawn

(1)–(5) (*amend* FA 2002 s 111(1), (3), *insert* sub-s (4A))

(6)–(8) (*amend* FA 2002 Sch 34 para 4)

(9) This section applies to instruments executed after 14th April 2003.

(10) But this section does not apply to an instrument giving effect to a contract made on or before 9th April 2003, unless—

(*a*) the instrument is made in consequence of the exercise after that date of any option, right of pre-emption or similar right, or

(*b*) the instrument transfers the property in question to, or vests it in, a person other than the purchaser under the contract because of an assignment (or, in Scotland, assignation) or further contract made after that date.

(11) This section shall be deemed to have come into force on 15th April 2003.

127 Circumstances in which relief for company acquisitions withdrawn

(1)–(5) (*amend* FA 2002 s 113(1), (3), *insert* sub-s (3A))

(6) (*amend* FA 2002 Sch 35 paras 3, 4)

(7) This section applies to instruments executed after 14th April 2003.

(8) But this section does not apply to an instrument giving effect to a contract made on or before 9th April 2003, unless—

(*a*) the instrument is made in consequence of the exercise after that date of any option, right of pre-emption or similar right, or (*b*) the instrument transfers the property in question to, or vests it in, a person other than the purchaser under the contract because of an assignment (or, in Scotland, assignation) or further contract made after that date.

(9) This section shall be deemed to have come into force on 15th April 2003.

128 Exemption of certain leases granted by registered social landlords

(1) No stamp duty is chargeable under Part 2 of Schedule 13 to the Finance Act 1999 (c 16) on a lease of a dwelling granted by a registered social landlord to one or more individuals in accordance with arrangements to which this section applies if the lease is for an indefinite term or is terminable by notice of a month or less.

(2) "Registered social landlord" means—

(*a*) in relation to England and Wales, a body registered in the register maintained under section 1(1) of the Housing Act 1996 (c 52);

(*b*) in relation to Scotland, a body registered in the register maintained under section 57 of the Housing (Scotland) Act 2001 (asp 10);

(*c*) in relation to Northern Ireland, a housing association registered in the register maintained under Article 14 of the Housing (Northern Ireland) Order 1992 (SI 1992/1725 (NI 15)).

(3) This section applies to arrangements between a registered social landlord and a housing authority under which the landlord provides, for individuals nominated by the authority in pursuance of its statutory housing functions, temporary rented accommodation which the landlord itself has obtained on a short-term basis.

The reference above to accommodation obtained by the landlord "on a short-term basis" is to accommodation leased to the landlord for a term of five years or less.

(4) A "housing authority" means—

(*a*) in relation to England and Wales—

(i) a principal council within the meaning of the Local Government Act 1972 (c 70), or

(ii) the Common Council of the City of London;

(*b*) in relation to Scotland, a council constituted under section 2 of the Local Government etc (Scotland) Act 1994 (c 39);

(*c*) in relation to Northern Ireland—

(i) the Department for Social Development in Northern Ireland, or

(ii) the Northern Ireland Housing Executive.

(5) An instrument on which stamp duty is not chargeable by virtue only of this section shall not be taken to be duly stamped unless—

(*a*) it is stamped with the duty to which it would be liable but for this section, or

(*b*) it has, in accordance with section 12 of the Stamp Act 1891 (c 39), been stamped with a particular stamp denoting that it is not chargeable with any duty.

(6) This section shall be construed as one with the Stamp Act 1891.

(7) This section applies to instruments executed after the day on which this Act is passed.

129 Relief for certain leases granted before section 128 has effect

(1) This section applies to instruments that—

(*a*) are executed in the period beginning with 1 January 2000 and ending with the day on which this Act is passed, and

(*b*) are instruments to which section 128 (exemption of certain leases granted by registered social landlords) would have applied if that provision had been in force when the instrument was executed.

(2) If the instrument is not stamped until after the day on which this Act is passed, the law in force at the time of its execution shall be deemed for stamp duty purposes to be what it would have been if section 128 had been in force at that time.

(3) If the Commissioners are satisfied that—

(*a*) the instrument was stamped on or before the day on which this Act is passed,

(*b*) stamp duty was chargeable in respect of it, and

(*c*) had it been stamped after that day stamp duty would, by virtue of section 128, not have been chargeable,

they shall pay to such person as they consider appropriate an amount equal to the duty (and any interest or penalty) that would not have been payable if that section had been in force at the time the instrument was executed.

(4) Any such payment must be claimed before 1st January 2004.

(5) Entitlement to a payment is subject to compliance with such conditions as the Commissioners may determine with respect to the production of the instrument, to its being stamped so as to indicate that it has been produced under this section or to other matters.

(6) For the purposes of [section 44 of the Commissioners for Revenue and Customs Act 2005 (payment into Consolidated Funds)][1] any amount paid under this section is a repayment.

(7) This section shall be construed as one with the Stamp Act 1891.

(8) For the purposes of this section as it applies in relation to instruments executed before the coming into force of section 57 of the Housing (Scotland) Act 2001 (asp 10), the references in section 128 to a registered social landlord shall be read in relation to Scotland as references to—

(*a*) a housing association registered in the register maintained under section 3(1) of the Housing Associations Act 1985 (c 69) by Scottish Homes, or

(*b*) a body corporate whose objects corresponded to those of a housing association and which, pursuant to a contract with Scottish Homes, was registered in a register kept for the purpose by Scottish Homes.

Amendments—[1] Words in sub-s (6) substituted by Commissioners for Revenue and Customs Act 2005 s 50, Sch 4 paras 125, 126 with effect from 18 April 2005 by virtue of the Commissioners for Revenue and Customs Act (Commencement) Order, SI 2005/1126, art 2(2).

130 Registered social landlords: treatment of certain leases granted between 1st January 1990 and 27th March 2000

(1) This section applies to a lease in relation to which the following conditions are met—

(*a*) it is a lease of a dwelling to one or more individuals;

(*b*) it is for an indefinite term or is terminable by notice of a month or less;

(*c*) it was executed on or after 1st January 1990 and before 28th March 2000;

(*d*) at the time it was executed the rate or average rate of the rent (whether reserved as a yearly rent or not) was £5,000 a year or less; and

(*e*) the landlord's interest has at any time before 26th June 2003 been held by a registered social landlord.

(2) A lease to which this section applies (whether or not presented for stamping) shall be treated—

(*a*) for the purposes of section 14 of the Stamp Act 1891 (c 39) (production of instrument in evidence) as it applies in relation to proceedings begun after the day on which this Act is passed, and

(*b*) for the purposes of section 17 of that Act (enrolment etc of instrument) as it applies to any act done after that day,

as if it had been duly stamped in accordance with the law in force at the time when it was executed.

(3) If in the case of a lease to which this section applies the Commissioners are satisfied—

(*a*) that the instrument was stamped on or before the day on which this Act is passed, and

(*b*) that stamp duty was charged in respect of it,

they shall pay to such person as they consider appropriate an amount equal to the duty (and any interest or penalty) so charged.

(4) Any such payment must be claimed before 1st January 2004.

(5) Entitlement to a payment under subsection (3) is subject to compliance with such conditions as the Commissioners may determine with respect to the production of the instrument, to its being stamped so as to indicate that it has been produced under this section or to other matters.

(6) For the purposes of [section 44 of the Commissioners for Revenue and Customs Act 2005 (payment into Consolidated Funds)][1] any amount paid under subsection (3) above is a repayment.

(7) This section shall be construed as one with the Stamp Act 1891.

(8) The reference in subsection (1) above to the landlord's interest being held by a "registered social landlord" is to its being held by a body that—

(*a*) is registered in a register maintained under—

(i) Article 124 of the Housing (Northern Ireland) Order 1981 (SI 1981/156 (NI 3)),

(ii) section 3(1) of the Housing Associations Act 1985 (c 69),

(iii) Article 14 of the Housing (Northern Ireland) Order 1992 (SI 1992/1725 (NI 15)),

(iv) section 1(1) of the Housing Act 1996 (c 52), or

(v) section 57 of the Housing (Scotland) Act 2001 (asp 10), or

(*b*) is a body corporate whose objects correspond to those of a housing association and which, pursuant to a contract with Scottish Homes, is registered in a register kept for the purposes by Scottish Homes.

(9) Section 129 of this Act (relief for certain leases granted on or after 1st January 2000) does not apply to a lease to which this section applies.

Amendments—[1] Words in sub-s (6) substituted by Commissioners for Revenue and Customs Act 2005 s 50, Sch 4 paras 125, 127 with effect from 18 April 2005 by virtue of the Commissioners for Revenue and Customs Act (Commencement) Order, SI 2005/1126, art 2(2).

PART 9

MISCELLANEOUS AND SUPPLEMENTARY PROVISIONS

Provisions consequential on changes to company law

195 Companies acquiring their own shares

(1) This section applies for the purposes of the Taxes Acts and the Inheritance Tax Act 1984 (c 51) where a company acquires any of its own shares (whether by purchase, the issuing of bonus shares or otherwise).

(2) The acquisition of any of those shares by the company is not to be treated as the acquisition of an asset.

(3) The company is not, by virtue of the acquisition or holding of any of those shares or its being entered in the company's register of members in respect of any of them, to be treated as a member of itself.

(4) Subject to subsection (5)—

(*a*) the company's issued share capital is to be treated as if it had been reduced by the nominal value of the shares acquired,

(*b*) such of those shares as are not cancelled on acquisition are to be treated as if they had been so cancelled, and

(*c*) any subsequent cancellation by the company of any of those shares is to be disregarded (and, accordingly, is not the disposal of an asset and does not give rise to an allowable loss within the meaning of the Taxation of Chargeable Gains Act 1992 (c 12)).

(5) Where the shares are issued to the company as bonus shares, subsection (4)(*a*) and (*b*) does not apply and the shares are to be treated as if they had not been issued.

(6) Where, disregarding subsections (2) to (5)—

(*a*) a company holds any of its own shares, and

(*b*) the company issues bonus shares in respect of those shares or any class of those shares ("the existing shares"),

nothing in this section prevents the existing shares being the company's holding of shares for the purposes of the application of section 126 of the Taxation of Chargeable Gains Act 1992 (application of sections 127 to 131 of that Act (company reorganisations etc)).

(7) In subsection (6) the reference to the application of section 126 of the Taxation of Chargeable Gains Act 1992 does not include a reference to the application of that section in a modified form by virtue of any enactment relating to chargeable gains.

(8) Where a company disposes of any of its own shares to a person in circumstances where, but for subsections (2) to (5), it would be regarded as holding the shares immediately before the disposal—

(*a*) subsections (4)(*b*) and (*c*) and (5) cease to apply in relation to the shares disposed of ("the relevant shares"),

(*b*) the relevant shares are to be treated as having been issued as new shares to that person by the company at the time of the disposal (and not as having been disposed of by the company at that time),

(*c*) that person is to be treated as having subscribed for the relevant shares,

(*d*) an amount equal to the amount or value of the consideration (if any) payable for the disposal of the relevant shares is to be treated as the amount subscribed for those shares,

(*e*) if the amount or value of that consideration does not exceed the nominal value of those shares, the share capital of those shares is to be treated for the purposes of [Part 23 of the Corporation Tax Act 2010][2] as if it were an amount equal to the amount or value of that consideration, and

(*f*) if the amount or value of that consideration exceeds their nominal value, the relevant shares are to be treated as if they had been issued at a premium representing that excess.

(9) Where—

(*a*) a company purchases its own shares, and

(*b*) the price payable by a company for the shares is taken into account in computing the profits of the company which are chargeable to tax [under Chapter 2 of Part 3 of the Corporation Tax Act 2009][1],

subsections (2) to (7) do not apply and subsection (8) does not apply in relation to any disposal by the company of any of the shares.

(10) Schedule 40 to this Act (which makes amendments relating to the acquisition and disposal by a company of its own shares) has effect.

(11) For the purposes of this section—

(*a*) a company issues "bonus shares" if it issues share capital as paid up otherwise than by the receipt of new consideration (within the meaning of [section 1115 of the Corporation Tax Act 2010][2]), and

(*b*) "the Taxes Acts" has the same meaning as in the Taxes Management Act 1970 (c 9),

and in this section references to a "company" are to a company with a share capital.

(12) The preceding provisions of this section and the provisions of Schedule 40 to this Act have effect in relation to any acquisition of shares by a company on or after such day as the Treasury may by order made by statutory instrument appoint.

Commentary—*Simon's Taxes* **D5.502; E3.211.**

Regulations—The Finance Act 2003, Section 195 and Schedule 40 (Appointed Day) Order, SI 2003/3077 (s 195 and Sch 40 have effect in relation to any acquisition of shares by a company on or after 1 December 2003).

Amendments—[1] In sub-s (9)(*b*) words substituted for words "in accordance with the provisions of the Taxes Act 1988 applicable to Case I or II of Schedule D" by CTA 2009 s 1322, Sch 1 paras 558, 565. CTA 2009 applies for accounting periods ending on or after 1 April 2009 (for corporation tax purposes) and for tax years 2009–10 onwards (for income and capital gains tax purposes).

2 In sub-s (8)(*e*) words "Part 6 of the Taxes Act 1988" substituted and in sub-s (11)(*a*) words "section 254 of the Taxes Act 1988" substituted by CTA 2010 s 1177, Sch 1 paras 400, 413. CTA 2010 has effect for corporation tax purposes for accounting periods ending on or after 1 April 2010, and for income and capital gains tax purposes for the tax year 2010–11 and subsequent tax years.

Administrative matters

206 Admissibility of evidence not affected by offer of settlement etc

...

(3), (4) (*amend* FA 1999 Sch 18 para 3)

(5) The above amendments have effect in relation to statements made, or documents produced, after the passing of this Act.

Commentary—*Simon's Taxes* **A4.165.**

Supplementary

215 Interpretation

In this Act "the Taxes Act 1988" means the Income and Corporation Taxes Act 1988 (c 1).

216 Repeals

(1) The enactments mentioned in Schedule 43 to this Act (which include provisions that are spent or of no practical utility) are repealed to the extent specified.

(2) The repeals specified in that Schedule have effect subject to the commencement provisions and savings contained or referred to in the notes set out in that Schedule.

217 Short title

This Act may be cited as the Finance Act 2003.

SCHEDULES

SCHEDULE 3

STAMP DUTY LAND TAX: TRANSACTIONS EXEMPT FROM CHARGE

Section 49

No chargeable consideration

1 A land transaction is exempt from charge if there is no chargeable consideration for the transaction.

Cross references—FA 2003 Sch 15 para 25 (this paragraph does not apply to cases where FA 2003 Sch 15 paras 10, 14, 17, 18 apply).

Grant of certain leases by registered social landlords

2—(1) The grant of a lease of a dwelling is exempt from charge if the lease—

(*a*) is granted by a [relevant housing provider][1] to one or more individuals in accordance with arrangements to which this paragraph applies, and

(*b*) is for an indefinite term or is terminable by notice of a month or less.

(2) This paragraph applies to arrangements between a [relevant housing provider][1] and a housing authority under which the [relevant housing provider][1] provides, for individuals nominated by the authority in pursuance of its statutory housing functions, temporary rented accommodation which the landlord itself has obtained on a short-term basis.

The reference above to accommodation obtained by the landlord "on a short-term basis" is to accommodation leased to the landlord for a term of five years or less.

[(2A) A "relevant housing provider" means—

(*a*) a non-profit registered provider of social housing, or

(*b*) a registered social landlord.][1]

(3) A "housing authority" means—

(*a*) in relation to England and Wales—

(i) a principal council within the meaning of the Local Government Act 1972 (c 70), or

(ii) the Common Council of the City of London;

(*b*) in relation to Scotland, a council constituted under section 2 of the Local Government etc (Scotland) Act 1994 (c 39);

(*c*) in relation to Northern Ireland—

(i) the Department for Social Development in Northern Ireland, or

(ii) the Northern Ireland Housing Executive.

Amendments—[1] In sub-ss (1), (2), words substituted for words "registered social landlord" and "landlord", and sub-s (2A) inserted, by the Housing and Regeneration Act 2008 s 277, Sch 9 paras 29, 31(1), (2) with effect from 1 April 2010 (by virtue of SI 2010/862 art 2 (subject to transitional provisions and savings in SI 2010/862 arts 2, 3, Schedule paras 1–4)).

Transactions in connection with divorce etc

3 A transaction between one party to a marriage and the other is exempt from charge if it is effected—

(*a*) in pursuance of an order of a court made on granting in respect of the parties a decree of divorce, nullity of marriage or judicial separation;

(*b*) in pursuance of an order of a court made in connection with the dissolution or annulment of the marriage, or the parties' judicial separation, at any time after the granting of such a decree;

(*c*) in pursuance of—

(i) an order of a court made at any time under section 22A, 23A or 24A of the Matrimonial Causes Act 1973 (c 18), or

(ii) an incidental order of a court made under section 8(2) of the Family Law (Scotland) Act 1985 (c 37) by virtue of section 14(1) of that Act;

(*d*) at any time in pursuance of an agreement of the parties made in contemplation or otherwise in connection with the dissolution or annulment of the marriage, their judicial separation or the making of a separation order in respect of them.

[Assents and appropriations by personal representatives

3A—(1) The acquisition of property by a person in or towards satisfaction of his entitlement under or in relation to the will of a deceased person, or on the intestacy of a deceased person, is exempt from charge.

(2) Sub-paragraph (1) does not apply if the person acquiring the property gives any consideration for it, other than the assumption of secured debt.

(3) Where sub-paragraph (1) does not apply because of sub-paragraph (2), the chargeable consideration for the transaction is determined in accordance with paragraph 8A(1) of Schedule 4.

(4) In this paragraph—

"debt" means an obligation, whether certain or contingent, to pay a sum of money either immediately or at a future date, and

"secured debt" means debt that, immediately after the death of the deceased person, is secured on the property.][1]

Amendments—[1] Paragraph 3A inserted by FA 2004 s 300 and deemed always to have had effect.

[Transactions in connection with dissolution of civil partnership etc

3A A transaction between one party to a civil partnership and the other is exempt from charge if it is effected—

(*a*) in pursuance of an order of a court made on granting in respect of the parties an order or decree for the dissolution or annulment of the civil partnership or their judicial separation;

(*b*) in pursuance of an order of a court made in connection with the dissolution or annulment of the civil partnership, or the parties' judicial separation, at any time after the granting of such an order or decree for dissolution, annulment or judicial separation as mentioned in paragraph (*a*);

(*c*) in pursuance of—

(i) an order of a court made at any time under any provision of Schedule 5 to the Civil Partnership Act 2004 that corresponds to section 22A, 23A or 24A of the Matrimonial Causes Act 1973, or

(ii) an incidental order of a court made under any provision of the Civil Partnership Act 2004 that corresponds to section 8(2) of the Family Law (Scotland) Act 1985 by virtue of section 14(1) of that Act of 1985;

(*d*) at any time in pursuance of an agreement of the parties made in contemplation of or otherwise in connection with the dissolution or annulment of the civil partnership, their judicial separation or the making of a separation order in respect of them.][1]

Amendments—[1] Second paragraph 3A inserted by Tax and Civil Partnership Regulations, SI 2005/3229, reg 174, with effect from 5 December 2005 (reg 1(1)).

Variation of testamentary dispositions etc

4—(1) A transaction following a person's death that varies a disposition (whether effected by will, under the law relating to intestacy or otherwise) of property of which the deceased was competent to dispose is exempt from charge if the following conditions are met.

(2) The conditions are—

(*a*) that the transaction is carried out within the period of two years after a person's death, and

(*b*) that no consideration in money or money's worth other than the making of a variation of another such disposition is given for it.

[(2A) Where the condition in sub-paragraph (2)(*b*) is not met, the chargeable consideration for the transaction is determined in accordance with paragraph 8A(2) of Schedule 4.][1]

(3) This paragraph applies whether or not the administration of the estate is complete or the property has been distributed in accordance with the original dispositions.

Amendments—[1] Sub-para (2A) inserted by FA 2004 s 301(1), (7) and deemed always to have had effect.

Power to add further exemptions

5—(1) The Treasury may by regulations provide that any description of land transaction specified in the regulations is exempt from charge.

(2) The regulations may contain such supplementary, incidental and transitional provision as appears to the Treasury to be appropriate.

Regulations—The Stamp Duty Land Tax (Exemption of Certain Acquisitions of Residential Property) Regulations, SI 2008/2339 (exemption from stamp duty land tax for relevant acquisitions of land for chargeable consideration of not more than £175,000, with effect in relation to acquisitions made on or after 3 September 2008 but before 3 September 2009).

SCHEDULE 4
STAMP DUTY LAND TAX: CHARGEABLE CONSIDERATION

Section 50

HMRC Manuals—Stamp Duty Land Tax Manual, SDLTM03700 (general meaning of chargeable consideration for SDLT purposes)

Money or money's worth

1—(1) The chargeable consideration for a transaction is, except as otherwise expressly provided, any consideration in money or money's worth given for the subject-matter of the transaction, directly or indirectly, by the purchaser or a person connected with him.

(2) [Section 1122 of the Corporation Tax Act 2010][1] (connected persons) applies for the purposes of sub-paragraph (1).

Amendments—[1] In sub-para (2) words "Section 839 of the Taxes Act 1988" substituted by CTA 2010 s 1177, Sch 1 paras 400, 414. CTA 2010 has effect for corporation tax purposes for accounting periods ending on or after 1 April 2010, and for income and capital gains tax purposes for the tax year 2010–11 and subsequent tax years.

Value added tax

2 The chargeable consideration for a transaction shall be taken to include any value added tax chargeable in respect of the transaction, other than value added tax chargeable by virtue of an [option to tax any land under Part 1 of Schedule 10][1] to the Value Added Tax Act 1994 (c 23) made after the effective date of the transaction.

Amendments—[1] Words substituted by the Value Added Tax (Buildings and Land) Order, SI 2008/1146, art 6, Sch 1 paras 10, 11 with effect in relation to supplies made on or after 1 June 2008, subject to savings in Sch 2 of the Order.

Postponed consideration

3 The amount or value of the chargeable consideration for a transaction shall be determined without any discount for postponement of the right to receive it or any part of it.

Just and reasonable apportionment

4—(1) For the purposes of this Part consideration attributable—

(*a*) to two or more land transactions, or

(*b*) in part to a land transaction and in part to another matter, or

(*c*) in part to matters making it chargeable consideration and in part to other matters,

shall be apportioned on a just and reasonable basis.

(2) If the consideration is not so apportioned, this Part has effect as if it had been so apportioned.

(3) For the purposes of this paragraph any consideration given for what is in substance one bargain shall be treated as attributable to all the elements of the bargain, even though—

(*a*) separate consideration is, or purports to be, given for different elements of the bargain, or

(*b*) there are, or purport to be, separate transactions in respect of different elements of the bargain.

HMRC Manuals—Stamp Duty Land Tax Manual, SDLTM04010a (just and reasonable apportionment – example)

Exchanges

5—(1) This paragraph applies to determine the chargeable consideration where one or more land transactions are entered into by a person as purchaser (alone or jointly) wholly or partly in consideration of one or more other land transactions being entered into by him (alone or jointly) as vendor.

(2) In this paragraph—

(*a*) "relevant transaction" means any of those transactions, and

(*b*) "relevant acquisition" means a relevant transaction entered into as purchaser and "relevant disposal" means a relevant transaction entered into as vendor.

(3) The following rules apply if the subject-matter of any of the relevant transactions is a major interest in land—

(*a*) where a single relevant acquisition is made, the chargeable consideration for the acquisition is—

(i) the market value of the subject-matter of the acquisition, and

(ii) if the acquisition is the grant of a lease at a rent, that rent;

(*b*) where two or more relevant acquisitions are made, the chargeable consideration for each relevant acquisition is—

(i) the market value of the subject-matter of that acquisition, and

(ii) if the acquisition is the grant of a lease at a rent, that rent.

(4) The following rules apply if the subject-matter of none of the relevant transactions is a major interest in land—

(*a*) where a single relevant acquisition is made in consideration of one or more relevant disposals, the chargeable consideration for the acquisition is the amount or value of any chargeable consideration other than the disposal or disposals that is given for the acquisition;

(*b*) where two or more relevant acquisitions are made in consideration of one or more relevant disposals, the chargeable consideration for each relevant acquisition is the appropriate proportion of the amount or value of any chargeable consideration other than the disposal or disposals that is given for the acquisitions.

(5) For the purposes of sub-paragraph (4)(*b*) the appropriate proportion is—

$$\frac{MV}{TMV}$$

where—

MV is the market value of the subject-matter of the acquisition for which the chargeable consideration is being determined, and

TMV is the total market value of the subject-matter of all the relevant acquisitions.

(6) This paragraph has effect subject to—

paragraph 6 of this Schedule (partition etc: disregard of existing interest) . . . [1]

. . . [2]

[(7) This paragraph does not apply in a case to which paragraph 17 applies.][2]

HMRC Manuals—Stamp Duty Land Tax Manual, SDLTM04020a (exchanges and chargeable consideration – examples)

Cross references—FA 2003 Sch 15 para 16(1), (2) (application of this paragraph where an interest in a partnership is acquired in consideration of entering into a land transaction with an existing partner).

Amendments—[1] Words ", and section 58 (relief for certain exchanges of residential property)" repealed by FA 2004 s 326, Sch 42 Pt 4(2) with effect in accordance with FA 2004 Sch 39 para 26. This repeal was previously made by the Stamp Duty and Stamp Duty Land Tax (Variation of the Finance Act 2003) (No 2) Regulations, SI 2003/2816 regs 1, 2, Schedule para 3(5) with effect from 1 December 2003. Those regulations have been revoked by FA 2004 Sch 39 para 14(2).

[2] Words in sub-para (6) repealed, and sub-para (7) inserted, by the SDLT (Amendment of Part 4 of the Finance Act 2003) Regulations, SI 2004/1069 regs 2, 4(1), (2) with effect from 7 April 2004.

Partition etc: disregard of existing interest

6 In the case of a land transaction giving effect to a partition or division of a chargeable interest to which persons are jointly entitled, the share of the interest held by the purchaser immediately before the partition or division does not count as chargeable consideration.

HMRC Manuals—Stamp Duty Land Tax Manual, SDLTM04030a (land partitioned – example)

Cross references—FA 2003 Sch 15 para 16(3) (disapplication of this paragraph where FA 2003 Sch 15 para 16 applies)

Valuation of non-monetary consideration

7 Except as otherwise expressly provided, the value of any chargeable consideration for a land transaction, other than—

(*a*) money (whether in sterling or another currency), or

(*b*) debt as defined for the purposes of paragraph 8 (debt as consideration),

shall be taken to be its market value at the effective date of the transaction.

Debt as consideration

8—(1) Where the chargeable consideration for a land transaction consists in whole or in part of—

(*a*) the satisfaction or release of debt due to the purchaser or owed by the vendor, or

(*b*) the assumption of existing debt by the purchaser,

the amount of debt satisfied, released or assumed shall be taken to be the whole or, as the case may be, part of the chargeable consideration for the transaction.

[(1A) Where—

(*a*) debt is secured on the subject-matter of a land transaction immediately before and immediately after the transaction, and

(*b*) the rights or liabilities in relation to that debt of any party to the transaction are changed as a result of or in connection with the transaction,

then for the purposes of this paragraph there is an assumption of that debt by the purchaser, and that assumption of debt constitutes chargeable consideration for the transaction.][1]

[(1B) Where in a case in which sub-paragraph (1)(*b*) applies—

(*a*) the debt assumed is or includes debt secured on the property forming the subject-matter of the transaction, and

(*b*) immediately before the transaction there were two or more persons each holding an undivided share of that property, or there are two or more such persons immediately afterwards,

the amount of secured debt assumed shall be determined as if the amount of that debt owed by each of those persons at a given time were the proportion of it corresponding to his undivided share of the property at that time.][1]

[(1C)For the purposes of sub-paragraph (1B), in England and Wales and Northern Ireland each joint tenant of property is treated as holding an equal undivided share of it.][1]

(2) If the effect of [this paragraph][1] would be that the amount of the chargeable consideration for the transaction exceeded the market value of the subject-matter of the transaction, the amount of the chargeable consideration is treated as limited to that value.

(3) In this paragraph—

(*a*) "debt" means an obligation, whether certain or contingent, to pay a sum of money either immediately or at a future date,

(*b*) "existing debt", in relation to a transaction, means debt created or arising before the effective date of, and otherwise than in connection with, the transaction, and

(*c*) references to the amount of a debt are to the principal amount payable or, as the case may be, the total of the principal amounts payable, together with the amount of any interest that has accrued due on or before the effective date of the transaction.

HMRC Manuals—Stamp Duty Land Tax Manual, SDLTM04040a (assumption of debt – example).

Cross references—Pension Protection Fund (Tax) Regulations, SI 2006/575 reg 43(1) (Pension Protection Fund: circumstances in which this paragraph does not apply).

Amendments—[1] Sub-paras (1A)–(1C) inserted, and in sub-para (2), words substituted for the words "sub-paragraph (1)" by FA 2004 s 301(2)–(4), (6) with effect for any transaction of which the effective date (within the meaning of FA 2003 Pt 4) is on or after 22 July 2004.

[Cases where conditions for exemption not fully met

8A—(1) Where a land transaction would be exempt from charge under paragraph 3A of Schedule 3 (assents and appropriations by personal representatives) but for sub-paragraph (2) of that paragraph (cases where person acquiring property gives consideration for it), the chargeable consideration for the transaction does not include the amount of any secured debt assumed.

"Secured debt" has the same meaning as in that paragraph.

(2) Where a land transaction would be exempt from charge under paragraph 4 of Schedule 3 (variation of testamentary dispositions etc) but for a failure to meet the condition in sub-paragraph (2)(*b*) of that paragraph (no consideration other than variation of another disposition), the chargeable consideration for the transaction does not include the making of any such variation as is mentioned in that sub-paragraph.][1]

Amendments—[1] This paragraph inserted by FA 2004 s 301(2), (5), (7) and deemed always to have had effect.

Conversion of amounts in foreign currency

9—(1) References in this Part to the amount or value of the consideration for a transaction are to its amount or value in sterling.

(2) For the purposes of this Part the sterling equivalent of an amount expressed in another currency shall be ascertained by reference to the London closing exchange rate on the effective date of the transaction (unless the parties have used a different rate for the purposes of the transaction).

Carrying out of works

10—(1) Where the whole or part of the consideration for a land transaction consists of the carrying out of works of construction, improvement or repair of a building or other works to enhance the value of land, then—

(*a*) to the extent that the conditions specified in sub-paragraph (2) are met, the value of the works does not count as chargeable consideration, and

(*b*) to the extent that those conditions are not met, the value of the works shall be taken into account as chargeable consideration.

(2) The conditions referred to in sub-paragraph (1) are—

(*a*) that the works are carried out after the effective date of the transaction,

(*b*) that the works are carried out on land acquired or to be acquired under the transaction or on other land held by the purchaser or a person connected with him, and

(*c*) that it is not a condition of the transaction that the works are carried out by the vendor or a person connected with him.

[(2A) [Where by virtue of—

(*a*) subsection (8) of section 44 (contract and conveyance),

(*b*) paragraph 12A of Schedule 17A (agreement for lease), or

(*c*) paragraph 19(3) to (6) of Schedule 17A (missives of let etc in Scotland),

there are two notifiable transactions (the first being the contract or agreement and the second being the transaction effected on completion or, as the case may be, the grant or execution of the lease),][3] the condition in sub-paragraph (2)(*a*) is treated as met in relation to the second transaction if it is met in relation to the first.][2]

(3) In this paragraph—

(*a*) references to the acquisition of land are to the acquisition of a major interest in it;

(*b*) the value of the works shall be taken to be the amount that would have to be paid in the open market for the carrying out of the works in question.

(4) Section 839 of the Taxes Act 1988 (connected persons) has effect for the purposes of this paragraph.

[(5) This paragraph is subject to paragraph 17 (arrangements involving public or educational bodies).][1]

HMRC Manuals—Stamp Duty Land Tax Manual, SDLTM04060a (construction works – example)

Amendments—[1] Sub-para (5) inserted by the SDLT (Amendment of Schedule 4 to the Finance Act 2003) Regulations, SI 2003/3293 reg 2(1), (3) with effect from 19 December 2003.

[2] Sub-para (2A) inserted by FA 2004 s 296, Sch 39 para 9(1), (2) with effect for any transaction of which the effective date is after 17 March 2004: FA 2004 Sch 39 para 13(3).

[3] Words in sub-para (2A) substituted for the words "Where subsection (8) of section 44 (contract and conveyance) applies, so that there are two notifiable transactions (the first being the contract and the second being the transaction effected on completion)," by FA 2004 s 297(1), (8), (9) with effect for any transaction of which the effective date is on or after 22 July 2004.

Provision of services

11[—(1)] [1] Where the whole or part of the consideration for a land transaction consists of the provision of services (other than the carrying out of works to which paragraph 10 applies), the value of that consideration shall be taken to be the amount that would have to be paid in the open market to obtain those services.

[(2) This paragraph is subject to paragraph 17 (arrangements involving public or educational bodies).][1]

Amendments—[1] Sub-para (1) numbered as such, and sub-para (2) inserted, by the SDLT (Amendment of Schedule 4 to the Finance Act 2003) Regulations, SI 2003/3293 reg 2(1), (4) with effect from 19 December 2003.

Land transaction entered into by reason of employment

12—(1) Where a land transaction is entered into by reason of the purchaser's employment, or that of a person connected with him, then—

(*a*) if the transaction gives rise to a charge to tax under Chapter 5 of Part 3 of the Income Tax (Earnings and Pensions) Act 2003 (c 1) (taxable benefits: living accommodation) and—

(i) no rent is payable by the purchaser, or

(ii) the rent payable by the purchaser is less than the cash equivalent of the benefit calculated under section 105 or 106 of that Act,

there shall be taken to be payable by the purchaser as rent an amount equal to the cash equivalent chargeable under those sections;

(*b*) if the transaction would give rise to a charge under that Chapter but for section 99 of that Act (accommodation provided for performance of duties), the consideration for the transaction is the actual consideration (if any);

(*c*) if neither paragraph (*a*) nor paragraph (*b*) applies, the consideration for the transaction shall be taken to be not less than the market value of the subject-matter of the transaction as at the effective date of the transaction.

(2) Section 839 of the Taxes Act 1988 (connected persons) has effect for the purposes of this paragraph.

13–15

Amendment—Repealed by FA 2004 s 326, Sch 42 Pt 4(2) with effect in accordance with FA 2004 Sch 39 para 26. This repeal was previously made by the Stamp Duty and Stamp Duty Land Tax (Variation of the Finance Act 2003) (No 2) Regulations, SI 2003/2816 regs 1, 2, Schedule para 8(11) with effect from 1 December 2003. Those regulations have been revoked by FA 2004 Sch 39 para 14(2).

Indemnity given by purchaser

16 Where the purchaser agrees to indemnify the vendor in respect of liability to a third party arising from breach of an obligation owed by the vendor in relation to the land that is the subject of the transaction, neither the agreement nor any payment made in pursuance of it counts as chargeable consideration.

[Purchaser bearing inheritance tax liability

16A Where—

(*a*) there is a land transaction that is—

(i) a transfer of value within section 3 of the Inheritance Tax Act 1984 (transfers of value), or

(ii) a disposition, effected by will or under the law of intestacy, of a chargeable interest comprised in the estate of a person immediately before his death,

and

(*b*) the purchaser is or becomes liable to pay, agrees to pay or does in fact pay any inheritance tax due in respect of the transfer or disposition,

his liability, agreement or payment does not count as chargeable consideration for the transaction.][1]

Amendments—[1] Paragraphs 16A–16C inserted by the SDLT (Amendment to the Finance Act 2003) Regulations, SI 2006/875 regs 2, 3. SI 2006/875 came into force on 12 April 2006, and the amendments have effect in relation to land transactions with an effective date on or after that date: SI 2006/875 reg 1.

[Purchaser bearing capital gains tax liability

16B—(1) Where—

(*a*) there is a land transaction under which the chargeable interest in question—

(i) is acquired otherwise than by a bargain made at arm's length, or

(ii) is treated by section 18 of the Taxation of Chargeable Gains Act 1992 (connected persons) as so acquired,

and

(*b*) the purchaser is or becomes liable to pay, or does in fact pay, any capital gains tax due in respect of the corresponding disposal of the chargeable interest,

his liability or payment does not count as chargeable consideration for the transaction.

(2) Sub-paragraph (1) does not apply if there is chargeable consideration for the transaction (disregarding the liability or payment referred to in sub-paragraph (1)(*b*)).][1]

Amendments—[1] Paragraphs 16A–16C inserted by the SDLT (Amendment to the Finance Act 2003) Regulations, SI 2006/875 regs 2, 3. SI 2006/875 came into force on 12 April 2006, and the amendments have effect in relation to land transactions with an effective date on or after that date: SI 2006/875 reg 1.

[Costs of enfranchisement

16C Costs borne by the purchaser under section 9(4) of the Leasehold Reform Act 1967 or section 33 of the Leasehold Reform, Housing and Urban Development Act 1993 (costs of enfranchisement) do not count as chargeable consideration.][1]

Amendments—[1] Paragraphs 16A–16C inserted by the SDLT (Amendment to the Finance Act 2003) Regulations, SI 2006/875 regs 2, 3. SI 2006/875 came into force on 12 April 2006, and the amendments have effect in relation to land transactions with an effective date on or after that date: SI 2006/875 reg 1.

[Arrangements involving public or educational bodies

17—(1) This paragraph applies in any case where arrangements are entered into under which—

[(*a*) there is a transfer, or the grant or assignment of a lease, of land by a qualifying body ("A") to a non-qualifying body ("B") ("the main transfer"),][2]

[(*b*) in consideration (whether in whole or in part) of the main transfer there is a grant by B to A of a lease or under-lease of the whole, or substantially the whole, of that land ("the leaseback"),][3]

(*c*) B undertakes to carry out works or provide services to A, and

(*d*) some or all of the consideration given by A to B for the carrying out of those works or the provision of those services is consideration in money, [whether or not there is also a transfer, or the grant or assignment of a lease, of any other land by A to B (a "transfer of surplus land").][2]

(2) The following are qualifying bodies—

(*a*) public bodies within section 66,

(*b*) institutions within the further education sector or the higher education sector within the meaning of 91 of the Further and Higher Education Act 1992,

(*c*) further education corporations within the meaning of section 17 of that Act,

(*d*) higher education corporations within the meaning section 90 of that Act,

(*e*) persons who undertake to establish and maintain, and carry on, or provide for the carrying on, of an Academy within the meaning of section 482 of the Education Act 1996, and

(*f*) in Scotland, institutions funded by the Scottish Further Education Funding Council or the Scottish Higher Education Funding Council.

[(3) The following shall not count as chargeable consideration for the main transfer or any transfer of surplus land—

(*a*) the lease-back;

(*b*) the carrying out of building works by B for A; or

(*c*) the provision of services by B to A.][2]

[(4) The chargeable consideration for the lease back does not include—

(*a*) the main transfer;

(*b*) any transfer of surplus land; or

(*c*) the consideration in money paid by A to B for the building works or other services referred to in sub-paragraph (3).][2]

[(4A) Sub-paragraphs (3) and (4) shall be disregarded for the purposes of determining whether the land transaction in question is notifiable.][4]

(5) This paragraph applies to Scotland as if—

(*a*) references to A transferring land to B were references to A transferring the interest of an owner of land to B, and

[(*b*) references in sub-paragraph (1) to assignment were references to assignation.][2]

Until the appointed day for the purposes of the Abolition of Feudal Tenure etc (Scotland) Act 2000 (asp 5), the reference in paragraph (a) to the interest of the owner shall be read, in relation to feudal property, as a reference to the estate or interest of the proprietor of the dominium utile.

(6) In this paragraph "under-lease" includes a sub-lease.][1]

Amendments—[1] This paragraph inserted by the SDLT (Amendment of Schedule 4 to the Finance Act 2003) Regulations, SI 2003/3293 reg 2(1), (5) with effect from 19 December 2003.

[2] Sub-para (1)(a), (b) and words at end of sub-para (1) substituted, and sub-paras (3), (4), (5)(b) substituted, by the SDLT (Amendment of Part 4 of the Finance Act 2003) Regulations, SI 2004/1069 regs 2, 4 with effect from 7 April 2004.

[3] Sub-para (1)(b) substituted by the SDLT (Amendment of Part 4 of the Finance Act 2003) (No 2) Regulations, SI 2004/1206 with effect from 27 April 2004.

[4] Sub-para (4A) inserted by FA 2004 s 296, Sch 39 para 9(1), (3) with effect for any transaction of which the effective date is after 17 March 2004: FA 2004 Sch 39 para 13(3).

SCHEDULE 5

STAMP DUTY LAND TAX: AMOUNT OF TAX CHARGEABLE: RENT

Section 56

Introduction

1 This Schedule provides for calculating the tax chargeable—

(*a*) in respect of a chargeable transaction for which the chargeable consideration consists of or includes rent, or

(*b*) where such a transaction is to be taken into account as a linked transaction.

[Amounts payable in respect of periods before grant of lease

1A For the purposes of this Part "rent" does not include any chargeable consideration for the grant of a lease that is payable in respect of a period before the grant of the lease.][1]

Amendments—[1] This paragraph inserted by FA 2004 s 296, Sch 39 para 10 with effect for any transaction of which the effective date is after 17 March 2004: FA 2004 Sch 39 para 13(3).

Calculation of tax chargeable in respect of rent

2—(1) Tax is chargeable under this Schedule in respect of so much of the chargeable consideration as consists of rent.

[(2) The tax chargeable is the total of the amounts produced by taking the relevant percentage of so much of the relevant rental value as falls within each rate band.][1]

[(3) The relevant percentages and rate bands are determined by reference to whether the relevant land—

(*a*) consists entirely of residential property (in which case Table A below applies), or

(*b*) consists of or includes land that is not residential property (in which case Table B below applies).

Table A: Residential

Rate bands	*Percentage*
£0 to [£125,000][2]	0%
Over [£125,000][2]	1%

Table B: Non-residential or mixed

Rate bands	*Percentage*
£0 to £150,000	0%
Over £150,000	1%][1]

[(4) For the purposes of sub-paragraphs (2) and (3)—

(*a*) the relevant rental value is the net present value of the rent payable over the term of the lease, and

(*b*) the relevant land is the land that is the subject of the lease.][1]

[(5) If the lease in question is one of a number of linked transactions for which the chargeable consideration consists of or includes rent, the above provisions are modified.][1]

[(6) In that case the tax chargeable is determined as follows.

First, calculate the amount of the tax that would be chargeable if the linked transactions were a single transaction, so that—

(*a*) the relevant rental value is the total of the net present values of the rent payable over the terms of all the leases, and

(*b*) the relevant land is all land that is the subject of any of those leases.

Then, multiply that amount by the fraction:

$$\frac{NPV}{TNPV}$$

where—

NPV is the net present value of the rent payable over the term of the lease in question, and

TNPV is the total of the net present values of the rent payable over the terms of the all the leases.][1]

Note—In sub-para (3) in Table A "£175,000" substituted for "£125,000" (in both places) in relation to transactions with an effective date on or after 22 April 2009 but before 1 January 2010; FA 2009 s 10(1)(*b*).

Modifications—FA 2003 Sch 15 para 11 (modification of this paragraph where there is a transfer of a chargeable interest to a partnership, and the chargeable consideration includes rent).

FA 2003 Sch 15 para 19 (modification of this paragraph where there is a transfer of a chargeable interest from a partnership, and the chargeable consideration includes rent).

Regulations—The Stamp Duty Land Tax (Exemption of Certain Acquisitions of Residential Property) Regulations, SI 2008/2339 (exemption from stamp duty land tax for relevant acquisitions of land for chargeable consideration of not more than £175,000, with effect in relation to acquisitions made on or after 3 September 2008 but before 3 September 2009).

Amendments—[1] Sub-paras (2)–(6) substituted for sub-paras (2)–(5) by the Stamp Duty Land Tax (Amendment of Schedule 5 to the Finance Act 2003) Regulations, SI 2003/2914 reg 2, Schedule para 1 with effect from 1 December 2003.

[2] "£125,000" substituted for "£120,000" by FA 2006 s 162(2), with effect in relation to any transaction of which the effective date (within the meaning of Part 4 of FA 2003) is after 22 March 2006. The figure of "£175,000" is substituted for "£125,000" (in both places) in Table A in relation to transactions with an effective date on or after 22 April 2009 but before 1 January 2010: FA 2009 s 10(1)(*b*).

Net present value of rent payable over term of lease

3 The net present value (v) of the rent payable over the term of a lease is calculated by applying the formula:

$$v = \sum_{i=1}^{n} \frac{r_i}{(1+T)^i}$$

where—

ri is the rent payable . . . [1] [in respect of year i][2],

i is the first, second, third, etc year of the term,

n is the term of the lease ...[1], and

T is the temporal discount rate (see paragraph 8).

Amendments—[1] Words "(see paragraphs 4 and 5)" and "(see paragraphs 6 and 7)" repealed by FA 2004 s 326, Sch 42 Pt 4(2) with effect in accordance with FA 2004 Sch 39 para 26. This repeal was previously made by the Stamp Duty and Stamp Duty Land Tax (Variation of the Finance Act 2003) (No 2) Regulations, SI 2003/2816 regs 1, 2, Schedule para 8(9) with effect from 1 December 2003. Those regulations have been revoked by FA 2004 Sch 39 para 14(2).

[2] Words substituted for the words "in year i" by FA 2006 s 164(2) with effect in relation to any lease granted or treated as granted on or after 19 July 2006.

4–7

Amendment—Repealed by FA 2004 s 326, Sch 42 Pt 4(2) with effect in accordance with FA 2004 Sch 39 para 26. This repeal was previously made by the Stamp Duty and Stamp Duty Land Tax (Variation of the Finance Act 2003) (No 2) Regulations, SI 2003/2816 regs 1, 2, Schedule para 8(11) with effect from 1 December 2003. Those regulations have been revoked by FA 2004 Sch 39 para 14(2).

Temporal discount rate

8—(1) For the purposes of this Schedule the "temporal discount rate" is 3.5% or such other rate as may be specified by regulations made by the Treasury.

(2) Regulations under this paragraph may make any such provision as is mentioned in subsection (3)(*b*) to (*f*) of section 178 of the Finance Act 1989 (c 26) (power of Treasury to set rates of interest).

(3) Subsection (5) of that section (power of Inland Revenue to specify rate by order in certain circumstances) applies in relation to regulations under this paragraph as it applies in relation to regulations under that section.

Tax chargeable in respect of consideration other than rent[: general][1]

9—(1) Where in the case of a transaction to which this Schedule applies there is chargeable consideration other than rent, the provisions of this Part apply in relation to that consideration as in relation to other chargeable consideration [(but see paragraph 9A)][1].

(2)–(3) . . . [1]

(4) Tax chargeable under this Schedule is in addition to any tax chargeable under section 55 in respect of consideration other than rent.

(5) Where a transaction to which this Schedule applies falls to be taken into account for the purposes of that section as a linked transaction, no account shall be taken of rent in determining the relevant consideration.

Amendments—[1] Words in sub-para (1) inserted, and whole of sub-paras (2)–(3), repealed, and word in heading inserted, by FA 2008 s 95(1), (2) with effect in relation to transactions with an effective date on or after 12 March 2008.

[Tax chargeable in respect of consideration other than rent: 0% band

9A—(1) This paragraph applies in the case of a transaction to which this Schedule applies where there is chargeable consideration other than rent.

(2) If—

(*a*) the relevant land consists entirely of land that is non-residential property, and

(*b*) the relevant rent is at least £1,000,

the 0% band in Table B in section 55(2) does not apply in relation to the consideration other than rent and any case that would have fallen within that band is treated as falling within the 1% band.

(3) Sub-paragraphs (4) and (5) apply if—

(*a*) the relevant land is partly residential property and partly non-residential property, and

(*b*) the relevant rent attributable, on a just and reasonable apportionment, to the land that is non-residential property is at least £1,000.

(4) For the purpose of determining the amount of tax chargeable under section 55 in relation to the consideration other than rent, the transaction (or, where it is one of a number of linked transactions, that set of transactions) is treated as if it were two separate transactions (or sets of linked transactions), namely—

(*a*) one whose subject-matter consists of all of the interests in land that is residential property, and

(*b*) one whose subject-matter consists of all of the interests in land that is non-residential property.

(5) For that purpose, the chargeable consideration attributable to each of those separate transactions (or sets of linked transactions) is the chargeable consideration so attributable on a just and reasonable apportionment.

(6) In this paragraph "the relevant rent" means—

(*a*) the annual rent in relation to the transaction in question, or

(*b*) if that transaction is one of a number of linked transactions for which the chargeable consideration consists of or includes rent, the total of the annual rents in relation to all of those transactions.

(7) In sub-paragraph (6) the "annual rent" means the average annual rent over the term of the lease or, if—

(*a*) different amounts of rent are payable for different parts of the term, and

(*b*) those amounts (or any of them) are ascertainable at the effective date of the transaction,

the average annual rent over the period for which the highest ascertainable rent is payable.

(8) In this paragraph "relevant land" has the meaning given in section 55(3) and (4).][1]

Amendments—[1] Paragraph 9A inserted by FA 2008 s 95(1), (3) with effect in relation to transactions with an effective date on or after 12 March 2008.

10, 11

Amendment—Repealed by FA 2004 s 326, Sch 42 Pt 4(2) with effect in accordance with FA 2004 Sch 39 para 26. This repeal was previously made by the Stamp Duty and Stamp Duty Land Tax (Variation of the Finance Act 2003) (No 2) Regulations, SI 2003/2816 regs 1, 2, Schedule para 8(11) with effect from 1 December 2003. Those regulations have been revoked by FA 2004 Sch 39 para 14(2).

SCHEDULE 6

STAMP DUTY LAND TAX: DISADVANTAGED AREAS RELIEF

Section 57

HMRC Manuals—Stamp Duty Land Tax Manual SDLTM20050–20100 (general explanation of disadvantaged relief).

Statement of Practice SP 1/04—(Disadvantaged areas relief, Stamp Office approach to borderline cases).

Modifications—FA 2003 Sch 15 para 26 (modification of this Schedule in its application to the transfer of an interest in a partnership that is a chargeable transaction by virtue of FA 2003 Sch 15 para 14 or 17).

PART 1

DISADVANTAGED AREAS

Meaning of "disadvantaged area"

1—(1) For the purposes of this Schedule a "disadvantaged area" means an area designated as a disadvantaged area by regulations made by the Treasury.

(2) The regulations may—

(*a*) designate specified areas as disadvantaged areas, or

(*b*) provide for areas of a description specified in the regulations to be designated as disadvantaged areas.

(3) If the regulations so provide, the designation of an area as a disadvantaged area shall have effect for such period as may be specified by or determined in accordance with the regulations.

(4) The regulations may—

(*a*) make different provision for different cases, and

(*b*) contain such incidental, supplementary, consequential or transitional provision as appears to the Treasury to be necessary or expedient.

Continuation of regulations made for purposes of stamp duty

2 Any regulations made by the Treasury—

(*a*) designating areas as disadvantaged areas for the purposes of section 92 of the Finance Act 2001 (c 9) (stamp duty exemption for land in disadvantaged areas), and

(*b*) in force immediately before the implementation date,

have effect for the purposes of this Schedule as if made under paragraph 1 above and may be varied or revoked accordingly.

PART 2

LAND WHOLLY SITUATED IN A DISADVANTAGED AREA

Introduction

3 This Part of this Schedule applies to a land transaction if—

[(*a*)] [1] the subject matter of the transaction is a chargeable interest in relation to land that is wholly situated in a disadvantaged area[, and (*b*) the land is wholly or partly residential property][1].

Modifications—FA 2003 Sch 15 para 26 (modification of this paragraph in its application to the transfer of an interest in a partnership that is a chargeable transaction by virtue of FA 2003 Sch 15 para 14 or 17).

Amendments—[1] Words inserted by FA 2005 s 96, Sch 9 paras 1(2), 4 with effect, subject to FA 2005 Sch 9 para 4(2), for any transaction of which the effective date (as defined by FA 2005 Sch 9 para 4(4)) is after 16 March 2005.

Land all non-residential

4 . . . [1]

Amendments—[1] Paragraph repealed by FA 2005 ss 96, 104, Sch 9 paras 1(3), 4 and Sch 11 Pt 3(2) with effect, subject to FA 2005 Sch 9 para 4(2), for any transaction of which the effective date (as defined by FA 2005 Sch 9 para 4(4)) is after 16 March 2005.

Land all residential

5—(1) This paragraph applies where all the land is residential property.

(2) If—

(*a*) the consideration for the transaction does not include rent and the relevant consideration does not exceed £150,000, or

(*b*) the consideration for the transaction consists only of rent and the relevant rental value does not exceed £150,000,

the transaction is exempt from charge.

(3) If the consideration for the transaction includes rent and the relevant rental value does not exceed £150,000, the rent does not count as chargeable consideration.

(4) If the consideration for the transaction includes consideration other than rent, then—

(*a*) if—

(i) . . . [1]

(ii) the relevant consideration does not exceed £150,000,

the consideration other than rent does not count as chargeable consideration;

(*b*) . . . [1]

Modifications—FA 2003 Sch 15 para 26 (modification of this paragraph in its application to the transfer of an interest in a partnership that is a chargeable transaction by virtue of FA 2003 Sch 15 para 14 or 17).

HMRC Manuals—Stamp Duty Land Tax Manual, SDLTM20060 (residential property – leases executed between 10.04.03 and 30.10.03, and those from 01.12.03)

Amendments—[1] Sub-para (4)(a)(i), (b) repealed by FA 2008 s 95(4)(a), (5) with effect in relation to transactions with an effective date on or after 12 March 2008.

Land partly non-residential and partly residential

6—(1) [This paragraph applies, where the land is partly non-residential property and partly residential property, in relation to the consideration attributable to land that is residential property.][1]

References in this paragraph to the consideration attributable to . . . [1] land that is residential property (or to the rent or annual rent so attributable) are to the consideration (or rent or annual rent) so attributable on a just and reasonable apportionment.

(2) . . . [1]

(3) . . . [1]

(4) If—

(*a*) the consideration so attributable does not include rent and the relevant consideration does not exceed £150,000, or

(*b*) the consideration so attributable consists only of rent and the relevant rental value does not exceed £150,000,

none of the consideration so attributable counts as chargeable consideration.

(5) If the consideration so attributable includes rent and the relevant rental value does not exceed £150,000, the rent so attributable does not count as chargeable consideration.

(6) If the consideration so attributable includes consideration other than rent, then—

(*a*) if—

(i) . . . [2]

(ii) the relevant consideration does not exceed £150,000,

the consideration other than rent does not count as chargeable consideration;

(*b*) . . . [2]

HMRC Manuals—Stamp Duty Land Tax Manual SDLTM20080 (apportionment under this paragraph might be on the basis of the percentage areas quoted in planning applications, where appropriate, or alternatively of floor space relating to the respective uses. Other methods of apportionment will be considered.)

Modifications—FA 2003 Sch 15 para 26 (modification of this paragraph in its application to the transfer of an interest in a partnership that is a chargeable transaction by virtue of FA 2003 Sch 15 para 14 or 17).

Amendments—[1] Words in sub-para (1) substituted and repealed; and sub-paras (2), (3) repealed by FA 2005 ss 96, 104, Sch 9 paras 1(4), 4 and Sch 11 Pt 3(2) with effect, subject to FA 2005 Sch 9 para 4(2), for any transaction of which the effective date (as defined by FA 2005 Sch 9 para 4(4)) is after 16 March 2005.

[2] Sub-para (6)(a)(i), (b) repealed by FA 2008 s 95(4)(b), (5) with effect in relation to transactions with an effective date on or after 12 March 2008.

PART 3
LAND PARTLY SITUATED IN A DISADVANTAGED AREA

Introduction

7—(1) This Part of this Schedule applies to a land transaction if—

[(*a*)] [1] the subject matter of the transaction is a chargeable interest in relation to land that is partly in a disadvantaged area and partly outside such an area[, and

(*b*) the land situated in a disadvantaged area is wholly or partly residential property][1].

(2) References in this Part to the consideration attributable to land situated in a disadvantaged area and to land not so situated (or to the rent or annual rent so attributable) are to the consideration (or rent or annual rent) so attributable on a just and reasonable apportionment.

Modifications—FA 2003 Sch 15 para 26 (modification of this paragraph in its application to the transfer of an interest in a partnership that is a chargeable transaction by virtue of FA 2003 Sch 15 para 14 or 17).

Amendments—[1] Words inserted by FA 2005 s 96, Sch 9 paras 1(5), 4 with effect, subject to FA 2005 Sch 9 para 4(2), for any transaction of which the effective date (as defined by FA 2005 Sch 9 para 4(4)) is after 16 March 2005.

Land all non-residential

8 . . . [1]

Amendments—[1] Paragraph repealed by FA 2005 ss 96, 104, Sch 9 paras 1(6), 4 and Sch 11 Pt 3(2) with effect, subject to FA 2005 Sch 9 para 4(2), for any transaction of which the effective date (as defined by FA 2005 Sch 9 para 4(4)) is after 16 March 2005.

Land all residential

9—(1) This paragraph applies where all the land situated in a disadvantaged area is residential property.

(2) If—

(*a*) the consideration attributable to land situated in a disadvantaged area does not include rent and the relevant consideration does not exceed £150,000, or

(*b*) the consideration so attributable consists only of rent and the relevant rental value does not exceed £150,000,

none of the consideration so attributable counts as chargeable consideration.

(3) If the consideration attributable to land situated in a disadvantaged area includes rent and the relevant rental value does not exceed £150,000, the rent so attributable does not count as chargeable consideration.

(4) If the consideration attributable to land in a disadvantaged area includes consideration other than rent ("non-rent consideration"), then—

(*a*) if—

(i) . . . [1]

(ii) the relevant consideration does not exceed £150,000,

the non-rent consideration so attributable does not count as chargeable consideration;

(*b*) . . . [1]

Modifications—FA 2003 Sch 15 para 19 (modification of this paragraph in its application to the transfer of a chargeable interest from a partnership: chargeable consideration including rent).

FA 2003 Sch 15 para 26 (modification of this paragraph in its application to the transfer of an interest in a partnership that is a chargeable transaction by virtue of FA 2003 Sch 15 para 14 or 17).

Amendments—[1] Sub-para (4)(a)(i), (b) repealed by FA 2008 s 95(4)(c), (5) with effect in relation to transactions with an effective date on or after 12 March 2008.

Land partly non-residential and partly residential

10—(1) [This paragraph applies, where the land situated in a disadvantaged area is partly non-residential property and partly residential property, in relation to the consideration attributable to land that is residential property.][1]

References in this paragraph to the consideration attributable to . . . [1] land that is residential property (or to the rent or annual rent so attributable) are to the consideration (or rent or annual rent) attributable to land in a disadvantaged area that is, on a just and reasonable apportionment, so attributable.

(2) . . . [1]

(3) . . .[1]

(4) If—

(*a*) the consideration so attributable does not include rent and the relevant consideration does not exceed £150,000, or

(*b*) the consideration so attributable consists only of rent and the relevant rental value does not exceed £150,000,

none of the consideration so attributable counts as chargeable consideration.

(5) If the consideration so attributable includes rent and the relevant rental value does not exceed £150,000, the rent so attributable does not count as chargeable consideration.

(6) If the consideration so attributable includes consideration other than rent, then—

(*a*) if—

(i) . . .[2]

(ii) the relevant consideration does not exceed £150,000,

the consideration other than rent does not count as chargeable consideration;

(*b*) . . .[2]

Modifications—FA 2003 Sch 15 para 26 (modification of this paragraph in its application to the transfer of an interest in a partnership that is a chargeable transaction by virtue of FA 2003 Sch 15 para 14 or 17).

Amendments—[1] Words in sub-para (1) substituted and repealed; and sub-paras (2), (3) repealed by FA 2005 ss 96, 104, Sch 9 paras 1(7), 4 and Sch 11 Pt 3(2) with effect, subject to FA 2005 Sch 9 para 4(2), for any transaction of which the effective date (as defined by FA 2005 Sch 9 para 4(4)) is after 16 March 2005.

[2] Sub-para (6)(*a*)(i), (*b*) repealed by FA 2008 s 95(4)(*d*), (5) with effect in relation to transactions with an effective date on or after 12 March 2008.

PART 4
[SUPPLEMENTARY][1]

Amendments—[1] Heading (which previously read "Interpretation") substituted by FA 2004 s 298(1), (5)(a) with effect from 22 July 2004.

Relevant consideration and relevant rental value

11—(1) References in this Schedule to the "relevant consideration" in relation to a transaction are to the amount falling to be taken into account for the purposes of section 55(2) in determining the rate of tax chargeable under that section in relation to the transaction apart from any relief under this Schedule (whether in relation to that or any other transaction).

(2) References in this Schedule to the "relevant rental value" in relation to a transaction are to the amount falling to be taken into account for the purposes of paragraph 2(3) of Schedule 5 in determining the rate of tax chargeable under that Schedule in relation to the transaction apart from any relief under this Schedule (whether in relation to that or any other transaction).

Modifications—FA 2003 Sch 15 para 26 (modification of this paragraph in its application to the transfer of an interest in a partnership that is a chargeable transaction by virtue of FA 2003 Sch 15 para 14 or 17).

Rent and annual rent

12 For the purposes of this Schedule "rent" has the same meaning as in Schedule 5 (amount of tax chargeable: rent) and "annual rent" has the same meaning as in paragraph [9A][1] of that Schedule.

Modifications—FA 2003 Sch 15 para 26 (modification of this paragraph in its application to the transfer of an interest in a partnership that is a chargeable transaction by virtue of FA 2003 Sch 15 para 14 or 17).

Amendments—[1] Reference substituted by FA 2008 s 95 (6) with effect in relation to transactions with an effective date on or after 12 March 2008.

[Notification of transactions

13 For the purposes of [sections 77 and 77A (which specify][2] what land transactions are notifiable) no account shall be taken of any provision of this Schedule to the effect that consideration does not count as chargeable consideration.][1]

Amendments—[1] This paragraph inserted by FA 2004 s 298 (1), (5)(b) with effect from 22 July 2004.

[2] Words substituted by FA 2008 s 94, Sch 30 para 6 with effect in relation to transactions with an effective date on or after 12 March 2008.

[SCHEDULE 6A
RELIEF FOR CERTAIN ACQUISITIONS OF RESIDENTIAL PROPERTY]

Section 58A][1]

HMRC Manuals—Stamp Duty Land Tax Manual SDLTM21000–21070 (explanation of scope of this relief).

Amendments—This Schedule inserted by FA 2004 s 296, Sch 39 para 17(2) with effect for any transaction of which the effective date (within the meaning of FA 2003 Pt 4) is on or after 22 July 2004: FA 2004 Sch 39 para 26. The insertion was previously made by the Stamp Duty and Stamp Duty Land Tax (Variation of the

Finance Act 2003) (No 2) Regulations, SI 2003/2816 regs 1, 2, Schedule para 3(2) with effect from 1 December 2003. Those regulations are revoked by FA 2004 Sch 39 para 14(2).

[Acquisition by house-building company from individual acquiring new dwelling

1—(1) Where a dwelling ("the old dwelling") is acquired by a house-building company from an individual (whether alone or with other individuals), the acquisition is exempt from charge if the following conditions are met.

(2) The conditions are—

(*a*) that the individual (whether alone or with other individuals) acquires from the house-building company a new dwelling,

(*b*) that the individual—

(i) occupied the old dwelling as his only or main residence at some time in the period of two years ending with the date of its acquisition, and

(ii) intends to occupy the new dwelling as his only or main residence,

(*c*) that each acquisition is entered into in consideration of the other, and

(*d*) that the area of land acquired by the house-building company does not exceed the permitted area.

(3) Where the conditions in sub-paragraph (2)(*a*) to (*c*) are met but the area of land acquired by the house-building company exceeds the permitted area, the chargeable consideration for the acquisition is taken to be the amount calculated by deducting the market value of the permitted area from the market value of the old dwelling.

(4) A "house-building company" means a company that carries on the business of constructing or adapting buildings or parts of buildings for use as dwellings.

References in this paragraph to such a company include any company connected with it.

(5) In this paragraph—

(*a*) references to the acquisition of the new dwelling are to the acquisition, by way of grant or transfer, of a major interest in the dwelling;

(*b*) references to the acquisition of the old dwelling are to the acquisition, by way of transfer, of a major interest in the dwelling; and

(*c*) references to the market value of the old dwelling and of the permitted area are, respectively, to the market value of that major interest in the dwelling and of that interest so far as it relates to that area.][1]

Amendments—[1] This Schedule inserted by FA 2004 s 296, Sch 39 para 17(2) with effect for any transaction of which the effective date (within the meaning of FA 2003 Pt 4) is on or after 22 July 2004: FA 2004 Sch 39 para 26. The insertion was previously made by the Stamp Duty and Stamp Duty Land Tax (Variation of the Finance Act 2003) (No 2) Regulations, SI 2003/2816 regs 1, 2, Schedule para 3(2) with effect from 1 December 2003. Those regulations are revoked by FA 2004 Sch 39 para 14(2).

[Acquisition by property trader from individual acquiring new dwelling

2—(1) Where a dwelling ("the old dwelling") is acquired by a property trader from an individual (whether alone or with other individuals), the acquisition is exempt from charge if the following conditions are met.

(2) The conditions are—

(*a*) that the acquisition is made in the course of a business that consists of or includes acquiring dwellings from individuals who acquire new dwellings from house-building companies,

(*b*) that the individual (whether alone or with other individuals) acquires a new dwelling from a house-building company,

(*c*) that the individual—

(i) occupied the old dwelling as his only or main residence at some time in the period of two years ending with the date of its acquisition, and

(ii) intends to occupy the new dwelling as his only or main residence,

(*d*) that the property trader does not intend—

(i) to spend more than the permitted amount on refurbishment of the old dwelling, or

(ii) to grant a lease or licence of the old dwelling, or

(iii) to permit any of its principals or employees (or any person connected with any of its principals or employees) to occupy the old dwelling, and

(*e*) that the area of land acquired by the property trader does not exceed the permitted area.

Paragraph (d)(ii) does not apply to the grant of lease or licence to the individual for a period of no more than six months.

(3) Where the conditions in sub-paragraph (2)(*a*) to (*d*) are met, but the area of land acquired by the property trader exceeds the permitted area, the chargeable consideration for the acquisition is taken to be the amount calculated by deducting the market value of the permitted area from the market value of the old dwelling.

(4) The provisions of paragraph 1(4) (meaning of "house-building company" etc) also have effect for the purposes of this paragraph.

(5) In this paragraph—

(*a*) references to the acquisition of a new dwelling are to the acquisition, by way of grant or transfer, of a major interest in the dwelling;

(*b*) references to the acquisition of the old dwelling are to the acquisition, by way of transfer, of a major interest in the dwelling; and

(*c*) references to the market value of the old dwelling and of the permitted area are, respectively, to the market value of that major interest in the dwelling and of that interest so far as it relates to that area.][1]

Amendments—[1] This Schedule inserted by FA 2004 s 296, Sch 39 para 17(2) with effect for any transaction of which the effective date (within the meaning of FA 2003 Pt 4) is on or after 22 July 2004: FA 2004 Sch 39 para 26. The insertion was previously made by the Stamp Duty and Stamp Duty Land Tax (Variation of the Finance Act 2003) (No 2) Regulations, SI 2003/2816 regs 1, 2, Schedule para 3(2) with effect from 1 December 2003. Those regulations are revoked by FA 2004 Sch 39 para 14(2).

[Acquisition by property trader from personal representatives

3—(1) Where a dwelling is acquired by a property trader from the personal representatives of a deceased individual, the acquisition is exempt from charge if the following conditions are met.

(2) The conditions are—

(*a*) that the acquisition is made in the course of a business that consists of or includes acquiring dwellings from personal representatives of deceased individuals,

(*b*) that the deceased individual occupied the dwelling as his only or main residence at some time in the period of two years ending with the date of his death,

(*c*) that the property trader does not intend—

(i) to spend more than the permitted amount on refurbishment of the dwelling, or

(ii) to grant a lease or licence of the dwelling, or

(iii) to permit any of its principals or employees (or any person connected with any of its principals or employees) to occupy the dwelling, and

(*d*) that the area of land acquired does not exceed the permitted area.

(3) Where the conditions in sub-paragraph (2)(*a*) to (*c*) are met, but the area of land acquired exceeds the permitted area, the chargeable consideration for the acquisition is taken to be the amount calculated by deducting the market value of the permitted area from the market value of the dwelling.

(4) In this paragraph—

(*a*) references to the acquisition of the dwelling are to the acquisition, by way of transfer, of a major interest in the dwelling; and

(*b*) references to the market value of the dwelling and of the permitted area are, respectively, to the market value of that major interest in the dwelling and of that interest so far as it relates to that area.][1]

Amendments—[1] This Schedule inserted by FA 2004 s 296, Sch 39 para 17(2) with effect for any transaction of which the effective date (within the meaning of FA 2003 Pt 4) is on or after 22 July 2004: FA 2004 Sch 39 para 26. The insertion was previously made by the Stamp Duty and Stamp Duty Land Tax (Variation of the Finance Act 2003) (No 2) Regulations, SI 2003/2816 regs 1, 2, Schedule para 3(2) with effect from 1 December 2003. Those regulations are revoked by FA 2004 Sch 39 para 14(2).

[Acquisition by property trader from individual where chain of transactions breaks down

4—(1) Where a dwelling ("the old dwelling") is acquired by a property trader from an individual (whether alone or with other individuals), the acquisition is exempt from charge if—

(*a*) the individual has made arrangements to sell a dwelling ("the old dwelling") and acquire another dwelling ("the second dwelling"),

(*b*) the arrangements to sell the old dwelling fail, and

(*c*) the acquisition of the old dwelling is made for the purpose of enabling the individual's acquisition of the second dwelling to proceed,

and the following conditions are met.

(2) The conditions are—

(*a*) that the acquisition is made in the course of a business that consists of or includes acquiring dwellings from individuals in those circumstances,

(*b*) that the individual—

(i) occupied the old dwelling as his only or main residence at some time in the period of two years ending with the date of its acquisition, and

(ii) intends to occupy the second dwelling as his only or main residence,

(*c*) that the property trader does not intend—

(i) to spend more than the permitted amount on refurbishment of the old dwelling, or

(ii) to grant a lease or licence of the old dwelling, or

(iii) to permit any of its principals or employees (or any person connected with any of its principals or employees) to occupy the old dwelling, and

(*d*) that the area of land acquired does not exceed the permitted area.

Paragraph (c)(ii) does not apply to the grant of a lease or licence to the individual for a period of no more than six months.

(3) Where the conditions in sub-paragraph (2)(*a*) to (*c*) are met, but the area of land acquired exceeds the permitted area, the chargeable consideration for the acquisition is taken to be the amount calculated by deducting the market value of the permitted area from the market value of the old dwelling.

(4) In this paragraph—

(*a*) references to the acquisition of the second dwelling are to the acquisition, by way of grant or transfer, of a major interest in the dwelling;

(*b*) references to the acquisition of the old dwelling are to the acquisition, by way of transfer, of a major interest in the dwelling; and

(*c*) references to the market value of the old dwelling and of the permitted area are, respectively, to the market value of that major interest in the dwelling and of that interest so far as it relates to that area.][1]

Amendments—[1] This Schedule inserted by FA 2004 s 296, Sch 39 para 17(2) with effect for any transaction of which the effective date (within the meaning of FA 2003 Pt 4) is on or after 22 July 2004: FA 2004 Sch 39 para 26. The insertion was previously made by the Stamp Duty and Stamp Duty Land Tax (Variation of the Finance Act 2003) (No 2) Regulations, SI 2003/2816 regs 1, 2, Schedule para 3(2) with effect from 1 December 2003. Those regulations are revoked by FA 2004 Sch 39 para 14(2).

[Acquisition by employer in case of relocation of employment

5—(1) Where a dwelling is acquired from an individual (whether alone or with other individuals) by his employer, the acquisition is exempt from charge if the following conditions are met.

(2) The conditions are—

(*a*) that the individual occupied the dwelling as his only or main residence at some time in the period of two years ending with the date of the acquisition,

(*b*) that the acquisition is made in connection with a change of residence by the individual resulting from relocation of employment,

(*c*) that the consideration for the acquisition does not exceed the market value of the dwelling, and

(*d*) that the area of land acquired does not exceed the permitted area.

(3) Where the conditions in sub-paragraph (2)(*a*) to (*c*) are met but the area of land acquired exceeds the permitted area, the chargeable consideration for the acquisition is taken to be the amount calculated by deducting the market value of the permitted area from the market value of the dwelling.

(4) In this paragraph "relocation of employment" means a change of the individual's place of employment due to—

(*a*) his becoming an employee of the employer,

(*b*) an alteration of the duties of his employment with the employer, or

(*c*) an alteration of the place where he normally performs those duties.

(5) For the purposes of this paragraph a change of residence is one "resulting from" relocation of employment if—

(*a*) the change is made wholly or mainly to allow the individual to have his residence within a reasonable daily travelling distance of his new place of employment, and

(*b*) his former residence is not within a reasonable daily travelling distance of that place.

The individual's "new place of employment" means the place where he normally performs, or is normally to perform, the duties of his employment after the relocation.

(6) In this paragraph—

(*a*) references to the acquisition of the dwelling are to the acquisition, by way of transfer, of a major interest in the dwelling;

(*b*) references to the market value of the dwelling and of the permitted area are, respectively, to the market value of that major interest in the dwelling and of that interest so far as it relates to that area; and

(*c*) references to an individual's employer include a prospective employer.][1]

Amendments—[1] This Schedule inserted by FA 2004 s 296, Sch 39 para 17(2) with effect for any transaction of which the effective date (within the meaning of FA 2003 Pt 4) is on or after 22 July 2004: FA 2004 Sch 39 para 26. The insertion was previously made by the Stamp Duty and Stamp Duty Land Tax (Variation of the Finance Act 2003) (No 2) Regulations, SI 2003/2816 regs 1, 2, Schedule para 3(2) with effect from 1 December 2003. Those regulations are revoked by FA 2004 Sch 39 para 14(2).

[Acquisition by property trader in case of relocation of employment

6—(1) Where a dwelling is acquired by a property trader from an individual (whether alone or with other individuals), the acquisition is exempt from charge if the following conditions are met.

(2) The conditions are—

(*a*) that the acquisition is made in the course of a business that consists of or includes acquiring dwellings from individuals in connection with a change of residence resulting from relocation of employment,

(*b*) that the individual occupied the dwelling as his only or main residence at some time in the period of two years ending with the date of the acquisition,

(*c*) that the acquisition is made in connection with a change of residence by the individual resulting from relocation of employment,

(*d*) that the consideration for the acquisition does not exceed the market value of the dwelling,

(*e*) that the property trader does not intend—

(i) to spend more than the permitted amount on refurbishment of the dwelling, or

(ii) to grant a lease or licence of the dwelling, or

(iii) to permit any of its principals or employees (or any person connected with any of its principals or employees) to occupy the dwelling, and

(*f*) that the area of land acquired does not exceed the permitted area.

Paragraph (e)(ii) does not apply to the grant of a lease or licence to the individual for a period of no more than six months.

(3) Where the conditions in sub-paragraph (2)(*a*) to (*e*) are met but the area of land acquired exceeds the permitted area, the chargeable consideration for the acquisition is taken to be the amount calculated by deducting the market value of the permitted area from the market value of the dwelling.

(4) In this paragraph "relocation of employment" means a change of the individual's place of employment due to—

(*a*) his becoming employed by a new employer,

(*b*) an alteration of the duties of his employment, or

(*c*) an alteration of the place where he normally performs those duties.

(5) For the purposes of this paragraph a change of residence is one "resulting from" relocation of employment if—

(*a*) the change is made wholly or mainly to allow the individual to have his residence within a reasonable daily travelling distance of his new place of employment, and

(*b*) his former residence is not within a reasonable daily travelling distance of that place.

An individual's "new place of employment" means the place where he normally performs, or is normally to perform, the duties of his employment after the relocation.

(6) In this paragraph—

(*a*) references to the acquisition of the dwelling are to the acquisition, by way of transfer, of a major interest in the dwelling; and

(*b*) references to the market value of the dwelling and of the permitted area are, respectively, to the market value of that major interest in the dwelling and of that interest so far as it relates to that area.][1]

Amendments—[1] This Schedule inserted by FA 2004 s 296, Sch 39 para 17(2) with effect for any transaction of which the effective date (within the meaning of FA 2003 Pt 4) is on or after 22 July 2004: FA 2004 Sch 39 para 26. The insertion was previously made by the Stamp Duty and Stamp Duty Land Tax (Variation of the Finance Act 2003) (No 2) Regulations, SI 2003/2816 regs 1, 2, Schedule para 3(2) with effect from 1 December 2003. Those regulations are revoked by FA 2004 Sch 39 para 14(2).

[Meaning of "dwelling", "new dwelling" and "the permitted area"

7—(1) "Dwelling" includes land occupied and enjoyed with the dwelling as its garden or grounds.

(2) A building or part of a building is a "new dwelling" if—

(*a*) it has been constructed for use as a single dwelling and has not previously been occupied, or

(*b*) it has been adapted for use as a single dwelling and has not been occupied since its adaptation.

(3) "The permitted area", in relation to a dwelling, means land occupied and enjoyed with the dwelling as its garden or grounds that does not exceed—

(*a*) an area (inclusive of the site of the dwelling) of 0.5 of a hectare, or

(*b*) such larger area as is required for the reasonable enjoyment of the dwelling as a dwelling having regard to its size and character.

(4) Where sub-paragraph (3)(*b*) applies, the permitted area is taken to consist of that part of the land that would be the most suitable for occupation and enjoyment with the dwelling as its garden or grounds if the rest of the land were separately occupied.][1]

Amendments—[1] This Schedule inserted by FA 2004 s 296, Sch 39 para 17(2) with effect for any transaction of which the effective date (within the meaning of FA 2003 Pt 4) is on or after 22 July 2004: FA 2004 Sch 39 para 26. The insertion was previously made by the Stamp Duty and Stamp Duty Land Tax (Variation of the Finance Act 2003) (No 2) Regulations, SI 2003/2816 regs 1, 2, Schedule para 3(2) with effect from 1 December 2003. Those regulations are revoked by FA 2004 Sch 39 para 14(2).

[Meaning of "property trader" and "principal"

8—(1) A "property trader" means—

(*a*) a company,

(*b*) a limited liability partnership, or

(*c*) a partnership whose members are all either companies or limited liability partnerships,

that carries on the business of buying and selling dwellings.

(2) In relation to a property trader a "principal" means—

(*a*) in the case of a company, a director;

(*b*) in the case of a limited liability partnership, a member;

(*c*) in the case of a partnership whose members are all either companies or limited liability partnerships, a member or a person who is a principal of a member.

(3) For the purposes of this Schedule—

(*a*) anything done by or in relation to a company connected with a property trader is treated as done by or in relation to that property trader, and

(*b*) references to the principals or employees of a property trader include the principals or employees of any such company.][1]

Amendments—[1] This Schedule inserted by FA 2004 s 296, Sch 39 para 17(2) with effect for any transaction of which the effective date (within the meaning of FA 2003 Pt 4) is on or after 22 July 2004: FA 2004 Sch 39 para 26. The insertion was previously made by the Stamp Duty and Stamp Duty Land Tax (Variation of the Finance Act 2003) (No 2) Regulations, SI 2003/2816 regs 1, 2, Schedule para 3(2) with effect from 1 December 2003. Those regulations are revoked by FA 2004 Sch 39 para 14(2).

[Meaning of "refurbishment" and "the permitted amount"

9—(1) "Refurbishment" of a dwelling means the carrying out of works that enhance or are intended to enhance the value of the dwelling, but does not include—

(*a*) cleaning the dwelling, or

(*b*) works required solely for the purpose of ensuring that the dwelling meets minimum safety standards.

(2) The "permitted amount", in relation to the refurbishment of a dwelling, is—

(*a*) £10,000, or

(*b*) 5% of the consideration for the acquisition of the dwelling, whichever is the greater, but subject to a maximum of £20,000.][1]

Amendments—[1] This Schedule inserted by FA 2004 s 296, Sch 39 para 17(2) with effect for any transaction of which the effective date (within the meaning of FA 2003 Pt 4) is on or after 22 July 2004: FA 2004 Sch 39 para 26. The insertion was previously made by the Stamp Duty and Stamp Duty Land Tax (Variation of the Finance Act 2003) (No 2) Regulations, SI 2003/2816 regs 1, 2, Schedule para 3(2) with effect from 1 December 2003. Those regulations are revoked by FA 2004 Sch 39 para 14(2).

[Connected companies etc

10 [Section 1122 of the Corporation Tax Act 2010][2] (connected persons) has effect for the purposes of this Schedule.][1]

Amendments—[1] This Schedule inserted by FA 2004 s 296, Sch 39 para 17(2) with effect for any transaction of which the effective date (within the meaning of FA 2003 Pt 4) is on or after 22 July 2004: FA 2004 Sch 39 para 26. The insertion was previously made by the Stamp Duty and Stamp Duty Land Tax (Variation of the Finance Act 2003) (No 2) Regulations, SI 2003/2816 regs 1, 2, Schedule para 3(2) with effect from 1 December 2003. Those regulations are revoked by FA 2004 Sch 39 para 14(2).

In sub-para

2 Words "Section 839 of the Taxes Act 1988" substituted by CTA 2010 s 1177, Sch 1 paras 400, 415. CTA 2010 has effect for corporation tax purposes for accounting periods ending on or after 1 April 2010, and for income and capital gains tax purposes for the tax year 2010–11 and subsequent tax years.

[Withdrawal of relief under this Schedule

11—(1) Relief under this Schedule is withdrawn in the following circumstances.

(2) Relief under paragraph 2 (acquisition by property trader from individual acquiring new dwelling) is withdrawn if the property trader—

(*a*) spends more than the permitted amount on refurbishment of the old dwelling, or

(*b*) grants a lease or licence of the old dwelling, or

(*c*) permits any of its principals or employees (or any person connected with any of its principals or employees) to occupy the old dwelling.

Paragraph (b) does not apply to the grant of lease or licence to the individual for a period of no more than six months.

(3) Relief under paragraph 3 (acquisition by property trader from personal representatives) is withdrawn if the property trader—

(*a*) spends more than the permitted amount on refurbishment of the dwelling, or

(*b*) grants a lease or licence of the dwelling, or

(*c*) permits any of its principals or employees (or any person connected with any of its principals or employees) to occupy the dwelling.

(4) Relief under paragraph 4 (acquisition by property trader from individual where chain of transactions breaks down) is withdrawn if the property trader—

(*a*) spends more than the permitted amount on refurbishment of the old dwelling, or

(*b*) grants a lease or licence of the old dwelling, or

(*c*) permits any of its principals or employees (or any person connected with any of its principals or employees) to occupy the old dwelling.

Paragraph (b) does not apply to the grant of lease or licence to the individual for a period of no more than six months.

(5) Relief under paragraph 6 (acquisition by property trader in case of relocation of employment) is withdrawn if the property trader—

(*a*) spends more than the permitted amount on refurbishment of the dwelling, or

(*b*) grants a lease or licence of the dwelling, or

(*c*) permits any of its principals or employees (or any person connected with any of its principals or employees) to occupy the dwelling.

Paragraph (b) does not apply to the grant of lease or licence to the individual for a period of no more than six months.

(6) Where relief is withdrawn the amount of tax chargeable is the amount that would have been chargeable in respect of the acquisition but for the relief.][1]

Amendments—[1] This Schedule inserted by FA 2004 s 296, Sch 39 para 17(2) with effect for any transaction of which the effective date (within the meaning of FA 2003 Pt 4) is on or after 22 July 2004: FA 2004 Sch 39 para 26. The insertion was previously made by the Stamp Duty and Stamp Duty Land Tax (Variation of the Finance Act 2003) (No 2) Regulations, SI 2003/2816 regs 1, 2, Schedule para 3(2) with effect from 1 December 2003. Those regulations are revoked by FA 2004 Sch 39 para 14(2).

SCHEDULE 7

STAMP DUTY LAND TAX: GROUP RELIEF AND RECONSTRUCTION AND ACQUISITION RELIEFS

Section 62

HMRC Manuals—Stamp Duty Land Tax Manual SDLTM23000–23280 (explanation of this relief).

PART 1

GROUP RELIEF

Group relief

1—(1) A transaction is exempt from charge if the vendor and purchaser are companies that at the effective date of the transaction are members of the same group.

(2) For the purposes of group relief—

(*a*) "company" means a body corporate, and

(*b*) companies are members of the same group if one is the 75% subsidiary of the other or both are 75% subsidiaries of a third company.

(3) For the purposes of group relief a company ("company A") is the 75% subsidiary of another company ("company B") if company B—

(*a*) is beneficial owner of not less than 75% of the ordinary share capital of company A,

(*b*) is beneficially entitled to not less than 75% of any profits available for distribution to equity holders of company A, and

(*c*) would be beneficially entitled to not less than 75% of any assets of company A available for distribution to its equity holders on a winding-up.

(4) The ownership referred to in sub-paragraph (3)(*a*) is ownership either directly or through another company or companies.

For the purposes of that provision the amount of ordinary share capital of company A owned by company B through another company or companies shall be determined in accordance with [sections 1155 to 1157 of the Corporation Tax Act 2010][2].

(5) In sub-paragraphs (3)(*a*) and (4) above "ordinary share capital", in relation to a company, means all the issued share capital (by whatever name called) of the company, other than capital the holders of which have a right to a dividend at a fixed rate but have no other right to share in the profits of the company.
[(6) Chapter 6 of Part 5 of the Corporation Tax Act 2010 (group relief: equity holders and profits or assets available for distribution) applies for the purposes of sub-paragraphs (3)(*b*) and (*c*) above as it applies for the purposes of section 151(4)(*a*) and (*b*) of that Act.
6A In that Chapter as it applies for the purposes of subparagraphs (3)(*b*) and (*c*) above, sections 171(1)(*b*) and (3), 173, 174 and 176 to 178 of that Act are to be treated as omitted.][2]
(7) This paragraph is subject to paragraph 2 (restrictions on availability of group relief) and [paragraphs 3 and 4A][1] (withdrawal of group relief).

Modifications—Pension Protection Fund (Tax) Regulations, SI 2006/575 reg 43(2) (this paragraph applies in relation to a group of companies of which the Board of the Pension Protection Fund is a member as if, in the case of each reference to 75 per cent, there were substituted a reference to 50 per cent.).

Amendments—[1] In sub-para (7), words substituted for the words "paragraph 3" by F(No 2)A 2005 s 49, Sch 10 paras 1, 3 with effect where the effective date of the relevant transaction (within the meaning of FA 2003 Sch 7 para 3 or 4A) is after 19 May 2005.

However, this amendment does not have effect—

(a) in relation to any transaction which is effected in pursuance of a contract entered into and substantially performed on or before the specified date (ie 16 March 2005), or

(b) subject to what follows below, in relation to any other transaction which is effected in pursuance of a contract entered into on or before the specified date (ie 16 March 2005).

The exclusion by para (*b*) above of transactions effected in pursuance of contracts entered into on or before the specified date does not apply—

(a) if there is any variation of the contract or assignment of rights under the contract after that date,

(b) if the transaction is effected in consequence of the exercise after that date of any option, right of pre-emption or similar right, or

(c) if after that date there is an assignment, subsale or other transaction (relating to the whole or part of the subject-matter of the contract) as a result of which a person other than the purchaser under the contract becomes entitled to call for a conveyance to him: F(No 2)A 2005 Sch 10 para 16(1), (6)–(8).

[2] In sub-para (4) words "section 838(5) to (10) of the Taxes Act 1988" substituted and sub-para (6) substituted for former sub-paras (6)-(6A) by CTA 2010 s 1177, Sch 1 paras 400, 416(1),(2). CTA 2010 has effect for corporation tax purposes for accounting periods ending on or after 1 April 2010, and for income and capital gains tax purposes for the tax year 2010–11 and subsequent tax years. Sub-para (6) previously read as follows—

"(6) Schedule 18 to the Taxes Act 1988 (equity holders and profits or assets available for distribution) applies for the purposes of subsection (3)(*b*) and (*c*) above as it applies for the purposes of section 413(7)(*a*) and (*b*) of that Act, but with the omission of paragraphs 5(3) and 5B to 5E."

Restrictions on availability of group relief

2—(1) Group relief is not available if at the effective date of the transaction there are arrangements in existence by virtue of which, at that or some later time, a person has or could obtain, or any persons together have or could obtain, control of the purchaser but not of the vendor.
This does not apply to arrangements entered into with a view to an acquisition of shares by a company ("the acquiring company")—

(*a*) in relation to which section 75 of the Finance Act 1986 (c 41) (stamp duty: acquisition relief) will apply,

(*b*) in relation to which the conditions for relief under that section will be met, and

(*c*) as a result of which the purchaser will be a member of the same group as the acquiring company.

[For another exception to this, see sub-paragraph (3A).][2]
(2) Group relief is not available if the transaction is effected in pursuance of, or in connection with, arrangements under which—

(*a*) the consideration, or any part of the consideration, for the transaction is to be provided or received (directly or indirectly) by a person other than a group company, or

(*b*) the vendor and the purchaser are to cease to be members of the same group by reason of the purchaser ceasing to be a 75% subsidiary of the vendor or a third company.

(3) Arrangements are within sub-paragraph (2)(*a*) if under them the vendor or the purchaser, or another group company, is to be enabled to provide any of the consideration, or is to part with any of it, by or in consequence of the carrying out of a transaction or transactions involving, or any of them involving, a payment or other disposition by a person other than a group company.
[(3A) Sub-paragraphs (1) and (2)(*b*) do not apply to arrangements in so far as they are for the purpose of facilitating a transfer of the whole or part of the business of a company to another company in relation to which—

(*a*) section 96 of the Finance Act 1997 is intended to apply (stamp duty relief: demutualisation of insurance companies), and

(*b*) the conditions for relief under that section are intended to be met.][2]

(4) In sub-paragraphs (2)(*a*) and (3) a "group company" means a company that at the effective date of the transaction is a member of the same group as the vendor or the purchaser.

[(4A) Group relief is not available if the transaction—

(*a*) is not effected for bona fide commercial reasons, or

(*b*) forms part of arrangements of which the main purpose, or one of the main purposes, is the avoidance of liability to tax.

"Tax" here means stamp duty, income tax, corporation tax, capital gains tax or tax under this Part.][1]

(5) In this paragraph—

"arrangements" includes any scheme, agreement or understanding, whether or not legally enforceable; and

"control" has the meaning given by [section 1124 of the Corporation Tax Act 2010][5].

Amendments—[1] Sub-para (4A) inserted by F(No 2)A 2005 s 49, Sch 10 paras 17, 19 with effect in relation to any transaction of which the effective date is on or after 20 July 2005.

However, this amendment does not have effect—

(a) in relation to any transaction which is effected in pursuance of a contract entered into and substantially performed on or before 16 March 2005, or

(b) (subject to what follows below) in relation to any other transaction which is effected in pursuance of a contract entered into on or before that date.

The exclusion by para (*b*) above of transactions effected in pursuance of contracts entered into on or before 16 March 2005 does not apply—

(a) if there is any variation of the contract or assignment of rights under the contract after that date,

(b) if the transaction is effected in consequence of the exercise after that date of any option, right of pre-emption or similar right, or

(c) if after that date there is an assignment, subsale or other transaction (relating to the whole or part of the subject-matter of the contract) as a result of which a person other than the purchaser under the contract becomes entitled to call for a conveyance to him: F(No 2)A 2005 Sch 10 para 22(1)–(3).

[2] Words at the end of sub-para (1) and the whole of sub-para (3A) inserted by FA 2006 s 167(2), (3) with effect in relation to any transfer which takes place, or is intended to take place, after 22 March 2006.

[3] In sub-para (5) in the definition of "control", words "section 840 of the Taxes Act 1988" substituted by CTA 2010 s 1177, Sch 1 paras 400, 416(1), (3). CTA 2010 has effect for corporation tax purposes for accounting periods ending on or after 1 April 2010, and for income and capital gains tax purposes for the tax year 2010–11 and subsequent tax years.

Withdrawal of group relief

3—(1) Where in the case of a transaction ("the relevant transaction") that is exempt from charge by virtue of paragraph 1 (group relief)—

(*a*) the purchaser ceases to be a member of the same group as the vendor—

(i) before the end of the period of three years beginning with the effective date of the transaction, or

(ii) in pursuance of, or in connection with, arrangements made before the end of that period,, and

(*b*) at the time the purchaser ceases to be a member of the same group as the vendor ("the relevant time"), it or a relevant associated company holds a chargeable interest—

(i) that was acquired by the purchaser under the relevant transaction, or

(ii) that is derived from a chargeable interest so acquired,

and that has not subsequently been acquired at market value under a chargeable transaction for which group relief was available but was not claimed,

group relief in relation to the relevant transaction, or an appropriate proportion of it, is withdrawn and tax is chargeable in accordance with this paragraph.

[(2) The amount chargeable is the tax that would have been chargeable in respect of the relevant transaction but for group relief if the chargeable consideration for that transaction had been an amount equal to—

(*a*) the market value of the subject-matter of the transaction, and

(*b*) if the acquisition was the grant of a lease at a rent, that rent,

or, as the case may be, an appropriate proportion of the tax that would have been so chargeable.][1]

(3) In sub-paragraphs (1) and (2) "an appropriate proportion" means an appropriate proportion having regard to the subject matter of the relevant transaction and what is held at the relevant time by the transferee company or, as the case may be, by that company and its relevant associated companies.

(4) In this paragraph—

"arrangements" includes any scheme, agreement or understanding, whether or not legally enforceable; and

"relevant associated company", in relation to the purchaser, means a company that—

(*a*) is a member of the same group as the purchaser immediately before the purchaser ceases to be a member of the same group as the vendor, and (*b*) ceases to be a member of the same group as the vendor in consequence of the purchaser so ceasing.

(5) This paragraph has effect subject to [paragraphs 4 and 4ZA][3] (cases in which group relief not withdrawn) [and paragraph 4A (withdrawal of group relief in certain cases involving successive transactions)][2].

Cross references—Pension Protection Fund (Tax) Regulations, SI 2006/575 reg 43(3) (for the purposes of sub-para (1) above, there is no withdrawal of group relief if the vendor is the Board of the Pension Protection Fund).

Mutual Societies (Transfers of Business) (Tax) Regulations, SI 2009/2971 reg 33 (preservation of exemption from SDLT where purchaser ceases to be member of same group as transferor).

Modifications—FA 2003 Sch 15 para 27 (modification of this paragraph in its application to the transfer of an interest in a partnership that is a chargeable transaction by virtue of FA 2003 Sch 15 para 17).

Amendments—[1] Sub-para (2) substituted by F(No 2)A 2005 s 49, Sch 10 paras 1, 4(a) with effect where the effective date of the relevant transaction (within the meaning of FA 2003 Sch 7 para 3 or 4A) is after 19 May 2005.

However, this amendment does not have effect—

(a) in relation to any transaction which is effected in pursuance of a contract entered into and substantially performed on or before the specified date (ie 19 May 2005), or

(b) subject to what follows below, in relation to any other transaction which is effected in pursuance of a contract entered into on or before the specified date (ie 19 May 2005).

The exclusion by para (*b*) above of transactions effected in pursuance of contracts entered into on or before the specified date does not apply—

(a) if there is any variation of the contract or assignment of rights under the contract after that date,

(b) if the transaction is effected in consequence of the exercise after that date of any option, right of pre-emption or similar right, or

(c) if after that date there is an assignment, subsale or other transaction (relating to the whole or part of the subject-matter of the contract) as a result of which a person other than the purchaser under the contract becomes entitled to call for a conveyance to him: F(No 2)A 2005 Sch 10 para 16(1), (6)–(8).

[2] Words in sub-para (5) inserted by F(No 2)A 2005 s 49, Sch 10 paras 1, 4(b) with effect where the effective date of the relevant transaction (within the meaning of FA 2003 Sch 7 para 3 or 4A) is after 19 May 2005. This amendment is also subject to the qualifications given in note [1] above, save that the "specified date" in this instance is 16 March 2005: F(No 2)A 2005 Sch 10 para 16(1), (6)–(8).

[3] Words in sub-para (5) substituted by FA 2008 s 96(1), (2) with effect in relation to transactions with an effective date on or after 13 March 2008.

Cases in which group relief not withdrawn

4—(1) Group relief is not withdrawn under paragraph 3 in the following cases.

(2), (3) . . . [3]

(4) The second case is where the purchaser ceases to be a member of the same group as the vendor by reason of anything done for the purposes of, or in the course of, winding up the vendor or another company that is above the vendor in the group structure.

(5) For [the purposes of [sub-paragraph (4)][3]][1] a company is "above" the vendor in the group structure if the vendor, or another company that is above the vendor in the group structure, is a 75% subsidiary of the company.

(6) The third case is where—

(*a*) the purchaser ceases to be a member of the same group as the vendor as a result of an acquisition of shares by another company ("the acquiring company") in relation to which—

(i) section 75 of the Finance Act 1986 (c 41) applies (stamp duty: acquisition relief), and

(ii) the conditions for relief under that section are met,

and

(*b*) the purchaser is immediately after that acquisition a member of the same group as the acquiring company.

[(6A) The fourth case is where—

(*a*) the purchaser ceases to be a member of the same group as the vendor as a result of the transfer of the whole or part of the vendor's business to another company ("the acquiring company") in relation to which—

(i) section 96 of the Finance Act 1997 applies (stamp duty relief: demutualisation of insurance companies), and

(ii) the conditions for relief under that section are met, and

(*b*) the purchaser is immediately after that transfer a member of the same group as the acquiring company.][2]

(7) But if in a case within sub-paragraph (6) [or (6A)][2]—

(*a*) the purchaser ceases to be a member of the same group as the acquiring company—

(i) before the end of the period of three years beginning with the effective date of the relevant transaction, or

(ii) in pursuance of, or in connection with, arrangements made before the end of that period,

and

(*b*) at the time the purchaser ceases to be a member of the same group as the acquiring company, it or a relevant associated company holds a chargeable interest—
(i) that was acquired by the purchaser under the relevant transaction, or
(ii) that is derived from an interest so acquired,
and that has not subsequently been acquired at market value under a chargeable transaction for which group relief was available but was not claimed,

the provisions of this Part relating to group relief apply as if the purchaser had then ceased to be a member of the same group as the vendor.

(8) In sub-paragraph (7)—

"arrangements" includes any scheme, agreement or understanding, whether or not legally enforceable; and

"relevant associated company", in relation to the purchaser, means a company that is a member of the same group as the purchaser that ceases to be a member of the same group as the acquiring company in consequence of the purchaser so ceasing.

Modifications—FA 2003 Sch 15 para 27 (modification of this paragraph in its application to the transfer of an interest in a partnership that is a chargeable transaction by virtue of FA 2003 Sch 15 para 17).

Amendments—[1] Sub-para (3)(b) substituted, and in sub-para (5), words substituted for the words "this purpose" by F(No 2)A 2005 s 49, Sch 10 paras 1, 5 with effect where the effective date of the relevant transaction (within the meaning of FA 2003 Sch 7 para 3 or 4A) is after 19 May 2005.

However, this amendment does not have effect—

(a) in relation to any transaction which is effected in pursuance of a contract entered into and substantially performed on or before the specified date (ie 16 March 2005), or

(b) subject to what follows below, in relation to any other transaction which is effected in pursuance of a contract entered into on or before the specified date (ie 16 March 2005).

The exclusion by para (*b*) above of transactions effected in pursuance of contracts entered into on or before the specified date does not apply—

(a) if there is any variation of the contract or assignment of rights under the contract after that date,

(b) if the transaction is effected in consequence of the exercise after that date of any option, right of pre-emption or similar right, or

(c) if after that date there is an assignment, subsale or other transaction (relating to the whole or part of the subject-matter of the contract) as a result of which a person other than the purchaser under the contract becomes entitled to call for a conveyance to him: F(No 2)A 2005 Sch 10 para 16(1), (6)–(8).

[2] Sub-para (6A) and words in sub-para (7) inserted by FA 2006 s 167(4) with effect in relation to any transfer which takes place, or is intended to take place, after 22 March 2006.

[3] Sub-paras (2), (3) repealed and words in sub-para (5) substituted, by FA 2008 s 96(1), (3) with effect in relation to transactions with an effective date on or after 13 March 2008.

[Group relief not withdrawn where vendor leaves group

4ZA—(1) Group relief is not withdrawn under paragraph 3 where the purchaser ceases to be a member of the same group as the vendor because the vendor leaves the group.

(2) The vendor is regarded as leaving the group if the companies cease to be members of the same group by reason of a transaction relating to shares in—
(*a*) the vendor, or
(*b*) another company that—
(i) is above the vendor in the group structure, and
(ii) as a result of the transaction ceases to be a member of the same group as the purchaser.

(3) For the purpose of sub-paragraph (2) a company is "above" the vendor in the group structure if the vendor, or another company that is above the vendor in the group structure, is a 75% subsidiary of the company.

(4) But if there is a change in the control of the purchaser after the vendor leaves the group, paragraphs 3, 4(6) and (7), 5 and 6 have effect as if the purchaser had then ceased to be a member of the same group as the vendor (but see sub-paragraph (7)).

(5) For the purposes of this paragraph there is a change in the control of the purchaser if—
(*a*) a person who controls the purchaser (alone or with others) ceases to do so,
(*b*) a person obtains control of the purchaser (alone or with others), or
(*c*) the purchaser is wound up.

(6) For the purposes of sub-paragraph (5) a person does not control, or obtain control of, the purchaser if that person is under the control of another person or other persons.

(7) Sub-paragraph (4) does not apply where—
(*a*) there is a change in the control of the purchaser because a loan creditor (within the meaning [given by section 453 of the Corporation Tax Act 2010][2]) obtains control of, or ceases to control, the purchaser, and
(*b*) the other persons who controlled the purchaser before that change continue to do so.

(8) In this paragraph references to "control" shall be interpreted in accordance with [sections 450 and 451 of the Corporation Tax Act 2010][2] (subject to sub-paragraph (6)).][1]

Amendments—[1] Para 4ZA inserted by FA 2008 s 96(1), (4) with effect in relation to transactions with an effective date on or after 13 March 2008.

[2] In sub-para (7)(*a*) words "of section 417(7) to (9) of the Taxes Act 1988" substituted and in sub-para (8) words "section 416 of the Taxes Act 1988" substituted by CTA 2010 s 1177, Sch 1 paras 400, 416(1), (4). CTA 2010 has effect for corporation tax purposes for accounting periods ending on or after 1 April 2010, and for income and capital gains tax purposes for the tax year 2010–11 and subsequent tax years.

[Withdrawal of group relief in certain cases involving successive transactions

4A—(1) Where, in the case of a transaction ("the relevant transaction") that is exempt from charge by virtue of paragraph 1 (group relief)—

(*a*) there is a change in the control of the purchaser,

(*b*) that change occurs—

(i) before the end of the period of three years beginning with the effective date of the relevant transaction, or

(ii) in pursuance of, or in connection with, arrangements made before the end of that period,

(*c*) apart from this paragraph, group relief in relation to the relevant transaction would not be withdrawn under paragraph 3, and

(*d*) any previous transaction falls within sub-paragraph (2),

paragraphs 3[, 4 and 4ZA][2] have effect in relation to the relevant transaction as if the vendor in relation to the earliest previous transaction falling within sub-paragraph (2) were the vendor in relation to the relevant transaction.

[(1A) Sub-paragraph (1) has effect subject to sub-paragraph (3A).][2]

(2) A previous transaction falls within this sub-paragraph if—

(*a*) the previous transaction is exempt from charge by virtue of paragraph 1, 7 or 8,

(*b*) the effective date of the previous transaction is less than three years before the date of the event falling within sub-paragraph (1)(*a*),

(*c*) the chargeable interest acquired under the relevant transaction by the purchaser in relation to that transaction is the same as, comprises, forms part of, or is derived from, the chargeable interest acquired under the previous transaction by the purchaser in relation to the previous transaction, and

(*d*) since the previous transaction, the chargeable interest acquired under that transaction has not been acquired by any person under a transaction that is not exempt from charge by virtue of paragraph 1, 7 or 8.

(3) For the purposes of [this paragraph][2] there is a change in the control of a company if—

(*a*) any person who controls the company (alone or with others) ceases to do so,

(*b*) a person obtains control of the company (alone or with others), or

(*c*) the company is wound up.

References to "control" in [this paragraph][2] shall be construed in accordance with [sections 450 and 451 of the Corporation Tax Act 2010][3].

[(3A) Sub-paragraph (1) does not apply where—

(*a*) there is a change in the control of the purchaser because a loan creditor (within the meaning [given by section 453 of the Corporation Tax Act 2010][3]) obtains control of, or ceases to control, the purchaser, and

(*b*) the other persons who controlled the purchaser before that change continue to do so.][2]

(4) If two or more transactions effected at the same time are the earliest previous transactions falling within sub-paragraph (2), the reference in sub-paragraph (1) to the vendor in relation to the earliest previous transaction is a reference to the persons who are the vendors in relation to the earliest previous transactions.

(5) In this paragraph "arrangements" includes any scheme, agreement or understanding, whether or not legally enforceable.][1]

Amendments—[1] Paragraph 4A inserted by F(No 2)A 2005 s 49, Sch 10 paras 1, 6 with effect where the effective date of the relevant transaction (within the meaning of FA 2003 Sch 7 para 3 or 4A) is after 19 May 2005.

However, this amendment does not have effect—

(a) in relation to any transaction which is effected in pursuance of a contract entered into and substantially performed on or before the specified date (ie 16 March 2005), or

(b) subject to what follows below, in relation to any other transaction which is effected in pursuance of a contract entered into on or before the specified date (ie 16 March 2005).

The exclusion by para (*b*) above of transactions effected in pursuance of contracts entered into on or before the specified date does not apply—

(a) if there is any variation of the contract or assignment of rights under the contract after that date,

(b) if the transaction is effected in consequence of the exercise after that date of any option, right of pre-emption or similar right, or

(c) if after that date there is an assignment, subsale or other transaction (relating to the whole or part of the subject-matter of the contract) as a result of which a person other than the purchaser under the contract becomes entitled to call for a conveyance to him: F(No 2)A 2005 Sch 10 para 16(1), (6)–(8).

[2] In sub-paras (1), (3) words substituted, sub-paras (1A), (3A) inserted, by FA 2008 s 96(1), (5) with effect in relation to transactions with an effective date on or after 13 March 2008.

[3] In sub-para (3) words "section 416 of the Taxes Act 1988" substituted and in sub-paragraph (3A)(*a*) words "of section 417(7) to (9) of the Taxes Act 1988" substituted by CTA 2010 s 1177, Sch 1 paras 400, 416(1) ,(5). CTA 2010 has effect for corporation tax purposes for accounting periods ending on or after 1 April 2010, and for income and capital gains tax purposes for the tax year 2010–11 and subsequent tax years.

Recovery of group relief from another group company or controlling director

5—(1) This paragraph applies where—

(*a*) tax is chargeable under paragraph 3 (withdrawal of group relief),

(*b*) the amount so chargeable has been finally determined, and

(*c*) the whole or part of the amount so chargeable is unpaid six months after the date on which it became payable.

(2) The following persons may, by notice under paragraph 6, be required to pay the unpaid tax—

(*a*) the vendor;

(*b*) any company that at any relevant time was a member of the same group as the purchaser and was above it in the group structure;

(*c*) any person who at any relevant time was a controlling director of the purchaser or a company having control of the purchaser.

(3) For the purposes of sub-paragraph (2)(*b*)—

(*a*) a "relevant time" means any time between effective date of the relevant transaction and the purchaser ceasing to be a member of the same group as the vendor; and

(*b*) a company ("company A") is "above" another company ("company B") in a group structure if company B, or another company that is above company B in the group structure, is a 75% subsidiary of company A.

(4) In sub-paragraph (2)(*c*)—

"director", in relation to a company, has the meaning given by section 67(1) of the Income Tax (Earnings and Pensions) Act 2003 (c 1) (read with subsection (2) of that section) and includes any person falling within [section 452(1) of the Corporation Tax Act 2010][1]; and

"controlling director", in relation to a company, means a director of the company who has control of it (construing control in accordance with [sections 450 and 451 of the Corporation Tax Act 2010][1]).

Modifications—FA 2003 Sch 15 para 27 (modification of this paragraph in its application to the transfer of an interest in a partnership that is a chargeable transaction by virtue of FA 2003 Sch 15 para 17).

Amendments—[1] In sub-para (4) in the definition of "director" words "section 417(5) of the Taxes Act 1988 (read with subsection (6) of that section)" substituted and in the definition of "controlling director" words "section 416 of the Taxes Act 1988" substituted by CTA 2010 s 1177, Sch 1 paras 400, 416(1),(6). CTA 2010 has effect for corporation tax purposes for accounting periods ending on or after 1 April 2010, and for income and capital gains tax purposes for the tax year 2010–11 and subsequent tax years.

Recovery of group relief: supplementary

6—(1) The Inland Revenue may serve a notice on a person within paragraph 5(2) above requiring him within 30 days of the service of the notice to pay the amount that remains unpaid.

(2) Any such notice must be served before the end of the period of three years beginning with the date of the final determination mentioned in paragraph 5(1)(*b*).

(3) The notice must state the amount required to be paid by the person on whom the notice is served.

(4) The notice has effect—

(*a*) for the purposes of the recovery from that person of the amount required to be paid and of interest on that amount, and

(*b*) for the purposes of appeals,

as if it were a notice of assessment and that amount were an amount of tax due from that person.

(5) A person who has paid an amount in pursuance of a notice under this paragraph may recover that amount from the purchaser.

(6) A payment in pursuance of a notice under this paragraph is not allowed as a deduction in computing any income, profits or losses for any tax purpose.

Modifications—FA 2003 Sch 15 para 27 (modification of this paragraph in its application to the transfer of an interest in a partnership that is a chargeable transaction by virtue of FA 2003 Sch 15 para 17).

PART 2

RECONSTRUCTION AND ACQUISITION RELIEFS

Reconstruction relief

7—(1) Where—

(*a*) a company ("the acquiring company") acquires the whole or part of the undertaking of another company ("the target company") in pursuance of a scheme for the reconstruction of the target company, and

(*b*) the first, second and third conditions specified below are met,

a land transaction entered into for the purposes of or in connection with the transfer of the undertaking or part is exempt from charge.

Relief under this paragraph is referred to in this Part as "reconstruction relief".

(2) The first condition is that the consideration for the acquisition consists wholly or partly of the issue of non-redeemable shares in the acquiring company to all the shareholders of the target company.

"Non-redeemable shares" means shares that are not redeemable shares.

(3) Where the consideration for the acquisition consists partly of the issue of non-redeemable shares as mentioned in the first condition, that condition is met only if the rest of the consideration consists wholly of the assumption or discharge by the acquiring company of liabilities of the target company.

(4) The second condition is that after the acquisition has been made—

(*a*) each shareholder of each of the companies is a shareholder of the other, and

(*b*) the proportion of shares of one of the companies held by any shareholder is the same, or as nearly as may be the same, as the proportion of shares of the other company held by that shareholder.

(5) The third condition is that the acquisition is effected for bona fide commercial reasons and does not form part of a scheme or arrangement of which the main purpose, or one of the main purposes, is the avoidance of liability to tax.

[(5A) If immediately before the acquisition the target company or the acquiring company holds any of its own shares, the shares are to be treated for the purposes of sub-paragraphs (2) and (4) as having been cancelled before the acquisition (and, accordingly, the company is to be treated as if it were not a shareholder of itself).][1]

"Tax" here means stamp duty, income tax, corporation tax, capital gains tax or tax under this Part.

(6) This paragraph is subject to paragraph 9 (withdrawal of reconstruction or acquisition relief).

Amendments—[1] Sub-para (5A) inserted by FA 2007 s 74(3), (5) with effect in relation to any land transaction of which the effective date is on or after 19 July 2007.

Acquisition relief

8—(1) Where—

(*a*) a company ("the acquiring company") acquires the whole or part of the undertaking of another company ("the target company"), and

(*b*) [all the conditions][1] specified below are met,

the rate of tax chargeable on a land transaction entered into for the purposes of or in connection with the transfer of the undertaking or part is limited to 0.5%.

Relief under this section is referred to in this Part as "acquisition relief".

(2) The first condition is that the consideration for the acquisition consists wholly or partly of the issue of non-redeemable shares in the acquiring company to—

(*a*) the target company, or

(*b*) all or any of the target company's shareholders.

"Non-redeemable shares" means shares that are not redeemable shares.

(3) Where the consideration for the acquisition consists partly of the issue of non-redeemable shares as mentioned in the first condition, that condition is met only if the rest of the consideration consists wholly of—

(*a*) cash not exceeding 10% of the nominal value of the non-redeemable shares so issued, or

(*b*) the assumption or discharge by the acquiring company of liabilities of the target company, or

(*c*) both of those things.

(4) The second condition is that the acquiring company is not associated with another company that is a party to arrangements with the target company relating to shares of the acquiring company issued in connection with the transfer of the undertaking or part.

[(5) For this purpose companies are associated if one has control of the other or both are controlled by the same person or persons.

The reference to control shall be construed in accordance with section 416 of the Taxes Act 1988.][2]

[(5A)The third condition is that the undertaking or part acquired by the acquiring company has as its main activity the carrying on of a trade that does not consist wholly or mainly of dealing in chargeable interests.

In this sub-paragraph "trade" has the same meaning as in the Taxes Act 1988.][1]

[(5B) The fourth condition is that the acquisition is effected for bona fide commercial reasons and does not form part of arrangements of which the main purpose, or one of the main purposes, is the avoidance of liability to tax.

"Tax" here means stamp duty, income tax, corporation tax, capital gains tax or tax under this Part.][2]
[(5C) In this paragraph "arrangements" include any scheme, agreement or understanding, whether or not legally enforceable.][2]
(6) This paragraph is subject to paragraph 9 (withdrawal of reconstruction or acquisition relief).

Amendments—[1] In sub-para (1)(b), words substituted for the words "the first and second conditions", and sub-para (5A) inserted; by F(No 2)A 2005 s 49, Sch 10 paras 1, 8 with effect in relation to any transaction of which the effective date is after 19th May 2005.
However, this amendment does not have effect—
(a) in relation to any transaction which is effected in pursuance of a contract entered into and substantially performed on or before the specified date (ie 16 March 2005), or
(b) subject to what follows below, in relation to any other transaction which is effected in pursuance of a contract entered into on or before the specified date (ie 16 March 2005).
The exclusion by para (*b*) above of transactions effected in pursuance of contracts entered into on or before the specified date does not apply—
(a) if there is any variation of the contract or assignment of rights under the contract after that date,
(b) if the transaction is effected in consequence of the exercise after that date of any option, right of pre-emption or similar right, or
(c) if after that date there is an assignment, subsale or other transaction (relating to the whole or part of the subject-matter of the contract) as a result of which a person other than the purchaser under the contract becomes entitled to call for a conveyance to him: F(No 2)A 2005 Sch 10 para 16(5)–(8).
[2] Sub-para (5) substituted, and sub-paras (5B), (5C) inserted, by F(No 2)A 2005 s 49, Sch 10 paras 17, 20 with effect in relation to any transaction of which the effective date is on or after the day on which F(No 2)A 2005 is passed.
However, this amendment does not have effect—
(a) in relation to any transaction which is effected in pursuance of a contract entered into and substantially performed on or before 16 March 2005, or
(b) (subject to what follows below) in relation to any other transaction which is effected in pursuance of a contract entered into on or before that date.
The exclusion by para (*b*) above of transactions effected in pursuance of contracts entered into on or before 16 March 2005 does not apply—
(a) if there is any variation of the contract or assignment of rights under the contract after that date,
(b) if the transaction is effected in consequence of the exercise after that date of any option, right of pre-emption or similar right, or
(c) if after that date there is an assignment, subsale or other transaction (relating to the whole or part of the subject-matter of the contract) as a result of which a person other than the purchaser under the contract becomes entitled to call for a conveyance to him: F(No 2)A 2005 Sch 10 para 22(1)–(3).

Withdrawal of reconstruction or acquisition relief

9—(1) Where in the case of a transaction ("the relevant transaction") that is exempt by virtue of reconstruction relief or is subject to a reduced rate of tax by virtue of acquisition relief—
(*a*) control of the acquiring company changes—
(i) before the end of the period of three years beginning with the effective date of the transaction, or
(ii) in pursuance of, or in connection with, arrangements made before the end of that period,
and
(*b*) at the time control of the acquiring company changes ("the relevant time"), it or a relevant associated company holds a chargeable interest—
(i) that was acquired by the acquiring company under the relevant transaction, or
(ii) that is derived from an interest so acquired,
and that has not subsequently been acquired at market value under a chargeable transaction in relation to which reconstruction or acquisition relief was available but was not claimed,
reconstruction or acquisition relief in relation to the relevant transaction, or an appropriate proportion of it, is withdrawn and tax is chargeable in accordance with this paragraph.
[(2) The amount chargeable is the tax that would have been chargeable in respect of the relevant transaction but for reconstruction or acquisition relief if the chargeable consideration for that transaction had been an amount equal to—
(*a*) the market value of the subject-matter of the transaction, and
(*b*) if the acquisition was the grant of a lease at a rent, that rent,
or, as the case may be, an appropriate proportion of the tax that would have been so chargeable.][1]
(3) In sub-paragraphs (1) and (2) "an appropriate proportion" means an appropriate proportion having regard to the subject-matter of the relevant transaction and what is held at the relevant time by the acquiring company or, as the case may be, by that company and any relevant associated companies.
(4) In this paragraph "relevant associated company", in relation to the acquiring company, means a company—
(*a*) that is controlled by the acquiring company immediately before the control of that company changes, and

(*b*) of which control changes in consequence of the change of control of that company.

(5) In this paragraph—

(*a*) "arrangements" includes any scheme, agreement or understanding, whether or not legally enforceable;

(*b*) "control" shall be construed in accordance with [sections 450 and 451 of the Corporation Tax Act 2010][2]; and

(*c*) references to control of a company changing are to the company becoming controlled—

(i) by a different person,

(ii) by a different number of persons, or

(iii) by two or more persons at least one of whom is not the person, or one of the persons, by whom the company was previously controlled.

(6) This paragraph has effect subject to paragraph 10 (cases in which reconstruction or acquisition relief not withdrawn).

Amendments—[1] Sub-para (2) substituted by F(No 2)A 2005 s 49, Sch 10 paras 1, 9 with effect where the effective date of the relevant transaction (within the meaning of this paragraph) is after 19 May 2005.

However, this amendment does not have effect—

(a) in relation to any transaction which is effected in pursuance of a contract entered into and substantially performed on or before the specified date (ie 19 May 2005), or

(b) subject to what follows below, in relation to any other transaction which is effected in pursuance of a contract entered into on or before the specified date (ie 19 May 2005).

The exclusion by para (*b*) above of transactions effected in pursuance of contracts entered into on or before the specified date does not apply—

(a) if there is any variation of the contract or assignment of rights under the contract after that date,

(b) if the transaction is effected in consequence of the exercise after that date of any option, right of pre-emption or similar right, or

(c) if after that date there is an assignment, subsale or other transaction (relating to the whole or part of the subject-matter of the contract) as a result of which a person other than the purchaser under the contract becomes entitled to call for a conveyance to him: F(No 2)A 2005 Sch 10 para 16(2), (6)–(8).

2 In sub-para (5)(*b*) words "section 416 of the Taxes Act 1988" substituted by CTA 2010 s 1177, Sch 1 paras 400, 416(1), (7). CTA 2010 has effect for corporation tax purposes for accounting periods ending on or after 1 April 2010, and for income and capital gains tax purposes for the tax year 2010–11 and subsequent tax years.

Cases in which reconstruction or acquisition relief not withdrawn

10—(1) Reconstruction or acquisition relief is not withdrawn under paragraph 9 in the following cases.

(2) The first case is where control of the acquiring company changes as a result of a share transaction that is effected as mentioned in any of paragraphs (*a*) to (*d*) of paragraph 3 of Schedule 3 (transactions in connection with divorce etc).

(3) The second case is where control of the acquiring company changes as a result of a share transaction that—

(*a*) is effected as mentioned in paragraph 4(1) of Schedule 3, and

(*b*) meets the conditions in paragraph 4(2) of that Schedule (variation of testamentary dispositions etc).

(4) The third case is where control of the acquiring company changes as a result of an exempt intra-group transfer.

An "exempt intra-group transfer" means a transfer of shares effected by an instrument that is exempt from stamp duty by virtue of section 42 of the Finance Act 1930 (c 28) or section 11 of the Finance Act (Northern Ireland) 1954 (c 23 (NI)) (transfers between associated bodies corporate).

But see paragraph 11 (withdrawal of relief in case of subsequent non-exempt transfer).

(5) The fourth case is where control of the acquiring company changes as a result of a transfer of shares to another company in relation to which share acquisition relief applies.

"Share acquisition relief" means relief under section 77 of the Finance Act 1986 (c 41) and a transfer is one in relation to which that relief applies if an instrument effecting the transfer is exempt from stamp duty by virtue of that provision.

But see paragraph 11 (withdrawal in case of subsequent non-exempt transfer).

(6) The fifth case is where—

(*a*) control of the acquiring company changes as a result of a loan creditor becoming, or ceasing to be, treated as having control of the company, and

(*b*) the other persons who were previously treated as controlling the company continue to be so treated.

"Loan creditor" here has the meaning given by [section 453 of the Corporation Tax Act 2010][1].

Amendments—[1] In sub-para (6) words "section 417(7) to (9) of the Taxes Act 1988" substituted by CTA 2010 s 1177, Sch 1 paras 400, 416(1) ,(8). CTA 2010 has effect for corporation tax purposes for accounting periods ending on or after 1 April 2010, and for income and capital gains tax purposes for the tax year 2010–11 and subsequent tax years.

Withdrawal of reconstruction or acquisition relief on subsequent non-exempt transfer

11—(1) Where paragraph 10(4) (change of control of acquiring company as a result of exempt intra-group transfer) has effect to prevent the withdrawal of reconstruction or acquisition relief on a change of control of the acquiring company, but—

(*a*) a company holding shares in the acquiring company to which the exempt intra-group transfer related, or that are derived from shares to which that transfer related, ceases to be a member of the same group as the target company—

(i) before the end of the period of three years beginning with the effective date of the relevant transaction, or

(ii) in pursuance of or in connection with arrangements made before the end of that period,

and

(*b*) the acquiring company or a relevant associated company, at that time ("the relevant time"), holds a chargeable interest—

(i) that was transferred to the acquiring company by the relevant transaction, or

(ii) that is derived from an interest that was so transferred, and that has not subsequently been transferred at market value by a chargeable transaction in relation to which reconstruction or acquisition relief was available but was not claimed,

reconstruction or acquisition relief in relation to the relevant transaction, or an appropriate proportion of it, is withdrawn and tax is chargeable in accordance with this paragraph.

(2) Where paragraph 10(5) (change of control of acquiring company as a result of a transfer to which share acquisition relief applies) has effect to prevent the withdrawal of reconstruction or acquisition relief on a change of control of the acquiring company, but—

(*a*) control of the other company mentioned in that provision changes—

(i) before the end of the period of three years beginning with the effective date of the relevant transaction, or

(ii) in pursuance of or in connection with arrangements made before the end of that period,

at a time when that company holds any shares transferred to it by the exempt transfer, or any shares derived from shares so transferred, and

(*b*) the acquiring company or a relevant associated company, at that time ("the relevant time"), holds a chargeable interest—

(i) that was transferred to the acquiring company by the relevant transaction, or

(ii) that is derived from an interest that was so transferred,

and that has not subsequently been transferred at market value by a chargeable transaction in relation to which reconstruction or acquisition relief was available but was not claimed,

reconstruction or acquisition relief in relation to the relevant transaction, or an appropriate proportion of it, is withdrawn and tax is chargeable in accordance with this paragraph.

(3) The amount chargeable is the tax that would have been chargeable in respect of the relevant transaction but for reconstruction or acquisition relief if the chargeable consideration for that transaction had been an amount equal to the market value of the subject matter of the transaction or, as the case may be, an appropriate proportion of the tax that would have been so chargeable.

(4) In sub-paragraphs (1), (2) and (3) "an appropriate proportion" means an appropriate proportion having regard to the subject-matter of the relevant transaction and what is held at the relevant time by the acquiring company or, as the case may be, by that company and any relevant associated companies.

(5) In this paragraph "relevant associated company", in relation to the acquiring company, means a company—

(*a*) that is controlled by the acquiring company immediately before the control of that company changes, and

(*b*) of which control changes in consequence of the change of control of that company.

(6) In this paragraph—

(*a*) "arrangements" includes any scheme, agreement or understanding, whether or not legally enforceable;

(*b*) "control" shall be construed in accordance with [sections 450 and 451 of the Corporation Tax Act 2010][1]; and

(*c*) references to control of a company changing are to the company becoming controlled—

(i) by a different person,

(ii) by a different number of persons, or

(iii) by two or more persons at least one of whom is not the person, or one of the persons, by whom the company was previously controlled.

Amendments—[1] In sub-para (6)(*b*) words "section 416 of the Taxes Act 1988" substituted by CTA 2010 s 1177, Sch 1 paras 400, 416(1) ,(9). CTA 2010 has effect for corporation tax purposes for accounting periods ending on or after 1 April 2010, and for income and capital gains tax purposes for the tax year 2010–11 and subsequent tax years.

Recovery of reconstruction or acquisition relief from another group company or controlling director

12—(1) This paragraph applies where—

(*a*) tax is chargeable under paragraph 9 or 11 (withdrawal of reconstruction or acquisition relief),

(*b*) the amount so chargeable has been finally determined, and

(*c*) the whole or part of the amount so chargeable is unpaid six months after the date on which it became payable.

(2) The following persons may, by notice under paragraph 13, be required to pay the unpaid tax—

(*a*) any company that at any relevant time was a member of the same group as the acquiring company and was above it in the group structure;

(*b*) any person who at any relevant time was a controlling director of the acquiring company or a company having control of the acquiring company.

(3) For the purposes of sub-paragraph (2) "relevant time" means any time between effective date of the relevant transaction and the change of control by virtue of which tax is chargeable.

(4) For the purposes of sub-paragraph (2)(*a*) a company ("company A") is "above" another company ("company B") in a group structure if company B, or another company that is above company B in the group structure, is a 75% subsidiary of company A.

(5) For the purposes of sub-paragraph (2)(*b*)—

(*a*) "director", in relation to a company, has the meaning given by section 67(1) of the Income Tax (Earnings and Pensions) Act 2003 (c 1) (read with subsection (2) of that section) and includes any person falling within [section 452(1) of the Corporation Tax Act 2010][1]; and

(*b*) "controlling director", in relation to a company, means a director of the company who has control of it (construing control in accordance with [sections 450 and 451 of the Corporation Tax Act 2010][1]).

Amendments—[1] In sub-para (5)(*a*) words "section 417(5) of the Taxes Act 1988 (read with subsection (6) of that section)" substituted and in sub-para (5)(*b*) words "section 416 of the Taxes Act 1988" substituted by CTA 2010 s 1177, Sch 1 paras 400, 416(1), (10). CTA 2010 has effect for corporation tax purposes for accounting periods ending on or after 1 April 2010, and for income and capital gains tax purposes for the tax year 2010–11 and subsequent tax years.

Recovery of reconstruction or acquisition relief: supplementary

13—(1) The Inland Revenue may serve a notice on a person within paragraph 12(2) above requiring him within 30 days of the service of the notice to pay the amount that remains unpaid.

(2) Any such notice must be served before the end of the period of three years beginning with the date of the final determination mentioned in paragraph 12(1)(*b*).

(3) The notice must state the amount required to be paid by the person on whom the notice is served.

(4) The notice has effect—

(*a*) for the purposes of the recovery from that person of the amount required to be paid and of interest on that amount, and

(*b*) for the purposes of appeals,

as if it were a notice of assessment and that amount were an amount of tax due from that person.

(5) A person who has paid an amount in pursuance of a notice under this paragraph may recover that amount from the acquiring company.

(6) A payment in pursuance of a notice under this paragraph is not allowed as a deduction in computing any income, profits or losses for any tax purpose.

SCHEDULE 8

STAMP DUTY LAND TAX: CHARITIES RELIEF

Section 68

HMRC Manuals—Stamp Duty Land Tax Manual SDLTM26000–26020 (explanation of this relief).

Modifications—FA 2003 Sch 15 para 28 (this Schedule applies to the transfer of an interest in a partnership that is a chargeable transaction by virtue of FA 2003 Sch 15 paras 14 or 17, with the insertion of para 3, and the modification of paras 1, 2).

Charities relief

1—(1) A land transaction is exempt from charge if the purchaser is a charity and the following conditions are met.

Relief under [this Schedule][1] is referred to in this Part as "charities relief".

(2) The first condition is that the purchaser must intend to hold the subject-matter of the transaction for qualifying charitable purposes, that is—

(*a*) for use in furtherance of the charitable purposes of the purchaser or of another charity, or (*b*) as an investment from which the profits are applied to the charitable purposes of the purchaser.

(3) The second condition is that the transaction must not have not been entered into for the purpose of avoiding tax under this Part (whether by the purchaser or any other person).

(4) In this section a "charity" means a body or trust established for charitable purposes only.

Modifications—FA 2003 Sch 15 para 28 (this Schedule applies to the transfer of an interest in a partnership that is a chargeable transaction by virtue of FA 2003 Sch 15 paras 14 or 17, with the insertion of para 3, and the modification of paras 1, 2).

Amendments—[1] In sub-para (1), words substituted for the words "this paragraph " by FA 2004 s 302(3), (7) with effect for any transaction of which the effective date (within the meaning of FA 2004 Pt 4) is on or after the day 22 July 2004.

Withdrawal of charities relief

2—(1) Where in the case of a transaction ("the relevant transaction") that is exempt by virtue of [this Schedule][1]—

(*a*) a disqualifying event occurs—

(i) before the end of the period of three years beginning with the effective date of the transaction, or

(ii) in pursuance of, or in connection with, arrangements made before the end of that period,

and

(*b*) at the time of the disqualifying event the purchaser holds a chargeable interest—

(i) that was acquired by the purchaser under the relevant transaction, or

(ii) that is derived from an interest so acquired,

charities relief in relation to the relevant transaction, or an appropriate proportion of it, is withdrawn and tax is chargeable in accordance with this paragraph.

(2) The amount chargeable is the amount that would have been chargeable in respect of the relevant transaction but for charities relief or, as the case may be, an appropriate proportion of the tax that would have been so chargeable.

(3) For the purposes of this paragraph a "disqualifying event" means—

(*a*) the purchaser ceasing to be established for charitable purposes only, or

(*b*) the subject-matter of the transaction, or any interest or right derived from it, being used or held by the purchaser otherwise than for qualifying charitable purposes.

(4) In sub-paragraphs (1) and (2) an "appropriate proportion" means an appropriate proportion having regard to—

(*a*) what was acquired by the purchaser under the relevant transaction and what is held by the purchaser at the time of the disqualifying event, and

(*b*) the extent to which what is held by the purchaser at that time becomes used or held for purposes other than qualifying charitable purposes.

(5) In this paragraph "qualifying charitable purposes" has the same meaning as in paragraph 1.

Modifications—FA 2003 Sch 8 para 3 (modification of this paragraph in relation to a transaction that, by virtue of FA 2003 Sch 8 para 3, is a disqualifying event for the purposes of this paragraph).

FA 2003 Sch 15 para 28 (this Schedule applies to the transfer of an interest in a partnership that is a chargeable transaction by virtue of FA 2003 Sch 15 paras 14 or 17, with the insertion of para 3, and the modification of paras 1, 2).

Amendments—[1] In sub-para (1), words substituted for the words "paragraph 1 (charities relief)" by FA 2004 s 302(4), (7) with effect for any transaction of which the effective date (within the meaning of FA 2004 Pt 4) is on or after 22 July 2004.

[Cases where first condition not fully met

3—(1) This paragraph applies where—

(*a*) a land transaction is not exempt from charge under paragraph 1 because the first condition in that paragraph is not met, but

(*b*) the purchaser ("C") intends to hold the greater part of the subject-matter of the transaction for qualifying charitable purposes.

(2) In such a case—

(*a*) the transaction is exempt from charge, but

(*b*) for the purposes of paragraph 2 (withdrawal of charities relief) "disqualifying event" includes—

(i) any transfer by C of a major interest in the whole or any part of the subject-matter of the transaction, or

(ii) any grant by C at a premium of a low-rental lease of the whole or any part of that subject-matter,

that is not made in furtherance of the charitable purposes of C.

(3) For the purposes of sub-paragraph (2)(*b*)(ii)—

(*a*) a lease is granted "at a premium" if there is consideration other than rent, and

(*b*) a lease is a "low-rental" lease if the annual rent (if any) [is less than £1,000][2] a year.

(4) In relation to a transaction that, by virtue of this paragraph, is a disqualifying event for the purposes of paragraph 2—

(*a*) the date of the event for those purposes is the effective date of the transaction;

(*b*) paragraph 2 has effect as if—

(i) in sub-paragraph (1)(*b*), for "at the time of" there were substituted "immediately before",

(ii) in sub-paragraph (4)(*a*), for "at the time of" there were substituted "immediately before and immediately after", and

(iii) sub-paragraph (4)(*b*) were omitted.

(5) In this paragraph—

"qualifying charitable purposes" has the same meaning as in paragraph 1;

"rent" has the same meaning as in Schedule 5 (amount of tax chargeable: rent) and "annual rent" has the same meaning as in paragraph [9A][2] of that Schedule.][1]

Modifications—FA 2003 Sch 15 para 28 (this Schedule applies to the transfer of an interest in a partnership that is a chargeable transaction by virtue of FA 2003 Sch 15 paras 14 or 17, with the insertion of para 3 (headed "Interpretation" as shown in FA 2003 Sch 15 para 28(2)), and the modification of paras 1, 2).

Amendments—[1] This paragraph inserted by FA 2004 s 302(1), (7) with effect for any transaction of which the effective date (within the meaning of FA 2004 Pt 4) is on or after 22 July 2004.

[2] Words in sub-paras (3)(b), (5) substituted by FA 2008 s 95(7) with effect in relation to transactions with an effective date on or after 12 March 2008.

[Charitable trusts

4—(1) This Schedule applies in relation to a charitable trust as it applies in relation to a charity.

(2) In this paragraph "charitable trust" means—

(*a*) a trust of which all the beneficiaries are charities, or

(*b*) a unit trust scheme in which all the unit holders are charities, and "charity" has the same meaning as in paragraph 1.

(3) In this Schedule as it applies by virtue of this paragraph—

(*a*) references to the purchaser in paragraphs (*a*) and (*b*) of paragraph 1(2) are to the beneficiaries or unit holders, or any of them;

(*b*) the reference to the purchaser in paragraph 2(3)(*a*) is to any of the beneficiaries or unit holders;

(*c*) the reference in paragraph 3(2)(*b*) to the charitable purposes of C is to those of the beneficiaries or unit holders, or any of them.][1]

Modifications—FA 2003 Sch 15 para 28 (this Schedule applies to the transfer of an interest in a partnership that is a chargeable transaction by virtue of FA 2003 Sch 15 paras 14 or 17, with the insertion of para 3, and the modification of paras 1, 2).

Amendments—[1] This paragraph inserted by FA 2004 s 302(2), (7) with effect for any transaction of which the effective date (within the meaning of FA 2004 Pt 4) is on or after 22 July 2004.

SCHEDULE 9

STAMP DUTY LAND TAX: RIGHT TO BUY, SHARED OWNERSHIP LEASES ETC

Section 70

HMRC Manuals—Stamp Duty Land Tax Manual SDLTM27000–27070 (explanation of this relief).

Right to buy transactions

1—(1) In the case of a right to buy transaction—

(*a*) section 51(1) (contingent consideration to be included in chargeable consideration on assumption that contingency will occur) does not apply, and

(*b*) any consideration that would be payable only if a contingency were to occur, or that is payable only because a contingency has occurred, does not count as chargeable consideration.

(2) A "right to buy transaction" means—

(*a*) the sale of a dwelling at a discount, or the grant of a lease of a dwelling at a discount, by a relevant public sector body, or

(*b*) the sale of a dwelling, or the grant of a lease of a dwelling, in pursuance of the preserved right to buy.

(3) The following are relevant public sector bodies for the purposes of sub-paragraph (2)(*a*):

Government

A Minister of the Crown
The Scottish Ministers
A Northern Ireland department

Local Government

A local housing authority within the meaning of the Housing Act 1985 (c 68)
A county council in England

A council constituted under section 2 of the Local Government etc (Scotland) Act 1994 (c 39), the common good of such a council or any trust under its control

A district council within the meaning of the Local Government Act (Northern Ireland) 1972 (c 9 (NI))

Social housing

[The Regulator of Social Housing][3]

Scottish Homes

The Northern Ireland Housing Executive

[A non-profit registered provider of social housing][3]

A registered social landlord

A housing action trust established under Part 3 of the Housing Act 1988 (c 50)

New towns and development corporations [etc][2]

The [Homes and Communities Agency][2]

A development corporation established by an order made, or having effect as if made, under the New Towns Act 1981 (c 64)

A development corporation established by an order made, or having effect as if made, under the New Towns (Scotland) Act 1968 (c 16)

A new town commission established under section 7 of the New Towns Act (Northern Ireland) 1965 (c 13 (NI))

An urban development corporation established by an order made under section 135 of the Local Government, Planning and Land Act 1980 (c 65)

...[1]

Police

A police authority within the meaning of section 101(1) of the Police Act 1996 (c 16)

A police authority within the meaning of section 2(1) or 19(9)(*b*) of the Police (Scotland) Act 1967 (c 77)

The Northern Ireland Policing Board

Miscellaneous

An Education and Libraries Board within the meaning of the Education and Libraries (Northern Ireland) Order 1986 (SI1986/594 (NI 3))

The United Kingdom Atomic Energy Authority

Any person mentioned in paragraphs (*g*), (*k*), (*l*) or (*n*) of section 61(11) of the Housing (Scotland) Act 1987 (c 26)

A body prescribed for the purposes of this sub-paragraph by Treasury order.

(4) For the purposes of sub-paragraph (2)(*b*) the transfer of a dwelling, or the grant of a lease of a dwelling, is made in pursuance of the preserved right to buy if—

(*a*) the vendor is—

(i) in England and Wales, a person against whom the right to buy under Part 5 of the Housing Act 1985 (c 68) is exercisable by virtue of section 171A of that Act, or

(ii) in Scotland, a person against whom the right to buy under section 61 of the Housing (Scotland) Act 1987 is exercisable by virtue of section 81A of that Act,

(which provide for the preservation of the right to buy on disposal to a private sector landlord),

(*b*) the purchaser is the qualifying person for the purposes of the preserved right to buy, and

(*c*) the dwelling is the qualifying dwelling-house in relation to the purchaser.

(5) A grant under section 20 or 21 of the Housing Act 1996 (c 52) (purchase grants in respect of disposals at a discount by registered social landlords) does not count as part of the chargeable consideration for a right to buy transaction in relation to which the vendor is a registered social landlord [or [private registered provider][4] of social housing][3].

[(6) A grant under section 19 of the Housing and Regeneration Act 2008 which—

(*a*) is made by virtue of section 35 of that Act, or

(*b*) is otherwise made to a relevant provider of social housing (within the meaning of section 35 of that Act) in respect of discounts given by the provider on disposals of dwellings to tenants,

does not count as part of the chargeable consideration for a right to buy transaction to which the vendor is a relevant provider of social housing.][3]

Modification—Transfer of Housing Corporation Functions (Modifications and Transitional Provisions) Order, SI 2008/2839 art 3, Schedule (any reference to the Housing Corporation shall be treated as if it were a reference to the Regulator of Social Housing).

Amendments—[1] Words in sub-para (3) omitted, repealed by the Welsh Development Agency (Transfer of Functions to the National Assembly for Wales and Abolition) Order, SI 2005/3226 art 7(1), Sch 2 para 14 with effect from 23 November 2005.

2 In sub-para (3), word inserted, and words substituted for words "Commission for the New Towns" by the Housing and Regeneration Act 2008 s 56, Sch 8 para 80 with effect from 1 December 2008 (by virtue of SI 2008/3068, arts 1(2), 2(1)(w), (3)).

3 In sub-para (3), words substituted for words "The Housing Corporation" and words inserted, in sub-para (5), words inserted, and whole of sub-para (6) inserted, by the Housing and Regeneration Act 2008 s 277, Sch 9 paras 29, 32(1), (3), (4) with effect from 1 April 2010 (by virtue of SI 2010/862 art 2 (subject to transitional provisions and savings in SI 2010/862 art 2, Schedule, paras 1–4)).

4 In sub-para (5), words substituted for words "registered provider" by the Housing and Regeneration Act 2008 (Registration of Local Authorities) Order, SI 2010/844 art 6, Sch 2 para 25(*a*) with effect from 1 April 2010.

Shared ownership lease: election for market value treatment

2—(1) This paragraph applies where—

(*a*) a lease is granted—

(i) by a qualifying body, or

(ii) in pursuance of the preserved right to buy,

(*b*) the conditions in sub-paragraph (2) are met, and

(*c*) the purchaser elects for tax to be charged in accordance with this paragraph.

(2) The conditions are as follows—

(*a*) the lease must be of a dwelling;

(*b*) the lease must give the lessee or lessees exclusive use of the dwelling;

(*c*) the lease must provide for the lessee or lessees to acquire the reversion;

(*d*) the lease must be granted partly in consideration of rent and partly in consideration of a premium calculated by reference to—

(i) the market value of the dwelling, or

(ii) a sum calculated by reference to that value;

(*e*) the lease must contain a statement of—

(i) the market value of the dwelling, or

(ii) the sum calculated by reference to that value,

by reference to which the premium is calculated.

(3) An election for tax to be charged in accordance with this paragraph must be included in the land transaction return made in respect of the grant of the lease, or in an amendment of that return, and is irrevocable, so that the return may not be amended so as to withdraw the election.

(4) Where this paragraph applies the chargeable consideration for the grant of the lease shall be taken to be the amount stated in the lease in accordance with sub-paragraph (2)(*e*)(i) or (ii).

[(4A) Where this paragraph applies no account shall be taken for the purposes of stamp duty land tax of the rent mentioned in sub-paragraph (2)(*d*).][1]

As to the tax treatment of the acquisition of the reversion in pursuance of the lease, see paragraph 3.

(5) Section 118 (meaning of "market value") does not apply in relation to the reference in sub-paragraph (2)(*e*) above to the market value of the dwelling.

Amendments—[1] Sub-para (4A) inserted by FA 2007 s 78 with effect from 19 July 2007.

Transfer of reversion under shared ownership lease where election made for market value treatment

3 The transfer of the reversion to the lessee or lessees under the terms of a lease to which paragraph 2 applies (shared ownership lease: election for market value treatment) is exempt from charge if—

(*a*) an election was made for tax to be charged in accordance with that paragraph, and

(*b*) any tax chargeable in respect of the grant of the lease has been paid.

Cross references—FA 2003 Sch 19 para 7(2) (in this paragraph as it applies in a case where the original lease was granted before the implementation date—

(a) the reference to a lease to which FA 2003 Sch 9 para 2 applies shall be read as a reference to a lease to which FA 1980 s 97 applied), and

(b) the reference to an election having been made for tax to be charged under that paragraph shall be read accordingly as a reference to a corresponding election having been in relation to stamp duty under that section.

For the implementation date, see FA 2003 Sch 19 para 2).

Shared ownership lease: election where staircasing allowed

4—(1) This paragraph applies where—

(*a*) a lease is granted by a qualifying body or in pursuance of the preserved right to buy,

(*b*) the conditions in sub-paragraph (2) below are met, and

(*c*) the purchaser elects for tax to be charged in accordance with this paragraph.

(2) The conditions are as follows—

(*a*) the lease must be of a dwelling;

(*b*) the lease must give the lessee or lessees exclusive use of the dwelling;

(*c*) the lease must provide that the lessee or lessees may, on the payment of a sum, require the terms of the lease to be altered so that the rent payable under it is reduced;

(*d*) the lease must be granted partly in consideration of rent and partly in consideration of a premium calculated by reference to—

(i) the premium obtainable on the open market for the grant of a lease containing the same terms as the lease but with the substitution of the minimum rent for the rent payable under the lease, or

(ii) a sum calculated by reference to that premium;

(*e*) the lease must contain a statement of the minimum rent and of—

(i) the premium obtainable on the open market, or

(ii) the sum calculated by reference to that premium,

by reference to which the premium is calculated.

(3) An election for tax to be charged in accordance with this paragraph must be included in the land transaction return made in respect of the grant of the lease, or in an amendment of that return, and is irrevocable, so that the return may not be amended so as to withdraw the election.

(4) Where this paragraph applies—

(*a*) the rent in consideration of which the lease is granted shall be taken to be the minimum rent stated in the lease in accordance with sub-paragraph (2)(*e*), and

(*b*) the chargeable consideration for the grant other than rent shall be taken to be the amount stated in the lease in accordance with sub-paragraph (2)(*e*)(i) or (ii).

(5) In this paragraph the "minimum rent" means the lowest rent which could become payable under the lease if it were altered as mentioned in sub-paragraph (2)(*c*) at the date when the lease is granted.

[Shared ownership lease: treatment of staircasing transaction

4A—(1) This paragraph applies where under a shared ownership lease—

(*a*) the lessee or lessees have the right, on the payment of a sum, to require the terms of the lease to be altered so that the rent payable under it is reduced, and

(*b*) by exercising that right the lessee or lessees acquire an interest, additional to one already held, calculated by reference to the market value of the dwelling and expressed as a percentage of the dwelling or its value (a "share of the dwelling").

(2) Such an acquisition is exempt from charge if—

(*a*) an election was made for tax to be charged in accordance with paragraph 2 or, as the case may be, paragraph 4 and any tax chargeable in respect of the grant of the lease has been paid, or

(*b*) immediately after the acquisition the total share of the dwelling held by the lessee or lessees does not exceed 80%.

(3) In this paragraph "shared ownership lease" means a lease granted—

(*a*) by a qualifying body, or

(*b*) in pursuance of the preserved right to buy,

in relation to which the conditions in paragraph 2(2) or 4(2) are met.

(4) Section 118 (meaning of "market value") does not apply in relation to the references in this paragraph to the market value of the dwelling.][1]

Amendments—[1] This paragraph inserted by FA 2004 s 303(1), (4) with effect for an acquisition after 17 March 2004.

[Shared ownership lease: grant not linked with staircasing transactions etc

4B—(1) For the purpose of determining the rate of tax chargeable on the grant of a shared ownership lease of a dwelling, the grant shall be treated as if it were not linked to—

(*a*) any acquisition of an interest in the dwelling to which paragraph 4A applies, or

(*b*) a transfer of the reversion to the lessee or lessees under the terms of the lease.

(2) In this paragraph "shared ownership lease" has the same meaning as in paragraph 4A.][1]

Amendments—[1] Para 4B inserted by FA 2008 s 95(8) with effect in relation to transactions with an effective date on or after 12 March 2008.

Shared ownership leases: meaning of "qualifying body" and "preserved right to buy"

5—(1) This paragraph has effect for the purposes of paragraphs [2, 4 and 4A][1] (shared ownership leases: election as to basis of taxation).

(2) A "qualifying body" means—

(*a*) a local housing authority within the meaning of the Housing Act 1985 (c 68);

(*b*) a housing association within the meaning of—

(i) the Housing Associations Act 1985 (c 69), or

(ii) Part 2 of the Housing (Northern Ireland) Order 1992 (SI 1992/1725 (NI 15));

(*c*) a housing action trust established under Part 3 of the Housing Act 1988 (c 50);

(*d*) the Northern Ireland Housing Executive;

[(*e*) the Homes and Communities Agency;][2]

(*f*) a development corporation established by an order made, or having effect as if made, under the New Towns Act 1981 (c 64);

[(*g*) a [private registered provider][5] of social housing that is not within paragraph (*b*) (subject to sub-paragraph (2A)).][3]

[(2A) A [private registered provider][5] of social housing within sub- paragraph (2)(*g*) ("R") is only a qualifying body in relation to a lease of premises if the following has been funded with the assistance of a grant or other financial assistance under section 19 of the Housing and Regeneration Act 2008—

(*a*) the purchase or construction of the premises by R (or a person connected with R), or

(*b*) the adaptation of the premises by R (or a person connected with R) for use as a dwelling.

(2B) [Section 1122 of the Corporation Tax Act 2010][4] (connected persons) has effect for the purposes of sub-paragraph (2A).][3]

(3) A lease is granted "in pursuance of the preserved right to buy" if—

(*a*) the vendor is a person against whom the right to buy under Part 5 of the Housing Act 1985 is exercisable by virtue of section 171A of that Act (preservation of right to buy on disposal to private sector landlord),

(*b*) the lessee is, or lessees are, the qualifying person for the purposes of the preserved right to buy, and

(*c*) the lease is of a dwelling that is the qualifying dwelling-house in relation to the purchaser.

Amendments—[1] References substituted by FA 2004 s 303(2), (4) with effect for an acquisition after 17 March 2004.

[2] Sub-para (2)(*e*) substituted by the Housing and Regeneration Act 2008 s 56, Sch 8 para 81 with effect from 1 December 2008 (by virtue of SI 2008/3068, arts 1(2), 2(1)(w), (3)).

[3] Sub-paras (2)(*g*), (2A), (2B) inserted by FA 2009 s 81(1), (5), (6) with effect in relation to transactions with an effective date on or after 21 July 2009.

[4] In sub-para (2B) words "Section 839 of the Taxes Act 1988" substituted by CTA 2010 s 1177, Sch 1 paras 400, 417(1), (2). CTA 2010 has effect for corporation tax purposes for accounting periods ending on or after 1 April 2010, and for income and capital gains tax purposes for the tax year 2010–11 and subsequent tax years.

[5] In sub-paras (2)(*g*), (2A), words substituted for words "registered provider" by the Housing and Regeneration Act 2008 (Registration of Local Authorities) Order, SI 2010/844 art 6, Sch 2 para 25(*b*) with effect from 1 April 2010.

Rent to mortgage or rent to loan: chargeable consideration

6—(1) The chargeable consideration for a rent to mortgage or rent to loan transaction is determined in accordance with this paragraph.

(2) A "rent to mortgage transaction" means—

(*a*) the transfer of a dwelling to a person, or

(*b*) the grant of a lease of a dwelling to a person,

pursuant to the exercise by that person of the right to acquire on rent to mortgage terms under Part 5 of the Housing Act 1985 (c 68).

(3) The chargeable consideration for such a transaction is equal to the price that, by virtue of section 126 of the Housing Act 1985, would be payable for—

(*a*) a transfer of the dwelling to the person (where the rent to mortgage transaction is a transfer), or

(*b*) the grant of a lease of the dwelling to the person (where the rent to mortgage transaction is the grant of a lease),

if the person were exercising the right to buy under Part 5 of that Act.

(4) A "rent to loan transaction" means the execution of a heritable disposition in favour of a person pursuant to the exercise by that person of the right to purchase a house by way of the rent to loan scheme in Part 3 of the Housing (Scotland) Act 1987 (c 26).

(5) The chargeable consideration for such a transaction is equal to the price that, by virtue of section 62 of the Housing (Scotland) Act 1987 (c 26), would be payable for the house if the person were exercising the right to purchase under section 61 of that Act.

[Shared ownership trust: introduction

7—(1) In this Schedule "shared ownership trust" means a trust of land, within the meaning of section 1 of the Trusts of Land and Appointment of Trustees Act 1996, which satisfies the following conditions.

(2) Condition 1 is that the trust property is—

(*a*) a dwelling, and

(*b*) in England or Wales.

(3) Condition 2 is that one of the beneficiaries ("the social landlord") is a qualifying body . . . [2].

(4) Condition 3 is that the terms of the trust—

(*a*) provide for one or more of the individual beneficiaries ("the purchaser") to have exclusive use of the trust property as the only or main residence of the purchaser,

(*b*) require the purchaser to make an initial payment to the social landlord ("the initial capital"),

(*c*) require the purchaser to make additional payments to the social landlord by way of compensation under section 13(6)(*a*) of the Trusts of Land and Appointment of Trustees Act 1996, ("rent-equivalent payments"),

(*d*) enable the purchaser to make other additional payments to the social landlord ("equity-acquisition payments"),

(*e*) determine the initial beneficial interests of the social landlord and of the purchaser by reference to the initial capital,

(*f*) specify a sum, equating or relating to the market value of the dwelling, by reference to which the initial capital was calculated, and

(*g*) provide for the purchaser's beneficial interest in the trust property to increase, and the social landlord's to diminish (or to be extinguished), as equity-acquisition payments are made.

(5) Section 118 (meaning of "market value") does not apply to this paragraph.

(6) In Condition 1 "dwelling" includes—

(*a*) a building which is being constructed or adapted for use as a dwelling,

(*b*) land which is to be used for the purpose of the construction of a dwelling, and

(*c*) land which is, or is to become, the garden or grounds of a dwelling.][1]

[(7) In Condition 2 "qualifying body" means—

(*a*) a qualifying body within the meaning of paragraph 5(2)(*a*) to (*f*), or

(*b*) a [private registered provider][4] of social housing within paragraph 5(2)(*g*) (subject to sub-paragraph (8)).

(8) A [private registered provider][4] of social housing within paragraph 5(2)(*g*) ("R") is only a qualifying body in relation to a shared ownership trust if the following has been or is being funded with the assistance of a grant or other financial assistance under section 19 of the Housing and Regeneration Act 2008—

(*a*) the purchase or construction of the trust property by R (or a person connected with R), or

(*b*) the adaptation of the trust property by R (or a person connected with R) for use as a dwelling.

(9) [Section 1122 of the Corporation Tax Act 2010][3] (connected persons) has effect for the purposes of sub-paragraph (8).][2]

Amendments—[1] Paragraphs 7–11 inserted by FA 2007 s 77 with effect in relation to land transactions with an effective date on or after 19 July 2007.

[2] In sub-para (3) words "(within the meaning of paragraph 5(2))" repealed and sub-paras (7)–(9) inserted by FA 2009 s 81(1), (7) with effect in relation to transactions with an effective date on or after 21 July 2009.

[3] In sub-para (9) words "Section 839 of the Taxes Act 1988" substituted by CTA 2010 s 1177, Sch 1 paras 400, 417(1),(3). CTA 2010 has effect for corporation tax purposes for accounting periods ending on or after 1 April 2010, and for income and capital gains tax purposes for the tax year 2010–11 and subsequent tax years.

[4] In sub-paras (7)(*b*), (8), words substituted for words "registered provider" by the Housing and Regeneration Act 2008 (Registration of Local Authorities) Order, SI 2010/844 art 6, Sch 2 para 25(*c*) with effect from 1 April 2010.

[Shared ownership trust: "purchaser"

8 For the purposes of the application of stamp duty land tax in relation to a shared ownership trust, the person (or persons) identified as the purchaser in accordance with paragraph 7, and not the social landlord or any other beneficiary, is (or are) to be treated as the purchaser of the trust property.][1]

Amendments—[1] Paragraphs 7–11 inserted by FA 2007 s 77 with effect in relation to land transactions with an effective date on or after 19 July 2007.

[Shared ownership trust: election for market value treatment

9—(1) This paragraph applies where—

(*a*) a shared ownership trust is declared, and

(*b*) the purchaser elects for tax to be charged in accordance with this paragraph.

(2) An election must be included in—

(*a*) the land transaction return for the declaration of the shared ownership trust, or

(*b*) an amendment of that return.

(3) An election may not be revoked.

(4) Where this paragraph applies—

(*a*) the chargeable consideration for the declaration of the shared ownership trust shall be taken to be the amount stated in accordance with paragraph 7(4)(*f*), and

(*b*) no account shall be taken for the purposes of stamp duty land tax of rent-equivalent payments.

(5) The transfer to the purchaser of an interest in the trust property upon the termination of the trust is exempt from charge if—

(*a*) an election was made under this paragraph, and

(*b*) any tax chargeable in respect of the declaration of the shared ownership trust has been paid.][1]

Amendments—[1] Paragraphs 7–11 inserted by FA 2007 s 77 with effect in relation to land transactions with an effective date on or after 19 July 2007.

[Shared ownership trust: treatment of staircasing transaction

10—(1) An equity-acquisition . . . [2] payment under a shared ownership trust, and the consequent increase in the purchaser's beneficial interest, shall be exempt from charge if—

(*a*) an election was made under paragraph 9, and

(*b*) any tax chargeable in respect of the declaration of trust has been paid.

(2) An equity-acquisition . . . [2] payment under a shared ownership trust, and the consequent increase in the purchaser's beneficial interest, shall also be exempt from charge if following the increase the purchaser's beneficial interest does not exceed 80% of the total beneficial interest in the trust property.][1]

Amendments—[1] Paragraphs 7–11 inserted by FA 2007 s 77 with effect in relation to land transactions with an effective date on or after 19 July 2007.

[2] In sub-paras (1), (2) word repealed by FA 2008 s 95(9) with effect in relation to transactions with an effective date on or after 12 March 2008.

[Shared ownership trust: treatment of additional payments where no election made

11—Where no election has been made under paragraph 9 in respect of a shared ownership trust—

(*a*) the initial capital shall be treated for the purposes of stamp duty land tax as chargeable consideration other than rent, and

(*b*) any rent-equivalent . . . [2] payment by the purchaser shall be treated for the purposes of stamp duty land tax as a payment of rent.][1]

Amendments—[1] Paragraphs 7–11 inserted by FA 2007 s 77 with effect in relation to land transactions with an effective date on or after 19 July 2007.

[2] In sub-para (b) word repealed by FA 2008 s 95(9) with effect in relation to transactions with an effective date on or after 12 March 2008.

[Shared ownership trust: declaration not linked with staircasing transactions etc

12 For the purpose of determining the rate of tax chargeable on the declaration of a shared ownership trust, the declaration shall be treated as if it were not linked to—

(*a*) any equity-acquisition payment under the trust or any consequent increase in the purchaser's beneficial interest in the trust property, or

(*b*) a transfer to the purchaser of an interest in the trust property upon the termination of the trust.][1]

Amendments—[1] Para 12 inserted by FA 2008 s 95(10) with effect in relation to transactions with an effective date on or after 12 March 2008.

[Rent to shared ownership lease: charge to tax

13—(1) The chargeable consideration for transactions forming part of a rent to shared ownership lease scheme is determined in accordance with this paragraph.

(2) A "rent to shared ownership lease scheme" means a scheme or arrangement under which a qualifying body—

(*a*) grants an assured shorthold tenancy of a dwelling to a person ("the tenant") or persons ("the tenants"), and

(*b*) subsequently grants a shared ownership lease of the dwelling or another dwelling to the tenant or one or more of the tenants.

(3) The following transactions are to be treated as if they were not linked to each other—

(*a*) the grant of the assured shorthold tenancy,

(*b*) the grant of the shared ownership lease, and

(*c*) any other land transaction between the qualifying body and the tenant, or any of the tenants, entered into as part of the scheme.

(4) For the purpose of determining the effective date of the grant of the shared ownership lease, the possession of the dwelling by the tenant or tenants pursuant to the assured shorthold tenancy is to be disregarded.

(5) In this paragraph—

"assured shorthold tenancy" has the same meaning as in Part 1 of the Housing Act 1988;

"qualifying body" has the same meaning as in paragraph 5;

"shared ownership lease" has the same meaning as in paragraph 4A.][1]

Amendments—[1] Paras 13 and 14 inserted by FA 2009 s 82(1) with effect in relation to cases in which the effective date of the grant of the shared ownership lease or the declaration of the shared ownership trust is on or after 22 April 2009.

[Rent to shared ownership trust: charge to tax

14—(1) The chargeable consideration for transactions forming part of a rent to shared ownership trust scheme is determined in accordance with this paragraph.

(2) A "rent to shared ownership trust scheme" means a scheme or arrangement under which—

(*a*) a qualifying body grants an assured shorthold tenancy of a dwelling to a person ("the tenant") or persons ("the tenants"), and

(*b*) the tenant, or one or more of tenants, subsequently becomes the purchaser under a shared ownership trust of the dwelling, or another dwelling, under which the qualifying body is the social landlord.

(3) The following transactions are to be treated as if they were not linked to each other—

(*a*) the grant of the assured shorthold tenancy,

(*b*) the declaration of the shared ownership trust, and

(*c*) any other land transaction between the qualifying body and the tenant, or any of the tenants, entered into as part of the scheme.

(4) For the purpose of determining the effective date of the declaration of the shared ownership trust, the possession of the dwelling by the tenant or tenants pursuant to the assured shorthold tenancy is to be disregarded.

(5) In this paragraph—

"assured shorthold tenancy" has the same meaning as in Part 1 of the Housing Act 1988;

"qualifying body" has the same meaning as in paragraph 5;

"social landlord" and "purchaser", in relation to a shared ownership trust, have the same meaning as in paragraph 7.][1]

Amendments—[1] Paras 13 and 14 inserted by FA 2009 s 82(1) with effect in relation to cases in which the effective date of the grant of the shared ownership lease or the declaration of the shared ownership trust is on or after 22 April 2009.

[First-time buyers

15 (1) This paragraph applies where—

(*a*) a lease is granted as mentioned in sub-paragraph (1)(*a*) of paragraph 2 and the conditions in sub-paragraph (2) of that paragraph are met but no election is made for tax to be charged in accordance with that paragraph,

(*b*) a lease is granted as mentioned in sub-paragraph (1)(*a*) of paragraph 4 and the conditions in sub-paragraph (2) of that paragraph are met but no election is made for tax to be charged in accordance with that paragraph,

(*c*) paragraph 4A applies in relation to the acquisition of an interest (but the acquisition is not exempt from charge by virtue of sub-paragraph (2) of that paragraph),

(*d*) a shared ownership trust is declared but no election is made for tax to be charged in accordance with paragraph 9, or

(*e*) an equity-acquisition payment is made under a shared ownership trust (but the equity-acquisition payment, and the consequential increase in the purchaser's beneficial interest, are not exempt from charge by virtue of paragraph 10).

(2) Neither section 57AA nor section 73CA applies in relation to—

(*a*) the acquisition of the lease,

(*b*) the acquisition of the interest,

(*c*) the declaration of the shared ownership trust, or

(*d*) the equity-acquisition payment and the consequential increase in the purchaser's beneficial interest.][1]

Amendments[1] Para 15 inserted by FA 2010 s 6(1), (5) with effect in relation to any land transaction of which the effective date is on or after 25 March 2010 but before 25 March 2012 (FA 2010 s 6(6)).

SCHEDULE 10

STAMP DUTY LAND TAX: RETURNS, ENQUIRIES, ASSESSMENTS AND APPEALS

Section 78

PART 1
LAND TRANSACTION RETURNS

Contents of return

1—(1) A land transaction return must—

(*a*) be in the prescribed form,

(*b*) contain the prescribed information, and

(*c*) include a declaration by the purchaser (or each of them) that the return is to the best of his knowledge correct and complete.

[(1A) Sub-paragraph (1)(*c*) is subject to paragraphs 1A and 1B.][1]

(2) In sub-paragraph (1) "prescribed" means prescribed by regulations made by the Inland Revenue.

(3) The regulations may make different provision for different kinds of return.

(4) Regulations under sub-paragraph (1)(*b*) may require the provision of information corresponding to any of the particulars formerly required under—

(*a*) Schedule 2 to the Finance Act 1931 (c 28) (requirement to deliver particulars of land transactions in Great Britain), or

(*b*) section 244 of the Finance Act 1994 (c 9) (corresponding provision for Northern Ireland).

(5) The return is treated as containing any information provided by the purchaser for the purpose of completing the return.

Amendments—[1] Sub-para (1A) inserted by the SDLT (Land Transaction Returns) Regulations, SI 2004/3208 regs 2, 3 with effect from 8 December 2004, in relation to a land transaction the effective date of which is on or after 8 December 2004.

[Declaration by agent

1A—(1) Where—

(*a*) the purchaser (or each of them) authorises an agent to complete a land transaction return,

(*b*) the purchaser (or each of them) makes a declaration that, with the exception of the effective date, the information provided in the return is to the best of his knowledge correct and complete, and

(*c*) the land transaction return includes a declaration by the agent that the effective date provided in the return is to the best of his knowledge correct,

the requirement in paragraph 1(1)(c) shall be deemed to be met.

(2) Sub-paragraph (1) applies only where the return is in a form specified by the Inland Revenue for the purposes of that sub-paragraph.

(3) Nothing in this paragraph affects the liability of the purchaser (or each of them) under this Part of this Act.][1]

Amendments—[1] Paragraphs 1A, 1B inserted by the SDLT (Land Transaction Returns) Regulations, SI 2004/3208 regs 2, 3 with effect from 8 December 2004, in relation to a land transaction the effective date of which is on or after 8 December 2004.

[Declaration by the relevant Official Solicitor

1B—(1) Where—

(*a*) the purchaser (or any of them) is a person under a disability,

(*b*) the Official Solicitor is acting for the purchaser (or any of them), and

(*c*) the land transaction return includes a declaration by the Official Solicitor that the return is to the best of his knowledge correct and complete,

the requirement in paragraph 1(1)(c) shall be deemed to be met.

(2) Sub-paragraph (1) applies only where the return is in a form specified by the Inland Revenue for the purposes of that sub-paragraph.

(3) Nothing in this paragraph affects the liability of the purchaser (or each of them) under this Part of this Act.

(4) In this paragraph "the Official Solicitor" means the Official Solicitor to the Supreme Court of England and Wales or the Official Solicitor to the Supreme Court of Northern Ireland (as the case requires).][1]

Amendments—[1] Paragraphs 1A, 1B inserted by the SDLT (Land Transaction Returns) Regulations, SI 2004/3208 regs 2, 3 with effect from 8 December 2004, in relation to a land transaction the effective date of which is on or after 8 December 2004.

Meaning of filing date and delivery of return

2—(1) References in this Part of this Act to the filing date, in relation to a land transaction return, are to the last day of the period within which the return must be delivered.

(2) References in this Part of this Act to the delivery of a land transaction return are to the delivery of a return that—

(*a*) complies with the requirements of paragraph 1(1) (contents of return), . . . [1]

(*b*) ...[1]

Amendments—[1] Sub-para (2)(b) and preceding word "and" repealed by FA 2007 ss 80(1), (7), (9)(f), 114, Sch 27 Pt 4(4) with effect in relation to land transactions with an effective date on or after 19 July 2007.

Failure to deliver return: flat-rate penalty

3—(1) A person who is required to deliver a land transaction return and fails to do so by the filing date is liable to a flat-rate penalty under this paragraph.

He may also be liable to a tax-related penalty under paragraph 4.

(2) The penalty is—

(*a*) £100 if the return is delivered within three months after the filing date, and

(*b*) £200 in any other case.

Failure to deliver return: tax-related penalty

4—(1) A purchaser who is required to deliver a land transaction return in respect of a chargeable transaction and fails to do so within twelve months after the filing date is liable to a tax-related penalty under this paragraph.

This is in addition to any flat-rate penalty under paragraph 3.

(2) The penalty is an amount not exceeding the amount of tax chargeable in respect of the transaction.

Formal notice to deliver return: daily penalty

5—(1) If it appears to the Inland Revenue—

(*a*) that a purchaser required to deliver a land transaction return in respect of a chargeable transaction has failed to do so, and

(*b*) that the filing date has now passed,

they may issue a notice requiring him to deliver a land transaction return in respect of the transaction.

(2) The notice must specify—

(*a*) the transaction to which it relates, and

(*b*) the period for complying with the notice (which must not be less than 30 days from the date of issue of the notice).

(3) If the purchaser does not comply with the notice within the specified period, the Inland Revenue may apply to the [tribunal][1] for an order imposing a daily penalty.

(4) On such an application the [tribunal][1] may direct that the purchaser shall be liable to a penalty or penalties not exceeding £60 for each day on which the failure continues after the day on which he is notified of the direction.

(5) This paragraph does not affect, and is not affected by, any penalty under paragraph 3 or 4 (flat-rate or tax-related penalty for failure to deliver return).

Amendments—[1] In sub-para(3) word substituted for the words "General or Special Commissioners"; in sub-para (4) word substituted for the word "Commissioners" by the Transfer of Tribunal Functions and Revenue and Customs Appeals Order, SI 2009/56 art 3, Sch 1 para 374 with effect from 1 April 2009.

Amendment of return by purchaser

6—(1) The purchaser may amend a land transaction return given by him by notice to the Inland Revenue.

(2) The notice must be in such form, and contain such information, as the Inland Revenue may require.

[(2A) If the effect of the amendment would be to entitle the purchaser to a repayment of tax, the notice must be accompanied by—

(*a*) the contract for the land transaction; and

(*b*) the instrument (if any) by which that transaction was effected.][1]

(3) Except as otherwise provided, an amendment may not be made more than twelve months after the filing date.

Amendments—[1] Sub-para (2A) inserted by the SDLT (Land Transaction Returns) Regulations, SI 2004/3208 regs 2, 3 with effect from 8 December 2004, in relation to a land transaction the effective date of which is on or after 8 December 2004.

Correction of return by Revenue

7—(1) The Inland Revenue may amend a land transaction return so as to correct obvious errors or omissions in the return (whether errors of principle, arithmetical mistakes or otherwise).

[(1A) The power under sub-paragraph (1) may, in such circumstances as the Commissioners for Her Majesty's Revenue and Customs may specify in regulations, be exercised—

(*a*) in relation to England and Wales, by the Chief Land Registrar;

(*b*) in relation to Scotland, by the Keeper of the Registers of Scotland;

(*c*) in relation to Northern Ireland, by the Registrar of Titles or the registrar of deeds;

(*d*) in any case, by such other persons with functions relating to the registration of land as the regulations may specify.][1]

(2) A correction under this paragraph is made by notice to the purchaser.

(3) No such correction may be made more than nine months after—

(*a*) the day on which the return was delivered, or

(*b*) if the correction is required in consequence of an amendment under paragraph 6, the day on which that amendment was made.

(4) A correction under this paragraph is of no effect if the purchaser—

(*a*) amends the return so as to reject the correction, or

(*b*) after the end of the period within which he may amend the return, but within three months from the date of issue of the notice of correction, gives notice rejecting the correction.

(5) Notice under sub-paragraph (4)(b) must be given to the officer of the Board by whom notice of the correction was given.

Amendments—[1] Sub-para (1A) inserted by F(No 2)A 2005 s 47(4) with effect from 20 July 2005.

Penalty for incorrect or uncorrected return

8—*(1) A purchaser who—*

(a) fraudulently or negligently delivers in respect of a chargeable transaction a land transaction return which is incorrect, or

(b) discovers that a land transaction return delivered by him in respect of a chargeable transaction (neither fraudulently nor negligently) is incorrect and does not remedy the error without unreasonable delay,

is liable to a tax-related penalty.

(2) The penalty is an amount not exceeding the amount of tax understated, that is, the difference between—

(a) the amount of tax chargeable in respect of the transaction, and

(b) the amount that would have been chargeable on the basis of the return delivered.[1]

HMRC Manuals—Stamp Duty Land Tax Manual SDLTM86190–86220 (Revenue practice on penalties under this paragraph).

Cross references—See FA 2004 s 313(4)(*f*) (disclosure of tax avoidance schemes: no liability to a penalty under this paragraph by reason of any failure to include in any return or account any reference number or other information required by virtue of FA 2004 s 313(3)(*a*)).

Amendments—[1] Para 8 repealed by FA 2008 s 122, Sch 40 para 21(k) with effect from 1 April 2009 (by virtue of SI 2009/571 art 2).

PART 2
DUTY TO KEEP AND PRESERVE RECORDS

Duty to keep and preserve records

9—(1) A purchaser who is required to deliver a land transaction return must—

(*a*) keep such records as may be needed to enable him to deliver a correct and complete return, and

(*b*) preserve those records in accordance with this paragraph.

(2) The records must be preserved [until the end of the later of the relevant day and the][1] date on which—

(*a*) an enquiry into the return is completed, or

(*b*) if there is no enquiry, the Inland Revenue no longer have power to enquire into the return.

[(2A) "The relevant day" means—

(*a*) the sixth anniversary of the effective date of the transaction, or

(*b*) such earlier day as may be specified in writing by the Commissioners for Her Majesty's Revenue and Customs (and different days may be specified for different cases).][1]

(3) The records required to be kept and preserved under this paragraph include—

(*a*) relevant instruments relating to the transaction, in particular, any contract or conveyance, and any supporting maps, plans or similar documents;

(*b*) records of relevant payments, receipts and financial arrangements.

[(4) The Commissioners for Her Majesty's Revenue and Customs may by regulations—

(*a*) provide that the records required to be kept and preserved under this paragraph include, or do not include, records specified in the regulations, and

(*b*) provide that those records include supporting documents so specified.

(5) Regulations under this paragraph may make provision by reference to things specified in a notice published by the Commissioners for Her Majesty's Revenue and Customs in accordance with the regulations (and not withdrawn by a subsequent notice).

(6) "Supporting documents" includes accounts, books, deeds, contracts, vouchers and receipts.][1]

Amendments—[1] In sub-para (2) words substituted for words "for six years after the effective date of the transaction and until any later", and sub-paras (2A), (4)–(6) inserted, by FA 2009 s 98, Sch 50 paras 3–5 with effect from 1 April 2010 (by virtue of SI 2010/815 art 2).

Preservation of information [etc][1]

[**10**—The duty under paragraph 9 to preserve records may be satisfied—

(*a*) by preserving them in any form and by any means, or

(*b*) by preserving the information contained in them in any form and by any means, subject to any conditions or exceptions specified in writing by the Commissioners for Her Majesty's Revenue and Customs.][1]

Amendments—[1] In the heading, word substituted for words "instead of original records", and para 10 substituted, by FA 2009 s 98, Sch 50 paras 3, 6, 7 with effect from 1 April 2010 (by virtue of SI 2010/815 art 2). Para 10 previously read as follows—

"**10**—(1) The duty under paragraph 9 to preserve records may be satisfied by the preservation of the information contained in them.

(2) Where information is so preserved a copy of any document forming part of the records is admissible in evidence in any proceedings before the [tribunal] to the same extent as the records themselves.".

Penalty for failure to keep and preserve records

11—(1) A person who fails to comply with paragraph 9 in relation to a transaction is liable to a penalty not exceeding £3,000, subject to the following exception.
(2) No penalty is incurred if the Inland Revenue are satisfied that any facts that they reasonably require to be proved, and that would have been proved by the records, are proved by other documentary evidence provided to them.

PART 3
ENQUIRY INTO RETURN

HMRC Manuals—Stamp Duty Land Tax Manual SDLTM80800–81500 (Revenue practice on opening an enquiry).
SDLTM81400–81940 (working an enquiry, including guidance on meetings and reassessing the tax payable).
SDLTM82400–82970 (concluding an enquiry).

Notice of enquiry

12—(1) The Inland Revenue may enquire into a land transaction return if they give notice of their intention to do so ("notice of enquiry")—
(*a*) to the purchaser,
(*b*) before the end of the enquiry period.
(2) The enquiry period is the period of nine months—
(*a*) after the filing date, if the return was delivered on or before that date;
(*b*) after the date on which the return was delivered, if the return was delivered after the filing date;
(*c*) after the date on which the amendment was made, if the return is amended under paragraph 6 (amendment by purchaser).
[This is subject to the following qualification.][1]
[(2A) If—
(*a*) the Inland Revenue give notice, within the period specified in sub-paragraph (2), of their intention to enquire into a land transaction return delivered under section 80 (adjustment where contingency ceases or consideration is ascertained), 81 (further return where relief withdrawn) or 81A (return or further return in consequence of later linked transaction), and
(*b*) it appears to the Inland Revenue to be necessary to give a notice under this paragraph in respect of an earlier land transaction return in respect of the same land transaction,
a notice may be given notwithstanding that the period referred to in sub-paragraph (2) has elapsed in relation to that earlier land transaction.][1]
(3) A return that has been the subject of one notice of enquiry may not be the subject of another, except one given in consequence of an amendment (or another amendment) of the return under paragraph 6.

Amendments—[1] Words in sub-para (2) inserted, and sub-para (2A) inserted, by the SDLT (Land Transaction Returns) Regulations, SI 2004/3208 regs 2, 4 with effect from 8 December 2004, in relation to a land transaction the effective date of which is on or after 8 December 2004.

Scope of enquiry

13—(1) An enquiry extends to anything contained in the return, or required to be contained in the return, that relates—
(*a*) to the question whether tax is chargeable in respect of the transaction, or
(*b*) to the amount of tax so chargeable.
This is subject to the following exception.
(2) If the notice of enquiry is given as a result of an amendment of the return under paragraph 6 (amendment by purchaser)—
(*a*) at a time when it is no longer possible to give notice of enquiry under paragraph 12, or
(*b*) after an enquiry into the return has been completed,

the enquiry into the return is limited to matters to which the amendment relates or that are affected by the amendment.

Notice to produce documents etc for purposes of enquiry

14—*(1) If the Inland Revenue give notice of enquiry into a land transaction return, they may by notice in writing require the purchaser—*

(*a*) to produce to them such documents in his possession or power, and

(*b*) to provide them with such information, in such form,

as they may reasonably require for the purposes of the enquiry.

(2) A notice under this paragraph (which may be given at the same time as the notice of enquiry) must specify the time (which must not be less than 30 days) within which the purchaser is to comply with it.

(3) In complying with a notice under this paragraph copies of documents may be produced instead of originals, but—

(*a*) the copies must be photographic or other facsimiles, and

(*b*) the Inland Revenue may by notice require the original to be produced for inspection.

A notice under paragraph (b) must specify the time (which must not be less than 30 days) within which the purchaser is to comply with it.

(4) The Inland Revenue may take copies of, or make extracts from, any documents produced to them under this paragraph.

(5) A notice under this paragraph does not oblige a purchaser to produce documents or provide information relating to the conduct of—

(*a*) any pending appeal by him, or

(*b*) any pending referral to the [tribunal][1] under paragraph 19 to which he is a party.[2]

HMRC Manuals—Stamp Duty Land Tax Manual SDLTM84570–84670 (Revenue guidance on requesting information from purchaser).

Amendments—[1] In sub-para (5)(b) word substituted for the words "Special Commissioners" by the Transfer of Tribunal Functions and Revenue and Customs Appeals Order, SI 2009/56 art 3, Sch 1 para 376 with effect from 1 April 2009.

[2] This para repealed by the Finance Act 2009, Section 96 and Schedule 48 (Appointed Day, Savings and Consequential Amendments) Order, SI 2009/3054 art 3, Schedule para 11(1), (4) with effect from 1 April 2010. Note that, in relation to a notice given under this para before 1 April 2010, paras 15, 16 continue to have effect on and after 1 April 2010 (SI 2009/3054 art 7(1), (2)).

Appeal against notice to produce documents etc

15—*(1) An appeal may be brought against a requirement imposed by a notice under paragraph 14 to produce documents or provide information.*

(2) Notice of appeal must be given—

(*a*) in writing,

(*b*) within 30 days after the issue of the notice appealed against,

(*c*) to the officer of the Board by whom that notice was given.

(3) An appeal under this paragraph shall be . . .[1] determined in the same way as an appeal against an assessment.

(4) On an appeal under this paragraph [that is notified to the tribunal, the tribunal][1]—

(*a*) shall set aside the notice so far as it requires the production of documents, or the provision of information, that appears . . .[1] not reasonably required for the purposes of the enquiry, and

(*b*) shall confirm the notice so far as it requires the production or documents, or the provision of information, that appears . . .[1] reasonably required for the purposes of the enquiry.

(5) A notice that is confirmed by the [tribunal][1] (or so far as it is confirmed) has effect as if the period specified in it for complying was 30 days from the determination of the appeal.

[(6) Notwithstanding the provisions of sections 11 and 13 of the Tribunals, Courts and Enforcement Act 2007 the decision of the tribunal on an appeal under this paragraph is final.][1], [2]

Amendments—[1] In sub-para (3) words "heard and" repealed; in sub-para (4) words substituted for the words "the Commissioners" and words "to them" repealed in both places; in sub-para (5) word substituted for the word "Commissioners"; sub-para (6) substituted by the Transfer of Tribunal Functions and Revenue and Customs Appeals Order, SI 2009/56 art 3, Sch 1 para 377 with effect from 1 April 2009. Sub-para (6) previously read as follows—

"(6) The decision of the Commissioners on an appeal under this paragraph is final.".

[2] This para repealed by the Finance Act 2009, Section 96 and Schedule 48 (Appointed Day, Savings and Consequential Amendments) Order, SI 2009/3054 art 3, Schedule para 11(1), (4) with effect from 1 April 2010. Note that, in relation to a notice given under para 14 before 1 April 2010, paras 15, 16 continue to have effect on and after 1 April 2010 (SI 2009/3054 art 7(1), (2)).

Penalty for failure to produce documents etc

16—*(1) A person who fails to comply with a notice under paragraph 14 (notice to produce documents etc for purposes of enquiry) is liable—*

(*a*) to a penalty of £50, and

(*b*) if the failure continues after a penalty is imposed under paragraph (*a*) above, to a further penalty or penalties not exceeding the amount specified in sub-paragraph (2) below for each day on which the failure continues.

(2) The amount referred to in sub-paragraph (1)(*b*) is—

(*a*) £30 if the penalty is determined by an officer of the Board, and

(*b*) £150 if the penalty is determined by the court.

(3) No penalty shall be imposed under this paragraph in respect of a failure at any time after the failure has been remedied.[1]

HMRC Manuals—Stamp Duty Land Tax Manual SDLTM86250–86300 (Revenue guidance on penalties under this paragraph).

Amendments—[1] This para repealed by the Finance Act 2009, Section 96 and Schedule 48 (Appointed Day, Savings and Consequential Amendments) Order, SI 2009/3054 art 3, Schedule para 11(1), (4) with effect from 1 April 2010. Note that, in relation to a notice given under para 14 before 1 April 2010, paras 15, 16 continue to have effect on and after 1 April 2010 (SI 2009/3054 art 7(1), (2)).

Amendment of self-assessment during enquiry to prevent loss of tax

17—(1) If at a time when an enquiry is in progress into a land transaction return the Inland Revenue form the opinion—

(*a*) that the amount stated in the self-assessment contained in the return as the amount of tax payable is insufficient, and

(*b*) that unless the assessment is immediately amended there is likely to be a loss of tax to the Crown,

they may by notice in writing to the purchaser amend the assessment to make good the deficiency.

(2) In the case of an enquiry that under paragraph 13(2) is limited to matters arising from an amendment of the return, sub-paragraph (1) above applies only so far as the deficiency is attributable to the amendment.

(3) For the purposes of this paragraph the period during which an enquiry is in progress is the whole of the period—

(*a*) beginning with the day on which notice of enquiry is given, and

(*b*) ending with the day on which the enquiry is completed.

HMRC Manuals—Stamp Duty Land Tax Manual SDLTM81900–81940 (Revenue practice on jeopardy assessments under this paragraph).

SDLTM81920 (circumstances where the Revenue consider making jeopardy assessments).

Amendment of return by taxpayer during enquiry

18—(1) This paragraph applies if a return is amended under paragraph 6 (amendment by purchaser) at a time when an enquiry is in progress into the return.

(2) The amendment does not restrict the scope of the enquiry but may be taken into account (together with any matters arising) in the enquiry.

(3) So far as the amendment affects the amount stated in the self-assessment included in the return as the amount of tax payable, it does not take effect while the enquiry is in progress and—

(*a*) if the Inland Revenue state in the closure notice that they have taken the amendments into account and that—

(i) the amendment has been taken into account in formulating the amendments contained in the notice, or

(ii) their conclusion is that the amendment is incorrect,

the amendment shall not take effect;

(*b*) otherwise, the amendment takes effect when the closure notice is issued.

(4) For the purposes of this paragraph the period during which an enquiry is in progress is the whole of the period—

(*a*) beginning with the day on which notice of enquiry is given, and

(*b*) ending with the day on which the enquiry is completed.

Referral of questions to [the tribunal][1] during enquiry

19—(1) At any time when an enquiry is in progress into a land transaction return any question arising in connection with the subject-matter of the enquiry may be referred [to the tribunal for determination][1].

(2) Notice of referral must be given—

(*a*) jointly by the purchaser and the Inland Revenue,

(*b*) . . .[1]

(*c*) to the [tribunal][1].

(3) . . .[1].

(4) More than one notice of referral may be given under this paragraph in relation to an enquiry.

(5) For the purposes of this paragraph the period during which an enquiry is in progress is the whole of the period—

(*a*) beginning with the day on which the notice of enquiry was given, and

(*b*) ending with the day on which the enquiry is completed.

Amendments—[1] In the heading, sub-para (2)(c) words substituted for the words "Special Commissioners"; in sub-para (1) words substituted for the words "to the Special Commissioners for their determination"; sub-paras (2)(b), (3) repealed; by the Transfer of Tribunal Functions and Revenue and Customs Appeals Order, SI 2009/56 art 3, Sch 1 para 378 with effect from 1 April 2009. Sub-paras (2)(b), (3) previously read as follows—

"(*b*) in writing,"

"(3) The notice of referral must specify the question or questions being referred.".

Withdrawal of notice of referral

20—(1) The Inland Revenue or the purchaser may withdraw a notice of referral under paragraph 19 . . . [1]

(2) . . . [1]

Amendments—[1] In sub-para (1) words "by notice in accordance with this paragraph" repealed; sub-para (2) repealed by the Transfer of Tribunal Functions and Revenue and Customs Appeals Order, SI 2009/56 art 3, Sch 1 para 379 with effect from 1 April 2009. Sub-para (2) previously read as follows—

"(2) Notice of withdrawal must be given—

(*a*) in writing,

(*b*) to the other party to the referral and to the Special Commissioners,

(*c*) before the first hearing by the Special Commissioners in relation to the referral.".

Effect of referral on enquiry

21—(1) While proceedings on a referral under paragraph 19 are in progress in relation to an enquiry—

(*a*) no closure notice shall be given in relation to the enquiry, and

(*b*) no application may be made for a direction to give such a notice.

(2) For the purposes of this paragraph proceedings on a referral are in progress where—

(*a*) notice of referral has been given,

(*b*) the notice has not been withdrawn, and

(*c*) the questions referred have not been finally determined.

(3) For the purposes of sub-paragraph (2)(*c*) a question referred is finally determined when—

(*a*) it has been determined by the [tribunal][1], and

(*b*) there is no further possibility of the determination being varied or set aside (disregarding any power to grant permission to appeal out of time).

Amendments—[1] In sub-para (3)(a) word substituted for the words "Special Commissioners" by the Transfer of Tribunal Functions and Revenue and Customs Appeals Order, SI 2009/56 art 3, Sch 1 para 380 with effect from 1 April 2009.

Effect of determination

22—(1) The determination of a question referred to the [tribunal][1] under paragraph 19 is binding on the parties to the referral in the same way, and to the same extent, as a decision on a preliminary issue in an appeal.

(2) The determination shall be taken into account by the Inland Revenue—

(*a*) in reaching their conclusions on the enquiry, and

(*b*) in formulating any amendments of the return required to give effect to those conclusions.

(3) Any right of appeal under paragraph 35 (appeals against assessments) may not be exercised so as to reopen the question determined except to the extent (if any) that it could be reopened if it had been determined as a preliminary issue in that appeal.

Amendments—[1] In sub-para (1) word substituted for the words "Special Commissioners" by the Transfer of Tribunal Functions and Revenue and Customs Appeals Order, SI 2009/56 art 3, Sch 1 para 381 with effect from 1 April 2009.

Completion of enquiry

23—(1) An enquiry under paragraph 12 is completed when the Inland Revenue by notice (a "closure notice") inform the purchaser that they have completed their enquiries and state their conclusions.

(2) A closure notice must either—

(*a*) state that in the opinion of the Inland Revenue no amendment of the return is required, or

(*b*) make the amendments of the return required to give effect to their conclusions.

(3) A closure notice takes effect when it is issued.

Direction to complete enquiry

24—(1) The purchaser may apply to the [tribunal][1] for a direction that the Inland Revenue give a closure notice within a specified period.
[(2) Any such application is to be subject to the relevant provisions of Part 5 of the Taxes Management Act 1970 (see, in particular, section 48(2)(*b*) of that Act).][1]
(3) The [tribunal][1] hearing the application shall give a direction unless . . . [1] satisfied that the Inland Revenue have reasonable grounds for not giving a closure notice within a specified period.

Amendments—[1] In sub-para (1) word substituted for the words "General or Special Commissioners"; sub-para (2) substituted; in sub-para (3) word substituted for the word "Commissioners" and words "they are" repealed by the Transfer of Tribunal Functions and Revenue and Customs Appeals Order, SI 2009/56 art 3, Sch 1 para 382 with effect from 1 April 2009. Sub-para (2) previously read as follows—

"(2) Any such application shall be heard and determined in the same way as an appeal.".

PART 4
REVENUE DETERMINATION IF NO RETURN DELIVERED

Cross references—Pension Protection Fund (Tax) Regulations, SI 2006/575 reg 43(4) (SI 2006/575 reg 43 to be construed as one with this Part).

Determination of tax chargeable if no return delivered

25—(1) If in the case of a chargeable transaction no land transaction return is delivered by the filing date, the Inland Revenue may make a determination (a "Revenue determination") to the best of their information and belief of the amount of tax chargeable in respect of the transaction.
(2) Notice of the determination must be served on the purchaser, stating the date on which it is issued.
(3) No Revenue determination may be made more than six years after the effective date of the transaction.

Cross references—FA 2009 Sch 56 (penalty for failure to make payments on time).

Prospective amendments—In sub-para (3) words "4 years" to be substituted for the words "six years" by FA 2009 s 99, Sch 51 paras 14, 15(1), (2) with effect from 1 April 2011 (SI 2010/867 art 2(2)).

Determination to have effect as a self-assessment

26—(1) A determination under paragraph 25 has effect for enforcement purposes as if were a self-assessment by the purchaser.
(2) In sub-paragraph (1) "for enforcement purposes" means for the purposes of the following provisions of this Part of this Act—

(*a*) the provisions of this Schedule providing for tax-related penalties;

(*b*) section 87 (interest on unpaid tax);

(*c*) section 91 and Schedule 12 (collection and recovery of unpaid tax etc).

(3) Nothing in this paragraph affects any liability of the purchaser to a penalty for failure to deliver a return.

Determination superseded by actual self-assessment

27—(1) If after a Revenue determination has been made the purchaser delivers a land transaction return in respect of the transaction, the self-assessment included in that return supersedes the determination.
(2) Sub-paragraph (1) does not apply to a return delivered—

(*a*) more than six years after the day on which the power to make the determination first became exercisable, or

(*b*) more than twelve months after the date of the determination,

whichever is the later.
(3) Where—

(*a*) proceedings have been begun for the recovery of any tax charged by a Revenue determination, and

(*b*) before the proceedings are concluded the determination is superseded by a self-assessment,

the proceedings may be continued as if they were proceedings for the recovery of so much of the tax charged by the self-assessment as is due and payable and has not been paid.

Prospective amendments—In sub-para (2)(*a*) words "4 years" to be substituted for the words "six years" by FA 2009 s 99, Sch 51 paras 14, 15(1), (3) with effect from 1 April 2011 (SI 2010/867 art 2(2)).

PART 5
REVENUE ASSESSMENTS

Assessment where loss of tax discovered

28—(1) If the Inland Revenue discover as regards a chargeable transaction that—
(*a*) an amount of tax that ought to have been assessed has not been assessed, or
(*b*) an assessment to tax is or has become insufficient, or
(*c*) relief has been given that is or has become excessive,
they may make an assessment (a "discovery assessment") in the amount or further amount that ought in their opinion to be charged in order to make good to the Crown the loss of tax.
(2) The power to make a discovery assessment in respect of a transaction for which the purchaser has delivered a return is subject to the restrictions specified in paragraph 30.

Assessment to recover excessive repayment of tax

29—(1) If an amount of tax has been repaid to any person that ought not to have been repaid to him, that amount may be assessed and recovered as if it were unpaid tax.
(2) Where the repayment was made with interest, the amount assessed and recovered may include the amount of interest that ought not to have been paid.
(3) The power to make an assessment under this paragraph in respect of a transaction for which the purchaser has delivered a land transaction return is subject to the restrictions specified in paragraph 30.

Restrictions on assessment where return delivered

30—(1) If the purchaser has delivered a land transaction return in respect of the transaction in question, an assessment under paragraph 28 or 29 in respect of the transaction—
(*a*) may only be made in the two cases specified in sub-paragraph (2) and (3) below, and
(*b*) may not be made in the circumstances specified in sub-paragraph (5) below.
(2) The first case is where the situation mentioned in paragraph 28(1) or 29(1) is attributable to fraudulent or negligent conduct on the part of—
(*a*) the purchaser,
(*b*) a person acting on behalf of the purchaser, or
(*c*) a person who was a partner of the purchaser at the relevant time.
(3) The second case is where the Inland Revenue, at the time they—
(*a*) ceased to be entitled to give a notice of enquiry into the return, or
(*b*) completed their enquiries into the return,
could not have been reasonably expected, on the basis of the information made available to them before that time, to be aware of the situation mentioned in paragraph 28(1) or 29(1).
(4) For this purpose information is regarded as made available to the Inland Revenue if—
(*a*) it is contained in a land transaction return made by the purchaser,
(*b*) it is contained in any documents produced or information provided to the Inland Revenue for the purposes of an enquiry into any such return, or
(*c*) it is information the existence of which, and the relevance of which as regards the situation mentioned in paragraph 28(1) or 29(1)—
(i) could reasonably be expected to be inferred by the Inland Revenue from information falling within paragraphs (*a*) or (*b*) above, or
(ii) are notified in writing to the Inland Revenue by the purchaser or a person acting on his behalf.
(5) No assessment may be made if—
(*a*) the situation mentioned in paragraph 28(1) or 29(1) is attributable to a mistake in the return as to the basis on which the tax liability ought to have been computed, and
(*b*) the return was in fact made on the basis or in accordance with the practice generally prevailing at the time it was made.

Time limit for assessment

31—(1) The general rule is that no assessment may be made more than six years after the effective date of the transaction to which it relates.
(2) In a case involving fraud or negligence on the part of—
(*a*) the purchaser, or
(*b*) a person acting on behalf of the purchaser, or
(*c*) a person who was a partner of the purchaser at the relevant time,
an assessment may be made up to 21 years after the effective date of the transaction to which it relates.

(3) An assessment under paragraph 29 (assessment to recover excessive repayment of tax) is not out of time—

(*a*) in a case where notice of enquiry is given into the land transaction return delivered by the person concerned, if it is made before the enquiry is completed;

(*b*) in any case, if it is made within one year after the repayment in question was made.

(4) Where the purchaser has died—

(*a*) any assessment on the personal representatives of the deceased must be made within three years after his death, and

(*b*) an assessment shall not be made by virtue of sub-paragraph (2) in respect of a transaction of which the effective date was more than six years before the death.

(5) Any objection to the making of an assessment on the ground that the time limit for making it has expired can only be made on an appeal against the assessment.

Prospective amendments—In sub-para (1) words "4 years" to be substituted for the words "six years", sub-paras (2), (2A) to be substituted for sub-para (2), in sub-para (4)(*a*) words "4 years" to be substituted for the words "three years", and sub-para (6) to be inserted, by FA 2009 s 99, Sch 51 paras 14, 15(1), (4)–(8) with effect from 1 April 2011 (SI 2010/867 art 2(2)). New sub-paras (2), (2A), (6) to read as follows—

"(2) An assessment of a person to tax in a case involving a loss of tax brought about carelessly by the purchaser or a related person may be made at any time not more than 6 years after the effective date of the transaction to which it relates (subject to sub-paragraph (2A)).

(2A) An assessment of a person to tax in a case involving a loss of tax—

(*a*) brought about deliberately by the purchaser or a related person,

(*b*) attributable to a failure by the person to comply with an obligation under section 76(1) or paragraph 3(3)(*a*), 4(3)(*a*) or 8(3)(*a*) of Schedule 17A, or

(*c*) attributable to arrangements in respect of which the person has failed to comply with an obligation under section 309, 310 or 313 of the Finance Act 2004 (obligation of parties to tax avoidance schemes to provide information to Her Majesty's Revenue and Customs),

may be made at any time not more than 20 years after the effective date of the transaction to which it relates.".

"(6) In this paragraph "related person", in relation to a purchaser, means—

(*a*) a person acting on behalf of the purchaser, or

(*b*) a person who was a partner of the purchaser at the relevant time.".

[Losses brought about carelessly or deliberately

31A—(1) This paragraph applies for the purposes of paragraph 31.

(2) A loss of tax is brought about carelessly by a person if the person fails to take reasonable care to avoid bringing about that loss.

(3) Where—

(*a*) information is provided to Her Majesty's Revenue and Customs,

(*b*) the person who provided the information, or the person on whose behalf the information was provided, discovers some time later that the information was inaccurate, and

(*c*) that person fails to take reasonable steps to inform Her Majesty's Revenue and Customs,

any loss of tax brought about by the inaccuracy is to be treated as having been brought about carelessly by that person.

(4) References to a loss of tax brought about deliberately by a person include a loss of tax brought about as a result of a deliberate inaccuracy in a document given to Her Majesty's Revenue and Customs by or on behalf of that person.]

Prospective amendments—This para to be inserted by FA 2009 s 99, Sch 51 paras 14, 15(1), (9) with effect from 1 April 2011 (SI 2010/867 art 2(2)).

Assessment procedure

32—(1) Notice of an assessment must be served on the purchaser.

(2) The notice must state—

(*a*) the tax due,

(*b*) the date on which the notice is issued, and

(*c*) the time within which any appeal against the assessment must be made.

(3) After notice of the assessment has been served on the purchaser, the assessment may not be altered except in accordance with the express provisions of this Part of this Act.

(4) Where an officer of the Board has decided to make an assessment to tax, and has taken all other decisions needed for arriving at the amount of the assessment, he may entrust to some other officer of the Board responsibility for completing the assessing procedure, whether by means involving the use of a computer or otherwise, including responsibility for serving notice of the assessment.

PART 6
RELIEF IN CASE OF EXCESSIVE ASSESSMENT

Relief in case of double assessment

33—(1) A person who believes he has been assessed to tax more than once in respect of the same matter may make a claim [to the Inland Revenue for relief against any double charge][1].

(2), (3) . . . [1]

[(4) An appeal may be made against a decision on a claim for relief under this paragraph.][2]

Amendments—[1] Words in sub-para (1) substituted for the words "for relief under this paragraph", and sub-paras (2), (3) repealed, by FA 2004 ss 299(1), (7), 326, Sch 42 Pt 4(2) with effect from 22 July 2004.

[2] Sub-para (4) substituted by the Transfer of Tribunal Functions and Revenue and Customs Appeals Order, SI 2009/56 art 3, Sch 1 para 383 with effect from 1 April 2009. Sub-para (4) previously read as follows—

"(4) An appeal against a decision of the Inland Revenue on a claim for relief under this paragraph may be brought to the Commissioners having jurisdiction to hear an appeal relating to the assessment, or the later of the assessments, to which the claim relates.".

Relief in case of mistake in return

34—(1) A person who believes he has paid tax under an assessment that was excessive by reason of some mistake in a land transaction return may make a claim [to the Inland Revenue for relief against any excessive charge][1].

(2) The claim must be made . . . [1] not more than six years after the effective date of the transaction.

(3) . . . [1]

(4) No relief shall be given under this paragraph—

(*a*) in respect of a mistake as to the basis on which the liability of the claimant ought to have been computed when the return was in fact made on the basis or in accordance with the practice generally prevailing at the time when it was made, or

(*b*) in respect of a mistake in a claim or election included in the return.

(5) In determining a claim under this paragraph the Inland Revenue shall have regard to all the relevant circumstances of the case.

They shall, in particular, consider whether the granting of relief would result in amounts being excluded from charge to tax.

(6) On an appeal against the Inland Revenue's decision on the claim, [that is notified to the tribunal, the tribunal shall][2] hear and determine the claim in accordance with the same principles as apply to the determination by the Inland Revenue of claims under this paragraph.

HMRC Manuals—Stamp Duty Land Tax Manual SDLTM52500–52550 (Revenue practice on this relief).

Amendments—[1] Words in sub-para (1) substituted for the words "for relief under this paragraph"; in para (2), words "by notice in writing given to the Inland Revenue" repealed; and sub-para (3) repealed, by FA 2004 ss 299(1), (8), 326, Sch 42 Pt 4(2) with effect from 22 July 2004.

[2] In sub-para (6) words substituted for the words "the Special Commissioners shall" by the Transfer of Tribunal Functions and Revenue and Customs Appeals Order, SI 2009/56 art 3, Sch 1 para 384 with effect from 1 April 2009.

Prospective amendments—In sub-para (2) words "4 years" to be substituted for the words "six years" by FA 2009 s 99, Sch 51 paras 14, 15(1), (10) with effect from 1 April 2011 (SI 2010/867 art 2(2)).

PART 7
[REVIEWS AND APPEALS][1]

Amendments—[1] Heading substituted for former heading "Appeals against Revenue decisions on tax" by the Transfer of Tribunal Functions and Revenue and Customs Appeals Order, SI 2009/56 art 3, Sch 1 para 385 with effect from 1 April 2009.

Right of appeal

35—(1) An appeal may be brought against—

(*a*) an amendment of a self-assessment under paragraph 17 (amendment by Revenue during enquiry to prevent loss of tax),

(*b*) a conclusion stated or amendment made by a closure notice,

(*c*) a discovery assessment, . . . [1]

(*d*) an assessment under paragraph 29 (assessment to recover excessive repayment)[, or

(*e*) a Revenue determination under paragraph 25 (determination of tax chargeable if no return delivered).][1]

(2) . . . [2]

(3) [If][2] an appeal under sub-paragraph (1)(*a*) against an amendment of a self-assessment [is][2] made while an enquiry is in progress [none of the steps mentioned in paragraph 36A(2)(*a*) to (*c*) may be taken in relation to the appeal][2] until the enquiry is completed.

Amendments—[1] Word in sub-para (1)(c) repealed, and sub-para (1)(e) inserted, by the SDLT (Land Transaction Returns) Regulations, SI 2004/3208 regs 2, 5(1), (2) with effect from 8 December 2004, in relation to a land transaction the effective date of which is on or after 8 December 2004.

[2] Sub-para (2) repealed; in sub-para (3) word in the first and second places inserted and in the third place words substituted for the words "shall not be heard and determined" by the Transfer of Tribunal Functions and Revenue and Customs Appeals Order, SI 2009/56 art 3, Sch 1 para 386 with effect from 1 April 2009. Sub-para (2) previously read as follows—

"(2) The appeal lies to the General or Special Commissioners.".

Notice of appeal

36—(1) Notice of an appeal under paragraph 35 must be given—

(*a*) in writing

(*b*) within 30 days after the specified date,

(*c*) to the relevant officer of the Board.

(2) In relation to an appeal under paragraph 35(1)(*a*)—

(*a*) the specified date is the date on which the notice of amendment was issued, and

(*b*) the relevant officer of the Board is the officer by whom the notice of amendment was given.

(3) In relation to an appeal under paragraph 35(1)(*b*)—

(*a*) the specified date is the date on which the closure notice was issued, and

(*b*) the relevant officer of the Board is the officer by whom the closure notice was given.

(4) In relation to an appeal under paragraph 35(1)(*c*) or (*d*)—

(*a*) the specified date is the date on which the notice of assessment was issued, and

(*b*) the relevant officer of the Board is the officer by whom the notice of assessment was given.

[(4A) In relation to an appeal under paragraph 35(1)(*e*)—

(*a*) the specified date is the date on which the Revenue determination was issued, and

(*b*) the relevant officer of the Board is the officer by whom the determination was made.][1]

(5) The notice of appeal must specify the grounds of appeal.

[(5A) The only grounds on which an appeal lies under paragraph 35(1)(*e*) are that—

(*a*) the purchase to which the determination relates did not take place,

(*b*) the interest in the land to which the determination relates has not been purchased,

(*c*) the contract for the purchase of the interest to which the determination relates has not been substantially performed, or

(*d*) the land transaction is [not notifiable][2] (for example, because the land transaction is exempt from charge under Schedule 3).][1]

(6) . . . [3]

Amendments—[1] Sub-paras (4A), (5A) inserted by the SDLT (Land Transaction Returns) Regulations, SI 2004/3208 regs 2, 5(1), (3) with effect from 8 December 2004, in relation to a land transaction the effective date of which is on or after 8 December 2004.

[2] Words in sub-para (5A)(d) substituted by FA 2008 s 94, Sch 30 para 7 with effect in relation to transactions with an effective date on or after 12 March 2008.

[3] Sub-para (6) repealed by the Transfer of Tribunal Functions and Revenue and Customs Appeals Order, SI 2009/56 art 3, Sch 1 para 387 with effect from 1 April 2009. Sub-para (6) previously read as follows—

"(6) On the hearing of the appeal the Commissioners may allow the appellant to put forward grounds not specified in the notice, and take them into consideration, if satisfied that the omission was not deliberate or unreasonable.".

[Appeal: HMRC review or determination by tribunal

36A—(1) This paragraph applies if notice of appeal has been given to HMRC.

(2) In such a case—

(a) the appellant may notify HMRC that the appellant requires HMRC to review the matter in question (see paragraph 36B),

(b) HMRC may notify the appellant of an offer to review the matter in question (see paragraph 36C), or

(c) the appellant may notify the appeal to the tribunal (see paragraph 36D).

(3) See paragraphs 36G and 36H for provision about notifying appeals to the tribunal after a review has been required by the appellant or offered by HMRC.

(4) This paragraph does not prevent the matter in question from being dealt with in accordance with paragraph 37(1) (settling of appeals by agreement).][1]

Amendments—[1] Paragraphs 36A–36I inserted by the Transfer of Tribunal Functions and Revenue and Customs Appeals Order, SI 2009/56 art 3, Sch 1 para 388 with effect from 1 April 2009.

[Appellant requires review by HMRC

36B—(1) Sub-paragraphs (2) and (3) apply if the appellant notifies HMRC that the appellant requires HMRC to review the matter in question.

(2) HMRC must, within the relevant period, notify the appellant of HMRC's view of the matter in question.
(3) HMRC must review the matter in question in accordance with paragraph 36E.
(4) The appellant may not notify HMRC that the appellant requires HMRC to review the matter in question and HMRC shall not be required to conduct a review if—

(*a*) the appellant has already given a notification under this paragraph in relation to the matter in question,

(*b*) HMRC have given a notification under paragraph 36C in relation to the matter in question, or

(*c*) the appellant has notified the appeal to the tribunal under paragraph 36D.

(5) In this paragraph "relevant period" means—

(*a*) the period of 30 days beginning with the day on which HMRC receive the notification from the appellant, or

(*b*) such longer period as is reasonable.][1]

Amendments—[1] Paragraphs 36A–36I inserted by the Transfer of Tribunal Functions and Revenue and Customs Appeals Order, SI 2009/56 art 3, Sch 1 para 388 with effect from 1 April 2009.

[HMRC offer review

36C—(1) Sub-paragraphs (2) to (6) apply if HMRC notify the appellant of an offer to review the matter in question.
(2) When HMRC notify the appellant of the offer, HMRC must also notify the appellant of HMRC's view of the matter in question.
(3) If, within the acceptance period, the appellant notifies HMRC of acceptance of the offer, HMRC must review the matter in question in accordance with paragraph 36E.
(4) If the appellant does not give HMRC such a notification within the acceptance period, HMRC's view of the matter in question is to be treated as if it were contained in an agreement in writing under paragraph 37(1) for the settlement of that matter.
(5) The appellant may not give notice under paragraph 37(2) (desire to withdraw from agreement) in a case where sub-paragraph (4) applies.
(6) Sub-paragraph (4) does not apply to the matter in question if, or to the extent that, the appellant notifies the appeal to the tribunal under paragraph 36H.
(7) HMRC may not notify the appellant of an offer to review the matter in question (and, accordingly, HMRC shall not be required to conduct a review) if—

(*a*) HMRC have already given a notification under this paragraph in relation to the matter in question,

(*b*) the appellant has given a notification under paragraph 36B in relation to the matter in question, or

(*c*) the appellant has notified the appeal to the tribunal under paragraph 36D.

(8) In this paragraph "acceptance period" means the period of 30 days beginning with the date of the document by which HMRC notify the appellant of the offer to review the matter in question.][1]

Amendments—[1] Paragraphs 36A–36I inserted by the Transfer of Tribunal Functions and Revenue and Customs Appeals Order, SI 2009/56 art 3, Sch 1 para 388 with effect from 1 April 2009.

[Notifying appeal to the tribunal

36D—(1) This paragraph applies in a case where paragraph 36A applies.
(2) The appellant may notify the appeal to the tribunal.
(3) If the appellant notifies the appeal to the tribunal, the tribunal is to decide the matter in question.
(4) Sub-paragraphs (2) and (3) do not apply in a case where—

(*a*) HMRC have given a notification of their view of the matter in question under paragraph 36B, or

(*b*) HMRC have given a notification under paragraph 36C in relation to the matter in question.

(5) In a case falling within sub-paragraph (4)(a) or (b), the appellant may notify the appeal to the tribunal, but only if permitted to do so by paragraph 36G or 36H.][1]

Amendments—[1] Paragraphs 36A–36I inserted by the Transfer of Tribunal Functions and Revenue and Customs Appeals Order, SI 2009/56 art 3, Sch 1 para 388 with effect from 1 April 2009.

[Nature of review etc

36E—(1) This paragraph applies if HMRC are required by paragraph 36B or 36C to review the matter in question.
(2) The nature and extent of the review are to be such as appear appropriate to HMRC in the circumstances.
(3) For the purpose of sub-paragraph (2), HMRC must, in particular, have regard to steps taken before the beginning of the review—

(*a*) by HMRC in deciding the matter in question, and

(*b*) by any person in seeking to resolve disagreement about the matter in question.

(4) The review must take account of any representations made by the appellant at a stage which gives HMRC a reasonable opportunity to consider them.

(5) The review may conclude that HMRC's view of the matter in question is to be—

(*a*) upheld,

(*b*) varied, or

(*c*) cancelled.

(6) HMRC must notify the appellant of the conclusions of the review and their reasoning within—

(*a*) the period of 45 days beginning with the relevant day, or

(*b*) such other period as may be agreed.

(7) In sub-paragraph (6) "relevant day" means—

(*a*) in a case where the appellant required the review, the day when HMRC notified the appellant of HMRC's view of the matter in question,

(*b*) in a case where HMRC offered the review, the day when HMRC received notification of the appellant's acceptance of the offer.

(8) Where HMRC are required to undertake a review but do not give notice of the conclusions within the period specified in sub-paragraph (6), the review is treated as having concluded that HMRC's view of the matter in question (see paragraphs 36B(2) and 36C(2)) is upheld.

(9) If sub-paragraph (8) applies, HMRC must notify the appellant of the conclusions which the review is treated as having reached.][1]

Amendments—[1] Paragraphs 36A–36I inserted by the Transfer of Tribunal Functions and Revenue and Customs Appeals Order, SI 2009/56 art 3, Sch 1 para 388 with effect from 1 April 2009.

[Effect of conclusions of review

36F—(1) This paragraph applies if HMRC give notice of the conclusions of a review (see paragraph 36E).

(2) The conclusions are to be treated as if they were an agreement in writing under paragraph 37(1) for the settlement of the matter in question.

(3) The appellant may not give notice under paragraph 37(2) (desire to withdraw from agreement) in a case where sub-paragraph (2) applies.

(4) Sub-paragraph (2) does not apply to the matter in question if, or to the extent that, the appellant notifies the appeal to the tribunal under paragraph 36G.][1]

Amendments—[1] Paragraphs 36A–36I inserted by the Transfer of Tribunal Functions and Revenue and Customs Appeals Order, SI 2009/56 art 3, Sch 1 para 388 with effect from 1 April 2009.

[Notifying appeal to tribunal after review concluded

36G—(1) This paragraph applies if—

(*a*) HMRC have given notice of the conclusions of a review in accordance with paragraph 36E, or

(*b*) the period specified in paragraph 36E(6) has ended and HMRC have not given notice of the conclusions of the review.

(2) The appellant may notify the appeal to the tribunal within the post-review period.

(3) If the post-review period has ended, the appellant may notify the appeal to the tribunal only if the tribunal gives permission.

(4) If the appellant notifies the appeal to the tribunal, the tribunal is to determine the matter in question.

(5) In this paragraph "post-review period" means—

(*a*) in a case falling with sub-paragraph (1)(*a*), the period of 30 days beginning with the date of the document in which HMRC give notice of the conclusions of the review in accordance with paragraph 36E(6), or

(*b*) in a case falling within sub-paragraph (1)(*b*), the period that—

(i) begins with the day following the last day of the period specified in paragraph 36E(6), and

(ii) ends 30 days after the date of the document in which HMRC give notice of the conclusions of the review in accordance with paragraph 36E(9).][1]

Amendments—[1] Paragraphs 36A–36I inserted by the Transfer of Tribunal Functions and Revenue and Customs Appeals Order, SI 2009/56 art 3, Sch 1 para 388 with effect from 1 April 2009.

[Notifying appeal to tribunal after review offered but not accepted

36H—(1) This paragraph applies if—

(*a*) HMRC have offered to review the matter in question (see paragraph 36C), and

(*b*) the appellant has not accepted the offer.

(2) The appellant may notify the appeal to the tribunal within the acceptance period.

(3) But if the acceptance period has ended, the appellant may notify the appeal to the tribunal only if the tribunal gives permission.
(4) If the appellant notifies the appeal to the tribunal, the tribunal is to determine the matter in question.
(5) In this paragraph "acceptance period" has the same meaning as in paragraph 36C.][1]

Amendments—[1] Paragraphs 36A–36I inserted by the Transfer of Tribunal Functions and Revenue and Customs Appeals Order, SI 2009/56 art 3, Sch 1 para 388 with effect from 1 April 2009.

[Other interpretation

36I—(1) In paragraphs 36A to 36H—

(*a*) "matter in question" means the matter to which an appeal relates;

(*b*) a reference to a notification is a reference to a notification in writing.

(2) In paragraphs 36A to 36H, a reference to the appellant includes a person acting on behalf of the appellant except in relation to—

(*a*) notification of HMRC's view under paragraph 36B(2),

(*b*) notification by HMRC of an offer of review (and of their view of the matter) under paragraph 36C,

(*c*) notification of the conclusions of a review under paragraph 36E(6), and

(*d*) notification of the conclusions of a review under paragraph 36E(9).

(3) But if a notification falling within any of the sub-paragraphs of paragraph (2) is given to the appellant, a copy of the notification may also be given to a person acting on behalf of the appellant.][1]

Amendments—[1] Paragraphs 36A–36I inserted by the Transfer of Tribunal Functions and Revenue and Customs Appeals Order, SI 2009/56 art 3, Sch 1 para 388 with effect from 1 April 2009.

Settling of appeals by agreement

37—(1) If, before an appeal under paragraph 35 is determined, the appellant and the Inland Revenue agree that the decision appealed against—

(*a*) should be upheld without variation,

(*b*) should be varied in a particular manner, or

(*c*) should be discharged or cancelled,

the same consequences shall follow, for all purposes, as would have followed if, at the time the agreement was come to, the [tribunal][1] had determined the appeal and had upheld the decision without variation, varied it in that manner or discharged or cancelled it, as the case may be.

(2) Sub-paragraph (1) does not apply if, within 30 days from the date when the agreement was come to, the appellant gives notice in writing to the Inland Revenue that he wishes to withdraw from the agreement.

(3) Where the agreement is not in writing—

(*a*) sub-paragraphs (1) and (2) do not apply unless the fact that an agreement was come to, and the terms agreed, are confirmed by notice in writing given by the Inland Revenue to the appellant or by the appellant to the Inland Revenue, and

(*b*) the references in those provisions to the time when the agreement was come to shall be read as references to the time when the notice of confirmation was given.

(4) Where—

(*a*) the appellant notifies the Inland Revenue, orally or in writing, that he does not wish to proceed with the appeal, and

(*b*) the Inland Revenue do not, within 30 days after that notification, give the appellant notice in writing indicating that they are unwilling that the appeal should be withdrawn,

the provisions of sub-paragraphs (1) to (3) have effect as if, at the date of the appellant's notification, the appellant and the Inland Revenue had come to an agreement (orally or in writing, as the case may be) that the decision under appeal should be upheld without variation.

(5) References in this paragraph to an agreement being come to with an appellant, and to the giving of notice or notification by or to the appellant, include references to an agreement being come to, or notice or notification being given by or to, a person acting on behalf of the appellant in relation to the appeal.

Amendments—[1] In sub-para (1) word substituted for the word "Commissioners" by the Transfer of Tribunal Functions and Revenue and Customs Appeals Order, SI 2009/56 art 3, Sch 1 para 389 with effect from 1 April 2009.

Recovery of tax not postponed by appeal

38—(1) Where there is an appeal . . . [1] under paragraph 35, the tax charged by the amendment or assessment in question remains due and payable as if there had been no appeal.

(2) Sub-paragraph (1) is subject to—

paragraph 39 (direction by [the tribunal][1] postponing payment), and paragraph 40 (agreement to postpone payment).

Amendments—[1] In sub-para (1) words "to the Commissioners" repealed; in sub-para (2) words substituted for the word "Commissioners" by the Transfer of Tribunal Functions and Revenue and Customs Appeals Order, SI 2009/56 art 3, Sch 1 para 390 with effect from 1 April 2009.

Direction by [the tribunal][1] to postpone payment

39—[(1) If the appellant has grounds for believing that the amendment or assessment overcharges the appellant to tax, or as a result of the conclusion stated in the closure notice the tax charged on the appellant is excessive, the appellant may—

(a) first apply by notice in writing to HMRC within 30 days of the specified date for a determination by them of the amount of tax the payment of which should be postponed pending the determination of the appeal;

(b) where such a determination is not agreed, refer the application for postponement to the tribunal within 30 days from the date of the document notifying HMRC's decision on the amount to be postponed.

An application under sub-paragraph (a) must state the amount believed to be overcharged to tax and the grounds for that belief.][1]

(2) . . . [1]

(3) An application may be made more than 30 days after the specified date if there is a change in the circumstances of the case as a result of which the appellant has grounds for believing that he is overcharged to tax by the decision appealed against.

(4) If, after any determination on such an application of the amount of tax the payment of which should be postponed, there is a change in the circumstances of the case as a result of which either party has grounds for believing that the amount so determined has become excessive or, as the case may be, insufficient, he may, [if the parties cannot agree on a revised determination, apply, at any time before the determination of the appeal, to the tribunal for a revised][1] determination of that amount.

[(5) An application under this paragraph is to be subject to the relevant provisions of Part 5 of the Taxes Management Act 1970 (see, in particular, section 48(2)(*b*) of that Act).][1]

The fact that any such application has been heard and determined by any Commissioners does not preclude them from hearing and determining the appeal or any further application under this paragraph.

(6) The amount of tax of which payment is to be postponed pending the determination of the appeal is the amount (if any) by which it appears . . . [1] that there are reasonable grounds for believing that the appellant is overcharged.

(7) Where an application is made under this paragraph, the date on which any tax of which payment is not postponed is due and payable shall be determined as if the tax were charged by an amendment or assessment of which notice was issued on the date on which the application was determined and against which there was no appeal.

(8) On the determination of the appeal—

(*a*) the date on which any tax payable in accordance with that determination is due and payable shall, so far as it is tax the payment of which had been postponed, or which would not have been charged by the amendment or assessment if there had been no appeal, be determined as if the tax were charged by an amendment or assessment—

(i) of which notice was issued on the date on which [HMRC][1] issues to the appellant a notice of the total amount payable in accordance with the determination, and

(ii) against which there had been no appeal, and

(*b*) any tax overpaid shall be repaid.

Amendments—[1] In heading, words substituted for the word "Commissioners"; sub-paras (1), (5) substituted; sub-para (2) repealed; in sub-para (4) words substituted for the words "by notice in writing given to the other party at any time before the determination of the appeal, apply to the Commissioners for a further"; in sub-para (6) words "to the Commissioners, having regard to the representations made and any evidence adduced," repealed; in sub-para (8) words substituted for the words "the Inland Revenue" by the Transfer of Tribunal Functions and Revenue and Customs Appeals Order, SI 2009/56 art 3, Sch 1 para 391 with effect from 1 April 2009. Sub-paras (1), (2), (5) previously read as follows—

"(1) If the appellant has grounds for believing that he is overcharged to tax by the decision appealed against, he may by notice in writing apply to the Commissioners for a direction that payment of an amount of tax shall be postponed pending the determination of the appeal.

(2) The notice must—

(*a*) be given to the relevant officer of the Board within 30 days after the specified date, and

(*b*) state the amount by which the appellant believes himself to be overcharged to tax, and his grounds for that belief.

(5) An application under this paragraph shall be heard and determined by the Commissioners in the same way as an appeal.".

Agreement to postpone payment of tax

40—(1) If the appellant and the relevant officer of the Board agree that payment of an amount of tax should be postponed pending the determination of the appeal, the same consequences shall follow, for all purposes, as would have followed if, at the time the agreement was come to, the [tribunal][1] had made a direction to the same effect.

This is without prejudice to the making of a further agreement or of a further direction.

(2) Where the agreement is not in writing—

(*a*) sub-paragraph (1) does not apply unless the fact that an agreement was come to, and the terms agreed, are confirmed by notice in writing given by the relevant officer of the Board to the appellant or by the appellant to that officer, and

(*b*) the reference in that provision to the time when the agreement was come to shall be read as a reference to the time when notice of confirmation was given.

(3) References in this paragraph to an agreement being come to with an appellant, and to the giving of notice to or by the appellant, include references to an agreement being come to, or notice being given to or by, a person acting on behalf of the appellant in relation to the appeal.

Amendments—[1] In sub-para (1) word substituted for the word "Commissioners" by the Transfer of Tribunal Functions and Revenue and Customs Appeals Order, SI 2009/56 art 3, Sch 1 para 392 with effect from 1 April 2009.

[Tribunal determinations

41 The determination of the tribunal in relation to any proceedings under the enactments relating to stamp duty land tax shall be final and conclusive except as otherwise provided in—

(*a*) sections 9 to 14 of the Tribunals, Courts and Enforcement Act 2007,

(*b*) the Taxes Management Act 1970 applied as modified, or

(*c*) the enactments relating to stamp duty land tax.][1]

Amendments—[1] Paragraphs 41–46 inserted by the Transfer of Tribunal Functions and Revenue and Customs Appeals Order, SI 2009/56 art 3, Sch 1 para 393 with effect from 1 April 2009.

[Assessments and self assessments

42—(1) In this paragraph any reference to an appeal means an appeal under paragraphs 33(4) or 35(1).

(2) If, on an appeal notified to the tribunal, the tribunal decides—

(*a*) that the appellant is overcharged by a self-assessment; or

(*b*) that the appellant is overcharged by an assessment other than a self-assessment,

the assessment shall be reduced accordingly, but otherwise the assessment shall stand good.

(3) If, on appeal it appears to the tribunal—

(*a*) that the appellant is undercharged to stamp duty land tax by a self-assessment; or

(*b*) that the appellant is undercharged by an assessment other than a self-assessment,

the assessment shall be increased accordingly.

(4) Where, on an appeal against an assessment other than a self-assessment which—

(*a*) assesses an amount which is chargeable to stamp duty land tax, and

(*b*) charges stamp duty land tax on the amount assessed,

it appears to the tribunal as mentioned in sub-paragraphs (2) or (3), it may, unless the circumstances of the case otherwise require, reduce or increase only the amount assessed; and where an appeal is so determined the stamp duty land tax charged by that assessment shall be taken to have been reduced or increased accordingly.][1]

Amendments—[1] Paragraphs 41–46 inserted by the Transfer of Tribunal Functions and Revenue and Customs Appeals Order, SI 2009/56 art 3, Sch 1 para 393 with effect from 1 April 2009.

[Payment of stamp duty land tax where there is a further appeal

43—(1) Where a party to an appeal to the tribunal under paragraph 35 makes a further appeal, notwithstanding that the further appeal is pending, stamp duty land tax shall nevertheless be payable or repayable in accordance with the determination of the tribunal or court as the case may be.

(2) But if the amount charged by the assessment is altered by the order or judgment of the Upper Tribunal or court—

(*a*) if too much stamp duty land tax has been paid, the amount overpaid shall be refunded with such interest, if any, as may be allowed by that order or judgment; and

(*b*) if too little stamp duty land tax has been charged, the amount undercharged shall be due and payable at the expiration of a period of thirty days beginning with the date on which HMRC issue to the other party a notice of the total amount payable in accordance with the order or judgment.][1]

Amendments—[1] Paragraphs 41–46 inserted by the Transfer of Tribunal Functions and Revenue and Customs Appeals Order, SI 2009/56 art 3, Sch 1 para 393 with effect from 1 April 2009.

[Late notice of appeal

44—(1) This paragraph applies in a case where—

(*a*) notice of appeal may be given to HMRC under this Schedule or any other provision of Part 4 of this Act, but

(*b*) no notice is given before the relevant time limit.

(2) Notice may be given after the relevant time limit if—

(*a*) HMRC agree, or

(*b*) where HMRC do not agree, the tribunal gives permission.

(3) If the following conditions are met, HMRC shall agree to notice being given after the relevant time limit.

(4) Condition A is that the appellant has made a request in writing to HMRC to agree to the notice being given.

(5) Condition B is that HMRC are satisfied that there was reasonable excuse for not giving the notice before the relevant time limit.

(6) Condition C is that HMRC are satisfied that request under sub-paragraph (4) was made without unreasonable delay after the reasonable excuse ceased.

(7) If a request of the kind referred to in sub-paragraph (4) is made, HMRC must notify the appellant whether or not HMRC agree to the appellant giving notice of appeal after the relevant time limit.

(8) In this paragraph "relevant time limit", in relation to notice of appeal, means the time before which the notice is to be given (but for this paragraph).][1]

Amendments—[1] Paragraphs 41–46 inserted by the Transfer of Tribunal Functions and Revenue and Customs Appeals Order, SI 2009/56 art 3, Sch 1 para 393 with effect from 1 April 2009.

[Questions to be determined by the relevant [tribunal][2]

45—(1) Where the question in any dispute on any appeal under paragraphs 34(6) or 35(1) is a question of the market value of the subject matter of the land transaction that question shall be determined on a reference by the relevant [tribunal][2].

(2) In this [paragraph "the relevant tribunal"][2] means—

(*a*) where the land is in England and Wales, the [Upper Tribunal][2];

(*b*) where the land is in Scotland, the Lands Tribunal for Scotland;

(*c*) where the land is in Northern Ireland, the Lands Tribunal for Northern Ireland.][1]

Amendments—[1] Paragraphs 41–46 inserted by the Transfer of Tribunal Functions and Revenue and Customs Appeals Order, SI 2009/56 art 3, Sch 1 para 393 with effect from 1 April 2009.

[2] In heading and sub-para (1), words substituted for words "Lands Tribunal", and in sub-para (2), words substituted for words "regulation 'the relevant Lands Tribunal' " and "Lands Tribunal" by the Transfer of Tribunal Functions (Lands Tribunal and Miscellaneous Amendments) Order, SI 2009/1307 art 5(1), (2), Sch 1 para 270 with effect from 1 June 2009.

[Meaning of HMRC

46 In this Schedule "HMRC" means Her Majesty's Revenue and Customs.][1]

Amendments—[1] Paragraphs 41–46 inserted by the Transfer of Tribunal Functions and Revenue and Customs Appeals Order, SI 2009/56 art 3, Sch 1 para 393 with effect from 1 April 2009.

SCHEDULE 11

STAMP DUTY LAND TAX: [RECORD-KEEPING WHERE TRANSACTION IS NOT NOTIFIABLE]

Section 79

Amendments—Words in heading substituted by FA 2008 s 94, Sch 30 para 11 with effect in relation to transactions with an effective date on or after 12 March 2008.

PART 1
GENERAL

Repeal—Part 1 repealed by FA 2008 s 94, Sch 30 para 8 with effect in relation to transactions with an effective date on or after 12 March 2008.

PART 2
DUTY TO KEEP AND PRESERVE RECORDS

Duty to keep and preserve records

4—[(A1) This paragraph applies where a transaction is not notifiable, unless the transaction is a transaction treated as taking place under a provision listed in section 79(2)(*a*) to (*d*).][1]

(1) [The purchaser][1] must—

(*a*) keep such records as may be needed to enable him [to demonstrate that the transaction is not notifiable][1], and (*b*) preserve those records in accordance with this paragraph.

(2) The records must be preserved [until the end of—

(*a*) the sixth anniversary of the effective date of the transaction, or

(*b*) such earlier day as may be specified in writing by the Commissioners for Her Majesty's Revenue and Customs (and different days may be specified for different cases).][2]

(3) The records required to be kept and preserved under this paragraph include—

(*a*) relevant instruments relating to the transaction, in particular, any contract or conveyance, and any supporting maps, plans or similar documents;

(*b*) records of relevant payments, receipts and financial arrangements.

[(4) The Commissioners for Her Majesty's Revenue and Customs may by regulations—

(*a*) provide that the records required to be kept and preserved under this paragraph include, or do not include, records specified in the regulations, and

(*b*) provide that those records include supporting documents so specified.

(5) Regulations under this paragraph may make provision by reference to things specified in a notice published by the Commissioners for Her Majesty's Revenue and Customs in accordance with the regulations (and not withdrawn by a subsequent notice).

(6) "Supporting documents" includes accounts, books, deeds, contracts, vouchers and receipts.][2]

Amendments—[1] Sub-para (A1) inserted, words in sub-para (1) substituted, by FA 2008 s 94, Sch 30 para 9 with effect in relation to transactions with an effective date on or after 12 March 2008.

[2] In sub-para (2), words substituted for words "for six years after the effective date of the transaction", and sub-paras (4)–(6) inserted, by FA 2009 s 98, Sch 50 paras 8, 9 with effect from 1 April 2010 (by virtue of SI 2010/815 art 2).

Preservation of information [etc][1]

[5—The duty under paragraph 4 to preserve records may be satisfied—

(*a*) by preserving them in any form and by any means, or

(*b*) by preserving the information contained in them in any form and by any means, subject to any conditions or exceptions specified in writing by the Commissioners for Her Majesty's Revenue and Customs.][1]

Amendments—[1] In heading word substituted for words "instead of original records", and para 5 substituted, by FA 2009 s 98, Sch 50 paras 8, 10, 11 with effect from 1 April 2010 (by virtue of SI 2010/815 art 2). Para 5 previously read as follows—

"5—

(1) The duty under paragraph 4 to preserve records may be satisfied by the preservation of the information contained in them.

(2) Where information is so preserved a copy of any document forming part of the records is admissible in evidence in any proceedings before the [tribunal] to the same extent as the records themselves."

Penalty for failure to keep and preserve records

6—(1) A person who fails to comply with paragraph 4 in relation to a transaction is liable to a penalty not exceeding £3,000, subject to the following exception.

(2) No penalty is incurred if the Inland Revenue are satisfied that any facts that they reasonably require to be proved, and that would have been proved by the records, are proved by other documentary evidence provided to them.

PART 3

ENQUIRY INTO SELF-CERTIFICATE

Repeal—Part 3 repealed by FA 2008 s 94, Sch 30 para 10 with effect in relation to transactions with an effective date on or after 12 March 2008.

[SCHEDULE 11A

STAMP DUTY LAND TAX: CLAIMS NOT INCLUDED IN RETURNS

Section 82A]

Amendments—This Schedule inserted by FA 2004 s 299(1), (3), Sch 40 with effect from 22 July 2004.

[Introductory

1 This Schedule applies to a claim under any provision of this Part other than a claim that is required to be made in, or by amendment to, a return under this Part.

References in this Schedule to a claim shall be read accordingly.][1]

Amendments—[1] This Schedule inserted by FA 2004 s 299(1), (3), Sch 40 with effect from 22 July 2004.

[Making of claims

2—(1) A claim must be made in such form as the Inland Revenue may determine.

(2) The form of claim must provide for a declaration to the effect that all the particulars given in the form are correctly stated to the best of the claimant's information and belief.

(3) The form of claim may require—

(*a*) a statement of the amount of tax that will be required to be discharged or repaid in order to give effect to the claim;

(*b*) such information as is reasonably required for the purpose of determining whether and, if so, the extent to which the claim is correct;

(*c*) the delivery with the claim of such statements and documents, relating to the information contained in the claim, as are reasonably required for the purpose mentioned in paragraph (*b*).

(4) A claim for repayment of tax may not be made unless the claimant has documentary evidence that the tax has been paid.][1]

Amendments—[1] This Schedule inserted by FA 2004 s 299(1), (3), Sch 40 with effect from 22 July 2004.

[Duty to keep and preserve records

3—(1) A person who may wish to make a claim must—

(*a*) keep such records as may be needed to enable him to make a correct and complete claim, and

(*b*) preserve those records in accordance with this paragraph.

(2) The records must be preserved until the latest of the following times—

(*a*) the end of the period of twelve months beginning with day on which the claim was made;

(*b*) where there is an enquiry into the claim, or into an amendment of the claim, the time when the enquiry is completed;

(*c*) where the claim is amended and there is there is no enquiry into the amendment, the time when the Inland Revenue no longer have power to enquire into the amendment.

(3) The duty under this paragraph to preserve records may be satisfied by the preservation of the information contained in them.

(4) Where information is so preserved a copy of any document forming part of the records is admissible in evidence in any proceedings before the [tribunal][2] to the same extent as the records themselves.[3]

[(4A) The Commissioners for Her Majesty's Revenue and Customs may by regulations—

(*a*) provide that the records required to be kept and preserved under this paragraph include, or do not include, records specified in the regulations, and

(*b*) provide that those records include supporting documents so specified.

(4B) Regulations under this paragraph may make provision by reference to things specified in a notice published by the Commissioners for Her Majesty's Revenue and Customs in accordance with the regulations (and not withdrawn by a subsequent notice).

(4C) "Supporting documents" includes accounts, books, deeds, contracts, vouchers and receipts.][3]

(5) A person who fails to comply with this paragraph in relation to a claim that he makes is liable to a penalty not exceeding £3,000, subject to the following exception.

(6) No penalty is incurred if the Inland Revenue are satisfied that any facts that they reasonably require to be proved, and that would have been proved by the records, are proved by other documentary evidence provided to them.][1]

Amendments—[1] This Schedule inserted by FA 2004 s 299(1), (3), Sch 40 with effect from 22 July 2004.

[2] In sub-para (4) word substituted for the word "Commissioners" by the Transfer of Tribunal Functions and Revenue and Customs Appeals Order, SI 2009/56 art 3, Sch 1 para 396 with effect from 1 April 2009.

[3] Sub-paras (3), (4) repealed, and sub-paras (4A)–(4C) inserted, by FA 2009 s 98, Sch 50 paras 12, 13 with effect from 1 April 2010 (by virtue of SI 2010/815 art 2).

[Preservation of information etc

3A The duty under paragraph 3 to preserve records may be satisfied—

(*a*) by preserving them in any form and by any means, or

(*b*) by preserving the information contained in them in any form and by any means,

subject to any conditions or exceptions specified in writing by the Commissioners for Her Majesty's Revenue and Customs.][1]

Amendments—[1] Para 3A inserted by FA 2009 s 98, Sch 50 paras 12, 14 with effect from 1 April 2010 (by virtue of SI 2010/815 art 2).

[Amendment of claim by claimant

4—(1) The claimant may amend his claim by notice to the Inland Revenue.

(2) No such amendment may be made—

(*a*) more than twelve months after the day on which the claim was made, or

(*b*) if the Inland Revenue give notice under paragraph 7 (notice of enquiry), during the period—

(i) beginning with the day on which notice is given, and

(ii) ending with the day on which the enquiry under that paragraph is completed.][1]

Amendments—[1] This Schedule inserted by FA 2004 s 299(1), (3), Sch 40 with effect from 22 July 2004.

[Correction of claim by Revenue

5—(1) The Inland Revenue may by notice to the claimant amend a claim so as to correct obvious errors or omissions in the claim (whether errors of principle, arithmetical mistakes or otherwise).

(2) No such correction may be made—

(*a*) more than nine months after the day on which the claim was made, or

(*b*) if the Inland Revenue give notice under paragraph 7 (notice of enquiry), during the period—

(i) beginning with the day on which notice is given, and

(ii) ending with the day on which the enquiry under that paragraph is completed.

(3) A correction under this paragraph is of no effect if, within three months from the date of issue of the notice of correction, the claimant gives notice rejecting the correction.

(4) Notice under sub-paragraph (3) must be given to the officer of the Board by whom the notice of correction was given.][1]

Amendments—[1] This Schedule inserted by FA 2004 s 299(1), (3), Sch 40 with effect from 22 July 2004.

[Giving effect to claims and amendments

6—(1) As soon as practicable after a claim is made, or is amended under paragraph 4 or 5, the Inland Revenue shall give effect to the claim or amendment by discharge or repayment of tax.

(2) Where the Inland Revenue enquire into a claim or amendment—

(*a*) sub-paragraph (1) does not apply until a closure notice is given under paragraph 11 (completion of enquiry), and then it applies subject to paragraph 13 (giving effect to amendments under paragraph 11), but

(*b*) the Inland Revenue may at any time before then give effect to the claim or amendment, on a provisional basis, to such extent as they think fit.][1]

Amendments—[1] This Schedule inserted by FA 2004 s 299(1), (3), Sch 40 with effect from 22 July 2004.

[Notice of enquiry

7—(1) The Inland Revenue may enquire into a person's claim or amendment of a claim if they give him notice of their intention to do so ("notice of enquiry") before the end of the period of nine months after the day on which the claim or amendment was made.

(2) A claim or amendment that has been the subject of one notice of enquiry may not be the subject of another.][1]

Amendments—[1] This Schedule inserted by FA 2004 s 299(1), (3), Sch 40 with effect from 22 July 2004.

[Notice to produce documents etc for purposes of enquiry

8—*(1) If the Inland Revenue give a person a notice of enquiry, they may by notice in writing require him—*

(*a*) to produce to them such documents in his possession or power, and

(*b*) to provide them with such information, in such form, as they may reasonably require for the purposes of the enquiry.

(2) A notice given to a person under this paragraph (which may be given at the same time as the notice of enquiry) must specify the time (which must not be less than 30 days) within which he is to comply with it.

(3) In complying with a notice under this paragraph copies of documents may be produced instead of originals, but—

(*a*) the copies must be photographic or other facsimiles, and

(*b*) the Inland Revenue may by notice require the original to be produced for inspection.

A notice under paragraph (b) must specify the time (which must not be less than 30 days) within which the person is to comply with it.

(4) The Inland Revenue may take copies of, or make extracts from, any documents produced to them under this paragraph.

(5) A notice under this paragraph does not oblige a person to produce documents or provide information relating to the conduct of any pending appeal by him.][1], [2]

Amendments—[1] This Schedule inserted by FA 2004 s 299(1), (3), Sch 40 with effect from 22 July 2004.

[2] This para repealed by the Finance Act 2009, Section 96 and Schedule 48 (Appointed Day, Savings and Consequential Amendments) Order, SI 2009/3054 art 3, Schedule para 11(1), (5) with effect from 1 April 2010. Note that, in relation to a notice given under para 8 before 1 April 2010, paras 9, 10 continue to have effect on and after 1 April 2010 (SI 2009/3054 art 7(1), (3)).

[Appeal against notice to produce documents etc

9—*(1) An appeal may be brought against a requirement imposed by a notice under paragraph 8 to produce documents or provide information.*

(2) Notice of appeal must be given—

(*a*) in writing,

(*b*) within 30 days after the issue of the notice appealed against,

(*c*) to the officer of the Board by whom that notice was given.

(3) An appeal under this paragraph shall be . . . [2] determined in the same way as an appeal against an assessment.

(4) On an appeal under this paragraph [that is notified to the tribunal, the tribunal][2]—

(*a*) shall set aside the notice so far as it requires the production of documents, or the provision of information, that appears . . . [2] not reasonably required for the purposes of the enquiry, and

(*b*) shall confirm the notice so far as it requires the production of documents, or the provision of information, that appears . . . [2] reasonably required for the purposes of the enquiry.

(5) A notice that is confirmed by the [tribunal][2] (or so far as it is confirmed) has effect as if the period specified in it for complying was 30 days from the determination of the appeal.

[(6) Notwithstanding the provisions of sections 11 and 13 of the Tribunals, Courts and Enforcement Act 2007, the decision of the tribunal on an appeal under this paragraph is final.][2]][1], [3]

Amendments—[1] This Schedule inserted by FA 2004 s 299(1), (3), Sch 40 with effect from 22 July 2004.

[2] In sub-para (3) words "heard and" repealed; in sub-para (4) words substituted for the words "the Commissioners" and words "to them" repealed in both places; in sub-para (5) word substituted for the word "Commissioners"; sub-para (6) substituted by the Transfer of Tribunal Functions and Revenue and Customs Appeals Order, SI 2009/56 art 3, Sch 1 para 397 with effect from 1 April 2009. Sub-para (6) previously read as follows—

"(6) The decision of the Commissioners on an appeal under this paragraph is final.".

[3] This para repealed by the Finance Act 2009, Section 96 and Schedule 48 (Appointed Day, Savings and Consequential Amendments) Order, SI 2009/3054 art 3, Schedule para 11(1), (5) with effect from 1 April 2010. Note that, in relation to a notice given under para 8 before 1 April 2010, paras 9, 10 continue to have effect on and after 1 April 2010 (SI 2009/3054 art 7(1), (3)).

[Penalty for failure to produce documents etc

10—*(1) A person who fails to comply with a notice under paragraph 8 (notice to produce documents etc for purposes of enquiry) is liable—*

(*a*) to a penalty of £50, and

(*b*) if the failure continues after a penalty is imposed under paragraph (*a*), to a further penalty or penalties not exceeding £30 for each day on which the failure continues.

(2) No penalty shall be imposed under this paragraph in respect of a failure at any time after the failure has been remedied.][1], [2]

Amendments—[1] This Schedule inserted by FA 2004 s 299(1), (3), Sch 40 with effect from 22 July 2004.

[2] This para repealed by the Finance Act 2009, Section 96 and Schedule 48 (Appointed Day, Savings and Consequential Amendments) Order, SI 2009/3054 art 3, Schedule para 11(1), (5) with effect from 1 April 2010. Note that, in relation to a notice given under para 8 before 1 April 2010, paras 9, 10 continue to have effect on and after 1 April 2010 (SI 2009/3054 art 7(1), (3)).

[Completion of enquiry

11—(1) An enquiry under paragraph 7 is completed when the Inland Revenue by notice (a "closure notice") inform the purchaser that they have completed their enquiries and state their conclusions.

(2) A closure notice must either—

(*a*) state that in the opinion of the Inland Revenue no amendment of the claim is required, or

(*b*) if in the Inland Revenue's opinion the claim is insufficient or excessive, amend the claim so as to make good or eliminate the deficiency or excess.

In the case of an enquiry into an amendment of a claim, paragraph (b) applies only so far as the deficiency or excess is attributable to the amendment.

(3) A closure notice takes effect when it is issued.][1]

Amendments—[1] This Schedule inserted by FA 2004 s 299(1), (3), Sch 40 with effect from 22 July 2004.

[Direction to complete enquiry

12—(1) The claimant may apply to the [tribunal][2] for a direction that the Inland Revenue give a closure notice within a specified period.

[(2) Any such application is to be subject to the relevant provisions of Part 5 of the Taxes Management Act 1970 (see, in particular, section 48(2)(*b*) of that Act).][2]

(3) The [tribunal][2] shall give a direction unless . . . [2] satisfied that the Inland Revenue have reasonable grounds for not giving a closure notice within a specified period.][1]

Amendments—[1] This Schedule inserted by FA 2004 s 299(1), (3), Sch 40 with effect from 22 July 2004.

[2] In sub-para (1) words substituted for the words "General or Special Commissioners"; sub-para (2) substituted; in sub-para (3) word substituted for the words "Commissioners hearing the application" and words "they are" repealed by the Transfer of Tribunal Functions and Revenue and Customs Appeals Order, SI 2009/56 art 3, Sch 1 para 397 with effect from 1 April 2009. Sub-para (2) previously read as follows—

"(2) Any such application shall be heard and determined in the same way as an appeal.".

[Giving effect to amendments under paragraph 11

13—(1) Within 30 days after the date of issue of a notice under paragraph 11(2)(*b*) (closure notice that amends claim), the Inland Revenue shall give effect to the amendment by making such adjustment as may be necessary, whether—

(*a*) by way of assessment on the claimant, or

(*b*) by discharge or repayment of tax.

(2) An assessment made under sub-paragraph (1) is not out of time if it is made within the time mentioned in that sub-paragraph.][1]

Amendments—[1] This Schedule inserted by FA 2004 s 299(1), (3), Sch 40 with effect from 22 July 2004.

[Appeals against amendments under paragraph 11

14—(1) An appeal may be brought against a conclusion stated or amendment made by a closure notice.

(2) Notice of the appeal must be given—

(*a*) in writing,

(*b*) within 30 days after the date on which the closure notice was issued,

(*c*) to the officer of the Board by whom the closure notice was given.

(3) The notice of appeal must specify the grounds of appeal.

(4) . . . [2]

(5) [Paragraphs 36A to 37 and 44][2] of Schedule 10 (settling of appeals by agreement) applies in relation to an appeal under this paragraph as [they apply][2] in relation to an appeal under paragraph 35 of that Schedule.

(6) On an appeal against an amendment made by a closure notice, the [tribunal][2] may vary the amendment appealed against whether or not the variation is to the advantage of the appellant.

(7) Where any such amendment is varied, whether by the [tribunal][2] or by the order of a court, paragraph 13 (giving effect to amendments under paragraph 11) applies (with the necessary modifications) in relation to the variation as it applied in relation to the amendment.][1]

Amendments—[1] This Schedule inserted by FA 2004 s 299(1), (3), Sch 40 with effect from 22 July 2004.

[2] Sub-para (4) repealed; in sub-para (5) words substituted for the words "Paragraph 37" and for the words "it applies"; in sub-paras (6), (7) word substituted for the word "Commissioners"; by the Transfer of Tribunal Functions and Revenue and Customs Appeals Order, SI 2009/56 art 3, Sch 1 para 399 with effect from 1 April 2009. Sub-para (4) previously read as follows—

"(4) On the hearing of the appeal the Commissioners may allow the appellant to put forward grounds not specified in the notice, and take them into consideration, if satisfied that the omission was not deliberate or unreasonable.".

[Jurisdiction of Commissioners

[15—*(1) An appeal against a conclusion stated or amendment made by a closure notice is to be made to the Special Commissioners if it relates to a claim made to the Board.*

(2) Subject to—

(a) sub-paragraph (1),

(b) paragraph 33(4) of Schedule 10 (appeal against decision on claim for relief in case of double assessment), and

(c) any right to elect to bring an appeal before the Special Commissioners conferred by regulations under Schedule 17 (General and Special Commissioners, appeals and other proceedings),

an appeal under any provision of this Schedule is to be made to the General Commissioners.][2]][1]

Amendments—[1] This Schedule inserted by FA 2004 s 299(1), (3), Sch 40 with effect from 22 July 2004.

[2] Para 15 repealed by the Transfer of Tribunal Functions and Revenue and Customs Appeals Order, SI 2009/56 art 3, Sch 1 para 400 with effect from 1 April 2009.

SCHEDULE 12

STAMP DUTY LAND TAX: COLLECTION AND RECOVERY OF TAX

Section 91

PART 1

GENERAL

Issue of tax demands and receipts

1—(1) Where tax is due and payable, a collector may make demand of the sum charged from the person liable to pay it.

(2) On payment of the tax, the collector shall if so requested give a receipt.

Prospective amendments—Para 1A to be inserted by the Tribunals, Courts and Enforcement Act 2007 s 62(3), Sch 13 para 147(1), (2) with effect from a date to be appointed. Para 1A to read as follows—

"*Recovery of tax by taking control of goods*

1A In England and Wales, if a person neglects or refuses to pay the sum charged, the collector may use the procedure in Schedule 12 to the Tribunals, Courts and Enforcement Act 2007 (taking control of goods) to recover the sum."

Para 1A to be repealed by FA 2008 s 129, Sch 43 para 9 with effect from a date to be appointed.

Recovery of tax by distraint

2—(1) In England and Wales or Northern Ireland, if a person neglects or refuses to pay the sum charged, upon demand made by the collector, the collector may distrain upon the goods and chattels of the person charged ("the person in default").

(2) For the purposes of levying such distress a justice of the peace, on being satisfied by information on oath that there is reasonable ground for believing that a person is neglecting or refusing to pay a sum charged, may issue a warrant in writing authorising a collector to break open, in the daytime, any house or premises, calling to his assistance any constable.

Every such constable shall, when so required, assist the collector in the execution of the warrant and in levying such distress in the house or premises.

(3) A levy or warrant to break open must be executed by, or under the direction of, and in the presence of, the collector.

(4) A distress levied by the collector shall be kept for five days, at the costs and charges of the person in default.

(5) If the person in default does not pay the sum due, together with the costs and charges, the distress shall be appraised by one or more independent persons appointed by the collector, and shall be sold by public auction by the collector for payment of the sum due and all costs and charges.

Any surplus resulting from the distress, after the deduction of the costs and charges and of the sum due, shall be restored to the owner of the goods distrained.

(6) The Treasury may by regulations make provision with respect to—

(*a*) the fees chargeable on or in connection with the levying of distress, and

(*b*) the costs and charges recoverable where distress has been levied.

Recovery of tax by diligence in Scotland

3—*(1) In Scotland, where any tax is due and has not been paid, the sheriff, on an application by the collector accompanied by a certificate by the collector—*

(*a*) stating that none of the persons specified in the application has paid the tax to him,

(*b*) stating that the collector has demanded payment under paragraph 1 from each such person of the amount due by him,

(*c*) stating that 14 days have elapsed since the date of such demand without payment of that amount, and

(*d*) specifying the amount due and unpaid by each such person,

shall grant a summary warrant in a form prescribed by Act of Sederunt authorising the recovery, by any of the diligences mentioned in sub-paragraph (2), of the amount remaining due and unpaid.

(2) The diligences referred to in sub-paragraph (1) are—

(*a*) an attachment;

(*b*) an earnings arrestment;

(*c*) an arrestment and action of furthcoming or sale.

(3) Subject to sub-paragraph (4), the sheriff officer's fees, together with the outlays necessarily incurred by him, in connection with the execution of a summary warrant are chargeable against the debtor.

(4) No fee is chargeable by the sheriff officer against the debtor for collecting, and accounting to the collector for, sums paid to him by the debtor in respect of the amount owing.[1]

Amendments—[1] This para repealed by FA 2008 s 129, Sch 43 para 16 with effect from 23 November 2009 (by virtue of SI 2009/3024 art 3). Note that if, before 23 November 2009, a warrant has been granted under—

- TMA 1970 s 63;
- Social Security Administration Act 1992 s 121B;
- FA 1997 s 52; or
- FA 2003 Sch 12 para 3;

that warrant shall continue to have effect according to the provisions under which it was granted (SI 2009/3024 art 4).

PART 2
COURT PROCEEDINGS

Civil proceedings in magistrates' court or court of summary jurisdiction

4—(1) An amount not exceeding £2,000 due and payable by way of tax is in England and Wales or Northern Ireland recoverable summarily as a civil debt in proceedings brought in the name of the collector.

(2) All or any of the sums recoverable under this paragraph that are—

(*a*) due from any one person, and

(*b*) payable to any one collector,

may be included in the same complaint, summons or other document required to be laid before or issued by justices.

Each such document shall, as respects each such sum, be construed as a separate document and its invalidity as respects any one such sum does not affect its validity as respects any other such sum.

(3) Proceedings under this paragraph in England and Wales may be brought at any time within one year from the time when the matter complained of arose.

(4) In sub-paragraph (1) the expression "recoverable summarily as a civil debt" in relation to proceedings in Northern Ireland means recoverable by proceedings under Article 62 of the Magistrates' Courts (Northern Ireland) Order 1981 (SI 1981/1675 (NI 26)).

(5) The Treasury may by order increase the sum specified in sub-paragraph (1).

Proceedings in county court or sheriff court

5—(1) Tax due and payable may be sued for and recovered from the person charged as a debt due to the Crown by proceedings *brought in the name of a collector*[1]—

(*a*) in a county court, or

(*b*) in a sheriff court.

(2) *An officer of the Board who is authorised by the Board to do so may address the court in any proceedings under this paragraph in England and Wales or Scotland.*[1]

(3) In Northern Ireland—

(*a*) the reference in sub-paragraph (1) to a county court is to a county court held for a division under the County Courts (Northern Ireland) Order 1980 (SI 1980/397 (NI 3));

(*b*) proceedings may not be brought under this paragraph if the amount exceeds the limit specified in Article 10(1) of that Order;

(*c*) Part III of that Order (general civil jurisdiction) applies for the purposes of this paragraph; and

(*d*) sections 21 and 42(2) of the Interpretation Act (Northern Ireland) 1954 (c 33 (NI)) apply as if any reference in those provisions to an enactment included this paragraph.

Amendments—[1] Words in sub-para (1), and whole of sub-para (2), repealed, by FA 2008 s 137(6) with effect from 21 July 2008. These amendments do not affect proceedings commenced or brought in the name of a collector or authorised officer before this date (FA 2008 s 137(7)).

Proceedings in High Court or Court of Session

6 Tax may be sued for and recovered from the person charged—

(*a*) as a debt due to the Crown, or

(*b*) by any other means by which a debt of record or otherwise due to the Crown may be sued for and recovered,

by proceedings in the High Court or, in Scotland, in the Court of Session sitting as the Court of Exchequer.

. . . [1]

7 . . . [1]

Amendments—[1] This para and preceding heading repealed by FA 2008 s 138, Sch 44 para 10 with effect from 21 July 2008.

SCHEDULE 13

STAMP DUTY LAND TAX: INFORMATION POWERS

Section 93

PART 1

POWER OF AUTHORISED OFFICER TO CALL FOR DOCUMENTS OR INFORMATION FROM TAXPAYER

Notice requiring taxpayer to deliver documents or provide information

1—*(1) An authorised officer of the Board may by notice in writing require a person—*

(*a*) to deliver to him such documents as are in that person's possession or power and (in the officer's reasonable opinion) contain, or may contain, information relevant to—

(*i*) any tax liability to which that person is or may be subject, or

(*ii*) the amount of any such liability, or

(*b*) to provide him with such information as he may reasonably require as being relevant to, or to the amount of, any such liability.

(2) An "authorised officer of the Board" means an officer of the Board authorised for the purposes of this Part of this Schedule.

(3) Before a person is given a notice under this paragraph he must be given a reasonable opportunity to deliver the documents or provide the information in question.

No application for consent under paragraph 2 shall be made unless he has been given that opportunity.[1]

Amendments—[1] Paras 1–13 repealed by the Finance Act 2009, Section 96 and Schedule 48 (Appointed Day, Savings and Consequential Amendments) Order, SI 2009/3054 art 3, Schedule para 11(1), (6)(*a*) with effect from 1 April 2010. Note that, in relation to a notice given under Part 1 or 2 of Sch 13 before 1 April 2010, s 93(3), (6) apply on and after 1 April 2010 disregarding the amendments made by the Schedule to SI 2009/3054 (SI 2009/3054 art 7(1), (4)).

Requirement of consent of [the tribunal][1]

2—*(1) The consent of [the tribunal]*[1] *is required for the giving of a notice under paragraph 1.*

(2) Consent shall not be given unless the Commissioner is satisfied that in all the circumstances the officer is justified in proceeding under that paragraph.

(3) . . . [1, 2]

Amendments—[1] In the heading, words substituted for the words "General or Special Commissioner"; in sub-para (1) words substituted for the words "a General or Special Commissioner"; in sub-para (2) word substituted for the word "Commissioner"; sub-para (3) and the word following, repealed by the Transfer of Tribunal Functions and Revenue and Customs Appeals Order, SI 2009/56 art 3, Sch 1 para 402 with effect from 1 April 2009. Text previously read as follows—

"(3) A Commissioner who has given such consent shall not take part in, or be present at, any proceedings on, or related to, any appeal brought by the person to whom the notice applies if the Commissioner has reason to believe that any of the required information is likely to be adduced in evidence in those proceedings.

The "required information" means any document or information that was the subject of the notice with respect to which the Commissioner gave his consent.".

[2] Paras 1–13 repealed by the Finance Act 2009, Section 96 and Schedule 48 (Appointed Day, Savings and Consequential Amendments) Order, SI 2009/3054 art 3, Schedule para 11(1), (6)(*a*) with effect from 1 April 2010. Note that, in relation to a notice given under Part 1 or 2 of Sch 13 before 1 April 2010, s 93(3), (6) apply on and after 1 April 2010 disregarding the amendments made by the Schedule to SI 2009/3054 (SI 2009/3054 art 7(1), (4)

Contents of notice under this Part

3—*(1) A notice under paragraph 1 must—*

(*a*) specify or describe the documents or information to which it relates, and

(*b*) require the documents to be delivered, or the information to be provided, within such time as may be specified in the notice.

(2) The period specified for complying with the notice must not be less than 30 days after the date of the notice.[1]

Amendments—[1] Paras 1–13 repealed by the Finance Act 2009, Section 96 and Schedule 48 (Appointed Day, Savings and Consequential Amendments) Order, SI 2009/3054 art 3, Schedule para 11(1), (6)(*a*) with effect from 1 April 2010. Note that, in relation to a notice given under Part 1 or 2 of Sch 13 before 1 April 2010, s 93(3), (6) apply on and after 1 April 2010 disregarding the amendments made by the Schedule to SI 2009/3054 (SI 2009/3054 art 7(1), (4)

Summary of reasons to be given

4—*(1) An officer who gives a notice under paragraph 1 must also give to the person to whom the notice applies a written summary of his reasons for applying for consent to the notice.*

(2) This does not require the disclosure of any information—

(*a*) that would, or might, identify any person who has provided the officer with any information which he took into account in deciding whether to apply for consent, or

(*b*) that the [tribunal][1] giving consent under paragraph 2 directs need not be disclosed.

(3) [The tribunal][1] shall not give any such direction unless . . . [1] satisfied that the officer has reasonable grounds for believing that disclosure of the information in question would prejudice the assessment or collection of tax.[2]

Amendments—[1] In sub-para (2)(b) word substituted for the words "General or Special Commissioner"; in sub-para (3) words substituted for the words "A Commissioner" and words "he is" repealed by the Transfer of Tribunal Functions and Revenue and Customs Appeals Order, SI 2009/56 art 3, Sch 1 para 403 with effect from 1 April 2009.

[2] Paras 1–13 repealed by the Finance Act 2009, Section 96 and Schedule 48 (Appointed Day, Savings and Consequential Amendments) Order, SI 2009/3054 art 3, Schedule para 11(1), (6)(*a*) with effect from 1 April 2010. Note that, in relation to a notice given under Part 1 or 2 of Sch 13 before 1 April 2010, s 93(3), (6) apply on and after 1 April 2010 disregarding the amendments made by the Schedule to SI 2009/3054 (SI 2009/3054 art 7(1), (4)

Power to take copies of documents etc

5 *The person to whom documents are delivered, or to whom information is provided, in pursuance of a notice under paragraph 1 may take copies of them or of extracts from them.*[1]

Amendments—[1] Paras 1–13 repealed by the Finance Act 2009, Section 96 and Schedule 48 (Appointed Day, Savings and Consequential Amendments) Order, SI 2009/3054 art 3, Schedule para 11(1), (6)(*a*) with effect from 1 April 2010. Note that, in relation to a notice given under Part 1 or 2 of Sch 13 before 1 April 2010, s 93(3), (6) apply on and after 1 April 2010 disregarding the amendments made by the Schedule to SI 2009/3054 (SI 2009/3054 art 7(1), (4)

PART 2
POWER OF AUTHORISED OFFICER TO CALL FOR DOCUMENTS FROM THIRD PARTY

Notice requiring documents to be delivered or made available

6—*(1) An authorised officer of the Board may for the purpose of enquiring into the tax liability of any person ("the taxpayer") by notice in writing require any other person—*

(*a*) to deliver to the officer, or

(*b*) if the person to whom the notice is given so elects, to make available for inspection by a named officer of the Board,

such documents as are in that person's possession or power and (in the officer's reasonable opinion) contain, or may contain, information relevant to any tax liability to which the taxpayer is or may be, or may have been, subject, or the amount of any such liability.

(2) An "authorised officer of the Board" means an officer of the Board authorised for the purposes of this Part of this Schedule.

(3) Before a person is given a notice under this paragraph he must be given a reasonable opportunity to deliver or make available the documents in question.

No application for consent under paragraph 7 shall be made unless he has been given that opportunity.

(4) The persons who may be treated as "the taxpayer" for the purposes of this paragraph include a company that has ceased to exist and an individual who has died.

But a notice in relation to a taxpayer who has died may not be given more than six years after his death.[1]

Amendments—[1] Paras 1–13 repealed by the Finance Act 2009, Section 96 and Schedule 48 (Appointed Day, Savings and Consequential Amendments) Order, SI 2009/3054 art 3, Schedule para 11(1), (6)(*a*) with effect from 1 April 2010. Note that, in relation to a notice given under Part 1 or 2 of Sch 13 before 1 April 2010, s 93(3), (6) apply on and after 1 April 2010 disregarding the amendments made by the Schedule to SI 2009/3054 (SI 2009/3054 art 7(1), (4)

Requirement of consent of [the tribunal][1]

7—*(1) The consent of [the tribunal]*[1] *is required for the giving of a notice under paragraph 6.*

(2) Consent shall not be given unless the [tribunal][1] *is satisfied that in all the circumstances the officer is justified in proceeding under that paragraph.*

(3) . . . [1, 2]

Amendments—[1] In the heading words substituted for the words "General or Special Commissioner"; in sub-para (1) words substituted for the words "a General or Special Commissioner"; in sub-para (2) word substituted for the word "Commissioner"; sub-para (3) repealed by the Transfer of Tribunal Functions and Revenue and Customs Appeals Order, SI 2009/56 art 3, Sch 1 para 404 with effect from 1 April 2009. Sub-para (3) previously read as follows—

> "(3) A Commissioner who has given such consent shall not take part in, or be present at, any proceedings on, or related to, any appeal brought by the taxpayer concerned if the Commissioner has reason to believe that any of the documents that were the subject of the notice is likely to be adduced in evidence in those proceedings.".

[2] Paras 1–13 repealed by the Finance Act 2009, Section 96 and Schedule 48 (Appointed Day, Savings and Consequential Amendments) Order, SI 2009/3054 art 3, Schedule para 11(1), (6)(*a*) with effect from 1 April 2010. Note that, in relation to a notice given under Part 1 or 2 of Sch 13 before 1 April 2010, s 93(3), (6) apply on and after 1 April 2010 disregarding the amendments made by the Schedule to SI 2009/3054 (SI 2009/3054 art 7(1), (4)

Contents of notice under paragraph 6

8—*(1) A notice under paragraph 6 must—*

(*a*) specify or describe the documents to which it relates, and

(*b*) require the documents to be delivered or made available within such time as may be specified in the notice.

(2) The period specified for complying with the notice must not be less than 30 days after the date of the notice.

(3) Subject to paragraph 11 (power to give notice in respect of unnamed taxpayer or taxpayers), a notice under this paragraph must name the taxpayer to whom it relates.[1]

Amendments—[1] Paras 1–13 repealed by the Finance Act 2009, Section 96 and Schedule 48 (Appointed Day, Savings and Consequential Amendments) Order, SI 2009/3054 art 3, Schedule para 11(1), (6)(*a*) with effect from 1 April 2010. Note that, in relation to a notice given under Part 1 or 2 of Sch 13 before 1 April 2010, s 93(3), (6) apply on and after 1 April 2010 disregarding the amendments made by the Schedule to SI 2009/3054 (SI 2009/3054 art 7(1), (4)

Copy of notice to be given to taxpayer

9—*(1) Where a notice is given to a person under this paragraph, the officer shall give a copy of the notice to the taxpayer to whom it relates.*

(2) This paragraph does not apply if, on application by the officer, [the tribunal][1] *directs that it shall not apply.*

(3) Such a direction shall only be given if the [tribunal][1] *is satisfied that the officer has reasonable grounds for suspecting the taxpayer of fraud.*[2]

Amendments—[1] In sub-para (2) words substituted for the words "a General or Special Commissioner"; in sub-para (3) word substituted for the word "Commissioner" by the Transfer of Tribunal Functions and Revenue and Customs Appeals Order, SI 2009/56 art 3, Sch 1 para 405 with effect from 1 April 2009.

[2] Paras 1–13 repealed by the Finance Act 2009, Section 96 and Schedule 48 (Appointed Day, Savings and Consequential Amendments) Order, SI 2009/3054 art 3, Schedule para 11(1), (6)(*a*) with effect from 1 April 2010. Note that, in relation to a notice given under Part 1 or 2 of Sch 13 before 1 April 2010, s 93(3), (6) apply on and after 1 April 2010 disregarding the amendments made by the Schedule to SI 2009/3054 (SI 2009/3054 art 7(1), (4)

Summary of reasons to be given

10—*(1) An officer who gives a notice under paragraph 6 must also give to the taxpayer concerned a written summary of his reasons for applying for consent to the notice.*

(2) This does not require the disclosure of any information—

(*a*) that would, or might, identify any person who has provided the officer with any information which he took into account in deciding whether to apply for consent, or

(*b*) that the [tribunal][1] giving consent under paragraph 7 directs need not be disclosed.

(3) [The tribunal][1] *shall not give such a direction unless . . .* [1] *satisfied that the officer has reasonable grounds for believing that disclosure of the information in question would prejudice the assessment or collection of tax.*

(4) This paragraph does not apply if under paragraph 9(2) a copy of the notice need not be given to the taxpayer.[2]

Amendments—[1] In sub-para (2)(b) word substituted for the words "General or Special Commissioner"; in sub-para (3) words substituted for the words "A Commissioner" and words "he is" repealed by the Transfer of Tribunal Functions and Revenue and Customs Appeals Order, SI 2009/56 art 3, Sch 1 para 406 with effect from 1 April 2009.

[2] Paras 1–13 repealed by the Finance Act 2009, Section 96 and Schedule 48 (Appointed Day, Savings and Consequential Amendments) Order, SI 2009/3054 art 3, Schedule para 11(1), (6)(*a*) with effect from 1 April 2010. Note that, in relation to a notice given under Part 1 or 2 of Sch 13 before 1 April 2010, s 93(3), (6) apply on and after 1 April 2010 disregarding the amendments made by the Schedule to SI 2009/3054 (SI 2009/3054 art 7(1), (4)

Power to give notice relating to unnamed taxpayer or taxpayers

11—*(1) If, on an application made by an officer of the Board and authorised by an order of the Board, [the tribunal gives consent]*[1]*, the officer may give such a notice as is mentioned in paragraph 6 without naming the taxpayer to whom the notice relates.*

(2) Consent shall not be given unless the [tribunal][1] *is satisfied—*

(*a*) that the notice relates—

(*i*) to a taxpayer whose identity is not known to the officer, or

(*ii*) to a class of taxpayers whose individual identities are not so known,

(*b*) that there are reasonable grounds for believing that the taxpayer, or any of the class of taxpayers, to whom the notice relates may have failed or may fail to comply with any provision of this Part of this Act,

(*c*) that any such failure is likely to have led or to lead to serious prejudice to the proper assessment or collection of tax, and

(*d*) that the information that is likely to be contained in the documents to which the notice relates is not readily available from another source.

(3) Before a person is given a notice under this paragraph he must be given a reasonable opportunity to deliver or make available the documents in question.
No application for consent under sub-paragraph (1) shall be made unless he has been given that opportunity.
(4) A person to whom there is given a notice under this paragraph may, by notice in writing given to the officer within 30 days after the date of the notice, object to it on the ground that it would be onerous for him to comply with it.
(5) If the matter is not resolved by agreement it shall be referred to the [tribunal][1] who may confirm, vary or cancel the notice.[2]

Amendments—[1] In sub-para (1) words substituted for the words "a Special Commissioner gives his consent"; in sub-para (2) word substituted for the word "Commissioner"; in sub-para (5) word substituted for the words "Special Commissioner" by the Transfer of Tribunal Functions and Revenue and Customs Appeals Order, SI 2009/56 art 3, Sch 1 para 407 with effect from 1 April 2009.
[2] Paras 1–13 repealed by the Finance Act 2009, Section 96 and Schedule 48 (Appointed Day, Savings and Consequential Amendments) Order, SI 2009/3054 art 3, Schedule para 11(1), (6)(*a*) with effect from 1 April 2010. Note that, in relation to a notice given under Part 1 or 2 of Sch 13 before 1 April 2010, s 93(3), (6) apply on and after 1 April 2010 disregarding the amendments made by the Schedule to SI 2009/3054 (SI 2009/3054 art 7(1), (4)

Contents of notice under paragraph 11

12—*(1) A notice under paragraph 11 must—*
(*a*) specify or describe the documents to which it relates, and
(*b*) require the documents to be delivered or made available within such time as may be specified in the notice.
(2) The period specified for complying with the notice must not be less than 30 days after the date of the notice.[1]

Amendments—[1] Paras 1–13 repealed by the Finance Act 2009, Section 96 and Schedule 48 (Appointed Day, Savings and Consequential Amendments) Order, SI 2009/3054 art 3, Schedule para 11(1), (6)(*a*) with effect from 1 April 2010. Note that, in relation to a notice given under Part 1 or 2 of Sch 13 before 1 April 2010, s 93(3), (6) apply on and after 1 April 2010 disregarding the amendments made by the Schedule to SI 2009/3054 (SI 2009/3054 art 7(1), (4)

Power to take copies of documents etc

13 *The person to whom documents are delivered or made available in pursuance of a notice under this Part of this Schedule may take copies of them or of extracts from them.*[1]

Amendments—[1] Paras 1–13 repealed by the Finance Act 2009, Section 96 and Schedule 48 (Appointed Day, Savings and Consequential Amendments) Order, SI 2009/3054 art 3, Schedule para 11(1), (6)(*a*) with effect from 1 April 2010. Note that, in relation to a notice given under Part 1 or 2 of Sch 13 before 1 April 2010, s 93(3), (6) apply on and after 1 April 2010 disregarding the amendments made by the Schedule to SI 2009/3054 (SI 2009/3054 art 7(1), (4)

PART 3
POWER TO CALL FOR PAPERS OF TAX ACCOUNTANT

Power to call for papers of tax accountant

14—(1) Where a person who has stood in relation to others as a tax accountant—
(*a*) is convicted of an offence in relation to tax by or before a court in the United Kingdom, or
(*b*) has a penalty imposed on him under section 96 (assisting in preparation of incorrect return etc),

an authorised officer of the Board may by notice in writing require that person to deliver to him such documents as are in his possession or power and (in the officer's reasonable opinion) contain information relevant to any tax liability to which any client of his is or has been, or may be or have been, subject, or to the amount of any such liability.
(2) An "authorised officer of the Board" means an officer of the Board authorised for the purposes of this Part of this Schedule.
(3) Before a person is given a notice under this paragraph he must be given a reasonable opportunity to deliver the documents in question.
No application for consent under paragraph 16 shall be made unless he has been given that opportunity.

When notice may be given

15—(1) No notice under paragraph 14 may be given for so long as an appeal is pending against the conviction or penalty.
(2) For the purposes of sub-paragraph (1)—
(*a*) an appeal is treated as pending (where one is competent but has not been brought) until the expiration of the time for bringing it or, in the case of a conviction in Scotland, until the expiration of 28 days from the date of conviction; and

(*b*) references to an appeal include a further appeal, but in relation to the imposition of a penalty do not include an appeal against the amount of the penalty.

(3) No notice may be given under paragraph 14 by reference to a person's conviction or the imposition on him of a penalty after the end of the period of twelve months beginning with the date on which the power to give such a notice was first exercisable in his case by virtue of that conviction or penalty.

Requirement of consent of appropriate judicial authority

16—(1) The consent of the appropriate judicial authority is required for the giving of a notice under paragraph 14.

(2) Consent shall not be given unless that authority is satisfied that in all the circumstances the officer is justified in proceeding under that paragraph.

(3) The appropriate judicial authority is—

(*a*) in England and Wales, a circuit judge;

(*b*) in Scotland, a sheriff;

(*c*) in Northern Ireland, a county court judge.

Contents of notice

17—(1) A notice under paragraph 14 must—

(*a*) specify or describe the documents to which it relates, and

(*b*) require the documents to be delivered within such time as may be specified in the notice.

(2) The period specified for complying with the notice must not be less than 30 days after the date of the notice.

Power to take copies of documents etc

18 The officer to whom documents are delivered in pursuance of a notice under paragraph 14 may take copies of them or of extracts from them.

PART 4
RESTRICTIONS ON POWERS UNDER PARTS 1 TO 3

Introduction

19 The provisions of [Part][1] 3 of this Schedule have effect subject to the following restrictions.

Amendments—[1] Word substituted for words "Parts 1 to" by the Finance Act 2009, Section 96 and Schedule 48 (Appointed Day, Savings and Consequential Amendments) Order, SI 2009/3054 art 3, Schedule para 11(1), (6)(*b*) with effect from 1 April 2010.

Personal records or journalistic material

20—(1) [Part 3 of this Schedule does][1] not apply—

(*a*) to documents that are personal records or journalistic material, or

(*b*) to information contained in any personal records or journalistic material.

(2) In sub-paragraph (1)—

"personal records" means personal records as defined in section 12 of the Police and Criminal Evidence Act 1984 (c 60) or, in Northern Ireland, in Article 14 of the Police and Criminal Evidence (Northern Ireland) Order 1989 (SI 1989/1341 (NI 12)); and

"journalistic material" means journalistic material as defined in section 13 of that Act or, in Northern Ireland, in Article 15 of that Order.

Amendments—[1] In sub-para (1), words substituted for words "Parts 1 to 3 of this Schedule do " by the Finance Act 2009, Section 96 and Schedule 48 (Appointed Day, Savings and Consequential Amendments) Order, SI 2009/3054 art 3, Schedule para 11(1), (6)(*c*) with effect from 1 April 2010.

Documents or information relating to pending appeal

21—*(1) A notice under Part 1 of this Schedule does not oblige a person to deliver documents or provide information relating to the conduct of any pending appeal by him.*[1]

(2) A notice under Part 2 of this Schedule does not oblige a person to deliver or make available documents relating to the conduct of a pending appeal by the taxpayer.[1]

(3) A notice under Part 3 of this Schedule does not oblige a person to deliver documents relating to the conduct of a pending appeal by the client.

(4) An "appeal" here means an appeal relating to tax.

Amendments—[1] Sub-paras (1), (2) repealed by the Finance Act 2009, Section 96 and Schedule 48 (Appointed Day, Savings and Consequential Amendments) Order, SI 2009/3054 art 3, Schedule para 11(1), (6)(*d*) with effect from 1 April 2010.

Barristers, advocates and solicitors

22—(1) A notice under Part . . . [2] 3 of this Schedule may not be given to a [relevant lawyer][1] by an authorised officer of the Board but only by the Board.
(2) Accordingly, in relation to a [relevant lawyer][1], the references in [that Part][2] to an authorised officer of the Board shall be read as references to the Board.
[(3) "Relevant lawyer" means a barrister, advocate, solicitor or other professional legal adviser communications with whom may be the subject of a claim to legal privilege.
(4) "Legal privilege" here has the same meaning as in paragraph 35 of this Schedule.][1]

Amendments—[1] In sub-para (1), words "2 or" repealed, and in sub-para (2), words substituted for words "those Parts", by the Finance Act 2009, Section 96 and Schedule 48 (Appointed Day, Savings and Consequential Amendments) Order, SI 2009/3054 art 3, Schedule para 11(1), (6)(*e*), (*f*) with effect from 1 April 2010.

[2] In sub-paras (1), (2), words substituted for words "barrister, advocate or solicitor", and sub-paras (3), (4) inserted, by the Legal Services Act 2007 s 208, Sch 21 para 138 with effect from 1 January 2010 (by virtue of SI 2009/3250, art 2(*h*)).

Provision of copies instead of original documents

23—(1) To comply with a notice under Part . . . [1] 3 of this Schedule . . . [1]copies of documents may be delivered instead of originals.
(2) The copies must be photographic or otherwise by way of facsimile.
(3) If so required by the officer (or, as the case may be, the Board) in the case of any documents specified in the requirement, the originals must be made available for inspection by a named officer of the Board.
(4) Failure to comply with such a requirement counts as failure to comply with the notice.

Amendments—[1] In sub-para (1), words "1 or" repealed, and in sub-para (2), words ", and as an alternative to delivering documents to comply with a notice under Part 2 of this Schedule, repealed, by the Finance Act 2009, Section 96 and Schedule 48 (Appointed Day, Savings and Consequential Amendments) Order, SI 2009/3054 art 3, Schedule para 11(1), (6)(*g*), with effect from 1 April 2010.

Documents originating more than six years before date of notice

24—*(1) A notice under Part 2 of this Schedule does not oblige a person to deliver or make available a document the whole of which originates more than six years before the date of the notice.*
(2) Sub-paragraph (1) does not apply where the notice is so expressed as to exclude the restrictions of that sub-paragraph.
(3) A notice may only be so expressed if—

(*a*) in the case of a notice given by an authorised officer, the [tribunal][1] giving consent to the notice has also given approval to the exclusion;
(*b*) in the case of a notice given by the Board, they have applied to [the tribunal][1] for, and obtained, that approval.

(4) Approval shall only be given if the [tribunal][1] is satisfied, on application by the officer or the Board, that tax has been, or may have been, lost to the Crown owing to the fraud of the taxpayer.[2]

Amendments—[1] In sub-para (3)(a) word substituted for the words "General or Special Commissioner"; in sub-para (3)(b) words substituted for the words "a General or Special Commissioner"; in sub-para (5) word substituted for the word "Commissioner" by the Transfer of Tribunal Functions and Revenue and Customs Appeals Order, SI 2009/56 art 3, Sch 1 para 408 with effect from 1 April 2009.

[2] Para repealed by the Finance Act 2009, Section 96 and Schedule 48 (Appointed Day, Savings and Consequential Amendments) Order, SI 2009/3054 art 3, Schedule para 11(1), (6)(*a*) with effect from 1 April 2010.

Documents subject to legal privilege

25—(1) A notice under Part . . . [2] 3 of this Schedule does not oblige a [relevant lawyer (within the meaning of paragraph 22(3))][1] to deliver or make available, without his client's consent, any document with respect to which a claim to legal privilege could be maintained.
(2) "Legal privilege" here has the same meaning as in paragraph 35 of this Schedule.

Amendments—[1] Words substituted for words "barrister, advocate or solicitor", by the Legal Services Act 2007 s 208, Sch 21 para 138(*c*) with effect from 1 January 2010 (by virtue of SI 2009/3250, art 2(*h*)).

[2] In sub-para (1), words "2 or" repealed, by the Finance Act 2009, Section 96 and Schedule 48 (Appointed Day, Savings and Consequential Amendments) Order, SI 2009/3054 art 3, Schedule para 11(1), (6)(*h*), with effect from 1 April 2010.

Documents belonging to auditor or tax adviser

26—*(1) A notice under Part 2 of this Schedule*—

(*a*) does not oblige a person who has been appointed as auditor for the purposes of any enactment to deliver or make available documents that are his property and were created by him or on his behalf for or in connection with the performance of his functions under that enactment, and
(*b*) does not oblige a tax adviser to deliver or make available documents that are his property and consist of relevant communications (as defined below).

(2) "Relevant communications" means communications between the tax adviser and—

(*a*) a person in relation to whose tax affairs he has been appointed, or

(*b*) any other tax adviser of such a person,

the purpose of which is the giving or obtaining of advice about any of those tax affairs.

(3) In this paragraph "tax adviser" means a person appointed to give advice about the tax affairs of another person (whether appointed directly by that other person or by another tax adviser of his).

(4) This paragraph has effect subject to paragraph 27 (documents belonging to auditor or tax adviser: information to be disclosed).[1]

Amendments—[1] Paras 26–31 repealed by the Finance Act 2009, Section 96 and Schedule 48 (Appointed Day, Savings and Consequential Amendments) Order, SI 2009/3054 art 3, Schedule para 11(1), (6)(*a*) with effect from 1 April 2010.

Documents belonging to auditor or tax adviser: information to be disclosed

27—*(1) This paragraph applies where a notice is given under Part 2 of this Schedule relating to a document that falls within paragraph 26 (documents belonging to auditor or tax adviser) but contains—*

(*a*) information explaining any information, return or other document that the person to whom the notice is given has, as tax accountant, assisted any client of his in preparing for, or for delivering to, the officer or the Board, or

(*b*) in the case of a notice under paragraph 11 (notice in respect of unnamed taxpayer or taxpayers), information as to the identity or address of any taxpayer to whom the notice relates or any person who has acted on behalf of any such person,

that has not otherwise been made available to the Inland Revenue.

(2) For this purpose information is regarded as having been made available to the Inland Revenue if it is contained in some other document and—

(*a*) that other document, or a copy of it, has been delivered to the officer or the Board, or

(*b*) that other document has been inspected by an officer of the Board.

(3) Where this paragraph applies the person to whom the notice is given must, if he does not deliver the document or make it available for inspection in accordance with the notice—

(*a*) deliver to the officer (or, as the case may be, the Board) a copy (photographic or otherwise by way of facsimile) of any parts of the document that contain such information as is mentioned in sub-paragraph (1), and

(*b*) if so required by the officer (or, as the case may be, the Board), make available for inspection by a named officer of the Board such parts of the original document as contain such information.

(4) Failure to comply with any such requirement counts as a failure to comply with the notice.[1]

Amendments—[1] Paras 26–31 repealed by the Finance Act 2009, Section 96 and Schedule 48 (Appointed Day, Savings and Consequential Amendments) Order, SI 2009/3054 art 3, Schedule para 11(1), (6)(*a*) with effect from 1 April 2010.

PART 5
POWERS OF BOARD TO CALL FOR DOCUMENTS OR INFORMATION

Notice requiring delivery of documents or provision of information

28—*(1) The Board may by notice in writing require a person—*

(*a*) to deliver to a named officer of the Board such documents as are in the person's possession or power and (in the Board's reasonable opinion) contain, or may contain, information relevant to—

(*i*) any tax liability to which the person is or may be subject, or

(*ii*) the amount of any such liability, or

(*b*) to provide to a named officer of the Board such information as the Board may reasonably require as being relevant to, or to the amount of, any such liability.

(2) Notice under this paragraph shall not be given unless the Board have reasonable grounds for believing—

(*a*) that the person to whom it relates may have failed, or may fail, to comply with any provision of this Part of this Act, and

(*b*) that any such failure is likely to have led, or to lead, to serious prejudice to the proper assessment or collection of tax.[1]

Amendments—[1] Paras 26–31 repealed by the Finance Act 2009, Section 96 and Schedule 48 (Appointed Day, Savings and Consequential Amendments) Order, SI 2009/3054 art 3, Schedule para 11(1), (6)(*a*) with effect from 1 April 2010.

Contents of notice

29 *A notice under paragraph 28 must—*

(*a*) specify or describe the documents or information to which it relates, and (*b*) require the documents to be delivered or the information to be provided within such time as may be specified in the notice.[1]

Amendments—[1] Paras 26–31 repealed by the Finance Act 2009, Section 96 and Schedule 48 (Appointed Day, Savings and Consequential Amendments) Order, SI 2009/3054 art 3, Schedule para 11(1), (6)(*a*) with effect from 1 April 2010.

Power to take copies of documents etc

30 *The person to whom documents are delivered, or to whom information is provided, in pursuance of a notice under paragraph 28 may take copies of them or of extracts from them.*[1]

Amendments—[1] Paras 26–31 repealed by the Finance Act 2009, Section 96 and Schedule 48 (Appointed Day, Savings and Consequential Amendments) Order, SI 2009/3054 art 3, Schedule para 11(1), (6)(*a*) with effect from 1 April 2010.

Exclusion of personal records or journalistic material

31—*(1) This Part of this Schedule does not apply to documents that are personal records or journalistic material.*

(2) In sub-paragraph (1)—

"personal records" means personal records as defined in section 12 of the Police and Criminal Evidence Act 1984 (c 60) or, in Northern Ireland, in Article 14 of the Police and Criminal Evidence (Northern Ireland) Order 1989 (SI 1989/1341 (NI 12)); and

"journalistic material" means journalistic material as defined in section 13 of that Act or, in Northern Ireland, in Article 15 of that Order.[1]

PART 6
ORDER OF JUDICIAL AUTHORITY FOR THE DELIVERY OF DOCUMENTS

Order for the delivery of documents

32—(1) The appropriate judicial authority may make an order under this paragraph if satisfied on information on oath given by an authorised officer of the Board—

(*a*) that there is reasonable ground for suspecting that an offence involving serious fraud in connection with, or in relation to, stamp duty land tax has been or is about to be committed, and

(*b*) that documents that may be required as evidence for the purposes of any proceedings in respect of such an offence are or may be in the power or possession of any person.

(2) An order under this paragraph is an order requiring the person who appears to the authority to have in his possession or power the documents specified or described in the order to deliver them to an officer of the Board within—

(*a*) ten working days after the day on which notice of the order is served on him, or

(*b*) such shorter or longer period as may be specified in the order.

For this purpose a "working day" means any day other than a Saturday, Sunday or public holiday.

(3) The appropriate judicial authority is—

(*a*) in England and Wales, a circuit judge;

(*b*) in Scotland, a sheriff;

(*c*) in Northern Ireland, a county court judge.

(4) Where in Scotland the information relates to persons residing or having places of business at addresses situated in different sheriffdoms—

(*a*) an application for an order may be made to the sheriff for the sheriffdom in which any of the addresses is situated, and

(*b*) where the sheriff makes an order in respect of a person residing or having a place of business in his own sheriffdom, he may also make orders in respect of all or any of the other persons to whom the information relates (whether or not they have an address within the sheriffdom).

(5) In sub-paragraph (1) an "authorised officer of the Board" means an officer of the Board authorised by the Board for the purposes of this Part of this Schedule.

(6) The Inland Revenue may make provision by regulations as to—

(*a*) the procedures for approving in any particular case the decision to apply for an order under this Part of this Schedule, and

(*b*) the descriptions of officer by whom such approval may be given.

Notice of application for order

33—(1) A person is entitled—

(*a*) to notice of the intention to apply for an order against him under paragraph 32, and

(*b*) to appear and be heard at the hearing of the application,

unless the appropriate judicial authority is satisfied that this would seriously prejudice the investigation of the offence.

(2) The Inland Revenue may make provision by regulations as to the notice to be given, the contents of the notice and the manner of giving it.

Obligations of person given notice of application

34—(1) A person who has been given notice of intention to apply for an order under paragraph 32 must not—

(*a*) conceal, destroy, alter or dispose of any document to which the application relates, or

(*b*) disclose to any other person information or any other matter likely to prejudice the investigation of the offence to which the application relates.

This is subject to the following qualifications.

(2) Sub-paragraph (1)(*a*) does not prevent anything being done—

(*a*) with the leave of the appropriate judicial authority,

(*b*) with the written permission of an officer of the Board,

(*c*) after the application has been dismissed or abandoned, or

(*d*) after any order made on the application has been complied with.

(3) Sub-paragraph (1)(*b*) does not prevent a professional legal adviser from disclosing any information or other matter—

(*a*) to, or to a representative of, a client of his in connection with the giving by the adviser of legal advice to the client, or

(*b*) to any person—

(i) in contemplation or, or in connection with, legal proceedings, and

(ii) for the purposes of those proceedings.

This sub-paragraph does not apply in relation to any information or other matter that is disclosed with a view to furthering a criminal purpose.

(4) A person who fails to comply with the obligation in sub-paragraph (1)(*a*) or (*b*) may be dealt with as if he had failed to comply with an order under paragraph 32.

Exception of items subject to legal privilege

35—(1) This Part of this Schedule does not apply to items subject to legal privilege.

(2) Items "subject to legal privilege" means—

(*a*) communications between a professional legal adviser and his client or any person representing his client made in connection with the giving of legal advice to the client;

(*b*) communications between a professional legal adviser and his client or any person representing his client, or between such an adviser or his client or any such representative and any other person, made in connection with or in contemplation of legal proceedings and for the purposes of such proceedings;

(*c*) items enclosed with or referred to in such communications and made—

(i) in connection with the giving of legal advice, or

(ii) in connection with or in contemplation of legal proceedings and for the purposes of such proceedings,

when they are in possession of a person entitled to possession of them.

(3) Items held with the intention of furthering a criminal purpose are not subject to legal privilege.

Resolution of disputes as to legal privilege

36—(1) The Inland Revenue may make provision by regulations for the purposes of this Part of this Schedule for the resolution of disputes as to whether a document, or part of a document, is an item subject to legal privilege.

(2) The regulations may, in particular, make provision as to—

(*a*) the custody of the document whilst its status is being decided,

(*b*) the appointment of an independent, legally qualified person to decide the matter,

(*c*) the procedures to be followed, and

(*d*) who is to meet the costs of the proceedings.

Complying with an order

37—(1) The Inland Revenue may make provision by regulations as to how a person is to comply with an order under paragraph 32.

(2) The regulations may, in particular, make provision as to—

(*a*) the officer of the Board to whom the documents are to be produced,

(*b*) the address to which the documents are to be taken or sent, and

(*c*) the circumstances in which sending documents by post complies with the order.

(3) Where an order relates to a document in electronic or magnetic form, the order shall be taken to require the person to deliver the information recorded in the document in a form in which it is visible and legible.

Document not to be retained if photograph or copy sufficient

38 Where a document delivered to an officer of the Board under this Part of this Schedule is of such a nature that a photograph or copy of it would be sufficient—

(*a*) for use as evidence at a trial for an offence, or

(*b*) for forensic examination or for investigation in connection with an offence,

it shall not be retained longer than is necessary to establish that fact and to obtain the photograph or copy.

Access to or supply of photograph or copy of documents delivered

39—(1) If a request for permission to be granted access to a document that—

(*a*) has been delivered to an officer of the Board under this Part of this Schedule, and

(*b*) is retained by the Board for the purposes of investigating an offence,

is made to the officer in overall charge of the investigation by a person who had custody or control of the document immediately before it was so delivered, or by someone acting on behalf of any such person, the officer shall allow the person who made the request access to it under the supervision of an officer of the Board.

(2) If a request for a photograph or copy of any such document is made to the officer in overall charge of the investigation by a person who had custody or control of the document immediately before it was so delivered, or by someone acting on behalf of any such person, the officer shall—

(*a*) allow the person who made the request access to it under the supervision of an officer of the Board for the purpose of photographing or copying it, or

(*b*) photograph or copy it, or cause it to be photographed or copied.

(3) Where a document is photographed or copied under sub-paragraph (2)(*b*) the photograph or copy shall be supplied to the person who made the request.

(4) The photograph or copy shall be supplied within a reasonable time from the making of the request.

(5) There is no duty under this paragraph to grant access to, or to supply a photograph or copy of, a document if the officer in overall charge of the investigation for the purposes of which it was delivered has reasonable grounds for believing that to do so would prejudice—

(*a*) that investigation,

(*b*) the investigation of an offence other than the offence for the purposes of the investigation of which the document was delivered, or

(*c*) any criminal proceedings that may be brought as a result of—

(i) the investigation of which he is in charge, or

(ii) any such investigation as is mentioned in paragraph (*b*).

(6) The references in this paragraph to the officer in overall charge of the investigation is to the person whose name and address are endorsed on the order concerned as being the officer so in charge.

Sanction for failure to comply with order

40—(1) A person who fails to comply with an order under this Part of this Schedule may be dealt with as if he had committed a contempt of the court.

(2) For this purpose "the court" means—

(*a*) in relation to an order made by a circuit judge, the Crown Court;

(*b*) in relation to an order made by a sheriff, a sheriff court;

(*c*) in relation to an order made by a county court judge in Northern Ireland, a county court in Northern Ireland.

Notice of order, etc

41 The Inland Revenue may make provision by regulations as to the circumstances in which notice of an order under paragraph 32, or of an application for such an order, is to be treated as having been given.

General provisions about regulations

42 Regulations under this Part of this Schedule may contain such incidental, supplementary and transitional provision as appears to the Inland Revenue to be appropriate.

PART 7
ENTRY WITH WARRANT TO OBTAIN EVIDENCE OF OFFENCE

Amendments—Part 7 (paras 43–52) repealed by FA 2007 ss 84(4), 114, Sch 22 paras 3, 16, Sch 27 Pt 5(1) with effect from 1 December 2007 by virtue of SI 2007/3166 art 3.

Note that, although SI 2007/3166 does not specifically commence FA 2007 Sch 22, the relevant Government department has confirmed to the publisher that the commencement of s 84(4) takes with it Sch 22.

Power to issue warrant

43—*(1) The appropriate judicial authority, if satisfied on information on oath given by an officer of the Board that—*

(a) there is reasonable ground for suspecting that an offence involving serious fraud in connection with, or in relation to, tax is being, has been or is about to be committed and that evidence of it is to be found on premises specified in the information, and

(b) in applying under this paragraph the officer acts with the approval of the Board given in relation to the particular case,

may issue a warrant in writing authorising an officer of the Board to enter the premises, if necessary by force, at any time within 14 days from the time of issue of the warrant, and search them.

(2) The appropriate judicial authority is—

(a) in England and Wales, a circuit judge;

(b) in Scotland, a sheriff;

(c) in Northern Ireland, a county court judge.

(3) Where in Scotland the information relates to premises situated in different sheriffdoms—

(a) petitions for the issue of warrants in respect of all the premises to which the information relates may be made to the sheriff for a sheriffdom in which any of the premises is situated, and

(b) where the sheriff issues a warrant in respect of premises situated in his own sheriffdom, he shall also have jurisdiction to issue warrants in respect of all or any of the other premises to which the information relates.

This does not affect any power or jurisdiction of a sheriff to issue a warrant in respect of an offence committed within his own sheriffdom.

Amendments—Part 7 (paras 43–52) repealed by FA 2007 ss 84(4), 114, Sch 22 paras 3, 16, Sch 27 Pt 5(1) with effect from 1 December 2007 by virtue of SI 2007/3166 art 3.

Note that, although SI 2007/3166 does not specifically commence FA 2007 Sch 22, the relevant Government department has confirmed to the publisher that the commencement of s 84(4) takes with it Sch 22.

Meaning of offence involving serious fraud

44—*(1) An offence that involves fraud is for the purposes of this Part of this Schedule an offence involving serious fraud if its commission has led, or is intended or likely to lead, either—*

(a) to substantial financial gain to any person, or

(b) to serious prejudice to the proper assessment or collection of tax.

(2) An offence that, if considered alone, would not be regarded as involving serious fraud may nevertheless be so regarded if there is reasonable ground for suspecting that it forms part of a course of conduct that is, or but for its detection would be, likely to result in serious prejudice to the proper assessment or collection of tax.

(3) Sub-paragraphs (1) and (2) are without prejudice to the general concept of serious fraud.

Amendments—Part 7 (paras 43–52) repealed by FA 2007 ss 84(4), 114, Sch 22 paras 3, 16, Sch 27 Pt 5(1) with effect from 1 December 2007 by virtue of SI 2007/3166 art 3.

Note that, although SI 2007/3166 does not specifically commence FA 2007 Sch 22, the relevant Government department has confirmed to the publisher that the commencement of s 84(4) takes with it Sch 22.

Approval of application by Board

45—*(1) The Board shall not approve an application for a warrant under this Part of this Schedule unless they have reasonable grounds for believing that use of the procedure under Part 6 of this Schedule (order for delivery of documents) might seriously prejudice the investigation.*

(2) Section 4A of the Inland Revenue Regulation Act 1890 (c 21) (Board's functions exercisable by an officer acting under their authority) does not apply to the giving of Board approval under this paragraph.

Amendments—Part 7 (paras 43–52) repealed by FA 2007 ss 84(4), 114, Sch 22 paras 3, 16, Sch 27 Pt 5(1) with effect from 1 December 2007 by virtue of SI 2007/3166 art 3.

Note that, although SI 2007/3166 does not specifically commence FA 2007 Sch 22, the relevant Government department has confirmed to the publisher that the commencement of s 84(4) takes with it Sch 22.

Extent of powers conferred by warrant

46 *The powers conferred by a warrant under this Part of this Schedule are not exercisable—*

(a) *by more than such number of officers of the Board as may be specified in the warrant,*
(b) *outside such times of day as may be so specified, and*
(c) *if the warrant so provides, otherwise than in the presence of a constable in uniform.*

Amendments—Part 7 (paras 43–52) repealed by FA 2007 ss 84(4), 114, Sch 22 paras 3, 16, Sch 27 Pt 5(1) with effect from 1 December 2007 by virtue of SI 2007/3166 art 3.

Note that, although SI 2007/3166 does not specifically commence FA 2007 Sch 22, the relevant Government department has confirmed to the publisher that the commencement of s 84(4) takes with it Sch 22.

Exercise of powers conferred by warrant

47—*(1) An officer of the Board seeking to exercise the powers conferred by a warrant under this Part of this Schedule or, if there is more than one such officer, the one who is in charge of the search—*
(a) *if the occupier of the premises concerned is present at the time the search is to begin, shall supply a copy of the warrant endorsed with his name to the occupier;*
(b) *if at that time the occupier is not present but a person who appears to the officer to be in charge of the premises is present, shall supply such a copy to that person; and*
(c) *if neither paragraph (a) nor paragraph (b) applies, shall leave such a copy in a prominent place on the premises.*

(2) An officer who enters the premises under the authority of a warrant under this Part of this Schedule may—
(a) *take with him such other persons as appear to him to be necessary,*
(b) *seize and remove any things whatsoever found there that he has reasonable cause to believe may be required as evidence for the purposes of proceedings in respect of such an offence as is mentioned in paragraph 43(1), and*
(c) *search or cause to be searched any person found on the premises whom he has reasonable cause to believe to be in possession of such things.*

But no person shall be searched except by a person of the same sex.

(3) In the case of information contained in a computer that—
(a) *an officer who enters the premises as mentioned in sub-paragraph (2) has reasonable cause to believe may be required as evidence for the purposes mentioned in paragraph (b) of that sub-paragraph, and*
(b) *is accessible from the premises,*

the power of seizure under that sub-paragraph includes a power to require the information to be produced in a form in which it can be taken away and in which it is visible and legible.

Amendments—Part 7 (paras 43–52) repealed by FA 2007 ss 84(4), 114, Sch 22 paras 3, 16, Sch 27 Pt 5(1) with effect from 1 December 2007 by virtue of SI 2007/3166 art 3.

Note that, although SI 2007/3166 does not specifically commence FA 2007 Sch 22, the relevant Government department has confirmed to the publisher that the commencement of s 84(4) takes with it Sch 22.

Items subject to legal privilege

48—*(1) Nothing in this Part of this Schedule authorises the seizure of items subject to legal privilege.*

(2) Items "subject to legal privilege" means—
(a) *communications between a professional legal adviser and his client or any person representing his client made in connection with the giving of legal advice to the client;*
(b) *communications between a professional legal adviser and his client or any person representing his client, or between such an adviser or his client or any such representative and any other person, made in connection with or in contemplation of legal proceedings and for the purposes of such proceedings;*
(c) *items enclosed with or referred to in such communications and made—*
  (i) in connection with the giving of legal advice, or
  (ii) in connection with or in contemplation of legal proceedings and for the purposes of such proceedings,

when they are in possession of a person entitled to possession of them.

(3) Items held with the intention of furthering a criminal purpose are not subject to legal privilege.

Amendments—Part 7 (paras 43–52) repealed by FA 2007 ss 84(4), 114, Sch 22 paras 3, 16, Sch 27 Pt 5(1) with effect from 1 December 2007 by virtue of SI 2007/3166 art 3.

Note that, although SI 2007/3166 does not specifically commence FA 2007 Sch 22, the relevant Government department has confirmed to the publisher that the commencement of s 84(4) takes with it Sch 22.

Procedure where documents etc are removed

49—*(1) An officer of the Board who removes anything in the exercise of the powers conferred by this Part of this Schedule shall, if so requested by a person showing himself—*

(a) to be the occupier of the premises from which it was removed, or

(b) to have had custody or control of it immediately before the removal,

provide that person with a record of what he removed.

(2) The officer of the Board shall provide the record within a reasonable time from the making of the request for it.

Amendments—Part 7 (paras 43–52) repealed by FA 2007 ss 84(4), 114, Sch 22 paras 3, 16, Sch 27 Pt 5(1) with effect from 1 December 2007 by virtue of SI 2007/3166 art 3.

Note that, although SI 2007/3166 does not specifically commence FA 2007 Sch 22, the relevant Government department has confirmed to the publisher that the commencement of s 84(4) takes with it Sch 22.

Document not to be retained if photograph or copy sufficient

50 *Where anything that has been removed by an officer of the Board as mentioned in paragraph 49 is of such a nature that a photograph or copy of it would be sufficient—*

(a) for use as evidence at a trial for an offence, or

(b) for forensic examination or for investigation in connection with an offence,

it shall not be retained longer than is necessary to establish that fact and to obtain the photograph or copy.

Amendments—Part 7 (paras 43–52) repealed by FA 2007 ss 84(4), 114, Sch 22 paras 3, 16, Sch 27 Pt 5(1) with effect from 1 December 2007 by virtue of SI 2007/3166 art 3.

Note that, although SI 2007/3166 does not specifically commence FA 2007 Sch 22, the relevant Government department has confirmed to the publisher that the commencement of s 84(4) takes with it Sch 22.

Access to or supply of photograph or copy of items removed

51—*(1) If a request for permission to be granted access to anything that—*

(a) has been removed by an officer of the Board, and

(b) is retained by the Board for the purposes of investigating an offence,

is made to the officer in overall charge of the investigation by a person who had custody or control of the thing immediately before it was so removed or by someone acting on behalf of any such person, the officer shall allow the person who made the request access to it under the supervision of an officer of the Board.

(2) If a request for a photograph or copy of any such thing is made to the officer in overall charge of the investigation by a person who has custody or control of the thing immediately before it was so removed, or by someone acting on behalf of any such person, the officer shall—

(a) allow the person who made the request access to it under the supervision of an officer of the Board for the purpose of photographing or copying it, or

(b) photograph or copy it, or cause it to be photographed or copied.

(3) Where anything is photographed or copied under sub-paragraph (2)(b) the photograph or copy shall be supplied to the person who made the request.

(4) The photograph or copy shall be supplied within a reasonable time from the making of the request.

(5) There is no duty under this paragraph to grant access to, or to supply a photograph or copy of, anything if the officer in overall charge of the investigation for the purposes of which it was removed has reasonable grounds for believing that to do so would prejudice—

(a) that investigation,

(b) the investigation of an offence other than the offence for the purposes of the investigation of which the thing was removed, or

(c) any criminal proceedings that may be brought as a result of—

(i) the investigation of which he is in charge, or

(ii) any such investigation as is mentioned in paragraph (b).

(6) The references in this paragraph to the officer in overall charge of the investigation is to the person whose name and address are endorsed on the warrant concerned as being the officer so in charge.

Amendments—Part 7 (paras 43–52) repealed by FA 2007 ss 84(4), 114, Sch 22 paras 3, 16, Sch 27 Pt 5(1) with effect from 1 December 2007 by virtue of SI 2007/3166 art 3.

Note that, although SI 2007/3166 does not specifically commence FA 2007 Sch 22, the relevant Government department has confirmed to the publisher that the commencement of s 84(4) takes with it Sch 22.

Endorsement and custody etc of warrant

52—*(1) Where entry has been made with a warrant under this Part of this Schedule, and the officer making the entry has seized any things under the authority of the warrant, he shall endorse on or attach to the warrant a list of the things seized.*

(2) The following provisions (which relate to return, retention and inspection of warrants), that is—

(a) in England and Wales, section 16(10) to (12) of the Police and Criminal Evidence Act 1984 (c 60), and

(b) in Northern Ireland, Article 18(10) to (12) of the Police and Criminal Evidence (Northern Ireland) Order 1989 (SI 1989/1341 (NI 12)),

apply to a warrant under this Part of this Schedule (together with any list endorsed on or attached to it under sub-paragraph (1)) as they apply to a warrant issued to a constable under any enactment.

Amendments—Part 7 (paras 43–52) repealed by FA 2007 ss 84(4), 114, Sch 22 paras 3, 16, Sch 27 Pt 5(1) with effect from 1 December 2007 by virtue of SI 2007/3166 art 3.

Note that, although SI 2007/3166 does not specifically commence FA 2007 Sch 22, the relevant Government department has confirmed to the publisher that the commencement of s 84(4) takes with it Sch 22.

PART 8

FALSIFICATION ETC OF DOCUMENTS

Falsification etc of documents

53—(1) A person commits an offence if he intentionally—

(*a*) falsifies, conceals, destroys or otherwise disposes of, or

(*b*) causes or permits the falsification, concealment, destruction or disposal of,

a document to which this paragraph applies.

(2) This paragraph applies to any document that the person—

(*a*) has been required by a notice under Part [3][2] of this Schedule, or an order under Part 6 of this Schedule, to deliver, or to deliver or make available for inspection, or

(*b*) has been given an opportunity in accordance with paragraph . . . [2] 14(3) to deliver, or to deliver or make available for inspection.

(3) A person does not commit an offence under this paragraph if he acts—

(*a*) with the written permission of [the tribunal][1] or an officer of the Board,

(*b*) . . . [2] or

(*c*) after a copy has been delivered in accordance with paragraph 23(1) or 27(3) and the original has been inspected.

(4) A person does not commit an offence under this paragraph as it applies by virtue of sub-paragraph (2)(*a*) if he acts after the end of the period of two years beginning with the date on which the notice is given or the order is made, unless before the end of that period an officer of the Board has notified the person, in writing, that the notice or order has not been complied with to his satisfaction.

(5) A person does not commit an offence under this paragraph as it applies by virtue of sub-paragraph (2)(*b*) if he acts—

(*a*) after the end of the period of six months beginning with the date on which an opportunity to deliver the document was given, or

(*b*) after an application for consent to a notice being given in relation to the document has been refused.

(6) A person guilty of an offence under this paragraph is liable—

(*a*) on summary conviction, to a fine not exceeding the statutory maximum;

(*b*) on conviction on indictment, to imprisonment for a term not exceeding two years or a fine or to both.

Amendments—[1] In sub-para (3)(a) words substituted for the words "a General or Special Commissioner" by the Transfer of Tribunal Functions and Revenue and Customs Appeals Order, SI 2009/56 art 3, Sch 1 para 409 with effect from 1 April 2009.

[2] In sub-para (2)(a), reference substituted for words "1, 2, 3 or 5", in sub-para (2)(b), words "1(3), 6(3), 11(3) or" repealed, and sub-para (3)(*b*) repealed, by the Finance Act 2009, Section 96 and Schedule 48 (Appointed Day, Savings and Consequential Amendments) Order, SI 2009/3054 art 3, Schedule para 11(1), (6)(*I*)–(*k*) with effect from 1 April 2010. Sub-para (3)(b) previously read as follows—

"(b) after the document has been delivered or, in a case within Part 2 of this Schedule, inspected,".

SCHEDULE 14

STAMP DUTY LAND TAX: DETERMINATION OF PENALTIES AND RELATED APPEALS

Section 99

HMRC Manuals—Stamp Duty Land Tax Manual SDLTM86530–86640 (Revenue practice on contract settlements and abatement).

SDLTM86710–86740 (determination of penalties under this Schedule).

Determination of penalties and appeals

1 The provisions of this Schedule apply in relation to penalties under this Part of this Act.

Determination of penalty by officer of the Board

2—(1) An officer of the Board authorised for the purposes of this paragraph may make a determination—

(*a*) imposing the penalty, and

(*b*) setting it at such amount as in the officer's opinion is correct or appropriate.

(2) Notice of the determination must be served on the person liable to the penalty.

(3) The notice must also state—

(*a*) the date on which the notice is issued, and

(*b*) the time within which an appeal against the determination may be made.

(4) A penalty determined under this paragraph is due and payable at the end of the period of 30 days beginning with the date of issue of the notice of determination.

(5) Where an officer of the Board has decided to impose a penalty, and has taken all other decisions needed for arriving at the amount of the penalty, he may entrust to any other officer of the Board responsibility for completing the determination procedure, whether by means involving the use of a computer or otherwise, including responsibility for serving notice of the determination.

Alteration of penalty determination

3—(1) After notice has been served of the determination of a penalty, the determination cannot be altered except in accordance with this paragraph or on appeal.

(2) If it is discovered by an authorised officer that the amount of the penalty is or has become insufficient, the officer may make a determination in a further amount so that the penalty is set at the amount which in the officer's opinion is correct or appropriate.

(3) If in the case of a tax-related penalty it is discovered by an authorised officer that the amount taken into account as the amount of tax is or has become excessive, he may revise the determination so that the penalty is set at the amount that is correct.

Where more than the correct amount has already been paid the appropriate amount shall be repaid.

(4) In this paragraph an "authorised officer" means an officer of the Board authorised by the Board for the purposes of this paragraph.

Liability of personal representatives

4 If a person liable to a penalty has died—

(*a*) any determination that could have been made in relation to that person may be made in relation to his personal representatives, and

(*b*) any penalty imposed on them is a debt due from and payable out of the person's estate.

Appeal against penalty determination

5—(1) An appeal [may be made][1] against the determination of a penalty.

(2) Notice of appeal must be given in writing to the officer of the Board by whom the determination was made within 30 days of the date of issue of the notice of determination.

[(3) The notice of appeal must specify the grounds of appeal.][1]

(4) On an appeal under this paragraph [that is notified to the First-tier Tribunal, the tribunal][1] may—

(*a*) if it appears . . . [1] that no penalty has been incurred, set the determination aside;

(*b*) if the amount determined appears . . . [1] to be appropriate, confirm the determination;

(*c*) if the amount determined appears to them to be excessive, reduce it to such other amount (including nil) as appears to them to be appropriate;

(*d*) if the amount determined appears to them to be insufficient, increase it to such amount, not exceeding the permitted maximum, [as the First-tier Tribunal considers appropriate][1].

[(5) The provisions of paragraphs 36A to 36I of Schedule 10 apply to appeals under this paragraph.][1]

Amendments—[1] In sub-para (1) words substituted for the words "lies to the General or Special Commissioners"; sub-para (3) substituted; in sub-para (4) words substituted for the words "the Commissioners"; in sub-para (4)(a), (b) words "to them" repealed in both places; in sub-para (4)(d) words substituted for the words "as they consider appropriate"; sub-para (5) inserted by the Transfer of Tribunal Functions and Revenue and Customs Appeals Order, SI 2009/56 art 3, Sch 1 para 411 with effect from 1 April 2009. Sub-para (3) previously read as follows—

"(3) The notice of appeal must specify the grounds of appeal, but on the hearing of the appeal the Commissioners may allow the appellant to put forward a ground not specified in the notice of appeal, and take it into consideration, if satisfied that the omission was not deliberate or unreasonable.".

Further appeal

6—[(1) In addition to any right of appeal on a point of law under section 11(2) of the Tribunals, Courts and Enforcement Act 2007, the person liable to the penalty may appeal to the Upper Tribunal against the amount of the penalty which has been determined under paragraph (5), but not against any decision which falls under section 11(5)(*d*) or (*e*) of that Act and was made in connection with the determination of the amount of the penalty.
(1A) Section 11(3) and (4) of the Tribunals, Courts and Enforcement Act 2007 applies to the right of appeal under sub-paragraph (1) as it applies to the right of appeal under section 11(2) of that Act.][1]
(2) On an appeal under this paragraph the [Upper Tribunal][1] has the same powers as are conferred on the [First-tier Tribunal][1] by paragraph 5(4) above.
(3) . . . [1]

Amendments—[1] Sub-paras (1), (1A) substituted for former sub-para (1); in sub-para (2) words in the first place substituted for the word "court" and in the second place substituted for the word "Commissioners"; sub-para (3) repealed by the Transfer of Tribunal Functions and Revenue and Customs Appeals Order, SI 2009/56 art 3, Sch 1 para 4128 with effect from 1 April 2009. Sub-paras (1), (3) previously read as follows—

"(1) An appeal lies against the amount of a penalty determined by the Commissioners on an appeal under paragraph 5, at the instance of the person liable to the penalty—
(*a*) to the High Court, or
(*b*) in Scotland, to the Court of Session sitting as the Court of Exchequer."

"(3) The right of appeal under this paragraph is in addition to any right of appeal conferred by regulations under paragraph 9 of Schedule 17 (general power to provide for appeals on points of law).".

Penalty proceedings before the court

7—(1) Where in the opinion of the Board the liability of a person for a penalty arises by reason of his fraud, or the fraud of another person, proceedings for the penalty may be brought—
(*a*) in the High Court, or
(*b*) in Scotland, in the Court of Session sitting as the Court of Exchequer.
(2) Proceedings under this paragraph in England and Wales shall be brought—
(*a*) by and in the name of the Board as an authorised department for the purposes of the Crown Proceedings Act 1947 (c 44), or
(*b*) in the name of the Attorney General.
Any such proceedings shall be deemed to be civil proceedings by the Crown within the meaning of Part 2 of the Crown Proceedings Act 1947.
(3) Proceedings under this paragraph in Scotland shall be brought in the name of the Advocate General for Scotland.
(4) Proceedings under this paragraph in Northern Ireland shall be brought—
(*a*) by and in the name of the Board as an authorised department for the purposes of the Crown Proceedings Act 1947 as for the time being in force in Northern Ireland, or
(*b*) in the name of the Advocate General for Northern Ireland.
Any such proceedings shall be deemed to be civil proceedings within the meaning of Part 2 of the Crown Proceedings Act 1947 as for the time being in force in Northern Ireland.
(5) If in proceedings under this paragraph the court does not find that fraud is proved but considers that the person concerned is nevertheless liable to a penalty, the court may determine a penalty notwithstanding that, but for the opinion of the Board as to fraud, the penalty would not have been a matter for the court.
(6) Paragraph 2 (determination of penalty by officer of the Board) does not apply where proceedings are brought under this paragraph.
(7) In relation to any time before the coming into force of section 2(1) of the Justice (Northern Ireland) Act 2002 (c 26), the reference in sub-paragraph (4)(*b*) to the Advocate General for Northern Ireland shall be read as a reference to the Attorney General for Northern Ireland.

Time limit for determination of penalties

8—(1) The following time limits apply in relation to the determination of penalties under this Schedule.
(2) The general rule is that—
(*a*) no penalty may be determined under paragraph 2 (determination by officer of Board), and
(*b*) no proceedings for a penalty may be brought under paragraph 7 (penalty proceedings before the court),
more than six years after the date on which the penalty was incurred or, in the case of a daily penalty, began to be incurred.
This rule is subject to the following provisions of this paragraph.

(3) Where the amount of a penalty is to be ascertained by reference to the tax chargeable in respect of a transaction, a penalty may be determined under paragraph 2, or proceedings for a penalty may be begun under paragraph 7, at any time within three years after the final determination of the amount of tax by reference to which the amount of the penalty is to be determined.

(4) Sub-paragraph (3) does not apply where a person has died and the determination would be made in relation to his personal representatives if the tax was charged in an assessment made more than six years after the effective date of the transaction to which it relates.

(5) A penalty under section 96 (penalty for assisting in preparation of incorrect return) may be determined by an officer of the Board, or proceedings for such a penalty may be commenced before a court, at any time within 20 years after the date on which the penalty was incurred.

Prospective amendments—In sub-para (2) words "4 years" to be substituted for the words "six years" and words "("the relevant date")" to be inserted after the words "began to be incurred", in sub-para (3) words "(subject to any of the following provisions of this paragraph allowing a longer period)" to be inserted at the end, and sub-paras (4A)–(4C) to be inserted, by FA 2009 s 99, Sch 51 paras 14, 16 with effect from 1 April 2011 (SI 2010/867 art 2(2)). New sub-paras (4A)–(4C) read as follows—

"(4A) Where a person is liable to a penalty in a case involving a loss of tax brought about carelessly by the person (or by another person acting on that person's behalf), the penalty may be determined, or the proceedings may be brought, at any time not more than 6 years after the relevant date (subject to sub-paragraphs (4B) and (5)).

(4B) Where a person is liable to a penalty in a case involving a loss of tax—

(*a*) brought about deliberately by the person (or by another person acting on that person's behalf),

(*b*) attributable to a failure by the person to comply with an obligation under section 76(1) or paragraph 3(3)(*a*), 4(3)(*a*) or 8(3)(*a*) of Schedule 17A, or

(*c*) attributable to arrangements in respect of which the person has failed to comply with an obligation under section 309, 310 or 313 of the Finance Act 2004 (obligation of parties to tax avoidance schemes to provide information to Her Majesty's Revenue and Customs),

the penalty may be determined, or the proceedings may be brought, at any time not more than 20 years after the relevant date.

(4C) Paragraph 31A of Schedule 10 (losses brought about carelessly or deliberately) applies for the purpose of this paragraph.".

Note that where a person incurs a penalty on or before 31 March 2011 under Part 4 of FA 2003, and the case involves a loss of tax arising in one of the circumstances specified in sub-para (4B) (as inserted from 1 April 2011), the amendments to sub-paras (2) and the insertion of sub-paras (4A)–(4C) by FA 2009 Sch 51 para 16(2), (4) are to be disregarded (SI 2010/867 art 7).

SCHEDULE 15

STAMP DUTY LAND TAX: PARTNERSHIPS

Section 104

PART 1

GENERAL PROVISIONS

Partnerships

1 In this Part of this Act a "partnership" means—

(*a*) a partnership within the Partnership Act 1890 (c 39),

(*b*) a limited partnership registered under the Limited Partnerships Act 1907 (c 24), or

(*c*) a limited liability partnership formed under the Limited Liability Partnerships Act 2000 (c 12) or the Limited Liability Partnerships Act (Northern Ireland) 2002 (c 12 (NI)),

or a firm or entity of a similar character to any of those mentioned above formed under the law of a country or territory outside the United Kingdom.

Legal personality of partnership disregarded

2—(1) For the purposes of this Part of this Act—

(*a*) a chargeable interest held by or on behalf of a partnership is treated as held by or on behalf of the partners, and

(*b*) a land transaction entered into for the purposes of a partnership is treated as entered into by or on behalf of the partners,

and not by or on behalf of the partnership as such.

(2) Sub-paragraph (1) applies notwithstanding that the partnership is regarded as a legal person, or as a body corporate, under the law of the country or territory under which it is formed.

Continuity of partnership

3 For the purposes of this Part of this Act a partnership is treated as the same partnership notwithstanding a change in membership if any person who was a member before the change remains a member after the change.

Partnership not to be regarded as unit trust scheme etc

4 A partnership is not to be regarded for the purposes of this Part of this Act as a unit trust scheme or an open ended investment company.

PART 2
ORDINARY PARTNERSHIP TRANSACTIONS

Introduction

5—(1) This Part of this Schedule applies to transactions entered into as purchaser by or on behalf of the members of a partnership, other than transactions within Part 3 of this Schedule [(transactions to which special provisions apply)][1].

Amendments—[1] Words substituted for the words "(transactions excluded from stamp duty land tax)" by FA 2004 s 304, Sch 41 paras 2(c), 3 with effect for any partnership transaction of which the effective date (within the meaning of FA 2003 Pt 4) is after 22 July 2004. A "partnership transaction" means a transaction mentioned in FA 2003 Sch 15 para 9(1): FA 2004 Sch 41 para 3(2).

Responsibility of partners

6—(1) Anything required or authorised to be done under this Part of this Act by or in relation to the purchaser under the transaction is required or authorised to be done by or in relation to all the responsible partners.

(2) The responsible partners in relation to a transaction are—

(*a*) the persons who are partners at the effective date of the transaction, and

(*b*) any person who becomes a member of the partnership after the effective date of the transaction.

(3) This paragraph has effect subject to paragraph 8 (representative partners).

Joint and several liability of responsible partners

7—(1) Where the responsible partners are liable—

(*a*) to make a payment of tax or to interest on unpaid tax,

(*b*) to make a payment in accordance with an assessment under paragraph 29 of Schedule 10 (recovery of excessive repayment), or

(*c*) to a penalty under this Part of this Act or to interest on such a penalty,

the liability is a joint and several liability of those partners.

[(1A) No amount may be recovered by virtue of sub-paragraph (1)(*a*) or (*b*) from a person who did not become a responsible partner until after the effective date of the transaction in respect of which the tax is payable.][1]

(2) No amount may be recovered by virtue of sub-paragraph (1)(*c*) from a person who did not become a responsible partner until after the relevant time.

(3) The relevant time for this purpose is—

(*a*) in relation to so much of a penalty as is payable in respect of any day, or to interest on so much of a penalty as is so payable, the beginning of that day;

(*b*) in relation to any other penalty, or interest on such a penalty, the time when the act or omission occurred that caused the penalty to become payable.

Amendments—[1] Sub-para (1A) inserted by FA 2004 s 305 with effect from 22 July 2004.

Representative partners

8—(1) Anything required or authorised to be done by or in relation to the responsible partners may instead be done by or in relation to any representative partner or partners.

(2) This includes making the declaration required by paragraph 1(1)(*c*) of Schedule 10 . . . [1] (declaration that return . . . [1] is complete and correct).

(3) A representative partner means a partner nominated by a majority of the partners to act as the representative of the partnership for the purposes of this Part of this Act.

(4) Any such nomination, or the revocation of such a nomination, has effect only after notice of the nomination, or revocation, has been given to the Inland Revenue.

Amendments—[1] Words in sub-para (2) repealed by FA 2008 s 94, Sch 30 para 12 with effect in relation to transactions with an effective date on or after 12 March 2008.

[PART 3
TRANSACTIONS TO WHICH SPECIAL PROVISIONS APPLY][1]

Amendments—[1] This Part substituted by FA 2004 s 304, Sch 41 paras 1, 3 with effect for any partnership transaction of which the effective date (within the meaning of FA 2003 Pt 4) is after 22 July 2004. A "partnership transaction" means a transaction mentioned in FA 2003 Sch 15 para 9(1): FA 2004 Sch 41 para 3(2).

[Introduction

9—(1) This Part of this Schedule applies to certain transactions involving—

(*a*) the transfer of a chargeable interest to a partnership (paragraph 10),

(*b*) the transfer of an interest in a partnership (paragraphs 14, 17, 31 and 32), or

(*c*) the transfer of a chargeable interest from a partnership (paragraph 18).

(2) References in this Part of this Schedule to the transfer of a chargeable interest include—

(*a*) the grant or creation of a chargeable interest,

(*b*) the variation of a chargeable interest, and

(*c*) the surrender, release or renunciation of a chargeable interest.][1]

Amendments—[1] This Part substituted by FA 2004 s 304, Sch 41 paras 1, 3 with effect for any partnership transaction of which the effective date (within the meaning of FA 2003 Pt 4) is after 22 July 2004. A "partnership transaction" means a transaction mentioned in sub para (1) above: FA 2004 Sch 41 para 3(2).

[Transfer of chargeable interest to a partnership: general

10—(1) This paragraph applies where—

(*a*) a partner transfers a chargeable interest to the partnership, or

(*b*) a person transfers a chargeable interest to a partnership in return for an interest in the partnership, or

(*c*) a person connected with—

(i) a partner, or

(ii) a person who becomes a partner as a result of or in connection with the transfer,

transfers a chargeable interest to the partnership.

It applies whether the transfer is in connection with the formation of the partnership or is a transfer to an existing partnership.

[(2) The chargeable consideration for the transaction shall (subject to paragraph 13) be taken to be equal to—

$$MV \times (100 - SLP)\%$$

where—

MV is the market value of the interest transferred, and

SLP is the sum of the lower proportions.][2]

(5) Paragraph 12 provides for determining the sum of the lower proportions.

(6) Paragraph 11 applies . . . [2] if the whole or part of the chargeable consideration for the transaction is rent.

(7) Paragraphs 6 to 8 (responsibility of partners) have effect in relation to a transaction to which this paragraph applies, but the responsible partners are—

(*a*) those who were partners immediately before the transfer and who remain partners after the transfer, and

(*b*) any person becoming a partner as a result of, or in connection with, the transfer.

[(8) This paragraph has effect subject to any election under paragraph 12A.][3]][1]

Cross references—See FA 2003 Sch 15 para 23 (sub-paras (2)–(5) above do not apply where there is a transfer of a chargeable interest from a partnership to a partnership, and none of the chargeable consideration is rent).

FA 2008 Sch 31 para 11 (application of sub-para (1)(*a*)–(*c*) to a transfer of a chargeable interest to a partnership where the effective date of the transaction is before 21 July 2008).

Modifications—FA 2003 Sch 15 para 13 (modification of this paragraph where there is a transfer of a chargeable interest to a partnership consisting wholly of bodies corporate).

Amendments—[1] This Part substituted by FA 2004 s 304, Sch 41 paras 1, 3 with effect for any partnership transaction of which the effective date (within the meaning of FA 2003 Pt 4) is after 22 July 2004. A "partnership transaction" means a transaction mentioned in FA 2003 Sch 15 para 9(1): FA 2004 Sch 41 para 3(2).

[2] Sub-para (2) substituted for sub-paras (2)–(4) and in sub-para (6), words "(instead of sub-paragraphs (2) to (5))" repealed by FA 2006 s 162, Sch 24 para 2, s 178, Sch 26 Pt 7(2) with effect in relation to any transfer of which the effective date (within the meaning of FA 2003 Pt 4) is on or after 19 July 2006.

[3] Sub-para (8) inserted by FA 2008 s 97, Sch 31 para 5 with effect from 21 July 2008.

[Transfer of chargeable interest to a partnership: chargeable consideration including rent

11—(1) This paragraph applies in relation to a transaction to which paragraph 10 applies where the whole or part of the chargeable consideration for the transaction is rent.

[(2) Schedule 5 (amount of tax chargeable: rent) has effect with the modifications set out in sub-paragraphs (2A) to (2C).

(2A) In paragraph 2—

(*a*) for "the net present value of the rent payable over the term of the lease" substitute "the relevant chargeable proportion of the net present value of the rent payable over the term of the lease", and (*b*) for "the net present values of the rent payable over the terms of all the leases" substitute "the relevant chargeable proportions of the net present values of the rent payable over the terms of all the leases".

(2B) In paragraph [9A(6)][3]—

(*a*) for "the annual rent" substitute "the relevant chargeable proportion of the annual rent", and

(*b*) for "the total of the annual rents" substitute "the relevant chargeable proportion of the total of the annual rents".

(2C) For paragraph 9(4) substitute—

"(4) Tax chargeable under this Schedule is in addition to any tax chargeable under section 55 as it has effect by virtue of paragraph 10 of Schedule 15.".

(2D) For the purposes of sub-paragraphs (2A) and (2B) the relevant chargeable proportion is—

$$(100 - SLP)\%$$

where SLP is the sum of the lower proportions.

. . .][2]

(8) Paragraph 12 provides for determining the sum of the lower proportions.

(9) This paragraph is subject to paragraph 13.][1]

Cross references—See FA 2003 Sch 15 para 23 (this paragraph does not apply where there is transfer of a chargeable interest from a partnership to a partnership, and the whole or part of the chargeable consideration is rent).

Modifications—FA 2003 Sch 15 para 13 (modification of this paragraph where there is a transfer of a chargeable interest to a partnership consisting wholly of bodies corporate).

Amendments—[1] This Part substituted by FA 2004 s 304, Sch 41 paras 1, 3 with effect for any partnership transaction of which the effective date (within the meaning of FA 2003 Pt 4) is after 22 July 2004. A "partnership transaction" means a transaction mentioned in FA 2003 Sch 15 para 9(1): FA 2004 Sch 41 para 3(2).

[2] Sub-paras (2)–(2D) substituted for former sub-paras (2)–(7) by FA 2006 s 162, Sch 24 para 3 with effect in relation to any transfer of which the effective date (within the meaning of FA 2003 Pt 4) is on or after 19 July 2006.

[3] Reference in sub-para (2B) substituted by FA 2008 s 95(11)(a) with effect in relation to transactions with an effective date on or after 12 March 2008.

[Transfer of chargeable interest to a partnership: sum of the lower proportions

12—(1) The sum of the lower proportions in relation to a transaction to which paragraph 10 applies is determined as follows:—

Step One

Identify the relevant owner or owners.

A person is a relevant owner if—

(*a*) immediately before the transaction, he was entitled to a proportion of the chargeable interest, and

(*b*) immediately after the transaction, he is a partner or connected with a partner.

Step Two

For each relevant owner, identify the corresponding partner or partners.

A person is a corresponding partner in relation to a relevant owner if, immediately after the transaction—

(*a*) he is a partner, and

(*b*) he is the relevant owner [or is an individual connected with the relevant owner][2].

[(If there is no relevant owner with a corresponding partner, the sum of the lower proportions is nil.)][2]

Step Three

For each relevant owner, find the proportion of the chargeable interest to which he was entitled immediately before the transaction.

Apportion that proportion between any one or more of the relevant owner's corresponding partners.

Step Four

Find the lower proportion for each person who is a corresponding partner in relation to one or more relevant owners.

The lower proportion is—

(*a*) the proportion of the chargeable interest attributable to the partner, or

(*b*) if lower, the partner's partnership share immediately after the transaction.

The proportion of the chargeable interest attributable to the partner is—

(i) if he is a corresponding partner in relation to only one relevant owner, the proportion (if any) of the chargeable interest apportioned to him (at Step Three) in respect of that owner;

(ii) if he is a corresponding partner in relation to more than one relevant owner, the sum of the proportions (if any) of the chargeable interest apportioned to him (at Step Three) in respect of each of those owners.

Step Five

Add together the lower proportions of each person who is a corresponding partner in relation to one or more relevant owners.

The result is the sum of the lower proportions.

(2) For the purposes of this paragraph persons who are entitled to a chargeable interest as beneficial joint tenants (or, in Scotland, as joint owners) shall be taken to be entitled to the chargeable interest as beneficial tenants in common (or, in Scotland, as owners in common) in equal shares.][1]

[(3) For the purpose of paragraph (*b*) of Step 2 a company is to be treated as an individual connected with the relevant owner in so far as it—

(*a*) holds property as trustee, and

(*b*) is connected with the relevant owner only because of [section 1122(6) of the Corporation Tax Act 2010][4].][3]

Amendments—[1] This Part substituted by FA 2004 s 304, Sch 41 paras 1, 3 with effect for any partnership transaction of which the effective date (within the meaning of FA 2003 Pt 4) is after 22 July 2004. A "partnership transaction" means a transaction mentioned in FA 2003 Sch 15 para 9(1): FA 2004 Sch 41 para 3(2).

[2] Words in sub-para (1) step two para (b) substituted, and words at end of step two para (b) inserted, by FA 2007 s 72(1)–(3) with effect in respect of transfers occurring on or after 19 July 2007: FA 2007 s 72(13).

The amendments are to this paragraph as it stood before amendment by the Stamp Duty Land Tax (Variation of the Finance Act 2003) Regulations, SI 2006/3237. The amendments, to the extent provided for by FA 2007 s 72(13)–(15), replace the amendments made by those regulations: see FA 2007 s 72(2), (16). However, the amendments by FA 2007 are subject to transitional provisions as provided by FA 2007 s 72(17).

[3] Sub-para (3) inserted by FA 2007 s 72(1), (2), (4) with effect in respect of transfers occurring on or after 19 July 2007: FA 2007 s 72(13).

[4] In sub-para (3)(*b*) words "section 839(3) of the Taxes Act 1988" substituted by CTA 2010 s 1177, Sch 1 paras 400, 418(1),(2). CTA 2010 has effect for corporation tax purposes for accounting periods ending on or after 1 April 2010, and for income and capital gains tax purposes for the tax year 2010–11 and subsequent tax years.

[Election by property-investment partnership to disapply paragraph 10

12A—(1) Paragraph 10 does not apply to a transfer of a chargeable interest to a property-investment partnership if the purchaser in relation to the transaction elects for that paragraph not to apply.

(2) Where an election under this paragraph is made in respect of a transaction—

(*a*) paragraph 18 (if relevant) is also disapplied,

(*b*) the chargeable consideration for the transaction shall be taken to be the market value of the chargeable interest transferred, and

(*c*) the transaction falls within Part 2 of this Schedule.

(3) An election under this paragraph must be included in the land transaction return made in respect of the transaction or in an amendment of that return.

(4) Such an election is irrevocable and a land transaction return may not be amended so as to withdraw the election.

(5) Where an election under this paragraph in respect of a transaction (the "main transaction") is made in an amendment of a land transaction return—

(*a*) the election has effect as if it had been made on the date on which the land transaction return was made, and

(*b*) any land transaction return in respect of an affected transaction may be amended (within the period allowed for amendment of that return) to take account of that election.

(6) In sub-paragraph (5) "affected transaction", in relation to the main transaction, means a transaction—

(*a*) to which paragraph 14 applied, and

(*b*) with an effective date on or after the effective date of the main transaction.

(7) In this paragraph "property-investment partnership" has the meaning given in paragraph 14(8).][1]

Amendments—[1] This para inserted by FA 2008 s 97, Sch 31 para 6 with effect from 21 July 2008.

[Transfer of chargeable interest to a partnership consisting wholly of bodies corporate

13 . . .

Amendment—This paragraph repealed by FA 2007 ss 72(1), (5), 114, Sch 27 Pt 4(1) with effect in respect of transfers occurring on or after 19 July 2007: FA 2007 s 72(13).

The repeal is in relation to this paragraph as it stood before amendment by the Stamp Duty Land Tax (Variation of the Finance Act 2003) Regulations, SI 2006/3237. The repeal, to the extent provided for by FA 2007 s 72(13)–(15), replaces the amendments made by those regulations: see FA 2007 s 72(2), (16). However, the repeal is subject to transitional provisions as provided by FA 2007 s 72(17).

[[Transfer . . . [3] of interest in property-investment partnership] [2]

14—(1) This paragraph applies where—

(*a*) there is a transfer of an interest in a [property-investment][2] partnership;

(*b*) ...[3]

(*c*) the relevant partnership property includes a chargeable interest.

(2) The transfer—

(*a*) shall be taken for the purposes of this Part to be a land transaction;

(*b*) is a chargeable transaction.

(3) The purchaser under the transaction is the person who acquires an increased partnership share or, as the case may be, becomes a partner in consequence of the transfer.

[(3A) A transfer to which this paragraph applies is a Type A transfer if it takes the form of arrangements entered into under which—

(*a*) the whole or part of a partner's interest as partner is acquired by another person (who may be an existing partner), and

(*b*) consideration in money or money's worth is given by or on behalf of the person acquiring the interest.

(3B) A transfer to which this paragraph applies is also a Type A transfer if it takes the form of arrangements entered into under which—

(*a*) a person becomes a partner,

(*b*) the interest of an existing partner in the partnership is reduced or an existing partner ceases to be a partner, and

(*c*) there is a withdrawal of money or money's worth from the partnership by the existing partner mentioned in paragraph (*b*) (other than money or money's worth paid from the resources available to the partnership prior to the transfer).

(3C) Any other transfer to which this paragraph applies is a Type B transfer.][4]

(4) ...[3]

(5) The "relevant partnership property", in relation to [a Type A transfer][4] of an interest in a partnership, is every chargeable interest held as partnership property immediately after the transfer, other than—

(*a*) any [chargeable][4] interest that was transferred to the partnership in connection with the transfer;

(*b*) a lease to which paragraph 15 (exclusion of market rent leases) applies[, and

(*c*) any chargeable interest that is not attributable economically to the interest in the partnership that is transferred][4].

[(5A) The "relevant partnership property", in relation to a Type B transfer of an interest in a partnership, is every chargeable interest held as partnership property immediately after the transfer, other than—

(*a*) any chargeable interest that was transferred to the partnership in connection with the transfer,

(*b*) a lease to which paragraph 15 (exclusion of market rent leases) applies,

(*c*) any chargeable interest that is not attributable economically to the interest in the partnership that is transferred,

(*d*) any chargeable interest that was transferred to the partnership on or before 22 July 2004,

(*e*) any chargeable interest in respect of whose transfer to the partnership an election has been made under paragraph 12A, and

(*f*) any other chargeable interest whose transfer to the partnership did not fall within paragraph 10(1)(*a*), (*b*) or (*c*).][4]

(6) The chargeable consideration for the transaction shall be taken to be equal to a proportion of the market value of the relevant partnership property.

(7) That proportion is—

(*a*) if the person acquiring the interest in the partnership was not a partner before the transfer, his partnership share immediately after the transfer;

(*b*) if he was a partner before the transfer, the difference between his partnership share before and after the transfer.][1]

[(8) In this paragraph—

"property-investment partnership" means a partnership whose sole or main activity is investing or dealing in chargeable interests (whether or not that activity involves the carrying out of construction operations on the land in question);

"construction operations" has the same meaning as in Chapter 3 of Part 3 of the Finance Act 2004 (see section 74 of that Act).][2]

[(9) An interest in respect of the transfer of which this paragraph applies shall be treated as a chargeable interest for the purposes of paragraph 3(1) of Schedule 7 to the extent that the relevant partnership property consists of a chargeable interest.][3]

Cross references—See FA 2003 Sch 15 para 30 (a transaction which is a chargeable transaction by virtue of this paragraph is a notifiable transaction if (but only if) the consideration for the transaction exceeds the zero rate threshold).

Amendments—[1] This Part substituted by FA 2004 s 304, Sch 41 paras 1, 3 with effect for any partnership transaction of which the effective date (within the meaning of FA 2003 Pt 4) is after 22 July 2004. A "partnership transaction" means a transaction mentioned in FA 2003 Sch 15 para 9(1): FA 2004 Sch 41 para 3(2).

2 Heading substituted for former heading "Transfer of partnership interest: consideration given and chargeable interest held", words in sub-para (1)(a) and the whole of sub-para (8) inserted by FA 2006 s 163, Sch 24 para 9 with effect in relation to any transfer that has (or, but for the amendment made by FA 2006 Sch 24 para 9, would have) an effective date (within the meaning of FA 2003 Pt 4) which is on or after 19 July 2006.

3 Sub-paras (1)(b), (4), and in Heading, words "for consideration" repealed, and sub-para (9) inserted, by FA 2007 ss 72(1), (2), (6), Sch 27 Pt 4(1) with effect in respect of transfers occurring on or after the day on which FA 2007 is passed: FA 2007 s 72(13).

The amendments are to this paragraph as it stood before amendment by the Stamp Duty Land Tax (Variation of the Finance Act 2003) Regulations, SI 2006/3237. The amendments, to the extent provided for by FA 2007 s 72(13)–(15), replace the amendments made by those regulations: see FA 2007 s 72(2), (16). However, the amendments by FA 2007 are subject to transitional provisions as set out by FA 2007 s 72(17).

But the amendments do not have effect in respect of anything done in respect of a property-investment partnership established before 19 July 2007 if—

(a) the partnership does not acquire a chargeable interest on or after that day, and

(b) stamp duty land tax was paid in respect of each chargeable interest acquired before that day, by reference to chargeable consideration of not less than the market value: FA 2007 s 72(14).

4 Sub-paras (3A)–(3C), (5A) inserted, words in sub-para (5) substituted (for words "a transfer") and inserted, and sub-para (5)(c) and preceding word "and" inserted, by FA 2008 s 97, Sch 31 para 1. These amendments have effect in respect of transfers occurring on or after 19 July 2007 and are treated as having come into force on that day.

FA 2007 s 72(14), (17) apply in relation to these amendments as they apply in relation to the amendments made by FA 2007 s 72(6), (10).

[Exclusion of market rent leases

15—(1) A lease held as partnership property immediately after a transfer of an interest in the partnership is not relevant partnership property for the purposes of paragraph 14(5) [or (5A)][2] if the following four conditions are met.

(2) The first condition is that—

(*a*) no chargeable consideration other than rent has been given in respect of the grant of the lease, and

(*b*) no arrangements are in place at the time of the transfer for any chargeable consideration other than rent to be given in respect of the grant of the lease.

(3) The second condition is that the rent payable under the lease as granted was a market rent at the time of the grant.

(4) The third condition is that—

(*a*) the term of the lease is 5 years or less, or

(*b*) if the term of the lease is more than 5 years—

(i) the lease provides for the rent payable under it to be reviewed at least once in every 5 years of the term, and

(ii) the rent payable under the lease as a result of a review is required to be a market rent at the review date.

(5) The fourth condition is that there has been no change to the lease since it was granted which is such that, immediately after the change has effect, the rent payable under the lease is less than a market rent.

(6) The market rent of a lease at any time is the rent which the lease might reasonably be expected to fetch at that time in the open market.

(7) A review date is a date from which the rent determined as a result of a rent review is payable.][1]

Amendments—[1] This Part substituted by FA 2004 s 304, Sch 41 paras 1, 3 with effect for any partnership transaction of which the effective date (within the meaning of FA 2003 Pt 4) is after 22 July 2004. A "partnership transaction" means a transaction mentioned in FA 2003 Sch 15 para 9(1): FA 2004 Sch 41 para 3(2).

2 Words in sub-para (1) inserted by FA 2008 s 97, Sch 31 para 2. This amendment has effect in respect of transfers occurring on or after 19 July 2007 and is treated as having come into force on that day.

FA 2007 s 72(14), (17) apply in relation to this amendment as they apply in relation to the amendments made by s FA 2007 s 72(6), (10).

[Partnership interests: application of provisions about exchanges etc.

16—(1) Where paragraph 5 of Schedule 4 (exchanges) applies to the acquisition of an interest in a partnership in consideration of entering into a land transaction with an existing partner, the interest in the partnership shall be treated as a major interest in land for the purposes of that paragraph if the relevant partnership property includes a major interest in land.

(2) In sub-paragraph (1) "relevant partnership property" has the meaning given by paragraph 14(5) [or (5A) (as appropriate)][2].

(3) The provisions of paragraph 6 of Schedule 4 (partition etc: disregard of existing interest) do not apply where this paragraph applies.][1]

Amendments—[1] This Part substituted by FA 2004 s 304, Sch 41 paras 1, 3 with effect for any partnership transaction of which the effective date (within the meaning of FA 2003 Pt 4) is after 22 July 2004. A "partnership transaction" means a transaction mentioned in FA 2003 Sch 15 para 9(1): FA 2004 Sch 41 para 3(2).

2 Words in sub-para (2) inserted by FA 2008 s 97, Sch 31 para 3. This amendment has effect in respect of transfers occurring on or after 19 July 2007 and is treated as having come into force on that day.
FA 2007 s 72(14), (17) apply in relation to this amendment as they apply in relation to the amendments made by s FA 2007 s 72(6), (10).

[Transfer of partnership interest pursuant to earlier arrangements

17—(1) This paragraph applies where—
(*a*) there is a transfer of a chargeable interest to a partnership ("the land transfer");
(*b*) the land transfer falls within paragraph (*a*), (*b*) or (*c*) of paragraph 10(1);
(*c*) there is subsequently a transfer of an interest in the partnership ("the partnership transfer");
(*d*) the partnership transfer is made—
(i) if the land transfer falls within paragraph 10(1)(*a*) or (*b*), by the person who makes the land transfer;
(ii) if the land transfer falls within paragraph 10(1)(*c*), by the partner concerned;
(*e*) the partnership transfer is made pursuant to arrangements that were in place at the time of the land transfer;
(*f*) the partnership transfer is not (apart from this paragraph) a chargeable transaction.
(2) The partnership transfer—
(*a*) shall be taken for the purposes of this Part to be a land transaction;
(*b*) is a chargeable transaction.
(3) The partners shall be taken to be the purchasers under the transaction.
(4) The chargeable consideration for the transaction shall be taken to be equal to a proportion of the market value, as at the date of the transaction, of the interest transferred by the land transfer.
(5) That proportion is—
(*a*) if the person making the partnership transfer is not a partner immediately after the transfer, his partnership share immediately before the transfer;
(*b*) if he is a partner immediately after the transfer, the difference between his partnership share before and after the transfer.
(6) The partnership transfer and the land transfer shall be taken to be linked transactions.
(7) Paragraphs 6 to 8 (responsibility of partners) have effect in relation to the partnership transfer, but the responsible partners are—
(*a*) those who were partners immediately before the transfer and who remain partners after the transfer, and
(*b*) any person becoming a partner as a result of, or in connection with, the transfer.][1]

Cross references—See FA 2003 Sch 15 para 30 (a transaction which is a chargeable transaction by virtue of this paragraph is a notifiable transaction if (but only if) the consideration for the transaction exceeds the zero rate threshold).

Amendments—[1] This Part substituted by FA 2004 s 304, Sch 41 paras 1, 3 with effect for any partnership transaction of which the effective date (within the meaning of FA 2003 Pt 4) is after 22 July 2004. A "partnership transaction" means a transaction mentioned in FA 2003 Sch 15 para 9(1): FA 2004 Sch 41 para 3(2).

[Withdrawal of money etc from partnership after transfer of chargeable interest

17A—(1) This paragraph applies where—
(*a*) there is a transfer of a chargeable interest to a partnership ("the land transfer");
(*b*) the land transfer falls within paragraph (*a*), (*b*) or (*c*) of paragraph 10(1);
(*c*) during the period of three years beginning with the date of the land transfer, a qualifying event occurs;
[(*d*) at the time of the qualifying event, an election has not been made in respect of the land transfer under paragraph 12A.][3]
(2) A qualifying event is—
(*a*) a withdrawal from the partnership of money or money's worth which does not represent income profit by the relevant person—
(i) withdrawing capital from his capital account,
(ii) reducing his interest, or
(iii) ceasing to be a partner, or
(*b*) in a case where the relevant person has made a loan to the partnership—
(i) the repayment (to any extent) by the partnership of the loan, or
(ii) a withdrawal by the relevant person from the partnership of money or money's worth which does not represent income profit.
(3) For this purpose the relevant person is—
(*a*) where the land transfer falls within paragraph 10(1)(*a*) or (*b*), the person who makes the land transfer, and
(*b*) where the land transfer falls within paragraph 10(1)(*c*), the partner concerned or a person connected with him.

(4) The qualifying event—

(*a*) shall be taken to be a land transaction, and

(*b*) is a chargeable transaction.

(5) The partners shall be taken to be the purchasers under the transaction.

(6) Paragraphs 6 to 8 (responsibility of partners) have effect in relation to the transaction.

(7) The chargeable consideration for the transaction shall be taken to be—

(*a*) in a case falling within sub-paragraph (2)(*a*), equal to the value of the money or money's worth withdrawn from the partnership, or

(*b*) in a case falling within sub-paragraph (2)(*b*)(i), equal to the amount repaid, and

(*c*) in a case falling within sub-paragraph (2)(*b*)(ii), equal to so much of the value of the money or money's worth withdrawn from the partnership as does not exceed the amount of the loan,

but (in any case) shall not exceed the market value, as at the effective date of the land transfer, of the chargeable interest transferred by the land transfer, reduced by any amount previously chargeable to tax.][1]

[(8) Where—

(*a*) a qualifying event gives rise to a charge under this paragraph, and

(*b*) the same event gives rise to a charge under paragraph 14 (transfer for consideration of interest in property- investment partnership),

the amount of the charge under this paragraph is reduced (but not below nil) by the amount of the charge under that paragraph.][2]

Amendments—[1] This paragraph inserted by F(No 2)A 2005 s 49, Sch 10 paras 1, 10 with effect where the effective date of the transaction transferring the chargeable interest to the partnership is after 19 May 2005.

However, this amendment does not have effect—

(a) in relation to any transaction which is effected in pursuance of a contract entered into and substantially performed on or before the specified date (ie 16 March 2005), or

(b) subject to what follows below, in relation to any other transaction which is effected in pursuance of a contract entered into on or before the specified date (ie 16 March 2005).

The exclusion by para (*b*) above of transactions effected in pursuance of contracts entered into on or before the specified date does not apply—

(a) if there is any variation of the contract or assignment of rights under the contract after that date,

(b) if the transaction is effected in consequence of the exercise after that date of any option, right of pre-emption or similar right, or

(c) if after that date there is an assignment, subsale or other transaction (relating to the whole or part of the subject-matter of the contract) as a result of which a person other than the purchaser under the contract becomes entitled to call for a conveyance to him: F(No 2)A 2005 Sch 10 para 16(3), (6)–(8).

[2] Sub-para (8) inserted by FA 2006 s 163, Sch 24 para 10 with effect in relation to any qualifying event of which the effective date (within the meaning of FA 2003 Pt 4) is on or after 19 July 2006.

[3] Sub-para (1)(d) inserted by FA 2008 s 97, Sch 31 para 8 with effect from 21 July 2008.

[Transfer of chargeable interest from a partnership: general

18—(1) This paragraph applies where a chargeable interest is transferred—

(*a*) from a partnership to a person who is or has been one of the partners, or

(*b*) from a partnership to a person connected with a person who is or has been one of the partners.

[(2) The chargeable consideration for the transaction shall (subject to paragraph 24) be taken to be equal to—

$$MV \times (100 - SLP)\%$$

where—

MV is the market value of the interest transferred, and

SLP is the sum of the lower proportions.

. . .][2]

(5) Paragraph 20 provides for determining the sum of the lower proportions.

(6) Paragraph 19 applies . . . [2] if the whole or part of the chargeable consideration for the transaction is rent.

(7) For the purposes of this paragraph property that was partnership property before the partnership was dissolved or otherwise ceased to exist shall be treated as remaining partnership property until it is distributed.

[(8) This paragraph has effect subject to any election under paragraph 12A.][3]][1]

Cross references—See FA 2003 Sch 15 para 23 (sub-paras (2)–(5) above do not apply where there is a transfer of a chargeable interest from a partnership to a partnership, and none of the chargeable consideration is rent).

Modifications—FA 2003 Sch 15 para 24 (modification of this paragraph in certain circumstances involving a transfer of a chargeable interest from a partnership consisting wholly of bodies corporate).

Amendments—[1] This Part substituted by FA 2004 s 304, Sch 41 paras 1, 3 with effect for any partnership transaction of which the effective date (within the meaning of FA 2003 Pt 4) is after 22 July 2004. A "partnership transaction" means a transaction mentioned in FA 2003 Sch 15 para 9(1): FA 2004 Sch 41 para 3(2).

2 Sub-para (2) substituted for former sub-paras (2)–(4) and in sub-para (6) words "(instead of sub-paragraphs (2) to (5))" repealed by FA 2006 s 162, Sch 24 para 5, s 178, Sch 26 Pt 7(2) with effect in relation to any transfer of which the effective date (within the meaning of FA 2003 Pt 4) is on or after 19 July 2006.

3 Sub-para (8) inserted by FA 2008 s 97, Sch 31 para 7 with effect from 21 July 2008.

[Transfer of chargeable interest from a partnership: chargeable consideration including rent

19—(1) This paragraph applies in relation to a transaction to which paragraph 18 applies where the whole or part of the chargeable consideration for the transaction is rent.

[(2) Schedule 5 (amount of tax chargeable: rent) has effect with the modifications set out in sub-paragraphs (2A) to (2C).

(2A) In paragraph 2—

(*a*) for "the net present value of the rent payable over the term of the lease" substitute "the relevant chargeable proportion of the net present value of the rent payable over the term of the lease", and

(*b*) for "the net present values of the rent payable over the terms of all the leases" substitute "the relevant chargeable proportions of the net present values of the rent payable over the terms of all the leases".

(2B) In paragraph [9A(6)][3]—

(*a*) for "the annual rent" substitute "the relevant chargeable proportion of the annual rent", and

(*b*) for "the total of the annual rents" substitute "the relevant chargeable proportion of the total of the annual rents".

(2C) For paragraph 9(4) substitute—

"(4) Tax chargeable under this Schedule is in addition to any tax chargeable under section 55 as it has effect by virtue of paragraph 18 of Schedule 15.".

(2D) For the purposes of sub-paragraphs (2A) and (2B) the relevant chargeable proportion is—

$$(100 - SLP)\%$$

where SLP is the sum of the lower proportions.

. . .][2]

(8) Paragraph 20 provides for determining the sum of the lower proportions.

(9) This paragraph is subject to paragraph 24.][1]

Cross references—See FA 2003 Sch 15 para 23 (this paragraph does not apply where there is transfer of a chargeable interest from a partnership to a partnership, and the whole or part of the chargeable consideration is rent).

Modifications—FA 2003 Sch 15 para 24 (modification of this paragraph in certain circumstances involving a transfer of a chargeable interest from a partnership consisting wholly of bodies corporate).

Amendments—1 This Part substituted by FA 2004 s 304, Sch 41 paras 1, 3 with effect for any partnership transaction of which the effective date (within the meaning of FA 2003 Pt 4) is after 22 July 2004. A "partnership transaction" means a transaction mentioned in FA 2003 Sch 15 para 9(1): FA 2004 Sch 41 para 3(2).

2 Sub-paras (2)–(2D) substituted for former sub-paras (2)–(7) by FA 2006 s 162, Sch 24 para 6 with effect in relation to any transfer of which the effective date (within the meaning of FA 2003 Pt 4) is on or after 19 July 2006.

3 Reference in sub-para (2B) substituted by FA 2008 s 95(11)(b) with effect in relation to transactions with an effective date on or after 12 March 2008.

[Transfer of chargeable interest from a partnership: sum of the lower proportions

20—(1) The sum of the lower proportions in relation to a transaction to which paragraph 18 applies is determined as follows:—

Step One

Identify the relevant owner or owners.

A person is a relevant owner if—

(*a*) immediately after the transaction, he is entitled to a proportion of the chargeable interest, and

(*b*) immediately before the transaction, he was a partner or connected with a partner.

Step Two

For each relevant owner, identify the corresponding partner or partners.

A person is a corresponding partner in relation to a relevant owner if, immediately before the transaction—

(*a*) he was a partner, and

(*b*) he was the relevant owner [or was an individual connected with the relevant owner][2].

[(If there is no relevant owner with a corresponding partner, the sum of the lower proportions is nil.)][2]

Step Three

For each relevant owner, find the proportion of the chargeable interest to which he is entitled immediately after the transaction.

Apportion that proportion between any one or more of the relevant owner's corresponding partners.

Step Four

Find the lower proportion for each person who is a corresponding partner in relation to one or more relevant owners.

The lower proportion is—

(*a*) the proportion of the chargeable interest attributable to the partner, or

(*b*) if lower, the partnership share attributable to the partner.

The proportion of the chargeable interest attributable to the partner is—

(i) if he is a corresponding partner in relation to only one relevant owner, the proportion (if any) of the chargeable interest apportioned to him (at Step Three) in respect of that owner;

(ii) if he is a corresponding partner in relation to more than one relevant owner, the sum of the proportions (if any) of the chargeable interest apportioned to him (at Step Three) in respect of each of those owners.

Paragraph 21 provides for determining the partnership share attributable to the partner.

Step Five

Add together the lower proportions of each person who is a corresponding partner in relation to one or more relevant owners.

The result is the sum of the lower proportions.

(2) For the purposes of this paragraph persons who are entitled to a chargeable interest as beneficial joint tenants (or, in Scotland, as joint owners) shall be taken to be entitled to the chargeable interest as beneficial tenants in common (or, in Scotland, as owners in common) in equal shares.][1]

[(3) For the purpose of paragraph (*b*) of Step 2 a company is to be treated as an individual connected with the relevant owner in so far as it—

(*a*) holds property as trustee, and

(*b*) is connected with the relevant owner only because of [section 1122(6) of the Corporation Tax Act 2010][4].][3]

Amendments—[1] This Part substituted by FA 2004 s 304, Sch 41 paras 1, 3 with effect for any partnership transaction of which the effective date (within the meaning of FA 2003 Pt 4) is after 22 July 2004. A "partnership transaction" means a transaction mentioned in FA 2003 Sch 15 para 9(1): FA 2004 Sch 41 para 3(2).

[2] Words in sub-para (1) step two para (b) substituted, and words at end of step two inserted, by FA 2007 s 72(1), (2), (7) with effect in respect of transfers occurring on or after 19 July 2007: FA 2007 s 72(13).

The amendments are to this paragraph as it stood before amendment by the Stamp Duty Land Tax (Variation of the Finance Act 2003) Regulations, SI 2006/3237.

The amendments, to the extent provided for by FA 2007 s 72(13)–(15), replace the amendments made by those regulations: see FA 2007 s 72(2), (16). However, the amendments by FA 2007 are subject to transitional provisions as provided by FA 2007 s 72(17).

[3] Sub-para (3) inserted by FA 2007 s 72(1), (2), (8) with effect in respect of transfers occurring on or after 19 July 2007: FA 2007 s 72(13).

[4] In sub-para (3)(*b*) words "section 839(3) of the Taxes Act 1988" substituted by CTA 2010 s 1177, Sch 1 paras 400, 418(1),(3). CTA 2010 has effect for corporation tax purposes for accounting periods ending on or after 1 April 2010, and for income and capital gains tax purposes for the tax year 2010–11 and subsequent tax years.

[Transfer of chargeable interest from a partnership: partnership share attributable to partner

21—(1) This paragraph provides for determining the partnership share attributable to a partner for the purposes of paragraph 20(1) (see Step Four).

(2) Paragraph 22 applies for determining the partnership share attributable to a partner where—

(*a*) the effective date of the transfer of the relevant chargeable interest to the partnership was before 20th October 2003, or

(*b*) the effective date of the transfer of the relevant chargeable interest to the partnership was on or after that date and—

(i) the instrument by which the transfer was effected has been duly stamped with *ad valorem* stamp duty, or

(ii) any tax payable in respect of the transfer has been duly paid under this Part.

(3) Where the effective date of the transfer of the relevant chargeable interest to the partnership was on or after 20th October 2003 but neither of the conditions in sub-paragraphs (i) and (ii) of sub-paragraph (2)(*b*) is met, the partnership share attributable to the partner is zero.

(4) The relevant chargeable interest is—

(*a*) the chargeable interest which ceases to be partnership property as a result of the transaction to which paragraph 18 applies, or

(*b*) where the transaction to which paragraph 18 applies is the grant or creation of a chargeable interest, the chargeable interest out of which that interest is granted or created.][1]

Amendments—[1] This Part substituted by FA 2004 s 304, Sch 41 paras 1, 3 with effect for any partnership transaction of which the effective date (within the meaning of FA 2003 Pt 4) is after 22 July 2004. A "partnership transaction" means a transaction mentioned in FA 2003 Sch 15 para 9(1): FA 2004 Sch 41 para 3(2).

[22—(1) Where this paragraph applies, the partnership share attributable to the partner is determined as follows:—

Step One

Find the partner's actual partnership share on the relevant date.
In a case falling within paragraph 21(2)(*a*), the relevant date—
(*a*) if the partner was a partner on 19th October 2003, is that date;
(*b*) if the partner became a partner after that date, is the date on which he became a partner.
In a case falling within paragraph 21(2)(*b*), the relevant date—
(*a*) if the partner was a partner on the effective date of the transfer of the relevant chargeable interest to the partnership, is that date;
(*b*) if the partner became a partner after that date, is the date on which he became a partner.
Step Two
Add to that partnership share any increases in the partner's partnership share which—
(*a*) occur in the period starting on the day after the relevant date and ending immediately before the transaction to which paragraph 18 applies, and
(*b*) count for this purpose.
The result is the increased partnership share.
An increase counts for the purpose of paragraph (*b*) only if—
(i) where the transfer which resulted in the increase took place on or before the date on which the Finance Act 2004 was passed, the instrument by which the transfer was effected has been duly stamped with *ad valorem* stamp duty under the enactments relating to stamp duty;
(ii) where the transfer which resulted in the increase took place after that date, any tax payable in respect of the transfer has been duly paid under this Part.
Step Three
Deduct from the increased partnership share any decreases in the partner's partnership share which occur in the period starting on the day after the relevant date and ending immediately before the transaction to which paragraph 18 applies.
The result is the partnership share attributable to the partner.
(2) If the effect of applying Step Three would be to reduce the partnership share attributable to the partner below zero, the partnership share attributable to the partner is zero.
(3) In a case falling within paragraph 21(2)(*a*), if the partner ceased to be a partner before 19th October 2003, the partnership share attributable to the partner is zero.
(4) In a case falling within paragraph 21(2)(*b*), if the partner ceased to be a partner before the effective date of the transfer of the relevant chargeable interest to the partnership, the partnership share attributable to the partner is zero.
(5) Paragraph 21(4) (relevant chargeable interest) applies for the purposes of this paragraph.][1]

Amendments—[1] This Part substituted by FA 2004 s 304, Sch 41 paras 1, 3 with effect for any partnership transaction of which the effective date (within the meaning of FA 2003 Pt 4) is after 22 July 2004. A "partnership transaction" means a transaction mentioned in FA 2003 Sch 15 para 9(1): FA 2004 Sch 41 para 3(2).

[Transfer of chargeable interest from a partnership to a partnership

23—(1) This paragraph applies where—
(*a*) there is a transfer of a chargeable interest from a partnership to a partnership, and
(*b*) the transfer is both—
(i) a transaction to which paragraph 10 applies, and
(ii) a transaction to which paragraph 18 applies.
[(2) Paragraphs 10(2) and 18(2) do not apply.
(2A) The chargeable consideration for the transaction shall be taken to be what it would have been if paragraph 10(2) had applied or, if greater, what it would have been if paragraph 18(2) had applied.
(3) Where the whole or part of the chargeable consideration for the transaction is rent—
(*a*) paragraphs 11 and 19 do not apply;
(*b*) the tax chargeable in respect of so much of the chargeable consideration as consists of rent shall be taken to be what it would have been if paragraph 11 had applied or, if greater, what it would have been if paragraph 19 had applied;
(*c*) the disapplication of the 0% band provided for by paragraph [9A][3] of Schedule 5 has effect if—
(i) it would have had effect if paragraph 11(2B) of this Schedule had applied, or
(ii) it would have had effect if paragraph 19(2B) of this Schedule had applied.][2]][1]

Modifications—FA 2003 Sch 15 para 24 (modification of this paragraph in certain circumstances involving a transfer of a chargeable interest from a partnership consisting wholly of bodies corporate).

Amendments—[1] This Part substituted by FA 2004 s 304, Sch 41 paras 1, 3 with effect for any partnership transaction of which the effective date (within the meaning of FA 2003 Pt 4) is after 22 July 2004. A "partnership transaction" means a transaction mentioned in FA 2003 Sch 15 para 9(1): FA 2004 Sch 41 para 3(2).

[2] Sub-paras (2)–(3) substituted for former sub-paras (2), (3) by FA 2006 s 162, Sch 24 para 8 with effect in relation to any transfer of which the effective date (within the meaning of FA 2003 Pt 4) is on or after 19 July 2006.

[3] Reference in sub-para (3)(c) substituted by FA 2008 s 95(11)(c) with effect in relation to transactions with an effective date on or after 12 March 2008.

[Transfer of chargeable interest from a partnership consisting wholly of bodies corporate

24—(1) This paragraph applies where—

(*a*) there is a transaction to which paragraph 18 applies;

(*b*) immediately before the transaction all the partners are bodies corporate;

(*c*) the sum of the lower proportions is 75 or more.

(2) Paragraphs 18, 19 and 23 have effect with these modifications.

(3) In paragraph 18, for [sub-paragraphs (2) and (5)][2] substitute—

"(2) The chargeable consideration for the transaction shall be taken to be equal to the market value of the interest transferred.".

[(4A) In paragraph 19(2), for "sub-paragraphs (2) to (2C)" substitute "sub-paragraph (2C)".

(5) In paragraph 19, omit sub-paragraphs (2A), (2B), (2D) and (8).

. . .][2]

(9) Paragraph 20 provides for determining the sum of the lower proportions.][1]

Amendments—[1] This Part substituted by FA 2004 s 304, Sch 41 paras 1, 3 with effect for any partnership transaction of which the effective date (within the meaning of FA 2003 Pt 4) is after 22 July 2004. A "partnership transaction" means a transaction mentioned in FA 2003 Sch 15 para 9(1): FA 2004 Sch 41 para 3(2).

[2] In sub-para (3) words substituted for "sub-paragraphs (2) to (5)" and sub-paras (4A), (5) substituted for former sub-paras (4)–(8) by FA 2006 s 162, Sch 24 para 7 with effect in relation to any transfer of which the effective date (within the meaning of FA 2003 Pt 4) is on or after 19 July 2006.

[Application of exemptions and reliefs

25—(1) Where paragraph 10, 14, 17 or 18 applies, paragraph 1 of Schedule 3 (exemption of transactions for which there is no chargeable consideration) does not apply.

(2) But (subject to paragraphs 26 to 28) this Part of this Schedule has effect subject to any other provision affording exemption or relief from stamp duty land tax.][1]

Amendments—[1] This Part substituted by FA 2004 s 304, Sch 41 paras 1, 3 with effect for any partnership transaction of which the effective date (within the meaning of FA 2003 Pt 4) is after 22 July 2004. A "partnership transaction" means a transaction mentioned in FA 2003 Sch 15 para 9(1): FA 2004 Sch 41 para 3(2).

[Application of disadvantaged areas relief

26—(1) Schedule 6 (disadvantaged areas relief) applies to the transfer of an interest in a partnership that is a chargeable transaction by virtue of paragraph 14 or 17 with these modifications.

(2) For paragraph 3 substitute—

"3—

(1) This Part of this Schedule applies to a transfer of an interest in a partnership that is a chargeable transaction by virtue of paragraph 14 of Schedule 15 if every chargeable interest comprising the relevant partnership property is a chargeable interest in relation to land that is wholly situated in a disadvantaged area.

(2) This Part of this Schedule applies to a transfer of an interest in a partnership that is a chargeable transaction by virtue of paragraph 17 of Schedule 15 if the subject matter of the land transfer is a chargeable interest in relation to land that is wholly situated in a disadvantaged area.".

(3) In paragraph 5, for sub-paragraphs (2) to (4) substitute—

"(2) If the relevant consideration does not exceed £150,000 the transaction is exempt from charge.".

(4) For paragraph 6 substitute—

"6—

(1) This paragraph applies where the land is partly non-residential property and partly residential property.

(2) The non-residential proportion of the chargeable consideration for the transaction does not count as chargeable consideration.

(3) The non-residential proportion is the proportion of the market value of the relevant property that, on a just and reasonable apportionment, is attributable to land that is non-residential property.

(4) If the relevant consideration does not exceed £150,000, none of the residential proportion of the chargeable consideration counts as chargeable consideration.

(5) The residential proportion is the proportion of the market value of the relevant property that, on a just and reasonable apportionment, is attributable to land that is residential property.".

(5) For paragraph 7 substitute—

"7—

(1) This Part of this Schedule applies to a transfer of an interest in a partnership that is a chargeable transaction by virtue of paragraph 14 of Schedule 15 if—

(*a*) some (but not all) of the chargeable interests comprising the relevant partnership property are chargeable interests in relation to land that is wholly situated in a disadvantaged area, or

(*b*) any chargeable interest comprised in the relevant partnership property is a chargeable interest in relation to land that is partly situated in a disadvantaged area and partly situated outside such an area.

(2) This Part of this Schedule applies to a transfer of an interest in a partnership that is a chargeable transaction by virtue of paragraph 17 of Schedule 15 if the subject matter of the land transfer is a chargeable interest in relation to land that is partly situated in a disadvantaged area and partly situated outside such an area.

(3) In this Part—

(*a*) references to the disadvantaged-area proportion are to the proportion of the market value of the relevant property that, on a just and reasonable apportionment, is attributable to land situated in a disadvantaged area;

(*b*) references to the advantaged-area proportion are to the proportion of the market value of the relevant property that, on a just and reasonable apportionment, is attributable to land that is situated outside a disadvantaged area.".

(6) In paragraph 8, for "consideration attributable to the land situated in the disadvantaged area" substitute "disadvantaged-area proportion of the chargeable consideration".

(7) In paragraph 9, for sub-paragraphs (2) to (4) substitute—

"(2) If the relevant consideration does not exceed £150,000 none of the disadvantaged-area proportion of the chargeable consideration counts as chargeable consideration.".

(8) For paragraph 10 substitute—

"10—

(1) This paragraph applies where the land situated in a disadvantaged area is partly non-residential property and partly residential property.

(2) The non-residential proportion of the disadvantaged-area proportion of the chargeable consideration for the transaction does not count as chargeable consideration [(subject to any election under paragraph 12A)][3].

(3) The non-residential proportion is the proportion of the disadvantaged-area proportion of the market value of the relevant property that, on a just and reasonable apportionment, is attributable to land that is not residential property.

(4) If the relevant consideration does not exceed £150,000, none of the residential proportion of the disadvantaged-area proportion of the chargeable consideration counts as chargeable consideration [(subject to any election under paragraph 12A)][3].

(5) The residential proportion is the proportion of the disadvantaged-area proportion of the market value of the relevant property that, on a just and reasonable apportionment, is attributable to land that is residential property.".

(9) After paragraph 11(1) insert—

"(1A) In this Schedule—

"the land transfer" means the transaction that is the land transfer for the purposes of paragraph 17 of Schedule 15;

"the relevant partnership property" has the meaning given by paragraph 14(5) [or (5A) (as appropriate)][2] of Schedule 15;

"the relevant property"—

(*a*) in the case of a transfer of an interest in a partnership that is a chargeable transaction by virtue of paragraph 14 of Schedule 15, means the relevant partnership property;

(*b*) in the case of a transfer of an interest in a partnership that is a chargeable transaction by virtue of paragraph 17 of Schedule 15, means the subject matter of the land transfer.

(1B) There is a transfer of an interest in a partnership for the purposes of this Schedule if there is such a transfer for the purposes of Part 3 of Schedule 15 (see paragraph 36 of that Schedule).".

(10) Omit paragraphs 11(2) and 12.][1]

Amendments—[1] This Part substituted by FA 2004 s 304, Sch 41 paras 1, 3 with effect for any partnership transaction of which the effective date (within the meaning of FA 2003 Pt 4) is after 22 July 2004. A "partnership transaction" means a transaction mentioned in FA 2003 Sch 15 para 9(1): FA 2004 Sch 41 para 3(2).

[2] In sub-para (9), in the inserted sub-para (1A), words in the definition of "the relevant partnership property" inserted, by FA 2008 s 97, Sch 31 para 4. This amendment has effect in respect of transfers occurring on or after 19 July 2007 and is treated as having come into force on that day.

FA 2007 s 72(14), (17) apply in relation to this amendment as they apply in relation to the amendments made by FA 2007 s 72(6), (10).

[3] Sub-para (8), in substituted para (10)(2), (4) words inserted by FA 2008 s 97, Sch 31 para 9 with effect from 21 July 2008.

[Application of group relief

27—(1) Part 1 of Schedule 7 (group relief) applies to—

(*a*) a transaction to which paragraph 10 applies, and

(*b*) a transaction that is a chargeable transaction by virtue of paragraph 17,

with these modifications.

(2) In paragraph 3(1)(*a*), for "the purchaser" substitute "a partner who was a partner at the effective date of the relevant transaction ("the relevant partner")".

(3) In paragraph 3(1), for paragraph (*b*) substitute—

"(*b*) at the time the relevant partner ceases to be a member of the same group as the vendor ("the relevant time"), a chargeable interest is held by or on behalf of the members of the partnership and that chargeable interest—

(i) was acquired by or on behalf of the partnership under the relevant transaction, or

(ii) is derived from a chargeable interest so acquired, and has not subsequently been acquired at market value under a chargeable transaction for which group relief was available but was not claimed,".

(4) In paragraph 3(3), for the words from "the transferee company" to the end substitute "or on behalf of the partnership and to the proportion in which the relevant partner is entitled at the relevant time to share in the income profits of the partnership.".

(5) In paragraph 3(4), omit the definition of "relevant associated company".

(6) In paragraphs 4 to 6, for "the purchaser" (wherever appearing) substitute "the relevant partner".][1]

Amendments—[1] This Part substituted by FA 2004 s 304, Sch 41 paras 1, 3 with effect for any partnership transaction of which the effective date (within the meaning of FA 2003 Pt 4) is after 22 July 2004. A "partnership transaction" means a transaction mentioned in FA 2003 Sch 15 para 9(1): FA 2004 Sch 41 para 3(2).

[27A—(1) This paragraph applies where in calculating the sum of the lower proportions in relation to a transaction (in accordance with paragraph 12)—

(*a*) a company ("the connected company") would have been a corresponding partner of a relevant owner ("the original owner") but for the fact that paragraph (*b*) of Step Two includes connected persons only if they are individuals, and

(*b*) the connected company and the original owner are members of the same group.

(2) The charge in respect of the transaction shall be reduced to the amount that would have been payable had the connected company been a corresponding partner of the original owner for the purposes of calculating the sum of the lower proportions.

(3) The provisions of Part 1 of Schedule 7 apply to group relief under sub-paragraph (2) above as to group relief under paragraph 1(1) of Schedule 7, but—

(*a*) with the omission of paragraph 2(2)(*a*),

(*b*) with the substitution for "the purchaser" in paragraph 3(1)(*a*) of "a partner who was, at the effective date of the transaction, a partner and a member of the same group as the transferor ("the relevant partner")", and

(*c*) with the other modifications specified in paragraph 27(3) to (6) above.][1]

Amendments—[1] This paragraph inserted by FA 2007 s 72(1), (2), (9) with effect in respect of transfers occurring on or after 19 July 2007: FA 2007 s 72(13).

The insertion, to the extent provided for by FA 2007 s 72(13)–(15), replaces that made by the Stamp Duty Land Tax (Variation of the Finance Act 2003) Regulations, SI 2006/3237: see FA 2007 s 72(2). However, this amendment is subject to transitional provisions as provided by FA 2007 s 72(17).

[Application of charities relief

28—(1) Schedule 8 (charities relief) applies to the transfer of an interest in a partnership that is a chargeable transaction by virtue of paragraph 14 or 17 with these modifications.

(2) In paragraph 1(1), for "A land transaction is exempt from charge if the purchaser is a charity" substitute "A transfer of an interest in a partnership that is a chargeable transaction by virtue of paragraph 14 or 17 of Schedule 15 is exempt from charge if the transferee is a charity".

(3) In paragraph 1(2)—

(*a*) for "the purchaser must intend to hold the subject-matter of the transaction" substitute "every chargeable interest held as partnership property immediately after the transfer must be held";

(*b*) in paragraphs (*a*) and (*b*) for "the purchaser" substitute "the transferee".

(4) In paragraph 1(3) for "the purchaser" substitute "the transferee".

(5) In paragraph 2(1), for paragraph (*b*) substitute—

"(*b*) at the time of the disqualifying event the partnership property includes a chargeable interest—

(i) that was held as partnership property immediately after the relevant transaction, or

(ii) that is derived from an interest held as partnership property at that time,".

(6) In paragraph 2(3)(*a*), for "the purchaser" substitute "the transferee".
(7) In paragraph 2(3), for paragraph (*b*) substitute—

"(*b*) any chargeable interest held as partnership property immediately after the relevant transaction, or any interest or right derived from it, being used or held otherwise than for qualifying charitable purposes.".

(8) For paragraph 2(4) substitute—
"(4) In sub-paragraphs (1) and (2) an "appropriate proportion" means an appropriate proportion having regard to—

(*a*) the chargeable interests held as partnership property immediately after the relevant transaction and the chargeable interests held as partnership property at the time of the disqualifying event, and

(*b*) the extent to which any chargeable interest held as partnership property at that time becomes used or held for purposes other than qualifying charitable purposes.".

(9) After paragraph 2 insert—

"Interpretation

3—

(1) There is a transfer of an interest in a partnership for the purposes of this Schedule if there is such a transfer for the purposes of Part 3 of Schedule 15 (see paragraph 36 of that Schedule).

(2) Paragraph 34(1) of Schedule 15 (meaning of references to partnership property) applies for the purposes of this Schedule as it applies for the purposes of Part 3 of that Schedule.".][1]

Amendments—[1] This Part substituted by FA 2004 s 304, Sch 41 paras 1, 3 with effect for any partnership transaction of which the effective date (within the meaning of FA 2003 Pt 4) is after 22 July 2004. A "partnership transaction" means a transaction mentioned in FA 2003 Sch 15 para 9(1): FA 2004 Sch 41 para 3(2).

[Acquisition of interest in partnership not chargeable except as specially provided

29 Except as provided by—

(*a*) paragraph 10 (transfer of chargeable interest to a partnership), or

(*b*) paragraph 14 (transfer of partnership interest: consideration given and chargeable interest held), or

(*c*) paragraph 17 (transfer of partnership interest pursuant to earlier arrangements),

the acquisition of an interest in a partnership is not a chargeable transaction, notwithstanding that the partnership property includes land.][1]

Amendments—[1] This Part substituted by FA 2004 s 304, Sch 41 paras 1, 3 with effect for any partnership transaction of which the effective date (within the meaning of FA 2003 Pt 4) is after 22 July 2004. A "partnership transaction" means a transaction mentioned in FA 2003 Sch 15 para 9(1): FA 2004 Sch 41 para 3(2).

[Transactions that are not notifiable

30—(1) A transaction which is a chargeable transaction by virtue of paragraph 14 or 17 (transfer of partnership interest) is a notifiable transaction if (but only if) the consideration for the transaction exceeds the zero rate threshold.

(2) The consideration for a transaction exceeds the zero rate threshold if either or both of the following conditions are met—

(*a*) the relevant consideration for the purposes of section 55 (amount of tax chargeable: general) is such that the rate of tax chargeable under that section is 1% or higher;

(*b*) the relevant rental value for the purposes of Schedule 5 (amount of tax chargeable: rent) is such that the rate of tax chargeable under that Schedule is 1% or higher.][1]

Amendments—[1] This Part substituted by FA 2004 s 304, Sch 41 paras 1, 3 with effect for any partnership transaction of which the effective date (within the meaning of FA 2003 Pt 4) is after 22 July 2004. A "partnership transaction" means a transaction mentioned in FA 2003 Sch 15 para 9(1): FA 2004 Sch 41 para 3(2).

[Stamp duty on transfers of partnership interests: continued application

31—(1) Nothing in section 125 (abolition of stamp duty except in relation to stock or marketable securities), or in Part 2 of Schedule 20 (amendments and repeals consequential on that section), affects the application of the enactments relating to stamp duty in relation to an instrument by which a transfer of an interest in a partnership is effected.

(2) In Part 1 of Schedule 20 (provisions supplementing section 125) references to stock or marketable securities shall be read as including any property that is the subject-matter of a transaction by which an interest in a partnership is transferred.

(3) In their application in relation to an instrument by which a transfer of an interest in a partnership is effected, the enactments relating to stamp duty have effect subject to paragraphs 32 and 33.][1]

Amendments—[1] This Part substituted by FA 2004 s 304, Sch 41 paras 1, 3 with effect for any partnership transaction of which the effective date (within the meaning of FA 2003 Pt 4) is after 22 July 2004. A "partnership transaction" means a transaction mentioned in FA 2003 Sch 15 para 9(1): FA 2004 Sch 41 para 3(2).

[Stamp duty on transfers of partnership interests: modification

32—(1) This paragraph applies where—

(*a*) stamp duty under Part 1 of Schedule 13 to the Finance Act 1999 (transfer on sale) is chargeable on an instrument effecting a transfer of an interest in a partnership, and

(*b*) the relevant partnership property includes a chargeable interest.

(2) The "relevant partnership property", in relation to a transfer of an interest in a partnership, is every chargeable interest held as partnership property immediately after the transfer, other than any interest that was transferred to the partnership in connection with the transfer.

(3) The consideration for the transaction shall (subject to sub-paragraph (8)) be taken to be equal to the actual consideration for the transaction less the excluded amount.

(4) The excluded amount is a proportion of the net market value of the relevant partnership property immediately after the transfer.

(5) That proportion is—

(*a*) if the person acquiring the interest in the partnership was not a partner before the transfer, his partnership share immediately after the transfer;

(*b*) if he was a partner before the transfer, the difference between his partnership share before and after the transfer.

(6) The net market value of a chargeable interest at a particular date is—

$$MV - SL$$

where—

MV is the market value of the chargeable interest at that date, and

SL is the amount outstanding at that date on any loan secured solely on the chargeable interest.

(7) If, in relation to a chargeable interest, SL is greater than MV, the net market value of the chargeable interest shall be taken to be nil.

(8) If the excluded amount is greater than the actual consideration for the transaction, the consideration for the transaction shall be taken to be nil.

(9) Where this paragraph applies in relation to an instrument, the instrument shall not be regarded as duly stamped unless it has been stamped in accordance with section 12 of the Stamp Act 1891.][1]

Amendments—[1] This Part substituted by FA 2004 s 304, Sch 41 paras 1, 3 with effect for any partnership transaction of which the effective date (within the meaning of FA 2003 Pt 4) is after 22 July 2004. A "partnership transaction" means a transaction mentioned in FA 2003 Sch 15 para 9(1): FA 2004 Sch 41 para 3(2).

[33—[(1) This paragraph applies where stamp duty under Part 1 of Schedule 13 to the Finance Act 1999 (transfer on sale) is, apart from this paragraph, chargeable on an instrument effecting a transfer of an interest in a partnership.][2]

[(1A) If the relevant partnership property does not include any stock or marketable securities, no stamp duty shall (subject to sub-paragraph (8)) be chargeable on the instrument.][2]

(3) [If the relevant partnership property includes stock or marketable securities,][2] the stamp duty chargeable on the instrument shall not exceed the stamp duty that would be chargeable if—

(*a*) the instrument were an instrument effecting a transfer of [that stock and those securities][2], and

[(*b*) the consideration for the transfer were equal to the appropriate proportion of the net market value of that stock and those securities immediately after the transfer.][2]

[(3A) The "relevant partnership property", in relation to a transfer of an interest in a partnership, is the partnership property immediately after the transfer, other than any partnership property that was transferred to the partnership in connection with the transfer.][2]

(4) . . .[2]

(5) [The appropriate][2] proportion is—

(*a*) if the person acquiring the interest in the partnership was not a partner before the transfer, his partnership share immediately after the transfer;

(*b*) if he was a partner before the transfer, the difference between his partnership share before and after the transfer.

(6) The net market value of stock or securities at a particular date is—

$$MV - SL$$

where—

MV is the market value of the stock or securities at that date, and

SL is the amount outstanding at that date on any loan secured solely on the stock or securities.

(7) If, in relation to any stock or securities, SL is greater than MV, the net market value of the stock or securities shall be taken to be nil.

(8) Where this paragraph applies in relation to an instrument, the instrument shall not be regarded as duly stamped unless it has been stamped in accordance with section 12 of the Stamp Act 1891.
(9) This paragraph shall be construed as one with the Stamp Act 1891.][1]

Amendments—[1] This Part substituted by FA 2004 s 304, Sch 41 paras 1, 3 with effect for any partnership transaction of which the effective date (within the meaning of FA 2003 Pt 4) is after 22 July 2004. A "partnership transaction" means a transaction mentioned in FA 2003 Sch 15 para 9(1): FA 2004 Sch 41 para 3(2).

[2] Sub-paras (1), (1A) substituted for sub-paras (1), (2); in sub-para (3), words inserted, and words substituted for the words "the stock and marketable securities comprised in the relevant partnership property"; sub-para (3)(b) substituted; sub-para (3A) inserted; sub-para (4) repealed; and in sub-para (5), words substituted for the word "That"; by F(No 2)A 2005 ss 49, 70, Sch 10 paras 17, 21, Sch 11 Pt 3(1) with effect in relation to any instrument executed on or after the day on which F(No 2)A 2005 is passed: F(No 2)A 2005 Sch 10 para 22.

[Interpretation: partnership property and partnership share

34—(1) Any reference in this Part of this Schedule to partnership property is to an interest or right held by or on behalf of a partnership, or the members of a partnership, for the purposes of the partnership business.
(2) Any reference in this Part of this Schedule to a person's partnership share at any time is to the proportion in which he is entitled at that time to share in the income profits of the partnership.][1]

Amendments—[1] This Part substituted by FA 2004 s 304, Sch 41 paras 1, 3 with effect for any partnership transaction of which the effective date (within the meaning of FA 2003 Pt 4) is after 22 July 2004. A "partnership transaction" means a transaction mentioned in FA 2003 Sch 15 para 9(1): FA 2004 Sch 41 para 3(2).

[Interpretation: transfer of chargeable interest to a partnership

35 For the purposes of this Part of this Schedule, there is a transfer of a chargeable interest to a partnership in any case where a chargeable interest becomes partnership property.][1]

Amendments—[1] This Part substituted by FA 2004 s 304, Sch 41 paras 1, 3 with effect for any partnership transaction of which the effective date (within the meaning of FA 2003 Pt 4) is after 22 July 2004. A "partnership transaction" means a transaction mentioned in FA 2003 Sch 15 para 9(1): FA 2004 Sch 41 para 3(2).

[Interpretation: transfer of interest in a partnership

[36 For the purposes of this Part of this Schedule, where a person acquires or increases a partnership share there is a transfer of an interest in the partnership (to that partner and from the other partners).][2]][1]

Amendments—[1] This Part substituted by FA 2004 s 304, Sch 41 paras 1, 3 with effect for any partnership transaction of which the effective date (within the meaning of FA 2003 Pt 4) is after 22 July 2004. A "partnership transaction" means a transaction mentioned in FA 2003 Sch 15 para 9(1): FA 2004 Sch 41 para 3(2).

[2] This paragraph substituted by FA 2007 s 72(1), (2), (10) with effect in respect of transfers occurring on or after 19 July 2007: FA 2007 s 72(13).
However, this substitution does not have effect in respect of anything done in respect of a property-investment partnership established before 19 July 2007 if—
(a) the partnership does not acquire a chargeable interest on or after that day, and
(b) stamp duty land tax was paid in respect of each chargeable interest acquired before that day, by reference to chargeable consideration of not less than the market value: FA 2007 s 72(14).

[Interpretation: transfer of chargeable interest from a partnership

37 For the purposes of this Part of this Schedule, there is a transfer of a chargeable interest from a partnership in any case where—
(*a*) a chargeable interest that was partnership property ceases to be partnership property, or
(*b*) a chargeable interest is granted or created out of partnership property and the interest is not partnership property.][1]

[1] This Part substituted by FA 2004 s 304, Sch 41 paras 1, 3 with effect for any partnership transaction of which the effective date (within the meaning of FA 2003 Pt 4) is after 22 July 2004. A "partnership transaction" means a transaction mentioned in FA 2003 Sch 15 para 9(1): FA 2004 Sch 41 para 3(2).

[Interpretation: market value of leases

38—(1) This paragraph applies in relation to a lease for the purposes of this Part of this Schedule if—
(*a*) the grant of the lease is or was a transaction to which paragraph 10 applies or applied (or a transaction to which paragraph 10 would have applied if that paragraph had been in force at the time of the grant), or
(*b*) the grant of the lease is a transaction to which paragraph 18 applies.
(2) In determining the market value of the lease, an obligation of the tenant under the lease is to be taken into account if (but only if)—
(*a*) it is an obligation such as is mentioned in paragraph 10(1) of Schedule 17A, or

(*b*) it is an obligation to make a payment to a person.][1]

Amendments—[1] This Part substituted by FA 2004 s 304, Sch 41 paras 1, 3 with effect for any partnership transaction of which the effective date (within the meaning of FA 2003 Pt 4) is after 22 July 2004. A "partnership transaction" means a transaction mentioned in FA 2003 Sch 15 para 9(1): FA 2004 Sch 41 para 3(2).

[Interpretation: connected persons

39—(1) [Section 1122 of the Corporation Tax Act 2010][3] (connected persons) has effect for the purposes of this Part of this Schedule.

(2) As applied by sub-paragraph (1), that section has effect with the omission of [subsection (7)][3] (partners connected with each other).][1]

[(3) As applied by sub-paragraph (1) for the purposes of paragraph 12 or 20, that section has effect with the omission of [subsection (6)(*c*) to (*e*)][3] (trustee connected with settlement).][2]

Amendments—[1] This Part substituted by FA 2004 s 304, Sch 41 paras 1, 3 with effect for any partnership transaction of which the effective date (within the meaning of FA 2003 Pt 4) is after 22 July 2004. A "partnership transaction" means a transaction mentioned in FA 2003 Sch 15 para 9(1): FA 2004 Sch 41 para 3(2).

[2] Sub-para (3) inserted by FA 2007 s 72(1), (2), (11) with effect in respect of transfers occurring on or after 19 July 2007: FA 2007 s 72(13).

[3] In sub-para (1) words "Section 839 of the Taxes Act 1988" substituted, in sub-para (2) words "subsection (4)" substituted and in sub-para (3) words "subsection (3)(*c*)" substituted by CTA 2010 s 1177, Sch 1 paras 400, 419. CTA 2010 has effect for corporation tax purposes for accounting periods ending on or after 1 April 2010, and for income and capital gains tax purposes for the tax year 2010–11 and subsequent tax years.

[Interpretation: arrangements

40 In this Part of this Schedule "arrangements" includes any scheme, agreement or understanding, whether or not legally enforceable.][1]

Amendments—[1] This Part substituted by FA 2004 s 304, Sch 41 paras 1, 3 with effect for any partnership transaction of which the effective date (within the meaning of FA 2003 Pt 4) is after 22 July 2004. A "partnership transaction" means a transaction mentioned in FA 2003 Sch 15 para 9(1): FA 2004 Sch 41 para 3(2).

SCHEDULE 16

STAMP DUTY LAND TAX: TRUSTS AND POWERS

Section 105

HMRC Manuals—Stamp Duty Land Tax Manual SDLTM31700–32500 (explanation of this Schedule).

Meaning of "settlement" and "bare trust"

1—(1) In this Part "settlement" means a trust that is not a bare trust.

(2) In this Part a "bare trust" means a trust under which property is held by a person as trustee—

(*a*) for a person who is absolutely entitled as against the trustee, or who would be so entitled but for being a minor or other person under a disability, or

(*b*) for two or more persons who are or would be jointly so entitled,

and includes a case in which a person holds property as nominee for another.

(3) In sub-paragraph (2)(*a*) and (*b*) the references to a person being absolutely entitled to property as against the trustee are references to a case where the person has the exclusive right, subject only to satisfying any outstanding charge, lien or other right of the trustee, to resort to the property for payment of duty, taxes, costs or other outgoings or to direct how the property is to be dealt with.

(4) In sub-paragraph (2) "minor", in relation to Scotland, means a person under legal disability by reason of nonage.

HMRC Manuals—Stamp Duty Land Tax Manual SDLTM31710 (the phrase "absolutely entitled" broadly means that the beneficiary may acquire or receive the trust property either immediately or by giving the requisite notice to the trustees in accordance with the terms of the trust; and the trustees have no power over or right to deal with the trust property without the permission of the beneficiary who enjoys absolute entitlement).

SDLTM31710a (Revenue example).

SDLTM31720 (common examples of settlements).

Interests of beneficiaries under certain trusts

2 Where property is held in trust under the law of Scotland, or of a country or territory outside the United Kingdom, on terms such that, if the trust had effect under the law of England and Wales, a beneficiary would be regarded as having an equitable interest in the trust property—

(*a*) that beneficiary shall be treated for the purposes of this Part as having such an interest notwithstanding that no such interest is recognised by the law of Scotland or, as the case may be, the country or territory outside the United Kingdom, and

(*b*) an acquisition of the interest of a beneficiary under the trust shall accordingly be treated as involving the acquisition of an interest in the trust property.

[Bare trustee

3—(1) Subject to sub-paragraph (2), where a person acquires a chargeable interest [or an interest in a partnership][2] as bare trustee, this Part applies as if the interest were vested in, and the acts of the trustee in relation to it were the acts of, the person or persons for whom he is trustee.
(2) Sub-paragraph (1) does not apply in relation to the grant of a lease.
(3) Where a lease is granted to a person as bare trustee, he is treated for the purposes of this Part, as it applies in relation to the grant of the lease, as purchaser of the whole of the interest acquired.
(4) Where a lease is granted by a person as bare trustee, he is to be treated for the purposes of this Part, as it applies in relation to the grant of the lease, as vendor of the whole of the interest disposed of.][1]

Amendments—[1] This paragraph substituted by F(No 2)A 2005 s 49, Sch 10 paras 1, 11 with effect where the effective date of the land transaction consisting of the grant of the lease is after 19th May 2005.
However, this amendment does not have effect—
(a) in relation to any transaction which is effected in pursuance of a contract entered into and substantially performed on or before the specified date (ie 16 March 2005), or
(b) subject to what follows below, in relation to any other transaction which is effected in pursuance of a contract entered into on or before the specified date (ie 16 March 2005).
The exclusion by para (*b*) above of transactions effected in pursuance of contracts entered into on or before the specified date does not apply—
(a) if there is any variation of the contract or assignment of rights under the contract after that date,
(b) if the transaction is effected in consequence of the exercise after that date of any option, right of pre-emption or similar right, or
(c) if after that date there is an assignment, subsale or other transaction (relating to the whole or part of the subject-matter of the contract) as a result of which a person other than the purchaser under the contract becomes entitled to call for a conveyance to him: F(No 2)A 2005 Sch 10 para 16(4), (6)–(8).
[2] Words in sub-para (1) inserted by FA 2007 s 72(1), (2), (12)(a) with effect in respect of acquisitions occurring on or after 19 July 2007: FA 2007 s 72(15). However, the commencement provision is subject to transitional provisions as set out in FA 2007 s 72(17).

Acquisition by trustees of settlement

4 Where persons acquire a chargeable interest [or an interest in a partnership][1] as trustees of a settlement, they are treated for the purposes of this Part, as it applies in relation to that acquisition, as purchasers of the whole of the interest acquired (including the beneficial interest).

Amendments—[1] Words inserted by FA 2007 s 72(1), (2), (12)(b) with effect in respect of acquisitions occurring on or after 19 July 2007: FA 2007 s 72(15). However, the commencement provision is subject to transitional provisions as set out in FA 2007 s 72(17).

Responsibility of trustees of settlement

5—(1) Where the trustees of a settlement are liable—
(*a*) to make a payment of tax or interest on unpaid tax,
(*b*) to make a payment in accordance with an assessment under paragraph 29 of Schedule 10 (recovery of excessive repayment), or
(*c*) to a penalty under this Part or to interest on such a penalty,
the payment, penalty or interest may be recovered (but only once) from any one or more of the responsible trustees.
(2) No amount may be recovered by virtue of sub-paragraph (1)(*c*) from a person who did not become a responsible trustee until after the relevant time.
(3) The responsible trustees, in relation to a land transaction, are the persons who are trustees at the effective date of the transaction and any person who subsequently becomes a trustee.
(4) The relevant time for this purpose is—
(*a*) in relation to so much of a penalty as is payable in respect of any day, or to interest on so much of a penalty as is so payable, the beginning of that day;
(*b*) in relation to any other penalty, or interest on such a penalty, the time when the act or omission occurred that caused the penalty to become payable.

Relevant trustees for purposes of return etc

6—(1) A return . . . [1] in relation to a land transaction may be made or given by any one or more of the trustees who are the responsible trustees in relation to the transaction.
The trustees by whom such a return or self-certificate is made are referred to below as "the relevant trustees".
(2) The declaration required by paragraph 1(1)(*c*) of Schedule 10 . . . [1] (declaration that return . . . [1] is complete and correct) must be made by all the relevant trustees.
(3) If the Inland Revenue give notice of an enquiry into the return . . . [1]—
(*a*) the notice must be given to each of the relevant trustees,

(*b*) the powers of the Inland Revenue as to the production of documents and provision of information for the purposes of the enquiry are exercisable separately (and differently) in relation to each of the relevant trustees,

(*c*) any of the relevant trustees may apply for a direction that a closure notice be given (and all of them are entitled to appear and be heard on the application), and

(*d*) the closure notice must be given to each of the relevant trustees.

Provided that a notice is not invalidated by virtue of paragraph (*a*) or (*d*) if it is given to each of the relevant trustees whose identity is known to the Inland Revenue.

(4) A Revenue determination or discovery assessment relating to the transaction must be made against all of the relevant trustees and is not effective against any of them unless notice of it is given to each of them whose identity is known to the Inland Revenue.

(5) In the case of an appeal arising from proceedings under this Part relating to the transaction—

(*a*) the appeal may be brought by any of the relevant trustees,

(*b*) notice of the appeal must be given to any of them by whom it is not brought,

(*c*) the agreement of all the relevant trustees is required if the appeal is to be settled by agreement,

(*d*) if it is not settled, any of them are entitled to appear and be heard, and

(*e*) the decision on the appeal binds all of them.

Amendments—[1] Words in sub-paras (1)–(3) repealed by FA 2008 s 94, Sch 30 para 13 with effect in relation to transactions with an effective date on or after 12 March 2008.

Consideration for exercise of power of appointment or discretion

7 Where a chargeable interest is acquired by virtue of—

(*a*) the exercise of a power of appointment, or

(*b*) the exercise of a discretion vested in trustees of a settlement,

there shall be treated as consideration for the acquisition of the interest or right by virtue of the exercise of the power or discretion any consideration given for the person in whose favour the appointment was made or the discretion was exercised becoming an object of the power or discretion.

[Reallocation of trust property as between beneficiaries

8 Where—

(*a*) the trustees of a settlement reallocate trust property in such a way that a beneficiary acquires an interest in certain trust property and ceases to have an interest in other trust property, and

(*b*) the beneficiary consents to ceasing to have an interest in that other property,

the fact that he gives consent does not mean that there is chargeable consideration for the acquisition.][1]

Amendments—[1] This paragraph inserted by FA 2006 s 165 with effect in relation to any acquisition of which the effective date (within the meaning of Part 4 of FA 2003) is on or after 19 July 2006.

[SCHEDULE 17

STAMP DUTY LAND TAX: GENERAL AND SPECIAL COMMISSIONERS, APPEALS AND OTHER PROCEEDINGS]

Section 115

Amendments—Schedule 17 repealed by the Transfer of Tribunal Functions and Revenue and Customs Appeals Order, SI 2009/56 art 3, Sch 1 para 413 with effect from 1 April 2009.

General and Special Commissioners: application of general provisions

1 *[Part 1 of the Taxes Management Act 1970 (c 9) (administration) has effect as if this Part of this Act were part of the Taxes Acts.]*[1]

Amendments—[1] Schedule 17 repealed by the Transfer of Tribunal Functions and Revenue and Customs Appeals Order, SI 2009/56 art 3, Sch 1 para 413 with effect from 1 April 2009.

Prescribed matters to be determined by Commissioners or Lands Tribunal

[2—*(1) The Lord Chancellor may make regulations providing that a question, dispute, appeal or other matter that is of a prescribed description and arises in relation to the provisions of this Part is to be determined—*

(a) by the General Commissioners,

(b) by the Special Commissioners,

(c) by the General or Special Commissioners, or

(d) by the relevant Lands Tribunal.

[(1A) The Lord Chancellor may make regulations under this paragraph only after consulting all of the following—

(a) the Lord Chief Justice of England and Wales;

(b) the Lord President of the Court of Session;

(c) the Lord Chief Justice of Northern Ireland.

(1B) The Lord Chief Justice of England and Wales may nominate a judicial office holder (as defined in section 109(4) of the Constitutional Reform Act 2005) to exercise his functions under this paragraph.

(1C) The Lord President of the Court of Session may nominate a judge of the Court of Session who is a member of the First or Second Division of the Inner House of that Court to exercise his functions under this paragraph.

(1D) The Lord Chief Justice of Northern Ireland may nominate any of the following to exercise his functions under this paragraph—

(a) the holder of one of the offices listed in Schedule 1 to the Justice (Northern Ireland) Act 2002;

(b) a Lord Justice of Appeal (as defined in section 88 of that Act).][1]

(2) In this paragraph—

"prescribed" means prescribed in regulations under this paragraph;

"relevant Lands Tribunal" means—

(a) in relation to land in England and Wales, the Lands Tribunal;

(b) in relation to land in Scotland, the Lands Tribunal for Scotland;

(c) in relation to land in Northern Ireland, the Lands Tribunal for Northern Ireland.][2]

Amendments—[1] Sub-paras (1A)–(1D) inserted by the Constitutional Reform Act 2005 s 15, Sch 4 para 307(1), (2) with effect from 3 April 2006 (by virtue of SI 2006/1014 art 2(a), Sch 1 para 11).

[2] Schedule 17 repealed by the Transfer of Tribunal Functions and Revenue and Customs Appeals Order, SI 2009/56 art 3, Sch 1 para 413 with effect from 1 April 2009.

General or Special Commissioners: jurisdiction

[**3**—*(1) Where the General or Special Commissioners have jurisdiction in respect of a matter, the Lord Chancellor may make regulations for determining—*

(a) whether the General or Special Commissioners, or both of them, are to have the jurisdiction, and

(b) if both of them are to have the jurisdiction, how it is to be divided between them.

(2) Where the General Commissioners have jurisdiction in respect of a matter, the General Commissioners for that division which is determined in accordance with regulations made by the Lord Chancellor under this paragraph are to have the jurisdiction.

(3) The Lord Chancellor may make regulations—

(a) providing that, in certain circumstances, the Special Commissioners are to have jurisdiction in respect of a matter instead of the General Commissioners or the General Commissioners are to have jurisdiction instead of the Special Commissioners;

(b) providing that, in certain circumstances, the General Commissioners for one division are have to jurisdiction in respect of a matter instead of the General Commissioners for another division.

[(4) The Lord Chancellor may make regulations under this paragraph only after consulting all of the following—

(a) the Lord Chief Justice of England and Wales;

(b) the Lord President of the Court of Session;

(c) the Lord Chief Justice of Northern Ireland.

(5) The Lord Chief Justice of England and Wales may nominate a judicial office holder (as defined in section 109(4) of the Constitutional Reform Act 2005) to exercise his functions under this paragraph.

(6) The Lord President of the Court of Session may nominate a judge of the Court of Session who is a member of the First or Second Division of the Inner House of that Court to exercise his functions under this paragraph.

(7) The Lord Chief Justice of Northern Ireland may nominate any of the following to exercise his functions under this paragraph—

(a) the holder of one of the offices listed in Schedule 1 to the Justice (Northern Ireland) Act 2002;

(b) a Lord Justice of Appeal (as defined in section 88 of that Act).]][1][2]

Amendments—[1] Sub-paras (4)–(7) inserted by the Constitutional Reform Act 2005 s 15, Sch 4 para 307(1), (3) with effect from 3 April 2006 (by virtue of SI 2006/1014 art 2(a), Sch 1 para 11).

[2] Schedule 17 repealed by the Transfer of Tribunal Functions and Revenue and Customs Appeals Order, SI 2009/56 art 3, Sch 1 para 413 with effect from 1 April 2009.

Proceedings brought out of time

[**4**—*(1) An appeal under this Part to the General or Special Commissioners may be brought out of time with the consent in writing of an officer of the Board or the Board.*

(2) Consent shall be given if the officer or, as the case may be, the Board are satisfied—

(a) that there was a reasonable excuse for not bringing the appeal within the time limit, and

(b) that an application for consent was made without unreasonable delay.

(3) If the officer or, as the case may be, the Board are not so satisfied, they shall refer the matter for determination by the Commissioners.

(4) If there is a right to elect to bring the appeal before the Special Commissioners instead of before the General Commissioners, the Commissioners to whom an application under this paragraph is to be referred are the General Commissioners, unless the election has been made before the application is referred.][1]

Amendments—[1] Schedule 17 repealed by the Transfer of Tribunal Functions and Revenue and Customs Appeals Order, SI 2009/56 art 3, Sch 1 para 413 with effect from 1 April 2009.

Quorum etc of the Commissioners

[5 *[(1)]* [1]*The Lord Chancellor may make regulations about the number of General or Special Commissioners required or permitted to perform functions in relation to a relevant matter.*

[(2) The Lord Chancellor may make regulations under this paragraph only after consulting all of the following—

(a) the Lord Chief Justice of England and Wales;

(b) the Lord President of the Court of Session;

(c) the Lord Chief Justice of Northern Ireland.

(3) The Lord Chief Justice of England and Wales may nominate a judicial office holder (as defined in section 109(4) of the Constitutional Reform Act 2005) to exercise his functions under this paragraph.

(4) The Lord President of the Court of Session may nominate a judge of the Court of Session who is a member of the First or Second Division of the Inner House of that Court to exercise his functions under this paragraph.

(5) The Lord Chief Justice of Northern Ireland may nominate any of the following to exercise his functions under this paragraph—

(a) the holder of one of the offices listed in Schedule 1 to the Justice (Northern Ireland) Act 2002;

(b) a Lord Justice of Appeal (as defined in section 88 of that Act).][1]][2]

Amendments—[1] Paragraph renumbered as such, and sub-paras (2)–(5) inserted, by the Constitutional Reform Act 2005 s 15, Sch 4 para 307(1), (4) with effect from 3 April 2006 (by virtue of SI 2006/1014 art 2(a), Sch 1 para 11).

[2] Schedule 17 repealed by the Transfer of Tribunal Functions and Revenue and Customs Appeals Order, SI 2009/56 art 3, Sch 1 para 413 with effect from 1 April 2009.

Procedure

[6—*(1) The Lord Chancellor may make regulations about the practice and procedure to be followed in connection with matters in respect of which the Special or General Commissioners have jurisdiction.*

(2) The regulations may, in particular, include provision—

(a) enabling the Commissioners to join as a party to the proceedings a person who would not otherwise be a party;

(b) for requiring a party to the proceedings to provide information and make documents available for inspection by—

(i) the Commissioners,

(ii) any party to the proceedings, or

(iii) an officer of the Board;

(c) for requiring persons to attend the hearing to give evidence and produce documents;

(d) as to evidence generally in relation to proceedings;

(e) enabling the Commissioners to review their decisions;

(f) for the imposition of penalties not exceeding an amount specified in the regulations;

(g) for the determination and recovery of penalties imposed by virtue of paragraph (f) and for appeals against such penalties.][1]

Amendments—[1] Schedule 17 repealed by the Transfer of Tribunal Functions and Revenue and Customs Appeals Order, SI 2009/56 art 3, Sch 1 para 413 with effect from 1 April 2009.

Consequences of determination by the Commissioners

[7 *The Lord Chancellor may make regulations prescribing the consequences of any determination by the General or Special Commissioners in respect of a relevant matter.*][1]

Amendments—[1] Schedule 17 repealed by the Transfer of Tribunal Functions and Revenue and Customs Appeals Order, SI 2009/56 art 3, Sch 1 para 413 with effect from 1 April 2009.

Costs

[8 *The Lord Chancellor may make regulations about—*

(a) the award by the General or Special Commissioners of the costs of, or incidental to, a determination by them in respect of a relevant matter;

(b) the recovery of costs so awarded.][1]

Amendments—[1] Schedule 17 repealed by the Transfer of Tribunal Functions and Revenue and Customs Appeals Order, SI 2009/56 art 3, Sch 1 para 413 with effect from 1 April 2009.

Finality of decisions of the Commissioners

[9—*(1) The Lord Chancellor may make regulations about the following matters—*

(a) the circumstances in which—

(i) a determination by the General or Special Commissioners in respect of a relevant matter, or

(ii) an award of costs under regulations under paragraph 8,

may or may not be questioned;

(b) if a determination or award may be questioned, how it may be questioned.

(2) The regulations may—

(a) authorise or require the Commissioners, in circumstances specified in the regulations, to state a case for the opinion of a court;

(b) make provision as to the practice and procedure to be followed in connection with cases so stated;

(c) make provision in relation to cases so stated corresponding to any provision made by section 56 of the Taxes Management Act 1970 (c 9) (statement of case for opinion of High Court) or by that section as modified in its application to Northern Ireland by section 58 of that Act.

(3) The regulations may—

(a) provide for an appeal to lie to a court on a question of law arising from a decision of the Commissioners;

(b) make provision as to the practice and procedure to be followed in connection with such appeals;

(c) make provision in relation to such appeals corresponding to any provision made by section 56A of the Taxes Management Act 1970 (appeals from the Special Commissioners) or by that section as modified in its application to Northern Ireland by section 58 of that Act.][1]

Amendments—[1] Schedule 17 repealed by the Transfer of Tribunal Functions and Revenue and Customs Appeals Order, SI 2009/56 art 3, Sch 1 para 413 with effect from 1 April 2009.

Publication of reports of decisions

[10—*(1) The Lord Chancellor may make regulations authorising the Special Commissioners to publish reports of such of their decisions as they consider appropriate.*

(2) The regulations shall provide that any report published that is not a report of proceedings heard in public must be in a form that so far as possible prevents the identification of any person whose affairs are dealt with in the report.

(3) No obligation of secrecy to which the Special Commissioners are subject prevents their publishing reports of their decisions in accordance with provision made by virtue of this paragraph.][1]

Amendments—[1] Schedule 17 repealed by the Transfer of Tribunal Functions and Revenue and Customs Appeals Order, SI 2009/56 art 3, Sch 1 para 413 with effect from 1 April 2009.

Supplementary provisions

[11—*[(1) Any power to make regulations under this Schedule is exercisable—*

(a) only with the consent of the Scottish Ministers;

(b) subject to any other provision of this Schedule.][1]

(2) Regulations under this Schedule shall be made by statutory instrument which shall be subject to annulment in pursuance of a resolution of either House of Parliament.

(3) Regulations under this Schedule may—

(a) apply any other enactment, with or without modifications;

(b) make different provision for different cases or different circumstances;

(c) contain such supplementary, incidental, consequential and transitional provision as the Lord Chancellor thinks appropriate.

(4) In this Schedule—

(*a*) *"relevant matter", in relation to the General or Special Commissioners, means a matter in respect of which they have jurisdiction;*

(*b*) *references to the provisions of this Part include any instrument made under such a provision;*

(*c*) *references to the General or Special Commissioners having jurisdiction are to the Commissioners having jurisdiction by virtue of the provisions of this Part;*

(*d*) *references to the General or Special Commissioners having jurisdiction in respect of a matter include cases where a question, dispute, appeal or other matter that arises in relation to the provisions of this Part is to be determined by the Commissioners.*][2]

Amendments—[1] Sub-para (1) substituted by the Constitutional Reform Act 2005 s 15, Sch 4 para 307(1), (5) with effect from 3 April 2006 (by virtue of SI 2006/1014 art 2(a), Sch 1 para 11).

[2] Schedule 17 repealed by the Transfer of Tribunal Functions and Revenue and Customs Appeals Order, SI 2009/56 art 3, Sch 1 para 413 with effect from 1 April 2009.

[SCHEDULE 17A

FURTHER PROVISIONS RELATING TO LEASES]

[Section 120]

Amendments—This Schedule inserted by FA 2004 s 296, Sch 39 para 22(2) with effect for any transaction of which the effective date (within the meaning of FA 2003 Pt 4) is on or after 22 July 2004: FA 2004 Sch 39 para 26. This insertion was previously made by the Stamp Duty and Stamp Duty Land Tax (Variation of the Finance Act 2003) (No 2) Regulations, SI 2003/2816 regs 1, 2, Schedule para 8(2) with effect from 1 December 2003. Those regulations are revoked by FA 2004 Sch 39 para 14(2).

[Meaning of "lease"

1 In the application of this Part to England and Wales or Northern Ireland "lease" means—

(*a*) an interest or right in or over land for a term of years (whether fixed or periodic), or

(*b*) a tenancy at will or other interest or right in or over land terminable by notice at any time.][1]

Amendments—[1] This Schedule inserted by FA 2004 s 296, Sch 39 para 22(2) with effect for any transaction of which the effective date (within the meaning of FA 2003 Pt 4) is on or after 22 July 2004: FA 2004 Sch 39 para 26. This insertion was previously made by the Stamp Duty and Stamp Duty Land Tax (Variation of the Finance Act 2003) (No 2) Regulations, SI 2003/2816 regs 1, 2, Schedule para 8(2) with effect from 1 December 2003. Those regulations are revoked by FA 2004 Sch 39 para 14(2).

[Leases for a fixed term

2 In the application of the provisions of this Part to a lease for a fixed term, no account shall be taken of—

(*a*) any contingency as a result of which the lease may determine before the end of the fixed term, or

(*b*) any right of either party to determine the lease or renew it.][1]

Amendments—[1] This Schedule inserted by FA 2004 s 296, Sch 39 para 22(2) with effect for any transaction of which the effective date (within the meaning of FA 2003 Pt 4) is on or after 22 July 2004: FA 2004 Sch 39 para 26. This insertion was previously made by the Stamp Duty and Stamp Duty Land Tax (Variation of the Finance Act 2003) (No 2) Regulations, SI 2003/2816 regs 1, 2, Schedule para 8(2) with effect from 1 December 2003. Those regulations are revoked by FA 2004 Sch 39 para 14(2).

[Leases that continue after a fixed term

3—(1) This paragraph applies to—

(*a*) a lease for a fixed term and thereafter until determined, or

(*b*) a lease for a fixed term that may continue beyond the fixed term by operation of law.

(2) For the purposes of this Part (except [sections 77 and 77A][3] (notifiable transactions)), a lease to which this paragraph applies is treated—

(*a*) in the first instance as if it were a lease for the original fixed term and no longer,

(*b*) if the lease continues after the end of that term, as if it were a lease for a fixed term one year longer than the original fixed term,

(*c*) if the lease continues after the end of the term resulting from the application of paragraph (*b*), as if it were a lease for a fixed term two years longer than the original fixed term,

and so on.

(3) Where the effect of sub-paragraph (2) in relation to the continuation of the lease after the end of a fixed term is that additional tax is payable in respect of a transaction or that tax is payable in respect of a transaction where none was payable before—

(*a*) the purchaser must deliver a return or further return in respect of that transaction before the end of the period of 30 days after the end of that term,

(*b*) the return must include a self-assessment of the amount of tax chargeable in respect of the transaction on the basis of the information contained in the return, (*c*) the tax so chargeable is to be calculated by reference to the rates in force at the effective date of the transaction, and

[(*d*) the tax or additional tax payable must be paid not later than the filing date for the return.][2]

(4) The provisions of Schedule 10 (returns, enquiries, assessments and other matters) apply to a return under this paragraph as they apply to a return under section 76 (general requirement to deliver land transaction return), with the adaptation that references to the effective date of the transaction shall be read as references to the day on which the lease becomes treated as being for a longer fixed term.

(5) For the purposes of [sections 77 and 77A][3] (notifiable transactions) a lease to which this paragraph applies is a lease for whatever is its fixed term.][1]

Modifications—Pensions Schemes (Taxable Property Provisions) Regulations, SI 2006/1958 reg 7 (application of this paragraph, subject to modifications for the purposes of FA 2004 Sch 29 para 34(2)).

Cross references—FA 2009 Sch 55 (penalty for failure to make returns etc).

Amendments—[1] This Schedule inserted by FA 2004 s 296, Sch 39 para 22(2) with effect for any transaction of which the effective date (within the meaning of FA 2003 Pt 4) is on or after 22 July 2004: FA 2004 Sch 39 para 26. This insertion was previously made by the Stamp Duty and Stamp Duty Land Tax (Variation of the Finance Act 2003) (No 2) Regulations, SI 2003/2816 regs 1, 2, Schedule para 8(2) with effect from 1 December 2003. Those regulations are revoked by FA 2004 Sch 39 para 14(2).

[2] Sub-para (3)(d) substituted by FA 2007 s 80(1), (8), (9)(g) with effect in respect of requirements to deliver a return or further return which arise on or after 19 July 2007.

[3] Words in sub-paras (2), (5) substituted by FA 2008 s 94, Sch 30 para 14 with effect in relation to transactions with an effective date on or after 12 March 2008.

[Treatment of leases for indefinite term

4—(1) For the purposes of this Part (except [sections 77 and 77A][3] (notifiable transactions))—

(*a*) a lease for an indefinite term is treated in the first instance as if it were a lease for a fixed term of a year,

(*b*) if the lease continues after the end of the term resulting from the application of paragraph (*a*), it is treated as if it were a lease for a fixed term of two years,

(*c*) if the lease continues after the end of the term resulting from the application of paragraph (*b*), it is treated as if it were a lease for a fixed term of three years,

and so on.

(2) No account shall be taken for the purposes of this Part of any other statutory provision in England and Wales or Northern Ireland deeming a lease for an indefinite period to be a lease for a different term.

(3) Where the effect of sub-paragraph (1) in relation to the continuation of the lease after the end of a deemed fixed term is that additional tax is payable in respect of a transaction or that tax is payable in respect of a transaction where none was payable before—

(*a*) the purchaser must deliver a return or further return in respect of that transaction before the end of the period of 30 days after the end of that term,

(*b*) the return must include a self-assessment of the amount of tax chargeable in respect of the transaction on the basis of the information contained in the return,

(*c*) the tax so chargeable is to be calculated by reference to the rates in force at the effective date of the transaction, and

[(*d*) the tax or additional tax payable must be paid not later than the filing date for the return.][2]

(4) The provisions of Schedule 10 (returns, enquiries, assessments and other matters) apply to a return under this paragraph as they apply to a return under section 76 (general requirement to deliver land transaction return), with the adaptation that references to the effective date of the transaction shall be read as references to the day on which the lease becomes treated as being for a longer fixed term.

(4A) For the purposes of [sections 77 and 77A][3] (notifiable transactions) a lease for an indefinite term is a lease for a term of less then seven years.

(5) References in this paragraph to a lease for an indefinite period include—

(*a*) a periodic tenancy or other interest or right terminable by a period of notice,

(*b*) a tenancy at will in England and Wales or Northern Ireland, or

(*c*) any other interest or right terminable by notice at any time.][1]

Modifications—Pensions Schemes (Taxable Property Provisions) Regulations, SI 2006/1958 reg 7 (application of this paragraph, subject to modifications for the purposes of FA 2004 Sch 29 para 34(2)).

Cross references—FA 2009 Sch 55 (penalty for failure to make returns etc).

Amendments—[1] This Schedule inserted by FA 2004 s 296, Sch 39 para 22(2) with effect for any transaction of which the effective date (within the meaning of FA 2003 Pt 4) is on or after 22 July 2004: FA 2004 Sch 39 para 26. This insertion was previously made by the Stamp Duty and Stamp Duty Land Tax (Variation of the Finance Act 2003) (No 2) Regulations, SI 2003/2816 regs 1, 2, Schedule para 8(2) with effect from 1 December 2003. Those regulations are revoked by FA 2004 Sch 39 para 14(2).

[2] Sub-para (3)(d) substituted by FA 2007 s 80(1), (8), (9)(g) with effect in respect of requirements to deliver a return or further return which arise on or after 19 July 2007.

[3] Words in sub-paras (1), (4A) substituted by FA 2008 s 94, Sch 30 para 14 with effect in relation to transactions with an effective date on or after 12 March 2008.

[Treatment of successive linked leases

5—(1) This paragraph applies where—

(*a*) successive leases are granted or treated as granted (whether at the same time or at different times) of the same or substantially the same premises, and

(*b*) those grants are linked transactions.

(2) This Part applies as if the series of leases were a single lease—

(*a*) granted at the time of the grant of the first lease in the series,

(*b*) for a term equal to the aggregate of the terms of all the leases, and

(*c*) in consideration of the rent payable under all of the leases.

(3) The grant of later leases in the series is accordingly disregarded for the purposes of this Part except section 81A (return or further return in consequence of later linked transaction).][1]

Amendments—[1] This Schedule inserted by FA 2004 s 296, Sch 39 para 22(2) with effect for any transaction of which the effective date (within the meaning of FA 2003 Pt 4) is on or after 22 July 2004: FA 2004 Sch 39 para 26. This insertion was previously made by the Stamp Duty and Stamp Duty Land Tax (Variation of the Finance Act 2003) (No 2) Regulations, SI 2003/2816 regs 1, 2, Schedule para 8(2) with effect from 1 December 2003. Those regulations are revoked by FA 2004 Sch 39 para 14(2).

[Rent

6—(1) For the purposes of this Part a single sum expressed to be payable in respect of rent, or expressed to be payable in respect of rent and other matters but not apportioned, shall be treated as entirely rent.

(2) Sub-paragraph (1) is without prejudice to the application of paragraph 4 of Schedule 4 (chargeable consideration: just and reasonable apportionment) where separate sums are expressed to be payable in respect of rent and other matters.][1]

Amendments—[1] This Schedule inserted by FA 2004 s 296, Sch 39 para 22(2) with effect for any transaction of which the effective date (within the meaning of FA 2003 Pt 4) is on or after 22 July 2004: FA 2004 Sch 39 para 26. This insertion was previously made by the Stamp Duty and Stamp Duty Land Tax (Variation of the Finance Act 2003) (No 2) Regulations, SI 2003/2816 regs 1, 2, Schedule para 8(2) with effect from 1 December 2003. Those regulations are revoked by FA 2004 Sch 39 para 14(2).

[Variable or uncertain rent

7—(1) This paragraph applies to determine the amount of rent payable under a lease where that amount—

(*a*) varies in accordance with provision in the lease, or

(*b*) is contingent, uncertain or unascertained.

(2) As regards rent payable in respect of any period before the end of the fifth year of the term of the lease—

(*a*) the provisions of this Part apply as in relation to other chargeable consideration, and

(*b*) the provisions of section 51(1) and (2) accordingly apply if the amount is contingent, uncertain or unascertained.

(3) As regards rent payable in respect of any period after the end of the fifth year of the term of the lease, the annual amount is assumed for the purposes of this Part to be, in every case, equal to the highest amount of rent payable in respect of any consecutive twelve month period in the first five years of the term.

In determining that amount take into account (if necessary) any amounts determined as mentioned in sub-paragraph (2)(*b*), but disregard [paragraphs 9(2) and 9A(3) (deemed reduction of rent, where further lease granted, for period during which rents overlap)][3].

(4) This paragraph has effect subject to paragraph 8 (adjustment where rent payable ceases to be uncertain).

[(4A) For the purposes of this paragraph and paragraph 8, the cases where the amount of rent payable under a lease is uncertain or unascertained include cases where there is a possibility of that amount being varied under—

(*a*) section 12, 13 or 33 of the Agricultural Holdings Act 1986,

(*b*) Part 2 of the Agricultural Tenancies Act 1995,

(*c*) section 13, 14, 15 or 31 of the Agricultural Holdings (Scotland) Act 1991, or

(*d*) section 9, 10 or 11 of the Agricultural Holdings (Scotland) Act 2003.][2]

(5) No account shall be taken for the purposes of this Part of any provision for rent to be adjusted in line with the retail prices index.][1]

Amendments—[1] This Schedule inserted by FA 2004 s 296, Sch 39 para 22(2) with effect for any transaction of which the effective date (within the meaning of FA 2003 Pt 4) is on or after 22 July 2004: FA 2004 Sch 39 para 26. This insertion was previously made by the Stamp Duty and Stamp Duty Land Tax (Variation of the Finance Act 2003) (No 2) Regulations, SI 2003/2816 regs 1, 2, Schedule para 8(2) with effect from 1 December 2003. Those regulations are revoked by FA 2004 Sch 39 para 14(2).

2 Sub-para (4A) inserted by FA 2006 s 164, Sch 25 para 2(1) with effect in relation to any lease granted or treated as granted on or after 19 July 2006 by virtue of FA 2006 Sch 25 para 9(6).

3 Words in sub-para (3) substituted for "paragraph 9(2) (deemed reduction of rent for overlap period in case of grant of further lease)" by FA 2006 s 164, Sch 25 para 3(2) with effect in relation to any case where—
(a) the grant of the old lease was chargeable to stamp duty land tax, and
(b) the new lease is granted on or after 19 July 2006 by virtue of FA 2006 Sch 25 para 9(6).
"The old lease" and "the new lease" mean the leases referred to in sub-paragraphs (1)(*a*) and (1)(*b*), respectively, of paragraph 9A of Schedule 17A to FA 2003 (inserted by paragraph 3).

[First rent review in final quarter of fifth year

7A Where—
(*a*) a lease contains provision under which the rent may be adjusted,
(*b*) under that provision the first (or only) such adjustment—
(i) is to an amount that (before the adjustment) is uncertain, and
(ii) has effect from a date (the "review date") that is expressed as falling five years after a specified date,
and
(*c*) the specified date falls within the three months before the beginning of the term of the lease,
this Schedule has effect as if references to the first five years of the term of the lease were to the period beginning with the start of the term of the lease and ending with the review date. References to the fifth year of the term of the lease shall be read accordingly.][1]

Amendments—[1] This Schedule inserted by FA 2004 s 296, Sch 39 para 22(2) with effect for any transaction of which the effective date (within the meaning of FA 2003 Pt 4) is on or after 22 July 2004: FA 2004 Sch 39 para 26. This insertion was previously made by the Stamp Duty and Stamp Duty Land Tax (Variation of the Finance Act 2003) (No 2) Regulations, SI 2003/2816 regs 1, 2, Schedule para 8(2) with effect from 1 December 2003. Those regulations are revoked by FA 2004 Sch 39 para 14(2).
This paragraph was however not contained in the original Schedule 17A as inserted by SI 2003/2816. FA 2004 Sch 39 para 11(1), (2) amends that version of the Schedule to insert the above paragraph. That insertion had effect for any transaction of which the effective date was after 17 March 2004 and before 22 July 2004: FA 2004 Sch 39 para 13(3), (5).

[Adjustment where rent ceases to be uncertain

8—(1) Where the provisions of section 51(1) and (2) (contingent, uncertain or unascertained consideration) apply in relation to a transaction by virtue of paragraph 7 (uncertain rent) and—
(*a*) the end of the fifth year of the term of the lease is reached, or
(*b*) the amount of rent payable in respect of the first five years of the term of the lease ceases to be uncertain at an earlier date,
the following provisions have effect to require or permit reconsideration of how this Part applies to the transaction (and to any transaction in relation to which it is a linked transaction).
(2) For the purposes of this paragraph the amount of rent payable ceases to be uncertain when—
(*a*) in the case of contingent rent, the contingency occurs or it becomes clear that it will not occur, and
(*b*) in the case of uncertain or unascertained rent, the amount becomes ascertained.
(3) If the result as regards the rent paid or payable in respect of the first five years of the term of the lease is that a transaction becomes notifiable, or that additional tax is payable in respect of a transaction or that tax is payable where none was payable before—
(*a*) the purchaser must make a return to the Inland Revenue within 30 days of the date referred to in sub-paragraph (1)(*a*) or (*b*),
(*b*) the return must contain a self-assessment of the tax chargeable in respect of the transaction on the basis of the information contained in the return,
(*c*) the tax so chargeable is to be calculated by reference to the rates in force at the effective date of the transaction, and
[(*d*) the tax or additional tax payable must be paid not later than the filing date for the return.][2]
(4) The provisions of Schedule 10 (returns, enquiries, assessment and other matters) apply to a return under this paragraph as they apply to a return under section 76 (general requirement to make land transaction return), subject to the adaptation that references to the effective date of the transaction shall be read as references to the date referred to in sub-paragraph (1)(*a*) or (*b*).
(5) If the result as regards the rent paid or payable in respect of the first five years of the term of the lease is that less tax is payable in respect of the transaction than has already been paid—
(*a*) the purchaser may, within the period allowed for amendment of the land transaction return, amend the return accordingly;
(*b*) after the end of that period he may (if the land transaction return is not so amended) make a claim to the Inland Revenue for repayment of the amount overpaid.][1]

Modifications—Pensions Schemes (Taxable Property Provisions) Regulations, SI 2006/1958 reg 8 (application of this paragraph, subject to modifications for the purposes of FA 2004 Sch 29 para 34(2)).

Cross references—FA 2009 Sch 55 (penalty for failure to make returns etc).

Amendments—[1] This Schedule inserted by FA 2004 s 296, Sch 39 para 22(2) with effect for any transaction of which the effective date (within the meaning of FA 2003 Pt 4) is on or after 22 July 2004: FA 2004 Sch 39 para 26. This insertion was previously made by the Stamp Duty and Stamp Duty Land Tax (Variation of the Finance Act 2003) (No 2) Regulations, SI 2003/2816 regs 1, 2, Schedule para 8(2) with effect from 1 December 2003. Those regulations are revoked by FA 2004 Sch 39 para 14(2).

[2] Sub-para (3)(*d*) substituted by FA 2007 s 80(1), (8), (9)(*g*) with effect in respect of requirements to deliver a return or further return which arise on or after the day on which FA 2007 is passed.

[Rent for overlap period in case of grant of further lease

9—(1) This paragraph applies where—

(*a*) A surrenders an existing lease to B ("the old lease") and in consideration of that surrender B grants a lease to A of the same or substantially the same premises ("the new lease"),

(*b*) the tenant under a lease ("the old lease") of premises to which Part 2 of the Landlord and Tenant Act 1954 or the Business Tenancies (Northern Ireland) Order 1996 applies makes a request for a new tenancy ("the new lease") which is duly executed,

(*c*) on termination of a lease ("the head lease") a sub-tenant is granted a lease ("the new lease") of the same or substantially the same premises as those comprised in his original lease ("the old lease")—

(i) in pursuance of an order of a court on a claim for relief against re-entry or forfeiture, or

(ii) in pursuance of a contractual entitlement arising in the event of the head lease being terminated,

or

(*d*) a person who has guaranteed the obligations of a lessee under a lease that has been terminated ("the old lease") is granted a lease of the same or substantially the same premises ("the new lease") in pursuance of the guarantee.

(2) For the purposes of this Part the rent payable under the new lease in respect of any period falling within the overlap period is treated as reduced by the amount of the rent that would have been payable in respect of that period under the old lease.

(3) The overlap period is the period between the date of grant of the new lease and what would have been the end of the term of the old lease had it not been terminated.

(4) The rent that would have been payable under the old lease shall be taken to be the amount taken into account in determining the stamp duty land tax chargeable in respect of the acquisition of the old lease.

(5) This paragraph does not have effect so as to require the rent payable under the new lease to be treated as a negative amount.][1]

Amendments—[1] This Schedule inserted by FA 2004 s 296, Sch 39 para 22(2) with effect for any transaction of which the effective date (within the meaning of FA 2003 Pt 4) is on or after 22 July 2004: FA 2004 Sch 39 para 26.

This paragraph was first inserted by the Stamp Duty and Stamp Duty Land Tax (Variation of the Finance Act 2003) (No 2) Regulations, SI 2003/2816 regs 1, 2, Schedule para 8(2) with effect from 1 December 2003. (Those regulations are revoked by FA 2004 Sch 39 para 14(2).) That version was amended by FA 2004 Sch 39 para 11(1) with effect for any transaction of which the effective date was after 17 March 2004 and before 22 July 2004: FA 2004 Sch 39 para 13(3), (5).

[Backdated lease granted to tenant holding over

9A—(1) This paragraph applies where—

(*a*) the tenant under a lease continues in occupation after the date on which, under its terms, the lease terminates ("the contractual termination date"),

(*b*) he is granted a new lease of the same or substantially the same premises, and

(*c*) the term of the new lease is expressed to begin on or immediately after the contractual termination date.

(2) The term of the new lease is treated for the purposes of this Part as beginning on the date on which it is expressed to begin.

(3) The rent payable under the new lease in respect of any period falling—

(*a*) after the contractual termination date, and

(*b*) before the date on which the new lease is granted,

is treated for the purposes of this Part as reduced by the amount of taxable rent that is payable in respect of that period otherwise than under the new lease.

(4) For the purposes of sub-paragraph (3) rent is "taxable" if or to the extent that it is taken into account in determining liability to stamp duty land tax.

(5) Sub-paragraph (3) does not have effect so as to require the rent payable under the new lease to be treated as a negative amount.][1]

Amendments—[1] This paragraph inserted by FA 2006 s 164, Sch 25 para 3(1) with effect in relation to any case where—

(a) the grant of the old lease was chargeable to stamp duty land tax, and

(b) the new lease is granted on or after 19 July 2006 by virtue of FA 2006 Sch 25 para 9(6).
"The old lease" and "the new lease" mean the leases referred to in FA 2003 Sch 17A para 9A(1)(*a*), (*b*), respectively.

[Tenants' obligations etc that do not count as chargeable consideration

10—(1) In the case of the grant of a lease none of the following counts as chargeable consideration—

(*a*) any undertaking by the tenant to repair, maintain or insure the demised premises (in Scotland, the leased premises);

(*b*) any undertaking by the tenant to pay any amount in respect of services, repairs, maintenance or insurance or the landlord's costs of management;

(*c*) any other obligation undertaken by the tenant that is not such as to affect the rent that a tenant would be prepared to pay in the open market;

(*d*) any guarantee of the payment of rent or the performance of any other obligation of the tenant under the lease;

(*e*) any penal rent, or increased rent in the nature of a penal rent, payable in respect of the breach of any obligation of the tenant under the lease;

[(*f*) any liability of the tenant for costs under section 14(2) of the Leasehold Reform Act 1967 or section 60 of the Leasehold Reform, Housing and Urban Development Act 1993 (costs to be borne by person exercising statutory right to be granted lease);][2]

[(*g*) any other obligation of the tenant to bear the landlord's reasonable costs or expenses of or incidental to the grant of a lease;][2]

[(*h*) any obligation under the lease to transfer to the landlord, on the termination of the lease, payment entitlements granted to the tenant under the single payment scheme (that is, the scheme of income support for farmers in pursuance of Title III of Council Regulation (EC) No 1782/2003) in respect of land subject to the lease.][2]

(2) Where sub-paragraph (1) applies in relation to an obligation, a payment made in discharge of the obligation does not count as chargeable consideration.

(3) The release of any such obligation as is mentioned in sub-paragraph (1) does not count as chargeable consideration in relation to the surrender of the lease.][1]

Amendments—[1] This Schedule inserted by FA 2004 s 296, Sch 39 para 22(2) with effect for any transaction of which the effective date (within the meaning of FA 2003 Pt 4) is on or after 22 July 2004: FA 2004 Sch 39 para 26. This insertion was previously made by the Stamp Duty and Stamp Duty Land Tax (Variation of the Finance Act 2003) (No 2) Regulations, SI 2003/2816 regs 1, 2, Schedule para 8(2) with effect from 1 December 2003. Those regulations are revoked by FA 2004 Sch 39 para 14(2).

[2] Sub-paras (1)(f)–(h) inserted by the SDLT (Amendment to the Finance Act 2003) Regulations, SI 2006/875 regs 2, 4. SI 2006/875 came into force on 12 April 2006, and this amendment has effect in relation to land transactions with an effective date on or after that date: SI 2006/875 reg 1.

[Cases where assignment of lease treated as grant of lease

11—[(1) This paragraph applies where the grant of a lease is exempt from charge by virtue of any of the provisions specified in sub-paragraph (3).][3]

(2) The first assignment of the lease that is not exempt from charge by virtue of any of the provisions specified in sub-paragraph (3), and in relation to which the assignee does not acquire the lease as a bare trustee of the assignor, is treated for the purposes of this Part as if it were the grant of a lease by the assignor—

(*a*) for a term equal to the unexpired term of the lease referred to in sub-paragraph (1), and

(*b*) on the same terms as those on which the assignee holds that lease after the assignment.

[(2A) Sub-paragraph (2) shall not apply where an assignment of a lease, but for the application of that sub-paragraph, would be exempt by virtue of Schedule 61 to the Finance Act 2009.][4]

(3) The provisions are—

(*a*) section 57A (sale and leaseback arrangements);

(*b*) Part 1 or 2 of Schedule 7 (group relief or reconstruction or acquisition relief);

(*c*) section 66 (transfers involving public bodies);

(*d*) Schedule 8 (charities relief);

(*e*) any such regulations as are mentioned in section 123(3) (regulations reproducing in relation to stamp duty land tax the effect of enactments providing for exemption from stamp duty).

[(*f*) Paragraphs 6 and 8 of Part 3 of Schedule 61 to the Finance Act 2009 (alternative finance investment bond relief)][4]

(4) This paragraph does not apply where the relief in question is group relief, reconstruction or acquisition relief or charities relief and is withdrawn as a result of a disqualifying event occurring before the effective date of the assignment.

(5) For the purposes of sub-paragraph (4) "disqualifying event" means—

(*a*) in relation to the withdrawal of group relief, [the event falling within paragraph 3(1)(*a*) of Schedule 7 (purchaser ceasing to be a member of the same group as the vendor), as read with paragraph 4A of that Schedule][2];

(*b*) in relation to the withdrawal of reconstruction or acquisition relief, the change of control of the acquiring company mentioned in paragraph 9(1)(*a*) of that Schedule or, as the case may be, the event mentioned in paragraph 11(1)(*a*) or (2)(*a*) of that Schedule;

(*c*) in relation to the withdrawal of charities relief, a disqualifying event as defined in paragraphs 2(3) or 3(2) of Schedule 8.][1]

Amendments—[1] This Schedule inserted by FA 2004 s 296, Sch 39 para 22(2) with effect for any transaction of which the effective date (within the meaning of FA 2003 Pt 4) is on or after 22 July 2004: FA 2004 Sch 39 para 26. This insertion was previously made by the Stamp Duty and Stamp Duty Land Tax (Variation of the Finance Act 2003) (No 2) Regulations, SI 2003/2816 regs 1, 2, Schedule para 8(2) with effect from 1 December 2003. Those regulations are revoked by FA 2004 Sch 39 para 14(2).

2 In sub-para (5)(a), words substituted for the words "the purchaser ceasing to be a member of the same group as the vendor (within the meaning of Part 1 of Schedule 7);" by F(No 2)A 2005 s 49, Sch 10 paras 1, 7 with effect where the effective date of the relevant transaction (within the meaning of FA 2003 Sch 7 para 3 or 4A) is after 19 May 2005.

However, this amendment does not have effect—

(a) in relation to any transaction which is effected in pursuance of a contract entered into and substantially performed on or before the specified date (ie 16 March 2005), or

(b) subject to what follows below, in relation to any other transaction which is effected in pursuance of a contract entered into on or before the specified date (ie 16 March 2005).

The exclusion by para (b) above of transactions effected in pursuance of contracts entered into on or before the specified date does not apply—

(a) if there is any variation of the contract or assignment of rights under the contract after that date,

(b) if the transaction is effected in consequence of the exercise after that date of any option, right of pre-emption or similar right, or

(c) if after that date there is an assignment, subsale or other transaction (relating to the whole or part of the subject-matter of the contract) as a result of which a person other than the purchaser under the contract becomes entitled to call for a conveyance to him: F(No 2)A 2005 Sch 10 para 16(1), (6)–(8).

3 Sub-para (1) substituted by F(No 2)A 2005 s 49, Sch 10 paras 1, 12 with effect where the effective date of the land transaction consisting of the grant of the lease is after 19 May 2005. However, this amendment is subject to the qualifications detailed in note **2** above: F(No 2)A 2005 Sch 10 para 16(4), (6)–(8).

4 Paras (2A), (3)(*f*) inserted by the SDLT (Alternative Finance Investment Bonds) Regulations, SI 2010/814 reg 2 with effect from 7 April 2010.

[Assignment of lease: responsibility of assignee for returns etc

12—(1) Where a lease is assigned, anything that but for the assignment would be required or authorised to be done by or in relation to the assignor under or by virtue of—

(*a*) section 80 (adjustment where contingency ceases or consideration is ascertained),

(*b*) section 81A (return or further return in consequence of later linked transaction),

(*c*) paragraph 3 or 4 of this Schedule (return or further return required where lease for indefinite period continues), or

(*d*) paragraph 8 of this Schedule (adjustment where rent ceases to be uncertain),

shall, if the event giving rise to the adjustment or return occurs after the effective date of the assignment, be done instead by or in relation to the assignee.

(2) So far as necessary for giving effect to sub-paragraph (1) anything previously done by or in relation to the assignor shall be treated as if it had been done by or in relation to the assignee.

(3) This paragraph does not apply if the assignment falls to be treated as the grant of a lease by the assignor (see paragraph 11).][1]

Amendments—[1] This Schedule inserted by FA 2004 s 296, Sch 39 para 22(2) with effect for any transaction of which the effective date (within the meaning of FA 2003 Pt 4) is on or after 22 July 2004: FA 2004 Sch 39 para 26. This insertion was previously made by the Stamp Duty and Stamp Duty Land Tax (Variation of the Finance Act 2003) (No 2) Regulations, SI 2003/2816 regs 1, 2, Schedule para 8(2) with effect from 1 December 2003. Those regulations are revoked by FA 2004 Sch 39 para 14(2).

[Agreement for lease

12A—(1) This paragraph applies where in England and Wales or Northern Ireland—

(*a*) an agreement for a lease is entered into, and

(*b*) the agreement is substantially performed without having been completed.

(2) The agreement is treated as if it were the grant of a lease in accordance with the agreement ("the notional lease"), beginning with the date of substantial performance.

The effective date of the transaction is that date.

(3) Where a lease is subsequently granted in pursuance of the agreement—

(*a*) the notional lease is treated as if it were surrendered at that time, and

(*b*) the lease itself is treated for the purposes of paragraph 9 (rent for overlap period in case of grant of further lease) as if it were granted in consideration of that surrender.

[Paragraph 5 does not apply so as to treat the notional lease and the lease itself as a single lease.][2]

(4) Where sub-paragraph (1) applies and the agreement is (to any extent) afterwards rescinded or annulled, or is for any other reason not carried into effect, the tax paid by virtue of that sub-paragraph shall (to that extent) be repaid by the Inland Revenue. Repayment must be claimed by amendment of the land transaction return made in respect of the agreement.

(5) In this paragraph "substantially performed" and "completed" have the same meanings as in section 44 (contract and conveyance).][1]

Amendments—[1] This Schedule inserted by FA 2004 s 296, Sch 39 para 22(2) with effect for any transaction of which the effective date (within the meaning of FA 2003 Pt 4) is on or after 22 July 2004: FA 2004 Sch 39 para 26. This insertion was previously made by the Stamp Duty and Stamp Duty Land Tax (Variation of the Finance Act 2003) (No 2) Regulations, SI 2003/2816 regs 1, 2, Schedule para 8(2) with effect from 1 December 2003. Those regulations are revoked by FA 2004 Sch 39 para 14(2).

Paragraphs 12A and 12B (below) were however not contained in the original Schedule 17A as inserted by SI 2003/2816. FA 2004 Sch 39 para 11(1), (4) amended that version of the Schedule to insert those paragraphs (identical to the paragraphs 12A and 12B as shown) with effect for any transaction of which the effective date is after 17 March 2004 and before 22 July 2004: FA 2004 Sch 39 para 13(3), (5).

[2] Words at the end of sub-para (3) inserted by FA 2006 s 164, Sch 25 para 4 with effect in relation to any agreement that is substantially performed on or after 19 July 2006 by virtue of FA 2006 Sch 25 para 9(6).

[Assignment of agreement for lease

12B—(1) This paragraph applies, in place of section 45 (contract and conveyance: effect of transfer of rights), where in England and Wales or Northern Ireland a person assigns his interest as lessee under an agreement for a lease.

(2) If the assignment occurs without the agreement having been substantially performed, section 44 (contract and conveyance) has effect as if—

(*a*) the contract were with the assignee and not the assignor, and

(*b*) the consideration given by the assignee for entering into the contract included any consideration given by him for the assignment.

(3) If the assignment occurs after the agreement has been substantially performed—

(*a*) the assignment is a separate land transaction, and

(*b*) the effective date of that transaction is the date of the assignment.

(4) Where there are successive assignments, this paragraph has effect in relation to each of them.][1]

Amendments—[1] This Schedule inserted by FA 2004 s 296, Sch 39 para 22(2) with effect for any transaction of which the effective date (within the meaning of FA 2003 Pt 4) is on or after 22 July 2004: FA 2004 Sch 39 para 26. This insertion was previously made by the Stamp Duty and Stamp Duty Land Tax (Variation of the Finance Act 2003) (No 2) Regulations, SI 2003/2816 regs 1, 2, Schedule para 8(2) with effect from 1 December 2003. Those regulations are revoked by FA 2004 Sch 39 para 14(2).

Paragraphs 12A (above) and 12B were however not contained in the original Schedule 17A as inserted by SI 2003/2816. FA 2004 Sch 39 para 11(1), (4) amended that version of the Schedule to insert those paragraphs (identical to the paragraphs 12A and 12B as shown) with effect for any transaction of which the effective date is after 17 March 2004 and before 22 July 2004: FA 2004 Sch 39 para 13(3), (5).

[Increase of rent treated as grant of new lease: variation of lease [in first five years][3]

13—(1) Where a lease is varied so as to increase the amount of the rent [as from a date before the end of the fifth year of the term of the lease][3], the variation is treated for the purposes of this Part as if it were the grant of a lease in consideration of the additional rent made payable by it.

(2) Sub-paragraph (1) does not apply to an increase of rent [in pursuance of—

(*a*) a provision contained in the lease, or

(*b*) a provision mentioned in any of paragraphs (*a*) to (*d*) of paragraph 7(4A)][2].][1]

Amendments—[1] This Schedule inserted by FA 2004 s 296, Sch 39 para 22(2) with effect for any transaction of which the effective date (within the meaning of FA 2003 Pt 4) is on or after 22 July 2004: FA 2004 Sch 39 para 26. This insertion was previously made by the Stamp Duty and Stamp Duty Land Tax (Variation of the Finance Act 2003) (No 2) Regulations, SI 2003/2816 regs 1, 2, Schedule para 8(2) with effect from 1 December 2003. Those regulations are revoked by FA 2004 Sch 39 para 14(2).

[2] In sub-para (2), words substituted for "in pursuance of a provision contained in the lease (but see paragraph 14)" by FA 2006 s 164, Sch 25 para 2(2) with effect in relation to any lease granted or treated as granted on or after 19 July 2006 by virtue of FA 2006 Sch 25 para 9(6).

[3] 3 In heading and sub-para (1), words inserted by FA 2006 s 164, Sch 25 para 6 with effect in relation to any variation of a lease made on or after 19 July 2006 by virtue of FA 2006 Sch 25 para 9(6).

[Increase of rent treated as grant of new lease: abnormal increase after fifth year

14—(1) This paragraph applies if, after the end of the fifth year of the term of a lease—

(*a*) the amount of rent payable increases (or is increased)[, whether in accordance with the provisions of the lease or otherwise][2], and

(*b*) the rent payable as a result ("the new rent") is such that the increase falls to be regarded as abnormal (see paragraph 15).

(2) The increase in rent is treated as if it were the grant of a lease in consideration of the excess rent.
(3) The excess rent is the difference between the new rent and the rent previously taxed.
[(4) Where the provisions of this paragraph have not previously applied to an increase in the rent payable under the lease, the rent previously taxed is—

(*a*) if paragraph (*b*) or (*c*) does not apply, the rent payable under the lease without the increase referred to in sub-paragraph (1);

(*b*) if the amount of rent payable under the lease is determined under paragraph 7 (variable or uncertain rent), the rent that is assumed to be payable after the fifth year of the term of the lease (in accordance with paragraph 7(3));

(*c*) if there has been a variation in the lease falling within paragraph 13 (increase of rent treated as grant of new lease: variation of lease in first five years), the rent payable as a result of the variation (or, if there has been more than one such variation, the most recent one).

(4A) Where the provisions of this paragraph have previously applied to an increase in the rent payable under the lease, the rent previously taxed is the rent payable as a result of the last increase in relation to which the provisions of this paragraph applied.
(4B) In determining the rent previously taxed, disregard paragraphs 9(2) and 9A(3) (deemed reduction of rent, where further lease granted, for period during which rents overlap).][2]
(5) The deemed grant is treated as—

(*a*) made on the date on which the increased rent first became payable, and

(*b*) for a term equal to the unexpired part of the original lease, and as linked with the grant of the original lease (and with any other transaction with which that transaction is linked).

(6) The assumption in paragraph 7(3) (that the rent does not change after the end of the fifth year of the term of a lease) does not apply for the purposes of this paragraph or paragraph 15 except for the purpose of determining the rent previously taxed.][1]
[(7) The reference to a lease in sub-paragraph (1) is to—

(*a*) a lease actually granted on or after the implementation date, or

(*b*) a lease that is treated as existing by reason of a deemed grant under paragraph 12A(2) or 19(3) of which the effective date is on or after the implementation date.][2]

Amendments—[1] This Schedule inserted by FA 2004 s 296, Sch 39 para 22(2) with effect for any transaction of which the effective date (within the meaning of FA 2003 Pt 4) is on or after 22 July 2004: FA 2004 Sch 39 para 26. This insertion was previously made by the Stamp Duty and Stamp Duty Land Tax (Variation of the Finance Act 2003) (No 2) Regulations, SI 2003/2816 regs 1, 2, Schedule para 8(2) with effect from 1 December 2003. Those regulations are revoked by FA 2004 Sch 39 para 14(2).

[2] Words in sub-para (1)(a) substituted for "in accordance with the provisions of the lease", sub-paras (4)–(4B) substituted for former sub-para (4), sub-para (7) inserted by FA 2006 s 164, Sch 25 para 7 with effect in relation to any increase of rent that takes effect or after 19 July 2006 by virtue of FA 2006 Sch 25 para 9(6).

[Increase of rent after fifth year: whether regarded as abnormal

15—Whether an increase in rent is to be regarded for the purposes of paragraph 14 as abnormal is determined as follows:—
[Step One
Find the start date.
Where the provisions of paragraph 14 have not previously applied to an increase in the rent payable under the lease, the start date is—

(*a*) if paragraph (*b*) or (*c*) does not apply, the beginning of the term of the lease;

(*b*) if the amount of rent payable under the lease is determined under paragraph 7 (variable or uncertain rent), the beginning of the period by reference to which the rent assumed to be payable after the fifth year of the term of the lease is determined in accordance with paragraph 7(3);

(*c*) if there has been a variation in the lease falling within paragraph 13 (increase of rent treated as grant of new lease: variation of lease in first five years), the date of the variation (or, if there has been more than one such variation, the date of the most recent one).

Where the provisions of paragraph 14 have previously applied to an increase in the rent payable under the lease, the start date is the date of the last increase in relation to which the provisions of that paragraph applied.
Step Two
Find the number of whole years in the period between the start date and the date on which the new rent first becomes payable.
Step Three

The rent increase is regarded as abnormal if the excess rent (see paragraph 14(3)) is greater than:

$$\frac{R \times Y}{5}$$

where—

R is the rent previously taxed (see paragraph 14(4) or (4A)), and

Y is the number of whole years found under Step Two.][2][1]

Amendments—[1] This Schedule inserted by FA 2004 s 296, Sch 39 para 22(2) with effect for any transaction of which the effective date (within the meaning of FA 2003 Pt 4) is on or after 22 July 2004: FA 2004 Sch 39 para 26. This insertion was previously made by the Stamp Duty and Stamp Duty Land Tax (Variation of the Finance Act 2003) (No 2) Regulations, SI 2003/2816 regs 1, 2, Schedule para 8(2) with effect from 1 December 2003. Those regulations are revoked by FA 2004 Sch 39 para 14(2).

[2] Steps One to Three substituted for former Steps One to Six by FA 2006 s 164, Sch 25 para 8 with effect in relation to any increase of rent that takes effect or after 19 July 2006 by virtue of FA 2006 Sch 25 para 9(6).

[[Reduction of rent or term or other variation of lease][2]

15A—(1) Where a lease is varied so as to reduce the amount of the rent, the variation is treated for the purposes of this Part as an acquisition of a chargeable interest by the lessee.

[1A) Where any consideration in money or money's worth (other than an increase in rent) is given by the lessee for any variation of a lease, other than a variation of the amount of the rent or of the term of the lease, the variation is treated for the purposes of this Part as an acquisition of a chargeable interest by the lessee.][2]

(2) Where a lease is varied so as to reduce the term, the variation is treated for the purposes of this Part as an acquisition of a chargeable interest by the lessor.][1]

Amendments—[1] This Schedule inserted by FA 2004 s 296, Sch 39 para 22(2) with effect for any transaction of which the effective date (within the meaning of FA 2003 Pt 4) is on or after 22 July 2004: FA 2004 Sch 39 para 26. This insertion was previously made by the Stamp Duty and Stamp Duty Land Tax (Variation of the Finance Act 2003) (No 2) Regulations, SI 2003/2816 regs 1, 2, Schedule para 8(2) with effect from 1 December 2003. Those regulations are revoked by FA 2004 Sch 39 para 14(2).

[2] Sub-para (1A) inserted, and Heading substituted, by F(No 2)A 2005 s 49, Sch 10 paras 1, 13 with effect in relation to any transaction of which the effective date is after 19 May 2005.

However, this amendment does not have effect—

(a) in relation to any transaction which is effected in pursuance of a contract entered into and substantially performed on or before the specified date (ie 16 March 2005), or

(b) subject to what follows below, in relation to any other transaction which is effected in pursuance of a contract entered into on or before the specified date (ie 16 March 2005).

The exclusion by para (*b*) above of transactions effected in pursuance of contracts entered into on or before the specified date does not apply—

(a) if there is any variation of the contract or assignment of rights under the contract after that date,

(b) if the transaction is effected in consequence of the exercise after that date of any option, right of pre-emption or similar right, or

(c) if after that date there is an assignment, subsale or other transaction (relating to the whole or part of the subject-matter of the contract) as a result of which a person other than the purchaser under the contract becomes entitled to call for a conveyance to him: F(No 2)A 2005 Sch 10 para 16(5)–(8).

[Surrender of existing lease in return for new lease

16—Where a lease is granted in consideration of the surrender of an existing lease between the same parties—

(*a*) the grant of the new lease does not count as chargeable consideration for the surrender, and

(*b*) the surrender does not count as chargeable consideration for the grant of the new lease.

Paragraph 5 (exchanges) of Schedule 4 (chargeable consideration) does not apply in such a case.][1]

Amendments—[1] This Schedule inserted by FA 2004 s 296 Sch 39 para 22(2) with effect for any transaction of which the effective date (within the meaning of FA 2003 Pt 4) is on or after 22 July 2004: FA 2004 Sch 39 para 26. This insertion was previously made by the Stamp Duty and Stamp Duty Land Tax (Variation of the Finance Act 2003) (No 2) Regulations, SI 2003/2816 regs 1, 2, Schedule para 8(2) with effect from 1 December 2003. Those regulations are revoked by FA 2004 Sch 39 para 14(2).

The final sentence of paragraph 16 above was however not contained in the original Schedule 17A as inserted by SI 2003/2816. FA 2004 Sch 39 para 11(1), (5) amended that version of the Schedule to insert that sentence. That insertion had effect for any transaction of which the effective date was after 17 March 2004 and before 22 July 2004: FA 2004 Sch 39 para 13(3), (5).

[Assignment of lease: assumption of obligations by assignee

17 In the case of an assignment of a lease the assumption by the assignee of the obligation—

(*a*) to pay rent, or

(*b*) to perform or observe any other undertaking of the tenant under the lease,

does not count as chargeable consideration for the assignment.][1]

Amendments—[1] This Schedule inserted by FA 2004 s 296, Sch 39 para 22(2) with effect for any transaction of which the effective date (within the meaning of FA 2003 Pt 4) is on or after 22 July 2004: FA 2004 Sch 39 para 26. This insertion was previously made by the Stamp Duty and Stamp Duty Land Tax (Variation of the Finance Act 2003) (No 2) Regulations, SI 2003/2816 regs 1, 2, Schedule para 8(2) with effect from 1 December 2003. Those regulations are revoked by FA 2004 Sch 39 para 14(2).

[Reverse premium

18—(1) In the case of the grant, assignment or surrender of a lease a reverse premium does not count as chargeable consideration.

(2) A "reverse premium" means—

(*a*) in relation to the grant of a lease, a premium moving from the landlord to the tenant;

(*b*) in relation to the assignment of a lease, a premium moving from the assignor to the assignee;

(*c*) in relation to the surrender of a lease, a premium moving from the tenant to the landlord.][1]

Amendments—[1] This Schedule inserted by FA 2004 s 296, Sch 39 para 22(2) with effect for any transaction of which the effective date is on or after 22 July 2004: FA 2004 Sch 39 para 26. This insertion was previously made by the Stamp Duty and Stamp Duty Land Tax (Variation of the Finance Act 2003) (No 2) Regulations, SI 2003/2816 regs 1, 2, Schedule para 8(2) with effect from 1 December 2003. Those regulations are revoked by FA 2004 Sch 39 para 14(2).

[Loan or deposit in connection with grant or assignment of lease

18A—(1) Where, under arrangements made in connection with the grant of a lease—

(*a*) the lessee, or any person connected with him or acting on his behalf, pays a deposit, or makes a loan, to any person, and

(*b*) the repayment of all or part of the deposit or loan is contingent on anything done or omitted to be done by the lessee or on the death of the lessee,

the amount of the deposit or loan (disregarding any repayment) is to be taken for the purposes of this Part to be consideration other than rent given for the grant of the lease.

(2) Where, under arrangements made in connection with the assignment of a lease—

(*a*) the assignee, or any person connected with him or acting on his behalf, pays a deposit, or makes a loan, to any person, and

(*b*) the repayment of all or part of the deposit or loan is contingent on anything done or omitted to be done by the assignee or on the death of the assignee,

the amount of the deposit or loan (disregarding any repayment) is to be taken for the purposes of this Part to be consideration other than rent given for the assignment of the lease.

(3) Sub-paragraph (1) or (2) does not apply in relation to a deposit if the amount that would otherwise fall within the sub-paragraph in question in relation to the grant or (as the case requires) assignment of the lease is not more than twice the relevant maximum rent.

(4) The relevant maximum rent is—

(*a*) in relation to the grant of a lease, the highest amount of rent payable in respect of any consecutive twelve month period in the first five years of the term;

(*b*) in relation to the assignment of a lease, the highest amount of rent payable in respect of any consecutive twelve month period in the first five years of the term remaining outstanding as at the date of the assignment,

the highest amount of rent being determined (in either case) in the same way as the highest amount of rent mentioned in paragraph 7(3).

(5) Tax is not chargeable by virtue of this paragraph—

(*a*) merely because of paragraph [9A][2] of Schedule 5 (which excludes the 0% band in [Table B][2] in section 55(2) in cases where [the relevant rent attributable to non-residential property is not less than £1,000][2] a year), or

(*b*) merely because of paragraph 5(4)(*b*), 6(6)(*b*), 9(4)(*b*) or 10(6)(*b*) of Schedule 6 (which make similar provision in relation to land which is wholly or partly residential property and is wholly or partly situated in a disadvantaged area).

(6) [Section 1122 of the Corporation Tax Act 2010][3] (connected persons) has effect for the purposes of this paragraph.][1]

Amendments—[1] This paragraph inserted by F(No 2)A 2005 s 49, Sch 10 paras 1, 14 with effect in relation to any transaction of which the effective date is after 19 May 2005.

However, this amendment does not have effect—

(a) in relation to any transaction which is effected in pursuance of a contract entered into and substantially performed on or before the specified date (ie 16 March 2005), or

(b) subject to what follows below, in relation to any other transaction which is effected in pursuance of a contract entered into on or before the specified date (ie 16 March 2005).

The exclusion by para (*b*) above of transactions effected in pursuance of contracts entered into on or before the specified date does not apply—

(a) if there is any variation of the contract or assignment of rights under the contract after that date,

(b) if the transaction is effected in consequence of the exercise after that date of any option, right of pre-emption or similar right, or

(c) if after that date there is an assignment, subsale or other transaction (relating to the whole or part of the subject-matter of the contract) as a result of which a person other than the purchaser under the contract becomes entitled to call for a conveyance to him: F(No 2)A 2005 Sch 10 para 16(5)–(8).

[2] In sub-para (5)(a), words substituted by FA 2008 s 95(12) with effect in relation to transactions with an effective date on or after 12 March 2008.

3 In sub-para (6) words "Section 839 of the Taxes Act 1988" substituted by CTA 2010 s 1177, Sch 1 paras 400, 419. CTA 2010 has effect for corporation tax purposes for accounting periods ending on or after 1 April 2010, and for income and capital gains tax purposes for the tax year 2010–11 and subsequent tax years.

[Provisions relating to leases in Scotland

19—(1) In the application of this Part to Scotland—

(*a*) any reference to the term of a lease is to the period of the lease, and

(*b*) any reference to the reversion on a lease is to the interest of the landlord in the property subject to the lease.

(2) Where in Scotland there is a lease constituted by concluded missives of let ("the first lease") and at some later time a lease is executed ("the second lease")—

(*a*) the first lease is treated as if it were surrendered at that time, and

(*b*) the second lease is treated for the purposes of paragraph 9 (rent for overlap period in case of grant of further lease) as if it were granted in consideration of that surrender.

[Paragraph 5 does not apply so as to treat the first lease and the second lease as a single lease.][2]

(3) Where in Scotland—

(*a*) there is an agreement (including missives of let not constituting a lease) under which a lease is to be executed, and

(*b*) the agreement is substantially performed without a lease having been executed,

the agreement is treated as if it were the grant of a lease in accordance with the agreement ("the notional lease"), beginning with the date of substantial performance.

The effective date of the transaction is when the agreement is substantially performed.

(4) Where sub-paragraph (3) applies and at some later time a lease is executed—

(*a*) the notional lease is treated as if it were surrendered at that time, and

(*b*) the lease itself is treated for the purposes of paragraph 9 as if it were granted in consideration of that surrender.

[Paragraph 5 does not apply so as to treat the notional lease and the lease itself as a single lease.][2]

(5) References in sub-paragraphs (2) to (4) to the execution of a lease are to the execution of a lease that either is in conformity with, or relates to substantially the same property and period as, the missives of let or other agreement.

(6) Where sub-paragraph (3) applies and the agreement is (to any extent) afterwards rescinded or annulled, or is for any other reason not carried into effect, the tax paid by virtue of that sub-paragraph shall (to that extent) be repaid by the Inland Revenue. Repayment must be claimed by amendment of the land transaction return made in respect of the agreement.][1]

Amendments—[1] This Schedule inserted by FA 2004 s 296, Sch 39 para 22(2) with effect for any transaction of which the effective date (within the meaning of FA 2003 Pt 4) is on or after 22 July 2004: FA 2004 Sch 39 para 26. This insertion was previously made by the Stamp Duty and Stamp Duty Land Tax (Variation of the Finance Act 2003) (No 2) Regulations, SI 2003/2816 regs 1, 2, Schedule para 8(2) with effect from 1 December 2003. Those regulations are revoked by FA 2004 Sch 39 para 14(2).

Sub-para (2) above read differently in the original Schedule 17A as inserted by SI 2003/2816. FA 2004 Sch 37 para 11(1), (6) amended that version of the Schedule by substituting sub-paras (2)–(6) for the original sub-para (2). The effect was that it read the same as the new version of the Schedule. That substitution had effect for any transaction of which the effective date was after 17 March 2004 and before 22 July 2004: FA 2004 Sch 39 para 13(3), (5).

2 Words in sub-paras (2), (4) inserted by FA 2006 s 164, Sch 25 para 5 with effect in relation to any agreement that is substantially performed on or after 19 July 2006 by virtue of FA 2006 Sch 25 para 9(6).

SCHEDULE 18

STAMP DUTY LAND TAX: CONSEQUENTIAL AMENDMENTS

Section 123

Provisional Collection of Taxes Act 1968

1 (*amends* PCTA 1968 s 1(1))

Inheritance Tax Act 1984

2 (*amends* IHTA 1984 s 190(4))

Income and Corporation Taxes Act 1988

3 (*amends* TA 1988 ss 209B, 213, 214, 215, 827; sub-paras (2)-(5) repealed by CTA 2010 Sch 3 Pt 1)

Finance Act 1989

4 (*amends* FA 1989 s 178(2))

Taxation of Chargeable Gains Act 1992

5 (*amends* TCGA 1992 s 38(2))

Income Tax (Earnings and Pensions) Act 2003

6 (*amends* ITEPA 2003 s 277(3))

SCHEDULE 19

STAMP DUTY LAND TAX: COMMENCEMENT AND TRANSITIONAL PROVISIONS

Section 124

HMRC Manuals—Stamp Duty Land Tax Manual SDLTM49000–49700 (explanation of this Schedule, with examples).

Introduction

1—(1) Subject to the provisions of this Schedule, the provisions of this Part come into force on the passing of this Act.

(2) The following provisions have effect as regards what transactions are SDLT transactions, that is, are chargeable or notifiable or are transactions in relation to which section 79 (registration etc) applies.

(3) Nothing in this Schedule shall be read as meaning that other transactions, whether effected before or after the passing of this Act, are to be disregarded in applying the provisions of this Part.

The implementation date

2—(1) A transaction is not an SDLT transaction unless the effective date of the transaction is on or after the implementation date.

(2) In this Part "the implementation date" means the date appointed by Treasury order as the implementation date for the purposes of stamp duty land tax.

Regulations—Stamp Duty Land Tax (Appointment of the Implementation Date) Order, SI 2003/2899 (appoints 1 December 2003 as the implementation date).

Contract entered into before first relevant date

3—(1) Subject to the following provisions of this paragraph, a transaction is not an SDLT transaction if it is effected in pursuance of a contract entered into before the first relevant date.

(2) The "first relevant date" is the day after the passing of this Act.

(3) The exclusion of transactions effected in pursuance of contracts entered into before the first relevant date does not apply—

(*a*) if there is any variation of the contract or assignment of rights under the contract on or after that date;

(*b*) if the transaction is effected in consequence of the exercise after that date of any option, right of pre-emption or similar right;

[(*c*) if on or after that date there is an assignment, subsale or other transaction (relating to the whole or part of the subject-matter of the contract) as a result of which a person other than the purchaser under the contract becomes entitled to call for a conveyance to him.][1]

Amendments—[1] Sub-para (3)(c) substituted by FA 2004 s 296, Sch 39 para 12 with effect for any transaction of which the effective date is after 17 March 2004. However, this amendment does not apply in relation to a contract that was substantially performed before 17 March 2004: FA 2004 Sch 39 para 13(3), (4).

Contract substantially performed before implementation date

4—(1) This paragraph applies where a transaction—

(*a*) is completed on or after the implementation date,

(*b*) is effected in pursuance of a contract entered into and substantially performed before that date, and

(*c*) is not excluded from being an SDLT transaction by paragraph 3.

(2) The transaction is not an SDLT transaction if the contract was substantially performed before the first relevant date.

(3) In any other case, the fact that the contract was substantially performed before the implementation date does not affect the matter.

Accordingly, the effective date of the transaction is the date of completion.

[Contracts substantially performed after implementation date

4A Where—

(*a*) a transaction is effected in pursuance of a contract entered into before the first relevant date,
(*b*) the contract is substantially performed, without having been completed, after the implementation date, and
(*c*) there is subsequently an event within paragraph 3(3) by virtue of which the transaction is an SDLT transaction,

the effective date of the transaction shall be taken to be the date of the event referred to in paragraph (c) (and not the date of substantial performance).][1]

Amendments—[1] Paragraphs 4A, 4B inserted by FA 2004 s 296, Sch 39 para 24 with effect for any transaction of which the effective date (within the meaning of FA 2003 Pt 4) is on or after 22 July 2004: FA 2004 Sch 39 para 26. This insertion was previously made by the Stamp Duty and Stamp Duty Land Tax (Variation of the Finance Act 2003) (No 2) Regulations, SI 2003/2816 regs 1, 2, Schedule para 10 with effect from 1 December 2003. Those regulations are revoked by FA 2004 Sch 39 para 14(2).

[Application of provisions in case of transfer of rights

4B—(1) This paragraph applies where section 44 (contract and conveyance) has effect in accordance with section 45 (effect of transfer of rights).
(2) Any reference in paragraph 3, 4 or 4A to the date when a contract was entered into (or made) shall be read, in relation to a contract deemed to exist by virtue of section 45(3) (deemed secondary contract with transferee), as a reference to the date of the assignment, subsale or other transaction in question.][1]

Amendments—[1] Paragraphs 4A, 4B inserted by FA 2004 s 296, Sch 39 para 24 with effect for any transaction of which the effective date (within the meaning of FA 2003 Pt 4) is on or after 22 July 2004: FA 2004 Sch 39 para 26. This insertion was previously made by the Stamp Duty and Stamp Duty Land Tax (Variation of the Finance Act 2003) (No 2) Regulations, SI 2003/2816 regs 1, 2, Schedule para 10 with effect from 1 December 2003. Those regulations are revoked by FA 2004 Sch 39 para 14(2).

Credit for ad valorem stamp duty paid

5—(1) Where a transaction chargeable to stamp duty land tax is effected in pursuance of a contract entered into before the implementation date, any *ad valorem* stamp duty paid on the contract shall go to reduce the amount of tax payable (but not so as to give rise to any repayment).
(2) Where the application or operation of any exemption or relief from stamp duty land tax turns on whether tax was paid or payable in respect of an earlier transaction, that requirement is treated as met if *ad valorem* stamp duty was paid or (as the case may be) payable in respect of the instrument by which that transaction was effected.

Effect for stamp duty purposes of stamp duty land tax being paid or chargeable

6—(1) ...[1]
(2) The references in section 111(1)(*c*) of, and paragraph 4(3) of Schedule 34 to, the Finance Act 2002 (c 23) (which relate to the circumstances in which stamp duty group relief is withdrawn) to a transfer at market value by a duly stamped instrument on which *ad valorem* duty was paid and in respect of which group relief was not claimed shall be read, on or after the implementation date, as including a reference to a transfer at market value by a chargeable transaction in respect of which relief under Part 1 of Schedule 7 to this Act was available but was not claimed.
(3) The references in section 113(1)(*c*) of, and in paragraph 3(3) or 4(3) of Schedule 35 to, the Finance Act 2002 (which relate to the circumstances in which stamp duty company acquisitions relief is withdrawn) to a transfer at market value by a duly stamped instrument on which *ad valorem* duty was paid and in respect of which section 76 relief was not claimed shall be read, on or after the implementation date, as including a reference to a transfer at market value by a chargeable transaction on which stamp duty land tax was chargeable and in respect of which relief under Part 2 of Schedule 7 to this Act was available but was not claimed.

Amendments—[1] Sub-para (1) repealed by FA 2004 s 326, Sch 42 Pt 4(2) with effect in accordance with FA 2004 Sch 39 para 26. This repeal was previously made by the Stamp Duty and Stamp Duty Land Tax (Variation of the Finance Act 2003) (No 2) Regulations, SI 2003/2816 regs 1, 2, Schedule para 11(1) with effect from 1 December 2003. Those regulations have been revoked by FA 2004 Sch 39 para 14(2).

Earlier related transactions under stamp duty

7—(1) In relation to a transaction that is not an SDLT transaction but which is linked to an SDLT transaction and accordingly falls to be taken into account in determining the rate of stamp duty land tax chargeable on the latter transaction, any reference in this Part to the chargeable consideration for the first-mentioned transaction shall be read as a reference to the consideration by reference to which *ad valorem* stamp duty was payable in respect of the instrument by which that transaction was effected.

[(2) In paragraph 3 of Schedule 9 (relief for transfer of reversion under shared ownership lease where election made for market value treatment) and paragraph 4A of that Schedule (shared ownership lease: treatment of staircasing transaction) as they apply in a case where the original lease was granted before the implementation date—

(*a*) a reference to a lease to which paragraph 2 of that Schedule applies shall be read as a reference to a lease to which section 97 of the Finance Act 1980 applied (which made provision for stamp duty corresponding to that paragraph), and

(*b*) a reference to an election having been made for tax to be charged in accordance with paragraph 2 or 4 of that Schedule shall be read as a reference to the lease having contained a statement of the parties' intention such as is mentioned in section 97(2)(*d*) of the Finance Act 1980 or, as the case may be, paragraph (*d*) of section 108(5) of the Finance Act 1981 (which made provision for stamp duty corresponding to paragraph 4).][2]

(3) In section 54 (exceptions from deemed market value rule for transactions with connected company) the reference in subsection (4)(*b*) to group relief having been claimed in respect of a transaction shall be read in relation to a transaction carried out before the implementation date as a reference to relief having been claimed under section 42 of the Finance Act 1930 (c 28), section 11 of the Finance Act (Northern Ireland) 1954 (c 23 (NI)) or section 151 of the Finance Act 1995 (c 4) in respect of stamp duty on the instrument by which the transaction was effected.

[(4) For the purposes of paragraph 5 of Schedule 17A (treatment of successive linked leases) no account shall be taken of any transaction that is not an SDLT transaction.][1]

Amendments—[1] Sub-para (4) inserted by FA 2004 s 296, Sch 39 para 22(8) with effect for any transaction of which the effective date (within the meaning of FA 2003 Pt 4) is on or after 22 July 2004: FA 2004 Sch 39 para 26. This insertion was previously made by the Stamp Duty and Stamp Duty Land Tax (Variation of the Finance Act 2003) (No 2) Regulations, SI 2003/2816 regs 1, 2, Schedule para 8(1) with effect from 1 December 2003. Those regulations are revoked by FA 2004 Sch 39 para 14(2).

[2] Sub-para (2) substituted by FA 2004 s 303(3), (5), and deemed to have come into force on 1 December 2003.

[Stamping of contract where transaction on completion subject to stamp duty land tax

7A—(1) This paragraph applies where—

(*a*) a contract that apart from paragraph 7 of Schedule 13 to the Finance Act 1999 (contracts chargeable as conveyances on sale) would not be chargeable with stamp duty is entered into before the implementation date,

(*b*) a conveyance made in conformity with the contract is effected on or after the implementation date, and

(*c*) the transaction effected on completion is an SDLT transaction or would be but for an exemption or relief from stamp duty land tax.

(2) If in those circumstances the contract is presented for stamping together with a Revenue certificate as to compliance with the provisions of this Part of this Act in relation to the transaction effected on completion—

(*a*) the payment of stamp duty land tax on that transaction or, as the case may be, the fact that no such tax was payable shall be denoted on the contract by a particular stamp, and

(*b*) the contract shall be deemed thereupon to be duly stamped.

(3) In this paragraph "conveyance" includes any instrument.][1]

Amendments—[1] Paragraph 7A inserted by FA 2004 s 296, Sch 39 para 25(1) with effect for any transaction of which the effective date (within the meaning of FA 2003 Pt 4) is on or after 22 July 2004: FA 2004 Sch 39 para 26. This insertion was previously made by the Stamp Duty and Stamp Duty Land Tax (Variation of the Finance Act 2003) (No 2) Regulations, SI 2003/2816 regs 1, 2, Schedule para 11(1) with effect from 1 December 2003. Those regulations are revoked by FA 2004 Sch 39 para 14(2).

[Stamping of agreement for lease where grant of lease subject to stamp duty land tax][1]

8—(1) [This paragraph applies where—][1]

(*a*) an agreement for a lease is entered into before the implementation date,

(*b*) a lease giving effect to the agreement is executed on or after that date, and

(*c*) the transaction effected on completion is an SDLT transaction or would be but for an exemption or relief from stamp duty land tax.

[(2) If in those circumstances the agreement is presented for stamping together with a Revenue certificate as to compliance with the provisions of this Part of this Act in relation to the grant of the lease—

(*a*) the payment of stamp duty land tax in respect of the grant of the lease or, as the case may be, the fact that no such tax was payable shall be denoted on the agreement by a particular stamp, and

(*b*) the agreement shall be deemed thereupon to be duly stamped.][1]

(3) For the purposes of this paragraph a lease gives effect to an agreement if the lease either is in conformity with the agreement or relates to substantially the same property and term as the agreement.

(4) References in this paragraph to an agreement for a lease include missives of let in Scotland.

Amendments—[1] Heading and words in sub-para (1) substituted, and sub-para (2) substituted, by FA 2004 s 296, Sch 39 para 25(2), (3) with effect for any transaction of which the effective date (within the meaning of FA 2003 Pt 4) is on or after 22 July 2004: FA 2004 Sch 39 para 26. These amendments were previously made by the Stamp Duty and Stamp Duty Land Tax (Variation of the Finance Act 2003) (No 2) Regulations, SI 2003/2816 regs 1, 2, Schedule para 11(2), (3) with effect from 1 December 2003. Those regulations are revoked by FA 2004 Sch 39 para 14(2).

Exercise of option or right of pre-emption acquired before implementation date

9—(1) This paragraph applies where—

(*a*) an option binding the grantor to enter into a land transaction, or

(*b*) a right of pre-emption preventing the grantor from entering into, or restricting the right of the grantor to enter into, a land transaction,

is acquired before the implementation date and exercised on or after that date.

(2) Where the option or right was acquired on or after 17th April 2003, any consideration for the acquisition is treated as part of the chargeable consideration for the transaction resulting from the exercise of the option or right.

(3) Where the option or right was varied on or after 17th April 2003 and before the implementation date, any consideration for the variation is treated as part of the chargeable consideration for the transaction resulting from the exercise of the option or right.

(4) Whether or not sub-paragraph (2) or (3) applies, the acquisition of the option or right and any variation of the option or right is treated as linked with the land transaction resulting from the exercise of the option or right.

But not so as to require the consideration for the acquisition or variation to be counted twice in determining the rate of tax chargeable on the land transaction resulting from the exercise of the option or right.

(5) Where this paragraph applies any *ad valorem* stamp duty paid on the acquisition or variation of the option or right shall go to reduce the amount of tax payable on the transaction resulting from the exercise of the option or right (but not so as to give rise to any repayment).

Supplementary

10 In this Schedule "contract" includes any agreement.

SCHEDULE 20

STAMP DUTY: RESTRICTION TO INSTRUMENTS RELATING TO STOCK OR MARKETABLE SECURITIES

Section 125

PART 1
SUPPLEMENTARY PROVISIONS

Cross references—See FA 2003 Sch 15 para 31(2) (in this Part, references to stock or marketable securities shall be read as including any property that is the subject matter of a transaction by which an interest in a partnership is transferred).

Reduction of stamp duty where instrument partly relating to stock or marketable securities

1—(1) This paragraph applies where stamp duty under Part 1 of Schedule 13 to the Finance Act 1999 (c 16) (transfer on sale) is chargeable on an instrument that relates partly to stock or marketable securities and partly to property other than stock or marketable securities.

(2) In such a case—

(*a*) the consideration in respect of which duty would otherwise be charged shall be apportioned, on a just and reasonable basis, as between the stock or marketable securities and the other property, and

(*b*) the instrument shall be charged only in respect of the consideration attributed to the stock or marketable securities.

Apportionment of consideration for stamp duty purposes

2—(1) Where part of the property referred to in section 58(1) of the Stamp Act 1891 (c 39) (consideration to be apportioned between different instruments as parties think fit) consists of stock or marketable securities, that provision shall have effect as if "the parties think fit" read "is just and reasonable".

(2) Where—

(*a*) part of the property referred to in section 58(2) of the Stamp Act 1891 (c 39) (property contracted to be purchased by two or more persons etc) consists of stock or marketable securities, and (*b*) both or (as the case may be) all the relevant persons are connected with one another,

that provision shall have effect as if the words from "for distinct parts of the consideration" to the end of the subsection read ", the consideration shall be apportioned in such manner as is just and reasonable, so that a distinct consideration for each part of the property transferred is set forth in the transfer relating to that part, and the transfer shall be charged with ad valorem duty in respect of that consideration.".

(3) If in a case where sub-paragraph (1) or (2) applies the consideration is apportioned in a manner that is not just and reasonable, the enactments relating to stamp duty shall have effect as if—

(*a*) the consideration had been apportioned in a manner that is just and reasonable, and

(*b*) the amount of any distinct consideration set forth in any transfer relating to a part of the property transferred were such amount as is found by a just and reasonable apportionment (and not the amount actually set forth).

(4) For the purposes of sub-paragraph (2)—

(*a*) a person is a relevant person if he is a person by or for whom the property is contracted to be purchased;

(*b*) the question whether persons are connected with one another shall be determined in accordance with [section 1122 of the Corporation Tax Act 2010][1].

Amendments—[1] In sub-para (4)(*b*) words "section 839 of the Taxes Act 1988" substituted by CTA 2010 s 1177, Sch 1 paras 400, 420. CTA 2010 has effect for corporation tax purposes for accounting periods ending on or after 1 April 2010, and for income and capital gains tax purposes for the tax year 2010–11 and subsequent tax years.

PART 2
CONSEQUENTIAL AMENDMENTS AND REPEALS

Cross references—See FA 2003 Sch 15 para 31(1) (nothing in this Part affects the application of enactments relating to stamp duty in relation to an instrument by which a transfer of an interest in a partnership is effected).

Removal of unnecessary references to "conveyance"

3 In the enactments relating to stamp duty for "conveyance or transfer", wherever occurring, substitute "transfer".

Finance Act 1895

4 (*amends* FA 1895 s 12)

Finance Act 1990

5 (*amends* FA 1990 s 108)

Finance Act 1999

6 (*amends* FA 1999 Sch 13 para 1)

Power to make further consequential amendments or repeals

7—(1) The Treasury may by regulations make such other amendments or repeals of enactments relating to stamp duty or stamp duty reserve tax as appear to them appropriate in consequence of the abolition of stamp duty except on instruments relating to stock or marketable securities.

(2) The regulations may include such transitional provisions and savings as appear to the Treasury to be appropriate.

(3) Regulations under this paragraph shall be made by statutory instrument which shall be subject to annulment in pursuance of a resolution of the House of Commons.

SCHEDULE 40
ACQUISITION BY COMPANY OF ITS OWN SHARES

Section 195

Commentary—*Simon's Taxes* **D5.502; E3.211.**

Regulations—The Finance Act 2003, Section 195 and Schedule 40 (Appointed Day) Order, SI 2003/3077 (s 195 and Sch 40 have effect in relation to any acquisition of shares by a company on or after 1st December 2003).

...

Stamp duty and stamp duty reserve tax

2–4 (*amend* FA 1986 ss 66, 90, 92: para 2(*b*) *repealed* by FA 2008 s 99, Sch 32 para 21 with effect in relation to instruments executed on or after 13 March 2008 and not stamped before 19 March 2008.)

5 (*amends* FA 1999 Sch 13 para 1)

FINANCE ACT 2004

(2004 Chapter 12)

ARRANGEMENT OF SECTIONS

PART 6
OTHER TAXES

Stamp duty land tax and stamp duty

An Act to Grant certain duties, to alter other duties, and to amend the law relating to the National Debt and the Public Revenue, and to make further provision in connection with finance.

[22 July 2004]

PART 6
OTHER TAXES

Stamp duty land tax and stamp duty

296 Miscellaneous amendments

Schedule 39 to this Act, which makes amendments to Part 4 (stamp duty land tax) and Part 5 (stamp duty) of the Finance Act 2003 (c 14), has effect.

Stamp duty land tax

297 Leases

(1), (2) (*amends* FA 2003 s 43(3))
(3) (*amends* FA 2003 s 48(7))
(4) (*substitutes* FA 2003 s 53(1))
(5)–(7) (*amends* FA 2003 s 79)
(8) (*amends* FA 2003 Sch 4 para 10(2A))
(9) Subsections (2) to (4) and (8) apply in relation to any transaction of which the effective date is on or after the day on which this Act is passed.
(10) Subsections (5) to (7) apply in relation to any transaction or deemed transaction of which the effective date is on or after 17th March 2004.
(11) In this section "effective date" has the same meaning as in Part 4 of the Finance Act 2003.

298 Notification, registration and penalties

(1) Part 4 of the Finance Act 2003 (c 14) (stamp duty land tax) is amended as follows.
(2) (*amends* FA 2003 s 77)
(3) (*amends* FA 2003 s 79(1))
(4) (*inserts* FA 2003 s 99(2A))
(5) (*amends* heading of FA 2003 Sch 6 Part 4; *inserts* FA 2003 Sch 6 para 13)

299 Claims not included in returns

(1) Part 4 of the Finance Act 2003 (c 14) (stamp duty land tax) is amended as follows.
(2) (*inserts* FA 2003 s 82A)
(3) After Schedule 11 insert the Schedule set out in Schedule 40 to this Act.
(4) (*amends* FA 2003 s 80(4))
(5) (*amends* FA 2003 s 111(1))
(6) (*inserts* FA 2003 s 113(3A))
(7) (*amends* FA 2003 Sch 10 para 33)
(8) (*amends* FA 2003 Sch 10 para 34)

300 Assents and appropriations by personal representatives

(1) (*inserts* FA 2003 Sch 3 para 3A)
(2) The amendment made by this section is deemed always to have had effect.

301 Chargeable consideration

(1) (*inserts* FA 2003 Sch 3 para 4(2A))
(2) Schedule 4 to that Act (stamp duty land tax: chargeable consideration) is amended as follows.
(3), (4) (*amends* FA 2003 Sch 4 para 8)
(5) (*inserts* FA 2003 Sch 4 para 8A)
(6) The amendments made by subsections (3) and (4) apply in relation to any transaction of which the effective date (within the meaning of Part 4 of the Finance Act 2003) is on or after the day on which this act is passed.
(7) The other amendments made by this section are deemed always to have had effect.

302 Charities relief

(1) (*inserts* FA 2003 Sch 8 para 3)
(2) (*inserts* FA 2003 Sch 8 para 4)
(3) (*amends* FA 2003 Sch 8 para 1(1))
(4) (*amends* FA 2003 Sch 8 para 2(1))
(5) (*amends* FA 2003 s 81(4))
(6) (*amends* FA 2003 s 87(4))
(7) This section applies in relation to any transaction of which the effective date (within the meaning of Part 4 of the Finance Act 2003 (c 14)) is on or after the day on which this Act is passed.

303 Shared ownership leases

(1) (*inserts* FA 2003 Sch 9 para 4A)
(2) (*amends* FA 2003 Sch 9 para 5)
(3) (*amends* FA 2003 Sch 19 para 7(2))
(4) Subsections (1) and (2) apply in relation to an acquisition after 17th March 2004.
(5) Subsection (3) is deemed to have come into force on 1st December 2003.

304 Application to certain partnership transactions

Schedule 41 to this Act (which makes provision with respect to the application of stamp duty land tax to certain transactions involving partnerships) has effect.

305 Liability of partners

(inserts FA 2003 Sch 15 para 7(1A))

PART 7
DISCLOSURE OF TAX AVOIDANCE SCHEMES

306 Meaning of "notifiable arrangements" and "notifiable proposal"

(1) In this Part "notifiable arrangements" means any arrangements which—

(*a*) fall within any description prescribed by the Treasury by regulations,

(*b*) enable, or might be expected to enable, any person to obtain an advantage in relation to any tax that is so prescribed in relation to arrangements of that description, and

(*c*) are such that the main benefit, or one of the main benefits, that might be expected to arise from the arrangements is the obtaining of that advantage.

(2) In this Part "notifiable proposal" means a proposal for arrangements which, if entered into, would be notifiable arrangements (whether the proposal relates to a particular person or to any person who may seek to take advantage of it).

307 Meaning of "promoter"

(1) For the purposes of this Part a person is a promoter—

(*a*) in relation to a notifiable proposal, if, in the course of a relevant business—

(i) he is to any extent responsible for the design of the proposed arrangements, or

(ii) he makes the notifiable proposal available for implementation by other persons, and

(*b*) in relation to notifiable arrangements, if he is by virtue of paragraph (*a*)(ii) a promoter in relation to a notifiable proposal which is implemented by those arrangements or if, in the course of a relevant business, he is to any extent responsible for—

(i) the design of the arrangements, or

(ii) the organisation or management of the arrangements.

(2) In this section "relevant business" means any trade, profession or business which—

(*a*) involves the provision to other persons of services relating to taxation, or

(*b*) is carried on by a bank, as defined by section 840A of the Taxes Act 1988, or by a securities house, as defined by section 209A(4) of that Act.

(3) For the purposes of this section anything done by a company is to be taken to be done in the course of a relevant business if it is done for the purposes of a relevant business falling within subsection (2)(*b*) carried on by another company which is a member of the same group.

(4) Section 170 of the Taxation of Chargeable Gains Act 1992 has effect for determining for the purposes of subsection (3) whether two companies are members of the same group, but as if in that section—

(*a*) for each of the references to a 75 per cent subsidiary there were substituted a reference to a 51 per cent subsidiary, and

(*b*) subsection (3)(*b*) and subsections (6) to (8) were omitted.

(5) A person is not to be treated as a promoter for the purposes of this Part by reason of anything done in prescribed circumstances.

308 Duties of promoter

(1) [A person who is a promoter in relation to a notifiable proposal][1] must, within the prescribed period after the relevant date, provide the Board with prescribed information relating to [the][1] notifiable proposal.

(2) In subsection (1) "the relevant date" means the earlier of the following—

(*a*) the date on which the promoter makes [the][1] notifiable proposal available for implementation by any other person, or

(*b*) the date on which the promoter first becomes aware of any transaction forming part of notifiable arrangements implementing the notifiable proposal.

(3) [A person who is a promoter in relation to notifiable arrangements][1] must, within the prescribed period after the date on which he first becomes aware of any transaction forming part of [the notifiable][1] arrangements, provide the Board with prescribed information relating to those arrangements, unless those arrangements implement a proposal in respect of which notice has been given under subsection (1).

[(4) Subsection (4A) applies where a person complies with subsection (1) in relation to a notifiable proposal for arrangements and another person is—

(*a*) also a promoter in relation to the notifiable proposal or is a promoter in relation to a notifiable proposal for arrangements which are substantially the same as the proposed arrangements (whether they relate to the same or different parties), or

(*b*) a promoter in relation to notifiable arrangements implementing the notifiable proposal or notifiable arrangements which are substantially the same as notifiable arrangements implementing the notifiable proposal (whether they relate to the same or different parties).

(4A) Any duty of the other person under subsection (1) or (3) in relation to the notifiable proposal or notifiable arrangements is discharged if—

(*a*) the person who complied with subsection (1) has notified the identity and address of the other person to HMRC or the other person holds the reference number allocated to the proposed notifiable arrangements under section 311, and (*b*) the other person holds the information provided to HMRC in compliance with subsection (1).

(4B) Subsection (4C) applies where a person complies with subsection (3) in relation to notifiable arrangements and another person is—

(*a*) a promoter in relation to a notifiable proposal for arrangements which are substantially the same as the notifiable arrangements (whether they relate to the same or different parties), or

(*b*) also a promoter in relation to the notifiable arrangements or notifiable arrangements which are substantially the same (whether they relate to the same or different parties).

(4C) Any duty of the other person under subsection (1) or (3) in relation to the notifiable proposal or notifiable arrangements is discharged if—

(*a*) the person who complied with subsection (3) has notified the identity and address of the other person to HMRC or the other person holds the reference number allocated to the notifiable arrangements under section 311, and

(*b*) the other person holds the information provided to HMRC in compliance with subsection (3).][1]

(5) Where a person is a promoter in relation to two or more notifiable proposals or sets of notifiable arrangements which are substantially the same (whether they relate to the same parties or different parties), he need not provide information under subsection (1) or (3) if he has already provided information under either of those subsections in relation to any of the other proposals or arrangements.

Amendments—[1] In sub-s (1), words substituted for words "The promoter", and word substituted for word "any"; in sub-s (2)(*a*), word substituted for word "a"; in sub-s (3), words substituted for words "The promoter", and words substituted for words "any notifiable"; and sub-ss (4)(4C) substituted for previous sub-s (4); by FA 2008 s 116, Sch 38 paras 1, 2 with effect from 1 April 2010 for the purposes of stamp duty land tax (by virtue of SI 2010/409 art 2).

309 Duty of person dealing with promoter outside United Kingdom

(1) Any person ("the client") who enters into any transaction forming part of any notifiable arrangements in relation to which—

(*a*) a promoter is resident outside the United Kingdom, and

(*b*) no promoter is resident in the United Kingdom,

must, within the prescribed period after doing so, provide the Board with prescribed information relating to the notifiable arrangements.

(2) Compliance with section 308(1) by any promoter in relation to the notifiable arrangements discharges the duty of the client under subsection (1).

310 Duty of parties to notifiable arrangements not involving promoter

Any person who enters into any transaction forming part of notifiable arrangements as respects which neither he nor any other person in the United Kingdom is liable to comply with section 308 (duties of promoter) or section 309 (duty of person dealing with promoter outside the United Kingdom) must at the prescribed time provide the Board with prescribed information relating to the notifiable arrangements.

311 Arrangements to be given reference number

(1) Where a person complies [or purports to comply][1] with section 308(1) or (3), 309(1) or 310 in relation to any notifiable proposal or notifiable arrangements, the Board . . . [1]—

(*a*) [may within 30 days][1] allocate a reference number to the notifiable arrangements or, in the case of a notifiable proposal, to the proposed notifiable arrangements, and

(*b*) if it does so, [must notify that number to the person and (where the person is one who has complied or purported to comply with section 308(1) or (3)) to any other person—

(i) who is a promoter in relation to the notifiable proposal (or arrangements implementing the notifiable proposal) or the notifiable arrangements (or proposal implemented by the notifiable arrangements), and

(ii) whose identity and address has been notified to HMRC by the person.][1]

(2) The allocation of a reference number to any notifiable arrangements (or proposed notifiable arrangements) is not to be regarded as constituting any indication by the Board that the arrangements could as a matter of law result in the obtaining by any person of a tax advantage.

(3) In this Part "reference number", in relation to any notifiable arrangements, means the reference number allocated under this section.

Amendments—[1] In sub-s (1), words inserted, words "may within 30 days" repealed, and words substituted for words "notify the person of that number", by FA 2008 s 116, Sch 38 paras 1, 3 with effect from 1 April 2010 for the purposes of stamp duty land tax (by virtue of SI 2010/409 art 2).

[312 Duty of promoter to notify client of number

(1) This section applies where a person who is a promoter in relation to notifiable arrangements is providing (or has provided) services to any person ("the client") in connection with the notifiable arrangements.

(2) The promoter must, within 30 days after the relevant date, provide the client with prescribed information relating to any reference number (or, if more than one, any one reference number) that has been notified to the promoter (whether by HMRC or any other person) in relation to—

(*a*) the notifiable arrangements, or

(*b*) any arrangements substantially the same as the notifiable arrangements (whether involving the same or different parties).

(3) In subsection (2) "the relevant date" means the later of—

(*a*) the date on which the promoter becomes aware of any transaction which forms part of the notifiable arrangements, and

(*b*) the date on which the reference number is notified to the promoter.

(4) But where the conditions in subsection (5) are met the duty imposed on the promoter under subsection (2) to provide the client with information in relation to notifiable arrangements is discharged.

(5) Those conditions are—

(*a*) that the promoter is also a promoter in relation to a notifiable proposal and provides services to the client in connection with them both,

(*b*) the notifiable proposal and the notifiable arrangements are substantially the same, and

(*c*) the promoter has provided to the client, in a form and manner specified by HMRC, prescribed information relating to the reference number that has been notified to the promoter in relation to the proposed notifiable arrangements.

(6) HMRC may give notice that, in relation to notifiable arrangements specified in the notice, promoters are not under the duty under subsection (2) after the date specified in the notice.][1]

Amendments—[1] Sections 312, 312A substituted for previous s 312 by FA 2008 s 116, Sch 38 paras 1, 4 with effect from 1 April 2010 for the purposes of stamp duty land tax (by virtue of SI 2010/409 art 2).

[312A Duty of client to notify parties of number

(1) This section applies where a person (a "client") to whom a person who is a promoter in relation to notifiable arrangements or a notifiable proposal is providing (or has provided) services in connection with the notifiable arrangements or notifiable proposal receives prescribed information relating to the reference number allocated to the notifiable arrangements or proposed notifiable arrangements.

(2) The client must, within the prescribed period, provide prescribed information relating to the reference number to any other person—

(*a*) who the client might reasonably be expected to know is or is likely to be a party to the arrangements or proposed arrangements, and

(*b*) who might reasonably be expected to gain a tax advantage in relation to any relevant tax by reason of the arrangements or proposed arrangements.

(3) For the purposes of subsection (1) a tax is a "relevant tax" in relation to arrangements or arrangements proposed in a proposal of any description if it is prescribed in relation to arrangements or proposals of that description by regulations under section 306.

(4) HMRC may give notice that, in relation to notifiable arrangements or a notifiable proposal specified in the notice, persons are not under the duty under subsection (2) after the date specified in the notice.

(5) The duty under subsection (2) does not apply in prescribed circumstances.][1]

Amendments—[1] Sections 312, 312A substituted for previous s 312 by FA 2008 s 116, Sch 38 paras 1, 4 with effect from 1 April 2010 for the purposes of stamp duty land tax (by virtue of SI 2010/409 art 2).

313 Duty of parties to notifiable arrangements to notify Board of number, etc

(1) Any person who is a party to any notifiable arrangements must provide the Board with prescribed information relating to—

(*a*) any reference number notified to him . . . [1], and

(*b*) the time when he obtains or expects to obtain by virtue of the arrangements an advantage in relation to any relevant tax.

(2) For the purposes of subsection (1) a tax is a "relevant tax" in relation to any notifiable arrangements if it is prescribed in relation to arrangements of that description by regulations under section 306.

(3) Regulations [made by HMRC][1] may—

(*a*) in prescribed cases, require the [information prescribed under subsection (1)][1] to be included in any return or account which the person is required by or under any enactment to deliver to the Board, and

(*b*) in prescribed cases, require the [information prescribed under subsection (1) and such other information as is prescribed][1] to be provided separately to the Board at the prescribed time or times.

(4) A person is not liable to a penalty under—

(*a*) section 95 of the Taxes Management Act 1970 (c 9) (incorrect return or accounts for income tax or capital gains tax),

(*b*) paragraph 8 of Schedule 2 to the Oil Taxation Act 1975 (c 22) (incorrect returns and accounts for purposes of petroleum revenue tax),

(*c*) section 247 of the Inheritance Tax Act 1984 (c 51) (provision of incorrect information for purposes of inheritance tax),

(*d*) any provision relating to incorrect or uncorrected returns made under section 98 of the Finance Act 1986 (c 41) (administration of stamp duty reserve tax),
(*e*) paragraph 20 of Schedule 18 to the Finance Act 1998 (c 36) (incorrect or uncorrected return for corporation tax),
(*f*) paragraph 8 of Schedule 10 to the Finance Act 2003 (incorrect or uncorrected return for purposes of stamp duty land tax), or
(*g*) any other prescribed provision,

by reason of any failure to include in any return or account any reference number or other information required by virtue of subsection (3)(a) (but see section 98C of the Taxes Management Act 1970 for the penalty for failure to comply with this section).

[(5) HMRC may give notice that, in relation to notifiable arrangements specified in the notice, persons are not under the duty under subsection (1) after the date specified in the notice.][1]

Amendments—[1] In sub-s (1)(*a*), words "under section 311 by the Board or under section 312 by the promoter" repealed; in sub-s (3), words substituted for words "under subsection (1)", in para (*a*), words substituted for words "number and other information", and in para (*b*), words substituted for words "number and other information"; and new sub-s (5) inserted; by FA 2008 s 116, Sch 38 paras 1, 5 with effect from 1 April 2010 for the purposes of stamp duty land tax (by virtue of SI 2010/409 art 2).

314 Legal professional privilege

(1) Nothing in this Part requires any person to disclose to the Board any privileged information.

(2) In this Part "privileged information" means information with respect to which a claim to legal professional privilege, or, in Scotland, to confidentiality of communications, could be maintained in legal proceedings.

315 Penalties

(1) (*inserts* TMA 1970 s 98C)
(2) (*amends* TMA 1970 s 100(2))
(3) (*inserts* TMA 1970 s 100C(1A))

[316 Information to be provided in form and manner specified by HMRC

(1) HMRC may specify the form and manner in which information required to be provided by any of the information provisions must be provided if the provision is to be complied with.

(2) The "information provisions" are sections 308(1) and (3), 309(1), 310, 312(2), 312A(2) and 313(1) and (3).][1]

Amendments—[1] This section substituted by FA 2008 s 116, Sch 38 paras 1, 6 with effect from 1 April 2010 for the purposes of stamp duty land tax (by virtue of SI 2010/409 art 2).

317 Regulations under Part 7

(1) Any power of the Treasury or the Board to make regulations under this Part is exercisable by statutory instrument.

(2) Regulations made by the Treasury or the Board under this Part may contain transitional provisions and savings.

(3) A statutory instrument containing regulations made by the Treasury or the Board under any provision of this Part is subject to annulment in pursuance of a resolution of the House of Commons.

318 Interpretation of Part 7

(1) In this Part—

"advantage", in relation to any tax, means—

(*a*) relief or increased relief from, or repayment or increased repayment of, that tax, or the avoidance or reduction of a charge to that tax or an assessment to that tax or the avoidance of a possible assessment to that tax,
(*b*) the deferral of any payment of tax or the advancement of any repayment of tax, or
(*c*) the avoidance of any obligation to deduct or account for any tax;

"arrangements" includes any scheme, transaction or series of transactions;

"corporation tax" includes any amount which, by virtue of any of the provisions mentioned in paragraph 1 of Schedule 18 to the Finance Act 1998 (c 36) (company tax returns, assessments and related matters) is assessable and chargeable as if it were corporation tax;

"notifiable arrangements" has the meaning given by section 306(1);

"notifiable proposal" has the meaning given by section 306(2);

"prescribed", except in section 306, means prescribed by regulations made by the Board;

"promoter", in relation to notifiable arrangements or a notifiable proposal, has the meaning given by section 307;

"reference number", in relation to notifiable arrangements, has the meaning given by section 311(3);

"tax" means—

(*a*) income tax,
(*b*) capital gains tax,
(*c*) corporation tax,

(*d*) petroleum revenue tax,
(*e*) inheritance tax,
(*f*) stamp duty land tax, or
(*g*) stamp duty reserve tax.

(2) Subject to subsection (1), expressions which are defined in the Taxes Act 1988 for the purposes of the Tax Acts, as defined in section 831(2) of that Act, have the same meaning in this Part.

319 Part 7: commencement and savings

(1) The following provisions of this Part come into force on the passing of this Act—

sections 306 to 315, so far as is necessary for enabling the making of any regulations for which they provide, and

sections 317 and 318 and this section.

(2) Except as provided by subsection (1), the provisions of this Part come into force on 1st August 2004.

(3) Section 308 does not apply to a promoter in the case of—

(*a*) any notifiable proposal as respects which the relevant date, as defined by subsection (2) of that section, fell before 18th March 2004,
(*b*) any notifiable arrangements which implement such a proposal, or
(*c*) any notifiable arrangements which include any transaction entered into before 18th March 2004.

(4) Sections 309 and 310 do not apply in relation to notifiable arrangements which include any transaction entered into before 23rd April 2004.

(5) Section 313 does not apply in relation to any notifiable arrangements in respect of which, by virtue of subsection (3) or (4), none of the duties imposed by sections 308 to 310 arises.

PART 9

SUPPLEMENTARY PROVISIONS

326 Repeals

(1) The enactments mentioned in Schedule 42 to this Act (which include provisions that are spent or of no practical utility) are repealed to the extent specified.

(2) The repeals specified in that Schedule have effect subject to the commencement provisions and savings contained or referred to in the notes set out in that Schedule.

327 Interpretation

In this Act "the Taxes Act 1988" means the Income and Corporation Taxes Act 1988 (c 1).

328 Short title

This Act may be cited as the Finance Act 2004.

SCHEDULES

SCHEDULE 39

STAMP DUTY LAND TAX AND STAMP DUTY

Section 296

PART 1

AMENDMENTS TO PART 4 OF THE FINANCE ACT 2003: GENERAL

Introduction

1 Part 4 of the Finance Act 2003 (c 14) (stamp duty land tax) is amended in accordance with this Part of this Schedule.

Variation of lease

2 (*amends* FA 2003 s 43(3))

Agreement for lease

3 (*inserts* FA 2003 s 44(9A))

Contract providing for conveyance to third party

4—(1) (*inserts* FA 2003 s 44A)
(2) (*inserts* FA 2003 s 48(7))
(3) (*inserts* FA 2003 s 77(5))

Contract and conveyance: effect of transfer of rights

5—(1)–(4) (*amends* FA 2003 s 45)
(5) (*inserts* FA 2003 s 45A)
(6) (*amends* FA 2003 s 122)

Relief for sale and leaseback arrangements

6 . . .

Amendment—This paragraph repealed by FA 2004 s 326, Sch 42 Pt 4(2) with effect in accordance with FA 2004 Sch 39 para 26.

Registration of land transactions

7 (*amends* FA 2003 s 79(2))

"Effective date" of a transaction

8 (*amends* FA 2003 s 119(2))

Chargeable consideration

9—(1) Schedule 4 (chargeable consideration) is amended as follows.
(2) (*inserts* FA 2003 Sch 4 para 10(2A))
(3) (*inserts* FA 2003 Sch 4 para 17(4A))

Provisions relating to leases

10 (*inserts* FA 2003 Sch 5 para 1A)

11 . . .

Amendment—This paragraph repealed by FA 2004 s 326, Sch 42 Pt 4(2) with effect in accordance with FA 2004 Sch 39 para 26.

Transfer of rights after 10th July 2003 relating to earlier contract: applicability of SDLT regime

12 (*amends* FA 2003 Sch 19 para 3(3))

Commencement

13—(1) Paragraph 4, and paragraphs 7 and 8 so far as relating to the section 44A inserted by that paragraph, apply in relation to any contract entered into after 17th March 2004.
(2) Paragraph 5, and paragraphs 7 and 8 so far as relating to the section 45A inserted by that paragraph, apply in relation to any transfer of rights occurring after that date.
(3) Subject to sub-paragraphs (4) and (5), the amendments made by the other provisions of this Part of this Schedule apply in relation to any transaction of which the effective date is after 17th March 2004.
(4) Paragraph 12 does not apply in relation to a contract that was substantially performed before 17th March 2004.
(5) Paragraphs 6 and 11 (which contain amendments the effect of which is reproduced in Part 2 of this Schedule) do not apply in relation to any transaction of which the effective date is on or after the day on which this Act is passed.
(6) In this paragraph—

"effective date" and "substantially performed" have the same meaning as in Part 4 of the Finance Act 2003 (as amended by this Part of this Schedule);

"transfer of rights" has the same meaning as in section 45 of that Act or, as the case may require, section 45A of that Act (inserted by paragraph 5(5)).

PART 2

RE-ENACTMENT, WITH CHANGES, OF AMENDMENTS MADE BY SECTION 109 REGULATIONS

Introduction and revocation

14—(1) This Part of this Schedule contains amendments to Parts 4 and 5 of the Finance Act 2003 (c 14) (stamp duty land tax and stamp duty) corresponding, subject to certain changes, to those made by the Stamp Duty and Stamp Duty Land Tax (Variation of the Finance Act 2003) (No. 2) Regulations 2003 (SI 2003/2816) (made under section 109 of that Act).
(2) Those regulations are revoked.

Meaning of taking possession

15—(1)–(4) (*amends* FA 2003 s 44)

Relief for sale and leaseback arrangements

16 (*inserts* FA 2003 s 57A)

Relief for certain acquisitions of residential property

17—(1) (*substitutes* FA 2003 s 58A for FA 2003 ss 58, 59)
(2) (*inserts* FA 2003 Sch 6A)
(3) (*amends* FA 2003 s 81(1), (4))
(4) (*amends* FA 2003 s 87(3), (4))

Initial transfer of assets to trustees of unit trust scheme

18 (*inserted* FA 2003 s 64A and *repealed by* FA 2006 s 178, Sch 26 Pt 7(3).)

Return or further return in consequence of later linked transaction

19—(1) (*inserts* FA 2003 s 81A)
(2) (*amends* FA 2003 s 81(3))
(3) (*amends* FA 2003 s 87(3))

Declaration by person authorised to act on behalf of purchaser

20 (*inserts* FA 2003 s 81B)

Crown application

21—(1)–(3) (*amends* FA 2003 s 107)

Further provision relating to leases

22—(1) (*substitutes* FA 2003 s 120)
(2) (*inserts* FA 2003 Sch 17A)
(3) (*inserts* FA 2003 s 51(5))
(4) (*amends* FA 2003 s 80)
(5) (*amends* FA 2003 s 87(3))
(6) (*inserts* FA 2003 s 90(7))
(7) (*amends* table in FA 2003 s 122)
(8) (*inserts* FA 2003 Sch 19 para 7(4))

Abolition of stamp duty: application to duplicates and counterparts

23 (*amends* FA 2003 s 125(5))

Application of transitional provisions to certain contracts

24 (*inserts* FA 2003 Sch 19 paras 4A, 4B)

Stamping of contract or agreement where transaction on completion or grant of lease subject to stamp duty land tax

25—(1) (*inserts* FA 2003 Sch 19 para 7A)
(2) (*amends* FA 2003 Sch 19 para 8)
(4) (*amends* FA 2003 s 122)

Commencement

26 This Part of this Schedule applies in relation to any transaction of which the effective date (within the meaning of Part 4 of the Finance Act 2003) is on or after the day on which this Act is passed.

SCHEDULE 40

STAMP DUTY LAND TAX: CLAIMS NOT INCLUDED IN RETURNS

Section 299

(*inserts* FA 2003 Sch 11A)

SCHEDULE 41

STAMP DUTY LAND TAX: APPLICATION TO CERTAIN PARTNERSHIP TRANSACTIONS

Section 304

1 (*substitutes* FA 2003 Sch 15 Pt 3)

2 (*amends* FA 2003 ss 104(2), 125(8), Sch 15 para 5)

3—(1) The preceding provisions of this Schedule have effect in relation to any partnership transaction of which the effective date (within the meaning of Part 4 of the Finance Act 2003 (c 14)) is after the day on which this Act is passed.
(2) "Partnership transaction" means a transaction mentioned in paragraph 9(1) of Schedule 15 to the Finance Act 2003 (as substituted by paragraph 1 of this Schedule).

SCHEDULE 42

REPEALS

Section 326

PART 4
OTHER TAXES

(2)

Stamp Duty Land Tax

Note—As the repeals are already in force, this table has been omitted.

FINANCE ACT 2005

(2005 Chapter 7)

An Act to Grant certain duties, to alter other duties, and to amend the law relating to the National Debt and the Public Revenue, and to make further provision in connection with finance.

[7 April 2005]

PART 3
STAMP TAXES

Stamp duty land tax

94 Alternative property finance
Schedule 8 (which makes amendments of Part 4 of FA 2003 relating to alternative property finance) has effect.

Stamp duty land tax and stamp duty

95 Raising of thresholds
. . . [1]

Amendments—[1] Section 95 repealed by FA 2006 s 178, Sch 26 Pt 7(1) in relation to any transaction of which the effective date (within the meaning of Part 4 of FA 2003) is after 22 March 2006 and to instruments executed after 22 March 2006, by virtue of FA 2006 s 162(4), (5).

96 Removal of disadvantaged areas relief for non-residential property
Schedule 9 (which provides for the removal, in relation to non-residential property, of relief from stamp duty land tax and stamp duty for land in disadvantaged areas) has effect.

Stamp duty and stamp duty reserve tax

97 Demutualisation of insurance companies
(1) Section 90 of FA 1986 (other exceptions to the principal charge to stamp duty reserve tax under section 87 of that Act) is amended as follows.
(2) (*amends* FA 1986 s 90(1A)).
(3) Schedule 19 to FA 1999 (stamp duty and stamp duty reserve tax: unit trusts) is amended as follows.
(4) (*amends* FA 1986 Sch 19 para 6(5)).
(5) The amendment in subsection (2) applies where the relevant day for the purposes of section 87 of FA 1986 falls on or after the day on which this Act is passed.
(6) The amendment in subsection (4) applies in relation to surrenders (within the meaning of Part 2 of Schedule 19 to FA 1999) occurring on or after the day on which this Act is passed.

PART 7
SUPPLEMENTARY PROVISIONS

104 Repeals
(1) The enactments mentioned in Schedule 11 (which include provisions that are spent or of no practical utility) are repealed to the extent specified.
(2) The repeals specified in that Schedule have effect subject to the commencement provisions and savings contained or referred to in the notes set out in that Schedule.

105 Interpretation

In this Act—

"ALDA 1979" means the Alcoholic Liquor Duties Act 1979 (c 4);
"CAA 2001" means the Capital Allowances Act 2001 (c 2);
"FA", followed by a year, means the Finance Act of that year;
"F(No 2)A", followed by a year, means the Finance (No 2) Act of that year;
"HODA 1979" means the Hydrocarbon Oil Duties Act 1979 (c 5);
"ICTA" means the Income and Corporation Taxes Act 1988 (c 1);
"IHTA 1984" means the Inheritance Tax Act 1984 (c 51);
"ITEPA 2003" means the Income Tax (Earnings and Pensions) Act 2003 (c 1);
"ITTOIA 2005" means the Income Tax (Trading and Other Income) Act 2005 (c 5);
"TCGA 1992" means the Taxation of Chargeable Gains Act 1992 (c 12);
"TMA 1970" means the Taxes Management Act 1970 (c 9);
"VERA 1994" means the Vehicle Excise and Registration Act 1994 (c 22).

106 Short title

This Act may be cited as the Finance Act 2005.

SCHEDULES

SCHEDULE 8

STAMP DUTY LAND TAX: ALTERNATIVE PROPERTY FINANCE

Section 94

Introduction

1 Part 4 of FA 2003 is amended in accordance with this Schedule.

Alternative property finance: England and Wales and Northern Ireland

2 (*inserts* FA 2003 s 71A).

Alternative property finance: Scotland

3—(1) Section 72 (alternative property finance: land sold to financial institution and leased to individual) is amended as follows.
(2) (*amends* FA 2003 s 72(1)).
(3) (*substitutes* FA 2003 s 72(7)).
(4) (*repeals* FA 2003 s 72(8)).
(5) (*inserts* FA 2003 s 72(10)).
(6) (*amends* heading to FA 2003 s 72).

4 (*inserts* FA 2003 s 72A).

Consequential amendments

5—(1) Section 73 (alternative property finance: land sold to individual and re-sold to individual) is amended as follows.
(2) (*amends* FA 2003 s 73(2)(*b*)).
(3) (*amends* FA 2003 s 73(5)(*a*)).

6 (*amends* FA 2003 s 122).

Commencement

7—(1) Paragraphs 2 and 3, and paragraphs 5 and 6 so far as relating to section 71A of FA 2003, have effect in any case where the effective date of the first transaction, within the meaning of section 71A of FA 2003 (as inserted by paragraph 2), falls on or after the day on which this Act is passed.
(2) Paragraph 4, and paragraphs 5 and 6 so far as relating to section 72A of FA 2003, have effect in any case where the effective date of the first transaction, within the meaning of section 72A of FA 2003 (as inserted by paragraph 4), falls on or after the day on which this Act is passed.
(3) In this paragraph "the effective date" has the same meaning as in Part 4 of FA 2003.

SCHEDULE 9

STAMP DUTY LAND TAX AND STAMP DUTY: REMOVAL OF DISADVANTAGED AREAS RELIEF FOR NON-RESIDENTIAL PROPERTY

Section 96

Stamp duty land tax

1—(1) Schedule 6 to FA 2003 (disadvantaged areas relief) is amended as follows.
(2) (*amends* FA 2003 Sch 6 para 3).
(3) (*repeals* FA 2003 Sch 6 para 4).
(4) (*amends* FA 2003 Sch 6 para 6).
(5) (*amends* FA 2003 Sch 6 para 7).
(6) (*repeals* FA 2003 Sch 6 para 8).
(7) (*amends* FA 2003 Sch 6 para 10).

Stamp duty

2—(1) The Stamp Duty (Disadvantaged Areas) (Application of Exemptions) Regulations 2003 (SI 2003/1056) are amended as follows.
(2) (*inserts* SI 2003/1056 reg 2A).
(3) (*inserts* SI 2003/1056 reg 5(3A)).

3 The insertion by paragraph 2 of provisions into the Stamp Duty (Disadvantaged Areas) (Application of Exemptions) Regulations 2003 is without prejudice to the power to amend or revoke those provisions by further regulations under section 92A of FA 2001.

Commencement and transitional provisions

4—(1) Subject to sub-paragraph (2), paragraph 1 applies in relation to any transaction of which the effective date is after 16th March 2005.
(2) That paragraph does not apply—

(*a*) in relation to any transaction that is effected in pursuance of a contract entered into and substantially performed on or before 16th March 2005, or

(*b*) (subject to sub-paragraph (3)) in relation to any other transaction that is effected in pursuance of a contract entered into on or before that date.

(3) The exclusion by sub-paragraph (2)(*b*) of transactions effected in pursuance of contracts entered into on or before 16th March 2005 does not apply—

(*a*) if there is any variation of the contract or assignment of rights under the contract after that date,

(*b*) if the transaction is effected in consequence of the exercise after that date of any option, right of pre-emption or similar right, or

(*c*) if after that date there is an assignment, subsale or other transaction (relating to the whole or part of the subject-matter of the contract) as a result of which a person other than the purchaser under the contract becomes entitled to call for a conveyance to him.

(4) In this paragraph "effective date" and "substantially performed" have the same meaning as in Part 4 of FA 2003.

5—(1) Subject to sub-paragraph (2), paragraph 2 applies in relation to instruments executed after 16th March 2005.
(2) That paragraph does not apply in relation to an instrument giving effect to a contract entered into on or before 16th March 2005, unless—

(*a*) the instrument is made in consequence of the exercise after that date of any option, right of pre-emption or similar right, or

(*b*) the instrument transfers the property in question to, or vests it in, a person other than the purchaser under the contract, because of an assignment (or, in Scotland, assignation) or further contract made after that date.

SCHEDULE 11

REPEALS

Section 104

PART 3

STAMP TAXES

(1)

Stamp Duty Land Tax: Alternative Property Finance

Short title and chapter	*Extent of repeal*
Finance Act 2003 (c 14)	In section 72, in subsection (1)(*c*) the words "or its successor in title", and subsection (8).

These repeals have effect in accordance with paragraph 7(1) of Schedule 8 to this Act.

(2)

Stamp Duty Land Tax: Disadvantaged Areas Relief

Short title and chapter	*Extent of repeal*
Finance Act 2003 (c 14)	In Schedule 6— (*a*) paragraph 4; (*b*) in the second sentence of paragraph 6(1), the words "land that is non-residential property or"; (*c*) paragraphs 6(2) and 6(3); (*d*) paragraph 8; (*e*) in the second sentence of paragraph 10(1), the words "land that is non-residential property or"; (*f*) paragraphs 10(2) and 10(3).

These repeals have effect in accordance with paragraph 4 of Schedule 9 to this Act.

COMMISSIONERS FOR REVENUE AND CUSTOMS ACT 2005

(2005 Chapter 11)

An Act to make provision for the appointment of Commissioners to exercise functions presently vested in the Commissioners of Inland Revenue and the Commissioners of Customs and Excise; for the establishment of a Revenue and Customs Prosecutions Office; and for connected purposes.

[7 April 2005]

Note—Please see VAT statutes for the text of this Act.

Regulations—See the Revenue and Customs (Inspections) Regulations, SI 2005/1133 (reproduced in the VAT statutory instruments section).

FINANCE (NO 2) ACT 2005

(2005 Chapter 22)

ARRANGEMENT OF SECTIONS

PART 3

STAMP TAXES

Stamp duty land tax

An Act to Grant certain duties, to alter other duties, and to amend the law relating to the National Debt and the Public Revenue, and to make further provision in connection with finance.

[20 July 2005]

PART 3
STAMP TAXES

Stamp duty land tax

47 E-conveyancing

(1) (*amends* Public Finance and Accountability (Scotland) Act 2000 s 9(1)).
(2) (*amends* FA 2003 s 79(1)).
(3) (*substitutes* FA 2003 s 119(1)(*a*), (*b*)).
(4) (*inserts* FA 2003 Sch 10 para 7(1A)).
(5) The Commissioners for Her Majesty's Revenue and Customs—
(*a*) may make regulations conferring administrative functions on a land registrar in connection with stamp duty land tax, and
(*b*) may make payments to land registrars in respect of the exercise of those functions.
(6) In subsection (5) "land registrar" means—
(*a*) in relation to England and Wales, the Chief Land Registrar,
(*b*) in relation to Scotland, the Keeper of the Registers of Scotland,
(*c*) in relation to Northern Ireland, the Registrar of Titles or the registrar of deeds, and
(*d*) in any case, such other persons with functions relating to the registration of land as regulations under subsection (5) may specify.
(7) Regulations under subsection (5)—
(*a*) shall be made by statutory instrument, and
(*b*) shall be subject to annulment in pursuance of a resolution of the House of Commons.

48 Disclosure of information contained in land transaction returns

(1) (*inserts* FA 2003 s 78A).
(2) (*substitutes* FA 1994 s 245(2)).
(3) (*substitutes* heading to FA 1994 Part 6).
(4) (*revokes* Stamp Duty Land Tax (Consequential Amendment of Enactments) Regulations, SI 2005/82, reg 3).
(5) Subsections (1) to (4) come into force on such day as the Treasury may by order appoint.
(6) Section 114(3) of FA 2003 (negative resolution procedure) does not apply to an order made under subsection (5).

Commencement—Finance (No 2) Act 2005, Sections 48(1) to 48(5), (Appointed Day) Order, SI 2009/2094 (appointed day for the purposes of sub-s (5) is 30 July 2009)

49 Miscellaneous amendments

Schedule 10 (which makes miscellaneous amendments of Part 4 of FA 2003) has effect.

Stamp duty and stamp duty reserve tax

50 Power to extend exceptions relating to recognised exchanges

(1) The Treasury may by regulations extend the application of the provisions mentioned in subsection (2) to any market (specified by name or by description) which—
(a) is not a recognised exchange, but

(b) is a multilateral trading facility (or, assuming compliance with the provisions of Title II of the Directive (authorisation and operating conditions), would be such a facility).

(2) The provisions referred to in subsection (1) are—

(a) sections 80A and 80C of FA 1986 (stamp duty: exceptions for sales to intermediaries and for repurchases and stock lending), and

(b) sections 88A and 89AA of that Act (stamp duty reserve tax: exceptions for intermediaries and for repurchases and stock lending).

(3) In this section—

"the Directive" means Directive 2004/39/EC of the European Parliament and of the Council of 21 April 2004 on markets in financial instruments;

"multilateral trading facility" has the same meaning as in the Directive (see Article 4(15));

"recognised exchange" means any of the following—

(a) an EEA exchange,

(b) a recognised foreign exchange,

(c) a recognised foreign options exchange,

within the meaning of the provisions mentioned in subsection (2).

(4) Regulations under this section may provide for the application of the provisions mentioned in subsection (2) subject to any adaptations appearing to the Treasury to be necessary or expedient.

(5) In subsection (1)(b) the words "(or, assuming compliance with the provisions of Title II of the Directive (authorisation and operating conditions), would be such a facility)" shall cease to have effect on such day as the Treasury may by order appoint.

(6) Section 117 of FA 2002 (power to extend the exceptions in subsection (2) to any market prescribed by order under section 118(3) of the Financial Services and Markets Act 2000) shall cease to have effect on such day as the Treasury may by order appoint.

(7) The power to make regulations or an order under this section is exercisable by statutory instrument.

(8) A statutory instrument containing—

(a) regulations under this section, or

(b) an order under subsection (5),

shall be subject to annulment in pursuance of a resolution of the House of Commons.

Regulations—Stamp Duty and Stamp Duty Reserve Tax (Extension of Exceptions relating to Recognised Exchanges) Regulations, SI 2005/1990; Stamp Duty and Stamp Duty Reserve Tax (Extension of Exceptions relating to Recognised Exchanges) Regulations, SI 2006/139.

Amendment—This section repealed by FA 2007 ss 73, 114, Sch 21 para 8, Sch 27 Pt 4(2) with effect from 1 November 2007.

PART 4
EUROPEAN COMPANY STATUTE

57 Stamp duty reserve tax

(1) (*amends* FA 1986 s 99(4)).

(2) Subsection (1) shall have effect for the purposes of determining, in relation to anything occurring on or after 1st April 2005, whether securities (whenever issued or raised) are chargeable securities for the purposes of Part IV of FA 1986.

58 Bearer instruments: stamp duty and stamp duty reserve tax

(1) (*amends* FA 1986 s 90(3C)(*a*)).

(2) (*amends* FA 1986 s 90(3E)(*a*)).

(3) (*amends* FA 1999 Sch 15 para 11).

(4) This section shall have effect for the purposes of determining whether or not stamp duty or stamp duty reserve tax is chargeable in respect of anything done on or after 1st April 2005.

PART 6
SUPPLEMENTARY PROVISIONS

70 Repeals

(1) The enactments mentioned in Schedule 11 (which include provisions that are spent or of no practical utility) are repealed to the extent specified.

(2) The repeals specified in that Schedule have effect subject to the commencement provisions and savings contained or referred to in the notes set out in that Schedule.

71 Interpretation

In this Act—

"CAA 2001" means the Capital Allowances Act 2001 (c 2);

"FA", followed by a year, means the Finance Act of that year;

"ICTA" means the Income and Corporation Taxes Act 1988 (c 1);

"ITEPA 2003" means the Income Tax (Earnings and Pensions) Act 2003 (c 1);

"ITTOIA 2005" means the Income Tax (Trading and Other Income) Act 2005 (c 5);

"TCGA 1992" means the Taxation of Chargeable Gains Act 1992 (c 12);

"VATA 1994" means the Value Added Tax Act 1994 (c 23);
"VERA 1994" means the Vehicle Excise and Registration Act 1994 (c 22).

72 Short title
This Act may be cited as the Finance (No 2) Act 2005.

SCHEDULES

SCHEDULE 10

STAMP DUTY LAND TAX: MISCELLANEOUS AMENDMENTS

Section 49

PART 1

AMENDMENTS COMING INTO FORCE IN ACCORDANCE WITH PARAGRAPH 16

Introduction

1 Part 4 of FA 2003 (stamp duty land tax) is amended in accordance with this Part of this Schedule.

Transfer of rights: exclusion of transaction to which alternative finance provisions apply

2 (*amends* FA 2003 s 45(3)).

Group relief

3 (*amends* FA 2003 Sch 7 para 1(7)).

4 (*amends* FA 2003 Sch 7 para 3).

5 (*amends* FA 2003 Sch 7 para 4).

6 (*inserts* FA 2003 Sch 7 para 4A).

7 (*amends* FA 2003 Sch 17A para 11(5)(*a*)).

Reconstruction and acquisition reliefs

8 (*amends* FA 2003 Sch 7 para 8).

9 (*substitutes* Sch 7 para 9(2)).

Withdrawal of money etc from partnership after transfer of chargeable interest

10 (*inserts* FA 2003 Sch 15 para 17A).

Grant of lease to bare trustee

11 (*substitutes* FA 2003 Sch 16 para 3).

12 (*substitutes* FA 2003 Sch 17A para 11(1)).

Variation of lease

13 (*amends* FA 2003 Sch 17A para 15A).

Loan or deposit in connection with grant or assignment of lease

14 (*inserts* FA 2003 Sch 17A para 18A).

15 (*inserts* FA 2003 s 80(4A)).

Commencement

16—(1) Subject to sub-paragraph (7), paragraphs 3 to 7 have effect where the effective date of the relevant transaction (within the meaning of paragraph 3 or 4A of Schedule 7 to FA 2003) is after 19th May 2005.
(2) Subject to sub-paragraph (7), paragraph 9 has effect where the effective date of the relevant transaction (within the meaning of paragraph 9 of Schedule 7 to FA 2003) is after 19th May 2005.
(3) Subject to sub-paragraph (7), paragraph 10 has effect where the effective date of the transaction transferring the chargeable interest to the partnership is after 19th May 2005.

(4) Subject to sub-paragraph (7), paragraphs 11 and 12 have effect where the effective date of the land transaction consisting of the grant of the lease is after 19th May 2005.
(5) Subject to sub-paragraph (7), the amendments made by the other provisions of this Part of this Schedule have effect in relation to any transaction of which the effective date is after 19th May 2005.
(6) In sub-paragraphs (7) and (8) "the specified date" means—
(*a*) in relation to the amendments made by paragraphs 4(*a*) and 9, 19th May 2005, and
(*b*) in relation to the amendments made by the other provisions of this Part of this Schedule, 16th March 2005.
(7) The amendments made by this Part of this Schedule do not have effect—
(*a*) in relation to any transaction which is effected in pursuance of a contract entered into and substantially performed on or before the specified date, or
(*b*) subject to sub-paragraph (8), in relation to any other transaction which is effected in pursuance of a contract entered into on or before the specified date.
(8) The exclusion by sub-paragraph (7)(*b*) of transactions effected in pursuance of contracts entered into on or before the specified date does not apply—
(*a*) if there is any variation of the contract or assignment of rights under the contract after that date,
(*b*) if the transaction is effected in consequence of the exercise after that date of any option, right of pre-emption or similar right, or
(*c*) if after that date there is an assignment, subsale or other transaction (relating to the whole or part of the subject-matter of the contract) as a result of which a person other than the purchaser under the contract becomes entitled to call for a conveyance to him.
(9) In this paragraph "assignment", "effective date" and "substantially performed" have the same meaning as in Part 4 of FA 2003.

PART 2
AMENDMENTS COMING INTO FORCE IN ACCORDANCE WITH PARAGRAPH 22

Introduction

17 Part 4 of FA 2003 (stamp duty land tax) is amended in accordance with this Part of this Schedule.

Transfers involving public bodies

18 (*inserts* FA 2003 s 66(6)).

Group relief: avoidance arrangements

19 (*inserts* FA 2003 Sch 7 para 2(4A)).

Acquisition relief: avoidance arrangements

20 (*substitutes* FA 2003 Sch 7 para 8(5), and *inserts* para 8(5B), (5C)).

Stamp duty on transfers of partnership interests

21—(1) In Schedule 15 (stamp duty land tax: partnerships), paragraph 33 (which relates to stamp duty on transfers of partnership interests) is amended as follows.
(2) (*substitutes* FA 2003 Sch 15 para 33(1), (1A)).
(3) (*amends* FA 2003 Sch 15 para 33(3)).
(4) (*inserts* FA 2003 Sch 15 para 33(3A)).
(5) (*repeals* FA 2003 Sch 15 para 33(4)).
(6) (*amends* FA 2003 Sch 15 para 33(5)).

Commencement

22—(1) Subject to sub-paragraph (2), paragraphs 18 to 20 have effect in relation to any transaction of which the effective date is on or after the day on which this Act is passed.
(2) Paragraphs 19 and 20 do not have effect—
(*a*) in relation to any transaction which is effected in pursuance of a contract entered into and substantially performed on or before 16th March 2005, or
(*b*) (subject to sub-paragraph (3)) in relation to any other transaction which is effected in pursuance of a contract entered into on or before that date.
(3) The exclusion by sub-paragraph (2)(*b*) of transactions effected in pursuance of contracts entered into on or before 16th March 2005 does not apply—
(*a*) if there is any variation of the contract or assignment of rights under the contract after that date,

(*b*) if the transaction is effected in consequence of the exercise after that date of any option, right of pre-emption or similar right, or

(*c*) if after that date there is an assignment, subsale or other transaction (relating to the whole or part of the subject-matter of the contract) as a result of which a person other than the purchaser under the contract becomes entitled to call for a conveyance to him.

(4) Paragraph 21 has effect in relation to any instrument executed on or after the day on which this Act is passed.

(5) In this paragraph "assignment", "effective date" and "substantially performed" have the same meaning as in Part 4 of FA 2003.

SCHEDULE 11
REPEALS
Section 70

PART 3
STAMP TAXES

(1)

Stamp Duty Land Tax: Miscellaneous

Short title and chapter	*Extent of repeal*
Finance Act 2003 (c 14)	In Schedule 15, paragraph 33(4).

This repeal has effect in relation to any instrument executed on or after the day on which this Act is passed.

(2)

Stamp Duty and Stamp Duty Reserve Tax: Extension of Exceptions

Short title and chapter	*Extent of repeal*
Finance Act 2002 (c 23)	Section 117.

This repeal has effect in accordance with section 50 of this Act.

FINANCE ACT 2006

(2006 Chapter 25)

ARRANGEMENT OF SECTIONS

Schedule 26—Repeals
Part 7—Stamp taxes

An Act to Grant certain duties, to alter other duties, and to amend the law relating to the National Debt and the Public Revenue, and to make further provision in connection with finance.

[19 July 2006]

PART 8
STAMP TAXES

Stamp duty and stamp duty land tax: thresholds

162 Raising of thresholds

(1) (*amends* FA 2003 s 55 Table A)
(2) (*amends* FA 2003 Sch 5 para 2(3) Table A)
(3) (*amends* FA 1999 Sch 13 para 4)
(4) The amendments made by subsections (1) and (2) have effect in relation to any transaction of which the effective date (within the meaning of Part 4 of FA 2003) is after 22nd March 2006.
(5) The amendment made by subsection (3) has effect in relation to instruments executed after 22nd March 2006.

Stamp duty land tax

163 Partnerships

Schedule 24 (amendments of Schedule 15 to FA 2003) has effect.

164 Leases

(1) (*substitutes* FA 2003 s 77(2A))
(2) (*amends* FA 2003 Sch 5 para 3)
(3) Subsection (1) has effect in relation to any assignment of which the effective date (within the meaning of Part 4 of FA 2003) is on or after the day on which this Act is passed.
(4) Subsection (2) has effect in relation to any lease granted or treated as granted on or after that day.
(5) Schedule 25 (amendments of Schedule 17A to FA 2003) has effect.

165 Reallocation of trust property as between beneficiaries

(1) (*inserts* FA 2003 Sch 16 para 8)
(2) Subsection (1) has effect in relation to any acquisition of which the effective date (within the meaning of Part 4 of FA 2003) is on or after the day on which this Act is passed.

166 Unit trust schemes

(1) Part 4 of FA 2003 (stamp duty land tax) is amended as follows.
(2) (*repeals* FA 2003 s 64A)
(3) In section 101 (unit trust schemes)—
  (*a*) (*amends* FA 2003 s 101(1))
  (*b*) (*amends* FA 2003 s 101(7))
(4) This section has effect in relation to any land transaction of which the effective date is, or is after, 22nd March 2006 (but see subsections (5) and (6)).
(5) This section does not have effect in relation to—
  (*a*) any land transaction which is effected in pursuance of a contract entered into and substantially performed before 2 p.m. on 22nd March 2006 ("the relevant time"), or
  (*b*) any other land transaction which is effected in pursuance of a contract entered into before the relevant time and which is not an excluded transaction.
(6) For this purpose, a land transaction effected in pursuance of a contract is an excluded transaction if—
  (*a*) any provision of the contract has effect by reference to a unit trust scheme and the scheme is not established before the relevant time,
  (*b*) at or after the relevant time the contract is varied in a way that significantly affects the land transaction (see subsection (7)),
  (*c*) the subject-matter of the land transaction is not identified in the contract in a way that would have enabled its acquisition before the relevant time,
  (*d*) rights under the contract are assigned at or after the relevant time,
  (*e*) the land transaction is effected in consequence of the exercise, at or after the relevant time, of any option, right of pre-emption or similar right, or
  (*f*) at or after the relevant time there is an assignment, subsale or other transaction (relating to the whole or part of the contract's subject-matter) as a result of which a person other than the purchaser under the contract becomes entitled to call for a conveyance to him.
(7) For the purposes of subsection (6)(*b*) the contract is varied in a way that significantly affects the land transaction if (and only if)—
  (*a*) it is varied so as to substitute a different purchaser in relation to the land transaction,
  (*b*) it is varied so as to alter the subject-matter of the land transaction, or
  (*c*) it is varied so as to alter the consideration for the land transaction.

(8) Expressions which are used in Part 4 of FA 2003 and in this section have the same meaning in this section as in that Part.

167 Demutualisation of insurance companies

(1) Schedule 7 to FA 2003 (stamp duty land tax: group relief etc) is amended as follows.

(2) (*amends* FA 2003 Sch 7 para 2)

(3) (*inserts* FA 2003 Sch 7 para 2(3A))

(4) In paragraph 4 (cases in which group relief not withdrawn under paragraph 3)—

(*a*) (*inserts* FA 2003 Sch 7 para 4(6A))

(*b*) (*amends* FA 2003 Sch 7 para 4(7))

(5) The amendments made by this section have effect in relation to any transfer which takes place, or is intended to take place, after 22nd March 2006.

168 Alternative finance

(1) (*amends* FA 2003 ss 71A to 73)

(2) (*repeals* FA 2003 ss 71A(6), 72(6), 72A(6) and 73(4))

(3) (*amends* FA 2003 s 73(3))

(4) (*inserts* FA 2003 s 73A)

(5) This section shall have effect in relation to arrangements in which the effective date of the first transaction (within the meaning of sections 71A to 73 of FA 2003) is on or after the date on which this Act is passed; and section 119(1) of FA 2003 shall have effect for determining the effective date for the purposes of this subsection.

Stamp duty

169 Reliefs for certain company acquisitions

(1) Part 3 of FA 1986 (stamp duty) is amended as follows.

(2) In section 75 (relief for acquisition of target company's undertaking in pursuance of reconstruction scheme)—

(*a*) (*amends* FA 1986 s 75(4))

(*b*) (*amends* FA 1986 s 75(5)(*c*))

(3) (*amends* FA 1986 s 76(3))

(4) In section 77 (relief for acquisition of target company's share capital), in subsection (3) (conditions for relief),—

(*a*) (*repeals* FA 1986 s 77(3)(*a*))

(*b*) (*amends* FA 1986 s 77(3)(*g*))

(*c*) (*amends* FA 1986 s 77(3)(*h*))

(5) The amendments made by this section have effect in relation to instruments executed after the day on which this Act is passed.

PART 10

SUPPLEMENTARY PROVISIONS

178 Repeals

(1) The enactments mentioned in Schedule 26 (which include provisions that are spent or of no practical utility) are repealed to the extent specified.

(2) The repeals specified in that Schedule have effect subject to the commencement provisions and savings contained or referred to in the notes set out in that Schedule.

179 Interpretation

In this Act—

. . .

"FA", followed by a year, means the Finance Act of that year;

. . .

SCHEDULES

SCHEDULE 24

STAMP DUTY LAND TAX: AMENDMENTS OF SCHEDULE 15 TO FA 2003

Section 163

Introduction

1 Schedule 15 to FA 2003 (stamp duty land tax: partnerships) is amended as follows.

Transfer of chargeable interest to a partnership

2—(1) (*substitutes* FA 2003 Sch 15 para 10(2))

(2) (*amends* FA 2003 Sch 15 para 10(6))

3 (*substitutes* FA 2003 Sch 15 para 11(2)–(2D))

4—(1) (*amends* FA 2003 Sch 15 para 13(3))
(2) (*substitutes* FA 2003 Sch 15 para 13(4A), (5))

Transfer of chargeable interest from a partnership

5—(1) (*substitutes* FA 2003 Sch 15 para 18(2))
(2) (*amends* FA 2003 Sch 15 para 18(6))

6 (*substitutes* FA 2003 Sch 15 para 19(2)–(2D))

7—(1) (*amends* FA 2003 Sch 15 para 24(3))
(2) (*substitutes* FA 2003 Sch 15 para 24(4A), (5))

Transfer of chargeable interest from a partnership to a partnership

8 (*substitutes* FA 2003 Sch 15 para 23(2)–(3))

Transfer of partnership interest: restriction of charge to property-investment partnerships

9—(1) (*substitutes* FA 2003 Sch 15 para 14 heading)
(2) (*amends* FA 2003 Sch 15 para 14(1)(*a*))
(3) (*inserts* FA 2003 Sch 15 para 14(8))

Prevention of double charge where money etc withdrawn from partnership

10 (*inserts* FA 2003 Sch 15 para 17A(8))

Commencement

11—(1) Paragraphs 2 to 8 have effect in relation to any transfer of which the effective date is on or after the day on which this Act is passed.
(2) Paragraph 9 has effect in relation to any transfer that has (or, but for the amendment made by that paragraph, would have) an effective date which is on or after that day.
(3) Paragraph 10 has effect in relation to any qualifying event of which the effective date is on or after that day.
(4) In this paragraph "effective date" has the same meaning as in Part 4 of FA 2003.

SCHEDULE 25

STAMP DUTY LAND TAX: AMENDMENTS OF SCHEDULE 17A TO FA 2003

Section 164

Introduction

1 Schedule 17A (stamp duty land tax: further provisions relating to leases) is amended as follows.

Agricultural tenancies variable under statutory provisions

2—(1) (*inserts* FA 2003 Sch 17A para 7(4A))
(2) (*substitutes* FA 2003 Sch 17A para 13(2)(*a*), (*b*))

Backdated lease granted to tenant holding over

3—(1) (*inserts* FA 2003 Sch 17A para 9A)
(2) (*amends* FA 2003 Sch 17A para 7(3))

Disapplication of "single lease" treatment where agreement for lease followed by grant

4 (*amends* FA 2003 Sch 17A para 12A(3))

5—(1) (*amends* FA 2003 Sch 17A para 19(2))
(2) (*amends* FA 2003 Sch 17A para 19(4))

Disapplication of "new lease" treatment for certain rent increases after fifth year

6—(1) (*amends* FA 2003 Sch 17A para 13 heading)
(2) (*amends* FA 2003 Sch 17A para 13(1))

Abnormal rent increase after fifth year

7—(1) (*amends* FA 2003 Sch 17A para 14(1)(*a*))
(2) (*substitutes* FA 2003 Sch 17A para 14(4)–(4B))

(3) (*inserts* FA 2003 Sch 17A para 14(7))

8—(1) (*substitutes* FA 2003 Sch 17A para 15 Steps One to Three)

Commencement

9—(1) Paragraph 2 has effect in relation to any lease granted or treated as granted on or after commencement day.
(2) Paragraph 3 has effect in relation to any case where—
(*a*) the grant of the old lease was chargeable to stamp duty land tax, and
(*b*) the new lease is granted on or after commencement day.
"The old lease" and "the new lease" mean the leases referred to in sub-paragraphs (1)(*a*) and (1)(*b*), respectively, of paragraph 9A of Schedule 17A to FA 2003 (inserted by paragraph 3).
(3) Paragraphs 4 and 5 have effect in relation to any agreement that is substantially performed on or after commencement day.
(4) Paragraph 6 has effect in relation to any variation of a lease made on or after commencement day.
(5) Paragraphs 7 and 8 have effect in relation to any increase of rent that takes effect on or after commencement day.
(6) In this paragraph "commencement day" means the day on which this Act is passed.

SCHEDULE 26

REPEALS

Section 178

PART 7
STAMP TAXES

(1) Stamp Duty and Stamp Duty Land Tax: Thresholds

Short title and chapter	*Extent of repeal*
Finance Act 2005 (c 7)	Section 95.

This repeal has effect in accordance with section 162 of this Act.

(2) Stamp Duty Land Tax: Partnerships

Short title and chapter	Extent of repeal
Finance Act 2003 (c 14)	In Schedule 15— (a) in paragraph 10(6), the words "(instead of sub-paragraphs (2) to (5))"; (b) in paragraph 18(6), the words "(instead of sub-paragraphs (2) to (5))".

These repeals have effect in relation to any transfer of which the effective date (within the meaning of Part 4 of FA 2003) is on or after the day on which this Act is passed.

(3) Stamp Duty Land Tax: Unit Trust Schemes

Short title and chapter	*Extent of repeal*
Finance Act 2003 (c 14)	Section 64A.
	In section 101(7), the words from "section 53" to "companies), or".
Finance Act 2004 (c 12)	In Schedule 39, paragraph 18.

These repeals have effect in accordance with section 166 of this Act.

(4) Stamp Duty Land Tax: Alternative Finance

Short title and chapter	*Extent of repeal*
Finance Act 2003 (c 14).	Section 71A(6).
	Section 72(6).

(5) Stamp Duty: Reliefs for Certain Company Acquisitions

Short title and chapter	*Extent of repeal*
Finance Act 1986 (c 41)	In section 75(4), the words "that the registered office of the acquiring company is in the United Kingdom and". In section 76(3), the words "that the registered office of the acquiring company is in the United Kingdom and". Section 77(3)(*a*).

These repeals have effect in accordance with section 169 of this Act.

FINANCE ACT 2007

(2007 Chapter 11)

PART 2

ENVIRONMENT

Energy-saving: houses

19 SDLT relief for new zero-carbon homes

(1) (*inserts* FA 2003 ss 58B, 58C)
(2) (*inserts* FA 2003 s 114(5), (6))

PART 5

SDLT, STAMP DUTY AND SDRT

SDLT: anti-avoidance provisions

71 Anti-avoidance

(1) (*inserts* FA 2003 ss 75A–75C)
(2) The amendment made by subsection (1) has effect in respect of disposals and acquisitions if the disposal mentioned in new section 75A(1)(*a*) (inserted by that subsection) takes place on or after 6th December 2006.
(3) But—
(*a*) the transitional provisions of sub-paragraphs (2) to (5) of paragraph 1 of the Schedule to the Stamp Duty Land Tax (Variation of the Finance Act 2003) Regulations 2006 (SI 2006/3237) continue to have effect in relation to this section as in relation to that paragraph, and
(*b*) a provision of new section 75C (inserted by subsection (1) above) shall not have effect where the disposal mentioned in new section 75A(1)(*a*) took place before the day on which this Act is passed, if or in so far as the provision would make a person liable for a higher amount of tax than would have been charged in accordance with those regulations.

72 Partnerships

(1) Schedule 15 to FA 2003 (stamp duty land tax: partnerships) is amended as follows.
(2) A reference in this section to a provision of that Schedule is to the provision as it had effect before variation by the Stamp Duty Land Tax (Variation of the Finance Act 2003) Regulations 2006.
(3) (*amends* FA 2003 Sch 15 para 12(1) Step Two)
(4) (*inserts* FA 2003 Sch 15 para 12(3))
(5) Omit paragraph 13 (transfer to partnership where all partners are companies).
(6) In paragraph 14 (transfer of interest in property-investment partnership)—
(*a*) (*repeals* FA 2003 Sch 15 para 14(1)(*b*), (4))
(*b*) (*inserts* FA 2003 Sch 15 para 14(9))
(amends italic cross-heading before FA 2003 Sch 15 para 14)
(7) (*amends* FA 2003 Sch 15 para 20(1) Step Two)
(8) (*inserts* FA 2003 Sch 15 para 20(3))
(9) (*inserts* FA 2003 Sch 15 para 27A)
(10) (*substitutes* FA 2003 Sch 15 para 36)
(11) (*inserts* FA 2003 Sch 15 para 39(3))
(12) In Schedule 16 to FA 2003 (trusts and powers)—
(*a*) (*amends* FA 2003 Sch 16 para 3(1))
(*b*) (*amends* FA 2003 Sch 16 para 4)
(13) The amendments made by subsections (1) to (11) have effect in respect of transfers occurring on or after the day on which this Act is passed.

(14) But the amendments made by subsections (6) and (10) do not have effect in respect of anything done in respect of a property-investment partnership established before the day on which this Act is passed if—

(a) the partnership does not acquire a chargeable interest on or after that day, and

(b) stamp duty land tax was paid in respect of each chargeable interest acquired before that day, by reference to chargeable consideration of not less than the market value.[1]

(15) The amendment made by subsection (12) has effect in respect of acquisitions occurring on or after the day on which this Act is passed.

(16) An amendment made by this section replaces, to the extent provided for by subsections (13) to (15), any variation made by the Stamp Duty Land Tax (Variation of the Finance Act 2003) Regulations 2006 (SI 2006/3237).

(17) Despite subsections (13) to (16), the transitional provisions of sub-paragraphs (8) to (10) of paragraph 2 of the Schedule to the Stamp Duty Land Tax (Variation of the Finance Act 2003) Regulations 2006 (SI 2006/3237) continue to have effect in relation to the amendments made by this section as in relation to that paragraph.

Amendments—[1] Sub-s (14) repealed by FA 2008 s 97, Sch 31 para 10 with effect from 21 July 2008.

Reliefs in relation to shares etc

73 Exemptions: intermediaries, repurchases etc

Schedule 21 contains provision in relation to exemptions from stamp duty and stamp duty reserve tax in cases involving intermediaries, repurchases, stock lending or recognised investment exchanges.

Prospective amendment—This section to be repealed by FA 2007 s 114, Sch 27 Pt 4(2) with effect in accordance with the provisions of FA 1990 ss 108, 110.

74 Acquisition relief: disregard of company holding own shares

(1) (*inserts* FA 1986 s 75(5A))

(2) (*inserts* FA 1986 s 77(3A))

(3) (*inserts* FA 2003 Sch 7 para 7(5A))

(4) The amendments made by subsections (1) and (2) have effect in relation to any instrument executed on or after the day on which this Act is passed.

(5) The amendment made by subsection (3) has effect in relation to any land transaction of which the effective date is on or after that day.

Other reliefs etc

75 SDLT: alternative finance arrangements

(1) (*inserts* FA 2003 s 73B)

(2) (*inserts* FA 2003 s 48(3A))

(3) (*substitutes* FA 2003 ss 71A(8), 72(7), 72A(8), 73(5)(*a*))

(4) The amendments made by this section—

(*a*) have effect in relation to anything that would, but for the exemption provided by new section 73B inserted by subsection (1) above, be a land transaction with an effective date on or after 22nd March 2007, and

(*b*) apply, in accordance with paragraph (*a*), to interests irrespective of the date of their creation.

76 SDLT: exchanges

(1) (*amends* FA 2003 s 47(1))

(2) (*inserts* FA 2003 s 108(4))

(3) The amendments made by this section have effect in relation to a set of land transactions if the effective date of any of them is on or after the day on which this Act is passed.

77 SDLT: shared ownership trusts

(1) (*inserts* FA 2003 Sch 9 paras 7–11)

(2) The amendment made by subsection (1) has effect in relation to land transactions with an effective date on or after the day on which this Act is passed.

78 SDLT: shared ownership lease

(*inserts* FA 2003 Sch 9 para 2(4A))

79 Certain transfers of school land

(1) In Chapter 7 of Part 2 of the School Standards and Framework Act 1998 (c 31) ("the 1998 Act") (new framework for maintained schools), omit sections 79 and 79A (no stamp duty or SDLT payable in respect of certain transfers).

(2) The repeal of—

(*a*) section 79A of the 1998 Act, and

(*b*) section 79 of that Act as it applies for the purposes of section 79A,

has effect in relation to any land transaction of which the effective date is on or after the day on which this Act is passed.

(3) Subject to that, the repeal of section 79 of the 1998 Act has effect in relation to any instrument executed on or after that day.

SDLT: administration

80 Payment of tax

(1) FA 2003 is amended as follows.
(2) (*repeals* FA 2003 s 76(3)(*b*))
(3) (*substitutes* FA 2003 s 80(2)(*d*))
(4) In section 81 (withdrawal of relief: further return)—
 (*a*) (*repeals* FA 2003 s 81(2)(*b*))
 (*b*) (*inserts* FA 2003 s 81(2A))
(5) (*substitutes* FA 2003 s 81A(1)(*d*))
(6) (*amends* FA 2003 s 86(1), (2))
(7) (*repeals* FA 2003 Sch 10 para 2(2)(*b*))
(8) (*substitutes* FA 2003 Sch 17A paras 3(3)(*d*), 4(3)(*d*) and 8(3)(*d*))
(9) The amendments made by this section have effect as follows—
 (*a*) the amendment made by subsection (2) has effect in relation to land transactions with an effective date on or after the day on which this Act is passed,
 (*b*) the amendment made by subsection (3) has effect in relation to returns where the event as a result of which the return is required occurs on or after the day on which this Act is passed,
 (*c*) the amendment made by subsection (4) has effect in relation to returns where the disqualifying event occurs on or after the day on which this Act is passed,
 (*d*) the amendment made by subsection (5) has effect in relation to returns where the effective date of the later transaction is on or after the day on which this Act is passed,
 (*e*) the amendment made by subsection (6) has effect in relation to land transactions with an effective date on or after the day on which this Act is passed,
 (*f*) the amendment made by subsection (7) has effect in relation to land transactions with an effective date on or after the day on which this Act is passed, and
 (*g*) the amendment made by subsection (8) has effect in respect of requirements to deliver a return or further return which arise on or after the day on which this Act is passed.

81 . . . [1]

Amendments—[1] This section repealed by FA 2008 s 94, Sch 30 para 15 with effect in relation to transactions with an effective date on or after 12 March 2008.

PART 7

MISCELLANEOUS

109 Meaning of "recognised stock exchange" etc

Schedule 26 contains—
 (*a*) new definitions of "recognised stock exchange" for the purposes of the Tax Acts and TCGA 1992,
 (*b*) provision for the valuation for the purposes of TCGA 1992 of certain shares or securities listed on recognised stock exchanges,
 (*c*) provision for the valuation for the purposes of Chapter 8 of Part 4 of ITTOIA 2005 of strips and securities exchanged for strips, and
 (*d*) minor and consequential amendments in relation to stock exchanges.

110 Mergers Directive: regulations

(1) The Treasury may by regulations make provision about—
 (*a*) the tax consequences of a merger to form an SE or SCE,
 (*b*) the tax consequences of a merger where—
  (i) each party to the merger is resident in a member State, and
  (ii) the parties are not all resident in the same member State,
 (*c*) the tax consequences of a transfer between companies of a business or part of a business, where—
  (i) each party to the transfer is resident in a member State, and
  (ii) the parties are not all resident in the same member State,
 (*d*) the tax consequences of a share exchange to which section 135 of TCGA 1992 (exchange of securities) applies where companies A and B are resident in different member States,
 (*e*) the residence of an SE or SCE.
(2) Regulations may, in particular, make provision—
 (*a*) about the taxation of chargeable gains (including conferring relief from taxation in relation to transfers or mergers which satisfy specified conditions),
 (*b*) conferring relief from taxation on a distribution of a company which satisfies specified conditions,

(*c*) about the treatment of securities issued on a transfer or merger,
(*d*) about the treatment of loan relationships,
(*e*) about the treatment of derivative contracts,
(*f*) about the treatment of intangible fixed assets, and
(*g*) about capital allowances.

(3) Regulations may make provision only if the Treasury think it necessary or expedient for the purposes of complying with the United Kingdom's obligations under the Mergers Directive.

(4) In this section—

"the Mergers Directive" means Council Directive 90/434/EEC,

"SCE" means an SCE formed in accordance with Council Regulation (EC) 1435/2003 on the Statute for a European Cooperative Society, and

"SE" means an SE formed in accordance with Council Regulation (EC) 2157/2001 on the Statute for a European Company.

(5) Regulations under this section may—
(*a*) amend the Taxes Acts,
(*b*) make incidental or consequential amendments of enactments other than the Taxes Acts,
(*c*) make provision having retrospective effect,
(*d*) make provision generally or only for specified cases or circumstances,
(*e*) make different provision for different cases or circumstances,
(*f*) make incidental, consequential or transitional provision.

(6) In this section "the Taxes Acts" has the meaning given by section 118(1) of TMA 1970.

112 Updating references to Standing Committees

(1) (*amends* PCTA 1968 s 1(4)(*b*))
(2) (*amends* FA 1973 s 50(2)(*a*))

SCHEDULES

SCHEDULE 21

EXEMPTIONS FROM STAMP DUTY AND SDRT: INTERMEDIARIES, REPURCHASES ETC

Section 73

Prospective amendment—This Schedule to be repealed by FA 2007 s 114, Sch 27 Pt 4(2) with effect in accordance with the provisions of FA 1990 ss 108, 110.

Intermediaries

1—(1) Section 80A of FA 1986 (exemption from stamp duty: sales to intermediaries) is amended as follows.
(2) (*substitutes* FA 1986 s 80A(1)–(2C))
(3) (*amends* FA 1986 s 80A(6))
(4) (*inserts* FA 1986 s 80A(6A))
(5) The amendments made by this paragraph have effect in relation to any instrument executed on or after 1st November 2007.

Prospective amendment—This Schedule to be repealed by FA 2007 s 114, Sch 27 Pt 4(2) with effect in accordance with the provisions of FA 1990 ss 108, 110.

2—(1) Section 80B of FA 1986 (exemption from stamp duty on sales to intermediaries: supplementary) is amended as follows.
(2) In subsection (2)—
(*a*) (*inserts* definition of "the Directive" in FA 1986 s 80B(2))
(*b*) (*repeals* definition of "EEA exchange" in FA 1986 s 80B(2))
(*c*) (*amends* FA 1986 s 80B(2) definition of "EEA State")
(3) (*inserts* FA 1986 s 80B(2A))
(4) (*inserts* FA 1986 s 80B(5A))
(5) (*amends* FA 1986 s 80B(7))
(6) The amendments made by this paragraph have effect in relation to any instrument executed on or after 1st November 2007.

Prospective amendment—This Schedule to be repealed by FA 2007 s 114, Sch 27 Pt 4(2) with effect in accordance with the provisions of FA 1990 ss 108, 110.

3—(1) Section 88A of FA 1986 (exemption from SDRT: sales to intermediaries) is amended as follows.
(2) (*substitutes* FA 1986 s 88A(1)–(2C))
(3) (*amends* FA 1986 s 88A(6))
(4) (*inserts* FA 1986 s 88A(6A))
(5) The amendments made by this paragraph have effect in relation to any agreement to transfer securities—

(*a*) in a case where the agreement is conditional, if the condition is satisfied on or after 1st November 2007, and

(*b*) in any other case, if the agreement is made on or after that date.

Prospective amendment—This Schedule to be repealed by FA 2007 s 114, Sch 27 Pt 4(2) with effect in accordance with the provisions of FA 1990 ss 108, 110.

4—(1) Section 88B of FA 1986 (exemption from SDRT on sales to intermediaries: supplementary) is amended as follows.

(2) In subsection (2)—

(*a*) (*inserts* definition of "the Directive" into FA 1986 s 88B(2))

(*b*) (*repeals* definition of "EEA exchange" in FA 1986 s 88B(2))

(*c*) (*amends* definition of "EEA State" in FA 1986 s 88B(2))

(3) (*inserts* FA 1986 s 88B(2A))

(4) (*inserts* FA 1986 s 88B(3A))

(5) (*amends* FA 1986 s 88B(5))

(6) (*amends* FA 1986 s 88B(7))

(7) The amendments made by this paragraph have effect in relation to any agreement to transfer securities—

(*a*) in a case where the agreement is conditional, if the condition is satisfied on or after 1st November 2007, and

(*b*) in any other case, if the agreement is made on or after that date.

Prospective amendment—This Schedule to be repealed by FA 2007 s 114, Sch 27 Pt 4(2) with effect in accordance with the provisions of FA 1990 ss 108, 110.

Repurchases and stock lending

5—(1) Section 80C of FA 1986 (exemption from stamp duty: repurchases and stock lending) is amended as follows.

(2) (*amends* FA 1986 s 80C(1))

(3) (*inserts* FA 1986 s 80C(2A))

(4) (*amends* FA 1986 s 80C(3))

(5) (*amends* FA 1986 s 80C(6))

(6) In subsection (7)—

(*a*) (*inserts* definitions of "the Directive" and "EEA State")

(*b*) (*repeals* definition of "EEA exchange")

(7) (*inserts* FA 1986 s 80C(7A))

(8) The amendments made by this paragraph have effect in relation to any instrument executed on or after 1st November 2007.

Prospective amendment—This Schedule to be repealed by FA 2007 s 114, Sch 27 Pt 4(2) with effect in accordance with the provisions of FA 1990 ss 108, 110.

6—(1) Section 89AA of FA 1986 (exemption from SDRT: repurchases and stock lending) is amended as follows.

(2) (*amends* FA 1986 s 89AA(1))

(3) (*inserts* FA 1986 s 89AA(2A))

(4) (*amends* FA 1986 s 89AA(3))

(5) (*amends* FA 1986 s 89AA(5))

(6) In subsection (6)—

(*a*) (*inserts* definitions of "the Directive" and "EEA State")

(*b*) (*repeals* definition of "EEA exchange")

(7) (*inserts* FA 1986 s 89AA(6A))

(8) The amendments made by this paragraph have effect in relation to any agreement to transfer securities—

(*a*) in a case where the agreement is conditional, if the condition is satisfied on or after 1st November 2007, and

(*b*) in any other case, if the agreement is made on or after that date.

Prospective amendment—This Schedule to be repealed by FA 2007 s 114, Sch 27 Pt 4(2) with effect in accordance with the provisions of FA 1990 ss 108, 110.

Exemptions from stamp duty and SDRT in cases involving recognised investment exchanges

7—(1) In section 116 of FA 1991 (stamp duty: investment exchanges and clearing houses), subsection (4) is amended as follows.

(2) (*inserts* FA 1991 s 116(4)(*aa*))

(3) (*amends* FA 1991 s 116(4)(*b*))

Prospective amendment—This Schedule to be repealed by FA 2007 s 114, Sch 27 Pt 4(2) with effect in accordance with the provisions of FA 1990 ss 108, 110.

Consequential repeal

8—(1) (*repeals* F(No 2)A 2005 s 50)
(2) This paragraph comes into force on 1st November 2007.

Prospective amendment—This Schedule to be repealed by FA 2007 s 114, Sch 27 Pt 4(2) with effect in accordance with the provisions of FA 1990 ss 108, 110.

SCHEDULE 26

MEANING OF "RECOGNISED STOCK EXCHANGE" ETC

Section 109

Meaning of "recognised stock exchange" etc in Tax Acts and TCGA 1992

1 (*substitutes* ITA 2007 s 1005)

2 (*substitutes* TA 1988 s 841)

3 (*inserts* TCGA 1992 s 288(5A), (5B))

Valuation of shares listed on recognised stock exchange for purposes of TCGA 1992 etc

4—(1) (*substitutes* TCGA 1992 s 272(3), (4))
(2) The amendment made by sub-paragraph (1) has effect where the date of valuation falls on or after such day as may be appointed by the Treasury by order; and different days may be appointed for different purposes.

5—(1) (*substitutes* ITTOIA 2005 s 450)
(2) The amendment made by sub-paragraph (1) has effect where the date of valuation falls on or after such day as may be appointed by the Treasury by order; and different days may be appointed for different purposes.

Minor and consequential amendments

6 (*substitutes* FA 1986 s 90(8)(*b*))

7—(1) ICTA is amended as follows.
(2) (*amends* TA 1988 s 210(4))
(3) (*amends* TA 1988 s 312(1E)(*a*))
(4) (*amends* TA 1988 s 415(1)(*b*))
(5) (*amends* TA 1988 s 576H(2)(*a*))
(6) (*amends* TA 1988 s 587B)
(7) (*amends* TA 1988 s 704)
(8) (*amends* TA 1988 s 828(2))
(9) (*amends* TA 1988 s 842(1)(*c*))
(10) (*amends* TA 1988 Sch 20 para 5)

8—(1) TCGA 1992 is amended as follows.
(2) (*amends* TCGA 1992 s 130(1)(*a*))
(3) (*amends* TCGA 1992 s 144(8)(*a*))
(4) (*amends* TCGA 1992 s 146(4)(*b*))
(5) (*amends* TCGA 1992 s 273(2))
(6) (*repeals* TCGA 1992 s 285)

9 (*amends* FA 2002 Sch 26 para 4(2C)(*b*))

10 (*amends* ITEPA 2003)

11 (*amends* ITTOIA 2005 ss 443(2), 460(3))

12—(1) ITA 2007 is amended as follows.
(2) (*amends* ITA 2007 s 143(2)(*a*))
(3) (*amends* ITA 2007 s 151(2))
(4) (*amends* ITA 2007 s 184(3), (6))
(5) (*amends* ITA 2007 s 257(5))
(6) (*amends* ITA 2007 s 274(2))
(7) (*amends* ITA 2007 s 295(3))
(8) (*amends* ITA 2007 s 382(2))
(9) (*amends* ITA 2007 s 397(6))
(10) (*amends* ITA 2007 s 432)
(11) (*amends* ITA 2007 s 691(1)(*b*))
(12) (*amends* ITA 2007 s 989)

(13) (*repeals* ITA 2007 s 1010)
(14) (*amends* ITA 2007 s 1014(2)(*g*))
(15) (*amends* ITA 2007 Sch 4)

SCHEDULE 27
REPEALS

Section 114

PART 4
SDLT, STAMP DUTY AND SDRT

(1) Anti-avoidance: Partnerships

Short title and chapter	*Extent of repeal*
Finance Act 2003 (c 14)	In Schedule 15— (*a*) paragraphs 13 and 14(1)(*b*) and (4), and (*b*) in the italic cross-heading before paragraph 14 the words "for consideration"

These repeals have effect in accordance with section 72 of this Act.

(2) Exemptions: Intermediaries, Repurchases etc

Short title and chapter	*Extent of repeal*
Finance Act 1986 (c 41)	In section 80B(2), the definition of "EEA exchange".
	In section 80C(7), the definition of "EEA exchange" (together with the word "and" at the end of it).
	In section 88B(2), the definition of "EEA exchange".
	In section 89AA(6), the definition of "EEA exchange".
Finance (No 2) Act 2005 (c 22)	Section 50.
Finance Act 2007 (c.)	Section 73.
	Schedule 21.

1 Subject to Note 2, these repeals have effect in accordance with Schedule 21 to this Act.

2 The repeals of section 73 of, and Schedule 21 to, this Act have effect in accordance with sections 108 and 110 of FA 1990.

(3) Certain Transfers of School Land

Short title and chapter	*Extent of repeal*
School Standards and Framework Act 1998 (c 31)	Sections 79 and 79A.
Education and Inspections Act 2006 (c 40)	In Part 3 of Schedule 4, paragraph 20.

These repeals have effect in accordance with section 79 of this Act.

(4) Payment of SDLT

Short title and chapter	*Extent of repeal*
Finance Act 2003 (c 14)	In section 76(3), paragraph (*b*) and the word "and" before it.
	In section 81(2), paragraph (*b*) and the word "and" before it.
	In Schedule 10, in paragraph 2(2), paragraph (*b*) and the word "and" before it.

These repeals have effect in accordance with section 80 of this Act.

PART 6
MISCELLANEOUS

(5) Meaning of "Recognised Stock Exchange" etc

Short title and chapter	*Extent of repeal*
Income and Corporation Taxes Act 1988 (c 1)	In Schedule 20, in paragraph 5, the words ", or which are dealt in on the Unlisted Securities Market".
Taxation of Chargeable Gains Act 1992 (c 12)	In section 130(1)(*a*), the words "in the United Kingdom or elsewhere".
	In section 146(4)(*b*), the words "in the United Kingdom or elsewhere".
	Section 285.
Finance Act 1996 (c 8)	In Schedule 38, paragraphs 7 and 12(1).
Financial Services and Markets Act 2000 (c 8)	In Schedule 20, paragraph 4(6).
Income Tax (Trading and Other Income) Act 2005 (c 5)	Section 443(2)(*g*).
Income Tax Act 2007 (c 3)	In section 460(3), the words "or 451".
	In section 295(3)(*c*), the words "on the Unlisted Securities Market or dealt in".
	Section 1010.
	In Schedule 1, paragraph 227.

FINANCE ACT 2008

(2008 Chapter 9)

CONTENTS

PART 5
STAMP TAXES

Stamp duty land tax

An Act to Grant certain duties, to alter other duties, and to amend the law relating to the National Debt and the Public Revenue, and to make further provision in connection with finance.

[21 July 2008]

PART 5
STAMP TAXES

Stamp duty land tax

93 Zero-carbon homes

(1) Sections 58B and 58C of FA 2003 (relief from SDLT on first acquisition of zero-carbon homes) are amended as follows.
(2) (*substitutes* FA 2003 s 58B(2))
(3) Section 58C is amended as follows.
(4) (*amends* FA 2003 s 58C(1))
(5) (*inserts* FA 2003 s 58C(2)(*d*))
(6) (*amends* FA 2003 s 58C(3))
(7) The amendments made by subsections (2), (4) and (6) are treated as always having had effect; and provision included in regulations by virtue of those amendments may be made so as to have effect in relation to acquisitions on or after 1 October 2007.

Regulations—Stamp Duty Land Tax (Zero-Carbon Homes Relief) (Amendment) Regulations 2008, SI 2008/1932.

94 Notification and registration of transactions

(1) Part 4 of FA 2003 (stamp duty land tax) is amended as follows.
(2) (*substitutes* FA 2003 ss 77, 77A)
(3) (*amends* FA 2003 s 79(2))
(4) Schedule 30 contains consequential provision.
(5) The amendments made by this section and that Schedule have effect in relation to transactions with an effective date on or after 12 March 2008.

95 Charge where consideration includes rent: 0% band

(1) Schedule 5 to FA 2003 (amount of SDLT chargeable: rent) is amended as follows.
(2) (*amends* FA 2003 Sch 5 para 9(1) and heading, *repeals* sub-paras (2)–(3))
(3) (*inserts* FA 2003 Sch 5 para 9A)
(4), (5) (*repeal* FA 2003 Sch 6 paras 5(4)(*a*)(i), (*b*), 6(6))(*a*)(i), (*b*), 9(4))(*a*)(i), (*b*), 10(6))(*a*)(i), (*b*))
(6) (*amends* FA 2003 Sch 6 para 12)
(7) (*amends* FA 2003 Sch 8 para 3(3)(*b*), (5))
(8) (*inserts* FA 2003 Sch 9 para 4B)
(9)) (*amends* FA 2003 Sch 9 paras 10(1), (2), 11(*b*))
(10) (*inserts* FA 2003 Sch 9 para 12)
(11) (*amends* FA 2003 Sch 15 paras 11(2B)(*a*), 19(2B), 23(3)(*c*))
(12) (*amends* FA 2003 Sch 17A para 18A(5)(*a*))
(13) The amendments made by this section have effect in relation to transactions with an effective date on or after 12 March 2008.

96 Withdrawal of group relief

(1) Part 1 of Schedule 7 to FA 2003 (group relief) is amended as follows.
(2) (*amends* FA 2003 Sch 7 para 3(5))
(3) (*repeals* FA 2003 Sch 7 para 4(2), (3), *amends* sub-para (5))
(4) (*inserts* FA 2003 Sch 7 para 4ZA)
(5) (*amends* FA 2003 Sch 7 para 4A(1), (3), *inserts* sub-paras (1A), (3A))
(6) The amendments made by this section have effect in relation to transactions with an effective date on or after 13 March 2008.

97 Transfers of interests in property-investment partnerships

(1) Schedule 31 contains provision relating to stamp duty land tax chargeable on transfers to, and of interests in, property-investment partnerships.
(2) Part 1 of that Schedule (transfer of interest in partnership: "relevant partnership property"), and this section so far as relating to that Part—
- (*a*) have effect in respect of transfers occurring on or after 19 July 2007 (subject to subsection (3)), and
- (*b*) are treated as having come into force on that day.

(3) Subsections (14) and (17) of section 72 of FA 2007 (partnerships) apply in relation to the amendments made by Part 1 of that Schedule as they apply in relation to the amendments made by subsections (6) and (10) of that section.

Stamp duty

98 Exemption from ad valorem stamp duty for low value transactions

(1) Paragraph 1 of Schedule 13 to FA 1999 (charge to stamp duty on conveyance or transfer on sale) is amended as follows.

(2) (*amends* FA 1999 Sch 13 para 1(3))
(3) (*inserts* FA 1999 Sch 13 para 1(3A))
(4) (*amends* FA 1999 Sch 13 para 6(1))
(5) The amendments made by this section have effect in relation to instruments executed on or after 13 March 2008 and not stamped before 19 March 2008.
(6) For the purposes of section 14(4) of the Stamp Act 1891 (c 39) (instruments not to be given in evidence etc unless stamped in accordance with the law in force at the time of first execution), the law in force at the time of execution of an instrument—

(*a*) executed on or after 13 March 2008 but before 19 March 2008, and
(*b*) not stamped before 19 March 2008,

shall be deemed to be the law as varied in accordance with this section.

99 Abolition of fixed stamp duty on certain instruments

(1) Schedule 32 contains provision abolishing fixed stamp duty on certain instruments.
(2) The amendments and saving made by that Schedule have effect in relation to instruments executed on or after 13 March 2008 and not stamped before 19 March 2008.
(3) For the purposes of section 14(4) of the Stamp Act 1891 (instruments not to be given in evidence etc unless stamped in accordance with the law in force at the time of first execution), the law in force at the time of execution of an instrument—

(*a*) executed on or after 13 March 2008 but before 19 March 2008, and
(*b*) not stamped before 19 March 2008,

shall be deemed to be the law as varied in accordance with Schedule 32.

100 Gifts inter vivos

(1) (*repeals* FA 1985 s 82(5), (9))
(2) (*repeals* FA 1999 Sch 14 para 9)
(3) The amendments made by this section have effect in relation to instruments executed on or after 13 March 2008, other than instruments effecting a land transaction (within the meaning of paragraph 22 of Schedule 32).
(4) For the purposes of section 14(4) of the Stamp Act 1891 (instruments not to be given in evidence etc unless stamped in accordance with the law in force at the time of first execution), the law in force at the time of execution of such an instrument shall be deemed to be the law as varied in accordance with this section.

101 Loan capital

(1) Section 79 of FA 1986 (stamp duty and loan capital) is amended as follows.
(2) (*amends* FA 1986 s 79(6))
(3) (*inserts* FA 1986 s 79(7B))
(4) (*inserts* FA 1986 s 79(13))
(5) The amendments made by this section have effect in relation to any instrument executed on or after the day on which this Act is passed.

PART 8
MISCELLANEOUS

Alternative finance arrangements

154 Stamp duty and stamp duty reserve tax: alternative finance investment bonds

(1) FA 1986 is amended as follows.
(2) (*inserts* FA 1986 s 78(7)(*d*))
(3) Section 79 (loan capital: instruments not chargeable to stamp duty) is amended as follows.
(4) (*inserts* FA 1986 s 79(8A))
(5) (*inserts* FA 1986 s 99(9A))
(6) The amendments made by subsections (2) to (4) have effect in relation to instruments executed on or after the day on which this Act is passed (and for this purpose it does not matter when the arrangements falling within section 48A of FA 2005 [or section 507 of CTA 2009][1] are made).
(7) The amendment made by subsection (5) has effect in relation to—

(*a*) agreements to transfer chargeable securities made on or after the day on which this Act is passed, and
(*b*) the transfer, issue or appropriation of chargeable securities after that day in pursuance of an agreement made after that day;

(and for this purpose it does not matter when the arrangements falling within section 48A of FA 2005 are made).

Amendments—[1] In sub-s (6), words inserted by CTA 2009 s 1322, Sch 1 paras 728, 732. CTA 2009 applies for accounting periods ending on or after 1 April 2009 (for corporation tax purposes) and for tax years 2009–10 onwards (for income and capital gains tax purposes).

155 Alternative property finance: anti-avoidance

(1) FA 2003 is amended as follows.
(2) (*amends* FA 2003 s 73A heading)

(3) (*inserts* FA 2003 s 73AB)
(4) The amendment made by subsection (3) has effect in relation to alternative finance arrangements entered into on or after 12 March 2008.

SCHEDULES

SCHEDULE 30

STAMP DUTY LAND TAX: NOTIFICATION ETC: CONSEQUENTIAL PROVISION

Section 94

FA 2003

1 Part 4 of FA 2003 (stamp duty land tax) is amended as follows.

2—(1) Section 79 (registration of land transactions) is amended as follows.
(2) (*amends* FA 2003 s 79(3))
(3) (*substitutes* FA 2003 s 79(5))
(4) (*amends* FA 2003 s 79(6)(*a*))

3 (*amends* FA 2003 s 81B(1))

4—(1) Section 103 (joint purchasers) is amended as follows.
(2) (*amends* FA 2003 s 103(4))
(3) (*amends* FA 2003 s 103(5))

5—(*amends* FA 2003 s 122)

6 (*amends* FA 2003 Sch 6 para 13)

7 (*amends* FA 2003 Sch 10 para 36(5A)(*d*))

8 (*repeals* FA 2003 Sch 11 Pt 1)

9—(1) In Part 2 of that Schedule (duty to keep and preserve records), paragraph 4 is amended as follows.
(2) (*inserts* FA 2003 Sch 11 para 4(A1))
(3) (*amends* FA 2003 Sch 11 para 4(1))
(4) (*amends* FA 2003 Sch 11 para 4(2))

10 (*repeals* FA 2003 Sch 11 Pt 3)

11 (*amends* FA 2003 Sch 11 heading)

12 (*amends* FA 2003 Sch 15 para 8(2))

13—(1) In Schedule 16 (SDLT: trusts and powers), paragraph 6 is amended as follows.
(2) (*amends* FA 2003 Sch 16 para 6(1), (3))
(3) (*amends* FA 2003 Sch 16 para 6(2))

14 (*amends* FA 2003 Sch 17A paras 3(2), (5) and 4(1), (4A))

FA 2007

15 (*repeals* FA 2007 s 81)

SCHEDULE 31

STAMP DUTY LAND TAX: SPECIAL PROVISIONS FOR PROPERTY-INVESTMENT PARTNERSHIPS

Section 97

PART 1

TRANSFER OF INTEREST IN PARTNERSHIP: "RELEVANT PARTNERSHIP PROPERTY"

Paragraph 14 of Schedule 15 to FA 2003

1—(1) Paragraph 14 of Schedule 15 to FA 2003 (transfer of interest in property-investment partnership) is amended as follows.
(2) (*inserts* FA 2003 Sch 15 para 14(3A)–(3C))
(3) (*amends* FA 2003 Sch 15 para 14(5), *inserts* sub-para (5)(*c*))
(4) (*inserts* FA 2003 Sch 15 para 14(5A))

Consequential provision

2 (*amends* FA 2003 Sch 15 para 15(1))

3 (*amends* FA 2003 Sch 15 para 16(2))

4 (*amends* FA 2003 Sch 15 para 26(9))

PART 2
ELECTIONS IN RESPECT OF INTEREST TRANSFERRED TO PARTNERSHIP

Election when interest transferred to partnership

5 (*amends* FA 2003 Sch 15 para 10)

6 (*inserts* FA 2003 Sch 15 para 12A)

7 (*inserts* FA 2003 Sch 15 para 18(8))

Consequential provision

8 (*inserts* FA 2003 Sch 15 para 17A(1)(*d*))

9 (*amends* FA 2003 Sch 15 para 26(8))

PART 3
TRANSITIONAL PROVISION

10 (*repeals* FA 2007 s 72(14))

11—(1) This paragraph applies in the case of a transfer of a chargeable interest to a partnership falling within paragraph 10(1)(*a*), (*b*) or (*c*) of Schedule 15 to FA 2003 where the effective date of the transaction is before the day on which this Act is passed.
(2) The purchaser in relation to the transaction may at any time before the end of the period of 12 months beginning with that day amend the land transaction return in respect of that transaction so as to make an election under paragraph 12A of Schedule 15 to FA 2003 (inserted by this Schedule).
(3) An election made in reliance on sub-paragraph (2) has effect as if it had been made on the date on which the land transaction return was made, even though paragraph 12A of Schedule 15 to FA 2003 was not in force at that time.
(4) Where an election is made in reliance on sub-paragraph (2), the power under section 12A(5)(*b*) of Schedule 15 to FA 2003 to amend a land transaction return in respect of an affected transaction to take account of that election may be exercised at any time before the end of the period of 12 months beginning with the day on which this Act is passed.

SCHEDULE 32
STAMP DUTY: ABOLITION OF FIXED DUTY ON CERTAIN INSTRUMENTS
Section 99

PART 1
ABOLITION OF FIXED DUTY

FA 1985

1 Part 3 of FA 1985 (stamp duty) is amended as follows.

2 (*repeals* FA 1985 s 83(2))

3 (*repeals* FA 1985 s 83(8), (9), *amends* (11))

FA 1986

4 Part 3 of FA 1986 (stamp duty) is amended as follows.

5 (*repeals* FA 1986 s 66(2A))

6 (*amends* FA 1986 s 67(9))

7 (*amends* FA 1986 s 70(9))

8 (*substitutes* FA 1986 s 72A(1)(*b*))

FA 1999

9 FA 1999 is amended as follows.

10—(1) Schedule 13 (instruments chargeable to stamp duty and rates of duty) is amended as follows.

(2) (*amends* FA 1999 Sch 13 para 1(5))
(3) (*repeals* FA 1999 Sch 13 paras 16, 17, 18(2), 10(1), 21(3), 22, 23)

11—(1) Schedule 15 (stamp duty: bearer instruments) is amended as follows.
(2) (*repeals* FA 1999 Sch 15 para 6)
(3) (*inserts* FA 1999 Sch 15 para 12A)
(4) (*substitutes* FA 1999 Sch 15 para 20(*b*))
(5) (*repeals* FA 1999 Sch 15 para 26(*b*))

PART 2
CONSEQUENTIAL PROVISIONS AND SAVING

FA 1982

12 (*repeals* FA 1982 s 129(1))

FA 1986

13 Part 3 of FA 1986 (stamp duty) is amended as follows.

14—(1) Section 67 (stamp duty on certain transfers to depositary receipt systems) is amended as follows.
(2) (*amends* FA 1986 s 67(1))
(3) (*amends* FA 1986 s 67(3))
(4) (*inserts* FA 1986 s 67(9A))

15—(1) Section 70 (stamp duty on certain transfers to a clearance system) is amended as follows.
(2) (*amends* FA 1986 s 70(1))
(3) (*amends* FA 1986 s 70(3))
(4) (*inserts* FA 1986 s 70(9A))

FA 1987

16 Part 3 of FA 1987 (stamp duty and stamp duty reserve tax) is amended as follows.

17 (*amends* FA 1987 s 50(1))

18 (*amends* FA 1987 s 55(1))

FA 1990

19 (*amends* FA 1990 s 108(1))

FA 1999

20 (*repeals* FA 1999 Sch 14 paras 10(*b*), 11(*b*), 12(3), 13(3))

FA 2003

21 (*repeals* FA 2003 Sch 40 para 2(*b*))

Saving for certain land transactions

22—(1) The following provisions of this Schedule do not have effect in relation to an instrument effecting a land transaction or a duplicate or counterpart of such an instrument—
(*a*) paragraphs 1 to 3,
(*b*) paragraph 10,
(*c*) paragraph 12,
(*d*) paragraph 18, and
(*e*) the repeal of paragraphs 10(*b*) and 11(*b*) of Schedule 14 to FA 1999.
(2) In sub-paragraph (1) "land transaction" has the same meaning as in Part 4 of FA 2003, except that it does not include a transfer of an interest in a property-investment partnership (within the meaning of Schedule 15 of that Act).

Repeals on abolition day

23 If a day is appointed under section 111 of FA 1990 (abolition day), paragraphs 14 and 15 of this Schedule cease to have effect in accordance with section 108 of that Act.

SCHEDULE 38

DISCLOSURE OF TAX AVOIDANCE SCHEMES

Section 116

Commencement—The Finance Act 2008, Schedule 38, (Appointed Day) Order, SI 2008/1935 art 2 (1 November 2008 appointed as the day on which the amendments made by this Schedule come into force). Note, however, that these amendments came into force for the purposes of stamp duty land tax on 1 April 2010, by virtue of the Finance Act 2008, Schedule 38, (Appointed Day) Order, SI 2010/409 art 2).

Amendments of Part 7 of FA 2004

1 Part 7 of FA 2004 (disclosure of tax avoidance schemes) is amended as follows.

2—(1) Section 308 (duties of promoter) is amended as follows.
(2) (*amends* FA 2004 s 308(1))
(3) (*amends* FA 2004 s 308(2)(*a*))
(4) (*amends* FA 2004 s 308(3))
(5) (*substitutes* FA 2004 s 308(4)–(4C))

3 (*amends* FA 2004 s 311(1))

4 (*substitutes* FA 2004 ss 312, 312A)

5—(1) Section 313 (duty of parties to notifiable arrangements to notify HMRC of number etc) is amended as follows.
(2) (*amends* FA 2004 s 313(1)(*a*))
(3) (*amends* FA 2004 s 313(3))
(4) (*inserts* FA 2004 s 313(5))

6 (*substitutes* FA 2004 s 316)

Amendments of TMA 1970

7—(*amends* TMA 1970 s 98C))

SCHEDULE 43

TAKING CONTROL OF GOODS ETC: CONSEQUENTIAL PROVISION

Section 129

PART 1

CONSEQUENTIAL PROVISION: TAKING CONTROL OF GOODS

FA 2003

9 (*repeals* FA 2003 Sch 12 para 1A)

Tribunals, Courts and Enforcement Act 2007 (c 15)

10—(1) Schedule 12 of the Tribunals, Courts and Enforcement Act 2007 (taking control of goods) is amended as follows.
(2) Omit paragraph 14(5) (relevant premises where enforcement agent acting under section 121A of Social Security Administration Act 1992).
(3) In paragraph 19(2) (powers to use reasonable force), for paragraphs (*b*) to (*e*) substitute—
"(*b*) section 127 of the Finance Act 2008."

Other repeals

11 In consequence of the preceding provisions of this Schedule, omit—
(*a*) paragraph 8 of Schedule 5 to the Social Security Contributions (Transfer of Functions, etc) Act 1999 (c 2),
(*b*) paragraph 6 of Schedule 11 to the Welfare Reform and Pensions Act 1999 (c 30),
(*c*) section 5(1) of the National Insurance Contributions and Statutory Payments Act 2004 (c 3), and
(*d*) paragraphs 33, 104(2), 114, 116(2), 119, 123, 126(2), 136, 140 and 147(2) of Schedule 13 to the Tribunals, Courts and Enforcement Act 2007 (c 15).

PART 2

CONSEQUENTIAL PROVISION: SUMMARY WARRANT

Commencement—Finance Act 2008, Section 128 and Part 2 of Schedule 43 (Appointed Day, Transitional Provision and Savings) Order, SI 2009/3024 art 3 (the appointed day for the coming into force of Sch 43 Part 2 is 23 November 2009).

FA 2003

16 In Schedule 12 to FA 2003 (stamp duty land tax: collection and recovery), omit paragraph 3 (recovery of tax in Scotland).

FINANCE ACT 2009

(2009 Chapter 10)

An Act to Grant certain duties, to alter other duties, and to amend the law relating to the National Debt and the Public Revenue, and to make further provision in connection with finance.

[21 July 2009]

PART 1
CHARGES, RATES, ALLOWANCES, ETC

Stamp duty land tax

10 Thresholds for residential property

(1) Part 4 of FA 2003 (stamp duty land tax) has effect in relation to transactions with an effective date on or after 22 April 2009 but before 1 January 2010 as if—

(*a*) in section 55(2) (amount of tax chargeable: general), in Table A (bands and percentages for residential property), for "£125,000" (in both places) there were substituted "£175,000", and

(*b*) in paragraph 2(3) of Schedule 5 (amount of tax chargeable: rent), in Table A (bands and percentages for residential property), for "£125,000" (in both places) there were substituted "£175,000".

(2) The following are revoked—

(*a*) the Stamp Duty Land Tax (Variation of Part 4 of the Finance Act 2003) Regulations 2008 (SI 2008/2338), and

(*b*) the Stamp Duty Land Tax (Exemption of Certain Acquisitions of Residential Property) Regulations 2008 (SI 2008/2339).

(3) The revocations made by subsection (2) have effect in relation to transactions with an effective date on or after 22 April 2009.

PART 3
PENSIONS

73 Financial assistance scheme

(1) The Treasury may by regulations make provision for and in connection with—

(*a*) the application of the relevant taxes in relation to the financial assistance scheme, and

(*b*) the application of the relevant taxes in relation to any person in connection with the financial assistance scheme.

(2) "The financial assistance scheme" means the scheme provided for by regulations under section 286 of the Pensions Act 2004.

(3) The provision that may be made by regulations under this section includes provision imposing any of the relevant taxes (as well as provisions for exemptions or reliefs).

(4) The relevant taxes are—

(*a*) income tax,

(*b*) capital gains tax,

(*c*) corporation tax,

(*d*) inheritance tax,

(*e*) value added tax,

(*f*) stamp duty land tax,

(*g*) stamp duty, and

(*h*) stamp duty reserve tax.

(5) Regulations under this section may, in particular, include provision for and in connection with the taxation of payments made by virtue of regulations under section 286 of the Pensions Act 2004.

(6) The exemptions and reliefs that may be given by regulations under this section include, in particular, exemption from charges to income tax, corporation tax or capital gains tax in respect of—

(*a*) income arising from any assets held or managed by, or receipts of, the person who manages the financial assistance scheme ("the scheme manager") and any chargeable gains arising from the disposal of any such assets, and

(*b*) the receipt of fraud compensation payments (within the meaning of Part 2 of the Pensions Act 2004: see section 182(1) of that Act).

(7) Regulations under this section may include provision having effect in relation to any time before they are made if the provision does not increase any person's liability to tax.

(8) The provision made by regulations under this section may be framed as provision applying with appropriate modifications provisions having effect in relation to registered pension schemes; and for this purpose "registered pension scheme" means a pension scheme within the meaning of Part 4 of FA 2004 which is registered under Chapter 2 of that Part of that Act.

(9) Regulations under this section may include—

(*a*) provision amending any enactment or instrument, and

(*b*) consequential, supplementary and transitional provision.

(10) Regulations under this section are to be made by statutory instrument.

(11) A statutory instrument containing regulations under this section is subject to annulment in pursuance of a resolution of the House of Commons.

74 FSCS intervention in relation to insurance in connection with pensions

(1) The Treasury may by regulations make provision for and in connection with the application of the relevant taxes in relation to circumstances in which there is relevant intervention under the FSCS.

(2) "Relevant intervention" means—

(*a*) anything done under, or while seeking to make, arrangements for securing continuity of insurance in connection with registered pension schemes,

(*b*) anything done as part of measures for safeguarding policyholders in connection with registered pension schemes, or

(*c*) the payment of compensation in connection with registered pension schemes.

(3) "The FSCS" means the Financial Services Compensation Scheme (established under Part 15 of the Financial Services and Markets Act 2000).

(4) The provision that may be made by regulations under this section includes provision imposing any of the relevant taxes (as well as provisions for exemptions or reliefs).

(5) The relevant taxes are—

(*a*) income tax,

(*b*) capital gains tax,

(*c*) corporation tax,

(*d*) inheritance tax,

(*e*) stamp duty land tax,

(*f*) stamp duty, and

(*g*) stamp duty reserve tax.

(6) Regulations under this section may include provision having effect in relation to any time before they are made if the provision does not increase any person's liability to tax.

(7) The provision made by regulations under this section may be framed as provision modifying, or applying with appropriate modifications, provisions having effect in relation to registered pension schemes.

(8) Regulations under this section may include—

(*a*) provision amending any enactment or instrument, and

(*b*) consequential, supplementary and transitional provision.

(9) Regulations under this section are to be made by statutory instrument.

(10) A statutory instrument containing regulations under this section is subject to annulment in pursuance of a resolution of the House of Commons.

(11) In this section "registered pension scheme" means a pension scheme within the meaning of Part 4 of FA 2004 which is registered under Chapter 2 of that Part of that Act.

PART 5
STAMP TAXES

Stamp duty land tax

80 Exercise of collective rights by tenants of flats

(1) Section 74 of FA 2003 (collective enfranchisement by leaseholders) is amended as follows.

(2) (*substitutes* FA 2003 s 74(1))

(3) In subsection (2)—

(*a*) omit "In that case,", and

(*b*) for "flats in respect of which the right of collective enfranchisement is being exercised" substitute "qualifying flats contained in the premises".

(4) (*substitutes* FA 2003 s 74(4))

(5) For the heading substitute "Exercise of collective rights by tenants of flats".

(6) Accordingly, in section 55(5) of that Act (amount of tax chargeable), for "collective enfranchisement by leaseholders" substitute "exercise of collective rights by tenants of flats".

(7) The amendments made by this section have effect in relation to transactions with an effective date on or after 22 April 2009.

81 Registered providers of social housing

(1) Part 4 of FA 2003 (stamp duty land tax) is amended as follows.

(2) Section 71 (certain acquisitions by registered social landlord) is amended as follows.

(3) (*inserts* FA 2003 s 71(A1))

(4) In subsection (4), for "subsection (1)(*c*)" substitute "this section".

(5) Schedule 9 (right to buy etc) is amended as follows.

(6) In paragraph 5 (shared ownership leases: "qualifying body" etc)—

(*a*) (*inserts* FA 2003 Sch 9 para 5(2)(*g*))

(*b*) (*inserts* FA 2003 Sch 9 para 5(2A), (2B))

(7) In paragraph 7 (shared ownership trusts: introduction)—

(*a*) in sub-paragraph (3), omit "(within the meaning of paragraph 5(2))", and

(*b*) (*inserts* FA 2003 Sch 9 para 7(7)–(9))

(8) The amendments made by this section have effect in relation to transactions with an effective date on or after the day on which this Act is passed.

82 Rent to shared ownership

(1) (*inserts* FA 2003 Sch 9 paras 13, 14)

(2) The amendment made by this section has effect in relation to cases in which the effective date of the grant of the shared ownership lease or the declaration of the shared ownership trust is on or after 22 April 2009.

(3) Paragraphs 13(4) and 14(4) of Schedule 9 to FA 2003 (inserted by this section) have effect for the purposes of subsection (2).

Stock lending arrangements

83 Stamp taxes in event of insolvency

(1) Schedule 37 contains provision amending Part 3 (stamp duty) and Part 4 (stamp duty reserve tax) of FA 1986 in respect of repurchase and stock lending arrangements in the event of the insolvency of one of the parties.

(2) The amendments made by that Schedule have effect where the insolvency in question occurs on or after 1 September 2008.

(3) This section and that Schedule cease to have effect—

(*a*) in relation to the amendments made to Part 3 of FA 1986, when the repeal of sections 80 to 85 of that Act (by Part 6 of Schedule 19 to, and in accordance with sections 107 to 109 of, FA 1990) comes into force, and

(*b*) in relation to the amendments made to Part 4 of FA 1986, when the repeal of that Part (by Part 7 of Schedule 19 to, and in accordance with section 110 of, FA 1990) comes into force.

PART 7
ADMINISTRATION

Information etc

96 Extension of information and inspection powers to further taxes

(1) In paragraph 63(1) of Schedule 36 to FA 2008 (information and inspection powers: meaning of "tax"), for paragraph (*e*) (and the "and" before it) substitute—

"(*e*) insurance premium tax,
(*f*) inheritance tax,
(*g*) stamp duty land tax,
(*h*) stamp duty reserve tax,
(*i*) petroleum revenue tax,
(*j*) aggregates levy,
(*k*) climate change levy,
(*l*) landfill tax, and
(*m*) relevant foreign tax,".

(2) Schedule 48 contains further amendments of that Schedule.

(3) The amendments made by this section and Schedule 48 come into force on such day as the Treasury may by order appoint.

(4) An order under subsection (3) may—

(*a*) appoint different days for different purposes, and

(*b*) contain transitional provision and savings.

(5) The Treasury may by order make any incidental, supplemental, consequential, transitional or transitory provision or saving which appears appropriate in consequence of, or otherwise in connection with, this section and Schedule 48.

(6) An order under subsection (5) may—

(*a*) make different provision for different purposes, and

(*b*) make provision amending, repealing or revoking an enactment or instrument (whenever passed or made).

(7) An order under this section is to be made by statutory instrument.

(8) A statutory instrument containing an order under subsection (5) is subject to annulment in pursuance of a resolution of the House of Commons.

98 Record-keeping

(1) Schedule 50 contains provision about obligations to keep records.

(2) The amendments made by that Schedule come into force on such day as the Treasury may by order made by statutory instrument appoint.

Order—Finance Act 2009, Schedule 50 (Record-keeping) (Appointed Day) Order 2010 (appoints 1 April 2010 as the date for the Sch 50 amendments to come into force).

Assessments, claims etc

99 Time limits for assessments, claims etc

(1) Schedule 51 contains provision about time limits for assessments, claims etc

(2) The amendments made by that Schedule come into force on such day as the Treasury may by order made by statutory instrument appoint.

(3) An order under subsection (2)—

(*a*) may make different provision for different purposes, and

(*b*) may include transitional provision and savings.

Order—Finance Act 2009, Schedule 51 (Time Limits for Assessments, Claims, etc) (Appointed Days and Transitional Provisions) Order 2010 (1 April 2011 is appointed as the date for Sch 51 paras 5–26 to come into force).

Penalties

106 Penalties for failure to make returns etc

(1) Schedule 55 contains provision for imposing penalties on persons in respect of failures to make returns and other documents relating to liabilities for tax.

(2) That Schedule comes into force on such day as the Treasury may by order appoint.

(3) An order under subsection (2)—

(*a*) may commence a provision generally or only for specified purposes, and

(*b*) may appoint different days for different provisions or for different purposes.

(4) The Treasury may by order make any incidental, supplemental, consequential, transitional, transitory or saving provision which may appear appropriate in consequence of, or otherwise in connection with, Schedule 55.

(5) An order under subsection (4) may include provision amending, repealing or revoking any provision of any Act or subordinate legislation whenever passed or made (including this Act and any Act amended by it).

(6) An order under subsection (4) may make different provision for different purposes.

(7) An order under this section is to be made by statutory instrument.

(8) A statutory instrument containing an order under subsection (4) which includes provision amending or repealing any provision of an Act is subject to annulment in pursuance of a resolution of the House of Commons.

107 Penalties for failure to pay tax

(1) Schedule 56 contains provision for imposing penalties on persons in respect of failures to comply with obligations to pay tax.

(2) That Schedule comes into force on such day as the Treasury may by order appoint.

(3) An order under subsection (2)—

(*a*) may commence a provision generally or only for specified purposes, and

(*b*) may appoint different days for different provisions or for different purposes.

(4) The Treasury may by order make any incidental, supplemental, consequential, transitional, transitory or saving provision which may appear appropriate in consequence of, or otherwise in connection with, Schedule 56.

(5) An order under subsection (4) may include provision amending, repealing or revoking any provision of any Act or subordinate legislation whenever passed or made (including this Act and any Act amended by it).

(6) An order under subsection (4) may make different provision for different purposes.

(7) An order under this section is to be made by statutory instrument.

(8) A statutory instrument containing an order under subsection (4) which includes provision amending or repealing any provision of an Act is subject to annulment in pursuance of a resolution of the House of Commons.

PART 8

MISCELLANEOUS

Other matters

123 Alternative finance investment bonds

Schedule 61 contains provision about the taxation of chargeable gains, stamp duty land tax and capital allowances for and in connection with arrangements falling within section 48A of FA 2005 (alternative finance investment bonds).

124 Mutual societies: tax consequences of transfers of business etc

(1) The Treasury may by regulations make provision for and in connection with—

(*a*) the tax consequences of a transfer of all or part of the business or engagements of a mutual society,

(*b*) the tax consequences of an amalgamation of mutual societies, and

(*c*) the tax consequences of the conversion of a mutual society into a company.

(2) "Mutual society" means—

(*a*) a building society incorporated (or deemed to be incorporated) under the Building Societies Act 1986,

(*b*) a friendly society within the meaning of the Friendly Societies Act 1992, or

(*c*) an industrial and provident society registered (or deemed to be registered) under the Industrial and Provident Societies Act 1965.

(3) Regulations under this section may, in particular, make provision about—

(*a*) relief from tax in respect of losses,

(*b*) capital allowances,

(*c*) the taxation of chargeable gains (including provision conferring relief for specified transfers and amalgamations),

(*d*) the treatment of intangible fixed assets and goodwill,

(*e*) the treatment of loan relationships (and matters treated as loan relationships),

(*f*) the treatment of derivative contracts (and contracts treated as derivative contracts),

(*g*) exemption or other relief from stamp duty, stamp duty reserve tax or stamp duty land tax, and

(*h*) the treatment of arrangements the purpose, or one of the main purposes, of which is to secure a tax advantage.

(4) Regulations under this section may, in particular—

(*a*) modify enactments and instruments relating to tax (whenever passed or made),

(*b*) make different provision for different cases or different purposes, and

(*c*) make incidental, consequential or transitional provision (including provision modifying enactments and instruments, whenever passed or made).

(5) Regulations under this section may include provision having effect in relation to any time before they are made if the provision does not increase any person's liability to tax.

(6) Regulations under this section are to be made by statutory instrument.

(7) A statutory instrument containing regulations under this section is subject to annulment in pursuance of a resolution of the House of Commons.

(8) In this section—

"arrangements" includes any arrangements, scheme or understanding of any kind, whether or not legally enforceable and whether involving a single transaction or two or more transactions;

"company" means a company formed and registered under the Companies Act 2006 (or treated as formed and registered under that Act);

"derivative contract" has the same meaning as in Part 7 of CTA 2009 (see section 576 of that Act);

"goodwill" and "intangible fixed asset" have the same meaning as in Part 8 of CTA 2009 (see sections 713 and 715 of that Act);

"loan relationship" has the same meaning as in the Corporation Tax Acts (see section 302(1) and (2) of CTA 2009);

"modify" includes amend, repeal or revoke;

"tax" includes stamp duty;

"tax advantage" means—

(*a*) a relief from tax (including a tax credit) or increased relief from tax,

(*b*) a repayment of tax or increased repayment of tax,

(*c*) the avoidance, reduction or delay of a charge to tax or an assessment to tax, or

(*d*) the avoidance of a possible assessment to tax.

SCHEDULES

SCHEDULE 37

STOCK LENDING: STAMP TAXES IN THE EVENT OF INSOLVENCY

Section 83

PART 1
STAMP DUTY

1 FA 1986 is amended as follows.

2 (inserts FA 1986 s 80D))

3—(1) In consequence of the amendment made by paragraph 2, section 88(1C) (disregard of certain instruments falling within section 80C(1)) is amended as follows.

(2) At the beginning of the words after paragraph (*c*) insert "then, if section 80D does not apply,".

PART 2
STAMP DUTY RESERVE TAX

4 Part 4 of FA 1986 (stamp duty reserve tax) is amended as follows.

5 (inserts FA 1986 s 89AB)

SCHEDULE 48

EXTENSION OF INFORMATION AND INSPECTION POWERS

Section 96

(*amends* FA 2008 Sch 36: see *VAT* section)

SCHEDULE 50

RECORD-KEEPING

Section 98

Order—Finance Act 2009, Schedule 50 (Record-keeping) (Appointed Day) Order 2010 (appoints 1 April 2010 as the date for the Sch 50 amendments to come into force).

Stamp duty land tax

3 Part 4 of FA 2003 (stamp duty land tax) is amended as follows.

4 Schedule 10 (stamp duty land tax: returns, enquiries, assessments and appeals) is amended in accordance with paragraphs 5 to 7.

5—(1) Paragraph 9 (duty to keep and preserve records) is amended as follows.
(2) In sub-paragraph (2), for "for six years after the effective date of the transaction and until any later" substitute "until the end of the later of the relevant day and the".
(3) (*inserts* FA 2003 Sch 10 para 9(2A))
(4) (*inserts* FA 2003 Sch 10 para 9(4)–(6))

6 (*substitutes* FA 2003 Sch 10 para 10)

7 Accordingly, in the heading before paragraph 10, for "*instead of original records*" substitute "*etc*".

8 Schedule 11 (record-keeping where transaction is not notifiable) is amended in accordance with paragraphs 9 to 11.

9—(1) Paragraph 4 (duty to keep and preserve records) is amended as follows.
(2) In sub-paragraph (2), for "for six years after the effective date of the transaction" substitute "until the end of—

(*a*) the sixth anniversary of the effective date of the transaction, or

(*b*) such earlier day as may be specified in writing by the Commissioners for Her Majesty's Revenue and Customs (and different days may be specified for different cases)."

(3) (*inserts* FA 2003 Sch 11 para 4(4)–(6))

10 (*substitutes* FA 2003 Sch 11 para 5)

11 Accordingly, in the heading before paragraph 5, for "*instead of original records*" substitute "*etc*".

12 Schedule 11A (claims not included in returns) is amended in accordance with paragraphs 13 and 14.

13—(1) Paragraph 3 (duty to keep and preserve records) is amended as follows.
(2) Omit sub-paragraphs (3) and (4).
(3) (*inserts* FA 2003 Sch 11A para 3(4A)–(4C))

14 (*inserts* FA 2003 Sch 11A para 3A)

SCHEDULE 51

TIME LIMITS FOR ASSESSMENTS, CLAIMS ETC

Section 99

Order—Finance Act 2009, Schedule 51 (Time Limits for Assessments, Claims, etc) (Appointed Days and Transitional Provisions) Order 2010 (1 April 2011 is appointed as the date for Sch 51 paras 5–26 to come into force).

Stamp duty land tax

14 Part 4 of FA 2003 (stamp duty land tax) is amended as follows.

15—(1) Schedule 10 (returns, enquiries, assessments and appeals) is amended as follows.
(2) In paragraph 25(3) (determination of tax chargeable if no return delivered), for "six years" substitute "4 years".

(3) In paragraph 27(2)(*a*) (determination superseded by actual self-assessment), for "six years" substitute "4 years".
(4) Paragraph 31 (time limit for assessment) is amended in accordance with sub-paragraphs (5) to (8).
(5) In sub-paragraph (1), for "six years" substitute "4 years".
(6) For sub-paragraph (2) substitute—

"(2) An assessment of a person to tax in a case involving a loss of tax brought about carelessly by the purchaser or a related person may be made at any time not more than 6 years after the effective date of the transaction to which it relates (subject to sub-paragraph (2A)).

(2A) An assessment of a person to tax in a case involving a loss of tax—

(*a*) brought about deliberately by the purchaser or a related person,

(*b*) attributable to a failure by the person to comply with an obligation under section 76(1) or paragraph 3(3)(*a*), 4(3)(*a*) or 8(3)(*a*) of Schedule 17A, or

(*c*) attributable to arrangements in respect of which the person has failed to comply with an obligation under section 309, 310 or 313 of the Finance Act 2004 (obligation of parties to tax avoidance schemes to provide information to Her Majesty's Revenue and Customs), may be made at any time not more than 20 years after the effective date of the transaction to which it relates."

(7) In sub-paragraph (4)(*a*), for "three years" substitute "4 years".
(8) After sub-paragraph (5) insert—

"(6) In this paragraph "related person", in relation to a purchaser, means—

(*a*) a person acting on behalf of the purchaser, or

(*b*) a person who was a partner of the purchaser at the relevant time."

(9) After paragraph 31 insert—

"Losses brought about carelessly or deliberately

31A—

(1) This paragraph applies for the purposes of paragraph 31.

(2) A loss of tax is brought about carelessly by a person if the person fails to take reasonable care to avoid bringing about that loss.

(3) Where—

(*a*) information is provided to Her Majesty's Revenue and Customs,

(*b*) the person who provided the information, or the person on whose behalf the information was provided, discovers some time later that the information was inaccurate, and

(*c*) that person fails to take reasonable steps to inform Her Majesty's Revenue and Customs,

any loss of tax brought about by the inaccuracy is to be treated as having been brought about carelessly by that person.

(4) References to a loss of tax brought about deliberately by a person include a loss of tax brought about as a result of a deliberate inaccuracy in a document given to Her Majesty's Revenue and Customs by or on behalf of that person."

(10) In paragraph 34(2) (relief in case of mistake in return), for "six years" substitute "4 years".

16—(1) Paragraph 8 of Schedule 14 (time limit for determination of penalties) is amended as follows.
(2) In sub-paragraph (2)—

(*a*) for "six years" substitute "4 years", and

(*b*) after "began to be incurred" insert "("the relevant date")".

(3) In sub-paragraph (3), insert at the end "(subject to any of the following provisions of this paragraph allowing a longer period)".
(4) After sub-paragraph (4) insert—

"(4A) Where a person is liable to a penalty in a case involving a loss of tax brought about carelessly by the person (or by another person acting on that person's behalf), the penalty may be determined, or the proceedings may be brought, at any time not more than 6 years after the relevant date (subject to sub-paragraphs (4B) and (5)).

(4B) Where a person is liable to a penalty in a case involving a loss of tax—

(*a*) brought about deliberately by the person (or by another person acting on that person's behalf),

(*b*) attributable to a failure by the person to comply with an obligation under section 76(1) or paragraph 3(3)(*a*), 4(3)(*a*) or 8(3)(*a*) of Schedule 17A, or (*c*) attributable to arrangements in respect of which the person has failed to comply with an obligation under section 309, 310 or 313 of the Finance Act 2004 (obligation of parties to tax avoidance schemes to provide information to Her Majesty's Revenue and Customs),

the penalty may be determined, or the proceedings may be brought, at any time not more than 20 years after the relevant date.

(4C) Paragraph 31A of Schedule 10 (losses brought about carelessly or deliberately) applies for the purpose of this paragraph."

SCHEDULE 55

PENALTY FOR FAILURE TO MAKE RETURNS ETC

Section 106

Penalty for failure to make returns etc'

1—(1) A penalty is payable by a person ("P") where P fails to make or deliver a return, or to deliver any other document, specified in the Table below on or before the filing date.

(2) Paragraphs 2 to 13 set out—

(*a*) the circumstances in which a penalty is payable, and

(*b*) subject to paragraphs 14 to 17, the amount of the penalty.

(3) If P's failure falls within more than one paragraph of this Schedule, P is liable to a penalty under each of those paragraphs (but this is subject to paragraph 17(3)).

(4) In this Schedule—

"filing date", in relation to a return or other document, means the date by which it is required to be made or delivered to HMRC;

"penalty date", in relation to a return or other document, means the date on which a penalty is first payable for failing to make or deliver it (that is to say, the day after the filing date).

(5) In the provisions of this Schedule which follow the Table—

(*a*) any reference to a return includes a reference to any other document specified in the Table, and

(*b*) any reference to making a return includes a reference to delivering a return or to delivering any such document.

	Tax to which return etc relates	*Return or other document*
1	Income tax or capital gains tax	(a) Return under section 8(1)(a) of TMA 1970
		(b) Accounts, statement or document required under section 8(1)(b) of TMA 1970
2	Income tax or capital gains tax	(a) Return under section 8A(1)(a) of TMA 1970
		(b) Accounts, statement or document required under section 8A(1)(b) of TMA 1970
3	Income tax or corporation tax	(a) Return under section 12AA(2)(a) or (3)(a) of TMA 1970
		(b) Accounts, statement or document required under section 12AA(2)(b) or (3)(b) of TMA 1970
4	Income tax	(a) Annual return of payments and net tax deducted for the purposes of PAYE regulations
		(b) Return of revised payments and net tax deducted for those purposes where those amounts are revised after end of tax year
5	Income tax	Return under section 254 of FA 2004 (pension schemes)
6	Deductions on account of tax under Chapter 3 of Part 3 of FA 2004 (construction industry scheme)	Return under regulations under section 70 of FA 2004
7	Corporation tax	Company tax return under paragraph 3 of Schedule 18 to FA 1998
8	Inheritance tax	Account under section 216 or 217 of IHTA 1984
9	Stamp duty land tax	Land transaction return under section 76 of FA 2003 or further return under section 81 of that Act

	Tax to which return etc relates	*Return or other document*
10	Stamp duty land tax	Return under paragraph 3, 4 or 8 of Schedule 17A to FA 2003
11	Stamp duty reserve tax	Notice of charge to tax under regulations under section 98 of FA 1986
12	Petroleum revenue tax	Return under paragraph 2 of Schedule 2 to OTA 1975
13	Petroleum revenue tax	Statement under section 1(1)(a) of PRTA 1980

Amount of penalty: occasional returns and annual returns

2 Paragraphs 3 to 6 apply in the case of a return falling within any of items 1 to 5 and 7 to 13 in the Table.

3 P is liable to a penalty under this paragraph of £100.

4— (1) P is liable to a penalty under this paragraph if (and only if)—

(*a*) P's failure continues after the end of the period of 3 months beginning with the penalty date,

(*b*) HMRC decide that such a penalty should be payable, and

(*c*) HMRC give notice to P specifying the date from which the penalty is payable.

(2) The penalty under this paragraph is £10 for each day that the failure continues during the period of 90 days beginning with the date specified in the notice given under sub-paragraph (1)(*c*).

(3) The date specified in the notice under sub-paragraph (1)(*c*)—

(*a*) may be earlier than the date on which the notice is given, but

(*b*) may not be earlier than the end of the period mentioned in sub-paragraph (1)(*a*).

5—(1) P is liable to a penalty under this paragraph if (and only if) P's failure continues after the end of the period of 6 months beginning with the penalty date.

(2) The penalty under this paragraph is the greater of—

(*a*) 5% of any liability to tax which would have been shown in the return in question, and

(*b*) £300.

6—(1) P is liable to a penalty under this paragraph if (and only if) P's failure continues after the end of the period of 12 months beginning with the penalty date.

(2) Where, by failing to make the return, P withholds information which would enable or assist HMRC to assess P's liability to tax, the penalty under this paragraph is determined in accordance with sub-paragraphs (3) and (4).

(3) If the withholding of the information is deliberate and concealed, the penalty is the greater of—

(*a*) 100% of any liability to tax which would have been shown in the return in question, and

(*b*) £300.

(4) If the withholding of the information is deliberate but not concealed, the penalty is the greater of—

(*a*) 70% of any liability to tax which would have been shown in the return in question, and

(*b*) £300.

(5) In any other case, the penalty under this paragraph is the greater of—

(*a*) 5% of any liability to tax which would have been shown in the return in question, and

(*b*) £300.

. . .

Reductions for disclosure

14—(1) Paragraph 15 provides for reductions in the penalty under paragraph 6(3) or (4) or 11(3) or (4) where P discloses information which has been withheld by a failure to make a return ("relevant information").

(2) P discloses relevant information by—

(*a*) telling HMRC about it,

(*b*) giving HMRC reasonable help in quantifying any tax unpaid by reason of its having been withheld, and

(*c*) allowing HMRC access to records for the purpose of checking how much tax is so unpaid.

(3) Disclosure of relevant information—

(*a*) is "unprompted" if made at a time when P has no reason to believe that HMRC have discovered or are about to discover the relevant information, and

(*b*) otherwise, is "prompted".

(4) In relation to disclosure "quality" includes timing, nature and extent.

15—(1) Where a person who would otherwise be liable to a 100% penalty has made an unprompted disclosure, HMRC must reduce the 100% to a percentage, not below 30%, which reflects the quality of the disclosure.
(2) Where a person who would otherwise be liable to a 100% penalty has made a prompted disclosure, HMRC must reduce the 100% to a percentage, not below 50%, which reflects the quality of the disclosure.
(3) Where a person who would otherwise be liable to a 70% penalty has made an unprompted disclosure, HMRC must reduce the 70% to a percentage, not below 20%, which reflects the quality of the disclosure.
(4) Where a person who would otherwise be liable to a 70% penalty has made a prompted disclosure, HMRC must reduce the 70% to a percentage, not below 35%, which reflects the quality of the disclosure.
(5) But HMRC must not under this paragraph—
(*a*) reduce a penalty under paragraph 6(3) or (4) below £300, or
(*b*) reduce a penalty under paragraph 11(3) or (4) below the amount set by paragraph 11(3)(*b*) or (4)(*b*) (as the case may be).

Special reduction

16—(1) If HMRC think it right because of special circumstances, they may reduce a penalty under any paragraph of this Schedule.
(2) In sub-paragraph (1) "special circumstances" does not include—
(*a*) ability to pay, or
(*b*) the fact that a potential loss of revenue from one taxpayer is balanced by a potential overpayment by another.
(3) In sub-paragraph (1) the reference to reducing a penalty includes a reference to—
(*a*) staying a penalty, and
(*b*) agreeing a compromise in relation to proceedings for a penalty.

Interaction with other penalties and late payment surcharges

17—(1) Where P is liable for a penalty under any paragraph of this Schedule which is determined by reference to a liability to tax, the amount of that penalty is to be reduced by the amount of any other penalty incurred by P, if the amount of the penalty is determined by reference to the same liability to tax.
(2) In sub-paragraph (1) the reference to "any other penalty" does not include—
(*a*) a penalty under any other paragraph of this Schedule, or
(*b*) a penalty under Schedule 56 (penalty for late payment of tax).
(3) Where P is liable for a penalty under more than one paragraph of this Schedule which is determined by reference to a liability to tax, the aggregate of the amounts of those penalties must not exceed 100% of the liability to tax.

Assessment

18—(1) Where P is liable for a penalty under any paragraph of this Schedule HMRC must—
(*a*) assess the penalty,
(*b*) notify P, and
(*c*) state in the notice the period in respect of which the penalty is assessed.
(2) A penalty under any paragraph of this Schedule must be paid before the end of the period of 30 days beginning with the day on which notification of the penalty is issued.
(3) An assessment of a penalty under any paragraph of this Schedule—
(*a*) is to be treated for procedural purposes in the same way as an assessment to tax (except in respect of a matter expressly provided for by this Schedule),
(*b*) may be enforced as if it were an assessment to tax, and
(*c*) may be combined with an assessment to tax.
(4) A supplementary assessment may be made in respect of a penalty if an earlier assessment operated by reference to an underestimate of the liability to tax which would have been shown in a return.

19—(1) An assessment of a penalty under any paragraph of this Schedule in respect of any amount must be made on or before the later of date A and (where it applies) date B.
(2) Date A is the last day of the period of 2 years beginning with the filing date.
(3) Date B is the last day of the period of 12 months beginning with—
(*a*) the end of the appeal period for the assessment of the liability to tax which would have been shown in the return, or
(*b*) if there is no such assessment, the date on which that liability is ascertained or it is ascertained that the liability is nil.

(4) In sub-paragraph (3)(*a*) "appeal period" means the period during which—
(*a*) an appeal could be brought, or
(*b*) an appeal that has been brought has not been determined or withdrawn.
(5) Sub-paragraph (1) does not apply to a re-assessment under paragraph 24(2)(*b*).

Appeal

20—(1) P may appeal against a decision of HMRC that a penalty is payable by P.
(2) P may appeal against a decision of HMRC as to the amount of a penalty payable by P.

21—(1) An appeal under paragraph 20 is to be treated in the same way as an appeal against an assessment to the tax concerned (including by the application of any provision about bringing the appeal by notice to HMRC, about HMRC review of the decision or about determination of the appeal by the First-tier Tribunal or Upper Tribunal).
(2) Sub-paragraph (1) does not apply—
(*a*) so as to require P to pay a penalty before an appeal against the assessment of the penalty is determined, or
(*b*) in respect of any other matter expressly provided for by this Act.

22—(1) On an appeal under paragraph 20(1) that is notified to the tribunal, the tribunal may affirm or cancel HMRC's decision.
(2) On an appeal under paragraph 20(2) that is notified to the tribunal, the tribunal may—
(*a*) affirm HMRC's decision, or
(*b*) substitute for HMRC's decision another decision that HMRC had power to make.
(3) If the tribunal substitutes its decision for HMRC's, the tribunal may rely on paragraph 16—
(*a*) to the same extent as HMRC (which may mean applying the same percentage reduction as HMRC to a different starting point), or
(*b*) to a different extent, but only if the tribunal thinks that HMRC's decision in respect of the application of paragraph 16 was flawed.
(4) In sub-paragraph (3)(*b*) "flawed" means flawed when considered in the light of the principles applicable in proceedings for judicial review.
(5) In this paragraph "tribunal" means the First-tier Tribunal or Upper Tribunal (as appropriate by virtue of paragraph 21(1)).

Reasonable excuse

23—(1) Liability to a penalty under any paragraph of this Schedule does not arise in relation to a failure to make a return if P satisfies HMRC or (on appeal) the First-tier Tribunal or Upper Tribunal that there is a reasonable excuse for the failure.
(2) For the purposes of sub-paragraph (1)—
(*a*) an insufficiency of funds is not a reasonable excuse, unless attributable to events outside P's control,
(*b*) where P relies on any other person to do anything, that is not a reasonable excuse unless P took reasonable care to avoid the failure, and
(*c*) where P had a reasonable excuse for the failure but the excuse has ceased, P is to be treated as having continued to have the excuse if the failure is remedied without unreasonable delay after the excuse ceased.

Determination of penalty geared to tax liability where no return made

24—(1) References to a liability to tax which would have been shown in a return are references to the amount which, if a complete and accurate return had been delivered on the filing date, would have been shown to be due or payable by the taxpayer in respect of the tax concerned for the period to which the return relates.
(2) In the case of a penalty which is assessed at a time before P makes the return to which the penalty relates—
(*a*) HMRC is to determine the amount mentioned in sub-paragraph (1) to the best of HMRC's information and belief, and
(*b*) if P subsequently makes a return, the penalty must be re-assessed by reference to the amount of tax shown to be due and payable in that return (but subject to any amendments or corrections to the return).
(3) In calculating a liability to tax which would have been shown in a return, no account is to be taken of any relief under subsection (4) of section 419 of ICTA (relief in respect of repayment etc of loan) which is deferred under subsection (4A) of that section.

Partnerships

25—(1) This paragraph applies where—

(*a*) the representative partner, or

(*b*) a successor of the representative partner,

fails to make a return falling within item 3 in the Table (partnership returns).

(2) A penalty in respect of the failure is payable by every relevant partner.

(3) In accordance with sub-paragraph (2), any reference in this Schedule to P is to be read as including a reference to a relevant partner.

(4) An appeal under paragraph 20 in connection with a penalty payable by virtue of this paragraph may be brought only by—

(*a*) the representative partner, or

(*b*) a successor of the representative partner.

(5) Where such an appeal is brought in connection with a penalty payable in respect of a failure, the appeal is to treated as if it were an appeal in connection with every penalty payable in respect of that failure.

(6) In this paragraph—

"relevant partner" means a person who was a partner in the partnership to which the return relates at any time during the period in respect of which the return was required;

"representative partner" means a person who has been required by a notice served under or for the purposes of section 12AA(2) or (3) of TMA 1970 to deliver any return;

"successor" has the meaning given by section 12AA(11) of TMA 1970.

Double jeopardy

26 P is not liable to a penalty under any paragraph of this Schedule in respect of a failure or action in respect of which P has been convicted of an offence.

Interpretation

27—(1) This paragraph applies for the construction of this Schedule.

(2) The withholding of information by P is—

(*a*) "deliberate and concealed" if P deliberately withholds the information and makes arrangements to conceal the fact that the information has been withheld, and

(*b*) "deliberate but not concealed" if P deliberately withholds the information but does not make arrangements to conceal the fact that the information has been withheld.

(3) "HMRC" means Her Majesty's Revenue and Customs.

(4) References to a liability to tax, in relation to a return falling within item 6 in the Table (construction industry scheme), are to a liability to make payments in accordance with Chapter 3 of Part 3 of FA 2004.

(5) References to an assessment to tax, in relation to inheritance tax and stamp duty reserve tax, are to a determination.

SCHEDULE 56

PENALTY FOR FAILURE TO MAKE PAYMENTS ON TIME

Section 107

Penalty for failure to pay tax

1—(1) A penalty is payable by a person ("P") where P fails to pay an amount of tax specified in column 3 of the Table below on or before the date specified in column 4.

(2) Paragraphs 3 to 8 set out—

(*a*) the circumstances in which a penalty is payable, and

(*b*) subject to paragraph 9, the amount of the penalty.

(3) If P's failure falls within more than one provision of this Schedule, P is liable to a penalty under each of those provisions.

(4) In the following provisions of this Schedule, the "penalty date", in relation to an amount of tax, means the date on which a penalty is first payable for failing to pay the amount (that is to say, the day after the date specified in or for the purposes of column 4 of the Table).

	Tax to which payment relates	*Amount of tax payable*	*Date after which penalty is incurred*
PRINCIPAL AMOUNTS			
1	Income tax or capital gains tax	Amount payable under section 59B(3) or (4) of TMA 1970	The date falling 30 days after the date specified in section 59B(3) or (4) of TMA 1970 as the date by which the amount must be paid

	Tax to which payment relates	*Amount of tax payable*	*Date after which penalty is incurred*
2	Income tax	Amount payable under PAYE regulations (except an amount falling within item 20)	The date determined by or under PAYE regulations as the date by which the amount must be paid
3	Income tax	Amount shown in return under section 254(1) of FA 2004	The date falling 30 days after the date specified in section 254(5) of FA 2004 as the date by which the amount must be paid
4	Deductions on account of tax under Chapter 3 of Part 3 of FA 2004 (construction industry scheme)	Amount payable under section 62 of FA 2004 (except an amount falling within item 17, 23 or 24)	The date determined by or under regulations under section 62 of FA 2004 as the date by which the amount must be paid
5	Corporation tax	Amount shown in company tax return under paragraph 3 of Schedule 18 to FA 1998	The filing date for the company tax return for the accounting period for which the tax is due (see paragraph 14 of Schedule 18 to FA 1998)
6	Corporation tax	Amount payable under regulations under section 59E of TMA 1970 (except an amount falling within item 17, 23 or 24)	The filing date for the company tax return for the accounting period for which the tax is due (see paragraph 14 of Schedule 18 to FA 1998)
7	Inheritance tax	Amount payable under section 226 of IHTA 1984 (except an amount falling within item 14 or 21)	The filing date (determined under section 216 of IHTA 1984) for the account in respect of the liability for that amount
8	Inheritance tax	Amount payable under section 227 or 229 of IHTA 1984 (except an amount falling within item 14 or 21)	For the first instalment, the filing date (determined under section 216 of IHTA 1984) for the account in respect of the liability for that amount For any later instalment, the date falling 30 days after the date determined under section 227 or 229 of IHTA 1984 as the date by which the instalment must be paid
9	Stamp duty land tax	Amount payable under section 86(1) or (2) of FA 2003	The date falling 30 days after the date specified in section 86(1) or (2) of FA 2003 as the date by which the amount must be paid
10	Stamp duty reserve tax	Amount payable under section 87, 93 or 96 of FA 1986 or Schedule 19 to FA 1999 (except an amount falling within item 17, 23 or 24)	The date falling 30 days after the date determined by or under regulations under section 98 of FA 1986 as the date by which the amount must be paid
11	Petroleum revenue tax	Amount charged in an assessment under paragraph 11(1) of Schedule 2 to OTA 1975	The date falling 30 days after the date determined in accordance with paragraph 13 of Schedule 2 to OTA 1975 as the date by which the amount must be paid
AMOUNTS PAYABLE IN DEFAULT OF A RETURN BEING MADE			
12	Income tax or capital gains tax	Amount payable under section 59B(5A) of TMA 1970	The date falling 30 days after the date specified in section 59B(5A) of TMA 1970 as the date by which the amount must be paid
13	Corporation tax	Amount shown in determination under paragraph 36 or 37 of Schedule 18 to FA 1998	The filing date for the company tax return for the accounting period for which the tax is due (see paragraph 14 of Schedule 18 to FA 1998)

	Tax to which payment relates	*Amount of tax payable*	*Date after which penalty is incurred*
14	Inheritance tax	Amount shown in a determination made by HMRC in the circumstances set out in paragraph 2	The filing date (determined under section 216 of IHTA 1984) for the account in respect of the liability for that amount
15	Stamp duty land tax	Amount shown in determination under paragraph 25 of Schedule 10 to FA 2003 (including that paragraph as applied by section 81(3) of that Act)	The date falling 30 days after the filing date for the return in question
16	Petroleum revenue tax	Amount charged in an assessment made where participator fails to deliver return for a chargeable period	The date falling 6 months and 30 days after the end of the chargeable period
17	Tax falling within any of items 1 to 6, 9 or 10	Amount (not falling within any of items 12 to 15) which is shown in an assessment or determination made by HMRC in the circumstances set out in paragraph 2	The date falling 30 days after the date by which the amount would have been required to be paid if it had been shown in the return in question
AMOUNT SHOWN TO BE DUE IN OTHER ASSESSMENTS, DETERMINATIONS, ETC			
18	Income tax or capital gains tax	Amount payable under section 55 of TMA 1970	The date falling 30 days after the date determined in accordance with section 55(3), (4), (6) or (9) of TMA 1970 as the date by which the amount must be paid
19	Income tax or capital gains tax	Amount payable under section 59B(5) or (6) of TMA 1970	The date falling 30 days after the date specified in section 59B(5) or (6) of TMA 1970 as the date by which the amount must be paid
20	Income tax	Amount shown in determination made by HMRC where it appears that tax payable under PAYE regulations has not been paid	The date determined by or under PAYE regulations as the date by which the amount must be paid
21	Inheritance tax	Amount shown in— (*a*) an amendment or correction of a return showing an amount falling within item 7 or 8, or (*b*) a determination made by HMRC in circumstances other than those set out in paragraph 2	The later of— (*a*) the filing date (determined under section 216 of IHTA 1984) for the account in respect of the liability for that amount, and (*b*) the date falling 30 days after the date on which the amendment, correction, assessment or determination is made
22	Petroleum revenue tax	Amount charged in an assessment, or an amendment of an assessment, made in circumstances other than those set out in items 11 and 16	The date falling 30 days after— (*a*) the date by which the amount must be paid, or (*b*) the date on which the assessment or amendment is made, whichever is later

	Tax to which payment relates	*Amount of tax payable*	*Date after which penalty is incurred*
23	Tax falling within any of items 1 to 6, 9 or 10	Amount (not falling within any of items 18 to 20) shown in an amendment or correction of a return showing an amount falling within any of items 1 to 6, 9 or 10	The date falling 30 days after— (*a*) the date by which the amount must be paid, or (*b*) the date on which the amendment or correction is made, whichever is later
24	Tax falling within any of items 1 to 6, 9 or 10	Amount (not falling within any of items 18 to 20) shown in an assessment or determination made by HMRC in circumstances other than those set out in paragraph 2	The date falling 30 days after— (*a*) the date by which the amount must be paid, or (*b*) the date on which the assessment or determination is made, whichever is later

. . .

Commencement—Finance Act 2009, Schedule 56 (Appointed Day and Consequential Provisions) Order, SI 2010/466 (appointed day for the coming into force of this Schedule is 6 April 2010, in relation only to the amounts of tax specified in column 3 of the Table for items 2, 3 and 4 (and items 17, 23 and 24, but only insofar as the tax falls within any of items 2, 3 or 4)).

Special reduction

9— (1) If HMRC think it right because of special circumstances, they may reduce a penalty under any paragraph of this Schedule.

(2) In sub-paragraph (1) "special circumstances" does not include—

(*a*) ability to pay, or

(*b*) the fact that a potential loss of revenue from one taxpayer is balanced by a potential over-payment by another.

(3) In sub-paragraph (1) the reference to reducing a penalty includes a reference to—

(*a*) staying a penalty, and

(*b*) agreeing a compromise in relation to proceedings for a penalty.

Suspension of penalty during currency of agreement for deferred payment

10—(1) This paragraph applies if—

(*a*) P fails to pay an amount of tax when it becomes due and payable,

(*b*) P makes a request to HMRC that payment of the amount of tax be deferred, and

(*c*) HMRC agrees that payment of that amount may be deferred for a period ("the deferral period").

(2) If P would (apart from this sub-paragraph) become liable, between the date on which P makes the request and the end of the deferral period, to a penalty under any paragraph of this Schedule for failing to pay that amount, P is not liable to that penalty.

(3) But if—

(*a*) P breaks the agreement (see sub-paragraph (4)), and

(*b*) HMRC serves on P a notice specifying any penalty to which P would become liable apart from sub-paragraph (2),

P becomes liable, at the date of the notice, to that penalty.

(4) P breaks an agreement if—

(*a*) P fails to pay the amount of tax in question when the deferral period ends, or

(*b*) the deferral is subject to P complying with a condition (including a condition that part of the amount be paid during the deferral period) and P fails to comply with it.

(5) If the agreement mentioned in sub-paragraph (1)(*c*) is varied at any time by a further agreement between P and HMRC, this paragraph applies from that time to the agreement as varied.

Assessment

11—(1) Where P is liable for a penalty under any paragraph of this Schedule HMRC must—

(*a*) assess the penalty,

(*b*) notify P, and

(*c*) state in the notice the period in respect of which the penalty is assessed.

(2) A penalty under any paragraph of this Schedule must be paid before the end of the period of 30 days beginning with the day on which notice of the assessment of the penalty is issued.

(3) An assessment of a penalty under any paragraph of this Schedule—

(*a*) is to be treated for procedural purposes in the same way as an assessment to tax (except in respect of a matter expressly provided for by this Schedule),

(*b*) may be enforced as if it were an assessment to tax, and

(*c*) may be combined with an assessment to tax.

(4) A supplementary assessment may be made in respect of a penalty if an earlier assessment operated by reference to an underestimate of an amount of unpaid tax.

(5) A supplementary assessment may be made in respect of a penalty under paragraph 6 if—

(*a*) notice of the assessment of the penalty was issued before the end of the tax year, and

(*b*) before the end of the year, P makes a further default (so that the penalty for the earlier default is increased).

12—(1) An assessment of a penalty under any paragraph of this Schedule in respect of any amount must be made on or before the later of date A and (where it applies) date B.

(2) Date A is the last day of the period of 2 years beginning with the date specified in or for the purposes of column 4 of the Table (that is to say, the last date on which payment may be made without incurring a penalty).

(3) Date B is the last day of the period of 12 months beginning with—

(*a*) the end of the appeal period for the assessment of the amount of tax in respect of which the penalty is assessed, or

(*b*) if there is no such assessment, the date on which that amount of tax is ascertained.

(4) In sub-paragraph (3)(*a*) "appeal period" means the period during which—

(*a*) an appeal could be brought, or

(*b*) an appeal that has been brought has not been determined or withdrawn.

Appeal

13—(1) P may appeal against a decision of HMRC that a penalty is payable by P.

(2) P may appeal against a decision of HMRC as to the amount of a penalty payable by P.

14—(1) An appeal under paragraph 13 is to be treated in the same way as an appeal against an assessment to the tax concerned (including by the application of any provision about bringing the appeal by notice to HMRC, about HMRC review of the decision or about determination of the appeal by the First-tier Tribunal or Upper Tribunal).

(2) Sub-paragraph (1) does not apply—

(*a*) so as to require P to pay a penalty before an appeal against the assessment of the penalty is determined, or

(*b*) in respect of any other matter expressly provided for by this Act.

15—(1) On an appeal under paragraph 13(1) that is notified to the tribunal, the tribunal may affirm or cancel HMRC's decision.

(2) On an appeal under paragraph 13(2) that is notified to the tribunal, the tribunal may—

(*a*) affirm HMRC's decision, or

(*b*) substitute for HMRC's decision another decision that HMRC had power to make.

(3) If the tribunal substitutes its decision for HMRC's, the tribunal may rely on paragraph 9—

(*a*) to the same extent as HMRC (which may mean applying the same percentage reduction as HMRC to a different starting point), or

(*b*) to a different extent, but only if the tribunal thinks that HMRC's decision in respect of the application of paragraph 9 was flawed.

(4) In sub-paragraph (3)(*b*) "flawed" means flawed when considered in the light of the principles applicable in proceedings for judicial review.

(5) In this paragraph "tribunal" means the First-tier Tribunal or Upper Tribunal (as appropriate by virtue of paragraph 14(1)).

Reasonable excuse

16—(1) Liability to a penalty under any paragraph of this Schedule does not arise in relation to a failure to make a payment if P satisfies HMRC or (on appeal) the First-tier Tribunal or Upper Tribunal that there is a reasonable excuse for the failure.

(2) For the purposes of sub-paragraph (1)—

(*a*) an insufficiency of funds is not a reasonable excuse unless attributable to events outside P's control,

(*b*) where P relies on any other person to do anything, that is not a reasonable excuse unless P took reasonable care to avoid the failure, and

(*c*) where P had a reasonable excuse for the failure but the excuse has ceased, P is to be treated as having continued to have the excuse if the failure is remedied without unreasonable delay after the excuse ceased.

Double jeopardy

17 P is not liable to a penalty under any paragraph of this Schedule in respect of a failure or action in respect of which P has been convicted of an offence.

Interpretation

18—(1) This paragraph applies for the construction of this Schedule.

(2) "HMRC" means Her Majesty's Revenue and Customs.

(3) References to tax include construction industry deductions under Chapter 3 of Part 3 of FA 2004.

(4) References to a determination, in relation to an amount payable under PAYE regulations or under Chapter 3 of Part 3 of FA 2004, include a certificate.

(5) References to an assessment to tax, in relation to inheritance tax and stamp duty reserve tax, are to a determination.

SCHEDULE 61

ALTERNATIVE FINANCE INVESTMENT BONDS

Section 123

PART 1
INTRODUCTORY

Interpretation

1—(1) In this Schedule—

"alternative finance investment bond" means arrangements within section 48A of FA 2005 (alternative finance investment bond: introduction);

"bond assets", "bond-holder", "bond-issuer" and "capital" have the meaning given by that section;

"HMRC" means Her Majesty's Revenue and Customs;

"prescribed" means prescribed in regulations made by HMRC;

"qualifying interest" means a major interest in land (within the meaning given by section 117 of FA 2003) except that it does not include a lease if the lease is for—

(*a*) a term of years of 21 years or less, or

(*b*) in Scotland, a period of 21 years or less.

(2) Except where the context otherwise requires, any expression which is used in this Schedule and in Part 4 of FA 2003 has the meaning which it has in that Part.

PART 2
ISSUE, TRANSFER AND REDEMPTION OF RIGHTS UNDER ARRANGEMENTS

Issue, transfer and redemption of rights under bond not be treated as chargeable transaction

2 Section 48B(2) of FA 2005 (effect of bond for purposes of tax) applies for the purposes of stamp duty land tax as it applies for the purposes of income tax and capital gains tax.

Relief not available where bond-holder acquires control of underlying asset

3—(1) Paragraph 2 does not apply if control of the underlying asset is acquired by—

(*a*) a bond-holder, or

(*b*) a group of connected bond-holders.

(2) A bond-holder ("BH"), or a group of connected bond-holders, acquires control of the underlying asset if—

(*a*) the rights of bond-holders under an alternative finance investment bond include the right of management and control of the bond assets, and

(*b*) BH, or the group, acquires sufficient rights to enable BH, or the members of the group acting jointly, to exercise the right of management and control of the bond assets to the exclusion of any other bond-holders.

4—(1) But paragraph 3(1) does not apply (and, accordingly, section 48B(2) of FA 2005 applies by virtue of paragraph 2) in either of the following cases.

(2) The first case is where—

(*a*) at the time that the rights were acquired BH (or all of the connected bond-holders) did not know and had no reason to suspect that the acquisition enabled the exercise of the right of management and control of the bond assets to the exclusion of other bond-holders, and

(*b*) as soon as reasonably practicable after BH (or any of the bond-holders) becomes aware that the acquisition enables that exercise, BH transfers (or some or all of the bond-holders transfer) sufficient rights for that exercise no longer to be possible.

(3) The second case is where BH—

(*a*) underwrites a public offer of rights under the bond, and

(*b*) does not exercise the right of management and control of the bond assets.

(4) In this paragraph—

"connected" is to be read in accordance with section 839 of ICTA, and

"underwrite", in relation to an offer of rights under a bond, means to agree to make payments of capital under the bond in the event that other persons do not make those payments.

PART 3

TRANSACTIONS RELATING TO UNDERLYING ASSETS CONSISTING OF LAND INTRODUCTORY

General conditions for operation of reliefs etc

5—(1) This paragraph defines conditions A to G for the purposes of paragraphs 6 to 18. Paragraphs 20 and 22 set out circumstances in which the reliefs provided by paragraphs 6 to 18 are not available even if conditions A to G are met.

(2) Condition A is that one person ("P") and another ("Q") enter into arrangements under which—

(*a*) P transfers to Q a qualifying interest in land ("the first transaction"), and

(*b*) P and Q agree that when the interest ceases to be held by Q as mentioned in sub-paragraph (3)(*b*), Q will transfer the interest to P.

(3) Condition B is that—

(*a*) Q, as bond-issuer, enters into an alternative finance investment bond (whether before or after entering into the arrangements mentioned in sub-paragraph (2)), and

(*b*) the interest in land to which those arrangements relate is held by Q as a bond asset.

(4) Condition C is that, for the purpose of generating income or gains for the alternative finance investment bond—

(*a*) Q and P enter into a leaseback agreement, or

(*b*) such other condition or conditions as may be specified in regulations made by the Treasury is or are met.

(5) For the purposes of condition C, Q and P enter into a leaseback agreement if Q grants to P, out of the interest transferred to Q,—

(*a*) a lease (if the interest transferred is freehold or, in Scotland, the interest of the owner), or

(*b*) a sub-lease (if the interest transferred is leasehold or, in Scotland, the tenant's right over or interest in a property subject to a lease).

(6) Condition D is that, before the end of the period of 120 days beginning with the effective date of the first transaction, Q provides HMRC with the prescribed evidence that—

(*a*) in England and Wales, a satisfactory legal charge has been entered in the register of title kept under section 1 of the Land Registration Act 2002,

(*b*) in Scotland, a satisfactory standard security has been registered in the Land Register of Scotland, or

(*c*) in Northern Ireland, a satisfactory charge has been entered in the register of titles kept under section 10 of the Land Registration Act (Northern Ireland) 1970.

(7) A charge or security is satisfactory for the purposes of condition D if it—

(*a*) is a first charge on, or a security ranking first granted over, the interest transferred to Q,

(*b*) is in favour of the Commissioners for Her Majesty's Revenue and Customs, and

(*c*) is for the amount mentioned in sub-paragraph (8).

(8) That amount is the total of—

(*a*) the amount of stamp duty land tax which would (apart from paragraph 6(2)) be chargeable on the first transaction if the chargeable consideration for that transaction had been the market value of the interest at that time, and

(*b*) any interest and any penalties which would for the time being be payable on or in respect of that amount of tax, if the tax had been due and payable (but not paid) in respect of the first transaction.

(9) Condition E is that the total of the payments of capital made to Q before the termination of the bond is not less than 60% of the value of the interest in the land at the time of the first transaction.

(10) Condition F is that Q holds the interest in the land as a bond asset until the termination of the bond.

(11) Condition G is that—

(*a*) before the end of the period of 30 days beginning with the date on which the interest in the land ceases to be held as a bond asset, that interest is transferred by Q to P ("the second transaction"), and

(*b*) the second transaction is effected not more than 10 years after the first transaction.

(12) The Treasury may by regulations amend sub-paragraph (11)(*b*) by substituting for the period mentioned there such other period as may be specified.

Cross-references—Alternative Finance Investment Bonds (Stamp Duty Land Tax) (Prescribed Evidence) Regulations, SI 2009/2052 reg 3 (for the purpose of sub-para (6) the prescribed evidence is all of the following—

(a) any document provided by the relevant Land Registry confirming the creation and registration of a legal charge or standard security in favour of the Commissioners for Her Majesty's Revenue and Customs in relation to that land, and

(b) the UTRN for the SDLT land transaction return on which relief from the tax was claimed on the transfer of the land from the original owner to the bond-issuer.

STAMP DUTY LAND TAX

Relief from stamp duty land tax: first transaction

6—(1) This paragraph applies if—

(*a*) the first transaction relates to an interest in land in the United Kingdom, and

(*b*) each of conditions A to C is met before the end of the period of 30 days beginning with the effective date of that transaction.

(2) Where this paragraph applies the first transaction is exempt from charge to stamp duty land tax.

(3) Where the interest in the land is replaced as the bond asset by an interest in other land, this paragraph is subject to paragraph 18.

(4) This paragraph is also subject to paragraph 20.

7—(1) This paragraph applies if—

(*a*) the interest in the land is transferred by Q to P without conditions E and F having been met,

(*b*) the period mentioned in paragraph 5(11)(*b*) expires without each of those conditions having been met, or

(*c*) at any time it becomes apparent for any other reason that any of conditions E to G cannot or will not be met.

(2) This paragraph also applies if condition D is not met.

(3) The relief provided by paragraph 6(2) is withdrawn and stamp duty land tax is chargeable on the first transaction in accordance with this paragraph.

(4) The amount chargeable is the tax that would have been chargeable in respect of the first transaction (but for relief under paragraph 6(2)) if the chargeable consideration for that transaction had been the market value of the interest at the time of that transaction.

(5) Interest is due and payable on the amount of that tax as from the end of the period of 30 days after the effective date of that transaction until the tax is paid.

(6) Q must deliver a further land transaction return before the end of the period of 30 days after the date on which this paragraph first applies.

(7) The return must include a self-assessment of the amount of tax chargeable.

(8) Tax payable must be paid not later than the filing date for the further return.

(9) Schedule 10 to FA 2003 (returns, assessments and other matters) applies to a return under this paragraph as it applies to a return under section 76 of that Act (general requirement to deliver land transaction return), with the following modifications—

(*a*) references to the transaction to which the return relates are to the event by virtue of which this paragraph applies, and

(*b*) references to the effective date of the transaction are to the date on which that event occurs.

Relief from stamp duty land tax: second transaction

8—(1) The second transaction is exempt from charge to stamp duty land tax if—

(*a*) each of conditions A to G is met, and

(*b*) the provisions of Part 4 of FA 2003 relating to the first transaction are complied with.

(2) Where the interest in the land is replaced as the bond asset by an interest in other land, this paragraph is subject to paragraph 18.
(3) This paragraph is also subject to paragraph 20.

Discharge of charge when conditions for relief met

9 If, after the effective date of the second transaction, Q provides HMRC with the prescribed evidence that each of conditions A to C and E to G has been met, the land ceases to be subject to the charge or security registered in pursuance of condition D.

. . .

Cross-references—Alternative Finance Investment Bonds (Stamp Duty Land Tax) (Prescribed Evidence) Regulations, SI 2009/2052 reg 4 (for the purpose of this para the prescribed evidence is all of the following—
(a) a statement from the bond-issuer, or a person authorised to act on behalf of the bond-issuer, that all conditions A to C and E to G in Part 3 of Schedule 61 have been met,
(b) the UTRN for the SDLT land transaction return on which relief from the tax was claimed on the transfer of the land from the original owner to the bond-issuer,
(c) the UTRN for the SDLT land transaction return on which relief from the tax was claimed on the transfer of the land from the bond-issuer to the original owner, and
(d) any document as provided by the relevant Land Registry confirming that the land has been registered in the name of the original owner.

Relief not available if purpose of arrangements is improper

22—(1) The reliefs provided by paragraphs 6 to 12 (and paragraph 18 so far as it relates to those paragraphs) are not available if the arrangements mentioned in paragraph 5(2)—
(*a*) are not effected for genuine commercial reasons, or
(*b*) form part of arrangements of which the main purpose, or one of the main purposes, is the avoidance of liability to tax.
(2) In sub-paragraph (1) "tax" means income tax, corporation tax, capital gains tax, stamp duty or stamp duty land tax.

Regulations

23—(1) Regulations under any paragraph of this Schedule—
(*a*) may make provision generally or only for specified purposes, or different provision for different purposes, and
(*b*) may make consequential, supplementary or incidental provision (including amendments of any enactment).
(2) Regulations under any paragraph of this Schedule are to be made by statutory instrument.
(3) A statutory instrument containing regulations under any paragraph of this Schedule is subject to annulment in pursuance of a resolution of the House of Commons.

PART 4
SUPPLEMENTARY

Consequential amendments of FA 2003

24 FA 2003 is amended as follows.

25 (*inserts* FA 2003 s 73C)—

26 (*inserts* FA 2003 s 86(5A))

FINANCE ACT 2010

(2010 Chapter 13)

[8 April 2010]

PART 1
CHARGES, RATES ETC

Stamp duty land tax

6 Relief for first-time buyers
(1) Part 4 of FA 2003 (stamp duty land tax) is amended as follows.
(2) After section 57A insert—

"57AA First-time buyers
(1) A land transaction is exempt from charge under section 55 if—
(*a*) it is a relevant acquisition of a major interest in land,

(*b*) the land consists entirely of residential property,

(*c*) the relevant consideration (see section 55) for the transaction (other than any consisting of rent) is more than £125,000 but not more than £250,000,

(*d*) the purchaser, or (if more than one) each of the purchasers, is a first-time buyer who intends to occupy the residential property as the purchaser's only or main residence, and

(*e*) (subject to subsection (4)) the transaction is not one of a number of linked transactions.

(2) In this section "first-time buyer" means a person who—

(*a*) has not previously been a purchaser in relation to a relevant acquisition of a major interest in land which consisted of or included residential property,

(*b*) has not previously acquired an equivalent interest in such land under the law of a territory outside the United Kingdom,

(*c*) has not previously been, or been one of the persons who was, "the person" for the purposes of section 71A, 72, 72A or 73 in a case where the first transaction within the meaning of the section concerned was a relevant acquisition of a major interest in land which consisted of or included residential property, and

(*d*) would not have been such a person for those purposes in such a case if the provisions mentioned in paragraph (*c*) had been in force, and had had effect in the territory concerned, at all material times (subject, where required, to appropriate modifications).

(3) In this section "relevant acquisition of a major interest in land" means an acquisition of a major interest in land other than—

(*a*) the grant of a lease for a term of less than 21 years, or

(*b*) the assignment of a lease which has less than 21 years to run.

(4) Subsection (1)(*e*) does not prevent a transaction being exempt from charge under section 55 if each of the linked transactions is one the subject-matter of which is land, or an interest in or right over land, which falls within section 116(1)(*a*), (*b*) or (*c*) by reason of its connection with the same building."

(3) After section 73C insert—

"73CA Sections 71A to 73: first-time buyers

(1) Where section 71A, 72, 72A or 73 applies, the first transaction within the meaning of the section concerned is exempt from charge under section 55 if—

(*a*) the transaction is a relevant acquisition of a major interest in land,

(*b*) the land consists entirely of residential property,

(*c*) the relevant consideration (see section 55) for the transaction (other than any consisting of rent) is more than £125,000 but not more than £250,000,

(*d*) the person (within the meaning of the section concerned), or (if more than one) each of them, is a first-time buyer who intends to occupy the residential property as the person's only or main residence, and

(*e*) (subject to subsection (3)) the transaction is not one of a number of linked transactions.

(2) In subsection (1)—

"first-time buyer", and

"relevant acquisition of a major interest in land",

have the same meaning as in section 57AA.

(3) Subsection (4) of section 57AA applies for the purposes of this section."

(4) In section 110 (approval of regulations under general power), insert at the end—

"(6) This section does not apply to regulations containing only provision varying section 57AA or 73CA, or paragraph 15 of Schedule 9, which does not increase any person's liability to tax."

(5) In Schedule 9 (right to buy, shared ownership leases etc), insert at the end—

"First-time buyers

15

(1) This paragraph applies where—

(*a*) a lease is granted as mentioned in sub-paragraph (1)(*a*) of paragraph 2 and the conditions in sub-paragraph (2) of that paragraph are met but no election is made for tax to be charged in accordance with that paragraph, (*b*) a lease is granted as mentioned in sub-paragraph (1)(*a*) of paragraph 4 and the conditions in sub-paragraph (2) of that paragraph are met but no election is made for tax to be charged in accordance with that paragraph,

(*c*) paragraph 4A applies in relation to the acquisition of an interest (but the acquisition is not exempt from charge by virtue of sub-paragraph (2) of that paragraph),

(*d*) a shared ownership trust is declared but no election is made for tax to be charged in accordance with paragraph 9, or

(*e*) an equity-acquisition payment is made under a shared ownership trust (but the equity-acquisition payment, and the consequential increase in the purchaser's beneficial interest, are not exempt from charge by virtue of paragraph 10).

(2) Neither section 57AA nor section 73CA applies in relation to—

(*a*) the acquisition of the lease,

(*b*) the acquisition of the interest,

(*c*) the declaration of the shared ownership trust, or

(*d*) the equity-acquisition payment and the consequential increase in the purchaser's beneficial interest."

(6) The amendments made by this section have effect in relation to any land transaction of which the effective date is on or after 25 March 2010 but before 25 March 2012.

7 Rate in respect of residential property where consideration over £1m

(1) In section 55(2) of FA 2003 (amount of SDLT chargeable), in Table A (bands and percentages for residential property), for the final entry (cases where relevant consideration is more than £500,000 to be chargeable at 4%) substitute—

"More than £500,000 but not more than £1,000,000	4%
More than £1,000,000	5%"

(2) The amendment made by subsection (1) has effect in relation to any land transaction of which the effective date is on or after 6 April 2011.

(3) But that amendment does not have effect in relation to any transaction—

(*a*) effected in pursuance of a contract entered into and substantially performed before 25 March 2010, or

(*b*) effected in pursuance of a contract entered into before that date and not excluded by subsection (4).

(4) A transaction effected in pursuance of a contract entered into before 25 March 2010 is excluded by this subsection if—

(*a*) there is any variation of the contract, or assignment (or assignation) of rights under the contract, on or after 25 March 2010,

(*b*) the transaction is effected in consequence of the exercise on or after that date of any option, right of pre-emption or similar right, or

(*c*) on or after that date there is an assignment (or assignation), subsale or other transaction relating to the whole or part of the subject-matter of the contract as a result of which a person other than the purchaser under the contract becomes entitled to call for a conveyance.

PART 2
ANTI-AVOIDANCE AND REVENUE PROTECTION
Stamp taxes

54 SDRT: depositary receipt systems and clearance services systems

(1) Part 4 of FA 1986 (stamp duty reserve tax) is amended as follows.

(2) In section 95(1) (depositary receipts: exceptions), before "there shall be" insert "subject to section 97C,".

(3) In section 97(1) (clearance services: exceptions), before "there shall be" insert "subject to section 97C,".

(4) In section 97B (transfer between depositary receipt system and clearance system), after subsection (1) insert—

"(1A) Subsection (1) is subject to section 97C."

(5) After that section insert—

"97C Transfers to non-EU depositary receipt and clearance services systems

(1) This section applies where arrangements are made in accordance with which chargeable securities are—

(*a*) issued to an EU system, and

(*b*) subsequently transferred from an EU system to a non-EU system.

(2) Nothing in section 95(1), 97(1) or 97B(1) disapplies a charge to tax under section 93 or 96 in respect of that transfer if—

(*a*) the chargeable securities have not previously been transferred, or

(*b*) where they have previously been transferred, the transfer (or, if more than one, each of them) was an exempt transfer.

(3) For the purposes of subsection (1)(*a*) chargeable securities are issued to an EU system if—

(*a*) pursuant to an arrangement of the kind mentioned in section 93(1), they are issued to a nominee in respect of an EU depositary receipt issuer, or

(*b*) pursuant to an arrangement of the kind mentioned in section 96(1), they are issued to a nominee in respect of an EU clearance service operator.

(4) For the purposes of subsection (1)(*b*)—

(*a*) a transfer is from an EU system if it is from a company which is incorporated under the law of a member State and at the time of the transfer falls within section 67(6) or 70(6), and

(*b*) a transfer is to a non-EU system if it is to a company which is not incorporated under the law of a member State and at the time of the transfer falls within section 67(6) or 70(6).

(5) In this section—

"arrangements" includes any agreement, understanding, scheme, transaction or series of transactions (whether or not legally enforceable);

"EU clearance service operator" means a person—

(*a*) whose business is or includes the provision of clearance services for the purchase and sale of chargeable securities, and

(*b*) who—

(i) if it is a company, is incorporated under the law of a member State, and

(ii) in any other case, is resident in a member State;

"EU depositary receipt issuer" means a person—

(*a*) whose business is or includes issuing depositary receipts for chargeable securities, and

(*b*) who—

(i) if it is a company, is incorporated under the law of a member State, and

(ii) in any other case, is resident in a member State;

"exempt transfer" means a transfer in respect of which, by reason of section 90(5), 95(1), 97(1) or 97B(1), no charge to stamp duty reserve tax arises;

"nominee"—

(*a*) in respect of an EU clearance service operator, means a person whose business is or includes holding chargeable securities as nominee for the EU clearance service operator, and

(*b*) in respect of an EU depositary receipt issuer, means a person whose business is or includes holding chargeable securities as nominee or agent for the EU depositary receipt issuer."

(6) The amendments made by this section have effect in relation to transfers of chargeable securities on or after 1 October 2009.

55 SDLT: partnerships

(1) In section 75C of FA 2003 (SDLT anti-avoidance: supplemental)—

(*a*) in subsection (8), omit paragraph (*b*) (and the "and" before it), and

(*b*) after that subsection insert—

"(8A) Nothing in Part 3 of Schedule 15 applies to the notional transaction under section 75A."

(2) The amendments made by subsection (1) have effect in relation to any notional transaction of which the effective date is on or after 24 March 2010.

(3) But those amendments do not have effect in relation to a notional transaction if any scheme transaction is—

(*a*) completed before that date,

(*b*) effected in pursuance of a contract entered into and substantially performed before that date, or

(*c*) effected in pursuance of a contract entered into before that date and not excluded by subsection (4).

(4) A scheme transaction effected in pursuance of a contract entered into before 24 March 2010 is excluded by this subsection if—

(*a*) there is any variation of the contract, or assignment (or assignation) of rights under the contract, on or after 24 March 2010, (*b*) the transaction is effected in consequence of the exercise on or after that date of any option, right of pre-emption or similar right, or

(*c*) it is a land transaction and on or after that date there is an assignment (or assignation), subsale or other transaction relating to the whole or part of the subject-matter of the contract as a result of which a person other than the purchaser under the contract becomes entitled to call for a conveyance.

PART 3
OTHER PROVISIONS

Miscellaneous

65 Stamp duty and SDRT: clearing houses

(1) In sections 116(1)(*b*) and 117(1)(*b*) of FA 1991 (investment exchanges and clearing houses: stamp duty and SDRT), for the words after "description) of such an exchange" substitute "or clearing house, or a nominee (or nominee of a prescribed description) of a member of such an exchange or clearing house, and".

(2) The amendments made by subsection (1) are treated as always having had effect.

Stamp Taxes
Statutory Instruments

Contents

List of printed Statutory Instruments

SI 2010/1818 Stamp Duty and Stamp Duty Reserve Tax (Investment Exchanges and Clearing Houses) Regulations 2010
SI 2010/1819 Stamp Duty and Stamp Duty Reserve Tax (Investment Exchanges and Clearing Houses) Regulations (No 2) 2010
SI 2010/1824 Stamp Duty and Stamp Duty Reserve Tax (Investment Exchanges and Clearing Houses) (Over the Counter) Regulations 2010
SI 2010/1877 Stamp Duty and Stamp Duty Reserve Tax (Investment Exchanges and Clearing Houses) Regulations (No 3) 2010
SI 2010/1897 Stamp Duty and Stamp Duty Reserve Tax (Investment Exchanges and Clearing Houses) Regulations (No 4) 2010

Chronological list of statutory instruments

SI 1985/1688 Stamp Duty (Exempt Instruments) Regulations.
SI 1986/1711 Stamp Duty Reserve Tax Regulations.
SI 1987/516 Stamp Duty (Exempt Instruments) Regulations.
SI 1988/268 Stamp Duty and Stamp Duty Reserve Tax (Definitions of Unit Trust Scheme) Regulations.
SI 1988/835 Stamp Duty Reserve Tax (Amendment) Regulations. (amending)
SI 1989/1297 Taxes (Interest Rate) Regulations.
SI 1989/1301 *Stamp Duty Reserve Tax (Amendment) Regulations.* (amending)
SI 1992/197 Stamp Duty and Stamp Duty Reserve Tax (Definition of Unit Trust Scheme) Regulations.
SI 1992/232 Electricity (Northern Ireland Consequential Amendments) Order.
SI 1992/570 *Stamp Duty and Stamp Duty Reserve Tax (Investment Exchanges and Clearing Houses) Regulations.* (revoked)
SI 1992/3286 FA 1986 (Stamp Duty and Stamp Duty Reserve Tax) (Amendment) Regulations. (amending)
SI 1992/3287 Stamp Duty Reserve Tax (Amendment) Regulations. (amending)
SI 1993/3110 Stamp Duty Reserve Tax (Amendment) Regulations. (amending)
SI 1994/1813 General and Special Commissioners (Amendment of Enactments) Regulations. (amending)
SI 1995/2051 Stamp Duty Reserve Tax ([SWX Europe Limited]) Regulations.
SI 1996/1584 Stamp Duty and Stamp Duty Reserve Tax (Pensions Funds Pooling Schemes) Regulations.
SI 1996/2348 Stamp Duty (Production of Documents) (Northern Ireland) Regulations.
SI 1996/3187 *Taxes (Interest Rate)(Amendment No 4) Regulations.* (amending)
SI 1997/1156 Stamp Duty and Stamp Duty Reserve Tax (Open-ended Investment Companies) Regulations.
SI 1997/2428 Finance Act 1997 (Stamp Duty and Stamp Duty Reserve Tax) (Appointed Day) Order
SI 1997/2429 Stamp Duty and Stamp Duty Reserve Tax (Investment Exchanges and Clearing Houses) Regulations 1997 (repealed)
SI 1997/2430 *Stamp Duty Reserve Tax (Amendment) Regulations 1997*. (amending)
SI 1997/2708 *Finance Act 1989 Section 178(1) (Appointed Day) Order 1997* (not reproduced)
SI 1998/311 *Finance Act 1989 Section 178(1) (Appointed Day) Order 1998* (not reproduced)
SI 1998/1517 Visiting Forces and Allied Headquarters (Stamp Duties) (Designation) Order 1998
SI 1998/1518 Visiting Forces (Stamp Duties) (Designation) Order 1998
SI 1998/2244 Government of Wales Act 1998 (Commencement No 1) Order 1998
SI 1998/3176 *Taxes (Interest Rate) (Amendment No 2) Regulations 1998* (amending)
SI 1998/3177 European Single Currency (Taxes) Regulations 1998
SI 1999/118 Government of Wales Act 1998 (Commencement No 3) Order 1999
SI 1999/527 Social Security Contributions (Transfer of Functions, etc) Act 1999 (Commencement No 1 and Transitional Provisions) Order 1999 (see *Yellow Tax Handbook* SIs)
SI 1999/679 Transfer of Functions (Lord Advocate and Advocate General for Scotland) Order 1999
SI 1999/782 Government of Wales Act 1998 (Commencement No 4) Order 1999
SI 1999/1467 *Stamp Duty and Stamp Duty Reserve Tax (Open-ended Investment Companies) (Amendment) Regulations 1999* (amending)
SI 1999/2383 *Stamp Duty Reserve Tax (UK Depositary Interests in Foreign Securities) Regulations 1999* (amending)
SI 1999/2536 *Stamp Duty Reserve Tax (Amendment) Regulations 1999* (amending)
SI 1999/2537 Stamp Duty (Collection and Recovery of Penalties) Regulations 1999

SI 2005/2007 *Finance Act 2002, Section 117 (Day Appointed for Cessation of Effect) Order 2005*
SI 2005/2462 *Taxes (Interest Rate) (Amendment) Regulations 2005*
SI 2006/139 Stamp Duty and Stamp Duty Reserve Tax (Extension of Exceptions relating to Recognised Exchanges) Regulations 2006
SI 2006/746 *Stamp Duty and Stamp Duty Reserve Tax (Definition of Unit Trust Scheme and Open-ended Investment Company) (Amendment) Regulations 2006* (amend SI 2001/964)
SI 2006/776 *Stamp Duty Land Tax (Administration) (Amendment) Regulations 2006* (amend SI 2003/2837)
SI 2006/875 *Stamp Duty Land Tax (Amendment to the Finance Act 2003) Regulations 2006*
SI 2006/3237 Stamp Duty Land Tax (Variation of the Finance Act 2003) Regulations 2006
SI 2006/3427 Stamp Duty Land Tax (Electronic Communications) (Amendment) Regulations 2006
SI 2007/12 SDRT (UK Depository Interest in Foreign Securities) (Amendment) Regulations 2007
SI 2007/126 Financial Services and Markets Act 2000 (Markets in Financial Instruments) Regulations 2007
SI 2007/458 Stamp Duty and Stamp Duty Reserve Tax (Extension of Exceptions relating to Recognised Exchanges) (Amendment) Regulations 2007
SI 2007/1097 Stamp Duty and Stamp Duty Reserve Tax (Investment Exchanges and Clearing Houses) (Eurex Clearing AG) Regulations 2007
SI 2007/1385 Finance Act 2003, Section 66 (Prescribed Statutory Provisions) Order 2007
SI 2007/3437 Stamp Duty Land Tax (Zero-Carbon Homes Relief) Regulations 2007
SI 2008/52 Stamp Duty Reserve Tax (Investment Exchanges and Clearing Houses) (The London Stock Exchange) Regulations 2008
SI 2008/164 *Stamp Duty and Stamp Duty Reserve Tax (Investment Exchanges and Clearing Houses) (Eurex Clearing AG) (Amendment) Regulations 2008*
SI 2008/710 Stamp Duty Land Tax (Open-ended Investment Companies) Regulations 2008
SI 2008/914 *Stamp Duty Reserve Tax (virt-x Exchange Limited) (Amendment) Regulations 2008*
SI 2008/1814 Stamp Duty and Stamp Duty Reserve Tax (Investment Exchanges and Clearing Houses) (European Central Counterparty Limited and the Turquoise Multilateral Trading Facility) Regulations 2008 (repealed)
SI 2008/1932 *Stamp Duty Land Tax (Zero-Carbon Homes Relief) (Amendment) Regulations 2008*
SI 2008/1935 *Finance Act 2008, Schedule 38, (Appointed Day) Order 2008*
SI 2008/2338 *Stamp Duty Land Tax (Variation of Part 4 of the Finance Act 2003) Regulations 2008* (revoked)
SI 2008/2339 *Stamp Duty Land Tax (Exemption of Certain Acquisitions of Residential Property) Regulations 2008* (revoked)
SI 2008/2777 Stamp Duty and Stamp Duty Reserve Tax (Investment Exchanges and Clearing Houses) Regulations 2008
SI 2008/3234 *Taxes and Duties (Interest Rate) (Amendment) Regulations 2008*
SI 2008/3235 Stamp Duty and Stamp Duty Reserve Tax (Investment Exchanges and Clearing Houses) Regulations (No 2) 2008
SI 2008/3236 *Stamp Duty Reserve Tax (Amendment of section 89AA of the Finance Act 1986) Regulations 2008*
SI 2009/35 Stamp Duty and Stamp Duty Reserve Tax (Investment Exchanges and Clearing Houses) Regulations 2009
SI 2009/56 *Transfer of Tribunal Functions and Revenue and Customs Appeals Order 2009*
SI 2009/194 Stamp Duty and Stamp Duty Reserve Tax (Investment Exchanges and Clearing Houses) Regulations (No 2) 2009 (repealed)
SI 2009/397 Stamp Duty and Stamp Duty Reserve Tax (Investment Exchanges and Clearing Houses) Regulations (No 3) 2009 (repealed)
SI 2009/1115 Stamp Duty and Stamp Duty Reserve Tax (Investment Exchanges and Clearing Houses) Regulations (No 4) 2009
SI 2009/1307 *Transfer of Tribunal Functions (Lands Tribunal and Miscellaneous Amendments) Order 2009*
SI 2009/1344 Stamp Duty and Stamp Duty Reserve Tax (Investment Exchanges and Clearing Houses) Regulations (No 5) 2009
SI 2009/1462 Stamp Duty and Stamp Duty Reserve Tax (Investment Exchanges and Clearing Houses) Regulations (No 6) 2009

Statutory Instruments

1985/1688

STAMP DUTY (EXEMPT INSTRUMENTS) REGULATIONS 1985

Made by the Commissioners of Inland Revenue under FA 1985 s 89

Made . . . .*4th November 1985*
Laid before the House of Commons . . . .*6th November 1985*
Coming into Operation . . . .*1st January 1986*

1 These regulations may be cited as the Stamp Duty (Exempt Instruments) Regulations 1985 and shall come into operation on 1st January 1986.

2 In these regulations unless the context otherwise requires:
"Her Majesty's Land Registry" and "Chief Land Registrar" have the same meaning as in section 126 (1) of the Land Registration Act 1925 and "Registered land" has the same meaning as in section 3 of that Act.

3 For the purposes of section 89 of the Finance Act 1985 the following class of instrument is prescribed—
Instruments by means of which any transfer on sale within the meaning of paragraphs (*a*) or (*c*) of section 28 (1) of the Finance Act 1931 is effected and in respect of which the following conditions are fulfilled—
(*a*) the instrument is executed on or after the 1st January 1986;
(*b*) the consideration for the sale in question is of an amount or value such that no stamp duty is chargeable and the instrument is certified in accordance with section 34 (4) of the Finance Act 1958; and
(*c*)
(i) the land in question is registered land; or
(ii) in the case of land which is not registered land it is an instrument—
(*a*) to which section 123 of the Land Registration Act 1925 applies, or
(*b*) which effects a transfer in the case of which under rule 72 of the Land Registration Rules 1925 the transferee is deemed to be the applicant for first registration.

4 Where the instrument is of the class of instrument to which regulation 3 above applies it shall be the duty of the applicant to deliver to the proper office of Her Majesty's Land Registry with his application for registration the instrument of transfer and a document signed by the transferee or by some person on his behalf and showing his address giving all the particulars set out in Schedule 2 to the Finance Act 1931.

5 The Chief Land Registrar shall furnish to the Commissioners of Inland Revenue the said particulars given to him under regulation 4 above.

1986/1711

STAMP DUTY RESERVE TAX REGULATIONS 1986

Made by the Treasury under FA 1986 s 98

Made . . . .*2nd October 1986*
Laid before the House of Commons . . . .*3rd October 1986*
Coming into Operation . . . .*27th October 1986*

ARRANGEMENT OF REGULATIONS

Citation and commencement

1 These Regulations may be cited as the Stamp Duty Reserve Tax Regulations 1986 and shall come into operation on 27th October 1986.

Interpretation

2 In these Regulations unless the context otherwise requires—

"Act" means Part IV of the Finance Act 1986;

["accountable date" means—

(*a*) in relation to a relevant transaction—

(i) in connection with which securities are transferred by means of a relevant system operated by the operator of that system, or

(ii) which is reported by means of a relevant system to [the Financial Services Authority][4] or an exchange by the operator of that system in a case where the securities to which the transaction relates are not transferred by means of a relevant system, or

(iii) which is reported, otherwise than by means of a relevant system, to an exchange, in a case where the securities to which the transaction relates are not transferred by means of a relevant system,

the date agreed between the Board and the operator or, if no such date is agreed, the date which is the fourteenth day following the date of the relevant transaction,

(*b*) in relation to interest on overdue tax arising in connection with a relevant transaction which, by virtue of a party to that transaction being a participant in a relevant system, or a member of an exchange, could have been, but was not, reported to [the Financial Services Authority][5] or an exchange by means of that system, or to an exchange otherwise than by means of a relevant system, the date which is the fourteenth day following the date of the relevant transaction, . . .[3]

(*c*) in relation to a relevant transaction to which neither paragraph (*a*) nor paragraph (*b*) applies, the date which is the seventh day of the month following the month in which the charge to tax occasioned by the relevant transaction is incurred;][2] [and

(*d*) in relation to a surrender, the date which is the fourteenth day of the month following the month in which the relevant two week period ends;][2]

"accountable person" means—

[(*a*) in relation to a charge under section 87 of the Act ("section 87")—

[(i) if the person mentioned as B in section 87(1) is a member of an exchange, or if a member of an exchange is acting as an agent for B who is not such a member, that member, and failing that

(ii) if the person mentioned as A in section 87(1) is a member of an exchange, or if a member of an exchange is acting as an agent for A who is not such a member; that member, and failing that][2]

(iii) if the person mentioned as B in section 87(1) is a qualified dealer, or if a qualified dealer is acting as an agent for B who is not a qualified dealer, the qualified dealer, and failing that

(iv) if the person mentioned as A in section 87(1) is a qualified dealer, or if a qualified dealer is acting as an agent for A who is not a qualified dealer, the qualified dealer, and failing that

(v) the person mentioned as B in section 87(1),][1]

(*b*) in relation to a charge under section 93(1) to (7) of the Act, the person mentioned in section 93(8) thereof:

Provided that if section 93(9) is applicable, then the accountable person means the person to whom the securities are transferred.

(*c*) in relation to a charge under section 93(10) of the Act, the person liable to pay the instalment,

(*d*) in relation to a charge under section 96(1) to (5) of the Act, the person mentioned in subsection (6) thereof:

Provided that if section 96(7) is applicable, then the accountable person means the person to whom the securities are transferred, . . . [3]

(*e*) in relation to a charge under section 96(8) of the Act, the person liable to pay the instalment; [and

(*f*) in relation to a charge on the surrender of a unit under paragraph 2(1) of Schedule 19 to the Finance Act 1999—

(i) the managers of the unit trust scheme and, failing that,

(ii) the trustees of the unit trust scheme;

(*g*) in relation to a charge on the surrender of a share in an open-ended investment company under paragraph 2(1) of Schedule 19 to the Finance Act 1999—

(i) the authorised corporate director of the company and, failing that,

(ii) the company;][3]

["authorised corporate director" and "open-ended investment company", have the meanings given by regulation 2 of the Stamp Duty and Stamp Duty Reserve Tax (Open-ended Investment Companies) Regulations 1997;][3]

"barrister" includes a member of the Faculty of Advocates;

["the Board" means the Commissioners of Inland Revenue;

"EEA regulated market" means a market of a kind described in [paragraph 36(2) of Part III of the Schedule to the Financial Services and Markets Act 2000 (Exemption) Order 2001][4];

"exchange" means—

(*a*) a recognised investment exchange within the meaning given by section [285(1)(*a*) of the Financial Services and Markets Act 2000][4], or

(*b*) an EEA regulated market;][2]

. . . [2]

. . . [4]

"General Commissioners" has the same meaning as in the Taxes Management Act 1970;

["HMRC" means Her Majesty's Revenue and Customs;][6]

["investment business" means business which consists of the carrying on of one or more of the activities specified in Articles 14, 21, 25, 37, 40, 45, 51 and 53 and, in so far as it applies to any of those Articles, Article 64 of the Financial Services and Markets Act 2000 (Regulated Activities) Order 2001;][4]

. . . [2]

"notice" means notice in writing;

["operator" means—

(*a*) a person approved by the Treasury under the Treasury Regulations as Operator of a relevant system;

(*b*) subject to paragraph (*c*), where a relevant transaction is reported to an exchange otherwise than by means of a relevant system, the operator of that exchange or, if there is no such operator, that exchange;

(*c*) where a relevant transaction is reported to more than one exchange otherwise than by means of a relevant system, the operator of the exchange of which the party who is the accountable person in relation to that transaction is a member or, if there is no such operator, that exchange;][2]

["qualified dealer" means a person who, not being a [member of an exchange][2]—

[(*a*) a person who has permission under Part 4 of the Financial Services and Markets Act 2000 to carry on investment business, or][4]

[(*c*) is authorised under a legislative provision of the government of a territory outside the United Kingdom to carry on investment business, or

(d) while not required to be authorised to do so, carries on investment business;][2]

. . . [4]

["relevant system" has the meaning given by regulation 2(1) of the Treasury Regulations;][2]

"relevant transaction" means—

(*a*) an agreement falling within section 87(1) of the Act,

(*b*) a transfer, issue or appropriation falling within section 93(1)(*b*) of the Act, or

(*c*) a transfer or issue falling within section 96(1)(*b*) of the Act,

and in respect of which there is a charge to tax;

["relevant two-week period" has the meaning given by paragraph 4(2) of Schedule 19 to the Finance Act 1999;][3]

"Special Commissioners" has the same meaning as in the Taxes Management Act 1970;

["surrender" shall be construed in accordance with paragraph 2(1) of Schedule 19 to the Finance Act 1999 (surrender of units to managers);][3]

"tax" means stamp duty reserve tax.

["the Treasury Regulations" means the [Uncertificated Securities Regulations 2001][5].][2]

["tribunal" has the same meaning as in the Taxes Management Act 1970;][6]

["unit" and "unit trust scheme" have the meanings given by paragraph 14 of Schedule 19 to the Finance Act 1999.][3]

Amendments—[1] Para (*a*) in the definition of "accountable person" substituted by the Stamp Duty Reserve Tax (Amendment) Regulations, SI 1988/835 with effect from 27 May 1988.

[2] Definitions of "broker and dealer" and "market maker" revoked, definition of "accountable date", paras (i), (ii) in the definition of "accountable person", words in definition of "qualified dealer" substituted and definitions of "the Board", "EEA regulated market", "exchange", "operator", "recognised professional body", "relevant system" and "the Treasury Regulations" inserted by the Stamp Duty Reserve Tax (Amendment) Regulations, SI 1997/2430 with effect from 20 October 1997.

[3] In definitions "accountable date" and "accountable person" words revoked, and words inserted, definitions "authorised corporate director" and "open-ended investment company", "relevant two-week period", "surrender" and "unit" and "unit trust scheme" inserted by the Stamp Duty Reserve Tax (Amendment No 2) Regulations, SI 1999/3264, reg 3, with effect from 6 February 2000.

[4] Words substituted in the definition of "accountable date", "EEA regulated market", and "exchange"; definition of "European Institution", "recognised professional body" and "recognised self-regulating organisation" revoked, definition of "investment business" substituted, and in definition of "qualified dealer", para (*a*) substituted for paras (*a*), (*b*), by the Financial Services and Markets Act 2000 (Consequential Amendments) (Taxes) Order, SI 2001/3629 arts 112, 113 with effect from 1 December 2001, immediately after the coming into force of the Financial Services and Markets Act 2000 ss 411, 432(1), Sch 20 (and SI 2001/3629 Pts 1 and 2).

[5] Words in definition of "the Treasury Regulations" substituted by the Uncertificated Securities Regulations, SI 2001/3755 reg 51, Sch 7 para 18 with effect from 26 November 2001.

[6] Definitions of "General Commissioners" and "Special Commissioners" revoked, and definitions of "HMRC" and "tribunal" inserted, by the Transfer of Tribunal Functions and Revenue and Customs Appeals Order, SI 2009/56 art 3, Sch 2 paras 12, 13 with effect from 1 April 2009.

Prospective amendment—Following definitions to be inserted by the SDRT (Amendment) Regulations, SI 2010/664, regs 7, 8, with effect from 1 April 2011:

""carelessly" has the same meaning as in section 118(5) and (6) of the Taxes Management Act 1970;

"deliberately" has the same meaning as in section 118(7) of the Taxes Management Act 1970;".

[2A References in these Regulations to any of the provisions of Schedule 19 to the Finance Act 1999 shall be construed as including references to those provisions as modified in relation to open-ended investment companies by the Stamp Duty and Stamp Duty Reserve Tax (Open-ended Investment Companies) Regulations 1997.][1]

Amendments—[1] This regulation inserted by the Stamp Duty Reserve Tax (Amendment No 2) Regulations, SI 1999/3264, reg 4, with effect from 6 February 2000.

Due date for payment

3 Tax charged under the Act[, or under paragraph 2(1) of Schedule 19 to the Finance Act 1999,][1] shall be due and payable on the accountable date.

Amendments—[1] Words inserted by the Stamp Duty Reserve Tax (Amendment No 2) Regulations, SI 1999/3264, reg 5, with effect from 6 February 2000.

Notice of charge and payment

4—(1) [Subject to paragraph (3), an accountable person, except where][1] different arrangements are authorised in writing by the Board, shall on or before the accountable date—

(*a*) give notice of each charge to tax to the Board, and

(*b*) pay the tax due.

(2) A notice under this regulation shall be in such form as the Board may prescribe or authorise and shall contain such information as they may reasonably require for the purposes of the Act.

[(3) This regulation shall not apply where—

(*a*) the tax in question has been accounted for by the operator under regulation 4A, or

(*b*) regulation 4B applies to the accountable person.][1]

Amendments—[1] Words in para (1) substituted, and para (3) inserted, by the Stamp Duty Reserve Tax (Amendment No 2) Regulations, SI 1999/3264, reg 6, with effect from 6 February 2000.

[4A—(1) An operator, except where different arrangements are authorised in writing by the Board, shall on or before the accountable date—

(*a*) give notice to the Board of each charge to tax arising—

(i) in respect of a relevant transaction in connection with which securities are transferred by means of a relevant system operated by him, or

(ii) in respect of a relevant transaction that is reported to [the Financial Services Authority][2] or an exchange by means of a relevant system operated by him, or

(iii) in respect of a relevant transaction that is reported otherwise than by means of a relevant system to an exchange in relation to which he is the operator, or (as the case may be) which itself is the operator, in a case where the securities to which the transaction relates are not transferred by means of a relevant system, and

(*b*) pay the tax due.

(2) A notice under this regulation shall be in such form as the Board may prescribe or authorise and shall contain such information as they may reasonably require for the purposes of the Act.

(3) The Board may, by notification in writing to an operator, impose such requirements, conditions or procedures as they consider necessary for the purposes of these Regulations.][1]

Amendments—[1] This regulation inserted by Stamp Duty Reserve Tax (Amendment) Regulations, SI 1997/2430 with effect from 20 October 1997.

[2] Words in sub-para (1)(*a*)(ii) substituted by the Financial Services and Markets Act 2000 (Consequential Amendments) (Taxes) Order, SI 2001/3629 arts 112, 114 with effect from 1 December 2001, immediately after the coming into force of the Financial Services and Markets Act 2000 ss 411, 432(1), Sch 20 (and SI 2001/3629 Pts 1 and 2).

[4B—(1) An accountable person in relation to a charge to tax on a surrender shall on or before the accountable date—

(*a*) give notice to the Board—

(i) detailing all surrenders for which the relevant two-week period ends in the month preceding that in which the accountable date falls, and

(ii) setting out the total of any reductions under paragraphs 4 and 5 of Schedule 19 to the Finance Act 1999 of the amounts of tax chargeable on those surrenders;

(iii) identifying those surrenders to which [paragraph 6A, 6][2] or 7 of Schedule 19 to the Finance Act 1999 applies, and

(iv) stating the total amount of tax due and payable, and

[(*aa*) give to the Board any certificate pursuant to paragraph 6A(2) of Schedule 19 to the Finance Act 1999 to be contained in, or provided with, the notice, and][2]

(*b*) pay the tax due.

(2) A notice under this regulation shall be given—

(*a*) in relation to each unit trust scheme of which the accountable person is the manager or trustee; and

(*b*) in relation to each open-ended investment company of which the accountable person is the authorised corporate director, or in relation to an open-ended investment company which is the accountable person.

(3) A notice under this regulation[, and any certificate pursuant to paragraph 6A(2) of Schedule 19 to the Finance Act 1999 to be contained in, or provided with, such a notice,][2] shall be in such form as the Board may prescribe or authorise and shall contain such information as they may reasonably require for the purposes of the Act and Part II of Schedule 19 to the Finance Act 1999.][1]

Amendments—[1] This regulation inserted by Stamp Duty Reserve Tax (Amendment No 2) Regulations, SI 1999/3264, reg 7, with effect from 6 February 2000.

[2] Words in para (1)(*a*)(iii) substituted, para (1)(*aa*) and words in para (3) inserted by the Stamp Duty and Stamp Duty Reserve Tax (Definition of Unit Trust Scheme and Open-ended Investment Company) Regulations, SI 2001/964 reg 5 with effect from 6 April 2001.

Power to require information

5—(1) The Board may by notice require any person to furnish them within such time, not being less than 30 days, as may be specified in the notice with such information (including documents or records) as the Board may reasonably require for the purposes of the Act.

(2) A barrister or solicitor shall not be obliged in pursuance of a notice under this regulation to disclose, without his client's consent, any information with respect to which a claim to professional privilege could be maintained.[1]

Amendments—[1] Reg 5 repealed by the SDRT (Amendment) Regulations, SI 2010/664 regs 2, 3 with effect from 1 April 2010.

Notice of determination

6—(1) Where it appears to the Board that a relevant transaction [or surrender][2] has taken place or where a claim is made to the Board in connection with a relevant transaction[or surrender][2], the Board may give notice to any person who appears to them in relation to that transaction [or surrender][2] to be the accountable person [or, having regard to regulation 4A(1), the operator][1], or the person liable for any of the tax charged or to the claimant, stating that they have determined the matters specified in the notice.

(2) If it appears to the Board that any such matter specified in a notice of determination is, or may be, material as respects any liability under the Act of two or more persons, they may give notice of the determination to each of those persons.

(3) Any matter that appears to the Board to be relevant for the purposes of the Act may be determined and specified in a notice under this regulation.

(4) A determination for the purposes of a notice under this regulation of any fact relating to a relevant transaction [or surrender][2] —

(*a*) shall, if that fact has been stated in a notice under regulation [4, 4A, or 4B][2] and the Board are satisfied that the notice is correct, be made by the Board in accordance with that notice, but

(*b*) may, in any other case, be made by the Board to the best of their judgment.

(5) A notice under this regulation shall state the time within which and the manner in which an appeal against any determination in it may be made.

(6) Subject to any variation by agreement in writing or on appeal, a determination in a notice under this regulation shall be conclusive for the purposes of the Act[, and, where appropriate, Part II of Schedule 19 to the Finance Act 1999][2] against a person on whom the notice is served.

Amendments—[1] Words in paras (1) inserted by Stamp Duty Reserve Tax (Amendment) Regulations, SI 1997/2430 with effect from 20 October 1997.

[2] In paras (1), (6) words inserted, and in para (4) first words inserted, and second words substituted, by the Stamp Duty Reserve Tax (Amendment No 2) Regulations, SI 1999/3264, reg 8, with effect from 6 February 2000.

Relief from accountability

7 [If on a claim—

(*a*) in relation to a charge under section 87 of the Act, an accountable person or an operator, other than a person liable under section 91 of the Act, or

(*b*) in relation to a charge under paragraph 2(1) of Schedule 19 to the Finance Act 1999, an accountable person, other than a person liable under paragraph 2(3) of that Schedule,][1]

proves to the Board's satisfaction that he has taken without success all reasonable steps, both before and after the date of the agreement, to recover from the person liable tax for which he is accountable under regulation [4, 4A or 4B][1], he shall be relieved of his liability to account for and pay that tax and any interest on that tax.

Amendments—[1] Words substituted by the Stamp Duty Reserve Tax (Amendment No 2) Regulations, SI 1999/3264, reg 9, with effect from 6 February 2000.

Appeals against determination

8—(1) A person on whom a notice under regulation 6 has been served may, within 30 days of the date of the notice, appeal against any determination specified in it by notice given to the Board and specifying the grounds of appeal.

[(2) Sections 49D, 49G and 49H of the Taxes Management Act 1970 provide for notification of the appeal to the tribunal.][3]

(3) Where—

(*a*) it is so agreed between the appellant and the Board, or

(*b*) the High Court, on an application made by the appellant, is satisfied that the matters to be decided on the appeal are likely to be substantially confined to questions of law and gives leave for that purpose,

the appeal may be [notified][3] to the High Court.

[(4) An appeal on any question as to the value of land in the United Kingdom may be [notified][3] to the appropriate . . . [4] tribunal.][1]

[(4ZA) The appeal may be notified under subsections (3) or (4) only if it could be notified to the tribunal under section 49D, 49G or 49H of the Taxes Management Act 1970.][3]

[(4A) If and so far as the question in dispute on any appeal under this section which has been notified to the tribunal or the High Court is a question as to the value of land in the United Kingdom, the question shall be determined on a reference to the appropriate . . . [4] tribunal.][3]

[(4B) In this regulation "the [appropriate][4] tribunal" means—

(*a*) where the land is in England or Wales, the [Upper Tribunal][4];

(*b*) where the land is in Scotland, the Lands Tribunal for Scotland;

(*c*) where the land is in Northern Ireland, the Lands Tribunal for Northern Ireland.][1]

[(4C) On the hearing of an appeal before them, the Special Commissioners may allow the appellant to put forward any ground of appeal not specified in the notice of appeal and take it into account if satisfied that the omission was not wilful or unreasonable.[3]

(4D) [On an appeal that is notified to the tribunal, the tribunal shall][3] confirm the determination appealed against unless . . . [3] satisfied that the determination ought to be varied or quashed.][2]

(5) In the application of this regulation to Scotland, for references to the High Court there shall be substituted references to the Court of Session.

Amendments—[1] Paras (4), (4B) substituted for para (4) by the Stamp Duty Reserve Tax (Amendment) Regulations, SI 1993/3110 regs 1–3 with effect from 1 January 1994.

[2] Paras (4C), (4D) renumbered by Stamp Duty Reserve Tax (Amendment) Regulations, SI 1997/2430 with effect from 20 October 1997. Prior to amendment, these paras were numbered as second paras (4A), (4B) and were inserted by the General and Special Commissioners (Amendment of Enactments) Regulations, SI 1994/1813 Sch 1 para 28, with effect from 1 September 1994.

[3] Para (2) substituted, words in paras (3), (4), inserted, para (4ZA) inserted, para (4A) substituted, para (4C) revoked, in para (4D), words substituted for words "The Special Commissioners shall on an appeal to them" and words "they are" revoked, by the Transfer of Tribunal Functions and Revenue and Customs Appeals Order, SI 2009/56 art 3, Sch 2 paras 12, 14 with effect from 1 April 2009. Paras (2), (4A) previously read as follows—

"(2) Subject to the following provisions of this regulation the appeal shall be to the Special Commissioners.".

"(4A) If and so far as the question in dispute on any appeal under this regulation to the Special Commissioners or the High Court is a question as to the value of land in the United Kingdom, the question shall be determined on a reference to the appropriate tribunal.".

[4] In paras (4), (4A), words "Lands" revoked, and in para (4B), words substituted for words "appropriate Lands" and "Lands Tribunal", by the Transfer of Tribunal Functions (Lands Tribunal and Miscellaneous Amendments) Order, SI 2009/1307 art 5(1), (3), Sch 2 para 25 with effect from 1 June 2009.

[Late notice of appeal

9—(1) This regulation applies in a case where—

(*a*) notice of appeal may be given to HMRC under regulation 8, but

(*b*) no notice is given before the relevant time limit.

(2) Notice may be given after the relevant time limit if—

(*a*) HMRC agree, or

(*b*) where HMRC do not agree, the tribunal gives permission.

(3) If the following conditions are met, HMRC shall agree to notice being given after the relevant time limit.

(4) Condition A is that the appellant has made a request in writing to HMRC to agree to the notice being given.

(5) Condition B is that HMRC are satisfied that there was reasonable excuse for not giving the notice before the relevant time limit.

(6) Condition C is that HMRC are satisfied that the request under paragraph (4) was made without unreasonable delay after the reasonable excuse ceased.

(7) If a request of the kind referred to in paragraph (4) is made, HMRC must notify the appellant whether or not HMRC agree to the appellant giving notice of appeal after the relevant time limit.

(8) In this regulation "relevant time limit", in relation to notice of appeal, means the time before which the notice is to be given (but for this regulation).][1]

Amendments—[1] Reg 9 substituted by the Transfer of Tribunal Functions and Revenue and Customs Appeals Order, SI 2009/56 art 3, Sch 2 paras 12, 15 with effect from 1 April 2009. This reg previously read as follows—

"Appeal out of time

9 An appeal under regulation 8 may be brought out of time with the consent of the Board or the Special Commissioners; and the Board—

(*a*) shall give that consent if satisfied, on an application for the purpose, that there was a reasonable excuse for not bringing the appeal within the time limited and that the application was made thereafter without unreasonable delay, and

(*b*) shall, if not so satisfied, refer the application for determination by the Special Commissioners.".

[Appeals from the Special Commissioners

10*—(1) Any party to an appeal, if dissatisfied in point of law with the determination of that appeal by the Special Commissioners, may appeal against that determination to the High Court.*

(2) The High Court shall hear and determine any question of law arising on an appeal under paragraph (1) above and may reverse, affirm or vary the determination of the Special Commissioners, or remit the matter to the Special Commissioners with the court's opinion on it, or make such other order in relation to the matter as the court thinks fit.

(3) This regulation shall have effect—

(a) in its application to Scotland, with the substitution of references to the Court of Session for references to the High Court; and

(b) in its application to Northern Ireland, with the substitution of references to the Court of Appeal in Northern Ireland for references to the High Court.][1,2]

Amendments—[1] This regulation substituted by the General and Special Commissioners (Amendments of Enactments) Regulations, SI 1994/1813 Sch 1 para 29, with effect from 1 September 1994.

[2] This regulation revoked by the Transfer of Tribunal Functions and Revenue and Customs Appeals Order, SI 2009/56 art 3, Sch 2 paras 12, 16 with effect from 1 April 2009.

Interest on overpaid tax

11—(1) Where tax repaid under regulation 14 is not less than £25 it shall be repaid with interest on it at the rate which is the [rate applicable under section 178 of the Finance Act 1989][1] for the purposes of section 92(2) of the Act from the time it was paid.

(2) Interest paid under this regulation shall not constitute income for the purposes of income tax or corporation tax.

Note—For the rate applicable under FA 1989 s 178, see SI 1989/1297 *post*.

Amendments—[1] Words in para (1) substituted by the Stamp Duty Reserve Tax (Amendment) Regulations, SI 1989/1301 reg 3 with effect from 18 August 1989.

Recovery of tax

12—(1) The Board shall not exercise any remedy or take any proceedings for the recovery of any amount of tax which is due from any person unless the amount has been agreed in writing between that person and the Board or has been determined and specified in a notice under regulation 6.

(2) Where an amount has been so determined and specified, but an appeal to which this paragraph applies is pending against the determination, the Board shall not exercise any remedy or take any legal proceedings to recover the amount determined except such part of it as may be agreed in writing or determined and specified in a further notice under regulation 6 to be a part not in dispute.

(3) Paragraph (2) applies to any appeal under regulation 8 but not to any further appeal; and regulation 8 shall have effect, in relation to a determination made in pursuance of paragraph (2) of this regulation, as if [paragraphs (4) to (4B)][1] of that regulation were omitted.

Amendments—[1] Words in para (3) substituted by the Stamp Duty Reserve Tax (Amendment) Regulations, SI 1993/3110 regs 1, 2, 4.

Underpayments

13—(1) Subject to paragraphs (2) and (3), where too little tax has been paid in respect of a relevant transaction [or surrender][2] the tax underpaid shall be payable with interest, whether or not the amount that has been paid was that stated as payable in a notice under regulation [4, 4A or 4B][2].

(2) Where tax charged under the Act [or under paragraph 2(1) of Schedule 19 to the Finance Act 1999,][2] is paid in accordance with a notice given to the Board under regulation [4, 4A or 4B][2] and the payment is made and accepted in full satisfaction of the tax so charged, no additional amount of tax shall be determined and specified in a notice under regulation 6 after the end of the period of 6 years beginning with the later of—

(*a*) the date on which the payment was made and accepted, and

(*b*) the relevant accountable date;

and, subject to paragraph (3), at the end of that period any liability for the additional tax shall be extinguished.

(3) In any case of [fraudulent or negligent conduct][1] by or on behalf of any person in connection with or in relation to tax the period mentioned in paragraph (2) shall be the period of 6 years beginning when the [fraudulent or negligent conduct][1] comes to the knowledge of the Board.

Amendments—[1] Words in para (3) substituted by the Stamp Duty Reserve Tax (Amendment) Regulations, SI 1993/3110 regs 1, 2, 5 with effect from 1 January 1994.

[2] In paras (1), (2) first words inserted, and second words substituted, by Stamp Duty Reserve Tax (Amendment) Regulations, SI 1999/3264, reg 10, with effect from 6 February 2000.

Prospective amendment—In para (2), "period of 4" to be substituted for "period of 6" and "paragraphs (2A) and (3)" to be substituted for "paragraph (3)", para (2A) to be inserted, and paras (3)–(5) to be substituted for para (3), by the SDRT (Amendment) Regulations, regs 7, 9, with effect from 1 April 2011, subject to transitional provision in SI 2010/664 reg 12. Paras (2A), (3)–(5) to read as follows:

"(2A) In any case of an underpayment of tax brought about carelessly by or on behalf of any person the period mentioned in paragraph (2) shall be the period of 6 years beginning with the date specified under paragraph (2)."

"(3) In any case of an underpayment of tax brought about deliberately by or on behalf of any person the period mentioned in paragraph (2) shall be the period of 20 years beginning with the date specified under paragraph (2).

(4) Paragraph (5) applies to any case not falling within paragraph (2) where too little tax has been paid in respect of a relevant transaction or surrender provided that the case does not involve a loss of tax brought about deliberately by a person liable for the tax (or a person acting on behalf of such a person).

(5) Where this paragraph applies—

(*a*) no proceedings are to be brought for the recovery of the tax after the end of the period of 20 years beginning with the date on which the relevant transaction or surrender was made; and

(*b*) at the end of that period any liability for the tax is extinguished."

Overpayments

14—(1) If on a claim it is proved to the Board's satisfaction that too much tax has been paid in respect of any relevant transaction [or surrender][1] the excess (and any interest paid thereon) shall be repaid by the Board.

(2) A claim under this regulation shall be made within a period of 6 years beginning with the later of—

(*a*) the date on which the payment was made, and

(*b*) the relevant accountable date.

Amendments—[1] Words inserted by the Stamp Duty Reserve Tax (Amendment) Regulations, SI 1999/3264, reg 11, with effect from 6 February 2000.

Prospective amendment—In para (2), "4" to be substituted for "6" by the SDRT (Amendment) Regulations, regs 7, 10, with effect from 1 April 2011.

Inspection of records

15—(1) Every accountable person [or operator][1] *shall, whenever [and wherever]*[1] *required to do so, make available for inspection by an officer of the Board authorised for that purpose all books, documents and other records in his possession or under his control containing information relating to any relevant transaction to which he was a party or in connection with which he acted.*

(2) Where records are maintained by computer the person required to make them available for inspection shall provide the officer making the inspection with all facilities necessary for obtaining information from them.[2]

Amendments—[1] Words in para (1) inserted by Stamp Duty Reserve Tax (Amendment) Regulations, SI 1997/2430 with effect from 20 October 1997.

[2] Reg 15 repealed by the SDRT (Amendment) Regulations, SI 2010/664 regs 2, 3 with effect from 1 April 2010.

Evidence

16—(1) For the purposes of the preceding provisions of these Regulations, a notice under regulation 6 specifying any determination which can no longer be varied or quashed on appeal shall be sufficient evidence of the matters specified.

(2) In any proceedings for the recovery of tax or interest on tax, a certificate by an officer of the Board—

(*a*) that the tax or interest is due, or

(*b*) that, to the best of his knowledge and belief, it has not been paid,

shall be sufficient evidence that the sum mentioned in the certificate is due or, as the case may be, unpaid; and a document purporting to be such a certificate shall be deemed to be such a certificate unless the contrary is proved.

Determination of questions on previous view of the law

17 Where any payment has been made and accepted in satisfaction of any liability for tax and on a view of the law then generally received or adopted in practice, any question whether too little or too much has been paid or what was the right amount of tax payable shall be determined on the same view, notwithstanding that it appears from a subsequent legal decision or otherwise that the view was or may have been wrong.

Recovery of over-repayment of tax, etc

18—(1) Where an amount of tax has been repaid, or interest has been paid, to any person which ought not to have been repaid or paid to him, that amount may be determined and recovered as if it were tax due from him.

(2) Subject to paragraph (3) a determination under this regulation may be made before the expiration of 6 years from the date on which the amount was repaid or paid.

(3) In any case of [fraudulent or negligent conduct][1] the period mentioned in paragraph (2) shall be 6 years from the date on which the [fraudulent or negligent conduct][1] comes to the knowledge of the Board.

(4) In this regulation an amount repaid or paid includes an amount allowed by way of set off.

Amendments—[1] Words in para (3) substituted by the Stamp Duty Reserve Tax (Amendment) Regulations, SI 1993/3110 regs 1, 2, 6 with effect from 1 January 1994.

Prospective amendment—In para (2), "and (3A)" to be inserted after "(3)", "4" to be substituted for "6", and paras (3), (3A) to be substituted for para (3), by the SDRT (Amendment) Regulations, regs 7, 11, with effect from 1 April 2011, subject to transitional provision in SI 2010/664 reg 12. Paras (3), (3A) to read as follows:

> "(3) In any case where a repayment is brought about carelessly the period mentioned in paragraph (2) shall be 6 years from the date specified in paragraph (2).
>
> (3A) In any case where a repayment is brought about deliberately the period mentioned in paragraph (2) shall be 20 years from the date specified in paragraph (2). "

Service of documents

19 A notice or other document which is to be served on or given to a person under these Regulations may be delivered to him or left at his usual or last known place of residence or served by post, addressed to him at his usual or last known place of residence or place of business or employment.

Taxes Management Act 1970: provisions to apply

20—(1) The provisions of the Taxes Management Act 1970 specified in the first column of the Table in Part I of the Schedule to these Regulations shall apply in relation to the tax as they apply in relation to a tax within the meaning of that Act subject to any modification specified in the second column of that Table.

(2) Any expression to which a meaning is given by the Act or in these Regulations and which is used in a provision of the Taxes Management Act 1970 as applied by this regulation shall in that provision, as so applied, have the same meaning as in the Act or these Regulations.

(3) The provisions of the Taxes Management Act 1970 specified in . . . [1] Part I of the Schedule (as modified where appropriate) are restated as so modified and applied in Part II of the Schedule.

Amendments—[1] Word revoked by the Stamp Duty Reserve Tax (Amendment) Regulations, SI 1988/835 regs 1, 2, 7 with effect from 27 May 1988.

Inland Revenue Regulation Act 1890: provisions not to apply

21 Sections 21, 22 and 35 of the Inland Revenue Regulation Act 1890 (proceedings for fines, etc) shall not apply in relation to stamp duty reserve tax.

SCHEDULE

Regulation 20

PART I

TABLE

Provision applied	*Modifications*
Section 23(1)	—
(2)	For the words "five shillings" substitute "25 pence".
(3)	For the word ""security"" substitute ""securities""; and for the words "includes shares, stock, debentures and debenture stock" substitute "means chargeable securities".
25(1)	For the words "chargeable gains an inspector" substitute "relevant transactions the Board"; and omit the words "in writing".
(2)	—
(3)	—
[(4)	For the words "stock exchange in the United Kingdom, other than a market maker," substitute "recognised investment exchange or a market of the kind described in [paragraph 36(2) of Part III of the Schedule to the Financial Services and Markets Act 2000 (Exemption) Order 2001][15] ("EEA regulated market")".][1]
(5)	For the words "a stock exchange in the United Kingdom" substitute ["a recognised investment exchange or an EEA regulated market"][2] and omit the words "after 5th April 1968 and".
(8)	—
(9)	For the words ""company"" to the end substitute ""shares or securities" means chargeable securities and "company" shall be construed accordingly".
26(1)	For the words "chargeable gains" substitute "relevant transactions"; omit the words "in writing"; and omit the words "or an inspector".
(2)	For the words "include" to the end substitute "are references to chargeable securities".
[47C	—][16]
[49A(1) to (3)	—][16]
[49B	—][16]
[49C	In subsection (4) from "is to be treated" to the end substitute "is to be treated as conclusive for the purposes of Part IV of the Finance Act 1986, and where appropriate, Part II of Schedule II to the Finance Act 1999 against a person on whom the notice is served."" and "omit subsection (5)][16]
[49D and 49E	—][16]
[49F	In subsection (2) from "are to be treated" to the end substitute "are to be treated as conclusive for the purposes of Part IV of the Finance Act 1986, and where appropriate, Part II of Schedule II to the Finance Act 1999 against a person on whom the notice is served"" and "omit subsection (3)][16]

[49G, 49H, 49I	—][16]
[46A(1)	*Omit paragraphs (a) and (b) and the words "General Commissioners or" in paragraph (c); and for the words "appeals or other proceedings under the Taxes Acts" substitute "an appeal against a determination".*[16]
(2)	*—*[16]
(3)	*—*[16]
(4)	*—]*[3,16]
. . .	. . .[4,16]
[53(1)	*Before the word "Commissioners" insert "special"*[16]
(2)	*—]*[5,16]
[56B(1)	*—*[16]
(2)	*Before the word "Commissioners" wherever it occurs insert "Special".*[16]
(3)	*Before the word "Commissioners" in both places where it occurs insert "Special".*[16]
(4)	*—*[16]
(5)	*—*[16]
(6)	*—*[16]
56C	*—*[16]
56D	*—*[16]
60	—][3]
61	—
[63(1)	—
(2)	—
63A(1)	—
(2)	—][6]
[65(1)	For paragraphs (a) and (b) there shall be substituted "the amount of any tax for the time being due and payable is less than £1,000,".][7]
(4)	—
[66(1)	For the words "any assessment" substitute "the Act".][7]
(2)	—
(2A)	—
(3)	—
(4)	—
67(1)	Omit the words "under any assessment".
(2)	—
68	—
69	For the words "Part IX of this" substitute "the"; omit the words "charged and"; and omit the words "under the assessment" to the end.
71(2)	For the words "chargeable to" substitute "accountable or liable for"; omit the word "income"; for the words "Income Tax Acts" substitute "Act"; and omit the words "for the purpose of the assessment of the body".
(3)	Omit the word "income"; for the words "charged on the body" substitute "for which the body is accountable or liable"; and for the words "Income Tax Acts" substitute "Act".
72(1)	For the words "assessable and chargeable to income" substitute "accountable or liable for"; and for the words "assessed and charged" substitute "accountable or liable".
(2)	For the word "chargeable" substitute "accountable or liable"; for the words "Income Tax Acts" substitute "Act"; and for the words "of assessment and payment of income tax" substitute "thereof".
(3)	For the words "has been charged" substitute "is accountable or liable"; for the words "Income Tax Acts" in both places in which they occur substitute "Act"; and for the word "charged" substitute "for which he is accountable or liable".
73	For the words "chargeable to income" substitute "accountable or liable for".

74(1)	For the words “chargeable to income” substitute “accountable or liable for”; and for the words “chargeable on such deceased person” substitute “for which such deceased person is accountable or liable”.
(2)	—
78(1)	Omit the words from the beginning to “(Schedule A etc)”; omit the words “whether a British subject or not”; for the words “assessable and chargeable to income” substitute “accountable or liable for”; omit the words from “whether the branch” to “or gains or not”; for the words “assessed and charged” substitute “accountable or liable”; and omit the words from “and in the actual receipt” to the end.
83(1)	For the words “in whose name” substitute “who is accountable or liable in respect of”; omit the words “is chargeable”; for the words “Income Tax Acts” substitute “Act”; and for the words “of assessment and payment of income tax” substitute “thereof”.
(2)	For the words “has been charged” substitute “is accountable or liable”; for the words “Income Tax Acts” in both places in which they occur substitute “Act”; and for the word “charged” substitute “for which he is accountable or liable”.
[86(1)	For the words “The following” to “section 55 or 59B of this Act,” substitute “Tax which becomes due and payable”; and for the words “the relevant date” substitute “1st October 1999 or the accountable date, whichever is the later,”.
(3)	For the word ‘relevant’ substitute ‘accountable’.][8]
89(1)	. . . [9]
(3)	. . . [9]
90	—
[93(1)	For the words “where” to “with the notice” substitute “where any person (the taxpayer) fails to give a notice which he is required to give under regulation [4, 4A or 4B][14] of the Stamp Duty Reserve Tax Regulations 1986”.][1]
[(2)	—][7]
(3)	*Omit the words “General or”.[16]*
[(5)	For the words “to (4)” substitute “and (3)”; and for the words from “if” to the end substitute “if the failure by the taxpayer to give the notice continues after the end of a period of one year beginning on the last day on which the notice should have been given, he shall be liable to a penalty of an amount not exceeding the amount of the tax which he should have paid by the date by which he should have given the notice”][7].
(6)	—.][1]
[95(1)	In paragraph (a) for the word “delivers” substitute “gives”; and for the words from “return” to “Act)” substitute “notice under regulation [4, 4A or 4B][14] of the Stamp Duty Reserve Tax Regulations 1986”; in paragraph (b) omit the word “return,”, for the words “in connection with” substitute “in, or in connection with,”; omit the words “for any allowance, deduction or relief”; and for the words “income tax or capital gains” substitute “stamp duty reserve”; omit paragraph (c) and the word “or” immediately preceding it.][O10_1]
(2)	In paragraph (a) for the words “income tax and capital gains” substitute “stamp duty reserve”; omit the words “for” to “assessment”; and omit the words “including” to “repayable”; in paragraph (b) for the word “return” substitute “notice”; after the word “statement” insert “or”; omit the words “or accounts”; after the word “as” insert “given or”; and omit the words “or substituted”.
97(1)	For the word “return” in both places in which it occurs substitute “notice”; after the word “statement” in both places in which it occurs insert “or”; omit the words “or accounts” in both places in which they occur; for the words “sections 95 and 96” substitute “section 95”; for the words “made or submitted” in both places in which they occur substitute “given or made”; and for the words “those sections” substitute “that section”.
[98(1)	Omit the words “Subject to the provisions of this section and section 98A below,”.
(2)	Omit the words “Subject to section 98A below”.
(3)	—
(4)	—
Table	Omit the provisions specified in the first and second columns of the Table and the words at the end of the Table and insert the following provisions—

	Section 23 of this Act;	The Stamp Duty Reserve Tax Regulations 1986 (other than [regulations [4, 4A and 4B][14]][10]).
	Section 25(1), (2), (3), (4), (5), (8) and (9) of this Act;	[The Stamp Duty Reserve Tax (UK Depositary Interests in Foreign Securities) Regulations 1999][11]
	Section 26 of this Act;	
	The Stamp Duty Reserve Tax Regulations 1986.][10]	

[99 For the words "preparation or delivery" substitute "giving"; for the words "information, return, accounts or other document" substitute "notice under regulation [4, 4A or 4B][14], . . .[17], of the Stamp Duty Reserve Tax Regulations 1986 [or Schedule 36 to the Finance Act 2008][17]; and omit paragraph (a).][12]

[100(1) Before the word "Commissioners" insert "Special"; and for the words "the Taxes Acts" substitute "this Act".

(2) In paragraph (a) for the words "section 93(1) above" onwards substitute "section 93(1)(a) above, or"; omit paragraph (b); in paragraph (c) for the words "section 98(1) above" onwards substitute "section 98(1)(i) above"; omit paragraphs (d) and (e).

(3) —

(4) —

(5) —

100A(1) —

(2) —

(3) Omit the words "in an assessment".

100B(1) For the words from "this Act" onwards substitute "the Stamp Duty Reserve Tax Regulations 1986 relating to appeals against determinations specified in notices under regulation 6 of those Regulations ("regulation 6 determinations") shall have effect in relation to an appeal against such a determination as they have effect in relation to appeals against regulation 6 determinations".

(2) Omit the words "section 50(6) to (8) of this Act shall not apply but"; and before the word "Commissioners" in both places where it occurs insert "Special".

(3) For the words "section 56 of this Act" substitute "regulation 10 of the Stamp Duty Reserve Tax Regulations 1986"; and before the word "Commissioners" in both places where it occurs insert "Special".

[100C —][16]

(2) Before the word "Commissioners" insert "Special".

(3) Before the word "Commissioners" insert "Special"; and omit the words "in an assessment".

(4) —

(5) —

100D —][12]

101 For the word "assessment" substitute "notice under regulation 6 of The Stamp Duty Reserve Tax Regulations 1986"; after the word "varied" insert "or quashed"; *for the word "any" in the second place in which it occurs substitute "the Special"*[16]*;* and for the word "that" to the end substitute "of the matters specified".

102 —

[103(1) Omit the words "Subject to subsection (2) below" and the words "for any period"; *and before the word "Commissioners" insert "Special"*[16].

(3) —

(4) Before the word "Commissioners" insert "Special".][7,16]

104 For the words "the Taxes Acts" substitute "this Act"; and for the word "misdemeanour" substitute "offence".

105 —

108(1) For the words "Taxes Acts" in both places in which they occur substitute "Act"; and omit the words "This subsection" to the end.

(2) For the words from the beginning to "on" substitute "Tax for which"; and after the word "Charter" insert "is accountable or liable".

(3) —

111(1) *Omit the words "Capital Gains Tax"; the words "1979"; and omit the words "inspector or other" in both places in which they occur.*

(2) *Omit the words "inspector or other"; and for the words "£5" substitute "level 1 on the standard scale as defined in section 75 of the Criminal Justice Act 1982.".*[17]

114(1) For the words ["An assessment or determination"][13] substitute "A notice of determination"; for the words "Taxes Acts" in both places in which they occur substitute "Act"; omit the words "or property charged or"; and the words "charged or".

(2) For the words ["An assessment or determination"][13] substitute "A notice of determination"; in paragraph (a)(i) omit the word "liable"; in paragraph (a)(ii) for the words "the description of any profits or property" substitute "any matter specified therein"; and omit the word "or"; omit paragraph (a)(iii); omit paragraph (b).

118(1) Omit the following expressions and the words which occur after them:
"the Board"
"chargeable gain"
"chargeable period"
"inspector"
"return"
"tax"
"the Taxes Acts"
"trade"; and in the words which occur after the expression "neglect" for the words "Taxes Act" substitute "Act".

(2) [After][16] the word "deemed" in the second place in which it occurs insert "not to have failed to do it unless the excuse ceased and, after the excuse ceased, he shall be deemed".

Amendments—[1] Sections 25(4), 93(1), 95(1) substituted by the Stamp Duty Reserve Tax (Amendment) Regulations, SI 1997/2430 reg 11(2)(4) in relation to any relevant transaction entered into from 19 October 1997.

[2] Words in s 25(5) substituted in relation to any relevant transaction entered into from 19 October 1997 by SI 1997/2430 reg 11(3).

[3] Sections 46A, 56B–D, 60 inserted by the Stamp Duty Reserve Tax (Amendment) Regulations, SI 1993/3110 reg 7(2), (3) with effect from 1 January 1994.

[4] Sections 50(3)–(6), 51(1), (2), 52(1)–(3) revoked by the General and Special Commissioners (Amendment of Enactments) Regulations, SI 1994/1813 reg 2, Sch 1 para 30(2), Sch 2 Pt II with effect from 1 September 1994.

[5] Section 53 substituted by SI 1994/1813 reg 2(1), Sch 1 para 30(3) with effect from 1 September 1994.

[6] Section 63 substituted by ss 63 and 63A by SI 1993/3110 reg 7(4) with effect from 1 January 1994.

[7] Sections 65(1), 66(1), 93(2), (5), 103 substituted by SI 1993/3110 reg 7(5), (6), (8), (12) with effect from 1 January 1994.

[8] Section 86 substituted by the Stamp Duty Reserve Tax (Amendment) Regulations, SI 1999/2536, reg 3(1), (2) with effect from 1 October 1999.

[9] Section 89(1), (3) revoked by SI 1989/1301 reg 4(*b*) with effect from 18 August 1989.

[10] Section 98 substituted by SI 1993/3110 reg 7(9), words revoked by SI 1994/1813 reg 2, Sch 1 para 30(4), Sch 2 Part II, and words substituted by SI 1997/2430 reg 11(6) in relation to any relevant transaction entered into with effect from after 20 October 1997.

[11] Words inserted by the Stamp Duty Reserve Tax (UK Depositary Interests in Foreign Securities) Regulations, SI 1999/2383 reg 5 with effect from 25 August 1999.

[12] Section 99 substituted by SI 1993/3110 reg 7(10), and words inserted by SI 1997/2430, reg 11(7) in relation to any relevant transaction entered into from 19 October 1997. Section 100 substituted and ss 100A, 100B, 100C and 100D inserted by SI 1993 reg 7(11) with effect from 1 January 1994.

[13] Words in s 114(1), (2) substituted by SI 1993/3110 reg 7(13) with effect from 1 January 1994.

[14] Words substituted by the Stamp Duty Reserve Tax (Amendment) Regulations, SI 1999/3264, reg 12, with effect from 6 February 2000.

[15] Words substituted by the Financial Services and Markets Act 2000 (Consequential Amendments) (Taxes) Order, SI 2001/3629 arts 112,115(1), (2) with effect from 1 December 2001, immediately after the coming into force of the Financial Services and Markets Act 2000 ss 411, 432(1), Sch 20 (and SI 2001/3629 Pts 1 and 2).

[16] Entries inserted, revoked and substituted, by the Transfer of Tribunal Functions and Revenue and Customs Appeals Order, SI 2009/56 art 3, Sch 2 paras 12, 18 with effect from 1 April 2009.

[17] In entry for s 99, words ", or any information under regulation 5," revoked, and words inserted, and entries for s 111 revoked, by the SDRT (Amendment) Regs, SI 2010/664, regs 2, 4, with effect from 1 April 2010.

PART II
TAXES MANAGEMENT ACT 1970

Note—This heading refers to Part II of this statutory instrument, ie SI 1986/1711. It restates the provisions of TMA 1970, Pt III below as modified by Part I of this Schedule.

PART III
OTHER RETURNS AND INFORMATION

Note—This heading refers to Part III of TMA 1970. The following text shows the modified provisions of TMA 1970 as introduced by reg 20(3) above.

23 Power to obtain copies of registers of securities

(1) The Board may cause to be served upon any body corporate a notice requiring them to deliver to the Board within a specified time, being not less than twenty-one days, a copy, certified by a duly authorised officer of such body, of the whole of, or any specified class of entries in, any register containing the names of the holders of any securities issued by them.

(2) On delivery of the copy in accordance with the notice payment shall be made therefor at the rate of 25 pence in respect of each one hundred entries.

(3) In this section "securities" means chargeable securities, and "entry" means, in relation to any register, so much thereof as relates to the securities held by any one person.

25 Issuing houses, stockbrokers, etc

(1) For the purpose of obtaining particulars of relevant transactions the Board may by notice require a return under any of the provisions of this section.

(2) An issuing house or other person carrying on a business of effecting public issues of shares or securities in any company, or placings of shares or securities in any company, either on behalf of the company, or on behalf of holders of blocks of shares or securities which have not previously been the subject of a public issue or placing, may be required to make a return of all such public issues or placings effected by that person in the course of the business in the period specified in the notice requiring the return, giving particulars of the persons to or with whom the shares or securities are issued, allotted or placed, and the number or amount of the shares or securities so obtained by them respectively.

(3) A person not carrying on such a business may be required to make a return as regards any such public issue or placing effected by that person and specified in the notice, giving particulars of the persons to or with whom the shares or securities are issued, allotted, or placed and the number or amount of the shares or securities so obtained by them respectively.

[(4) A member of a recognised investment exchange or a market of the kind described in [paragraph 36(2) of Part III of the Schedule to the Financial Services and Markets Act 2000 (Exemption) Order 2001][2] (EEA Regulated Markets) (Exemption) Order 1995 ("EEA regulated market") may be required to make a return giving particulars of any transactions effected by him in the course of his business in the period specified in the notice requiring the return and giving particulars of—

(*a*) the parties to the transactions,

(*b*) the number or amount of the shares or securities dealt with in the respective transactions, and

(*c*) the amount or value of the consideration.

(5) A person (other than a member of a recognised investment exchange or an EEA regulated market) who acts as an agent or broker in the United Kingdom in transactions in shares or securities may be required to make a return giving particulars of any such transactions effected by him in the period specified in the notice, and giving particulars of—

(*a*) the parties to the transactions,

(*b*) the number or amount of the shares or securities dealt with in the respective transactions, and

(*c*) the amount or value of the consideration.][1]

(8) No person shall be required under this section to include in a return particulars of any transaction effected more than three years before the service of the notice requiring him to make the return.

(9) In this section "shares or securities" means chargeable securities and "company" shall be construed accordingly.

Amendments—[1] Sub-ss (4) and (5) substituted by the Stamp Duty Reserve Tax (Amendment) Regulations, SI 1997/2430 reg 12(2) with effect from 20 October 1997.

[2] Words substituted by the Financial Services and Markets Act 2000 (Consequential Amendments) (Taxes) Order, SI 2001/3629 arts 112, 115(1), (3) with effect from 1 December 2001, immediately after the coming into force of the Financial Services and Markets Act 2000 ss 411, 432(1), Sch 20.

26 Nominee shareholders

(1) If, for the purpose of obtaining particulars of relevant transactions, any person in whose name any shares of a company are registered is so required by notice by the Board, he shall state whether or not he is the beneficial owner of those shares and, if not the beneficial owner of those shares or any of them, shall furnish the name and address of the person or persons on whose behalf the shares are registered in his name.

(2) In this section references to shares are references to chargeable securities.

PART V
APPEAL AND OTHER PROCEEDINGS

Amendments—This Part substituted by the Transfer of Tribunal Functions and Revenue and Customs Appeals Order, SI 2009/56 art 3, Sch 2 paras 12, 19 with effect from 1 April 2009.

[47C Meaning of tribunal

In this Act "tribunal" means the First-tier Tribunal or, where determined by or under Tribunal Procedure Rules, the Upper Tribunal.][1]

Amendments—[1] This Part substituted by the Transfer of Tribunal Functions and Revenue and Customs Appeals Order, SI 2009/56 art 3, Sch 2 paras 12, 19 with effect from 1 April 2009.

[49A Appeal: HMRC review or determination by tribunal

(1) This section applies if notice of appeal has been given to HMRC.

(2) In such a case—

(*a*) the appellant may notify HMRC that the appellant requires HMRC to review the matter in question (see section 49B),

(*b*) HMRC may notify the appellant of an offer to review the matter in question (see section 49C), or

(*c*) the appellant may notify the appeal to the tribunal (see section 49D).

(3) See sections 49G and 49H for provision about notifying appeals to the tribunal after a review has been required by the appellant or offered by HMRC.][1]

Amendments—[1] This Part substituted by the Transfer of Tribunal Functions and Revenue and Customs Appeals Order, SI 2009/56 art 3, Sch 2 paras 12, 19 with effect from 1 April 2009.

[49B Appellant requires review by HMRC

(1) Subsections (2) and (3) apply if the appellant notifies HMRC that the appellant requires HMRC to review the matter in question.

(2) HMRC must, within the relevant period, notify the appellant of HMRC's view of the matter in question.

(3) HMRC must review the matter in question in accordance with section 49E.

(4) The appellant may not notify HMRC that the appellant requires HMRC to review the matter in question and HMRC shall not be required to conduct a review if—

(*a*) the appellant has already given a notification under this section in relation to the matter in question,

(*b*) HMRC have given a notification under section 49C in relation to the matter in question, or

(*c*) the appellant has notified the appeal to the tribunal under section 49D.

(5) In this section "relevant period" means—

(*a*) the period of 30 days beginning with the day on which HMRC receive the notification from the appellant, or

(*b*) such longer period as is reasonable.][1]

Amendments—[1] This Part substituted by the Transfer of Tribunal Functions and Revenue and Customs Appeals Order, SI 2009/56 art 3, Sch 2 paras 12, 19 with effect from 1 April 2009.

[49C HMRC offer review

(1) Subsections (2) to (6) apply if HMRC notify the appellant of an offer to review the matter in question.

(2) When HMRC notify the appellant of the offer, HMRC must also notify the appellant of HMRC's view of the matter in question.

(3) If, within the acceptance period, the appellant notifies HMRC of acceptance of the offer, HMRC must review the matter in question in accordance with section 49E.

(4) If the appellant does not give HMRC such a notification within the acceptance period HMRC's view of the matter in question is to be treated as conclusive for the purposes of Part IV of the Finance Act 1986, and where appropriate, Part II of Schedule II to the Finance Act 1999 against a person on whom the notice is served.

(6) Subsection (4) does not apply to the matter in question if, or to the extent that, the appellant notifies the appeal to the tribunal under section 49H.

(7) HMRC may not notify the appellant of an offer to review the matter in question (and, accordingly, HMRC shall not be required to conduct a review) if—

(*a*) HMRC have already given a notification under this section in relation to the matter in question,

(*b*) the appellant has given a notification under section 49B in relation to the matter in question, or

(*c*) the appellant has notified the appeal to the tribunal under section 49D.

(8) In this section "acceptance period" means the period of 30 days beginning with the date of the document by which HMRC notify the appellant of the offer to review the matter in question.][1]

Amendments—[1] This Part substituted by the Transfer of Tribunal Functions and Revenue and Customs Appeals Order, SI 2009/56 art 3, Sch 2 paras 12, 19 with effect from 1 April 2009.

[49D Notifying appeal to the tribunal

(1) This section applies if notice of appeal has been given to HMRC.

(2) The appellant may notify the appeal to the tribunal.

(3) If the appellant notifies the appeal to the tribunal, the tribunal is to decide the matter in question.

(4) Subsections (2) and (3) do not apply in a case where—

(*a*) HMRC have given a notification of their view of the matter in question under section 49B, or

(*b*) HMRC have given a notification under section 49C in relation to the matter in question.

(5) In a case falling within subsection (4)(*a*) or (*b*), the appellant may notify the appeal to the tribunal, but only if permitted to do so by section 49G or 49H.][1]

Amendments—[1] This Part substituted by the Transfer of Tribunal Functions and Revenue and Customs Appeals Order, SI 2009/56 art 3, Sch 2 paras 12, 19 with effect from 1 April 2009.

[49E Nature of review etc

(1) This section applies if HMRC are required by section 49B or 49C to review the matter in question.

(2) The nature and extent of the review are to be such as appear appropriate to HMRC in the circumstances.

(3) For the purpose of subsection (2), HMRC must, in particular, have regard to steps taken before the beginning of the review—

(*a*) by HMRC in deciding the matter in question, and

(*b*) by any person in seeking to resolve disagreement about the matter in question.

(4) The review must take account of any representations made by the appellant at a stage which gives HMRC a reasonable opportunity to consider them.

(5) The review may conclude that HMRC's view of the matter in question is to be—

(*a*) upheld,

(*b*) varied, or

(*c*) cancelled.

(6) HMRC must notify the appellant of the conclusions of the review and their reasoning within—

(*a*) the period of 45 days beginning with the relevant day, or

(*b*) such other period as may be agreed.

(7) In subsection (6) "relevant day" means—

(*a*) in a case where the appellant required the review, the day when HMRC notified the appellant of HMRC's view of the matter in question,

(*b*) in a case where HMRC offered the review, the day when HMRC received notification of the appellant's acceptance of the offer.

(8) Where HMRC are required to undertake a review but do not give notice of the conclusions within the time period specified in subsection (6), the conclusion of the review is deemed to be that HMRC's view of the matter in question (see sections 49B(2) and 49C(2)) is upheld.

(9) If subsection (8) applies, HMRC must notify the appellant of the conclusion which the review is treated as having reached.][1]

Amendments—[1] This Part substituted by the Transfer of Tribunal Functions and Revenue and Customs Appeals Order, SI 2009/56 art 3, Sch 2 paras 12, 19 with effect from 1 April 2009.

[49F Effect of conclusions of review

(1) This section applies if HMRC give notice of the conclusions of a review (see section 49E(6) and (9)).

(2) The conclusions are to be treated as conclusive for the purposes of Part IV of the Finance Act 1986, and where appropriate, Part II of Schedule II to the Finance Act 1999 against a person on whom the notice is served.

(4) Subsection (2) does not apply to the matter in question if, or to the extent that, the appellant notifies the appeal to the tribunal under section 49G.][1]

Amendments—[1] This Part substituted by the Transfer of Tribunal Functions and Revenue and Customs Appeals Order, SI 2009/56 art 3, Sch 2 paras 12, 19 with effect from 1 April 2009.

[49G Notifying appeal to tribunal after review concluded

(1) This section applies if—

(*a*) HMRC have given notice of the conclusions of a review in accordance with section 49E, or

(*b*) the period specified in section 49E(6) has ended and HMRC have not given notice of the conclusions of the review.

(2) The appellant may notify the appeal to the tribunal within the post-review period.

(3) If the post-review period has ended, the appellant may notify the appeal to the tribunal only if the tribunal gives permission.

(4) If the appellant notifies the appeal to the tribunal, the tribunal is to determine the matter in question.

(5) In this section "post-review period" means—

(*a*) in a case falling within subsection (1)(*a*) the period of 30 days beginning with the date of the document in which HMRC give notice of the conclusions of the review in accordance with section 49E(6), or

(*b*) in a case falling within subsection (1)(*b*), the period that—

(i) begins with the day following the last day of the period specified in section 49E(6), and

(ii) ends 30 days after the date of the document in which HMRC give notice of the conclusions of the review in accordance with section 49E(9).][1]

Amendments—[1] This Part substituted by the Transfer of Tribunal Functions and Revenue and Customs Appeals Order, SI 2009/56 art 3, Sch 2 paras 12, 19 with effect from 1 April 2009.

[49H Notifying appeal to tribunal after review offered but not accepted

(1) This section applies if—

(*a*) HMRC have offered to review the matter in question (see section 49C), and

(*b*) the appellant has not accepted the offer.

(2) The appellant may notify the appeal to the tribunal within the acceptance period.

(3) But if the acceptance period has ended, the appellant may notify the appeal to the tribunal only if the tribunal gives permission.

(4) If the appellant notifies the appeal to the tribunal, the tribunal is to determine the matter in question.

(5) In this section "acceptance period" has the same meaning as in section 49C.][1]

Amendments—[1] This Part substituted by the Transfer of Tribunal Functions and Revenue and Customs Appeals Order, SI 2009/56 art 3, Sch 2 paras 12, 19 with effect from 1 April 2009.

[49I Interpretation of sections 49A to 49H

(1) In sections 49A to 49H—

(*a*) "matter in question" means the matter to which an appeal relates;

(*b*) a reference to a notification is a reference to a notification in writing.

(2) In sections 49A to 49H a reference to the appellant includes a person acting on behalf of the appellant except in relation to—

(*a*) notification of HMRC's view under section 49B(2);

(*b*) notification by HMRC of an offer of review (and of their view of the matter) under section 49C;

(*c*) notification of the conclusions of a review under section 49E(6); and

(*d*) notification of the deemed conclusions of a review under section 49E(9).

(3) But if a notification falling within any of the paragraphs of subsection (2) is given to the appellant, a copy of the notification may also be given to a person acting on behalf of the appellant.][1]

Amendments—[1] This Part substituted by the Transfer of Tribunal Functions and Revenue and Customs Appeals Order, SI 2009/56 art 3, Sch 2 paras 12, 19 with effect from 1 April 2009. This Part previously read as follows—

"46A Regulations about jurisdiction

(1) The Lord Chancellor may, with the consent of the Lord Advocate, make regulations—

(*c*) as to the number of Special Commissioners required or permitted to hear, or perform other functions in relation to, an appeal against a determination.

(2) The Regulations may—

(*a*) make different provision for different cases or different circumstances, and

(*b*) contain such supplementary, incidental, consequential and transitional provision as the Lord Chancellor thinks appropriate.

(3) Provision made by virtue of subsection (1) or (2) above may include provision amending this or any other Act or any instrument made under an Act.

(4) Regulations under this section shall be made by statutory instrument subject to annulment in pursuance of a resolution of either House of Parliament.

Procedure before Special Commissioners

53 Appeals against summary determination of penalties

(1) An appeal shall lie to the High Court or, in Scotland, the Court of Session as the Court of Exchequer in Scotland, against the summary determination by the Special Commissioners of any penalty pursuant to regulations under section 56B of this Act.

(2) On any such appeal the court may either confirm or reverse the determination of the Commissioners or reduce or increase the sum determined.

Jurisdiction

56B Regulations about practice and procedure

(1) The Lord Chancellor may, with the consent of the Lord Advocate, make regulations about the practice and procedure to be followed in connection with appeals.

(2) The regulations may in particular include provision—

(*a*) enabling the Special Commissioners to join as a party to an appeal a person who would not otherwise be a party;

(*b*) for requiring any party to an appeal to provide information and make documents available for inspection by the Special Commissioners or by officers of the Board;

(*c*) for requiring persons to attend the hearing of an appeal to give evidence and produce documents;

(*d*) as to evidence generally in relation to appeals;

(*e*) enabling the Special Commissioners to review their decisions;

(*f*) for the imposition of penalties not exceeding an amount specified in the regulations;

(*g*) for the determination and recovery of penalties (imposed by virtue of paragraph (*f*) above or any other enactment) and for appeals against penalties.

(3) The regulations may also include provision—

(*a*) authorising or requiring the Special Commissioners, in circumstances prescribed in the regulations, to state a case for the opinion of a court;

(*b*) for an appeal to lie to a court on a question of law arising from a decision of the Special Commissioners;

(*c*) as to the practice and procedure to be followed in connection with cases so stated or such appeals.

(4) The regulations may—

(*a*) make different provision for different cases or different circumstances, and

(*b*) contain such supplementary, incidental, consequential and transitional provision as the Lord Chancellor thinks appropriate.

(5) Provision made by virtue of any of subsections (1) to (4) above may include provision amending this or any other Act or any instrument made under an Act.

(6) Regulations under this section shall be made by statutory instrument subject to annulment in pursuance of a resolution of either House of Parliament.

56C Power of Special Commissioners to order costs

(1) Regulations made under section 56B above may include provision for—

(*a*) the award by the Special Commissioners of the costs of, or incidental to, appeal hearings before them,

(*b*) the recovery of costs so awarded, and

(*c*) appeals against such awards.

(2) Any provision made by virtue of subsection 1(*a*) above shall provide that the Special Commissioners shall not award costs against a party to an appeal unless they consider that he has acted wholly unreasonably in connection with the hearing in question.

56D Power of Special Commissioners to publish reports of decisions

(1) Regulations made under section 56B above may include provision for the Special Commissioners to publish reports of such of their decisions as they consider appropriate.

(2) Any provision made by virtue of subsection (1) above shall provide that any report published, other than a report of an appeal that was heard in public, shall be in a form that so far as possible prevents the identification of any person whose affairs are dealt with in the report.

(3) No obligation of secrecy to which the Special Commissioners are subject (by virtue of this Act or otherwise) shall prevent their publishing reports of their decisions in accordance with any provision made by virtue of subsection (1) above.".

PART VI
COLLECTION AND RECOVERY

[60 Issue of demand notes and receipts

(1) Every collector shall, when the tax becomes due and payable, make demand of the respective sums given to him in charge to collect, from the persons charged therewith, or at the places of their last abode, or on the premises in respect of which the tax is charged, as the case may require.

(2) On payment of the tax, the collector shall if requested give a receipt.][1]

Amendments—[1] This section inserted by the Stamp Duty Reserve Tax (Amendment) Regulations, SI 1993/3110 regs 1, 2, 8 with effect from 1 January 1994.

Distraint and poinding

61 Distraint by collectors

(1) If a person neglects or refuses to pay the sum charged, upon demand made by the collector, the collector shall, for non-payment thereof, distrain upon the lands, tenements and premises in respect of which the tax is charged, or distrain the person charged by his goods and chattels, and all such other goods and chattels as the collector is hereby authorised to distrain.

(2) For the purpose of levying any such distress, a collector may, after obtaining a warrant for the purpose signed by the General Commissioners, break open, in the daytime, any house or premises, calling to his assistance any constable.
Every such constable shall, when so required, aid and assist the collector in the execution of the warrant and in levying the distress in the house or premises.
(3) A levy or warrant to break open shall be executed by, or under the direction of, and in the presence of, the collector.
(4) A distress levied by the collector shall be kept for five days, at the costs and charges of a person neglecting or refusing to pay.
(5) If the person aforesaid does not pay the sum due, together with the costs and charges within the said five days, the distress shall be appraised by two or more inhabitants of the parish in which the distress is taken, or by other sufficient persons, and shall be sold by public auction by the collector for payment of the sum due and all costs and charges.
The costs and charges of taking, keeping and selling the distress shall be retained by the collector, and any overplus coming by the distress, after the deduction of the costs and charges and of the sum due, shall be restored to the owner of the goods distrained.

[63 Recovery of tax in Scotland

(1) Subject to subsection (3) below, in Scotland, where any tax is due and has not been paid, the sheriff, on an application by the collector accompanied by a certificate by the collector—

(*a*) stating that none of the persons specified in the application has paid the tax due by him;

(*b*) stating that the collector has demanded payment under section 60 of this Act from each such person of the amount due by him;

(*c*) stating that 14 days have elapsed since the date of such demand without payment of the said amount; and

(*d*) specifying the amount due and unpaid by each such person,

shall grant a summary warrant in a form prescribed by Act of Sederunt authorising the recovery, by any of the diligences mentioned in subsection (2) below, of the amount remaining due and unpaid.
(2) The diligences referred to in subsection (1) above are—

[(*a*) an attachment;][2]

(*b*) an earnings arrestment;

(*c*) an arrestment and action of furthcoming or sale.][1]

Amendments—[1] This section substituted by the Stamp Duty Reserve Tax (Amendment) Regulations, SI 1993/3110 regs 1, 2, 7 with effect from 1 January 1994.

[2] Sub-s (2)(*a*) substituted by the Debt Arrangement and Attachment (Scotland) Act 2002 s 61, Sch 3 para 30(1), (2) with effect from 30 December 2002.

[63A Sheriff officer's fees and outlays

(1) Subject to subsection (2) below and without prejudice to [section 39(1) of the Debt Arrangement and Attachment (Scotland) Act 2002 (asp 17) (expenses of attachment)][2], the sheriff officer's fees, together with the outlays necessarily incurred by him, in connection with the execution of a summary warrant shall be chargeable against the debtor.
(2) No fee shall be chargeable by the sheriff officer against the debtor for collecting, and accounting to the collector for, sums paid to him by the debtor in respect of the amount owing.][1]

Amendments—[1] This section inserted by the Stamp Duty Reserve Tax (Amendment) Regulations, SI 1993/3110 regs 1, 2, 8 with effect from 1 January 1994.

[2] Words in sub-s (1) substituted by the Debt Arrangement and Attachment (Scotland) Act 2002 s 61, Sch 3 para 30(1), (3) with effect from 30 December 2002.

Court proceedings

65 Magistrates' courts

[(1) Where the amount of any tax for the time being due and payable is less than £1,000, the tax shall, without prejudice to any other remedy, be recoverable summarily as a civil debt by proceedings commenced in the name of a collector.][1]
(4) It is hereby declared that in subsection (1) above the expression "recoverable summarily as a civil debt" in respect of proceedings in Northern Ireland means recoverable in proceedings under Article 62 of the Magistrates' Courts (Northern Ireland) Order 1981.

Amendments—[1] Sub-s (1) substituted by the Stamp Duty Reserve Tax (Amendment) Regulations, SI 1993/3110 regs 1, 2, 7 with effect from 1 January 1994.

66 County courts

[(1) Tax due and payable under the Act may, in England and Wales, and in Northern Ireland where the amount does not exceed the limit specified in Article 10(1) of the County Courts (Northern Ireland) Order 1980, without prejudice to any other remedy, be sued for and recovered from the person charged therewith as a debt due to the Crown by proceedings in a county court commenced in the name of a collector.][3]

(2) An officer of the Board who is authorised by the Board to do so may address the court in any proceedings under this section in a county court in England and Wales.

(2A) . . . [1]

[(3) In this section as it applies in Northern Ireland the expression "county court" shall mean a county court held for a division under the County Courts (Northern Ireland) Order 1980.][2]

(4) Sections 21 and 42(2) of the Interpretation Act (Northern Ireland) 1954 shall apply as if any reference in those provisions to any enactment included a reference to this section, and Part III of the County Courts (Northern Ireland) Order 1980 (general civil jurisdiction) shall apply for the purposes of this section in Northern Ireland.

Amendments—[1] Sub-s (2A) repealed by the High Court and County Courts Jurisdiction Order, SI 1991/724 with effect from 1 July 1991.

[2] Sub-s (3) substituted by the High Court and County Courts Jurisdiction Order, SI 1991/724 with effect from 1 July 1991.

[3] Sub-s (1) substituted by the Stamp Duty Reserve Tax (Amendment) Regulations, SI 1993/3110 regs 1, 2, 7 with effect from 1 January 1994.

67 Inferior courts in Scotland

(1) In Scotland, where the amount of tax for the time being due and payable does not exceed the sum for the time being specified in section 35(1)(*a*) of the Sheriff Courts (Scotland) Act 1971 the tax may, without prejudice to any other remedy, be sued for and recovered from the person charged therewith as a debt due to the Crown by proceedings commenced in the name of a collector in the sheriff court.

(2) Sections 65 and 66 above shall not apply in Scotland.

68 High Court, etc

(1) Any tax may be sued for and recovered from the person charged therewith in the High Court as a debt due to the Crown, or by any other means whereby any debt of record or otherwise due to the Crown can, or may at any time, be sued for and recovered, as well as by the other means specially provided by this Act for levying the tax.

(2) All matters within the jurisdiction of the High Court under this section shall be assigned in Scotland to the Court of Session sitting as the Court of Exchequer.

Supplemental

69 Interest on tax

Interest charged under the Act shall be treated for the purposes—

(*a*) of sections 61, 63 and 65 to 68 above, and

(*b*) of section 35(2)(*g*) (i) of the Crown Proceedings Act 1947 (rules of court to impose restrictions on set-off and counterclaim where the proceedings or set-off or counterclaim relate to taxes) and of any rules of court (including county court rules) for England and Wales or Northern Ireland, which impose such a restriction, and

(*c*) of section 35(2)(*b*) of the said Act of 1947 as set out in section 50 of that Act (which imposes corresponding restrictions in Scotland),

as if it were tax due and payable.

PART VII

PERSONS CHARGEABLE IN A REPRESENTATIVE CAPACITY, ETC

71 Bodies of persons

(2) Subject to section 108 of this Act, the chamberlain or other officer acting as treasurer, auditor or receiver for the time being of any body of persons accountable or liable for tax shall be answerable for doing all such acts as are required to be done under the Act and for payment of the tax.

(3) Every such officer as aforesaid may from time to time retain, out of any money coming into his hands on behalf of the body, so much thereof as is sufficient to pay the tax for which the body is accountable or liable, and shall be indemnified for all such payments made in pursuance of the Act.

72 Trustees, guardians, etc, of incapacitated persons

(1) The trustee, guardian, tutor, curator or committee or any incapacitated person having the direction, control or management of the property or concern of any such person, whether such person resides in the United Kingdom or not, shall be accountable or liable for tax in like manner and to the like amount as that person would be accountable or liable if he were not an incapacitated person.

(2) The person who is accountable or liable in respect of an incapacitated person shall be answerable for all matters required to be done under the Act for the purpose thereof.

(3) Any person who is accountable or liable under the Act in respect of any incapacitated person as aforesaid may retain, out of money coming into his hands on behalf of any such person, so much thereof from time to time as is sufficient to pay the tax for which he is accountable or liable, and shall be indemnified for all such payments made in pursuance of the Act.

73 Further provision as to infants

If a person accountable or liable for tax is an infant, then his parent, guardian or tutor—

(*a*) shall be liable for the tax in default of payment by the infant, and

(*b*) on neglect or refusal of payment, may be proceeded against in like manner as any other defaulter, and

(*c*) if he makes such payment, shall be allowed all sums so paid in his accounts.

74 Personal representatives

(1) If a person accountable or liable for tax dies, the executor or administrator of the person deceased shall be liable for the tax for which such deceased person is accountable or liable, and may deduct any payments made under this section out of the assets and effects of the person deceased.

(3) On neglect or refusal of payment, any person liable under this section may be proceeded against in like manner as any other defaulter.

PART VIII

CHARGES ON NON-RESIDENTS

78 Method of charging non-residents

(1) A person not resident in the United Kingdom shall be accountable or liable for tax in the name of any such trustee, guardian, tutor, curator or committee as is mentioned in section 72 of this Act, or of any branch or agent, in like manner and to the like amount as such non-resident person would be accountable or liable if he were resident in the United Kingdom.

83 Responsibilities and indemnification of persons in whose name a non-resident person is chargeable

(1) A person who is accountable or liable in respect of a non-resident person shall be answerable for all matters required to be done under the Act for the purpose thereof.

(2) A person who is accountable or liable under the Act in respect of any non-resident person as aforesaid may retain, out of money coming into his hands on behalf of any such person, so much thereof from time to time as is sufficient to pay the tax for which he is accountable or liable, and shall be indemnified for all such payments made in pursuance of the Act.

PART IX

INTEREST ON OVERDUE TAX

[86 Interest on overdue tax

(1) Tax which becomes due and payable shall carry interest at the rate applicable under section 178 of the Finance Act 1989 from 1st October 1999 or the accountable date, whichever is the later, until payment.

(3) Subsection (1) above applies even if the accountable date is a non-business day within the meaning of section 92 of the Bills of Exchange Act 1882.][1]

Note—For the rate applicable under FA 1989 s 178, see SI 1989/1297 *post*.

Amendments—[1] This section substituted by the Stamp Duty Reserve Tax (Amendment) Regulations, SI 1999/2536, reg 4(1), (2) with effect from 1 October 1999.

89 The prescribed rate of interest

Amendments—This section repealed by the Stamp Duty Reserve Tax (Amendment) Regulations, SI 1989/1301 reg 5(*b*) with effect from 18 August 1989.

90 Disallowance of relief for interest on tax

Interest payable under this Part of this Act shall be paid without any deduction of income tax and shall not be allowed as a deduction in computing any income, profits or losses for any tax purposes.

PART X

PENALTIES, ETC

93 Failure to give notice for stamp duty reserve tax

[(1) This section applies where any person (the taxpayer) fails to give a notice which he is required to give under regulation [4, 4A or 4B][2] of the Stamp Duty Reserve Tax Regulations 1986.

(2) The taxpayer shall be liable to a penalty which shall be £100.

(3) If, on an application made to them by an officer of the Board, the Special Commissioners so direct, the taxpayer shall be liable to a further penalty or penalties not exceeding £60 for each day on which the failure continues after the day on which he is notified of the direction (but excluding any day for which a penalty under this subsection has already been imposed).[3]

(5) Without prejudice to any penalties under subsections (2) and (3) above, if the failure by the taxpayer to give the notice continues after the end of a period of one year beginning on the last day on which the notice should have been given, he shall be liable to a penalty of an amount not exceeding the amount of the tax which he should have paid by the date by which he should have given the notice.

(6) No penalty shall be imposed under subsection (3) above in respect of a failure at any time after the failure has been remedied.][1]

Amendments—[1] This section substituted by the Stamp Duty Reserve Tax (Amendment) Regulations, SI 1997/2430 reg 12(3) with effect from 20 October 1997.

[2] Words substituted by the Stamp Duty Reserve Tax (Amendment) Regulations, SI 1999/3264, reg 13, with effect from 6 February 2000.

[3] Sub-s (3) repealed by the Transfer of Tribunal Functions and Revenue and Customs Appeals Order, SI 2009/56 art 3, Sch 2 paras 12, 20 with effect from 1 April 2009.

95 Incorrect notice, etc for stamp duty reserve tax

[(1) Where a person fraudulently or negligently—

(*a*) gives any incorrect notice under regulation [4, 4A or 4B][2] of the Stamp Duty Reserve Tax Regulations 1986, or

(*b*) makes any incorrect statement or declaration in, or in connection with, any claim in respect of stamp duty reserve tax,

he shall be liable to a penalty not exceeding the amount of the difference specified in subsection (2) below.][1]

(2) The difference is that between—

(*a*) the amount of stamp duty reserve tax payable by the said person, and

(*b*) the amount which would have been the amount so payable if the notice, statement or declaration as given or made by him had been correct.

Amendments—[1] Sub-s (1) substituted by the Stamp Duty Reserve Tax (Amendment) Regulations, SI 1997/2430 reg 12(4) with effect from 20 October 1997.

[2] Words substituted by the Stamp Duty Reserve Tax (Amendment) Regulations, SI 1999/3264, reg 13, with effect from 6 February 2000.

97 Incorrect notice; supplemental

(1) Where any such notice, statement or declaration as are mentioned in section 95 above were given or made by any person neither fraudulently nor negligently and it comes to his notice (or, if he has died, to the notice of his personal representatives) that they were incorrect, then, unless the error is remedied without unreasonable delay, the notice, statement or declaration shall be treated for the purposes of that section as having been negligently given or made by him.

[98 Special returns, etc

(1) Where any person—

(*a*) has been required, by a notice served under or for the purposes of any of the provisions specified in the first column of the Table below, to deliver any return or other document, to furnish any particulars, to produce any document, or to make anything available for inspection, and he fails to comply with the notice, or

(*b*) fails to furnish any information, give any certificate or produce any document or record in accordance with any of the provisions specified in the second column of the Table below,

he shall be liable, subject to subsections (3) and (4) below—

(i) to a penalty not exceeding £300, and

(ii) if the failure continues after a penalty is imposed under paragraph (i) above, to a further penalty or penalties not exceeding £60 for each day on which the failure continues after the day on which the penalty under paragraph (i) above was imposed (but excluding any day for which a penalty under this paragraph has already been imposed).

(2) Where a person fraudulently or negligently furnishes, gives, produces or makes any incorrect information, certificate, document, record or declaration of a kind mentioned in any of the provisions specified in either column of the Table below, he shall be liable to a penalty not exceeding £3,000.

(3) No penalty shall be imposed under subsection (1) above in respect of a failure within paragraph (*a*) of that subsection at any time after the failure has been remedied.

(4) No penalty shall be imposed under paragraph (ii) of subsection (1) above in respect of a failure within paragraph (*b*) of that subsection at any time after the failure has been remedied.

[TABLE

1	2
Section 23 of this Act;	The Stamp Duty Reserve Tax Regulations 1986 (other than [regulations [4, 4A and 4B][5]][3]).
Section 25 (1), (2), (3), (4), (5), (8) and (9) of this Act;	[The Stamp Duty Reserve Tax (UK Depositary Interests in Foreign Securities) Regulations 1999][4]
Section 26 of this Act;	
The Stamp Duty Reserve Tax Regulations 1986.][2]][1]	

Amendments—[1] This section substituted by the Stamp Duty Reserve Tax (Amendment) Regulations, SI 1993/3110 regs 1, 2, 7 with effect from 1 January 1994.

[2] Table substituted by the General and Special Commissioners (Amendment of Enactments) Regulations, SI 1994/1813 Sch 1 para 31(4) with effect from 1 September 1994.

[3] Words in Table substituted by the Stamp Duty Reserve Tax (Amendment) Regulations, SI 1997/2430 reg 12(5) with effect from 20 October 1997.

[4] Words inserted by the Stamp Duty Reserve Tax (UK Depositary Interests in Foreign Securities) Regulations, SI 1999/2383 reg 5 with effect from 25 August 1999.

[5] Words substituted by the Stamp Duty Reserve Tax (Amendment) Regulations, SI 1999/3264, reg 13, with effect from 6 February 2000.

[99 Assisting in giving incorrect notice, etc

Any person who assists in or induces the giving of any notice under regulation [4, 4A or 4B][2], . . . [3], of the Stamp Duty Reserve Tax Regulations 1986 [or Schedule 36 to the Finance Act 2008][3] which he knows to be incorrect shall be liable to a penalty not exceeding £3,000.][1]

Amendments—[1] This section substituted by the Stamp Duty Reserve Tax (Amendment) Regulations, SI 1993/3110 regs 1, 2, 7 with effect from 1 January 1994.

[2] Words substituted by the Stamp Duty Reserve Tax (Amendment) Regulations, SI 1999/3264, reg 13, with effect from 6 February 2000.

[3] Words ", or any information under regulation 5," repealed, and words inserted, by the SDRT (Amendment) Regulations, SI 2010/664, regs 2, 5, with effect from 1 April 2010.

[100 Determination of penalties by officer of Board

(1) Subject to subsection (2) below and except where proceedings for a penalty have been instituted under section 100D below or a penalty has been imposed by the Special Commissioners under section 53 of this Act, an officer of the Board authorised by the Board for the purposes of this section may make a determination imposing a penalty under any provision of this Act and setting it at such amount as, in his opinion, is correct or appropriate.

(2) Subsection (1) above does not apply where the penalty is a penalty under—

(*a*) section 93(1)(*a*) above, or

(*c*) section 98(1)(i) above.

(3) Notice of a determination of a penalty under this section shall be served on the person liable to the penalty and shall state the date on which it is issued and the time within which an appeal against the determination may be made.

(4) After the notice of a determination under this section has been served the determination shall not be altered except in accordance with this section or on appeal.

(5) If it is discovered by an officer of the Board authorised by the Board for the purposes of this section that the amount of a penalty determined under this section is or has become insufficient the officer may make a determination in a further amount so that the penalty is set at the amount which, in his opinion, is correct or appropriate.][1]

Amendments—[1] Sections 100, 100A–100D substituted for s 100 by the Stamp Duty Reserve Tax (Amendment) Regulations, SI 1993/3110 regs 1, 2, 7 with effect from 1 January 1994.

[100A Provisions supplementary to section 100

(1) Where a person who has incurred a penalty has died, a determination under section 100 above which could have been made in relation to him may be made in relation to his personal representatives, and any penalty imposed on personal representatives by virtue of this subsection shall be a debt due from and payable out of his estate.

(2) A penalty determined under section 100 above shall be due and payable at the end of the period of thirty days beginning with the date of the issue of the notice of determination.

(3) A penalty determined under section 100 above shall for all purposes be treated as if it were tax charged and due and payable.][1]

Amendments—[1] Sections 100, 100A–100D substituted for s 100 by the Stamp Duty Reserve Tax (Amendment) Regulations, SI 1993/3110 regs 1, 2, 7 with effect from 1 January 1994.

[100B Appeals against penalty determinations

(1) An appeal may be brought against the determination of a penalty under section 100 above and, subject to the following provisions of this section, the provisions of the Stamp Duty Reserve Tax Regulations 1986 relating to appeals against determinations specified in notices under regulation 6 of those Regulations ("regulation 6 determinations") shall have effect in relation to an appeal against such a determination as they have effect in relation to appeals against regulation 6 determinations.

(2) On an appeal against the determination of a penalty under section 100 above—

(*a*) in the case of a penalty which is required to be of a particular amount, the [First-tier Tribunal][2] may—

(i) if it appears . . . [2] that no penalty has been incurred, set the determination aside,

(ii) if the amount determined appears . . . [2] to be correct, confirm the determination, or

(iii) if the amount determined appears . . . [2] to be incorrect, increase or reduce it to the correct amount,

(*b*) in the case of any other penalty, the [First-tier Tribunal][2] may—

(i) if it appears . . . [2] that no penalty has been incurred, set the determination aside,

(ii) if the amount determined appears . . . [2] to be appropriate, confirm the determination,

(iii) if the amount determined appears . . . [2] to be excessive, reduce it to such other amount (including nil) [as it considers][2] appropriate, or

(iv) if the amount determined appears . . . [2] to be insufficient, increase it to such amount not exceeding the permitted maximum [as it considers][2] appropriate.

[(3) In addition to any right of appeal on a point of law under section 11(2) of the TCEA 2007, the person liable to the penalty may appeal to the Upper Tribunal against the amount of the penalty which had been determined under subsection (2), but not against any decision which falls under section 11(5)(*d*) or (*e*) of that Act and was made in connection with the determination of the amount of the penalty.

(3A) Section 11(3) and (4) of the TCEA 2007 applies to the right of appeal under subsection (3) as it applies to the right of appeal under section 11(2) of that Act.

(3B) On an appeal under this section the Upper Tribunal has the same powers as are conferred on the First-tier Tribunal by virtue of this section.][2]][1]

Amendments—[1] Sections 100, 100A–100D substituted for s 100 by the Stamp Duty Reserve Tax (Amendment) Regulations, SI 1993/3110 regs 1, 2, 7 with effect from 1 January 1994.

[2] In sub-s (2), words substituted for words "Special Commissioners" in each place and "as they consider" in both places, words "to them" repealed in each place, and sub-ss (3)–(3B) substituted for previous sub-s (3), by the Transfer of Tribunal Functions and Revenue and Customs Appeals Order, SI 2009/56 art 3, Sch 2 paras 12, 20(1), (3) with effect from 1 April 2009. Sub-s (3) previously read as follows—

"(3) Without prejudice to regulation 10 of the Stamp Duty Reserve Tax Regulations 1986, an appeal from a decision of the Special Commissioners against the amount of a penalty which has been determined under section 100 above or this section shall lie, at the instance of the person liable to the penalty, to the High Court or, in Scotland, to the Court of Session as the Court of Exchequer in Scotland; and on that appeal the court shall have the like jurisdiction as is conferred on the Special Commissioners by virtue of this section.".

[100C Penalty proceedings before [First-tier Tribunal][2]

(1) An officer of the Board authorised by the Board for the purposes of this section may commence proceedings before the [First-tier Tribunal][2] for any penalty to which subsection (1) of section 100 above does not apply by virtue of subsection (2) of that section.

[(2) the person liable to the penalty shall be a party to the proceedings.][2]

(3) Any penalty determined by the [First-tier Tribunal][2] in proceedings under this section shall for all purposes be treated as if it were tax charged and due and payable.

[(4) In addition to any right of appeal on a point of law under section 11(2) of the TCEA 2007, the person liable to the penalty may appeal to the Upper Tribunal against the amount of the penalty which had been determined under subsection (1), but not against any decision which falls under section 11(5)(d) or (e) of that Act and was made in connection with the determination of the amount of the penalty.

(4A) section 11(3) and (4) of the TCEA 2007 applies to the right of appeal under subsection (4) as it applies to the right of appeal under section 11(2) of that Act.][2]

(5) On any such appeal the [Upper Tribunal][2] may—

(*a*) if it appears that no penalty has been incurred, set the determination aside,

(*b*) if the amount determined appears to be appropriate, confirm the determination,

(*c*) if the amount determined appears to be excessive, reduce it to such other amount (including nil) as the [Upper Tribunal][2] considers appropriate, or

(*d*) if the amount determined appears to be insufficient, increase it to such amount not exceeding the permitted maximum as the [Upper Tribunal][2] considers appropriate.][1]

Amendments—[1] Sections 100, 100A–100D substituted for s 100 by the Stamp Duty Reserve Tax (Amendment) Regulations, SI 1993/3110 regs 1, 2, 7 with effect from 1 January 1994.

[2] In heading, words substituted for words "Commissioners", in sub-ss (1), (3) words substituted for words "Special Commissioners", sub-s (2) substituted, sub-ss (4), (4A) substituted for previous sub-s (4), in sub-s (5), words substituted for words "court" in each place, by the Transfer of Tribunal Functions and Revenue and Customs Appeals Order, SI 2009/56 art 3, Sch 2 paras 12, 20(1), (4) with effect from 1 April 2009. Sub-ss (2), (4) previously read as follows—

"(2) Proceedings under this section shall be by way of information in writing, made to the Special Commissioners, and upon summons issued by them to the defendant (or defender) to appear before them at a time and place stated in the summons; and they shall hear and decide each case in a summary way.".

"(4) An appeal against the determination of a penalty in proceedings under this section shall lie to the High Court or, in Scotland, the Court of Session as the Court of Exchequer in Scotland—

(*a*) by any party on a question of law, and

(*b*) by the defendant (or, in Scotland, the defender) against the amount of the penalty.".

[100D Penalty proceedings before court

(1) Where in the opinion of the Board the liability of any person for a penalty arises by reason of the fraud of that or any other person, proceedings for the penalty may be instituted before the High Court or, in Scotland, the Court of Session as the Court of Exchequer in Scotland.

(2) Proceedings under this section which are not instituted (in England, Wales or Northern Ireland) under the Crown Proceedings Act 1947 by and in the name of the Board as an authorised department for the purposes of that Act shall be instituted—

(*a*) in England and Wales, in the name of the Attorney General,

(*b*) in Scotland, in the name of the Lord Advocate, and

(*c*) in Northern Ireland, in the name of the Attorney General for Northern Ireland.

(3) Any proceedings under this section instituted in England and Wales shall be deemed to be civil proceedings by the Crown within the meaning of Part II of the Crown Proceedings Act 1947 and any such proceedings instituted in Northern Ireland shall be deemed to be civil proceedings within the meaning of that Part of that Act as for the time being in force in Northern Ireland.

(4) If in proceedings under this section the court does not find that fraud is proved but consider that the person concerned is nevertheless liable to a penalty, the court may determine a penalty notwithstanding that, but for the opinion of the Board as to fraud, the penalty would not have been a matter for the court.][1]

Amendments—[1] Sections 100, 100A–100D substituted for s 100 by the Stamp Duty Reserve Tax (Amendment) Regulations, SI 1993/3110 regs 1, 2, 7 with effect from 1 January 1994.

101 Evidence for purposes of preceding provisions of Part X

For the purposes of the preceding provisions of this Part of this Act, any notice under regulation 6 of The Stamp Duty Reserve Tax Regulations 1986 which can no longer be varied or quashed by [a tribunal on an appeal notified to it][1] or by order of any court shall be sufficient evidence of the matters specified.

Amendments—[1] Words substituted for words "the Special Commissioners on appeal", by the Transfer of Tribunal Functions and Revenue and Customs Appeals Order, SI 2009/56 art 3, Sch 2 paras 12, 20(1), (5) with effect from 1 April 2009.

102 Mitigation of penalties

The Board may in their discretion mitigate any penalty, or stay or compound any proceedings for recovery thereof, and may also, after judgment, further mitigate or entirely remit the penalty.

[103 Time limits for penalties

(1) Where the amount of a penalty is to be ascertained by reference to tax payable by a person, the penalty may be determined by an officer of the Board, or proceedings for the penalty may be commenced before the [tribunal][2] or a court—

(*a*) at any time within six years after the date on which the penalty was incurred, or

(*b*) at any later time within three years after the final determination of the amount of tax by reference to which the amount of the penalty is to be ascertained.

(3) A penalty under section 99 of this Act may be determined by an officer of the Board, or proceedings for such a penalty may be commenced before a court, at any time within twenty years after the date on which the penalty was incurred.

(4) A penalty to which neither subsection (1) nor subsection (3) above applies may be so determined, or proceedings for such a penalty may be commenced before the [tribunal][2] or a court, at any time within six years after the date on which the penalty was incurred or began to be incurred.][1]

Amendments—[1] This section substituted by the Stamp Duty Reserve Tax (Amendment) Regulations, SI 1993/3110 regs 1, 2, 7 with effect from 1 January 1994.

[2] In sub-ss (1), (4), words substituted for words "Special Commissioners", by the Transfer of Tribunal Functions and Revenue and Customs Appeals Order, SI 2009/56 art 3, Sch 2 paras 12, 20(1), (6) with effect from 1 April 2009.

104 Saving for criminal proceedings

The provisions of this Act shall not, save so far as is otherwise provided, affect any criminal proceedings for any offence.

105 Evidence in cases of fraud or wilful default

(1) Statements made or documents produced by or on behalf of a person shall not be inadmissible in any such proceedings as are mentioned in subsection (2) below by reason only that it has been drawn to his attention that—

(*a*) in relation to tax, the Board may accept pecuniary settlements instead of instituting proceedings, and

(*b*) though no undertaking can be given as to whether or not the Board will accept such a settlement in the case of any particular person, it is the practice of the Board to be influenced by the fact that a person has made a full confession of any fraud or default to which he had been a party and has given full facilities for investigation,

and that he was or may have been induced thereby to make the statements or produce the documents.

(2) The proceedings mentioned in subsection (1) above are—

(*a*) any criminal proceedings against the person in question for any form of fraud or wilful default in connection with or in relation to tax, and

(*b*) any proceedings against him for the recovery of any sum due from him, whether by way of tax or penalty, in connection with or in relation to tax.

PART XI
MISCELLANEOUS AND SUPPLEMENTAL

Companies

108 Responsibility of company officers

(1) Everything to be done by a company under the Act shall be done by the company acting through the proper officer of the company, and service on a company of any document under or in pursuance of the Act may be effected by serving it on the proper officer.

(2) Tax for which a company which is not a body corporate, or which is a body corporate not incorporated under [any][1] enactment forming part of the law of the United Kingdom, or by Charter, is accountable or liable, may, at any time after the tax becomes due, and without prejudice to any other method of recovery, be recovered from the proper officer of the company, and that officer may retain out of any money coming into his hands on behalf of the company sufficient sums to pay that tax, and, so far as he is not so reimbursed, shall be entitled to be indemnified by the company in respect of the liability so imposed on him.

(3) For the purposes of this section—

(*a*) the proper officer of a company which is a body corporate shall be the secretary or person acting as secretary of the company, except that if a liquidator has been appointed for the company the liquidator shall be the proper officer,

(*b*) the proper officer of a company which is not a body corporate or for which there is no proper officer within paragraph (*a*) above, shall be the treasurer or the person acting as treasurer, of the company.

Amendments—[1] In sub-s (2), word substituted for words "the Companies Act 1985 or any other", by the Companies Act 2006 (Consequential Amendments) (Taxes and National Insurance) Order, SI 2009/1890 art 3(3)(*a*) with effect from 1 October 2009.

Valuation

111 Valuation of assets: power to inspect

(1) If for the purposes of the Act the Board authorise an officer of the Board to inspect any property for the purpose of ascertaining its market value the person having the custody or possession of that property shall permit the officer so authorised to inspect it at such reasonable times as the Board may consider necessary.

(2) If any person wilfully delays or obstructs an officer of the Board acting in pursuance of this section he shall be liable on summary conviction to a fine not exceeding level 1 on the standard scale as defined in section 75 of the Criminal Justice Act 1982.[1]

Amendments—[1] Section 111 repealed by the SDRT (Amendment) Regulations, SI 2010/664, regs 2, 6, with effect from 1 April 2010.

Documents

114 Want of form or errors not to invalidate notice of determination, etc

(1) A notice of determination, warrant or other proceeding which purports to be made in pursuance of any provision of the Act shall not be quashed, or deemed to be void or voidable, for want of form, or be affected by reason of a mistake, defect or omission therein, if the same is in substance and effect in conformity with or according to the intent and meaning of the Act, and if the person intended to be affected thereby is designated therein according to common intent and understanding.

(2) A notice of determination shall not be impeached or affected—

(*a*) by reason of a mistake therein as to—

(i) the name or surname of a person, or

(ii) any matter specified therein.

Interpretation

118 Interpretation

(1) In this Act, unless the context otherwise requires—

"Act" includes an Act of the Parliament of Northern Ireland and "enactment" shall be construed accordingly,

"body of persons" means any body politic, corporate or collegiate, and any company, fraternity, fellowship and society of persons, whether corporate or not corporate,

"branch or agency" means any factorship, agency, receivership, branch or management, and "branch or agent" shall be construed accordingly,

"collector" means any collector of taxes,

"company" has the meaning given by section [832(1)][1] of the principal Act (with section [468][1] of that Act),

["HMRC" means "Her Majesty's Revenue and Customs;][2]

"incapacitated person" means any infant, person of unsound mind, lunatic, idiot or insane person,

"neglect" means negligence or a failure to give any notice, make any return or to produce or furnish any document or other information required by or under the Act,

"the principal Act" means the Income and Corporation Taxes Act [1988][1]

["the TCEA 2007" means the Tribunals, Courts and Enforcement Act 2007;][2]

["tribunal" is to be read in accordance with section 47C][2].

(2) For the purposes of this Act, a person shall be deemed not to have failed to do anything required to be done within a limited time if he did it within such further time, if any, as the Board or the [tribunal][2] or officer concerned may have allowed; and where a person had a reasonable excuse for not doing anything required to be done he shall be deemed not to have failed to do it unless the excuse ceased and, after the excuse ceased, he shall be deemed not to have failed to do it if he did it without unreasonable delay after the excuse had ceased.

Amendments—[1] Numbers and year in sub-s (1) substituted by TA 1988 Sch 29 para 32 Table.

[2] In sub-s (1), definitions of "HMRC", "the TCEA 2007" and "tribunal" inserted, and in sub-s (2), word substituted for words "Special Commissioners", by the Transfer of Tribunal Functions and Revenue and Customs Appeals Order, SI 2009/56 art 3, Sch 2 paras 12, 21 with effect from 1 April 2009.

1987/516

STAMP DUTY (EXEMPT INSTRUMENTS) REGULATIONS 1987

Made by the Treasury under FA 1985 s 87(2)

Made . . . . *24th March 1987*
Laid before the House of Commons . . . . *26th March 1987*
Coming into Force . . . . *1st May 1987*

Statement of Practice SP 6/90—Conveyances and transfers of property subject to a debt: express covenants.

1 These regulations may be cited as the Stamp Duty (Exempt Instruments) Regulations 1987 and shall come into force on 1st May 1987.

[1A In these Regulations "life policy" means—

(*a*) any policy of insurance on a human life, or on the happening of a contingency dependent upon a human life, except a policy of insurance for a payment only upon the death of a person otherwise than from a natural cause, or

(*b*) a grant or contract for the payment of an annuity upon a human life.][1]

Amendments—[1] This regulation inserted by the Stamp Duty (Exempt Instruments)(Amendment) Regulations, SI 1999/2539 reg 3 with effect from 1 October 1999.

2—(1) An instrument which—

(*a*) is executed on or after 1st May 1987,

(*b*) is a kind specified in the Schedule hereto for the purposes of this regulation, and

(*c*) is certified by a certificate which fulfils the conditions of regulation 3 to be an instrument of that kind,

shall be exempt from duty under the provisions specified in paragraph (2) of this regulation.

(2) The provisions specified are—

[(*a*) the following paragraphs of Part III of Schedule 13 to the Finance Act 1999—

(i) paragraph 16 (conveyance or transfer otherwise than on sale),

(ii) paragraph 17 (declaration of use or trust),

(iii) paragraph 18 (dispositions in Scotland);][1]

(*b*) sections 83(2) and 84 (8) of the Finance Act 1985.

Amendments—[1] Para (2)(*a*) substituted by the Stamp Duty (Exempt Instruments) (Amendment) Regulations, SI 1999/2539 reg 4 with effect from 1 October 1999.

3 The certificate—

(*a*) shall be in writing and—

(i) be included as part of the instrument, or

(ii) be endorsed upon or, where separate, be physically attached to the instrument concerned;

(*b*) shall contain a sufficient description of—

(i) the instrument concerned where the certificate is separate but physically attached to the instrument, and

(ii) the category in the Schedule hereto into which the instrument falls;

(*c*)

(i) shall be signed by the transferor or grantor or by his solicitor or duly authorised agent, and

(ii) where it is not signed by the transferor or grantor or by his solicitor, it shall contain a statement by the signatory of the capacity in which he signs, that he is authorised so to sign and that he gives the certificate from his own knowledge of the facts stated in it.

Modification—The term "solicitor" to be construed as including reference to recognised bodies within the meaning of the Administration of Justice Act 1985 s 9, see the Solicitors' Incorporated Practices Order, SI 1991/2684.

4 The Schedule to these regulations shall have effect for the specification of instruments for the purposes of regulation 2.

5 An instrument which is certified in accordance with these regulations shall not be required under section 82(5) or section 84(9) of the Finance Act 1985 to be stamped in accordance with section 12 of the Stamp Act 1891 with a particular stamp denoting that it is duly stamped or that it is not chargeable with any duty.

SCHEDULE

Regulation 4

An instrument which effects any one or more of the following transactions only is an instrument specified for the purposes of regulation 2—

A. The vesting of property subject to a trust in the trustees of the trust on the appointment of a new trustee, or in the continuing trustees on the retirement of a trustee.

B. The conveyance or transfer of property the subject of a specific devise or legacy to the beneficiary named in the will (or his nominee).

C. The conveyance or transfer of property which forms part of an intestate's estate to the person entitled on intestacy (or his nominee).

D. The appropriation of property within section 84(4) of the Finance Act 1985 (death: appropriation in satisfaction of a general legacy of money) or section 84(5) or (7) of that Act (death: appropriation in satisfaction of any interest of surviving spouse [or civil partner][2] and in Scotland also of any interest of issue).

E. The conveyance or transfer of property which forms part of the residuary estate of a testator to a beneficiary (or his nominee) entitled solely by virtue of his entitlement under the will.

F. The conveyance or transfer of property out of a settlement in or towards satisfaction of a beneficiary's interest, not being an interest acquired for money or money's worth, being a conveyance or transfer constituting a distribution of property in accordance with the provisions of the settlement.

G. The conveyance or transfer of property on and in consideration only of marriage to a party to the marriage (or his nominee) or to trustees to be held on the terms of a settlement made in consideration only of the marriage.

[GG. The conveyance or transfer of property on and in consideration only of the formation of a civil partnership to a party to the civil partnership (or his nominee) or to trustees to be held on the terms of a settlement made in consideration only of the civil partnership.][2]

H. The conveyance or transfer of property within section 83(1) [or (1A)][2] of the Finance Act 1985 (transfers in connection with divorce [or dissolution of civil partnership][2] etc).

I. The conveyance or transfer by the liquidator of property which formed part of the assets of the company in liquidation to a shareholder of that company (or his nominee) in or towards satisfaction of the shareholder's rights on a winding-up.

J. The grant in fee simple of an easement in or over land for no consideration in money or money's worth.

K. The grant of a servitude for no consideration in money or money's worth.

L. The conveyance or transfer of property operating as a voluntary disposition inter vivos for no consideration in money or money's worth nor any consideration referred to in section 57 of the Stamp Act 1891 (conveyance in consideration of a debt etc).

M. The conveyance or transfer of property by an instrument within section 84(1) of the Finance Act 1985 (death: varying disposition).

[N. The declaration of any use or trust of or concerning a life policy, or property representing, or benefits arising under, a life policy.][1]

Amendments—[1] Entry N inserted by the Stamp Duty (Exempt Instruments) (Amendment) Regulations, SI 1999/2539 reg 5 with effect from 1 October 1999.

[2] Words inserted by Tax and Civil Partnership (No 2) Regulations, SI 2005/3230 reg 2, with effect from 5 December 2005 (reg 1).

1988/268

STAMP DUTY AND STAMP DUTY RESERVE TAX (DEFINITIONS OF UNIT TRUST SCHEME) REGULATIONS 1988

Made by the Treasury under FA 1946 s 57 and F(No 2)A (NI) 1946 s 28

Made . . . . 18th February 1988
Laid before the House of Commons . . . . 18th February 1988
Coming into Force . . . . 11th March 1988

Citation and commencement

1 These Regulations may be cited as the Stamp Duty and Stamp Duty Reserve Tax (Definitions of Unit Trust Scheme) Regulations 1988 and shall come into force on 11th March 1988.

Interpretation

2 In these Regulations unless the context otherwise requires—

"limited partnership" means a limited partnership registered under the Limited Partnerships Act 1907 and "general partner" and "limited partner" have the same meanings as in that Act;

"limited partnership scheme" means a unit trust scheme of the description specified in regulation 4;

"Part III" means Part III of the Finance (No 2) Act (Northern Ireland) 1946;

"Part VII" means Part VII of the Finance Act 1946;

["participant", in relation to a unit trust scheme, shall be construed in accordance with section 235 of the Financial Services and Markets Act 2000;][1]

"scheme property" means, in relation to a unit trust scheme, property of any description, including money, which is held on trust for the participants in the scheme;

"unit trust scheme" means a scheme which, apart from these Regulations, is a unit trust scheme for the purposes of Part VII or Part III as the case may be.

Amendments—[1] Definition of "participant" substituted by the Financial Services and Markets Act 2000 (Consequential Amendments) (Taxes) Order, SI 2001/3629 art 118 with effect from 1 December 2001, immediately after the coming into force of the Financial Services and Markets Act 2000 ss 411, 432(1), Sch 20 (and SI 2001/3629 Pts 1 and 2).

Exception of certain unit trust schemes from Part VII and Part III

3 A unit trust scheme which is—

(*a*) a limited partnership scheme, or

(*b*) a profit sharing scheme which has been approved in accordance with Part I of Schedule 9 to the Finance Act 1978 [or

(*c*) an employee share ownership plan approved under Schedule 8 to the Finance Act 2000,][1];

shall be treated as not being a unit trust scheme for the purposes of Part VII or Part III as the case may be.

Amendments—[1] Words inserted by the Stamp Duty and Stamp Duty Reserve Tax (Definitions of Unit Trust Scheme) (Amendment) Regulations, SI 2000/2549 with effect from 11 October 2000.

Description of a limited partnership scheme

4 A unit trust scheme is a limited partnership scheme when the scheme property is held on trust for the general partners and the limited partners in a limited partnership.

1989/1297

TAXES (INTEREST RATE) REGULATIONS 1989

Made by the Treasury under FA 1989 s 178

Made . . . .*27 July 1989*
Laid before the House of Commons . . . .*28 July 1989*
Coming into Force . . . .*18 August 1989*

Commentary—*Simon's Taxes* **A4.523, D1.1348, D1.1349; E4.632; I11.405, I11.532.**

Citation and commencement

1 These Regulations may be cited as the Taxes (Interest Rate) Regulations 1989 and shall come into force on 18th August 1989.

Interpretation

2—(1) In these Regulations unless the context otherwise requires—

["the 1998 Regulations" means the Corporation Tax (Instalment Payments Regulations 1998;][1]

"established rate" means—

(*a*) on the coming into force of these Regulations, 14 per cent per annum; and

(*b*) in relation to any date after the first reference date after the coming into force of these Regulations, the reference rate found on the immediately preceding reference date;

["operative date" means—

(*a*) the [twelfth][3] working day after the reference date, or

(*b*) where regulation 3ZA or 3BA applies—

(i) where the reference date is the first Tuesday, the day which is the Monday next following the first Tuesday, or

(ii) where the reference date is the second Tuesday, the day which is the Monday next following the second Tuesday;][2]

["reference date" means—

(*a*) the . . . [3] working day following the day on which the most recent meeting of the Monetary Policy Committee of the Bank of England took place, or

(*b*) where regulation 3ZA or 3BA applies—

(i) the day which is the Tuesday next following the day on which that meeting took place ("the first Tuesday"), and

(ii) the day which is the Tuesday ("the second Tuesday") occurring two weeks after the first Tuesday;][2]

"section 178" means section 178 of the Finance Act 1989;

"working day" means any day other than a non-business day within the meaning of section 92 of the Bills of Exchange Act 1882.

[(2) In these Regulations the reference rate found on a reference date is the official bank rate determined by the most recent meeting of the Monetary Policy Committee of the Bank of England.][3]

Amendments—[1] Words in para (1) inserted by the Taxes (Interest Rate) (Amendment No 2) Regulations, SI 1998/3176 reg 3 with effect for accounting periods ending on or after 1 July 1999 by virtue of the Finance Act 1994, Section 199 (Appointed Day) Order, SI 1998/3173 art 2.

[2] In para (1), definitions of "operative date" and "reference date" substituted by the Taxes and Duties (Interest Rate) (Amendment) Regulations, SI 2008/3234 reg 2 with effect from 7 January 2009.

[3] In definition of "operative date" word substituted for word "eleventh", in definition of "reference date" word "second" revoked, and para (2) substituted, by the Taxes and Duties (Interest Rate) (Amendment) Regulations, SI 2009/2032 regs 2, 3 with effect from 12 August 2009. Para (2) previously read as follows—

"(2) In these Regulations the reference rate found on a reference date is the percentage per annum found by averaging the base lending rates at close of business on that date of—

(*a*) Bank of Scotland,

(*b*) Barclays Bank plc,

(*c*) Lloyds Bank plc,

(*d*) Midland Bank plc,

(*e*) National Westminster Bank plc, and

(*f*) (The Royal Bank of Scotland plc,

and—

(i) where regulation 3ZA applies, if the result is not a multiple of one-quarter, rounding the result up to the nearest amount which is such a multiple,

(ii) where regulation 3BA applies, if the result is not a multiple of one-quarter, rounding the result down to the nearest amount which is such a multiple,

(iii) in any other case, if the result is not a whole number, rounding the result to the nearest such number, with any result midway between two whole numbers rounded down.".

[Applicable rate of interest equal to zero

2A *In determining the rate of interest applicable under section 178 for any purposes mentioned in these Regulations, if the result is less than zero the rate shall be treated as zero for those purposes.]*[1,2]

Amendments—[1] This para inserted by the Taxes and Duties (Interest Rate) (Amendment) Regulations, SI 2008/3234 reg 2 with effect from 7 January 2009.

[2] This reg revoked by the Taxes and Duties (Interest Rate) (Amendment) Regulations, SI 2009/2032 regs 2, 4 with effect from 12 August 2009.

[Applicable rates of interest on unpaid tax, tax repaid and repayment supplement]1

[**3**—(1) For the purposes of—

(*a*) [section 86 (except where regulation 3AA(1)(*aa*) applies) and section 88][5] of the Taxes Management Act 1970,

[(*aa*) section 59C of the Taxes Management Act 1970, as it applies to any income tax or capital gains tax which has become payable in accordance with—

(i) section 55 of that Act, so far as it relates to an amendment or an assessment referred to in paragraphs (*a*) and (*b*) of subsection (1) of that section, or

(ii) section 59B of that Act,

(*ab*) section 103A of the Taxes Management Act 1970, so far as it relates to—

(i) any person who may be required by a notice under section 8, 8A or 12AA of that Act (or under any of those sections as extended by section 12 of that Act) to make and deliver a return for a year of assessment or other period, and

(ii) income tax or capital gains tax.][3]

(*b*) [section 118F of, and paragraph 6B of Schedule 3 to][2] the Income and Corporation Taxes Act 1988, . . . [4]

[(*ba*) section 71(8A) of the Social Security Administration Act 1992 and section 69(8A) of the Social Security Administration (Northern Ireland) Act 1992, as they have effect in any case where the amount recoverable referred to in each of those sections is in respect of working families' tax credit or disabled person's tax credit, and paragraph 8 of Schedule 4 to the Tax Credits Act 1999;][6]

(*c*) paragraph 6(2)(*a*) of Schedule 1 to the Social Security Contributions and Benefits Act 1992, [. . . [7]

(*d*) section 15A of the Stamp Act 1891,][4][; and][7]

[(*e*) sections 87 and 88 of the Finance Act 2003.][7]

the rate applicable under section 178 shall, subject to paragraph (2), be 8.5 per cent per annum.

(2) Where, on a reference date after 1st January 1997, the reference rate found on that date differs from the established rate, the rate applicable under section 178 for the purposes of the enactments referred to in paragraph (1) shall, on and after the next operative date, be the percentage per annum found by applying the formula specified in paragraph (3).

(3) The formula specified in this paragraph is—

$$RR + 2.5$$

,

where RR is the reference rate referred to in paragraph (2).][1]

Note—The rate of interest under this Regulation changes periodically in accordance with the specified formula. Changes are announced by HMRC press release. The rate applicable at any given time can be obtained from *Simon's Taxes*, Binder 1 and from *Simon's Weekly Tax Intelligence*.

Amendments—[1] This regulation substituted by the Taxes (Interest Rate) (Amendment No 4) Regulations, SI 1996/3187, with effect from 31 January 1997.

[2] Words in sub-para (1)(*b*) inserted by the Taxes (Interest Rate) (Amendment No 2) Regulations, SI 1997/2707 with effect from 9 December 1997.

[3] Sub-paragraphs 3(1)(*aa*) and (*ab*) inserted by the Taxes (Interest Rate) (Amendment) Regulations, SI 1998/310, with effect from 9 March 1998.

[4] In para (1), word "and" in sub-para (*b*) revoked, word "and" in sub-para (*c*), and the whole of sub-para (*d*) inserted by the Taxes (Interest Rate) (Amendment No 3) Regulations, SI 1999/2538 reg 3 with effect from 1 October 1999.

[5] Words in para (1)(*a*) substituted by the Taxes (Interest Rate) (Amendment No 1) Regulations, SI 2001/204 reg 3, with effect from 6 March 2001. Words previously read "sections 86 and 88".

6 Para (1)(*ba*) inserted by the Taxes (Interest Rate) (Amendment No 2) Regulations, SI 2001/254 reg 3, with effect from 7 March 2001.

7 In para (1), words in sub-para (*c*) revoked, word in sub-para (*d*) inserted, and sub-para (*e*) inserted, by the Taxes (Interest Rate) (Amendment) Regulations, SI 2005/2462 regs 2, 3 with effect from 26 September 2005.

[3AA—(1) For the purposes of—

(*a*) sections 86A and 87 of the Taxes Management Act 1970,

[(*aa*) section 86 of the Taxes Management Act 1970 as it has effect in relation to accounting periods of companies ending before 1st October 1993 (interest on unpaid assessed corporation tax),][4]

(*b*) paragraph 3 of Schedule 16A to the Finance Act 1973,

(*c*) paragraphs 15 . . . [5]of Schedule 2, and paragraph 8 of Schedule 5, to the Oil Taxation Act 1975,

(d) paragraph 59 of Schedule 8 to the Development Land Tax Act 1976,[5]

(*e*) . . . [2]

(f) section 825 of, and paragraph 3 of Schedule 19A to, the Income and Corporation Taxes Act 1988,[5]

rate applicable under section 178 shall, [except where regulation 3AC applies and][3] subject to paragraph (2), [be—

(i) where paragraph (*aa*) above applies, 6.5 per cent per annum;

(ii) in all other cases, 6.25 per cent per annum.][4]

(2) Where, on a reference date after 1st January 1997, the reference rate found on that date differs from the established rate, the rate applicable under section 178 for the purposes of the enactments referred to in paragraph (1) shall, on and after the next operative date, be the percentage per annum found by applying the formula specified in paragraph (3) . . . [5].

[(3) The formula specified in this paragraph is—

$$RR + 2.5$$

,

where RR is the reference rate referred to in paragraph (2).][5]][1]

Note—The rate of interest under this Regulation changes periodically in accordance with the specified formula. Changes are announced by HMRC press release. The rate applicable at any given time can be obtained from *Simon's Taxes*, Binder 1 and from *Simon's Weekly Tax Intelligence*.

Amendments—[1] This regulation inserted by Taxes (Interest Rate) (Amendment No 4) Regulations, SI 1996/3187, with effect from 31 January 1997.

2 Sub-para (1)(*e*) revoked by the Taxes (Interest Rate) (Amendment No 3) Regulations, SI 1999/2538 reg 4 with effect from 1 October 1999.

3 Words inserted by Taxes (Interest Rate) (Amendment No 4) Regulations, SI 1999/2637 reg 4 with effect from 14 October 1999.

4 Para (1)(*aa*) inserted and words at end of para (1) substituted by the Taxes (Interest Rate) (Amendment No 1) Regulations, SI 2001/204 reg 4, with effect from 6 March 2001. Words previously read "be 6.25% per annum".

5 In para (1)(*c*), words "and 16" revoked, para (1)(*d*), (*f*) revoked, in para (2), words revoked, and para (3) substituted, by the Taxes and Duties (Interest Rate) (Amendment) Regulations, SI 2009/2032 regs 2, 5 with effect from 12 August 2009. Revoked words in para (2) previously read as follows—

"and, if the result is not a multiple of one-quarter, rounding the result down to the nearest amount which is such a multiple".

Para (3) previously read as follows—

"(3) The formula specified in this paragraph is—

$$(RR + 2.5)\frac{(100 - BR)}{100}$$

where RR is the reference rate referred to in paragraph (2) and BR is the percentage at which income tax at the basic rate is charged for the year of assessment in which the reference date referred to in that paragraph falls.".

[3AB—(1) For the purposes of—

(*a*) section 824 of the Income and Corporation Taxes Act 1988,

(*b*) paragraph 6(2)(*b*) of Schedule 1 to the Social Security Contributions and Benefits Act 1992, . . . [2]

(*c*) section 283 of the Taxation of Chargeable Gains Act 1992.

[(*d*) section 92 of the Finance Act 1986, . . . [3]

(*e*) section 110 of the Finance Act 1999,][2] [; and][3]

[(*f*) section 89 of the Finance Act 2003.][3]

the rate applicable under section 178 shall, subject to paragraph (2), be 4 per cent per annum.

(2) Where, on a reference date after 1st January 1997, the reference rate found on that date differs from the established rate, the rate applicable under section 178 for the purposes of the enactments referred to in paragraph (1) shall, on and after the next operative date, be the [higher of—

(*a*) 0.5% per annum, and

(*b*) the percentage per annum found by applying the formula specified in paragraph (3).][4]
[(3) The formula specified in this paragraph is—

$$RR - 1$$

,
where RR is the reference rate referred to in paragraph (2).][4]][1]

Note—The rate of interest under this Regulation changes periodically in accordance with the specified formula. Changes are announced by HMRC press release. The rate applicable at any given time can be obtained from *Simon's Taxes*, Binder 1 and from *Simon's Weekly Tax Intelligence*.

Amendments—[1] This regulation inserted by the Taxes (Interest Rate) (Amendment No 4) Regulations, SI 1996/3187, with effect from 31 January 1997.

[2] Word "and" in sub-para (1)(*b*) revoked, and sub-paras (1)(*d*), (*e*) inserted, by the Taxes (Interest Rate) (Amendment No 3) Regulations, SI 1999/2538 reg 5 with effect from 1 October 1999.

[3] In para (1), word in sub-para (*d*) revoked, word in sub-para (*e*) inserted, and sub-para (*f*) inserted, by the Taxes (Interest Rate) (Amendment) Regulations, SI 2005/2462 regs 2, 4 with effect from 26 September 2005.

[4] In para (2), words substituted, and para (3) substituted, by the Taxes and Duties (Interest Rate) (Amendment) Regulations, SI 2009/2032 regs 2, 7 with effect from 12 August 2009. Substituted words in para (2) previously read as follows—

"percentage per annum found by applying the formula specified in paragraph (3) and, if the result is not a multiple of one-quarter, rounding the result down to the nearest amount which is such a multiple.".

Para (3) previously read as follows—

"(3) The formula specified in this paragraph is—

$$(RR - 1) \times ((100 - BR) / 100)$$

where RR is the reference rate referred to in paragraph (2) and [BR is the percentage at which income tax at the basic rate is charged for the year of assessment in which the reference date referred to in that paragraph falls.".

[3AC—(1) For the purposes of section 87 of the Taxes Management Act 1970 in so far as it relates to tax that becomes due and payable on or after 14th October 1999, the rate applicable under section 178 shall, subject to paragraph (2), be 7.5 per cent per annum.
(2) Where on a reference date after 14th October 1999 the reference rate found on that date differs from the established rate, the rate applicable under section 178 for the purposes mentioned in paragraph (1) shall, on and after the next operative date, be the percentage per annum found by applying the formula specified in paragraph (3).
(3) The formula specified in this paragraph is—

$$RR + 2.5$$

,
where RR is the reference rate referred to in paragraph (2).][1]

Amendments—[1] This regulation inserted by Taxes (Interest Rate) (Amendment No 4) Regulations, SI 1999/2637 reg 4 with effect from 14 October 1999.

[Applicable rate of interest on overdue corporation tax

[3A—(1) For the purposes of section 87A of the Taxes Management Act 1970 the rate applicable under section 178 shall, [except where regulation 3ZA or 3ZB applies and][2] subject to paragraph(2), be 6.25 per cent per annum.
(2) Where, on a reference date after 1st October 1993, the reference rate found on that date differs from the established rate, the rate applicable under section 178 for the purposes of the enactment referred to in paragraph (1) shall, on and after the next operative date, be the percentage per annum found by applying the formula specified in paragraph (3) . . . [3]
[(3) The formula specified in this paragraph is—

$$RR + 2.5$$

,
where RR is the reference rate referred to in paragraph (2).][3]][1]

Note—The rate of interest under this Regulation changes periodically in accordance with the specified formula. Changes are announced by HMRC press release. The rate applicable at any given time can be obtained from *Simon's Taxes*, Binder 1 and from *Simon's Weekly Tax Intelligence*.

Amendments—[1] This regulation inserted by the Taxes (Interest Rate) (Amendment No 3) Regulations, SI 1993/2212 with effect from 1 October 1993.

[2] Words in para (1) inserted by the Taxes (Interest Rate) (Amendment No 2) Regulations, SI 1998/3176 reg 5 with effect for accounting periods ending on or after 1 July 1999 by virtue of FA 1994 s 199 (Appointed Day) Order, SI 1998/3173 art 2.

[3] In para (2), words revoked, and para (3) substituted, by the Taxes and Duties (Interest Rate) (Amendment) Regulations, SI 2009/2032 regs 2, 8 with effect from 12 August 2009. Revoked words in para (2) previously read as follows—

"and, if the result is not a multiple of one-quarter, rounding the result down to the nearest amount which is such a multiple.".

Para (3) previously read as follows—

"(3) The formula specified in this paragraph is—

$$RR + 2.5$$

,

where RR is the reference rate referred to in paragraph (2) and SCR is the percentage at which corporation tax at the small companies' rate is charged for the financial year in which the reference date referred to in that paragraph falls.".

[3AAA—(1) For the purposes of—

(*a*) paragraph 16 of Schedule 2 to the Oil Taxation Act 1975,

(*b*) paragraph 59 of Schedule 8 to the Development Land Tax Act 1976, and

(*c*) section 825 of, and paragraph 3 of Schedule 19A to, the Income and Corporation Taxes Act 1988,

the rate applicable under section 178 shall, subject to paragraph (3), be the percentage per annum found by applying the formula specified in paragraph (2), but if the result is not a multiple of one-quarter the result shall be rounded down to the nearest amount which is such a multiple.

(2) The formula specified for the purposes of paragraph (1) is—

$$((RR + 2.5) \times 80) / 100$$

where RR is the official bank rate determined at the meeting of the Monetary Policy Committee of the Bank of England which immediately preceded the coming into force of these Regulations.

(3) Where on a reference date after the coming into force of these Regulations, the reference rate found on that date differs from the established rate, the rate applicable under section 178 for the purposes of the enactments referred to in paragraph (1) shall, on and after the next operative date, be the higher of—

(*a*) 0.5% per annum, and

(*b*) the percentage per annum found by applying the formula specified in paragraph (4).

(4) The formula specified in this paragraph is—

$$RR - 1$$

,

where RR is the reference rate referred to in paragraph (3).][1]

Amendments—[1] Regulation inserted, by the Taxes and Duties (Interest Rate) (Amendment) Regulations, SI 2009/2032 regs 2, 6 with effect from 12 August 2009.

[3ZA—(1) For the purposes of section 87A of the Taxes Management Act 1970 in so far as it relates, by virtue of subsection (1A) of that section, to an amount or amounts treated as becoming due and payable in respect of the total liability of a large company for an accounting period ending on or after 1st July 1999 in accordance with regulation 5 of the 1998 Regulations, the rate applicable under section 178 shall, subject to paragraph (2), be 8.25 per cent per annum.

(2) Where on a reference date after 7th January 1999 the reference rate found on that date differs from the established rate, the rate applicable under section 178 for the purposes mentioned in paragraph (1) shall, on and after the next operative date and as respects the period specified in paragraph (3), be the percentage per annum found by applying the formula specified in paragraph (4).

(3) The period specified in this paragraph is any period falling between—

(*a*) the date on which the first instalment payment is treated as becoming due and payable for the accounting period concerned under regulation 5 of the 1998 Regulations, and

(*b*) the day following the expiry of nine months from the end of that accounting period,

during which any amount treated as becoming due and payable in accordance with regulation 5 of those Regulations for that accounting period remains unpaid.

(4) The formula specified in this paragraph is—

$$[RR + 1]$$

,[2]

where RR is the reference rate referred to in paragraph (2).][1]

Amendments—[1] This regulation inserted by the Taxes (Interest Rate) (Amendment No 2) Regulations, SI 1998/3176 reg 6 with effect for accounting periods ending on or after 1 July 1999 by virtue of FA 1994 s 199 (Appointed Day) Order, SI 1998/3173 art 2.

[2] Formula substituted by the Taxes (Interest Rate) (Amendment) Regulations, SI 2000/893 reg 2(1), with effect as from 20 April 2000 in relation to interest running from before that day as well as to interest running from, or from after, that day.

[3ZB—(1) For the purposes of section 87A of the Taxes Management Act 1970 in so far as it relates to an unpaid amount in respect of the total liability of a company for an accounting period ending on or after 1st July 1999, other than an amount to which regulation 3ZA applies, the rate applicable under section 178 shall, subject to paragraph (2), be 8.5 per cent per annum.

(2) Where on a reference date after 7th January 1999 the reference rate found on that date differs from the established rate, the rate applicable under section 178 for the purposes mentioned in paragraph (1) shall, on and after the next operative date, be the percentage per annum found by applying the formula specified in paragraph (3).

(3) The formula specified in this paragraph is—

$$RR + 2.5$$

,

where RR is the reference rate referred to in paragraph (2).] [1]

Amendments—[1] This regulation inserted by the Taxes (Interest Rate) (Amendment No 2) Regulations, SI 1998/3176 reg 6 with effect for accounting periods ending on or after 1 July 1999 by virtue of FA 1994 s 199 (Appointed Day) Order, SI 1998/3173 art 2.

[Applicable rate of interest on tax overpaid][1]

[3B—(1) For the purposes of section 826 of the Income and Corporation Taxes Act 1988 the rate applicable under section 178 shall, [except where regulation 3BA or 3BB applies and][2] subject to paragraph(2), be 3·25 per cent per annum.

(2) Where, on a reference date after 1st October 1993, the reference rate found on that date differs from the established rate, the rate applicable under section 178 for the purposes of the enactment referred to in paragraph (1) shall, on and after the next operative date, be the [higher of—

(*a*) 0.5% per annum, and

(*b*) the percentage per annum found by applying the formula specified in paragraph (3).][3]

[(3) The formula specified in this paragraph is—

$$RR - 1$$

,

where RR is the reference rate referred to in paragraph (2).][3]][1]

Note—The rate of interest under this Regulation changes periodically in accordance with the specified formula. Changes are announced by HMRC press release. The rate applicable at any given time can be obtained from *Simon's Taxes*, Binder 1 and from *Simon's Weekly Tax Intelligence*.

Amendments—[1] This regulation inserted by the Taxes (Interest Rate) (Amendment No 3) Regulations, SI 1993/2212 with effect from 1 October 1993.

[2] Words in para (1) inserted by the Taxes (Interest Rate) (Amendment No 2) Regulations, SI 1998/3176 reg 5 with effect for accounting periods ending on or after 1 July 1999 by virtue of FA 1994 s 199 (Appointed Day) Order, SI 1998/3173 art 2.

[3] In para (2), words substituted, and para (3) substituted, by the Taxes and Duties (Interest Rate) (Amendment) Regulations, SI 2009/2032 regs 2, 9 with effect from 12 August 2009. Substituted words in para (2) previously read as follows—

> "percentage per annum found by applying the formula specified in paragraph (3) and, if the result is not a multiple of one-quarter, rounding the result down to the nearest amount which is such a multiple.".

Para (3) previously read as follows—

> "(3) The formula specified in this paragraph is—
>
> $$RR + 2.5$$
>
> ,
>
> where RR is the reference rate referred to in paragraph (2) and CTR is the percentage at which corporation tax is charged for the financial year in which the reference date referred to in that paragraph falls.".

[3BA—(1) For the purposes of section 826 of the Income and Corporation Taxes Act 1988 in so far as it relates to an amount paid by a company in respect of its total liability for an accounting period ending on or after 1st July 1999, being an amount falling within paragraph (*d*) of subsection (1) of that section (overpayment of instalment by large company under regulation 5 of the 1998 Regulations) or an amount falling within paragraph (*e*) of that subsection (payment by company other than large company prior to the day following the expiry of nine months from the end of the accounting period concerned), the rate applicable under section 178 shall, subject to paragraph (2), be 6 per cent per annum.

(2) Where on a reference date after 7th January 1999 the reference rate found on that date differs from the established rate, the rate applicable under section 178 for the purposes mentioned in paragraph (1) shall, on and after the next operative date and as respects the period specified in paragraph (3), be the [higher of—

(*a*) 0.5% per annum, and

(*b*) the percentage per annum found by applying the formula specified in paragraph (4).][2]

(3) The period specified in this paragraph is any period falling between—

(*a*) the date on which the first instalment payment is treated as becoming due and payable for the accounting period concerned under regulation 5 of the 1998 Regulations or, in the case of a company other than a large company, the date on which the first instalment payment would be so treated if the company were a large company, and

(*b*) the day following the expiry of nine months from the end of that accounting period,

during which there exists an amount paid by the company in respect of its total liability to which paragraph (1) applies.

(4) The formula specified in this paragraph is—

$$RR - 0.25$$

,

where RR is the reference rate referred to in paragraph (2).] [1]

Amendments—[1] This regulation inserted by the Taxes (Interest Rate) (Amendment No 2) Regulations, SI 1998/3176 reg 8 with effect for accounting periods ending after 30 June 1999 by virtue of FA 1994 s 199 (Appointed Day) Order, SI 1998/3173 art 2.

[2] In para (2), words substituted, by the Taxes and Duties (Interest Rate) (Amendment) Regulations, SI 2009/2032 regs 2, 10 with effect from 12 August 2009. Substituted words in para (2) previously read as follows—

"percentage per annum found by applying the formula specified in paragraph (4).".

[3BB—(1) For the purposes of section 826 of the Income and Corporation Taxes Act 1988 in so far as it relates to an amount overpaid by a company in respect of its total liability for an accounting period ending on or after 1st July 1999, being an amount paid[, or which remains overpaid,][2] on or after the day following the expiry of nine months from the end of that period, the rate applicable under section 178 shall, subject to paragraph (2) [and on and after that day][2], be 5 per cent per annum.

(2) Where on a reference date after 7th January 1999 the reference rate found on that date differs from the established rate, the rate applicable under section 178 for the purposes mentioned in paragraph (1) shall, on and after the next operative date, be the [higher of—

(*a*) 0.5% per annum, and

(*b*) the percentage per annum found by applying the formula specified in paragraph (3).][3]

(3) The formula specified in this paragraph is—

$$RR - 1$$

,

where RR is the reference rate referred to in paragraph (2).][1]

Amendments—[1] This regulation inserted by the Taxes (Interest Rate) (Amendment No 2) Regulations, SI 1998/3176 reg 8 with effect for accounting periods ending on or after 1 July 1999 by virtue of FA 1994 s 199 (Appointed Day) Order, SI 1998/3173 art 2.

[2] Words in para (1) inserted by the Taxes (Interest Rate) (Amendment No 2) Regulations, SI 1999/1928 regs 1, 3 with effect from 28 July 1999.

[3] In para (2), words substituted, by the Taxes and Duties (Interest Rate) (Amendment) Regulations, SI 2009/2032 regs 2, 11 with effect from 12 August 2009. Substituted words in para (2) previously read as follows—

"percentage per annum found by applying the formula specified in paragraph (3).".

4 . . .

Note—This regulation is reproduced in the IHT section of this publication.

[Applicable rate of official rate of interest

5—[(1) Subject to paragraph (2), the rate applicable under section 178 for the purposes of Chapter 7 of Part 3 of the Income Tax (Earnings and Pensions) Act 2003 ("Chapter 7") shall, [on and after 6th April 2010, be 4.00 per cent per annum][4] .][3]

(2) In relation to a loan outstanding for the whole or part of a year of assessment where—

(*a*) the loan was made in the currency of a country or territory specified in the Table below,

(*b*) the benefit of the loan is obtained by reason of the employment of a person who normally lives in that country or territory, and

(*c*) that person has lived in that country or territory at some time in the period of six years ending with that year,

the rate applicable under section 178 for the purposes of [Chapter 7][3] and the date on and after which that rate has effect shall be ascertained from the entries in the Table below relating to the country or territory concerned.

TABLE

Country or territory	*Date on and after which applicable rate has effect*	*Applicable rate*
Japan	6th June 1994	3·9 per cent per annum
Switzerland	[6th July 1994][2]	[5·5 per cent per annum][2]][1]

Notes—The rate of interest under this Regulation is subject to occasional changes made by statutory instruments. The rate applicable at any given time may be obtained from *Simon's Taxes*, Binder 1 and from *Simon's Weekly Tax Intelligence*.

TA 1988 s 160 has been replaced by ITEPA 2003 s 181.

Amendments—[1] This regulation substituted by the Taxes (Interest Rate) (Amendment) Regulations, SI 1994/1307.

[2] Words and percentage in Table substituted by SI 1994/1567.

[3] Para (1) substituted, and in para (2), words substituted for words "section 181", by the Taxes (Interest Rate) (Amendment) Regulations, SI 2009/199 reg 2 with effect from 1 March 2009. Para (1) previously read as follows—

"(1) For the purposes of section 181 of the Income Tax (Earnings and Pensions) Act 2003 ("section 181") the rate applicable under section 178 shall, on and after 6th April 2007 and subject to paragraph (2), be 6.25 per cent per annum.".

[4] Words in para (1) substituted for "on and after 1st March 2009, be 4.75 per cent per annum" by the Taxes (Interest Rate) (Amendment) Regulations, SI 2010/415, with effect from 6 April 2010.

Effect of change in applicable rate

6 Where the rate applicable under section 178 for the purpose of any of the enactments referred to in [these Regulations][1] changes on an operative date by virtue of these Regulations, that change shall have effect for periods beginning on or after the operative date in relation to interest running from before that date as well as from or from after that date.

Amendments—[1] Words substituted for words "regulation 3(1) or 4(1)", by the Taxes and Duties (Interest Rate) (Amendment) Regulations, SI 2009/2032 regs 2, 14 with effect from 12 August 2009.

1992/197

STAMP DUTY AND STAMP DUTY RESERVE TAX (DEFINITION OF UNIT TRUST SCHEME) REGULATIONS 1992

Made by the Treasury under FA 1946 s 57(1A), (1B)

Made . . . . *6th February 1992*
Laid before the House of Commons . . . . *7th February 1992*
Coming into force . . . . *1st March 1992*

1 These Regulations may be cited as the Stamp Duty and Stamp Duty Reserve Tax (Definition of Unit Trust Scheme) Regulations 1992 and shall come into force on 1st March 1992.

2 A scheme made by the Lord Chancellor in exercise of the powers conferred on him by section 42(1) of the Administration of Justice Act 1982 shall be treated as not being a unit trust scheme for the purposes of Part VII of the Finance Act 1946.

1992/232

ELECTRICITY (NORTHERN IRELAND CONSEQUENTIAL AMENDMENTS) ORDER 1992

Made under the Northern Ireland Constitution Act 1973 s 38(2) 1973 as extended by paragraph 1(7) of Schedule 1 to the Northern Ireland Act 1974

Made . . . . *11 February 1992*
Coming into operation in accordance with . . . . *Article 1(2)*

Title, commencement and extent

1—(1) This Order may be cited as the Electricity (Northern Ireland Consequential Amendments) Order 1992.

(2) This Order comes into force on such day or days as may be appointed by order made under Article 1(2) of the Electricity (Northern Ireland) Order 1992.

(3) Article 2 extends to Northern Ireland only, . . .

Stamp duty exemption for certain contracts

2 Electricity shall be treated as goods for the purposes of section 59 of the Stamp Act 1891 (certain contracts chargeable as conveyances on sale).

3–5 . . .

Note—Articles 3–5 and words omitted from art 1(3) are not relevant for stamp duty.

1995/2051

STAMP DUTY RESERVE TAX ([SWX EUROPE LIMITED]) REGULATIONS 1995

Made by the Treasury under FA 1991 ss 116(3), (4) and 117

Made . . . . *1st August 1995*
Laid before the House of Commons . . . . *4th August 1995*
Coming into force . . . . *25th August 1995*

Citation and commencement

1 These Regulations may be cited as the Stamp Duty Reserve Tax ([SWX Europe Limited][1]) Regulations 1995 and shall come into force on 25th August 1995.

Amendment—[1] Words substituted by the Stamp Duty Reserve Tax (virt-x Exchange Limited) (Amendment) Regulations, SI 2008/914 reg 2 with effect from 18 April 2008.

Interpretation

2 In these Regulations unless the context otherwise requires—

"Board of directors" means the Board of directors of [SWX Europe Limited][3];

"clearing participant" means a member (as defined by this regulation) who is also a member of [a relevant clearing service][2] and who as such is permitted by the Board of directors and [the relevant clearing service][2] to clear transactions made on the Exchange for a traded security;

"client" means a person who gives instructions to a participant for equity securities to be purchased or, as the case may be, sold on the Exchange;

"equity securities" means stocks and shares which are issued or raised by a company but does not include stocks and shares issued or raised by a company not incorporated in the United Kingdom unless—

(*a*) they are registered in a register kept in the United Kingdom by or on behalf of the company, or

(*b*) in the case of shares, they are paired, within the meaning of section 99(6A) of the Finance Act 1986, with shares issued by a company incorporated in the United Kingdom;

"the Exchange" means [the exchange operated by [SWX Europe Limited][3]][1];

"member" in relation to [SWX Europe Limited][3] means a person approved by the Board of directors as a participant;

"nominee" means a person whose business is or includes holding equity securities as a nominee for [a relevant clearing service][2] acting in its capacity as a person providing clearing services in connection with a transaction made on the Exchange, or as a nominee for a clearing participant (as the case may be);

"non-clearing participant" means a participant other than a clearing participant;

"participant" means a participant in the Exchange;

["relevant clearing service" means—

(*a*) The London Clearing House Limited; or

(*b*) SIS x-clear Aktiengesellschaft for as long as it is a member (as defined by this regulation);][2]

"section 117" means section 117 of the Finance Act 1991;

. . . [1]

Amendments—[1] Words in the definition "member" substituted, and the definition of "Tradepoint" repealed by the Stamp Duty Reserve Tax (Tradepoint) (Amendment) Regulations, SI 2001/2267 reg 2(3) with effect from 25 June 2001.

[2] Words substituted in the definitions of "clearing participant" and "nominee", and the definition of "relevant clearing service" inserted; by the Stamp Duty Reserve Tax (virt-x Exchange Limited) (Amendment) Regulations, SI 2003/2078 regs 2, 3 with effect from 17 November 2003.

[3] Words in definitions of "Board of directors", "the Exchange" and "member" substituted by the Stamp Duty Reserve Tax (virt-x Exchange Limited) (Amendment) Regulations, SI 2008/914 reg 3 with effect from 18 April 2008.

Prescribed persons for the purposes of section 117

3 For the purposes of section 117—

(*a*) The London Clearing House Limited is a recognised clearing house which is prescribed;

(*b*) [SWX Europe Limited][1] is a recognised investment exchange which is prescribed and, in relation to that exchange, a member who is a clearing participant is prescribed as a description of member of that exchange.

Amendment—[1] Words in reg (3)(*b*) substituted by the Stamp Duty Reserve Tax (virt-x Exchange Limited) (Amendment) Regulations, SI 2008/914 reg 4 with effect from 18 April 2008.

Prescribed circumstances for the purposes of section 117

4—(1) In the circumstances prescribed by paragraph (2) below, a charge to stamp duty reserve tax shall be treated as not arising.

(2) The circumstances prescribed are where, in connection with a transaction made on the Exchange—

(*a*) equity securities of a particular kind are agreed to be transferred—

(i) from a clearing participant or a nominee of a clearing participant to another clearing participant or nominee, or

(ii) from a non-clearing participant or a client to a clearing participant or a nominee of a clearing participant, or

(iii) from a clearing participant or a nominee of a clearing participant to [a relevant clearing service][1] or to a nominee of [a relevant clearing service][1], or

(iv) from a person other than a clearing participant to [a relevant clearing service][1] or to a nominee of [a relevant clearing service][1], as a result of a failure by a clearing participant to fulfil his obligations in respect of the transaction concerned to transfer equity securities to [the relevant clearing service][1] or to a nominee of [the relevant clearing service][1], or

(v) from [a relevant clearing service][1] or a nominee of [a relevant clearing service][1] a clearing participant or a nominee of a clearing participant; and

(*b*) the person to whom those securities are agreed to be transferred under any of the agreements specified in sub-paragraph (*a*) above ("the relevant agreement") is required on receipt of those shares to transfer equity securities under a matching agreement to another person or, in the case of an agreement falling within paragraph (iv) of that sub-paragraph, would have been so required if the failure referred to in that paragraph had not occurred.

(3) In paragraph (2) above—

(*a*) "matching agreement" means an agreement under which—

(i) the equity securities agreed to be transferred are of the same kind as the equity securities agreed to be transferred under the relevant agreement, and

(ii) the number and transfer price of the equity securities agreed to be transferred are identical to the number and transfer price of the equity securities agreed to be transferred under the relevant agreement;

(*b*) references to [a relevant clearing service][1] are references to [a relevant clearing service][1] in its capacity as a person providing clearing services in connection with a transaction made on the Exchange;

(*c*) references to a clearing participant are references to a clearing participant in his capacity as such.

Press releases etc—Inland Revenue 4-8-95 (exemption from stamp duty reserve tax of Tradepoint).

Amendments—[1] Words in paras (2)(*a*), (3)(*b*) substituted by the Stamp Duty Reserve Tax (virt-x Exchange Limited) (Amendment) Regulations, SI 2003/2078 regs 2, 4 with effect from 17 November 2003.

Consequential provision

5—(1) Equity securities which are the subject of an agreement specified in regulation 4(2)(*a*) shall be dealt with by a clearing participant who is a party to the agreement in a separate designated account, and not otherwise.

(2) In paragraph (1) above "designated account" means an account designated by [the relevant clearing service of which the clearing participant is a member][1] for a clearing participant in connection with the equity securities concerned.

Amendments—[1] Words in para (2) substituted by the Stamp Duty Reserve Tax (virt-x Exchange Limited) (Amendment) Regulations, SI 2003/2078 regs 2, 5 with effect from 17 November 2003.

1996/1584

STAMP DUTY AND STAMP DUTY RESERVE TAX (PENSION FUNDS POOLING SCHEMES) REGULATIONS 1996

Made by the Treasury under FA 1946 s 57(1A) and F(No 2)A (NI) 1946 s 28

Made . . . . *19th June 1996*

Laid before the House of Commons . . . . *19th June 1996*

Coming into force . . . . *11th July 1996*

1 These Regulations may be cited as the Stamp Duty and Stamp Duty Reserve Tax (Pension Funds Pooling Schemes) Regulations 1996 and shall come into force on 11th July 1996.

2 In these Regulations—

"pension funds pooling scheme" means a unit trust scheme of the description specified in regulation 4 of the Income Tax (Pension Funds Pooling Schemes) Regulations 1996;

"unit trust scheme" has the meaning given by section [237(1) of the Financial Services and Markets Act 2000][1].

Amendments—[1] Words substituted by the Financial Services and Markets Act 2000 (Consequential Amendments) (Taxes) Order, SI 2001/3629 art 144 with effect from 1 December 2001, immediately after the coming into force of the Financial Services and Markets Act 2000 ss 411, 432(1), Sch 20 (and SI 2001/3629 Pts 1, 2).

3 A unit trust scheme which is a pension funds pooling scheme shall be treated as not being a unit trust scheme for the purposes of Part VII of the Finance Act 1946 or Part III of the Finance (No 2) Act (Northern Ireland) 1946 as the case may be.

1996/2348

STAMP DUTY (PRODUCTION OF DOCUMENTS) (NORTHERN IRELAND) REGULATIONS 1996

Made by the Commissioners of Inland Revenue under FA 1994 ss 244(2) and 245(1), (5), (7)

Made . . . .*9th September 1996*
Laid before the House of Commons . . . .*11th September 1996*
Coming into force . . . .*4th November 1996*

Citation and commencement

1 These Regulations may be cited as the Stamp Duty (Production of Documents) (Northern Ireland) Regulations 1996 and shall come into force on 4th November 1996.

Interpretation

2 In these Regulations unless the context otherwise requires—
"exempt instrument" shall be construed in accordance with regulation 4(1);
"grant", "lease" and "lessee" shall be construed in accordance with section 245(2) of the Finance Act 1994;
"long leasehold interest", in relation to a transaction, means a leasehold interest which, at the time of that transaction, was for a term of 25 years or more before expiry;
"registered land" has the meaning given by section 45(1) of the Interpretation Act (Northern Ireland) 1954;
"relevant instrument" means an instrument which a transferee, lessee or proposed lessee is required to produce to the Commissioners of Inland Revenue under subsection (1) of section 244;
"section 244" means section 244 of the Finance Act 1994;
"short leasehold interest", in relation to a transaction, means a leasehold interest which, at the time of that transaction, was for a term of less than 25 years before expiry.

Prescribed particulars

3 The particulars to be given in a document produced pursuant to subsection (2) of section 244 are those prescribed by the Schedule to these Regulations.

Classes of exempt instrument

4—(1) Paragraphs (2) and (3) prescribe classes of instrument which are exempt instruments for the purposes of section 245(1) of the Finance Act 1994.
(2) The class of instrument prescribed by this paragraph is any instrument effecting any transfer on sale of any freehold interest in land in Northern Ireland where the instrument has the characteristics specified in paragraph (4).
(3) The class of instrument prescribed by this paragraph is any instrument effecting any transfer on sale of any lease of land in Northern Ireland where the instrument has the characteristics specified in paragraph (4).
(4) The characteristics specified are that—
(*a*) the instrument is executed on or after 4th November 1996;
(*b*) by reason of the amount or value of the consideration for the transfer effected by the instrument, no stamp duty is chargeable on the instrument; and
(*c*) the instrument is certified in accordance with section 7(4) of the Finance Act (Northern Ireland), 1958.

Furnishing of documents relating to registered land

5—(1) This regulation applies in the case of an exempt instrument which effects a transfer—
(*a*) of land which is registered land, or
(*b*) of land which is not registered land, and the case is one in which, as a result of the transfer, the first registration of the ownership of the land becomes compulsory by virtue of section 24 of the Land Registration Act (Northern Ireland) 1970.
(2) The transferee shall produce to the Registrar of Titles with the exempt instrument such a document as is mentioned in subsection (2) of section 244 and contains the particulars prescribed by the Schedule to these Regulations; and the Registrar of Titles shall furnish that document to the Commissioner of Valuation for Northern Ireland.
(3) In paragraph (2) "the Registrar of Titles" shall be construed in accordance with section 1(4) of the Land Registration Act (Northern Ireland) 1970.

Furnishing of documents relating to unregistered land

6—(1) This regulation applies in the case of an exempt instrument which effects a transfer of land which is not registered land, and the case is one in which, as a result of the transfer, the first registration of the ownership of that land does not become compulsory by virtue of section 24 of the Land Registration Act (Northern Ireland) 1970.
(2) The transferee shall produce to the Registrar of Deeds with the exempt instrument such a document as is mentioned in subsection (2) of section 244 and contains the particulars prescribed by the Schedule to these Regulations; and the Registrar of Deeds shall furnish that document to the Commissioner of Valuation for Northern Ireland.
(3) In paragraph (2) "the Registrar of Deeds" means the officer having the control and management of the registry of deeds; and "the registry of deeds" has the meaning given by section 46(2) of the Interpretation Act (Northern Ireland) 1954.

SCHEDULE

PRESCRIBED PARTICULARS TO BE GIVEN IN A DOCUMENT PRODUCED PURSUANT TO SUBSECTION (2) OF SECTION 244 OR REGULATION 5(2) OR 6(2)

Regulations 3, 5(2), 6(2)

The particulars prescribed are particulars—

(1) of the description of the relevant instrument;
(2) of the date of the relevant instrument;
(3) of the names and addresses of the transferor and the transferee or the lessor and the lessee;
(4) of the situation and postal address of the land to which the transaction relates, including—
 (*a*) in any case relating to registered land, the Folio Number, County, Townland and Area,
 (*b*) in any case relating to unregistered land or land which is part of a Folio, the Folio Number and Townland, and
 (*c*) if necessary for the identification of the land, a photocopy of a plan indicating boundaries and areas, and stating the size of the areas and whether those areas are measured in acres or hectares;
(5) showing whether the interest transferred or granted by the transaction is a freehold interest, a long leasehold interest or a short leasehold interest;
(6) showing whether the transfer or grant relates to—
 (*a*) a dwelling house,
 (*b*) commercial property,
 (*c*) development land,
 (*d*) farmland, or
 (*e*) other land,

 and, in the case of a transfer or grant which relates to other land, specifying the nature of that other land;
(7) in any case where the transfer or grant relates to commercial property, showing whether that transfer or grant relates to a single plot of land for the construction of a dwelling;
(8) in any case where the interest transferred or granted is a freehold interest or a long leasehold interest, specifying the amount of the consideration, and in any case where that amount relates to a number of separate items, the allocation of that amount among those items;
(9) showing whether the consideration for the transaction includes value added tax, and if so the amount of that value added tax;
(10) in any case where the interest transferred or granted is a short leasehold interest, specifying—
 (*a*) the term of the lease,
 (*b*) the date of commencement of the term,
 (*c*) the rent reserved,
 (*d*) the dates on which the rent is payable,
 (*e*) any capital payment made in connection with the transfer or grant of the lease,
 (*f*) whether the lease makes provision for rent reviews, and if so the dates of those rent reviews,
 (*g*) whether the lessee is responsible for repairs and insurance,
 (*h*) whether the lessee is responsible for any other matters and, if so, specifying those other matters, and
 (*i*) any other covenants affecting the value of the lease;
(11) of any debt released by the transaction, the amount of that debt and the person to whom that debt was owed;
(12) of the name and address of any selling or letting agent;

(13) of the name of the solicitor for the transferor or lessor;

(14) in a case where the document is signed by an individual who is not the transferee, lessee or proposed lessee, of the name, address and telephone number of that individual.

1997/1156

STAMP DUTY AND STAMP DUTY RESERVE TAX (OPEN-ENDED INVESTMENT COMPANIES) REGULATIONS 1997

Made by the Treasury under FA 1995 s 152

Made . . . . *3rd April 1997*
Laid before the House of Commons . . . . *7th April 1997*
Coming into force . . . . *28th April 1997*

Citation and commencement

1 These Regulations may be cited as the Stamp Duty and Stamp Duty Reserve Tax (Open-ended Investment Companies) Regulations 1997 and shall come into force on 28th April 1997.

Interpretation

2 In these Regulations—

["authorised corporate director", "open-ended investment company", "owner of shares" and "scheme property" have the meanings given by subsection (10) of section 468 of the Income and Corporation Taxes Act 1988, read with subsections (11) to (18) of that section, as those subsections are added in relation to open-ended investment companies by regulation 10(4) of the Open-ended Investment Companies (Tax) Regulations 1997; and accordingly references in subsections (11) to (16) of that section to the "Tax Acts" shall be construed as if they included references both to the enactments relating to stamp duty and to the enactments relating to stamp duty reserve tax;][1]

"authorised unit trust" means a unit trust scheme in the case of which an order under section [243 of the Financial Services and Markets Act 2000][2] is in force;

. . .[1]

["the enactments relating to stamp duty" and "the enactments relating to stamp duty reserve tax" have the meanings given by section 152(6) of the Finance Act 1995;

"the relevant enactments relating to stamp duty or stamp duty reserve tax" means—

(*a*) sections 88(1), 90(1) to (1B), 99(5A) and (5B) of the Finance Act 1986, and

(*b*) section 122(1) and (2) of, and paragraphs 1 to 9, 14 and 17 of Schedule 19 to, the Finance Act 1999;][1]

. . .[1]

["trust instrument", "trust property", "unit", "unit holder" and "unit trust scheme" have the meanings given by paragraph 14 of Schedule 19 to the Finance Act 1999.][1]

Amendments—[1] Definitions of "the Board", "open-ended investment company" and "authorised corporate director", and "the Taxes Act" revoked, definitions "authorised corporate director", "open-ended investment company", "owner of shares" and "scheme property", and "the enactments relating to stamp duty" and "the enactments relating to stamp duty reserve tax" and "the relevant enactments relating to stamp duty or stamp duty reserve tax" inserted, and definitions of "trust instrument", "trust property", "unit", "unit holder" and "unit trust scheme" substituted for original definition "unit" and "unit trust scheme", by the Stamp Duty and Stamp Duty Reserve Tax (Open-ended Investment Companies) (Amendment No 2) Regulations, SI 1999/3261, reg 3, with effect from 6 February 2000.

[2] Words in definition of "authorised unit trust" substituted by the Financial Services and Markets Act 2000 (Consequential Amendments) (Taxes) Order, SI 2001/3629 art 167 with effect from 1 December 2001, immediately after the coming into force of the Financial Services and Markets Act 2000 ss 411, 432(1), Sch 20 (and SI 2001/3629 Pts 1 and 2).

[Stamp duty and stamp duty reserve tax treatment of open-ended investment companies

3 Subject to the modifications set out in regulations 4 to 4B, the relevant enactments relating to stamp duty or stamp duty reserve tax shall have effect in relation to open-ended investment companies in a manner corresponding to that in which they have effect in relation to unit trust schemes.][1]

Amendments—[1] This regulation substituted by the Stamp Duty and Stamp Duty Reserve Tax (Open-ended Investment Companies) (Amendment No 2) Regulations, SI 1999/3261, reg 4, with effect from 6 February 2000.

[General modifications of the relevant enactments relating to stamp duty or stamp duty reserve tax

4—(1) Subject to the modifications specified in regulations 4A and 4B, the relevant enactments relating to stamp duty or stamp duty reserve tax shall be modified as follows in relation to open-ended investment companies.

(2) References, however expressed, to—

(*a*) a unit trust scheme, or

(*b*) the trustees of a unit trust scheme,

shall have effect as if they were references to an open-ended investment company.

(3) References, however expressed, to the managers of a unit trust scheme shall have effect as if they were references to the authorised corporate director of an open-ended investment company.

(4) References, however expressed, to—

(*a*) a unit under a unit trust scheme, or

(*b*) an entitlement to a share of the trust property,

shall have effect as if they were references to a share in an open-ended investment company.

(5) References, however expressed, to—

(*a*) a unit holder, or

(*b*) a person entitled to a unit,

shall have effect as if they were references to the owner of a share in an open-ended investment company.

(6) References, however expressed, to trust property shall have effect as if they were references to scheme property.

(7) References, however expressed, to a trust instrument shall have effect as if they were references to an instrument incorporating an open-ended investment company.][1]

Amendments—[1] This regulation substituted, together with regs 4A, 4B, for original reg 4, by the Stamp Duty and Stamp Duty Reserve Tax (Open-ended Investment Companies) (Amendment No 2) Regulations, SI 1999/3261, reg 5, with effect from 6 February 2000.

[Modifications of Schedule 19 to the Finance Act 1999

4A—(1) Schedule 19 to the Finance Act 1999 shall be modified as follows in relation to open-ended investment companies.

(2) In paragraph 4—

(*a*) in sub-paragraph (1)—

(i) for the words "units of the same class as the unit in question" there shall be substituted the word "shares", and

(ii) for the words "units of that class" there shall be substituted the word "shares";

(*b*) in sub-paragraph (3) for the words "units of the class" in both places where they occur there shall be substituted the word "shares";

(*c*) in sub-paragraph (4) for the words "units of the class in question" there shall be substituted the word "shares";

(*d*) after sub-paragraph (5) there shall be added the following sub-paragraph—

"(6) Where there is more than one class of shares in an open-ended investment company, the proportionate reduction of tax under this paragraph shall be calculated as if all the shares in the company had been converted into shares of a single class."

(3) In paragraph 14—

(*a*) for sub-paragraph (2) there shall be substituted the following sub-paragraph—

"(2) 'Open-ended investment company' has, subject to paragraph 17, the meaning given by subsection (10) of section 468 of the Income and Corporation Taxes Act 1988, read with subsections (11) to (18) of that section, as those subsections are added in relation to open-ended investment companies by regulation 10(4) of the Open-ended Investment Companies (Tax) Regulations 1997; and accordingly references in subsection (11) to (16) of that section to the 'Tax Acts' shall be construed as if they included references both to the enactments relating to stamp duty and to the enactments relating to stamp duty reserve tax; and those enactments shall have effect accordingly."

(*b*) in sub-paragraph (3) the definitions of "trust instrument", "trust property", "unit" and "unit holder" shall be omitted.

(4) In paragraph 17 sub-paragraph (4) shall be omitted.][1]

Amendments—[1] This regulation substituted, together with regs 4, 4B, for original reg 4, by the Stamp Duty and Stamp Duty Reserve Tax (Open-ended Investment Companies) (Amendment No 2) Regulations, SI 1999/3261, reg 5, with effect from 6 February 2000.

[Modifications of the Finance Act 1986

4B—(1) Section 99 of the Finance Act 1986 (general interpretation provisions) shall be modified as follows in relation to open-ended investment companies.

(2) In subsection (5A) paragraph (*a*) and the word 'or' following it shall be omitted.][1]

[(3) After subsection (5B) insert—

"(5C) "Chargeable securities" does not include shares in a company which is treated as not being an open-ended investment company by regulations made under paragraph 17 of Schedule 19 to the Finance Act 1999 ("paragraph 17").

In this subsection the reference to paragraph 17 is a reference to that paragraph as it has effect in relation to open-ended investment companies by virtue of regulations 3 to 4A of the Stamp Duty and Stamp Duty Reserve Tax (Open-ended Investment Companies) Regulations 1997."][2]

Amendments—[1] This regulation substituted, together with regs 4, 4A, for original reg 4, by the Stamp Duty and Stamp Duty Reserve Tax (Open-ended Investment Companies) (Amendment No 2) Regulations, SI 1999/3261, reg 5, with effect from 6 February 2000.

[2] Para (3) inserted by the Stamp Duty and Stamp Duty Reserve Tax (Definition of Unit Trust Scheme and Open-ended Investment Company) Regulations, SI 2001/964 with effect from 6 April 2001.

Bearer securities issued by an open-ended investment company in a foreign currency

5 Bearer securities issued by an open-ended investment company in a currency other than sterling shall be treated, for the purposes of the enactments relating to stamp duty and[the enactments relating to stamp duty reserve tax][1], as if the securities had been issued in sterling.

Amendments—[1] Words substituted by the Stamp Duty and Stamp Duty Reserve Tax (Open-ended Investment Companies) (Amendment No 2) Regulations, SI 1999/3261, reg 6, with effect from 6 February 2000.

Shares in open-ended investment companies dealing in interest-bearing investments

6 . . .

Amendments—This regulation revoked by the Stamp Duty and Stamp Duty Reserve Tax (Open-ended Investment Companies) (Amendment No 2) Regulations, SI 1999/3261, reg 7, with effect from 6 February 2000.

Conversion of an authorised unit trust to an open-ended investment company—exemption from stamp duty charge

7—(1) Stamp duty shall not be chargeable on an instrument transferring any property which is subject to the trusts of an authorised unit trust ("the target trust") to an open-ended investment company ("the acquiring company") if the conditions set out in paragraph (2) are fulfilled.

(2) Those conditions are that—

(*a*) the transfer forms part of an arrangement for the conversion of an authorised unit trust to an open-ended investment company, whereby the whole of the available property of the target trust becomes the whole of the property of the acquiring company;

(*b*) under the arrangement all the units in the target trust are extinguished;

(*c*) the consideration under the arrangement consists of or includes the issue of shares ("the consideration shares") in the acquiring company to the persons who held the extinguished units;

(*d*) the consideration shares are issued to those persons in proportion to their holdings of the extinguished units; and

(*e*) the consideration under the arrangement does not include anything else other than the assumption or discharge by the acquiring company of liabilities of the trustees of the target trust.

(3) An instrument on which stamp duty is not chargeable by virtue only of this regulation shall not be taken to be duly stamped unless it is stamped with the duty to which it would be liable but for this regulation or it has, in accordance with section 12 of the Stamp Act 1891, been stamped with a particular stamp denoting that it is not chargeable with any duty.

(4) In this regulation and in regulations 8 to 10 "the whole of the available property of the target trust" means the whole of the property subject to the trusts of the target trust, other than any property which is retained for the purpose of discharging liabilities of the trustees of the target trust.

(5) For the purposes of this regulation and regulations 8 to 10 each of the parts of an umbrella scheme (and not the scheme as a whole) shall be regarded as an authorised unit trust; and "umbrella scheme" has the same meaning as in section 468 of the Income and Corporation Taxes Act 1988.

Conversion of an authorised unit trust to an open-ended investment company—exemption from stamp duty reserve tax charge

8—(1) Section 87 of the Finance Act 1986 shall not apply as regards an agreement to transfer securities which constitute property which is subject to the trusts of an authorised unit trust ("the target trust") to an open-ended investment company ("the acquiring company") if the conditions set out in paragraph (2) are fulfilled.

(2) Those conditions are that—

(*a*) the agreement forms part of an arrangement for the conversion of an authorised unit trust to an open-ended investment company, whereby the whole of the available property of the target trust becomes the whole of the property of the acquiring company;

(*b*) under the arrangement all the units in the target trust are extinguished;

(*c*) the consideration under the arrangement consists of or includes the issue of shares ("the consideration shares") in the acquiring company to the persons who held the extinguished units;

(*d*) the consideration shares are issued to those persons in proportion to their holdings of the extinguished units; and (*e*) the consideration under the arrangement does not include anything else other than the assumption or discharge by the acquiring company of liabilities of the trustees of the target trust.

(3) Where—

(*a*) stamp duty is not chargeable on an instrument by virtue of regulation 7(1), or

(*b*) section 87 of the Finance Act 1986 does not apply as regards an agreement by virtue of paragraph (1) of this regulation,

section 87 of the Finance Act 1986 shall not apply as regards an agreement, or a deemed agreement, to transfer a unit to the managers of the target trust which is made in order that the unit may be extinguished under the arrangement mentioned in regulation 7(2)(b) or, as the case may be, paragraph (2)(b) of this regulation.

Amalgamation of an authorised unit trust with an open-ended investment company—exemption from stamp duty charge

9—(1) Stamp duty shall not be chargeable on an instrument transferring any property which is subject to the trusts of an authorised unit trust ("the target trust") to an open-ended investment company ("the acquiring company") if the conditions set out in paragraph (2) are fulfilled.

(2) Those conditions are that—

(*a*) the transfer forms part of an arrangement for the amalgamation of an authorised unit trust with an open-ended investment company, whereby the whole of the available property of the target trust becomes part (but not the whole) of the property of the acquiring company;

(*b*) under the arrangement all the units in the target trust are extinguished;

(*c*) the consideration under the arrangement consists of or includes the issue of shares ("the consideration shares") in the acquiring company to the persons who held the extinguished units;

(*d*) the consideration shares are issued to those persons in proportion to their holdings of the extinguished units; and

(*e*) the consideration under the arrangement does not include anything else other than the assumption or discharge by the acquiring company of liabilities of the trustees of the target trust.

(3) An instrument on which stamp duty is not chargeable by virtue only of this section shall not be taken to be duly stamped unless it is stamped with the duty to which it would be liable but for this regulation or it has, in accordance with section 12 of the Stamp Act 1891, been stamped with a particular stamp denoting that it is not chargeable with any duty.

(4) This regulation applies to any instrument which is executed—

(*a*) on or after the date of coming into force of these Regulations; . . .[1]

(*b*) . . .[1]

Amendments—[1] Word "but" in sub-para (4)(*a*) and sub-para (4)(*b*) omitted by Stamp Duty and Stamp Duty Reserve Tax (Open-ended Investment Companies) (Amendment) Regulations, SI 1999/1467 with effect from 16 June 1999.

Amalgamation of an authorised unit trust with an open-ended investment company—exemption from stamp duty reserve tax charge

10—(1) Section 87 of the Finance Act 1986 shall not apply as regards an agreement to transfer securities which constitute property which is subject to the trusts of an authorised unit trust ("the target trust") to an open-ended investment company ("the acquiring company") if the conditions set out in paragraph (2) are fulfilled.

(2) Those conditions are that—

(*a*) the agreement forms part of an arrangement for the amalgamation of an authorised unit trust with an open-ended investment company, whereby the whole of the available property of the target trust becomes part (but not the whole) of the property of the acquiring company;

(*b*) under the arrangement all the units in the target trust are extinguished;

(*c*) the consideration under the arrangement consists of or includes the issue of shares ("the consideration shares") in the acquiring company to the persons who held the extinguished units;

(*d*) the consideration shares are issued to those persons in proportion to their holdings of the extinguished units; and

(*e*) the consideration under the arrangement does not include anything else other than the assumption or discharge by the acquiring company of liabilities of the trustees of the target trust.

(3) Where—

(*a*) stamp duty is not chargeable on an instrument by virtue of regulation 9(1), or

(*b*) section 87 of the Finance Act 1986 does not apply as regards an agreement by virtue of paragraph (1) of this regulation,

section 87 of the Finance Act 1986 shall not apply as regards an agreement, or a deemed agreement, to transfer a unit to the managers of the target trust which is made in order that the unit may be extinguished under the arrangement mentioned in regulation 9(2)(b) or, as the case may be, paragraph (2)(b) of this regulation.

(4) This regulation applies—

(*a*) to an agreement which is not conditional, if the agreement is made on or after the date of coming into force of these Regulations . . . [1]; and

(*b*) to a conditional agreement, if the condition is satisfied on or after the date of coming into force of these Regulations . . . [1].

Amendments—[1] Words "but before 1st July 1999" in sub-paras (4)(*a*)(*b*) revoked by Stamp Duty and Stamp Duty Reserve Tax (Open-ended Investment Companies) (Amendment) Regulations, SI 1999/1467 with effect from 16 June 1999.

Disapplication of section 42 of the Finance Act 1930

11 Section 42 of the Finance Act 1930 (relief from transfer stamp duty in case of transfer of property as between associated companies) shall not apply as regards any beneficial interest in property that is conveyed or transferred to or from an open-ended investment company.

Disapplication of sections 75 to 77 of the Finance Act 1986

12 Sections 75 to 77 of the Finance Act 1986 (acquisition by a company of another company's undertaking) shall not apply as regards open-ended investment companies.

1997/2428

FINANCE ACT 1997 (STAMP DUTY AND STAMP DUTY RESERVE TAX) (APPOINTED DAY) ORDER 1997

Made by the Treasury under FA 1997 ss 97(6), 98(4), 102(6) and 103(8)

Made . . . . 8th October 1997

1 This Order may be cited as the Finance Act 1997 (Stamp Duty and Stamp Duty Reserve Tax) (Appointed Day) Order 1997.

2—(1) The day appointed for the purposes of each of the enactments specified in paragraph (2) is 20th October 1997.

(2) The enactments specified are sections 97, 98, 102 and 103 of the Finance Act 1997.

1997/2429

STAMP DUTY AND STAMP DUTY RESERVE TAX (INVESTMENT EXCHANGES AND CLEARING HOUSES) REGULATIONS 1997

Made by the Treasury under FA 1991 ss 116 and 117

Made . . . . 8th October 1997

Amendment—These regulations revoked by the Stamp Duty and Stamp Duty Reserve Tax (Investment Exchanges and Clearing Houses) Regulations (No 9), SI 2009/1828, reg 6, with effect:

(a) for the purposes of the charge to stamp duty, in relation to instruments executed on or after 30 July 2009

(b) for the purposes of the charge to stamp duty reserve tax:

(i) in the case of agreements to transfer traded securities which are not conditional, in relation to agreements made on or after 30 July 2009;

(ii) in the case of agreements to transfer traded securities which are conditional, in relation to agreements where the condition is satisfied on or after that date.

Citation, commencement and effect

***1**—(1) These Regulations may be cited as the Stamp Duty and Stamp Duty Reserve Tax (Investment Exchanges and Clearing Houses) Regulations 1997 and shall come into force on 20th October 1997.*

(2) These Regulations shall have effect—

(a) as respects the charge to stamp duty, in relation to instruments executed on or after 20th October 1997;

(b) as respects the charge to stamp duty reserve tax—

(i) in the case of an agreement to transfer equity securities which is not conditional, where the agreement is made on or after 20th October 1997;

(ii) in the case of an agreement to transfer equity securities which is conditional, where the condition is satisfied on or after that date.

Interpretation

2 *In these Regulations unless the context otherwise requires—*

"the Board of directors" means the Board of directors of LIFFE (A & M);

"clearing member" means a member (as defined by this regulation) who is also a member of The London Clearing House Limited and who as such is permitted by the Board of directors and that clearing house to clear transactions made on LIFFE for an equity security;
"equity securities" means stocks and shares which are issued or raised by a company but does not include stocks and shares issued or raised by a company not incorporated in the United Kingdom unless—
(*a*) they are registered in a register kept in the United Kingdom by or on behalf of the company, or
(*b*) in the case of shares, they are paired, within the meaning of section 99(6A) of the Finance Act 1986, with shares issued by a company incorporated in the United Kingdom;
"LIFFE" means The London International Financial Futures and Options Exchange;
"LIFFE (A & M)" means LIFFE Administration and Management;
"member" means a member of LIFFE (A & M) who is recognised as such by the Board of directors;
"non-clearing member" means a member other than a clearing member;
"option" means an option to buy or sell securities which is listed by and traded on LIFFE.

Prescription of recognised investment exchange and recognised clearing house

3 *For the purposes of sections 116 and 117 of the Finance Act 1991—*
(a) LIFFE (A & M) is a recognised investment exchange which is prescribed;
(b) The London Clearing House Limited is a recognised clearing house which is prescribed.

Transfers of securities to The London Clearing House Limited—prescribed circumstances

4—*(1) In the circumstances prescribed by paragraph (2), a charge to stamp duty or to stamp duty reserve tax shall be treated as not arising.*
(2) The circumstances prescribed are where, as a result of the exercise of options, equity securities of a particular kind are transferred or issued or agreed to be transferred or issued—
(a) to The London Clearing House Limited; or
(b) to a person whose business is or includes holding such securities as a nominee for The London Clearing House Limited.
(3) References in this regulation and in regulation 5 to The London Clearing House Limited are references to that clearing house in its capacity as a person providing clearing services in connection with a transaction made on LIFFE.

Transfers of securities to or from members of LIFFE—prescribed circumstances

5—*(1) In the circumstances prescribed by paragraph (2), a charge to stamp duty or to stamp duty reserve tax shall be treated as not arising.*
(2) The circumstances prescribed are where, in order to meet an obligation to receive securities resulting from the exercise of options, equity securities of a particular kind are transferred or agreed to be transferred—
(a) from a non-clearing member or a nominee of a non-clearing member to a clearing member or a nominee of a clearing member; or
(b) from The London Clearing House Limited or a nominee of that clearing house to a clearing member or a nominee of a clearing member.
(3) References in paragraph (2) to a clearing member are references to a clearing member in his capacity as such.

Revocation of the Stamp Duty and Stamp Duty Reserve Tax (Investment Exchanges and Clearing Houses) Regulations 1992

6 *The Stamp Duty and Stamp Duty Reserve Tax (Investment Exchanges and Clearing Houses) Regulations 1992 are hereby revoked as respects instruments and agreements referred to in regulation 1(2).*

Note—This Statutory Instrument revokes the Stamp Duty and Stamp Duty Reserve Tax (Investment Exchanges and Clearing Houses) Regulations, SI 1992/570, in relation to the charge to stamp duty for instruments executed on or after 20 October 1997, and in relation to the charge to stamp duty reserve tax for the transfer of equity securities which are not conditional made on or after 20 October 1997 and for conditional transfers where the condition is satisfied on or after 20 October 1997.

1998/1517

VISITING FORCES AND ALLIED HEADQUARTERS (STAMP DUTIES) (DESIGNATION) ORDER 1998

Made under FA 1960 s 74

Made .... *24 June 1998*
Coming into force .... *24 June 1998*

1 This Order may be cited as the Visiting Forces and Allied Headquarters (Stamp Duties) (Designation) Order 1998 and shall come into force on 24th June 1998.

2 Each of the countries specified in the First Schedule to this Order and each of the allied headquarters specified in the Second Schedule to this Order is hereby designated for the purposes of section 74 of the Finance Act 1960.

FIRST SCHEDULE

Albania, Bulgaria, the Czech Republic, Estonia, Hungary, Latvia, Lithuania, Poland, Romania, the Slovak Republic, Slovenia, Spain and Sweden.

SECOND SCHEDULE

Headquarters of the Supreme Allied Commander Atlantic (SACLANT).
Headquarters Eastern Atlantic (EASTLANT).
Headquarters Maritime Air Eastern Atlantic (MARAIREASTLANT).
Headquarters Submarine Forces Eastern Atlantic (SUBEASTLANT).
Headquarters Allied Forces North Western Europe (AFNORTHWEST).
Headquarters Allied Naval Forces North Western Europe (NAVNORTHWEST).
Headquarters Allied Air Forces North Western Europe (AIRNORTHWEST).
NATO Airborne Early Warning Force Headquarters and NATO E-3A Component.

1998/1518

VISITING FORCES (STAMP DUTIES) (DESIGNATION) ORDER 1998

Made under FA 1960 s 74

Made .... *24 June 1998*
Coming into force in relation to each country specified in article 2, the date determined in accordance with .... *article 1(2)*

1—(1) This Order may be cited as the Visiting Forces (Stamp Duties) (Designation) Order 1998 and shall come into force in accordance with the following provisions of this article.

(2) This Order shall come into force, in relation to each of the countries specified in article 2, on whichever is the later of the following dates—

(*a*) the date on which its Government becomes a party to the Agreement among the States Parties to the North Atlantic Treaty and the Other States Participating in the Partnership for Peace regarding the Status of their Forces dated 19th June 1995; and

(*b*) the day after the date on which this Order is made.

(3) The date on which this Order comes into force in relation to each of the countries specified in article 2 shall be notified in the London, Edinburgh and Belfast Gazettes.

2 The following countries are hereby designated for the purposes of section 74 of the Finance Act 1960—

Armenia, Austria, Azerbaijan, Belarus, Finland, Georgia, Kazakhstan, Kyrgyzstan, the Former Yugoslav Republic of Macedonia, Moldova, Russia, Switzerland, Turkmenistan, Ukraine, and Uzbekistan.

1998/2244

GOVERNMENT OF WALES ACT 1998 (COMMENCEMENT NO 1) ORDER 1998

Made by the Secretary of State for Wales under the Government of Wales Act 1998 s 158

Made .... *1st September 1998*

1 This Order may be cited as the Government of Wales Act 1998 (Commencement No 1) Order 1998.

2 In this Order, references to "the Act" are to the Government of Wales Act 1998.

3 The date of 2nd September 1998 is appointed for the coming into force of the following provisions of the Act—

Section 130(4) and (5) (transfer of Development Board for Rural Wales staff).
Section 132(1) and (6) (preparatory work for winding-down of Development Board for Rural Wales).
Section 133(3) and (4) (Development Board for Rural Wales—consequential etc provisions).
Section 136(4) and (5) (transfer of Land Authority for Wales Staff).
Section 138(1) and (6) (preparatory work for winding-down of Land Authority for Wales).
Section 139(3) and (4) (Land Authority for Wales—consequential etc provisions).
Section 140(5) and (6) (transfer of Housing for Wales staff).
Section 142(1), (7) and (8) (preparatory work for winding-down of Housing for Wales).
Section 143(3) and (4) (Housing for Wales—consequential etc provisions).
Section 150 (abolition of Residuary Body for Wales).
Schedule 18 Part VII and section 152 so far as relating thereto (repeals relating to Residuary Body for Wales).

4 The date of 1st October 1998 is appointed for the coming into force of the following provisions of the Act—

Sections 126 to 128 including all provisions of Schedules 13 and 14 (extension of functions of Welsh Development Agency).
Section 129 including all provisions of Schedule 15, and section 130(1) to (3) (cessation of functions and transfer of property etc of Development Board for Rural Wales).
Section 131 (Development Board for Rural Wales—transitional provisions).
Section 132(2) to (5) and (7) (winding-down of Development Board for Rural Wales).
Section 133(1) and (2) (abolition of Development Board for Rural Wales).
Section 134, 135 and 136(1) to (3) (Land Authority for Wales—cessation of functions, consequential amendment and transfer of property etc).
Section 137 (Land Authority for Wales—transitional provisions).
Section 138(2) to (5) and (7) (winding-down of Land Authority for Wales).
Section 139(1) and (2) (abolition of Land Authority for Wales).
Schedule 18 Parts III to V and section 152 so far as relating thereto (repeals relating to Welsh Development Agency, Development Board for Rural Wales and Land Authority for Wales).

5 The date of 1st November 1998 is appointed for the coming into force of the following provisions of the Act—

Section 140(1) to (4) including all provisions of Schedule 16, and section 141 (Housing for Wales—transfer of functions and transitional provisions).
Section 142(2) to (6) (winding-down of Housing for Wales).
Section 143(1) and (2) (abolition of Housing for Wales).
Schedule 18 Part VI and section 152 so far as relating thereto (repeals relating to Housing for Wales).

1998/3177

EUROPEAN SINGLE CURRENCY (TAXES) REGULATIONS 1998

Made . . . . *17th December 1998*
Laid before the House of Commons . . . . *17th December 1998*
Coming into force . . . . *1st January 1999*

ARRANGEMENT OF REGULATIONS

PART I
INTRODUCTORY

PART VI
REPURCHASES AND STOCK LENDING—STAMP DUTY AND STAMP DUTY RESERVE TAX

PART I
INTRODUCTORY

Citation and commencement

1 These Regulations may be cited as the European Single Currency (Taxes) Regulations 1998 and shall come into force on 1st January 1999.

Interpretation

2—(1) In these Regulations unless the context otherwise requires—

"commodity or financial futures" has the meaning given by subsection (2)(*a*) of section 143 of the 1992 Act, and references in these Regulations to commodity or financial futures include references to a commodity or financial futures contract referred to in subsection (7)(*a*) or (*b*);

"debt", other than a debt on a security, includes a debt owed by a bank which is not in sterling and which is represented by a sum standing to the credit of a person in an account in the bank;

"derivative" means any commodity or financial futures or an option;

"ecu" shall be construed in accordance with section 95(5) of the Finance Act 1993;

"euro" means the single currency adopted or proposed to be adopted as its currency by a member State in accordance with the Treaty establishing the European Community;

"euroconversion" has the meaning given by regulation 3;

. . . [1]

"member State" means a member State other than the United Kingdom;

"participating member State" means a member State that adopts the euro as its currency;

. . . [1]

"reconventioning" in relation to a relevant asset means a change, consequent on simple redenomination, in the terms of the asset as a result of which the new terms become aligned to the prevailing terms of equivalent marketable relevant assets denominated in euro;

"relevant asset" means a debt (whether or not a debt on a security), [an option][1] or any commodity or financial futures;

"renominalisation" in relation to a relevant asset means a change, consequent on simple redenomination, in the minimum nominal amount in which the asset can be held or traded to a new round amount;

"security" has the meaning given by section 132(3)(*b*) of the 1992 Act;

"simple redenomination" means the conversion of the currency in which an asset, liability, contract or instrument is expressed from the currency of a participating member State into euro, and any rounding of the resulting amount to the nearest euro cent;

"the Taxes Act" means the Income and Corporation Taxes Act 1988;

"the 1992 Act" means the Taxation of Chargeable Gains Act 1992.

(2) In these Regulations references to an option, without more, are references to an option to which section 144 or 144A of the 1992 Act applies.

Amendments—[1] Definitions of "long-term capital asset" and "long-term capital liability", and "qualifying contract" revoked, and words in definition of "relevant asset" substituted, by the European Single Currency (Taxes) (Amendment) Regulations, SI 2002/1971 regs 2, 3 with effect for accounting periods beginning after 30 September 2002.

Definition of euroconversion

3—(1) "Euroconversion" means—

(*a*) in relation to any currency, or an amount expressed in any currency, of a participating member State, the conversion or restating of that currency or that amount into euro and any rounding of the resulting amount within a euro;

(*b*) in relation to any asset, liability, contract or instrument—

(i) the simple redenomination of that asset, liability, contract or instrument, or

(ii) in the case of a relevant asset, the simple redenomination of that asset accompanied by either or both of renominalisation and reconventioning, or

(iii) the substitution (whether by way of exchange, conversion, replacement or otherwise) for the asset, liability, contract or instrument of an equivalent replacement asset, liability, contract or instrument.

(2) An equivalent replacement asset, liability, contract or instrument means an asset, liability, contract or instrument whose amount, terms and conditions are identical to what is reasonable to assume would be the amount, terms and conditions of the original asset, liability, contract or instrument were it to undergo a simple redenomination, or (in the case of a relevant asset) a simple redenomination accompanied by either or both of renominalisation and reconventioning.

(3) For the purposes of paragraphs (1) and (2) a simple redenomination is accompanied (in the case of a relevant asset) by renominalisation or reconventioning if either—

(*a*) the renominalisation or reconventioning is effected simultaneously, or

(*b*) it is effected within a period of time following the simple redenomination which is such as to enable it reasonably to be inferred that the renominalisation or reconventioning is associated with the simple redenomination.

. . .

PART VI
REPURCHASES AND STOCK LENDING—STAMP DUTY AND STAMP DUTY RESERVE TAX

Interpretation

24 In this Part of these Regulations "capital payment" means any payment on the euroconversion of securities other than any interest, dividend or other annual payment payable in respect of the securities.

Replacement of stock in a euroconversion

25—(1) This regulation applies in a case where—

(*a*) there is an arrangement involving the transfer of stock to which subsection (1)(*a*) of section 80C of the Finance Act 1986 (repurchases and stock lending—exemption from stamp duty) applies, and

(*b*) there is a euroconversion of that stock ("the old stock"), effected wholly or in part by the issue of new stock to replace the old stock.

(2) The new stock shall be regarded, for the purposes of section 80C of the Finance Act 1986, as stock of the same kind and amount as the old stock.

Replacement of chargeable securities in a euroconversion

26—(1) This regulation applies in a case where—

(*a*) there is an arrangement involving the transfer of chargeable securities to which subsection (1)(*a*) of section 89AA of the Finance Act 1986 (repurchases and stock lending—exemption from stamp duty reserve tax) applies, and

(*b*) there is a euroconversion of those chargeable securities ("the old chargeable securities"), effected wholly or partly by the issue of new chargeable securities to replace the old chargeable securities.

(3) The new chargeable securities shall be regarded, for the purposes of section 89AA of the Finance Act 1986, as chargeable securities of the same kind and amount as the old chargeable securities.

Payment or benefit received by transferee on euroconversion

27—(1) This regulation applies in a case where—

(*a*) there is an arrangement involving the transfer of stock to which subsection (1) of section 80C of the Finance Act 1986 applies,

(*b*) a capital payment would, but for the arrangement, be received by the person referred to as B in that section or by his nominee on the euroconversion of that stock,

(*c*) neither the person referred to as A in that section nor his nominee is required under the arrangement to pay to B or to B's nominee an amount equivalent to the amount of that capital payment, and an amount equivalent to the amount of that capital payment is not required under the arrangement to be taken into account in computing the price of stock to be transferred to B or his nominee under the arrangement, and

(*d*) the amount of the capital payment would not exceed 500 euros.

(2) A shall not be regarded, for the purposes of section 80C of the Finance Act 1986, as a person to whom a benefit consisting of an amount equal to the capital payment referred to in paragraph (1) accrues as mentioned in subsection (4)(*b*) of that section.

Payment or benefit received by transferee of chargeable securities on euroconversion

28—(1) This regulation applies in a case where—

(*a*) there is an arrangement involving the transfer of chargeable securities to which subsection (1) of section 89AA of the Finance Act 1986 applies,

(*b*) a capital payment would, but for the arrangement, be received by the person referred to as Q in that section or by his nominee on the euroconversion of those chargeable securities,

(*c*) neither the person referred to as P in that section nor his nominee is required under the arrangement to pay to Q or to Q's nominee an amount equivalent to the amount of that capital payment, and an amount equivalent to the amount of that capital payment is not required under the arrangement to be taken into account in computing the price of the chargeable securities to be transferred to Q or his nominee under the arrangement, and (*d*) the amount of the capital payment would not exceed 500 euros.

(2) P shall not be regarded, for the purposes of section 89AA of the Finance Act 1986, as a person to whom a benefit consisting of an amount equal to the capital payment referred to in paragraph (1) accrues as mentioned in subsection (4)(*b*) of that section.

Renominalisation resulting in new minimum denomination in which stock can be held or traded

29—(1) This regulation applies in a case where—

(*a*) there is an arrangement involving the transfer of stock to which subsection (1) of section 80C of the Finance Act 1986 applies,

(*b*) there is a euroconversion of that stock prior to the transfer of stock under the arrangement by A or his nominee to B or his nominee as mentioned in subsection (1)(*b*) of that section,

(*c*) the aggregate nominal value (expressed in euros) of the stock transferred by B to A or his nominee as mentioned in subsection (1)(*a*) of that section, or of stock issued to replace that stock in a euroconversion is, as a result of renominalisation, not a whole multiple of the new minimum denomination in which that stock can be traded at the time of the transfer of stock referred to in sub-paragraph (*b*),

(*d*) stock the aggregate nominal value of which is equal to the largest whole multiple of the new minimum denomination which does not exceed the aggregate nominal value referred to in sub-paragraph (*c*) is required under the arrangement to be transferred by A or his nominee to B or his nominee, and

(*e*) A or his nominee is required under the arrangement to pay to B or his nominee an amount which either—

(i) is equal to the amount of what would, but for the arrangement, have been the proceeds of disposal of the remainder of the stock on the renominalisation received by B, or

(ii) is equal to the value, at the time of the transfer of stock referred to in sub-paragraph (*b*), of the remainder of the stock if the remainder could still be held at that time though not traded.

(2) Where this regulation applies, the requirement for payment of the amount specified in paragraph (1)(*e*) is to be regarded, for the purposes of section 80C of the Finance Act 1986, as equivalent to a requirement for the remainder of the stock to be transferred by A or his nominee to B or his nominee.

(3) the value referred to in paragraph (1)(*e*)(ii) is the appropriate proportion (based on nominal value) of the market value of the minimum amount of the original stock that, at the time of the transfer of stock referred to in sub-paragraph (*b*), could be traded.

(4) Where the amount calculated in accordance with sub-paragraph (*e*) of paragraph (1) does not exceed 500 euros, and the arrangement does not require payment of a sum equal to this amount, this regulation shall have effect as if the amount calculated in accordance with that sub-paragraph were nil and the requirement specified in that sub-paragraph were satisfied.

Renominalisation resulting in new minimum denomination in which chargeable securities can be held or traded

30—(1) This regulation applies in a case where—

(*a*) there is an arrangement involving the transfer of chargeable securities to which subsection (1) of section 89AA of the Finance Act 1986 applies,

(*b*) there is a euroconversion of those chargeable securities prior to the transfer of chargeable securities under the arrangement by P or his nominee to Q to his nominee as mentioned in subsection (1)(*b*) of that section,

(*c*) the aggregate nominal value (expressed in euros) of the chargeable securities transferred by Q to P or his nominee as mentioned in subsection (1)(*a*) of that section, or of chargeable securities issued to replace those chargeable securities in a euroconversion is, as a result of renominalisation, not a whole multiple of the new minimum denomination in which those chargeable securities can be traded at the time of the transfer of chargeable securities referred to sub-paragraph (*b*),

(*d*) chargeable securities the aggregate nominal value of which is equal to the largest whole multiple of the new minimum denomination which does not exceed the aggregate nominal value referred to in sub-paragraph (*c*) are required under the arrangement to be transferred by P or his nominee to Q or his nominee, and

(*e*) P or his nominee is required under the arrangement to pay to Q or his nominee an amount which either—

(i) is equal to the amount of what would, but for the arrangement, have been the proceeds of disposal of the remainder of the chargeable securities on the renominalisation received by Q, or

(ii) is equal to the value, at the time of the transfer of chargeable securities referred to in sub-paragraph (*b*), of the remainder of the chargeable securities if the remainder could still be held at that time though not traded.

(2) Where this regulation applies, the requirement for payment of the amount specified in paragraph (1)(*e*) is to be regarded, for the purposes of section 89AA of the Finance Act 1986, as equivalent to a requirement for the remainder of the chargeable securities to be transferred by P or his nominee to Q or his nominee.
(3) The value referred to in paragraph (1)(*e*)(ii) is the appropriate proportion (based on nominal value) of the market value of the minimum amount of the original chargeable securities that, at the time of the transfer of chargeable securities referred to in paragraph (1)(*b*), could be traded.
(4) Where the amount calculated in accordance with sub-paragraph (*e*) of paragraph (1) does not exceed 500 euros, and the arrangement does not require payment of a sum equal to this amount, this regulation shall have effect as if the amount calculated in accordance with that sub-paragraph were nil and the requirement specified in that sub-paragraph were satisfied.

1999/118

GOVERNMENT OF WALES ACT 1998 (COMMENCEMENT NO 3) ORDER 1999

Made by the Secretary of State for Wales under the Government of Wales Act 1998 s 158

Made . . . .*11th January 1999*

1 This Order may be cited as the Government of Wales Act 1998 (Commencement No 3) Order 1999.

2 The date of 1st February 1999 is appointed for the coming into force of the following provisions of the Government of Wales Act 1998—

Section 111(1). (Welsh Administration Ombudsman).

Schedule 9 Part I and section 111(2) so far as relating thereto. (Welsh Administration Ombudsman—appointment, staff etc.).

Schedule 12 paragraphs 1, 18, 19, 31 and 32, and section 125 so far as relating thereto. (Minor and consequential amendments).

Schedule 18 Part I in respect of the repeal in the Finance Act 1989, and section 152 so far as relating thereto. (Repeals—Welsh Administration Ombudsman and Health Service Commissioner for Wales).

1999/2383

STAMP DUTY RESERVE TAX (UK DEPOSITARY INTERESTS IN FOREIGN SECURITIES) REGULATIONS 1999

Made by the Treasury under FA 1986 s 98 and FA 1999 ss 119, 121

Made . . . .*24th August 1999*
Laid before the House of Commons . . . .*24th August 1999*
Coming into force . . . .*25th August 1999*

Citation and commencement

1 These Regulations may be cited as the Stamp Duty Reserve Tax (UK Depositary Interests in Foreign Securities) Regulations 1999 and shall come into force on 25 August 1999.

Interpretation

2 In these Regulations—

"the Board" means the Commissioners of Inland Revenue;

. . .[3]

"depositary interest" means a security which—

(*a*) consists of the rights of a person in or relating to securities of a particular kind which, or entitlements to which, are held on trust for the benefit of that person by another person, and

(*b*) under the terms of its issue, can only be transferred in accordance with regulations under [section 785 of the Companies Act 2006 (provision enabling procedures for evidencing and transferring title)][4] or by means of a transfer within section 186(1) of the Finance Act 1996 (transfer of securities to member of electronic transfer system);

"foreign securities" means securities falling within the definition of "securities" in regulation 3(1) of the Uncertificated Securities Regulations 1995 which—

(*a*) are issued or raised by a body corporate that is not incorporated, and whose central management and control is not exercised, in the United Kingdom;
(*b*) are not registered in a register kept in the United Kingdom by or on behalf of the body corporate by which they are issued or raised;
(*c*) . . . [3]
(*d*) are of the same class in the body corporate as securities which [—
(i) are listed on a recognised stock exchange, or
(ii) are of a type which would have been treated as so listed immediately before 28th November 2001;][2] . . . [1];

"the Management Act" means the Taxes Management Act 1970;
"operator" has the meaning given by regulation 2 of the principal Regulations;
["recognised stock exchange" has the meaning given by section 841 of the Income and Corporation Taxes Act 1988;][1]
"the principal Regulations" means the Stamp Duty Reserve Tax Regulations 1986;
"relevant day" has the meaning given by section 87(3) of the Finance Act 1986;
"the Schedule" means the Schedule to the principal Regulations;
"UK depositary interest" means a depositary interest which is issued in the United Kingdom or registered on a register kept in the United Kingdom.

Amendments—[1] Words in definition "foreign securities" repealed and definition of "recognised stock exchange" substituted for original definition of "recognised stock exchange overseas" by the SDRT (UK Depositary Interests in Foreign Securities) (Amendment) Regulations, SI 2000/1871 regs 3, 4 with effect from 7 August 2000.
[2] In definition of "foreign securities", in para (*d*) words substituted by the SDRT (UK Depositary Interests in Foreign Securities) (Amendment) Regulations, SI 2001/3779 reg 2 with effect from 19 December 2001.
[3] Definition of "collective investment scheme", and para (*c*) in definition of "foreign securities", revoked by the SDRT (UK Depository Interest in Foreign Securities) (Amendment) Regulations, SI 2007/12 reg 2 with effect from 1 February 2007.
[4] Words in definition of "depository interest" substituted by the Companies Act 2006 (Consequential Amendments) (Taxes and National Insurance) Order, SI 2008/954 art 48 with effect from 6 April 2008.

Exclusion of a UK depositary interest in foreign securities from the definition of "chargeable securities" in Part IV of the Finance Act 1986

3—(1) Subject to paragraph (2), a UK depositary interest in foreign securities is not a chargeable security for the purposes of Part IV of the Finance Act 1986.
(2) Paragraph (1) does not apply to an agreement to transfer a security where the security ceases to be a UK depositary interest in foreign securities on or before the relevant day.

Notice relating to UK depositary interests in foreign securities

4—(1) This regulation applies to an operator in circumstances where, for the first time, a depositary interest in a particular foreign security is issued and the operator intends to treat the depositary interest as one to which regulation 3(1) applies.
(2) An operator shall, on or before the date which is the fourteenth day following the date of issue, give notice to the Board of—
(*a*) the date of issue, and
(*b*) the depositary interest issued.
(3) A notice under this regulation shall be in such form as the Board may prescribe or authorise and shall contain such information as they may reasonably require for the purposes of the Finance Act 1986.

5, 6 (*Amend SI 1986/1711, Schedule.*)

1999/2537

STAMP DUTY (COLLECTION AND RECOVERY OF PENALTIES) REGULATIONS 1999

Made by the Treasury under FA 1999 Sch 17 paras 16 and 17

Made . . . . 9th September 1999
Laid before the House of Commons . . . . 9th September 1999
Coming into force . . . . 1st October 1999

Citation, commencement and effect

1—(1) These Regulations may be cited as the Stamp Duty (Collection and Recovery of Penalties) Regulations 1999 and shall come into force on 1st October 1999.
(2) These Regulations have effect in relation to penalties in respect of things done or omitted on or after 1st October 1999.

Interpretation

2 In these Regulations—

"the enactments relating to stamp duty" means the Stamp Act 1891 and any enactment amending, or which is to be construed as one with, that Act;

"the Management Act" means the Taxes Management Act 1970;

"stamp duty penalty" means a penalty under the enactments relating to stamp duty, other than a penalty under section 15B of the Stamp Act 1891.

The Management Act: provisions to apply

3—(1) The provisions of the Management Act specified in the first column of the Table in Part I of the Schedule to these Regulations shall apply in relation to stamp duty penalties as they apply in relation to taxes within the meaning of that Act subject to any modification specified in the second column of that Table.

(2) Any expression which is used in a provision of the Management Act as applied by this regulation, and to which a meaning is not given by that Act as so applied, shall in that provision have the same meaning as in the enactments relating to stamp duty or these Regulations.

(3) The provisions of the Management Act which are applied subject to modifications by this regulation are restated (as modified where appropriate) in Part II of the Schedule to these Regulations.

SCHEDULE

Regulation 3

PART I—

TABLE

Provision applied	*Modifications*
Section 60(1)	For the words "the tax" in the first place where they occur substitute "a stamp duty penalty"; and omit the words "or on the premises in respect of which the tax is charged,".
(2)	For the word "tax" substitute "penalty".
61	—
63	For the side-note to the section substitute "Recovery of stamp duty penalties in Scotland".
(1)	Omit the words "Subject to subsection (3) below,"; for the word "tax" in the first place where it occurs substitute "stamp duty penalty"; and in paragraph (*a*) for the word "tax" substitute "penalty".
(2)	—
63A	—
65(1)	For the words "income tax, capital gains tax or corporation tax" substitute "a stamp duty penalty".
(2)	For the word "tax" substitute "stamp duty penalties"; and for the words "under one assessment" substitute "in respect of the same act or omission".
(3)	—
(4)	—
(5)	—
66(1)	For the word "Tax" substitute "A stamp duty penalty"; and omit the words "under any assessment".
(2)	—
(3)	—
(4)	—
67(1)	For the word "tax" substitute "a stamp duty penalty"; and omit the words "under any assessment".
(1A)	—
(2)	—
68(1)	For the word "tax" in the first place where it occurs substitute "stamp duty penalty"; and for the word "tax" in the second place where it occurs substitute "penalty".

(2) —

69 For the side-note to the section substitute "Interest on stamp duty penalties". For the words from "A penalty" to "as if it were interest so charged" substitute "Interest charged under section 103A of this Act on a stamp duty penalty"; and for the words from "as if it were tax" in the first place where they occur to the end substitute "as if it were a stamp duty penalty due and payable in respect of the same act or omission as that to which the stamp duty penalty on which the interest is charged relates".

70(2) In paragraph (*a*) before the word "penalty" insert "stamp duty"; and omit the words from "under Part II, VA or X" to "under Part IX of this Act"; in paragraph (*b*) omit the words ", surcharge or interest".

103A For the side-note to the section substitute "Interest on stamp duty penalties". For the words from "penalty" to "Finance Act 1998," substitute "stamp duty penalty"; and after the words "Finance Act 1989" insert "for the purpose of section 15A of the Stamp Act 1891".

107A For the side-note to the section substitute "Trustees".

(2) Omit the word "relevant"; for the words from "liable" to "section 86 of this Act" substitute "liable to a stamp duty penalty, or to interest under section 103A of this Act on such a penalty,"; and for the words ", interest, payment or surcharge" substitute "or interest".

(3) Omit "(*a*) or (*c*)"; for the words "a relevant trustee" substitute "a trustee"; and for the words from "the relevant time" to the end substitute "the time when the act or omission which caused the penalty to become payable occurred".

108(1) For the words "Taxes Acts" in both places where they occur substitute "relevant enactments relating to stamp duty"; and omit the words from "This subsection" to the end.

(2) For the words from the beginning to "Corporation Tax Acts on" substitute "A stamp duty penalty for which"; after the word "Charter," insert "is liable,"; for the words "the tax becomes due" substitute "the penalty becomes due"; and for the words "that tax" substitute "that penalty".

(3) —

112 For the side-note to the section substitute "Loss, destruction or damage to notices of determination, etc".

(1) For the words from "assessment to tax" to "or any return" substitute "notice of determination,"; for the words "relating to tax" substitute "relating to a stamp duty penalty"; . . . [1]; for the words "in relation to tax" substitute "in relation to the penalty"; for the words "assessment or duplicate of assessment" substitute "notice of determination"; for the words "the return or" substitute "the"; omit the words "made or" in both places where they occur; for the words "charged with tax" substitute "charged with a stamp duty penalty"; and for the words from "any tax for the same chargeable period" to "so charged" substitute "an amount in respect of that same penalty".

(2) *Omit the words "General or"; and omit the word "concerned".*[1]

113 For the side-note to the section substitute "Form of determinations and other documents".

(1D) For the words "a penalty under section 100 of this Act" substitute "a stamp duty penalty".

(3) For the words from "Every assessment" to "of determination" substitute "Every determination, warrant, notice of determination"; omit the word "assessing,"; and for the words "and levying tax or determining a penalty" substitute ", levying or determining a stamp duty penalty".

114 For the side-note to the section substitute "Want of form or errors not to invalidate determinations, etc".

(1) For the words "An assessment or determination" substitute "A determination"; after the word "proceeding" insert "in relation to a stamp duty penalty"; for the words "the Taxes Acts" in both places where they occur substitute "the relevant enactments relating to stamp duty"; and omit the words "or property".

(2) For the words "An assessment or determination" substitute "A determination"; in paragraph (*a*)(ii) for the words "the description of any profits or property" substitute "the amount of the penalty"; in paragraph (*a*)(iii) for the words "the amount of the tax charged" substitute "any other matter specified therein"; and in paragraph (*b*) omit the words "assessment or".

115(1)	For the word "form" substitute "other document"; and for the words "the Taxes Acts" substitute "the relevant enactments relating to stamp duty".
(2)	For the words "the Taxes Acts" substitute "the relevant enactments relating to stamp duty"; before the words "by any officer of the Board" insert "or"; omit the words "or by or on behalf of any body of Commissioners"; in paragraph (*b*) omit the words "in the case of a company, at any other prescribed place, and"; omit the words "or any other prescribed place".
(5)	*Omit the words "the General Commissioners Regulations or".*[1]
118(1)	Omit the following definitions— "Act" "branch or agency" "chargeable gain" "chargeable period" *"the General Commissioners Regulations"*[1] "incapacitated person" "infant" "inspector" "the relevant trustees" "return" "successor" "tax" "the Taxes Acts" "the 1992 Act" "trade"; and after the definition of "the principal Act" insert the following definition— " 'the relevant enactments relating to stamp duty' means this Act and— (a) Part II of Schedule 17 to the Finance Act 1999, and (b) the Stamp Duty (Collection and Recovery of Penalties) Regulations 1999,".

Amendments—[1] In table, in entry for s 112(1), words "omit the word "inspectors,"" revoked, entries for ss 112(2), 115(5), and in entry for s 118 words "the General Commissioners Regulations", revoked, by the Transfer of Tribunal Functions and Revenue and Customs Appeals Order, SI 2009/56 art 3, Sch 2 paras 68–70 with effect from 1 April 2009.

PART II
TAXES MANAGEMENT ACT 1970

Note—This Part restates the provisions of TMA 1970, Pt VI as modified by Part I of this Schedule.

PART VI
COLLECTION AND RECOVERY

60 Issue of demand notes and receipts

(1) Every collector shall, when a stamp duty penalty becomes due and payable, make demand of the respective sums given to him in charge to collect, from the persons charged therewith, or at the places of their last abode, as the case may require.

(2) On payment of the penalty, the collector shall if so requested give a receipt.

Distraint and poinding

61 Distraint by collectors

(1) If a person neglects or refuses to pay the sum charged, upon demand made by the collector, the collector may distrain upon the goods and chattels of the person charged (in this section referred to as "the person in default").

(2) For the purpose of levying any such distress, a justice of the peace, on being satisfied by information on oath that there is reasonable ground for believing that a person is neglecting or refusing to pay a sum charged, may issue a warrant in writing authorising a collector to break open, in the daytime, any house or premises, calling to his assistance any constable.

Every such constable shall, when so required, aid and assist the collector in the execution of the warrant and in levying the distress in the house or premises.

(3) A levy or warrant to break open shall be executed by, or under the direction of, and in the presence of, the collector.

(4) A distress levied by the collector shall be kept for five days, at the costs and charges of the person in default.

(5) If the person in default does not pay the sum due, together with the costs and charges, the distress shall be appraised by one or more independent persons appointed by the collector, and shall be sold by public auction by the collector for payment of the sum due and all costs and charges.

Any overplus coming by the distress, after the deduction of the costs and charges and of the sum due, shall be restored to the owner of the goods distrained.

(6) The Treasury may by regulations make provision with respect to—

(*a*) the fees chargeable on or in connection with the levying of distress, and

(*b*) the costs and charges recoverable where distress has been levied;

and any such regulations shall be made by statutory instrument which shall be subject to annulment in pursuance of a resolution of the House of Commons.

63 Recovery of stamp duty penalties in Scotland

(1) In Scotland, where any stamp duty penalty is due and has not been paid, the sheriff, on an application by the collector accompanied by a certificate by the collector—

(*a*) stating that none of the persons specified in the application has paid the penalty due by him;

(*b*) stating that the collector has demanded payment under section 60 of this Act from each such person of the amount due by him;

(*c*) stating that 14 days have elapsed since the date of such demand without payment of the said amount; and

(*d*) specifying the amount due and unpaid by each such person,

shall grant a summary warrant in a form prescribed by Act of Sederunt authorising the recovery, by any of the diligences mentioned in subsection (2) below, of the amount remaining due and unpaid.

(2) The diligences referred to in subsection (1) above are—

[(*a*) an attachment;][1]

(*b*) an earnings arrestment;

(*c*) an arrestment and action of furthcoming or sale.

Amendments—[1] Sub-s (2)(*a*) substituted by the Debt Arrangement and Attachment (Scotland) Act 2002 s 61, Sch 3 para 37(1), (2) with effect from 30 December 2002.

63A Sheriff officer's fees and outlays

(1) Subject to subsection (2) below and without prejudice to [section 39(1) of the Debt Arrangement and Attachment (Scotland) Act 2002 (asp 17) (expenses of attachment)][1], the sheriff officer's fees, together with the outlays necessarily incurred by him, in connection with the execution of a summary warrant shall be chargeable against the debtor.

(2) No fee shall be chargeable by the sheriff officer against the debtor for collecting, and accounting to the collector for, sums paid to him by the debtor in respect of the amount owing.

Amendments—[1] In sub-s (1), words substituted by the Debt Arrangement and Attachment (Scotland) Act 2002 s 61, Sch 3 para 37(1), (3) with effect from 30 December 2002.

Court proceedings

65 Magistrates' courts

(1) Any amount due and payable by way of a stamp duty penalty which does not exceed £2,000 shall, without prejudice to any other remedy, be recoverable summarily as a civil debt by proceedings commenced in the name of the collector.

(2) All or any of the sums due in respect of stamp duty penalties from any one person and payable to any one collector (being sums which are by law recoverable summarily) may, whether or not they are due in respect of the same act or omission, be included in the same complaint, summons, order, warrant or other document required by law to be laid before justices or to be issued by justices, and every such document as aforesaid shall, as respects each such sum, be construed as a separate document and its invalidity as respects any one such sum shall not affect its validity as respects any other such sum.

(3) Proceedings under this section may be brought in England and Wales at any time within one year from the time when the matter complained of arose.

(4) It is hereby declared that in subsection (1) above the expression "recoverable summarily as a civil debt" in respect of proceedings in Northern Ireland means recoverable in proceedings under Article 62 of the Magistrates' Courts (Northern Ireland) Order 1981.

(5) The Treasury may by order made by statutory instrument increase the sum specified in subsection (1) above; and any such statutory instrument shall be subject to annulment in pursuance of a resolution of the Commons House of Parliament.

66 County courts

(1) A stamp duty penalty due and payable may, in England and Wales, and in Northern Ireland where the amount does not exceed the limit specified in Article 10(1) of the County Courts (Northern Ireland) Order 1980, without prejudice to any other remedy, be sued for and recovered from the person charged therewith as a debt due to the Crown by proceedings in a county court commenced in the name of a collector.

(2) An officer of the Board who is authorised by the Board to do so may address the court in proceedings under this section in a county court in England and Wales.

(3) In this section as it applies in Northern Ireland the expression "county court" shall mean a county court held for a division under the County Courts (Northern Ireland) Order 1980.

(4) Sections 21 and 42(2) of the Interpretation Act (Northern Ireland) 1954 shall apply as if any reference in those provisions to any enactment included a reference to this section, and Part III of the County Courts (Northern Ireland) Order 1980 (general civil jurisdiction) shall apply for the purposes of this section in Northern Ireland.

67 Inferior courts in Scotland

(1) In Scotland, a stamp duty penalty due and payable may, without prejudice to any other remedy, be sued for and recovered from the person charged therewith as a debt due to the Crown by proceedings commenced in the name of a collector in the sheriff court.

(1A) An officer of the Board who is authorised by the Board to do so may address the court in any proceedings under this section.

(2) Sections 65 and 66 above shall not apply in Scotland.

68 High Court, etc

(1) Any stamp duty penalty may be sued for and recovered from the person charged therewith in the High Court as a debt due to the Crown, or by any other means whereby any debt of record or otherwise due to the Crown can, or may at any time, be sued for and recovered, as well as by the other means specially provided by this Act for levying the penalty.

(2) All matters within the jurisdiction of the High Court under this section shall be assigned in Scotland to the Court of Session sitting as the Court of Exchequer.

Supplemental

69 Interest on stamp duty penalties

Interest charged under section 103A of this Act on a stamp duty penalty shall be treated for the purposes—

(*a*) of sections 61, 63 and 65 to 68 above, and

(*b*) of section 35(2)(*g*)(i) of the Crown Proceedings Act 1947 (rules of court to impose restrictions on set-off and counterclaim where the proceedings or set-off or counterclaim relate to taxes) and of any rules of court (including county court rules) for England and Wales or Northern Ireland, which impose such a restriction, and

(*c*) of section 35(2)(*b*) of the said Act of 1947 as set out in section 50 of that Act (which imposes corresponding restrictions in Scotland),

as if it were a stamp duty penalty due and payable in respect of the same act or omission as that to which the stamp duty penalty on which the interest is charged relates.

70 Evidence

(2) A certificate of a collector—

(*a*) that a stamp duty penalty is payable, and

(*b*) that payment of the penalty has not been made to him or, to the best of his knowledge and belief, to any other collector or to any person acting on his behalf or on behalf of another collector,

shall be sufficient evidence that the sum mentioned in the certificate is unpaid and is due to the Crown, and any document purporting to be such a certificate as is mentioned in this subsection shall be deemed to be such a certificate unless the contrary is proved.

PART X

PENALTIES, ETC

103A Interest on stamp duty penalties

A stamp duty penalty shall carry interest at the rate applicable under section 178 of the Finance Act 1989 for the purpose of section 15A of the Stamp Act 1891 from the date on which it becomes due and payable until payment.

PART XI
MISCELLANEOUS AND SUPPLEMENTAL

Settlements

107A Trustees

(2) Subject to subsection (3) below, where the trustees of a settlement are liable to a stamp duty penalty, or to interest under section 103A of this Act on such a penalty, the penalty or interest may be recovered (but only once) from any one or more of those trustees.
(3) No amount may be recovered by virtue of subsection (2) above from a person who did not become a trustee until after the time when the act or omission which caused the penalty to become payable occurred.

Companies

108 Responsibility of company officers

(1) Everything to be done by a company under the relevant enactments relating to stamp duty shall be done by the company acting through the proper officer of the company, or, except where a liquidator has been appointed for the company, through such other person as may for the time being have the express, implied or apparent authority of the company to act on its behalf for the purpose, and service on a company of any document under or in pursuance of the relevant enactments relating to stamp duty may be effected by serving it on the proper officer.
(2) A stamp duty penalty for which a company which is not a body corporate, or which is a body corporate not incorporated under [any][1] enactment forming part of the law of the United Kingdom, or by Charter, is liable, may, at any time after the penalty becomes due, and without prejudice to any other method of recovery, be recovered from the proper officer of the company, and that officer may retain out of any money coming into his hands on behalf of the company sufficient sums to pay that penalty, and, so far as he is not so reimbursed, shall be entitled to be indemnified by the company in respect of the liability so imposed on him.
(3) For the purposes of this section—

(*a*) the proper officer of a company which is a body corporate shall be the secretary or person acting as secretary of the company, except that if a liquidator has been appointed for the company the liquidator shall be the proper officer,

(*b*) the proper officer of a company which is not a body corporate or for which there is no proper officer within paragraph (*a*) above, shall be the treasurer or the person acting as treasurer, of the company.

Amendments—[1] In sub-s (2), word substituted for words "the Companies Act 1985 or any other", by the Companies Act 2006 (Consequential Amendments) (Taxes and National Insurance) Order, SI 2009/1890 art 3(3)(*a*) with effect from 1 October 2009.

112 Loss, destruction or damage to notices of determination, etc

(1) Where any notice of determination, or other document relating to a stamp duty penalty, has been lost or destroyed, or been so defaced or damaged as to be illegible or otherwise useless, [HMRC][1] may, notwithstanding anything in any enactment to the contrary, do all such acts and things as they might have done, and all acts and things done under or in pursuance of this section shall be as valid and effectual for all purposes as they would have been, if the notice of determination had not been made, or the other document had not been furnished or required to be furnished:
Provided that, where any person who is charged with a stamp duty penalty in consequence or by virtue of any act or thing done under or in pursuance of this section proves to the satisfaction of [tribunal][1] that he has already paid an amount in respect of that same penalty, relief shall be given to the extent to which the liability of that person has been discharged by the payment so made either by abatement from the charge or by repayment, as the case may require.
(2) *In this section, "the Commissioners" means, as the case may require, either the Board or the Special Commissioners.*[1]

Amendments—[1] In sub-s (1), words substituted for words "the Commissioners, collectors and other officers having powers in relation to the penalty" and "the Commissioners having jurisdiction in the case", and sub-s (2) revoked, by the Transfer of Tribunal Functions and Revenue and Customs Appeals Order, SI 2009/56 art 3, Sch 2 paras 68, 71(1), (2) with effect from 1 April 2009.

113 Form of determinations and other documents

(1D) Where an officer of the Board has decided to impose a stamp duty penalty and has taken all other decisions needed for arriving at the amount of the penalty, he may entrust to any other officer of the Board responsibility for completing the determination procedure, whether by means involving the use of a computer or otherwise, including responsibility for serving notice of the determination on the person liable to the penalty.

(3) Every determination, warrant, notice of determination or of demand, or other document required to be used in charging, collecting, levying or determining a stamp duty penalty shall be in accordance with the forms prescribed from time to time in that behalf by the Board, and a document in the form prescribed and supplied or approved by them shall be valid and effectual.

114 Want of form or errors not to invalidate determinations, etc

(1) A determination, warrant or other proceeding in relation to a stamp duty penalty which purports to be made in pursuance of any provision of the relevant enactments relating to stamp duty shall not be quashed, or deemed to be void or voidable, for want of form, or be affected by reason of a mistake, defect or omission therein, if the same is in substance and effect in conformity with or according to the intent and meaning of the relevant enactments relating to stamp duty, and if the person charged or intended to be charged or affected thereby is designated therein according to common intent and understanding.

(2) A determination shall not be impeached or affected—

(*a*) by reason of a mistake therein as to—

(i) the name or surname of a person liable, or

(ii) the amount of the penalty, or

(iii) any other matter specified therein, or

(*b*) by reason of any variance between the notice and the determination.

115 Delivery and service of documents

(1) A notice or other document which is to be served under the relevant enactments relating to stamp duty on a person may be either delivered to him or left at his usual or last known place of residence.

(2) Any notice or other document to be given, sent, served, or delivered under the relevant enactments relating to stamp duty may be served by post, and, if to be given, sent, served or delivered to or on any person by the Board, or by any officer of the Board, may be so served addressed to that person—

(*a*) at his usual or last known place of residence, or his place of business or employment, or

(*b*) in the case of a liquidator of a company, at his address for the purposes of the liquidation.

(5) Nothing in this section applies to any notice or other document required or authorised by the Special Commissioners Regulations to be sent or delivered to, or served on, any person.[1]

Amendments—[1] Sub-s (5) revoked by the Transfer of Tribunal Functions and Revenue and Customs Appeals Order, SI 2009/56 art 3, Sch 2 paras 68, 71(1), (3) with effect from 1 April 2009.

118 Interpretation

(1) In this Act, unless the context otherwise requires—

"the Board" means the Commissioners of Inland Revenue,

"body of persons" means any body politic, corporate or collegiate, and any company, fraternity, fellowship and society of persons, whether corporate or not corporate,

"collector" means any collector of taxes,

"company" has the meaning given by section 832(1) of the principal Act (with section 468 of that Act),

"the principal Act" means the Income and Corporation Taxes Act 1988,

"the relevant enactments relating to stamp duty" means this Act and—

(*a*) Part II of Schedule 17 to the Finance Act 1999, and

(*b*) the Stamp Duty (Collection and Recovery of Penalties) Regulations 1999,

"the Special Commissioners Regulations" means the Special Commissioners (Jurisdiction and Procedure) Regulations 1994.[1]

Amendments—[1] Entry for "the Special Commissioners Regulations" revoked by the Transfer of Tribunal Functions and Revenue and Customs Appeals Order, SI 2009/56 art 3, Sch 2 paras 68, 71(1), (4) with effect from 1 April 2009.

1999/3262

STAMP DUTY AND STAMP DUTY RESERVE TAX (INVESTMENT EXCHANGES AND CLEARING HOUSES) (OM LONDON EXCHANGE LIMITED) REGULATIONS 1999

Made by the Treasury under FA 1991 ss 116, 117

Made . . . . *7th December 1999*

Laid before the House of Commons . . . . *8th December 1999*

Coming into force . . . . *29th December 1999*

Citation, commencement and effect

1—(1) These Regulations may be cited as the Stamp Duty and Stamp Duty Reserve Tax (Investment Exchanges and Clearing Houses) (OM London Exchange Limited) Regulations 1999 and shall come into force on 29th December 1999.

(2) These Regulations shall have effect—

(*a*) as respects the charge to stamp duty, in relation to instruments executed on or after 29th December 1999;

(*b*) as respects the charge to stamp duty reserve tax—

(i) in the case of an agreement to transfer equity securities which is not conditional, where the agreement is made on or after 29th December 1999;

(ii) in the case of an agreement to transfer equity securities which is conditional, where the condition is satisfied on or after that date.

Interpretation

2 In these Regulations—

"clearing member" means a member who is permitted by the rules of OM London Exchange Limited to clear transactions made on that exchange for an equity security;

"equity securities" means stocks and shares which are issued or raised by a company but does not include stocks and shares issued by a company not incorporated in the United Kingdom unless—

(*a*) they are registered in a register kept in the United Kingdom by or on behalf of the company, or

(*b*) in the case of shares, they are paired, within the meaning of section 99(6A) of the Finance Act 1986, with shares issued by a company incorporated in the United Kingdom;

"member" means a member of OM London Exchange Limited who is recognised as such by the rules of that exchange;

"non-clearing member" means a member other than a clearing member;

"option" means an option to buy or sell securities which is listed by and traded on OM London Exchange Limited;

"futures contract" means a futures, or a forward, contract conferring rights and obligations to buy or sell securities which is listed by and traded on OM London Exchange Limited.

Prescription of recognised investment exchange

3 For the purposes of sections 116 and 117 of the Finance Act 1991 OM London Exchange Limited is a recognised investment exchange which is prescribed.

Transfers and issues of securities to OM London Exchange Limited—prescribed circumstances

4—(1) In the circumstances prescribed by paragraph (2), a charge to stamp duty or to stamp duty reserve tax shall be treated as not arising.

(2) The circumstances prescribed are where, as a result of the exercise of options, or under futures contracts, equity securities of a particular kind are transferred or issued or agreed to be transferred or issued—

(*a*) to OM London Exchange Limited; or

(*b*) to a person whose business is or includes holding such securities as a nominee for OM London Exchange Limited.

(3) References in this regulation and in regulation 5 to OM London Exchange Limited are references to that exchange in its capacity as a person providing clearing services in connection with a transaction made on that exchange.

Transfers of securities to or from members of OM London Exchange Limited—prescribed circumstances

5—(1) In the circumstances prescribed by paragraph (2), a charge to stamp duty or to stamp duty reserve tax shall be treated as not arising.

(2) The circumstances prescribed are where, in order to meet an obligation to receive securities resulting from the exercise of options, or under futures contracts, equity securities of a particular kind are transferred or agreed to be transferred—

(*a*) from a non-clearing member or a nominee of a non-clearing member to a clearing member or the nominee of a clearing member; or

(*b*) from OM London Exchange Limited or a nominee of OM London Exchange Limited to a clearing member or a nominee of a clearing member.

(3) In paragraph (2) references to a clearing member are references to a clearing member in his capacity as such.

1999/3263

DISTRAINT BY COLLECTORS (FEES, COSTS AND CHARGES) (STAMP DUTY PENALTIES) REGULATIONS 1999

Made by the Treasury under TMA 1970 s 61(6)

Made . . . .*7th December 1999*
Laid before the House of Commons . . . .*8th December 1999*
Coming into force . . . .*29th December 1999*

Citation, commencement and effect

1—(1) These Regulations may be cited as the Distraint by Collectors (Fees, Costs and Charges) (Stamp Duty Penalties) Regulations 1999 and shall come into force on 29th December 1999.
(2) These Regulations have effect in relation to the levying of distress under section 61 of the Taxes Management Act 1970 where, upon demand made by a collector, a person has neglected or refused to pay a sum in respect of a stamp duty penalty.

Interpretation

2 In these Regulations—
"close possession" means physical possession by the distrainor or a person acting on his behalf of the goods and chattels distrained;
"the enactments relating to stamp duty" means the Stamp Act 1891 and any enactment amending, or which is to be construed as one with, that Act;
"stamp duty penalty" means a penalty under the enactments relating to stamp duty, other than a penalty under section 15B of the Stamp Act 1891;
"walking possession" means possession in accordance with an agreement between the distrainor and the distrainee whereby, in consideration of the distrainor not remaining in close possession, the distrainor undertakes not to dispose of the goods distrained or any part thereof, or permit their removal by any person not authorised by the distrainor to remove them.

Ascertainment of fees, costs and charges

3 The fees chargeable on or in connection with the levying of distress and the costs recoverable where the distress has been levied shall be those specified in the Schedule to these Regulations, but subject to any provision of that Schedule.

Deduction of fees, costs and charges by the collector

4 The fees, costs and charges specified in the Schedule to these Regulations shall be deducted by the collector from the sums received on or in connection with the levying of distress or where distress has been levied.

Disputes as to fees, costs and charges

5—(1) In the case of dispute as to any fees chargeable, or costs and charges recoverable under the Schedule to these Regulations, the amount of those fees, costs and charges shall be taxed.
(2) Such a taxation shall be carried out by the district judge of the county court for the district in which the distress is or is intended to be levied, and he may give such directions as to the costs of taxation as he thinks fit.
(3) In the application of paragraph (2) to Northern Ireland, there shall be substituted for the words "by the district judge of the county court for the district in which the distress is or is intended to be levied" the words "by the Master (Taxing Office)".

SCHEDULE

Regulation 3

Action taken	*Fees, costs and charges*
On or in connection with the levying of distress	Fees
For making a visit to premises with a view to levying distress (whether the levy is made or not).	A sum not exceeding £12·50.
Levying distress where the total sum charged is £100 or less.	£12·50

Levying distress where the total sum charged is more than £100.	12½ per cent on the first £100 of the amount to be recovered; 4 per cent on the next £400; 2½ per cent on the next £1,500; 1 per cent on the next £8,000; ¼ per cent on any additional sum.
Where distress has been levied	*Costs and Charges*
1 Taking possession	
Where close possession is taken.	£4·50 for the day of levy only.
Where walking possession is taken.	45p per day, payable for the day the distress is levied and up to 14 days thereafter.
2 Removal and storage of goods	The reasonable costs and charges of removal and storage.
3 Appraisement	The reasonable fees, charges and expenses of the person appraising.
4 Sale	
Where the sale is held on the auctioneer's premises, for the auctioneer's commission (to include all out-of-pocket expenses other than charges for advertising, removal and storage).	15 per cent on the sum realised plus the reasonable cost of advertising, removal and storage.
Where the sale is held on the debtor's premises, for the auctioneer's commission (not to include out-of-pocket expenses or charges for advertising).	7½ per cent on the sum realised plus out-of-pocket expenses actually and reasonably incurred and the reasonable costs of advertising.

1 In any case where close possession is taken, an individual left in possession must provide his own board.

2 For the purpose of calculating any percentage fees, costs and charges, a fraction of £1 is to be reckoned as £1, but any fraction of a penny in the total amount so calculated is to be disregarded.

3 In addition to any amount authorised by this Schedule in respect of the supply of goods or services on which value added tax is chargeable there may be added a sum equivalent to value added tax at the appropriate rate on that amount.

2000/2995

STAMP DUTY AND STAMP DUTY RESERVE TAX (INVESTMENT EXCHANGES AND CLEARING HOUSES) (JIWAY LIMITED) REGULATIONS 2000

Made by the Treasury under FA 1991, ss 116 and 117

Made . . . . .8 November 2000
Laid before the House of Commons . . . . .9 November 2000
Coming into force . . . . .10 November 2000

Citation and commencement

1 These Regulations may be cited as the Stamp Duty and Stamp Duty Reserve Tax (Investment Exchanges and Clearing Houses) (Jiway Limited) Regulations 2000 and shall come into force on 10th November 2000.

Interpretation

2 In these Regulations, "equity securities" means stocks and shares which are issued or raised by a company but does not include stocks and shares issued by a company not incorporated in the United Kingdom unless—

(*a*) they are registered in a register kept in the United Kingdom by or on behalf of the company, or

(*b*) in the case of shares, they are paired, within the meaning of section 99(6A) of the Finance Act 1986, with shares issued by a company incorporated in the United Kingdom.

Prescription of recognised investment exchange

3 For the purposes of sections 116 and 117 of the Finance Act 1991, Jiway Limited is a recognised investment exchange which is prescribed.

Transfers of securities to Jiway Limited—prescribed circumstances

4—(1) In the circumstances prescribed by paragraph (2), a charge to stamp duty or to stamp duty reserve tax shall be treated as not arising.

(2) The circumstances prescribed by this paragraph are where, in connection with a transaction or transactions made or to be made on the exchange operated by Jiway Limited, equity securities are transferred or agreed to be transferred—

(*a*) to Jiway Limited; or

(*b*) to a person whose business is or includes holding equity securities as a nominee of Jiway Limited.

(3) In paragraph (2), references to Jiway Limited are references to that company in its capacity as a person providing clearing services in connection with transactions made on the exchange which it operates.

2001/255

STAMP DUTY RESERVE TAX (INVESTMENT EXCHANGES AND CLEARING HOUSES) (THE LONDON STOCK EXCHANGE) REGULATIONS 2001

Made by the Treasury under ss 116(3), (4) and 117 of FA 1991

Made . . . . *1 February 2001*
Laid before the House of Commons . . . . *2 February 2001*
Coming into force . . . . *26 February 2001*

Citation and commencement

1 These Regulations may be cited as the Stamp Duty Reserve Tax (Investment Exchanges and Clearing Houses) (The London Stock Exchange) Regulations 2001 and shall come into force on 26th February 2001.

Interpretation

2 In these Regulations unless the context otherwise requires—

"Board of directors" means the Board of directors of London Stock Exchange plc;

"clearing participant" means a member (as defined by this regulation) who is also a member of The London Clearing House Limited and who as such is permitted by the Board of directors and that clearing house to clear transactions made on the Exchange for a traded security;

"client" means a person who gives instructions to a participant for equity securities to be purchased or, as the case may be, sold on the Exchange;

"equity securities" means stocks and shares which are issued or raised by a company but does not include stocks and shares issued or raised by a company not incorporated in the United Kingdom unless—

(*a*) they are registered in a register kept in the United Kingdom by or on behalf of the company, or

(*b*) in the case of shares, they are paired, within the meaning of section 99(6A) of the Finance Act 1986, with shares issued by a company incorporated in the United Kingdom;

"the Exchange" means the London Stock Exchange;

"member" in relation to London Stock Exchange plc means a person approved by the Board of directors as a participant;

"nominee" means a person whose business is or includes holding equity securities as a nominee for The London Clearing House Limited acting in its capacity as a person providing clearing services in connection with a transaction made on the Exchange, or as a nominee for a clearing participant (as the case may be);

"non-clearing participant" means a participant other than a clearing participant;

"participant" means a participant in the Exchange;

"section 117" means section 117 of the Finance Act 1991.

Prescribed persons for the purposes of section 117

3 For the purposes of section 117—

(*a*) The London Clearing House Limited is a recognised clearing house which is prescribed;

(*b*) London Stock Exchange plc is a recognised investment exchange which is prescribed and, in relation to that exchange, a member who is a clearing participant is prescribed as a description of member of that exchange.

Prescribed circumstances for the purposes of section 117

4—(1) In the circumstances prescribed by paragraph (2) below, a charge to stamp duty reserve tax shall be treated as not arising.

(2) The circumstances prescribed are where, in connection with a transaction made on the Exchange—

(*a*) equity securities of a particular kind are agreed to be transferred—

(i) from a clearing participant or a nominee of a clearing participant to another clearing participant or nominee, or

(ii) from a non-clearing participant or a client to a clearing participant or a nominee of a clearing participant, or

(iii) from a clearing participant or a nominee of a clearing participant to The London Clearing House Limited or to a nominee of that clearing house, or

(iv) from a person other than a clearing participant to The London Clearing House Limited or to a nominee of that clearing house, as a result of a failure by a clearing participant to fulfil his obligations in respect of the transaction concerned to transfer equity securities to The London Clearing House Limited or to a nominee of that clearing house, or

(v) from The London Clearing House Limited or a nominee of that clearing house to a clearing participant or a nominee of a clearing participant; and

(*b*) the person to whom those securities are agreed to be transferred under any of the agreements specified in sub-paragraph (*a*) above ("the relevant agreement") is required on receipt of those shares to transfer equity securities under a matching agreement to another person or, in the case of an agreement falling within paragraph (iv) of that sub-paragraph, would have been so required if the failure referred to in that paragraph had not occurred.

(3) In paragraph (2) above—

(*a*) "matching agreement" means an agreement under which—

(i) the equity securities agreed to be transferred are of the same kind as the equity securities agreed to be transferred under the relevant agreement, and

(ii) the number and transfer price of the equity securities agreed to be transferred are identical to the number and transfer price of the equity securities agreed to be transferred under the relevant agreement;

(*b*) references to The London Clearing House Limited are references to that clearing house in its capacity as a person providing clearing services in connection with a transaction made on the Exchange;

(*c*) references to a clearing participant are references to a clearing participant in his capacity as such.

Consequential provision

5—(1) Equity securities which are the subject of an agreement specified in regulation 4(2)(*a*) shall be dealt with by a clearing participant who is a party to the agreement in a separate designated account, and not otherwise.

(2) In paragraph (1) above "designated account" means an account designated by The London Clearing House Limited for a clearing participant in connection with the equity securities concerned.

2001/964

STAMP DUTY AND STAMP DUTY RESERVE TAX (DEFINITION OF UNIT TRUST SCHEME AND OPEN-ENDED INVESTMENT COMPANY) REGULATIONS 2001

Made by the Treasury under FA 1986 s 98, FA 1995 s 152, and FA 1999 s 121, Sch 19 para 17

Made . . . .*14 March 2001*
Laid before the House of Commons . . . .*14 March 2001*
Coming into force . . . .*6 April 2001*

Citation and commencement

1 These Regulations may be cited as the Stamp Duty and Stamp Duty Reserve Tax (Definition of Unit Trust Scheme and Open-ended Investment Company) Regulations 2001 and shall come into force on 6th April 2001.

Interpretation

[2—(1) In these Regulations—

"feeder fund" means a feeder fund within the meaning of (and complying with the requirements) of paragraph 2 of Part 1 of Schedule 1 to the Personal Pension Schemes (Appropriate Schemes) Regulations 1997 (including a constituent part of an umbrella registered pension unit trust which is regarded as a feeder fund for the purposes of those Regulations);

"open-ended investment company" has the meaning given in section 236 of the Financial Services and Markets Act 2000;

"qualifying EEA investment company" means a company—

(*a*) which is formed under the law of an EEA State and complies with the requirements specified in [section 833(2) of the Companies Act 2006][2],

(*b*) which may lawfully offer its shares to the public in an EEA State, and

(*c*) in relation to which, on the basis of its last published annual accounts, the ratio between the company's loan capital and the value of its ordinary shares is 50% per cent or less;

"qualifying EEA open-ended investment company" means an open-ended investment company within the meaning given by section 236 of the Financial Services and Markets Act 2000 which—

(*a*) is formed under the law of an EEA state,

(*b*) is not a UCITS, and

(*c*) may lawfully offer its shares to the public in an EEA State;

"recognised scheme" has the meaning given in section 264 of the Financial Services and Markets Act 2000;

"registered pension scheme" has the meaning given in section 150(2) of the Finance Act 2004;

"registered pension unit trust" means a registered pension scheme which is an authorised unit trust scheme of a kind mentioned in Part 1 of Schedule 1 to the Personal Pension Schemes (Appropriate Schemes) Regulations 1997;

"trust instrument" has the meaning given by paragraph 14 of Schedule 19 to the Finance Act 1999;

"UCITS" means an undertaking for collective investment in transferable securities within the meaning of Article 1 of Council Directive 85/611/EEC, as last amended by European Parliament and Council Directive 2001/108/EC;

"umbrella registered pension unit trust" means a registered pension unit trust which is constituted as an umbrella fund within the meaning of the Financial Services (Regulated Scheme) Regulations 1991;

"units" and "unit trust scheme" have the meanings given by section 237 of the Financial Services and Markets Act 2000.

(2) In these Regulations "individual pension account" means an account within which investments may be held and which satisfies the following conditions:

Condition 1

The funds of the account consist only of—

(*a*) monies received from the trustees, managers or administrators of registered pension schemes, or monies held for the purposes of registered pension schemes that are designated to be held within the account, and

(*b*) income and gains arising from those monies when held as funds of the account.

Condition 2

Any monies received in accordance with Condition 1 consist of one or more of the following—

(*a*) contributions to a registered pension scheme by a member, or the employer of a member, of that registered pension scheme,

(*b*) amounts transferred to a registered pension scheme from another registered pension scheme,

(*c*) minimum contributions referred to in section 188(3)(*c*) of the Finance Act 2004,

(*d*) minimum payments within the meaning given by section 8(2) of the Pension Schemes Act 1993.

Condition 3

The funds and other assets of the account—

(*a*) are held—

(i) by the trustees, managers or administrators of the registered pension schemes whose members subscribe to the account as account holders, and

(ii) on behalf of the individual account holders as beneficial owners subject to the account rules, or

(*b*) in the case of assets consisting of units in a registered pension unit trust or, where the registered pension unit trust is an umbrella registered pension unit trust, in the respective parts of the umbrella registered pension unit trust—

(i) are registered in the names of the individual account holders, and

(ii) are issued subject to the terms of the trust deed and the rules constituting the registered pension unit trust.

Condition 4

The funds and other assets of the account are used only to provide benefits in respect of individual account holders under registered pension schemes and subject to the limits and rules of those registered pension schemes.

Condition 5

The assets of the account, other than cash awaiting investment, consist of one or more of the following investments—

(*a*) units in an authorised unit trust scheme or in a unit trust scheme that is a recognised scheme,
(*b*) shares in a qualifying EEA open-ended investment company,
(*c*) units in a UCITS formed under the laws of a member state other than the United Kingdom which has been authorised by the competent authorities of that member state and is a recognised scheme,
(*d*) shares in a body corporate which is a qualifying UK investment company,
(*e*) shares in a body corporate which is a qualifying EEA investment company,
(*f*) shares in an investment company with variable capital, and
(*g*) investments falling within paragraph 13 of Part 2 of Schedule 2 to the Financial Services and Markets Act 2000 (government and public securities).

The reference in head (*a*) to units in an authorised unit trust scheme, where the authorised unit trust scheme is an umbrella registered pension unit trust that is constituted as a feeder fund or comprises feeder funds, comprises both the units in the feeder fund or feeder funds that are issued to the individual account holder and the underlying units held by the feeder fund or feeder funds.

Condition 6

If monies are received by the account that comprise an individual's investment in more than one registered pension scheme the amount relating to each registered pension scheme is separately identified by the administrator of the account.

Condition 7

Whenever required to do so by an officer of Revenue and Customs, the administrator of the account has provided to that officer the following information—

(*a*) the names of individuals who are the account holders,
(*b*) details of the registered pension schemes of which those individuals are members,
(*c*) the amount of the funds, and the description and value of the assets, held on behalf of each account holder,
(*d*) the amount of income and gains accruing to each account holder from funds and assets held on that individual's behalf,
(*e*) transfers of funds to another individual pension account on behalf of an account holder.

Condition 8

Whenever required to do so by an officer of Revenue and Customs, the administrator of the account has enabled that officer to audit and inspect all aspects of the management and administration of the account, including records and systems relating to the management or administration of the account.][1]

Amendments—[1] Regulation 2 substituted by the Stamp Duty and Stamp Duty Reserve Tax (Definition of Unit Trust Scheme and Open-ended Investment Company) (Amendment) Regulations, SI 2006/746 with effect from 6 April 2006.

[2] In para (1), words in definition of "qualifying EEA investment company" substituted by the Companies Act 2006 (Consequential Amendments) (Taxes and National Insurance) Order, SI 2008/954 art 49 with effect from 6 April 2008.

Schemes to be treated as not being unit trust schemes

3—(1) A scheme of the description specified in paragraph (2) shall be treated as not being a unit trust scheme for the purposes of the enactments relating to stamp duty and the enactments relating to stamp duty reserve tax.

(2) The description of scheme specified in this paragraph is a unit trust scheme the units under which are required by the terms of the trust instrument to be held only within individual pension accounts.

Companies to be treated as not being open-ended investment companies

4—(1) A company of the description specified in paragraph (2) shall be treated as not being an open-ended investment company for the purposes of the enactments relating to stamp duty and the enactments relating to stamp duty reserve tax.

(2) The description of company specified in this paragraph is an open-ended investment company the shares in which are required by the terms of the instrument incorporating the company to be held only within individual pension accounts.

Amendments to the Stamp Duty Reserve Tax Regulations 1986

5 (*amends* the Stamp Duty Reserve Tax Regulations, SI 1986/1711).

Amendment to the Stamp Duty and Stamp Duty Reserve Tax (Open-ended Investment Companies) Regulations 1997

6 (*amends* the Stamp Duty and Stamp Duty Reserve Tax (Open-ended Investment Companies) Regulations, SI 1997/1156).

2001/3746

VARIATION OF STAMP DUTIES REGULATIONS 2001

Made by the Treasury under FA 2000 Sch 33 para 1

Amendments—These regulations revoked by the Stamp Duty (Disadvantaged Areas) (Application of Exemptions) Regulations, SI 2003/1056 reg 8 with effect for instruments executed after 9 April 2003.

2001/3747

STAMP DUTY (DISADVANTAGED AREAS) REGULATIONS 2001

Made by the Treasury under FA 2001 s 92(4) and (9)

Made . . . . *29 November 2001*
Laid before the House of Commons . . . . *29 November 2001*
Coming into force . . . . *30 November 2001*

Citation and commencement

1 These Regulations may be cited as the Stamp Duty (Disadvantaged Areas) Regulations 2001 and shall come into force on 30th November 2001.

Designation of disadvantaged areas

2 The following are designated as disadvantaged areas for the purposes of section 92 of, and Schedule 30 to, the Finance Act 2001—

(*a*) the areas in England specified in Schedule 1 to these Regulations;
(*b*) the areas in Wales specified in Schedule 2 to these Regulations;
(*c*) the areas in Scotland specified in Schedule 3 to these Regulations;
(*d*) the areas in Northern Ireland specified in Schedule 4 to these Regulations.

TABLE A—ENGLAND—EAST MIDLANDS
TABLE B—EASTERN ENGLAND
TABLE C—ENGLAND—LONDON
TABLE D—NORTH EASTERN ENGLAND
TABLE E—NORTH WESTERN ENGLAND
TABLE F—SOUTH EASTERN ENGLAND
TABLE G—SOUTH WESTERN ENGLAND
TABLE H—ENGLAND—WEST MIDLANDS
TABLE I—ENGLAND—YORKSHIRE AND HUMBERSIDE
TABLE J—WALES
TABLE K—SCOTLAND
TABLE L—NORTHERN IRELAND

SCHEDULE 1

Regulation 2

AREAS IN ENGLAND DESIGNATED AS DISADVANTAGED AREAS

The areas in England specified in this Schedule are—

(*a*) the wards and electoral divisions, as at 7th May 1998, which are—
  (i) listed as wards in the Index of Multiple Deprivation 2000 published by the Department of the Environment, Transport and the Regions, and
  (ii) listed in Tables A to I below; and
(*b*) any land which—
  (i) as at 7th May 1998, did not fall within any of the wards and electoral divisions mentioned in paragraph (*a*), but
  (ii) as at 27th November 2001, had a postcode which was identical to the full postcode of land which, as at 7th May 1998, did fall within one of those wards and electoral divisions.

TABLE A—ENGLAND—EAST MIDLANDS

Local authority	*Ward*
Amber Valley	Aldercar
	Alfreton West
Ashfield	Kirkby in Ashfield East
	Sutton in Ashfield East
	Sutton in Ashfield Central
	Kirkby in Ashfield West
	Kirkby in Ashfield Central
	Sutton in Ashfield West
Bassetlaw	Worksop South East
	Rampton
	Hodsock
	Harworth East
	Harworth West
	East Retford North
Bolsover	Shirebrook North-West
	Scarcliffe North
	Shirebrook South
	Shirebrook North
	Shirebrook East
	Elmton-with-Creswell
	Bolsover Central
	Scarcliffe East
	Shirebrook South-West
	Pleasley
	Bolsover North
	Bolsover West
	Ault Hucknall
	Whitwell
Boston	Fenside
	Holland Fen
Broxtowe	Eastwood South
Chesterfield	Markham
	Rother
	Middlecroft
	St. Helen's
	Barrow Hill and Hollingwood
	Lowgates and Woodthorpe
	Dunston
	Old Whittington
Corby	Kingswood
	Hazelwood
Derby	Litchurch
	Osmaston
	Babington
	Derwent
	Normanton
	Sinfin
East Lindsey	Ingoldmells
	Mablethorpe

	Sutton and Trusthorpe
	Winthorpe
	Scarbrough
	Trinity
	St. Clements
	New Leake
	Chapel St. Leonards
	Theddlethorpe St. Helen
Erewash	Ilkeston North
Gedling	Oxclose
High Peak	Gamesley
Leicester	North Braunstone
	Wycliffe
	Spinney Hill
	Saffron
	New Parks
	West Humberstone
	Mowmacre
	Belgrave
	Eyres Monsell
	Coleman
	Beaumont Leys
	Latimer
	Charnwood
	Thurncourt
Lincoln	Tritton
	Minster
	Abbey
	Castle
	Longdales
Mansfield	Northfield
	Pleasleyhill
	Meden
	Cumberlands
	Titchfield
	Ladybrook
	Birklands
	Sherwood
	Ravensdale
	Broomhill
	Oak Tree
Newark and Sherwood	Devon
	Clipstone
	Ollerton North
	Bilsthorpe
	Boughton
	Blidworth
North East Derbyshire	Holmewood and Heath
	Hasland
	Clay Cross South
North West Leicestershire	Greenhill

Northampton	Dallington and Kings Heath
	St. Crispin
	Castle
Nottingham	Strelley
	Manvers
	Radford
	Trent
	Aspley
	St. Ann's
	Bulwell West
	Bridge
	Bestwood Park
	Lenton
	Forest
	Beechdale
	Bulwell East
	Byron
	Bilborough
	Robin Hood
	Clifton East
	Basford
	Portland
	Greenwood
South Kesteven	Earlesfield
Wellingborough	Queensway
	Croyland
West Lindsey	Gainsborough East
	Gainsborough South-West

TABLE B—EASTERN ENGLAND

Local Authority	*Ward*
Basildon	Vange
	Fryerns East
	Pitsea West
	Fryerns Central
Bedford	Kingsbrook
	Cauldwell
	Queens Park
Breckland	Thetford-Abbey
Colchester	St. Andrew's
Fenland	Wisbech North
Great Yarmouth	Regent
	Nelson
	Northgate
	Lichfield and Cobholm
	Magdalen West
	Magdalen East
	Claydon
	Yarmouth North
Harlow	Hare Street and Town Centre
Ipswich	Gainsborough

	Town
	Chantry
King's Lynn and West Norfolk	Lynn North
	St. Margarets
	Gaywood South
	Lynn South West
	Lynn Central
Luton	Dallow
	Biscot
Norwich	Mile Cross
	Mancroft
	Catton Grove
	Bowthorpe
	Lakenham
Peterborough	Central
	Dogsthorpe
	Ravensthorpe
	East
	North
St. Edmundsbury	Clements
Tendring	Golf Green
	St. James
	Rush Green
	St. Marys
	Harwich East
Thurrock	Tilbury Riverside
	Tilbury St. Chads
	Belhus
	Chadwell St. Mary
	West Thurrock
Waveney	Harbour
	Kirkley
	Normanston
	St. Margarets
	Whitton

TABLE C—ENGLAND—LONDON

Local authority	*Ward*
Barking and Dagenham	Gascoigne
	Fanshawe
	Abbey
	Manor
	Alibon
	Marks Gate
	Village
	Thames
	Heath
	Becontree
	Parsloes
	Triptons
	Goresbrook

	Cambell
Bexley	Thamesmead East
Brent	Carlton
	Stonebridge
	St. Raphael's
	Roundwood
	Harlesden
	Church End
	St. Andrew's
	Willesden Green
Bromley	Anerley
	Penge
Camden	St. Pancras
	Somers Town
	Castlehaven
	Grafton
	Caversham
	Gospel Oak
	Priory
	King's Cross
	Holborn
	Regent's Park
	Camden
	Kilburn
Croydon	Fieldway
	New Addington
Ealing	Dormers Wells
	Northcote
	Glebe
	Heathfield
Enfield	Angel Road
	Craig Park
	Latymer
	St. Peters
	Weir Hall
	Ponders End
	St. Alphege
Greenwich	St. Mary's
	Arsenal
	Glyndon
	Nightingale
	Middle Park
	Sherard
	Eynsham
	Ferrier
	Hornfair
	West
	Woolwich Common
	Herbert
	Burrage
	Rectory Field

	Lakedale
	Kidbrooke
	Charlton
	Thamesmead Moorings
	Plumstead Common
Hackney	Queensbridge
	Wenlock
	Chatham
	Haggerston
	Westdown
	Eastdown
	Northfield
	New River
	Leabridge
	Dalston
	Springfield
	Kings Park
	Rectory
	Moorfields
	Homerton
	Northwold
	De Beauvoir
	Brownswood
	Victoria
	Clissold
	Wick
	South Defoe
	North Defoe
Hammersmith and Fulham	White City and Shepherds Bush
	College Park and Old Oak
	Broadway
	Wormholt
	Coningham
Haringey	Coleraine
	White Hart Lane
	Park
	Tottenham Central
	Bruce Grove
	High Cross
	South Tottenham
	Seven Sisters
	Noel Park
	West Green
	Green Lanes
	Woodside
	Harringay
	South Hornsey
Havering	Hilldene
Hounslow	Hanworth
Islington	Hillmarton
	Sussex

	Tollington
	Junction
	Highview
	Thornhill
	Bunhill
	Holloway
	Canonbury West
	Canonbury East
	Highbury
	Mildmay
	Quadrant
	Barnsbury
	Clerkenwell
	St. Peter
	Hillrise
	St. George's
Kensington and Chelsea	Golborne
	St. Charles
	Avondale
Lambeth	Angell
	Vassall
	Gipsy Hill
	Larkhall
	Bishop's
	Stockwell
	Ferndale
	St. Martin's
	Tulse Hill
	Prince's
	Oval
	Knight's Hill
	Town Hall
Lewisham	Evelyn
	Grinling Gibbons
	Bellingham
	Downham
	Churchdown
	Whitefoot
	Marlowe
	Grove Park
	Rushey Green
	Sydenham West
	Drake
	Hither Green
Newham	Ordnance
	Beckton
	Canning Town and Grange
	St. Stephens
	Stratford
	Park
	Little Ilford

	Plaistow
	Manor Park
	Plashet
	West Ham
	Hudsons
	Upton
	Custom House and Silvertown
	Kensington
	Castle
	Monega
	New Town
	Wall End
	Forest Gate
	South
	Central
	Bemersyde
	Greatfield
Redbridge	Loxford
Southwark	Friary
	Consort
	Liddle
	Brunswick
	Rotherhithe
	Chaucer
	Barset
	The Lane
	Burgess
	St. Giles
	Cathedral
	Browning
	Faraday
	Abbey
	Newington
	Waverley
	Bellenden
	Bricklayers
Tower Hamlets	Spitalfields
	Lansbury
	Weavers
	Blackwall
	Limehouse
	Redcoat
	East India
	St. Dunstan's
	St. James'
	Park
	Holy Trinity
	Bromley
	Shadwell
	St. Peter's
	Bow

	St. Mary's
	St. Katherine's
	Millwall
Waltham Forest	Leyton
	Higham Hill
	Cathall
	Cann Hall
	Lea Bridge
	Hoe Street
	St. James Street
Wandsworth	Latchmere
	Roehampton
Westminster	Queen's Park
	Church Street
	Westbourne
	Harrow Road

TABLE D—NORTH EASTERN ENGLAND

Local Authority	*Ward*
Alnwick	Alnwick Clayport
Berwick-upon-Tweed	Tower
Blyth Valley	Cowpen
	Croft
	Hartford and West Cramlington
	Kitty Brewster
	Plessey
	Cramlington East
	Isabella
Castle Morpeth	Lynemouth
	Chevington
Chester-le-Street	Chester West
	Grange Villa
	Edmondsley
	Pelton Fell
Darlington	Central
	Eastbourne South
	Cockerton West
	Eastbourne North
	Park East
	Lascelles
	Northgate South
	Bank Top
	Northgate North
Derwentside	South Stanley
	Craghead
	Consett South
	South Moor
	Catchgate
	Delves Lane
	Burnhope
	Stanley Hall

	Leadgate
	Dipton Annfield Plain
Durham	Pelaw
	New Brancepeth
	Shadforth
	Bearpark
Easington	Eden Hill
	Deneside
	Dawdon
	Shotton
	Easington Colliery
	Acre Rigg
	Haswell
	Wheatley Hill
	Horden North
	Horden South
	Wingate
	Dene House
	High Colliery
	Thornley
	Blackhalls
	Howletch
	South
	Hutton Henry
	Murton West
	South Hetton
	Deaf Hill
	Passfield
Gateshead	Bede
	Felling
	Bensham
	High Fell
	Teams
	Deckham
	Saltwell
	Leam
	Lamesley
	Blaydon
Hartlepool	Owton
	Dyke House
	Stranton
	St. Hilda
	Brus
	Jackson
	Rossmere
	Brinkburn
	Park
	Fens
Middlesbrough	Thorntree
	Pallister
	St. Hilda's

	Park End
	Beckfield
	Beechwood
	Berwick Hills
	North Ormesby
	Westbourne
	Grove Hill
	Easterside
	Southfield
	Ayresome
	Gresham
	Stainton and Thornton
	Hemlington
Newcastle upon Tyne	Walker
	Monkchester
	Elswick
	West City
	Byker
	Scotswood
	Benwell
	Woolsington
	Moorside
	Fawdon
	Blakelaw
	Kenton
	Wingrove
	Fenham
	Newburn
	Walkergate
	Denton
North Tyneside	Chirton
	Riverside
	Collingwood
	Longbenton
	Howdon
	Wallsend
	Valley
Redcar and Cleveland	Grangetown
	South Bank
	Kirkleatham
	Coatham
	Newcomen
	Dormanstown
	Eston
	Lockwood and Skinningrove
	Loftus
Sedgefield	West
	Thickley
	Cornforth
	Old Trimdon
	Sunnydale

	New Trimdon and Trimdon Grange
	Chilton
	Broom
	Fishburn
	Tudhoe
	Ferryhill
South Tyneside	Rekendyke
	Bede
	Cleadon Park
	Tyne Dock and Simonside
	Biddick Hall
	Primrose
	Beacon and Bents
	All Saints
	Hebburn South
	Harton
	Whiteleas
	Monkton
	Fellgate and Hedworth
	Horsley Hill
	Hebburn Quay
	Whitburn and Marsden
Stockton-on-Tees	Portrack and Tilery
	Hardwick
	Parkfield
	Newtown
	Roseworth
	Mile House
	Blue Hall
	Victoria
	Charltons
	Mandale
	Grange
	Stainsby
	St. Aidan's
Sunderland	Southwick
	Town End Farm
	Thorney Close
	South Hylton
	Grindon
	Castletown
	Colliery
	Hendon
	Washington North
	Central
	Hetton
	Houghton
	Eppleton
	Thornholme
	Ryhope
	Pallion

Teesdale	Evenwood with Ramshaw
	Cockfield
Tynedale	Prudhoe North
Wansbeck	Hirst
	Newbiggin East
	Choppington
	Central
	Park
	College
	Sleekburn
	Newbiggin West
Wear Valley	Woodhouse Close
	St. Helen's
	Coundon
	Henknowle
	Stanley
	Willington East
	Wheatbottom and Helmington Row
	Coundon Grange
	Tow Law
	Willington West
	West Auckland

TABLE E—NORTH WESTERN ENGLAND

Local Authority	*Ward*
Allerdale	Salterbeck
	Ewanrigg
	Westfield
	Northside
	Moorclose
	Ellenborough
	Clifton
	Netherhall
Barrow-in-Furness	Central
	Risedale
	Hindpool
	Barrow Island
	Ormsgill
	Walney North
Blackburn with Darwen	Audley
	Shadsworth
	Higher Croft
	Wensley Fold
	Shear Brow
	Queen's Park
	Bastwell
	Little Harwood with Whitebirk
	Mill Hill
	Sudell
	Meadowhead
	Corporation Park

Blackpool	Park
	Alexandra
	Claremont
	Talbot
	Foxhall
	Clifton
	Brunswick
	Victoria
	Tyldesley
	Warbreck
	Waterloo
Bolton	Central
	Derby
	Farnworth
	Tonge
	Halliwell
	Burnden
	Harper Green
	Breightmet
Burnley	Daneshouse
	Bank Hall
	Barclay
	Trinity
	Fulledge
	Brunshaw
	Coal Clough with Deerplay
Bury	Redvales
	East
	Besses
Carlisle	Upperby
	Botcherby
	Morton
Chester	Blacon Hall
	Dee Point
Chorley	Chorley East
Copeland	Mirehouse West
	Sandwith
	Cleator Moor South
	Mirehouse East
	Distington
	Frizington
	Harbour
	Cleator Moor North
	Hensingham
Crewe & Nantwich	Maw Green
Ellesmere Port and Neston	Westminster
	Stanlow
	Grange
	Central
	Wolverham
	Rivacre

Halton	Castlefields
	Riverside
	Kingsway
	Murdishaw
	Palace Field
	Grange
	Brookvale
	Halton Brook
	Norton
	Mersey
	Broadheath
	Hough Green
	Ditton
Hyndburn	Central
	Church
	Spring Hill
	Barnfield
Knowsley	Princess
	Longview
	Cherryfield
	Kirkby Central
	Northwood
	Cantril Farm
	Tower Hill
	Knowsley Park
	St. Michaels
	St. Gabriels
	Halewood South
	Whitefield
	Page Moss
	Park
	Halewood West
	Prescot East
	Whiston South
	Whiston North
Lancaster	Alexandra
	Poulton
	Skerton Central
	Skerton East
Liverpool	Speke
	Everton
	Vauxhall
	Granby
	Pirrie
	Breckfield
	Melrose
	Clubmoor
	Smithdown
	Dovecot
	Netherley
	Kensington

	St. Mary's
	Valley
	Abercromby
	County
	Dingle
	Tuebrook
	Fazakerley
	Anfield
	Broadgreen
	Picton
	Old Swan
	Gillmoss
	Warbreck
	Arundel
	Croxteth
	Allerton
Manchester	Benchill
	Harpurhey
	Beswick and Clayton
	Bradford
	Ardwick
	Central
	Newton Heath
	Gorton South
	Woodhouse Park
	Moss Side
	Longsight
	Hulme
	Cheetham
	Lightbowne
	Baguley
	Blackley
	Sharston
	Gorton North
	Charlestown
	Brooklands
	Burnage
	Moston
	Crumpsall
	Northenden
	Rusholme
	Fallowfield
	Whalley Range
	Levenshulme
	Barlow Moor
	Old Moat
Oldham	Coldhurst
	Werneth
	Alexandra
	St. Marys
	Hollinwood

	St. James
	Lees
	St. Pauls
	Chadderton South
Pendle	Whitefield
	Bradley
	Waterside
	Walverden
	Southfield
	Brierfield
	Marsden
	Vivary Bridge
Preston	Fishwick
	Ribbleton
	Deepdale
	St. Matthew's
	Brookfield
	Avenham
	Central
Rochdale	Central and Falinge
	Middleton West
	Smallbridge and Wardleworth
	Newbold
	Middleton Central
	Brimrod and Deeplish
	Balderstone
	Heywood West
Rossendale	Worsley
	Greensclough
	Stacksteads
	Longholme
Salford	Broughton
	Little Hulton
	Blackfriars
	Ordsall
	Pendleton
	Langworthy
	Winton
	Weaste and Seedley
	Barton
	Walkden North
	Pendlebury
Sefton	Linacre
	Orrell
	Derby
	Netherton
	Ford
	Litherland
	St. Oswald
	Church
South Ribble	Seven Stars

St. Helens	Parr and Hardshaw
	Broad Oak
	West Sutton
	Marshalls Cross
	Queen's Park
	Thatto Heath
	Grange Park
	Newton West
	Sutton and Bold
	Haydock
Stockport	Brinnington
Tameside	Ashton St. Peters'
	Hyde
	Godley
	Longdendale Denton South
	Ashton St. Michael's
	Hyde Newton
Trafford	Clifford
	Bucklow
	Talbot
Vale Royal	Over Two
	Wharton
	Vale Royal
Warrington	Westy
	Bewsey and Whitecross
	Orford
	Hulme
	Poplars
West Lancashire	Tanhouse
	Digmoor
	Moorside
	Birch Green
	Skelmersdale North
Wigan	Norley
	Ince
	Newtown
	Abram
	Leigh Central
	Atherton
	Whelley
	Hindley
Wirral	Bidston
	Birkenhead
	Tranmere
	Seacombe
	Leasowe
	Egerton
	Liscard
	New Brighton
	Claughton
	Bromborough

Wyre	Pharos
	Park
	Mount

TABLE F—SOUTH EASTERN ENGLAND

Local authority	*Ward/Electoral division*
Arun	Littlehampton River
	Littlehampton Ham
Ashford	Stanhope
	Ashford Brookfield
	Ashford Hampden
Brighton and Hove	Marine
	Moulsecoomb
	Queen's Park
Dartford	Joyce Green
Dover	Buckland
	St. Radigunds
	Town and Pier
	Castle
	Tower Hamlets
Gravesham	Riverside
Hastings	Central St. Leonards
	Castle
	Gensing
	Hollington
	Broomgrove
	Mount Pleasant
	Maze Hill
	Ore
	Braybrooke
	Wishing Tree
Havant	Warren Park
	Barncroft
	Bondfields
	Battins
Isle of Wight	St. Johns -1
	Pan
	Ryde North East
	Ventnor-1
Maidstone	Shepway West
	Park Wood
Medway	Twydall
Milton Keynes	Woughton
	Eaton Manor
Oxford	Blackbird Leys
Portsmouth	Charles Dickens
	Paulsgrove
Reading	Whitley
Shepway	Folkestone Central
	St. Mary in the Marsh
	Folkestone East

	Folkestone Harbour
Southampton	Redbridge
	Bargate
Swale	Sheerness West
	Eastern
	Sheerness East
Thanet	Pier
	Ethelbert
	Newington
	Northdown Park
	Cecil
	Marine
	Central Eastcliff
	Northwood
	Central Westcliff

TABLE G—SOUTH WESTERN ENGLAND

Local authority	*Ward*
Bath and North East Somerset	Twerton
Bournemouth	Boscombe West
	Wallisdown
Bristol, City of	Lawrence Hill
	Filwood
	Southmead
	Knowle
	Ashley
	Whitchurch Park
	Bishopsworth
	Hartcliffe
	Easton
	Lockleaze
	Kingsweston
Carrick	Penwerris
Exeter	Wonford
Gloucester	Barton
	Westgate
	Matson
Kerrier	Illogan South
	Camborne North
	Camborne West
	Redruth North
	Camborne South
North Devon	Trinity
	Ilfracombe Central
	St. Mary's
	Ilfracombe East
North Somerset	Weston-Super-Mare South
	Weston-Super-Mare Ellenborough
Penwith	Penzance East
	Penzance West
	Hayle-Gwithian

	Marazion
	St. Ives North
	St. Just
	Hayle-Gwinear
Plymouth	St. Peter
	Ham
	Budshead
	Honicknowle
	Sutton
	St. Budeaux
	Keyham
Swindon	Whitworth
	Park
Taunton Deane	Taunton Halcon
	Taunton Lyngford
Torbay	Tormohun
	Torwood
	Blatchcombe
	Coverdale
Torridge	Westward Hol
West Somerset	Williton
Weymouth and Portland	Melcombe Regis

TABLE H—ENGLAND—WEST MIDLANDS

Local authority	*Ward*
Birmingham	Aston
	Sparkbrook
	Small Heath
	Nechells
	Soho
	Washwood Heath
	Handsworth
	Sparkhill
	Ladywood
	Shard End
	Kingstanding
	Bartley Green
	Fox Hollies
	Longbridge
	Kingsbury
	King's Norton
	Stockland Green
	Weoley
	Yardley
	Sandwell
	Hodge Hill
	Acock's Green
	Billesley
Cannock Chase	Broomhill
County of Herefordshire	Belmont
Coventry	Foleshill

	St. Michael's
	Longford
	Henley
	Binley and Willenhall
	Radford
	Holbrook
	Upper Stoke
Dudley	Castle and Priory
	St. Thomas's
	Netherton and Woodside
	Brockmoor & Pensett
	Brierley Hill
	Lye and Wollescote
East Staffordshire	Victoria
	Waterside
	Uxbridge
	Burton
	Broadway
	Eton
Newcastle-under-Lyme	Holditch
	Cross Heath
	Silverdale
Nuneaton & Bedworth	Camp Hill
Redditch	Batchley
Sandwell	Soho and Victoria
	St. Pauls
	Greets Green and Lyng
	Friar Park
	Smethwick
	West Bromwich Central
	Hateley Heath
	Princes End
	Great Bridge
	Oldbury
	Tipton Green
	Wednesbury North
	Wednesbury South
	Bristnall
	Rowley
Solihull	Chelmsley Wood
	Fordbridge
	Smith's Wood
	Kingshurst
South Staffordshire	Huntington
Staffordshire Moorlands	Biddulph East
Stoke-on-Trent	Brookhouse
	Blurton
	Burslem Grange
	Longton South
	Tunstall North
	Great Fenton

	Chell
	Shelton
	Burslem Central
	Berryhill
	Abbey
	Norton and Bradeley
	Meir Park
	Fenton Green
Tamworth	Glascote
Telford & Wrekin	Woodside
	Malinslee and Langley
	Cuckoo Oak
	Brookside
	Donnington
	Arleston
Walsall	Blakenall
	St. Matthew's
	Birchills Leamore
	Pleck
	Darlaston South
	Bentley and Darlaston Nth
	Palfrey
	Bloxwich East
	Willenhall South
	Bloxwich West
	Brownhills
Wolverhampton	Low Hill
	East Park
	St. Peter's
	Heath Town
	Ettingshall
	Bilston East
	Blakenhall
	Bilston North
	Graiseley
	Bushbury
	Fallings Park
Worcester	St. Barnabas
Wyre Forest	Oldington and Foley Park

TABLE I—ENGLAND—YORKSHIRE AND HUMBERSIDE

Local authority	*Ward*
Barnsley	Dearne Thurnscoe
	Athersley
	Monk Bretton
	Brierley
	Dearne South
	Ardsley
	Worsbrough
	Cudworth
	Park

	Hoyland West
	North West
	Darfield
	Royston
	Hoyland East
Bradford	Little Horton
	Bradford Moor
	University
	Bowling
	Toller
	Tong
	Undercliffe
	Keighley South
	Heaton
	Eccleshill
	Shipley East
	Odsal
	Keighley West
	Great Horton
Calderdale	St. John's
	Ovenden
	Mixenden
Doncaster	Conisbrough
	Central
	Bentley Central
	Thorne
	Mexborough
	Adwick
	Balby
	Askern
	Town Field
	Intake
	Wheatley
	Rossington
	Stainforth
East Riding of Yorkshire	Bridlington South
Kingston upon Hull, City of	Noddle Hill
	Orchard Park
	Myton
	Marfleet
	St. Andrews
	University
	Newington
	Longhill
	Pickering
	Southcoates
	Ings
	Stoneferry
Kirklees	Deighton
	Thornhill
	Dewsbury West

	Crosland Moor
	Newsome
	Batley West
	Batley East
	Dewsbury East
Leeds	City and Holbeck
	Seacroft
	Harehills
	Burmantofts
	Richmond Hill
	Hunslet
	University
	Chapel Allerton
	Beeston
North East Lincolnshire	North East
	South
	Marsh
	Park (Cleethorpes)
	Croft Baker
North Lincolnshire	Brumby
	Frodingham and Town
Rotherham	Central
	Herringthorpe
	Park
	Dalton, Hooton Roberts and Thrybergh
	Brampton, Melton and Wentworth
	Greasbrough
	Rawmarsh West
	Maltby
	Rawmarsh East
	Boston
	Swinton
	Wath
	Thurcroft and Whiston
Scarborough	Castle
	Eastfield
	Falsgrave
Selby	Selby South
	Selby North
Sheffield	Southey Green
	Burngreave
	Manor
	Park
	Firth Park
	Castle
	Nether Shire
	Darnall
	Owlerton
	Brightside
	Sharrow
	Norton

Wakefield	Hemsworth
	Castleford Ferry Fryston
	South Kirkby
	Wakefield East
	South Elmsall
	Wakefield Central
	Normanton and Sharlston
	Castleford Whitwood
	Knottingley
	Featherstone
	Wakefield North
	Castleford Glasshoughton

SCHEDULE 2

Regulation 2

AREAS IN WALES DESIGNATED AS DISADVANTAGED AREAS

The areas in Wales specified in this Schedule are—

(*a*) the electoral divisions, as at 1st April 1998, which are—

(i) contained in the Welsh Index of Multiple Deprivation 2000 published by the National Assembly for Wales, and

(ii) listed in Table J below; and

(*b*) any land which—

(i) as at 1st April 1998, did not fall within any of the electoral divisions mentioned in paragraph (*a*), but

(ii) as at 27th November 2001, had a postcode which was identical to the full postcode of land which, as at 1st April 1998, did fall within one of those electoral divisions.

TABLE J—WALES

Unitary authority	*Electoral division*
Blaenau Gwent	Nantyglo
	Tredegar Central and West
	Llanhilleth
	Sirhowy
	Rassau
	Cwmtillery
	Blaina
	Cwm
	Ebbw Vale South
	Ebbw Vale North
	Brynmawr
	Six Bells
	Abertillery
	Beaufort
	Georgetown
	Badminton
Bridgend	Caerau
	Bettws
	Blackmill
	Llangeinor
	Blaengarw
	Cornelly
	Maesteg West
	Morfa

	Nantyffyllon
	St. Bride's Minor
	Pontycymmer
	Nant-y-moel
	Pyle
	Maesteg East
	Ogmore Vale
	Cefn Cribwr
Caerphilly	New Tredegar
	Aberbargoed
	Darran Valley
	Twyn
	Carno
	Tir-Phil
	Pontlottyn
	Bargoed
	Moriah
	Argoed
	Hengoed
	Aber Valley
	Gilfach
	Abertysswg
	St. Cattwg
	Cefn Fforest
	St. James
	Machen
	Bedwas and Trethomas
	Crumlin
	Pengam
	Ynysddu
	Newbridge
	Penyrheol
	Pontllanfraith
	Abercarn
	Nelson
	Crosskeys
Cardiff	Butetown
	Ely
	Caerau
	Splott
	Adamsdown
	Llanrumney
	Trowbridge
	Grangetown
	Llandaff North
	Fairwater
	Riverside
Carmarthenshire	Glanymor
	Llwynhendy
	Felinfoel
	Tyisha

	Pantyffynnon
	Glanamman
	Bigyn
	Bynea
	Garnant
	Kidwelly
	Burry Port
	Trimsaran
	Dafen
	Pembrey
	Quarter Bach Llynfell
	Brynamman
	Elli
	Ammanford
	Llangyndeyrn
	Tumble
	Saron
	Cross Hands
	Myddynfych
	Lliedi
	Hengoed
	Pontyberem
	Betws
	Penygroes
	Glyn
	Llangeler
	Llandybie and Heolddu
	Llangennech
Ceredigion	Aberystwyth South
	Llangeitho
	Cardigan
	Llandyfriog
	Llandysul Town
	Llanarth
	Lledrod
	Troedyraur
	Llangybi
	Penbryn
	Capel Dewi
	Llanfihangel Ystrad
	Tregaron
	New Quay
Conwy	Pant-yr-afon/Penmaenan
	Tudno
	Bryn
	Glyn
	Towyn
	Kinmel Bay
	Pentre Mawr
	Llysfaen
	Gogarth

	Mostyn
Denbighshire	Rhyl West
	Rhyl South West
	Meliden
	Denbigh Upper/Henllan
	Rhyl East
	Bodelwyddan
	Denbigh Central
	Prestatyn North
Flintshire	Flint Castle
	Ffynnongroyw
	Mold West
	Bagillt West
	Higher and East Shotton
	Mostyn
	Holywell West
	Sealand
	Greenfield
	Gronant
	Holywell East
	Connah's Quay Central
	Flint
	Oakenholt
	Queensferry
	Saltney
Gwynedd	Peblig
	Marchog
	Talysarn
	Bowydd and Rhiw
	Barmouth
	Pwllheli South
	Rachub
	Cadnant
	Ogwen
	Deiniolen
	Penygroes
	Conglywal and Maenofferen
	Llanaelhaearn/Pistyll
	Pwllheli North
	Corris/Mawddwy
	Aberdaron
	Arthog
	Seiont
	Llanllyfni
	Hirael
	Gerlan
	Hendre
	Cynfal and Teigl
	Clynnog
	Tudweiliog
	Botwnnog

	Deiniol
	Trawsfynydd
	Penisarwaun
	Llanberis
	Llanbedrog
	Llanrug
	Abersoch
Isle of Anglesey	Morawelon
	Holyhead Town
	Tudur
	Maeshyfryd
	Amlwch Port
	Porthyfelin
	Llannerch-y-medd
	Aberffraw
	Rhosneigr
	Kingsland
	London Road
	Bryngwran
	Llanbadrig
	Moelfre
	Mechell
	Amlwch Rural
	Llanfaethlu
	Bodorgan
	Llaneilian
	Rhosyr
	Parc a'r Mynydd
	Llanidan
Merthyr Tydfil	Gurnos
	Penydarren
	Dowlais
	Merthyr Vale
	Bedlinog
	Cyfarthfa
	Vaynor
	Plymouth
	Town
	Park
	Treharris
Monmouthshire	Lansdown
Neath Port Talbot	Cymmer
	Gwynfi
	Sandfields West
	Glyncorrwg
	Onllwyn
	Sandfields East
	Ystalyfera
	Briton Ferry West
	Neath East
	Lower Brynamman

	Pelenna
	Seven Sisters
	Godre'r graig
	Gwaun-Cae-Gurwen
	Aberdulais
	Aberavon
	Neath South
	Cwmllynfell
	Blaengwrach
	Bryn and Cwmavon
	Glynneath
	Dyffryn
	Crynant
	Trebanos
	Taibach
	Neath North
	Resolven
	Margam
	Pontardawe
	Coedffranc Central
	Port Talbot
	Briton Ferry East
Newport	Pillgwenlly
	Tredegar Park
	Bettws
	Ringland
	Alway
	Victoria
	Stow Hill
	Gaer
	Shaftesbury
Pembrokeshire	Pembroke—Monkton
	Pembroke Dock—Llanion
	Pembroke Dock—Central
	Pembroke—St. Mary
	Neyland West
	Garth
	Milford North and West
	Pembroke Dock—Market
	Hakin
	Pembroke Dock—Pennar
	Goodwick
	Neyland East
	Castle
	Milford Central and East
	Merlin's Bridge
	Maenclochog
	St. Dogmaels
Powys	Ystradgynlais
	Tawe-Uchaf/Ystradfellte
	Aber-craf

	Newtown South
	Cwm-twrch
	Newtown Central
	Ynyscedwyn
	Welshpool Castle
Rhondda, Cynon, Taff	Pen-y-waun
	Maerdy
	Tylorstown
	Glyncoch
	Llwyn-y-pia
	Penrhiwceiber
	Treherbert
	Cwm Clydach
	Rhydfelen Central/Ilan
	Gilfach Goch
	Mountain Ash West
	Cymmer
	Ynyshir
	Trealaw
	Aberaman South
	Tonyrefail West
	Pen-y-graig
	Ystrad
	Cwmbach
	Ferndale
	Tonypandy
	Abercynon
	Tonyrefail East
	Aberaman North
	Hirwaun
	Pentre
	Rhigos
	Rhydfelen Lower
	Porth
	Llanharry
	Treorchy
	Mountain Ash East
	Cilfynydd
	Aberdare East
	Graig
	Ynysybwl
	Tyn-y-nant
	Rhondda
	Aberdare West/Llwydcoed
Swansea	Townhill
	Penderry
	Graigfelen
	Castle
	Bonymaen
	Landore
	Gorseinon East

	St. Thomas
	Dulais East
	Cockett
	Penllergaer
	Mynyddbach
	Lower Loughor
The Vale of Glamorgan	Castleland
	Gibbonsdown
	Court
	Cadoc
	Buttrills
Torfaen	Trevethin
	St. Cadocs and Penygarn
	Cwmyniscoy
	Abersychan
	Upper Cwmbran
	Brynwern
	St. Dials
	Snatchwood
	Greenmeadow
	Blaenavon
	Pontnewynydd
Wrexham	Plas Madoc
	Queensway
	Caia Park
	Gwenfro
	Pant
	Penycae
	Brymbo
	Cefn
	Gwersyllt North
	Whitegate
	Ruabon
	Maesydre
	Ponciau
	Acton

SCHEDULE 3

Regulation 2

AREAS IN SCOTLAND DESIGNATED AS DISADVANTAGED AREAS

The areas in Scotland specified in this Schedule are—

(*a*) the areas which, as at 21st April 1991, had any of the postcodes which are-

(i) contained in Revising the Scottish Area Deprivation Index published by the Scottish Executive, and

(ii) listed in Table K below; and

(*b*) any land which—

(i) as at 21st April 1991, did not fall within any of the areas mentioned in paragraph (*a*), but

(ii) as at 27th November 2001, had a postcode which was identical to the full postcode of land which, as at 21st April 1991, did fall within one of those areas.

TABLE K—SCOTLAND

Postcode	*Local authority*
AB1 3	Aberdeen

AB2 1	Aberdeen
AB2 2	Aberdeen
DD1 5	Dundee
DD11 1	Dundee
DD2 3	Dundee
DD2 4	Dundee
DD3 0	Dundee
DD3 7	Dundee
DD4 0	Dundee/Angus
DD4 6	Dundee
DD4 8	Dundee
DD4 9	Dundee
DG1 2	Dumfries and Galloway
DG9 7	Dumfries and Galloway
EH11 3	Edinburgh
EH14 2	Edinburgh
EH16 4	Edinburgh
EH3 8	Edinburgh
EH4 4	Edinburgh
EH5 1	Edinburgh
EH54 5	West Lothian
EH6 6	Edinburgh
EH8 8	Edinburgh
FK2 7	Falkirk
FK8 1	Stirling
FK10 1	Clackmannanshire
G1 5	Glasgow
G11 6	Glasgow
G13 2	Glasgow
G13 3	Glasgow
G13 4	Glasgow
G14 0	Glasgow
G15 7	Glasgow
G15 8	Glasgow
G20 0	Glasgow
G20 7	Glasgow
G20 8	Glasgow
G20 9	Glasgow
G21 1	Glasgow
G21 2	Glasgow
G21 3	Glasgow
G21 4	Glasgow
G22 5	Glasgow
G22 6	Glasgow
G22 7	Glasgow
G23 5	Glasgow
G3 8	Glasgow
G31 1	Glasgow
G31 2	Glasgow
G31 3	Glasgow
G31 4	Glasgow

G31 5	Glasgow
G32 6	Glasgow
G32 7	Glasgow
G32 8	Glasgow
G33 1	Glasgow
G33 3	Glasgow
G33 4	Glasgow
G33 5	Glasgow
G34 0	Glasgow
G34 9	Glasgow
G4 0	Glasgow
G40 1	Glasgow
G40 2	Glasgow
G40 3	Glasgow
G40 4	Glasgow
G41 1	Glasgow
G42 0	Glasgow
G42 7	Glasgow
G42 8	Glasgow
G42 9	Glasgow
G43 1	Glasgow
G45 0	Glasgow
G45 9	Glasgow
G46 8	Glasgow/East Renfrewshire
G5 0	Glasgow
G5 9	Glasgow
G51 1	Glasgow
G51 2	Glasgow
G51 3	Glasgow
G51 4	Glasgow
G52 1	Glasgow
G52 4	Glasgow
G53 5	Glasgow
G53 6	Glasgow
G53 7	Glasgow/East Renfrewshire
G66 2	East Dunbartonshire
G71 5	North Lanarkshire
G72 0	South Lanarkshire
G72 7	South Lanarkshire
G73 1	South Lanarkshire
G81 1	West Dunbartonshire
G81 2	West Dunbartonshire
G81 4	West Dunbartonshire
G81 5	West Dunbartonshire
KA1 4	East Ayrshire
KA18 3	East Ayrshire
KA18 4	East Ayrshire
KA3 1	East Ayrshire
KA3 2	East Ayrshire/North Ayrshire
KA6 7	East Ayrshire
KA7 1	South Ayrshire

KA8 0	South Ayrshire
KA8 9	South Ayrshire
KY1 2	Fife
KY1 3	Fife
KY5 8	Fife
KY8 2	Fife
KY8 3	Fife
ML1 4	North Lanarkshire
ML2 0	North Lanarkshire
ML2 7	North Lanarkshire
ML2 9	North Lanarkshire
ML3 0	South Lanarkshire
ML4 2	North Lanarkshire
ML5 2	North Lanarkshire
ML5 4	North Lanarkshire
ML5 5	North Lanarkshire
ML6 0	North Lanarkshire
ML6 6	North Lanarkshire
ML6 7	North Lanarkshire
PA1 1	Renfrewshire
PA1 2	Renfrewshire
PA14 6	Inverclyde/Renfrewshire
PA15 2	Inverclyde
PA15 3	Inverclyde
PA15 4	Inverclyde
PA16 0	Inverclyde
PA2 0	Renfrewshire
PA3 1	Renfrewshire
PA3 2	Renfrewshire
PA3 4	Renfrewshire
PA4 8	Renfrewshire
PH1 5	Perth & Kinross

SCHEDULE 4

Regulation 2

AREAS IN NORTHERN IRELAND DESIGNATED AS DISADVANTAGED AREAS

The areas in Northern Ireland specified in this Schedule are—

(*a*) the wards, as at 21st April 1991, which are—

(i) contained in Measures of Deprivation in Northern Ireland 2001 published by the Northern Ireland Statistics and Research Agency, and

(ii) listed in Table L below; and

(*b*) any land which—

(i) as at 21st April 1991, did not fall within any of those wards, but

(ii) as at 27th November 2001, had a postcode which was identical to the full postcode of land which, as at 21st April 1991, did fall within one of those wards.

TABLE L—NORTHERN IRELAND

Local government district	*Ward*
Antrim	Rathenraw
	Fountain Hill
	New Park
Ards	West Winds
	Central

Armagh	Callan Bridge
	Abbey Park
	Downs
	Keady
	Carrigatuke
Ballymena	Ballykeel
	Ballee
	Fair Green
	Moat
	Dunclug
	Castle Demesne
Ballymoney	Newhill
	Ballyhoe & Corkey
	Benvardin
	Stranocum
	Route
	Killoquin Lower
	Carnany
Banbridge	Edenderry
	Gilford
Belfast	Crumlin
	Falls
	Whiterock
	St. Annes
	Ballymacarrett
	Woodvale
	New Lodge
	The Mount
	Shankill
	Upper Springfield
	Ardoyne
	Shaftesbury
	Water Works
	Duncairn
	Clonard
	Woodstock
	Beechmount
	Blackstaff
	Glencairn
	Island
	Glencolin
	Glen Road
	Highfield
	Botanic
	Ballysillan
	Legoniel
	Falls Park
	Andersonstown
	Cliftonville
	Bloomfield
	Ladybrook

	Bellevue
	Sydenham
	Chichester Park
Carrickfergus	Northland
	Gortalee
	Sunnylands
	Killycrot
	Love Lane
	Clipperstown
Castlereagh	Tullycarnet
	Enler
	Cregagh
	Minnowburn
Coleraine	Ballysally
	Churchland
	Cross Glebe
	Royal Portrush
	Central
	Kilrea
Cookstown	Ardboe
	Pomeroy
	Dunnamore
	Killycolpy
	Killymoon
	Newbuildings
	Gortalowry
	Stewartstown
	The Loop
	Moneymore
Craigavon	Court
	Drumgask
	Drumgor
	Corcrain
	Church
	Tullygally
	Drumnamoe
	Ballybay
	Taghnevan
	Tavanagh
	Ballyoran
Derry	Brandywell
	Creggan South
	The Diamond
	St. Peter's
	Victoria
	Creggan Central
	Shantallow East
	Shantallow West
	Westland
	Glen
	Rosemount

	Carn Hill
	Beechwood
	Corrody
	Strand
	Caw
	Clondermot
	Enagh
	Culmore
	Crevagh & Springtown
	Ebrington
	Banagher
	Claudy
	Faughan
Down	Flying Horse
	Cathedral
	Murlough
	Killyleagh
	Castlewellan
	Ardglass
Dungannon	Ballysaggart
	Coalisland South
	Altmore
	Fivemiletown
	Clogher
	Ballygawley
	Mullaghmore
	Washing Bay
	Drumglass
	Augher
	Coalisland West & Newmil
	Coalisland North
	Donaghmore
Fermanagh	Newtownbutler
	Devenish
	Lisnaskea
	Irvinestown
	Rosslea
	Brookeborough
	Belleek & Boa
	Ederny & Lack
	Erne
Larne	Central
	Ballyloran
	Craigy Hill
	Blackcave
	Carnlough
Limavady	Binevenagh
	Coolessan
	Feeny
	Magilligan
	Glack

	Dungiven
	The Highlands
	Upper Glenshane
	Enagh
Lisburn	Twinbrook
	Collin Glen
	Kilwee
	Old Warren
	Knockmore
Magherafelt	Maghera
	Town Parks East
	Upperlands
	Castledawson
	Draperstown
Moyle	Glentaisie
	Bushmills
	Armoy
	Knocklayd
	Bonamargy & Rathlin
	Kinbane
	Glendun
Newry and Mourne	Daisy Hill
	Ballybot
	Crossmaglen
	St. Patrick's
	Creggan
	Derrymore
	Drumgullion
	Camlough
	St. Mary's
	Newtownhamilton
	Silver Bridge
	Beesbrook
	Spelga
	Rathfriland
	Forkhill
	Kilkeel South
	Clonallan
	Kilkeel Central
	Lisnascree
	Fathom
Newtownabbey	Braden
	Dunanney
	Coole
	Whitehouse
	Valley
	Monkstown
North Down	Dufferin
	Whitehill
	Conlig
	Harbour

Omagh	Termon
	Fintona
	Owenkillew
	Sixmilecross
	Dromore
	Drumquin
	Gortrush
	Lisanelly
	Drumnakilly
	Camowen
	Newtownsaville
	Trillick
	Dergmoney
Strabane	East
	Castlederg
	Glenderg
	Clare
	Newtownstewart
	Sion Mills
	Dunnamanagh
	West
	Plumbridge
	Victoria Bridge
	South
	Artigarvan
	Slievekirk
	Finn
	North

2002/1975

STAMP DUTY AND STAMP DUTY RESERVE TAX (EXTENSION OF EXCEPTIONS RELATING TO RECOGNISED EXCHANGES) REGULATIONS 2002

Made by the Treasury under FA 2002 s 117(1)

Made . . . .*25 July 2002*
Laid before the House of Commons . . . .*25 July 2002*
Coming into force . . . .*26 July 2002*

1 These Regulations may be cited as the Stamp Duty and Stamp Duty Reserve Tax (Extension of Exceptions relating to Recognised Exchanges) Regulations 2002 and shall come into force on 26th July 2002.

2 The application of the provisions specified in section 117(2) of the Finance Act 2002 is extended to the market known as OFEX.

2003/1056

STAMP DUTY (DISADVANTAGED AREAS) (APPLICATION OF EXEMPTIONS) REGULATIONS 2003

Made by the Treasury under FA 2001 ss 92A, 92B(6), FA 2002 s 110(6)

Made . . . .*9th April 2003*
Laid before the House of Commons . . . .*9th April 2003*
Coming into force . . . .*10th April 2003*

Citation, commencement and effect

1—(1) These Regulations may be cited as the Stamp Duty (Disadvantaged Areas) (Application of Exemptions) Regulations 2003 and shall come into force on 10th April 2003.
(2) These Regulations have effect in relation to instruments executed on or after 10th April 2003.

Interpretation

2—(1) In these Regulations—
"conveyance on sale" has the same meaning as in Part 1 of Schedule 13 to the Finance Act 1999 (see paragraph 1(2) of that Schedule);
"instrument" and "executed" have the meanings given by section 122(1) of the Stamp Act 1891;
"lease of land" has the same meaning as in Part 2 of Schedule 13 to the Finance Act 1999;
"the rate or average rate of rent" means the rate of rent by reference to which stamp duty is determined under paragraph 12(3) of Schedule 13 to the Finance Act 1999;
"relevant consideration" means—
(*a*) in the case of a conveyance or transfer on sale, the consideration for the sale;
(*b*) in the case of a lease of land, the consideration in respect of which, under paragraph 12(2) of Schedule 13 to the Finance Act 1999, the stamp duty is the same as that on a conveyance on a sale for the same consideration;
"residential property" has the meaning given by section 92B read together with regulation 7.
(2) In these Regulations—
(*a*) unless the context otherwise requires, any reference to a numbered section is a reference to the section of the Finance Act 2001 bearing that number; and
(*b*) any reference to "Schedule 30" is a reference to Schedule 30 to that Act.

[Disapplication of exemptions conferred by section 92 or by Schedule 30 where all of land is non-residential property

2A An exemption conferred by section 92 or by Schedule 30 shall not apply where none of the land in question is residential property.][1]

Amendments—[1] Regulation inserted by FA 2005 s 96, Sch 9 paras 2(2), 5 with effect, subject to FA 2005 Sch 9 para 5(2), for instruments executed after 16 March 2005. This insertion is without prejudice to the power to amend or revoke these provisions by further regulations under FA 2001 s 92A: FA 2005 Sch 9 para 3.

Application of exemptions conferred by section 92 or by Schedule 30 where all the land is residential property

3—(1) Subject to paragraph (3), an exemption conferred by section 92 or by Schedule 30 shall not apply in the cases specified by paragraph (2) below.
(2) The cases specified by this paragraph are cases where—
(*a*) all the land in question is residential property, and
(*b*) subject to regulation 6, the amount or value of relevant consideration is more than £150,000.
(3) Where the instrument in question is a lease of land, nothing in this regulation affects the application of an exemption conferred by section 92 or by Schedule 30 in relation to stamp duty chargeable in respect of the rate or average rate of rent.

Leases of land: further provision as to the application of exemptions conferred by section 92 or by Schedule 30

4—(1) This regulation applies where the instrument in question is a lease of land.
(2) Subject to paragraph (4), an exemption conferred by section 92 or by Schedule 30 shall not apply in the cases specified by paragraph (3) below.
(3) The cases specified by this paragraph are cases where—
(*a*) all the land in question is residential property, and
(*b*) subject to regulation 6, the rate or average rate of rent is more than £15,000.
(4) Nothing in this regulation affects the application of an exemption conferred by section 92 or by Schedule 30 in relation to stamp duty chargeable in respect of the amount or value of relevant consideration.

Application of exemptions conferred by section 92 or by Schedule 30 where land only partly residential property

5—(1) This regulation (which includes provisions corresponding to those contained in Schedule 30) applies where the land in question is—
(*a*) a building or land part of which falls within subsection (1)(*a*) or (*b*) of section 92B (meaning of "residential property"), or
(*b*) an interest in or right over land that subsists only partly as mentioned in subsection (1)(c) of that section.

(2) Where the land in question falls wholly or partly within a disadvantaged area, liability to stamp duty under Part 1 or 2 of Schedule 13 to the Finance Act 1999 on—

(*a*) a conveyance or transfer on sale of an estate or interest in land, or

(*b*) a lease of land, shall be determined in accordance with the following paragraphs of this regulation.

(3) Subject to regulation 6, the consideration in respect of which duty would be chargeable, but for the provisions of section 92 or paragraphs 1 and 3 of Schedule 30, shall be apportioned, on such basis as is just and reasonable, as between the land in question to the extent that it is residential property and the land in question to the extent that it is not.

[(3A) An exemption conferred by section 92 or by Schedule 30 shall not apply in relation to any duty chargeable in respect of relevant consideration, or the rate or average rate of rent, attributed to the land in question to the extent that it is not residential property.][1]

(4) An exemption conferred by section 92 or by Schedule 30 shall have effect in relation to any duty otherwise chargeable in respect of relevant consideration attributed to the land in question to the extent that it is residential property only where the amount or value of the consideration so attributed is £150,000 or less.

(5) An exemption conferred by section 92 or by Schedule 30 shall have effect in relation to any duty otherwise chargeable in respect of the rate or average rate of rent attributed to the land in question to the extent that it is residential property only where the rate or average rate so attributed is £15,000 or less.

Determination of consideration for the purposes of regulations 3, 4 and 5: land situated partly in a disadvantaged area and partly outside such an area

Amendments—[1] Para (3A) inserted by FA 2005 s 96, Sch 9 paras 2(3), 5 with effect, subject to FA 2005 Sch 9 para 5(2), for instruments executed after 16 March 2005. This insertion is without prejudice to the power to amend or revoke these provisions by further regulations under FA 2001 s 92A: FA 2005 Sch 9 para 3.

6—(1) In determining the amount of any consideration for the purposes of regulation 3, 4 or 5, the provisions of section 92 and paragraphs 1 and 3 of Schedule 30 shall be disregarded save to the extent mentioned in the following paragraphs of this regulation.

(2) Paragraphs (3) and (4) apply where the land in question is situated partly in a disadvantaged area and partly outside such an area.

(3) For the purposes of regulations 3(2)(*b*) and 4(3)(*b*), the consideration shall be treated as being the attributed consideration.

(4) For the purposes of regulation 5(3), the consideration to be apportioned shall be treated as being the attributed consideration and the apportionment shall be made as between—

(*a*) the land in question to the extent that it is situated in a disadvantaged area and is residential property; and

(*b*) the land in question to the extent that it is it is situated in a disadvantaged area and is not residential property.

(5) "The attributed consideration" means the consideration which would be attributed under paragraph 1(2) of Schedule 30 to such part of the land as is situated in the disadvantaged area.

Land comprising or including six or more separate dwellings

7 Where there is a single contract for the conveyance, transfer or lease of land comprising or including six or more separate dwellings, none of that land counts as residential property for the purposes of these Regulations.

Revocation of the Variation of Stamp Duties Regulations 2001

8 The Variation of Stamp Duties Regulations 2001 are hereby revoked.

2003/2837

STAMP DUTY LAND TAX (ADMINISTRATION) REGULATIONS 2003

Made by the Commissioners of Inland Revenue under FA 2003 ss 79(4), 90(2), (3), (6) and 113(2), Sch 10 para 1, Sch 11 para 2, and Sch 13 paras 33(2), 36, 37(1) and (2), 41 and 42, and the Treasury, in exercise of the powers conferred upon them by FA 2003 Sch 12 para 2(6)

Made . . . .*7 November 2003*
Laid before the House of Commons . . . .*10 November 2003*
Coming into force . . . .*1 December 2003*

ARRANGEMENT OF REGULATIONS

PART 1
GENERAL

PART 1
GENERAL

Citation and commencement

1—(1) These Regulations may be cited as the Stamp Duty Land Tax (Administration) Regulations 2003 and shall come into force on 1st December 2003.

Interpretation

2—(1) In these Regulations—

"the 2003 Act" means the Finance Act 2003;

"the Board" means the Commissioners of Inland Revenue;

["HMRC" means Her Majesty's Revenue and Customs;][1]

"land transaction return" has the meaning given by section 76(1).

(2) In these Regulations, a reference to a numbered section without more is a reference to the section of the 2003 Act bearing that number.

Amendments—[1] Definition of "HMRC" inserted by the Transfer of Tribunal Functions and Revenue and Customs Appeals Order, SI 2009/56 art 3, Sch 2 paras 112, 113 with effect from 1 April 2009.

PART 2
REVENUE CERTIFICATES AND SELF-CERTIFICATES

Interpretation of Part 2

3 In this Part—

"the Inland Revenue" means any officer of the Board;

"Revenue certificate" has the meaning given by section 79(3)(*a*);

"purchaser" has the meaning given by section 43(4);

"self-certificate" has the meaning given by section 79(3)(*b*);

"vendor" has the meaning given by section 43(4).

Conditions to be met before a Revenue certificate is issued

4—(1) The conditions specified in paragraphs (2) to (5) must be met before a Revenue certificate is issued.

(2) The first condition is that a land transaction return in respect of the transaction must have been received by the Inland Revenue.

(3) The second condition is that the return (together with any other returns that are required)—

(*a*) has been completed; and

(*b*) includes any declaration required by paragraph 1(1)(*c*) of Schedule 10 to the 2003 Act.

(4) The third condition is that—

(*a*) as required by section 76(3)(*a*), a self-assessment is included in the return; and

(*b*) on the basis of the information contained in the return, the self-assessment appears to be correct.

(5) The fourth condition is that, as required by section 76(3)(*b*), payment of the amount of tax chargeable in respect of the transaction accompanies the return.

Form and contents of Revenue certificates

5—(1) A Revenue certificate must be in writing and must contain the information prescribed by paragraphs (2) to (7).

(2) The information prescribed by this paragraph is the address of the land to which the transaction relates.

(3) The information prescribed by this paragraph is any number recorded—

(*a*) as the title number of the land—

(i) for England and Wales, in the register of title maintained by the Chief Land Registrar;

(ii) for Scotland, in the Land Register of Scotland maintained by the Keeper of the Registers of Scotland;

(*b*) for Northern Ireland, as the folio number of the land in any registry maintained by the Land Registry of Northern Ireland.

(4) The information prescribed by this paragraph is any National Land and Property Gazetteer Unique Property Reference Number.

(5) The information prescribed by this paragraph is a description of the transaction.

(6) The information prescribed by this paragraph is the effective date in relation to the transaction (within the meaning given by section 119).

(7) The information prescribed by this paragraph is—

(*a*) the name of the purchaser; and

(*b*) the name of the vendor.

Duplicate Revenue certificates

6—(1) If the Inland Revenue are satisfied that a Revenue certificate has been lost or destroyed ("the original certificate"), a duplicate Revenue certificate may be issued.

(2) The duplicate Revenue certificate may be issued in the form of—

(*a*) a Revenue certificate equivalent to, and replacing, the original certificate; or

(*b*) a new Revenue certificate superseding the original certificate.

Multiple Revenue certificates

7—(1) This regulation applies where a land transaction return is made relating to more than one transaction.

(2) Subject to paragraph (3), the Inland Revenue shall issue one Revenue certificate in respect of the transactions to which the return relates.

(3) If the purchaser requests on the return that separate Revenue certificates be issued in respect of each of the transactions to which the return relates, the Inland Revenue may provide separate certificates in respect of any of those transactions.

Form and contents of self-certificate

8—(1) A self-certificate must be in writing and—

(*a*) on the form prescribed by Schedule 1; or

(*b*) in a form that has been approved by the Board.

(2) A self-certificate must contain the information required by the form prescribed by Schedule 1.

PART 3
LAND TRANSACTION RETURNS

Form and contents of land transaction return

9—(1) A land transaction return must be in writing and completed in black ink.

(2) A land transaction return must be—

(*a*) on the form prescribed by Part 1 of Schedule 2 together with any of the forms prescribed by Parts 2 to 4 of that Schedule which are relevant; or

(*b*) in a form that has been approved by the Board.

(3) A land transaction return must contain the information required by the forms prescribed by Schedule 2.

PART 4
DEFERRED PAYMENTS

Interpretation of this Part

10—(1) In this Part—

"application" means an application under section 90;

"the Inland Revenue" means any officer of the Board;

"relevant events" has the meaning given by regulation 12(2)(*c*).

When application to be made

11 An application must be made on or before the last day of the period within which the land transaction return relating to the transaction in question must be delivered.

Form and contents of application

12—(1) An application must be in writing.

(2) An application must set out all the facts and circumstances relevant to it and, in particular, must specify—

(*a*) the consideration to which it relates;

(*b*) the respects in which that consideration is contingent or uncertain; and

(*c*) the events ("relevant events") on the occurrence of which the whole or any part of that consideration will—

(i) cease to be contingent, or

(ii) become ascertained.

Additional contents of application where consideration consists of works or services

13—(1) This regulation applies where the consideration to which an application relates, or any element of that consideration, consists of—

(*a*) the carrying out of works of construction, improvement or repair of a building or other works to enhance the value of land; or (*b*) the provision of services (other than the carrying out of such works).

(2) The application must contain a scheme for payment of tax which must include—

(*a*) a proposal for the payment of tax in respect of the consideration, or element of the consideration, consisting of the carrying out of such works or the provision of such services within 30 days after the carrying out or provision is substantially completed;

(*b*) if the carrying out of such works or the provision of such services is expected to last for more than 6 months, proposals for a scheme of payment of tax at intervals of not more than 6 months.

Provision of information

14—(1) The Inland Revenue may by notice in writing require a person by whom an application is made to provide such information as they may reasonably require for the purposes of determining whether to accept the application.

(2) A notice given under this regulation must specify the time (which must not be less than 30 days from the date of issue of the notice) within which the applicant must comply with it.

Recovery of tax not postponed by application

15—(1) This regulation applies where an application has been made but has not been accepted by the Inland Revenue (including where there is an appeal under regulation 19 against the refusal of the application).

(2) The tax in respect of the chargeable consideration to which the application relates remains due and payable as if there had been no application (and, if relevant, no appeal).

This is subject to—

(*a*) the following paragraphs of this regulation;

(*b*) regulation 22 (direction by [tribunal][1] postponing payment); and

(*c*) regulation 23 (agreement to postpone payment).

(3) Payment of an amount of such tax as would not be due and payable if the application were accepted shall be postponed pending the reaching of a decision on the application.

(4) If an application is refused by the Inland Revenue, and there is no appeal under regulation 19 against the refusal of the application, the date on which any tax the payment of which had been postponed under paragraph (3) is due and payable shall be determined as if it were charged by an assessment of which notice was issued on the date on which the Inland Revenue issues to the applicant a notice of the total amount payable in consequence of the refusal of the application.

This is subject to—

(*a*) regulation 22 (direction by [tribunal][1] postponing payment); and

(*b*) regulation 23 (agreement to postpone payment).

Amendments—[1] Word substituted for word "Commissioners", in both places, by the Transfer of Tribunal Functions and Revenue and Customs Appeals Order, SI 2009/56 art 3, Sch 2 paras 112, 114 with effect from 1 April 2009.

Notice of decision on an application

16—(1) The Inland Revenue must give notice in writing to the person by whom the application was made of their decision whether to accept or refuse an application.

(2) Where the Inland Revenue accept an application, the notice must set out the terms on which the application has been accepted and, in particular, must—

(*a*) specify—

(i) any tax payable in accordance with a land transaction return relating to the transaction in question;

(ii) the nature of any relevant events; and

(iii) the dates of any relevant events (if known); and

(*b*) state that tax is payable within 30 days after the occurrence of a relevant event and in accordance with Part 4 of these Regulations.

(3) Where the Inland Revenue refuse an application, the notice must set out—

(*a*) the grounds for the refusal; and

(*b*) the total amount of tax payable in consequence of the refusal.

Grounds on which application may be refused

17—An application may be refused by the Inland Revenue if—

(*a*) the conditions for making an application specified in section 90(1) are not met;

(*b*) the application does not comply with the requirements of regulation 12 or 14;

(*c*) there are tax avoidance arrangements in relation to the transaction in question (see regulation 18);

(*d*) the application, or information provided in connection with it, is incorrect; or (*e*) information required to be provided under regulation 14 is not provided within such time as the Inland Revenue reasonably required.

Tax avoidance arrangements

18—(1) For the purposes of regulation 17(*c*), arrangements are tax avoidance arrangements in relation to a transaction if their main object or one of their main objects is—

(*a*) to enable payment of the tax payable in respect of the transaction to be deferred; or

(*b*) to avoid the amount or value of the whole or part of the chargeable consideration for the transaction being determined for the purposes of Part 4 of the Finance Act 2003 in accordance with section 51(1).

(2) In this regulation, "arrangements" includes any scheme, agreement or understanding, whether or not legally enforceable.

Right of appeal

19—(1) An appeal may be brought against a refusal by the Inland Revenue to accept an application.

(2) The appeal lies to the General or Special Commissioners ("the Commissioners").[1]

Amendments—[1] Para (2) revoked by the Transfer of Tribunal Functions and Revenue and Customs Appeals Order, SI 2009/56 art 3, Sch 2 paras 112, 115 with effect from 1 April 2009.

Notice of appeal

20—(1) Notice of an appeal under regulation 19 must be given—

(*a*) in writing;

(*b*) within 30 days after the date on which the notice of the decision to refuse the application was issued; and

(*c*) to the officer of the Board by whom that notice was given.

(2) The notice of appeal must specify the grounds of appeal.

[(3) The provisions of paragraphs 36A to 36I of Schedule 10 to the 2003 Act apply to appeals under this regulation.][1]

Amendments—[1] Para (3) substituted by the Transfer of Tribunal Functions and Revenue and Customs Appeals Order, SI 2009/56 art 3, Sch 2 paras 112, 116 with effect from 1 April 2009. Para (3) previously read as follows—

"(3) On the hearing of the appeal the Commissioners may allow the appellant to put forward grounds not specified in the notice, and take them into consideration, if satisfied that the omission was not deliberate or unreasonable.".

Settling of appeals by agreement

21—(1) If before an appeal under regulation 19 is determined, the appellant and the Inland Revenue agree that the decision appealed against—

(*a*) should be upheld without variation,

(*b*) should be varied in a particular manner, or

(*c*) should be discharged or cancelled,

the same consequences shall follow, for all purposes, as would have followed if, at the time the agreement was come to, the [tribunal][1] had determined the appeal and had upheld the decision without variation, varied it in that manner or discharged or cancelled it, as the case may be.

(2) Paragraph (1) does not apply if, within 30 days from the date when the agreement was come to, the appellant gives notice in writing to the Inland Revenue that he wishes to withdraw from the agreement.

(3) Where the agreement is not in writing—

(*a*) paragraphs (1) and (2) do not apply unless the fact that an agreement was come to, and the terms agreed, are confirmed by notice in writing given by the Inland Revenue to the appellant or by the appellant to the Inland Revenue; and

(*b*) the references in those paragraphs to the time when agreement was come to shall be read as references to the time when the notice of confirmation was given.

(4) Where—

(*a*) the appellant notifies the Inland Revenue, orally or in writing, that he does not wish to proceed with the appeal, and

(*b*) the Inland Revenue do not, within 30 days after that notification, give the appellant notice in writing indicating that they are unwilling that the appeal should be withdrawn,

paragraphs (1) to (3) have effect as if, at the date of the appellant's notification, the appellant and the Inland Revenue had come to an agreement (orally or in writing, as the case may be) that the decision under appeal should be upheld without variation.

(5) References in this regulation to an agreement being come to with an appellant, and to the giving of notice or notification by or to the appellant, include references to an agreement being come to, or notice or notification being given by or to, a person acting on behalf of the appellant in relation to the appeal.

Amendments—[1] In para (1), words substituted for word "Commissioners", by the Transfer of Tribunal Functions and Revenue and Customs Appeals Order, SI 2009/56 art 3, Sch 2 paras 112, 117 with effect from 1 April 2009.

Direction by [the tribunal][1] postponing payment

22—[(1) If the appellant has grounds for believing that the amendment or assessment overcharges the appellant to tax, or as a result of the conclusion stated in the closure notice the tax charged on the appellant is excessive, the appellant may—

(*a*) first apply by notice in writing to HMRC within 30 days of the specified date for a determination by them of the amount of tax the payment of which should be postponed pending the determination of the appeal;

(*b*) where such a determination is not agreed, refer the application for postponement to the tribunal within 30 days from the date of the document notifying HMRC's decision on the amount to be postponed;

an application under sub-paragraph (*a*) must state the amount believed to be overcharged to tax and the grounds for that belief.][1]

(2) The notice must—

(a) be given within 30 days after the date on which the notice of the decision to refuse the application was issued and to the officer of the Board by whom that notice was given; and

(b) *state the amount of tax to be postponed.*[1]

(3) If, after any determination on such an application of the amount of tax payment of which should be postponed, there is a change in the circumstances of the case as a result of which either party has grounds for believing that the amount so determined has become excessive or, as the case may be, insufficient, he may, [if the parties cannot agree on a revised determination, apply, at any time before the determination of the appeal, to the tribunal for a revised][1] determination of that amount.

[(4) Any such application is to be subject to the relevant provisions of Part 5 of the Taxes Management Act 1970 (see, in particular, section 48(2)(*b*) of that Act).][1]

(5) The amount of tax of which payment is to be postponed pending the determination of the appeal is the amount (if any) which appears . . . [1] to be appropriate.

(6) Where an application is made under this regulation, the date on which any tax of which payment is not postponed is due and payable shall be determined as if the tax were charged by an assessment of which notice was issued on the date on which the application was determined.

(7) On the determination of the appeal—

(*a*) the date on which any tax payable in accordance with that determination is due and payable shall, so far as it is tax the payment of which had been postponed, be determined as if the tax were charged by an assessment of which notice was issued on the date on which [HMRC][1] issues to the appellant a notice of the total amount payable in accordance with the determination; and

(*b*) any tax overpaid shall be repaid.

Amendments—[1] In heading, words substituted for word "Commissioners", paras (1), (4) substituted, para (2) revoked, in para (3), words substituted for words "by notice in writing given to the other party at any time before the determination of the appeal, apply to the Commissioners for a further", in para (5), words "to the Commissioners, having regard to the representations made and any evidence adduced," revoked, and in para (7)(*a*), word substituted for words "the Inland Revenue", by the Transfer of Tribunal Functions and Revenue and Customs Appeals Order, SI 2009/56 art 3, Sch 2 paras 112, 118 with effect from 1 April 2009. Paras (1), (4) previously read as follows—

"(1) An appellant may by notice in writing apply to the Commissioners for a direction that payment of an amount of tax—

(*a*) in respect of the chargeable consideration to which the application relates, and

(*b*) which would not have been due and payable had the application been accepted,

shall be postponed pending the determination of the appeal.".

"(4) An application under this regulation shall be heard and determined by the Commissioners in the same way as an appeal.

The fact that any such application has been heard and determined by any Commissioners does not preclude them from hearing and determining the appeal or any further application under this regulation.".

Agreement to postpone payment

23—(1) If the appellant and the officer of the Board by whom the notice of the decision to refuse the application was given agree that payment of an amount of tax should be postponed pending the determination of the appeal, the same consequences shall follow, for all purposes, as would have followed if, at the time the agreement was come to, the [tribunal][1] had made a direction to the same effect.

This is without prejudice to the making of a further agreement or of a further direction.

(2) Where the agreement is not in writing—

(*a*) paragraph (1) does not apply unless the fact that an agreement was come to, and the terms agreed, are confirmed by notice in writing given by the officer of the Board in question to the appellant or by the appellant to that officer; and (*b*) the reference in that paragraph to the time when the agreement was come to shall be read as a reference to the time when notice of confirmation was given.

(3) References in this regulation to an agreement being come to with an appellant, and to the giving of notice to or by the appellant, include references to an agreement being come to, or notice being given to or by a person acting on behalf of the appellant in relation to the appeal.

Amendments—[1] In para (1), word substituted for word "Commissioners" by the Transfer of Tribunal Functions and Revenue and Customs Appeals Order, SI 2009/56 art 3, Sch 2 paras 112, 119 with effect from 1 April 2009.

Payments and returns

24—(1) This regulation applies where the Inland Revenue accepts an application.

(2) If the application relates to deferring the payment of tax that has already been paid, the amount already paid shall be repaid together with interest as from the date of payment.

(3) The purchaser must make a return or further return ("the return") to the Inland Revenue—

(*a*) within 30 days after the occurrence of a relevant event;

(*b*) if relevant—

(i) within the period of 30 days mentioned in regulation 13(2)(*a*);

(ii) subject to regulation 27, in accordance with the scheme for payment mentioned in regulation 13(2)(*b*); or

(iii) after the final payment has been made in accordance with that scheme, within 30 days after the purchaser obtains new information the effect of which is that additional tax or less tax is payable in respect of the transaction than has already been paid.

(4) The return must be accompanied by payment of any tax or additional tax payable.

(5) If the effect of the return is that less tax is payable in respect of a transaction than has already been paid, the amount overpaid shall on a claim by the purchaser be repaid together with interest as from the date of payment.

Form and contents of returns

25—(1) A return under regulation 24(3) must be in writing and must contain the following information—

(*a*) a self-assessment of the amount of tax chargeable in respect of the transaction as a whole on the basis of information contained in the return;

(*b*) a statement of the amount of tax payable in respect of so much of the chargeable consideration for the transaction as is not, or is no longer, contingent or uncertain.

(2) The amounts mentioned in paragraph (1) must be calculated by reference to the rates in force at the effective date of the transaction.

Adjustment of payments made as mentioned in section 90(5)

26 Where—

(*a*) a payment is made as mentioned in section 90(5), and

(*b*) an application is accepted in respect of other chargeable consideration taken into account in calculating the amount of payment,

section 80 (adjustment where contingency ceases or consideration is ascertained) does not apply in relation to the payment and, instead, any necessary adjustment shall be made in accordance with these Regulations.

Returns and payments where consideration consists of works or services

27—(1) This regulation applies where a return or further return is required to be made in accordance with regulation 24(3)(*b*)(ii) and the carrying out of the works or provision of the services in question is expected to be substantially completed within a period of less than 6 months after the date on which the return or further return is required.

(2) Where this regulation applies, the applicant and the Inland Revenue may agree that the scheme of payment mentioned in regulation 13(2)(*b*) should be varied so that the next return or further return due to be made in respect of the consideration, or element of the consideration, consisting of the carrying out of such works or the provision of such services may be made within 30 days after the substantial completion of the carrying out of the works or the provision of the services.

(3) If the carrying out of the works or provision of the services in question is not substantially completed within a period of less than 6 months after the date on which, apart from the variation of the scheme of payment, the return or further return would have been required—

(*a*) the variation shall cease to have effect; and

(*b*) returns or further returns must continue to be made in accordance with regulation 24(3)(*b*)(ii).

Applications accepted by the Inland Revenue having no effect

28—For the purposes of Part 4 of the Finance Act 2003 and these Regulations, an application which has been accepted by the Inland Revenue—

(*a*) shall have no effect if—
  (i) it contains false or misleading information; or
  (ii) any facts or circumstances relevant to it are not disclosed to the Inland Revenue; and
(*b*) shall cease to have any effect if the facts and circumstances relevant to it materially change.

PART 5
DISTRAINT BY COLLECTORS: FEES, COSTS AND CHARGES

Interpretation of Part 4

29 In this Part—
"close possession" means physical possession by a distrainor or a person acting on his behalf of the goods and chattels distrained;
"walking possession" means possession in accordance with an agreement between a distrainor and a distrainee by which, in consideration of the distrainor not remaining in close possession, the distrainee undertakes neither—
  (*a*) to dispose of any of the goods and chattels distrained; nor
  (*b*) to permit their removal by any person not authorised by the distrainor to remove them.

Ascertainment of fees, costs and charges

30—(1) The fees chargeable on or in connection with the levying of distress under paragraph 2 of Schedule 12 to the 2003 Act are those specified in the Table in Part 1 of Schedule 3.
(2) The costs and charges recoverable where such distress has been levied are those specified in the Table in Part 2 of that Schedule.
(3) This is subject to the provisions of Part 3 of that Schedule.

Deduction of fees, costs and charges by the collector

31 The fees, costs and charges specified in Schedule 3 shall be deducted by the collector from the sums received on or in connection with the levying of distress or where distress has been levied.

Disputes as to fees, costs and charges

32—(1) In any case of dispute as to the fees chargeable, or costs and charges recoverable, under Schedule 3, the amount of those fees, costs and charges shall be assessed in accordance with this regulation.
(2) The relevant authority shall carry out any such assessment and may give such directions as to the costs of the assessment as he thinks fit.
(3) In paragraph (2), "the relevant authority" means—
  (*a*) in England and Wales, the district judge of the county court for the district in which the distress is, or is intended to be, levied;
  (*b*) in Northern Ireland, the Master (Taxing Office).

PART 6
INTERPRETATION OF PART 5

33 In this Part—
"the appropriate judicial authority" has the meaning given by paragraph 32(3) of Schedule 13 to the 2003 Act;
"the court" has the meaning given by paragraph 40(2) of Schedule 13 to the 2003 Act;
"items subject to legal privilege" has the meaning given by paragraph 35(2) of Schedule 13 to the 2003 Act;
"notice of application" means the notice of intention to apply for an order to which a person is entitled under paragraph 33(1) of Schedule 13 to the 2003 Act;
"order" means an order under paragraph 32 of Schedule 13 to the 2003 Act;
"working day" means any day other than a Saturday, Sunday or public holiday.

Approval of decision to apply for an order

34—Before the hearing of an application for an order, an officer of [Revenue and Customs][1] who is a member of the Senior Civil Service in—
  (*a*) [the Cross-Cutting Policy branch of Her Majesty's Revenue and Customs][1], or
  (*b*) [the Special Compliance Office of Her Majesty's Revenue and Customs][1],
must approve in writing the decision to apply for that order.

Amendment—[1] Words substituted by the SDLT (Administration) (Amendment) Regulations, SI 2005/1132 reg 2(1), (2) with effect from 18 April 2005.

Notice of application

35—(1) Notice of application must be given in writing and must contain the following details—

(*a*) the date, time and place of the hearing of the application;

(*b*) the specifications or descriptions of documents which are the subject of the application;

(*c*) a description of the suspected offence to which the application relates; and

(*d*) the name of the person suspected of committing, having committed or being about to commit the suspected offence.

(2) Notice of application must be given to the person entitled to it not less than five working days before the hearing of the application.

Notice of an order, or notice of an application, treated as having been given

36—(1) Where notice of an order, or notice of application, is delivered to a person, or left at his proper address, notice shall be treated as having been given to that person on the day on which it is delivered or left or, where that day is not a working day, on the next working day.

(2) Where notice of application, or notice of an order, is sent to a person's proper address by facsimile transmission or other similar means which produce a document containing a text of the communication, notice shall be treated as given when the text is received in a legible form.

(3) For the purposes of this regulation, a person's proper address is—

(*a*) the usual or last known place of residence, or the place of business or employment, of that person; or

(*b*) in the case of a company, the address of the company's registered office; or

(*c*) in the case of a liquidator of a company, the liquidator's address for the purposes of the liquidation.

Complying with an order

37—(1) A person complies with an order by producing the documents specified or described in the order to the officer of [Revenue and Customs][1] specified in the order within—

(*a*) the period mentioned in paragraph 32(2) of Schedule 13 to the 2003 Act; or

(*b*) such further period, if any, as is agreed with that officer.

(2) For the purposes of paragraph (1), documents are produced to an officer of [Revenue and Customs][1] if they are either—

(*a*) delivered to the officer; or

(*b*) left for the officer at an address specified in the relevant order.

(3) Where documents are sent to an officer of [Revenue and Customs][1] at the address specified in the relevant order by post, they shall be treated, unless the contrary is proved, as having been produced to the officer—

(*a*) if first class post is used, on the second working day after posting;

(*b*) if second class post is used, on the fourth working day after posting.

Amendment—[1] Words substituted by the SDLT (Administration) (Amendment) Regulations, SI 2005/1132 reg 2(1), (3) with effect from 18 April 2005.

Resolution of disputes as to legal privilege

38—(1) This regulation applies where there is a dispute between [the Commissioners for Her Majesty's Revenue and Customs][1] and a person against whom an order has been made as to whether a document, or part of a document, is an item subject to legal privilege.

(2) The person against whom an order has been made may apply to the appropriate judicial authority to resolve the dispute.

(3) All the documents to which an application under paragraph (2) relates must be lodged in the court at the same time as the application is made and shall be held by the court until the appropriate judicial authority resolves the dispute.

(4) The court shall give [the Commissioners for Her Majesty's Revenue and Customs][1] notice of an application made under paragraph (2) not less than five working days before the hearing of the application, and [the Commissioners for Her Majesty's Revenue and Customs][1] shall be entitled to appear and be heard at that hearing in addition to the person making the application.

(5) On the hearing of an application made under paragraph (2), the appropriate judicial authority shall—

(*a*) resolve the dispute by confirming whether the document, or part of the document, is or is not an item subject to legal privilege; and

(*b*) order the costs of the application to be met by [the Commissioners for Her Majesty's Revenue and Customs][1] except where it holds that no document, or no part of any document, to which the application relates is an item subject to legal privilege.

(6) Where a person makes an application under paragraph (2) within the period mentioned in regulation 37(1), he shall be treated as having complied with the order in relation to the documents to which the application relates until the appropriate judicial authority resolves the dispute.

(7) A dispute may be resolved at any time by [the Commissioners for Her Majesty's Revenue and Customs][1] and the person against whom an order has been made reaching an agreement, whether in writing or otherwise, and, for all purposes, the consequences of such an agreement shall be the same as those which would have ensued if, at the time when the agreement was reached, the appropriate judicial authority had resolved the dispute.

Amendment—[1] Words substituted by the SDLT (Administration) (Amendment) Regulations, SI 2005/1132 reg 2(1), (4) with effect from 18 April 2005.

SCHEDULE 1

SELF-CERTIFICATE

Regulation 8

HM Revenue
& Customs

Stamp duty land tax

Certification that no Land Transaction Return is required for a land transaction

This is a self-certificate under Section 79(3) of Finance Act 2003

Effective date of transaction

/ /

Title number/folio number

Property or land address

Name and address of purchaser's solicitor/agent

Name(s) and address of purchaser

Name(s) and address of vendor

Please turn over

Reason no Land Transaction Return is required

✓

☐ Transfer or conveyance of a freehold interest in land for no chargeable consideration.

☐ Grant of a lease in England & Wales or Northern Ireland for a term of seven years or more and for no chargeable consideration (that is, no premium and no rent of any monetary value).

☐ Transfer or assignment of a lease for no chargeable consideration.

☐ Grant of a lease where all the following are satisfied:
- the term of the lease is less than seven years, and
- the amount of any premium is not such as to attract a charge to SDLT at a rate of 1% or higher (ignoring the availability of any relief), and
- the amount of any rent is not such as to attract a charge to SDLT at a rate of 1% or higher (ignoring the availability of any relief).

☐ Transfer or assignment of a lease where both the following are satisfied:
- the term of the lease when granted was less than seven years, and
- the amount of any consideration for the assignment is not such as to attract a charge to SDLT at a rate of 1% or higher (ignoring the availability of any relief).

☐ Land transaction (other than the transfer of a freehold interest in land, or grant or assignment of a lease) where the amount of the consideration is not such as to attract a charge to SDLT at a rate of 1% or higher (ignoring the availability of any relief).

☐ Land transaction exempt from SDLT under Schedule 3 paragraph 3 Finance Act 2003 (transactions in connection with divorce or dissolution of a civil partnership formed under the Civil Partnership Act 2004).

☐ Land transaction exempt from SDLT under Schedule 3 paragraph 4 Finance Act 2003 (variation of testamentary dispositions).

☐ Transfer or conveyance of a freehold interest in land consisting entirely of residential property where the chargeable consideration, together with that of any linked transaction(s), is less than £1,000.

☐ Acquisition by a beneficiary entitled under a will or on intestacy, where the only consideration given is the assumption of 'secured debt' as defined in paragraph 3A of Schedule 3 Finance Act 2003.

☐ Transfer of interest in a partnership for chargeable consideration not exceeding the zero rate threshold.

Note: in Scotland
- for 'a freehold interest in land' read 'ownership of land'
- 'a lease' includes missives of let constituting a lease
- for 'assignment of a lease' read 'assignation of a tenant's interest under a lease (including missives of let constituting a lease)'

Declaration

This certificate must be signed by the person acquiring the interest. Signature by an agent is not acceptable. Where there is more than one transferee all of them must sign the certificate, except in certain circumstances (please refer to guidance notes).

I certify that for the reason given (as ticked) I do not need to submit a Land Transaction Return to HM Revenue & Customs.

If you give false information in this certificate you may face financial penalties and prosecution.

I declare that the information I have given in this form is true and complete to the best of my knowledge and belief.

Signature of purchaser(s)

[ ]

Name (printed)

[ ]

Capacity in which signing

[ ]

Date

[/ /]

Amendments—Form substituted by the SDLT (Administration) (Amendment) Regulations, SI 2006/776 with effect from 17 April 2006. However, in relation to forms delivered before 16 April 2007, the requirement to deliver a self certificate in the form prescribed by this Schedule containing the information required by that form, is satisfied by delivering a certificate—

(a) on the form prescribed in this Schedule containing the information required by that form, or

(b) on the form formerly prescribed by this Schedule containing the information required by that form.

SCHEDULE 2

LAND TRANSACTION RETURN

Regulation 9

PART 1

MAIN FORM

HM Revenue & Customs — **Land Transaction Return**

For official use only

Your transaction return

How to fill in this return

The guidance notes that come with this return will help you answer the questions.

- Write inside the boxes. Use black ink and CAPITAL letters.
- If you make a mistake, please cross it out and write the correct information underneath.
- **Leave blank any boxes that don't apply to you – please don't strike through anything irrelevant.**
- Show amounts in whole pounds only, rounded down to the nearest pound. Ignore the pence.
- Fill out the payslip on page 7.
- Do not fold the return. Send it back to us unfolded in the envelope provided.
- **Photocopies are not acceptable.**

If you need help with any part of this return or with anything in the guidance notes, please phone the Stamp Taxes enquiry line on **0845 603 0135**, open 8:30am to 5:00pm Monday to Friday, except Bank Holidays. You can get further copies of this return and any supplementary returns from the Orderline on **0845 302 1472.**

Starting your return

ABOUT THE TRANSACTION

1 Type of property

Enter code from the guidance notes

2 Description of transaction

Enter code from the guidance notes

3 Interest transferred or created

Enter code from the guidance notes

4 Effective date of transaction

D D M M Y Y Y Y

5 Any restrictions, covenants or conditions affecting the value of the interest transferred or granted? Put 'X' in one box

Yes No

If 'yes' please provide details

6 Date of contract or conclusion of missives

D D M M Y Y Y Y

7 Is any land exchanged or part-exchanged? Put 'X' in one box

Yes No

If 'yes' please complete address of location

Postcode

House or building number

Rest of address, including house name, building name or flat number

8 Is the transaction pursuant to a previous option agreement? Put 'X' in one box

Yes No

Stamp Taxes

ABOUT THE TAX CALCULATION

9 Are you claiming relief? Put 'X' in one box

Yes No

If 'yes' please show the reason

Enter code from the guidance notes

Enter the charity's registered number, if available, or the company's CIS number

For relief claimed on part of the property only, please enter the amount remaining chargeable

£ . 0 0

10 What is the total consideration in money or money's worth, including any VAT actually payable for the transaction notified?

£ . 0 0

11 If the total consideration for the transaction includes VAT, please state the amount

£ . 0 0

12 What form does the consideration take?
Enter the relevant codes from the guidance notes

13 Is this transaction linked to any other(s)?
Put 'X' in one box

Yes No

Total consideration or value in money or money's worth, including VAT paid for all of the linked transactions

£ . 0 0

14 Total amount of tax due for this transaction

£ . 0 0

15 Total amount paid or enclosed with this notification

£ . 0 0

Does the amount paid include payment of any penalties and any interest due? Put 'X' in one box

Yes No

ABOUT LEASES

If this doesn't apply, go straight to box 26 on page 3.

16 Type of lease

Enter code from the guidance notes

17 Start date as specified in lease

D D M M Y Y Y Y

18 End date as specified in lease

D D M M Y Y Y Y

19 Rent-free period
Number of months

20 Annual starting rent inclusive of VAT (actually) payable

£ . 0 0

End date for starting rent

D D M M Y Y Y Y

Later rent known? Put 'X' in one box

Yes No

21 What is the amount of VAT, if any?

£ . 0 0

22 Total premium payable

£ . 0 0

23 Net present value upon which tax is calculated

£ . 0 0

24 Total amount of tax due – premium

£ . 0 0

25 Total amount of tax due – NPV

£ . 0 0

Check the guidance notes to see if you will need to complete supplementary return 'Additional details about the transaction, including leases', SDLT4.

ABOUT THE LAND including buildings

Where more than one piece of land is being sold or you cannot complete the address field in the space provided, please complete the supplementary return 'Additional details about the land', SDLT3.

26 **Number of properties included**

27 **Where more than one property is involved, do you want a certificate for each property?** Put 'X' in one box

Yes No

28 **Address or situation of land**

Postcode

House or building number

Rest of address, including house name, building name or flat number

Is the rest of the address on the supplementary return 'Additional details about the land', SDLT3?

Put 'X' in one box

Yes No

29 **Local authority number**

30 **Title number, if any**

31 **NLPG UPRN**

32 **If agricultural or development land, what is the area (if known)?** Put 'X' in one box

Hectares Square metres

Area

33 **Is a plan attached?** Please note that the form reference number should be written/displayed on map. Put 'X' in one box

Yes No

ABOUT THE VENDOR including transferor, lessor

34 **Number of vendors included** (Note: if more than one vendor, complete boxes 45 to 48)

35 **Title** Enter MR, MRS, MISS, MS or other title

Note: only complete for an individual

36 **Vendor (1) surname or company name**

37 **Vendor (1) first name(s)** Note: only complete for an individual

38 **Vendor (1) address**

Postcode

House or building number

Rest of address, including house name, building name or flat number

Stamp Taxes

ABOUT THE VENDOR CONTINUED

39 **Agent's name**

40 **Agent's address**
Postcode

Building number

Rest of address, including building name

41 **Agent's DX number and exchange**

42 **Agent's e-mail address**

43 **Agent's reference**

44 **Agent's telephone number**

ADDITIONAL VENDOR

Details of other people involved (including transferor, lessor), other than vendor (1). If more than one additional vendor please complete supplementary return 'Land Transaction Return – Additional vendor/purchaser details', SDLT2.

45 **Title** Enter MR, MRS, MISS, MS or other title
Note: only complete for an individual

46 **Vendor (2) surname or company name**

47 **Vendor (2) first name(s)**
Note: only complete for an individual

48 **Vendor (2) address**

Put 'X' in this box if the same as box 38.

If not, please give address below
Postcode

House or building number

Rest of address, including house name, building name or flat number

ABOUT THE PURCHASER including transferee, lessee

49 **Number of purchasers included** (Note: if more than one purchaser is involved, complete boxes 65 to 69)

50 **National Insurance number (purchaser 1), if you have one.** Note: only complete for an individual

51 **Title** Enter MR, MRS, MISS, MS or other title
Note: only complete for an individual

52 **Purchaser (1) surname or company name**

53 **Purchaser (1) first name(s)**
Note: only complete for an individual

54 **Purchaser (1) address**

Put 'X' in this box if the same address as box 28.

If not, please give address below

Postcode

House or building number

Rest of address, including house name, building name or flat number

55 **Is the purchaser acting as a trustee?** Put 'X' in one box

Yes No

56 **Please give a daytime telephone number** – this will help us if we need to contact you about your return

57 **Are the purchaser and vendor connected?**
Put 'X' in one box

Yes No

58 **To which address shall we send the certificate?**
Put 'X' in one box

Property (box 28) Purchaser's (box 54)

Agent's (box 61)

59 **I authorise my agent to handle correspondence on my behalf.** Put 'X' in one box

Yes No

60 **Agent's name**

61 **Agent's address**
Postcode

Building number

Rest of address, including building name

62 **Agent's DX number and exchange**

63 **Agent's reference**

64 **Agent's telephone number**

ADDITIONAL PURCHASER

Details of other people involved (including transferee, lessee), other than purchaser (1). If more than one additional purchaser, please complete supplementary return 'Land Transaction Return – Additional vendor/purchaser details', SDLT2.

65 **Title** Enter MR, MRS, MISS, MS or other title
Note: only complete for an individual

66 **Purchaser (2) surname or company name**

67 **Purchaser (2) first name(s)**
Note: only complete for an individual

68 **Purchaser (2) address**

Put 'X' in this box if the same as purchaser (1) (box 54).

If not, please give address below
Postcode

House or building number

Rest of address, including house name, building name or flat number

69 **Is purchaser (2) acting as a trustee?** Put 'X' in one box

Yes

No

ADDITIONAL SUPPLEMENTARY RETURNS

70 **How many supplementary returns have you enclosed with this return?** Write the number in each box. If none, please put '0'.

Additional vendor/purchaser details, SDLT2

Additional details about the land, SDLT3

Additional details about the transaction, including leases, SDLT4

DECLARATION

71 **The purchaser(s) must sign this return.** Read the guidance notes in booklet SDLT6, in particular the section headed *'Who should complete and sign the Land Transaction Return?'.*

If you give false information, you may face financial penalties and prosecution.
The information I have given on this return is correct and complete to the best of my knowledge and belief.

Signature of purchaser 1

Signature of purchaser 2

Please keep a copy of this return and a note of the unique transaction reference number, which is in the 'Reference' box on the payslip.

Finally, please send your completed return to:
HM Revenue & Customs, Stamp Taxes/SDLT, Comben House, Farriers Way, NETHERTON, Merseyside, Great Britain, L30 4RN, or the DX address is: Rapid Data Capture Centre, DX725593, Bootle 9

Please don't fold it – keep it flat and use the envelope provided. Fill out the payslip on the next page and pay in accordance with the 'How to pay' instructions.

PART 2
ADDITIONAL VENDOR/PURCHASER DETAILS

Inland Revenue

Land Transaction Return

Additional vendor/purchaser details

When to fill in this return

You must fill in this return for each additional vendor and/or purchaser. The guidance notes will help you answer the questions.

If you need help with any part of this return or with anything in the guidance notes, please phone the Stamp Taxes enquiry line on **0845 603 0135**, open 8:30am to 5:00pm Monday to Friday, except Bank Holidays. Calls are charged at local rates. You can get further copies of this return from the Orderline on **0845 302 1472.**

For official use only

☐☐ ☐☐ ☐☐☐☐

VENDOR OR PURCHASER

1 **Please indicate if this return is for an additional vendor or an additional purchaser.** Put 'X' in one box

☐ **Vendor** Complete section below only

☐ **Purchaser** Complete section below and the section over the page

COMPLETE IN ALL CASES

2 **Title** Enter MR, MRS, MISS, MS or other title
Note: only complete for an individual

3 **Surname or company name**

4 **First name(s)**
Note: only complete for an individual

5 **Address**
Postcode

House or building number

Rest of address, including house name, building name or flat number

Please turn over for additional purchaser details.

ADDITIONAL PURCHASER DETAILS

Only complete this section if this return is for an additional purchaser.

6 **Are the purchaser and vendor connected?**
Put 'X' in one box

☐ Yes ☐ No

7 **Is the purchaser acting as a trustee?** Put 'X' in one Box

☐ Yes ☐ No

8 **Declaration**

The purchaser(s) must sign this return
Read the notes in Section 1 of the guidance notes, SDLT6
'Who should complete the Land Transction Return?'

If you give false information, you may face financial penalties and prosecution.

The information I have given on this form is correct and complete to the best of my knowledge and belief.

Signature of purchaser.

PART 3
ADDITIONAL DETAILS ABOUT THE LAND

Inland Revenue

Land Transaction Return
Additional details about the land

When to fill in this return
Fill in this return when you cannot fit all the details on the main Land Transaction Return, SDLT1. The guidance notes will help you answer the questions.

If you need help with any part of this return or with anything in the guidance notes, please phone the Stamp Taxes enquiry line on **0845 603 0135**, open 8:30am to 5:00pm Monday to Friday, except Bank Holidays. Calls are charged at local rates. You can get further copies of this return from the Orderline on **0845 302 1472**.

REFERENCE
Insert the reference number from the payslip on page 7 of the Land Transaction Return, SDLT1, here.

For official use only

ABOUT THE LAND

1 **Type of property**
Enter code from the guidance notes

2 **Local authority number**

3 **Title number, if any**

4 **NLPG UPRN**

5 **Address or situation of land**
Postcode

House or building number

Rest of address, including house name, building name, flat number or continuation from the SDLT1

Please turn over

Stamp Taxes

ABOUT THE LAND CONTINUED

6 If agricultural or development land, what is the area (if known)?

Hectares Square metres

Area

7 If there are any minerals or mineral rights reserved enter the code below

Enter code from the guidance notes

8 Is a plan attached? Please note that the form reference number should be written/displayed on map. Put 'X' in one box

Yes No

9 Interest transferred or created

Enter code from the guidance notes

PART 4
ADDITIONAL DETAILS ABOUT THE TRANSACTION, INCLUDING LEASES

Inland Revenue

Land Transaction Return

Additional details about the transaction, including leases

When to fill in this return
You must fill in this return where additional information about the transaction and/or lease can be provided.
The guidance notes will help you answer the questions.

If you need help with any part of this return or with anything in the guidance notes, please phone the Stamp Taxes enquiry line on **0845 603 0135**, open 8:30am to 5:00pm Monday to Friday, except Bank Holidays. Calls are charged at local rates. You can get further copies of this return from the Orderline on **0845 302 1472**.

REFERENCE
Insert the reference number from the payslip on page 7 of the Land Transaction Return, SDLT1, here.

For official use only

ABOUT THE TRANSACTION

1 **If this transaction is part of the sale of business, please say if the sale includes** Put 'X' in relevant boxes

Stock
Goodwill
Other
Chattels and moveables

What is the total amount of the consideration for the sale of the business apportioned to these items?

£ . 0 0

2 **If the property is for commercial use, what is it?** Put 'X' in the appropriate box(es)

Office
Hotel
Shop
Warehouse
Factory
Other
Other industrial unit

3 **Have you applied for and received a post transaction ruling in accordance with Code of Practice 10, or asked us for advice on the application of the law to this transaction?** Put 'X' in one box

Yes
No

If 'yes' have you followed it when completing this return? Put 'X' in one box

Yes
No
Ruling not received

4 **Is any part of the consideration contingent or dependent on uncertain future events?**

Yes
No

5 **Have you agreed with the Inland Revenue that you will pay on a deferred basis?**

Yes
No

6 **If there are any minerals or mineral rights reserved enter the code below**

Enter code from the guidance notes

7 **If the purchaser is VAT registered, give their VAT reference number**

8 **If the purchaser is a company please give the following details**

Tax reference number

Company registration number

If registered abroad, give its place of registration

Please turn over

ABOUT THE TRANSACTION CONTINUED

9 **Give a description of the purchaser**
Enter code from the guidance notes

ABOUT LEASES

Complete if the transaction notified on SDLT1 is for the grant of more than one lease

10 **Type of property**

Enter code from the guidance notes

11 **Address or situation of land**

Put 'X' in this box if the same as box 28 on SDLT1

If not, please give address below

Postcode

House or building number

Rest of address, including house name, building name, flat number or continuation from the SDLT1

continued at the top of the next column

12 **Local authority number**

13 **Title number, if any**

14 **NLPG UPRN**

15 **If the transaction is for land, what is the unit and area of measurement?** Put 'X' in one box

Hectares Square metres

Area

16 **Is a plan attached? Please note that the form reference number should be written/displayed on the map.**
Put X in one box

Yes No

17 **Interest transferred or created**

Enter code from the guidance notes

18 **Type of lease**

Enter code from the guidance notes

ABOUT LEASES CONTINUED

19 **Start date as specified in lease**

D D M M Y Y Y Y

20 **End date as specified in lease**

D D M M Y Y Y Y

21 **Rent free period**
Number of months

22 **Annual starting rent inclusive of VAT (actually) payable**

£ · 0 0

End date for starting rent

D D M M Y Y Y Y

Later rent known? Put 'X' in one box

Yes No

23 **What is the amount of VAT, if any?**

£ · 0 0

24 **Total premium payable**

£ · 0 0

25 **Net present value upon which tax is calculated**

£ · 0 0

26 **Total amount of tax due - premium**

£ · 0 0

27 **Total amount of tax due - NPV**

£ · 0 0

28 **Any terms surrendered**

29 **Break clause type** Put 'X' in one box

Landlord Tenant only

Either

30 **What is the date of the break clause?**

D D M M Y Y Y Y

31 **Which of the following relate to this lease?**
Put 'X' in relevant boxes. If none, leave blank

Option to renew

Market rent

Turnover rent

Unascertainable rent

Contingent reserved rent

32 **Rent review frequency**

33 **Date of first review**

D D M M Y Y Y Y

34 **Rent review clause (type)** Put 'X' in one box

Open market RPI

Other

35 **If Schedule 17A para 7FA 2003 has been used in calculating the NPV, what is the date of the rent change?**

D D M M Y Y Y Y

Please turn over

ABOUT LEASES CONTINUED

36 Service charge amount if known

£ . 0 0

37 Service charge frequency Put 'X' in one box

Monthly

Annually

Quarterly

Other

38 Other consideration – tenant to landlord

(for example, services, building works)

Enter the relevant codes from the guidance notes

39 Other consideration – landlord to tenant

(for example, services, building works)

Enter the relevant codes from the guidance notes

SDLT 4 V2 PG 4

Amendments—Form substituted by the SDLT (Administration) (Amendment) Regulations, SI 2004/3124 with effect from 6 December 2004. However, in relation to forms delivered before 1 April 2005, the requirement to make a land transaction return on the form prescribed by this Part containing the information required by that form, is satisfied by making a return—

(a) on the prescribed substituted form containing the information required by that form, or

(b) on the form formerly prescribed by this Part containing the information required by that form.

SCHEDULE 3
FEES, COSTS AND CHARGES

Regulation 30

PART 1
FEES CHARGEABLE ON OR IN CONNECTION WITH THE LEVYING OF DISTRESS

Action taken in connection with the levying of distress	*Fees*
For making a visit to premises with a view to levying distress (whether the levy is made or not)	A sum not exceeding £12.50.
Levying distress where the total sum charged is £100 or less.	£12.50
Levying distress where the total sum charged is more than £100.	12½ per cent on the first £100 of the amount to be recovered; 4 per cent on the next £400; 2½ per cent on the next £1500; 1 per cent on the next £8000; ¼ per cent on any additional sum.

PART 2
COSTS AND CHARGES RECOVERABLE WHERE DISTRESS HAS BEEN LEVIED

Action taken where distress has been levied	*Costs and charges*
1. Taking possession	
Where close possession is taken.	£4.50 for the day of levy only.
Where walking possession is taken.	45p per day, payable for the day the distress is levied and up to 14 days thereafter.
2. Removal and storage of goods.	The reasonable costs and charges of removal and storage.
3.Appraisement.	The reasonable fees, charges and expenses of the person appraising.
4.Sale.	
Where the sale is held on the auctioneer's premises, for the reasonable cost of advertising, auctioneer's commission (to include all out of pocket expenses other than charges for advertising, removal and storage).	15 per cent on the sum realised plus the reasonable cost of advertising, removal and storage.
Where the sale is held on the debtor's premises, for the auctioneer's commission (not to include out-of-pocket expenses or charges for advertising).	7½ per cent on the sum realised plus out-of-pocket expenses actually and reasonably incurred and the reasonable costs of advertising.

PART 3
MISCELLANEOUS PROVISIONS RELATING TO FEES, COSTS AND CHARGES

1 In any case where close possession is taken, an individual left in possession must provide his own board.

2 For the purpose of calculating any percentage fees, costs and charges, a fraction of £1 is to be reckoned as £1, but any fraction of a penny in the total amount so calculated is to be disregarded.

3 In addition to any amount authorised by this Schedule in respect of the supply of goods or services on which value added tax is chargeable there may be added a sum equivalent to value added tax at the appropriate rate on that amount.

2003/2899

STAMP DUTY LAND TAX (APPOINTMENT OF THE IMPLEMENTATION DATE) ORDER 2003

Made by the Treasury under FA 2003 Sch 19 para 2(2)

Made . . . . 12th November 2003

Citation

1 This Order may be cited as the Stamp Duty Land Tax (Appointment of the Implementation Date) Order 2003.

Implementation date

2 The date appointed as the implementation date for the purposes of stamp duty land tax is 1st December 2003.

2004/1363

STAMP DUTY LAND TAX (APPEALS) REGULATIONS 2004

Revocation—These Regulations revoked by the Transfer of Tribunal Functions and Revenue and Customs Appeals Order, SI 2009/56 art 3, Sch 2 para 187(*r*) with effect from 1 April 2009.

2004/1864

TAX AVOIDANCE SCHEMES (INFORMATION) REGULATIONS 2004

Made by the Treasury under FA 1999 s 132, FA 2002 s 135, FA 2004 ss 308(1), (3), 309(1), 310, 312, 313(1), (3), (4)(g), 317(2), 318(1)

Made . . . . 22 July 2004
Laid before the House of Commons . . . . 22 July 2004
Coming into force . . . . 1 August 2004

Citation, commencement and effect

1—(1) These Regulations may be cited as the Tax Avoidance Schemes (Information) Regulations 2004 and shall come into force on 1st August 2004.

(2) These Regulations do not have effect in respect of proposals or arrangements (as the case may be) which are notifiable by virtue of any of the provisions of Part 2 of the Schedule to the Arrangements Regulations—

(*a*) for the purposes of section 308(1), if the relevant date in relation to a proposal falls before 22nd June 2004;

(*b*) for the purposes of section 308(3), if the date on which the promoter first becomes aware of any transaction forming part of arrangements falls before that date;

(*c*) for the purposes of sections 309 and 310, if the date on which any transaction forming part of arrangements is entered into falls before that date.

Interpretation

2 In the Regulations—

"the Act" means the Finance Act 2004, and a reference to a numbered section (without more) is a reference to the section of the Act which is so numbered;

"the Arrangements Regulations" means the Tax Avoidance Schemes (Prescribed Descriptions of Arrangements) Regulations 2004;

["the SDLT Arrangements Regulations" means the Stamp Duty Land Tax Avoidance Schemes (Prescribed Descriptions of Arrangements) Regulations 2005;][1]

"corporation tax" shall be construed in accordance with section 318(1);

"employment" has the same meaning as it has for the purposes of the employment income Parts of the Income Tax (Earnings and Pensions) Act 2003 (see section 4 of that Act) and includes offices to which the provisions of those Parts that are expressed to apply to employments apply equally (see section 5 of that Act); and "employee" and "employer" have corresponding meanings;

"notifiable arrangements" has the meaning given by section 306(1);

"notifiable proposal" has the meaning given by section 306(2);

"promoter" has the meaning given by section 307;

"the prescribed taxes" means capital gains tax, corporation tax[, income tax and stamp duty land tax][1];

"the relevant date" has the meaning given by section 308(2).

Amendments—[1] Definition of "the SDLT Arrangements Regulations" inserted, and words in the definition of "the prescribed taxes" substituted, by the Tax Avoidance Schemes (Information) (Amendment) Regulations, SI 2005/1869 regs 2, 3 with effect from 1 August 2005.

However, these amendments do not have effect in respect of proposals or arrangements (as the case may be) which are notifiable by virtue of the Stamp Duty Land Tax Avoidance Schemes (Prescribed Descriptions of Arrangements) Regulations, SI 2005/1868—

(a) for the purposes of FA 2004 s 308(1), if the relevant date in relation to a proposal falls before 1 August 2005;

(b) for the purposes of FA 2004 s 308(3), if the date on which the promoter first becomes aware of any transaction forming part of the arrangements falls before that date;

(c) for the purposes of FA 2004 s 309 or 310, the date on which any transaction forming part of the arrangements is entered into falls before that date: SI 2005/1869 reg 1.

Prescribed information in respect of notifiable proposals and arrangements

3—(1) The information which must be provided to the Board by a promoter under section 308(1) in respect of a notifiable proposal is sufficient information as might reasonably be expected to enable an officer of the Board to comprehend the manner in which the proposal is intended to operate, including—

(*a*) the promoter's name and address;

(*b*) details of the provision of the Arrangements Regulations [or the SDLT Arrangement Regulations][1] by virtue of which the proposal is notifiable;

(*c*) a summary of the proposal and the name (if any) by which it is known;

(*d*) information explaining each element of the proposed arrangements (including the way in which they are structured) from which the tax advantage expected to be obtained under those arrangements arises; and

(*e*) the statutory provisions, relating to any of the prescribed taxes, on which that tax advantage is based.

(2) The information which must be provided to the Board by a promoter under section 308(3) in respect of notifiable arrangements is sufficient information as might reasonably be expected to enable an officer of the Board to comprehend the manner in which the arrangements are intended to operate, including—

(*a*) the promoter's name and address;

(*b*) details of the provision of the Arrangements Regulations [or the SDLT Arrangement Regulations][1] by virtue of which the arrangements are notifiable;

(*c*) a summary of the arrangements and the name (if any) by which they are known;

(*d*) information explaining each element of the arrangements (including the way in which they are structured) from which the tax advantage expected to be obtained under the arrangements arises; and

(*e*) the statutory provisions, relating to any of the prescribed taxes, on which that tax advantage is based.

(3) The information which must be provided to the Board by a client under section 309 (duty of person dealing with promoter outside the United Kingdom) in respect of notifiable arrangements is sufficient information as might reasonably be expected to enable an officer of the Board to comprehend the manner in which the arrangements are intended to operate, including—

(*a*) the client's name and address;

(*b*) the name and address of the promoter;

(*c*) details of the provision of the Arrangements Regulations [or the SDLT Arrangement Regulations][1] by virtue of which the arrangements are notifiable;

(*d*) a summary of the arrangements, and the name (if any) by which they are known;

(*e*) information explaining each element of the arrangements (including the way in which they are structured) from which the tax advantage expected to be obtained under the arrangements arises; and

(*f*) the statutory provisions, relating to any of the prescribed taxes, on which that tax advantage is based.

(4) The information which must be provided to the Board by a person obliged to do so by section 310 (duty of parties to notifiable arrangements not involving promoter) is sufficient information as might reasonably be expected to enable an officer of the Board to comprehend the manner in which the arrangements of which that transaction forms part are intended to operate, including—

(*a*) the name and address of the person entering into the transaction;

(*b*) details of the provision of the Arrangements Regulations [or the SDLT Arrangement Regulations][1] by virtue of which the arrangements are notifiable;

(*c*) a summary of the arrangements and the name (if any) by which they are known;

(*d*) information explaining each element of the arrangements (including the way in which they are structured) from which the tax advantage expected to be obtained under the arrangements arises; and

(*e*) the statutory provisions, relating to any of the prescribed taxes, on which that tax advantage is based.

[(5) If, but for this paragraph—

(*a*) a person would be obliged to provide information in relation to two or more notifiable arrangements,

(*b*) those arrangements are substantially the same (whether they relate to the same parties or different parties), and

(*c*) he has already provided information under paragraph (4) in relation to any of the other arrangements, he need not provide further information under paragraph (4).][1]

Commentary—*Simon's Taxes* **A7.230, A7.232.**

Amendments—[1] Words inserted, and para (5) inserted, by the Tax Avoidance Schemes (Information) (Amendment) Regulations, SI 2005/1869 regs 2, 4 with effect from 1 August 2005.

However, these amendments do not have effect in respect of proposals or arrangements (as the case may be) which are notifiable by virtue of the Stamp Duty Land Tax Avoidance Schemes (Prescribed Descriptions of Arrangements) Regulations, SI 2005/1868—

(a) for the purposes of FA 2004 s 308(1), if the relevant date in relation to a proposal falls before 1 August 2005;

(b) for the purposes of FA 2004 s 308(3), if the date on which the promoter first becomes aware of any transaction forming part of the arrangements falls before that date;

(c) for the purposes of FA 2004 s 309 or 310, the date on which any transaction forming part of the arrangements is entered into falls before that date: SI 2005/1869 reg 1.

[Time for providing information under section 308, 308A, 309 or 310][4]

4—(1) The period or time (as the case may be) [within which—

(*a*) the prescribed information under section 308, 309 or 310, and

(*b*) the information or documents which will support or explain the prescribed information under section 308A,][4]

must be provided to the Board is found in accordance with the following paragraphs of this regulation.

[(1A) Where a proposal or arrangements (not being otherwise notifiable) is or are treated as notifiable by virtue of an order under section 306A(1), the prescribed period is the period of 10 days beginning on the day after that on which the order is made.][4]

(2) In the case of a notification under section 308(1), the prescribed period is the period of 5 days beginning with the day after the relevant date.

(3) In the case of a notification under section 308(3), the prescribed period is the period of 5 days beginning with the day after that on which the promoter first becomes aware of any transaction forming part of arrangements to which that subsection applies.

[(3A) Neither paragraph (2) nor (3) applies in a case falling within paragraph (1A) or (3B).

(3B) In the case of a requirement to provide specified information about, or documents relating to, the notifiable proposal or arrangements which arises by virtue of an order under section 308A(2), the prescribed period is the period of 10 days beginning on the day after that on which the order is made.][4]

(4) In the case of a notification under section 309(1), the prescribed period is the period of 5 days beginning with the day after that on which the client enters into the first transaction forming part of notifiable arrangements to which that subsection applies.

(5) In the case of a notification under section 310 the prescribed time is any time [during the period of 30 days beginning with the day after that on which the person enters into the first transaction forming part of the notifiable arrangements.][3]

[This is subject to [paragraph (5A)][2].][1]

[(5ZA) In the case of a notification under section 310 in relation to stamp duty land tax, the prescribed time is any time during the period of 30 days beginning with the day after [that on][4] which the person enters into the first transaction forming part of the notifiable arrangements.][2]

[(5A) In the case of a notification under section 310 which arises by virtue of the application of regulation 6 of the Tax Avoidance Schemes (Promoters and Prescribed Circumstances) Regulations 2004 (persons not to be treated as promoters: legal professional privilege), the prescribed time is any time during the period of 5 days beginning with the day after [that on][4] which the person enters into the first transaction forming part of the notifiable arrangements.][1]

(6) In reckoning any period under this regulation or regulation 5 any day which is a non-business day within the meaning of section 92 of the Bills of Exchange Act 1882 shall be disregarded.

(7) Where paragraph (2), (3) or (4) applies, if the prescribed period referred to in that paragraph would otherwise end before 30th September 2004, it shall instead end upon that date.

(8) This regulation is subject to regulations 5 (statutory clearances) and 6 (transitional provisions).

Commentary—*Simon's Taxes* **A7.213, A7.231.**

Amendments—[1] Words in para (5) inserted, and para (5A) inserted, by the Tax Avoidance Schemes (Promoters, Prescribed Circumstances and Information) (Amendment) Regulations, SI 2004/2613 reg 3 with effect from 14 October 2004. However, in any case where the latest time at which a person would by virtue of para (5A) above, be required to provide information to the Board under FA 2004 s 310 would be earlier than 19 November 2004, the latest time at which that information shall be required to be provided shall instead be 19 November 2004: SI 2004/2613 reg 1.

[2] Words in para (5) substituted for words "paragraphs (5ZA) and (5A)", and para (5ZA) revoked, by the Tax Avoidance Schemes (Information) (Amendment) Regulations, SI 2010/410, regs 2, 3, with effect from 1 April 2010.

[3] Words in para (5) substituted by the Tax Avoidance Schemes (Information) (Amendment) Regulations, SI 2006/1544 regs 2, 4 with effect from 1 August 2006.

The substituted text previously read as follows—

"during the period—

(*a*) beginning with the day after that on which the person enters into the first transaction forming part of the notifiable arrangements; and

(*b*) ending with the latest time at which he would first have had to provide the Board with information under section 313 in accordance with regulation 8.".

[4] Heading, and words in paras (1), (5ZA), (5A), substituted, and paras (1A), (3A) inserted, by the Tax Avoidance Schemes (Information) (Amendment) Regulations, SI 2007/2153 regs 2, 3 with effect from 1 September 2007: SI 2007/2153 reg 1.

Statutory clearances

5—(1) If—

(*a*) a promoter must provide information under subsection (1) of section 308;

(*b*) the relevant date by reference to which he must provide that information is that referred to in subsection (2)(*a*) of that section; and

(*c*) he reasonably expects to make an application on behalf of a client under any of the provisions listed in paragraph (3) ("a clearance application");

the prescribed period is that beginning with the day after the relevant date and ending with the applicable date.

(2) The applicable date is—

(*a*) the date on which the first transaction occurs in pursuance of the arrangements, or

(*b*) if the promoter ceases to hold the reasonable expectation referred to in paragraph (1)(*c*) 5 days after he ceases to hold it.

(3) The provisions are—

(*a*) sections 215, 225, 444A and 707 of the Income and Corporation Taxes Act 1988; and

(*b*) sections 138, 139, 140B and 140D of the Taxation of Chargeable Gains Act 1992.

Commentary—*Simon's Taxes* **A7.231**.

Time for providing information under section 308, 309 or 310: transitional provisions

6—(1) Where paragraph (2) or (3) applies, the prescribed period or time (as the case may be) to be found in accordance with regulation 4 shall end upon 31st October 2004 instead of the day on which it would end by virtue of that regulation.

(2) This paragraph applies in respect of proposals or arrangements (as the case may be) that are notifiable by virtue of any of the provisions of Part 1 of the Schedule to the Arrangements Regulations—

(*a*) for the purposes of section 308(1), if the relevant date in relation to a proposal falls within the period beginning with 18th March 2004 and ending with 31st July 2004;

(*b*) for the purposes of section 308(3), if the date on which the promoter first becomes aware of any transaction forming part of arrangements falls within the period beginning with 18th March 2004 and ending with 31st July 2004;

(*c*) for the purposes of sections 309 and 310, if the date on which any transaction forming part of arrangements is entered into falls within the period beginning with 23rd April 2004 and ending with 31st July 2004.

(3) This paragraph applies in relation to proposals or arrangements that are notifiable by virtue of any of the provisions of Part 2 of the Schedule to the Arrangements Regulations—

(*a*) for the purposes of section 308(1), if the relevant date in relation to a proposal falls within the period beginning with 22nd June 2004 and ending with 31st July 2004;

(*b*) for the purposes of section 308(3), if the date on which the promoter first becomes aware of any transaction forming part of arrangements falls within the period beginning with 22nd June 2004 and ending with 31st July 2004;

(*c*) for the purposes of sections 309 and 310, if the date on which any transaction forming part of arrangements is entered into falls within the period beginning with 22nd June 2004 and ending with 31st July 2004.

Commentary—*Simon's Taxes* **A7.228**.

Prescribed information under section 312

7 For the purposes of section 312 (duty of promoter to notify client of number), the prescribed information is the reference number referred to in subsection (1) of that section.

Commentary—*Simon's Taxes* **A7.233.**

Prescribed information under section 313: timing and manner of delivery

[8—(1) For the purposes of section 313(1) (duty of parties to notifiable arrangements to notify HMRC of number etc) the prescribed information is that specified in whichever of paragraphs (4)[, (5) or (5A)][2] is applicable.

(2) For the purposes of section 313(3)(*a*) (cases in which the prescribed information is to be included in returns) the prescribed cases are those specified at paragraphs (6) to (8).

(3) For the purposes of section 313(3)(*b*) (cases in which the prescribed information is to be provided separately)—

(*a*) the prescribed cases are those specified at paragraphs (10) to [(14A)][2]; and

(*b*) the prescribed times are those specified at paragraph (15).

(4) In the cases prescribed at paragraphs (6) to (8) the prescribed information is—

(*a*) the reference number allocated by HMRC under section 311 to the notifiable arrangements or proposed notifiable arrangements; and

(*b*) the year of assessment, tax year or accounting period (as the case may be) in which, or the date on which, the person providing the information expects a tax advantage to be obtained.

(5) In the cases prescribed at paragraphs (10) to (14) the prescribed information is—

(*a*) the name and address of the person providing it;

(*b*) any National Insurance number, tax reference number, PAYE reference number or other personal identifier allocated by HMRC to the person to whom the information relates;

(*c*) the reference number allocated to the scheme by HMRC under section 311 to the notifiable arrangements or proposed notifiable arrangements;

(*d*) the year of assessment, tax year or accounting period (as the case may be) in which, or the date on which, the person providing the information or, in the case of paragraph (10), an employee of that person, expects to obtain a tax advantage by virtue of the notifiable arrangements;

(*e*) the name of the person providing the declaration as to the accuracy and completeness of the notification; and

(*f*) the capacity in which the person mentioned in sub-paragraph (*e*) is acting.

[(5A) In the case prescribed at paragraph (14A) the prescribed information is—

(*a*) the name and address of the purchaser;

(*b*) the reference number (or, if more than one, any one reference number) allocated under the provisions of section 311;

(*c*) the address of the property forming the subject of the arrangements ("the property");

(*d*) the title number of the property (if any is allocated);

(*e*) the unique transaction reference number(if a land transaction return has been submitted to HMRC at the time the prescribed information is provided);

(*f*) the market value of the property, taking into account all chargeable interests in the property held by the same person or connected persons;

(*g*) the effective date of the first land transaction which forms part of the arrangements;

(*h*) the name of the person providing the declaration as to the accuracy and completeness of the notification; and

(i) the capacity in which that person is acting.][2]

(6) Subject to paragraphs (10), (12) and (13), in the case of a person who—

(*a*) expects an advantage to arise in respect of his liability to pay, entitlement to a repayment of, or to a deferment of his liability to pay, income tax or capital gains tax as a result of notifiable arrangements; and

(*b*) is required to make a return to HMRC by a notice under section 8 or 8A of the Taxes Management Act 1970 (income tax and capital gains tax: personal return and trustee's return), in respect of income tax or capital gains tax,

the prescribed information shall be included in the return under that section which relates to the year of assessment in which the person first enters into a transaction forming part of the notifiable arrangements and in the return for each subsequent year of assessment until the advantage ceases to apply to that person.

This paragraph does not apply if the advantage arises in respect of a partner's share of partnership profits or gains.

(7) Subject to paragraphs (10), (12) and (13), in the case of a company which—

(*a*) expects a tax advantage to arise in respect of its liability to pay, entitlement to a repayment of, or to a deferment of its liability to pay, corporation tax as a result of notifiable arrangements; and

(*b*) is required to make a return to HMRC by a notice under paragraph 3 of Schedule 18 to the Finance Act 1998 (company tax return), in respect of corporation tax,

the prescribed information shall be notified to HMRC in the return under that paragraph covering the period in which the company first enters into a transaction forming part of the notifiable arrangements and in the return covering each subsequent period until the tax advantage ceases to apply to the company.

This paragraph does not apply if the advantage arises in respect of a partner's share of partnership profits or gains.

(8) Subject to paragraphs (10) to (13) [and (14A)][2], in the case of a partnership—

(*a*) which expects an advantage to arise in respect of a partner's liability to pay, entitlement to a repayment of, or to a deferment of the partner's liability to pay any of the prescribed taxes in respect of partnership profits or gains as a result of notifiable arrangements; and

(*b*) in respect of which a return is required to be made to the Board by virtue of a notice under section 12AA of the Taxes Management Act 1970 (partnership return) in respect of any of the prescribed taxes,

the prescribed information shall be included in the returns specified in paragraph (9) covering the period in which the partnership first enters into a transaction forming part of the notifiable arrangements and in the returns covering each subsequent period until the tax advantage ceases to apply to the partner in question.

(9) The returns referred to in paragraph (8) are—

(*a*) the partnership's return under section 12AA of the Taxes Management Act 1970; and

(*b*) the return under section 8 or 8A of that Act, or under paragraph 3 of Schedule 18 to the Finance Act 1998, of the partner in respect of whom an advantage is expected.

(10) In the case of a person who is the employer of an employee, by reason of whose employment a tax advantage is expected to arise to any person in respect of income tax, corporation tax or capital gains tax as a result of notifiable arrangements—

(*a*) paragraphs (6) to (8) shall not apply; and

(*b*) the prescribed information shall be provided separately to HMRC in such form and manner as they may specify by the time in paragraph (15).

(11) In the case of a person who would be obliged to comply with a duty under paragraphs (6) to (8), but is not required, in respect of a year of assessment, accounting period or tax year—

(*a*) in the case of notifiable arrangements to which paragraph (6) applies, to make a return under either of the provisions mentioned in paragraph (6)(*b*);

(*b*) in the case of notifiable arrangements to which paragraph (7) applies, to make a return under the provision referred to in paragraph (7)(b); or

(*c*) in the case of notifiable arrangements to which paragraph (8) applies, to make a return under any of the provisions in paragraph (9);

the person must provide the information specified in paragraph (5) separately to HMRC in such form and manner as they may specify by the time in paragraph (15).

(12) In a case of a person who is obliged to comply with a duty under paragraphs (6) to (8) and—

(*a*) the relevant return is not delivered by the filing date; or

(*b*) the relevant return is delivered by the filing date but does not include the prescribed information;

paragraphs (6) to (8) shall not apply and the prescribed information shall be provided separately to HMRC in such form and manner as they may specify by the time in paragraph (15).

(13) In a case where—

(*a*) a person is required to provide information relating to more than one reference number;

(*b*) the information is included in a return under paragraphs (6) to (8); and

(*c*) the number of reference numbers in relation to which information is required exceeds the number of spaces allocated to the information on the return form;

the information relating to so many of the reference numbers as exceeds the number of allocated spaces shall be provided separately to HMRC in such form and manner as they may specify by the time in paragraph (15).

(14) In addition to the duty under any other paragraph above, in a case where the arrangements give rise to a claim submitted separately from the return under—

(*a*) section 261B of the Taxation of Chargeable Gains Act 1992 (treating trade loss etc as CGT loss); or

(*b*) Part 4 of the Income Tax Act 2007 (loss relief);

the prescribed information shall be provided separately to HMRC in such form and manner as they may specify at the time in paragraph (15).

[(14A) In a case where a purchaser expects an advantage to arise in respect of his liability to pay, entitlement to a repayment of, or to a deferment of his liability to pay stamp duty land tax as a result of notifiable arrangements the prescribed information shall be provided separately to HMRC in such form and manner as they may specify by the time in paragraph (15).

(14B) If paragraph 14A applies in relation to a land transaction entered into as purchaser by or on behalf of a partnership notification of the prescribed information by or in relation to the responsible partners may instead be done by or in relation to a representative partner or partners.][2]

(15) The prescribed times for providing information separately under paragraphs (10) to [(14A)][2] are—

(*a*) in the case of paragraph (10), any time during the period ending on the date on which—

(i) the return under regulation 73 of the Income Tax (Pay As You Earn) Regulations 2003 is or would be due in respect of the tax year in which the employer first enters into a transaction forming part of the notifiable arrangements; and

(ii) the return for each subsequent year is or would be due until an advantage ceases to apply to any person;

(*b*) in the case of paragraph (11)—

(i) for sub-paragraph (*a*), any time during the period ending on 31st January next following the end of the year of assessment in question;

(ii) for sub-paragraph (*b*), any time during the period ending on the date defined as the filing date for the purposes of paragraph 14 of Schedule 18 to the Finance Act 1998 in respect of the period of account in question;

(iii) for sub-paragraph (*c*), any time during the period ending on the earliest date by which the person in question could be required to file a return under section 12AA of the Taxes Management Act 1970, determined in accordance with whichever of subsections (4) and (5) of that section is applicable;

(*c*) in the case of paragraphs (12) and (13), any time during the period ending on the filing date for the relevant return;

(*d*) in the case of paragraph (14), the time that the claim is made;

[(*e*) in the case of paragraph (14A) no later than 30 days following the later of—

(i) the effective date of the first land transaction which forms part of the arrangements; or

(ii) the receipt of the reference number allocated under the provisions of section 311.][2]

(16) For the purposes of paragraph (15)(*c*) "the filing date" is whichever date in paragraph (i) to (iii) of paragraph (15)(*b*) applies to the relevant return.

[(16A) In paragraphs (5A), (14A), (14B) and (15), expressions which are used in Part 4 of the Finance Act 2003 have the same meaning as in that Part.][2]

(17) This regulation does not apply to information provided in respect of the SDLT Arrangement Regulations.[2]][1]

Commentary—*Simon's Taxes* **A7.233**.

Amendments—[1] This regulation substituted by the Tax Avoidance Schemes (Information) (Amendment) Regulations, SI 2009/611 regs 2, 4 with effect in relation to—

(a) reference numbers notified to a person under FA 2004 ss 311, 312 or 312A on or after 1 April 2009, where that person has a duty under FA 2004 s 313; and

(b) claims under either of the provisions mentioned in para (14) of the substituted reg 8 above, made on or after 1 April 2009 (SI 2009/611 reg 1(3)).

[2] Words in paras (1), (3)(a), (15) substituted, words in para (8), and paras (5A), (14A), (14B), (16A) inserted, and para (17) revoked, by the Tax Avoidance Schemes (Information) (Amendment) Regulations, SI 2010/410, regs 2, 3, with effect from 1 April 2010.

Exemption from liability for penalty

9 For the purposes of section 313(4)(*g*) (exemption from liability to penalty under other provisions about returns in respect of duty to notify Board of reference number for notifiable arrangements) section 98A(4) of the Taxes Management Act 1970 is prescribed.

Electronic delivery of information

10—(1) Information required to be delivered to the Board or to any other person by virtue of these Regulations may be delivered in such form and by such means of electronic communications as are for the time being authorised for that purpose.

(2) The use of a particular means of electronic communications is authorised for the purposes of paragraph (1) only if—

(*a*) it is authorised by directions given by the Board under section 132(5) of the Finance Act 1999 (voluntary filing by electronic means of returns and other documents); and

(*b*) the user complies with any conditions imposed by the Board under that section.

(3) Nothing in this regulation prevents the delivery of information by electronic communications if the information is contained in a return which is—

(*a*) authorised to be delivered electronically by virtue of regulations under section 132 of the Finance Act 1999; or

(*b*) required to be so delivered by virtue of regulations under section 135 of the Finance Act 2002 (mandatory e-filing).

2004/2421

STAMP DUTY AND STAMP DUTY RESERVE TAX (EXTENSION OF EXCEPTIONS RELATING TO RECOGNISED EXCHANGES) REGULATIONS 2004

Made . . . . *15 September 2004*
Laid before the House of Commons . . . . *16 September 2004*
Coming into force . . . . *12 October 2004*

Made by the Treasury under Finance Act 2002 s 117(1)

Citation and commencement

1 These Regulations may be cited as the Stamp Duty and Stamp Duty Reserve Tax (Extension of Exceptions relating to Recognised Exchanges) Regulations 2004 and shall come into force on 12th October 2004.

Extended application of provisions specified in section 117(2) of the Finance Act 2002

2 The application of the provisions specified in section 117(2) of the Finance Act 2002 is extended to the market known as the Alternative Investment Market established under the rules of the London Stock Exchange plc.

2004/3218

STAMP DUTY AND STAMP DUTY RESERVE TAX (INVESTMENT EXCHANGES AND CLEARING HOUSES) REGULATIONS 2004

Made by the Treasury under FA 1991 ss 116, 117

Made . . . . *8 December 2004*
Laid before the House of Commons . . . . *8 December 2004*
Coming into force . . . . *1 February 2005*

Citation, commencement and effect

1—(1) These regulations may be cited as the Stamp Duty and Stamp Duty Reserve Tax (Investment Exchanges and Clearing Houses) Regulations 2004 and shall come into force on 1st February 2005.

(2) These Regulations have effect—

(*a*) for the purposes of stamp duty, in relation to instruments executed on or after 1st February 2005;

(*b*) for the purposes of stamp duty reserve tax—

(i) in the case of an agreement to transfer equities which is not conditional, where the agreement is made on or after 1st February 2005;

(ii) in the case of an agreement to transfer equities which is conditional, where the condition is satisfied on or after that date.

Interpretation

2 In these Regulations, except where otherwise provided—

"clearing member" means a member of EDX London who is also a member of LCH.Clearnet and who as such is permitted by EDX London and that clearing house to clear futures and options contracts registered by LCH.Clearnet resulting from transactions relating to equities executed on EDX London or reported to it under the rules of EDX London;

"EDX London" means EDX London Limited, a company registered in England and Wales (registered number 4567917) which is a recognised investment exchange under the Financial Services and Markets Act 2000;

"equities" means stocks and shares which are issued or raised by a company but does not include stocks and shares issued or raised by a company not incorporated in the United Kingdom unless—

(*a*) they are registered in a register kept in the United Kingdom by or on behalf of the company; or

(*b*) in the case of shares, they are paired, within the meaning of section 99(6A) of the Finance Act 1986, with shares issued by a company incorporated in the United Kingdom;

"futures contract" means a futures contract or a forward contract conferring rights and obligations to buy or sell equities which is listed by or traded on EDX London or which may be reported to EDX London under the rules of EDX London;

"LCH.Clearnet" means LCH.Clearnet Limited, a company registered in England and Wales (registered number 4743602) which is a recognised clearing house under the Financial Services and Markets Act 2000;

"member" means a member of EDX London;
"non-clearing member" means a member who is not a clearing member;
"option" means an option, to buy or sell securities, which is listed by and traded on EDX London or which may be reported to EDX under the rules of EDX London.

Prescription of recognised investment exchange and recognised clearing house

3 For the purposes of sections 116 and 117 of the Finance Act 1991—
(*a*) EDX London is a prescribed recognised investment exchange;
(*b*) LCH.Clearnet is a prescribed recognised clearing house.

Transfers of securities to LCH.Clearnet — prescribed circumstances

4 No charge to stamp duty or to stamp duty reserve tax arises where, as a result of the exercise of options or the expiration of a futures contract, equities of a particular kind are transferred or issued or agreed to be transferred or issued to—
(*a*) LCH.Clearnet; or
(*b*) a person whose business is or includes holding such securities as a nominee for LCH.Clearnet.

Here, and in regulation 5, references to LCH.Clearnet are references to that clearing house in its capacity as a person providing clearing services in connection with a transaction made on EDX London or reported to EDX London pursuant to the rules of EDX London.

Transfers of securities to or from members of EDX London — prescribed circumstances

5 No charge to stamp duty or to stamp duty reserve tax arises where, in order to meet an obligation to receive securities resulting from the exercise of options or the expiration of a futures contract, equity securities of a particular kind are transferred or agreed to be transferred from—
(*a*) a non-clearing member or a nominee of a non-clearing member to a clearing member or a nominee of a clearing member; or
(*b*) LCH.Clearnet or a nominee for LCH.Clearnet to a clearing member or a nominee of a clearing member.

Here, references to a clearing member are references to a clearing member in his capacity as such.

2005/83

FINANCE ACT 2003, SECTION 66 (PRESCRIBED PERSONS) ORDER 2005

Made . . . . *20 January 2005*
Laid before the House of Commons . . . . *21 January 2005*
Coming into force . . . . *11 February 2005*

Made by the Treasury under FA 2003 s 66(4)

Citation and commencement

1 This Order may be cited as the Finance Act 2003, Section 66 (Prescribed Persons) Order 2005 and shall come into force on 11th February 2005.

NHS foundation trusts prescribed for purposes of s.66 of Finance Act 2003

2 For the purposes of section 66 of the Finance Act 2003 (stamp duty land tax: public bodies), NHS foundation trusts constituted in accordance with Schedule 1 to the Health and Social Care (Community Health and Standards) Act 2003, are prescribed.

2005/645

FINANCE ACT 2003, SECTION 66 (PRESCRIBED TRANSACTIONS) ORDER 2005

Made . . . . *10 March 2005*
Laid before the House of Commons . . . . *10 March 2005*
Coming into force . . . . *1 April 2005*

Made by the Treasury under Finance Act 2003 s 66(2)

Citation and commencement

1 This Order may be cited as the Finance Act 2003, Section 66 (Prescribed Transactions) Order 2005 and shall come into force on 1st April 2005.

Prescribed transactions

2 Any land transaction is exempt from stamp duty land tax if—

(a) it is effected under section 38 of the Energy Act 2004 (nuclear transfer schemes), and

(b) either the purchaser or the vendor is a public body.

2005/844

STAMP DUTY LAND TAX (ELECTRONIC COMMUNICATIONS) REGULATIONS 2005

Made . . . .*21 March 2005*

Laid before the House of Commons . . . .*21 March 2005*

Coming into force . . . .*11 April 2005*

Made by the Commissioners of Inland Revenue under Finance Act 1999 ss 132, 133(2)

PART 1
INTRODUCTION

Citation, commencement and interpretation

1—(1) These Regulations may be cited as the Stamp Duty Land Tax (Electronic Communications) Regulations 2005 and shall come into force on 11th April 2005.

(2) In these Regulations—

["ARTL System" has the meaning given by section 12(1) of the Requirements of Writing (Scotland) Act 1995;][1]

["the Board" means the Commissioners for Her Majesty's Revenue and Customs;][1]

["the Keeper" means the Keeper of the Registers of Scotland;][1]

"land transaction return" means a return complying with the requirements imposed by Part 1 of Schedule 10 to the Finance Act 2003 (stamp duty land tax: land transaction returns) and regulations under that Part; and

"official computer system" means a computer system maintained by or on behalf of the Board—

(*a*) to send or receive information or payments, or

(*b*) to process or store information.

(3) References in these Regulations to information and to the delivery of information shall be construed in accordance with section 132(8) of the Finance Act 1999.

Amendment—[1] Definitions "ARTL System" and "the Keeper" inserted, and definition "the Board" substituted, by the SDLT (Electronic Communications) (Amendment) Regulations, SI 2006/3427 arts 2, 3 with effect from 31 January 2007.

Scope of these Regulations

2—[(1)] [1] These Regulations [apply to][1]—

[(*a*) the delivery of a land transaction return to the Board;

(*ab*) the delivery of a land transaction return, by means of the ARTL System, to the Keeper; and][1]

(*b*) the making of any payment or repayment of tax or other sums in connection with the delivery of such a return.

[(2) Part 2 sets out general provisions as to the use of electronic communications in connection with the delivery to the Board of information and payments in relation to stamp duty land tax.

(3) Part 2 does not apply to stamp duty land tax in connection with a land transaction which—

(*a*) falls to be registered in the Land Register of Scotland; and

(*b*) is to be registered by means of the ARTL System.

Instead Part 2A applies to stamp duty land tax, and any land transaction return, in respect of such a land transaction, and in these Regulations—

"an ARTL transaction" means such a land transaction; and

"an ARTL application" means an application for the registration of such a land transaction.

(4) Part 3 contains provisions about evidence in connection with the use of electronic communications in respect of payments of stamp duty land tax and the delivery of land transaction returns.][1]

Amendment—[1] Para (1) numbered as such; words in para (1), and para (1)(*a*), substituted; para (1)(*ab*), and paras (2)–(4) inserted, by the SDLT (Electronic Communications) (Amendment) Regulations, SI 2006/3427 arts 2, 4 with effect from 31 January 2007.

PART 2
ELECTRONIC COMMUNICATIONS—GENERAL PROVISIONS

Restriction on the use of electronic communications

3—(1) The Board may only use electronic communications in connection with the matters referred to in [regulation 2(1)][1] if—

(*a*) the recipient has indicated that he consents to the Board using electronic communications in connection with those matters; and

(*b*) the Board have not been informed that that consent has been withdrawn.

(2) A person other than the Board may only use electronic communications in connection with the matters referred to in [regulation 2(1)][1] if the conditions specified in paragraphs (3) to (6) are satisfied.

(3) The first condition is that the person is for the time being permitted to use electronic communications for the purpose in question by an authorisation given by means of a direction of the Board.

(4) The second condition is that the person uses—

(*a*) an approved method for authenticating the identity of the sender of the communication;

(*b*) an approved method of electronic communications; and

(*c*) an approved method for authenticating any information delivered by means of electronic communications.

(5) The third condition is that any information or payment sent by means of electronic communications is in a form approved for the purpose of these Regulations.

Here "form" includes the manner in which the information is presented.

(6) The fourth condition is that the person maintains such records in written or electronic form as may be specified in a general or specific direction of the Board.

(7) In this regulation "approved" means approved, for the purposes of these Regulations and for the time being, by means of a general or specific direction of the Board.

Note—*Directions under Reg 3 of the SDLT (Electronic Communications) Regulations,* SI 2005/844

Returns under Part 1 of Schedule 10 to the Finance Act 2003

The Commissioners for Her Majesty's Revenue and Customs ("the Commissioners") direct that, on and after 13 July 2005, a person who is required to deliver a land transaction return under Part 1 of Schedule 10 to the Finance Act 2003 ("the relevant information") is authorised to do so over the Internet.

The Commissioners further direct that —

(a) the methods approved by them for —
  (i) authenticating the identity of the person sending the relevant information,
  (ii) delivery of the relevant information, and
  (iii) authenticating the relevant information; and

(b) the form approved by them in which the relevant information is to be delivered; are the methods and form set out, at the time of, and for the purposes of, the delivery of the relevant information, in the terms and conditions for use of the Stamp Taxes Online Land Transaction Return on the website of Her Majesty's Revenue and Customs (www.hmrc.gov.uk).

Agents acting on behalf of purchasers – returns under Part 1 of Schedule 10 to the Finance Act 2003

The Commissioners for Her Majesty's Revenue and Customs further direct that, on and after 13 July 2005, an agent who delivers information on behalf of a person who is required to deliver the relevant information is authorised to do so over the Internet provided that the following conditions are met.

The first condition is that —

(a) the agent makes a copy of the relevant information before it is sent; and

(b) the person, who is required to deliver the land transaction return, makes a declaration to the agent, before the return is sent, that either
  (i) the relevant information contained is correct to the best of his knowledge and belief, or
  (ii) the relevant information, with the exception of the effective date, is correct to the best of his knowledge and belief.

The second condition is that the agent completes the appropriate declaration within the Stamp Taxes Online computer application.

The Commissioners further direct that —

(a) the methods approved by them for —
  (i) authenticating the identity of the person sending the relevant information,
  (ii) delivery of the relevant information, and
  (iii) authenticating the relevant information; and

(b) the form approved by them in which the relevant information is to be delivered; are the methods and form set out, at the time of, and for the purposes of, the delivery of the relevant information, in the terms and conditions for use of the Stamp Taxes Online Land Transaction Return on the Inland Revenue website (www.hmrc.gov.uk).

Amendment—[1] Words in paras (1), (2) substituted by the SDLT (Electronic Communications) (Amendment) Regulations, SI 2006/3427 arts 2, 5 with effect from 31 January 2007.

Use of intermediaries

4 The Board may use intermediaries in connection with—

(*a*) the delivery of information or the making of payments or repayments by means of electronic communications in connection with the matters referred to in regulation 2(1), and

(*b*) the authentication or security of anything transmitted by such means,
and may require other persons to use intermediaries in connection with those matters.

[PART 2A
ELECTRONIC COMMUNICATIONS AND THE ARTL SYSTEM

Administrative functions of Keeper

4A—(1) The Keeper shall have the following functions in respect of stamp duty land tax—

(*a*) receiving, on behalf of the Board, land transaction returns in respect of ARTL transactions;

(*b*) receiving, on behalf of the Board, payments of any stamp duty land tax in respect of ARTL transactions; and

(*c*) transmitting to the Board those land transaction returns and any payment of stamp duty land tax in respect of the ARTL transactions to which they relate.

(2) The Keeper is the intermediary of the Board in respect of the matters mentioned in sub-paragraphs (*a*) and (*b*) of paragraph (1).][1]

Amendment—[1] Part 2A inserted by the SDLT (Electronic Communications) (Amendment) Regulations, SI 2006/3427 arts 2, 6 with effect from 31 January 2007.

Information to be delivered about compliance with Part 4 of the Finance Act 2003

4B—(1) If a land transaction return is delivered to the Keeper in connection with an ARTL transaction by means of the ARTL system, it must be accompanied by the following information as to compliance—

(*a*) a declaration by the person completing the return ("the responsible person") that the information which it contains has been approved by the purchaser; and

(*b*) a digital signature identifying the responsible person which is included in, or logically associated with, the communication containing the land transaction return.

(2) In this regulation—

"digital signature" means data in electronic form which serves as a method of authentication and which is—

(*a*) uniquely linked to the signatory;

(*b*) capable of identifying the signatory;

(*c*) created using a signature-creation device that the signatory can maintain under the signatory's sole control; and

(*d*) linked to the data to which it relates in such a manner that any subsequent change of data is detectable;

"signature-creation data" means unique data (including, but not limited to, codes or private cryptographic keys) which are used by the signatory to create an electronic signature; and

"signature-creation device" means configured software or hardware used to implement the signature-creation data.][1]

Amendment—[1] Part 2A inserted by the SDLT (Electronic Communications) (Amendment) Regulations, SI 2006/3427 arts 2, 6 with effect from 31 January 2007.

PART 3
ELECTRONIC COMMUNICATIONS—EVIDENTIAL PROVISIONS

Effect of delivering information by means of electronic communications

5—(1) Information to which these Regulations apply, and which is delivered by means of electronic communications, shall be treated as having been delivered, in the manner or form required by Part 4 of the Finance Act 2003 and the Stamp Duty Land Tax (Land Transaction Returns) Regulations 2003 if, but only if, all the conditions imposed by—

(*a*) these Regulations,

(*b*) any other applicable enactment (except to the extent that the condition thereby imposed is incompatible with these Regulations), and

(*c*) any specific or general direction given by the Board,

are satisfied.

(2) Information delivered by means of electronic communications shall be treated as having been delivered on the day on which the last of the conditions imposed as mentioned in paragraph (1) is satisfied.

This is subject to [paragraphs (2A), (3) and (4)][1].

[(2A) Information contained in a land transaction return delivered by electronic communications through the ARTL System to the Keeper in connection with an ARTL application shall be treated as delivered to the Board on the date on which it is delivered to the Keeper.

This is subject to paragraphs (3) and (4).][1]

(3) The Board may by a general or specific direction provide for information to be treated as delivered upon a different date (whether earlier or later) than that given by paragraph (2).

(4) Information shall not be taken to have been delivered to an official computer system [or the ARTL System][1] by means of electronic communications unless it is accepted by the system to which it is delivered.

Amendment—[1] Words in para (2) substituted; para (2A), and words in para (4), inserted; by the SDLT (Electronic Communications) (Amendment) Regulations, SI 2006/3427 arts 2, 7 with effect from 31 January 2007.

Proof of content

6—(1) A document certified by an officer of the Board to be a printed-out version of any information delivered by means of electronic communications under these Regulations on any occasion shall be evidence, unless the contrary is proved, that that information—

(*a*) was delivered by means of electronic communications on that occasion; and

(*b*) constitutes the entirety of what was delivered on that occasion.

[This paragraph does not apply to information delivered by means of electronic communications to the Keeper through the ARTL System.][1]

[(1A) A document certified by the Keeper to be a printed-out version of any information delivered by means of electronic communications through the ARTL System in connection with stamp duty land tax on any occasion shall be evidence, unless the contrary is proved that that information—

(*a*) was delivered by means of electronic communications on that occasion; and

(*b*) constitutes the entirety of what was delivered in that connection on that occasion.][1]

(2) A document purporting to be a certificate given in accordance with paragraph (1) [or (1A)][1] shall be presumed to be such a certificate unless the contrary is proved.

Amendment—[1] Words in para (1), para (1A), and words in para (2), inserted by the Stamp Duty Land Tax (Electronic Communications) (Amendment) Regulations, SI 2006/3427 arts 2, 8 with effect from 31 January 2007.

Proof of sender or recipient

7—[(1)] [1] The identity of—

(*a*) the sender of any information delivered to an official computer system by means of electronic communications under these Regulations, or

(*b*) the recipient of any information delivered by means of electronic communications from an official computer system,

shall be presumed, unless the contrary is proved, to be the person recorded as such on an official computer system.

[This paragraph does not apply to information delivered by means of electronic communications to the Keeper through the ARTL System.][1]

[(2) The sender of any information delivered to the Keeper through the ARTL System in connection with stamp duty land tax shall be presumed, unless the contrary is proved, to be the person recorded as such on that system.][1]

Amendment—[1] Para (1) numbered as such, words at end of para (1), and para (2), inserted, by the SDLT (Electronic Communications) (Amendment) Regulations, SI 2006/3427 arts 2, 9 with effect from 31 January 2007.

Information delivered electronically on another's behalf

8 Any information delivered by an approved method of electronic communications on behalf of any person shall be deemed to have been delivered by him unless he proves that it was delivered without his knowledge or connivance.

Proof of delivery of information and payments

9—(1) The use of an authorised method of electronic communications shall be presumed, unless the contrary is proved, to have resulted in the making of a payment or the delivery of information—

(*a*) in the case of information falling to be delivered, or a payment falling to be made, to the Board, if the making of the payment or the delivery of the information has been recorded on an official computer system; and

(*b*) in the case of information falling to be delivered, or a payment falling to be made, by the Board, if the despatch of that payment or information has been recorded on an official computer system.

(2) The use of an authorised method of electronic communications shall be presumed, unless the contrary is proved, not to have resulted in the making of a payment, or the delivery of information—

(*a*) in the case of information falling to be delivered, or a payment falling to be made, to the Board, if the making of the payment or the delivery of the information has not been recorded on an official computer system; and

(*b*) in the case of information falling to be delivered, or a payment falling to be made, by the Board, if the despatch of that payment or information has not been recorded on an official computer system.

(3) The time of receipt of any information or payment sent by an authorised means of electronic communications shall be presumed, unless the contrary is proved, to be that recorded on an official computer system.

[(4) Nothing in this regulation applies to information or a payment delivered by means of electronic communications to the Keeper through the ARTL System in connection with stamp duty land tax.][1]

Amendment—[1] Para (4) inserted by the SDLT (Electronic Communications) (Amendment) Regulations, SI 2006/3427 arts 2, 10 with effect from 31 January 2007.

Use of unauthorised means of electronic communications

10—(1) Paragraph (2) applies to information which is required to be delivered to the Board in connection with the matters mentioned in regulation 2.

(2) The use of a means of electronic communications, for the purpose of delivering any information to which this paragraph applies, shall be conclusively presumed not to have resulted in the delivery of that information, unless—

(*a*) that means of electronic communications is for the time being approved for delivery of information of that kind; and

(*b*) the sender is approved for the use of that means of electronic communications in relation to information of that kind.

2005/1868

STAMP DUTY LAND TAX AVOIDANCE SCHEMES (PRESCRIBED DESCRIPTIONS OF ARRANGEMENTS) REGULATIONS 2005

Made . . . . 11 July 2005
Laid before the House of Commons . . . . 11 July 2005
Coming into force . . . . 1 August 2005

Made by the Treasury under Finance Act 2004 ss 306(1)(a), (b) and 318

Citation, commencement and interpretation

1—(1) These Regulations may be cited as the Stamp Duty Land Tax Avoidance Schemes (Prescribed Descriptions of Arrangements) Regulations 2005 and shall come into force on 1st August 2005.

(2) In these Regulations—

"chargeable interests" has the meaning given by section 48 of the Finance Act 2003;

"residential" and "non-residential property" have the meanings given in section 116 of the Finance Act 2003; and

a reference (without more) to a numbered section is a reference to the section of the Finance Act 2004 which is so numbered.

(3) For the purposes of these Regulations, section 839 of the Income and Corporation Taxes Act 1988 applies to determine whether persons are connected.

Prescribed description of arrangements in relation to stamp duty land tax

2—(1) For the purposes of Part 7 (disclosure of tax avoidance schemes) the arrangements specified in paragraph (3) are prescribed in relation to stamp duty land tax.

(2) In this regulation—

"the applicable value" means the aggregate market value of all of the chargeable interests in [property (whether residential or non-residential)][1] subject to the arrangements;

"the Commissioners" means the Commissioners for Her Majesty's Revenue and Customs (see section 1 of the Commissioners for Revenue and Customs Act 2005); and

"market value" shall be construed in accordance with section 118 of the Finance Act 2003, and for the purposes of ascertaining that value, all chargeable interests held by the same person or connected persons shall be taken into account.

[(3) The arrangements are those whose subject matter is one of the following—

(*a*) wholly non-residential property in respect of which the applicable value is at least £5,000,000;

(*b*) wholly residential property in respect of which the applicable value is at least £1,000,000;

(*c*) a mixture of non-residential and residential property where either—

(i) the applicable value of the residential property is at least £1,000,000; or

(ii) the applicable value of all the property is at least £5,000,000.

(3A) The time for establishing the applicable value in paragraph (3) is to be the time any requirement to notify would arise under section 308, 309 or 310 (as the case may be).

(3B) Arrangements are excepted from disclosure under this regulation if—

(*a*) they are excluded by virtue of the provisions in the Schedule to these Regulations; or

(*b*) they are of the same, or substantially the same, description as arrangements which were first made available for implementation before 1st April 2010.][1]

[(4) If a promoter makes a notifiable proposal available generally but does not know whether a proposal will result in arrangements, it shall be assumed, for the purposes of these Regulations, that the subject matter of any resulting arrangements will consist of—

(*a*) wholly non-residential property in respect of which the applicable value is at least £5,000,000;
(*b*) wholly residential property in respect of which the applicable value is at least £1,000,000; or
(*c*) a mixture of non-residential and residential property where either—
(i) the applicable value of the residential property is at least £1,000,000; or
(ii) the applicable value of all the property is at least £5,000,000.][1]

(5) If a promoter makes a notifiable proposal available generally, it shall be assumed that the applicable value is £5,000,000 or more.[1]

(6) In any case where—
(*a*) a promoter makes available a proposal for arrangements in circumstances where he knows the identity of at least one of the persons who it is proposed should be a party to the arrangements;
(*b*) a promoter becomes aware of a transaction entered into in pursuance of arrangements of the kind described in sub-paragraph (*a*); or
(*c*) a person becomes a party to any transaction forming part of notifiable arrangements; and liable to comply with—
(i) section 309 (duty of person dealing with promoter outside the United Kingdom); or
(ii) section 310 (duty of parties to notifiable arrangements not involving promoter);

if the person under a duty to provide the Commissioners with prescribed information does not know the applicable value, it shall be assumed to be at least [the applicable value provided in whichever of paragraph (3)(*a*), (*b*) or (*c*) applies][1].

Amendments—[1] Words in para (2) substituted for words "non-residential property", paras (3)–(3B) substituted for previous para (3), para (4) substituted, para (5) revoked, and words in para (6) substituted for figure "£5,000,000", by the Stamp Duty Land Tax Avoidance Schemes (Prescribed Descriptions of Arrangements) (Amendment) Regulations, SI 2010/407 reg 2, with effect from 1 April 2010. Paras (3), (4) previously read as follows:

"(3) The arrangements are those—
(*a*) whose subject matter does not consist wholly of residential property;
(*b*) in respect of which the applicable value is at least £5,000,000 at the time any requirement to notify would (but for this sub-paragraph) arise under section 308, 309 or 310 (as the case may be), and
(*c*) are not excluded by virtue of the provisions of the Schedule to these Regulations.

(4) If a promoter does not know whether proposals will result in arrangements, the subject matter of which will consist at least in part of non-residential property, it shall be assumed, for the purposes of these Regulations, that the subject matter of any resulting arrangements will so consist."

SCHEDULE

Regulation 2(3)(c)

Excluded Arrangements

Arrangements are excluded from being prescribed arrangements for the purposes of these Regulations if they—
(*a*) comprise one or more of steps A to F listed below (subject to Rules 1 and 2 which specify arrangements involving combinations of those steps which are not excluded arrangements); but
(*b*) do not include any step, which is necessary for the purpose of securing a tax advantage, other than one listed below.

Rule 1

Arrangements involving Steps B, D, E and F are excluded arrangements unless rule 2 applies.

Rule 2

Arrangements are not excluded arrangements if they—
(*a*) include all, or at least two of, steps A, C and D; or
(*b*) involve more than one instance of step A, C or D.

The steps are as follows.

Step A: Acquisition of a chargeable interest by special purpose vehicle

The acquisition of a chargeable interest in land by a company created for that purpose ("a special purpose vehicle").

Step B: Claims to relief

Making—
(*a*) a single claim to relief under any of the following provisions of the Finance Act 2003—
(i) section 57A (sale and leaseback arrangements);
(ii) section 60 (compulsory purchase facilitating development);
(iii) section 61 (compliance with planning obligation);
(iv) section 64 (demutualisation of building society);
(v) section 64A (initial transfer of assets to trustees of unit trust scheme);

(vi) section 65 (incorporation of limited liability partnership);
(vii) section 66 (transfers involving public bodies);
(viii) section 67 (transfer in consequence of reorganisation of parliamentary constituencies);
(ix) section 69 (acquisition by bodies established for national purposes);
(x) section 71 (certain acquisitions by registered social landlords);
(xi) section 74 (collective enfranchisement by leaseholders);
(xii) section 75 (crofting community right to buy);
(xiii) Schedule 6 (disadvantaged areas relief);
(xiv) Schedule 6A (relief for certain acquisitions of residential property);
(xv) Schedule 7 (group relief and reconstruction acquisition reliefs);
(xvi) Schedule 8 (charities relief); or
(xvii) Schedule 9 (right to buy, shared ownership leases etc.);

(*b*) one or more claims to relief under any one of the following provisions of the Finance Act 2003—
(i) section 71A (alternative property finance: land sold to financial institution and leased to individual);
(ii) section 72 (alternative property finance in Scotland: land sold to financial institution and leased to individual);
(iii) section 72A (alternative property finance in Scotland: land sold to financial institution and individual in common); or
(iv) section 73 (alternative property finance: land sold to financial institution and resold to individual).

Step C: Sale of shares in special purpose vehicle

The sale of shares in a special purpose vehicle, which holds a chargeable interest in land, to a person with whom neither the special purpose vehicle, nor the vendor, is connected.

Step D: Not exercising election to waive exemption from VAT

No election is made to waive exemption from value added tax contained in paragraph 2 of Schedule 10 to the Value Added Tax Act 1994 (treatment of buildings and land for value added tax purposes).

Step E: Transfer of a business as a going concern

Arranging the transfer of a business, connected with the land which is the subject of the arrangements, in such a way that it is treated for the purposes of value added tax as the transfer of a going concern.

Step F: Undertaking a joint venture

The creation of a partnership (within the meaning of paragraph 1 of Schedule 15 to the Finance Act 2003) to which the property which subject to a land transaction is to be transferred.

2005/1990

STAMP DUTY AND STAMP DUTY RESERVE TAX (EXTENSION OF EXCEPTIONS RELATING TO RECOGNISED EXCHANGES) REGULATIONS 2005

Made . . . . .20 July 2005
Laid before the House of Commons .21 July 2005
Coming into force . . . . .11 August 2005

The Treasury, in exercise of the powers conferred upon them by section 50(1) and (4) of the Finance (No.2) Act 2005, make the following Regulations;

Citation and commencement

1 These Regulations may be cited as the Stamp Duty and Stamp Duty Reserve Tax (Extension of Exceptions relating to Recognised Exchanges) Regulations 2005 and shall come into force on 11th August 2005.

Extended application of provisions specified in section 50(2) of the Finance (No 2) Act 2005

2 The application of the provisions specified in section 50(2) of the Finance (No 2) Act 2005 ("the relevant provisions") is extended to the following markets, which are multilateral trading facilities (or, assuming compliance with the provisions of Title II of the Directive (authorisation and operating conditions), would be such facilities), namely—

(*a*) the market known as AIM established under the rules of London Stock Exchange plc;
(*b*) the market known as OFEX;

(*c*) the market known as POSIT and operated by Investment Technology Group Limited. The markets specified in sub-paragraphs (*a*) to (*c*) are referred to in these Regulations as "prescribed multilateral trading facilities".

Application of the relevant provisions to prescribed multilateral trading facilities

3 (1) In their application to prescribed multilateral trading facilities, the relevant provisions as adapted as follows.

(2) In the following provisions of these Regulations a reference to a numbered section is a reference to the section of the Finance Act 1986 bearing that number.

Adaptation of section 80A

4 (1) Section 80A (stamp duty—exceptions for sales to intermediaries) is adapted as follows.

(2) In subsection (1)—

(*a*) in paragraph (*a*) for "an EEA exchange, or a recognised foreign exchange," substitute "a prescribed multilateral trading facility"; and

(*b*) in paragraphs (*b*) and (*c*) for "the exchange" substitute "the facility".

(3) In subsection (2)—

(*a*) in paragraph (*a*) for "an EEA exchange, or a recognised foreign options exchange," substitute "a prescribed multilateral trading facility";

(*b*) in paragraph (*b*) for "that exchange" substitute "that facility" (in both places);

(*c*) in paragraph (*c*) for "that exchange" substitute "that facility"; and

(*d*) in paragraph (*d*)—

(i) for "exchange, or a" substitute "exchange, a"; and

(ii) after "foreign exchange" insert "or a prescribed multilateral trading facility".

(4) In subsection (3)—

(*a*) in paragraph (*a*) for "an EEA exchange, or a recognised foreign options exchange," substitute "a prescribed multilateral trading facility"; and

(*b*) in paragraph (*b*) for "that exchange" substitute "that facility" (in both places).

(5) In subsection (6)—

(*a*) in the words before paragraph (*a*) for "an exchange" substitute "a prescribed multilateral trading facility"; and

(*b*) in paragraphs (*a*) and (*b*) for "the exchange" (in each place) substitute "the facility".

(6) At the end of the section add—

"(8) In this section 'prescribed multilateral trading facility' has the meaning given by regulation 2 of the Stamp Duty and Stamp Duty Reserve Tax (Extension of Exceptions relating to Recognised Exchanges) Regulations 2005 (SI 2005/1990).".

Adaptation of section 80C

5 (1) Section 80C (stamp duty—exceptions for repurchases and stock lending) is adapted as follows.

(2) In subsection (3)—

(*a*) in paragraph (*a*) for "an EEA exchange or a recognised foreign exchange" substitute "a prescribed multilateral trading facility";

(*b*) in paragraph (*b*) for "that exchange" substitute "that facility".

(3) In subsection (6)—

(*a*) in the words before paragraph (*a*) for "an exchange" substitute "a prescribed multilateral trading facility"; and

(*b*) in paragraphs (*a*) and (*b*) for "the exchange" (in each place) substitute "the facility".

(4) For subsection (7) substitute—

"(7) In this section 'prescribed multilateral trading facility' has the meaning given by regulation 2 of the Stamp Duty and Stamp Duty Reserve Tax (Extension of Exceptions relating to Recognised Exchanges) Regulations 2005.".

Adaptation of section 88A

6 (1) Section 88A (stamp duty reserve tax—exceptions from the principal charge for transactions involving intermediaries) is adapted as follows.

(2) In subsection (1)—

(*a*) in paragraph (*a*) for "an EEA exchange, or a recognised foreign exchange" substitute "a prescribed multilateral trading facility";

(*b*) in paragraphs (*b*) and (*c*) for "the exchange" (in each place) substitute "the facility".

(3) In subsection (2)—

(*a*) in paragraph (*a*) for "an EEA exchange or a recognised foreign options exchange" substitute "a prescribed multilateral trading facility";

(*b*) in paragraphs (*b*) and (*c*) for "that exchange" (in each place) substitute "that facility";

(*c*) in paragraph (*d*)—
(i) for "exchange, or a" substitute "exchange, a"; and
(ii) after "foreign exchange" insert ", or a prescribed multilateral trading facility".

(4) In subsection (3)—
(*a*) in paragraph (*a*) for "an EEA exchange, or a recognised foreign options exchange" substitute "a prescribed multilateral trading facility"
(*b*) in paragraph (*b*) for "that exchange" (in each place) substitute "that facility".

(5) In subsection (6)—
(*a*) in the words preceding paragraph (*a*) for "an exchange" substitute "a facility"; and
(*b*) in paragraphs (*a*) and (*b*) (in each place) for "the exchange" substitute "the facility".

(6) At the end of the section add—

"(7) In this section 'prescribed multilateral trading facility' has the meaning given by regulation 2 of the Stamp Duty and Stamp Duty Reserve Tax (Extension of Exceptions relating to Recognised Exchanges) Regulations 2005.".

Adaptation of section 89AA

7 (1) Section 89AA (stamp duty reserve tax—exceptions from the principal charge for transactions involving repurchase and stock lending) is adapted as follows.

(2) In subsection (3)—
(*a*) in paragraph (*a*)for "on an EEA exchange or a recognised foreign exchange" substitute "a prescribed multilateral trading facility"; and
(*b*) in paragraph (*b*) for "that exchange" substitute "that facility".

(3) In subsection (5)—
(*a*) in the words preceding paragraph (*a*) for "an exchange" substitute "a facility"; and
(*b*) in paragraphs (*a*) and (*b*) for "the exchange" (in each place) substitute "the facility".

(4) For subsection (6) substitute—

"(6) In this section 'prescribed multilateral trading facility' has the meaning given by regulation 2 of the Stamp Duty and Stamp Duty Reserve Tax (Extension of Exceptions relating to Recognised Exchanges) Regulations 2005.".

2006/139

STAMP DUTY AND STAMP DUTY RESERVE TAX (EXTENSION OF EXCEPTIONS RELATING TO RECOGNISED EXCHANGES) REGULATIONS 2006

Made by the Treasury under F(No 2)A 2005 s 50(1), (4)

Made . . . .*25 January 2006*
Laid before the House of Commons . . . .*26 January 2006*
Coming into force . . . .*16 February 2006*

Commentary—*Sergeant and Sims on Stamp Duties* **A16.3**.

Citation and commencement

1 These Regulations may be cited as the Stamp Duty and Stamp Duty Reserve Tax (Extension of Exceptions relating to Recognised Exchanges) Regulations 2006 and shall come into force on 16th February 2006.

Extended application of provisions specified in section 50(2) of the Finance (No 2) Act 2005

2—(1) The application of the provisions specified in section 50(2) of the Finance (No 2) Act 2005 ("the relevant provisions") is extended to the following market, which is a multilateral trading facility (or, assuming compliance with the provisions of Title II of the Directive (authorisation and operating conditions), would be such a facility), namely the market known as [Instinet Chi-X and operated by Instinet Chi-X Limited][1].

(2) Regulations 3 to 7 of the Stamp Duty Reserve Tax (Extension of Exceptions relating to Recognised Exchanges) Regulations 2005 apply to the market mentioned in paragraph (1) as they apply to the multilateral trading facilities listed in paragraphs (*a*) to (*c*) of regulation 2 of those Regulations.

Amendments—[1] Words in para (1) substituted by the Stamp Duty and Stamp Duty Reserve Tax (Extension of Exceptions relating to Recognised Exchanges) (Amendment) Regulations, SI 2007/458 reg 2 with effect from 13 March 2007.

2006/3237

STAMP DUTY LAND TAX (VARIATION OF THE FINANCE ACT 2003) REGULATIONS 2006

Made 11.00 am on . . . .*6th December 2006*

Laid before the House of Commons 2.00 pm on . . . . . . .6th December 2006

Coming into force 2.00 pm on .6th December 2006

The Treasury consider it expedient in the public interest to make the provision made by these Regulations.

Accordingly, the Treasury, in exercise of the power conferred upon them by section 109 of the Finance Act 2003, make the following Regulations.

1 Citation and commencement

These Regulations may be cited as The Stamp Duty Land Tax (Variation of the Finance Act 2003) Regulations 2006 and shall come into force at 2 pm on 6th December 2006.

2 Variation of the Finance Act 2003

(1) Part 4 of the Finance Act 2003 is varied—

(*a*) in its application to land transactions which are scheme transactions, within the meaning of the new section 75A set out in paragraph 1 of the Schedule to these Regulations, in accordance with that paragraph (which inserts new section 75A and provides for the charge in respect of those transactions to be computed by reference to a notional land transaction), and

(*b*) in its application to land transactions involving a partnership, in accordance with paragraph 2 of the Schedule to these Regulations.

(2) In these Regulations—

(*a*) expressions which are used in Part 4 of the Finance Act 2003 have the same meaning in the Schedule as in that Part; and

(*b*) "the relevant time" means 2 pm on 6th December 2006.

SCHEDULE

AMENDMENT OF PART 4 OF THE FINANCE ACT 2003

Regulation 2

Stamp Duty Land Tax: anti-avoidance

1—(1) After section 75 of the Finance Act 2003 (stamp duty land tax: crofting) insert—

"75A Anti-avoidance

(1) This section applies where—

(*a*) one person (V) disposes of a chargeable interest and another person (P) acquires either it or a chargeable interest deriving from it,

(*b*) a number of transactions are involved in connection with the disposal and acquisition ("the scheme transactions"), and

(*c*) the sum of the amounts of stamp duty land tax payable in respect of the scheme transactions is less than would be payable on a notional land transaction effecting the acquisition of V's chargeable interest by P on its disposal by V.

(2) In subsection (1) "transaction" includes in particular—

(*a*) a non-land transaction,

(*b*) an agreement, offer or undertaking not to take specified action,

(*c*) any kind of arrangement whether or not it could otherwise be described as a transaction, and

(*d*) a transaction which takes place after the acquisition by P of the chargeable interest.

(3) The scheme transactions may include, for example—

(*a*) the acquisition by P of a lease deriving from a freehold owned or formerly owned by V;

(*b*) a sub-sale to a third person;

(*c*) the grant of a lease to a third person subject to a right to terminate;

(*d*) the exercise of a right to terminate a lease or to take some other action;

(*e*) an agreement not to exercise a right to terminate a lease or to take some other action;

(*f*) the variation of a right to terminate a lease or to take some other action,

(4) Where this section applies—

(*a*) any of the scheme transactions which is a land transaction shall be disregarded for the purposes of this Part, but

(*b*) there shall be a notional land transaction for the purposes of this Part effecting the acquisition of V's chargeable interest by P on its disposal by V.

(5) The chargeable consideration on the notional land transaction mentioned in subsections (1)(*c*) and (4)(*b*) is the largest amount (or aggregate amount) given or received by or on behalf of any one person in respect of the scheme transactions.

(6) The effective date of the notional land transaction is—

(*a*) the last date of completion for the scheme transactions, or

(*b*) if earlier, the date on which a contract in respect of the scheme transactions is substantially performed.

(7) The notional transaction attracts any relief under this Part which it would attract if it were an actual transaction.

(8) This section does not apply where subsection (1)(*c*) is satisfied only by reason of—

(*a*) sections 71A to 73, or

(*b*) a provision of Schedule 9.

(9) For the purposes of this section an interest in a partnership is a chargeable interest in so far as it concerns land owned by the partnership.".

(2) This paragraph has effect in respect of disposals and acquisitions if—

(*a*) the disposal mentioned in the new section 75A(1)(*a*) (inserted by sub-paragraph (1) above) takes place after the relevant time, and

(*b*) all the scheme transactions (within the meaning of the new section 75A(1)(*b*)) take place after that time.

(3) This paragraph does not have effect in relation to—

(*a*) any scheme transaction which is effected in pursuance of a contract entered into and substantially performed before the relevant time.

(*b*) any other scheme transaction which is effected in pursuance of a contract entered into before the relevant time and which is not an excluded transaction.

(4) For this purpose, a scheme transaction effected in pursuance of a contract is an excluded transaction if—

(*a*) at or after the relevant time the contract is varied in a way that significantly affects the scheme transaction (see sub-paragraph (5)),

(*b*) the subject-matter of the scheme transaction is not identified in the contract in a way that would have enabled its acquisition before the relevant time,

(*c*) rights under the contract are assigned at or after the relevant time,

(*d*) the scheme transaction is effected in consequence of the exercise, at or after the relevant time, of any option, right of pre-emption or similar right, or

(*e*) at or after the relevant time there is an assignment, sub-sale or other transaction (relating to the whole or part of the contract's subject-matter) as a result of which a person other than the purchaser under the contract becomes entitled to call for a conveyance to him.

(5) For the purposes of sub-paragraph (4)(*a*) the contract is varied in a way that significantly affects the scheme transaction if (and only if)—

(*a*) it is varied so as to substitute a different purchaser in relation to the scheme transaction,

(*b*) it is varied so as to alter the subject-matter of the scheme transaction, or

(*c*) it is varied so as to alter the consideration for the scheme transaction.

Stamp Duty Land Tax: partnerships

2—(1) Schedule 15 to the Finance Act 2003 (stamp duty land tax: partnerships) is amended as follows.

(2) In Step Two of paragraph 12(1) (transfer to partnership: how to calculate the "sum of the lower proportions")—

(*a*) in paragraph (*b*) for "or is connected with the relevant owner" substitute "or is an individual connected with the relevant owner", and

(*b*) at the end add—

"(If there is no relevant owner with a corresponding partner, the sum of the lower proportions is nil.)".

(3) Omit paragraph 13 (transfer of partnership where all partners are companies).

(4) In paragraph 14 (transfer of interest in property-investment partnership)—

(*a*) for sub-paragraph (1)(*b*) substitute—

"(*b*) either—

(i) the transferee is a person, other than an individual, connected with the transferor, or

(ii) consideration is given for the transfer,",

(*b*) at the end add—

"(9) An interest in respect of the transfer to which this paragraph applies shall be treated as a chargeable interest for the purposes of paragraph 3(1) of Schedule 7 to the extent that the relevant partnership property consists of a chargeable interest.", and

(*c*) in the italic cross-heading omit "for consideration".

(5) In Step Two of paragraph 20(1) (transfer from partnership: how to calculate the "sum of the lower proportions")—

(*a*) in paragraph (*b*) for "or was connected with the relevant owner" substitute "or was an individual connected with the relevant owner", and

(*b*) at the end add—

"(If there is no relevant owner with a corresponding partner, the sum of the lower proportions is nil.)".

(6) After paragraph 27 (application of group relief) insert—

"27A—

(1) This paragraph applies where in calculating the sum of the lower proportions in relation to a transaction (in accordance with paragraph 12)—

(*a*) a company ("the connected company") would have been a corresponding partner of a relevant owner ("the original owner") but for the fact that paragraph (*b*) of Step Two includes connected persons only if they are individuals, and

(*b*) the connected company and the original owner are members of the same group.

(2) The charge in respect of the transaction shall be reduced to the amount that would have been payable had the connected company been a corresponding partner of the original owner for the purposes of calculating the sum of the lower proportions.

(3) The provisions of Part 1 of Schedule 7 apply to group relief under sub-paragraph (2) above as to group relief under paragraph 1(1) of Schedule 7 but—

(*a*) with the omission of paragraph 2(2)(*a*),

(*b*) with the substitution for "the purchaser" in paragraph 3(1)(*a*) of "a partner who was, at the effective date of the transaction, a partner and a member of the same group as the transferor ("the relevant partner"); and

(*c*) with the other modifications specified in paragraph 27(3) to (6) above.".

(7) This paragraph has effect in relation to any land transaction of which the effective date is, or is after, 6th December 2006 (but see sub-paragraph (8)).

(8) This paragraph does not have effect in relation to—

(*a*) any land transaction which is effected in pursuance of a contract entered into and substantially performed before the relevant time, or

(*b*) any other land transaction which is effected in pursuance of a contract entered into before the relevant time and which is not an excluded transaction.

(9) For this purpose, a land transaction effected in pursuance of a contract is an excluded transaction if—

(*a*) at or after the relevant time the contract is varied in a way that significantly affects the land transaction (see sub-paragraph (10)),

(*b*) the subject-matter of the land transaction is not identified in the contract in a way that would have enabled its acquisition before the relevant time,

(*c*) rights under the contract are assigned at or after the relevant time,

(*d*) the land transaction is effected in consequence of the exercise, at or after the relevant time, of any option, right of pre-emption or similar right, or

(*e*) at or after the relevant time there is an assignment, sub-sale or other transaction (relating to the whole or part of the contract's subject-matter) as a result of which a person other than the purchaser under the contract becomes entitled to call for a conveyance to him.

(10) For the purposes of sub-section (9)(*a*) the contract is varied in a way that significantly affects the land transaction if (and only if)—

(*a*) it is varied so as to substitute a different purchaser in relation to the land transaction,

(*b*) it is varied so as to alter the subject-matter of the land transaction, or

(*c*) it is varied so as to alter the consideration for the land transaction.

2007/1097

STAMP DUTY AND STAMP DUTY RESERVE TAX (INVESTMENT EXCHANGES AND CLEARING HOUSES) (EUREX CLEARING AG) REGULATIONS 2007

Made by the Treasury under FA 1991 ss 116 and 117

Made . . . .*29th March 2007*
Laid before the House of Commons . . . .*30th March 2007*
Coming into force . . . .*23rd April 2007*

1 Citation, commencement and effect

(1) These Regulations may be cited as the Stamp Duty and Stamp Duty Reserve Tax (Investment Exchanges and Clearing Houses) (Eurex Clearing AG) Regulations 2007 and shall come into force on 23rd April 2007.

(2) These Regulations shall have effect—

(*a*) for the purposes of the charge to stamp duty, in relation to instruments executed on or after 23rd April 2007;

(*b*) for the purposes of the charge to stamp duty reserve tax—

(i) in the case of agreements to transfer equities which are not conditional, in relation to agreements made on or after 23rd April 2007;

(ii) in the case of agreements to transfer equities which are conditional, in relation to agreements where the condition is satisfied on or after that date.

2 Interpretation

(1) In these Regulations—

"clearing member" means—

(*a*) a member of Eurex Clearing AG who—

(i) is also a member of the Eurex exchange (as defined by this regulation); and

(ii) is permitted by that exchange and that clearing house to clear options contracts; or

(*b*) a member of Eurex Clearing AG who—

(i) is not a member of the Eurex exchange; and

(ii) is permitted by that clearing house to clear options contracts on behalf of [a non-clearing member][1] (as defined by this regulation),

in his capacity as such a member;

"equities" means stocks and shares which are issued or raised by a company but does not include stocks and shares issued or raised by a company not incorporated in the United Kingdom unless—

(*a*) they are registered in a register kept in the United Kingdom by or on behalf of the company; or

(*b*) in the case of shares, they are paired, within the meaning of section 99(6A) of the Finance Act 1986, with shares issued by a company incorporated in the United Kingdom;

"Eurex Clearing AG" means Eurex Clearing Aktiengesellschaft, a company registered in Germany which is a recognised clearing house under the Financial Services and Markets Act 2000 . . .[1];

"the Eurex exchange" means either one of the investment exchanges known as Eurex Deutschland and Eurex Zurich;

["non-clearing member" means a member of the Eurex exchange who is not a clearing member, in his capacity as such or in his capacity as a person who is a party to a transaction with a clearing member which is otherwise permitted to be cleared by the rules of Eurex Clearing AG;][1]

"option" means an option, to buy or sell equities, which—

(*a*) is listed by and traded on the Eurex exchange (as defined by this regulation); or

(*b*) is otherwise permitted to be cleared by the rules of Eurex Clearing AG.

Amendments—[1] Words in definition of "clearing member" substituted, words in definition of "Eurex Clearing AG" revoked, and definition of "non-clearing member" inserted, by the Stamp Duty and Stamp Duty Reserve Tax (Investment Exchanges and Clearing Houses) (Eurex Clearing AG) (Amendment) Regulations, SI 2008/164 regs 3, 4 with effect as follows—

- for the purposes of the charge to stamp duty, in relation to instruments executed on or after 19 February 2008;
- for the purposes of the charge to stamp duty reserve tax—

(i) in the case of agreements to transfer equities which are not conditional, in relation to agreements made on or after 19 February 2008;

(ii) in the case of agreements to transfer equities which are conditional, in relation to agreements where the condition is satisfied on or after 19 January 2008.

[3 Prescription of recognised investment exchanges and recognised clearing house

For the purposes of sections 116 and 117 of the Finance Act 1991—

(*a*) Eurex Deutschland is prescribed as a recognised investment exchange;

(*b*) Eurex Zurich is prescribed as a recognised investment exchange; and

(*c*) Eurex Clearing AG is prescribed as a recognised clearing house.][1]

Amendments—[1] Regulation 3 substituted by the Stamp Duty and Stamp Duty Reserve Tax (Investment Exchanges and Clearing Houses) (Eurex Clearing AG) (Amendment) Regulations, SI 2008/164 regs 3, 5 with effect as follows—

- for the purposes of the charge to stamp duty, in relation to instruments executed on or after 19 February 2008;
- for the purposes of the charge to stamp duty reserve tax—

(i) in the case of agreements to transfer equities which are not conditional, in relation to agreements made on or after 19 February 2008;

(ii) in the case of agreements to transfer equities which are conditional, in relation to agreements where the condition is satisfied on or after 19 January 2008.

4 Transfers of securities to Eurex Clearing AG—prescribed circumstances

A charge to stamp duty or to stamp duty reserve tax shall be treated as not arising where, as a result of the exercise of an option, equities are transferred or issued, or agreed to be transferred or issued, to—

(*a*) Eurex Clearing AG, or

(*b*) a person whose business is or includes holding such equities as a nominee for Eurex Clearing AG.

[Here, and in regulation 5, references to Eurex Clearing AG are references to that clearing house in its capacity as a person providing clearing services in connection with a transaction made on the Eurex exchange or otherwise permitted to be cleared by the rules of that clearing house.][1]

Amendments—[1] Words inserted by the Stamp Duty and Stamp Duty Reserve Tax (Investment Exchanges and Clearing Houses) (Eurex Clearing AG) (Amendment) Regulations, SI 2008/164 regs 3, 6 with effect as follows—

– for the purposes of the charge to stamp duty, in relation to instruments executed on or after 19 February 2008;

– for the purposes of the charge to stamp duty reserve tax—

(i) in the case of agreements to transfer equities which are not conditional, in relation to agreements made on or after 19 February 2008;

(ii) in the case of agreements to transfer equities which are conditional, in relation to agreements where the condition is satisfied on or after 19 January 2008.

5 Transfers of securities from Eurex Clearing AG [or a non-clearing member][1]—prescribed circumstances

A charge to stamp duty or to stamp duty reserve tax shall be treated as not arising where, in order to meet an obligation to receive equities resulting from the exercise of an option, equities are transferred, or agreed to be transferred, from—

(*a*) Eurex Clearing AG, . . . [1]

(*b*) a person whose business is or includes holding such equities as a nominee for Eurex Clearing AG,

(*c*) a non-clearing member, or

(*d*) a person whose business is or includes holding such equities as a nominee for a non-clearing member,][1]

to a clearing member or a nominee of a clearing member.

Amendments—[1] Word "or" in para (*a*) revoked, paras (*c*), (*d*), and words in heading, inserted, by the Stamp Duty and Stamp Duty Reserve Tax (Investment Exchanges and Clearing Houses) (Eurex Clearing AG) (Amendment) Regulations, SI 2008/164 regs 3, 7 with effect as follows—

– for the purposes of the charge to stamp duty, in relation to instruments executed on or after 19 February 2008;

– for the purposes of the charge to stamp duty reserve tax—

(i) in the case of agreements to transfer equities which are not conditional, in relation to agreements made on or after 19 February 2008;

(ii) in the case of agreements to transfer equities which are conditional, in relation to agreements where the condition is satisfied on or after 19 January 2008.

2007/1385

FINANCE ACT 2003, SECTION 66 (PRESCRIBED STATUTORY PROVISIONS) ORDER 2007

Made by the Treasury under FA 2003 s 66(2)

Made . . . .*2nd May 2007*

Laid before the House of Commons . . . .*3rd May 2007*

Coming into force . . . .*25th May 2007*

1 Citation and commencement

This Order may be cited as the Finance Act 2003, Section 66 (Prescribed Statutory Provisions) Order 2007 and shall come into force on 25th May 2007.

2 Prescribed Statutory Provisions

A land transaction that is not entered into as mentioned in section 66(1) of the Finance Act 2003 is exempt from charge to stamp duty land tax if—

(*a*) the transaction is effected—

(i) under paragraph A23(2), 4(2), 5(4B) or 8(2)(*b*) of Schedule 22 to the School Standards and Framework Act 1998 (transfer of land to local education authority), or

(ii) by a transfer required by virtue of regulations made under section 27(2)(*b*) of the Education and Inspections Act 2006 (transfer of land on removal of foundation or reduction in foundation governors), and

(*b*) either the purchaser or the vendor is a public body.

2007/3437

STAMP DUTY LAND TAX (ZERO-CARBON HOMES RELIEF) REGULATIONS 2007

Made by the Treasury under FA 2003 ss 58B and 58C and approved by a resolution of the House of Commons under FA 2003 s 114(5)

Made . . . . *6 December 2007*
Coming into force . . . . *7 December 2007*

1 Citation, commencement and effect

(1) These Regulations may be cited as the Stamp Duty Land Tax (Zero-Carbon Homes Relief) Regulations 2007 and shall come into force on the day after the day on which they are made.

(2) These Regulations shall have effect in relation to acquisitions—

(*a*) made on or after 1st October 2007, and

(*b*) before 1st October 2012.

2 Interpretation

In these Regulations—

"accredited assessor" means—

(*a*) in England or Wales, either—

(i) a person who is a member of an accreditation scheme approved by the Secretary of State in relation to newly erected dwellings for the purposes of regulation 17F (1) to (3) of the Building Regulations 2000, or

(ii) where no accreditation scheme as described in paragraph (i) has yet been approved, a person who is authorised to issue ratings calculated by the Government's Standard Assessment Procedure for Energy Rating of Dwellings ("the SAP") by the holder of a licence granted by the Department for Environment, Food and Rural Affairs to certify that the ratings assessed under the SAP have been issued by a body authorised by the Secretary of State;

(*b*) in Scotland, the Scottish Ministers or a person who is approved by the Scottish Ministers to issue certificates for the purposes of these Regulations; and

(*c*) in Northern Ireland, a person who is a member of an accreditation scheme approved by the Department of Finance and Personnel or the Department for Social Development for the purpose of assessing the energy performance of dwellings by reference to the approved methodology;

"the approved methodology" means—

(*a*) the methodology for the calculation of the energy performance of buildings approved by the Secretary of State for the purposes of regulation 17A of the Building Regulations 2000; and

(*b*) any further methodology for the calculation of energy performance of buildings approved by the Secretary of State under regulation 7;

"zero-carbon home" has the meaning given in regulation 5; and

"zero-carbon home certificate" means a certificate issued under regulation 6(1).

3 Scope of Regulations

These Regulations apply to a land transaction which is the first acquisition of a dwelling which is a zero-carbon home.

4 Relief

(1) Relief from charge to stamp duty land tax shall be granted in relation to a land transaction to which these Regulations apply as follows.

This is subject to paragraph (5).

(2) Where the chargeable consideration is not more than £500,000 and does not consist of or include rent, the transaction is exempt from charge.

(3) Where the chargeable consideration includes rent and consideration other than rent and the consideration other than rent is not more than £500,000, no tax shall be chargeable in respect of the consideration other than rent.

(4) Where the chargeable consideration does not include rent and is more than £500,000, or the consideration other than rent is more than £500,000, the amount of tax chargeable shall be reduced by £15,000.

(5) Her Majesty's Revenue and Customs may refuse relief if they have reasonable grounds to think that a dwelling is not a zero-carbon home within the meaning of these Regulations, notwithstanding that a zero-carbon home certificate has been issued in relation to that dwelling.

5 Zero-Carbon Home

(1) "Zero-carbon home" means a dwelling that is energy efficient in relation to the aspects of energy efficiency in column 1 of the table.

(2) The evidence to be adduced to show that a dwelling satisfies each relevant aspect of energy efficiency is set out in column 2 of the table.

(3) Whether the requirements in column 2 are met shall be determined by an assessment of the dwelling by an accredited assessor.

1 Aspects of energy efficiency	*2 Evidence*
Heat loss parameter ("HLP").	The HLP of the dwelling calculated in accordance with the approved methodology must be no more than 0.8 Watts per square metre Kelvin (W/m^2K).
Dwelling CO2 emission rate ("DER").	The DER over the course of a year calculated in accordance with the approved methodology must be no more than zero kilograms per square metre ($kg/m^2/year$).
Net CO2 emissions.	The net CO2 emissions from the dwelling over the course of a year calculated in accordance with the approved methodology must be no more than zero kilograms per square metre ($kg/m^2/year$).

(4) In this regulation—

"dwelling CO2 emission rate" means the annual CO2 emissions per unit floor area for space heating, water heating, ventilation and lighting, less the emissions saved by energy generation technologies in or on the dwelling;

"heat loss parameter" means the heat loss per unit of temperature difference per unit floor area determined by the internal dimensions of surfaces bounding the dwelling, the thermal performance of the materials used in construction and the air permeability of the dwelling envelope;

"net CO2 emissions" means—

(*a*) the annual CO2 emissions per unit floor area for space heating, water heating, ventilation and lighting, and those associated with appliances and cooking, less

(*b*) the emissions saved by the use of energy generation technologies in or on the dwelling and additional allowable electricity.

(5) For the purposes of the definition of "net CO2 emissions"—

"allowable electricity" means electricity generated from a zero-carbon energy source designed to serve the dwelling and which is conveyed to the dwelling, or to a sub-station connected directly to the dwelling, by cables used exclusively for the conveyance of electricity from that source;

"zero-carbon energy source" includes wind, photovoltaic and hydro-electric power.

6 Certification

(1) If the dwelling satisfies the definition of zero-carbon home the accredited assessor who carried out the assessment in accordance with regulation 5(3) shall issue a zero-carbon home certificate.

[(1A) The accredited assessor may charge a reasonable fee in respect of the assessment of the dwelling in accordance with regulation 5(3) and production of a zero-carbon home certificate.][1]

(2) A zero-carbon home certificate must state—

(*a*) in relation to the dwelling—

(i) the address . . .[1], including postcode,

(ii) that the dwelling is a zero-carbon home within the meaning of these Regulations, and

(iii) in relation to dwellings in England and Wales only, the unique identifying number from the energy performance certificate if an energy performance certificate has been produced;

(*b*) in relation to the accredited assessor issuing the certificate—

(i) the accredited assessor's full name,

(ii) the name and address of the accredited assessor's employer, or if he is self-employed, the name under which he trades and his address, and

(iii) in relation to dwellings in England and Wales only, the accreditation scheme, if any, to which the accredited assessor belongs;

(*c*) the date on which it was issued.

(3) Within the relevant time, the vendor shall

(*a*) obtain a zero-carbon home certificate from an accredited assessor, and

(*b*) give that certificate to the purchaser.

(4) In this regulation—

"energy performance certificate" has the meaning given in regulation 2 of the Energy Performance of Buildings (Certificates and Inspections) (England and Wales) Regulations 2007;

"relevant time" means—

(*a*) in respect of a first acquisition of a zero-carbon home occurring after the coming into force of these Regulations on or before the acquisition, . . . [1]

(*b*) in respect of a first acquisition of a zero-carbon home occurring before the coming into force of these Regulations but to which these Regulations apply, as soon as practicable following the coming into force of these Regulations[, and

(*c*) in respect of a first acquisition of a zero-carbon home, which is part of a building constructed for use as a single dwelling, occurring before 13 August 2008, as soon as practicable following that date.][1]

Amendments—[1] Para (1A) inserted, in para (2)(*a*)(i) words "of the building" revoked, in para (4), in the definition of "relevant time", in para (*a*) word "and" revoked and para (*c*) and preceding word "and" inserted, by the Stamp Duty Land Tax (Zero-Carbon Homes Relief) (Amendment) Regulations, SI 2008/1932 reg 2 with effect as follows—

– the insertion of para (1A), and amendment to para (2)(*a*)(i), from 13 August 2008; and

– the amendments to para (4), in relation to acquisitions made on or after 1 October 2007 and before 1 October 2012.

7 Approval of methodology

The Secretary of State may approve a methodology for the calculation of the energy performance of dwellings for the purposes of these Regulations.

8 Claiming Relief

Any relief under these Regulations must be claimed in a land transaction return or an amendment of such a return.

9 Linked transactions including the first acquisition of a zero-carbon home

Where the first acquisition of one or more zero-carbon homes is one of a number of linked transactions—

(*a*) section 55(4) of the Finance Act 2003 shall not apply to that acquisition for the purpose of these Regulations; but

(*b*) that acquisition shall continue to form part of the set of transactions for other purposes.

2008/52

STAMP DUTY RESERVE TAX (INVESTMENT EXCHANGES AND CLEARING HOUSES) (THE LONDON STOCK EXCHANGE) REGULATIONS 2008

Made by the Treasury under FA 1991 ss 116(3) and (4) and 117

Made . . . . *14 January 2008*

Laid before the House of Commons . . . . *14 January 2008*

Coming into force . . . . *4 February 2008*

1 Citation, commencement and effect

(1) These Regulations may be cited as the Stamp Duty Reserve Tax (Investment Exchanges and Clearing Houses) (The London Stock Exchange) Regulations 2008 and shall come into force on 4th February 2008.

(2) These Regulations shall have effect—

(*a*) in the case of agreements to transfer equities which are not conditional, in relation to agreements made on or after 4th February 2008;

(*b*) in the case of agreements to transfer equities which are conditional, in relation to agreements where the condition is satisfied on or after that date.

2 Interpretation

(1) In these Regulations—

"Board of directors" means the Board of directors of London Stock Exchange plc;

"clearing participant" means a member (as defined by this regulation) who is also a member of x-clear and who as such is permitted by the Board of directors and that clearing house to clear transactions made on the Exchange for a traded security;

"client" means a person who gives instructions to a participant for equity securities to be purchased or, as the case may be, sold on the Exchange;

"equity securities" means stocks and shares which are issued or raised by a company but does not include stocks and shares issued by a company not incorporated in the United Kingdom unless—

(*a*) they are registered in a register kept in the United Kingdom by or on behalf of the company; or

(*b*) in the case of shares, they are paired, within the meaning of section 99(6A) of the Finance Act 1986, with shares issued by a company incorporated in the United Kingdom;

"the Exchange" means the London Stock Exchange;

"member" in relation to London Stock Exchange plc means a person approved by the Board of directors as a participant;

"nominee" means a person whose business is or includes holding equity securities as a nominee for x-clear acting in its capacity as a person providing clearing services in connection with a transaction made on the Exchange, or as a nominee for a clearing participant (as the case may be);

"non-clearing participant" means a participant other than a clearing participant;

"participant" means a participant in the Exchange;

"section 117" means section 117 of the Finance Act 1991;

"x-clear" means SIS x-clear *Aktiengesellschaft*, a company registered in Switzerland which is a recognised clearing house under the Financial Services and Markets Act 2000.

3 Prescription of recognised clearing house

For the purposes of section 117 x-clear is a recognised clearing house which is prescribed.

4 Prescribed circumstances for the purposes of section 117

(1) In the circumstances prescribed by paragraph (2) below, a charge to stamp duty reserve tax shall be treated as not arising.

(2) The circumstances prescribed are where, in connection with a transaction made on the Exchange—

(*a*) equity securities of a particular kind are agreed to be transferred from—

(i) a clearing participant or a nominee of a clearing participant to another clearing participant or nominee, or

(ii) a non-clearing participant or a client to a clearing participant or a nominee of a clearing participant, or

(iii) a clearing participant or a nominee of a clearing participant to x-clear or to a nominee of that clearing house, or

(iv) a person other than a clearing participant to x-clear or to a nominee of that clearing house, as a result of a failure by a clearing participant to fulfil his obligations in respect of the transaction concerned to transfer equity securities to x-clear or to a nominee of that clearing house, or

(v) The London Clearing House Limited or a nominee of that clearing house to x-clear or a nominee of that clearing house, or

(vi) x-clear or a nominee of that clearing house to The London Clearing House Limited or a nominee of that clearing house, or

(vii) x-clear or a nominee of that clearing house to a clearing participant or a nominee of a clearing participant; and

(*b*) the person to whom those securities are agreed to be transferred under any of the agreements specified in sub-paragraph (*a*) above ("the relevant agreement") is required on receipt of those shares to transfer equity securities under a matching agreement to another person or, in the case of an agreement falling within paragraph (iv) of that sub-paragraph, would have been so required if the failure referred to in that paragraph had not occurred.

(3) In paragraph (2) above—

(*a*) "matching agreement" means an agreement under which—

(i) the equity securities agreed to be transferred are of the same kind as the equity securities agreed to be transferred under the relevant agreement, and

(ii) the number and transfer price of the equity securities agreed to be transferred are identical to the number and transfer price of the equity securities agreed to be transferred under the relevant agreement;

(*b*) references to x-clear and to The London Clearing House Limited are references to those clearing houses in their capacity as persons providing clearing services in connection with a transaction made on the Exchange;

(*c*) references to a clearing participant are references to a clearing participant in his capacity as such.

5 Consequential provision

(1) Equity securities which are the subject of an agreement specified in regulation 4(2)(*a*) shall be dealt with by a clearing participant who is a party to the agreement in a separate designated account, and not otherwise.

(2) In paragraph (1) above "designated account" means an account designated by x-clear for a clearing participant in connection with the equity securities concerned.

2008/710

STAMP DUTY LAND TAX (OPEN-ENDED INVESTMENT COMPANIES) REGULATIONS 2008

Made by the Treasury under FA 2003 ss 102 and 123(2), (3)

Made . . . . *12 March 2008*

Laid before the House of Commons . . . . *12 March 2008*

Coming into force . . . . *6 April 2008*

1 Citation and commencement

These Regulations may be cited as the Stamp Duty Land Tax (Open-ended Investment Companies) Regulations 2008 and shall come into force on 6th April 2008.

2 Interpretation

In these Regulations—

"authorised unit trust" means a unit trust scheme in the case of which an order under section 243 of the Financial Services and Markets Act 2000 is in force;

"land transaction" has the meaning given by section 43(1) of the Finance Act 2003; and

"land transaction return" has the meaning given by section 76(1) of that Act.

3 Conversion of an authorised unit trust to an open-ended investment company—exemption from stamp duty land tax charge

(1) A land transaction transferring any property which is subject to the trusts of an authorised unit trust ("the target trust") to an open-ended investment company ("the acquiring company") is exempt from charge to stamp duty land tax if the conditions set out in paragraph (2) are fulfilled.

(2) Those conditions are that—

(*a*) the transfer forms part of an arrangement for the conversion of an authorised unit trust to an open-ended investment company, whereby the whole of the available property of the target trust becomes the whole of the property of the acquiring company;

(*b*) under the arrangement all the units in the target trust are extinguished;

(*c*) the consideration under the arrangement consists of or includes the issue of shares ("the consideration shares") in the acquiring company to the persons who held the extinguished units;

(*d*) the consideration shares are issued to those persons in proportion to their holdings of the extinguished units; and

(*e*) the consideration under the arrangement does not include anything else, other than the assumption or discharge by the acquiring company of liabilities of the trustees of the target trust.

(3) Relief under this regulation must be claimed in a land transaction return or an amendment of such a return.

(4) In this regulation and in regulation 4 "the whole of the available property of the target trust" means the whole of the property subject to the trusts of the target trust, other than any property which is retained for the purpose of discharging liabilities of the trustees of the target trust.

(5) For the purposes of this regulation and regulation 4, each of the parts of an umbrella scheme (and not the scheme as a whole) shall be regarded as an authorised unit trust, and "umbrella scheme" has the same meaning as in section 468 of the Income and Corporation Taxes Act 1988.

4 Amalgamation of an authorised unit trust with an open-ended investment company—exemption from stamp duty land tax charge

(1) A land transaction transferring any property which is subject to the trusts of an authorised unit trust ("the target trust") to an open-ended investment company ("the acquiring company") is exempt from charge to stamp duty land tax if the conditions set out in paragraph (2) are fulfilled.

(2) Those conditions are that—

(*a*) the transfer forms part of an arrangement for the amalgamation of an authorised unit trust with an open-ended investment company, whereby the whole of the available property of the target trust becomes part (but not the whole) of the property of the acquiring company;
(*b*) under the arrangement all the units in the target trust are extinguished;
(*c*) the consideration under the arrangement consists of or includes the issue of shares ("the consideration shares") in the acquiring company to the persons who held the extinguished units;
(*d*) the consideration shares are issued to those persons in proportion to their holdings of the extinguished units; and
(*e*) the consideration under the arrangement does not include anything else, other than the assumption or discharge by the acquiring company of liabilities of the trustees of the target trust.

(3) Relief under this regulation must be claimed in a land transaction return or an amendment of such a return.

2008/1814

STAMP DUTY AND STAMP DUTY RESERVE TAX (INVESTMENT EXCHANGES AND CLEARING HOUSES) (EUROPEAN CENTRAL COUNTERPARTY LIMITED AND THE TURQUOISE MULTILATERAL TRADING FACILITY) REGULATIONS 2008

Made by the Treasury under FA 1991 ss 116, 117

Made . . . . 8 *July 2008*
Laid before the House of Commons . . . . 9 *July 2008*
Coming into force . . . . 30 *July 2008*

Amendment—These regulations revoked by the Stamp Duty and Stamp Duty Reserve Tax (Investment Exchanges and Clearing Houses) Regulations (No 8), SI 2009/1827, reg 6, with effect:
(a) for the purposes of the charge to stamp duty, in relation to instruments executed on or after 4 August 2009
(b) for the purposes of the charge to stamp duty reserve tax:
(i) in the case of agreements to transfer traded securities which are not conditional, in relation to agreements made on or after 4 August 2009;
(ii) in the case of agreements to transfer traded securities which are conditional, in relation to agreements where the condition is satisfied on or after that date.

1 Citation, commencement and effect

(1) These Regulations may be cited as the Stamp Duty and Stamp Duty Reserve Tax (Investment Exchanges and Clearing Houses) (European Central Counterparty Limited and the Turquoise Multilateral Trading Facility) Regulations 2008 and shall come into force on 30th July 2008.

(2) These Regulations shall have effect—
(a) for the purposes of the charge to stamp duty, in relation to instruments executed on or after 30th July 2008;
(b) for the purposes of the charge to stamp duty reserve tax—
(i) in the case of agreements to transfer traded securities which are not conditional, in relation to agreements made on or after 30th July 2008;
(ii) in the case of agreements to transfer traded securities which are conditional, in relation to agreements where the condition is satisfied on or after that date.

2 *Interpretation*

(1) In these Regulations—

"clearing participant" means a member of EuroCCP who as such is permitted by the Rules of EuroCCP to clear transactions made on the Facility for a traded security and who may or may not also be a participant in the Facility;

"client" means a person who gives instructions to a non-clearing firm for traded securities to be sold on the Facility;

"EuroCCP" means European Central Counterparty Limited, a company which is a recognised clearing house under the Financial Services and Markets Act 2000;

"the Facility" means the multilateral trading facility operated by Turquoise Services Limited, a company which is permitted to operate a multilateral trading facility for the purposes of Part IV of the Financial Services and Markets Act 2000;

"nominee" means a person whose business is or includes holding traded securities as a nominee for EuroCCP acting in its capacity as a person providing clearing services in connection with a transaction made on the Facility, or as a nominee for a clearing participant (as the case may be);

"non-clearing firm" means a participant in the Facility other than a clearing participant;

"traded securities" means stocks and shares which are issued or raised by a company but does not include stocks and shares issued by a company not incorporated in the United Kingdom unless—

(a) they are registered in a register kept in the United Kingdom by or on behalf of the company; or

(b) in the case of shares, they are paired, within the meaning of section 99(6A) of the Finance Act 1986, with shares issued by a company incorporated in the United Kingdom.

3 *Prescription of recognised clearing house*

For the purposes of sections 116 and 117 of the Finance Act 1991—

(a) Turquoise Multilateral Trading Facility ("the Facility") is prescribed as a recognised investment exchange; and

(b) EuroCCP is prescribed as a recognised clearing house.

4 *Prescribed circumstances for the purposes of sections 116 and 117*

(1) In the circumstances prescribed by paragraph (2) below, a charge to stamp duty or stamp duty reserve tax shall be treated as not arising.

(2) The circumstances prescribed are where, in connection with a transaction made on the Facility—

(a) traded securities of a particular kind are transferred, or agreed to be transferred, from—

(i) a clearing participant or a nominee of a clearing participant to another clearing participant or nominee, or

(ii) a non-clearing firm or its client to a clearing participant or a nominee of a clearing participant, or

(iii) a clearing participant or a nominee of a clearing participant to EuroCCP or to a nominee of that clearing house, or

(iv) a person other than a clearing participant to EuroCCP or to a nominee of that clearing house, as a result of a failure by a clearing participant to fulfil his obligations in respect of the transaction concerned to transfer traded securities to EuroCCP or to a nominee of that clearing house, or

(v) EuroCCP or a nominee of that clearing house to a clearing participant or a nominee of a clearing participant; and

(b) the person to whom those securities are agreed to be transferred under any of the agreements specified in sub-paragraph (a) above ("the relevant agreement") is required on receipt of those securities to transfer traded securities under a matching agreement to another person or, in the case of an agreement falling within paragraph (iv) of that sub-paragraph, would have been so required if the failure referred to in that paragraph had not occurred.

(3) In paragraph (2) above—

(a) "matching agreement" means an agreement under which—

(i) the traded securities agreed to be transferred are of the same kind as the traded securities agreed to be transferred under the relevant agreement, and

(ii) the number and transfer price of the traded securities agreed to be transferred are identical to the number and transfer price of the traded securities agreed to be transferred under the relevant agreement;

(b) references to EuroCCP are references to that clearing houses in its capacity as a person providing clearing services in connection with a transaction made on the Facility;

(c) references to a clearing participant are references to a clearing participant in his capacity as such.

5 *Consequential provision*

(1) Traded securities which are the subject of an agreement specified in regulation 4(2)(a) shall be dealt with by a clearing participant who is a party to the agreement in a separate designated account, and not otherwise.

(2) In paragraph (1) above "designated account" means an account designated by EuroCCP for a clearing participant in connection with the traded securities concerned.

2008/2339

STAMP DUTY LAND TAX (EXEMPTION OF CERTAIN ACQUISITIONS OF RESIDENTIAL PROPERTY) REGULATIONS 2008

Made by the Treasury under FA 2003 Sch 3 para 5

Made . . . .*2 September 2008*

Laid before the House of Commons . . . .*2 September 2008*

Coming into force . . . .*3 September 2008*

Amendments—These regulations revoked by FA 2009 s 10(2) with effect in relation to transactions with an effective date on or after 22 April 2009.

1 Citation, commencement and effect

(1) *These Regulations may be cited as the Stamp Duty Land Tax (Exemption of Certain Acquisitions of Residential Property) Regulations 2008 and shall come into force on 3rd September 2008.*

(2) *These Regulations shall have effect in relation to transactions with an effective date—*

(a) *on or after 3rd September 2008, and*

(b) *before 3rd September 2009.*

2 Interpretation

In these Regulations expressions which are used in Part 4 of the Finance Act 2003 have the same meaning as in that Part.

3 Exemption for acquisitions of residential property at not more than £175,000

(1) *A land transaction is exempt from the charge to stamp duty land tax if—*

(a) *it is a relevant acquisition of land which consists entirely of residential property, and*

(b) *the relevant chargeable consideration for the transaction is not more than £175,000.*

(2) *In paragraph (1)(a) a "relevant acquisition of land" means an acquisition of a major interest in land other than—*

(a) *the grant of a lease for a term of less than 21 years, or*

(b) *the assignment of a lease which has less than 21 years to run.*

(3) *In paragraph (1)(b) the "relevant chargeable consideration for the transaction" means—*

(a) *the chargeable consideration for the transaction, or*

(b) *where the transaction is one of a number of linked transactions, the total of the chargeable consideration for all those transactions.*

2008/2777

STAMP DUTY AND STAMP DUTY RESERVE TAX (INVESTMENT EXCHANGES AND CLEARING HOUSES) REGULATIONS 2008

Made by the Treasury under FA 1991 ss 116, 117

Made . . . . *22 October 2008*

Laid before the House of Commons . . . . *23 October 2008*

Coming into force . . . . *13 November 2008*

1 Citation and commencement

(1) These Regulations may be cited as the Stamp Duty and Stamp Duty Reserve Tax (Investment Exchanges and Clearing Houses) Regulations 2008 and shall come into force on 13th November 2008.

(2) These Regulations shall have effect—

(*a*) for the purposes of the charge to stamp duty, in relation to instruments executed on or after 13th November 2008;

(*b*) for the purposes of the charge to stamp duty reserve tax—

(i) in the case of agreements to transfer traded securities which are not conditional, in relation to agreements made on or after 13th November 2008;

(ii) in the case of agreements to transfer traded securities which are conditional, in relation to agreements where the condition is satisfied on or after that date.

2 Interpretation

(1) In these Regulations—

"clearing participant" means a member of LCH Clearnet Limited who as such is permitted by the Rules of LCH Clearnet Limited to clear transactions made on the Facility for a traded security and who may or may not also be a participant in the Facility;

"client" means a person who gives instructions to a non-clearing firm for traded securities to be sold on the Facility;

"LCH Clearnet Limited" is a company which is a recognised clearing house under the Financial Services and Markets Act 2000;

"Equiduct Trading" is the electronic trading system used by Borse Berlin AG;

"the Facility" means Equiduct Trading operated by Borse Berlin AG, a business which is permitted to operate a trading facility under Article 36 of the Directive;

"nominee" means a person whose business is or includes holding trading securities as a nominee for LCH Clearnet Limited acting in its capacity as a person providing clearing services in connection with a transaction made on the Facility, or as a nominee for a clearing participant (as the case may be);

"non-clearing firm" means a participant in the Facility other than a clearing participant;
"traded securities" means stocks and shares which are issued or raised by a company but does not include stocks and shares issued by a company not incorporated in the United Kingdom unless—

(*a*) the stocks and shares are registered in a register kept in the United Kingdom by or on behalf of the company; or

(*b*) in the case of shares, they are paired, within the meaning of section 99(6A) of the Finance Act 1986, with shares issued by a company incorporated in the United Kingdom.

3 Prescription of recognised investment exchanges and recognised clearing houses

For the purpose of sections 116 and 117 of the Finance Act 1991—

(*a*) Borse Berlin AG is prescribed as a recognised investment exchange; and

(*b*) LCH Clearnet Limited is prescribed as a recognised clearing house.

4 Prescribed circumstances for the purposes of sections 116 and 117

(1) In the circumstances prescribed in this regulation, a charge to stamp duty or stamp duty reserve tax shall be treated as not arising.

(2) The circumstances prescribed are where, in connection with a transaction made on the Facility conditions A and B are met.

(3) Condition A is that traded securities of a particular kind are transferred, or agreed to be transferred, from—

(*a*) a clearing participant or a nominee of a clearing participant to another clearing participant or nominee,

(*b*) a non-clearing firm or its client to a clearing participant or a nominee of a clearing participant,

(*c*) a clearing participant or a nominee of a clearing participant to LCH Clearnet Limited or to a nominee of that clearing house,

(*d*) a person other than a clearing participant to LCH Clearnet Limited or to a nominee of that clearing house, as a result of a failure by a clearing participant to fulfil his obligations in respect of the transaction concerned to transfer traded securities to LCH Clearnet Limited or to a nominee of that clearing house, or

(*e*) LCH Clearnet Limited or a nominee of that clearing house to a clearing participant or a nominee of a clearing participant.

(4) Condition B is that the person to whom those securities are agreed to be transferred under any of the agreements specified in paragraph (3) ("the relevant agreement") is required on receipt of those securities to transfer traded securities under a matching agreement to another person or, in the case of an agreement falling within paragraph (3)(*d*), would have been so required if the failure referred to in that paragraph had not occurred.

(5) In paragraph (4)—

(*a*) a "matching agreement" means an agreement under which—

(i) the traded securities agreed to be transferred are of the same kind as the traded securities agreed to be transferred under the relevant agreement, and

(ii) the number and transfer price of the traded securities agreed to be transferred are identical to the number and transfer price of the traded securities agreed to be transferred under the relevant agreement;

(*b*) references to LCH Clearnet Limited are references to that clearing house in its capacity as a person providing clearing services in connection with a transaction made on the Facility;

(*c*) references to a clearing participant are references to a clearing participant in his capacity as such.

5 Consequential provision

(1) Traded securities which are the subject of an agreement specified in regulation 4(3) shall be dealt with by a clearing participant who is party to the agreement in a separate designated account, and not otherwise.

(2) In paragraph (1) "designated account" means an account designated by LCH Clearnet Limited for a clearing participant in connection with the traded securities concerned.

2008/3235

STAMP DUTY AND STAMP DUTY RESERVE TAX (INVESTMENT EXCHANGES AND CLEARING HOUSES) REGULATIONS (NO 2) 2008

Made by the Treasury under FA 1991 ss 116 and 117

Made . . . . *16 December 2008*

Laid before the House of Commons . . . . *17 December 2008*

Coming into force . . . .*7 January 2009*

1 Citation and commencement

(1) These Regulations may be cited as the Stamp Duty and Stamp Duty Reserve Tax (Investment Exchanges and Clearing Houses) Regulations (No 2) 2008 and shall come into force on 7th January 2009.

(2) These Regulations shall have effect—

(*a*) for the purposes of the charge to stamp duty, in relation to instruments executed on or after 7th January 2009;

(*b*) for the purposes of the charge to stamp duty reserve tax—

(i) in the case of agreements to transfer traded securities which are not conditional, in relation to agreements made on or after 7th January 2009;

(ii) in the case of agreements to transfer traded securities which are conditional, in relation to agreements where the condition is satisfied on or after that date.

2 Interpretation

(1) In these Regulations—

"clearing participant" means a member of LCH Clearnet Limited who as such is permitted by the Rules of LCH Clearnet Limited to clear transactions made on the Facility for a traded security and who may or may not also be a participant in the Facility;

"client" means a person who gives instructions to a non-clearing firm for traded securities to be sold on the Facility;

"LCH Clearnet Limited" is a company which is a recognised clearing house under the Financial Services and Markets Act 2000;

"the Facility" means the investment exchange operated by PLUS Markets plc, a company which is permitted to operate as an investment exchange under the Financial Services and Markets Act 2000;

"nominee" means a person whose business is or includes holding trading securities as a nominee for LCH Clearnet Limited acting in its capacity as a person providing clearing services in connection with a transaction made on the Facility, or as a nominee for a clearing participant (as the case may be);

"non-clearing firm" means a participant in the Facility other than a clearing participant;

"traded securities" means stocks and shares which are issued or raised by a company but does not include stocks and shares issued by a company not incorporated in the United Kingdom unless—

(*a*) the stocks and shares are registered in a register kept in the United Kingdom by or on behalf of the company; or

(*b*) in the case of shares, they are paired, within the meaning of section 99(6A) of the Finance Act 1986, with shares issued by a company incorporated in the United Kingdom.

3 Prescription of recognised investment exchanges and recognised clearing houses

For the purpose of sections 116 and 117 of the Finance Act 1991—

(*a*) PLUS Markets plc is prescribed as a recognised investment exchange; and

(*b*) LCH Clearnet Limited is prescribed as a recognised clearing house.

4 Prescribed circumstances for the purposes of sections 116 and 117

(1) In the circumstances prescribed in this regulation, a charge to stamp duty or stamp duty reserve tax shall be treated as not arising.

(2) The circumstances prescribed are where, in connection with a transaction made on the Facility conditions A and B are met.

(3) Condition A is that traded securities of a particular kind are transferred, or agreed to be transferred, from—

(*a*) a clearing participant or a nominee of a clearing participant to another clearing participant or nominee,

(*b*) a non-clearing firm or its client to a clearing participant or a nominee of a clearing participant,

(*c*) a clearing participant or a nominee of a clearing participant to LCH Clearnet Limited or to a nominee of that clearing house,

(*d*) a person other than a clearing participant to LCH Clearnet Limited or to a nominee of that clearing house, as a result of a failure by a clearing participant to fulfil his obligations in respect of the transaction concerned to transfer traded securities to LCH Clearnet Limited or to a nominee of that clearing house, or

(*e*) LCH Clearnet Limited or a nominee of that clearing house to a clearing participant or a nominee of a clearing participant.

(4) Condition B is that the person to whom those securities are agreed to be transferred under any of the agreements specified in paragraph (3) ("the relevant agreement") is required on receipt of those securities to transfer traded securities under a matching agreement to another person or, in the case of an agreement falling within paragraph (3)(*d*), would have been so required if the failure referred to in that paragraph had not occurred.

(5) In paragraph (4)—

(*a*) a "matching agreement" means an agreement under which—

(i) the traded securities agreed to be transferred are of the same kind as the traded securities agreed to be transferred under the relevant agreement, and

(ii) the number and transfer price of the traded securities agreed to be transferred are identical to the number and transfer price of the traded securities agreed to be transferred under the relevant agreement;

(*b*) references to LCH Clearnet Limited are references to that clearing house in its capacity as a person providing clearing services in connection with a transaction made on the Facility;

(*c*) references to a clearing participant are references to a clearing participant in his capacity as such.

5 Consequential provision

(1) Traded securities which are the subject of an agreement specified in regulation 4(3) shall be dealt with by a clearing participant who is party to the agreement in a separate designated account, and not otherwise.

(2) In paragraph (1) "designated account" means an account designated by LCH Clearnet Limited for a clearing participant in connection with the traded securities concerned.

2009/35

STAMP DUTY AND STAMP DUTY RESERVE TAX (INVESTMENT EXCHANGES AND CLEARING HOUSES) REGULATIONS 2009

Made by the Treasury under FA 1991 ss 116, 117

Made . . . . *15 January 2009*
Laid before the House of Commons . . . . *16 January 2009*
Coming into force . . . . *9 February 2009*

1 Citation and commencement

(1) These Regulations may be cited as the Stamp Duty and Stamp Duty Reserve Tax (Investment Exchanges and Clearing Houses) Regulations 2009 and shall come into force on 9th February 2009.

(2) These Regulations shall have effect—

(*a*) for the purposes of the charge to stamp duty, in relation to instruments executed on or after 9th February 2009;

(*b*) for the purposes of the charge to stamp duty reserve tax—

(i) in the case of agreements to transfer traded securities which are not conditional, in relation to agreements made on or after 9th February 2009;

(ii) in the case of agreements to transfer traded securities which are conditional, in relation to agreements where the condition is satisfied on or after that date.

2 Interpretation

(1) In these Regulations—

"clearing participant" means a member of X-Clear who as such is permitted by the Rules of X-CLEAR to clear transactions made on the Facility for a traded security and who may or may not also be a participant in the Facility;

"client" means a person who gives instructions to a non-clearing firm for traded securities to be sold on the Facility;

"X-Clear" means SIX X-Clear AG, a company which is a recognised clearing house under the Financial Services and Markets Act 2000;

"the Facility" means the multilateral trading facility Euro Millennium, operated by NYFIX International Limited, a company which is authorised to operate a multilateral trading facility for the purposes of Part IV of the Financial Services and Markets Act 2000;

"nominee" means a person whose business is or includes holding trading securities as a nominee for X-CLEAR acting in its capacity as a person providing clearing services in connection with a transaction made on the Facility, or as a nominee for a clearing participant (as the case may be);

"non-clearing firm" means a participant in the Facility other than a clearing participant;

"traded securities" means stocks and shares which are issued or raised by a company but does not include stocks and shares issued by a company not incorporated in the United Kingdom unless—

(*a*) the stocks and shares are registered in a register kept in the United Kingdom by or on behalf of the company; or

(*b*) in the case of shares, they are paired, within the meaning of section 99(6A) of the Finance Act 1986, with shares issued by a company incorporated in the United Kingdom.

3 Prescription of recognised investment exchanges and recognised clearing houses

For the purpose of sections 116 and 117 of the Finance Act 1991—

(*a*) Euro Millennium Multilateral Trading Facility ("the Facility") is prescribed as a recognised investment exchange; and

(*b*) SIX X-CLEAR AG is prescribed as a recognised clearing house.

4 Prescribed circumstances for the purposes of sections 116 and 117

(1) In the circumstances prescribed in this regulation, a charge to stamp duty or stamp duty reserve tax shall be treated as not arising.

(2) The circumstances prescribed are where, in connection with a transaction made on the Facility conditions A and B are met.

(3) Condition A is that traded securities of a particular kind are transferred, or agreed to be transferred, from—

(*a*) a clearing participant or a nominee of a clearing participant to another clearing participant or nominee,

(*b*) a non-clearing firm or its client to a clearing participant or a nominee of a clearing participant,

(*c*) a clearing participant or a nominee of a clearing participant to X-CLEAR or to a nominee of that clearing house,

(*d*) a person other than a clearing participant to X-CLEAR or to a nominee of that clearing house, as a result of a failure by a clearing participant to fulfil his obligations in respect of the transaction concerned to transfer traded securities to X-CLEAR or to a nominee of that clearing house, or

(*e*) X-CLEAR or a nominee of that clearing house to a clearing participant or a nominee of a clearing participant.

(4) Condition B is that the person to whom those securities are agreed to be transferred under any of the agreements specified in paragraph (3) ("the relevant agreement") is required on receipt of those securities to transfer traded securities under a matching agreement to another person or, in the case of an agreement falling within paragraph (3)(*d*), would have been so required if the failure referred to in that paragraph had not occurred.

(5) In paragraph (4)—

(*a*) a "matching agreement" means an agreement under which—

(i) the traded securities agreed to be transferred are of the same kind as the traded securities agreed to be transferred under the relevant agreement, and

(ii) the number and transfer price of the traded securities agreed to be transferred are identical to the number and transfer price of the traded securities agreed to be transferred under the relevant agreement;

(*b*) references to X-CLEAR are references to that clearing house in its capacity as a person providing clearing services in connection with a transaction made on the Facility;

(*c*) references to a clearing participant are references to a clearing participant in his capacity as such.

5 Consequential provision

(1) Traded securities which are the subject of an agreement specified in regulation 4(3) shall be dealt with by a clearing participant who is party to the agreement in a separate designated account, and not otherwise.

(2) In paragraph (1) "designated account" means an account designated by X-CLEAR for a clearing participant in connection with the traded securities concerned.

2009/194

STAMP DUTY AND STAMP DUTY RESERVE TAX (INVESTMENT EXCHANGES AND CLEARING HOUSES) REGULATIONS (NO 2) 2009

Made by the Treasury under FA 1991 ss 116, 117

Made . . . . *4 February 2009*

Laid before the House of Commons . . . . *4 February 2009*

Coming into force . . . . *23 February 2009*

Amendment—These regulations revoked by the Stamp Duty and Stamp Duty Reserve Tax (Investment Exchanges and Clearing Houses) Regulations (No 15) 2009, SI 2009/2977, reg 6, with effect:

(a) for the purposes of the charge to stamp duty, in relation to instruments executed on or after 4 December 2009

(b) for the purposes of the charge to stamp duty reserve tax:

(i) in the case of agreements to transfer traded securities which are not conditional, in relation to agreements made on or after 4 December 2009;

(ii) in the case of agreements to transfer traded securities which are conditional, in relation to agreements where the condition is satisfied on or after that date.

1 Citation, commencement and effect

(1) These Regulations may be cited as the Stamp Duty and Stamp Duty Reserve Tax (Investment Exchanges and Clearing Houses) Regulations (No 2) 2009 and shall come into force on 23rd February 2009.

(2) These Regulations shall have effect—

(a) for the purposes of the charge to stamp duty, in relation to instruments executed on or after 23rd February 2009;

(b) for the purposes of the charge to stamp duty reserve tax—

(i) in the case of agreements to transfer traded securities which are not conditional, in relation to agreements made on or after 23rd February 2009;

(ii) in the case of agreements to transfer traded securities which are conditional, in relation to agreements where the condition is satisfied on or after that date.

2 Interpretation

In these Regulations—

"clearing participant" means a member of EuroCCP who as such is permitted by the Rules of EuroCCP to clear transactions made on the Facility for a traded security and who may or may not also be a participant in the Facility;

"client" means a person who gives instructions to a non-clearing firm for traded securities to be sold on the Facility;

"EuroCCP" means European Central Counterparty Limited, a body corporate which is a recognised clearing house under the Financial Services and Markets Act 2000;

"the Facility" means the multilateral trading facility operated by Smartpool Trading Limited, a body corporate which is permitted to operate a multilateral trading facility for the purposes of Part 4 of the Financial Services and Markets Act 2000;

"nominee" means a person whose business is or includes holding traded securities as a nominee for EuroCCP acting in its capacity as a person providing clearing services in connection with a transaction made on the Facility, or as a nominee for a clearing participant (as the case may be);

"non-clearing firm" means a participant in the Facility other than a clearing participant;

"traded securities" means stocks and shares which are issued or raised by a body corporate but does not include stocks and shares issued by a body corporate not incorporated in the United Kingdom unless—

(a) the stocks and shares are registered in a register kept in the United Kingdom by or on behalf of the body corporate; or

(b) in the case of shares, they are paired, within the meaning of section 99(6A) of the Finance Act 1986, with shares issued by a body corporate incorporated in the United Kingdom.

3 Prescription of recognised investment exchange and recognised clearing house

For the purposes of sections 116 and 117 of the Finance Act 1991—

(a) the SmartPool Multilateral Trading Facility ("the Facility") is prescribed as a recognised investment exchange; and

(b) EuroCCP is prescribed as a recognised clearing house.

4 Prescribed circumstances for the purposes of sections 116 and 117

(1) In the circumstances prescribed by paragraph (2) below, the charge to stamp duty and the charge to stamp duty reserve tax shall be treated as not arising.

(2) The circumstances prescribed are where, in connection with a transaction made on the Facility conditions A and B are met.

(3) Condition A is that traded securities of a particular kind are transferred, or agreed to be transferred, from—

(a) a clearing participant or a nominee of a clearing participant to another clearing participant or nominee, or

(b) a non-clearing firm or its client to a clearing participant or a nominee of a clearing participant, or

(c) a clearing participant or a nominee of a clearing participant to EuroCCP or to a nominee of that clearing house, or

(d) a person other than a clearing participant to EuroCCP or to a nominee of that clearing house, as a result of a failure by a clearing participant to fulfil his obligations in respect of the transaction concerned to transfer traded securities to EuroCCP or to a nominee of that clearing house, or

(e) EuroCCP or a nominee of that clearing house to a clearing participant or a nominee of a clearing participant.

(4) Condition B is that the person to whom those securities are agreed to be transferred under any of the agreements specified in paragraph (3) above ("the relevant agreement") is required on receipt of those securities to transfer traded securities under a matching agreement to another person or, in the case of an agreement falling within sub-paragraph (d), would have been so required if the failure referred to in that sub-paragraph had not occurred.

(5) In paragraph (4)—

(a) "matching agreement" means an agreement under which—

(i) the traded securities agreed to be transferred are of the same kind as the traded securities agreed to be transferred under the relevant agreement, and

(ii) the number and transfer price of the traded securities agreed to be transferred are identical to the number and transfer price of the traded securities agreed to be transferred under the relevant agreement;

(b) references to EuroCCP are references to that clearing houses in its capacity as a person providing clearing services in connection with a transaction made on the Facility;

(c) references to a clearing participant are references to a clearing participant in his capacity as such.

5 Consequential provision

(1) Traded securities which are the subject of an agreement specified in regulation 4(3) shall be dealt with by a clearing participant who is a party to the agreement in a separate designated account, and not otherwise.

(2) In paragraph (1) "designated account" means an account designated by EuroCCP for a clearing participant in connection with the traded securities concerned.

2009/397

STAMP DUTY AND STAMP DUTY RESERVE TAX (INVESTMENT EXCHANGES AND CLEARING HOUSES) REGULATIONS (NO 3) 2009

Made by the Treasury under FA 1991 ss 116, 117

Made . . . .*26 February 2009*

Laid before the House of Commons . . . .*2 March 2009*

Coming into force . . . .*23 March 2009*

Amendment—These regulations revoked by the Stamp Duty and Stamp Duty Reserve Tax (Investment Exchanges and Clearing Houses) Regulations (No 14) 2009, SI 2009/2976, reg 6, with effect:

(a) for the purposes of the charge to stamp duty, in relation to instruments executed on or after 4 December 2009

(b) for the purposes of the charge to stamp duty reserve tax:

(i) in the case of agreements to transfer traded securities which are not conditional, in relation to agreements made on or after 4 December 2009;

(ii) in the case of agreements to transfer traded securities which are conditional, in relation to agreements where the condition is satisfied on or after that date.

1 Citation and commencement

(1) These Regulations may be cited as the Stamp Duty and Stamp Duty Reserve Tax (Investment Exchanges and Clearing Houses) Regulations (No 3) 2009 and shall come into force on 23rd March 2009.

(2) These Regulations shall have effect—

(a) for the purposes of the charge to stamp duty, in relation to instruments executed on or after 23rd March 2009;

(b) for the purposes of the charge to stamp duty reserve tax—

(i) in the case of agreements to transfer traded securities which are not conditional, in relation to agreements made on or after 23rd March 2009;

(ii) in the case of agreements to transfer traded securities which are conditional, in relation to agreements where the condition is satisfied on or after that date.

2 Interpretation

(1) In these Regulations—

"clearing participant" means a member of EuroCCP who as such is permitted by the Rules of EuroCCP to clear transactions made on the Facility for a traded security and who may or may not also be a participant in the Facility;
"client" means a person who gives instructions to a non-clearing firm for traded securities to be sold on the Facility;
"EuroCCP" means European Central Counterparty Limited, a company which is a recognised clearing house under the Financial Services and Markets Act 2000;
"NYSE Arca Europe" or "the Facility" means the multilateral trading facility operated by Euronext Amsterdam NV, a market operator which is permitted to operate a trading facility pursuant to the Directive;
"nominee" means a person whose business is or includes holding traded securities as a nominee for EuroCCP acting in its capacity as a person providing clearing services in connection with a transaction made on the Facility, or as a nominee for a clearing participant (as the case may be);
"non-clearing firm" means a participant in the Facility other than a clearing participant;
"traded securities" means stocks and shares which are issued or raised by a body corporate but does not include stocks and shares issued by a body corporate not incorporated in the United Kingdom unless—
(a) the stocks and shares are registered in a register kept in the United Kingdom by or on behalf of the body corporate; or
(b) in the case of shares, they are paired, within the meaning of section 99(6A) of the Finance Act 1986, with shares issued by a body corporate incorporated in the United Kingdom.

3 Prescription of recognised investment exchanges and recognised clearing houses
For the purpose of sections 116 and 117 of the Finance Act 1991—
(a) NYSE Arca Europe is prescribed as a recognised investment exchange; and
(b) EuroCCP is prescribed as a recognised clearing house.

4 Prescribed circumstances for the purposes of sections 116 and 117
(1) In the circumstances prescribed in this regulation, a charge to stamp duty and the charge to stamp duty reserve tax shall be treated as not arising.
(2) The circumstances prescribed are where, in connection with a transaction made on the Facility conditions A and B are met.
(3) Condition A is that traded securities of a particular kind are transferred, or agreed to be transferred, from—
(a) a clearing participant or a nominee of a clearing participant to another clearing participant or nominee,
(b) a non-clearing firm or its client (or a nominee of a non-clearing firm or of a client of a non-clearing firm) to a clearing participant or a nominee of a clearing participant,
(c) a clearing participant or a nominee of a clearing participant to EuroCCP or to a nominee of that clearing house,
(d) a person other than a clearing participant to EuroCCP or to a nominee of that clearing house, as a result of a failure by a clearing participant to fulfil his obligations in respect of the transaction concerned to transfer traded securities to EuroCCP or to a nominee of that clearing house, or
(e) EuroCCP or a nominee of that clearing house to a clearing participant or a nominee of a clearing participant.
(4) Condition B is that the person to whom those securities are agreed to be transferred under any of the agreements specified in paragraph (3) ("the relevant agreement") is required on receipt of those securities to transfer traded securities under a matching agreement to another person or, in the case of an agreement falling within paragraph (3)(d), would have been so required if the failure referred to in that paragraph had not occurred.
(5) In paragraph (4)—
(a) a "matching agreement" means an agreement under which—
(i) the traded securities agreed to be transferred are of the same kind as the traded securities agreed to be transferred under the relevant agreement, and
(ii) the number and transfer price of the traded securities agreed to be transferred are identical to the number and transfer price of the traded securities agreed to be transferred under the relevant agreement;
(b) references to EuroCCP are references to that clearing house in its capacity as a person providing clearing services in connection with a transaction made on the Facility;
(c) references to a clearing participant are references to a clearing participant in his capacity as such.

5 Consequential provision

(1) Traded securities which are the subject of an agreement specified in regulation 4(3) shall be dealt with by a clearing participant who is party to the agreement in a separate designated account, and not otherwise.

(2) In paragraph (1) "designated account" means an account designated by EuroCCP for a clearing participant in connection with the traded securities concerned.

2009/1115

STAMP DUTY AND STAMP DUTY RESERVE TAX (INVESTMENT EXCHANGES AND CLEARING HOUSES) REGULATIONS (NO 4) 2009

Made by the Treasury under FA 1991 ss 116, 117

Made . . . . *30 April 2009*
Laid before the House of Commons . . . . *1 May 2009*
Coming into force . . . . *22 May 2009*

1 Citation, commencement and effect

(1) These Regulations may be cited as the Stamp Duty and Stamp Duty Reserve Tax (Investment Exchanges and Clearing Houses) Regulations (No 4) 2009 and shall come into force on 22nd May 2009.

(2) These Regulations shall have effect—

(*a*) for the purposes of the charge to stamp duty, in relation to instruments executed on or after 22nd May 2009;

(*b*) for the purposes of the charge to stamp duty reserve tax—

(i) in the case of agreements to transfer traded securities which are not conditional, in relation to agreements made on or after 22nd May 2009;

(ii) in the case of agreements to transfer traded securities which are conditional, in relation to agreements where the condition is satisfied on or after that date.

2 Interpretation

In these Regulations—

"clearing participant" means a member of EuroCCP who as such is permitted by the Rules of EuroCCP to clear transactions made on the Facility for a traded security and who may or may not also be a participant in the Facility;

"client" means a person who gives instructions to a non-clearing firm for traded securities to be sold on the Facility;

"EuroCCP" means European Central Counterparty Limited, a body corporate which is a recognised clearing house under the Financial Services and Markets Act 2000;

"the Facility" means "Block Board" the multilateral trading facility operated by Pipeline Financial Group Limited, a body corporate which is permitted to operate a multilateral trading facility for the purposes of Part 4 of the Financial Services and Markets Act 2000;

"nominee" means a person whose business is or includes holding traded securities as a nominee for EuroCCP acting in its capacity as a person providing clearing services in connection with a transaction made on the Facility, or as a nominee for a clearing participant (as the case may be);

"non-clearing firm" means a participant in the Facility other than a clearing participant;

"traded securities" means stocks and shares which are issued or raised by a body corporate but does not include stocks and shares issued by a body corporate not incorporated in the United Kingdom unless—

(*a*) the stocks and shares are registered in a register kept in the United Kingdom by or on behalf of the body corporate; or

(*b*) in the case of shares, they are paired, within the meaning of section 99(6A) of the Finance Act 1986, with shares issued by a body corporate incorporated in the United Kingdom.

3 Prescription of recognised investment exchange and recognised clearing house

For the purposes of sections 116 and 117 of the Finance Act 1991—

(*a*) "Block Board" is prescribed as a recognised investment exchange; and

(*b*) EuroCCP is prescribed as a recognised clearing house.

4 Prescribed circumstances for the purposes of sections 116 and 117

(1) In the circumstances prescribed by paragraph (2) below, the charge to stamp duty and the charge to stamp duty reserve tax shall be treated as not arising.

(2) The circumstances prescribed are where, in connection with a transaction made on the Facility, conditions A and B are met.

(3) Condition A is that traded securities of a particular kind are transferred, or agreed to be transferred, from—

(*a*) a clearing participant or a nominee of a clearing participant to another clearing participant or nominee, or

(*b*) a non-clearing firm or its client (or a nominee of a non-clearing firm or of a client of a non-clearing firm) to a clearing participant or a nominee of a clearing participant, or

(*c*) a clearing participant or a nominee of a clearing participant to EuroCCP or to a nominee of that clearing house, or

(*d*) a person other than a clearing participant to EuroCCP or to a nominee of that clearing house, as a result of a failure by a clearing participant to fulfil his obligations in respect of the transaction concerned to transfer traded securities to EuroCCP or to a nominee of that clearing house, or

(*e*) EuroCCP or a nominee of that clearing house to a clearing participant or a nominee of a clearing participant.

(4) Condition B is that the person to whom those securities are agreed to be transferred under any of the agreements specified in paragraph (3) above ("the relevant agreement") is required on receipt of those securities to transfer traded securities under a matching agreement to another person or, in the case of an agreement falling within sub-paragraph (3) (*d*), would have been so required if the failure referred to in that sub-paragraph had not occurred.

(5) In paragraph (4)—

(*a*) "matching agreement" means an agreement under which—

(i) the traded securities agreed to be transferred are of the same kind as the traded securities agreed to be transferred under the relevant agreement, and

(ii) the number and transfer price of the traded securities agreed to be transferred are identical to the number and transfer price of the traded securities agreed to be transferred under the relevant agreement;

(*b*) references to EuroCCP are references to that clearing houses in its capacity as a person providing clearing services in connection with a transaction made on the Facility;

(*c*) references to a clearing participant are references to a clearing participant in his capacity as such.

5 Consequential provision

(1) Traded securities which are the subject of an agreement specified in regulation 4(3) shall be dealt with by a clearing participant who is a party to the agreement in a separate designated account, and not otherwise.

(2) In paragraph (1) "designated account" means an account designated by EuroCCP for a clearing participant in connection with the traded securities concerned.

2009/1344

STAMP DUTY AND STAMP DUTY RESERVE TAX (INVESTMENT EXCHANGES AND CLEARING HOUSES) REGULATIONS (NO 5) 2009

Made by the Treasury under FA 1991 ss 116, 117

Made . . . . *1 June 2009*
Laid before the House of Commons . . . . *2 June 2009*
Coming into force . . . . *30 June 2009*

1 Citation and commencement

(1) These Regulations may be cited as the Stamp Duty and Stamp Duty Reserve Tax (Investment Exchanges and Clearing Houses) Regulations (No 5) 2009 and shall come into force on 30th June 2009.

(2) These Regulations shall have effect—

(*a*) for the purposes of the charge to stamp duty, in relation to instruments executed on or after 30th June 2009;

(*b*) for the purposes of the charge to stamp duty reserve tax—

(i) in the case of agreements to transfer traded securities which are not conditional, in relation to agreements made on or after 30th June 2009;

(ii) in the case of agreements to transfer traded securities which are conditional, in relation to agreements where the condition is satisfied on or after that date.

2 Interpretation

(1) In these Regulations—

"clearing participant" means a member of X-CLEAR who as such is permitted by the Rules of X-CLEAR to clear transactions made on the Facility for a traded security and who may or may not also be a participant in the Facility;

"client" means a person who gives instructions to a non-clearing firm for traded securities to be sold on the Facility;

"X-CLEAR" means SIX X-CLEAR AG, a company which is a recognised clearing house under the Financial Services and Markets Act 2000;

"the Facility" means the Liquidnet H2O multilateral trading facility, operated by Liquidnet Europe Limited, a company which is authorised to operate a multilateral trading facility for the purposes of Part IV of the Financial Services and Markets Act 2000;

"nominee" means a person whose business is or includes holding traded securities as a nominee for X-CLEAR acting in its capacity as a person providing clearing services in connection with a transaction made on the Facility, or as a nominee for a clearing participant (as the case may be);

"non-clearing firm" means a participant in the Facility other than a clearing participant;

"traded securities" means stocks and shares which are issued or raised by a company but does not include stocks and shares issued by a company not incorporated in the United Kingdom unless—

(*a*) the stocks and shares are registered in a register kept in the United Kingdom by or on behalf of the company; or

(*b*) in the case of shares, they are paired, within the meaning of section 99(6A) of the Finance Act 1986, with shares issued by a company incorporated in the United Kingdom.

3 Prescription of recognised investment exchanges and recognised clearing houses

For the purpose of sections 116 and 117 of the Finance Act 1991—

(*a*) Liquidnet H2O Multilateral Trading Facility ("the Facility") is prescribed as a recognised investment exchange; and

(*b*) SIX X-CLEAR AG is prescribed as a recognised clearing house.

4 Prescribed circumstances for the purposes of sections 116 and 117

(1) In the circumstances prescribed in this regulation, a charge to stamp duty or stamp duty reserve tax shall be treated as not arising.

(2) The circumstances prescribed are where, in connection with a transaction made on the Facility conditions A and B are met.

(3) Condition A is that traded securities of a particular kind are transferred, or agreed to be transferred, from—

(*a*) a clearing participant or a nominee of a clearing participant to another clearing participant or nominee,

(*b*) a non-clearing firm or its client to a clearing participant or a nominee of a clearing participant,

(*c*) a clearing participant or a nominee of a clearing participant to X-CLEAR or to a nominee of that clearing house,

(*d*) a person other than a clearing participant to X-CLEAR or to a nominee of that clearing house, as a result of a failure by a clearing participant to fulfil his obligations in respect of the transaction concerned to transfer traded securities to X-CLEAR or to a nominee of that clearing house, or

(*e*) X-CLEAR or a nominee of that clearing house to a clearing participant or a nominee of a clearing participant.

(4) Condition B is that the person to whom those securities are agreed to be transferred under any of the agreements specified in paragraph (3) ("the relevant agreement") is required on receipt of those securities to transfer traded securities under a matching agreement to another person or, in the case of an agreement falling within paragraph (3)(*d*), would have been so required if the failure referred to in that paragraph had not occurred.

(5) In paragraph (4)—

(*a*) a "matching agreement" means an agreement under which—

(i) the traded securities agreed to be transferred are of the same kind as the traded securities agreed to be transferred under the relevant agreement, and

(ii) the number and transfer price of the traded securities agreed to be transferred are identical to the number and transfer price of the traded securities agreed to be transferred under the relevant agreement;

(*b*) references to X-CLEAR are references to that clearing house in its capacity as a person providing clearing services in connection with a transaction made on the Facility;

(*c*) references to a clearing participant are references to a clearing participant in his capacity as such.

5 Consequential provision

(1) Traded securities which are the subject of an agreement specified in regulation 4(3) shall be dealt with by a clearing participant who is party to the agreement in a separate designated account, and not otherwise.

(2) In paragraph (1) "designated account" means an account designated by X-CLEAR for a clearing participant in connection with the traded securities concerned.

2009/1462

STAMP DUTY AND STAMP DUTY RESERVE TAX (INVESTMENT EXCHANGES AND CLEARING HOUSES) REGULATIONS (NO 6) 2009

Made by the Treasury under FA 1991 ss 116 and 117

Made . . . . *11 June 2009*
Laid before the House of Commons . . . . *12 June 2009*
Coming into force . . . . *5 July 2009*

Amendments—Revoked by Stamp Duty and Stamp Duty Reserve Tax (Investment Exchanges and Clearing Houses) Regulations (No 3) 2010, SI 2010/1877 with effect from 13 August 2010.

1 Citation and commencement

(1) These Regulations may be cited as the Stamp Duty and Stamp Duty Reserve Tax (Investment Exchanges and Clearing Houses) Regulations (No 6) 2009 and shall come into force on 5th July 2009.

(2) These Regulations shall have effect—

- *(a) for the purposes of the charge to stamp duty, in relation to instruments executed on or after 5th July 2009;*
- *(b) for the purposes of the charge to stamp duty reserve tax—*
  - *(i) in the case of agreements to transfer traded securities which are not conditional, in relation to agreements made on or after 5th July 2009;*
  - *(ii) in the case of agreements to transfer traded securities which are conditional, in relation to agreements where the condition is satisfied on or after that date.*

2 Interpretation

(1) In these Regulations—

"clearing participant" means a member of (a) LCH Clearnet Limited who as such is permitted by the Rules of LCH Clearnet Limited or (*b*) X-CLEAR who as such is permitted by the Rules of X-CLEAR or (*c*) European Multilateral Clearing Facility NV (EMCF) who as such is permitted by the Rules of EMCF to clear transactions made on the Facility for a traded security and who may or may not also be a participant in the Facility;

"client" means a person who gives instructions to a non-clearing firm for traded securities to be sold on the Facility;

"LCH Clearnet Limited" is a company which is a recognised clearing house under the Financial Services and Markets Act 2000;

"X-CLEAR" means SIX X-CLEAR AG, a company which is a recognised clearing house under the Financial Services and Markets Act 2000

"EMCF" means European Multilateral Clearing Facility NV, a company which is a recognised clearing house under the Financial Services and Markets Act 2000

"the Facility" means the multilateral trading facility operated by BATS Trading Limited, a company which is authorised to operate a multilateral trading facility for the purposes of Part IV of the Financial Services and Markets Act 2000;

"nominee" means a person whose business is or includes holding traded securities as a nominee for LCH Clearnet Limited or X-CLEAR or EMCF acting in its capacity as a person providing clearing services in connection with a transaction made on the Facility, or as a nominee for a clearing participant (as the case may be);

"non-clearing firm" means a participant in the Facility other than a clearing participant;

"traded securities" means stocks and shares which are issued or raised by a company but does not include stocks and shares issued by a company not incorporated in the United Kingdom unless—

- *(a) the stocks and shares are registered in a register kept in the United Kingdom by or on behalf of the company; or*
- *(b) in the case of shares, they are paired, within the meaning of section 99(6A) of the Finance Act 1986, with shares issued by a company incorporated in the United Kingdom.*

3 Prescription of recognised investment exchanges and recognised clearing houses

For the purpose of sections 116 and 117 of the Finance Act 1991—

- *(a) BATS Trading Limited multilateral trading facility ("the Facility") is prescribed as a recognised investment exchange; and*
- *(b) LCH Clearnet Limited is prescribed as a recognised clearing house; and*
- *(c) SIX X-CLEAR AG is prescribed as a recognised clearing house; and*

(d) European Multilateral Clearing Facility NV is prescribed as a recognised clearing house.

4 Prescribed circumstances for the purposes of sections 116 and 117

(1) In the circumstances prescribed in this regulation, a charge to stamp duty or stamp duty reserve tax shall be treated as not arising.

(2) The circumstances prescribed are where, in connection with a transaction made on the Facility conditions A and B are met.

(3) Condition A is that traded securities of a particular kind are issued or transferred, or agreed to be issued or transferred, from—

- *(a) a clearing participant or a nominee of a clearing participant to another clearing participant or nominee,*
- *(b) a non-clearing firm or its client to a clearing participant or a nominee of a clearing participant,*
- *(c) a clearing participant or a nominee of a clearing participant to LCH Clearnet Limited, X-CLEAR or EMCF, or to a nominee of either LCH Clearnet Limited, X-CLEAR or EMCF.*
- *(d) a person other than a clearing participant to LCH Clearnet Limited, X-CLEAR or EMCF or to a nominee of either LCH Clearnet Limited, X-CLEAR or EMCF as a result of a failure by a clearing participant to fulfil his obligations in respect of the transaction concerned to transfer traded securities to LCH Clearnet Limited, X-CLEAR or EMCF, or to a nominee of either LCH Clearnet Limited, X-CLEAR or EMCF, or*
- *(e) LCH Clearnet Limited, X-CLEAR or EMCF, or a nominee of either LCH Clearnet Limited, X-CLEAR or EMCF to a clearing participant or a nominee of a clearing participant.*
- *(f) LCH Clearnet Limited or a nominee of that clearing house to X-CLEAR or EMCF or a nominee of that clearing house, or*
- *(g) X-CLEAR or a nominee of that clearing house to LCH Clearnet Limited or EMCF or a nominee of that clearing house.*
- *(h) EMCF or a nominee of that clearing house to LCH Clearnet Limited or X-CLEAR or a nominee of that clearing house.*

(4) Condition B is that the person to whom those securities are agreed to be transferred under any of the agreements specified in paragraph (3) ("the relevant agreement") is required on receipt of those securities to transfer traded securities under a matching agreement to another person or, in the case of an agreement falling within paragraph (3)(d), would have been so required if the failure referred to in that paragraph had not occurred.

(5) In paragraph (4)—

- *(a) a "matching agreement" means an agreement under which—*
  - *(i) the traded securities agreed to be transferred are of the same kind as the traded securities agreed to be transferred under the relevant agreement, and*
  - *(ii) the number and transfer price of the traded securities agreed to be transferred are identical to the number and transfer price of the traded securities agreed to be transferred under the relevant agreement;*
- *(b) references to LCH Clearnet Limited, X-CLEAR or EMCF are references to that clearing house in its capacity as a person providing clearing services in connection with a transaction made on the Facility;*
- *(c) references to a clearing participant are references to a clearing participant in its capacity as such.*

5 Consequential provision

(1) Traded securities which are the subject of an agreement specified in regulation 4(3) shall be dealt with by a clearing participant who is party to the agreement in a separate designated account, and not otherwise.

(2) In paragraph (1) "designated account" means an account designated by LCH Clearnet Limited, X-CLEAR or EMCF for a clearing participant in connection with the traded securities concerned.

2009/1601

STAMP DUTY AND STAMP DUTY RESERVE TAX (INVESTMENT EXCHANGES AND CLEARING HOUSES) REGULATIONS (NO 7) 2009

Made by the Treasury under FA 1991 ss 116, 117

Made . . . . *1 July 2009*
Laid before the House of Commons . . . . *2 July 2009*
Coming into force . . . . *3 August 2009*

Amendments—Revoked by Stamp Duty and Stamp Duty Reserve Tax (Investment Exchanges and Clearing Houses) Regulations (No 2) 2010, SI 2010/1819 with effect from 10 August 2010.

1 Citation and commencement

(1) These Regulations may be cited as the Stamp Duty and Stamp Duty Reserve Tax (Investment Exchanges and Clearing Houses) Regulations (No 7) 2009 and shall come into force on 3rd August 2009.

(2) These Regulations shall have effect—

(a) for the purposes of the charge to stamp duty, in relation to instruments executed on or after 3rd August 2009;

(b) for the purposes of the charge to stamp duty reserve tax—

(i) in the case of agreements to transfer traded securities which are not conditional, in relation to agreements made on or after 3rd August 2009;

(ii) in the case of agreements to transfer traded securities which are conditional, in relation to agreements where the condition is satisfied on or after that date.

2 Interpretation

(1) In these Regulations—

"clearing participant" means a member of (a) LCH.Clearnet Limited who as such is permitted by the Rules of LCH.Clearnet Limited or (*b*) X-CLEAR who as such is permitted by the Rules of X-CLEAR or (*c*) European Multilateral Clearing Facility NV (EMCF) who as such is permitted by the Rules of EMCF to clear transactions made on the Facility for a traded security and who may or may not also be a participant in the Facility;

"client" means a person who gives instructions to a non-clearing firm for traded securities to be sold on the Facility;

"LCH.Clearnet Limited" is a company which is a recognised clearing house under the Financial Services and Markets Act 2000;

"X-CLEAR" means SIX X-CLEAR AG, a company which is a recognised clearing house under the Financial Services and Markets Act 2000;

"EMCF" means European Multilateral Clearing Facility NV, a company which is a recognised clearing house under the Financial Services and Markets Act 2000;

"the Facility" means the multilateral trading facility operated by Chi-X Europe Limited, a company which is authorised to operate a multilateral trading facility for the purposes of Part IV of the Financial Services and Markets Act 2000;

"nominee" means a person whose business is or includes holding traded securities as a nominee for LCH.Clearnet Limited or X-CLEAR or EMCF acting in its capacity as a person providing clearing services in connection with a transaction made on the Facility, or as a nominee for a clearing participant (as the case may be);

"non-clearing firm" means a participant in the Facility other than a clearing participant;

"traded securities" means stocks and shares which are issued or raised by a company but does not include stocks and shares issued by a company not incorporated in the United Kingdom unless—

(a) the stocks and shares are registered in a register kept in the United Kingdom by or on behalf of the company; or

(b) in the case of shares, they are paired, within the meaning of section 99(6A) of the Finance Act 1986, with shares issued by a company incorporated in the United Kingdom.

3 Prescription of recognised investment exchanges and recognised clearing houses

For the purpose of sections 116 and 117 of the Finance Act 1991—

(a) Chi-X Europe Limited ("the Facility") is prescribed as a recognised investment exchange; and

(b) LCH.Clearnet Limited is prescribed as a recognised clearing house; and

(c) SIX X-CLEAR AG is prescribed as a recognised clearing house; and

(d) European Multilateral Clearing Facility NV is prescribed as a recognised clearing house.

4 Prescribed circumstances for the purposes of sections 116 and 117

(1) In the circumstances prescribed in this regulation, a charge to stamp duty or stamp duty reserve tax shall be treated as not arising.

(2) The circumstances prescribed are where, in connection with a transaction made on the Facility conditions A and B are met.

(3) Condition A is that traded securities of a particular kind are issued or transferred, or agreed to be issued or transferred, from—

(a) a clearing participant or a nominee of a clearing participant to another clearing participant or nominee,

(b) a non-clearing firm or its client to a clearing participant or a nominee of a clearing participant,

(c) a clearing participant or a nominee of a clearing participant to LCH.Clearnet Limited, X-CLEAR or EMCF, or to a nominee of either LCH.Clearnet Limited, X-CLEAR or EMCF.

(d) a person other than a clearing participant to LCH.Clearnet Limited, X-CLEAR or EMCF or to a nominee of either LCH.Clearnet Limited, X-CLEAR or EMCF as a result of a failure by a clearing participant to fulfil his obligations in respect of the transaction concerned to transfer traded securities to LCH.Clearnet Limited, X-CLEAR or EMCF, or to a nominee of either LCH.Clearnet Limited, X-CLEAR or EMCF, or

(e) LCH.Clearnet Limited, X-CLEAR or EMCF, or a nominee of either LCH.Clearnet Limited, X-CLEAR or EMCF to a clearing participant or a nominee of a clearing participant.

(f) LCH.Clearnet Limited or a nominee of that clearing house to X-CLEAR or EMCF or a nominee of that clearing house, or

(g) X-CLEAR or a nominee of that clearing house to LCH.Clearnet Limited or EMCF or a nominee of that clearing house.

(h) EMCF or a nominee of that clearing house to LCH.Clearnet Limited or X-CLEAR or a nominee of that clearing house.

(4) Condition B is that the person to whom those securities are agreed to be transferred under any of the agreements specified in paragraph (3) ("the relevant agreement") is required on receipt of those securities to transfer traded securities under a matching agreement to another person or, in the case of an agreement falling within paragraph (3)(d), would have been so required if the failure referred to in that paragraph had not occurred.

(5) In paragraph (4)—

(a) a "matching agreement" means an agreement under which—

(i) the traded securities agreed to be transferred are of the same kind as the traded securities agreed to be transferred under the relevant agreement, and

(ii) the number and transfer price of the traded securities agreed to be transferred are identical to the number and transfer price of the traded securities agreed to be transferred under the relevant agreement;

(b) references to LCH.Clearnet Limited, X-CLEAR or EMCF are references to that clearing house in its capacity as a person providing clearing services in connection with a transaction made on the Facility;

(c) references to a clearing participant are references to a clearing participant in its capacity as such.

5 Consequential provision

(1) Traded securities which are the subject of an agreement specified in regulation 4(3) shall be dealt with by a clearing participant who is party to the agreement in a separate designated account, and not otherwise.

(2) In paragraph (1) "designated account" means an account designated by LCH.Clearnet Limited, X-CLEAR or EMCF for a clearing participant in connection with the traded securities concerned.

2009/1827

STAMP DUTY AND STAMP DUTY RESERVE TAX (INVESTMENT EXCHANGES AND CLEARING HOUSES) REGULATIONS (NO 8) 2009

Made by the Treasury under FA 1991 ss 116, 117

Made . . . . *8 July 2009*

Laid before the House of Commons . . . . *9 July 2009*

Coming into force . . . . *4 August 2009*

Revocation—Revoked by Stamp Duty and Stamp Duty Reserve Tax (Investment Exchanges and Clearing Houses) Regulations, SI 2010/1818 with effect from 10 August 2010.

1 Citation and commencement

(1) These Regulations may be cited as the Stamp Duty and Stamp Duty Reserve Tax (Investment Exchanges and Clearing Houses) Regulations (No 8) 2009 and shall come into force on 4th August 2009.

(2) These Regulations shall have effect—

(a) for the purposes of the charge to stamp duty, in relation to instruments executed on or after 4th August 2009;

(b) for the purposes of the charge to stamp duty reserve tax—

(i) in the case of agreements to transfer traded securities which are not conditional, in relation to agreements made on or after 4th August 2009;

(ii) in the case of agreements to transfer traded securities which are conditional, in relation to agreements where the condition is satisfied on or after that date.

Revocation—Revoked by Stamp Duty and Stamp Duty Reserve Tax (Investment Exchanges and Clearing Houses) Regulations, SI 2010/1818 with effect from 10 August 2010.

2 *Interpretation*

(1) In these Regulations—

"clearing participant" means a member of (a) EuroCCP who as such is permitted by the Rules of EuroCCP or *(b)* LCH.Clearnet Limited who as such is permitted by the Rules of LCH.Clearnet Limited or *(c)* X-CLEAR who as such is permitted by the Rules of X-CLEAR to clear transactions made on the Facility for a traded security and who may or may not also be a participant in the Facility;

"client" means a person who gives instructions to a non-clearing firm for traded securities to be sold on the Facility;

"EuroCCP" means European Central Counterparty Limited, a company which is a recognised clearing house under the Financial Services and Markets Act 2000;

"LCH.Clearnet Limited" is a company which is a recognised clearing house under the Financial Services and Markets Act 2000;

"X-CLEAR" means SIX X-CLEAR AG, a company which is a recognised clearing house under the Financial Services and Markets Act 2000;

"Facility" means the multilateral trading facility operated by Turquoise Services Limited, a company which is authorised to operate a multilateral trading facility for the purposes of Part IV of the Financial Services and Markets Act 2000;

"nominee" means a person whose business is or includes holding traded securities as a nominee for EuroCCP or LCH.Clearnet Limited or X-CLEAR acting in its capacity as a person providing clearing services in connection with a transaction made on the Facility, or as a nominee for a clearing participant (as the case may be);

"non-clearing firm" means a participant in the Facility other than a clearing participant;

"traded securities" means stocks and shares which are issued or raised by a company but does not include stocks and shares issued by a company not incorporated in the United Kingdom unless—

(a) the stocks and shares are registered in a register kept in the United Kingdom by or on behalf of the company; or

(b) in the case of shares, they are paired, within the meaning of section 99(6A) of the Finance Act 1986, with shares issued by a company incorporated in the United Kingdom.

Revocation—Revoked by Stamp Duty and Stamp Duty Reserve Tax (Investment Exchanges and Clearing Houses) Regulations, SI 2010/1818 with effect from 10 August 2010.

3 *Prescription of recognised investment exchange and recognised clearing houses*

For the purposes of sections 116 and 117 of the Finance Act 1991—

(a) Turquoise Services Limited is prescribed as a recognised investment exchange; and

(b) EuroCCP is prescribed as a recognised clearing house,

(c) LCH.Clearnet Limited is prescribed as a recognised clearing house, and,

(d) X-CLEAR is prescribed as a recognised clearing house.

Revocation—Revoked by Stamp Duty and Stamp Duty Reserve Tax (Investment Exchanges and Clearing Houses) Regulations, SI 2010/1818 with effect from 10 August 2010.

4 *Prescribed circumstances for the purposes of sections 116 and 117*

(1) In the circumstances prescribed by paragraph (2), a charge to stamp duty or stamp duty reserve tax shall be treated as not arising.

(2) The circumstances prescribed are where, in connection with a transaction made on the Facility, conditions A and B are met.

(3) Condition A is that traded securities of a particular kind are issued or transferred, or agreed to be issued or transferred, from—

(a) a clearing participant or a nominee of a clearing participant to another clearing participant or nominee,

(b) a non-clearing firm or its client to a clearing participant or a nominee of a clearing participant,

(c) a clearing participant or a nominee of a clearing participant to EuroCCP, LCH.Clearnet Limited or X-CLEAR, or to a nominee of either EuroCCP, LCH.Clearnet Limited or X-CLEAR.

(d) a person other than a clearing participant to EuroCCP, LCH.Clearnet Limited or X-CLEAR or to a nominee of either EuroCCP, LCH.Clearnet Limited or X-CLEAR as a result of a failure by a clearing participant to fulfil his obligations in respect of the transaction concerned to transfer traded securities to EuroCCP, LCH.Clearnet Limited or X-CLEAR, or to a nominee of either EuroCCP, LCH.Clearnet Limited or X-CLEAR, or

(e) EuroCCP, LCH.Clearnet Limited or X-CLEAR, or a nominee of either EuroCCP, LCH.Clearnet Limited or X-CLEAR to a clearing participant or a nominee of a clearing participant.

(f) EuroCCP or a nominee of that clearing house to LCH.Clearnet Limited or X-CLEAR or a nominee of either clearing house, or

(g) *LCH.Clearnet Limited or a nominee of that clearing house to EuroCCP or X-CLEAR or a nominee of either clearing house.*

(h) *X-CLEAR or a nominee of that clearing house to EuroCCP or LCH.Clearnet Limited or a nominee of either clearing house.*

(4) Condition B is that the person to whom those securities are agreed to be transferred under any of the agreements specified in paragraph (3) above ("the relevant agreement") is required on receipt of those securities to transfer traded securities under a matching agreement to another person or, in the case of an agreement falling within sub-paragraph (3)(d), would have been so required if the failure referred to in that paragraph had not occurred.

(5) In paragraph (4)—

(a) *"matching agreement" means an agreement under which—*

(i) *the traded securities agreed to be transferred are of the same kind as the traded securities agreed to be transferred under the relevant agreement, and*

(ii) *the number and transfer price of the traded securities agreed to be transferred are identical to the number and transfer price of the traded securities agreed to be transferred under the relevant agreement;*

(b) *references to EuroCCP, LCH.Clearnet Limited or X-CLEAR are references to that clearing house in its capacity as a person providing clearing services in connection with a transaction made on the Facility;*

(c) *references to a clearing participant are references to a clearing participant in its capacity as such.*

Revocation—Revoked by Stamp Duty and Stamp Duty Reserve Tax (Investment Exchanges and Clearing Houses) Regulations, SI 2010/1818 with effect from 10 August 2010.

5 *Consequential provision*

(1) Traded securities which are the subject of an agreement specified in regulation 4(3) shall be dealt with by a clearing participant who is a party to the agreement in a separate designated account, and not otherwise.

(2) In paragraph (1) "designated account" means an account designated by EuroCCP, LCH.Clearnet Limited or X-CLEAR for a clearing participant in connection with the traded securities concerned.

Revocation—Revoked by Stamp Duty and Stamp Duty Reserve Tax (Investment Exchanges and Clearing Houses) Regulations, SI 2010/1818 with effect from 10 August 2010.

6 Revocation of the Stamp and Stamp Duty Reserve Tax (Investment Exchanges and Clearing Houses) (European Central Counterparty Limited and the Turquoise Multilateral Trading Facility) Regulations 2008 (SI 2008/1814)

The Stamp Duty and Stamp Duty Reserve Tax (Investment Exchanges and Clearing Houses) (European Central Counterparty Limited and the Turquoise Multilateral Trading Facility) Regulations 2008 (SI 2008/1814) are hereby revoked as respects instruments and agreements referred to in regulation 1(2).

Revocation—Revoked by Stamp Duty and Stamp Duty Reserve Tax (Investment Exchanges and Clearing Houses) Regulations, SI 2010/1818 with effect from 10 August 2010.

2009/1828

STAMP DUTY AND STAMP DUTY RESERVE TAX (INVESTMENT EXCHANGES AND CLEARING HOUSES) REGULATIONS (NO 9) 2009

Made by the Treasury under FA 1991 ss 116, 117

Made . . . . 8 July 2009
Laid before the House of Commons . . . . 9 July 2009
Coming into force . . . . 30 July 2009

1 Citation and commencement

(1) These Regulations may be cited as the Stamp Duty and Stamp Duty Reserve Tax (Investment Exchanges and Clearing Houses) Regulations (No 9) 2009 and shall come into force on 30th July 2009.

(2) These Regulations shall have effect—

(*a*) for the purposes of the charge to stamp duty, in relation to instruments executed on or after 30th July 2009;

(*b*) for the purposes of the charge to stamp duty reserve tax—

(i) in the case of agreements to transfer traded securities which are not conditional, in relation to agreements made on or after 30th July 2009;

(ii) in the case of agreements to transfer traded securities which are conditional, in relation to agreements where the condition is satisfied on or after that date.

2 Interpretation

(1) In these Regulations—

"clearing participant" means (*a*) a member of LIFFE who as such is permitted by the Rules of LIFFE to clear transactions made on the Exchange of traded securities or (*b*) LCH.Clearnet Limited, when required by the applicable Rules of LIFFE to clear transactions made on the Exchange;

"the Exchange" means the London International Financial Futures and Options Exchange ("LIFFE") which is operated by LIFFE A&M;

"LCH.Clearnet Limited" is a company which is a recognised clearing house under the Financial Services and Markets Act 2000;

"LIFFE A&M" means LIFFE Administration and Management, an unlimited company having a share capital, which is a recognised investment exchange authorised to provide clearing services under the Financial Services and Markets Act 2000;

"nominee" means a person whose business is or includes holding traded securities as a nominee for LCH.Clearnet Limited or LIFFE A&M, in each case acting in its capacity as a person providing clearing services in connection with a transaction made on the Exchange, or as a nominee for a clearing participant, or as a nominee for a non-clearing firm (as the case may be);

"non-clearing firm" means a member of LIFFE other than a clearing participant;

"option" means an option to buy or sell traded securities where such option is listed by and made on or under the Rules of LIFFE.

"traded securities" means options, stocks, shares or loan capital, or interests in stocks, shares or loan capital, issued or raised by a body corporate but does not include stocks and shares issued by a body corporate not incorporated in the United Kingdom unless—

(*a*) the stocks and shares are registered in a register kept in the United Kingdom by or on behalf of the body corporate; or

(*b*) in the case of shares, they are paired, within the meaning of section 99(6A) of the Finance Act 1986, with shares issued by a body corporate incorporated in the United Kingdom;

3 Prescription of recognised investment exchanges and recognised clearing houses

For the purpose of sections 116 and 117 of the Finance Act 1991—

(*a*) LIFFE A&M is prescribed as a recognised investment exchange; and

(*b*) LCH.Clearnet Limited is prescribed as a recognised clearing house.

4 Prescribed circumstances for the purposes of sections 116 and 117

(1) In the circumstances prescribed in this regulation, the charge to stamp duty and the charge to stamp duty reserve tax shall be treated as not arising.

(2) The circumstances prescribed are where, in connection with a transaction made on the Exchange conditions A and B are met.

(3) Condition A is that traded securities of a particular kind are issued or transferred, or agreed to be issued or transferred, from—

(*a*) a clearing participant or a nominee of a clearing participant to another clearing participant or nominee,

(*b*) a non-clearing firm or a nominee of a non-clearing firm to a clearing participant or a nominee of a clearing participant,

(*c*) a clearing participant or a nominee of a clearing participant to LIFFE A&M, or to LCH.Clearnet Limited, or to a nominee of either LIFFE A&M or LCH.Clearnet Limited,

(*d*) a person other than a clearing participant to LIFFE A&M, or to LCH.Clearnet Limited, or to a nominee of either LIFFE A&M or LCH.Clearnet Limited, as a result of a failure by a clearing participant to fulfil his obligations in respect of the transaction concerned to transfer traded securities to LIFFE A&M, or to LCH.Clearnet Limited, or to a nominee of either LIFFE A&M or LCH.Clearnet Limited, or

(*e*) LIFFE A&M, or LCH.Clearnet Limited, or a nominee of either LIFFE A&M or LCH.Clearnet Limited to a clearing participant or a nominee of a clearing participant.

(4) Condition B is that the person to whom those securities are agreed to be issued or transferred under any of the agreements specified in paragraph (3) ("the relevant agreement") is required on receipt of those securities to transfer traded securities under a matching agreement to another person or, in the case of an agreement falling within paragraph (3)(*d*), would have been so required if the failure referred to in that paragraph had not occurred.

(5) In paragraph (4)—

(*a*) a "matching agreement" means an agreement under which—

(i) the traded securities agreed to be transferred are of the same kind as the traded securities agreed to be transferred under the relevant agreement, and

(ii) the number and transfer price of the traded securities agreed to be transferred are identical to the number and transfer price of the traded securities agreed to be transferred under the relevant agreement;

(*b*) references to LCH.Clearnet Limited are references to that clearing house in its capacity as a person providing clearing services in connection with a transaction made on the Exchange;

(*c*) references to LIFFE A&M are references to LIFFE A&M acting in its capacity as a self-clearing recognised investment exchange providing clearing services in connection with a transaction made on the Exchange;

(*d*) references to a clearing participant are references to a clearing participant in its capacity as such.

5 Consequential provision

(1) Traded securities which are the subject of an agreement specified in regulation 4(3) shall be dealt with by a clearing participant who is party to the agreement in a separate designated account, and not otherwise.

(2) In paragraph (1) "designated account" means an account designated by LIFFE A&M, acting in its capacity as a self-clearing recognised investment exchange in connection with the traded securities concerned.

6 Revocation of the Stamp and Stamp Duty Reserve Tax (Investment Exchanges and Clearing Houses) Regulation 1997/2429

The Stamp Duty and Stamp Duty Reserve Tax (Investment Exchanges and Clearing Houses) Regulations 1997/2429 are hereby revoked as respects instruments and agreements referred to in regulation 1(2).

2009/1831

STAMP DUTY AND STAMP DUTY RESERVE TAX (INVESTMENT EXCHANGES AND CLEARING HOUSES) REGULATIONS (NO 10) 2009

Made by the Treasury under FA 1991 ss 116, 117

Made . . . .*9 July 2009*

Laid before the House of Commons . . . .*9 July 2009*

Coming into force . . . .*3 August 2009*

Amendment—These regulations revoked by the Stamp Duty and Stamp Duty Reserve Tax (Investment Exchanges and Clearing Houses) Regulations (No 13) 2009, SI 2009/2975, reg 6, with effect:

(a) for the purposes of the charge to stamp duty, in relation to instruments executed on or after 2 December 2009

(b) for the purposes of the charge to stamp duty reserve tax:

(i) in the case of agreements to transfer traded securities which are not conditional, in relation to agreements made on or after 2 December 2009;

(ii) in the case of agreements to transfer traded securities which are conditional, in relation to agreements where the condition is satisfied on or after that date.

1 Citation and commencement

(1) These Regulations may be cited as the Stamp Duty and Stamp Duty Reserve Tax (Investment Exchanges and Clearing Houses) Regulations (No 10) 2009 and shall come into force on 3rd August 2009.

(2) These Regulations shall have effect—

(a) for the purposes of the charge to stamp duty, in relation to instruments executed on or after 3rd August 2009;

(b) for the purposes of the charge to stamp duty reserve tax—

(i) in the case of agreements to transfer traded securities which are not conditional, in relation to agreements made on or after 3rd August 2009;

(ii) in the case of agreements to transfer traded securities which are conditional, in relation to agreements where the condition is satisfied on or after that date.

2 Interpretation

(1) In these Regulations—

"clearing participant" means a member of (a) European Multilateral Clearing Facility NV (EMCF) who as such is permitted by the Rules of EMCF or (b) X-CLEAR who as such is permitted by the Rules of X-CLEAR to clear transactions made on the Facility for a traded security and who may or may not also be a participant in the Facility;

"client" means a person who gives instructions to a non-clearing firm for traded securities to be sold on the Facility;

"EMCF" means European Multilateral Clearing Facility NV, a company which is a recognised clearing house under the Financial Services and Markets Act 2000;
"X-CLEAR" means SIX X-CLEAR AG, a company which is a recognised clearing house under the Financial Services and Markets Act 2000;
"the Facility" means the multilateral trading facility operated by NASDAQ OMX Europe Limited, a company which is authorised to operate a multilateral trading facility for the purposes of Part IV of the Financial Services and Markets Act 2000;
"nominee" means a person whose business is or includes holding traded securities as a nominee for EMCF or X-CLEAR acting in its capacity as a person providing clearing services in connection with a transaction made on the Facility, or as a nominee for a clearing participant (as the case may be);
"non-clearing firm" means a participant in the Facility other than a clearing participant;
"traded securities" means stocks and shares which are issued or raised by a company but does not include stocks and shares issued by a company not incorporated in the United Kingdom unless—

(a) the stocks and shares are registered in a register kept in the United Kingdom by or on behalf of the company; or
(b) in the case of shares, they are paired, within the meaning of section 99(6A) of the Finance Act 1986, with shares issued by a company incorporated in the United Kingdom.

3 Prescription of recognised investment exchanges and recognised clearing houses
For the purpose of sections 116 and 117 of the Finance Act 1991—

(a) NASDAQ OMX Europe Limited ("the Facility") is prescribed as a recognised investment exchange; and
(b) European Multilateral Clearing Facility NV is prescribed as a recognised clearing house; and
(c) SIX X-CLEAR AG is prescribed as a recognised clearing house.

4 Prescribed circumstances for the purposes of sections 116 and 117
(1) In the circumstances prescribed in this regulation, a charge to stamp duty or stamp duty reserve tax shall be treated as not arising.
(2) The circumstances prescribed are where, in connection with a transaction made on the Facility conditions A and B are met.
(3) Condition A is that traded securities of a particular kind are issued or transferred, or agreed to be issued or transferred, from—

(a) a clearing participant or a nominee of a clearing participant to another clearing participant or nominee,
(b) a non-clearing firm or its client to a clearing participant or a nominee of a clearing participant,
(c) a clearing participant or a nominee of a clearing participant to EMCF or X-CLEAR, or to a nominee of either EMCF or X-CLEAR.
(d) a person other than a clearing participant to EMCF or X-CLEAR, or to a nominee of EMCF or X-CLEAR, as a result of a failure by a clearing participant to fulfil his obligations in respect of the transaction concerned to transfer traded securities to EMCF or X-CLEAR, or to a nominee of either EMCF or X-CLEAR, or
(e) X-CLEAR or EMCF, or a nominee of either X-CLEAR or EMCF to a clearing participant or a nominee of a clearing participant.
(f) X-CLEAR or a nominee of that clearing house to EMCF or a nominee of that clearing house.
(g) EMCF or a nominee of that clearing house to X-CLEAR or a nominee of that clearing house.

(4) Condition B is that the person to whom those securities are agreed to be transferred under any of the agreements specified in paragraph (3) ("the relevant agreement") is required on receipt of those securities to transfer traded securities under a matching agreement to another person or, in the case of an agreement falling within paragraph (3)(d), would have been so required if the failure referred to in that paragraph had not occurred.
(5) In paragraph (4)—

(a) a "matching agreement" means an agreement under which—
  (i) the traded securities agreed to be transferred are of the same kind as the traded securities agreed to be transferred under the relevant agreement, and
  (ii) the number and transfer price of the traded securities agreed to be transferred are identical to the number and transfer price of the traded securities agreed to be transferred under the relevant agreement;
(b) references to X-CLEAR or EMCF are references to that clearing house in its capacity as a person providing clearing services in connection with a transaction made on the Facility;
(c) references to a clearing participant are references to a clearing participant in its capacity as such.

5 Consequential provision

(1) Traded securities which are the subject of an agreement specified in regulation 4(3) shall be dealt with by a clearing participant who is party to the agreement in a separate designated account, and not otherwise.

(2) In paragraph (1) "designated account" means an account designated by X-CLEAR or EMCF for a clearing participant in connection with the traded securities concerned.

2009/1832

STAMP DUTY AND STAMP DUTY RESERVE TAX (INVESTMENT EXCHANGES AND CLEARING HOUSES) REGULATIONS (NO 11) 2009

Made by the Treasury under FA 1991 ss 116, 117

Made . . . . *9 July 2009*

Laid before the House of Commons . . . . *9 July 2009*

Coming into force . . . . *3 August 2009*

1 Citation and commencement

(1) These Regulations may be cited as the Stamp Duty and Stamp Duty Reserve Tax (Investment Exchanges and Clearing Houses) Regulations (No 11) 2009 and shall come into force on 3rd August 2009.

(2) These Regulations shall have effect—

(*a*) for the purposes of the charge to stamp duty, in relation to instruments executed on or after 3rd August 2009;

(*b*) for the purposes of the charge to stamp duty reserve tax—

(i) in the case of agreements to transfer traded securities which are not conditional, in relation to agreements made on or after 3rd August 2009;

(ii) in the case of agreements to transfer traded securities which are conditional, in relation to agreements where the condition is satisfied on or after that date.

2 Interpretation

(1) In these Regulations—

"clearing participant" means a member of either (*a*) CC&G who as such is permitted by the Rules of CC&G or (*b*) EMCF who as such is permitted by the Rules of EMCF, to clear transactions made on the Facility for a traded security and who may or may not also be a participant in the Facility;

"client" means a person who gives instructions to a non-clearing firm for traded securities to be sold on the Facility;

"CC&G" means Cassa di Compensazione e Garanzia SpA, a company which is a recognised clearing house under the Financial Services and Markets Act 2000;

"EMCF" means European Multilateral Clearing Facility NV, a company which is a recognised clearing house under the Financial Services and Markets Act 2000;

"the Facility" means the multilateral trading facility operated by Baikal Global Limited, a company which is permitted to operate a multilateral trading facility for the purposes of Part IV of the Financial Services and Markets Act 2000;

"nominee" means a person whose business is or includes holding traded securities as a nominee for either CC&G or EMCF acting in their capacity as a person providing clearing services in connection with a transaction made on the Facility, or as a nominee for a clearing participant (as the case may be);

"non-clearing firm" means a participant in the Facility other than a clearing participant; and

"traded securities" means stocks and shares which are issued or raised by a company but does not include stocks and shares issued by a company not incorporated in the United Kingdom unless—

(*a*) the stocks and shares are registered in a register kept in the United Kingdom by or on behalf of the company; or

(*b*) in the case of shares, they are paired, within the meaning of section 99(6A) of the Finance Act 1986, with shares issued by a company incorporated in the United Kingdom.

3 Prescription of recognised investment exchanges and recognised clearing houses

For the purpose of sections 116 and 117 of the Finance Act 1991—

(*a*) The Facility is prescribed as a recognised investment exchange;

(*b*) CC&G is prescribed as a recognised clearing house; and

(*c*) EMCF is prescribed as a recognised clearing house.

4 Prescribed circumstances for the purposes of sections 116 and 117

(1) In the circumstances prescribed in this regulation, a charge to stamp duty or stamp duty reserve tax shall be treated as not arising.

(2) The circumstances prescribed are where, in connection with a transaction made on the Facility, conditions A and B below are met.

(3) Condition A is that traded securities of a particular kind are issued or transferred, or agreed to be issued or transferred, from—

(*a*) a clearing participant or a nominee of a clearing participant to another clearing participant or a nominee of another clearing participant;

(*b*) a non-clearing firm or its client to a clearing participant or a nominee of a clearing participant;

(*c*) a clearing participant or a nominee of a clearing participant to CC&G or EMCF, or to a nominee of either CC&G or EMCF;

(*d*) a person other than a clearing participant to CC&G or EMCF, or to a nominee of CC&G or EMCF, as a result of a failure by a clearing participant to fulfil his obligations in respect of the transaction concerned to transfer traded securities to CC&G or EMCF, or to a nominee of either CC&G or EMCF;

(*e*) CC&G or EMCF, or a nominee of either CC&G or EMCF, to a clearing participant or a nominee of a clearing participant;

(*f*) CC&G or a nominee of CC&G to EMCF or a nominee of EMCF; or

(*g*) EMCF or a nominee of EMCF to CC&G or a nominee of CC&G.

(4) Condition B is that the person to whom those securities are agreed to be transferred under any of the agreements specified in paragraph (3) ("the relevant agreement") is required on receipt of those securities to transfer traded securities under a matching agreement to another person or, in the case of an agreement falling within paragraph (3)(*d*), would have been so required if the failure referred to in that paragraph had not occurred.

(5) In paragraph (4)—

(*a*) a "matching agreement" means an agreement under which—

(i) the traded securities agreed to be transferred are of the same kind as the traded securities agreed to be transferred under the relevant agreement, and

(ii) the number and transfer price of the traded securities agreed to be transferred are identical to the number and transfer price of the traded securities agreed to be transferred under the relevant agreement;

(*b*) references to CC&G or EMCF are references to that clearing house in its capacity as a person providing clearing services in connection with a transaction made on the Facility;

(*c*) references to a clearing participant are references to a clearing participant in its capacity as such.

5 Consequential provision

(1) Traded securities which are the subject of an agreement specified in regulation 4(3) shall be dealt with by a clearing participant who is party to the agreement in a separate designated account, and not otherwise.

(2) In paragraph (1) "designated account" means an account designated by CC&G or EMCF for a clearing participant in connection with the traded securities concerned.

2009/2052

ALTERNATIVE FINANCE INVESTMENT BONDS (STAMP DUTY LAND TAX) (PRESCRIBED EVIDENCE) REGULATIONS 2009

Made by the Commissioners for HMRC under FA 2009 Sch 61 paras 5(6), 9, 18(5), 18(6) and 23(1)

Made . . . .*23 July 2009*
Laid before the House of Commons . . . .*23 July 2009*
Coming into force . . . .*13 August 2009*

1 Citation and commencement

These Regulations may be cited as the Alternative Finance Investment Bonds (Stamp Duty Land Tax) (Prescribed Evidence) Regulations 2009 and shall come into force on 13th August 2009.

2 Interpretation

(1) In these Regulations—

"Schedule 61" means Schedule 61 to the Finance Act 2009,

"SDLT" means Stamp Duty Land Tax,

"The original owner" is "P" as provided for by paragraph 5(2) of Schedule 61,

"UTRN" means the unique transaction reference number allocated by HMRC to a land transaction for the purposes of stamp duty land tax.

(2) In these Regulations the relevant Land Registry is defined as—

(*a*) in relation to land in England and Wales—Her Majesty's Land Registry,

(*b*) in relation to land in Scotland—Registrars of Scotland,

(*c*) in relation to land in Northern Ireland—The Land Registry of Northern Ireland.

3 Prescribed evidence for the purpose of paragraph 5(6) of Schedule 61

For the purpose of paragraph 5(6) of Schedule 61 (condition D for operation of reliefs) the prescribed evidence is all of the following—

(*a*) any document provided by the relevant Land Registry confirming the creation and registration of a legal charge or standard security in favour of the Commissioners for Her Majesty's Revenue and Customs in relation to that land, and

(*b*) the UTRN for the SDLT land transaction return on which relief from the tax was claimed on the transfer of the land from the original owner to the bond-issuer.

4 Prescribed evidence for the purpose of paragraph 9 of Schedule 61

For the purpose of paragraph 9 of Schedule 61 (discharge of charge when conditions for relief met) the prescribed evidence is all of the following—

(*a*) a statement from the bond-issuer, or a person authorised to act on behalf of the bond-issuer, that all conditions A to C and E to G in Part 3 of Schedule 61 have been met,

(*b*) the UTRN for the SDLT land transaction return on which relief from the tax was claimed on the transfer of the land from the original owner to the bond-issuer,

(*c*) the UTRN for the SDLT land transaction return on which relief from the tax was claimed on the transfer of the land from the bond-issuer to the original owner, and

(*d*) any document as provided by the relevant Land Registry confirming that the land has been registered in the name of the original owner.

5 Prescribed evidence for the purpose of paragraph 18(5) of Schedule 61

For the purposes of paragraph 18(5) of Schedule 61 (Substitution of asset) the prescribed evidence is all of the following—

(*a*) the UTRN for the SDLT land transaction return on which relief from the tax was claimed on the transfer of the land from the original owner to the bond-issuer,

(*b*) the UTRN for the SDLT land transaction return on which relief from the tax was claimed on the transfer of the land from the bond-issuer to the original owner, and

(*c*) any document as provided by the relevant Land Registry confirming that the land has been registered in the name of the original owner.

6 Prescribed evidence for the purpose of paragraph 18(6) of Schedule 61

For the purposes of paragraph 18(6) of Schedule 61 (Substitution of asset) the prescribed evidence is all of the following—

(*a*) the UTRN for the SDLT land transaction return on which relief from the tax was claimed on the transfer of the land from the original owner to the bond-issuer,

(*b*) the UTRN for the SDLT land transaction return on which relief from the tax was claimed on the transfer of the land from the bond-issuer to the original owner,

(*c*) any document that confirms that the replacement land is not in the United Kingdom and that conditions A to C in Part 3 of Schedule 61 have been met in relation to that land, and;

(*d*) any document as provided by the relevant Land Registry confirming that the land has been registered in the name of the original owner.

2009/2095

STAMP DUTY LAND TAX (USE OF INFORMATION CONTAINED IN LAND TRANSACTION RETURNS) REGULATIONS 2009

Made by the Treasury under FA 2003 ss 78A(1)(d) and 114(6)

Made . . . . *30 July 2009*
Laid before the House of Commons . . . . *31 July 2009*
Coming into force . . . . *21 August 2009*

1 Citation and commencement

These Regulations may be cited as the Stamp Duty Land Tax (Use of Information Contained in Land Transaction Returns) Regulations 2009 and shall come into force on 21st August 2009.

2 Interpretation

In these Regulations—

"land transaction return" means a return complying with the requirements imposed by Part 1 of Schedule 10 to the Finance Act 2003 (stamp duty land tax: land transaction returns) and regulations under that Part;

"DFP" means Department of Finance and Personnel as set out in the Departments (Northern Ireland) Order 1999.

3 Disclosure and use of land transaction information to and by the Commissioner of Valuation for Northern Ireland and District Valuers in Northern Ireland

(1) Relevant information may be made available for use by the Commissioner of Valuation for Northern Ireland and District Valuers in Northern Ireland for the purposes of, the exercise of any statutory function of the Commissioner or District Valuers (as the case may be).

(2) Relevant information made available for use by the Commissioner of Valuation for Northern Ireland or District Valuers in Northern Ireland under this regulation may be disclosed by the Commissioner of Valuation for Northern Ireland or District Valuers in Northern Ireland to DFP for the purposes of regulation 4.

4 Disclosure and use of land transaction information to and by the Department of Finance and Personnel

(1) Relevant information may be available for use by DFP for the purposes of any lawful function of DFP but must not be used in any way which would permit any person other than an officer of DFP to identify the vendor or the purchaser.

(2) Relevant information made available for use by DFP under this regulation must not be disclosed outside DFP without the consent of the Commissioners for Her Majesty's Revenue and Customs. Such consent may be general or specific.

2009/2954

STAMP DUTY AND STAMP DUTY RESERVE TAX (INVESTMENT EXCHANGES AND CLEARING HOUSES) REGULATIONS (NO 12) 2009

Made . . . .*5 November 2009*

Laid before the House of Commons . . . .*6 November 2009*

Coming into force . . . .*29 November 2009*

The Treasury make the following Regulations in exercise of the powers conferred on them by sections 116 and 117 of the Finance Act 1991.

1 Citation and commencement

(1) These Regulations may be cited as the Stamp Duty and Stamp Duty Reserve Tax (Investment Exchanges and Clearing Houses) Regulations (No 12) 2009 and shall come into force on 29th November 2009.

(2) These Regulations shall have effect—

(*a*) for the purposes of the charge to stamp duty, in relation to instruments executed on or after 29th November 2009;

(*b*) for the purposes of the charge to stamp duty reserve tax—

(i) in the case of agreements to transfer traded securities which are not conditional, in relation to agreements made on or after 29th November 2009;

(ii) in the case of agreements to transfer traded securities which are conditional, in relation to agreements where the condition is satisfied on or after that date.

2 Interpretation

(1) In these Regulations—

"clearing participant" means a member of Eurex Clearing AG who as such is permitted by the Rules of Eurex Clearing AG to clear transactions made on the Exchange for a traded security and who may or may not also be a participant in the Exchange;

"client" means a person who gives instructions to a non-clearing firm for traded securities to be sold on the Exchange;

"Eurex Clearing AG" is a company registered in Germany which is a recognised clearing house under the Financial Services and Markets Act 2000;

"the Exchange" means the Irish Stock Exchange, which is permitted to operate as a recognised investment exchange under Article 36 of the Directive;

"nominee" means a person whose business is or includes holding trading securities as a nominee for Eurex Clearing AG acting in its capacity as a person providing clearing services in connection with a transaction made on the Exchange, or as a nominee for a clearing participant (as the case may be);

"non-clearing firm" means a participant in the Exchange other than a clearing participant;

"traded securities" means stocks and shares which are issued or raised by a company but does not include stocks and shares issued by a company not incorporated in the United Kingdom unless—

(*a*) the stocks and shares are registered in a register kept in the United Kingdom by or on behalf of the company; or

(*b*) in the case of shares, they are paired, within the meaning of section 99(6A) of the Finance Act 1986, with shares issued by a company incorporated in the United Kingdom.

3 Prescription of recognised investment exchanges and recognised clearing houses

For the purpose of sections 116 and 117 of the Finance Act 1991—

(*a*) The Irish Stock Exchange is prescribed as a recognised investment exchange; and

(*b*) Eurex Clearing AG is prescribed as a recognised clearing house.

4 Prescribed circumstances for the purposes of sections 116 and 117

(1) In the circumstances prescribed in this regulation, a charge to stamp duty or stamp duty reserve tax shall be treated as not arising.

(2) The circumstances prescribed are where, in connection with a transaction made on the Exchange, conditions A and B are met.

(3) Condition A is that traded securities of a particular kind are transferred, or agreed to be transferred, from—

(*a*) a clearing participant or a nominee of a clearing participant to another clearing participant or nominee,

(*b*) a non-clearing firm or its client to a clearing participant or a nominee of a clearing participant,

(*c*) a clearing participant or a nominee of a clearing participant to Eurex Clearing AG or to a nominee of that clearing house,

(*d*) a person other than a clearing participant to Eurex Clearing AG or to a nominee of that clearing house, as a result of a failure by a clearing participant to fulfil his obligations in respect of the transaction concerned to transfer traded securities to Eurex Clearing AG or to a nominee of that clearing house, or

(*e*) Eurex Clearing AG or a nominee of that clearing house to a clearing participant or a nominee of a clearing participant.

(4) Condition B is that the person to whom those securities are agreed to be transferred under any of the agreements specified in paragraph (3) ("the relevant agreement") is required on receipt of those securities to transfer traded securities under a matching agreement to another person or, in the case of an agreement falling within paragraph (3)(*d*), would have been so required if the failure referred to in that paragraph had not occurred.

(5) In this regulation—

(*a*) a "matching agreement" means an agreement under which—

(i) the traded securities agreed to be transferred are of the same kind as the traded securities agreed to be transferred under the relevant agreement, and

(ii) the number and transfer price of the traded securities agreed to be transferred are identical to the number and transfer price of the traded securities agreed to be transferred under the relevant agreement;

(*b*) references to Eurex Clearing AG are references to that clearing house in its capacity as a person providing clearing services in connection with a transaction made on the Exchange;

(*c*) references to a clearing participant are references to a clearing participant in his capacity as such.

5 Consequential provision

(1) Traded securities which are the subject of an agreement specified in regulation 4(3) shall be dealt with by a clearing participant who is party to the agreement in a separate designated account, and not otherwise.

(2) In paragraph (1) "designated account" means an account designated by Eurex Clearing AG for a clearing participant in connection with the traded securities concerned.

2009/2971

MUTUAL SOCIETIES (TRANSFERS OF BUSINESS) (TAX) REGULATIONS 2009

Made by the Treasury under FA 2009 s 124

Made . . . . 9 November 2009

Laid before the House of Commons . . . . 10 November 2009

Coming into force . . . .*1 December 2009*

PART 1

PRELIMINARY PROVISIONS AND INTERPRETATION

1 Citation, commencement and effect

(1) These Regulations may be cited as the Mutual Societies (Transfers of Business) (Tax) Regulations 2009 and shall come into force on 1st December 2009.

(2) Regulations 2 to 11, 15 to 25, and 31 to 34 shall have effect—

(*a*) in relation to any relevant transfer which takes place on or after 22 April 2009; and

(*b*) in relation to any land transaction which forms part of a relevant transfer to which these Regulations apply where the effective date of that land transaction is on or after 22 April 2009.

(3) Regulations 12 to 14, 26 to 30, and 35 shall have effect in relation to any relevant transfer which takes place on or after 1st December 2009.

2 Interpretation

(1) In these Regulations—

"CTA" means the Corporation Tax Act 2009;

"FA, followed by a year" means the Finance Act of that year;

"ICTA" means the Income and Corporation Taxes Act 1988;

"TCGA" means the Taxation of Chargeable Gains Act 1992;

"75% subsidiary" has the meaning given by section 838 of ICTA;

"business" includes engagements;

"chargeable intangible asset" has the meaning given by section 741 of CTA (meaning of "chargeable intangible asset");

"commercial company" means a company formed and registered under the Companies Act 2006 (or treated as formed and registered under that Act) which is a public company limited by shares;

"creditor relationship" has the meaning given by section 302(5) of CTA ("loan relationship", "creditor relationship", "debtor relationship");

"debtor relationship" has the meaning given by section 302(6) of CTA ("loan relationship", "creditor relationship", "debtor relationship");

"effective date" has the meaning given by section 119 of FA 2003 (meaning of "effective date" of a transaction);

"fair value accounting" has the meaning given by section 313 of CTA (basis of accounting);

"land transaction" has the meaning given by section 43(1) of FA 2003 (land transactions);

"loan relationship" includes matters treated as a loan relationship by Part 6 of CTA (relationships treated as loan relationships);

"relevant transfer" has the meaning given by regulation 3;

"subsidiary of a mutual society" means a company within the meaning of the Companies Act 2006—

(*a*) in which a building society, an industrial and provident society or a friendly society, as the case may be, holds a majority of the voting rights or of which that society is a member and alone controls, pursuant to an agreement with other shareholders or members, a majority of the voting rights; and

(*b*) in relation to which that society has the right to appoint or remove a majority of the company's board of directors;

"tax-neutral" has the meaning given by section 776 of CTA (meaning of tax neutral transfer).

(2) In regulations 5 to 7 and 16 to 18 "asset" has the meaning given by section 21 of TCGA (assets and disposals).

(3) In regulations 6, 7, 9, 17, 18 and 25 references to a company being a member of a group of companies are to be read in accordance with section 170 of TCGA (interpretation of sections 171 to 181).

(4) In regulations 13 and 29 "group" has the meaning given by Chapter 8 of Part 8 of CTA (intangible fixed assets).

(5) In these Regulations references to a person being connected with another are to be read in accordance with section 839 of ICTA (connected persons).

3 Meaning of relevant transfer

(1) A "relevant transfer" by a building society is—

(*a*) an amalgamation of two or more building societies ("the transferor") by the establishment of a successor building society ("the transferee") in accordance with section 93 of the Building Societies Act 1986 (amalgamations);

(*b*) a transfer by a building society ("the transferor") of the whole of its business to another building society ("the transferee") in accordance with section 94 of the Building Societies Act 1986 (transfers of engagements);

(*c*) a transfer by a building society ("the transferor") of part of its business to another building society ("the transferee") in accordance with section 94 (transfers of engagements) of the Building Societies Act 1986;

(*d*) a transfer by a building society ("the transferor") of the whole of its business to a commercial company ("the transferee") in accordance with section 97 of the Building Societies Act 1986 (transfers of business to commercial company); or

(*e*) a transfer by a building society ("the transferor") of the whole of its business to a subsidiary of a mutual society ("the transferee") in accordance with section 97 of the Building Societies Act 1986 (transfers of business to commercial company).

(2) A "relevant transfer" by an industrial and provident society is—

(*a*) an amalgamation of two or more industrial and provident societies ("the transferor") into one industrial and provident society ("the transferee") in accordance with section 50 of the Industrial and Provident Societies Act 1965 (amalgamation of societies);

(*b*) a transfer by an industrial and provident society ("the transferor") of the whole of its business to another industrial and provident society ("the transferee") in accordance with section 51 of the Industrial and Provident Societies Act 1965 (transfer of engagements between societies);

(*c*) a transfer by an industrial and provident society ("the transferor") of part of its business to one or more industrial and provident societies ("the transferee") in accordance with section 51 of the Industrial and Provident Societies Act 1965 (transfer of engagements between societies);

(*d*) a conversion of an industrial and provident society ("the transferor") into a company ("the transferee") in accordance with section 52 of the Industrial and Provident Societies Act 1965 (conversion into, amalgamation with, or transfer of engagements to company);

(*e*) an amalgamation of an industrial and provident society ("the transferor") with a company ("the transferee") in accordance with section 52 of the Industrial and Provident Societies Act 1965 (conversion into, amalgamation with, or transfer of engagements to company); or

(*f*) a transfer by an industrial and provident society ("the transferor") of the whole of its business to a company ("the transferee") in accordance with section 52 of the Industrial and Provident Societies Act 1965 (conversion into, amalgamation with, or transfer of engagements to company).

(3) A "relevant transfer" by a friendly society is—

(*a*) an amalgamation of two or more friendly societies ("the transferor") by the establishment of a successor society ("the transferee") in accordance with section 85 of the Friendly Societies Act 1992 (amalgamation of friendly societies);

(*b*) a transfer by a friendly society ("the transferor") of the whole of its business to a person ("the transferee") referred to in section 86 of the Friendly Societies Act 1992 (transfer of engagements by or to friendly society);

(*c*) a transfer by a friendly society ("the transferor") of part of its business to a person ("the transferee") referred to in section 86 of the Friendly Societies Act 1992 (transfer of engagements by or to friendly society);

(*d*) a transfer by a friendly society ("the transferor") of the whole of its business to a person ("the transferee") specified by the Financial Services Authority in accordance with section 90 of the Friendly Societies Act 1992 (power of authority to effect transfer of engagements); or

(*e*) a conversion of a friendly society ("the transferor") into a company ("the transferee") in accordance with section 91 of the Friendly Societies Act 1992 (conversion of friendly society into company).

PART 2
BUILDING SOCIETIES

4 Relevant transfer by a building society

(1) This regulation applies if there is a relevant transfer by a building society.

(2) The Corporation Tax Acts shall have effect in relation to the relevant transfer subject to paragraphs (3) to (18).

(3) For the purposes of the allowances and charges provided for by the Capital Allowances Act 2001 a trade which is transferred or amalgamated as a result of the relevant transfer shall not be treated as permanently discontinued nor shall a new trade be treated as set up and commenced, and—

(*a*) there shall be made to or on the transferee in accordance with that Act all such allowances and charges as would, if the transferor had continued to carry on the trade, have fallen to be made to or on the transferor; and

(*b*) the amount of any such allowance or charge shall be computed as if—

(i) the transferee had been carrying on the trade since the transferor began to do so, and

(ii) everything done to or by the transferor had been done to or by the transferee (but so that no sale or transfer which, on the transfer of the trade, is made to the transferee by the transferor of any assets in use for the purpose of the trade shall be treated as giving rise to any such allowance or charge).

(4) The transferee shall be entitled to such relief under section 393(1) of ICTA (losses other than terminal losses), as for a loss sustained by the transferee in carrying on the trade, for any amount for which the transferor would have been entitled to relief if it had continued to carry on the trade. This paragraph is subject to paragraph (5) and to any claim made by the transferor under section 393A(1) of ICTA (losses: set off against profits of the same, or an earlier, accounting period).

(5) If the amount of relevant liabilities exceeds the value of relevant assets, the transferee shall be entitled to relief by virtue of paragraph (4) only if, and only to the extent that, the amount of that excess is less than the amount mentioned in that paragraph.

(6) For the purposes of paragraph (5)—

(*a*) the value of assets (other than money) shall be taken to be the price which they might reasonably be expected to have fetched on a sale in the open market immediately before the predecessor ceased to carry on the trade; and

(*b*) the amount of liabilities shall be taken to be their amount at that time.

(7) Subsection (2A) of section 393A of ICTA (losses: set off against profits of the same, or an earlier, accounting period) shall not apply to any loss which (but for this paragraph) would fall within subsection (2B) of that section by virtue of the transferor ceasing to carry on the trade, and subsection (7) of that section shall not apply for the computation of any such loss.

(8) If, on the transferor ceasing to carry on the trade, the transferee begins to carry on the activities of the trade as part of its trade, then that part of the trade carried on by the transferee shall be treated for the purposes of this regulation as a separate trade, if the effect of so treating it is that paragraph (2) has effect on that event in relation to that separate trade.

(9) If, on the transferor ceasing to carry on part of a trade, the transferee begins to carry on the activities of that part as its trade or part of its trade, the transferor shall for the purposes of this regulation be treated as having carried on that part of its trade as a separate trade if the effect of so treating it is that paragraph (2) has effect on that event in relation to that separate trade.

(10) If, under paragraphs (8) or (9), any activities of the transferor fall, on that transferor ceasing or beginning to carry them on, to be treated as a separate trade, such apportionments of receipts, expenses, assets or liabilities shall be made as may be just and reasonable.

(11) If, by virtue of paragraph (10), any item falls to be apportioned and, at the time of the apportionment, it appears that it is material as respects the liability to tax (for whatever period) of two or more building societies or a commercial company or a subsidiary of a mutual society, any question which arises as to the manner in which the item shall be apportioned shall be determined, for the purposes of the tax of those building societies, commercial company or subsidiary of a mutual in like manner as an appeal, and all those companies shall be entitled to be a party to those proceedings.

(12) If the amount of relevant liabilities does not exceed the value of relevant assets—

(*a*) paragraph (10) shall have effect as if for the words following "separate trade," to the end of the paragraph there were substituted "any necessary apportionment shall be made of receipts or expenses."; and

(*b*) paragraph (11) shall have effect as if for "item" there were substituted "sum".

(13) In this regulation—

"relevant assets" means—

(*a*) assets vested in the transferor immediately before it ceased to carry on the trade, which were not transferred to the transferee; and

(*b*) consideration given to the transferor by the transferee in respect of the relevant transfer or change of the entity carrying on the business as a consequence of the relevant transfer;

and for the purposes of sub-paragraph (*b*) the assumption by the transferee of any liabilities of the transferor shall not be treated as the giving of consideration to the transferor by the transferee;

"relevant liabilities" means liabilities outstanding and vested in the transferor immediately before it ceased to carry on the trade which were not transferred to the transferee; but a liability representing the transferor's share capital, share premium account, reserves or relevant loan stock is not a relevant liability.

(14) Where the transferor transferred a liability to the transferee but the creditor concerned agreed to accept settlement of part of the liability as settlement of the whole, the liability shall be treated for the purposes of paragraph (13) as not having been transferred to the transferee except as to that part.

(15) For the purposes of paragraph (13), a liability representing the transferor's share capital, share premium account, reserves or relevant loan stock shall be treated as not doing so, if, in the period of one year ending with the day on which the transferor ceased to carry on the trade, the liability arose on a conversion of a liability not representing its share capital, share premium account, reserves or relevant loan stock.

(16) Where a liability of the transferor representing its relevant loan stock is not a relevant liability for the purposes of paragraph (5) but is secured on an asset of the transferor not yet transferred to the transferee, the value of the asset shall, for the purposes of paragraph (5), be reduced by an amount equal to the amount of the liability.

(17) In this regulation "relevant loan stock" means any loan stock or similar security (whether secured or unsecured) except any in the case of which paragraph (18) applies.

(18) This paragraph applies where, at the time the liability giving rise to the loan stock or other security was incurred, the person who was the creditor was carrying on a trade of lending money.

5 Transfer of an asset—taxation of chargeable gains

If—

(*a*) there is a relevant transfer within regulation 3(1)(*e*); and

(*b*) there is a disposal of an asset by the transferor to the transferee,

the transferor and the transferee shall be treated for the purposes of corporation tax in respect of chargeable gains as if the asset were acquired from the transferor for a consideration of such amount as would secure that on the disposal neither a gain nor a loss would accrue to the transferor.

6 Transfer of an asset—taxation of chargeable gains—company ceasing to be member of group

If—

(*a*) there is a relevant transfer within regulation 3(1)(*a*), (*b*) or (*e*);

(*b*) the transferor and the transferee are not members of the same group at the time of the relevant transfer; and

(*c*) as a result of the relevant transfer, a company ceases to be a member of the same group as the transferor,

section 179 of TCGA (company ceasing to be a member of group: post-appointed day cases) shall not apply in respect of any asset acquired by the company referred to in paragraph (*c*) from the transferor or from any other member of the same group as the transferor.

7 Transfer of an asset—company ceasing to be a member of a group—further provisions

(1) This regulation applies if there is a relevant transfer within regulation 3(1)(*a*), (*b*) or (*e*).

(2) If this regulation applies and the transferor and the transferee—

(*a*) as a result of the relevant transfer become members of the same group; but

(*b*) subsequently cease to be members of the same group,

paragraph (3) applies.

(3) If paragraph (2) is satisfied, section 179 of TCGA (company ceasing to be a member of group: post-appointed day cases) shall not have effect as respects—

(*a*) any asset acquired by the transferee as a consequence of the relevant transfer from the transferor or any other member of the same group; or

(*b*) any asset acquired as a consequence of the relevant transfer from the transferor, or any other member of the same group, by any company which is a member of the same group as the transferor at the time of the relevant transfer.

(4) If this regulation applies and, as a result of the relevant transfer, a company which was a member of the same group as the transferor at the time of the relevant transfer—

(*a*) ceases to be a member of that group;

(*b*) becomes a member of the same group as the transferee; and

(*c*) subsequently ceases to be a member of that group,

section 179 of TCGA shall have effect when the company ceases to be a member of the same group as the transferee as respects any relevant asset acquired by that company otherwise than from the transferee as if that asset had been acquired from the transferee.

This paragraph is subject to paragraph (6).

(5) In paragraph (4) "relevant asset" means any asset acquired by the company referred to in that paragraph from—

(*a*) the transferor; or

(*b*) any other company which is a member of the same group as the transferor at the time of the relevant transfer,

when the company referred to in that paragraph and the transferor, or the company referred to in that paragraph, the transferor and the other company, were members of the same group.

(6) Paragraph (4) shall not apply if the company referred to in that paragraph which acquired that asset and the company from which that asset was acquired (one being a 75 per cent subsidiary of the other) cease simultaneously to be members of the same group as the transferee but continue to be members of the same group as one another.

8 Transfer of loan relationship or derivative contract

(1) This regulation applies if—

(*a*) there is a relevant transfer by a building society;

(*b*) the transferor has consistently applied appropriate accounting treatment in accordance with generally accepted accounting practice up to and including the date of the relevant transfer in respect of all loan relationships and derivative contracts shown in its balance sheet; and

(*c*) as a result of the relevant transfer the transferee directly or indirectly replaces the transferor as a party to—

(i) the loan relationships; or

(ii) the derivative contracts.

(2) The transferee shall bring into account, in accordance with paragraphs (3) to (15), amounts in respect of the transfer adjustment.

(3) The "transfer adjustment" is the difference, if any, that arises on a comparison of the closing accounting balance sheet figure, adjusted for tax as appropriate, in respect of the loan relationships or the derivative contracts in the transferor's accounts and the opening accounting balance sheet figure, adjusted for tax as appropriate, in respect of the loan relationships or derivative contracts in the transferee's accounts.

(4) If the transferor carries out simultaneous relevant transfers of its business, within regulation 3(1)(*c*) of part of its business the "transfer adjustment" in respect of each transferee is to be computed by reference to the difference between the opening accounting balance sheet figure, adjusted for tax as appropriate, for the transferred loan relationships and derivative contracts in each transferee's accounts and the closing accounting balance sheet figure, adjusted for tax as appropriate, for those same loan relationships and derivative contracts in the transferor's accounts.

(5) For the purposes of paragraphs (3) and (4), where, in the Tax Acts, an accounting balance sheet figure is adjusted for tax, it is that adjusted figure that is to be used when calculating the transfer adjustment.

(6) The credits and debits to be brought into account as profits or deficits or losses for the purposes of Part 3, 5, 6 or 7 of CTA in respect of the transferee's transfer adjustment shall be determined in accordance with this regulation.

(7) The transferee shall bring one-sixth of the transfer adjustment ("the applicable amount") into account for each year of a six year period ("the prescribed period") beginning with the day on which the relevant transfer takes place. This is subject to paragraphs (8), (10) and (16).

(8) If there are two or more accounting periods falling in a year, the applicable amount for the year shall be apportioned between the accounting periods.

(9) An apportionment between accounting periods of an applicable amount in accordance with paragraph (8) shall be made according to the proportion of the year which is included in each accounting period.

(10) If the transferee ceases to be within the charge to corporation tax before the end of the prescribed period, the whole of the applicable amounts, so far as they have not been brought into account in an earlier accounting period, shall be brought into account as a credit or debit for the period ending when the transferee ceases to be within that charge. This paragraph is subject to paragraph (11).

(11) If before the end of the prescribed period—

(*a*) the transferee transfers the business by way of a relevant transfer within regulation 3(1)(*a*) or (*b*) to a successor building society ("A"); and,

(*b*) as a result of the transfer, the transferee ceases to be within the charge to corporation tax,

that relevant transfer will not cause the whole of the applicable amounts, so far as they have not been brought into account in an earlier period, to be brought into account for the period in which that relevant transfer takes place.

(12) Where there is a relevant transfer to which paragraph (11) applies, paragraph (7) will apply to the applicable amounts which have not been brought into account by the transferee as if references to "the transferee" were references to "A".

(13) If this regulation applies and the transferor has been bringing debits and credits into account in accordance with regulation 3A of the Loan Relationships and Derivative Contracts (Change of Accounting Practice) Regulations 2004, the relevant transfer shall be treated for the purposes of regulation 3A(6) of those Regulations as though it were a qualifying transfer.

(14) In paragraph (1)(*c*) the reference to "the transferee directly or indirectly replaces the transferor as a party" has the same meaning given by—

(*a*) regulation 10 in the case of a loan relationship; and

(*b*) regulation 11 in the case of a derivative contract.

(15) Paragraph (7) does not apply if the transferee has made an election under paragraph (16).

(16) If the amount of the transfer adjustment does not exceed £1.5 million, the transferee may elect to bring into account the full amount of the transfer adjustment in the accounting period in which the relevant transfer takes place.

(17) An election under paragraph (16)—

(*a*) must be made—

(i) by notice in writing to an officer of Revenue and Customs; and

(ii) no later than 12 months after the end of the accounting period in which the relevant transfer took place;

(*b*) must specify the amount of the transfer adjustment; and

(*c*) is irrevocable.

(18) In this regulation—

"generally accepted accounting practice" has the meaning given by section 50(1) of FA 2004 (generally accepted accounting practice);

"officer of Revenue and Customs" has the meaning given by section 2 of the Commissioners for Revenue and Customs Act 2005 (officers of revenue and customs).

9 Transfer of loan relationship or derivative contract—further provisions

(1) This regulation applies if—

(*a*) there is a relevant transfer within regulation 3(1)(*a*), (*b*), (*d*) or (*e*); and

(*b*) before the date of the relevant transfer there had been a transfer to a company of—

(i) a loan relationship to which section 336 of CTA (transfers of loans on group transactions) applied; or

(ii) a derivative contract to which section 625 of CTA (group member replacing another as party to a derivative contract) applied;

but this is subject to paragraph (6).

(2) Paragraph (3) applies if, as a result of the relevant transfer, the company referred to in paragraph (1)(*b*) ceases to be a member of the same group as the transferor—

(*a*) before the end of the relevant six year period referred to in—

(i) section 344(4) of CTA (transferee leaving group after replacing transferor as party to loan relationship); or

(ii) section 630(4) of CTA (introduction to sections 631 and 632); and

(*b*) whilst still a party to the relevant loan relationship or derivative contract.

(3) If paragraph (2) is satisfied—

(*a*) the company referred to in paragraph (1)(*b*) shall be treated as not having ceased to be a member of the same group as the transferor;

(*b*) in the case of a loan relationship, section 345 of CTA (transferee leaving group otherwise than because of an exempt distribution) shall not apply to the loan relationship as a result of the relevant transfer; and

(*c*) in the case of a derivative contract, section 631 of CTA (transferee leaving group otherwise than because of exempt distribution) shall not apply to the derivative contract as a result of the relevant transfer.

(4) Paragraph (5) applies if the company referred to in paragraph (1)(*b*) ceases to be a member of the same group as the transferee—

(*a*) before the end of the relevant six year period referred to in—

(i) section 344(4) of CTA (transferee leaving group after replacing transferor as party to loan relationship); or

(ii) section 630(4) of CTA (introduction to sections 631 and 632); and

(*b*) whilst still a party to the relevant loan relationship or derivative contract.

(5) If paragraph (4) is satisfied—

(*a*) in the case of a loan relationship, section 345 of CTA (transferee leaving group otherwise than because of an exempt distribution) shall apply to the loan relationship as a result of the relevant transfer; and

(*b*) in the case of a derivative contract, section 631 of CTA (transferee leaving group otherwise than because of exempt distribution) shall apply to the derivative contract as a result of the relevant transfer.

(6) This regulation does not apply where a transferor of a loan relationship is regarded as using fair value accounting in respect of that loan relationship.

(7) A transferor shall be regarded for the purposes of this regulation as using fair value accounting in respect of a loan relationship only if the credits and debits to be brought into account for the purposes of these Regulations as respects that loan relationship are determined on that basis.

(8) It does not matter for the purposes of paragraph (7) if the transferor does not otherwise use fair value accounting in respect of the loan relationship.

10 Meaning of transferee replacing building society as party to a loan relationship

(1) References in regulation 8 to a transferee replacing a transferor as a party to a loan relationship include references to a transferee becoming party to a loan relationship which—

(*a*) confers rights within paragraph (2);

(*b*) imposes obligations within paragraph (2); or

(*c*) both confers such rights and imposes such obligations.

(2) Rights or obligations are within this paragraph if they are equivalent to those of the transferor under a loan relationship to which that transferor has ceased to be a party as a result of the relevant transfer.

(3) For the purposes of paragraph (2), a transferor's rights under a creditor relationship are equivalent to rights under another creditor relationship if each set of rights gives the holder of an asset representing the relationship in question—

(*a*) the same rights against the same persons as to capital, interest and dividends; and

(*b*) the same remedies to enforce those rights.

(4) For the purposes of paragraph (3), any difference in—

(*a*) the total nominal amounts of the assets representing each loan relationship;

(*b*) the form in which they are held; or

(*c*) the way in which they can be transferred,

is ignored.

(5) For the purposes of paragraph (2), a transferee's obligations under a debtor relationship are equivalent to obligations under another debtor loan relationship if under each set of obligations the holder of the liability representing the loan relationship in question has—

(*a*) the same obligations to the same persons as to capital, interest and dividends; and

(*b*) the same remedies to enforce those obligations.

(6) For the purposes of paragraph (5), any difference in—

(*a*) the total nominal amounts of the assets representing the creditor loan relationship corresponding to each relationship;

(*b*) the form in which they are held; or

(*c*) the way in which they can be transferred,

is ignored.

11 Meaning of transferee replacing building society as a party to a derivative contract

(1) References in regulation 8 to a transferee replacing a transferor as a party to a derivative contract include references to the transferee becoming party to a derivative contract which—

(*a*) confers rights within paragraph (2);

(*b*) imposes obligations within paragraph (2); or

(*c*) both confers such rights and imposes such obligations.

(2) Rights or obligations are within this paragraph if they are equivalent to those of the transferor under a derivative contract to which that transferor has ceased to be a party as a result of the relevant transfer.

12 Transfer of intangible fixed assets

(1) This regulation applies if—

(*a*) there is a relevant transfer within regulation 3(1)(*e*) which includes intangible fixed assets;

(*b*) those assets are chargeable intangible assets in relation to the transferor immediately before the relevant transfer; and

(*c*) those assets are chargeable intangible assets in relation to the transferee immediately after the relevant transfer.

(2) The transfer of those assets is tax-neutral for the purposes of—

(*a*) these Regulations; and

(*b*) Part 8 of CTA (intangible fixed assets).

(3) For the application of sections 780 (deemed realisation and reacquisition at market value) and 785 (principal company becoming member of another group) of CTA where this regulation applies, see regulation 13.

(4) This regulation and regulations 13 and 14 apply to goodwill as they apply to intangible fixed assets.

13 Transfer of intangible fixed assets—further provisions

(1) This regulation applies if—

(*a*) there is a relevant transfer within regulation 3(1)(*a*), (*b*) or (*e*) which includes intangible fixed assets;

(*b*) those assets are—

(i) chargeable intangible assets in relation to the transferor immediately before the relevant transfer; and

(ii) chargeable intangible assets in relation to the transferee immediately after the relevant transfer; and

(*c*) the transfer of those assets is tax-neutral for the purposes of these Regulations or Part 8 of CTA (intangible fixed assets).

(2) If because of the relevant transfer a company ceases to be a member of the same group as the transferor, that event does not cause—

(*a*) section 780 of CTA (deemed realisation and reacquisition at market value); or

(*b*) section 785 of that Act (principal company becoming member of another group), to apply as respects any assets acquired by the company from the transferor or any other member of the same group as the transferor.

(3) If the transferor and transferee are members of the same group at the time of the relevant transfer but later cease to be, that later event does not cause section 780 or 785 of CTA to apply in relation to any asset to which this regulation applies.

(4) Paragraph (3) applies to—

(*a*) any asset acquired by the transferee on or before the relevant transfer from the transferor, or from any other member of the same group; or

(*b*) any asset acquired from the transferor or from any other member of the same group by a company (other than the transferee) that is a member of that group at the time of the relevant transfer.

(5) Paragraph (6) applies if a company which is a member of the same group as the transferor at the time of the relevant transfer—

(*a*) ceases to be a member of that group and becomes a member of the same group as the transferee, and

(*b*) later ceases to be a member of that group.

(6) Section 780 of CTA (deemed realisation and reacquisition at market value) applies on that later event as if any asset to which this paragraph applies that has not been acquired from the transferee had been so acquired.

(7) Paragraph (6) applies to—

(*a*) any asset acquired by the company referred to in paragraph (5) from the transferor when that company and the transferor were members of the same group, or

(*b*) any asset acquired by the company referred to in paragraph (5) from another company which is a member of the same group at the time of the relevant transfer when the company referred to in paragraph (5), the transferor and the other company were members of the same group.

(8) Paragraph (6) does not apply if—

(*a*) the company which acquired the asset is a 75% subsidiary of the company from which it was acquired or vice versa;

(*b*) those companies cease simultaneously to be members of the same group as the transferee; and

(*c*) those companies continue to be members of the same group as one another.

14 Intangible fixed assets transferred as if at no gain or no loss

(1) This regulation applies if—

(*a*) there is a relevant transfer by a building society; and

(*b*) the transferor is treated—

(i) for the purposes of these Regulations; or

(ii) by virtue of the provisions referred to in paragraph (2),

as disposing of any assets for a consideration of such amount as would secure that neither a gain nor a loss would accrue to the transferor on that disposal.

(2) The provisions referred to in this paragraph are—

(*a*) section 215 of TCGA (disposal of assets on amalgamation of building societies); and

(*b*) section 216 of that Act (assets transferred from society to company).

(3) The assets, in the hands of the transferee, shall be treated as not satisfying the general rule set out in section 882(1) of CTA (application of Part 8 to assets created or acquired on or after 1 April 2002).

PART 3

INDUSTRIAL AND PROVIDENT SOCIETIES

15 Interpretation

In this Part—

"carrying value" has the meaning given by section 317 of CTA (carrying value);

"discount" has the meaning given by section 480(5) of CTA (relevant non-lending relationships involving discounts);

"notional carrying value" in relation to an asset or liability has the same meaning as it has for section 340(6) of CTA (group transfers and transfers of insurance business: transfer at notional carrying value).

16 Transfer of an asset—taxation of chargeable gains

If—

(*a*) there is a relevant transfer within regulation 3(2)(*d*), (*e*) or (*f*); and

(*b*) there is a disposal of an asset by the transferor to the transferee,

the transferor and the transferee shall be treated for the purposes of corporation tax in respect of chargeable gains as if the asset were acquired from the transferor for a consideration of such amount as would secure that on the disposal neither a gain nor a loss would accrue to the transferor.

17 Transfer of an asset—taxation of chargeable gains—company ceasing to be a member of group

If—

(*a*) there is a relevant transfer within regulation 3(2)(*a*), (*b*), (*d*), (*e*) or (*f*);

(*b*) the transferor and the transferee are not members of the same group at the time of the relevant transfer; and

(*c*) as a result of the relevant transfer, a company ceases to be a member of the same group as the transferor,

section 179 of TCGA (company ceasing to be a member of group: post-appointed day cases) shall not apply in respect of any asset acquired by the company referred to in paragraph (*c*) as a consequence of the relevant transfer from the transferor or from any other member of the same group as the transferor.

18 Transfer of an asset—company ceasing to be a member of a group—further provisions

(1) This regulation applies if there is a relevant transfer within regulation 3(2)(*a*), (*b*), (*d*), (*e*) or (*f*).

(2) If there is a relevant transfer to which this regulation applies, and the transferor and the transferee—

(*a*) are members of the same group at the time of the relevant transfer; but

(*b*) subsequently cease to be members of the same group,

paragraph (3) applies.

(3) If paragraph (2) is satisfied, section 179 of TCGA (company ceasing to be a member of group: post-appointed day cases) shall not have effect as respects—

(*a*) any asset acquired by the transferee as a consequence of the relevant transfer from the transferor or any other member of the same group; or

(*b*) any asset acquired as a consequence of the transfer from the transferor, or any other member of the same group, by any company which is a member of the same group as the transferor at the time of the relevant transfer.

(4) If this regulation applies and, as a result of the relevant transfer, a company which was a member of the same group as the transferor at the time of the relevant transfer—

(*a*) ceases to be a member of that group;

(*b*) becomes a member of the same group as the transferee; and

(*c*) subsequently ceases to be a member of that group,

section 179 of TCGA shall have effect when the company ceases to be a member of the same group as the transferee as respects any relevant asset acquired by that company otherwise than from the transferee as if that asset had been acquired from the transferee.

This paragraph is subject to paragraph (6).

(5) In paragraph (4) "relevant asset" means any asset acquired by the company referred to in that paragraph from—

(*a*) the transferor; or

(*b*) any other company which is a member of the same group as the transferor at the time of the relevant transfer,

when the company referred to in that paragraph and the transferor, or the company referred to in that paragraph, the transferor and the other company, were members of the same group.

(6) Paragraph (4) shall not apply if the company referred to in that paragraph which acquired that asset and the company from which that asset was acquired (one being a 75 per cent subsidiary of the other) cease simultaneously to be members of the same group as the transferee but continue to be members of the same group as one another.

19 Transfer of loan relationship

(1) Subject to paragraph (7), this regulation applies if—

(*a*) there is a relevant transfer by an industrial and provident society; and

(*b*) as a result of that transfer, the transferee directly or indirectly replaces the transferor as a party to a loan relationship (as to which see regulation 20).

(2) The credits and debits to be brought into account for the purposes of Parts 3, 5 and 6 of CTA as a result of the relevant transfer shall be determined in accordance with paragraphs (3) to (10).

(3) Subject to paragraph (5), for the accounting period in which the relevant transfer takes place, the transferor shall be treated as having entered into the relevant transfer for consideration of an amount equal to the notional carrying value of the asset or liability representing the loan relationship at the time of the relevant transfer.

(4) For any accounting period in which the transferee is a party to the loan relationship, the transferee shall be treated as if it had acquired the asset or liability representing the loan relationship for consideration of an amount equal to the notional carrying value of the asset or liability in the accounts of the transferor at the time of the relevant transfer.

(5) If a discount arises in respect of the relevant transfer, the consideration referred to in paragraph (3) shall be treated as increased by the amount of that discount.
(6) Schedule 28AA to ICTA (provision not at arm's length) does not apply in relation to the amounts in respect of which credits or debits are to be brought into account under this regulation.
(7) This regulation does not apply where the transferor is regarded as using fair value accounting in respect of the loan relationship (as to which see regulation 21).
(8) The transferor shall be regarded for the purposes of this Part as using fair value accounting in respect of a loan relationship only if the credits and debits to be brought into account for the purposes of these Regulations as respects the relationship are determined on that basis.
(9) It does not matter for the purposes of paragraph (8) if the transferor does not otherwise use fair value accounting in respect of the loan relationship.
(10) For the purposes of this regulation, subsection (5) of section 480 of CTA (relevant non-lending relationships involving discounts) applies as it applies for the purposes of that section.
(11) This regulation is subject to—
(*a*) section 332 of CTA (repo, stock lending and other transactions); and
(*b*) regulation 26.

20 Meaning of transferee replacing transferor as a party to a loan relationship
(1) References in regulation 19 to a transferee replacing a transferor as a party to a loan relationship include references to a transferee becoming party to a relationship which—
(*a*) confers rights within paragraph (2);
(*b*) imposes obligations within paragraph (2); or
(*c*) both confers such rights and imposes such obligations.
(2) Rights or obligations are within this paragraph if they are equivalent to those of the transferor under a loan relationship to which that transferor ceased to be a party as a result of the relevant transfer.
(3) For the purposes of paragraph (2), a transferor's rights under a creditor relationship are equivalent to rights under another creditor relationship if each set of rights gives the holder of an asset representing the relationship in question—
(*a*) the same rights against the same persons as to capital, interest and dividends; and
(*b*) the same remedies to enforce those rights.
(4) For the purposes of paragraph (3), any difference in—
(*a*) the total nominal amounts of the assets representing each relationship;
(*b*) the form in which they are held; or
(*c*) the way in which they can be transferred,
is ignored.
(5) For the purposes of paragraph (2), a transferee's obligations under a debtor relationship are equivalent to obligations under another debtor relationship if under each set of obligations the holder of the liability representing the relationship in question has—
(*a*) the same obligations to the same persons as to capital, interest and dividends; and
(*b*) the same remedies to enforce those obligations.
(6) For the purposes of paragraph (5), any difference in—
(*a*) the total nominal amounts of the assets representing the creditor relationship corresponding to each relationship;
(*b*) the form in which they are held; or
(*c*) the way in which they can be transferred,
is ignored.

21 Transfer of loan relationship where fair value accounting is used
(1) This regulation applies if regulation 19 would apply but for the fact that the transferor is regarded as using fair value accounting in respect of the loan relationship.
(2) The credits and debits to be brought into account for the purposes of Parts 3, 5 and 6 of CTA as a result of the relevant transfer shall be determined in accordance with paragraphs (3) to (5).
(3) The amount which is to be brought into account by the transferor in respect of the relevant transfer ("the transferor's amount") is—
(*a*) if the amount relates to an asset, either—
(i) the fair value of the asset as at the date when the transferee becomes party to the loan relationship; or
(ii) the fair value of the rights under or interest in the loan relationship as at that date; and
(*b*) if the amount relates to a liability, the fair value of the liability as at that date.
(4) Subject to paragraph (5), for any accounting period in which the transferee is a party to the loan relationship, for the purpose of determining the credits and debits to be brought into account in respect of the relationship for the purposes of these Regulations, the transferee shall be treated as if it had acquired the asset or liability representing the relationship for consideration of an amount equal to the transferor's amount.

(5) If a discount arises in respect of the transfer, the transferor's amount shall be treated as increased by the amount of the discount.
(6) This regulation is subject to—
(*a*) section 332 of CTA (repo, stock lending and other transactions); and
(*b*) regulation 26.

22 Replacement of industrial and provident society as party to a derivative contract
(1) Subject to paragraph (7), this regulation applies if—
(*a*) there is a relevant transfer by an industrial and provident society; and
(*b*) as a result of that transfer the transferee directly or indirectly replaces the transferor as a party to a derivative contract (as to which see regulation 23).
(2) The credits and debits to be brought into account for the purposes of Part 3 or 7 of CTA as a result of the relevant transfer shall be determined in accordance with paragraphs (3) to (6).
(3) Subject to paragraph (5), for the accounting period in which the relevant transfer takes place, the transferor shall be treated as having entered into the derivative contract for consideration of an amount equal to the notional carrying value of that contract (as to which see paragraph (8)).
(4) For any accounting period in which the transferee is a party to the derivative contract, the transferee shall be treated as if it had acquired that derivative contract for consideration of an amount equal to the notional carrying value of that contract in the accounts of the transferor (as to which see paragraph (8)).
(5) If a discount arises in respect of the relevant transfer, the consideration referred to in paragraph (3) shall be treated for the purposes of that paragraph as increased by the amount of the discount.
(6) Schedule 28AA to ICTA (provision not at arm's length) does not apply in relation to the amounts in respect of which credits or debits are to be brought into account under this regulation.
(7) This regulation does not apply where the transferor is regarded as using fair value accounting in respect of the derivative contract (as to which see regulation 24).
(8) For the purposes of this regulation the notional carrying value of a derivative contract is the amount which would have been its carrying value in the accounts of the transferor if a period of account had ended immediately before the date on which the transferor had ceased to be a party to that derivative contract.
(9) For the purposes of this regulation, subsection (5) of section 480 of CTA (relevant non-lending relationships involving discounts) applies as it applies for the purposes of that section.
(10) This regulation is subject to regulation 27.

23 Meaning of transferee replacing transferor as party to a derivative contract
(1) References in regulation 22 to a transferee replacing a transferor as a party to a derivative contract include references to the transferee becoming party to a derivative contract which—
(*a*) confers rights within paragraph (2),
(*b*) imposes liabilities within paragraph (2), or
(*c*) both confers such rights and imposes such liabilities.
(2) Rights or liabilities are within this paragraph if they are equivalent to those of the transferor under a derivative contract to which the transferor has ceased to be a party as a result of the relevant transfer.

24 Transfer of derivative contract where fair value accounting is used
(1) This regulation applies in a case where regulation 22 would apply but for the fact that the transferor is regarded as using fair value accounting as respects the derivative contract.
(2) Subject to paragraph (4), the amount which is to be brought into account by the transferor in respect of a relevant transfer is the fair value of the derivative contract as at the date of that transfer.
(3) For any accounting period in which the transferee is a party to the derivative contract, for the purpose of determining the credits and debits to be brought into account in respect of the contract for the purposes of these Regulations, the transferee shall be treated as if it had acquired the contract for consideration of an amount equal to the fair value of the contract as at the date of the transfer.
(4) If a discount arises in respect of the relevant transfer, the amount to be brought into account under paragraph (2) shall be treated as increased by the amount of the discount.
(5) For the purposes of this regulation, subsection (5) of section 480 of CTA (relevant non-lending relationships involving discounts) applies as it applies for the purposes of that section.
(6) This regulation is subject to regulation 27.

25 Transfer of loan relationship or derivative contract—further provisions
(1) This regulation applies if—
(*a*) there is a relevant transfer within regulation 3(2)(*a*), (*b*), (*d*), (*e*) or (*f*); and
(*b*) before the date of the relevant transfer there had been a transfer to a company of—
(i) a loan relationship to which section 336 of CTA (transfers of loans on group transactions) applied; or

(ii) a derivative contract to which section 625 of CTA (group member replacing another as party to derivative contract) applied,

but this is subject to paragraph (6).

(2) Paragraph (3) applies if as a result of the relevant transfer the company referred to in paragraph (1)(*b*) ceases to be a member of the same group as the transferor—

(*a*) before the end of the relevant six year period referred to in—

(i) section 344(4) of CTA (transferee leaving group after replacing transferor as party to loan relationship); or

(ii) section 630(4) of CTA (introduction to sections 631 and 632); and

(*b*) whilst still a party to the relevant loan relationship or derivative contract.

(3) If paragraph (2) is satisfied—

(*a*) the company referred to in paragraph (1)(*b*) shall be treated as not having ceased to be a member of the same group as the transferor;

(*b*) in the case of a loan relationship, section 345 of CTA (transferee leaving group otherwise than because of exempt distribution) shall not apply to the loan relationship as a result of the relevant transfer; and

(*c*) in the case of a derivative contract, section 631 of CTA (transferee leaving group otherwise than because of exempt distribution) shall not apply to the derivative contract as a result of the relevant transfer.

(4) Paragraph (5) applies if the company referred to in paragraph (1)(*b*) ceases to be a member of the same group as the transferee—

(*a*) before the end of the relevant six year period referred to in—

(i) section 344(4) of CTA (transferee leaving group after replacing transferor as party to loan relationship); or

(ii) section 630(4) of CTA (introduction to sections 631 and 632); and

(*b*) whilst still a party to the relevant loan relationship or derivative contract.

(5) If paragraph (4) is satisfied—

(*a*) in the case of a loan relationship, section 345 of CTA (transferee leaving group otherwise than because of exempt distribution) shall apply to the loan relationship as a result of the relevant transfer; and

(*b*) in the case of a derivative contract, section 631 of CTA (transferee leaving group otherwise than because of exempt distribution) shall apply to the derivative contract as a result of the relevant transfer.

(6) This regulation does not apply where the transferor of a loan relationship is regarded as using fair value accounting in respect of that loan relationship.

(7) The transferor shall be regarded for the purposes of this Part as using fair value accounting in respect of a loan relationship only if the credits and debits to be brought into account for the purposes of these Regulations as respects that loan relationship are determined on that basis.

(8) It does not matter for the purposes of paragraph (7) if the transferor does not otherwise use fair value accounting in respect of the loan relationship.

(9) This regulation is subject to—

(*a*) regulation 26 if there has been a transfer of a loan relationship to which section 336 of CTA (transfers of loans on group transactions) applied; or

(*b*) regulation 27 if there has been a transfer of a derivative contract to which section 625 of CTA (group member replacing another as party to a derivative contract) applied.

26 Transferor of loan relationship is party to avoidance

(1) Regulations 19, 21 and 25 do not apply if conditions A and B are met.

(2) Condition A is that the transferor is a party to arrangements under which there is likely to be a transfer of rights or liabilities under the loan relationship by the transferee to another person in circumstances in which—

(*a*) sections 336 and 340 of CTA; or

(*b*) regulation 19, 21 or 25,

would not apply.

(3) Condition B is that the purpose, or one of the main purposes, of the arrangements is to obtain a tax advantage for the transferor or a person connected with the transferor.

(4) In this regulation "transfer" includes any arrangement which equates in substance to a transfer.

27 Transferor of derivative contract is party to avoidance

(1) Regulations 22, 24 and 25 do not apply if conditions A and B are met.

(2) Condition A is that the transferor is a party to arrangements under which there is likely to be a transfer of rights or liabilities under the derivative contract by the transferee to another person in circumstances in which—

(*a*) section 625 of CTA; or

(*b*) regulation 22, 24 or 25,

would not apply.

(3) Condition B is that the purpose, or one of the main purposes, of the arrangements is to obtain a tax advantage for the transferor or a person connected with the transferor.

(4) In this regulation "transfer" includes any arrangement which equates in substance to a transfer.

28 Transfer of intangible fixed assets

(1) This regulation applies if—

(*a*) there is a relevant transfer within regulation 3(2)(*a*), (*b*), (*d*), (*e*) or (*f*) which includes intangible fixed assets;

(*b*) those assets are chargeable intangible assets in relation to the transferor immediately before the relevant transfer; and

(*c*) those assets are chargeable intangible assets in relation to the transferee immediately after the relevant transfer.

(2) The transfer of those assets is tax-neutral for the purposes of—

(*a*) these Regulations; and

(*b*) Part 8 of CTA (intangible fixed assets).

(3) For the application of sections 780 (deemed realisation and reacquisition at market value) and 785 (principal company becoming member of another group) of CTA where this regulation applies, see regulation 29.

(4) This regulation and regulations 29 and 30 apply to goodwill as they apply to intangible fixed assets.

29 Transfer of intangible fixed assets—further provisions

(1) This regulation applies if—

(*a*) there is a relevant transfer within regulation 3(2)(*a*), (*b*), (*d*), (*e*) or (*f*) which includes intangible fixed assets;

(*b*) those assets are—

(i) chargeable intangible assets in relation to the transferor immediately before the relevant transfer; and

(ii) chargeable intangible assets in relation to the transferee immediately after the relevant transfer; and

(*c*) the transfer is tax-neutral for the purposes of these Regulations or Part 8 of CTA (intangible fixed assets).

(2) If because of the relevant transfer a company ceases to be a member of the same group as the transferor, that event does not cause—

(*a*) section 780 of CTA (deemed realisation and reacquisition at market value); or

(*b*) section 785 of that Act (principal company becoming member of another group),

to apply as respects any assets acquired by the company from the transferor or any other member of the same group as the transferor.

(3) If the transferor and transferee are members of the same group at the time of the relevant transfer but later cease to be, that later event does not cause section 780 or 785 of CTA to apply in relation to any asset to which this regulation applies.

(4) Paragraph (3) applies to—

(*a*) any asset acquired by the transferee on or before the relevant transfer from the transferor, or from any other member of the same group; or

(*b*) any asset acquired from the transferor or from any other member of the same group by a company (other than the transferee) that is a member of that group at the time of the relevant transfer.

(5) Paragraph (6) applies if a company which is a member of the same group as the transferor at the time of the relevant transfer—

(*a*) ceases to be a member of that group and becomes a member of the same group as the transferee, and

(*b*) later ceases to be a member of that group.

(6) Section 780 of CTA (deemed realisation and reacquisition at market value) applies on that later event as if any asset to which this paragraph applies that has not been acquired from the transferee had been so acquired.

(7) Paragraph (6) applies to—

(*a*) any asset acquired by the company referred to in paragraph (5) from the transferor when that company and the transferor were members of the same group; or

(*b*) any asset acquired by the company referred to in paragraph (5) from another company which is a member of the same group at the time of the relevant transfer when the company referred to in paragraph (5), the transferor and the other company were members of the same group.

(8) Paragraph (6) does not apply if—

(*a*) the company which acquired the asset is a 75% subsidiary of the company from which it was acquired or vice versa;

(*b*) those companies cease simultaneously to be members of the same group as the transferee; and

(*c*) those companies continue to be members of the same group as one another.

30 Intangible fixed assets transferred as if at no gain or no loss

(1) This regulation applies if—

(*a*) there is a relevant transfer by an industrial and provident society; and

(*b*) the transferor is treated—

(i) for the purposes of these Regulations; or

(ii) by virtue of section 486 of ICTA (industrial and provident societies and co-operative associations),

as disposing of any assets for a consideration of such amount as would secure that neither a gain nor a loss would accrue to the transferor on that disposal.

(2) The assets, in the hands of the transferee, shall be treated as not satisfying the general rule set out in section 882(1) of CTA (application of Part 8 to assets created or acquired on or after 1 April 2002).

31 Exemption from stamp duty land tax

A land transaction made in connection with a relevant transfer within regulation 3(2)(*b*), (*c*), (*d*), (*e*) or (*f*) shall be exempt from charge under Part 4 of FA 2003.

32 Exemption from stamp duty

Any instrument, document or agreement required to give effect to a relevant transfer by an industrial and provident society shall not be chargeable to stamp duty under the Stamp Act 1891.

PART 4

FURTHER PROVISIONS RELATING TO RELEVANT TRANSFERS

33 Stamp duty land tax—group relief

(1) Paragraph 3 of Schedule 7 to FA 2003 (withdrawal of group relief) does not apply if—

(*a*) there is a relevant transfer;

(*b*) before the date of that relevant transfer there had been a land transaction to which Part 1 of Schedule 7 to FA 2003 applied; and

(*c*) as a result of that relevant transfer, the purchaser in relation to the land transaction referred to in sub-paragraph (*b*) ceases to be a member of the same group as the transferor—

(i) before the end of the period of three years beginning with the effective date of that land transaction; or

(ii) in pursuance of, or in connection with, arrangements made before the end of that three year period.

(2) In this regulation, references to a company being a member of a group of companies are to be read in accordance with paragraph 1 of Schedule 7 to FA 2003.

34 Transitional provision

(1) This regulation applies if a relevant transfer takes place on or after 22 April 2009 but before the date on which these Regulations come into force.

(2) Subject to paragraph (4) nothing in these Regulations shall have effect so as to—

(*a*) impose a charge to tax (or increase a charge to tax) on a party to the relevant transfer;

(*b*) reduce a relief from tax, including a tax credit, available to a party to the relevant transfer; or

(*c*) reduce losses available to a party to the relevant transfer;

where that charge or reduction arises only as a result of the application of these Regulations.

(3) If paragraph (2) applies—

(*a*) any charge to tax (or increase in a charge to tax) on a party to the relevant transfer;

(*b*) any reduction in relief from tax available to a party to the relevant transfer; or

(*c*) any reduction in losses available to a party to the relevant transfer;

shall be disregarded.

(4) Paragraphs (2) and (3) do not apply in relation to—

(*a*) any charge to tax (or increase in a charge to tax);

(*b*) any reduction in relief from tax; or

(*c*) any reduction in losses;

which may arise as a result of anything done or occurring on or after the date on which these Regulations come into force.

35 Arrangements the purpose of which is to secure a tax advantage

(1) This regulation applies if a relevant transfer forms part of an unallowable arrangement.

(2) If paragraph (1) is satisfied the following Cases shall apply.

Case 1

Case 1 is where as a result of the arrangement any party to the relevant transfer obtains a relief from tax (including a tax credit) or an increased relief from tax.

Where Case 1 applies, the relief from tax, or increased relief from tax, shall not be allowed.
Case 2
Case 2 is where as a result of the arrangement any party to the relevant transfer obtains a repayment of tax or an increased repayment of tax.
Where Case 2 applies, the repayment of tax, or the increased repayment, shall not be allowed.
Case 3
Case 3 is where as a result of the arrangement any party to the relevant transfer avoids, reduces or delays a charge or assessment to tax.
Where Case 3 applies, a charge or an assessment to tax may be made upon that party.
Case 4
Case 4 is where as a result of the arrangement any party to the relevant transfer avoids a possible assessment to tax.
Where Case 4 applies, an assessment to tax may be made upon that party.
(3) For the purposes of this regulation an arrangement is an unallowable arrangement where the purpose, or one of the main purposes, of a person in being a party to the relevant transfer is to obtain a tax advantage as a result of that transfer for that person or any other person.

2009/2975

STAMP DUTY AND STAMP DUTY RESERVE TAX (INVESTMENT EXCHANGES AND CLEARING HOUSES) REGULATIONS (NO 13) 2009

Made . . . . *10 November 2009*
Laid before the House of Commons . . . . *11 November 2009*
Coming into force . . . . *2 December 2009*

The Treasury make the following Regulations in exercise of the powers conferred on them by sections 116 and 117 of the Finance Act 1991.

1 Citation and commencement

(1) These Regulations may be cited as the Stamp Duty and Stamp Duty Reserve Tax (Investment Exchanges and Clearing Houses) Regulations (No 13) 2009 and shall come into force on 2nd December 2009.
(2) These Regulations shall have effect—
- (*a*) for the purposes of the charge to stamp duty, in relation to instruments executed on or after 2nd December 2009;
- (*b*) for the purposes of the charge to stamp duty reserve tax—
  - (i) in the case of agreements to transfer traded securities which are not conditional, in relation to agreements made on or after 2nd December 2009;
  - (ii) in the case of agreements to transfer traded securities which are conditional, in relation to agreements where the condition is satisfied on or after that date.

2 Interpretation

(1) In these Regulations—
"clearing participant" means a member of—
- (*a*) EMCF, who as such is permitted by the rules of EMCF to clear transactions made on the facility for a traded security, and who may or may not also be a participant in the facility;
- (*b*) X-CLEAR, who as such is permitted by the rules of X-CLEAR to clear transactions made on the facility for a traded security, and who may or may not also be a participant in the facility; or
- (*c*) LCH, who as such is permitted by the rules of LCH to clear transactions made on the facility for a traded security, and who may or may not also be a participant in the facility;

"client" means a person who gives instructions to a non-clearing firm for traded securities to be sold on the facility;
"EMCF" means European Multilateral Clearing Facility NV, a company which is a recognised clearing house under the Financial Services and Markets Act 2000;
"the facility" means the multilateral trading facility operated by NASDAQ OMX Europe Limited, a company which is authorised to operate a multilateral trading facility for the purposes of Part IV of the Financial Services and Markets Act 2000;
"LCH" means LCH.Clearnet Limited, a company which is a recognised clearing house under the Financial Services and Markets Act 2000;
"nominee" means a person whose business is or includes holding traded securities as a nominee for EMCF, X-CLEAR or LCH acting in its capacity as a person providing clearing services in connection with a transaction made on the facility, or as a nominee for a clearing participant (as the case may be);
"non-clearing firm" means a participant in the facility other than a clearing participant;

"traded securities" means stocks and shares which are issued or raised by a company but does not include stocks and shares issued by a company not incorporated in the United Kingdom unless—

(*a*) the stocks and shares are registered in a register kept in the United Kingdom by or on behalf of the company; or

(*b*) in the case of shares, they are paired, within the meaning of section 99(6A) of the Finance Act 1986, with shares issued by a company incorporated in the United Kingdom.

"X-CLEAR" means SIX X-CLEAR AG, a company which is a recognised clearing house under the Financial Services and Markets Act 2000;

3 Prescription of recognised investment exchanges and recognised clearing houses

For the purpose of sections 116 and 117 of the Finance Act 1991—

(*a*) the facility is prescribed as a recognised investment exchange;

(*b*) EMCF is prescribed as a recognised clearing house;

(*c*) X-CLEAR is prescribed as a recognised clearing house; and

(*d*) LCH is prescribed as a recognised clearing house.

4 Prescribed circumstances for the purposes of sections 116 and 117

(1) In the circumstances prescribed in this regulation, a charge to stamp duty or stamp duty reserve tax shall be treated as not arising.

(2) The circumstances prescribed are where, in connection with a transaction made on the facility, conditions A and B are met.

(3) Condition A is that traded securities of a particular kind are issued or transferred, or agreed to be issued or transferred, from—

(*a*) a clearing participant or a nominee of a clearing participant to another clearing participant or nominee,

(*b*) a non-clearing firm or its client to a clearing participant or a nominee of a clearing participant,

(*c*) a clearing participant or a nominee of a clearing participant to EMCF, X-CLEAR or LCH, or to a nominee of any of those clearing houses,

(*d*) a person other than a clearing participant to EMCF, X-CLEAR or LCH, or to a nominee of any of those clearing houses, as a result of a failure by a clearing participant to fulfil his obligations in respect of transferring those securities to EMCF, X-CLEAR or LCH, or to a nominee of any of those clearing houses,

(*e*) X-CLEAR, EMCF or LCH, or a nominee of any of those clearing houses, to a clearing participant or a nominee of a clearing participant,

(*f*) X-CLEAR or a nominee of that clearing house to EMCF or LCH or a nominee of either clearing house,

(*g*) EMCF or a nominee of that clearing house to X-CLEAR or LCH or a nominee of either clearing house, or

(*h*) LCH or a nominee of that clearing house to X-CLEAR or EMCF or a nominee of either clearing house.

(4) Condition B is that the person to whom those securities are agreed to be transferred under any of the agreements specified in paragraph (3) ("the relevant agreement") is required on receipt of those securities to transfer traded securities under a matching agreement to another person or, in the case of an agreement falling within paragraph (3)(*d*), would have been so required if the failure referred to in that paragraph had not occurred.

(5) In this regulation—

(*a*) a "matching agreement" means an agreement under which—

(i) the traded securities agreed to be transferred are of the same kind as the traded securities agreed to be transferred under the relevant agreement, and

(ii) the number and transfer price of the traded securities agreed to be transferred are identical to the number and transfer price of the traded securities agreed to be transferred under the relevant agreement;

(*b*) references to X-CLEAR, EMCF or LCH are references to that clearing house in its capacity as a person providing clearing services in connection with a transaction made on the facility;

(*c*) references to a clearing participant are references to a clearing participant in its capacity as such.

5 Consequential provision

(1) Traded securities which are the subject of an agreement specified in regulation 4(3) shall be dealt with by a clearing participant who is party to the agreement in a separate designated account, and not otherwise.

(2) In paragraph (1) "designated account" means an account designated by X-CLEAR, EMCF or LCH for a clearing participant in connection with the traded securities concerned.

6 Revocation of the Stamp Duty and Stamp Duty Reserve Tax (Investment Exchanges and Clearing Houses) Regulations (No 10) 2009

The Stamp Duty and Stamp Duty Reserve Tax (Investment Exchanges and Clearing Houses) Regulations (No 10) 2009 (SI 2009/1831) are hereby revoked as respects instruments and agreements referred to in regulation 1(2) of these regulations.

2009/2976

STAMP DUTY AND STAMP DUTY RESERVE TAX (INVESTMENT EXCHANGES AND CLEARING HOUSES) REGULATIONS (NO 14) 2009

Made . . . . .10 November 2009

Laid before the House of Commons . . . . .11 November 2009

Coming into force . . . . 4 December 2009

The Treasury make the following Regulations in exercise of the powers conferred by sections 116 and 117 of the Finance Act 1991.

1 Citation and commencement

(1) These Regulations may be cited as the Stamp Duty and Stamp Duty Reserve Tax (Investment Exchanges and Clearing Houses) Regulations (No 14) 2009 and shall come into force on 4th December 2009.

(2) These Regulations shall have effect—

(*a*) for the purposes of the charge to stamp duty, in relation to instruments executed on or after 4th December 2009;

(*b*) for the purposes of the charge to stamp duty reserve tax—

(i) in the case of agreements to transfer traded securities which are not conditional, in relation to agreements made on or after 4th December 2009;

(ii) in the case of agreements to transfer traded securities which are conditional, in relation to agreements where the condition is satisfied on or after that date.

2 Interpretation

In these Regulations—

"clearing participant" means a member of a Relevant Clearing House who as such is permitted by the Rules of that Relevant Clearing House to clear transactions made on the Facility for a traded security and who may or may not also be a participant in the Facility;

"client" means a person who gives instructions to a non-clearing firm for traded securities to be sold on the Facility;

"EuroCCP" means European Central Counterparty Limited, a company which is a recognised clearing house under the Financial Services and Markets Act 2000;

"LCH.Clearnet" means LCH.Clearnet Limited, a company which is a recognised clearing house under the Financial Services and Markets Act 2000;

"NYSE Arca Europe" or "the Facility" means the multilateral trading facility operated by Euronext Amsterdam NV, a market operator which is permitted to operate a trading facility pursuant to the Directive;

"Relevant Clearing House" means any of EuroCCP, LCH.Clearnet and X-CLEAR, each in its capacity as a person providing clearing services in connection with a transaction made on the Facility;

"X-CLEAR" means SIX X-CLEAR AG, a company which is a recognised clearing house under the Financial Services and Markets Act 2000;

"nominee" means a person whose business is or includes holding traded securities as a nominee for a Relevant Clearing House acting in its capacity as a person providing clearing services in connection with a transaction made on the Facility, or as a nominee for a clearing participant (as the case may be);

"non-clearing firm" means a participant in the Facility other than a clearing participant;

"traded securities" means stocks and shares which are issued or raised by a body corporate but does not include stocks and shares issued by a body corporate not incorporated in the United Kingdom unless—

(*a*) the stocks and shares are registered in a register kept in the United Kingdom by or on behalf of the body corporate; or

(*b*) in the case of shares, they are paired, within the meaning of section 99(6A) of the Finance Act 1986, with shares issued by a body corporate incorporated in the United Kingdom.

3 Prescription of recognised investment exchanges and recognised clearing houses

For the purpose of sections 116 and 117 of the Finance Act 1991—

(*a*) NYSE Arca Europe is prescribed as a recognised investment exchange;

(*b*) EuroCCP is prescribed as a recognised clearing house;
(*c*) LCH.Clearnet is prescribed as a recognised clearing house; and
(*d*) X-CLEAR is prescribed as a recognised clearing house.

4 Prescribed circumstances for the purposes of sections 116 and 117

(1) In the circumstances prescribed in this regulation, the charge to stamp duty and the charge to stamp duty reserve tax shall be treated as not arising.

(2) The circumstances prescribed are where, in connection with a transaction made on the Facility conditions A and B are met.

(3) Condition A is that traded securities of a particular kind are transferred, or agreed to be transferred, from—

(*a*) a clearing participant or a nominee of a clearing participant to another clearing participant or nominee,
(*b*) a non-clearing firm or its client (or a nominee of a non-clearing firm or its client) to a clearing participant or a nominee of a clearing participant,
(*c*) a clearing participant or a nominee of a clearing participant to a Relevant Clearing House or to a nominee of that Relevant Clearing House,
(*d*) a person other than a clearing participant to a Relevant Clearing House or to a nominee of a Relevant Clearing House, as a result of a failure by a clearing participant to fulfil their obligations in respect of the transaction concerned to transfer traded securities to a Relevant Clearing House or to a nominee of a Relevant Clearing House,
(*e*) a Relevant Clearing House or a nominee of Relevant Clearing House to a clearing participant or a nominee of a clearing participant, or
(*f*) a Relevant Clearing House or a nominee of Relevant Clearing House to another a Relevant Clearing House or a nominee of another Relevant Clearing House.

(4) Condition B is that the person to whom those securities are agreed to be transferred under any of the agreements specified in paragraph (3) above ("the relevant agreement") is required on receipt of those securities to transfer traded securities under a matching agreement to another person or, in the case of an agreement falling within paragraph (3)(*d*), would have been so required if the failure referred to in that paragraph had not occurred.

(5) In this regulation—

(*a*) a "matching agreement" means an agreement under which—
(i) the traded securities agreed to be transferred are of the same kind as the traded securities agreed to be transferred under the relevant agreement, and
(ii) the number and transfer price of the traded securities agreed to be transferred are identical to the number and transfer price of the traded securities agreed to be transferred under the relevant agreement;
(*b*) references to a clearing participant are references to a clearing participant in their capacity as such.

5 Consequential provision

(1) Traded securities which are the subject of an agreement specified in regulation 4(3) shall be dealt with by a clearing participant who is party to the agreement in a separate designated account, and not otherwise.

(2) In paragraph (1) "designated account" means an account designated by a Relevant Clearing House for a clearing participant in connection with the traded securities concerned.

6 Revocation of the Stamp Duty and Stamp Duty Reserve Tax (Investment Exchanges and Clearing Houses) Regulations (No 3) 2009 (SI 2009/397)

The Stamp Duty and Stamp Duty Reserve Tax (Investment Exchanges and Clearing Houses) Regulations (No 3) 2009 (SI 2009/397) are hereby revoked as respects instruments and agreements referred to in regulation 1(2) of these regulations.

2009/2977

STAMP DUTY AND STAMP DUTY RESERVE TAX (INVESTMENT EXCHANGES AND CLEARING HOUSES) REGULATIONS (NO 15) 2009

Made . . . . *10 November 2009*
Laid before the House of Commons . . . . *11 November 2009*
Coming into force. . . . . *4 December 2009*

The Treasury make the following Regulations in exercise of the powers conferred by sections 116 and 117 of the Finance Act 1991.

1 Citation, commencement and effect

(1) These Regulations may be cited as the Stamp Duty and Stamp Duty Reserve Tax (Investment Exchanges and Clearing Houses) Regulations (No 15) 2009 and shall come into force on 4th December 2009.

(2) These Regulations shall have effect—

(*a*) for the purposes of the charge to stamp duty, in relation to instruments executed on or after 4th December 2009;

(*b*) for the purposes of the charge to stamp duty reserve tax—

(i) in the case of agreements to transfer traded securities which are not conditional, in relation to agreements made on or after 4th December 2009;

(ii) in the case of agreements to transfer traded securities which are conditional, in relation to agreements where the condition is satisfied on or after that date.

2 Interpretation

In these Regulations—

"clearing participant" means a member of EuroCCP or X-CLEAR who as such is permitted by the Rules of that clearing house to clear transactions made on the Facility for a traded security and who may or may not also be a participant in the Facility;

"client" means a person who gives instructions to a non-clearing firm for traded securities to be sold on the Facility;

"EuroCCP" means European Central Counterparty Limited, a company which is a recognised clearing house under the Financial Services and Markets Act 2000;

"the Facility" means the multilateral trading facility operated by Smartpool Trading Limited, a body corporate which is permitted to operate a multilateral trading facility for the purposes of Part 4 of the Financial Services and Markets Act 2000;

"X-CLEAR" means SIX X-CLEAR AG, a company which is a recognised clearing house under the Financial Services and Markets Act 2000;

"nominee" means a person whose business is or includes holding traded securities as a nominee for EuroCCP or X-CLEAR acting in its capacity as a person providing clearing services in connection with a transaction made on the Facility, or as a nominee for a clearing participant (as the case may be);

"non-clearing firm" means a participant in the Facility other than a clearing participant;

"traded securities" means stocks and shares which are issued or raised by a body corporate but does not include stocks and shares issued by a body corporate not incorporated in the United Kingdom unless—

(*a*) the stocks and shares are registered in a register kept in the United Kingdom by or on behalf of the body corporate; or

(*b*) in the case of shares, they are paired, within the meaning of section 99(6A) of the Finance Act 1986, with shares issued by a body corporate incorporated in the United Kingdom.

3 Prescription of recognised investment exchange and recognised clearing house

For the purposes of sections 116 and 117 of the Finance Act 1991—

(*a*) the SmartPool Multilateral Trading Facility ("the Facility") is prescribed as a recognised investment exchange;

(*b*) EuroCCP is prescribed as a recognised clearing house; and

(*c*) X-CLEAR is prescribed as a recognised clearing house.

4 Prescribed circumstances for the purposes of sections 116 and 117

(1) In the circumstances prescribed by paragraph (2), the charge to stamp duty and the charge to stamp duty reserve tax shall be treated as not arising.

(2) The circumstances prescribed are where, in connection with a transaction made on the Facility conditions A and B are met.

(3) Condition A is that traded securities of a particular kind are transferred, or agreed to be transferred, from—

(*a*) a clearing participant or a nominee of a clearing participant to another clearing participant or nominee,

(*b*) a non-clearing firm or its client (or a nominee of a non-clearing firm or its client) to a clearing participant or a nominee of a clearing participant,

(*c*) a clearing participant or a nominee of a clearing participant to EuroCCP or X-CLEAR or to a nominee of EuroCCP or X-CLEAR,

(*d*) a person other than a clearing participant to EuroCCP or X-CLEAR or to a nominee of EuroCCP or X-CLEAR, as a result of a failure by a clearing participant to fulfil their obligations in respect of the transaction concerned to transfer traded securities to EuroCCP or X-CLEAR or to a nominee of EuroCCP or X-CLEAR,

(*e*) EuroCCP or X-CLEAR or a nominee of EuroCCP or X-CLEAR to a clearing participant or a nominee of a clearing participant,
(*f*) EuroCCP or a nominee of EuroCCP to X-CLEAR or a nominee of X-CLEAR, or
(*g*) X-CLEAR or a nominee of X-CLEAR to EuroCCP or a nominee of EuroCCP.

(4) Condition B is that the person to whom those securities are agreed to be transferred under any of the agreements specified in paragraph (3) above ("the relevant agreement") is required on receipt of those securities to transfer traded securities under a matching agreement to another person or, in the case of an agreement falling within paragraph (3)(*d*), would have been so required if the failure referred to in that paragraph had not occurred.

(5) In this regulation—
(*a*) "matching agreement" means an agreement under which—
(i) the traded securities agreed to be transferred are of the same kind as the traded securities agreed to be transferred under the relevant agreement, and
(ii) the number and transfer price of the traded securities agreed to be transferred are identical to the number and transfer price of the traded securities agreed to be transferred under the relevant agreement;
(*b*) references to EuroCCP and X-CLEAR are references to those clearing houses in their capacity as persons providing clearing services in connection with a transaction made on the Facility;
(*c*) references to a clearing participant are references to a clearing participant in his capacity as such.

5 Consequential provision

(1) Traded securities which are the subject of an agreement specified in regulation 4(3) shall be dealt with by a clearing participant who is a party to the agreement in a separate designated account, and not otherwise.

(2) In paragraph (1) "designated account" means an account designated by EuroCCP or X-CLEAR for a clearing participant in connection with the traded securities concerned.

6 Revocation of the Stamp Duty and Stamp Duty Reserve Tax (Investment Exchanges and Clearing Houses) Regulations (No 2)

The Stamp Duty and Stamp Duty Reserve Tax (Investment Exchanges and Clearing Houses) Regulations (No 2) 2009 (SI 2009/194) are hereby revoked as respects instruments and agreements referred to in regulation 1(2) of these regulations.

2009/3024

FINANCE ACT 2008, SECTION 128 AND PART 2 OF SCHEDULE 43 (APPOINTED DAY, TRANSITIONAL PROVISION AND SAVINGS) ORDER 2009

Made . . . . 9 November 2009

The Commissioners for Her Majesty's Revenue and Customs, in exercise of the powers conferred by section 129(4) and (5) of the Finance Act 2008 make the following Order:

Citation and interpretation

1—(1) This Order may be cited as The Finance Act 2008, Section 128 and Part 2 of Schedule 43 (Appointed Day, Transitional Provision and Savings) Order 2009.

2 In this Order "FA 2008" means the Finance Act 2008.

Appointed day

3 The day appointed for the coming into force of Section 128 of, and Part 2 of Schedule 43 to, FA 2008 is 23rd November 2009.

Transitional Provision and Savings

4—(1) If, before the commencement date, a warrant has been granted under—
(*a*) section 63 of the Taxes Management Act 1970 (recovery of tax in Scotland);
(*b*) section 121B of the Social Security Administration Act 1992 (recovery of contributions etc in Scotland);
(*c*) section 52 of the Finance Act 1997 (recovery of relevant tax in Scotland); or
(*d*) paragraph 3 of Schedule 12 to the Finance Act 2003 (recovery of stamp duty land tax by diligence in Scotland).

that warrant shall continue to have effect according to the provisions under which it was granted.

5 (1) The amendments made by paragraph 13(1) and (2) of Schedule 43 to FA 2008 to the Debtors (Scotland) Act 1987 shall not have effect in relation to—

(*a*) actions commenced under section 1 (time to pay directions); or

(*b*) applications made under section 5 (time to pay orders);

before the commencement date.

(2) The amendment made by paragraph 13(3) of Schedule 43 to FA 2008 to the definition of "summary warrant" in section 106 (interpretation) of the Debtors (Scotland) Act 1987 shall not apply to summary warrants granted before the commencement date.

2009/3088

STAMP DUTY AND STAMP DUTY RESERVE TAX (INVESTMENT EXCHANGES AND CLEARING HOUSES) (OVER THE COUNTER) REGULATIONS 2009

Made . . . . *25 November 2009*

Laid before the House of Commons . . . . *26 November 2009*

Coming into force . . . . *18 December 2009*

The Treasury make the following Regulations in exercise of the powers conferred on them by sections 116 and 117 of the Finance Act 1991.

1 Citation, commencement and effect

(1) These Regulations may be cited as the Stamp Duty and Stamp Duty Reserve Tax (Investment Exchanges and Clearing Houses) (Over the Counter) Regulations 2009 and shall come into force on 18th December 2009.

(2) These Regulations shall have effect—

(*a*) for the purposes of the charge to stamp duty, in relation to instruments executed on or after 18th December 2009;

(*b*) for the purposes of the charge to stamp duty reserve tax—

(i) in the case of agreements to transfer traded securities which are not conditional, in relation to agreements made on or after 18th December 2009;

(ii) in the case of agreements to transfer traded securities which are conditional, in relation to agreements where the condition is satisfied on or after that date.

2 Interpretation

In these Regulations—

"clearing participant" means a member of EuroCCP who as such is permitted by the Rules of EuroCCP to clear transactions made over the counter for a traded security;

"client" means a person who gives instructions to a non-clearing firm for traded securities to be sold or transferred over-the-counter;

the "Directive" means Directive 2004/39/EC of the European Parliament and of the Council of 21 April 2004 on markets in financial instruments, as amended from time to time;

"EuroCCP" means European Central Counterparty Limited, a body corporate which is a recognised clearing house under the Financial Services and Markets Act 2000;

"nominee" means a person whose business is or includes holding traded securities as a nominee for EuroCCP acting in its capacity as a person providing clearing services in connection with a transaction made over the counter, or as a nominee for a clearing participant, non-clearing firm or client (as the case may be);

"non-clearing firm" means any person who uses a clearing participant for the purpose of clearing over the counter transactions in traded securities through EuroCCP;

"over the counter" means a transaction in traded securities made other than on a recognised investment exchange;

"recognised investment exchange" means a recognised investment exchange within the meaning of the Financial Services and Markets Act 2000, a regulated market within the meaning of the Directive or a multilateral trading facility within the meaning of the Directive; and

"traded securities" means stocks and shares which are issued or raised by a body corporate but does not include stocks and shares issued by a body corporate not incorporated in the United Kingdom unless—

(*a*) the stocks and shares are registered in a register kept in the United Kingdom by or on behalf of the body corporate; or

(*b*) in the case of shares, they are paired, within the meaning of section 99(6A) of the Finance Act 1986, with shares issued by a body corporate incorporated in the United Kingdom.

3 Prescription of recognised clearing house

For the purposes of sections 116 and 117 of the Finance Act 1991 EuroCCP is prescribed as a recognised clearing house.

4 Prescribed circumstances for the purposes of sections 116 and 117

(1) In the circumstances prescribed by paragraph (2) below, the charge to stamp duty and the charge to stamp duty reserve tax shall be treated as not arising.

(2) The circumstances prescribed are where, in connection with a transaction made over the counter, conditions A and B are met.

(3) Condition A is that traded securities of a particular kind are transferred, or agreed to be transferred, from—

(*a*) a clearing participant or a nominee of a clearing participant to another clearing participant or nominee,

(*b*) a non-clearing firm or its client (or a nominee of a non-clearing firm or of a client of a non-clearing firm) to a clearing participant or a nominee of a clearing participant,

(*c*) a clearing participant or a nominee of a clearing participant to EuroCCP or to a nominee of that clearing house,

(*d*) a person other than a clearing participant to EuroCCP or to a nominee of that clearing house, as a result of a failure by a clearing participant to fulfil his obligations in respect of the transaction concerned to transfer traded securities to EuroCCP or to a nominee of that clearing house, or

(*e*) EuroCCP or a nominee of that clearing house to a clearing participant or a nominee of a clearing participant.

(4) Condition B is that the person to whom those securities are agreed to be transferred under any of the agreements specified in paragraph (3) above ("the relevant agreement") is required on receipt of those securities to transfer traded securities under a matching agreement, or matching agreements, to another person or, in the case of an agreement falling within sub-paragraph (*d*), would have been so required if the failure referred to in that sub-paragraph had not occurred.

(5) In this regulation—

(*a*) "matching agreement or matching agreements" means an agreement or agreements under which—

(i) the traded securities agreed to be transferred are of the same kind as the traded securities agreed to be transferred under the relevant agreement, and

(ii) the number and transfer price of the traded securities agreed to be transferred are in total identical to the number and transfer price of the traded securities agreed to be transferred under the relevant agreement;

(*b*) references to EuroCCP are references to that clearing house in its capacity as a person providing clearing services in connection with a transaction made over the counter;

(*c*) references to a clearing participant are references to a clearing participant in his capacity as such.

5 Consequential provision

(1) Traded securities which are the subject of an agreement specified in regulation 4(3) shall be dealt with by a clearing participant who is a party to the agreement in a separate designated account, and not otherwise.

(2) In paragraph (1) "designated account" means an account designated by EuroCCP for a clearing participant in connection with the traded securities concerned.

2009/3227

NORTHERN ROCK PLC (TAX CONSEQUENCES) REGULATIONS 2009

Made by the Treasury under Banking (Special Provisions) Act 2008 s 10

Made . . . . *8 December 2009*

Laid before the House of Commons . . . . *8 December 2009*

Coming into force . . . . *1 January 2010*

1 Citation and commencement

These Regulations may be cited as the Northern Rock plc (Tax Consequences) Regulations 2009 and shall come into force on 1st January 2010.

2 Interpretation

In these Regulations—

"ACo" means Northern Rock plc, company registered number 03273685, or, except in relation to regulation 7, any wholly owned subsidiary of that company;

"BCo" means Gosforth Subsidiary No1 plc, company registered number 06952311, or any wholly owned subsidiary of that company;

"CTA 2009" means the Corporation Tax Act 2009;

"relevant time" means any time when both ACo and BCo are wholly owned by the Treasury;

"relevant transfer" means—

(*a*) a transfer or novation of any securities, or of any property, rights or liabilities, between ACo and BCo, or

(*b*) the grant of a lease, sublease, licence or sub-licence by ACo to BCo or by BCo to ACo,

in relation to, in connection with, or by or under, the Northern Rock plc Transfer Order 2009 at a relevant time.

3 Chargeable gains: no gain or loss disposal

(1) For the purposes of the Taxation of Chargeable Gains Act 1992, a disposal constituted by a relevant transfer is to be treated in relation to ACo and BCo as being for a consideration such that neither a gain nor a loss accrues to the transferor.

(2) For the purposes of any tax provision, paragraph (1) is to be treated as one of the no gain/no loss provisions in section 288(3A) of the Taxation of Chargeable Gains Act 1992 (meaning of "the no gain/no loss provisions").

4 Corporation tax: trading assets and trading liabilities

(1) For the purposes of Part 3 of CTA 2009 (trading income) ("Part 3"), a relevant transfer of a trading asset or a trading liability is to be treated in relation to ACo and BCo as being for a consideration such that neither a profit nor a loss accrues to the transferor.

(2) For the purposes of this regulation—

"trading asset" means an asset the proceeds of disposal of which would, but for this regulation, be brought into account as a receipt under Part 3 otherwise than in accordance with section 297 (trading credits and debits to be brought into account under Part 3), section 573 (trading credits and debits to be brought into account under Part 3) or section 747 (assets held for purposes of trade) of CTA 2009;

"trading liability" means a liability the payment for the assumption of which would, but for this regulation, be brought into account as an expense under Part 3 otherwise than in accordance with section 297 or section 573 of CTA 2009.

(3) Schedule 28AA to the Income and Corporation Taxes Act 1988 (provisions not at arm's length) does not apply in relation to a relevant transfer to which paragraph (1) applies.

5 Corporation tax: loan relationships

(1) For the purposes of Chapter 4 of Part 5 of CTA 2009 (continuity of treatment on transfers within groups or on reorganisations), in relation to a relevant transfer, ACo and BCo are to be treated as if, for the purposes of the transfer, they were members of the same group.

(2) But a relevant transfer within paragraph (1) is not to be treated as a case within section 336 of CTA 2009 (transfers of loans on group transactions) for the purposes of section 344 of the Act (introduction).

6 Corporation tax: intangible assets

(1) For the purposes of Part 8 of CTA 2009 (intangible fixed assets), a relevant transfer of a chargeable intangible asset is to be treated as tax-neutral.

(2) Schedule 28AA to the Income and Corporation Taxes Act 1988 (provisions not at arm's length) does not apply in relation to a relevant transfer to which paragraph (1) applies.

(3) For the purposes of section 882 of CTA 2009 (application of Part 8 to assets created or acquired on or after 1st April 2002), assets acquired by ACo or BCo on a relevant transfer are to be treated as if they were acquired from a person who at the time of the acquisition is a related party.

(4) Expressions used in this regulation and Part 8 of CTA 2009 have the same meaning in this regulation as they have in that Part.

7 Income tax: interest paid by banks

(1) For the purposes of section 878 of the Income Tax Act 2007 (interest paid by banks), ACo is to be treated as a bank in relation to payments of interest made by ACo after 31st December 2009 on any securities or liabilities to which this regulation applies.

(2) This regulation applies to—

(*a*) securities issued by ACo on or before 31st December 2009, and

(*b*) liabilities incurred under an agreement entered into by ACo on or before that date,

which are not transferred by a relevant transfer and in relation to which section 878 of the Income Tax Act 2007 applied to payments of interest made on or before 31st December 2009, or would have applied if a payment of interest had been made on or before that date.

8 Stamp duty

No stamp duty is chargeable on an instrument effecting or implementing a relevant transfer.

9 Stamp duty reserve tax

(1) No stamp duty reserve tax is chargeable on an agreement to transfer chargeable securities made in relation to, in connection with, or by or under, the Northern Rock plc Transfer Order 2009.

(2) In paragraph (1) "chargeable securities" has the meaning given in section 99 of the Finance Act 1986 (interpretation).

2010/466

FINANCE ACT 2009, SCHEDULE 56 (APPOINTED DAY AND CONSEQUENTIAL PROVISIONS) ORDER 2010

Made . . . .*25 February 2010*
Laid before the House of Commons. . . . .*26 February 2010*
Coming into force. . . . .*6 April 2010*

The Treasury make the following Order in exercise of the powers conferred by section 107 of the Finance Act 2009.

1 Citation, commencement and interpretation

This Order may be cited as the Finance Act 2009, Schedule 56 (Appointed Day and Consequential Provisions) Order 2010 and shall come into force on 6th April 2010.

2 In this Order—

"Schedule 56" means Schedule 56 to the Finance Act 2009;

"tax quarter" means any of the following (inclusive) periods—

6th April to 5th July, 6th July to 5th October, 6th October to 5th January and 6th January to 5th April;

"tax month" means the period beginning on the 6th day of a calendar month and ending on the 5th day of the following calendar month;

"tax period" means a tax quarter or tax month;

"section 254 period" means each period of three months ending with 31st March, 30th June, 30th September or 31st December as provided for in section 254(2) of the Finance Act 2004.

3 Appointed day

(1) In relation to those amounts of tax which are specified in paragraph (2), and are—

(*a*) chargeable in respect of a tax period starting on or after 6th April 2010, or

(*b*) chargeable in respect of a section 254 period ending on or after 30th September 2010

the day appointed for the coming into force of Schedule 56 is 6th April 2010.

(2) The amounts of tax referred to in paragraph (1) are the following amounts specified in column 3 of the Table in paragraph 1 of Schedule 56—

(*a*) items 2, 3 and 4, and

(*b*) items 17, 23 and 24 but only insofar as the tax falls within any of items 2,3 or 4.

4 Consequential provisions and savings

(1) Regulations 203 (default surcharge) and 204 (surcharge notice and appeal) of the Income Tax (Pay As You Earn) Regulations 2003 are omitted subject to the savings set out in paragraph (3).

(2) Regulations 48 (default surcharge) and 49 (surcharge notice and appeal) of the Income Tax (Construction Industry Scheme) Regulations 2005 are omitted subject to the savings set out in paragraph (3).

(3) The regulations referred to in paragraphs (1) and (2) shall continue to have effect in relation to surcharges arising in respect of late payments of tax where the tax was chargeable in respect of a tax period ending on or before 5th April 2010.

(4) Paragraph 110 of Schedule 2 (consequential amendments and supplemental provisions—secondary legislation) to the Transfer of Tribunal Functions and Revenue and Customs Appeals Order 2009 is omitted.

2010/664

STAMP DUTY RESERVE TAX (AMENDMENT) REGULATIONS 2010

Made . . . .*9 March 2010*
Laid before the House of Commons. . . . .*10 March 2010*
Coming into force. . . . .*1 April 2010*

The Treasury make the following regulations in exercise of the powers conferred by section 98 of the Finance Act 1986.

1 Citation and commencement

(1) These Regulations may be cited as the Stamp Duty Reserve Tax (Amendment) Regulations 2010.

(2) Regulations 2 to 6 come into force on 1st April 2010.

(3) Regulations 7 to 12 come into force on 1st April 2011.

2 Amendment of the Stamp Duty Reserve Tax Regulations 1986 coming into force on 1st April 2010

Amend the Stamp Duty Reserve Tax Regulations 1986 as follows.

3 Omit regulations 5 (power to require information) and 15 (inspection of records).

4 (1) Amend the Table in Part 1 of the Schedule (which applies the provisions of the Taxes Management Act 1970 specified in the first column of that Table, subject to any modification specified in the second column of that Table) as follows.
(2) In the entry for section 99 in the second column—
(*a*) omit ", or any information under regulation 5,"; and
(*b*) after "1986" insert "or Schedule 36 to the Finance Act 2008".
(3) Omit the entries in both columns for section 111.

5 (1) Amend Part II of the Schedule (which restates the provisions of the Taxes Management Act 1970 specified in Part I of the Schedule as modified where appropriate) as follows.
(2) In section 99 (as modified)—
(*a*) omit ", or any information under regulation 5,"; and
(*b*) after "1986" insert "or Schedule 36 to the Finance Act 2008".

6 Omit section 111 (as modified).

7 Amendment of the Stamp Duty Reserve Tax Regulations 1986 coming into force on 1st April 2011
Amend the Stamp Duty Reserve Tax Regulations 1986 as follows.

8 In regulation 2 (interpretation) after the definition of "the Board" insert—
""carelessly" has the same meaning as in section 118(5) and (6) of the Taxes Management Act 1970;
"deliberately" has the same meaning as in section 118(7) of the Taxes Management Act 1970;".

9 (1) Amend regulation 13 (underpayments) as follows.
(2) In paragraph (2)—
(*a*) for "period of 6" substitute "period of 4"; and
(*b*) for "paragraph (3)" substitute "paragraphs (2A) and (3)".
(3) After paragraph (2) insert—
"(2A) In any case of an underpayment of tax brought about carelessly by or on behalf of any person the period mentioned in paragraph (2) shall be the period of 6 years beginning with the date specified under paragraph (2).".
(4) For paragraph (3) substitute—
"(3) In any case of an underpayment of tax brought about deliberately by or on behalf of any person the period mentioned in paragraph (2) shall be the period of 20 years beginning with the date specified under paragraph (2).
(4) Paragraph (5) applies to any case not falling within paragraph (2) where too little tax has been paid in respect of a relevant transaction or surrender provided that the case does not involve a loss of tax brought about deliberately by a person liable for the tax (or a person acting on behalf of such a person).
(5) Where this paragraph applies—
(*a*) no proceedings are to be brought for the recovery of the tax after the end of the period of 20 years beginning with the date on which the relevant transaction or surrender was made; and
(*b*) at the end of that period any liability for the tax is extinguished.".

10 In regulation 14(2) (overpayments) for "6" substitute "4".

11 (1) Amend regulation 18 (recovery of over-repayment of tax, etc) as follows.
(2) In paragraph (2)—
(*a*) after "(3)" insert "and (3A)"; and
(*b*) for "6" substitute "4".
(3) For paragraph (3) substitute—
"(3) In any case where a repayment is brought about carelessly the period mentioned in paragraph (2) shall be 6 years from the date specified in paragraph (2).
(3A) In any case where a repayment is brought about deliberately the period mentioned in paragraph (2) shall be 20 years from the date specified in paragraph (2). ".

12 Transitional provision
In any case under regulation 13(2) or 18(2) of the Stamp Duty Reserve Tax Regulations 1986 where—
(*a*) a relevant transaction or surrender took place before 1st April 2011; and

(*b*) an underpayment or repayment was brought about by fraudulent or negligent conduct by or on behalf of any person;

the period in which a determination may be made is the earlier of the period of 6 years beginning when the fraudulent or negligent conduct comes to the knowledge of Her Majesty's Revenue and Customs or the period of 20 years provided in regulation 13(3) or 18(3A).

2010/814

STAMP DUTY LAND TAX (ALTERNATIVE FINANCE INVESTMENT BONDS) REGULATIONS 2010

Made . . . . *16 March 2010*
Laid before the House of Commons . . . . *17 March 2010*
Coming into force . . . . *7 April 2010*

The Treasury, in exercise of the powers conferred by paragraph 5 of Schedule 3 to the Finance Act 2003, make the following Regulations:

1 Citation and commencement

These Regulations may be cited as the Stamp Duty Land Tax (Alternative Finance Investment Bonds) Regulations 2010 and shall come into force on 7th April 2010.

2 Alternative finance investment bonds

(1) Paragraph 11, Schedule 17A to the Finance Act 2003 (cases where assignment of lease treated as grant of lease) must be treated as if including the following provisions—

(2) After paragraph 11(2)—

"(2A) Sub-paragraph (2) shall not apply where an assignment of a lease, but for the application of that sub-paragraph, would be exempt by virtue of Schedule 61 to the Finance Act 2009".

(3) In paragraph 11(3) after paragraph (*e*)—

"(*f*) Paragraphs 6 and 8 of Part 3 of Schedule 61 to the Finance Act 2009 (alternative finance investment bond relief)".

2010/867

FINANCE ACT 2009, SCHEDULE 51 (TIME LIMITS FOR ASSESSMENTS, CLAIMS, ETC) (APPOINTED DAYS AND TRANSITIONAL PROVISIONS) ORDER 2010

Made . . . . *18 March 2010*

The Treasury make the following Order in exercise of the powers conferred by sections 99(2) and 99(3) of the Finance Act 2009.

PART 1
APPOINTED DAYS AND PRELIMINARY PROVISIONS

1 Citation and interpretation

(1) This Order may be cited as the Finance Act 2009, Schedule 51 (Time Limits for Assessments, Claims, etc) (Appointed Days and Transitional Provisions) Order 2010.

(2) In this Order a reference to a paragraph (without more) is a reference to that paragraph of Schedule 51 to the Finance Act 2009.

(3) In this Order—

"The Commissioners" means the Commissioners for Her Majesty's Revenue and Customs;

"FA", followed by a year, means the Finance Act of that year.

"IHTA 1984" means the Inheritance Tax Act 1984;

2 Appointed days

(1) The day appointed as the day on which the amendments made by paragraphs 1 to 4 and 27 to 43 (insurance premium tax, aggregates levy, climate change levy, landfill tax and minor and consequential provision) come into force is 1st April 2010.

(2) The day appointed as the day on which the amendments made by paragraphs 5 to 26 (inheritance tax, stamp duty land tax and petroleum revenue tax) come into force is 1st April 2011.

PART 2
TRANSITIONAL PROVISION

3–6 (not relevant to stamp taxes)

7 Stamp duty land tax: determination of penalties

Where a person incurs a penalty on or before 31st March 2011 under Part 4 of FA 2003, and the case involves a loss of tax arising in one of the circumstances specified in paragraph 8(4B) of Schedule 14 to that Act (deliberately, etc), the amendments made by paragraph 16(2) and (4) are disregarded.

8–28(not relevant to stamp taxes)

2010/1818

STAMP DUTY AND STAMP DUTY RESERVE TAX (INVESTMENT EXCHANGES AND CLEARING HOUSES) REGULATIONS 2010

Made . . . . *15 July 2010*
Laid before the House of Commons . . . . *16 July 2010*
Coming into force . . . . *10 August 2010*

The Treasury make the following Regulations in exercise of the powers conferred by sections 116 and 117 of the Finance Act 1991.

1 Citation, commencement and effect

(1) These Regulations may be cited as the Stamp Duty and Stamp Duty Reserve Tax (Investment Exchanges and Clearing Houses) Regulations 2010 and come into force on 10th August 2010.

(2) These Regulations have effect—

(*a*) for the purposes of the charge to stamp duty, in relation to instruments executed on or after 10th August 2010;

(*b*) for the purposes of the charge to stamp duty reserve tax—

(i) in the case of agreements to transfer traded securities which are not conditional, in relation to agreements made on or after 10th August 2010;

(ii) in the case of agreements to transfer traded securities which are conditional, in relation to agreements where the condition is satisfied on or after that date.

2 Interpretation

In these Regulations—

"clearing participant" means a member of—

(*a*) EMCF who as such is permitted by the Rules of EMCF,

(*b*) EuroCCP who as such is permitted by the Rules of EuroCCP,

(*c*) LCH.Clearnet who as such is permitted by the Rules of LCH.Clearnet, or

(*d*) X-CLEAR who as such is permitted by the Rules of X-CLEAR,

to clear transactions made on the Turquoise MTF for a traded security and who may or may not also be a participant on the Turquoise MTF;

"client" means a person who gives instructions to a non-clearing firm for traded securities to be sold on the Turquoise MTF;

"EMCF" means European Multilateral Clearing Facility N.V.;

"EuroCCP" means European Central Counterparty Limited;

"LCH.Clearnet" means LCH.Clearnet Limited;

"X-CLEAR" means SIX X-CLEAR AG;

"nominee" means a person whose business is or includes holding traded securities as a nominee for EMCF, EuroCCP, LCH.Clearnet or X-CLEAR acting in its capacity as a person providing clearing services in connection with a transaction made on the Turquoise MTF, or as a nominee for a clearing participant;

"non-clearing firm" means a participant on the Turquoise MTF other than a clearing participant;

"traded securities" means stocks and shares which are issued or raised by a body corporate but does not include stocks and shares issued or raised by a body corporate not incorporated in the United Kingdom unless—

(*e*) the stocks and shares are registered in a register kept in the United Kingdom by or on behalf of the body corporate; or

(*f*) in the case of shares, they are paired, within the meaning of section 99(6A) of the Finance Act 1986, with shares issued by a body corporate incorporated in the United Kingdom;

"Turquoise MTF" is a multilateral trading facility operated by Turquoise Services Limited.

3 Prescription of recognised investment exchanges and recognised clearing houses

For the purposes of sections 116 and 117 of the Finance Act 1991—

(*a*) Turquoise MTF is prescribed as a recognised investment exchange;

(*b*) EMCF is prescribed as a recognised clearing house;

(*c*) EuroCCP is prescribed as a recognised clearing house;

(*d*) LCH.Clearnet is prescribed as a recognised clearing house; and
(*e*) X-CLEAR is prescribed as a recognised clearing house.

4 Prescribed circumstances for the purposes of sections 116 and 117

(1) In the circumstances prescribed by paragraph (2), the charges to stamp duty and stamp duty reserve tax shall be treated as not arising.

(2) The circumstances prescribed are where, in connection with a transaction made on the Turquoise MTF, conditions A, B and C are met.

(3) Condition A is that traded securities are transferred, or agreed to be transferred, from—

(*a*) a clearing participant or its nominee to another clearing participant or its nominee;
(*b*) a non-clearing firm or its client, or nominee of a non-clearing firm or its client, to a clearing participant or its nominee;
(*c*) a clearing participant or its nominee to either EMCF, EuroCCP, LCH.Clearnet or X-CLEAR, or to their nominees;
(*d*) a person other than a clearing participant to either EMCF, EuroCCP, LCH.Clearnet or X-CLEAR, or to their nominees, as a result of a failure by a clearing participant to fulfil its obligations in respect of the transaction concerned to transfer traded securities to either EMCF, EuroCCP, LCH.Clearnet or X-CLEAR, or to their nominees;
(*e*) either EMCF, EuroCCP, LCH.Clearnet or X-CLEAR, or their nominees, to a clearing participant or its nominee;
(*f*) EMCF or its nominee to either EuroCCP, LCH.Clearnet or X-CLEAR or to their nominees;
(*g*) EuroCCP or its nominee to either EMCF, LCH.Clearnet or X-CLEAR or to their nominees;
(*h*) LCH.Clearnet or its nominee to either EMCF, EuroCCP or X-CLEAR or to their nominees; or
(i) X-CLEAR or its nominee to either EMCF, EuroCCP or LCH.Clearnet or to their nominees.

(4) Condition B is that the person to whom those securities are agreed to be transferred under any of the agreements specified in paragraph (3) ("the relevant agreement") is required on receipt of those securities to transfer traded securities under a matching agreement to another person or, in the case of an agreement falling within paragraph 3(*d*), would have been so required if the failure referred to in that paragraph had not occurred.

(5) Condition C is that traded securities which are the subject of a relevant agreement shall be dealt with by a clearing participant, who is a party to the relevant agreement, in a separate designated account.

(6) In this regulation—

(*a*) "designated account" means an account designated by EMCF, EuroCCP, LCH.Clearnet or X-CLEAR, for a clearing participant, in connection with the traded securities concerned;
(*b*) a "matching agreement" means an agreement under which—
(i) the traded securities agreed to be transferred are of the same kind as the traded securities agreed to be transferred under the relevant agreement; and
(ii) the number and transfer price of the traded securities agreed to be transferred are identical to the number and transfer price of the traded securities agreed to be transferred under the relevant agreement.

5 Revocation of the Stamp Duty and Stamp Duty Reserve Tax (Investment Exchanges and Clearing Houses) Regulations (No 8) 2009

The Stamp Duty and Stamp Duty Reserve Tax (Investment Exchanges and Clearing Houses) Regulations (No 8) 2009 are revoked.

2010/1819

STAMP DUTY AND STAMP DUTY RESERVE TAX (INVESTMENT EXCHANGES AND CLEARING HOUSES) REGULATIONS (NO 2) 2010

Made . . . . *15 July 2010*
Laid before the House of Commons . . . . *16 July 2010*
Coming into force . . . . *10 August 2010*

The Treasury make the following Regulations in exercise of the powers conferred by sections 116 and 117 of the Finance Act 1991.

1 Citation, commencement and effect

(1) These Regulations may be cited as the Stamp Duty and Stamp Duty Reserve Tax (Investment Exchanges and Clearing Houses) Regulations (No 2) 2010 and come into force on 10th August 2010.

(2) These Regulations have effect—

(*a*) for the purposes of the charge to stamp duty, in relation to instruments executed on or after 10th August 2010;
(*b*) for the purposes of the charge to stamp duty reserve tax—

(i) in the case of agreements to transfer traded securities which are not conditional, in relation to agreements made on or after 10th August 2010;

(ii) in the case of agreements to transfer traded securities which are conditional, in relation to agreements where the condition is satisfied on or after that date.

2 Interpretation

In these Regulations—

"Chi-X Europe MTF" means the multilateral trading facility operated by Chi-X Europe Limited;

"clearing participant" means a member of—

(*a*) EMCF who as such is permitted by the Rules of EMCF,

(*b*) EuroCCP who as such is permitted by the Rules of EuroCCP,

(*c*) LCH.Clearnet who as such is permitted by the Rules of LCH.Clearnet, or

(*d*) X-CLEAR who as such is permitted by the Rules of X-CLEAR,

to clear transactions made on the Chi-X Europe MTF for a traded security and who may or may not also be a participant on the Chi-X Europe MTF;

"client" means a person who gives instructions to a non-clearing firm for traded securities to be sold on the Chi-X Europe MTF;

"EMCF" means European Multilateral Clearing Facility NV;

"EuroCCP" means European Central Counterparty Limited;

"LCH.Clearnet" means LCH.Clearnet Limited;

"X-CLEAR" means SIX X-CLEAR AG;

"nominee" means a person whose business is or includes holding traded securities as a nominee for EMCF, EuroCCP, LCH.Clearnet or X-CLEAR acting in its capacity as a person providing clearing services in connection with a transaction made on the Chi-X Europe MTF, or as a nominee for a clearing participant;

"non-clearing firm" means a participant on the Chi-X Europe MTF other than a clearing participant;

"traded securities" means stocks and shares which are issued or raised by a body corporate but does not include stocks and shares issued or raised by a body corporate not incorporated in the United Kingdom unless—

(*e*) the stocks and shares are registered in a register kept in the United Kingdom by or on behalf of the body corporate; or

(*f*) in the case of shares, they are paired, within the meaning of section 99(6A) of the Finance Act 1986, with shares issued by a body corporate incorporated in the United Kingdom.

3 Prescription of recognised investment exchanges and recognised clearing houses

For the purposes of sections 116 and 117 of the Finance Act 1991—

(*a*) Chi-X Europe Limited is prescribed as a recognised investment exchange;

(*b*) EMCF is prescribed as a recognised clearing house;

(*c*) EuroCCP is prescribed as a recognised clearing house;

(*d*) LCH.Clearnet is prescribed as a recognised clearing house; and

(*e*) X-CLEAR is prescribed as a recognised clearing house.

4 Prescribed circumstances for the purposes of sections 116 and 117

(1) In the circumstances prescribed by paragraph (2), the charges to stamp duty and stamp duty reserve tax shall be treated as not arising.

(2) The circumstances prescribed are where, in connection with a transaction made on the Chi-X Europe MTF, conditions A, B and C are met.

(3) Condition A is that traded securities are transferred, or agreed to be transferred, from—

(*a*) a clearing participant or its nominee to another clearing participant or its nominee;

(*b*) a non-clearing firm or its client, or nominee of a non-clearing firm or its client, to a clearing participant or its nominee;

(*c*) a clearing participant or its nominee to either EMCF, EuroCCP, LCH.Clearnet or X-CLEAR, or to their nominees;

(*d*) a person other than a clearing participant to either EMCF, EuroCCP, LCH.Clearnet or X-CLEAR, or to their nominees, as a result of a failure by a clearing participant to fulfil its obligations in respect of the transaction concerned to transfer traded securities to either EMCF, EuroCCP, LCH.Clearnet or X-CLEAR, or to their nominees;

(*e*) either EMCF, EuroCCP, LCH.Clearnet or X-CLEAR, or their nominees, to a clearing participant or its nominee;

(*f*) EMCF or its nominee to either EuroCCP, LCH.Clearnet or X-CLEAR or to their nominees;

(*g*) EuroCCP or its nominee to either EMCF, LCH.Clearnet or X-CLEAR or to their nominees;

(*h*) LCH.Clearnet or its nominee to either EMCF, EuroCCP or X-CLEAR or to their nominees; or

(i) X-CLEAR or its nominee to either EMCF, EuroCCP or LCH.Clearnet or to their nominees.

(4) Condition B is that the person to whom those securities are agreed to be transferred under any of the agreements specified in paragraph (3) ("the relevant agreement") is required on receipt of those securities to transfer traded securities under a matching agreement to another person or, in the case of an agreement falling within paragraph 3(*d*), would have been so required if the failure referred to in that paragraph had not occurred.

(5) Condition C is that traded securities which are the subject of a relevant agreement shall be dealt with by a clearing participant, who is a party to the relevant agreement, in a separate designated account.

(6) In this regulation—

(*a*) "designated account" means an account designated by EMCF, EuroCCP, LCH.Clearnet or X-CLEAR, for a clearing participant, in connection with the traded securities concerned;

(*b*) a "matching agreement" means an agreement under which—

(i) the traded securities agreed to be transferred are of the same kind as the traded securities agreed to be transferred under the relevant agreement; and

(ii) the number and transfer price of the traded securities agreed to be transferred are identical to the number and transfer price of the traded securities agreed to be transferred under the relevant agreement.

5 Revocation of the Stamp Duty and Stamp Duty Reserve Tax (Investment Exchanges and Clearing Houses) Regulations (No 7) 2009

The Stamp Duty and Stamp Duty Reserve Tax (Investment Exchanges and Clearing Houses) Regulations (No 7) 2009 are revoked.

2010/1824

STAMP DUTY AND STAMP DUTY RESERVE TAX (INVESTMENT EXCHANGES AND CLEARING HOUSES) (OVER THE COUNTER) REGULATIONS 2010

Made .... *15 July 2010*

Laid before the House of Commons .... *19 July 2010*

Coming into force .... *10 August 2010*

The Treasury make the following Regulations in exercise of the powers conferred on them by sections 116 and 117 of the Finance Act 1991.

1 Citation, commencement and effect

(1) These Regulations may be cited as the Stamp Duty and Stamp Duty Reserve Tax (Investment Exchanges and Clearing Houses) (Over the Counter) Regulations 2010 and come into force on 10th August 2010.

(2) These Regulations have effect—

(*a*) for the purposes of the charge to stamp duty, in relation to instruments executed on or after 10th August 2010;

(*b*) for the purposes of the charge to stamp duty reserve tax—

(i) in the case of agreements to transfer traded securities which are not conditional, in relation to agreements made on or after 10th August 2010;

(ii) in the case of agreements to transfer traded securities which are conditional, in relation to agreements where the condition is satisfied on or after that date.

2 Interpretation

In these Regulations—

"clearing participant" means a member of LCH.Clearnet Limited who as such is permitted by the Rules of LCH.Clearnet Limited to clear transactions made over the counter for a traded security;

"client" means a person who gives instructions to a non-clearing firm for traded securities to be sold or transferred over the counter;

"nominee" means a person whose business is or includes holding traded securities as a nominee for LCH.Clearnet Limited acting in its capacity as a person providing clearing services in connection with a transaction made over the counter, or as a nominee for a clearing participant, non-clearing firm or client;

"non-clearing firm" means any person who uses a clearing participant for the purpose of clearing over the counter transactions in traded securities through LCH.Clearnet Limited;

"over the counter" means a transaction in traded securities made other than on a recognised investment exchange;

"traded securities" means stocks and shares which are issued or raised by a body corporate but does not include stocks and shares issued or raised by a body corporate not incorporated in the United Kingdom unless—

(*a*) the stocks and shares are registered in a register kept in the United Kingdom by or on behalf of the body corporate; or

(*b*) in the case of shares, they are paired, within the meaning of section 99(6A) of the Finance Act 1986, with shares issued by a body corporate incorporated in the United Kingdom.

3 Prescription of recognised clearing house

For the purposes of sections 116 and 117 of the Finance Act 1991 LCH.Clearnet Limited is prescribed as a recognised clearing house.

4 Prescribed circumstances for the purposes of sections 116 and 117

(1) In the circumstances prescribed by paragraph (2) below, the charges to stamp duty and stamp duty reserve tax shall be treated as not arising.

(2) The circumstances prescribed are where, in connection with a transaction made over the counter, conditions A, B and C are met.

(3) Condition A is that traded securities are transferred, or agreed to be transferred, from—

(*a*) a clearing participant or its nominee to another clearing participant or its nominee;

(*b*) a non-clearing firm or its nominee or client to a clearing participant or its nominee;

(*c*) a clearing participant or its nominee to LCH.Clearnet Limited or its nominee;

(*d*) a person other than a clearing participant to LCH.Clearnet Limited or its nominee, as a result of a failure by a clearing participant to fulfil its obligations in respect of the transaction concerned to transfer traded securities to LCH.Clearnet Limited or its nominee; or

(*e*) LCH.Clearnet Limited or its nominee to a clearing participant or its nominee.

(4) Condition B is that the person to whom those securities are agreed to be transferred under any of the agreements specified in paragraph (3) above ("the relevant agreement") is required on receipt of those securities to transfer traded securities under a matching agreement, to another person or, in the case of an agreement falling within paragraph 3(*d*), would have been so required if the failure referred to in that sub-paragraph had not occurred.

(5) Condition C is that traded securities which are the subject of a relevant agreement shall be dealt with by a clearing participant, who is a party to the relevant agreement, in a separate designated account.

(6) In this regulation—

(*a*) "designated account" means an account designated by LCH.Clearnet Limited for a clearing participant, in connection with the traded securities concerned;

(*b*) "matching agreement" means an agreement under which—

(i) the traded securities agreed to be transferred are of the same kind as the traded securities agreed to be transferred under the relevant agreement; and

(ii) the number and transfer price of the traded securities agreed to be transferred are in total identical to the number and transfer price of the traded securities agreed to be transferred under the relevant agreement.

2010/1877

STAMP DUTY AND STAMP DUTY RESERVE TAX (INVESTMENT EXCHANGES AND CLEARING HOUSES) REGULATIONS (NO 3) 2010

Made . . . . *21 July 2010*

Laid before the House of Commons . . . . *22 July 2010*

Coming into force . . . . *13 August 2010*

The Treasury make the following Regulations in exercise of the powers conferred by sections 116 and 117 of the Finance Act 1991.

1 Citation, commencement and effect

(1) These Regulations may be cited as the Stamp Duty and Stamp Duty Reserve Tax (Investment Exchanges and Clearing Houses) Regulations (No 3) 2010 and come into force on 13th August 2010.

(2) These Regulations have effect—

(*a*) for the purposes of the charge to stamp duty, in relation to instruments executed on or after 13th August 2010;

(*b*) for the purposes of the charge to stamp duty reserve tax—

(i) in the case of agreements to transfer traded securities which are not conditional, in relation to agreements made on or after 13th August 2010;

(ii) in the case of agreements to transfer traded securities which are conditional, in relation to agreements where the condition is satisfied on or after that date.

2 Interpretation

In these Regulations—

"BATS MTF" means a multilateral trading facility operated by BATS Trading Limited;

"clearing participant" means a member of—

(*a*) EMCF who as such is permitted by the Rules of EMCF,

(*b*) EuroCCP who as such is permitted by the Rules of EuroCCP,

(*c*) LCH.Clearnet who as such is permitted by the Rules of LCH.Clearnet, or

(*d*) X-CLEAR who as such is permitted by the Rules of X-CLEAR,

to clear transactions made on the BATS MTF for a traded security and who may or may not also be a participant on the BATS MTF;

"client" means a person who gives instructions to a non-clearing firm for traded securities to be sold on the BATS MTF;

"EMCF" means European Multilateral Clearing Facility N.V.;

"EuroCCP" means European Central Counterparty Limited;

"LCH.Clearnet" means LCH.Clearnet Limited;

"X-CLEAR" means SIX X-CLEAR AG;

"nominee" means a person whose business is or includes holding traded securities as a nominee for EMCF, EuroCCP, LCH.Clearnet or X-CLEAR acting in its capacity as a person providing clearing services in connection with a transaction made on the BATS MTF, or as a nominee for a clearing participant;

"non-clearing firm" means a participant on the BATS MTF other than a clearing participant;

"traded securities" means stocks and shares which are issued or raised by a body corporate but does not include stocks and shares issued or raised by a body corporate not incorporated in the United Kingdom unless—

(*e*) the stocks and shares are registered in a register kept in the United Kingdom by or on behalf of the body corporate; or

(*f*) in the case of shares, they are paired, within the meaning of section 99(6A) of the Finance Act 1986, with shares issued by a body corporate incorporated in the United Kingdom.

3 Prescription of recognised investment exchanges and recognised clearing houses

For the purposes of sections 116 and 117 of the Finance Act 1991—

(*a*) BATS Trading Limited is prescribed as a recognised investment exchange;

(*b*) EMCF is prescribed as a recognised clearing house;

(*c*) EuroCCP is prescribed as a recognised clearing house;

(*d*) LCH.Clearnet is prescribed as a recognised clearing house; and

(*e*) X-CLEAR is prescribed as a recognised clearing house.

4 Prescribed circumstances for the purposes of sections 116 and 117

(1) In the circumstances prescribed by paragraph (2), the charges to stamp duty and stamp duty reserve tax shall be treated as not arising.

(2) The circumstances prescribed are where, in connection with a transaction made on the BATS MTF, conditions A, B and C are met.

(3) Condition A is that traded securities are transferred, or agreed to be transferred, from—

(*a*) a clearing participant or its nominee to another clearing participant or its nominee;

(*b*) a non-clearing firm or its client, or nominee of a non-clearing firm or its client, to a clearing participant or its nominee;

(*c*) a clearing participant or its nominee to either EMCF, EuroCCP, LCH.Clearnet or X-CLEAR, or to their nominees;

(*d*) a person other than a clearing participant to either EMCF, EuroCCP, LCH.Clearnet or X-CLEAR, or to their nominees, as a result of a failure by a clearing participant to fulfil its obligations in respect of the transaction concerned to transfer traded securities to either EMCF, EuroCCP, LCH.Clearnet or X-CLEAR, or to their nominees;

(*e*) either EMCF, EuroCCP, LCH.Clearnet or X-CLEAR, or their nominees, to a clearing participant or its nominee;

(*f*) EMCF or its nominee to either EuroCCP, LCH.Clearnet or X-CLEAR or to their nominees;

(*g*) EuroCCP or its nominee to either EMCF, LCH.Clearnet or X-CLEAR or to their nominees;

(*h*) LCH.Clearnet or its nominee to either EMCF, EuroCCP or X-CLEAR or to their nominees; or

(i) X-CLEAR or its nominee to either EMCF, EuroCCP or LCH.Clearnet or to their nominees.

(4) Condition B is that the person to whom those securities are agreed to be transferred under any of the agreements specified in paragraph (3) ("the relevant agreement") is required on receipt of those securities to transfer traded securities under a matching agreement to another person or, in the case of an agreement falling within paragraph 3(*d*), would have been so required if the failure referred to in that paragraph had not occurred.

(5) Condition C is that traded securities which are the subject of a relevant agreement shall be dealt with by a clearing participant, who is a party to the relevant agreement, in a separate designated account.

(6) In this regulation—

(*a*) "designated account" means an account designated by EMCF, EuroCCP, LCH.Clearnet or X-CLEAR, for a clearing participant, in connection with the traded securities concerned;

(*b*) a "matching agreement" means an agreement under which—

(i) the traded securities agreed to be transferred are of the same kind as the traded securities agreed to be transferred under the relevant agreement; and

(ii) the number and transfer price of the traded securities agreed to be transferred are identical to the number and transfer price of the traded securities agreed to be transferred under the relevant agreement.

5 Revocation of the Stamp Duty and Stamp Duty Reserve Tax (Investment Exchanges and Clearing Houses) Regulations (No 6) 2009

The Stamp Duty and Stamp Duty Reserve Tax (Investment Exchanges and Clearing Houses) Regulations (No 6) 2009 are revoked.

2010/1897

STAMP DUTY AND STAMP DUTY RESERVE TAX (INVESTMENT EXCHANGES AND CLEARING HOUSES) REGULATIONS (NO 4) 2010

Made .... *22 July 2010*

Laid before the House of Commons .... *26 July 2010*

Coming into force .... *17 August 2010*

The Treasury make the following Regulations in exercise of the powers conferred by sections 116 and 117 of the Finance Act 1991.

1 Citation, commencement and effect

(1) These Regulations may be cited as the Stamp Duty and Stamp Duty Reserve Tax (Investment Exchanges and Clearing Houses) Regulations (No 4) 2010 and come into force on 17th August 2010.

(2) These Regulations have effect—

(*a*) for the purposes of the charge to stamp duty, in relation to instruments executed on or after 17th August 2010;

(*b*) for the purposes of the charge to stamp duty reserve tax—

(i) in the case of agreements to transfer traded securities which are not conditional, in relation to agreements made on or after 17th August 2010;

(ii) in the case of agreements to transfer traded securities which are conditional, in relation to agreements where the condition is satisfied on or after that date.

2 Interpretation

In these Regulations—

"Frankfurt Stock Exchange" means a regulated market operated by Deutsche Borse AG;

"Open Market MTF" means a multilateral trading facility operated by Deutsche Borse AG;

"clearing participant" means a member of Eurex Clearing who as such is permitted by the Rules of Eurex to clear transactions made on the Deutsche Borse AG exchange for a traded security and who may or may not also be a participant on the Deutsche Borse AG exchange;

"client" means a person who gives instructions to a non-clearing firm for traded securities to be sold on the Deutsche Borse AG exchange;

"Deutsche Borse AG exchange" means either the Frankfurt Stock Exchange or the Open Market MTF.

"Eurex Clearing" means Eurex Clearing AG;

"nominee" means a person whose business is or includes holding traded securities as a nominee for Eurex Clearing acting in its capacity as a person providing clearing services in connection with a transaction made on the Deutsche Borse AG exchange, or as a nominee for a clearing participant;

"non-clearing firm" means a participant on the Deutsche Borse AG exchange other than a clearing participant;

"traded securities" means stocks and shares which are issued or raised by a body corporate but does not include stocks and shares issued or raised by a body corporate not incorporated in the United Kingdom unless—

(*a*) the stocks and shares are registered in a register kept in the United Kingdom by or on behalf of the body corporate; or (*b*) in the case of shares, they are paired, within the meaning of section 99(6A) of the Finance Act 1986, with shares issued by a body corporate incorporated in the United Kingdom.

3 Prescription of recognised investment exchanges and recognised clearing houses

For the purposes of sections 116 and 117 of the Finance Act 1991—

(*a*) the Frankfurt Stock Exchange is prescribed as a recognised investment exchange;
(*b*) Open Market MTF is prescribed as a recognised investment exchange;
(*c*) Eurex is prescribed as a recognised clearing house.

4 Prescribed circumstances for the purposes of sections 116 and 117

(1) In the circumstances prescribed by paragraph (2), the charges to stamp duty and stamp duty reserve tax shall be treated as not arising.

(2) The circumstances prescribed are where, in connection with a transaction made on the Deutsche Borse AG exchange, conditions A, B and C are met.

(3) Condition A is that traded securities are transferred, or agreed to be transferred, from—

(*a*) a clearing participant or its nominee to another clearing participant or its nominee;
(*b*) a non-clearing firm or its client, or nominee of a non-clearing firm or its client, to a clearing participant or its nominee;
(*c*) a clearing participant or its nominee to Eurex Clearing or to its nominee;
(*d*) a person other than a clearing participant to Eurex Clearing or to its nominee, as a result of a failure by a clearing participant to fulfil its obligations in respect of the transaction concerned to transfer traded securities to Eurex Clearing or to its nominee;
(*e*) Eurex Clearing or its nominee to a clearing participant or its nominee;
(*f*) a clearing participant or its nominee to a non-clearing firm.

(4) Condition B is that the person to whom those securities are agreed to be transferred under any of the agreements specified in paragraph (3) ("the relevant agreement") is required on receipt of those securities to transfer traded securities under a matching agreement to another person or, in the case of an agreement falling within paragraph 3(*d*), would have been so required if the failure referred to in that paragraph had not occurred.

(5) Condition C is that traded securities which are the subject of a relevant agreement shall be dealt with by a clearing participant, who is a party to the relevant agreement, in a separate designated account.

(6) In this regulation—

(*a*) "designated account" means an account designated by Eurex Clearing, for a clearing participant, in connection with the traded securities concerned;
(*b*) a "matching agreement" means an agreement under which—
  (i) the traded securities agreed to be transferred are of the same kind as the traded securities agreed to be transferred under the relevant agreement; and
  (ii) the number and transfer price of the traded securities agreed to be transferred are identical to the number and transfer price of the traded securities agreed to be transferred under the relevant agreement.

Extra-Statutory Concessions

Contents

Concessions

G1 STAMP ALLOWANCE ON LOST DOCUMENTS

Note—This Concession has been classified as obsolete. See now SDMA 1891, s 12A.

G2 STAMPING OF REPLICAS OF DOCUMENTS WHICH HAVE BEEN SPOILT OR LOST

Note—This Concession has been classified as obsolete. See now SDMA 1891, s 12A.

G3 GROUP LIFE AND PENSION POLICIES

Note—This Concession has been classified as obsolete: see FA 1989 s 173.

G4 REPAYMENT OF DUTY ON CANCELLED POLICIES OF INSURANCE

Note—This Concession has been classified as obsolete: see FA 1989 s 173.

G5 TRANSFER OF STOCK FROM PERSONS TO THEMSELVES OPERATING AS AN EXECUTOR'S ASSENT

Stamp duty is not claimed on transfer of stock in a company registered in England, Wales or Northern Ireland from a person to himself (or from two or more persons to themselves) which operates as an executor's assent. The point does not arise in relation to companies registered in Scotland.

G6 TRANSFERS OF ASSETS BETWEEN NON-PROFIT MAKING BODIES WITH SIMILAR OBJECTS

When the reconstruction of a non-profit making body with objects in a field of public interest such as education, community work or scientific research, or the amalgamation of two or more such bodies involves a transfer to the successor body of assets for which there passes no consideration in money or money's worth, the instruments of transfer are treated as exempt from ad valorem stamp duty and charged to £5 fixed duty only. There must be sufficient identity between the members of the transferor and transferee bodies and the rules of both must prohibit the distribution of assets to members and provide that on a winding-up the assets can only be transferred to a similar body subject to like restrictions.

Note—This text of this Concession is as reproduced in IR 1 (August 2002).

G7 TRANSFERS OF STOCK INTO SEPON

Note—This Concession was replaced by FA 1996 s 191.

G8 STOCK LOAN RETURNS

Note—This Concession was replaced by FA 1996 s 191.

G9 TRANSFERS OF COLLATERAL

Note—This Concession was replaced by FA 1996 s 191.

Stamp Taxes
Statements of Practice

Notes—Statements of Practice which are obsolete or obsolescent or are not applicable in the current year are listed in italics, but not printed.

Before 18 July 1978 information on administrative practice was issued in various forms including Parliamentary statements and written answers, and letters to professional bodies and journals. An index of those statements issued before 18 July 1978 which remained valid was published in a Revenue Press Release on 18 June 1979 and revised by further Press Releases dated 29 October 1980 and 23 March 1982.

These statements have no binding force and do not affect a taxpayer's right of appeal on points concerning his liability to tax.

HMRC note—The Civil Partnership Act (CPA) received Royal Assent on 18/11/2004 and became effective from 5 December 2005. The Government's commitment is that, for all tax purposes, same-sex couples who form a civil partnership will be treated the same as married couples.

As part of this commitment to tax parity, from 5 December 2005 all Statements of Practice should be taken as extended to apply equally to civil partners and married couples.

Currency—These Statements were updated by HMRC in August 2005. Please note that references to the "Inland Revenue" should now be considered as referring to "HM Revenue and Customs" and references to the "Board of the Inland Revenue" should be read as the "Commissioners for HM Revenue and Customs".

Contents

Statements of Practice

SP 5/78 CONVEYANCE IN CONSIDERATION OF A DEBT (8 NOVEMBER 1978)

Note—This Statement was classified as obsolete by IR 131 (August 2002).

SP 3/84 STAMP DUTY: CONVERTIBLE LOAN STOCK (13 MARCH 1984)

Transfers of certain loan capital are exempted from stamp duty by FA 1986 s 79. [Subsection (5)] provides that the exemption is not available where the loan capital carries an unexpired right of conversion into shares or other securities or to the acquisition of shares or other securities, including loan capital of the same description. The Commissioners for HMRC are advised that [subsection (5)] does not exclude from the exemption loan capital which carries an unexpired right of conversion into or acquisition of loan capital which itself comes within terms of the exemption.

Note—This statement was revised in Booklet IR 131 Supp (November 2000).

SP 9/84 STAMP DUTY: TREATMENT OF SECURITIES DEALT IN ON THE STOCK EXCHANGE UNLISTED SECURITIES MARKET

Note—This Statement was classified as obsolete by IR 131 (August 2002).

SP 10/87 STAMP DUTY: CONVEYANCES AND LEASES OF BUILDING PLOTS (22 DECEMBER 1987)

Note—This statement is superseded by SP 8/93.

SP 6/90 CONVEYANCES AND TRANSFERS OF PROPERTY SUBJECT TO A DEBT: SA 1891 S 57 (27 APRIL 1990)

INTRODUCTION

1 Since the abolition of the duty on voluntary dispositions in 1985, many enquiries have been received about the stamp duty chargeable on conveyances etc subject to a debt where *no* chargeable consideration (*eg* money or stock) unrelated to the debt is given by the transferee. This Statement of Practice sets out the Commissioners for HMRC's view of the correct stamp duty treatment of such conveyances.

2 For the sake of completeness it should be noted that where chargeable consideration unrelated to debt *is* given by the transferee, s 57 renders the conveyance liable to ad valorem duty on the aggregate of that consideration and the debt whether the transferee assumes liability for the debt or not (*IRC v City of Glasgow Bank* (1881) 8 R (Ct of Sess) 389, 18 SLR 242).

SA 1891 S 57

3 The most commonly misunderstood applications of s 57 arise where:

– a mortgaged property held in the name of one spouse is transferred into the joint names of both spouses;
– a mortgaged property held in the name of one spouse or in their joint names is transferred into the sole name of the other;
– a mortgaged business property, frequently farmland, is conveyed from a sole proprietor to a family partnership or from a family partnership to a fresh partnership bringing in other members of the family.

4 The critical question is whether the transaction to which the conveyance gives effect is or is not a sale. If it is, s 57 will apply and the conveyance will be chargeable to ad valorem duty on the amount of the debt assumed. If it is not, then s 57 will not apply and ad valorem duty will not be payable.

EXPRESS COVENANTS

5 Where property is transferred subject to a debt, the transferee may covenant, either in the instrument or by means of a separate written undertaking, to pay the debt or indemnify the transferor against his personal liability to the lender. Such a covenant or undertaking constitutes valuable consideration and, in view of s 57, establishes the transaction as a sale for stamp duty purposes.

6 Where the transferor covenants to pay the debt and the transferee does not assume any liability for it, no chargeable consideration has been given and there is no sale. The transfer would then be a voluntary disposition—ie an unencumbered gift capable of being certified as Category L under the Stamp Duty (Exempt Instruments) Regulations 1987 (SI 1987/516)—and so exempt from the 50p charge that would otherwise arise.

IMPLIED COVENANTS

7 Where no express covenant or undertaking is given by the transferee, the Commissioners for HMRC are advised that, except in Scotland, a covenant by the transferee may be implied. That makes the transaction a sale, as in para 4 above.

8 Such an implied covenant may be negated if there is evidence that it was the intention of the parties at the time of the transfer that the transferor should continue to be liable for the whole of the mortgage debt. Where evidence of such a contrary intention exists, the transfer would again be treated for stamp duty purposes as a voluntary disposition.

9 Where property in joint names subject to a debt is transferred to one of the joint holders (though with no cash passing), a covenant by the transferee to indemnify the transferor may be implied even where both parties were jointly liable on the mortgage.

AMOUNT CHARGEABLE

10 Where a conveyance of property subject to a debt is chargeable to ad valorem duty and the express or implied covenant by the transferee relates only to part of the debt, only the amount of that part is treated as chargeable consideration within s 57. A certificate of value under [FA 1999 Sch 13 para 6] may, where appropriate, be included in the conveyance where the relevant amount of the debt does not exceed the amount certified.

OTHER PROVISIONS

11 The foregoing does not affect any statutory exemption from duty that may apply, *eg* that for transfers to a charity (FA 1982 s 129) and that available for certain transfers of property from one party to a marriage to the other in connection with their divorce or separation (FA 1985 s 83(1) and Stamp Duty (Exempt Instruments) Regulations 1987, Category H).

PROCEDURE

12 Where the applicant is satisfied that the conveyance or transfer is made on sale, it may be sent or taken for stamping with a remittance for the duty payable. If the transfer contains an appropriate certificate of value—see para 10 above—it may be sent direct to the Land Registry in the usual way if appropriate. In either case, if the amount of the debt outstanding is not given in the conveyance or transfer the amount should be stated in a covering letter.

13 Where the conveyance or transfer contains a covenant by the transferor to pay the debt (see para 6) and is certified as within the Stamp Duty (Exempt Instruments) Regulations 1987, Category L it should also be sent direct to the Land Registry if appropriate.

14 In any other case where the applicant believes that the conveyance or transfer effects a voluntary disposition—see para 8 above—it should be presented for adjudication accompanied by a statement of the facts and any supporting evidence.

Note—This statement was revised in Booklet IR 131 Supp (November 2000).

SP 6/91 STAMP DUTY AND VALUE ADDED TAX (VAT): INTERACTION (22 JULY 1991)

Note—Superseded by SP 11/91.

SP 11/91 STAMP DUTY AND VAT—INTERACTION (12 SEPTEMBER 1991)

1 This statement is a revised version of the statement about stamp duty and VAT issued on 22 July 1991, SP 6/91, and replaces it.

INTRODUCTION

2 To comply with a judgment of the European Court of Justice in June 1988, standard rate UK VAT has been applied to non-residential construction with effect from 1 April 1989 (FA 1989 s 18). VAT is compulsory on sales of buildings treated as new for this purpose, which are mainly buildings under three years old that have been completed after March 1989. And owners of non-residential property were given the option from 1 August 1989 of charging VAT on sales of old buildings and on leases.

3 These new charges have prompted a number of enquiries about the relationship between stamp duty and VAT where both taxes arise on a sale or lease of commercial property or, occasionally, other assets.

SALES OF NEW NON-DOMESTIC BUILDINGS

4 The Commissioners for HMRC are advised that for stamp duty purposes the amount or value of the consideration for a sale is the gross amount inclusive of VAT. Therefore where VAT is payable on the sale of new non-residential property, stamp duty is calculated on the VAT-inclusive consideration.

OTHER NON-DOMESTIC TRANSACTIONS

5 Transactions in non-residential property other than sales of new buildings are exempt from VAT. These include—

– sales of old buildings
– the assignment of existing leases, or the creation of new leases, in old or new property.

However, the vendor or lessor can elect to waive the exemption.

6 The Commissioners for HMRC have received legal advice that—

– where the election has already been exercised at the time of the transaction, stamp duty is chargeable on the purchase price, premium or rent including VAT;
– where the election has not been exercised at that time, VAT should similarly be included in any payments to which an election could still apply (which will depend on the facts of each case).

7 The Commissioners for HMRC propose to follow this advice, which will result in a change of practice: in the past, the Stamp Office did not seek to include the VAT element in the stamp duty charge in cases where an election to waive the exemption from VAT had not yet been exercised. The new practice applies to documents executed on or after 1 August 1991.

8 Neither a formal notice of election made to HM Customs & Excise, nor any notification to the purchaser or lessee that such an election has been made, will attract stamp duty.

RENT

9 Where VAT is charged on the rent under a lease, and is itself treated as rent under the lease, stamp duty at the appropriate rate according to the length of the term will be charged on the VAT-inclusive figure. If the lease provides for payment of VAT on the rent otherwise than as rent, duty will be charged on the VAT element as consideration payable periodically (Stamp Act 1891 s 56). In either case the rate of VAT in force at the date of execution of the lease will be used in the calculation.

10 In the case of a formal Deed of Variation or similar document varying the terms of the original lease so as to provide for payment of VAT by way of additional rent, further stamp duty may be payable (Stamp Act 1891 s 77(5)).

AGREEMENTS FOR LEASES

11 Paragraphs 5 to 10 above also apply to an agreement for lease if that is the instrument to be stamped [FA 1999 Sch 13 para 14].

PROCEDURE

12 Applicants for stamping are requested to make clear, either in the conveyance or lease document itself, or in a covering letter to the Stamp Office, whether the property is commercial or residential.

13 Deeds of Variation etc (para 10 above) should be presented for adjudication together with a copy of the original lease.

NO VAT ON STAMP DUTY

14 It is sometimes suggested that stamp duty might itself attract a charge to VAT. This is not the case. The value for VAT depends on the amount (consideration) obtained by the supplier from the purchaser, less the included VAT itself. Stamp duty is paid by the purchaser/lessee of property direct to HMRC and not to the supplier; it does not therefore form part of the consideration for VAT purposes.

Note—This statement was revised in Booklet IR 131 Supp (November 2000).

SP 8/93 STAMP DUTY: NEW BUILDINGS (12 JULY 1993)

This statement sets out the practice the Commissioners for HMRC will apply in relation to the stamp duty chargeable in certain circumstances on the conveyance or lease of a new or partly constructed building. It affects transactions where, at the date of the contract for sale or lease of a building plot, building work has not commenced or has been only partially completed on that site but where that work has started or has been completed at the time the conveyance or lease is executed.

This statement reflects the advice the Commissioners for HMRC have received on this subject in the light of the decision in the case of *Prudential Assurance Company Ltd v IRC* ([1992] STC 863; [1993] 1 WLR 211). The statement does not apply to the common situation where the parties have entered into a contract for the sale of a new house and that contract is implemented by a conveyance of the whole property. This statement replaces the statements of practice issued in 1957 and 1987 (SP 10/87) on this subject which are now withdrawn.

The Commissioners for HMRC are advised that, whilst each case will clearly depend on its own facts, the law is as follows—

1 TWO TRANSACTIONS/TWO CONTRACTS

Where the purchaser or lessee is entitled under the terms of a contract to a conveyance or lease of land alone in consideration of the purchase price or rent of the site and a second genuine contract for building works is entered into as a separate transaction, the *ad valorem* duty on the conveyance or lease will be determined by the amount of the purchase price or rent which the purchaser or lessee is obliged to pay under the terms of the first contract. In these circumstances it does not matter whether any building work has commenced at the date of the conveyance or lease. The consideration chargeable to *ad valorem* duty will still be only that passing for the land.

2 ONE TRANSACTION/TWO CONTRACTS

Where there is one transaction between the parties but this is implemented by two contracts, one for the sale or lease of the building plot and one for the building works themselves, the amount of ad valorem duty charged on the instrument will depend on the amount of the consideration, which in turn will depend on whether those contracts can be shown to be genuinely independent of each other.

(i) if the two contracts are so interlocked that they cannot be said to be genuinely capable of independent completion (and in particular where if default occurs on either contract, the other is then not enforceable) ad valorem duty will be charged on the total consideration for the land and buildings, whether completed or not, as if the parties had entered into only one contract.

(ii) if the two contracts are shown to be genuinely independent of each other, ad valorem duty will be charged by reference to the consideration paid or payable for the land and any building works on that land at the date of execution of the instrument. It follows that, where the instrument is executed after the building works are completed, ad valorem duty will be charged on the consideration for the land and the completed building(s).

3 SHAM OR ARTIFICIAL TRANSACTIONS

This statement does not apply to cases where the transaction concerned, or any part of it, involves a sham or artificial transaction.

CONTRACTS ALREADY ENTERED INTO

Where unconditional contracts have been entered into before or within 28 days of the date of this Statement and the duty payable on the resulting conveyance or lease would have been less under the earlier Statements of Practice, the Stamp Office will accept duty in the lesser amount. In such cases the instrument should be submitted together with all the evidence to support the claim that unconditional contracts were entered into within this transitional period.

PROCEDURE FOR SUBMITTING DOCUMENTS

Where a person accepts that a conveyance or lease of a building plot is chargeable on the total price paid or payable for the land and the completed building, it should be submitted for stamping in the usual way together with a covering letter giving the aggregate price and a payment for the duty appropriate to that price.

Where the total price does not exceed the amount up to which the instrument is liable to nil duty (currently £60,000) and a certificate of value is included in the instrument, a conveyance may be sent direct to the Land Registry in England and Wales or, in Scotland, to the Keeper of the Registers of Scotland. A lease will need to be stamped in respect of the rent.

Where the total price exceeds the threshold at which duty becomes payable but the taxpayer takes the view that duty is payable on some smaller sum, the instrument should be submitted to the Stamp Office. This applies even where the taxpayer believes that the amount potentially chargeable to *ad valorem* duty is below the threshold and a certificate of value is included in the instrument. The instrument should be accompanied by a copy of the agreement(s) for sale etc and a letter stating the amount which the taxpayer regards as chargeable consideration, identifying separately any amount attributable to building work. Details of any contractual arrangements not covered by the agreement(s) should also be given in the covering letter.

Note—This statement was revised in Booklet IR 131 (August 2002).

SP 3/98 STAMP DUTY—GROUP RELIEF (13 OCTOBER 1998)

1 FA 1930 s 42 gives relief from stamp duty for transfers of property between members of the same group of companies. FA 1995 s 151 similarly gives relief from duty on the grant of a lease between members of the same group.

2 FA 1967 s 27(3) and FA 1995 s 151(3) are designed to prevent the use of group relief to avoid stamp duty when property, or an economic interest in it, passes out of the group.

3 This statement sets out the Stamp Office's current general practice in order to assist practitioners in determining whether claims to relief might qualify. The treatment of a particular case will of course depend on the precise facts. This statement is for general guidance only; and the facts of a particular transaction may, exceptionally, place it outside the guidelines. It applies also to the equivalent Northern Ireland legislation.

GENERAL

4 Broadly, s 27(3) and the corresponding provisions in s 151, provide that relief is not to be given if the transfer was made in pursuance of, or in connection with, an arrangement under which—

(a) all or part of the consideration for the transfer was to be provided or received, directly or indirectly, by a person outside the group; or

(b) the interest being transferred was previously transferred by a person outside the group; or

(c) the transferor and transferee were no longer to be part of the same group.

5 The person claiming the relief when the relevant instrument is adjudicated has the onus of satisfying the Stamp Office that the intra-group transaction is not carried out in pursuance of, or in connection with, an arrangement of a kind which disqualifies the transaction from relief—*Escoigne Properties Ltd v IRC* [1958] AC 549, 564.

"ARRANGEMENT"

6 In this context, arrangement means the plan or scheme in pursuance of which the things identified in ss 27(3), 151(3) have been or are to be done—*Shop and Store Developments Ltd v IRC* [1967] 1 AC 472, 493, 494. The arrangement need not be based in contract. It is sufficient if the intra-group transaction is made in connection with that plan or scheme. The intra-group transaction may be the first bi-lateral step by which legal rights and obligations are created in pursuance of the arrangement. If there is an expectation that a disqualifying event will happen in accordance with the arrangement and no likelihood in practice that it will not, relief will be refused.

7 The words "in connection with" are very broad. In *Escoigne*, there was a gap of four years between the two steps in issue.

PROVISION OR RECEIPT OF CONSIDERATION BY A PERSON OUTSIDE THE GROUP—FA 1967 S 27(3)(A); FA 1995 S 151(3)(A), (4)

8 Section 27(3)(*a*) denies relief where the instrument was executed in pursuance of or in connection with an arrangement under which any of the consideration is to be provided or received, directly or indirectly, by a person outside the group. It also denies relief if the arrangement is one under which the transferor or transferee (or a member of the same group as either of them) is to be enabled to provide any of the consideration, or is to part with it, in consequence of a transaction involving a payment or other disposition by a person outside the group. Section 151 lays down similar rules for leases.

9 In some cases, the question arises whether loan finance for the purchase or lease will disqualify an intra-group transaction from relief. It is necessary to look at all the facts of the individual case, but the Stamp Office will interpret the provisions in the light of their general purpose of denying relief where the intra-group transaction is a means of saving stamp duty when the property, or an interest in it, moves out of the group. Accordingly, the Stamp Office are likely to be satisfied that relief is due if the intra-group transaction is not to be followed by a sale of the property transferred, or an underlease, to a person outside the group. If the intra-group transaction is to be followed by a sale or underlease to a person outside the group, but the claimant can demonstrate that stamp duty will be paid in respect of that transaction in approximately the same amount as would have been payable if the intra-group transferor or lessor had itself sold the property or granted the underlease, the Stamp Office are likely to be satisfied that the intra-group transaction and the transfer or lease out are independent for stamp duty purposes and grant the relief sought.

10 A transaction is not disqualified merely because the transferee within the group obtains a specific loan for the purchase of the asset; or the loan is secured on the asset; or arrangements are made to replace or novate an existing charge on the property transferred. It will be necessary to consider the facts as a whole, especially if the loan finance is not straightforward finance on ordinary commercial terms.

11 Intra-group transactions will be very carefully scrutinised, and relief may be refused, where, for example, the intra-group transaction involves or is to be followed by—

- the creation or transfer of loan stock or equity capital;
- a capital reorganisation of the transferee;
- a guarantee by a third party not associated with the group;
- the creation of a new charge or financial arrangement whereby title to the property is, or may be, vested in the lender otherwise than in satisfaction of all or part of the debt; or
- the assignment of the freehold reversion or the intra-group lease to a person outside the group.

12 Similarly transactions will be very carefully scrutinised where—

- all or part of the consideration for the transaction is to remain outstanding or is represented by intra-group debt, (as the aim and effect may be to reduce the value of the transferee company on a possible future sale outside the group); or

– the existing shareholders of the transferee include shareholders outside the group and the transaction is to be followed by the declaration of a dividend in *specie*, or by the liquidation of the transferee.

13 Further assurances by way of statutory declaration—the document in which the claim is made to the Stamp Office—will be required in any case in which the property transferred or vested intra-group is the only, or only substantial, asset of the transferee. Information to that effect should be provided in the statutory declaration submitted with the documents.

14 Where group member A has granted a lease to a person outside the group, and subsequently grants an underlease to its fellow group member B, so that the rent already payable by the lessee becomes payable to B rather than A, relief is likely to be given for the intra-group underlease, provided there are no other factors which suggest that relief should be denied.

PROPERTY PREVIOUSLY CONVEYED BY A PERSON OUTSIDE THE GROUP—FA 1967 S 27(3)(B)

15 Section 27(3)(*b*) was intended to prevent the avoidance of duty on the transfer of property into a group by means of a sub-sale, so as to take advantage of the Stamp Act 1891 s 58(4). For example, suppose the property is sold to a group member by a vendor outside the group, but the sale rests in contract without a transfer of the legal title. The group member then sells the property to another member of its own group, and directs the vendor to transfer the legal title to that other member. In accordance with s 58(4) the transfer completing the sale and the sub-sale is chargeable to duty only in relation to the sub-sale (thus relieving the effect of s 4 of the Stamp Act). However, s 27(3)(*b*) would deny group relief for that transfer.

16 The Stamp Office will continue to apply s 27(3)(*b*) to schemes of this type and to any other scheme where an attempt has been made to avoid the duty payable on the acquisition by the group. However, where an outside vendor sells a property to a member of the group, the sale is completed by a transfer and stamp duty is paid on that transfer, the Stamp Office will normally regard any subsequent intra-group transfer as independent, and grant relief for the transfer within the purchaser's group.

DISSOCIATION OR DEMERGER OF TRANSFEREE—FA 1967 S 27(3)(C): FA 1995 S 151(3)(B)

17 Before the introduction of s 27(3), almost all the avoidance devices encountered in this area involved the transfer of property to a subsidiary, often created solely as a vehicle for that property, followed by the transfer of the shares in the subsidiary out of the group. Compared with a transfer of the property out of the group, a substantial amount of duty could be avoided even where the subsidiary paid for the property from its own resources. If the consideration for the intra-group transaction remained outstanding or was represented by debt, duty could be reduced further by reducing the value of the shares—hence s 27(3)(*a*).

18 Section 27(3)(*c*) was introduced to counter this avoidance in relation to conveyances and transfers on sale. Section 151(3)(*b*) deals with leases on similar lines.

19 In cases of this kind, the Stamp Office will need to be satisfied that the intra-group transfer or lease is not a step in pursuance of an arrangement to demerge the transferee. The existence of such an arrangement may be apparent from company documents, correspondence and other dealings between members of the group and professional advisers, or from discussions or negotiations with the potential purchasers, underwriters or minority shareholders.

20 In practice, the Stamp Office will apply these provisions so as to preclude group relief if there is evidence of a plan or scheme to dispose of the subsidiary and there is no practical likelihood that the scheme will not be carried through. It will not be regarded as sufficient for the claimant to contend that such an arrangement which is less than contractual may possibly be frustrated by unforeseen events or unlikely occurrences. Even a contract may be frustrated.

21 As the liability of the relevant instrument must, as a matter of general principle, be determined as at the date of the instrument, the question whether an arrangement of the relevant kind exists must also be determined at that time, although the Stamp Office may have regard to what is said and done thereafter to establish the true position (*Wm Cory and Son Ltd v IRC* [1965] AC 1088). For the purposes of stamp duty, it is therefore the existence of the scheme or plan to which these provisions direct attention, not the ultimate outcome of steps, which may be taken to implement that scheme. Accordingly, statements of practice in relation to other taxes have no application in this context.

SP 1/03 STAMP DUTY—DISADVANTAGED AREAS RELIEF (APRIL 2003)

This Statement of Practice is intended as guidance for those claiming exemption from stamp duty in respect of transfers of property situated in designated areas ("Disadvantaged Areas Relief") and explains how Inland Revenue Stamp Taxes will interpret the extension to the relief introduced with effect from 10 April 2003.

The relief is one of a number of measures set out in the Government's Urban White Paper "*Our Towns and Cities—The Future—Delivering an Urban Renaissance*" published in November 2000. The measure is designed to stimulate the physical, economic and social regeneration of the UK's most disadvantaged areas by attracting development and by encouraging the purchase of residential and commercial property by individuals and businesses. The areas eligible for relief were designated "Enterprise Areas" by the Chancellor in his 2002 Pre-Budget Report. In addition to the relief, a range of other Government policies designed to support enterprise and economic regeneration, including the Community Investment Tax Relief, will benefit these areas, helping to support the development of new and existing businesses.

INTRODUCTION

1 Disadvantaged Areas Relief (provided for by section 92 of, and Schedule 30 to, the Finance Act 2001) was introduced on 30 November 2001 and was initially only available for conveyances or transfers on sale (of both residential and commercial property) for which the consideration did not exceed £150,000. Stamp duty in respect of conveyances or transfers of commercial property in disadvantaged areas was abolished in consequence of the Stamp Duty (Disadvantaged Areas) (Application of Exemptions) Regulations 2003 ("the Regulations"), which have effect in relation to instruments executed on or after 10 April 2003. Thereafter the £150,000 limit applies only in relation to residential property.

2 Finance Act 2002 inserted the following provisions in Finance Act 2001 to distinguish residential from other property and to provide for differing stamp duty exemptions—

- Section 92A which enables stamp duty relief in designated disadvantaged areas in respect of all properties to be varied depending on whether or not the property is "residential";
- Section 92B which defines "residential property" for the purposes of the relief. Non-residential property, in respect of which unlimited relief is available, is therefore defined in the Act by exclusion. The section also sets out particular building uses that are specifically included within, or specifically excluded from, the definition.

3 In most cases there will be no difficulty in practice in establishing whether or not a property is "residential". This statement sets out in more detail the Stamp Office's approach to borderline cases and gives guidance on the practical application of the legislation. The annexed flowchart provides a quick guide for simpler cases as to whether property constitutes "residential property".

CERTIFICATION

4 Claims for unlimited relief must be accompanied by a certificate stating either that none of the land in question is residential property or, if part is residential, the proportion that is non-residential (together with the usual certificate of value for the remainder).

- Residential property—Section 92A(4) of Finance Act 2001, together with the Regulations, provides that the exemption will only apply if the document is certified to the effect that the amount or value of the consideration does not exceed £150,000.
- Non-residential property—Subsection (2) of section 92 of Finance Act 2001 provides that the exemption will only apply if the document is certified to the Commissioners as being an instrument on which stamp duty is not chargeable by virtue of subsection (1) of that section.

5 The following are suggested forms of words for particular certificates—

- Residential Property— "I/We hereby certify that the transaction effected by this instrument does not form part of a larger transaction or series of transactions in respect of which the amount or value of the consideration exceeds £150,000 and that stamp duty is not chargeable thereon by virtue of the provisions of sections 92 and 92A of the Finance Act 2001."
- Non-residential Property— "I/We hereby certify that this is an instrument in respect of non-residential property on which stamp duty is not chargeable by virtue of the provisions of section 92 of the Finance Act 2001."

– Mixed Use Property— "I/We hereby certify that the transaction effected by this instrument is in respect of property part of which is residential property, and which does not form part of a larger transaction or series of transactions in respect of which the amount or value of the consideration relating to the residential part exceeds £150,000 so that stamp duty is not chargeable by virtue of sections 92 and 92A of the Finance Act 2001, and part of which is non-residential property on which stamp duty is not chargeable by virtue of the provisions of section 92 of the Finance Act 2001. The basis upon which the allocation between residential and non-residential parts has been made is as follows: . . . "

6 While the legislation does not specifically require the certificate to be included as part of the document, it is suggested that it should be so included. If the person submitting the document for stamping does not provide a certificate, either in the document or separately in writing, exemption will not be granted.

7 Appropriate contemporaneous evidence should be retained to support any certificate provided. Estate agents' specifications, site plans, planning applications or permissions, marketing material and photographs may all provide relevant information.

8 Anyone falsely certifying a document with a view to obtaining relief that is not due will be committing a stamp duty fraud.

THE MEANING OF RESIDENTIAL PROPERTY

9 Section 92B defines "residential property" as a building which—

– is used as a dwelling, or
– is suitable for use as a dwelling, or
– is in the process of being constructed or adapted for such use.

If a property meets any one of these separate tests it will be treated as residential property and be subject to the £150,000 limit for relief, as will any garden or grounds belonging to it or any interests or rights attaching to it. Each element of the definition is considered in turn below.

The question of whether and to what extent a building and grounds are defined as residential property for stamp duty purposes may also have implications for its treatment for capital gains tax and local authority rates.

USE AS A DWELLING

10 Where a building is in use at the date of execution of the relevant instrument, it will be a question of fact whether and to what extent it is used as a dwelling. Use at the date the instrument is executed overrides any past or intended future uses for this purpose.

11 Where the property in question is in use as a dwelling at the date of execution, it is residential property for the purposes of the relief unless it is part of a multiple transaction qualifying for relief under the Regulations (see paragraphs 35 to 39 below).

12 For the treatment of buildings put to both residential and non-residential use, see paragraphs 17 and 18 below.

SUITABLE FOR USE AS A DWELLING

13 The suitability test applies to the state of the building at the time the instrument is executed, having regard to the facilities available and any history of use. For example, HMRC will not regard an office block as "suitable for use as a dwelling", but a house which has been used as an office without particular adaptation may well be so.

14 If a building is not in use at the date of execution but its last use was as a dwelling, it will be taken to be 'suitable for use as a dwelling' and treated as residential property for the purposes of the relief, unless evidence is produced to the contrary (see paragraph 15).

15 Whether a building is suitable for use as a dwelling will depend upon the precise facts and circumstances. The simple removal of, for example, a bathroom suite or kitchen facilities will not be regarded as rendering a building unsuitable for use as a dwelling. Where it is claimed that a previously residential property is no longer suitable for use as a dwelling, perhaps because it is derelict or has been substantially altered, the claimant will need to provide evidence that this is the case. See also paragraph 29.

16 Where a building has been used partly for residential purposes and partly for another purpose, its overall suitability for use as a dwelling will be judged from the facilities available at the date of execution of the relevant document. For example, if two rooms of a house were in use as a dentist's surgery and waiting room at the date of execution, HMRC would nevertheless normally consider this property suitable for use as a dwelling unless the claimant provided evidence to the contrary. In other words, the interaction of the Regulations with section 92B(1) enables a building that is used only partly as a dwelling to be nevertheless suitable for use wholly as a dwelling, with the effect that the £150,000 limit applies to the whole of the consideration. Where only a distinct part of the building is used and suitable for use as a dwelling, that part will be residential property for the purposes of the relief and the mixed use provisions will apply (paragraphs 17 and 18 below).

MIXED USE

17 Where only part of a building (and land or interest relating to it) is "residential property" within section 92B(1), the consideration "shall be apportioned on such basis as is just and reasonable" between the residential and non-residential elements. The £150,000 limit is then applied only to the residential portion, in accordance with the appropriate certification (regulation 5 of the Regulations). For example—

A property situated wholly within a disadvantaged area is bought for:

(a) £200,000
(b) £400,000

50% of the property is "residential property" on the basis of a just and reasonable apportionment.

Relief is conferred by FA 2001 s 92, applied in conjunction with regulation 5 of the Regulations. Paragraph (3) of regulation 5 calls for an apportionment of the total consideration between residential and non-residential elements. Paragraph (4) confirms that relief applies to the residential property element only where the consideration attributed to it does not exceed £150,000. In these examples—

(a) £100,000 is attributed to the residential property element, so relief is due. The part of the land that is not residential property is also exempt under the normal operation of FA 2001 s 92. So no duty is payable.
(b) the £200,000 attributed to the residential property element is not exempt, because of regulation 5(4), but attracts duty at the rate of 1% (stamp duty payable £2,000). The non-residential property element is exempt as above.

18 The "just and reasonable" test is necessarily subjective, and each case will be considered on its merits. Apportionment might be on the basis of the percentage areas quoted in planning applications, where appropriate, or alternatively of floor space relating to the respective uses. Other methods of apportionment will be considered as part of a claim.

SPECIFIC CASES

19 Some types of communal or institutional building are used neither as dwellings nor for commercial purposes. The legislation therefore outlines how these are classified for the purposes of relief, specifically *including* some such buildings within the definition of "dwelling" (section 92B(2)) and specifically *excluding* others (section 92B(3)). If they do not fall within any of the specific categories of section 92B(3), most residential institutions will come within section 92B(2)(*d*) and will be treated as dwellings by default.

20 Categories of building use specifically included within the definition of "use as a dwelling" (so that transfers of such buildings only qualify for relief if the consideration does not exceed £150,000) (section 92B(2)) are—

(a) residential accommodation for school pupils, for example accommodation blocks in boarding schools;
(b) residential accommodation for students, other than that within section 92B(3)(*b*). Student accommodation provided by private landlords is 'a dwelling', as is accommodation leased to students by universities or colleges in flats or houses rather than in halls of residence (see section 92B(3)(*b*));
(c) residential accommodation for members of any of the armed forces, including accommodation for their families (section 92B(2)(*c*));

(d) an institution that is the sole or main residence of at least 90% of its residents and does not fall within any of the categories referred to in section 92B(3) (see section 92B(2)(*d*) and also paragraph 21 below). This would include, for example,
- sheltered accommodation for the elderly where no nursing or personal care is provided
- accommodation for religious communities (subject to the rules regarding mixed use; see paragraphs 17 and 18).

21 Categories of building use specifically excluded from the definition of 'use as a dwelling' (so that transfers of such buildings in a disadvantaged area will qualify for unlimited relief) (section 92B(3)) are—

(a) a home or other institution providing residential accommodation for children;
(b) a hall of residence for students in further or higher education. This is not defined in the legislation but in practice property provided by a university or similar establishment will be judged on the facts (number of inhabitants, type of facilities, availability of communal areas);
(c) a home or other institution providing residential accommodation with personal care for persons in need of personal care by reason of old age, disablement, past or present dependence on alcohol or drugs or past or present mental disorder;
(d) a hospital or hospice;
(e) a prison or similar establishment, or
(f) a hotel or inn or similar establishment.

22 The specific inclusions and exclusions set out in paragraphs 20 and 21 above apply not only to a building's actual use at the date of the transfer, but to the uses for which it is suitable at that date. Where, however, a building is being put to one of the non-residential uses specified in section 92B(3), this overrides any suitability for another use (section 92B(4)). For example, a building used as a children's home may also be suitable for use as a school boarding house, but this will not preclude a claim to unlimited relief.

23 Where a vacant building is suitable for at least one of the uses specified in section 92B(2) and at least one specified in section 92B(3), the tiebreaker in section 92B(5) determines, for the purposes of the relief, the use for which it is "most suitable". Whether or not a vacant building has one or more uses for which it is most suitable is a question of fact. Evidence supporting such uses should be provided with the claim for relief.

24 Where there is a single use for which a building is most suitable, the fact that it is also suitable for another use will be discounted.

25 If there are a number of uses for which a building is most suitable and they all come within either of the two subsections, any other use for which the building is suitable will be discounted.

26 Where no most suitable use can be shown, the default will be to classify the building as residential property and apply the £150,000 limit.

27 Land and buildings that are not suitable for any use at the date of execution will be treated as residential property if they are "in the process of being constructed or adapted for such use"- see paragraphs 28 and 29 below.

PROCESS OF BEING CONSTRUCTED OR ADAPTED FOR USE AS A DWELLING

28 Undeveloped land is in essence non-residential, but land may be "residential property" for the purposes of disadvantaged areas relief if a residential building is being built on it at the date the instrument is executed. The process of construction is taken as commencing when the builders first start work. A development of six or more dwellings is deemed to be non-residential under regulation 6 of the Regulations, even if in the process of construction at the date of the instrument (see paragraph 35 below).

29 Where (at the date the relevant instrument is executed) an existing building is being adapted for, or restored to, domestic use, it is "residential property" for the purposes of the relief. This may apply, for example, where a derelict building is being made fit for habitation, or where a previously non-residential building is being converted to a dwelling. Again, the process is taken as commencing when the builders start work.

THE GARDEN OR GROUNDS OF A BUILDING USED ETC. AS A DWELLING

30 Section 92B(1)(*b*) includes within the definition of residential property "land that is or forms part of the garden or grounds of a building within paragraph (*a*) (including any building or structure on such land)". The test HMRC will apply is similar to that applied for the purposes of the capital gains tax relief for main residences (section 222(3) of the Taxation of Chargeable Gains Act 1992). The land will include that which is needed for the reasonable enjoyment of the dwelling having regard to the size and nature of the dwelling.

31 A caravan or houseboat is not a "building" for this purpose.

32 Commercial farmland is not within the definition of residential property. A farmhouse situated on agricultural land would be dealt with under the mixed use provisions (paragraphs 17 and 18 above).

33 Outhouses on land within the section 92B(1)(*b*) definition will also be "residential property" unless it can be demonstrated that they have a specific non-residential purpose. Where a distinct non-residential use can be demonstrated, the mixed use provisions will apply.

INTEREST IN OR RIGHTS OVER RESIDENTIAL PROPERTY

34 The treatment of interests in, or rights over, land or buildings for the purposes of disadvantaged areas relief will follow that of the land or buildings to which they relate.

SIX OR MORE SEPARATE DWELLINGS TRANSFERRED BY SINGLE CONTRACT

35 The Regulations provide that "where there is a single contract for the conveyance, transfer or lease of land comprising or including six or more separate dwellings, none of that land counts as residential property . . . " Accordingly the transaction will qualify for unlimited relief. This recognises that commercial developers and institutional landlords, for example, frequently deal in numerous properties at one time. The fact that those properties may individually be "residential property" does not detract from the inherently commercial nature of the transaction itself.

36 To qualify as "separate", the dwellings must be self-contained. So for example, flats within a block, sharing some common areas but each with their own amenities, will qualify as separate dwellings. Rooms let within a house will not constitute separate dwellings if tenants share amenities such as a kitchen and bathroom.

37 A transaction in respect of six or more such dwellings must be carried out by means of a single contract in order to qualify for relief. Several instruments may however be presented for stamping if the properties are held under separate title.

38 Qualifying multiple transactions will be treated as non-residential property for the purposes of relief, even where the proportionate consideration for individual dwellings exceeds the £150,000 limit for residential property. It is not a condition of relief that multiple transactions comprise only dwellings.

39 The fact that some of the six or more dwellings within the single contract are outside a designated disadvantaged area will not prevent them from constituting a non-residential transaction. However relief will only be available for the portion of the land situated within the disadvantaged area.

PROPERTY ONLY PARTLY WITHIN A DISADVANTAGED AREA

40 Schedule 30 to Finance Act 2001, together with the Regulations, determines how property situated partly within and partly outside a designated disadvantaged area is to be treated for the purposes of the relief. Such cases are relatively rare in practice. Queries may be referred to Inland Revenue (Stamp Taxes) for guidance.

LEASE DUTY

41 Relief is also available from duty on the rental element of new leases executed on or after 10 April 2003. Rental leases of residential property shall be eligible for relief where the average annual rent is no more than £15,000 and/ or where any premium does not exceed £150,000. For non- residential property, full relief is available for the rental element of leases as well as for any premium.

OTHER ISSUES

42 The extended relief applies to documents executed on or after 10 April 2003, irrespective of whether the contract was entered into before or after that date. There is no scope to reclaim stamp duty already paid in respect of transfers executed on or before 9 April 2003.

FLOW CHART TO DETERMINE WHETHER PROPERTY IS OR IS NOT 'RESIDENTIAL PROPERTY'

Is the subject of the conveyance/transfer/lease . . .

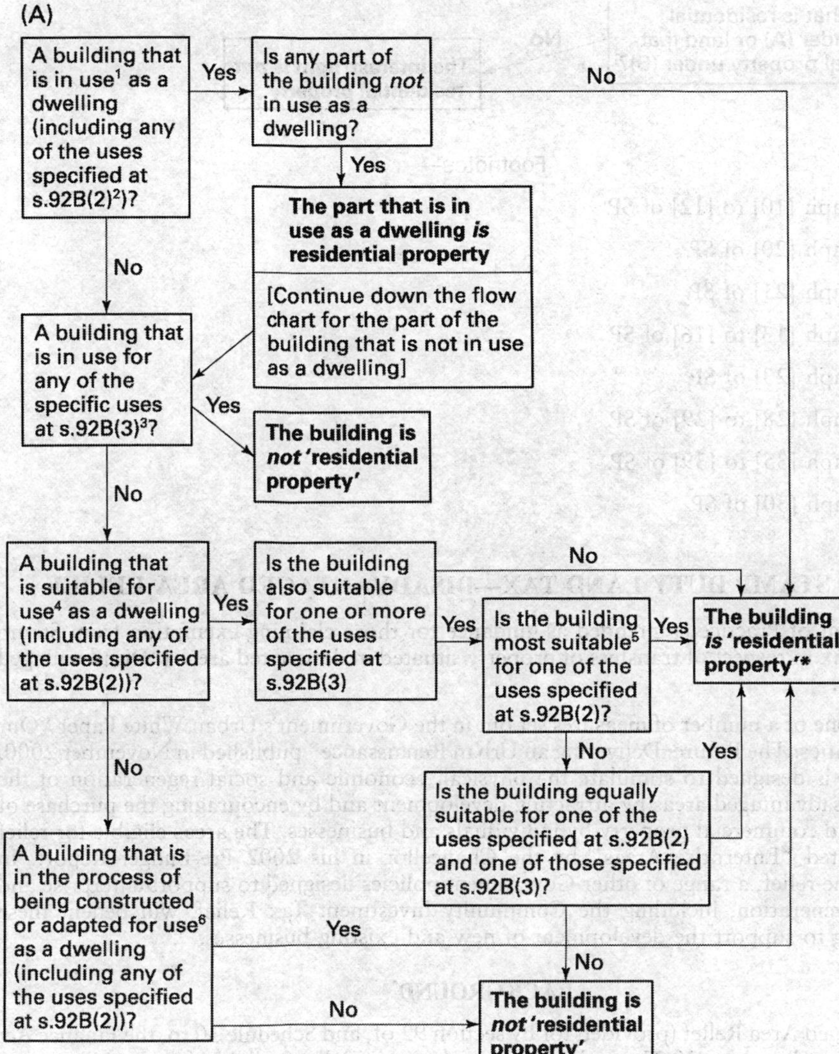

*unless the conveyance, transfer or lease comprises or includes six or more separate dwellings[7] made persuant to a single contract, in which circumstances none of the land will be 'residential property'

Is the subject of the conveyance/transfer/lease . . .

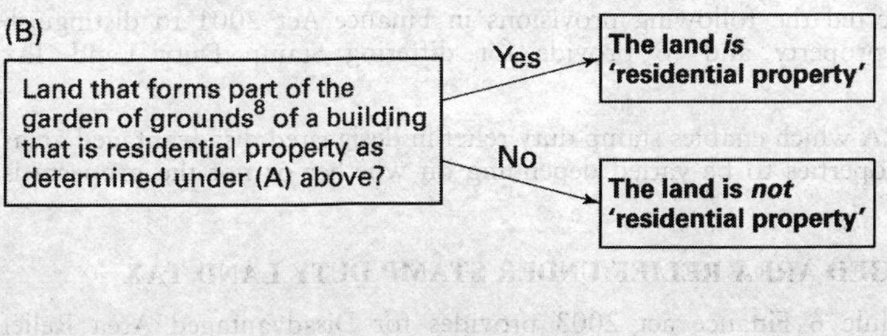

(C)

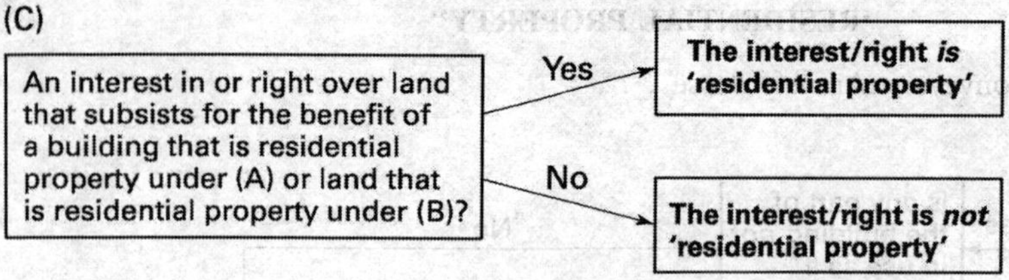

Footnotes—

1 See paragraph [10] to [12] of SP.

2 See paragraph [20] of SP.

3 See paragraph [21] of SP.

4 See paragraph [13] to [16] of SP.

5 See paragraph [23] of SP.

6 See paragraph [28] to [29] of SP.

7 See paragraph [35] to [39] of SP.

8 See paragraph [30] of SP.

SP 1/04 STAMP DUTY LAND TAX—DISADVANTAGED AREA RELIEF

This Statement of Practice is intended as guidance for those claiming exemption from Stamp Duty Land Tax in respect of transfers of property situated in designated areas ("Disadvantaged Area Relief").

The relief is one of a number of measures set out in the Government's Urban White Paper "Our Towns and Cities: The Future: Delivering an Urban Renaissance" published in November 2000. The measure is designed to stimulate the physical, economic and social regeneration of the UK's most disadvantaged areas by attracting development and by encouraging the purchase of residential and commercial property by individuals and businesses. The areas eligible for relief were designated "Enterprise Areas" by the Chancellor in his 2002 Pre-Budget Report. In addition to the relief, a range of other Government policies designed to support enterprise and economic regeneration, including the Community Investment Tax Relief, will benefit these areas, helping to support the development of new and existing businesses.

BACKGROUND

1 Disadvantaged Area Relief (provided for by section 92 of, and Schedule 30 to, the Finance Act 2001) was introduced on 30 November 2001 and was initially available for conveyances or transfers on sale (of both residential and commercial property) for which the consideration did not exceed £150,000. Stamp duty in respect of conveyances or transfers of commercial property in disadvantaged areas was abolished in consequence of the Stamp Duty (Disadvantaged Areas) (Application of Exemptions) Regulations 2003 ("the Regulations"), which have effect in relation to instruments executed on or after 10 April 2003. Thereafter the £150,000 limit applies only in relation to residential property.

2 Finance Act 2002 inserted the following provisions in Finance Act 2001 to distinguish residential from other property and to provide for differing Stamp Duty Land Tax exemptions—

– FA 2001 Section 92A which enables stamp duty relief in designated disadvantaged areas in respect of all properties to be varied depending on whether or not the property is "residential".

DISADVANTAGED AREA RELIEF UNDER STAMP DUTY LAND TAX

3 Section 57 and Schedule 6 Finance act 2003 provides for Disadvantaged Area Relief under Stamp Duty Land Tax.

4 The definition of residential property under Stamp Duty Land Tax is provided at section 116 FA 2003. Non-residential property is therefore defined in the Act by exclusion. Section 116 also sets out particular building uses that are specifically included within, or specifically excluded from, the definition.

5 In most cases there will be no difficulty in practice in establishing whether or not a property is "residential". This statement sets out in more detail the Stamp Office's approach to borderline cases and gives guidance on the practical application of the legislation. The annexed flowchart provides a quick guide for simpler cases as to whether property constitutes "residential property".

CLAIMING THE RELIEF

6 The way in which relief is claimed is different under Stamp Duty Land Tax.

FA 2003 Section 76 requires that most land transactions, including those that qualify for Disadvantaged Area Relief, must be notified to HMRC on a Land Transaction Return Form (SDLT 1).

7 Relief is claimed by simply completing a box within this form. Certificates of Value are no longer required and no supporting evidence or documentation is required at this point. Once the return has been submitted and we are satisfied with the information provided, the purchaser is issued with a certificate which they must present with documents when applying for registration of title at Land Registry, Registers of Scotland or Land Registry of Northern Ireland.

8 FA 2003 Schedule 10 Part 3 gives HMRC the power to enquire into a Land Transaction Return. These provisions permit HMRC to open an enquiry into any aspect of a Land Transaction Return, including claims to reliefs.

Appropriate contemporaneous evidence should be retained to support any claim to the relief. There is no need to create records that would otherwise not be available. Estate agents' specifications, site plans, planning applications or permissions, marketing material, photographs and print outs of an internet post code search may all provide relevant information should there be an enquiry into a land tax return.

9 As with all claims the onus is on the purchaser to check whether or not the relief is due.

THE MEANING OF RESIDENTIAL PROPERTY

10 FA 2003 Section 116(1) defines "residential property" as a building which:

– is used as a dwelling,
– or is suitable for use as a dwelling,
– or is in the process of being constructed or adapted for such use.

If a property meets any one of these separate tests it will be treated as residential property and be subject to the £150,000 limit for relief, as will any garden or grounds belonging to it or any interests or rights attaching to it. Each element of the definition is considered in turn below. The question of whether and to what extent a building and grounds are defined as residential property for stamp duty purposes may also have implications for its treatment for capital gains tax and local authority rates.

USE AS A DWELLING

11 Where a building is in use at the effective date of the transaction it will be a question of fact whether and to what extent it is used as a dwelling.

Use at the effective date overrides any past or intended future uses for this purpose. For example, a purchaser is buying a house with the intention to refurbish it to create, in its place, an alternative therapy treatment centre. For the purposes of the relief the house in considered to be a dwelling because it was suitable for that use at the effective date of the transaction. (For another example see paragraph 34)

12 Where the property in question is in use as a dwelling at the effective date of the transaction, it is residential property for the purposes of the relief unless it is part of a multiple transaction qualifying for relief under FA 2003 s 116(7) (see paragraphs 40 to 44 below).

13 There is no motive test applicable to the usage of land or buildings, so where a residential property is purchased with the owner intending to use it as a non-residential business the building is considered residential, under the suitability test, for the purposes of the relief.

14 For the treatment of buildings put to both residential and non-residential use, see paragraphs 19 and 20 below.

SUITABLE FOR USE AS A DWELLING

15 The suitability test applies to the state of the building at the effective date of the transaction, having regard to the facilities available and any history of use. For example, HMRC will not regard an office block as "suitable for use as a dwelling", but a house which has been used as an office without particular adaptation may well be so.

16 If a building is not in use at the effective date of the transaction but its last use was as a dwelling, it will be taken to be "suitable for use as a dwelling" and treated as residential property for the purposes of the relief, unless evidence is produced to the contrary (see paragraph 17).

17 Whether a building is suitable for use as a dwelling will depend upon the precise facts and circumstances. The simple removal of, for example, a bathroom suite or kitchen facilities will not be regarded as rendering a building unsuitable for use as a dwelling. Where it is claimed that a previously residential property is no longer suitable for use as a dwelling, perhaps because it is derelict or has been substantially altered, the claimant will need to provide evidence that this is the case. See also paragraph 34.

18 Where a building has been used partly for residential purposes and partly for another purpose, its overall suitability for use as a dwelling will be judged from the facilities available at the effective date of the transaction. For example, if two rooms of a house were in use as a dentist's surgery and waiting room at the effective date of the transaction, HMRC would nevertheless normally consider this property suitable for use as a dwelling unless the claimant provided evidence to the contrary. A building that is used only partly as a dwelling may nevertheless be suitable for use wholly as a dwelling, with the effect that the £150,000 limit applies to the whole of the consideration. Where only a distinct part of the building is used and suitable for use as a dwelling, that part will be residential property for the purposes of the relief and the mixed use provisions will apply (See paragraphs 19 and 20 below).

MIXED USE

19 Where only part of a building (and land or interest relating to it) is "residential property" within section 116(1), the consideration "shall be apportioned on such basis as is just and reasonable" between the residential and non-residential elements. The £150,000 limit is then applied only to the residential portion (Schedule 6 FA 2003). For example:

A property situated wholly within a disadvantaged area is bought for:

(a) £200,000
(b) £400,000

50% of the property is "residential property" on the basis of a just and reasonable apportionment.

In these examples:

(a) £100,000 is attributed to the residential property element, so relief is due. The part of the land that is not residential property is also exempt. So no duty is payable.
(b) the £200,000 attributed to the residential property element is not exempt, because of Schedule 6 paragraph 6, but attracts duty at the rate of 1% (Stamp Duty Land Tax payable £2,000). The non-residential property element is exempt as above.

Where a transaction involves six or more mixed use properties, under S116(7) FA 2003, providing certain conditions are met, the residential element is exempt and no Stamp Duty Land Tax is payable. See paragraphs 40 to 44.

20 The "just and reasonable" test is necessarily subjective, and each case will be considered on its merits. Apportionment might be on the basis of the percentage areas quoted in planning applications, where appropriate, or alternatively of floor space relating to the respective uses. Other methods of apportionment will be considered as part of a claim.

SPECIFIC CASES

21 Some types of communal or institutional building are used neither as dwellings nor for commercial purposes. The legislation therefore outlines how these are classified for the purposes of relief, specifically including some such buildings within the definition of "dwelling" (section 116(2)) and specifically excluding others (section 116(3)). If they do not fall within any of the specific categories of section 116(3), most residential institutions will come within section 116(2)(d) and will be treated as dwellings by default.

22 Categories of building use specifically included within the definition of "use as a dwelling" (so that transfers of such buildings only qualify for relief if the consideration does not exceed £150,000) (section 116(2)) are:

(a) residential accommodation for school pupils, for example accommodation blocks in boarding schools;
(b) residential accommodation for students, other than that within section 116(3)(b). Student accommodation provided by private landlords is "a dwelling", as is accommodation leased to students by universities or colleges in flats or houses rather than in halls of residence (see section 116(3)(b));
(c) residential accommodation for members of any of the armed forces, including accommodation for their families (section 116(2)(c));
(d) an institution that is the sole or main residence of at least 90% of its residents and does not fall within any of the categories referred to in section 116(3) (see section 116(2)(d) and also paragraph 23 below).

This would include, for example:

– sheltered accommodation for the elderly where no nursing or personal care is provided. An example of this would be where an elderly person purchases a home on a warden-assisted housing development.
– accommodation for religious communities (subject to the rules regarding mixed use; see paragraphs 19 and 20).

23 Categories of building use specifically excluded from the definition of "use as a dwelling" (so that transfers of such buildings in a disadvantaged area will qualify for unlimited relief) (section 116(3)) are:

(a) a home or other institution providing residential accommodation for children;
(b) a hall of residence for students in further or higher education. This is not defined in the legislation but in practice property provided by a university or similar establishment will be judged on the facts (number of inhabitants, type of facilities, availability of communal areas);
(c) a home or other institution providing residential accommodation with personal care for persons in need of personal care by reason of old age, disablement, past or present dependence on alcohol or drugs or past or present mental disorder (for example, an institution that provides accommodation as part of a wider care service such as residential care homes or residential drug treatment centres);
(d) a hospital or hospice;
(e) a prison or similar establishment, or
(f) a hotel or inn or similar establishment.

BED AND BREAKFASTS/GUEST HOUSES

24 Each case will be taken on its merits, however, paragraph 25 below provides general examples of the treatment of B&Bs/guest houses.

25 A property providing a Bed and Breakfast (B&B) service, which has amenities installed in each room such as bathing facilities, telephone lines etc and is available all year round as the rooms do not need any further adaptation, would be considered non residential for the purposes of the relief. Example—

– Mr and Mrs Boyd run a bed and breakfast in a disadvantaged area of Blackpool. They live on the premises and it is open all year round but trade declines during the winter months. Under section 116(3) FA 2003, the Boyd's B&B is a "hotel or inn or similar establishment" and is therefore not used as a dwelling.
– Mrs Leaver lives in Southwest London and lets out two spare rooms on a B&B basis during the fortnight of the Wimbledon tennis tournament. She doesn't make any

adaptations to the rooms other than the removal of some of her personal items. For the purposes of the relief Mrs Leaver's property is, at all times, considered to be in use as and suitable for use as a dwelling.

26 Buy-to-let properties suitable for use as a dwelling are residential unless they are a development of six or more dwellings whereby they would be non-residential under S116(7).

27 The specific inclusions and exclusions set out in paragraphs 22 and 23 above apply not only to a building's actual use at the effective date of the transaction, but to the uses for which it is suitable at that date. Where, however, a building is being put to one of the non-residential uses specified in section 116(3), this overrides any suitability for another use (section 116(4)). For example, a building used as a children's home may also be suitable for use as a school boarding house, but this will not preclude a claim to unlimited relief.

28 Where a vacant building is suitable for at least one of the uses specified in section 116(2) and at least one specified in section 116(3), section 116(5) determines, for the purposes of the relief, the use for which it is "most suitable". Whether or not a vacant building has one or more uses for which it is most suitable is a question of fact. Evidence supporting such uses should be retained.

29 Where there is a single use for which a building is most suitable, the fact that it is also suitable for another use will be discounted.

30 If there are a number of uses for which a building is most suitable and they all come within either of the two subsections, any other use for which the building is suitable will be discounted.

31 Where no most suitable use can be shown, the default will be to classify the building as residential property and apply the £150,000 limit.

32 Land and buildings that are not suitable for any use at the effective date of the transaction will be treated as residential property if they are "in the process of being constructed or adapted for such use"—see paragraphs 33 and 34 below.

PROCESS OF BEING CONSTRUCTED OR ADAPTED FOR USE AS A DWELLING

33 Undeveloped land is in essence non-residential, but land may be "residential property" for the purposes of Disadvantaged Area Relief if a residential building is being built on it at the effective date of the transaction. A development of six or more dwellings is deemed to be non-residential under S116(7), even if in the process of construction or marketing has not at the effective date of the transaction (see paragraph 40).

34 Where (at the effective date of the transaction) an existing building is being adapted for, marketed for, or restored to, domestic use, it is residential for the purposes of the relief. The process is taken as commencing when the developer begins marketing the properties for sale or starts physical work on the site which ever is earlier.

This may apply, for example, where a derelict building is being made fit for habitation, or where a previously non-residential building is being converted to a dwelling. For example:

Kristian is buying an apartment, in what will be a converted church, off-plan. The sale is completed on 15th March 2004, the properties were marketed for sale on 3 January 2004 and work on converting the church commenced on 2nd February 2004. For the purposes of this transaction the church is considered to be a dwelling, even though it has yet to be fully converted, from 3rd January. If the consideration is greater than £150,000 Kristian will have to pay the appropriate rate of Stamp Duty Land Tax.

In the above example the developer that initially purchased the church will have bought it as a non-residential property regardless of the intention to turn the building into residential units.

THE GARDEN OR GROUNDS OF A BUILDING USED ETC AS A DWELLING

35 Section 116(1)(*b*) includes within the definition of residential property "land that is or forms part of the garden or grounds of a building within paragraph (*a*) (including any building or structure on such land)". The test HMRC will apply is similar to that applied for the purposes of the capital gains tax relief for main residences (section 222(3) of the Taxation of Chargeable Gains Act 1992). The land will include that which is needed for the reasonable enjoyment of the dwelling having regard to the size and nature of the dwelling.

36 A caravan or houseboat is not a "building" for this purpose.

37 Commercial farmland is not within the definition of residential property. A farmhouse situated on agricultural land would be dealt with under the mixed use provisions (paragraphs 19 and 20 above).

It may often be the case that farmhouses will occupy only a small fraction of the total land and will therefore, when apportioned, fall below the £150,000 consideration limit thus attracting the residential relief.

38 Outhouses on land within the section 116(1)(b) definition will also be "residential property" unless it can be demonstrated that they have a specific non-residential purpose. Where a distinct non-residential use can be demonstrated, the mixed use provisions will apply.

INTEREST IN OR RIGHTS OVER RESIDENTIAL PROPERTY

39 The treatment of interests in, or rights over, land or buildings for the purposes of Disadvantaged Area Relief will follow that of the land or buildings to which they relate.

SIX OR MORE SEPARATE DWELLINGS TRANSFERRED BY A SINGLE TRANSACTION

40 Section 116(7) FA 2003 provides that "where six or more separate dwellings are the subject of a single transaction involving the transfer of a major interest in, or the grant of a lease over, them, then . . . those dwellings are treated as not being residential property". This recognises that commercial developers and institutional landlords, for example, frequently deal in numerous properties at one time. The fact that those properties may individually be "residential property" does not detract from the inherently commercial nature of the transaction itself.

41 To qualify as "separate", the dwellings must be self-contained. So for example, flats within a block, sharing some common areas but each with their own amenities will qualify as separate dwellings. Rooms let within a house will not constitute separate dwellings if tenants share amenities such as a kitchen and bathroom.

42 A transaction in respect of six or more such dwellings must be carried out by means of a single transaction in order to qualify for relief.

43 Qualifying multiple transactions will be treated as non-residential property for the purposes of relief, even where the proportionate consideration for individual dwellings exceeds the £150,000 limit for residential property. It is not a condition of relief that multiple transactions comprise only dwellings. One example of this would be where a purchaser is buying eight houses and four shops. Mixed use properties, such as pubs with self-contained residential accommodation, are also treated as non-residential.

44 The fact that some of the six or more dwellings within the single transaction are outside a designated disadvantaged area will not prevent them from constituting a non-residential transaction. However relief will only be available for the portion of the land situated within the disadvantaged area.

PROPERTY ONLY PARTLY WITHIN A DISADVANTAGED AREA

45 Schedule 6, Part 3, FA 2003 determines how property situated partly within and partly outside a designated disadvantaged area is to be treated for the purposes of the relief. Such cases are relatively rare in practice. Queries may be referred to Inland Revenue (Stamp Taxes) for guidance.

GRANTS OF NEW LEASES

46 FA 2003 Schedule 6 Part 2 deals with the charge to Stamp Duty Land Tax on the grant of a new lease.

Land all non-residential

47 If all of the land is non-residential it is exempt from any charge to Stamp Duty Land Tax.

Land all residential

48 The general rule is that:

(a) if the premium (and any other consideration than rent) does not exceed £150,000 then this is exempt from Stamp Duty Land Tax, and
(b) if the "net present value" of the rental payments does not exceed £150,000 then this is exempt from Stamp Duty Land Tax.

"Net present value" is, broadly speaking, the total rental payments due under the lease, discounted to reflect the fact that future rental payments are of less value than current rental payments. There is a tool for calculating net present value on the HMRC website. There is a special rule where the average annual rent exceeds £600. In such a case there is no relief or exemption for any premium. Any premium, however small, will be charged at 1% (or at higher rates if it exceeds £250,000).

49 Where there is mixed use apportionment is applied. The non-residential portion is exempt from lease duty.

If the consideration includes rent and the relevant rental value does not exceed £150,000, the rent does not count as chargeable consideration.

50 If the consideration includes consideration other than rent then:

(a) If the annual rent does not exceed £600 and the relevant consideration does not exceed £150,000, the consideration other than rent does not count as chargeable consideration
(b) If the annual rent exceeds £600, the consideration other than rent is counted as chargeable consideration

The "annual rent" is the average annual rent over the term of the lease.

FURTHER RESOURCES

Information can be found on our website, which also contains:

– A postcode search tool [www.hmrc.gov.uk/so/dar/dar-search.htm] to help identify whether a property falls within a disadvantaged area, and
– an intelligent decision-maker [www.hmrc.gov.uk/so/decisionmaker2.pdf] to help you decide whether a property is residential or non-residential.
– a lease duty calculator [http://ldcalculator.inlandrevenue.gov.uk/] which provides the amount of Stamp Duty Land Tax payable on a lease transaction.

Stamp Taxes

Stamp Taxes
HMRC Interpretations

Note—This Interpretation was published in HMRC's *Tax Bulletin*. HMRC state that the Interpretations will normally be applied in relevant cases, but that this is subject to a number of qualifications. Particular cases may turn on their own facts or context and there may be circumstances in which an Interpretation will not apply. There may also be circumstances in which the Board would find it necessary to argue for a different Interpretation in appeal proceedings.

The number before the interpretation (ie RI 174) does not appear in the Tax Bulletin. It has been added by the publishers to facilitate identification for the purpose of cross references.

Please note that references to the 'Inland Revenue' should now be considered as referring to 'HM Revenue and Customs' and references to the 'Board of the Inland Revenue' should be read as the 'Commissioners for HM Revenue and Customs'.

RI 174 (AUGUST 1997) STAMP DUTY LITIGATION

PARINV (HATFIELD) LTD V IRC [1996] STC 933—OFF-SHORE DECLARATION OF TRUST INEFFECTIVE TO AVOID AD VALOREM DUTY ON SUBSEQUENT TRANSFERS

This case concerned the effectiveness of an off-shore declaration of trust in avoiding ad valorem stamp duty on subsequent transfers. The High Court held that the device was ineffective. The taxpayer has lodged an appeal. In the meantime, the Stamp Office will continue to apply the law on the basis of the High Court's decision.

In the Parinv case, the taxpayer sought to rely on a copy of an unstamped overseas document to argue that the Stamp Office should stamp a transfer of property to a purchaser at 50p rather than 1%, on the basis that the transfer transferred only bare legal title and that the equitable interest in the property was transferred by the unstamped document. This argument was rejected by the Court on the grounds that the unstamped document was not admissible as evidence, in view of the Stamp Act 1891 s 14(4).

UNSTAMPED DOCUMENTS—INLAND REVENUE PRACTICE

Following enquiries from customers, the Revenue has decided to publicise its current practice with regard to unstamped documents. Under the terms of Stamp Act 1891 s 14(4)—

"an instrument executed in any part of the United Kingdom, or relating wheresoever executed, to any property situate, or to any matter or thing done or to be done, in any part of the United Kingdom, shall not, except in criminal proceedings, be given in evidence, or be available for any purpose whatever, unless it is duly stamped in accordance with the law in force at the time when it was first executed".

It has been the Revenue's view that an unstamped document cannot be offered in evidence in any legal proceedings other than criminal proceedings, and that this includes hearings before the Special or General Commissioners. Following the case of *Parinv (Hatfield) Ltd v IRC*, the Revenue's current practice will be as follows.

In the *Parinv* case, the Revenue argued that an unstamped instrument was itself excluded from being used in civil proceedings, a view accepted by Lindsay J. Furthermore he took the view that a true copy, sometimes called a conformed copy, of an original unstamped document cannot be used to provide information or material or evidence of the original to the court.

The court then went on to consider the Revenue's position in connection with copy documents. In his analysis of Stamp Act 1891 s 14(4) Lindsay J considered the words "shall not . . . be available for any purpose whatever". He indicated that these words were not an absolute prohibition because this would prevent an unstamped document being examined even in order to determine what should be the appropriate stamp. The Court referred to a judgement in an earlier case and endorsed the view that the words mean that one person cannot compel another person to rely on and accept an unstamped document.

The Revenue in addition, argued that it was able to look at the copy document with the purpose of establishing the liability to duty of another document. The Court held that because the taxpayer is obliged by s 5 of the Act to provide all facts and circumstances affecting the liability to duty of a document including all such evidence deemed necessary by the Board to form a view if adjudication or assessment is required, the Revenue was not obliged by the Act to exclude from its consideration the contents of a copy of an unstamped document which had been supplied to it in order to meet that obligation. It was unlikely that Parliament would have imposed a fine for non-disclosure (ie a fraudulent act) and yet required the Revenue to ignore the disclosure. So the Revenue can have regard to a document for the purpose of an assessment of duty. But that does not compel the Revenue to go any further.

The Revenue is aware that documents executed overseas are frequently retained there with a view to deferral or avoidance of payment of stamp duty. It will not be the Revenue's practice to request sight of original documents in these or other circumstances, merely to check whether they have been duly stamped or not. However, if the documents are to be relied on by a person in support of any claim to relief, or otherwise used in evidence in relation to any liability to tax, or the amount thereof, that person should be aware that the Revenue cannot be compelled to accept in support of such claim or as evidence unstamped original or conformed unstamped copies of documents.

PENALTY FOR FRAUD

Stamp Act 1891 s 5 requires that all the facts and circumstances affecting the liability of an instrument to duty, or the amount of the duty chargeable, shall be fully and truly set forth in the instrument, and that any failure to do so by the parties or their advisers with intent to defraud the Crown, shall attract a fine. The Stamp Office takes the view that a failure to disclose the fact that the parties are attempting to rely on an unstamped instrument, contrary to Stamp Act 1891 s 14(4) in executing a transfer which purports to convey the bare legal estate, will constitute a breach of s 5, and appropriate action will be taken.

The Stamp Office also takes the view that any attempt by the parties to an instrument containing a certificate under the exempt instruments legislation which relied on another instrument executed overseas which was not duly stamped, would constitute a breach of s 5.

LM TENANCIES 1 PLC V IRC [1996] STC 880—CONSIDERATION CALCULATED IN ACCORDANCE WITH A FORMULA ASCERTAINED BY APPLICATION OF CONTINGENCY PRINCIPLE

This case concerned the application of the contingency principle. The High Court held that where the calculation of duty relied on a future value, (the price of a gilt some time after execution of the document) the Stamp Office could rely on the last published figure.

The taxpayer has lodged an appeal against this decision. In the meantime the Stamp Office will apply the law on the basis of the Court's decision, subject to the normal right of appeal in any individual case. On that basis, duty is payable on an ascertainable amount where the contingency principle can be applied in the way outlined above.

The Stamp Office is of the view that the contingency principle, as it was held to apply in this case, will apply to other reference values which are unknown at the date of execution. An example is the practice of making future rent increases subject to an increase in an index, typically the RPI. The Stamp Office will apply the published increase in RPI over the twelve months prior to execution of the lease or agreement for lease to calculate the average annual rent.

Where the contingency principle does not apply, FA 1994 s 242 now provides that where the consideration for an interest in land is unascertainable, ad valorem stamp duty is chargeable on the basis of the value of the property conveyed.

Commentary—*Simon's Taxes* **I3.602**.

Stamp Taxes
Press releases etc

Contents

Press releases, etc

STAMP DUTY ON LEASES

2 January 1963. *Controller of Stamps*

THE BASIS OF ASSESSMENT

The Revenue have recently given consideration to the basis of assessment of duty on leases which contain one or more of the following provisions:

(a) a known rent not exceeding £100 pa and a further unascertainable rent;
(b) a term commencing from a date prior to the date of execution;
(c) a rent or rents fixed for part only of the term, the rent for the remainder of the term to be agreed subsequently.

The question under consideration in regard to leases of type (*a*) . . . [NB This question was rendered obsolete by FA 1963, which repealed FA 1947 s 54(2).]

In regard to leases of type (*b*) the Board's view is that, in computing the length of the term, any period prior to the date of the lease is to be left out of account on the authority of *Shaw v Kay* (1847) 1 Ex 412, *Cadogan v Guiness* (1936) Ch 515, and *Colton v Becollda Property Investments Ltd* [1950] 1 KB 216. These cases do not, however, provide any authority as to the treatment of rent payable in respect of a period prior to the date of the lease: for the sake of consistency and simplicity, the Board have decided that such rent shall be left out of account, so that the treatment approved by the courts in relation to the term will in practice also be applied to the rent. This means, in effect, a continuation of existing practice, although this practice may not have been applied consistently in individual cases in the past.

Leases of type (*c*) . . .

Note—The treatment of leases of type (c) no longer applies: see Revenue Bulletin (August 1995).

GRANTS OF REPRESENTATION

28 February 1978. *Practice Direction of the Principal Registry of the Family Division*

1 Where, for the purposes of applying for a grant of representation, it is necessary for the applicant to produce to the Principal or a District Probate Registry an original deed or other instrument, it is the practice of the Registry to examine the instrument to ensure that it has been properly executed and duly stamped under SA 1891 before proceeding with the application. Where there is any doubt whether the instrument is duly stamped, the applicant will be asked to present the instrument to the Controller of Stamps (Inland Revenue) for adjudication before the issue of the grant.

2 To avoid delay in the issue of the grant in such cases, the Commissioners of Inland Revenue have agreed that the applicant may, if so desired, submit the original instrument to the Adjudication Section of the Office of the Controller of Stamps for preliminary noting, endorsement and return, providing that a written undertaking is at the same time given to the Controller by the solicitor applying for the grant of representation that he will, on or immediately after the issue of the grant, re-submit the original instrument to the Controller for formal adjudication and pay the stamp duty (if any) to which the instrument is adjudged liable.

3 In every case on the application for a grant, the original instrument (after inspection) will be returned as soon as practicable to the applicant, or his solicitor, by the probate registry. Practitioners are reminded, however, that where the application is for a grant to an assignee or assignees under the Non-Contentious Probate Rules 1954 Rule 22, a copy of the original instrument of assignment must be lodged in the registry (see Rule 22(3)).

STAMP DUTY: PURCHASE BY A COMPANY OF ITS OWN SHARES

1 May 1984. *Inland Revenue*

In reply to a Parliamentary Question the Financial Secretary to the Treasury gave the following Written Answer yesterday:

> "The Companies Act 1981 enables companies to purchase their own shares. A specific exemption from *ad valorem* stamp duty was not provided although it was intended that s 52 of the Act (Disclosure of Particulars of Purchase and Authorised Contracts) should effectively provide for this. Doubts have arisen as to whether s 52 achieved this objective.
>
> *Ad valorem* duty is payable on any conveyance or transfer on sale and SA 1891 s 54, provides that the expression 'conveyance on sale' includes every instrument whereby any property sold is transferred or vested in the purchaser. The Revenue are advised that although the matter is not free from doubt there are grounds for holding that this section does not apply when a company purchases its own shares. This is the view that the Board proposes to adopt. A Secretary or Registrar of a company may accordingly amend the register without requiring that any delivery statement is stamped with *ad valorem* duty.
>
> The Companies Act 1981 provides an exemption from capital duty for future re-issues of the repurchased shares."

NOTE

The Financial Secretary has clarified the stamp duty treatment on the purchase by a company of its own shares.

The Companies Act 1981 enabled companies to purchase their own shares. An exemption from capital duty was provided to cover any future issues of the cancelled shares but nothing was said in the Act about transfer duty. The Bill however was amended to remove the need for a document which would attract stamp duty. Doubts have arisen as to whether the amendments achieved their objective. The Financial Secretary has informed the House that the Revenue has been advised that although the position is not free from doubt there are grounds for holding that *ad valorem* duty is not payable. This is the view that the Revenue proposes to adopt.

[NB The Companies Act 1981 s 52 is now reproduced as the Companies Act 1985 s 169. Note that Form 169 is itself chargeable under FA 1986 s 66.]

STAMP DUTY ON SHARES TO BE ABOLISHED

20 March 1990. *Inland Revenue*

The Chancellor proposes in his Budget to abolish all stamp duties on transactions in shares from a date late in 1991–92 to coincide as far as possible with the introduction of paperless dealing under the Stock Exchange's new share transfer system ("TAURUS").

Abolition of these duties will also:

(a) enhance London's competitiveness as an international centre for equity trading;
(b) boost wider share ownership by reducing transaction costs and benefit savers.

This is the sixth major tax to be abolished since 1983. It makes a significant contribution to the overall simplification of the tax system and the reduction of compliance burdens on taxpayers.

DETAILS

Stamp duties on shares: main duties

1 The main duties to be abolished are:

(a) stamp duty on individual share transfers, which is levied on UK securities at a rate since 1986 of, broadly, 0·5 per cent of the price paid;
(b) stamp duty of 1·5 per cent, which is payable where UK shares are converted into depositary receipts ("ADRs") or transferred into clearance services;
(c) stamp duty reserve tax, which applies, at the same rates as stamp duty, to some share transactions which are outside the stamp duty net.

Stamp duties on shares: associated charges

2 Also to be abolished are:

(a) the stamp duty charges on bearer shares;

(b) the 50p fixed duty on share transfers other than sales;
(c) stamp duty on all transfers of units under a unit trust scheme.

Timing

3 Legislation to abolish these duties will be in the 1990 Finance Bill. The Chancellor proposes that abolition should be triggered by Treasury Order in due course. He has indicated that this Order will broadly coincide with the start of paperless trading under the Stock Exchange's planned TAURUS system—*ie* towards the end of 1991–92 on the current timetable [but see the Revenue Press Release of 19 December 1991]. Until then, duty continues to apply at the existing rates.

Effects of abolition

4 The Government believes abolition of these taxes will:
(a) smooth the path for cheaper and more efficient paperless share dealing, by removing the need for the systems involved to take account of stamp duty;
(b) increase the liquidity and efficiency of the London equity market, and maintain its competitiveness in the face of planned tax reductions in other financial centres;
(c) encourage investment in UK equities and so foster wider share ownership;
(d) benefit savers, including beneficiaries of pension funds and life policies;
(e) further simplify the tax system and ease the compliance burden on individual shareholders, the equity market and company registrars.

Cost

5 The timing means that no cost will arise until late in 1991–92. The cost that year will depend on precisely when the duty is abolished; a 1 January 1992 start would for example produce a 1991–92 cost of £120 million. The full year cost will be around £800 million.

Stamp duty on property

6 The Chancellor is not proposing to make any changes to the stamp duty on the transfer of land and property (including houses).

NOTES

Abolition of duties

1 This Government has already abolished
(a) In vestment income surcharge (1984);
(b) National insurance surcharge (1984);
(c) Development land tax (1985);
(d) the tax on lifetime gifts (1986);
(e) capital duty and the associated unit trust instrument duty (1988)

as well as a number of minor duties. Abolition of stamp duty on shares carries this process forward, making a significant contribution to the overall simplification of the tax system.

Stamp duty on shares

2 The *ad valorem* stamp duty on individual transfers of UK companies' shares is currently charged at 50p per £100 or part thereof, *ie* broadly at 0·5 per cent. There are exemptions for purchases by market-makers and charities. Government stock and most commercial loan capital are outside the scope of the charge.

3 Conversion of UK shares into depositary receipts ("ADRs") or their transfer into a clearance service attracts a 1·5 per cent "season ticket" charge—see para 8 below.

4 Bearer instruments are normally charged at 15 per cent on a once-and-for-all basis, either on issue (for instruments issued in the UK) or on their first transfer in Great Britain.

5 Certain transfers of shares otherwise than on sale can give rise to a fixed 50p charge—for example transfers where there is no change of beneficial ownership.

Stamp duty reserve tax

6 This tax was introduced in 1986 in order to broaden the base of stamp duty on shares, by charging a wider range of transactions. Stamp duty is a tax on *documents*, but stamp duty reserve tax applies to most *agreements* to sell UK securities. It therefore brings within the scope of the charge:

(a) the purchase and resale of a security within the same Stock Exchange account;
(b) the purchase of renounceable letters of allotment or acceptance;
(c) the purchase of shares registered in the name of a nominee acting for seller and purchaser;
(d) the purchase of shares which are resold before they are taken into the purchaser's name.

7 Stamp duty reserve tax on individual share transfers is charged at the same rate, 0·5 per cent, as stamp duty on shares. For conversion into ADR form etc there is again a 1·5 per cent charge to parallel the higher rate of stamp duty—see 8 below.

Depositary receipts and clearance services—the higher rate charges

8 Where shares are transferred into depositary receipt form or into a clearance service, the higher rate of 1·5 per cent stamp duty or stamp duty reserve tax applies on the initial transfer. This charge is in the nature of a "season ticket"—subsequent transfers of depositary receipts, or of shares within a clearance service, then take place free of stamp duty or stamp duty reserve tax.

Unit trusts

9 Stamp duty arises on the purchase of units by one unit holder from another, and in the more common situation of a surrender for cash of units to the managers. The rates are broadly the same as the *ad valorem* charge on shares, but special reliefs apply.

STAMP DUTY ADJUDICATION

18 July 1990. *The Law Society*

The Stamp Office has announced a change in its adjudication procedures. Following examination of an instrument for adjudication, the Stamp Office's practice is to notify the applicant of the amount of duty estimated to be payable.

It will continue to allow 28 days for applicants to respond to estimates of duty payable. If no response has been received after the 28 days, only one reminder will be issued. The office will consider the request for adjudication as having been withdrawn once a further 14 days have elapsed after the issue of the reminder, and will then return the instrument unstamped to the applicant.

This will not prevent the applicant from re-presenting the instrument for adjudication. However, SA 1891 ss 14(4) (instrument not duly stamped not to be given in evidence), 15 (penalty upon stamping instruments after execution) might apply in the event of delay [*Law Society's Gazette*, 18 July 1990, p 13].

STAMP DUTY: CHARGES TO BE ABOLISHED

19 March 1991. *Inland Revenue*

The Chancellor proposes in his Budget to abolish stamp duty charges on property other than land and buildings. The intention is to abolish these charges at the same time as the duty on shares (likely to be late in 1991–92).

The stamp duty on Northern Ireland bank notes will be abolished from 1 January 1992.

Abolition of these charges will:

(a) relieve from stamp duty a variety of types of property, such as patents, goodwill and debt, including sovereign debt;
(b) further simplify the tax system, and reduce the compliance burden on taxpayers.

DETAILS

1 At present stamp duty is charged on transactions in various types of property. FA 1990 included provisions abolishing all the stamp duty charges (including stamp duty reserve tax) on transactions in shares, from a date to be fixed by Treasury order. The date will be fixed to coincide as closely as possible with the introduction of paperless share dealing under the Stock Exchange's automated share transfer system ("TAURUS").

2 The new proposals will remove the 1 per cent and fixed (mainly 50p) stamp duty charges on documents relating to all other types of property except land and buildings (including houses).

3 The only charges that will remain are the 1 per cent sale duty on land and buildings, and the associated fixed charges; and the charge on the premium and rent of new leases, known as lease duty. The Chancellor is not proposing changes to these duties.

4 The Government intend to introduce the legislation at the Committee Stage of the Finance Bill.

5 The full-year cost will be £15 million.

NOTES

Existing stamp duties

1 Stamp duty is a tax on documents. There are a number of separate duties, under different heads of charge.

2 The main stamp duty is a charge at 1 per cent of the price paid on a conveyance or transfer of property by means of a document. In addition, fixed (generally 50p) duties arise on certain deeds where no money usually changes hands—for example, declarations of trust and exchanges.

Stamp duty reforms

3 In addition to the FA 1990 provisions to abolish the duties on shares, this Government has already abolished:

- stamp duty on gifts (1985);
- capital duty (1988);
- unit trust instrument duty (1988);
- life assurance policy duty (1989);

and a number of the fixed duties have been removed.

4 Since 1979 the rate of duty on land and buildings has been reduced, and the threshold below which no stamp duty is payable on land and buildings raised three times. The current threshold is £30,000.

Stamp duty on Northern Ireland bank notes

5 Northern Ireland bank notes, unlike those issued in Great Britain, attract stamp duty under the "Bank Note" head of charge in SA 1891 Sch 1. The duty is charged, at 50p per £100, on the average value of notes in circulation each half year. The duty on bank notes in Great Britain was abolished in 1972.

Cross-reference—Revenue press release 20-3-90 (abolition of stamp duty on shares).

STAMP DUTY—MITIGATION OF PENALTIES

29 May 1991. *The Law Society*

A letter from the Inland Revenue Stamp Office (published in the *Law Society's Gazette*, 29 May 1991) sets out the Revenue practice as regards mitigation of the statutory penalties (SA 1891 s 15(2)(*c*)) for late presentation of documents liable to stamp duty as follows:

> "In addition to the duty payable, the price to be paid for late stamping is—
>
> - £10 (SA 1891 s 15(1)), plus
> - interest at 5 per cent per annum on the duty outstanding where this is more than £10 (SA 1891 s 15(1)), plus
> - a sum equal to the amount of duty outstanding (SA 1891 s 15(2)(*c*)).
>
> In all but those cases of deliberate withholding of duty, avoidance or extreme delay (over one year late), this could be said to be a disproportionately high price to pay. We would not dissent from this view and our practice will be to invoke the authority provided by SA 1891 s 15(3)(*b*) and mitigate the penalty. The degree of mitigation will be influenced by the reasons for and length of delay. However the minimum level to which a penalty can be expected to be mitigated will reflect interest rates prevailing during the period of delay.
>
> Our offices are instructed in general to mitigate penalties to a level equivalent to an interest rate charge of 12 per cent to 15 per cent per annum for a delay of up to three months, 15 per cent to 20 per cent per annum for three to six months delay, and 20 per cent to 25 per cent for six to 12 months."

[See further the letter published in the Law Society's Gazette on 9 June 1993, referred to below.]

FINANCE BILL: STAMP DUTY: ABOLITION OF CHARGES

14 June 1991. *Inland Revenue*

The Government has tabled six new clauses to the Finance Bill containing its proposals for abolishing stamp duty charges on all property other than land and buildings, as announced in the Chancellor's Budget.

DETAILS

1 Under the new proposals all stamp duty charges will be abolished except where the property being transferred is:

(a) land;
(b) an interest in the proceeds of sale of land held on trust for sale; or
(c) a licence to occupy land.

2 "Land" includes buildings.

3 The property to be exempted includes goodwill, patents and debt, including sovereign debt. The charges to be abolished are the 1 per cent duty on sales of such property, and the fixed (mainly 50p) charges on certain other transactions where none of the property being transferred is land.

4 No change is proposed to the duties on land. So the 1 per cent sale duty on houses and land where the price is above £30,000 [but see FA 1963 s 55, and the Stamp Duty (Temporary Provisions) Act 1992], and the charges on the premium and rent of new leases, remain the same.

5 The rules for cases where property is transferred subject to a debt, or in consideration of a debt, will also remain unchanged.

6 The new clauses provide that, where land and exempt property are transferred together, the purchase price is to be apportioned fairly between them. For example, a business may be transferred at a price which includes both the business premises and goodwill. The provisions will ensure that the chargeable property does not attract either too much or too little stamp duty.

7 With one exception the changes will come into effect at the same time as the abolition of stamp duties on shares, which will be fixed to coincide as closely as possible with the introduction of paperless share dealing ("TAURUS"). The exception is the duty on Northern Ireland banknotes, which will be abolished from 1 January 1992. The TAURUS system is expected to be introduced in May 1992.

Notes

1 The Chancellor's Budget proposals for stamp duty were set out in a press release "Stamp duty: Charges to be abolished" issued on Budget Day, 19 March 1991.

2 Under FA 1990 the abolition date of stamp duties on shares is to be fixed by Treasury Order.

Cross-reference—Revenue press release 20-3-90 (abolition of stamp duty on shares).

PROPOSED MERGER OF LIFFE AND LTOM: NEW TAX RULES

18 October 1991. *Inland Revenue*

The Financial Secretary to the Treasury, Francis Maude, announced yesterday proposed new tax and stamp duty rules for the new market formed from the merger of the London International Financial Futures Exchange (LIFFE) and the London Traded Options Market (LTOM).

In a written reply to a Parliamentary Question (HC Written Answer, 17 October 1991, Vol 196, col 214), the Financial Secretary said—

> "The rules for certain tax reliefs which are available at present to market-makers in traded options assume that the London Traded Options Market is part of the Stock Exchange. When the proposed merger of the London Traded Options Market with the London International Financial Futures Exchange takes place, this will no longer be so. New regulations will be made to adapt the present

reliefs accordingly, and to widen them in some respects to take account of the structure of the new market, once the arrangements for the merger have been finalised.

The new regulations will provide stamp duty and stamp duty reserve tax reliefs for members of the new merged market acting as principal traders in equity options. The reliefs will apply, within certain prescribed limits, to transactions in equities which are necessary to hedge positions in options to buy or sell securities which members enter into on their own account and not on behalf of clients.

Stock lending reliefs, and exemption in certain circumstances from the anti-bond-washing legislation, will also apply to such transactions and to transactions where stock is borrowed or purchased to meet a delivery obligation arising from the exercise or assignment of an option, again within certain prescribed limits.

For members of the merged market acting as principal traders in option contracts, regulations will be made to place them on a comparable basis to Stock Exchange market-makers when required to manufacture a dividend."

DETAILS

Stamp duty/SDRT

1 Currently, market-makers in options to buy or sell securities get relief from stamp duty reserve tax (SDRT) on agreements to purchase securities in the ordinary course of their market-making business, provided the options—

(a) are quoted on the Stock Exchange; and
(b) relate to the same securities as the securities purchased.

This relief—which does not extend to other options dealers—mirrors the SDRT relief for market-makers in shares quoted on the Stock Exchange.

2 The merger of the markets will mean that the traded options market will no longer be part of the Stock Exchange. The regulations will adapt the current stamp duty and SDRT provisions to cater for the merged market. By giving a relief to principal traders on the new market (subject to a more restrictive limitation than market-makers) they will broaden the scope of the present exemption.

3 The regulations will make other provisions about stamp duty and SDRT arising out of the merger. For example, they will ensure that the stamp duty relief for stock-borrowing transactions is extended to members of the merged market subject to the relevant limits; and that delivery of stock on the exercise of an option under the new arrangements does not lead to multiple charges to SDRT.

Stock lending

4 Stock lending is a long established practice that enables securities dealers, in return for a fee, to "borrow" securities (including shares) from institutions such as insurance companies or pension funds when they need them in order to deliver on sales. The dealer undertakes to replace the borrowed stock at a later date with securities of the same kind and amount.

5 Although termed "stock lending" the process involves the transfer of ownership of the securities. Under present law, if securities are borrowed under an approved stock lending arrangement by a market-maker in those securities, both borrower and lender are exempt from tax charges which would otherwise arise when the securities were transferred. These exemptions currently apply only where the borrower is a market maker. This is because such market-makers provide liquidity, and so assist the efficiency of the market, by taking on an obligation to deal at all times at the prices they quote. This may involve selling securities which they do not have, so they may need to borrow securities to enable them to meet their obligations to deliver on the sale.

6 Traded options dealers, whether or not they are market-makers, may be faced with an obligation to deliver securities on which they have entered into options contracts. In the new traded options market it is envisaged that dealers who are not market-makers will play an important role in providing liquidity. The Government has therefore decided to allow tax relief on stock borrowed to hedge positions they have taken in options. Limitations will be prescribed to ensure that the reliefs are restricted to genuine hedging transactions or transactions entered into to enable a delivery obligation to be fulfilled. These limitations will be more restricted for non-market-making principal traders (who can choose whether or not to deal in a particular

option) than for market-makers (who have to deal and who therefore require a more flexible regime). Nevertheless the limitations will in each case recognise the need to hedge, and to maintain a hedge, against options positions.

Manufactured dividends

7 Where stock is lent, payments made by the borrower to the lender to compensate the lender for the dividends that would have been received had the securities not been lent are known as "manufactured dividends". The rules for accounting for tax on manufactured dividends include provisions to prevent relief for the tax in respect of manufactured dividends paid outside approved procedures. These rules will apply to members of the new merged market who borrow stock in the same way as they currently apply to equivalent market makers on the Stock Exchange.

Bond-washing

8 Bond-washing is the practice whereby shares are sold with an accrued dividend and bought back immediately after the shares have gone ex dividend so that the payment for the accrued dividend is treated as a capital gain rather than as income and so receives more favourable tax treatment. TA 1988 s 732 discourages securities dealers from entering into such transactions by reducing the amount which they can deduct for tax purposes in respect of the accrued dividend.

9 At present market-makers in securities are exempted from the anti-bond-washing provisions of TA 1988 s 732. This is because a market-maker's business involves buying and selling securities at all times, regardless of whether they are cum or ex dividend.

10 The exemption for market-makers reflects the existing market structure of the Stock Exchange (of which LTOM is presently part). The options and futures market to be formed from the merger of LIFFE and LTOM, however, will rely for its liquidity on a wider category of principal traders than just market-makers, and it has therefore been decided that they too should benefit from the exemption. As with the stock lending reliefs, there will be prescribed limitations to restrict the exemption to hedging transactions, and transactions entered into, to enable a delivery obligation to be fulfilled.

NOTES

Stamp duty/SDRT

1 The regulations will be made under the powers in FA 1991 ss 116, 117.

2 The existing exemption from SDRT for market-makers in options is in FA 1986 s 89(1A).

3 Stamp duty on shares and SDRT are due to be abolished under legislation in FA 1990. The abolition date will be fixed by Treasury Order.

Stock lending

4 The regulations will be made under the powers contained in TA 1988 s 129(4).

5 The existing arrangements for the approval of stock lending arrangements are set out in TA 1988 s 129 and SI 1989/1299 (as amended by SI 1990/2552).

Manufactured dividends

6 The regulations will be made under the powers contained in TA 1988 Sch 23A.

Bondwashing

7 The regulations will be made under TA 1988 s 732 as amended by FA 1991 s 56.

STAMP DUTY AND VAT

4 March 1992. *Law Society*

Following the publication of Statement of Practice SP 11/91 on the interaction between stamp duty and VAT, the Law Society's revenue law committee raised a number of points of uncertainty in correspondence with the Inland Revenue. The Revenue's views on the points raised are noted below.

[AMOUNT ON WHICH STAMP DUTY IS PAYABLE]

It has emerged from [the correspondence that the Revenue's] view, as a result of the legal advice it has received, and in the light of which SP 11/91 was published, is first that the contingency principle will apply to any transaction in respect of a property which could be affected by an election to waive exemption from VAT, where the election has not been exercised by a landlord at the time that a lease is entered into (and there is no contemporaneous or binding agreement between the parties to the lease that the election will not be exercised). Accordingly in calculating the duty payable VAT should therefore in the Revenue's view be added to any payments to be made by the purchaser or lessee to which an election could still apply.

Secondly, in the cases which deal with the so-called contingency principle it was held that stamp duty is chargeable on a *prima facie* sum regardless of whether that sum might increase or decrease depending on the occurrence of some contingency.

The Revenue considers that the calculation should be based on current rates of VAT, notwithstanding that there may be a fluctuation in the rate of VAT in the period which elapses between the date when the lease is granted and when any election is made.

Apart from the correspondence on the quantum of duty [the Law Society's revenue law committee reports that the correspondence to date has also established the Revenue's views on the following points].

[AGREEMENT BY LESSOR NOT TO ELECT TO WAIVE EXEMPTION]

If, having entered into an agreement for a lease which made no reference to the intending lessor making an election to waive exemption from VAT, the intending lessor subsequently agreed that he or she would not make the election, on what basis would the agreement for lease be stamped, ie what would be the value of the consideration?

[Revenue view] A binding undertaking by a lessor, after an agreement for lease is entered into but before it is stamped, not to exercise an option to charge VAT, would be effective to exclude any stamp duty on VAT that might otherwise be charged on that agreement.

[TRANSFER OF BUSINESS AS A GOING CONCERN]

[The revenue law committee] assume that where the transferor has elected to charge VAT in relation to land (so it will be necessary for the transferee to make a similar election), if the transfer is to be treated as a supply of neither goods nor services for VAT purposes, then conveyances or transfers will be stamped as if no VAT is due, provided the agreement itself or any covering letter to the local stamp office makes it clear that the parties expect such treatment to be available or can confirm that Customs & Excise will apply the transfers of going concerns provisions to the transaction. This would save having to delay submission of documents until it is clear (or has been confirmed post-transfer) that such treatment will apply. Could the Stamp Office confirm that this procedure would be adopted?

[Revenue view] Yes. Such documents can be dealt with at any stamp office and do not need to be sent for adjudication on those grounds alone.

[GROUPS OF COMPANIES]

Where a lease is made between two companies in a VAT group registration (and so the supply is to be ignored for VAT purposes) will the possibility of an election being made at a later date be ignored?

[Revenue view] Yes.

[SUB-SALES]

With sub-sales, is the additional amount that would be payable, had an election to charge VAT been made prior to A agreeing to transfer land to B, ignored in determining whether the consideration provided by C to B upon a sub-sale of the property was less than its value (Stamp Act 1891 s 58(4)(*a*), (7))?

[Revenue view] Yes.

Law Society's Gazette, 4 March 1992, p 16.

STAMP DUTY—MITIGATION OF PENALTIES

9 June 1993. *Law Society*

[The following statutory penalties may be imposed for the late presentation of documents liable to stamp duty—

- £10 (Stamp Act 1891 s 15(1)), plus
- interest at 5 per cent per annum on the duty outstanding where this is more than £10 (Stamp Act 1891 s 15(1)), plus
- a sum equal to the amount of duty outstanding (Stamp Act 1891 s 15(2)(*c*)).

In practice, except in cases of deliberate withholding of duty, avoidance or delays exceeding one year, the Revenue exercises its authority to mitigate penalties (Stamp Act 1891 s 15(3)(*b*)).]

In the *Law Society's Gazette* of 29 May 1991, a letter from the Controller of Stamps, Keith Hodgson, was published, which gave details of the scale of charges which the Stamp Office would apply where instruments were not presented for stamping at the proper time.

Since then, there has been a reduction in the level of interest charged, to reflect the general reduction in interest rates, and Stamp Offices are now instructed to mitigate penalties to a level equivalent to an interest rate charge of around 10 per cent per annum for delays of up to three months, and 10 per cent to 15 per cent for three to 12 months: *Law Society's Gazette*, 9 June 1993 p 32.

STAMP DUTY—NEW BUILDINGS

12 July 1993. *Inland Revenue*

The Inland Revenue have today published a statement of practice (SP 8/93) setting out their view of how the law on stamp duty applies to certain transactions involving new buildings. The transactions concerned are where there purport to be separate contracts for the construction of the buildings and the purchase of the land on which they are to stand. The statement does not affect the common situation where a contract for the sale of a new house on a plot of land is subsequently given effect by a conveyance of the whole property, in the same way as most ordinary sales of new houses. A copy of the statement is reproduced in Appendix 2.

The statement reflects legal advice given to the Board following the High Court decision in the case of the *Prudential Assurance Company Ltd v IRC* ([1992] STC 863; [1993] 1 WLR 211). It replaces previous statements on this subject published in 1957 and 1987 (SP 10/87).

DETAILS

1 The statement applies only where—

- there is a contract for the sale or lease of a building plot and the builder or developer is to construct buildings on the site for the purchaser; and
- at the date of the contract, building work on the plot has either not been started or is incomplete; and
- at the time the conveyance or lease is executed, building work on the plot has begun (and perhaps been completed).

2 The statement sets out the stamp duty consequences of a number of different arrangements. The stamp duty treatment in a particular case will depend on the precise facts of the case. But in broad terms—

(i) where there is a contract for a conveyance or lease of land and, as a separate transaction, a further contract for building works, stamp duty on the conveyance or lease will be calculated without regard to the further contract.

(ii) where within a single transaction there are separate contracts for the sale or lease of a building plot, and for building works on that plot, the stamp duty charge depends on whether the contracts are genuinely independent. If the contracts are independent, duty will be charged on the price paid or payable for both the land itself and for any building that is on the land at the time the instrument is executed, including partly completed buildings. If the contracts are not independent, stamp duty will be charged on the total price for the land and completed buildings.

3 The statement does not apply where there is evidence of a sham or artificial transaction.

Transitional arrangements

4 Stamp duty can be paid on the basis which applied before this Statement, where that is more beneficial, if unconditional contracts have been entered into either before the Statement or within 28 days after it.

Procedure

5 If stamp duty is offered on the total price paid for a building plot and the completed building, the documents should be submitted to the Stamp Office in the usual way.

6 If the total price does not exceed the stamp duty threshold (£60,000 for documents executed on or after 16 March) the documents (except for new leases) can be submitted direct to the Land Registry (in Scotland, the Keeper of the Registers) provided the usual certificate can be included. New leases will need to be stamped in respect of the rent.

7 If the total price paid exceeds the threshold but duty is offered on a lesser amount, the documents should be sent to the Stamp Office together with a full explanation.

STAMP DUTY (CLAUSE 226)

17 March 1994. *Hansard*

Mr Andrew Smith: Would not it have been better if the Government had structured the law so that there was equity between the different ways of organising transactions, rather than leaving it to members of the public to organise their affairs so that they can structure the transaction in a way that takes advantage of the ambiguous position of that important aspect of the law?

. . .

Mr Nelson: I think and hope that the Government have got it right, but to be fair to the Hon Gentleman, I asked the same question when I examined the original proposals. The answer is that stamp duty is a tax on documents, and it is important to consider the substance of the documents involved. Of course, one seeks and hopes for clarity in the imposition of tax so that those who construct documents know exactly what their liabilities are. One cannot, however, avoid considering the nature of the document to ascertain whether duty will arise.

To clarify matters for my Hon Friend the Member for Slough, under the new rules, where a property worth £100,000 is exchanged for another worth £70,000 plus £30,000 cash, it is true that stamp duty will fall on the full £100,000 value on both sides of that exchange. There is no need, however, for that to happen where a cash equality sum is involved, and it can be obviated in two ways. One way is that the exchange contract should have a clause apportioning an amount of £70,000, as in the example, which relates to the value. So it could be said that in exchange for a property worth £100,000, the other party will hand over another which is assumed to have a notional value of £70,000 of the total. Where the value of the property is apportioned in that exchange, I understand that that is the only amount that is liable to stamp duty.

That is not necessarily the only way of getting round a problem that might arise where there is a cash equality sum and stamp duty might otherwise be liable. The better way is for there to be a contract of sale. There is little difference between the effect of a contract of exchange and a contract of sale, but the latter would essentially say, "I sell to you this property worth £100,000 and you will pay me a property worth £70,000 and cash of £30,000." Where it is a sale document, the stamp duty will apply on only one side of that and it would not be necessary to pay full stamp duty the other way round.

House developers and others who take properties in part exchange will be able to do that, only with the imposition of the nominal 50p stamp duty, and then they can sell them. When a part exchange property was sold, its purchaser would have to pay stamp duty in the normal way. That is what would happen if it involved three parties instead of two.

. . .

Mr Nelson: . . . The stamp duty office is willing to advise practitioners, or others who are in doubt, about how to structure a contract to ensure that it is effective and that people do not have to pay stamp duty on a value over and above that of the property which is being transferred. That is the right way to proceed.

. . .

Mr Butterfill: Does my Hon Friend agree that it is almost inconceivable that a house builder of any substance who was operating a part-exchange scheme would fail to point out to a purchaser the way in which the matter should be structured so as to minimise the liability?

Mr Nelson: My Hon Friend is right. I can tell him and the Hon Member for Christchurch (Mrs Maddock), who rightly referred to the propensity of people to part exchange their properties, that the House Builders Federation made representations and explained its concern about the impact that the measure would have on its marketing and on the form of part-exchange deals that are such an essential part of the marketplace. The Government clarified that that would be permitted. I believe that that was broadly welcome by the House Builders Federation.

Mr Andrew Smith: I beg to move amendment No 361, in page 194, line 40 [clause 226(5)], at end insert—

> (5A) "For the purposes of section 34(4) of the Finance Act 1958 (certificates of value) a transaction shall not be regarded as forming part of a larger transaction solely because it is or comprises part of the consideration for the transfer or vesting of another estate or interest in land or the grant of any lease or tack.".

The amendment would make it clear that the £60,000 threshold below which duty is payable applies to both legs of the transaction or exchange. I understand that once again conflicting advice has been issued by different stamp offices on the application of the threshold to exchange transactions following the Budget. Some have said that the threshold will apply to the combined value of the two properties, others that it will apply to each property individually.

. . .

The treatment of a particular case will depend on all the facts, but where one property is exchanged for another, the stamp office would apply the thresholds to each separately. For example, if a property worth £50,000 was being exchanged for a house worth £50,000, the threshold would apply separately to each property and neither would be liable for duty. Therefore, the amendment is unnecessary.

Mr Smith: I am grateful to the Minister for clarifying that he understands that that is the case. Would any compensation be payable to people who have been advised differently by the Stamp Office on that matter?

. . .

Mr Nelson: . . . People can claim repayment if the stamp office has charged them incorrectly. I hope and believe that they have not.

HC Official Report, Standing Committee A (Thirteenth Sitting), cols 714, 715, 718–722.

Note—This has been superseded by Tax Bulletin 18 (August 1995).

LAND REGISTRY ANNOUNCES CHANGE IN STAMP DUTY ADJUDICATION PROCEDURES

5 April 1994. *HM Land Registry*

As a means of improving customer service and after discussion with the Stamp Office, the Chief Land Registrar has decided to revise the practice under which an original instrument requiring adjudication must, to gain priority, be lodged at the Land Registry prior to its submission to the Stamp Office.

With effect from 5 April 1994, it will no longer be a requirement for an applicant to lodge the original instrument with an application for registration when that instrument requires adjudication by the Stamp Office.

Instead, a certified copy of the instrument may be lodged with the application, together with a letter to the Land Registry explaining the position and confirming that the original instrument will be lodged with the Land Registry promptly on its return from the Stamp Office.

When the original instrument has been stamped, it must be sent without delay to the district land registry where the application was lodged, with a covering letter of explanation.

STAMP DUTY—PROPERTY TRANSACTIONS

18 April 1994. *Inland Revenue*

This Press Release gives guidance, in response to enquiries and representations, about some aspects of the stamp duty changes introduced by the 1994 Finance Bill [clauses 237–243 of the 1994 Finance Bill as amended]. They are—

(a) the calculation of duty on an exchange of properties, particularly where the properties are of unequal value and a payment of money (known as equality money) is also made;

(b) the application of the £60,000 threshold to exchanges;

(c) the treatment of sales where one property is sold and another property is given in part payment of the sale price. The guidance makes clear that in these circumstances duty at 1 per cent. is charged (subject to the threshold) on the consideration for the property being sold; the transfer of the other property which is given in part payment is liable only to the fixed duty of 50p.

DETAILS

Exchanges

1 Clause 239 of the 1994 Finance Bill [as amended] (originally clause 226) introduces new rules for stamp duty on exchanges of interests in land or buildings. Under the new rules duty is charged on each transfer. The duty in each case is calculated by reference to the "consideration" (*ie* the value) given for the transfer; where the consideration consists of property, its open market value will be taken. For example, if one house worth £100,000 is exchanged for another house worth £100,000, duty of £1,000 (1 per cent of £100,000) is charged on each transfer. The £60,000 threshold is applied separately to each side of the exchange. For example, if there is a straightforward exchange of one house worth £50,000 for another worth £50,000, both transfers are within the threshold and so no duty would be payable on either (see para 10 below).

2 Where the market values of the two properties being exchanged are not equal, a payment of money (or some other consideration) may often be given with the lower value property, so as to equalise the bargain. The treatment of such cases for stamp duty purposes will depend on the facts and the effect of the relevant documents.

Examples

3 For example, where one house worth £100,000 is exchanged for another worth £80,000 plus £20,000 money, the conveyance for the transfer of the £100,000 house will normally say that the consideration for the transfer consists of the £80,000 house and the £20,000 money; and the conveyance will be stamped accordingly with duty on £100,000.

4 On the conveyance of the £80,000 house, the Stamp Office have charged duty under the new rules by reference to the consideration expressed in the conveyance—

(a) where the conveyance provides that the consideration for the transfer of the cheaper property is the appropriate proportion of the value of the more expensive property, stamp duty is applied accordingly. Thus if the conveyance provides that the consideration for the £80,000 house is the appropriate proportion of the £100,000 house, the amount charged to duty on the transfer of the £80,000 house is limited to £80,000;

(b) more commonly the conveyance may say simply that the consideration for the transfer of the £80,000 house consists of the £100,000 house. In these circumstances, the Stamp Office will have charged duty by reference to the value of the £100,000 house.

Representations

5 Representations have been made that in many cases the wording of the conveyance of the cheaper property may not fully reflect the consideration expressed in the initial contract or agreement. It has been suggested that where the contract provides for an exchange and also provides for money to be paid as equality money by one party to the other, the equality money should be taken into account in deciding how much of the more expensive property is regarded as consideration for the cheaper property (even though the equality money has not been mentioned in the conveyance of the cheaper property).

Revised practice

6 The Revenue have taken legal advice on this. The conclusion is that where it is clear from the contract that the intention of the parties to the transaction is that the cheaper property

should be transferred for the more expensive property *less* the equality money, the Stamp Office will limit the charge to duty accordingly. For example, if the initial contract provided for an £80,000 house to be exchanged for a £100,000 house, and for £20,000 to be paid as equality money, the amount charged to duty on the transfer of the £80,000 property would be limited to £80,000. The result in an individual case will depend on the facts of the case and the relevant documents. The Stamp Office will need to see the relevant contract with the conveyance which is to be stamped.

7 Where there is a multiple exchange of properties, an apportionment on similar lines may be made to determine how much of the consideration is attributable to each of the transfers. For example, two or more properties may be exchanged for one larger property, with or without a payment of equality money. Here again, the precise result will depend on the facts of the case.

Past cases

8 Where the transfer of a cheaper property has already been stamped by reference to the full value of a more expensive property, but the person who has paid the duty thinks that the duty would be reduced on the basis explained in paras 6 or 7 above, the Stamp Office will be prepared to review the case. Applicants should resubmit the relevant conveyance, and the contract (or a certified copy of the contract). (If it is not possible to obtain the original stamped document from the relevant Registrar, the Stamp Office should be consulted about alternative arrangements.) Where appropriate, excess duty will be repaid provided the claim is made within the two-year time limit laid down by the Stamp Duties Management Act 1891 s 10.

9 Claims for repayment should be made to the Stamp Office at Worthing (for England, Wales and Northern Ireland), or Edinburgh (for Scotland).

Application of £60,000 threshold

10 Sales of property (other than shares) for a price not exceeding the £60,000 threshold are exempted from duty, provided that a "certificate of value" is given stating that the transfer is not part of a larger transaction, or a series of transactions, for a total price of more than £60,000. The threshold is applied separately to each side of an exchange of properties. If in a particular case the threshold has not been applied separately to each side of an exchange (or to two sales where the purchase prices have been set off against each other), and the person who paid the duty believes that too much duty was paid, the documents (with the certificate of value) may be returned for reconsideration to the Stamp Office on the same basis as in paras 8 and 9 above.

11 Where there is a multiple exchange—for example, properties A and B are exchanged for property C—the transfers of properties A and B would be regarded as parts of a larger transaction, and the threshold would not apply to either of them if the total consideration for both was more than £60,000. The threshold would be applied separately to the transfer of property C.

Sales

12 In many cases, transactions which in the past have been structured and documented as exchanges could equally well be carried out as sales for a price which may be partly satisfied in kind. For example, when a builder offers a property for sale, he may receive the price from the buyer in the form either of money, or partly of money and partly of the buyer's old house. Such a transaction can be carried out and documented (commencing with the initial contract) as a sale. Stamp duty is charged on the consideration for the sale. So if, for example, the buyer is buying a new house for £100,000, and pays for it with £30,000 in cash plus his old house worth £70,000, duty of £1,000 (1 per cent of £100,000) would be charged on the transfer of the £100,000 house. The house which the builder accepts as part payment for the sale would not be regarded as a separate sale for stamp duty purposes. It would be charged only to the fixed duty of 50p. The threshold would not be of relevance to this transfer as it is not a conveyance on sale.

General

13 In cases of doubt about how a particular document of the types mentioned above would be treated by the Stamp Office for stamp duty purposes, the Technical Section, The Stamp Office, Ridgeworth House, Liverpool Gardens, Worthing BN11 1XP, will be willing to help.

Note—This has been superseded by Tax Bulletin 18 (August 1995).

STAMP DUTY: GROUP RELIEF

29 November 1994. *Inland Revenue*

The Chancellor proposes in his Budget to make two changes to the stamp duty relief for transfers between companies in the same group. Under these measures,

– companies within a group will, subject to conditions, be able to grant new leases to each other free from stamp duty;
– the test for group membership for the purpose of the relief will be changed from 90 per cent ownership of issued share capital to 75 per cent ownership of ordinary share capital.

The changes will apply to documents executed on or after the day on which the Finance Bill receives Royal Assent.

The Chancellor's intention is to extend stamp duty group relief to new leases, in line with representations; and to bring the group control test for this relief closer to the test for corporation tax purposes.

DETAILS

New leases

1 Sales of land or shares by one company to another company in the same group are exempt from stamp duty, subject to anti-avoidance provisions designed to discourage exploitation of the relief. Assignments of existing leases are similarly exempt. But grants of new leases are outside the scope of these provisions. A number of representations have been received for the relief to be extended to grants of new leases.

2 Under the new rules, new leases will qualify for group relief in the same way as sales and assignments of existing leases. Agreements for lease will similarly qualify (provided they are executed on or after the date of Royal Assent).

Test for group membership

3 Under the present rules, companies are associated for the purpose of the stamp duty group relief if either one company owns 90 per cent of the other, or both are 90 per cent owned by a third company. Ownership is measured by reference to issued share capital.

4 The new rules will be different in two respects. The requirement of 90 per cent ownership will be changed to 75 per cent ownership; and only ordinary shares will be taken into account, instead of the whole of the issued share capital.

5 These changes will broadly align the group control test for stamp duty with that for corporation tax. More transfers between companies will be exempt from stamp duty. In a few cases, the new rules will preclude relief where it would currently be available.

STAMP DUTY: FA 1994

3 August 1995. *Tax Bulletin 18*

1 We have received a number of enquiries about the stamp duty provisions in FA 1994 ss 240–243. This article aims to give some general guidance on these points. The precise treatment of a particular document will, of course, depend on all the facts of the case and the legal effect of the document.

EXCHANGES ETC—FA 1994 S 241

2 Section 241 introduced new rules of stamp duty on exchanges of interest in land or buildings. Section 241 operates in a similar manner to SA 1891 ss 6, 55 and 57. These provisions impose a charge on instruments which implement transactions which would not be characterised as a sale at common law because the consideration is something other than a price in money paid or promised. Pursuant to these provisions, certain kinds of consideration are to be treated for the purposes of the charge as equivalent to a money price, the charge being imposed by reference to the value of the consideration to be given. (In relation to s 57, Statement of Practice SP 6/90 remains effective).

3 For the purposes of the charge to duty under the "conveyance or transfer on sale" heading in SA 1891 s 241(1) attributes a value to the consideration and states that "the instrument shall be charged with *ad valorem* duty under that heading" where a charge is not imposed in respect of that consideration by virtue of any other provision.

4 As stamp duty is charged on instruments, rather than transactions, s 241(1) falls to be applied to each instrument which satisfies the terms of the provision. Accordingly, if, for example, the consideration for the transfer of an interest in land is the transfer of an interest in land, each transfer is chargeable by reference to the market value of the interest transferred by the other.

THE £60,000 THRESHOLD

5 The £60,000 threshold is applied separately to each side of the exchange. For example, if there is a straightforward exchange of one house worth £50,000 for another worth £50,000, both transfers are within the threshold and no duty would be payable on either provided each is certified in accordance with FA 1958 s 34(4).

6 Where there is a multiple exchange—for example, properties A and B are exchanged for property C—the transfers of properties A and B would be regarded as parts of a larger transaction (under FA 1958 s 34(4)). The threshold would not apply to either of them if the total consideration for both was more than £60,000, but would be applied separately to the transfer of property C.

EQUALITY MONEY

7 Where the market values of two properties being exchanged are not equal, a payment of money (or some other consideration) is often given with the lower value property, so as to equalise the bargain. In many cases the wording of the conveyance of the lower value property may not fully reflect the consideration expressed in the original contract or agreement. Where it is clear from the contract that the lower value property has been transferred for the higher value property less the equality money, the Stamp Office will limit the charge to duty accordingly. For example, if the initial contract provided for an £80,000 house to be exchanged for a £100,000 house, and for £20,000 to be paid as equality money, the amount charged to duty on the transfer of the £80,000 house would be limited to £80,000. In these cases the Stamp Office needs to see the relevant contract as well as the conveyance.

8 Where there is a multiple exchange of properties, an apportionment on similar lines may be made to determine how much of the consideration is attributable to each of the transfers. For example, two or more properties may be exchanged for one larger property, with or without a payment of equality money.

SALES

9 In many cases, transactions which in the past have been structured and documented as an exchange could equally well be carried out as a sale for a price which may be partly satisfied in kind. For example, when a person offers a property for sale, he may receive the price from the buyer in the form either of money, or partly of money and partly of the buyer's existing house. Such a transaction can be carried out and documented (commencing with the initial contract) as a sale. Section 241 does not apply where duty is already imposed under the conveyance on sale head of charge. Accordingly, if the transaction is within the common law concept of "sale", s 241 is excluded and duty is simply charged by reference to the price of the sale.

10 Although a sale ordinarily involves a price in money paid or promised (*Littlewoods Mail Order Stores Limited v IRC* [1963] AC 135 at page 152), the Courts have held that the transaction is still a "sale" if property is taken in satisfaction of part of the purchase price: *Simpson v Connolly* [1953] 2 All ER 474 p 477; *Connell Estate Agents v Begej* [1993] 2 EGLR 35. In the Connell case, the purchaser had agreed to purchase land for £109,000. In satisfaction of this price the vendor was "to receive ownership of 10 Milner Road, Finedon, plus balance of £53,000". The Court of Appeal held that the transaction was a sale of the more valuable property for the price of £109,000 and that the purchaser's property was part of that price. The Court confirmed however, that a transaction cannot be characterised as a sale unless some money is paid by the purchaser to the vendor and the cash element is more than merely nominal. So if, for example, the buyer is buying a house for £100,000, and pays for it with £30,000 in cash plus his existing house worth £70,000, duty of £1,000 (1 per cent of £100,000) would be charged on the transfer of the £100,000 house.

11 The house which the vendor accepts as part payment for the sale would not be regarded as a separate sale for stamp duty purposes. The consideration for the purchaser's property is not the vendor's property but merely the discharge of a potential obligation to pay part of the purchase price on completion. Accordingly, s 241 does not apply to the transfer of the purchaser's property. SA 1891 s 57 does not apply to the transfer of the purchaser's property because the purchaser's property is not conveyed to the vendor in consideration, wholly or in part, of any "debt due" to the vendor. The word "due" when used in relation to a debt means due and payable (*Re European Life Assurance* [1869] LR 9 Eq 122, and the other cases cited in Stroud's Judicial Dictionary 5th Ed Vol 2 pp 781–783). As the purchase price is not payable until completion, a transfer of property by the purchaser on or before completion cannot be said to be in

consideration of a debt due. Ordinarily, on completion, the transfer of the purchaser's property will be handed to the vendor's solicitor, together with a cheque or other means of payment, at the same time as the vendor's solicitor hands over the transfer of the vendor's property. For there to be a debt due to the vendor, the purchaser would have to be put in the position of having taken a transfer of the vendor's property without having paid for it.

12 On the basis that there is a sale for cash to be satisfied in part by the transfer of another property, *ad valorem* stamp duty is charged on the consideration for the sale, but not on the transfer of the other property. That transfer would only be charged to the fixed duty of 50 pence. The threshold would not be relevant to this transfer as it is not a conveyance on sale.

SURRENDER AND REGRANT OF LEASES

13 Where a lease is granted in consideration only of the surrender or abandonment of an existing lease of the same property, SA 1891 s 77(1) provides exemption from duty. If the new lease is granted in consideration of a premium and/or rent as well as the surrender of the existing lease, there is a grant of a lease which is partly exempt (the surrender) and partly chargeable to duty (the premium and/or rent). The Stamp Office would not seek to refuse exemption under SA 1891 s 77(1) merely on the grounds that there were some minor changes in the property subject to the lease, provided that these could be regarded as de minimis. The same treatment would apply where a variation of a lease takes effect in law as a surrender and regrant.

14 Where the lease on one property is being replaced by a lease on another property, the stamp duty treatment will depend on the facts of the case and the effect of the document. But if, for example, the document granted a new lease on one property and the consideration was the surrender of a lease on another property, duty would be charged on the grant of the new lease, by reference to the market value of the lease surrendered (as premium/consideration) and any other payment by way of premium or rent.

15 The stamp duty treatment of the surrender of the old lease will similarly depend on the facts and the documents. In most cases where there is a surrender and regrant, the Stamp Office's experience is that no deed of surrender is submitted for stamping, either because the new lease simply supersedes the old one by operation of law and there is no surrender document, or possibly because any surrender document is not submitted for stamping.

SALE AND LEASEBACK

16 Where there is a sale and leaseback, the Stamp Office normally sees a contract of sale for a price, and an agreement for lease (followed by the grant of a lease), rather than an exchange of one for the other. In that case, the sale would be liable to duty in the normal way by reference to the price and the agreement for lease would be charged by reference to any premium and rent.

17 If, however, the property is transferred in consideration of a leaseback of the same property, alone or together with a sum of money, duty would be assessed on the transfer by reference to the value (if any) of the lease plus any cash element. Duty would also be assessed on the lease by reference to any amount by which the value of the property transferred exceeded the cash consideration.

UNASCERTAINABLE CONSIDERATION—FA 1994 S 242

18 Section 242 deals with sales of land or buildings where the price is not ascertainable at the time the relevant document is executed. In these circumstances, the open market value of the property is to be taken as the consideration for stamp duty purposes. Similarly, where the rent under a new lease is not ascertainable the open market rent is to be taken.

19 That rule does not, however, apply where the amount of the consideration can already be determined by reference to the "contingency principle"—s 242(3)(*a*). Under this principle, if the consideration agreed between the parties and specified in the instrument is subject to possible future variation, the specified figure would be taken for stamp duty purposes (*Independent Television Authority v IR Comrs* [1961] AC 427 p 443). Thus if the consideration is 25 per cent of profits over 5 years, but not to be less than £100,000, the consideration for stamp duty purposes would be £100,000. The existence of additional but unascertainable consideration would bring the transaction within s 242.

20 The ascertainable figure produced by the contingency principle may be a maximum or minimum, or a basic sum which is subject to future variation. But a minimum figure which was merely a nominal figure inserted in a lease to avoid s 242, or which did not represent the agreed consideration or rent, would not satisfy s 242(3)(*a*) as it would not be a minimum rent for the purpose of the contingency principle as formulated by Lord Radcliffe in the Independent

Television Authority case. We consider that for this purpose a minimum rent must be an amount genuinely agreed between the parties as such, ie, as an amount which is contemplated by the parties and accepted by the landlord as compensation for the use and occupation of the premises by the tenant(s). It is therefore necessary to consider all the facts in order to ascertain the true nature and intended purpose of the instrument (*Oughtred v IR Comrs* [1958] Ch 678 page 688; [1960] AC 206).

21 The market value rule applies where part of the consideration or rent is unascertainable. Duty would then be charged on the market value or rent (but not the market value or rent **plus** the ascertainable consideration). Where the rent under a lease is unascertainable for only part of the term, the market rent will be taken for the whole term in order to calculate the average annual rent. In establishing the market rent, all the terms and conditions of the actual lease will be taken into account under normal valuation principles, s 242(3)(*b*). It is the market rent for the particular **lease** and not merely the market rent for the land at a particular time which must be established for the purposes of s 242(2).

22 It has been suggested to us that s 242 is ineffective on the grounds that if there is a valid contract, the consideration will be ascertainable, even though it may not be immediately quantifiable. For a contract to be valid, it is sufficient that the consideration is ascertainable either at the time of the contract or subsequently. Section 242 by contrast applies where the consideration is not ascertainable at the time the document is executed. The section has to be read in conjunction with FA 1963 s 55, which refers to the amount or value of the consideration, and the words "cannot . . . be ascertained" clearly mean "cannot be ascertained for the purpose of the charge", rather than "cannot be ascertained as a matter of contract law". Our view is that the wording of s 242(1) is apt to cover the case where the amount or value of the consideration cannot be ascertained at the relevant time for the purposes of stamp duty chargeable under the conveyance on sale head of charge.

23 It has also been suggested that some transactions could come within both s 241 and s 242, on the grounds that where the amount or value of the consideration is not ascertainable, the right to it might be "property" within s 241(1). In general, the two sections deal with distinct types of cases. There may be some cases which could fall within both sections, but the precise treatment will depend on the facts of the case. In practice, where the transfer is for full value, it should make little or no difference to the amount of duty whether s 241 or s 242 applies. Where there is a difference, duty would be charged under the provision which produces the higher amount of duty (following the principle in *Speyer Bros v IR Comrs* [1908] AC 92).

24 The treatment of split-term leases set out in our letter of 2 January 1963 to the Law Society's Gazette (where they are described as leases of type (*c*)) no longer applies. The annex on page 237 reproduces the relevant part of the 1963 letter.

SURRENDERS—FA 1994 S 243

25 Section 243 provides that where, in pursuance of an agreement, a lease is surrendered or renounced without a deed of surrender, the agreement is liable to duty as if it were a deed.

26 We have been asked what particular types of document would be regarded as an "agreement". In an individual case, it would of course be necessary to consider the facts and the terms of the relevant document. The case of *Fleetwood-Hesketh v IR Comrs* [1936] 1 KB 351 shows that a document recording or implementing an agreement may itself be treated as an agreement for stamp duty purposes whether there is a previous oral agreement or an oral agreement contemporaneous with the written agreement. Where such a document satisfies the requirements of the Law of Property (Miscellaneous Provisions) Act 1989 s 2, it will be an agreement within s 243.

VALUATIONS

27 Although the stamp duty legislation does not provide for appeals on valuation to go to the Lands Tribunal, a reference by consent could be made to the Tribunal under the Lands Tribunal Act 1949 s 1(5) on a question of land valuation. We would normally consent. However, where questions of both law and valuation arise in relation to an appeal relating to liability and quantum respectively, we would wish to resolve the legal issue in the High Court prior to any determination of value by the Lands Tribunal. In contrast, a valuation issue would after appeal go to the Lands Tribunal.

AGREEMENT FOR LEASE—FA 1994 S 240

28 Section 240 provides that if an agreement for lease and the lease which gives effect to the agreement, are presented for stamping at the same time, and any duty chargeable on the agreement is paid, the agreement shall be treated as having been executed at the same time as the lease for the purposes of the provisions relating to penalties for late stamping. We have been asked whether FA 1931 s 28 means that the agreement must nevertheless be produced to

the Stamp Office within 30 days of execution. Presentation of the agreement with the lease, within 30 days after the execution of the lease, will be accepted as satisfying the requirement under s 28 to produce the agreement.

GENERAL

29 This article supersedes the relevant parts of the Press Releases of 30 November 1993 and 18 April 1994 and the Stamp Office guidance notes issued in December 1993.

Extract from the Controller of Stamps' letter of 2 January 1963 to the Law Society's Gazette

"The Board of Inland Revenue have recently given consideration to the basis of assessment of duty on leases which contain one or more of the following provisions:

. . .

(*c*) a rent or rents fixed for part only of the term, the rent for the remainder of the term to be agreed subsequently.

Leases of type (*c*) present great difficulty and the Board are advised that in the absence of authority, it cannot be said with certainty how the provisions of the lease head of charge should properly be applied. In the absence of such authority and with the object of securing a consistent practice, hitherto lacking, and to bring the assessment of duty as far as possible into line with the facts, the Board have decided that such leases shall be assessed by treating separately the part of the term in respect of which the rent is known from that in respect of which it is unknown; *ad valorem* duty under 'Lease (3)' will be assessed in respect of the former part as if it were a lease at the known rate or average rate of rent for a term of that length, and fixed duty under 'Lease (4)' will be assessed in respect of the latter part.

The practice explained above in relation to leases of type (*c*) will not affect the basis of assessment of leases where there is a rent of one description (eg a ground rent) of known amount for the whole of the term and a further rent of another description (eg a service rent) ascertainable for part only of the term. In such cases the basis of assessment will continue to be *ad valorem* duty under 'Lease (3)' on the average ascertainable annual rent payable throughout the term and fixed duty under 'Lease (4)' on the further uncertain rent."

TRADEPOINT—TAX AND STAMP DUTY RESERVE TAX RELIEFS

4 August 1995. *Inland Revenue*

Regulations have been laid today to remove the tax obstacles which might otherwise have prevented effective trading by Tradepoint (a new screen-based market for dealing in equities).

DETAILS

1 These regulations are the Income Tax (Dealers in Securities) (Tradepoint) Regulations 1995, the Income Tax (Manufactured Dividends) (Tradepoint) Regulations 1995 and the Stamp Duty Reserve Tax (Tradepoint) Regulations 1995. They will allow the London Clearing House in its capacity as the clearing house for Tradepoint to be exempt from Stamp Duty Reserve Tax (SDRT) and the anti-bondwashing legislation. They will also allow favourable treatment in respect of manufactured dividends. These three benefits will also apply to certain members of Tradepoint in particular circumstances. Copies of the regulations will be available shortly from Her Majesty's Stationery Office.

2 Bond washing is a device for turning income into capital gains and so, in certain cases, avoiding tax. This is countered by legislation which does not apply to Stock Exchange market makers acting in the ordinary course of market making business. It would also be inappropriate for it to apply to the London Clearing House and to certain members of Tradepoint where they are taking no proprietary interest in Tradepoint transactions but are simply involved as part of Tradepoint's clearing process. These regulations ensure this.

3 Manufactured dividends are paid to compensate recipients for real dividends that are not received. They can be paid when stock is lent over a period which straddles a dividend date or where sales of cum-dividend stock are satisfied by delivery of ex-dividend stock. Unless such payments are approved, the payer is penalised for tax purposes. When made by Stock Exchange market makers such payments are normally treated as approved. These regulations will ensure that the same applies for the London Clearing House and for members of Tradepoint when they are involved only as part of Tradepoint's clearing process.

4 SDRT is a tax on certain agreements to transfer securities, which supplements the stamp duty on shares. Stamp duty applies only where there is a transfer document. Without these regulations, Tradepoint's clearing arrangements could result in more than one charge to stamp duty/SDRT for a single purchase by a Tradepoint client. The regulations ensure that extra charges to SDRT under such arrangements will not arise. In line with transactions on other exchanges, a single charge to stamp duty or SDRT will occur on the transfer of the shares to the purchaser.

Note—Tradepoint received recognition as an investment exchange from the Securities and Investment Board on 7 June 1995.

STOCK LENDING: STAMP DUTY RESERVE TAX

2 October 1995. *Inland Revenue*

The Inland Revenue have today published three Concessions giving relief from stamp duty reserve tax on certain stock lending transactions [see Concessions G7, G8 and G9 *ante*].

DETAILS

1 In the ordinary course of their business Stock Exchange market makers borrow shares from institutions for the purpose of their market making operations. In return, the lender is given security. These transactions are carried out under standard agreements substantially in a form approved by the Stock Exchange and the Inland Revenue.

2 The Stock Exchange propose to introduce a new Dematerialised Stock Lending Service on 2 October. Stock lenders will be permitted to hold their stock in SEPON (the Stock Exchange's nominee company), so that stock loans (and returns of borrowed stock) can be carried out by electronic transfer within SEPON rather than by paper transfers. Under the new service, the Stock Exchange will collect stamp duty reserve tax (SDRT) on transfers within SEPON where appropriate.

3 The first two concessions relate to the SDRT treatment of the new service.

4 The first concession is concerned with the transfers of stock by lenders into SEPON for the purpose of the new service. Under present legislation transfers into SEPON are exempt from stamp duty but are liable to SDRT at 0·5 per cent, unless they qualify for a specific exemption. Thus if a lender transferred his existing holding of shares into SEPON, the transfer would be liable to 0·5 per cent SDRT. The concession will reduce the SDRT in those circumstances to 50p (in line with the stamp duty charge on a transfer to a nominee in similar circumstances).

5 The second concession is concerned with the return of stock from the market maker to the lender at the end of the loan. Present legislation limits the stamp duty charge on the transfer to 50p. But under the dematerialised service, the return will no longer be a paper transfer. It would therefore be liable to SDRT rather than stamp duty, but there is at present no corresponding SDRT relief limiting the charge to 50p. The concession will limit the SDRT charge to 50p in circumstances where stamp duty would have been limited to 50p if there had been a paper transfer.

6 The third concession stems from changes made in December 1990 to the terms of the standard stock lending agreements to strengthen the security given to stock lenders. These were technical changes but would strictly result in a liability to SDRT in certain circumstances where no stamp duty or SDRT was charged under the previous agreements. The concession, which is already in operation, gives relief from these extra charges.

Note—The concessions will be superseded when the FA 1997 reform of the repurchase and stock lending regime is brought into effect (due to be in 1997–98).

STAMP DUTY ON SHARES

28 November 1995. *Inland Revenue*

Changes to the present rules for stamp duty on shares and stamp duty reserve tax (SDRT) were announced by the Chancellor today. Under the proposals:

– the present rules will be adapted to cater for the introduction of paperless share transfers under the CREST system, due to start in July 1996;
– an optional alternative to the present regime for clearance services will be provided.

The changes will apply from 1 July 1996.

DETAILS

1 Stamp duty is charged on documents transferring shares. A company registrar cannot register the transfer of ownership unless the transfer document has been stamped with the

appropriate duty (or has been certified as exempt from duty). The Stock Exchange collect duty on transactions involving Stock Exchange members. SDRT is charged on certain agreements to transfer securities, where there is no transfer document and so no liability to stamp duty.

2 The Treasury have laid draft regulations before Parliament to amend company law to permit shares to be held in uncertificated form and to be transferred through an approved paperless transfer system. The proposed CREST system for paperless share transfers is expected to start in July 1996. Paperless transfers will be liable to SDRT rather than stamp duty, and the present stamp duty and SDRT rules need some amendment to cater for them. CREST (and any other system approved under the Treasury regulations) will be required by the tax rules to collect SDRT on relevant transactions settled within the system or reported through it for regulatory purposes.

3 Legislation will be included in the Finance Bill to make a number of changes:

(i) as the law stands, a transfer which is not on sale is liable to 50p stamp duty. There is no corresponding 50p rate of SDRT, and a 50p rate is not being introduced. Deposits of certificated shares into CREST will be exempted from the 50p stamp duty charge. They will not be liable to SDRT unless the 0·5 per cent or 1·5 per cent SDRT charge applies—for example because they are transfers for consideration in money or money's worth;

(ii) at present, a charge to SDRT does not arise until two months after the agreement to transfer the shares. This allows time for a transfer document to be produced and stamped, as will normally happen under the present system. The stamp duty then franks the SDRT liability. With paperless transfers, there will generally be no stamped document, and the two-month delay will no longer be appropriate. The two-month gap will be removed to avoid a cash-flow loss to the Exchequer. Where there is still a stamped transfer document, the stamp duty paid on it will cancel the SDRT charge;

(iii) at present, the rates of SDRT round the tax up to the next 50p—eg 50p per £100 or part of £100. To simplify the calculations, the rates will be changed to a flat percentage—eg 0·5 per cent. (The stamp duty rates will however remain unchanged; the machines used to stamp documents are designed to cater for the present form of rates);

(iv) the territorial scope of SDRT will be clarified. The practice up to now has been to regard agreements made overseas between persons not resident in the United Kingdom (UK) as outside the scope of the tax. Recent legal advice, however, suggests that these agreements are chargeable to SDRT. The legislation will be amended to confirm that. Thus, transfers between non-residents which are settled through CREST will be liable to SDRT (just as they are liable to stamp duty at present where there is a paper transfer). The present practice will however continue to be operated in relation to unconditional agreements which are made before 1 July 1996;

(v) where stock is borrowed by a Stock Exchange market-maker, the stamp duty charge on a transfer of borrowed stock back to the lender is limited to 50p. In the case of dematerialised stock lending, the SDRT charge on the return of stock to the lender is limited to 50p by extra-statutory concession (Inland Revenue Press Release, 2 October). These stock loan returns will be exempted from SDRT from 1 July 1996. The legislation will also provide in statutory form the SDRT relief given at present by extra-statutory concession for transfers of collateral under stock lending arrangements;

(vi) stamp duty and SDRT are charged at 1·5 per cent on transfers of shares into "clearance services"—ie broadly, systems where the shares are held indefinitely by a nominee and rights are bought and sold by book entry transfer without a transfer of the shares themselves. An option will be introduced to enable clearance services to opt for the normal SDRT charges to apply to transactions within the service, instead of the 1·5 per cent charge on transfers into the service. It will be a condition of the option that satisfactory arrangements are made by the clearance service operator for the collection of SDRT and for compliance with the requirements of the SDRT legislation. Where the clearance service has no UK presence, the appointment of a UK tax representative may be required as a condition of the option, unless satisfactory alternative arrangements are made;

(vii) the present rules for the 1·5 per cent SDRT charge on transfers of shares into depositary receipt schemes assume that the shares will be held by a nominee rather than by the issuer of depositary receipts. The legislation will be amended so as to apply also where the shares are held by the issuer of the depositary receipts itself.

4 CREST (and any other paperless system approved under the Treasury regulations) will have a statutory obligation to collect SDRT on relevant transactions carried out within its system or reported through it for regulatory purposes. Firms which are market-makers, brokers and dealers or "qualified dealers" for the purpose of the SDRT regulations—ie broadly firms which are regulated—will be able to obtain any reliefs to which they (or their clients) are entitled, by identifying the relevant transactions in CREST rather than by claiming repayment from the Stamp Office. The present regulations governing the assessment and collection of SDRT are being reviewed and will be amended in due course to make any changes needed to take account of the introduction of paperless share transfers.

TRANSFER OF SECURITIES TO MEMBERS OF ELECTRONIC TRANSFER SYSTEMS ETC [FA 1996 S 186]

27 February 1996. *Hansard.*

Ms Dawn Primarolo: There are issues to be considered when UK shares are traded on foreign stock exchanges. However, there are exemptions where shares are traded abroad—in New York, for instance—in depository form or where settlement is within a clearance system to which a 1·5 per cent clearance system charge applies. Those exemptions will not necessarily cover every case. In some circumstances, the beneficial ownership of shares changes and the stamp duty-related tax that arises from that will not be covered by the exemptions.

Mrs Angela Knight: The variation is that although the 1·5 per cent remains for depository receipts, an alternative is provided for the clearance system. In future, a clearance system can either charge 1·5 per cent on shares that go into the clearance system and then have the transactions take place free of duty, or it will be able to elect, if it so wishes, to pay no charge as shares go into the clearance system but it pays 0·5 per cent as the shares are transferred.

HC Official Report, Standing Committee E (seventeenth sitting), cols 558, 559, 561, 562

STOCK LENDING AND COLLATERAL SECURITY ARRANGEMENTS [FA 1996 S 191]

27 February 1996. *Hansard.*

Ms Primarolo: Could the Minister explain what happens if the stock exchange has got it wrong and the CREST system does not operate properly even with the new clause?

. . .

Mrs Knight: If CREST did not go ahead, the current system would continue to operate. Therefore, we would have the stock-lending process that we have now. On the other hand, if the stock exchange decided that it would not remove the requirement for a broker-dealer—the middle man, an intermediary—but would retain an individual who had to be part of the stock-lending process, the new clause covers that. If the stock exchange decided that, following the implementation of CREST, there would never again be any requirement for an intermediary, the clause covers that as well. Therefore, all rule-change eventualities are covered.

HC Official Report, Standing Committee E (seventeenth sitting), col 564

OPEN-ENDED INVESTMENT COMPANIES AND AUTHORISED UNIT TRUSTS—STAMP DUTY

9 May 1996. *Inland Revenue*

The Economic Secretary to the Treasury, Mrs Angela Knight MP, today announced proposals to relax the stamp duty and stamp duty reserve tax rules for authorised unit trusts converting into open-ended investment companies, and for mergers between authorised unit trusts. The proposals will facilitate the introduction of OEICs and at the same time will provide a window of opportunity for rationalisation in the unit trust industry. In reply to a Parliamentary Question, she said:—

> "In response to the consultative document which the Treasury published last year with draft regulations to permit the creation of open-ended investment companies (OEICs), the Treasury have received a number of representations that conversions of authorised unit trusts into OEICs should be exempted from stamp duty and stamp duty reserve tax (SDRT), including conversions of two or more trusts into a single OEIC.
>
> When regulations are made to deal with the stamp duty and SDRT treatment of OEICs, I intend to include in them an exemption for conversions of an authorised unit trust into an OEIC or a single sub-fund of an umbrella OEIC. The regulations will also contain an exemption from stamp duty and SDRT, for a period of some two years, for conversions which involve a merger (such as the conversion of two or more authorised unit trusts into a single OEIC or sub-fund, or the merger of an authorised unit trust with an OEIC).
>
> We also intend to introduce legislation in the next Finance Bill to exempt mergers between authorised unit trusts from stamp duty and SDRT if the merger is carried out after the Bill becomes law and within a period of some two years thereafter.

These measures will give unit trust groups a unique opportunity to rationalise their range of authorised unit trusts, and to convert some or all of them into OEICs if they wish. At the same time, the introduction of OEICs will continue to widen the opportunities for share ownership for the investing public."

DETAILS

1 Open-ended investment companies (OEICs) cannot currently be formed under UK company law. Last year the Treasury issued for consultation a draft of regulations which would permit OEICs to be set up, and the Securities and Investments Board issued draft product regulations for consultation. FA 1995 included powers to make regulations for the tax treatment of OEICs.

2 When an authorised unit trust (AUT) is converted into an OEIC, the transfer of the trust's investments to the OEIC would, as the law stands, generally be liable to stamp duty or stamp duty reserve tax (SDRT). When regulations are made later this year, they will include an exemption from stamp duty and SDRT for the conversion of an AUT into an OEIC, or into a sub-fund of an umbrella OEIC. They will also include an exemption, for a period of some two years, for a merger of two or more AUTs into an OEIC (or a sub-fund of an umbrella OEIC).

3 The Chancellor also proposes to introduce legislation in the next Finance Bill to exempt mergers between authorised unit trusts from stamp duty and SDRT if the merger is carried out after the Bill becomes law and within a period of some two years thereafter.

Notes

Open-ended investment companies are open-ended in the sense that their shares will be continually created or redeemed depending on the net demand by investors to acquire shares or to redeem their existing holdings. As with existing authorised unit trusts, these transactions will be undertaken at a price derived from the net asset value of the OEIC's underlying investments. An OEIC may take "umbrella" form, ie incorporating a number of subfunds in which shareholders can invest separately.

STAMP DUTY—UNIT TRUSTS AND OPEN-ENDED INVESTMENT COMPANIES

26 November 1996. *Inland Revenue*

The temporary stamp duty exemption announced in May for mergers between authorised unit trusts, and mergers of authorised unit trusts into open-ended investment companies (OEICs), is to run until 30 June 1999, under the Chancellor's proposals today. The Government also wishes to simplify the present stamp duty regime for repurchases of units by unit trust managers.

DETAILS

Conversions and mergers

1 The Economic Secretary to the Treasury, Angela Knight MP, announced in May that—

- when regulations were made in due course to deal with the stamp duty and stamp duty reserve tax (SDRT) treatment of OEICs, she intended to include in them an exemption for conversions of an authorised unit trust into an OEIC (or a single sub-fund of an umbrella OEIC);
- the regulations would also provide an exemption, for a period of some two years, for conversions which involve a merger (such as a conversion of two or more authorised unit trusts into a single OEIC);
- legislation would be introduced in the next Finance Bill to exempt mergers between unit trusts if the merger was carried out after the bill became law and within a period of some two years thereafter (Inland Revenue Press Release, 9 May 1996 [see above]).

2 The temporary exemptions will run until 30 June 1999. This will help to facilitate the introduction of OEICs, and will also provide an opportunity for rationalisation in the unit trust industry.

Repurchase of units

3 Under the present stamp duty rules for unit trusts, there is 0.5 per cent charge on the repurchase of units by the manager from investors, but the duty can be repaid if the units are

cancelled within the next two months and the underlying investments are sold. This is, however, complex to operate, and is unlikely to fit easily with single pricing of units. It may be uncertain at the time of the repurchase whether the units will in due course be cancelled and the duty repaid.

4 The Government therefore intends to introduce a simpler regime which will apply both for units in unit trusts (whether authorised or unauthorised) and for shares in OEICs. They have in mind to replace the present rule by a lower charge on repurchases, but with no repayment when units (or shares I OEICs) are cancelled. The details are under discussion with representative of the industry, and a further announcement will be made in the near future.

Notes

1 Open-ended investment companies are open-ended in the sense that their shares can be continually created or redeemed depending on the net demand by investors to acquire shares or redeem their existing holdings. As with authorised unit trusts, these transactions will be undertaken at a price derived from the net asset value of the OEIC's underlying investments. An OEIC may take "umbrella" form, with a number of sub-funds with different investment objectives.

2 OEICs cannot currently be formed under UK company law, but the Treasury have made regulations to permit OEICs to be set up (The Open-Ended Investment Companies (Investment Companies with Variable Capital) Regulations 1996 SI 1996/2827). The regulations will come into effect on 6 January 1997. The Securities and Investments Board have issued a final draft of product regulations for OEICs. These are also expected to take effect in January 1997. Regulations for the tax treatment of OEICs will keep in step with that timetable.

3 When an authorised unit trust is converted into an OEIC, the transfer of the trust's investment to the OEIC, would as the law stands, generally be liable to stamp duty or SDRT. Similarly there would be a stamp duty or SDRT liability when unit trusts merge with each other.

STAMP DUTY ON LEASES

8 January 1997. *Law Society's Gazette*

A change in practice by the Stamp Office in its approach to calculation of stamp duty on new leases which contain provision for future rent increases in line with RPI (retail price index) changes has resulted in the Law Society's revenue law committee receiving a number of inquiries from solicitors.

The Stamp Office is relying upon the decision in *LM Tenancies plc v IR Comrs* [1996] STC 880 to apply the contingency principle to rent reserved under a lease so that stamp duty is calculated by reference to RPI changes in the year ending with the date of execution of the lease. This approach has led to some excessive estimates of liability.

The revenue law committee has taken up the issue wit the Stamp Office and has made two main points. Firstly, it does not consider that the new approach is justified. *L M Tenancies* was concerned with stamp duty avoidance; to apply the decision in that case across the board to any lease with a rent review clause linked to the RPI is unjustified. Secondly, this is an extremely important change in practice which the Stamp Office has not apparently published effectively.

In response, the Stamp Office has assured the committee that it will examine the facts of each case and give careful consideration to the application of the *LM Tenancies* decision.

The Stamp Office points out that a public announcement of the new practice was made in *Hansard* in a reply given by the Economic Secretary to the Treasury to a parliamentary written question asked by a Conservative MP. It followed representations from the House Builders Federation, the Manufacturing and Construction Industries Alliance and individual property owners.

This reply states:

> "Stamp duty is charges on the grant of a new lease of property by reference to the premium paid for the lease and the average annual rent. Duty on the premium is charged at 1 per cent but there is no charge on the premium where the premium is £60,000 or less and the average annual rent is £6,000 or less. Duty is charged on the average annual rent by reference to a sliding scale of rates which depend on the length of the lease. For example, for a lease of over 100 years, the rate is 24 per cent (£12 per £50 or part of £50 of the average annual rent.)

Where an existing lease is sold by the leaseholder to someone else, duty is charged at 1 per cent on the price paid, in the same way as with the sale of a freehold. No duty is charged on the rent. I have received representations from the House Builders Federation, the Manufacturing and Construction Industries Alliance, and McCarthy and Stone about the treatment of a grant of a new lease under which the rent is to be adjusted in future in line with RPI changes.

Where the terms of a lease lay down specific figures for future rent payments, or provide for the rent to be increased by a fixed percentage each year, there is no difficulty in calculating what the average annual rent is for the purpose of the stamp duty charge. The calculation is more difficult where the rent is to depend on the future movement of an index such as the RPI. Decisions of the courts, including the recent case *L M Tenancies plc v IR Comrs*, have given some guidance on the calculation of the charge to duty where an element is not ascertainable at the outset.

The Inland Revenue has reviewed its practice on the stamp duty treatment of leases of this type then in light of representations that have been made. It accepts that in some cases the calculations made by Stamp Offices produce too high a figure. In the *LM Tenancies* case, the premium paid for a lease was to be calculated by reference to the market price of a Treasury loan stock 25 days after the execution of the lease. The Court decided that duty should be calculated by reference to the value of the stock at the date of execution of the lease.

The Inland Revenue's view, in the light of the court's decision in *LM Tenancies*, is that where the rent under a lease is to be adjusted by reference to RPI changes the duty should be calculated by reference to the change in the year ending with the date of execution of the lease. The precise method of adjustment may depend on the terms of the lease and on the way they provide for the calculation to be made. For example, whether the rent is to be increased annually or only at longer intervals. Generally, where the adjustment is to be made by comparing the value of the RPI at different dates, the difference between the two values over the latest year will be used to measure the rent increase for stamp duty purposes.

For example, if the initial rent is £300 a year and is to be adjusted annually, and the RPI has gone up from 150 to 153, equivalent to 2 per cent over the relevant 12 month period, it would be assumed that the rent would go up by £6 (2 per cent of £300) each year. Thus, the rent would be taken as £306 in the second year, £312 in the third year, and so on, in order to calculate the average annual rent under the lease.

The Inland Revenue is issuing instructions to Stamp Offices accordingly, to ensure that individual cases are dealt with on a consistent basis. A taxpayer who disagrees with the Stamp Office's calculation of the duty in a particular case will, of course, have the normal rights of appeal."

One firm of solicitors has already obtained counsel's opinion on this issue, to the effect that the Stamp Office's approach is "not sustainable". If there are any changes in this area the revenue law committee will ensure they are reported as soon as possible.

This note was written by Jill Hallpike, the secretary to the Law Society's revenue law committee.

SDRT ON UK SHARE TRANSFERS

16 January 1997. *Tax Journal. Letter from Macfarlanes with extract from Inland Revenue letter*

. . . the FA 1996 changes to the stamp duty reserve tax (SDRT) regime. Most of these were designed to deal with the charging and collection of SDRT within CREST. Some of the changes, however, have implications for all transfers of shares in UK companies.

If we ignore, for present purposes, the changes made (in FA 1996 s 187(1)) to the territorial scope of SDRT, the principal changes are as follows—

- The two month delay before the charge to SDRT arises has been repealed and SDRT charge arises immediately when the agreement to transfer shares is entered into or, in the case of a conditional agreement, when that agreement becomes unconditional (see the amendments made to FA 1986 s 87(2) by FA 1996 s 88(1). The accountable date for SDR is therefore correspondingly earlier.
- The SDRT charge is not automatically cancelled until a stock transfer form is executed. If the charge is to be cancelled, it must be shown "to the Board's satisfaction" that two conditions have been fulfilled. Those two conditions are (i) that a stock transfer form (or

other transfer document) has been executed and (ii) that the stock transfer form has been properly stamped. Until it is so proved, the duty to notify the inland Revenue of the charge and to pay the SDRT will continue to exist.

Those changes took effect on 1 July 1996.

In correspondence with the Inland Revenue, we have raised the question of how these provisions will affect Stamp Office practice. We referred in particular to cases in which it was not possible to stamp a stock transfer form before the accountable date (and therefore it is not possible to apply for the SDRT charge to be cancelled within that timescale).

This position could, of course, occur in several situations but, in our correspondence, we specifically raised the following circumstances.

The first set of circumstances was where the stock transfer form has been submitted for adjudication and the adjudication has not been completed by the accountable date for SDRT. This might occur (i) where an exemption is being claimed (eg, intra group relief under FA 1930 s 42 or relief for transfers in a reconstruction or amalgamation under FA 1986 s 75) or (ii) where the amount of the consideration is not ascertained or has to be valued (eg, completion accounts being drawn up or the consideration is not in cash).

The accountable date might also be passed without a stampable document being created where completion of the agreement is deferred.

The Inland Revenue's response goes some way to clarifying the practice which the Inland Revenue will adapt in relation to the FA 1996 changes. The Inland Revenue has agreed to the publication of the following extracts from its letter.

"The revisions introduced by the Finance Act 1996 mean that unless an agreement to transfer chargeable securities for money or money's worth is conditional, the charge to SDRT will arise immediately and will not be cancelled until 'it is proved to the Board's satisfaction' that instruments of transfer have been executed and correctly stamped—FA 1986 s 92 (as amended).

In practice it is likely that, in most cases, the relevant transfer document will have been stamped before the SDRT accountable date is reached. In these cases, the Inland Revenue will not expect a separate application for cancellation of SDRT to be made and will accept that stamping itself is sufficient to cancel the SDRT charge, although it may be necessary at a later date to check on selected cases to ensure that documents have been correctly stamped.

There are no provisions in the legislation for postponing or waiving the payment of SDRT where documents have not been stamped by the accountable date. Late payments will incur interest and penalties can be imposed where the tax is over one year late (TMA 1970 ss 86, 93 and 95). The correct procedure is to pay the SDRT by the accountable date. This will be refunded with interest if documents are subsequently stamped. A refund of penalties cannot, however, be guaranteed.

In your letter, you referred to circumstances in which a document cannot be stamped by the accountable date either because it is subject to adjudication or because completion is deferred. The scenarios outlined in your letter fall into two distinct categories:

(i) those where the consideration is not ascertainable by the accountable date or completion will not be possible by this date, although full *ad valorem* stamp duty will eventually be paid; and
(ii) those where the stamp duty is likely to be nominal or nil (eg, because an exemption is being claimed) but the adjudication process will not be concluded by the accountable date.

In the first scenario, SDRT should be paid on the basis of a reasonable estimate of the likely sum of consideration to be paid; it will not be acceptable to estimate the SDRT as nil simply on the basis that stamp duty will eventually be paid and the SDRT cancelled. Once the consideration has been ascertained and the documents are ready for stamping, provided that the SDRT and accrued interest is not less than the sum required to conclude the stamping process, we would be prepared to transfer the sum paid as SDRT (with interest) to the stamp duty account to facilitate stamping. This will remove the need to pay separately for stamp duty and later claim a refund of SDRT. Please note that once out of the SDRT account, the sum would cease to earn interest. Any overpayment would be refunded by your local stamp office.

Where the sum paid as SDRT and accrued interest is less than the sum required for stamping, there will be no facility for transferring funds internally and accountable persons will be required to produce stamped documents before SDRT can be refunded.

We do not envisage many cases falling into the second scenario because the Stamp Office is usually able to respond quickly to routine applications. If these are made in good time, documents are likely to be stamped before the SDRT accountable date. To the extent that this is not possible, we will be prepared to wait for the documents to be adjudicated on the following conditions—

– The accountable person acknowledges in writing liability for the SDRT due and recognises that the Inland Revenue can pursue him for payment with interest at any time subject to any future production of stamped documents or pending stamping.

– The Shares Unit must be given the adjudication case reference number so that the progress of the case can be monitored.

– If the documents are not stamped within three months of the accountable date, the SDRT should be paid in full with interest.

– If the claim for exemption or nominal stamp fails before the end of three months, SDRT should be paid immediately with any interest due.

The Inland Revenue does not waive its right to impose penalties.

Applications will be considered on a case by case basis and the Inland Revenue reserves the right to exclude any case from the above arrangement.

Subject to agreement with these conditions, SDRT does not need to be paid on the accountable date."

STAMP DUTY RESERVE TAX NOTES FOR GUIDANCE

February 1998. *Inland Revenue Stamp Office*

Note—The Guidance Notes were superseded by the Stamp Office Manual, published April 2000. SDRT is covered in Chapters 10–15 of the Manual.

CHANGE IN PRACTICE: VALUE FOR STAMP DUTY WHEN BUSINESS TRANSFERRED AS A GOING CONCERN AND ACTION IF VAT BECOMES PAYABLE.

16 September 1998. *Law Society Gazette. Article reproduced from Stamp Office Customer News Letter and later amended, 15 January 1999.*

The Stamp Office is publicising a change in practice on the sale of a business as a going concern on behalf of HM Customs and Excise. The following is reproduced from the Stamp Office Customer Newsletter.

BUSINESS SALES AND VAT

Sales of businesses often involve the payment of VAT, and we will charge stamp duty on the consideration including that VAT.

If the sale relates to a going concern this is exempt from VAT, which means stamp duty is payable only on the consideration without the addition of VAT.

When you present a business sale document to us, we need to find out whether VAT is payable or not, and whether Custom & Excise accepts that the business qualifies for VAT relief as a transfer of a going concern.

In the past this has often taken the form of advance clearance from Customs & Excise confirming the position.

NEW ARRANGEMENTS

Most Customs & Excise offices will no longer issue these letters, but will instead refer you to the guidance in Public Notice 700/9 (November 1996). Clearance will generally only now be given after the sale has taken place.

DOES THIS MEAN STAMP DUTY WILL BE CHARGED ON THE CONSIDERATION PLUS VAT?

No. Provided that the document does relates to a going concern and there in no clause which allows VAT to be charged at a later date, then duty is payable on the consideration exclusive of VAT.

WHAT IF VAT CAN BE CHARGED?

If the document allows for VAT to be charged later on, for instance, if Customs & Excise refuse clearance, then we will stamp the document on the initial consideration stated and ask you to confirm that—

- the transaction is believed to involve the transfer of a going concern and consequently no VAT has been added to the consideration stated in the document;
- you have advised your client that they are obliged to tell the Stamp Office if that position changes, in line with their obligations under s 5 of the Stamp Act 1891; and
- that the client undertakes to arrange for the document to be returned to the Stamp Office and to pay the extra duty due if VAT does become payable.

A written undertaking from the client to that effect should be enclosed with your letter. The Stamp Office has special arrangements with the Land Registry for the release of documents direct to the Stamp Office where they are held by the Registry but are required for adjustment of the stamp duty they bear.

WHAT CERTIFICATE OF VALUE DO I INCLUDE?

Documents should be certified in respect of the initial consideration paid which is exclusive of VAT.

If a subsequent charge to VAT increases the total amount paid so that the threshold is exceeded, duty will be payable on the VAT-inclusive sum at the higher rate.

STAMP DUTY—NEW LEASES WITH INDEXED RENT LEVELS

14 May 1999.

The Economic Secretary to the Treasury, Patricia Hewitt, today announced that the Inland Revenue have reviewed their practice in relation to the stamp duty treatment of new leases under which future rent levels are expressed to be dependent on future movements in an index such as the retail prices index (RPI).

The change in practice, based on recent legal advice, means that in general less stamp duty will be payable in these cases. Many people who have paid stamp duty on such leases under the current basis will be entitled to a repayment. The new basis takes effect from today.

In a reply to a Parliamentary Question, Mrs Hewitt said—

> "In the light of recent legal advice given to the Inland Revenue the treatment of these leases for stamp duty is to be changed.
>
> When a new lease is taken out, stamp duty is charged by reference to both the premium and the rent under the lease. The premium attracts duty at the same rates as the selling price on the sale of a freehold interest. The premium gets the benefit of the £60,000 nil rate band provided that the rent does not exceed a ceiling, currently £600 per annum. The average annual rent is charged at rates of between 1% and 24%, depending on the length of the lease.
>
> Many leases provide that the rent is to increase by a fixed percentage at annual or other intervals, or they lay down the actual amounts of the increases. The average annual rent, and therefore the stamp duty, is straightforward to calculate in these cases. But if future rent levels are expressed in terms of future movements in a index, like the RPI, it is less clear how a figure for the average annual rent can be calculated at the time the lease is taken out. In the light of representations, on 6 November 1996 the then Economic Secretary made a statement to this House by way of Written Answer, setting out how the Stamp Office would apply stamp duty in such cases for the future, on the basis of legal advice (HC Written Answer, Vol 284 cols 541–543).
>
> Broadly, where the rent under a lease was to be adjusted by reference to future changes in an index, stamp duty would be calculated by reference to changes in that index during the year ending with the date of execution of the lease.

However, the legal validity of this approach has been challenged. Further legal advice given to the Inland Revenue is that the current system of applying a formula to allow for increases in an index number after the date of execution of a lease is not appropriate. So this practice will cease.

In future, where there is a formula expressed in the lease for rent reviews based on the RPI, only any change in the RPI up to the date of its execution will be taken into account for stamp duty purposes. This is expected to result, in most cases, in the average rent being little more than the initial rent.

This change means that people who have paid stamp duty on this type of lease may have paid more duty than they should have done. The Inland Revenue will invite those who paid duty on a lease of this kind to contact the Stamp Office and claim any repayment due to them. Details of the arrangements for repayments are set out in an Inland Revenue press release and on the Inland Revenue web-site."

DETAILS

The Inland Revenue will make repayments of excess stamp duty paid under the practice announced in 1996 as follows—

– repayments will be made to those who made appeals against the assessment of stamp duty pending the outcome of litigation challenging the Stamp Office's practice;
– repayments will also be made to those affected who present a claim to the Stamp Office within the two years of execution of the relevant lease provided for under the Stamp Duties Management Act 1891; and
– in the exceptional circumstances of this change of practice, the Stamp Office will also consider claims in respect of similar leases executed on or after 25 February 1995, provided that such claims are made within one year of the date of this press release.

NOTES

1 Stamp duty on a new lease is based on two elements of payment—the initial payment (premium) and the rent. Any premium is treated like a sale price and attracts duty at the standard scale if it is over £60,000 (1%, 2% and 3% in 1998–99). And the average annual rent bears duty at between 1% and 24%, depending on the terms of the lease.

2 If the annual rent exceeds £600 then the premium loses the advantage of the £60,000 threshold. This is in order to discourage artificial fragmentation of property deals which are close to the threshold.

3 When a fixed cash sum for instance is stated as the rent to be paid over the term of the lease then there is no difficulty in determining the average rent over the life of the lease. But if the lease specifies that the rent for future years will increase in line with an external index such as the retail price index the mechanism for uprating the rent with respect to that index was not as clear as it should be. Hence today's change.

4 In future where rent reviews are to be based on an external index such as the RPI only any change in the RPI up to the date of the execution of the lease will be taken into account for stamp duty.

5 In most cases this will result in the average rent being little more than the initial rent.

6 Under stamp duty law, repayments of excess duty are made by adjusting the stamps impressed on the document, so as to reflect the correct amount due.

7 Applicants for repayments should contact the Stamp Office at the following address—Stamp Allowance Claims Section, Manchester Stamp Office, Alexandra House, Parsonage, Manchester M60 9BT. DX 14430 Manchester 2.

Applications should where possible be accompanied by the original stamped document. If that is not in the applicant's possession, for example because it is held by a solicitor, building society or land registry, the Stamp Office should be consulted as to alternative arrangements. Duplicate and copy documents are not acceptable.

STAMP DUTY RESERVE TAX—DEPOSITARY INTERESTS IN FOREIGN SECURITIES

25 August 1999.

UK depositary interests in foreign securities will be exempt from stamp duty reserve tax (SDRT) following Treasury regulations laid yesterday.

This will allow the operator of an electronic settlement system, which is approved under the Uncertificated Securities Regulations 1995, to provide a settlement service in foreign shares, without purchasers incurring a liability to SDRT.

When UK securities are transferred within such an electronic settlement service, SDRT is charged to match the stamp duty charge on equivalent transfers in paper form. FA 1999 s 119, which provides for these regulations to be made, allows a new kind of security—known as a UK depositary interest in foreign securities—to be transferred within such an electronic settlement service free of SDRT.

Rather than the foreign shares being traded, depositary interests will be issued and traded.

The regulations define the precise scope of these UK depositary interests and ensure that the underlying securities are—

- shares in a foreign company—that is, a company which is neither incorporated in the UK nor centrally managed and controlled in the UK;
- not held on a register in the UK;
- of the same class in the company concerned, as shares that are listed on a stock exchange outside the UK and recognised under TA 1988 s 841;
- not units or shares in a collective investment scheme.

DETAILS

1 The new regulations are the Stamp Duty Reserve Tax (UK Depositary Interests in Foreign Securities) Regulations, SI 1999/2383.

2 The Uncertificated Securities Regulations, SI 1995/3272, made under the Companies Act 1989 s 207, allow relevant securities to be evidenced otherwise than by certificate and transferred by an approved operator within an electronic settlement service, without the use of written instruments.

3 The new regulations, which enable UK depositary interests in foreign securities to be settled within such an electronic settlement service free of SDRT, come into force today.

STAMP DUTY—SEVEN YEAR LEASES

17 September 1999.

The rate of stamp duty applying to the rental element of new leases for exactly seven years is to be confirmed in the Finance Bill 2000.

This will reaffirm the Government's intention of ensuring that new leases of exactly seven years are subject to stamp duty on the rent paid under the lease, and will correct a technical omission in FA 1999, putting an end to any uncertainty.

Annual revenue from stamp duty on the rental element of leases of seven years and below is about £1 million.

DETAILS

1 FA 1999 s 112 and Sch 13 re-state the schedule of rates of stamp duty in percentage terms to correspond to the rates of duty generally in force. This is done to introduce a standardised provision for rounding up amounts of duty to multiples of £5 to streamline administration, with effect from 1 October 1999. The stamp duty rates on leases for periods of less than seven years and those for more than seven years are set at percentages of the rental which correspond to the current rates of duty. But there is no explicit reference to the rate of duty for new leases for a period of exactly seven years, although the current legislation sets the stamp duty for the rental element of such leases at 50p for each £50 or part thereof (or zero in the case of annual rents of no more than £500).

2 The effect of this would be that from 1 October 1999 leases for exactly seven years would not be subject to stamp duty on the rent paid under the lease instead of being liable to the current 1% of the average annual rent—though the duty on any premium paid for the lease would not be reduced.

3 A measure will be brought forward in next year's Finance Bill, effective from 1 October 1999, to ensure that the Government's intention (which was set out in the published explanatory notes to FA 1999) is met. This will again put leases for exactly seven years onto the same footing as those for under seven years.

4 There will be two possibilities for relevant documents for seven year leases executed on or after 1 October 1999 arising in the interim—

(a) They may be presented for stamping in accordance with the lower amounts of duty specified in FA 1999. In such cases—
- the document will be considered to be "duly stamped" for legal purposes until the new measures take effect (after the vote on Resolutions is taken at the end of next year's Budget debates);
- at this point the document will cease to be duly stamped until it is again presented for stamping so that the duty is topped up to the intended 1%;
- interest and penalties for late stamping will apply to the second stamping only if, and to the extent that, the extra duty is paid or a document is presented (again) more than 30 days after the new measures take effect.

(b) Taxpayers may, if they wish, have their documents stamped in the first place at the full 1% to ensure that the documents concerned will remain duly stamped after the new measures take effect. This entirely voluntary procedure will avoid the need for a second presentation for stamping.

NOTES

FA 1999 s 112(3) and Sch 13 include a restatement in percentage terms of the rates of stamp duty in the first schedule to the Stamp Act 1891. An Inland Revenue Budget Day Press Release describes the change to the rounding provisions for stamp duty. The rental element of new leases is charged to stamp duty at a percentage of the average annual rent depending on the length of the lease. Under current legislation, leases for periods not exceeding seven years are charged at 1% and those for between seven and thirty-five years are charged at 2%.

WHEN IS A FIXTURE NOT A FIXTURE?

DEDUCTIONS FOR CHATTELS (OR MOVEABLES IN SCOTLAND)

August 2001. *Stamp Taxes Bulletin*

Where the consideration for the conveyance or transfer on sale of a property includes an amount attributed by the parties to chattels (or moveables in Scotland), that amount will not normally be charged to stamp duty provided the chattels pass by delivery and are not conveyed in the document.

Case law provides that where assets of different character are agreed to be sold for one consideration for the whole, an apportionment between the chargeable and non-chargeable property must be a bona fide one. This is taken to mean that it must be based on the commercial value of the property concerned. A contract for sale based on a false apportionment may be unenforceable because of its improper intent and can therefore have more far-reaching consequences.

Over the last year or so, Stamp Taxes has seen a steady increase in the number of cases where the amount of consideration attributed to items claimed to be chattels is more than a small percentage of the total consideration. This is especially the case where this brings the chargeable amount just below the £250,000 or £500,000 thresholds.

Customers should note that in cases where it appears that an excessive amount of the consideration has been artificially attributed to non-chargeable items a full inventory and breakdown of the consideration will be requested by Stamp Taxes. This is to ensure that all the items claimed as chattels are properly within that description and that the allocation of the consideration is bona fide and not in breach of Section 5 of the Stamp Act 1891.

Stamp Taxes does not provide a comprehensive list of items which are accepted as chattels or moveables since many cases need to be considered on their own merits and case law is evolving in this area all the time. However items which will generally be accepted as chattels or moveables include—carpets, curtains, light shades, pot plants, free-standing kitchen white goods and portable electric or gas fires.

Items which are generally unacceptable as chattels are—fitted kitchen cabinets and cupboards, fitted kitchen white goods, fitted bathroom sanitary ware, central heating systems, plants growing in the soil, central heating systems and gas fires connected to a piped gas supply.

LOOSE PLANT AND MACHINERY

Plant and machinery may in certain circumstances be treated as "goods, wares and merchandise" and will then fall within the exception to the charge to stamp duty under Paragraph 7, Sch 13, Finance Act 1999.

The requirement for plant and machinery to be in an actual state of severance at the date of the agreement for sale for it to fall within the "goods, wares and merchandise" description is an historical one. It stems from case law based on circumstances involving mortgagees in possession. The two main tests as to whether plant and machinery constitutes goods, wares and merchandise are essentially the same as for chattels, namely (1) the degree of annexation to the building or land and (2) the purpose or object of annexation. Stamp Taxes has for many years required customers to certify that plant and machinery claimed as loose plant must be in an actual state of severance if it is to be considered as goods and therefore outside the charge to duty on an agreement for sale. We will no longer insist upon this certification being given.

Where it would be possible for plant and machinery to be relatively easily severed from the property to which it is fixed, say for example by the simple expedient of removing some bolts securing it to the floor or walls, we will no longer insist that this is actually done before it will be considered to be 'loose plant and machinery'.

The position in law has not changed nor does this mean that all plant and machinery suddenly falls within the exception. As in the past, the consideration attributed to fixed plant will be chargeable to stamp duty on the agreement for sale document [Editor's Note: the consideration is actually chargeable to stamp duty at the conveyance stage]. Heavy plant and machinery which is integral to a building and plant where its removal would damage the building or land will still be considered fixed plant. This will be particularly relevant in respect of plant such as, for example, escalators and elevators, boilers, furnaces, walk-in refrigerators and restaurant cooking stations, none of which would be likely to be classed as loose plant for stamp duty purposes. Each case will be considered on its own merits. The Stamp Taxes form Stamps 22 will be amended to reflect this new treatment. The equivalent forms used in Scotland and Northern Ireland do not require amendment since they did not previously include the certification requirement.

Archie Brown—Technical Adviser

Note—This article was published in the Stamp Taxes Bulletin (Issue 1, August 2001).

DISADVANTAGED AREAS—STAMP DUTY EXEMPTION

February 2002. *Stamp Taxes Bulletin*

On 30 November 2001, the Government introduced the first phase of a stamp duty exemption for property transactions in designated disadvantaged areas. The exemption applies to all transfers, conveyances and leases of land, or interests in land, executed on or after 30 November 2001, where the consideration or premium does not exceed £150,000.

BACKGROUND

In the Pre-Budget Report in November 2000 the Chancellor announced that a stamp duty exemption for land transactions in disadvantaged areas would form part of a fiscal package, worth £1 billion over five years, designed to encourage investment and stimulate regeneration in deprived areas. The primary legislation to implement this relief was enacted as Section 92 and Schedule 30 Finance Act 2001. The effect of this legislation was restricted to transactions up to £150,000 by regulations made on 28 November (SI 2001/3746), immediately following the 2001 Pre-Budget Report. The regulations to specify the qualifying areas (SI 2001/3747) and to confirm the date of commencement of the relief (SI 2001/3748) were made on 29 November 2001. This package of regulations reflects the fact that the relief is being implemented in two stages. The next phase, which is subject to approval as state aid by the European Union, is to increase substantially or remove the limit for non-residential property transactions. Before this can be done it is necessary to introduce a definition of residential property in the next Finance Bill.

THE QUALIFYING AREAS: WHERE ARE THEY AND HOW WERE THEY SELECTED?

The areas that qualify for the relief are the most deprived, as determined by the indices of deprivation in each of the four nations that comprise the United Kingdom. In England and

Scotland the poorest 15% of wards and postcodes qualify. In Wales and Northern Ireland the poorest 42% of wards are designated as disadvantaged.

In England, Wales and Northern Ireland, the indices refer to electoral wards or divisions. In Scotland the index uses postcode areas. The regulations use wards and postcode areas accordingly.

We have published the qualifying wards and postcode areas in Scotland on our website at www.inlandrevenue.gov.uk/so. In total there are nearly 2,000 qualifying areas.

WHAT HAPPENS IF THE ELECTORAL WARD OR POSTCODE AREA HAS BEEN ABOLISHED OR CHANGED?

From time to time, reorganisations of local government can result in changes to ward boundaries. Postcode areas can also be subject to revision. The ward and postcode areas specified in the regulations match the ward boundaries and postcodes used in each country's most recent index of deprivation. In England and Wales the indices were compiled in 1998, using the wards and electoral divisions that existed at that time. In Northern Ireland the index of deprivation was compiled in 2001 using the electoral boundaries that existed in 1991.

The Scottish index was updated in 1998, using 1991 postcodes. The question of whether a particular property falls within an area that qualifies for relief therefore depends on whether the property is situated in a qualifying area as determined by boundaries current at:

- 7 May 1998 for England
- 1 April 1998 for Wales
- 21 April 1991 for Scotland & Northern Ireland.

HOW SHOULD CLAIMS FOR THE RELIEF BE MADE?

When you are satisfied that a property falls within an area that qualifies for relief from stamp duty, you should submit a claim to one of our offices. The London office offers a counter service for personal callers and cannot accept postal applications. The exemption is an adjudicated relief and documents on which the relief is claimed must be presented for formal adjudication. To assist us in dealing with claims it would help if the following are provided at the time the document is presented for stamping—

- **a certificate confirming that it is a document on which duty is not chargeable by virtue of Section 92 Finance Act 2001.**
  The certificate may be within the document itself or in an accompanying letter. Section 92 (2) Finance Act 2002 provides that the exemption will only apply if the document is so certified.
- **the full postcode for the property on which the relief is claimed**
  Reference to the postcode is the quickest way for us to confirm that the property is in a qualifying area. The Royal Mail Postcode Enquiry Line 08457 111 222 will supply the postcode for any postal address. For properties that are newly constructed, or for land on which no buildings have been erected, there will be a recently allocated postcode or no postcode at all. We will not in these circumstances, be able to confirm that the property is in a qualifying area. Claims for relief in such cases should be made naming the ward in which the property was located at the qualifying date. A map showing the location of the property and the ward boundaries should be supplied. If this is not possible we will accept a map showing the location of the property in relation to established adjacent properties. The status of the surrounding properties will enable us to confirm that the property, on which relief is claimed, falls within a qualifying area.
- **a completed form L(A)451**
- **a photocopy of the document**
- **a copy of the relevant contract**
- **a certificate of value for £250,000 (not £150,000)**
  It was not possible to use the regulations that limit the effect of Section 92 Finance Act 2001 (SI 2001/3746) to alter the various levels of certificates of value, as set out in the Finance Act 1999. Instead the regulations provide that relief only applies if the document could have included a £150,000 certificate of value if that had been one of the levels of certificate in the 1999 Finance Act. Thus the requirement to provide a certificate of value for £250,000 still holds good.
- **the duty payable on the rental element, if the document is a lease and/or agreement for lease.**

The exemption applies only to lease premiums up to £150,000 and duty is payable on ground rents at usual rates.

– **a note of whether the property is residential or non-residential.**
We need this for statistical and evaluation purposes.

You are reminded that if an examination of your claim results in a decision that relief under Section 92 Finance Act 2001 is not due, and as a consequence, stamp duty is paid after the due date for payment, an interest charge may be incurred.

WHAT IS HAPPENING ABOUT THE NEXT PHASE?

The Government announced an intention to raise significantly, or abolish entirely, the £150,000 limit for transactions in "non-residential" property, probably during this year, subject to approval from the European Union as state aid. The current limit will remain in force for "residential" properties.

Before this second phase can be implemented it is necessary to distinguish "residential" and "non-residential" property in the statute.

On 21 December 2001 we issued a consultation document setting out a draft clause for inclusion in the Finance Bill 2002 to define "residential property" for the purposes of the second phase of the stamp duty exemption for land transactions in disadvantaged areas. Comments on the draft clause are invited by 22 February 2002.

Copies of the press release and consultation document are available in paper form from the Visitor Centre, South West Wing, Bush House, Strand, London WC2B 4QN. An electronic version of the consultation document can be obtained at our web site: www.inlandrevenue.gov.uk/so.

FURTHER INFORMATION

If any further information is needed we have published a detailed customer newsletter, which is available from any of our offices. If your question has not been answered in this article, nor in the newsletter, a member of our telephone helpline staff on 0845 603 0135 (Monday to Friday 08.30–17.00) will be pleased to assist you.

Note—This article was published in the Stamp Taxes Bulletin (Issue 2, February 2002).

OPTIONS—A RESPONSE TO PRESS ARTICLES

October 2002. *Stamp Taxes Bulletin.*

Stamp Offices have received a significant number of telephone enquiries following the publication of certain newspaper articles that promoted the use of options as a stamp duty saving scheme. Callers have been asking us to confirm that the scheme works in the manner described in the articles.

The Inland Revenue considers that these articles contain serious errors in stamp duty law. We are therefore publishing this item to clarify the issues.

The articles suggested that stamp duty on a purchase of a property at a price of £700,000 could be reduced by structuring the transaction so that the purchaser paid a price of £210,000 for an option to acquire the property at a price of £490,000. It was suggested that by doing so the duty of £28,000 that would apply to a purchase at £700,000 would be reduced to £14,700 (ie duty at 3 per cent on the consideration of £490,000 only).

Under Stamp Act 1891 s 5, all relevant facts and circumstances affecting the liability of an instrument to duty or the amount of that duty must be "fully and truly set forth in the instrument". To comply with Section 5 it would therefore be necessary when presenting a transfer document reciting a purchase price of £490,000, to produce the Option Agreement for stamping. An Agreement granting an option to purchase property made for consideration, is a document liable to ad valorem conveyance on sale duty (*George Wimpey & Co Ltd v IRC* [1975] 2 All ER 45).

The transfer of the property at a price of £490,000 would not be stampable at the 3 per cent rate as suggested in the press articles. Since it stems from the Option Agreement, it forms part of a larger series of transactions at an aggregate value exceeding £500,000. A certificate of value for £500,000 could not be validly inserted in the transfer document and duty would, accordingly, be payable at 4 per cent.

The question also arises as to the rate of duty that should apply to the stamping of the option agreement. In any transaction structured in the manner set out in the articles the Stamp Office will require full disclosure of all correspondence surrounding the negotiations and the manner in which the purchase money or monies was paid. Each case will be treated on its merits, but it should be borne in mind that, in some cases, the Stamp Office are likely to contend that the Option Agreement is itself part of a series of transactions, so that any certificate of value to be included in it must take into account the price to be paid upon exercise of the option.

Note—This article was published in the Stamp Taxes Bulletin (Issue 3, October 2002).
Commentary—*Sergeant and Sims on Stamp Duties* **A4.9**.

DISADVANTAGED AREAS—FA 2001 S 92

13 March 2003. *Stamp Taxes Bulletin (extract).*

Since the postcode search tool has been available on our website we have received a number of follow up telephone calls from customers seeking further advice about this exemption.

In response to this we have compiled a list of frequently asked questions (FAQs) and the answers to these questions that we hope you find helpful.

DO I HAVE TO CLAIM THIS RELIEF FROM STAMP DUTY?

Yes as an adjudicated relief the onus is on the customer to make a claim for exemption from stamp duty.

Once you are satisfied that you meet all the qualifying criteria you should submit all the relevant information and documentation to your local stamp office. You should not submit any payments.

WHAT HAPPENS IF I MAKE A CLAIM FOR RELIEF AND IT FAILS?

In the event that you fail to meet all the qualifying criteria your claim for exemption will fail and we will request payment of the stamp duty together with any interest that may be due.

WHAT HAPPENS IF I HAVE PAID THE STAMP DUTY AND LATER FIND OUT THAT THE PROPERTY QUALIFIES FOR EXEMPTION FROM STAMP DUTY?

Providing that you find this out within two years from the date of the document you will be able to claim back any stamp duty paid in error. If we agree with your claim we will add interest to any monies that we repay. You should in the first instance contact the office that dealt with the stamping of your document.

WHAT HAPPENS IF THE RESULT OF MY POSTCODE SEARCH IS NEGATIVE AND THE MESSAGE SAYS THAT THE POSTCODE HAS NOT BEEN "FOUND"?

The result of your postcode search may be negative because your property/land—

- is part of a new development and/or has been allocated a postcode recently which does not appear on our postcode database yet
- has yet to be allocated a postcode

In cases such as this if you are claiming exemption from stamp duty you should tell us that the postcode has not been found or no postcode is available.

You should name the ward in which the property was located as at the qualifying date.

A map showing the location of the property and the ward boundaries should be supplied. If this is not possible we will accept a map showing the location of the property, in relation to established adjacent properties. The status of the surrounding properties will enable us to confirm that the property, on which relief is claimed, falls within a qualifying area.

A list of the qualifying wards (postcode areas in Scotland) as at the qualifying dates is available on our website).

WHAT ARE THE CURRENT RATES OF INTEREST?

The current rates of interest which came into effect from 6 November 2001 are 6.5 per cent on duty that has been paid late and 2.5 per cent on any monies that is due for repayment.

Commentary—*Sergeant and Sims on Stamp Duties* **A1.1, A17.5.**

THE SWITCH TO "STAMP DUTY LAND TAX" PLANNED TO TAKE PLACE ON 1 DECEMBER 2003

June 2003. *SDLT Customer Newsletter—Issue 1*

Welcome to the first of a series of newsletters designed to provide guidance on the introduction of stamp duty land tax later this year.

BACKGROUND

In Budget 2002, the Government announced its intention to modernise the stamp duty charge on UK land and buildings. Current legislation was considered outdated, incompatible with modern commercial practice and the move to e-business. A modernised regime is needed to support the automated electronic systems that the land registries intend to introduce in the next 3–8 years. There has also been increasing evidence of widespread avoidance of duty in large commercial transactions.

In April 2002 a consultative document was published outlining proposals of how the duty might be modernised. A number of consultative committees were established and met regularly through the summer and autumn of last year. The responses to the Consultative Document and the contributions of the various committees informed the next stage of the modernisation project. In November 2002 we published draft legislation to stimulate further debate.

Following from this, the publication of the Finance Bill 2003 on 16 April sets out the statutory framework for the modernised tax, which the Chancellor has announced is planned for introduction from 1 December 2003.

Not all aspects of the tax have been finalised and there is to be a further round of consultation about how it will apply in a number of complex commercial areas. But the basic fundamentals that will apply to the vast majority of transactions are set out in the primary legislation. This newsletter provides information about them and how the changes will affect our customers.

THE KEY CHANGES

Stamp duty has always been a tax on documents. But stamp duty land tax will be a tax on transactions involving interests in land in the UK. The tax will not be triggered by the execution of a document. Instead, tax will become payable automatically on the due date, which will be 30 days after the effective date of the transaction. The effective date is generally the date that the purchaser acquires the subject matter of the transaction, which may be in advance of legal completion of the transfer.

Another major change is that the tax will become mandatory. Stamp duty has sometimes been regarded as a "voluntary tax" because it was not directly enforceable against any person and the Stamp Office could not compel payment of it. Payment of duty has traditionally been made as a result of the pressures that stem from having an unstamped document, the chief ones being the inadmissibility of such documents in court in civil proceedings and the fact that registrars, particularly the land registries, cannot register stampable documents that have not been stamped. The legislation introducing the tax will provide that the purchaser, or person acquiring the subject-matter of the transaction must notify the Stamp Office of the transaction by making a land transaction return together with a self-assessment of the tax due. For this purpose "purchaser" includes a lessee where the transaction in question is the grant or assignment of a lease.

HOW WILL THE PROCESS WORK IN PRACTICE?

There are specific transitional rules that will apply to contracts entered into prior to the implementation date but which are completed after it. These will be covered in a separate newsletter. But generally from 1 December 2003, the purchaser will be required to deliver a land transaction return, giving particulars of the transaction and paying the tax that is due. The Land Transaction Return and payment should be sent to our Processing Centre at Netherton. It will not be necessary to send any supporting documentation such as the contract or the actual transfer. The return can also be submitted to local stamp offices, but this will result in a slower service, as the return has to be processed in the central location. The Processing Centre will process the return and issue a stamp duty land tax certificate. The certificate will be required by the land registries before they will accept documents as evidencing a change of ownership. In effect therefore, the certificate replaces the traditional duty stamps that are currently impressed on documents.

The issuing of the stamp duty land tax certificate does not necessarily mean that the matter is finalised. We will be operating a 'process now, check later system'. We can open an enquiry into a transaction notified to us at any time within nine months of the date that the return is due, or is actually notified to us, if later, (the 'filing date').

As now, some transactions will not be liable to the tax either because they are below the threshold or because the transaction qualifies for a relief. These will still have to be notified to us on a land transaction return if chargeable consideration has been provided and the transaction is the transfer of a freehold, the assignment or transfer of an existing lease or the grant of a new lease for a term of seven years or more. By contrast, certain transactions will not require notification and documents can be self certified as being exempt from the tax and sent direct to the land registries. These will be subject to audits and the same enquiry process. Further guidance will be issued on this in a later newsletter.

Eventually we plan to streamline the system further. The introduction of electronic conveyancing and land registration systems should allow the tax to be paid at the time of registration.

ARE THERE ANY CHANGES TO THE RATES OF DUTY?

For conveyances and transfers of land, tax will continue to be charged as a percentage of the "chargeable consideration". The definition of chargeable consideration has been widened so that it is now defined as "money or money's worth". The present rates of stamp duty will continue to apply to purchases of residential property and the threshold remains at £60,000. But for transactions in non-residential and mixed- use properties the threshold will be increased to £150,000 from the implementation of stamp duty land tax.

For leases, tax on premiums will be calculated in exactly the same way as now, that is as a percentage of the amount paid. Again the threshold for non-residential and mixed-use properties will be increased to £150,000. But the Finance Bill includes legislation that provides for an entirely different method of calculating tax on new lease rents. The new charge will be levied at 1% of the net present value of rental payments payable under the terms of the lease. However, the Government has stated that it will consult further on this proposal and will not implement it if an acceptable alternative basis can be found.

LATE NOTIFICATION OF TRANSACTIONS AND LATE PAYMENT OF TAX

A land transaction return must be delivered and payment of the tax must be made within 30 days of the effective date of the transaction. Penalties are payable if the transaction is notified late and interest is payable on tax paid late.

FURTHER INFORMATION

More information will be provided in later customer newsletters. We recognise that the changes represent a major reform of part of the conveyancing system and that our customers need to be fully informed. For this reason we have developed a customer education programme that was launched in Somerset House on 16 May. We will follow this up with further customer newsletters, information bulletins and articles in Solicitors' and Conveyancers' journals and magazines. We will be enhancing our Internet site and publishing revised leaflets.

In addition, we are planning a series of regional training events for the legal profession in partnership with the Law Societies of England & Wales, Scotland and Northern Ireland.

In the meantime, you may like to consult our website at www.inlandrevenue.gov.uk/so/index.htm for the details published on Budget Day and when the Finance Bill was issued.

TRANSACTIONS IN SHARES

It is stressed that the information in this leaflet applies only to interests in UK land. Transactions in shares are not affected by the changes and they will continue to be liable to stamp duty or stamp duty Reserve Tax exactly as they are now.

THE SWITCH TO "STAMP DUTY LAND TAX" PLANNED TO TAKE PLACE ON 1 DECEMBER 2003

July 2003. *SDLT Customer Newsletter—Issue 2*

Welcome to the second of our newsletters designed to provide guidance on the introduction of stamp duty land tax later this year. This issue focuses on customer awareness and customer education issues.

We are committed to helping to make the changeover as smooth as possible. We will be keeping our customers informed of developments throughout the next few months using a variety of methods, which will be explained later in this newsletter.

WHAT CAN YOU DO NOW?

It is important that our customers are prepared for the changes. Practitioners can do this by ensuring that they consider the legal and practical implications for both themselves and their clients.

CURRENT AWARENESS OF MODERNISATION OF STAMP DUTY

We recently commissioned a study conducted by the British Market Research Bureau to ascertain current awareness levels of the modernisation of stamp duty. 1100 telephone interviews were conducted with a range of solicitors and Licensed Conveyancers from both large and small firms.

The overall level of awareness was 45% but a more detailed breakdown showed that London practitioners were slightly more aware of the changes than those elsewhere—49% compared to 44%. And the more employees in the firm, the greater the level of awareness.

The 493 respondents who were aware of the changes, were asked how they became aware of modernisation. The main sources were the law societies and industry journals at 44% and 42% respectively.

Respondents were then asked whether they felt they had received enough information and a fairly significant 72% said that they hadn't.

In order to assist in the development of an awareness campaign, respondents were asked about their preferred method of receiving information. Leaflets came out well on top at 53%.

HOW WE WILL HELP YOU PREPARE FOR THE CHANGES

On 16 May we hosted an open morning for solicitors, accountants and representatives from various groups affected by the changes to mark the launch of our customer education campaign. The event featured an overview of the new processes and their impact on customers together with a presentation on preparing customers for the changes. The event was very well attended and well received. We intend to hold similar presentations over the next few months. Details and invitations will appear on our website.

The first two issues in a series of **Information Bulletins** have been produced and mailed to around 10,000 firms of solicitors who have had contact with us in the past. These bulletins will continue to be produced in the run up to the commencement of the changes. If people want to be added to the list they should contact Des Newman on 020 7438 7762. The aim of these bulletins is to keep customers informed of developments on an ongoing basis. They will be produced every 4 to 6 weeks.

This series of **Customer Newsletters** will contain more detailed information about technical changes. Again they will be produced every 4 to 6 weeks and will be enclosed when documents are returned from Stamp Offices to Conveyancers.

Eight weeks prior to implementation of the changes, **flyers** will be enclosed with all returned documents reminding Conveyancers about what they need to do from 1 December. This message will focus on a different issue each week.

The above documents will also be available on the Stamp Taxes website.

The market research demonstrated that **industry journals** were one of the key ways in which people obtained information and therefore we will be proactively contacting various magazines and journals with a view to having articles placed.

An exhibition stand has been produced which we are willing to take to any relevant exhibitions and events.

TRAINING

Actual training for solicitors will be delivered by ourselves working in partnership with the three law societies (England & Wales, Scotland and Northern Ireland). Training will be rolled out from September onwards and dates and venues are available from the respective law societies.

The events will be organised by the law societies who will be responsible for the administration and advertising. The actual training material will be produced by us and we will provide the speakers at the sessions which will last around two hours.

The training will cover—

- an overview of the main legislative changes
- details of the enquiry process from opening through to closure
- completion of the new Land Transaction Return
- the various ways in which customers can obtain advice and guidance.

CUSTOMER ASSISTANCE

Customers will be helped with their obligations both before and after go live in a variety of ways.

The existing stamp duty **leaflets** are being reviewed and it is likely that there will be one main SDLT leaflet covering all aspects which will be available only on the Internet. There will then be a simple quick reference guide to SDLT aimed at the public but this will be available in hard copy as well.

In line with other taxes, there will be a **Code of Practice** to support the enquiry process. This will automatically be enclosed when a letter is issued to notify the customer that an enquiry is to take place.

A number of **calculation tools for the Internet** are being developed. An SDLT calculator will allow users to input the price, the date of their purchase in order to obtain the amount of SDLT due (including SDLT on leases). In addition a digital mapping tool for disadvantaged areas is being developed which will allow users to search for, and identify, land and property that qualifies for disadvantaged area relief.

The introduction of SDLT will bring with it a requirement for new **guidance** and an SDLT Manual will be produced covering three areas—technical, procedural and compliance. In accordance with the Code of Practice on Access to Government information the manual will be published on the Internet.

WHERE CAN I FIND FURTHER INFORMATION?

The **Enquiry Line** has already been expanded and there is the capacity to add additional resources should they be required. The Enquiry Line is open from Monday to Friday from 8.30am to 5pm and the number is 0845 6030135. All calls are charged at local rates.

Further information can be found on the Stamp Taxes website.

Additional details are available in the Finance Bill 2003 press notice (REV 55) and the budget day press notice, PN05—Modernising the taxation of property. These can also be found on our website.

THE SWITCH TO STAMP DUTY LAND TAX PLANNED TO TAKE PLACE ON 1 DECEMBER 2003

August 2003. *SDLT Customer Newsletter—Issue 3*

COMMENCEMENT AND TRANSITIONAL PROVISIONS

This issue of the newsletter is concerned with the introduction of stamp duty land tax on 1 December 2003. It provides guidance on whether transactions that may have been entered into prior to that date but which are completed at a later date are within the existing stamp duty regime, or come within the scope of stamp duty land tax.

In this article we focus on general principles and the main points that are likely to arise. It is not possible to cover every possible scenario. We have already published on our web site a flow chart that can be used to determine whether or not a transaction is a stamp duty or stamp duty land tax matter [reproduced in the Annex below].

More detailed guidance will be available in the new stamp duty land tax manual that will be published in electronic form. A draft version of the manual will be published on the Internet in the beginning of October 2003. We would welcome comments on the content of the manual. Please send comments by post to—

Vivienne Scrimshire, Room 116, New Wing, Somerset House, London WC2B 1 LR, or alternatively these may be e-mailed to Vivienne.Scrimshire@ir.gsi.gov.uk

The legislation dealing with the commencement and transitional provisions is contained in Finance Act 2003 Sch 19. The Finance Act 2003 received Royal Assent on **10 July 2003** and this is an important date in considering whether or not a transaction is to be subject to stamp duty or stamp duty land tax.

THE BASIC CHARGE TO STAMP DUTY LAND TAX

As a general rule, a land transaction falls within the scope of stamp duty land tax if the "effective date" of the transaction is on or after "implementation date". The "effective date" of a transaction is the earlier of the transaction being completed by a conveyance, or the date that the contract is "substantially performed". Substantial performance of a contract occurs when—

- the purchaser (which includes a lessee under the terms of a lease) has paid any rent, or
- the purchaser has paid the whole or substantially the whole (not normally less than 90%) of any consideration other than rent, or
- the purchaser has taken possession, or become entitled to possession of the property. This includes receipt of, or entitlement to receipt of, rents and profits.

Implementation date means 1 December 2003.

Example 1

A contracts to sell a property to B on 15 December 2003. The transaction is completed by the purchase price being paid in full on 15 January 2004 and a transfer is executed the same day. This is a stamp duty land tax transaction as the effective date of the transaction is after "implementation date", 1 December 2003.

Accordingly the transaction will be notifiable as a stamp duty land tax transaction on a Land Transaction Return. (For guidance on this please refer to Customer Newsletter 1 [reproduced above]).

In example 1 both the contract and the effective date of the transaction were after implementation date. It is not necessary however for the contract to have been entered into after 1 December 2003 for a transaction to be subject to stamp duty land tax. Contracts entered into prior to 1 December 2003 may give rise to a stamp duty land tax charge (see example 2).

Example 2

A contracts to sell a property to B on 18 September 2003. The transaction is completed by the purchase price being paid on 7 December 2003 and a transfer is executed the same day. As the effective date of the transaction is after "implementation date", the transaction is a stamp duty land tax transaction.

CONTRACTS ENTERED INTO ON OR BEFORE 10 JULY 2003

There are however, special rules that apply for land transactions that implement contracts entered into on or before 10 July 2003. The key points are as follows—

- Contracts that are substantially performed on or before 10 July 2003 are not stamp duty land tax transactions (see example 3).
- Contracts that are not substantially performed on or before 10 July 2003 are not stamp duty land tax transactions (see example 4) unless—
  - (a) there is any variation of the contract or assignment of rights under the contract after 10 July 2003; or
  - (b) the transaction is effected in consequence of the exercise after 10 July 2003 of any option, right of pre-emption or similar right; or

(c) the purchaser under the transaction is a person other than the purchaser under the contract because of a further contract (for example a sub-sale contract) made after 10 July 2003.

A variation of a contract under (*a*) does not include minor matters peripheral to the contract such as changes to colour schemes or pets being permitted on premises. It does however, include any changes to the following; the parties to the transaction, the subject matter of the sale, the contractual consideration or in an agreement for lease, the length of the term.

Example 3

On 1 May 2003, A contracted to sell a property to B. On 1 June 2003, B paid the purchase price in full (an act of substantial performance). The contract is completed by a conveyance dated 1 March 2004. This is not a stamp duty land tax transaction because it was substantially performed on or before 10 July 2003. The conveyance is liable to stamp duty.

Example 4

A contracts to sell a property to B on 1 July 2003. The contract is not substantially performed in advance of completion and none of the exceptions listed at (*a*) to (*c*) above apply. A conveyance of the property is made to the contracting purchaser, B, on 7 March 2004. This is not a stamp duty land tax transaction but the conveyance is liable to stamp duty.

VARIATIONS AND CONTRACTS ENTERED INTO ON OR AFTER 10 JULY 2003

Finance Act 2003 Sch 19 para 4(3) makes special provisions for contracts entered into prior to implementation date. These include a contract made on or before 10 July 2003 which has not been substantially performed before 10 July 2003, a similar contract that has been varied after that date, or where the contracting purchaser has sub-sold or transferred his rights after that date. It also makes provision for contracts entered into in the period between 10 July 2003 and 1 December 2003.

The substantial performance of such contracts before implementation is disregarded. Consequently a charge to stamp duty land tax can only arise on completion. The following examples illustrate this.

Example 5

A contracts to sell a property to B on 1 October 2003. Substantial performance of the contract takes place on 20 November 2003 when B pays the purchase price in full. The contract is completed by the conveyance of the property to B on 1 July 2006. A charge to stamp duty land tax arises on 1 July 2006.

Example 6

A contracts to sell a property to B on 1 September 2003 and substantial performance occurs on 15 October 2003 when B pays the purchase price in full. On 1 November 2003 B contracts to sell the property to C. The contract is completed on 1 February 2004, when A transfers the property direct to C. There is no charge to stamp duty Land tax on B because the conveyance to the ultimate purchaser does not trigger a stamp duty land tax charge. C incurs a stamp duty land tax liability on 1 February 2004.

In the example above, B has been able to benefit from the availability of a modified form of sub-sale relief. But it should be borne in mind that this relief was available only because substantial performance of the A-B contract occurred before 1 December 2003. Sub-sale relief will only be available in respect of contracts entered into after 10 July 2003 in very limited circumstances. More guidance on sub-sales will be provided in a later Newsletter.

Example 7

A contracts to sell a property to B on 1 November 2003, which is substantially performed (for the first time) on 1 March 2004 in advance of completion when B pays the purchase price. As substantial performance occurred after 1 December 2003 a stamp duty land tax charge arises on B, on 1 March 2004.

STAMP DUTY CREDIT AVAILABLE TO OFFSET AGAINST STAMP DUTY LAND TAX CHARGE

Where a stamp duty land tax transaction is effected pursuant to a contract entered into before 1 December 2003 any ad valorem stamp duty paid on the contract is available for crediting against the stamp duty land tax liability that arises when the transaction is substantially performed or completed. There is however, no entitlement to a refund if it transpires that the stamp duty liability exceeds the stamp duty Land tax charge.

Examples of contracts liable to ad valorem stamp duty are pre-implementation date—

- Agreements for Lease, and
- Contracts for sale chargeable under FA 2002 s115 (consideration exceeding £10 million).

STAMP DUTY PROVISIONS AFFECTING LAND TRANSACTIONS.

- An instrument effecting a land transaction is not subject to stamp duty if the transaction is a stamp duty land tax transaction (FA 2003 s125 (5)(*a*))—See example 2 above.
- If a conveyance is within the charge to stamp duty there is no charge to stamp duty land tax—See example 4 above.
- Sch 19 para 8 makes special provisions that broadly replicate the provisions of FA 1994 s 240 as amended, relating to Agreements for Lease and leases. The following is an example of this.

Example 8

An agreement for lease is entered into on 1 October 2003,which is completed when the lease is executed on 1 March 2004. The Agreement for Lease is a stamp duty transaction because at the time that it was executed it did not effect a stamp duty land tax transaction. It is liable to stamp duty under FA 1999 Sch 13 para 14. Under the provisions of FA 1994 s 240 as amended, stamping of the Agreement can be deferred until 30 days after the execution of the lease without the penalty or interest provisions applying.

In these circumstances the delivery of a stamp duty land tax Return, the Agreement for Lease and payment within 30 days of 1 March 2004 will not give rise to the Agreement incurring a stamp duty penalty or interest charge. Procedural guidance will be issued at a later date regarding the manner that the Return and the Agreement should be presented to Stamp Taxes.

If the Agreement for Lease had been stamped prior to the lease being granted, the duty paid on the Agreement would be credited against the stamp duty land tax charge. Again further guidance will be provided at a later date regarding the procedural arrangements.

An important point to note is that the timing differences of the Agreement for Lease and lease, which straddle the "implementation date", means that an entirely different basis of calculation is used to determine the amount of stamp duty payable on the Agreement, and the amount of stamp duty land tax payable when the lease is granted. This is because lease rents are charged to stamp duty on the average annual rent, whereas stamp duty land tax calculates tax on the net present value of the lease rents over the term. Additional information will be provided on how stamp duty land tax on lease rents is calculated in a later newsletter.

ADDITIONAL MISCELLANEOUS PROVISIONS

In this newsletter we have attempted to concentrate on the main issues that are likely to arise on the more routine transactions. It is not proposed to comment in greater detail on the following, which are, nevertheless, listed for information.

- Contracts liable to stamp duty under FA 1999 Sch 13 para 7 (equitable interests) are deemed to have been duly stamped if they are completed by a stamp duty land tax transaction (FA 2003 Sch 19 para 6(1)).
- Transitional provisions that apply in relation to group relief and acquisition relief are provided at FA 2003 Sch 19 paras 6(2) and 6(3).
- FA 2003 Sch 19 para 7 makes provisions for transactions which are not themselves stamp duty land tax transactions but are "linked" to stamp duty land tax transactions.
- FA 2003 Sch 19 para 9 makes provisions for options and rights of pre-emption acquired before implementation date but exercised on or after implementation date.

In addition to the further Newsletters that will be published in the run up to implementation further guidance will be given at a number of regional training events. For further information on these please refer to Newsletter issue 2 [reproduced above].

ANNEX

Is my transaction subject to SDLT?

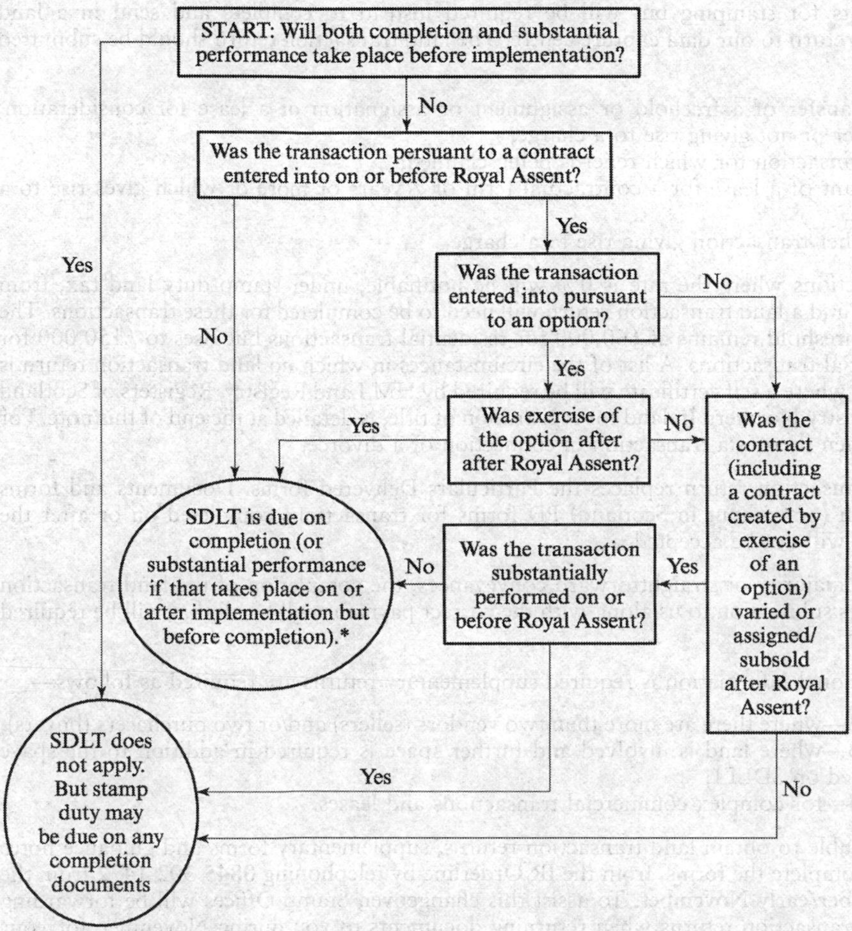

* Stamp duty may still be due on an agreement for lease or contract for over £10 million entered into before implementation. Credit is available against the SDLT due on subsequent completion or substantial performance.

NEW PROCESS FOR SDLT THAT WILL APPLY FOR THE MAJORITY OF TRANSACTIONS COMPLETED ON OR AFTER 1 DECEMBER 2003

September 2003. *Stamp Duty Information Bulletin—Issue 4*

This issue covers the new process for stamp duty land tax that will apply for the majority of transactions completed on or after 1 December 2003 and answer some frequently asked questions to help you to understand the changes that are taking place. Further information on stamp duty land tax is available on [the Inland Revenue website: http://www.inlandrevenue.go-v.uk/so/land_tax_changes.htm].

More detailed guidance will be available in the new stamp duty land tax manual that will be published in electronic form. A draft version of the manual [was] published in the week commencing 22 September 2003 and may be accessed from our website. We would welcome comments on the content of the manual. Please send comments by post to Vivienne Scrimshire, Room 116, New Wing, Somerset House, London WC2B 1LR; or alternatively these may be e-mailed to—Vivienne.Scrimshire@ir.gsi.gov.uk.

THE NEW PROCESS FROM 1 DECEMBER 2003

Stamp duty land tax is a tax on transactions, not documents. For transactions in land and buildings in the UK, completed on or after 1 December 2003 you will no longer need to send in documents for stamping but will be required instead to complete and send in a land transaction return to our data capture centre. The land transaction return should be submitted to notify—

- any transfer of a freehold or assignment or assignation of a lease for consideration, whether or not giving rise to a charge;
- any transaction for which relief is being claimed;
- the grant of a lease for a contractual term of 7 years or more or which gives rise to a charge;
- any other transaction giving rise to a charge.

NB: Transactions where the rate is 0% will be notifiable, under stamp duty land tax, from 1 December and a land transaction return will need to be completed for these transactions. The 0% upper threshold remains at £60,000 for residential transactions but rises to £150,000 for non-residential transactions. A list of the circumstances in which no land transaction return is required but where a self certificate will be required by HM Land Registry, Registers of Scotland or Land Registry Northern Ireland for registration of title, is detailed at the end of this note. For example, when there is a transaction in connection of a divorce.

The land transaction return replaces the Particulars Delivered forms. Documents and forms received with (or without in Scotland) PD forms for transactions completed on or after the 1 December will not be accepted.

For the vast majority of straightforward conveyances, the completion of the land transaction return and its submission to us along with the correct payment will be all that will be required of you.

Where additional information is required supplementary returns are required as follows—

- SDLT2—where there are more than two vendors (sellers) and/or two purchasers (buyers);
- SDLT3—where land is involved and further space is required in addition to the space provided on SDLT1;
- SDLT4—for complex commercial transactions and leases.

You will be able to obtain land transaction returns, supplementary forms and guidance notes on how to complete the forms, from the IR Orderline by telephoning **0845 302 1472** from the end of **October/early November**. To assist this changeover, Stamp Offices will be forwarding blank land transaction returns when returning documents to you during November, for your use from 1 December for transactions within the scope of stamp duty land tax.

Submission of plans

Accurate identification of property is of vital importance. If you are able to find out the National Land and Property Gazetteer Unique Property Reference Number (box 31 on the land transaction return), you should enter it on the return, as this will assist greatly in ensuring the correct identification of the property.

However, a plan submitted with the return can also be of great help in the identification process for certain types of property. Plans are required for development land, agricultural land and small "garden" plots. You do not need to submit plans for domestic property—this includes new housing developments where properties are often referred to by plot numbers.

Completing and signing the land transaction return

The detailed guidance notes should be used when completing the form which must be completed in ***black ink***. The completed land transaction return **must legally be signed by the purchaser (buyer). If there is more than one purchaser it must be signed by all purchasers.** The return **may not** be signed by the purchaser's solicitor or agent. It is the purchaser's responsibility to ensure that the information contained in the land transaction return is correct and complete. The purchaser may request that their agent be authorised to handle correspondence on their behalf, by completing box 59 of the land transaction return, however the purchaser remains responsible for the return and the payment of the stamp duty land tax

Each form has a unique reference number, so photocopies may not be used.

Where to send the land transaction return

The land transaction return must be sent to the Inland Revenue's rapid data capture centre within 30 days of the effective date of the transaction. The full address is: Inland Revenue, Stamp Taxes, Comben House, Farriers Way, Netherton, Merseyside, L30 4RN.

It is important not to send the returns to local Stamp Offices as this will delay the issue of a certificate. Local offices will not be able to process land transaction returns and will re-direct them to the data capture centre. You should send payment of stamp duty land tax at the same time as you submit the land transaction return. Payment may be made by—

- Cheque, enclosed with the return;
- electronic payment (BACS, CHAPS etc);
- at your bank, Post Office or by Alliance and Leicester/Giro account using the payslip.

The certificate will be based solely on information contained on the land transaction return (and where appropriate supplementary forms). Any additional information provided by way of covering letter or documents will not be considered. Therefore no covering letter, other information or documents should be submitted with the return unless you are submitting a plan because the land is for development, is agricultural or is a small "garden" plot.

Envelopes will be available, via the Orderline, with the Netherton DX (Document exchange) number provided for those firms that have this postal service.

What happens at the rapid data capture centre?

The completed land transaction return is scanned and the data optically- captured The return will only be processed if it contains—

- a unique reference number;
- the liable person's name and address (the liable person is generally the purchaser);
- a signed declaration, signed by all purchasers;
- the effective date of the transaction (an explanation of what is an effective date is described in the frequently asked questions).

Land transaction returns that do not meet these basic requirements cannot be processed and so will be returned to customers. If other areas of the form are not completed, although we may be able to accept the form for processing we will seek that additional information through a follow up letter. To assist us in providing you with a quality service, we would urge you to complete the return as fully as possible to avoid delays.

Land transaction return certificate

A certificate will be issued once the land transaction return has been processed at our data capture centre if—

- all relevant information is provided;
- our own system check verifies the calculation of stamp duty land tax due;
- payment is enclosed.

The certificate replaces the impressed stamp and provides you with valid proof that stamp duty land tax has been paid. The certificate must be presented to HM Land Registry, Registers of Scotland or Land Registry Northern Ireland when applying for registration of title.

Late returns

The Finance Act 2003 introduced a penalty for late notification and payment of stamp duty land tax. Where the land transaction return and/or payment is not received within 30 days of the effective date of the transaction (the filing date) but within three months of the 30 day limit, a penalty of £100 will be charged automatically. A penalty of £200 will be automatically charged in all other cases. Any late payment will also give rise to an interest charge.

Amended returns

Where customers wish to query or amend information captured, they should write to a local Stamp Office who will have a facility to amend the original notification. An amendment may not be made more than 12 months after the filing date.

Circumstances when no land transaction return is required

The following transactions do not need to be notified for stamp duty land tax purposes. However, you will need to certify that the transaction is exempt and submit, as now, that self-certificate to HM Land Registry, Registers of Scotland or Land Registry Northern Ireland when applying for registration of title. We have provided a special form for this purpose which is available from the Orderline.

(1) transfer or conveyance of a freehold interest in land (in Scotland, ownership of land or the interest of the proprietor of the *dominium utile* of land) for no chargeable consideration;
(2) transfer or assignment of a leasehold interest in land (in Scotland, assignation of a tenant's interest under a lease of land) for no chargeable consideration;
(3) grant of lease (in Scotland, exchange of missives of let) where all the following are satisfied—
- the term of the lease is less than seven years;
- the amount of any premium is not such as to attract a charge to stamp duty land tax at a rate of 1% or more (ignoring the availability of any relief);
- the amount of any rent is not such as to attract a charge to stamp duty land tax at a rate of 1% or higher (ignoring the availability of any relief);

(4) other land transaction (for example, the grant of an easement or servitude) where the chargeable consideration is not such as to attract a charge to stamp duty land tax at a rate of 1% or higher (ignoring the availability of any relief);
(5) land transaction exempt from stamp duty land tax under Schedule 3 paragraph 3 Finance Act 2003 (transactions in connection with divorce);
(6) land transaction exempt from stamp duty land tax under Schedule 3 paragraph 4 Finance Act 2003 (variation of testamentary dispositions).

Self-certificate forms will be available from the IR Orderline and HM Land Registry, Registers of Scotland and Land Registry of Northern Ireland from 1 December. You can use photocopies of this form.

FREQUENTLY ASKED QUESTIONS

1. Why do I have to send the form to Netherton?

The Inland Revenue's rapid data capture centre in Netherton, near Liverpool, is one of the sites used for scanning a variety of Inland Revenue forms. This is where completed land transaction returns will be scanned in order to produce a stamp duty land tax certificate, the equivalent of the stamping process undertaken now. This certificate is the document you submit to HM Land Registry, the Registers of Scotland or the Land Registers of Northern Ireland in order to apply for registration of title. Centralising and automating the process in this way will streamline the capture of your property information data and the production of the certificate with the aim of providing rapid and consistent turnaround times for you throughout the year. It is worth noting that our local Stamp Offices will not have this scanning facility so will be unable to offer an alternative service to that provided by the Netherton centre.

2. Why does the form need to be signed by the purchaser(s)?

Unlike the current stamp duty regime, Stamp duty Land Tax introduces a clearly identifiable liable person—usually the purchaser or lessee. This person is legally responsible, for notification and payment of stamp duty land tax. They will also be liable to pay any additional tax, interest or penalties arising as a result of a formal enquiry into the return. It is therefore important that the liable person satisfies him/herself that the information being provided on the land transaction return is complete and correct to the best of their knowledge. Following precedents in other taxes where there is a liable person, the best way for a liable person to confirm to Inland Revenue that they are satisfied with the information being provided is by way of signature on the return. This is a statutory requirement under stamp duty land tax and returns which are not signed will not be accepted.

3. Why is the land transaction return (SDLT1) longer than the LA451 ("Particulars Delivered")?

The new form replaces the information included on the LA451 and the supporting documents provided with it, which can be scrutinised by the Stamp Office. Although there are six pages to the new form, for most straightforward transactions (eg simple residential conveyances), less than half the boxes will need to be completed. The information requested is necessary for the correct liability to be established and for the tax to be properly and fairly administered. Comprehensive and accurate data supplied to us will be invaluable in building up a detailed picture of the property market and will help inform possible future policy and operational decisions on Stamp duty Land Tax.

4. Why do I have to supply National Insurance numbers?

The purchaser's National Insurance number is only required where the purchaser, or one of the purchaser's, is an individual. The Inland Revenue's main record system uses National Insurance numbers and as part of our modernisation programme we are linking into this system. This will allow stamp duty land tax to be administered more efficiently and fairly in line with our other mainstream taxes. We do however appreciate that not all individual purchasers may have a National Insurance number for example if the purchaser is a non-UK national. Our guidance notes to the form cover what you need to do in these circumstances.

5. Why can't I send in documents as previously?

In the vast majority of cases all the necessary data will have been provided on the form so it will no longer be necessary to send in documents as well. This will reduce the amount of paper to be sent through the post to us and should avoid any chance of valuable original documents going astray. The new process also represents a first step towards more streamlined ways of submitting data to us and helps prepare the way for possible future changes, such as the plans for an electronic conveyancing system to co-ordinate the electronic delivery of various aspects of the conveyancing process.

6. Can I complete the form electronically?

We are currently looking at a number of ways to allow the form to be completed on-screen and are working closely with representative bodies and others. We'll keep you informed of our progress as we appreciate that many of you would welcome the opportunity to complete the form this way. Please look out for information about this in future bulletins and on our website.

7. What are the transitional provisions for land and property transactions that take place around the December 2003 changeover date?

The transitional provisions are contained in Schedule 19 Finance Act 2003. This Schedule provides the rules for determining whether a transaction, entered into prior to 1 December 2003, which is completed after 1 December, is chargeable to stamp duty or stamp duty land tax.

A flowchart is available to help you decide if the transaction is subject to stamp duty land tax on our website at—www.inlandrevenue.gov.uk/so/sdlt_flowchart.pdf. Also, information and examples our provided in our Customer Newsletter Issue 3 available at: www.inlandrevenue.gov.uk/so/newsletter3.pdf.

8. What is the effective date of a transaction?

For the majority of transactions the effective date is the date of completion of the transaction, whether or not this is evidenced by a document. However if a contract is substantially performed before completion, the date on which substantial performance takes place is the effective date. Broadly substantial performance is the point at which—

- payment of a substantial amount of the consideration (generally 90% of the total amount) is made;
- the purchaser is entitled to possession of the property;
- the first payment of rent is made);
- option or right of pre-emption—is when the option or right is acquired.

9. What records covering transactions need to be retained and for how long?

The new arrangements for stamp duty land tax are built on the basis of a "process now—check later" system. This is again in line with the way that the Inland Revenue administers other taxes. In order to undertake the "check later" part of this, we will select a small number of transactions for enquiry. In those cases we will ask for supporting evidence concerning the particular property transaction. All records supporting transactions should be kept for six financial years. It is the responsibility of the purchaser to ensure records are kept. Examples of the types of records that need to be retained are detailed below but the list is not exhaustive—

– a contract/agreement for sale and any related papers;
– professional valuations of both the land and any apportionments of fixed fixtures and loose fittings, if such valuations were obtained at the time;
– relevant instruments relating to the transaction, in particular any contract or conveyance, and any supporting maps, plans or similar documents.

10. How do I find out if the property is in a disadvantaged area and qualifies relief?

There is an on-line "postcode tool" on our website at—http://inlandrevenue.gov.uk/so/pcode_search.htm.

This will enable you to determine whether a property is in a disadvantaged area from the postcode. Where exceptionally the answer cannot be found, for example for a new property that has only just received a postcode, you can gain further guidance from our Enquiry Line by telephoning 0845 603 0135.

We are looking at other ways of improving how this information is provided to you. Full details will be provided on our website.

Note

We would also like to clarify a point arising from an overview of the changes that we made in issue 3.

In the previous bulletin where an overview of some of the changes to stamp duty was provided including the point that for transactions completed on or after 1 December 2003, legal practitioners will no longer need to submit documents, on behalf of purchasers, to the Inland Revenue for stamping. Instead they will have to notify liability to tax using the new land transaction return. Payment should be sent at the same time as the return to the Inland Revenue processing centre in Netherton. Provided information and payment are submitted in full, the Inland Revenue will issue a stamp duty land certificate which they or their agents will need to submit to land registries in order to register ownership of land or to record a deed, as appropriate. The certificate replaces the current stamped impressions, which are made onto documents.

We would like to clarify that this is subject to transitional provisions under which certain transactions effected in pursuance of contracts entered into on or before Royal Assent of the Finance Act (10 July 2003) remain subject to stamp duty.

MODERNISING STAMP DUTY ON LAND TRANSACTIONS

20 October 2003. *IR News Release*

The Government today announced the next steps in the process of modernising stamp duty on land transactions, following the announcement of the main proposals in Budget 2003.

These include—

– A significant change to the proposed charge on the rental element when a new lease is granted ("lease duty"), reducing tax bills by £1500 per lease on commercial transactions (£600 per lease on residential transactions), which will be of special benefit to smaller businesses.
– A new relief for businesses raising finance through the sale and leaseback of their land and buildings and relief for "chain-breaking" and similar companies which help to ensure an active housing market
– Further consultation on how the new regime might apply to partnerships. The announcement follows extensive consultation on the process throughout the earlier part of this year.

Ruth Kelly MP, Financial Secretary to the Treasury, said—

> "Stamp duty land tax is on course for implementation on 1 December 2003. The proposals announced today, along with those announced in Budget 2003, will help to achieve the

Government's aim of a modern, efficient, system of taxing land transactions which promotes fairness between taxpayers, reduces distortions and prevents avoidance. I am also pleased that our proposals, which follow extensive and valuable consultation with interested parties, will be of particular help to small and medium-sized enterprises and business start-ups."

The Government will shortly be laying regulations before the House of Commons to give effect to the changes to lease duty, sale and leaseback, chain-breaking and other reliefs. The regulations will also make some technical corrections and clarifications which are set out in the attached Technical Note. The Government has today published draft clauses for consultation on partnerships.

DETAILS

The story so far

1 In his Budget Statement on 9 April 2003 the Chancellor of the Exchequer announced that a modernised system of stamp duty, renamed "stamp duty land tax", would apply to most land transactions on or after 1 December 2003. This system will replace the current archaic system of impressing a physical stamp on documents with a regime in line with that for other taxes. People acquiring interests in land will be required to submit a "land transaction return" to the Inland Revenue along with payment of the duty. This will substantially reduce the scope for avoidance since liability will depend on the nature of the transaction and not on the technicality of which particular document was used.

2 The Chancellor also announced that on or after 1 December 2003 the threshold below which no stamp duty is payable would be raised, for commercial transactions, to £150,000 from the current £60,000. Furthermore, as an aid to regeneration, commercial transactions in designated disadvantaged areas would be entirely exempt from stamp duty.

3 Stamp duty land tax is on course for implementation on 1 December 2003. The Inland Revenue has launched a substantial customer education programme aimed at ensuring in particular that solicitors, licensed conveyancers and other professional advisers are aware of the significance of the change for their practices.

4 The announcements made today cover stamp duty land tax on the rental element of newly granted leases ("lease duty"), further reliefs for particular commercial transactions and stamp duty land tax on partnership transactions.

Lease duty

5 In his Budget Statement the Chancellor announced his decision that a new structure for lease duty should come into force on 1 December. The current structure, with its arbitrary "cliff edges" and reliance on average annual rent, created distortions, encouraged decisions which were tax-driven rather than business-driven, and gave opportunities for avoidance.

6 The Government is keen that any new structure should—

– minimise potential scope for avoidance,
– reduce the distortions inherent in the current system to achieve greater fairness in the treatment of different transactions,
– better reflect modern commercial practice,
– be based on clear economic principles and in line with modern valuation and accounting principles, and
– be more in line with the charge on freehold transfers (transfers of ownership).

7 A structure which in the Government's view achieves these aims was accordingly included in Finance Act 2003. However the Chancellor made it clear that consultation on a new structure would continue and that changes might be made before implementation of the new structure on 1 December 2003.

8 The Government is extremely grateful to all who participated in the consultation process. A good deal of valuable information and data was provided by participants and some important work was done in partnership. Throughout the consultation process the Government has been particularly keen to have regard to the effect of any new structure on small and medium-sized enterprises and business start-ups.

9 Having considered all the contributions made the Government now proposes to modify the structure contained in Finance Act 2003 as follows—

– The Finance Act charges stamp duty land tax on the "Net Present Value" ("NPV") of rent payable under a lease. NPV sums the discounted values of the rents. This discount recognises that future rent payments will be of less value. The Government believes that NPV represents a fair way of assessing the amount on which stamp duty land tax should be charged and proposes to retain it.

– The Finance Act sets a threshold of £150,000 for commercial leases, £60,000 for residential leases. If the NPV does not exceed the threshold no stamp duty land tax is charged on the rental element. These thresholds mean that 60% of commercial leases and 93% of residential leases will pay no stamp duty land tax on the rental element. The Government believes these thresholds are fair and intend to retain them.
– The Finance Act provides that once the threshold is exceeded stamp duty land tax is charged at 1% of the full amount of the NPV. The Government proposes to modify this so that stamp duty land tax is charged at 1% of the excess over the threshold. This means that on any commercial lease chargeable to stamp duty land tax the tax payable on the rental element will be £1,500 less than under the Finance Act provisions. Similarly for residential leases, the stamp duty land tax payable on the rental element will be £600 less.

Example

A lease of commercial property for 18 years at an annual rent of £15,000 will have an NPV of £197,845. Under the Finance Act provisions stamp duty land tax of £1,978 would be payable. Under the Government's proposals only £478 will be payable.

10 The Government also proposes to clarify the stamp duty land tax treatment of leases with uncertain rents, so as to avoid an undue compliance burden on tenants, and to provide that rent increases more than five years after the start of a lease are ignored (subject to anti-avoidance provisions). Details are set out in the attached Technical Note.

11 The changes to lease duty are estimated to reduce the expected yield from stamp duty land tax by £20 million in a full year.

Other reliefs

12 The Finance Act already provides for many reliefs from stamp duty land tax, for example for property acquired by charities or let by registered social landlords. There are reliefs for house-builders who take houses in part exchange (which benefits in particular those providing retirement homes) and companies which assist in employee relocation.

13 The Government proposes, in line with commitments given by the Chief Secretary to the Treasury, the right Hon Paul Boateng MP, during the passage of Finance Bill 2003 through Parliament, to widen these reliefs to include companies who help to ensure an active housing market, by "chain-breaking" (buying property when a prospective sale falls through) and by buying houses from the personal representatives of people who have died. Details are set out in the attached Technical Note.

14 The Government also proposes to give relief for sale and lease-back transactions (where a company raises finance by selling a property for a capital sum and leasing it back at an annual rent). Provided certain conditions are met the "lease-back" leg of the transaction will not be charged to stamp duty land tax.

15 The cost of and yield from these reliefs is expected to be negligible.

Technical corrections and clarifications

16 The attached Technical Note sets out a number of technical corrections and clarifications. The Government is grateful to all those who made representations on these issues. The cost of and yield from these changes is expected to be negligible.

Partnerships

17 In his Budget statement the Chancellor announced that certain transactions involving partnerships would remain within the existing stamp duty regime until at least 2004 to give time for further consultation. These are: transactions between a partnership and a partner or an incoming partner, changes in partnership interests and transactions between a partnership and a departing partner.

18 The Government is today publishing draft clauses which bring these transactions, so far as they involve dealings in land, within the scope of stamp duty land tax. As with the Government's other proposals the aim is to give fairness between taxpayers, reduce distortions and prevent avoidance.

19 The Government will be meeting interested parties to discuss these proposals but would welcome comments from others. The Government's intention is that the clauses will be included in Finance Bill 2004 and will take effect from the date of Royal Assent to Finance Bill 2004.

NOTES

1 Stamp duty land tax applies (subject to some transitional provisions) to all "land transactions" completed on or after 1 December 2003. "Land transaction" includes the conveyance or transfer of a freehold (in Scotland, transfer of ownership), the assignment or assignation of an existing lease and the grant of a new lease. It replaces stamp duty, which is abolished except for instruments relating to stock and marketable securities, and for instruments relating to some partnership transactions.

2 Where a land transaction takes place the purchaser (including a new tenant) must submit a "land transaction return" to the Inland Revenue (there are exceptions for some transactions which do not have to be notified, for example where there is no consideration in any form chargeable to tax). This replaces the current procedure whereby documents are presented to the Inland Revenue for stamping.

3 The rates and thresholds for stamp duty land tax are the same as they currently are under stamp duty, except that—

(a) Under stamp duty the rate is nil for land transactions where the purchase price does not exceed £60,000. For non-residential transactions this threshold will be raised to £150,000 under stamp duty land tax
(b) There will be a new regime for charging stamp duty land tax on the rental element of new leases ("lease duty") as described above.

4 The current rates of lease duty under stamp duty are based on Average Annual Rent ("AAR") and on the term of the lease. They are—

(1) Term not more than 7 years (including indefinite leases and periodic tenancies)—
  (a) if the rent is £5,000 or less Nil,
  (b) if the rent is more than £5,000 1%.
(2) Term more than 7 years but not more than 35 years 2%.
(3) Term more than 35 years but not more than 100 years 12%.
(4) Term more than 100 years 24%.

STAMP DUTY LAND TAX: TECHNICAL NOTE

20 October 2003. *IR Technical Note*

1 This Note supplements the News Release of 20 October 2003 [reproduced above]. It gives further details of—

– The technical changes to stamp duty land tax on the rental element of leases ("lease duty").
– The reliefs being given for sale and lease-back transactions and acquisitions by "chain-breaking" and similar companies.
– Other technical corrections and clarifications.

2 These changes will be effected by way of regulations made under FA 2003 s 109. The regulations require approval by the House of Commons.

STAMP DUTY LAND TAX ON LEASES

3 The News Release gives details of the main change proposed for the charging structure. The changes set out below supplement this in order to—

– remove uncertainty in the treatment of some leases;
– keep the compliance burden to a minimum; and
– ensure that taxpayers know what duty they will have to pay.

4 The amendments are as follows.

POST 5 YEAR RENT CHANGES

5 Currently, where rent changes are known and included in the terms of a lease from the outset, they are fully taken into account in calculating the Net Present Value ("NPV") of the lease (unless they are increases only to reflect RPI). However, where rent changes are made, after two years, to reflect market rents, these changes are ignored for the purposes of calculating the NPV.

6 The proposed changes remove this disparity of treatment. They provide that all rent changes after 5 years are ignored for the purposes of the NPV calculation and, for rental due after 5 years, the highest rent paid in any previous period of 12 months is substituted and used in the calculation. This will provide comparability of treatment for these types of lease.

LEASES WITH UNCERTAIN RENT

7 Where rent is expressed as relating to turnover, or where there are rent sharing or similar measures in place, the lessee is required to make a reasonable estimate of the rent due and include this estimate in their land transaction return. When any part of this estimated rent is determined, they must make an amended return including that part of the rent which is now determined. Representations have been received that this could place a severe compliance burden on many small businesses whose rent is determined by monthly turnover.

8 To simplify this area, it is proposed to amend Finance Act 2003 so that, where a lease has a rent which is still uncertain after five years (eg a turnover based lease for 15 years), *one and only one additional return* is required at the five year point. This return will base the NPV on the actual rent paid in the first five years and (for any post five year rent due) will apply the amendment at paragraph 6 above ie the highest rent paid in any 12 month period over the previous five years will be used in the NPV calculation.

9 Where all the uncertainty in the rental of a lease is determined before five years, *one and only one* additionally return is required at that point.

10 These measures will provide certainty and substantially reduce the compliance burden for small businesses.

CONTINGENCIES

11 Amendments will be made to clarify that break and forfeiture clauses in a lease do not operate to artificially shorten the term of a lease in the NPV calculation. Similarly, options to renew, contained in the lease, will not be treated as a contingency extending the term of a lease.

EXTENSIONS TO LEASES DURING THEIR TERM

12 An amendment will be introduced so that where a lease is extended during the currency of its term, this extension is treated as the grant of a new lease for the period by which the term of the lease is extended. This will be treated as a transaction linked with the original grant and, if not already notifiable, should the total term then extend to seven or more years, the whole transaction will be notifiable.

CONTINUATION OF LEASES AND LEASES FOR AN INDEFINITE TERM

13 Currently, where there is a lease for a fixed term and thereafter, this term is defined as the term plus such further period as must elapse before the earliest date at which the lease can be determined. This will be amended so that the term is defined as the term specified in the lease.

14 Where a lease comes to the end of its term but the landlord does not require possession of the property, this extension is treated, in England and Wales, as a periodic tenancy which extends the term of the lease. In Scotland, there is a similar treatment called tacit relocation. Currently, the treatment of this extension is unclear and an amendment will be introduced to clarify the situation. Where a lease continues after the end of its term, this extension will be deemed to be the grant of a new lease for the period of 12 months (or the original term of the previous lease if shorter). Should this continue past this period, it will be deemed to be another lease of similar length and so on. These leases will be linked transactions. This will also apply in Scotland, where the lease is for an unspecified period at the outset. The original period of such a lease will be deemed to be 12 months.

15 Where a lease is granted for an indefinite term, for example if it is for life of until repayment of a debt, the term of these leases will be deemed to be for a period of 12 months. As above, should the lease continue after this period, the continuation will be deemed as the grant of another lease for 12 months and so on with each deemed grant being treated as a linked transaction with those previously.

16 For all these leases and deemed leases, treated as linked transactions, there will be notification requirements, so that, whenever the total NPV of the rents means that stamp duty land tax is due or where the total term of the leases is seven years or more, the series of deemed leases will be notifiable transactions.

ANTI-AVOIDANCE

17 To prevent avoidance of stamp duty land tax using these amendments, it is proposed that, after the five year point when rent changes are not taken into account in the NPV, if the rent rises by more than 5% + RPI annually, this rent increase is deemed to be the grant of a new lease in a similar way to the way Paragraph 10 Schedule 5 already treats rent increases not included in the terms of a lease.

18 Currently, assignments or assignations of leases where the payment of a premium is not involved are stamp duty land tax transactions but the assumption of the obligation to pay rent is not treated as consideration. Therefore, no duty is paid on these type of assignments or assignations. It is proposed to change this treatment in a limited variety of circumstances. Where the lease, at the previous transaction, benefited from a relief, so that the duty payable was reduced or eliminated, assignment or assignation of such a lease will be deemed to be the grant of a lease by the assignor to the assignee. This will prevent the use of reliefs to avoid stamp duty land tax.

OTHER RELIEFS

19 In accordance with commitments made by the Chief Secretary to the Treasury during Standing Committee debates on Finance Bill 2003, the Government has consulted with interested parties with a view to widening the scope of the relief package to include full or partial reliefs from stamp duty land tax for sale and leaseback transactions, certain types of exchange transactions involving house-building companies and for purchases of residential property by "chain-breaking" companies. The following additional reliefs are now proposed:

SALES AND LEASEBACKS

20. Partial relief will be given for the leaseback element of a sale and leaseback of commercial property. These transactions take the form of a sale of premises (or the assignment or assignation of an existing lease of premises) followed by a leaseback of those premises by the purchaser to the vendor. They are commonly entered into as a means of raising finance by companies or other commercial entities. The leaseback element of the transaction will be relieved from a charge to stamp duty land tax, provided that certain conditions are met. These are that the sale and leaseback arrangement does not involve residential property, that the leaseback is of the same premises that were the subject of the sale or assignment (or assignation) and that the consideration for the sale or assignment (or assignation) element of the transaction consists only of cash or the release or assumption of a liability.

EXCHANGE TRANSACTIONS INVOLVING HOUSE-BUILDING COMPANIES

21 Finance Act 2003 s 58 provides for relief where a house-building company acquires a dwelling from individuals in consideration of their agreeing to purchase a new dwelling from the house-building company. However, if the house-building company uses an unconnected company to acquire the individuals' former dwelling, no relief from stamp duty land tax exists in respect of that acquisition. Such an arrangement may commonly occur where the selling individuals are seeking to move to a retirement home. Relief will be introduced in these circumstances where the unconnected company acquires the individuals' former dwelling in the course of carrying on a trade as a property trader, does not spend more than a permitted amount on refurbishments, does not grant a lease or licence over the acquired property and does not permit any officer or employee to occupy the property. If these conditions are met, it is right that the role of the property trading company in providing liquidity to the housing market should not suffer a charge to stamp duty land tax. A charge to tax as provided for under stamp duty land tax legislation enacted in Finance Act 2003 will arise when the property trading company on-sells the property.

22 A similar relief will be provided for companies who specialise in purchasing residential properties from personal representatives of deceased individuals and then on-sell the property. These companies provide liquidity to the residential housing market and, subject to conditions, relief from stamp duty land tax will be given on the acquisition.

CHAIN-BREAKING COMPANIES

23 Relief from stamp duty land tax will be introduced for companies part or all of whose trade consists of buying residential property in order to keep a chain of residential transactions from failing. Individuals looking to move house are often dependent on selling their own house before buying their target home. If their prospective purchaser pulls out, then their own purchase cannot go ahead. In these circumstances, a chain-breaking company would acquire the individuals' current property so that the move can still take place. The chain-breaking company purchases the property and then sells on in a short space of time. The purchase by the chain-breaking company will relieved from stamp duty land tax, provided that it is acting in the course of a trade of buying properties in these circumstances, does not spend more than a permitted amount on refurbishments, does not grant a lease or licence over the acquired property and does not permit any officer or employee to occupy the property. stamp duty land tax will be paid on the eventual sale by the chain-breaking company.

SURRENDERS AND REGRANTS

24 The law will be clarified so that the surrender of any lease will not be consideration for the grant of another and the grant will not be consideration for the surrender. When a new lease is

granted the charge to stamp duty land tax will be on the premium and rent due and not on the value of any interest surrendered. Where a lease is surrendered to the landlord, then as long as the surrendered lease is for a fixed rent credit will be given in computing the stamp duty land tax due on the new lease for the amount of rent that was due for the surrendered years. This will help many commercial arrangements for surrenders and regrants.

Example

A commercial lease ("lease 1") is granted for 10 years, rent £100,000 per year. The NPV is £831,660 so stamp duty land tax of £6,816 is chargeable. After 5 years it is surrendered and a new lease ("lease 2") of 10 years with rent of £150,000 per year is granted. Without any relief the NPV of lease 2 would be £1,247,490 and so stamp duty land tax of £10,794 would be chargeable. The relief recognises that rent paid for the first five years of lease 2 has already been partially taken into account in taxing lease 1. So the rent payable under lease 2 is taken to be £50,000 per year for the first five years and £150,000 per year thereafter. This reduces the NPV to £795,985 and the stamp duty land tax chargeable to £6,459.

TECHNICAL CORRECTIONS AND CLARIFICATIONS

25 These are—

(a) Clarification of the interpretation of "taking possession" in section 44, and provision that this includes possession by a person connected with the purchaser;

(b) Clarification that fixed duty is abolished on duplicates and counterparts of instruments that effect a land transaction which is an stamp duty land tax transaction;

(c) Clarification as to the operation of the transitional provisions where a contract is entered into on or before 10 July 2003 in two respects—

- Where a contract is entered into on or before 10 July 2003 but the contracting purchaser sub-sells or assigns his rights after that date the proposed changes make it clear that the sub-sale or assignment (or assignation), if completed or substantially performed on or after 1 December 2003, is an stamp duty land tax transaction.
- Where the transaction provided for in the contract becomes an stamp duty land tax transaction by virtue of FA 2003 Sch 19 para 3(3) the "effective date" is the date of that event if it is later than the date the contract is substantially performed. There are examples of the operation of the transitional provisions at the end of this Note.

(d) Confirmation that the holder of a Power of Attorney can sign a land transaction return

(e) Clarification of the obligation to submit a further land transaction return when stamp duty land tax becomes chargeable, or chargeable at a higher rate, as a result of a later "linked transaction". The purchaser will need to submit a further land transaction return in respect of the earlier transaction(s) and for this purpose the "effective date" will be the date of the later transaction.

(f) Clarification that stamp duty land tax applies to the Crown in the same way as stamp duty does, but subject to the specific exemptions for Government departments and similar bodies (FA 2003 s 107(2)) and for certain transactions by other public bodies (FA 2003 s 66).

(g) A change to the way in which agreements for leases entered into before 1 December 2003 are dealt with for stamp duty purposes if the execution of the lease is an stamp duty land tax transaction. FA 2003 Sch 19 paragraph 8 provides that the agreement for lease can be presented for stamping and the stamp duty is then credited against stamp duty land tax due on the execution of the lease. It has been pointed out to us that this causes delay in being able to deliver the land transaction return. We propose to reverse the procedure so that the stamp duty land tax is paid first and the agreement for lease can then be stamped with a "denoted" stamp.

TRANSITIONAL PROVISIONS: EXAMPLES

Examples 1–5 show the current operation of the transitional provisions and no change is proposed. Example 6 relates to the proposed new provision.

(1) A enters into a contract with B on 1 January 2003. The contract is completed on 1 January 2004 without any paragraph 3(3) event having occurred. This is not an stamp duty land tax transaction and the conveyance is chargeable to stamp duty.

(2) A enters into a contract with B on 1 January 2003. The contract is varied on 1 September 2003 and completed on 1 January 2004 without having first been substantially performed. The variation is a paragraph 3(3) event and accordingly this is an stamp duty land tax transaction. The effective date is the date of completion.

(3) A enters into a contract with B on 1 January 2003. The contract is varied on 1 September 2003, substantially performed on 1 October 2003 and completed on 1 January 2004. The variation is a paragraph 3(3) event and accordingly this is an stamp duty land tax transaction. The effective date is the date of completion because substantial performance pre-implementation is disregarded (FA 2003 Sch 19 para 4(3)).

(4) A enters into a contract with B on 1 January 2003. The contract is varied on 1 September 2003, substantially performed on 1 January 2004 and completed on 1 February 2004. The variation is a paragraph 3(3) event and accordingly this is an stamp duty land tax transaction. The effective date is the date of substantial performance (FA 2003 s 44(4)).

(5) A enters into a contract with B on 1 January 2003. The contract is substantially performed on 1 November 2003, varied on 1 July 2004 and completed on 1 December 2004. The variation is a paragraph 3(3) event and accordingly this is an stamp duty land tax transaction. The effective date is the date of completion because substantial performance pre-implementation is disregarded (FA 2003 Sch 19 para 4(3)).

(6) A enters into a contract with B on 1 January 2003. The contract is substantially performed on 1 January 2004, varied on 1 July 2004 and completed on 1 December 2004. The variation is a paragraph 3(3) event and accordingly this is an stamp duty land tax transaction. By virtue of the changes now being proposed the effective date will be 1 July 2004.

WRITTEN MINISTERIAL STATEMENT BY THE FINANCIAL SECRETARY

20 October 2003. *Ministerial Statement.*

STAMP DUTY LAND TAX

I am pleased to announce the next steps in the process of modernising stamp duty on land transactions. These include—

– A significant change to the proposed charge on the rental element when a new lease is granted ("lease duty"), reducing tax bills by £1500 per lease on commercial transactions (£600 per lease on residential transactions), which will be of significant benefit to smaller businesses
– A new relief for businesses raising finance through the sale and leaseback of their land and buildings and relief for "chain-breaking" and similar companies which help to ensure an active housing market

Further consultation on how the new regime might apply to partnerships. The announcement follows extensive consultation on the process throughout the earlier part of this year. Theses proposals along with those announced in Budget 2003, will help to achieve the Government's aim of a modern, efficient, system of taxing land transactions which promotes fairness between taxpayers, reduces distortions and prevents avoidance. I am also pleased that our proposals, which follow extensive and valuable consultation with interested parties, will be of particular help to small and medium-sized enterprises and business start-ups. The Inland Revenue is today publishing a News Release, supplemented by a Technical Note [reproduced above], giving details of the proposed changes. I will be laying regulations to give effect to the changes before the House shortly. The Inland Revenue is also publishing for consultation draft clauses on the Stamp Duty Land tax treatment of partnership transactions. The Government's proposals on lease duty follow extensive consultation over the last 18 months. I am extremely grateful to all who participated in the consultation process. A good deal of valuable information and data was provided by participants and some important work was done in partnership. Throughout the consultation process the Government has been particularly keen to have regard to the effect of any new structure on small and medium-sized enterprises and business start-ups.

Having considered all the contributions made I now propose to modify the structure contained in Finance Act 2003, by way of regulations under section 112 of that Act, as follows:

– The Finance Act charges stamp duty land tax on the "Net Present Value" ("NPV") of rent payable under a lease. NPV sums the discounted values of the rents. This discount recognises that future rent payments will be of less value. The Government believes that NPV represents a fair way of assessing the amount on which stamp duty land tax should be charged and proposes to retain it.
– The Finance Act sets a threshold of £150,000 for commercial leases, £60,000 for residential leases. If the NPV does not exceed the threshold no stamp duty land tax is charged on the rental element. These thresholds mean that 60% of commercial leases and 90% of residential leases will pay no stamp duty land tax on the rental element. The Government believes these thresholds are fair and intend to retain them.
– The Finance Act provides that once the threshold is exceeded stamp duty land tax is charged at 1% of the full amount of the NPV. The Government proposes to modify this so that stamp duty land tax is charged at 1% of the excess over the threshold. This means that on any commercial lease chargeable to stamp duty land tax the tax payable will be £1,500 less than under the Finance Act provisions.

EXAMPLE—

A lease for 18 years at an annual rent of £15000 will have an NPV of £197,845. Under the Finance Act provisions stamp duty land tax of £1,978 would be payable. Under the Government's proposals only £478 will be payable.

I also propose to clarify the stamp duty land tax treatment of leases with uncertain rents, so as to avoid an undue compliance burden on tenants, and to provide that rent increases more than five years after the start of a lease are ignored. I also propose (by way of regulations made under section 109 Finance Act 2003) to widen the reliefs in sections 58 and 59 of that Act to include companies who help to ensure an active housing market, by "chain-breaking" (buying property when a prospective sale falls through) and by buying houses from the personal representatives of people who have died. I also propose to give relief for sale and lease-back transactions (where a company raises finance by selling a property for a capital sum and leasing it back at an annual rent).

In his Budget statement my Right Hon Friend the Chancellor of the Exchequer announced that certain transactions involving partnerships would remain within the existing stamp duty regime until at least 2004 to give time for further consultation. These are: transactions between a partnership and an incoming partner, changes in partnership interests and transactions between a partnership and a departing partner.

The Inland Revenue is today publishing draft clauses [see below] which bring these transactions, so far as they involve dealings in land, within the scope of stamp duty land tax. As with the Government's other proposals the aim is to give fairness between taxpayers, reduce distortions and prevent avoidance. My officials will be meeting interested parties to discuss these proposals but would welcome comments from others. The Government's intention is that the clauses will be included in Finance Bill 2004 and will take effect from the date of royal assent to Finance Bill 2004.

HM TREASURY
20 October 2003

SDLT—GUIDANCE NOTES ON SELF-CERTIFICATION

November 2003.

Form SDLT60 (Certification that no Land Transaction Return is required for a land transaction) is available at http://www.inlandrevenue.gov.uk/so/sdlt60-self-certificate.pdf.

WHAT IS "SELF-CERTIFICATION"?

Most land transactions, including all transactions where a payment of stamp duty land tax is required, must be notified to the Inland Revenue on a Land Transaction Return form (Form SDLT 1). On receipt of the return the Inland Revenue will issue a certificate. The certificate must accompany any application for registration of the transaction (or of a document) at the appropriate land registry.

Some land transactions, however, where no stamp duty land tax is payable do not have to be notified to the Inland Revenue. For such transactions the purchaser can give a "self-certificate" to the appropriate land registry.

For the purposes of SDLT, "purchaser" is defined as the person acquiring the interest even if no consideration is paid.

WHAT LAND TRANSACTIONS MUST BE NOTIFIED TO THE INLAND REVENUE ON A FORM SDLT 1?

These transactions cannot be self-certified and an Inland Revenue certificate must accompany any application for registration.

- The acquisition of a freehold or leasehold interest in land (in Scotland, the acquisition of ownership of land, including the interest of the proprietor of the *dominium utile*, or of the tenant's interest in property subject to a lease) where there is chargeable consideration, **whether or not any stamp duty land tax is payable.** In particular such acquisitions must be notified even if the chargeable consideration is £60,000 or less (£150,000 or less for non-residential property) so that stamp duty land tax is chargeable at 0%. The only exceptions are for some transactions in connection with divorce and some variations of testamentary dispositions (see below).

- The grant of a lease (including, in Scotland, exchange of missives of let) for a term of seven years or more, **whether or not any stamp duty land tax is payable.**
- Any other land transaction which attracts a charge to stamp duty land tax at a rate of 1% or more, or would do so but for some relief.

WHAT LAND TRANSACTIONS DO NOT HAVE TO BE NOTIFIED TO THE INLAND REVENUE, AND SO CAN BE SELF-CERTIFIED?

- The acquisition of a freehold or leasehold interest in land (in Scotland, the acquisition of ownership of land, including the interest of the proprietor of the *dominium utile*, or of the tenant's interest in property subject to a lease) where there is **no chargeable consideration** (see below on what constitutes chargeable consideration).
- The grant of a lease (including, in Scotland, the exchange of missives of let) where **all** the following conditions are satisfied:
  - The term of the lease is less than seven years.
  - The amount of any premium (in Scotland, grassum) is not such as to attract a charge to stamp duty land tax at a rate of 1% or more, ignoring the availability of any relief.
  - The amount of any rent is not such as to attract a charge to stamp duty land tax at a rate of 1% or more, ignoring the availability of any relief.
- Any other acquisition of an interest in land (for example, the acquisition of an easement or servitude) where the chargeable consideration is not such as to attract a charge to stamp duty land tax at a rate of 1% or more, ignoring the availability of any relief.
- Transactions exempt from charge under Finance Act 2003 Schedule 3 paragraph 3 (transactions in connection with divorce).
- Transactions exempt from charge under Finance Act 2003 Schedule 3 paragraph 4 (variations of testamentary dispositions).

WHAT IS CHARGEABLE CONSIDERATION?

The basic rule is that anything given in money or money's worth for the subject-matter of a land transaction is chargeable consideration. There are three special cases (in each case "property" means the subject-matter of a land transaction):

- There is chargeable consideration where a property is transferred subject to an existing debt such as a mortgage (but, in Scotland, only where the transferee assumes liability for the obligation). So a "gift" of property subject to a mortgage is a notifiable transaction and cannot be self-certified.
- There are special rules when one property is exchanged for another which mean that there will normally be chargeable consideration on both transactions.
- There are special rules when property is transferred to a company wholly or partly in exchange for shares which mean that there will normally be chargeable consideration.

There is more detail on chargeable consideration and the special rules in the Guidance Notes for the Land Transaction Return. You can obtain a copy from the Orderline.

WHO CAN SIGN THE SELF-CERTIFICATE?

The purchaser or transferee must sign. If there is more than one purchaser or transferee then all must sign. Signature by an agent such as a solicitor, licensed conveyancer or accountant is not acceptable unless the purchaser has been recognised by a Court as mentally incapable of understanding their affairs. A parent or guardian may sign on behalf of a minor.

Where the purchaser or transferee is a company the Company Secretary or any person having express, implied or apparent authority to act on behalf of the company may sign. However where the company is in liquidation the liquidator must sign.

Where the purchaser or transferee is a partnership the self-certificate may be signed by one or more nominated partners.

Where the purchasers or transferees enter into the transaction as trustees (other than bare trustees as defined in Finance Act 2003 Schedule 16) then any one or more of them may sign.

SPECIAL ARRANGEMENTS FOR ADMINISTRATION OF SDLT FROM 1 DECEMBER 2003

12 November 2003. *Stamp Duty Information Bulletin—Issue 6.*

INTRODUCTION

From 1 December 2003, stamp duty land tax (SDLT) replaces existing stamp duty for UK land and buildings transactions. In line with other taxes, SDLT will introduce a "process now, check later" system, as well as introducing the new concept of a "liable person".

A key aspect of the new system will be the clear requirement to notify relevant transactions by completing a Land Transaction Return (LTR) within 30 days of the effective date of the transaction. In response, the Stamp Office will issue an SDLT certificate that can be presented to a Land Registry (replacing the current need to get documents stamped).

As with all significant changes, it may take practitioners and their clients some time to get used to the new guidelines, processes and forms. So, after consultation with the Law Society, the Law Society for Scotland and the Law Society for Northern Ireland and other key interested parties, we have put special arrangements in place to help the transition in the first few months.

DETAILS

In the early days of any new system, there can sometimes be failures by practitioners on behalf of their clients that are not deliberate; rather they result from misunderstanding, error or lack of familiarity with the new rules and guidance. Therefore, for a short period we will:

– Look wherever possible to process and issue SDLT certificates even if the Land Transaction Returns (LTRs) have been completed unsatisfactorily and contain some omissions or errors.
– Forego late filing penalties for LTRs that have been submitted more than 30 days but not more than 40 days after the effective date of the transaction. Wherever possible, in these instances the LTR will be processed as normal and a SDLT certificate issued.

Nevertheless, forms that contain critical errors or omissions will not receive a certificate. Instead, they will be sent back, with a letter identifying the boxes on the LTR that need to be corrected and re-submitted (see below).

WHAT WILL BE SENT BACK?

LTRs will be sent back where the basic information is missing, such as—

– The correct payment of tax is not enclosed (or paid via the other payment options, as described on the payslip)
– Where it has not been signed by the purchaser or person holding a purchaser's power of attorney
– Key pieces of data including the name of the purchaser(s) or the address of the property being bought which mean a certificate simply cannot be issued.

Where returns are sent back (primarily to practitioners), we will aim to return them immediately and ask that they are remedied and re-submitted quickly. We will also issue a letter with the rejected LTR detailing the omitted item(s) that are required under law. The aim is to help to identify any misunderstandings and avoid future occurrences.

FUTURE DEVELOPMENTS

This "light touch" approach will be constantly monitored and evaluated commencing on 1 December 2003. It is hoped that within a short period of time, the majority of errors and omissions will be reduced and a high proportion of the LTRs will be submitted accurately.

Comprehensive guidance on stamp duty land tax is available on our website at http://www.inlandrevenue.gov.uk/so/. Alternatively our customer service office in Worthing and our enquiry line staff are available to help customers understand the requirements of the new legislation. The telephone number is 0845 6030135.

Even though a LTR may have qualified for a certificate under this relaxed period it should be stressed that the issue of a certificate (and the non-rejection of the LTR), does not mean that we have "accepted" that the tax payable on the LTR is the correct amount. We will not have prejudiced our right to enquire into the transaction within the time limit allowed by the legislation.

A formal announcement will be made (at least 4 weeks) in advance of the date on which this concession is brought to a close.

FIXTURES AND CHATTELS—STAMP DUTY LAND TAX

The same general legal principles which apply to deductions for chattels for stamp duty will also apply to stamp duty land tax.

Stamp duty land tax differs from stamp duty in that it is a tax on the transaction and not on the document that implements it. Stamp duty land tax is charged on transactions.

For an item to be regarded as a fixture or part of the land (chargeable to tax), as opposed to a chattel or moveable in Scotland, (not chargeable) the item must, as a starting point, be annexed to the property. The issue then turns on the degree and purpose of the annexation, with greater emphasis being placed (in the more recent cases) to purpose. Where a purchaser agrees to buy a property for a price that includes an amount properly attributed to chattels or moveables, that amount will not be charged to stamp duty land tax.

In recent times, IR Stamp Taxes has seen an increasing number of cases in which the amount of consideration attributed to chattels is more than a small percentage of the total consideration. This has been particularly noticeable where, as a result of the apportionment, the chargeable consideration is brought just below the £250,000 or £500,000 stamp duty thresholds.

Under the stamp duty land tax regime the purchaser is responsible for the accurate completion of the Land Transaction Return, including the entry in Box 10 of form SDLT 1 of the consideration for the land transaction. Under paragraph (4) of Schedule 4 Finance Act 2003, a "just and reasonable apportionment" is required where a price is paid partly for a land transaction and partly for a non-land transaction such as the purchase of chattels. It does not matter that the parties to a transaction may agree a particular apportionment, which is then documented in the contract. The apportionment will not be correct unless it was arrived at on a "just and reasonable" basis.

We have the right to make enquiries into the accuracy of a Land Transaction Return and the apportionment of the purchase price may well be one of the aspects on which we will make enquiries. Similarly it is quite possible that we will also undertake enquiries into cases where a deduction has been made for chattels to confirm that those items properly fall within the definition of chattels.

We are unable to provide a comprehensive list of items that we accept as chattels or moveables. This is because each case must be considered on its own merits and because this is an area of the law that continues to evolve.

The following are, however, confirmed as being items that will normally fall to be regarded as chattels—

- Carpets (fitted or otherwise);
- Curtains and blinds;
- Free standing furniture;
- Kitchen white goods;
- Electric and gas fires (provided that they can be removed by disconnection from the power supply without causing damage to the property);
- Light shades and fittings (unless recessed).

On the other hand, the following will not normally be regarded as chattels—

- Fitted kitchen units, cupboards and sinks;
- Agas and wall mounted ovens;
- Fitted bathroom sanitary ware;
- Central heating systems;
- Intruder alarm systems.

Externally any plants, shrubs or trees growing in the soil form part of the land and are not regarded as chattels. A deduction would, however, be possible for amounts properly apportioned to any plants growing in pots or containers.

The above guidance is written primarily in the context of sales of residential property. The same principles apply when considering the purchase of industrial or commercial property in which the sale may also involve the acquisition of plant, machinery or equipment.

Further information is available on our website at www.inlandrevenue.gov.uk/so/sdlt_index.htm.

The SDLT Manual also available on our website will be updated shortly.

CALCULATION OF STAMP DUTY LAND TAX ON LEASES

When a lease is entered into, the stamp duty land tax (SDLT) due on that lease depends on the premium payable (if any), the rent due under the lease and the term (period) of the lease. SDLT is payable by the lessee (tenant) and **not** by the landlord.

Notifiable lease transactions

A lease transaction is notifiable if—

– the lease is for a term of seven years or more (or treated as being for a term of seven years or more); **or**
– SDLT is due (at more than 0%) on either the premium element or rental element or both of the lease;

If a lease transaction is notifiable, a land transaction return **must** be completed by the tenant and sent into the processing centre at Netherton.

Calculation of the SDLT due

The SDLT due on a lease transaction (if any) depends on the premium payable, the rent due under the lease and the term of the lease. The SDLT is calculated in two separate parts, the SDLT due on the premium and the SDLT due on the rental element. These are added together and entered onto the land transaction return as a total figure of these two elements.

A) SDLT due on the premium

SDLT is due on the premium part of a lease if the premium payable is more than the relevant threshold. The relevant threshold depends on whether the **average annual rent** is more than £600 per year.

Average annual rent is determined by the **ascertainable** rent each year. Rent is ascertainable if you know you are going to have to pay at least this amount for the year. For example—

(i) if the rent you have to pay depends **entirely** on the turnover of your business, that is there is no minimum amount of rent you have to pay, then there is no **ascertainable** rent as there is no amount you know you will have to pay;
(ii) if the rent you have to pay depends on the turnover of your business and you have a minimum amount you have to pay, whether or not your turnover meets a certain figure, the minimum rent due is the **ascertainable** rent;
(iii) if the rent you have to pay is a fixed amount plus an amount based on percentage of turnover, the **ascertainable** rent is the fixed amount you have to pay, excluding any percentage amount;
(iv) if your rent is fixed, or any increases in the rent are known from the outset, the **ascertainable** rent is the amount known from the outset.

Average annual rent is calculated by adding all the **ascertainable** rent together and dividing it by the term (period) of the lease.

If the average annual rent is **less than or equal** to £600, the relevant thresholds are—

Residential leases	*Commercial or mixed-use leases*
£60,000	£150,000

If the average annual rent is **more than** £600, the relevant threshold is £0, that is, all the premium is taxable.

If the premium is taxable, the **rate** of tax depends on the amount of premium as follows—

Up to (and including) threshold	0%
From threshold to £250,000	1%
From £250,001 to £500,000	3%
From £500,001	4%

B) SDLT due on the rental element

SDLT is **also** due on the rental element of a lease and is charged at a flat rate of 1% of the **Net Present Value** (NPV) of the rental stream over the term (period) of the lease. NPV depends on the term (period) of the lease and the amount of rent payable in the first five years.

To calculate the NPV, determine what the amount of rent payable for each of the first five years of the term (period) of the lease is. If this cannot be determined, for example, if it depends fully or to some extent on turnover, or some other unknown amount, you should make a reasonable estimate of what you expect the rent to be each year. Once you have determined what the rental payments in the first five years are (or are likely to be) you need to determine what the highest rent payable in any continuous twelve-month period is (this will usually, but not always, be the highest annual rent payable). This amount should be used in the calculation for all years after the first five.

The tables in Annex 1 give factors to apply for all years from 1 to 99 for leases of up to 99 years. There are two columns: individual year factor and cumulative factor.

The column called **individual year factor** should be used where the rent payable in the first five years varies, that is, the yearly rent is not the same in the first five years of the lease.

The column called **cumulative factor** should be used where the rent does not vary in the first five years, that is, the same amount of rent is payable for each of the first five years of the lease.

How to use the column called individual year factor

(1) Determine the rental payable for each of the first five years—
  (i) Apply year one factor (0.966183575) to the rent for year one. So, for example, if the rent payable in year one was £20,000 the figure to use would be £20,000 × 0.966183575 = £19323.71;
  (ii) Apply year two factor (0.9335107) to the rent for year two. So for example, if the rent payable in year two was £25,000 the figures to use would be £25,000 × 0.9335107 = £23,337.76;
  (iii) Continue similarly until year six is reached.

(2) For years six onwards only one calculation is needed—
  – The **rent used for year six** should be the highest rent payable in any continuous twelve-month period in the first five years. This will normally (but not always) be the highest rent payable in any of the first five years. This rent applies for all subsequent years. The factor to apply to this rent depends on the term (period) of the lease. If you have a six-year lease, apply the factor for year six (0.81350064) to the **rent used for year six**. So, for example, if the **rent used for year six** was £32,500, the figure to use would be £32,500 × 0.81350064 = £26,438.77. If you have a twenty-year lease, apply the factor for year twenty (9.69735093) to the **rent used for year six**. So, for example, if the **rent used for year six** was £32,500, the figure to use would be £315,163.90.

(3) Calculate the NPV—
  – Add together the figures obtained for years one to five (five figures) and the figure obtained for year six onwards. **This will be a maximum of six figures to add together.** This total is the NPV of the rent.

(4) Calculate the SDLT due on the NPV—
  – If the NPV (calculated at step (3) above) is greater than the relevant threshold (£60,000 for residential leases and £150,000 for commercial and mixed-use leases), SDLT is due at 1% of the **excess** of the NPV above the relevant threshold. For example, if a residential lease has an NPV of £72,500 (the residential threshold being £60,000) tax would be due on £72,500 – £60,000 = £15,000 × 1% = £150. **Go to step C.**

How to use the column called cumulative factor

This column should **only** be used where the rent doesn't vary during the first five years, that is, it is the same amount for each of the first five years of the lease.

Use the factor for the term (period) of the lease with the rent payable in year one. For example, if you have a six-year lease, the factor is 5.32855302. The NPV of a lease paying a rent of £30,000 for six years is, therefore, £159,856. If the lease was for twenty years, the factor is 9.697350926 and the NPV is £426,372.

C) Calculate the SDLT due

Add the SDLT calculated on the premium (Step A) to the SDLT calculated on the rent (Step B). This is the total SDLT due for the lease.

Quick guide

The table below gives a guide as to whether SDLT will be due on the premium (if any) and/or the rental element of a lease. This is for guidance only and cannot be relied upon t give accurate amounts due. If the entry is in bold, it is probable that SDLT is due on that element of the payment for the lease.

Quick guide table

Premium	*NPV**	*AAR***	*Tax on*
Below threshold	Below threshold	Below or equal to £600	—
Below threshold	Below threshold	Greater than £600	Premium
Below threshold	Above threshold	Below or equal to £600	NPV
Below threshold	Above threshold	Greater than £600	Premium/NPV
Above threshold	Below threshold	Below or equal to £600	Premium
Above threshold	Below threshold	Greater than £600	Premium
Above threshold	Above threshold	Below or equal to £600	Premium/NPV
Above threshold	Above threshold	Greater than £600	Premium/NPV

* NPV = Net Present Value

** AAR = Average Annual Rent

Examples

(1) A residential lease for 99 years with a premium of £50,000 and an annual rent of £200 for the first 25 years, £400 for the next 25 years and £800 thereafter.

(A) The average annual rent is £547 and so the premium thresholds aren't affected. The premium is below the residential threshold and so no SDLT is due on the premium.

(B) As the rent doesn't change in the first five years, use the cumulative table. The factor for 99 years is 27.62336529 and the rent to be used for year six is £200. The NPV is, therefore, £5,524. As this is below the residential threshold, no SDLT is due on the rental element.

(C) The total SDLT due is nil. However, a land transaction return is still required as the term of the lease is for seven years or more.

(2) A residential lease for 25 years with a premium of £50,000 and an annual rent of £1,000 reviewable after five years

(A) The average annual rent is £1,000 (which is more than £600) and so the premium threshold becomes £0. SDLT is due on the premium at a rate of 1% (as the premium is not more than £250,000). The SDLT due is £500.

(B) As the rent doesn't change in the first five years, use the cumulative table. The factor for 25 years is 16.48151459 and the rent to be used for year six is £1,000. The NPV is, therefore, £16,481. As this is below the residential threshold, no SDLT is due on the rental element.

(C) The total SDLT due is £500. This should be included on a land transaction return.

(3) A commercial lease for 20 years with a premium of £50,000 and an annual rent of 10% of turnover. There is no minimum rent. Rent payable in the first five years is estimated to be £100,000 each year.

(A) The average annual rent is £0 (as there is no ascertainable rent) and so the premium thresholds aren't affected. The premium is below the commercial threshold and so no SDLT is due on the premium.

(B) As the rent doesn't change in the first five years, use the cumulative table. The factor for 20 years is 14.2124033 and the rent to be used for year six is £100,000. The NPV is, therefore, £1,421,240. This is above the commercial threshold and SDLT is due on the excess of (£1,421,240 – £150,000 = £1,271,240) at 1%, that is SDLT of £12,712.40 is due.

(C) The total SDLT due is £12,712.40 (rounded down to £12,712). This should be included on a land transaction return.

(4) A commercial lease for 35 years with a premium of £125,000 and an annual rent based on 10 % of turnover or £38,000, whichever is the greater. Rent payable in the first five years is estimated to be £38,000 for years one and two £40,000 for year three and £45,000 for years four and five.

(A) The average annual rent is £38,000 (as this is the ascertainable rent) and so the premium threshold becomes £0. SDLT is due on the premium at a rate of 1% (as the premium is not more than £250,000). The SDLT due is £1,250.

(B) As the rent changes in the first five years, use the Individual year table. The factor for year one is 0.96618357 and the NPV for this year is £38,000 × 0.96618357 = £36,714.97. The factor for year two is 0.9335107 and the NPV for this year is £38,000 × 0.9335107 = £35,473.40. The factor for year three is 0.90194271 and the NPV for this year is £40,000 × 0.90194271 = £36,077.70. The factor for year four is 0.87144223 and the NPV for this year is £45,000 × 0.87144223 = £39,214.90. The factor for year five is 0.84197317 and the NPV for this year is £45,000 × 0.84197317 = £37,888.79. The highest rent payable in any twelve month period is £45,000 and this is used as the rent for year six onwards. The factor for a thirty-five year lease is 15.48560872 and the NPV for the balance of the term of the lease is £45,000 × 15.48560872 = £696,852.39. The total NPV is, therefore, £36,714.97 + £35,473.40 + £36,077.70 + £39,214,.90 + £37,888.79 + £696,852.39 = £882222.15. This is above the commercial threshold and SDLT is due on the excess of (£882,222–£150,000 = £732,222) at 1%, that is SDLT of £7,322.22 is due.

(C) C) The total SDLT due is £1,250.00 + £7,322.22 = £8,572.22 (rounded down to £8,572). This should be included on a land transaction return.

Tables of individual year factors and cumulative factors

Year	*Individual year factor*	*Cumulative factor*
1	0.96618357	0.96618357
2	0.93351070	1.89969428
3	0.90194271	2.80163698
4	0.87144223	3.67307921
5	0.84197317	4.51505238
6	0.81350064	5.32855302
7	1.59949160	6.11454398
8	2.35890316	6.87395554
9	3.09263413	7.60768651
10	3.80155295	8.31660532
11	4.48649866	9.00155104
12	5.14828196	9.66333433
13	5.78768611	10.30273849
14	6.40546790	10.92052028
15	7.00235852	11.51741090
16	7.57906443	12.09411681
17	8.13626821	12.65132059
18	8.67462935	13.18968173
19	9.19478504	13.70983742
20	9.69735093	14.21240330
21	10.18292183	14.69797420
22	10.65207246	15.16712484
23	11.10535809	15.62041047
24	11.54331523	16.05836760
25	11.96646222	16.48151459
26	12.37529989	16.89035226
27	12.77031213	17.28536451
28	13.15196647	17.66701885
29	13.52071463	18.03576700
30	13.87699304	18.39204541
31	14.22122338	18.73627576
32	14.55381309	19.06886547
33	14.87515581	19.39020818
34	15.18563186	19.70068423
35	15.48560872	20.00066110

36	15.77544144	20.29049381
37	16.05547305	20.57052542
38	16.32603499	20.84108736
39	16.58744749	21.10249987
40	16.84001996	21.35507234
41	17.08405133	21.59910371
42	17.31983043	21.83488281
43	17.54763633	22.06268870
44	17.76773864	22.28279102
45	17.98039788	22.49545026
46	18.18586575	22.70091813
47	18.38438543	22.89943780
48	18.57619188	23.09124425
49	18.76151212	23.27656450
50	18.94056550	23.45561787
51	19.11356392	23.62861630
52	19.28071217	23.79576454
53	19.44220805	23.95726043
54	19.59824272	24.11329510
55	19.74900086	24.26405323
56	19.89466089	24.40971327
57	20.03539523	24.55044760
58	20.17137043	24.68642281
59	20.30274744	24.81779981
60	20.42968174	24.94473412
61	20.55232358	25.06737596
62	20.67081812	25.18587049
63	20.78530559	25.30035796
64	20.89592150	25.41097388
65	21.00279678	25.51784916
66	21.10605792	25.62111030
67	21.20582714	25.72087951
68	21.30222252	25.81727489
69	21.39535815	25.91041052
70	21.48534427	26.00039664
71	21.57228738	26.08733975
72	21.65629038	26.17134275
73	21.73745270	26.25250508
74	21.81587040	26.33092278
75	21.89163630	26.40668868
76	21.96484006	26.47989244
77	22.03556834	26.55062072
78	22.10390484	26.61895721
79	22.16993044	26.68498281
80	22.23372329	26.74877567
81	22.29535890	26.81041127
82	22.35491021	26.86996258
83	22.41244770	26.92750008
84	22.46803949	26.98309186
85	22.52175136	27.03680373
86	22.57364688	27.08869926

87	22.62378749	27.13883986
88	22.67223252	27.18728489
89	22.71903931	27.23409168
90	22.76426326	27.27931564
91	22.80795790	27.32301028
92	22.85017494	27.36522732
93	22.89096436	27.40601673
94	22.93037442	27.44542680
95	22.96845178	27.48350415
96	23.00524149	27.52029387
97	23.04078711	27.55583948
98	23.07513070	27.59018308
99	23.10831292	27.62336529

Previous issues of the Information Bulletin are available from our website at www.inlandrevenue-.gov.uk/so/bull_news_flyers_sdlt.htm.

STAMP DUTY LAND TAX: TREATMENT OF PRIVATE FINANCE INITIATIVE PROJECTS

19 December 2003. *IR press release 102/03*

The Government has today made Regulations clarifying the stamp duty land tax treatment of land transactions forming part of a Private Finance Initiative (PFI) project. These Regulations will take effect from 19 December 2003.

Ruth Kelly MP, Financial Secretary to the Treasury, said: "The Government recognises the importance of PFI transactions and the economic benefits which they bring. Having consulted at length with interested parties, our proposals will ensure that the treatment of these transactions under current stamp duty will be continued for the present under stamp duty land tax".

DETAILS

1 The Regulations are The Stamp Duty Land Tax (Amendment of Schedule 4 to the Finance Act 2003) Regulations 2003 (SI 2003/3923).

2 The Regulations clarify the stamp duty land tax treatment of certain land transactions in PFI projects. The Regulations apply to "qualifying transactions", defined as transactions between certain public and educational bodies ("qualifying bodies") and a private sector supplier under a global agreement which provides for—

– the provision of services or the carrying out of works by the private sector supplier;
– payment for those services by the qualifying body;
– the transfer of land or the grant (or assignment) of a lease by the qualifying body;
– the grant of a lease back to the qualifying body; and
– in some cases, the transfer of land (sometimes termed "Surplus Land") by the qualifying body.

3 The Regulations provide that where a transaction is a qualifying transaction—

– neither the lease back to the public body nor the carrying out of works nor the provision of services is chargeable consideration for the transfer or grant of the lease by the qualifying body, or for the transfer of the Surplus Land (in other words tax will generally be charged only on any cash premium or rent paid by the private sector supplier);
– there is no chargeable consideration for the lease back (in other words there is no charge on the qualifying body); and
– the stamp duty land tax provisions relating to exchanges (which normally charge tax on the market value of the property) do not apply to qualifying transactions.

NOTES

1 Stamp duty land tax applies (subject to some transitional provisions) to all "land transactions" completed on or after 1 December 2003. "Land transaction" includes the

conveyance or transfer of a freehold (in Scotland, transfer of ownership), the assignment or assignation of an existing lease and the grant of a new lease. It replaces stamp duty, which is abolished except for instruments relating to stock and marketable securities, and for instruments relating to some partnership transactions.

2 Stamp duty land tax is charged on the "chargeable consideration" given for the transaction. It does not matter whether the consideration is in the form of money or some other form.

3 A PFI transaction is an agreement under which a private sector supplier performs services for a public sector or educational body such as—

(i) the design and construction of a building or complex of buildings (eg a hospital, school, university accommodation, army garrison, bus station, leisure centre, care homes and other buildings or facilities that may be publicly owned);
(ii) the financing of the design and construction of the buildings in (a) above;
(iii) the management and delivery of various services within or related to the buildings constructed at (i) above on a continuous basis.

4 The treatment of PFI transactions under the old stamp duty regime was set out in Tax Bulletin 43C (parts 1–6) published by the Inland Revenue in October 1999.

STAMP DUTY LAND TAX: GROUP RELIEF

April 2004. *Inland Revenue Tax Bulletin Issue 70*

1. This article gives practical and technical guidance on claims for group relief in stamp duty land tax under Schedule 7 to the Finance Act 2003. It deals with material which was previously covered by the Statement of Practice issued for stamp duty group relief, SP3/98 published on 13 October 1998. That Statement does not apply to stamp duty land tax but will continue to apply to stamp duty.

HOW TO CLAIM GROUP RELIEF IN STAMP DUTY LAND TAX

2. In contrast to stamp duty, documents must not be submitted with a claim. The claim should be made on form SDLT1 by putting a cross at box 9 and inserting code 12.

3. Following procedures for other returns within stamp duty land tax, the certificate that enables title to be registered will be issued provided that the return is complete. Certificates will not be delayed simply because the Inland Revenue may wish to enquire into particular aspects of the return including a claim to group relief.

4. The relief is self-assessed and will be dealt with on a 'process now/check later' basis along with all other stamp duty land tax matters. Under stamp duty land tax the Inland Revenue does not require the preparation and submission of the letter of claim (see paragraph 6.641 of the Inland Revenue Stamp Taxes manual).

5. This means that companies must judge the admissibility of the claim themselves. Under stamp duty land tax the Inland Revenue has the power to assess and collect under-declared tax and seek penalties in cases where errors in returns (including errors in group relief claims) are the result of negligence or fraud.

ENQUIRIES INVOLVING GROUP RELIEF CLAIMS

6. If the decision is taken to enquire into a return where the transaction is subject to a group relief claim, the Inland Revenue will open an enquiry under paragraph 12 of Schedule 10 FA 2003. The enquiry must be made within 9 months of the filing date. Enquiries may cover all aspects of the return and will not necessarily be limited to the group relief claim itself.

7. The decision to enquire into a transaction will be made after the certificate (form SDLT5) is issued and will not therefore delay registration of title. But the issue of the certificate should not be taken as an indication that the Inland Revenue either accepts the validity of a group relief claim or has chosen not to enquire into that return.

8. Enquiries will consider all aspects of the transaction, including the group relief claim. Documents may be called for and these may include the instruments of transfer and related documents. The Inland Revenue may also ask for more information about the claim. In particular, evidence may be sought to show that the tests in paragraphs 1 and 2 of Schedule 7 were met.

9. If the evidence presented does not support the claim the self assessment will be amended to remove the relief.

PARAGRAPH 1 OF SCHEDULE 7

10. Paragraph 1 of Schedule 7 to FA 2003 provides exemption from stamp duty land tax where, at the effective date of the transaction, the companies are members of the same group. Exemption extends to the grant of leases between group companies.

MEANING OF COMPANY

11. Relief is extended to any 'body corporate' through the definition of 'company' in section 100(1) FA 2003. To determine whether an entity qualifies as a body corporate the Inland Revenue will follow the guidelines for stamp duty set out at paragraph 6.124 of the Stamp Taxes Manual.

MEANING OF SUBSIDIARY

12. Paragraph 1(2)(b) requires that the companies claiming relief must be 75% subsidiaries of one another or 75% subsidiaries of a third company.

13. Paragraph 1(3) provides that for a company (A) to be a 75% subsidiary of another company (B) if:

- company B is the beneficial owner of at least 75% of the ordinary share capital of company A;
- it is beneficially entitled to not less than 75% of profits available for distribution to equity holders; and
- it would be entitled to not less than 75% of any assets of A available for distribution to equity holders on winding up.

14. Paragraph 1(4) provides that 'ownership' for these purposes is either directly or indirectly through another company or group of companies. The rules in section 838(5) to (10) ICTA 1988 apply to determine the amount of ordinary share capital. Paragraph 1(5) defines 'ordinary share capital'.

15. Paragraph 1(6) applies Schedule 18 ICTA 1988 which defines 'equity holder'.

16. The meaning of subsidiary is also relevant to the arrangements test in paragraph 2(2)(b) of Schedule 7 (see 19 below).

17. The tests in paragraph 1 of Schedule 7 apply independently of the tests in paragraph 2 and claims are not allowable if these tests are not met.

PARAGRAPH 2 OF SCHEDULE 7

18. Paragraph 2 provides anti-avoidance rules which restrict the availability of group relief. It will prevent relief being allowable in circumstances where certain 'arrangements' are in place.

MEANING OF ARRANGEMENTS

19. 'Arrangements is defined generally for the purposes of paragraph 2 in paragraph 2(5) to include any scheme, arrangement or understanding, whether or not legally enforceable'. This definition is used in section 76(6A)(b) FA 1986 (inserted by section 112(6) FA 2002) but 'arrangements' was not defined for the equivalent stamp duty provisions in section 42(2) FA 1930 or section 27(2) FA 1967. Under this new definition, 'arrangements' will include schemes, arrangements or understandings not in writing and the existence of arrangements in a particular claim will depend on a consideration of all of the facts relating to the claim and the surrounding circumstances.

20. In considering whether arrangements exist that might disqualify the claim, the Inland Revenue will seek to establish whether there was any scheme arrangement or understanding.

PARAGRAPH 2(1): ARRANGEMENTS FOR CHANGE OF CONTROL OF PURCHASER

21. Paragraph 2(1) prevents a claim to group relief if arrangements are in existence at the time of the claim for a person (or persons together) to obtain control of the purchaser but not the vendor. Arrangements under paragraph 2(1) have to be in existence at the effective date of the transaction.

22. Where there is a change of control, paragraph 2(1) is intended to prevent avoidance of stamp duty land tax by passing property, or an economic interest in it, out of the group.

23. The statements of the Economic Secretary during debate in Parliament on the equivalent stamp duty provision in Finance Act 2000 are still relevant. The Economic Secretary said:

> 'I have received representations expressing concern about the blocking of relief for transfers from the company about to leave the group to another group member—in other words, when the company leaving the group is the transferor. I am persuaded that there are commercial situations in which an asset is transferred to another group company after arrangements are in place for the transferor company to leave the group. In a sense, therefore, the asset never leaves the original group. I am willing to make a concession for such cases, which will be useful to businesses, as their legal advisers have suggested.
>
> I have some worry that it might be possible to construct avoidance devices from the concession, so I have asked the Stamp Office to monitor carefully the use of the relief. If the concession is abused, the Government will not hesitate to act swiftly.'

(See Hansard 18 July 2000, column 253.)

24. The Inland Revenue will not argue that paragraph 2(1) denies group relief in cases where the transferor is to leave the group having transferred the land to other group members.

25. Furthermore, paragraph 2(1) does not apply if the arrangements that are in place are those for the acquisition of shares by a company under a reconstruction as long as the conditions in paragraph 2(1)(a), (b) and (c) are met. These are:

– that section 75 FA 1986 will apply to the acquisition and the conditions for relief under that section will be met;
– that after the acquisition the purchaser will be a member of the same group as the acquiring company.

PARAGRAPH 2(2) OF SCHEDULE 7

26. Paragraph 2(2)(a) denies relief where there are arrangements under which consideration is to be provided or received (directly or indirectly) by a person other than a group company.

27. Where group relief is claimed the Inland Revenue will consider all of the facts and interpret paragraph 2(2)(a) as not denying relief unless the loan finance is provided as part of a scheme to save stamp duty land tax when the property or an interest in it leaves the group.

28. For example, it is unlikely that there will be arrangements within paragraph 2(2)(a) if:

– the claim is not to be followed by a sale or underlease outside the group; or
– the claim is followed by a sale or underlease outside the group but stamp duty land tax is to be paid by the purchaser outside the group on consideration close to market value (or is deemed to be a grant of a lease under paragraph 11 of Schedule 17A FA 2003), then again it is unlikely that relief will be prevented by paragraph 2(2)(a).

29. Loans from commercial lenders on ordinary commercial terms to facilitate the transfer between group members will also not normally disqualify a claim for the purposes of the arrangements test in paragraph 2(2)(a). For example, a claim can be accepted if:

– a specific loan is taken for the purchase of the asset; or
– the loan is secured on the asset; or
– arrangements are made to replace or novate an existing charge on the property transferred.

30. Paragraphs 27 to 29 above are limited to paragraph 2(2)(a) of Schedule 7. They do not mean that if other tests in paragraphs 1 and 2 of Schedule 7 are not met the claim is acceptable.

31. When an enquiry is opened the case will be considered on their particular facts. Some examples of the type of circumstances which the Inland Revenue might want to examine in more detail during an enquiry are where the claim is part of (or is to be followed by):

– the creation or transfer of loan stock or equity capital;
– a capital reorganisation of the transferee;
– a guarantee by a third party not associated with the group;
– the creation of a new charge or financial arrangement whereby title to the property is, or may be, vested in the lender otherwise than in satisfaction of all or part of the debt; or
– the assignment of the freehold reversion or the intra-group lease to a person outside the group.

32. Other circumstances which can indicate that the claim is not admissible include where:

– all or part of the consideration for the transaction is to remain outstanding or is represented by intra-group debt, (as the aim and effect may be to reduce the value of the transferee company on a possible future sale outside the group); or
– the existing shareholders of the transferee include shareholders outside the group and the transaction is to be followed by the declaration of a dividend in specie, or by the liquidation of the transferee.

SUBSALES AND GROUP RELIEF IN STAMP DUTY LAND TAX

33. Paragraph 2(2) provides rules for stamp duty land tax based on those for stamp duty in section 27(3) FA 1967. Section 27(3)(b) FA 1967 (intended to prevent acquisitions of land from outside the group without stamp duty being paid) is not included in Schedule 7 and this is because the problem it seeks to address, resting on contracts, is not relevant to stamp duty land tax. It is not possible to 'rest on contract' to avoid stamp duty land tax because of the 'substantial' performance rule in section 44 FA 2003.

PARAGRAPH 2(2)(B): ARRANGEMENTS FOR THE PURCHASER TO CEASE TO BE A MEMBER OF THE SAME GROUP

34. A claim for relief is not appropriate if there are arrangements for the purchaser to cease to be a 75% subsidiary of the vendor or a third company. In deciding whether there are any such arrangements, the practical likelihood of the scheme being carried through is not in itself relevant.

35. But the Inland Revenue will not take the view that just because land is transferred to a group company which does nothing other than hold property it follows that there are arrangements for the purchaser to leave the group. We recognise that there are many commercial reasons why groups may transfer property internally. It is necessary to consider the full circumstances of the case to decide whether such arrangements are in place.

36. Whether such arrangements were or were not in place must be decided at the time of the return and Inland Revenue enquiries will seek to establish the facts at the effective date of the transaction.

RELEVANCE OF ARRANGEMENTS UNDER PARAGRAPH 2 TO A RECOVERY OF TAX UNDER PARAGRAPH 3 ('CLAWBACK')

37. Paragraph 3 of Schedule 7 is independent of paragraph 2. When an enquiry is made into a claim the question will be the admissibility of the claim itself in accordance with the statutory provisions. The fact that the arrangements, if carried out as planned, could lead to a recovery or will be exempt from a recovery will not mean that claim itself is allowable except as provided in paragraph 2.

PARAGRAPH 3(1)(A)(II): ARRANGEMENTS DURING THE THREE YEAR RECOVERY PERIOD

38. Paragraph 3 imposes a requirement to make a return (under section 81 FA 2003) for the withdrawal of relief when the purchaser ceases to be a member of the same group within three years of the effective date of the transaction.

39. Paragraph 3(1)(a) deals with the recovery period. Paragraph 3(1)(a)(ii) provides that group relief will be recovered if the transfer outside the group after the end of the period is under arrangements made before the end of the period.

40. 'Arrangements' is defined in paragraph 3(4) with the same definition as in paragraph 2.

41. When there is a transfer outside the group, companies will need to decide whether to make a return under section 81. If the transfer outside the group is after the end of the three year period, companies will still need to consider whether there were arrangements in place for the transfer during the three year period. To make this decision a proper consideration of all of the circumstances will be required.

42. The Inland Revenue will not assume that just because a company is transferred outside the group shortly after the end of the three year period it will be in accordance with arrangements made within the three year period. We will only seek to argue that there should have been a recovery return if the facts of the case point to there having been such arrangements.

SECTION 54(4) FA 2003: EXCEPTION FROM THE CONNECTED COMPANY CHARGE ON A WINDING UP

43. Section 54(4) FA 2003 provides the third case of exception from the deemed market value rule in section 53 FA 2003. The exception applies to the distribution of assets on the winding up of a company, as long as the subject matter of the transaction or an interest from which that interest is derived, has not been the subject of a transaction in respect of which a claim to group relief was made by the vendor. But it is not the Inland Revenue's intention that section 54(4) should be prevented from applying where a group relief claim was made by the vendor but recovered under paragraph 3 of Schedule 7 either at the time of or before the effective date of the transaction.

SDLT—SALE OF LAND WITH ASSOCIATED CONSTRUCTION, &C, CONTRACT

April 2004. *Inland Revenue statement.*

We have been asked how to determine the chargeable consideration for stamp duty land tax purposes where V agrees to sell land to P and V also agrees to carry out work (commonly works of construction, improvement or repair) on the land sold. Our view is that the decision in *Prudential Assurance Co Ltd v IRC* [1992] STC 863 applies for the purposes of stamp duty land tax as it does for stamp duty. This is because the basis of the decision was the identification of the subject matter of the transaction and this is as relevant for stamp duty land tax as it is for stamp duty.

It follows that SP 8/93 will be applied for stamp duty land tax as it was for stamp duty. The paragraphs on "contracts already entered into" and "procedure for submitting documents" are, however, not relevant to stamp duty land tax.

Where, however, the sale of land and the construction, &c, contract are in substance one bargain (as they were in the Prudential case) there must be a just and reasonable apportionment of the total consideration given for all elements of the bargain in order to arrive at the chargeable consideration for stamp duty land tax purposes.

The SDLT Manual will be amended in due course to reflect this.

STAMP DUTY LAND TAX AND NIL-RATE BAND DISCRETIONARY TRUSTS

12 November 2004. *Inland Revenue Guidance Note.*

1 We have received a number of enquiries about the interaction between stamp duty land tax and 'nil-rate band discretionary trusts' ('NRB Trusts'). This note should enable taxpayers and their advisers to decide on the stamp duty land tax consequences of transactions with NRB Trusts. This note does not cover any taxes other than stamp duty land tax. Neither does it cover the powers or fiduciary responsibilities of trustees of NRB Trusts, or of personal representatives, under general law. Trustees and personal representatives may wish to take independent legal advice on those aspects.

2 An NRB Trust is commonly established under the Will of a deceased person. The typical form is a pecuniary legacy, not exceeding the nil-rate band for inheritance tax, to be held by the trustees of the NRB Trust ('the NRB trustees') on discretionary trusts for a specified class of beneficiaries. The residue of the estate, often including the matrimonial home, commonly passes to the surviving spouse, although it may pass to residuary trustees.

3 Where the personal representatives discharge the pecuniary legacy by payment of the specified sum to the trustees no stamp duty land tax issue arises. However in many cases the personal representatives satisfy the legacy otherwise than by payment of the specified sum. It is in these cases that a stamp duty land tax liability may arise on the transfer of the matrimonial home or other land to the surviving spouse or residuary trustees.

4 The transfer of an interest in land, whether to a residuary beneficiary or to any other person, and whether in satisfaction of an entitlement under a Will or not, is a land transaction for stamp duty land tax purposes. The question is whether the transferee gives any chargeable consideration for the transfer. Very often a beneficiary gives no chargeable consideration for the transfer of land under a Will. However transactions in connection with NRB Trusts may result in the beneficiary giving chargeable consideration.

5 The commonest examples of such transactions, and their stamp duty land tax consequences, are as follows:

- The NRB trustees accept the surviving spouse's promise to pay in satisfaction of the pecuniary legacy and in consideration of that promise land is transferred to the surviving spouse. The promise to pay is chargeable consideration for stamp duty land tax purposes.
- The NRB trustees accept the personal representatives' promise to pay in satisfaction of the pecuniary legacy and land is transferred to the surviving spouse in consideration of the spouse accepting liability for the promise. The acceptance of liability for the promise is chargeable consideration for stamp duty land tax purposes. The amount of chargeable consideration is the amount promised (not exceeding the market value of the land transferred)
- Land is transferred to the surviving spouse and the spouse charges the property with payment of the amount of the pecuniary legacy. The NRB trustees accept this charge in satisfaction of the pecuniary legacy. The charge is money's worth and so is chargeable consideration for stamp duty land tax purposes

– The personal representatives charge land with the payment of the pecuniary legacy. The personal representatives and NRB trustees also agree that the trustees have no right to enforce payment of the amount of the legacy personally against the owner of the land for the time being. The NRB trustees accept this charge in satisfaction of the legacy. The property is transferred to the surviving spouse subject to the charge. There is no chargeable consideration for stamp duty land tax purpose provided that there is no change in the rights or liabilities of any person in relation to the debt secured by the charge.

6 We have also been asked about the consequences for stamp duty land tax purposes of a Deed of Variation made by beneficiaries after the death of the deceased person. A Deed of Variation may effect a land transaction if it alters the beneficial interests in land, for example by settling land in trust. However, placing a charge on land is not in itself a land transaction. In addition paragraph 4 of Schedule 3 FA 2003 provides that under certain conditions a land transaction effected by a Deed of Variation is exempt from charge.

BUDGET 2005 PROVISIONS ON STAMP DUTY LAND TAX

14 April 2005. *Inland Revenue Notice.*

THE BUDGET 2005 PROVISIONS

1 A number of stamp duty land tax measures were announced on Budget Day, 16 March 2005. This note summarises the effect that subsequent developments have had on these measures. In particular it explains that in some circumstances a repayment may be due to purchasers who have paid tax on the basis of measures announced in the Budget (see paragraph 8 below).

2 All the Budget measures were included in the Finance Bill published on 22 March 2005. However that Bill has now been withdrawn. Instead the Finance (No 2) Bill, containing some but not all of the provisions in the original Finance Bill, was passed by the House of Commons on 6 April and received Royal Assent as Finance Act 2005 on 7 April 2005.

Increase in the threshold for residential transactions from £60,000 to £120,000

3 This measure has been included in Finance Act 2005 (as section 95) and will have effect as announced, that is, for land transactions the effective date of which was on or after 17 March 2005.

Withdrawal of disadvantaged areas relief on non-residential transactions

4 This measure has been included in Finance Act 2005 (as section 96 and Schedule 9) and will have effect as announced, that is, for land transactions the effective date of which was on or after 17 March 2005, subject to transitional provisions for some contracts entered into on or before 16 March 2005.

Extension of reliefs for alternative property finance

5 This measure has been included in Finance Act 2005 (as section 94 and Schedule 8) and will have effect for land transactions where the effective date of the 'first transaction' is on or after 7 April 2005.

Miscellaneous amendments

6 Budget Resolution 46 gave provisional statutory effect under the Provisional Collection of Taxes Act 1968 ('the 1968 Act') to a number of miscellaneous amendments to the legislation governing stamp duty land tax. These amendments were summarised in a Technical Note published by the Inland Revenue on 16 March 2005. Broadly speaking the Resolution had effect for transactions the effective date of which was on or after 17 March 2005.

7 Provisions giving effect to Budget Resolution 46 were included (as Part 1 of Schedule 17) in the original Finance Bill, now withdrawn. However Finance Act 2005 does not contain any provisions giving effect to Budget Resolution 46. It follows that by virtue of section 1(5) of the 1968 Act the Resolution ceased to have statutory effect when Parliament was prorogued on 7 April 2005.

8 If you have paid tax which would not have been payable but for the provisional statutory effect of Budget Resolution 46 a repayment is due to you. Any requests for repayment should be sent, along with an explanation of why you think a repayment is due to you, to:

Complex Transactions Unit
Manchester Stamp Office
Upper 5th Floor
Royal Exchange
Exchange Street
MANCHESTER M2 7EB

If you are in doubt as to whether a repayment is due please contact the Complex Transactions Unit with an explanation of the circumstances.

STATEMENTS MADE DURING THE DEBATE ON THE FINANCE (NO 2) BILL

9 Purchasers and their advisers will wish to be aware of the statements made by the front-bench spokesmen during debate on the Finance (No 2) Bill, which concern measures in the original Bill which were not included in Finance Act 2005, including the measures in Budget Resolution 46:

Paul Boateng MP (Labour): 'It is therefore our full intention to introduce a second Finance Bill after the election – should it be the wish of the British people – in which the measures not included in this revised version will be brought back. We will, of course, aim to ensure that the statutory dates for these measures will continue to apply, as announced in the Budget.' (Hansard, 6 April 2005, col. 1432)

George Osborne MP (Conservative): 'We agree with the Government about the need to tackle tax avoidance and we agree on principle with the many measures that they have introduced to close tax loopholes. However, the detail of such measures requires the closest possible examination, to ensure that we do not inadvertently damage the competitiveness of UK industry and further increase burdens on business. Indeed, many anti-tax avoidance measures are retrospective, as they would come into force on the day on which they were announced. There would therefore be no revenue implications if we considered them after the election in a Conservative Finance Bill or, in the unlikely event that Labour wins, a Labour one.' (Hansard, 6 April 2005, col 1444)

Dr Vincent Cable MP (Liberal Democrat): 'On the major change, the anti-avoidance measures, we need a great deal more time for reflection. We are all committed to such measures where they are effective, but they are at the core of the Government's budgetary arithmetic, as the Chief Secretary knows. They propose to raise £3 billion over three years, so the ability to make the measures stick is central to the Budget's credibility. For the reasons that have partly been given, it is right that we be given further time for reflection.' (Hansard, 6 April 2005, col 1448)

INTERMEDIARY AND STOCK LENDING RELIEFS—FA 2007, SCH 21

14 December 2007. *HMRC Guidance Note.*

Transaction reporting to a Multilateral Trading Facility, Recognised Foreign Exchange or Recognised Foreign Options Exchange.

HM Revenue and Customs (HMRC) has been asked to clarify the operation of the stamp duty and stamp duty reserve tax rules for intermediary and stock lending relief, as amended with effect from 1 November 2007, in respect of transactions involving stocks other than those that are regularly traded on a regulated market.

The intermediary relief legislation covering stocks regularly traded on a multilateral trading facility (MTF), recognised foreign exchange (RFE) or recognised foreign options exchange (RFOE) provides that relief is only available where the transaction is subject to the rules of the particular MTF/exchange and is reported to the MTF/exchange in accordance with those rules (see sections 80A(6) and 88A(6) FA 1986). The stock lending relief provisions contain a similar requirement (see sections 80C(6) and 89AA(5) FA 1986).

HMRC understands that the rules of some MTFs/exchanges may, following the implementation of the Directive on Markets in Financial Instruments (MiFID), no longer contain a requirement to report a transaction to the MTF/exchange. This means that members of those organisations are strictly unable to fulfil the requirement in the legislation that transactions must be reported to the MTF/exchange.

HMRC recognises that a strict reading of the legislation would result in intermediary or stock lending relief not being granted. It therefore intends to amend the legislation to address this at the earliest opportunity. In the meantime, HMRC will not refuse relief where the rules of an MTF/exchange are either silent about the need to report transactions or specifically state that a report is not required. Nor will stock lending relief be denied if the stock loan is reported to CREST for settlement and the Trade System of Origin (TSO) field completed in accordance with the rules of the market/MTF/exchange.

For trading transactions on the Alternative Investment Market (AIM) of the London Stock Exchange (LSE), the trade report that AIM members are required to make to the LSE will be regarded as satisfying the reporting condition for the purposes of section 80A(6) and 88A(6).

STAMP TAXES ONLINE—TRANSACTIONS WITH MORE THAN 100 PROPERTIES

4 February 2008. *HMRC Notice.*

The online service can accept transactions of up to 100 properties. We want to extend this, but know that an IT solution is at least 12 months away. In the meantime, we're introducing a new process which we hope will encourage even more people to use online filing.

Currently, if transactions have more than 100 properties, paper returns must be sent to Birmingham Stamp Office, where hand-written certificates are produced for practitioners to submit for registration purposes. The new process will still have a manual element, but should make life easier.

From 1 February 2008 the process will be:

- complete the online return for the first 100 properties
- submit a schedule to Birmingham Stamp Office, by email to: Shujina Bibi for only the properties that exceed 100.

There is no "template" for this schedule. You should simply ensure that all the relevant information is given (see below).

For example:

- If the transaction includes 150 properties, the schedule submitted to Birmingham should include the last 50 properties.
- Birmingham will save the schedule and allocate a reference number in SDLTMP-9999999 format. They will keep a record of the reference number and email this to you, with the agent reference.
- Complete the return online and enter the allocated reference number in the 'Property Address' field, at the end of the address details for the first property.
- Add the remaining 99 properties not included in the schedule and submit the return.
- Send the online certificate(s) and/or the 99 PDFs (if appropriate to the online product being used) together with a copy of the schedule to the appropriate land registry. The reference number allocated by Birmingham will appear on the certificate, under the first property address.

Information required on the schedule for each property is:

- Property address
- Title number
- NLPG UPRN (National Land Property Gazette Unique Property Registration Number)

The schedule must also include:

- First purchaser name
- Description of transaction
- Effective date
- Agents reference

Before the schedule is passed onto the appropriate land registry, you should add:

- Reference number issued by Birmingham
- UTRN

STAMP DUTY ON SHARED OWNERSHIP HOMES

31 March 2008. *HMRC Information Sheet.*

BACKGROUND

Shared ownership purchasers acquire a lease, for which they pay a premium representing a percentage of the market value of the property, and rent in respect of the remainder. They may be able to make further capital payments (which will increase their share and reduce the rent payable) and ultimately to acquire the freehold. This is known as "staircasing".

SDLT AND SHARED OWNERSHIP

– Shared ownership purchasers can elect to pay SDLT at the outset on the market value of the property. In this case there will be no further SDLT charges at any stage.
– If no election is made, SDLT will be charged on the initial purchase in the normal way — that is, on the premium and the net present value of the rent payable under the lease. (In practice it is very unlikely that any tax will be due on the rent.)
– There is then a special SDLT relief which means staircasing payments are not charged to SDLT until an 80 percent share of the property is reached.
– Any further "staircasing" payments which take the purchaser above this level — including the acquisition of the freehold, will attract SDLT

BUDGET MEASURE

– The measure announced in the Budget abolishes, from Budget Day, the so called "£600 rule" for residential leases. This rule meant that, where the annual rent under the lease (not the NPV) exceeded £600, SDLT applied at 1 per cent on the premium even where this was below the SDLT threshold (£125,000, or £150,000 in a disadvantaged area).
– The special rules for shared ownership purchasers have not changed, but in practice these purchasers were often hit by the £600 rule because their initial payment was below the threshold but their annual rent was more than £600.

EFFECT OF THE MEASURE FOR SHARED OWNERSHIP PURCHASERS

– Where a market value election is not made, no SDLT will be payable on the premium where this does not exceed the SDLT threshold (£125,000, or £150,000 in a disadvantaged area), whatever the annual rent paid. If the premium is more than this, SDLT will still be charged on the whole premium at 1 per cent (and at higher rates in the unlikely event that the premium exceeds £250,000).
– No tax will be payable on "staircasing" payments which do not take the purchaser above an 80 per cent share of the property.
– Any further "staircasing" payments which take the purchaser above this level – including the acquisition of the freehold, will attract SDLT. Tax will be payable on the amount actually paid at the appropriate rate in force at the time the payment is made.
– The rate of tax charged on these further "staircasing" payments will be based on the total capital payments made to date – that is, on the initial premium and all "staircasing" payments, regardless of whether any tax has previously been paid on them. This is because the various payments are treated as "linked transactions" for SDLT purposes.

Example 1

Market value of the property is £220,000.

Initial lease premium is £110,000, representing a 50 per cent share of the property. SDLT payable is nil (because this amount is below the SDLT threshold).

First "staircasing" payment is £55,000, taking the purchaser's share to 75 per cent. SDLT payable is nil (this payment attracts relief as it doesn't take the purchaser's share over 80 per cent).

Final "staircasing" payment is £55,000, taking the purchaser's share to 100 per cent including acquisition of the freehold. SDLT is payable at 1 per cent on £55,000 (because the rate of SDLT is determined by the total of all payments made, that is £220,000).

Example 2

Market value of the property is £220,000.

Initial lease premium is £165,000, representing a 75 per cent share of the property. SDLT is payable at 1 per cent on £165,000 (because this amount is above the SDLT threshold).

Final staircasing payment is £55,000, taking the purchaser's share to 100 per cent including acquisition of the freehold. SDLT is payable at 1 per cent on £55,000 (because the rate of SDLT is determined by the total of all payments made, that is £220,000).

SDLT—BUDGET CHANGES TO NOTIFICATION REQUIREMENTS

17 April 2008. *HMRC Notice*

Following on from the announcement of changes in the Stamp Duty Land Tax (SDLT) notification thresholds in Budget 2008 [BN57 and Finance Bill clause 91], the various Land Registries and HM Revenue & Customs (HMRC) have agreed to produce this note which conveyancers and others involved in land transactions may find helpful in explaining how these changes will work in practice.

As you know, Budget 2008 announced changes in requirements for notification of land transactions to HMRC. These changes will have effect for transactions with an effective date on and after 12 March 2008.

The changes raise the threshold for notification of non-leasehold transactions involving major interests in land from a chargeable consideration of £1,000 to £40,000. The changes also affect transactions involving leases for a term of seven years or more, which will now only have to be notified where any chargeable consideration other than rent is equal to or more than £40,000 or where any rent is equal to or more than £1,000.

As a result of these changes it will no longer be necessary to complete either form SDLT 1 Land Transaction Return or form SDLT 60 Self certificate if the transaction is below the new notification threshold.

The new notification system is we hope, much simpler and easier to understand for customers.

Some people have asked whether there are any circumstances in which a certificate that no SDLT is due (form SDLT 60) is now required. We are happy to confirm that there are now no circumstances in which an SDLT 60 is required in order for documents to be registered. Indeed, the current Finance Bill legislates to remove all reference to this form. Subject to Parliamentary approval, these consequential amendments will become law when the Bill receives Royal assent later this summer.

It may also help to mention that the acquisition of a chargeable interest other than a major interest in land remains notifiable only where there is chargeable consideration for which SDLT is due at a rate of 1 per cent or more. The acquisition of an easement, for example, is an acquisition of a chargeable interest other than a major interest in land. So, if the chargeable consideration on it was at the rate of 1 per cent or higher, the transaction would be notifiable.

It will be noted that the new notification threshold differs in two major respects from the previous rules. First, the threshold for notification in relation to major interests in residential property has risen from £1,000 to £40,000. Second, there is now a threshold for mixed and non-residential property, where none previously existed.

HMRC and the land registries will be working together over the coming months to update published guidance and will be happy to advise on any queries you might have.

STAMP DUTY EXEMPTION FOR RESIDENTIAL PROPERTY

2 September 2008. *HM Treasury*

The Chancellor of the Exchequer has today announced that stamp duty land tax will not apply to purchases of residential property of £175,000 or less.

This will provide an exemption from stamp duty land tax for land transactions consisting entirely of residential property where the chargeable consideration is not more than £175,000.

This relief will apply to transactions with an effective date on or after 3rd September 2008 and before 3rd September 2009.

Note—See also FA 2009 s 10 (extended zero-rate threshold continues to apply in relation to transactions with an effective date on or after 22 April 2009 but before 1 January 2010).

STAMP DUTY AND STAMP DUTY RESERVE TAX (SDRT)—INVESTMENT EXCHANGES AND CLEARING HOUSES; REGULATIONS MADE UNDER SECTIONS 116 AND 117 FINANCE ACT 1991

21 October 2009.*HMRC Notice*

HM Revenue & Customs (HMRC) Stamp Taxes has recently received a number of enquiries seeking clarification as to whether securities transactions that are reported to, and cleared via, an investment exchange or a multilateral trading facility, are eligible for clearing relief from Stamp Duty or Stamp Duty Reserve Tax (SDRT) under existing Investment Exchange and Clearing House regulations.

BACKGROUND

HM Treasury has the power under Sections 116 and 117 FA 1991 to make regulations which provide for transactions involving prescribed recognised investment exchanges (which, for the purposes of these regulations, include regulated markets and multilateral trading facilities) or their members or nominees, or prescribed recognised clearing houses (or their nominee) to be relieved from Stamp Duty and SDRT charges in certain prescribed circumstances. This relief is often referred to as "clearing relief".

A clearing house is essentially a "middleman" standing between an ultimate seller and an ultimate purchaser of securities, acting as a "buyer" of securities from the seller and a "seller" of the same securities and quantity to the purchaser. In this way the delivery of securities, and payment for them, is guaranteed because the clearing house and its clearing members assume all the risks of the transaction. The clearing process does, however, create a series of transfers for what is essentially a single purchase and sale. Each transfer of securities to a clearing house member and to the clearing house itself potentially attracts a charge to Stamp Duty or SDRT in addition to that falling on the ultimate purchaser. Regulations made under Sections 116 and 117 FA 1991 provide, however, for the intervening charges to be relieved from Stamp Duty or SDRT whilst leaving the charge falling on the ultimate purchaser in place.

CLARIFICATION

The regulations commonly provide that there shall be no charge to Stamp Duty or SDRT where securities are transferred between the entities in the prescribed circumstances "in connection with a transaction made on the facility [or exchange]". The meaning of the word "made" is not defined in the regulations. Following representations and after taking advice, HMRC considers that "made" in these regulations includes all transactions that are performed on an investment exchange or multilateral trading facility in accordance with the rules of that exchange or facility. This means that transactions "made" on a platform will include transactions conducted away from the central trading mechanism but executed in accordance with the rules of the trading platform (referred to as "negotiated transactions" in the Markets in Financial Instruments Directive).

Any enquiry relating to this Guidance Note should be made to the HMRC Stamp Taxes Policy Team (telephone Simon English: 020 7147 2808 or Andrew Hewitt: 020 7147 0092).

STAMP DUTY RESERVE TAX—REFUNDS FOLLOWING HSBC HOLDINGS AND VIDACOS NOMINEES LTD V HMRC

18 January 2010. *HMRC Notice*

Following the judgment in HSBC Holdings by the ECJ on 1 October 2009, HMRC has invited statutory claims for repayment from persons who have paid SDRT pursuant to the issue of shares in a UK incorporated company to a depositary receipt issuer or a clearance service located within the European Union.

[See also Stamp Duty and Stamp Duty Reserve Tax: Implications of the ECJ Decision in HSBC Holdings Plc and Vidacos Nominees Ltd v Commissioners for Her Majesty's Revenue & Customs (C560–07)]

BACKGROUND

On 1 October 2009, the European Court of Justice released its judgment in Case C–569/07 HSBC Holdings Ltd and Vidacos Nominees v The Commissioners for HM Revenue & Customs

[2009] All ER (D) 03 (Oct). In the light of the ruling HM Revenue & Customs (HMRC) accepts that Article 11(a) of Council Directive 69/335/EEC of 17 July 1969 concerning indirect taxes on the raising of capital, as amended by Council Directive 85/303/EEC of 10 June 1985 (now Council Directive 2008/7/EC) ("the EC Capital Directive"), must be interpreted as meaning that it prohibits the levying of a duty such as the charge to SDRT imposed by section 96 Finance Act 1986 on the issue of shares into a Community clearance service.

IMPLICATIONS

HMRC invites statutory claims for repayment under Regulation 14 of the Stamp Duty Reserve Tax Regulations 1986 ("the SDRT Regulations") from persons who pursuant to sections 93 or 96 Finance Act 1986 have paid SDRT pursuant to the issue of shares in a United Kingdom incorporated company to a depositary receipt issuer or a clearance service located within the European Union.

TIME LIMIT FOR REPAYMENT CLAIMS

Regulation 14 of the SDRT Regulations requires any claim for a refund of SDRT to be sent to HMRC Stamp Taxes within a period of six years beginning with the later of the date on which the payment was made and the relevant accountable date for payment of SDRT under the SDRT Regulations. Any claims made after the expiry of that period will be time–barred.

INTEREST ON SDRT REFUNDS

Where the amount of SDRT to be refunded is £25 or more, interest calculated at the rate applicable under section 178 Finance Act 1989 will be paid on the amount of any repayment, calculated from the time at which the SDRT was paid.

MAKING A CLAIM

In the first instance the information and documents listed in the Appendix to this statement should accompany any claim for repayment. It may be that in certain circumstances further information is required by HMRC before a given claim will be processed.

Claims should state the subject matter as "Claim made as a result of the ECJ decision in HSBC and Vidacos Nominees v HMRC" and should be addressed to Adam Shooter at HMRC Stamp Taxes, 9th Floor, City Centre House, Union Street, Birmingham B2 4AR.

APPENDIX

Information and documents required in support of a claim to SDRT paid at 1.5% on the issue of shares to a clearance service or depositary receipt issuer within the EU

A claim must include the information and documents set out below:

1 Transactions reported to and settled in the CREST system:

a) The reason(s) to support the request for a refund of SDRT, which includes copy evidence/information to demonstrate that shares were issued (rather than transferred),

b) the CREST transaction reference ID,

c) the trade date,

d) the intended settlement date,

e) the full name of issuer,

f) the full name of purchaser/transferee i.e. name of clearance service (or depositary receipt issuer) within the European Union (see below),

g) the full name and description of security,

h) the share quantity,

i) the agreed price per share,

j) the consideration paid (if any)

k) the amount of SDRT debited in CREST,

l) a signed declaration (see below)

2 Transactions reported outside of the CREST system to HMRC Stamp Taxes:

a) The reason(s) to support the request for a refund of SDRT, which includes copy evidence/information to demonstrate that shares were issued (rather than transferred),

b) the trade date,

c) the intended settlement date,

d) the full name of issuer,

e) the full name of purchaser/transferee, i.e. name of clearance service (or depositary receipt issuer) within the European Union (see below),

f) the full name and description of security,

g) the share quantity,

h) the agreed price per share,

i) the consideration paid (if any),

j) the amount of SDRT originally paid,

k) the date when notification and payment of SDRT was sent to HMRC Stamp Taxes,

l) the original (not a paper copy, fax, facsimile or email of the original) SDRT receipt issued by Stamp Taxes,

m) A signed declaration (in the attached form)

A declaration must be included in the claim which has been signed by an appointed officer of the claimant organisation to confirm that 1.5% SDRT has been paid on the issues of UK securities in respect of the transactions outlined in the claim and that no earlier claim and subsequent refund (either partially or in full) in respect of those transactions has been received by the organisation from HMRC Stamp Taxes or Euroclear UK and Ireland.

EU Clearance Services and Depositary Receipt Issuer

Nominee	Clearance Service
Vidacos Nominees Ltd	Clearstream Frankfurt Germany (formerly DBC)
Euroclear 2	Euroclear Bank (formerly Euroclear France)
Askas Nominees Ltd	Amsterdam Stock Exchange (KAS Associates)
VPC	Swedish CSD
Necigef	Netherlands CSD
HSBC	VaerdiPapircentralen (VP) – Danish Clearance Service

Depositary Receipt Issuer (within the European Union)

HSBC Issuer Services (Depositary) Nominees Ltd

Company Declaration

Declaration

I declare that, in relation to the claim for repayment from HMRC of Stamp Duty Reserve Tax (SDRT), all of the following is true in relation to each and every aspect of the claim:

– That the SDRT to be reclaimed was paid on the issue of UK securities into a clearance service or depositary receipt issuer established in a European Union (EU) member state

(and that the country was a member of the EU at the time the securities were issued into the clearance service or depositary receipt issuer),
- That the SDRT to be reclaimed was paid at the rate of 1.5%,
- That the SDRT claim is made within 6 years beginning with the later of the date on which the payment was made, and the relevant accountable date,
- That no previous refund of SDRT has been made either by HMRC or Euroclear UK and Ireland, whether in part or fully, in respect of the transactions to which this refund of SDRT is claimed.

Signature:

Name (printed):

Position held in claiming organisation:

Date:

RELIEF FROM STAMP DUTY ON INTRA-GROUP TRANSFERS OF STOCK OR MARKETABLE SECURITIES

30 March 2010. *HMRC Notice*

HMRC has issued a short guide on how to make a claim to relief from Stamp Duty in respect of instruments effecting certain transactions between companies in the same group.

SECTION 42 FINANCE ACT 1930, AS AMENDED

This note is a short guide on how to make a claim to relief from Stamp Duty in respect of instruments effecting certain transactions between companies in the same group. It does not cover all the points that can arise, so if further information is required please contact the Stamp Office. Alternatively, more detailed information is in the Stamp Taxes Manual which is available on the HMRC internet site www.hmrc.gov.uk/so

INTRA-GROUP TRANSFERS

An instrument which has the effect of passing a beneficial interest in property between bodies corporate in the same group, which would otherwise be chargeable with ad valorem Stamp Duty as a transfer on sale, will not be chargeable with duty provided that a valid claim for relief is made under the provisions of Section 42 Finance Act 1930, as amended by Section 27 Finance Act 1967 and Section 123 Finance Act 2000.

BODY CORPORATE

A "body corporate" is one which has perpetual succession and a legal personality distinct from that of its members. In the United Kingdom a body corporate includes companies with limited or unlimited liability, companies limited by guarantee, charter companies and bodies created by statute. The relief is not restricted to a body corporate situated in the United Kingdom and is available to non-UK companies which the applicant can show are bodies corporate within the meaning of the legislation.

ASSOCIATED BODIES CORPORATE

One body corporate is associated with another if the following conditions are met—

(a) the first is the beneficial owner of not less than 75% of the ordinary share capital of the second, or a third body corporate is the beneficial owner of not less than 75% of the ordinary share capital of each;

(b) the first is beneficially entitled to not less than 75% of any profits available for distribution to equity holders of the second body; and

(c) the first would be beneficially entitled to not less than 75% of any assets of the second available for distribution to its equity holders on a winding up.

Ordinary share capital means all the issued share capital of whatever description except capital the holders of which are entitled to a fixed dividend but have no other right to a share in the profits of the body corporate.

The association can be direct or through intermediate companies. A claim can, for example, be made for transactions between A and B if there is a direct relationship or between B and C which are both associated with A provided that the relationship with A meets the required test.

In cases of doubt applicants are encouraged to read the section 'Bars to Relief' in the Stamp Duty Manual 6.169

HOW TO CLAIM STAMP DUTY RELIEF

Write to the Stamp Office. The letter of claim needs to be signed either by a named board member of the company through which the associated company relationship is being established, or a named solicitor or accountant acting on behalf of the parent company who is aware of the full facts and circumstances of the transaction as set out in the letter from personal knowledge. Phrases such as "I am advised" or "To the best of my knowledge and belief" are not acceptable.

With your letter include

– the instrument or instruments in respect of which relief is being claimed.
– the supporting evidence See the section below on what you need to provide

All instruments on which a claim to relief under Section 42 is made need to be lodged with the Stamp Office for formal adjudication under Section 12 of the Stamp Act 1891, together with all relevant supporting documentation. One consequence of the provisions of Section 12 is that the Stamp Office may require the evidence in support of a claim to relief to be provided in the form of a Statutory Declaration, rather than in plain letter form. In general the Stamp Office will not insist that a Statutory Declaration is sworn in support of a group relief claim although we do reserve the right to require this where we deem it to be necessary.

INFORMATION TO INCLUDE IN THE CLAIM

The letter of claim needs to include all of the following:-

(1) It should state that a claim for relief from Transfer on Sale duty is made under Section 42 Finance Act 1930, as amended, in respect of specified instruments.

(2) Details of the dates of all instruments on which relief is claimed.

(3) Details of the authorised and issued share capital of the parent and subsidiary companies and of any intermediate companies through which the relationship required under the legislation is traced. In the case of non-UK companies, include sufficient information to show that they qualify as bodies corporate for the purposes of the relief. A list of non-UK entities previously accepted as bodies corporate can be found in section 6.124 of the Stamp taxes manual. If the parties to the document(s) on which relief is claimed are indirectly associated a family tree diagram should also be supplied, showing percentage of ownership for each branch.

(4) State whether any class of share detailed at 3 above carries a right to only a fixed dividend and no other share in the profits.

(5) If there is more than one class of share in issue, set out the profit rights attached to each class of share and set out the asset distribution rights attached to each class of share in any winding up of the company.

(6) State whether any of the bodies corporate is in liquidation.

(7) Show details of the shareholders of all the issued shares in each subsidiary company and any intermediate company through which the relationship required under the legislation is traced. If the relationship between companies is dependant upon shares held by nominees, documentary evidence of the beneficial ownership of the shares should be provided.

(8) Confirm that at the date of execution of the instrument on which relief is being claimed no arrangement was in existence by virtue of which at that or some later time any person had or could obtain, or any persons together had or could obtain, control of the transferee but not the transferor.

(9) Say whether it is intended that:
– the relationship required by the legislation is to be maintained
– the transferee body corporate will retain the beneficial ownership of the transferred property

(10) Give the amount of the consideration and say whether it was satisfied from cash resources (see note 4 below), through an inter-company loan account or by way of a third party loan (see note 5 below).

(11) Give an assurance that none of the documents were executed in pursuance of or in connection with an arrangement described in Section 27(3) Finance Act 1967.

SUPPORTING EVIDENCE NEEDED FOR THE CLAIM

The completed and signed letter of claim should be accompanied by:-

(1) The original of all documents and instruments referred to in the letter.
(2) Certified copies all the documents and instruments.
(3) A certified extract from the Register of Members of all subsidiary and intermediate companies as at the date of the instrument(s) on which relief is being claimed, so that the relationship between the transferor and the transferee can be easily established.
(4) A copy of the latest accounts of the transferee company if the consideration was provided from cash resources.
(5) Copies of any agreement with a third party relating to the provision of consideration.
(6) Copies of correspondence, agreements, board minutes or any other writings, etc., if the relationship between the parties or the ownership of the transferred property is not intended to continue or there was any possibility that it might not continue.

WHERE TO SEND THE CLAIM

Send your claim marked "Stamp duty – Group relief claim" to: Birmingham Stamp Office, 9th Floor, City Centre House, 30 Union Street, Birmingham B2 4AR, or DX 15001 Birmingham 1.

Stamp Taxes Index

Defined words and phrases are listed separately at the end.

Stamp Taxes

R

V

W

Words and Phrases

Words in brackets indicate the context in which the word or phrase is used.

accountable date (stamp duty reserve tax), SI 1986/1711 reg 2
accountable person (stamp duty reserve tax), SI 1986/1711 reg 2
accredited assessor, SI 2007/3437 reg 2
allied headquarters, FA 1960 s 74(6)(*aa*)
appeal, SI 2004/1363 reg 2
approved methodology, SI 2007/3437 reg 2
assignment, FA 2003 s 121
associated (bodies corporate), FA 1930 s 42(2A), FA 1967 s 27(2)
authorised corporate director, SI 1997/1156 reg 2
authorised unit trust, SI 2008/710 reg 2
bare trust, FA 2003 Sch 15 para 1
barrister (stamp duty reserve tax), SI 1986/1711 reg 2
bearer instrument, FA 1999 Sch 15 para 3
bearer instrument by usage, FA 1999 Sch 15 para 10
body of persons (stamp duty reserve tax), SI 1986/1711 Sch para 118
branch or agency (stamp duty reserve tax), SI 1986/1711 Sch para 118
broker and dealer (stamp duty reserve tax), FA 1986 s 89, SI 1986/1711 reg 2
capital market instrument, FA 1996 s 79(13)
capital payment, SI 1998/3177 reg 24
CC&G, SI 2009/1832 reg 2(1)
certificate to bearer (unit trust scheme), FA 1999 Sch 19 para 14(3)
chargeable interest, FA 2003 s 48(1)
chargeable securities (stamp duty reserve tax), FA 1986 s 99 (3)–(6), (6A), (10)–(12)
charter-party, SA 1891 s 49
chief office, SDMA 1891 s 27
clearing member, SI 1999/3262 reg 2
clearing participant, SI 1995/2051 regs 2, 4(3)(*cc*), SI 2008/52 reg 2(1), SI 2008/2777 reg 2(1), SI 2008/3235 reg 2(1), SI 2009/35 reg 2(1), SI 2009/194 reg 2(1), SI 2009/397 reg 2(1), SI 2009/115 reg 2(1), SI 2009/1344 reg 2(1), , SI 2009/1462 reg 2(1), SI 2009/1601 reg 2(1), SI 2009/1827 reg 2(1), SI 2009/1828 reg 2(1), SI 2009/1831 reg 2(1), SI 2009/1832 reg 2(1), SI 2009/2954 reg 2(1); SI 2009/2954 reg 2(1); SI 2009/2976 reg 2, SI 2009/2977 reg 2, SI 2009/3088 reg 2
close possession, SI 1999/3263 reg 2; SI 2003/2837 reg 29
collective investment scheme, FA 1986 ss 80B(2), 88B(2); FSMA 2000 s 235
collector (stamp duty reserve tax), SI 1986/1711 Sch para 118
Commissioners, SDMA 1891 s 27, SA 1891 s 122(1)
commodity or financial futures, SI 1998/3177 reg 2(1)
company (bearer instrument), FA 1999 Sch 15 para 11
company (stamp duty reserve tax), SI 1986/1711 Sch para 118
company's place of business, SI 2004/1363 reg 8
completion, FA 2003 s 121
compulsory purchase facilitating development, FA 2003 s 60
contingent consideration, FA 2003 s 51(3)
contract of insurance, FA 1997 s 96(8)
conveyance on sale, FA 1999 Sch 13 para 1(2)
conveyance or transfer other than on sale, FA 1999 Sch 13 para 16
day of The Stock Exchange reforms, FA 1986 s 85(5)(*aa*)
debt, SI 1998/3177 reg 2(1)
Delta number, SI 1992/570 reg 2
Deltapluslong limit, SI 1992/570 reg 9(1)
Deltaplusshort limit, SI 1992/570 reg 9(2)
deposit certificate (bearer instrument), FA 1999 Sch 15 para 9
depositary interest, SI 1999/2383 reg 2
depositary receipt, FA 1986 ss 69(1), (2), 94(1), (2), 99(7), (8)
derivative, SI 1998/3177 reg 2(1)
die, SDMA 1891 s 27
disadvantaged area, FA 2003 Sch 6 para 1
duty, SDMA 1891 s 27
dwelling, FA 2003 Sch 6A para 7(1)
dwelling CO_2 emission rate, SI 2007/3437 reg 5(4)
ecu, SI 1998/3177 reg 2(1)
EEA State, FA 1986 ss 80B(2), 88B(2)
EMCF, SI 2009/1462 reg 2(1), SI 2009/1601 reg 2(1), SI 2009/1831 reg 2(1), SI 2009/1832 reg 2(1); SI 2009/2975 reg 2(1)
employee, FA 2003 s 121
enactments relating to stamp duty, FA 1995 s 152(6); SI 1999/3263 reg 2
Equiduct Trading, SI 2008/2777 reg 2(1)
equity securities, SI 1992/570 reg 2, SI 1995/2051 reg 2, SI 1999/3262 reg 2; SI 2000/2995 reg 2; SI 2008/52 reg 2(1)
EU clearance service operator, FA 1986 s 97C(5)
EU depositary receipt issuer, FA 1986 s 97C(5)
Eurex Clearing AG, SI 2009/2954 reg 2(1)
euro, SI 1998/3177 reg 2(1)

Insurance Premium Tax

Contents

Insurance Premium Tax Statutes

IPT

Contents

PROVISIONAL COLLECTION OF TAXES ACT 1968

(1968 Chapter 2)

1 Temporary statutory effect of House of Commons resolutions affecting . . . , [insurance premium tax][2], . . .

(1) This section applies only to . . . , [insurance premium tax][2], . . .

(2) Subject to that, and to the provisions of subsections (4) to (8) below, where the House of Commons passes a resolution which—

(*a*) provides for the renewal for a further period of any tax in force or imposed during the previous financial year (whether at the same or a different rate, and whether with or without modifications) or for the variation or abolition of any existing tax, and

(*b*) contains a declaration that it is expedient in the public interest that the resolution should have statutory effect under the provisions of this Act,

the resolution shall, for the period specified in the next following subsection, have statutory effect as if contained in an Act of Parliament and, where the resolution provides for the renewal of a tax, all enactments which were in force with reference to that tax as last imposed by Act of Parliament shall during that period have full force and effect with respect to the tax as renewed by the resolution. In this section references to the renewal of a tax include references to its reimposition, and references to the abolition of a tax include references to its repeal.

(3) The said period is—

(*a*) in the case of a resolution passed in [November or December][3] in any year, one expiring with [5th May in the next calendar year][3];

[(*aa*) in the case of a resolution passed in February or March in any year, one expiring with 5th August in the same calendar year; and][5]

(*b*) in the case of any other resolution, one expiring at the end of four months after the date on which it is expressed to take effect or, if no such date is expressed, after the date on which it is passed.

(4) A resolution shall cease to have statutory effect under this section unless within the next [thirty][4] days on which the House of Commons sits after the day on which the resolution is passed—

(*a*) a Bill renewing, varying or, as the case may be, abolishing the tax is read a second time by the House, or

(*b*) a Bill is amended by the House [in Committee or on Report, or by any [Public Bill Committee][6] of the House][1] so as to include provision for the renewal, variation or, as the case may be, abolition of the tax.

(5) A resolution shall also cease to have statutory effect under this section if—

(*a*) the provisions giving effect to it are rejected during the passage of the Bill containing them through the House, or

(*b*) an Act comes into operation renewing, varying or, as the case may be, abolishing the tax, or

(*c*) Parliament is dissolved or prorogued.

(6) Where, in the case of a resolution providing for the renewal or variation of a tax, the resolution ceases to have statutory effect by virtue of subsection (4) or (5) above, or the period specified in subsection (3) above terminates, before an Act comes into operation renewing or varying the tax, any money paid in pursuance of the resolution shall be repaid or made good, and any deduction made in pursuance of the resolution shall be deemed to be an unauthorised deduction.

(7) Where any tax as renewed or varied by a resolution is modified by the Act renewing or varying the tax, any money paid in pursuance of the resolution which would not have been payable under the new conditions affecting the tax shall be repaid or made good, and any deduction made in pursuance of the resolution shall, so far as it would not have been authorised under the new conditions affecting the tax, be deemed to be an unauthorised deduction.

(8) When during any session a resolution has had statutory effect under this section, statutory effect shall not be again given under this section in the same session to the same resolution or to a resolution having the same effect.

Note—Words and any subsection not relevant for the purposes of IPT have been omitted.

Cross reference—See FA 1994 Sch 7 para 34 (insurance premium tax paid by virtue of a resolution under this Act becoming repayable under sub-s (6) or (7) above).

Amendments—[1] Words in sub-s (4)(*b*) added by FA 1968 s 60.

[2] Words in the heading and in sub-s (1) added by virtue of FA 1994 Sch 7 para 33.

[3] Words in sub-s (3)(*a*) substituted by FA 1993 s 205 in relation to resolutions passed after 27 July 1993.

[4] Word in sub-s (4) substituted by FA 1993 s 205 in relation to resolutions passed after 27 July 1993.

[5] Words in sub-s (3) inserted by F(No 2)A 1997 s 50 in relation to resolutions passed after 31 July 1997.

[6] Words in sub-s (4)(*b*) substituted by FA 2007 s 112(1) with effect from 19 July 2007.

5 House of Commons resolution giving provisional effect to motions affecting taxation

(1) This section shall apply if the House of Commons resolves that provisional statutory effect shall be given to one or more motions to be moved by the Chancellor of the Exchequer, or some other Minister, and which, if agreed to by the House, would be resolutions—

(*a*) to which statutory effect could be given under section 1 of this Act, or

IPT

(*b*), (c) . . .

(2) Subject to subsection (3) below, on the passing of the resolution under subsection (1) above, sections 1 . . . of this Act, . . . shall apply as if each motion to which the resolution applies had then been agreed to by a resolution of the House.

(3) Subsection (2) above shall cease to apply to a motion if that motion, or a motion containing the same proposals with modifications, is not agreed to by a resolution of the House (in this section referred to as "a confirmatory resolution") within the next ten days on which the House sits after the resolution under subsection (1) above is passed, and, if it ceases to apply, all such adjustments, whether by way of discharge or repayment of tax, or discharge of security, or otherwise, shall be made as may be necessary to restore the position to what it would have been if subsection (2) above had never applied to that motion, and to make good any deductions which have become unauthorised deductions.

(4) . . .

Note—Sub-ss (1)(*b*), (4) and words omitted from sub-s (2) are not relevant to insurance premium tax; sub-s (1)(*c*) is repealed.

Cross reference—See FA 1994 Sch 7 para 34 (insurance premium tax paid by virtue of a resolution under this Act becoming repayable under sub-s (3) above).

6 Short title, repeals and saving as respects Northern Ireland

(1) This Act may be cited as the Provisional Collection of Taxes Act 1968.

(2) . . .

(3) . . . [1]

Note—Sub-s (2) repeals enactments specified in Schedule.

Amendments—[1] Sub-s (3) repealed by Northern Ireland Constitution Act 1973 s 41(1)(*a*) and Sch 6 Pt I, with effect from 18 July 1973.

INTERPRETATION ACT 1978

(1978 Chapter 30)

Note—See VAT Statutes, *ante*.

INCOME AND CORPORATION TAXES ACT 1988

(1988 Chapter 1)

PART XIX

SUPPLEMENTAL

Miscellaneous

827 VAT penalties etc

Note—This section repealed by CTA 2009 ss 1322, 1326, Sch 1 paras 1, 268, Sch 3 Part 1. CTA 2009 applies for accounting periods ending on or after 1 April 2009 (for corporation tax purposes) and for tax years 2009–10 onwards (for income and capital gains tax purposes).

Relevant provisions rewritten to CTA 2009 ss 1303(1), (2), 1306(1).

FINANCE ACT 1994

(1994 Chapter 9)

ARRANGEMENT OF SECTIONS

PART III

INSURANCE PREMIUM TAX

The basic provisions

An Act to grant certain duties, to alter other duties, and to amend the law relating to the National Debt and the Public Revenue, and to make further provision in connection with Finance.

[3rd May 1994]

PART III
INSURANCE PREMIUM TAX

The basic provisions

48 Insurance premium tax

(1) A tax, to be known as insurance premium tax, shall be charged in accordance with this Part.

(2) The tax shall be under the care and management of the Commissioners of Customs and Excise.

49 Charge to tax

Tax shall be charged on the receipt of a premium by an insurer if the premium is received—

(*a*) under a taxable insurance contract, and

(*b*) on or after 1st October 1994.

50 Chargeable amount

(1) Tax shall be charged by reference to the chargeable amount.

(2) For the purposes of this Part, the chargeable amount is such amount as, with the addition of the tax chargeable, is equal to the amount of the premium.

IPT

(3) [Subsections (1) and (2)][1] above shall have effect subject to section 69 below.

Commentary—*De Voil Indirect Tax Service* **V18.101**.

Amendments—[1] Words substituted by FA 1997 s 23(2) with effect as provided by FA 1997, s 24.

[51 Rate of tax

(1) Tax shall be charged—

(*a*) at the higher rate, in the case of a premium which is liable to tax at that rate; and

(*b*) at the standard rate, in any other case.

(2) For the purposes of this Part—

(*a*) for the higher rate is [20 per cent][2]; and

(*b*) the standard rate is [6 per cent][2].][1]

Commentary—*De Voil Indirect Tax Service* **V18.111**.

Press releases etc—C & E News Release 4/97 6-2-97 (by concession, the higher rate will not apply to ordinary motor insurance sold by car or motor cycle dealers or to home contents insurance when sold by retailers).

Amendments—[1] This section substituted by FA 1997 s 21(1) with effect as provided by FA 1997 s 24.

[2] In sub-s (2)(*b*), words substituted for words "17.5 per cent", and in sub-s (2)(*b*), words substituted for words "5 per cent" by F(No 2)A 2010 s 4(1) with effect in relation to a premium falling to be regarded for the purposes of FA 1994 Part 3 as received under a taxable insurance contract by an insurer on or after 4 January 2011.

[51A Premiums liable to tax at the higher rate

(1) A premium received under a taxable insurance contract by an insurer is liable to tax at the higher rate if it falls within one or more of the paragraphs of Part II of Schedule 6A to this Act.

(2) Part I of Schedule 6A to this Act shall have effect with respect to the interpretation of that Schedule.

(3) Provision may be made by order amending Schedule 6A as it has effect for the time being.

(4) This section is subject to section 69 below.]

Commentary—*De Voil Indirect Tax Service* **V18.112**.

OrdersInsurance Premium Tax (Amendment of Schedule 6A to the Finance Act 1994) Order 2009.

Simon's Tax Cases—*R v C&E Comrs, ex p Lunn Poly Ltd* [1999] STC 350.

Amendments—This section inserted by FA 1997 s 22(1) with effect as provided by FA 1997 s 24.

52 Liability to pay tax

(1) Tax shall be payable by the person who is the insurer in relation to the contract under which the premium is received.

(2) Subsection (1) above shall have effect subject to any regulations made under section 65 below.

Commentary—*De Voil Indirect Tax Service* **V18.126, 127**.

[52A Certain fees to be treated as premiums under higher rate contracts

(1) This section applies where—

(*a*) at or about the time when a higher rate contract is effected, and

(*b*) in connection with that contract,

a fee in respect of an insurance-related service is charged by a taxable intermediary to a person who is or becomes the insured (or one of the insured) under the contract or to a person who acts for or on behalf of such a person.

(2) Where this section applies—

(*a*) a payment in respect of the fee shall be treated for the purposes of this Part as a premium received under a taxable insurance contract by an insurer, and

(*b*) that premium—

(i) shall be treated for the purposes of this Part as so received at the time when the payment is made, and

(ii) shall be chargeable to tax at the higher rate.

(3) Tax charged by virtue of subsection (2) above shall be payable by the taxable intermediary as if he were the insurer under the contract mentioned in paragraph (*a*) of that subsection.

(4) For the purposes of this section, a contract of insurance is a "higher rate contract" if—

(*a*) it is a taxable insurance contract; and

(*b*) the whole or any part of a premium received under the contract by the insurer is (apart from this section) liable to tax at the higher rate.

(5) For the purposes of this Part a "taxable intermediary" is a person falling within subsection (6) [or (6A)][2] below who—

(*a*) at or about the time when a higher rate contract is effected, and

(*b*) in connection with that contract,

charges a fee in respect of an insurance-related service to a person who is or becomes the insured (or one of the insured) under the contract or to a person who acts for or on behalf of such a person.

[(6) A person falls within this subsection if the higher rate contract mentioned in subsection (1) above falls within paragraph 2 or 3 of Schedule 6A to this Act (motor cars or motor cycles, or relevant goods) and the person is—

(*a*) within the meaning of the paragraph in question, a supplier of motor cars or motor cycles or, as the case may be, of relevant goods; or

(*b*) a person connected with a person falling within paragraph (*a*) above; or
(*c*) a person who in the course of his business pays—
(i) the whole or any part of the premium received under that contract, or
(ii) a fee connected with the arranging of that contract,
to a person falling within paragraph (a) or (b) above.

(6A) A person falls within this subsection if the higher rate contract mentioned in subsection (1) above falls within paragraph 4 of Schedule 6A to this Act (travel insurance) and the person is—
(*a*) the insurer under that contract; or
(*b*) a person through whom that contract is arranged in the course of his business; or
(*c*) a person connected with the insurer under that contract; or
(*d*) a person connected with a person falling within paragraph (*b*) above; or
(*e*) a person who in the course of his business pays—
(i) the whole or any part of the premium received under that contract, or
(ii) a fee connected with the arranging of that contract,
to a person falling within any of paragraphs (a) to (d) above.][3]

(7) . . . [3]

(8) For the purposes of this section, any question whether a person is connected with another shall be determined in accordance with [section 1122 of the Corporation Tax Act 2010][5].

(9) In this section—
"insurance-related service" means any service which is related to, or connected with, insurance;
. . . [4]][1]

Commentary—*De Voil Indirect Tax Service* **V18.114.**

Amendments—[1] This section inserted by FA 1997 s 25 in relation to payments in respect of fees charged after 18 March 1997.
[2] Words in sub-s (5) inserted by FA 1998 s 147(2) in relation to payments in respect of fees charged on or after 1 August 1998.
[3] Sub-ss (6), (6A) substituted for sub-ss (6), (7) by FA 1998 s 147(3) in relation to payments in respect of fees charged on or after 1 August 1998.
[4] In sub-s (9) the words "tour operator" and "travel agent" omitted by FA 1998 s 147(4) in relation to payments in respect of fees charged on or after 1 August 1998.
[5] In sub-s (8) words substituted for words "section 839 of the Taxes Act 1988" by CTA 2010 s 1177, Sch 1 para 281. CTA 2010 has effect for corporation tax purposes for accounting periods ending on or after 1 April 2010, and for income and capital gains tax purposes for the tax year 2010–11 and subsequent tax years.

Administration

53 Registration of insurers

(1) A person who—
(*a*) receives, as insurer, premiums in the course of a taxable business, and
(*b*) is not registered,
is liable to be registered.

[(1A) The register kept under this section may contain such information as the Commissioners think is required for the purposes of the care and management of the tax.][1]

(2) A person who—
(*a*) at any time forms the intention of receiving, as insurer, premiums in the course of a taxable business, and
(*b*) is not already receiving, as insurer, premiums in the course of another taxable business,
shall notify the Commissioners of those facts.

(3) A person who at any time—
(*a*) ceases to have the intention of receiving, as insurer, premiums in the course of a taxable business, and
(*b*) has no intention of receiving, as insurer, premiums in the course of another taxable business,
shall notify the Commissioners of those facts.

(4) Where a person is liable to be registered by virtue of subsection (1) above the Commissioners shall register him with effect from the time when he begins to receive premiums in the course of the business concerned; and it is immaterial whether or not he notifies the Commissioners under subsection (2) above.

(5) Where a person—
(*a*) notifies the Commissioners under subsection (3) above, [and][2]
(*b*) satisfies them of the facts there mentioned, . . . [3]
(*c*) . . . [3]
the Commissioners shall cancel his registration with effect from the earliest practicable time after he ceases to receive, as insurer, premiums in the course of any taxable business.

[(5A) In a case where—
(*a*) the Commissioners are satisfied that a person has ceased to receive, as insurer, premiums in the course of any taxable business, but
(*b*) he has not notified them under subsection (3) above,
they may cancel his registration with effect from the earliest practicable time after he so ceased.][4]

IPT

(6) For the purposes of this section regulations may make provision—

(*a*) as to the time within which a notification is to be made;

(*b*) as to the circumstances in which premiums are to be taken to be received in the course of a taxable business;

(*c*) as to the form and manner in which any notification is to be made and as to the information to be contained in or provided with it;

(*d*) requiring a person who has made a notification to notify the Commissioners if any information contained in or provided in connection with it is or becomes inaccurate;

(*e*) as to the correction of entries in the register.

(7) References in this section to receiving premiums are to receiving premiums on or after 1st October 1994.

Commentary—*De Voil Indirect Tax Service* **V18.131, 136.**

Regulations—Insurance Premium Tax Regulations, SI 1994/1774.
Insurance Premium Tax (Amendment) Regulations, SI 1995/1587
Insurance Premium Tax (Amendment) Regulations, SI 2006/2700
Insurance Premium Tax (Amendment) Regulations, SI 2008/1945

Cross references—See Insurance Premium Tax Regulations, SI 1994/1774 reg 4(1) (notification of liability to register),
SI 1994/1774 reg 6 (notification of liability to be de-registered),
SI 1994/1774 reg 7 (transfer of a going concern),
SI 1994/1774 reg 11 (death, bankruptcy or incapacity of registrable persons),
SI 1994/1774 reg 19(2) (claim for credit following cancellation of registration).

Amendments—[1] Sub-s (1A) inserted by FA 1995 s 34, Sch 5 para 3.

[2] Word "and" at end of sub-s (5)(*a*) inserted by FA 1995 s 34, Sch 5 para 2(2), (4) with effect for notifications under sub-s (3) made on or after 1 May 1995.

[3] Word "and" at end of sub-s (5)(*b*), and sub-s (5)(*c*), repealed by FA 1995 s 34, Sch 5 para 2(2), (4), Sch 29 Pt VII with effect for notifications under sub-s (3) made after 30 April 1995.

[4] Sub-s (5A) inserted by FA 1995 s 34, Sch 5 para 3.

[53AA Registration of taxable intermediaries

(1) A person who—

(*a*) is a taxable intermediary, and

(*b*) is not registered,

is liable to be registered.

(2) The register kept under this section may contain such information as the Commissioners think is required for the purposes of the care and management of the tax.

(3) A person who—

(*a*) at any time forms the intention of charging taxable intermediary's fees, and

(*b*) is not already charging such fees in the course of another business,

shall notify the Commissioners of those facts.

(4) A person who at any time—

(*a*) ceases to have the intention of charging taxable intermediary's fees in the course of his business, and

(*b*) has no intention of charging such fees in the course of another business of his,

shall notify the Commissioners of those facts.

(5) Where a person is liable to be registered by virtue of subsection (1) above, the Commissioners shall register him with effect from the time when he begins to charge taxable intermediary's fees in the course of the business concerned; and it is immaterial whether or not he notifies the Commissioners under subsection (3) above.

(6) Where a person—

(*a*) notifies the Commissioners under subsection (4) above, and

(*b*) satisfies them of the facts there mentioned,

the Commissioners shall cancel his registration with effect from the earliest practicable time after he ceases to charge taxable intermediary's fees in the course of any business of his.

(7) In a case where—

(*a*) the Commissioners are satisfied that a person has ceased to charge taxable intermediary's fees in the course of any business of his, but

(*b*) he has not notified them under subsection (4) above,

they may cancel his registration with effect from the earliest practicable time after he so ceased.

(8) For the purposes of this section regulations may make provision—

(*a*) as to the time within which a notification is to be made;

(*b*) as to the form and manner in which any notification is to be made and as to the information to be contained in or provided with it;

(*c*) requiring a person who has made a notification to notify the Commissioners if any information contained in or provided in connection with it is or becomes inaccurate;

(*d*) as to the correction of entries in the register.

(9) In this Part "taxable intermediary's fees" means fees which, to the extent of any payment in respect of them, are chargeable to tax by virtue of section 52A above.]

Commentary—*De Voil Indirect Tax Service* **V18.135, 137**.
Regulations—Insurance Premium Tax (Amendment) Regulations, SI 1997/1157
Insurance Premium Tax (Amendment) Regulations, SI 2006/2700.
Amendments—This section inserted by FA 1997 s 26 with effect from 19 March 1997.

[53A Information required to keep register up to date

(1) Regulations may make provision requiring a registrable person to notify the Commissioners of particulars which—

(*a*) are of changes in circumstances relating to the registrable person or any business carried on by him,

(*b*) appear to the Commissioners to be required for the purpose of keeping the register kept under section 53 [or 53AA][2] above up to date, and

(*c*) are of a prescribed description.

(2) Regulations may make provision—

(*a*) as to the time within which a notification is to be made;

(*b*) as to the form and manner in which a notification is to be made;

(*c*) requiring a person who has made a notification to notify the Commissioners if any information contained in it is inaccurate.][1]

Regulations—Insurance Premium Tax (Amendment) Regulations, SI 1995/1587.
Insurance Premium Tax (Amendment) Regulations, SI 1997/1157.
Amendments—[1] This section inserted by FA 1995 s 34, Sch 5 para 4.
[2] Words in sub-s(1)(*b*) inserted by FA 1997 s 27(2) with effect from 19 March 1997.

54 Accounting for tax and time for payment

Regulations may provide that a registrable person shall—

(*a*) account for tax by reference to such periods (accounting periods) as may be determined by or under the regulations;

(*b*) make, in relation to accounting periods, returns in such form as may be prescribed and at such times as may be so determined;

(*c*) pay tax at such times and in such manner as may be so determined.

Commentary—*De Voil Indirect Tax Service* **V18.146**.
Regulations—Insurance Premium Tax Regulations, SI 1994/1774.

55 Credit

(1) Regulations may provide that where an insurer [or taxable intermediary][1] has paid tax and all or part of the premium [or taxable intermediary's fee (as the case may be)][1] is repaid, the insurer [or taxable intermediary][1] shall be entitled to credit of such an amount as is found in accordance with prescribed rules.

(2) Regulations may provide that where—

(*a*) by virtue of regulations made under section 68 below tax is charged in relation to a premium which is shown in the accounts of an insurer as due to him,

(*b*) that tax is paid, and

(*c*) it is shown to the satisfaction of the Commissioners that the premium, or part of it, will never actually be received by or on behalf of the insurer,

the insurer shall be entitled to credit of such an amount as is found in accordance with prescribed rules.

(3) Regulations may make provision as to the manner in which an insurer [or taxable intermediary][1] is to benefit from credit, and in particular may make provision—

(*a*) that an insurer [or taxable intermediary][1] shall be entitled to credit by reference to accounting periods;

(*b*) that an insurer [or taxable intermediary][1] shall be entitled to deduct an amount equal to his total credit for an accounting period from the total amount of tax due from him for the period;

(*c*) that if no tax is due from an insurer [or taxable intermediary][1] for an accounting period but he is entitled to credit for the period, the amount of the credit shall be paid to him by the Commissioners;

(*d*) that if the amount of credit to which an insurer [or taxable intermediary][1] is entitled for an accounting period exceeds the amount of tax due from him for the period, an amount equal to the excess shall be paid to him by the Commissioners;

(*e*) for the whole or part of any credit to be held over to be credited for a subsequent accounting period;

(*f*) as to the manner in which a person who has ceased to be registrable [(whether under section 53 or section 53AA)][1] is to benefit from credit.

(4) Regulations under subsection (3)(*c*) or (*d*) above may provide that where at the end of an accounting period an amount is due to an insurer [or taxable intermediary][1] who has failed to submit returns for an earlier period as required by this Part, the Commissioners may withhold payment of the amount until he has complied with that requirement.

IPT

(5) Regulations under subsection (3)(*e*) above may provide for credit to be held over either on the insurer's [or taxable intermediary's][1] application or in accordance with general or special directions given by the Commissioners from time to time.

(6) Regulations may provide that—

(*a*) no deduction or payment shall be made in respect of credit except on a claim made in such manner and at such time as may be determined by or under regulations;

(*b*) payment in respect of credit shall be made subject to such conditions (if any) as the Commissioners think fit to impose, including conditions as to repayment in specified circumstances;

(*c*) deduction in respect of credit shall be made subject to such conditions (if any) as the Commissioners think fit to impose, including conditions as to the payment to the Commissioners, in specified circumstances, of an amount representing the whole or part of the amount deducted.

(7) Regulations may require a claim by an insurer [or taxable intermediary][1] to be made in a return required by provision made under section 54 above.

(8) Regulations may provide that where—

(*a*) all or any of the tax payable in respect of a premium [or taxable intermediary's fee][1] has not been paid, and

(*b*) the circumstances are such that a person would be entitled to credit if the tax had been paid,

prescribed adjustments shall be made as regards any amount of tax due from any person.

Commentary—*De Voil Indirect Tax Service* **V18.121**.

Regulations—Insurance Premium Tax Regulations, SI 1994/1774.

Insurance Premium Tax (Amendment) Regulations, SI 1997/1157.

Cross references—See Insurance Premium Tax Regulations, SI 1994/1774 reg 18(3) (claims for credit: directions under sub-s (5) of this section).

Amendments—[1] Words inserted by FA 1997 s 27(3) with effect from 19 March 1997.

56 Power to assess

(1) In a case where—

(*a*) a person has failed to make any returns required to be made under this Part,

(*b*) a person has failed to keep any documents necessary to verify returns required to be made under this Part,

(*c*) a person has failed to afford the facilities necessary to verify returns required to be made under this Part, or

(*d*) it appears to the Commissioners that returns required to be made by a person under this Part are incomplete or incorrect, the Commissioners may assess the amount of tax due from the person concerned to the best of their judgment and notify it to him.

(2) Where a person has for an accounting period been paid an amount to which he purports to be entitled under regulations made under section 55 above, then, to the extent that the amount ought not to have been paid or would not have been paid had the facts been known or been as they later turn out to be, the Commissioners may assess the amount as being tax due from him for that period and notify it to him accordingly.

(3) Where a person is assessed under subsections (1) and (2) above in respect of the same accounting period the assessments may be combined and notified to him as one assessment.

(4) Where the person failing to make a return, or making a return which appears to the Commissioners to be incomplete or incorrect, was required to make the return as a personal representative, trustee in bankruptcy, trustee in sequestration, receiver, liquidator or person otherwise acting in a representative capacity in relation to another person, subsection (1) above shall apply as if the reference to tax due from him included a reference to tax due from that other person.

(5) An assessment under subsection (1) or (2) above of an amount of tax due for an accounting period shall not be made after the later of the following—

(*a*) two years after the end of the accounting period;

(*b*) one year after evidence of facts, sufficient in the Commissioners' opinion to justify the making of the assessment, comes to their knowledge; but where further such evidence comes to their knowledge after the making of an assessment under subsection (1) or (2) above another assessment may be made under the subsection concerned in addition to any earlier assessment.

(6) In a case where—

(*a*) as a result of a person's failure to make a return for an accounting period the Commissioners have made an assessment under subsection (1) above for that period,

(*b*) the tax assessed has been paid but no proper return has been made for the period to which the assessment related, and

(*c*) as a result of a failure to make a return for a later accounting period, being a failure by the person referred to in paragraph (*a*) above or a person acting in a representative capacity in relation to him, as mentioned in subsection (4) above, the Commissioners find it necessary to make another assessment under subsection (1) above, then, if the Commissioners think fit, having regard to the failure referred to in paragraph (*a*) above, they may specify in the assessment referred to in paragraph (*c*) above an amount of tax greater than that which they would otherwise have considered to be appropriate.

(7) Where an amount has been assessed and notified to any person under subsection (1) or (2) above it shall be deemed to be an amount of tax due from him and may be recovered accordingly unless, or except to the extent that, the assessment has subsequently been withdrawn or reduced.

(8) For the purposes of this section notification to—

(*a*) a personal representative, trustee in bankruptcy, trustee in sequestration, receiver or liquidator, or (*b*) a person otherwise acting in a representative capacity in relation to another person, shall be treated as notification to the person in relation to whom the person mentioned in paragraph (*a*) above, or the first person mentioned in paragraph (*b*) above, acts.

57–58

Amendment—Repealed by FA 2008 s 142 with effect from 21 July 2008.

Review and appeal

59 [Appeals][4]

(1) [Subject to section 60, an appeal shall lie to an appeal tribunal from any person who is or will be affected by any decision of HMRC with respect to the any of the following matters—][4]

(*a*) the registration or cancellation of registration of any person under this Part;

(*b*) whether tax is chargeable in respect of a premium or how much tax is chargeable;

[(*bb*) whether a payment falls to be treated under section 52A(2) above as a premium received under a taxable insurance contract by an insurer and chargeable to tax at the higher rate;][3]

(*c*) whether a person is entitled to credit by virtue of regulations under section 55 above or how much credit a person is entitled to or the manner in which he is to benefit from credit;

(*d*) an assessment [falling within subsection (1A) below][1] or the amount of such an assessment;

(*e*) any refusal of an application under section 63 below;

(*f*) whether a notice may be served on a person by virtue of regulations made under section 65 below;

(*g*) an assessment under regulations made under section 65 below or the amount of such an assessment;

(*h*) whether a scheme established by regulations under section 68 below applies to an insurer as regards an accounting period;

(*i*) the requirement of any security under paragraph 24 of Schedule 7 to this Act or its amount;

(*j*) any liability to a penalty under paragraphs 12 to 19 of Schedule 7 to this Act;

(*k*) the amount of any penalty or interest specified in an assessment under paragraph 25 of Schedule 7 to this Act;

(*l*) a claim for the repayment of an amount under paragraph 8 of Schedule 7 to this Act;

(*m*) any liability of the Commissioners to pay interest under paragraph 22 of Schedule 7 to this Act or the amount of the interest payable.

[(1A) An assessment falls within this subsection if it is an assessment under section 56 above in respect of an accounting period in relation to which a return required to be made by virtue of regulations under section 54 above has been made.][2]

(2) Any person who is or will be affected by any decision to which this section applies may by notice in writing to the Commissioners require them to review the decision.

(3) The Commissioners shall not be required under this section to review any decision unless the notice requiring the review is given before the end of the period of 45 days beginning with the day on which written notification of the decision, or of the assessment containing the decision, was first given to the person requiring the review.

(4) For the purposes of subsection (3) above it shall be the duty of the Commissioners to give written notification of any decision to which this section applies to any person who—

(a) requests such a notification,

(b) has not previously been given written notification of that decision, and

(c) if given such a notification, will be entitled to require a review of the decision under this section.

(5) A person shall be entitled to give a notice under this section requiring a decision to be reviewed for a second or subsequent time only if—

(a) the grounds on which he requires the further review are that the Commissioners did not, on any previous review, have the opportunity to consider certain facts or other matters, and

(b) he does not, on the further review, require the Commissioners to consider any facts or matters which were considered on a previous review except in so far as they are relevant to any issue not previously considered.

(6) Where the Commissioners are required in accordance with this section to review any decision, it shall be their duty to do so; and on the review they may withdraw, vary or confirm the decision.

(7) In a case where—

(a) it is the duty under this section of the Commissioners to review any decision, and

IPT

(b) they do not, within the period of 45 days beginning with the day on which the review was required, give notice to the person requiring it of their determination on the review,

they shall be assumed for the purposes of this Part to have confirmed the decision.

(8) The Commissioners shall not by virtue of any requirement under this section to review a decision have any power, apart from their power in pursuance of paragraph 13 of Schedule 7 to this Act, to mitigate the amount of any penalty imposed under this Part.[4]

Commentary—*De Voil Indirect Tax Service* **V18.152, 153.**

Note—This section was brought into force on 1 October 1994, by virtue of the FA 1994 (Appointed Day) Order, SI 1994/1773.

Cross references—See Insurance Premium Tax Regulations, SI 1994/1774 reg 42 (distress),
SI 1994/1774 reg 43 (diligence).
FA 1997 Sch 5 para 19(2) (review of decision contained in an assessment under FA 1997 Sch 5 para 14, 15 or 17).

Simon's Tax Cases—59(1)(*b*), (*l*), (2), *C&E Comrs v Cresta Holidays Ltd and others* [2001] STC 386.

Amendments—[1] Words in sub-s (1)(*d*) substituted by FA 1995 s 34, Sch 5 para 5(2), (4) with effect for assessments made after 30 April 1995.

[2] Sub-s (1A) inserted by FA 1995 s 34, Sch 5 para 5(3), (4) with effect for assessments made after 30 April 1995.

[3] Sub-s (1)(*bb*) inserted by FA 1997 s 27(6) with effect from 19 March 1997.

[4] Heading substituted for the former heading "Review of Commissioners' decisions"; words in sub-s (1) first paragraph substituted for the words "This section applies to any decision of the Commissioners with respect to any of the following matters—"; sub-ss (2)–(8) repealed by the Transfer of Tribunal Functions and Revenue and Customs Appeals Order, SI 2009/56 art 3, Sch 1 para 205(3), (4) with effect from 1 April 2009, subject to transitional and savings provisions in Sch 3 paras 2, 3, 9.

[59A Offer of review

(1) HMRC must offer a person (P) a review of a decision that has been notified to P if an appeal lies under section 59 in respect of the decision.

(2) The offer of the review must be made by notice given to P at the same time as the decision is notified to P.

(3) This section does not apply to the notification of the conclusions of a review.][1]

Amendments—[1] Sections 59A–59G inserted by the Transfer of Tribunal Functions and Revenue and Customs Appeals Order, SI 2009/56 art 3, Sch 1 para 206 with effect from 1 April 2009.

[59B Right to require review

(1) Any person (other than P) who has the right of appeal under section 59 against a decision may require HMRC to review that decision if that person has not appealed to the appeal tribunal under section 59G.

(2) A notification that such a person requires a review must be made within 30 days of that person becoming aware of the decision.][1]

Amendments—[1] Sections 59A–59G inserted by the Transfer of Tribunal Functions and Revenue and Customs Appeals Order, SI 2009/56 art 3, Sch 1 para 206 with effect from 1 April 2009.

[59C Review by HMRC

(1) HMRC must review a decision if—

(a) they have offered a review of the decision under section 59A, and

(b) P notifies HMRC accepting the offer within 30 days from the date of the document containing the notification of the offer.

(2) But P may not notify acceptance of the offer if P has already appealed to the appeal tribunal under section 59G.

(3) HMRC must review a decision if a person other than P notifies them under section 59B.

(4) HMRC shall not review a decision if P, or another person, has appealed to the appeal tribunal under section 59G in respect of the decision.][1]

Amendments—[1] Sections 59A–59G inserted by the Transfer of Tribunal Functions and Revenue and Customs Appeals Order, SI 2009/56 art 3, Sch 1 para 206 with effect from 1 April 2009.

[59D Extensions of time

(1) If under section 59A HMRC have offered P a review of a decision, HMRC may within the relevant period notify P that the relevant period is extended.

(2) If under section 59B another person may require HMRC to review a matter, HMRC may within the relevant period notify the other person that the relevant period is extended.

(3) If notice is given the relevant period is extended to the end of 30 days from—

(*a*) the date of the notice, or

(*b*) any other date set out in the notice or a further notice.

(4) In this section "relevant period" means—

(*a*) the period of 30 days referred to in—

(i) section 59C(1)(*b*) (in a case falling within subsection (1)), or

(ii) section 59B(2) (in a case falling within subsection (2)), or

(*b*) if notice has been given under subsection (1) or (2), that period as extended (or as most recently extended) in accordance with subsection (3).][1]

Amendments—[1] Sections 59A–59G inserted by the Transfer of Tribunal Functions and Revenue and Customs Appeals Order, SI 2009/56 art 3, Sch 1 para 206 with effect from 1 April 2009.

[59E Review out of time

(1) This section applies if—

(*a*) HMRC have offered a review of a decision under section 59A and P does not accept the offer within the time allowed under section 59C(1)(*b*) or 59D(3); or

(*b*) a person who requires a review under section 59B does not notify HMRC within the time allowed under that section or section 59D(3).

(2) HMRC must review the decision under section 59C if—

(*a*) after the time allowed, P, or the other person, notifies HMRC in writing requesting a review out of time,

(*b*) HMRC are satisfied that P, or the other person, had a reasonable excuse for not accepting the offer or requiring review within the time allowed, and

(*c*) HMRC are satisfied that P, or the other person, made the request without unreasonable delay after the excuse had ceased to apply.

(3) HMRC shall not review a decision if P, or another person, has appealed to the appeal tribunal under section 59G in respect of the decision.][1]

Amendments—[1] Sections 59A–59G inserted by the Transfer of Tribunal Functions and Revenue and Customs Appeals Order, SI 2009/56 art 3, Sch 1 para 206 with effect from 1 April 2009.

[59F Nature of review etc

(1) This section applies if HMRC are required to undertake a review under section 59C or 59E.

(2) The nature and extent of the review are to be such as appear appropriate to HMRC in the circumstances.

(3) For the purpose of subsection (2), HMRC must, in particular, have regard to steps taken before the beginning of the review—

(*a*) by HMRC in reaching the decision, and

(*b*) by any person in seeking to resolve disagreement about the decision.

(4) The review must take account of any representations made by P, or the other person, at a stage which gives HMRC a reasonable opportunity to consider them.

(5) The review may conclude that the decision is to be—

(*a*) upheld,

(*b*) varied, or

(*c*) cancelled.

(6) HMRC must give P, or the other person, notice of the conclusions of the review and their reasoning within—

(*a*) a period of 45 days beginning with the relevant date, or

(*b*) such other period as HMRC and P, or the other person, may agree.

(7) In subsection (6) "relevant date" means—

(*a*) the date HMRC received P's notification accepting the offer of a review (in a case falling within section 59A), or

(*b*) the date HMRC received notification from another person requiring review (in a case falling within section 59B), or

(*c*) the date on which HMRC decided to undertake the review (in a case falling within section 59E).

(8) Where HMRC are required to undertake a review but do not give notice of the conclusions within the time period specified in subsection (6), the review is to be treated as having concluded that the decision is upheld.

(9) If subsection (8) applies, HMRC must notify P or the other person of the conclusion which the review is treated as having reached.][1]

Amendments—[1] Sections 59A–59G inserted by the Transfer of Tribunal Functions and Revenue and Customs Appeals Order, SI 2009/56 art 3, Sch 1 para 206 with effect from 1 April 2009.

[59G Bringing of appeals

(1) An appeal under section 59 is to be made to the appeal tribunal before—

(*a*) the end of the period of 30 days beginning with—

(i) in a case where P is the appellant, the date of the document notifying the decision to which the appeal relates, or

(ii) in a case where a person other than P is the appellant, the date that person becomes aware of the decision, or

(*b*) if later, the end of the relevant period (within the meaning of section 59D).

(2) But that is subject to subsections (3) to (5).

(3) In a case where HMRC are required to undertake a review under section 59C—

(*a*) an appeal may not be made until the conclusion date, and

(*b*) any appeal is to be made within the period of 30 days beginning with the conclusion date.

(4) In a case where HMRC are requested to undertake a review by virtue of section 59E—

(*a*) an appeal may not be made—

(i) unless HMRC have decided whether or not to undertake a review, and

IPT

(ii) if HMRC decide to undertake a review, until the conclusion date; and

(*b*) any appeal is to be made within the period of 30 days beginning with—

(i) the conclusion date (if HMRC decide to undertake a review), or

(ii) the date on which HMRC decide not to undertake a review.

(5) In a case where section 59F(8) applies, an appeal may be made at any time from the end of the period specified in section 59F(6) to the date 30 days after the conclusion date.

(6) An appeal may be made after the end of the period specified in subsection (1), (3)(*b*), (4)(*b*) or (5) if the appeal tribunal gives permission to do so.

(7) In this section "conclusion date" means the date of the document notifying the conclusion of the review.][1]

Amendments—[1] Sections 59A–59G inserted by the Transfer of Tribunal Functions and Revenue and Customs Appeals Order, SI 2009/56 art 3, Sch 1 para 206 with effect from 1 April 2009.

60 [Further provisions relating to appeals][1]

(1) . . . [1]

(2) Without prejudice to paragraph 13 of Schedule 7 to this Act, nothing in [section 59][1] above shall be taken to confer on a tribunal any power to vary an amount assessed by way of penalty or interest except in so far as it is necessary to reduce it to the amount which is appropriate under paragraphs 12 to 21 of that Schedule.

(3) . . . [1]

[(4) Subject to subsections (4A) and (4B), where the appeal is against the decisions with respect to any of the matters mentioned in section 59(1)(*b*) and (*d*), it shall not be entertained unless the amount which HMRC have determined to be payable as tax has been paid or deposited with them.

(4A) In a case where the amount determined to be payable as tax has not been paid or deposited an appeal shall be entertained if—

(*a*) HMRC are satisfied (on the application of the appellant), or

(*b*) the appeal tribunal decides (HMRC not being so satisfied and on the application of the appellant),

that the requirement to pay or deposit the amount determined would cause the appellant to suffer hardship.

(4B) Notwithstanding the provisions of sections 11 and 13 of the Tribunals, Courts and Enforcement Act 2007, the decision of the appeal tribunal as to the issue of hardship is final.][1]

(5) Where on an appeal against a decision with respect to any of the matters mentioned in section 59(1)(*d*) above—

(*a*) it is found that the amount specified in the assessment is less than it ought to have been, and

(*b*) the tribunal gives a direction specifying the correct amount,

the assessment shall have effect as an assessment of the amount specified in the direction and that amount shall be deemed to have been notified to the appellant.

(6) Where on an appeal under this section it is found that the whole or part of any amount paid or deposited in pursuance of subsection (4) above is not due, so much of that amount as is found not to be due shall be repaid with interest [at the rate applicable under section 197 of the Finance Act 1996][1].

(7) Where on an appeal under this section it is found that the whole or part of any amount due to the appellant by virtue of regulations under section 55(3)(*c*) or (*d*) or (*f*) above has not been paid, so much of that amount as is found not to have been paid shall be paid with interest [at the rate applicable under section 197 of the Finance Act 1996][1].

(8) Where an appeal under this section has been entertained notwithstanding that an amount determined by [HMRC][1] to be payable as tax has not been paid or deposited and it is found on the appeal that that amount is due [it shall be paid with interest at the rate applicable under section 197 of the Finance Act 1996][1]

[(8A) Interest under subsection (8) shall be paid without any deduction of income tax.][1]

(9) On an appeal against an assessment to a penalty under paragraph 12 of Schedule 7 to this Act, the burden of proof as to the matters specified in paragraphs (*a*) and (*b*) of sub-paragraph (1) of paragraph 12 shall lie upon [HMRC][1].

[(10) Sections 85 and 85B of the Value Added Tax Act 1994 (settling of appeals by agreement and payment of tax where there is a further appeal) shall have effect as if—

(*a*) the references to section 83 of that Act included references to section 59 above, and

(*b*) the references to value added tax included references to insurance premium tax.][1]

Commentary—*De Voil Indirect Tax Service* **V18.152.**

Notes—This section was brought into force on 1 October 1994, by virtue of the FA 1994 (Appointed Day) Order, SI 1994/1773.
FA 1985 ss 25, 29 have been consolidated as VATA 1994 ss 85, 87.
VATA 1983 s 40 has been consolidated as VATA 1994 ss 83, 84.

Cross references—See FA 1997 Sch 5 para 19(2) (appeal following decision by Commissioners contained in an assessment under FA 1997 Sch 5 para 14, 15 or 17).

Amendments—[1] The following amendments made by the Transfer of Tribunal Functions and Revenue and Customs Appeals Order, SI 2009/56 art 3, Sch 1 para 207 with effect from 1 April 2009, subject to transitional and savings provisions in Sch 3 paras 2, 3, 9—

- heading substituted for former heading "Appeals";
- sub-ss (1), (3) repealed;
- – in sub-s (2) words substituted for the words "subsection (1)";
- sub-ss (4)–(4B) substituted for former sub-s (4);
- words in sub-ss (6), (7) substituted on both places for the words "at such rate as the tribunal may determine";
- in sub-s (8) word substituted for the words "the Commissioners" and words in the second place substituted for the words "the tribunal may, if it thinks fit, direct that that amount shall be paid with interest at such rate as may be specified in the direction";
- sub-s (8A) inserted;
- in sub-s (9) word substituted for the words "the Commissioners";
- sub-s 10 substituted.

Sub-ss (1), (3), (4), 10 previously read as follows—

(1) Subject to the following provisions of this section, an appeal shall lie to an appeal tribunal with respect to any of the following decisions—

(*a*) any decision by the Commissioners on a review under section 59 above (including a deemed confirmation under subsection (7) of that section);

(*b*) any decision by the Commissioners on such review of a decision referred to in section 59(1) above as the Commissioners have agreed to undertake in consequence of a request made after the end of the period mentioned in section 59(3) above.

(3) Where an appeal is made under this section by a person who is required to make returns by virtue of regulations under section 54 above, the appeal shall not be entertained unless the appellant—

(*a*) has made all the returns which he is required to make by virtue of those regulations, and

(*b*) has paid the amounts shown in those returns as payable by him;

but the restriction in paragraph (*b*) above shall not apply in the case of an appeal against a decision with respect to the matter mentioned in section 59(1)(*i*) above.

(4) Where the appeal is against a decision with respect to any of the matters mentioned in paragraphs (*b*) and (*d*) of section 59(1) above it shall not be entertained unless—

(*a*) the amount which the Commissioners have determined to be payable as tax has been paid or deposited with them, or

(*b*) on being satisfied that the appellant would otherwise suffer hardship the Commissioners agree or the tribunal decides that it should be entertained notwithstanding that that amount has not been so paid or deposited.

(10) Sections 25 and 29 of the Finance Act 1985 (settling of appeals by agreement and enforcement of certain decisions of tribunal) shall have effect as if—

(*a*) the references to section 40 of the Value Added Tax Act 1983 included references to this section, and

(*b*) the references to value added tax included references to insurance premium tax.

61 Review and appeal: commencement

Sections 59 and 60 above shall come into force on such day as may be appointed by order.

Miscellaneous

62 Partnership, bankruptcy, transfer of business, etc

(1) Regulations may make provision for determining by what persons anything required by this Part to be done by an insurer [or taxable intermediary][1] is to be done where the business concerned is carried on in partnership or by another unincorporated body.

(2) The registration under this Part of an unincorporated body other than a partnership may be in the name of the body concerned; and in determining whether premiums are received by such a body no account shall be taken of any change in its members.

(3) Regulations may make provision for determining by what person anything required by this Part to be done by an insurer is to be done in a case where insurance business is carried on by persons who are underwriting members of Lloyd's and are members of a syndicate of such underwriting members.

(4) Regulations may—

(*a*) make provision for the registration for the purposes of this Part of a syndicate of underwriting members of Lloyd's;

(*b*) provide that for purposes prescribed by the regulations no account shall be taken of any change in the members of such a syndicate;

and regulations under paragraph (a) above may modify section 53 above.

(5) As regards any case where a person carries on a business of an insurer [or taxable intermediary][1] who has died or become bankrupt or incapacitated or been sequestrated, or of an insurer [or taxable intermediary][1] which is in liquidation or receivership or [administration][1], regulations may—

(*a*) require the person to inform the Commissioners of the fact that he is carrying on the business and of the event that has led to his carrying it on;

(*b*) make provision allowing the person to be treated for a limited time as if he were the insurer [or taxable intermediary][1];

(*c*) make provision for securing continuity in the application of this Part where a person is so treated.

(6) Regulations may make provision for securing continuity in the application of this Part in cases where a business carried on by a person is transferred to another person as a going concern.

(7) Regulations under subsection (6) above may in particular provide—

(*a*) for liabilities and duties under this Part of the transferor to become, to such extent as may be provided by the regulations, liabilities and duties of the transferee;

(*b*) for any right of either of them to repayment or credit in respect of tax to be satisfied by making a repayment or allowing a credit to the other;

but the regulations may provide that no such provision as is mentioned in paragraph (a) or (b) of this subsection shall have effect in relation to any transferor and transferee unless an application in that behalf has been made by them under the regulations.

Commentary—*De Voil Indirect Tax Service* **V18.134**.

Regulations—Insurance Premium Tax Regulations, SI 1994/1774.

Insurance Premium Tax (Amendment) Regulations, SI 1997/1157.

Amendments—[1] Words in sub-s (1) and (5) inserted by FA 1997 s 27(7) with effect from 19 March 1997.

[2] Words in sub-s (5) substituted by the Enterprise Act 2002 (Insolvency) Order, SI 2003/2096 art 4, Schedule para 23 with effect from 15 September 2003. However, this amendment does not apply in relation to any case where a petition for an administration order was presented before that date: SI 2003/2096 arts 1(1), 6.

63 Groups of companies

(1) Where under the following provisions of this section any bodies corporate are treated as members of a group, for the purposes of this Part—

(*a*) any taxable business carried on by a member of the group shall be treated as carried on by the representative member,

[(*aa*) any business carried on by a member of the group who is a taxable intermediary shall be treated as carried on by the representative member,][1]

(*b*) the representative member shall be taken to be the insurer in relation to any taxable insurance contract as regards which a member of the group is the actual insurer,

[(*bb*) the representative member shall be taken to be the taxable intermediary in relation to any taxable intermediary's fees as regards which a member of the group is the actual taxable intermediary,] [1]

(*c*) any receipt by a member of the group of a premium under a taxable insurance contract shall be taken to be a receipt by the representative member, and

(*d*) all members of the group shall be jointly and severally liable for any tax due from the representative member.

(2) Two or more bodies corporate are eligible to be treated as members of a group if each of them falls within subsection (3) below and—

(*a*) one of them controls each of the others,

(*b*) one person (whether a body corporate or an individual) controls all of them, or

(*c*) two or more individuals carrying on a business in partnership control all of them.

(3) A body falls within this subsection if it is resident in the United Kingdom or it has an established place of business in the United Kingdom.

(4) Where an application to that effect is made to the Commissioners with respect to two or more bodies corporate eligible to be treated as members of a group, then—

(*a*) from the beginning of an accounting period they shall be so treated, and

(*b*) one of them shall be the representative member,

unless the Commissioners refuse the application; and the Commissioners shall not refuse the application unless it appears to them necessary to do so for the protection of the revenue.

(5) Where any bodies corporate are treated as members of a group and an application to that effect is made to the Commissioners, then, from the beginning of an accounting period—

(*a*) a further body eligible to be so treated shall be included among the bodies so treated,

(*b*) a body corporate shall be excluded from the bodies so treated,

(*c*) another member of the group shall be substituted as the representative member, or

(*d*) the bodies corporate shall no longer be treated as members of a group,

unless the application is to the effect mentioned in paragraph (a) or (c) above and the Commissioners refuse the application.

(6) The Commissioners may refuse an application under subsection (5)(*a*) or (*c*) above only if it appears to them necessary to do so for the protection of the revenue.

(7) Where a body corporate is treated as a member of a group as being controlled by any person and it appears to the Commissioners that it has ceased to be so controlled, they shall, by notice given to that person, terminate that treatment from such date as may be specified in the notice.

(8) An application under this section with respect to any bodies corporate must be made by one of those bodies or by the person controlling them and must be made not less than 90 days before the date from which it is to take effect, or at such later time as the Commissioners may allow.

(9) For the purposes of this section a body corporate shall be taken to control another body corporate if it is empowered by statute to control that body's activities or if it is that body's holding company within the meaning of section [1159 of and Schedule 6 to][2] the Companies Act [2006][2]; and an individual or individuals shall be taken to control a body corporate if he or they, were he or they a company, would be that body's holding company within the meaning of [those sections][2].

Commentary—*De Voil Indirect Tax Service* **V18.140.**

Amendments—[1] Sub-s (1)(*aa*) and (*bb*) inserted by FA 1997 s 27(8) with effect from 19 March 1997.

[2] In para (9), words substituted for words "736 of", "1985" and "that section", by the Companies Act 2006 (Consequential Amendments) (Taxes and National Insurance) Order, SI 2009/1890 art 4(1)(*b*) with effect from 1 October 2009.

64 Information, powers, penalties, etc

Schedule 7 to this Act (which contains provisions relating to information, powers, penalties and other matters) shall have effect.

65 Liability of insured in certain cases

(1) Regulations may make provision under this section with regard to any case where at any time [the insurer—

(*a*) does not have any business establishment or other fixed establishment in the United Kingdom, and

(*b*) is established in a country or territory in respect of which it appears to the Commissioners that the condition in subsection (1A) below is met.][1]

[(1A) The condition mentioned in subsection (1)(*b*) above is that—

(*a*) the country or territory is neither a member State nor a part of a member State, and

(*b*) there is no provision for mutual assistance between the United Kingdom and the country or territory similar in scope to the assistance provided for between the United Kingdom and each other member State by the mutual assistance provisions.

(1B) In subsection (1A) above "the mutual assistance provisions" means—

(*a*) section 134 of, and Schedule 39 to, the Finance Act 2002 (recovery of taxes etc due in other member States), and

(*b*) section 197 of the Finance Act 2003 (exchange of information between tax authorities of member States).][1]

(2) Regulations may make provision allowing notice to be served in accordance with the regulations on—

(*a*) the person who is insured under a taxable insurance contract, if there is one insured person, or

(*b*) one or more of the persons who are insured under a taxable insurance contract, if there are two or more insured persons;

and a notice so served is referred to in this section as a liability notice.

(3) Regulations may provide that if a liability notice has been served in accordance with the regulations—

(*a*) the Commissioners may assess to the best of their judgment the amount of any tax due in respect of premiums received by the insurer under the contract concerned after the material date and before the date of the assessment, and

(*b*) that amount shall be deemed to be the amount of tax so due.

(4) The material date is—

(*a*) where there is one person on whom a liability notice has been served in respect of the contract, the date when the notice was served or such later date as may be specified in the notice;

(*b*) where there are two or more persons on whom liability notices have been served in respect of the contract, the date when the last of the notices was served or such later date as may be specified in the notices.

(5) Regulations may provide that where—

(*a*) an assessment is made in respect of a contract under provision included in the regulations by virtue of subsection (3) above, and

(*b*) the assessment is notified to the person, or each of the persons, on whom a liability notice in respect of the contract has been served,

the persons mentioned in subsection (6) below shall be jointly and severally liable to pay the tax assessed, and that tax shall be recoverable accordingly.

(6) The persons are—

(*a*) the person or persons mentioned in subsection (5)(*b*) above, and

(*b*) the insurer.

(7) Where regulations make provision under subsection (5) above they must also provide that any provision made under that subsection shall not apply if, or to the extent that, the assessment has subsequently been withdrawn or reduced.

(8) Regulations may make provision as to the time within which, and the manner in which, tax which has been assessed is to be paid.

IPT

(9) Where any amount is recovered from an insured person by virtue of regulations made under this section, the insurer shall be liable to pay to the insured person an amount equal to the amount recovered; and regulations may make provision requiring an insurer to pay interest where this subsection applies.

(10) Regulations may make provision for adjustments to be made of a person's liability in any case where—

(*a*) an assessment is made under section 56 above in relation to the insurer, and

(*b*) an assessment made by virtue of regulations under this section relates to premiums received (or assumed for the purposes of the assessment to be received) within a period which corresponds to any extent with the accounting period to which the assessment under section 56 relates.

(11) Regulations may make provision as regards a case where—

(*a*) an assessment made in respect of a contract by virtue of regulations under this section relates to premiums received (or assumed for the purposes of the assessment to be received) within a given period, and

(*b*) an amount of tax is paid by the insurer in respect of an accounting period which corresponds to any extent with that period;

and the regulations may include provision for determining whether, or how much of, any of the tax paid as mentioned in paragraph (b) above is attributable to premiums received under the contract in the period mentioned in paragraph (a) above.

(12) Regulations may—

(*a*) make provision requiring the Commissioners, in prescribed circumstances, to furnish prescribed information to an insured person;

(*b*) make provision requiring any person on whom a liability notice has been served to keep records, to furnish information, or to produce documents for inspection or cause documents to be produced for inspection;

(*c*) make such provision as the Commissioners think is reasonable for the purpose of facilitating the recovery of tax from the persons having joint and several liability (rather than from the insurer alone);

(*d*) modify the effect of any provision of this Part.

(13) Regulations may provide for an insured person to be liable to pay tax assessed by virtue of the regulations notwithstanding that he has already paid an amount representing tax as part of a premium.

Commentary—*De Voil Indirect Tax Service* **V18.128**.

Regulations—Insurance Premium Tax Regulations, SI 1994/1774.

Insurance Premium Tax (Amendment) Regulations, SI 2008/1945.

Cross reference—See Insurance Premium Tax Regulations, SI 1994/1774 reg 39(1) (interest on reimbursements under sub-s (9) of this section).

Amendments—[1] Sub-s (1)(*a*), (*b*) (which was repealed by FA 2008 s 142 with effect from 21 July 2008) substituted, and sub-ss (1A), (1B) inserted, by FA 2008 s 143 with effect from 21 July 2008.

66 Directions as to amounts of premiums

(1) This section applies where—

(*a*) anything is received by way of premium under a taxable insurance contract, and

(*b*) the amount of the premium is less than it would be if it were received under the contract in open market conditions.

(2) The Commissioners may direct that the amount of the premium shall be taken for the purposes of this Part to be such amount as it would be if it were received under the contract in open market conditions.

(3) A direction under subsection (2) above shall be given by notice in writing to the insurer, and no direction may be given more than three years after the time of the receipt.

(4) Where the Commissioners make a direction under subsection (2) above in the case of a contract they may also direct that if—

(*a*) anything is received by way of premium under the contract after the giving of the notice or after such later date as may be specified in the notice, and

(*b*) the amount of the premium is less than it would be if it were received under the contract in open market conditions,

the amount of the premium shall be taken for the purposes of this Part to be such amount as it would be if it were received under the contract in open market conditions.

(5) For the purposes of this section a premium is received in open market conditions if it is received—

(*a*) by an insurer standing in no such relationship with the insured person as would affect the premium, and

(*b*) in circumstances where there is no other contract or arrangement affecting the parties.

(6) For the purpose of this section it is immaterial whether what is received by way of premium is money or something other than money or both.

Commentary—*De Voil Indirect Tax Service* **V18.106**.

67 Deemed date of receipt of certain premiums

(1) In a case where—

(*a*) a premium under a contract of insurance is received by the insurer after 30th November 1993 and before 1st October 1994, and

(*b*) the period of cover for the risk begins on or after 1st October 1994,

for the purposes of this Part the premium shall be taken to be received on 1st October 1994.

(2) Subsection (3) below applies where—

(*a*) a premium under a contract of insurance is received by the insurer after 30th November 1993 and before 1st October 1994,

(*b*) the period of cover for the risk begins before 1st October 1994 and ends after 30th September 1995, and

(*c*) the premium, or any part of it, is attributable to such of the period of cover as falls after 30th September 1995.

(3) For the purposes of this Part—

(*a*) so much of the premium as is attributable to such of the period of cover as falls after 30th September 1995 shall be taken to be received on 1st October 1994;

(*b*) so much as is so attributable shall be taken to be a separate premium.

(4) If a contract relates to more than one risk subsection (1) above shall have effect as if the reference in paragraph (*b*) to the risk were to any given risk.

(5) If a contract relates to more than one risk, subsections (2) and (3) above shall apply as follows—

(*a*) so much of the premium as is attributable to any given risk shall be deemed for the purposes of those subsections to be a separate premium relating to that risk;

(*b*) those subsections shall then apply separately in the case of each given risk and the separate premium relating to it;

and any further attribution required by those subsections shall be made accordingly.

(6) Subsections (1) and (4) above do not apply in relation to a contract if the contract belongs to a class of contract as regards which the normal practice is for a premium to be received by or on behalf of the insurer before the date when cover begins.

(7) Subsections (2), (3) and (5) above do not apply in relation to a contract if the contract belongs to a class of contract as regards which the normal practice is for cover to be provided for a period exceeding twelve months.

(8) Any attribution under this section shall be made on such basis as is just and reasonable.

Commentary—*De Voil Indirect Tax Service* **V18.106**.

Cross reference—See Insurance Premium Tax Regulations, SI 1994/1774 reg 23 (deemed date of receipt of certain premiums).

[67A Announced increase in rate of tax: certain premiums treated as received on date of increase

(1) This section applies in any case where a proposed increase is announced by a Minister of the Crown in the rate at which tax is to be charged on a premium if it is received by the insurer on or after a date specified in the announcement ("the date of the change").

(2) In a case where—

(*a*) a premium under a contract of insurance is received by the insurer on or after the date of the announcement but before the date of the change, and

(*b*) the period of cover for the risk begins on or after the date of the change,

for the purposes of this Part the premium shall be taken to be received on the date of the change.

(3) Subsection (4) below applies where—

(*a*) a premium under a contract of insurance is received by the insurer on or after the date of the announcement but before the date of the change;

(*b*) the period of cover for the risk begins before the date of the change and ends on or after the first anniversary of the date of the change; and

(*c*) the premium, or any part of it, is attributable to such of the period of cover as falls on or after the first anniversary of the date of the change.

(4) For the purposes of this Part—

(*a*) so much of the premium as is attributable to such of the period of cover as falls on or after the first anniversary of the date of the change shall be taken to be received on the date of the change; and

(*b*) so much as is so attributable shall be taken to be a separate premium.

(5) In determining whether the condition in subsection (2)(*a*) or (3)(*a*) above is satisfied, the provisions of regulations made by virtue of subsection (3) or (7) of section 68 below apply as they would apart from this section; but, subject to that, where subsection (2) or (4) above applies—

(*a*) that subsection shall have effect notwithstanding anything in section 68 below or regulations made under that section; and

(*b*) any regulations made under that section shall have effect as if the entry made in the accounts of the insurer showing the premium as due to him had been made as at the date of the change.

(6) Any attribution under this section shall be made on such basis as is just and reasonable.

(7) In this section—

IPT

"increase", in relation to the rate of tax, includes the imposition of a charge to tax by adding to the descriptions of contract which are taxable insurance contracts;
"Minister of the Crown" has the same meaning as in the Ministers of the Crown Act 1975.][1]

Commentary—*De Voil Indirect Tax Service* **V18.116**.
Cross references—See F(No 2)A 2010 s 4(3) (in the application of this section in relation to increases in IPT made by F(No 2)A 2010 s 4, for the purposes of sub-s (1) the announcement is taken to have been made on 22 June 2010 and the date of the change is 4 January 2011).
Amendments—[1] This section inserted by FA 1997 s 29(1) with effect from 26 November 1996.

[67B Announced increase in rate of tax: certain contracts treated as made on date of increase

(1) This section applies in any case where—
(*a*) an announcement falling within section 67A(1) above is made; but
(*b*) a proposed exception from the increase in question is also announced by a Minister of the Crown; and
(*c*) the proposed exception is to apply in relation to a premium only if the conditions described in subsection (2) below are satisfied in respect of the premium.

(2) Those conditions are—
(*a*) that the premium is in respect of a contract made before the date of the change;
(*b*) that the premium falls, by virtue of regulations under section 68 below, to be regarded for the purposes of this Part as received under the contract by the insurer before such date ("the concessionary date") as is specified for the purpose in the announcement.

(3) In a case where—
(*a*) a premium under a contract of insurance is received by the insurer on or after the date of the announcement but before the concessionary date, and
(*b*) the period of cover for the risk begins on or after the date of the change,

the rate of tax applicable in relation to the premium shall be determined as if the contract had been made on the date of the change.

(4) Subsection (5) below applies where—
(*a*) a premium under a contract of insurance is received by the insurer on or after the date of the announcement but before the concessionary date;
(*b*) the period of cover for the risk begins before the date of the change and ends on or after the first anniversary of the date of the change; and
(*c*) the premium, or any part of it, is attributable to such of the period of cover as falls on or after the first anniversary of the date of the change.

(5) Where this subsection applies—
(*a*) the rate of tax applicable in relation to so much of the premium as is attributable to such of the period of cover as falls on or after the first anniversary of the date of the change shall be determined as if the contract had been made on the date of the change; and
(*b*) so much of the premium as is so attributable shall be taken to be a separate premium.

(6) Any attribution under this section shall be made on such basis as is just and reasonable.

(7) In this section—
"the date of the change" has the same meaning as in section 67A above;
"Minister of the Crown" has the same meaning as in section 67A above.][1]

Commentary—*De Voil Indirect Tax Service* **V18.116**.
Amendments—[1] This section inserted by FA 1997 s 29(1) with effect from 26 November 1996.

[67C Announced increase in rate of tax: exceptions and apportionments

(1) Sections 67A(2) and 67B(3) above do not apply in relation to a premium if the risk to which that premium relates belongs to a class of risk as regards which the normal practice is for a premium to be received by or on behalf of the insurer before the date when cover begins.

(2) Sections 67A(3) and (4) and 67B(4) and (5) above do not apply in relation to a premium if the risk to which that premium relates belongs to a class of risk as regards which the normal practice is for cover to be provided for a period exceeding twelve months.

(3) If a contract relates to more than one risk, then, in the application of section 67A(2), 67A(3) and (4), 67B(3) or 67B(4) and (5) above—
(*a*) the reference in section 67A(2)(*b*) or (3)(*b*) or 67B(3)(*b*) or (4)(*b*), as the case may be, to the risk shall be taken as a reference to any given risk,
(*b*) so much of the premium as is attributable to any given risk shall be taken for the purposes of section 67A(2), 67A(3) and (4), 67B(3) or 67B(4) and (5) above, as the case may be, to be a separate premium relating to that risk,
(*c*) those provisions shall then apply separately in the case of each given risk and the separate premium relating to it, and
(*d*) any further attribution required by section 67A(3) and (4) or 67B(4) and (5) above shall be made accordingly,

and subsections (1) and (2) above shall apply accordingly.

(4) Any attribution under this section shall be made on such basis as is just and reasonable.][1]

Commentary—*De Voil Indirect Tax Service* **V18.116**.

Cross reference—See F(No 2)A 2010 s 4(3) (in the application of this section in relation to increases in IPT made by F(No 2)A 2010 s 4, for the purposes of sub-s (1) the announcement is taken to have been made on 22 June 2010 and the date of the change is 4 January 2011).

Amendments—[1] This section inserted by FA 1997 s 29(1) with effect from 26 November 1996.

68 Special accounting schemes

(1) Regulations may make provision establishing a scheme in accordance with the following provisions of this section; and in this section "a relevant accounting period", in relation to an insurer, means an accounting period as regards which the scheme applies to the insurer.

(2) Regulations may provide that if an insurer notifies the Commissioners that the scheme should apply to him as regards accounting periods beginning on or after a date specified in the notification and prescribed conditions are fulfilled, then, subject to any provision made under subsection (9) below, the scheme shall apply to the insurer as regards accounting periods beginning on or after that date.

(3) Regulations may provide that where—

(*a*) an entry is made in the accounts of an insurer showing a premium under a taxable insurance contract as due to him, and

(*b*) the entry is made as at a particular date which falls within a relevant accounting period,

then (whether or not that date is one on which the premium is actually received by the insurer or on which the premium would otherwise be treated for the purposes of this Part as received by him) the premium shall for the purposes of this Part be taken to be received by the insurer on that date or, in prescribed circumstances, to be received by him on a different date determined in accordance with the regulations.

(4) Where regulations make provision under subsection (3) above they may also provide that, for the purposes of this Part, the amount of the premium shall be taken to be the amount which the entry in the accounts treats as its amount.

(5) Regulations may provide that provision made under subsections (3) and (4) above shall apply even if the premium, or part of it, is never actually received by the insurer or on his behalf; and the regulations may include provision that, where the premium is never actually received because the contract under which it would have been received is never entered into or is terminated, the premium is nonetheless to be taken for the purposes of this Part to be received under a taxable insurance contract.

(6) Regulations may provide that any provision made under subsection (4) above shall be subject to any directions made under section 66 above.

(7) Regulations may provide that where a premium is treated as received on a particular date by virtue of provision made under subsection (3) above and there is another date on which the premium—

(*a*) is actually received by the insurer, or

(*b*) would, apart from the regulations, be treated for the purposes of this Part as received by him,

the premium shall be taken for the purposes of this Part not to be received by him on that other date.

(8) Regulations may provide that provision made under subsection (7) above shall apply only to the extent that there is no excess of the actual amount of the premium over the amount which, by virtue of regulations under this section or of a direction under section 66 above, is to be taken for the purposes of this Part to be its amount; and the regulations may include provision that where there is such an excess, the excess amount shall be taken for the purposes of this Part to be a separate premium and to be received by the insurer on a date determined in accordance with the regulations.

(9) Regulations may provide that if a notification has been given in accordance with provision made under subsection (2) above and subsequently—

(*a*) the insurer gives notice to the Commissioners that the scheme should not apply to him as regards accounting periods beginning on or after a date specified in the notice, or

(*b*) the Commissioners give notice to the insurer that the scheme is not to apply to him as regards accounting periods beginning on or after a date specified in the notice,

then, if prescribed conditions are fulfilled, the scheme shall not apply to the insurer as regards an accounting period beginning on or after the date specified in the notice mentioned in paragraph (a) or (b) above unless the circumstances are such as may be prescribed.

(10) Regulations may include provision—

(*a*) enabling an insurer to whom the scheme applies as regards an accounting period to account for tax due in respect of that period on the assumption that the scheme will apply to him as regards subsequent accounting periods;

(*b*) designed to secure that, where the scheme ceases to apply to an insurer, any tax which by virtue of provision made under paragraph (*a*) above has not been accounted for is accounted for and paid.

(11) Regulations may provide that where—

(*a*) an entry in the accounts of an insurer shows a premium as due to him,

(*b*) the entry is made as at a date falling before 1st October 1994, (*c*) tax in respect of the receipt of the premium would, apart from the regulations, be charged by reference to a date (whether or not the date on which the premium is actually received by the insurer) falling on or after 1st October 1994,

(*d*) the date by reference to which tax would be charged falls within a relevant accounting period, and

(*e*) prescribed conditions are fulfilled,

the premium, or such part of it as may be found in accordance with prescribed rules, shall be taken for the purposes of this Part to have been received by the insurer before 1st October 1994.

(12) Without prejudice to subsection (13) below, regulations may include provision modifying any provision made under this section so as to secure the effective operation of the provision in a case where a premium consists wholly or partly of anything other than money.

(13) Regulations may modify the effect of any provision of this Part.

(14) The reference in subsection (3)(*a*) above to a premium under a taxable insurance contract includes a reference to anything that, although not actually received by or on behalf of the insurer, would be such a premium if it were so received.

Commentary—*De Voil Indirect Tax Service* **V18.127**.
Regulations—Insurance Premium Tax Regulations, SI 1994/1774.
Concession ESC 4.1—Special accounting scheme—introductory provisions.

[69 Charge to tax where different rates apply

(1) This section applies for the purpose of determining the chargeable amount in a case where a contract provides cover falling within any one of the following paragraphs, that is to say—

(*a*) cover for one or more exempt matters,

(*b*) cover for one or more standard rate matters, or

(*c*) cover for one or more higher rate matters,

and also provides cover falling within another of those paragraphs.

(2) In the following provisions of this section "the non-exempt premium" means the difference between—

(*a*) the amount of the premium; and

(*b*) such part of the premium as is attributable to any exempt matter or matters or, if no part is so attributable, nil.

(3) If the contract provides cover for one or more exempt matters and also provides cover for either—

(*a*) one or more standard rate matters, or

(*b*) one or more higher rate matters,

the chargeable amount is such amount as, with the addition of the tax chargeable at the standard rate or (as the case may be) the higher rate, is equal to the non-exempt premium.

(4) If the contract provides cover for both—

(*a*) one or more standard rate matters, and

(*b*) one or more higher rate matters,

the higher rate element and the standard rate element shall be found in accordance with the following provisions of this section.

(5) For the purposes of this section—

(*a*) "the higher rate element" is such portion of the non-exempt premium as is attributable to the higher rate matters (including tax at the higher rate); and

(*b*) "the standard rate element" is the difference between—

(i) the non-exempt premium; and

(ii) the higher rate element.

(6) In a case falling within subsection (4) above, tax shall be charged separately—

(*a*) at the standard rate, by reference to the standard rate chargeable amount, and

(*b*) at the higher rate, by reference to the higher rate chargeable amount,

and the tax chargeable in respect of the premium is the aggregate of those amounts of tax.

(7) For the purposes of this section—

"the higher rate chargeable amount" is such amount as, with the addition of the tax chargeable at the higher rate, is equal to the higher rate element;

"the standard rate chargeable amount" is such amount as, with the addition of the tax chargeable at the standard rate, is equal to the standard rate element.

(8) References in this Part to the chargeable amount shall, in a case falling within subsection (4) above, be taken as referring separately to the standard rate chargeable amount and the higher rate chargeable amount.

(9) In applying subsection (2)(*b*) above, any amount that is included in the premium as being referable to tax (whether or not the amount corresponds to the actual amount of tax payable in respect of the premium) shall be taken to be wholly attributable to the non-exempt matter or matters.

(10) In applying subsection (5)(*a*) above, any amount that is included in the premium as being referable to tax at the higher rate (whether or not the amount corresponds to the actual amount of tax payable at that rate in respect of the premium) shall be taken to be wholly attributable to the higher rate element.

(11) Subject to subsections (9) and (10) above, any attribution under subsection (2)(*b*) or (5)(*a*) above shall be made on such basis as is just and reasonable.

(12) For the purposes of this section—

(*a*) an "exempt matter" is any matter such that, if it were the only matter for which the contract provided cover, the contract would not be a taxable insurance contract;

(*b*) a "non-exempt matter" is a matter which is not an exempt matter;

(*c*) a "standard rate matter" is any matter such that, if it were the only matter for which the contract provided cover, tax at the standard rate would be chargeable on the chargeable amount;

(*d*) a "higher rate matter" is any matter such that, if it were the only matter for which the contract provided cover, tax at the higher rate would be chargeable on the chargeable amount.

(13) If the contract relates to a lifeboat and lifeboat equipment, the lifeboat and the equipment shall be taken together in applying this section.

(14) For the purposes of this section "lifeboat" and "lifeboat equipment" have the same meaning as in paragraph 6 of Schedule 7A to this Act.][1]

Commentary—*De Voil Indirect Tax Service* **V18.105**.

Simon's Tax Cases—*Manchester and Salford Hospital Saturday Fund v C&E Comrs* [1999] STC 649.

Amendments—[1] This section substituted by FA 1997 s 23(1) with effect as provided by FA 1997 s 24.

Supplementary

70 Interpretation: taxable insurance contracts

(1) Subject to [subsection (1A) below][1], any contract of insurance is a taxable insurance contract.

[(1A) A contract is not a taxable insurance contract if it falls within one or more of the paragraphs of Part I of Schedule 7A to this Act.][2]

[(1B) Part II of Schedule 7A to this Act (interpretation of certain provisions of Part I) shall have effect.][2]

(2)–(10) . . . [3]

(11) This section has effect subject to section 71 below.

(12) This section and section 71 below have effect for the purposes of this Part.

Commentary—*De Voil Indirect Tax Service* **V18.103**.

Amendments—[1] Words in sub-s (1) substituted by the Insurance Premium Tax (Taxable Insurance Contracts) Order, SI 1994/1698 arts 1, 4 with effect from 1 October 1994.

[2] Sub-ss (1A), (1B) inserted by the Insurance Premium Tax (Taxable Insurance Contracts) Order, SI 1994/1698, arts 1, 4 with effect from 1 October 1994.

[3] Sub-ss (2)–(10) repealed by the Insurance Premium Tax (Taxable Insurance Contracts) Order, SI 1994/1698, arts 1, 4 with effect from 1 October 1994.

71 Taxable insurance contracts: power to change definition

(1) Provision may be made by order that—

(*a*) a contract of insurance that would otherwise not be a taxable insurance contract shall be a taxable insurance contract if it falls within a particular description;

(*b*) a contract of insurance that would otherwise be a taxable insurance contract shall not be a taxable insurance contract if it falls within a particular description.

(2) A description referred to in subsection (1) above may be by reference to the nature of the insured or by reference to such other factors as the Treasury think fit.

(3) Provision under this section may be made in such way as the Treasury think fit, and in particular may be made by amending this Part.

(4) An order under this section may amend or modify the effect of section 69 above in such way as the Treasury think fit.

Commentary—*De Voil Indirect Tax Service* **V18.104**.

Orders—Insurance Premium Tax (Taxable Insurance Contracts) Order, SI 1996/2955.
Insurance Premium Tax (Taxable Insurance Contracts) Order, SI 1997/1627.

72 Interpretation: premium

(1) In relation to a taxable insurance contract, a premium is any payment received under the contract by the insurer, and in particular includes any payment wholly or partly referable to—

(*a*) any risk,

(*b*) costs of administration,

(*c*) commission,

(*d*) any facility for paying in instalments or making deferred payment (whether or not payment for the facility is called interest), or

(*e*) tax.

IPT

[(1A) Where an amount is charged to the insured by any person in connection with a taxable insurance contract, any payment in respect of that amount is to be regarded as a payment received under that contract by the insurer unless—

(*a*) the payment is chargeable to tax at the higher rate by virtue of section 52A above; or

(*b*) the amount is charged under a separate contract and is identified in writing to the insured as a separate amount so charged.][1]

[(1AA) A contract ("the relevant contract") is not to be regarded as a separate contract for the purposes of subsection (1A) above if conditions A to D are met.

(1AB) Condition A is that the insured is an individual ("I") and enters into the taxable insurance contract in a personal capacity.

(1AC) Condition B is that I—

(*a*) is required to enter into the relevant contract by, or as a condition of entering into, the taxable insurance contract, or

(*b*) would be unlikely to enter into the relevant contract without also entering into the taxable insurance contract.

(1AD) Condition C is that—

(*a*) the amount charged to I under the relevant contract in respect of any particular services is not open to negotiation by I, or

(*b*) the other terms on which particular services are to be provided to I under the relevant contract are not open to such negotiation.

(1AE) Condition D is that the amount charged to I under the taxable insurance contract is arrived at without a comprehensive assessment having been undertaken of the individual circumstances of I which might affect the level of risk.][4]

[(1B) Where—

(*a*) an amount is charged (to the insured or any other person) in respect of the acquisition of a right (whether of the insured or any other person) to require the insurer to provide, or offer to provide, any of the cover included in a taxable insurance contract, and

(*b*) any payment in respect of that amount is not regarded as a payment received under that contract by the insurer by virtue of subsection (1A) above,

the payment is to be regarded as a payment received under that contract by the insurer unless it is chargeable to tax at the higher rate by virtue of section 52A above.][3]

(2) A premium may consist wholly or partly of anything other than money, and references to payment in subsection (1) above shall be construed accordingly.

(3) Where a premium is to any extent received in a form other than money, its amount shall be taken to be—

(*a*) an amount equal to the value of whatever is received in a form other than money, or

(*b*) if money is also received, the aggregate of the amount found under paragraph (*a*) above and the amount received in the form of money.

(4) The value to be taken for the purposes of subsection (3) above is open market value at the time of the receipt by the insurer.

(5) The open market value of anything at any time shall be taken to be an amount equal to such consideration in money as would be payable on a sale of it at that time to a person standing in no such relationship with any person as would affect that consideration.

(6) Where (apart from this subsection) anything received under a contract by the insurer would be taken to be an instalment of a premium, it shall be taken to be a separate premium.

(7) Where anything is received by any person on behalf of the insurer—

(*a*) it shall be treated as received by the insurer when it is received by the other person, and

(*b*) the later receipt of the whole or any part of it by the insurer shall be disregarded.

[(7A) Where any person is authorised by or on behalf of an employee to deduct from anything due to the employee under his contract of employment an amount in respect of a payment due under a taxable insurance contract, subsection (7) above shall not apply to the receipt on behalf of the insurer by the person so authorised of the amount deducted.][2]

(8) In a case where—

(*a*) a payment under a taxable insurance contract is made to a person (the intermediary) by or on behalf of the insured, and

(*b*) the whole or part of the payment is referable to commission to which the intermediary is entitled,

in determining for the purposes of subsection (7) above whether, or how much of, the payment is received by the intermediary on behalf of the insurer any of the payment that is referable to that commission shall be regarded as received by the intermediary on behalf of the insurer notwithstanding the intermediary's entitlement.

[(8A) Where, by virtue of subsection (7A) above, subsection (7) above does not apply to the receipt of an amount by a person and the whole or part of the amount is referable to commission to which he is entitled—

(*a*) if the whole of the amount is so referable, the amount shall be treated as received by the insurer when it is deducted by that person; and

(*b*) otherwise, the part of the amount that is so referable shall be treated as received by the insurer when the remainder of the payment concerned is or is treated as received by him.][2]

(9) References in subsection (8) above to a payment include references to a payment in a form other than money.

[(9A) Provision may be made by order amending subsections (1AA) to (1AE) above.][5]

(10) This section has effect for the purposes of this Part.

Commentary—*De Voil Indirect Tax Service* **V18.101**.

Simon's Tax Cases—s 72(1A)(*b*), *Homeserve Membership Ltd v R&C Comrs* [2009] STC 2366.

Amendments—[1] Sub-s (1A) inserted by FA 1997 s 28(1) in relation to payments received in respect of amounts charged on or after 1 April 1997.

[2] Sub-ss (7A) and (8A) inserted by FA 1997 s 30 in relation to amounts deducted on or after 19 March 1997.

[3] Sub-s (1B) inserted by FA 2007 s 101 with effect in relation to amounts charged on or after 22 March 2007.

[4] Sub-ss (1AA)–(1AE) inserted by FA 2010 s 51(1)–(3) with effect in relation to payments made on or after 24 March 2010 (FA 2010 s 51(6)).

[5] Sub-s (9A) inserted by FA 2010 s 51(1), (2), (4) with effect from 8 April 2010.

73 Interpretation: other provisions

(1) Unless the context otherwise requires—

"accounting period" shall be construed in accordance with section 54 above;

"appeal tribunal" means [the First-tier Tribunal or, where determined by or under Tribunal Procedure Rules, the Upper Tribunal][8];

"authorised person" means any person acting under the authority of the Commissioners;

"the Commissioners" means the Commissioners of Customs and Excise;

"conduct" includes any act, omission or statement;

["the higher rate" shall be construed in accordance with section 51 above;][3]

["HMRC" means Her Majesty's Revenue and Customs;][8]

["insurance business" means a business which consists of or includes the provision of insurance;][2]

"insurer" means a person or body of persons (whether incorporated or not) carrying on insurance business;

"legislation relating to insurance premium tax" means this Part (as defined by subsection (9) below), any other enactment (whenever passed) relating to insurance premium tax, and any subordinate legislation made under any such enactment;

"prescribed" means prescribed by an order or regulations under this Part;

["the standard rate" shall be construed in accordance with section 51 above;][3]

"tax" means insurance premium tax;

["tax representative" shall be construed in accordance with section 57 above;][7]

"taxable business" means a business which consists of or includes the provision of insurance under taxable insurance contracts;

"taxable insurance contract" shall be construed in accordance with section 70 above;

["taxable intermediary" shall be construed in accordance with section 52A above;][4]

["taxable intermediary's fees" has the meaning given by section 53AA(9) above.][4]

(2) . . . [1]

(3) [subject to subsection (3A) below,][5] a registrable person is a person who—

(*a*) is registered under section 53 above, or

(*b*) is liable to be registered under that section.

[(3A) Reference in sections 53A and 54 above and paragraphs 1,9 and 12 of Schedule 7 to this Act to a registrable person include a reference to a person who—

(*a*) is registered under section 53AA above; or

(*b*) is liable to be registered under that section.][6]

(4)–(8) . . . [1]

(9) A reference to this Part includes a reference to any order or regulations made under it and a reference to a provision of this Part includes a reference to any order or regulations made under the provision, unless otherwise required by the context or any order or regulations.

(10) This section has effect for the purposes of this Part.

Commentary—*De Voil Indirect Tax Service* **V18.131, 181**.

Amendments—[1] Sub-ss (2) and (4)–(8) repealed by the Insurance Premium Tax (Taxable Insurance Contracts) Order, SI 1994/1698 arts 1, 6 with effect from 1 October 1994.

[2] Definition of "insurance business" inserted by FA 1995 s 34, Sch 5 para 6.

[3] Definitions of "the higher rate" and "the standard rate" inserted by FA 1997 s 21(2) with effect as provided by FA 1997 s 24.

[4] Definitions of "taxable intermediary" and "taxable intermediary's fees" inserted by FA 1997 s 27(9) with effect from 19 March 1997.

[5] Words in sub-s (3) inserted by FA 1997 s 27 (10) with effect from 19 March 1997.

[6] Sub-s (3A) inserted by FA 1997 s 27(10) with effect from 19 March 1997.

[7] The definition of "tax representative" repealed by FA 2008 s 142 with effect from 21 July 2008.

IPT

8 In sub-s (1) words in definition of "appeal tribunal" substituted for the words "a VAT and duties tribunal"; definition of "HMRC" inserted; by the Transfer of Tribunal Functions and Revenue and Customs Appeals Order, SI 2009/56 art 3, Sch 1 para 208 with effect from 1 April 2009.

74 Orders and regulations

(1) The power to make an order under section 61 above shall be exercisable by the Commissioners, and the power to make an order under any other provision of this Part shall be exercisable by the Treasury.

(2) Any power to make regulations under this Part shall be exercisable by the Commissioners.

(3) Any power to make an order or regulations under this Part shall be exercisable by statutory instrument.

(4) An order under section [5IA][1][, 71 or 72][2] above shall be laid before the House of Commons; and unless it is approved by that House before the expiration of a period of 28 days beginning with the date on which it was made it shall cease to have effect on the expiration of that period, but without prejudice to anything previously done under the order or to the making of a new order.

(5) In reckoning any such period as is mentioned in subsection (4) above no account shall be taken of any time during which Parliament is dissolved or prorogued or during which the House of Commons is adjourned for more than four days.

(6) A statutory instrument containing an order or regulations under this Part (other than an order under section [5IA][1][, 71 or 72][2] above) shall be subject to annulment in pursuance of a resolution of the House of Commons.

(7) Any power to make an order or regulations under this Part—

(*a*) may be exercised as regards prescribed cases or descriptions of case;

(*b*) may be exercised differently in relation to different cases or descriptions of case.

(8) An order or regulations under this Part may include such supplementary, incidental, consequential or transitional provisions as appear to the Treasury or the Commissioners (as the case may be) to be necessary or expedient.

(9) No specific provision of this Part about an order or regulations shall prejudice the generality of subsections (7) and (8) above.

Order—Insurance Premium Tax (Prescribed Rates of Interest) Order, SI 1994/1819.

Regulations—Insurance Premium Tax Regulations, SI 1994/1774.

Amendments—[1] Words in sub-s (4), (6) inserted by FA 1997 s 22(2) with effect as provided by FA 1997, s 24.

2 In sub-ss (4), (6), words substituted for words "or 71", by FA 2010 s 51(1), (5) with effect from 8 April 2010.

[SCHEDULE 6A

PREMIUMS LIABLE TO TAX AT THE HIGHER RATE][1]

Section 51A

Commentary—*De Voil Indirect Tax Service* **V18.112.**

Amendments—[1] This Schedule inserted by FA 1997 s 22(3), Sch 4 with effect as provided by FA 1997 s 24.

[PART I

INTERPRETATION

[1—(1) In this Schedule—

"insurance-related service" means any service which is related to, or connected with, insurance;

"supply" includes all forms of supply; and "supplier" shall be construed accordingly.

(2) For the purposes of this Schedule, any question whether a person is connected with another shall be determined in accordance with [section 1122 of the Corporation Tax Act 2010][2].][1]

Amendments—[1] This Schedule inserted by FA 1997 s 22(3), Sch 4 with effect as provided by FA 1997 s 24.

2 In sub-para (2) words substituted for words "section 839 of the Taxes Act 1988" by CTA 2010 s 1177, Sch 1 para 284. CTA 2010 has effect for corporation tax purposes for accounting periods ending on or after 1 April 2010, and for income and capital gains tax purposes for the tax year 2010–11 and subsequent tax years.

[PART II

DESCRIPTIONS OF PREMIUM

Insurance relating to motor cars or motor cycles

[2—(1) A premium under a taxable insurance contract relating to a motor car or motor cycle falls within this paragraph if—

(*a*) the contract is arranged through a person falling within sub-paragraph (2) below, or

(*b*) the insurer under the contract is a person falling within that sub-paragraph,

unless the insurance is provided to the insured free of charge.

(2) A person falls within this sub-paragraph if—

(*a*) he is a supplier of motor cars or motor cycles;

(*b*) he is connected with a supplier of motor cars or motor cycles; or

(*c*) he pays—

(i) the whole or any part of the premium received under the taxable insurance contract, or

(ii) a fee connected with the arranging of that contract,

to a supplier of motor cars or motor cycles or to a person who is connected with a supplier of motor cars or motor cycles.

[(2A)A premium does not fall within this paragraph if it is—

(*a*) payable under a taxable insurance contract relating to a motor car or motor cycle which is supplied by way of sale, and

(*b*) attributable to cover of the kind generally known as—

(i) fully comprehensive,

(ii) third party, fire and theft, or

(iii) third party.][2]

(3) Where a taxable insurance contract relating to a motor car or motor cycle is arranged through a person who is connected with a supplier of motor cars or motor cycles, the premium does not fall within this paragraph by virtue only of sub-paragraph (2)(*b*) above except to the extent that the premium is attributable to cover for a risk which relates to a motor car or motor cycle supplied by a supplier of motor cars or motor cycles with whom that person is connected.

(4) Where the insurer under a taxable insurance contract relating to a motor car or motor cycle is connected with a supplier of motor cars or motor cycles, the premium does not fall within this paragraph by virtue only of sub-paragraph (2)(*b*) above except to the extent that the premium is attributable to cover for a risk which relates to a motor car or motor cycle supplied by a supplier of motor cars or motor cycles with whom the insurer is connected.

(5) For the purposes of this paragraph, the cases where insurance is provided to the insured free of charge are those cases where no charge (whether by way of premium or otherwise) is made—

(*a*) in respect of the taxable insurance contract, or

(*b*) at or about the time when the taxable insurance contract is made and in connection with that contract, in respect of any insurance-related service,

by any person falling within sub-paragraph (2) above to any person who is or becomes the insured (or one of the insured) under the contract or to any person who acts, otherwise than in the course of a business, for or on behalf of such a person.

(6) In this paragraph—

"motor car" and "motor cycle" have the meaning given—

(*a*) by section 185(1) of the Road Traffic Act 1988; or

(*b*) in Northern Ireland, by Article 3(1) of the Road Traffic (Northern Ireland) Order 1995;

["sale", in relation to a motor car or motor cycle, means—

(*a*) a sale under which title to the motor car or motor cycle passes to the purchaser immediately on purchase, or

(*b*) a sale pursuant to a hire purchase agreement (within the meaning of the Consumer Credit Act 1974) under which it is intended at the outset of the agreement that the title to the motor car or motor cycle is to pass to the purchaser, whether on conclusion of the agreement or at the end of a period specified in the agreement.][2]

"supplier" does not include an insurer who supplies a car or motor cycle as a means of discharging liabilities arising by reason of a claim under an insurance contract.][1]

Amendments—[1] This Schedule inserted by FA 1997 s 22(3), Sch 4 with effect as provided by FA 1997 s 24.

[2] Sub-para (2A), and in sub-para (6) definition of "sale", inserted, by the Insurance Premium Tax (Amendment of Schedule 6A to the Finance Act 1994) Order, SI 2009/219 art 2 with effect in relation to taxable insurance contracts made or coming into operation on or after 1 April 2009.

Press releases etc—C & E News release 4/97 6-2-97 (by concession, the higher rate will not apply to ordinary motor insurance sold by car or motor cycle dealers).

Insurance relating to domestic appliances etc

[3—(1) A premium under a taxable insurance contract relating to relevant goods falls within this paragraph if—

(*a*) the contract is arranged through a person falling within sub-paragraph (2) below, or

(*b*) the insurer under the contract is a person falling within that sub-paragraph,

unless the insurance is provided to the insured free of charge.

(2) A person falls within this sub-paragraph if—

(*a*) he is a supplier of relevant goods;

(*b*) he is connected with a supplier of relevant goods; or

(*c*) he pays—

(i) the whole or any part of the premium received under the taxable insurance contract, or

(ii) a fee connected with the arranging of that contract,

to a supplier of relevant goods or to a person who is connected with a supplier of relevant goods.

(3) Where a taxable insurance contract relating to relevant goods is arranged through a person who is connected with a supplier of relevant goods, the premium does not fall within this paragraph by virtue only of sub-paragraph (2)(*b*) above except to the extent that the premium is attributable to cover for a risk which relates to relevant goods supplied by a supplier of relevant goods with whom that person is connected.

(4) Where the insurer under a taxable insurance contract relating to relevant goods is connected with a supplier of relevant goods, the premium does not fall within this paragraph by virtue only of sub-paragraph (2)(*b*) above except to the extent that the premium is attributable to cover for a risk which relates to relevant goods supplied by a supplier of relevant goods with whom the insurer is connected.

(5) For the purposes of this paragraph, the cases where insurance is provided to the insured free of charge are those cases where no charge (whether by way of premium or otherwise) is made—

(*a*) in respect of the taxable insurance contract, or

(*b*) at or about the time when the taxable insurance contract is made and in connection with that contract, in respect of any insurance-related service,

by any person falling within sub-paragraph (2) above to any person who is or becomes the insured (or one of the insured) under the contract or to any person who acts, otherwise than in the course of a business, for or on behalf of such a person.

(6) In this paragraph—

"relevant goods" means any electrical or mechanical appliance of a kind—

(*a*) which is ordinarily used in or about the home; or

(*b*) which is ordinarily owned by private individuals and used by them for the purposes of leisure, amusement or entertainment;

"supplier" does not include an insurer who supplies relevant goods as a means of discharging liabilities arising by reason of a claim under an insurance contract.

(7) In sub-paragraph (6) above—

"appliance" includes any device, equipment or apparatus;

"the home" includes any private garden and any private garage or private workshop appurtenant to a dwelling.][1]

Amendments—[1] This Schedule inserted by FA 1997 s 22(3), Sch 4 with effect as provided by FA 1997 s 24.

Press releases etc—C & E News release 4/97 6-2-97 (by concession, the higher rate will not apply to home contents insurance when sold by retailers).

[Insurance provided by divided company

3A—(1) A premium under a taxable insurance contract relating to a motor car or motor cycle also falls within paragraph 2 above if—

(*a*) the insurance to be provided under the contract is provided by a divided company, and

(*b*) any division of that company would, if it were a separate company, be a person connected with a supplier of motor cars or motor cycles.

(2) A premium under a taxable insurance contract relating to relevant goods also falls within paragraph 3 above if—

(*a*) the insurance to be provided under the contract is provided by a divided company, and

(*b*) any division of that company would, if it were a separate company, be a person connected with a supplier of relevant goods.

(3) Sub-paragraph (1) or (2) above does not apply if the insurance is provided to the insured free of charge.

(4) A premium falls within paragraph 2 above by virtue of this paragraph only to the extent that it is attributable to cover for a risk which relates to a motor car or motor cycle supplied by a supplier of motor cars or motor cycles with whom the division in question would, if it were a separate company, be connected.

(5) A premium falls within paragraph 3 above by virtue of this paragraph only to the extent that it is attributable to cover for a risk which relates to relevant goods supplied by a supplier of relevant goods with whom the division would, if it were a separate company, be connected.

(6) For the purposes of this paragraph—

(*a*) a company is a "divided company" if under the law under which the company is formed, under the company's constitution or under arrangements entered into by or in relation to the company—

(i) some or all of the assets of the company are available primarily, or only, to meet particular liabilities of the company, and

(ii) some or all of the members of the company, and some or all of its creditors, have rights primarily, or only, in relation to particular assets of the company;

(*b*) a "division" of such a company means an identifiable part of it (by whatever name known) that carries on distinct business activities and to which particular assets and liabilities of the company are primarily or wholly attributable.

(7) In this paragraph "provided to the insured free of charge" has the meaning given by sub-paragraph (5) of paragraph 2 or 3 above.

In determining for this purpose whether a divided company by whom insurance is provided is a person falling within sub-paragraph (2) of paragraph 2 or 3 above, the company shall be treated as connected with any person with whom a division of that company would be connected if it were a separate company.

(8) Other expressions defined for the purposes of paragraph 2 or 3 above have the same meaning in this paragraph.][1]

Amendments—[1] This paragraph inserted by FA 2003 s 194 with effect for a premium that falls to be regarded for the purposes of FA 1994 Pt 3 as received under a taxable insurance contract by an insurer after 9 July 2003.

Travel insurance

[4—(1) A premium under a taxable insurance contract falls within this paragraph if it is in respect of the provision of cover against travel risks for a person travelling.

(2) Where—

(*a*) a contract of insurance provides cover against both travel risks and risks other than travel risks,

(*b*) the premium attributable to the cover against travel risks does not exceed 10 per cent of the total premium payable under the contract, and

(*c*) the contract does not provide cover for a person travelling against travel risks falling within two or more of the paragraphs of sub-paragraph (3) below,

the premium, so far as attributable to the cover against travel risks, does not fall within this paragraph by virtue of sub-paragraph (1) above.

(3) The travel risks mentioned in sub-paragraph (2)(*c*) above are—

(*a*) liability in respect of cancellation of travel or of accommodation arranged in connection with travel;

(*b*) delayed or missed departure;

(*c*) curtailment of travel or of the use of accommodation arranged in connection with travel;

(*d*) loss or delayed arrival of baggage;

(*e*) personal injury or illness or expenses of repatriation.

(4) A premium does not fall within this paragraph by virtue of sub-paragraph (1) above if it is payable under a taxable insurance contract relating to a motor vehicle and is attributable to cover of the kind generally known as—

(*a*) fully comprehensive,

(*b*) third party, fire and theft,

(*c*) third party, or

(*d*) roadside assistance,

or if it is payable under a taxable insurance contract relating to a caravan, boat or aircraft and is attributable to cover of a description broadly corresponding to any of those set out in paragraphs (a) to (d) above (so far as applicable) provided in respect of the caravan, boat or aircraft for a period of at least one month for the person travelling.

(5) In this paragraph—

"person travelling" includes a person intending to travel;

"travel risks" means risks associated with, or related to, travel or intended travel—

(*a*) outside the United Kingdom,

(*b*) by air within the United Kingdom,

(*c*) within the United Kingdom in connection with travel falling within paragraph (*a*) or (*b*) above, or

(*d*) which involves absence from home for at least one night,

or risks to which a person travelling may be exposed during, or at any place at which he may be in the course of, any such travel.][1]

Press releases etc—Hansard 6-2-97 (Standing Committee B (Sixth sitting): Finance Bill debate) ("The definition of travel agents and tour operators is deliberately drafted to include hotels and caravan sites because we have seen that there is already the potential to value shift . . . Insurance products are sometimes linked with hotel products and there is a potential for growth in value shifting, which we want to stamp out.")

Hansard 11-2-97 (Standing Committee B (Seventh sitting): Finance Bill debate) (in a situation in which a travel agent sells a package of different holidays, one of which he offers directly as a tour operator while the other is offered by another tour operator on whose behalf he sells the insurance, so long as there is a margin on that sale to the travel agent, the insurance premium tax would be at full rate).

Simon's Tax Cases—*R v C&E Comrs, ex p Lunn Poly Ltd* [1999] STC 350.

IPT

Amendments—[1] This Schedule originally inserted by FA 1997 s 22(3), Sch 4 with effect as provided by FA 1997 s 24. Para 4 substituted by FA 1998 s 146(2) in relation to a premium which falls to be regarded as received under a taxable insurance contract by an insurer on or after 1 August 1998.

SCHEDULE 7
INSURANCE PREMIUM TAX

Section 64

PART I
INFORMATION

Commentary—*De Voil Indirect Tax Service* **V18.176, V18.177**.

Records

1—(1) Regulations may require registrable persons to keep records.

(2) Regulations under sub-paragraph (1) above may be framed by reference to such records as may be specified in any notice published by the Commissioners in pursuance of the regulations and not withdrawn by a further notice.

(3) Regulations may require any records kept in pursuance of the regulations to be preserved for such period not exceeding six years as may[—

(*a*)] [1]be specified in the regulations

[(*b*) authorise the Commissioners to direct that any such records need only be preserved for a shorter period than that specified in the regulations, and

(*c*) authorise a direction to be made so as to apply generally or in such cases as the Commissioners may stipulate.][1]

[(4) A duty under the regulations to preserve records may be discharged—

(*a*) by preserving them in any form and by any means, or

(*b*) by preserving the information contained in them in any form and by any means, subject to any conditions or exceptions specified in writing by the Commissioners.][1]

Regulations—Insurance Premium Tax Regulations, SI 1994/1774.

Amendments—[1] In sub-para (3), para (a) designated as such, and paras (*b*), (*c*) and preceding word "and" inserted, and sub-para (4) substituted for previous sub-paras (4)–(6), by FA 2009 s 98, Sch 50 para 1 with effect from 1 April 2010 (by virtue of SI 2010/815 art 2). Sub-paras (4)–(6) previously read as follows—

"(4) Any duty under regulations to preserve records may be discharged by the preservation of the information contained in them by such means as the Commissioners may approve; and where that information is so preserved a copy of any document forming part of the records shall (subject to the following provisions of this paragraph) be admissible in evidence in any proceedings, whether civil or criminal, to the same extent as the records themselves.

subject to any conditions or exceptions specified in writing by the Commissioners."

(5) The Commissioners may, as a condition of approving under sub-paragraph (4) above any means of preserving information contained in any records, impose such reasonable requirements as appear to them necessary for securing that the information will be as readily available to them as if the records themselves had been preserved.

(6) A statement contained in a document produced by a computer shall not by virtue of sub-paragraph (4) above be admissible in evidence—

(*a*) . . .

(*b*) . . .

(*c*) in civil proceedings in Scotland, except in accordance with sections 5 and 6 of the Civil Evidence (Scotland) Act 1988;

(*d*) in criminal proceedings in Scotland, except in accordance with Schedule 8 to the Criminal Procedure (Scotland) Act 1995

(*e*) . . .

(*f*) . . . ".

Other provisions

2—(1) Every person who is concerned (in whatever capacity) in [an insurance business][1] shall furnish to the Commissioners such information relating to [contracts of insurance][2] entered into in the course of the business as the Commissioners may reasonably require.

(2) Every person who makes arrangements for other persons to enter into any [contract of insurance][3] shall furnish to the Commissioners such information relating to that contract as the Commissioners may reasonably require.

(3) Every person who—

(*a*) is concerned in a business that is not [an insurance business][1], and

(*b*) has been involved in the entry into any [contract of insurance][3] providing cover for any matter associated with the business,

shall furnish to the Commissioners such information relating to that contract as the Commissioners may reasonably require.

(4) The information mentioned in sub-paragraph (1), (2) or (3) above shall be furnished within such time and in such form as the Commissioners may reasonably require.[4]

Amendments—[1] Words in sub-paras (1), (3)(*a*) substituted by FA 1995 s 34, Sch 5 para 7 with effect for contracts entered into both before and after the passing of FA 1995 (1 May 1995).

[2] Words in sub-para (1) substituted by FA 1995 s 34, Sch 5 para 7.

[3] Words in sub-paras (2), (3)(*b*) substituted by FA 1995 s 34, Sch 5 para 7.

[4] This para repealed by the Finance Act 2009, Section 96 and Schedule 48 (Appointed Day, Savings and Consequential Amendments) Order, SI 2009/3054 art 3, Schedule para 6(*a*) with effect from 1 April 2010.

3—*(1) Every person who is concerned (in whatever capacity) in [an insurance business]*[1] *shall upon demand made by an authorised person produce or cause to be produced for inspection by that person any documents relating to [contracts of insurance]*[2] *entered into in the course of the business.*

(2) Every person who makes arrangements for other persons to enter into any [contract of insurance][3] *shall upon demand made by an authorised person produce or cause to be produced for inspection by that person any documents relating to that contract.*

(3) Every person who—

(*a*) is concerned in a business that is not [an insurance business][1], and

(*b*) has been involved in the entry into any [contract of insurance][3] providing cover for any matter associated with the business,

shall upon demand made by an authorised person produce or cause to be produced for inspection by that person any documents relating to that contract.

(4) Where, by virtue of any of sub-paragraphs (1) to (3) above, an authorised person has power to require the production of any documents from any person, he shall have the like power to require production of the documents concerned from any other person who appears to the authorised person to be in possession of them; but where any such other person claims a lien on any document produced by him, the production shall be without prejudice to the lien.

(5) The documents mentioned in sub-paragraphs (1) to (4) above shall be produced—

(*a*) at the principal place of business of the person on whom the demand is made or at such other place as the authorised person may reasonably require, and

(*b*) at such time as the authorised person may reasonably require.

(6) An authorised person may take copies of, or make extracts from, any document produced under any of sub-paragraphs (1) to (4) above.

(7) If it appears to him to be necessary to do so, an authorised person may, at a reasonable time and for a reasonable period, remove any document produced under any of sub-paragraphs (1) to (4) above and shall, on request, provide a receipt for any document so removed; and where a lien is claimed on a document produced under sub-paragraph (4) above the removal of the document under this sub-paragraph shall not be regarded as breaking the lien.

(8) Where a document removed by an authorised person under sub-paragraph (7) above is reasonably required for the proper conduct of a business he shall, as soon as practicable, provide a copy of the document, free of charge, to the person by whom it was produced or caused to be produced.

(9) Where any documents removed under the powers conferred by this paragraph are lost or damaged the Commissioners shall be liable to compensate their owner for any expenses reasonably incurred by him in replacing or repairing the documents.[4]

Amendments—[1] Words in sub-paras (1), (3)(*a*) substituted by FA 1995 s 34, Sch 5 para 7 with effect for contracts entered into both before and after the passing of FA 1995 (1 May 1995).

[2] Words in sub-para (1) substituted by FA 1995 s 34, Sch 5 para 7.

[3] Words in sub-paras (2), (3)(*b*) substituted by FA 1995 s 34, Sch 5 para 7.

[4] This para repealed by the Finance Act 2009, Section 96 and Schedule 48 (Appointed Day, Savings and Consequential Amendments) Order, SI 2009/3054 art 3, Schedule para 6(*a*) with effect from 1 April 2010.

PART II
POWERS

Commentary—*De Voil Indirect Tax Service* **V18.181–185**.

Entry, arrest, etc

4—*(1) For the purpose of exercising any powers under this Part of this Act an authorised person may at any reasonable time enter premises used in connection with the carrying on of a business.*[2]

(2)–(7) . . . [1],

Cross references—Criminal Justice and Police Act 2001 s 50, Sch 1 Pt 1 (s 50 of that Act which provides additional powers of seizure from premises applies to the power of seizure conferred under sub-para (3) above; for the relevant provisions of the Criminal Justice and Police Act 2001, see the *VAT* section of this publication ante).

Amendments—[1] Sub-paras (2)–(7) repealed by FA 2007 ss 84, 114, Sch 22 paras 3, 9, Sch 27 Pt 5(1) with effect from 1 December 2007 (by virtue of SI 2007/3166 art 3(*a*)).

[2] Sub-para (1) repealed by the Finance Act 2009, Section 96 and Schedule 48 (Appointed Day, Savings and Consequential Amendments) Order, SI 2009/3054 art 3, Schedule para 6(*a*) with effect from 1 April 2010.

[Order for access to recorded information etc

4A—(1) Where, on an application by an authorised person, a justice of the peace or, in Scotland, a justice (within the meaning of section 462 of the Criminal Procedure (Scotland) Act 1975) is satisfied that there are reasonable grounds for believing—

(*a*) that an offence in connection with tax is being, has been or is about to be committed, and

(*b*) that any recorded information (including any document of any nature whatsoever) which may be required as evidence for the purpose of any proceedings in respect of such an offence is in the possession of any person,

he may make an order under this paragraph.

(2) An order under this paragraph is an order that the person who appears to the justice to be in possession of the recorded information to which the application relates shall—

(*a*) give an authorised person access to it, and

(*b*) permit an authorised person to remove and take away any of it which he reasonably considers necessary,

not later than the end of the period of 7 days beginning on the date of the order or the end of such longer period as the order may specify.

(3) The reference in sub-paragraph (2)(*a*) above to giving an authorised person access to the recorded information to which the application relates includes a reference to permitting the authorised person to take copies of it or to make extracts from it.

(4) Where the recorded information consists of information [stored in any electronic form][2], an order under this paragraph shall have effect as an order to produce the information in a form in which it is visible and legible [or from which it can readily be produced in a visible and legible form][2] and, if the authorised person wishes to remove it, in a form in which it can be removed.

(5) This paragraph is without prejudice to paragraphs 3 and 4 above.][1]

Amendments—[1] This para inserted by FA 1995 s 34, Sch 5 para 8(1).

[2] Words in sub-para (4) substituted and inserted by the Criminal Justice and Police Act 2001 ss 70, 138, Sch 2 Pt 2 para 13 with effect from 1 April 2003 (by virtue of SI 2003/708).

Removal of documents etc

5—(1) An authorised person who removes anything in the exercise of a power conferred by or under paragraph 4 [or 4A][1] above shall, if so requested by a person showing himself—

(*a*) to be the occupier of premises from which it was removed, or

(*b*) to have had custody or control of it immediately before the removal,

provide that person with a record of what he removed.

(2) The authorised person shall provide the record within a reasonable time from the making of the request for it.

(3) Subject to sub-paragraph (7) below, if a request for permission to be allowed access to anything which—

(*a*) has been removed by an authorised person, and

(*b*) is retained by the Commissioners for the purposes of investigating an offence,

is made to the officer in overall charge of the investigation by a person who had custody or control of the thing immediately before it was so removed or by someone acting on behalf of such a person, the officer shall allow the person who made the request access to it under the supervision of an authorised person.

(4) Subject to sub-paragraph (7) below, if a request for a photograph or copy of any such thing is made to the officer in overall charge of the investigation by a person who had custody or control of the thing immediately before it was so removed, or by someone acting on behalf of such a person, the officer shall—

(*a*) allow the person who made the request access to it under the supervision of an authorised person for the purpose of photographing it or copying it, or

(*b*) photograph or copy it, or cause it to be photographed or copied.

(5) Subject to sub-paragraph (7) below, where anything is photographed or copied under sub-paragraph (4)(*b*) above the officer shall supply the photograph or copy, or cause it to be supplied, to the person who made the request.

(6) The photograph or copy shall be supplied within a reasonable time from the making of the request.

(7) There is no duty under this paragraph to allow access to, or to supply a photograph or copy of, anything if the officer in overall charge of the investigation for the purposes of which it was removed has reasonable grounds for believing that to do so would prejudice—

(*a*) that investigation,

(*b*) the investigation of an offence other than the offence for the purposes of the investigation of which the thing was removed, or (*c*) any criminal proceedings which may be brought as a result of the investigation of which he is in charge or any such investigation as is mentioned in paragraph (*b*) above.

(8) Any reference in this paragraph to the officer in overall charge of the investigation is a reference to the person whose name and address are endorsed on the warrant concerned as being the officer so in charge.

Amendments—[1] Words in sub-para (1) inserted by FA 1995 s 34, Sch 5 para 8(2).

6—(1) Where, on an application made as mentioned in sub-paragraph (2) below, the appropriate judicial authority is satisfied that a person has failed to comply with a requirement imposed by paragraph 5 above, the authority may order that person to comply with the requirement within such time and in such manner as may be specified in the order.

(2) An application under sub-paragraph (1) above shall be made—

(*a*) in the case of a failure to comply with any of the requirements imposed by sub-paragraphs (1) and (2) of paragraph 5 above, by the occupier of the premises from which the thing in question was removed or by the person who had custody or control of it immediately before it was so removed, and

(*b*) in any other case, by the person who had such custody or control.

(3) In this paragraph "the appropriate judicial authority" means—

(*a*) in England and Wales, a magistrates' court;

(*b*) in Scotland, the sheriff;

(*c*) in Northern Ireland, a court of summary jurisdiction, as defined in Article 2(2)(*a*) of the Magistrates' Court (Northern Ireland) Order 1981.

(4) In England and Wales and Northern Ireland, an application for an order under this paragraph shall be made by way of complaint; and sections 21 and 42(2) of the Interpretation Act (Northern Ireland) 1954 shall apply as if any reference in those provisions to any enactment included a reference to this paragraph.

PART III
RECOVERY

Commentary—*De Voil Indirect Tax Service* **V18.174**.

Recovery of tax etc

7—(1) Tax due from any person shall be recoverable as a debt due to the Crown.

(2) (*Amends* Insolvency Act 1986 s 386(1) and *inserts* Insolvency Act 1986 Sch 6 para 3A).

(3) In the Bankruptcy (Scotland) Act 1985 Schedule 3 (preferred debts) shall be amended as mentioned in sub-paragraphs (4) and (5) below.

(4) (*Inserts* Bankruptcy (Scotland) Act 1985 Sch 3 para 2(1A)).

(5) (*Inserts* Bankruptcy (Scotland) Act 1985 Sch 3 para 8A).

(6) (*Amends* Insolvency (Northern Ireland) Order, SI 1989/2405 art 346(1) and *inserts* Insolvency (Northern Ireland) Order, SI 1989/2405 Sch 4 para 3A).

(7)–(12) . . . [1]

Amendments—[1] Sub-paras (7)–(12) repealed by FA 1997 Sch 18 Part V(2) with effect from 1 July 1997 (See SI 1997/1433). Sub-paras (8)–(12) were previously substituted for sub-para (8) by FA 1995 s 34, Sch 5 para 9.

Recovery of overpaid tax

8—(1) Where a person has paid an amount to the Commissioners by way of tax which was not tax due to them, they shall be liable to repay the amount to him.

(2) The Commissioners shall only be liable to repay an amount under this paragraph on a claim being made for the purpose.

(3) It shall be a defence, in relation to a claim under this paragraph, that repayment of an amount would unjustly enrich the claimant.

[(4) The Commissioners shall not be liable, on a claim made under this paragraph, to repay any amount paid to them more than [4 years][2] before the making of the claim.][1]

(5) . . . [1]

(6) A claim under this paragraph shall be made in such form and manner and shall be supported by such documentary evidence as may be prescribed by regulations.

(7) Except as provided by this paragraph, the Commissioners shall not be liable to repay an amount paid to them by way of tax by virtue of the fact that it was not tax due to them.

Regulations—Insurance Premium Tax Regulations, SI 1994/1774.

Cross reference—See Insurance Premium Tax Regulations, SI 1994/1774 reg 14 (claims for overpaid tax: form of claim).
FA 1997 Sch 5 Part I (unjust enrichment).
FA 1997 Sch 5 para 14 (assessment of excessive repayment).

Amendments—[1] Sub-para (4) substituted for sub-paras (4) and (5) by FA 1997 s 50, Sch para 5(2) with effect from 19 March 1997.

[2] In sub-para (4) words substituted for words "three years" by FA 2009 s 99, Sch 51 paras 1, 2 with effect from 1 April 2010 (by virtue of SI 2010/867 art 2(1)). However, this amendment is disregarded where claims made under this para are for the repayment of amounts paid to the Commissioners on or before 31 March 2007 (SI 2010/867 art 3).

PART IV
PENALTIES

Commentary—*De Voil Indirect Tax Service* **V18.161–165**.

Criminal offences

9—(1) A person is guilty of an offence if—

(*a*) being a registrable person, he is knowingly concerned in, or in the taking of steps with a view to, the fraudulent evasion of tax by him or another registrable person, or

(*b*) not being a registrable person, he is knowingly concerned in, or in the taking of steps with a view to, the fraudulent evasion of tax by a registrable person.

(2) Any reference in sub-paragraph (1) above to the evasion of tax includes a reference to the obtaining of a payment under regulations under section 55(3)(*c*) or (*d*) or (*f*) of this Act.

(3) A person is guilty of an offence if with the requisite intent—

(*a*) he produces, furnishes or sends, or causes to be produced, furnished or sent, for the purposes of this Part of this Act any document which is false in a material particular, or

(*b*) he otherwise makes use for those purposes of such a document;

and the requisite intent is intent to deceive or to secure that a machine will respond to the document as if it were a true document.

(4) A person is guilty of an offence if in furnishing any information for the purposes of this Part of this Act he makes a statement which he knows to be false in a material particular or recklessly makes a statement which is false in a material particular.

(5) A person is guilty of an offence by virtue of this sub-paragraph if his conduct during any specified period must have involved the commission by him of one or more offences under the preceding provisions of this paragraph; and the preceding provisions of this sub-paragraph apply whether or not the particulars of that offence or those offences are known.

(6) A person is guilty of an offence if—

(*a*) he enters into a taxable insurance contract, or

(*b*) he makes arrangements for other persons to enter into a taxable insurance contract,

with reason to believe that tax in respect of the contract will be evaded.

(7) A person is guilty of an offence if he enters into taxable insurance contracts without giving security (or further security) he has been required to give under paragraph 24 below.

Criminal penalties

10—(1) A person guilty of an offence under paragraph 9(1) above shall be liable—

(*a*) on summary conviction, to a penalty of the statutory maximum or of three times the amount of the tax, whichever is the greater, or to imprisonment for a term not exceeding six months or to both;

(*b*) on conviction on indictment, to a penalty of any amount or to imprisonment for a term not exceeding seven years or to both.

(2) The reference in sub-paragraph (1) above to the amount of the tax shall be construed, in relation to tax itself or a payment falling within paragraph 9(2) above, as a reference to the aggregate of—

(*a*) the amount (if any) falsely claimed by way of credit, and

(*b*) the amount (if any) by which the gross amount of tax was falsely understated.

(3) A person guilty of an offence under paragraph 9(3) or (4) above shall be liable—

(*a*) on summary conviction, to a penalty of the statutory maximum or, where sub-paragraph (4) below applies, to the alternative penalty there specified if it is greater, or to imprisonment for a term not exceeding six months or to both;

(*b*) on conviction on indictment, to a penalty of any amount or to imprisonment for a term not exceeding seven years or to both.

(4) In a case where—

(*a*) the document referred to in paragraph 9(3) above is a return required under this Part of this Act, or

(*b*) the information referred to in paragraph 9(4) above is contained in or otherwise relevant to such a return,

the alternative penalty is a penalty equal to three times the aggregate of the amount (if any) falsely claimed by way of credit and the amount (if any) by which the gross amount of tax was understated.

(5) A person guilty of an offence under paragraph 9(5) above shall be liable—

(*a*) on summary conviction, to a penalty of the statutory maximum or (if greater) three times the amount of any tax that was or was intended to be evaded by his conduct, or to imprisonment for a term not exceeding six months or to both;

(*b*) on conviction on indictment, to a penalty of any amount or to imprisonment for a term not exceeding seven years or to both;

and paragraph 9(2) and sub-paragraph (2) above shall apply for the purposes of this sub-paragraph as they apply respectively for the purposes of paragraph 9(1) and sub-paragraph (1) above.

(6) A person guilty of an offence under paragraph 9(6) above shall be liable on summary conviction to a penalty of level 5 on the standard scale or three times the amount of the tax, whichever is the greater.

(7) A person guilty of an offence under paragraph 9(7) above shall be liable on summary conviction to a penalty of level 5 on the standard scale.

(8) In this paragraph—

(*a*) "credit" means credit for which provision is made by regulations under section 55 of this Act;

(*b*) "the gross amount of tax" means the total amount of tax due before taking into account any deduction for which provision is made by regulations under section 55(3) of this Act.

Criminal proceedings etc

11 Sections 145 to 155 of the Customs and Excise Management Act 1979 (proceedings for offences, mitigation of penalties and certain other matters) shall apply in relation to offences under paragraph 9 above and penalties imposed under paragraph 10 above as they apply in relation to offences and penalties under the customs and excise Acts as defined in that Act.

Notes—For CEMA 1979 ss 145–155, see VAT division.
Level 5 on the standard scale, and the statutory maximum is £5,000, with effect from 1 October 1992.

Civil penalties

12—*(1) In a case where—*

(a) for the purpose of evading tax, a registrable person does any act or omits to take any action, and

(b) his conduct involves dishonesty (whether or not it is such as to give rise to criminal liability),

he shall be liable to a penalty equal to the amount of tax evaded, or (as the case may be) sought to be evaded, by his conduct; but this is subject to sub-paragraph (7) below.

(2) The reference in sub-paragraph (1)(a) above to evading tax includes a reference to obtaining a payment under regulations under section 55(3)(c) or (d) or (f) of this Act in circumstances where the person concerned is not entitled to the sum.

(3) The reference in sub-paragraph (1) above to the amount of tax evaded or sought to be evaded is a reference to the aggregate of—

(a) the amount (if any) falsely claimed by way of credit, and

(b) the amount (if any) by which the gross amount of tax was falsely understated.

(4) In this paragraph—

(a) "credit" means credit for which provision is made by regulations under section 55 of this Act;

(b) "the gross amount of tax" means the total amount of tax due before taking into account any deduction for which provision is made by regulations under section 55(3) of this Act.

(5) Statements made or documents produced by or on behalf of a person shall not be inadmissible in any such proceedings as are mentioned in sub-paragraph (6) below by reason only that it has been drawn to his attention—

(a) that, in relation to tax, the Commissioners may assess an amount due by way of a civil penalty instead of instituting criminal proceedings and, though no undertaking can be given as to whether the Commissioners will make such an assessment in the case of any person, it is their practice to be influenced by the fact that a person has made a full confession of any dishonest conduct to which he has been a party and has given full facilities for investigation, and

(b) that the Commissioners or, on appeal, an appeal tribunal have power under paragraph 13 below to reduce a penalty under this paragraph,

and that he was or may have been induced thereby to make the statements or produce the documents.

(6) The proceedings referred to in sub-paragraph (5) above are—

(a) any criminal proceedings against the person concerned in respect of any offence in connection with or in relation to tax, and

(b) any proceedings against him for the recovery of any sum due from him in connection with or in relation to tax.

IPT

(7) Where, by reason of conduct falling within sub-paragraph (1) above, a person is convicted of an offence (whether under this Part of this Act or otherwise) that conduct shall not also give rise to liability to a penalty under this paragraph.[1]

Amendments—[1] This para repealed by FA 2008 s 122, Sch 40 para 21(*d*) with effect from 1 April 2009 (by virtue of SI 2009/571 art 2).

This para repealed only in so far as it relates to conduct involving dishonesty which relates to—

(a) an inaccuracy in a document, or

(b) a failure to notify HMRC of an under-assessment by HMRC (SI 2009/571 art 6).

13—*(1) Where a person is liable to a penalty under paragraph 12 above the Commissioners or, on appeal, an appeal tribunal may reduce the penalty to such amount (including nil) as they think proper.*

(2) In the case of a penalty reduced by the Commissioners under sub-paragraph (1) above an appeal tribunal, on an appeal relating to the penalty, may cancel the whole or any part of the reduction made by the Commissioners.

(3) None of the matters specified in sub-paragraph (4) below shall be matters which the Commissioners or any appeal tribunal shall be entitled to take into account in exercising their powers under this paragraph.

(4) Those matters are—

(a) the insufficiency of the funds available to any person for paying any tax due or for paying the amount of the penalty;

(b) the fact that there has, in the case in question or in that case taken with any other cases, been no or no significant loss of tax.[1]

Amendments—[1] This para repealed by FA 2008 s 122, Sch 40 para 21(*d*) with effect from 1 April 2009 (by virtue of SI 2009/571 art 2).

This para repealed only in so far as it relates to conduct involving dishonesty which relates to—

(a) an inaccuracy in a document, or

(b) a failure to notify HMRC of an under-assessment by HMRC (SI 2009/517 art 6).

14—(1) A person who fails to comply with section 53(2) [or 53AA (3)][1] of this Act shall be liable to a penalty equal to 5 per cent of the relevant tax or, if it is greater or the circumstances are such that there is no relevant tax, to a penalty of £250; but this is subject to sub-paragraphs (3) and (4) below.

(2) In sub-paragraph (1) above "relevant tax" means the tax (if any) for which the person concerned is liable for the period which—

(*a*) begins on the date with effect from which he is, in accordance with section 53 [or, as the case may be, section 53AA][2] of this Act, required to be registered, and

(*b*) ends on the date on which the Commissioners received notification of his liability to be registered.

(3) Conduct falling within sub-paragraph (1) above shall not give rise to liability to a penalty under this paragraph if the person concerned satisfies the Commissioners or, on appeal, an appeal tribunal that there is a reasonable excuse for his conduct.

(4) Where, by reason of conduct falling within sub-paragraph (1) above—

(*a*) a person is convicted of an offence (whether under this Part of this Act or otherwise), or

(*b*) a person is assessed to a penalty under paragraph 12 above [or to a penalty for a deliberate inaccuracy under Schedule 24 to the Finance Act 2007 (penalties for errors)][3],

that conduct shall not also give rise to liability to a penalty under this paragraph.

(5) If it appears to the Treasury that there has been a change in the value of money since the passing of this Act or, as the case may be, the last occasion when the power conferred by this sub-paragraph was exercised, they may by order substitute for the sum for the time being specified in sub-paragraph (1) above such other sum as appears to them to be justified by the change.

(6) An order under sub-paragraph (5) above shall not apply in relation to a failure which ended on or before the date on which the order comes into force.

Amendments—[1] Words in sub-s (1) inserted by FA 1997 s 27 (11).

[2] Words in sub-s (2)(*a*) inserted by FA 1997 s 27 (11) with effect from 19 March 1997.

[3] Words in sub-s (4)(*b*) inserted by the Finance Act 2008, Schedule 40 (Appointed Day, Transitional Provisions and Consequential Amendments) Order, SI 2009/571 art 8, Sch 1 para 11(1), (2) with effect from 1 April 2009.

Prospective amendments—This para to be repealed by FA 2008 s 123, Sch 41 para 25 with effect from 1 April 2010 (by virtue of SI 2009/511 art 2).

15—(1) This paragraph applies if a person fails to comply with—

(*a*) a requirement imposed by regulations made under section 54 of this Act to pay the tax due in respect of any period within the time required by the regulations, or

(*b*) a requirement imposed by regulations made under that section to furnish a return in respect of any period within the time required by the regulations;

and sub-paragraphs (2) and (3) below shall have effect subject to sub-paragraphs (5) and (6) below and paragraph 25(7) below.

(2) The person shall be liable to a penalty equal to 5 per cent of the tax due or, if it is greater, to a penalty of £250.
(3) The person—

(*a*) shall be liable, in addition to an initial penalty under sub-paragraph (2) above, to a penalty of £20 for every relevant day when he fails to pay the tax or furnish the return, but

(*b*) shall not in respect of the continuation of the failure be liable to further penalties under sub-paragraph (2) above;

and a relevant day is any day falling after the time within which the tax is required to be paid or the return is required to be furnished.
(4) For the purposes of sub-paragraph (2) above the tax due—

(*a*) shall, if the person concerned has furnished a return, be taken to be the tax shown in the return as that for which he is accountable in respect of the period in question, and

(*b*) shall, in any other case, be taken to be such tax as has been assessed for that period and notified to him under section 56(1) of this Act.

(5) A failure falling within sub-paragraph (1) or (3) above shall not give rise to liability to a penalty under this paragraph if the person concerned satisfies the Commissioners or, on appeal, an appeal tribunal that there is a reasonable excuse for the failure.
(6) Where, by reason of a failure falling within sub-paragraph (1) or (3) above—

(*a*) a person is convicted of an offence (whether under this Part of this Act or otherwise), or

(*b*) a person is assessed to a penalty under paragraph 12 above [or to a penalty for a deliberate inaccuracy under Schedule 24 to the Finance Act 2007 (penalties for errors)][1],

that failure shall not also give rise to liability to a penalty under this paragraph.
(7) If it appears to the Treasury that there has been a change in the value of money since the passing of this Act or, as the case may be, the last occasion when the power conferred by this sub-paragraph was exercised, they may by order substitute for the sums for the time being specified in sub-paragraphs (2) and (3) above such other sums as appear to them to be justified by the change.
(8) An order under sub-paragraph (7) above shall not apply in relation to a failure which began before the date on which the order comes into force.

Cross reference—FA 2009 s 108 (suspension of penalties during currency of agreement for deferred payment).
Amendments—[1] Words in sub-s (6)(*b*) inserted by the Finance Act 2008, Schedule 40 (Appointed Day, Transitional Provisions and Consequential Amendments) Order, SI 2009/571 art 8, Sch 1 para 11(1), (3) with effect from 1 April 2009.

16—(1) This paragraph applies where—

(*a*) by virtue of regulations made under section 65 of this Act a liability notice (within the meaning of that section) is served on an insured person,

(*b*) by virtue of such regulations that person is liable to pay an amount of tax which has been assessed in accordance with the regulations, and

(*c*) that tax is not paid within the time required by the regulations;

and sub-paragraphs (2) and (3) below shall have effect subject to sub-paragraphs (4) and (5) below and paragraph 25(7) below.
(2) The person shall be liable to a penalty equal to 5 per cent of the tax assessed as mentioned in sub-paragraph (1) above or, if it is greater, to a penalty of £250.
(3) The person—

(*a*) shall be liable, in addition to an initial penalty under sub-paragraph (2) above, to a penalty of £20 for every relevant day when the tax is unpaid, but

(*b*) shall not in respect of the continuation of the non-payment of the tax be liable to further penalties under sub-paragraph (2) above;

and a relevant day is any day falling after the time within which the tax is required to be paid.
(4) A person shall not be liable to a penalty by virtue of this paragraph if he satisfies the Commissioners or, on appeal, an appeal tribunal that he took all reasonable steps to ensure that the tax mentioned in sub-paragraph (1)(*b*) above was paid within the time required by the regulations.
(5) Where, by reason of a failure to pay tax, a person is convicted of an offence (whether under this Part of this Act or otherwise), that failure shall not also give rise to liability to a penalty under this paragraph.
(6) If it appears to the Treasury that there has been a change in the value of money since the passing of this Act or, as the case may be, the last occasion when the power conferred by this sub-paragraph was exercised, they may by order substitute for the sums for the time being specified in sub-paragraphs (2) and (3) above such other sums as appear to them to be justified by the change.
(7) An order under sub-paragraph (6) above shall not apply in relation to any failure to pay tax that was required to be paid before the date on which the order comes into force.

17—(1) If a person fails to comply with—

(*a*) section 53(3) of this Act,

(*b*) *any provision of paragraph 2 or 3 above, or*[2]

(*c*) a requirement imposed by any regulations made under this Part of this Act, other than a requirement falling within sub-paragraph (2) below,

he shall be liable to a penalty of £250; but this is subject to sub-paragraphs (3) and (4) below.

(2) A requirement falls within this sub-paragraph if it is—

(*a*) a requirement imposed by regulations made under section 54 of this Act to pay the tax due in respect of any period within the time required by the regulations,

(*b*) a requirement imposed by regulations made under that section to furnish a return in respect of any period within the time required by the regulations,

(*c*) a requirement imposed by regulations made under section 65 of this Act to pay tax within the time required by the regulations, or

(*d*) a requirement specified for the purposes of this sub-paragraph by regulations.

(3) A failure falling within sub-paragraph (1) above shall not give rise to liability to a penalty under this paragraph if the person concerned satisfies the Commissioners or, on appeal, an appeal tribunal that there is a reasonable excuse for the failure.

(4) Where by reason of a failure falling within sub-paragraph (1) above—

(*a*) a person is convicted of an offence (whether under this Part of this Act or otherwise), or

(*b*) a person is assessed to a penalty under paragraph 12 above [or to a penalty for a deliberate inaccuracy under Schedule 24 to the Finance Act 2007 (penalties for errors)][1],

that failure shall not also give rise to liability to a penalty under this paragraph.

(5) If it appears to the Treasury that there has been a change in the value of money since the passing of this Act or, as the case may be, the last occasion when the power conferred by this sub-paragraph was exercised, they may by order substitute for the sum for the time being specified in sub-paragraph (1) above such other sum as appears to them to be justified by the change.

(6) An order under sub-paragraph (5) above shall not apply in relation to a failure which began before the date on which the order comes into force.

Amendments—[1] Words in sub-s (4)(*b*) inserted by the Finance Act 2008, Schedule 40 (Appointed Day, Transitional Provisions and Consequential Amendments) Order, SI 2009/571 art 8, Sch 1 para 11(1), (3) with effect from 1 April 2009.

[2] Sub-para (1)(*b*) repealed by the Finance Act 2009, Section 96 and Schedule 48 (Appointed Day, Savings and Consequential Amendments) Order, SI 2009/3054 art 3, Schedule para 6(*b*) with effect from 1 April 2010. Note, word "or" following sub-para (1)(*b*) is not repealed. Note that, where HMRC have requested information or documents before 1 April 2010, sub-para (1)(*b*) continues to have effect on and after that date (SI 2009/3054 art 6(*a*)).

18 . . . [1]

Amendments—[1] Para 18 repealed by FA 2008 s 142 with effect from 21 July 2008.

Prospective amendments—Para 18A to be inserted by the Tribunals, Courts and Enforcement Act 2007 s 62(3), Sch 13 paras 113, 116(1), (2) with effect from a date to be appointed. Para 18A to be repealed by FA 2008 s 129, Sch 43 para 3 with effect from such day as the Commissioners may by statutory instrument appoint. Para 18A as inserted to read—

"18A—(1) This paragraph applies where an enforcement agent acting under the power conferred by section 51(A1) of the Finance Act 1997 (power to use the procedure in Schedule 12 to the Tribunals, Courts and Enforcement Act 2007) has entered into a controlled goods agreement with the person against whom the power is exercisable ("the person in default").

(2) In this paragraph, "controlled goods agreement" has the meaning given by paragraph 13(4) of that Schedule.

(3) Subject to sub-paragraph (4) below, if the person in default removes or disposes of goods (or permits their removal or disposal) in breach of the controlled goods agreement, he is liable to a penalty equal to half of the tax or other amount recoverable under section 51(A1) of the Finance Act 1997.

(4) The person in default shall not be liable to a penalty under sub-paragraph (3) above if he satisfies the Commissioners or, on appeal, an appeal tribunal, that there is a reasonable excuse for the breach in question.

(5) This paragraph extends only to England and Wales."

19—(1) This paragraph applies where—

(*a*) in accordance with regulations under [section 51 of the Finance Act 1997 (enforcement by distress)][1] above a distress is authorised to be levied on the goods and chattels of a person (a person in default) who has refused or neglected to pay any tax due from him or any amount recoverable as if it were tax due from him, and

(*b*) the person levying the distress and the person in default have entered into a walking possession agreement.

(2) For the purposes of this paragraph a walking possession agreement is an agreement under which, in consideration of the property distrained upon being allowed to remain in the custody of the person in default and of the delaying of its sale, the person in default—

(*a*) acknowledges that the property specified in the agreement is under distraint and held in walking possession, and

(*b*) undertakes that, except with the consent of the Commissioners and subject to such conditions as they may impose, he will not remove or allow the removal of any of the specified property from the premises named in the agreement.

(3) Subject to sub-paragraph (4) below, if the person in default is in breach of the undertaking contained in a walking possession agreement, he shall be liable to a penalty equal to half of the tax or other amount referred to in sub-paragraph (1)(*a*) above.
(4) The person in default shall not be liable to a penalty under sub-paragraph (3) above if he satisfies the Commissioners or, on appeal, an appeal tribunal that there is a reasonable excuse for the breach in question.
(5) This paragraph does not extend to Scotland.

Amendments—[1] The words in sub-s (1)(*a*) substituted for the words "paragraph 7(7) above" by FA 1997 s 53(5) with effect from 1 July 1997 (see SI 1997/1432).

Prospective amendments—Sub-para (5) to be substituted by the Tribunals, Courts and Enforcement Act 2007 s 50, Sch 10 para 116(1), (3) with effect from a date to be appointed. Sub-para (5) as substituted to read—

"(5) This paragraph extends only to Northern Ireland.".

20 For the purposes of paragraphs . . . [2], 15(5), 17(3) . . . [1] and 19(4) above—
(*a*) an insufficiency of funds available for paying any amount is not a reasonable excuse, and
(*b*) where reliance is placed on any other person to perform any task, neither the fact of that reliance nor any conduct of the person relied upon is a reasonable excuse.

Amendments—[1] Reference ", 18(2)" in para 20 repealed by FA 2008 s 142 with effect from 21 July 2008.
[2] Reference "14(3)" repealed by the Finance Act 2008 (Penalties for Errors and Failure to Notify etc) (Consequential Amendments) Order, SI 2010/530 art 2, Schedule paras 1, 4 with effect from 1 April 2010.

PART V
INTEREST

Commentary—*De Voil Indirect Tax Service* **V18.171–173**.

Interest on tax etc

21—(1) Where an assessment is made under any provision of section 56 of this Act, the whole of the amount assessed shall carry interest at [the rate applicable under section 197 of the Finance Act 1996][1] from the reckonable date until payment; but this is subject to sub-paragraph (2) and paragraph 25(7) below.
(2) Sub-paragraph (1) above shall not apply in relation to an assessment under section 56(1) of this Act unless at least one of the following conditions is fulfilled, namely—
(*a*) that the assessment relates to an accounting period in respect of which either a return has previously been made, or an earlier assessment has already been notified to the person concerned;
(*b*) that the assessment relates to an accounting period which exceeds three months and begins on the date with effect from which the person was, or was required to be, registered under this Part of this Act.
(3) In a case where—
(*a*) the circumstances are such that a relevant assessment could have been made, but
(*b*) before such an assessment was made the tax due or other amount concerned was paid (so that no such assessment was necessary),
the whole of the amount paid shall carry interest at [the rate applicable under section 197 of the Finance Act 1996][1] from the reckonable date until the date on which it was paid; and for the purposes of this sub-paragraph a relevant assessment is an assessment in relation to which sub-paragraph (1) above would have applied if the assessment had been made.
(4) The references in sub-paragraphs (1) and (3) above to the reckonable date shall be construed as follows—
(*a*) where the amount assessed or paid is such an amount as is referred to in subsection (2) of section 56 of this Act, the reckonable date is the seventh day after the day on which a written instruction was issued by the Commissioners directing the making of the payment of the amount which ought not to have been paid to the person concerned;
(*b*) in all other cases the reckonable date is the latest date on which (in accordance with regulations under this Part of this Act) a return is required to be made for the accounting period to which the amount assessed or paid relates;
and interest under this paragraph shall run from the reckonable date even if that date is a non-business day, within the meaning of section 92 of the Bills of Exchange Act 1882.
(5) . . . [2]
(6) Interest under this paragraph shall be paid without any deduction of income tax.

IPT

Note—The rate of interest for the purposes of this section has been prescribed as follows—

Commencement date	*Rate*	*SI No*
1 October 1994	5.5%	1994/1819
6 February 1996	6.25%	1996/166, 1997/1016
6 July 1998	9.5%	1998/1461

Cross-references—See FA 2009 s 101, Sch 54 (interest payable to HMRC).

Amendments—[1] Words in sub-paras (1) and (3) substituted for words "the prescribed rate" by FA 1996 s 197(6)(*b*), (7) with effect for periods beginning on or after 1 April 1997 (see SI 1997/1015). This para has effect in relation to interest running from before that day, as well as in relation to interest running from, or from after, that day.

[2] Sub-s (5) repealed by FA 1996 Sch 41 Pt VIII(1) with effect for periods beginning on or after 1 April 1997 (see SI 1997/1105).

Interest payable by Commissioners

22—(1) Where, due to an error on the part of the Commissioners, a person—

(*a*) has paid to them by way of tax an amount which was not tax due and which they are in consequence liable to repay to him,

(*b*) has failed to claim payment of an amount to the payment of which he was entitled in pursuance of provision made under section 55(3)(*c*), (*d*) or (*f*) of this Act, or

(*c*) has suffered delay in receiving payment of an amount due to him from them in connection with tax,

then, if and to the extent that they would not be liable to do so apart from this paragraph, they shall (subject to the following provisions of this paragraph) pay interest to him on that amount for the applicable period.

[(1A) In sub-paragraph (1) above—

(*a*) the reference in paragraph (*a*) to an amount which the Commissioners are liable to repay in consequence of the making of a payment that was not due is a reference to only so much of that amount as is the subject of a claim that the Commissioners are required to satisfy or have satisfied; and

(*b*) the amounts referred to in paragraph (*c*) do not include any amount payable under this paragraph.][2]

(2) Interest under this paragraph shall be payable at [the rate applicable under section 197 of the Finance Act 1996][1].

(3) The applicable period, in a case falling within sub-paragraph (1)(*a*) above, is the period—

(*a*) beginning with the date on which the payment is received by the Commissioners, and

(*b*) ending with the date on which they authorise payment of the amount on which the interest is payable.

(4) The applicable period, in a case falling within sub-paragraph (1)(*b*) or (*c*) above, is the period—

(*a*) beginning with the date on which, apart from the error, the Commissioners might reasonably have been expected to authorise payment of the amount on which the interest is payable, and

(*b*) ending with the date on which they in fact authorise payment of that amount.

[(5) In determining the applicable period for the purposes of this paragraph there shall be left out of account any period by which the Commissioner's' authorisation of the payment of interest is delayed by the conduct of the person who claims the interest.][4]

[(5A) The reference in sub-paragraph (5) above to a period by which the Commissioner's' authorisation of the payment of interest is delayed by the conduct of the person who claims it includes, in particular, any period which is referable to—

(*a*) any unreasonable delay in the making of the claim for interest or in the making of any claim for the payment or repayment of the amount on which interest is claimed;

(*b*) any failure by that person or a person acting on his behalf or under his influence to provide the Commissioners—

(i) at or before the time of the making of a claim, or

(ii) subsequently in response to a request for information by the Commissioners,

with all the information required by them to enable the existence and amount of the claimant's entitlement to a payment or repayment, and to interest on that payment or repayment, to be determined; and

(*c*) the making, as part of or in association with either—

(i) the claim for interest, or

(ii) any claim for the payment or repayment of the amount on which interest is claimed,

of a claim to anything to which the claimant was not entitled.][4]

(6) In determining for the purposes of sub-paragraph (5A) above whether any period of delay is referable to a failure by any person to provide information in response to a request by the Commissioners, there shall be taken to be so referable, except so far as may be provided for by regulation, any period which—

(*a*) begins with the date on which the Commissioners require that person to provide information which they reasonably consider relevant to the matter to be determined; and

(*b*) ends with the earliest date on which it would be reasonable for the Commissioners to conclude—

(i) that they have received a completed answer to their request for information;

(ii) that they have received all that they need in answer to that request; or

(iii) that it is unnecessary for them to be provided with any new information in answer to that request.][4]

(7) . . .[4]

(8) The Commissioners shall only be liable to pay interest under this paragraph on a claim made in writing for that purpose.

[(9) A claim under this paragraph shall not be made more than [4 years][5] after the end of the applicable period to which it relates.][3]

[(10) References in this paragraph to the authorisation by the Commissioners of the payment of any amount include references to the discharge by way of set-off the Commissioners' liability to pay that amount.][3]

Note—The rate of interest for the purposes of this section has been prescribed as follows—

Commencement date	*Rate*	*SI No*
1 October 1994	8%	1994/1819
1 April 1997	6%	1997/1016, 1998/1461
1 April 2000	5%	2000/631

Cross references—See FA 1997 Sch 5 para 15 (assessments of overpayment of interest).
See FA 2009 s 102, Sch 54 (repayment of interest by HMRC).

Amendments—[1] Words in para (2) substituted for words "such rate as may from time to time be prescribed by order, and—

(a) any such order may prescribe different rates for different purposes;

(b) any such order shall apply to interest for periods beginning on or after the date on which the order is expressed to come into force, whether or not interest runs from before that date.",

by FA 1996 s 197(6)(*c*), (7) with effect for periods beginning on or after 1 April 1997 (see SI 1997/1015) and has effect in relation to interest running from before that day as well as in relation to interest running from, or from after, that day.

[2] Sub-para (1A) inserted by FA 1997 s 50, Sch 5 para 9(2) and deemed always to have had effect.

[3] Sub-paras (9) and (10) substituted by FA 1997 s 50, Sch 5 para 9(3), (4) and deemed always to have had effect.

[4] Sub-paras (5), (5A) and (6) substituted for sub-paras (5) to (7) by FA 1997 s 50, Sch 5 para 10 for the purposes of determining whether any period beginning on or after 19 March 1997 is left out of account.

[5] In sub-para (9) words substituted for words "three years" by FA 2009 s 99, Sch 51 paras 1, 3 with effect from 1 April 2010 (by virtue of SI 2010/867 art 2(1)). However, this amendment is disregarded where claims made under this para are for the repayment of amounts paid to the Commissioners on or before 31 March 2007 (SI 2010/867 art 4).

23— (1) In a case where—

(*a*) any interest is payable by the Commissioners to a person on a sum due to him under this Part of this Act, and

(*b*) he is a person to whom regulations under section 55 of this Act apply,

the interest shall be treated as an amount to which he is entitled by way of credit in pursuance of the regulations.

(2) Sub-paragraph (1) above shall be disregarded for the purpose of determining a person's entitlement to interest or the amount of interest to which he is entitled.

PART VI
MISCELLANEOUS

Security for tax

24 Where it appears to the Commissioners requisite to do so for the protection of the revenue they may require a registrable person, as a condition of his entering into taxable insurance contracts, to give security (or further security) of such amount and in such manner as they may determine for the payment of any tax which is or may become due from him.

Assessments to penalties etc

25—(1) Where a person is liable—

(*a*) to a penalty under any of paragraphs 12 to 19 above, or (*b*) for interest under paragraph 21 above,

the Commissioners may, subject to sub-paragraph (2) below, assess the amount due by way of penalty or interest (as the case may be) and notify it to him accordingly; and the fact that any conduct giving rise to a penalty under any of paragraphs 12 to 19 above may have ceased before an assessment is made under this paragraph shall not affect the power of the Commissioners to make such an assessment.

(2) In the case of the penalties and interest referred to in the following paragraphs of this sub-paragraph, the assessment under this paragraph shall be of an amount due in respect of the accounting period which in the paragraph concerned is referred to as the relevant period—

(*a*) in the case of a penalty under paragraph 12 above relating to the evasion of tax, the relevant period is the accounting period for which the tax evaded was due;

(*b*) in the case of a penalty under paragraph 12 above relating to the obtaining of a payment under regulations under section 55(3)(*c*) or (*d*) or (*f*) of this Act, the relevant period is the accounting period in respect of which the payment was obtained;

(*c*) in the case of interest under paragraph 21 above, the relevant period is the accounting period in respect of which the tax (or amount assessed as tax) was due.

(3) In a case where the amount of any penalty or interest falls to be calculated by reference to tax which was not paid at the time it should have been and that tax cannot be readily attributed to any one or more accounting periods, it shall be treated for the purposes of this Part of this Act as tax due for such period or periods as the Commissioners may determine to the best of their judgment and notify to the person liable for the tax and penalty or interest.

(4) Where a person is assessed under this paragraph to an amount due by way of any penalty or interest falling within sub-paragraph (2) above and is also assessed under subsection (1) or (2) of section 56 of this Act for the accounting period which is the relevant period under sub-paragraph (2) above, the assessments may be combined and notified to him as one assessment, but the amount of the penalty or interest shall be separately identified in the notice.

(5) Sub-paragraph (6) below applies in the case of—

(*a*) an amount due by way of penalty under paragraph 15 or 16 above;

(*b*) an amount due by way of interest under paragraph 21 above.

(6) Where this sub-paragraph applies in the case of an amount—

(*a*) a notice of assessment under this paragraph shall specify a date, being not later than the date of the notice, to which the aggregate amount of the penalty or, as the case may be, the amount of interest which is assessed is calculated, and

(*b*) if the penalty or interest continues to accrue after that date, a further assessment or further assessments may be made under this paragraph in respect of amounts which so accrue.

(7) If, within such period as may be notified by the Commissioners to the person liable to the penalty under paragraph 15 or 16 above or for the interest under paragraph 21 above—

(*a*) a failure falling within paragraph 15(3) above is remedied,

(*b*) the tax referred to in paragraph 16(1) above is paid, or

(*c*) the amount referred to in paragraph 21(1) above is paid,

it shall be treated for the purposes of paragraph 15, 16 or 21 above (as the case may be) as remedied or paid on the date specified as mentioned in sub-paragraph (6)(a) above.

(8) Where an amount has been assessed and notified to any person under this paragraph it shall be recoverable as if it were tax due from him unless, or except to the extent that, the assessment has subsequently been withdrawn or reduced.

(9) Subsection (8) of section 56 of this Act shall apply for the purposes of this paragraph as it applies for the purposes of that section.

Cross references—See the Recovery of Duties and Taxes Etc Due in Other Member States (Corresponding UK Claims, Procedure and Supplementary) Regulations, SI 2004/674 Sch 2 para 4 (modification of the application of this paragraph in respect of recovery of insurance premium tax interest).

Assessments: time limits

26—(1) Subject to the following provisions of this paragraph, an assessment under—

(*a*) any provision of section 56 of this Act, or

(*b*) paragraph 25 above,

shall not be made more than [4 years after the relevant event][2].

[(1A) In this paragraph "the relevant event", in relation to an assessment, means—

(*a*) the end of the accounting period concerned, or

(*b*) in the case of an assessment under paragraph 25 of an amount due by way of a penalty other than a penalty referred to in paragraph 25(2), the event giving rise to the penalty.][2]

(2) An assessment under paragraph 25 above of—

(*a*) an amount due by way of any penalty referred to in sub-paragraph (2) of that paragraph, or

(*b*) an amount due by way of interest,

may be made at any time before the expiry of the period of two years beginning with the time when the amount of tax due for the accounting period concerned has been finally determined.

(3) In relation to an assessment under paragraph 25 above, any reference in [sub-paragraph (1A)][2] or (2) above to the accounting period concerned is a reference to that period which, in the case of the penalty or interest concerned, is the relevant period referred to in sub-paragraph (2) of that paragraph.

[(4) An assessment of an amount due from a person in a case involving a loss of tax—

(*a*) brought about deliberately by the person (or by another person acting on that person's behalf), or

(*b*) attributable to a failure by the person to comply with an obligation under section 53(1) or (2) or 53AA(1) or (3), may be made at any time not more than 20 years after the relevant event.

(5) In sub-paragraph (4)(*a*) the reference to a loss brought about deliberately by the person includes a loss brought about as a result of a deliberate inaccuracy in a document given to Her Majesty's Revenue and Customs by or on behalf of that person.][2]

Amendments—[1] Words in sub-para (1) substituted for words "six years" by FA 1997 s 50, Sch 5 para 6 with effect from 19 March 1997.

[2] In sub-para (1) words substituted, sub-s (1A) inserted, in sub-para (3) words substituted for words "sub-paragraph (1)", and sub-paras (4), (5) substituted for previous sub-para (4), by FA 2009 s 99, Sch 51 para 4 with effect from 1 April 2010 (by virtue of SI 2010/867 art 2(1)). However, this amendment is to be disregarded where, for the purposes of this para the "relevant event" occurred on or before 31 March 2007 (SI 2010/867 art 5). Substituted words in sub-para (1), previously read as follows—

"three years after the end of the accounting period concerned or, in the case of an assessment under paragraph 25 above of an amount due by way of a penalty which is not a penalty referred to in sub-paragraph (2) of that paragraph, three years after the event giving rise to the penalty.".

Sub-para (4) previously read as follows—

"(4) If tax has been lost—

(*a*) as a result of conduct falling within paragraph 12(1) above or for which a person has been convicted of fraud, or

(*b*) in circumstances giving rise to liability to a penalty under paragraph 14 above,

an assessment may be made as if, in sub-paragraph (1) above, each reference to [three years] were a reference to twenty years."

Supplementary assessments

27 If, otherwise than in circumstances falling within subsection (5)(*b*) of section 56 of this Act, it appears to the Commissioners that the amount which ought to have been assessed in an assessment under any provision of that section or under paragraph 25 above exceeds the amount which was so assessed, then—

(*a*) under the like provision as that assessment was made, and

(*b*) on or before the last day on which that assessment could have been made,

the Commissioners may make a supplementary assessment of the amount of the excess and shall notify the person concerned accordingly.

Disclosure of information

28—(1) Notwithstanding any obligation not to disclose information that would otherwise apply, the Commissioners may disclose information—

(*a*) to the Secretary of State, or

(*b*) to an authorised officer of the Secretary of State,

for the purpose of assisting the Secretary of State in the performance of his duties.

(2) Notwithstanding any such obligation as is mentioned in sub-paragraph (1) above—

(*a*) the Secretary of State, or

(*b*) an authorised officer of the Secretary of State,

may disclose information to the Commissioners or to an authorised officer of the Commissioners for the purpose of assisting the Commissioners in the performance of duties in relation to tax.

(3) Information that has been disclosed to a person by virtue of this paragraph shall not be disclosed by him except—

(*a*) to another person to whom (instead of him) disclosure could by virtue of this paragraph have been made, or

(*b*) for the purpose of any proceedings connected with the operation of any provision of, or made under, any enactment in relation to insurance or to tax.

(4) References in the preceding provisions of this paragraph to an authorised officer of the Secretary of State are to any person who has been designated by the Secretary of State as a person to and by whom information may be disclosed under this paragraph.

(5) The Secretary of State shall notify the Commissioners in writing of the name of any person designated under sub-paragraph (4) above.

IPT

[28A—(1) Notwithstanding any obligation not to disclose information that would otherwise apply, the Commissioners may disclose information—

(*a*) to the Treasury, or

(*b*) to an authorised officer of the Treasury,

for the purpose of assisting the Treasury in the performance of their duties.

(2) Notwithstanding any such obligation as is mentioned in sub-paragraph (1) above—

(*a*) the Treasury, or

(*b*) an authorised officer of the Treasury,

may disclose information to the Commissioners or to an authorised officer of the Commissioners for the purpose of assisting the Commissioners in the performance of duties in relation to tax.

(3) Information that has been disclosed to a person by virtue of this paragraph shall not be disclosed by him except—

(*a*) to another person to whom (instead of him) disclosure could by virtue of this paragraph have been made, or

(*b*) for the purpose of any proceedings connected with the operation of any provision of, or made under, any enactment in relation to insurance or to tax.

(4) References in the preceding provisions of this paragraph to an authorised officer of the Treasury are to any person who has been designated by the Treasury as a person to and by whom information may be disclosed under this paragraph.

(5) The Treasury shall notify the Commissioners in writing of the name of any person designated under sub-paragraph (4) above.][1]

Amendments—[1] Inserted by SI 1997/2781 with effect from 5 January 1998.

[28B—(1) Notwithstanding any obligation not to disclose information that would otherwise apply, the Commissioners may disclose information to the Financial Services Authority ("the Authority") for the purpose of assisting the Authority in the performance of its functions.

(2) Information that has been disclosed to the Authority pursuant to this paragraph shall not be disclosed by the Authority except for the purpose of any proceedings connected with the operation of any provision of, or made under, any enactment in relation to insurance or to tax.][1]

Amendments—[1] This paragraph inserted by the Financial Services and Markets Act 2000 (Consequential Amendments) Order, SI 2004/355 art 4 with effect from 4 March 2004.

Evidence by certificate

29—(1) A certificate of the Commissioners—

(*a*) that a person was or was not at any time registered under section 53 of this Act, [or][1]

(*b*) that any return required by regulations under section 54 of this Act has not been made or had not been made at any time, . . .[1]

(*c*) . . .[1]

shall be sufficient evidence of that fact until the contrary is proved.

(2) Any document purporting to be a certificate under sub-paragraph (1) above shall be taken to be such a certificate until the contrary is proved.

Amendments—[1] Words inserted and repealed by FA 2008 s 138, Sch 44 para 5 with effect from 21 July 2008. Para (*c*) previously read as follows—

"(*c*) that any tax shown as due in a return made in pursuance of regulations made under section 54 of this Act, or in an assessment made under section 56 of this Act, has not been paid,".

Service of notices etc

30 Any notice, notification or requirement to be served on, given to or made of any person for the purposes of this Part of this Act may be served, given or made by sending it by post in a letter addressed to that person or his tax representative at the last or usual residence or place of business of that person or representative.

No deduction of penalties or interest

31 (*inserts* TA 1988 s 827(1B)).

Destination of receipts

32 *All money and securities for money collected or received for or on account of the tax shall*—

(a) if collected or received in Great Britain, be placed to the general account of the Commissioners kept at the Bank of England under section 17 of the Customs and Excise Management Act 1979;

(b) if collected or received in Northern Ireland, be paid into the Consolidated Fund of the United Kingdom in such manner as the Treasury may direct.

Amendment—Paragraph repealed by the Commissioners for Revenue and Customs Act 2005 ss 50, 52, Sch 4 para 53 and Sch 5 with effect from 18 April 2005 by virtue of the Commissioners for Revenue and Customs Act (Commencement) Order, SI 2005/1126, art 2(2).

Provisional collection of tax

33 (*amends* PCTA 1968 s 1(1)).

34—(1) In a case where—

(*a*) by virtue of a resolution having effect under the Provisional Collection of Taxes Act 1968 tax has been paid at a rate specified in the resolution, and

(*b*) by virtue of section 1(6) or (7) or 5(3) of that Act any of that tax is repayable in consequence of the restoration in relation to the premium concerned of a lower rate,

the amount repayable shall be the difference between the tax paid by reference to the actual chargeable amount at the rate specified in the resolution and the tax that would have been payable by reference to the actual chargeable amount at the lower rate.

(2) In sub-paragraph (1) above the "actual chargeable amount" means the chargeable amount by reference to which tax was paid.

(3) In a case where—

(*a*) by virtue of a resolution having effect under the Provisional Collection of Taxes Act 1968 tax is chargeable at a rate specified in the resolution, but

(*b*) before the tax is paid it ceases to be chargeable at that rate in consequence of the restoration in relation to the premium concerned of a lower rate,

the tax chargeable at the lower rate shall be charged by reference to the same chargeable amount as that by reference to which tax would have been chargeable at the rate specified in the resolution.

Adjustment of contracts

35—(1) Where, after the making of a contract of insurance and before a given premium is received by the insurer under the contract, there is a change in the tax chargeable on the receipt of the premium, then, unless the contract otherwise provided, there shall be added to or deducted from the amount payable as the premium an amount equal to the difference between—

(*a*) the tax chargeable had the change not been made, and

(*b*) the tax in fact chargeable.

(2) References in sub-paragraph (1) above to a change in the tax chargeable include references to a change to or from no tax being chargeable.

(3) Where this paragraph applies, the amount of the premium shall not be treated as altered for the purposes of calculating tax.

[SCHEDULE 7A

INSURANCE PREMIUM TAX: CONTRACTS THAT ARE NOT TAXABLE][1]

Section 70

Commentary—*De Voil Indirect Tax Service* **V18.103.**

Amendments—This Schedule inserted by the Insurance Premium Tax (Taxable Insurance Contracts) Order, SI 1994/1698 arts 1, 5 with effect from 1 October 1994.

PART I
DESCRIPTIONS OF CONTRACT

Contracts of reinsurance

1 A contract falls within this paragraph if it is a contract of reinsurance

Contracts constituting long term business

2—(1) [Subject to sub-paragraph (3) below][1] a contract falls within this paragraph [if it is exclusively a contract of long-term insurance.][2]

[(2) In deciding whether a contract is exclusively a contract of long-term insurance, as is mentioned in sub-paragraph (1) above, where—

(*a*) the contract includes cover for risks relating to accident or sickness;

(*b*) the contract contains related and subsidiary provisions such that it might also be regarded as a contract of general insurance, but is treated as a contract of long-term insurance for the purposes of any relevant order made under section 22 of the Financial Services and Markets Act 2000; and

(*c*) the contract was not entered into after 30th November 1993,

the inclusion of such cover shall be ignored.][2]

[(3) A contract which would otherwise fall within this paragraph does not do so if it is for medical insurance.

(4) Subject to sub-paragraph (5) below, for the purposes of this paragraph a contract is a contract for medical insurance if it provides one or more of the following benefits, whether or not their provision is subject to conditions or limitations—

(*a*) medical, dental or optical, consultation, diagnosis or treatment;

(*b*) alternative or complementary medical treatment or therapy;

(*c*) convalescent care;

(*d*) goods or services related to any of the above;

(*e*) payment or reimbursement of, or a grant towards, the whole or part of the cost of any of the above;

(*f*) payment of a specified sum for optical, dental or medical appointments;

(*g*) payment of a specified sum for each specified period of treatment as a hospital in-patient;

(*h*) payment of a specified sum for each specified period of convalescent care; or

(*i*) payment of a specified sum, except one to which sub-paragraph (6) below applies, when a person is diagnosed as requiring or has undergone a specified medical procedure.

(5) A benefit which would apart from this sub-paragraph fall within sub-paragraph (4) above shall not do so if, before he can become entitled to the benefit, the insured is required—

(*a*) to be suffering from a disability which so impairs his ability to carry out normal activities of daily living that he requires long term care, supervision or assistance; and

(*b*) to have been suffering from the disability for a continuous period of not less than 4 weeks.

(6) This sub-paragraph applies to a payment of a specified sum if the contract under which it is payable provides that only one such payment in relation to each specified medical procedure will be made in respect of each person in relation to whom benefit is payable under the contract.][1]

Amendments—[1] Words in sub-para (1) above and sub-paras (3)–(6) above inserted by the Insurance Premium Tax (Taxable Insurance Contracts) Order, SI 1997/1627 in relation to premiums received or treated as received on or after 1 October 1997.
[2] Words in sub-para (1) substituted, and sub-para (2) substituted, by the Financial Services and Markets Act 2000 (Consequential Amendments and Repeals) Order, SI 2001/3649 art 346(1)–(3) with effect from 1 December 2001.

Contracts relating to motor vehicles for use by handicapped persons

3—(1) A contract falls within this paragraph if it relates only to a motor vehicle and the conditions mentioned in sub-paragraph (2) below are satisfied.

(2) The conditions referred to in sub-paragraph (1) above are that—

(*a*) the vehicle is used, or intended for use, by a handicapped person in receipt of a disability living allowance by virtue of entitlement to the mobility component or of a mobility supplement;

(*b*) the insured lets such vehicles on hire to such persons in the course of a business consisting predominantly of the provision of motor vehicles to such persons; and

(*c*) the insured does not in the course of the business let such vehicles on hire to such persons on terms other than qualifying terms.

(3) For the purposes of sub-paragraph (2)(*c*) above a vehicle is let on qualifying terms to a person (the lessee) if the consideration for the letting consists wholly or partly of sums paid to the insured by—

[(*a*) the Department for Work and Pensions;][1]

(*b*) the Department of Health and Social Services for Northern Ireland; or

(*c*) the Ministry of Defence,

on behalf of the lessee in respect of the disability living allowance or mobility supplement to which the lessee is entitled.

(4) For the purposes of this paragraph—

(*a*) "handicapped" means chronically sick or disabled;

(*b*) "disability living allowance" means a disability living allowance within the meaning of section 71 of the Social Security Contributions and Benefits Act 1992 or section 71 of the Social Security Contributions and Benefits (Northern Ireland) Act 1992;

(*c*) "mobility supplement" means a mobility supplement within the meaning of article 26A of the Naval, Military and Air Forces etc (Disablement and Death) Service Pensions Order 1983, article 25A of the Personal Injuries (Civilians) Scheme 1983, article 3 of the Motor Vehicles (Exemption from Vehicles Excise Duty) Order 1985 or article 3 of the Motor Vehicles (Exemption from Vehicles Excise Duty) (Northern Ireland) Order 1985.

Amendments—[1] Sub-para (3)(*a*) substituted by the Secretaries of State for Education and Skills and for Work and Pensions Order, SI 2002/1397 art 12, Schedule para 10 with effect from 27 June 2002.

Contracts relating to commercial ships

4—(1) A contract falls within this paragraph if it relates only to a commercial ship and is [a contract of general insurance of a relevant class.][1]

[(2) For the purposes of this paragraph, a contract of general insurance is of a relevant class if it insures against risks arising from or in relation to—

(*a*) accidents,

(*b*) ships, or

(*c*) liabilities of ships,

(and no other risks).][1]

(3) For the purposes of this paragraph a commercial ship is a ship which is—

(*a*) of a gross tonnage of 15 tons or more; and

(*b*) not designed or adapted for use for recreation or pleasure.

Amendments—[1] Words in sub-para (1) substituted, and sub-para (2) substituted, by the Financial Services and Markets Act 2000 (Consequential Amendments and Repeals) Order, SI 2001/3649 art 346(4) with effect from 1 December 2001.

Contracts relating to lifeboats and lifeboat equipment

5—(1) A contract falls within this paragraph if it relates only to a lifeboat and is [a contract of general insurance of a relevant class.][1]

[(2) For the purposes of this paragraph, a contract of general insurance is of a relevant class if it insures against risks arising from or in relation to—

(*a*) accidents,

(*b*) ships, or

(*c*) liabilities of ships,

(and no other risks).][1]

(3) For the purposes of this paragraph, a lifeboat is a vessel used or to be used solely for rescue or assistance at sea.

Amendments—[1] Words in sub-para (1) substituted, and sub-para (2) substituted, by the Financial Services and Markets Act 2000 (Consequential Amendments and Repeals) Order, SI 2001/3649 art 346(5) with effect from 1 December 2001.

6—(1) A contract falls within this paragraph if it relates only to a lifeboat and lifeboat equipment and is such that, if it related only to a lifeboat, it would fall within paragraph 5 above.

(2) In deciding whether a contract relates to lifeboat equipment the nature of the risks concerned is immaterial, and they may (for example) be risks of dying or sustaining injury or of loss or damage.

(3) For the purposes of this paragraph—

(*a*) "lifeboat" has the meaning given by paragraph 5(3) above; and

(*b*) "lifeboat equipment" means anything used or to be used solely in connection with a lifeboat.

Contracts relating to commercial aircraft

7—(1) A contract falls within this paragraph if it relates only to a commercial aircraft and is [a contract of general insurance of a relevant class.][1]

[(2) For the purposes of this paragraph, a contract of general insurance is of a relevant class if it insures against risks arising from or in relation to—

(*a*) accidents,

(*b*) aircraft, or

(*c*) aircraft liability,

(and no other risks).][1]

(3) For the purposes of this paragraph a commercial aircraft is an aircraft which is—

(*a*) of a weight of 8,000 kilograms or more; and

(*b*) not designed or adapted for use for recreation or pleasure.

Amendments—[1] Words in sub-para (1) substituted, and sub-para (2) substituted, by the Financial Services and Markets Act 2000 (Consequential Amendments and Repeals) Order, SI 2001/3649 art 346(6) with effect from 1 December 2001.

Contracts relating to risks outside the United Kingdom

8—(1) A contract falls within this paragraph if it relates only to a risk which is situated outside the United Kingdom.

[(2) The question of whether a risk is situated in the United Kingdom shall be determined in accordance with regulations made under section 424(3) of the Financial Services and Markets Act 2000; but in determining that question as respects a contract which relates to a building it shall be irrelevant whether or not the contract also covers the contents of the building.][1]

Amendments—[1] Sub-para (2) substituted, by the Financial Services and Markets Act 2000 (Consequential Amendments and Repeals) Order, SI 2001/3649 art 346(7) with effect from 1 December 2001.

Contracts relating to foreign or international railway rolling stock

9—(1) A contract falls within this paragraph if it relates only to foreign or international railway rolling stock and is [a contract of general insurance of a relevant class.][1]
[(2) For the purposes of this paragraph, a contract of general insurance is of a relevant class if it insures against risks arising from or in relation to—
(*a*) railway rolling stock, or
(*b*) general liability to third parties,
(and no other risks).][1]
(3) For the purposes of this paragraph foreign or international railway rolling stock is railway rolling stock used principally for journeys taking place wholly or partly outside the United Kingdom.

Amendments—[1] Words in sub-para (1) substituted, and sub-para (2) substituted, by the Financial Services and Markets Act 2000 (Consequential Amendments and Repeals) Order, SI 2001/3649 art 346(8) with effect from 1 December 2001.

Contracts relating to the Channel tunnel

10—(1) A contract falls within this paragraph if it relates only to the Channel tunnel system and is [a contract of general insurance of a relevant class.][1]
[(2) For the purposes of this paragraph, a contract of general insurance is of a relevant class if it insures against risks arising from or in relation to—
(*a*) fire or natural forces,
(*b*) damage to property, or
(*c*) general liability to third parties,
(and no other risks).][1]
(3) For the purposes of this paragraph "the Channel tunnel system" means—
(*a*) the tunnels described in section 1(7)(*a*) of the Channel Tunnel Act 1987;
(*b*) the control towers situated in the terminal areas described in section 1(7)(*b*) of that Act; and
(*c*) the shuttle crossovers, wherever situated.

Amendments—[1] Words in sub-para (1) substituted, and sub-para (2) substituted, by the Financial Services and Markets Act 2000 (Consequential Amendments and Repeals) Order, SI 2001/3649 art 346(9) with effect from 1 December 2001.

11—(1) A contract falls within this paragraph if it relates only to relevant Channel tunnel equipment and is [a contract of general insurance of a relevant class.][1]
[(2) For the purposes of this paragraph, a contract of general insurance is of a relevant class if it insures against risks arising from or in relation to—
(*a*) fire or natural forces,
(*b*) damage to property, or
(*c*) general liability to third parties,
(and no other risks).][1]
(3) For the purposes of this paragraph "the Channel tunnel system" has the meaning given by paragraph 10(3) above.
(4) For the purposes of this paragraph "relevant Channel tunnel equipment" means, subject to sub-paragraph (5) below, the fixed or movable equipment needed for the operation of the Channel tunnel system or for the operation of trains through any tunnel forming part of it and in particular includes—
(*a*) any ventilation, cooling or electrical plant used or to be used in connection with any such operation; and
(*b*) any safety, signalling and control equipment which is or is to be so used.
(5) Equipment which consists of or forms part of—
(*a*) roads, bridges, platforms, ticket offices and other facilities for the use of passengers or motor vehicles;
(*b*) administrative buildings and maintenance facilities; and
(*c*) railway track or signalling equipment which is not situated in any part of the Channel tunnel system,
is not relevant Channel tunnel equipment for the purposes of this paragraph.

Amendments—[1] Words in sub-para (1) substituted, and sub-para (2) substituted, by the Financial Services and Markets Act 2000 (Consequential Amendments and Repeals) Order, SI 2001/3649 art 346(10) with effect from 1 December 2001.

Contracts relating to goods in foreign or international transit

12—(1) A contract falls within this paragraph if it relates only to loss of or damage to goods in foreign or international transit and the insured enters into the contract in the course of a business carried on by him.
(2) For the purposes of this paragraph goods in foreign or international transit are goods in transit, and any container in which they are carried, where their carriage—
(*a*) begins and ends outside the United Kingdom;

(*b*) begins outside but ends in the United Kingdom; or

(*c*) ends outside but begins in the United Kingdom.

(3) For the purposes of sub-paragraph (2) above "container" has the same meaning as in regulation 38(3) of the Value Added Tax (General) Regulations 1985.

Contracts relating to credit

13—(1) A contract falls within this paragraph if it relates only to credit granted in relation to goods or services supplied under a relevant contract by a person carrying on business in the United Kingdom.

(2) For the purposes of this paragraph a relevant contract is—

(*a*) a contract to make a relevant supply of goods, or a supply of services, or both, to an overseas customer;

(*b*) a contract to supply goods to a person who is to—

(i) export those goods; or

(ii) incorporate those goods in other goods which he is to export,

where the condition mentioned in sub-paragraph (3) below is satisfied;

(*c*) a contract to supply to a person who is to export goods services consisting of the valuation or testing of, or other work carried out on, those goods where the condition mentioned in sub-paragraph (3) below is satisfied;

(*d*) a contract to supply services to a person in order that he may comply with a legally binding obligation to make a supply of services to an overseas customer.

(3) The condition referred to in sub-paragraph (2)(*b*) and (*c*) above is that the goods to be exported are to be exported in order that the person exporting them may comply with a legally binding obligation to make a relevant supply of goods to an overseas customer.

(4) For the purposes of this paragraph—

(*a*) "export" means export from the United Kingdom and cognate expressions shall be construed accordingly; and

(*b*) any reference to a person who is to export goods shall be taken as including a reference to a person at whose direction the insured is to export them and the reference in sub-paragraph (3) above to the person exporting goods shall be construed accordingly.

(5) Where a contract relates to—

(*a*) credit of the description in sub-paragraph (1) above; and

(*b*) loss resulting from the insured or any third party being required to pay the amount of any bond or guarantee against non-performance by the insured of the contract which involves him making the supply,

the contract shall be treated for the purposes of sub-paragraph (1) above as if it did not relate to loss of the description in paragraph (b) above.

Contracts relating to exchange losses

14—(1) A contract falls within this paragraph if—

(*a*) it relates only to loss resulting from a change in the rate at which the price for a supply which is or may be made by the insured may be exchanged for another currency; and

(*b*) the conditions mentioned in sub-paragraph (2) below are satisfied.

(2) The conditions referred to in sub-paragraph (1) above are that—

(*a*) the insured is a person carrying on business in the United Kingdom;

(*b*) the contract of insurance concerns a contract to make a relevant supply of goods, or a supply of services, or both, to an overseas customer (whether or not the contract to make the supply is one into which the insured has entered, or one for which he has tendered or intends to tender); and

(*c*) the period of cover for the risk expires no later than the date by which the whole of the price for the supply is to be paid or, where the contract has not been entered into, would be required to be paid.

(3) Where the contract relates to—

(*a*) loss of the description in sub-paragraph (1)(*a*) above; and

(*b*) loss relating from a change in the rate at which the price of goods which the insured imports into the United Kingdom for the purpose of enabling him to make the supply concerned may be exchanged for another currency,

the contract shall be treated for the purposes of sub-paragraphs (1) and (2) above as if it did not relate to loss of the description in paragraph (b) above.

IPT

Contracts relating to the provision of financial facilities

15—(1) A contract falls within this paragraph if it relates only to the provision of a relevant financial facility and the conditions mentioned in sub-paragraph (2) below are satisfied.

(2) The conditions referred to in sub-paragraph (1) above are that—

(*a*) the person to whom the relevant financial facility is provided is an overseas customer;

(*b*) it is provided in order that he may comply with a legally binding obligation to receive a relevant supply of goods, or a supply of services, or both, from a person carrying on business . . . [1]; and

[(*c*) the contract of insurance insures against risks arising from or in relation to either or both—

(i) credit,

(ii) suretyship.][2]

(3) For the purposes of this paragraph a relevant financial facility is—

(*a*) the making of an advance;

(*b*) the issue of a letter of credit or acceptance of a bill of exchange;

(*c*) the giving of a guarantee or bond; or

(*d*) any other similar transaction entered into in order to provide a customer with the means to pay, or a supplier with the right to call upon a third party for, the consideration for goods or services.

Amendments—[1] Words in sub-para (2)(*b*) deleted by Insurance Premium Tax (Taxable Insurance Contracts) Order, SI 1996/2955, Art 2 with effect from 1 January 1997.

[2] Sub-para (2)(*c*) substituted by the Financial Services and Markets Act 2000 (Consequential Amendments and Repeals) Order, SI 2001/3649 art 346(11) with effect from 1 December 2001.

PART II
INTERPRETATION

16—(1) This Part of this Schedule applies for the purposes of Part I of this Schedule.

(2) A relevant supply of goods is any supply of goods where the supply is to be made outside the United Kingdom or where the goods are to be exported from the United Kingdom.

(3) An overseas customer, in relation to a supply of goods or services, is a person who—

(*a*) does not have any business establishment in the United Kingdom but has such an establishment elsewhere;

(*b*) has such establishments both in the United Kingdom and elsewhere, provided that the establishment at which, or for the purposes of which, the goods or services which are to be supplied to him are most directly to be used is not in the United Kingdom; or

(*c*) has no such establishment in any place and does not have his usual place of residence in the United Kingdom.

[16A Paragraphs 2, 4, 5, 7, 10, 11 and 15 must be read with—

(*a*) section 22 of the Financial Services and Markets Act 2000;

(*b*) any relevant order under that section; and

(*c*) Schedule 2 to that Act.][1]

Amendments—[1] Para 16A added by the Financial Services and Markets Act 2000 (Consequential Amendments and Repeals) Order, SI 2001/3649 art 346(12) with effect from 1 December 2001.

FINANCE ACT 1996

(1996 Chapter 8)

An Act to grant certain duties, to alter other duties, and to amend the law relating to the National Debt and the Public Revenue, and to make further provision in connection with Finance.

[29th April 1996]

PART VII
MISCELLANEOUS AND SUPPLEMENTAL

Miscellaneous: indirect taxation

197 Setting of rates of interest

(1) The rate of interest applicable for the purposes of an enactment to which this section applies shall be the rate which for the purposes of that enactment is provided for by regulations made by the Treasury under this section.

(2) This section applies to—

(*a*) . . .

(*b*) [sections 60(6), (7) and (8) of and][3] paragraphs 21 and 22 of Schedule 7 to that Act (interest on amounts of insurance premium tax and on amounts payable by the Commissioners in respect of that tax);

(*c*), (*d*) . . .

[(*e*) paragraph 17 of Schedule 5 to the Finance Act 1997 (interest on amounts repayable in respect of overpayments by the Commissioners in connection with excise duties, insurance premium tax and landfill tax);][1]

(*f*) –(*i*) . . .

(3) Regulations under this section may—

(*a*) make different provision for different enactments or for different purposes of the same enactment,

(*b*) either themselves specify a rate of interest for the purposes of an enactment or make provision for any such rate to be determined, and to change from time to time, by reference to such rate or the average of such rates as may be referred to in the regulations,

(*c*) provide for rates to be reduced below, or increased above, what they otherwise would be by specified amounts or by reference to specified formulae,

(*d*) provide for rates arrived at by reference to averages or formulae to be rounded up or down,

(*e*) provide for circumstances in which changes of rates of interest are or are not to take place, and

(*f*) provide that changes of rates are to have effect for periods beginning on or after a day determined in accordance with the regulations in relation to interest running from before that day, as well as in relation to interest running from, or from after, that day.

(4) The power to make regulations under this section shall be exercisable by statutory instrument subject to annulment in pursuance of a resolution of the House of Commons.

(5) Where—

(a) regulations under this section provide, without specifying the rate determined in accordance with the regulations, for a new method of determining the rate applicable for the purposes of any enactment, or

(b) the rate which, in accordance with regulations under this section, is the rate applicable for the purposes of any enactment changes otherwise than by virtue of the making of regulations specifying a new rate,[2]

the Commissioners of Customs and Excise shall make an order specifying the new rate and the day from which, in accordance with the regulations, it has effect.

(6) The words "the rate applicable under section 197 of the Finance Act 1996" shall be substituted—

(*a*) . . .

(*b*) for the words "the prescribed rate" in each of sub-paragraphs (1) and (3) of paragraph 21 of Schedule 7 to that Act (insurance premium tax);

(*c*) for the words from "such rate" onwards in sub-paragraph (2) of paragraph 22 of that Schedule; and

(*d*) . . .

(7) Subsections (1) and (6) above shall have effect for periods beginning on or after such day as the Treasury may by order made by statutory instrument appoint and shall have effect in relation to interest running from before that day, as well as in relation to interest running from, or from after, that day; and different days may be appointed under this subsection for different purposes.

Note—Sub-ss (2)(*a*), (*c*), (*d*), (*f*), (*g*)–(*i*), (6)(*a*), (*d*) are not relevant to IPT.

Reference to "that Act" in sub-s s (2), (6) are to FA 1994.

Sub-ss (1), (6) have effect for periods beginning on or after 1 April 1997 (see FA 1996 s 197 (Appointed Day) Order, SI 1997/1015).

Orders—Finance Act 1996, section 197, (Appointed Day) Order 1997, SI 1997/1015.

Air Passenger Duty and Other Indirect Taxes (Interest Rate) Regulations 1998, SI 1998/1461.

Air Passenger Duty and Other Indirect Taxes (Interest Rate) (Amendment) Regulations 2000, SI 2000/631.

Air Passenger Duty and Other Indirect Taxes (Interest Rate) (Amendment) Regulations 2001, SI 2001/3337.

Air Passenger Duty and Other Indirect Taxes (Interest Rate) (Amendment) Regulations 2003, SI 2003/230.

Taxes and Duties (Interest Rate) (Amendment) Regulations 2008, SI 2008/3234.

Taxes and Duties (Interest Rate) (Amendment) Regulations 2009, SI 2009/2032.

Taxes and Duties (Interest Rate) Regulations 2010, SI 2010/1879.

Amendments—[1] Sub-s (2)(*e*) inserted by FA 1997 s 50, Sch 5 para 21.

[2] Sub-s (5) repealed by FA 2009 s 105(6)(*b*) with effect from 21 July 2009.

[3] In sub-s (2)(*b*) words inserted by the Transfer of Tribunal Functions and Revenue and Customs Appeals Order, SI 2009/56 art 3(1), Sch 1 paras 232, 239(1), (2)(*b*) with effect from 1 April 2009.

Supplemental

205 Repeals

(1) The enactments mentioned in Schedule 41 to this Act (which include spent provisions) are hereby repealed to the extent specified in the third column of that Schedule.

(2) The repeals specified in that Schedule have effect subject to the commencement provisions and savings contained in, or referred to, in the notes set out in that Schedule.

FINANCE ACT 1997

(1997 Chapter 16)

ARRANGEMENT OF SECTIONS

An Act to grant certain duties, to alter other duties, and to amend the law relating to the National Debt and the Public Revenue, and to make further provision in connection with Finance.

[19 March 1997]

PART II
INSURANCE PREMIUM TAX

New rates of tax

21 Rate of tax

(1) (*substitutes* FA 1994, s 51).
(2) (*amends* FA 1994 s 73(1)).

22 Premiums liable to tax at the higher rate

(1) (*inserts* FA 1994 s 51A).
(2) (*amends* FA 1994 s 74).
(3) (*inserts* FA 1994 Sch 6A).

23 Charge to tax where different rates apply

(1) (*substitutes* FA 1994 s 69).
(2) (*amends* FA 1994 s 50).

24 Commencement of sections 21 to 23

(1) Except as provided by subsection (2) below, sections 21 to 23 above have effect in relation to a premium which falls to be regarded for the purposes of Part III of the Finance Act 1994 as received under a taxable insurance contract by an insurer on or after 1st April 1997.

(2) Sections 21 to 23 above do not have effect in relation to a premium if the premium—

(*a*) is in respect of a contract made before 1st April 1997; and (*b*) falls, by virtue of regulations under section 68 of the Finance Act 1994 (special accounting scheme), to be regarded for the purposes of Part III of that Act as received under the contract by the insurer on a date before 1st August 1997.

(3) Subsection (2) above does not apply in relation to a premium if the premium—

(*a*) is an additional premium under the contract;

(*b*) falls as mentioned in subsection (2)(*b*) above to be regarded as received under the contract by the insurer on or after 1st April 1997; and

(*c*) is in respect of a risk which was not covered by the contract before 1st April 1997.

(4) Without prejudice to the generality of subsections (1) to (3) above, those subsections shall be construed in accordance with sections 67A to 67C of the Finance Act 1994 (which are inserted by section 29 below).

Taxable intermediaries and their fees

25 Certain fees to be treated as premiums under higher rate contracts

(1) (*inserts* FA 1994 s 52A).

(2) The amendment made by subsection (1) above has effect in relation to payments in respect of fees charged on or after the day on which this Act is passed.

26 Registration of taxable intermediaries

(*inserts* FA 1994 s 53AA).

27 Supplementary provisions

(*amends* FA 1994 ss 53A(1)(*b*), 55, 57, 58, 59(*bb*), 62, 63(1)(*aa*), (*bb*), 73(1), (3), Sch 7 para 14 and *inserts* s 73(1A).

Amendments—Sub-s (11) repealed by FA 2008 s 123, Sch 41 para 25 with effect from 1 April 2010 (by virtue of SI 2009/511 art 2).

Miscellaneous

28 Amounts charged by other intermediaries

(1) (*inserts* FA 1994 s 72(1A)).

(2) The amendment made by subsection (1) above has effect in relation to payments received in respect of amounts charged on or after 1st April 1997.

29 Prevention of pre-emption

(1) (*inserts* FA 1994 ss 67A, 67B and 67C).

(2) In the application of sections 67A to 67C of the Finance Act 1994 in relation to the increases in insurance premium tax effected by this Part and the exceptions from those increases—

(*a*) the announcement relating to those increases, as described in section 67A(1), and to those exceptions, as described in section 67B(1), shall be taken to have been made on 26th November 1996;

(*b*) "the date of the change" is 1st April 1997; and

(*c*) "the concessionary date" is 1st August 1997.

(3) The amendment made by subsection (1) above has effect on and after 26th November 1996.

30 Tax point for payroll deductions

(1), (2) (*insert* FA 1994 s 72(7A), (8A)).

(3) This section applies in relation to amounts deducted on or after the day on which this Act is passed.

PART IV

PAYMENTS AND OVERPAYMENTS IN RESPECT OF INDIRECT TAXES

Excise duties and other indirect taxes

50 Overpayments, interest, assessments, etc

(1) Schedule 5 to this Act (which makes provision in relation to excise duties, insurance premium tax and landfill tax which corresponds to that made for VAT by sections 44 to 48 above) shall have effect.

(2) (*not relevant to IPT*).

Enforcement of payment

51 Enforcement by distress

(1) The Commissioners may by regulations make provision—

(*a*) for authorising distress to be levied on the goods and chattels of any person refusing or neglecting to pay—

(i) any amount of relevant tax due from him, or

(ii) any amount recoverable as if it were relevant tax due from him;

(*b*) for the disposal of any goods or chattels on which distress is levied in pursuance of the regulations; and

(*c*) for the imposition and recovery of costs, charges, expenses and fees in connection with anything done under the regulations.

IPT

(2) The provision that may be contained in regulations under this section shall include, in particular—

(*a*) provision for the levying of distress, by any person authorised to do so under the regulations, on goods or chattels located at any place whatever (including on a public highway); and

(*b*) provision authorising distress to be levied at any such time of the day or night, and on any such day of the week, as may be specified or described in the regulations.

(3) Regulations under this section may—

(*a*) make different provision for different cases, and

(*b*) contain any such incidental, supplemental, consequential or transitional provision as the Commissioners think fit;

and the transitional provision that may be contained in regulations under this section shall include transitional provision in connection with the coming into force of the repeal by this Act of any other power by regulations to make provision for or in connection with the levying of distress.

(4) The power to make regulations under this section shall be exercisable by statutory instrument subject to annulment in pursuance of a resolution of the House of Commons.

(5) The following are relevant taxes for the purposes of this section, that is to say—

(*a*), (*b*) . . .

(*c*) insurance premium tax;

(*d*) –(*f*) . . .

(6) In this section "the Commissioners" means the Commissioners of Customs and Excise.

(7) Regulations made under this section shall not have effect in Scotland.

Notes—Sub-ss (5)(*a*), (*b*), (*d*)–(*f*) are not relevant to IPT.

Prospective amendments—Sub-s (A1) to be inserted, in sub-s (1) words "not having effect in England and Wales or Scotland" to be inserted after words "by regulations", and sub-s (7) to be repealed, by the Tribunals, Courts and Enforcement Act 2007 ss 62(3), 146, Sch 13 para 126, Sch 23 Pt 3, with effect from a date to be appointed. Sub-s (A1) to read as follows—

"(A1) The Commissioners may, in England and Wales, use the procedure in Schedule 12 to the Tribunals, Courts and Enforcement Act 2007 (taking control of goods) to recover any of these that a person refuses or neglects to pay—

(*a*) any amount of relevant tax due from him;

(*b*) any amount recoverable as if it were relevant tax due from him.".

52 Enforcement by diligence

(1) Where any amount of relevant tax or any amount recoverable as if it were relevant tax is due and has not been paid, the sheriff, on an application by the Commissioners accompanied by a certificate by them—

(a) stating that none of the persons specified in the application has paid the amount due from him;

(b) stating that payment of the amount due from each such person has been demanded from him; and

(c) specifying the amount due from and unpaid by each such person,

shall grant a summary warrant in a form prescribed by Act of Sederunt authorising the recovery, by any of the diligences mentioned in subsection (2) below, of the amount remaining due and unpaid.

(2) The diligences referred to in subsection (1) above are—

[(a) an attachment][1];

(b) an earnings arrestment;

(c) an arrestment and action of forthcoming or sale.

(3) Subject to subsection (4) below and without prejudice to [section 39(1) of the Debt Arrangement and Attachment (Scotland) Act 2002 (asp 17) (expenses of attachment)][2] the sheriff officer's fees, together with the outlays necessarily incurred by him, in connection with the execution of a summary warrant shall be chargeable against the debtor.

(4) No fees shall be chargeable by the sheriff officer against the debtor for collecting, and accounting to the Commissioners for, sums paid to him by the debtor in respect of the amount owing.

(5) The following are relevant taxes for the purposes of this section, that is to say—

(a), (b) . . .

(c) insurance premium tax;

(d)–(f) . . .

(6) In this section "the Commissioners" means the Commissioners of Customs and Excise.

(7) This section shall come into force on such day as the Commissioners of Customs and Excise may by order made by statutory instrument appoint, and different days may be appointed under this subsection for different purposes.

(8) This section extends only to Scotland.[3]

Notes—Sub-ss (5)(*a*), (*b*), (*d*)–(*f*) are not relevant to IPT.

The appointed day under sub-s (7) above is 1 July 1997 (see SI 1997/1432).

Amendments—[1] Sub-s (2)(*a*) substituted by the Debt Arrangement and Attachment (Scotland) Act 2002, s 61, Sch 3, Pt 1, para 26(*a*) with effect from 30 December 2002; see the Debt Arrangement and Attachment (Scotland) Act 2002, s 64(2).

2 Words in sub-s (3) substituted by the Debt Arrangement and Attachment (Scotland) Act 2002, s 61, Sch 3, Pt 1, para 26(*b*) with effect from 30 December 2002; see the Debt Arrangement and Attachment (Scotland) Act 2002, s 64(2).

3 This section repealed by FA 2008 s 129(2), Sch 43 para 15 with effect from 23 November 2009 (by virtue of SI 2009/3024 art 3). Note that if before the commencement date a warrant has been granted under this section, that warrant shall continue to have effect according to the provisions under which it was granted (SI 2009/3024 art 4(1)(c)).

53 Amendments consequential on sections 51 and 52

. . .

(5) (Amends FA 1994 Sch 7 para 19(1)(*a*)).

. . .

(9) This section shall come into force on such day as the Commissioners of Customs and Excise may by order made by statutory instrument appoint, and different days may be appointed under this subsection for different purposes.

Notes—Words omitted are not relevant for the purposes of IPT.
The appointed day under sub-s (9) above is 1 July 1997 (see SI 1997/1432).

SCHEDULES

SCHEDULE 4

INSURANCE PREMIUM TAX: THE HIGHER RATE

Section 22

(*inserts* FA 1994 Sch 6A).

SCHEDULE 5

INDIRECT TAXES: OVERPAYMENTS ETC

Section 50

PART I
UNJUST ENRICHMENT

Application of Part I

1—(1) This Part of this Schedule has effect for the purposes of the following provisions (which make it a defence to a claim for repayment that the repayment would unjustly enrich the claimant), namely—

(*a*) section 137A(3) of the Customs and Excise Management Act 1979 (excise duties);
(*b*) paragraph 8(3) of Schedule 7 to the Finance Act 1994 (insurance premium tax); and
(*c*) paragraph 14(3) of Schedule 5 to the Finance Act 1996 (landfill tax).

(2) Those provisions are referred to in this Part of this Schedule as unjust enrichment provisions.

(3) In this Part of this Schedule—

"the Commissioners" means the Commissioners of Customs and Excise;

"relevant repayment provision" means—

(*a*) section 137A of the Customs and Excise Management Act 1979 (recovery of overpaid excise duty);
(*b*) paragraph 8 of Schedule 7 to the Finance Act 1994 (recovery of overpaid insurance premium tax); or
(*c*) paragraph 14 of Schedule 5 to the Finance Act 1996 (recovery of overpaid landfill tax);

"relevant tax" means any duty of excise, insurance premium tax or landfill tax; and

"subordinate legislation" has the same meaning as in the Interpretation Act 1978.

Disregard of business losses

2—(1) This paragraph applies where—

(*a*) there is an amount paid by way of relevant tax which (apart from an unjust enrichment provision) would fall to be repaid under a relevant repayment provision to any person ("the taxpayer"), and
(*b*) the whole or a part of the cost of the payment of that amount to the Commissioners has, for practical purposes, been borne by a person other than the taxpayer.

(2) Where, in a case to which this paragraph applies, loss or damage has been or may be incurred by the taxpayer as a result of mistaken assumptions made in his case about the operation of any provisions relating to a relevant tax, that loss or damage shall be disregarded, except to the extent of the quantified amount, in the making of any determination—

(*a*) of whether or to what extent the repayment of an amount to the taxpayer would enrich him; or
(*b*) of whether or to what extent any enrichment of the taxpayer would be unjust.

IPT

(3) In sub-paragraph (2) above "the quantified amount" means the amount (if any) which is shown by the taxpayer to constitute the amount that would appropriately compensate him for loss or damage shown by him to have resulted, for any business carried on by him, from the making of the mistaken assumptions.

(4) The reference in sub-paragraph (2) above to provisions relating to a relevant tax is a reference to any provisions of—

(*a*) any enactment, subordinate legislation or Community legislation (whether or not still in force) which relates to that tax or to any matter connected with it; or

(*b*) any notice published by the Commissioners under or for the purposes of any such enactment or subordinate legislation.

(5) This paragraph has effect for the purposes of making any repayment on or after the day on which this Act is passed, even if the claim for that repayment was made before that day.

Reimbursement arrangements

3—(1) The Commissioners may by regulations make provision for reimbursement arrangements made by any person to be disregarded for the purposes of any or all of the unjust enrichment provisions except where the arrangements—

(*a*) contain such provision as may be required by the regulations; and

(*b*) are supported by such undertakings to comply with the provisions of the arrangements as may be required by the regulations to be given to the Commissioners.

(2) In this paragraph "reimbursement arrangements" means any arrangements for the purposes of a claim under a relevant repayment provision which—

(*a*) are made by any person for the purpose of securing that he is not unjustly enriched by the repayment of any amount in pursuance of the claim; and

(*b*) provide for the reimbursement of persons who have for practical purposes borne the whole or any part of the cost of the original payment of that amount to the Commissioners.

(3) Without prejudice to the generality of sub-paragraph (1) above, the provision that may be required by regulations under this paragraph to be contained in reimbursement arrangements includes—

(*a*) provision requiring a reimbursement for which the arrangements provide to be made within such period after the repayment to which it relates as may be specified in the regulations;

(*b*) provision for the repayment of amounts to the Commissioners where those amounts are not reimbursed in accordance with the arrangements;

(*c*) provision requiring interest paid by the Commissioners on any amount repaid by them to be treated in the same way as that amount for the purposes of any requirement under the arrangements to make reimbursement or to repay the Commissioners;

(*d*) provision requiring such records relating to the carrying out of the arrangements as may be described in the regulations to be kept and produced to the Commissioners, or to an officer of theirs.

(4) Regulations under this paragraph may impose obligations on such persons as may be specified in the regulations—

(*a*) to make the repayments to the Commissioners that they are required to make in pursuance of any provisions contained in any reimbursement arrangements by virtue of sub-paragraph (3)(*b*) or (*c*) above;

(*b*) to comply with any requirements contained in any such arrangements by virtue of sub-paragraph (3)(*d*) above.

(5) Regulations under this paragraph may make provision for the form and manner in which, and the times at which, undertakings are to be given to the Commissioners in accordance with the regulations; and any such provision may allow for those matters to be determined by the Commissioners in accordance with the regulations.

(6) Regulations under this paragraph may—

(*a*) contain any such incidental, supplementary, consequential or transitional provision as appears to the Commissioners to be necessary or expedient; and

(*b*) make different provision for different circumstances.

(7) Regulations under this paragraph may have effect (irrespective of when the claim for repayment was made) for the purposes of the making of any repayment by the Commissioners after the time when the regulations are made; and, accordingly, such regulations may apply to arrangements made before that time.

(8) Regulations under this paragraph shall be made by statutory instrument subject to annulment in pursuance of a resolution of the House of Commons.

Regulations—Insurance Premium Tax (Amendment) Regulations 1998, SI 1998/60.

Contravention of requirement to repay Commissioners

4—(1) Where any obligation is imposed by regulations made by virtue of paragraph 3(4) above, a contravention or failure to comply with that obligation shall, to the extent that it relates to amounts repaid under section 137A of the Customs and Excise Management Act 1979, attract a penalty under section 9 of the Finance Act 1994 (penalties in connection with excise duties).

(2) For the purposes of Schedule 7 to the Finance Act 1994 (insurance premium tax), a contravention or failure to comply with an obligation imposed by regulations made by virtue of paragraph 3(4) above shall be deemed, to the extent that it relates to amounts repaid under paragraph 8 of that Schedule (recovery of overpaid insurance premium tax), to be a failure to comply with a requirement falling within paragraph 17(1)(*c*) of that Schedule (breach of regulations).

(3) Paragraph 23 of Schedule 5 to the Finance Act 1996 (power to provide for penalty) shall have effect as if an obligation imposed by regulations made by virtue of paragraph 3(4) above were, to the extent that it relates to amounts repaid under paragraph 14 of that Schedule (recovery of overpaid landfill tax), a requirement imposed by regulations under Part III of that Act; and the provisions of that Schedule in relation to penalties under Part V of that Schedule shall have effect accordingly.

PART II

TIME LIMITS

Repayments

5—(1) (*not relevant to IPT*)

(2) (*Substitutes* FA 1994 Sch 7 para 8(4), (5)).

(3) (*not relevant to IPT*)

Assessments

6—(1) In each of the enactments specified in sub-paragraph (2) below (which provide for the time limits applying to the making of assessments), for the words "six years", wherever they occur, there shall be substituted the words "three years".

(2) Those enactments are—

(*a*) (*amends* FA 1994 s 12(4)(*a*), (5)).

(*b*) (*amended* FA 1994 Sch 7 para 26(1), (4)); *repealed by* FA 2009 s 99, Sch 51 para 43.

(*c*) (*amended* FA 1996 Sch 5 para 33(1), (4)); *repealed by* FA 2009 s 99, Sch 51 para 43.

Amendments—Sub-para (2)(*b*), (*c*) repealed by FA 2009 s 99(1), Sch 51 para 43(*b*) with effect from 1 April 2010 (by virtue of SI 2010/867, art 2(1)).

PART III

INTEREST

Interest on overpaid insurance premium tax

9—(1) Paragraph 22 of Schedule 7 to the Finance Act 1994 (interest payable by the Commissioners in connection with insurance premium tax) shall have effect, and be deemed always to have had effect, with the amendments for which this paragraph provides.

(2) (*inserts* FA 1994 Sch 7 para 22(1A)).

(3) (*substitutes* FA 1994 Sch 7 para 22(9)).

(4) (*substitutes* FA 1994 Sch 7 para 22(10)).

10—(1) (*substitutes* FA 1994 Sch 7 para 22 (5) to (7)).

(2) Sub-paragraph (1) above shall have effect for the purposes of determining whether any period beginning on or after the day on which this Act is passed is left out of account.

PART V

RECOVERY OF EXCESS PAYMENTS BY THE COMMISSIONERS

Assessment for excessive repayment

14—(1) Where—

(*a*) any amount has been paid at any time to any person by way of a repayment under a relevant repayment provision, and

(*b*) the amount paid exceeded the amount which the Commissioners were liable at that time to repay to that person,

the Commissioners may, to the best of their judgement, assess the excess paid to that person and notify it to him.

IPT

(2) Where any person is liable to pay any amount to the Commissioners in pursuance of an obligation imposed by virtue of paragraph 3(4)(*a*) above, the Commissioners may, to the best of their judgement, assess the amount due from that person and notify it to him.

(3) In this paragraph "relevant repayment provision" means—

(*a*) section 137A of the Customs and Excise Management Act 1979 (recovery of overpaid excise duty);

(*b*) paragraph 8 of Schedule 7 to the Finance Act 1994 (recovery of overpaid insurance premium tax); . . . [1]

(*c*) paragraph 14 of Schedule 5 to the Finance Act 1996 (recovery of overpaid landfill tax) [or

(*d*) Part I of Schedule 3 to the Finance Act 2001 (payments made and rebates disallowed in error)][1].

Amendments—[1] Words in sub-para (3)(*b*) repealed, and sub-para (3)(*d*) inserted, by FA 2001 ss 15, 110, Sch 3, Pt 4, para 19(1), (2), Sch 33 Pt 1(4) with effect from 1 November 2001 (by virtue of SI 2001/3300).

Assessment for overpayments of interest

15—(1) Where—

(*a*) any amount has been paid to any person by way of interest under a relevant interest provision, but

(*b*) that person was not entitled to that amount under that provision,

the Commissioners may, to the best of their judgement, assess the amount so paid to which that person was not entitled and notify it to him.

(2) In this paragraph "relevant interest provision" means—

(*a*) . . . [1]

(*b*) paragraph 22 of Schedule 7 to that Act (interest payable by the Commissioners on overpayments etc of insurance premium tax); . . . [1]

(*c*) paragraph 29 of Schedule 5 to the Finance Act 1996 (interest payable by the Commissioners on overpayments etc of landfill tax) [or

(*d*) Part II of Schedule 3 to the Finance Act 2001 (interest)][1].

Amendments—[1] Sub-para (2)(*a*) and words in sub-para (2(*b*) repealed, and sub-para (2)(*d*) inserted, by FA 2001 ss 15, 110, Sch 3, Pt 4, para 19(1), (3), Sch 33 Pt 1(4) with effect from1 November 2001 (by virtue of SI 2001/3300).

Assessments under paragraphs 14 and 15

16—(1) An assessment under paragraph 14 or 15 above shall not be made more than two years after the time when evidence of facts sufficient in the opinion of the Commissioners to justify the making of the assessment comes to the knowledge of the Commissioners.

(2) Where an amount has been assessed and notified to any person under paragraph 14 or 15 above, it shall be recoverable (subject to any provision having effect in accordance with paragraph 19 below) as if it were relevant tax due from him.

(3) Sub-paragraph (2) above does not have effect if, or to the extent that, the assessment in question has been withdrawn or reduced.

Interest on amounts assessed

17—(1) Where an assessment is made under paragraph 14 or 15 above, the whole of the amount assessed shall carry interest at the rate applicable under section 197 of the Finance Act 1996 from the date on which the assessment is notified until payment.

(2) Where any person is liable to interest under sub-paragraph (1) above the Commissioners may assess the amount due by way of interest and notify it to him.

(3) Without prejudice to the power to make assessments under this paragraph for later periods, the interest to which an assessment under this paragraph may relate shall be confined to interest for a period of no more than two years ending with the time when the assessment under this paragraph is made.

(4) Interest under this paragraph shall be paid without any deduction of income tax.

(5) A notice of assessment under this paragraph shall specify a date, being not later than the date of the notice, to which the amount of interest is calculated; and, if the interest continues to accrue after that date, a further assessment or assessments may be made under this paragraph in respect of amounts which so accrue.

(6) If, within such period as may be notified by the Commissioners to the person liable for interest under sub-paragraph (1) above, the amount referred to in that sub-paragraph is paid, it shall be treated for the purposes of that sub-paragraph as paid on the date specified as mentioned in sub-paragraph (5) above.

(7) Where an amount has been assessed and notified to any person under this paragraph it shall be recoverable as if it were relevant tax due from him.

(8) Sub-paragraph (7) above does not have effect if, or to the extent that, the assessment in question has been withdrawn or reduced.

Supplementary assessments

18 If it appears to the Commissioners that the amount which ought to have been assessed in an assessment under paragraph 14, 15 or 17 above exceeds the amount which was so assessed, then—

(*a*) under the same paragraph as that assessment was made, and

(*b*) on or before the last day on which that assessment could have been made,

the Commissioners may make a supplementary assessment of the amount of the excess and shall notify the person concerned accordingly.

Review of decisions and appeals

19— . . .

(2) Sections [59 to 60][1] of that Act of 1994 (review and appeal in the case of insurance premium tax) shall have effect in relation to any decision which—

(*a*) is contained in an assessment under paragraph 14, 15 or 17 above,

(*b*) is a decision about whether any amount is due to the Commissioners or about how much is due, and

(*c*) is made in a case in which the relevant repayment provision is paragraph 8 of Schedule 7 to that Act or the relevant interest provision is paragraph 22 of that Schedule,

as if that decision were a decision to which section 59 of that Act applies.

. . .

Amendments—[1] In sub-para (2) words substituted for words "59 and 60" by the Transfer of Tribunal Functions and Revenue and Customs Appeals Order, SI 2009/56, art 3(1), Sch 1 paras 241, 244(1), (3) with effect from 1 April 2009.

Interpretation of Part V

20—(1) In this Part of this Schedule "the Commissioners" means the Commissioners of Customs and Excise.

(2) In this Part of this Schedule "relevant tax", in relation to any assessment, means—

(*a*) a duty of excise if the assessment relates to—

(i) a repayment of an amount paid by way of such a duty,

(ii) an overpayment of interest under [Part II of Schedule 3 to the Finance Act 2001][1], or

(iii) interest on an amount specified in an assessment in relation to which the relevant tax is a duty of excise;

(*b*) insurance premium tax if the assessment relates to—

(i) a repayment of an amount paid by way of such tax,

(ii) an overpayment of interest under paragraph 22 of Schedule 7 to the Finance Act 1994, or

(iii) interest on an amount specified in an assessment in relation to which the relevant tax is insurance premium tax;

and

(*c*) landfill tax if the assessment relates to—

(i) a repayment of an amount paid by way of such tax,

(ii) an overpayment of interest under paragraph 29 of Schedule 5 to the Finance Act 1996, or

(iii) interest on an amount specified in an assessment in relation to which the relevant tax is landfill tax.

(3) For the purposes of this Part of this Schedule notification to a personal representative, trustee in bankruptcy, interim or permanent trustee, receiver, liquidator or person otherwise acting in a representative capacity in relation to another shall be treated as notification to the person in relation to whom he so acts.

Amendments—[1] Words in sub-para (2)(*a*)(ii) substituted by FA 2001 s 15, Sch 3, Pt 4, para 19(1), (5) with effect from1 November 2001 (by virtue of SI 2001/3300).

Consequential amendment

21 (*inserts* FA 1996 s 197(2)(*e*)).

SCHEDULE 18

REPEALS

Section 113

PART V

INDIRECT TAXES

Note—Details of repeals already in effect have been omitted from this Schedule.

IPT

FINANCE ACT 1998

(1998 Chapter 36)

An Act to grant certain duties, to alter other duties, and to amend the law relating to the National Debt and the Public Revenue, and to make further provision in connection with Finance.

[31 July 1998]

PART V

OTHER TAXES

Insurance premium tax

146 Travel insurance: higher rate tax

(1) Schedule 6A to the Finance Act 1994 (premiums liable to tax at the higher rate) shall be amended as follows.

(2) (*substitutes* FA 1994 Sch 6A para 4).

(3) Except as provided by subsection (4) below, subsections (1) and (2) above have effect in relation to a premium which falls to be regarded for the purposes of Part III of the Finance Act 1994 as received under a taxable insurance contract by an insurer on or after 1st August 1998.

(4) Subsections (1) and (2) above do not have effect in relation to a premium if the premium—

(*a*) is in respect of a contract made before 1st August 1998; and

(*b*) falls, by virtue of regulations under section 68 of the Finance Act 1994 (special accounting scheme), to be regarded for the purposes of Part III of that Act as received under the contract by the insurer on a date before 1st February 1999.

(5) In the application of sections 67A to 67C of the Finance Act 1994 in relation to the increase in insurance premium tax effected by this section and the exception from that increase—

(*a*) the announcement relating to that increase, as described in section 67A(1), and to that exception, as described in section 67B(1), shall be taken to have been made on 17th March 1998;

(*b*) "the date of the change" is 1st August 1998; and

(*c*) "the concessionary date" is 1st February 1999.

147 Taxable intermediaries

(1) Section 52A of the Finance Act 1994 (certain fees to be treated as premiums under higher rate contracts) shall be amended as follows.

(2) (*amends* FA 1994 s 52A(5)).

(3) (*substitutes* FA 1994 s 52A(6)(7)).

(4) (*amends* FA 1994 s 52A(9)).

(5) The amendments made by this section have effect in relation to payments in respect of fees charged on or after 1st August 1998.

PART VI

MISCELLANEOUS AND SUPPLEMENTAL

Supplemental

165 Repeals

(1) The enactments mentioned in Schedule 27 to this Act (which include spent provisions) are hereby repealed to the extent specified in the third column of that Schedule.

(2) The repeals specified in that Schedule have effect subject to the commencement provisions and savings contained or referred to in the notes set out in that Schedule.

SCHEDULE 27

REPEALS

PART V

OTHER TAXES

INSURANCE PREMIUM TAX

Note—This repeal is already in force and has therefore been omitted.

HUMAN RIGHTS ACT 1998

(1998 Chapter 42)

An Act to give further effect to rights and freedoms guaranteed under the European Convention on Human Rights; to make provision with respect to holders of certain judicial offices who become judges of the European Court of Human Rights; and for connected purposes.

[9th November 1998]

Note—Please see VAT Statutes *ante* for the text of this Act.

FINANCE ACT 1999

(1999 Chapter 16)

An Act to grant certain duties, to alter other duties, and to amend the law relating to the National Debt and the Public Revenue, and to make further provision in connection with Finance.

[27 July 1999]

PART VII
OTHER TAXES

Insurance premium tax

125 Rate of insurance premium tax

(1) In section 51(2)(b) of the Finance Act 1994 (4 per cent standard rate of insurance premium tax), for "4 per cent" there shall be substituted "5 per cent"

(2) Subsection (1) above has effect in relation to a premium which falls to be regarded for the purposes of Part III of the Finance Act 1994 (insurance premium tax) as received under a taxable insurance contract by an insurer on or after 1st July 1999.

(3) Subsection (1) above does not have effect in relation to a premium which—

(a) is in respect of a contract made before 1st July 1999, and

(b) falls to be regarded for the purposes of Part III of that Act as received under the contract by the insurer on a date before 1st January 2000, by virtue of regulations under section 68 of that Act (special accounting schemes).

(4) Subsection (3) above does not apply in relation to a premium which—

(a) is an additional premium under a contract,

(b) falls to be regarded for the purposes of Part III of that Act as received under the contract by the insurer on or after 1st July 1999, by virtue of regulations under section 68 of that Act, and

(c) is in respect of a risk which was not covered by the contract before 1st July 1999.

(5) In the application of sections 67A to 67C of that Act (announced increase in rate of insurance premium tax) in relation to the increase under subsection (1) above and the exception under subsection (3) above—

(a) the announcement for the purpose of sections 67A(1) and 67B(1) shall be taken to have been made on 9th March 1999,

(b) the date of the change is 1st July 1999, and

(c) the concessionary date is 1st January 2000.[1]

Amendments—[1] This section repealed by F(No 2)A 2010 s 4(4) with effect in relation to a premium falling to be regarded for the purposes of FA 1994 Part 3 as received under a taxable insurance contract by an insurer on or after 4 January 2011.

FINANCIAL SERVICES AND MARKETS ACT 2000

(2000 Chapter 8)

An Act to make provision about the regulation of financial services and markets; to provide for the transfer of certain statutory functions relating to building societies, friendly societies, industrial and provident societies and certain other mutual societies; and for connected purposes.

[14 June 2000]

PART II
REGULATED AND PROHIBITED ACTIVITIES

Regulated activities

22 The classes of activity and categories of investment

(1) An activity is a regulated activity for the purposes of this Act if it is an activity of a specified kind which is carried on by way of business and—

(*a*) relates to an investment of a specified kind; or

IPT

(*b*) in the case of an activity of a kind which is also specified for the purposes of this paragraph, is carried on in relation to property of any kind.

(2) Schedule 2 makes provision supplementing this section.

(3) Nothing in Schedule 2 limits the powers conferred by subsection (1).

(4) "Investment" includes any asset, right or interest.

(5) "Specified" means specified in an order made by the Treasury.

Note—This section came into force on 25 February 2001 (by virtue of SI 2001/516).

Regulations—Financial Services and Markets Act 2000 (Regulated Activities) Order, SI 2001/544 (as amended).
Financial Services and Markets Act 2000 (Financial Promotion and Miscellaneous Amendments) Order, SI 2002/1310.

PART XXX
SUPPLEMENTAL

433 Short title

This Act may be cited as the Financial Services and Markets Act 2000.

SCHEDULE 2
REGULATED ACTIVITIES

Section 22(2)

Note—This Schedule came into force on 25 February 2001 (by virtue of SI 2001/516).

Regulations—Financial Services and Markets Act 2000 (Regulated Activities) Order, SI 2001/544 (as amended by SI 2001/3544).

[PART I
REGULATED ACTIVITIES: GENERAL][1]

Amendments—[1] Part heading substituted by the Dormant Bank and Building Society Accounts Act 2008 s 15, Sch 2 para 1(1), (2) with effect from 12 March 2009 (by virtue of SI 2009/490 art 2).

General

1 The matters with respect to which provision may be made under section 22(1) in respect of activities include, in particular, those described in general terms in this Part of this Schedule.

Dealing in investments

2—(1) Buying, selling, subscribing for or underwriting investments or offering or agreeing to do so, either as a principal or as an agent.

(2) In the case of an investment which is a contract of insurance, that includes carrying out the contract.

Arranging deals in investments

3 Making, or offering or agreeing to make—

(*a*) arrangements with a view to another person buying, selling, subscribing for or underwriting a particular investment;

(*b*) arrangements with a view to a person who participates in the arrangements buying, selling, subscribing for or underwriting investments.

Deposit taking

4 Accepting deposits.

Safekeeping and administration of assets

5—(1) Safeguarding and administering assets belonging to another which consist of or include investments or offering or agreeing to do so.

(2) Arranging for the safeguarding and administration of assets belonging to another, or offering or agreeing to do so.

Managing investments

6 Managing, or offering or agreeing to manage, assets belonging to another person where—

(*a*) the assets consist of or include investments; or

(*b*) the arrangements for their management are such that the assets may consist of or include investments at the discretion of the person managing or offering or agreeing to manage them.

Investment advice

7 Giving or offering or agreeing to give advice to persons on—

(*a*) buying, selling, subscribing for or underwriting an investment; or
(*b*) exercising any right conferred by an investment to acquire, dispose of, underwrite or convert an investment.

Establishing collective investment schemes

8 Establishing, operating or winding up a collective investment scheme, including acting as—
(*a*) trustee of a unit trust scheme;
(*b*) depositary of a collective investment scheme other than a unit trust scheme; or
(*c*) sole director of a body incorporated by virtue of regulations under section 262.

Using computer-based systems for giving investment instructions

9—(1) Sending on behalf of another person instructions relating to an investment by means of a computer-based system which enables investments to be transferred without a written instrument.
(2) Offering or agreeing to send such instructions by such means on behalf of another person.
(3) Causing such instructions to be sent by such means on behalf of another person.
(4) Offering or agreeing to cause such instructions to be sent by such means on behalf of another person.

[PART 1A
REGULATED ACTIVITIES: RECLAIM FUNDS]

Activities of reclaim funds

9A—(1) The matters with respect to which provision may be made under section 22(1) in respect of activities include, in particular, any of the activities of a reclaim fund.
(2) "Reclaim fund" has the meaning given by section 5(1) of the Dormant Bank and Building Society Accounts Act 2008.][1]

Amendments—[1] This Part inserted by the Dormant Bank and Building Society Accounts Act 2008 s 15, Sch 2 para 1(1), (3) with effect from 12 March 2009 (by virtue of SI 2009/490 art 2).

PART II
INVESTMENTS

General

10 The matters with respect to which provision may be made under section 22(1) in respect of investments include, in particular, those described in general terms in this Part of this Schedule.

Securities

11—(1) Shares or stock in the share capital of a company.
(2) "Company" includes—
(*a*) any body corporate (wherever incorporated), and
(*b*) any unincorporated body constituted under the law of a country or territory outside the United Kingdom,

other than an open-ended investment company.

Instruments creating or acknowledging indebtedness

12 Any of the following—
(*a*) debentures;
(*b*) debenture stock;
(*c*) loan stock;
(*d*) bonds;
(*e*) certificates of deposit;
(*f*) any other instruments creating or acknowledging a present or future indebtedness.

Government and public securities

13—(1) Loan stock, bonds and other instruments—
(*a*) creating or acknowledging indebtedness; and
(*b*) issued by or on behalf of a government, local authority or public authority.
(2) "Government, local authority or public authority" means—
(*a*) the government of the United Kingdom, of Northern Ireland, or of any country or territory outside the United Kingdom;

IPT

(*b*) a local authority in the United Kingdom or elsewhere;
(*c*) any international organisation the members of which include the United Kingdom or another member State.

Instruments giving entitlement to investments

14—(1) Warrants or other instruments entitling the holder to subscribe for any investment.
(2) It is immaterial whether the investment is in existence or identifiable.

Certificates representing securities

15 Certificates or other instruments which confer contractual or property rights—
(*a*) in respect of any investment held by someone other than the person on whom the rights are conferred by the certificate or other instrument; and
(*b*) the transfer of which may be effected without requiring the consent of that person.

Units in collective investment schemes

16—(1) Shares in or securities of an open-ended investment company.
(2) Any right to participate in a collective investment scheme.

Options

17 Options to acquire or dispose of property.

Futures

18 Rights under a contract for the sale of a commodity or property of any other description under which delivery is to be made at a future date.

Contracts for differences

19 Rights under—
(*a*) a contract for differences; or
(*b*) any other contract the purpose or pretended purpose of which is to secure a profit or avoid a loss by reference to fluctuations in—
(i) the value or price of property of any description; or
(ii) an index or other factor designated for that purpose in the contract.

Contracts of insurance

20 Rights under a contract of insurance, including rights under contracts falling within head C of Schedule 2 to the Friendly Societies Act 1992.

Participation in Lloyd's syndicates

21—(1) The underwriting capacity of a Lloyd's syndicate.
(2) A person's membership (or prospective membership) of a Lloyd's syndicate.

Deposits

22 Rights under any contract under which a sum of money (whether or not denominated in a currency) is paid on terms under which it will be repaid, with or without interest or a premium, and either on demand or at a time or in circumstances agreed by or on behalf of the person making the payment and the person receiving it.

Loans secured on land

23—(1) Rights under any contract under which—
(*a*) one person provides another with credit; and
(*b*) the obligation of the borrower to repay is secured on land.
(2) "Credit" includes any cash loan or other financial accommodation.
(3) "Cash" includes money in any form.

[Other finance arrangements involving land

23A—(1) Rights under any arrangement for the provision of finance under which the person providing the finance either—
(*a*) acquires a major interest in land from the person to whom the finance is provided, or

(*b*) disposes of a major interest in land to that person,

as part of the arrangement.

(2) References in sub-paragraph (1) to a "major interest" in land are to—

(*a*) in relation to land in England or Wales—

(i) an estate in fee simple absolute, or

(ii) a term of years absolute,

whether subsisting at law or in equity;

(*b*) in relation to land in Scotland—

(i) the interest of an owner of land, or

(ii) the tenant's right over or interest in a property subject to a lease;

(*c*) in relation to land in Northern Ireland—

(i) any freehold estate, or

(ii) any leasehold estate,

whether subsisting at law or in equity.

(3) It is immaterial for the purposes of sub-paragraph (1) whether either party acquires or (as the case may be) disposes of the interest in land—

(*a*) directly, or

(*b*) indirectly.][1]

Amendments—[1] Para 23A inserted by the Regulation of Financial Services (Land Transactions) Act 2005 s 1 with effect from 19 February 2006 (Regulation of Financial Services (Land Transactions) Act 2005 s 2(2)).

Rights in investments

24 Any right or interest in anything which is an investment as a result of any other provision made under section 22(1).

PART III
SUPPLEMENTAL PROVISIONS

The order-making power

25—(1) An order under section 22(1) may—

(*a*) provide for exemptions;

(*b*) confer powers on the Treasury or the Authority;

(*c*) authorise the making of regulations or other instruments by the Treasury for purposes of, or connected with, any relevant provision;

(*d*) authorise the making of rules or other instruments by the Authority for purposes of, or connected with, any relevant provision;

(*e*) make provision in respect of any information or document which, in the opinion of the Treasury or the Authority, is relevant for purposes of, or connected with, any relevant provision;

(*f*) make such consequential, transitional or supplemental provision as the Treasury consider appropriate for purposes of, or connected with, any relevant provision.

(2) Provision made as a result of sub-paragraph (1)(f) may amend any primary or subordinate legislation, including any provision of, or made under, this Act.

(3) "Relevant provision" means any provision—

(*a*) of section 22 or this Schedule; or

(*b*) made under that section or this Schedule.

Parliamentary control

26—(1) This paragraph applies to the first order made under section 22(1).

(2) This paragraph also applies to any subsequent order made under section 22(1) which contains a statement by the Treasury that, in their opinion, the effect (or one of the effects) of the proposed order would be that an activity which is not a regulated activity would become a regulated activity.

(3) An order to which this paragraph applies—

(*a*) must be laid before Parliament after being made; and

(*b*) ceases to have effect at the end of the relevant period unless before the end of that period the order is approved by a resolution of each House of Parliament (but without that affecting anything done under the order or the power to make a new order).

(4) "Relevant period" means a period of twenty-eight days beginning with the day on which the order is made.

(5) In calculating the relevant period no account is to be taken of any time during which Parliament is dissolved or prorogued or during which both Houses are adjourned for more than four days.

Interpretation

27—(1) In this Schedule—

"buying" includes acquiring for valuable consideration;

"offering" includes inviting to treat;

"property" includes currency of the United Kingdom or any other country or territory; and

"selling" includes disposing for valuable consideration.

(2) In sub-paragraph (1) "disposing" includes—

(*a*) in the case of an investment consisting of rights under a contract—

(i) surrendering, assigning or converting those rights; or

(ii) assuming the corresponding liabilities under the contract;

(*b*) in the case of an investment consisting of rights under other arrangements, assuming the corresponding liabilities under the contract or arrangements;

(*c*) in the case of any other investment, issuing or creating the investment or granting the rights or interests of which it consists.

(3) In this Schedule references to an instrument include references to any record (whether or not in the form of a document).

FINANCE ACT 2003

(2003 Chapter 14)

An Act to grant certain duties, to alter other duties, and to amend the law relating to the National Debt and the Public Revenue, and to make further provision in connection with finance.

[10 July 2003]

PART 8
OTHER TAXES

Insurance premium tax

194 Higher rate of tax: divided companies

(1) (*inserts* FA 1994 Sch 6A para 3A)

(2) Subsection (1) applies in relation to a premium that falls to be regarded for the purposes of Part 3 of the Finance Act 1994 (c 9) (insurance premium tax) as received under a taxable insurance contract by an insurer on or after the day on which this Act is passed.

FINANCE ACT 2007

(2007 Chapter 11)

PART 7
MISCELLANEOUS

101 IPT: meaning of "premium"

(1) (*inserts* FA 1994 s 72(1B))

(2) The amendment made by subsection (1) has effect in relation to amounts charged on or after 22nd March 2007.

SCHEDULE

SCHEDULE 24
PENALTIES FOR ERRORS

Note—Please see *VAT Statutes* ante for the text of this Schedule.

FINANCE ACT 2008

(2008 Chapter 9)

An Act to Grant certain duties, to alter other duties, and to amend the law relating to the National Debt and the Public Revenue, and to make further provision in connection with finance.

[21 July 2008]

PART 7

ADMINISTRATION

Press releases—HMRC Guidance Note, 18 July 2008 (HMRC set-off across taxes following Finance Bill 2008).

CHAPTER 1

INFORMATION ETC

New information etc powers

114 Computer records etc

Note—Please see *VAT Statutes* ante for the text of this Section.

CHAPTER 3

PENALTIES

122 Penalties for errors

Note—Please see *VAT Statutes* ante for the text of this Section.

123 Penalties for failure to notify etc

Note—Please see *VAT Statutes* ante for the text of this Section.

CHAPTER 4

APPEALS ETC

Reviews and appeals etc: general

124 HMRC decisions etc: reviews and appeals

Note—Please see *VAT Statutes* ante for the text of this Section.

CHAPTER 5

PAYMENT AND ENFORCEMENT

Taking control of goods etc

127 Enforcement by taking control of goods: England and Wales

Note—Please see *VAT Statutes* ante for the text of this Section.

128 Summary warrant: Scotland

Note—Please see *VAT Statutes* ante for the text of this Section.

129 Consequential provision and commencement

Note—Please see *VAT Statutes* ante for the text of this Section.

Set off

130 Set-off: England and Wales and Northern Ireland

Note—Please see *VAT Statutes* ante for the text of this Section.

131 No set-off where insolvency procedure has been applied

Note—Please see *VAT Statutes* ante for the text of this Section.

133 Set-off etc where right to be paid a sum has been transferred

Note—Please see *VAT Statutes* ante for the text of this Section.

Other measures

135 Interest on unpaid tax in case of disaster etc of national significance

Note—Please see *VAT Statutes* ante for the text of this Section.

136 Fee for payment

Note—Please see *VAT Statutes* ante for the text of this Section.

Supplementary

139 Interpretation of Chapter

Note—Please see *VAT Statutes* ante for the text of this Section.

PART 8
MISCELLANEOUS

Insurance premium tax

142 Tax representatives

(1) (*amends* FA 1994 ss 57, 58, 65(1), 73(1), Sch 7 paras 18, 20).
(2) (*repeals* FA 1997 s 27(4), (5)).

143 Overseas insurers

(1) Section 65 of FA 1994 (insurance premium tax: liability of insured where insurer not established in United Kingdom) is amended as follows.
(2) (*amends* FA 1994 s 65(1)).
(3) (*inserts* FA 1994 s 65(1A), (1B))

Payments from Exchequer accounts

158 Power of Treasury to make payments

Note—Please see *VAT Statutes* ante for the text of this Section.

159 Payments from certain Exchequer accounts: mechanism

Note—Please see *VAT Statutes* ante for the text of this Section.

Other matters

160 Power to give statutory effect to concessions

Note—Please see *VAT Statutes* ante for the text of this Section.

PART 9
FINAL PROVISIONS

165 Interpretation

166 Short title

Note—Please see *VAT Statutes* ante for the text of these Sections.

SCHEDULES

SCHEDULE 36

INFORMATION AND INSPECTION POWERS

Section 113

Note—Please see *VAT Statutes* ante for the text of this Schedule.

SCHEDULE 41

PENALTIES: FAILURE TO NOTIFY AND CERTAIN VAT AND EXCISE WRONGDOING

Section 123

Note—Please see *VAT Statutes* ante for the text of this Schedule.

FINANCE ACT 2009

(2009 Chapter 10)

An Act to Grant certain duties, to alter other duties, and to amend the law relating to the National Debt and the Public Revenue, and to make further provision in connection with finance.

[21 July 2009]

PART 7
ADMINISTRATION

Standards and values

92 HMRC Charter

Note—Please see *VAT Statutes* ante for the text of this Section.

93 Duties of senior accounting officers of qualifying companies

Note—Please see *VAT Statutes* ante for the text of this Section.

94 Publishing details of deliberate tax defaulters

Note—Please see *VAT Statutes* ante for the text of this Section.

Information etc

95 Amendment of information and inspection powers

Note—Please see *VAT Statutes* ante for the text of this Section.

96 Extension of information and inspection powers to further taxes

(1) In paragraph 63(1) of Schedule 36 to FA 2008 (information and inspection powers: meaning of "tax"), for paragraph (*e*) (and the "and" before it) substitute—

"(*e*) insurance premium tax,
(*f*) inheritance tax,
(*g*) stamp duty land tax,
(*h*) stamp duty reserve tax,
(*i*) petroleum revenue tax,
(*j*) aggregates levy,
(*k*) climate change levy,
(*l*) landfill tax, and
(*m*) relevant foreign tax,".

(2) Schedule 48 contains further amendments of that Schedule.

(3) The amendments made by this section and Schedule 48 come into force on such day as the Treasury may by order appoint.

(4) An order under subsection (3) may—

(*a*) appoint different days for different purposes, and
(*b*) contain transitional provision and savings.

(5) The Treasury may by order make any incidental, supplemental, consequential, transitional or transitory provision or saving which appears appropriate in consequence of, or otherwise in connection with, this section and Schedule 48.

(6) An order under subsection (5) may—

(*a*) make different provision for different purposes, and
(*b*) make provision amending, repealing or revoking an enactment or instrument (whenever passed or made).

(7) An order under this section is to be made by statutory instrument.

(8) A statutory instrument containing an order under subsection (5) is subject to annulment in pursuance of a resolution of the House of Commons.

Order—Finance Act 2009, Section 96 and Schedule 48 (Appointed Day, Savings and Consequential Amendments) Order, SI 2009/3054 (appointed day is 1 April 2010).

97 Powers to obtain contact details for debtors

Note—Please see *VAT Statutes* ante for the text of this Section.

98 Record-keeping

(1) Schedule 50 contains provision about obligations to keep records.

(2) The amendments made by that Schedule come into force on such day as the Treasury may by order made by statutory instrument appoint.

Order—Finance Act 2009, Schedule 50 (Record-keeping) (Appointed Day) Order, SI 2010/815 (appoints 1 April 2010 as the date for the Sch 50 amendments to come into force).

Assessments, claims etc

99 Time limits for assessments, claims etc

(1) Schedule 51 contains provision about time limits for assessments, claims etc

(2) The amendments made by that Schedule come into force on such day as the Treasury may by order made by statutory instrument appoint.

(3) An order under subsection (2)—

(*a*) may make different provision for different purposes, and
(*b*) may include transitional provision and savings.

Order—Finance Act 2009, Schedule 51 (Time Limits for Assessments, Claims, etc) (Appointed Days and Transitional Provisions) Order, SI 2010/867 (1 April 2010 is appointed as the date for Sch 51 paras 1–4, 27–43 to come into force).

Interest

101 Late payment interest on sums due to HMRC

Note—Please see *VAT Statutes* ante for the text of this Section.

Order—Finance Act 2009, Sections 101 to 103 (Appointed Day and Supplemental Provision) Order, SI 2010/1878 (the appointed day on which ss 101–103 come into force for the purposes of bank payroll tax (including any penalties assessed in relation to that tax) is 31 August 2010).

102 Repayment interest on sums to be paid by HMRC

Note—Please see *VAT Statutes* ante for the text of this Section.

Order—Finance Act 2009, Sections 101 to 103 (Appointed Day and Supplemental Provision) Order, SI 2010/1878 (the appointed day on which ss 101–103 come into force for the purposes of bank payroll tax (including any penalties assessed in relation to that tax) is 31 August 2010).

103 Rates of interest

Note—Please see *VAT Statutes* ante for the text of this Section.

Order—Finance Act 2009, Sections 101 to 103 (Appointed Day and Supplemental Provision) Order, SI 2010/1878 (the appointed day on which ss 101–103 come into force for the purposes of bank payroll tax (including any penalties assessed in relation to that tax) is 31 August 2010).

104 Supplementary

Note—Please see *VAT Statutes* ante for the text of this Section.

108 Suspension of penalties during currency of agreement for deferred payment

Note—Please see *VAT Statutes* ante for the text of this Section.

109 Miscellaneous amendments

Note—Please see *VAT Statutes* ante for the text of this Section.

SCHEDULES

SCHEDULE 46

DUTIES OF SENIOR ACCOUNTING OFFICERS OF QUALIFYING COMPANIES

Section 93

Note—Please see *VAT Statutes* ante for the text of this Schedule.

SCHEDULE 47

AMENDMENT OF INFORMATION AND INSPECTION POWERS

Section 95

Note—Please see *VAT Statutes* ante for the text of this Schedule.

SCHEDULE 48

EXTENSION OF INFORMATION AND INSPECTION POWERS

Section 96

Note—Please see *VAT Statutes* ante for the text of this Schedule.

SCHEDULE 49

POWERS TO OBTAIN CONTACT DETAILS FOR DEBTORS

Section 97

Note—Please see *VAT Statutes* ante for the text of this Schedule.

SCHEDULE 50

RECORD-KEEPING

Section 98

Order—Finance Act 2009, Schedule 50 (Record-keeping) (Appointed Day) Order 2010 (appoints 1 April 2010 as the date for the Sch 50 amendments to come into force).

Insurance premium tax

1 (1) Paragraph 1 of Schedule 7 to FA 1994 (insurance premium tax: records) is amended as follows.

(2) In sub-paragraph (3)—

(*a*) after "may" insert

"—

(*a*) ", and

(*b*) *inserts* FA 1994 Sch 7 para 1(3)(*b*), (*c*))

(3) (*substitutes* FA 1994 Sch 7 para 1(4))

2 In consequence of the amendment made by paragraph 1(3), in the Criminal Procedure (Consequential Provisions) (Scotland) Act 1995, in Schedule 4, omit paragraph 89(4)(*a*).

SCHEDULE 51

TIME LIMITS FOR ASSESSMENTS, CLAIMS ETC

Section 99

Order—Finance Act 2009, Schedule 51 (Time Limits for Assessments, Claims, etc) (Appointed Days and Transitional Provisions) Order 2010 (1 April 2010 is appointed as the date for Sch 51 paras 1–4, 27–43 to come into force).

Insurance premium tax

1 Schedule 7 to FA 1994 (insurance premium tax) is amended as follows.

2 In paragraph 8(4) (recovery of overpaid tax), for "three years" substitute "4 years".

3 In paragraph 22(9) (interest payable by Commissioners), for "three years" substitute "4 years".

4—(1) Paragraph 26 (assessments: time limits) is amended as follows.
(2) In sub-paragraph (1), for the words from "three years after" (in the first place) to the end substitute "4 years after the relevant event".
(3) (*inserts* FA 1994 Sch 7 para 26(1A))
(4) In sub-paragraph (3), for "sub-paragraph (1)" substitute "sub-paragraph (1A)".
(5) (*substitutes* FA 1994 Sch 7 para 26(4), (5))

SCHEDULE 53

LATE PAYMENT INTEREST

Section 101

Note—Please see *VAT Statutes* ante for the text of this Schedule.

SCHEDULE 54

REPAYMENT INTEREST

Section 102

Note—Please see *VAT Statutes* ante for the text of this Schedule.

SCHEDULE 57

AMENDMENTS RELATING TO PENALTIES

Section 109

Note—Please see *VAT Statutes* ante for the text of this Schedule.

IPT

FINANCE ACT 2010

(2010 Chapter 13)

[8 April 2010]

PART 2
ANTI-AVOIDANCE AND REVENUE PROTECTION

Value added tax and insurance premium tax

51 Insurance premium tax: separate contracts
(1) Part 3 of FA 1994 (insurance premium tax) is amended as follows.
(2) Section 72 (meaning of "premium") is amended as follows.
(3) After subsection (1A) insert—

"(1AA) A contract ("the relevant contract") is not to be regarded as a separate contract for the purposes of subsection (1A) above if conditions A to D are met.

(1AB) Condition A is that the insured is an individual ("I") and enters into the taxable insurance contract in a personal capacity.

(1AC) Condition B is that I—

(*a*) is required to enter into the relevant contract by, or as a condition of entering into, the taxable insurance contract, or

(*b*) would be unlikely to enter into the relevant contract without also entering into the taxable insurance contract.

(1AD) Condition C is that—

(*a*) the amount charged to I under the relevant contract in respect of any particular services is not open to negotiation by I, or

(*b*) the other terms on which particular services are to be provided to I under the relevant contract are not open to such negotiation.

(1AE) Condition D is that the amount charged to I under the taxable insurance contract is arrived at without a comprehensive assessment having been undertaken of the individual circumstances of I which might affect the level of risk."

(4) After subsection (9) insert—

"(9A) Provision may be made by order amending subsections (1AA) to (1AE) above."

(5) In section 74(4) and (6) (orders which need to be approved by House of Commons), for "or 71" substitute ", 71 or 72".
(6) The amendment made by subsection (3) has effect in relation to payments made on or after 24 March 2010.

FINANCE (NO 2) ACT 2010

(2010 Chapter 31)

[27 July 2010]

PART 1
RATES, ETC

Insurance premium tax

4 Rates of insurance premium tax

(1) In section 51(2) of FA 1994 (rates of insurance premium tax)—

(*a*) in paragraph (*a*) (higher rate), for "17.5 per cent" substitute "20 per cent", and

(*b*) in paragraph (*b*) (standard rate), for "5 per cent" substitute "6 per cent".

(2) The amendments made by subsection (1) have effect in relation to a premium falling to be regarded for the purposes of Part 3 of FA 1994 as received under a taxable insurance contract by an insurer on or after 4 January 2011.

(3) In the application of sections 67A and 67C of FA 1994 (announced increase in rate) in relation to the increases made by this section—

(*a*) the announcement for the purposes of section 67A(1) is to be taken to have been made on 22 June 2010, and

(*b*) the date of the change is 4 January 2011.

(4) In FA 1999, omit section 125; and the repeal of that section comes into force in accordance with the provision made by this section for the coming into force of the amendments made by subsection (1).

Insurance Premium Tax Statutory Instruments

Contents

1994/1774

INSURANCE PREMIUM TAX REGULATIONS 1994

Made by the Commissioners of Customs and Excise under FA 1994 ss 53(6), 54, 55(1)–(8), 57(15), 58(2), (4), 62(1), (3)–(7), 65(1)–(3), (5), (7)–(13), 68(1)–(11), 74(2), (7), (8), and Sch 7 paras 1(1)–(3), 7(7), (8), 8(6).

Made . . . . *6th July 1994*
Laid before the House of Commons . . . . *7th July 1994*
Coming into force . . . . *1st August 1994*

ARRANGEMENT OF REGULATIONS

PART I
PRELIMINARY

PART II

REGISTRATION AND PROVISION FOR SPECIAL CASES

PART III

ACCOUNTING, PAYMENT AND RECORDS

PART IV

CLAIMS IN RESPECT OF CREDIT

PART IVA

REIMBURSEMENT ARRANGEMENTS

PART V

SPECIAL ACCOUNTING SCHEME

PART VI

TAX REPRESENTATIVES

PART VII

LIABILITY OF INSURED PERSONS

PART VIII

DISTRESS AND DILIGENCE

PART I
PRELIMINARY

Citation and commencement

1 These Regulations may be cited as the Insurance Premium Tax Regulations 1994 and shall come into force on 1st August 1994.

Interpretation

2—(1) In these Regulations—

"accounting period" means—

(*a*) in the case of a registered person, each period of three months ending on the dates notified to him by the Commissioners, whether by means of a certificate of registration issued by them or otherwise;

(*b*) in the case of a registrable person who is not registered, each quarter; or

(*c*) in the case of any registrable person, such other period in relation to which he is required by or under regulation 12 to make a return;

and, in every case, the first accounting period of a registrable person shall commence on the effective date determined in accordance with section 53 [or 53AA][1] of the Act upon which the person was or should have been registered;

"the Act" means Part III of the Finance Act 1994;

"Collector" means a Collector, Deputy Collector or Assistant Collector of Customs and Excise;

"Lloyd's" means the society incorporated by section 3 of Lloyd's Act 1871;

"managing agent" has the same meaning as in section 12(1) of Lloyd's Act 1982;

"registered person" means a person who is registered under section 53 [or 53AA][1] of the Act and, except in regulation 30, "register" and "registration" shall be construed accordingly;

"registration number" means the unique identifying number allocated to a registered person and notified to him by the Commissioners;

"return" means a return which is required to be made in accordance with regulation 12;

["taxable intermediary's fees" means fees which, to the extent of any payment in respect of them, are chargeable to tax by virtue of section 52A of the Finance Act 1994 and references in these regulations to "fee" or "fees" shall be construed accordingly;][1]

"underwriting member" has the same meaning as in section 2(1) of Lloyd's Act 1982.

(2) Any reference in these Regulations to "this Part" is a reference to the Part of these Regulations in which that reference is made.
(3) Any reference in these Regulations to a form prescribed in the Schedule to these Regulations shall include a reference to a form which the Commissioners are satisfied is a form to the like effect.

Amendments—[1] Words "or 53AA" in definitions of "accounting period" and "registered person" and definition of "taxable intermediary's fees" inserted by the Insurance Premium Tax (Amendment) Regulations, SI 1997/1157 with effect from 1 May 1997.

Requirement, direction, demand or approval

3 Any requirement, direction, demand or approval by the Commissioners under or for the purposes of these Regulations shall be made or given by a notice in writing.

PART II
REGISTRATION AND PROVISIONS FOR SPECIAL CASES

Notification of liability to register

4—(1) A person who is required by section 53(2) of the Act to notify the Commissioners of the facts there mentioned shall do so on the form numbered 1 in the Schedule to these Regulations.
(2) Where the notification referred to in this regulation is made by a partnership, it shall include the particulars set out on the form numbered 2 in the Schedule to these Regulations.
(3) The notification referred to in this regulation shall be made within thirty days of the earliest date after 31st July 1994 on which the person either forms or continues to have the intention to receive premiums in the course of a taxable business.

Commentary—*De Voil Indirect Tax Service* **V18.132.**

[Notification of liability to register—taxable intermediaries

4A—(1) A person who is required by section 53AA(3) of the Act to notify the Commissioners of the facts there mentioned shall do so on the form numbered 1 in the Schedule to these Regulations.
(2) Where the notification referred to in this regulation is made by a partnership, it shall include the particulars set out on the form numbered 2 in the Schedule to these Regulations.
(3) The notification referred to in this regulation shall be made within thirty days of the earliest date after 30th April 1997 on which the person either forms or continues to have the intention to charge taxable intermediary's fees in the course of any business of his.][1]

Amendments—[1] Reg 4A and the immediately preceding heading inserted by the Insurance Premium Tax (Amendment) Regulations, SI 1997/1157 with effect from 1 May 1997.

Changes in particulars

[5—(1) A person who has made a notification under regulation 4 [or 4A][2], whether or not it was made in accordance with paragraph (3) [of regulation 4 or 4A above][2], shall, within thirty days of—
(*a*) discovering any inaccuracy in; or
(*b*) any change occurring which causes to become inaccurate,

any information contained in or provided with the notification, notify the Commissioners in writing and furnish them with full particulars thereof.
(2) Without prejudice to paragraph (1) above, a registrable person shall, within thirty days of any change occurring in any of the circumstances referred to in paragraph (4) below, notify the Commissioners in writing and furnish them with particulars of—
(*a*) the change; and
(*b*) the date on which the change occurred.
(3) A registrable person who discovers that any information contained in or provided with a notification under paragraph (2) above is inaccurate shall, within thirty days of his discovering the inaccuracy, notify the Commissioners and furnish them with particulars of—
(*a*) the inaccuracy;
(*b*) the date on which the inaccuracy was discovered;
(*c*) why the information was inaccurate; and
(*d*) the correct information.
(4) The circumstances mentioned in paragraph (2) above are the following circumstances relating to the registrable person[, any insurance business carried on by him or any business in the course of which he charges taxable intermediary's fees][2]—
(*a*) his name, his trading name (if different) and address;
(*b*) the name, the trading name (if different) and address of his tax representative;
(*c*) his status, namely whether he carries on business as a sole proprietor, body corporate, partnership or other unincorporated body;
(*d*) in the case of a partnership, the name and address of the partners;
(*e*) in the case of a syndicate of underwriting members of Lloyd's which has been registered as such, the number or other identifying feature by reference to which it was registered.

IPT

(5) Where in relation to a registrable person the Commissioners are satisfied that any of the information recorded in the register kept under section 53 [or 53AA][2] of the Act is or has become inaccurate they may correct the register accordingly.

(6) For the purposes of paragraph (5) above it is immaterial whether or not the registrable person has made any notification he was required to make under this regulation.][1]

Commentary—*De Voil Indirect Tax Service* **V18.132.**

Amendments—[1] Para (5) substituted by the Insurance Premium Tax (Amendment) Regulations, SI 1995/1587 with effect from 17 July 1995.

[2] First words in para (1) and words in para (5) inserted and second words in para (1) and words in para (4) substituted by the Insurance Premium Tax (Amendment) Regulations, SI 1997/1157 with effect from 1 May 1997.

Notification of liability to be de-registered

6 A person who is required by section 53(3) of the Act to notify the Commissioners of the facts there mentioned shall, within thirty days of his having ceased to have the intention to receive premiums in the course of any taxable business, notify the Commissioners in writing and shall therein inform them of—

(*a*) the date on which he ceased to have the intention of receiving premiums in the course of any taxable business; and

(*b*) if different, the date on which the last such premium was received.

Commentary—*De Voil Indirect Tax Service* **V18.136.**

[Notification of liability to be de-registered— taxable intermediaries

6A A person who is required by section 53AA(4) of the Act to notify the Commissioners of the facts there mentioned shall, within thirty days of his having ceased to have the intention of charging taxable intermediary's fees, give notice to the Commissioners in writing—

(*a*) of the date on which he ceased to charge taxable intermediary's fees in the course of any business of his; and

(*b*) if different, the date on which the last such fee was received.][1]

Commentary—*De Voil Indirect Tax Service* **V18.187.**

Amendments—[1] Reg 6A and the immediately preceding heading inserted by the Insurance Premium Tax (Amendment) Regulations, SI 1997/1157 with effect from 1 May 1997.

Transfer of a going concern

7—(1) Where—

(*a*) a taxable business is transferred as a going concern;

(*b*) the registration of the transferor has not already been cancelled;

(*c*) as a result of the transfer of the business the registration of the transferor is to be cancelled and the transferee becomes liable to be registered; and

(*d*) an application is made on the form numbered 3 in the Schedule to these Regulations by both the transferor and the transferee,

the Commissioners may with effect from the date of the transfer cancel the registration of the transferor and register the transferee with the registration number previously allocated to the transferor.

(2) An application under paragraph (1) above shall be treated as the notification referred to in regulation 6.

(3) Where the transferee of a business has been registered under paragraph (1) above with the registration number previously allocated to the transferor—

(*a*) any liability of the transferor existing at the date of the transfer to make a return or account for or pay any tax under Part III of these Regulations shall become the liability of the transferee;

(*b*) any entitlement of the transferor, whether or not existing at the date of the transfer, to credit or payment under Part IV of these Regulations shall become the entitlement of the transferee.

(4) In addition to the provisions set out in paragraph (3) above, where the transferee of a business has been registered under paragraph (1) above with the registration number previously allocated to the transferor during an accounting period subsequent to that in which the transfer took place (but with effect from the date of the transfer) and any—

(*a*) return has been made;

(*b*) tax has been accounted for; or

(*c*) entitlement to credit has been claimed,

by either the transferor or the transferee, it shall be treated as having been done by the transferee.

(5) Where—

(*a*) a taxable business is transferred as a going concern;

(*b*) the transferee makes a payment to a person which represents the repayment of any premium or part of a premium received in the course of that business; and

(*c*) the transferor has paid tax on that premium or part,

then, whether or not the transferee has been registered under paragraph (1) above with the registration number previously allocated to the transferor, any entitlement to credit under Part IV of these Regulations shall become the entitlement of the transferee.

Commentary—*De Voil Indirect Tax Service* **V18.133.**

Registration of Lloyd's syndicates

8—(1) Where a taxable business is carried on by persons who are underwriting members of Lloyd's who are members of a syndicate of such underwriting members the registration of those persons for the purposes of the Act may be by reference to the syndicate; and, where such a syndicate is not known by any name, the registration may be by reference to any number or other identifying feature of the syndicate.

(2) In determining whether premiums are received by any syndicate which has been registered in the manner described in paragraph (1) above no account shall be taken of any change in the members of the syndicate.

Commentary—*De Voil Indirect Tax Service* **V18.134.**

Representation of Lloyd's syndicates

9—(1) Anything required to be done by or under the Act (whether by these Regulations or otherwise) by or on behalf of a syndicate of underwriting members of Lloyd's shall be the joint and several responsibility of the persons mentioned in paragraph (2) below; but if it is done by any of those persons it shall be sufficient compliance with any such requirement.

(2) The persons are—

(*a*) the underwriting members of the syndicate;

(*b*) the managing agent of the syndicate; and

(*c*) as regards any accounting period for which it is required by paragraph (3) below to act as the syndicate's representative, Lloyd's.

(3) Where a syndicate of underwriting members of Lloyd's has made an election that Lloyd's shall act as its representative Lloyd's shall so act in relation to any accounting period as regards which—

(*a*) that election has effect;

(*b*) the syndicate is registered as described in regulation 8; and

(*c*) the scheme established by Part V of these Regulations applies to the syndicate.

(4) An election under paragraph (3) above shall be made in writing and shall specify the first accounting period of the syndicate in respect of which the election is to have effect, being an accounting period beginning on or after the date the election is made.

(5) Subject to paragraphs (6) and (7) below, an election under paragraph (3) above shall have effect for the accounting period specified in the election and all subsequent accounting periods.

(6) An election under paragraph (3) above shall not have effect unless written notification of the election is given to the Commissioners before the beginning of the accounting period specified in the election.

(7) An election under paragraph (3) above shall cease to have effect with effect from the accounting period specified in any notice in writing given by the syndicate to the Commissioners for this purpose, being an accounting period beginning after the date the notice is given.

Commentary—*De Voil Indirect Tax Service* **V18.138.**

Representation of unincorporated body

10—(1) Where anything is required to be done by or under the Act (whether by these Regulations or otherwise) by or on behalf of an unincorporated body other than a partnership, it shall be the joint and several responsibility of—

(*a*) every member holding office as president, chairman, treasurer, secretary or any similar office; or

(*b*) if there is no such office, every member holding office as a member of a committee by which the affairs of the body are managed; or

(*c*) if there is no such office or committee, every member;

but, subject to paragraph (2) below, if it is done by any of the persons referred to above that shall be sufficient compliance with any such requirement.

(2) Where an unincorporated body other than a partnership is required to make any notification such as is referred to in regulations 4 to 6, it shall not be sufficient compliance unless the notification is made by a person upon whom a responsibility for making it is imposed by paragraph (1) above.

(3) Where anything is required to be done by or under the Act (whether by these Regulations or otherwise) by or on behalf of a partnership, it shall be the joint and several responsibility of every partner; but if it is done by one partner or, in the case of a partnership whose principal place of business is in Scotland, by any other person authorised by the partnership with respect thereto that shall be sufficient compliance with any such requirement.

Death, bankruptcy or incapacity of registrable persons

11—(1) If a registrable person dies or becomes bankrupt or incapacitated, the Commissioners may, from the date on which he died or became bankrupt or incapacitated, as the case may be, treat as a registrable person any person carrying on any taxable business of his [or any business in the course of which he charged taxable intermediary's fees][1] and any legislation relating to insurance premium tax shall apply to any person so treated as though he were a registered person.
(2) Any person carrying on such business as aforesaid shall, within thirty days of commencing to do so, inform the Commissioners in writing of that fact and of the date of the death or bankruptcy or of the nature of the incapacity and the date on which it began.
(3) Where the Commissioners have treated a person carrying on a business as a registrable person under paragraph (1) above, they shall cease so to treat him if—
(*a*) the registration of the registrable person is cancelled, whether or not any other person is registered with the registration number previously allocated to him;
(*b*) the bankruptcy is discharged or the incapacity ceases; or
(*c*) he ceases carrying on the business of the registrable person.
(4) In relation to a registrable person which is a company, the references in this regulation to the registrable person becoming incapacitated shall be construed as references to its going into liquidation or receivership or to [entering administration][2]; and references to the incapacity ceasing shall be construed accordingly.

Commentary—*De Voil Indirect Tax Service* **V18.141.**

Amendments—[1] Words in para (1) inserted by the Insurance Premium Tax (Amendment) Regulations, SI 1997/1157 with effect from 1 May 1997.

[2] Words in para (4) substituted by the Enterprise Act 2002 (Insolvency) Order, SI 2003/2096 art 5, Schedule para 54 with effect from 15 September 2003. However, this amendment does not apply in any case where a petition for an administration order was presented before that date: SI 2003/2096 art 6.

PART III
ACCOUNTING, PAYMENT AND RECORDS

Making of returns

12—(1) Subject to paragraphs (2) and (4) below and save as the Commissioners may otherwise allow, a registrable person shall, in respect of each accounting period, make a return to the Controller, Central Collection Unit (IPT) on the form numbered 4 in the Schedule to these Regulations.
(2) Lloyd's may, in respect of any two or more syndicates of underwriting members of Lloyd's for which it is required by regulation 9(3) to act as representative as regards an accounting period which, as regards each such syndicate, begins on the same date and ends on the same date, make a return on the form numbered 5 in the Schedule to these Regulations; and, provided it is accompanied by a summary schedule on the form numbered 6 in the Schedule to these Regulations, the making of a return under this paragraph shall be treated as sufficient compliance with paragraph (1) above in relation to the accounting period of each of the syndicates concerned.
(3) Subject to paragraph (4) below, a registrable person shall make each return not later than the last day of the month next following the end of the period to which it relates.
(4) Where the Commissioners consider it necessary in the circumstances of any particular case, they may—
(*a*) vary the length of any accounting period or the date on which it begins or ends or by which any return must be made;
(*b*) allow or direct the registrable person to make a return in accordance with sub-paragraph (*a*) above;
(*c*) allow or direct a registrable person to make returns to a specified address;
and any person to whom the Commissioners give any direction such as is referred to in this regulation shall comply therewith.

Commentary—*De Voil Indirect Tax Service* **V18.146.**

Correction of errors

13—(1) In this regulation—
"credit" means credit to which a person is entitled under Part IV of these Regulations;
"overdeclaration" means, in relation to any return, the amount (if any) which was wrongly treated as tax due for the accounting period concerned and which caused either the amount of tax which was payable to be overstated or the entitlement to a payment under regulation 19(1) to be understated or both or would have caused such an overstatement or understatement were it not for the existence of an underdeclaration in relation to that return;
"underdeclaration" means, in relation to any return, the aggregate of—
(*a*) the amount (if any) of tax due for the accounting period concerned which was not taken into account; and
(*b*) the amount (if any) which was wrongly deducted as credit,

and which caused either the amount of tax which was payable to be understated or the entitlement to a payment under regulation 19(1) to be overstated or both or would have caused such an understatement or overstatement were it not for the existence of an overdeclaration in relation to that return.

(2) This regulation applies where a registrable person has made a return which was inaccurate as the result of an overdeclaration or underdeclaration.

(3) Where, in relation to any overdeclarations or underdeclarations that are discovered by the registrable person in an accounting period—

(*a*) the total of the overdeclarations discovered does not exceed [£50,000][1], he may enter that total in [Boxes 6 to 8 (overdeclarations), as appropriate,][1] in the return for that accounting period;

(*b*) the total of the underdeclarations discovered does not exceed [£50,000][1], he may enter that total in [Boxes 3 and 4 (underdeclarations), as appropriate,][1] in the return for that accounting period;

and, where he does so, he shall calculate the tax payable by him or the payment to which he is entitled accordingly.

[But if Box 10 of the registrable person's return for the accounting period requires an entry for net value of taxable premiums (excluding tax) that is less than £5,000,000 (see regulation 12 and Forms 4 and 5 in the Schedule), the total mentioned in sub-paragraph (*a*) or (*b*) must not for these purposes exceed 1% of that net value unless the respective total is [£10,000 or less][2].][1]

(4) Where the return for the accounting period in which the overdeclaration or underdeclaration was discovered is made by Lloyd's in accordance with regulation 12(2), paragraph (3) above shall apply as if the references to the totals of the overdeclarations or underdeclarations . . . [1] were references to each such total for each syndicate in respect of which the return is made . . . [1].

(5) No amount shall be entered in any return in respect of any overdeclaration or underdeclaration except in accordance with this regulation.

(6) Where any amount has been entered in a return in accordance with this regulation, that return shall be regarded as correcting any earlier return to which that amount relates.

Commentary—*De Voil Indirect Tax Service* **V18.147.**

Amendments—[1] In para (3)(*a*), (*b*), words substituted and final sentence inserted, and in para (4), words revoked, by the Value Added Tax, etc (Correction of Errors, etc) Regulations, SI 2008/1482 reg 3 with effect in relation to the overdeclarations or underdeclarations in reg 13(3) which registrable persons first discover in their accounting periods that begin on 1 July 2008 or later. Paras (3), (4) previously read as follows—

"(3) Where, in relation to any overdeclarations or underdeclarations that are discovered by the registrable person in an accounting period—

(*a*) the total of the overdeclarations discovered does not exceed £2,000, he may enter that total in the box opposite the legend "Overdeclarations from previous periods" in the return for that accounting period;

(*b*) the total of the underdeclarations discovered does not exceed £2,000, he may enter that total in the box opposite the legend "Underdeclarations from previous periods" in the return for that accounting period;

and, where he does so, he shall calculate the tax payable by him or the payment to which he is entitled accordingly.

(4) Where the return for the accounting period in which the overdeclaration or underdeclaration was discovered is made by Lloyd's in accordance with regulation 12(2), paragraph (3) above shall apply as if the references to the totals of the overdeclarations or underdeclarations not exceeding £2,000 were references to each such total for each syndicate in respect of which the return is made not exceeding £2,000.".

[2] In para (3), words substituted for words "less than £10,000" by the Amusement Machine Licence Duty, etc (Amendments) Regulations, SI 2008/2693 reg 4(1)(*a*) with effect for a discovery first made on 1 November 2008 or later.

Claims for overpaid tax

14 Except where the amount to which the claim relates has been entered in a return in accordance with regulation 13 or is included in an amount so entered, any claim under paragraph 8 of Schedule 7 to the Act shall be made in writing to the Commissioners and shall, by reference to such documentary evidence as is in the possession of the claimant, state the amount of the claim and the method by which that amount was calculated.

Commentary—*De Voil Indirect Tax Service* **V18.185.**

Payment of tax

15 Save as the Commissioners may otherwise allow or direct, any person required to make a return shall pay to the Controller, Central Collection Unit (IPT) such amount of tax as is payable by him in respect of the accounting period to which the return relates no later than the last day on which he was required to make the return.

Commentary—*De Voil Indirect Tax Service* **V18.146.**

Records

16—(1) Every registrable person shall, for the purpose of accounting for tax, keep and preserve the following—

(*a*) his business and accounting records;

(*b*) policy documents, cover notes, endorsements and similar documents, and copies of such documents that are issued by him;

(*c*) copies of all invoices, renewal notices and similar documents issued by him;

(*d*) all credit or debit notes or other documents received by him which evidence an increase or decrease in the amount of any premium [or fee][1], and copies of such documents that are issued by him;

(*e*) such other records as the Commissioners may specify in a notice published by them and not withdrawn by them.

(2) Every registrable person shall keep and preserve the records specified in paragraph (1) above for a period of six years.

(3) The reference in paragraph (1)(*d*) above to any premium shall be construed for the purposes of that paragraph as it would be construed for the purposes of Part V of these Regulations.

Commentary—*De Voil Indirect Tax Service* **V18.171.**

Amendments—[1] Words in para (1)(*d*) inserted by the Insurance Premium Tax (Amendment) Regulations, SI 1997/1157 with effect from 1 May 1997.

PART IV
CLAIMS IN RESPECT OF CREDIT

Scope

[**17**—(1) This Part applies where—

(*a*) an insurer has paid tax and all or part of the premium on which the tax was charged is repaid; or

(*b*) a taxable intermediary has paid tax and all or part of the fee on which the tax was charged is repaid.

(2) Where—

(*a*) an insurer receives a premium in an accounting period and repays that premium or part of it in that accounting period; or

(*b*) a taxable intermediary receives a fee in an accounting period and repays that fee or part of it in that accounting period,

this Part shall apply as if the tax on the premium or fee (as the case may be) had already been paid by him.][1]

(3) This Part applies subject to regulation 7.

Commentary—*De Voil Indirect Tax Service* **V18.121.**

Amendments—[1] Paras (1), (2) substituted by the Insurance Premium Tax (Amendment) Regulations, SI 1997/1157 with effect from 1 May 1997.

Claims in returns

18—(1) Where this Part applies, the insurer [or, as the case may be, taxable intermediary][1] shall be entitled to credit of an amount which represents the difference between the amount of tax paid by him and the amount of tax he would have been liable to pay had the premium [or fee][1] received by him been reduced or extinguished, as the case may be, by the amount of the repayment.

(2) Subject to paragraph (3) below, an insurer [or taxable intermediary][1] who is entitled to credit under this Part may claim it by deducting its amount from any tax due from him for the accounting period in which the premium [or fee][1] was repaid or any subsequent accounting period and, where he does so, he shall make his return for that accounting period accordingly.

(3) Where the Commissioners have given a special or general direction under section 55(5) of the Act prescribing rules according to which any credit may or shall be held over to an accounting period subsequent to that in which the [premium or fee, or part of such premium or fee][1] was repaid, that credit, subject to any subsequent such direction varying or withdrawing the rules, may only be claimed in accordance with those rules.

Commentary—*De Voil Indirect Tax Service* **V18.121.**

Amendments—[1] Words in paras (1), (2) inserted and words in para (3) substituted by the Insurance Premium Tax (Amendment) Regulations, SI 1997/1157 with effect from 1 May 1997.

Payments in respect of credit

19—(1) Subject to paragraph (5) below, where the total credit claimed by the insurer [or taxable intermediary][1] in accordance with this Part exceeds the total of the tax due from him for the accounting period, the Commissioners shall pay to him an amount equal to the excess.

(2) Where the Commissioners have cancelled the registration of an insurer [or taxable intermediary][1] in accordance with section 53(5) [or 53AA(c)][1] of the Act, and he is not a registrable person, he shall make any claim in respect of credit to which this Part applies by making an application in writing.

(3) An insurer [or taxable intermediary][1] making an application under paragraph (2) above shall furnish to the Commissioners full particulars in relation to the credit claimed, including (but not restricted to)—

(*a*) the return in which the relevant tax was accounted for;

(*b*) the date and manner of payment of that tax;

(*c*) the date of the repayment of the [premium or fee, or part of such premium or fee][1]; and

(*d*) the amounts of both the tax which was paid and the repayment.

(4) Subject to paragraph (5) below, where the Commissioners are satisfied that the insurer [or taxable intermediary as the case may be][1] is entitled to credit as claimed by him, and that he has not previously had the benefit of that credit, they shall pay to him an amount equal to the credit.

(5) The Commissioners shall not be liable to make any payment under this regulation unless and until the insurer [or taxable intermediary][1] has made all the returns which he was required to make.

Commentary—*De Voil Indirect Tax Service* **V18.121.**

Amendments—[1] Words in paras (1)–(5) inserted and words in para (3)(*c*) substituted by the Insurance Premium Tax (Amendment) Regulations, SI 1997/1157 with effect from 1 May 1997.

[PART IVA
REIMBURSEMENT ARRANGEMENTS][1]

Commentary—*De Voil Indirect Tax Service* **V18.185.**

Amendments—[1] Part IVA (regs 19A–19H) inserted by the Insurance Premium Tax (Amendment) Regulations, SI 1998/60 with effect from 11 February 1998.

[Interpretation of Part IVA

19A In this Part—

"claim" means a claim made (irrespective of when it was made) under paragraph 8 of Schedule 7 to the Act for repayment of an amount paid to the Commissioners by way of tax which was not tax due to them; and "claimed" and "claimant" shall be construed accordingly;

"reimbursement arrangements" means any arrangements (whether made before, on or after 30th January 1998) for the purposes of a claim which—

(*a*) are made by a claimant for the purpose of securing that he is not unjustly enriched by the repayment of any amount in pursuance of the claim; and

(*b*) provide for the reimbursement of persons (consumers) who have, for practical purposes, borne the whole or any part of the cost of the original payment of that amount to the Commissioners;

"relevant amount" means that part (which may be the whole) of the amount of a claim which the claimant has reimbursed or intends to reimburse to consumers.][1]

Amendments—[1] Part IVA (regs 19A–19H) inserted by the Insurance Premium Tax (Amendment) Regulations, SI 1998/60 with effect from 11 February 1998.

[Reimbursement arrangements—general

19B Without prejudice to regulation 19H below, for the purposes of paragraph 8(3) of Schedule 7 to the Act (defence by the Commissioners that repayment by them of an amount claimed would unjustly enrich the claimant) reimbursement arrangements made by a claimant shall be disregarded except where they—

(*a*) include the provisions described in regulation 19C below; and

(*b*) are supported by the undertakings described in regulation 19G below.][1]

Amendments—[1] Part IVA (regs 19A–19H) inserted by the Insurance Premium Tax (Amendment) Regulations, SI 1998/60 with effect from 11 February 1998.

[Reimbursement arrangements—provisions to be included

19C The provisions referred to in regulation 19B(a) above are that—

(*a*) reimbursement for which the arrangements provide will be completed by no later than 90 days after the repayment to which it relates;

(*b*) no deduction will be made from the relevant amount by way of fee or charge (howsoever expressed or effected);

(*c*) reimbursement will be made only in cash or by cheque;

(*d*) any part of the relevant amount that is not reimbursed by the time mentioned in paragraph (*a*) above will be repaid by the claimant to the Commissioners;

(*e*) any interest paid by the Commissioners on any relevant amount repaid by them will also be treated by the claimant in the same way as the relevant amount falls to be treated under paragraphs (*a*) and (*b*) above; and

(*f*) the records described in regulation 19E below will be kept by the claimant and produced by him to the Commissioners, or to an officer of theirs in accordance with regulation 19F below.][1]

Amendments—[1] Part IVA (regs 19A–19H) inserted by the Insurance Premium Tax (Amendment) Regulations, SI 1998/60 with effect from 11 February 1998.

[Repayments to the Commissioners

19D The claimant shall, without prior demand, make any repayment to the Commissioners that he is required to make by virtue of regulation 19C(*d*) and (*e*) above within 14 days of the expiration of the period of 90 days referred to in regulation 19C(*a*) above.][1]

Amendments—[1] Part IVA (regs 19A–19H) inserted by the Insurance Premium Tax (Amendment) Regulations, SI 1998/60 with effect from 11 February 1998.

[Records

19E The claimant shall keep records of the following matters—

(*a*) the names and addresses of those consumers whom he has reimbursed or whom he intends to reimburse;
(*b*) the total amount reimbursed to each such consumer;
(*c*) the amount of interest included in each total amount reimbursed to each consumer;
(*d*) the date that each reimbursement is made.][1]

Amendments—[1] Part IVA (regs 19A–19H) inserted by the Insurance Premium Tax (Amendment) Regulations, SI 1998/60 with effect from 11 February 1998.

[Production of records

19F—(1) Where a claimant is given notice in accordance with paragraph (2) below, he shall, in accordance with such notice produce to the Commissioners, or to an officer of theirs, the records that he is required to keep pursuant to regulation 19E above.

(2) A notice given for the purposes of paragraph (1) above shall—

(*a*) be in writing;
(*b*) state the place and time at which, and the date on which the records are to be produced; and
(*c*) be signed and dated by the Commissioners, or by an officer of theirs,

and may be given before or after, or both before and after the Commissioners have paid the relevant amount to the claimant.][1]

Amendments—[1] Part IVA (regs 19A–19H) inserted by the Insurance Premium Tax (Amendment) Regulations, SI 1998/60 with effect from 11 February 1998.

[Undertakings

19G—(1) Without prejudice to regulation 19H(*b*) below, the undertakings referred to in regulation 19B(*b*) above shall be given to the Commissioners by the claimant no later than the time at which he makes the claim for which the reimbursement arrangements have been made.

(2) The undertakings shall be in writing, shall be signed and dated by the claimant, and shall be to the effect that—

(*a*) at the date of the undertakings he is able to identify the names and addresses of those consumers whom he has reimbursed or whom he intends to reimburse;
(*b*) he will apply the whole of the relevant amount repaid to him, without any deduction by way of fee or charge or otherwise, to the reimbursement in cash or by cheque, of such consumers by no later than 90 days after his receipt of that amount (except insofar as he has already so reimbursed them);
(*c*) he will apply any interest paid to him on the relevant amount repaid to him wholly to the reimbursement of such consumers by no later than 90 days after his receipt of that interest;
(*d*) he will repay to the Commissioners without demand the whole or such part of the relevant amount repaid to him or of any interest paid to him as he fails to apply in accordance with the undertakings mentioned in sub-paragraphs (*b*) and (*c*) above;
(*e*) he will keep the records described in regulation 19E above; and
(*f*) he will comply with any notice given to him in accordance with regulation 19F above concerning the production of such records.][1]

Amendments—[1] Part IVA inserted (regs 19A–19H) by the Insurance Premium Tax (Amendment) Regulations, SI 1998/60 with effect from 11 February 1998.

[Reimbursement arrangements made before 11th February 1998

19H Reimbursement arrangements made by a claimant before 11th February 1998 shall not be disregarded for the purposes of paragraph 8(3) of Schedule 7 to the Act if, not later than 11th March 1998—

(*a*) he includes in those arrangements (if they are not already included) the provisions described in regulation 19C above; and
(*b*) gives the undertakings described in regulation 19G above.][1]

Amendments—[1] Part IVA inserted (regs 19A–19H) by the Insurance Premium Tax (Amendment) Regulations, SI 1998/60 with effect from 11 February 1998.

PART V
SPECIAL ACCOUNTING SCHEME

Interpretation

20—(1) In this Part—

"date of receipt", in relation to any premium, means the date on which apart from the operation of the scheme the premium is received or taken to be received by the provisions of the Act;

"initial period" means the first of the accounting periods which begin on or after the date specified in a notification made under regulation 21(1);

"premium written date", in relation to any premium, means the date as at which the insurer makes an entry in his accounts showing the premium as due to him.

(2) Any reference in this Part to the accounts of any person shall be construed as a reference to—

(*a*) the books, accounts or other similar records which he maintains in whatever form for the purpose of enabling him to show the premiums receivable by him in the revenue account he is required to prepare [in accordance with rules made under Part 10 of the Financial Services and Markets Act 2000][1]; and "premiums receivable" has the same meaning as [in those rules][1]; or

(*b*) where he is not required to prepare the revenue account referred to in sub-paragraph (*a*) above, any books, accounts or other records which would enable him to prepare one.

(3) Any reference in this Part to a premium shall be construed as including a reference to anything that, although not actually received by or on behalf of an insurer, would be a premium if it were so received.

(4) In deciding whether and (if it does) how the scheme applies to an accounting period of an insurer to whom the scheme has previously applied as regards one or more accounting periods ending before the beginning of the initial period specified in a notification he has made under regulation 21(1), the fact of such previous application of the scheme shall be ignored.

Commentary—*De Voil Indirect Tax Service* **V18.127.**

Amendments—[1] Words in para (2)(*a*) substituted by the Financial Services and Markets Act 2000 (Consequential Amendments and Repeals) Order, SI 2001/3649 art 462 with effect from 1 December 2001.

Notification by insurer that scheme to apply

21—(1) An insurer who is a registrable person and—

(*a*) is required to prepare the revenue account referred to in regulation 20(2)(*a*); or

(*b*) not being required to prepare such a revenue account, keeps accounts as described in regulation 20(2)(*b*),

may notify the Commissioners in writing that the scheme should apply to him as regards accounting periods beginning on or after a date specified in the notification, being a date falling after the date the notification is made.

(2) An insurer who has made a notification under paragraph (1) above may notify the Commissioners in writing that he wishes to withdraw the notification and, provided he makes the notification referred to in this paragraph no later than the last day by which he is required to make the return for the initial period and before he has made that return, the scheme shall not apply to him as regards any accounting period.

(3) The fact that an insurer has on a previous occasion withdrawn or been expelled from the scheme under regulation 26 or 27 or withdrawn a notification under paragraph (2) above shall not prevent him making a notification under paragraph (1) above.

Commentary—*De Voil Indirect Tax Service* **V18.127.**

Relevant accounting periods

22 Subject to regulations 21(2), 26 and 27, the scheme shall apply as regards all the accounting periods of an insurer who has made a notification under regulation 21(1) with effect from the initial period.

Premiums treated as received on premium written date

23—(1) Subject to paragraph (8) below, any premium in relation to which—

(*a*) an insurer has made an entry in his accounts showing the premium as due to him;

(*b*) the premium written date falls within a relevant accounting period; and

(*c*) the date of receipt does not fall within an accounting period which is earlier than the initial period and which is not a relevant accounting period,

shall be treated for the purposes of the Act as received by the insurer on the premium written date; and the insurer shall account for tax due in respect of the relevant accounting period concerned accordingly.

IPT

(2) Paragraph (1) above shall apply even if the premium or any part of it is never actually received by the insurer; and, where it is never actually received because the contract under which it is or would have been received is terminated or is not entered into, the premium shall nonetheless be taken for the purposes of the Act to have been received under the contract (including, where appropriate, a taxable insurance contract) under which the insurer treated it as due.

(3) Where in relation to any premium to which paragraph (1) above applies the premium written date is a date other than the date of receipt, the premium shall be treated for the purposes of the Act as not having been received by the insurer on the date of receipt; but this is subject to paragraph (4) below.

(4) Paragraph (3) above shall not apply to any excess which falls to be treated as a separate premium in accordance with regulation 24(2).

(5) An insurer to whom the scheme applies as regards an accounting period may assume that the scheme will apply as regards all subsequent accounting periods and account for tax due in respect of that period accordingly.

(6) Subject to paragraph (7) below, where in relation to a premium—

(*a*) the premium written date falls before 1st October 1994;

(*b*) the premium was actually received by the insurer on or after 1st October 1994; and

(*c*) the contract under which the premium was received is not a contract to which, if the premium had actually been received on the premium written date, section 67(3) of the Act would have applied,

the premium shall be treated for the purposes of the Act as received before 1st October 1994 and the insurer shall accordingly not account for any tax on that premium.

(7) Paragraph (6) above shall not apply to any premium where—

(*a*) the contract under which the premium was received relates to a risk the period of cover for which begins on or after 1st October 1994; and

(*b*) it is not the normal practice as regards the class of contract to which that contract belongs for an insurer to make an entry in his accounts showing the premium as due as at a date before the period of cover begins.

(8) Where the initial period begins on 1st October 1994, nothing in this regulation shall be taken as requiring a premium—

(*a*) which was actually received by the insurer before 1st October 1994;

(*b*) in respect of which the premium written date falls within a relevant accounting period;

(*c*) which is not taken by virtue of section 67 of the Act to be received on 1st October 1994; and

(*d*) which was received under a contract which relates to a risk the period of cover for which begins before 1st October 1994,

to be treated as received on a date other than the date of receipt.

(9) Where in relation to any premium—

(*a*) an insurer has made an entry in his accounts showing the premium as due to him;

(*b*) the entry was made on a date falling within a relevant accounting period; and

(*c*) the premium written date would, apart from this paragraph, fall in a relevant accounting period which is earlier than the accounting period referred to in paragraph (*b*) above,

the insurer shall be treated for the purposes of this regulation as if he had made the entry showing the premium as due to him as at the date on which the entry was made and that date (and no other date) shall be the premium written date accordingly.

Commentary—*De Voil Indirect Tax Service* **V18.127.**

Amount of premium

24—(1) Subject to any direction made under section 66 of the Act, where in relation to any premium to which regulation 23(1) applies the amount which is entered in the accounts as due (the initial amount) is not the amount which is or would be found apart from the operation of the scheme to be the amount of the premium in accordance with the provisions of the Act the amount of the premium shall be taken to be the initial amount.

(2) Where paragraph (1) above applies and the amount of the premium which is received exceeds the initial amount, the excess shall be treated as a separate premium and shall be treated as received on a date determined in accordance with paragraphs (3) and (4) below.

(3) Where an amount of premium is treated as a separate premium in accordance with paragraph (2) above and—

(*a*) the initial amount is not less than the amount which has been agreed with the insured by the insurer or his agent as the amount which, as at the date the entry is made, is due under the contract; and

(*b*) the insurer makes an entry in his accounts showing the excess as due,

it shall be treated as received on the date he makes that entry in his accounts.

(4) In any case where an amount of premium is treated as a separate premium in accordance with paragraph (2) above and paragraph (3) above does not apply, the excess shall be treated as received on the date as at which the initial amount is entered in the accounts as due.

(5) An insurer who intends to enter in his accounts as due any excess over the initial amount of any premium which, if he were to make such an entry, would be treated as received on a date determined in accordance with paragraph (3) above may assume that it will be so treated until such time as he ceases to have that intention.

(6) Where in relation to an amount of premium which is treated as a separate premium in accordance with paragraph (2) above the date of receipt is a date other than the date determined in accordance with paragraphs (3) and (4) above, it shall be treated as not having been received by the insurer on the date of receipt.

Commentary—*De Voil Indirect Tax Service* **V18.127.**

Credit

25—(1) Subject to paragraph (2) below, where tax has been paid—

(*a*) in respect of a premium to which regulation 24(1) applies and the initial amount exceeds the amount which is or would be found apart from the operation of the scheme to be the amount of the premium in accordance with the provisions of the Act; or

(*b*) in respect of a premium or part of a premium which has not been received,

then, if it is shown to the satisfaction of the Commissioners that that excess, premium or part, as the case may be, will never actually be received, the amount of that excess, premium or part shall be treated as an amount of premium which the insurer has repaid on the date upon which the Commissioners are so satisfied and he shall be entitled to credit for the amount concerned in accordance with Part IV of these Regulations.

(2) It shall be a condition of any claim being made by an insurer in reliance upon paragraph (1) above that, if the excess, premium or part (as the case may be) or any part thereof is in fact received by the insurer, he shall pay to the Commissioners an amount equal to the tax chargeable on the amount received; and any amount which the insurer is liable to pay under this paragraph shall be treated as tax due for the accounting period in which the amount of excess or premium was received.

Commentary—*De Voil Indirect Tax Service* **V18.127.**

Concession IPT3—Special accounting scheme: introductory provisions.

Withdrawal from the scheme

26—(1) An insurer may notify the Commissioners in writing that the scheme should not apply to him as regards accounting periods beginning on or after a date specified in the notification (being a date falling after the date the notification is made) and the scheme shall cease to apply to him accordingly.

(2) The scheme shall nonetheless continue to apply to an insurer who has made a notification under paragraph (1) above unless and until—

(*a*) he has made all the returns which he was required to make;

(*b*) he has paid all the tax which was payable in respect of the accounting periods for which he was required to make those returns; and

(*c*) the scheme has applied as regards such number of relevant accounting periods as is required in order for the scheme to have applied to him for a period of not less than twelve consecutive months beginning with the first day of the initial period;

and, when he has complied with sub-paragraphs (a) to (c) above and with any requirement to make returns or pay tax arising since the date the notification was made, the scheme shall cease to apply with effect from the first of his accounting periods which begin on or after the date of such compliance.

Commentary—*De Voil Indirect Tax Service* **V18.127.**

Expulsion from the scheme

27—(1) In any case where the Commissioners consider it necessary for the protection of the revenue, including (but not restricted to) a case where the revenue is prejudiced by reason of the premium written date in relation to premiums falling in accounting periods later than those in which falls the date of receipt, they may give notice to an insurer who has made the notification under regulation 21(1) that the scheme is not to apply to him; and the scheme shall accordingly not apply or cease to apply, as the case may be.

(2) Where a notice is given under paragraph (1) above before the last day of the initial period, the scheme shall not apply to any of the accounting periods of the insurer.

(3) Where a notice is given under paragraph (1) above on or after the last day of the initial period, the notice shall specify the accounting period of the insurer with effect from which the scheme is not to apply to him, being an accounting period the last day of which falls after the date the notice is given.

Commentary—*De Voil Indirect Tax Service* **V18.127.**

Tax to be accounted for on cessation

28—(1) Where the scheme has ceased to apply to an insurer by virtue of regulation 26 or 27, he shall account for and pay any tax chargeable on premiums in relation to which the date of receipt falls within a relevant accounting period and for which he has not accounted and which he has not paid in reliance upon the assumption referred to in regulation 23(5) as if the premiums were received in the accounting period with effect from which the scheme has ceased to apply to him.
(2) Where the Commissioners have cancelled the registration of an insurer and the last of his accounting periods is a relevant accounting period, paragraph (1) above shall apply as if—
(*a*) the scheme had ceased to apply to him by virtue of regulation 26 or 27; and
(*b*) the reference to the accounting period with effect from which the scheme has ceased to apply to him were a reference to the last of his accounting periods.

Commentary—*De Voil Indirect Tax Service* **V18.127.**

PART VI
TAX REPRESENTATIVES

Notification in certain cases

29—*(1) Where the Commissioners approve a person as an insurer's [or taxable intermediary's][1] tax representative in a case where action has been taken as mentioned in section 57(4) of the Act or a request has been made as mentioned in section 57(10) of the Act, as the case may be, they shall be taken to have given such approval on the date they serve on the insurer [or taxable intermediary][1] a notice in writing confirming their approval or on such later date as may be specified in the notice.*
(2) Where the Commissioners inform an insurer [or taxable intermediary][1] that they have received a notification such as is referred to in section 57(8) of the Act, they shall be taken to have so informed him on the date they serve on him a notice in writing to that effect.
(3) Where the Commissioners make a direction such as is described in section 57(11) of the Act, they shall be taken to have made the direction—
(a) on the date they serve on both the insurer [or, as the case may be, taxable intermediary][1] and the person who is to be his tax representative a notice in writing confirming that that person shall be his tax representative;
(b) where such notices are served on different dates, the later of them; or
(c) where such notices specify a date falling after the date on which the later of them is served, the date specified in the notices.[2]

Commentary—*De Voil Indirect Tax Service* **V18.127.**
Amendments—[1] Words in paras (1)–(3) inserted by the Insurance Premium Tax (Amendment) Regulations, SI 1997/1157 with effect from 1 May 1997.
[2] This regulation revoked by the Insurance Premium Tax (Amendment) Regulations, SI 2008/1945 regs 2, 3 with effect from 1 September 2008.

Registration

30—*(1) The Commissioners shall register alongside the name of an insurer [or taxable intermediary][1] the name of any tax representative of his for the time being.*
(2) Where the Commissioners withdraw their approval of a tax representative who has been registered by them under paragraph (1) above, they shall cancel that registration.[2]

Amendments—[1] Words inserted by the Insurance Premium Tax (Amendment) Regulations, SI 1997/1157 with effect from 1 May 1997.
[2] This regulation revoked by the Insurance Premium Tax (Amendment) Regulations, SI 2008/1945 regs 2, 3 with effect from 1 September 2008.

Liability to notify

31 *A tax representative shall not—*
(a) be jointly and severally liable with the insurer [or taxable intermediary][1]; or
(b) be required to secure the insurer's [or taxable intermediary's][1] compliance with or the discharge of his obligation,

in relation to any requirement that the insurer [or taxable intermediary][1] make a notification such as is referred to in regulation 4 or 6.[2]

Amendments—[1] Words inserted by the Insurance Premium Tax (Amendment) Regulations, SI 1997/1157 with effect from 1 May 1997.
[2] This regulation revoked by the Insurance Premium Tax (Amendment) Regulations, SI 2008/1945 regs 2, 3 with effect from 1 September 2008.

PART VII
LIABILITY OF INSURED PERSONS

Interpretation

32 In this Part—

"contract" means a taxable insurance contract;

"liability notice" means a notice served under regulation 34;

"material date" has the same meaning as in section 65(4) of the Act;

"tax debt" means a liability to pay an amount which is tax or is deemed to be or recoverable as if it were tax which, at the time of any payment, has not been discharged.

Scope

[33 This Part applies where an insurer who is a registrable person—

(*a*) does not have any business establishment or other fixed establishment in the United Kingdom, and

(*b*) is established in a country or territory in respect of which it appears to the Commissioners that the condition in section 65(1A) of the Act is met.][1]

Amendments—[1] This regulation substituted by the Insurance Premium Tax (Amendment) Regulations, SI 2008/1945 regs 2, 4 with effect from 1 September 2008. This regulation previously read as follows—

"**33**

This Part applies where—

(*a*) an insurer who is a registrable person does not have any business establishment or other fixed establishment in the United Kingdom, and

(*b*) no person is that insurer's tax representative by virtue of section 57 of the Act.".

Liability notices

34 Where this Part applies, the Commissioners may serve a notice on the person who is insured under a contract or, where there are two or more such persons, one or more of them.

Power to assess tax due

35—(1) This regulation applies where—

(*a*) the Commissioners have served a liability notice or notices; and

(*b*) the insurer—

(i) has failed to make any return he was required to make or any such return appears to the Commissioners to be incomplete or incorrect; or

(ii) has failed to pay any tax or amount deemed to be tax, including an amount which he was liable to pay by virtue of this Part.

(2) Where this regulation applies—

(*a*) the Commissioners may assess to the best of their judgment the amount of any tax due in respect of premiums received by the insurer under the contract after the material date and before the date of the assessment; and

(*b*) the amount so assessed shall be deemed to be the amount of tax due in respect of that contract for the period by reference to which the assessment is made.

Commentary—*De Voil Indirect Tax Service* **V18.128.**

Persons liable for tax assessed

36—(1) Where the Commissioners make an assessment under regulation 35 and notify it to the insured person, or each of the insured persons, on whom a liability notice in respect of the contract has been served—

(*a*) the insurer; and

(*b*) the insured persons mentioned in this regulation,

shall be jointly and severally liable to pay the amount of tax assessed, to the extent that the assessment has not subsequently been reduced or withdrawn, and that tax shall be recoverable accordingly.

(2) An insured person who has been notified of an assessment made under regulation 35 shall be liable in accordance with this regulation to pay the tax so assessed notwithstanding that he has already paid an amount representing that tax or any part of it as part of a premium.

Commentary—*De Voil Indirect Tax Service* **V18.128.**

Adjustment of assessments

37—(1) Where—

(*a*) an amount of tax has been assessed under regulation 35; and (*b*) the amount of that tax, or any part of it, has also been assessed under section 56 of the Act and notified to the insurer,

the assessment which has been made under regulation 35 shall be treated as reduced to the extent that the amount referred to in sub-paragraph (b) above has been included in the amount thereof.

(2) Where an assessment such as is referred to in paragraph (1)(*a*) or (*b*) above is subsequently withdrawn, that paragraph shall not apply; and where the assessment is reduced, it shall apply as if any reference to the amount of tax which has been assessed were a reference to the reduced amount.

Commentary—*De Voil Indirect Tax Service* **V18.128.**

Time for payment

38—Any insured person who is liable to pay an amount of tax which has been assessed under regulation 35 shall do so no later than thirty days after the date on which it was notified to him.

Commentary—*De Voil Indirect Tax Service* **V18.128.**

Interest on reimbursements

39—(1) Where an insurer is liable by virtue of section 65(9) of the Act to pay to an insured person an amount equal to the amount which has been recovered from him, then, if and to the extent that the insurer would not be liable to do so apart from this regulation, he shall pay interest to him.

(2) The interest payable under paragraph (1) above shall be paid at the rate of 8 per cent per annum for the period beginning with the date on which the amount was recovered from the insured person and ending with the date the insurer paid to him an amount equal to that amount.

Commentary—*De Voil Indirect Tax Service* **V18.128.**

Allocation of payments

40—(1) This regulation applies where an insurer pays an amount of tax to the Commissioners and—

(*a*) at the time of the payment there exists a tax debt of his by virtue of his being liable to pay tax which has been assessed under regulation 35;

(*b*) at the time of the payment there exists a tax debt of his which—

(i) is not within sub-paragraph (*a*) above; and

(ii) relates to an accounting period which corresponds to any extent with the period by reference to which the assessment referred to in sub-paragraph (*a*) above was made; and

(*c*) the amount of the payment is not sufficient to satisfy all his tax debts in full.

(2) Where this regulation applies and the payment would not otherwise be applied as described in this paragraph, the payment shall be applied to reduce or extinguish the tax debt within paragraph (1)(*a*) above before it is applied to any other tax debt.

(3) Where—

(*a*) this regulation applies;

(*b*) there are two or more tax debts within paragraph (1)(*a*) above; and

(*c*) the payment is not sufficient to satisfy those tax debts in full,

there shall be applied to each such tax debt such proportion of the payment as bears the same relationship to the whole of the payment as does the tax debt to the total of those tax debts.

Commentary—*De Voil Indirect Tax Service* **V18.128.**

Records

41—(1) Where—

(*a*) an insured person has been served with a liability notice;

(*b*) he is carrying on a business; and

(*c*) the contract provides cover for any matter associated with that business,

the insured person shall keep and preserve the records specified in paragraph (2) below.

(2) The records which an insured person shall keep and preserve are such of the following as relate to the contract—

(*a*) his business and accounting records;

(*b*) policy documents, cover notes, endorsements and similar documents;

(*c*) all invoices, renewal notices and similar documents issued to him;

(*d*) all credit or debit notes or other documents received by him which evidence an increase or decrease in the premium, and copies of such documents that are issued by him.

(3) Every insured person who is required to keep and preserve records by paragraph (1) above shall do so for a period of six years.

(4) The reference in paragraph (2)(*d*) above to any premium shall be construed for the purposes of that paragraph as it would be construed for the purposes of Part V of these Regulations.

Commentary—*De Voil Indirect Tax Service* **V18.128.**

PART VIII
DISTRESS AND DILIGENCE

[A42 In this Part—

"Job Band" followed by a number between "1" and "12" means the band for the purposes of pay and grading in which the job an officer performs is ranked in the system applicable to Customs and Excise.]

Amendments—Inserted by Insurance Premium Tax (Amendment) Regulations, SI 1996/2099, Reg 3 with effect from 2 September 1996.

42 . . .

Amendments—This regulation revoked by the Distress for Customs and Excise Duties and Other Indirect Taxes Regulations, SI 1997/1431 with effect from 1 July 1997. See SI 1997/1431 for the replacement provisions.

Diligence

[43 In Scotland, the following provisions have effect:

(*a*) where the Commissioners are empowered to apply to the sheriff for a warrant to authorise a sheriff officer to recover any amount of tax or sum recoverable as if it were tax remaining due and unpaid, any application, and any certificate required to accompany that application, may be made on their behalf by a Collector or an officer of rank not below that of [Job Band 7][2];

(*b*) where, during the course of [an attachment][3] the Commissioners are entitled as a creditor to do any act, then any such act, with the exception of the exercise of the power contained in [section 30(4) of the Debt Arrangement and Attachment (Scotland) Act (asp 17)][3], may be done on their behalf by a Collector or an officer of rank not below that of [Job Band 7][2].][1]

Amendments—[1] This regulation substituted by the Insurance Premium Tax (Amendment) Regulations, SI 1995/1587 with effect from 17 July 1995.

[2] Words substituted by Insurance Premium Tax (Amendments) Regulations, SI 1996/2099, Reg 4 with effect from 2 September 1996.

[3] Words in para (*b*) substituted by the Debt Arrangement and Attachment (Scotland) Act 2002 s 61, Sch 3 Pt 2 para 34 with effect from 30 December 2002.

Note—In Schedule, Forms 1, 4, 5 and 6 substituted by Insurance Premium Tax (Amendment) Regulations, SI 1997/1157, reg 15, Sch with effect from 1 May 1997. Form 1 subsequently substituted by the Insurance Premium Tax (Amendment) Regulations, SI 2006/2700 reg 2, Schedule, with effect from 1 December 2006.

IPT

SCHEDULE

Regulation 4(1)

FORM 1

HM Revenue & Customs

Insurance Premium Tax

Application for Registration

When you have filled in this form and signed it, please send it to:

The Controller
Central Collection Unit (IPT)
HM Revenue & Customs
Alexander House
21 Victoria Avenue
Southend-on-Sea X
SS99 1AA

For official use

Date of receipt

Insurance Premium Tax

Application for Registration

Before you start, please read the Registration sections of the notice 'Insurance Premium Tax'. Write clearly in ink and use capital letters.

1 Please give your full name and your business address.

Name

Business address

Postcode

Phone Fax no

2 Please give your trading name if it is different from the name given at question **1**.

Only complete question **3** if you do not have a business establishment in the United Kingdom (UK). Otherwise, go to question 4.

3 (a) Do you wish to appoint an agent to act on your behalf in the UK?

Please tick ☑

Yes ☐ Go to **3**(b).

No ☐ Go to **4**.

(b) If you wish to appoint an agent in the UK to act on your behalf, please complete this authority and provide the agent's details. This authority allows us to exchange and disclose information about you with your agent and to deal with them on matters within the responsibility of HM Revenue & Customs (HMRC) as specified on this form. We will hold this authority until you tell us that the details have changed.

I,*(print your name)*

of *(name of your business, company or partnership if appropriate)*

authorise HMRC to disclose information to
(agent's business name)

who is acting on my/our behalf. This authorisation is limited to IPT matters only.

Signature

Date

Give **your agent's** details here

Address

Postcode

Phone Fax

Client reference

4 What is the legal status of your business?
If you are a partnership, please remember to complete form IPT 2 as well as this form.

Please tick ☑

Sole proprietor ☐ Partnership ☐

Limited Company ☐ Give details from your certificate of incorporation:

Certificate number | Date of certificate

Unincorporated Body (other than partnership) ☐ Specify type of body

Lloyd's syndicate ☐

IPT

5 Do you wish to use this form to notify that you are going to use the special accounting scheme from the first of your accounting periods? (Use of the scheme is mandatory for a Lloyd's syndicate wishing to elect Lloyd's to act on its behalf.)

Please tick ☑
Yes ☐ No ☐

Only complete **6** if you are a Lloyd's syndicate. Otherwise go straight to 7.

6 (a) Please give your syndicate number.

(b) Are you electing that Lloyd's may act for you from the first of your accounting periods?

Please tick ☑
Yes ☐ No ☐

(c) Are all your premiums processed through Lloyd's Policy Signing Office (LPSO)?

Please tick ☑
Yes ☐ Go to **6**(e).
No ☐ Go to **6**(d).

(d) What percentage (%) of your premium income is not processed through LPSO?

%

(e) Who will be responsible for submitting IPT returns?

Please tick ☑
Lloyd's ☐
Managing agent ☐

(f) Please give your managing agent's name and address.

Name
Address
Postcode
Phone Fax

(g) Are you involved in Mirror Syndicate activity?

Please tick ☑
Yes ☐ No ☐

(h) Are you reinsured to close?

Please tick ☑
Yes ☐ Give the number of the syndicate which has taken over your liability.
No ☐

7 Are you in run off?

Please tick ☑
Yes ☐ No ☐

8 Please tick the box that best describes your business.

Please tick ☑
UK Insurer ☐ Branch of non-UK Insurer ☐
Captive ☐ Representative Office ☐
Other ☐ Taxable Intermediary ☐
Please give details

9 (a) Are you applying to register because a business has been transferred to you as a going concern?

Please tick ☑
Yes ☐ Give details below:
Date of transfer | IPT registration no. of previous owner
No ☐ Go to 10.

(b) Do you wish to keep the IPT number of the previous owner?
If you wish to keep the number, please remember to complete form IPT 68.

Please tick ☑
Yes ☐
No ☐

10 Please give the date you expect to receive your first taxable premium.
The term premium includes any fee, charged by an intermediary, which is subject to IPT.

11 What class(es) of insurance business do you intend to provide?
See Section 5 of the notice 'Insurance Premium Tax' which will help you to answer this question.

Please continue on a separate sheet of paper if necessary, and attach it to this form.

12 Please give the expected value of your taxable premium income for the 12 month period commencing from the date that you have given in question 10.
If you do not have completely accurate figures, please give an estimate instead.

£

13 Are you registered for VAT in the UK?

Please tick ☑
Yes ☐ Give your VAT registration no.
No ☐

14 Please indicate your preferred method of payment.
If you wish to pay by direct debit, please complete the accompanying mandate form. Mandate forms can be obtained from the Central Collection Unit.

Please tick ☑
Direct debit ☐ Credit transfer ☐
Cheque ☐ Postal order ☐
Cash ☐

15 Please complete and sign the declaration

Declaration

I,

(enter your full name in capital letters) declare that the information given on this form and contained in any accompanying document is true and complete.

Please tick ☑ Signature Date

Sole proprietor ☐ Partner ☐ Director ☐ Company Secretary ☐ Authorised Official ☐ Other ☐
Please give details below

For official use only

LVO code and reg no

Stagger ☐ Group reg ☐ Lloyd's return ☐

	Registration	Tax Rep	TOGC
Approved - Initials/date			
Refused - Initials/date			
Letter of approval issued			

Amendments—Form 1 substituted by the Insurance Premium Tax (Amendment) Regulations, SI 2008/1945 regs 2, 5, Schedule, with effect from 1 September 2008.

Regulation 4(2)

FORM 2

HM Customs and Excise

Insurance Premium Tax

Partnership Details

SPECIMEN

When you have filled in this form and signed it please send it to:

The Controller
Central Collection Unit (IPT)
HM Customs and Excise
Alexander House
21 Victoria Avenue
Southend-on-Sea X
SS99 1AA

For official use only
Date of receipt
IPT reg no:

IPT 2 CD 3679/1/NB(05/94)

These details form part of your application to register.

Please make sure that every partner completes and signs one of the sections below.

Please use CAPITAL LETTERS and write clearly in ink.

Full name of Partner:

Home address:

Postcode:

Home telephone:

Signature: Date:

Full name of Partner:

Home address:

Postcode:

Home telephone:

Signature: Date:

Full name of Partner:

Home address:

Postcode.

Home telephone:

Signature: Date:

CD 3679/1R/NB(05/94)

Full name of Partner:

Home address:

Postcode:

Home telephone:

Signature: Date:

Full name of Partner:

Home address:

Postcode:

Home telephone:

Signature: Date:

Full name of Partner:

Home address:

Postcode:

Home telephone:

Signature: Date:

CD 3679/2/NB(05/94)

Full name of Partner:

Home address:

Postcode:

Home telephone:

Signature: Date:

Full name of Partner:

Home address:

Postcode:

Home telephone:

Signature: Date:

Full name of Partner:

Home address:

Postcode:

Home telephone:

Signature: Date:

CD 3679/2R/NB(05/94)

IPT

Regulation 7(1)

FORM 3

HM Customs
and Excise

Insurance Premium Tax

Request for Transfer of a Registration Number

When you have filled in this form and signed it please send it to:

The Controller
Central Collection Unit (IPT)
HM Customs and Excise
Alexander House
21 Victoria Avenue
Southend-on-Sea X
SS99 1AA

If this form is not returned by .... , we will assume that you do not want the registration number to be transferred.

IPT 68 IB(January 2001)

Part 2: If you are the previous owner of a business, please read this form carefully and answer all the questions in Part 2.

1. Please give your full name, **and** your trading name if you have one:

2. I transferred my business / changed my legal status on

   The new owner is

3. From the above date, I wish to cancel my IPT registration because I will stop receiving taxable insurance premiums from that date. I agree to transfer my number to the new owner. The IPT registration number is

4. If this application is allowed, I agree to the following conditions:
   - the new owner will be entitled to any money or credit which Customs & Excise would normally have paid to me if the number had not been transferred; and
   - I will have no right to claim any money paid by Customs to the new owner.

5. Please give an address where we can contact you after the business has been taken over by the new owner.

Postcode Telephone number

Signature(s)

Please tick one box

☐ Sole Proprietor ☐ Partner (Remember, all partners must sign)

☐ Director ☐ Company Secretary

☐ Authorised Official ☐ Other - please give details below

IPT 68 Page 2 (01/01)

IPT

Before you begin, please read the notes overleaf.
Remember to complete both parts of the form.

Part 1: If you are the new owner of a business, please read this form carefully and answer all the questions in Part 1.

1. Please give your full name:

2. I took over a business as a going concern on

3. I apply to use the previous owner's IPT registration number which is

4. If this application is allowed, I agree to the following conditions:
   - I will send in my first IPT return form to Customs and Excise, with all the tax owing for the period shown on the form;
   - I will send in any outstanding returns which are due from the previous owner;
   - I will pay any IPT still owing on premiums received by the previous owner before the business was transferred;
   - any IPT return made by the previous owner for a period after the transfer date will be treated as made by me; and
   - I will have no right to claim any money paid by Customs to the previous owner, before the IPT registration number is transferred.

Signature(s)

Please tick one box

- ☐ Sole Proprietor
- ☐ Partner (Remember, all partners must sign)
- ☐ Director
- ☐ Company Secretary
- ☐ Authorised Official
- ☐ Other - please give details below

Important: Before you start, please read these notes

Who can ask for a number to be transferred?

Anyone taking over a business as a going concern (buying a business, without causing a significant break in trading) or changing their legal status - eg from a sole trader to a partnership - can ask to keep the registration number already used by the business. But the previous owner of the business must also agree.

When can I ask for a number to be transferred?

You can ask for a number to be transferred if:

- the previous owner will stop receiving taxable insurance premiums from the transfer date and will therefore be cancelling the registration;
- the new owner will be receiving taxable insurance premiums after taking over the business and is not registered for IPT;
- you both agree to the transfer of the number; and
- you both agree to the conditions on the application form overleaf.

How to apply, and when

The application form is in two parts. Part 1 should be filled in by the new owner and Part 2 by the previous owner. If you decide to apply, fill in the form as soon as the transfer takes place and before the registration is cancelled. We will also treat the form as the previous owner's request for the registration to be cancelled.

Who has to sign the form?

The form must be signed by both the old owner and the new owner. If you sign the form, and we agree to transfer the number, this forms a legal agreement which cannot be broken at a later date.

If you are changing the legal status of your business, the same person may have to sign both parts of the form. This can happen where you are acting as both the new owner and the previous owner at the same time. If a partnership is involved in the transfer of a number, all partners must sign the form. If the previous owner was a sole proprietor, or a partner, who has died, the executor must sign.

What to do when you have filled in the form

Please send it to the address on the front of the form. The new owner must also send in a Form IPT 1 to register, and a Form IPT 2 if the business is a partnership. When we have considered your application, we will write to tell you whether the number can be transferred.

Data Protection Act 1998

HM Customs and Excise collects, information in order to administer the taxes for which it is responsible (such as VAT, insurance premium tax, excise duties, air passenger duty, landfill tax), and for detecting and preventing crime.

Where the law permits we may also get information about you from third parties, or give information to them, for example in order to check its accuracy, prevent or detect crime or protect public funds in other ways. These third parties may include the police, other government departments and agencies.

IPT 68 Page 2R (01/01)

IPT

Regulation 12(1)

FORM 4

HM Revenue & Customs

Insurance Premium Tax Return

For the Period

to

For Official Use

IPT Registration Number | Period

You could be liable to a financial penalty if your completed return and all IPT payable are not received by the due date.

Due Date:

For official use D O R only

Fold here

Before you fill in this form please read the notes on the back.
Fill in all boxes clearly in ink, and write 'none' where necessary. Don't put a dash or leave any box blank. If there are no pence write '**00**' in the pence column. **Do not** enter more than one amount in any box.

For Official Use

		£	p
1	Standard rate IPT due for this period		
2	Higher rate IPT due for this period		
3	Underdeclarations of standard rate IPT from previous periods		
4	Underdeclarations of higher rate IPT from previous periods		
5	Total (in the sum of boxes 1 to 4)		
6	Underdeclarations of standard rate IPT from previous periods		
7	Underdeclarations of higher rate IPT from previous periods		
8	Total overdeclarations from previous periods		
9	Net tax payable or repayable (the difference between box 5 and box 8)		
10	Net value of taxable premiums (excluding tax)		

Special accounting scheme - please tick this box if you are using the scheme ☐

if you are enclosing a payment please tick this box. ☐

DECLARATION: You, or someone on your behalf, must sign below:

I, ______________________ declare that the

(Full name of signatory in BLOCK LETTERS)

information given above is true and complete.

Signature ______________ Date ______________

A false declaration can result in prosecution.

IPT100 Draft v0 2 Page 1 HMRC 05/08

Amendments—Form 4 and Form 5 substituted by the Value Added Tax, etc (Correction of Errors, etc) Regulations, SI 2008/1482 reg 3(3) with effect in respect of or as regards accounting periods that begin on 1 July 2008 or later.

Regulation 12(2)

FORM 5

HM Revenue & Customs

Lloyd's Composite IPT return for Syndicates

For the Period

to

For Official Use

IPT Registration number Period

You could be liable to a financial penalty if your completed return and all the IPT payable are not received by the due date.

Due Date:

For official use DOR only

Fold here

Fill in all boxes clearly in ink, and write 'none' where necessary. Don't put a dash or leave any box blank. If there are no pence write '00' in the pence column. **Do not** enter more than one amount in any box.

For Official Use

		£	p
1	Standard rate IPT due for this period		
2	Higher rate IPT due for this period		
3	Underdeclarations of standard rate IPT from previous periods		
4	Underdeclarations of higher rate IPT from previous periods		
5	Total (the sum of boxes 1 to 4)		
6	Overdeclarations of standard rate IPT from previous periods		
7	Overdeclarations of higher rate IPT from previous periods		
8	Total overdeclarations from previous periods		
9	Net tax payable or repayable (the difference between box 5 and box 8)		
10	Net value of taxable premiums (excluding tax)		

If you are enclosing a payment please tick this box.

DECLARATION by the representatives of Syndicates, as defined in Regulation 9 of the Insurance Premium Tax Regulations 1994.

I, ______________________ declare that the

(Full name of signatory in BLOCK LETTERS)

information given above is true and complete.

Signature ____________ Date ____________

A false declaration can result in prosecution.

IPT100L Page 1 HMRC 05/08

Amendments—Form 4 and Form 5 substituted by the Value Added Tax, etc (Correction of Errors, etc) Regulations, SI 2008/1482 reg 3(3) with effect in respect of or as regards accounting periods that begin on 1 July 2008 or later.

IPT

Regulation 12(2)

FORM 6

Regulation 12(2)

Form 6

Lloyd's Composite Return - Schedule of Participating Syndicates

Period .... to ....

Lloyd's Syndicate number	IPT registration number	Standard rate IPT due for this period 1 £ p	Higher rate IPT due for this period 2 £ p	Underdeclarations of standard rate IPT from previous periods 3 £ p	Underdeclarations of higher rate IPT from previous periods 4 £ p	Total (the sum of boxes 1 to 4) 5 £ p	Overdeclarations of standard rate IPT from previous periods 6 £ p	Overdeclarations of higher rate IPT from previous periods 7 £ p	Total Overdeclarations from previous periods 8 £ p	Net tax payable or repayable (the difference between box 5 and box 8) 9 £ p	Net value of taxable premiums (excluding tax) 10 £ p
	Totals										

IPT 100L(S)

Amendment—Form 6 substituted by Insurance Premium Tax (Amendment) Regulations, SI 1997/1157, reg 15, Sch with effect from 1 May 1997.

1997/1431

DISTRESS FOR CUSTOMS AND EXCISE DUTIES AND OTHER INDIRECT TAXES REGULATIONS 1997

Made by the Commissioners of Customs and Excise under FA 1997 ss 51(1), (2), (3)

Made . . . . *9th June 1997*
Laid before House of Commons . . . . *9th June 1997*
Coming into force . . . . *1st July 1997*

Citation and commencement

1 These Regulations may be cited as The Distress for Customs and Excise Duties and Other Indirect Taxes Regulations 1997 and shall come into force on 1st July 1997.

Interpretation

2—(1) In these Regulations—

"authorised person" means a person acting under the authority of the Commissioners;

"costs" means any costs, charges, expenses and fees;

"officer" means, subject to section 8(2) of the Customs and Excise Management Act 1979, a person commissioned by the Commissioners pursuant to section 6(3) of that Act;

"person in default" means a person who has refused or neglected to pay any relevant tax due from him;

"relevant tax" means any of the following—

. . .

(*c*) insurance premium tax;

. . .

"walking possession agreement" means an agreement under which, in consideration of any goods and chattels distrained upon being allowed to remain in the custody of the person in default and of the delaying of their sale, that person—

(*a*) acknowledges that the goods and chattels specified in the agreement are under distraint and held in walking possession; and

(*b*) undertakes that, except with the consent of the Commissioners and subject to such conditions as they may impose, he will not remove or allow the removal of any of the specified goods and chattels from the place named in the agreement;

"1994 Act" means Part III of the Finance Act 1994;

"1996 Act" means Part III of the Finance Act 1996;

(2) Any reference in these Regulations to an amount of relevant tax includes a reference to any amount recoverable as if it were an amount of that relevant tax.

Note—Words omitted are not relevant for the purposes of IPT.

Revocations and transitional provisions

3—(1) The Regulations specified in Schedule 3 are hereby revoked to the extent set out there.

(2) Where a warrant is signed before the coming into force of these Regulations, these Regulations shall apply to anything done, after these Regulations come into force, in relation to that warrant or as a consequence of distress being levied.

Levying distress

4—(1) Subject to regulation 5 below, if upon written demand a person neglects or refuses to pay any relevant tax due from him an officer may levy distress on the goods and chattels of that person and by warrant signed by him direct any authorised person to levy such distress.

(2) Where a warrant has been signed, distress shall be levied by or under the direction of, and in the presence of, the authorised person.

(3) Subject to regulation 6 below, distress may be levied on any goods and chattels located at any place whatever including on a public highway.

Restrictions on levying distress

5—(1) Where—

. . .

(*b*) an amount of insurance premium tax is due and the Commissioners may be required under section 59 of the 1994 Act to review a decision which, if that decision were varied or withdrawn, would cause the amount to be reduced or extinguished; or

. . .

no distress shall be levied before expiry of the last day on which the person who is liable to pay the amount concerned is required, by rules made under paragraph 9 of Schedule 12 to the VAT Act, to serve a notice of appeal with respect to that decision.

. . .

Note—Words omitted are not relevant for the purposes of IPT.

Goods and chattels not subject to levy

6 No distress shall be levied on any goods and chattels mentioned in Schedule 1 which at the time of levy are located in a place and used for a purpose mentioned in that Schedule.

Times for levying distress

7—(1) Subject to paragraph (2) below, a levy of distress shall commence only during the period between eight o'clock in the morning and eight o'clock at night on any day of the week but it may be continued thereafter outside that period until the levy is completed.

(2) Where a person holds himself out as conducting any profession, trade or business during hours which are partly within and partly outside, or wholly outside the period mentioned in paragraph (1) above, a levy of distress may be commenced at any time during that period or during the hours of any day in which he holds himself out as conducting that profession, trade or business and it may be continued thereafter outside that period or those hours until the levy is completed.

Costs

8—(1) A person in respect of whose goods and chattels a warrant has been signed shall be liable to pay to an officer or authorised person all costs, in connection with anything done under these Regulations described in column 1 of Schedule 2, as determined in accordance with column 2 of that Schedule.

(2) An authorised person may, after deducting and accounting for the amount of relevant tax to the Commissioners, retain costs from any amount received.

Sale

9 If any person upon whose goods and chattels distress has been levied does not pay the amount of relevant tax due together with costs within 5 days of a levy, an officer or authorised person may sell the distress for payment of the amount of relevant tax and costs; and the officer or authorised person, after deducting and retaining the amount of relevant tax and costs shall restore any surplus to the owner of the goods upon which distress was levied.

Disputes as to costs

10—(1) In the case of any dispute as to costs, the amount of those costs shall be taxed by a district judge of the county court of the district where the distress was levied, and he may make such order as he thinks fit as to the costs of the taxation.

(2) In the application of this regulation to Northern Ireland, in the case of any dispute as to costs, the amount of those costs shall be taxed in the same manner as costs in equity suits or proceedings in the county court in Northern Ireland.

SCHEDULE 1

GOODS AND CHATTELS NOT SUBJECT TO LEVY

Regulation 6

1 Any of the following goods and chattels which are located in a dwelling house at which distress is being levied and are reasonably required for the domestic needs of any person residing in that dwelling house—

(*a*) beds and bedding;
(*b*) household linen;
(*c*) chairs and settees;
(*d*) tables;
(*e*) food;
(*f*) lights and light fittings;
(*g*) heating appliances;
(*h*) curtains;
(*i*) floor coverings;
(*j*) furniture, equipment and utensils used for cooking, storing or eating food;
(*k*) refrigerators;
(*l*) articles used for cleaning, mending, or pressing clothes;
(*m*) articles used for cleaning the home;
(*n*) furniture used for storing—
 (i) clothing, bedding or household linen;
 (ii) articles used for cleaning the home;
 (iii) utensils used for cooking or eating food;
(*o*) articles used for safety in the home;
(*p*) toys for the use of any child within the household;
(*q*) medical aids and medical equipment.

2 Any of the following items which are located in premises used for the purposes of any profession, trade or business—

(*a*) fire fighting equipment for use on the premises;
(*b*) medical aids and medical equipment for use on the premises.

SCHEDULE 2

SCALE OF COSTS

Regulation 8(1)

Matter (1)	Costs (2)
1 For attending to levy distress where payment is made of an amount of relevant tax due and distress is not levied:	£12.50.
2 For levying distress—	
(a) where an amount of relevant tax demanded and due does not exceed £100:	£12.50.
(b) where an amount of relevant tax demanded and due exceeds £100:	12½% on the first £100, 4% on the next £400, 2½% on the next £1,500, 1% on the next £8,000, ¼% on any additional sum.
3 For taking possession of distrained goods—	
(a) where a person remains in physical possession of goods at the place where distress was levied (the person to provide his own food and lodgings):	£4.50 per day.
(b) where possession is taken under a walking possession agreement:	£7.00.
4 For appraising goods upon which distress has been levied:	Reasonable costs of appraisement.
5 For arranging removal and storage of goods upon which distress has been levied:	Reasonable costs of arrangement.
6 For removing and storing goods upon which distress has been levied:	Reasonable costs of removal and storage.
7 For advertising the sale of goods upon which distress has been levied:	Reasonable costs of advertising.
8 For selling the distress—	
(a) where a sale by auction is held at the auctioneer's premises:	15% of the sum realised.
(b) where a sale by auction is held elsewhere:	7½% of the sum realised and the auctioneer's reasonable costs.
(c) where a sale by other means is undertaken:	7½% of the sum realised and reasonable costs.

9 In addition to any amount specified in this scale in respect of the supply of goods or services on which value added tax is chargeable there may be added a sum equivalent to value added tax at the appropriate rate on that amount.

SCHEDULE 3

REVOCATIONS

Regulation 3 (1)

Note—The IPT repeals made under this Schedule are already in effect and have therefore been omitted.

1998/1461

AIR PASSENGER DUTY AND OTHER INDIRECT TAXES (INTEREST RATE) REGULATIONS 1998

Made by the Treasury under FA 1996 s 197

Made . . . . *15th June 1998*

Laid before the House of Commons . . . . *15th June 1998*

Coming into force . . . . *6th July 1998*

Citation and commencement

1 These Regulations may be cited as the Air Passenger Duty and Other Indirect Taxes (Interest Rate) Regulations 1998 and shall come into force on 6th July 1998.

Interpretation

2—(1) In these Regulations unless the context otherwise requires—
"established rate" means—
(*a*) on the coming into force of these Regulations, [6 per cent][1] per annum; and
(*b*) in relation to any day after the first reference day after the coming into force of these Regulations, the reference rate found on the immediately preceding reference day;
"operative day" means the [[twelfth][3] working day after the reference day][2];
"reference day" means the [. . . [3] working day following the day on which the most recent meeting of the Monetary Policy Committee of the Bank of England took place][2];
"section 197" means section 197 of the Finance Act 1996;
the "relevant enactments" are those referred to in regulations 4(1) and 5(1) below;
"working day" means any day other than a non-business day within the meaning of section 92 of the Bills of Exchange Act 1882.

[(2) In these Regulations the reference rate found on a reference date is the official bank rate determined by the most recent meeting of the Monetary Policy Committee of the Bank of England.][3]

Amendments—[1] Words substituted by the Air Passenger Duty and Other Indirect Taxes (Interest Rate) (Amendment) Regulations, SI 2000/631 regs 2, 3 with effect from 1 April 2000.

[2] In para (1), in definition of "operative day" words substituted for words "sixth day of each month", and in definition of "reference day" words substituted for words "twelfth working day before the next operative day" by the Taxes and Duties (Interest Rate) (Amendment) Regulations, SI 2008/3234 reg 3(1), (2) with effect from 7 January 2009.

[3] In para (1), in definition of "operative day" word substituted for word "eleventh" and in definition of "reference day", word "second" revoked, and para (2) substituted, by the Taxes and Duties (Interest Rate) (Amendment) Regulations, SI 2009/2032 regs 15, 16 with effect from 12 August 2009. Para (2) previously read as follows—

"(2) In these Regulations the reference rate found on a reference day is the percentage per annum found by averaging the base lending rates at close of business on that day of—
(*a*) Bank of Scotland,
(*b*) Barclays Bank plc,
(*c*) Lloyds Bank plc,
(*d*) [HSBC Bank plc],
(*e*) National Westminster Bank plc, and
(*f*) The Royal Bank of Scotland plc,

and, if the result is not a whole number, rounding the result to the nearest such number, with any result midway between two whole numbers rounded down.".

[2A *In determining the rate of interest applicable under section 197 for the purposes of any enactments referred to in these Regulations, if the result is less than zero the rate shall be treated as zero for those purposes.]*[1]

Amendments—[1] Reg 2A inserted by the Taxes and Duties (Interest Rate) (Amendment) Regulations, SI 2008/3234 reg 3(1), (3) with effect from 7 January 2009, and revoked by the Taxes and Duties (Interest Rate) (Amendment) Regulations, SI 2009/2032 regs 15, 17 with effect from 12 August 2009.

3 The Air Passenger Duty and Other Indirect Taxes (Interest Rate) Regulations 1997 are hereby revoked.

[Applicable rate of interest payable to the Commissioners of Customs and Excise in connection with excise duties, insurance premium tax, VAT, landfill tax, and customs duty

4—(1) For the purposes of—
(*a*) [section 60(8) of, and paragraphs 7 and 8(1) of Schedule 6 to,][4] the Finance Act 1994,
(*b*) paragraph 21 of Schedule 7 to that Act,
(*c*) [sections 74 and 85A(3)][4] of the Value Added Tax Act 1994,
(*d*) [section 56(5) of and][4] paragraph 26 of Schedule 5 to the Finance Act 1996,
(*e*) paragraph 17 of Schedule 5 to the Finance Act 1997, . . . [2]
(*f*) section 126 of the Finance Act 1999, [. . . [3]
(*g*) paragraphs 41(2)(*f*), 70(1)(*b*)[, 81(3) and 123(6)][4] of Schedule 6 to the Finance Act 2000 (climate change levy),][2] [and
(*h*) sections 25(2)(*f*)[, 30(3)(*f*) and 42(6)][4] of, and paragraphs 6 and 8(3)(*a*) of Schedule 5 to, the Finance Act 2001 (aggregates levy),][3]

the rate applicable under section 197 shall, subject to paragraph (2) below, be 8.5 per cent per annum.

(2) Where, on any reference day after the coming into force of these Regulations, the reference rate found on that day differs from the established rate, the rate applicable under section 197 of the Finance Act 1996 for the purposes of the enactments referred to in paragraph (1) above shall, from the next operative day, be the percentage per annum determined in accordance with the formula specified in paragraph (3) below.

(3) The formula specified in this paragraph is—

$$RR + 2.5,$$

where RR is the reference rate referred to in paragraph (2) above.][1]

[(4) With effect from 1st November 2001 the rate of interest prescribed in paragraph (1) above for the purposes of paragraph 17 of Schedule 5 to the Finance Act 1997 also applies in the application of that paragraph to assessments under paragraph 14 or 15 of that Schedule as amended by paragraph 19 of Schedule 3 to the Finance Act 2001.][2]

Amendments—[1] This regulation substituted by the Air Passenger Duty and Other Indirect Taxes (Interest Rate) (Amendment) Regulations, SI 2000/631 regs 2, 4 with effect from 1 April 2000.

[2] Word "and" in para (1)(*e*) revoked, and para (1)(*f*) and para (4) inserted, by the Air Passenger Duty and Other Indirect Taxes (Interest Rate) (Amendment) Regulations, SI 2001/3337 reg 2 with effect from 1 November 2001.

[3] Word "and" in para (1)(*f*) revoked, and para (1)(*h*) inserted, by the Air Passenger Duty and Other Indirect Taxes (Interest Rate) (Amendment) Regulations, SI 2003/230 regs 2, 3 with effect from 1 April 2003.

[4] In para (1), in sub-para (a), words substituted for words "paragraph 7 of Schedule 6 to ", in sub-para (*c*), words substituted for words "section 74", in sub-para (*d*), words inserted, in sub-para (*g*), words substituted for words "and 81(3)", and in sub-para (*h*), words substituted for words "and 30(3)(*f*)", by the Transfer of Tribunal Functions and Revenue and Customs Appeals Order, SI 2009/56 art 3, Sch 2 paras 38, 39 with effect from 1 April 2009.

IPT

[Applicable rate of interest payable by the Commissioners of Customs and Excise in connection with air passenger duty, insurance premium tax, VAT, landfill tax, and customs duty

5—(1) For the purposes of—

(*a*) [Parts 2 and 3 of Schedule 3 to the Finance Act 2001 (interest payable on repayments etc),][2]

(*b*) paragraph 22 of Schedule 7 to that Act,

[(*ba*) section 60(6) of the Finance Act 1994,][4]

(*c*) section 78 of the Value Added Tax Act 1994,

(*d*) [section 56(3) and (4) of and][4] paragraph 29 of Schedule 5 to the Finance Act 1996, . . . [2]

(*e*) section 127 of the Finance Act 1999, [. . . [3]

(*f*) paragraphs 62(3)(*f*)[, 66, 123(4) and 123(5)][4] of Schedule 6 to the Finance Act 2000 (climate change levy)][2] [and

(*g*) [section 42(4) and (5) of and][4] paragraphs 2 and 6(1)(*b*) of Schedule 8 to the Finance Act 2001 (aggregates levy),][3]

the rate applicable under section 197 of the Finance Act 1996 shall be 5 per cent per annum.

(2) Where, on a reference day after the coming into force of these Regulations, the reference rate found on that date differs from the established rate, the rate applicable under section 197 for the purposes of the enactments referred to in paragraph (1) above shall, from the next operative day, be the [higher of—

(*a*) 0.5% per annum, and

(*b*) the percentage per annum found by applying the formula specified in paragraph (3).][5]

[(3) The formula specified in this paragraph is—

$$RR - 1,$$

where RR is the reference rate referred to in paragraph (2).][5]

Amendments—[1] This regulation substituted by the Air Passenger Duty and Other Indirect Taxes (Interest Rate) (Amendment) Regulations, SI 2000/631 regs 2, 5 with effect from 1 April 2000.

[2] In para (1), words in sub-para (*a*) substituted, word "and" in sub-para (*d*) revoked, and sub-para (*f*) added by the Air Passenger Duty and Other Indirect Taxes (Interest Rate) (Amendment) Regulations, SI 2001/3337 regs 1, 3 with effect from 1 November 2001.

[3] Word "and" in para (1)(*e*) revoked, and para (1)(*g*) inserted, by the Air Passenger Duty and Other Indirect Taxes (Interest Rate) (Amendment) Regulations, SI 2003/230 regs 2, 4 with effect from 1 April 2003.

[4] In para (1), sub-para (*ba*) inserted, in sub-para (*c*) words substituted for words "section 78", in sub-paras (*d*), (*g*) words inserted, and in sub-para (*f*) words substituted for words "and 66", by the Transfer of Tribunal Functions and Revenue and Customs Appeals Order, SI 2009/56 art 3, Sch 2 paras 38, 40 with effect from 1 April 2009.

[5] In para (2), words substituted, and para (3) substituted, by the Taxes and Duties (Interest Rate) (Amendment) Regulations, SI 2009/2032 regs 15, 18 with effect from 12 August 2009. Words in para (2) previously read as follows—

"percentage per annum determined in accordance with the formula specified in paragraph (3) below.".

Para (3) previously read as follows—

"(3) The formula specified in this paragraph is—

$$RR - 1,$$

where RR is the reference rate referred to in paragraph (2) above.".

Effect of change in applicable rate

6 Where the rate applicable under section 197 for the purposes of any of the relevant enactments changes on an operative day by virtue of these Regulations, that change shall have effect for periods beginning on or after the operative day in relation to interest running from before that day as well as in relation to interest running from, or from after that day.

7 Where the rate applicable under section 197 for the purposes of any of the relevant enactments changes on an operative day by virtue of these Regulations, the rate in force immediately prior to any change shall continue to have effect for periods immediately prior to the change and so on in the case of any number of successive changes.

Applicable rate of interest prior to the coming into force of these Regulations

8 The rate applicable under section 197 for interest running from before the date these Regulations come into force in relation to periods prior to that date shall be specified for the relevant enactments in the following Tables—

Table 2
Paragraph 21 of Schedule 7 to the Finance Act 1994

Interest for any period	*Rate*
From 1st October 1994 and before 6th February 1996	5·5 per cent
After 5th February 1996 and before 6th July 1998	6·25 per cent

Table 6
Paragraph 22 of Schedule 7 to the Finance Act 1994

Interest for any period	*Rate*
after 1st October 1994 and before 1st April 1997	8 per cent
after 31st March 1997 and before 6th July 1998	6 per cent

9 . . .

Note—This regulation is not relevant for the purposes of IPT.

2001/2635

FINANCIAL SERVICES AND MARKETS ACT 2000 (LAW APPLICABLE TO CONTRACTS OF INSURANCE) REGULATIONS 2001

Made by the Treasury under FSMA 2000 ss 424(3), 417(1), 428(3).

Made . . . . *19 July 2001*
Laid before Parliament . . . . *20 July 2001*
Coming into force in accordance with regulation 1

PART I
GENERAL

Citation and commencement

1 These Regulations may be cited as the Financial Services and Markets Act 2000 (Law Applicable to Contracts of Insurance) Regulations 2001 and come into force on the day on which section 19 of the Act comes into force.

Interpretation

2—(1) In these Regulations—

"the Act" means the Financial Services and Markets Act 2000;

"the 1990 Act" means the Contracts (Applicable Law) Act 1990;

"applicable law", in relation to a contract of insurance, means the law that is applicable to that contract;

"contract of general insurance" and "contract of long-term insurance" have the meanings given by the Regulated Activities Order;

"EEA State of the commitment" means, in relation to a contract of long-term insurance entered into on a date—

(*a*) if the policyholder is an individual, the EEA State in which he resides on that date; or
(*b*) otherwise, the EEA State in which the establishment of the policyholder to which the contract relates is situated on that date;

"establishment", in relation to a person ("A"), means—
(*a*) A's head office;
(*b*) any of A's agencies;
(*c*) any of A's branches; or
(*d*) any permanent presence of A in an EEA State, which need not take the form of a branch or agency and which may consist of an office managed by A's staff or by a person who is independent of A but has permanent authority to act for A as if he were an agency;

"large risk" has the meaning given by Article 5(d) of the first non-life insurance directive and includes risks specified by paragraph (iii) of that definition insured by professional associations, joint ventures or temporary groups;

"mandatory rules" means the rules from which the law allows no derogation by way of contract;

"the Regulated Activities Order" means the Financial Services and Markets Act 2000 (Regulated Activities) Order 2001.

(2) References to the EEA State where the risk covered by a contract of insurance is situated are to—
(*a*) if the contract relates to buildings or to buildings and their contents (in so far as the contents are covered by the same contract of insurance), the EEA State in which the property is situated;
(*b*) if the contract relates to vehicles of any type, the EEA State of registration;
(*c*) if the contract covers travel or holidays risks and has a duration of four months or less, the EEA State in which the policyholder entered into the contract;
(*d*) in any other case—
(i) if the policyholder is an individual, the EEA State in which he resides on the date the contract is entered into;
(ii) otherwise, the EEA State in which the establishment of the policyholder to which the contract relates is situated on that date.

[(2A) If the contract of insurance relates to a vehicle dispatched from one EEA State to another, in respect of the period of 30 days beginning with the day on which the purchaser accepts delivery a reference to the EEA State in which a risk is situated is a reference to the State of destination (and not, as provided by paragraph (2)(*b*), to the State of registration).][1]

(3) References to the country in which a person resides are to—
(*a*) if he is an individual, the country in which he has his habitual residence;
(*b*) in any other case, the country in which he has his central administration.

(4) Where an EEA State (including the United Kingdom) includes several territorial units, each of which has its own laws concerning contractual obligations, each unit is to be considered as a separate state for the purposes of identifying the applicable law under these Regulations.

Amendments—[1] Sub-para (2A) inserted by the Financial Services and Markets Act 2000 (Motor Insurance) Regulations, SI 2007/2403 reg 3 with effect from 5 September 2007.

3–10 . . .

Note—Regulations beyond the scope of this publication have been omitted.

2010/867

FINANCE ACT 2009, SCHEDULE 51 (TIME LIMITS FOR ASSESSMENTS, CLAIMS, ETC) (APPOINTED DAYS AND TRANSITIONAL PROVISIONS) ORDER 2010

Made . . . .*18 March 2010*

The Treasury make the following Order in exercise of the powers conferred by sections 99(2) and 99(3) of the Finance Act 2009.

PART 1
APPOINTED DAYS AND PRELIMINARY PROVISIONS

1 Citation and interpretation

(1) This Order may be cited as the Finance Act 2009, Schedule 51 (Time Limits for Assessments, Claims, etc) (Appointed Days and Transitional Provisions) Order 2010.

(2) In this Order a reference to a paragraph (without more) is a reference to that paragraph of Schedule 51 to the Finance Act 2009.

(3) In this Order—

"The Commissioners" means the Commissioners for Her Majesty's Revenue and Customs;

"FA", followed by a year, means the Finance Act of that year.

IPT

"IHTA 1984" means the Inheritance Tax Act 1984;

2 Appointed days

(1) The day appointed as the day on which the amendments made by paragraphs 1 to 4 and 27 to 43 (insurance premium tax, aggregates levy, climate change levy, landfill tax and minor and consequential provision) come into force is 1st April 2010.

(2) The day appointed as the day on which the amendments made by paragraphs 5 to 26 (inheritance tax, stamp duty land tax and petroleum revenue tax) come into force is 1st April 2011.

PART 2

TRANSITIONAL PROVISION

3 Insurance premium tax: claims

The amendment made by paragraph 2 is disregarded where claims made under paragraph 8 of Schedule 7 to FA 1994 (recovery of overpaid tax) are for the repayment of amounts paid to the Commissioners on or before 31st March 2007.

4 The amendment made by paragraph 3 is disregarded where claims made under paragraph 22 of Schedule 7 to FA 1994 (interest payable by Commissioners) are for the repayment of amounts paid to the Commissioners on or before 31st March 2007.

5 Insurance premium tax: assessments

The amendments made by paragraph 4 are disregarded where, for the purposes of paragraph 26 of Schedule 7 to FA 1994 (assessments: time limits), the "relevant event" occurred on or before 31st March 2007.

6–28(not relevant to IPT)

Insurance Premium Tax Extra-Statutory Concessions

Note—These Concessions are numbered as they appear in HMRC VAT Notice 48, section 4, *IPT: Concessions designed to remove inequities or anomalies in administration.*

IPT

Contents

VAT Notice 48

July 2009.

This notice cancels and replaces Notice 48 (March 2002). Details of any changes to the previous version can be found in paragraph 1.1 of this notice.

Section 4: IPT—Concessions designed to remove inequities or anomalies in administration

4.1 IPT—SPECIAL ACCOUNTING INTRODUCTORY PROVISIONS

4.1.1 (PART I) INCEPTION WRITTEN OPTION

1—(1) Where the special accounting scheme applies to an insurer for the accounting period beginning on 1 October 1994, he need not account for any tax due on a premium—

(a) *actually received on or after 1 October 1994 and in a relevant accounting period;*

(b) *received under a contract that relates to a risk the period of cover for which begins before 1 October 1994; and*

(c) *for which the tax point applicable under the special accounting scheme falls before 1 October 1995.*

(2) Where (1)(a) and (b) above apply, but the tax point adopted by the insurer under the special accounting scheme falls on or after 1 October 1995, the insurer need not account for tax where the total premium received or written relates entirely to a risk the period of cover for which began before 1 October 1994.

Note—This concession will be withdrawn with effect from 1 April 2010. See the HMRC Technical Note, 'Withdrawal of Extra-statutory Concessions', published April 2009.

4.1.2 (PART II) STRICT WRITTEN PREMIUM OPTION

2—(1) Where the special accounting scheme applies to an insurer for the accounting period beginning on 1 October 1994 and the insurer—

(a) *treats as tax due one forty-first of all premiums written on or after 1 October 1994 that are received (or due) under a taxable insurance contract but on which tax is not chargeable; and*

(b) *does not include such amounts treated as tax in claims for overdeclarations or make a claim for refund of overpaid tax in respect of them,*

then he may claim as a credit against tax due one forty-first of any refund written on or after 1 October 1994 of all or part of a premium that was originally received under a taxable insurance contract but on which tax was not due.

(2) For the purposes of this paragraph, regulation 25 of the Insurance Premium Tax Regulations 1994 shall apply to premiums written on or after 1 October 1994 that are due under taxable insurance contracts but on which tax was not chargeable.

(3) For the purposes of this paragraph, a premium is written on or after 1 October 1994 if the tax point applicable under the special accounting scheme falls on or after that date; and a refund is written on or after 1 October 1994 if it is entered in the insurer's accounts as at a date falling on or after that date.

3. Nothing in this part shall require an insurer to account for tax on the portion of a premium that is attributable to exempt matters in accordance with section 69 of the Finance Act 1994, or prevent him from taking advantage of any de minimis rules.

IPT

4.1.3 (PART III)

4. An insurer may elect to use one or both options described in Parts I and II above but, where he chooses to use both options each option must be applied to the entirety of a clearly defined sector of business.

5. The Commissioners may withdraw or restrict the application of any part of this Concession to an individual insurer if they consider it is being used to avoid tax.

Note—This concession will be withdrawn with effect from 1 April 2010. See the HMRC Technical Note, 'Withdrawal of Extra-statutory Concessions', published April 2009.

4.2 IPT—DE MINIMIS PROVISIONS

1. Where an insurer is able to demonstrate that the total premium for a taxable insurance contract which provides cover for both exempt and non-exempt matters is below the de minimis limits set out in paragraph 3 below, then—

(a) that contract may be treated as though it were exempt; and
(b) credit may be claimed in respect of any tax that has already been accounted for on premiums received or written under that contract (subject to the normal provisions as to the manner in which an insurer is able to claim and benefit from such credit).

2. Where an insurer applies this concession to a taxable insurance contract he must monitor payments received or due in relation to that contract. If a premium written or received by an insurer takes the total premium relating to a contract over the limits set out in paragraph 3 below, the insurer must account for tax on that total premium at the tax point applicable to the additional premium which takes the total premium over the limits set out in paragraph 3.

3. A total premium for a taxable insurance contract is below the de minimis limits if it is £500,000 or less, and 10 per cent or less of it is attributable to non-exempt matters.

4. Where the only taxable contracts under which an insurer intends to provide insurance are those in respect of which, to the best of the insurer's knowledge, the total premiums will each be below the de minimis limits, then provided—

(a) application has been made in writing to the Commissioners for exemption from the requirement to make returns;
(b) any information as may reasonably be requested by the Commissioners about the number and value of taxable insurance contracts entered into by the insurer has been supplied to them; and
(c) the Commissioners approve that insurer's application

the insurer will be exempted from the requirements of registrable persons to make returns.

5. For the purposes of this concession the "total premium" for a taxable insurance contract is the total of all premiums which have been received under that contract once there can be no more premium payments (either by or to the insurer) made under it.

4.3 IPT—INSURANCE RELATING TO MOTOR CARS OR MOTOR CYCLES

For the purposes of Finance Act 1994 Sch 6A, a premium under a taxable insurance policy relating to a motor car or motor cycle (other than a motor car or motor cycle on hire) will not be regarded as falling within paragraph 2(1) to the extent that it relates to a policy of motor vehicle insurance which provides cover of the kind generally known as—

— fully comprehensive,
— third party, fire and theft, or
— third party.

The Commissioners may withdraw or restrict the application of this concession to an individual insurer if they consider it is being used to avoid tax.

4.4 IPT—HOME CONTENTS INSURANCE

For the purposes of Schedule 6A to the Finance Act 1994 a premium under a taxable insurance contract relating to relevant goods will not fall within paragraph 3(1) to the extent that it relates to insurance of the kind generally known as household contents insurance and which principally relates to risks arising in connection with items in the private dwellings of individuals.

"Relevant goods" are as defined in FA 1994 Sch 6A para 3(6).

The Commissioners may withdraw or restrict the application of this concession to an individual insurer if they consider it is being used to avoid tax.

Note—This concession will be withdrawn with effect from 1 April 2010. See the HMRC Technical Note, 'Withdrawal of Extra-statutory Concessions', published April 2009.

4.5 IPT—ARRANGEMENTS FOR DISCOUNTED INSURANCE

1. By concession, where—

(a) a premium under a taxable insurance contract is liable to insurance premium tax at the higher rate; and
(b) the insurance is arranged or provided by one of the persons in Finance Act 1994 Sch 6A paras 2(2) or 3(2) for less than the actual cost of providing that insurance to the insured,

the higher rate element of any premium received by the insurer will be the amount paid by the insured (or any person on his behalf).

2. For the purposes of paragraph 1 above—

(a) "higher rate element" is as defined in FA 1994 s 69(5) (as amended); and
(b) references to payments being made on behalf of the insured shall not be taken to include any sum paid to the insurer or any person acting on behalf of the insurer by a person mentioned in FA 1994 Sch 6A paras 2(2) or 3(2).

The Commissioners may withdraw or restrict the application of this concession to an individual insurer if they consider it is being used to avoid tax.

Insurance Premium Tax
Press releases

IPT

Contents

Press Releases etc

IMPLEMENTATION OF CUSTOMS' RULING ON THE LIABILITY OF THE "REINSURANCE" OF SURETY BONDS

9 December 2003. *Business Brief 25/03*

Customs has recently completed a review of the insurance premium tax (IPT) liability of premiums receivable under contracts covering risks guaranteed by way of surety bonds (ie contracts for the "reinsurance" of surety bonds).

As a result of the review, Customs has concluded that these "reinsurance" contracts are in fact contracts of primary insurance for IPT purposes (the bond contracts falling outside the scope of IPT because they are contracts of guarantee and not written as contracts of insurance). Therefore, premiums receivable under these contracts are liable to UK IPT when the risk covered (ie the surety bond provider) is located in the UK.

IMPLEMENTATION

Due to the uncertainty over the treatment of these products both before and during the period of Customs' review, it was agreed at the start of the review that any ruling would take effect from a current date. To allow a reasonable period for businesses to register for IPT if necessary and make the necessary adjustments to their systems, Customs has decided to delay implementation of their ruling until 1 April 2004.

As a result, all insurers or reinsurers underwriting surety bond "reinsurance" contracts as described above will be required to register for IPT (if not already registered) and account for IPT on all premiums with a tax point that falls on or after the 1 April 2004 which are receivable in respect of contracts that incept on or after that date.

Customs are aware that many of the companies liable to account for IPT as a result of this ruling are located outside the UK and are not currently IPT registered. In such circumstances, UK bond provider companies should notify their "reinsurers" of the liability to account for IPT and advise them to contact Customs on the number shown below as soon as possible. It is important to note that, in certain instances of non-compliance, Customs are able to recover unpaid IPT from the insured parties.

Note—See now Business Brief 13/05 below for a reversal of this ruling.

REVISED TREATMENT OF GUARANTEED ASSET PROTECTION (GAP) INSURANCE

12 February 2004. *Business Brief 5/04*

Customs have recently completed a review of the IPT treatment of credit protection and gap insurance (ie "guaranteed asset protection" insurance covering the gap between an asset's sale value and write-off value) both of which are currently excluded from the higher rate. As a result of this review, it has been decided that a certain type of gap insurance has been excluded incorrectly from the higher rate and this brief explains the revised treatment to take effect from 1 April 2004.

BACKGROUND

When the higher rate of IPT was introduced in 1997 it was decided that it did not apply to credit protection and gap insurance. This decision was published in the revised IPT Notice issued in 1997 and has been included in subsequent rewrites. The decision was taken on the understanding that gap and credit protection insurance could only be sold through motor dealers in connection with finance arrangements and therefore fell outside the higher rate because they were not taxable insurance contracts " . . . relating to a motor car or motor cycle . . . ".

Since this decision was taken, however, a new type of insurance, which is also known as "gap" insurance, has come onto the market. This particular type of gap insurance (sometimes referred to as "vehicle replacement" or "return to invoice" insurance) relates to the motor vehicle itself and is not linked to any finance arrangements. Furthermore, it often allows the dealer a great deal of pricing flexibility, therefore lending itself to VAT avoidance.

REVISED TREATMENT

In view of this, it has been decided that only credit protection and financial gap insurance (ie gap insurance sold as part of finance arrangements to cover the gap between the amount owed on a loan for a vehicle and the amount paid out under the motor insurance policy if the vehicle is written off) properly fall within the exclusion.

This means that non-financial gap insurance is now liable to the higher rate of IPT when sold through suppliers of motor vehicles or persons connected to them. This revised liability applies to premiums received on or after 1 April 2004 and, for businesses using the special accounting scheme, to premiums written in respect of annual contracts incepting on or after that date (the treatment of any contracts normally written for a period other than one year will be considered on a case by case basis).

FURTHER HELP AND ADVICE

General guidance on IPT can be found in Customs' Notice IPT1 "Insurance Premium Tax".

The views expressed in this Business Brief are those of HM Customs and Excise.

IMPLEMENTATION OF TRIBUNAL DECISION REGARDING THE LIABILITY OF THE REINSURANCE OF SURETY BONDS

5 July 2005. *Business Brief 13/05*

This Business Brief article announces HM Revenue & Customs' (HMRC) decision not to appeal a recent Tribunal decision (*Travellers Casualty & Surety and others*), which found that the reinsurance of surety bonds is exempt from Insurance Premium Tax (IPT). It reverses the ruling given in Business Brief 25/03.

BACKGROUND

Following a lengthy review, Customs (now HMRC) concluded in 2003 that the reinsurance of surety bonds was in fact primary insurance and therefore liable to IPT (unlike reinsurance which is exempt from IPT). This conclusion was based upon the fact that the underlying bond contracts were written as contracts of guarantee rather than contracts of insurance and therefore fell outside the scope of IPT. Customs took the view that to be 'reinsurance' for IPT, the underlying risk being 'reinsured' must be written under a contract of insurance.

This ruling was announced in Business Brief 25/03 and implemented from 1 April 2004, requiring businesses writing this type of reinsurance to register and account for IPT on premiums with a tax point falling after this date.

The ruling was subsequently appealed to a Tribunal by seven of the principal UK surety bond underwriters (ie the recipients of the reinsurance). They were supported by the Association of British Insurers (ABI) who represented the industry during the period of review.

THE TRIBUNAL DECISION

The Tribunal found that the insurance of surety bonds was clearly a specialist sector of the reinsurance market and there was no case law or textbook that specifically covers its status or otherwise as 'reinsurance'. On balance, however, it decided that the insurance of surety risks did fall within the definition of reinsurance for IPT, on the basis that the wider reinsurance markets regard the transfer of an insurer's surety risk to other insurers as reinsurance, and the interpretation of terms of statute should not conflict with commercial usage without good reason.

HMRC has decided not to appeal this decision.

PRACTICAL IMPLICATIONS

As a result of this decision, the reinsurance of surety bonds and similar products is exempt from IPT, irrespective of whether the underlying contract is one of insurance or one of guarantee.

Businesses that were registered for IPT solely because of the ruling contained in our earlier Business Brief may now apply to be deregistered. Businesses that have already accounted for IPT on premiums received under surety reinsurance contracts may claim a refund from HMRC as detailed below.

INFORMATION ON MAKING CLAIMS OR ADJUSTMENTS

Businesses that think this decision applies to them and have already accounted for IPT may claim any resulting repayment due to them from HMRC by using one of the following methods:

(1) where, during the course of an accounting period, you discover previous errors not exceeding £2000 net, an adjustment may be made on your IPT return for the period of discovery (or, if the business is to deregister, the final return) or,

(2) if, during the course of an accounting period, you discover previous errors exceeding £2000 net, a separate claim should be submitted to HMRC (in these cases, the errors must not be corrected through your IPT returns). Details of where to send your claim can be obtained from HM Revenue & Customs' National Advice Service on 0845 010 9000.

All adjustments or claims are limited to a three-year period and will be subject to the conditions set out below.

– Businesses must be able to produce suitable evidence that they accounted for IPT on the basis outlined above, and must be able to substantiate the amount claimed.
– HMRC may reject all or part of a claim if repayment would unjustly enrich the claimant. For example, if a business has passed the tax on to the customer but is unable, or does not intend, to pass on the repayment.

A notification to HMRC that a business intends making a claim in the future is not a valid claim.

NOTICE OF REQUIREMENT TO GIVE SECURITY FOR ENVIRONMENTAL TAXES

April 2008. *Notice ET1*

1. INTRODUCTION

1.1 What is this notice about?

There is provision in the laws on Insurance Premium Tax, Landfill Tax, Aggregates Levy and Climate Change Levy for us to require you to provide an amount of security if we consider that tax is at risk of being unpaid by your business.

This Notice is our Statement of Practice on the circumstances where we may require security for Insurance Premium Tax, Landfill Tax, Aggregates Levy and Climate Change Levy. For our Statement of Practice on VAT Security see Notice 700/52 Notice of Requirement to give security to HM Revenue and Customs.

This notice and others mentioned are available both on paper and on our website.

2. WHEN WILL YOU ISSUE A NOTICE OF REQUIREMENT TO GIVE SECURITY?

We may issue a Notice of Requirement to you for example if:

– you have in your previous or current business, failed to comply with your tax obligations
– your business is run by disqualified directors or by undischarged bankrupts
– you have previously been prosecuted or penalised for a tax offence, or
– other persons concerned in the current registration of your business are connected with past failures to pay tax due.

There may also be other circumstances when we may ask you to provide security.

2.1 Will I receive any warning before you require security?

Not always. Where we have strong grounds to suspect that revenue is at risk of being unpaid by your business we may require security without warning.

3. HOW MUCH SECURITY WILL YOU REQUIRE FROM ME?

We base the amount of security on a long-standing and well-tested formula that is approved by the independent VAT & Duties Tribunals. This formula reflects the minimum time it would take us to recover the debt if, in future, you do not pay your tax. We calculate the amount of security using the most accurate information available to us at the time which may include the:

- tax declared on tax returns from your current business
- tax declared on tax returns from your previous businesses
- tax declared on tax returns from businesses of a similar size, with similar customers and in the same trade class, or
- taxable turnover/premium declared on your application to register.

We may also add any outstanding tax from your current registered business to our calculation before issuing a Notice of Requirement.

If you make quarterly returns, we will require an amount of security based on the tax we estimate you would have to pay over six months.

If you make monthly returns, we will accept a lower amount of security based on the tax we estimate you would have to pay over four months.

4. WHAT FORMS OF SECURITY WILL YOU ACCEPT?

We will normally accept security in the following forms:

- cash or bankers draft
- bank or building society guarantee, or
- a joint bank or building society account.

However, we will only accept a guarantee from a financial institution approved by us. Please contact the address shown on the Notice of Requirement and we will advise you whether the guarantor is acceptable.

4.1 When will I have to provide the security?

The security is required immediately. Please contact us if you need time to make the necessary arrangements.

5. WHAT WILL HAPPEN IF I DON'T PROVIDE THE SECURITY?

It is a **criminal offence** to continue to trade without providing the security and we may prosecute you.

A person is guilty of a criminal offence if he:

	Description
Landfill tax	Carries out taxable activities (as defined in section 69(1) of the Finance Act 1996) without giving security he has been required to give.
Aggregates levy	Is responsible for any aggregate being subjected to commercial exploitation in the United Kingdom where, at the time it is so subjected, he has been required to give security and he has not complied with that requirement.
Climate change levy	Is liable to account for the levy on a taxable supply that he makes where, at the time the supply is made, he has been required to give security and has not complied with that requirement.
Climate change levy	Is liable to account for the levy on a taxable supply that another person makes to him where, if he makes any arrangements for the making of the supply at a time when he as been required to give security and he has not complied with that requirement.
Insurance premium tax	Enters into taxable insurance contracts (as defined by section 73(1) of the Finance Act 1994) without giving security.

You may be liable to a penalty of up to **£5,000 for each taxable supply/taxable activity/taxable insurance contract** you make or enter into without providing the security.

If you do not provide the security, we may prosecute you for the whole period of trading from the date the Notice of Requirement was issued.

5.1 Can I be prosecuted as well as my company?

Yes. If you are involved in a business that continues to trade without providing the security you may be prosecuted individually. You may also be personally responsible for paying any fines and compensation awarded by the court.

6. HOW LONG WILL YOU HOLD THE SECURITY FOR?

We will regularly review the requirement and will return the security when we consider you are no longer a risk to the collection of tax. If you have any information that you feel may alter our decision to hold security, please contact us and we will reconsider the requirement.

At the very least, we will review the requirement within 12 months of you providing the security (if you make monthly returns) or 2 years (if you make quarterly returns).

6.1 When will you use the security?

If you fall behind with payments of your tax we may offset the security against the amount you owe. We may then ask you to provide a further amount of security.

7. STATUTORY REVIEW AND APPEAL

7.1 What if I disagree with the decision to require security?

If you disagree with our decision to require security as described in Section 2 of this notice you have the right to require us to review our decision. You should do this within 45 days of receiving the Notice of Requirement to give security. You should contact us as soon as possible if you:

– think there are facts that may not have been fully considered, or
– can provide further information.

It is in your interests to provide any further information as soon as possible.

You must ask for a statutory review of your case prior to lodging an appeal at independent tribunal.

7.2 Your right to appeal to tribunal

If you are not satisfied with the outcome of a review you can appeal to an independent VAT & Duties Tribunal. You have 30 days from the date of the review decision to lodge your appeal. Where your 30-days time limit has expired you must apply direct to the appropriate Tribunal Centre. For more information see Notice 990: Excise and Customs Appeals.

7.3 Can I continue to make taxable supplies/carry out taxable activities/enter into taxable insurance contracts if I appeal?

If you have been served with a Notice of Requirement for security, you continue to trade at your own risk. Your appeal does not affect your ongoing liability to prosecution should you continue to trade without providing the security.

However, in order to allow time for your appeal to be heard, we may agree to await the decision of the Tribunal before taking steps to begin or continue any proposed or ongoing prosecution of you or your business. We will write to you if we agree to await the decision of the Tribunal.

If the Tribunal dismisses your appeal, or you withdraw it, we may decide to commence or re-commence immediately our prosecution of you or your business.

Commentary—*De Voil Indirect Tax Service* **V5.186.**

REVISED REGISTRATION PROCEDURES FOR OVERSEAS INSURERS

19 August 2008. *HMRC Brief 39/08*

This Revenue & Customs brief outlines the revised procedures for non-UK based insurers to register and account for Insurance Premium Tax (IPT). It also explains the revised circumstances under which we would seek to recover tax directly from an insured person. These changes were announced in Budget 2008 and come into effect from 21 July 2008.

BACKGROUND

All insurers underwriting taxable insurance in respect of risks located in the UK are required to register and account for IPT, regardless of where the insurer is based. Prior to the changes announced in the Budget, insurers based in another EU member state or outside the EU, were required to appoint a UK tax representative to deal with their IPT affairs. The tax representative was jointly and severally liable so that, in the event of a failure by the insurer, the representative assumed legal responsibility for the insurer's IPT obligations, such as submitting returns and paying any tax due.

Following representations from the insurance industry, a review of the tax representative requirement, including a formal consultation exercise, was carried out in 2007. It was clear from this that the requirement was difficult and onerous to operate and, in extreme cases, resulted in non-compliance by overseas insurers, putting their UK counterparts at a competitive disadvantage. Furthermore, recent European Court of Justice judgments have caused us to consider its approach to the issues.

As a result, measures were announced in Budget 2008 to remove the compulsory requirement to appoint a joint and severally liable tax representative. Our power to recover IPT from the insured person was also restricted to circumstances where the insurer is based outside the EU and is not covered by a Mutual Assistance provision or similar agreement.

REVISED PROCEDURES FOR NON-UK BASED INSURERS

From 21 July 2008, non-UK based insurers will have two options for dealing with their UK IPT affairs. They can either appoint an agent to act on their behalf, or they can deal with us directly.

APPOINTING AN AGENT

Whilst it would be preferable to have an agent based in the UK, we recognise that non-UK based insurers may prefer to use an agent based elsewhere in the EU to represent its tax affairs in both the UK and in other member states. We will, therefore, allow non-UK based insurers to appoint an agent based anywhere in the EU. We cannot, however, accept an agent based outside the EU.

We will require written authorisation from the insurer to deal with an agent on their behalf and will need a new authorisation each time there is a change of agent. The authorisation must give full details of the agent and the date on which they begin to act for the insurer. Existing tax representatives can continue to act for insurers and neither they nor the insurer they act for needs to take any action in respect of the IPT registration. The tax representative continues to be jointly and severally liable for any tax due before 21 July 2008.

Where an agent is appointed all documents, such as returns etc, will be sent to the agent rather than to the insurer. While the agent will be expected to deal with the insurer's day to day IPT affairs, such as compiling and submitting returns or making payments etc, they will not be liable for any tax due. However, in the future, agents may be liable to civil penalties in respect of certain errors on returns or other documents. Insurers need to ensure that whoever they nominate to act as agent is fully capable of handling their IPT affairs. The insurer may not, for example, be able to rely on any failure by the agent as an excuse for failure to discharge their own IPT responsibilities. In particular, the insurer and their agent will need to ensure that there are suitable arrangements in place for the relevant business records to be made available in the UK, should we need to see them.

DEALING DIRECTLY WITH HMRC

As an alternative to appointing an agent, non-UK insurers may decide to deal with us directly. This option is available to newly registered insurers or insurers who are already registered and are currently using a tax representative. In the case of existing registrations, the insurer simply needs to notify us in writing of the date from which they will be dealing with their own IPT affairs. Insurers who deal with their own IPT affairs will need to ensure that, as far as possible, arrangements are in place for records to be produced in the UK should we need to see them. In most cases, this will involve the insurer posting a selection of requested records to us for examination. The records would be returned on completion of our enquiries.

REGISTRATION FORM

The IPT registration form, IPT1, will be amended to reflect these changes. There will be a space on the form for non-UK insurers, who are registering for the first time, to indicate whether they intend to appoint an agent or to deal with us directly. There will also be a space to record the agent's particulars and a declaration that we can deal with the agent in respect of the insurer's UK IPT affairs. Insurers who are already registered need take no action unless they wish to change their current arrangements, in which case they should write in to advise us at the address shown below.

RETURNS AND PAYMENTS

Where an agent is based in another member state, or where the insurer is dealing with their own IPT affairs, contact with the insurer will be via one of our offices in London. Return forms will be issued to the agent or insurer as required via the London office, but should be sent back to the normal address shown on the back of the IPT return form:

HM Revenue & Customs
Central Collection Unit (IPT)
21 Victoria Avenue
Southend on Sea X SS99 1AS

Because of the additional time involved in posting correspondence to a non-UK address, insurers or agents will have less time in which to complete and submit the returns, but hopefully this will be kept to no more than a few days. Payments can be made in any currency. We accept payment via direct debit, from a UK bank account. We are also able to accept payments directly from a UK or overseas bank account using BACS or CHAPS. Where possible we would encourage insurers or agents to make direct electronic transfers between bank accounts using one of the methods mentioned above.

Where payment is not made by electronic means, we can accept cheques, preferably drawn on a UK bank account, which should accompany the return form. While we will also accept cheques drawn on an overseas account, insurers or agents should bear in mind that these may take longer to clear through the banking system. Insurers or agents should also note that any exchange rate fluctuations between Sterling and other currencies will be borne by the business.

LIABILITY OF INSURED PERSON TO ACCOUNT FOR IPT

Prior to the changes announced in the Budget, we were able to recover IPT directly from an insured person in instances where a non-UK based insurer, had underwritten a taxable risk in the UK but had either failed to register and/or account for tax due. This provision applied to customers of all non-UK insurers irrespective of where the insurer was based. The Mutual Assistance Directives enable us to exchange information with the fiscal authorities in other EU member states and, where necessary, ask them to recover tax on our behalf. In addition, the UK has similar agreements in place with several countries outside the EU. With effect from 21 July 2008, therefore, the power to recover tax from the insured person has been restricted to customers of insurers based in countries where no such arrangements exist.

The IPT guidance and public notice will be amended shortly to reflect these changes.

For further help or advice please contact the National Advice Service on 0845 010 9000 or 0845 000 0200 (text phone).

Commentary—*De Voil Indirect Tax Service* **V18.128**, **V18.132**.

ACTION FOLLOWING THE HIGH COURT JUDGMENT IN THE HOME-SERVE IPT APPEAL

18 August 2009 *HMRC Brief 47/2009*

HMRC has decided not to appeal the Homeserve judgment on Insurance Premium Tax and will pay claims from businesses that have been accounting for that tax on fees charged under similar arrangements. However, it will take action to close the loophole exposed by the litigation.

On 18 June the High Court released its judgment in the Homeserve Membership Ltd (Homeserve) Insurance Premium Tax (IPT) appeal 2009 EWHC 1311(Ch), [2009] All ER (D) 264 (Jun). Homeserve arranges domestic plumbing and electrical breakdown insurance for householders. In 2004 Homeserve restructured its arrangements so that it charged part of what would ordinarily be considered the insurance premium as an "arrangement and administration fee" under a separate contract with the insured.

The High Court found in favour of Homeserve, that is that the contract between Homeserve and the insured person fell outside the scope of IPT, being a separate contract to the taxable insurance contract.

HMRC has decided not to appeal this judgment. Claims from businesses that have been accounting for IPT on fees charged under arrangements such as those adopted by Homeserve (that is, charging fees under separate contracts with the insured parties and notifying the insured in writing that the fee is an amount so charged) will be paid subject to the normal repayment, capping and unjust enrichment rules.

HMRC's view, however, is that where fees are artificially carved out of what would ordinarily be taxable insurance premium, IPT is properly due. Action will be taken to close the loophole exposed by the outcome of the Homeserve litigation.

HMRC will be consulting informally with the ABI and other insurance industry representatives to ensure the proposed changes to IPT legislation are properly targeted.

FURTHER INFORMATION

Please contact the National Advice Service on Tel 0845 010 9000 or your nominated HM Revenue & Customs' contact should you have one.

Commentary—*De Voil Indirect Tax Service* **V18.101**.

CHANGES TO TIME LIMITS FOR ASSESSMENTS AND CLAIMS

19 March 2010 *HMRC Brief 16/10*

This Brief is a reminder of the new four-year time limit coming into effect on 1 April 2010 for direct taxes claims and assessments under self-assessment. This date also marks the convergence of the rules governing normal time limits for all the main direct and indirect taxes. For people outside self-assessment, the new time limits for repayment claims don't take effect until 1 April 2012.

INTRODUCTION

The compliance checks legislation introduced a new normal four year time limit for assessments and **claims**, from 1 April 2010, in schedule 39 of the Finance Act 2008.

Initially this affects:

- capital gains tax;
- corporation tax;
- income tax;
- PAYE;
- VAT.

Aligning these time limits where possible reduces compliance costs for customers and makes our compliance checks easier.

The new time limits come into effect on 1 April 2010 for direct taxes. The normal time limits for these taxes are decreasing from six years, or five years from the 31 January immediately following the tax year, to four years.

The new time limits came into effect on 1 April 2009 for VAT because the normal time limits for VAT are increasing from three to four years. There are transitional provisions for VAT. These provisions prevent out of time periods from coming back in time by disregarding a prescribed accounting period that ends on or before 31 March 2006. This means that by 1 April 2010 the four year time limit for VAT assessments will apply in full.

The new time limits apply to assessments and **claims** for the above taxes that are made after these dates regardless of the period the assessment or **claim** relates to.

REPAYMENT CLAIMS – SELF ASSESSMENT AND PAYE

. . .

CHANGES TO ASSESSMENT TIME LIMITS

. . .

The new limits from 01 April 2010 for VAT assessments and **claims** are:

– Normal time limit – four years;
– Careless behaviour – four years;
– Deliberate behaviour – 20 years;

from the end of the relevant tax period.

In particular, HMRC will no longer have 20 years to assess where a tax loss was attributable to negligent conduct which now equates to careless behaviour. However the 20 year time limit will still apply to cases of failure to notify, and certain failures in respect of tax avoidance schemes.

The new time limits do not affect:

– periods already out of date under the old time limits;
– the time limits for making enquiries into SA or CTSA returns;
– the time limits for making penalty determinations for direct tax;
– the time limits for assessing Class 1, 1A and 2 National Insurance Contributions; or
– the two-year rule and the evidence of facts rules for VAT assessments.

While the normal time limit for most assessments and determinations will be four years from the end of the relevant tax period, there are however many variations from this norm. The tables of time limits (www.hmrc.gov.uk/manuals/chmanual/ch56000.htm) in the appendices of the Compliance Handbook give a full summary.

For more information see the Compliance Handbook (www.hmrc.gov.uk/manuals/chmanual/ch50000.htm) chapter 50000.

Further indirect tax changes

For Indirect Tax the Finance Act 2009 schedule 51 introduced a new normal four-year time limit for assessments and **claims**, from 1 April 2010. This affects:

– Aggregates Levy
– Climate Change Levy
– Insurance Premium Tax
– Landfill Tax

The new limits from 1 April 2010 for the above taxes are:

– Normal time limit – four years
– Careless behaviour – four years
– Deliberate behaviour – 20 years

from the end of the relevant tax period.

The time limit for assessments and making **claims** was therefore increased with effect from 1 April 2010 from three years to four. However, in order to ensure that accounting periods that were out of time on 31 March 2010 are not brought back in time by the change, transitional arrangements have been put in place.

The technical guidance in the Compliance Handbook will be updated in due course to cover these further changes.

Commentary—*Simon's Taxes* **A6.708**.

NEW PENALTY FOR FAILURE TO NOTIFY

18 June 2010 *HMRC Brief 30/10*

This Brief provides information on the penalty for failing to notify which applies to most taxes from 1 April 2010.

INTRODUCTION

This Business Brief explains the failure to notify penalty contained in Sch 41 of the 2008 Finance Act (FA 2008) which from 1 April 2010 can be applied to most taxes. There is full guidance on this penalty at CH70000 and CH500000 in the Compliance Handbook (www.hmrc.gov.uk/manuals/chmanual/index.htm).

FROM 1 APRIL 2010 THE PENALTY COULD BE APPLIED TO A FAILURE TO NOTIFY FOR:

Aggregates Levy	Climate Change Levy	Insurance Premium Tax
Air Passenger Duty	Corporation Tax	Landfill Tax
Alcoholic Liquor Duty	Excise Duties	Lottery Duty
Amusement Machine Licence Duty	Gaming Duty	Pool Betting Duty
	General Betting Duty	Remote Gaming Duty
Bingo Duty	Hydrocarbon Oils Duty	Tobacco Products Duty
Capital Gains Tax	Income Tax	VAT

BACKGROUND

Under the review of HMRC's powers, deterrents and safeguards (www.hmrc.gov.uk/about/powers-appeal.htm) legislation has been introduced to align and modernise the framework under which we administer the taxes and duties formerly handled by Customs and Excise and the Inland Revenue.

We inherited a number of different penalty regimes from Customs and Excise and the Inland Revenue. The law and practice relating to penalties varied not only between the two former departments but also between the various taxes and duties for which each department was responsible.

Finance Act 2007, section 97 and Schedule 24 introduced a simpler and more consistent penalty system for inaccuracies in tax returns and other documents.

Finance Act 2008, section 123 and Schedule 41 has extended and adapted the new penalty framework to introduce:

– A standard penalty across most our taxes where a customer fails to register or notify us and as a result tax is due. Paragraph 1 of Schedule 41.
– Various VAT and Excise wrongdoing penalties. Paragraphs 2, 3 and 4 of Schedule 41 – see Revenue and Customs Brief 52/09.

FAILURE TO NOTIFY

Failure to notify occurs when someone fails to tell us on time that an event has happened that:

– gives rise to additional liability
– gives rise to chargeability
– means they need to register with us

These events could include:

– where a person has Income Tax, Capital Gains Tax or Corporation Tax to pay and we have not given them a notice to make a return
– when a person starts a new taxable activity
– when the turnover from an existing activity has reached a certain level
– when the nature of the activity changes

We will not charge a penalty if the person has a reasonable excuse for not telling us at the appropriate time, provided that they tell us without unreasonable delay after the excuse had ended.

DATES AND TIMES

The new failure to notify penalty regime applies to failures occurring on or after 1 April 2010. When you must notify us by depends on the type of tax and the declaration method involved.

Examples are given in Appendix 1 at the end of this Brief of the most common taxes a self-employed person or small business is likely to encounter.

SIZE OF PENALTY

The amount of the penalty is a percentage of the tax that is unpaid at a specified date, or to which the person is liable for the relevant period. This tax is known as the "potential lost revenue".

The percentage is determined by the behaviour that led to the failure to notify and the behaviour after the failure has been established. Higher penalties are charged if the failure was deliberate, but the percentage can be reduced from the maximum for disclosure and the amount of help the person gives us in establishing the amount of tax unpaid.

BEHAVIOUR THAT LED TO THE FAILURE

The new penalty is designed to address the behaviour that caused the failure so that, within the deliberate category, the law provides for higher penalties in the most serious cases where the person has failed to notify us and has taken steps to conceal the need to notify.

The definition of the behaviour that led to the failure to notify will be:

	Maximum %	Prompted Minimum %	Unprompted Minimum %
Non-deliberate	30	20	10
Deliberate but not concealed	70	35	20
Deliberate and concealed	100	50	30

A disclosure is unprompted if at the time it is made the person had no reason to believe that we had discovered or were about to discover the failure. Otherwise it is a prompted disclosure.

We want to encourage people to join the tax system. If the failure is notified within 12 months of the tax becoming unpaid, the penalty for a non-deliberate failure to notify may be reduced for:

- a prompted disclosure from 20 per cent to 10 per cent
- an unprompted disclosure from 10 per cent to 0 per cent

BEHAVIOUR AFTER THE FAILURE HAS BEEN ESTABLISHED

The maximum penalty percentage is reduced by an amount that represents the quality of disclosure. The term "reduction for disclosure" replaces the terms "abatement" and "mitigation" used in previous penalty regimes. The first thing to consider about the quality of the disclosure is whether the disclosure was prompted or unprompted.

To calculate the reduction for disclosure you need to consider another three elements of disclosure:

- telling us about it – which involves admitting the failure, making a full disclosure and explaining how and why the failure occurred
- giving us help – which involves giving active assistance and actively engaging in quantifying the amount, as opposed to passive acceptance or obstruction
- volunteering any information relevant to the disclosure, such as allowing us access to records

APPEALING AGAINST A FAILURE TO NOTIFY PENALTY

When we have decided on the penalty we will issue a penalty assessment. The person is entitled to a review of, and can appeal against, our decision:

- that a penalty is payable
- the amount of the penalty

IPT

MORE INFORMATION

Compliance Handbook (www.hmrc.gov.uk/manuals/chmanual/index.htm).

New penalties internet page (www.hmrc.gov.uk/about/new-penalties/index.htm).

Q and A briefing on all penalty changes (www.hmrc.gov.uk/about/new-penalties/faqs.htm) Appendix 1.

EXAMPLES OF LATE NOTIFICATION

Below are some examples of when a failure to notify penalty may apply for the most common taxes.

INCOME THAT NEEDS TO BE DECLARED ON A SELF ASSESSMENT RETURN

. . .

VAT

A business that has exceeded the VAT registration threshold over the past 12 months, or expects to turnover the whole VAT threshold in the next 30 days, must tell us within 30 days.

Find out how and when to register for VAT (www.hmrc.gov.uk/vat/start/register/index.htm).

. . .

Commentary—*Simon's Taxes* **A6.612**.

Insurance Premium Tax Index

Defined words and phrases are listed separately at the end.

IPT

IPT

IPT

U

W

Words and Phrases

Words in brackets indicate the context in which the word or phrase is used.

accounting period, FA 1994 ss 54, 73(1), SI 1994/1774 reg 2(1)
accounts (special accounting scheme), SI 1994/1774 reg 20(2)
aircraft tribunal, FA 1994 s 73(1)
applicable period (interest on tax repaid), FA 1994 Sch 7 para 22(3)–(7)
authorised person, FA 1993 s 73(1)
buying, FSMA 2000 Sch 22 para 27
Channel tunnel equipment, FA 1994 Sch 7A para 11(4), (5)
Channel tunnel system, FA 1994 Sch 7A para 10(3)
chargeable amount, FA 1994 s 50
collector, SI 1994/1774 reg 2(1)
commercial aircraft, FA 1994 Sch 7A para 7(3)
commercial ship, FA 1994 Sch 7A para 4(3)
Commissioners, FA 1994 s 73(1)
conduct, FA 1994 s 73(1)
control (groups of companies), FA 1994 s 63(9)
disability allowance, FA 1994 Sch 7A para 3(4)(*b*)
disposing, FSMA 2000 Sch 22 para 27
established rate, SI 1998/1461, reg 2(1)
exempt matter, FA 1994 s 69(3)
export, FA 1994 Sch 7A para 13(4)
financial facility, FA 1994 Sch 7A para 15(3)
foreign or international railway rolling stock, FA 1994 Sch 7A para 9(3)
handicapped, FA 1994 Sch 7A para 3(4)(*a*)
higher rate matter, FA 1994 s 69 (12)(*a*)–(*d*)
increase (tax), FA 1994 s 67A
initial amount (special accounting scheme), SI 1994/1774 reg 24(1)
initial period (special accounting scheme), SI 1994/1774 reg 20(1)
insurance business, FA 1994 s 73(1)
insurance premium, FA 1994 s 72(1)
insurance related service, FA 1994 s 52A(9), Sch 6A para 1(1)
insurer, FA 1994 s 73(1)
investment, FSMA 2000 s 22(4)
Job Band, SI 1994/1774 reg A42
legislation relating to insurance premium tax, FA 1994 s 73(1)
lifeboat, FA 1994 Sch 7A para 5(3)
lifeboat equipment, FA 1994 Sch 7A para 6(3)
Lloyd's, SI 1994/1774 reg 2(1)
managing agent, SI 1994/1774 reg 2(1)
mobility supplement, FA 1994 Sch 7A para 3(4)(*c*)
non-exempt matter, FA 1994 s 69(4)
offering, FSMA 2000 Sch 22 para 27
overdeclaration, SI 1994/1774 reg 13(1)
overseas customer, FA 1994 Sch 7A para 16(3)
premium, FA 1994 s 72(1)
premium (special accounting scheme), SI 1994/1774 reg 20(3)
premium written date (special accounting scheme), SI 1994/1774 reg 20(1)
prescribed, FA 1994 s 73(1)
prescribed rate (interest on unpaid tax), FA 1994 Sch 7 para 21(5)
property, FSMA 2000 Sch 22 para 27
railway rolling stock, foreign or international, FA 1994 Sch 7A para 9(3)
reckonable date (interest on unpaid tax), FA 1994 Sch 7 para 21(4)
registered person, SI 1994/1774 reg 2(1)
registrable person, FA 1994 s 73(3)
registration number, SI 1994/1774 reg 2(1)
relevant accounting period (special accounting schemes), FA 1994 s 68(1)
relevant supply of goods, FA 1994 Sch 7A para 16(2)
return, SI 1994/1774 reg 2(1)
selling, FSMA 2000 Sch 22 para 27
ship, commercial, FA 1994 Sch 7A para 4(3)
supply, FA 1994 Sch 6A para 1(1)
tax, FA 1994 s 73(1)
tax representative, FA 1994 ss 57, 73(1)
taxable business, FA 1994 s 73(1)
taxable insurance contract, FA 1994 ss 70, 71
taxable intermediary, SI 1994/1774 reg 2 (1)
underdeclaration, SI 1994/1774 reg 13(1)
underwriting member, SI 1994/1774 reg 2(1)
walking possession agreement, FA 1994 Sch 7 para 19(2)

Landfill tax

Contents

Landfill Tax Statutes

Contents

PROVISIONAL COLLECTION OF TAXES ACT 1968

(1968 Chapter 2)

1 Temporary statutory effect of House of Commons resolutions affecting . . . , [landfill tax][2], . . .

(1) This section applies only to . . . , [landfill tax][2]

(2) Subject to that, and to the provisions of subsections (4) to (8) below, where the House of Commons passes a resolution which—

(*a*) provides for the renewal for a further period of any tax in force or imposed during the previous financial year (whether at the same or a different rate, and whether with or without modifications) or for the variation or abolition of any existing tax, and

(*b*) contains a declaration that it is expedient in the public interest that the resolution should have statutory effect under the provisions of this Act,

the resolution shall, for the period specified in the next following subsection, have statutory effect as if contained in an Act of Parliament and, where the resolution provides for the renewal of a tax, all enactments which were in force with reference to that tax as last imposed by Act of Parliament shall during that period have full force and effect with respect to the tax as renewed by the resolution.

In this section references to the renewal of a tax include references to its reimposition, and references to the abolition of a tax include references to its repeal.

(3) The said period is—

(*a*) in the case of a resolution passed in [November or December][3] in any year, one expiring with [5th May in the next calendar year][3];

[(*aa*) in the case of a resolution passed in February or March in any year, one expiring with 5th August in the same calendar year; and][5]

(*b*) in the case of any other resolution, one expiring at the end of four months after the date on which it is expressed to take effect or, if no such date is expressed, after the date on which it is passed.

(4) A resolution shall cease to have statutory effect under this section unless within the next [thirty][4] days on which the House of Commons sits after the day on which the resolution is passed—

(*a*) a Bill renewing, varying or, as the case may be, abolishing the tax is read a second time by the House, or

(*b*) a Bill is amended by the House [in Committee or on Report, or by any [Public Bill Committee][6] of the House][1] so as to include provision for the renewal, variation or, as the case may be, abolition of the tax.

(5) A resolution shall also cease to have statutory effect under this section if—

(*a*) the provisions giving effect to it are rejected during the passage of the Bill containing them through the House, or

(*b*) an Act comes into operation renewing, varying or, as the case may be, abolishing the tax, or

(*c*) Parliament is dissolved or prorogued.

(6) Where, in the case of a resolution providing for the renewal or variation of a tax, the resolution ceases to have statutory effect by virtue of subsection (4) or (5) above, or the period specified in subsection (3) above terminates, before an Act comes into operation renewing or varying the tax, any money paid in pursuance of the resolution shall be repaid or made good, and any deduction made in pursuance of the resolution shall be deemed to be an unauthorised deduction.

(7) Where any tax as renewed or varied by a resolution is modified by the Act renewing or varying the tax, any money paid in pursuance of the resolution which would not have been payable under the new conditions affecting the tax shall be repaid or made good, and any deduction made in pursuance of the resolution shall, so far as it would not have been authorised under the new conditions affecting the tax, be deemed to be an unauthorised deduction.

(8) When during any session a resolution has had statutory effect under this section, statutory effect shall not be again given under this section in the same session to the same resolution or to a resolution having the same effect.

Note—Words and any subsection not relevant for the purposes of landfill tax have been omitted.

Amendments—[1] Words in sub-s (4)(*b*) added by FA 1968 s 60.

[2] Words in the heading and in sub-s (1) added by virtue of FA 1998 s 148.

[3] Words in sub-s (3)(*a*) substituted by FA 1993 s 205 in relation to resolutions passed after 27 July 1993.

[4] Word in sub-s (4) substituted by FA 1993 s 205 in relation to resolutions passed after 27 July 1993.

[5] Words in sub-s (3) inserted by F(No 2)A 1997 s 50 in relation to resolutions passed after 31 July 1997.

[6] Words in sub-s (4)(*b*) substituted by FA 2007 s 112(1) with effect from 19 July 2007.

5 House of Commons resolution giving provisional effect to motions affecting taxation

(1) This section shall apply if the House of Commons resolves that provisional statutory effect shall be given to one or more motions to be moved by the Chancellor of the Exchequer, or some other Minister, and which, if agreed to by the House, would be resolutions—

(*a*) to which statutory effect could be given under section 1 of this Act, or

(*b*) . . .

(*c*) . . .

(2) Subject to subsection (3) below, on the passing of the resolution under subsection (1) above, sections 1 . . . of this Act, . . . shall apply as if each motion to which the resolution applies had then been agreed to by a resolution of the House.

(3) Subsection (2) above shall cease to apply to a motion if that motion, or a motion containing the same proposals with modifications, is not agreed to by a resolution of the House (in this section referred to as "a confirmatory resolution") within the next ten days on which the House sits after the resolution under subsection (1) above is passed, and, if it ceases to apply, all such adjustments, whether by way of discharge or repayment of tax, or discharge of security, or otherwise, shall be made as may be necessary to restore the position to what it would have been if subsection (2) above had never applied to that motion, and to make good any deductions which have become unauthorised deductions.

(4) . . .

Note—Sub-ss (1)(*b*), (4) and words omitted from sub-s (2) are not relevant to landfill tax; sub-s (1)(*c*) is repealed.

6 Short title, repeals and saving as respects Northern Ireland

(1) This Act may be cited as the Provisional Collection of Taxes Act 1968.

(2) . . .

(3) . . . [1]

Note—Sub-s (2) repeals enactments specified in Schedule.

Amendments—[1] Sub-s (3) repealed by Northern Ireland Constitution Act 1973 s 41(1)(*a*) and Sch 6 Pt I, with effect from 18 July 1973.

INTERPRETATION ACT 1978

(1978 Chapter 30)

Note—See VAT Statutes, *ante*.

INCOME AND CORPORATION TAXES ACT 1988

(1988 Chapter 1)

PART XIX

SUPPLEMENTAL

Miscellaneous

827 VAT penalties etc

Note—This section repealed by CTA 2009 ss 1322, 1326, Sch 1 paras 1, 268, Sch 3 Part 1. CTA 2009 applies for accounting periods ending on or after 1 April 2009 (for corporation tax purposes) and for tax years 2009–10 onwards (for income and capital gains tax purposes).

Relevant provisions rewritten to CTA 2009 ss 1303(1), (2), 1306(1).

FINANCE ACT 1996

(1996 Chapter 8)

ARRANGEMENT OF SECTIONS

PART III

LANDFILL TAX

The basic provisions

Exemptions

An Act to grant certain duties, to alter other duties, and to amend the law relating to the National Debt and the Public Revenue, and to make further provision in connection with Finance.

[29th April 1996]

PART III
LANDFILL TAX

The basic provisions

Press releases etc—C & E Business Brief 18/96 27-8-96 (guidance notes issued to help registrable landfill site operators).
IR Tax Bulletin June 1996 p 317 (Revenue views on treatment of payments of landfill tax for purposes of Schedule D Cases I and II.

39 Landfill tax

(1) A tax, to be known as landfill tax, shall be charged in accordance with this Part.

(2) The tax shall be under the care and management of the Commissioners of Customs and Excise.

40 Charge to tax

(1) Tax shall be charged on a taxable disposal.

(2) A disposal is a taxable disposal if—

(*a*) it is a disposal of material as waste,

(*b*) it is made by way of landfill,

(*c*) it is made at a landfill site, and

(*d*) it is made on or after 1st October 1996.

(3) For this purpose a disposal is made at a landfill site if the land on or under which it is made constitutes or falls within land which is a landfill site at the time of the disposal.

Commentary—*De Voil Indirect Tax Service* **V20.103**.

Simon's Tax Cases—s 40(2), *C&E Comrs v Parkwood Landfill Ltd* [2002] STC 417; *Waste Recycling Group Ltd v R&C Comrs* [2009] STC 200.

41 Liability to pay tax

(1) The person liable to pay tax charged on a taxable disposal is the landfill site operator.

(2) The reference here to the landfill site operator is to the person who is at the time of the disposal the operator of the landfill site which constitutes or contains the land on or under which the disposal is made.

42 Amount of tax

(1) The amount of tax charged on a taxable disposal shall be found by taking—

(*a*) [£48][2] for each whole tonne disposed of and a proportionately reduced sum for any additional part of a tonne, or

(*b*) a proportionately reduced sum if less than a tonne is disposed of.

(2) Where the material disposed of consists entirely of qualifying material this section applies as if the reference to [[£48][2] were to £2.50][1].

(3) Qualifying material is material for the time being listed for the purposes of this section in an order.

(4) The Treasury must have regard to the object of securing that material is listed if it is of a kind commonly described as inactive or inert.

Press releases etc—C & E News Release 48/96 18-9-96 (Foundry sand is chargeable at £2 per tonne).

Regulations—See Landfill Tax (Qualifying Material) Order, SI 1996/1528.

Amendments—[1] Words in sub-s (2) substituted by FA 2007 s 15(4) with effect in relation to disposals made, or treated as made, on or after 1 April 2008.

[2] Figures in sub-ss (1)(*a*), (2) substituted by FA 2009 s 18(1) with effect in relation to disposals made, or treated as made, on or after 1 April 2010.

Prospective amendments—In sub-ss (1), (2), figure "56" to be substituted for figure "48" by FA 2010 s 15(1) with effect in relation to disposals made, or treated as made, on or after 1 April 2011.

Exemptions

43 Material removed from water

(1) A disposal is not a taxable disposal for the purposes of this Part if it is shown to the satisfaction of the Commissioners that the disposal is of material all of which—

(*a*) has been removed (by dredging or otherwise) from water falling within subsection (2) below, and

(*b*) formed part of or projected from the bed of the water concerned before its removal.

(2) Water falls within this subsection if it is—

(*a*) a river, canal or watercourse (whether natural or artificial), or

(*b*) a dock or harbour (whether natural or artificial).

(3) A disposal is not a taxable disposal for the purposes of this Part if it is shown to the satisfaction of the Commissioners that the disposal is of material all of which—

(*a*) has been removed (by dredging or otherwise) from water falling within the approaches to a harbour (whether natural or artificial),

(*b*) has been removed in the interests of navigation, and

(*c*) formed party of or projected from the bed of the water concerned before its removal.

(4) A disposal is not a taxable disposal for the purposes of this Part if it is shown to the satisfaction of the Commissioners that the disposal is of material all of which—

(*a*) consists of naturally occurring mineral material, and

(*b*) has been removed (by dredging or otherwise) from the sea in the course of commercial operations carried out to obtain substances such as sand or gravel from the seabed.

[(5) A disposal is not a taxable disposal for the purposes of this Part if it is shown to the satisfaction of the Commissioners that the disposal is of material all of which comprises material falling within subsection (1) or (3) and other material which has been added to that material for the purpose of securing that it is not liquid waste.][1]

Commentary—*De Voil Indirect Tax Service* **V20.122.**

Amendments—[1] Sub-s (5) inserted by the Landfill Tax (Material Removed from Water) Order, SI 2007/2909 art 2 with effect from 30 October 2007: SI 2007/2909 art 1.

[43A Contaminated land

(1) A disposal is not a taxable disposal for the purposes of this Part if it is a disposal within subsection (2) below.

(2) A disposal is within this subsection if—

(*a*) it is of material all of which has been removed from land in relation to which a certificate issued under section 43B below was in force at the time of the removal;

(*b*) none of that material has been removed from a part of the land in relation to which, as at the time of the removal, the qualifying period has expired;

(*c*) it is a disposal in relation to which any conditions to which the certificate was made subject are satisfied; and

(*d*) it is not a disposal within subsection (4) below.

(3) For the purpose of subsection (2)(*b*) above the qualifying period expires, in relation to the part of the land in question—

(*a*) in the case of a reclamation which qualified under section 43B(7)(*a*) below, where the object involves the construction of—

(i) a building; or

(ii) a civil engineering work,

when the construction commences;

(*b*) in any other case of a reclamation which qualified under section 43B(7)(*a*) below, when pollutants have been cleared to the extent that they no longer prevent the object from being fulfilled; or

(*c*) in the case of a reclamation which qualified under section 43B(7)(*b*) below, when pollutants have been cleared to the extent that the potential for harm has been removed.

(4) Subject to subsection (5) below, a disposal is within this subsection if it is of material the removal of any of which is required in order to comply with—

(*a*) a works notice served under section 46A of the Control of Pollution Act 1974;

(*b*) an enforcement notice served under section 13 of the Environmental Protection Act 1990;

(*c*) a prohibition notice served under section 14 of the Environmental Protection Act 1990;

(*d*) an order under section 26 of the Environmental Protection Act 1990;

(*e*) a remediation notice served under section 78E of the Environmental Protection Act 1990;

(*f*) an enforcement notice served under section 90B of the Water Resources Act 1991; . . . [2]

(*g*) a works notice served under section 161A of the Water Resources Act 1991;

[(*h*) an enforcement notice served under regulation 36 of the Environmental Permitting (England and Wales) Regulations 2007;

(*j*) a suspension notice served under regulation 37 of those Regulations; or

(*k*) an order under regulation 44 of those Regulations.][5]

(*l*) a notice served under regulation 28(2) of the Water Environment (Controlled Activities) (Scotland) Regulations 2005.][4]

(5) A disposal shall not be regarded as falling within subsection (4) above where the removal of the material has been carried out by or on behalf of any of the following bodies:

(*a*) a local authority;

(*b*) a development corporation;

(*c*) the Environment Agency;

(*d*) the Scottish Environment Protection Agency;

(*e*) . . . [6]

(*f*) Scottish Enterprise;

(*g*) Highlands and Islands Enterprise;

(*h*) . . . [3]

(6) In this section—

"development corporation" means—

(*a*) in England and Wales, a corporation established under section 135 of the Local Government, Planning and Land Act 1980;

Landfill Tax

(*b*) in Scotland, a corporation established under section 2 of the New Towns (Scotland) Act 1968;

. . . [6]

"Highlands and Islands Enterprise" means the body established by section 1(*b*) of the Enterprise and New Towns (Scotland) Act 1990;

"land" includes land covered by water;

"Scottish Enterprise" means the corporation established by section 1(*a*) of the Enterprise and New Towns (Scotland) Act 1990;

. . . [3]

(7) For the purposes of this section—

(*a*) the removal of material includes its removal from one part of the land for disposal on another part of the same land;

(*b*) the clearing of pollutants includes their being cleared from one part of the land for disposal on another part of the same land.][1]

Commentary—*De Voil Indirect Tax Service* **V20.125**.

Amendments—[1] This section inserted by Landfill Tax (Contaminated Land) Order, SI 1996/1529 art 3, with effect from 1 August 1996.

[2] In sub-s (4) word in para (*f*) repealed with effect in England and Wales by the Pollution Prevention and Control (England and Wales) Regulations, SI 2000/1973 reg 39, Sch 10 para 21 with effect from 1 August 2000. With effect in Scotland, paras (*h*)–(*k*) are inserted as follows by virtue of the Pollution Prevention and Control (Scotland) Regulations, SI 2000/323 reg 36, Sch 10 para 6 with effect from 28 September 2000—

"(*h*) an enforcement notice served under regulation 19 of the Pollution Prevention and Control (Scotland) Regulations 2000;

(*j*) a suspension notice served under regulation 20 of those Regulations; or

(*k*) an order under regulation 33 of those Regulations."

[3] Words in sub-s (5)(*h*), and in sub-s (6) definition of "Welsh Development Agency", repealed by the Welsh Development Agency (Transfer of Functions to the National Assembly for Wales and Abolition) Order, SI 2005/3226 art 7(1), Sch 2 para 10 with effect from 23 November 2005.

[4] In sub-s (4) word "or" omitted from after para (*j*) repealed, and para (*l*) and preceding word "or" inserted, by the Water Environment and Water Services (Scotland) Act 2003 (Consequential Provisions and Modifications) Order, SI 2006/1054 art 2, Sch 1 para 2 with effect from 1 April 2006.

[5] Sub-s (4)(*h*)–(*k*) substituted by the Environmental Permitting (England and Wales) Regulations, SI 2007/3538 reg 73, Sch 21 para 25 with effect, in relation to England and Wales, from 6 April 2008.

[6] Sub-s (5)(*e*), and in sub-s (6) definition of "English Partnerships", repealed by the Housing and Regeneration Act 2008 ss 56, 321(1), Sch 8 para 64, Sch 16, with effect from 1 December 2008 (by virtue of SI 2008/3068 arts 1(2), 2(1)(*w*), (3)).

Prospective amendments—Sub-ss (4)(*b*)–(*d*) repealed by the Pollution Prevention and Control Act 1999 Sch 3 with effect from a day to be appointed.

Section 43A to be repealed by the Landfill Tax (Material from Contaminated Land) (Phasing out of Exemption) Order, SI 2008/2669 art 4(a) with effect from 1 April 2012.

[43B Contaminated land: certificates

(1) Subject to subsection (2) below, the Commissioners shall issue a certificate in relation to any land where—

(a) an application in writing is made by a person carrying out, or intending to carry out, a reclamation of that land (the applicant);

(b) the applicant provides to them such information as they may direct, whether generally or as regards that particular case[, within such time as they may direct][2];

(c) the application is made not less than 30 days before the date from which the certificate is to take effect; and

(d) the reclamation qualifies under subsection (7) below.

(2) The Commissioners shall not refuse an application for a certificate in a case where the conditions specified in subsection (1)(a) to (d) above are satisfied unless it appears to them—

(a) necessary to do so for the protection of the revenue; or

(b) except where the applicant is one of the bodies mentioned in subsection (5) of section 43A above, that all or part of the reclamation of land to which the application relates is required in order to comply with a notice or order mentioned in subsection (4) of that section.

(3) The Commissioners may make a certificate subject to such conditions set out in the certificate as they think fit, including (but not restricted to) conditions—

(a) that the certificate is to be in force only in relation to a particular quantity of material;

(b) that the certificate is to be in force only in relation to disposals made at a particular landfill site or sites;

(c) that the certificate is to be in force in relation to part only of the land to which the application relates.[3]

(4) A certificate issued under this section—

(*a*) shall have effect from the date it is issued to the applicant or such later date as the Commissioners may specify in the certificate; and (*b*) shall cease to have effect on such date as the Commissioners may set out in the certificate, but in any event no later than the day on which the person to whom the certificate was issued ceases to have the intention to carry out any activity involving reclamation of the land in relation to which the certificate was issued.

(5) Where a certificate has been issued to a person, the Commissioners—

(*a*) may vary it by issuing a further certificate to that person; or

(*b*) may withdraw it by giving notice in writing to that person; but this is subject to subsection (6) below.

(6) The Commissioners shall not withdraw a certificate unless it appears to them—

(*a*) necessary to do so for the protection of the revenue;

(*b*) that the reclamation did not in fact qualify under subsection (7) below or no longer so qualifies;

(*c*) that there will not be any or any more disposals within section 43A(2) above of material from the land to which the certificate relates; or

(*d*) except where the person to whom the certificate was issued is one of the bodies mentioned in subsection (5) of section 43A above, that the removal of material from the land to which the certificate relates is required in order to comply with a notice or order mentioned in subsection (4) of that section.

(7) A reclamation qualifies under this subsection if—

(*a*) it is, or is to be, carried out with the object of facilitating development, conservation, the provision of a public park or other amenity, or the use of the land for agriculture or forestry; or

(*b*) in a case other than one within paragraph (*a*) above, it is, or is to be, carried out with the object of reducing or removing the potential of pollutants to cause harm,

and, in either case, the conditions specified in subsection (8) below are satisfied.

(8) The conditions mentioned in subsection (7) above are—

(*a*) that the reclamation constitutes or includes cleaning the land of pollutants which are causing harm or have the potential for causing harm;

(*b*) that, in a case within subsection (7)(*a*) above, those pollutants would (unless cleared) prevent the object concerned being fulfilled; and

(*c*) that all relevant activities have ceased or have ceased to give rise to any pollutants in relation to that land.

(9) For the purposes of subsection (8) above the clearing of pollutants—

(*a*) need not be such that all pollutants are removed;

(*b*) need not be such that pollutants are removed from every part of the land in which they are present;

(*c*) may involve their being cleared from one part of the land and disposed of on another part of the same land.

(10) For the purposes of subsection (8)(*c*) above an activity is relevant if—

(*a*) it has at any time resulted in the presence of pollutants in, on or under the land in question otherwise than—

(i) without the consent of the person who was the occupier of the land at the time, or

(ii) by allowing pollutants to be carried onto the land by air or water, and

(*b*) at that time it was carried out—

(i) by the applicant or a person connected with him, or

(ii) by any person on the land in question.

(11) For the purposes of subsection (10) above—

(*a*) any question whether a person is connected with another shall be determined in accordance with section 839 of the Taxes Act 1988;

(*b*) the occupier of land that is not in fact occupied is the person entitled to occupy it.

(12) In this section "land" has the meaning given by section 43A(6) above.][1]

Commentary—*De Voil Indirect Tax Service* **V20.125**.

Simon's Tax Cases—43B(8)(*c*), *Augean plc v R&C Comrs* [2008] STC 2894.

Amendments—[1] This section inserted by Landfill Tax (Contaminated Land) Order, SI 1996/1529 art 3, with effect from 1 August 1996.

[2] Words in sub-s (1)(*b*) inserted by the Landfill Tax (Material from Contaminated Land) (Phasing out of Exemption) Order, SI 2008/2669 art 2(1) with effect from 15 November 2008. This amendment applies in relation to applications made before 15 November 2008 (as well as those made on or after that date) (SI 2008/2669 art 2(2).

[3] Sub-ss (1)–(3) repealed by the Landfill Tax (Material from Contaminated Land) (Phasing out of Exemption) Order, SI 2008/2669 art 3(1)(*a*) with effect from 1 December 2008. This amendment does not have effect until 1 April 2012 in relation to applications made before 1 December 2008.

Prospective amendments—Sub-ss (4)–(12) to be repealed by the Landfill Tax (Material from Contaminated Land) (Phasing out of Exemption) Order, SI 2008/2669 art 4(*b*) with effect from 1 April 2012.

[43C Site restoration

Commentary—*De Voil Indirect Tax Service* **V20.126**.

Amendments—This section repealed by FA 2009 s 119, Sch 60 paras 1, 10 with effect from 1 September 2009.

44 Mining and quarrying

(1) A disposal is not a taxable disposal for the purposes of this Part if it is shown to the satisfaction of the Commissioners that the disposal is of material all of which fulfils each of the conditions set out in subsections (2) to (4) below.

(2) The material must result from commercial mining operations (whether the mining is deep or open-cast) or from commercial quarrying operations.

(3) The material must be naturally occurring material extracted from the earth in the course of the operations.

(4) The material must not have been subjected to, or result from, a non-qualifying process carried out at any stage between the extraction and the disposal.

(5) A non-qualifying process is—

(*a*) a process separate from the mining or quarrying operations, or

(*b*) a process forming part of those operations and permanently altering the material's chemical composition.

Commentary—*De Voil Indirect Tax Service* **V20.123**.

[44A Quarries

(1) A disposal is not a taxable disposal for the purposes of this Part if it is—

(*a*) of material all of which is treated for the purposes of section 42 above as qualifying material,

(*b*) made at a qualifying landfill site, and

(*c*) made, or treated as made, on or after 1st October 1999.

(2) A landfill site is a qualifying landfill site for the purposes of this section if at the time of the disposal—

(*a*) the landfill site is or was a quarry,

(*b*) subject to subsection (3) below, it is a requirement of planning consent in respect of the land in which the quarry or former quarry is situated that it be wholly or partially refilled, and

(*c*) subject to subsection (4) below, the licence[, permit][2] or, as the case may require, resolution authorising disposals on or in the land comprising the site permits only the disposal of material which comprises qualifying material.

(3) Where a quarry—

(*a*) was in existence before 1st October 1999, and

(*b*) quarrying operations ceased before that date,

the requirement referred to in subsection (2)(b) must have been imposed on or before that date.

(4) Where a licence [or permit][2] authorising disposals on or in the land does not (apart from the application of this subsection) meet the requirements of subsection (2)(*c*) above and an application has been made to vary the licence [or permit][2] in order to meet them, it shall be deemed to meet them for the period before—

(*a*) the application is disposed of, or

(*b*) the second anniversary of the making of the application if it occurs before the application is disposed of.

(5) For the purposes of subsection (4) an application is disposed of if—

(*a*) it is granted,

(*b*) it is withdrawn,

(*c*) it is refused and there is no right of appeal against the refusal,

(*d*) a time limit for appeal against refusal expires without an appeal having been commenced, or

(*e*) an appeal against refusal is dismissed or withdrawn and there is no further right of appeal.][1]

Commentary—*De Voil Indirect Tax Service* **V20.123**.

Simon's Tax Cases—44A(2)(*b*), *C&E Comrs v Ebbcliff Ltd* [2004] STC 391.

Amendments—[1] This section inserted by Landfill Tax (Site Restoration and Quarries) Order, SI 1999/2075, art 2(*b*), with effect from 1 October 1999.

[2] Words in sub-ss (2)(*c*), (4) inserted by Landfill Tax (Site Restoration, Quarries and Pet Cemeteries) Order, SI 2005/725 arts 2, 4 with effect from 6 April 2005.

45 Pet cemeteries

(1) A disposal is not a taxable disposal for the purposes of this Part if—

(*a*) the disposal is of material consisting entirely of the remains of dead domestic pets, and

(*b*) the landfill site at which the disposal is made fulfils the test set out in subsection (2) below.

(2) The test is that during the relevant period—

(*a*) no landfill disposal was made at the site, or

(*b*) the only landfill disposals made at the site were of material consisting entirely of the remains of dead domestic pets.

(3) For the purposes of subsection (2) above the relevant period—

(*a*) begins with 1st October 1996 or (if later) with the coming into force in relation to the site of the licence[, resolution or permit][1] mentioned in section 66 below, and

(*b*) ends immediately before the disposal mentioned in subsection (1) above.

Commentary—*De Voil Indirect Tax Service* **V20.124**.

Amendment—[1] Words in sub-s (3)(*a*) substituted by Landfill Tax (Site Restoration, Quarries and Pet Cemeteries) Order, SI 2005/725 arts 2, 5 with effect from 6 April 2005.

46 Power to vary

(1) Provision may be made by order to produce the result that—

(*a*) a disposal which would otherwise be a taxable disposal (by virtue of this Part as it applies for the time being) is not a taxable disposal;

(*b*) a disposal which would otherwise not be a taxable disposal (by virtue of this Part as it applies for the time being) is a taxable disposal.

(2) Without prejudice to the generality of subsection (1) above, an order under this section may—

(*a*) confer exemption by reference to certificates issued by the Commissioners and to conditions set out in certificates;

(*b*) allow the Commissioners to direct requirements to be met before certificates can be issued;

[(*c*) provide for reviews and appeals relating to decisions about certificates.][1]

(3) Provision may be made under this section in such way as the Treasury think fit (whether by amending this Part or otherwise).

Order—Landfill Tax (Contaminated Land) Order 1996, SI 1996/1529.
Landfill Tax (Site Restoration and Quarries) Order 1999, SI 1999/2075.
Landfill Tax (Site Restoration, Quarries and Pet Cemeteries) Order 2005, SI 2005/725.
Landfill Tax (Material Removed from Water) Order 2007, SI 2007/2909.
Landfill Tax (Material from Contaminated Land) (Phasing out of Exemption) Order 2008, SI 2008/2669.

Amendment—[1] Sub-s (2)(*c*) substituted by the Transfer of Tribunal Functions and Revenue and Customs Appeals Order, SI 2009/56 art 3, Sch 1 para 233 with effect from 1 April 2009.

Administration

47 Registration

(1) The register kept under this section may contain such information as the Commissioners think is required for the purposes of the care and management of the tax.

(2) A person who—

(*a*) carries out taxable activities, and

(*b*) is not registered,

is liable to be registered.

(3) Where—

(*a*) a person at any time forms the intention of carrying out taxable activities, and

(*b*) he is not registered,

he shall notify the Commissioners of his intention.

(4) A person who at any time ceases to have the intention of carrying out taxable activities shall notify the Commissioners of that fact.

(5) Where a person is liable to be registered by virtue of subsection (2) above the Commissioners shall register him with effect from the time when he begins to carry out taxable activities; and this subsection applies whether or not he notifies the Commissioners under subsection (3) above.

(6) Where the Commissioners are satisfied that a person has ceased to carry out taxable activities they may cancel his registration with effect from the earliest practicable time after he so ceased; and this subsection applies whether or not he notifies the Commissioners under subsection (4) above.

(7) Where—

(*a*) a person notifies the Commissioners under subsection (4) above,

(*b*) they are satisfied that he will not carry out taxable activities,

(*c*) they are satisfied that no tax which he is liable to pay is unpaid,

(*d*) they are satisfied that no credit to which he is entitled under regulations made under section 51 below is outstanding, and

(*e*) subsection (8) below does not apply,

the Commissioners shall cancel his registration with effect from the earliest practicable time after he ceases to carry out taxable activities.

(8) Where—

(*a*) a person notifies the Commissioners under subsection (4) above, and

(*b*) they are satisfied that he has not carried out, and will not carry out, taxable activities,

the Commissioners shall cancel his registration with effect from the time when he ceased to have the intention to carry out taxable activities.

(9) For the purposes of this section regulations may make provision—

(*a*) as to the time within which a notification is to be made;

(*b*) as to the form and manner in which any notification is to be made and as to the information to be contained in or provided with it;

(*c*) requiring a person who has made a notification to notify the Commissioners if any information contained in or provided in connection with it is or becomes inaccurate;

(*d*) as to the correction of entries in the register.

(10) References in this Part to a registrable person are to a person who—

(*a*) is registered under this section, or

(*b*) is liable to be registered under this section.

Commentary—*De Voil Indirect Tax Service* **V20.161**.
Regulations—Land fill Tax Regulations, SI 1996/1527.
Cross references—See Landfill Tax Regulations, SI 1996/1527 reg 4 (notification of liability to be registered), SI 1996/1597 reg 5 (changes in particulars), SI 1996/1527 reg 6 (notification of cessation of taxable activities).

48 Information required to keep register up to date

(1) Regulations may make provision requiring a registrable person to notify the Commissioners of particulars which—

(*a*) are of changes in circumstances relating to the registrable person or any business carried on by him,
(*b*) appear to the Commissioners to be required for the purpose of keeping the register kept under section 47 above up to date, and
(*c*) are of a prescribed description.

(2) Regulations may make provision—

(*a*) as to the time within which a notification is to be made;
(*b*) as to the form and manner in which a notification is to be made;
(*c*) requiring a person who has made a notification to notify the Commissioners if any information contained in it is inaccurate.

Regulations—Landfill Tax Regulations, SI 1996/1527.
Cross references—See Landfill Tax Regulations, SI 1996/1527 reg 5 (changes in particulars).

49 Accounting for tax and time for payment

Regulations may provide that a registrable person shall—

(*a*) account for tax by reference to such periods (accounting periods) as may be determined by or under the regulations;
(*b*) make, in relation to accounting periods, returns in such form . . . [1]and at such times as may be so determined;
(*c*) pay tax at such times and in such manner as may be so determined.

Regulations—Landfill Tax Regulations, SI 1996/1527.
Cross references—See Landfill Tax Regulations, SI 1996/1527 reg 11 (making of returns), SI 1996/1527 reg 15 (payment of tax).
Amendments—[1] Words "as may be prescribed" in s 49(*b*) repealed by FA 2009 s 119, Sch 60 para 12 with effect from 21 July 2009. The omission of these words does not affect any regulation made under this provision before the passing of FA 2009, and does not prevent the powers conferred by the provision from being used after the passing of FA 2009 to revoke any regulations made under the powers before that time; FA 2009 s 119, Sch 60 para 13(3).

50 Power to assess

(1) Where—

(*a*) a person has failed to make any returns required to be made under this Part,
(*b*) a person has failed to keep any documents necessary to verify returns required to be made under this Part,
(*c*) a person has failed to afford the facilities necessary to verify returns required to be made under this Part, or
(*d*) it appears to the Commissioners that returns required to be made by a person under this Part are incomplete or incorrect,

the Commissioners may assess the amount of tax due from the person concerned to the best of their judgment and notify it to him.

(2) Where a person has for an accounting period been paid an amount to which he purports to be entitled under regulations made under section 51 below, then, to the extent that the amount ought not to have been paid or would not have been paid had the facts been known or been as they later turn out to be, the Commissioners may assess the amount as being tax due from him for that period and notify it to him accordingly.

(3) Where a person is assessed under subsections (1) and (2) above in respect of the same accounting period the assessments may be combined and notified to him as one assessment.

(4) Where the person failing to make a return, or making a return which appears to the Commissioners to be incomplete or incorrect, was required to make the return as a personal representative, trustee in bankruptcy, receiver, liquidator or person otherwise acting in a representative capacity in relation to another person, subsection (1) above shall apply as if the reference to tax due from him included a reference to tax due from that other person.

(5) An assessment under subsection (1) or (2) above of an amount of tax due for an accounting period shall not be made after the later of the following—

(*a*) two years after the end of the accounting period;
(*b*) one year after evidence of facts, sufficient in the Commissioners' opinion to justify the making of the assessment, comes to their knowledge;

but where further such evidence comes to their knowledge after the making of an assessment under subsection (1) or (2) above another assessment may be made under the subsection concerned in addition to any earlier assessment.

(6) Where—

(*a*) as a result of a person's failure to make a return in relation to an accounting period the Commissioners have made an assessment under subsection (1) above for that period,

(*b*) the tax assessed has been paid but no proper return has been made in relation to the period to which the assessment related, and

(*c*) as a result of a failure to make a return in relation to a later accounting period, being a failure by the person referred to in paragraph (*a*) above or a person acting in a representative capacity in relation to him, as mentioned in subsection (4) above, the Commissioners find it necessary to make another assessment under subsection (1) above,

then, if the Commissioners think fit, having regard to the failure referred to in paragraph (a) above, they may specify in the assessment referred to in paragraph (c) above an amount of tax greater than that which they would otherwise have considered to be appropriate.

(7) Where an amount has been assessed and notified to any person under subsection (1) or (2) above it shall be deemed to be an amount of tax due from him and may be recovered accordingly unless, or except to the extent that, the assessment has subsequently been withdrawn or reduced.

(8) For the purposes of this section notification to—

(*a*) a personal representative, trustee in bankruptcy, receiver or liquidator, or

(*b*) a person otherwise acting in a representative capacity in relation to another person,

shall be treated as notification to the person in relation to whom the person mentioned in paragraph (a) above, or the first person mentioned in paragraph (b) above, acts.

(9) Subsection (5) above has effect subject to paragraph 33 of Schedule 5 to this Act.

(10) In this section "trustee in bankruptcy" means, as respects Scotland, an interim or permanent trustee (within the meaning of the Bankruptcy (Scotland) Act 1985) or a trustee acting under a trust deed (within the meaning of that Act).

Cross-reference—Banking Act 2009 (Parts 2 and 3 Consequential Amendments) Order, SI 2009/317 art 3, Schedule (modification of this section in so far as it relates to bank insolvency or administration under Banking Act 2009 Pts 2, 3).

Credit

51 Credit: general

(1) Regulations may provide that where—

(*a*) a person has paid or is liable to pay tax, and

(*b*) prescribed conditions are fulfilled,

the person shall be entitled to credit of such an amount as is found in accordance with prescribed rules.

(2) Regulations may make provision as to the manner in which a person is to benefit from credit, and in particular may make provision—

(*a*) that a person shall be entitled to credit by reference to accounting periods;

(*b*) that a person shall be entitled to deduct an amount equal to his total credit for an accounting period from the total amount of tax due from him for the period;

(*c*) that if no tax is due from a person for an accounting period but he is entitled to credit for the period, the amount of the credit shall be paid to him by the Commissioners;

(*d*) that if the amount of credit to which a person is entitled for an accounting period exceeds the amount of tax due from him for the period, an amount equal to the excess shall be paid to him by the Commissioners;

(*e*) for the whole or part of any credit to be held over to be credited for a subsequent accounting period;

(*f*) as to the manner in which a person who has ceased to be registrable is to benefit from credit.

(3) Regulations under subsection (2)(*c*) or (*d*) above may provide that where at the end of an accounting period an amount is due to a person who has failed to submit returns for an earlier period as required by this Part, the Commissioners may withhold payment of the amount until he has complied with that requirement.

(4) Regulations under subsection (2)(*e*) above may provide for credit to be held over either on the person's application or in accordance with directions given by the Commissioners from time to time; and the regulations may allow directions to be given generally or with regard to particular cases.

(5) Regulations may provide that—

(*a*) no benefit shall be conferred in respect of credit except on a claim made in such manner and at such time as may be determined by or under regulations;

(*b*) payment in respect of credit shall be made subject to such conditions (if any) as the Commissioners think fit to impose, including conditions as to repayment in specified circumstances;

(*c*) deduction in respect of credit shall be made subject to such conditions (if any) as the Commissioners think fit to impose, including conditions as to the payment to the Commissioners, in specified circumstances, of an amount representing the whole or part of the amount deducted.

(6) Regulations may require a claim by a person to be made in a return required by provision made under section 49 above.

(7) Nothing in section 52 or 53 below shall be taken to derogate from the power to make regulations under this section (whether with regard to bad debts, the environment or any other matter).

Commentary—*De Voil Indirect Tax Service* **V20.145**.

Regulations—Landfill Tax Regulations, SI 1996/1527.

Cross references—See Landfill Tax Regulations, SI 1996/1527 regs 17–20 (credit: general), SI 1996/1527 reg 21 (credit permanent removals etc).

52 Bad debts

(1) Regulations may be made under section 51 above with a view to securing that a person is entitled to credit if—

(*a*) he carries out a taxable activity as a result of which he becomes entitled to a debt which turns out to be bad (in whole or in part), and

(*b*) such other conditions as may be prescribed are fulfilled.

(2) The regulations may include provision under section 51(5)(*b*) or (*c*) above requiring repayment or payment if it turns out that it was not justified to regard a debt as bad (or to regard it as bad to the extent that it was so regarded).

(3) The regulations may include provision for determining whether, and to what extent, a debt is to be taken to be bad.

Commentary—*De Voil Indirect Tax Service* **V20.146**.

Regulations—Landfill Tax Regulations, SI 1996/1527.

Cross references—See Landfill Tax Regulations, SI 1996/1527 reg 22–29 (credit: bad debts).

53 Bodies concerned with the environment

(1) Regulations may be made under section 51 above with a view to securing that a person is entitled to credit if—

(*a*) he pays a sum to a body whose objects are or include the protection of the environment, and

(*b*) such other conditions as may be prescribed are fulfilled.

(2) The regulations may in particular prescribe conditions—

(*a*) requiring bodies to which sums are paid (environmental bodies) to be approved by another body (the regulatory body);

(*b*) requiring the regulatory body to be approved by the Commissioners;

(*c*) requiring sums to be paid with the intention that they be expended on such matters connected with the protection of the environment as may be prescribed.

(3) The regulations may include provision under section 51(5)(*b*) or (*c*) above requiring repayment or payment if—

(*a*) a sum is not in fact expended on matters prescribed under subsection (2)(*c*) above, or

(*b*) a prescribed condition turns out not to have been fulfilled.

(4) The regulations may include—

(*a*) provision for determining the amount of credit (including provision for limiting it);

(*b*) provision that matters connected with the protection of the environment include such matters as overheads (including administration) of environmental bodies and the regulatory body;

(*c*) provision as to the matters by reference to which an environmental body or the regulatory body can be, and remain, approved (including matters relating to the functions and activities of any such body);

[(*ca*) provision for an environmental body to be and remain approved only if it complies with conditions imposed from time to time by the regulatory body or for the regulatory body to be and remain approved only if it complies with conditions imposed from time to time by the Commissioners (including provision for the variation or revocation of such conditions);][1]

(*d*) provision allowing [the withdrawal of approval of an environmental body by the Commissioners or by the regulatory body, and the withdrawal of approval of the regulatory body by the Commissioners,][2] (whether prospectively or retrospectively);

(*e*) provision that, if approval of the regulatory body is withdrawn, another body may be approved in its place or its functions may be performed by the Commissioners;

(*f*) provision allowing the Commissioners to disclose to the regulatory body information which relates to the tax affairs of persons carrying out taxable activities and which is relevant to the credit scheme established by the regulations.

Commentary—*De Voil Indirect Tax Service* **V20.148**.

Regulations—Landfill Tax Regulations, SI 1996/1527.

Cross references—See Landfill Tax Regulations, SI 1996/1527 regs 30–36 (credit: bodies concerned with the environment).

Amendments—[1] Sub-s (4)(*ca*) inserted by FA 2007 s 24. This amendment is deemed to have come into force on 22 March 2007.

[2] Words in sub-s (4)(*d*) substituted by FA 2008 s 151(2). This amendment is treated as having come into force on 19 March 2008.

[Appeals][4]

54 Review of Commissioners' decisions

(1) [Subject to section 55, an appeal shall lie to an appeal tribunal from any person who is or will be affected by any of the following decisions—][4]

(*a*) a decision as to the registration or cancellation of registration of any person under this Part;
(*b*) a decision as to whether tax is chargeable in respect of a disposal or as to how much tax is chargeable;
[(*ba*) a decision to [withdraw a certificate under section 43B above][3];
(bb) a decision to make a certificate issued under section 43B above subject to a condition that it is to be in force in relation to part only of the land to which the application for the certificate related;][1,3]
(*c*) a decision as to whether a person is entitled to credit by virtue of regulations under section 51 above or as to how much credit a person is entitled to or as to the manner in which he is to benefit from credit;
[(*ca*) a decision to withdraw approval of an environmental body under any provision contained in regulations by virtue of section 53(4)(*d*) above;][2]
(*d*) a decision as to an assessment falling within subsection (2) below or as to the amount of such an assessment;
(*e*) a decision to refuse a request under section 58(3) below;
(*f*) a decision to refuse an application under section 59 below;
(*g*) a decision as to whether conditions set out in a specification under the authority of provision made under section 68(4)(*b*) below are met in relation to a disposal;
(*h*) a decision to give a direction under any provision contained in regulations by virtue of section 68(5) below;
(*i*) a decision as to a claim for the repayment of an amount under paragraph 14 of Schedule 5 to this Act;
(*j*) a decision as to liability to a penalty under Part V of that Schedule or as to the amount of such a penalty;
(*k*) a decision under paragraph 19 of that Schedule (as mentioned in paragraph 19(5));
(*l*) a decision as to any liability to pay interest under paragraph 26 or 27 of that Schedule or as to the amount of the interest payable;
(*m*) a decision as to any liability to pay interest under paragraph 29 of that Schedule or as to the amount of the interest payable;
(*n*) a decision to require any security under paragraph 31 of that Schedule or as to its amount;
(*o*) a decision as to the amount of any penalty or interest specified in an assessment under paragraph 32 of that Schedule.

(2) An assessment falls within this subsection if it is an assessment under section 50 above in respect of an accounting period in relation to which a return required to be made by virtue of regulations under section 49 above has been made.

(3)–(8) . . .[4]

Commentary—*De Voil Indirect Tax Service* **V20.174**.

Cross references—See FA 1997 Sch 5 para 19(3) (review of a decision contained in an assessment under FA 1997 Sch 5 para 14, 15 or 17).

Amendments—[1] Sub-paras (1)(*ba*), (*bb*) inserted by the Landfill Tax (Contaminated Land) Order, SI 1996/1529 art 4, with effect from 1 October 1996 (see s 57 below and SI 1996/1529 art 1).
[2] Sub-s (1)(*ca*) inserted by FA 2008 s 151(3). This amendment is treated as having come into force on 19 March 2008.
[3] In sub-s (1)(*ba*), words substituted for words "refuse an application for a certificate under section 43B above, or to withdraw such a certificate", and sub-s (1)(*bb*) repealed, by the Landfill Tax (Material from Contaminated Land) (Phasing out of Exemption) Order, SI 2008/2669 art 3(1)(*b*), (*c*) with effect from 1 December 2008. These amendments do not have effect until 1 April 2012 in relation to applications made before 1 December 2008.
[4] Heading substituted for previous heading "Review and appeal"; words at the beginning of sub-s (1) substituted for the words "This section applies to the following decisions of the Commissioners"; sub-ss (3)–(8) repealed, by the Transfer of Tribunal Functions and Revenue and Customs Appeals Order, SI 2009/56 art 3, Sch 1 para 234 with effect from 1 April 2009, subject to transitional and savings provisions in Sch 3 paras 2, 3.

Prospective amendments—Sub-ss (1)(*ba*) to be repealed by the Landfill Tax (Material from Contaminated Land) (Phasing out of Exemption) Order, SI 2008/2669 art 4(*c*) with effect from 1 April 2012.

[54A Offer of review

(1) HMRC must offer a person (P) a review of a decision that has been notified to P if an appeal lies under section 54 in respect of the decision.

(2) The offer of the review must be made by notice given to P at the same time as the decision is notified to P.

(3) This section does not apply to the notification of the conclusions of a review.][1]

Amendment—[1] Sections 54A–54G inserted by the Transfer of Tribunal Functions and Revenue and Customs Appeals Order, SI 2009/56 art 3, Sch 1 para 235 with effect from 1 April 2009.

[54B Right to require review

(1) Any person (other than P) who has the right of appeal under section 54 against a decision may require HMRC to review that decision if that person has not appealed to the appeal tribunal under section 54G.

(2) A notification that such a person requires a review must be made within 30 days of that person becoming aware of the decision.][1]

Amendment—[1] Sections 54A–54G inserted by the Transfer of Tribunal Functions and Revenue and Customs Appeals Order, SI 2009/56 art 3, Sch 1 para 235 with effect from 1 April 2009.

[54C Review by HMRC

(1) HMRC must review a decision if—

(*a*) they have offered a review of the decision under section 54A, and

(*b*) P notifies HMRC accepting the offer within 30 days from the date of the document containing the notification of the offer.

(2) But P may not notify acceptance of the offer if P has already appealed to the appeal tribunal under section 54G.

(3) HMRC must review a decision if a person other than P notifies them under section 54B.

(4) HMRC shall not be required to review a decision if P, or another person, has appealed to the appeal tribunal under section 54G in respect of the decision.][1]

Amendment—[1] Sections 54A–54G inserted by the Transfer of Tribunal Functions and Revenue and Customs Appeals Order, SI 2009/56 art 3, Sch 1 para 235 with effect from 1 April 2009.

[54D Extensions of time

(1) If under section 54A, HMRC have offered P a review of a decision, HMRC may within the relevant period notify P that the relevant period is extended.

(2) If under section 54B another person may require HMRC to review a matter, HMRC may within the relevant period notify the other person that the relevant period is extended.

(3) If notice is given the relevant period is extended to the end of 30 days from—

(*a*) the date of the notice, or

(*b*) any other date set out in the notice or a further notice.

(4) In this section "relevant period" means—

(*a*) the period of 30 days referred to in—

(i) section 54C(1)(*b*) (in a case falling within subsection (1)), or

(ii) section 54B(2) (in a case falling within subsection (2)), or

(*b*) if notice has been given under subsection (1) or (2), that period as extended (or as most recently extended) in accordance with subsection (3).][1]

Amendment—[1] Sections 54A–54G inserted by the Transfer of Tribunal Functions and Revenue and Customs Appeals Order, SI 2009/56 art 3, Sch 1 para 235 with effect from 1 April 2009.

[54E Review out of time

(1) This section applies if—

(*a*) HMRC have offered a review of a decision under section 54A and P does not accept the offer within the time allowed under section 54C(1)(*b*) or 54D(3); or

(*b*) a person who requires a review under section 54B does not notify HMRC within the time allowed under that section or section 54D(3).

(2) HMRC must review the decision under section 54C if—

(*a*) after the time allowed, P, or the other person, notifies HMRC in writing requesting a review out of time,

(*b*) HMRC are satisfied that P, or the other person, had a reasonable excuse for not accepting the offer or requiring review within the time allowed, and

(*c*) HMRC are satisfied that P, or the other person, made the request without unreasonable delay after the excuse had ceased to apply.

(3) HMRC shall not be required to review a decision if P, or another person, has appealed to the appeal tribunal under section 54G in respect of the decision.][1]

Amendment—[1] Sections 54A–54G inserted by the Transfer of Tribunal Functions and Revenue and Customs Appeals Order, SI 2009/56 art 3, Sch 1 para 235 with effect from 1 April 2009.

[54F Nature of review etc

(1) This section applies if HMRC are required to undertake a review under section 54C or 54E.

(2) The nature and extent of the review are to be such as appear appropriate to HMRC in the circumstances.

(3) For the purpose of subsection (2), HMRC must, in particular, have regard to steps taken before the beginning of the review—

(*a*) by HMRC in reaching the decision, and

(*b*) by any person in seeking to resolve disagreement about the decision.

(4) The review must take account of any representations made by P, or the other person, at a stage which gives HMRC a reasonable opportunity to consider them.

(5) The review may conclude that the decision is to be—

(*a*) upheld,

(*b*) varied, or

(*c*) cancelled.

(6) HMRC must give P, or the other person, notice of the conclusions of the review and their reasoning within—

(*a*) a period of 45 days beginning with the relevant date, or (*b*) such other period as HMRC and P, or the other person, may agree.

(7) In subsection (6) "relevant date" means—

(*a*) the date HMRC received P's notification accepting the offer of a review (in a case falling within section 54A), or

(*b*) the date HMRC received notification from another person requiring review (in a case falling within section 54B), or

(*c*) the date on which HMRC decided to undertake the review (in a case falling within section 54E).

(8) Where HMRC are required to undertake a review but do not give notice of the conclusions within the time period specified in subsection (6), the conclusion of the review is deemed to be that the decision is upheld.

(9) HMRC must notify the appellant of any conclusion under subsection (8).][1]

Amendment—[1] Sections 54A–54G inserted by the Transfer of Tribunal Functions and Revenue and Customs Appeals Order, SI 2009/56 art 3, Sch 1 para 235 with effect from 1 April 2009.

[54G Bringing of appeals

(1) An appeal under section 54 is to be made to the appeal tribunal before—

(*a*) the end of the period of 30 days beginning with—

(i) in a case where P is the appellant, the date of the document notifying the decision to which the appeal relates, or

(ii) in a case where a person other than P is the appellant, the date that person becomes aware of the decision, or

(*b*) if later, the end of the relevant period (within the meaning of section 54D).

(2) But that is subject to subsections (3) to (5).

(3) In a case where HMRC are required to undertake a review under section 54C—

(*a*) an appeal may not be made until the conclusion date, and

(*b*) any appeal is to be made within the period of 30 days beginning with the conclusion date.

(4) In a case where HMRC are requested to undertake a review by virtue of section 54E—

(*a*) an appeal may not be made—

(i) unless HMRC have decided whether or not to undertake a review, and

(ii) if HMRC decide to undertake a review, until the conclusion date; and

(*b*) any appeal is to be made within the period of 30 days beginning with—

(i) the conclusion date (if HMRC decide to undertake a review), or

(ii) the date on which HMRC decide not to undertake a review.

(5) In a case where section 54F(8) applies, an appeal may be made at any time from the end of the period specified in section 54F(6) to the date 30 days after the conclusion date.

(6) An appeal may be made after the end of the period specified in subsection (1), (3)(*b*), (4)(*b*) or (5) if the appeal tribunal gives permission to do so.

(7) In this section "conclusion date" means the date of the document notifying the conclusions of the review.][1]

Amendment—[1] Sections 54A–54G inserted by the Transfer of Tribunal Functions and Revenue and Customs Appeals Order, SI 2009/56 art 3, Sch 1 para 235 with effect from 1 April 2009.

55 [Appeals: further provisions][1]

(1), (2) . . . [1]

[(3) Subject to subsections (3A) and (3B), where an appeal under section 54 relates to a decision falling within section 54(1)(*b*) or (*d*), it shall not be entertained unless the amount which HMRC have determined to be payable as tax has been paid or deposited with them.

(3A) In a case where the amount determined to be payable as tax has not been paid or deposited an appeal may be entertained if—

(*a*) HMRC are satisfied (on the application of the appellant), or

(*b*) the appeal tribunal decides (HMRC not being so satisfied and on the application of the appellant),

that the requirement to pay or deposit the amount determined would cause the appellant to suffer hardship.

(3B) Notwithstanding the provisions of sections 11 and 13 of the Tribunals, Courts and Enforcement Act 2007, the decision of the tribunal as to the issue of hardship is final.][1]

(4) On an appeal under this section against an assessment to a penalty under paragraph 18 of Schedule 5 to this Act, the burden of proof as to the matters specified in paragraphs (*a*) and (*b*) of sub-paragraph (1) of paragraph 18 shall lie upon the Commissioners.

Cross references—See FA 1997 Sch 5 para 19(3) (appeal following decision by Commissioners contained in an assessment under FA 1997 Sch 5 para 14, 15 or 17).

Amendment—[1] Heading substituted for former heading "Appeals: general"; sub-ss (1), (2) repealed; sub-s (3) substituted, sub-ss (3A), (3B) inserted by the Transfer of Tribunal Functions and Revenue and Customs Appeals Order, SI 2009/56 art 3, Sch 1 para 236 with effect from 1 April 2009, subject to transitional and savings provisions in Sch 3 paras 2, 3.

56 Appeals: other provisions

(1) . . . [1]

(2) [Where on an appeal under section 54][1]—

(*a*) it is found that the amount specified in the assessment is less than it ought to have been, and

(*b*) the tribunal gives a direction specifying the correct amount,

the assessment shall have effect as an assessment of the amount specified the direction and that amount shall be deemed to have been notified to the appellant.

(3) Where on an appeal under section 55 above it is found that the whole or part of any amount paid or deposited in pursuance of section 55(3) above is not due, so much of that amount as is found not to be due shall be repaid with interest [at the rate applicable under section 197 of this Act][1].

(4) Where on an appeal under section 55 above it is found that the whole or part of any amount due to the appellant by virtue of regulations under section 51(2)(*c*) or (*d*) or (*f*) above has not been paid, so much of that amount as is found not to have been paid shall be paid with interest [at the rate applicable under section 197 of this Act][1].

(5) Where an appeal under section 55 above has been entertained notwithstanding that an amount determined by the Commissioners to be payable as tax has not been paid or deposited and it is found on the appeal that that amount is due [it shall be paid with interest at the rate applicable under section 197 of this Act][1].

[(5A) Interest under subsection (5) shall be paid without any deduction of income tax.][1]

(6) Without prejudice to paragraph 25 of Schedule 5 to this Act, nothing in section 55 above shall be taken to confer on a tribunal any power to vary an amount assessed by way of penalty except in so far as it is necessary to reduce it to the amount which is appropriate under paragraphs 18 to 24 of that Schedule.

(7) Without prejudice to paragraph 28 of Schedule 5 to this Act, nothing in section 55 above shall be taken to confer on a tribunal any power to vary an amount assessed by way of interest except in so far as it is necessary to reduce it to the amount which is appropriate under paragraph 26 or 27 of that Schedule.

[(8) Sections 85 and 85B of the Value Added Tax Act 1994 (settling of appeals by agreement and payment of tax where there is a further appeal) shall have effect as if—

(*a*) the references to section 83 of that Act included references to section 54 of this Act, and

(*b*) the references to value added tax included references to landfill tax.][1]

Cross references—See FA 1997 Sch 5 para 19(3) (appeal following decision by Commissioners contained in an assessment under FA 1997 Sch 5 para 14, 15 or 17).

Amendment—[1] The following amendments made by the Transfer of Tribunal Functions and Revenue and Customs Appeals Order, SI 2009/56 art 3, Sch 1 para 237 with effect from 1 April 2009, subject to transitional and savings provisions in Sch 3 paras 2, 3, 9—

- sub-s (1) repealed;
- in sub-s (2) words substituted for the words "Where on the appeal";
- in sub-ss (3), (4) words substituted for the words "at such rate as the tribunal may determine";
- in sub-s (5) words substituted for the words "the tribunal may, if it thinks fit, direct that that amount shall be paid with interest at such rate as may be specified in the direction";
- sub-s (5A) inserted;
- sub-s (8) substituted.

57 Review and appeal: commencement

Sections 54 to 56 above shall come into force on—

(*a*) 1st October 1996, or

(*b*) such earlier day as may be appointed by order.

Miscellaneous

58 Partnership, bankruptcy, transfer of business, etc

(1) As regards any case where a business is carried on in partnership or by another unincorporated body, regulations may make provision for determining by what persons anything required by this Part to be done by a person is to be done.

(2) The registration under this Part of an unincorporated body other than a partnership may be in the name of the body concerned; and in determining whether taxable activities are carried out by such a body no account shall be taken of any change in its members.

(3) The registration under this Part of a body corporate carrying on a business in several divisions may, if the body corporate so requests and the Commissioners see fit, be in the names of those divisions.

(4) As regards any case where a person carries on a business of a person who has died or become bankrupt or incapacitated or whose estate has been sequestrated, or of a person which is in liquidation or receivership or [administration][1], regulations may—

(*a*) require the first-mentioned person to inform the Commissioners of the fact that he is carrying on the business and of the event that has led to his carrying it on;

(*b*) make provision allowing the person to be treated for a limited time as if he were the other person;

(*c*) make provision for securing continuity in the application of this Part where a person is so treated.

(5) Regulations may make provision for securing continuity in the application of this Part in cases where a business carried on by a person is transferred to another person as a going concern.

(6) Regulations under subsection (5) above may in particular—

(*a*) require the transferor to inform the Commissioners of the transfer;

(*b*) provide for liabilities and duties under this Part of the transferor to become, to such extent as may be provided by the regulations, liabilities and duties of the transferee;

(*c*) provide for any right of either of them to repayment or credit in respect of tax to be satisfied by making a repayment or allowing a credit to the other;

but the regulations may provide that no such provision as is mentioned in paragraph (b) or (c) of this subsection shall have effect in relation to any transferor and transferee unless an application in that behalf has been made by them under the regulations.

Regulations—Landfill Tax Regulations, SI 1996/1527.

Cross references—See Landfill Tax Regulations, SI 1996/1527 reg 7 (transfer of a going concern), SI 1996/1527 reg 8 (representation of an unincorporated body), SI 1996/1527 reg 9 (bankruptcy or incapacity of registrable persons).

Banking Act 2009 (Parts 2 and 3 Consequential Amendments) Order, SI 2009/317 art 3, Schedule (modification of this section in so far as it relates to bank insolvency or administration under Banking Act 2009 Pts 2, 3).

Amendments—[1] Words in sub-s (4) substituted by the Enterprise Act 2002 (Insolvency) Order, SI 2003/2096 art 4, Schedule paras 27, 28 with effect from 15 September 2003. This amendment does not apply in relation to any case where a petition for an administration order was presented before that date: SI 2003/2096, arts 1(1), 6.

59 Groups of companies

(1) Where under the following provisions of this section any bodies corporate are treated as members of a group, for the purposes of this Part—

(*a*) any liability of a member of the group to pay tax shall be taken to be a liability of the representative member;

(*b*) the representative member shall be taken to carry out any taxable activities which a member of the group would carry out (apart from this section) by virtue of section 69 below;

(*c*) all members of the group shall be jointly and severally liable for any tax due from the representative member.

(2) Two or more bodies corporate are eligible to be treated as members of a group if the condition mentioned in subsection (3) below is fulfilled and—

(*a*) one of them controls each of the others,

(*b*) one person (whether a body corporate or an individual) controls all of them, or

(*c*) two or more individuals carrying on a business in partnership control all of them.

(3) The condition is that the prospective representative member has an established place of business in the United Kingdom.

(4) Where an application to that effect is made to the Commissioners with respect to two or more bodies corporate eligible to be treated as members of a group, then—

(*a*) from the beginning of an accounting period they shall be so treated, and

(*b*) one of them shall be the representative member,

unless the Commissioners refuse the application; and the Commissioners shall not refuse the application unless it appears to them necessary to do so for the protection of the revenue.

(5) Where any bodies corporate are treated as members of a group and an application to that effect is made to the Commissioners, then, from the beginning of an accounting period—

(*a*) a further body eligible to be so treated shall be included among the bodies so treated,

(*b*) a body corporate shall be excluded from the bodies so treated,

(*c*) another member of the group shall be substituted as the representative member, or

(*d*) the bodies corporate shall no longer be treated as members of a group,

unless the application is to the effect mentioned in paragraph (a) or (c) above and the Commissioners refuse the application.

(6) The Commissioners may refuse an application under subsection (5)(*a*) or (*c*) above only if it appears to them necessary to do so for the protection of the revenue.

(7) Where a body corporate is treated as a member of a group as being controlled by any person and it appears to the Commissioners that it has ceased to be so controlled, they shall, by notice given to that person, terminate that treatment from such date as may be specified in the notice.

(8) An application under this section with respect to any bodies corporate must be made by one of those bodies or by the person controlling them and must be made not less than 90 days before the date from which it is to take effect, or at such later time as the Commissioners may allow.

(9) For the purposes of this section a body corporate shall be taken to control another body corporate if it is empowered by statute to control that body's activities or if it is that body's holding company within the meaning of section [1159 of and Schedule 6 to][1] the Companies Act [2006][1]; and an individual or individuals shall be taken to control a body corporate if he or they, were he or they a company, would be that body's holding company within the meaning of [those sections][1].

Amendments—[1] In sub-s (9), words substituted for words "736 of", "1985" and "that section", by the Companies Act 2006 (Consequential Amendments) (Taxes and National Insurance) Order, SI 2009/1890 art 4(1)(c) with effect from 1 October 2009.

60 Information, powers, penalties, [secondary liability,][1] etc

Schedule 5 to this Act (which contains provisions relating to information, powers, penalties[, secondary liability][1] and other matters) shall have effect.

Amendments—[1] Words inserted by FA 2000 s 142(1), (2) with effect from 28 July 2000.

61 Taxable disposals: special provisions

(1) Where—

(*a*) a taxable disposal is in fact made on a particular day,

(*b*) within the period of 14 days beginning with that day the person liable to pay tax in respect of the disposal issues a landfill invoice in respect of the disposal, and

(*c*) he has not notified the Commissioners in writing that he elects not to avail himself of this subsection,

for the purposes of this Part the disposal shall be treated as made at the time the invoice is issued.

(2) The reference in subsection (1) above to a landfill invoice is to a document containing such particulars as regulations may prescribe for the purposes of that subsection.

(3) The Commissioners may at the request of a person direct that subsection (1) above shall apply—

(*a*) in relation to disposals in respect of which he is liable to pay tax, or

(*b*) in relation to such of them as may be specified in the direction,

as if for the period of 14 days there were substituted such longer period as may be specified in the direction.

Regulations—Landfill Tax Regulations, SI 1996/1527.

Cross references—See Landfill Tax Regulations, SI 1996/1527 reg 37 (contents of a landfill invoice).

62 Taxable disposals: regulations

(1) For the purposes of this Part, regulations may make provision under this section in relation to a disposal which is a taxable disposal (or would be apart from the regulations).

(2) The regulations may provide that if particular conditions are fulfilled—

(a) the disposal shall be treated as not being a taxable disposal, or

(b) the disposal shall, to the extent found in accordance with prescribed rules, be treated as not being a taxable disposal.

(3) The regulations may provide that if particular conditions are fulfilled—

(a) the disposal shall be treated as made at a time which is found in accordance with prescribed rules and which falls after the time when it would be regarded as made apart from the regulations, or

(b) the disposal shall, to the extent found in accordance with prescribed rules, be treated as made at a time which is found in accordance with prescribed rules and which falls after the time when it would be regarded as made apart from the regulations.

(4) In finding the time when the disposal would be regarded as made apart from the regulations, section 61(1) above and any direction under section 61(3) above shall be taken into account.

(5) The regulations may be framed by reference to—

(a) conditions specified in the regulations or by the Commissioners or by an authorised person, or

(b) any combination of such conditions;

and the regulations may specify conditions, or allow conditions to be specified, generally or with regard to particular cases.

(6) The regulations may make provision under subsections (2)(b) and (3)(b) above in relation to the same disposal.

(7) The regulations may only provide that a disposal is to be treated as not being a taxable disposal if or to the extent that—

[(a) the material comprised in the disposal is held temporarily pending one or more of the following—

(i) the incineration or recycling of the material, or

(ii) the removal of the material for use elsewhere, or

(iii) the use of the material, if it is qualifying material within the meaning of section 42(3) above, for the restoration to use of the site at which the disposal takes place, or any part of that site, upon completion of waste disposal operations at the site, or as the case may be, that part of the site, or

(iv) the sorting of the material with a view to its removal elsewhere or its eventual disposal, and][1]

(*b*) *[the material in question is held temporarily]*[1] *in an area designated for the purpose by an authorised person.*[2]

Regulations—Landfill Tax Regulations, SI 1996/1527.

Cross references—See Landfill Tax Regulations, SI 1996/1527 regs 38–40 (temporary disposals).

Amendments—[1] Sub-s (7)(*a*) and words in sub-s (7)(*b*) substituted by FA 2000 s 141(1)–(3), with effect from 28 July 2000.

[2] Section 62 repealed by FA 2009 s 119, Sch 60 para 4 with effect from 21 July 2009. The repeal of s 62 does not affect any regulation made under it before the passing of FA 2009, and does not prevent the powers conferred by the repealed provision from being used after the passing of FA 2009 to revoke any regulations made under the powers before that time: FA 2009 s 119, Sch 60 para 13(3).

63 Qualifying material: special provisions

(1) This section applies for the purposes of section 42 above.

(2) The Commissioners may direct that where material is disposed of it must be treated as qualifying material if it would in fact be such material but for a small quantity of non-qualifying material; and whether a quantity of non-qualifying material is small must be determined in accordance with the terms of the direction.

(3) The Commissioners may at the request of a person direct that where there is a disposal in respect of which he is liable to pay tax the material disposed of must be treated as qualifying material if it would in fact be such material but for a small quantity of non-qualifying material, and—

(*a*) a direction may apply to all disposals in respect of which a person is liable to pay tax or to such of them as are identified in the direction;

(*b*) whether a quantity of non-qualifying material is small must be determined in accordance with the terms of the direction.

(4) If a direction under subsection (3) above applies to a disposal any direction under subsection (2) above shall not apply to it.

(5) An order may provide that material must not be treated as qualifying material unless prescribed conditions are met.

(6) A condition may relate to any matter the Treasury think fit (such as the production of a document which includes a statement of the nature of the material).

Order—Landfill Tax (Qualifying Material) Order, SI 1996/1528.

Interpretation

64 Disposal of material as waste

(1) A disposal of material is a disposal of it as waste if the person making the disposal does so with the intention of discarding the material.

(2) The fact that the person making the disposal or any other person could benefit from or make use of the material is irrelevant.

(3) Where a person makes a disposal on behalf of another person, for the purposes of subsections (1) and (2) above the person on whose behalf the disposal is made shall be treated as making the disposal.

(4) The reference in subsection (3) above to a disposal on behalf of another person includes references to a disposal—

(*a*) at the request of another person;

(*b*) in pursuance of a contract with another person.

Commentary—*De Voil Indirect Tax Service* **V20.104**.

Simon's Tax Cases—*C&E Comrs v Parkwood Landfill Ltd* [2002] STC 417; Waste Recycling Group Ltd v R&C Comrs [2009] STC 200.

65 Disposal by way of landfill

(1) There is a disposal of material by way of landfill if—

(*a*) it is deposited on the surface of land or on a structure set into the surface, or

(*b*) it is deposited under the surface of land.

(2) Subsection (1) above applies whether or not the material is placed in a container before it is deposited.

(3) Subsection (1)(*b*) above applies whether the material—

(*a*) is covered with earth after it is deposited, or

(*b*) is deposited in a cavity (such as a cavern or mine).

(4) If material is deposited on the surface of land (or on a structure set into the surface) with a view to it being covered with earth the disposal must be treated as made when the material is deposited and not when it is covered.

(5) An order may provide that the meaning of the disposal of material by way of landfill (as it applies for the time being) shall be varied.

(6) An order under subsection (5) above may make provision in such way as the Treasury think fit, whether by amending any of subsections (1) to (4) above or otherwise.

(7) In this section "land" includes land covered by water where the land is above the low water mark of ordinary spring tides.

(8) In this section "earth" includes similar matter (such as sand or rocks).

Commentary—*De Voil Indirect Tax Service* **V20.105**.

Simon's Tax Cases—s 65(1), *C&E Comrs v Parkwood Landfill Ltd* [2002] STC 417.

[65A Prescribed landfill site activities to be treated as disposals

(1) An order may prescribe a landfill site activity for the purposes of this section.

(2) If a prescribed landfill site activity is carried out at a landfill site, the activity is to be treated—

(*a*) as a disposal at the landfill site of the material involved in the activity,

(*b*) as a disposal of that material as waste, and

(*c*) as a disposal of that material made by way of landfill.

(3) Connected provision may be made by order.

(4) Provision may be made under this section in such way as the Treasury think fit.

(5) An order under subsection (1) may prescribe a landfill site activity by reference to conditions.

(6) Those conditions may, in particular, relate to either or both of the following—

(*a*) whether the landfill site activity is carried out in a designated area of a landfill site, and

(*b*) whether there has been compliance with a requirement to give information relating to—

(i) the landfill site activity, or

(ii) the material involved in the landfill site activity, including information relating to whether the activity is carried out in a designated area of a landfill site.

(7) An order under this section—

(*a*) may amend, or otherwise modify, this Part or any other enactment relating to landfill tax, but

(*b*) may not alter any rate at which landfill tax is charged.

(8) Subsections (5) to (7) do not limit the generality of subsection (4).

(9) In this section—

"connected provision" means provision which appears to the Treasury to be necessary or expedient in connection with provision made under subsection (1);

"designated area" means an area of a landfill site designated in accordance with—

(*a*) an order under this section, or

(*b*) regulations under Part 1 of Schedule 5;

"landfill site activity" means any of the following descriptions of activity, or an activity that falls within any of the following descriptions—

(*a*) using or otherwise dealing with material at a landfill site;

(*b*) storing or otherwise having material at a landfill site.][1]

Order—Landfill Tax (Prescribed Landfill Site Activities) Order, SI 2009/1929.

Amendment—[1] Section 65A inserted by FA 2009 s 119, Sch 60 paras 1, 2 with effect from 21 July 2009.

66 Landfill sites

Land is a landfill site at a given time if at that time—

(*a*) a licence which is a site licence for the purposes of Part II of the Environmental Protection Act 1990 (waste on land) is in force in relation to the land and authorises disposals in or on the land,

(*b*) a resolution under section 54 of that Act (land occupied by waste disposal authorities in Scotland) is in force in relation to the land and authorises deposits or disposals in or on the land,

[(*ba*) a permit under regulations under section 2 of the Pollution Prevention and Control Act 1999 is in force in relation to the land and authorises deposits or disposals in or on the land,][1]

(*c*) a disposal licence issued under Part II of the Pollution Control and Local Government (Northern Ireland) Order 1978 (waste on land) is in force in relation to the land and authorises deposits on the land,

(*d*) a resolution passed under Article 13 of that Order (land occupied by district councils in Northern Ireland) is in force in relation to the land and relates to deposits on the land, or

(*e*) a licence under any provision for the time being having effect in Northern Ireland and corresponding to section 35 of the Environmental Protection Act 1990 (waste management licences) is in force in relation to the land and authorises disposals in or on the land.

Commentary—*De Voil Indirect Tax Service* **V20.105**.

Amendment—[1] Para (*ba*) inserted by the Pollution Prevention and Control Act 1999 s 6(1) Sch 2 para 19 with effect from 21 March 2000 (by virtue of SI 2000/800).

67 Operators of landfill sites

The operator of a landfill site at a given time is—

(*a*) the person who is at the time concerned the holder of the licence, where section 66(*a*) above applies;

(*b*) the waste disposal authority which at the time concerned occupies the landfill site, where section 66(*b*) above applies;

[(*ba*) the person who is at the time concerned the holder of the permit, where section 66(*ba*) above applies;][1]

(*c*) the person who is at the time concerned the holder of the licence, where section 66(*c*) above applies;

(*d*) the district council which passed the resolution, where section 66(*d*) above applies;

(*e*) the person who is at the time concerned the holder of the licence, where section 66(*e*) above applies.

Amendments—[1] Para (*ba*) inserted with effect in England and Wales by the Pollution Prevention and Control (England and Wales) Regulations, SI 2000/1973 reg 39, Sch 10 para 22 with effect from 1 August 2000, and with effect in Scotland by the Pollution Prevention and Control (Scotland) Regulations, SI 2000/323 reg 36, Sch 10 para 6 with effect from 28 September 2000.

68 Weight of material disposed of

(1) The weight of the material disposed of on a taxable disposal shall be determined in accordance with regulations.

(2) The regulations may—

(*a*) prescribe rules for determining the weight;

(*b*) authorise rules for determining the weight to be specified by the Commissioners in a prescribed manner;

(*c*) authorise rules for determining the weight to be agreed by the person liable to pay the tax and an authorised person.

(3) The regulations may in particular prescribe, or authorise the specification or agreement of, rules about—

(*a*) the method by which the weight is to be determined;

(*b*) the time by reference to which the weight is to be determined;

(*c*) the discounting of constituents (such as water).

(4) The regulations may include provision that a specification authorised under subsection (2)(*b*) above may provide—

(*a*) that it is to have effect only in relation to disposals of such descriptions as may be set out in the specification;

(*b*) that it is not to have effect in relation to particular disposals unless the Commissioners are satisfied that such conditions as may be set out in the specification are met in relation to the disposals;

and the conditions may be framed by reference to such factors as the Commissioners think fit (such as the consent of an authorised person to the specification having effect in relation to disposals).

(5) The regulations may include provision that—

(*a*) where rules are agreed as mentioned in subsection (2)(*c*) above, and

(*b*) the Commissioners believe that they should no longer be applied because they do not give an accurate indication of the weight or they are not being fully observed or for some other reason,

the Commissioners may direct that the agreed rules shall no longer have effect.

(6) The regulations shall be so framed that where in relation to a given disposal—

(*a*) no specification of the Commissioners has effect, and

(*b*) no agreed rules have effect,

the weight shall be determined in accordance with rules prescribed in the regulations.

Commentary—*De Voil Indirect Tax Service* **V20.141, 142.**

Regulations—Landfill Tax Regulations, SI 1996/1527.

Cross references—See Landfill Tax Regulations, SI 1996/1527 regs 41–44 (determination of weight of material disposed of).

69 Taxable activities

(1) A person carries out a taxable activity if—

(*a*) he makes a taxable disposal in respect of which he is liable to pay tax, or

(*b*) he permits another person to make a taxable disposal in respect of which he (the first-mentioned person) is liable to pay tax.

(2) Where—

(*a*) a taxable disposal is made, and

(*b*) it is made without the knowledge of the person who is liable to pay tax in respect of it,

that person shall for the purposes of this section be taken to permit the disposal.

70 Interpretation: other provisions

(1) Unless the context otherwise requires—

"accounting period" shall be construed in accordance with section 49 above;

"appeal tribunal" means a [the First-tier Tribunal or, where determined by or under Tribunal Procedure Rules, the Upper Tribunal;][2];

"authorised person" means any person acting under the authority of the Commissioners;

"the Commissioners" means the Commissioners of Customs and Excise;

"conduct" includes any act, omission or statement;

["the Environment Agency" means the body established by section 1 of the Environment Act 1995;][1]

Landfill Tax

["HMRC" means Her Majesty's Revenue and Customs;][2]
"material" means material of all kinds, including objects, substances and products of all kinds;
"prescribed" means prescribed by an order or regulations under this Part;
"registrable person" has the meaning given by section 47(10) above;
["the Scottish Environment Protection Agency" means the body established by section 20 of the Environment Act 1995;][1]
"tax" means landfill tax;
"taxable disposal" has the meaning given by section 40 above.

(2) A landfill disposal is a disposal—
(*a*) of material as waste, and
(*b*) made by way of landfill.

[(2A) A local authority is—
(*a*) the council of a county, county borough, district, London borough, parish or group of parishes (or, in Wales, community or group of communities);
(*b*) the Common Council of the City of London;
(*c*) as respects the Temples, the Sub-Treasurer of the Inner Temple and the Under-Treasurer of the Middle Temple respectively;
(*d*) the council of the Isles of Scilly;
(*e*) any joint committee or joint board established by two or more of the foregoing;
(*f*) in relation to Scotland, a council constituted under section 2 of the Local Government etc (Scotland) Act 1994, any two or more such councils and any joint committee or joint board within the meaning of section 235(1) of the Local Government (Scotland) Act 1973.][1]

(3) A reference to this Part includes a reference to any order or regulations made under it and a reference to a provision of this Part includes a reference to any order or regulations made under the provision, unless otherwise required by the context or any order or regulations.

(4) This section and sections 64 to 69 above apply for the purposes of this Part.

Amendments—[1] Definitions of the "Environment Agency" and the "Scottish Environment Protection Agency" in sub-s (1), and sub-s (2A), inserted by the Landfill Tax (Contaminated Land) Order, SI 1996/1529 art 5, with effect from 1 August 1996.
[2] In sub-s (1) words in the definition of "appeal tribunal" substituted for the words "VAT and duties tribunal"; definition of "HMRC" inserted by the Transfer of Tribunal Functions and Revenue and Customs Appeals Order, SI 2009/56 art 3, Sch 1 para 238 with effect from 1 April 2009.

Supplementary

71 Orders and regulations

(1) The power to make an order under section 57 above shall be exercisable by the Commissioners, and the power to make an order under any other provision of this Part shall be exercisable by the Treasury.

(2) Any power to make regulations under this Part shall be exercisable by the Commissioners.

(3) Any power to make an order or regulations under this Part shall be exercisable by statutory instrument.

(4) An order to which this subsection applies shall be laid before the House of Commons; and unless it is approved by that House before the expiration of a period of 28 days beginning with the date on which it was made it shall cease to have effect on the expiration of that period, but without prejudice to anything previously done under the order or to the making of a new order.

(5) In reckoning any such period as is mentioned in subsection (4) above no account shall be taken of any time during which Parliament is dissolved or prorogued or during which the House of Commons is adjourned for more than four days.

(6) A statutory instrument containing an order or regulations under this Part (other than an order under section 57 above or an order to which subsection (4) above applies) shall be subject to annulment in pursuance of a resolution of the House of Commons.

(7) Subsection (4) above applies to—
(*a*) an order under section 42(3) above providing for material which would otherwise be qualifying material not to be qualifying material;
(*b*) an order under section 46 above which produces the result that a disposal which would otherwise not be a taxable disposal is a taxable disposal;
(*c*) an order under section 63(5) above other than one which provides only that an earlier order under section 63(5) is not to apply to material;
[(*ca*) an order under section 65A above which produces the result that a landfill site activity which would not otherwise be prescribed for the purposes of section 65A is so prescribed;
(*cb*) an order under section 65A above which amends this Part or any enactment contained in an Act;][1]
(*d*) an order under section 65(5) above providing for anything which would otherwise not be a disposal of material by way of landfill to be such a disposal.

(8) Any power to make an order or regulations under this Part—
(*a*) may be exercised as regards prescribed cases or descriptions of case;
(*b*) may be exercised differently in relation to different cases or descriptions of case.

(9) An order or regulations under this Part may include such supplementary, incidental, consequential or transitional provisions as appear to the Treasury or the Commissioners (as the case may be) to be necessary or expedient.

(10) No specific provision of this Part about an order or regulations shall prejudice the generality of subsections (8) and (9) above.

Amendments—[1] Sub-sections (7)(*ca*) and (*cb*) inserted by FA 2009 s 119, Sch 60 paras 1, 3 with effect from 21 July 2009.

PART VII
MISCELLANEOUS AND SUPPLEMENTAL

Miscellaneous: indirect taxation

197 Setting of rates of interest

(1) The rate of interest applicable for the purposes of an enactment to which this section applies shall be the rate which for the purposes of that enactment is provided for by regulations made by the Treasury under this section.

(2) This section applies to—

(*a*) –(*c*) . . .

(*d*) [sections 56(3) to (5) of and][2] paragraphs 26 and 29 of Schedule 5 to this Act (interest payable to or by the Commissioners in connection with landfill tax).

[(*e*) paragraph 17 of Schedule 5 to the Finance Act 1997 (interest on amounts repayable in respect of overpayments by the Commissioners in connection with . . . landfill tax).][1]

(*f*), (*g*) . . .

(3) Regulations under this section may—

(*a*) make different provision for different enactments or for different purposes of the same enactment,

(*b*) either themselves specify a rate of interest for the purposes of an enactment or make provision for any such rate to be determined, and to change from time to time, by reference to such rate or the average of such rates as may be referred to in the regulations,

(*c*) provide for rates to be reduced below, or increased above, what they otherwise would be by specified amounts or by reference to specified formulae,

(*d*) provide for rates arrived at by reference to averages or formulae to be rounded up or down,

(*e*) provide for circumstances in which changes of rates of interest are or are not to take place, and

(*f*) provide that changes of rates are to have effect for periods beginning on or after a day determined in accordance with the regulations in relation to interest running from before that day, as well as in relation to interest running from, or from after, that day.

(4) The power to make regulations under this section shall be exercisable by statutory instrument subject to annulment in pursuance of a resolution of the House of Commons.

(5) Where—

(a) regulations under this section provide, without specifying the rate determined in accordance with the regulations, for a new method of determining the rate applicable for the purposes of any enactment, or

(b) the rate which, in accordance with regulations under this section, is the rate applicable for the purposes of any enactment changes otherwise than by virtue of the making of regulations specifying a new rate,

the Commissioners of Customs and Excise shall make an order specifying the new rate and the day from which, in accordance with the regulations, it has effect.[3]

(6) . . .

(7) Subsections (1) and (6) above shall have effect for periods beginning on or after such day as the Treasury may by order made by statutory instrument appoint and shall have effect in relation to interest running from before that day, as well as in relation to interest running from, or from after, that day; and different days may be appointed under this subsection for different purposes.

Note—Sub-ss (2)(*a*)–(*c*), (*f*), (*g*), (6) are not relevant to landfill tax.

Sub-s (1) has effect for periods beginning on or after 1 April 1997 (see FA 1996, s 197 (Appointed Day) Order, SI 1997/1015.

Amendments—[1] Inserted by FA 1997 s 50, Sch 5 para 21.

[2] In sub-s (2)(*d*) words inserted by the Transfer of Tribunal Functions and Revenue and Customs Appeals Order, SI 2009/56 art 3, Sch 1 para 239 with effect from 1 April 2009.

[3] Sub-s (5) repealed by FA 2009 s 105(6)(*b*) with effect from 21 July 2009.

Supplemental

206 Short title

This Act may be cited as the Finance Act 1996.

SCHEDULE 5
LANDFILL TAX
Section 60

PART I
INFORMATION

[Information: general][1]

1—*(1) Every person who is concerned (in whatever capacity) with any landfill disposal shall furnish to the Commissioners such information relating to the disposal as the Commissioners may reasonably require.*

(2) The information mentioned in sub-paragraph (1) above shall be furnished within such time and in such form as the Commissioners may reasonably require.[2]

Amendments—[1] Heading substituted by FA 2009 s 119, Sch 60 paras 5, 6 with effect from 21 July 2009.

[2] This para repealed by the Finance Act 2009, Section 96 and Schedule 48 (Appointed Day, Savings and Consequential Amendments) Order, SI 2009/3054 art 3, Schedule para 7 with effect from 1 April 2010.

[Information: material at landfill sites

1A—(1) Regulations may make provision about giving the Commissioners information relating to material at a landfill site or a part of a landfill site.

(2) Regulations under this paragraph may require a person to give information.

(3) Regulations under this paragraph may—

(*a*) require a person, or authorise an officer of Revenue and Customs to require a person, to designate a part of a landfill site (an "information area"), and

(*b*) require material, or prescribed descriptions of material, to be deposited in an information area.

(4) Regulations under this paragraph may make provision about information relating to what is done with material.

(5) Sub-paragraphs (2) to (4) do not prejudice the generality of sub- paragraph (1).][1]

Amendments—[1] Heading and para (1A) inserted by FA 2009 s 119, Sch 60 paras 5, 7 with effect from 21 July 2009.

[Information: site restoration

1B—(1) Before commencing restoration of all or part of a landfill site, the operator of the site must—

(*a*) notify the Commissioners in writing that the restoration is to commence, and

(*b*) provide such other written information as the Commissioners may require generally or in the particular case.

(2) In this paragraph "restoration" means work, other than capping waste, which is required by a relevant instrument to be carried out to restore a landfill site to use on completion of waste disposal operations.

(3) The following are relevant instruments—

(*a*) a planning consent,

(*b*) a waste management licence, and

(*c*) a permit authorising the disposal of waste on or in land.][1]

Amendments—[1] Heading and para (1B) inserted by FA 2009 s 119, Sch 60 paras 5, 7 with effect in relation to restoration of landfill sites commencing on or after 1 September 2009; FA 2009 s 119, Sch 60 para 13(2).

[Records; registrable persons][2]

2—(1) Regulations may require registrable persons to make records.

(2) Regulations under sub-paragraph (1) above may be framed by reference to such records as may be stipulated in any notice published by the Commissioners in pursuance of the regulations and not withdrawn by a further notice.

(3) Regulations may—

(*a*) require registrable persons to preserve records of a prescribed description (whether or not the records are required to be made in pursuance of regulations) for such period not exceeding six years as may be specified in the regulations;

(*b*) authorise the Commissioners to direct that any such records need only be preserved for a shorter period than that specified in the regulations;

(*c*) authorise a direction to be made so as to apply generally or in such cases as the Commissioners may stipulate.

[(4) A duty under regulations under this paragraph to preserve records may be discharged—

(*a*) by preserving them in any form and by any means, or

(*b*) by preserving the information contained in them in any form and by any means, subject to any conditions or exceptions specified in writing by the Commissioners.][1]

Regulations—Landfill Tax Regulations, SI 1996/1527.

Cross references—See Landfill Tax Regulations, SI 1996 1527 reg 12 (landfill tax account), SI 1996/1527 reg 16 (records).

Amendments—[1] Sub-paragraph (4) substituted for previous sub-paras (4)–(7) by FA 2009 s 98, Sch 50 para 21 with effect from 1 April 2010 (by virtue of SI 2010/815 art 2). Sub-paras (4)–(7) previously read as follows—

"(4) Any duty under regulations to preserve records may be discharged by the preservation of the information contained in them by such means as the Commissioners may approve; and where that information is so preserved a copy of any document forming part of the records shall (subject to the following provisions of this paragraph) be admissible in evidence in any proceedings, whether civil or criminal, to the same extent as the records themselves.

(5) The Commissioners may, as a condition of approving under sub-paragraph (4) above any means of preserving information contained in any records, impose such reasonable requirements as appear to them necessary for securing that the information will be as readily available to them as if the records themselves had been preserved.

(6) A statement contained in a document produced by a computer shall not by virtue of sub-paragraph (4) above be admissible in evidence—

(*a*) . . .

(*b*) in civil proceedings in Scotland, except in accordance with sections 5 and 6 of the Civil Evidence (Scotland) Act 1988;

(*c*) in criminal proceedings in Scotland, except in accordance with Schedule 8 to the Criminal Procedure (Scotland) Act 1995;

(*d*) . . .

(*e*) . . .

(7) In the case of civil proceedings in England and Wales to which sections 5 and 6 of the Civil Evidence Act 1968 apply, a statement contained in a document produced by a computer shall not be admissible in evidence by virtue of sub-paragraph (4) above except in accordance with those sections."

[2] Heading substituted by FA 2009 s 119, Sch 60 paras 5, 8 with effect from 21 July 2009.

[Records: material at landfill sites

2A—(1) Regulations may require a person to make records relating to material at a landfill site or a part of a landfill site.

(2) Regulations under this paragraph may make provision about records relating to what is done with material.

(3) Sub-paragraphs (2) to (7) of paragraph 2 apply in relation to regulations under this paragraph as they apply in relation to regulations under paragraph 2.

(4) But, in the application of paragraph 2(3)(*a*) in relation to regulations under this paragraph, the reference to registrable persons has effect as a reference to persons.][1]

Amendments—[1] Heading and paragraph (2A) inserted by FA 2009 s 119, Sch 60 paras 5, 9 with effect from 21 July 2009.

Documents

3—*(1) Every person who is concerned (in whatever capacity) with any landfill disposal shall upon demand made by an authorised person produce or cause to be produced for inspection by that person any documents relating to the disposal.*

(2) Where, by virtue of sub-paragraph (1) above, an authorised person has power to require the production of any documents from any person, he shall have the like power to require production of the documents concerned from any other person who appears to the authorised person to be in possession of them; but where any such other person claims a lien on any document produced by him, the production shall be without prejudice to the lien.

(3) The documents mentioned in sub-paragraphs (1) and (2) above shall be produced—

(*a*) at such place as the authorised person may reasonably require, and

(*b*) at such time as the authorised person may reasonably require.

(4) An authorised person may take copies of, or make extracts from, any document produced under sub-paragraph (1) or (2) above.

(5) If it appears to him to be necessary to do so, an authorised person may, at a reasonable time and for a reasonable period, remove any document produced under sub-paragraph (1) or (2) above and shall, on request, provide a receipt for any document so removed; and where a lien is claimed on a document produced under sub-paragraph (2) above the removal of the document under this sub-paragraph shall not be regarded as breaking the lien.

(6) Where a document removed by an authorised person under sub-paragraph (5) above is reasonably required for any purpose he shall, as soon as practicable, provide a copy of the document, free of charge, to the person by whom it was produced or caused to be produced.

(7) Where any documents removed under the powers conferred by this paragraph are lost or damaged the Commissioners shall be liable to compensate their owner for any expenses reasonably incurred by him in replacing or repairing the documents.[1]

Amendments—[1] This para repealed by the Finance Act 2009, Section 96 and Schedule 48 (Appointed Day, Savings and Consequential Amendments) Order, SI 2009/3054 art 3, Schedule para 7 with effect from 1 April 2010.

PART II
POWERS

Entry and inspection

4 For the purpose of exercising any powers under this Part of this Act an authorised person may at any reasonable time enter and inspect premises used in connection with the carrying on of a business.[1]

Amendments—[1] This para repealed by the Finance Act 2009, Section 96 and Schedule 48 (Appointed Day, Savings and Consequential Amendments) Order, SI 2009/3054 art 3, Schedule para 7 with effect from 1 April 2010.

Entry and search

5 . . .[1]

Cross references—Criminal Justice and Police Act 2001 s 50, Sch 1 Pt 1 (s 50 of that Act which provides additional powers of seizure from premises applies to the power of seizure conferred under sub-para (2) above; for the relevant provisions of the Criminal Justice and Police Act 2001, see the *VAT* section of this publication, ante).

Amendments—[1] This para repealed by FA 2007 ss 84, 114, Sch 22 paras 3, 10(*a*), Sch 27 Pt 5(1) with effect from 1 December 2007 (by virtue of SI 2007/3166 art 3(*a*)).

Arrest

6 . . .[1]

Amendments—[1] This para repealed by FA 2007 ss 84, 114, Sch 22 paras 3, 10(*b*), Sch 27 Pt 5(1) with effect from 1 December 2007 (by virtue of SI 2007/3166 art 3(*a*)).

Order for access to recorded information etc

7—(1) Where, on an application by an authorised person, a justice of the peace or, in Scotland, a justice (within the meaning of section 307 of the Criminal Procedure (Scotland) Act 1995) is satisfied that there are reasonable grounds for believing—

(*a*) that an offence in connection with tax is being, has been or is about to be committed, and

(*b*) that any recorded information (including any document of any nature whatsoever) which may be required as evidence for the purpose of any proceedings in respect of such an offence is in the possession of any person,

he may make an order under this paragraph.

(2) An order under this paragraph is an order that the person who appears to the justice to be in possession of the recorded information to which the application relates shall—

(*a*) give an authorised person access to it, and

(*b*) permit an authorised person to remove and take away any of it which he reasonably considers necessary,

not later than the end of the period of 7 days beginning with the date of the order or the end of such longer period as the order may specify.

(3) The reference in sub-paragraph (2)(*a*) above to giving an authorised person access to the recorded information to which the application relates includes a reference to permitting the authorised person to take copies of it or to make extracts from it.

(4) Where the recorded information consists of information [stored in any electronic form][1], an order under this paragraph shall have effect as an order to produce the information in a form in which it is visible and legible [or from which it can readily be produced in a visible and legible form][1] and, if the authorised person wishes to remove it, in a form in which it can be removed.

(5) This paragraph is without prejudice to paragraphs 3 to 5 above.

Amendments—[1] In sub-para (4), words substituted and words inserted by Criminal Justice and Police Act 2001 ss 70, 138, Sch 2 Pt 2 para 13 with effect from 1 April 2003 (by virtue of SI 2003/708).

Removal of documents etc

8—(1) An authorised person who removes anything in the exercise of a power conferred by or under paragraph 5 or 7 above shall, if so requested by a person showing himself—

(*a*) to be the occupier of premises from which it was removed, or

(*b*) to have had custody or control of it immediately before the removal,

provide that person with a record of what he removed.

(2) The authorised person shall provide the record within a reasonable time from the making of the request for it.

(3) Subject to sub-paragraph (7) below, if a request for permission to be allowed access to anything which—

(*a*) has been removed by an authorised person, and

(*b*) is retained by the Commissioners for the purposes of investigating an offence,

is made to the officer in overall charge of the investigation by a person who had custody or control of the thing immediately before it was so removed or by someone acting on behalf of such a person, the officer shall allow the person who made the request access to it under the supervision of an authorised person.

(4) Subject to sub-paragraph (7) below, if a request for a photograph or copy of any such thing is made to the officer in overall charge of the investigation by a person who had custody or control of the thing immediately before it was so removed, or by someone acting on behalf of such a person, the officer shall—

(*a*) allow the person who made the request access to it under the supervision of an authorised person for the purpose of photographing it or copying it, or

(*b*) photograph or copy it, or cause it to be photographed or copied.

(5) Subject to sub-paragraph (7) below, where anything is photographed or copied under sub-paragraph (4)(*b*) above the officer shall supply the photograph or copy, or cause it to be supplied, to the person who made the request.

(6) The photograph or copy shall be supplied within a reasonable time from the making of the request.

(7) There is no duty under this paragraph to allow access to, or to supply a photograph or copy of, anything if the officer in overall charge of the investigation for the purposes of which it was removed has reasonable grounds for believing that to do so would prejudice—

(*a*) that investigation,

(*b*) the investigation of an offence other than the offence for the purposes of the investigation of which the thing was removed, or

(*c*) any criminal proceedings which may be brought as a result of the investigation of which he is in charge or any such investigation as is mentioned in paragraph (*b*) above.

(8) Any reference in this paragraph to the officer in overall charge of the investigation is a reference to the person whose name and address are endorsed on the warrant concerned as being the officer so in charge.

9—(1) Where, on an application made as mentioned in sub-paragraph (2) below, the appropriate judicial authority is satisfied that a person has failed to comply with a requirement imposed by paragraph 8 above, the authority may order that person to comply with the requirement within such time and in such manner as may be specified in the order.

(2) An application under sub-paragraph (1) above shall be made—

(*a*) in the case of a failure to comply with any of the requirements imposed by sub-paragraphs (1) and (2) of paragraph 8 above, by the occupier of the premises from which the thing in question was removed or by the person who had custody or control of it immediately before it was so removed, and

(*b*) in any other case, by the person who had such custody or control.

(3) In this paragraph "the appropriate judicial authority" means—

(*a*) in England and Wales, a magistrates' court;

(*b*) in Scotland, the sheriff;

(*c*) in Northern Ireland, a court of summary jurisdiction, as defined in Article 2(2)(*a*) of the Magistrates' Court (Northern Ireland) Order 1981.

(4) In England and Wales and Northern Ireland, an application for an order under this paragraph shall be made by way of complaint; and sections 21 and 42(2) of the Interpretation Act (Northern Ireland) 1954 shall apply as if any reference in those provisions to any enactment included a reference to this paragraph.

Power to take samples

10—(1) An authorised person, if it appears to him necessary for the protection of the revenue against mistake or fraud, may at any time take, from material which he has reasonable cause to believe is intended to be, is being, or has been disposed of as waste by way of landfill, such samples as he may require with a view to determining how the material ought to be or to have been treated for the purposes of tax.

(2) Any sample taken under this paragraph shall be disposed of in such manner as the Commissioners may direct.

PART III
RECOVERY

General

11 Tax due from any person shall be recoverable as a debt due to the Crown.

Preferential and preferred debts

12—(1) . . .[1]
(2) . . .[1]
(3) (*inserts* Bankruptcy (Scotland) Act 1985 Sch 3 para 2 (1B)).
(4) (*inserts* Bankruptcy (Scotland) Act 1985 Sch 3 para 8B).
(5) (*amends* Insolvency (Northern Ireland) Order, SI 1989/2405 art 346(1) and *inserts* Insolvency (Northern Ireland) Order, SI 1989/2405 Sch 4 para 3B).

Amendments—[1] Sub-paras (1), (2) repealed by the Enterprise Act 2002 ss 278(2), 279, Sch 26 with effect 15 September 2003 (by virtue of SI 2003/2093).

Distress and diligence

13 . . .

Amendments—This paragraph repealed by FA 1997 Sch 18 Part V(2) with effect from 1 July 1997 (by virtue of SI 1997/1433).

Recovery of overpaid tax

14—(1) Where a person has paid an amount to the Commissioners by way of tax which was not tax due to them, they shall be liable to repay the amount to him.
(2) The Commissioners shall only be liable to repay an amount under this paragraph on a claim being made for the purpose.
(3) It shall be a defence, in relation to a claim under this paragraph, that repayment of an amount would unjustly enrich the claimant.
[(4) The Commissioners shall not be liable, on a claim made under this paragraph, to repay any amount paid to them more than [4 years][2] before the making of the claim.][1]
(5) A claim under this paragraph shall be made in such form and manner and shall be supported by such documentary evidence as may be prescribed by regulations.
(6) Except as provided by this paragraph, the Commissioners shall not be liable to repay an amount paid to them by way of tax by virtue of the fact that it was not tax due to them.

Cross references—See FA 1997 Sch 5 Part I (unjust enrichment).
FA 1997 Sch 5, para 14 (assessment of excessive repayment).
Landfill Tax Regulations, SI 1996/1527 reg 13 (correction of errors), SI 1996/1527 reg 14 (claims for overpaid tax).

Amendments—[1] Sub-para (4) substituted by FA 1997 s 50, Sch 5 para 5(3) with effect from 19 March 1997.
[2] In sub-para (4) words substituted for the words "three years" by FA 2009 s 99, Sch 51 paras 37, 38 with effect from 1 April 2010 (SI 2010/867 art 2). However, this amendment is disregarded where claims made under para 14 are for the repayment of an amount paid to the Commissioners on or before 31 March 2007 (see SI 2010/867 art 24).

PART IV
CRIMINAL PENALTIES

Criminal offences

15—(1) A person is guilty of an offence if—
(*a*) being a registrable person, he is knowingly concerned in, or in the taking of steps with a view to, the fraudulent evasion of tax by him or another registrable person, or
(*b*) not being a registrable person, he is knowingly concerned in, or in the taking of steps with a view to, the fraudulent evasion of tax by a registrable person.
(2) Any reference in sub-paragraph (1) above to the evasion of tax includes a reference to the obtaining of a payment under regulations under section 51(2)(*c*) or (*d*) or (*f*) of this Act.
(3) A person is guilty of an offence if with the requisite intent—
(*a*) he produces, furnishes or sends, or causes to be produced, furnished or sent, for the purposes of this Part of this Act any document which is false in a material particular, or
(*b*) he otherwise makes use for those purposes of such a document;
and the requisite intent is intent to deceive or to secure that a machine will respond to the document as if it were a true document.
(4) A person is guilty of an offence if in furnishing any information for the purposes of this Part of this Act he makes a statement which he knows to be false in a material particular or recklessly makes a statement which is false in a material particular.
(5) A person is guilty of an offence by virtue of this sub-paragraph if his conduct during any specified period must have involved the commission by him of one or more offences under the preceding provisions of this paragraph; and the preceding provisions of this sub-paragraph apply whether or not the particulars of that offence or those offences are known.
(6) A person is guilty of an offence if—
(*a*) he enters into a taxable landfill contract, or
(*b*) he makes arrangements for other persons to enter into such a contract,
with reason to believe that tax in respect of the disposal concerned will be evaded.

(7) A person is guilty of an offence if he carries out taxable activities without giving security (or further security) he has been required to give under paragraph 31 below.
(8) For the purposes of this paragraph a taxable landfill contract is a contract under which there is to be a taxable disposal.

Criminal penalties

16—(1) A person guilty of an offence under paragraph 15(1) above is liable—
(*a*) on summary conviction, to a penalty of the statutory maximum or of three times the amount of the tax, whichever is the greater, or to imprisonment for a term not exceeding six months or to both;
(*b*) on conviction on indictment, to a penalty of any amount or to imprisonment for a term not exceeding seven years or to both.
(2) The reference in sub-paragraph (1) above to the amount of the tax shall be construed, in relation to tax itself or a payment falling within paragraphs 15(2) above, as a reference to the aggregate of—
(*a*) the amount (if any) falsely claimed by way of credit, and
(*b*) the amount (if any) by which the gross amount of tax was falsely understated.
(3) A person guilty of an offence under paragraph 15(3) or (4) above is liable—
(*a*) on summary conviction, to a penalty of the statutory maximum (or, where sub-paragraph (4) below applies, to the alternative penalty there specified if it is greater) or to imprisonment for a term not exceeding six months or to both;
(*b*) on conviction on indictment, to a penalty of any amount or to imprisonment for a term not exceeding seven years or to both.
(4) Where—
(*a*) the document referred to in paragraph 15(3) above is a return required under this Part of this Act, or
(*b*) the information referred to in paragraph 15(4) above is contained in or otherwise relevant to such a return,
the alternative penalty is a penalty equal to three times the aggregate of the amount (if any) falsely claimed by way of credit and the amount (if any) by which the gross amount of tax was understated.
(5) A person guilty of an offence under paragraph 15(5) above is liable—
(*a*) on summary conviction, to a penalty of the statutory maximum (or, if greater, three times the amount of any tax that was or was intended to be evaded by his conduct) or to imprisonment for a term not exceeding six months or to both;
(*b*) on conviction on indictment, to a penalty of any amount or to imprisonment for a term not exceeding seven years or to both;
and paragraph 15(2) and sub-paragraph (2) above shall apply for the purposes of this sub-paragraph as they apply respectively for the purposes of paragraph 15(1) and sub-paragraph (1) above.
(6) A person guilty of an offence under paragraph 15(6) above is liable on summary conviction to a penalty of level 5 on the standard scale or three times the amount of the tax, whichever is the greater.
(7) A person guilty of an offence under paragraph 15(7) above is liable on summary conviction to a penalty of level 5 on the standard scale.
(8) In this paragraph—
(*a*) "credit" means credit for which provision is made by regulations under section 51 of this Act;
(*b*) "the gross amount of tax" means the total amount of tax due before taking into account any deduction for which provision is made by regulations under section 51(2) of this Act.

Criminal proceedings etc

17 Sections 145 to 155 of the Customs and Excise Management Act 1979 (proceedings for offences, mitigation of penalties and certain other matters) shall apply in relation to offences under paragraph 15 above and penalties imposed under paragraph 16 above as they apply in relation to offences and penalties under the customs and excise Acts as defined in that Act.

PART V

CIVIL PENALTIES

Evasion

18—*(1) Where—*
(a) for the purpose of evading tax, a registrable person does any act or omits to take any action, and
(b) his conduct involves dishonesty (whether or not it is such as to give rise to criminal liability), he is liable to a penalty equal to the amount of tax evaded, or (as the case may be) sought to be evaded, by his conduct; but this is subject to sub-paragraph (7) below.

(2) The reference in sub-paragraph (1)(a) above to evading tax includes a reference to obtaining a payment under regulations under section 51(2)(c) or (d) or (f) of this Act in circumstances where the person concerned is not entitled to the sum.

(3) The reference in sub-paragraph (1) above to the amount of tax evaded or sought to be evaded is a reference to the aggregate of—

(a) the amount (if any) falsely claimed by way of credit, and

(b) the amount (if any) by which the gross amount of tax was falsely understated.

(4) In this paragraph—

(a) "credit" means credit for which provision is made by regulations under section 45 of this Act;

(b) "the gross amount of tax" means the total amount of tax due before taking into account any deduction for which provision is made by regulations under section 45(2) of this Act.

(5) Statements made or documents produced by or on behalf of a person shall not be inadmissible in any such proceedings as are mentioned in sub-paragraph (6) below by reason only that it has been drawn to his attention—

(a) that, in relation to tax, the Commissioners may assess an amount due by way of a civil penalty instead of instituting criminal proceedings and, though no undertaking can be given as to whether the Commissioners will make such an assessment in the case of any person, it is their practice to be influenced by the fact that a person has made a full confession of any dishonest conduct to which he has been a party and has given full facilities for investigation, and

(b) that the Commissioners or, on appeal, an appeal tribunal have power under paragraph 25 below to reduce a penalty under this paragraph,

and that he was or may have been induced thereby to make the statements or produce the documents.

(6) The proceedings referred to in sub-paragraph (5) above are—

(a) any criminal proceedings against the person concerned in respect of any offence in connection with or in relation to tax, and

(b) any proceedings against him for the recovery of any sum due from him in connection with or in relation to tax.

(7) Where, by reason of conduct falling within sub-paragraph (1) above, a person is convicted of an offence (whether under this Part of this Act or otherwise) that conduct shall not also give rise to liability to a penalty under this paragraph.[1]

Amendments—[1] This para repealed by FA 2008 s 122, Sch 40 para 21(*e*) with effect from 1 April 2009 (by virtue of SI 2009/571 art 2).

This para repealed only in so far as it relates to conduct involving dishonesty which relates to—

(a) an inaccuracy in a document, or

(b) a failure to notify HMRC of an under-assessment by HMRC (SI 2009/571 art 6).

19—*(1) Where it appears to the Commissioners—*

(a) that a body corporate is liable to a penalty under paragraph 18 above, and

(b) that the conduct giving rise to that penalty is, in whole or in part, attributable to the dishonesty of a person who is, or at the material time was, a director or managing officer of the body corporate (a named officer),

the Commissioners may serve a notice under this paragraph on the body corporate and on the named officer.

(2) A notice under this paragraph shall state—

(a) the amount of the penalty referred to in sub-paragraph (1)(a) above (the basic penalty), and

(b) that the Commissioners propose, in accordance with this paragraph, to recover from the named officer such portion (which may be the whole) of the basic penalty as is specified in the notice.

(3) Where a notice is served under this paragraph, the portion of the basic penalty specified in the notice shall be recoverable from the named officer as if he were personally liable under paragraph 18 above to a penalty which corresponds to that portion; and the amount of that penalty may be assessed and notified to him accordingly under paragraph 32 below.

(4) Where a notice is served under this paragraph—

(a) the amount which, under paragraph 32 below, may be assessed as the amount due by way of penalty from the body corporate shall be only so much (if any) of the basic penalty as is not assessed on and notified to a named officer by virtue of sub-paragraph (3) above, and

(b) the body corporate shall be treated as discharged from liability for so much of the basic penalty as is so assessed and notified.

(5) No appeal shall lie against a notice under this paragraph as such but—

(a) where a body corporate is assessed as mentioned in sub-paragraph (4)(a) above, the body corporate may [appeal against][2] *of the Commissioners' decision as to its liability to a penalty and as to the amount of the basic penalty as if it were specified in the assessment;*

(b) where an assessment is made on a named officer by virtue of sub-paragraph (3) above, the named officer may [appeal against][2] require a review of the Commissioners' decision that the conduct of the body corporate referred to in sub-paragraph (1)(b) above is, in whole or in part, attributable to his dishonesty and of their decision as to the portion of the penalty which the Commissioners propose to recover from him;

[(c) sections 54 to 56 of this Act shall apply accordingly.][2]

(6) In this paragraph a "managing officer", in relation to a body corporate, means any manager, secretary or other similar officer of the body corporate or any person purporting to act in any such capacity or as a director; and where affairs of a body corporate are managed by its members, this paragraph shall apply in relation to the conduct of a member in connection with his functions of management as if he were a director of the body corporate.[1]

Amendments—[1] This para repealed by FA 2008 s 122, Sch 40 para 21(*e*) with effect from 1 April 2009 (by virtue of SI 2009/571 art 2).

This para repealed only in so far as it relates to conduct involving dishonesty which relates to—

(a) an inaccuracy in a document, or

(b) a failure to notify HMRC of an under-assessment by HMRC (SI 2009/571 art 6).

[2] In so far as this para continues to apply, words in sub-para (5)(*a*), (*b*) substituted for the words "require a review"; sub-para (5)(*c*) substituted by the Transfer of Tribunal Functions and Revenue and Customs Appeals Order, SI 2009/56 art 3, Sch 1 para 240 with effect from 1 April 2009. Sub-para (5)(*c*) previously read as follows—

"(*c*) sections 49 and 50 of this Act shall apply accordingly."

Misdeclaration or neglect

20—*(1) Where, for an accounting period—*

(a) a return is made which understates a persons liability to tax or overstates his entitlement to credit, or

(b) an assessment is made which understates a person's liability to tax and, at the end of the period of 30 days beginning on the date of the assessment, he has not taken all such steps as are reasonable to draw the understatement to the attention of the Commissioners,

the person concerned is liable, subject to sub-paragraphs (3) and (4) below, to a penalty equal to 5 per cent. of the amount of the understatement of liability or (as the case may be) overstatement of entitlement.

(2) Where—

(a) a return for an accounting period overstates or understates to any extent a person's liability to tax or his entitlement to credit, and

(b) that return is corrected, in such circumstances and in accordance with such conditions as may be prescribed by regulations, by a return for a later accounting period which understates or overstates, to the corresponding extent, that liability or entitlement,

it shall be assumed for the purposes of this paragraph that the statement made by each such return is a correct statement for the accounting period to which the return relates.

(3) Conduct falling within sub-paragraph (1) above shall not give rise to liability to a penalty under this paragraph if the person concerned furnishes full information with respect to the inaccuracy concerned to the Commissioners—

(a) at a time when he has no reason to believe that enquiries are being made by the Commissioners into his affairs, so far as they relate to tax, and

(b) in such form and manner as may be prescribed by regulations or specified by the Commissioners in accordance with provision made by regulations.

(4) Where, by reason of conduct falling within sub-paragraph (1) above—

(a) a person is convicted of an offence (whether under this Part of this Act or otherwise), or

(b) a person is assessed to a penalty under paragraph 18 above,

that conduct shall not also give rise to liability to a penalty under this paragraph.

(5) In this paragraph "credit" means credit for which provision is made by regulations under section 51 of this Act.[1]

Regulations—Landfill Tax Regulations, SI 1996/1527.

Cross references—See Landfill Tax Registrations, SI 1996/1527 reg 13(7) (correction of errors).

Amendments—[1] This para repealed by FA 2008 s 122, Sch 40 para 21(*e*) with effect from 1 April 2009 (by virtue of SI 2009/571 art 2)

Registration

21—*(1) A person who fails to comply with section 47(3) of this Act is liable to a penalty equal to 5 per cent of the relevant tax or, if it is greater or the circumstances are such that there is no relevant tax, to a penalty of £250; but this is subject to sub-paragraph (4) below.*

(2) In sub-paragraph (1) above "relevant tax" means the tax (if any) for which the person concerned is liable for the period which—

Landfill Tax

(*a*) begins on the date with effect from which he is, in accordance with section 47 of this Act, required to be registered, and

(*b*) ends on the date on which the Commissioners received notification of, or otherwise became aware of, his liability to be registered.

(3) A person who fails to comply with section 47(4) of this Act is liable to a penalty of £250.

(4) Where, by reason of conduct falling within sub-paragraph (1) above—

(*a*) a person is convicted of an offence (whether under this Part of this Act or otherwise), or

(*b*) a person is assessed to a penalty under paragraph 18 above,

that conduct shall not also give rise to liability to a penalty under this paragraph.

Amendments—Para 21(1), (2), (4) repealed by FA 2008 s 123, Sch 41 para 25(*h*)(ii) with effect from 1 April 2010 (by virtue of SI 2009/511 art 2).

Information

22—(1) If a person—

(*a*) *fails to comply with any provision of paragraph 1 or 3 above, or*[2]

(*b*) fails to make records as required by any provision of regulations made under paragraph 2 above,

he is liable to a penalty of £250; but this is subject to sub-paragraph (4) below.

(2) Where—

(*a*) a penalty (an initial penalty) is imposed on a person under sub-paragraph (1) above, and

(*b*) the failure which led to the initial penalty continues after its imposition,

he is (subject to sub-paragraph (4) below) liable to a further penalty of £20 for each day during which (or any part of which) the failure continues after the day on which the initial penalty was imposed.

(3) A person who fails to preserve records in compliance with any provision of regulations made under paragraph 2 above (read with that paragraph and any direction given under the regulations) is liable to a penalty of £250; but this is subject to sub-paragraph (4) below.

(4) Where by reason of a failure falling within sub-paragraph (1) or (3) above—

(*a*) a person is convicted of an offence (whether under this Part of this Act or otherwise), or

(*b*) a person is assessed to a penalty under paragraph 18 above [or a penalty for a deliberate inaccuracy under Schedule 24 to the Finance Act 2007 (penalties for errors) [or a penalty under Schedule 41 to the Finance Act 2008 (penalties: failure to notify and certain VAT and excise wrongdoing)]3,]1,

that failure shall not also give rise to liability to a penalty under this paragraph.

Amendments—[1] Words in sub-para (4)(*b*) inserted by the Finance Act 2008, Schedule 40 (Appointed Day, Transitional Provisions and Consequential Amendments) Order, SI 2009/571 art 8, Sch 1 paras 18, 19 with effect from 1 April 2009.

[2] Sub-para (1)(*a*) and following word "or" repealed, by the Finance Act 2009, Section 96 and Schedule 48 (Appointed Day, Savings and Consequential Amendments) Order, SI 2009/3054 art 3, Schedule para 7(*b*) with effect from 1 April 2010. Note that, where HMRC have requested information or documents before 1 April 2010, sub-para (1)(*a*) continues to have effect on and after that date (SI 2009/3054 art 6(*b*)).

[3] In sub-s (4)(*b*) words inserted by the Finance Act 2008 (Penalties for Errors and Failure to Notify etc) (Consequential Amendments) Order, SI 2010/530 art 2, Schedule para 6 with effect from 1 April 2010.

Breach of regulations

23—(1) Where regulations made under this Part of this Act impose a requirement on any person, they may provide that if the person fails to comply with the requirement he shall be liable to a penalty of £250; but this is subject to sub-paragraphs (2) and (3) below.

(2) Where by reason of any conduct—

(*a*) a person is convicted of an offence (whether under this Part of this Act or otherwise), or

(*b*) a person is assessed to a penalty under paragraph 18 above [or a penalty for a deliberate inaccuracy under Schedule 24 to the Finance Act 2007 (penalties for errors) [or a penalty under Schedule 41 to the Finance Act 2008 (penalties: failure to notify and certain VAT and excise wrongdoing)]2,]1,

that conduct shall not also give rise to liability to a penalty under the regulations.

(3) Sub-paragraph (1) above does not apply to any failure mentioned in paragraph 22 above.

Cross references—See FA 1997 Sch 5 para 4(3) (contravention of requirement to repay Commissioners).

Amendments—[1] Words in sub-para (2)(*b*) inserted by the Finance Act 2008, Schedule 40 (Appointed Day, Transitional Provisions and Consequential Amendments) Order, SI 2009/571 art 8, Sch 1 paras 28, 29 with effect from 1 April 2009.

[2] In sub-s (2)(*b*) words inserted by the Finance Act 2008 (Penalties for Errors and Failure to Notify etc) (Consequential Amendments) Order, SI 2010/530 art 2, Schedule para 6 with effect from 1 April 2010.

Prospective amendments—Para 23A to be inserted by the Tribunals, Courts and Enforcement Act 2007 s 62(3), Sch 13 paras 122, 123 with effect from a date to be appointed. Para 23A to be repealed by FA 2008 s 129, Sch 43 para 5 with effect from such day as the Commissioners may by statutory instrument appoint.

Para 23A to read—

"Controlled Goods Agreements

23A—(1)This paragraph applies where an enforcement agent acting under the power conferred by section 51(A1) of the Finance Act 1997 (power to use the procedure in Schedule 12 to the Tribunals, Courts and Enforcement Act 2007) has entered into a controlled goods agreement with the person against whom the power is exercisable ("the person in default").

(2) In this paragraph, "controlled goods agreement" has the meaning given by paragraph 13(4) of that Schedule.

(3) If the person in default removes or disposes of goods (or permits their removal or disposal) in breach of the controlled goods agreement, he is liable to a penalty equal to half of the tax or other amount recoverable under section 51(A1) of the Finance Act 1997.

(4) The person in default shall not be liable to a penalty under subparagraph

(3) above if he satisfies the Commissioners or, on appeal, an appeal tribunal, that there is a reasonable excuse for the breach in question.

(5) This paragraph extends only to England and Wales.".

Walking possession agreements

24—(1) This paragraph applies where—

(*a*) in accordance with regulations under [section 51 of the Finance Act 1997 (enforcement by distress)][1] a distress is authorised to be levied on the goods and chattels of a person (a person in default) who has refused or neglected to pay any tax due from him or any amount recoverable as if it were tax due from him, and

(*b*) the person levying the distress and the person in default have entered into a walking possession agreement.

(2) For the purposes of this paragraph a walking possession agreement is an agreement under which, in consideration of the property distrained upon being allowed to remain in the custody of the person in default and of the delaying of its sale, the person in default—

(*a*) acknowledges that the property specified in the agreement is under distraint and held in walking possession, and

(*b*) undertakes that, except with the consent of the Commissioners and subject to such conditions as they may impose, he will not remove or allow the removal of any of the specified property from the premises named in the agreement.

(3) If the person in default is in breach of the undertaking contained in a walking possession agreement, he is liable to a penalty equal to half of the tax or other amount referred to in sub-paragraph (1)(*a*) above.

(4) This paragraph does not extend to Scotland.

Amendments—[1] Words in sub-s (1)(*a*) above substituted for words "paragraph 13(1) above" by FA 1997 s 53(8) with effect from 1 July 1997 (see SI 1997/1432).

Prospective amendments—Sub-para (4) to be substituted by the Tribunals, Courts and Enforcement Act 2007 s 62(3), Sch 13 paras 122, 124 with effect from a date to be appointed. That sub-para as substituted, to read—

"(4) This paragraph extends only to Northern Ireland.".

Mitigation of penalties

25—(1) Where a person is liable to a penalty under this Part of this Schedule the Commissioners or, on appeal, an appeal tribunal may reduce the penalty to such amount (including nil) as they think proper.

(2) Where the person concerned satisfies the Commissioners or, on appeal, an appeal tribunal that there is a reasonable excuse for any breach, failure or other conduct, that is a factor which (among other things) may be taken into account under sub-paragraph (1) above.

(3) In the case of a penalty reduced by the Commissioners under sub-paragraph (1) above an appeal tribunal, on an appeal relating to the penalty, may cancel the whole or any part of the reduction made by the Commissioners.

PART VI
INTEREST

Interest on under-declared tax

26—(1) Sub-paragraph (2) below applies where—

(*a*) under section 50(1) of this Act the Commissioners assess an amount of tax due from a registrable person for an accounting period and notify it to him, and

(*b*) the assessment is made on the basis that the amount (the additional amount) is due from him in addition to any amount shown in a return made in relation to the accounting period.

(2) The additional amount shall carry interest for the period which—

(*a*) begins with the day after that on which the person is required by provision made under section 49 of this Act to pay tax due from him for the accounting period, and

(*b*) ends with the day before the relevant day.

(3) For the purposes of sub-paragraph (2) above the relevant day is the earlier of—

(*a*) the day on which the assessment is notified to the person;

(*b*) the day on which the additional amount is paid.

(4) Sub-paragraph (5) below applies where under section 50(2) of this Act the Commissioners assess an amount as being tax due from a registrable person for an accounting period and notify it to him.

(5) The amount shall carry interest for the period which—

(*a*) begins with the day after that on which the person is required by provision made under section 49 of this Act to pay tax due from him for the accounting period, and

(*b*) ends with the day before the relevant day.

(6) For the purposes of sub-paragraph (5) above the relevant day is the earlier of—

(*a*) the day on which the assessment is notified to the person;

(*b*) the day on which the amount is paid.

(7) Interest under this paragraph shall be payable at the rate applicable under section 197 of this Act.

(8) Interest under this paragraph shall be paid without any deduction of income tax.

(9) Sub-paragraph (10) below applies where—

(*a*) an amount carries interest under this paragraph (or would do so apart from that sub-paragraph), and

(*b*) all or part of the amount turns out not to be due.

(10) In such a case—

(*a*) the amount or part (as the case may be) shall not carry interest under this paragraph and shall be treated as never having done so, and

(*b*) all such adjustments as are reasonable shall be made, including adjustments by way of repayment by the Commissioners where appropriate.

Note—The rate of interest for the purposes of this section has been prescribed as follows—

Commencement date	*Rate*	*Order No*
1 April 1997	6.25%	1997/1016
6 July 1998	9.5%	1998/1461
1 April 2000	8.5%	2000/631

Cross-reference—See FA 2009 s 101, Sch 54 (interest payable to HMRC).

Interest on unpaid tax etc

27—(1) Sub-paragraph (2) below applies where—

(*a*) a registrable person makes a return under provision made under section 49 of this Act (whether or not he makes it at the time required by such provision), and

(*b*) the return shows that an amount of tax is due from him for the accounting period in relation to which the return is made.

(2) The amount shall carry interest for the period which—

(*a*) begins with the day after that on which the person is required by provision made under section 49 of this Act to pay tax due from him for the accounting period, and

(*b*) ends with the day before that on which the amount is paid.

(3) Sub-paragraph (4) below applies where—

(*a*) under section 50(1) of this Act the Commissioners assess an amount of tax due from a registrable person for an accounting period and notify it to him, and

(*b*) the assessment is made on the basis that no return required by provision made under section 49 of this Act has been made by the person in relation to the accounting period.

(4) The amount shall carry interest for the period which—

(*a*) begins with the day after that on which the person is required by provision made under section 49 of this Act to pay tax due from him for the accounting period, and

(*b*) ends with the day before that on which the amount is paid.

(5) Sub-paragraph (6) below applies where—

(*a*) under section 50(1) of this Act the Commissioners assess an amount of tax due from a registrable person for an accounting period and notify it to him, and

(*b*) the assessment (the supplementary assessment) is made on the basis that the amount (the additional amount) is due from him in addition to any amount shown in a return, or in any previous assessment, made in relation to the accounting period.

(6) The additional amount shall carry interest for the period which—

(*a*) begins with the day on which the supplementary assessment is notified to the person, and

(*b*) ends with the day before that on which the additional amount is paid.

(7) Sub-paragraph (8) below applies where under section 50(2) of this Act the Commissioners assess an amount as being tax due from a registrable person for an accounting period and notify it to him.

(8) The amount shall carry interest for the period which—
 (*a*) begins with the day on which the assessment is notified to the person, and
 (*b*) ends with the day before that on which the amount is paid.
(9) Sub-paragraph (10) below applies where under paragraph 32 below the Commissioners—
 (*a*) assess an amount due from a person by way of penalty under Part V of this Schedule [or under Schedule 41 to the Finance Act 2008][1] and notify it to him, or
 (*b*) assess an amount due from a person by way of interest under paragraph 26 above and notify it to him.
(10) The amount shall carry interest for the period which—
 (*a*) begins with the day on which the assessment is notified to the person, and
 (*b*) ends with the day before that on which the amount is paid.
(11) Interest under this paragraph shall be compound interest calculated—
 (*a*) at the penalty rate, and
 (*b*) with monthly rests;
and the penalty rate is the rate found by taking the rate at which interest is payable under paragraph 26 above and adding 10 percentage points to that rate.
(12) Interest under this paragraph shall be paid without any deduction of income tax.
(13) Where—
 (*a*) the Commissioners assess and notify an amount as mentioned in sub-paragraph (5)(*a*) or (7) or (9)(*a*) or (*b*) above,
 (*b*) they also specify a date for the purposes of this sub-paragraph, and
 (*c*) the amount concerned is paid on or before that date,
the amount shall not carry interest by virtue of sub-paragraph (6) or (8) or (10) above (as the case may be).
(14) Sub-paragraph (15) below applies where—
 (*a*) an amount carries interest under this paragraph (or would do so apart from that sub-paragraph), and
 (*b*) all or part of the amount turns out not to be due.
(15) In such a case—
 (*a*) the amount or part (as the case may be) shall not carry interest under this paragraph and shall be treated as never having done so, and
 (*b*) all such adjustments as are reasonable shall be made, including adjustments by way of repayment by the Commissioners where appropriate.

Cross reference—
Cross-reference—See FA 2009 s 101, Sch 54 (interest payable to HMRC).
FA 2009 s 108 (suspension of penalties during currency of agreement for deferred payment).
Amendments—[1] In sub-s (9)(*a*) words inserted by the Finance Act 2008 (Penalties for Errors and Failure to Notify etc) (Consequential Amendments) Order, SI 2010/530 art 2, Schedule para 6 with effect from 1 April 2010.

28—(1) Where a person is liable to pay interest under paragraph 27 above the Commissioners or, on appeal, an appeal tribunal may reduce the amount payable to such amount (including nil) as they think proper.
(2) Where the person concerned satisfies the Commissioners or, on appeal, an appeal tribunal that there is a reasonable excuse for the conduct giving rise to the liability to pay interest, that is a factor which (among other things) may be taken into account under sub-paragraph (1) above.
(3) In the case of interest reduced by the Commissioners under sub-paragraph (1) above an appeal tribunal, on an appeal relating to the interest, may cancel the whole or any part of the reduction made by the Commissioners.

Interest payable by Commissioners

29—(1) Where, due to an error on the part of the Commissioners, a person—
 (*a*) has paid to them by way of tax an amount which was not tax due and which they are in consequence liable to repay to him,
 (*b*) has failed to claim payment of an amount to the payment of which he was entitled in pursuance of provision made under section 51(2)(*c*) or (*d*) or (*f*) of this Act, or
 (*c*) has suffered delay in receiving payment of an amount due to him from them in connection with tax,
then, if and to the extent that they would not be liable to do so apart from this paragraph, they shall (subject to the following provisions of this paragraph) pay interest to him on that amount for the applicable period.
[(1A) In sub-paragraph (1) above—

(*a*) the reference in paragraph (*a*) to an amount which the Commissioners are liable to repay in consequence of the making of a payment that was not due is a reference to only so much of that amount as is the subject of a claim that the Commissioners are required to satisfy or have satisfied; and

(*b*) the amounts referred to in paragraph (*c*) do not include any amount payable under this paragraph.][1]

(2) The applicable period, in a case falling within sub-paragraph (1)(*a*) above, is the period—

(*a*) beginning with the date on which the payment is received by the Commissioners, and

(*b*) ending with the date on which they authorise payment of the amount on which the interest is payable.

(3) The applicable period, in a case falling within sub-paragraph (1)(*b*) or (*c*) above, is the period—

(*a*) beginning with the date on which, apart from the error, the Commissioners might reasonably have been expected to authorise payment of the amount on which the interest is payable, and

(*b*) ending with the date on which they in fact authorise payment of that amount.

[(4) In determining the applicable period for the purposes of this paragraph there shall be left out of account any period by which the Commissioners' authorisation of the payment of interest is delayed by the conduct of the person who claims the interest.] [3]

[(4A) The reference in sub-paragraph (4) above to a period by which the Commissioners' authorisation of the payment of interest is delayed by the conduct of the person who claims it includes, in particular, any period which is referable to—

(*a*) any unreasonable delay in the making of the claim for interest or in the making of any claim for the payment or repayment of the amount on which interest is claimed;

(*b*) any failure by that person or a person acting on his influence to provide the Commissioners—

(i) at or before the time of the making of a claim, or

(ii) subsequently in response to a request for information by the Commissioners.

with all the information required by them to enable the existence and amount of the claimant's entitlement to a payment or repayment, and to interest on that payment or repayment, to be determined; and

(*c*) the making, as part of or in association with either—

(i) the claim for interest, or

(ii) any claim for the payment or repayment of the amount on which interest is claimed, of a claim to anything to which the claimant was not entitled.][3]

[(5) In determining for the purposes of sub-paragraph (4A) above whether any period of delay is referable to a failure by any person to provide information in response to a request by the Commissioners, there shall be taken to be so referable, except so far as may be provided for by regulations, any period which—

(*a*) begins with the date on which the Commissioners require that person to provide information which they reasonably consider relevant to the matter to be determined; and

(*b*) ends with the earliest date on which it would be reasonable for the Commissioners to conclude—

(i) that they have received a complete answer to their request for information;

(ii) that they have received all that they need in answer to that request; or

(iii) that it is unnecessary for them to be provided with any information in answer to that request.][3]

(6) . . . [3]

(7) The Commissioners shall only be liable to pay interest under this paragraph on a claim made in writing for that purpose.

[(8) A claim under this paragraph shall not be made more than [4 years][4] after the end of the applicable period to which it relates.][2]

[(9) References in this paragraph—

(*a*) to receiving payment of any amount from the Commissioners, or

(*b*) to the authorisation by the Commissioners of the payment of any amount

include references to the discharge by way of set-off (whether in accordance with regulations under paragraph 42 or 43 below or otherwise) of the Commissioners' liability to pay that amount.][2]

(10) Interest under this paragraph shall be payable at the rate applicable under section 197 of this Act.

Note—The rate of interest for the purposes of this section has been prescribed as follows—

Commencement date	*Rate*	*Order No*
1 April 1997	6%	1997/1016 and 1998/1461
1 April 2000	5%	2000/631

Cross references—See FA 1997 Sch 5 para 15 (assessments of overpayments of interest.)
See FA 2009 s 102, Sch 54 (repayment of interest by HMRC).
Amendments—[1] Sub-para (1A) inserted by FA 1997 s 50, Sch 5 para 11(2) and always deemed to have had effect.
[2] Sub-paras (8) and (9) substituted by FA 1997 s 50, Sch 5 para 11(3), (4) and always deemed to have had effect.
[3] Sub-paras (4), (4A), (5) substituted for sub-paras (4)–(6) by FA 1997 s 50, Sch 5 para 12 with effect for the purposes of determining whether any period beginning or after the day of passing FA 1997 (19 March 1997) is left out of account.
[4] In sub-para (8) words substituted for "three years" by FA 2009 s 99, Sch 51 paras 37, 39 with effect from 1 April 2010 (SI 2010/867 art 2). However, this amendment is disregarded where claims made under para 29 relate to an applicable period which ends on or before 31 March 2007 (see SI 2010/867 art 25).

30—(1) Where—

(*a*) any interest is payable by the Commissioners to a person on a sum due to him under this Part of this Act, and

(*b*) he is a person to whom regulations under section 51 of this Act apply,

the interest shall be treated as an amount to which he is entitled by way of credit in pursuance of the regulations.

(2) Sub-paragraph (1) above shall be disregarded for the purpose of determining a person's entitlement to interest or the amount of interest to which he is entitled.

PART VII
MISCELLANEOUS

Security for tax

31 Where it appears to the Commissioners requisite to do so for the protection of the revenue they may require a registrable person, as a condition of his carrying out taxable activities, to give security (or further security) of such amount and in such manner as they may determine for the payment of any tax which is or may become due from him.

Assessments to penalties etc

32—(1) Where a person is liable—

(*a*) to a penalty under Part V of this Schedule, or

(*b*) for interest under paragraph 26 or 27 above,

the Commissioners may, subject to sub-paragraph (2) below, assess the amount due by way of penalty or interest (as the case may be) and notify it to him accordingly; and the fact that any conduct giving rise to a penalty under Part V of this Schedule may have ceased before an assessment is made under this paragraph shall not affect the power of the Commissioners to make such an assessment.

(2) In the case of the penalties and interest referred to in the following paragraphs of this sub-paragraph, the assessment under this paragraph shall be of an amount due in respect of the accounting period which in the paragraph concerned is referred to as the relevant period—

(*a*) in the case of a penalty under paragraph 18 above relating to the evasion of tax, and in the case of interest under paragraph 27 above on an amount due by way of such a penalty, the relevant period is the accounting period for which the tax evaded was due;

(*b*) in the case of a penalty under paragraph 18 above relating to the obtaining of a payment under regulations under section 51(2)(*c*) or (*d*) or (*f*) of this Act, and in the case of interest under paragraph 27 above on an amount due by way of such a penalty, the relevant period is the accounting period in respect of which the payment was obtained;

(*c*) in the case of interest under paragraph 26 above, and in the case of interest under paragraph 27 above on an amount due by way of interest under paragraph 26 above, the relevant period is the accounting period in respect of which the tax was due;

(*d*) in the case of interest under paragraph 27 above on an amount of tax, the relevant period is the accounting period in respect of which the tax was due.

(3) In a case where the amount of any penalty or interest falls to be calculated by reference to tax which was not paid at the time it should have been and that tax cannot be readily attributed to any one or more accounting periods, it shall be treated for the purposes of this Part of this Act as tax due for such period or periods as the Commissioners may determine to the best of their judgment and notify to the person liable for the tax and penalty or interest.

(4) Where a person is assessed under this paragraph to an amount due by way of any penalty or interest falling within sub-paragraph (2) above and is also assessed under subsection (1) or (2) of section 50 of this Act for the accounting period which is the relevant period under sub-paragraph (2) above, the assessments may be combined and notified to him as one assessment, but the amount of the penalty or interest shall be separately identified in the notice.

(5) Sub-paragraph (6) below applies in the case of an amount due by way of interest under paragraph 27 above.

(6) Where this sub-paragraph applies in the case of an amount—

Landfill Tax

(*a*) a notice of assessment under this paragraph shall specify a date, being not later than the date of the notice, to which the amount of interest which is assessed is calculated, and

(*b*) if the interest continues to accrue after that date, a further assessment or further assessments may be made under this paragraph in respect of amounts which so accrue.

(7) If, within such period as may be notified by the Commissioners to the person liable for the interest under paragraph 27 above, the amount referred to in paragraph 27(2), (4), (6), (8) or (10) above (as the case may be) is paid, it shall be treated for the purposes of paragraph 27 above as paid on the date specified as mentioned in sub-paragraph (6)(*a*) above.

(8) Where an amount has been assessed and notified to any person under this paragraph it shall be recoverable as if it were tax due from him unless, or except to the extent that, the assessment has subsequently been withdrawn or reduced.

(9) Subsection (8) of section 50 of this Act shall apply for the purposes of this paragraph as it applies for the purposes of that section.

Assessments: time limits

33—(1) Subject to the following provisions of this paragraph, an assessment under—

(*a*) any provision of section 50 of this Act, or

(*b*) paragraph 32 above,

shall not be made more than [4 years][1] after [the relevant event][1].

[(1A) In this paragraph "the relevant event", in relation to an assessment, means—

(*a*) the end of the accounting period concerned, or

(*b*) in the case of an assessment under paragraph 32 of an amount due by way of a penalty other than a penalty referred to in paragraph 32(2), the event giving rise to the penalty.][1]

(2) Subject to sub-paragraph (5) below, an assessment under paragraph 32 above of—

(*a*) an amount due by way of any penalty referred to in sub-paragraph (2) of that paragraph, or

(*b*) an amount due by way of interest,

may be made at any time before the expiry of the period of two years beginning with the time when the amount of tax due for the accounting period concerned has been finally determined.

(3) In relation to an assessment under paragraph 32 above, any reference in [sub-paragraph (1A)][1] or (2) above to the accounting period concerned is a reference to that period which, in the case of the penalty or interest concerned, is the relevant period referred to in sub-paragraph (2) of that paragraph.

[(4) An assessment of an amount due from a person in a case involving a loss of tax—

(*a*) brought about deliberately by the person (or by another person acting on that person's behalf), or

(*b*) attributable to a failure by the person to comply with an obligation under section 47(2) or (3),

may be made at any time not more than 20 years after the relevant event (subject to sub-paragraph (5)).

(4A) In sub-paragraph (4)(*a*) the reference to a loss brought about deliberately by the person includes a loss brought about as a result of a deliberate inaccuracy in a document given to Her Majesty's Revenue and Customs by or on behalf of that person.][1]

(5) Where after a person's death the Commissioners propose to assess an amount as due by reason of some conduct of the deceased—

(*a*) the assessment shall not be made more than [4 years][1] after the death, *and*

(*b*) *if the circumstances are as set out in sub-paragraph (4) above, the modification of sub-paragraph (1) above contained in that sub-paragraph shall not apply but any assessment which (from the point of view of time limits) could have been made immediately after the death may be made at any time within three years after it.*[1]

Amendments—[1] In sub-paras (1), (5)(*a*) words substituted for "three years", in sub-para (1) words substituted; sub-para (1A) inserted; in sub-para (3) words substituted for "sub-paragraph (1)"; sub-paras (4), (4A) substituted for previous sub-para (4); and sub-para (5)(*b*) and preceding word "and" repealed, by FA 2009 s 99, Sch 51 paras 37, 40 with effect from 1 April 2010 (SI 2010/867 art 2(1)). Substituted words in sub-para (1) previously read as follows—

"the end of the accounting period concerned or, in the case of an assessment under paragraph 32 above of an amount due by way of a penalty which is not a penalty referred to in sub-paragraph (2) of that paragraph, [three years] after the event giving rise to the penalty".

Sub-para (4) previously read as follows—

"(4) Subject to sub-paragraph (5) below, if tax has been lost—

(*a*) as a result of conduct falling within paragraph 18(1) above or for which a person has been convicted of fraud, or

(*b*) in circumstances giving rise to liability to a penalty under paragraph 21 above,

an assessment may be made as if, in sub-paragraph (1) above, each reference to [three years] were a reference to twenty years."

The following transitional provisions apply

- The amendments made to sub-paras (1), (3) and the insertion of sub-para (1A), are disregarded where, for the purposes of sub-paras (1), (3) the "relevant event" occurred on or before 31 March 2007 (SI 2010/867 art 26).
- The substitution of sub-para (4) is disregarded where, for the purposes of sub-para (4), the "relevant event" occurred on or before 31 March 2007 (SI 2010/867 art 27).
- The amendments made to sub-para (5) are disregarded where, for the purposes of sub-para (5), the death occurred on or before 31 March 2007 (SI 2010/867 art 28).

Supplementary assessments

34—If, otherwise than in circumstances falling within subsection (5)(*b*) of section 50 of this Act, it appears to the Commissioners that the amount which ought to have been assessed in an assessment under any provision of that section or under paragraph 32 above exceeds the amount which was so assessed, then—

(*a*) under the like provision as that assessment was made, and

(*b*) on or before the last day on which that assessment could have been made,

the Commissioners may make a supplementary assessment of the amount of the excess and shall notify the person concerned accordingly.

Disclosure of information

35—(1) Notwithstanding any obligation not to disclose information that would otherwise apply, the Commissioners may disclose information to—

(*a*) the Secretary of State,

(*b*) the Environment Agency,

(*c*) the Scottish Environment Protection Agency,

(*d*) the Department of the Environment for Northern Ireland,

(*e*) a district council in Northern Ireland, or

(*f*) an authorised officer of any person (a principal) mentioned in paragraphs (*a*) to (*e*) above,

for the purpose of assisting the principal concerned in the performance of the principal's duties.

(2) Notwithstanding any such obligation as is mentioned in sub-paragraph (1) above, any person mentioned in sub-paragraph (1)(*a*) to (*f*) above may disclose information to the Commissioners or to an authorised officer of the Commissioners for the purpose of assisting the Commissioners in the performance of duties in relation to tax.

(3) Information that has been disclosed to a person by virtue of this paragraph shall not be disclosed by him except—

(*a*) to another person to whom (instead of him) disclosure could by virtue of this paragraph have been made, or

(*b*) for the purpose of any proceedings connected with the operation of any provision of, or made under, any enactment in relation to the environment or to tax.

(4) References in the preceding provisions of this paragraph to an authorised officer of any person (the principal) are to any person who has been designated by the principal as a person to and by whom information may be disclosed by virtue of this paragraph.

(5) The Secretary of State shall notify the Commissioners in writing of the name of any person designated by the Secretary of State under sub-paragraph (4) above.

(6) No charge may be made for a disclosure made by virtue of this paragraph.

The register: publication

36—(1) The Commissioners may publish, by such means as they think fit, information which—

(*a*) is derived from the register kept under section 47 of this Act, and

(*b*) falls within any of the descriptions set out below.

(2) The descriptions are—

(*a*) the names of registered persons;

(*b*) the addresses of any sites or other premises at which they carry on business;

(*c*) the registration numbers assigned to them in the register;

(*d*) the fact (where it is the case) that the registered person is a body corporate which under section 59 of this Act is treated as a member of a group;

(*e*) the names of the other bodies corporate treated under that section as members of the group;

(*f*) the addresses of any sites or other premises at which those other bodies carry on business.

(3) Information may be published in accordance with this paragraph notwithstanding any obligation not to disclose the information that would otherwise apply.

Evidence by certificate etc

37—(1) A certificate of the Commissioners—

(*a*) that a person was or was not at any time registered under section 47 of this Act, [or][1] (*b*) that any return required by regulations made under section 49 of this Act has not been made or had not been made at any time, . . . [1]

(*c*) . . . [1]

shall be sufficient evidence of that fact until the contrary is proved.

(2) A photograph of any document furnished to the Commissioners for the purposes of this Part of this Act and certified by them to be such a photograph shall be admissible in any proceedings, whether civil or criminal, to the same extent as the document itself.

(3) Any document purporting to be a certificate under sub-paragraph (1) or (2) above shall be taken to be such a certificate until the contrary is proved.

Amendments—[1] Words inserted and repealed by FA 2008 s 138, Sch 44 para 7 with effect from 21 July 2008. Sub-para (1)(*c*) previously read as follows—

"(*c*) that any tax shown as due in a return made in pursuance of regulations made under section 49 of this Act, or in an assessment made under section 50 of this Act, has not been paid,".

Service of notices etc

38 Any notice, notification or requirement to be served on, given to or made of any person for the purposes of this Part of this Act may be served, given or made by sending it by post in a letter addressed to that person at his last or usual residence or place of business.

39—(1) This paragraph applies to directions, specifications and conditions which the Commissioners or an authorised person may give or impose under any provision of this Part.

(2) A direction, specification or condition given or imposed by the Commissioners may be withdrawn or varied by them.

(3) A direction, specification or condition given or imposed by an authorised person may be withdrawn or varied by him or by another authorised person.

(4) No direction, specification or condition shall have effect as regards any person it is intended to affect unless—

(*a*) a notice containing it is served on him, or

(*b*) other reasonable steps are taken with a view to bringing it to his attention.

(5) No withdrawal or variation of a direction, specification or condition shall have effect as regards any person the withdrawal or variation is intended to affect unless—

(*a*) a notice containing the withdrawal or variation is served on him, or

(*b*) other reasonable steps are taken with a view to bringing the withdrawal or variation to his attention.

No deduction of penalties or interest

40 (*inserts* TA 1988 s 827(1C)).

Destination of receipts

41

Amendments—Paragraph repealed by Commissioners for Revenue and Customs Act 2005 ss 50, 52, Sch 4 para 65 and Sch 5 with effect from 18 April 2005 by virtue of the Commissioners for Revenue and Customs Act (Commencement) Order, SI 2005/1126, art 2(2).

Set-off of amounts

42—(1) Regulations may make provision in relation to any case where—

(*a*) a person is under a duty to pay to the Commissioners at any time an amount or amounts in respect of landfill tax, and

(*b*) the Commissioners are under a duty to pay to that person at the same time an amount or amounts in respect of any tax (or taxes) under their care and management.

(2) The regulations may provide that if the total of the amount or amounts mentioned in sub-paragraph (1)(*a*) above exceeds the total of the amount or amounts mentioned in sub-paragraph (1)(*b*) above, the latter shall be set off against the former.

(3) The regulations may provide that if the total of the amount or amounts mentioned in sub-paragraph (1)(*b*) above exceeds the total of the amount or amounts mentioned in sub-paragraph (1)(*a*) above, the Commissioners may set off the latter in paying the former.

(4) The regulations may provide that if the total of the amount or amounts mentioned in sub-paragraph (1)(*a*) above is the same as the total of the amount or amounts mentioned in sub-paragraph (1)(*b*) above no payment need be made in respect of the former or the latter.

[(4A) The regulations may provide for any limitation on the time within which the Commissioners are entitled to take steps for recovering any amount due to them in respect of landfill tax to be disregarded, in such cases as may be described in the regulations, in determining whether any person is under such a duty to pay as is mentioned in sub-paragraph (1)(*a*) above.][1]

(5) The regulations may include provision treating any duty to pay mentioned in sub-paragraph (1) above as discharged accordingly.

(6) References in sub-paragraph (1) above to an amount in respect of a particular tax include references not only to an amount of tax itself but also to other amounts such as interest and penalty.

(7) In this paragraph "tax" includes "duty".

Regulations—Landfill Tax Regulations, SI 1996/1527.

Cross references—See Landfill Tax Regulations, SI 1996/1527 regs 45, 47 (set-off of amounts).

Amendments—[1] Sub-para (4A) inserted by FA 1997 s 50, Sch 5 para 13(1).

43 . . . [1]

Regulations—Landfill Tax Regulations, SI 1996/1527.

Cross references—See Landfill Tax Regulations, SI 1996/1527 regs 46, 47 (set-off of amounts).

Amendments—[1] Para 43 repealed by FA 2009 s 119, Sch 60 paras 5, 10 with effect from 1 September 2009 by virtue of FA 2009 s 119, Sch 60 para 13(1). Prior to that date, para 43 read as follows:

"43—

(1) Regulations may make provision in relation to any case where—

(*a*) a person is under a duty to pay to the Commissioners at any time an amount or amounts in respect of any tax (or taxes) under their care and management, and

(*b*) the Commissioners are under a duty to pay to that person at the same time an amount or amounts in respect of landfill tax.

(2) The regulations may provide that if the total of the amount or amounts mentioned in sub-paragraph (1)(*a*) above exceeds the total of the amount or amounts mentioned in sub-paragraph (1)(*b*) above, the latter shall be set off against the former.

(3) The regulations may provide that if the total of the amount or amounts mentioned in sub-paragraph (1)(*b*) above exceeds the total of the amount or amounts mentioned in sub-paragraph (1)(*a*) above, the Commissioners may set off the latter in paying the former.

(4) The regulations may provide that if the total of the amount or amounts mentioned in sub-paragraph (1)(*a*) above is the same as the total of the amount or amounts mentioned in sub-paragraph (1)(*b*) above no payment need be made in respect of the former or the latter.

[(4A) The regulations may provide for any limitation on the time within which the Commissioners are entitled to take steps for recovering any amount due to them in respect of any of the taxes under their care and management to be disregarded, in such cases as may be described in the regulations, in determining whether any person is under such a duty to pay as is mentioned in sub-paragraph (1)(*a*) above.]

(5) The regulations may include provision treating any duty to pay mentioned in sub-paragraph (1) above as discharged accordingly.

(6) References in sub-paragraph (1) above to an amount in respect of a particular tax include references not only to an amount of tax itself but also to other amounts such as interest and penalty.

(7) In this paragraph "tax" includes "duty"."

Amounts shown as tax on invoices

44—(1) Where—

(*a*) a registrable person issues an invoice showing an amount as tax chargeable on an event, and

(*b*) no tax is in fact chargeable on the event,

an amount equal to the amount shown as tax shall be recoverable from the person as a debt due to the Crown.

(2) Where—

(*a*) a registrable person issues an invoice showing an amount as tax chargeable on a taxable disposal, and

(*b*) the amount shown as tax exceeds the amount of tax in fact chargeable on the disposal,

an amount equal to the excess shall be recoverable from the person as a debt due to the Crown.

(3) References in this paragraph to an invoice are to any invoice, whether or not it is a landfill invoice within the meaning of section 61 of this Act.

Adjustment of contracts

45—(1) This paragraph applies where—

(*a*) material undergoes a landfill disposal,

(*b*) a payment falls to be made under a disposal contract relating to the material, and

(*c*) after the making of the contract there is a change in the tax chargeable on the landfill disposal.

(2) In such a case the amount of the payment mentioned in sub-paragraph (1)(*b*) above shall be adjusted, unless the disposal contract otherwise provides, so as to reflect the tax chargeable on the landfill disposal.

(3) For the purposes of this paragraph a disposal contract relating to material is a contract providing for the disposal of the material, and it is immaterial—

(*a*) when the contract was made;

(*b*) whether the contract also provides for other matters;

(*c*) whether the contract provides for a method of disposal and (if it does) what method it provides for.

(4) The reference in sub-paragraph (1) above to a change in the tax chargeable is a reference to a change—

(*a*) to or from no tax being chargeable, or

(*b*) in the amount of tax chargeable.

46—(1) This paragraph applies where—

(*a*) work is carried out under a construction contract,

(*b*) as a result of the work, material undergoes a landfill disposal,

(*c*) the contract makes no provision as to the disposal of such material, and

(*d*) the contract was made on or before 29th November 1994 (when the proposal to create tax was announced).

(2) In such a case the amount of any payment which falls to be made—

(*a*) under the construction contract, and

(*b*) in respect of the work,

shall be adjusted, unless the contract otherwise provides, so as to reflect the tax (if any) chargeable on the disposal.

(3) For the purposes of this paragraph a construction contract is a contract under which all or any of the following work is to be carried out—

(*a*) the preparation of a site;

(*b*) demolition;

(*c*) building;

(*d*) civil engineering.

Adjustment of rent etc

47—(1) This paragraph applies where—

(*a*) an agreement with regard to any sum payable in respect of the use of land (whether the sum is called rent or royalty or otherwise) provides that the amount of the sum is to be calculated by reference to the turnover of a business,

(*b*) the agreement was made on or before 29th November 1994 (when the proposal to create tax was announced), and

(*c*) the circumstances are such that (had the agreement been made after that date) it can reasonably be expected that it would have provided that tax be ignored in calculating the turnover.

(2) In such a case the agreement shall be taken to provide that tax be ignored in calculating the turnover.

[PART VIII

SECONDARY LIABILITY: CONTROLLERS OF LANDFILL SITES][1]

[Meaning of controller

48—(1) For the purposes of this Part of this Schedule a person is the controller of the whole, or a part, of a landfill site at a given time if he determines, or is entitled to determine, what disposals of material, if any, may be made—

(*a*) at every part of the site at that time, or

(*b*) at that part of the site at that time,

as the case may be.

(2) But a person who, because he is an employee or agent of another, determines or is entitled to determine what disposals may be made at a landfill site or any part of a landfill site is not the controller of that site or, as the case may be, that part of that site.

(3) Where a person is the controller of the whole or a part of a landfill site, that site or, as the case may be, that part of the site is referred to in this Part of this Schedule as being under his control.

(4) Any reference in this Part of this Schedule to a controller (without more) is a reference to a controller of the whole or a part of a landfill site.][1]

Amendments—[1] Pt VIII of this Schedule inserted by FA 2000 s 142(3), Sch 37, with effect for taxable disposals made after 27 July 2000.

[Secondary liability

49—(1) Where—

(*a*) a taxable disposal is made at a landfill site,

(*b*) at the time when that disposal is made a person is the operator of the landfill site by virtue of section 67(*a*), (*c*) or (*e*) of this Act, and

(*c*) at that time a person other than the operator mentioned in paragraph (*b*) above is the controller of the whole or a part of the landfill site,

the controller shall be liable to pay to the Commissioners an amount of the landfill tax chargeable on the disposal.

(2) The amount which the controller is liable to pay shall be determined in accordance with the following provisions of this paragraph.

(3) In a case where the whole of the landfill site is under the control of the controller, he shall be liable to pay the whole of the landfill tax chargeable.

(4) In a case where a part of the landfill site is under the control of the controller, he shall be liable to pay an amount of the landfill tax calculated in accordance with sub-paragraphs (5) and (6) below.

(5) The amount of landfill tax which the controller is liable to pay is the amount which would have been chargeable had a separate taxable disposal consisting of the amount of material referred to in sub-paragraph (6) below been made at the time of the disposal mentioned in sub-paragraph (1)(*a*) above.

(6) That amount of material is the amount by weight of the material comprised in the disposal mentioned in sub-paragraph (1)(*a*) above which was disposed of on the part of the landfill site under the control of the controller.

(7) If the amount mentioned in sub-paragraph (6) above is nil, the controller shall have no liability under sub-paragraph (1) above in relation to landfill tax chargeable on the disposal.

(8) For the purposes of sub-paragraph (1)(*b*) and (*c*) above—

(*a*) section 61 of this Act, and

(*b*) any regulations made under section 62 of this Act,

shall not apply for determining the time when the disposal in question is made.][1]

Amendments—[1] Pt VIII of this Schedule inserted by FA 2000 s 142(3), Sch 37, with effect for taxable disposals made after 27 July 2000.

[Operator entitled to credit

50—(1) This paragraph applies where—

(*a*) the operator of a landfill site is liable to pay landfill tax on a taxable disposal by reference to a particular accounting period,

(*b*) a controller of the whole or a part of that site is (apart from this paragraph) liable under paragraph 49 above to pay an amount of that tax, and

(*c*) for the accounting period in question the operator is entitled to credit under regulations made under section 51 of this Act.

(2) The amount of the tax which the controller is (apart from this sub-paragraph) liable to pay shall be reduced by the amount calculated in accordance with the following formula—

$$\frac{A \times C}{G}$$

where—

A is the amount of tax mentioned in sub-paragraph (1)(*b*) above;

C is the amount of credit mentioned in sub-paragraph (1)(*c*) above; and

G is the operator's gross tax liability for the accounting period in question.

(3) For the purposes of sub-paragraph (2) above, the operator's gross tax liability for the accounting period in question is the gross amount of landfill tax—

(*a*) which is chargeable on disposals made at all landfill sites of which he is the operator, and

(*b*) for which he is required to account by reference to that accounting period.

(4) In sub-paragraph (3) above, the gross amount of landfill tax means the amount of tax before any credit or any other adjustment is taken into account in the period in question.

(5) If the amount calculated in accordance with the formula in sub-paragraph (2) above is greater than the amount of tax mentioned in sub-paragraph (1)(*b*) above, the amount of the tax which the controller is liable to pay shall be reduced to nil.][1]

Amendments—[1] Pt VIII of this Schedule inserted by FA 2000 s 142(3), Sch 37, with effect for taxable disposals made after 27 July 2000.

[Payment of secondary liability

51—(1) This paragraph applies where a controller is liable under paragraph 49 above (after taking account of any reduction under paragraph 50 above) to pay an amount of landfill tax ("the relevant amount").

(2) The controller is required to pay the relevant amount to the Commissioners only if—

(*a*) a notice containing the required information is served on him, or

(*b*) other reasonable steps are taken with a view to bringing the required information to his attention,

before the end of the period of two years beginning with the day immediately following the relevant accounting day.

(3) The relevant accounting day is the last day of the accounting period by reference to which the landfill site operator liable to pay the landfill tax in question is required to account for that tax.

(4) If the controller is required to pay the relevant amount by virtue of this paragraph, the amount shall be paid before the end of the period of thirty days beginning with the day immediately following the notification day.

(5) The notification day is—

(*a*) in a case where notice is served on a controller as mentioned in sub-paragraph (2)(*a*) above, the day on which the notice is served, or

(*b*) in a case where other reasonable steps are taken as mentioned in sub-paragraph (2)(*b*) above, the day on which the last of those steps is taken.

(6) For the purposes of sub-paragraph (2) above the required information is the relevant amount and, if that amount is one reduced in accordance with paragraph 50 above, also—

(*a*) the amount of the controller's liability under paragraph 49 above apart from the reduction,

(*b*) the amount of credit to which the operator is entitled, and

(*c*) the operator's gross tax liability.][1]

Amendments—[1] Pt VIII of this Schedule inserted by FA 2000 s 142(3), Sch 37, with effect for taxable disposals made after 27 July 2000.

[Assessments

52—(1) Where an amount of landfill tax is—

(*a*) assessed under section 50 of this Act, and

(*b*) notified to a licensed operator,

the Commissioners may also determine that a controller of the whole or a part of any landfill site operated by the licensed operator shall be liable to pay so much of the amount assessed as they consider just and equitable.

(2) A controller is required to pay an amount determined under sub-paragraph (1) above only if—

(*a*) a notice stating the amount is served on him, or

(*b*) other reasonable steps are taken with a view to bringing the amount of the liability to his attention,

before the expiry of the period of two years beginning with the day immediately following the assessment day.

(3) The assessment day is the day on which the assessment in question is notified to the licensed operator.

(4) If a controller is required to pay an amount by virtue of this paragraph, it shall be paid before the end of the period of thirty days beginning with the day immediately following the notification day.

(5) The notification day is—

(*a*) in a case where notice is served on a controller as mentioned in sub-paragraph (2)(*a*) above, the day on which the notice is served, or

(*b*) in a case where other reasonable steps are taken as mentioned in sub-paragraph (2)(*b*) above, the day on which the last of those steps is taken.

(6) For the purposes of this paragraph a licensed operator is a person who is the operator of a landfill site by virtue of section 67(*a*), (*c*) or (*e*) of this Act.][1]

Amendments—[1] Pt VIII of this Schedule inserted by FA 2000 s 142(3), Sch 37, with effect for taxable disposals made after 27 July 2000.

[Assessment withdrawn or reduced

53—(1) Where—

(*a*) a controller is liable to pay an amount determined under paragraph 52 above, and

(*b*) the assessment notified to the licensed operator is withdrawn or reduced,

the Commissioners may determine that the controller's liability is to be cancelled or to be reduced to such an amount as they consider just and equitable.

(2) Sub-paragraphs (3) to (5) below apply where the Commissioners make a determination under sub-paragraph (1) above that the controller's liability is to be reduced (but not cancelled).

(3) In such a case they shall—

(*a*) serve the controller with notice stating the amount of the reduced liability, or

(*b*) take other reasonable steps with a view to bringing the reduced amount to the controller's attention.

(4) If the controller has already been served with notice of the amount determined under paragraph 52 above, or if other steps have already been taken to bring that amount to his attention—

(*a*) the Commissioners shall serve the notice mentioned in sub-paragraph (3)(*a*) above, or take the steps mentioned in sub-paragraph (3)(*b*) above, before the end of the period of thirty days beginning with the day immediately following that on which they make the determination under sub-paragraph (1) above, and

(*b*) the reduced amount shall be payable, or treated as having been payable, on or before the day on which the amount referred to in sub-paragraph (1)(*a*) above would have been payable apart from this paragraph.

(5) In a case where the controller has not been served with notice of the amount determined under paragraph 52 above, or no other steps have been taken to bring that amount to his attention, he shall be liable to pay the reduced amount only if—

(*a*) the notice mentioned in sub-paragraph (3)(*a*) above is served, or

(*b*) the other steps mentioned in sub-paragraph (3)(*b*) above are taken,

before the expiry of the period of two years beginning with the day immediately following that on which the Commissioners make the determination under sub-paragraph (1) above.

(6) Sub-paragraph (7) below applies where—

(*a*) the Commissioners make a determination under sub-paragraph (1) above that the controller's liability is to be cancelled, and

(*b*) the controller has already been served with notice of the amount determined under paragraph 52 above, or other steps have already been taken to bring that amount to his attention.

(7) In such a case the Commissioners shall—

(*a*) serve the controller with notice stating that the liability has been cancelled, or

(*b*) take other reasonable steps with a view to bringing the cancellation to the controller's attention,

before the end of the period of thirty days beginning with the day immediately following that on which they make the determination that the liability is to be cancelled.][1]

Amendments—[1] Pt VIII of this Schedule inserted by FA 2000 s 142(3), Sch 37, with effect for taxable disposals made after 27 July 2000.

[Adjustments

54—(1) This paragraph applies in any case where the liability of a licensed operator to pay landfill tax is adjusted otherwise than by—

(*a*) his being entitled to credit under regulations made under section 51 of this Act,

(*b*) his being notified of an amount assessed under section 50 of this Act, or

(*c*) the withdrawal or reduction of an assessment under section 50 of this Act which was notified to him.

(2) In such a case the Commissioners may determine that a controller of the whole or any part of a landfill site operated by the licensed operator—

(*a*) shall be liable to pay to the Commissioners such an amount as they consider just and equitable, or

(*b*) shall be entitled to an allowance of such an amount as they consider just and equitable.

(3) A controller is required to pay an amount determined under sub-paragraph (2)(*a*) above only if—

(*a*) a notice stating the amount is served on him, or

(*b*) other reasonable steps are taken with a view to bringing the amount of the liability to his attention,

before the end of the period of two years beginning with the day immediately following the relevant accounting day.

(4) The relevant accounting day is the last day of the accounting period of the operator within which the adjustment in question was taken into account.

(5) If a controller is required to pay an amount by virtue of sub-paragraph (3) above, it shall be paid before the end of the period of thirty days beginning with the day immediately following the notification day.

(6) The notification day is—

(*a*) in a case where notice is served on a controller as mentioned in sub-paragraph (3)(*a*) above, the day on which the notice is served, or

(*b*) in a case where other reasonable steps are taken as mentioned in sub-paragraph (3)(*b*) above, the day on which the last of those steps is taken.

(7) The Commissioners may determine in what manner a controller is to benefit from an allowance determined under sub-paragraph (2)(*b*) above.

(8) For the purposes of this paragraph a licensed operator is a person who is the operator of a landfill site by virtue of section 67(*a*), (*c*) or (*e*) of this Act.][1]

Amendments—[1] Pt VIII of this Schedule inserted by FA 2000 s 142(3), Sch 37, with effect for taxable disposals made after 27 July 2000.

[Amounts payable to be treated as tax

55 An amount which a controller is required to pay under paragraph 52, 53 or 54(2)(*a*) above or under paragraph 58 below shall be deemed to be an amount of tax due from him and shall be recoverable accordingly.][1]

Amendments—[1] Pt VIII of this Schedule inserted by FA 2000 s 142(3), Sch 37, with effect for taxable disposals made after 27 July 2000.

[Controller not carrying out taxable activity

56 A controller is not to be treated for the purposes of this Act as carrying out a taxable activity by reason only of any liability under this Part of this Schedule.][1]

Amendments—[1] Pt VIII of this Schedule inserted by FA 2000 s 142(3), Sch 37, with effect for taxable disposals made after 27 July 2000.

[Joint and several liability

57—(1) In any case where the condition in sub-paragraph (4), (5) or (6) below is satisfied, the controller and the operator shall be jointly and severally liable for the principal liability.

(2) But the amount which may be recovered from the controller in consequence of such liability shall not exceed the amount of the secondary liability.

(3) For the purposes of this paragraph—

(*a*) the principal liability is the amount referred to in sub-paragraph (4)(*a*), (5)(*a*) or (6)(*a*) below, as the case may be, and

(*b*) the secondary liability is the amount referred to in sub-paragraph (4)(*b*), (5)(*b*) or (6)(*b*) below, as the case may be.

(4) The condition in this sub-paragraph is satisfied if—

(*a*) the operator of a landfill site is liable under section 41 of this Act for landfill tax, and

(*b*) a controller is liable under paragraph 49 above, after taking account of any reduction under paragraph 50 above, to pay an amount of that tax.

(5) The condition in this sub-paragraph is satisfied if—

(*a*) the operator of a landfill site is notified of the amount of an assessment made under section 50 of this Act, and

(*b*) in consequence of a determination made under paragraph 52 above by the Commissioners in connection with the assessment, a controller is liable to pay an amount (after taking account of any reduction under paragraph 53 above).

(6) The condition in this sub-paragraph is satisfied if—

(*a*) the liability of the operator of a landfill site to pay landfill tax is adjusted in such a way that paragraph 54 above applies, and

(*b*) in consequence of a determination made under paragraph 54(2)(*a*) above by the Commissioners in connection with the adjustment, a controller is liable to pay an amount.][1]

Amendments—[1] Pt VIII of this Schedule inserted by FA 2000 s 142(3), Sch 37, with effect for taxable disposals made after 27 July 2000.

[Interest payable by a controller

58—(1) This paragraph applies where—

(*a*) the operator of a landfill site and the controller of the whole or a part of that site are by virtue of paragraph 57 above jointly and severally liable for an amount, and

(*b*) that amount carries interest by virtue of any provision of this Schedule.

(2) The controller and the operator shall be jointly and severally liable to pay the interest.

(3) But the amount which may be recovered from the controller in consequence of such liability shall not exceed the amount calculated in accordance with the following formula—

$$\frac{(I-[A+B])\times S}{P}$$

where—

I is the total amount of interest in question;

A is the amount of interest carried for the period which—

(*a*) begins with the first day of the period for which interest is carried, and

(*b*) ends with the day on which the controller becomes liable to pay the secondary liability;

B is the amount of interest carried for any day falling after that on which the secondary liability is met in full;

S is the amount of the secondary liability;

P is the amount of the principal liability.

In this paragraph secondary liability and principal liability have the same meaning as in paragraph 57 above.

(4) The controller is liable for an amount of interest only if—

(*a*) a notice stating the amount is served on him, or

(*b*) other reasonable steps are taken with a view to bringing the amount of the liability to his attention,

before the end of the period of two years beginning with the day immediately following the final day.

(5) The final day is the last day of the period for which the interest in question is carried.

(6) If the controller is required to pay an amount in accordance with this paragraph, it shall be paid before the end of the period of thirty days beginning with the day immediately following the notification day.

(7) The notification day is—

(*a*) in a case where notice is served on a controller as mentioned in sub-paragraph (4)(*a*) above, the day on which the notice is served, or

(*b*) in a case where other reasonable steps are taken as mentioned in sub-paragraph (4)(*b*) above, the day on which the last of those steps is taken.

(8) Where by virtue of sub-paragraph (2) above a controller is liable to pay interest which arises under paragraph 27 above, paragraph 28 above shall apply in relation to that interest as it applies to interest which a person is liable under paragraph 27 above to pay.][1]

Amendments—[1] Pt VIII of this Schedule inserted by FA 2000 s 142(3), Sch 37, with effect for taxable disposals made after 27 July 2000.

[Reviews and Appeals][2]

59 [Sections 54 to 56][2] of this Act shall apply to a decision of the Commissioners under this Part of this Schedule—

(*a*) that a person is a controller,

(*b*) that a person is liable under this Part of this Schedule to pay any amount (including a penalty under paragraph 60 below),

(*c*) that a person is not entitled under this Part of this Schedule to an allowance, or

(*d*) as to the amount of any liability or any allowance under this Part of this Schedule,

[as they apply][2] to the other decisions of the Commissioners specified in [section 54(1)][2].][1]

Amendments—[1] Pt VIII of this Schedule inserted by FA 2000 s 142(3), Sch 37, with effect for taxable disposals made after 27 July 2000.

[2] Heading substituted for the previous heading "Reviews"; words at beginning substituted for the words "Section 54"; words at end substituted in the first place for the words "as it applies" and in the second place for the words "subsection (1) of that section" by the Transfer of Tribunal Functions and Revenue and Customs Appeals Order, SI 2009/56 art 3, Sch 1 para 240(3), (4) with effect from 1 April 2009.

[Notice that person is, or is no longer, a controller

60—(1) This paragraph applies where—

(*a*) on the date when this paragraph comes into force, a person is a controller of the whole or a part of a landfill site, or

(*b*) after that date, a person becomes or ceases to be a controller of the whole or a part of a landfill site.

(2) The controller, and the operator of the landfill site in question, shall be under a duty to secure that notice which complies with the requirements of sub-paragraph (3) below appropriate to the case in question is given to the Commissioners.

(3) The requirements of this sub-paragraph are that the notice—

(*a*) states that a person is, has become or has ceased to be a controller,

(*b*) identifies that person and the site under his control or formerly under his control,

(*c*) states the date when he became or ceased to be the controller, and

(*d*) is given within the period of thirty days beginning with the day immediately following—

(i) the day when this paragraph comes into force, in a case falling within sub-paragraph (1)(*a*) above, or

(ii) the day when the person in question becomes or ceases to be the controller, in a case falling within sub-paragraph (1)(*b*) above.

(4) If a person fails to comply with sub-paragraph (2) above, he is liable to a penalty of £250.

(5) Paragraph 25 above applies to a penalty under sub-paragraph (4) above as it applies to a penalty under Part V of this Schedule.][1]

Amendments—[1] Pt VIII of this Schedule inserted by FA 2000 s 142(3), Sch 37, with effect for taxable disposals made after 27 July 2000.

[Extension of time limits where notice not served

61—(1) This paragraph applies where—

(*a*) a person is liable under paragraph 49 above to pay an amount of landfill tax or liable under paragraph 58 above to pay interest, or

(*b*) the Commissioners are entitled under paragraph 52, 53 or 54 above to determine an amount which a person is liable to pay.

(2) The reference to two years in paragraph 51(2), 52(2), 53(5), 54(3) or 58(4) above (as the case may be) shall be treated as a reference to twenty years if the requirement of paragraph 60(2) above to give notice to the Commissioners in relation to the person mentioned in sub-paragraph (1) above being or becoming a controller has not been complied with.][1]

Amendments—[1] Pt VIII of this Schedule inserted by FA 2000 s 142(3), Sch 37, with effect for taxable disposals made after 27 July 2000.

FINANCE ACT 1997

(1997 Chapter 16)

An act to grant certain duties, to alter other duties, and to amend the law relating to the National Debt and the Public Revenue, and to make further provision in connection with finance.

[19 March 1997]

PART IV

PAYMENTS AND OVERPAYMENTS IN RESPECT OF INDIRECT TAXES

Excise duties and other indirect taxes

50 Overpayments, interest, assessments, etc

(1) Schedule 5 to this Act (which makes provision in relation to excise duties, insurance premium tax and landfill tax which corresponds to that made for VAT by sections 44 to 48 above) shall have effect.

(2) . . .

Notes—Provisions omitted not relevant to landfill tax.

Enforcement of payment

51 Enforcement by distress

(1) The Commissioners may by regulations make provision—

(*a*) for authorising distress to be levied on the goods and chattels of any person refusing or neglecting to pay—

(i) any amount of relevant tax due from him, or

(ii) any amount recoverable as if it were relevant tax due from him;

(*b*) for the disposal of any goods or chattels on which distress is levied in pursuance of the regulations; and

(*c*) for the imposition and recovery of costs, charges, expenses and fees in connection with anything done under the regulations.

(2) The provision that may be contained in regulations under this section shall include, in particular—

(*a*) provision for the levying of distress, by any person authorised to do so under the regulations, on goods or chattels located at any place whatever (including on a public highway); and

(*b*) provision authorising distress to be levied at any such time of the day or night, and on any such day of the week, as may be specified or described in the regulations.

(3) Regulations under this section may—

(*a*) make different provision for different cases, and

(*b*) contain any such incidental, supplemental, consequential or transitional provision as the Commissioners think fit;

and the transitional provision that may be contained in regulations under this section shall include transitional provision in connection with the coming into force of the repeal by this Act of any other power by regulations to make provision for or in connection with the levying of distress.

(4) The power to make regulations under this section shall be exercisable by statutory instrument subject to annulment in pursuance of a resolution of the House of Commons.

(5) The following are relevant taxes for the purposes of this section, that is to say—

(*a*) –(*c*) . . .

(*d*) landfill tax;

(*e*), (*f*) . . .

(6) In this section "the Commissioners" means the Commissioners of Customs and Excise.

(7) Regulations made under this section shall not have effect in Scotland.

Note—Provisions omitted are not relevant to landfill tax.

Prospective amendments—Sub-s (A1) to be inserted by the Tribunals, Courts and Enforcement Act 2007 s 62(3), Sch 13 para 126(1), (2) with effect from a date to be appointed. Sub-s (A1) to be repealed by FA 2008 s 129(1), Sch 43 para 6 with effect from a date to be appointed. That sub-s to read as follows—

"(A1) The Commissioners may, in England and Wales, use the procedure in Schedule 12 to the Tribunals, Courts and Enforcement Act 2007 (taking control of goods) to recover any of these that a person refuses or neglects to pay—

(*a*) any amount of relevant tax due from him;

(*b*) any amount recoverable as if it were relevant tax due from him.".

In sub-s (1), words "not having effect in England and Wales or Scotland" to be inserted after word "regulations" by the Tribunals, Courts and Enforcement Act 2007, s 62(3), Sch 13 para 126(1), (3) with effect from a date to be appointed.

Sub-s (7) to be repealed by the Tribunals, Courts and Enforcement Act 2007 ss 62(3), 146, Sch 13 para 126(1), (4), Sch 23 Pt 3 with effect from a date to be appointed.

52 Enforcement by diligence

(1) Where any amount of relevant tax or any amount recoverable as if it were relevant tax is due and has not been paid, the sheriff, on an application by the Commissioners accompanied by a certificate by them—

(a) stating that none of the persons specified in the application has paid the amount due from him;

(b) stating that payment of the amount due from each such person has been demanded from him; and

(c) specifying the amount due from and unpaid by each such person,

shall grant a summary warrant in a form prescribed by Act of Sederunt authorising the recovery, by any of the diligences mentioned in subsection (2) below, of the amount remaining due and unpaid.

(2) The diligences referred to in subsection (1) above are—

[(a) an attachment][1]*;*

(b) an earnings arrestment;

(c) an arrestment and action of furthcoming or sale.

(3) Subject to subsection (4) below and without prejudice to [section 39(1) of the Debt Arrangement and Attachment (Scotland) Act 2002 (asp 17) (expenses of attachment)][2] *the sheriff officer's fees, together with the outlays necessarily incurred by him, in connection with the execution of a summary warrant shall be chargeable against the debtor.*

(4) No fees shall be chargeable by the sheriff officer against the debtor for collecting, and accounting to the Commissioners for, sums paid to him by the debtor in respect of the amount owing.

(5) The following are relevant taxes for the purposes of this section, that is to say—

(a) –(c) . . .

(d) landfill tax;

(e), (f) . . .

(6) In this section "the Commissioners" means the Commissioners of Customs and Excise.

(7) This section shall come into force on such day as the Commissioners of Customs and Excise may by order made by statutory instrument appoint, and different days may be appointed under this subsection for different purposes.

(8) This section extends only to Scotland.[3]

Notes—Provisions omitted are not relevant to landfill tax. The appointed day under sub-s (7) above is 1 July 1997 (see SI 1997/1432).

Amendments—[1] Sub-s (2)(*a*) substituted by the Debt Arrangement and Attachment (Scotland) Act 2002, s 61, Sch 3, Pt 1, para 26(*a*) with effect from 30 December 2002; see the Debt Arrangement and Attachment (Scotland) Act 2002, s 64(2).

[2] Words in sub-s 3 substituted by the Debt Arrangement and Attachment (Scotland) Act 2002, s 61, Sch 3, Pt 1, para 26(*b*) with effect from 30 December 2002; see the Debt Arrangement and Attachment (Scotland) Act 2002, s 64(2).

[3] This section repealed by FA 2008 s 129(2), Sch 43 para 15 with effect from 23 November 2009 (by virtue of SI 2009/3024 art 3). Note that if before the commencement date a warrant has been granted under this section, that warrant shall continue to have effect according to the provisions under which it was granted (SI 2009/3024 art 4(1)(c)).

53 Amendments consequential on sections 51 and 52

. . .

(8) In paragraph 24(1)(*a*) of Schedule 5 to the Finance Act 1996 (walking possession agreements in connection with enforcement of landfill tax), for "paragraph 13(1) above" there shall be substituted "section 51 of the Finance Act 1997 (enforcement by distress)".

(9) This section shall come into force on such day as the Commissioners of Customs and Excise may by order made by statutory instrument appoint, and different days may be appointed under this subsection for different purposes.

Notes—Words omitted not relevant for the purposes of landfill tax. The appointed day under sub-s (9) above is 1 July 1997 (see SI 1997/1432).

SCHEDULES

SCHEDULE 5

INDIRECT TAXES: OVERPAYMENTS ETC

Section 50

PART I

UNJUST ENRICHMENT

Application of Part I

1—(1) This Part of this Schedule has effect for the purposes of the following provisions (which make it a defence to a claim for repayment that the repayment would unjustly enrich the claimant), namely—

(*a*) section 137A(3) of the Customs and Excise Management Act 1979 (excise duties);

(*b*) paragraph 8(3) of Schedule 7 to the Finance Act 1994 (insurance premium tax); and

(*c*) paragraph 14(3) of Schedule 5 to the Finance Act 1996 (landfill tax).

(2) Those provisions are referred to in this Part of this Schedule as unjust enrichment provisions.

(3) In this Part of this Schedule—

"the Commissioners" means the Commissioners of Customs and Excise;

"relevant repayment provision" means—

(*a*) section 137A of the Customs and Excise Management Act 1979 (recovery of overpaid excise duty);

(*b*) paragraph 8 of Schedule 7 to the Finance Act 1994 (recovery of overpaid insurance premium tax); or

(*c*) paragraph 14 of Schedule 5 to the Finance Act 1996 (recovery of overpaid landfill tax);

"relevant tax" means any duty of excise, insurance premium tax or landfill tax; and

"subordinate legislation" has the same meaning as in the Interpretation Act 1978.

Disregard of business losses

2—(1) This paragraph applies where—

(*a*) there is an amount paid by way of relevant tax which (apart from an unjust enrichment provision) would fall to be repaid under a relevant repayment provision to any person ("the taxpayer"), and

(*b*) the whole or a part of the cost of the payment of that amount to the Commissioners has, for practical purposes, been borne by a person other than the taxpayer.

(2) Where, in a case to which this paragraph applies, loss or damage has been or may be incurred by the taxpayer as a result of mistaken assumptions made in his case about the operation of any provisions relating to a relevant tax, that loss or damage shall be disregarded, except to the extent of the quantified amount, in the making of any determination—

(*a*) of whether or to what extent the repayment of an amount to the taxpayer would enrich him; or

(*b*) of whether or to what extent any enrichment of the taxpayer would be unjust.

(3) In sub-paragraph (2) above "the quantified amount" means the amount (if any) which is shown by the taxpayer to constitute the amount that would appropriately compensate him for loss or damage shown by him to have resulted, for any business carried on by him, from the making of the mistaken assumptions.

(4) The reference in sub-paragraph (2) above to provisions relating to a relevant tax is a reference to any provisions of—

(*a*) any enactment, subordinate legislation or Community legislation (whether or not still in force) which relates to that tax or to any matter connected with it; or

(*b*) any notice published by the Commissioners under or for the purposes of any such enactment or subordinate legislation.

(5) This paragraph has effect for the purposes of making any repayment on or after the day on which this Act is passed, even if the claim for that repayment was made before that day.

Reimbursement arrangements

3—(1) The Commissioners may by regulations make provision for reimbursement arrangements made by any person to be disregarded for the purposes of any or all of the unjust enrichment provisions except where the arrangements—

(*a*) contain such provision as may be required by the regulations; and

(*b*) are supported by such undertakings to comply with the provisions of the arrangements as may be required by the regulations to be given to the Commissioners.

(2) In this paragraph "reimbursement arrangements" means any arrangements for the purposes of a claim under a relevant repayment provision which—

(*a*) are made by any person for the purpose of securing that he is not unjustly enriched by the repayment of any amount in pursuance of the claim; and

(*b*) provide for the reimbursement of persons who have for practical purposes borne the whole or any part of the cost of the original payment of that amount to the Commissioners.

(3) Without prejudice to the generality of sub-paragraph (1) above, the provision that may be required by regulations under this paragraph to be contained in reimbursement arrangements includes—

(*a*) provision requiring a reimbursement for which the arrangements provide to be made within such period after the repayment to which it relates as may be specified in the regulations;

(*b*) provision for the repayment of amounts to the Commissioners where those amounts are not reimbursed in accordance with the arrangements;

(*c*) provision requiring interest paid by the Commissioners on any amount repaid by them to be treated in the same way as that amount for the purposes of any requirement under the arrangements to make reimbursement or to repay the Commissioners;

(*d*) provision requiring such records relating to the carrying out of the arrangements as may be described in the regulations to be kept and produced to the Commissioners, or to an officer of theirs.

(4) Regulations under this paragraph may impose obligations on such persons as may be specified in the regulations—

(*a*) to make the repayments to the Commissioners that they are required to make in pursuance of any provisions contained in any reimbursement arrangements by virtue of sub-paragraph (3)(*b*) or (*c*) above;

(*b*) to comply with any requirements contained in any such arrangements by virtue of sub-paragraph (3)(*d*) above.

(5) Regulations under this paragraph may make provision for the form and manner in which, and the times at which, undertakings are to be given to the Commissioners in accordance with the regulations; and any such provision may allow for those matters to be determined by the Commissioners in accordance with the regulations.

(6) Regulations under this paragraph may—

(*a*) contain any such incidental, supplementary, consequential or transitional provision as appears to the Commissioners to be necessary or expedient; and

(*b*) make different provision for different circumstances.

(7) Regulations under this paragraph may have effect (irrespective of when the claim for repayment was made) for the purposes of the making of any repayment by the Commissioners after the time when the regulations are made; and, accordingly, such regulations may apply to arrangements made before that time.

(8) Regulations under this paragraph shall be made by statutory instrument subject to annulment in pursuance of a resolution of the House of Commons.

Contravention of requirement to repay Commissioners

4—(1) Where any obligation is imposed by regulations made by virtue of paragraph 3(4) above, a contravention or failure to comply with that obligation shall, to the extent that it relates to amounts repaid under section 137A of the Customs and Excise Management Act 1979, attract a penalty under section 9 of the Finance Act 1994 (penalties in connection with excise duties).

(2) For the purposes of Schedule 7 to the Finance Act 1994 (insurance premium tax), a contravention or failure to comply with an obligation imposed by regulations made by virtue of paragraph 3(4) above shall be deemed, to the extent that it relates to amounts repaid under paragraph 8 of that Schedule (recovery of overpaid insurance premium tax), to be a failure to comply with a requirement falling within paragraph 17(1)(*c*) of that Schedule (breach of regulations).

(3) Paragraph 23 of Schedule 5 to the Finance Act 1996 (power to provide for penalty) shall have effect as if an obligation imposed by regulations made by virtue of paragraph 3(4) above were, to the extent that it relates to amounts repaid under paragraph 14 of that Schedule (recovery of overpaid landfill tax), a requirement imposed by regulations under Part III of that Act; and the provisions of that Schedule in relation to penalties under Part V of that Schedule shall have effect accordingly.

PART II
TIME LIMITS

Repayments

5—(1), (2) . . .

(3) (*substitutes* FA 1996 Sch 5 para 14(4)).

Notes—Omitted provisions not relevant to landfill tax.

Assessments

6—(1) In each of the enactments specified in sub-paragraph (2) below (which provide for the time limits applying to the making of assessments), for the words "six years", wherever they occur, there shall be substituted the words "three years".

(2) Those enactments are—

(*a*) (*amends* FA 1994, s 12(4)(*a*), (5)].

(*b*) (*amended* FA 1994 Sch 7 para 26(1), (4); *repealed* by FA 2009 s 99(1), Sch 51 para 43(*b*)).

(*c*) (*amended* FA 1996 Sch 5 para 33(1), (4) *repealed* by FA 2009 s 99(1), Sch 51 para 43(*b*)).

PART III
INTEREST

Interest on overpaid landfill tax

11—(1) Paragraph 29 of Schedule 5 to the Finance Act 1996 (interest payable by the Commissioners in connection with landfill tax) shall have effect, and be deemed always to have had effect, with the amendments for which this paragraph provides.

(2) (*inserts* FA 1996 Sch 5 para 29(1A)).

(3), (4) (*substitute* FA 1996 Sch 5 para 29(8), (9)).

12—(1) (*substitutes* FA 1996 Sch 5 para 29(4)–(6)).

(2) Sub-paragraph (1) above shall have effect for the purposes of determining whether any period beginning on or after the day on which this Act is passed is left out of account.

PART IV
SET-OFF INVOLVING LANDFILL TAX

13 (*inserts* FA 1996 Sch 5 para 42(4A), 43(4A)).

PART V
RECOVERY OF EXCESS PAYMENTS BY THE COMMISSIONERS

Assessment for excessive repayment

14—(1) Where—

(*a*) any amount has been paid at any time to any person by way of a repayment under a relevant repayment provision, and

(*b*) the amount paid exceeded the amount which the Commissioners were liable at that time to repay to that person,

the Commissioners may, to the best of their judgement, assess the excess paid to that person and notify it to him.

(2) Where any person is liable to pay any amount to the Commissioners in pursuance of an obligation imposed by virtue of paragraph 3(4)(*a*) above, the Commissioners may, to the best of their judgement, assess the amount due from that person and notify it to him.

(3) In this paragraph "relevant repayment provision" means—

(*a*) section 137A of the Customs and Excise Management Act 1979 (recovery of overpaid excise duty);

(*b*) paragraph 8 of Schedule 7 to the Finance Act 1994 (recovery of overpaid insurance premium tax); . . . [1]

(*c*) paragraph 14 of Schedule 5 to the Finance Act 1996 (recovery of overpaid landfill tax) [or

(*d*) Part I of Schedule 3 to the Finance Act 2001 (payments made and rebates disallowed in error)][1]

Amendments—[1] Word in sub-para (3)(*b*) repealed, and sub-para (3)(*d*) and word preceding inserted, by FA 2001 ss 15, 110, Sch 3 para 19(1), (2), Sch 33 Pt 1(4) with effect from 1 November 2001 (by virtue of SI 2001/3300).

Assessment for overpayments of interest

15—(1) Where—

(*a*) any amount has been paid to any person by way of interest under a relevant interest provision, but

(*b*) that person was not entitled to that amount under that provision,

the Commissioners may, to the best of their judgement, assess the amount so paid to which that person was not entitled and notify it to him.

(2) In this paragraph "relevant interest provision" means—

(*a*) . . . [1]

(*b*) paragraph 22 of Schedule 7 to that Act (interest payable by the Commissioners on overpayments etc of insurance premium tax); . . . [1]

(*c*) paragraph 29 of Schedule 5 to the Finance Act 1996 (interest payable by the Commissioners on overpayments etc of landfill tax) [or

(*d*) Part II of Schedule 3 to the Finance Act 2001 (interest)][1]

Amendments—[1] Sub-para (2)(*a*) repealed, word in sub-para (2)(*b*) repealed, and sub-para (2)(*d*) and word preceding inserted, by FA 2001 ss 15, 110, Sch 3 para 19(1), (3), Sch 33 Pt 1(4) with effect from 1 November 2001 (by virtue of SI 2001/3300).

Assessments under paragraphs 14 and 15

16—(1) An assessment under paragraph 14 or 15 above shall not be made more than two years after the time when evidence of facts sufficient in the opinion of the Commissioners to justify the making of the assessment comes to the knowledge of the Commissioners.

(2) Where an amount has been assessed and notified to any person under paragraph 14 or 15 above, it shall be recoverable (subject to any provision having effect in accordance with paragraph 19 below) as if it were relevant tax due from him.

(3) Sub-paragraph (2) above does not have effect if, or to the extent that, the assessment in question has been withdrawn or reduced.

Interest on amounts assessed

17—(1) Where an assessment is made under paragraph 14 or 15 above, the whole of the amount assessed shall carry interest at the rate applicable under section 197 of the Finance Act 1996 from the date on which the assessment is notified until payment.

(2) Where any person is liable to interest under sub-paragraph (1) above the Commissioners may assess the amount due by way of interest and notify it to him.

(3) Without prejudice to the power to make assessments under this paragraph for later periods, the interest to which an assessment under this paragraph may relate shall be confined to interest for a period of no more than two years ending with the time when the assessment under this paragraph is made.

(4) Interest under this paragraph shall be paid without any deduction of income tax.

(5) A notice of assessment under this paragraph shall specify a date, being not later than the date of the notice, to which the amount of interest is calculated; and, if the interest continues to accrue after that date, a further assessment or assessments may be made under this paragraph in respect of amounts which so accrue.

(6) If, within such period as may be notified by the Commissioners to the person liable for interest under sub-paragraph (1) above, the amount referred to in that sub-paragraph is paid, it shall be treated for the purposes of that sub-paragraph as paid on the date specified as mentioned in sub-paragraph (5) above.

(7) Where an amount has been assessed and notified to any person under this paragraph it shall be recoverable as if it were relevant tax due from him.

(8) Sub-paragraph (7) above does not have effect if, or to the extent that, the assessment in question has been withdrawn or reduced.

Supplementary assessments

18 If it appears to the Commissioners that the amount which ought to have been assessed in an assessment under paragraph 14, 15 or 17 above exceeds the amount which was so assessed, then—

(*a*) under the same paragraph as that assessment was made, and

(*b*) on or before the last day on which that assessment could have been made,

the Commissioners may make a supplementary assessment of the amount of the excess and shall notify the person concerned accordingly.

Review of decisions and appeals

19—(1), (2) . . .

(3) Sections 54 to 56 of the Finance Act 1996 (review and appeal in the case of landfill tax) shall have effect in relation to any decision which—

(*a*) is contained in an assessment under paragraph 14, 15 or 17 above,

(*b*) is a decision about whether any amount is due to the Commissioners or about how much is due, and

(*c*) is made in a case in which the relevant repayment provision is paragraph 14 of Schedule 5 to that Act or the relevant interest provision is paragraph 29 of that Schedule,

as if that decision were a decision to which section 54 of that Act applies.

Notes—Provisions omitted not relevant to landfill tax.

Interpretation of Part V

20—(1) In this Part of this Schedule "the Commissioners" means the Commissioners of Customs and Excise.

(2) In this Part of this Schedule "relevant tax", in relation to any assessment, means—

(*a*) a duty of excise if the assessment relates to—

(i) a repayment of an amount paid by way of such a duty,

(ii) an overpayment of interest under [Part II of Schedule 3 to the Finance Act 2001][1], or

(iii) interest on an amount specified in an assessment in relation to which the relevant tax is a duty of excise;

(*b*) insurance premium tax if the assessment relates to—

(i) a repayment of an amount paid by way of such tax,

(ii) an overpayment of interest under paragraph 22 of Schedule 7 to the Finance Act 1994, or

(iii) interest on an amount specified in an assessment in relation to which the relevant tax is insurance premium tax;

and

(*c*) landfill tax if the assessment relates to—

(i) a repayment of an amount paid by way of such tax,

(ii) an overpayment of interest under paragraph 29 of Schedule 5 to the Finance Act 1996, or

(iii) interest on an amount specified in an assessment in relation to which the relevant tax is landfill tax.

(3) For the purposes of this Part of this Schedule notification to a personal representative, trustee in bankruptcy, interim or permanent trustee, receiver, liquidator or person otherwise acting in a representative capacity in relation to another shall be treated as notification to the person in relation to whom he so acts.

Amendments—[1] Words in sub-para (2)(*a*)(ii) substituted by FA 2001 s 15, Sch 3 para 19(1), (5) with effect from 1 November 2001 (by virtue of SI 2001/3300).

Consequential amendment

21 (*inserts* FA 1996 s 197(2)(*e*)).

SCHEDULE 18

REPEALS

Section 113

PART V

INDIRECT TAXES

(2) (*repeals* FA 1996 Sch 5 para 13).

FINANCE ACT 1998

(1998 Chapter 36)

An Act to grant certain duties, to alter other duties, and to amend the law relating to the National Debt and the Public Revenue, and to make further provision in connection with Finance.

[31 July 1998]

PART V

OTHER TAXES

Landfill tax

148 Provisional collection of landfill tax

(1) (*amends* PCTA 1968 s 1(1)).

(2)–(4) . . . [1]

Amendments—[1] Sub-ss (2)–(4) repealed by FA 2001 s 110, Sch 33 Pt 3(3) with effect from 11 May 2001.

HUMAN RIGHTS ACT 1998

(1998 Chapter 42)

An Act to give further effect to rights and freedoms guaranteed under the European Convention on Human Rights; to make provision with respect to holders of certain judicial offices who become judges of the European Court of Human Rights; and for connected purposes.

[9th November 1998]

Note—Please see VAT Statutes *ante* for the text of this Act.

FINANCE ACT 2000

(2000 Chapter 17)

An act to grant certain duties, to alter other duties, and to amend the law relating to the National Debt and the Public Revenue, and to make further provision in connection with finance.

[28 July 2000]

PART V

OTHER TAXES

Landfill tax

140 Rate

(1) (*spent*).

(2) This section has effect in relation to taxable disposals made, or treated as made, on or after 1st April 2000.

141 Disposals which are not taxable

(1) In section 62 of the Finance Act 1996 (regulations about taxable disposals) amend subsection (7) (limit on power to make regulations providing that a disposal is not taxable) as follows.

(2) (substitutes FA 1996 s 62(7)(*a*)).

(3) (*amends FA 1996 s 62(7)(b)*).

142 Secondary liability

(1) (*amends FA 1996 s 60*).

(2) (*amends sidenote to FA 1986 s 60*).

(3) (*adds FA 1986 Sch 5 Part VIII*).

(4) Subsection (3) has effect in relation to taxable disposals made on or after the day on which this Act is passed.

SCHEDULES

SCHEDULE 37

LANDFILL TAX: NEW PART VIII OF SCHEDULE 5 TO THE FINANCE ACT 1996

Section 142

Note—This Schedule sets out FA 1996 Sch 5 Part VIII inserted by FA 2000 s 142(3).

FINANCE ACT 2001

(2001 Chapter 9)

An Act to grant certain duties, to alter other duties, and to amend the law relating to the National Debt and the Public Revenue, and to make further provision in connection with Finance.

[11 May 2001]

PART 4

OTHER TAXES

Landfill tax

104 Landfill tax: rate

(*spent*)

PART 5

MISCELLANEOUS AND SUPPLEMENTARY PROVISIONS

Supplementary

. . .

Landfill Tax

110 Repeals and revocations

(1) The enactments mentioned in Schedule 33 to this Act (which include provisions that are spent or of no practical utility) are repealed or revoked to the extent specified.

(2) The repeals and revocations specified in that Schedule have effect subject to the commencement provisions and savings contained or referred to in the notes set out in that Schedule.

SCHEDULES

SCHEDULE 33

REPEALS

Section 110

PART 3

OTHER TAXES

(3) LANDFILL TAX AND CLIMATE CHANGE LEVY

Note—As the repeals are already in force, this table has been omitted.

FINANCE ACT 2005

(2005 Chapter 7)

An Act to Grant certain duties, to alter other duties, and to amend the law relating to the National Debt and the Public Revenue, and to make further provision in connection with finance.

[7 April 2005]

PART 4

OTHER TAXES

Landfill tax

99 Rate of landfill tax

(1) *(spent)*

(2) The amendments made by this section have effect in relation to taxable disposals made, or treated as made, on or after 1st April 2005.

FINANCE ACT 2006

(2006 Chapter 25)

An Act to Grant certain duties, to alter other duties, and to amend the law relating to the National Debt and the Public Revenue, and to make further provision in connection with finance.

[19 July 2006]

PART 9

MISCELLANEOUS PROVISIONS

Landfill tax

170 Rate of landfill tax

(1) *(spent)*

(2) The amendments made by this section have effect in relation to taxable disposals made, or treated as made, on or after 1st April 2006.

FINANCE ACT 2007

(2007 Chapter 11)

PART 1

CHARGES, RATES, THRESHOLDS ETC

Environment

15 Rates of landfill tax

(1) *(spent)*.

(2) . . .

(3) The amendments made by subsection (2) have effect in relation to disposals made (or treated as made) on or after 1st April 2007 (but before 1st April 2008).

(4) (*amends* FA 1996 s 42(1)(*a*))

(5) The amendments made by subsection (4) come into force on 1st April 2008 and have effect in relation to disposals made (or treated as made) on or after that date.

PART 2

ENVIRONMENT

Other measures

24 Landfill tax: bodies concerned with the environment

(1) (*inserts* FA 1996 s 53(4)(*ca*))

(2) The amendment made by subsection (1) is deemed to have come into force on 22nd March 2007.

SCHEDULES

SCHEDULE 24

PENALTIES FOR ERRORS

Note—Please see *VAT Statutes* ante for the text of this Schedule.

FINANCE ACT 2008

(2008 Chapter 9)

An Act to Grant certain duties, to alter other duties, and to amend the law relating to the National Debt and the Public Revenue, and to make further provision in connection with finance.

[21 July 2008]

PART 1

CHARGES, RATES, ALLOWANCES, RELIEFS ETC

Environmental taxes and duties

18 Standard rate of landfill tax

(1) (*spent*)

(2) The amendments made by subsection (1) come into force on 1 April 2009 and have effect in relation to disposals made (or treated as made) on or after that date.

PART 7

ADMINISTRATION

Press releases—HMRC Guidance Note, 18 July 2008 (HMRC set-off across taxes following Finance Bill 2008).

CHAPTER 1

INFORMATION ETC

New information etc powers

114 Computer records etc

Note—Please see *VAT Statutes* ante for the text of this Section.

CHAPTER 3

PENALTIES

122 Penalties for errors

Note—Please see *VAT Statutes* ante for the text of this Section.

123 Penalties for failure to notify etc

Note—Please see *VAT Statutes* ante for the text of this Section.

CHAPTER 4

APPEALS ETC

Reviews and appeals etc: general

124 HMRC decisions etc: reviews and appeals

Note—Please see *VAT Statutes* ante for the text of this Section.

CHAPTER 5
PAYMENT AND ENFORCEMENT

Taking control of goods etc

127 Enforcement by taking control of goods: England and Wales

Note—Please see *VAT Statutes* ante for the text of this Section.

128 Summary warrant: Scotland

Note—Please see *VAT Statutes* ante for the text of this Section.

129 Consequential provision and commencement

Note—Please see *VAT Statutes* ante for the text of this Section.

Set off

130 Set-off: England and Wales and Northern Ireland

Note—Please see *VAT Statutes* ante for the text of this Section.

131 No set-off where insolvency procedure has been applied

Note—Please see *VAT Statutes* ante for the text of this Section.

133 Set-off etc where right to be paid a sum has been transferred

Note—Please see *VAT Statutes* ante for the text of this Section.

Other measures

135 Interest on unpaid tax in case of disaster etc of national significance

Note—Please see *VAT Statutes* ante for the text of this Section.

136 Fee for payment

Note—Please see *VAT Statutes* ante for the text of this Section.

Supplementary

139 Interpretation of Chapter

Note—Please see *VAT Statutes* ante for the text of this Section.

PART 8
MISCELLANEOUS

Climate change levy and landfill tax

151 Landfill tax credit: withdrawing approval of environmental bodies

(1) Part 3 of FA 1996 (landfill tax) is amended as follows.
(2) (*amends* FA 1996 s 53(4)(*d*)).
(3) (*inserts* FA 1996 s 54(1)(*ca*)).
(4) The amendments made by this section are treated as having come into force on 19 March 2008.

Payments from Exchequer accounts

158 Power of Treasury to make payments

Note—Please see *VAT Statutes* ante for the text of this Section.

159 Payments from certain Exchequer accounts: mechanism

Note—Please see *VAT Statutes* ante for the text of this Section.

Other matters

160 Power to give statutory effect to concessions

Note—Please see *VAT Statutes* ante for the text of this Section.

PART 9
FINAL PROVISIONS

165 Interpretation

Note—Please see *VAT Statutes* ante for the text of this Section.

166 Short title

Note—Please see *VAT Statutes* ante for the text of this Section.

SCHEDULES

SCHEDULE 36
INFORMATION AND INSPECTION POWERS

Section 113

Note—Please see *VAT Statutes* ante for the text of this Section.

SCHEDULE 41

PENALTIES: FAILURE TO NOTIFY AND CERTAIN VAT AND EXCISE WRONGDOING

Section 123

Note—Please see *VAT Statutes* ante for the text of this Section.

FINANCE ACT 2009

(2009 Chapter 10)

An Act to Grant certain duties, to alter other duties, and to amend the law relating to the National Debt and the Public Revenue, and to make further provision in connection with finance.

[21 July 2009]

PART 1

PART 1 CHARGES, RATES, ALLOWANCES, ETC

Other environmental taxes and duties

18 Standard rate of landfill tax

(1) In section 42(1)(*a*) and (2) of FA 1996 (amount of landfill tax), for "£40" substitute "£48".

(2) The amendments made by subsection (1) have effect in relation to disposals made (or treated as made) on or after 1 April 2010.

PART 7

ADMINISTRATION

Standards and values

92 HMRC Charter

Note—Please see *VAT Statutes* ante for the text of this Section.

93 Duties of senior accounting officers of qualifying companies

Note—Please see *VAT Statutes* ante for the text of this Section.

94 Publishing details of deliberate tax defaulters

Note—Please see *VAT Statutes* ante for the text of this Section.

Information etc

95 Amendment of information and inspection powers

Note—Please see *VAT Statutes* ante for the text of this Section.

96 Extension of information and inspection powers to further taxes

(1) (*substitutes* FA 2008 Sch 36 para 63(1)(*e*)–(*m*))

(2) Schedule 48 contains further amendments of that Schedule.

(3) The amendments made by this section and Schedule 48 come into force on such day as the Treasury may by order appoint.

(4) An order under subsection (3) may—

(*a*) appoint different days for different purposes, and

(*b*) contain transitional provision and savings.

(5) The Treasury may by order make any incidental, supplemental, consequential, transitional or transitory provision or saving which appears appropriate in consequence of, or otherwise in connection with, this section and Schedule 48.

(6) An order under subsection (5) may—

(*a*) make different provision for different purposes, and

(*b*) make provision amending, repealing or revoking an enactment or instrument (whenever passed or made).

(7) An order under this section is to be made by statutory instrument.

(8) A statutory instrument containing an order under subsection (5) is subject to annulment in pursuance of a resolution of the House of Commons.

Order—Finance Act 2009, Section 96 and Schedule 48 (Appointed Day, Savings and Consequential Amendments) Order 2009, SI 2009/3054 (appointed day is 1 April 2010).

97 Powers to obtain contact details for debtors

Note—Please see *VAT Statutes* ante for the text of this Section.

98 Record-keeping

(1) Schedule 50 contains provision about obligations to keep records.

(2) The amendments made by that Schedule come into force on such day as the Treasury may by order made by statutory instrument appoint.

Order—Finance Act 2009, Schedule 50 (Record-keeping) (Appointed Day) Order 2010 (appoints 1 April 2010 as the date for the Sch 50 amendments to come into force).

Assessments, claims etc

99 Time limits for assessments, claims etc

(1) Schedule 51 contains provision about time limits for assessments, claims etc

(2) The amendments made by that Schedule come into force on such day as the Treasury may by order made by statutory instrument appoint.

(3) An order under subsection (2)—

(*a*) may make different provision for different purposes, and

(*b*) may include transitional provision and savings.

Order—Finance Act 2009, Schedule 51 (Time Limits for Assessments, Claims, etc) (Appointed Days and Transitional Provisions) Order 2010 (1 April 2010 is appointed as the date for Sch 51 paras 1–4, 27–43 to come into force).

Interest

101 Late payment interest on sums due to HMRC

Note—Please see *VAT Statutes* ante for the text of this Section.

102 Repayment interest on sums to be paid by HMRC

Note—Please see *VAT Statutes* ante for the text of this Section.

103 Rates of interest

Note—Please see *VAT Statutes* ante for the text of this Section.

104 Supplementary

Note—Please see *VAT Statutes* ante for the text of this Section.

108 Suspension of penalties during currency of agreement for deferred payment

Note—Please see *VAT Statutes* ante for the text of this Section.

109 Miscellaneous amendments

Note—Please see *VAT Statutes* ante for the text of this Section.

PART 8

MISCELLANEOUS

Other environmental taxes and duties

119 Landfill tax: prescribed landfill site activities

Schedule 60 contains provision about charging landfill tax on prescribed activities at landfill sites.

SCHEDULES

SCHEDULE 46

DUTIES OF SENIOR ACCOUNTING OFFICERS OF QUALIFYING COMPANIES

Section 93

Note—Please see *VAT Statutes* ante for the text of this Schedule.

SCHEDULE 47

AMENDMENT OF INFORMATION AND INSPECTION POWERS

Section 95

Note—Please see *VAT Statutes* ante for the text of this Schedule.

SCHEDULE 48

EXTENSION OF INFORMATION AND INSPECTION POWERS

Section 96

Note—Please see *VAT Statutes* ante for the text of this Schedule.

SCHEDULE 49

POWERS TO OBTAIN CONTACT DETAILS FOR DEBTORS

ection 97

Note—Please see *VAT Statutes* ante for the text of this Schedule.

SCHEDULE 50

RECORD-KEEPING

Section 98

Order—Finance Act 2009, Schedule 50 (Record-keeping) (Appointed Day) Order, SI 2010/815 (appoints 1 April 2010 as the date for the Sch 50 amendments to come into force).

Landfill tax

21 (*substitutes* FA 1996 Sch 5 para 2(4))

SCHEDULE 51

TIME LIMITS FOR ASSESSMENTS, CLAIMS ETC

Section 99

Order—Finance Act 2009, Schedule 51 (Time Limits for Assessments, Claims, etc) (Appointed Days and Transitional Provisions) Order, SI 2010/867 (1 April 2010 is appointed as the date for Sch 51 paras 1–4, 27–43 to come into force).

Landfill tax

37 Schedule 5 to FA 1996 (landfill tax) is amended as follows.

38 (*amends* FA 1996 Sch 5 para 14(4))

39 (*amends* FA 1996 Sch 5 para 29(8))

40—(*amends*) FA 1996 Sch 5 para 33)

SCHEDULE 53

LATE PAYMENT INTEREST

Section 101

Note—Please see *VAT Statutes* ante for the text of this Schedule.

SCHEDULE 54

REPAYMENT INTEREST

Section 102

Note—Please see *VAT Statutes* ante for the text of this Schedule.

SCHEDULE 57

AMENDMENTS RELATING TO PENALTIES

Section 109

Note—Please see *VAT Statutes* ante for the text of this Schedule.

SCHEDULE 60

LANDFILL TAX: PRESCRIBED LANDFILL SITE ACTIVITIES

Section 119

Introduction

1 Part 3 of FA 1996 (landfill tax) is amended as follows.

Prescribed landfill site activities to be treated as disposals

2 (*inserts* FA 1996 s 65A)

3 (*inserts* FA 1996 s 71(7)(*ca*), (*cb*))

Material temporarily held

4 Omit section 62 (taxable disposals: regulations about material temporarily held at a landfill site).

Material at landfill sites

5 Part 1 of Schedule 5 (information) is amended as follows.

6 For the heading before paragraph 1 substitute—*"Information: general"*

7 (*inserts* FA 1995 Sch 5 para 1A)

8 For the heading before paragraph 2 substitute—*"Records: registrable persons"*

9 (*inserts* FA 1995 Sch 5 para 2A)

Site restoration

10 Omit section 43C (site restoration).

11 (*inserts* FA 1995 Sch 5 para 1B)

Landfill tax returns

12 In section 49(*b*) (accounting for tax and time for payment), omit "as may be prescribed".

Commencement and savings

13—(1) The repeal made by paragraph 10 comes into force on 1 September 2009.
(2) The amendment made by paragraph 11 (information about site restoration) has effect in relation to restoration of landfill sites commencing on or after 1 September 2009.
(3) The repeal of section 62 made by paragraph 4, and the repeal in section 49 made by paragraph 12—

(*a*) do not affect any regulations made under the repealed provisions before the passing of this Act, and

(*b*) do not prevent the powers conferred by the repealed provisions from being used after the passing of this Act to revoke any regulations made under the powers before that time.

FINANCE ACT 2010

(2010 Chapter 13)

[8 April 2010]

PART 1
CHARGES, RATES ETC

Other environmental taxes

15 Standard rate of landfill tax

(1) In section 42(1) and (2) of FA 1996 (standard amount of landfill tax), for "£48" substitute "£56".
(2) The amendments made by subsection (1) have effect in relation to disposals made (or treated as made) on or after 1 April 2011.

Landfill tax
Statutory Instruments

Contents

1996/1527

LANDFILL TAX REGULATIONS 1996

Made by the Commissioners of Customs and Excise under FA 1996 ss 47(9), 48(1), (2), 49, 51(1)–(6), 52(1)–(3), 53(1)–(4), 58(1), (4)–(6), 61(2), 62(1)–(3), (5), (6), 68(1)–(6) and Sch 5 paras 2(1)–(3), 13(1), (6), 14(5), 20(3), 23(1), 42(1)–(5), 43(1)–(5)

Made . . . . *12 June 1996*
Laid before the House of Commons . . . . *12 June 1996*
Coming into force . . . . *1 August 1996*

ARRANGEMENT OF REGULATIONS

PART I
PRELIMINARY

Citation and commencement

1 These Regulations may be cited as the Landfill Tax Regulations 1996 and shall come into force on 1st August 1996.

Interpretation

2—(1) In these Regulations—

"accounting period" means—

(*a*) in the case of a registered person, each period of three months ending on the dates notified to him by the Commissioners, whether by means of a registration certificate issued by them or otherwise;

(*b*) in the case of a registrable person who is not registered, each quarter; or

(*c*) in the case of any registrable person, such other period in relation to which he is required by or under regulation 11 to make a return;

and, in every case, the first accounting period of a registrable person shall begin on the effective date of registration;

"the Act" means the Finance Act 1996;

"Collector" means a Collector, Deputy Collector or Assistant Collector of Customs and Excise;

"credit", except where the context otherwise requires, means credit which a person is entitled to claim under Part IV of these Regulations;

"disposal" means a landfill disposal (which expression has the meaning given in section 70(2) of the Act) made on or after 1st October 1996 and "disposed of " shall be construed accordingly;

"effective date of registration" means the date determined in accordance with section 47 of the Act upon which the person was or should have been registered;

"landfill invoice" means an invoice of the description in regulation 37;
"landfill site" has the meaning given in section 66 of the Act;
"landfill tax account" has the meaning given in regulation 12;
"landfill tax bad debt account" has the meaning given in regulation 26;
"quarter" means a period of three months ending at the end of March, June, September or December;
"registered person" means a person who is registered under section 47 of the Act and "register" and "registration" shall be construed accordingly;
"registrable person" has the meaning given in section 47(10) of the Act;
"registration number" means the identifying number allocated to a registered person and notified to him by the Commissioners;
"return" means a return which is required to be made in accordance with regulation 11;
"taxable business" means a business or part of a business in the course of which taxable activities are carried out;
["transfer note" is a transfer note within the meaning of—

(*a*) the Environmental Protection (Duty of Care) Regulations 1991; or

(*b*) the Controlled Waste (Duty of Care) Regulations (Northern Ireland) 2002;][1]

"working day" means any day of the week except Saturday and Sunday and a bank holiday or public holiday, in either case, for England.

(2) In these Regulations any question whether a person is connected with another shall be determined in accordance with section 839 of the Taxes Act 1988.

(3) Any reference in these Regulations to "this Part" is a reference to the Part of these Regulations in which that reference is made.

(4) Any reference in these Regulations to a form prescribed in the Schedule to these Regulations shall include a reference to a form which the Commissioners are satisfied is a form to the like effect.

Amendments—[1] In sub-para (1), definition of "transfer note" substituted by the Landfill Tax (Amendment) Regulations, SI 2004/769 reg 2 with effect from 1 May 2004. That definition previously read as follows—

" 'transfer note' has the same meaning as in the Environmental Protection (Duty of Care) Regulations 1991;".

Designation, direction or approval

3 Any designation, direction or approval by the Commissioners under or for the purposes of these Regulations shall be made or given by a notice in writing.

PART II
REGISTRATION AND PROVISION FOR SPECIAL CASES

Notification of liability to be registered

4—(1) A person who is required by section 47(3) of the Act to notify the Commissioners of his intention to carry out taxable activities shall do so on the form numbered 1 in the Schedule to these Regulations.

(2) Where the notification referred to in this regulation is made by a person who operates or intends to operate more than one landfill site, it shall include the particulars set out on the form numbered 2 in the Schedule to these Regulations.

(3) Where the notification referred to in this regulation is made by a partnership, it shall include the particulars set out on the form numbered 3 in the Schedule to these Regulations.

(4) The notification referred to in this regulation shall be made within 30 days of the earliest date after 1st August 1996 on which the person either forms or continues to have the intention to carry out taxable activities.

Changes in particulars

5—(1) A person who has made a notification under regulation 4, whether or not it was made in accordance with paragraph (4) of that regulation, shall, within 30 days of—

(*a*) discovering any inaccuracy in; or

(*b*) any change occurring which causes to become inaccurate,

any of the information which was contained in or provided with the notification, notify the Commissioners in writing and furnish them with full particulars.

(2) Without prejudice to paragraph (1) above, a registrable person shall, within 30 days of any change occurring in any of the circumstances referred to in paragraph (4) below, notify the Commissioners in writing and furnish them with particulars of—

(*a*) the change; and

(*b*) the date on which the change occurred.

(3) A registrable person who discovers that any information contained in or provided with a notification under paragraph (1) or (2) above was inaccurate shall, within 30 days of his discovering the inaccuracy, notify the Commissioners in writing and furnish them with particulars of—

(*a*) the inaccuracy;

(*b*) the date on which the inaccuracy was discovered;
(*c*) how the information was inaccurate; and
(*d*) the correct information.

(4) The circumstances mentioned in paragraph (2) above are the following circumstances relating to the registrable person or any taxable business carried on by him:

(*a*) his name, his trading name (if different), his address and the landfill sites he operates;
(*b*) his status, namely whether he carries on business as a sole proprietor, body corporate, partnership or other unincorporated body;
(*c*) in the case of a partnership, the name and address of any partner.

(5) Any person failing to comply with a requirement imposed in any of paragraphs (1) to (3) above shall be liable to a penalty of £250.

(6) Where in relation to a registered person the Commissioners are satisfied that any of the information recorded in the register is or has become inaccurate they may correct the register accordingly.

(7) For the purposes of paragraph (6) above, it is immaterial whether or not the registered person has notified the Commissioners of any change which has occurred in accordance with paragraphs (1) to (3) above.

Notification of cessation of taxable activities

6 A person who is required by section 47(4) of the Act to notify the Commissioners of his having ceased to have the intention to carry out taxable activities shall, within 30 days of his so having ceased, notify the Commissioners in writing and shall therein inform them of—

(*a*) the date on which he ceased to have the intention of carrying out taxable activities; and
(*b*) if different, the date on which he ceased to carry out taxable activities.

Transfer of a going concern

7—(1) Where—

(*a*) a taxable business is transferred as a going concern;
(*b*) the registration of the transferor has not already been cancelled;
(*c*) as a result of the transfer of the business the registration of the transferor is to be cancelled and the transferee has become liable to be registered; and
(*d*) an application is made on the form numbered 4 in the Schedule to these Regulations by both the transferor and the transferee,

the Commissioners may with effect from the date of the transfer cancel the registration of the transferor and register the transferee with the registration number previously allocated to the transferor.

(2) An application under paragraph (1) above shall be treated as the notification referred to in regulation 6.

(3) Where the transferee of a business has been registered under paragraph (1) above with the registration number previously allocated to the transferor—

(*a*) any liability of the transferor existing at the date of the transfer to make a return or account for or pay any tax under Part III of these Regulations shall become the liability of the transferee;
(*b*) any entitlement of the transferor, whether or not existing at the date of the transfer, to credit or payment under Part IV of these Regulations shall become the entitlement of the transferee.

(4) In addition to the provisions set out in paragraph (3) above, where the transferee of a business has been registered under paragraph (1) above with the registration number previously allocated to the transferor during an accounting period subsequent to that in which the transfer took place (but with effect from the date of the transfer) and any—

(*a*) return has been made;
(*b*) tax has been accounted for; or
(*c*) entitlement to credit has been claimed,

by either the transferor or the transferee, it shall be treated as having been done by the transferee.

(5) Where—

(*a*) a taxable business is transferred as a going concern;
(*b*) the transferee removes material as described in regulation 21(2) or (4); and
(*c*) the transferor has paid tax on the disposal concerned,

then, whether or not the transferee has been registered under paragraph (1) above with the registration number previously allocated to the transferor, any entitlement to credit arising under Part V of these Regulations shall become the entitlement of the transferee.

Representation of unincorporated body

8—(1) Where anything is required to be done by or under the Act (whether by these Regulations or otherwise) by or on behalf of an unincorporated body other than a partnership, it shall be the joint and several responsibility of—

(*a*) every member holding office as president, chairman, treasurer, secretary or any similar office; or

(*b*) if there is no such office, every member holding office as a member of a committee by which the affairs of the body are managed; or

(*c*) if there is no such office or committee, every member;

but, subject to paragraph (2) below, if it is done by any of the persons referred to above that shall be sufficient compliance with any such requirement.

(2) Where an unincorporated body other than a partnership is required to make any notification such as is referred to in regulations 4 to 6, it shall not be sufficient compliance unless the notification is made by a person upon whom a responsibility for making it is imposed by paragraph (1) above.

(3) Where anything is required to be done by or under the Act (whether by these Regulations or otherwise) by or on behalf of a partnership, it shall be the joint and several responsibility of every partner; but if it is done by one partner or, in the case of a partnership whose principal place of business is in Scotland, by any other person authorised by the partnership with respect thereto that shall be sufficient compliance with any such requirement.

Bankruptcy or incapacity of registrable persons

9—(1) If a registrable person becomes bankrupt or incapacitated, the Commissioners may, from the date on which he became bankrupt or incapacitated, as the case may be, treat as a registrable person any person carrying on any taxable business of his; and any legislation relating to landfill tax shall apply to any person so treated as though he were a registered person.

(2) Any person carrying on such business as aforesaid shall, within 30 days of commencing to do so, inform the Commissioners in writing of that fact and the date of the bankruptcy order or of the nature of the incapacity and the date on which it began.

(3) Where the Commissioners have treated a person carrying on a business as a registrable person under paragraph (1) above, they shall cease so to treat him if—

(*a*) the registration of the registrable person is cancelled, whether or not any other person is registered with the registration number previously allocated to him;

(*b*) the bankruptcy is discharged or the incapacity ceases; or

(*c*) he ceases carrying on the business of the registrable person.

(4) In relation to a registrable person which is a company, the references in this regulation to the registrable person becoming incapacitated shall be construed as references to its going into liquidation or receivership or [entering administration][1]; and references to the incapacity ceasing shall be construed accordingly.

Amendments—[1] Words in para (4) substituted by the Enterprise Act 2002 (Insolvency) Order, SI 2003/605 art 5, Schedule paras 65, 66 with effect from 15 September 2003. However, this amendment does not apply in relation to any case where a petition for an administration order was presented before that date: SI 2003/2096 at 6.

PART III
ACCOUNTING, PAYMENT[, RECORDS AND INFORMATION AREAS][1]

Amendments—[1] In heading to Part III, words substituted for words "and records" by the Landfill Tax (Amendment) Regulations, SI 2009/1930 reg 2(1), (2) with effect from 1 September 2009.

Interpretation

10 In this Part, "accounting period" has the meaning given in regulation 2(1).

Making of returns

11—(1) Subject to paragraph (3) below and save as the Commissioners may otherwise allow, a registrable person shall, in respect of each accounting period, make a return to the Controller, Central Collection Unit (LT), [in a form that is determined by the Commissioners in a public notice.][1]

(2) Subject to paragraph (3) below, a registrable person shall make each return not later than the last working day of the month next following the end of the period to which it relates.

(3) Where the Commissioners consider it necessary in the circumstances of any particular case, they may—

(*a*) vary the length of any accounting period or the date on which it begins or ends or by which any return must be made;

(*b*) allow or direct the registrable person to make a return in accordance with sub-paragraph (*a*) above;

(*c*) allow or direct a registrable person to make returns to a specified address,

and any person to whom the Commissioners give any direction such as is referred to in this regulation shall comply therewith.

Amendments—[1] In para (1), words substituted for words "on the form numbered 5 in the Schedule to these Regulations" by the Landfill Tax (Amendment) Regulations, SI 2009/1930 reg 2(1), (3) with effect from 1 September 2009.

Landfill tax account

12—(1) Every registrable person shall make and maintain an account to be known as "the landfill tax account".

(2) The landfill tax account shall be in such form and contain such particulars as may be stipulated in a notice published by the Commissioners and not withdrawn by a further notice.

Correction of errors

13—(1) In this regulation—

"overdeclaration" means, in relation to any return, the amount (if any) which was wrongly treated as tax due for the accounting period concerned and which caused the amount of tax which was payable to be overstated, or the entitlement to a payment under regulation 20 to be understated (or both) or would have caused such an overstatement or understatement were it not for the existence of an underdeclaration in relation to that return;

"underdeclaration" means, in relation to any return, the aggregate of—

(*a*) the amount (if any) of tax due for the accounting period concerned which was not taken into account; and

(*b*) the amount (if any) which was wrongly deducted as credit,

and which caused the amount of tax which was payable to be understated, or the entitlement to a payment under regulation 20 to be overstated (or both) or would have caused such an understatement or overstatement were it not for the existence of an overdeclaration in relation to that return.

(2) This regulation applies where a registrable person has made a return which was inaccurate as the result of an overdeclaration or underdeclaration.

(3) . . . [1]

(4) Where in any accounting period—

(*a*) a registrable person discovers one or more [overdeclarations or][1] underdeclarations; and

(*b*) having treated the amount of those [overdeclarations or][1] underdeclarations as reduced by the amount [respectively of any underdeclarations or overdeclarations][1] for the same accounting periods, the total of those [overdeclarations or][1] underdeclarations does not exceed [£50,000][1],

he may enter the [overdeclarations or][1] underdeclarations in his return for the accounting period in which they were discovered by including their amount in [the boxes for underdeclarations and overdeclarations as appropriate in the form referred to in regulation 11(1)][4].

[But if the registrable person's VAT turnover is small, the total mentioned in sub-paragraph (*b*) must not for these purposes exceed 1% of that turnover unless the total is [£10,000 or less][3].

And if that person is not registered for VAT, the total mentioned in sub-paragraph (*b*) must not for these purposes exceed £10,000.][1]

"[The VAT turnover is small only if Box 6 of that person's value added tax return for the prescribed accounting period in which the discovery is made must contain a total less than £5,000,000 (total value of sales and all other outputs excluding any value added tax).][2]

(5) Where a registrable person enters an amount in a return in accordance with paragraph . . . [1] (4) above he shall calculate the tax payable by him or the payment to which he is entitled accordingly.

(6) Where an amount has been entered in accordance with this regulation in a return which has been made—

(*a*) the return shall be regarded as correcting any earlier return to which that amount relates; and

(*b*) the registrable person shall be taken to have furnished information with respect to the inaccuracy in the prescribed form and manner for the purposes of paragraph 20 of Schedule 5 to the Act.

(7) No amount shall be entered in a return in respect of any overdeclaration or underdeclaration except in accordance with this regulation; and as regards any underdeclaration that cannot be corrected under paragraph (4) above a person shall not be taken to have furnished information with respect to an inaccuracy in the prescribed form and manner for the purposes of paragraph 20 of Schedule 5 to the Act unless he provides such information to the Commissioners in writing.

Amendments—[1] Para (3) revoked, words in para (4) inserted, and words "(3) or" in para (5) revoked, by the he Value Added Tax, etc (Correction of Errors, etc) Regulations, SI 2008/1482 reg 5 with effect in relation to overdeclarations or underdeclarations in reg 13 which registrable persons first discover in their accounting periods that begin on 1 July 2008 or later.

[2] In para (4), words inserted by the Value Added Tax, etc (Correction of Errors, etc) Regulations, SI 2008/1482 reg 8(1) with effect from 1 July 2008.

[3] In para (4), words substituted for words "less than £10,000" by the Amusement Machine Licence Duty, etc (Amendments) Regulations, SI 2008/2693 reg 4(1)(*b*) with effect for a discovery first made on 1 November 2008 or later.

4 In para (4), words substituted for words "Box 2 (underdeclarations) or Box 4 (overdeclarations), as appropriate (see Form 5 in the Schedule)" by the Landfill Tax (Amendment) Regulations, SI 2009/1930 reg 2(1), (4) with effect from 1 September 2009.

Claims for overpaid tax

14 Except where the amount to which the claim relates has been entered in a return in accordance with regulation 13 or is included in an amount so entered, any claim under paragraph 14 of Schedule 5 to the Act shall be made in writing to the Commissioners and shall, by reference to such documentary evidence as is in the possession of the claimant, state the amount of the claim and the method by which that amount was calculated.

[Interpretation of regulations 14A to 14H

14A In this regulation and in regulations 14B to 14H below—

"claim" means a claim made (irrespective of when it was made) under paragraph 14 of Schedule 5 to the Act for repayment of an amount paid to the Commissioners by way of tax which was not tax due to them; and "claimed" and "claimant" shall be construed accordingly;

"reimbursement arrangements" means any arrangements (whether made before, on or after 30th January 1998) for the purposes of a claim which—

(*a*) are made by a claimant for the purpose of securing that he is not unjustly enriched by the repayment of any amount in pursuance of the claim; and

(*b*) provide for the reimbursement of persons (consumers) who have, for practical purposes, borne the whole or any part of the cost of the original payment of that amount to the Commissioners;

"relevant amount" means that part (which may be the whole) of the amount of a claim which the claimant has reimbursed or intends to reimburse to consumers.][1]

Amendments—[1] This regulation inserted by the Landfill Tax (Amendment) Regulations, SI 1998/61 with effect from 11 February 1998.

[Reimbursement arrangements—general

14B Without prejudice to regulation 14H below, for the purposes of paragraph 14(3) of Schedule 5 to the Act (defence by the Commissioners that repayment by them of an amount claimed would unjustly enrich the claimant) reimbursement arrangements made by a claimant shall be disregarded except where they—

(*a*) include the provisions described in regulation 14C below; and

(*b*) are supported by the undertakings described in regulation 14G below.][1]

Amendments—[1] This regulation inserted by the Landfill Tax (Amendment) Regulations, SI 1998/61 with effect from 11 February 1998.

[Reimbursement arrangements—provisions to be included

14C The provisions referred to in regulation 14B(*a*) above are that—

(*a*) reimbursement for which the arrangements provide will be completed by no later than 90 days after the repayment to which it relates;

(*b*) no deduction will be made from the relevant amount by way of fee or charge (howsoever expressed or effected);

(*c*) reimbursement will be made only in cash or by cheque;

(*d*) any part of the relevant amount that is not reimbursed by the time mentioned in paragraph (*a*) above will be repaid by the claimant to the Commissioners;

(*e*) any interest paid by the Commissioners on any relevant amount repaid by them will also be treated by the claimant in the same way as the relevant amount falls to be treated under paragraphs (*a*) and (*b*) above; and

(*f*) the records described in regulation 14E below will be kept by the claimant and produced by him to the Commissioners, or to an officer of theirs in accordance with regulation 14F below.][1]

Amendments—[1] This regulation inserted by the Landfill Tax (Amendment) Regulations, SI 1998/61 with effect from 11 February 1998.

[Repayments to the Commissioners

14D The claimant shall, without prior demand, make any repayment to the Commissioners that he is required to make by virtue of regulation 14C(*d*) and (*e*) above within 14 days of the expiration of the period of 90 days referred to in regulation 14C(*a*) above.][1]

Amendments—[1] This regulation inserted by the Landfill Tax (Amendment) Regulations, SI 1998/61 with effect from 11 February 1998.

[Records

14E The claimant shall keep records of the following matters—

(*a*) the names and addresses of those consumers whom he has reimbursed or whom he intends to reimburse;
(*b*) the total amount reimbursed to each such consumer;
(*c*) the amount of interest included in each total amount reimbursed to each consumer;
(*d*) the date that each reimbursement is made.][1]

Amendments—[1] This regulation inserted by the Landfill Tax (Amendment) Regulations, SI 1998/61 with effect from 11 February 1998.

[Production of records

14F—(1) Where a claimant is given notice in accordance with paragraph (2) below, he shall, in accordance with such notice produce to the Commissioners, or to an officer of theirs, the records that he is required to keep pursuant to regulation 14E above.

(2) A notice given for the purposes of paragraph (1) above shall—
(*a*) be in writing;
(*b*) state the place and time at which, and the date on which the records are to be produced; and
(*c*) be signed and dated by the Commissioners, or by an officer of theirs,

and may be given before or after, or both before and after the Commissioners have paid the relevant amount to the claimant.][1]

Amendments—[1] This regulation inserted by the Landfill Tax (Amendment) Regulations, SI 1998/61 with effect from 11 February 1998.

[Undertakings

14G—(1) Without prejudice to regulation 14H(*b*) below, the undertakings referred to in regulation 14B(*b*) above shall be given to the Commissioners by the claimant no later than the time at which he makes the claim for which the reimbursement arrangements have been made.

(2) The undertakings shall be in writing, shall be signed and dated by the claimant, and shall be to the effect that—
(*a*) at the date of the undertakings he is able to identify the names and addresses of those consumers whom he has reimbursed or whom he intends to reimburse;
(*b*) he will apply the whole of the relevant amount repaid to him, without any deduction by way of fee or charge or otherwise, to the reimbursement in cash or by cheque, of such consumers by no later than 90 days after his receipt of that amount (except insofar as he has already so reimbursed them);
(*c*) he will apply any interest paid to him on the relevant amount repaid to him wholly to the reimbursement of such consumers by no later than 90 days after his receipt of that interest;
(*d*) he will repay to the Commissioners without demand the whole or such part of the relevant amount repaid to him or of any interest paid to him as he fails to apply in accordance with the undertakings mentioned in sub-paragraphs (*b*) and (*c*) above;
(*e*) he will keep the records described in regulation 14E above; and
(*f*) he will comply with any notice given to him in accordance with regulation 14F above concerning the production of such records.][1]

Amendments—[1] This regulation inserted by the Landfill Tax (Amendment) Regulations, SI 1998/61 with effect from 11 February 1998.

[Reimbursement arrangements made before 11th February 1998

14H Reimbursement arrangements made by a claimant before 11th February 1998 shall not be disregarded for the purposes of paragraph 14(3) of Schedule 5 to the Act if, not later than 11th March 1998—
(*a*) he includes in those arrangements (if they are not already included) the provisions described in regulation 14C above; and
(*b*) gives the undertakings described in regulation 14G above.][1]

Amendments—[1] This regulation inserted by the Landfill Tax (Amendment) Regulations, SI 1998/61 with effect from 11 February 1998.

Payment of tax

15 Save as the Commissioners may otherwise allow or direct, any person required to make a return shall pay to the Controller, Central Collection Unit (LT), such amount of tax as is payable by him in respect of the accounting period to which the return relates no later than the last day on which he was required to make the return.

Records

16—(1) Every registrable person shall, for the purpose of accounting for tax, preserve the following—
(*a*) his business and accounting records;
(*b*) his landfill tax account;

(*c*) transfer notes and any other original or copy records in relation to material brought onto or removed from the landfill site (including any record made [on or before 31st August 2009][1] for the purpose of Part IX of these Regulations [before that Part was revoked with effect from 1st September 2009, or for the purpose of regulation 16A(4) below][1]);

(*d*) all invoices (including landfill invoices) and similar documents issued to him and copies of such invoices and similar documents issued by him;

(*e*) all credit or debit notes or other documents received by him which evidence an increase or decrease in the amount of any consideration for a relevant transaction, and copies of such documents that are issued by him;

(*f*) such other records as the Commissioners may specify in a notice published by them and not withdrawn by a further notice.

(2) Subject to paragraphs (3) and (4) below, every registrable person shall preserve the records specified in paragraph (1) above for a period of six years.

(3) Subject to paragraph (4) below, a registrable person who has made a landfill tax bad debt account shall preserve that account for a period of five years from the date of the claim made under Part VI of these Regulations.

(4) The Commissioners may direct that registrable persons shall preserve the records specified in paragraph (1) above for a shorter period than that specified in this regulation; and such direction may be made so as to apply generally or in such cases as the Commissioners may stipulate.

(5) In paragraph (1) above—

(*a*) the reference to material being brought onto a landfill site is a reference to material that is brought onto the site for the purpose of a relevant transaction;

(*b*) the reference to material being removed from a landfill site is a reference to material being removed that has at some previous time fallen wholly or partly within paragraph (*a*) above.

(6) In this regulation "relevant transaction" means a disposal or anything that would be a disposal but for the fact that the material is not disposed of as waste.

Amendments—[1] In para (1)(*c*), words inserted by the Landfill Tax (Amendment) Regulations, SI 2009/1930 reg 2(1), (5) with effect from 1 September 2009.

[Information areas

16A—(1) An officer of Revenue and Customs is authorised to require a person to designate a part of a landfill site (an "information area"), and a person must designate an information area if so required.

(2) Where material at a landfill site is not going to be disposed of as waste and the Commissioners consider, or an officer of theirs considers, there to be a risk to the revenue—

(*a*) the material must be deposited in an information area; and

(*b*) a registrable person must give the Commissioners, or an officer of theirs, information and maintain a record in accordance with paragraph 4 below.

(3) A designation ceases to have effect if a notice in writing to that effect is given to a registrable person by the Commissioners or by an officer of Revenue and Customs.

(4) A registrable person must maintain a record in relation to the information area of the following information, and give this information to the Commissioners or an officer of theirs if requested—

(*a*) the weight and description of all material deposited there;

(*b*) the intended destination or use of all such material and, where any material has been removed or used, the actual destination or use of that material;

(*c*) the weight and description of any such material sorted or removed.][1]

Amendments—[1] This reg inserted by the Landfill Tax (Amendment) Regulations, SI 2009/1930 reg 2(1), (6) with effect from 1 September 2009.

PART IV
CREDIT: GENERAL

Interpretation

17 In this Part—

"relevant accounting period" means—

(*a*) in the case of an entitlement to credit arising under Part V of these Regulations, the accounting period in which the reuse condition or, as the case may be, the enforced removal condition was satisfied;

(*b*) in the case of an entitlement to credit arising under Part VI of these Regulations, the accounting period in which the period of one year from the date of the issue of the landfill invoice expired;

(*c*) in the case of an entitlement arising under Part VII of these Regulations, the accounting period in which the qualifying contribution was made;

"relevant amount" means the amount of the credit as determined in accordance with Part V, VI or VII of these Regulations, as the case may be;

Landfill tax

"relevant tax" means the tax, if any, that was required to have been paid as a condition of the entitlement to credit.

Scope

18—(1) This Part applies to entitlements to credit arising under Part V, VI or VII of these Regulations.

(2) No credit arising under any provisions of these Regulations may be claimed except in accordance with this Part.

Claims in returns

19—(1) Subject to paragraphs (2) and (3) below, a person entitled to credit may claim it by deducting its amount from any tax due from him for the relevant accounting period or any subsequent accounting period and, where he does so, he shall make his return for that accounting period accordingly.

(2) Where the entitlement to credit arises under Part VII of these Regulations paragraph (1) above shall apply as if there were substituted for "or any subsequent accounting period" the words "or any subsequent accounting period in the same contribution year as determined in relation to that person under regulation 31".

(3) The Commissioners may make directions generally or with regard to particular cases prescribing rules in accordance with which credit may or shall be held over to be credited in an accounting period subsequent to the relevant accounting period; and where such a direction has been made that credit, subject to any subsequent such direction varying or withdrawing the rules, may only be claimed in accordance with those rules.

Payments in respect of credit

20—(1) Subject to paragraph (5) below, where the total credit claimed by a registrable person in accordance with this Part exceeds the total of the tax due from him for the accounting period, the Commissioners shall pay to him an amount equal to the excess.

(2) Where the Commissioners have cancelled the registration of a person in accordance with section 47(6) of the Act, and he is not a registrable person, he shall make any claim in respect of credit to which this Part applies by making an application in writing.

(3) A person making an application under paragraph (2) above shall furnish to the Commissioners full particulars in relation to the credit claimed, including (but not restricted to)—

(*a*) except in the case of an entitlement to credit arising under Part VII of these Regulations, the return in which the relevant tax was accounted for;

(*b*) except in the case of an entitlement to credit arising under Part VII of these Regulations, the amount of the tax and the date and manner of its payment;

(*c*) the events by virtue of which the entitlement to credit arose.

(4) Subject to paragraph (5) below, where the Commissioners are satisfied that a person who has made a claim in accordance with paragraphs (2) and (3) above is entitled to credit, and that he has not previously had the benefit of that credit, they shall pay to him an amount equal to the credit.

(5) The Commissioners shall not be liable to make any payment under this regulation unless and until the person has made all the returns which he was required to make.

PART V
CREDIT: PERMANENT REMOVALS ETC

Entitlement to credit

21—(1) An entitlement to credit arises under this Part where—

(*a*) a registered person has accounted for an amount of tax and, except where the removal by virtue of which sub-paragraph (*b*) below is satisfied takes place in the accounting period in which credit arising under this Part is claimed in accordance with Part IV of these Regulations, he has paid that tax; and

(*b*) in relation to the disposal on which that tax was charged, either—

(i) the reuse condition has been satisfied; or

(ii) the enforced removal condition has been satisfied.

(2) The reuse condition is satisfied where—

(*a*) the disposal has been made with the intention that the material comprised in it—

(i) would be recycled or incinerated; or

(ii) removed for use (other than by way of a further disposal) at a place other than a relevant site; [or

(iii) removed for use in restoration of a relevant site and the material involved has previously been used to create or maintain temporary hard standing, to create or maintain a temporary screening bund or to create or maintain a temporary haul road;][2]

(*b*) that material, or some of it, has been recycled, incinerated or permanently removed from the landfill site, as the case may be, in accordance with that intention;

(*c*) that recycling, incineration or removal—

(i) has taken place no later than one year after the date of the disposal; or

(ii) where water had been added to the material in order to facilitate its disposal, has taken place no later than five years after the date of the disposal; and

(*d*) the registered person has, before the disposal, notified the Commissioners in writing that he intends to make one or more removals of material in relation to which sub-paragraphs (*a*) to (*c*) above will be satisfied.

(3) For the purpose of paragraph (2)(*a*)(ii) above a relevant site is the landfill site at which the disposal was made or any other landfill site.

(4) The enforced removal condition is satisfied where—

(*a*) the disposal is in breach of the terms of the licence[, resolution or permit][1], as the case may be, by virtue of which the land constitutes a landfill site;

(*b*) the registered person has been directed to remove the material comprised in the disposal, or some of it, by a relevant authority and he has removed it, or some of it; and

(*c*) a further taxable disposal of the material has been made and, except where the registered person is the person liable for the tax chargeable on that further disposal, he has paid to the site operator an amount representing that tax.

(5) For the purpose of paragraph (4)(*b*) above the following are relevant authorities—

(*a*) the Environment Agency;

(*b*) the Scottish Environment Protection Agency;

(*c*) the Department of the Environment for Northern Ireland;

(*d*) a district council in Northern Ireland.

(6) The amount of the credit arising under this Part shall be equal to the tax that was charged on the disposal; except that where only some of the material comprised in that disposal is removed, the amount of the credit shall be such proportion of that tax as the material removed forms of the total of the material.

[(7) In this Regulation—

"disposal area" means any area of a landfill site where any disposal takes place;

"haul road" means any road within the landfill site which gives access to a disposal area;

"hard standing" means a base within a landfill site on which any landfill site activity such as sorting, treatment, processing, storage or recycling is carried out;

"screening bund" means any structure on a landfill site (whether below or above ground) put in place to protect or conceal any landfill site activity or to reduce nuisance from noise.][2]

Amendments—[1] Words substituted by the Landfill Tax (Amendment) Regulations, SI 2005/759 regs 2, 3 with effect from 6 April 2005.

[2] Para (2)(*a*)(iii) and preceding word "or", and para (7), inserted by the Landfill Tax (Amendment) Regulations, SI 2009/1930 reg 2(1), (7), (8) with effect from 1 September 2009.

PART VI
CREDIT: BAD DEBTS

Interpretation

22 In this Part—

"claim" means a claim in accordance with Part IV of these Regulations for an amount of credit arising under this Part and "claimant" shall be construed accordingly;

"customer" means a person for whom a taxable activity is carried out by the claimant;

"outstanding amount" means, in relation to any claim—

(*a*) if at the time of the claim the claimant has received no payment in respect of the amount written off in his accounts, the amount so written off; or

(*b*) if at that time he has received a payment, the amount by which the amount written off exceeds the payment (or the aggregate of the payments);

"relevant disposal" means any taxable disposal upon which a claim is based;

"security" means—

(*a*) in relation to England, Wales and Northern Ireland, any mortgage, charge, lien or other security; and

(*b*) in relation to Scotland, any security (whether heritable or moveable), any floating charge and any right of lien or preference and right of retention (other than a right of compensation or set-off).

Scope

23 An entitlement to credit arises under this Part where—

(*a*) a registered person has carried out a taxable activity for a consideration in money for a customer with whom he is not connected;

(*b*) he has accounted for and paid tax on the disposal concerned;

(*c*) the whole or any part of the consideration for the disposal has been written off in his accounts as a bad debt;

(*d*) he has issued a landfill invoice in respect of the disposal which shows the amount of tax chargeable;

(*e*) that invoice was issued—

(i) within 14 days of the date of the disposal, or

(ii) within such other period as may have been specified in a direction of the Commissioners made under section 61(3) of the Act;

(*f*) a period of one year (beginning with the date of the issue of that invoice) has elapsed; and

(*g*) the following provisions of this Part have been complied with.

Amount of credit

24 The credit arising under this Part shall be of an amount equal to such proportion of the tax charged on the relevant disposal as the outstanding amount forms of the total consideration.

Evidence required in support of claim

25 The claimant, before he makes a claim, shall hold in respect of each relevant disposal—

(*a*) a copy of the landfill invoice issued by him;

(*b*) records or any other documents showing that he has accounted for and paid tax on the disposal; and

(*c*) records or any other documents showing that the consideration has been written off in his accounts as a bad debt.

Records required to be kept

26—(1) Any person who makes a claim shall make a record of that claim.

(2) The record referred to in paragraph (1) above shall contain the following information in respect of each claim made:

(*a*) in respect of each relevant disposal—

(i) the amount of tax charged;

(ii) the return in which that tax was accounted for and when it was paid;

(iii) the date and identifying number of the landfill invoice that was issued;

(iv) any consideration that has been received (whether before the claim was made or subsequently);

(v) the details of any transfer note;

(*b*) the outstanding amount;

(*c*) the amount of the claim;

(*d*) the return in which the claim was made.

(3) Any records made in pursuance of this regulation shall be kept in a single account known as "the landfill tax bad debt account".

Attribution of payments

27—(1) Where—

(*a*) the claimant has carried out a taxable activity for a customer;

(*b*) there exist one or more other matters in respect of which the claimant is entitled to a debt owed by the customer (whether they involve a taxable disposal or not and whether they are connected with waste or not); and

(*c*) a payment has been received by the claimant from the customer,

the payment shall be attributed to the taxable activity and the other matters in accordance with the rule set out in paragraphs (2) and (3) below (and the debts arising in respect of the taxable activity and the other matters are collectively referred to in those paragraphs as debts).

(2) The payment shall be attributed to the debt which arose earliest and, if not wholly attributed to that debt, thereafter to debts in the order of the dates on which they arose, except that attribution under this paragraph shall not be made if the payment was allocated to a debt by the customer at the time of payment and the debt was paid in full.

(3) Where—

(*a*) the earliest debt and the other debts to which the whole of the payment could be attributed arose on the same day; or

(*b*) the debts to which the balance of the payment could be attributed in accordance with paragraph (2) above arose on the same day,

the payment shall be attributed to those debts by multiplying, for each such debt, the payment made by a fraction of which the numerator is the amount remaining unpaid in respect of that debt and the denominator is the amount remaining unpaid in respect of all those debts.

Repayment of credit

28—(1) Where a claimant—

(*a*) has benefited from an amount of credit to which he was entitled under this Part; and

(*b*) either—

(i) a payment for the relevant disposal is subsequently received; or

(ii) a payment is, by virtue of regulation 27, treated as attributed to the relevant disposal,

he shall repay to the Commissioners such amount as equals the amount of the credit, or the balance thereof, multiplied by a fraction of which the numerator is the amount so received or attributed, and the denominator is the amount of the outstanding consideration.

(2) Where the claimant—

(*a*) fails to comply with the requirements of regulation 26; or

(*b*) in relation to the documents mentioned in that regulation, fails to comply with either—

(i) regulation 16; or

(ii) any obligation arising under paragraph 3 of Schedule 5 to the Act,

he shall repay to the Commissioners the amount of the claim to which the failure to comply relates.

Writing off debts

29—(1) This regulation shall apply for the purpose of determining whether, and to what extent, the consideration is to be taken to have been written off as a bad debt.

(2) The whole or any part of the consideration for a taxable activity shall be taken to have been written off as a bad debt where—

(*a*) the claimant has written it off in his accounts as a bad debt; and

(*b*) he has made an entry in relation to that activity in the landfill tax bad debt account in accordance with regulation 26 (and this shall apply regardless of whether a claim can be made in relation to that activity at that time).

(3) Where the claimant owes an amount of money to the customer which can be set off, the consideration written off in the landfill tax bad debt account shall be reduced by the amount so owed.

(4) Where the claimant holds in relation to the customer an enforceable security, the consideration written off in the landfill tax bad debt account shall be reduced by the value of the security.

PART VII

CREDIT: BODIES CONCERNED WITH THE ENVIRONMENT

Interpretation and general provisions

30—(1) In this Part—

"approved body" means a body approved for the time being under regulation 34;

"approved object" has the meaning given in regulation 33;

["contributing third party" means a person who has made or agreed to make (whether or not under a legally binding agreement) a payment to a registered person to secure the making by him of a qualifying contribution or to reimburse him, in whole or in part, for any such contribution he has made;][1]

"income" includes interest;

"qualifying contribution" has the meaning given in regulation 32;

"the regulatory body" means such body, if any, as in relation to which an approval of the Commissioners under regulation 35 has effect for the time being;

"running costs" includes any cost incurred in connection with the management and administration of a body or its assets.

(2) A body shall only be taken to spend a qualifying contribution in the course or furtherance of its approved objects—

(*a*) in a case where the contribution is made subject to a condition that it may only be invested for the purpose of generating income, where the body so spends all of that income;

(*b*) in a case not falling within sub-paragraph (*a*) above, where the body becomes entitled to income, where it so spends both the whole of the qualifying contribution and all of that income;

(*c*) in a case not falling within either of sub-paragraphs (*a*) and (*b*) above, where the body so spends the whole of the qualifying contribution; or

(*d*) where—

(i) it transfers any qualifying contribution or income derived therefrom to another approved body, and

(ii) that transfer is subject to a condition that the sum transferred shall be spent only in the course or furtherance of that other body's approved objects.

Landfill tax

(3) Any approval, or revocation of such approval, by the Commissioners or the regulatory body shall be given by notice in writing to the body affected and shall take effect from the date the notice is given or such later date as the Commissioners or, as the case may be, the regulatory body may specify in it.

Amendments—[1] Definition "contributing third party" inserted by the Landfill Tax (Amendment) Regulations, SI 1999/3270, regs 2, 3, with effect from 1 January 2000.

Entitlement to credit

31—(1) Subject to the following provisions of this regulation, an entitlement to credit arises under this Part in respect of qualifying contributions made by registered persons.

(2) Subject to paragraph (3) below, a person shall be entitled to credit in respect of 90 per cent of the amount of each qualifying contribution made by him in any accounting period; and for this purpose a qualifying contribution made—

[(*a*) in one accounting period;][1]

(*b*) before the return for the previous accounting period has been made; and

(*c*) before the period within which that return is required to be made has expired,

shall be treated as having been made in the accounting period mentioned in sub-paragraph (b) above (and not in the accounting period in which it was in fact made).

(3) In respect of the qualifying contributions made in each contribution year, a person shall not be entitled to credit of an amount greater than [5.5][3] per cent of his relevant tax liability.

[(4) For the purpose of paragraphs (2) and (3) the contribution year of a person is his first contribution year and then each period of 12 months beginning on 1st April][2].

[(5) The reference in paragraph (4) to the first contribution year of a person is a reference to the period beginning with his effective date of registration and ending on the day immediately preceding the first day of the next contribution year][2].

[(6)Where one contribution year ends and another contribution year begins in an accounting period, the amount of any qualifying contribution which, by virtue of paragraph (2) is treated as made in that period shall be apportioned, in accordance with paragraph (6A), between those contribution years][2].

[(6A) The apportionment shall be on the basis of either?

(*a*) the number of days of the accounting period that fall before 1st April and the number of days that fall on and after that day; or

(*b*) the amount of tax charged on taxable disposals made in the accounting period before 1st April and the amount of tax charged on taxable disposals made in that period on and after that day,

whichever the registered person may choose][2].

(6B)–(6E) . . . [2]

(7) Subject to [paragraph (10)][1] below, the reference in paragraph (3) above to the relevant tax liability of a person is a reference to the aggregate of—

(*a*) the tax payable by him, if any, in respect of the accounting period in relation to which that liability falls to be determined; and

(*b*) the tax payable by him, if any, in respect of any earlier accounting period or periods which fall within the same contribution year as that accounting period;

and where in respect of any accounting period he is entitled to a payment under regulation 20 the aggregate of the tax payable by him in respect of the accounting periods mentioned in sub-paragraphs (a) and (b) above shall be reduced by the amount of that payment.

(8), (9) . . . [1]

(10) For the purposes of [paragraph (7)][1] above any entitlement to credit arising under this Part shall be disregarded in determining the tax payable by a person in respect of any period.

Note—Landfill Tax (Amendment) Regulations, SI 2003/605 reg 5 (any contribution year of a person that commenced before 1 April 2003 and, but for SI 2003/605, would end after that day shall end when SI 2003/605 comes into force).

Amendments—[1] Para (2)(*a*) and words in paras (4), (7), (10) substituted, words in para (5) and paras (6A)–(6E) inserted, and paras (8), (9) revoked, by the Landfill Tax (Amendment) Regulations, SI 1999/3270, regs 2, 4, with effect from 1 January 2000.

[2] Paras (4), (5), (6), (6A) and figure in para (3) substituted, and paras (6B)–(6E) revoked, by the Landfill Tax (Amendment) Regulations, SI 2003/605 regs 2, 3, with effect from 1 April 2003. However, nothing in SI 2003/605 affects a qualifying contribution that was made, or treated as made, before the coming into force of SI 2003/605: SI 2003/605 reg 6. Note that reg 6 is revoked by the Landfill Tax (Amendment) Regulations, SI 2007/965 reg 6 with effect from 1 April 2007, save that it will continue to have effect with respect to a qualifying contribution that was made, or treated as made, before 1 April 2003 if, but only if, the condition specified in SI 2007/965 reg 6(3) is satisfied: SI 2007/965 reg 6(2).

[3] Figure in para (3) substituted for figure "6.0" by the Landfill Tax (Amendment) Regulations, SI 2010/924 reg 2, with effect from 1 April 2010.

Qualifying contributions

32—(1) A payment is a qualifying contribution if—

(*a*) it is made by a registered person to an approved body;

(*b*) it is made subject to a condition that the body shall spend the sum paid or any income derived from it or both only in the course or furtherance of its approved objects;

(*c*) the requirements of [paragraphs (2) to (2B)][1] below have been complied with in relation to that payment; and

(*d*) it is not repaid to him[, or to a contributing third party,][1] in the same accounting period as that in which it was made.

(2) A person claiming credit arising under this Part shall make a record containing the following information—

(*a*) the amount and date of each payment he has made to an approved body;

(*b*) the name and enrolment number of that body;

[(*c*) the name and address of any contributing third party; and

(*d*) the amount of the payment made or to be made by the contributing third party and the date, or as the case may require, dates on which payment of the whole or any part of that amount—

(i) was received, or

(ii) is expected to be received][1].

[(2A) A person claiming credit under this Part for a contribution in relation to which there is a contributing third party shall have provided to the regulatory body or, if they are performing the functions specified in regulation 34(1) below, to the Commissioners the following information—

(*a*) the name and address of the contributing third party;

(*b*) the amount of the payment made or to be made by the contributing third party and the date, or as the case may require, dates on which payment of the whole or any part of that amount—

(i) was received, or

(ii) is expected to be received;

(*c*) the enrolment number of the approved body to whom the contribution was made.

(2B) A person claiming credit under this Part for a contribution in relation to which there is a contributing third party shall have informed the approved body to which the contribution is made of the name and address of the contributing third party.][1]

[(3) For the purposes of this Part where any qualifying contribution or income derived therefrom is transferred to a body as described in regulation 30(2)(*d*)—

(*a*) the body to whom the sum is transferred shall be treated as having received qualifying contributions of the amount concerned; and

(*b*) that body shall be treated as having received those qualifying contributions from the registered person or persons who originally paid them (but this shall not give rise to any further entitlement to credit in respect of those contributions).][1]

Amendments—[1] Words in para (1)(*c*), and whole of para (3) substituted, words in para (1)(*d*) and whole of paras (2)(*c*), (2A), (2B) inserted, by the Landfill Tax (Amendment) Regulations, SI 1999/3270, regs 2, 5, with effect from 1 January 2000.

Bodies eligible for approval

33—(1) [A body is eligible to be approved if—][1]

(*a*) it is—

(i) a body corporate, or

(ii) a trust, partnership or other unincorporated body;

(*b*) its objects are or include any of the objects within paragraph (2) below (approved objects);

(*c*) it is precluded from distributing and does not distribute any profit it makes or other income it receives;

(*d*) it applies any profit or other income to the furtherance of its objects (whether or not approved objects);

[(*e*) it is precluded from applying any of its funds for the benefit of any of the persons—

(i) who have made qualifying contributions to it, or

(ii) who were a contributing third party in relation to such contributions,

except that such persons may benefit where they belong to a class of persons that benefits generally;][1] . . . [1]

[(*f*) it is not controlled by one or more of the persons and bodies listed in paragraphs (1A) and (1B) below;

(*g*) none of the persons or bodies listed in paragraph (1B) below is concerned in its management; and

(*h*) it pays to the regulatory body an application fee of £100 or such lesser sum as the regulatory body may require.][1]

[(1A) The persons and bodies mentioned in paragraph (1)(*f*) above are—

(*a*) a local authority;

(*b*) a body corporate controlled by one or more local authorities;

(*c*) a registered person;

(*d*) a person connected with any of the persons or bodies mentioned in sub-paragraphs (*a*) to (*c*) above.

(1B) The persons and bodies mentioned in paragraph (1)(*f*) and (*g*) above are—

(*a*) a person who controlled or was concerned in the management of a body the approval of which was revoked otherwise than under regulation 34(1)(*ee*);
(*b*) a person who has been convicted of an indictable offence;
(*c*) a person who is disqualified for being a charity trustee or a trustee for a charity by virtue of section 72 of the Charities Act 1993;
(*d*) a person connected with any of the persons or bodies mentioned in sub-paragraphs (*a*) to (*c*) above;
(*e*) a person who is incapable by reason of mental disorder.

(1C) For the purpose of paragraph 1(B)(*e*) above, a person shall be treated as incapable by reason of mental disorder where—
(*a*) in England and Wales, the judge has exercised any of his functions under Part VII of the Mental Health Act 1983;
(*b*) in Scotland, the court has appointed a curator bonis, tutor or judicial factor; or
(*c*) in Northern Ireland, the court has exercised any of its powers under Part VIII of the Mental Health (Northern Ireland) Order 1986 (whether or not by virtue of Article 97(2) of that Order),

but shall cease to be so treated where the judge or court concerned has made a finding that he is not or is no longer incapable of managing and administering his property and affairs.][1]

(2) The objects of a body are approved objects insofar as they are any of the following objects—
(*a*) in relation to any land the use of which for any economic, social or environmental purpose has been prevented or restricted because of the carrying on of an activity on the land which has ceased—
(i) reclamation, remediation or restoration; or
(ii) any other operation intended to facilitate economic, social or environmental use;

but this is subject to paragraph (3) below;
(*b*) in relation to any land the condition of which, by reason of the carrying on of an activity on the land which has ceased, is such that pollution (whether of that land or not) is being or may be caused—
(i) any operation intended to prevent or reduce any potential for pollution; or
(ii) any operation intended to remedy or mitigate the effects of any pollution that has been caused,

but this is subject to paragraph (3) below;
(*c*), (*cc*) . . .[3]
(*d*) where it is for the protection of the environment, the provision, maintenance or improvement of—
(i) a public park; or
(ii) another public amenity,

in the vicinity of a landfill site, provided the conditions in paragraph (6) below are satisfied;
[(*da*) where it is for the protection of the environment, and subject to paragraph (3A) below, the conservation or promotion of biological diversity through—
(i) the provision, conservation, restoration or enhancement of a natural habitat; or
(ii) the maintenance or recovery of a species in its natural habitat,

on land or in water situated in the vicinity of a landfill site;][4]
(*e*) where it is for the protection of the environment, the maintenance, repair or restoration of a building or other structure which—
(i) is a place of religious worship or of historic or architectural interest,
(ii) is open to the public, and
(iii) is situated in the vicinity of a landfill site,

provided the conditions in paragraph (6) below are satisfied;
(*f*) the provision of financial, administration and other similar services to bodies which are within this regulation and only such bodies.

[(2A) In paragraph (2)(*da*) above "biological diversity" has the same meaning as in the United Nations Environmental Programme Convention on Biological Diversity of 1992.][4]

(3) An object shall not be, or shall no longer be, regarded as falling within paragraph (2)(*a*) or (*b*) above if the reclamation, remediation, restoration or other operation—
(*a*) is such that any benefit from it will accrue to any person who has carried out or knowingly permitted the activity which has ceased;
(*b*) involves works which are required to be carried out by a notice or order within paragraph (4) below; or
(*c*) is wholly or partly required to be carried out by a relevant condition.

[(3A) An object shall not be, or shall no longer be, regarded as falling within paragraph (2)(*da*) above if it involves works which—

(*a*) are required to be carried out by a notice or order within paragraph (4) below;
(*b*) are required to be carried out in accordance with an agreement made under section 16 of the National Parks and Access to the Countryside Act 1949;
(*c*) are required to be carried out in accordance with an agreement made under section 15 of the Countryside Act 1968;
(*d*) give effect to any provision of a management scheme under section 28J of the Wildlife and Countryside Act 1981 or are required to be carried out by a notice served under section 28K of that Act;
(*e*) are wholly or partly required to be carried out by a relevant condition; or
(*f*) are carried out with a view to profit.][4]

(4) The notices and order mentioned in paragraph (3) above are—
(*a*) a works notice served under section 46A of the Control of Pollution Act 1974;
(*b*) an enforcement notice served under section 13 of the Environmental Protection Act 1990;
(*c*) a prohibition notice served under section 14 of the Environmental Protection Act 1990;
(*d*) an order under section 26 of the Environmental Protection Act 1990;
(*e*) a remediation notice served under section 78E of the Environmental Protection Act 1990;
(*f*) . . .[8]
(*g*) a works notice served under section 161A of the Water Resources Act 1991;
[(*h*) an enforcement notice served under regulation 36 of the Environmental Permitting (England and Wales) Regulations [2010][8];
(*i*) a suspension notice served under regulation 37 of those Regulations; or
(*j*) an order under regulation 44 of those Regulations;][6]
[(*k*) a notice served under regulation 28(2) of the Water Environment (Controlled Activities) (Scotland) Regulations 2005.][5]

(5) . . .[3]

(6) The conditions mentioned in sub-paragraphs (*d*) and (*e*) of paragraph (2) above are—
(*a*) in a case falling within sub-paragraph (*d*), that the provision of the park or amenity is not required by a relevant condition; and
(*b*) in a case falling within either of those sub-paragraphs, that the park, amenity, building or structure (as the case may be) is not to be operated with a view to profit.

(7) Where the objects of a body are or include any of the objects set out in paragraph (2) above, the following shall also be regarded as objects within that paragraph—
(*a*) the use of qualifying contributions in paying the running costs of the body, but this is subject to paragraph (8) below;
(*b*) . . .[1] the use of qualifying contributions in paying a contribution to the running costs of the regulatory body.

(8) The use of qualifying contributions in paying the running costs of the body shall only be regarded as an approved object if the body determines so to use no more than such proportion of the total of qualifying contributions, together with any income derived from them, (or, in the case of a contribution within regulation 30(2)(*a*), only that income) as the proportion of that total forms of the total funds at its disposal and does not in fact use a greater amount.

(9) For the purposes of paragraph (1) above [a body or person (in either case, for the purposes of this paragraph, "the person")][1] shall be taken to control a body where—
(*a*) in the case of a body which is a body corporate, the person is empowered by statute to control that body's activities or if he is that body's holding company within the meaning of section [1159 of and Schedule 6 to][7] the Companies Act [2006][7], and an individual shall be taken to control a body corporate if he, were he a company, would be that body's holding company within the meaning of that Act;
(*b*) in the case of a body which is a trust or a partnership, where—
(i) the person, taken together with any nominee of his, or
(ii) any nominee of the person, taken together with any nominee of that nominee or any other nominee of the person,

forms a majority of the total number of trustees or partners, as the case may be;
(*c*) in the case of any other body, where the person, whether directly or through any nominee, has the power—
(i) to appoint or remove any officer of the body;
(ii) to determine the objects of the body;
(iii) to determine how any of the body's funds may be applied.

(10) For the purposes of paragraphs (3)[, (3A)][4] and (6) above a condition is relevant if it is—
(*a*) a condition of any planning permission or other statutory consent or approval granted on the application of any person making a qualifying contribution to the body, or
[(*b*) a term of an agreement made under—
(i) section 106 of the Town and Country Planning Act 1990,
(ii) section 75 of the Town and Country Planning (Scotland) Act 1997, or

(iii) article 40 of the Planning (Northern Ireland) Order 1991,

to which such a person is a party.][1]

Note—Landfill Tax (Amendment) Regulations, SI 2003/605 reg 5 (any contribution year of a person that commenced before 1st April 2003 and, but for SI 2003/605, would end after that day shall end when SI 2003/605 comes into force).

Amendments—[1] Words in paras (1), (9) and whole of paras (1)(*e*), (*f*), (10)(*b*) substituted, words in para (1)(*e*), (7)(*b*) revoked, and whole of paras (1A)–(1C), (2)(*cc*), and words in para (5) inserted, by the Landfill Tax (Amendment) Regulations, SI 1999/3270, regs 2, 6, with effect from 1 January 2000.

[2] Sub-paras (4)(*h*)–(*k*) inserted with effect in England and Wales by the Pollution Prevention and Control (England and Wales) Regulations, SI 2000/1973 reg 39, Sch 10 para 21 with effect from 1 August 2000. With effect in Scotland, sub-paras (4)(*h*)–(*k*) inserted as follows by the Pollution Prevention and Control (Scotland) Regulations, SI 2000/323 reg 36, Sch 10 para 14 with effect from 28 September 2000:

"(*h*) an enforcement notice served under regulation 19 of the Pollution Prevention and Control (Scotland) Regulations 2000;

(*i*) a suspension notice served under regulation 20 of those Regulations;

(*j*) an order under regulation 33 of those Regulations.".

[3] Sub-paras (2)(*c*), (*cc*) and para (5) revoked, by the Landfill Tax (Amendment) Regulations, SI 2003/605 reg 2, 4, with effect from 1 April 2003. However, nothing in SI 2003/605 affects a qualifying contribution that was made, or treated as made, before the coming into force of SI 2003/605: SI 2003/605 reg 6. Note that reg 6 is revoked by the Landfill Tax (Amendment) Regulations, SI 2007/965 reg 6 with effect from 1 April 2007, save that it will continue to have effect with respect to a qualifying contribution that was made, or treated as made, before 1 April 2003 if, but only if, the condition specified in SI 2007/965 reg 6(3) is satisfied: SI 2007/965 reg 6(2).

[4] Sub-paras (2)(*da*), (2A) and (3A) inserted, and reference in sub-para (10) inserted, by the Landfill Tax (Amendment) (No 2) Regulations, SI 2003/2313 with effect from 1 October 2003.

[5] Sub-para (4)(*k*) inserted by the Water Environment and Water Services (Scotland) Act 2003 (Consequential Provisions and Modifications) Order, SI 2006/1054 art 2, Sch 1 para 3 with effect from 1 April 2006.

[6] Sub-paras (4)(*h*)–(*j*) substituted, in relation to England and Wales, by the Environmental Permitting (England and Wales) Regulations, SI 2007/3538 reg 73, Sch 21 para 37(1), (2) with effect from 6 April 2008.

[7] In para (9)(*a*), words substituted for words "736 of" and "1985", by the Companies Act 2006 (Consequential Amendments) (Taxes and National Insurance) Order, SI 2009/1890 art 4(1)(*h*) with effect from 1 October 2009.

[8] Sub-para (4)(*f*) revoked, and figure in sub-para (4)(*h*) substituted by the Environmental Permitting (England and Wales) Regulations, SI 2010/675 reg 107, Sch 26 para 11 with effect from 6 April 2010 (immediately after the coming into force of the Environmental Permitting (England and Wales) (Amendment) (No 2) Regulations, SI 2009/3381).

[Obligations of approved bodies

33A—(1) An approved body shall—

(*a*) continue to meet all the requirements of regulation 33 above;

[(*aa*) comply with such conditions as the regulatory body may impose from time to time under regulation 34(1)(*aa*) (including any conditions varied under regulation 34(1)(*ab*));][3]

(*b*) apply qualifying contributions and any income derived therefrom only to approved objects;

(*c*) not apply any of its funds for the benefit of any of the persons who have made qualifying contributions to it or who were contributing third parties in relation to such contributions (except to the extent that they benefit by virtue of belonging to a class of persons that benefits generally);

(*d*) make and retain records of the following—

(i) the name, address and registration number of each registered person making a qualifying contribution to the body;

(ii) the name and address of any contributing third party in relation to a qualifying contribution received by the body;

(iii) the amount and date of receipt of each qualifying contribution and the amount and date of receipt of any income derived therefrom;

(iv) in the case of a transfer of the whole or part of any qualifying contribution or income derived therefrom to or from the body, the date of the transfer, the amount transferred, the name and enrolment number of the body from or, as the case may require, to which it was transferred, the name, address and registration number of the person who made the qualifying contribution and the name and address of any contributing third party in relation to the qualifying contribution;

(v) in respect of each qualifying contribution and any income derived therefrom, including any such amount transferred to the body by another approved body, the date of and all other details relating to its expenditure;

(*e*) provide the following information to the regulatory body or, if they are performing the functions specified in regulation 34(1) below, to the Commissioners within 7 days of the receipt by it of any qualifying contribution—

(i) the amount of the contribution;

(ii) the date it was received;

(iii) the name and registration number of the person making the contribution;

(iv) the name and address of any contributing third party in relation to the contribution notified to it by virtue of regulation 32(2B) above;

(*f*) notify the regulatory body within 7 days of any [transfer by that approved body][3] of qualifying contributions or of income derived therefrom of—
(i) the date of the transfer;
(ii) the enrolment number of the approved body by . . . [3] which the transfer was made;
(iii) the amount transferred;
(iv) the name and registration number of the person who made the qualifying contribution;
(v) the name and address of any contributing third party in relation to the contribution; and
(vi) the approved objects to which the transferred funds are to be applied;

(*g*) provide the regulatory body or, if they are performing the functions specified in regulation 34(1) below, the Commissioners with information from or access to the records referred to in [sub-paragraph (*d*)][2] above within 14 days (or such longer period as the regulatory body or, as the case may require, the Commissioners may allow) of a request being made for such information or access;

(*h*) submit to the regulatory body or, if they are performing the functions specified in regulation 34(1) below, to the Commissioners within [28][4] days of the end of the relevant period determined in accordance with paragraph (2) below details of—
(i) qualifying contributions and any other income or profit whatsoever received by it,
(ii) any expenditure made by it during the period, and
(iii) any balances held by it at the end of the period;

[(*ha*) submit to the regulatory body at its request, not later than the day specified in paragraph (3), so many of the following details as it requires at any time during the relevant period—
(i) qualifying contributions and any other income or profit whatsoever received by it during the period,
(ii) any expenditure made by it during the period, and
(iii) any balances held during the period;

(*hb*) if the Commissioners are performing the functions specified in regulation 34(1) instead of the regulatory body, submit, at their request, not later than the day specified in paragraph (3), so many of the following details as they may require at any time during the relevant period—
(i) qualifying contributions and any other income or profit whatsoever received by it during the period,
(ii) any expenditure made by it during the period, and
(iii) any balances held during the period;][3]

[(*i*) submit to the regulatory body at its request, not later than [fourteenth day following the day on which the request is made][4], independently audited financial accounts for the approved body's last financial year; but such a request may not be made earlier than 10 months following the end of that financial year; and][3]

(*j*) pay to the regulatory body an amount equal to 5 per cent of each qualifying contribution it receives, or such lesser amount as the regulatory body may require, towards its running costs within 14 days of receipt of a demand for payment.

[(2) For the purposes of paragraphs (1)(*h*), (1)(*ha*) and (1*hb*) the relevant period in respect of an approved body is—
(*a*) in the case of the first such period, the period commencing with the date on which the body was approved and ending on the following 31st March; and
(*b*) in the case of subsequent periods, the period of 12 months commencing with the day after the end of the first or, as the case may require, a subsequent period.][3]

[(3) The day referred to in paragraphs [(1)(*ha*) and (1)(*hb*) is the twenty-eighth][4] day following the day on which a request is made.

(4) Where an approved body submits details in accordance with a request made under paragraph (1)(*ha*) or paragraph (1)(*hb*) the requirement in paragraph (1)(*h*) shall not apply in respect of those details.][3]][1]

Amendments—[1] This regulation inserted by the Landfill Tax (Amendment) Regulations, SI 1999/3270, regs 2, 7, with effect from 1 January 2000.

[2] Words substituted by the Landfill Tax (Amendment) Regulations, SI 2002/1 regs 2, 3 with effect from 1 February 2002.

[3] In para (1), sub-paras (*aa*), (*ha*), (*hb*) inserted, words in sub-para (*f*) substituted and revoked, sub-para (*i*) substituted; para (2) substituted and paras (3), (4) inserted; by the Landfill Tax (Amendment) Regulations, SI 2007/965 reg 3 with effect from 1 April 2007.

[4] Words in paras (1)(*h*), (*i*), (3) substituted, by the Landfill Tax (Amendment) Regulations, SI 2008/770 reg 3 with effect from 1 April 2008.

Functions of the regulatory body

34—(1) The regulatory body—
[(*a*) shall, on application being made to it by a body which is eligible to be approved under regulation 33 above, approve that body;][1]
[(*aa*) may—

Landfill tax

(i) at the time a body is approved, or
(ii) subsequently, by notice delivered to that body,

impose such conditions as it sees fit;

(*ab*) may, by notice delivered to a body, vary or revoke any condition of the approval;][2]
(*b*)–(*d*) . . . [1]
[(*e*) . . . [3]
(*ee*) shall revoke the approval of any body which applies for its approval to be revoked;][1]
(*f*) shall maintain a roll of bodies which it has approved;
(*g*) shall allocate an identifying number (the enrolment number) to each such body;
(*h*) shall remove from the roll any body whose approval [has been revoked under sub-paragraph (*ee*) or regulation 35(1)(*h*)][3];
(*i*) shall satisfy itself, by reference to such records or other documents or information it thinks fit, that the qualifying contributions received by the body have been spent by it only in the course or furtherance of its approved objects; . . . [1]
(*j*) shall publish information regarding which bodies it has approved and which approvals [has been revoked under sub-paragraph (*ee*) or regulation 35(1)(*h*)][3][; . . . [2]
[(*k*) shall, when notified by an approved body of the transfer to or by it of the whole or part of a qualifying contribution or of income derived therefrom, notify the registered person who made the qualifying contribution, and any contributing third party in relation to it, of—
(i) the date of the transfer,
(ii) the name and enrolment number of the body by or, as the case may require, to whom the transfer was made;
(iii) the amount transferred; and
(iv) the approved objects to which the transferred funds are to be applied][1][; and][2]
[(*l*) shall comply with such conditions as the Commissioners may impose from time to time under regulation 35(1)(*aa*) (including any conditions varied under regulation 35(1)(*ab*)).][2]

(2) Where—
(*a*) the Commissioners revoke their approval of the regulatory body without approving another body with effect from the day after the revocation takes effect; and
(*b*) they have not given notice in writing to each body which has been enrolled (and which has not been removed from the roll), no later than the date such revocation takes effect, that they [will be] [1] performing any of the functions specified in paragraph (1) above,

the approval of all such bodies shall be deemed to have been revoked on the day the Commissioners revoked their approval.

Amendments—[1] Paras (1)(*a*), (*e*), and words in para (2)(*b*) substituted, paras (1)(*b*)–(*d*) and word in para (1)(*i*) revoked, and para (1)(*k*) and word "and" immediately preceding it inserted, by the Landfill Tax (Amendment) Regulations, SI 1999/3270, regs 2, 8, with effect from 1 January 2000.

[2] Paras (1)(*aa*), (*ab*) inserted, word "and" in para (1)(*j*) revoked, and para (1)(*l*) and preceding word "and" inserted, by the Landfill Tax (Amendment) Regulations, SI 2007/965 reg 4 with effect from 1 April 2007.

[3] Words in para (1)(*e*) revoked, and words in para (1)(*h*), (*j*) substituted, by the Landfill Tax (Amendment) Regulations, SI 2008/770 reg 4 with effect from 1 April 2008.

Functions of the Commissioners

35—(1) The Commissioners—
[(*a*) may approve a body to carry out the functions prescribed by regulation 34(1) above;][1]
[(*aa*) may—
(i) at the time the body is approved, or
(ii) subsequently, by notice delivered to that body,

impose such conditions as they see fit;

(*ab*) may, by notice delivered to the body, vary or revoke any condition of the approval;][2]
(*b*) . . . [1]
(*c*) may revoke the approval;
(*d*) shall not approve a body without first revoking the approval for any other body with effect from a time earlier than that for which the new approval is to take effect;
(*e*) for any time as regards which no approval has effect, may perform any of the functions specified in regulation 34(1);
(*f*) may disclose to the [relevant][1] body information which relates to the tax affairs of registered persons and which is relevant to the credit scheme established by this Part; . . . [3]
(*g*) having regard to any information received from the [relevant][1] body, may serve notices [under regulation 36; and][3].
[(*h*) may, with respect to the approval of a body approved under regulation 34(1)(*a*), revoke that approval if the approved body fails to comply with any requirement of regulation 33A(1).][3]

[(2) Without prejudice to the generality of paragraph (1)(*c*) above, the Commissioners may revoke their approval of the regulatory body where it appears to them necessary to do so for the proper operation of the credit scheme established by this Part.][1]

Amendments—[1] Paras (1)(*a*), (2), substituted, para (1)(*b*) revoked, and words in paras (1)(*f*), (*g*) inserted, by the Landfill Tax (Amendment) Regulations, SI 1999/3270, regs 2, 9, with effect from 1 January 2000.

[2] Paras (1)(*aa*), (*ab*) inserted by the Landfill Tax (Amendment) Regulations, SI 2007/965 reg 5 with effect from 1 April 2007.

[3] Word in para (1)(*f*) revoked, words in para (1)(*g*) substituted, and para (1)(*h*) inserted, by the Landfill Tax (Amendment) Regulations, SI 2008/770 reg 5 with effect from 1 April 2008.

Repayment of credit

36—(1) Where a person has benefited from an amount of credit to which he was entitled under this Part and the Commissioners serve upon him a notice in relation to a qualifying contribution paid to an approved body—

(*a*) specifying that—

(i) they are not satisfied that the contribution has been spent by the body only in the course or furtherance of its approved objects; or

(ii) they are not satisfied that any income derived from the contribution has been so spent by the body;

(*b*) specifying a breach of a condition to which the approval of the body was made subject and which occurred before the contribution was spent by the body; or

(*c*) specifying that—

(i) the approval of the body has been revoked; and

(ii) the contribution had not been spent by the body before that revocation took effect,

he shall repay to the Commissioners the credit claimed in respect of the qualifying contribution.

(2) For the purpose of paragraph (1) above where—

(*a*) repayment is required in relation to credit that has been claimed in respect of more than one qualifying contribution in an accounting period; and

(*b*) regulation 31(3) applied so that the amount of credit was restricted,

the person shall be deemed to have claimed credit in respect of such proportion of each contribution made in that accounting period as the total credit claimed in accordance with that regulation forms of the total of the contributions made.

[(3) Where—

(*a*) a person has benefited from an amount of credit to which he was entitled under this Part; and

(*b*) the whole or a part of the qualifying contribution in respect of which the entitlement to credit arose has been repaid to him or a person who was a contributing third party in relation to the qualifying contribution,

he shall pay to the Commissioners an amount equal to 90 per cent of the amount repaid to him or, as the case may require, to the contributing third party.][1]

(4) Paragraph (5) below applies where—

(*a*) a person has benefited from an amount of credit to which he was entitled under this Part; and

(*b*) he is entitled to a payment under regulation 20 in respect of a later accounting period in the same contribution year as the accounting period in respect of which that credit was claimed.

(5) Where this paragraph applies the person shall pay to the Commissioners an amount equal to the difference between—

(*a*) the aggregate of—

(i) the amount of the credit from which he has benefited, and

(ii) any other amounts of credit arising under this Part which he is or was entitled to claim, in respect of that contribution year; and

(*b*) the amount of credit which he would have been entitled to claim if he had in fact claimed the aggregate amount mentioned in sub-paragraph (*a*) above in the return for the accounting period in respect of which he was entitled to the payment under regulation 20.

(6) Where—

(*a*) a person has benefited from an amount of credit to which he was entitled under this Part;

(*b*) he acquires an asset from a body to which he has made a qualifying contribution for—

(i) no consideration, or

(ii) a consideration which is less than the open market value of the asset,

he shall pay to the Commissioners an amount equal to 90 per cent of the amount by which the open market value exceeds the consideration; but this is subject to paragraph (7) below.

(7) A person required to pay an amount to the Commissioners by paragraph (6) above—

(*a*) shall not be required to pay more than the total amount of relevant credit;

(*b*) shall not be entitled to claim any further amounts of credit in respect of qualifying contributions made by him to the body in question on or after the date on which he acquired the asset.

(8) For the purposes of paragraphs (6) and (7) above—

(*a*) "asset" includes land, goods or services and any interest in any of these;

(*b*) the open market value of an asset is the amount of the consideration in money that would be payable for the asset by a person standing in no such relationship with any person as would affect that consideration;

(*c*) "relevant credit" means credit arising under this Part—

(i) from which a person has benefited, and

(ii) which has arisen in respect of qualifying contributions made by him to the body in question or treated by virtue of regulation 32(3) as having been received by that body from him.

Amendments—[1] Para (3) substituted by the Landfill Tax (Amendment) Regulations, SI 1999/3270, regs 2, 10, with effect from 1 January 2000.

PART VIII
LANDFILL INVOICES

Contents of a landfill invoice

37—(1) An invoice is a landfill invoice if it contains the following information:

(*a*) an identifying number;

(*b*) the date of its issue;

(*c*) the date of the disposal or disposals in respect of which it is issued or, where a series of disposals is made for the same person, the dates between which the disposals were made;

(*d*) the name, address and registration number of the person issuing it;

(*e*) the name and address of the person to whom it is issued;

(*f*) the weight of the material disposed of;

(*g*) a description of the material disposed of;

(*h*) the rate of tax chargeable in relation to the disposal or, if the invoice relates to more than one disposal and the rate of tax for each of them is not the same, the rate of tax chargeable for each disposal;

(*i*) the total amount payable for which the invoice is issued; and

(*j*) where the amount of tax is shown separately, a statement confirming that that tax may not be treated as the input tax of any person.

(2) In paragraph (1)(*j*) above "input tax" has the same meaning as in section 24(1) of the Value Added Tax Act 1994.

PART IX
TEMPORARY DISPOSALS

Amendments—Part IX (paras 38–40) revoked by the Landfill Tax (Amendment) Regulations, SI 2009/1930 reg 2(1), (9) with effect from 1 September 2009.

PART X
DETERMINATION OF WEIGHT OF MATERIAL DISPOSED OF

Scope

41 This Part applies for the purpose of determining the weight of material comprised in a disposal; and references in this Part to weight shall be construed as references to the weight of such material.

Basic method

42—(1) Except where regulation 43 or 44 applies and subject to paragraph (2) below, a registrable person shall determine weight by weighing the material concerned.

(2) The weighing of the material shall be carried out at the time of the disposal; and for this purpose any time at which section 61 of the Act [requires][1] the disposal to be treated as made shall be disregarded.

Amendments—[1] In para (2), word substituted for words "or Part IX of these Regulations require", by the Landfill Tax (Amendment) Regulations, SI 2009/1930 reg 2(1), (10) with effect from 1 September 2009.

Specified methods

43—(1) Except where regulation 44 applies, this regulation applies where the Commissioners have specified rules for determining weight in a notice published by them and not withdrawn by a further notice.

(2) A specification made by the Commissioners as described in paragraph (1) above may make provision for—

(*a*) the method by which weight is to be determined;

(*b*) the time by reference to which weight is to be determined.

(3) A specification made by the Commissioners as described in paragraph (1) above may provide—

(*a*) that it is to have effect only in relation to disposals of such descriptions as may be set out in the specification;

(*b*) that it is not to have effect in relation to particular disposals unless the Commissioners are satisfied that such conditions as may be set out in the specification are met in relation to the disposals.

(4) Where this regulation applies the registrable person shall determine weight in accordance with the rules in the specification (and not in accordance with the rule in regulation 42).

Agreed methods

44—(1) This regulation applies where—

(*a*) the registrable person and an authorised person have agreed in writing that weight shall be determined in accordance with rules other than those described in regulation 42 or specified under regulation 43; and

(*b*) a direction under paragraph (3) below has not been made.

(2) Rules may be agreed under this regulation as regards—

(*a*) the method by which weight is to be determined;

(*b*) the time by reference to which weight is to be determined;

(*c*) the discounting of water forming a constituent of material disposed of, but this is subject to paragraph (5) below.

(3) Where rules have been agreed under this regulation and the Commissioners believe that they should no longer be applied because they do not give an accurate indication of the weight or they are not being fully observed or for some other reason they may direct that the agreed rules shall no longer have effect.

(4) Where this regulation applies the registrable person shall determine weight in accordance with the rules agreed (and not in accordance with the rule in regulation 42 or 43).

(5) Subject to paragraphs (6) to (8) below, rules may be agreed regarding the discounting of water if, and only if—

(*a*) no water is present in the material naturally and the water is present because—

(i) it has been added for the purpose of enabling the material to be transported for disposal;

(ii) it has been used for the purpose of extracting any mineral; or

(iii) it has arisen, or has been added, in the course of an industrial process; or

(*b*) the material is the residue from the treatment of effluent or sewage by a water treatment works.

(6) Rules may not be agreed under paragraph (5) above where any of the material is capable of escaping from the landfill site concerned by leaching unless—

(*a*) it is likely to do so in the form of water only; or

(*b*) the leachate is to be collected on the site concerned and treated in order to eliminate any potential it has to cause harm.

(7) Where the material falls within paragraph (5)(*a*) above rules may not be agreed under paragraph (5) above unless the total water which has been added, or (in a case falling within paragraph (5)(*a*)(iii) above) has arisen or has been added or both, constitutes 25 per cent or more of the weight at the time of the disposal.

(8) Where the material falls within paragraph (5)(*b*) above rules may not be agreed under paragraph (5) above except for the discounting of water which has been added prior to disposal (and not of water which is present in the material naturally).

(9) For the purposes of paragraph (8) above any water which has been extracted prior to disposal shall be deemed to be water that has been added, except that where the water extracted exceeds the quantity of water added that excess shall be deemed to have been present naturally.

PART XI
SET-OFF OF AMOUNTS

Landfill tax amount owed to Commissioners

45—(1) Subject to regulation 47, this regulation applies where—

(*a*) a person is under a duty to pay to the Commissioners at any time an amount or amounts in respect of landfill tax; and

(*b*) the Commissioners are under a duty to pay to that person at the same time an amount or amounts in respect of any tax or taxes under their care and management.

(2) Where the total of the amount or amounts mentioned in paragraph (1)(*a*) above exceeds the total of the amount or amounts mentioned in paragraph (1)(*b*) above, the latter shall be set off against the former.

(3) Where the total of the amount or amounts mentioned in paragraph (1)(*b*) above exceeds the total of the amount or amounts mentioned in paragraph (1)(*a*) above, the Commissioners may set off the latter in paying the former.

(4) Where the total of the amount or amounts mentioned in paragraph (1)(*a*) above is the same as the total of the amount or amounts mentioned in paragraph (1)(*b*) above, no payment need be made in respect of either.

(5) Where this regulation applies and an amount has been set off in accordance with any of paragraphs (2) to (4) above, the duty of both the person and the Commissioners to pay the amount or amounts concerned shall be treated as having been discharged accordingly.
(6) References in paragraph (1) above to an amount in respect of a particular tax include references not only to an amount of tax itself but also to amounts of penalty, surcharge or interest.
(7) In this regulation "tax" includes "duty".

Landfill tax amount owed by Commissioners

46—(1) Subject to regulation 47, this regulation applies where—
(*a*) a person is under a duty to pay to the Commissioners at any time an amount or amounts in respect of any tax or taxes under their care and management; and
(*b*) the Commissioners are under a duty to pay to that person at the same time an amount or amounts in respect of landfill tax.
(2) Where the total of the amount or amounts mentioned in paragraph (1)(*a*) above exceeds the total of the amount or amounts mentioned in paragraph (1)(*b*) above, the latter shall be set off against the former.
(3) Where the total of the amount or amounts mentioned in paragraph (1)(*b*) above exceeds the total of the amount or amounts mentioned in paragraph (1)(*a*) above, the Commissioners may set off the latter in paying the former.
(4) Where the total of the amount or amounts mentioned in paragraph (1)(*a*) above is the same as the total of the amount or amounts mentioned in paragraph (1)(*b*) above, no payment need be made in respect of either.
(5) Where this regulation applies and an amount has been set off in accordance with any of paragraphs (2) to (4) above, the duty of both the person and the Commissioners to pay the amount or amounts concerned shall be treated as having been discharged accordingly.
(6) Paragraphs (6) and (7) of regulation 45 shall apply in relation to this regulation as they apply in relation to that regulation.

No set-off where insolvency procedure applied

47—(1) Neither regulation 45 nor 46 shall require any such amount as is mentioned in paragraph (1)(*b*) of those regulations (in either case, "the credit") to be set against any such sum as is mentioned in paragraph (1)(*a*) of those regulations (in either case, "the debit") in any case where—
(*a*) an insolvency procedure has been applied to the person entitled to the credit;
(*b*) the credit became due after that procedure was so applied;
(*c*) the liability to pay the debit either arose before that procedure was so applied or (having risen afterwards) relates to, or to matters occurring in the course of—
(i) the carrying on of any business; or
(ii) in the case of any sum such as is mentioned in regulation 46(1)(*b*), the carrying out of taxable activities,

at times before the procedure was so applied.
(2) Subject to paragraph (3) below, the following are the times when an insolvency procedure is to be taken, for the purposes of this regulation, to have been applied to any person, that is to say—
(*a*) when a bankruptcy order, winding-up order, . . . [1] or award of sequestration is made in relation to that person [or that person entering administration][1];
(*b*) when that person is put into administrative receivership;
(*c*) when that person, being a corporation, passes a resolution for voluntary winding-up;
(*d*) when any voluntary arrangement approved in accordance with Part I or Part VIII of the Insolvency Act 1986, or Part II or Chapter II of Part VIII of the Insolvency (Northern Ireland) Order 1989, comes into force in relation to that person;
(*e*) when a deed of arrangement registered in accordance with the Deeds of Arrangement Act 1914 or Chapter I of Part VIII of that Order of 1989 takes effect in relation to that person;
(*f*) when that person's estate becomes vested in any other person as that person's trustee under a trust deed.
(3) References in this regulation, in relation to any person, to the application of an insolvency procedure to that person shall not include—
(*a*) the making of a bankruptcy order, winding-up order, . . . [1] or award of sequestration [or that person entering administration][1] at a time when any such arrangements or deed as is mentioned in paragraph (2)(*d*) to (*f*) above is in force in relation to that person;
(*b*) the making of a winding-up order at any of the following times—
(i) immediately upon [the appointment of the administrator ceasing to have effect][1];
(ii) when that person is being wound-up voluntarily;
(iii) when that person is in administrative receivership; or
(*c*) the making of an administration order in relation to that person at any time when that person is in administrative receivership.

(4) For the purposes of this regulation a person shall be regarded as being in administrative receivership throughout any continuous period for which (disregarding any temporary vacancy in the office of receiver) there is an administrative receiver of that person, and the reference in paragraph (2) above to a person being put into administrative receivership shall be construed accordingly.

Amendments—[1] Words in para (2) revoked and inserted, and words in para (3) revoked, inserted and substituted, by the Enterprise Act 2002 (Insolvency) Order, SI 2003/605 art 5, Schedule paras 65, 67 with effect from 15 September 2003. However, these amendments do not apply in relation to any case where a petition for an administration order was presented before that date: SI 2003/2096 art 6.

PART XII
DISTRESS AND DILIGENCE

[A48 In this Part—

"Job Band" followed by a number between "1" and "12" means the band for the purposes of pay and grading in which the job an officer performs is ranked in the system applicable to Customs and Excise.]

Amendments—[1] Inserted by Landfill Tax (Amendment) Regulations, SI 1996/2100 reg 3 with effect from 2 September 1996.

48 . . .

Amendments—This regulation revoked by the Distress for Customs and Excise Duties and Other Indirect Taxes Regulations, SI 1997/1431 with effect from 1 July 1997. See SI 1997/1431 for the replacement provisions.

Diligence

49 In Scotland the following provisions shall have effect:

(*a*) where the Commissioners are empowered to apply to the sheriff for a warrant to authorise a sheriff officer to recover any amount of tax or sum recoverable as if it were tax remaining due and unpaid, any application, and any certificate required to accompany that application, may be made on their behalf by a Collector or an officer of rank not below that of [Job Band 7][1];

(*b*) where during the course of [an attachment][2] the Commissioners are entitled as a creditor to do any act, then any such act, with the exception of the exercise of the power contained in [section 30(4) of the Debt Arrangement and Attachment (Scotland) Act 2002 (asp 17)][2], may be done on their behalf by a Collector or an officer of rank not below that of [Job Band 7][1]

Amendments—[1] 1 Words in paras (*a*) and (*b*) substituted by Landfill Tax (Amendment) Regulations, SI 1996/2100 reg 4 with effect from 2 September 1996.

[2] 2 Words in para (*b*) substituted by the Debt Arrangement and Attachment (Scotland) Act 2002 s 61, Sch 3 Pt 2 para 36 with effect from 30 December 2002.

SCHEDULE

Regulation 4(1)

FORM 1

H M Customs
and Excise

Landfill Tax

Application for Registration

When you have filled in and signed this form,
please send it using the official reply
envelope provided to:

The Controller
Central Collection Unit (LT)
H M Customs and Excise
Alexander House
21 Victoria Avenue
Southend-on-Sea
SS99 1AY

For official use only:

LVO Code

Reg No.

LT 1A

Date of receipt

Initials

Keyer .... Checker ....

LT 1 Page 1 IB (December 2000)

Landfill Tax

Application for Registration

The general notes, included with this form, will help you to answer the following questions.
Please write clearly in ink and use BLOCK LETTERS.

Remember you should also complete form LT 1A, or LT 50 and LT 51 if you are applying to be registered as a group.

1 Please give the full name of the business.

- *if you are a sole proprietor please give your full name*
- *if your business is a limited company please give the company's name*
- *if your business is a partnership please give its trading name.*
  The names of partners must be shown on form LT 2

2 Please give your trading name (if different from the name given at **1**)

3 Please give the address of your principal place of business

- *Your landfill tax return forms will be sent to this address, unless you specify an alternative communication address at 4*
- *If this address is a landfill site it should also be included on the form LT 1A, or LT 50/51 if you are applying for group registration*

Postcode: ....

Tel no:

Fax no:

4 Please specify an alternative communications address, if appropriate.

- *Return forms and other correspondence are normally sent to the principal place of business, as at **3** above.*
- *Exceptionally you may ask for correspondence to be issued to another address.*

Name:

Business address

Postcode: ....

Tel no:

Fax no:

LT 1 Page 2 (12/00)

Landfill tax

5 Are you applying for group registration?

- *If **Yes**, please ensure that you complete forms LT 50 and LT 51*

Please tick ☑
Yes ☐ No ☐

6 Are you applying to be registered in divisions?

- *Each division of your company to be registered separately, must complete forms LT 1 and LT 1A*

Please tick ☑
Yes ☐ No ☐

7 What is the legal status of your business?

Please tick ☑
Sole proprietor ☐ Partnership ☐
Limited Company ☐

Give details from your certificate of incorporation:
Certificate no. Date of certificate

Other ☐ If other, please give details below:

8 Has your landfill activity been transferred to you as a going concern?

Only complete this box if:

- *you are taking over an existing landfill operation from someone else; or*
- *you have changed the legal status of your business*

Please tick ☑
No ☐ **Go to 10** **Yes** ☐ **Give details below then go to 9**

Date of transfer

Business name of previous owner

Landfill tax registration number of previous owner

9 Do you want to keep the previous owner's landfill tax registration number?

- *If you are applying to keep the number please complete form LT 68*

Please tick ☑
Yes ☐ No ☐

10 Please give your preferred method of payment.

Please tick ☑
Credit transfer ☐ Cheque ☐
Other ☐
(please specify)

11 How many landfill sites do you operate?

- *Please give details on the enclosed form LT 1A, or LT 50 and LT 51 if you are applying to be registered as part of a group*
- *Please see general notes for further information*

Number of sites [ ]

- This number should agree with the number shown on LT 1A, or LT 50 and LT 51 for group registrations.
- If you are applying to be registered as a group, this must be the total number of sites operated by the group as a whole as stated on forms LT 50 and LT 51.
- If the address at question 3 is a landfill site it *must* be entered on form LT 1A or LT 50 and LT 51 for group registrations.

12 Please give the date of your first expected taxable disposal:

- *Please see general notes for further information on taxable disposals*

Date: [ ]

13 Are you registered for VAT in the UK?

Please tick ☑

Yes ☐ Give your VAT registration no. [ ]

No ☐

14 Are there any other landfill business(es) you are, or have been, involved in in the last 24 months? This excludes any sites included in this application.

- *Please give the landfill tax registration numbers of any businesses you are or have been involved in. If you are a partnership or a limited company this means any businesses in which any partners or directors have been involved*
- *Please continue on a separate sheet if necessary*

Please tick ☑

Yes ☐ No ☐

Landfill tax registration numbers of other businesses:

[ ]

[ ]

[ ]

15 Please complete and sign the declaration

Declaration

I, [ ]

(enter your full name in BLOCK LETTERS) declare that the information given on this form and contained in any accompanying document is true and complete.

Signature [ ] Date [ ]

Please tick ☑

Sole proprietor	☐	Director	☐	Trustee	☐
Partner	☐	Company secretary	☐	Authorised official	☐

Data Protection Act 1998

HM Customs and Excise collects information in order to administer the taxes for which it is responsible (such as VAT, insurance premium tax, excise duties, air passenger duty, landfill tax), and for detecting and preventing crime.

Where the law permits we may also get information about you from third parties, or give information to them, for example in order to check its accuracy, prevent or detect crime or protect public funds in other ways. These third parties may include the police, other government departments and agencies.

LT 1 Page 4 (12/00)

Regulation 4(2)

FORM 2

Landfill Tax

Application for Registration

Landfill site details

Please complete this form with the details of all the sites you operate. If you are applying to be registered as a group, you may wish to include your site details on forms L T 50 and LT 51 instead of this form. The general notes will help you. If you require a continuation sheet please photocopy this form.

Do not include any sites which will not receive further waste.

Trading name of site (if different from those entered in boxes 1 and 2 on form LT 1)

Licence No:

Name:

Site address:
....
....
....
....
Postcode: ....

Tel no:

Fax no:

Is a weighbridge used to establish the weight of waste on this site?

Please tick ☑

Yes ☐ No ☐

Type of waste landfilled and estimated tonnes in a year (see note).

Estimated Tonnes

Standard:

Lower:

Exempt:

Controller. Does a person other than the operator determine what materials are disposed of at this site, or part of this site?

Please tick ☑

Yes ☐ No ☐

Trading name of site (if different from those entered in boxes 1 and 2 on form LT 1)

Licence No:

Name:

Site address:
....
....
....
....
Postcode: ....

Tel no:

Fax no:

Is a weighbridge used to establish the weight of waste on this site?

Please tick ☑

Yes ☐ No ☐

Type of waste landfilled and estimated tonnes in a year (see note).

Estimated Tonnes

Standard:

Lower:

Exempt:

Controller. Does a person other than the operator determine what materials are disposed of at this site, or part of this site?

Please tick ☑

Yes ☐ No ☐

LT 1A Page 1 **(Substitute)(LexisNexis)** IB (December 2000)

Trading name of site (if different from those entered in boxes 1 and 2 on form LT 1)

Licence No:

Name:

Site address: ....

Postcode: ....

Tel no:

Fax no:

Type of waste landfilled and estimated tonnes in a year (see note).

Estimated Tonnes

Standard:

Lower:

Exempt:

Is a weighbridge used to establish the weight of waste on this site?

Please tick ☑

Yes ☐ No ☐

Controller. Does a person other than the operator determine what materials are disposed of at this site, or part of this site?

Please tick ☑

Yes ☐ No ☐

Trading name of site (if different from those entered in boxes 1 and 2 on form LT 1)

Licence No:

Name:

Site address: ....

Postcode: ....

Tel no:

Fax no:

Type of waste landfilled and estimated tonnes in a year (see note).

Estimated Tonnes

Standard:

Lower:

Exempt:

Is a weighbridge used to establish the weight of waste on this site?

Please tick ☑

Yes ☐ No ☐

Controller. Does a person other than the operator determine what materials are disposed of at this site, or part of this site?

Please tick ☑

Yes ☐ No ☐

LT 1A Page 2 (12/00)

Trading name of site (if different from those entered in boxes 1 and 2 on form LT 1)

Licence No:

Name:

Site address: ....

....

....

....

Postcode: ....

Tel no:

Fax no:

Is a weighbridge used to establish the weight of waste on this site?

Please tick ☑

Yes ☐ No ☐

Type of waste landfilled and estimated tonnes in a year (see note).

Estimated Tonnes

Standard:

Lower:

Exempt:

Controller. Does a person other than the operator determine what materials are disposed of at this site, or part of this site?

Please tick ☑

Yes ☐ No ☐

Trading name of site (if different from those entered in boxes 1 and 2 on form LT 1)

Licence No:

Name:

Site address: ....

....

....

....

Postcode: ....

Tel no:

Fax no:

Is a weighbridge used to establish the weight of waste on this site?

Please tick ☑

Yes ☐ No ☐

Type of waste landfilled and estimated tonnes in a year (see note).

Estimated Tonnes

Standard:

Lower:

Exempt:

Controller. Does a person other than the operator determine what materials are disposed of at this site, or part of this site?

Please tick ☑

Yes ☐ No ☐

LT 1A Page 3 (12/00)

Trading name of site (if different from those entered in boxes 1 and 2 on form LT 1)

Licence No:

Name:

Site address: ....

Postcode: ....

Tel no:

Fax no:

Is a weighbridge used to establish the weight of waste on this site?

Please tick ☑

Yes ☐ No ☐

Type of waste landfilled and estimated tonnes in a year (see note).

Estimated Tonnes

Standard:

Lower:

Exempt:

Controller. Does a person other than the operator determine what materials are disposed of at this site, or part of this site?

Please tick ☑

Yes ☐ No ☐

Data Protection Act 1998

HM Customs and Excise collects information in order to administer the taxes for which it is responsible (such as VAT, insurance premium tax, excise duties, air passenger duty, landfill tax), and for detecting and preventing crime.

Where the law permits we may also get information about you from third parties, or give information to them, for example in order to check its accuracy, prevent or detect crime or protect public funds in other ways. These third parties may include the police, other government departments and agencies.

LT 1A Page 4 (12/00)

Regulation 4(3)

FORM 3

H M Customs
and Excise

Landfill Tax

Partnership Details

When you have filled in and signed this form, please send it together with form LT 1 using the official envelope provided to:

The Controller
Central Collection Unit (LT)
H M Customs and Excise
Alexander House
21 Victoria Avenue
Southend-on-Sea
SS99 1AY

For official use only

Date of receipt:

Landfill Tax Reg. No.

LT 2 Page 1 IB (September 2000)

These details form part of your application to be registered for landfill tax.

Trading name of Partnership:

Please make sure that **every** partner completes and signs one of the sections below. If there is insufficient space to include all partners, please photocopy this form or contact the Central Collection Unit (see page 1) for additional copies. Please use BLOCK LETTERS and write clearly in ink.

Full name of partner:

Home address:

Postcode: ....

Home telephone:

Signature:

Date:

Full name of partner:

Home address:

Postcode: ....

Home telephone:

Signature:

Date:

LT 2 Page 2 (09/00)

Full name of partner:

Home address: ....
....
....
....
Postcode: ....

Home telephone:

Signature: Date:

Full name of partner:

Home address: ....
....
....
....
Postcode: ....

Home telephone:

Signature: Date:

LT 2 Page 3(09/00)

Full name of partner:

Home address:
....
....
....
....
Postcode: ....

Home telephone:

Signature: Date:

Full name of partner:

Home address:
....
....
....
....
Postcode: ....

Home telephone:

Signature: Date:

Data Protection Act 1998

HM Customs and Excise collects information in order to administer the taxes for which it is responsible (such as VAT, insurance premium tax, excise duties, air passenger duty, landfill tax), and for detecting and preventing crime.

Where the law permits we may also get information about you from third parties, or give information to them, for example in order to check its accuracy, prevent or detect crime or protect public funds in other ways. These third parties may include the police, other government departments and agencies.

LT 2 Page 4(09/00)

Regulation 7(1)

FORM 4

H M Customs
and Excise

Landfill Tax

Request for Transfer of a Registration Number

When Parts 1 and 2 have been completed, the form is to be sent, together with forms LT 1 and LT 1A to:

The Controller
Central Collection Unit (LT)
HM Customs and Excise
Alexander House
21 Victoria Avenue
Southend-on-Sea X
SS99 1AY

Important: You must complete this form if you want to keep the registration number of the previous owner. If the form is not returned by .... , we will assume that you do not want the registration number to be transferred.

Once the transfer of the number has been allowed, it cannot be revoked.

Official use

Date of receipt

Keyer initials ....

Checker initials ....

LT 68 IB (July 2000)

The following notes will help you to fill in this form. Remember both parts of the form must be completed - the first part by the previous owner and the second part by the new owner.

Who can ask for a number to be transferred?

Anyone taking over a business as a going concern (buying a business, without causing a significant break in trading) can ask to keep the registration number already used by the business, but the previous owner of the business must also agree. Where there is a change in legal status eg from a sole trader to a partnership or limited company , the number can also be transferred.

When can a request be made for a number to be transferred?

A request can be made if:

- the previous owner will stop operating the landfill site from the transfer date and will therefore be cancelling their registration;
- the new owner will be operating the landfill site after taking over the business and is not already registered for landfill tax;
- both the previous owner and the new owner agree to the transfer of the number; and
- both the previous owner and the new owner agree to the conditions on this form.

Who can apply, and when?

The application form is in two parts. Part 1 should be filled in by the previous owner and Part 2 by the new owner. The form should be filled in as soon as the transfer takes place and **before** the registration is cancelled. We will also treat the form as the previous owner's request for the registration to be cancelled.

Who has to sign the form?

The form must be signed by both the previous owner and the new owner. If the new owner signs the form, and we agree to transfer the number, this forms a legal agreement which cannot be broken at a later date.

If the legal status of the business is changing, the same person may have to sign both parts of the form. This can happen where one person is acting as both the new owner and the previous owner at the same time. If a partnership is involved in the transfer of a number, all partners must sign the form. If the previous owner was a sole proprietor who has died, the executor must sign. If the previous owner was a partnership, the executor must sign on behalf of a partner who has died.

Where should the form be sent?

The new owner should send it to the address on the front of the form along with forms L T 1 and LT 1A to be registered, and form LT 2 if the business is a partnership. When we have considered the application, we will write to tell the new owner whether the number can be transferred.

LT 68 Page 1R (07/00)

Landfill tax

Remember that both parts of the form need to be completed

Part 1: If you are the previous owner of the landfill business, please read this form carefully and answer all the following questions.

1 Please give your full name, **and** your trading name if you have one:

2 I transferred my business/changed my legal status on:

3 The new owner is:

4 From the above date, I wish to cancel my landfill tax registration because I will cease operating a landfill business from that date. I agree to transfer my number to the new owner. The landfill tax registration number is:

5 If this application is allowed, I agree to the following conditions:

- the new owner will be entitled to any money or credit which Customs and Excise would normally have paid to me if the number had not been transferred; and
- I will have no right to claim any money paid by Customs and Excise to the new owner.

6 Please give an address where we can contact you after the business has been taken over by the new owner.

....

....

....

....

Postcode .... Telephone no. ....

Please tick one box only

☐ Sole Proprietor ☐ Company Secretary

☐ Director ☐ Executor

☐ Partner (All partners must sign).

If there are insufficient boxes on this form, please use a photocopy.

☐ Other - please give details

Signature(s)

Part 2: If you are the new owner of a landfill business, please read this form carefully and answer all the following questions.

1 Please give your full name:

2 I took over a business as a going concern on:

3 I apply to use the previous owner's landfill tax registration number which is:

4 If this application is approved, I agree to the following conditions:

- I will send my first and subsequent landfill tax return form to Customs and Excise no later than the due date, with all the tax shown on the form as due for the period which it covers;
- I will send in any outstanding returns which are due from the previous owner;
- I will pay any landfill tax, interest and penalties due (and not paid) from the previous owner before the business was transferred;
- any landfill tax return made by the previous owner for a period after the transfer date will be treated as made by me; and
- I will have no right to claim any money paid by Customs to the previous owner, before the landfill tax registration number is transferred.

Please tick one box only

☐ Sole Proprietor ☐ Company Secretary

☐ Director ☐ Executor

☐ Partner (All partners must sign).

If there are insufficient boxes on this form, please use a photocopy.

☐ Other - please give details below

Signature(s)

Checklist for the new owner:

- Have you and the previous owner signed the form?
- Have you already filled in and returned forms L T 1 and L T 1A to cover this change of ownership? If not, please send them in with this form. Your application for the number to be transferred to you cannot be processed without an accompanying LT 1 and LT 1A.
- Have all the partners signed the form?
- If you are a partnership, have you completed a form L T 2?
- If you are a limited company, have you included a copy of the certificate of incorporation?

Remember, if the transfer is agreed:

- Your registration will cover all your landfill business activities.
- You will become liable for any landfill tax still owing from the previous owner before the business was transferred.
- The previous owner will no longer have any right to repayments of tax, even if they refer to the period prior to the transfer.

The new owner should return the completed form to the address shown on the front of this form.

Complaints

The Adjudicator reviews complaints not settled to your satisfaction by Customs. The recommendations of the Adjudicator are independent and the service is free. The Adjudicator only looks at complaints, not general enquiries. Telephone the Adjudicator on (020) 7930 2292.

Data Protection Act 1998

HM Customs and Excise collects information in order to administer the taxes for which it is responsible (such as VAT , insurance premium tax, excise duties, air passenger duty, landfill tax), and for detecting and preventing crime.

Where the law permits we may also get information about you from third parties, or give information to them, for example in order to check its accuracy, prevent or detect crime or protect public funds in other ways. These third parties may include the police, other government departments and agencies.

LT 68 page 2R (07/00)

Regulation 11(1)

FORM 5

HM Customs and Excise

Landfill Tax Return

For the period

to

For Official Use

Landfill tax registration number	Period

Warning

You could be liable to penalty interest if all the landfill tax payable is not received by the due date

Due date:

For official use D O R only	

Before you complete this form please read the enclosed general notes. Both sides should be completed.
Fill in all boxes clearly in ink, and write "none" where necessary. Do not put a dash or leave any box blank. If there are no pence write **"00"** in the pence column. **Do not** enter more than one amount in any box.

Fold Here

For Official Use

		£	p
1	Tax due for this period		
2	Underdeclarations from previous periods (must not exceed £2000, see general notes)		
3	**Total** (the sum of boxes 1 and 2)		
4	Overdeclarations from previous periods (no limit)		
5	Tax credit claimed in respect of contributions to environmental bodies		
6	Please specify the amount of bad debt relief claimed for landfill tax in this period		
7	Other credits (see general notes)		
8	**Total credits** (the sum of boxes 4, 5, 6 and 7)		
9	Net tax due or repayable box 3 minus box 8)		

If you have made any contributions to environmental bodies, please ensure that boxes 13 - 20 on the reverse of this form are completed otherwise your claim may be rejected.

If you are enclosing a payment please tick this box (✓) ☐

Official use

LT 100 IB(July 2000)

For official use only

Please give the weight of waste in tonnes, per category, landfilled in this return period **Tonnes**

		Tonnes
10	Standard rate waste	
11	Lower rate waste	
12	Exempt waste	

Please provide information on any environmental bodies to which contributions have been made and for which a rebate is being claimed in box 5 overleaf.

	Environmental body enrolment number(s)	Amount of contribution £	p
13			
14			
15			
16			
17			
18			
19			
20			

SPECIMEN ONLY

Declaration:

You must sign below:

I, ____________________ declare that the

(Full name of signatory in BLOCK LETTERS)

information given is true and complete.

Signature ____________________ Date __________

A false declaration can result in prosecution.

Complaints:

The Adjudicator reviews complaints not settled to your satisfaction by Customs. The recommendations of the Adjudicator are independent and the service is free. The Adjudicator only looks at complaints, not general enquiries. Telephone the Adjudicator on (020) 7930 2292.

Data Protection Act 1998

HM Customs and Excise collects information in order to administer the taxes for which it is responsible (such as VAT, insurance premium tax, excise duties, air passenger duty, landfill tax), and for detecting and preventing crime.

Where the law permits we may also get information about you from third parties, or give information to them, for example in order to check its accuracy, prevent or detect crime or protect public funds in other ways. These third parties may include the police, other government departments and agencies.

LT100 (07/00)

Amendments—Form 5 substituted by the Value Added Tax, etc (Correction of Errors, etc) Regulations, SI 2008/1482 reg 5(6) with effect in relation to returns that relate to periods that begin on 1 July 2008 or later.

Form 5 revoked by the Landfill Tax (Amendment) Regulations, SI 2009/1930 reg 2(1), (11) with effect from 1 September 2009.

1996/1528

THE LANDFILL TAX (QUALIFYING MATERIAL) ORDER 1996

Made . . . . *12th June 1996*

Laid before the House of Commons . . . . *12th June 1996*

Coming into force . . . . *1st October 1996*

Landfill tax

Whereas section 42(2) of the Finance Act 1996 provides for a lower rate of landfill tax to be charged where the material disposed of consists entirely of qualifying material:

Whereas section 42(3) of that Act provides that qualifying material is material for the time being listed in an Order made by the Treasury:

Whereas section 42(4) of that Act requires the Treasury to have regard to the object of securing that material is listed in that Order if it is of a kind commonly described as inactive or inert:

Whereas the Treasury have had regard to that object:

Now the Treasury, in exercise of the powers conferred on them by sections 42(3) and 63(5) and (6) of the Finance Act 1996 and of all other powers enabling them in that behalf, hereby make the following Order:

1 This Order may be cited as the Landfill Tax (Qualifying Material) Order 1996 and shall come into force on 1st October 1996.

2 Subject to articles 3 to 5 below, the material listed in column 2 of the Schedule to this Order is qualifying material for the purpose of section 42 of the Act.

3 The Schedule to this Order shall be construed in accordance with the notes contained in it.

4 The material listed in column 2 of the Schedule to this Order must not be treated as qualifying material unless any condition set out alongside the description of the material in column 3 of that Schedule is satisfied.

5 Where the owner of the material immediately prior to the disposal and the operator of the landfill site at which the disposal is made are not the same person, material must not be treated as qualifying material unless it satisfies the relevant condition.

6 In the case of a disposal at a landfill site in Great Britain, the relevant condition is that a transfer note includes in relation to each type of material of which the disposal consists—

(*a*) a description of the material—

(i) which accords with its description in column 2 of the Schedule to this Order, or

(ii) where a note contained in that Schedule lists the material (other than by way of exclusion), which accords with that description, or

(iii) which is some other accurate description; or

(*b*) where the material is water within Group 9 of the Schedule to this Order—

(i) the description "water", and

(ii) a description of the material held in suspension which, if that material had been disposed of separately, would comply with the requirements of paragraph (*a*) above.

7 In the case of a disposal at a landfill site in Northern Ireland, the relevant condition is that any document produced to evidence the transfer of the material includes, in relation to each type of material of which the disposal consists, a description of that material as specified in paragraph (*a*) or, as the case may be, paragraph (*b*) of article 6 above.

8 In article 6 above "transfer note" has the same meaning as in the Environmental Protection (Duty of Care) Regulations 1991.

SCHEDULE

Article 2

Column 1	*Column 2*	*Column 3*
Group	*Description of material*	*Conditions*
Group 1	Rocks and soils	Naturally occurring
Group 2	Ceramic or concrete materials	
Group 3	Minerals	Process or prepared, not used
Group 4	Furnace slags	
Group 5	Ash	
Group 6	Low activity inorganic compounds	
Group 7	Calcium sulphate	Disposed of either at site not licensed to take putrescible waste or in containment cell which takes only calcium sulphate
Group 8	Calcium hydroxide and brine	Deposited in brine cavity

Column 1 *Group*	*Column 2* *Description of material*	*Column 3* *Conditions*
Group 9	Water	Containing other qualifying material in suspension

Notes:

(1) Group 1 includes clay, sand, gravel, sandstone, limestone, crushed stone, china clay, construction stone, stone from the demolition of buildings or structures, slate, topsoil, peat, silt and dredgings.

(2) Group 2 comprises only the following—

(*a*) glass;

(*b*) ceramics;

(*c*) concrete.

(3) For the purposes of Note (2) above—

(*a*) glass includes fritted enamel, but excludes glass fibre and glass-reinforced plastic;

(*b*) ceramics includes bricks, bricks and mortar, tiles, clay ware, pottery, china and refractories;

(*c*) concrete includes reinforced concrete, concrete blocks, breeze blocks and aircrete blocks, but excludes concrete plant washings.

(4) Group 3 comprises only the following—

(*a*) moulding sands;

(*b*) clays;

(*c*) mineral absorbents;

(*d*) man-made mineral fibres;

(*e*) silica;

(*f*) mica;

(*g*) mineral abrasives.

(5) For the purposes of Note (4) above—

(*a*) moulding sands excludes sands containing organic binders;

(*b*) clays includes moulding clays and clay absorbents, including Fuller's earth and bentonite;

(*c*) man-made mineral fibres includes glass fibres, but excludes glass-reinforced plastic and asbestos.

(6) Group 4 includes—

(*a*) vitrified wastes and residues from thermal processing of minerals where, in either case, the residue is both fused and insoluble;

(*b*) slag from waste incineration.

(7) Group 5—

(*a*) comprises only bottom ash and fly ash from wood, coal or waste combustion; and

(*b*) excludes fly ash from municipal, clinical and hazardous waste incinerators and sewage sludge incinerators.

(8) Group 6 comprises only titanium dioxide, calcium carbonate, magnesium carbonate, magnesium oxide, magnesium hydroxide, iron oxide, ferric hydroxide, aluminium oxide, aluminium hydroxide and zirconium dioxide.

(9) Group 7 includes gypsum and calcium sulphate based plasters, but excludes plasterboard.

1997/1431

DISTRESS FOR CUSTOMS AND EXCISE DUTIES AND OTHER INDIRECT TAXES REGULATIONS 1997

Made by the Commissioners of Customs and Excise under FA 1997 ss 51(1), (2), (3)

Made . . . . *9 June 1997*
Laid before House of Commons . . . . *9 June 1997*
Coming into force . . . . *1 July 1997*

Citation and commencement

1 These Regulations may be cited as The Distress for Customs and Excise Duties and Other Indirect Taxes Regulations 1997 and shall come into force on 1st July 1997.

Interpretation

2—(1) In these Regulations—

"authorised person" means a person acting under the authority of the Commissioners;

"costs" means any costs, charges, expenses and fees;
"officer" means, subject to section 8(2) of the Customs and Excise Management Act 1979, a person commissioned by the Commissioners pursuant to section 6(3) of that Act;
"person in default" means a person who has refused or neglected to pay any relevant tax due from him;
"relevant tax" means any of the following—

. . .

(*d*) landfill tax;

. . .

"walking possession agreement" means an agreement under which, in consideration of any goods and chattels distrained upon being allowed to remain in the custody of the person in default and of the delaying of their sale, that person—

(*a*) acknowledges that the goods and chattels specified in the agreement are under distraint and held in walking possession; and

(*b*) undertakes that, except with the consent of the Commissioners and subject to such conditions as they may impose, he will not remove or allow the removal of any of the specified goods and chattels from the place named in the agreement;

"1994 Act" means Part III of the Finance Act 1994;
"1996 Act" means Part III of the Finance Act 1996;

(2) Any reference in these Regulations to an amount of relevant tax includes a reference to any amount recoverable as if it were an amount of that relevant tax.

Note—Words omitted are not relevant for the purposes of landfill tax.

Revocations and transitional provisions

3—(1) The Regulations specified in Schedule 3 are hereby revoked to the extent set out there.
(2) Where a warrant is signed before the coming into force of these Regulations, these Regulations shall apply to anything done, after these Regulations come into force, in relation to that warrant or as a consequence of distress being levied.

Levying distress

4—(1) Subject to regulation 5 below, if upon written demand a person neglects or refuses to pay any relevant tax due from him an officer may levy distress on the goods and chattels of that person and by warrant signed by him direct any authorised person to levy such distress.
(2) Where a warrant has been signed, distress shall be levied by or under the direction of, and in the presence of, the authorised person.
(3) Subject to regulation 6 below, distress may be levied on any goods and chattels located at any place whatever including on a public highway.

Restrictions on levying distress

5—(1) Where—

. . .

(*c*) an amount of landfill tax is due and the Commissioners may be required under section 54 of the 1996 Act to review a decision which, if that decision were varied or withdrawn, would cause the amount to be reduced or extinguished,

no distress shall be levied before expiry of the last day on which the person who is liable to pay the amount concerned is required, by rules made under paragraph 9 of Schedule 12 to the VAT Act, to serve a notice of appeal with respect to that decision.

. . .

Note—Words omitted are not relevant for the purposes of landfill tax.

Goods and chattels not subject to levy

6 No distress shall be levied on any goods and chattels mentioned in Schedule 1 which at the time of levy are located in a place and used for a purpose mentioned in that Schedule.

Times for levying distress

7—(1) Subject to paragraph (2) below, a levy of distress shall commence only during the period between eight o'clock in the morning and eight o'clock at night on any day of the week but it may be continued thereafter outside that period until the levy is completed.
(2) Where a person holds himself out as conducting any profession, trade or business during hours which are partly within and partly outside, or wholly outside the period mentioned in paragraph (1) above, a levy of distress may be commenced at any time during that period or during the hours of any day in which he holds himself out as conducting that profession, trade or business and it may be continued thereafter outside that period or those hours until the levy is completed.

Costs

8—(1) A person in respect of whose goods and chattels a warrant has been signed shall be liable to pay to an officer or authorised person all costs, in connection with anything done under these Regulations described in column 1 of Schedule 2, as determined in accordance with column 2 of that Schedule.

(2) An authorised person may, after deducting and accounting for the amount of relevant tax to the Commissioners, retain costs from any amount received.

Sale

9 If any person upon whose goods and chattels distress has been levied does not pay the amount of relevant tax due together with costs within 5 days of a levy, an officer or authorised person may sell the distress for payment of the amount of relevant tax and costs; and the officer or authorised person, after deducting and retaining the amount of relevant tax and costs shall restore any surplus to the owner of the goods upon which distress was levied.

Disputes as to costs

10—(1) In the case of any dispute as to costs, the amount of those costs shall be taxed by a district judge of the county court of the district where the distress was levied, and he may make such order as he thinks fit as to the costs of the taxation.

(2) In the application of this regulation to Northern Ireland, in the case of any dispute as to costs, the amount of those costs shall be taxed in the same manner as costs in equity suits or proceedings in the county court in Northern Ireland.

SCHEDULE 1

GOODS AND CHATTELS NOT SUBJECT TO LEVY

Regulation 6

1 Any of the following goods and chattels which are located in a dwelling house at which distress is being levied and are reasonably required for the domestic needs of any person residing in that dwelling house—

- (*a*) beds and bedding;
- (*b*) household linen;
- (*c*) chairs and settees;
- (*d*) tables;
- (*e*) food;
- (*f*) lights and light fittings;
- (*g*) heating appliances;
- (*h*) curtains;
- (*i*) floor coverings;
- (*j*) furniture, equipment and utensils used for cooking, storing or eating food;
- (*k*) refrigerators;
- (*l*) articles used for cleaning, mending, or pressing clothes;
- (*m*) articles used for cleaning the home;
- (*n*) furniture used for storing—
  - (i) clothing, bedding or household linen;
  - (ii) articles used for cleaning the home;
  - (iii) utensils used for cooking or eating food;
- (*o*) articles used for safety in the home;
- (*p*) toys for the use of any child within the household;
- (*q*) medical aids and medical equipment.

2 Any of the following items which are located in premises used for the purposes of any profession, trade or business—

- (*a*) fire fighting equipment for use on the premises;
- (*b*) medical aids and medical equipment for use on the premises.

SCHEDULE 2

SCALE OF COSTS

Regulation 8(1)

Matter	*Costs*

Landfill tax

(1)	*(2)*
1 For attending to levy distress where payment is made of an amount of relevant tax due and distress is not levied:	£12.50.
2 For levying distress—	
(a) where an amount of relevant tax demanded and due does not exceed £100:	£12.50.
(b) where an amount of relevant tax demanded and due exceeds £100:	12½% on the first £100 4% on the next £400, 2½% on the next £1,500, 1% on the next £8,000, ¼% on any additional sum.
3 For taking possession of distrained goods—	
(a) where a person remains in physical possession of goods at the place where distress was levied (the person to provide his own food and lodging):	£4.50 per day.
(b) where possession is taken under a walking possession agreement:	£7.00.
4 For appraising goods upon which distress has been levied:	Reasonable costs of appraisement.
5 For arranging removal and storage of goods upon which distress has been levied:	Reasonable costs of arrangement.
6 For removing and storing goods upon which distress has been levied:	Reasonable costs of removal and storage.
7 For advertising the sale of goods upon which distress has been levied:	Reasonable costs of advertising.
8 For selling the distress—	
(a) where a sale by auction is held at the auctioneer's premises:	15% of the sum realised.
(b) where a sale by auction is held elsewhere:	7½% of the sum realised and auctioneer's reasonable costs.
(c) where a sale by other means is undertaken:	7½% of the sum realised and reasonable costs.

1998/1461

AIR PASSENGER DUTY AND OTHER INDIRECT TAXES (INTEREST RATE) REGULATIONS 1998

Made by the Treasury under FA 1996 s 197

Made . . . . *15th June 1998*
Laid before the House of Commons . . . . *15th June 1998*
Coming into force . . . . *6th July 1998*

Citation and commencement

1 These Regulations may be cited as the Air Passenger Duty and Other Indirect Taxes (Interest Rate) Regulations 1998 and shall come into force on 6th July 1998.

Interpretation

2—(1) In these Regulations unless the context otherwise requires—

"established rate" means—

(*a*) on the coming into force of these Regulations, [6 per cent][1] per annum; and

(*b*) in relation to any day after the first reference day after the coming into force of these Regulations, the reference rate found on the immediately preceding reference day;

"operative day" means the [[twelfth][3] working day after the reference day][2];

"reference day" means the [. . . [3] working day following the day on which the most recent meeting of the Monetary Policy Committee of the Bank of England took place][2];

"section 197" means section 197 of the Finance Act 1996;
the "relevant enactments" are those referred to in regulations 4(1) and 5(1) below;
"working day" means any day other than a non-business day within the meaning of section 92 of the Bills of Exchange Act 1882.

[(2) In these Regulations the reference rate found on a reference date is the official bank rate determined by the most recent meeting of the Monetary Policy Committee of the Bank of England.][3]

Amendments—[1] Words substituted by the Air Passenger Duty and Other Indirect Taxes (Interest Rate) (Amendment) Regulations, SI 2000/631 regs 2, 3 with effect from 1 April 2000.

[2] In para (1), in definition of "operative day" words substituted for words "sixth day of each month", and in definition of "reference day" words substituted for words "twelfth working day before the next operative day" by the Taxes and Duties (Interest Rate) (Amendment) Regulations, SI 2008/3234 reg 3(1), (2) with effect from 7 January 2009.

[3] In para (1), in definition of "operative day" word substituted for word "eleventh" and in definition of "reference day", word "second" revoked, and para (2) substituted, by the Taxes and Duties (Interest Rate) (Amendment) Regulations, SI 2009/2032 regs 15, 16 with effect from 12 August 2009.

[Applicable rate of interest equal to zero

2A *In determining the rate of interest applicable under section 197 for the purposes of any enactments referred to in these Regulations, if the result is less than zero the rate shall be treated as zero for those purposes.]*[1]

Amendments—[1] Regulation 2A inserted by the Taxes and Duties (Interest Rate) (Amendment) Regulations, SI 2008/3234 reg 3(1), (3) with effect from 7 January 2009 and revoked by the Taxes and Duties (Interest Rate) (Amendment) Regulations, SI 2009/2032 regs 15, 17 with effect from 12 August 2009.

3 The Air Passenger Duty and Other Indirect Taxes (Interest Rate) Regulations 1997 are hereby revoked.

[Applicable rate of interest payable to the Commissioners of Customs and Excise in connection with excise duties, insurance premium tax, VAT, landfill tax, and customs duty

4—(1) For the purposes of—
(*a*) [section 60(8) of, and paragraphs 7 and 8(1) of Schedule 6 to,][4] the Finance Act 1994,
(*b*) paragraph 21 of Schedule 7 to that Act,
(*c*) [sections 74 and 85A(3)][4] of the Value Added Tax Act 1994,
(*d*) [section 56(5) of and][4] paragraph 26 of Schedule 5 to the Finance Act 1996,
(*e*) paragraph 17 of Schedule 5 to the Finance Act 1997, . . . [2]
(*f*) section 126 of the Finance Act 1999, [. . . [3],
(*g*) paragraphs 41(2)(f), 70(1)(*b*)[, 81(3) and 123(6)][4] of Schedule 6 to the Finance Act 2000 (climate change levy),][2] [and
(*h*) sections 25(2)(*f*)[, 30(3)(*f*) and 42(6)][4] of, and paragraphs 6 and 8(3)(a) of Schedule 5 to, the Finance Act 2001 (aggregates levy),][3]

the rate applicable under section 197 shall, subject to paragraph (2) below, be 8.5 per cent per annum.
(2) Where, on any reference day after the coming into force of these Regulations, the reference rate found on that day differs from the established rate, the rate applicable under section 197 of the Finance Act 1996 for the purposes of the enactments referred to in paragraph (1) above shall, from the next operative day, be the percentage per annum determined in accordance with the formula specified in paragraph (3) below.
(3) The formula specified in this paragraph is—

$$RR + 2.5,$$

where RR is the reference rate referred to in paragraph (2) above.][1]
[(4) With effect from 1st November 2001 the rate of interest prescribed in paragraph (1) above for the purposes of paragraph 17 of Schedule 5 to the Finance Act 1997 also applies in the application of that paragraph to assessments under paragraph 14 or 15 of that Schedule as amended by paragraph 19 of Schedule 3 to the Finance Act 2001.][2]

Amendments—[1] This regulation substituted by the Air Passenger Duty and Other Indirect Taxes (Interest Rate) (Amendment) Regulations, SI 2000/631 regs 2, 4 with effect from 1 April 2000.

[2] Word "and" in para (1)(*e*) revoked, and para (1)(*g*) and para (4) inserted, by the Air Passenger Duty and Other Indirect Taxes (Interest Rate) (Amendment) Regulations, SI 2001/3337 reg 2 with effect from 1 November 2001.

[3] Word "and" in para (1)(*f*) revoked, and para (1)(*h*) inserted, by the Air Passenger Duty and Other Indirect Taxes (Interest Rate) (Amendment) Regulations, SI 2003/230 regs 2, 3 with effect from 1 April 2003.

[4] In para (1), in sub-para (*a*), words substituted for words "paragraph 7 of Schedule 6 to", in sub-para (*c*), words substituted for words "section 74", in sub-para (*d*), words inserted, in sub-para (*g*), words substituted for words "and 81(3)", and in sub-para (*h*), words substituted for words "and 30(3)(*f*)", by the Transfer of Tribunal Functions and Revenue and Customs Appeals Order, SI 2009/56 art 3, Sch 2 paras 38, 39 with effect from 1 April 2009.

[Applicable rate of interest payable by the Commissioners of Customs and Excise in connection with air passenger duty, insurance premium tax, VAT, landfill tax, and customs duty

5—(1) For the purposes of—
(*a*) [Parts 2 and 3 of Schedule 3 to the Finance Act 2001 (interest payable on repayments etc)][2],

(*b*) paragraph 22 of Schedule 7 to that Act,
[(*ba*) section 60(6) of the Finance Act 1994,][4]
(*c*) section 78 of the Value Added Tax Act 1994,
(*d*) [section 56(3) and (4) of and][4] paragraph 29 of Schedule 5 to the Finance Act 1996, . . . [2]
(*e*) section 127 of the Finance Act 1999, [. . . [3]
(*f*) paragraphs 62(3)(*f*)[, 66, 123(4) and 123(5)][4] of Schedule 6 to the Finance Act 2000 (climate change levy)][2] [and
(*g*) [section 42(4) and (5) of and][4] paragraphs 2 and 6(1)(*b*) of Schedule 8 to the Finance Act 2001 (aggregates levy),][3]

the rate applicable under section 197 of the Finance Act 1996 shall be 5 per cent per annum.

(2) Where, on a reference day after the coming into force of these Regulations, the reference rate found on that date differs from the established rate, the rate applicable under section 197 for the purposes of the enactments referred to in paragraph (1) above shall, from the next operative day, be the [higher of—

(*a*) 0.5% per annum, and
(*b*) the percentage per annum found by applying the formula specified in paragraph (3).][5]

[(3) The formula specified in this paragraph is—

$$RR - 1,$$

where RR is the reference rate referred to in paragraph (2).][1]

Amendments—[1] This regulation substituted by the Air Passenger Duty and Other Indirect Taxes (Interest Rate) (Amendment) Regulations, SI 2000/631 regs 2, 5 with effect from 1 April 2000.

[2] In para (1), words in sub-para (*a*) substituted, word "and" in sub-para (*d*) revoked, and sub-para (*f*) added by the Air Passenger Duty and Other Indirect Taxes (Interest Rate) (Amendment) Regulations, SI 2001/3337 regs 1, 3 with effect from 1 November 2001.

[3] Word "and" in para (1)(*e*) revoked, and para (1)(*g*) inserted, by the Air Passenger Duty and Other Indirect Taxes (Interest Rate) (Amendment) Regulations, SI 2003/230 regs 2, 4 with effect from 1 April 2003.

[4] In para (1), sub-para (*ba*) inserted, in sub-para (*c*) words substituted for words "section 78", in sub-paras (*d*), (*g*) words inserted, and in sub-para (*f*) words substituted for words "and 66", by the Transfer of Tribunal Functions and Revenue and Customs Appeals Order, SI 2009/56 art 3, Sch 2 paras 38, 40 with effect from 1 April 2009.

[5] In para (2), words substituted, and para (3) substituted, by the Taxes and Duties (Interest Rate) (Amendment) Regulations, SI 2009/2032 regs 15, 17 with effect from 12 August 2009.

Effect of change in applicable rate

6 Where the rate applicable under section 197 for the purposes of any of the relevant enactments changes on an operative day by virtue of these Regulations, that change shall have effect for periods beginning on or after the operative day in relation to interest running from before that day as well as in relation to interest running from, or from after that day.

7 Where the rate applicable under section 197 for the purposes of any of the relevant enactments changes on an operative day by virtue of these Regulations, the rate in force immediately prior to any change shall continue to have effect for periods immediately prior to the change and so on in the case of any number of successive changes.

Applicable rate of interest prior to the coming into force of these Regulations

8 The rate applicable under section 197 for interest running from before the date these Regulations come into force in relation to periods prior to that date shall be specified for the relevant enactments in the following Tables—

TABLE 4

Paragraph 26 of Schedule 5 to the Finance Act 1996

Interest for any period	*Rate*
from 1st April 1997 and before 6th July 1998	6·25 per cent

Table 8

Paragraph 29 of Schedule 5 to the Finance Act 1996

Interest for any period	*Rate*
from 1st April 1997 and before 6th July 1998	6 per cent

9 . . .

Note—This regulation not relevant for the purposes of landfill tax.

2007/965

LANDFILL TAX (AMENDMENT) REGULATIONS 2007

Made by the Commissioners for Her Majesty's Revenue and Customs under FA 1996 ss 51(1), 53(1), 53(4)(a), (b), (c) and (ca) and 71(9)

Made . . . . *22nd March 2007*
Laid before the House of Commons . . . . *22nd March 2007*
Coming into force . . . . *1st April 2007*

1 Citation commencement and interpretation

(1) These Regulations may be cited as the Landfill Tax (Amendment) Regulations 2007 and come into force on 1st April 2007.

(2) In these Regulations—

"the Principal Regulations" means the Landfill Tax Regulations 1996;

"the 2003 Regulations" means the Landfill Tax (Amendment) Regulations 2003.

2–5 (*amend* the Landfill Tax Regulations 1996, SI 1996/1527)

6 Revocation of regulation 6 of the 2003 Regulations with saving

(1) Omit regulation 6 of the 2003 Regulations.

(2) Regulation 6 of the 2003 Regulations (saving for contributions made before 1st April 2003) shall continue to have effect with respect to a qualifying contribution that was made, or treated as made, before 1st April 2003 if, but only if, the condition specified in paragraph (3) is satisfied.

(3) The condition referred to in paragraph (2) is that the approved body to which such a qualifying contribution was given or transferred is required to spend that contribution on one or more of the objects described in paragraph (4) pursuant to a written agreement made before the coming into force of these Regulations.

(4) The objects referred to in paragraph (3) are—

(*a*) for the purpose of encouraging the use of more sustainable waste management practices—

(i) research and development

(ii) education; or

(iii) collection and dissemination of information about waste management practices generally;

(*b*) for the purpose of encouraging the development of products from waste or the development of markets for recycled waste—

(i) research and development

(ii) education; or

(iii) collection and dissemination of information about the development of products from waste or the development of markets for recycled waste.

(5) In paragraph 4(*a*) "waste management practices" includes waste minimisation, minimisation of pollution and harm from waste, reuse of waste, waste recovery activities and the clearing of pollutants from contaminated land.

2009/1929

LANDFILL TAX (PRESCRIBED LANDFILL SITE ACTIVITIES) ORDER 2009

Made by the Treasury under FA 1996 s 65A

Made . . . . *21 July 2009*
Laid before the House of Commons . . . . *23 July 2009*
Coming into force . . . . *1 September 2009*

1 Citation and commencement

This Order may be cited as The Landfill Tax (Prescribed Landfill Site Activities) Order 2009 and comes into force on 1st September 2009.

2 Interpretation

In this Order—

"cell bund" means a structure within a disposal area which separates units of waste;

"disposal area" means any area of a landfill site where any landfill disposal takes place;

"hard standing" means a base within a landfill site on which any landfill site activity such as sorting, treatment, processing, storage or recycling is carried out;

"haul road" means any road within a landfill site which gives access to a disposal area;

Landfill tax

"screening bund" means any structure on a landfill site (whether below or above ground) put in place to protect or conceal any landfill site activity or to reduce nuisance from noise.

3 Prescribed landfill site activities

(1) The following landfill site activities are prescribed for the purposes of section 65A of the Finance Act 1996 (activities to be treated as disposals):

(*a*) the use of material to cover the disposal area during a short term cessation in landfill disposal activity;

(*b*) the use of material to create or maintain a temporary haul road;

(*c*) the use of material to create or maintain temporary hard standing;

(*d*) the use of material to create or maintain a cell bund;

(*e*) the use of material to create or maintain a temporary screening bund except where the material so used is naturally occurring material extracted from the landfill site in which the temporary screening bund is located;

(*f*) the temporary storage of ashes (including pulverised fuel ash and furnace bottom ash);

(*g*) the use of material placed against the drainage layer or liner of the disposal area to prevent damage to that layer or liner;

(*h*) any other landfill site activity if in relation to that activity—

(i) paragraph 1B of Part 1 of Schedule 5 to the Finance Act 1996 requires a person to notify or give information, or under regulation 16A of the Landfill Tax Regulations 1996 a person is required to designate a part of a landfill site as an "information area", give information or maintain a record in respect of the area; and

(ii) that requirement is not complied with.

(2) Paragraph (1) does not apply to any landfill site activity if, or to the extent that, it involves material that is or has been otherwise chargeable to landfill tax or exempted from landfill tax.

2010/867

FINANCE ACT 2009, SCHEDULE 51 (TIME LIMITS FOR ASSESSMENTS, CLAIMS, ETC) (APPOINTED DAYS AND TRANSITIONAL PROVISIONS) ORDER 2010

Made . . . . 18 March 2010

The Treasury make the following Order in exercise of the powers conferred by sections 99(2) and 99(3) of the Finance Act 2009.

PART 1
APPOINTED DAYS AND PRELIMINARY PROVISIONS

1 Citation and interpretation

(1) This Order may be cited as the Finance Act 2009, Schedule 51 (Time Limits for Assessments, Claims, etc) (Appointed Days and Transitional Provisions) Order 2010.

(2) In this Order a reference to a paragraph (without more) is a reference to that paragraph of Schedule 51 to the Finance Act 2009.

(3) In this Order—

"The Commissioners" means the Commissioners for Her Majesty's Revenue and Customs;

"FA", followed by a year, means the Finance Act of that year.

"IHTA 1984" means the Inheritance Tax Act 1984;

2 Appointed days

(1) The day appointed as the day on which the amendments made by paragraphs 1 to 4 and 27 to 43 (insurance premium tax, aggregates levy, climate change levy, landfill tax and minor and consequential provision) come into force is 1st April 2010.

(2) The day appointed as the day on which the amendments made by paragraphs 5 to 26 (inheritance tax, stamp duty land tax and petroleum revenue tax) come into force is 1st April 2011.

PART 2
TRANSITIONAL PROVISION

3–23(not relevant to LFT)

24 Landfill tax: claims

The amendment made by paragraph 38 is disregarded where claims made under paragraph 14 of Schedule 5 to FA 1996 (recovery of overpaid tax) are for the repayment of an amount paid to the Commissioners on or before 31st March 2007.

25 The amendment made by paragraph 39 is disregarded where claims made under paragraph 29 of Schedule 5 to FA 1996 (interest payable by the Commissioners) relate to an applicable period which ends on or before 31st March 2007.

26 Landfill tax: assessments

The amendments made by paragraph 40(2), (3) and (4) are disregarded where, for the purposes of paragraph 33(1) and (3) of Schedule 5 to FA 1996 (assessments: time limits), the "relevant event" occurred on or before 31st March 2007.

27 The amendments made by paragraph 40(5) are disregarded where, for the purposes of paragraph 33(4) of Schedule 5 to FA 1996 (assessments: time limits), the "relevant event" occurred on or before 31st March 2007.

28 The amendments made by paragraph 40(6) are disregarded where, for the purposes of paragraph 33(5) of Schedule 5 to FA 1996 (assessments: time limits), the death occurred on or before 31st March 2007.

Landfill Tax
Extra-Statutory Concessions

Note—These Concessions are numbered as they appear in VAT Notice 48.

Contents

NOTICE 48

July 2009.

This notice cancels and replaces Notice 48 (March 2002). Details of any changes to the previous version can be found in paragraph 1.1 of this notice.

SECTION 5: LANDFILL TAX—CONCESSIONS DESIGNED TO REMOVE INEQUITIES OR ANOMALIES IN ADMINISTRATION

5.1 Landfill tax—Used foundry sand

By way of concession, used foundry sand shall be treated as falling within Group 3 (Minerals) of the Landfill Tax (Qualifying Material) Order 1996. This means that used foundry sand, when disposed to landfill, shall attract the lower rate of landfill tax.

SECTION 10: CONCESSIONS OBSOLETE SINCE LAST EDITION OF UPDATE 1 TO NOTICE 48 (PUBLISHED OCTOBER 2000)

10.3 Landfill tax—Temporary disposal of material in designated areas for storage or sorting pending use in site restoration

1. For the purposes of Part IX of the Landfill Tax Regulations 1996—

(a) *the following may be treated as a qualifying use—*

— *storage of qualifying material for later use in restoration of the landfill site, and*
— *sorting of material into qualifying material for storage for use, or for immediate use, in restoration of the landfill site and other material for disposal; and*
— *the relevant period as defined in regulation 38(5)(c) for the purposes of the application of regulation 38(2)(c) in respect of such use may be treated as being 3 years.*

2. The concession applies only to disposals of material made on or after 1 October 1999.

3. Before applying this concession to any disposal, a site operator must apply to the Commissioners for an area to be designated under regulation 38 for, or in the case of an existing designated area for its designation to be amended to permit, the temporary disposal of material in the area pending all the material being put to the qualifying use set out in the concession.

4. Application of this concession is subject to compliance with all conditions imposed by or under Part IX of the above regulations applicable to, and to the operation of, the area designated for temporary disposals of material pending its being put to the qualifying use specified in the concession, including the record keeping requirement imposed by regulation 39.

Landfill Tax
Press releases etc

Contents

Press Releases etc

LANDFILL TAX—FURTHER AMENDMENTS TO MEET INDUSTRY CONCERNS

21 March 1996. *News Release 18/96*

The Government today tabled a number of amendments to the landfill tax provisions in the Finance Bill [see below] for debate at Report Stage on 27 and 28 March. They deal mainly with exemptions from the tax and the adjustment of contracts provisions and reflect the close and helpful dialogue that continues to take place with industry in the run up to the introduction of the tax on 1 October.

DREDGINGS

The Paymaster General announced in Committee that dredgings from inland waterways, harbours and ports will be exempt from landfill tax. The waste is naturally occurring and exists only through natural forces. Dredging also has the beneficial effect of keeping waterways clear for navigation and preventing floods. Customs & Excise have consulted with the dredging industry on the precise wording of the clause to ensure that it does not give rise to any ambiguity, and the wording of the new clause to the Finance Bill reflects the industry's concerns.

MINES AND QUARRIES WASTE

The Paymaster General also announced in committee that waste from mines and quarries would be exempt. The exemption will apply to all naturally occurring waste arising from mining and quarrying operations which has not been processed in a way which permanently alters its chemical characteristics, whether it is landfilled at the point of production or elsewhere. As with dredgings, Customs & Excise have consulted with representatives of the industry on the precise terms of the exemption to ensure their concerns are reflected.

CONTAMINATED LAND

Customs & Excise have also consulted widely about a proposed exemption from the tax for waste from historically contaminated land. The consultation took place on a draft clause linking the exemption to planning approval, in order to provide an objective criterion for eligibility to the exemption. However, following the consultation exercise, it was clear that it was not possible to proceed in this way as too many clearance projects do not require planning permission or do not have as part of the planning approval a requirement to clear polluted land.

The Government now intends to provide an exemption for waste from the clearance of contaminated land where clearance of all or part of the contamination is necessary to allow the land to be used for the intended purpose when the development or work on the land is complete. The exemption will apply to waste arising from the reclamation of the land, but current polluters will not be able to benefit from it.

The Government has not tabled a Report Stage amendment to provide for an exemption based on this alternative approach as time constraints would not have allowed for any further consultation. However, under another new clause tabled today, the Treasury will be able to make orders to add to, delete or vary the definition of waste exempt from the tax. The Government intends to use this order-making power to introduce the exemption for historically contaminated land. This will enable Customs & Excise to consult further over any difficulties with a view to putting a draft order out for consultation early in April.

ADJUSTMENT OF CONTRACTS

The Finance Bill as published allows contracts relating to material which is disposed of to landfill, or to be transported or otherwise handled before such disposal, to be adjusted to take account of the introduction of the tax or any future change in rate. Under the Bill as published, the payment under the contract could be adjusted to the amount "which can reasonably be expected the parties would have agreed". There was concern that the "reasonableness" test could have led to a great deal of litigation. Following consultation with those involved, the Government has tabled an amendment to simplify the provision so that landfill tax can be passed on automatically unless the contract specifically provides otherwise.

To meet concerns of those in the construction industry, the Government has tabled a second amendment to the adjustment of contracts provisions. This will enable constructors contracts for the redevelopment of sites, including the preparation of the site, to be adjusted in such a way that the tax can be passed on to the company on whose behalf the construction company is undertaking the work.

TECHNICAL AMENDMENTS

A number of minor amendments of a more technical nature have also been tabled—

- to extend the adjustment of rent provisions so that where a landfill site lease describes payments related to turnover as royalties or a similar term, the tax can be ignored;
- to clarify the definition of a landfill site and landfill site operator for tax purposes;
- to limit the period during which any repayment of overpaid landfill tax can be claimed to six years from the date the overpayment occurred; and
- to allow Customs & Excise to require the preservation of records which a landfill site operator has not been required to create under landfill tax regulations.

GOVERNMENT ANNOUNCES OUTCOME OF CONSULTATION ON SCOPE OF LOWER RATE OF LANDFILL TAX

26 March 1996. *News Release 21/96*

In response to a Parliamentary Question from Matthew Banks, MP for Southport, the Paymaster General, David Heathcoat-Amory, has announced today the outcome of the Customs & Excise consultation exercise on the scope of the lower rate of landfill tax.

The Chancellor announced in the last Budget that, when the tax is introduced on 1 October, inactive or inert waste would be liable to landfill tax at a lower rate of £2 per tonne and all other taxable waste would be liable at £7 per tonne. Customs & Excise issued a consultation paper on 15 December 1995 setting out the Government's proposals for what wastes would be liable at £2 per tonne.

Customs & Excise have now analysed the replies which they received to the consultation exercise. On the basis of the information provided and representations made, the Government has concluded that the lower rate of landfill tax should apply to the wastes listed below. Mixtures consisting only of listed wastes will qualify for the lower rate, as will water with suspended solids consisting only of listed wastes.

In order to be taxable at the lower rate, listed wastes (or mixtures of such wastes) must not contain or be contaminated with any material which is not listed below. But a *de minimis* level will apply to enable wastes to qualify for the lower rate if they consist wholly of listed wastes, apart from a small quantity of material which is not listed, provided that that material does not lead to any potential for pollution. Where wastes appear on the lower rate list and are also covered by an exemption, the exemption will apply.

1 *Naturally occurring rocks and soils*—including clay, sand, gravel, sandstone, limestone, crushed stone, china clay, clean building or demolition stone such as sandstone, limestone or slate, topsoil, peat, silt and dredgings.

2 *Ceramic or cemented materials*—glass; ceramics—including bricks, tiles, clay ware, pottery, china, bricks and mortar; concrete including reinforced concrete, concrete blocks, breeze blocks and thermalite blocks.

3 *Processed or prepared mineral materials, which have not been used or contaminated*—moulding sands and clays; clay absorbents, including Fuller's earth and bentonite and other mineral absorbents; man-made mineral fibres, including glass fibre; silica; mica; abrasives.

4 *Furnace slags.*

5 *Certain ash*—bottom ash and fly ash from wood or coal combustion (including pulverised fuel ash from coal combustion).

6 *Low activity inorganic compounds*—titanium dioxide; calcium carbonate; magnesium carbonate; magnesium oxide; magnesium hydroxide; ferric oxide; ferric hydroxide; aluminium oxide.

7 *Gypsum and plaster*—these will be subject to the lower rate only if disposed of in landfill sites licensed only to take inactive or inert waste.

8 *Other wastes*—there are, in addition to the above, a few wastes on which Customs & Excise are seeking further information before a conclusion is reached as to whether the lower rate is appropriate.

CUSTOMS & EXCISE PUBLISH INFORMATION NOTES ABOUT LANDFILL TAX

27 August 1996. *Business Brief 18/96*

Customs & Excise have published a series of information notes on the landfill tax (see below). The notes will help registrable landfill site operators who will be responsible for accounting for and paying landfill tax to Customs & Excise.

Landfill tax is introduced on 1 October 1996. From that date most waste disposed of at a registrable landfill site is liable to landfill tax. There are two rates of tax—£2 per tonne if the waste is inactive (this means it is less likely to cause pollution) and £7 per tonne for active waste.

Every business produces waste that it pays to have collected and disposed of, some of which goes to landfill. Therefore, the costs of waste disposal will probably increase after October 1996. Businesses may want to investigate the sort of waste they generate and consider whether they can do anything to reduce those costs. They may, for example, think about recycling or reuse rather than landfill. Therefore, the information notes may also be of interest to others involved in the disposal of waste, such as waste producers and waste carriers.

Some of the tax can be used to fund environmental purposes by allowing credit of landfill tax to operators of landfill sites who make contributions to approved environmental bodies. Information note 8/96 explains how this scheme works and will be of interest to those concerned about environmental issues.

The list of information notes are as follows—

Note	*Subject*
1/96 (revised)	Introduction to landfill tax
2/96	Registration
3/96	Tax liability
4/96	Calculating the weight of waste
5/96	Tax points
6/96	Records
7/96	Accounting for tax
8/96	Environmental bodies
9/96	Penalties and interest
10/96	Reviews and appeals
11/96	Contaminated land

For further information or copies of the information notes please contact the Landfill Tax Helpdesk, HM Customs & Excise, Dobson House, Regent Centre, Gosforth, Newcastle upon Tyne NE3 3PF. Telephone number 0645 128 484 or fax number 0645 129 595 (both at local call rate).

FOUNDRY SAND AND THE LANDFILL TAX

18 September 1996. *News Release 48/96*

Foundry sand will initially attract the lower rate of £2 per tonne of landfill tax, Customs & Excise announced today.

Customs & Excise's announcement follows an extensive consultation exercise with the foundry industry and will allow landfill site operators and producers to plan with certainty for the introduction of the tax on 1 October 1996. This decision will be reviewed when the results of further tests on foundry sand are available. Sand is used in the foundry industry for casting and is eventually discarded to landfill sites.

Landfill tax was first announced in the Chancellor's 1994 Budget and there has been extensive consultation with all sectors of the industry and individual producers on the basis and structure of the tax.

The standard rate of landfill tax is £7 per tonne.

INTRODUCTION OF LANDFILL TAX

30 September 1996. *News Release 51/96*

A new and imaginative way to encourage more environmentally friendly ways of waste disposal, while helping to create more jobs, comes into place tomorrow.

The landfill tax will help motivate waste producers to reduce their use of landfill sites and find better ways of dealing with their waste. The money raised from the tax will be used to reduce employers' national insurance contributions by £500 million from next April. This will help to create and maintain existing jobs.

The Exchequer Secretary, Phillip Oppenheim, welcomed the introduction of this new initiative—

"After extensive debate and consultation, both in Parliament and with those involved, I believe we have struck the right balance. We are helping to protect the environment while reducing the cost of employment. This shows the Government is keen to use sensible economic ways to achieve its environmental aims."

Environmental Minister James Clappison said—

"The landfill tax represents a significant new policy. The shift from taxing employment to taxing resources has rightly been an aim of the EU but it is the UK that is setting the pace. It marks an important step in extending the use of economic instruments to achieve environmental objectives. The central purpose of the tax is to ensure that landfill costs reflect the full cost of the environmental impact of the activity. By doing this business and consumers are encouraged, in a cost effective and non-regulatory manner, to produce less waste, and to reuse or recover value from more waste."

Department of Social Security Minister Oliver Heald said—

"The 0·2% reduction in the main rate of employers' national insurance contributions proposed for April 1997 comes on top of the substantial reductions of employers' contribution rates we have made in recent years. These demonstrate the Government's determination to help businesses and jobs by driving down employers' non-wage labour costs which are already amongst the lowest in Europe."

The tax will be administered by Customs & Excise who will collect it from landfill site operators. It will be levied per tonne of waste at two rates, £2 per tonne for inactive waste such as builders rubble, and £7 per tonne for active waste such as plastic packaging. There will be an incentive for landfill site operators to fund environmental trusts set up for approved environmental purposes. Site operators making payments to these bodies will be able to claim a tax credit of 90 per cent of their contributions, up to a maximum of 20 per cent of their landfill tax bill in a 12 month period.

NOTES

Landfill tax was announced by the Chancellor in the 1994 Budget and is expected to raise £450 million. The rates and other details were announced in the 1995 Budget, following an eight month consultation by Customs & Excise with groups affected by the tax on how it should be implemented. There are two rates, £2 per tonne for inactive waste, £7 per tonne for other taxable wastes.

The Government proposes to reduce the main rate of national insurance contributions for employers from 10·2 per cent to 10 per cent on 6 April 1997, saving businesses £500 million.

This year Customs & Excise have run a series of trade seminars around the country explaining details of the tax to affected businesses.

CLEARANCE OF CONTAMINATED LAND

5 June 1997. *Business Brief 12/97*

Customs have agreed to grant extra-statutory remission of landfill tax to late applications for the contaminated land exemption, provided certain conditions are satisfied.

Exemption from landfill tax of qualifying wastes from contaminated land reclamation depends on Customs issuing an exemption certificate to the reclaimant. However, an exemption certificate cannot be back dated so that reclaimants applying too late will have had to pay landfill tax on some of their wastes which were disposed of to landfill. In a number of cases applicants have claimed they were late applying for the exemption due to unfamiliarity with, or misunderstanding of, the legal provisions relating to landfill tax.

Claims for remission of tax will only be considered for waste that clearly would have qualified for exemption and that was charged landfill tax at disposal. Such waste must have come from reclamations which have had at least some of their wastes certified to ensure that the application would have been subject to verification by a local Customs Officer.

The Extra Statutory Class Concession (ESCC) applies to exemption certificates issued before 30 June 1997 and claims for remission must be made to Customs by 30 September 1997.

Further details of the ESCC are contained in a Landfill Tax Briefing issued on 26 May 1997. Copies are available from the Landfill Tax Help Desk, HM Customs & Excise, Dobson House, Regent Centre, Gosforth, Newcastle-upon-Tyne, NE3 3PF. Telephone 0645 128484 or Fax 0645 129595.

CHANGES TO THE LANDFILL TAX CREDIT SCHEME (LTCS) FROM 1 APRIL 2003

20 December 2002. *Information note.*

PRE-BUDGET REPORT (PBR) 2002

The pre-Budget report 2002, which may be found on the HM Treasury web site at www.hm-treasury.gov.uk, announced changes to the Landfill Tax Credit Scheme (LTCS) as set out below.

The Government has reviewed the role of the scheme in consultation with key stakeholders. The Government recognises that the scheme has supported many worthwhile community and environment projects that have improved the quality of the environment at the local level. The scheme has also been successful in generating local community involvement in such projects. However, there is less evidence that the LTCS has delivered a step change towards more sustainable waste management, and it has also been criticised for its administrative complexity and for failing to deliver value for money for the tax which is forgone. Recent changes have improved the administration of the scheme, but will not deliver the strategic and coherent approach to waste management which is needed.

The Government has therefore decided to reform the LTCS from 1 April 2003. The level of funding for the replacement schemes will be capped at the value of the tax which would have been forgone in 2002–03 if all the available tax credits had been claimed by landfill operators. Approximately one third of the funding, around £47 million, will continue to be made available through a reformed tax credit scheme for spending on local community environmental projects, ensuring that the current level of support for these types of projects is maintained. The remainder, around £100 million in 2003–04 rising to £110 million in 2004–05 and 2005–06, will be allocated to public spending to encourage sustainable waste management.

The Government will announce its final decisions on sustainable waste management spending over the coming months. Reducing the rate of growth of waste volumes and increasing recycling through kerbside recycling schemes and secondary market development will be priorities for additional investment. The Devolved Administrations will be responsible for the waste spending programmes in their regions.

The Government will also announce further decisions on the administration of the tax credit scheme for local community environmental projects over the coming months. Meanwhile, tax

Landfill Tax

credits which have already been claimed by landfill operators, or which may be claimed until 31 March 2003, will need to be spent under the existing LTCS arrangements. This will ensure that projects which have been allocated tax credit funding will continue to benefit until such time as they are completed.

WHAT THIS MEANS IF YOU ARE A LANDFILL SITE OPERATOR WHO HAS DONATED MONEY THROUGH THE LTCS, OR INTEND TO DO SO IN THE FUTURE.

Up to 31 March 2003 you may continue to claim credit for contributions to environmental bodies (EBs) in the way that you do now. Your contribution can be in respect of a project falling into any of the currently approved objects, including those in categories C and CC. However, from 1 April next year you will no longer be able to claim any credit for a contribution to a project under categories C and CC. An EB that has received a contribution from you up to 31 March 2003, in respect of projects in categories C and CC, may spend that contribution after 31 March 2003.

If you are committed to making contributions to a C or CC project after 31 March 2003, you may wish to consider bringing forward your contribution subject of course to not exceeding your maximum entitlement of 20 per cent of your annual landfill tax liability.

Also from 1 April 2003, the maximum credit of 20 per cent of your annual landfill tax liability that you are entitled to claim in a contribution year will be reduced to ensure that the scheme is capped at a maximum value of around £47 million. This means that from 1 April 2003 you will need to ensure that your contributions do not exceed the revised figure for the maximum allowable credit during a contribution year. As a guide we anticipate that this figure will be around 6 per cent however a precise figure will be announced before 1 April 2003. If your landfill tax accounting period straddles 1 April you will need to pro-rata your contribution so that it reflects the different maximum entitlements. You may calculate this precisely on the basis of your actual liabilities before and after 1 April 2003 or use a simplified calculation based on the number of days in the accounting period each side of 1 April 2003.

The revised maximum entitlement may mean that you need to review commitments you have made to the future funding of projects other than those in categories C and CC.

ALTERNATIVE FUNDING FOR CATEGORY C AND CC PROJECTS AFTER 1 APRIL 2003

Projects which already have tax credits allocated, and where the tax credits are already available, will continue to be able to be funded from those tax credits until they are spent or the project is completed. Decisions on the criteria or scope of the replacement spending scheme will be made in due course. However, the Government is conscious of the need to make announcements in good time for 1 April. Depending on the scope of the replacement spending scheme, it may be possible that projects which are currently eligible for funding under the LTCS will be able to be considered for funding under it.

Commentary—*De Voil Indirect Tax Service* **V20.148.**

CHANGES TO THE LANDFILL TAX CREDIT SCHEME—FURTHER INFORMATION

21 February 2003. *Information Note*

This note gives further information on the changes to the landfill tax credit scheme that were announced at the pre-Budget report last November and should be read in conjunction with the information note issued on 20 December 2002. This information supersedes any previous agreements or previously issued information.

DETAILED CHANGES TO THE LANDFILL TAX CREDIT SCHEME

The following changes will come into effect from 1 April—

- The reduction of the maximum percentage credit of annual landfill tax liability for a landfill site operator from 20% to 6·5%. If your accounting period covers time before and after 1 April then you will need to apportion your maximum percentage credit eg if your accounting period covers March, April and May then you are entitled to a maximum percentage credit in respect of March of 20% of your liability while for April and May that entitlement is 6·5%.

- Landfill site operators will not be able to claim credit in respect of contributions made to object c & cc projects after the 31 March 2003. However there are arrangements for covering that part of an accounting period that falls before 1 April 2003 where the end of the accounting period is not until after 1 April 2003 so that any entitlement to credit can be apportioned. For example, if your accounting period covers March, April and May then when you decide on how much you wish to contribute and to which project it should go, you should be aware that you can claim credit for March at up to 20% of your landfill tax liability. (For April and May it will be at 6·5%). In addition this contribution can go to an object c & cc project if you wish. In respect of April and May it cannot go to a c & cc project. If you do not make it clear to the environmental body that you wish your contribution to go to a c & cc project then any contribution from that accounting period will be assumed to be ineligible for object c & cc projects.
- All current contribution years will end on 31 March 2003 and from that date all operators' contribution years will run from 1 April to 31 March every year.
- Environmental bodies (EBs) will need to account separately for funds that were received in respect of contributions made before and after the end of March. It may be that EBs will ask operators to provide some sort of indicator to them as to what proportion of a contribution is in respect of the period before 1 April and what proportion is in respect of the period on or after that date.

Commentary—*De Voil Indirect Tax Service* **V20.148.**

LANDFILL TAX RATE FROM APRIL 2003

31 Mar 2003. *Written Ministerial Statement (Col 38WS)*

The Economic Secretary to the Treasury (John Healey): Legislation will be introduced in the Finance Bill 2003, to take effect from 1 April 2003, which will increase the standard rate of landfill tax from £13 per tonne to £14 per tonne. The increase is part of a series of £1 per tonne escalator increases, announced in Budget 1999. These increases have been publicised in the landfill public notice (LFT1). HM Customs and Excise is writing to all landfill operators registered for the tax to confirm the date of the change.

INTRODUCTION OF NEW BIODIVERSITY RELATED OBJECT FOR THE LANDFILL TAX CREDIT SCHEME (LTCS)

1 October 2003. *Business Brief 19/03*

In this year's Budget the Government announced changes to the Landfill Tax Credit Scheme (LTCS) including the introduction of a new object to encourage biodiversity. This refers to biodiversity in conservation on a specific habitat or species at a specific site in England, Scotland, Wales or Northern Ireland. The legal term for this change to the LTCS is the "biodiversity object".

From 1 October 2003 a new object will be introduced to the LTCS by amending Regulations. This new object allows contributions to be made by landfill site operators towards biodiversity related projects (including projects where public access to the habitat is not available). The introduction of this new object follows consultation by Customs with stakeholders in the LTCS.

The Government has also been working with Entrust, the regulator of the scheme, and other stakeholders to improve the scheme's operation. Administration of the scheme is being simplified through a reduction in the level of information required from projects and through the use of common systems wherever possible. Better information will be recorded on project funding and audit processes have been improved. The Government will also improve monitoring and evaluation of the scheme and has developed measures of value for money.

FURTHER INFORMATION

The amendment to the Landfill Tax Regulations 1996 is made by the Landfill Tax (Amendment) (No 2) Regulations, SI 2003/2313. Entrust, the LTCS regulator, is able to provide further information on the operation of the scheme and the new object. Details of the scheme and how Entrust can be contacted can be found at www.ltcs.org.uk.

Commentary—*De Voil Indirect Tax Service* **V20.148.**

LANDFILL TAX CREDIT SCHEME

19 March 2004. *Business Brief 9/04*

1 INCREASE IN THE MAXIMUM CREDIT CLAIMABLE

In Budget 2004 the Chancellor announced an increase in the maximum credit claimable under the Landfill Tax Credit Scheme. Landfill site operators who make contributions to bodies with objects concerned with the environment, enrolled under the landfill tax credit scheme, may claim a credit against their annual landfill tax liability. The maximum credit that they may claim currently is 6.5 per cent of that liability. With effect from the start of the new landfill tax contribution year, 1 April 2004, the percentage is to be increased from 6.5 per cent to 6.8 per cent, in line with the Government's commitment to maintain the real value of the scheme.

Landfill site operators whose accounting period covers time before and after 1 April will need to apportion their maximum percentage credit so that it reflects the different entitlements. They may calculate this precisely on the basis of their liabilities before and from 1 April 2004, or use a simplified calculation based on the number of days in the accounting period each side of 1 April 2004.

For example, if their accounting period covers March, April and May then they are entitled to a maximum percentage credit in respect of March of 6.5 per cent of their liability, while for April and May that entitlement is 6.8 per cent.

2 LANDFILL SITE OPERATORS IN NORTHERN IRELAND—WASTE TRANSFER NOTES

The Chancellor also announced changes to record-keeping requirements for landfill site operators in Northern Ireland. Since 1 October 2002, under Northern Ireland environmental law, it has been a general requirement that waste transfer notes are preserved for a period of two years. However, with effect from 1 May 2004, for Customs' purposes, landfill site operators in Northern Ireland will have to preserve waste transfer notes for six years, unless a shorter period has been agreed with Customs.

The change brings the requirements for landfill site operators in Northern Ireland, on the preservation of records and evidence to support a claim to bad debt relief, into line with those for Great Britain.

3 RATES OF LANDFILL TAX

The standard rate of landfill tax, which applies to active waste disposed of to landfill, will increase to £15 per tonne from 1 April 2004, as announced in Budget 1999. The Government announced in Budget 2003 that the rate would increase to £18 per tonne in 2005–06 and by at least £3 per tonne in the years thereafter on the way to a medium-to-long-term rate of £35 per tonne.

Budget 2004 announced that the lower rate, which applies to inactive waste disposed of to landfill, remains at £2 per tonne.

TAX LIABILITY OF MATERIALS RE-USED ON LANDFILL SITES

22 March 2004. *Business Brief 10/04*

Customs wish to announce a change in policy relating to material used on landfill sites.

BACKGROUND

For landfill tax purposes, material is disposed of as waste, if, when disposing of it or having it disposed of on his behalf, the producer intends to discard or throw it away. The fact that someone else uses it or intends to use it, or would have done so is irrelevant. It is the original producer's intention that determines if the material is waste. Only if the material is recycled is the original producer's intention no longer relevant.

DETAILS OF THE CHANGE

Up to now, for the purposes of landfill tax, Customs' guidance has been that material had to undergo a chemical change to be considered to have been recycled. With immediate effect,

Customs will accept that if a material is processed, changing it to a useable material, the process does not have to change the material's chemical properties in order for it to be considered to have been recycled.

The tax liability will now hinge on the intention of the recycler, as evidenced by the nature of the transaction. If a landfill site operator can demonstrate to Customs' satisfaction that the material he uses in site engineering is not discarded by its producer, it will not be subject to the tax.

Currently, one of the provisions for which landfill site operators can apply in order to operate a tax-free area is if they intend to carry out recycling of waste (which includes composting). Customs' revised interpretation of what constitutes recycling widens the scope of this qualifying use with immediate effect.

LANDFILL TAX–COURT OF APPEAL JUDGMENT IN THE CASE OF *EBBCLIFF LTD* SUPPORTS CUSTOMS' INTERPRETATION OF THE EXEMPTION FOR RESTORING LANDFILL SITES

8 September 2004. *Business Brief 24/04*

This Business Brief article reports on the end of litigation following the Court of Appeal's decision to dismiss Ebbcliff's appeal that most of the waste deposited at its site qualified for an exemption from landfill tax.

BACKGROUND

Ebbcliff operate a landfill facility. They registered for landfill tax, and paid tax on waste material deposited at the site. In October 1999 a landfill tax exemption was introduced for inert material, such as soil, used in the restoration of landfill sites. The scheme adopted by Ebbcliff for filling and contouring the site involves the disposal of inert waste into the landfill phase, clay for the capping layer (the impermeable layer of clay or artificial membrane near the top of the site that prevents rainwater from entering and helps to capture landfill gas) and restoration soils above that.

THE LAW AND CUSTOMS' INTERPRETATION

Certain work ('restoration') at a landfill site can qualify for an exemption from landfill tax. The term 'restoration' is defined as work, other than capping waste, which is required by a waste management licence or a planning consent to be carried out to restore a landfill site to use on completion of waste disposal operations. Ebbcliff's view was the exemption applies to all of the inert waste deposited on site above and below the capping layer. Customs' view, which the High Court and the Court of Appeal agreed with, is that restoration means only that work which amounts to waste disposal above the capping layer, ie the restoration soils. The judgment makes the point that "If the exemption was designed to cover all disposals of inert waste made for the purposes of restoring a derelict site to beneficial use, it is hard to see what policy reason there would be for excluding the capping layer from the exemption while including both the waste below and the soil above in the 'exemption'.

LANDFILL SITES WITHOUT A CAP

The Court of Appeal said that in such a case 'it will be a question of fact to be determined in the light of the evidence the point at which the filling of the site ends and the restoration of the site commences.'

Simon's Tax Cases—*C&E Comrs v Ebbcliff Ltd* [2004] STC 1496.

LANDFILL TAX—EXTENSION OF LANDFILL TAX EXEMPTIONS AND A TAX CREDIT FROM 6 APRIL 2005

4 April 2005. *Business Brief 9/05*

This Business Brief article provides information on the extension of exemptions and a tax credit to those landfill site operators whose sites are covered by waste management permits. It also gives details on where to claim, for those landfill site operators who have been unable to claim the exemptions and credit in the past. This article is not relevant to those whose sites are covered by waste management licences or resolutions, as they are already entitled to claim the exemptions and tax credit. Although the majority of permits will be issued in the period 2006 to 2007, some are being issued before then. Permits will ultimately replace waste management licences and resolutions.

BACKGROUND

Section 66 of the Finance Act 1996 defines which landfill sites fall within the scope of the landfill tax. Its original scope included only sites that were covered by a waste management licence or a resolution. This section was amended by the Pollution Prevention and Control Act 1999 and the Environment (Northern Ireland) Order 2002, which added to the list land which is covered by a permit under regulations under section 2 of that Act or Article 4 of that Order.

The above amendments did not insert all the necessary references to permits elsewhere in the Finance Act 1996 and the Landfill Tax Regulations. The changes set out below will rectify these omissions. Budget Notice CE14, paragraph 10, published on 16 March 2005, gives details of the sections of the Finance Act 1996 and the Landfill Tax Regulations 1996 to be amended.

CHANGES

The changes are contained in two Statutory Instruments that come into force on 6 April 2005. These will extend to permit holders the following exemptions and credit:

(a) The exemption for restoring a landfill site with qualifying material (see Note below);
(b) The exemption for filling quarries with qualifying material;
(c) The exemption for the disposal of the remains of dead domestic pets at pet cemeteries;
(d) The entitlement to credit when directed by a relevant authority, for example, the Environment Agency, to remove waste to another landfill site from the site where it was originally deposited; and
(e) The entitlement to temporarily dispose of qualifying material tax free for site restoration purposes.

Note: If the restoration at a) above is required under the terms of planning consent rather than the permit (as is currently the case in the majority, if not all, sites covered by licences) then the current, unamended, law already allows for the exemption.

CLAIMS

Landfill site operators who have been unable to claim the exemptions and credit in the past should send full details to:

Environmental Taxes UoE,
HM Customs & Excise,
Dobson House,
Regent Centre,
Gosforth,
Newcastle upon Tyne, NE3 3PF.

NOTICE OF REQUIREMENT TO GIVE SECURITY FOR ENVIRONMENTAL TAXES

April 2008. *Notice ET1*

Note—See under *IPT* section, ante, for the full text of this notice which is HMRC's Statement of Practice on the circumstances where they may require security for Insurance Premium Tax, Landfill Tax, Aggregates Levy and Climate Change Levy.

USE OF MATERIAL ON LANDFILL SITES—COURT OF APPEAL JUDGMENT IN WASTE RECYCLING GROUP LIMITED CASE

22 December 2008. *HMRC Brief 58/08*

1. This brief is for landfill site operators and is our response to the judgment of the Court of Appeal in *Commissioners for Her Majesty's Revenue and Customs v Waste Recycling Group Limited* [2008] All ER (D) 300 (Jul).

BACKGROUND

2. On 22 July 2008 the Court ruled in favour of Waste Recycling Group Limited in their action relating to landfill tax liability. The Court found that where material received on a landfill site is put to a use on the site (for example, for the daily coverage of sites required under environmental regulation, and construction of on-site haul roads), it is not taxable, as there is not, at the relevant time, a disposal with the intention of discarding the material.

3. We accepted the Court's decision and did not seek leave to appeal to the House of Lords.

DESCRIPTION OF USE OF MATERIAL

4. Notwithstanding any possible future changes to landfill tax legislation that the Government might decide to introduce, the judgment means that materials put to use on a landfill site are not taxable. Illustrative non-taxable uses of material include:

Cell engineering

– Mineral material (including clay) used as part of an artificially established (geological) barrier on the bottom, sides or top (cap) of a landfill. Materials used to protect from damage any geosynthetic product used for landfill containment on the base, sides or top of the landfill.
– Drainage material at the base and up the sides of the site used to collect leachate and allow its transport to a low point for collection/ extraction.
– Material used beneath the landfill cap and up the sides of the site to allow landfill gas to accumulate for extraction. Material used as a preferential drainage layer above the cap to encourage surface water run off.
– Mineral material (including clay) used to protect the cap and provide a restoration layer for planting.

Daily cover

Material used to cover waste during operations and/or at the end of the working day to reduce emissions of odour, dust etc and to reduce the risk of waste disturbance by birds, vermin or insects.

Temporary site haul roads

Material used for the construction of roads within the waste disposal area which give access to the landfill working areas.

Temporary hard-standing

Material used for the construction of bases/surfaces within the waste disposal area on which activities, for example treatment or recycling operations, take place.

Permanent site haul roads

Material used for constructing roads prior to the commencement of landfilling on the site or off the waste disposal area (characterised by construction in tarmac or concrete and incorporating drains, kerbs etc).

Permanent hard standing

Material used for constructing hard-standing areas prior to the commencement of landfilling on the site or off the waste disposal area (characterised by construction in tarmac or concrete with sealed drainage).

Cell bunds—part of the engineering structure

Mineral material including clay used to form separate cells on the base of the landfill as part of the engineered containment.

Cell bunds—not part of the engineering structure

Material used for the construction of bunds within the waste disposal area to separate individual cells, except on the base of the landfill as part of the engineered containment.

Temporary screening bunds

Material used as a temporary shield while landfill or recovery activities take place.

Permanent noise/visual screening bunds or mounds

Material used for the construction of permanent noise or visual screening structures that are intended to remain after the end of landfilling operations.

Gas and leachate pipes and boreholes

Material used to "backfill" the space between the edge of the hole drilled to extract or monitor landfill gas or leachate and the pipe inserted into that hole.

MAKING A CLAIM FOR TAX

5. We will not expect or require operators to correct past declaration errors, which were made on the basis of our prevailing interpretation of the law. Operators will, however, be required to apply the new interpretation of the law from the date of this Brief. Where a landfill site operator wishes to correct past errors and make a claim to us for a repayment of tax incorrectly paid, they may do so, subject to the conditions set out in this section of the Brief.

6. We may reject all or part of a claim if repayment would unjustly enrich the claimant. Broadly speaking, unjust enrichment means that a claimant would get a windfall profit, because the tax or duty that they are seeking to recover was, in effect, paid by the consumer or consumers (their customer or customers) and the claimant is not planning to pass the refund back to the consumer(s).

7. Landfill tax legislation sets out the rules for claiming overpaid tax. Claims can be made in two ways: by adjustment to the current landfill tax return, or by submitting a written claim to us.

8. Where the operator is registered for VAT, an adjustment may be made to their current landfill tax return, but the value of the errors must not exceed the greater of:

- £10,000
- 1 per cent of the box 6 figure on the claimant's VAT return for the VAT return period of discovery, subject to an upper limit of £50,000

9. For operators not liable to be registered for VAT there is a single error limit on the current landfill tax return of £10,000.

10. Where the errors exceed the limits set out in paragraphs 8 and 9, a written claim should be submitted to us (in these cases the errors must not be corrected through the claimant's returns). Any operator (even one eligible to do so) may opt not to seek a repayment through an adjustment to their landfill tax return. An operator that is any of the following:

- ineligible to adjust their landfill tax returns (see paragraph 8 and 9)
- currently deregistered for landfill tax
- does not wish to make a claim by adjusting their returns

should submit a written claim to us with the following information included:

- a statement of the amount being claimed
- the method of calculation in as much detail as possible

The following information should also be included to substantiate the claim:

- the reason for the claim
- the prescribed accounting periods in respect of which claims are being made, allocating amounts to periods
- the dates on which any overpayments, over-declarations or under-claims were made and, if the overpayment was made pursuant to an assessment or voluntary disclosure, the date on which the assessment or disclosure was made
- details of all documents, schedules, etc used in support of the claim

along with:

- a claim for statutory, simple interest under paragraph 29 to Schedule 5 of the Finance Act 1996 (where the claimant considers they are entitled to make one)
- the operator's bank account name, number and sort code (where the claimant wishes a repayment to be credited to their bank account)

11. We are not liable to repay any amount paid to us more than 3 years before the making of the claim and operators must be able to produce evidence that they overpaid the tax on material used on the landfill site for uses described in paragraph 4 above, and must be able to substantiate the amount claimed. Please note that notification to us that an operator intends making a claim in the future will not be treated as a valid claim for time limit purposes. Subject to the three-year limitation period, any claim should also be for all prescribed accounting periods in which the overpayment(s) occurred. Should a claim not take into account all errors or all affected accounting periods, we will seek to set-off amounts owed for these periods against amounts claimed in other periods.

12. Contributions to environmental bodies made as a result of any overpayment of tax will be taken into account and credits in respect of such contributions will not operate to reduce the amount of tax that can be claimed. Otherwise, claims will be paid or credited on a net basis, that is, those amounts paid to us. If, for instance, in a given accounting period the tax due to us was reduced, because the operator has subsequently claimed a credit in respect of bad debts or other credits, the amount of tax claimed should be reduced accordingly.

13. Claimants may be asked to supply information to verify the accuracy of their claim. Where claims have been submitted prior to the publication of this Brief, they will now be considered and information for the purposes of verification may be sought.

14. Advice on the guidance for making a claim set out in this Brief should be sought from our Environmental Taxes Unit of Expertise (address and phone number below).

WHERE TO SEND THE CLAIMS

15. All claims should be sent to:

The Environmental Taxes Unit of Expertise (UoE)
HM Revenue & Customs
Dobson House
Regent Centre
Gosforth
Newcastle upon Tyne NE3 3PF

Enquiries in relation to the submission of claims or to claims that have already been submitted to the UoE should be made by telephone to 0191 201 1749 or by email.

Commentary—*De Voil Indirect Tax Service* **V20.104**.

Landfill tax index

Defined words and phrases are listed separately at the end.

Landfill Tax

D

E

S

T

Words and Phrases

Words in brackets indicate the context in which the word or phrase is used.

accounting period, FA 1996 ss 49, 70(1), SI 1996/1527 reg 2(1)
appeal tribunal, FA 1996 s 70(1)
authorised person, FA 1996 s 70(1)
claim, SI 1996/1527 reg 22
Collector, SI 1996/1527 reg 2(1)
Commissioners, the, FA 1996 s 70(1)
conduct, FA 1996 s 70(1)
contributing third party, SI 1996/1527 reg 30
controller, FA 1996 Sch 5 para 48
credit, SI 1996/1527 reg 2(1)
customer, SI 1996/1527 reg 22
development corporation, FA 1996 s 43(6)
disposal, SI 1996/1527 reg 2(1)
disposal of material as waste, FA 1996 s 64(1)
disposal of material by way of landfill, FA 1996 s 65(1)
earth, FA 1996 s 65(8)
effective date of registration, SI 1996/1527 reg 2(1)
Environment Agency, FA 1996 s 70(1)
established rate, SI 1998/1461 reg 2(1)
group of companies, FA 1996 s 59(2)
Highlands and Islands Enterprise, FA 1996 s 43(6)
Job Band, SI 1996/1527 reg A48
land, FA 1996 s 65(7)
landfill disposal, FA 1996 s 70(2)
landfill invoice, FA 1996 s 61(2), SI 1996/1527 reg 37
landfill site, FA 1996 s 66
landfill site operator, FA 1996 s 41(2)
landfill tax, FA 1996 s 39(1)
landfill tax account, SI 1996/1527 reg 12
landfill tax bad debt account, SI 1996/1527 reg 26
local authority, FA 1996 s 70(2A)
material, FA 1996 s 70(1)
non-qualifying process, FA 1996 s 44(5)
outstanding amounts, SI 1996/1527 reg 22
overdeclaration, SI 1996/1527 reg 13(1)
prescribed, FA 1996 s 70(1)
qualifying material, FA 1996 s 42(3)
quarter, SI 1996/1527 reg 2(1)
register, SI 1996/1527 reg 2(1)
registered person, SI 1996/1527 reg 2(1)
registrable person, FA 1996 ss 47(10), 70(1)
registration, SI 1996/1527 reg 2(1)
registration number, SI 1996/1527 reg 2(1)
relevant accounting period, SI 1996/1527 reg 17
relevant amount, SI 1996/1527 reg 17
relevant disposal, SI 1996/1527 reg 22
relevant tax, SI 1996/1527 reg 17
restoration, FA 1996 s 43C
return, SI 1996/1527 reg 11
running costs, SI 1996/1527 reg 30
Scottish Enterprise, FA 1996 s 43(6)
Scottish Environment Protection Agency, FA 1996 s 70(1)
security, SI 1996/1527 reg 22
tax, FA 1996 s 70(1)
taxable activity, FA 1996 s 69(1)
taxable business, SI 1996/1527 reg 2(1)
taxable disposal, FA 1996 ss 40, 70(1)
taxable landfill contract, FA 1996 Sch 5 para 15(8)
transfer note, SI 1996/1527 reg 2(1), SI 1996/1528 art 8
trustee in bankruptcy, FA 1996 s 50(10)
underdeclaration, SI 1996/1527 reg 13(1)
waste management practices, SI 1996/1527 reg 33(5)
working day, SI 1996/1527 reg 2(1)

Aggregates Levy

Contents

Aggregates Levy Statutes

Contents

PROVISIONAL COLLECTION OF TAXES ACT 1968

(1968 Chapter 2)

1 Temporary statutory effect of House of Commons resolutions . . .

(1) This section applies only to . . . [aggregates levy][7] . . .

(1A) . . .[2]

(2) Subject to that, and to the provisions of subsections (4) to (8) below, where the House of Commons passes a resolution which—

(*a*) provides for the renewal for a further period of any tax in force or imposed during the previous financial year (whether at the same or a different rate, and whether with or without modifications) or for the variation or abolition of any existing tax, and

(*b*) contains a declaration that it is expedient in the public interest that the resolution should have statutory effect under the provisions of this Act,

the resolution shall, for the period specified in the next following subsection, have statutory effect as if contained in an Act of Parliament and, where the resolution provides for the renewal of a tax, all enactments which were in force with reference to that tax as last imposed by Act of Parliament shall during that period have full force and effect with respect to the tax as renewed by the resolution.

In this section references to the renewal of a tax include references to its reimposition, and references to the abolition of a tax include references to its repeal.

(3) The said period is—

(*a*) in the case of a resolution passed in [November or December][3] in any year, one expiring with [5th May in the next calendar year][4];

[(*aa*) in the case of a resolution passed in February or March in any year, one expiring with 5th August in the same calendar year; and][6]

(*b*) in the case of any other resolution, one expiring at the end of four months after the date on which it is expressed to take effect or, if no such date is expressed, after the date on which it is passed.

(4) A resolution shall cease to have statutory effect under this section unless within the next [thirty][5] days on which the House of Commons sits after the day on which the resolution is passed—

(*a*) a Bill renewing, varying or, as the case may be, abolishing the tax is read a second time by the House, or

(*b*) a Bill is amended by the House [in Committee or on Report, or by any [Public Bill Committee][8] of the House][1] so as to include provision for the renewal, variation or, as the case may be, abolition of the tax.

(5) a resolution shall also cease to have statutory effect under this section if—

(*a*) the provisions giving effect to it are rejected during the passage of the Bill containing them through the House, or

(*b*) an Act comes into operation renewing, varying or, as the case may be, abolishing the tax, or

(*c*) Parliament is dissolved or prorogued.

(6) Where, in the case of a resolution providing for the renewal or variation of a tax, the resolution ceases to have statutory effect by virtue of subsection (4) or (5) above, or the period specified in subsection (3) above terminates, before an Act comes into operation renewing or varying the tax, any money paid in pursuance of the resolution shall be repaid or made good, and any deduction made in pursuance of the resolution shall be deemed to be an unauthorised deduction.

(7) Where any tax as renewed or varied by a resolution is modified by the Act renewing or varying the tax, any money paid in pursuance of the resolution which would not have been payable under the new conditions affecting the tax shall be repaid or made good, and any deduction made in pursuance of the resolution shall, so far as it would not have been authorised under the new conditions affecting the tax, be deemed to be an unauthorised deduction.

(8) When during any session a resolution has had statutory effect under this section, statutory effect shall not be again given under this section in the same session to the same resolution or to a resolution having the same effect.

Note—Words omitted from the heading and sub-s (1) are not relevant for the purposes of aggregates levy.

Amendments—[1] Words in sub-s (4)(*b*) added by FA 1968 s 60.

[2] Sub-s (1A) repealed by FA 1993 ss 205(3), 213, Sch 23 Pt VI in relation to resolutions passed after 27 July 1993.

[3] Words in sub-s (3)(*a*) substituted for the words "March or April" by FA 1993 s 205 (4), (7) in relation to resolutions passed after 27 July 1993.

[4] Words in sub-s (3)(*a*) substituted for the words "5th August in the same calendar year" by FA 1993 s 205 (4), (7) in relation to resolutions passed after 27 July 1993.

[5] Word in sub-s (4) substituted for the word "twenty-five" by FA 1993 s 205(5), (7) in relation to resolutions passed after 27 July 1993.

[6] Words in sub-s (3) inserted by F(No 2)A 1997 s 50 in relation to resolutions passed after 31 July 1997.

[7] Words in sub-s (1) inserted by FA 2001 s 49(1) with effect from 11 May 2001.

[8] Words in sub-s (4)(*b*) substituted by FA 2007 s 112(1) with effect from 19 July 2007.

INCOME AND CORPORATION TAXES ACT 1988

(1988 Chapter 1)

827 VAT penalties etc

Note—This section repealed by CTA 2009 ss 1322, 1326, Sch 1 paras 1, 268, Sch 3 Part 1. CTA 2009 applies for accounting periods ending on or after 1 April 2009 (for corporation tax purposes) and for tax years 2009–10 onwards (for income and capital gains tax purposes).
Relevant provisions rewritten to CTA 2009 ss 1303(1), (2), 1306(1).

FINANCE ACT 1996

(1996 Chapter 8)

PART VII
MISCELLANEOUS AND SUPPLEMENTAL

Miscellaneous: indirect taxation

197 Setting of rates of interest

(1) The rate of interest applicable for the purposes of an enactment to which this section applies shall be the rate which for the purposes of that enactment is provided for by regulations made by the Treasury under this section.

(2) This section applies to—

(*a*)–(*g*) . . .

[(*h*) the following provisions of the Finance Act 2001 (interest payable to or by the Commissioners in connection with aggregates levy), that is to say—

(i) sections 25(2)(*f*) [, 30(3)(*f*) and 42(4) to (6)][3];

(ii) [paragraphs 6 and 8(3)(*a*)][2] of Schedule 5; and

(iii) paragraphs 2 and 6(1)(*b*) of Schedule 8.][1]

(*i*) . . .

(3) Regulations under this section may—

(*a*) make different provision for different enactments or for different purposes of the same enactment,

(*b*) either themselves specify a rate of interest for the purposes of an enactment or make provision for any such rate to be determined, and to change from time to time, by reference to such rate or the average of such rates as may be referred to in the regulations,

(*c*) provide for rates to be reduced below, or increased above, what they otherwise would be by specified amounts or by reference to specified formulae,

(*d*) provide for rates arrived at by reference to averages or formulae to be rounded up or down,

(*e*) provide for circumstances in which changes of rates of interest are or are not to take place, and

(*f*) provide that changes of rates are to have effect for periods beginning on or after a day determined in accordance with the regulations in relation to interest running from before that day, as well as in relation to interest running from, or from after, that day.

(4) The power to make regulations under this section shall be exercisable by statutory instrument subject to annulment in pursuance of a resolution of the House of Commons.

(5) Where—

(*a*) regulations under this section provide, without specifying the rate determined in accordance with the regulations, for a new method of determining the rate applicable for the purposes of any enactment, or

(*b*) the rate which, in accordance with regulations under this section, is the rate applicable for the purposes of any enactment changes otherwise than by virtue of the making of regulations specifying a new rate,

the Commissioners of Customs and Excise shall make an order specifying the new rate and the day from which, in accordance with the regulations, it has effect.

(6) . . .

(7) Subsections (1) and (6) above shall have effect for periods beginning on or after such day as the Treasury may by order made by statutory instrument appoint and shall have effect in relation to interest running from before that day, as well as in relation to interest running from, or from after, that day; and different days may be appointed under this subsection for different purposes.

Commentary—*De Voil Indirect Tax Service* **V5.196, V5.361–5.365**.

Note—Sub-ss (2)(*a*)–(*g*), (*i*), (6) are not relevant to aggregates levy.

Sub-s (1) has effect for periods beginning on or after 1 April 1997 (see FA 1996 s 197 (Appointed Day) Order, SI 1997/1015).

Amendments—[1] Sub-s (2)(*h*) inserted by FA 2001 s 49(2) with effect from 11 May 2001.

[2] Words in sub-s (2)(*h*) substituted by FA 2002 s 132(2), (3). This amendment is deemed to have come into force on 1 April 2002.

[3] In sub-s (2)(*h*)(i), words substituted for words "and 30(3)(*f*)" by the Transfer of Tribunal Functions and Revenue and Customs Appeals Order, SI 2009/56 art 3(1), Sch 1 paras 232, 239(1), (2)(*f*)) with effect from 1 April 2009.

FINANCE ACT 2001

(2001 Chapter 9)

ARRANGEMENT OF SECTIONS

PART 2

AGGREGATES LEVY

Supplemental

49 Minor and consequential amendments
Schedules:
Schedule 4—Aggregates levy: registration
Schedule 5—Aggregates levy: recovery and interest
Schedule 6—Aggregates levy: evasion, misdeclaration and neglect
Part 1—criminal offences
Part 2—civil penalties
Part 3—interpretation of Schedule
Schedule 7—Aggregates levy: information and evidence etc
Schedule 8—Aggregates levy: repayments and credits
Schedule 9—Aggregates levy: group treatment
Schedule 10—Aggregates levy: assessment of civil penalties and interest on them

An Act to grant certain duties, to alter other duties, and to amend the law relating to the National Debt and the Public Revenue, and to make further provision in connection with Finance.

[11 May 2001]

PART 2
AGGREGATES LEVY

Charging provisions

16 Charge to aggregates levy

(1) [A tax][1], to be known as aggregates levy, shall be charged in accordance with this Part on aggregate subjected to commercial exploitation.
(2) The charge to the levy shall arise whenever a quantity of taxable aggregate is subjected, on or after the commencement date, to commercial exploitation in the United Kingdom.
(3) The person charged with the levy arising on any occasion on a quantity of aggregate subjected to commercial exploitation shall be the person responsible for its being so subjected on that occasion.
(4) The levy shall be charged at the rate of [£2][2] per tonne of aggregate subjected to commercial exploitation; and the amount of levy charged on a part of a tonne of aggregate shall be the proportionately reduced amount.
(5) The levy shall be under the care and management of the Commissioners of Customs and Excise (in this Part referred to as "the Commissioners").
(6) In this Part "the commencement date" means such date as the Treasury may by order made by statutory instrument appoint for the purposes of this section.

Regulations—Finance Act 2001, section 16, (Appointed Day) Order, SI 2002/809 (the date appointed as the commencement date for the purposes of this section is 1 April 2002).
Simon's Tax Cases—*C&E Comrs v East Midlands Aggregates Ltd* [2004] STC 1582.
Amendments—[1] Words in sub-s (1) substituted by FA 2002 s 132(1), (3), Sch 38 para (2). These amendments are deemed to have come into force on 1 April 2002.
[2] In sub-s (4), figure substituted for previous figure "£1.95" by FA 2008 s 20 with effect in relation to aggregate subjected to commercial exploitation on or after 1 April 2009.
Prospective amendments—In sub-s (4), amount "£2.10" to be substituted for amount "£2" by FA 2010 s 16(1) with effect in relation to aggregate subjected to commercial exploitation on or after 1 April 2011.

17 Meanings of "aggregate" and "taxable aggregate"

(1) In this Part "aggregate" means (subject to section 18 below) any rock, gravel or sand, together with whatever substances are for the time being incorporated in the rock, gravel or sand or naturally occur mixed with it.
(2) For the purposes of this Part any quantity of aggregate is, in relation to any occasion on which it is subjected to commercial exploitation, a quantity of taxable aggregate except to the extent that—
(*a*) it is exempt under this section;
(*b*) it has previously been used for construction purposes (whether before or after the commencement date);
(*c*) it is, or derives from, any aggregate that has already been subjected to a charge to aggregates levy;
[(*d*) it is aggregate that on the commencement date is on a site other than—
(i) its originating site; or
(ii) a site that is required to be registered under the name of a person who is the operator, or one of the operators, of that originating site.][4]
(3) For the purposes of this Part aggregate is exempt under this section if—
(*a*) . . . [3]
(*b*) it consists wholly of aggregate won by being removed from the ground on the site of any building or proposed building in the course of excavations lawfully carried out—
(i) in connection with the modification or erection of the building; and
(ii) exclusively for the purpose of laying foundations or of laying any pipe or cable;
(*c*) it consists wholly of aggregate won—

(i) by being removed from the bed of any river, canal or watercourse (whether natural or artificial) or of any channel in or approach to any port or harbour (whether natural or artificial); and

(ii) in the course of the carrying out of any dredging undertaken exclusively for the purpose of creating, restoring, improving or maintaining that river, canal, watercourse, channel or approach;

(*d*) it consists wholly of aggregate won by being removed from the ground along the line or proposed line of any highway or proposed highway and in the course of excavations carried out—

(i) for the purpose of improving or maintaining the highway or of constructing the proposed highway; and

(ii) [not][4] for the purpose of extracting that aggregate; . . .[5]

[(*da*) it consists wholly of aggregate won by being removed from the ground along the line or proposed line of any railway, tramway or monorail or proposed railway, tramway or monorail and in the course of excavations carried out—

(i) for the purpose of improving or maintaining the railway, tramway or monorail or of constructing the proposed railway, tramway or monorail; and

(ii) not for the purpose of extracting that aggregate;][6]

(*e*) it consists wholly of the spoil, waste or other by-products[, not including the overburden,][2] resulting from the extraction or other separation from any quantity of aggregate of any china clay or ball clay; [or][5]

[(*f*) it consists wholly of the spoil from any process by which—

(i) coal, lignite, slate or shale; or

(ii) a substance listed in section 18(3) below,

has been separated from other rock after being extracted or won with that other rock;][2]

(4) For the purposes of this Part a quantity of any aggregate shall be taken to be a quantity of aggregate that is exempt under this section if it consists wholly or mainly of any one or more of the following, or is part of anything so consisting, namely—

(*a*) coal, lignite, slate or shale;

(*b*) . . .[2]

(*c*) the spoil or waste from, or other by-products of—

(i) any industrial combustion process, or

(ii) the smelting or refining of metal;

(*d*) the drill-cuttings resulting from any operations carried out in accordance with a licence granted under the Petroleum Act 1998 [or the Petroleum (Production) Act (Northern Ireland) 1964][4] . . .[4];

(*e*) anything resulting from works carried out in exercise of powers which are required to be exercised in accordance with, or are conferred by, provision made by or under the New Roads and Street Works Act 1991, the Roads (Northern Ireland) Order 1993 or the Street Works (Northern Ireland) Order 1995;

(*f*) clay, soil or vegetable or other organic matter.

(5) For the purposes of this section aggregate subjected to exploitation in the United Kingdom is aggregate that has already been subjected to a charge to aggregates levy if, and only if—

(*a*) there has been a previous occasion on which a charge to aggregates levy on that aggregate has arisen; and

(*b*) at least some of the aggregates levy previously charged on that aggregate is either—

(i) levy in respect of which there is or was no entitlement to a tax credit; or

(ii) levy in respect of which any entitlement to a tax credit is or was an entitlement to a tax credit of an amount less than the amount of the levy charged on it.

(6) For the purposes of subsection (5)(*b*) above, any credit the entitlement to which arises in a case which—

(*a*) falls within section 30(1)(*c*) [or 30A][1] below, and

(*b*) is prescribed for the purposes of this subsection,

shall be disregarded.

(7) In this section—

"coal" has the same meaning as in the Coal Industry Act 1994; and

"highway" includes any road within the meaning of the Roads (Scotland) Act 1984 or the Road Traffic (Northern Ireland) Order 1995.

Commentary—*De Voil Indirect Tax Service* **V22.108**.

Simon's Tax Cases—*C&E Comrs v East Midlands Aggregates Ltd* [2004] STC 1582; *MMC Midlands Ltd v R&C Comrs* [2009] STC 1969.

Amendments—[1] Words in sub-s (6)(*a*) inserted by FA 2002 s 129(2) with effect from 24 July 2002.

[2] Words in sub-s (3)(*e*) inserted, sub-s (3)(*f*) inserted, and sub-s (4)(*b*) repealed, by FA 2002 ss 130, 141, Sch 40 Pt 4(3). These amendments are deemed to have come into force on 1 April 2002.

Aggregates Levy

3 Sub-s (3)(*a*) repealed by FA 2002 ss 131(1), (4), 141, Sch 40 Pt 4(3). This amendment is deemed to have come into force on 1 April 2002.

4 Sub-s (2)(*d*) substituted, words in sub-s (3)(*d*) substituted, and in sub-s (4)(*d*), words inserted and repealed, by FA 2002 ss 132(1), (3), 141, Sch 38 para 3, Sch 40 Pt 4(3). These amendments are deemed to have come into force on 1 April 2002.

5 In sub-s (3) word "or" in para (*d*) repealed, and word in para (*e*) inserted, by FA 2007 ss 22(1), (2), (4), 114, Sch 27 Pt 1(1) with effect from 19 July 2007.

6 Sub-s (3)(*da*) inserted by FA 2007 s 22(1), (3), (5) with effect from 1 August 2007 (by virtue of the Finance Act 2007 section 22(3) (Appointed Day) Order, SI 2007/2118 art 2).

18 Exempt processes

(1) In this Part references to aggregate—

(*a*) include references to the spoil, waste, off-cuts and other by-products resulting from the application of any exempt process to any aggregate; but

(*b*) do not include references to anything else resulting from the application of any such process to any aggregate.

(2) In this Part "exempt process" means—

(*a*) the cutting of any rock to produce [stone with one or more flat surfaces][1];

(*b*) any process by which a relevant substance is extracted or otherwise separated (whether as part of the process of winning it from any land or otherwise) from any aggregate;

(*c*) any process for the production of lime or cement from limestone or from limestone and [anything else][2].

(3) In this section "relevant substance" means any of the following—

(*a*) anhydrite;

(*b*) ball clay;

(*c*) barytes;

(*d*) . . . [2];

(*e*) china clay;

(*f*) feldspar;

(*g*) fireclay;

(*h*) . . . [2];

(*i*) fluorspar;

(*j*) fuller's earth;

(*k*) gems and semi-precious stones;

(*l*) gypsum;

(*m*) any metal or the ore of any metal;

(*n*) muscovite;

(*o*) perlite;

(*p*) potash;

(*q*) pumice;

(*r*) rock phosphates;

(*s*) sodium chloride;

(*t*) talc;

(*u*) vermiculite.

(4) The Treasury may by order made by statutory instrument—

(*a*) modify the list of substances in subsection (3) above by adding any substance to that list or by removing any substance from it; and

(*b*) make any such transitional provision in connection with the modification of that list under this subsection as they may think fit.

(5) The Treasury shall not make an order under subsection (4) above by virtue of which any substance ceases to be a relevant substance unless a draft of the order has been laid before Parliament and approved by resolution of the House of Commons.

(6) A statutory instrument containing an order under subsection (4) above that has not had to be approved in draft for the purposes of subsection (5) above shall be subject to annulment in pursuance of a resolution of the House of Commons.

Amendments—[1] Words in sub-s (2)(*a*) substituted by FA 2002 s 131(2), (4). This amendment is deemed to have come into force on 1 April 2002.

2 Words in sub-s (2)(*c*) substituted, and words in sub-s (3)(*d*) and (*h*) repealed, by FA 2002 ss 132(1), (3), 141, Sch 38 para 4, Sch 40 Pt 4(3). These amendments are deemed to have come into force on 1 April 2002.

19 Commercial exploitation

(1) For the purposes of this Part a quantity of aggregate is subjected to exploitation if, and only if—

(*a*) it is removed from a site falling within subsection (2) below;

(*b*) it becomes subject to an agreement to supply it to any person;

(*c*) it is used for construction purposes; or

(*d*) it is mixed, otherwise than in permitted circumstances, with any material or substance other than water.

(2) The sites which, in relation to any quantity of aggregate, fall within this subsection are—

(*a*) the originating site of the aggregate;

(*b*) any site which is not the originating site of the aggregate but is registered under the name of a person [under whose name that originating site is also registered][1];

(*c*) any site not falling within paragraph (*a*) or (*b*) above to which the quantity of aggregate had been removed for the purpose of having an exempt process applied to it on that site but at which no such process has been applied to it.

(3) For the purposes of this Part the exploitation to which a quantity of aggregate is subjected shall be taken to be commercial exploitation if, and only if—

(*a*) it is subjected to exploitation in the course or furtherance of a business carried on by the person, or one of the persons, responsible for subjecting it to exploitation;

(*b*) the exploitation to which it is subjected does not consist in its removal from one registered site to another in a case where both sites are registered under the name of the same person;

(*c*) the exploitation to which it is subjected does not consist in or require its removal to a registered site for the purpose of having an exempt process applied to it on that site;

(*d*) the exploitation to which it is subjected does not consist in or require its removal to any premises for the purpose of having china clay or ball clay extracted or otherwise separated from it on that site; and

(*e*) the exploitation to which it is subjected is not such that, as a result and without its being subjected to any process involving its being mixed with any other substance or material (apart from water), it again becomes part of the land at the site from which it was won.

[(3A) For the purposes of subsection (3)(*a*) above "business" includes any activity of a Government department, local authority or charity.][1]

(4) Where, at the time when any aggregate is won from any site, the same person is in occupation of both—

(*a*) that site, and

(*b*) [other land][1] which is occupied, together with that site—

(i) for the purposes of the carrying on of any agricultural business, or

(ii) for the purposes of the carrying on of any forestry business or otherwise for the purposes of forestry,

subsection (3)(e) above shall have effect as if the reference to the land at the site from which the aggregate was won included the [other land][1], so long as it and that site continue to be occupied by that person for such purposes.

(5) For the purposes of this Part where a quantity of aggregate is subjected to exploitation, the exploitation shall be taken to be in the United Kingdom if, and only if, the aggregate is in the United Kingdom or United Kingdom waters when it is subjected to exploitation.

(6) For the purposes of this section a quantity of aggregate becomes subject to an agreement to supply it to any person—

(*a*) except to the extent that it is not separately identifiable at the time when the agreement is entered into, at that time; and

(*b*) to that extent, at the time when it is appropriated to the agreement;

but references in this Part to the supply of a quantity of aggregate do not include references to any supply which is effected, or is to be effected, by the transfer or creation of any interest or right in or over land.

(7) For the purposes of this section a quantity of aggregate is mixed with a material or substance in permitted circumstances if—

(*a*) the material or substance with which it is mixed consists wholly of a quantity of taxable aggregate that has not previously been subjected to commercial exploitation in the United Kingdom; and

(*b*) the mixing takes place on a site which, in a case where it falls within subsection (2) above in relation to any part of the aggregate included in the mixture, so falls in relation to every part of it.

Simon's Tax Cases—*C&E Comrs v East Midlands Aggregates Ltd* [2004] STC 1582.

Amendments—[1] Words in sub-ss (2), (4) substituted, and sub-s (3A) inserted, by FA 2002 s 132(1), (3), Sch 38 para 5. These amendments are deemed to have come into force on 1 April 2002.

20 Originating sites

(1) In this Part references, in relation to any aggregate, to its originating site are references (subject to subsection (2) below)—

(*a*) in the case of aggregate which has been won from the seabed of any area of sea in the United Kingdom or United Kingdom waters . . . [1], to the site where it is first landed after being so won;

(*b*) in the case of aggregate which results from the application of an exempt process to any aggregate . . . [1], to the site where that process was so applied;

(*c*) . . . [1]

(*d*) in any other case, to the site from which the aggregate was won or, as the case may be, from which it was most recently won.

(2) Where any aggregate which is on its originating site on the commencement date has been mixed before that date with aggregate the originating site of which would (but for this subsection) be different, the site where the mixture is situated on that date shall be deemed for the purposes of this Part to be the originating site of all the aggregate comprised in the mixture.

Amendments—[1] Words in sub-s (1)(*a*), (*b*) repealed, and sub-s (1)(*c*) repealed, by FA 2002 ss 131(3)(*a*), (4), 141, Sch 40 Pt 4(3). These amendments are deemed to have come into force on 1 April 2002.

21 Operators of sites

(1) For the purposes of this Part the persons operating a site are each of the following—

(*a*) the person who occupies the site; and

(*b*) if a person other than the occupier exercises any right to exercise control over aggregate on that site, that other person;

and "operator", in relation to a site, shall be construed accordingly.

(2) In subsection (1) above the reference to exercising control over aggregate on a site is a reference to doing any of the following, that is to say—

(*a*) winning aggregate from land at that site;

(*b*) . . .[1]

(*c*) carrying out any exempt process at that site;

(*d*) storing aggregate at that site.

Amendments—[1] Sub-s (2)(*b*) repealed by FA 2002 ss 131(3)(*b*), (4), 141, Sch 40 Pt 4(3). These amendments are deemed to have come into force on 1 April 2002.

22 Responsibility for exploitation of aggregate

(1) Subject to subsection (2) below, the persons who shall be taken for the purposes of this Part to be responsible for subjecting a quantity of aggregate to exploitation are each of the following—

(*a*) in a case of the exploitation of a quantity of aggregate by its removal from its originating site or from a connected site, the operator of that site;

(*b*) in a case of the exploitation of a quantity of aggregate by its removal from a site falling within section 19(2)(*c*) above, the operator of the site and (if different) the owner of the aggregate at the time when the removal takes place;

(*c*) in a case of the exploitation of a quantity of aggregate—

(i) by its being subjected, at a time when it is not on its originating site or a connected site, to any agreement, or

(ii) by its being used at such a time for construction purposes,

the person agreeing to supply it or using it for construction purposes;

(*d*) in a case of the exploitation of a quantity of aggregate—

(i) by its being subjected, at a time when it is on its originating site or a connected site, to any agreement, or

(ii) by its being used at such a time for construction purposes,

the person mentioned in paragraph (c) above and (if different) the operator of that site;

(*e*) in a case of the exploitation of a quantity of aggregate by its being mixed at premises that are not comprised in its originating site or a connected site with any material or substance, the owner of the aggregate at the time when the mixing takes place and the occupier of the premises where it takes place;

(*f*) in a case of the exploitation of a quantity of aggregate by its being mixed at its originating site or a connected site with any material or substance, the owner of the aggregate at the time when the mixing takes place and (if different) the operator of the site.

(2) A person who is responsible for subjecting a quantity of aggregate to exploitation shall not be taken for the purposes of this Part to be responsible for subjecting it to commercial exploitation unless that takes place in the course or furtherance of a business carried on by him.

[For the purposes of this subsection "business" includes any activity of a Government department, local authority or charity.][1]

(3) Where by virtue of this section more than one person is charged with aggregates levy, their liabilities under this Part as persons charged with the levy shall be joint and several.

(4) In this section "connected site", in relation to any quantity of aggregate, means any site that falls in relation to that quantity of aggregate within section 19(2)(*b*).

Amendments—[1] Words in sub-s (2) inserted by FA 2002 s 132(1), (3), Sch 38 para 6. This amendment is deemed to have come into force on 1 April 2002.

23 Weight of aggregate

(1) The Commissioners may make regulations for determining the weight of any aggregate for the purposes of aggregates levy.

(2) The regulations may—

(*a*) prescribe rules for determining the weight;

(*b*) authorise rules for determining the weight to be specified by the Commissioners in a prescribed manner;

(*c*) authorise rules for determining the weight to be agreed between the person charged with the levy and a person acting under the authority of the Commissioners.

(3) The regulations may, in particular, provide for the rules prescribed or authorised under the regulations to include rules about—

(*a*) the method by which the weight is to be determined;

(*b*) the time by reference to which the weight is to be determined;

(*c*) the discounting of constituents (such as water).

(4) The regulations may include provision that rules specified by virtue of subsection (2)(*b*) above—

(*a*) are to have effect only in such cases as may be described in the rules; and

(*b*) are not to have effect in particular cases unless the Commissioners are satisfied that such conditions as may be set out in the rules are met in those cases.

(5) Conditions for which provision is made by virtue of subsection (4)(*b*) above may be framed by reference to such factors as the Commissioners think fit (such as the consent, in a particular case, of a person acting under the authority of the Commissioners).

(6) The regulations may include provision that—

(*a*) where rules are agreed as mentioned in subsection (2)(*c*) above, and

(*b*) the Commissioners believe that they should no longer be applied (whether because they do not give an accurate indication of the weight or are not being fully observed or for some other reason),

the Commissioners may direct that the agreed rules shall no longer have effect.

Administration and enforcement

24 The register

(1) It shall be the duty of the Commissioners to establish and maintain a register of persons who are required to be registered for the purposes of aggregates levy.

(2) A person is required to be registered for the purposes of aggregates levy if he—

(*a*) carries out taxable activities, and

(*b*) is not exempted from registration by regulations under subsection (4) below.

(3) For the purposes of subsection (2) above a person carries out a taxable activity if a quantity of aggregate is subjected to commercial exploitation in the United Kingdom in circumstances in which he is responsible for its being so subjected.

(4) The Commissioners may by regulations provide for persons carrying out taxable activities to be, to such extent and subject to such conditions or restrictions as may be prescribed, either—

(*a*) exempt from the requirement of registration; or

(*b*) exempt from such obligations or liabilities imposed by or under this Part on persons required to be registered for the purposes of aggregates levy as may be prescribed.

(5) The Commissioners shall keep such information in the register as they consider it appropriate so to keep for the purposes of the care and management of aggregates levy.

(6) In particular, where it appears to the Commissioners that any person is operating or using any premises, or intends to operate or use any premises—

(*a*) for winning any aggregate,

(*b*) . . . [1]

(*c*) for applying an exempt process to any aggregate,

[(*ca*) for mixing, otherwise than in permitted circumstances (within the meaning given by section 19(7)), any aggregate with any material or substance other than water,][2]

(*d*) for storing any aggregate, or

(*e*) for the first landing in the United Kingdom of aggregate won from the seabed of any area of sea in the United Kingdom or United Kingdom waters,

they may, if they think fit, register those premises, in any entry relating to that person and under his name, as a registered site.

(7) Where any premises are registered in accordance with subsection (6) above as a registered site, the particulars included in the register shall set out as the boundaries of the site such boundaries as appear to the Commissioners best to secure that avoidance of levy is not facilitated by the registration of any part of any premises that is not used or operated as mentioned in subsection (6) above.

(8) Where any entry in the register at any time specifies that any premises registered under a person's name as a registered site are to be taken to be the originating site of—

(*a*) . . . [1]

(*b*) any aggregate resulting from the carrying out of any exempt process there, or

(*c*) any aggregate won or landed there,

any question for the purposes of this Part as to the boundaries at that time of the originating site of any such aggregate shall be conclusively determined in accordance with that entry.

(9) Schedule 4 to this Act (provisions with respect to registration for the purposes of aggregates levy) shall have effect.

(10) The preceding provisions of this section and the provisions of Schedule 4 to this Act shall come into force on such date as the Treasury may by order made by statutory instrument appoint; and different days may be appointed under this subsection for different purposes.

Regulations—Finance Act 2001, section 24 and Schedule 4, (Appointed Day) Order, SI 2001/4033 (the appointed day for entry into force of this section is 11 January 2002).

Simon's Tax Cases—*C&E Comrs v East Midlands Aggregates Ltd* [2004] STC 1582.

Amendments—[1] Sub-ss (6)(*b*) and (8)(*a*) repealed by FA 2002 ss 131(3)(*c*), (4), 141, Sch 40 Pt 4(3). These amendments are deemed to have come into force on 1 April 2002.

[2] Sub-s (6)(*ca*) inserted by FA 2002 s 132(1), (3), Sch 38 para 7. This amendment is deemed to have come into force on 1 April 2002.

25 Returns and payment of levy

(1) The Commissioners may by regulations make provision—

(*a*) for persons charged with aggregates levy to be liable to account for it by reference to such periods ("accounting periods") as may be determined by or under the regulations;

(*b*) for persons who are or are required to be registered for the purposes of aggregates levy to be subject to such obligations to make returns for those purposes for such periods, at such times and in such form as may be so determined; and

(*c*) for persons who are required to account for aggregates levy for any period to become liable to pay the amounts due from them at such times and in such manner as may be so determined.

(2) Without prejudice to the generality of the powers conferred by subsection (1) above, regulations under this section may contain provision—

(*a*) for aggregates levy falling in accordance with the regulations to be accounted for by reference to one accounting period to be treated in prescribed circumstances, and for prescribed purposes, as levy due for a different period;

(*b*) for the correction of errors made when accounting for aggregates levy by reference to any period;

(*c*) for the entries to be made in any accounts in connection with the correction of any such errors and for the financial adjustments to be made in that connection;

(*d*) for a person, for purposes connected with the making of any such entry or financial adjustment, to be required to provide to any prescribed person, or to retain, a document in the prescribed form containing prescribed particulars of the matters to which the entry or adjustment relates;

(*e*) for enabling the Commissioners, in such cases as they may think fit, to dispense with or relax a requirement imposed by regulations made by virtue of paragraph (*d*) above;

(*f*) for the amount of levy which, in accordance with the regulations, is treated as due for a later period than that by reference to which it should have been accounted for to be treated as increased by an amount representing interest at the rate applicable under section 197 of the Finance Act 1996 for such period as may be determined in accordance with the regulations.

(3) Subject to the following provisions of this section, if any person ("the taxpayer") fails—

(*a*) to comply with so much of any regulations under this section as requires him, at or before a particular time, to make a return for any accounting period, or

(*b*) to comply with so much of any regulations under this section as requires him, at or before a particular time, to pay an amount of aggregates levy due from him,

he shall be liable to a penalty of £250.

(4) Liability to a penalty under subsection (3) above shall not arise if the taxpayer satisfies the Commissioners or, on appeal, an appeal tribunal—

(*a*) that there is a reasonable excuse for the failure to make the return or to pay the levy in accordance with regulations; and

(*b*) that there is not an occasion after the last day on which the return or payment was required by the regulations to be made when there was a failure without reasonable excuse to make it.

(5) Where, by reason of any failure falling within paragraph (*a*) or (*b*) of subsection (3) above—

(*a*) a person is convicted of an offence (whether under this Act or otherwise), or

(*b*) a person is assessed to a penalty under paragraph 7 of Schedule 6 to this Act (penalty for evasion) [or a penalty for a deliberate inaccuracy under Schedule 24 to the Finance Act 2007 (penalties for errors)][1],

that person shall not, by reason of that failure, be liable also to a penalty under that subsection (3).

(6) In subsection (1)(*b*) above the reference to a person who is required to be registered for the purposes of aggregates levy includes a reference to a person who would be so required but for any exemption conferred by regulations under section 24(4) above.

Amendment—[1] Words in sub-s (5)(*b*) inserted by the Finance Act 2008, Schedule 40 (Appointed Day, Transitional Provisions and Consequential Amendments) Order, SI 2009/571 art 8, Sch 1 paras 21, 22 with effect from 1 April 2009.

26 Security for levy

(1) Where it appears to the Commissioners necessary to do so for the protection of the revenue they may require any person who is or is required to be registered to give security, or further security, for the payment of any aggregates levy which is or may become due from him.

(2) The power of the Commissioners to require any security, or further security, under this section shall be a power to require security, or further security, of such amount and in such manner as they may determine.

(3) A person who is responsible for any aggregate being subjected to commercial exploitation in the United Kingdom is guilty of an offence if, at the time it is so subjected—

(*a*) he has been required to give security under this section; and

(*b*) he has not complied with that requirement.

(4) A person guilty of an offence under this section shall be liable, on summary conviction, to a penalty of level 5 on the standard scale.

(5) Sections 145 to 155 of the Customs and Excise Management Act 1979 (proceedings for offences, mitigation of penalties and certain other matters) shall apply in relation to an offence under this section as they apply in relation to offences and penalties under the customs and excise Acts.

(6) In subsection (1) above the reference to a person who is required to be registered for the purposes of aggregates levy includes a reference to a person who would be so required but for any exemption conferred by regulations under section 24(4) above.

27 Recovery and interest

Schedule 5 to this Act (which makes provision for the recovery of amounts of aggregates levy due from any person and for the interest payable on such amounts) shall have effect.

28 Evasion, misdeclaration and neglect

Schedule 6 to this Act (which makes provision for and in connection with the imposition of criminal and civil penalties for the evasion of aggregates levy and for related misconduct) shall have effect.

29 Information and evidence

Schedule 7 to this Act (which provides for the supply of information to the Commissioners, for the powers under which the Commissioners may collect information for enforcement purposes and about evidence) shall have effect.

Credits and repayments

30 Credit for aggregates levy

(1) The Commissioners may, in accordance with the following provisions of this section, by regulations make provision in relation to cases where, after a charge to aggregates levy has arisen on any quantity of aggregate—

(*a*) any of that aggregate is exported from the United Kingdom in the form of aggregate;

(*b*) an exempt process is applied to any of that aggregate;

(*c*) any of that aggregate is used in a prescribed industrial or agricultural process;

(*d*) any of that aggregate is disposed of (by dumping or otherwise) in such manner not constituting its use for construction purposes as may be prescribed; or

(*e*) the whole or any part of a debt due to a person responsible for subjecting the aggregate to commercial exploitation is written off in his accounts as a bad debt.

(2) The provision that may be made in relation to any such case as is mentioned in subsection (1) above is provision—

(*a*) for such person as may be specified in the regulations to be entitled to a tax credit in respect of any aggregates levy charged on the aggregate in question;

(*b*) for a tax credit to which any person is entitled under the regulations to be brought into account when he is accounting for aggregates levy due from him for such accounting period or periods as may be determined in accordance with the regulations; and

(*c*) for a person entitled to a tax credit to be entitled, in any prescribed case where he cannot bring the tax credit into account so as to set it against a liability to aggregates levy, to a repayment of levy of an amount so determined.

(3) Regulations under this section may contain any or all of the following provisions—

(*a*) provision making any entitlement to a tax credit conditional on the making of a claim by such person, within such period and in such manner as may be prescribed;

(*b*) provision making entitlement to bring a tax credit into account, or to receive a repayment in respect of such a credit, conditional on compliance with such requirements as may be determined in accordance with the regulations;

(*c*) provision requiring a claim for a tax credit to be evidenced and quantified by reference to such records and other documents as may be so determined;

(*d*) provision requiring a person claiming any entitlement to a tax credit to keep, for such period and in such form and manner as may be so determined, those records and documents and a record of such information relating to the claim as may be so determined;

(*e*) provision for the withdrawal of a tax credit where any requirement of the regulations is not complied with;

(*f*) provision for interest at the rate applicable under section 197 of the Finance Act 1996 to be treated as added, for such period and for such purposes as may be prescribed, to the amount of any tax credit;

(*g*) provision for anything falling to be determined in accordance with the regulations to be determined by reference to a general or specific direction given in accordance with the regulations by the Commissioners.

(4) Without prejudice to the generality of the preceding provisions of this section, regulations under this section may also contain—

(*a*) provision for ascertaining whether, when and to what extent an amount is to be taken for the purposes of any regulations under this section to have been written off in any accounts as a bad debt;

(*b*) provision requiring a person who for the purposes of any such regulations is taken to have written off any amount as a bad debt to keep, for such period and in such form and manner as may be prescribed, information relating to anything subsequently paid in respect of the amount written off;

(*c*) provision for the withdrawal of the whole or an appropriate part of any tax credit relating to an amount taken to have been written off as a bad debt where the whole or any part (or further part) of the amount written off is subsequently paid;

(*d*) provision for ascertaining whether, and to what extent, anything received by any person is to be taken as a payment of, or of a part of, an amount taken, for the purposes of any regulations under this section, to have been written off;

(*e*) provision for determining the value for the purposes of provision made by virtue of paragraph (*d*) above of things received otherwise than in the form of money.

(5) Regulations made under this section shall have effect subject to the provisions of section 32 below.

[30A Transitional tax credit in Northern Ireland

(1) The Commissioners may by regulations make provision of the kind described in section 30(2) above (entitlement to tax credit) in relation to cases within subsection (2) below.

(2) The cases are those where a charge to aggregates levy has arisen on a quantity of aggregate which has been subjected to commercial exploitation in Northern Ireland during a period—

(*a*) starting on the prescribed date, and

(*b*) ending on 31st March 2011.

(3) The date prescribed for the purposes of subsection (2)(*a*) above may be earlier than the date on which this section comes into force.

(4) The amount of a tax credit to which a person is entitled under the regulations must not be more than 80% of any aggregates levy charged on the aggregate in question.

(5) Regulations under this section may in particular make provision—

(*a*) for a person operating a site to be entitled to a tax credit under the regulations in respect of a period for which he holds an aggregates levy credit certificate which has been issued in respect of the site and which has not been withdrawn;

(*b*) for an aggregates levy credit certificate to be issued to a person in respect of a site only if an aggregates levy credit agreement is in force in respect of the site;

(*c*) for the withdrawal of an aggregates levy credit certificate where the aggregates levy credit agreement in respect of which it was issued is no longer in force;

(*d*) for the form and content of aggregates levy credit certificates and aggregates levy credit agreements.

(6) Regulations under this section which make provision such as is mentioned in subsection (5)(*d*) above may be framed by reference to any provisions of a notice published by the Commissioners in pursuance of the regulations and not withdrawn by a further notice.

(7) If regulations under this section make provision such as is mentioned in subsection (5) above, the Commissioners or the Northern Ireland Department may—

(*a*) enter into aggregates levy credit agreements;

(*b*) issue and withdraw aggregates levy credit certificates;

(*c*) take such other steps as the Commissioners or the Northern Ireland Department consider appropriate in relation to aggregates levy credit agreements and aggregates levy credit certificates.

(8) Regulations under this section which make provision such as is mentioned in subsection (5) above must include provision requiring the Northern Ireland Department to inform the Commissioners if the Northern Ireland Department issues or withdraws an aggregates levy credit certificate.

(9) Subsections (3) to (5) of section 30 above apply to regulations under this section as they apply to regulations under that section.

(10) The Treasury may by order made by statutory instrument amend subsection (4) above by substituting for the percentage for the time being specified in that subsection a percentage lower than 80%.

(11) An order under subsection (10) above shall not be made unless a draft of the order has been laid before Parliament and approved by a resolution of the House of Commons.

(12) Any expenses of the Northern Ireland Department under this section shall be charged on the Consolidated Fund of Northern Ireland.

(13) In this section—

"aggregates levy credit agreement" means an agreement entered into in respect of a site by the person operating the site and the Commissioners or the Northern Ireland Department;

"aggregates levy credit certificate" means a certificate issued to the person operating a site by the Commissioners or the Northern Ireland Department as evidence of the fact that an aggregates levy credit agreement has been entered into in respect of the site;

"the Northern Ireland Department" means the Department of the Environment in Northern Ireland.][1]

Amendments—[1] Section 30A substituted by FA 2004 s 291(1), (2), (4), (5) with effect from 23 July 2004 by virtue of Finance Act 2004, section 291, (Appointed Day) Order, SI 2004/1942 art 2.

31 Repayments of overpaid levy

(1) Where a person has paid an amount to the Commissioners by way of aggregates levy which was not levy due to them, they shall be liable to repay the amount to him.

(2) The Commissioners shall not be liable to repay an amount under this section except on the making of a claim for that purpose.

(3) A claim under this section must be made in such form and manner, and must be supported by such documentary evidence, as may be required by regulations made by the Commissioners.

(4) The preceding provisions of this section are subject to the provisions of section 32 below.

(5) Except as provided by this section, the Commissioners shall not, by virtue of the fact that it was not levy due to them, be liable to repay any amount paid to them by way of aggregates levy.

32 Supplemental provisions about repayments etc

(1) The Commissioners shall not be liable, on any claim for a repayment of aggregates levy, to repay any amount paid to them more than [4 years] before the making of the claim.

(2) In the case of any claim for a repayment of an amount of aggregates levy other than a claim to a repayment to which a person is entitled by virtue of tax credit regulations, it shall be a defence to that claim that the repayment of that amount would unjustly enrich the claimant.

(3) Subsection (4) below applies for the purposes of subsection (2) above where—

(*a*) there is an amount paid by way of aggregates levy which (apart from subsection (2) above) would fall to be the subject of a repayment of aggregates levy to any person ("the taxpayer"); and

(*b*) the whole or a part of the cost of the payment of that amount to the Commissioners has, for practical purposes, been borne by a person other than the taxpayer.

(4) Where, in a case to which this subsection applies, loss or damage has been or may be incurred by the taxpayer as a result of mistaken assumptions made in his case about the operation of any provisions relating to aggregates levy, that loss or damage shall be disregarded, except to the extent of the quantified amount, in the making of any determination as to—

(*a*) whether or to what extent the repayment of an amount to the taxpayer would enrich him; or

(*b*) whether or to what extent any enrichment of the taxpayer would be unjust.

(5) In subsection (4) above "the quantified amount" means the amount (if any) which is shown by the taxpayer to constitute the amount that would appropriately compensate him for loss or damage shown by him to have resulted, for any business carried on by him, from the making of the mistaken assumptions.

(6) The reference in subsection (4) above to provisions relating to aggregates levy is a reference to any provisions of—

(*a*) any enactment or subordinate legislation (whether or not still in force) which relates to that levy or to any matter connected with it; or

(*b*) any notice published by the Commissioners under or for the purposes of any enactment or subordinate legislation relating to aggregates levy.

(7) Schedule 8 to this Act (which contains further provision about payments and repayments by the Commissioners and about the setting off of amounts due to or from the Commissioners under this Part and the setting of other amounts against such amounts) shall have effect.

Amendments—In sub-s (1) words substituted for the words "three years" by FA 2009 s 99, Sch 51 paras 27, 28 with effect from 1 April 2010. However, this amendment is disregarded where, for the purposes of sub-s (1), a claim is for the repayment of an amount paid to the Commissioners on or before 31 March 2007 (see SI 2010/867 arts 2(1), (8)).

Non-resident taxpayers

33 Appointment of tax representatives

(1) The Commissioners may by regulations make provision for securing that every non-resident taxpayer has a person resident in the United Kingdom to act as his tax representative for the purposes of aggregates levy.

(2) Regulations under this section may, in particular, contain any or all of the following—

(*a*) provision requiring notification to be given to the Commissioners where a person becomes a non-resident taxpayer;
(*b*) provision requiring the appointment of tax representatives by non-resident taxpayers;
(*c*) provision for the appointment of a person as a tax representative to take effect only where the person appointed is approved by the Commissioners;
(*d*) provision authorising the Commissioners to give a direction requiring the replacement of a tax representative;
(*e*) provision authorising the Commissioners to give a direction requiring a person specified in the direction to be treated as the appointed tax representative of a non-resident taxpayer so specified;
(*f*) provision about the circumstances in which a person ceases to be a tax representative and about the withdrawal by the Commissioners of their approval of a tax representative;
(*g*) provision enabling a tax representative to act on behalf of the person for whom he is the tax representative through an agent of the representative;
(*h*) provision for the purposes of any provision made by virtue of paragraphs (*a*) to (*g*) above regulating the procedure to be followed in any case and imposing requirements as to the information and other particulars to be provided to the Commissioners;
(*i*) provision as to the time at which things done under or for the purposes of the regulations are to take effect.

(3) Subject to subsection (4) below, a person who—
(*a*) becomes subject, in accordance with any regulations under this section, to an obligation to request the Commissioners' approval for any person's appointment as his tax representative, but
(*b*) fails (with or without making the appointment) to make the request as required by the regulations,

shall be liable to a penalty of £10,000.

(4) A failure such as is mentioned in subsection (3) above shall not give rise to liability to a penalty under this section if the person concerned satisfies the Commissioners or, on appeal, an appeal tribunal that there is a reasonable excuse for the failure.

34 Effect of appointment of tax representatives

(1) The tax representative of a non-resident taxpayer shall be entitled to act on the non-resident taxpayer's behalf for the purposes of any provision made by or under this Part.

(2) The tax representative of a non-resident taxpayer shall be under a duty, except to such extent as the Commissioners by regulations otherwise provide, to secure the non-resident taxpayer's compliance with, and discharge of, the obligations and liabilities to which the non-resident taxpayer is subject by virtue of any provision made by or under this Part (including obligations and liabilities arising or incurred before he became the non-resident taxpayer's tax representative).

(3) A person who is or has been the tax representative of a non-resident taxpayer shall be personally liable—
(*a*) in respect of any failure while he is or was the non-resident taxpayer's tax representative to secure compliance with, or the discharge of, any obligation or liability to which subsection (2) above applies, and
(*b*) in respect of anything done in the course of, or for purposes connected with, acting on the non-resident taxpayer's behalf,

as if the obligations and liabilities to which subsection (2) above applies were imposed jointly and severally on the tax representative and the non-resident taxpayer.

(4) A tax representative shall not be liable by virtue of this section to be registered for the purposes of aggregates levy; but the Commissioners may by regulations—
(*a*) require the registration of the names of tax representatives against the names of the non-resident taxpayers of whom they are the representatives;
(*b*) make provision for the deletion of the names of persons who cease to be tax representatives.

(5) A tax representative shall not by virtue of this section be guilty of any offence except in so far as—
(*a*) he has consented to, or connived in, the commission of the offence by the non-resident taxpayer;
(*b*) the commission of the offence by the non-resident taxpayer is attributable to any neglect on the part of the tax representative; or
(*c*) the offence consists in a contravention by the tax representative of an obligation which, by virtue of this section, is imposed both on the tax representative and on the non-resident taxpayer.

Other special cases

35 Groups of companies etc

(1) Schedule 9 to this Act (which provides for two or more bodies corporate to be treated as members of the same group for the purposes of this Part) shall have effect.

(2) Any aggregates levy with which a body corporate is charged in respect of aggregate subjected to commercial exploitation at a time when the body is a member of a group shall be treated for the purposes of this Part as if it were the representative member for that group (instead of that body) which is charged with the levy.

(3) All the bodies corporate who are members of a group when any aggregates levy becomes due from the representative member, together with any bodies corporate who become members of the group while any such levy remains unpaid, shall be jointly and severally liable for any aggregates levy due from the representative member.

(4) Subject to subsections (2) and (3) above, the Commissioners may by regulations make such provision as they consider appropriate about—

(*a*) the person by whom any obligation or liability imposed by or under this Part is to be performed or discharged, and

(*b*) the manner in which it is to be performed or discharged,

in a case where the person who (apart from the regulations) would be subject to the obligation or liability is one of a number of bodies corporate registered in the name of the representative member for a group.

(5) References in this section to aggregates levy being or becoming due from the representative member include references to any amounts being or becoming recoverable as if they were aggregates levy due from that member.

(6) For the purposes of this Part—

(*a*) a body corporate is a member of a group at any time in relation to which it falls to be treated as such a member in accordance with Schedule 9 to this Act; and

(*b*) the body corporate which is to be taken to be the representative member for a group at any time is the member of the group which in relation to that time is the representative member under that Schedule in the case of that group.

36 Partnerships and other unincorporated bodies

(1) The Commissioners may by regulations make provision for determining by what persons anything required to be done under this Part is to be done where, apart from those regulations, that requirement would fall on—

(*a*) persons carrying on business in partnership; or

(*b*) persons carrying on business together as an unincorporated body;

but any regulations under this subsection must be construed subject to the following provisions of this section.

(2) In determining for the purposes of this Part who at any time is the person chargeable with any aggregates levy where the persons responsible for subjecting any aggregate to commercial exploitation are persons carrying on any business—

(*a*) in partnership, or

(*b*) as an unincorporated body,

the firm or body shall be treated, for the purposes of that determination (and notwithstanding any changes from time to time in the members of the firm or body), as the same person and as separate from its members.

(3) Without prejudice to section 36 of the Partnership Act 1890 (rights of persons dealing with firm against apparent members of firm), where—

(*a*) persons have been carrying on in partnership any business in the course or furtherance of which any aggregate has been subjected to commercial exploitation, and

(*b*) a person ceases to be a member of the firm,

that person shall be regarded for the purposes of this Part (including subsection (7) below) as continuing to be a partner until the date on which the change in the partnership is notified to the Commissioners.

(4) Where a person ceases to be a member of a firm during an accounting period (or is treated as so ceasing by virtue of subsection (3) above) any notice, whether of assessment or otherwise, which—

(*a*) is served on the firm under or for the purposes of any provision made by or under this Part, and

(*b*) relates to, or to any matter arising in, that period or any earlier period during the whole or part of which he was a member of the firm,

shall be treated as served also on him.

(5) Without prejudice to section 16 of the Partnership Act 1890 (notice to acting partner to be notice to the firm), any notice, whether of assessment or otherwise, which—

(*a*) is addressed to a firm by the name in which it is registered, and (*b*) is served in accordance with this Part,

shall be treated for the purposes of this Part as served on the firm and, accordingly, where subsection (4) above applies, as served also on the former partner.

(6) Subject to subsection (7) below, nothing in this section shall affect the extent to which, under section 9 of the Partnership Act 1890 (liability of partners for debts of the firm), a partner is liable for aggregates levy owed by the firm.

(7) Where a person is a partner in a firm during part only of an accounting period, his personal liability for aggregates levy incurred by the firm in respect of aggregate subjected to commercial exploitation in that period shall include, but shall not exceed, such proportion of the firm's liability as may be just and reasonable in the circumstances.

37 Insolvency etc

(1) The Commissioners may by regulations make provision in accordance with the following provisions of this section for the application of this Part in cases in which an insolvency procedure is applied to a person or to a deceased person's estate.

(2) The provision that may be contained in regulations under this section may include any or all of the following—

(*a*) provision requiring any such person as may be prescribed to give notification to the Commissioners, in the prescribed manner, of the prescribed particulars of any relevant matter;

(*b*) provision requiring a person to be treated, to the prescribed extent, as if, for the purposes of this Part or such of its provisions as may be prescribed, he were the same person as the subject of the procedure; and

(*c*) provision for securing continuity in the application of any of the provisions of this Part where, by virtue of any regulations under this section, any person is treated as if he were the same person as the subject of the procedure.

(3) In subsection (2) above "relevant matter", in relation to a case in which an insolvency procedure is applied to any person or estate, means—

(*a*) the application of that procedure to that person or estate;

(*b*) the appointment of any person for the purposes of the application of that procedure;

(*c*) any other matter relating to—

(i) the application of that procedure to the subject of the procedure or to his estate;

(ii) the holding of an appointment made for the purposes of that procedure; or

(iii) the exercise or discharge of any powers or duties conferred or imposed on any person by virtue of such an appointment.

(4) Regulations made by virtue of subsection (2)(*b*) above may include provision for a person to cease, on the occurrence of such an event as may be prescribed, to be treated as if he were the same person as the subject of the procedure.

(5) Regulations under this section prescribing the manner in which any notification is to be given to the Commissioners may require it to be given in such manner and to contain such particulars as may be specified in a general notice published by the Commissioners in accordance with the regulations.

(6) Regulations under this section may provide that the extent to which, and the purposes for which, a person is to be treated under the regulations as if he were the same person as the subject of the procedure may be determined by reference to a notice given in accordance with the regulations to the person so treated.

(7) For the purposes of this section, an insolvency procedure is applied to a person if—

(*a*) a bankruptcy order, winding-up order or administration order is made [or an administrator is appointed][2] in relation to that person or a partnership of which he is a member;

(*b*) an award of sequestration is made in relation to that person's estate or the estate of a partnership of which he is a member;

(*c*) that person is put into administrative receivership;

(*d*) that person passes a resolution for voluntary winding up;

(*e*) any voluntary arrangement approved in accordance with—

(i) Part I or VIII of the Insolvency Act 1986, or

(ii) Part II or Chapter II of Part VIII of the Insolvency (Northern Ireland) Order 1989,

comes into force in relation to that person or a partnership of which that person is a member;

(*f*) a deed of arrangement registered in accordance with—

(i) the Deeds of Arrangement Act 1914, or

(ii) Chapter I of Part VIII of that Order,

takes effect in relation to that person;

(*g*)–(*j*) . . . [1]

(*k*) that person's estate becomes vested in any other person as that person's trustee under a trust deed (within the meaning of the Bankruptcy (Scotland) Act 1985).

(8) For the purposes of this section, an insolvency procedure is applied to a deceased person's estate if—

(*a*) after that person's death—

(i) a bankruptcy order, or

(ii) an order with corresponding effect but a different name,

is made in relation to that person's estate under any of the provisions of the Insolvency Act 1986 or the Insolvency (Northern Ireland) Order 1989 as they are applied to the administration of the insolvent estates of deceased persons; or

(*b*) an award of sequestration is made on that person's estate after his death.

(9) In subsection (7) above—

(*a*) the reference to any administration order is a reference to an administration order under [Schedule B1 to][2] the Insolvency Act 1986 or Article 21 of the Insolvency (Northern Ireland) Order 1989;

(*b*) the reference to a person being put into administrative receivership is a reference to the appointment in relation to him of an administrative receiver, within the meaning of section 251 of that Act of 1986 or Article 5(1) of that Order of 1989; and

(*c*) references to a member of a partnership include references to any person who is liable as a partner under section 14 of the Partnership Act 1890 (persons liable by "holding out").

(10) In this section "the subject of the procedure", in relation to the application of any insolvency procedure, means the person to whom, or to whose estate, the procedure is applied.

Amendments—[1] Sub-s (7)(*g*)–(*j*) repealed by FA 2002 ss 132(1), 141, Sch 38 para 8, Sch 40 Pt 4(3). These amendments are deemed to have come into force on 1 April 2002.

[2] Words in sub-s (7)(*a*) inserted, and words in sub-s (9)(*a*) substituted, by the Enterprise Act 2002 (Insolvency) Order, SI 2003/2096 art 4, Schedule paras 35, 36 with effect from 15 September 2003, except in relation to any case where a petition for an administration order was presented before that date: SI 2003/2096, arts 1(1), 6.

38 Death and incapacity

(1) The Commissioners may, in accordance with subsection (2) below, by regulations make provision for the purposes of aggregates levy in relation to cases where a person carries on a business of an individual who has died or become incapacitated.

(2) The provisions that may be contained in regulations under this section are—

(*a*) provision requiring the person who is carrying on the business to inform the Commissioners of the fact that he is carrying on the business and of the event that has led to his carrying it on;

(*b*) provision allowing that person to be treated for a limited time as if he and the person who has died or become incapacitated were the same person; and

(*c*) such other provision as the Commissioners think fit for securing continuity in the application of this Part where a person is so treated.

39 Transfer of a business as a going concern

(1) The Commissioners may by regulations make provision for securing continuity in the application of this Part in cases where any business carried on by a person is transferred to another person as a going concern.

(2) Regulations under this section may, in particular, include any or all of the following—

(*a*) provision requiring the transferor to inform the Commissioners of the transfer;

(*b*) provision for liabilities and duties under this Part of the transferor to become, to such extent as may be provided by the regulations, liabilities and duties of the transferee;

(*c*) provision for any right of either of them to a tax credit or repayment of aggregates levy to be satisfied by allowing the credit or making the repayment to the other;

(*d*) provision as to the preservation of any records or accounts relating to the business which, by virtue of any regulations under paragraph 2 of Schedule 7 to this Act, are required to be preserved for any period after the transfer.

(3) Regulations under this section may provide that no such provision as is mentioned in paragraph (*b*) or (*c*) of subsection (2) above shall have effect in relation to any transferor and transferee unless an application for the purpose has been made by them under the regulations.

Review and appeal

40 [Appeals][1]

(1) [Subject to section 41, an appeal shall lie to an appeal tribunal from any person who is or will be affected by any decision of HMRC with respect to any of the following matters—][1]

(*a*) whether or not a person is charged in any case with an amount of aggregates levy;

(*b*) the amount of aggregates levy charged in any case and the time when the charge is to be taken as having arisen;

(*c*) the registration of any person or premises for the purposes of aggregates levy or the cancellation of any registration;

(*d*) the person liable to pay the aggregates levy charged in any case, the amount of a person's liability to aggregates levy and the time by which he is required to pay an amount of that levy;

(*e*) the imposition of a requirement on any person to give security, or further security, under section 26 above and the amount and manner of providing any security required under that section;

(*f*) whether or not liability to a penalty or to interest on any amount arises in any person's case under any provision made by or under this Part, and the amount of any such liability;

(*g*) any matter the decision as to which is [appealable][1] under this section in accordance with paragraph 8(6) or (7) of Schedule 6 to this Act;

(*h*) the extent of any person's entitlement to any tax credit or to a repayment in respect of a tax credit and the extent of any liability of the Commissioners under this Part to pay interest on any amount;

(*i*) whether or not any person is required to have a tax representative by virtue of any regulations under section 33 above;

(*j*) the giving, withdrawal or variation, for the purposes of any such regulations, of any approval or direction with respect to the person who is to act as another's tax representative;

(*k*) whether a body corporate is to be treated, or is to cease to be treated, as a member of a group, the times at which a body corporate is to be so treated and the body corporate which is, in relation to any time, to be the representative member for a group;

(*l*) any matter not falling within the preceding paragraphs the decision with respect to which is contained in

[(i) an assessment under paragraphs 2 or 3 of Schedule 5 in respect of an accounting period in relation to which any return required to be made by virtue of regulations under section 25 has been made; or

(ii) an assessment under any provision of Schedule 5 other than paragraphs 2 or 3.][1]

[*(2) Any person who is or will be affected by any decision to which this section applies may by notice in writing to the Commissioners require them to review the decision.*

(3) The Commissioners shall not be required under this section to review any decision unless the notice requiring the review is given before the end of the period of forty-five days beginning with the day on which written notification of the decision, or of an assessment containing or giving effect to the decision, was first given to the person requiring the review.

(4) For the purposes of subsection (3) above it shall be the duty of the Commissioners to give written notification of any decision to which this section applies to any person who—

(a) requests such a notification;

(b) has not previously been given written notification of that decision; and

(c) if given such a notification, will be entitled to require a review of the decision under this section.

(5) A person shall be entitled to give a notice under this section requiring a decision to be reviewed for a second or subsequent time only if—

(a) the grounds on which he requires the further review are that the Commissioners did not, on any previous review, have the opportunity to consider certain facts or other matters; and

(b) he does not, on the further review, require the Commissioners to consider any facts or matters which were considered on a previous review except in so far as they are relevant to any issue to which the facts or matters not previously considered relate.

(6) Where the Commissioners are required by a notice under this section to review any decision, it shall be their duty to do so.

(7) On a review under this section the Commissioners may (subject to subsection (9) below) withdraw, vary or confirm the decision reviewed.

(8) Where—

(a) it is the duty under this section of the Commissioners to review any decision, and

(b) they do not, within the period of forty-five days beginning with the day on which the review was required, give notice to the person requiring it of their determination on the review,

they shall be deemed to have confirmed the decision.

(9) Where the Commissioners decide, on a review under this section, that a liability to a penalty or to an amount of interest arises, they shall not be entitled to modify the amount payable in respect of that liability except—

(a) in exercise of a power conferred by section 46(1) below (penalties) or paragraph 10(3) of Schedule 5 to this Act, paragraph 6(6) of Schedule 8 to this Act or paragraph 5(5) of Schedule 10 to this Act (penalty interest); or

(b) for the purpose of making the amount payable conform to the amount of the liability imposed by this Part.][1]

(10) This section has effect subject to paragraph 8(5) of Schedule 6 to this Act.

Amendments—[1] Heading substituted for former heading "Review of Commissioners' decisions"; in sub-s (1) words at the beginning substituted for the words "This section applies to any decision of the Commissioners with respect to any of the following matters—"; word in sub-(1)(*g*) substituted for the word "reviewable"; sub-s (1)(*l*)(i), (ii) substituted for the words "any assessment under this Part."; sub-ss (2)–(9) repealed by the Transfer of Tribunal Functions and Revenue and Customs Appeals Order, SI 2009/56 art 3, Sch 1 para 303 with effect from 1 April 2009, subject to transitional and savings provisions in Sch 3 paras 2, 3.

[40A Offer of review

(1) HMRC must offer a person (P) a review of a decision that has been notified to P if an appeal lies under section 40 in respect of the decision.

(2) The offer of the review must be made by notice given to P at the same time as the decision is notified to P.

(3) This section does not apply to the notification of the conclusions of a review.][1]

Amendment—[1] Sections 40A–40G inserted by the Transfer of Tribunal Functions and Revenue and Customs Appeals Order, SI 2009/56 art 3, Sch 1 para 304 with effect from 1 April 2009.

[40B Right to require review

(1) Any person (other than P) who has the right of appeal under section 40 against a decision may require HMRC to review that decision if that person has not appealed to the appeal tribunal under section 40G.

(2) A notification that such a person requires a review must be made within 30 days of that person becoming aware of the decision.][1]

Amendment—[1] Sections 40A–40G inserted by the Transfer of Tribunal Functions and Revenue and Customs Appeals Order, SI 2009/56 art 3, Sch 1 para 304 with effect from 1 April 2009.

[40C Review by HMRC

(1) HMRC must review a decision if—

(*a*) they have offered a review of the decision under section 40A, and

(*b*) P notifies HMRC accepting the offer within 30 days from the date of the document containing the notification of the offer.

(2) But P may not notify acceptance of the offer if P has already appealed to the appeal tribunal under section 40G.

(3) HMRC must review a decision if a person other than P notifies them under section 40B.

(4) HMRC shall not review a decision if P, or another person, has appealed to the appeal tribunal under section 40G in respect of the decision.][1]

Amendment—[1] Sections 40A–40G inserted by the Transfer of Tribunal Functions and Revenue and Customs Appeals Order, SI 2009/56 art 3, Sch 1 para 304 with effect from 1 April 2009.

[40D Extensions of time

(1) If under section 40A, HMRC have offered P a review of a decision, HMRC may within the relevant period notify P that the relevant period is extended.

(2) If under section 40B another person may require HMRC to review a matter, HMRC may within the relevant period notify the other person that the relevant period is extended.

(3) If notice is given the relevant period is extended to the end of 30 days from—

(*a*) the date of the notice, or

(*b*) any other date set out in the notice or a further notice.

(4) In this section "relevant period" means—

(*a*) the period of 30 days referred to in—

(i) section 40C(1)(*b*) (in a case falling within subsection (1)), or

(ii) section 40B(2) (in a case falling within subsection (2)), or

(*b*) if notice has been given under subsection (1) or (2), that period as extended (or as most recently extended) in accordance with subsection (3).][1]

Amendment—[1] Sections 40A–40G inserted by the Transfer of Tribunal Functions and Revenue and Customs Appeals Order, SI 2009/56 art 3, Sch 1 para 304 with effect from 1 April 2009.

[40E Review out of time

(1) This section applies if—

(*a*) HMRC have offered a review of a decision under section 40A and P does not accept the offer within the time allowed under section 40C(1)(*b*) or 40D(3); or

(*b*) a person who requires a review under section 40B does not notify HMRC within the time allowed under that section or section 40D(3).

(2) HMRC must review the decision under section 40C if—

(*a*) after the time allowed, P, or the other person, notifies HMRC in writing requesting a review out of time,

(*b*) HMRC are satisfied that P, or the other person, had a reasonable excuse for not accepting the offer or requiring review within the time allowed, and

(*c*) HMRC are satisfied that P, or the other person, made the request without unreasonable delay after the excuse had ceased to apply.

(3) HMRC shall not review a decision if P, or another person, has appealed to the appeal tribunal under section 40G in respect of the decision.][1]

Amendment—[1] Sections 40A–40G inserted by the Transfer of Tribunal Functions and Revenue and Customs Appeals Order, SI 2009/56 art 3, Sch 1 para 304 with effect from 1 April 2009.

[40F Nature of review etc

(1) This section applies if HMRC are required to undertake a review under section 40C or 40E.

(2) The nature and extent of the review are to be such as appear appropriate to HMRC in the circumstances.

(3) For the purpose of subsection (2), HMRC must, in particular, have regard to steps taken before the beginning of the review—

(*a*) by HMRC in reaching the decision, and

(*b*) by any person in seeking to resolve disagreement about the decision.

(4) The review must take account of any representations made by P, or the other person, at a stage which gives HMRC a reasonable opportunity to consider them.

(5) The review may conclude that the decision is to be—

(*a*) upheld,

(*b*) varied, or

(*c*) cancelled.

(6) HMRC must give P, or the other person, notice of the conclusions of the review and their reasoning within—

(*a*) a period of 45 days beginning with the relevant date, or

(*b*) such other period as HMRC and P, or the other person, may agree.

(7) In subsection (6) "relevant date" means—

(*a*) the date HMRC received P's notification accepting the offer of a review (in a case falling within section 40A), or

(*b*) the date HMRC received notification from another person requiring review (in a case falling within section 40B), or

(*c*) the date on which HMRC decided to undertake the review (in a case falling within section 40E).

(8) Where HMRC are required to undertake a review but do not give notice of the conclusions within the time period specified in subsection (6), the review is to be treated as having concluded that the decision is upheld.

(9) If subsection (8) applies, HMRC must notify P or the other person of the conclusion which the review is treated as having reached.][1]

Amendment—[1] Sections 40A–40G inserted by the Transfer of Tribunal Functions and Revenue and Customs Appeals Order, SI 2009/56 art 3, Sch 1 para 304 with effect from 1 April 2009.

[40G Bringing of appeals

(1) An appeal under section 40 is to be made to the appeal tribunal before—

(*a*) the end of the period of 30 days beginning with—

(i) in a case where P is the appellant, the date of the document notifying the decision to which the appeal relates, or

(ii) in a case where a person other than P is the appellant, the date that person becomes aware of the decision, or

(*b*) if later, the end of the relevant period (within the meaning of section 40D).

(2) But that is subject to subsections (3) to (5).

(3) In a case where HMRC are required to undertake a review under section 40C—

(*a*) an appeal may not be made until the conclusion date, and

(*b*) any appeal is to be made within the period of 30 days beginning with the conclusion date.

(4) In a case where HMRC are requested to undertake a review by virtue of section 40E—

(*a*) an appeal may not be made—

(i) unless HMRC have decided whether or not to undertake a review, and

(ii) if HMRC decide to undertake a review, until the conclusion date; and

(*b*) any appeal is to be made within the period of 30 days beginning with—

(i) the conclusion date (if HMRC decide to undertake a review), or

(ii) the date on which HMRC decide not to undertake a review.

(5) In a case where section 40F(8) applies, an appeal may be made at any time from the end of the period specified in section 40F(6) to the date 30 days after the conclusion date.

(6) An appeal may be made after the end of the period specified in subsection (1), (3)(*b*), (4)(*b*) or (5) if the appeal tribunal gives permission to do so.

(7) In this section "conclusion date" means the date of the document notifying the conclusion of the review.][1]

Amendment—[1] Sections 40A–40G inserted by the Transfer of Tribunal Functions and Revenue and Customs Appeals Order, SI 2009/56 art 3, Sch 1 para 304 with effect from 1 April 2009.

41 [Appeals: further provisions][1]

(1) . . . [1]

[(2) Subject to subsections (2A) and (2B), where an appeal under section 40 relates to a decision (whether or not contained in an assessment) that an amount of aggregates levy is due from any person, it shall not be entertained unless the amount which HMRC have determined to be due has been paid or deposited with them.][1]

[(2A) In a case where the amount determined to be payable as aggregates levy has not been paid or deposited an appeal shall be entertained if—

(*a*) HMRC are satisfied (on the application of the appellant), or

(*b*) the appeal tribunal decides (HMRC not being so satisfied and on the application of the appellant),

that the requirement to pay or deposit the amount determined would cause the appellant to suffer hardship.

(2B) Notwithstanding the provisions of sections 11 and 13 of the Tribunals, Courts and Enforcement Act 2007, the decision of the appeal tribunal as to the issue of hardship is final.][1]

(3) On an appeal [under section 40][1] relating to a penalty under paragraph 7 of Schedule 6 to this Act (evasion), the burden of proof as to the matters specified in paragraphs (*a*) to (*c*) of sub-paragraph (1) of that paragraph shall lie upon the Commissioners.

Amendments—[1] Heading substituted for former heading "Appeals against reviewed decisions; sub-s (1) repealed"; sub-s (2) substituted; sub-ss (2A), (2B) inserted; words in sub-s (3) substituted for the words "under this section" by the Transfer of Tribunal Functions and Revenue and Customs Appeals Order, SI 2009/56 art 3, Sch 1 para 305 with effect from 1 April 2009, subject to transitional and savings provisions in Sch 3 paras 2, 3.

42 Determinations on appeal

(1) Where, on an appeal under section [40][1] above—

(*a*) it is found that an assessment of the appellant . . . [1] is an assessment for an amount that is less than it ought to have been, and

(*b*) the tribunal give a direction specifying the correct amount,

the assessment shall have effect as an assessment of the amount specified in the direction and (without prejudice to any power under this Part to reduce the amount of interest payable on the amount of an assessment) as if it were an assessment notified to the appellant in that amount at the same time as the original assessment.

(2) On an appeal under section [40][1] above, the powers of the appeal tribunal in relation to any decision of the Commissioners shall include a power, where the tribunal allow an appeal on the ground that the Commissioners could not reasonably have arrived at the decision, either—

(*a*) to direct that the decision, so far as it remains in force, is to cease to have effect from such time as the tribunal may direct; or

(*b*) to require the Commissioners to conduct, in accordance with the directions of the tribunal, [a review or][1] a further review of the original decision [as appropriate][1].

(3) Where, on an appeal under section [40][1] above, the appeal tribunal find that a liability to a penalty or to an amount of interest arises, the tribunal shall not give any direction for the modification of the amount payable in respect of that liability except—

(*a*) in exercise of a power conferred on the tribunal by section 46(1) below (penalties) or paragraph 10(3) or (6) of Schedule 5 to this Act, paragraph 6(6) or (9) of Schedule 8 to this Act or paragraph 5(5) or (8) of Schedule 10 to this Act (penalty interest); or

(*b*) for the purpose of making the amount payable conform to the amount of the liability imposed by this Part.

(4) Where, on an appeal under section [40][1] above, it is found that the whole or part of any amount paid or deposited in pursuance of section 41(2) above is not due, so much of that amount as is found not to be due shall be repaid with interest [at the rate applicable under section 197 of the Finance Act 1996][1].

(5) Where, on an appeal under section [40][1] above, it is found that the whole or part of any amount due to the appellant by way of any repayment in respect of a tax credit has not been paid, so much of that amount as is found not to have been paid shall be paid with interest [at the rate applicable under section 197 of the Finance Act 1996][1].

(6) Where—

(*a*) an appeal under section [40][1] above has been entertained notwithstanding that an amount determined by the Commissioners to be payable as aggregates levy has not been paid or deposited, and

(*b*) it is found on the appeal that that amount is due,

[it shall be paid with interest at the rate applicable under section 197 of the Finance Act 1996][1].

[(6A) Interest under subsection (6) shall be paid without any deduction of income tax.][1]

[(7) Sections 85 and 85B of the Value Added Tax Act 1994 (settling of appeals by agreement and payment of tax where there is a further appeal) shall have effect as if—

(*a*) the references to section 83 of that Act included references to section 40 above, and

(*b*) the references to value added tax included references to aggregates levy.]1

Amendment—[1] The following amendments made by the Transfer of Tribunal Functions and Revenue and Customs Appeals Order, SI 2009/56 art 3, Sch 1 para 306 with effect from 1 April 2009, subject to transitional and savings provisions in Sch 3 paras 2, 3, 9—

- in sub-ss (1)–(5), (6)(*a*) figures substituted for figures "41";
- in sub-(1)(*a*) words "made, confirmed or treated as confirmed by the Commissioners on a review under section 40 above ("the original assessment")" repealed;
- in sub-s (2)(*b*) words inserted in both places;
- in sub-ss (4), (5) words at the end substituted for the words "at such rate as the tribunal may determine";
- in sub-s (6) words at the end substituted for the words "the tribunal may, if they think fit, direct that that amount shall be paid with interest at such rate as may be specified in the direction";
- sub-s (6A) inserted;
- sub-s (7) substituted.

43 Adjustments of contracts

(1) Where—

(*a*) an agreement to supply a quantity of aggregate to any person has been entered into at any time before the commencement date, and

(*b*) on or after that date aggregates levy is charged on that quantity of aggregate,

so much of the agreement as requires any payment to be made to the supplier at the time when or after the charge to levy on that quantity of aggregate arises shall be adjusted so as to secure that the cost of discharging the liability to pay the levy, to the extent that it would otherwise have been borne by the supplier, is borne by the person making the payment.

(2) Where—

(*a*) an agreement with regard to any sum payable in respect of the use of land (whether the sum is called rent or royalty or otherwise) provides that the amount of the sum is to be calculated by reference to—

(i) the turnover of a business, or

(ii) the price received for minerals extracted from the land,

(*b*) the agreement was entered into before commencement date, and

(*c*) the circumstances are such that (had the agreement been made on or after that date) it might reasonably be expected that it would have provided that aggregates levy charged in particular circumstances be ignored in calculating the turnover or price,

the agreement shall be taken to provide that aggregates levy charged in those circumstances shall be ignored in calculating the turnover or, as the case may be, price.

General provisions

44 Destination of receipts

All money and securities for money collected or received for or on account of aggregates levy shall—

(*a*) if collected or received in Great Britain, be placed to the general account of the Commissioners kept at the Bank of England under section 17 of the Customs and Excise Management Act 1979; and

(*b*) if collected or received in Northern Ireland, be paid into the Consolidated Fund of the United Kingdom in such manner as the Treasury may direct.

45 Regulations and orders

(1) The powers of the Commissioners under this Part to make regulations shall be exercisable by statutory instrument subject to annulment in pursuance of a resolution of the House of Commons.

(2) Where regulations made under this Part impose a relevant requirement on any person, they may provide that if the person fails to comply with the requirement he shall be liable, subject to subsection (3) below, to a penalty of £250.

(3) Where by reason of any conduct—

(*a*) a person is convicted of an offence (whether under this Act or otherwise), or

(*b*) a person is assessed to a penalty under paragraph 7 of Schedule 6 to this Act [or a penalty for a deliberate inaccuracy under Schedule 24 to the Finance Act 2007 (penalties for errors)][1],

that person shall not by reason of that conduct be liable also to a penalty under any regulations under this Part.

(4) In subsection (2) above "relevant requirement" means any requirement other than one the penalty for a contravention of which is specified in section 25(3) or 33(3) above or in paragraph 2 of Schedule 7 to this Act.

(5) Subject to subsection (6) below, a power under this Part to make any provision by order or regulations—

(*a*) may be exercised so as to apply the provision only in such cases as may be described in the order or regulations;

(*b*) may be exercised so as to make different provision for different cases or descriptions of case; and (*c*) shall include power by the order or regulations to make such supplementary, incidental, consequential or transitional provision as the Treasury or, as the case may be, the Commissioners may think fit.

(6) Subsection (5) above does not apply to an order under section 16(6) or 24(10) above.

Amendment—[1] Words in sub-s (3)(*b*) inserted by the Finance Act 2008, Schedule 40 (Appointed Day, Transitional Provisions and Consequential Amendments) Order, SI 2009/571 art 8, Sch 1 paras 21, 23 with effect from 1 April 2009.

46 Civil penalties

(1) Where a person is liable to a civil penalty imposed by or under this Part—

(*a*) the Commissioners or, on appeal, an appeal tribunal may reduce the penalty to such amount (including nil) as they think proper; but

(*b*) on an appeal relating to any penalty reduced by the Commissioners, an appeal tribunal may cancel the whole or any part of the Commissioners' reduction.

(2) In determining whether a civil penalty should be, or should have been, reduced under subsection (1) above, no account shall be taken of any of the following matters, that is to say—

(*a*) the insufficiency of the funds available to any person for paying any aggregates levy due or for paying the amount of the penalty;

(*b*) the fact that there has, in the case in question or in that case taken with any other cases, been no or no significant loss of aggregates levy;

(*c*) the fact that the person liable to the penalty or a person acting on his behalf has acted in good faith.

(3) For the purposes of any provision made by or under this Part under which liability to a civil penalty does not arise in respect of conduct for which there is shown to be a reasonable excuse—

(*a*) an insufficiency of funds available for paying any amount is not a reasonable excuse; and

(*b*) where reliance has been placed on any other person to perform any task, neither the fact of that reliance nor any conduct of the person relied upon is a reasonable excuse.

(4) Schedule 10 to this Act (which makes provision about the assessment of civil penalties imposed and about interest on such penalties) shall have effect.

(5) If it appears to the Treasury that there has been a change in the value of money since the time when the amount of a civil penalty provided for by this Part was fixed, they may by order made by statutory instrument substitute, for the amount for the time being specified as the amount of that penalty, such other sum as appears to them to be justified by the change.

(6) In subsection (5) above the reference to the time when the amount of a civil penalty was fixed is a reference—

(*a*) in the case of a penalty which has not previously been modified under that subsection, to the time of the passing of this Act; and

(*b*) in any other case, to the time of the making of the order under that subsection that made the most recent modification of the amount of that penalty.

(7) An order under subsection (5) above—

(*a*) shall not be made unless a draft of the order has been laid before Parliament and approved by resolution of the House of Commons; and

(*b*) shall not apply to the penalty for any conduct before the coming into force of the order.

(8) In this section "civil penalty" means any penalty liability to which arises otherwise than in consequence of a person's conviction for a criminal offence.

47 Service of notices etc

(1) Any notice, notification or requirement that is to be or may be served on, given to or imposed on any person for the purposes of any provision made by or under this Part may be served, given or imposed by sending it to that person or his tax representative by post in a letter addressed to that person or representative at the latest or usual residence or place of business of that person or representative.

(2) Any direction required or authorised by or under this Part to be given by the Commissioners may be given by sending it by post in a letter addressed to each person affected by it at his latest or usual residence or place of business.

(3) Any direction, notice or notification required or authorised by or under this Part to be given by the Commissioners may be withdrawn or varied by them by a direction, notice or notification given in the same manner as the one withdrawn or varied.

48 Interpretation of Part

(1) In this Part—

"accounting period" means a period which, in pursuance of any regulations under section 25(1) above, is an accounting period for the purposes of aggregates levy;

"aggregate" shall be construed in accordance with sections 17(1) and 18 above;

"agreement" includes any arrangement or understanding (whether or not legally enforceable), and cognate expressions shall be construed accordingly;

"agricultural" means agricultural within the meaning of the Agriculture Act 1967 or the Agriculture Act (Northern Ireland) 1949;

"appeal tribunal" means [the First-tier Tribunal or, where determined by or under Tribunal Procedure Rules, the Upper Tribunal;][2];
"the commencement date" has the meaning given by section 16(6) above;
"commercial exploitation" shall be construed in accordance with section 19 above;
"the Commissioners" means the Commissioners of Customs and Excise;
"conduct" includes acts and omissions;
"construction purposes" shall be construed in accordance with subsection (2) below;
"exempt process" shall be construed in accordance with section 18(2) above;
"forestry" includes the cultivation, maintenance and care of trees or woodland of any description;
"gravel" includes gravel comprising or containing pebbles or stones or both;
["HMRC" means Her Majesty's Revenue and Customs;][2]
"limestone" includes chalk and dolomite;
"member", in relation to a group, shall be construed in accordance with section 35(6) above;
"mixed" includes blended, and cognate expressions shall be construed accordingly;
"non-resident taxpayer" means a person who—

(*a*) is or is required to be registered for the purposes of aggregates levy, or would be so required but for an exemption by virtue of regulations under section 24(4) above; and

(*b*) is not resident in the United Kingdom;

"operate" and "operator", in relation to any site, shall be construed in accordance with section 21 above;
"originating site" shall be construed in accordance with section 20 above;
"prescribed" means prescribed by regulations made by the Commissioners under this Part;
"registered" means registered in the register maintained under section 24 above;
"representative member", in relation to a group, shall be construed in accordance with section 35(6) above;
"rock" does not include any rock contained in a quantity of aggregate consisting wholly or mainly of gravel or sand;
"structure" includes roads and paths, the way on which any railway track is or is to be laid and embankments;
"subordinate legislation" has the same meaning as in the Interpretation Act 1978;
"tax credit" means a tax credit for which provision is made by tax credit regulations;
"tax credit regulations" means regulations under section 30 [or 30A][1] above;
"tax representative", in relation to any person, means the person who, in accordance with any regulations under section 33 above, is for the time being that person's tax representative for the purposes of aggregates levy;
"taxable aggregate" shall be construed in accordance with section 17(2) to (4) above;
"United Kingdom waters" means—

(*a*) the territorial sea adjacent to the United Kingdom; or

(*b*) any area designated by Order in Council under section 1(7) of the Continental Shelf Act 1964.

(2) References in this Part to the use of anything for construction purposes are references to either of the following, except in so far as it consists in the application to it of an exempt process, that is to say—

(*a*) using it as material or support in the construction or improvement of any structure;

(*b*) mixing it with anything as part of the process of producing mortar, concrete, tarmacadam, coated roadstone or any similar construction material.

(3) References in this Part to winning any aggregate are references to winning it—

(*a*) by quarrying, dredging, mining or collecting it from any land or area of the seabed; or

(*b*) by separating it in any other manner from any land or area of the seabed in which it is comprised.

(4) References in this Part, in relation to any accounting period, to aggregates levy due from any person for that period are references (subject to any regulations made by virtue of section 25(2)(*a*) above) to the aggregates levy for which that person is required, in accordance with regulations under section 25 above, to account by reference to that period.

(5) References in this Part to a repayment of aggregates levy or of an amount of aggregates levy are references to any repayment of an amount to any person by virtue of—

(*a*) any tax credit regulations;

(*b*) section 31 above;

(*c*) paragraph 11(3) of Schedule 5 to this Act; or

(*d*) paragraph 6(3) of Schedule 10 to this Act.

(6) For the purposes of this Part a person is resident in the United Kingdom at any time if, at that time—

(*a*) that person has an established place of business in the United Kingdom;

(*b*) that person has a usual place of residence in the United Kingdom; or (*c*) that person is a firm or unincorporated body which (without being resident in the United Kingdom by virtue of paragraph (*a*) above) has amongst its partners or members at least one individual with a usual place of residence in the United Kingdom.

Amendments—[1] In sub-s (1), in the definition of "tax credit regulations", words inserted by FA 2004 s 291(1), (3)–(5) with effect from 23 July 2004 (by virtue of SI 2004/1942).

[2] In sub-s (1), in the definition of "appeal tribunal", words substituted for the words "a VAT and duties tribunal"; definition of "HMRC" inserted by the Transfer of Tribunal Functions and Revenue and Customs Appeals Order, SI 2009/56 art 3, Sch 1 para 307 with effect from 1 April 2009.

Supplemental

49 Minor and consequential amendments

(1) (*amends* PCTA 1968 s 1(1)).

(2) (*adds* FA 1996 s 197(2)(*h*)).

(3) (*inserts* TA 1988 s 827(1E)).

SCHEDULES

SCHEDULE 4

AGGREGATES LEVY: REGISTRATION

Section 24

Notification of registrability etc

[1—(1) An unregistered person who—

(*a*) is required to be registered for the purposes of aggregates levy; or

(*b*) has formed the intention of carrying out taxable activities that are registrable,

shall notify the Commissioners of that fact.

(1A) An unregistered person who—

(*a*) would be required to be registered for the purposes of aggregates levy but for an exemption by virtue of regulations under section 24(4) of this Act; or

(*b*) has formed the intention of carrying out taxable activities that would be registrable but for such an exemption,

shall, in such cases or circumstances as may be prescribed in the regulations, notify the Commissioners of that fact.

(1B)For the purposes of sub-paragraphs (1) and (1A) above, taxable activities are "registrable" if a person carrying them out is, by reason of doing so, required by section 24(2) of this Act to be registered for the purposes of aggregates levy.][1]

(2) Subject to sub-paragraphs (5) and (6) below, a person who fails to comply with sub-paragraph (1) [or (1A)][1] *above shall be liable to a penalty.*

(3) The amount of the penalty shall be—

(a) the amount equal to 5 per cent of the relevant levy; or

(b) if it is greater or the circumstances are such that there is no relevant levy, £250.

(4) In sub-paragraph (3) above "relevant levy" means the aggregates levy (if any) to which the person in question is liable in respect of aggregate subjected to commercial exploitation in the period which—

(a) begins with the date with effect from which he is required to be registered for the purposes of that levy or, as the case may be, would be so required but for an exemption by virtue of regulations under section 24(4) of this Act; and

(b) ends with the date on which the Commissioners received notification of, or otherwise first became aware of, the fact that that person was required to be registered or is a person who would be so required but for such an exemption.

(5) A failure to comply with sub-paragraph (1) [or (1A)][1] *above shall not give rise to any liability to a penalty under this paragraph if the person concerned satisfies the Commissioners or, on appeal, an appeal tribunal that there is a reasonable excuse for the failure.*

(6) Where, by reason of any conduct falling within sub-paragraph (2) above—

(a) a person is convicted of an offence (whether under this Act or otherwise), or

(b) a person is assessed to a penalty under paragraph 7 of Schedule 6 to this Act (penalty for evasion) [or a penalty for a deliberate inaccuracy under Schedule 24 to the Finance Act 2007 (penalties for errors)][2]*,*

that person shall not by reason of that conduct be liable also to a penalty under this paragraph.[3]

Regulations—Finance Act 2001, section 24 and Schedule 4, (Appointed Day) Order, SI 2001/4033 (appointed day for entry into force of this paragraph is 11 January 2002).

Amendments—[1] Sub-paras (1), (1A) and (1B) substituted for sub-para (1), and words in sub-paras (2), and (5) inserted, by FA 2002 s 132(1), (3), Sch 38 para 9. These amendments are deemed to have come into force on 1 April 2002.

[2] Words in sub-para (6)(*b*) inserted by the Finance Act 2008, Schedule 40 (Appointed Day, Transitional Provisions and Consequential Amendments) Order, SI 2009/571 art 8, Sch 1 paras 21, 24 with effect from 1 April 2009.

[3] Para 1(2) to (6) repealed by FA 2008 s 123, Sch 41 para 25(*l*) with effect from 1 April 2010 (by virtue of SI 2009/511 art 2).

Form of registration

2—(1) The Commissioners shall register a person who is required to be registered for the purposes of aggregates levy with effect from the time when the requirement arose.
(2) Where any two or more bodies corporate are members of the same group they shall be registered together as one person in the name of the representative member.
(3) The registration of a body corporate carrying on a business in several divisions may, if the body corporate so requests and the Commissioners see fit, be in the names of those divisions.
(4) The registration of—

(*a*) any two or more persons carrying on a business in partnership, or
(*b*) an unincorporated body,

may be in the name of the firm or body concerned.

Regulations—Finance Act 2001, section 24 and Schedule 4, (Appointed Day) Order, SI 2001/4033 (appointed day for entry into force of this paragraph is 11 January 2002).

Notification of loss or prospective loss of registrability

3—(1) A person who, having become liable to give a notification by virtue of paragraph 1 above, ceases (whether before or after being registered) to have the intention of carrying out taxable activities shall notify the Commissioners of that fact.
(2) A person who fails to comply with sub-paragraph (1) above shall be liable to a penalty of £250.

Regulations—Finance Act 2001, section 24 and Schedule 4, (Appointed Day) Order, SI 2001/4033 (appointed day for entry into force of this paragraph is 11 January 2002).

Cancellation of registration

4—(1) If the Commissioners are satisfied that a registered person—

(*a*) has ceased to carry out taxable activities, and
(*b*) does not have the intention of carrying out taxable activities,

they may cancel his registration with effect from such time after he last carried out such activities as appears to them to be appropriate.
(2) Sub-paragraph (1) above applies whether or not the registered person has notified the Commissioners under paragraph 3 above.
(3) Where a registered person is exempted from the requirement to be registered by virtue of regulations under section 24(4), the Commissioners may cancel his registration with effect from the time when he became so exempted or such later time as appears to them to be appropriate.
(4) The Commissioners shall be under a duty to exercise the power conferred by sub-paragraph (1) or (3) above with effect from any time if, where the power is exercisable, they are satisfied that the conditions specified in sub-paragraph (5) below are satisfied and were or will be satisfied at that time.
(5) Those conditions are—

(*a*) that the person in question—
   (i) has given a notification under paragraph 3 above; or
   (ii) is exempted from the requirement to be registered by virtue of regulations under section 24(4) of this Act;
(*b*) that no aggregates levy due from that person, and no amount recoverable as if it were such levy, remains unpaid;
(*c*) that no tax credit to which that person is entitled by virtue of any tax credit regulations is outstanding; and
(*d*) that that person is not subject to any outstanding liability to make a return for the purposes of aggregates levy.

(6) Where—

(*a*) a registered person notifies the Commissioners under paragraph 3 above, and
(*b*) they are satisfied that (if he had not been registered) he would not have been required to be registered at any time since the time when he was registered,

they shall cancel his registration with effect from the date of his registration.
(7) Where—

(*a*) a registered person is exempted from the requirement to be registered by virtue of regulations under section 24(4) of this Act, and
(*b*) the Commissioners are satisfied that he has been so exempted at all times since being registered,

they shall cancel his registration with effect from the date of his registration.

Regulations—Finance Act 2001, section 24 and Schedule 4, (Appointed Day) Order, SI 2001/4033 (appointed day for entry into force of this paragraph is 11 January 2002).

Correction of the register etc

5—(1) The Commissioners may by regulations make provision for and with respect to the correction of entries in the register.

(2) Regulations under this paragraph may, to such extent as appears to the Commissioners appropriate for keeping the register up to date, make provision requiring—

(*a*) registered persons, and

(*b*) persons who are required to be registered, and

(*c*) persons who would be so required but for any exemption by virtue of regulations under section 24(4) of this Act,

to notify the Commissioners of changes in circumstances relating to themselves, their businesses or any other matter with respect to which particulars are contained in the register (or would be, were the person registered).

Regulations—Finance Act 2001, section 24 and Schedule 4, (Appointed Day) Order, SI 2001/4033 (appointed day for entry into force of this paragraph is 20 December 2001).

Supplemental regulations about notifications

6—(1) For the purposes of any provision made by or under section 24 of this Act or this Schedule for any matter to be notified to the Commissioners, regulations made by the Commissioners may make provision—

(*a*) as to the time within which the notification is to be given;

(*b*) as to the form and manner in which the notification is to be given; and

(*c*) as to the information and other particulars to be contained in or provided with any notification.

(2) For those purposes the Commissioners may also by regulations impose obligations requiring a person who has given a notification to notify the Commissioners if any information contained in or provided in connection with that notification is or becomes inaccurate.

(3) The power under this paragraph to make regulations as to the time within which any notification is to be given shall include power to authorise the Commissioners to extend the time for the giving of a notification.

Regulations—Finance Act 2001, section 24 and Schedule 4, (Appointed Day) Order, SI 2001/4033 (appointed day for entry into force of this paragraph is 20 December 2001).

Publication of information on the register

7—(1) The Commissioners may publish, by such means as they think fit, any information which—

(*a*) is derived from the register; and

(*b*) falls within any of the descriptions set out below.

(2) The descriptions are—

(*a*) the names of registered persons;

(*b*) particulars of registered sites;

(*c*) the fact (where it is the case) that the registered person is a body corporate which is a member of a group;

(*d*) the names of the other bodies corporate which are members of the group.

(3) Information may be published in accordance with this paragraph notwithstanding any obligation not to disclose the information that would otherwise apply.

Regulations—Finance Act 2001, section 24 and Schedule 4, (Appointed Day) Order, SI 2001/4033 (appointed day for entry into force of this paragraph is 11 January 2002).

Interpretation of Schedule

8—(1) In this Schedule—

(*a*) references to the register are references to the register maintained under section 24 of this Act;

(*b*) references to registering a person are references to registering him in that register; and

(*c*) references to a person's registration are references to his registration in that register;

and "unregistered" shall be construed accordingly.

(2) For the purposes of this Schedule a person carries out a taxable activity if a quantity of aggregate is subjected to commercial exploitation in the United Kingdom in circumstances in which he is responsible for its being so subjected.

Regulations—Finance Act 2001, section 24 and Schedule 4, (Appointed Day) Order, SI 2001/4033 (appointed day for entry into force of this paragraph is 11 January 2002).

SCHEDULE 5
AGGREGATES LEVY: RECOVERY AND INTEREST
Section 27

Recovery of levy as debt due

1 Aggregates levy shall be recoverable as a debt due to the Crown.

Assessments of amounts of levy due

2—(1) Where it appears to the Commissioners—

(*a*) that any period is an accounting period by reference to which a person is liable to account for aggregates levy,

(*b*) that any aggregates levy for which that person is liable to account by reference to that period has become due, and

(*c*) that there has been a default by that person that falls within sub-paragraph (2) below,

they may assess the amount of the levy due from that person for that period to the best of their judgement and notify that amount to that person.

(2) The defaults falling within this sub-paragraph are—

(*a*) any failure to make a return required to be made by any provision made by or under this Part of this Act;

(*b*) any failure to keep any documents necessary to verify returns required to be made under any such provision;

(*c*) any failure to afford the facilities necessary to verify returns required to be made under any such provision;

(*d*) the making, in purported compliance with any requirement of any such provision to make a return, of an incomplete or incorrect return;

(*e*) any failure to comply with a requirement imposed by or under Schedule 4 to this Act.

(3) Where it appears to the Commissioners that a default falling within sub-paragraph (2) above is a default by a person on whom the requirement to make a return is imposed in his capacity as the representative of another person, sub-paragraph (1) above shall apply as if the reference to the amount of aggregates levy due included a reference to any aggregates levy due from that other person.

(4) In a case where—

(*a*) the Commissioners have made an assessment for any accounting period as a result of any person's failure to make a return for that period,

(*b*) the levy assessed has been paid but no proper return has been made for that period,

(*c*) as a result of a failure (whether by that person or a representative of his) to make a return for a later accounting period, the Commissioners find it necessary to make another assessment under this paragraph in relation to the later period, and

(*d*) the Commissioners think it appropriate to do so in the light of the absence of a proper return for the earlier period,

they may, in the assessment in relation to the later period, specify an amount of aggregates levy due that is greater than the amount that they would have considered to be appropriate had they had regard only to the later period.

(5) Where an amount has been assessed and notified to any person under this paragraph, it shall be recoverable on the basis that it is an amount of aggregates levy due from him.

(6) Sub-paragraph (5) above does not have effect if, or to the extent that, the assessment in question has been withdrawn or reduced.

Supplementary assessments

3—(1) If, where an assessment has been notified to any person under paragraph 2 above or this paragraph, it appears to the Commissioners that the amount which ought to have been assessed as due for any accounting period exceeds the amount that has already been assessed, the Commissioners may make a supplementary assessment of the amount of the excess and notify that person accordingly.

(2) Where an amount has been assessed and notified to any person under this paragraph it shall be recoverable on the basis that it is an amount of aggregates levy due from him.

(3) Sub-paragraph (2) above does not have effect if, or to the extent that, the assessment in question has been withdrawn or reduced.

Time limits for assessments

4—(1) An assessment under paragraph 2 or 3 above of an amount of aggregates levy due for any accounting period—

(*a*) shall not be made more than two years after the end of the accounting period unless it is made within the period mentioned in sub-paragraph (2) below; and

(*b*) subject to sub-paragraph (3) below, shall not in any event be made more than [4 years] after the end of that accounting period.

(2) The period referred to in sub-paragraph (1)(*a*) above is the period of one year after evidence of facts sufficient in the Commissioners' opinion to justify the making of the assessment first came to their knowledge.

[(3) An assessment of an amount due from a person in a case involving a loss of aggregates levy—

(*a*) brought about deliberately by the person (or by another person acting on that person's behalf), or

(*b*) attributable to a failure by the person to comply with an obligation under section 24(2) or paragraph 1 of Schedule 4,

may be made at any time not more than 20 years after the end of the accounting period to which it relates (subject to sub-paragraph (4)).

(3A) In sub-paragraph (3)(*a*) the reference to a loss brought about deliberately by the person includes a loss brought about as a result of a deliberate inaccuracy in a document given to Her Majesty's Revenue and Customs by or on behalf of that person.]

(4) Where, after a person's death, the Commissioners propose to assess an amount of aggregates levy as due by reason of some conduct of the deceased—

(*a*) the assessment shall not be made more than [4 years] after the death; *and*

(*b*) *if the circumstances are as set out in sub-paragraph (3) above—*

(*i*) the modification of sub-paragraph (1) above contained in that sub-paragraph shall not apply; but

(*ii*) any assessment which (applying that modification) could have been made immediately after the death may be made at any time within three years after it.

(5) Nothing in this paragraph shall prejudice the powers of the Commissioners under paragraph 2(4) above.

Amendments—In sub-paras (1)(*b*), (4)(*a*) words substituted for words "three years", sub-para (4)(*b*) and the word "and" before it repealed, and sub-paras (3), (3A) substituted for previous sub-para (3), by FA 2009 s 99, Sch 51 paras 27, 29, with effect from 1 April 2010 (by virtue of SI 2010/867 art 2(1)).

Note that the following transitional provisions apply (SI 2010/867 arts 10–12)—

– The amendment made to sub-para (1)(*b*) is disregarded where, for the purposes of sub–para (1)(*b*) the end of the accounting period was on or before 31 March 2007.

– The substitution of sub-para (3) is disregarded where, for the purposes of sub-para (3) the end of the accounting period to which the assessment relates was on or before 31 March 2007.

– The amendments made to sub–para (4) are disregarded where, for the purposes of sub-para (4) the death was on or before 31 March 2007.

Penalty interest on unpaid levy

5—(1) Where—

(*a*) a person makes a return for the purposes of any regulations made under section 25 of this Act (whether or not at the time required by the regulations), and

(*b*) the return shows that an amount of aggregates levy is due from him for the accounting period for which the return is made,

that amount shall carry penalty interest for the period specified in sub-paragraph (2) below.

(2) That period is the period which—

(*a*) begins with the day after that on which the person is required in accordance with regulations under section 25 of this Act to pay aggregates levy due from him for the accounting period in question; and

(*b*) ends with the day before that on which the amount shown in the return is paid.

Interest on overdue levy paid before assessment

6—(1) Where—

(*a*) the circumstances are such that there was a time when an assessment could have been made under paragraph 2 or 3 above of an amount of levy due from any person, but

(*b*) before the making and notification to that person of any assessment of that amount, the amount was paid,

the whole of the amount paid shall be taken to have carried interest for the period specified in sub-paragraph (2).

(2) That period is the period which—

(*a*) begins with the day after that on which the person is required in accordance with regulations under section 25 of this Act to pay aggregates levy due from him for the accounting period to which the amount in question relates; and

(*b*) ends with the day before that on which that amount was paid.

(3) The interest payable by virtue of this paragraph shall be payable at the rate applicable under section 197 of the Finance Act 1996.

Penalty interest on levy where no return made

7—(1) Where—

(*a*) the Commissioners make an assessment under paragraph 2 or 3 above of an amount of aggregates levy due from any person for any accounting period and notify it to him, and

(*b*) the assessment is made at a time after the time by which a return is required by regulations under section 25 of this Act to be made by that person for that accounting period and before any such return has been made,

that amount shall carry penalty interest for the period specified in sub-paragraph (2) below.

(2) That period is the period which—

(*a*) begins with the day after that on which the person is required in accordance with regulations under section 25 of this Act to pay aggregates levy due from him for the accounting period in question; and

(*b*) ends with the day before that on which the assessed amount is paid.

Ordinary and penalty interest on under-declared levy

8—(1) Subject to sub-paragraph (4) below, where—

(*a*) the Commissioners make an assessment under paragraph 2 or 3 above of an amount of aggregates levy due from any person for any accounting period and notify it to him,

(*b*) the assessment is made after a return for the purposes of any regulations under section 25 has been made by that person for that accounting period, and

(*c*) the assessment is made on the basis that the amount ("the additional amount") is due from him in addition to any amount shown in the return, or in a previous assessment made in relation to the accounting period,

the additional amount shall carry interest for the period specified in sub-paragraph (2) below.

(2) That period is the period which—

(*a*) begins with the day after that on which the person is required in accordance with regulations under section 25 of this Act to pay aggregates levy due from him for the accounting period in question; and

(*b*) ends with the day before the day on which the additional amount is paid.

(3) Interest under this paragraph—

(*a*) in respect of so much of the period specified in sub-paragraph (2) above as falls before the day on which the assessment is notified to the person in question, shall be payable at the rate applicable under section 197 of the Finance Act 1996; and

(*b*) in respect of the remainder (if any) of that period, shall be penalty interest.

(4) Where—

(*a*) the Commissioners make an assessment under paragraph 2 or 3 above of an amount of aggregates levy due from any person for any accounting period and notify it to him,

(*b*) they also specify a date for the purposes of this sub-paragraph, and

(*c*) the amount assessed is paid on or before that date,

the only interest carried by that amount under this paragraph shall be interest, at the rate given by sub-paragraph (3)(a) above, for the period before the day on which the assessment is notified.

Penalty interest on unpaid ordinary interest

9—(1) Subject to sub-paragraph (2) below, where the Commissioners make an assessment under paragraph 12 below of an amount of interest payable at the rate given by paragraph 8(3)(*a*) above, that amount shall carry penalty interest for the period which—

(*a*) begins with the day on which the assessment is notified to the person on whom the assessment is made; and

(*b*) ends with the day before the day on which the assessed interest is paid.

(2) Where—

(*a*) the Commissioners make an assessment under paragraph 12 below of an amount of interest due from any person,

(*b*) they also specify a date for the purposes of this sub-paragraph, and

(*c*) the amount of interest assessed is paid on or before that date,

the amount paid before that date shall not carry penalty interest under this paragraph.

Penalty interest

10—(1) Penalty interest under any of paragraphs 5 to 9 above shall be compound interest calculated—

(*a*) at the penalty rate; and

(*b*) with monthly rests.

(2) For this purpose the penalty rate is the rate found by—

(*a*) taking the rate applicable under section 197 of the Finance Act 1996 for the purposes of paragraph 8(3)(*a*) above; and

(*b*) adding 10 percentage points to that rate.

(3) Where a person is liable under any of paragraphs 5 to 9 above to pay any penalty interest, the Commissioners or, on appeal, an appeal tribunal may reduce the amount payable to such amount (including nil) as they think proper.

(4) Subject to sub-paragraph (5) below, where the person concerned satisfies the Commissioners or, on appeal, an appeal tribunal that there is a reasonable excuse for the conduct giving rise to the liability to pay penalty interest, that is a matter which (among other things) may be taken into account under sub-paragraph (3) above.

(5) In determining whether there is a reasonable excuse for the purposes of sub-paragraph (4) above, no account shall be taken of any of the following matters, that is to say—

(*a*) the insufficiency of the funds available to any person for paying any aggregates levy due or for paying the amount of the interest;

(*b*) the fact that there has, in the case in question or in that case taken with any other cases, been no or no significant loss of aggregates levy;

(*c*) the fact that the person liable to pay the interest or a person acting on his behalf has acted in good faith.

(6) In the case of interest reduced by the Commissioners under sub-paragraph (3) above an appeal tribunal, on an appeal relating to the interest, may cancel the whole or any part of the reduction made by the Commissioners.

Supplemental provisions about interest

11—(1) Interest under any of paragraphs 5 to 9 above shall be paid without any deduction of income tax.

(2) Sub-paragraph (3) below applies where—

(*a*) an amount carries interest under any of paragraphs 5 to 9 above (or would do so apart from that sub-paragraph); and

(*b*) all or part of the amount turns out not to be due.

(3) In such a case—

(*a*) the amount or part that turns out not to be due shall not carry interest under the applicable paragraph and shall be treated as never having done so; and

(*b*) all such adjustments as are reasonable shall be made, including (subject to section 32 of, and Schedule 8 to, this Act) adjustments by way of repayment.

Assessments to interest

12—(1) Where a person is liable for interest under any of paragraphs 5 to 9 above, the Commissioners may assess the amount due by way of interest and notify it to him accordingly.

(2) If, where an assessment has been notified to any person under sub-paragraph (1) above or this sub-paragraph, it appears to the Commissioners that the amount which ought to have been assessed exceeds the amount that has already been assessed, the Commissioners may make a supplementary assessment of the amount of the excess and notify that person accordingly.

(3) Where an amount has been assessed and notified to any person under this paragraph, it shall be recoverable as if it were aggregates levy due from him.

(4) Sub-paragraph (3) above—

(*a*) shall not apply so as to require any interest to be payable on interest except—

(i) in accordance with paragraph 9 above; or

(ii) in so far as it falls to be compounded in accordance with paragraph 10 above;

and

(*b*) shall not have effect if, or to the extent that, the assessment in question has been withdrawn or reduced.

(5) Paragraph 4 above shall apply in relation to assessments under this paragraph as if any assessment to interest were an assessment under paragraph 2 above to aggregates levy due for the period which is the relevant accounting period in relation to that interest.

(6) Subject to sub-paragraph (7) below, where a person—

(*a*) is assessed under this paragraph to an amount due by way of any interest, and

(*b*) is also assessed under paragraph 2 or 3 above for the accounting period which is the relevant accounting period in relation to that interest,

the assessments may be combined and notified to him as one assessment.

(7) A notice of a combined assessment under sub-paragraph (6) above must separately identify the interest being assessed.

(8) The relevant accounting period for the purposes of this paragraph is—

(*a*) in the case of interest on the levy due for any accounting period, that accounting period; and

(*b*) in the case of interest on interest (whether under paragraph 9 above or by virtue of any compounding under paragraph 10 above) the period which is the relevant accounting period for the interest on which the interest is payable.

(9) In a case where—

(*a*) the amount of any interest falls to be calculated by reference to aggregates levy which was not paid at the time when it should have been, and

(*b*) that levy cannot be readily attributed to any one or more accounting periods,

that levy shall be treated for the purposes of interest on any of that levy as aggregates levy due for such period or periods as the Commissioners may determine to the best of their judgement and notify to the person liable.

Further assessments to penalty interest

13—(1) Where an assessment is made under paragraph 12 above to an amount of penalty interest under any of paragraphs 5 to 9 above—

(*a*) the notice of assessment shall specify a date, not later than the date of the notice of assessment, to which the amount of interest which is assessed is calculated; and

(*b*) if the interest continues to accrue after that date, a further assessment or further assessments may be made under paragraph 12 above in respect of the amounts so accruing.

(2) Where—

(*a*) an assessment to penalty interest is made specifying a date for the purposes of sub-paragraph (1)(*a*) above, and

(*b*) within such period as may for the purposes of this sub-paragraph have been notified by the Commissioners to the person liable for the interest, the amount on which the interest is payable is paid,

that amount shall be deemed for the purposes of any further liability to interest to have been paid on the specified date.

Recovery by distress

14 In section 51(5) of the Finance Act 1997 (definition of relevant taxes for the purposes of the power to make provision by regulations for enforcement by distress of the relevant taxes), after paragraph (*d*) there shall be inserted—

"(*da*) aggregates levy;".

Prospective amendments—Para 14A to be inserted by the Tribunals, Courts and Enforcement Act 2007 s 62(3), Sch 13 paras 139, 140 with effect from a date to be appointed. Para 14A to be repealed by FA 2008 s 129, Sch 43 para 8 with effect from such day as the Commissioners may by statutory instrument appoint.

Para 14A to read—

"Controlled goods agreements

14A—(1)This paragraph applies where an enforcement agent acting under the power conferred, by virtue of paragraph 14 above, by section 51(A1) of the Finance Act 1997 (power to use the procedure in Schedule 12 to the Tribunals, Courts and Enforcement Act 2007) has entered into a controlled goods agreement with the person against whom the power is exercisable ("the person in default").

(2) In this paragraph, "controlled goods agreement" has the meaning given by paragraph 13(4) of that Schedule.

(3) Subject to sub-paragraph (4), if the person in default removes or disposes of goods (or permits their removal or disposal) in breach of the controlled goods agreement, he is liable to a penalty equal to half of the levy or other amount recoverable under section 51(A1) of the Finance Act 1997.

(4) The person in default shall not be liable to a penalty under subparagraph (3) above if he satisfies the Commissioners or, on appeal, an appeal tribunal, that there is a reasonable excuse for the breach in question.

(5) This paragraph extends only to England and Wales.".

Walking possession agreements

15—(1) This paragraph applies where—

(*a*) in accordance with regulations made by virtue of paragraph 14 above a distress is authorised to be levied on the goods and chattels of a person;

(*b*) that person ("the person in default") has refused or neglected to pay an amount of aggregates levy due from him or an amount recoverable from him as if it were aggregates levy; and

(*c*) the person levying the distress and the person in default have entered into a walking possession agreement.

(2) For the purposes of this paragraph a walking possession agreement is an agreement under which, in consideration of the property distrained upon being allowed to remain in the custody of the person in default and of the delaying of its sale, the person in default—

(*a*) acknowledges that the property specified in the agreement is under distraint and held in walking possession; and

(*b*) undertakes that, except with the consent of the Commissioners and subject to such conditions as they may impose, he will not remove or allow the removal of any of the specified property from the premises named in the agreement.

(3) Subject to sub-paragraph (4) below, if the person in default is in breach of the undertaking contained in a walking possession agreement, he shall be liable to a penalty equal to one half of the levy or other amount referred to in sub-paragraph (1)(*b*) above.

(4) The person in default shall not be liable to a penalty under sub-paragraph (3) above if he satisfies the Commissioners or, on appeal, an appeal tribunal that there is a reasonable excuse for the breach in question.

(5) This paragraph does not extend to Scotland.

Prospective amendments—Sub-para (5) to be substituted by the Tribunals, Courts and Enforcement Act 2007 s 62(3), Sch 13 paras 139, 141 with effect from a date to be appointed. Sub-para (5) as substituted, to read—

"(5) This paragraph extends only to Northern Ireland.".

Recovery by diligence

16 In section 52(5) of the Finance Act 1997 (definition of relevant taxes for the purposes of the power to make provision by regulations for enforcement by diligence of the relevant taxes), after paragraph (*d*) there shall be inserted—

"(*da*) aggregates levy;".

Preferential debts in England and Wales and Northern Ireland

17 (1), (2) . . . [1]

(3), (4) . . . [2]

Amendments—[1] Sub-paras (1), (2) repealed by the Enterprise Act 2002 ss 278(2), 279, Sch 26 with effect 15 September 2003 (by virtue of SI 2003/3093).

[2] Sub-paras (3), (4) repealed by the Insolvency (Northern Ireland) Order, SI 2005/1455 art 31, Sch 9 with effect from 27 March 2006..

Preferred debts in Scotland

18

Amendment—This paragraph repealed by the Enterprise Act 2002 ss 278(2), 279, Sch 26 with effect from 15 September 2003 (by virtue of SI 2003/3093).

Interpretation of Schedule etc

19—(1) In this Schedule "penalty interest" shall be construed in accordance with paragraph 10 above.

(2) Any notification of an assessment under any provision of this Schedule to a person's representative shall be treated for the purposes of this Part of this Act as notification to the person in relation to whom the representative acts.

(3) In this Schedule "representative", in relation to any person, means—

(*a*) any of that person's personal representatives;

(*b*) that person's trustee in bankruptcy or liquidator;

(*c*) any person holding office as a receiver in relation to that person or any of his property;

(*d*) that person's tax representative or any other person for the time being acting in a representative capacity in relation to that person.

(4) In this paragraph "trustee in bankruptcy" includes, as respects Scotland—

(*a*) an interim or permanent trustee (within the meaning of the Bankruptcy (Scotland) Act 1985); and

(*b*) a trustee acting under a trust deed (within the meaning of that Act).

SCHEDULE 6

AGGREGATES LEVY: EVASION, MISDECLARATION AND NEGLECT

Section 28

PART 1

CRITICAL OFFENCES

Evasion

1—(1) A person is guilty of an offence if he is knowingly concerned in, or in the taking of steps with a view to—

(*a*) the fraudulent evasion by that person of any aggregates levy with which he is charged; or

(*b*) the fraudulent evasion by any other person of any aggregates levy with which that other person is charged.

(2) The references in sub-paragraph (1) above to the evasion of aggregates levy include references to obtaining, in circumstances where there is no entitlement to it, either a tax credit or a repayment of aggregates levy.

(3) A person guilty of an offence under this paragraph shall be liable (subject to sub-paragraph (4) below)—

(*a*) on summary conviction, to a penalty of the statutory maximum or to imprisonment for a term not exceeding six months, or to both;

(*b*) on conviction on indictment, to a penalty of any amount or to imprisonment for a term not exceeding seven years, or to both.

(4) In the case of any offence under this paragraph, where the statutory maximum is less than three times the sum of the amounts of aggregates levy which are shown to be amounts that were or were intended to be evaded, the penalty on summary conviction shall be the amount equal to three times that sum (instead of the statutory maximum).

(5) For the purposes of sub-paragraph (4) above the amounts of levy that were or were intended to be evaded shall be taken to include—

(*a*) the amount of any tax credit, and

(*b*) the amount of any repayment of aggregates levy,

which was, or was intended to be, obtained in circumstances where there was no entitlement to it.

(6) In determining for the purposes of sub-paragraph (4) above how much aggregates levy (in addition to any amount falling within sub-paragraph (5) above) was or was intended to be evaded, no account shall be taken of the extent (if any) to which any liability to aggregates levy of any person fell, or would have fallen, to be reduced by the amount of any tax credit or repayment of aggregates levy to which he was, or would have been, entitled.

Misstatements

2—(1) A person is guilty of an offence if, with the requisite intent and for purposes connected with aggregates levy—

(*a*) he produces or provides, or causes to be produced or provided, any document which is false in a material particular; or

(*b*) he otherwise makes use of such a document;

and in this sub-paragraph "the requisite intent" means the intent to deceive any person or to secure that a machine will respond to the document as if it were a true document.

(2) A person is guilty of an offence if, in providing any information under any provision made by or under this Part of this Act—

(*a*) he makes a statement which he knows to be false in a material particular; or

(*b*) he recklessly makes a statement which is false in a material particular.

(3) A person guilty of an offence under this paragraph shall be liable (subject to sub-paragraph (4) below)—

(*a*) on summary conviction, to a penalty of the statutory maximum or to imprisonment for a term not exceeding six months, or to both;

(*b*) on conviction on indictment, to a penalty of any amount or to imprisonment for a term not exceeding seven years, or to both.

(4) In the case of any offence under this paragraph, where—

(*a*) the document referred to in sub-paragraph (1) above is a return required under any provision made by or under this Part of this Act, or

(*b*) the information referred to in sub-paragraph (2) above is contained in or otherwise relevant to such a return,

the amount of the penalty on summary conviction shall be whichever is the greater of the statutory maximum and the amount equal to three times the sum of the amounts (if any) by which the return understates any person's liability to aggregates levy.

(5) In sub-paragraph (4) above the reference to the amount by which any person's liability to aggregates levy is understated shall be taken to be equal to the sum of—

(*a*) the amount (if any) by which his gross liability was understated; and

(*b*) the amount (if any) by which any entitlements of his to tax credits and repayments of aggregates levy were overstated.

(6) In sub-paragraph (5) above "gross liability" means liability to aggregates levy before any deduction is made in respect of any entitlement to any tax credit or repayments of aggregates levy.

Conduct involving evasions or misstatements

3—(1) A person is guilty of an offence under this paragraph if his conduct during any particular period must have involved the commission by him of one or more offences under the preceding provisions of this Schedule.

(2) For the purposes of any proceedings for an offence under this paragraph it shall be immaterial whether the particulars of the offence or offences that must have been committed are known.

(3) A person guilty of an offence under this paragraph shall be liable (subject to sub-paragraph (4) below)—

(*a*) on summary conviction, to a penalty of the statutory maximum or to imprisonment for a term not exceeding six months, or to both;

(*b*) on conviction on indictment, to a penalty of any amount or to imprisonment for a term not exceeding seven years, or to both.

(4) In the case of any offence under this paragraph, where the statutory maximum is less than three times the sum of the amounts of aggregates levy which are shown to be amounts that were or were intended to be evaded by the conduct in question, the penalty on summary conviction shall be the amount equal to three times that sum (instead of the statutory maximum).

(5) For the purposes of sub-paragraph (4) above the amounts of levy that were or were intended to be evaded by any conduct shall be taken to include—

(*a*) the amount of any tax credit, and

(*b*) the amount of any repayment of aggregates levy,

which was, or was intended to be, obtained in circumstances where there was no entitlement to it.

(6) In determining for the purposes of sub-paragraph (4) above how much aggregates levy (in addition to any amount falling within sub-paragraph (5) above) was or was intended to be evaded, no account shall be taken of the extent (if any) to which any liability to aggregates levy of any person fell, or would have fallen, to be reduced by the amount of any tax credit or repayments of aggregates levy to which he was, or would have been, entitled.

Preparations for evasion

4—(1) Where a person—

(*a*) becomes a party to any agreement under or by means of which a quantity of taxable aggregate is or is to be subjected to commercial exploitation in the United Kingdom, or

(*b*) makes arrangements for any other person to become a party to such an agreement,

he is guilty of an offence if he does so in the belief that aggregates levy chargeable on the aggregate in question will be evaded.

(2) Subject to sub-paragraph (3) below, a person guilty of an offence under this paragraph shall be liable, on summary conviction, to a penalty of level 5 on the standard scale.

(3) In the case of any offence under this paragraph, where level 5 on the standard scale is less than three times the sum of the amounts of aggregates levy which are shown to be amounts that were or were intended to be evaded in respect of the aggregate in question, the penalty shall be the amount equal to three times that sum (instead of level 5 on the standard scale).

(4) For the purposes of sub-paragraph (3) above the amounts of levy that were or were intended to be evaded shall be taken to include—

(*a*) the amount of any tax credit, and

(*b*) the amount of any repayment of aggregates levy,

which was, or was intended to be, obtained in circumstances where there was no entitlement to it.

(5) In determining for the purposes of sub-paragraph (3) above how much aggregates levy (in addition to any amount falling within sub-paragraph (4) above) was or was intended to be evaded, no account shall be taken of the extent (if any) to which any liability to aggregates levy of any person fell, or would have fallen, to be reduced by the amount of any tax credit or repayments of aggregates levy to which he was, or would have been, entitled.

Criminal proceedings etc

5 *Sections 145 to 155 of the Customs and Excise Management Act 1979 (proceedings for offences, mitigation of penalties and certain other matters) shall apply in relation to offences and penalties under this Part of this Schedule as they apply in relation to offences and penalties under the customs and excise Acts.*

Arrest

6—(1) Where an authorised person has reasonable grounds for suspecting that a fraud offence has been committed he may arrest anyone whom he has reasonable grounds for suspecting to be guilty of the offence.

(2) In this paragraph—

"authorised person" means any person acting under the authority of the Commissioners; and

"a fraud offence" means an offence under any of paragraphs 1 to 3 above.1

Amendments—[1] This para repealed by FA 2007 ss 84, 114, Sch 22 paras 3, 12(*a*), Sch 27 Pt 5(1) with effect from 1 December 2007 (by virtue of SI 2007/3166 art 3(*a*)).

PART 2
CIVIL PENALTIES

Evasion

7—*(1) Subject to sub-paragraph (5) below, where—*

(a) any person engages in any conduct for the purpose of evading aggregates levy [and][1]

(b) . . . [1]

(c) that conduct involves dishonesty (whether or not it is such as to give rise to criminal liability),

that person shall be liable to a penalty . . . [1]

[(1A) The amount of the penalty shall be—

(a) equal to the amount of the levy evaded, or (as the case may be) intended to be evaded, by the person's conduct if at the time of engaging in that conduct he was or was required to be registered;

(b) equal to twice that amount if at that time the person neither was nor was required to be registered.][1]

(2) The references in sub-paragraph (1) above to evading aggregates levy include references to obtaining, in circumstances where there is no entitlement to it, either—

(a) a tax credit; or

(b) a repayment of aggregates levy.

(3) For the purposes of [sub-paragraph (1A)][1] *above the amount of levy that was or was intended to be evaded by any conduct shall be taken to include—*

(a) the amount of any tax credit, and

(b) the amount of any repayment of aggregates levy,

which was, or was intended to be, obtained in circumstances where there was no entitlement to it.

(4) In determining for the purposes of [sub-paragraph (1A)][1] *above how much aggregates levy (in addition to any amount falling within sub-paragraph (3) above) was or was intended to be evaded, no account shall be taken of the extent (if any) to which any liability to aggregates levy of any person fell, or would have fallen, to be reduced by the amount of any tax credit or repayments of aggregates levy to which he was, or would have been, entitled.*

(5) Where, by reason of conduct falling within sub-paragraph (1) above, a person is convicted of an offence (whether under this Act or otherwise) that person shall not by reason of that conduct be liable also to a penalty under this paragraph.[2]

Amendments—[1] Word in sub-para (1) inserted, and words repealed, sub-para (1A) inserted, and words in sub-paras (3), (4) substituted, by FA 2002 ss 133(1)–(4), (6), 141, Sch 40 Pt 4(3). These amendments are deemed to have come into force on 1 May 2002.

[2] Para 7 repealed by FA 2008 s 122, Sch 40 para 21(*i*) with effect from 1 April 2009 (by virtue of SI 2009/571 art 2). This para repealed only in so far as it relates to conduct involving dishonesty which relates to—

(a) an inaccuracy in a document, or

(b) a failure to notify HMRC of an under-assessment by HMRC (SI 2009/571 art 6).

Liability of directors etc for civil penalties

8—*(1) Where it appears to the Commissioners—*

(a) that a body corporate is liable to a penalty under paragraph 7 above, and

(b) that the conduct giving rise to that penalty is, in whole or in part, attributable to the dishonesty of a person who is, or at the material time was, a director or managing officer of the body corporate (a "named officer"),

the Commissioners may serve a notice under this paragraph on the body corporate and on the named officer.

(2) A notice under this paragraph shall state—

(a) the amount of the penalty referred to in sub-paragraph (1)(a) above ("the basic penalty"); and

(b) that the Commissioners propose, in accordance with this paragraph, to recover from the named officer such portion of the basic penalty (which may be the whole of it) as is specified in the notice.

(3) Where a notice is served under this paragraph, the portion of the basic penalty specified in the notice shall be recoverable from the named officer as if he were personally liable under paragraph 7 above to a penalty which corresponds to that portion.

(4) Where a notice is served under this paragraph—

(a) the amount which may be assessed under Schedule 10 to this Act as the amount due by way of penalty from the body corporate shall be only so much (if any) of the basic penalty as is not assessed on and notified to a named officer; and

(b) the body corporate shall be treated as discharged from liability for so much of the basic penalty as is so assessed and notified.

(5) Subject to the following provisions of this paragraph, the giving of a notice under this paragraph as such shall not be a decision which may be [appealed under section 40][2] of this Act.

(6) Where a body corporate is assessed as mentioned in sub-paragraph (4)(a) above, the decisions of the Commissioners that may be [appealed under section 40][2] of this Act shall include their decision—

(a) as to the liability of the body corporate to a penalty; and

(b) as to the amount of the basic penalty that is specified in the assessment;

and sections [40A to 42][2] of this Act shall apply accordingly.

(7) Where an assessment is made on a named officer by virtue of this paragraph, the decisions which may be [appealed under section 40][2] of this Act at the request of the named officer shall include—

(a) the Commissioners' decisions in the case of the body corporate as to the matters mentioned in sub-paragraph (6)(a) and (b) above;

(b) their decision that the conduct of the body corporate referred to in sub-paragraph (1)(b) above is, in whole or in part, attributable to the dishonesty of the named officer; and

(c) their decision as to the portion of the penalty which the Commissioners propose to recover from him;

and sections [40A to 42][2] of this Act shall apply accordingly.

(8) In this paragraph a "managing officer", in relation to a body corporate, means—

(a) any manager, secretary or other similar officer of the body corporate; or

(b) any person purporting to act in any such capacity or as a director.

(9) Where the affairs of a body corporate are managed by its members, this paragraph shall apply in relation to the conduct of a member in connection with his functions of management as if he were a director of the body corporate.[1]

Amendments—[1] Para 8 repealed by FA 2008 s 122, Sch 40 para 21(*i*) with effect from 1 April 2009 (by virtue of SI 2009/571 art 2).

This para repealed only in so far as it relates to conduct involving dishonesty which relates to—

(a) an inaccuracy in a document, or

(b) a failure to notify HMRC of an under-assessment by HMRC (SI 2009/571 art 6).

[2] Insofar as it continues to apply, in sub-paras (5), (7) words substituted for the words "reviewed under section 40", in sub-para (6) words substituted for the words "reviewed in accordance with section 40"; in sub-paras (6), (7), figures substituted for the figures "41 and 42" by the Transfer of Tribunal Functions and Revenue and Customs Appeals Order, SI 2009/56 art 3, Sch 1 para 309 with effect from 1 April 2009.

Misdeclaration or neglect

9—*(1) Subject to sub-paragraphs (3) to (5) below, where for an accounting period—*

(a) a return is made which understates a person's liability to aggregates levy or overstates his entitlement to any tax credit or repayment of aggregates levy, or

(b) at the end of the period of 30 days beginning on the date of the making of any assessment which understates a person's liability to aggregates levy, that person has not taken all such steps as are reasonable to draw the understatement to the attention of the Commissioners,

the person concerned shall be liable to a penalty equal to 5 per cent of the amount of the understatement of liability or (as the case may be) overstatement of entitlement.

(2) Where—

(a) a return for an accounting period—

Aggregates Levy

(*i*) overstates or understates to any extent a person's liability to aggregates levy, or

(*ii*) understates or overstates to any extent his entitlement to any tax credits or repayments of aggregates levy,

and

(b) that return is corrected—

(*i*) in such circumstances as may be prescribed by regulations made by the Commissioners, and

(*ii*) in accordance with such conditions as may be so prescribed,

by a return for a later accounting period which understates or overstates, to the corresponding extent, any liability or entitlement for the later period,

it shall be assumed for the purposes of this paragraph that the statement made by each such return is a correct statement for the accounting period to which the return relates.

(3) Conduct falling within sub-paragraph (1) above shall not give rise to liability to a penalty under this paragraph if the person concerned provides the Commissioners with full information with respect to the inaccuracy concerned—

(a) at a time when he has no reason to believe that enquiries are being made by the Commissioners into his affairs, so far as they relate to aggregates levy; and

(b) in such form and manner as may be prescribed by regulations made by the Commissioners or specified by them in accordance with any such regulations.

(4) Conduct falling within sub-paragraph (1) above shall not give rise to liability to a penalty under this paragraph if the person concerned satisfies the Commissioners or, on appeal, an appeal tribunal that there is a reasonable excuse for his conduct.

(5) Where, by reason of conduct falling within sub-paragraph (1) above—

(a) a person is convicted of an offence (whether under this Act or otherwise), or

(b) a person is assessed to a penalty under paragraph 7 above,

that person shall not by reason of that conduct be liable also to a penalty under this paragraph.[1]

Amendments—[1] Para 9 repealed by FA 2008 s 122, Sch 40 para 21(*i*) with effect from 1 April 2009 (by virtue of SI 2009/571 art 2).

[Incorrect records etc evidencing claim for tax credit

9A—(1) This paragraph applies where—

(*a*) a claim is made for a tax credit in such a case as is mentioned in—

(i) section 30(1)(*c*) of this Act (aggregate used in a prescribed industrial or agricultural process), or

(ii) section 30A of this Act (transitional tax credit in Northern Ireland);

(*b*) a record or other document is provided to the Commissioners as evidence for the claim; and

(*c*) the record or document is incorrect.

(2) The person who provided the document to the Commissioners, and any person who provided it to anyone else with a view to its being used as evidence for a claim for a tax credit, shall be liable to a penalty.

(3) The amount of the penalty shall be equal to 105 per cent of the difference between—

(*a*) the amount of tax credit that would have been due on the claim if the record or document had been correct, and

(*b*) the amount (if any) of tax credit actually due on the claim.

(4) The providing of a record or other document shall not give rise to a penalty under this paragraph if the person who provided it satisfies the Commissioners or, on appeal, an appeal tribunal that there is a reasonable excuse for his having provided it.

(5) Where by reason of providing a record or other document—

(*a*) a person is convicted of an offence (whether under this Act or otherwise), *or*[2]

(b) a person is assessed to a penalty under paragraph 7 or 9 above,[2]

that person shall not by reason of the providing of the record or document be liable also to a penalty under this paragraph.][1]

Amendments—[1] This paragraph inserted by FA 2002 s 133(5), (6). This amendment is deemed to have come into force on 1 May 2002.

[2] Para 9A(5)(*b*) and preceding word "or" repealed by FA 2008 s 122, Sch 40 para 21(*i*) with effect from 1 April 2009 (by virtue of SI 2009/571 art 2). Sub-para (5)(*b*) repealed only in so far as it relates to conduct involving dishonesty which relates to—

(a) an inaccuracy in a document, or

(b) a failure to notify HMRC of an under-assessment by HMRC (SI 2009/571 art 6).

PART 3
INTERPRETATION OF SCHEDULE

10—*(1) References in this Schedule to obtaining a tax credit are references to bringing an amount into account as a tax credit for the purposes of aggregates levy on the basis that that amount is an amount which may be so brought into account in accordance with tax credit regulations.*

(2) References in this Schedule to obtaining a repayment of aggregates levy are references to obtaining either—

(*a*) the payment or repayment of any amount, or

(*b*) the acknowledgement of a right to receive any amount,

on the basis that that amount is the amount of a repayment of aggregates levy to which there is an entitlement.

SCHEDULE 7
AGGREGATES LEVY: INFORMATION AND EVIDENCE ETC

Section 29

Provision of information

1—*(1) Every person involved (in whatever capacity) in subjecting any aggregate to exploitation in the United Kingdom, or in any connected activities, shall provide the Commissioners with such information relating to the matters in which he is or has been involved as the Commissioners may reasonably require.*

(2) Information required under sub-paragraph (1) above shall be provided to the Commissioners within such period after being required, and in such form, as the Commissioners may reasonably require.

(3) Subject to sub-paragraphs (4) and (5) below and to paragraph 3(5) of Schedule 10 to this Act (which relates to supplementary assessments of daily penalties), if a person fails to provide information which he is required to provide under this paragraph, he shall be liable—

(*a*) to a penalty of £250; and

(*b*) to a further penalty of £20 for every day after the last relevant date and before the day after that on which the required information is provided.

(4) Liability to a penalty specified in sub-paragraph (3) above shall not arise if the person required to provide the information satisfies the Commissioners or, on appeal, an appeal tribunal—

(*a*) in the case of the penalty under paragraph (*a*) of that sub-paragraph that there is a reasonable excuse—

(*i*) for the initial failure to provide the required information on or before the last relevant date; and

(*ii*) for every subsequent failure to provide it;

and

(*b*) in the case of any penalty under paragraph (*b*) of that sub-paragraph for any day, that there is a reasonable excuse for the failure to provide the information on or before that day.

(5) Where, by reason of any failure by any person to provide information required under this paragraph—

(*a*) that person is convicted of an offence (whether under this Act or otherwise), or

(*b*) that person is assessed to a penalty under paragraph 7 of Schedule 6 to this Act (penalty for evasion) [or a penalty for a deliberate inaccuracy under Schedule 24 to the Finance Act 2007 (penalties for errors)][1],

that person shall not by reason of that failure be liable also to a penalty under this paragraph.

(6) In this paragraph "the last relevant date" means the last day of the period within which the person in question was required to provide the information.[2]

Amendments—[1] Words in sub-para (5)(*b*) inserted by the Finance Act 2008, Schedule 40 (Appointed Day, Transitional Provisions and Consequential Amendments) Order, SI 2009/571 art 8, Sch 1 paras 21, 25 with effect from 1 April 2009.

[2] This para repealed by the Finance Act 2009, Section 96 and Schedule 48 (Appointed Day, Savings and Consequential Amendments) Order, SI 2009/3054 art 3, Schedule para 9 with effect from 1 April 2010. Note that, where HMRC have requested information or documents before 1 April 2010, sub-paras (3)–(6) continue to have effect on and after that date (SI 2009/3054 art 6(*d*)).

Records

2—(1) The Commissioners may by regulations impose obligations to keep records on persons who are or are required to be registered and on persons who would be so required but for an exemption by virtue of regulations under section 24(4) of this Act.

(2) Regulations under this paragraph may be framed by reference to such records as may be stipulated in any notice published by the Commissioners in pursuance of the regulations and not withdrawn by a further notice.

(3) Regulations under this paragraph may—

(*a*) require any records kept in pursuance of the regulations to be preserved for such period, not exceeding six years, as may be specified in the regulations;

(*b*) authorise the Commissioners to direct that any such records need only be preserved for a shorter period than that specified in the regulations;

(*c*) authorise a direction to be made so as to apply generally or in such cases as the Commissioners may stipulate.

[(4) A duty under regulations under this paragraph to preserve records may be discharged—

(*a*) by preserving them in any form and by any means, or

(*b*) by preserving the information contained in them in any form and by any means,

subject to any conditions or exceptions specified in writing by the Commissioners.][2]

(5) . . . [2]

(6) Subject to sub-paragraphs (7) and (8) below, a person who fails to preserve any record in compliance with—

(*a*) any regulations under this paragraph, or

(*b*) any notice, direction or requirement given or imposed under such regulations,

shall be liable to a penalty of £250.

(7) A failure such as is mentioned in sub-paragraph (6) above shall not give rise to any penalty under that sub-paragraph if the person required to preserve the record satisfies the Commissioners or, on appeal, an appeal tribunal that there is a reasonable excuse for the failure.

(8) Where, by reason of any such failure by any person as is mentioned in sub-paragraph (6) above—

(*a*) that person is convicted of an offence (whether under this Act or otherwise), or

(*b*) that person is assessed to a penalty under paragraph 7 of Schedule 6 to this Act (penalty for evasion) [or a penalty for a deliberate inaccuracy under Schedule 24 to the Finance Act 2007 (penalties for errors)][1],

that person shall not by reason of that failure be liable also to a penalty under this paragraph.

(9) The Commissioners may if they think fit at any time modify or withdraw any . . . [2] requirement . . . [2] imposed for the purposes of this paragraph.

Amendments—[1] Words in sub-para (8)(*b*) inserted by the Finance Act 2008, Schedule 40 (Appointed Day, Transitional Provisions and Consequential Amendments) Order, SI 2009/571 art 8, Sch 1 paras 21, 25 with effect from 1 April 2009.

[2] Sub-para (4) substituted for previous sub-paras (4), (5), and in sub-para (9) words "approval or" and "given or" repealed, by FA 2009 s 98, Sch 50 paras 15, 16, with effect from 1 April 2010 (by virtue of SI 2010/815 art 2).

Evidence of records that are required to be preserved

3—*(1) Subject to the following provisions of this paragraph, where any obligation to preserve records is discharged in accordance with paragraph 2(4) above, a copy of any document forming part of the records shall be admissible in evidence in any proceedings, whether civil or criminal, to the same extent as the records themselves.*

(2) A statement contained in a document produced by a computer shall not by virtue of this paragraph be admissible in evidence—

(*a*) . . . [1]

(*b*) in civil proceedings in Scotland, except in accordance with sections 5 and 6 of the Civil Evidence (Scotland) Act 1988;

(*c*) in criminal proceedings in Scotland, except in accordance with Schedule 8 to the Criminal Procedure (Scotland) Act 1995; or

(*d*) . . . [2], [3]

Amendments—[1] Sub-para (2)(*a*) repealed by the Criminal Justice Act 2003 ss 332, 336(3), Sch 37 Pt 6 with effect from 4 April 2005 (by virtue of SI 2005/950).

[2] Sub-para (2)(*d*) repealed by the Criminal Justice (Evidence) (Northern Ireland) Order, SI 2004/1501 art 46(2), Sch 2 with effect from 3 April 2006 (by virtue of the Criminal Justice (Evidence) (Northern Ireland) Order 2004 (Commencement No 3) Order, SR 2006/63, art 2).

[3] Para 3 repealed by FA 2009 s 98, Sch 50 paras 15, 17 with effect from 1 April 2010 (by virtue of SI 2010/815 art 2).

Production of documents

4—*(1) Every person involved (in whatever capacity) in subjecting any aggregate to exploitation in the United Kingdom, or in any connected activities, shall upon demand made by an authorised person produce or cause to be produced for inspection by that person any documents relating to the matters in which he is or has been involved.*

(2) Where, by virtue of sub-paragraph (1) above, an authorised person has power to require the production of any documents from any person—

(*a*) he shall have the like power to require production of the documents concerned from any other person who appears to the authorised person to be in possession of them; and (*b*) the production of any document by that other person in pursuance of a requirement under this sub-paragraph shall be without prejudice to any lien claimed by that other person on that document.

(3) The documents mentioned in sub-paragraphs (1) and (2) above shall be produced at such time and place as the authorised person may reasonably require.

(4) Subject to sub-paragraphs (5) and (6) below and to paragraph 3(5) of Schedule 10 to this Act (which relates to supplementary assessments of daily penalties), if a person fails to produce any document which he is required to produce under this paragraph, he shall be liable—

(*a*) to a penalty of £250; and

(*b*) to a further penalty of £20 for every day after the last relevant date and before the day after that on which the document is produced.

(5) Liability to a penalty specified in sub-paragraph (4) above shall not arise if the person required to produce the document in question satisfies the Commissioners or, on appeal, an appeal tribunal—

(*a*) in the case of the penalty under paragraph (*a*) of that sub-paragraph, that there is a reasonable excuse—

(*i*) for the initial failure to produce the document at the required time; and

(*ii*) for every subsequent failure to produce it;

and

(*b*) in the case of any penalty under paragraph (*b*) of that sub-paragraph for any day, that there is a reasonable excuse for the failure to produce the document on or before that day.

(6) Where, by reason of any failure by any person to provide information required under this paragraph—

(*a*) that person is convicted of an offence (whether under this Act or otherwise), or

(*b*) that person is assessed to a penalty under paragraph 7 of Schedule 6 to this Act (penalty for evasion) [or a penalty for a deliberate inaccuracy under Schedule 24 to the Finance Act 2007 (penalties for errors)][1],

that person shall not by reason of that failure be liable also to a penalty under this paragraph.

(7) In this paragraph "the last relevant date" means the last day of the period within which the person in question was required to produce the document.[2]

Amendments—[1] Words in sub-para (6)(*b*) inserted by the Finance Act 2008, Schedule 40 (Appointed Day, Transitional Provisions and Consequential Amendments) Order, SI 2009/571 art 8, Sch 1 paras 21, 25 with effect from 1 April 2009.

[2] This para repealed by the Finance Act 2009, Section 96 and Schedule 48 (Appointed Day, Savings and Consequential Amendments) Order, SI 2009/3054 art 3, Schedule para 9 with effect from 1 April 2010. Note that, where HMRC have requested information or documents before 1 April 2010, sub-paras (4)–(7) continue to have effect on and after that date (SI 2009/3054 art 6(*d*)).

Powers in relation to documents produced

5—*(1) An authorised person may take copies of, or make extracts from, any document produced under paragraph 4 above.*

(2) If it appears to him to be necessary to do so, an authorised person may, at a reasonable time and for a reasonable period, remove any document produced under paragraph 4 above.

(3) An authorised person who removes any document under sub-paragraph (2) above shall, if requested to do so, provide a receipt for the document so removed.

(4) Where a lien is claimed on a document produced under paragraph 4(2) above, the removal of the document under sub-paragraph (2) above shall not be regarded as breaking the lien.

(5) Where a document removed by an authorised person under sub-paragraph (2) above is reasonably required for any purpose he shall, as soon as practicable, provide a copy of the document, free of charge, to the person by whom it was produced or caused to be produced.

(6) Where any documents removed under the powers conferred by this paragraph are lost or damaged, the Commissioners shall be liable to compensate their owner for any expenses reasonably incurred by him in replacing or repairing the documents.[1]

Amendments—[1] This para repealed by the Finance Act 2009, Section 96 and Schedule 48 (Appointed Day, Savings and Consequential Amendments) Order, SI 2009/3054 art 3, Schedule para 9 with effect from 1 April 2010.

Entry and inspection

6 For the purpose of exercising any powers under this Part of this Act an authorised person may at any reasonable time enter and inspect premises used in connection with the carrying on of a business.[1]

Amendments—[1] This para repealed by the Finance Act 2009, Section 96 and Schedule 48 (Appointed Day, Savings and Consequential Amendments) Order, SI 2009/3054 art 3, Schedule para 9 with effect from 1 April 2010.

Entry and search

7—*(1) Where—*

(a) a justice of the peace is satisfied on information on oath that there is reasonable ground for suspecting that a fraud offence which appears to be of a serious nature is being, has been or is about to be committed on any premises or that evidence of the commission of such an offence is to be found there, or

(b) in Scotland a justice (within the meaning of section 307 of the Criminal Procedure (Scotland) Act 1995) is satisfied by evidence on oath as mentioned in paragraph (a) above,

he may issue a warrant in writing authorising any authorised person to enter those premises, if necessary by force, at any time within one month from the time of the issue of the warrant and to search them.

(2) A person who enters the premises under the authority of the warrant may—

(a) take with him such other persons as appear to him to be necessary;

(b) seize and remove any such documents or other things at all found on the premises as he has reasonable cause to believe may be required as evidence for the purposes of proceedings in respect of a fraud offence which appears to him to be of a serious nature;

(c) search, or cause to be searched, any person found on the premises whom he has reasonable cause to believe to be in possession of any documents or other things which may be so required.

(3) Sub-paragraph (2) above shall not authorise any person to be searched by a member of the opposite sex.

(4) The powers conferred by a warrant under this paragraph shall not be exercisable—

(a) by more than such number of authorised persons as may be specified in the warrant;

(b) outside such periods of the day as may be so specified; or

(c) if the warrant so provides, otherwise than in the presence of a constable in uniform.

(5) An authorised person seeking to exercise the powers conferred by a warrant under this paragraph or, if there is more than one such authorised person, such one of them as is in charge of the search shall provide a copy of the warrant endorsed with his name as follows—

(a) if the occupier of the premises concerned is present at the time the search is to begin, the copy shall be supplied to the occupier;

(b) if at that time the occupier is not present but a person who appears to the authorised person to be in charge of the premises is present, the copy shall be supplied to that person;

(c) if neither paragraph (a) nor paragraph (b) above applies, the copy shall be left in a prominent place on the premises.

(6) In this paragraph "a fraud offence" means an offence under any of paragraphs 1 to 3 of Schedule 6 to this Act.[1]

Amendments—[1] This para repealed by FA 2007 ss 84, 114, Sch 22 paras 3, 12(*b*), Sch 27 Pt 5(1) with effect from 1 December 2007 (by virtue of SI 2007/3166 art 3(*a*)).

Order for access to recorded information etc

8—(1) Where, on an application by an authorised person, a justice of the peace or, in Scotland, a justice (within the meaning of section 307 of the Criminal Procedure (Scotland) Act 1995) is satisfied that there are reasonable grounds for believing—

(*a*) that an offence in connection with aggregates levy is being, has been or is about to be committed, and

(*b*) that any recorded information (including any document of any nature at all) which may be required as evidence for the purpose of any proceedings in respect of such an offence is in the possession of any person,

he may make an order under this paragraph.

(2) An order under this paragraph is an order that the person who appears to the justice to be in possession of the recorded information to which the application relates shall—

(*a*) give an authorised person access to it, and

(*b*) permit an authorised person to remove and take away any of it which he reasonably considers necessary,

not later than the end of the period of seven days beginning with the date of the order, or the end of such longer period as the order may specify.

(3) The reference in sub-paragraph (2)(*a*) above to giving an authorised person access to the recorded information to which the application relates includes a reference to permitting the authorised person to take copies of it or to make extracts from it.

(4) Where the recorded information consists of information contained in a computer, an order under this paragraph shall have effect as an order to produce the information—

(*a*) in a form in which it is visible and legible; and

(*b*) if the authorised person wishes to remove it, in a form in which it can be removed.

(5) This paragraph is without prejudice to the preceding paragraphs of this Schedule.

Removal of documents etc

9—(1) An authorised person who removes anything in the exercise of a power conferred by or under paragraph 7 or 8 above shall, if so requested by a person showing himself—

(*a*) to be the occupier of premises from which it was removed, or

(*b*) to have had custody or control of it immediately before the removal,

provide that person with a record of what he removed.

(2) The authorised person shall provide the record within a reasonable time from the making of the request for it.

(3) Subject to sub-paragraph (7) below, if a request for permission to be allowed access to anything which—

(*a*) has been removed by an authorised person, and

(*b*) is retained by the Commissioners for the purposes of investigating an offence,

is made to the officer in overall charge of the investigation by a person who had custody or control of the thing immediately before it was so removed, or by someone acting on behalf of such a person, the officer shall allow the person who made the request access to it under the supervision of an authorised person.

(4) Subject to sub-paragraph (7) below, if a request for a photograph or copy of any such thing is made to the officer in overall charge of the investigation by a person who had custody or control of the thing immediately before it was so removed, or by someone acting on behalf of such a person, the officer shall—

(*a*) allow the person who made the request access to it under the supervision of an authorised person for the purpose of photographing it or copying it; or

(*b*) photograph or copy it, or cause it to be photographed or copied.

(5) Subject to sub-paragraph (7) below, where anything is photographed or copied under sub-paragraph (4)(*b*) above, the officer shall supply the photograph or copy, or cause it to be supplied, to the person who made the request.

(6) The photograph or copy shall be supplied within a reasonable time from the making of the request.

(7) There is no duty under this paragraph to allow access to anything, or to supply a photograph or copy of anything, if the officer in overall charge of the investigation for the purposes of which it was removed has reasonable grounds for believing that to do so would prejudice—

(*a*) that investigation;

(*b*) the investigation of an offence other than the offence for the purposes of the investigation of which the thing was removed; or

(*c*) any criminal proceedings which may be brought as a result of the investigation of which he is in charge or any such investigation as is mentioned in paragraph (*b*) above.

(8) Any reference in this paragraph to the officer in overall charge of the investigation is a reference to the person whose name and address are endorsed on the warrant concerned as being the officer so in charge.

Enforcement of paragraph 9

10—(1) Where, on an application made as mentioned in sub-paragraph (2) below, the appropriate judicial authority is satisfied that a person has failed to comply with a requirement imposed by paragraph 9 above, the authority may order that person to comply with the requirement within such time and in such manner as may be specified in the order.

(2) An application under sub-paragraph (1) above shall not be made except—

(*a*) in the case of a failure to comply with any of the requirements imposed by paragraph 9(1) and (2) above—

(i) by the occupier of the premises from which the thing in question was removed; or

(ii) by the person who had custody or control of it immediately before it was so removed;

(*b*) in any other case, by the person who had such custody or control.

(3) In this paragraph "the appropriate judicial authority" means—

(*a*) in England and Wales, a magistrates' court;

(*b*) in Scotland, the sheriff;

(*c*) in Northern Ireland, a court of summary jurisdiction, as defined in Article 2(2)(*a*) of the Magistrates' Courts (Northern Ireland) Order 1981.

(4) In England and Wales and Northern Ireland, an application for an order under this paragraph shall be made by way of complaint; and sections 21 and 42(2) of the Interpretation Act (Northern Ireland) 1954 shall apply as if any reference in those provisions to any enactment included a reference to this paragraph.

Power to take samples

11—(1) An authorised person, if it appears to him necessary for the protection of the revenue against mistake or fraud, may at any time take, from material which he has reasonable cause to believe is aggregate which is intended to be, is being, or has been subjected to exploitation in the United Kingdom, such samples as he may require with a view to determining how the material ought to be treated, or to have been treated, for the purposes of aggregates levy.

(2) Any sample taken under this paragraph shall be disposed of in such manner as the Commissioners may direct.

Evidence by certificate

12—(1) In any proceedings a certificate of the Commissioners—

(*a*) that a person was or was not at any time registered [or][1],

(*b*) that any return required by regulations made under section 25 of this Act has not been made or had not been made at any time,

(*c*)

(*d*) . . . [1]

shall be evidence or, in Scotland, sufficient evidence of that fact.

(2) A photograph of any document provided to the Commissioners for the purposes of this Part of this Act and certified by them to be such a photograph shall be admissible in any proceedings, whether civil or criminal, to the same extent as the document itself.

(3) In any proceedings any document purporting to be a certificate under sub-paragraph (1) or (2) above shall be taken to be such a certificate unless the contrary is shown.

Amendments—[1] Words inserted and repealed by FA 2008 s 138, Sch 44 para 9 with effect from 21 July 2008.

Inducements to provide information

13—(1) This paragraph applies—

(*a*) to any criminal proceedings against a person in respect of an offence in connection with or in relation to aggregates levy; and

(*b*) to any proceedings against a person for the recovery of any sum due from him in connection with or in relation to that levy.

(2) Statements made or documents produced or provided by or on behalf of a person shall not be inadmissible in any proceedings to which this paragraph applies by reason only that—

(*a*) a matter falling within sub-paragraph (3) or (4) below has been drawn to that person's attention; and

(*b*) he was or may have been induced, as a result, to make the statements or to produce or provide the documents.

(3) The matters falling within this sub-paragraph are—

(*a*) that, in relation to aggregates levy, the Commissioners may assess an amount due by way of a civil penalty instead of instituting criminal proceedings;

(*b*) that it is the practice of the Commissioners (without giving any undertaking as to whether they will make such an assessment in any case) to be influenced by whether a person—

(i) has made a full confession of any dishonest conduct to which he has been a party; and

(ii) has otherwise co-operated to the full with any investigation.

(4) The matter falling within this sub-paragraph is the fact that the Commissioners or, on appeal, an appeal tribunal have power under any provision of this Part of this Act to reduce a penalty.

Disclosure of information

14—(1) Notwithstanding any obligation not to disclose information that would otherwise apply but subject to sub-paragraph (2) below, the Commissioners may disclose any information obtained or held by them in or in connection with the carrying out of their functions in relation to aggregates levy to any of the following—

(*a*) any Minister of the Crown;

(*b*) the Scottish Ministers;

(*c*) any Minister, within the meaning of the Northern Ireland Act 1998, or any Northern Ireland department;

(*d*) the National Assembly for Wales;

(*e*) the Environment Agency;

(*f*) the Scottish Environment Protection Agency;

(*g*) a mineral planning authority in England and Wales (within the meaning of the Town and Country Planning Act 1990);

(*h*) a planning authority in Scotland;

(*i*) a district council in Northern Ireland;

(*j*) an authorised officer of any person mentioned in paragraphs (*a*) to (i) above.

(2) Information shall not be disclosed under sub-paragraph (1) above except for the purpose of assisting a person falling within paragraphs (*a*) to (*j*) of that sub-paragraph in the performance of his duties.

(3) Notwithstanding any such obligation as is mentioned in sub-paragraph (1) above, any person mentioned in sub-paragraph (1)(*a*) to (*j*) above may disclose information—

(*a*) to the Commissioners, or

(*b*) to an authorised officer of the Commissioners,

for the purpose of assisting the Commissioners in the performance of duties in relation to aggregates levy.

(4) Information that has been disclosed to a person by virtue of this paragraph shall not be disclosed by him except—

(*a*) to another person to whom (instead of him) disclosure could by virtue of this paragraph have been made; or

(*b*) for the purpose of any proceedings connected with the operation of any provision made by or under any enactment relating to the environment or to aggregates levy.

(5) References in the preceding provisions of this paragraph to an authorised officer of any person ("the principal") are to any person who has been designated by the principal as a person to and by whom information may be disclosed by virtue of this paragraph.

(6) Where the principal is a person falling within any of paragraphs (*a*) to (*c*) above, the principal shall notify the Commissioners in writing of the name of any person designated by the principal for the purposes of this paragraph.

(7) No charge may be made for any disclosure made by virtue of this paragraph.

(8) In this paragraph "enactment" includes an enactment contained in an Act of the Scottish Parliament or in any Northern Ireland legislation.

Interpretation of Schedule

15 In this Schedule—

"authorised person" means any person acting under the authority of the Commissioners;

"connected activities", in relation to the exploitation of aggregate in the United Kingdom, means any activities carried out—

(*a*) for purposes connected with the carrying out of any such exploitation or with any transaction involving the carrying out of any such exploitation; or

(*b*) for the purposes of, in connection with or in relation to the carrying on of any business involving any such exploitation.

SCHEDULE 8

AGGREGATES LEVY: REPAYMENTS AND CREDITS

Section 32

Reimbursement arrangements

1—(1) The Commissioners may by regulations make provision for reimbursement arrangements made by any person to be disregarded for the purposes of section 32(2) of this Act except where the arrangements—

(*a*) contain such provision as may be required by the regulations; and

(*b*) are supported by such undertakings to comply with the provisions of the arrangements as may be required by the regulations to be given to the Commissioners.

(2) In this paragraph "reimbursement arrangements" means any arrangements for the purposes of a claim to a repayment of aggregates levy which—

(*a*) are made by any person for the purpose of securing that he is not unjustly enriched by the repayment of any amount in pursuance of the claim; and

(*b*) provide for the reimbursement of persons who have for practical purposes borne the whole or any part of the cost of the original payment of that amount to the Commissioners.

(3) Without prejudice to the generality of sub-paragraph (1) above, the provision that may be required by regulations under this paragraph to be contained in reimbursement arrangements includes—

(*a*) provision requiring a reimbursement for which the arrangements provide to be made within such period after the repayment to which it relates as may be specified in the regulations;

(*b*) provision for the repayment of amounts to the Commissioners where those amounts are not reimbursed in accordance with the arrangements;

(*c*) provision requiring interest paid by the Commissioners on any amount repaid by them to be treated in the same way as that amount for the purposes of any requirement under the arrangements to make reimbursement or to repay the Commissioners;

(*d*) provision requiring such records relating to the carrying out of the arrangements as may be described in the regulations to be kept and produced to the Commissioners, or to an officer of theirs.

(4) Regulations under this paragraph may impose obligations on such persons as may be specified in the regulations—

(*a*) to make the repayments to the Commissioners that they are required to make in pursuance of any provisions contained in any reimbursement arrangements by virtue of sub-paragraph (3)(*b*) or (*c*) above;

(*b*) to comply with any requirements contained in any such arrangements by virtue of sub-paragraph (3)(*d*) above.

(5) Regulations under this paragraph may make provision for the form and manner in which, and the times at which, undertakings are to be given to the Commissioners in accordance with the regulations; and any such provision may allow for those matters to be determined by the Commissioners in accordance with the regulations.

Interest payable by the Commissioners

2—(1) Where, due to an error on the part of the Commissioners, a person—

(*a*) has paid to them by way of aggregates levy an amount which was not levy due and which they are in consequence liable to repay to him,

(*b*) has failed to claim a repayment of levy to which he was entitled, under tax credit regulations, in respect of any tax credits, or

(*c*) has suffered delay in receiving payment of an amount due to him from them in connection with aggregates levy,

then, if and to the extent that they would not be liable to do so apart from this paragraph, they shall (subject to the following provisions of this paragraph) pay interest to him on that amount for the applicable period.

(2) In sub-paragraph (1) above, the reference in paragraph (*a*) to an amount which the Commissioners are liable to repay in consequence of the making of a payment that was not due is a reference to only so much of that amount as is the subject of a claim that the Commissioners are required to satisfy or have satisfied.

(3) In that sub-paragraph the amounts referred to in paragraph (*c*)—

(*a*) do not include any amount payable under this paragraph;

(*b*) do not include the amount of any interest for which provision is made by virtue of section 30(3)(*f*) of this Act; but

(*c*) do include any amount due (in respect of an adjustment of overpaid interest) by way of a repayment under—

(i) paragraph 11(3) of Schedule 5 to this Act; or

(ii) paragraph 6(3) of Schedule 10 to this Act.

(4) The applicable period, in a case falling within sub-paragraph (1)(*a*) above, is the period—

(*a*) beginning with the date on which the payment is received by the Commissioners; and

(*b*) ending with the date on which they authorise payment of the amount on which the interest is payable.

(5) The applicable period, in a case falling within sub-paragraph (1)(*b*) or (*c*) above, is the period—

(*a*) beginning with the date on which, apart from the error, the Commissioners might reasonably have been expected to authorise payment of the amount on which the interest is payable; and

(*b*) ending with the date on which they in fact authorise payment of that amount.

(6) In determining the applicable period for the purposes of this paragraph there shall be left out of account any period by which the Commissioners' authorisation of the payment of interest is delayed by circumstances beyond their control.

(7) The reference in sub-paragraph (6) above to a period by which the Commissioners' authorisation of the payment of interest is delayed by circumstances beyond their control includes, in particular, any period which is referable to—

(*a*) any unreasonable delay in the making of any claim for the payment or repayment of the amount on which interest is claimed;

(*b*) any failure by any person to provide the Commissioners—

(i) at or before the time of the making of a claim, or

(ii) subsequently in response to a request for information by the Commissioners,

with all the information required by them to enable the existence and amount of the claimant's entitlement to a payment or repayment to be determined; and (*c*) the making, as part of or in association with any claim for the payment or repayment of the amount on which interest is claimed, of a claim to anything to which the claimant was not entitled.

(8) In determining for the purposes of sub-paragraph (7) above whether any period of delay is referable to a failure by any person to provide information in response to a request by the Commissioners, there shall be taken to be so referable, except so far as may be provided for by regulations, any period which—

(*a*) begins with the date on which the Commissioners require that person to provide information which they reasonably consider relevant to the matter to be determined; and

(*b*) ends with the earliest date on which it would be reasonable for the Commissioners to conclude—

(i) that they have received a complete answer to their request for information;

(ii) that they have received all that they need in answer to that request; or

(iii) that it is unnecessary for them to be provided with any information in answer to that request.

(9) The Commissioners shall not be liable to pay interest under this paragraph except on the making of a claim for that purpose.

(10) A claim under this paragraph must be in writing and must be made not more than [4 years] after the end of the applicable period to which it relates.

(11) References in this paragraph—

(*a*) to receiving payment of any amount from the Commissioners, or

(*b*) to the authorisation by the Commissioners of the payment of any amount,

include references to the discharge by way of set-off (whether in accordance with regulations under paragraph 9 or 10 below or otherwise) of the Commissioners' liability to pay that amount.

(12) Interest under this paragraph shall be payable at the rate applicable under section 197 of the Finance Act 1996.

Amendments—In sub-para (10) words substituted for words "three years" by FA 2009 s 99, Sch 51 paras 27, 30 with effect from 1 April 2010 (SI 2010/867 art 2(1)). However, this amendment is disregarded where claims made under para 2 are for the repayment of amounts relating to an applicable period which ends on or before 31 March 2007 (see SI 2010/867 arts 2, 9).

Assessment for excessive repayment

3—(1) Where—

(*a*) any amount has been paid at any time to any person by way of a repayment of aggregates levy, and

(*b*) the amount paid exceeded the amount which the Commissioners were liable at that time to repay to that person,

the Commissioners may, to the best of their judgement, assess the excess paid to that person and notify it to him.

(2) Where—

(*a*) any amount has been paid to any person by way of repayment of levy,

(*b*) the repayment is in respect of a tax credit the entitlement to which arose in a case falling within section 30(1)(*e*) (bad debts),

(*c*) the whole or any part of the credit is withdrawn on account of the payment of the whole or any part of the debt taken as bad,

(*d*) the amount of the repayment exceeded the amount which the Commissioners would have been liable to repay had the withdrawal taken place before the determination of the amount of the repayment,

the Commissioners may, to the best of their judgement, assess the excess repaid to that person and notify it to him.

(3) Where any person is liable to pay any amount to the Commissioners in pursuance of an obligation imposed by virtue of paragraph 1(4)(*a*) above, the Commissioners may, to the best of their judgement, assess the amount due from that person and notify it to him.

(4) Subject to sub-paragraph (5) below, where—

(*a*) an assessment is made on any person under this paragraph in respect of a repayment of levy made in relation to any accounting period, and

(*b*) the Commissioners have power under Schedule 5 to this Act to make an assessment on that person to an amount of aggregates levy due from that person for that period,

the assessments may be combined and notified to him as one assessment.

(5) A notice of a combined assessment under sub-paragraph (4) above must separately identify the amount being assessed in respect of repayments of levy.

Assessment for overpayments of interest

4 Where—

(*a*) any amount has been paid to any person by way of interest under paragraph 2 above, but
(*b*) that person was not entitled to that amount under that paragraph,

the Commissioners may, to the best of their judgement, assess the amount so paid to which that person was not entitled and notify it to him.

Assessments under paragraphs 3 and 4

5—(1) An assessment under paragraph 3 or 4 above shall not be made more than two years after the time when evidence of facts sufficient in the opinion of the Commissioners to justify the making of the assessment comes to the knowledge of the Commissioners.

(2) Where an amount has been assessed and notified to any person under paragraph 3 or 4 above, it shall be recoverable as if it were aggregates levy due from him.

(3) Sub-paragraph (2) above does not have effect if, or to the extent that, the assessment in question has been withdrawn or reduced.

Interest on amounts assessed

6—(1) Where an assessment is made under paragraph 3 or 4 above, the whole of the amount assessed shall carry interest, for the period specified in sub-paragraph (2) below, as follows—
(*a*) so much of that amount as represents the amount of a tax credit claimed by a person who was not entitled to it shall carry penalty interest; and
(*b*) so much of that amount as does not carry penalty interest under paragraph (*a*) above shall carry interest at the rate applicable under section 197 of the Finance Act 1996.

(2) That period is the period which—
(*a*) begins with the day after that on which the person is notified of the assessment; and
(*b*) ends with the day before that on which payment is made of the amount assessed.

(3) Interest under this paragraph shall be paid without any deduction of income tax.

(4) Penalty interest under this paragraph shall be compound interest calculated—
(*a*) at the penalty rate; and
(*b*) with monthly rests.

(5) For this purpose the penalty rate is the rate found by—
(*a*) taking the rate applicable under section 197 of the Finance Act 1996 for the purposes of sub-paragraph (1)(*b*) above; and
(*b*) adding 10 percentage points to that rate.

(6) Where a person is liable under this paragraph to pay any penalty interest, the Commissioners or, on appeal, an appeal tribunal may reduce the amount payable to such amount (including nil) as they think proper.

(7) Subject to sub-paragraph (8) below, where the person concerned satisfies the Commissioners or, on appeal, an appeal tribunal that there is a reasonable excuse for the conduct giving rise to the liability to pay penalty interest, that is a matter which (among other things) may be taken into account under sub-paragraph (6) above.

(8) In determining whether there is a reasonable excuse for the purposes of sub-paragraph (7) above, no account shall be taken of any of the following matters, that is to say—
(*a*) the insufficiency of the funds available to any person for paying any aggregates levy due or for paying the amount of the interest;
(*b*) the fact that there has, in the case in question or in that case taken with any other cases, been no or no significant loss of aggregates levy;
(*c*) the fact that the person liable to pay the interest or a person acting on his behalf has acted in good faith.

(9) In the case of interest reduced by the Commissioners under sub-paragraph (6) above an appeal tribunal, on an appeal relating to the interest, may cancel the whole or any part of the reduction made by the Commissioners.

Assessments to interest under paragraph 6

7—(1) Where any person is liable to interest under paragraph 6 above the Commissioners may assess the amount due by way of interest and notify it to him accordingly.

(2) Without prejudice to the power to make assessments under this paragraph for later periods, the interest to which an assessment under this paragraph may relate shall be confined to interest for a period of no more than two years ending with the time when the assessment under this paragraph is made.

(3) Where an amount has been assessed and notified to any person under this paragraph it shall be recoverable as if it were aggregates levy due from him.

(4) Sub-paragraph (3) above does not have effect if, or to the extent that, the assessment in question has been withdrawn or reduced.

(5) Where an assessment is made under this paragraph to an amount of interest under paragraph 6 above—

(*a*) the notice of assessment shall specify a date, not later than the date of the notice of assessment, to which the amount of interest which is assessed is calculated; and

(*b*) if the interest continues to accrue after that date, a further assessment or further assessments may be made under this paragraph in respect of the amounts so accruing.

(6) Where—

(*a*) an assessment to interest is made specifying a date for the purposes of sub-paragraph (5)(*a*) above, and

(*b*) within such period as may for the purposes of this sub-paragraph have been notified by the Commissioners to the person liable for the interest, the amount on which the interest is payable is paid,

that amount shall be deemed for the purposes of any further liability to interest to have been paid on the specified date.

Supplementary assessments

8 If it appears to the Commissioners that the amount which ought to have been assessed in an assessment under paragraph 3, 4 or 7 above exceeds the amount which was so assessed, then—

(*a*) under the same paragraph as that assessment was made, and

(*b*) on or before the last day on which that assessment could have been made,

the Commissioners may make a supplementary assessment of the amount of the excess and notify the person concerned accordingly.

Set-off of or against amounts due under this Part of this Act

9—(1) The Commissioners may by regulations make provision in relation to any case where—

(*a*) a person is under a duty to pay to the Commissioners at any time an amount or amounts in respect of aggregates levy; and

(*b*) the Commissioners are under a duty to pay to that person at the same time an amount or amounts in respect of that levy or any of the other taxes under their care and management.

(2) Regulations under this paragraph may provide that if the total of the amount or amounts mentioned in sub-paragraph (1)(*a*) above exceeds the total of the amount or amounts mentioned in sub-paragraph (1)(*b*) above, the latter shall be set off against the former.

(3) Regulations under this paragraph may provide that if the total of the amount or amounts mentioned in sub-paragraph (1)(*b*) above exceeds the total of the amount or amounts mentioned in sub-paragraph (1)(*a*) above, the Commissioners may set off the latter in paying the former.

(4) Regulations under this paragraph may provide that if the total of the amount or amounts mentioned in sub-paragraph (1)(*a*) above is the same as the total of the amount or amounts mentioned in sub-paragraph (1)(*b*) above no payment need be made in respect of the former or the latter.

(5) Regulations under this paragraph may provide for any limitation on the time within which the Commissioners are entitled to take steps for recovering any amount due to them in respect of aggregates levy to be disregarded, in such cases as may be described in the regulations, in determining whether any person is under such a duty to pay as is mentioned in sub-paragraph (1)(*a*) above.

(6) Regulations under this paragraph may include provision treating any duty to pay mentioned in sub-paragraph (1) above as discharged accordingly.

(7) References in sub-paragraph (1) above to an amount in respect of a particular tax include references not only to an amount of tax itself but also to other amounts such as interest and penalties that are or may be recovered as if they were amounts of tax.

(8) In this paragraph "tax" includes levy or duty.

Set-off of or against other taxes and duties

10—(1) The Commissioners may by regulations make provision in relation to any case where—

(*a*) a person is under a duty to pay to the Commissioners at any time an amount or amounts in respect of any tax (or taxes) under their care and management other than aggregates levy; and

(*b*) the Commissioners are under a duty, at the same time, to make any repayment of aggregates levy to that person or to make any other payment to him of any amount or amounts in respect of aggregates levy.

(2) Regulations under this paragraph may provide that if the total of the amount or amounts mentioned in sub-paragraph (1)(*a*) above exceeds the total of the amount or amounts mentioned in sub-paragraph (1)(*b*) above, the latter shall be set off against the former.

(3) Regulations under this paragraph may provide that if the total of the amount or amounts mentioned in sub-paragraph (1)(*b*) above exceeds the total of the amount or amounts mentioned in sub-paragraph (1)(*a*) above, the Commissioners may set off the latter in paying the former.

(4) Regulations under this paragraph may provide that if the total of the amount or amounts mentioned in sub-paragraph (1)(*a*) above is the same as the total of the amount or amounts mentioned in sub-paragraph (1)(*b*) above no payment need be made in respect of the former or the latter.
(5) Regulations under this paragraph may provide for any limitation on the time within which the Commissioners are entitled to take steps for recovering any amount due to them in respect of any of the taxes under their care and management to be disregarded, in such cases as may be described in the regulations, in determining whether any person is under such a duty to pay as is mentioned in sub-paragraph (1)(*a*) above.
(6) Regulations under this paragraph may include provision treating any duty to pay mentioned in sub-paragraph (1) above as discharged accordingly.
(7) References in sub-paragraph (1) above to an amount in respect of a particular tax include references not only to an amount of tax itself but also to other amounts such as interest and penalties that are or may be recovered as if they were amounts of tax.
(8) In this paragraph "tax" includes levy or duty.

Restriction on powers to provide for set-off

11—(1) Regulations made under paragraph 9 or 10 above shall not require any such amount or amounts as are mentioned in sub-paragraph (1)(*b*) of that paragraph ("the credit") to be set against any such amount or amounts as are mentioned in sub-paragraph (1)(*a*) of that paragraph ("the debit") in any case where—

(*a*) an insolvency procedure has been applied to the person entitled to the credit;
(*b*) the credit became due after that procedure was so applied; and
(*c*) the liability to pay the debit either arose before that procedure was so applied or (having arisen afterwards) relates to, or to matters occurring in the course of, the carrying on of any business at times before the procedure was so applied.

(2) For the purposes of this paragraph, an insolvency procedure is applied to a person if—

(*a*) a bankruptcy order, winding-up order or administration order is made [or an administrator is appointed][2] in relation to that person or an award of sequestration is made on that person's estate;
(*b*) that person is put into administrative receivership;
(*c*) that person passes a resolution for voluntary winding up;
(*d*) any voluntary arrangement approved in accordance with—
(i) Part I or VIII of the Insolvency Act 1986, or
(ii) Part II or Chapter II of Part VIII of the Insolvency (Northern Ireland) Order 1989,
comes into force in relation to that person;
(*e*) a deed of arrangement registered in accordance with—
(i) the Deeds of Arrangement Act 1914, or
(ii) Chapter I of Part VIII of that Order,
takes effect in relation to that person;
(*f*)–(*h*) . . .[1]
(*i*) that person's estate becomes vested in any other person as that person's trustee under a trust deed (within the meaning of the Bankruptcy (Scotland) Act 1985).

(3) In this paragraph references, in relation to any person, to the application of an insolvency procedure to that person shall not include—

(*a*) the making of a bankruptcy order, winding-up order...[2] or award of sequestration [or the appointment of an administrator][2] at a time when any such arrangement or deed as is mentioned in paragraph (*d*), (*e*) or (*i*) of sub-paragraph (2) above is in force in relation to that person;
(*b*) the making of a winding-up order at any of the following times, that is to say—
[(i) immediately upon the appointment of an administrator in respect of the person ceasing to have effect;][2]
(ii) when that person is being wound up voluntarily;
(iii) when that person is in administrative receivership;

or

(*c*) the making of an administration order in relation to that person at any time when that person is in administrative receivership.

(4) For the purposes of this paragraph a person shall be regarded as being in administrative receivership throughout any continuous period for which (disregarding any temporary vacancy in the office of receiver) there is an administrative receiver of that person.
(5) In this paragraph—

"administration order" means an administration order under [Schedule B1 to][2] the Insolvency Act 1986 or Article 21 of the Insolvency (Northern Ireland) Order 1989;

"administrative receiver" means an administrative receiver within the meaning of section 251 of that Act of 1986 or Article 5(1) of that Order of 1989.

Amendments—[1] Sub-para (2)(*f*)–(*h*) repealed by FA 2002 ss 132(1), (3), 141, Sch 38 para 10, Sch 40 Pt 4(3). These amendments are deemed to have come into force on 1 April 2002.

[2] Words in sub-paras (2)(*a*), (3)(*a*) inserted, words in sub-para (3)(*a*) repealed, and sub-para (3)(*b*)(i) and words in sub-para (5) substituted, by the Enterprise Act (Insolvency) Order, SI 2003/2096 art 4, Schedule paras 35, 37 with effect from 15 September 2003 (except in relation to any case where a petition for an administration order was presented before that date): SI 2003/2096, arts 1(1), 6.

Supplemental provisions of Schedule

12—(1) Any notification of an assessment under any provision of this Schedule to a person's representative shall be treated for the purposes of this Part of this Act as notification to the person in relation to whom the representative acts.

(2) In this paragraph "representative", in relation to any person, means—

(*a*) any of that person's personal representatives;

(*b*) that person's trustee in bankruptcy or liquidator;

(*c*) any person holding office as a receiver in relation to that person or any of his property;

(*d*) that person's tax representative or any other person for the time being acting in a representative capacity in relation to that person.

(3) In this paragraph "trustee in bankruptcy" includes, as respects Scotland—

(*a*) an interim or permanent trustee (within the meaning of the Bankruptcy (Scotland) Act 1985); and

(*b*) a trustee acting under a trust deed (within the meaning of that Act).

(4) The powers conferred by paragraphs 9 and 10 of this Schedule are without prejudice to any power of the Commissioners to provide by tax credit regulations for any amount to be set against another.

SCHEDULE 9

AGGREGATES LEVY: GROUP TREATMENT

Section 35

Eligibility for group treatment

1 Two or more bodies corporate are eligible to be treated as members of a group for the purposes of this Part of this Act if—

(*a*) each of them has an established place of business in the United Kingdom; and

(*b*) they are all under the same control.

Application for group treatment

2—(1) Subject to sub-paragraph (3) below, where an application is made to the Commissioners with respect to two or more bodies corporate and those bodies are all eligible to be treated as members of the same group, then, from the specified time—

(*a*) they shall be so treated for the purposes of this Part of this Act; and

(*b*) such one of them as is specified in the application shall be the representative member.

(2) Subject to sub-paragraph (3) below, where—

(*a*) any bodies corporate are treated as members of a group for the purposes of this Part of this Act, and

(*b*) an application is made to the Commissioners for the addition to the group of a body corporate that is eligible to be treated as a member of the group,

then, from the specified time, that body shall be included among the bodies so treated.

(3) The Commissioners may refuse an application under sub-paragraph (1) or (2) above if, and only if, it appears to them necessary to do so for the protection of the revenue; and an application that is refused under this sub-paragraph shall be, and be treated as always having been, ineffective.

(4) Where—

(*a*) it appears to the Commissioners that an application has been made for the purposes of this paragraph for a body corporate to be treated as a member of a group, but

(*b*) that body is not eligible to be treated as a member of that group,

the Commissioners shall give notice to the applicant that the application is ineffective.

(5) The Commissioners shall not refuse an application under sub-paragraph (3) above after the end of the period of ninety days beginning with the day on which the application is received by the Commissioners.

Modification of group treatment

3—(1) Subject to sub-paragraph (2) below, where any bodies corporate are treated as members of a group for the purposes of this Part of this Act and an application for the purpose is made to the Commissioners, then, from the specified time—

(*a*) a body corporate shall be excluded from the bodies so treated;

(*b*) one of those bodies corporate shall be substituted for another body corporate as the representative member; or

(*c*) the bodies corporate shall no longer be treated as members of a group.

(2) The Commissioners may refuse an application made for the purpose mentioned in sub-paragraph (1)(*a*) or (*c*) above if, and only if—

(*a*) the case is not one appearing to them to fall within paragraph 4(2)(*a*) and (*b*) below; and

(*b*) it appears to them necessary to refuse the application for the protection of the revenue.

(3) The Commissioners may refuse an application made for the purpose mentioned in sub-paragraph (1)(*b*) above if, and only if, it appears to them necessary to do so for the protection of the revenue.

(4) An application that is refused under this paragraph shall be, and be treated as always having been, ineffective.

(5) The specified time for the purposes of an application under sub-paragraph (1) above shall not be before the beginning of the accounting period which is current when the application is made.

Termination of group treatment

4—(1) If it appears to the Commissioners necessary to do so for the protection of the revenue, the Commissioners may, by notice given to any body corporate that is treated as a member of a group and to the representative member, terminate that treatment from such time as may be specified in the notice.

(2) Where—

(*a*) a body corporate is treated as a member of a group, and

(*b*) it appears to the Commissioners that it is not eligible to be treated as a member of that group,

they shall, by notice given to the body corporate and the representative member, terminate that treatment from such time as may be specified in the notice.

(3) Where—

(*a*) a body corporate ceases as from any time to be treated as a member of a group,

(*b*) immediately before that time that body was the representative member,

(*c*) there are two or more other bodies corporate which will continue after that time to be treated as members of the group, and

(*d*) none of those bodies corporate is substituted from that time, or from before that time, as the representative member of the group under paragraph 3(1)(*b*) above,

the Commissioners shall, by notice given to such one of the bodies corporate mentioned in paragraph (c) above as they think fit, substitute that body corporate as the representative member as from that time.

(4) The time specified in a notice under sub-paragraph (1) above shall not be a time before the day on which the notice is given to the representative member.

(5) Subject to sub-paragraph (6) below, the time specified in a notice under sub-paragraph (2) or (3) above may be a time before the giving of the notice.

(6) In the case of a notice given under sub-paragraph (2) above in respect of a body corporate's having ceased to be eligible to be treated as a member of a group, the time specified in the notice shall not be before the time when it so ceased.

Applications relating to group treatment

5 An application under this Schedule with respect to any bodies corporate must be made by one of those bodies or by the person controlling them.

Notifications relating to group treatment

6—(1) Where—

(*a*) two or more bodies corporate are treated as members of a group for the purposes of this Part of this Act, and

(*b*) any of those bodies ceases to be eligible to be so treated,

the body corporate which ceases to be so eligible shall notify the Commissioners of that fact.

(2) A body corporate which is designated as representative member in relation to any other bodies corporate shall not cease to have an established place of business in the United Kingdom without first notifying the Commissioners of that fact.

(3) A body corporate which fails to comply with sub-paragraph (1) or (2) above shall be liable to a penalty of £250.

Supplemental regulations about applications and notifications

7—(1) For the purposes of any provision made by or under this Schedule for an application to be made to the Commissioners, regulations made by the Commissioners may make provision—

(*a*) as to the time within which the application is to be made;

(*b*) as to the form and manner in which the application is to be made;

(*c*) as to the information and other particulars to be contained in or provided with any application.

(2) For those purposes the Commissioners may also by regulations impose obligations requiring a person who has made an application to notify the Commissioners if any information contained in or provided in connection with that application is or becomes inaccurate.

(3) The power under this paragraph to make regulations as to the time within which any application is to be made shall include power to authorise the Commissioners to extend the time for the making of an application.

(4) Sub-paragraphs (1) to (3) above shall apply for the purposes of any provision made by or under this Schedule for any matter to be notified to the Commissioners as they apply for the purposes of any provision so made for an application to be made to them; and for this purpose references to the making of the application shall be construed as references to the giving of the notification.

Interpretation of Schedule

8—(1) For the purposes of this Schedule two or more bodies are under the same control if—

(*a*) one of them controls each of the others;

(*b*) one person (whether a body corporate or an individual) controls all of them; or

(*c*) two or more individuals carrying on a business in partnership control all of them.

(2) For the purposes of this Schedule a body corporate shall be taken to control another body corporate if, and only if—

(*a*) it is empowered by statute to control that body's activities; or

(*b*) it is that body's holding company within the meaning of section [1159 of and Schedule 6 to][1] the Companies Act [2006 (c 46)][1].

(3) For the purposes of this Schedule an individual or individuals shall be taken to control a body corporate if, and only if (were he or they a company) he or they would be that body's holding company within the meaning of [those provisions][1].

(4) In this Schedule "the specified time", in relation to an application made under paragraph 2(1) or (2) or 3(1) above, means the beginning of such accounting period as may be specified in the application.

Amendments—[1] In para (2)(*b*), words substituted for words "736 of" and "1985", and in para (3), words substituted for words "section 736 of the Companies Act 1985", by the Companies Act 2006 (Consequential Amendments) (Taxes and National Insurance) Order, SI 2009/1890 art 4(1)(*e*), (2) with effect from 1 October 2009.

SCHEDULE 10

AGGREGATES LEVY: ASSESSMENT OF CIVIL PENALTIES AND INTEREST ON THEM

Section 46

Preliminary

1—(1) In this Schedule "civil penalty" means any penalty liability to which—

(*a*) is imposed by or under this Part of this Act; and

(*b*) arises otherwise than in consequence of a person's conviction for a criminal offence.

(2) In this Schedule—

(*a*) references to a person's being liable to a civil penalty include references to his being a person from whom the whole or any part of a civil penalty is recoverable by virtue of paragraph 8 of Schedule 6 to this Act; and

(*b*) references, in relation to a person from whom the whole or any part of a civil penalty is so recoverable, to the penalty to which he is liable are references to so much of the penalty as is recoverable from him.

(3) Any notification of an assessment under any provision of this Schedule to a person's representative shall be treated for the purposes of this Part of this Act as notification to the person in relation to whom the representative acts.

(4) In this paragraph "representative", in relation to any person, means—

(*a*) any of that person's personal representatives;

(*b*) that person's trustee in bankruptcy or liquidator;

(*c*) any person holding office as a receiver in relation to that person or any of his property;

(*d*) that person's tax representative or any other person for the time being acting in a representative capacity in relation to that person.

(5) In this paragraph "trustee in bankruptcy" includes, as respects Scotland—

(*a*) an interim or permanent trustee (within the meaning of the Bankruptcy (Scotland) Act 1985); and

(*b*) a trustee acting under a trust deed (within the meaning of that Act).

Assessments to penalties etc

2—(1) Where a person is liable to a civil penalty, the Commissioners may assess the amount due by way of penalty and notify it to him accordingly.

(2) If, where an assessment has been notified to any person under sub-paragraph (1) above or this sub-paragraph, it appears to the Commissioners that the amount which ought to have been assessed exceeds the amount that has already been assessed, the Commissioners may make a supplementary assessment of the amount of the excess and notify that person accordingly.

(3) The fact that any conduct giving rise to a civil penalty may have ceased before an assessment is made under this paragraph shall not affect the power of the Commissioners to make such an assessment.

(4) Where an amount has been assessed and notified to any person under this paragraph, it shall be recoverable as if it were aggregates levy due from him.

(5) Sub-paragraph (4) above—

(*a*) shall not apply so as to require any interest to be payable on a penalty otherwise than in accordance with this Schedule; and

(*b*) shall not have effect if, or to the extent that, the assessment in question has been withdrawn or reduced.

(6) Subject to sub-paragraph (7) below, where a person—

(*a*) is assessed under this paragraph to an amount due by way of a penalty, and

(*b*) is also assessed under any one or more provisions of Schedule 5 to this Act for an accounting period to which the conduct attracting the penalty is referable,

the assessments may be combined and notified to him as one assessment.

(7) A notice of a combined assessment under sub-paragraph (6) above must separately identify the penalty being assessed.

(8) The power to make an assessment under this paragraph is subject to paragraph 8(4) of Schedule 6 to this Act.

Further assessments to daily penalties

3—(1) This paragraph applies where an assessment is made under paragraph 2 above to an amount of a civil penalty to which any person is liable—

(*a*) under paragraph 1(3) of Schedule 7 to this Act (failure to provide information); or

(*b*) under paragraph 4(4) of that Schedule (failure to produce a document).

(2) The notice of assessment shall specify a time, not later than the end of the day of the giving of the notice of assessment, to which the amount of any daily penalty is calculated.

(3) For the purposes of sub-paragraph (2) above "daily penalty" means—

(*a*) in a case within sub-paragraph (1)(*a*) above, a penalty imposed by virtue of paragraph 1(3)(*b*) of Schedule 7 to this Act; and

(*b*) in a case within sub-paragraph (1)(*b*) above, a penalty imposed by virtue of paragraph 4(4)(*b*) of that Schedule.

(4) If further penalties accrue in respect of a continuing failure after that date to provide the information or, as the case may be, produce the document, a further assessment or further assessments may be made under paragraph 2 above in respect of the amounts so accruing.

(5) Where—

(*a*) an assessment to a civil penalty is made specifying a date for the purposes of sub-paragraph (2) above, and

(*b*) the failure in question is remedied within such period as may for the purposes of this sub-paragraph have been notified by the Commissioners to the person liable for the penalty,

the failure shall be deemed for the purposes of any further liability to civil penalties to have been remedied on the specified date.

Time limits on penalty assessments

4—(1) Subject to sub-paragraphs (2) and (3) below, an assessment under paragraph 2 above to a civil penalty shall not be made more than [4 years] after the conduct to which the penalty relates.

[(2) An assessment of a person to a civil penalty in a case involving a loss of aggregates levy—

(*a*) brought about deliberately by the person (or by another person acting on that person's behalf), or

(*b*) attributable to a failure by the person to comply with an obligation under section 24(2) or paragraph 1 of Schedule 4,

may be made at any time not more than 20 years after the conduct to which the penalty relates (subject to sub-paragraph (3)).

(2A) In sub-paragraph (2)(*a*) the reference to a loss brought about deliberately by the person includes a loss brought about as a result of a deliberate inaccuracy in a document given to Her Majesty's Revenue and Customs by or on behalf of that person.]

(3) Where, after a person's death, the Commissioners propose to assess an amount of a civil penalty due by reason of some conduct of the deceased—

(*a*) the assessment shall not be made more than [4 years] after the death; *and*

(*b*) *if the circumstances are as set out in sub-paragraph (2) above—*

(*i*) the modification of sub-paragraph (1) above contained in that sub-paragraph shall not apply; but

(*ii*) any assessment which (applying that modification) could have been made immediately after the death may be made at any time within three years after it.

Amendments—In sub-paras (1), (3)(*a*) words substituted for words "three years", sub-para (3)(*b*) and the word "and" preceding it, repealed and sub-paras (2), (2A) substituted for previous sub-para (2), by FA 2009 s 99, Sch 51 paras 27, 31, with effect from 1 April 2010 (SI 2010/867 art 2(1)).

Note that the following transitional provisions apply—

- The amendment made to sub-para (1) is disregarded where, for the purposes of sub-para (1), the conduct to which the penalty relates occurred on or before 31st March 2007 (SI 2010/867 art 13).
- The substitution of sub-para (2) is disregarded where, for the purposes of sub-para (2), the conduct to which the penalty relates occurred on or before 31 March 2007 (SI 2010/867 art 14).
- The amendments made to sub-para (3) are disregarded where, for the purposes of sub-para (3), the death was on or before 31 March 2007 (SI 2010/867 art 15).

Penalty interest on unpaid penalties

5—(1) Subject to sub-paragraph (2) below, where the Commissioners make an assessment under paragraph 2 above of any civil penalty to which a person is liable the amount of that penalty shall carry penalty interest for the period which—

(*a*) begins with the day on which the assessment is notified to the person on whom the assessment is made; and

(*b*) ends with the day before the day on which the assessed penalty is paid.

(2) Where—

(*a*) the Commissioners make an assessment under paragraph 2 above of an amount of any civil penalty to which any person is liable,

(*b*) they also specify a date for the purposes of this sub-paragraph, and

(*c*) the amount of the penalty assessed is paid on or before that date,

the amount paid before that date shall not carry penalty interest under this paragraph.

(3) Penalty interest under this paragraph shall be compound interest calculated—

(*a*) at the penalty rate; and

(*b*) with monthly rests.

(4) For this purpose the penalty rate is the rate found by—

(*a*) taking the rate applicable under section 197 of the Finance Act 1996 for the purposes of paragraph 8(3)(*a*) of Schedule 5 to this Act; and

(*b*) adding 10 percentage points to that rate.

(5) Where a person is liable under this paragraph to pay any penalty interest, the Commissioners or, on appeal, an appeal tribunal may reduce the amount payable to such amount (including nil) as they think proper.

(6) Subject to sub-paragraph (7) below, where the person concerned satisfies the Commissioners or, on appeal, an appeal tribunal that there is a reasonable excuse for the conduct giving rise to the liability to pay penalty interest, that is a matter which (among other things) may be taken into account under sub-paragraph (5) above.

(7) In determining whether there is a reasonable excuse for the purposes of sub-paragraph (6) above, no account shall be taken of any of the following matters, that is to say—

(*a*) the insufficiency of the funds available to any person for paying any aggregates levy or penalty due or for paying the amount of the interest;

(*b*) the fact that there has, in the case in question or in that case taken with any other cases, been no or no significant loss of aggregates levy;

(*c*) the fact that the person liable to pay the interest or a person acting on his behalf has acted in good faith.

(8) In the case of interest reduced by the Commissioners under sub-paragraph (5) above, an appeal tribunal, on an appeal relating to the interest, may cancel the whole or any part of the reduction made by the Commissioners.

Supplemental provisions about interest

6—(1) Interest under paragraph 5 above shall be paid without any deduction of income tax.

(2) Sub-paragraph (3) below applies where—

(*a*) an amount carries interest under paragraph 5 above (or would do so apart from that sub-paragraph); and

(*b*) all or part of the amount turns out not to be due.

(3) In such a case—

(*a*) the amount or part that turns out not to be due shall not carry interest under paragraph 5 above and shall be treated as never having done so; and

(*b*) all such adjustments as are reasonable shall be made, including (subject to section 32 of, and Schedule 8 to, this Act) adjustments by way of repayment.

Assessments to penalty interest on unpaid penalties

7—(1) Where a person is liable for interest under paragraph 5 above, the Commissioners may assess the amount due by way of interest and notify it to him accordingly.

(2) If, where an assessment has been notified to any person under sub-paragraph (1) above or this sub-paragraph, it appears to the Commissioners that the amount which ought to have been assessed exceeds the amount that has already been assessed, the Commissioners may make a supplementary assessment of the amount of the excess and notify that person accordingly.

(3) Where an amount has been assessed and notified to any person under this paragraph, it shall be recoverable as if it were aggregates levy due from him.

(4) Sub-paragraph (3) above—

(*a*) shall not apply so as to require any interest to be payable on interest (except in so far as it falls to be compounded in accordance with paragraph 5(3) above); and

(*b*) shall not have effect if, or to the extent that, the assessment in question has been withdrawn or reduced.

(5) Paragraph 4 above shall apply in relation to assessments under this paragraph as if any assessment to interest on a penalty were an assessment under paragraph 2 above to the penalty in question.

(6) Subject to sub-paragraph (7) below, where a person—

(*a*) is assessed under this paragraph to an amount due by way of any interest on a penalty, and

(*b*) is also assessed under any one or more provisions of Schedule 5 to this Act for the accounting period to which the conduct attracting the penalty is referable,

the assessments may be combined and notified to him as one assessment.

(7) A notice of a combined assessment under sub-paragraph (6) above must separately identify the interest being assessed.

Further assessments to interest on penalties

8—(1) Where an assessment is made under paragraph 7 above to an amount of penalty interest under paragraph 5 above—

(*a*) the notice of assessment shall specify a date, not later than the date of the notice of assessment, to which the amount of interest which is assessed is calculated; and

(*b*) if the interest continues to accrue after that date, a further assessment or further assessments may be made under paragraph 7 above in respect of the amounts so accruing.

(2) Where—

(*a*) an assessment to penalty interest is made specifying a date for the purposes of sub-paragraph (1)(*a*) above, and

(*b*) within such period as may for the purposes of this sub-paragraph have been notified by the Commissioners to the person liable for the interest, the amount on which the interest is payable is paid,

that amount shall be deemed for the purposes of any further liability to interest to have been paid on the specified date.

FINANCE ACT 2002

(2002 Chapter 23)

An Act to grant certain duties, to alter other duties, and to amend the law relating to the National Debt and the Public Revenue, and to make further provision in connection with finance.

[24 July 2002]

PART 5
OTHER TAXES

Aggregates levy

129 Aggregates levy: transitional relief for Northern Ireland

(1) (*inserts* FA 2001 s 30A).
(2) (*amends* FA 2001 s 17(6)(*a*)).

130 Aggregates levy: amendments to provisions exempting spoil etc

(1) (*amends* FA 2001 s 17(3)(*e*) and *inserts* FA 2001 s 17(3)(*f*)).
(2) (*repeals* FA 2001 s 17(4)(*b*)).
(3) This section shall be deemed to have come into force on 1st April 2002.

131 Aggregates levy: crushing and cutting rock

(1) (*repeals* FA 2001 s 17(3)(*a*)).
(2) (*amends* FA 2001 s 18(2)(*a*).
(3) (*amends* FA 2001 s 20(1), and *repeals* FA 2001 s 20(1)(*c*), 21(2)(*b*), 24(6)(*b*), and 24(8)(*a*)).
(4) This section shall be deemed to have come into force on 1st April 2002.

132 Aggregates levy: miscellaneous amendments

(1) Schedule 38 to this Act, which makes amendments to provisions in Part 2 of the Finance Act 2001 (aggregates levy), has effect.
(2) (*amends* FA 1996 s 197(2)(*h*)(ii)).
(3) This section shall be deemed to have come into force on 1st April 2002.

133 Aggregates levy: amendments to provisions about civil penalties

(1) Part 2 of Schedule 6 to the Finance Act 2001 (c 9) (aggregates levy: civil penalties) is amended as follows.
(2) *(amends FA 2001 Sch 6 para 7(1)(a) and repeals sub-para 7(1)(b)).*
(3) *(inserts FA 2001 Sch 6 para 7(1A)).*
(4) *(amends FA 2001 Sch 6 para 7(3) and (4)).*[1]
(5) (*inserts* FA 2001 Sch 6 para 9A).
(6) This section shall be deemed to have come into force on 1st May 2002.

Amendments—[1] Sub-ss (2)–(4) repealed by FA 2008 s 122, Sch 40 para 21(*j*) with effect from 1 April 2009 (by virtue of SI 2009/571 art 2). Sub-ss (2)–(4) repealed only in so far as they relate to conduct involving dishonesty which relates to—
(a) an inaccuracy in a document, or
(b) a failure to notify HMRC of an under-assessment by HMRC (SI 2009/571 art 6).

PART 6
MISCELLANEOUS AND SUPPLEMENTARY PROVISIONS

Supplementary

141 Repeals

(1) The enactments mentioned in Schedule 40 to this Act (which include provisions that are spent or of no practical utility) are repealed to the extent specified.
(2) The repeals specified in that Schedule have effect subject to the commencement provisions and savings contained or referred to in the notes set out in that Schedule.

SCHEDULES

SCHEDULE 38
AGGREGATES LEVY AMENDMENTS

Section 132

Introduction

1 This Schedule makes amendments to provisions of Part 2 of the Finance Act 2001 (c 9) (aggregates levy).

The charge

2 In section 16(1) (charge to aggregates levy), for "A levy" substitute "A tax".

Meaning of "aggregate" etc

3—(1) Section 17 (meaning of "aggregate" etc) is amended as follows.
(2) (*substitutes* FA 2001 s 17(2)(*d*)).
(3) (*amends* FA 2001 s 17(3)(*d*)(ii)).
(4) (*amends* FA 2001 s 17(4)(*d*)).

Exempt processes

4 (*amends* FA 2001 s 18(2)(*c*) and repeals s 18(3)(*d*) and (*h*)).

Commercial exploitation

5—(1) Section 19 (commercial exploitation) is amended as follows.
(2) (*amends* FA 2001 s 19(2)(*b*)).
(3) (*inserts* FA 2001 s 19(3A)).
(4) In subsection (4) (exemption in certain cases where aggregate is won from one site and incorporated into a neighbouring site), for the words "adjacent land" in both places substitute "other land".

Responsibility for commercial exploitation

6 (*amends* FA 2001 s 22(2)).

The register

7 (*inserts* FA 2001 s 24(6)(*ca*)).

Insolvency etc

8 In section 37 (regulations about cases of insolvency etc), in subsection (7) (meaning of "insolvency procedure) omit paragraphs (*g*) to (*j*) (appointment of receiver and other interim or provisional orders).

Notification of registrability etc

9—(1) Paragraph 1 of Schedule 4 (notification of registrability etc) is amended as follows.
(2) (*substitutes* FA 2001, Sch 4, para 1(1)–(1B)).
(3) In sub-paragraphs (2) and (5), after "sub-paragraph (1)" insert "or (1A)".

Restriction on powers to provide for set-off

10 In paragraph 11 of Schedule 8 (restriction on powers to provide for set-off), in sub-paragraph (2) (meaning of "insolvency procedure") omit paragraphs (*f*), (*g*) and (*h*) (appointment of receiver and other interim or provisional orders).

SCHEDULE 40

REPEALS

Section 141

PART 4

OTHER TAXES

(3) AGGREGATES LEVY

Note—All repeals relevant to aggregates levy are in effect and have therefore been omitted.

FINANCE ACT 2004

(2004 Chapter 12)

An Act to Grant certain duties, to alter other duties, and to amend the law relating to the National Debt and the Public Revenue, and to make further provision in connection with finance.

[22 July 2004]

PART 6

OTHER TAXES

Aggregates levy

290 Transitional tax credit in Northern Ireland: changes to existing scheme

(1) (*amended* FA 2001 s 30A(4))
(2) This section shall be deemed to have come into force on 1st April 2004.

291 Transitional tax credit in Northern Ireland: new scheme

(1) Part 2 of the Finance Act 2001 (c 9) (aggregates levy) is amended as set out in subsections (2) and (3).

(2) (*substitutes* FA 2001 s 30A)

(3) (*amends* FA 2001 s 48(1))

(4) The preceding provisions of this section come into force on such day as the Treasury may by order made by statutory instrument appoint.

(5) An order under subsection (4) may—

(*a*) make different provision for different purposes;

(*b*) make incidental, consequential, supplemental or transitional provision and savings.

Order—Finance Act 2004, Section 291 (Appointed Day) Order, SI 2004/1942 (appointed day is 23 July 2004).

FINANCE ACT 2007

(2007 Chapter 11)

PART 1

CHARGES, RATES, THRESHOLDS ETC

Environment

14 Rate of aggregates levy

(1) (*amends* FA 2001 s 16(4))

(2) The amendment made by subsection (1) has effect in relation to aggregate subjected to commercial exploitation on or after 1st April 2008.

PART 2

ENVIRONMENT

Other measures

22 Aggregates levy: exemption for aggregate removed from railways etc

(1) Section 17(3) of FA 2001 (exempt aggregate) is amended as follows.

(2)–(4) (*insert* FA 2001 s 17(3)(*da*))

(5) The amendment made by subsection (3) comes into force on such day as the Treasury may by order made by statutory instrument appoint.

Orders—Finance Act 2007 section 22(3) (Appointed Day) Order, SI 2007/2118 (appoints 1 August 2007 as the date on which the amendment in sub-s (3) comes into force).

SCHEDULE 24

PENALTIES FOR ERRORS

Note—Please see *VAT Statutes* ante for the text of this Schedule.

FINANCE ACT 2008

(2008 Chapter 9)

An Act to Grant certain duties, to alter other duties, and to amend the law relating to the National Debt and the Public Revenue, and to make further provision in connection with finance.

[21 July 2008]

PART 1

CHARGES, RATES, ALLOWANCES, RELIEFS ETC

Environmental taxes and duties

20 Rate of aggregates levy

(1) (*amends* FA 2001 s 16(4))

(2) The amendment made by subsection (1) has effect in relation to aggregate subjected to commercial exploitation on or after 1 April 2009.

PART 7

ADMINISTRATION

Press releases—HMRC Guidance Note, 18 July 2008 (HMRC set-off across taxes following Finance Bill 2008).

CHAPTER 1

INFORMATION ETC

New information etc powers

114 Computer records etc

Note—Please see *VAT Statutes* ante for the text of this Section.

CHAPTER 3

PENALTIES

122 Penalties for errors

Note—Please see *VAT Statutes* ante for the text of this Section.

123 Penalties for failure to notify etc

Note—Please see *VAT Statutes* ante for the text of this Section.

CHAPTER 4

APPEALS ETC

Reviews and appeals etc: general

124 HMRC decisions etc: reviews and appeals

Note—Please see *VAT Statutes* ante for the text of this Section.

CHAPTER 5

PAYMENT AND ENFORCEMENT

Taking control of goods etc

127 Enforcement by taking control of goods: England and Wales

Note—Please see *VAT Statutes* ante for the text of this Section.

128 Summary warrant: Scotland

Note—Please see *VAT Statutes* ante for the text of this Section.

129 Consequential provision and commencement

Note—Please see *VAT Statutes* ante for the text of this Section.

Set off

130 Set-off: England and Wales and Northern Ireland

Note—Please see *VAT Statutes* ante for the text of this Section.

131 No set-off where insolvency procedure has been applied

Note—Please see *VAT Statutes* ante for the text of this Section.

133 Set-off etc where right to be paid a sum has been transferred

Note—Please see *VAT Statutes* ante for the text of this Section.

Other measures

135 Interest on unpaid tax in case of disaster etc of national significance

Note—Please see *VAT Statutes* ante for the text of this Section.

136 Fee for payment

Note—Please see *VAT Statutes* ante for the text of this Section.

Supplementary

139 Interpretation of Chapter

Note—Please see *VAT Statutes* ante for the text of this Section.

PART 8

MISCELLANEOUS

Payments from Exchequer accounts

158 Power of Treasury to make payments

Note—Please see *VAT Statutes* ante for the text of this Section.

159 Payments from certain Exchequer accounts: mechanism

Note—Please see *VAT Statutes* ante for the text of this Section.

Other matters

160 Power to give statutory effect to concessions

Note—Please see *VAT Statutes* ante for the text of this Section.

PART 9

FINAL PROVISIONS

165 Interpretation

Note—Please see *VAT Statutes* ante for the text of this Section.

166 Short title

This Act may be cited as the Finance Act 2008.

SCHEDULES

SCHEDULE 36

INFORMATION AND INSPECTION POWERS

Section 113

Note—Please see *VAT Statutes* ante for the text of this Section.

SCHEDULE 41

PENALTIES: FAILURE TO NOTIFY AND CERTAIN VAT AND EXCISE WRONGDOING

Section 123

Note—Please see *VAT Statutes* ante for the text of this Section.

FINANCE ACT 2009

(2009 Chapter 10)

An Act to Grant certain duties, to alter other duties, and to amend the law relating to the National Debt and the Public Revenue, and to make further provision in connection with finance.

[21 July 2009]

PART 7

ADMINISTRATION

Standards and values

92 HMRC Charter

Note—Please see *VAT Statutes* ante for the text of this Section.

93 Duties of senior accounting officers of qualifying companies

Note—Please see *VAT Statutes* ante for the text of this Section.

94 Publishing details of deliberate tax defaulters

Note—Please see *VAT Statutes* ante for the text of this Section.

Information etc

95 Amendment of information and inspection powers

Note—Please see *VAT Statutes* ante for the text of this Section.

96 Extension of information and inspection powers to further taxes

(1) In paragraph 63(1) of Schedule 36 to FA 2008 (information and inspection powers: meaning of "tax"), for paragraph (*e*) (and the "and" before it) substitute—

"(*e*) insurance premium tax,
(*f*) inheritance tax,
(*g*) stamp duty land tax,
(*h*) stamp duty reserve tax,
(*i*) petroleum revenue tax,
(*j*) aggregates levy,
(*k*) climate change levy,
(*l*) landfill tax, and
(*m*) relevant foreign tax,".

(2) Schedule 48 contains further amendments of that Schedule.

(3) The amendments made by this section and Schedule 48 come into force on such day as the Treasury may by order appoint.

(4) An order under subsection (3) may—

(*a*) appoint different days for different purposes, and

(*b*) contain transitional provision and savings.

(5) The Treasury may by order make any incidental, supplemental, consequential, transitional or transitory provision or saving which appears appropriate in consequence of, or otherwise in connection with, this section and Schedule 48.

(6) An order under subsection (5) may—

(*a*) make different provision for different purposes, and

(*b*) make provision amending, repealing or revoking an enactment or instrument (whenever passed or made).

(7) An order under this section is to be made by statutory instrument.

(8) A statutory instrument containing an order under subsection (5) is subject to annulment in pursuance of a resolution of the House of Commons.

Order—Finance Act 2009, Section 96 and Schedule 48 (Appointed Day, Savings and Consequential Amendments) Order 2009, SI 2009/3054 (appointed day is 1 April 2010).

97 Powers to obtain contact details for debtors

Note—Please see *VAT Statutes* ante for the text of this Section.

98 Record-keeping

(1) Schedule 50 contains provision about obligations to keep records.

(2) The amendments made by that Schedule come into force on such day as the Treasury may by order made by statutory instrument appoint.

Order—Finance Act 2009, Schedule 50 (Record-keeping) (Appointed Day) Order 2010 (appoints 1 April 2010 as the date for the Sch 50 amendments to come into force).

Assessments, claims etc

99 Time limits for assessments, claims etc

(1) Schedule 51 contains provision about time limits for assessments, claims etc

(2) The amendments made by that Schedule come into force on such day as the Treasury may by order made by statutory instrument appoint.

(3) An order under subsection (2)—

(*a*) may make different provision for different purposes, and

(*b*) may include transitional provision and savings.

Order—Finance Act 2009, Schedule 51 (Time Limits for Assessments, Claims, etc) (Appointed Days and Transitional Provisions) Order 2010 (1 April 2010 is appointed as the date for Sch 51 paras 1–4, 27–43 to come into force).

Interest

101 Late payment interest on sums due to HMRC

Note—Please see *VAT Statutes* ante for the text of this Section.

102 Repayment interest on sums to be paid by HMRC

Note—Please see *VAT Statutes* ante for the text of this Section.

103 Rates of interest

Note—Please see *VAT Statutes* ante for the text of this Section.

104 Supplementary

Note—Please see *VAT Statutes* ante for the text of this Section.

108 Suspension of penalties during currency of agreement for deferred payment

Note—Please see *VAT Statutes* ante for the text of this Section.

109 Miscellaneous amendments

Note—Please see *VAT Statutes* ante for the text of this Section.

SCHEDULES

SCHEDULE 46

DUTIES OF SENIOR ACCOUNTING OFFICERS OF QUALIFYING COMPANIES

Section 93

Note—Please see *VAT Statutes* ante for the text of this Schedule.

SCHEDULE 47

AMENDMENT OF INFORMATION AND INSPECTION POWERS

Section 95

Note—Please see *VAT Statutes* ante for the text of this Schedule.

SCHEDULE 48

EXTENSION OF INFORMATION AND INSPECTION POWERS

Section 96

Note—Please see *VAT Statutes* ante for the text of this Schedule.

SCHEDULE 49

POWERS TO OBTAIN CONTACT DETAILS FOR DEBTORS

Section 97

Note—Please see *VAT Statutes* ante for the text of this Schedule.

SCHEDULE 50

RECORD-KEEPING

Section 98

. . .

Order—Finance Act 2009, Schedule 50 (Record-keeping) (Appointed Day) Order 2010 (appoints 1 April 2010 as the date for the Sch 50 amendments to come into force).

Aggregates levy

15 Schedule 7 to FA 2001 (aggregates levy: information and evidence etc) is amended as follows.

16—(1) Paragraph 2 (records) is amended as follows.
(2) (*substitutes* FA 2001 Sch 7 para 2(4))
(3) In sub-paragraph (9), omit "approval or" and "given or".

17 Omit paragraph 3 (evidence of records that are required to be preserved).

SCHEDULE 51

TIME LIMITS FOR ASSESSMENTS, CLAIMS ETC

Section 99

Order—Finance Act 2009, Schedule 51 (Time Limits for Assessments, Claims, etc) (Appointed Days and Transitional Provisions) Order 2010 (1 April 2010 is appointed as the date for Sch 51 paras 27–43 to come into force).

. . .

Aggregates levy

27 Part 2 of FA 2001 (aggregates levy) is amended as follows.

Order—Finance Act 2009, Schedule 51 (Time Limits for Assessments, Claims, etc) (Appointed Days and Transitional Provisions) Order 2010 (1 April 2010 is appointed as the date for Sch 51 paras 27–43 to come into force).

28 In section 32(1) (repayments of overpaid aggregates levy), for "three years" substitute "4 years".

Order—Finance Act 2009, Schedule 51 (Time Limits for Assessments, Claims, etc) (Appointed Days and Transitional Provisions) Order 2010 (1 April 2010 is appointed as the date for Sch 51 paras 27–43 to come into force).

29—(1) Paragraph 4 of Schedule 5 (time limits for assessments) is amended as follows.
(2) In sub-paragraph (1)(*b*), for "three years" substitute "4 years".
(3) (*substitutes* FA 2001 Sch 5 para 4(3), (3A))
(4) In sub-paragraph (4)—

(*a*) in paragraph (*a*), for "three years" substitute "4 years", and

(*b*) omit paragraph (*b*) (and the "and" before it).

Order—Finance Act 2009, Schedule 51 (Time Limits for Assessments, Claims, etc) (Appointed Days and Transitional Provisions) Order 2010 (1 April 2010 is appointed as the date for Sch 51 paras 27–43 to come into force).

30 In paragraph 2(10) of Schedule 8 (interest payable by Commissioners), for "three years" substitute "4 years".

Order—Finance Act 2009, Schedule 51 (Time Limits for Assessments, Claims, etc) (Appointed Days and Transitional Provisions) Order 2010 (1 April 2010 is appointed as the date for Sch 51 paras 27–43 to come into force).

31—(1) Paragraph 4 of Schedule 10 (time limits on penalty assessments) is amended as follows.
(2) In sub-paragraph (1), for "three years" substitute "4 years".
(3) (*substitutes* FA 2001 Sch 10 para 4(2), (2A))
(4) In sub-paragraph (3)—

(*a*) in paragraph (*a*), for "three years" substitute "4 years", and

(*b*) omit paragraph (*b*) (and the "and" before it).

Order—Finance Act 2009, Schedule 51 (Time Limits for Assessments, Claims, etc) (Appointed Days and Transitional Provisions) Order 2010 (1 April 2010 is appointed as the date for Sch 51 paras 27–43 to come into force).

SCHEDULE 53
LATE PAYMENT INTEREST
Section 101

Note—Please see *VAT Statutes* ante for the text of this Schedule.

SCHEDULE 54
REPAYMENT INTEREST
Section 102

Note—Please see *VAT Statutes* ante for the text of this Schedule.

SCHEDULE 57
AMENDMENTS RELATING TO PENALTIES
Section 109

Note—Please see *VAT Statutes* ante for the text of this Schedule.

FINANCE ACT 2010

(2010 Chapter 13)

[8 April 2010]

PART 1
CHARGES, RATES ETC

Other environmental taxes

16 Rate of aggregates levy

(1) In section 16(4) of FA 2001 (rate of aggregates levy), for "£2" substitute "£2.10".

(2) The amendment made by subsection (1) has effect in relation to aggregate subjected to commercial exploitation on or after 1 April 2011.

Aggregates Levy Statutory Instruments

Contents

Statutory Instruments

1997/1431

DISTRESS FOR CUSTOMS AND EXCISE DUTIES AND OTHER INDIRECT TAXES REGULATIONS 1997

Made by the Commissioners of Customs and Excise under FA 1997 ss 51(1), (2), (3)

Made . . . . *9th June 1997*
Laid before House of Commons . . . . *9th June 1997*
Coming into force . . . . *1st July 1997*

Citation and commencement

1 These Regulations may be cited as The Distress for Customs and Excise Duties and Other Indirect Taxes Regulations 1997 and shall come into force on 1st July 1997.

Interpretation

2—(1) In these Regulations—

"authorised person" means a person acting under the authority of the Commissioners;

"costs" means any costs, charges, expenses and fees;

"officer" means, subject to section 8(2) of the Customs and Excise Management Act 1979, a person commissioned by the Commissioners pursuant to section 6(3) of that Act;

"person in default" means a person who has refused or neglected to pay any relevant tax due from him;

"relevant tax" means any of the following—

. . .

[(*g*) aggregates levy;][1]

"walking possession agreement" means an agreement under which, in consideration of any goods and chattels distrained upon being allowed to remain in the custody of the person in default and of the delaying of their sale, that person—

(*a*) acknowledges that the goods and chattels specified in the agreement are under distraint and held in walking possession; and

(*b*) undertakes that, except with the consent of the Commissioners and subject to such conditions as they may impose, he will not remove or allow the removal of any of the specified goods and chattels from the place named in the agreement;

"1994 Act" means Part III of the Finance Act 1994;

"1996 Act" means Part III of the Finance Act 1996;

(2) Any reference in these Regulations to an amount of relevant tax includes a reference to any amount recoverable as if it were an amount of that relevant tax.

Note—Words omitted are not relevant for the purposes of aggregates levy.

Amendments—[1] Para (1)(*g*) added by the Aggregates Levy (General) Regulations, SI 2002/761 reg 39 with effect from 1 April 2002.

Revocations and transitional provisions

3—(1) The Regulations specified in Schedule 3 are hereby revoked to the extent set out there.

(2) Where a warrant is signed before the coming into force of these Regulations, these Regulations shall apply to anything done, after these Regulations come into force, in relation to that warrant or as a consequence of distress being levied.

Levying distress

4—(1) Subject to regulation 5 below, if upon written demand a person neglects or refuses to pay any relevant tax due from him an officer may levy distress on the goods and chattels of that person and by warrant signed by him direct any authorised person to levy such distress.

(2) Where a warrant has been signed, distress shall be levied by or under the direction of, and in the presence of, the authorised person.

(3) Subject to regulation 6 below, distress may be levied on any goods and chattels located at any place whatever including on a public highway.

Goods and chattels not subject to levy

6 No distress shall be levied on any goods and chattels mentioned in Schedule 1 which at the time of levy are located in a place and used for a purpose mentioned in that Schedule.

Times for levying distress

7—(1) Subject to paragraph (2) below, a levy of distress shall commence only during the period between eight o'clock in the morning and eight o'clock at night on any day of the week but it may be continued thereafter outside that period until the levy is completed.
(2) Where a person holds himself out as conducting any profession, trade or business during hours which are partly within and partly outside, or wholly outside the period mentioned in paragraph (1) above, a levy of distress may be commenced at any time during that period or during the hours of any day in which he holds himself out as conducting that profession, trade or business and it may be continued thereafter outside that period or those hours until the levy is completed.

Costs

8—(1) A person in respect of whose goods and chattels a warrant has been signed shall be liable to pay to an officer or authorised person all costs, in connection with anything done under these Regulations described in column 1 of Schedule 2, as determined in accordance with column 2 of that Schedule.
(2) An authorised person may, after deducting and accounting for the amount of relevant tax to the Commissioners, retain costs from any amount received.

Sale

9 If any person upon whose goods and chattels distress has been levied does not pay the amount of relevant tax due together with costs within five days of a levy, an officer or authorised person may sell the distress for payment of the amount of relevant tax and costs; and the officer or authorised person, after deducting and retaining the amount of relevant tax and costs shall restore any surplus to the owner of the goods upon which distress was levied.

Disputes as to costs

10—(1) In the case of any dispute as to costs, the amount of those costs shall be taxed by a district judge of the county court of the district where the distress was levied, and he may make such order as he thinks fit as to the costs of the taxation.
(2) In the application of this regulation to Northern Ireland, in the case of any dispute as to costs, the amount of those costs shall be taxed in the same manner as costs in equity suits or proceedings in the county court in Northern Ireland.

SCHEDULE 1

GOODS AND CHATTELS NOT SUBJECT TO LEVY

Regulation 6

1 Any of the following goods and chattels which are located in a dwelling house at which distress is being levied and are reasonably required for the domestic needs of any person residing in that dwelling house—

(*a*) beds and bedding;
(*b*) household linen;
(*c*) chairs and settees;
(*d*) tables;
(*e*) food;
(*f*) lights and light fittings;
(*g*) heating appliances;
(*h*) curtains;
(*i*) floor coverings;
(*j*) furniture, equipment and utensils used for cooking, storing or eating food;
(*k*) refrigerators;
(*l*) articles used for cleaning, mending, or pressing clothes;
(*m*) articles used for cleaning the home;
(*n*) furniture used for storing—
  (i) clothing, bedding or household linen;
  (ii) articles used for cleaning the home;
  (iii) utensils used for cooking or eating food;
(*o*) articles used for safety in the home;
(*p*) toys for the use of any child within the household;
(*q*) medical aids and medical equipment.

2 Any of the following items which are located in premises used for the purposes of any profession, trade or business—

(*a*) fire fighting equipment for use on the premises;
(*b*) medical aids and medical equipment for use on the premises.

SCHEDULE 2
SCALE OF COSTS
Regulation 8(1)

Matter	*Costs*
(1)	*(2)*
1 For attending to levy distress where payment is made of an amount of relevant tax due and distress is not levied:	£12.50.
2 For levying distress—	
(a) where an amount of relevant tax demanded and due does not exceed £100:	£12.50.
(b) where an amount of relevant tax demanded and due exceeds £100:	12½% on the first £100
	4% on the next £400,
	2½% on the next £1,500,
	1% on the next £8,000,
	¼% on any additional sum.
3 For taking possession of distrained goods—	
(a) where a person remains in physical possession of goods at the place where distress was levied (the person to provide his own food and lodging):	£4.50 per day.
(b) where possession is taken under a walking possession agreement:	£7.00.
4 For appraising goods upon which distress has been levied:	Reasonable costs of appraisement.
5 For arranging removal and storage of goods upon which distress has been levied:	Reasonable costs of arrangement.
6 For removing and storing goods upon which distress has been levied:	Reasonable costs of removal and storage.
7 For advertising the sale of goods upon which distress has been levied:	Reasonable costs of advertising.
8 For selling the distress—	
(*a*) where a sale by auction is held at the auctioneer's premises:	15% of the sum realised.
(*b*) where a sale by auction is held elsewhere:	7½% of the sum realised and auctioneer's reasonable costs.
(*c*) where a sale by other means is undertaken:	7½% of the sum realised and reasonable costs.

2001/4027

AGGREGATES LEVY (REGISTRATION AND MISCELLANEOUS PROVISIONS) REGULATIONS 2001

Made by the Commissioners of Customs and Excise under FA 2001 ss 24(4), 33(1), 33(2), 34(2), 34(4), 35(4), 36(1), 45, Sch 4 paras 5, 6, and Sch 9 para 7; and FA 1999 s 132

Made . . . . *19 December 2001*
Laid before the House of Commons . . . . *20 December 2001*
Coming into force . . . . *11 January 2002*

PART I
PRELIMINARY

1 These Regulations may be cited as the Aggregates Levy (Registration and Miscellaneous Provisions) Regulations 2001 and come into force on 11th January 2002.

PART II
REGISTRATION

Notification of registrability—form, manner, timing, etc

2—(1) A person who is required to notify the Commissioners under paragraph 1(1)(*a*) or (*b*) of Schedule 4 to the Act (notification of registrability for aggregates levy) shall do so on Form AL 1.
(2) But a partner so required shall do so on Form AL 1 and Form AL 2.
(3) All persons who notify their registrability under paragraph (1) or (2) above shall in addition notify the Commissioners of their site details on Form AL 1A.
(4) A person may make the notification required by paragraph (1), (2) or (3) above on either—
(*a*) a version of a relevant form completed (other than in respect of the inclusion of the requisite signature) by telephone; or
(*b*) subject to his possession of an approved digital certificate, an electronic version of a relevant form;
and, in either case, the version used shall not differ in any material respect from Form AL 1, Form AL 2 or Form AL 1A but may include relevant modifications.
(5) In all cases the required notification must contain and provide full information and particulars about every matter referred to in Form AL 1, Form AL 1A and, in the case of a partner, Form AL 2, together with such further details as the Commissioners may require.
(6) A person so required on 11th January 2002 must deliver the notification to the Commissioners no later than 1st March 2002.
(7) A person to whom paragraph (6) above does not apply, but who becomes so required after 11th January 2002, must deliver the notification to the Commissioners within 30 days starting from the day after becoming so required.
(8) A person who is required but fails to comply with this regulation remains subject to paragraph 1(1) of Schedule 4 to the Act.
(9) In this regulation—
"approved digital certificate" means a digital certificate which is accepted by the Commissioners as identifying a person for the purpose of their authorisation of his use of an electronic communication in respect of an assigned matter;
"assigned matter" has the meaning given in section 1(1) of the Customs and Excise Management Act 1979;
"electronic communication" has the same meaning as in section 15(1) of the Electronic Communications Act 2000;
"electronic version" means the version which is submitted by means of an electronic communication;
"notify" and "notification" are to be construed according to the context so as to cover notification by post, telephone and by means of an electronic communication according to the context;
"relevant form" means Form AL 1, Form AL 2 and Form AL 1A.

Exemption from registration

[**3**—(1) Where the only taxable activities that a person carries out or intends to carry out are relevant taxable activities, that person shall be exempt from the requirement of registration and all consequent obligations and liabilities.
(2) For the purposes of this regulation, a "relevant taxable activity" is the commercial exploitation of aggregate which is exempt under section 17(3)(*b*), (*c*), (*d*), [(*da*),][2] (*e*) or (*f*) or section 17(4)(*a*), (*c*), (*d*), (*e*) or (*f*) of the Act.
(3) Where at least one of the relevant taxable activities which such a person carries out is the commercial exploitation of aggregate which is exempt under section 17(3)(*e*) or (*f*) or section 17(4)(*a*) of the Act or clay (exempt under section 17(4)(*f*) of the Act), that person shall notify the Commissioners (notification under paragraph 1A of Schedule 4 to the Act) of this fact in writing in such a manner and providing such information as may be directed by the Commissioners or stipulated by them in a published notice.
(4) A person who has notified the Commissioners under paragraph (3) above shall also notify them of any change in circumstance in writing in such a manner and providing such information as may be directed by the Commissioners or stipulated by them in a published notice.
(5) In this regulation—
"aggregate" has the meaning given in section 17(1) of the Act;
"commercial exploitation" has the meaning given in section 19 of the Act;
"published notice" refers to a notice published by the Commissioners and not withdrawn or replaced by a further notice.][1]

Commentary—*De Voil Indirect Tax Service* **V22.108**.
Press releases etc—C&E Business Brief 34/02 24-12-02 (exemption from registration and other obligations).

Amendments—[1] This regulation substituted by the Aggregates Levy (Registration and Miscellaneous Provisions) (Amendment) Regulations, SI 2003/465 with effect from 1 April 2003.

[2] In para (2), reference inserted by the Aggregates Levy (Registration and Miscellaneous Provisions) (Amendment) Regulations, SI 2007/2168 reg 2(1). This amendment only has effect in relation to the commercial exploitation on or after 16 August 2007 of aggregate which is exempt under FA 2001 s 17(3)(*da*).

Changes in particulars

4—(1) A person who has made a notification (the "original notification") to the Commissioners under regulation 2(1), 2(2), 2(3) or 2(4) at any time shall also, as appropriate, notify them about the following matters.

(2) The first such matter is any inaccuracy or inadequacy in the information, particulars or details contained in or provided with the original notification.

(3) The second such matter is any change in circumstances that causes that information or those particulars or details to become inaccurate or inadequate.

(4) The third such matter is any change in circumstances relating to that person, that person's business or any other matter with respect to which particulars are contained in the register.

(5) A notification required by this regulation must—

(*a*) be given in writing;

(*b*) provide full particulars enabling the register kept by the Commissioners to be kept up to date; and

(*c*) be delivered to the Commissioners within 30 days.

(6) The first of those 30 days begin, as the case requires, on—

(*a*) the day after the person discovers that the original notification was inaccurate or is in a position to rectify the inadequacy in that notification (see paragraph (2) above); or

(*b*) the day after the change in circumstances occurred (see paragraphs (3) and (4) above).

(7) The full particulars referred to in paragraph (5)(*b*) above include (but are not limited to)—

(*a*) the nature of the relevant inaccuracy, inadequacy or change;

(*b*) the date on which the inaccuracy in the original notification was discovered or the inadequacy could be rectified;

(*c*) the date on which the change occurred;

(*d*) the nature of the inaccuracy, inadequacy or change;

(*e*) the correct information, particulars or details.

(8) A relevant change of circumstances under paragraph (3) or (4) above includes (but is not limited to)—

(*a*) the person's name, trading name, address or principal place of business;

(*b*) the person's status (namely, as sole proprietor, partner, unincorporated body, or body corporate);

(*c*) the name and address of a partner or a change in the membership of a partnership;

(*d*) the name and address of a trustee or beneficiary of a trust;

(*e*) the site details.

(9) The Commissioners may, on their own initiative or following a notification under this regulation, correct an entry in the register in a case where they are satisfied that it should be corrected or otherwise brought up to date.

(10) Where a person makes a notification under this regulation that is or becomes inaccurate, inadequate or misleading, the provisions of paragraphs (1) to (9) above shall apply to that notification as if it were the original notification.

Cessation of taxable activities

5—(1) This regulation applies to a person who has become liable to notify the Commissioners under either regulation 2 or 3.

(2) Where such a person ceases to have the intention of carrying on taxable activities (paragraph 3(1) of Schedule 4 to the Act) he shall notify the Commissioners of that fact.

(3) Such a person shall make that notification in writing setting out—

(*a*) the day on which he ceased to have the intention, and

(*b*) the day on which he carried out his final taxable activity.

(4) This notification must be delivered to the Commissioners within 30 days starting from the day after the later of the days referred to in paragraph (3) above.

PART III

GROUPS

References to groups, etc

6—(1) For the purposes of this Part—

(*a*) a body corporate is a member of a group at any time in relation to which it falls to be treated as such a member in accordance with Schedule 9 to the Act; and (*b*) the body corporate which is to be taken as the representative member for a group at any time is the member of the group which in relation to that time is the representative member under that Schedule in the case of that group.

(2) A body corporate that is a member of a group shall, under section 24 of and Schedule 4 to the Act, be registered in the name of the representative member.

Liability for returns

7 The obligation of a member of a group to make a return under regulations made under section 25 of the Act shall be discharged by the representative member making a return representing the cumulative total of what would be the individual returns for the group members were it not for the group treatment.

Group treatment

8—(1) An application for group treatment under paragraph 2(1) of Schedule 9 to the Act shall be made to the Commissioners in writing.

(2) In addition, each body corporate which is applying to be treated as a member of the group shall make an application to the Commissioners to that effect in writing.

(3) Any application under paragraphs (1) or (2) above shall include such information and declaration as the Commissioners may require.

Applications and notifications

9—(1) An application under paragraph 2(2) or 3(1) of Schedule 9 to the Act to add a body corporate to a group, exclude a body corporate from a group, change the representative member for a group or to cease group treatment shall be made in writing to the Commissioners and include such information and declaration as they may require.

(2) A notification under paragraph 6(1) or 6(2) of Schedule 9 to the Act in relation to a body corporate ceasing to be eligible to be treated as a member of a group or a body corporate which is the representative member for a group ceasing to have an established place of business in the United Kingdom shall be made in writing to the Commissioners and include such information and declaration as they may require.

(3) The notification required by paragraph (2) above shall be delivered to the Commissioners no later than the earlier of 30 days after the body corporate becomes aware that it will cease to be eligible to be treated as a member of a group or that it will cease to have an established place of business in the United Kingdom or 30 days after the body corporate ceases to be so eligible or ceases to have such an established place of business, as the case may require.

(4) The first of the 30 days referred to in paragraph (3) above is the first day after the one on which the body corporate becomes aware that it will cease to be so eligible or that it will cease to have an established place of business in the United Kingdom or the day after the one on which the body corporate ceases to be so eligible or ceases to have an established place of business in the United Kingdom, as the case may require.

Modifications etc

10 A person who has made an application or notification to the Commissioners under this Part shall notify them immediately should any information contained in or provided in connection with that application or notification be or become inaccurate.

Miscellaneous

11 In this Part, "member" and "representative member" have the same meanings as in section 48(1) of the Act.

PART IV
PARTNERSHIPS AND OTHER SPECIAL CASES

Partnerships

12—(1) This regulation applies for determining by what person anything required to be done by or under the Act is to be done where, apart from this regulation, that requirement would fall on persons carrying on business in partnership.

(2) Any such requirement shall be the joint and several responsibility of every partner.

(3) Subject to paragraphs (4) and (5) below—

(*a*) compliance with such a requirement by at least one of the partners shall suffice as compliance by all of them; and

(*b*) in the case of a partnership whose principal place of business is in Scotland, such compliance by a person duly authorised by the partnership shall suffice as compliance by the partners.

(4) Each partner shall comply with the requirement imposed by regulation 2 in relation to Form AL 2.

(5) A person joining or leaving a partnership, as the case requires, shall comply with the requirements imposed by regulation 4 so far as they apply to any change in the membership of a partnership.

Other unincorporated associations

13—(1) This regulation applies for determining by what persons anything required to be done by or under the Act is to be done where, apart from this regulation, that requirement would fall on persons carrying on business together as an unincorporated body other than a partnership.

(2) Any such requirement shall be the joint and several responsibility of—

(*a*) first, every person holding office in that body as president, chairman, treasurer, secretary or other similar office; or

(*b*) secondly, if there is no such office holder, every person who is a member of a committee by which the affairs of that body are managed; or

(*c*) thirdly, if there is no such office holder or member, every person carrying on that business.

(3) Compliance with such a requirement by one or more of the persons referred to in paragraph (2) above shall suffice as compliance with that requirement by all of them.

(4) But a purported notification under regulation 2(1), 2(2), 2(3) or 2(4) shall not be treated as complying with any of those regulations unless it is made by a person required to do so under paragraph (2)(*a*), (2)(*b*) or (2)(*c*) above, as appropriate.

Non resident taxpayers—requirement and provision for tax representatives

14—(1) This regulation applies to a person (a "non-resident taxpayer") who—

(*a*) is or is required to be registered for the purposes of the levy, and

(*b*) is not resident in the United Kingdom.

(2) A person who falls within this description shall notify the Commissioners in writing of this fact.

(3) Such notification shall be delivered to the Commissioners within 30 days starting from the day after the first day on which the person falls within the description.

(4) The Commissioners may—

(*a*) require or permit such a taxpayer to appoint some person resident in the United Kingdom to act as his tax representative for the purposes of the levy with effect from a date they specify, and

(*b*) oblige the taxpayer to request them, no later than such earlier date than the date in (*a*) above as they may specify, to approve the appointment of that person as the tax representative.

(5) Any appointment of a person as a tax representative shall take effect only if, and from the date, approved by the Commissioners.

(6) A request for approval under paragraph (4)(*b*) above shall be in writing and contain such information and particulars, and corresponding declaration by the taxpayer and the proposed tax representative, as the Commissioners may require.

15—(1) A non-resident may appoint a different tax representative as a replacement for a tax representative whose appointment has taken effect.

(2) Such appointment shall take effect only if, and from the date, approved by the Commissioners.

(3) A request to the Commissioners for the purposes of paragraph (2) above shall be in writing and contain such information and particulars, and corresponding declaration by the taxpayer and the proposed replacement tax representative, as the Commissioners may require.

16—(1) The Commissioners may, with effect from a date or dates they specify, for good cause and by way of written notice served on the non-resident taxpayer—

(*a*) withdraw their approval of any person appointed as a tax representative for that non-resident taxpayer;

(*b*) require that non-resident taxpayer to replace any tax representative with a different tax representative; and

(*c*) oblige that non-resident taxpayer to request their approval for a person's appointment as a replacement tax representative.

(2) Regulations 14(5) and (6) shall apply for the purposes of this regulation in corresponding manner as they apply for the purposes of regulation 14(4).

17—(1) This regulation applies in a case where the Commissioners require the appointment of a tax representative under regulation 14(4)(*a*) and the non-resident taxpayer—

(*a*) becomes liable to a penalty under section 33(3) of the Act (penalty for failing in obligation to request the Commissioners' approval of tax representative), or

(*b*) unreasonably fails to obtain the Commissioners' approval in accordance with regulation 14(4)(*b*) (approval of tax representative).

(2) Where this regulation applies, the Commissioners may give a direction requiring a specified person to be treated as the appointed and approved tax representative of that non-resident taxpayer from a specified date.

(3) Accordingly, a person specified in a direction under paragraph (2) above shall be treated as the tax representative of the non-resident taxpayer from the specified date until such date as the Commissioners may specify in a further direction.

(4) The Commissioners may only specify a person under paragraph (2) above who—

(*a*) is eligible to act as a tax representative, and

(*b*) is suitable in all the circumstances to be the tax representative for the relevant non-resident taxpayer.

(5) The Commissioners may give a direction requiring a specified person to be treated as the appointed and approved tax representative of a non-resident taxpayer as a replacement for a person specified in a direction under paragraph (2) above.

(6) Paragraphs (3) and (4) above apply in relation to paragraph (5) above in corresponding manner as they apply to paragraph (2) above.

(7) Regulations 15 and 16 do not apply in relation to a person specified in a direction under this regulation.

18—(1) A person shall cease to be the tax representative for a non-resident taxpayer from the time when—

(*a*) the non-resident taxpayer ceases to be registered;

(*b*) the non-resident taxpayer replaces that person with a different tax representative under regulation 15 or 16;

(*c*) the Commissioners so direct under regulation 17;

(*d*) the person dies, becomes incapacitated or becomes subject to an insolvency procedure;

(*e*) the person ceases to be eligible to act as a tax representative;

(*f*) the person delivers to the Commissioners notification in writing that he withdraws as tax representative for the non-resident taxpayer; or

(*g*) the non-resident taxpayer delivers to the Commissioners notification in writing that he withdraws an appointment that they permitted but did not require.

(2) A person who is specified in a direction under regulation 17 shall not—

(*a*) cease to be (or be treated as) the tax representative except in accordance with that regulation; or

(*b*) be permitted to withdraw under paragraph (1)(*f*) above.

(3) The name of a tax representative (or a person treated as such) shall be registered against the name of the non-resident taxpayer of whom that person is (or is treated as) the representative (section 24(1) of the Act).

(4) That name shall be deleted from the register if the person ceases to be the tax representative for that non-resident taxpayer and the Commissioners consider it appropriate to do so.

19—(1) A tax representative (or a person treated as such) shall notify and provide full particulars to the Commissioners in writing about any of the following matters.

(2) Such notification must be delivered to the Commissioners no later than 30 days starting from the first day after the matter arises.

(3) The first matter is any change in the name, constitution or ownership of the tax representative's business, any change in the site details or any event that may require the register to be varied.

(4) The second matter is the tax representative lawfully ceasing to be the appointed tax representative of the relevant non-resident taxpayer.

(5) The third matter is the tax representative ceasing to be eligible to act as a tax representative.

20 In this Part "eligible to act as a tax representative" is to be construed with reference to section 33(1) of the Act which provides that a tax representative must be resident in the United Kingdom.

PART V
PENALTIES

21 A person who fails to comply with a requirement imposed on him by or under any of the following regulations shall be liable to a penalty of £250 for each such failure—

(*a*) regulation 2(1), 2(2), 2(3), 2(5), 2(6) or 2(7) (form, manner and timing of notification about registrability);

(*b*) regulation 4(1) or (5) (notification of changes in particulars);

(*c*) regulation 10 (notification of changes in relation to groups);

(*d*) regulation 14(2) or 14(3) (notification by non-resident taxpayer);

(*e*) regulation 19(1) or 19(2) (notification by tax representative).

PART VI
INTERPRETATION

22—(1) In these Regulations, except where the context requires otherwise—

"the Act" refers to sections 16 to 49 of and Schedules 4 to 10 to the Finance Act 2001 and any reference to a section of, a Schedule to or a paragraph of a Schedule to the Act refers to the appropriate section of, Schedule to or paragraph of a Schedule to that Act;

"Form AL 1", "Form AL 2" and "Form AL 1A" refer respectively to the forms numbered 1, 2 and 3 in the Schedule to these Regulations;

"levy" refers to aggregates levy;

"Part", "regulation" or "regulations" refers to the appropriate Part, regulation or regulations of these Regulations;

"partner" refers to a person carrying on a business in partnership with at least one other person;

"taxable activity" and "taxable activities" are to be construed in accordance with the provisions of section 24(3) and paragraph 8(2) of Schedule 4 to the Act.

(2) A reference in these Regulations to a form prescribed in the Schedule to these Regulations shall include a reference to a form which the Commissioners are satisfied is to like effect.

SCHEDULE

FORM 1

Application for Registration

HM Revenue & Customs

Aggregates Levy
Application for Registration

Completing this form

Before you complete this form please make sure that you read *AL1 Notes* to help you complete your Aggregates Levy Application for Registration.

You must also complete form *AL1A* with your site details.

Please use capital letters and write clearly in black ink. Please make sure that you complete all boxes. Failure to do so may result in delays processing your application.

1 If your business is registered for VAT please give your VAT registration number

2 What is the legal status of your business?

If your business is a partnership, you must complete and return form *AL2* as well as this form.

If your business is a trust, you must complete and return form *AL6* as well as this form. Form *AL1* should be completed by a trustee if the business is run by the trustees. If the business is run by the beneficiaries all beneficiaries should complete form *AL1*.

Sole Proprietor

Partnership

Local Authority

Non-profit making body/unincorporated body

Public Corporation

Trust

Corporate body (for example, Limited Company)

If corporate body, please give incorporation details

Certificate number

Date of incorporation *DD MM YYYY*

3 Are you applying for group registration as the representative member of an aggregates levy group?

No Yes

If yes, you must provide the additional information set out on forms *AL50* and *AL51*

4 Are you applying to be registered in divisions?

No Yes

If yes, you must provide the additional information set out in the Aggregates Levy Public Notice *AGL1*

5 Full name of business

6 Give the trading name of your business *if different from the name given at question 5*

7 Give the address of your principal place of business

Postcode

Phone number

Fax number

Mobile phone number

email address

Website address

8 Please give an alternative communication address, if appropriate.

Return forms and other correspondence are normally sent to the principal place of business, shown at question 7.

Exceptionally you may ask for all your returns and correspondence to be issued to a different address.

Name

Address

Postcode

Phone number

Fax number

email address

9 Please indicate, by ticking the relevant box(es), which aggregates activities your business(es) is involved in, indicating what percentage of your total sales each activity represents.

If you are applying as the representative member of an aggregates levy group please indicate the business activities of all group members.

	✓	%
Quarry extraction		
Sand/gravel extraction		
The importation of aggregate from outside the UK		
Use of a mobile crusher to commercially extract aggregates		

Other, please explain and show a percentage

10 Please give the date of your first commercial exploitation of aggregate.

If you are applying as the representative member of an aggregates levy group, please show the date or anticipated date of the first occasion aggregate will be subjected to commercial exploitation by any group member including the representative member.

DD MM YYYY

11 Estimate the tonnage of aggregate you will commercially exploit in the next 12 months (excluding exempt supplies)

If you are applying as the representative member of an aggregates levy group please give the estimated tonnage for all group members.

tonnes

12 Do you expect any of your commercial activity to be exempt from the levy or subject to relief?

If you are applying as the representative member of an aggregates levy group please give the estimated tonnage for all group members.

No Yes

If yes, estimate the tonnage of exempt, relieved or exported supplies you expect to make in the next 12 months

Exempt

tonnes

Relieved

tonnes

Export

tonnes

13 Please indicate the preferred stagger for your returns by ticking the appropriate box.

If you intend to apply for non-standard tax periods tick the box provided and tick the stagger period most closely matching your non-standard periods.

Stagger 0
Monthly Returns

Stagger 1
Quarters Ending Mar/Jun/Sept/Dec

Stagger 2
Quarters Ending Jan/Apr/Jul/Oct

Stagger 3
Quarters Ending Feb/May/Aug/Nov

Do you wish to apply for non-standard tax periods?

No Yes

14 Please give details of the bank or building society account that you use for the aggregates levy business.

If you have a Girobank Account give the sort code and account number for making payments into your account - shown on the front of your cheque book

Sort code

☐☐ – ☐☐ – ☐☐

Account number

☐☐☐☐☐☐☐☐☐☐☐

Girobank Account number

☐☐☐☐☐☐☐☐☐☐☐

Account title

15 Will you account for aggregates levy using a computerised system?

No ☐ Yes ☐

If yes, please give details

Accounting software

Version

16 Have you taken over a business registrable for aggregates levy as a going concern, or changed the legal entity that owns the business (for example, from a sole proprietor to a limited company)?

No ☐ Yes ☐

If yes, what date did the transfer take place?
DD MM YYYY

☐☐ ☐☐ ☐☐☐☐

Business name of previous owner

Aggregates Registration number of previous owner

☐☐☐☐☐ ☐☐☐☐

Do you want to keep this number? If yes, you and the previous owner must also complete and return form *AL68*. If you do keep the registration number, remember that you will become liable for the previous owner's aggregates levy debts.

No ☐ Yes ☐

17 Is your business involved in any other activities registered, approved or authorised by HM Revenue & Customs?

Please tick boxes as appropriate and give the registration number

Landfill Tax ☐

Registration number

Excise Duties ☐

Registration number

Imports or Exports ☐

Other ☐

Give details

18 Are there any other aggregates business(es) you are, or have been, involved in during the last 24 months?

Please give the Aggregates Levy Registration numbers of any businesses you are or have been involved in. If you are a partnership or a limited company this means any businesses in which partners or directors have been involved.

Continue on a separate sheet if necessary.

No ☐ Yes ☐

Aggregates Levy Registration numbers of other businesses

☐☐☐☐☐ ☐☐☐☐

☐☐☐☐☐ ☐☐☐☐

☐☐☐☐☐ ☐☐☐☐

☐☐☐☐☐ ☐☐☐☐

☐☐☐☐☐ ☐☐☐☐

☐☐☐☐☐ ☐☐☐☐

☐☐☐☐☐ ☐☐☐☐

Declaration

Please sign and date the declaration below. (For corporate bodies, a director or company secretary must sign the form.) Please tick the appropriate box.

Sole Proprietor ☐

Partner ☐

Company Secretary ☐

Director ☐

Beneficiary of a Trust ☐

Trustee ☐

Authorised Official ☐

I declare that the information given on this form and in any attached sheets is true and complete.

Name in full *use capital letters*

Signature

Date *DD MM YYYY*

For official use

Date of receipt

Registration number

EDR

Keyer's initials

Checker's initials

Please send this form to:
HM Revenue & Customs
Central Collection Unit (AL)
21 Victoria Avenue
Southend-on-Sea
Essex
SS99 1AA

Please remember that you must advise us if any of the information provided in this application changes.

Form 2
Partnership Details

Full name of partner

Home Address

Postcode

Home Telephone Number

Signature

Date (if you are registering for the first time give the date you completed this section. If you are changing your partnership details give the date you joined or left the partnership)

Joined partnership

Left partnership

Full name of partner

Home Address

Postcode

Home Telephone Number

Signature

Date (if you are registering for the first time give the date you completed this section. If you are changing your partnership details give the date you joined or left the partnership)

Joined partnership

Left partnership

Form 3
Site Details

❷ **complete with the site details**

Site ID, for official use only:

If you are changing your site details please indicate the reason by ticking the appropriate box — New site ☐ Amend existing site ☐ Site closed ☐ Date D D M M Y Y Y Y

Trading name of site

Business Name
(This should be the same as supplied on the AL 1 or AL 51)

Site Address

Postcode

Ordnance Survey grid reference

Telephone number

Fax number

E-Mail:

Is a weighbridge used to establish the weight of aggregate at this site? Yes ☐ No ☐

Please give the reason for site closure (if appropriate)

If you have taken over this site from another operator please give their business name and aggregates levy registration number here. Name — Registration number

❸ **Please sign and complete the declaration:**

Declaration,

I,

(*enter your full name in BLOCK LETTERS*)

declare that the information given on this form and contained in any accompanying document is true and complete.

Signature: Date: D D M M Y Y Y Y

Mr,Mrs, Miss, Ms

Sole proprietor ☐ Director ☐ Trustee ☐

Partner ☐ Company Secretary ☐ Authorised Official ☐

AL 1A Page 3 PT2 (05/03)

2001/4033

FINANCE ACT 2001, SECTION 24 AND SCHEDULE 4, (APPOINTED DAY) ORDER 2001

Made by the Treasury under FA 2001 s 24(10)

Made . . . .*19 December 2001*

1 This Order may be cited as the Finance Act 2001, section 24 and Schedule 4, (Appointed Day) Order 2001.

2 The date appointed as the day on which paragraphs 5 and 6 of Schedule 4 to the Finance Act 2001 come into force is 20th December 2001.

3 The date appointed as the day on which section 24 of and paragraphs 1, 2, 3, 4, 7 and 8 of Schedule 4 to the Finance Act 2001 come into force is 11th January 2002.

2002/761

AGGREGATES LEVY (GENERAL) REGULATIONS 2002

Made by the Commissioners of Customs and Excise under FA 2001 ss 17(6), 23, 25(1) and (2), 30, 31(3), 37, 38, 39, 45, Sch 6 paras 9(2), (3), Sch 7 para 2, Sch 8 paras 1, 9, 10 and 11, FA 1997 s 51, FA 1999 s 132

Made . . . . *21 March 2002*
Laid before the House of Commons . . . . *21 March 2002*
Coming into force . . . . *1 April 2002*

ARRANGEMENT OF REGULATIONS

PART I
PRELIMINARY

Citation and commencement

1 These Regulations may be cited as the Aggregates Levy (General) Regulations 2002 and come into force on 1st April 2002.

General interpretation

2 In these Regulations except where the context requires otherwise—

"the Act" refers to sections 16 to 49 of and Schedules 4 to 10 to the Finance Act 2001 and any reference to a section of, Schedule to or paragraph of a Schedule to the Act refers to the appropriate section of, Schedule to or paragraph of a Schedule to that Act;

"aggregate" has the meaning given in section 17(1) of the Act;

"AL" refers to aggregates levy;

"commercial exploitation" and "commercially exploited" are to be construed in accordance with section 19 of the Act;

"disposed of to landfill" is to be interpreted in accordance with sections 65 and 70(2) of the Finance Act 1996;

"exempt aggregate" means aggregate which is not taxable aggregate;

"exempt process" has the meaning given in section 18(2) of the Act;

"originating site" has the meaning given in section 20(1) of the Act;

"Part", "regulation" or "regulations" refers to the appropriate Part, regulation or regulations of these Regulations;

"published notice" refers to a notice published by the Commissioners and not withdrawn or replaced by a further notice;

"registrable person" refers to a person who is registered or required to be registered under section 24 of and Schedule 4 to the Act other than a person who is exempt from the requirement of registration under regulations made under section 24(4) of the Act;

"Schedule" refers to the Schedule to these Regulations;

"taxable aggregate" is to be construed in accordance with section 17 of the Act;

"working day" excludes Saturday, Sunday and any bank or public holiday.

PART II
WEIGHT OF AGGREGATE

Determination of the weight of aggregate

3—(1) Subject to regulation 4, the weight of any quantity of aggregate shall be determined by the use of a weighbridge at a site covered by section 19(2) of the Act.

(2) The terms and conditions attached to the use of a weighbridge shall be stipulated by the Commissioners in a published notice and shall include provisions relating to the records to be kept and the discounting of constituents (such as water).

(3) Where this regulation applies, the weight of any quantity of aggregate is to be determined at the time when it is first subjected to commercial exploitation.

4—(1) Where the use of a weighbridge is not practicable, the weight of any quantity of aggregate is to be determined in accordance with a method approved by the Commissioners ("approved method").

(2) Any such approval shall be in writing, shall be subject to such terms and conditions as the Commissioners may specify, including (but not limited to) the records to be kept, the time at which the weight of any quantity of aggregate is to be determined and the discounting of constituents (such as water).

(3) Where it appears to the Commissioners that an approved method is not being applied correctly or that it produces an inaccurate result, they may direct that it shall no longer have effect.

(4) In the absence of an approved method, the Commissioners may prescribe the method to be used.

(5) Any direction made or method prescribed under this regulation shall be in writing and shall take effect from a specified date.

PART III
ACCOUNTING, PAYMENT, RECORDS, TAX CREDITS, REPAYMENTS, SET-OFF, ETC

Accounting periods

5—(1) A registrable person shall be subject to accounting periods.

(2) In the case of a registered person, these shall be each three month period ending on the dates notified to him at any time by the Commissioners for this purpose.

(3) In the case of any other registrable person, these shall be each three month period ending on 31 March, 30 June, 30 September or 31 December.

(4) However, in such cases and subject to such conditions as may be stipulated by the Commissioners in a published notice, the Commissioners may vary the start, end and length of any accounting period.

Returns

6—(1) A registrable person is obliged to make a return to the Commissioners covering each of his accounting periods.
(2) The registrable person is obliged to make that return no later than the last working day of the month immediately following the end of the period to which it relates.
(3) In the case of an accounting period that does not end on the last day of a month, the registrable person is obliged to make that return no later than the due day directed by the Commissioners.
(4) The Commissioners may allow the registrable person extra time in which to make that return.
(5) The registrable person must make that return in a form that is prescribed by the Commissioners in a published notice ("prescribed form").
(6) Subject to his possession of an approved digital certificate, the registrable person may make that return in a prescribed form using an electronic version of the return.
(7) The registrable person must make that return by securing that it is delivered either to the address prescribed by the Commissioners in a published notice or to any other address that they may direct or allow.
(8) In this regulation—

"approved digital certificate" means a digital certificate which is accepted by the Commissioners as identifying a person for the purpose of their authorisation of his use of an electronic communication in respect of an assigned matter;
"assigned matter" has the meaning given in section 1(1) of the Customs and Excise Management Act 1979;
"delivered" is to be construed according to the context so as to cover delivery by post and by means of an electronic communication as appropriate;
"electronic communication" has the same meaning as in section 15(1) of the Electronic Communications Act 2000;
"electronic version" means the version which is submitted by means of an electronic communication.

Content of returns

7—(1) The registrable person must declare in the return the AL due from him for the relevant accounting period, taking into consideration—

(*a*) the AL due on the commercial exploitation of taxable aggregate—
(i) the time of which falls in that accounting period, and
(ii) for which he is liable to account; and,
(*b*) any authorised or required adjustment or any correction of errors (see regulations 15(4), 18(3), 28 and 29).

(2) The registrable person must provide in the return accurate information about every matter that the prescribed form requires.
(3) The registrable person must sign, date and declare on the document forming his return that the information provided in it is true and complete.
(4) The registrable person must comply with paragraphs (1), (2) and (3) above in the manner prescribed by the Commissioners in a published notice.
(5) In this regulation, "sign" is to be construed according to the context so as to cover signatures in writing and signatures in electronic form as appropriate.

Payment

8—(1) A registrable person must pay to the Commissioners the amount of AL due from him for a given accounting period no later than the due date for the return for that period (see regulations 6(2), 6(3) and 6(4)).
(2) The registrable person must make that payment by securing that it is delivered either to the address or bank account prescribed by the Commissioners in a published notice or to any other address or bank account that they may direct or allow.
(3) The Commissioners may allow a registrable person who has made arrangements with them for the payment of any amount of AL due from him by means of direct debit an extra 7 days in which the payment may be made.
(4) The Commissioners shall only act pursuant to paragraph (3) above in accordance with such conditions as they shall stipulate in a published notice.

Records

9—(1) A registrable person is obliged to keep a record to be known as the "aggregates levy account" (periodic summary of AL due).

(2) A registrable person who makes a claim under regulations 12 and 15(1) (tax credits in respect of bad debts) is obliged to keep a record to be known as the "aggregates levy bad debts account".
(3) A registrable person who makes a claim under regulations 13 and 15(1) (other tax credits) is obliged to keep a record to be known as the "aggregates levy tax credits account".
(4) A record within this regulation must be kept in the manner stipulated in a published notice.

10 A registrable person is obliged to keep the following records—
(*a*) his business and accounting records;
(*b*) his stock record;
(*c*) copies of all invoices issued by him;
(*d*) all invoices received by him;
(*e*) copies of all credit and debit notes or similar documents issued by him;
(*f*) all credit and debit notes or similar documents received by him;
(*g*) documentary evidence (including the workings and all relevant background documents) to explain and support any calculation of the weight of—
(i) taxable aggregate which has been subject to commercial exploitation; and
(ii) exempt aggregate;
(*h*) documentary evidence regarding the adjustment of an entry concerning the amount of AL for which he is liable to account;
(*i*) documentary evidence regarding any claim by him for a tax credit under regulation 12 (bad debts) including, as appropriate, evidence of insolvency or liquidation and, in each case, regarding any relevant surrounding circumstances;
(*j*) documentary evidence regarding any claim by him for a tax credit under regulation 13 (other tax credits) including, as appropriate, evidence of export and end use and, in each case, regarding any relevant surrounding circumstances;
(*k*) documentary evidence regarding amounts of aggregate which have been dumped or disposed of to landfill;
(*l*) a record of the information he relies on in making each return pursuant to regulation 7;
(*m*) any other record that may be directed by the Commissioners or stipulated in a published notice.

11—(1) Subject to paragraph (2) below, a registrable person is required to preserve any record required by regulation 9 or 10 for a period of six years.
(2) The Commissioners may direct that any such record need only be preserved for such lesser period as they specify.
(3) For the purposes of paragraph (1) above, a record within regulation 9 need only be preserved in relation to events taking place not more than six years earlier.

Bad debts: entitlement to tax credit

12—(1) Paragraph (3) below applies where—
(*a*) a person has commercially exploited taxable aggregate within the meaning of section 19(1)(*a*) or (*b*) of the Act ("relevant commercial exploitation") and has accounted for and paid the AL chargeable in respect of that relevant commercial exploitation;
(*b*) that person has made a charge to a third party ("the customer") in respect of that relevant commercial exploitation;
(*c*) that person and the customer are not connected;
(*d*) the whole or any part of the consideration which represents the charge for that relevant exploitation ("the consideration") has been written off in his accounts as a bad debt; and
(*e*) the customer has become insolvent or gone into liquidation.
(2) Any question whether a person is connected with another for the purposes of paragraph (1) above shall be determined in accordance with section 839 of the Income and Corporation Taxes Act 1988.
(3) Subject to paragraph (4) below, the person shall be entitled to a tax credit in respect of the amount of AL accounted for and paid by him in respect of the outstanding amount (subject to the provisions of this Part including those provisions relating to the making of a relevant claim to the Commissioners).
(4) Where the charge made for the relevant commercial exploitation in question is less than twice the amount of AL accounted for and paid by a person in respect of that relevant commercial exploitation, the amount of the tax credit which he can claim under paragraph (3) above shall be restricted to half the outstanding amount.
(5) In this regulation and regulation 18—
"claim" refers to a claim in accordance with regulation 15 or 16 and "claimant" shall be construed accordingly;
"the outstanding amount" refers to—

(*a*) if at the time of the claim no part of the consideration written off in the claimant's accounts as a bad debt has been received, an amount equal to the amount of the consideration so written off;

(*b*) if at that time any part of the consideration so written off has been received, an amount by which that part is exceeded by the amount of the consideration written off.

(6) In paragraph (5) above, "received" refers to receipt either by the claimant or by a person to whom a right to receive the whole or any part of the consideration written off has been assigned.

(7) Accordingly, subject to paragraph (4) above, the tax credit arising under this regulation shall be of an amount equal to such proportion of the AL accounted for and paid in respect of the relevant commercial exploitation as the outstanding amount forms of the total consideration.

(8) The whole or any part of the consideration shall be taken to have been written off as a bad debt when an entry is made in relation to that supply in the claimant's aggregates levy bad debts account (see regulation 9(2)).

(9) Where the claimant owes an amount of money to the customer which can be set off, the amount of the consideration written off in the accounts shall be reduced by the amount so owed.

(10) Where the claimant holds in relation to the customer an enforceable security, the amount of the consideration written off in the claimant's accounts shall be reduced by the value of that security.

(11) In paragraph (10) above, "security" refers to—

(*a*) in England, Wales or Northern Ireland, any mortgage, charge, lien or other security;

(*b*) in Scotland, any security (whether heritable or moveable), any floating charge and right of lien or preference and right of retention (other than a right of compensation or set-off).

Other tax credits: entitlement

13—(1) This regulation applies to a person who has commercially exploited taxable aggregate and who has accounted for the AL chargeable on that commercial exploitation.

(2) Such a person is entitled to a tax credit in respect of any AL accounted for in respect of that commercial exploitation where the taxable aggregate in question—

(*a*) is exported or removed from the United Kingdom without further processing;

(*b*) is used in an exempt process;

(*c*) is used in any of the industrial or agricultural processes listed in the Schedule;

(*d*) is disposed of (by dumping or otherwise) in any of the following ways:

(i) it is returned without further processing to its originating site or any site which is not its originating site but is registered under the same name;

(ii) it is disposed of to landfill;

(iii) it is gravel or sand and is used for beach restoration purposes at a site which is not its originating site.

(3) This regulation is subject to the provisions of this Part including those provisions relating to the making of a relevant claim to the Commissioners and the keeping of records including any records that are directed by the Commissioners or stipulated in a published notice.

(4) For the purposes of subsection (6) of section 17 of the Act, all the processes listed in the Schedule are prescribed for the purposes of that subsection.

Tax credits: general

14 A tax credit shall only arise under regulation 12 or 13 if a claim is made by a person so entitled acting in accordance with regulation 15 or 16, as the case requires.

15—(1) Subject to paragraph (6) below, a person shall claim any such tax credit by bringing it into account when he is accounting for AL due from him for any accounting period.

(2) Subject to paragraph (3) below, a person shall not be entitled to make such a claim unless he is in possession of the records required by paragraphs (*i*), (*j*) and (*k*) of regulation 10 as appropriate.

(3) In the case of a claim for a tax credit under regulation 13(2)(*a*) (export or removal from the United Kingdom), a person shall be entitled to make such a claim in accordance with paragraph (1) above despite the fact that he is not in possession of the records required by paragraph (*j*) of regulation 10 provided that he obtains such records within three months of his making such a claim. If not, he shall make the appropriate adjustment to cancel the tax credit claimed in his next AL return. Any further claim will be subject to paragraphs (1) and (2) above.

(4) Accordingly—

(*a*) the requirements of regulation 7 (content of returns), regulation 8 (payment) and regulation 9 (accounts) apply subject to paragraph (1) above; but

(*b*) paragraph (1) above applies subject to regulation 28 (corrections) and regulation 29 (corrections of errors not exceeding [£50,000][1]).

(5) A claim subject to paragraphs (1) to (4) above shall be regarded as a claim for repayment of AL for the purposes of section 32 of the Act (supplemental provisions about repayments, etc) (and see paragraph (7) below).

(6) Where the total tax credit claimed by a person exceeds the total of the AL due from him for the accounting period in question, the Commissioners shall repay to him an amount equal to the excess (but see regulations 30 and 31).

(7) Given the provision made by section 30(5) of the Act, this regulation has effect subject to section 32 of the Act (application of supplemental provisions about repayments: [4 year time limit][2], unjust enrichment etc).

Amendments—[1] Figure in para (4)(*b*) substituted for figure "£2,000" by the Value Added Tax, etc (Correction of Errors, etc) Regulations, SI 2008/1482 reg 7(1) with effect in relation to under-calculations or over-calculations respectively, in the Aggregates Levy (General) Regulations, SI 2002/761 reg 29(2), (3), which registrable persons first discover in their accounting periods that start on 1 July 2008 or later: SI 2008/1482 reg 7(3).

[2] Words in para (7) substituted for "three year time limit" by the Aggregates Levy (General) (Amendment) Regulations, SI 2010/642 regs 2, 3, with effect from 1 April 2010. However, this amendment to be disregarded for the purposes of FA 2001 s 32(1) where a claim is for the repayment of an amount paid to the Commissioners on or before 31 March 2007.

16—(1) Where the Commissioners have cancelled the registration of a person in accordance with paragraph 4 of Schedule 4 to the Act, and he is not a registrable person, the Commissioners shall repay to him the amount of any tax credit if they are satisfied that he has made a proper claim to them in writing for this purpose.

(2) A claim under paragraph (1) above may be combined with a claim under regulation 15(1) if appropriate.

(3) A person making a claim under paragraph (1) above must furnish to the Commissioners full particulars in relation to the tax credit claimed including (but not restricted to)—

(*a*) the return in which the relevant AL was accounted for;

(*b*) the amount of the AL in question and the date and manner of its payment to the Commissioners;

(*c*) the events by virtue of which the bad debt or other entitlement to a tax credit arose; and

(*d*) any supporting documentary or other evidence.

(4) Where the Commissioners are satisfied that a person who has made a claim in accordance with paragraphs (1) and (3) above is entitled to a tax credit and that he has not previously had the benefit of that credit, they shall repay to him an amount equal to the credit (but see regulations 30 and 31).

(5) The Commissioners shall not be liable to make any repayment under this regulation unless and until the person has made all the returns which he was required to make (and see regulations 30 and 31).

(6) Given the provision made by section 30(5) of the Act, this regulation has effect subject to section 32 of the Act (application of supplemental provisions about repayments: [4 year time limit][1], unjust enrichment etc).

Amendments—[1] Words in para (6) substituted for "three year time limit" by the Aggregates Levy (General) (Amendment) Regulations, SI 2010/642 regs 2, 3, with effect from 1 April 2010. However, this amendment to be disregarded for the purposes of FA 2001 s 32(1) where a claim is for the repayment of an amount paid to the Commissioners on or before 31 March 2007.

Bad debts and other tax credits: supplementary provisions

17—(1) Where—

(*a*) a claimant in relation to regulation 12 has engaged in a relevant commercial exploitation of taxable aggregate,

(*b*) there exist one or more other matters in respect of which the claimant is entitled to a debt owed by the customer (whether or not they involve further charges in respect of the relevant commercial exploitation of taxable aggregate), and

(*c*) a payment has been received by the claimant from or on behalf of the customer,

the payment shall be attributed to the relevant commercial exploitation in respect of which the claim is made under regulation 12 ("the appropriate commercial exploitation") and the other matters in accordance with the rules set out in paragraphs (3) and (5) below.

(2) The debts arising in respect of the relevant commercial exploitation and the other matters are collectively referred to as debts in paragraphs (3) to (5) below.

(3) The payment shall be attributed to the debt that arose earliest and, if not wholly attributable to that debt, to the other debts in the order of the dates on which they arose.

(4) Attribution under paragraph (3) above shall not be made to the extent that the payment was allocated to a debt by the customer at the time of payment.

(5) Where—

(*a*) the earliest debt and the other debts to which the whole of the payment could be attributed arose on the same day, or

(*b*) the debts to which the balance of the payment could be attributed in accordance with paragraph (3) above arose on the same day,

the payment shall be attributed to each remaining debt according to the proportion that the debt in question contributes to the total remaining debt.

18—(1) Where a person—

(*a*) has received the benefit of a tax credit provided for by regulation 12 (bad debts), and

(*b*) a payment—

(i) for the relevant commercial exploitation in question is subsequently received by him (or by a person to whom a right to receive the whole or any part of the consideration written off has been assigned), or

(ii) is attributed to that relevant commercial exploitation by virtue of regulation 17,

that tax credit shall be withdrawn with effect from the time when sub-paragraph (b)(i) or (b)(ii) above is satisfied, as the case requires.

(2) Where a person—

(*a*) has received the benefit of a tax credit provided for by regulation 13 (tax credits other than bad debts), and

(*b*) it subsequently transpires that any relevant requirement of this Part is not complied with,

that tax credit shall be withdrawn with effect from the time when he received that benefit.

(3) Where a tax credit is withdrawn under this regulation—

(*a*) the requirements of regulation 7 (content of returns), regulation 8 (payment) and regulation 9 (accounts) apply subject to this regulation; but

(*b*) this regulation applies subject to regulation 28 (corrections) and regulation 29 (corrections of errors not exceeding [£50,000][1]).

(4) Paragraph (3) above applies subject to paragraph 3 of Schedule 8 to the Act (assessment for excessive repayment).

Amendments—[1] Figure in para (3)(*b*) substituted for figure "£2,000" by the Value Added Tax, etc (Correction of Errors, etc) Regulations, SI 2008/1482 reg 7(1) with effect in relation to under-calculations or over-calculations respectively, in the Aggregates Levy (General) Regulations, SI 2002/761 reg 29(2), (3), which registrable persons first discover in their accounting periods that start on 1 July 2008 or later: SI 2008/1482 reg 7(3).

Form and manner of claim for repayment of overpaid AL

19 A claim under section 31 of the Act (claim for repayment of AL which was not AL due) shall be made in writing to the Commissioners and shall, by reference to such documentary evidence as is in the possession of the claimant, state the amount of the claim and the method by which that amount was calculated.

Tax credits and other repayments: unjust enrichment—reimbursement arrangements to be disregarded

20 In this regulation and in regulations 21 to 26—

"claim" refers to a claim made under section 31 of the Act (claim for repayment of AL which was not AL due);

"reimbursement arrangements" refers to any arrangements for the purposes of the claim which—

(*a*) are made by the claimant for the purpose of securing that he is not unjustly enriched by the repayment of any amount in pursuance of the claim; and

(*b*) provide for the reimbursement of persons (recipients) who have for practical purposes borne the whole or any part of the cost of the original payment of that amount to the Commissioners;

"relevant amount" refers to that part (which may be the whole) of the amount of the claim which the claimant has reimbursed or intends to reimburse to other persons (recipients).

21 For the purposes of section 32(2) of the Act (defence by the Commissioners that repayment by them of an amount claimed would unjustly enrich the claimant) reimbursement arrangements made by a claimant shall be disregarded except where they—

(*a*) include the provisions described in regulation 22, and

(*b*) are supported by the undertakings described in regulation 26.

22 The provisions referred to in regulation 21(*a*) are that—

(*a*) reimbursement for which the arrangements provide will be completed by no later than 90 days after the repayment to which it relates;

(*b*) no deduction will be made from the relevant amount by way of fee or charge (however expressed or effected);

(*c*) reimbursement will be made only in cash or by cheque;

(*d*) any part of the relevant amount that is not reimbursed by the time mentioned in paragraph (*a*) above will be repaid by the claimant to the Commissioners;

(*e*) any interest paid by the Commissioners on any relevant amount repaid by them will also be treated by the claimant in the same way as the relevant amount falls to be treated under paragraphs (*a*) and (*b*) above; and (*f*) the records described in regulation 24 will be kept by the claimant and produced by him to the Commissioners in accordance with regulation 25.

23 The claimant shall, without prior demand, make any repayment to the Commissioners that he is required to make by virtue of regulation 22(*d*) or 22(*e*) within 14 days of the expiry of the period of 90 days referred to in regulation 22(*a*).

24 The claimant shall keep records of the following matters—

(*a*) the names and addresses of those persons (recipients) whom he has reimbursed or whom he intends to reimburse;

(*b*) the total amount reimbursed to each such person (recipient);

(*c*) the amount of interest included in each total amount reimbursed to each person (recipient);

(*d*) the date that each reimbursement is made.

25—(1) Where a claimant is given notice in accordance with paragraph (2) below he shall, in accordance with such notice, produce to the Commissioners the records that he is required to keep pursuant to regulation 24.

(2) A notice given for the purposes of paragraph (1) above shall—

(*a*) be in writing;

(*b*) state the date on which and the place and time at which the records are to be produced; and

(*c*) be signed and dated by the Commissioners.

(3) Such a notice may be given before or after, or before and after, the Commissioners have paid the relevant amount to the claimant.

26—(1) The undertakings referred to in regulation 21(*b*) shall be given to the Commissioners by the claimant no later than the time at which he makes the claim for which the reimbursement arrangements have been made.

(2) The undertakings shall be in writing and shall be signed and dated by the claimant.

(3) The undertakings shall be to the effect that—

(*a*) at the date of the undertakings he is able to identify the names and addresses of those persons (recipients) whom he has reimbursed or whom he intends to reimburse;

(*b*) he will apply the whole of the relevant amount repaid to him (without any deduction by way of fee, charge or otherwise) to the reimbursement in cash or by cheque of such persons (recipients) no later than 90 days after he receives that amount (unless he has properly reimbursed them already);

(*c*) he will apply any interest paid to him on the relevant amount repaid to him wholly to the reimbursement of such persons (recipients) no later than 90 days after he receives that interest;

(*d*) he will repay to the Commissioners without demand the whole or such part of the relevant amount repaid to him or of any interest paid to him as he fails to apply in accordance with the undertakings mentioned in sub-paragraph (*b*) or (*c*) above;

(*e*) he will keep the records described in regulation 24; and

(*f*) he will comply with any notice given to him in accordance with regulation 25 concerning the production of such records.

Correction of errors in AL returns

27 A registrable person—

(*a*) shall only be taken as providing full information in the prescribed or specified form and manner for the purposes of paragraph 9(3) of Schedule 6 to the Act (disclosure about inaccurate AL return),

(*b*) with respect to any inaccuracy to which paragraph 9(1)(*a*) of Schedule 6 to the Act applies (civil penalty for misdeclaration or neglect in relation to inaccurate return),

if he delivers that information in writing to the Commissioners, or acts in accordance with regulation 29, at a time to which paragraph 9(3)(*a*) of Schedule 6 to the Act applies (no reason to believe enquiries being made into his AL affairs).

28—(1) A registrable person shall correct any error made by him in accounting for AL or in connection with his AL account and, as appropriate, make any adjustment required by regulation 7(1)(*b*) (adjustment of AL returns).

(2) That correction or adjustment shall be made within such time and by means of such payment, financial adjustment, entry in accounts or other method as the Commissioners may require.

(3) This regulation has effect subject to, as the case requires—

(*a*) the time limit applying to regulations 15(1), 18(1) and 18(2) (tax credits) (see regulations 15(7) and 18(4)—amounts paid more than [4 years][1] before claim made and assessment subject to time limit in paragraph 5 of Schedule 8 to the Act);

(*b*) a time limit of [4 years][1] after the end of the accounting period in relation to which the error was made or the adjustment became required; or

(*c*) any time limit for an assessment in relation to the error (see paragraphs 2(1), 2(2)(*d*), 3 and 4 of Schedule 5 to the Act).

Amendments—[1] Words in para (3) substituted for "three years" by the Aggregates Levy (General) (Amendment) Regulations, SI 2010/642 regs 2, 4, with effect from 1 April 2010. However, this amendment to be disregarded for the purposes of FA 2001 s 32(1) where a claim is for the repayment of an amount paid to the Commissioners on or before 31 March 2007.

29—(1) This regulation applies by way of an exception to regulation 28 but only in relation to errors.

(2) Where a registrable person discovers that any return or returns which he has previously made is or are based on an under-calculation, he must correct the error or errors by adding the appropriate amount to the AL due for the accounting period in which the discovery is made under regulation 7(1)(*b*).

(3) Where a registrable person discovers that any return or returns which he has previously made is or are based on an over-calculation, he must correct the error or errors by deducting the appropriate amount from the AL due for the accounting period in which the discovery is made under regulation 7(1)(*b*).

(4) For the purposes of paragraphs (2) and (3) above—

"under-calculation" refers to the total amount of AL due in accordance with regulation 7(1) in the accounting period or periods to which the previous return or returns related which was not properly taken into consideration for that period or those periods as appropriate ("understated AL");

"over-calculation" refers to the total amount that was wrongly taken as AL due in accordance with regulation 7(1) in the accounting period or periods to which the previous return or returns related and which was wrongly taken into consideration for that period or those periods as appropriate ("overstated AL").

(5) For the purposes of paragraph (4) above—

(*a*) in reckoning the total amount constituting the under-calculation, an allowance must be made for any overstated AL;

(*b*) in reckoning the total amount constituting the over-calculation, an allowance must be made for any understated AL.

(6) In any case, the total net amount of any under-calculation or over-calculation corrected under this regulation shall not exceed [£50,000][1].

[But if the registrable person's VAT turnover is small, this total must not for these purposes exceed 1% of that turnover unless the total is [£10,000 or less][3].

And if that person is not registered for VAT, the total net amount must not for these purposes exceed £10,000.][1]

[The VAT turnover is small only if Box 6 of that person's value added tax return for the prescribed accounting period in which the discovery is made must contain a total less than £5,000,000 (total value of sales and all other outputs excluding any value added tax).][2]

(7) A registrable person making a correction under paragraph (2) or (3) above shall make proper allowance for that correction for the purposes of complying with regulation 9(1) (AL account) or 9(3) (AL tax credits account) as appropriate.

(8) Where an error in a return has to any extent been corrected under this regulation—

(*a*) that return shall be regarded as having been corrected to that extent, and

(*b*) the registrable person shall to that extent be taken to have provided full information with respect to the inaccuracy in the prescribed form and manner for the purposes of paragraph 9(3) of Schedule 6 to the Act (disclosure about inaccurate AL return).

(9) A person shall not correct an error in a return (where that error is the result of an under-calculation or over-calculation) except in accordance with this regulation.

(10) This regulation has effect subject to, as the case requires—

(*a*) any requirement of the Commissioners under regulation 28(2), and

(*b*) any applicable time limit specified in regulation 28(3).

Amendments—[1] In para (6), figure substituted for figure "£2,000", and final two sentences inserted, by the Value Added Tax, etc (Correction of Errors, etc) Regulations, SI 2008/1482 reg 7(1), (2) with effect in relation to under-calculations or over-calculations respectively, in the Aggregates Levy (General) Regulations, SI 2002/761 reg 29(2), (3), which registrable persons first discover in their accounting periods that start on 1 July 2008 or later: SI 2008/1482 reg 7(3).

[2] In para (6), words inserted by the Value Added Tax, etc (Correction of Errors, etc) Regulations, SI 2008/1482 reg 8(1) with effect in relation to under-calculations or over-calculations respectively, in the Aggregates Levy (General) Regulations, SI 2002/761 reg 29(2), (3), which registrable persons first discover in their accounting periods that start on 1 July 2008 or later: SI 2008/1482 reg 7(3).

[3] In para (6), words substituted for words "less than £10,000" by the Amusement Machine Licence Duty, etc (Amendments) Regulations, SI 2008/2693 reg 4(1)(*d*) with effect for a discovery first made on 1 November 2008 or later.

Set-off

30—(1) This regulation applies where—

(*a*) a person is under a duty to pay to the Commissioners at any time an amount or amounts in respect of AL; and

(*b*) the Commissioners are under a duty to pay to that person at the same time an amount or amounts in respect of any AL (or other tax or duty) under their care and management.

(2) Where the total of the amount or amounts mentioned in paragraph (1)(*a*) above exceeds the total of the amount or amounts mentioned in paragraph (1)(*b*) above, the latter shall be set off against the former.

(3) Where the total of the amount or amounts mentioned in paragraph (1)(*b*) above exceeds the total of the amount or amounts mentioned in paragraph (1)(*a*) above, the Commissioners may set off the latter in paying the former.

(4) Where the total of the amount or amounts mentioned in paragraph (1)(*a*) above is the same as the total of the amount or amounts mentioned in paragraph (1)(*b*) above, no payment need be made in respect of either.

(5) Where this regulation applies and an amount has been set off in accordance with any of paragraphs (2) to (4) above, the duty of both the person in question and the Commissioners to pay the amount concerned shall be treated as having been discharged accordingly.

31—(1) This regulation applies where—

(*a*) a person is under a duty to pay to the Commissioners at any time an amount or amounts in respect of any tax or duty (other than AL) under their care and management; and

(*b*) the Commissioners are under a duty, at the same time, to make a payment or repayment to that person of an amount or amounts of or in respect of AL.

(2) Where the total of the amount or amounts mentioned in paragraph (1)(*a*) above exceeds the total of the amount or amounts mentioned in paragraph (1)(*b*) above, the latter shall be set off against the former.

(3) Where the total of the amount or amounts mentioned in paragraph (1)(*b*) above exceeds the total of the amount or amounts mentioned in paragraph (1)(*a*) above, the Commissioners may set off the latter in paying the former.

(4) Where the total of the amount or amounts mentioned in paragraph (1)(*a*) above is the same as the total of the amount or amounts mentioned in paragraph (1)(*b*) above, no payment need be made in respect of either.

(5) Where this regulation applies and an amount has been set off in accordance with any of paragraphs (2) to (4) above, the duty of both the person in question and the Commissioners to pay the amount concerned shall be treated as having been discharged accordingly.

32—(1) Neither regulation 30 or 31 shall require any such amount as is mentioned in paragraph (1)(*b*) of either regulation ("the credit") to be set off against any item mentioned in paragraph (1)(*a*) of either regulation ("the debit") where—

(*a*) an insolvency procedure has been applied to the person entitled to the credit;

(*b*) the credit became due after that procedure was applied; and

(*c*) the liability to pay the debt either arose before that procedure was so applied or (having arisen afterwards) relates to, or to matters occurring in the course of, the carrying on of any business relevant for AL purposes at times before the procedure was so applied.

(2) An insolvency procedure is applied to a person for the purposes of this regulation in the circumstances described by sub-paragraphs (2) to (5) of paragraph 11 of Schedule 8 to the Act (insolvency procedures for the purposes of this regulation).

33 A reference in regulation 30 or 31 to an amount in respect of tax or duty includes a reference to an amount of any related penalty, surcharge or interest that may be recovered as if it was an amount of tax or duty.

PART IV
DEATH, INCAPACITY, INSOLVENCY, TRANSFERS

Individuals: death or incapacity

34—(1) The Commissioners may, for AL purposes and subject to this regulation, treat a person who carries on relevant activities on behalf of an individual who has died or become temporarily incapacitated as if they were the same person.

(2) Such treatment may continue pending someone other than that individual being registered under section 24 of and Schedule 4 to the Act in relation to those activities or the incapacity ceasing.

(3) A person who carries on relevant activities in the circumstances described in paragraph (1) above must notify the Commissioners of this in writing and that notification must also include the date of death or the date and nature of the incapacity.

(4) This notification must be delivered to the Commissioners within 21 days starting with the day after the person begins carrying on the relevant activities.

(5) In this regulation, "relevant activities" refers to any activities in relation to which the individual in question is or was a registrable person.

Insolvency

35—(1) The Commissioners may, for AL purposes and subject to this regulation, treat a person who carries on relevant activities of a registrable person to whom an insolvency procedure is applied as if they were the same person.

(2) Such treatment may continue pending someone other than that registrable person being registered under section 24 of and Schedule 4 to the Act in relation to those activities or the insolvency procedure no longer being applied.

(3) A person who carries on relevant activities in the circumstances described in paragraph (1) above must notify the Commissioners of this in writing and that notification must also include the date when the insolvency procedure was first applied.

(4) This notification must be delivered to the Commissioners within 21 days starting with the day after the person begins carrying on the relevant activities.

(5) In this regulation—

"relevant activities" refers to any activities in relation to which the individual in question is or was a registrable person;

"registrable person" may include, as appropriate, the estate of a deceased individual.

(6) An insolvency procedure is applied to a person for the purposes of this regulation in the circumstances described by sub-sections (7) to (9) of section 37 of the Act (insolvency procedures for the purposes of this regulation).

Representatives: death, incapacity or insolvency

36—(1) If the Commissioners so require, a representative who controls the assets of a registrable person because of death, incapacity or the application of an insolvency procedure shall, for the purposes of AL and subject to this regulation, be treated as if he was the registrable person.

(2) Any requirement resulting from paragraph (1) above for the representative to pay AL shall only apply to the extent of the assets he controls.

(3) Any other requirement resulting from paragraph (1) above shall apply in the same way as it would have applied to the registrable person but for the death, incapacity or insolvency procedure.

(4) In this regulation "registrable person" may include, as appropriate, the estate of a deceased individual.

(5) An insolvency procedure is applied to a person for the purposes of this regulation in the circumstances described by sub-sections (7) to (9) of section 37 of the Act (insolvency procedures for the purposes of this regulation).

Transfers of going concerns

37—(1) Where—

(*a*) a business carried on by a person who is registered under section 24 of and Schedule 4 to the Act is transferred to another person as a going concern,

(*b*) the registration of the transferor has not been cancelled,

(*c*) the transfer requires that the transferor's registration be cancelled and that the transferee either be registered for AL or notify the Commissioners that he is registrable for AL, and

(*d*) a written application for this purpose is made to the Commissioners by the transferor and transferee,

the Commissioners may, with effect from the date of the transfer, cancel the registration of the transferor and register the transferee in his place with the registration number previously allocated to the transferor.

(2) Should the Commissioners cancel the registration of the transferor and register the transferee in his place under paragraph (1) above then, in order to secure continuity in the application of the Act—

(*a*) any liability of the transferor existing at the date of the transfer to make a return or account for or pay AL shall become the liability of the transferee;

(*b*) any entitlement of the transferor, whether or not existing at the date of the transfer, to a tax credit or repayment under the Act or Part III of these Regulations shall become the entitlement of the transferee;

(*c*) any other provision by or under the Act relating to AL that applied to the transferor before his registration was cancelled (or any such provision that continues to apply to the transferor after that cancellation) shall apply to the transferee; and

(*d*) any circumstances relating to the application of the Act (or any provision made under the Act) to the AL affairs of the transferor before his registration was cancelled (or any such circumstances that continue to apply to the transferor after that cancellation) shall apply to the transferee.

(3) In addition to the provisions set out in paragraph (2) above, where—

(*a*) the Commissioners cancel the registration of the transferor and register the transferee in his place under paragraph (1) above with effect from a date earlier than the accounting period in which they do so, and (*b*) either the transferor or the transferee has, in relation to any time on or after that date but before the start of that accounting period—

(i) made a return,

(ii) accounted for AL, or

(iii) claimed a relevant tax credit,

the matters referred to in sub-paragraphs (b)(i) to (b)(iii) above shall be treated as having been done by the transferee.

PART V
PENALTIES

38—(1) A person who fails to comply with a requirement imposed on him by or under any of the following provisions of these Regulations shall be liable to a penalty of £250 for each such failure—

(*a*) regulation 7(1), 7(2), 7(3) or 7(4);

(*b*) regulation 8(2);

(*c*) regulation 9(1), 9(2), 9(3) or 9(4);

(*d*) regulation 10;

(*e*) regulation 28(1) or 28(2);

(*f*) regulation 29(7) or 29(9);

(*g*) regulation 34(3) or 34(4);

(*h*) regulation 35(3) or 35(4).

(2) A specific act or omission shall attract only one such penalty if the circumstances are such that, but for this paragraph, it would attract more than one penalty.

PART VI
CONSEQUENTIAL AMENDMENTS

39 (*amends the Distress for Customs and Excise Duties and Other Indirect Taxes Regulations, SI 1997/1431*).

SCHEDULE
INDUSTRIAL AND AGRICULTURAL PROCESSES

Regulation 13

A Industrial processes

Code	*Description*
001	Iron, steel and non-ferrous metal manufacture and smelting processing including foundry processes, investment casting, sinter plants and wire drawing.
002	Alloying.
003	Emission abatement for air, land and water.
004	[Drinking water, air and oil][1] filtration and purification.
005	Sewage treatment.
006	Production of energy.
007	Ceramic processes.
008	Refractory processes.
009	Manufacture of glass and glass products.
010	Manufacture of fibre glass.
011	Manufacture of man-made fibres.
012	[Production and processing of food and drink][1] eg sugar refining, production of gelatin.
013	Manufacture of plastics, rubber and PVC.
014	Chemical manufacturing eg soda ash, sea water magnesia, alumina.
015	Manufacture of precipitated calcium carbonate.
016	Manufacture of pharmaceuticals, bleaches, toiletries and detergents.
017	Aerating processes.
018	Manufacture of fillers for coating, sealants, adhesives, paints, grouts, mastics, putties and other binding or modifying media.
019	Manufacture of pigments, varnishes and inks.

Aggregates Levy

020	Production of [growing media and][1] line markings for sports pitches [and other leisure facilities][1].
021	Incineration.
022	Manufacture of desiccant.
023	Manufacture of carpet backing, underlay and foam.
024	Resin processes.
025	Manufacture of lubricant additives.
026	Leather tanning.
027	Paper manufacture.
028	Production of art materials.
029	Production of play sand eg for children's sand pits.
030	Clay pigeon manufacture.
031	Abrasive processes: specialist sand blasting, iron free grinding (pebble mills) and sandpaper manufacture.
032	Use as [a propping agent][1] in oil exploration eg fracture sands and drilling fluids.
033	Flue gas desulphurisation and flue gas scrubbing.
034	Manufacture of mine suppressant.
035	Manufacture of fire extinguishers.
036	Manufacture of materials used for fireproofing.
037	Acid neutralisation.
038	Manufacture of friction materials eg automotive.

B Agricultural processes

Code	*Description*
039	Manufacture of additives to soil [eg agricultural lime][1].
040	Manufacture of animal feeds.
041	Production of animal bedding material.
042	Production of fertiliser.
043	Manufacture of pesticides and herbicides.
044	Production of growing media[, including compost, for agricultural and horticultural use only][1].
045	Soil treatment, including mineral enrichment and reduction of acidity.

Press releases etc—C&E Business Brief 29/02 14-11-02 (changes to industrial and agricultural reliefs).

Amendments—[1] Words in Codes 004, 012, 032 substituted, and words in Codes 020, 039 and 044 inserted, by the Aggregates Levy (General) (Amendment) Regulations, SI 2003/466 with effect from 1 April 2003.

2004/1959

AGGREGATES LEVY (NORTHERN IRELAND TAX CREDIT) REGULATIONS 2004

Made . . . .*23 July 2004*
Laid before the House of Commons . . . .*26 July 2004*
Coming into force . . . .*1 September 2004*

The Commissioners of Customs and Excise, in exercise of the powers conferred upon them by sections 17(6), 30A and 45 of, and paragraph 2 of Schedule 7 to, the Finance Act 2001 and of all other powers enabling them in that behalf, hereby make the following Regulations:

1 These Regulations may be cited as the Aggregates Levy (Northern Ireland Tax Credit) Regulations 2004 and come into force on 1st September 2004.

2 In these Regulations—

"the Act" refers to sections 16 to 49 of, and Schedules 4 to 10 to, the Finance Act 2001;
"aggregates levy credit agreement" has the meaning given in regulation 7;
"aggregates levy credit certificate" has the meaning given in regulation 5;

"AL" refers to aggregates levy;

"the AL General Regulations" means The Aggregates Levy (General) Regulations 2002;

"commercial exploitation" and "commercially exploited" are to be construed in accordance with section 19 of the Act;

"published notice" refers to a notice published by the Commissioners and not withdrawn or replaced by a further notice;

"registered site" has the meaning given in section 24 of the Act;

"regulation" refers to the appropriate regulation of these Regulations;

"site operator" is to be construed in accordance with section 21 of the Act;

"taxable aggregate" is to be construed in accordance with section 17 of the Act;

"United Kingdom" means Great Britain and Northern Ireland.

3—(1) This regulation applies to an eligible person within the meaning of paragraph (6) below who on or after 1st April 2004 and before 1st April 2011 has commercially exploited within Northern Ireland taxable aggregate which has been extracted from a registered site in Northern Ireland and has accounted for the AL chargeable on that commercial exploitation.

(2) Subject to regulation 4, such a person is entitled to a tax credit as prescribed at paragraph (3) below in respect of any AL accounted for in respect of that commercial exploitation.

(3) The amount of any tax credit to which a person is entitled under this regulation is fixed at 80% of the AL due on the aggregate in question.

(4) This regulation supplements the provisions of Part III of the AL General Regulations (accounting, payment, records, tax credits, repayments, set-off etc).

(5) The tax credit prescribed by this regulation is prescribed for the purposes of subsection (6) of section 17 of the Act.

(6) In this regulation, an "eligible person" is a person who—

(*a*) is registered for AL under section 24 of, and Schedule 4 to, the Act in relation to a registered site situated in Northern Ireland;

(*b*) has entered into an aggregates levy credit agreement with the Commissioners in respect of any of the registered sites of which he is the site operator; and

(*c*) is in possession of an aggregates levy credit certificate issued to him by the Commissioners which relates to the registered site from which the aggregate in respect of which the claim is made was extracted, covers the period of that claim and has not been withdrawn.

4—(1) Regulation 3(2) shall not apply where any aggregate in respect of which a claim for a tax credit might otherwise be made under regulation 3 is or is to be transferred from Northern Ireland to another part of the United Kingdom in any form.

(2) However, regulation 3(2) shall apply where the claimant can demonstrate to the satisfaction of the Commissioners that such a transfer is only the first stage of an onward export of that aggregate without further processing from the United Kingdom.

5—(1) In these Regulations, an "aggregates levy credit certificate" is a certificate which—

(*a*) relates to a single specified registered site in Northern Ireland;

(*b*) is issued by the Commissioners to a site operator as evidence of the existence of an aggregates levy credit agreement between the Commissioners and that site operator in respect of that registered site and of the site operator's continued compliance with the terms of that agreement; and

(*c*) is not transferable.

(2) The Commissioners may make further provision as to the form and content of an aggregates levy credit certificate in a published notice.

6—(1) An aggregates levy credit certificate may be withdrawn by the Commissioners at any time if the site operator to whom it has been issued fails to comply with any of the terms of the related aggregates levy credit agreement which he has entered into in respect of the same registered site.

(2) The withdrawal of an aggregates levy credit certificate must be notified to the site operator in writing and will take effect from the date of such notification or such later date as it may specify.

7—(1) In these Regulations an "aggregates levy credit agreement" is an agreement between a site operator in Northern Ireland and the Commissioners which relates to a specified registered site and is evidence that the site operator has agreed to comply with the Code of Practice for the Aggregates Industry in Northern Ireland (an environmental improvement scheme for quarrying) and to be monitored in respect of such compliance.

(2) An aggregates levy credit agreement shall set out the obligations of the site operator in relation to the commissioning of environmental audits and the meeting of specified targets for improvements in environmental practice for the registered site to which it relates within specified time limits.

(3) The Commissioners may make further provision as to the form and content of an aggregates levy credit agreement in a published notice.

8 Where a person is eligible to claim a tax credit under regulation 3 or a tax credit under section 30(1)(a) of the Act (export in the form of aggregate), he is entitled to make only one such claim in respect of any quantity of aggregate.

9 A person who makes a claim under these Regulations is obliged to keep the following records in addition to those required under Part III of the AL General Regulations:
(*a*) a record to be known as the "aggregates levy Northern Ireland tax credit account";
(*b*) the relevant aggregates levy credit certificate;
(*c*) documentary evidence regarding any claim by him for a tax credit under regulation 3; and
(*d*) documentary evidence relating to environmental audits and improvement works.

10—(1) A tax credit shall only arise under regulation 3 if a claim is made by a person so entitled acting in accordance with regulation 15 or 16 of the AL General Regulations as the case requires.
(2) A person shall not be entitled to make such a claim unless he is in possession of the records required by regulation 9.

11 A person who fails to comply with any requirement imposed on him by regulation 9 shall be liable to a penalty of £250.

12 The Aggregates Levy (Northern Ireland Tax Credit) Regulations 2002 are revoked.

2010/867

FINANCE ACT 2009, SCHEDULE 51 (TIME LIMITS FOR ASSESSMENTS, CLAIMS, ETC) (APPOINTED DAYS AND TRANSITIONAL PROVISIONS) ORDER 2010

Made . . . . *18 March 2010*

The Treasury make the following Order in exercise of the powers conferred by sections 99(2) and 99(3) of the Finance Act 2009.

PART 1
APPOINTED DAYS AND PRELIMINARY PROVISIONS

1 Citation and interpretation

(1) This Order may be cited as the Finance Act 2009, Schedule 51 (Time Limits for Assessments, Claims, etc) (Appointed Days and Transitional Provisions) Order 2010.
(2) In this Order a reference to a paragraph (without more) is a reference to that paragraph of Schedule 51 to the Finance Act 2009.
(3) In this Order—
"The Commissioners" means the Commissioners for Her Majesty's Revenue and Customs;
"FA", followed by a year, means the Finance Act of that year.
"IHTA 1984" means the Inheritance Tax Act 1984;

2 Appointed days

(1) The day appointed as the day on which the amendments made by paragraphs 1 to 4 and 27 to 43 (insurance premium tax, aggregates levy, climate change levy, landfill tax and minor and consequential provision) come into force is 1st April 2010.
(2) The day appointed as the day on which the amendments made by paragraphs 5 to 26 (inheritance tax, stamp duty land tax and petroleum revenue tax) come into force is 1st April 2011.

PART 2
TRANSITIONAL PROVISION

3–7 (not relevant to aggregates levy)

8 Aggregates levy: claims

The amendment made by paragraph 28 is disregarded where, for the purposes of section 32(1) of FA 2001 (repayments of overpaid aggregates levy), a claim is for the repayment of an amount paid to the Commissioners on or before 31st March 2007.

9 The amendment made by paragraph 30 is disregarded where claims made under paragraph 2 of Schedule 8 to FA 2001 (interest payable by the Commissioners) are for the repayment of amounts relating to an applicable period which ends on or before 31st March 2007.

10 Aggregates levy: assessments

The amendment made by paragraph 29(2) is disregarded where, for the purposes of paragraph 4(1)(*b*) of Schedule 5 to FA 2001 (time limits for assessments), the end of the accounting period was on or before 31st March 2007.

11

The amendments made by paragraph 29(3) are disregarded where, for the purposes of paragraph 4(3) of Schedule 5 to FA 2001 (time limits for assessments), the end of the accounting period to which the assessment relates was on or before 31st March 2007.

12 The amendments made by paragraph 29(4) are disregarded where, for the purposes of paragraph 4(4) of Schedule 5 to FA 2001 (time limits for assessments), the death was on or before 31st March 2007.

13 The amendment made by paragraph 31(2) is disregarded where, for the purposes of paragraph 4(1) of Schedule 10 to FA 2001 (time limits on penalty assessments), the conduct to which the penalty relates occurred on or before 31st March 2007.

14 The amendments made by paragraph 31(3) are disregarded where, for the purposes of paragraph 4(2) of Schedule 10 to FA 2001 (time limits on penalty assessments), the conduct to which the penalty relates occurred on or before 31st March 2007.

15 The amendments made by paragraph 31(4) are disregarded where, for the purposes of paragraph 4(3) of Schedule 10 to FA 2001 (time limits on penalty assessments), the death was on or before 31st March 2007.

16–28(not relevant to aggregates levy)

Aggregates Levy
Press releases

Contents

Press releases, etc

CHANGES TO PRIMARY LEGISLATION

28 November 2001. *Business Brief 17/01*

The aggregates levy, a new tax on the commercial exploitation of aggregate in the UK, will come into effect on 1 April 2002. As a result of consultation with industry, and in addition to the changes announced in the pre-Budget report, the Government intends to make a number of technical changes to the aggregates levy provisions contained within FA 2001, subject to Parliamentary approval. These technical changes are detailed below.

The first draft of the secondary legislation for the levy will shortly be released for comment.

(I) UNCRUSHED ROCK

The current legislation exempts aggregate that has not been subjected to an industrial crushing process. However, it is now recognised that aggregate is sometimes produced without being crushed.

Given that the environmental effects of aggregate extraction are the same, regardless of whether that aggregate is crushed or not, the legislation will be amended to bring uncrushed rock within the scope of the levy. However, the current exemption for the production of dimension stone will still apply and will be amended to clarify that it also applies to building stone.

(II) TECHNICAL AMENDMENTS

(a) Aggregate, which is removed from its originating site before the commencement date

Currently, aggregate which is removed from its originating site before the commencement date will not be subject to the levy. However an amendment will be made to ensure that the levy cannot be avoided merely by removing aggregate from its originating site to a different site within the same registration before 1 April 2002.

(b) Aggregate necessarily arising from a road construction project

Aggregate, which is necessarily arising from the line of the road in a road construction project, will be exempt from the levy. However, the inclusion of the words "wholly or mainly" in s 17(3)(*d*)(ii) of the law could be interpreted as meaning that the exemption might still apply even if some of the extraction taking place was to obtain aggregate, rather than the aggregate being only a necessary by- product of this non-quarrying activity. It is therefore planned to amend the law to clarify the original policy intention and ensure that the exemption only applies to aggregate necessarily arising from within the line of the road in a road building project.

(c) Lime and cement manufacture

The current exemption for lime and cement manufacture in s 18(2)(*c*) will be amended to make clear that all inputs into lime or cement manufacture will be exempt, not just the limestone.

(d) Treatment of calcite

It is proposed that calcite is removed from the list of exempt relevant substances at s 18(3)(*d*) to ensure a level playing field between the markets for calcite and calcium carbonate, while at the same time removing the potential assurance difficulties relating to definitional issues between the two substances. The effect of this change is that while calcite will no longer have an outright exemption from the levy, both calcite and calcium carbonate used in non-aggregate, industrial applications will be eligible for a tax credit under s 30 of the law.

(e) Treatment of flint

The law will be amended to ensure that flint will be subject to the levy when it is used as an aggregate. However, flint will remain exempt if it is cut and used as a type of building stone. Also, flint used in non-aggregate applications, such as in the agriculture and animal feed sectors, will be eligible for a tax credit under s 30 of the law.

(f) Commercial exploitation of aggregate

As the law currently stands, aggregate can be moved tax free to another site owned by someone who is an operator on an originating site, but who is not necessarily a registered operator of that site. In order to maintain a clear audit trail, it is proposed that the law is amended to restrict the provision to movement of aggregate between sites that are registered under the name of the same person.

(g) Definition of "business"

The law will be amended to reflect the policy that "business", for the purposes of aggregates levy, includes local authorities and charities. This is to clarify that the levy will also apply to aggregate used by such non-profit making organisations.

(h) Registration of sites

It is proposed that the law is amended to ensure that the Commissioners have the power to register premises where mixing of aggregate takes place, given that mixing is one of the four tax points for the levy.

(i) Insolvency and set off provisions

It is proposed that the insolvency provisions contained at s 37(7)(*g*)(*h*)(*i*) and (*j*) and the set off provisions contained at Sch 8 para 11(2)(*f*)(*g*) and (*h*) will be removed. This is to reflect the fact that they are interim procedures which are not regarded as formal insolvency's by the Commissioners for VAT purposes.

If you have any questions about any of these issues, please contact our aggregate levy helpline numbers on 0161 827 0906 or 0161 827 0321. A public notice containing further technical details about the aggregates levy will be available in early January.

PHASED INTRODUCTION IN NORTHERN IRELAND

22 February 2002. *Business Brief 4/02*

The Government announced in the pre-Budget report that it is minded to phase in the aggregates levy in Northern Ireland, where aggregates are used in processed products. This recognises the potential effects of the levy on this specific sector. Phasing in the levy, including 100% relief for use of aggregates in processed products in 2002–03, will be subject to EU state aid approval.

A note on the broad scope of the phased introduction was included with all registration packs issued to those businesses in Northern Ireland who might be required to register for the levy. If you did not receive a registration pack but believe you may be liable to register, because for instance your business produces aggregate or imports it from the Republic of Ireland, please call Customs & Excise on 0845 7585831.

This business brief provides further information on the manner in which the phased introduction will operate if state aid approval is granted. In particular, it provides further detail on the uses of aggregate that will be eligible for relief and the proposed mechanism by which the relief will operate. The necessary legislation is currently being prepared and Customs & Excise will consult with representatives of local industry once a draft is available.

(A) USES OF AGGREGATE ELIGIBLE FOR RELIEF

Any aggregate used to make the following in Northern Ireland will be entitled to the relief—

– concrete (whether pre-cast, ready-mix or prepared on site);

- mortar;
- asphalt (whether delivered pre-mixed or mixed on site eg slurry seal);
- coated roadstone and coated chippings; and
- surface dressing (where dry aggregate chippings are rolled into bitumen on site).

Aggregate put to uses other than those listed above in Northern Ireland will not be entitled to this relief. Nor will any dry aggregate that is transported from Northern Ireland to Great Britain. There is already provision within the legislation for the relief of all exports of aggregate from the UK.

The entitlement to relief will not be affected by the origin of the aggregate (whether extracted in Northern Ireland or Great Britain or imported), nor will it be affected by the ultimate destination of products manufactured for onward sale, so long as they are manufactured in Northern Ireland.

(B) EXTENT OF THE RELIEF

In the first year of the levy's operation there will be 100% relief from tax for aggregates used in Northern Ireland to make the products specified above. In subsequent years the amount of levy to be paid will increase according to the following timetable—

2003–04 = 20% of the levy;

2004–05 = 40% of the levy;

2005–06 = 60% of the levy;

2006–07 = 80% of the levy; and

2007–08 and subsequent years = 100% of the levy.

(C) OPERATION OF THE RELIEF

The Northern Ireland relief will operate in the same manner as the relief for aggregate used in prescribed industrial or agricultural processes. The only extra requirement envisaged is that suppliers of aggregate must keep a separate account for the reliefs claimed under this scheme.

Full details of how this relief system operates is contained in "A general guide to the aggregates levy" section 5 which is available from Customs & Excise in Belfast. General information on the levy is available at www.hmce.gov.uk.

(D) FURTHER GUIDANCE

We intend to issue an information note that will provide detailed guidance on the precise operation of the proposed relief when the legislation has been drafted.

If you have any questions about any of these issues or aspects of the levy, please contact Customs & Excise in Northern Ireland on 028 9056 2271/2838.

CHANGES TO INDUSTRIAL AND AGRICULTURAL RELIEFS

14 November 2002. *Business Brief 29/02*

Aggregates Levy is a tax on the commercial exploitation of aggregate in the UK, and came into effect on 1 April 2002. Any aggregate that is used in prescribed industrial and agricultural processes is relieved from the levy. The list of relieved processes was drawn up through consultation with industry and is set out in the Aggregates Levy (General) Regulations 2002.

Continuing dialogue with industry and experience of the levy to date has identified a number of areas, which lack clarity or require amendment. Customs & Excise therefore intend to amend the Regulations to provide greater clarity and ensure that the list of prescribed processes reflects their policy objectives.

These changes are set out below and will take effect from 1 April 2003.

(A) CODE 004—WATER FILTRATION

Water and air filtration and purification becomes—

"Drinking water, air and oil filtration and purification"

This makes it clear that water filtration can only be relieved if it is a part of the process of providing drinking water, and also adds oil filtration to the list of relieved processes.

(B) CODE 012—FOOD PROCESSING

Production of food and food processing eg sugar refining, production of gelatin becomes—
"Production and processing of food and drink eg sugar refining, production of gelatin"

This is merely a change in wording to provide greater clarity.

(C) CODE 032—OIL EXPLORATION

Use of proppart in oil exploration eg fracture sands and drilling fluids becomes—

"Use as a propping agent in oil exploration eg fracture sands and drilling fluids"

This replaces "proppart" with "propping agent", as the latter is the correct technical term.

(D) CODE 039—ADDITIVES TO SOIL

Manufacture of additives to soil becomes—

"Manufacture of additives to soil eg agricultural lime"

This change is to remove any confusion as to which code to use when claiming relief in respect of agricultural lime.

(E) CODE 044—GROWING MEDIA

Production of growing media becomes—

"Production of growing media, including compost, for agricultural and horticultural use only"

This makes it clear that relief is limited to use in growing media for the agricultural sector, which includes horticulture. Relief will not be claimable where aggregate is used in growing media for non-agricultural processes such as the laying of sports pitches. This change more accurately reflects the wording of the primary legislation (FA 2001 s 30(1)(*c*)).

If you have any questions about the Aggregates Levy, please contact the National Advice Service on 0845 010 9000. A public notice will be available in April 2003 giving full technical details of all of the prescribed industrial and agricultural processes.

EXEMPTION FROM REGISTRATION AND OTHER OBLIGATIONS

24 December 2002. *Business Brief 34/02*

Aggregates Levy is a tax on the commercial exploitation of aggregate in the UK and came into effect on 1 April 2002. Any person responsible for commercially exploiting aggregate, including exempt aggregate, must register for the levy and carry out certain obligations of registered persons unless specifically exempted from doing so under The Aggregates Levy (Registration and Miscellaneous Provisions) Regulations 2001.

Subject to Parliamentary approval, Customs and Excise intend to amend the Regulations so that any person who exploits solely exempt aggregate will not have to register for aggregates levy nor carry out certain obligations such as submitting nil returns.

These changes are set out below and will take effect from 1 April 2003.

A) FULL EXEMPTION FROM REGISTRATION AND ALL OBLIGATIONS

This will apply to any person who commercially exploits only—

- soil, vegetable matter or other organic matter; or
- spoil, waste or other by-products of any industrial combustion process, or the smelting or refining of metal; or
- drill-cuttings from licensed oil exploration; or
- arisings from roads when utilities work is carried out.

B) EXEMPTION FROM REGISTRATION AND CONSEQUENT OBLIGATIONS BUT REQUIRED TO NOTIFY CUSTOMS OF ACTIVITIES

Any person who exploits only—

- coal, lignite, slate or shale; or
- spoil, waste or other by-products resulting from the separation of coal, lignite, slate or shale after extraction; or
- spoil, waste or other by-products resulting from the separation of specified minerals after extraction; or
- china clay and ball clay and spoil or waste resulting from its extraction; or
- any other clay

shall be exempt from registration and consequent obligations such as submitting returns but will be required to notify Customs of site details, activities undertaken and responsible persons. Notifications should be sent to—

HM Customs and Excise, Aggregates Levy Team, Dobson House, Regent Centre, Gosforth, Newcastle Upon Tyne, NE3 3PF.

If you have any questions about the Aggregates Levy, please contact the National Advice Service on 0845 010 9000. A public notice will be available in April 2003 and will include these changes.

EXTENDED RELIEF FOR NORTHERN IRELAND

10 December 2003. *Business Brief 27/03*

The Chancellor made the following announcement in today's pre-Budget Report (PBR)?

> "Since Budget 2003, the Government and the aggregates and construction industries in Northern Ireland have worked hard to improve the analysis of the operation of the levy and the aggregates market in the Province, including an independent study, *Assessment of the State of the Construction Aggregates Sector in Northern Ireland*, that the Government commissioned which is published alongside the pre-Budget Report. The Government has also examined proposals for an extension to the current five-year scheme, which provides relief from the levy for aggregate used in processed products in Northern Ireland.
>
> Following discussions with stakeholders and the evidence from the study, and subject to state aid approval, the Government intends to extend the scope and length of the current relief for aggregates in Northern Ireland, providing aggregates businesses in Northern Ireland that wish to benefit from the extended relief agree to implement environmental improvements to their operations. The relief will continue to cover aggregate in processed products and be extended to cover virgin aggregate, coming into effect during 2004 and fixed at the current level of 80 per cent of the full rate until 31 March 2012. The environmental improvements that quarry operators will need to sign up to will be regularly monitored and reviewed and enforcement activity will be stepped up."

This Business Brief article provides information on how the new relief scheme will operate if European Commission state aid approval is granted.

1 WHO WILL BE ELIGIBLE TO CLAIM THE NEW RELIEF?

Businesses which are registered for the aggregates levy and commercially exploit virgin aggregate extracted in Northern Ireland. Eligibility will be conditional upon claimants entering into and complying with the terms of a Negotiated Agreement (see question 11 for details).

"Commercial exploitation" is defined in Notice AGL1 "Aggregates Levy" available on the Customs and Excise website www.hmce.gov.uk/forms/notices/agl1 or in hard copy from the National Advice Service on 0845 010 9000.

2 WHAT WILL THE NEW SCHEME APPLY TO?

The relief will continue to cover aggregate in processed products (concrete, asphalt etc) and be extended to cover virgin aggregate.

3 WHAT WILL THE RATE OF RELIEF BE?

The relief will be 80% of the full rate of levy (as at present), which will apply for the duration of the new scheme, until 31 March 2012.

4 SO HOW MUCH TAX WILL BE PAYABLE PER TONNE?

The full rate of levy on aggregate exploited in the UK is currently £1.60 per tonne. If this remains unchanged in Budget 2004, relieved aggregate in Northern Ireland would be liable at 20% of that rate ie 32 pence per tonne.

5 WHEN WILL THE NEW SCHEME COME INTO EFFECT?

The introduction of the new scheme is still subject to state aid approval from the European Commission. The scheme will start shortly after that approval is received but in any case will not be earlier than 1 April 2004.

6 WILL AGGREGATE USED OUTSIDE NORTHERN IRELAND BE ELIGIBLE FOR RELIEF?

The new scheme will not affect current arrangements for exports of virgin aggregate from the UK, which will remain eligible for 100% relief from the levy.

Aggregate used to manufacture processed products in Northern Ireland which is subsequently exported from the UK will be eligible for the 80% relief under the new scheme.

Aggregate or products made from aggregate sent from Northern Ireland to Great Britain will not be eligible for the relief and will be subject to the full rate of levy upon first commercial exploitation.

7 WILL IMPORTS OF AGGREGATE INTO NORTHERN IRELAND BE LIABLE TO RELIEF?

This is an issue that will be explored with the European Commission but Customs expects that, under EU law, the relief will have to be extended to imports of aggregate into Northern Ireland.

8 IS THIS NEW SCHEME PERMANENT?

No. The new scheme will operate until 31 March 2012.

9 WHAT HAPPENS AFTER 31 MARCH 2012?

It is too early to say. The impact of the new scheme will be kept under review and this will inform what happens after 31 March 2012.

10 WILL I STILL BE ABLE TO CLAIM RELIEF UNDER THE CURRENT RELIEF SCHEME?

No. The current scheme will be abolished and replaced by the new scheme.

11 WHAT IS A NEGOTIATED AGREEMENT?

The detail of the form and content of Negotiated Agreements is still being discussed by the Department of Environment Northern Ireland (DoENI) and main industry representative bodies in Northern Ireland, the Quarry Products Association Northern Ireland (QPANI) and the British Aggregates Association (BAA).

Broadly, however, these agreements will set targets for improvement in environmental performance of quarrying operations; among the areas of performance likely to be covered are air quality, blasting, dust, energy efficiency, groundwater and waste management. Each agreement will be individually tailored to the circumstances of the quarry, taking into account, for example, current standards and scope for improvement.

Once discussions between DoENI and the QPANI and BAA have been finalised, all aggregates levy registered businesses in Northern Ireland will be sent details of how to set up a Negotiated Agreement and thus claim relief under the new scheme.

12 DO I HAVE TO BELONG TO THE QPANI OR BAA TO BE ELIGIBLE FOR RELIEF?

No. Eligibility to relief is based on the criteria outlined in question 1 above.

13 HOW CAN I CONTRIBUTE TO THE DOENI–TRADE DISCUSSIONS ABOUT NEGOTIATED AGREEMENTS IF I AM NOT A MEMBER OF THE QPANI OR THE BAA?

DoENI will be launching shortly a public consultation exercise on the HELM report, which is to be used as the basis for trade discussions about the form and content of Negotiated Agreements. If you would like to take part in these discussions, please write to:

Department of the Environment, Environmental Policy Division
River House, 48 High Street,
Belfast, BT1 2AW.

14 WHO WILL BE RESPONSIBLE FOR MONITORING COMPLIANCE WITH NEGOTIATED AGREEMENTS?

The DoENI will be responsible for conducting the initial assessment of a quarry's environmental standards and monitoring performance against the targets set out in the agreement. Compliance will be reflected by the issue/renewal of a certificate by DoENI, which, in turn, will be used by the business to support claims to relief during the period of the certificate's validity.

15 WHAT WOULD HAPPEN IF A BUSINESS DID NOT MEET THE TERMS OF ITS NEGOTIATED AGREEMENT?

This has yet to be decided but it is likely that failure to meet agreed targets would result in punitive action, including rendering the business concerned ineligible to claim relief for a specified period.

16 WHAT WILL THE GOVERNMENT DO IF STATE AID APPROVAL IS NOT GRANTED?

It is too early to say but the Government will keep the industry updated of progress and work with it to try to overcome any potential obstacles.

17 WHERE CAN I OBTAIN A COPY OF THE SYMONDS' REPORT ON THE STATE OF THE QUARRYING INDUSTRY IN NORTHERN IRELAND?

It is available from the aggregates levy pages of the Customs and Excise website at www.hmce.gov.uk/business/othertaxes/agg-levy.

EXTENDED RELIEF FOR NORTHERN IRELAND

10 May 2004. *Business Brief 13/04*

The Government has confirmed that the scope and duration of the aggregates levy relief scheme in Northern Ireland has been extended. This follows notification from the European Commission that the Government's proposals for such an extended scheme have received state aid clearance. Further details are available in HM Treasury news release 44/04.

This Business Brief article provides information on how the new relief scheme will operate.

1. WHAT IS THE AGGREGATES LEVY?

Aggregates levy is an environmental tax on the commercial exploitation in the UK of virgin aggregate (rock, sand and gravel) and was introduced across the UK on 1 April 2002 at a rate of 1.60 per tonne (this rate remained unchanged in Budgets 2003 and 2004). Anybody who commercially exploits aggregate in the UK is liable to register and account for the levy to Customs and Excise. 710 traders are currently registered for the tax across the UK, 140 of which are registered in Northern Ireland.

2. WHO IS ELIGIBLE TO CLAIM THE NEW RELIEF?

Relief is available to businesses which are registered for the aggregates levy with Customs and commercially exploit virgin aggregate extracted in Northern Ireland. Eligibility is conditional upon the claimant being in possession of an Aggregates Levy Credit Certificate. The certificate will be issued to an operator in Northern Ireland by the Department of the Environment (acting as Customs' agent) if he can demonstrate to the Department's satisfaction that he either holds or has applied for the relevant regulatory authorisations, and if he enters into an agreement with the Department committing the business to implementing environmental improvements to its operations. More details about these arrangements, including special arrangements for the start of the scheme, are set out in the answer to question 12 below.

"Commercial exploitation" is defined in Notice AGL1 "Aggregates Levy" available on the Customs and Excise website www.hmce.gov.uk/forms/notices/agl1 or in hard copy from the National Advice Service on 0845 010 9000.

3. WHAT DOES THE SCHEME APPLY TO?

The relief covers aggregate in processed products (concrete, asphalt etc.) and virgin aggregate in its raw state.

4. WHAT IS THE LEVEL OF RELIEF?

The relief is 80% of the full rate of levy for the duration of the new scheme—until 31 March 2011.

5. HOW MUCH TAX IS PAYABLE PER TONNE?

The full rate of levy on aggregate exploited in the UK is currently 1.60 per tonne. Relieved aggregate in Northern Ireland is liable at 20% of that rate, i.e. currently 32 pence per tonne.

6. FROM WHAT DATE IS THE EXTENDED SCHEME EFFECTIVE?

1 April 2004.

7. SO CAN I CLAIM RELIEF FROM THIS DATE?

Quarry operators in Northern Ireland will be able to claim the extended relief from the date set out on their Aggregates Levy Credit Certificate issued to them by the Department of the Environment in Northern Ireland. Details about the circumstances in which such a certificate will be issued are set out in the answer to question 12 below.

Retroactive legal cover for the relief will be provided by the Finance Bill currently before Parliament and by regulations made under the Finance Bill provisions, which will be laid before Parliament once the Bill receives Royal Assent later in the year.

8. SO THE NEW SCHEME IS NOT PERMANENT. WHAT HAPPENS AFTER 31 MARCH 2011?

It is too early to say. The impact of the new scheme will be kept under review and this will inform what happens after 31 March 2011.

9. IS AGGREGATE USED OUTSIDE NORTHERN IRELAND ELIGIBLE FOR RELIEF?

The new scheme does not affect arrangements for exports of virgin aggregate from the UK, which remain eligible for 100% relief from the levy.

Aggregate used to manufacture processed products in Northern Ireland which is subsequently exported from the UK is eligible for the 80% relief.

Aggregate or products made from aggregate sent from Northern Ireland to Great Britain is not eligible for the relief and is subject to the full rate of levy upon first commercial exploitation. (NB relief may be claimed if the aggregate or processed products are merely transiting Great Britain as part of an export movement.)

10. ARE IMPORTS OF AGGREGATE INTO NORTHERN IRELAND LIABLE TO RELIEF?

No. Those importing such aggregate will not be subject to the cost of complying with the environmental improvements provided for under the scheme so it would not be fair on operators in Northern Ireland to extend the relief to such imports.

11. DO I HAVE TO BELONG TO A TRADE ASSOCIATION TO BE ELIGIBLE FOR RELIEF?

No. Eligibility to relief is based on the criteria outlined at question 2 above.

12. WHAT WILL ENTITLE ME TO RELIEF?

To qualify for relief, a business will need to be registered with Customs and Excise for the aggregates levy. It will also need to exploit virgin aggregate extracted in Northern Ireland and be in possession of an Aggregates Levy Credit Certificate. The issue of certificates by the Department of the Environment in Northern Ireland, and therefore entitlement to relief, will be conditional on a business/operator signing and complying with an Aggregates Levy Credit Agreement with that Department. This agreement will commit the business to making improvements to the way it operates and set targets for improvement in environmental performance of quarrying operations.

It will take a few months to sort out agreements with all operators in Northern Ireland. Initially therefore a business will need to satisfy the Department of the Environment in Northern Ireland that it either holds or has applied for the relevant regulatory authorisations, and agrees to enter into an Aggregates Levy Credit Agreement with the Department, which will commit the business to compliance with the Code of Practice for the aggregates industry in Northern Ireland. The business will also have to arrange for an audit of its site to be completed by an accredited environmental consultant. Once these commitments have been made, the Department of the Environment will issue an Aggregates Levy Credit Certificate and the business will be able to claim relief from aggregates levy from the date set out on that certificate (regardless of when it is received by the operator).

The Department of the Environment will be able to enter a date on the certificate that is on or after 1 April 2004. For applications received in the first few weeks, where it is satisfied that an operator holds or has applied for relevant regulatory authorisations and has made the necessary commitments outlined above, the Department of the Environment will provide for claims to be backdated to 1 April when it completes the certificates. This provides strong incentives for operators to join the scheme as soon as possible.

The audit mentioned above will have to be returned to the Department of the Environment by a specified date. The Department will review all audits and set site-specific targets for improvement in the light of them. Continued eligibility to relief will be dependent on businesses meeting such targets, which will be regularly monitored and reviewed.

13. WHAT WILL THE AGGREGATES LEVY CREDIT AGREEMENTS BETWEEN OPERATORS AND DEPARTMENT OF THE ENVIRONMENT DO?

These agreements will set targets for improvement in environmental performance of quarrying operations; among the areas of performance that will be covered are air quality, blasting, dust, energy efficiency, groundwater and waste management. Each agreement will be individually tailored to the circumstances of the quarry, taking into account, for example, current standards and scope for improvement.

All aggregates levy registered businesses in Northern Ireland have been sent guidance on exactly how the new relief scheme will work.

14. WHO WILL BE RESPONSIBLE FOR MONITORING COMPLIANCE WITH THE AGREEMENTS?

The Department of the Environment in Northern Ireland will be responsible for conducting the initial assessment of a quarry's environmental standards based on information provided by applicant businesses, drawing up an agreement with each business and monitoring performance against the targets set out in the agreement. Compliance will be reflected by the issue/renewal of the Aggregates Levy Credit Certificate by the Department of the Environment, which, in turn, will be used by the business to support claims to relief during the period of the certificate's validity.

15. WHAT HAPPENS IF A BUSINESS DOES NOT MEET THE TERMS OF ITS AGREEMENT?

Failure to meet agreed targets will result in punitive action, including rendering the business concerned ineligible to claim relief.

16. CAN BUSINESSES IN NORTHERN IRELAND CONTINUE TO CLAIM RELIEF UNDER THE OLD 5-YEAR DEGRESSIVE SCHEME—WHICH STILL HAD NEARLY 3 YEARS LEFT TO RUN?

No. The old 5-year scheme has been abolished and replaced by the new scheme. Any business that does not have a valid Aggregates Levy Credit Certificate covering the period from the start of the new scheme will be liable to pay the full rate of aggregates levy on all aggregate they commercially exploit until they obtain such a certificate.

FURTHER INFORMATION

Further details are available in Treasury news release 44/04. For further information on the aggregates levy please contact the Customs National Advice Service on 0845 010 9000. For further information about the credit agreements, please contact: Department of the Environment, Environmental Policy Group, 20–21 Donegall Street, Belfast BT1 2GP; E-mail: Evelyn.Hoy@doeni.gov.uk; Phone 028 9054 4570 or 4511.

UPDATE TO NOTICE AGL1 AGGREGATES LEVY (JULY 2006) – CHANGE TO WATER DISCOUNT CALCULATION

7 July 2006. *Business Brief 08/06*

This Business Brief article provides information about an update to Notice AGL1 Aggregates Levy that makes changes to the section on added water discount.

HMRC has reviewed the standard water discounting arrangements in place since 1 July 2005 for water added to aggregates. There are a couple of areas that require clarification to ensure that the moisture content discounts are reasonable and consistent.

DUST DAMPENING OF AGGREGATE

From 1 September 2006, businesses cannot use the standard percentages for dust dampening of aggregate, where this involves no more than spraying stockpiles of aggregate. The standard percentages are not appropriate in this case, as it would, in effect, amount to a refund or reduction of the rate of the levy for businesses.

For such dust dampening, businesses (if they had changed to using standard percentages), will have to revert to the pre-July 2005 position of providing evidence and agreeing a more exact percentage of added water with their local aggregates officer.

MARINE DREDGED AGGREGATE

Aggregate extracted from the seabed, that is, marine dredged aggregate or 'ballast as dredged' has been eligible for the standard discount percentages since 1 July 2005.

After discussion with industry, including the British Marine Aggregate Producers Association, HM Revenue & Customs confirm that the standard percentage discounts, 7% for washed sand, and 3.5% for washed gravel, may be applied to marine dredged aggregate.

REVISED TEXT

The revised paragraph 11.7 to Notice AGL1 Aggregates Levy that was introduced into the notice in Update 1 dated May 2005 now reads as follows:

11.7 How do I calculate the added water discount?

From 1 July 2005 there are two options. First, you can use our standard added water percentages, which means that you do not have to weigh pre-washed and washed samples regularly to determine the weight as accurately as possible. This could save you time and expense. These percentages are:

Washed sand:	7%
Washed gravel:	3.5%
Washed rock / aggregate:	4%

Alternatively, you can agree a more exact percentage of added water, in which case you must provide evidence of the weight of the water. This second option was in fact the only one available up until 1 July 2005.

Whichever option you choose, you must first obtain written agreement to the proposed option and method from your local aggregates levy officer.

From 1 September 2006 you can only use the second option (ie agreeing with an officer a percentage allowable) for dust dampening of aggregate, as this involves no more than spraying stockpiles of aggregate and does not count as washing.

NOTICE OF REQUIREMENT TO GIVE SECURITY FOR ENVIRONMENTAL TAXES

April 2008. *Notice ET1*

Note—See under *IPT* section, ante, for the full text of this notice which is HMRC's Statement of Practice on the circumstances where they may require security for Insurance Premium Tax, Landfill Tax, Aggregates Levy and Climate Change Levy.

Aggregates Levy Index

Defined words and phrases are listed separately at the end.

Words and Phrases

Words in brackets indicate the context in which the word or phrase is used.

accounting period, FA 2001 s 48(1)
aggregate, FA 2001 s 17(1)
aggregates levy credit agreement, FA 2001 s 30A(13)
aggregates levy credit certificate, FA 2001 s 30A(13)
agreement, FA 2001 s 48(1)
agricultural, FA 2001 s 48(1)
appeal tribunal, FA 2001 s 48(1)
approved digital certificate, SI 2001/4027 reg 2(9), SI 2002/761 reg 6(8)
assigned matter, SI 2002/761 reg 6(8)
authorised person, FA 2001 Sch 7 para 15, SI 1997/1431 reg 2(1)
civil penalty, FA 2001 s 46(8), Sch 10 para 1(1)
connected activities, FA 2001 Sch 7 para 15
exempt aggregate, SI 2002/761 reg 2
exempt processes, FA 2001 s 18(2)
forestry, FA 2001 s 48(1)
gravel, FA 2001 s 48(1)
highway, FA 2001 s 17(7)
limestone, FA 2001 s 48(1)
mixed, FA 2001 s 48(1)
non-resident tax-payer, FA 2001 s 48(1)
operator, FA 2001 s 21(1)
originating site, FA 2001 s 20
person in default, SI 1997/1431 reg 2(1)
published notice, SI 2002/761 reg 2
registrable person, SI 2002/761 reg 2
reimbursement arrangements, SI 2002/761 reg 20
relevant substance, FA 2001 s 18(3)
representative, FA 2001 Sch 5 para 19(3), Sch 8 para 12(2), Sch 10 para 1(4)
rock, FA 2001 s 48(1)
structure, FA 2001 s 48(1)
tax credit, FA 2001 s 48(1)
tax representative, FA 2001 s 48(1)
trustee in bankruptcy, FA 2001 Sch 5 para 19(4), Sch 8 para 12(3), Sch 10 para 1(5)
United Kingdom waters, FA 2001 s 48(1)
walking possession agreement, SI 1997/1431 reg 2(1)

Climate Change Levy

Contents

Climate Change Levy Statutes

Contents

PROVISIONAL COLLECTION OF TAXES ACT 1968

(1968 Chapter 2)

An Act to consolidate the Provisional Collection of Taxes Act 1913 and certain other enactments relating to the provisional collection of taxes or matters connected therewith.

[1st February 1968]

1 Temporary statutory effect of House of Commons resolutions affecting . . . , [climate change levy][5], . . .

(1) This section applies only to . . . [, climate change levy][5] . . .

(2) Subject to that, and to the provisions of subsections (4) to (8) below, where the House of Commons passes a resolution which—

(*a*) provides for the renewal for a further period of any tax in force or imposed during the previous financial year (whether at the same or a different rate, and whether with or without modifications) or for the variation or abolition of any existing tax, and

(*b*) contains a declaration that it is expedient in the public interest that the resolution should have statutory effect under the provisions of this Act,

the resolution shall, for the period specified in the next following subsection, have statutory effect as if contained in an Act of Parliament and, where the resolution provides for the renewal of a tax, all enactments which were in force with reference to that tax as last imposed by Act of Parliament shall during that period have full force and effect with respect to the tax as renewed by the resolution.

In this section references to the renewal of a tax include references to its reimposition, and references to the abolition of a tax include references to its repeal.

(3) The said period is—

(*a*) in the case of a resolution passed in [November or December][2] in any year, one expiring with [5th May in the next calendar year][2];

[(*aa*) in the case of a resolution passed in February or March in any year, one expiring with 5th August in the same calendar year; and][4]

(*b*) in the case of any other resolution, one expiring at the end of four months after the date on which it is expressed to take effect or, if no such date is expressed, after the date on which it is passed.

(4) A resolution shall cease to have statutory effect under this section unless within the next [thirty][3] days on which the House of Commons sits after the day on which the resolution is passed—

(*a*) a Bill renewing, varying or, as the case may be, abolishing the tax is read a second time by the House, or

(*b*) a Bill is amended by the House [in Committee or on Report, or by any [Public Bill Committee][6] of the House][1] so as to include provision for the renewal, variation or, as the case may be, abolition of the tax.

(5) A resolution shall also cease to have statutory effect under this section if—

(*a*) the provisions giving effect to it are rejected during the passage of the Bill containing them through the House, or

(*b*) an Act comes into operation renewing, varying or, as the case may be, abolishing the tax, or

(*c*) Parliament is dissolved or prorogued.

(6) Where, in the case of a resolution providing for the renewal or variation of a tax, the resolution ceases to have statutory effect by virtue of subsection (4) or (5) above, or the period specified in subsection (3) above terminates, before an Act comes into operation renewing or varying the tax, any money paid in pursuance of the resolution shall be repaid or made good, and any deduction made in pursuance of the resolution shall be deemed to be an unauthorised deduction.

(7) Where any tax as renewed or varied by a resolution is modified by the Act renewing or varying the tax, any money paid in pursuance of the resolution which would not have been payable under the new conditions affecting the tax shall be repaid or made good, and any deduction made in pursuance of the resolution shall, so far as it would not have been authorised under the new conditions affecting the tax, be deemed to be an unauthorised deduction.

(8) When during any session a resolution has had statutory effect under this section, statutory effect shall not be again given under this section in the same session to the same resolution or to a resolution having the same effect.

Commentary—*Simon's Taxes* **A1.104.**

Note—Words omitted from the heading and sub-s (1) are not relevant for the purposes of climate change levy.

Amendments—[1] Words in sub-s (4)(*b*) added by FA 1968 s 60.

[2] Words in sub-s (3)(*a*) substituted by FA 1993 s 205 in relation to resolutions passed after 27 July 1993.

[3] Words in sub-s (4) substituted by FA 1993 s 205 in relation to resolutions passed after 27 July 1993.

[4] Sub-s(3)(*aa*) inserted by F(No 2)A 1997 s 50(1), (3) in relation to resolutions passed after 31 July 1997.

[5] Words in heading and sub-s (1) inserted by FA 2000 s 30, Sch 7 para 1 with effect from 28 July 2000.

[6] Words in sub-s (4)(*b*) substituted by FA 2007 s 112(1) with effect from 19 July 2007.

5 House of Commons resolution giving provisional effect to motions affecting taxation

(1) This section shall apply if the House of Commons resolves that provisional statutory effect shall be given to one or more motions to be moved by the Chancellor of the Exchequer, or some other Minister, and which, if agreed to by the House, would be resolutions—

(*a*) to which statutory effect could be given under section 1 of this Act, or

(*b*) , (*c*) . . . [1]

(2) Subject to subsection (3) below, on the passing of the resolution under subsection (1) above, sections 1 . . . of this Act . . . shall apply as if each motion to which the resolution applies had then been agreed to by a resolution of the House.

(3) Subsection (2) above shall cease to apply to a motion if that motion, or a motion containing the same proposals with modifications, is not agreed to by a resolution of the House (in this section referred to as "a confirmatory resolution") within the next ten days on which the House sits after the resolution under subsection (1) above is passed, and, if it ceases to apply, all such adjustments, whether by way of discharge or repayment of tax, or discharge of security, or otherwise, shall be made as may be necessary to restore the position to what it would have been if subsection (2) above had never applied to that motion, and to make good any deductions which have become unauthorised deductions.

(4) . . .

Commentary—*Simon's Taxes* **A1.104**.

Note—Sub-s (1)(*b*), (4) and words omitted from sub-s (2) are not relevant to climate change levy.

Amendments—[1] Words in sub-s (2) substituted and sub-s (1)(*c*), and word immediately preceding it, repealed by FA 1993 s 205(1), (6), (7) Sch 23 Pt VI in relation to resolutions passed after 27 July 1993.

6 Short title, repeals and saving as respects Northern Ireland

(1) This Act may be cited as the Provisional Collection of Taxes Act 1968.

(2), (3) . . . [1]

Note—Sub-s (2) repeals enactments specified in Schedule. Effect has been given to these repeals where applicable in the relevant provisions of the earlier enactments.

Amendments—[1] Sub-s (3) repealed by Northern Ireland Constitution Act 1973 s 41(1)(*a*) and Sch 6 Pt 1, with effect from 18 July 1973.

FINANCE ACT 1996

(1996 Chapter 8)

An Act to grant certain duties, to alter other duties, and to amend the law relating to the National Debt and the Public Revenue, and to make further provision in connection with Finance.

[29th April 1996]

PART VII
MISCELLANEOUS AND SUPPLEMENTAL

Miscellaneous: indirect taxation

197 Setting of rates of interest

(1) The rate of interest applicable for the purposes of an enactment to which this section applies shall be the rate which for the purposes of that enactment is provided for by regulations made by the Treasury under this section.

(2) This section applies to—

(*a*)–(*f*) . . .

[(*g*) the following provisions of Schedule 6 to the Finance Act 2000 (interest payable to or by the Commissioners in connection with climate change levy), that is to say, paragraphs 41(2)(*f*), 62(3)(*f*), 66, 70(1)(*b*)[, 81(3) and 123(4) to (6)][2].][1]

(*h*) , (*i*) . . .

(3) Regulations under this section may—

(*a*) make different provision for different enactments or for different purposes of the same enactment,

(*b*) either themselves specify a rate of interest for the purposes of an enactment or make provision for any such rate to be determined, and to change from time to time, by reference to such rate or the average of such rates as may be referred to in the regulations,

(*c*) provide for rates to be reduced below, or increased above, what they otherwise would be by specified amounts or by reference to specified formulae,

(*d*) provide for rates arrived at by reference to averages or formulae to be rounded up or down,

(*e*) provide for circumstances in which changes of rates of interest are or are not to take place, and

(*f*) provide that changes of rates are to have effect for periods beginning on or after a day determined in accordance with the regulations in relation to interest running from before that day, as well as in relation to interest running from, or from after, that day.

(4) The power to make regulations under this section shall be exercisable by statutory instrument subject to annulment in pursuance of a resolution of the House of Commons.

(5) Where—

(*a*) regulations under this section provide, without specifying the rate determined in accordance with the regulations, for a new method of determining the rate applicable for the purposes of any enactment, or

(*b*) the rate which, in accordance with regulations under this section, is the rate applicable for the purposes of any enactment changes otherwise than by virtue of the making of regulations specifying a new rate,

the Commissioners of Customs and Excise shall make an order specifying the new rate and the day from which, in accordance with the regulations, it has effect.

(6) (*amends FA 1994 Schs 6, 7 and VATA 1994 s 74*).

(7) Subsections (1) and (6) above shall have effect for periods beginning on or after such day as the Treasury may by order made by statutory instrument appoint and shall have effect in relation to interest running from before that day, as well as in relation to interest running from, or from after, that day; and different days may be appointed under this subsection for different purposes.

Note—Sub-ss (2)(*a*)–(*f*), (*h*), (*i*), (6) are not relevant to climate change levy.

Sub-s (1) has effect for periods beginning on or after 1 April 1997 (see FA 1996 s 197 (Appointed Day) Order, SI 1997/1015).

Amendments—[1] Sub-s (2)(*g*) inserted by FA 2000 Sch 7 para 6 with effect from 28 July 2000.

[2] Words in sub-s (2)(*g*) substituted for words "and 81(3)" by the Transfer of Tribunal Functions and Revenue and Customs Appeals Order, SI 2009/56 art 3(1), Sch 1 paras 232, 239(1), (2)(*e*) with effect from 1 April 2009.

FINANCE ACT 2000

(2000 Chapter 17)

An act to grant certain duties, to alter other duties, and to amend the law relating to the National Debt and the Public Revenue, and to make further provision in connection with finance.

[28 July 2000]

30 Climate change levy

(1) Schedule 6 to this Act (which makes provision for a new tax that is to be known as climate change levy) shall have effect.

(2) Schedule 7 to this Act (climate change levy: consequential amendments) shall have effect.

(3) Part V of Schedule 6 to this Act (registration for the purposes of climate change levy) shall not come into force until such date as the Treasury may appoint by order made by statutory instrument; and different days may be appointed under this subsection for different purposes.

Regulations—Climate Change Levy (Registration and Miscellaneous Provisions) Regulations, SI 2001/7.

Climate Change Levy (General) Regulations, SI 2001/838.

Climate Change Levy (Electricity and Gas) Regulations, SI 2001/1136.

Climate Change Levy (Combined Heat and Power Stations) Regulations, SI 2005/1714.

Climate Change Levy (Fuel Use and Recycling Processes) Regulations, SI 2005/1715.

Climate Change Agreements (Energy-intensive Installations) Regulations, SI 2006/59.

SCHEDULES

SCHEDULE 6

CLIMATE CHANGE LEVY

Section 30

Cross references—See the Climate Change Levy (Combined Heat and Power Stations) Exemption Certificate Regulations, SI 2001/486 (exemption certificates for combined heat and power stations).

Climate Change Agreements (Eligible Facilities) Regulations, SI 2001/662.

Climate Change Levy (General) Regulations, SI 2001/838.

Climate Change Levy (Electricity and Gas) Regulations, SI 2001/1136.

Climate Change Agreements (Energy-intensive Installations) Regulations, SI 2001/1139.

Climate Change Levy (Combined Heat and Power Stations) Regulations, SI 2005/1714.

Climate Change Levy (Fuel Use and Recycling Processes) Regulations, SI 2005/1715.

Climate Change Agreements (Energy-intensive Installations) Regulations, SI 2006/59.

Climate Change Agreements (Eligible Facilities) Regulations, SI 2006/60.

Climate Change Agreements (Eligible Facilities) (Amendment) Regulations, SI 2006/1931.

Climate Change Levy (Solid Fuel) (Revocation) Regulations, SI 2009/3338.

PART I
THE LEVY

Climate change levy

1—(1) A tax to be known as climate change levy ("the levy") shall be charged in accordance with this Schedule.
(2) The levy is under the care and management of the Commissioners of Customs and Excise.

Levy charged on taxable supplies

2—(1) The levy is charged on taxable supplies.
(2) Any supply of a taxable commodity is a taxable supply, subject to the provisions of Part II of this Schedule.

Meaning of "taxable commodity"

3—(1) The following are taxable commodities for the purposes of this Schedule, subject to sub-paragraph (2) and to any regulations under sub-paragraph (3)—
(*a*) electricity;
(*b*) any gas in a gaseous state that is of a kind supplied by a gas utility;
(*c*) any petroleum gas, or other gaseous hydrocarbon, in a liquid state;
(*d*) coal and lignite;
(*e*) coke, and semi-coke, of coal or lignite;
(*f*) petroleum coke.
(2) The following are not taxable commodities—
(*a*) hydrocarbon oil or road fuel gas within the meaning of the Hydrocarbon Oil Duties Act 1979;
(*b*) waste within the meaning of Part II of the Environmental Protection Act 1990 or the meaning given by Article 2(2) of the Waste and Contaminated Land (Northern Ireland) Order 1997.
(3) The Treasury may by regulations provide that a commodity of a description specified in the regulations is, or is not, a taxable commodity for the purposes of this Schedule.

PART II
TAXABLE SUPPLIES

Introduction

4—(1) A supply of a taxable commodity (or part of such a supply) is a taxable supply for the purposes of the levy if levy is chargeable on the supply under—
paragraph 5 (supplies of electricity),
paragraph 6 (supplies of gas), or
paragraph 7 (other supplies in course or furtherance of business),
and the supply (or part) is not excluded under paragraphs 8 to 10 or exempt under paragraphs 11 to 22.
(2) In this Schedule—
(*a*) references to a supply of a taxable commodity include a supply that is deemed to be made under paragraph 23, and
(*b*) references to a taxable supply include a supply that is deemed to be made under paragraph 24 [or 45A][1],
but paragraphs 23 and 24 have effect subject to any exceptions provided for under paragraph 21.

Amendments—[1] Words in sub-para (2)(*b*) inserted by FA 2007 s 23, Sch 2 paras 1, 2 with effect from 1 November 2007: SI 2007/2902 art 2(1).

Supplies of electricity

5—(1) Levy is chargeable on a supply of electricity if—
(*a*) the supply is made by an electricity utility, and
(*b*) the person to whom the supply is made—
(i) is not an electricity utility, or
(ii) is the utility itself.
(2) Levy is chargeable on a supply made from a combined heat and power station of electricity produced in the station if—
(*a*) the station is a partly exempt combined heat and power station,
(*b*) the supply is not one that is deemed to be made under paragraph 23(3) (self-supply by producer), and

(*c*) the person to whom the supply is made is not an electricity utility.

(3) Levy is chargeable on a supply of electricity that is deemed to be made under [paragraph 20(6)(*a*), 20B(6)(*a*), 23(3)[, 24 or 45A][2]][1].

(4) Except as provided by sub-paragraphs (1) to (3), levy is not chargeable on a supply of electricity.

Amendments—[1] Words in sub-para (3) substituted by FA 2003 s 191(1), (2) with effect for supplies deemed to be made after 30 March 2003.

[2] In sub-para (3), words substituted for the words "or 24" by FA 2007 s 23, Sch 2 paras 1, 3 with effect from 1 November 2007: SI 2007/2902 art 2(1).

Supplies of gas

6—(1) Levy is chargeable on a supply of any gas if—

(*a*) the supply is made by a gas utility, and

(*b*) the person to whom the supply is made—

(i) is not a gas utility, or

(ii) is the utility itself.

(2) Levy is chargeable on a supply of gas that is deemed to be made under paragraph 23(3) (self-supply by producer) if the gas—

(*a*) is held in a gaseous state immediately prior to being released for burning, and

(*b*) is of a kind supplied by a gas utility.

[(2A) Levy is chargeable on a supply of gas that is deemed to be made under paragraph 24 [or 45A][2].][1]

(3) Except as provided by [sub-paragraph (1), (2) or (2A)][1], levy is not chargeable on a supply of any gas that is supplied in a gaseous state.

Amendments—[1] Sub-para (2A) inserted, and words in sub-para (3) substituted, by FA 2003 s 191(1), (3) with effect for supplies deemed to be made after 9 July 2003.

[2] Words in sub-para (2A) inserted by FA 2007 s 23, Sch 2 paras 1, 4 with effect from 1 November 2007: SI 2007/2902 art 2(1).

Other supplies made in course or furtherance of business

7—(1) This paragraph applies to a supply of a taxable commodity other than—

(*a*) electricity, or

(*b*) gas in a gaseous state.

(2) Levy is chargeable on any such supply if the supply is made in the course or furtherance of a business.

Excluded supplies: supply for domestic or charity use

8—(1) A supply is excluded from the levy if it is—

(*a*) for domestic use (see paragraph 9), or

(*b*) for charity use.

(2) For the purposes of this paragraph, a supply is for charity use if the commodity supplied is for use by a charity otherwise than in the course or furtherance of a business.

(3) If a supply is partly for domestic or charity use and partly not, the part of the supply that is for domestic or charity use is excluded from the levy.

(4) Where a supply of a commodity is partly for domestic or charity use and partly not—

(*a*) if at least 60 per cent of the commodity is supplied for domestic or charity use, the whole supply is treated as a supply for domestic or charity use, and

(*b*) in any other case, an apportionment shall be made to determine the extent to which the supply is for domestic or charity use.

Excluded supplies: meaning of "for domestic use"

9—(1) For the purposes of paragraph 8 the following supplies are always for domestic use—

(*a*) a supply of not more than one tonne of coal or coke held out for sale as domestic fuel;

(*b*) a supply to a person at any premises of—

(i) any gas in a gaseous state that is provided through pipes and is of a kind supplied by a gas utility, or

(ii) petroleum gas in a gaseous state provided through pipes,

where the gas or petroleum gas (together with any other gas or petroleum gas provided through pipes to him at the premises by the same supplier) was not provided at a rate exceeding 4397 kilowatt hours a month;

(*c*) a supply of petroleum gas in a liquid state where the petroleum gas is supplied in cylinders the net weight of each of which is less than 50 kilogrammes and either the number of cylinders supplied is 20 or fewer or the petroleum gas is not intended for sale by the recipient;

(*d*) a supply of petroleum gas in a liquid state, otherwise than in cylinders, to a person at any premises at which he is not able to store more than two tonnes of such petroleum gas;

(*e*) a metered supply of electricity to a person at any premises where the electricity (together with any other electricity provided to him at the premises by the same supplier) was not provided at a rate exceeding 1000 kilowatt hours a month;

(*f*) an unmetered supply of electricity to a person where the electricity (together with any other unmetered electricity provided to him by the same supplier) was not provided at a rate exceeding 1000 kilowatt hours a month.

(2) For the purposes of paragraph 8, supplies not within sub-paragraph (1) are for domestic use if and only if the commodity supplied is for use in—

(*a*) a building, or part of a building, which consists of a dwelling or number of dwellings,

(*b*) a building, or part of a building, used for a relevant residential purpose,

(*c*) self-catering holiday accommodation (including any accommodation advertised or held out as such),

(*d*) a caravan,

(*e*) a houseboat (that is to say, a boat or other floating decked structure designed or adapted for use solely as a place of permanent habitation and not having means of, or capable of being readily adapted for, self-propulsion), or

(*f*) an appliance that—

(i) is not part of a combined heat and power station,

(ii) is located otherwise than in premises of a description mentioned in any of paragraphs (*a*) to (*e*), and

(iii) is used to heat air or water that, when heated, is supplied to premises of, or each of, such a description.

(3) For the purposes of this paragraph use for a relevant residential purpose means use as—

(*a*) a home or other institution providing residential accommodation for children,

(*b*) a home or other institution providing residential accommodation with personal care for persons in need of personal care by reason of old age, disablement, past or present dependence on alcohol or drugs or past or present mental disorder,

(*c*) a hospice,

(*d*) residential accommodation for students or school pupils,

(*e*) residential accommodation for members of any of the armed forces,

(*f*) a monastery, nunnery or similar establishment, or

(*g*) an institution which is the sole or main residence of at least 90 per cent of its residents,

except use as a hospital, a prison or similar institution or an hotel or inn or similar establishment.

[(4) The power to make provision by order under section 2(1C) of the Value Added Tax Act 1994 varying, or varying any provision contained in, Schedule A1 to that Act (supplies for domestic use and non-business use by a charity that attract reduced VAT rate) includes power to make provision for any appropriate corresponding variation of, or of any provision contained in, this paragraph.][2]

[(5) The power to make provision under section 29A(3) of the Value Added Tax Act 1994 varying Schedule 7A to that Act (charge at reduced rate) includes power to make provision for any appropriate corresponding variation of this paragraph.][1]

Amendments—[1] Sub-para (5) inserted by FA 2001 s 99(6), Sch 31 para 7 with effect from 11 May 2001.
[2] Sub-para (4) repealed by FA 2001 s 110, Sch 33 Pt III(1) with effect from 1 November 2001.

Excluded supplies: supply before 1st April 2001

10 Any supply made before 1st April 2001 is excluded from the levy.

Exemption: supply not for burning in the UK

11—(1) A supply of a taxable commodity to which this sub-paragraph applies is exempt from the levy if the person to whom the supply is made . . .[1]—

(*a*) . . .[1] intends to use the commodity in making supplies of it to any other person, or

(*b*) . . .[1] intends to cause the commodity to be exported from the United Kingdom and has no intention to cause it to be thereafter brought back into the United Kingdom.

(2) Sub-paragraph (1) applies to supplies of a taxable commodity other than—

(*a*) electricity, or

(*b*) any gas in a gaseous state.

(3) A supply of electricity, or of gas in a gaseous state, is exempt from the levy if the person to whom the supply is made . . .[1]—

(*a*) . . .[1] intends to cause the commodity to be exported from the United Kingdom, and

(*b*) has no intention to cause it to be thereafter brought back into the United Kingdom.

(4) Regulations under paragraph 22 may, in particular, include provision as to the application of sub-paragraph (3) in cases where a person who is both an exporter and an importer of a commodity intends to be a net exporter of the commodity.

Amendment—[1] Words in sub-paras (1), (3) repealed by FA 2007 ss 23, 114, Sch 2 paras 1, 11, Sch 27 Pt 1(1) with effect from 19 July 2007.

Words repealed in sub-para (1) previously read as follows—

"has, before the supply is made, notified the supplier", and "that he" (in two places).

Words repealed in sub-para (3) previously read as follows—

"has, before the supply is made, notified the supplier that", and "he".

[Exemption: Northern Ireland gas supplies

11A A supply of gas is exempt from the levy if—

(*a*) the supply is made by a gas utility, and

(*b*) the person to whom the supply is made intends to cause the gas to be burned in Northern Ireland.][1]

Amendments—[1] This paragraph inserted by FA 2001 s 105(2), (7) with effect for supplies made after 31 March 2001.

Exemption: supply used in transport

12—(1) A supply of a taxable commodity is exempt from levy if the commodity is to be burned (or, in the case of electricity, consumed)—

(*a*) in order to propel a train,

(*b*) in order to propel a non-railway vehicle while it is being used for, or for purposes connected with, transporting passengers,

(*c*) in a railway vehicle, or a non-railway vehicle, while it is being used for, or for purposes connected with, transporting passengers,

(*d*) in a railway vehicle while it is being used for, or for purposes connected with, transporting goods, or

(*e*) in a ship while it is engaged on a journey any part of which is beyond the seaward limit of the territorial sea.

Paragraphs (*a*) to (*c*) are subject to the exception in sub-paragraph (3).

(2) In this paragraph—

"railway vehicle" and "train" have the meaning given by section 83 of the Railways Act 1993;

"non-railway vehicle" means—

(*a*) any vehicle other than a railway vehicle, or

(*b*) any ship,

that is designed or adapted to carry not less than 12 passengers.

(3) Sub-paragraph (1)(*a*) to (*c*) does not apply in relation to the transporting of passengers to, from or within—

(*a*) a place of entertainment, recreation or amusement, or

(*b*) a place of cultural, scientific, historical or similar interest,

that is a place to which rights of admission, or where rights to use facilities at it, are supplied by the person to whom the commodity is supplied or by a person connected with him within the meaning of [section 1122 of the Corporation Tax Act 2010][1].

Amendments—[1] In sub-para (3) words substituted for words "section 839 of the Taxes Act 1988" by CTA 2010 s 1177, Sch 1 para 314(1), (2). CTA 2010 has effect for corporation tax purposes for accounting periods ending on or after 1 April 2010, and for income and capital gains tax purposes for the tax year 2010–11 and subsequent tax years.

Exemption: supplies to producers of commodities other than electricity

13 A supply of a taxable commodity to a person is exempt from the levy if—

(*a*) the supply is not a supply of electricity that is deemed to be made under paragraph 23(3), and

(*b*) the commodity is to be used by that person—

(i) in producing taxable commodities other than electricity,

(ii) in producing hydrocarbon oil or road fuel gas,

[(ii a) in producing biodiesel for chargeable use within the meaning of section 6AA of the Hydrocarbon Oil Duties Act 1979 (excise duty on biodiesel),][1]

[(ii b) in producing bioblend for delivery for home use from any place mentioned in section 6AB(1)(*b*) of that Act (excise duty on bioblend),][1]

[(ii c) in producing bioethanol for chargeable use within the meaning of section 6AD of that Act (excise duty on bioethanol),][1] [(ii d) in producing bioethanol blend for delivery for home use from any place mentioned in section 6AE(1)(*b*) of that Act (excise duty on bioethanol blend),][1]

(iii) in producing, for chargeable use within the meaning of section 6A of the Hydrocarbon Oil Duties Act 1979 (fuel substitutes), [liquids (within the meaning of that section) in respect of which a charge is capable of arising under that section][1], or

(iv) in producing uranium for use in an electricity generating station.

[Expressions which are used in this paragraph and the Hydrocarbon Oil Duties Act 1979 have the same meaning in this paragraph as they have in that Act][1].

Amendments—[1] Sub-paras (*b*)(iia)–(iid) inserted; in sub-para (*b*)(iii), words substituted for the words "liquids that are not hydrocarbon oil"; and the final sentence substituted, by FA 2004 s 289(2)–(4), (6) with effect—

(a) as regards biodiesel and bioblend, in relation to supplies made after 21 July 2004; and

(b) as regards bioethanol and bioethanol blend, in relation to supplies made after 31 December 2004.

The final sentence previously read as follows—

"For this purpose 'hydrocarbon oil' and 'road fuel gas' have the same meaning as in the Hydrocarbon Oil Duties Act 1979 and 'liquid' has the same meaning as in section 6A of that Act.".

[13A—(1) The Commissioners may by regulations make provision amending paragraph 13 for the purpose of—

(*a*) extending the circumstances in which a supply of a taxable commodity is exempt from the levy, or

(*b*) restricting the circumstances in which a supply of a taxable commodity is exempt from the levy.

(2) Regulations under this paragraph that include provision made for the purpose mentioned in sub-paragraph (1)(*a*) may provide for the provision to have retrospective effect.

(3) A statutory instrument that contains (whether alone or with other provisions) regulations under this paragraph made for the purpose mentioned in sub-paragraph (1)(*b*) shall not be made unless a draft of the instrument has been laid before Parliament and approved by a resolution of the House of Commons.][1]

Amendments—[1] This paragraph inserted by FA 2004 s 289(5) with effect from 22 July 2004.

Exemption: supplies (other than self-supplies) to electricity producers

14—(1) A supply of a taxable commodity to a person is exempt from the levy if—

(*a*) the commodity is to be used by that person in producing electricity in a generating station that is neither—

(i) a fully exempt combined heat and power station, nor

(ii) a partly exempt combined heat and power station,

and

(*b*) the supply is not a supply of electricity that is deemed to be made under paragraph 23(3).

(2) Sub-paragraph (1) does not exempt a supply where the person to whom the supply is made—

(*a*) is an exempt unlicensed electricity supplier of a description prescribed by regulations made by the Treasury, . . . [2]

(*b*) uses the commodity supplied in producing electricity[, and

(*c*) uses the electricity produced otherwise than in exemption-retaining ways.][1]

(3) Sub-paragraph (1) does not exempt a supply where the person to whom the supply is made—

(*a*) is an auto-generator,

(*b*) uses the commodity supplied in producing electricity, and

[(*c*) uses the electricity produced otherwise than in exemption-retaining ways.][1]

[(3A) For the purposes of this paragraph, electricity is used in an "exemption-retaining" way if it is used—

(*a*) in making supplies that are excluded under paragraphs 8 to 10 or exempt under any of paragraphs 11, 12 [, 18 and 18A][3], or

(*b*) in any of the ways mentioned in sub-paragraphs (i) to (iv) of paragraph 13(*b*).][1]

(4) In this paragraph "exempt unlicensed electricity supplier" means a person—

(*a*) to whom an exemption from section 4(1)(*c*) of the Electricity Act 1989 (persons supplying electricity to premises) has been granted by an order under section 5 of that Act, or

(*b*) to whom an exemption from Article 8(1)(*c*) of the Electricity Supply (Northern Ireland) Order 1992 has been granted by an order under Article 9 of that Order,

except where he is acting otherwise than for purposes connected with the carrying on of activities authorised by the exemption.

(5) Sub-paragraph (4) applies subject to—

(*a*) any direction under paragraph 151(1), and

(*b*) any regulations under paragraph 151(2).

Amendments—[1] Word "and", sub-paras (2)(*c*), and (3A) inserted, and sub-para (3)(*c*) substituted by FA 2001 s 105(3)–(5), (7) with effect for supplies made after 31 March 2001.
[2] In para (2)(*a*), the word "and" repealed by FA 2001 s 110, Sch 33 Pt 3(3) with effect from 11 May 2001.
[3] Words in sub-para (3A)(*a*) substituted by FA 2003 s 188(2)(*a*) with effect from 10 July 2003.

Exemption: supplies (other than self-supplies) to combined heat and power stations

15—(1) A supply of a taxable commodity to a person is exempt from the levy if—
(*a*) [that person intends to cause the commodity to be used][1] in—
(i) a fully exempt combined heat and power station, or
(ii) a partly exempt combined heat and power station,
in producing any outputs of the station, and
(*b*) the supply is not a supply of electricity that is deemed to be made under paragraph 23(3).
For this purpose "outputs" has the meaning given by paragraph 148(9).
(2) Where—
(*a*) a supply of a taxable commodity to a person would (apart from this sub-paragraph) be exempted in full by sub-paragraph (1), and
(*b*) at the time the supply is made, the efficiency percentage for the combined heat and power station in which the commodity is to be used . . .[2] is less than the threshold efficiency percentage for the station,
sub-paragraph (1) only exempts the relevant fraction of the supply.
(3) For the purposes of sub-paragraph (2), the "relevant fraction" of a supply of a taxable commodity that is to be used in a combined heat and power station is the fraction—
(*a*) whose numerator is the efficiency percentage for the station at the time the supply is made, and
(*b*) whose denominator is the threshold efficiency percentage for the station at that time.
(4) For the purposes of this paragraph—
(*a*) the "threshold efficiency percentage" for a combined heat and power station is the percentage set as the threshold efficiency percentage for the station by regulations made by the Treasury;
[(*b*) the "efficiency percentage" for a combined heat and power station shall be determined in accordance with regulations under paragraph 149.][3]
(5) . . .[3]

Amendments—[1] Words in sub-para (1)(*a*) substituted by FA 2001 s 105(6), (7) with effect for supplies made after 31 March 2001.
[2] In para (2)(*b*), the words "by that person" repealed by FA 2001 s 110, Sch 33 Pt 3(3) with effect for supplies made after 31 March 2001.
[3] Sub-para (4)(*b*) substituted, and sub-para (5) repealed, by FA 2003 ss 189(1), (2), 216, Sch 43 Pt 4 with effect for supplies made on or after 22 July 2005 (by virtue of SI 2005/1713).

Exemption: supplies (other than self-supplies) of electricity from partly exempt combined heat and power stations

16—(1) This paragraph applies to a supply that—
(*a*) is a supply made from a partly exempt combined heat and power station of electricity produced in the station, and
(*b*) is not a supply that is deemed to be made under paragraph 23(3).
(2) The supply is exempt from the levy if the quantity of electricity supplied by the supply is not such as causes the exceeding of any specified limit that, by virtue of regulations made by the Treasury, applies in relation to the station for any specified period.
(3) In this paragraph "specified" means prescribed by, or determined in accordance with, regulations made by the Treasury.

Exemption: self-supplies by electricity producers

17—(1) This paragraph applies to a supply of electricity that is deemed to be made under paragraph 23(3) by a person ("the producer") to himself.
(2) If the producer is an auto-generator, the supply is exempt from the levy unless—
(*a*) it is a supply from a partly-exempt combined heat and power station of electricity produced in the station, and
(*b*) the quantity of electricity supplied by the supply is such as causes the exceeding of any such limit as is mentioned in paragraph 16(2) that applies in relation to the station.
(3) If the producer is not an auto-generator, the supply is exempt from the levy if it is a supply made from a fully exempt combined heat and power station of electricity produced in the station.
(4) If the producer is not an auto-generator, the supply is exempt from the levy if—
(*a*) it is a supply from a partly-exempt combined heat and power station of electricity produced in the station, and

(*b*) the quantity of electricity supplied by the supply is not such as causes the exceeding of any such limit as is mentioned in paragraph 16(2) that applies in relation to the station.

Exemption: supply not used as fuel

18—(1) A supply of a taxable commodity is exempt from the levy if the person to whom the supply is made intends to cause the commodity to be used otherwise than as fuel.

(2) The Treasury may by regulations specify, in relation to any commodity, uses of that commodity that, for the purposes of sub-paragraph (1), are to be taken as being, or as not being, uses of that commodity as fuel.

(3) The uses of a commodity that may be specified under sub-paragraph (2) as being uses of that commodity as, or otherwise than as, fuel include uses ("mixed uses") of the commodity that involve it being used partly as fuel and partly not; but the Treasury must have regard to the object of securing that a mixed use is not specified as being a use of the commodity otherwise than as fuel if it involves the use of the commodity otherwise than as fuel in a way that is merely incidental to its use as fuel.

Exemption: supply for use in recycling processes

[18A—(1) A supply of a taxable commodity is exempt from the levy if the person to whom the supply is made intends to cause the commodity to be used as fuel in a prescribed recycling process falling within sub-paragraph (2).

(2) A recycling process falls within this sub-paragraph if there is another process ("the competing process") that—

(*a*) is not a recycling process,

(*b*) uses taxable commodities otherwise than as fuel,

(*c*) produces a product of the same kind as one produced by the recycling process,

(*d*) uses a greater amount of energy than the recycling process to produce a given quantity of that product, and

(*e*) involves a lesser charge to levy for a given quantity of that product than would, but for this paragraph, be the case for the recycling process.

(3) For the purposes of sub-paragraph (2)(*b*) taxable commodities are used "otherwise than as fuel" only if the supplies of those commodities to the person using them are exempted from the levy by virtue of paragraph 18.

(4) Sub-paragraphs (5) and (6) apply where the recycling process or the competing process, as well as producing a product that is of the same kind as one produced by the other process ("the corresponding product"), also produces one or more products that are not ("different products").

(5) If the production of the different products is merely incidental to the production of the corresponding product, the different products shall be treated for the purposes of sub-paragraph (2)(*d*) and (*e*) as being of the same kind as the corresponding product.

(6) If the production of the different products is not merely incidental to the production of the corresponding product—

(*a*) the amounts of energy referred to in sub-paragraph (2)(*d*), and the amounts of the charge to levy referred to in sub-paragraph (2)(*e*), shall be determined on a just and reasonable apportionment;

(*b*) the exemption conferred by sub-paragraph (1) shall be restricted to the proportion of the supply that is the same as the proportion of the energy used by the recycling process to produce the corresponding product (as determined for the purposes of paragraph (*a*)).

(7) In this paragraph "prescribed" means prescribed by regulations made by the Treasury.][1]

Amendments—[1] This paragraph inserted by FA 2003 s 188(1) with effect from 10 July 2003.

Exemption: electricity from renewable sources

19—(1) A supply of electricity is exempt from the levy if—

(*a*) the supply is not one that is deemed to be made under paragraph 23(3),

(*b*) the supply is made under a contract that contains a renewable source declaration given by the supplier,

(*c*) prescribed conditions are fulfilled, and

(*d*) the supplier, and each other person (if any) who is a generator of any renewable source electricity allocated by the supplier to supplies under the contract, has in a written notice given to the Commissioners agreed that he will fulfil those conditions so far as they may apply to him.

(2) In this paragraph "renewable source declaration" means a declaration that, in each averaging period, the amount of electricity supplied by exempt renewable supplies made by the supplier in the period will not exceed the difference between—

(*a*) the total amount of renewable source electricity that during that period is either acquired or generated by the supplier, and (*b*) so much of that total amount as is allocated by the supplier otherwise than to exempt renewable supplies made by him in the period.

In this sub-paragraph "averaging period" has the same meaning as in paragraph 20 and "exempt renewable supplies" means supplies made on the basis that they are exempt under this paragraph.

(3) For the purposes of this paragraph and paragraph 20, electricity is "renewable source electricity" if—

(*a*) it is generated in a prescribed manner, and

(*b*) prescribed conditions are fulfilled.

A manner of generating electricity may be prescribed by reference to the means by which the electricity is generated or the materials from which it is generated (or both).

(4) In prescribing a manner of generating electricity under sub-paragraph (3), the Commissioners must have regard to the object of securing that exemption under this paragraph is only available for supplies of electricity that has a renewable source.

[(4A) For the purposes of this paragraph, coal mine methane shall be regarded as a renewable source.][1,2]

(5) The conditions that may be prescribed under sub-paragraph (1)(*c*) include, in particular, conditions in connection with—

(*a*) the giving of effect to renewable source declarations;

(*b*) the supply of information;

(*c*) the inspection of records and, for that purpose, the production of records in legible form and entry into premises;

(*d*) monitoring by the Gas and Electricity Markets Authority, or the Director General of Electricity Supply for Northern Ireland, of the application of provisions of, or made under, this paragraph;

(*e*) the doing of things to or by a person authorised by the Authority or the Director General (as well as to or by the Authority or the Director General);

(*f*) things being done at times or in ways specified by the Authority, the Director General or such an authorised person.

(6) A condition prescribed under sub-paragraph (1)(*c*) may be one that is required to be fulfilled throughout a period, including a period ending after the time when a supply whose exemption turns on the fulfilment of the condition is treated as being made.

(7) The conditions that may be prescribed under sub-paragraph (3)(*b*) include, in particular, conditions in connection with—

(*a*) the generation of the electricity;

(*b*) the materials from which the electricity is generated;

(*c*) any of the matters mentioned in paragraphs (*b*) to (*f*) of sub-paragraph (5).

(8) Each of—

(*a*) the Gas and Electricity Markets Authority, and

(*b*) the Director General of Electricity Supply for Northern Ireland,

shall supply the Commissioners with such information (whether or not obtained under this paragraph), and otherwise give the Commissioners such co-operation, as the Commissioners may require in connection with the application (whether generally or in relation to any particular case) of any relevant provisions.

(9) In sub-paragraph (8) "relevant provisions" means provisions of or made under—

(*a*) this paragraph or paragraph 20, or

(*b*) paragraph 23(3) so far as relating to electricity, or paragraph 23(4).

(10) None of—

(*a*) section 57(1) of the Electricity Act 1989,

(*b*) section 42(1) of the Gas Act 1986, and

(*c*) Article 61(1) of the Electricity (Northern Ireland) Order 1992,

(provisions restricting disclosure of information) applies to any disclosure of information made in pursuance of sub-paragraph (8).

Amendments—[1] Sub-para (4A) inserted by FA 2002 s 126 with effect for supplies of electricity made on or after 1 November 2003 (by virtue of SI 2003/2622).

[2] Sub-para (4A) repealed by FA 2008 s 149 in relation to electricity generated on or after 1 November 2008.

Exemption under paragraph 19: averaging periods

20—(1) This paragraph applies where a person ("the supplier") makes supplies of electricity on the basis that they are exempt under paragraph 19 ("exempt renewable supplies").

(2) The rules about balancing and averaging periods are—

(*a*) a balancing period is a period of 3 months;

(*b*) when a balancing period ends, a new one begins;

(*c*) the first balancing period and the first averaging period begin at the same time;
(*d*) unless the supplier specifies an earlier time, that time is the time when he is treated as making the first of the exempt renewable supplies;
(*e*) when an averaging period ends, a new one begins;
(*f*) an averaging period ends once it has run for 2 years (but may end sooner under paragraph (*g*) or sub-paragraph (4)(*a*) or (5)(*a*));
(*g*) if the supplier stops making exempt renewable supplies, the end of the balancing period in which he makes the last exempt renewable supply is also the end of the averaging period in which that balancing period falls.

(3) At the end of each balancing period calculate—
(*a*) the total of—
(i) the quantity of renewable source electricity that the supplier acquired or generated in that period, and
(ii) any balancing credit carried forward to that balancing period; and
(*b*) the total of—
(i) the quantity of electricity supplied by exempt renewable supplies made by him in that period, and
(ii) any balancing debit carried forward to that balancing period.

(4) If the total mentioned in sub-paragraph (3)(*a*) exceeds that mentioned in sub-paragraph (3)(*b*)—
(*a*) the averaging period within which the balancing period fell ends at the end of the balancing period, and
(*b*) a balancing credit equal to the difference between the two totals is carried forward to the next balancing period.

(5) If the totals mentioned in paragraphs (*a*) and (*b*) of sub-paragraph (3) are the same—
(*a*) the averaging period within which the balancing period fell ends at the end of the balancing period, and
(*b*) no balancing credit or debit is carried forward to the next balancing period.

[(6) If the total mentioned in sub-paragraph (3)(*b*) exceeds that mentioned in sub-paragraph (3)(*a*), then—
(*a*) in a case where, at the time when the balancing period ends, an averaging period also ends because of sub-paragraph (2)(*f*) or (*g*), the supplier is for the purposes of this Schedule deemed to make at that time a taxable supply of a quantity of electricity equal to the excess;
(*b*) in any other case, a balancing debit equal to the excess is carried forward to the next balancing period.][1]

Amendments—[1] Sub-para (6) substituted for sub-paras (6)–(8) by FA 2003 s 193(1), (2), (4) with effect where the end of the balancing period referred to in sub-para (6)(*a*) as substituted falls after 30 March 2003.

[Exemption: electricity produced in combined heat and power stations

20A—(1) A supply of electricity is exempt from the levy chargeable under paragraph 5(1) if—
(*a*) the supply is not one that is deemed to be made under paragraph 23(3);
(*b*) the supply is made under a contract that contains a CHP declaration given by the supplier;
(*c*) prescribed conditions are fulfilled; and
(*d*) the supplier, and each other person (if any) who is a generator of any CHP electricity allocated by the supplier to supplies under the contract, has in a written notice given to the Commissioners agreed that he will fulfil those conditions so far as they may apply to him.

(2) Sub-paragraph (1) does not apply in relation to a supply to a person of electricity produced in a wholly or partly exempt combined heat and power station where the supply is made to that person from the station.

(3) In this paragraph "CHP declaration" means a declaration that, in each averaging period, the amount of electricity supplied by exempt CHP supplies made by the supplier in the period will not exceed the difference between—
(*a*) the total amount of CHP electricity that during that period is either acquired or generated by the supplier; and
(*b*) so much of that total amount as is allocated by the supplier otherwise than to exempt CHP supplies made by him in the period.

In this sub-paragraph "averaging period" has the same meaning as in paragraph 20B; and "exempt CHP supplies" means supplies made on the basis that they are exempt under this paragraph.

(4) For the purposes of this paragraph and paragraph 20B, electricity is "CHP electricity" if—
(*a*) the electricity was—
(i) produced in a fully exempt combined heat and power station, or
(ii) produced in a partly exempt combined heat and power station and originally supplied from the station without causing the limit referred to in paragraph 16(2) to be exceeded,

(*b*) the electricity is not renewable source electricity (within the meaning of paragraph 19); and
(*c*) prescribed conditions are fulfilled.

(5) The conditions that may be prescribed under sub-paragraph (1)(*c*) include, in particular, conditions in connection with—

(*a*) the giving of effect to CHP declarations;
(*b*) the supply of information;
(*c*) the inspection of records and, for that purpose, the production of records in legible form and entry into premises;
(*d*) monitoring by the Gas and Electricity Markets Authority, or the Director General of Electricity Supply for Northern Ireland, of the application of provisions of, or made under, this paragraph;
(*e*) the doing of things to or by a person authorised by the Authority or the Director General (as well as the doing of things to or by the Authority or the Director General);
(*f*) things being done at times or in ways specified by the Authority, the Director General or such an authorised person.

(6) A condition prescribed under sub-paragraph (1)(*c*) may be one that is required to be fulfilled throughout a period, including a period ending after the time when a supply whose exemption turns on the fulfilment of the condition is treated as being made.

(7) The conditions that may be prescribed under sub-paragraph (4)(*c*) include, in particular, conditions in connection with any of the matters mentioned in paragraphs (*b*) to (*f*) of sub-paragraph (5).

(8) Each of—

(*a*) the Gas and Electricity Markets Authority, and
(*b*) the Director General of Electricity Supply for Northern Ireland,

shall supply the Commissioners with such information (whether or not obtained under this paragraph), and otherwise give the Commissioners such co-operation, as the Commissioners may require in connection with the application of this paragraph (whether generally or in relation to any particular case).

(9) Paragraph 19(10) (disclosure of information) applies in relation to sub-paragraph (8) above as it applies in relation to paragraph 19(8).][1]

Amendments—[1] This paragraph inserted by FA 2002 s 123 with effect for supplies of electricity made after 31 March 2003 (by virtue of SI 2003/603).

[Exemption under paragraph 20A: averaging periods

20B—(1) This paragraph applies where a person ("the supplier") makes supplies of electricity on the basis that they are exempt under paragraph 20A ("exempt CHP supplies").

(2) The rules about balancing and averaging periods are—

(*a*) a balancing period is a period of three months;
(*b*) when a balancing period ends, a new one begins;
(*c*) the first balancing period and the first averaging period begin at the same time;
(*d*) unless the supplier specifies an earlier time, that time is the time when he is treated as making the first of the exempt CHP supplies;
(*e*) when an averaging period ends, a new one begins;
(*f*) an averaging period ends once it has run for two years (but may end sooner under paragraph (*g*) or sub-paragraph (4)(*a*) or (5)(*a*));
(*g*) if the supplier stops making exempt CHP supplies, the end of the balancing period in which he makes the last exempt CHP supply is also the end of the averaging period in which the balancing period falls.

(3) At the end of each balancing period calculate—

(*a*) the total of—
  (i) the quantity of CHP electricity that the supplier acquired or generated in that period, and
  (ii) any balancing credit carried forward to that balancing period; and
(*b*) the total of—
  (i) the quantity of electricity supplied by exempt CHP supplies made by him in that period, and
  (ii) any balancing debit carried forward to that balancing period.

(4) If the total mentioned in sub-paragraph (3)(*a*) exceeds that mentioned in sub-paragraph (3)(*b*)—

(*a*) the averaging period within which the balancing period fell ends at the end of the balancing period, and
(*b*) a balancing credit equal to the difference between the two totals is carried forward to the next balancing period.

(5) If the totals mentioned in paragraphs (*a*) and (*b*) of sub-paragraph (3) are the same—

(*a*) the averaging period within which the balancing period fell ends at the end of the balancing period, and

(*b*) no balancing credit or debit is carried forward to the next balancing period.

[(6) If the total mentioned in sub-paragraph (3)(*b*) exceeds that mentioned in sub-paragraph (3)(*a*), then—

(*a*) in a case where, at the time when the balancing period ends, an averaging period also ends because of sub-paragraph (2)(*f*) or (*g*), the supplier is for the purposes of this Schedule deemed to make at that time a taxable supply of a quantity of electricity equal to the excess;

(*b*) in any other case, a balancing debit equal to the excess is carried forward to the next balancing period.][2]][1]

Amendments—[1] This paragraph inserted by FA 2002 s 123 with effect for supplies of electricity made after 31 March 2003 (by virtue of SI 2003/603).

[2] Sub-para (6) substituted for sub-paras (6)–(8) by FA 2003 s 192(1), (3), (5) with effect where the end of the balancing period referred to in sub-para (6)(*a*) as substituted falls after 31 March 2003.

Regulations to avoid double charges to levy

21—(1) The Commissioners may by regulations make provision for avoiding, counteracting or mitigating double charges to levy.

(2) For the purposes of this paragraph there is a double charge to levy where—

(*a*) a supply of a taxable commodity ("the produced commodity") is a taxable supply, and

(*b*) a taxable commodity used directly or indirectly in producing the produced commodity has been the subject of a taxable supply.

(3) Regulations under this paragraph may, in particular, make provision for a supply of a taxable commodity to be wholly or to any extent—

(*a*) exempt from the levy, or

(*b*) deemed not a supply of the commodity.

(4) The provision mentioned in sub-paragraph (3) includes provision for exceptions to any of sub-paragraphs (1) to (3) of paragraph 23 or paragraph 24(3).

(5) The powers conferred by this paragraph are in addition to the powers to make provision by tax credit regulations in relation to any such case as is mentioned in paragraph 62(1)(*g*).

Regulations giving effect to exemptions

22—(1) The Commissioners may by regulations make provision for giving effect to the exclusions and exemptions provided for by paragraphs 8 to 21.

(2) Regulations under this paragraph may, in particular, include provision for—

(*a*) determining the extent to which a supply of a taxable commodity is, or is to be treated as being, a taxable supply;

(*b*) authorising a person making supplies of a taxable commodity to another person to treat the supplies to that other person as being taxable supplies only to an extent certified by the Commissioners.

Deemed supply: use of commodities by utilities and producers

23—(1) Where an electricity utility—

(*a*) has electricity available to it, and

(*b*) as regards a quantity of the electricity, makes no supply of that quantity to another person but causes it to be consumed in the United Kingdom,

the utility is for the purposes of this Schedule deemed to make a supply to itself of that quantity of the electricity.

(2) Where a gas utility—

(*a*) holds gas in a gaseous state, and

(*b*) as regards a quantity of the gas, makes no supply of that quantity to another person but causes it to be burned in the United Kingdom,

the utility is for the purposes of this Schedule deemed to make a supply to itself of that quantity of the gas.

(3) Where—

(*a*) a person has produced a taxable commodity,

(*b*) the commodity is either—

(i) a taxable commodity other than electricity, or

(ii) electricity that has been produced from taxable commodities, and

(*c*) as regards a quantity of the commodity, the person makes no supply of that quantity to another person but causes it to be burned (or, in the case of electricity, consumed) in the United Kingdom, the person is for the purposes of this Schedule deemed to make a supply to himself of that quantity of the commodity.

(4) The Commissioners may by regulations make provision for electricity to be treated for the purposes of sub-paragraph (3)(*b*)(ii)—

(*a*) as produced from taxable commodities unless prescribed conditions are fulfilled, or

(*b*) as produced otherwise than from taxable commodities only where prescribed conditions are fulfilled.

(5) The conditions that may be prescribed under sub-paragraph (4) include, in particular, conditions in connection with the materials from which the electricity is produced.

Deemed supply: [change of circumstances etc][1]

24—[(1) This paragraph applies in the following cases.][1]

[(1A) The first case is where—

(*a*) a supply of a taxable commodity has been made,

(*b*) the supply was not a taxable supply, and

(*c*) there is such a change in circumstances or any person's intentions that, if the changed circumstances or intentions had existed at the time the supply was made, the supply would have been a taxable supply.][1]

[(1B) The second case is where—

(*a*) a supply of a taxable commodity has been made,

(*b*) the supply was made on the basis that it was not a taxable supply, and

(*c*) it is later determined that the supply was (to any extent) a taxable supply.][1]

[(2) This paragraph does not apply where the reason that—

(*a*) the supply was not a taxable supply, or

(*b*) the supply was made on the basis that it was not a taxable supply,

is that it was, or was thought to be, exempt from the levy under paragraph 19 or 20A (exemption for supply of electricity produced from renewable sources or in combined heat and power stations) (but see paragraph 20 or 20B).][1]

(3) [Where this paragraph applies][1] the person to whom the supply was made is for the purposes of this Schedule deemed to make a taxable supply of the commodity to himself.

[(3A) Where—

(*a*) had matters been as mentioned in sub-paragraph (1A)(*c*), only part of the supply would have been a taxable supply, or

(*b*) the determination referred to in sub-paragraph (1B)(*c*) is that only part of the supply was a taxable supply,

the reference in sub-paragraph (3) to the commodity shall be read as a reference to a corresponding part of it.][1]

(4) Where—

(*a*) a supply of a taxable commodity was not a taxable supply by virtue of being supplied for use in premises of a description mentioned in any of paragraphs (*a*) to (*f*) of paragraph 9(2), and

(*b*) those premises cease to be premises of any of those descriptions,

sub-paragraph (3) only applies to so much (if any) of the commodity supplied as was not used in the premises before they ceased to be premises of any of those descriptions.

(5) The Commissioners may by regulations make provision specifying descriptions of occurrences and non-occurrences that are to be taken as being, or as not being, changes of circumstances or intentions for the purposes of [sub-paragraph (1A)(*c*)][1].

Amendments—[1] Words in Heading substituted; sub-paras (1)–(2) substituted for sub-paras (1), (2); words in sub-para (3) inserted; sub-para (3A) inserted; and words in sub-para (5) substituted, by FA 2003 s 190(1)–(6), (8) with effect for supplies made on or after 22 July 2005 (by virtue of SI 2005/1713).

PART III
TIME OF SUPPLY

Introduction

25 This Part of this Schedule applies to determine when a supply of a taxable commodity is treated as taking place.

Electricity or gas: supply when climate change levy accounting document issued

26—(1) This paragraph applies—

(*a*) to supplies of electricity, and

(*b*) to supplies of gas where the gas is supplied in a gaseous state and is of a kind supplied by a gas utility.

(2) Where this paragraph applies, a supply is treated as taking place each time a climate change levy accounting document in respect of a supply is issued by the person making the supply.
(3) A supply that is treated as taking place under this paragraph is a supply of the electricity or gas covered by the accounting document.
(4) Nothing in this paragraph applies to any electricity or gas that is covered by a special utility scheme (see paragraph 29).

Electricity or gas: duty to issue climate change levy accounting document

27—(1) This paragraph applies where on any day—
(*a*) electricity, or gas that is in a gaseous state and is of a kind supplied by a gas utility, is actually supplied to a person ("the consumer"),
(*b*) the supply by which the electricity or gas is supplied is a taxable supply, and
(*c*) the person liable to account for the levy on that supply is the person making the supply ("the supplier").
(2) A climate change levy accounting document covering the electricity or gas actually supplied on that day must be issued by the supplier no later than—
(*a*) the end of the period of 15 weeks beginning with that day, if on that day the consumer is a small-scale user of the commodity supplied;
(*b*) the end of the period of 6 weeks beginning with that day, if on that day the consumer is not a small-scale user of the commodity supplied.
(3) A climate change levy accounting document issued under this paragraph that covers the electricity, or the gas of any kind, actually supplied on any day must also cover any electricity or (as the case may be) any gas of that kind that—
(*a*) has been actually supplied by the supplier to the consumer on any earlier day, and
(*b*) has not been covered by a previous climate change levy accounting document.
(4) For the purposes of this paragraph—
(*a*) an accounting document shall be taken to cover the electricity or gas actually supplied on a day if it covers the electricity or gas actually supplied during a period that includes that day; and
(*b*) an accounting document shall be taken to cover the electricity or gas actually supplied on a day or during a period if it is an accounting document for a quantity of electricity or gas that is a reasonable estimate of the quantity actually supplied.
(5) A climate change levy accounting document issued under this paragraph must contain a statement of—
(*a*) the quantity of electricity or gas that it covers,
(*b*) the period during which, or during which it is estimated that, that quantity was actually supplied,
(*c*) the supplier's name and address,
(*d*) the customer's name and address, and
(*e*) the reference number used by the supplier for the customer.
(6) For the purposes of this paragraph a person is, on any day, a small-scale user of a commodity if the rate at which he is taken to be supplied with that commodity on that day does not exceed the prescribed rate.
(7) The Commissioners may make provision by regulations as to the rate at which a person is, for the purposes of sub-paragraph (6), taken to be supplied with a commodity on any day.
(8) Regulations under sub-paragraph (7) may, in particular, include provision for—
(*a*) rates to be determined or estimated in accordance with the regulations;
(*b*) rates to be so determined or estimated by reference to the quantity of a commodity actually supplied, or estimated to have been actually supplied, during a period ending with, or at any time before or after, the day in question;
(*c*) cases where a person is supplied with a commodity of any kind by two or more suppliers.
(9) Nothing in this paragraph applies to any electricity or gas—
(*a*) that is covered by a special utility scheme (see paragraph 29), or
(*b*) that is actually supplied before 1st April 2001.
(10) This paragraph applies subject to paragraph 36(5).

Electricity or gas: actual supply not followed by climate change levy accounting document

28—(1) This paragraph applies where on any day—
(*a*) electricity, or gas that is in a gaseous state and is of a kind supplied by a gas utility, is actually supplied to a person ("the consumer"),
(*b*) the supply by which the electricity or gas is supplied is a taxable supply,
(*c*) the person liable to account for the levy on that supply is the person making the supply ("the supplier"), and

(*d*) the supplier does not within the period applicable under sub-paragraph (2) of paragraph 27 issue a climate change levy accounting document under that paragraph covering the electricity or gas.

(2) Where this paragraph applies, a supply is treated as taking place at the end of that period.

(3) A supply that is treated as taking place under this paragraph is a supply of all the electricity or (as the case may be) gas of the same kind that—

(*a*) has been actually supplied by the supplier to the consumer before the end of that period, and

(*b*) has not been covered by a climate change levy accounting document.

(4) Sub-paragraph (4) of paragraph 27 (interpretation of "covered by an accounting document") applies for the purposes of this paragraph as for those of that paragraph.

(5) Nothing in this paragraph applies to any electricity or gas—

(*a*) that is covered by a special utility scheme (see paragraph 29),

(*b*) that is actually supplied before 1st April 2001, or

(*c*) that is treated under paragraph 36(3) as supplied on that day.

Electricity or gas: special utility schemes

29—(1) For the purposes of this Schedule a "special utility scheme" is a scheme for determining when—

(*a*) a supply of electricity, or

(*b*) a supply of gas that is in a gaseous state and is of a kind supplied by a gas utility,

is treated as taking place in cases where the electricity or gas is covered by the scheme.

(2) If in the opinion of the Commissioners it is reasonable to do so, they may in accordance with the provisions of this paragraph prepare a special utility scheme for a utility or for two or more utilities.

In this paragraph "utility" includes a person who makes supplies on which levy is chargeable by virtue of paragraph 5(2) (partly exempt combined heat and power stations).

(3) A special utility scheme shall specify the period for which it is to have effect.

(4) No special utility scheme shall be of any effect in relation to any electricity or gas supplied by a utility unless the utility elects in writing to be bound by it for the specified period.

(5) If a utility makes such an election—

(*a*) the scheme shall have effect for the specified period in relation to such electricity or gas supplied by the utility as is covered by the scheme, and

(*b*) during the specified period the scheme applies to determine when a supply of a taxable commodity is treated as taking place if the commodity is electricity or gas covered by the scheme.

(6) A special utility scheme may—

(*a*) cover all or any of the electricity or gas supplied by a utility for which the scheme is prepared;

(*b*) provide for paragraph 36 or 37 not to apply, or to apply with modifications, to electricity or gas covered by the scheme.

(7) The Commissioners may by regulations make further provision with respect to special utility schemes, including (in particular) provision amending this paragraph.

Other commodities: general rules for supply by UK residents

30—(1) This paragraph applies to supplies that are not of either of the descriptions mentioned in paragraphs (*a*) and (*b*) of paragraph 26(1) (electricity and gas in a gaseous state).

(2) The general rules as to when such supplies are taken to be made are, in cases where the supply is made by a person resident in the United Kingdom, as follows—

(*a*) if the commodity is to be removed, the supply takes place at the time of the removal;

(*b*) if the commodity is not to be removed, the supply takes place when the commodity is made available to the person to whom it is supplied;

(*c*) if the commodity (being sent or taken on approval or sale or return or similar terms) is removed before it is known whether a supply will take place, the supply takes place when it becomes certain that the supply has taken place or, if sooner, 12 months after the removal.

(3) These general rules are subject to—

paragraph 31 (earlier invoice),

paragraph 32 (later invoice),

paragraph 34 (deemed supplies), and

paragraph 36 (directions by Commissioners).

Other commodities: earlier invoice

31—(1) If before the time applicable under paragraph 30(2) the person making the supply—

(*a*) issues an invoice in respect of the supply, or

(*b*) receives a payment in respect of it,

the supply is treated, to the extent that it is covered by the invoice or payment, as taking place when the invoice is issued or the payment is received.

(2) Sub-paragraph (1) does not apply where the commodity (being sent or taken on approval or sale or return or similar terms) is removed before it is known whether a supply will take place.

(3) Sub-paragraph (1) applies subject to any direction under paragraph 35(3).

Other commodities: later invoice

32—(1) If within 14 days after the time applicable under paragraph 30(2) the person making the supply issues an invoice in respect of it, the supply is treated as taking place at the time the invoice is issued.

(2) This does not apply—

(*a*) to the extent that the supply is treated as taking place at the time mentioned in paragraph 31(1) (earlier invoice), or

(*b*) if the person liable to account for any levy charged on the supply has notified the Commissioners in writing that he elects not to avail himself of sub-paragraph (1).

(3) The Commissioners may, at the request of a person liable to account for any levy charged on any supplies, direct that sub-paragraph (1) shall apply—

(*a*) in relation to those supplies, or

(*b*) in relation to such of those supplies as may be specified in the direction,

with the substitution for the period of 14 days of such longer period as may be specified in the direction.

(4) Sub-paragraphs (1) to (3) apply subject to any direction under paragraph 35.

Other commodities: supply by non-UK residents

33—(1) This paragraph applies to supplies that—

(*a*) are not of either of the descriptions mentioned in paragraphs (*a*) and (*b*) of paragraph 26(1) (electricity and gas in a gaseous state), and

(*b*) are made by a person who is not resident in the United Kingdom.

(2) The supply is treated as taking place—

(*a*) when the commodity is delivered to the person to whom it is supplied, or

(*b*) if earlier, when it is made available in the United Kingdom to that person.

(3) Sub-paragraph (2) applies subject to—

(*a*) sub-paragraph (4),

(*b*) paragraph 34 (deemed supplies), and

(*c*) any direction under paragraph 35.

(4) If within 14 days after the time applicable under sub-paragraph (2) the person to whom the supply is made elects in writing for the supply to be treated as taking place at the time the election is made, the supply is treated as taking place at the time the election is made.

Other commodities: deemed supplies

34—(1) This paragraph applies to supplies that—

(*a*) are not of either of the descriptions mentioned in paragraphs (*a*) and (*b*) of paragraph 26(1) (electricity and gas in a gaseous state), and

(*b*) are deemed to be made under paragraph 23[, 24 or 45A][3].

(2) A supply that is deemed to be made under paragraph 23 is treated as taking place when the commodity is burned [. . .][2].

(3) A supply that is deemed to be made under paragraph 24 is treated as taking place upon the occurrence of the change in circumstances or intentions [or, as the case may be, upon the later determination][1].

[(4) A supply that is deemed to be made under paragraph 45A is treated as taking place upon the later determination.][3]

Amendments—[1] Words in sub-para (3) inserted by FA 2003 s 190(7), (8) with effect for supplies made on or after 22 July 2005 (by virtue of SI 2005/1713).

[2] Words in sub-para (2) omitted by FA 2006 ss 172(7), 178, Sch 26 Pt 8(1) (being unnecessary because the paragraph does not apply in the case of electricity).

[3] In sub-para (1)(*b*), words substituted for the words "or 24", and sub-para (4) inserted, by FA 2007 s 23, Sch 2 paras 1, 5 with effect from 1 November 2007: SI 2007/2902 art 2(1).

Other commodities: directions by Commissioners

35—(1) This paragraph applies to supplies that are not of either of the descriptions mentioned in paragraphs (*a*) and (*b*) of paragraph 26(1) (electricity and gas in a gaseous state).

(2) The Commissioners may, at the request of the person liable to account for any levy charged on any supplies to which this paragraph applies, make a direction under sub-paragraph (3) or (4) altering the time at which those supplies (or such of those supplies as may be specified in the direction) are to be treated as taking place.

(3) The Commissioners may direct that the supplies shall be treated as taking place—

(*a*) at times or on dates determined by or by reference to the occurrence of some event described in the direction, or

(*b*) at times or on dates determined by or by reference to the time when some event so described would in the ordinary course of events occur,

provided the resulting times or dates are in every case earlier than would otherwise apply.

(4) The Commissioners may direct that the supplies shall be treated as taking place—

(*a*) at the beginning of the relevant working period (as defined in the case of the person making the request in and for the purposes of the direction), or

(*b*) at the end of the relevant working period (as so defined).

(5) A direction under sub-paragraph (4) shall not apply to the extent that the time when the supplies in question are made is determined by paragraph 31(1).

Supplies invoiced or paid for before 1st April 2001

36—(1) This paragraph applies where—

(*a*) the taxable commodities covered by an invoice issued, or payment received, before 1st April 2001 are to any extent commodities that have not been burned (or, in the case of electricity, consumed) before the invoice is issued or payment is received, and

(*b*) the advance invoicing or payment is not acceptable normal practice.

It does not matter whether the invoice mentioned in paragraph (*a*) is, or is not, a climate change levy accounting document.

(2) A fair apportionment shall be made to determine the quantity of the taxable commodities covered by the invoice or payment that will not be, or was not, burned (or consumed) before 1st April 2001.

(3) Where this paragraph applies, a supply is treated as taking place on 1st April 2001.

That supply is a supply of the quantity of the taxable commodities that is mentioned in, and determined under, sub-paragraph (2).

(4) For the purposes of this paragraph advance invoicing or payment is "acceptable normal practice" if—

(*a*) the supply is of a kind in the case of which it is normal practice for invoices to be issued, or payments made, in respect of taxable commodities not already burned (or consumed),

(*b*) that practice does not involve issuing invoices, or making payments, more than 15 weeks in advance of the burning (or consumption) of any of the taxable commodities in respect of which the invoice is issued or payment is made, and

(*c*) the advance invoicing or payment is in accordance with the practice.

(5) Nothing in paragraph 27 requires a climate change levy accounting document to be issued to cover any commodities that are supplied by a supply that, under sub-paragraph (3), is treated as made on 1st April 2001.

(6) This paragraph applies to invoices issued, and payments received, before the passing of this Act (as well as to those issued or received after its passing).

Supplies of electricity or gas spanning change of rate etc

37—(1) This paragraph applies in the case of a supply of electricity, or of gas that is in a gaseous state and is of a kind supplied by a gas utility, affected by—

(*a*) a change in the descriptions of supplies that are taxable supplies,

(*b*) a change in any rate of levy in force,

(*c*) a change consisting in the rate of levy applicable to the supply ceasing to be, or becoming, the rate that is applicable to . . . [1] reduced-rate supplies, or

(*d*) the change consisting in the transition from 31st March 2001 to 1st April 2001.

(2) For the purposes of this paragraph a supply is affected by a change if the electricity or gas of which it is a supply ("the supplied commodity") is actually supplied partly before the change and partly after.

However, this paragraph does not apply in the case of a supply that, under paragraph 36(3), is treated as made on 1st April 2001.

(3) If the person liable to account for any levy on the supply so elects—

(*a*) the rate at which levy is chargeable on any part of the supply, or

(*b*) any question whether, or to what extent, the supply is a taxable supply,

shall be determined in accordance with sub-paragraph (5) or (6).

(4) An election for determination in accordance with sub-paragraph (6) may be made only where—

(*a*) there is such a change as is mentioned in sub-paragraph (1)(*c*), and

(*b*) all the supplied commodity is actually supplied before the supply is treated as taking place.

(5) Where the election is for determination in accordance with this sub-paragraph, the rules are—

"A Treat the fraction of the supplied commodity actually supplied before the change ("the pre-change fraction") as supplied by a supply made before the change and treat the fraction of the supplied commodity actually supplied after the change ("the post-change fraction") as supplied by a supply made after the change.

B Where the pre-change and post-change fractions are not known (because, for example, there are no relevant meter readings available)—

"the pre-change fraction" is calculated by dividing—

(*a*) the number of days in the period over which the supply is actually made that fall before the change, by

(*b*) the number of days in that period; and

"the post-change fraction" is the difference between 1 and the pre-change fraction.

C If use of the fractions given by rule B would produce an inequitable result, the pre-change and post-change fractions may be derived from a reasonable estimate of the fractions of the supplied commodity actually supplied before and after the change.

(6) Where the election is for determination in accordance with this sub-paragraph, treat the change as taking place immediately after the time at which the last of the supplied commodity was actually supplied.

Amendment—[1] In sub-para (1)(*c*), words "half-rate supplies or" omitted by FA 2006 ss 172(9), 178, Sch 26 Pt 8(1) with effect from 1 November 2007: SI 2007/2901 art 2(1).

This amendment does not apply in relation to a half-rate supply made before 1 April 2006: SI 2007/2901 art 2(2). For this purpose, "half-rate supply" carries the meaning it has in this Schedule before 1 November 2007. FA 2006 s 172(3)–(6) applies for determining when a supply is to be regarded as made: SI 2007/2901 art 2(3).

Other supplies spanning change of rate etc

38—(1) This paragraph applies where there is—

(*a*) a change in the descriptions of supplies that are taxable supplies,

(*b*) a change in the rate of levy in force,

(*c*) a change consisting in the rate of levy applicable to any supply ceasing to be, or becoming, the rate that is applicable to . . . [1] reduced-rate supplies, or

(*d*) the change consisting in the transition from 31st March 2001 to 1st April 2001.

(2) Where—

(*a*) a supply affected by the change would apart from special provisions be treated under paragraph 30(2) or 33(2) as made wholly or partly at a time when it would not have been affected by the change, or

(*b*) a supply not so affected would apart from special provisions be treated under paragraph 30(2) or 33(2) as made wholly or partly at a time when it would have been so affected,

the rate at which levy is chargeable on the supply, or any question whether it is a taxable supply, shall, if the person liable to account for any levy on the supply so elects, be determined without regard to the special provisions.

(3) In this paragraph "special provisions" means the provisions of paragraphs 31, 32, 33(4) and 35.

Amendment—[1] In sub-para (1)(*c*) words "half-rate supplies or" omitted by FA 2006 ss 172(10), 178, Sch 26 Pt 8(1) with effect from 1 November 2007.

This amendment does not apply in relation to a half-rate supply made before 1 April 2006: SI 2007/2901 art 2(2). For this purpose, "half-rate supply" carries the meaning it has in this Schedule before 1 November 2007. FA 2006 s 172(3)–(6) applies for determining when a supply is to be regarded as made: SI 2007/2901 art 2(3).

Regulations as to time of supply

39—(1) The Commissioners may make provision by regulations as to the time at which a supply is to be treated as taking place—

(*a*) in cases where the supply is for a consideration and the whole or part of the consideration—

(i) is determined or payable periodically, or from time to time, or at the end of any period, or

(ii) is determined at the time when the commodity is appropriated for any purpose;

(*b*) in the case of a supply otherwise than for consideration;

(*c*) in the case of any supply that is deemed to be made under paragraph 23[, 24 or 45A][1].

(2) In any such case as is mentioned in sub-paragraph (1) the regulations may provide that a taxable commodity shall be treated as separately and successively supplied at prescribed times or intervals.

(3) Paragraphs 26 to 36 (main rules as to time of supply) have effect subject to any regulations under this paragraph.

(4) The power to make regulations under this paragraph includes power to provide for specified provisions of the regulations to be treated as special provisions for the purposes of paragraph 38 (supplies spanning change of rate etc).

Amendments—[1] Words in sub-para (1)(*c*) substituted for the words "or 24" by FA 2007 s 23, Sch 2 paras 1, 6 with effect from 1 November 2007: SI 2007/2902 art 2(1).

PART IV
PAYMENT AND RATE OF LEVY

Persons liable to account for levy

40—(1) The person liable to account for the levy charged on a taxable supply is, except in a case where sub-paragraph (2) [or (3)][1] applies, the person making the supply.

(2) In the case of a taxable supply made by a person who—

(*a*) is not resident in the United Kingdom, and

(*b*) is not a utility,

the person liable to account for the levy charged on the supply is the person to whom the supply is made.

[(3)In the case of levy charged on a taxable supply under paragraph 45B, the person liable to account for the levy is the operator of the facility to which the supply was made.][1]

Amendments—[1] Sub-para (3) and consequential amendments inserted by FA 2009 s 118, Sch 59 paras 2, 3 with effect where the certification period begins on or after 1 April 2009.

Returns and payment of levy

41—(1) The Commissioners may by regulations make provision—

[(*a*) for persons liable to account for levy to do so—

(i) by reference to such periods ("accounting periods") as may be determined by or under the regulations, or

(ii) in such other way as may be so determined;][1]

(*b*) for persons who are or are required to be registered for the purposes of the levy to be subject to such obligations to make returns for those purposes for such periods, at such times and in such form as may be so determined; and

(*c*) for persons who are required to account for levy . . . [1] to become liable to pay the amounts due from them at such times and in such manner as may be so determined.

(2) Without prejudice to the generality of the powers conferred by sub-paragraph (1), regulations under this paragraph may contain provision—

(*a*) for levy falling in accordance with the regulations to be accounted for by reference to one accounting period to be treated in prescribed circumstances, and for prescribed purposes, as levy due for a different period;

(*b*) for the correction of errors made when accounting for levy by reference to any period;

(*c*) for the entries to be made in any accounts in connection with the correction of any such errors and for the financial adjustments to be made in that connection;

(*d*) for a person, for purposes connected with the making of any such entry or financial adjustment, to be required to provide to any prescribed person, or to retain, a document in the prescribed form containing prescribed particulars of the matters to which the entry or adjustment relates;

(*e*) for enabling the Commissioners, in such cases as they may think fit, to dispense with or relax a requirement imposed by regulations made by virtue of paragraph (*d*);

(*f*) for the amount of levy which, in accordance with the regulations, is treated as due for a later period than that by reference to which it should have been accounted for to be treated as increased by an amount representing interest at the rate applicable under section 197 of the Finance Act 1996 for such period as may be determined in accordance with the regulations.

[(2A) Paragraph 91(5) provides for the application of Part 7 of this Schedule (recovery and interest) in relation to cases where, by virtue of regulations under sub-paragraph (1)(*a*)(ii) above [or by virtue of paragraph 45B(8)][3], a person is liable to account for levy otherwise than by reference to accounting periods.

(2B) Regulations under this paragraph may provide for the application of any provision of this Schedule in relation to such cases.][1]

(3) Subject to the following provisions of this paragraph, if any person ("the taxpayer") fails—

(*a*) to comply with so much of any regulations under this paragraph as requires him, at or before a particular time, to make a return for any accounting period, or

(*b*) to comply with so much of any regulations under this paragraph as requires him, at or before a particular time, to pay an amount of levy due from him,

he shall be liable to a penalty of £250.

(4) Liability to a penalty under sub-paragraph (3) shall not arise if the taxpayer satisfies the Commissioners or, on appeal, an appeal tribunal—

(*a*) that there is a reasonable excuse for the failure to make the return or to pay the levy in accordance with the regulations; and

(*b*) that there is not an occasion after the last day on which the return or payment was required by the regulations to be made when there was a failure without a reasonable excuse to make it.

(5) Where, by reason of any failure falling within paragraph (*a*) or (*b*) of sub-paragraph (3)—

(*a*) a person is convicted of an offence (whether under this Schedule or otherwise), or

(*b*) a person is assessed to a penalty under paragraph 98 (penalty for evasion) [or to a penalty for a deliberate inaccuracy under Schedule 24 to the Finance Act 2007 (penalties for errors)][2],

that person shall not, by reason of that failure, be liable also to a penalty under that sub-paragraph (3).

Amendments—[1] Sub-para (1)(*a*) substituted, words "for any period" in sub-para (1)(*c*) repealed, and sub-paras (2A) and (2B) inserted, by FA 2003 ss 192(1), (2), 216, Sch 43 Pt 4 with effect from 10 July 2003.

[2] Words in sub-para (5)(*b*) inserted by the Finance Act 2008, Schedule 40 (Appointed Day, Transitional Provisions and Consequential Amendments) Order, SI 2009/571 art 8, Sch 1 para 20(1), (2) with effect from 1 April 2009.

[3] Words in sub-para (2A) inserted by FA 2009 s 118, Sch 59 paras 2, 4 with effect where the certification period begins on or after 1 April 2009.

Amount payable by way of levy

42—(1) The amount payable by way of levy on a taxable supply is—

(*a*) if the supply is [not][2] a reduced-rate supply, the amount ascertained from the Table in accordance with sub-paragraph (2);

(b) . . .[2]

(*c*) if the supply is a reduced-rate supply, 20 per cent of the amount that would be payable if the supply were [not][2] a reduced-rate supply.

[Table

Taxable commodity supplied	*Rate at which levy payable if supply is not a reduced-rate supply*
Electricity	£0.00470 per kilowatt hour
Gas supplied by a gas utility or any gas supplied in a gaseous state that is of a kind supplied by a gas utility	£0.00164 per kilowatt hour
Any petroleum gas, or other gaseous hydrocarbon, supplied in a liquid state	£0.01050 per kilogram
Any other taxable commodity	£0.01281 per kilogram][1]

[(1A) Sub-paragraph (1) is subject to paragraph 45B.][3]

(2) The levy payable on a fraction of a quantity of a commodity is that fraction of the levy payable on that quantity of the commodity.

[(3) If a reduced-rate supply is part of an aid scheme within Article 25 of Commission Regulation (EC) No 800/2008, sub-paragraph (4) cites the title and publication reference of that Regulation for the purpose of complying with Article 3(1) of that Regulation.

(4) That citation is Commission Regulation (EC) No 800/2008 of 6 August 2008 declaring certain categories of aid compatible with the common market in application of Articles 87 and 88 of the Treaty (General block exemption Regulation) (OJ 2008 No L214/3) (with the reference to Articles 87 and 88 being read, as a result of the Treaty of Lisbon, as a reference to Articles 107 and 108 of the Treaty on the Functioning of the European Union).][4]

Amendments—[1] Table substituted by FA 2008 s 19(1), with effect in relation to supplies treated as taking place on or after 1 April 2009.

[2] In sub-paras (1)(*a*), (*c*), the words "neither a half-rate supply nor" substituted, and sub-para (1)(*b*) omitted, by FA 2006 ss 172(11), 178, Sch 26 Pt 8(1) with effect from 1 November 2007: SI 2007/2901 art 2(1).

These amendments do not apply in relation to a half-rate supply made before 1 April 2006: SI 2007/2901 art 2(2). For this purpose, "half-rate supply" carries the meaning it has in this Schedule before 1 November 2007. FA 2006 s 172(3)–(6) applies for determining when a supply is to be regarded as made: SI 2007/2901 art 2(3).

[3] Sub-para (1A) inserted by FA 2009 s 118, Sch 59 paras 2, 5 with effect in relation to certification periods beginning on or after 1 April 2009.

[4] Sub-paras (3), (4) inserted by FA 2010 s 67 with effect from 8 April 2010.

Prospective amendments—In sub-para (1), the table to be substituted, and words "35 per cent" to be substituted for words "20 per cent", by FA 2010 ss 17(1), 18(1) with effect in relation to supplies treated as taking place on or after 1 April 2011. The table to read as follows—

"TABLE

Taxable commodity supplied	*Rate at which levy payable if supply is not a reduced-rate supply*
Electricity	£0.00485 per kilowatt hour
Gas supplied by a gas utility or any gas supplied in a gaseous state that is of a kind supplied by a gas utility	£0.00169 per kilowatt hour
Any petroleum gas, or other gaseous hydrocarbon, supplied in a liquid state	£0.01083 per kilogram
Any other taxable commodity	£0.01321 per kilogram".

Half-rate for supplies to horticultural producers

43—*(1) For the purposes of this Schedule a half-rate supply is a taxable supply in respect of which the following conditions are satisfied—*

(a) the first condition is that the person to whom the supply is made is a horticultural producer;

(b) the second condition is that the horticultural producer intends to use the taxable commodity supplied—

(i) in the heating, for the growth of horticultural produce primarily with a view to the production of horticultural produce for sale, of any building or structure, or of the earth or other growing medium in it,

(ii) in the lighting, for the growth of horticultural produce primarily with a view to the production of horticultural produce for sale, of any building or structure, or

(iii) in the sterilisation of the earth or other growing medium to be used for the growth of horticultural produce as mentioned in sub-paragraph (i) in any building or structure.

(2) In this paragraph "horticultural producer" means a person growing horticultural produce primarily for sale.

(3) In this paragraph "horticultural produce" means—

(a) fruit;

(b) vegetables of a kind grown for human consumption, including fungi, but not including maincrop potatoes or peas grown for seed, for harvesting dry or for vining;

(c) flowers, pot plants and decorative foliage;

(d) herbs;

(e) seeds other than pea seeds, and bulbs and other material, being seeds, bulbs or material for sowing or planting for the production of—

(i) fruit,

(ii) vegetables falling within paragraph (b),

(iii) flowers, plants or foliage falling within paragraph (c), or

(iv) herbs,

or for reproduction of the seeds, bulbs or other material planted; or

(f) trees and shrubs, other than trees grown for the purpose of afforestation;

but does not include hops.

(4) The Commissioners may by regulations make provision for facilitating the enjoyment of the reduced rate of levy payable on half-rate supplies.

(5) Regulations under sub-paragraph (4) may, in particular, include provision—

(a) for determining the extent to which a taxable supply is, or is to be treated as being, a half-rate supply;

(b) for authorising a person making taxable supplies to another person to treat the supplies to that other person as being half-rate supplies only to an extent certified by the Commissioners;

(c) for a person making half-rate supplies ("the supplier") to account for levy on those supplies as if the supplies were neither half-rate supplies nor reduced-rate supplies.

(6) Provision such as is mentioned in sub-paragraph (5)(c) may be made only where tax credit regulations provide for a horticultural producer to be entitled to a tax credit in respect of 50 per cent of the levy accounted for by the supplier on any half-rate supplies—

(a) that are made by the supplier to the horticultural producer, and

(b) on which the supplier has accounted for levy on the basis mentioned in sub-paragraph (5)(c).[1]

Amendment—[1] This paragraph repealed by FA 2006 ss 172(12), 178, Sch 26 Pt 8(1) with effect from 1 November 2007: SI 2007/2901 art 2(1).

This amendment does not apply in relation to a half-rate supply made before 1 April 2006: SI 2007/2901 art 2(2). For this purpose, "half-rate supply" carries the meaning it has in this Schedule before 1 November 2007. FA 2006 s 172(3)–(6) applies for determining when a supply is to be regarded as made: SI 2007/2901 art 2(3).

Regulations made under this para made before 1 November 2007 are unaffected by the repeal of this para: SI 2004/2901 art 2(4).

Reduced-rate for supplies covered by climate change agreement

[**44**—(1) For the purposes of this Schedule, a taxable supply is a reduced-rate supply if—

(*a*) the taxable commodity is supplied to a facility specified in a certificate given by the Secretary of State to the Commissioners as a facility which is to be taken as being covered by a climate change agreement for a period specified in the certificate, and

(*b*) the supply is made at a time falling in that period.

(2) Sub-paragraph (1) has effect subject to [sub-paragraphs (2A) to (2D) and][2][paragraphs 45 and 45B][3].

[(2A) The Secretary of State may—

(*a*) give a certificate that includes provision specifying one or more descriptions of taxable commodity as being ineligible for reduced-rate supply,

(*b*) vary a certificate so that it includes provision (or further provision) specifying one or more descriptions of taxable commodity as being ineligible for reduced-rate supply, or

(*c*) vary a certificate so that it ceases to include the provision (or some of the provision) specifying one or more descriptions of taxable commodity as being ineligible for reduced-rate supply.

(2B) A taxable supply of a taxable commodity to a facility is not a reduced-rate supply if, at the time of the supply, the commodity falls within a description that is specified (by virtue of sub-paragraph (2A)(*a*) or (*b*)) in the certificate relating to the facility.

(2C) The Secretary of State may only include provision in a certificate by virtue of sub-paragraph (2A)(*a*) or (*b*)—

(*a*) if the Treasury consents in writing to the specification before the specification is made, and

(*b*) if, and for as long as, the result is compatible with the common market by virtue of Commission Regulation (EC) No 800/2008 of 6 August 2008 declaring certain categories of aid compatible with the common market in application of Articles 87 and 88 of the Treaty establishing the European Community (General block exemption Regulation) (OJ 2008 No L214/3).

(2D) In sub-paragraphs (2A) to (2C) "certificate" means such a certificate as is mentioned in sub-paragraph (1)(*a*).][2]

(3) The Commissioners may by regulations make provision for giving effect to sub-paragraph (1).

(4) Regulations under this paragraph may, in particular, include provision for determining whether any taxable commodity is supplied to a facility.

(5) The provision that may be made by virtue of sub-paragraph (4) includes, in particular, provision for a taxable commodity of any description specified in the regulations to be taken as supplied to a facility only if the commodity is delivered to the facility.][1]

Amendments—[1] This paragraph substituted by FA 2007 s 23, Sch 2 paras 1, 7 with effect from 1 November 2007: SI 2007/2902 art 2(1). This amendment only applies in relation to a supply actually made on or after 1 November 2007: SI 2007/2902 art 2(2).

This paragraph previously read as follows—

"44—

(1) Where the Secretary of State gives a certificate to the Commissioners stating that, for a period specified in the certificate, a facility is to be taken as being covered by a climate change agreement, the Commissioners shall publish a notice in respect of the facility.

(2) Such a notice shall—

(*a*) state the day on which it is published,

(*b*) identify the facility or facilities in respect of which it is published,

(*c*) for each facility—

(i) set out the first and last days of the period specified for the facility in the Secretary of State's certificate, and

(ii) indicate the effect of sub-paragraph (3),

and

(*d*) indicate that the notice may be varied by later notices.

(3) For the purposes of this Schedule, a reduced-rate supply is a taxable supply in respect of which the following conditions are satisfied—

(*a*) the first condition is that the taxable commodity supplied by the supply is supplied to a facility identified in a notice published under sub-paragraph (1);

(*b*) the second condition is that the supply is made at a time falling in the period that begins with the later of—

(i) the first day set out for the facility under sub-paragraph (2)(*c*), and

(ii) the day on which the notice is published,

and ends with the last day set out for the facility under sub-paragraph (2)(*c*).

(4) Sub-paragraph (3) has effect subject to paragraph 45.

(5) The Commissioners may, for the purposes of sub-paragraph (3), by regulations make provision for determining whether any taxable commodity is supplied to a facility.

(6) The provision that may be made by regulations under sub-paragraph (5) includes, in particular, provision for a taxable commodity of any description specified in the regulations to be taken as supplied to a facility only if the commodity is delivered to the facility.".

[2] Sub-paras (2A)–(2D) and consequential amendment inserted by FA 2009 s 117(1), (2) with effect from 21 July 2009.

[3] Words substituted by FA 2009 s 118, Sch 59 paras 2, 6 with effect where the certification period begins on or after 1 April 2009.

[Reduced-rate supplies: variation of certificates under paragraph 44][1]

45—(1) This paragraph applies where the Secretary of State, after having given in respect of a facility such a certificate as is mentioned in paragraph 44(1) ("the original certificate"), gives a certificate (a "variation certificate") to the Commissioners stating—

(*a*) that, throughout the period ("the original period") specified for the facility in the original certificate, the facility is to be taken as not being covered by a climate change agreement; or

(*b*) that, for so much of the original period as falls on or after a day specified in the variation certificate (being a day falling within the original period), the facility is to be taken as no longer being covered by a climate change agreement.

(2)–(4) . . . [1]

(5) If—

(*a*) the statement in the variation certificate in respect of the facility is of the type described in sub-paragraph (1)(*a*), and

(*b*) the day on which [the variation certificate is given][1] falls before the beginning of the original period,

[the original certificate has effect as if the facility had never been specified in it][1].

(6) If—

(*a*) the statement in the variation certificate in respect of the facility is of the type described in sub-paragraph (1)(*a*), and

(*b*) the day on which [the variation certificate is given][1] falls during the original period,

[the original certificate has effect as if the last day of the period specified for the facility in the original certificate were the day on which the variation certificate is given][1].

(7) If the statement in the variation certificate in respect of the facility is of the type described in sub-paragraph (1)(*b*), [the original certificate has effect as if the last day of the period specified for the facility in the original certificate were the later of—

(*a*) the day on which the variation certificate is given, and

(*b*) the day specified in the variation certificate.][1]

Amendments—[1] Sub-paras (2)–(4) repealed; words in sub-paras (5), (6), (7) substituted; and Heading substituted, by FA 2007 ss 23, 114, Sch 2 paras 1, 8, Sch 27 Pt 1(1) with effect from 1 November 2007: SI 2007/2902 art 2(1).

Sub-paras (2)–(4) previously read as follows—

"(2) Where the Commissioners receive a variation certificate in respect of a facility before they have published a notice under paragraph 44(1) in response to the original certificate so far as relating to the facility, their obligation to publish a notice under paragraph 44(1) in respect of the facility shall have effect as an obligation to publish such a notice in response to the original certificate as varied by the variation certificate.

(3) Where the Commissioners receive a variation certificate but sub-paragraph (2) does not apply, they shall publish a notice (a "variation notice") that—

(*a*) states the day on which it is published,

(*b*) identifies the facility or facilities in respect of which it is published,

(*c*) sets out, for each facility in respect of which the statement in the variation certificate is of the type described in sub-paragraph (1)(*b*), the date specified for the facility in the variation certificate, and

(*d*) for each facility, indicates the effect of sub-paragraphs (4) to (7) as they apply in the case of the facility.

(4) Sub-paragraphs (5) to (7) set out the effect of a variation notice being published in respect of a facility.".

The words substituted in sub-para (5) previously read as follows—

"the variation notice is published", and "the notice ("the original notice") published under paragraph 44(1) in response to the original certificate has effect as if the facility had never been identified in it".

The words substituted in sub-para (6) previously read as follows—

"the variation notice is published", and "the original notice has effect as if the last day set out for the facility under paragraph 44(2)(*c*) were the day on which the variation notice is published".

The words substituted in sub-para (7) previously read as follows—

"the original notice has effect as if the last day set out for the facility under paragraph 44(2)(*c*) were the later of—

(*a*) the day on which the variation notice is published, and

(*b*) the day set out in the variation notice for the facility under sub-paragraph (3)(*c*).".

The Heading previously read as follows—

"Reduced-rate supplies: variation of notices under paragraph 44".

[Reduced-rate supplies: deemed supply

45A—(1) This paragraph applies where—

(*a*) a taxable supply has been made to any person ("the recipient"),

(*b*) the supply was made on the basis that it was a reduced-rate supply, and

(*c*) it is later determined that the supply was not a reduced-rate supply.

(2) For the purposes of this Schedule—

(*a*) the recipient is deemed to make a taxable supply to itself of the taxable commodity, and

(*b*) the amount payable by way of levy on that deemed supply is 80 per cent. of the amount that would be payable if the supply were not a reduced-rate supply.][1]

[(3) This paragraph does not apply where a supply is treated as not being a reduced-rate supply by virtue of paragraph 45B.][2]

Amendments—[1] This paragraph inserted by FA 2007 s 23, Sch 2 paras 1, 9 with effect from 1 November 2007: SI 2007/2902 art 2(1). This amendment only applies in relation to a supply actually made on or after 1 November 2007 and on the basis that it is a reduced-rate supply: SI 2007/2902 art 2(3).

[2] Sub-para (3) inserted by FA 2009 s 118, Sch 59 paras 2, 7 with effect where the certification period begins on or after 1 April 2009.

[Removal of reduced rate where targets set by climate change agreement not met

45B—(1) This paragraph applies where, by virtue of such a certificate as is mentioned in paragraph 44(1), a facility is to be taken as being covered by a climate change agreement for a period specified in that certificate ("the certification period").

(2) If it appears to the Secretary of State that the progress made in the certification period towards meeting targets set for the facility by the agreement has been such as under the provisions of the agreement is unsatisfactory, the Secretary of State may issue a certificate under this paragraph.

(3) The certificate must (in addition to specifying the facility, agreement and certification period to which it applies) specify—

(*a*) T, that is, the value (expressed in terms of a reduction in tonnes of carbon dioxide equivalent) of achieving the targets set for the facility by the agreement, and

(*b*) P, that is, the value (expressed in the same terms) of the progress made by the facility, during the certification period, towards meeting those targets.

(4) Where a certificate has been issued under this paragraph—

(*a*) each taxable supply made to the facility at any time falling within the certification period is to be treated as not being a reduced-rate supply, and

(*b*) accordingly, an amount (determined in accordance with sub-paragraph (5)) is payable by way of levy on that taxable supply.

(5) The amount payable under this paragraph on a taxable supply is—

$$\frac{T-P}{T} \times 0.8R$$

where—

T and P have the values mentioned in sub-paragraph (3);

R is the amount which would have been payable by way of levy on the supply (had it not been a reduced-rate supply) at the time that it was made, in accordance with paragraph 42(1)(*a*).

(6) The Secretary of State must send the certificate to—

(*a*) the Commissioners, and

(*b*) the person who is the operator of the facility.

(7) A certificate under this paragraph may be issued after the certification period ends.

(8) A person liable to account for levy under this paragraph—

(*a*) is liable to account for it otherwise than by reference to an accounting period, and

(*b*) must not (by virtue of regulations under paragraph 41) become liable to pay it as from a date before the date on which the certificate under this paragraph is issued.

(9) Levy due under this paragraph is payable in addition to any levy already payable on any supply made in the certification period.

(10) In this paragraph—

"certification period", in a case where the certificate referred to in sub-paragraph (1) has been varied under paragraph 45, means the period for which that certificate has effect as varied;

"tonne of carbon dioxide equivalent" has the meaning given in the Climate Change Act 2008.][1]

Amendments—[1] This paragraph inserted by FA 2009 s 118, Sch 59 para 1 with effect where the certification period begins on or after 1 April 2009.

Climate change agreements

46 In this Schedule "climate change agreement" means—

(*a*) an agreement that falls within paragraph 47, or

(*b*) a combination of agreements that falls within paragraph 48.

Climate change agreements: direct agreement with Secretary of State

47—(1) An agreement (including one entered into before the passing of this Act) falls within this paragraph if it is an agreement—

(*a*) entered into with the Secretary of State,

(*b*) expressed to be entered into for the purposes of the reduced rate of climate change levy,

(*c*) identifying the facilities to which it applies,

(*d*) to which a representative of each facility to which it applies is a party,

(*e*) setting, or providing for the setting of, targets for the facilities to which it applies,

(*f*) specifying certification periods (as to which see paragraph 49(1)) for the facilities to which it applies, and

(*g*) providing for five-yearly (or more frequent) reviews by the Secretary of State of targets set by or under the agreement for those facilities and for giving effect to outcomes of such reviews.

(2) In this paragraph and paragraph 48 "representative", in relation to a facility to which an agreement applies, means—

(*a*) the person who is the operator of the facility at—

(i) the time the agreement is entered into, or

(ii) if later, the time the facility last became a facility to which the agreement applies,

or

(*b*) a person authorised by that operator to agree to the facility being a facility to which the agreement applies.

Climate change agreement: combination of umbrella and underlying agreements

48—(1) A combination of agreements falls within this paragraph if the following conditions are satisfied.

(2) The first condition is that the combination is a combination of—

(*a*) an umbrella agreement (including one entered into before the passing of this Act), and

(*b*) an agreement (including one entered into before the passing of this Act) that, in relation to the umbrella agreement, is an underlying agreement.

(3) The second condition is that between them the two agreements—

(*a*) set, or provide for the setting of, targets for the facilities to which the underlying agreement applies,

(*b*) specify certification periods (as to which see paragraph 49(1)) for the facilities to which the underlying agreement applies, and

(*c*) provide for five-yearly (or more frequent) reviews by the Secretary of State of targets set by or under the agreements for those facilities and for giving effect to outcomes of such reviews.

(4) For the purposes of this paragraph an "umbrella agreement" is an agreement—

(*a*) entered into with the Secretary of State,

(*b*) expressed to be entered into for the purposes of the reduced rate of climate change levy,

(*c*) identifying the facilities to which it applies, and

(*d*) to which a representative of each facility to which it applies is a party.

(5) For the purposes of this paragraph an agreement is an "underlying agreement" in relation to an umbrella agreement if it is an agreement—

(*a*) expressed to be entered into for the purposes of the umbrella agreement,

(*b*) entered into—

(i) with the Secretary of State, or

(ii) with a party to the umbrella agreement other than the Secretary of State,

(*c*) approved by the Secretary of State if he is not a party to it,

(*d*) identifying which of the facilities to which the umbrella agreement applies are the facilities to which it applies, and

(*e*) to which a representative of each facility to which it applies is a party.

(6) In the case of a climate change agreement that is a combination of agreements that falls within this paragraph, references to the facilities to which the climate change agreement applies are references to the facilities to which the underlying agreement applies.

Climate change agreement: supplemental provisions

49—(1) The first certification period specified by a climate change agreement for a facility to which it applies shall begin with the later of—

(*a*) the date on which the agreement, so far as relating to the facility, is expressed to take effect, and

(*b*) 1st April 2001;

and each subsequent certification period so specified shall begin immediately after the end of a previous certification period.

(2) Where a climate change agreement (the "new agreement") applies to a facility to which another climate change agreement previously applied, the first certification period specified by the new agreement for the facility shall be—

(*a*) a period beginning as provided by sub-paragraph (1), or

(*b*) a period that—

(i) begins earlier than that, and

(ii) is a period that was a certification period specified for the facility by any climate change agreement that previously applied to the facility.

A period such as is mentioned in paragraph (*b*) includes a period beginning, or beginning and ending, before the date on which the new agreement, so far as relating to the facility, is expressed to take effect.

(3) For the purposes of giving certificates such as are mentioned in paragraphs 44(1) and 45(1), the Secretary of State may take a facility as being covered by a climate change agreement for a period if the facility is one to which the agreement applies and either—

(*a*) that period is the first certification period specified by the agreement for the facility, or

(*b*) that period is a subsequent certification period for the facility and it appears to the Secretary of State that progress made in the immediately preceding certification period towards meeting targets set for the facility by the agreement or by a climate change agreement that previously applied to the facility is, or is likely to be, such as under the provisions of the agreement in question is to be taken as being satisfactory.

(4) For the purposes of sub-paragraph (3)(*b*) a climate change agreement may (in particular) provide that progress towards meeting any targets for a facility is to be taken as being satisfactory if, in the absence (or partial absence) of any such progress required under the agreement, alternative requirements provided for by the agreement are satisfied.

(5) For the purposes of sub-paragraphs (2) and (3), the circumstances in which a facility to which a climate change agreement applies is one to which another such agreement previously applied include those where the facility is—

(*a*) a part, or a combination of parts, of a facility to which another such agreement previously applied,

(*b*) a combination of two or more such facilities,

(*c*) any combination of parts of such facilities, or

(*d*) any combination of such facilities and parts of such facilities.

(6) Paragraphs 47 and 48 and sub-paragraph (4) above are not to be taken as meaning that an agreement, or combination of agreements, containing provision in addition to any mentioned in those paragraphs and that sub-paragraph is not a climate change agreement.

(7) For the purposes of paragraphs 47 and 48 and this paragraph "target", in relation to a facility to which a climate change agreement applies, means a target relating to—

(*a*) energy, or energy derived from a source of any description, used in the facility or an identifiable group of facilities within which the facility falls, or

(*b*) emissions, or emissions of any description, from the facility or such a group of facilities;

and for this purpose "identifiable group" means a group that is identified in the agreement or that at any relevant time can be identified under the agreement.

(8) Nothing in this Schedule is to be taken as requiring the Secretary of State to—

(*a*) enter into any climate change agreement,

(*b*) enter into a climate change agreement with any particular person or persons, in respect of any particular facility or facilities or on any particular terms, or

(*c*) approve any, or any particular, proposed climate change agreement.

Facilities to which climate change agreements can apply

50—(1) This paragraph applies where, in connection with concluding or varying a climate change agreement, it falls to be determined whether a facility is to be, or is to continue to be, identified in the agreement as a facility to which the agreement applies.

(2) For the purposes of such a determination "facility" is (subject to any regulations under sub-paragraph (3) or (4)) to be taken as meaning—

(*a*) an installation covered by paragraph 51; or

(*b*) a site on which there is or are—

(i) such an installation or two or more such installations,

(ii) a part, or parts, of such an installation,

(iii) a part, or parts, of each of two or more such installations, or

(iv) any combination of such installations and parts of such installations.

(3) The Secretary of State may by regulations make provision for an installation covered by paragraph 51 to be taken to be a facility for those purposes only if—

(*a*) the taxable commodities supplied to the installation by taxable supplies are intended to be burned (or, in the case of electricity, consumed)—

(i) in the installation, or

(ii) on the site where the installation is situated but not in the installation,

and

(*b*) the amounts of taxable commodities, and of any other commodities specified in the regulations, subject to each of those intentions are such that any conditions specified in the regulations are satisfied.

(4) The Secretary of State may by regulations make provision for a site to be taken to be a facility for those purposes only if—

(*a*) the taxable commodities supplied to the site by taxable supplies are intended to be burned (or, in the case of electricity, consumed)—

(i) in installations on the site that are covered by paragraph 51 (or in parts of such installations), or

(ii) on the site but not in any such installation (or part of such an installation),

and

(*b*) the amounts of taxable commodities, and of any other commodities specified in the regulations, subject to each of those intentions are such that any conditions specified in the regulations are satisfied.

(5) Regulations under sub-paragraph (3) or (4) may make provision for deeming, for the purposes of the regulations, commodities to be intended to be burned (or, in the case of electricity, consumed) in circumstances specified in the regulations.

(6) In this paragraph and paragraph 51 "installation" means a stationary technical unit.

Energy-intensive installations

51—(1) An installation is covered by this paragraph if it falls within any one or more of the descriptions of installation set out in the Table.

[(2) Sub-paragraph (2A) applies where—

(*a*) an installation falls within any one or more of those descriptions, and

(*b*) there is, on the same site as the installation, a location at which ancillary activities are carried out.][1]

[(2A) The installation (taken alone) is not covered by this paragraph, but the combination—

(*a*) of the installation and that location, or

(*b*) where there is more than one such location, of the installation and all of those locations,

is to be taken as being an installation covered by this paragraph.][1]

[(2B) In sub-paragraph (2) "ancillary activities" means activities that—

(*a*) are directly associated with any of the primary activities carried out in the installation,

(*b*) have a technical connection with those primary activities, and

(*c*) could have an effect on environmental pollution.][1]

(3) [Sub-paragraphs (1) to (2B)][1] are subject to any regulations under paragraph 52.

(4) . . .[1]

(5) . . .[1]

(6) In [sub-paragraph (2B)][1]—

"environmental pollution" has the same meaning as in the Pollution Prevention and Control Act 1999;

"primary activity", in relation to an installation falling within any one or more of the descriptions of installation set out in the Table, means an activity the carrying out of which at the installation results in the installation falling within one or more of those descriptions.

TABLE

DESCRIPTIONS OF ENERGY-INTENSIVE INSTALLATIONS

[Installations regulated under the Environmental Permitting (England and Wales) Regulations 2007][2]

1 Part A installations.

Installations that would be so regulated but for a threshold or exception

2 Installations that would be Part A installations but for—

(*a*) a relevant numeric threshold, or

(*b*) a relevant exception.

Installations that would be so regulated if certain modifications were made to the Regulations

3 Installations that would be Part A installations if the relevant modifications were made.

Corresponding installations in Scotland and Northern Ireland

4 Installations that are situated in Scotland or Northern Ireland, but if situated in England and Wales—

(*a*) would be Part A installations,

(*b*) would be Part A installations but for—

(i) a relevant numeric threshold, or

(ii) a relevant exception, or

(*c*) would be Part A installations if the relevant modifications were made.

Interpretation of entries 1 to 4

5—(1) [In this entry "the Schedule" means Schedule 1 to the Environmental Permitting (England and Wales) Regulations 2007.][2]

(2) In entries 1 to 4—

(*a*) ["Part A installation" has the meaning given in regulation 3(2) of the Environmental Permitting (England and Wales) Regulations 2007;][2]

(*b*) "relevant exception" means—

(i) the exception in paragraph (*b*)(i) of Part A(1) of Section 2.1 of [Part 2 of the Schedule][2],

(ii) the exceptions in paragraph (*c*) of Part A(1) of Section 5.1 of [Part 2 of the Schedule][2] for activities falling within Part B of that Section and for the incineration of specified hazardous waste in an exempt incineration plant, or

(iii) the exception in paragraph (*e*) of Part A(1) of Section 5.1 of [Part 2 of the Schedule][2] for incineration as part of a Part B activity in so far as this exception relates to the activities referred to in paragraphs (*a*) and (*b*) of Part B of that Section;

(*c*) "the relevant modifications" means the omission of the following provisions of [Part 2 of the Schedule][2]:

(i) the final twelve words of paragraph (*b*) of Part A(1) of Section 4.4;

(ii) the final twelve words of paragraph (*b*) of Part A(1) of Section 4.5;

(iii) [paragraph 1 of the Interpretation and application of Part A(1) of Section 5.4;][2]

(iv) the final fourteen words of paragraph (*c*) of Part A(1) of Section 6.1;

(v) the final fourteen words of paragraph (*c*) of Part A(1) of Section 6.4; and

(vi) the final fourteen words of paragraph (*f*)(ii) of Part A(1) of Section 6.8; and

(*d*) "relevant numeric threshold" means a numeric threshold specified in any of the following provisions of [Part 2 of the Schedule][2]:

(i) paragraphs (*c*) and (*d*) of Part A(1) of Section 2.1;

(ii) Part A(2) of Section 2.1;

(iii) paragraph (*b*) of Part A(1) of Section 2.2;

(iv) Part A(1) of Section 2.3;

(v) paragraph (*b*) of Part A(1) of Section 3.1;

(vi) paragraph (*b*) of Part A(2) of Section 3.1;

(vii) paragraph (*b*) of Part A(1) of Section 3.3;

(viii) Part A(2) of Section 3.3;

(ix) paragraph (*a*) of Part A(1) of Section 3.4;

(x) Part A(2) of Section 3.6;

(xi) paragraphs (*c*) and (*d*) of Part A(1) of Section 4.1;

(xii) paragraphs (*d*) and (*e*) of Part A(1) of Section 5.1;

(xiii) Part A(1) of Section 5.2;

(xiv) Part A(1) of Section 5.3;

(xv) paragraph (c) of Part A(1) of Section 5.4;

(xvi) paragraph (b) of Part A(1) of Section 6.1;

(xvii) Part A(1) of Section 6.3;

(xviii) paragraphs (*a*) and (*b*) of Part A(1) of Section 6.4;

(xix) Part A(2) of Section 6.4;
(xx) Part A(2) of Section 6.7;
(xxi) paragraphs (*a*) to (*e*) of Part A(1) of Section 6.8;
(xxii) Part A(2) of Section 6.8; and
(xxiii) Part A(1) of Section 6.9; and

(*e*) any reference to a part of the United Kingdom includes the territorial waters adjacent to that part.][1]

Regulations—Climate Change Agreements (Energy-intensive Installations) Regulations, SI 2006/59; Climate Change Agreements (Eligible Facilities) Regulations, SI 2006/60.

Amendments—[1] Sub-paras (2), (2A), and (2B) substituted for sub-para (2), words in sub-paras (3), (6) substituted, sub-paras (4), (5) repealed, and entries in the Table substituted by the Climate Change Agreements (Energy-intensive Installations) Regulations, SI 2001/1139 with effect from 23 March 2001.

[2] Cross-heading, entries 5(1), 5(2)(*a*), 5(2)(*c*)(iii), and words in entries 5(2)(*b*)–(*d*), substituted, by the Environmental Permitting (England and Wales) Regulations, SI 2007/3538 reg 73, Sch 21 para 27 with effect from 6 April 2008 in relation to England and Wales.

Power to vary the installations covered by paragraph 51

52—(1) The Treasury may make provision by regulations for varying the installations covered by paragraph 51.

(2) The provision that may be made by regulations under this paragraph includes, in particular, provision—

(*a*) for the installations covered by paragraph 51 to include, or not to include, any installation of a description specified in the regulations;

(*b*) amending the Table in paragraph 51 by adding a description of installation to the Table, removing a description of installation from the Table or altering a description of installation set out in the Table;

(*c*) amending paragraph 51.

PART V
REGISTRATION

Note—Paragraphs 59, 60 come into force on 2 January 2001 and ss 53–58, 61 come into force on 29 January 2001 by virtue of SI 2000/3350 arts 2, 3.

Requirement to be registered

53—(1) A person is required to be registered with the Commissioners for the purposes of the levy if a taxable supply is made in respect of which he is the person liable to account for the levy charged.

(2) The Commissioners shall, for the purposes of sub-paragraph (1) and in accordance with the provisions of this Part of this Schedule, establish and maintain a register of persons liable to account for levy.

(3) The Commissioners shall keep such information in the register as they consider appropriate for the care and management of the levy.

[(4) Regulations made by the Commissioners may provide that, in such cases or circumstances and subject to such conditions or requirements as may be prescribed in the regulations, the Commissioners may exempt a person from the requirement to be registered.][1]

Amendments—[1] Sub-para (4) inserted by FA 2003 s 192(1), (3) with effect from 10 July 2003.

Interpretation of Part V

54 In this Part of this Schedule—

(*a*) references to the register are references to the register maintained under paragraph 53(2);

(*b*) references to registering a person are references to registering him in that register; and

(*c*) references to a person's registration are references to his registration in that register.

Notification of registrability etc

55—(1) A person who—

(*a*) intends to make, or have made to him, any taxable supply in respect of which (if made) he will be the person liable to account for the levy charged, or

(*b*) is required to be registered for the purposes of the levy,

shall (if he is not so registered) notify the Commissioners of that fact.

(2) Subject to sub-paragraphs (5) and (6), a person who fails to comply with sub-paragraph (1) shall be liable to a penalty.

(3) The amount of the penalty shall be—

(*a*) the amount equal to 5 per cent of the relevant levy; or (*b*) if it is greater or the circumstances are such that there is no relevant levy, £250.

(4) In sub-paragraph (3) "relevant levy" means the levy (if any) for which the person in question is liable to account in respect of taxable supplies made in the period which—

(*a*) begins with the date with effect from which he is required to be registered for the purposes of the levy; and

(*b*) ends with the date on which the Commissioners received notification of, or otherwise first became aware of, the fact that he was required to be registered.

(5) A failure to comply with sub-paragraph (1) shall not give rise to any liability to a penalty under this paragraph if the person concerned satisfies the Commissioners or, on appeal, an appeal tribunal that there is a reasonable excuse for the failure.

(6) Where, by reason of any conduct falling within sub-paragraph (2)—

(*a*) a person is convicted of an offence (whether under this Act or otherwise), or

(*b*) a person is assessed to a penalty under paragraph 98 (penalty for evasion) [or to a penalty for a deliberate inaccuracy under Schedule 24 to the Finance Act 2007 (penalties for errors)][1],

that person shall not by reason of that conduct be liable also to a penalty under this paragraph.

Amendments—[1] Words in sub-para (6)(*b*) inserted by the Finance Act 2008, Schedule 40 (Appointed Day, Transitional Provisions and Consequential Amendments) Order, SI 2009/571 art 8, Sch 1 para 20(1), (3) with effect from 1 April 2009.

Prospective amendments—Para 55(2)–(6) to be repealed by FA 2008 s 123, Sch 41 para 25(*k*) with effect from 1 April 2010 (by virtue of SI 2009/511 art 2).

Form of registration

56—(1) The Commissioners shall register a person if—

(*a*) they receive from him a notification given in pursuance of paragraph 55, or

(*b*) although they have not received from him such a notification, it appears to them that he is required to be registered.

Where the Commissioners register a person who is required to be registered, they shall register him with effect from the time when the requirement arose.

(2) Where any two or more bodies corporate are members of the same group they shall be registered together as one person in the name of the representative member.

(3) The registration of a body corporate carrying on a business in several divisions may, if the body corporate so requests and the Commissioners see fit, be in the names of those divisions.

(4) The registration of—

(*a*) any two or more persons carrying on a business in partnership, or

(*b*) an unincorporated body,

may be in the name of the firm or body concerned.

Notification of loss or prospective loss of registrability

57—(1) Where a person who has become liable to give a notification by virtue of paragraph 55 ceases (whether before or after being registered for the purposes of the levy) to intend to make, or to intend to have made to him, taxable supplies in respect of which (if made) he would be the person liable to account for the levy charged, he shall notify the Commissioners of that fact.

(2) A person who fails to comply with sub-paragraph (1) shall be liable to a penalty of £250.

Cancellation of registration

58—(1) If the Commissioners are satisfied that a registered person—

(*a*) has ceased to make, or have made to him, taxable supplies on which he is liable to account for the levy charged, and

(*b*) does not intend to make, or have made to him, any such supplies,

they may cancel his registration with effect from such time after he last made, or had made to him, taxable supplies as appears to them to be appropriate.

(2) Sub-paragraph (1) applies whether or not the registered person has notified the Commissioners under paragraph 57.

(3) The Commissioners shall be under a duty to exercise the power conferred by sub-paragraph (1) with effect from any time if, where the power is exercisable, they are satisfied that the conditions specified in sub-paragraph (4) are satisfied and were or will be satisfied at that time.

(4) Those conditions are—

(*a*) that the person in question has given a notification under paragraph 57;

(*b*) that no levy due from that person, and no amount recoverable as if it were levy, remains unpaid;

(*c*) that no tax credit to which that person is entitled by virtue of any tax credit regulations is outstanding; and

(*d*) that that person is not subject to any outstanding liability to make a return for the purposes of the levy.

(5) Where—

(*a*) a registered person notifies the Commissioners under paragraph 57, and

(*b*) they are satisfied that (if he had not been registered) he would not have been required to be registered at any time since the time when he was registered,

they shall cancel his registration with effect from the date of his registration.

Correction of the register etc

59—(1) The Commissioners may by regulations make provision for and with respect to the correction of entries in the register.

(2) Regulations under this paragraph may, to such extent as appears to the Commissioners appropriate for keeping the register up to date, make provision requiring—

(*a*) registered persons, and

(*b*) persons who are required to be registered,

to notify the Commissioners of changes in circumstances relating to themselves, their businesses or any other matter with respect to which particulars are contained in the register (or would be, were the person registered).

Supplemental regulations about notifications

60—(1) For the purposes of any provision made by or under this Part of this Schedule for any matter to be notified to the Commissioners, regulations made by the Commissioners may make provision—

(*a*) as to the time within which the notification is to be given;

(*b*) as to the form and manner in which the notification is to be given; and

(*c*) as to the information and other particulars to be contained in or provided with any notification.

(2) For those purposes the Commissioners may also by regulations impose obligations requiring a person who has given a notification to notify the Commissioners if any information contained in or provided in connection with that notification is or becomes inaccurate.

(3) The power under this paragraph to make regulations as to the time within which any notification is to be given shall include power to authorise the Commissioners to extend the time for the giving of a notification.

Publication of information on the register

61—(1) The Commissioners may publish, by such means as they think fit, any information which—

(*a*) is derived from the register; and

(*b*) falls within any of the descriptions set out below.

(2) The descriptions are—

(*a*) the names of registered persons;

(*b*) the fact (where it is the case) that the registered person is a body corporate which is a member of a group;

(*c*) the names of the other bodies corporate which are members of the group.

(3) Information may be published in accordance with this paragraph notwithstanding any obligation not to disclose the information that would otherwise apply.

PART VI

CREDITS AND REPAYMENTS

Tax credits

62—(1) The Commissioners may, in accordance with the following provisions of this paragraph, by regulations make provision in relation to cases where—

(*a*) after a taxable supply has been made, there is such a change in circumstances or any person's intentions that, if the changed circumstances or intentions had existed at the time the supply was made, the supply would not have been a taxable supply;

(*b*) after a supply of a taxable commodity is made on the basis that it is a taxable supply, it is determined that the supply was not (to any extent) a taxable supply;

(*c*) after a taxable supply has been made on the basis that it was [not][2] a reduced-rate supply, it is determined that the supply was (to any extent) a . . . [2] reduced-rate supply;

(*d*) *levy is accounted for on a half-rate supply as if the supply were neither a half-rate supply nor a reduced-rate supply;*[2]

(*e*) after a charge to levy has arisen on a supply of a taxable commodity ("the original commodity") to a person who uses the commodity supplied in producing taxable commodities primarily for his own consumption, that person makes supplies of any of the commodities in whose production he has used the original commodity;

(*f*) after a person has become entitled to a debt as a result of making a taxable supply, the debt turns out to be bad (in whole or in part);

(*g*) the making of a taxable supply gives rise to a double charge to levy within the meaning of paragraph 21.

(2) The provision that may be made in relation to any such case as is mentioned in sub-paragraph (1) is provision—

(*a*) for such person as may be specified in the regulations to be entitled to a tax credit in respect of any levy charged on the supply (or, in such a case as is mentioned in sub-paragraph (1)(*g*), one of the supplies) in question;

(*b*) for a tax credit to which any person is entitled under the regulations to be brought into account when he is accounting for [such levy due from him][1] as may be determined in accordance with the regulations; and

(*c*) for a person entitled to a tax credit to be entitled, in any prescribed case where he cannot bring the tax credit into account so as to set it against a liability to levy, to a repayment of levy of an amount so determined.

(3) Regulations under this paragraph may contain any or all of the following provisions—

(*a*) provision making any entitlement to a tax credit conditional on the making of a claim by such person, within such period and in such manner as may be prescribed;

(*b*) provision making entitlement to bring a tax credit into account, or to receive a repayment in respect of such a credit, conditional on compliance with such requirements (including the making of a claim) as may be determined in accordance with the regulations;

(*c*) provision requiring a claim for a tax credit to be evidenced and quantified by reference to such records and other documents as may be so determined;

(*d*) provision requiring a person claiming any entitlement to a tax credit to keep, for such period and in such form and manner as may be so determined, those records and documents and a record of such information relating to the claim as may be so determined;

(*e*) provision for the withdrawal of a tax credit where any requirement of the regulations is not complied with;

(*f*) provision for interest at the rate applicable under section 197 of the Finance Act 1996 to be treated as added, for such period and for such purposes as may be prescribed, to the amount of any tax credit;

(*g*) provision for determining whether, and to what extent, a debt is to be taken as bad;

(*h*) provision for the withdrawal of a tax credit to which a person has become entitled in a case within sub-paragraph (1)(*f*) where any part of the debt that has been taken to be bad falls to be regarded as not having been bad;

(*i*) provision for determining whether, and to what extent, any part of a debt that has been taken to be bad should be regarded as not having been bad;

(*j*) provision for anything falling to be determined in accordance with the regulations to be determined by reference to a general or specific direction given in accordance with the regulations by the Commissioners.

(4) Regulations made under this paragraph shall have effect subject to the provisions of paragraph 64.

Amendments—[1] Words in sub-para (2)(*b*) substituted for the words "levy due from him for such accounting period or periods" by FA 2003 s 192(1), (4) with effect from 10 July 2003.

[2] In sub-s (1)(*c*), words "neither a half-rate supply nor" substituted, words "half-rate or" repealed, and sub-s (1)(*d*) repealed, by FA 2006 ss 172(13), 178, Sch 26 Pt 8(1) with effect from 1 November 2007: SI 2007/2901 art 2(1).

These amendments do not apply in relation to a half-rate supply made before 1 April 2006: SI 2007/2901 art 2(2). For this purpose, "half-rate supply" carries the meaning it has in this Schedule before 1 November 2007. FA 2006 s 172(3)–(6) applies for determining when a supply is to be regarded as made: SI 2007/2901 art 2(3).

Regulations made under this para made before 1 November 2007 are unaffected by the above amendments: SI 2004/2901 art 2(4).

Repayments of overpaid levy

63—(1) Where a person has paid an amount to the Commissioners by way of levy which was not levy due to them, they shall be liable to repay the amount to him.

(2) The Commissioners shall not be liable to repay an amount under this paragraph if, or to the extent that, any person has become entitled to a tax credit in respect of that amount by virtue of tax credit regulations.

(3) The Commissioners shall not be liable to repay an amount under this paragraph except on the making of a claim for that purpose.

(4) A claim under this paragraph must be made in such form and manner, and must be supported by such documentary evidence, as may be required by regulations made by the Commissioners.

(5) The preceding provisions of this paragraph are subject to the provisions of paragraph 64.

(6) Except as provided by this paragraph or tax credit regulations, the Commissioners shall not, by virtue of the fact that it was not levy due to them, be liable to repay any amount paid to them by way of levy.

Supplemental provisions about repayments etc

64—(1) The Commissioners shall not be liable, on any claim for a repayment of levy, to repay any amount paid to them more than [4 years] before the making of the claim.

(2) It shall be a defence to any claim for a repayment of an amount of levy that the repayment of that amount would unjustly enrich the claimant.

(3) Sub-paragraph (4) applies for the purposes of sub-paragraph (2) where—

(*a*) there is an amount paid by way of levy which (apart from sub-paragraph (2)) would fall to be the subject of a repayment of levy to any person ("person A"); and

(*b*) the whole or a part of the cost of the payment of that amount to the Commissioners has, for practical purposes, been borne by a person other than person A.

(4) Where, in a case to which this sub-paragraph applies, loss or damage has been or may be incurred by person A as a result of mistaken assumptions made in his case about the operation of any provisions relating to levy, that loss or damage shall be disregarded, except to the extent of the quantified amount, in the making of any determination as to—

(*a*) whether or to what extent the repayment of an amount to person A would enrich him; or

(*b*) whether or to what extent any enrichment of person A would be unjust.

(5) In sub-paragraph (4) "the quantified amount" means the amount (if any) which is shown by person A to constitute the amount that would appropriately compensate him for loss or damage shown by him to have resulted, for any business carried on by him, from the making of the mistaken assumptions.

(6) The reference in sub-paragraph (4) to provisions relating to levy is a reference to any provisions of—

(*a*) any enactment or subordinate legislation (whether or not still in force) which relates to the levy or to any matter connected with it; or

(*b*) any notice published by the Commissioners under or for the purposes of any enactment or subordinate legislation relating to the levy.

Amendments—In sub-para (1), words substituted for the words "three years" by FA 2009 s 99, Sch 51 paras 32, 33 with effect from 1 April 2010 (SI 2010/867 art 2(1)). However, this amendment is disregarded where, for the purpose of sub-para (1), claims made are for the repayment of amounts paid to the Commissioners on or before 31 March 2007 (see SI 2010/867 art 16).

Reimbursement arrangements

65—(1) The Commissioners may by regulations make provision for reimbursement arrangements made by any person to be disregarded for the purposes of paragraph 64(2) except where the arrangements—

(*a*) contain such provision as may be required by the regulations; and

(*b*) are supported by such undertakings to comply with the provisions of the arrangements as may be required by the regulations to be given to the Commissioners.

(2) In this paragraph "reimbursement arrangements" means any arrangements for the purposes of a claim to a repayment of levy which—

(*a*) are made by any person for the purpose of securing that he is not unjustly enriched by the repayment of any amount in pursuance of the claim; and

(*b*) provide for the reimbursement of persons who have for practical purposes borne the whole or any part of the cost of the original payment of that amount to the Commissioners.

(3) Without prejudice to the generality of sub-paragraph (1), the provision that may be required by regulations under this paragraph to be contained in reimbursement arrangements includes—

(*a*) provision requiring a reimbursement for which the arrangements provide to be made within such period after the repayment to which it relates as may be specified in the regulations;

(*b*) provision for the repayment of amounts to the Commissioners where those amounts are not reimbursed in accordance with the arrangements;

(*c*) provision requiring interest paid by the Commissioners on any amount repaid by them to be treated in the same way as that amount for the purposes of any requirement under the arrangements to make reimbursement or to repay the Commissioners;

(*d*) provision requiring such records relating to the carrying out of the arrangements as may be described in the regulations to be kept and produced to the Commissioners, or to an officer of theirs.

(4) Regulations under this paragraph may impose obligations on such persons as may be specified in the regulations—

(*a*) to make the repayments to the Commissioners that they are required to make in pursuance of any provisions contained in any reimbursement arrangements by virtue of sub-paragraph (3)(*b*) or (*c*);

(*b*) to comply with any requirements contained in any such arrangements by virtue of sub-paragraph (3)(*d*).

(5) Regulations under this paragraph may make provision for the form and manner in which, and the times at which, undertakings are to be given to the Commissioners in accordance with the regulations; and any such provision may allow for those matters to be determined by the Commissioners in accordance with the regulations.

Interest payable by the Commissioners

66—(1) Where, due to an error on the part of the Commissioners, a person—

(*a*) has paid to them by way of levy an amount which was not levy due and which they are in consequence liable to repay to him,

(*b*) has failed to claim a repayment of levy to which he was entitled, under any tax credit regulations, in respect of any tax credits, or

(*c*) has suffered delay in receiving payment of an amount due to him from them in connection with levy,

then, if and to the extent that they would not be liable to do so apart from this paragraph, they shall (subject to the following provisions of this paragraph) pay interest to him on that amount for the applicable period.

(2) In sub-paragraph (1), the reference in paragraph (*a*) to an amount which the Commissioners are liable to repay in consequence of the making of a payment that was not due is a reference to only so much of that amount as is the subject of a claim that the Commissioners are required to satisfy or have satisfied.

(3) In that sub-paragraph the amounts referred to in paragraph (*c*)—

(*a*) do not include any amount payable under this paragraph;

(*b*) do not include the amount of any interest for which provision is made by virtue of paragraph 62(3)(*f*); but

(*c*) do include any amount due (in respect of an adjustment of overpaid interest) by way of a repayment under paragraph 87(3) or 110(3).

(4) The applicable period, in a case falling within sub-paragraph (1)(*a*), is the period—

(*a*) beginning with the date on which the payment is received by the Commissioners; and

(*b*) ending with the date on which they authorise payment of the amount on which the interest is payable.

(5) The applicable period, in a case falling within sub-paragraph (1)(*b*) or (*c*), is the period—

(*a*) beginning with the date on which, apart from the error, the Commissioners might reasonably have been expected to authorise payment of the amount on which the interest is payable; and

(*b*) ending with the date on which they in fact authorise payment of that amount.

(6) In determining the applicable period for the purposes of this paragraph there shall be left out of account any period by which the Commissioners' authorisation of the payment of interest is delayed by circumstances beyond their control.

(7) The reference in sub-paragraph (6) to a period by which the Commissioners' authorisation of the payment of interest is delayed by circumstances beyond their control includes, in particular, any period which is referable to—

(*a*) any unreasonable delay in the making of any claim for the payment or repayment of the amount on which interest is claimed;

(*b*) any failure by any person to provide the Commissioners—

(i) at or before the time of the making of a claim, or

(ii) subsequently in response to a request for information by the Commissioners,

with all the information required by them to enable the existence and amount of the claimant's entitlement to a payment or repayment, and to interest on that payment or repayment, to be determined; and

(*c*) the making, as part of or in association with any claim for the payment or repayment of the amount on which interest is claimed, of a claim to anything to which the claimant was not entitled.

(8) In determining for the purposes of sub-paragraph (7) whether any period of delay is referable to a failure by any person to provide information in response to a request by the Commissioners, there shall be taken to be so referable, except so far as may be provided for by regulations, any period which—

(*a*) begins with the date on which the Commissioners require that person to provide information which they reasonably consider relevant to the matter to be determined; and

(*b*) ends with the earliest date on which it would be reasonable for the Commissioners to conclude—

(i) that they have received a complete answer to their request for information;

(ii) that they have received all that they need in answer to that request; or

(iii) that it is unnecessary for them to be provided with any information in answer to that request.

(9) The Commissioners shall not be liable to pay interest under this paragraph except on the making of a claim for that purpose.

(10) A claim under this paragraph must be in writing and must be made not more than [4 years] after the end of the applicable period to which it relates.

(11) References in this paragraph—

(*a*) to receiving payment of any amount from the Commissioners, or

(*b*) to the authorisation by the Commissioners of the payment of any amount,

include references to the discharge by way of set-off (whether in accordance with regulations under paragraph 73 or 74 or otherwise) of the Commissioners' liability to pay that amount.

(12) Interest under this paragraph shall be payable at the rate applicable under section 197 of the Finance Act 1996.

Amendments—In sub-s (10), words substituted for the words "three years" by FA 2009 s 99, Sch 51 paras 32, 34 with effect from 1 April 2010 (SI 2010/867 art 2(1)). However, this amendment is disregarded where, for the purpose of para 66, claims made for the repayment of interest relate to an applicable period which ended on or before 31 March 2007 (see SI 2010/867 art 17).

Assessment for excessive repayment

67—(1) Where—

(*a*) any amount has been paid at any time to any person by way of a repayment of levy, and

(*b*) the amount paid exceeded the amount which the Commissioners were liable at that time to repay to that person,

the Commissioners may, to the best of their judgement, assess the excess paid to that person and notify it to him.

(2) Where—

(*a*) any amount has been paid to any person by way of repayment of levy,

(*b*) the repayment is in respect of a tax credit the entitlement to which arose in a case falling within paragraph 62(1)(*f*) (tax credit where all or part of a debt is bad),

(*c*) the whole or any part of the credit is withdrawn on account of any part of the debt taken as bad falling to be regarded as not having been bad, and

(*d*) the amount paid exceeded the amount which the Commissioners would have been liable to repay to that person had that withdrawal been taken into account,

the Commissioners may, to the best of their judgement, assess the excess paid to that person and notify it to him.

(3) Where any person is liable to pay any amount to the Commissioners in pursuance of an obligation imposed by virtue of paragraph 65(4)(*a*), the Commissioners may, to the best of their judgement, assess the amount due from that person and notify it to him.

(4) Subject to sub-paragraph (5), where—

(*a*) an assessment is made on any person under this paragraph in respect of a repayment of levy made in relation to any accounting period, and

(*b*) the Commissioners have power under Part VII of this Schedule to make an assessment on that person to an amount of levy due from that person for that period,

the assessments may be combined and notified to him as one assessment.

(5) A notice of a combined assessment under sub-paragraph (4) must separately identify the amount being assessed in respect of repayments of levy.

Assessment for overpayments of interest

68 Where—

(*a*) any amount has been paid to any person by way of interest under paragraph 66, but

(*b*) that person was not entitled to that amount under that paragraph,

the Commissioners may, to the best of their judgement, assess the amount so paid to which that person was not entitled and notify it to him.

Assessments under paragraphs 67 and 68

69—(1) An assessment under paragraph 67 or 68 shall not be made more than two years after the time when evidence of facts sufficient in the opinion of the Commissioners to justify the making of the assessment comes to the knowledge of the Commissioners.

(2) Where an amount has been assessed and notified to any person under paragraph 67 or 68, it shall be recoverable as if it were levy due from him.

(3) Sub-paragraph (2) does not have effect if, or to the extent that, the assessment in question has been withdrawn or reduced.

Interest on amounts assessed

70—(1) Where an assessment is made under paragraph 67 or 68, the whole of the amount assessed shall carry interest, for the period specified in sub-paragraph (2), as follows—

(*a*) so much of that amount as represents the amount of a tax credit claimed by a person who was not entitled to it (but not any amount assessed under paragraph 67(2)) shall carry penalty interest;

(*b*) so much of that amount as does not carry penalty interest under paragraph (*a*) shall carry interest at the rate applicable under section 197 of the Finance Act 1996.

(2) That period is the period which—

(*a*) begins with the day after that on which the person is notified of the assessment; and

(*b*) ends with the day before that on which payment is made of the amount assessed.

(3) Interest under this paragraph shall be paid without any deduction of income tax.

(4) Penalty interest under this paragraph shall be compound interest calculated—

(*a*) at the penalty rate, and

(*b*) with monthly rests.

(5) For this purpose the penalty rate is the rate found by—

(*a*) taking the rate applicable under section 197 of the Finance Act 1996 for the purposes of sub-paragraph (1)(*b*); and

(*b*) adding 10 percentage points to that rate.

(6) Where a person is liable under this paragraph to pay any penalty interest, the Commissioners or, on appeal, an appeal tribunal may reduce the amount payable to such amount (including nil) as they think proper.

(7) Subject to sub-paragraph (8), where the person concerned satisfies the Commissioners or, on appeal, an appeal tribunal that there is a reasonable excuse for the conduct giving rise to the liability to pay penalty interest, that is a matter which (among other things) may be taken into account under sub-paragraph (6).

(8) In determining whether there is a reasonable excuse for the purposes of sub-paragraph (7), no account shall be taken of any of the following matters, that is to say—

(*a*) the insufficiency of the funds available to any person for paying any levy due or for paying the amount of the interest;

(*b*) the fact that there has, in the case in question or in that case taken with any other cases, been no or no significant loss of levy;

(*c*) the fact that the person liable to pay the interest or a person acting on his behalf has acted in good faith.

(9) In the case of interest reduced by the Commissioners under sub-paragraph (6) an appeal tribunal, on an appeal relating to the interest, may cancel the whole or any part of the reduction made by the Commissioners.

Assessments to interest under paragraph 70

71—(1) Where any person is liable to interest under paragraph 70 the Commissioners may assess the amount due by way of interest and notify it to him accordingly.

(2) Without prejudice to the power to make assessments under this paragraph for later periods, the interest to which an assessment under this paragraph may relate shall be confined to interest for a period of no more than two years ending with the time when the assessment under this paragraph is made.

(3) Where an amount has been assessed and notified to any person under this paragraph it shall be recoverable as if it were levy due from him.

(4) Sub-paragraph (3) does not have effect if, or to the extent that, the assessment in question has been withdrawn or reduced.

(5) Where an assessment is made under this paragraph to an amount of interest under paragraph 70—

(*a*) the notice of assessment shall specify a date, not later than the date of the notice of assessment, to which the amount of interest which is assessed is calculated; and

(*b*) if the interest continues to accrue after that date, a further assessment or further assessments may be made under this paragraph in respect of the amounts so accruing.

(6) Where—

(*a*) an assessment to interest is made specifying a date for the purposes of sub-paragraph (5)(*a*), and

(*b*) within such period as may for the purposes of this sub-paragraph have been notified by the Commissioners to the person liable for the interest, the amount on which the interest is payable is paid,

that amount shall be deemed for the purposes of any further liability to interest to have been paid on the specified date.

Supplementary assessments

72 If it appears to the Commissioners that the amount which ought to have been assessed in an assessment under paragraph 67, 68 or 71 exceeds the amount which was so assessed, then—

(*a*) under the same paragraph as that assessment was made, and

(*b*) on or before the last day on which that assessment could have been made,

the Commissioners may make a supplementary assessment of the amount of the excess and notify the person concerned accordingly.

Set-off of or against amounts due under this Schedule

73—(1) The Commissioners may by regulations make provision in relation to any case where—

(*a*) a person is under a duty to pay to the Commissioners at any time an amount or amounts in respect of levy; and

(*b*) the Commissioners are under a duty to pay to that person at the same time an amount or amounts in respect of levy or any of the other taxes under their care and management.

(2) Regulations under this paragraph may provide that if the total of the amount or amounts mentioned in sub-paragraph (1)(*a*) exceeds the total of the amount or amounts mentioned in sub-paragraph (1)(*b*), the latter shall be set off against the former.

(3) Regulations under this paragraph may provide that if the total of the amount or amounts mentioned in sub-paragraph (1)(*b*) exceeds the total of the amount or amounts mentioned in sub-paragraph (1)(*a*), the Commissioners may set off the latter in paying the former.

(4) Regulations under this paragraph may provide that if the total of the amount or amounts mentioned in sub-paragraph (1)(*a*) is the same as the total of the amount or amounts mentioned in sub-paragraph (1)(*b*) no payment need be made in respect of the former or the latter.

(5) Regulations under this paragraph may provide for any limitation on the time within which the Commissioners are entitled to take steps for recovering any amount due to them in respect of levy to be disregarded, in such cases as may be described in the regulations, in determining whether any person is under such a duty to pay as is mentioned in sub-paragraph (1)(*a*).

(6) Regulations under this paragraph may include provision treating any duty to pay mentioned in sub-paragraph (1) as discharged accordingly.

(7) References in sub-paragraph (1) to an amount in respect of a particular tax include references not only to an amount of tax itself but also to other amounts such as interest and penalties that are or may be recovered as if they were amounts of tax.

(8) In this paragraph "tax" includes duty.

Set-off of or against other taxes and duties

74—(1) The Commissioners may by regulations make provision in relation to any case where—

(*a*) a person is under a duty to pay to the Commissioners at any time an amount or amounts in respect of any tax (or taxes) under their care and management other than levy; and

(*b*) the Commissioners are under a duty, at the same time, to make any repayment of levy to that person or to make any other payment to him of any amount or amounts in respect of levy.

(2) Regulations under this paragraph may provide that if the total of the amount or amounts mentioned in sub-paragraph (1)(*a*) exceeds the total of the amount or amounts mentioned in sub-paragraph (1)(*b*), the latter shall be set off against the former.

(3) Regulations under this paragraph may provide that if the total of the amount or amounts mentioned in sub-paragraph (1)(*b*) exceeds the total of the amount or amounts mentioned in sub-paragraph (1)(*a*), the Commissioners may set off the latter in paying the former.

(4) Regulations under this paragraph may provide that if the total of the amount or amounts mentioned in sub-paragraph (1)(*a*) is the same as the total of the amount or amounts mentioned in sub-paragraph (1)(*b*) no payment need be made in respect of the former or the latter.

(5) Regulations under this paragraph may provide for any limitation on the time within which the Commissioners are entitled to take steps for recovering any amount due to them in respect of any of the taxes under their care and management to be disregarded, in such cases as may be described in the regulations, in determining whether any person is under such a duty to pay as is mentioned in sub-paragraph (1)(*a*).

(6) Regulations under this paragraph may include provision treating any duty to pay mentioned in sub-paragraph (1) as discharged accordingly.

(7) References in sub-paragraph (1) to an amount in respect of a particular tax include references not only to an amount of tax itself but also to other amounts such as interest and penalties that are or may be recovered as if they were amounts of tax.

(8) In this paragraph "tax" includes duty.

Restriction on powers to provide for set-off

75—(1) Regulations made under paragraph 73 or 74 shall not require any such amount or amounts as are mentioned in sub-paragraph (1)(*b*) of that paragraph ("the credit") to be set against any such amount or amounts as are mentioned in sub-paragraph (1)(*a*) of that paragraph ("the debit") in any case where—

(*a*) an insolvency procedure has been applied to the person entitled to the credit;

(*b*) the credit became due after that procedure was so applied; and

(*c*) the liability to pay the debit either arose before that procedure was so applied or (having arisen afterwards) relates to, or to matters occurring in the course of, the carrying on of any business at times before the procedure was so applied.

(2) For the purposes of this paragraph, an insolvency procedure is applied to a person if—

(*a*) a bankruptcy order, winding-up order or administration order is made [or an administrator is appointed][1] in relation to that person or an award of sequestration is made on that person's estate;

(*b*) that person is put into administrative receivership;

(*c*) that person passes a resolution for voluntary winding up;

(*d*) any voluntary arrangement approved in accordance with—

(i) Part I or VIII of the Insolvency Act 1986, or

(ii) Part II or Chapter II of Part VIII of the Insolvency (Northern Ireland) Order 1989,

comes into force in relation to that person;

(*e*) a deed of arrangement registered in accordance with—

(i) the Deeds of Arrangement Act 1914, or

(ii) Chapter I of Part VIII of that Order,

takes effect in relation to that person;

(*f*) a person is appointed as the interim receiver of some or all of that person's property under section 286 of the Insolvency Act 1986 or Article 259 of the Insolvency (Northern Ireland) Order 1989;

(*g*) a person is appointed as the provisional liquidator in relation to that person under section 135 of that Act or Article 115 of that Order;

(*h*) an interim order is made under Part VIII of that Act, or Chapter II of Part VIII of that Order, in relation to that person; or

(*i*) that person's estate becomes vested in any other person as that person's trustee under a trust deed (within the meaning of the Bankruptcy (Scotland) Act 1985).

(3) In this paragraph references, in relation to any person, to the application of an insolvency procedure to that person shall not include—

(*a*) the making of a bankruptcy order, winding-up order . . . [1] or award of sequestration [or the appointment of an administrator][1] at a time when any such arrangement or deed as is mentioned in paragraph (*d*), (*e*) or (*i*) of sub-paragraph (2) is in force in relation to that person;

(*b*) the making of a winding-up order at any of the following times, that is to say—

[(i) immediately upon the appointment of an administrator in respect of the person ceasing to have effect;][1]

(ii) when that person is being wound up voluntarily;

(iii) when that person is in administrative receivership;

or

(*c*) the making of an administration order in relation to that person at any time when that person is in administrative receivership.

(4) For the purposes of this paragraph a person shall be regarded as being in administrative receivership throughout any continuous period for which (disregarding any temporary vacancy in the office of receiver) there is an administrative receiver of that person.

(5) In this paragraph—

"administration order" means an administration order under [Schedule B1 to][1] the Insolvency Act 1986 or Article 21 of the Insolvency (Northern Ireland) Order 1989;

"administrative receiver" means an administrative receiver within the meaning of section 251 of that Act or Article 5(1) of that Order.

Amendments—[1] Words in sub-para (2)(*a*) inserted, in sub-para (3)(*a*), words repealed and words inserted, sub-para (3)(*b*)(i) substituted, and words in sub-para (5) substituted, by the Enterprise Act 2002 (Insolvency) Order, SI 2003/2096 art 4, Schedule paras 31, 32 with effect from 15 September 2003. These amendments do not apply in relation to any case where a petition for an administration order was presented before 15 September 2003: SI 2003/2096 arts 1(1), 6.

Part VI: supplemental provisions

76—(1) Any notification of an assessment under any provision of this Part of this Schedule to a person's representative shall be treated for the purposes of this Schedule as notification to the person in relation to whom the representative acts.

(2) In this paragraph "representative", in relation to any person, means—

(*a*) any of that person's personal representatives;

(*b*) that person's trustee in bankruptcy or liquidator;

(*c*) any person holding office as a receiver in relation to that person or any of his property;

(*d*) that person's tax representative or any other person for the time being acting in a representative capacity in relation to that person.

(3) In this paragraph "trustee in bankruptcy" includes, as respects Scotland—

(*a*) an interim or permanent trustee (within the meaning of the Bankruptcy (Scotland) Act 1985); and

(*b*) a trustee acting under a trust deed (within the meaning of that Act).

(4) The powers conferred by paragraphs 73 and 74 are without prejudice to any power of the Commissioners to provide by tax credit regulations for any amount to be set against another.

PART VII

RECOVERY AND INTEREST

Recovery of levy as debt due

77 Levy shall be recoverable as a debt due to the Crown.

Assessments of amounts of levy due

78—(1) Where it appears to the Commissioners—

(*a*) that any period is an accounting period by reference to which a person is liable to account for levy,

(*b*) that any levy for which that person is liable to account by reference to that period has become due, and

(*c*) that there has been a default by that person that falls within sub-paragraph (2),

they may assess the amount of levy due from that person for that period to the best of their judgement and notify that amount to that person.

[(1A) Where it appears to the Commissioners—

(*a*) that any levy for which a person is liable to account otherwise than by reference to an accounting period has become due, and

(*b*) that there has been a default by that person that falls within sub-paragraph (2),

they may assess the amount of that levy to the best of their judgement and notify it to him.][1]

(2) The defaults falling within this sub-paragraph are—

(*a*) any failure to make a return required to be made by any provision made by or under this Schedule;

(*b*) any failure to keep any documents necessary to verify returns required to be made under any such provision;

(*c*) any failure to afford the facilities necessary to verify returns required to be made under any such provision;

(*d*) the making, in purported compliance with any requirement of any such provision to make a return, of an incomplete or incorrect return;

(*e*) any failure to comply with a requirement imposed by or under Part V of this Schedule (registration).

(3) Where it appears to the Commissioners that a default falling within sub-paragraph (2) is a default by a person on whom the requirement to make a return is imposed in his capacity as the representative of another person, sub-paragraph (1) shall apply as if the reference to the amount of levy due included a reference to any levy due from that other person.

(4) In a case where—

(*a*) the Commissioners have made an assessment for any accounting period as a result of any person's failure to make a return for that period,

(*b*) the levy assessed has been paid but no proper return has been made for that period,

(*c*) as a result of a failure (whether by that person or a representative of his) to make a return for a later accounting period, the Commissioners find it necessary to make another assessment under this paragraph in relation to the later period, and

(*d*) the Commissioners think it appropriate to do so in the light of the absence of a proper return for the earlier period,

they may, in the assessment in relation to the later period, specify an amount of levy due that is greater than the amount that they would have considered to be appropriate had they had regard only to the later period.
(5) Where an amount has been assessed and notified to any person under this paragraph, it shall be recoverable on the basis that it is an amount of levy due from him.
(6) Sub-paragraph (5) does not have effect if, or to the extent that, the assessment in question has been withdrawn or reduced.

Amendments—[1] Sub-para (1A) inserted by FA 2003 s 192(1), (5) with effect from 10 July 2003.

Supplementary assessments

79—(1) If, where an assessment has been notified to any person under paragraph 78 or this paragraph, it appears to the Commissioners that the amount which ought to have been assessed as due for any accounting period exceeds the amount that has already been assessed, the Commissioners may make a supplementary assessment of the amount of the excess and notify that person accordingly.
(2) Where an amount has been assessed and notified to any person under this paragraph it shall be recoverable on the basis that it is an amount of levy due from him.
(3) Sub-paragraph (2) does not have effect if, or to the extent that, the assessment in question has been withdrawn or reduced.

Time limits for assessments

80—(1) An assessment under paragraph 78 or 79 of an amount of levy due for any accounting period—

(*a*) shall not be made more than two years after the end of the accounting period unless it is made within the period mentioned in sub-paragraph (2); and

(*b*) subject to sub-paragraph (3), shall not in any event be made more than [4 years] after the end of that accounting period.

(2) The period referred to in sub-paragraph (1)(*a*) is the period of one year after evidence of facts sufficient in the Commissioners' opinion to justify the making of the assessment first came to their knowledge.
[(3) An assessment of an amount due from a person in a case involving a loss of levy—

(*a*) brought about deliberately by the person (or by another person acting on that person's behalf), or

(*b*) attributable to a failure by the person to comply with an obligation under paragraph 53 or 55,

may be made at any time not more than 20 years after the end of the accounting period to which it relates (subject to sub-paragraph (4)).
(3A) In sub-paragraph (3)(*a*) the reference to a loss brought about deliberately by the person includes a loss brought about as a result of a deliberate inaccuracy in a document given to Her Majesty's Revenue and Customs by or on behalf of that person.]
(4) Where, after a person's death, the Commissioners propose to assess an amount of levy as due by reason of some conduct of the deceased—

(*a*) the assessment shall not be made more than [4 years] after the death; *and*

(*b*) *if the circumstances are as set out in sub-paragraph (3)—*

(*i*) the modification of sub-paragraph (1) contained in that sub-paragraph shall not apply; but

(*ii*) any assessment which (applying that modification) could have been made immediately after the death may be made at any time within three years after it.

(5) Nothing in this paragraph shall prejudice the powers of the Commissioners under paragraph 78(4).

Amendments—In sub-paras (1)(*b*), (4)(*a*) words substituted for the words "three years"; sub-para (4)(*b*) and preceding word "and" repealed, and sub-paras (3), (3A) substituted for previous sub-para (3), by FA 2009 s 99, Sch 51 paras 32, 35 with effect from 1 April 2010 (SI 2010/867 art 2(1)). Sub-para (3) previously read as follows:

"(3) Subject to sub-paragraph (4), where levy has been lost—

(*a*) as a result of any conduct for which a person has been convicted of an offence involving fraud,

(*b*) in circumstances giving rise to liability to a penalty under paragraph 55 (failure to notify of registrability etc), or

(*c*) as a result of conduct falling within paragraph 98(1) (evasion),

that levy may be assessed under paragraph 78 or 79 as if, in sub-paragraph (1)(b) above, for "three years" there were substituted "twenty years"."

The following transitional provisions apply—

– The amendment made to sub-para (1)(*b*) is disregarded where, for the purposes of sub-para (1)(*b*), the end of the prescribed accounting period or the date when the levy is due occurred on or before 31 March 2007 (SI 2010/867 art 18).
– The substitution of sub-para (3) is disregarded where, for the purposes of sub-para (3), the end of the prescribed accounting period occurred on or before 31 March 2007 (SI 2010/867 art 19).

– The amendments made to sub-para (4) are disregarded where, for the purposes of sub-para (4), the death occurred on or before 31 March 2007 (SI 2010/867 art 20).

Ordinary interest on overdue levy paid before assessment

81—(1) Where—

(*a*) the circumstances are such that an assessment could have been made under paragraph 78 or 79 of an amount of levy due from any person, but

(*b*) before such an assessment was made and notified to that person that amount was paid (so that no such assessment was necessary),

the whole of the amount paid shall carry interest for the period specified in sub-paragraph (2).

(2) That period is the period which—

(*a*) begins with the day after that on which the person is required in accordance with regulations under paragraph 41 to pay levy due from him for the accounting period to which the amount paid relates; and

(*b*) ends with the day before that on which the amount is paid.

(3) Interest under this paragraph shall be payable at the rate applicable under section 197 of the Finance Act 1996.

Penalty interest on unpaid levy

82—(1) Where—

(*a*) a person makes a return for the purposes of any regulations made under paragraph 41 (whether or not at the time required by the regulations), and

(*b*) the return shows that an amount of levy is due from him for the accounting period for which the return is made,

that amount shall carry penalty interest for the period specified in sub-paragraph (2).

(2) That period is the period which—

(*a*) begins with the day after that on which the person is required in accordance with regulations under paragraph 41 to pay levy due from him for the accounting period in question; and

(*b*) ends with the day before that on which the amount shown in the return is paid.

Penalty interest on levy where no return made

83—(1) Where—

(*a*) the Commissioners make an assessment under paragraph 78 or 79 of an amount of levy due from any person for any accounting period and notify it to him, and

(*b*) the assessment is made at a time after the time by which a return is required by regulations under paragraph 41 to be made by that person for that accounting period and before any such return has been made,

that amount shall carry penalty interest for the period specified in sub-paragraph (2).

(2) That period is the period which—

(*a*) begins with the day after that on which the person is required in accordance with regulations under paragraph 41 to pay levy due from him for the accounting period in question; and

(*b*) ends with the day before that on which the assessed amount is paid.

(3) Where the person, after the assessment is made, makes for the purposes of any regulations under paragraph 41 a return for the accounting period in question, the assessed amount shall not carry penalty interest under this paragraph to the extent that that amount is shown in the return as an amount of levy due from him for that accounting period (and, accordingly, carries penalty interest under paragraph 82).

Ordinary and penalty interest on under-declared levy

84—(1) Subject to sub-paragraph (4), where—

(*a*) the Commissioners make an assessment under paragraph 78 or 79 of an amount of levy due from any person for any accounting period and notify it to him,

(*b*) the assessment is made after a return for the purposes of any regulations under paragraph 41 has been made by that person for that accounting period, and

(*c*) the assessment is made on the basis that the amount ("the additional amount") is due from him in addition to any amount shown in the return, or in a previous assessment made in relation to the accounting period,

the additional amount shall carry interest for the period specified in sub-paragraph (2).

(2) That period is the period which—

(*a*) begins with the day after that on which the person is required in accordance with regulations under paragraph 41 to pay levy due from him for the accounting period in question; and (*b*) ends with the day before the day on which the additional amount is paid.

(3) Interest under this paragraph—

(*a*) in respect of so much of the period specified in sub-paragraph (2) as falls before the day on which the assessment is notified to the person in question, shall be payable at the rate applicable under section 197 of the Finance Act 1996 for the purposes of paragraph 81(3); and

(*b*) in respect of the remainder (if any) of that period, shall be penalty interest.

(4) Where—

(*a*) the Commissioners make an assessment under paragraph 78 or 79 of an amount of levy due from any person for any accounting period and notify it to him,

(*b*) they also specify a date for the purposes of this sub-paragraph, and

(*c*) the amount assessed is paid on or before that date,

the only interest carried by that amount under this paragraph shall be interest, at the rate given by sub-paragraph (3)(a), for the period before the day on which the assessment is notified.

Penalty interest on unpaid ordinary interest

85—(1) Subject to sub-paragraph (2), where the Commissioners make an assessment under paragraph 88 of an amount of interest payable at the rate given by paragraph 81(3), that amount shall carry penalty interest for the period which—

(*a*) begins with the day on which the assessment is notified to the person on whom the assessment is made; and

(*b*) ends with the day before the day on which the assessed interest is paid.

(2) Where—

(*a*) the Commissioners make an assessment under paragraph 88 of an amount of interest due from any person,

(*b*) they also specify a date for the purposes of this sub-paragraph, and

(*c*) the amount of interest assessed is paid on or before that date,

the amount paid before that date shall not carry penalty interest under this paragraph.

Penalty interest

86—(1) Penalty interest under any of paragraphs 82 to 85 shall be compound interest calculated—

(*a*) at the penalty rate, and

(*b*) with monthly rests.

(2) For this purpose the penalty rate is the rate found by—

(*a*) taking the rate applicable under section 197 of the Finance Act 1996 for the purposes of paragraph 81(3); and

(*b*) adding 10 percentage points to that rate.

(3) Where a person is liable under any of paragraphs 82 to 85 to pay any penalty interest, the Commissioners or, on appeal, an appeal tribunal may reduce the amount payable to such amount (including nil) as they think proper.

(4) Subject to sub-paragraph (5), where the person concerned satisfies the Commissioners or, on appeal, an appeal tribunal that there is a reasonable excuse for the conduct giving rise to the liability to pay penalty interest, that is a matter which (among other things) may be taken into account under sub-paragraph (3).

(5) In determining whether there is a reasonable excuse for the purposes of sub-paragraph (4), no account shall be taken of any of the following matters, that is to say—

(*a*) the insufficiency of the funds available to any person for paying any levy due or for paying the amount of the interest;

(*b*) the fact that there has, in the case in question or in that case taken with any other cases, been no or no significant loss of levy;

(*c*) the fact that the person liable to pay the interest or a person acting on his behalf has acted in good faith.

(6) In the case of interest reduced by the Commissioners under sub-paragraph (3) an appeal tribunal, on an appeal relating to the interest, may cancel the whole or any part of the reduction made by the Commissioners.

Supplemental provisions about interest

87—(1) Interest under any of paragraphs 81 to 85 shall be paid without any deduction of income tax.

(2) Sub-paragraph (3) applies where—

(*a*) an amount carries interest under any of paragraphs 81 to 85 (or would do so apart from that sub-paragraph); and

(*b*) all or part of the amount turns out not to be due.

(3) In such a case—

(*a*) the amount or part that turns out not to be due shall not carry interest under the applicable paragraph and shall be treated as never having done so; and

(*b*) all such adjustments as are reasonable shall be made, including (subject to paragraphs 64 to 76) adjustments by way of repayment.

Assessments to interest

88—(1) Where a person is liable for interest under any of paragraphs 81 to 85, the Commissioners may assess the amount due by way of interest and notify it to him accordingly.

(2) If, where an assessment has been notified to any person under sub-paragraph (1) or this sub-paragraph, it appears to the Commissioners that the amount which ought to have been assessed exceeds the amount that has already been assessed, the Commissioners may make a supplementary assessment of the amount of the excess and shall notify that person accordingly.

(3) Where an amount has been assessed and notified to any person under this paragraph, it shall be recoverable as if it were levy due from him.

(4) Sub-paragraph (3)—

(*a*) shall not apply so as to require any interest to be payable on interest except—

(i) in accordance with paragraph 85, or

(ii) in so far as it falls to be compounded in accordance with paragraph 86;

and

(*b*) shall not have effect if, or to the extent that, the assessment in question has been withdrawn or reduced.

(5) Paragraph 80 shall apply in relation to assessments under this paragraph as if any assessment to interest were an assessment under paragraph 78 to levy due for the period which is the relevant accounting period in relation to that interest.

(6) Subject to sub-paragraph (7), where a person—

(*a*) is assessed under this paragraph to an amount due by way of any interest, and

(*b*) is also assessed under paragraph 78 or 79 for the accounting period which is the relevant accounting period in relation to that interest,

the assessments may be combined and notified to him as one assessment.

(7) A notice of a combined assessment under sub-paragraph (6) must separately identify the interest being assessed.

(8) The relevant accounting period for the purposes of this paragraph is—

(*a*) in the case of interest on levy due for any accounting period, that accounting period; and

(*b*) in the case of interest on interest (whether under paragraph 85 or by virtue of any compounding under paragraph 86), the period which is the relevant accounting period for the interest on which the interest is payable.

(9) In a case where—

(*a*) the amount of any interest falls to be calculated by reference to levy which was not paid at the time when it should have been, and

(*b*) that levy cannot be readily attributed to any one or more accounting periods,

that levy shall be treated for the purposes of interest on any of that levy as levy due for such period or periods as the Commissioners may determine to the best of their judgement and notify to the person liable.

Further assessments to penalty interest

89—(1) Where an assessment is made under paragraph 88 to an amount of penalty interest under any of paragraphs 82 to 85—

(*a*) the notice of assessment shall specify a date, not later than the date of the notice of assessment, to which the amount of interest which is assessed is calculated; and

(*b*) if the interest continues to accrue after that date, a further assessment or further assessments may be made under paragraph 88 in respect of the amounts so accruing.

(2) Where—

(*a*) an assessment to penalty interest is made specifying a date for the purposes of sub-paragraph (1)(*a*), and

(*b*) within such period as may for the purposes of this sub-paragraph have been notified by the Commissioners to the person liable for the interest, the amount on which the interest is payable is paid,

that amount shall be deemed for the purposes of any further liability to interest to have been paid on the specified date.

Prospective amendment—Para 89A to be inserted by the Tribunals, Courts and Enforcement Act 2007 s 62(3), Sch 13 paras 135, 136, with effect from a date to be appointed. Para 89A to be repealed by FA 2008 s 129, Sch 43 para 7 with effect from such day as the Commissioners may by statutory instrument appoint.

Para 89A to read—

"Controlled goods agreements

89A—(1)This paragraph applies where an enforcement agent acting under the power conferred by section 51(A1) of the Finance Act 1997 (power to use the procedure in Schedule 12 to the Tribunals, Courts and Enforcement Act 2007) has entered into a controlled goods agreement with the person against whom the power is exercisable ("the person in default").

(2) In this paragraph, "controlled goods agreement" has the meaning given by paragraph 13(4) of that Schedule.

(3) Subject to sub-paragraph (4), if the person in default removes or disposes of goods (or permits their removal or disposal) in breach of the controlled goods agreement, he is liable to a penalty equal to half of the levy or other amount recoverable under section 51(A1) of the Finance Act 1997.

(4) The person in default shall not be liable to a penalty under subparagraph (3) above if he satisfies the Commissioners or, on appeal, an appeal tribunal, that there is a reasonable excuse for the breach in question.

(5) This paragraph extends only to England and Wales.".

Walking possession agreements

90—(1) This paragraph applies where—

(*a*) in accordance with regulations under section 51 of the Finance Act 1997 (enforcement by distress), a distress is authorised to be levied on the goods and chattels of a person ("the person in default") who has refused or neglected to pay an amount of levy due from him or an amount recoverable from him as if it were levy; and

(*b*) the person levying the distress and the person in default have entered into a walking possession agreement.

(2) For the purposes of this paragraph a walking possession agreement is an agreement under which, in consideration of the property distrained upon being allowed to remain in the custody of the person in default and of the delaying of its sale, the person in default—

(*a*) acknowledges that the property specified in the agreement is under distraint and held in walking possession; and

(*b*) undertakes that, except with the consent of the Commissioners and subject to such conditions as they may impose, he will not remove or allow the removal of any of the specified property from the premises named in the agreement.

(3) Subject to sub-paragraph (4), if the person in default is in breach of the undertaking contained in a walking possession agreement, he shall be liable to a penalty equal to one half of the levy or other amount referred to in sub-paragraph (1)(*a*).

(4) The person in default shall not be liable to a penalty under sub-paragraph (3) if he satisfies the Commissioners or, on appeal, an appeal tribunal that there is a reasonable excuse for the breach in question.

(5) This paragraph does not extend to Scotland.

Prospective amendments—Sub-para (5) to be substituted by the Tribunals, Courts and Enforcement Act 2007 s 62(3), Sch 13 paras 135, 137, with effect from a date to be appointed. Sub-para (5) as substituted, to read—

"(5) This paragraph extends only to Northern Ireland.".

Interpretation etc of Part VII

91—(1) In this Part of this Schedule "penalty interest" shall be construed in accordance with paragraph 86.

(2) Any notification of an assessment under any provision of this Part of this Schedule to a person's representative shall be treated for the purposes of this Schedule as notification to the person in relation to whom the representative acts.

(3) In this Part of this Schedule "representative", in relation to any person, means—

(*a*) any of that person's personal representatives;

(*b*) that person's trustee in bankruptcy or liquidator;

(*c*) any person holding office as a receiver in relation to that person or any of his property;

(*d*) that person's tax representative or any other person for the time being acting in a representative capacity in relation to that person.

(4) In this paragraph "trustee in bankruptcy" includes, as respects Scotland—

(*a*) an interim or permanent trustee (within the meaning of the Bankruptcy (Scotland) Act 1985); and

(*b*) a trustee acting under a trust deed (within the meaning of that Act).

[(5) In relation to cases where, by virtue of regulations under paragraph 41(1)(*a*)(ii) [or by virtue of paragraph 45B(8)][2], a person is liable to account for levy otherwise than by reference to accounting periods, this Part of this Schedule shall have effect as if—

(*a*) references to levy due for "an" or "any" accounting period were references simply to levy due;

(*b*) references to levy due for a specified accounting period were references to the levy in question;

(*c*) references to an assessment for a specified accounting period were references to an assessment in respect of the levy in question;

(*d*) any time limit framed by reference to the end of the accounting period for which levy is due were framed by reference to the date on which payment of the levy is due;

(*e*) references to the making of a return for an accounting period were references to the payment of the levy in question;

(*f*) references to the amount shown in such a return were references to the amount of levy paid;

(*g*) paragraph 88(8) and (9) were omitted.][1]

Amendments—[1] Sub-para (5) inserted by FA 2003 s 192(1), (6) with effect from 10 July 2003.

[2] Words in sub-para (5) inserted by FA 2009 s 118, Sch 59 paras 2, 8 with effect where the certification period begins on or after 1 April 2009.

PART VIII
EVASION, MISDECLARATION AND NEGLECT

Criminal offences: Evasion

92—(1) A person is guilty of an offence if he is knowingly concerned in, or in the taking of steps with a view to—

(*a*) the fraudulent evasion by that person of any levy with which he is charged; or

(*b*) the fraudulent evasion by any other person of any levy with which that other person is charged.

(2) The references in sub-paragraph (1) to the evasion of levy include references to obtaining, in circumstances where there is no entitlement to it, either a tax credit or a repayment of levy.

(3) A person guilty of an offence under this paragraph shall be liable (subject to sub-paragraph (4))—

(*a*) on summary conviction, to a penalty of the statutory maximum or to imprisonment for a term not exceeding six months, or to both;

(*b*) on conviction on indictment, to a penalty of any amount or to imprisonment for a term not exceeding seven years, or to both.

(4) In the case of any offence under this paragraph, where the statutory maximum is less than three times the sum of the amounts of levy which are shown to be amounts that were or were intended to be evaded, the penalty on summary conviction shall be the amount equal to three times that sum (instead of the statutory maximum).

(5) For the purposes of sub-paragraph (4) the amounts of levy that were or were intended to be evaded shall be taken to include—

(*a*) the amount of any tax credit, and

(*b*) the amount of any repayment of levy,

which was, or was intended to be, obtained in circumstances where there was no entitlement to it.

(6) In determining for the purposes of sub-paragraph (4) how much levy (in addition to any amount falling within sub-paragraph (5)) was or was intended to be evaded, no account shall be taken of the extent (if any) to which any liability to levy of any person fell, or would have fallen, to be reduced by the amount of any tax credit or repayment of levy to which he was, or would have been, entitled.

Criminal offences: Misstatements

93—(1) A person is guilty of an offence if, with the requisite intent and for purposes connected with the levy—

(*a*) he produces or provides, or causes to be produced or provided, any document which is false in a material particular, or

(*b*) he otherwise makes use of such a document;

and in this sub-paragraph "the requisite intent" means the intent to deceive any person or to secure that a machine will respond to the document as if it were a true document.

(2) A person is guilty of an offence if, in providing any information under any provision made by or under this Schedule—

(*a*) he makes a statement which he knows to be false in a material particular; or

(*b*) he recklessly makes a statement which is false in a material particular.

(3) A person guilty of an offence under this paragraph shall be liable (subject to sub-paragraph (4))—

(*a*) on summary conviction, to a penalty of the statutory maximum or to imprisonment for a term not exceeding six months, or to both;

(*b*) on conviction on indictment, to a penalty of any amount or to imprisonment for a term not exceeding seven years, or to both.

(4) In the case of any offence under this paragraph, where—

(*a*) the document referred to in sub-paragraph (1) is a return [or other notification][1] required under any provision made by or under this Schedule, or

(*b*) the information referred to in sub-paragraph (2) is contained in or otherwise relevant to such a return [or notification][1],

the amount of the penalty on summary conviction shall be whichever is the greater of the statutory maximum and the amount equal to three times the sum of the amounts (if any) by which the return [or notification][1] understates any person's liability to levy.

(5) In sub-paragraph (4) the reference to the amount by which any person's liability to levy is understated shall be taken to be equal to the sum of—

(*a*) the amount (if any) by which his gross liability was understated; and

(*b*) the amount (if any) by which any entitlements of his to tax credits and repayments of levy were overstated.

(6) In sub-paragraph (5) "gross liability" means liability to levy before any deduction is made in respect of any entitlement to any tax credit or repayments of levy.

Amendments—[1] Words in sub-para (4) inserted by FA 2003 s 191(1), (7) with effect from 10 July 2003.

Criminal offences: Conduct involving evasions or misstatements

94—(1) A person is guilty of an offence under this paragraph if his conduct during any particular period must have involved the commission by him of one or more offences under the preceding provisions of this Part of this Schedule.

(2) For the purposes of any proceedings for an offence under this paragraph it shall be immaterial whether the particulars of the offence or offences that must have been committed are known.

(3) A person guilty of an offence under this paragraph shall be liable (subject to sub-paragraph (4))—

(*a*) on summary conviction, to a penalty of the statutory maximum or to imprisonment for a term not exceeding six months, or to both;

(*b*) on conviction on indictment, to a penalty of any amount or to imprisonment for a term not exceeding seven years, or to both.

(4) In the case of any offence under this paragraph, where the statutory maximum is less than three times the sum of the amounts of levy which are shown to be amounts that were or were intended to be evaded by the conduct in question, the penalty on summary conviction shall be the amount equal to three times that sum (instead of the statutory maximum).

(5) For the purposes of sub-paragraph (4) the amounts of levy that were or were intended to be evaded by any conduct shall be taken to include—

(*a*) the amount of any tax credit, and

(*b*) the amount of any repayment of levy,

which was, or was intended to be, obtained in circumstances where there was no entitlement to it.

(6) In determining for the purposes of sub-paragraph (4) how much levy (in addition to any amount falling within sub-paragraph (5)) was or was intended to be evaded, no account shall be taken of the extent (if any) to which any liability to levy of any person fell, or would have fallen, to be reduced by the amount of any tax credit or repayments of levy to which he was, or would have been, entitled.

Criminal offences: Preparations for evasion

95—(1) Where a person—

(*a*) becomes a party to any agreement under or by means of which a supply of a taxable commodity is or is to be made, or

(*b*) makes arrangements for any other person to become a party to such an agreement,

he is guilty of an offence if he does so in the belief that levy chargeable on the supply will be evaded.

(2) Subject to sub-paragraph (3), a person guilty of an offence under this paragraph shall be liable, on summary conviction, to a penalty of level 5 on the standard scale.

(3) In the case of any offence under this paragraph, where level 5 on the standard scale is less than three times the sum of the amounts of levy which are shown to be amounts that were or were intended to be evaded in respect of the supply in question, the penalty shall be the amount equal to three times that sum (instead of level 5 on the standard scale).

(4) For the purposes of sub-paragraph (3) the amounts of levy that were or were intended to be evaded shall be taken to include—

(*a*) the amount of any tax credit, and

(*b*) the amount of any repayment of levy,

which was, or was intended to be, obtained in circumstances where there was no entitlement to it.

(5) In determining for the purposes of sub-paragraph (3) how much levy (in addition to any amount falling within sub-paragraph (4)) was or was intended to be evaded, no account shall be taken of the extent (if any) to which any liability to levy of any person fell, or would have fallen, to be reduced by the amount of any tax credit or repayments of levy to which he was, or would have been, entitled.

Offences under paragraphs 92 to 95: procedural matters

96 *Sections 145 to 155 of the Customs and Excise Management Act 1979 (proceedings for offences, mitigation of penalties and certain other matters) shall apply in relation to offences and penalties under paragraphs 92 to 95 as they apply in relation to offences and penalties under the customs and excise Acts.*

Arrest for offences under paragraphs 92 to 94

97—*(1) Where an authorised person has reasonable grounds for suspecting that a fraud offence has been committed he may arrest anyone whom he has reasonable grounds for suspecting to be guilty of the offence.*

(2) In this paragraph—

"authorised person" means any person acting under the authority of the Commissioners; and

"a fraud offence" means an offence under any of paragraphs 92 to 94.

Amendments—[1] This para repealed by FA 2007 ss 84, 114, Sch 22 paras 3, 11(*a*), Sch 27 Pt 5(1) with effect from 1 December 2007 (by virtue of SI 2007/3166 art 3(*a*)).

Civil penalties: Evasion

98—*(1) Subject to sub-paragraph (5), where—*

(a) any person engages in any conduct for the purpose of evading levy, and

(b) that conduct involves dishonesty (whether or not it is such as to give rise to criminal liability),

that person shall be liable to a penalty.

(2) The amount of the penalty shall be—

(a) equal to the amount of levy evaded, or (as the case may be) intended to be evaded, by the person's conduct if at the time of engaging in that conduct he was or was required to be registered for the purposes of the levy;

(b) equal to twice that amount if at that time the person neither was nor was required to be registered for those purposes.

(3) The references in sub-paragraph (1) to evading levy include references to obtaining, in circumstances where there is no entitlement to it, either—

(a) a tax credit; or

(b) a repayment of levy.

(4) For the purposes of sub-paragraph (2) the amount of levy that was or was intended to be evaded by any conduct shall be taken to include—

(a) the amount of any tax credit, and

(b) the amount of any repayment of levy,

which was, or was intended to be, obtained in circumstances where there was no entitlement to it.

(5) In determining for the purposes of sub-paragraph (2) how much levy (in addition to any amount falling within sub-paragraph (4)) was or was intended to be evaded, no account shall be taken of the extent (if any) to which any liability to levy of any person fell, or would have fallen, to be reduced by the amount of any tax credit or repayments of levy to which he was, or would have been, entitled.

(6) Where, by reason of conduct falling within sub-paragraph (1), a person is convicted of an offence (whether under this Act or otherwise) that person shall not by reason of that conduct be liable also to a penalty under this paragraph.[1]

Amendments—[1] Para 98 repealed by FA 2008 s 122, Sch 40 para 21(*h*) with effect from 1 April 2009 (by virtue of SI 2009/571 art 2).

This para repealed only in so far as it relates to conduct involving dishonesty which relates to—

(a) an inaccuracy in a document, or

(b) a failure to notify HMRC of an under-assessment by HMRC (SI 2009/571 art 6).

Liability of directors etc for penalties under paragraph 98

99—*(1) Where it appears to the Commissioners—*

(a) that a body corporate is liable to a penalty under paragraph 98, and

(b) that the conduct giving rise to that penalty is, in whole or in part, attributable to the dishonesty of a person who is, or at the material time was, a director or managing officer of the body corporate (a "named officer"),

the Commissioners may serve a notice under this paragraph on the body corporate and on the named officer.

(2) A notice under this paragraph shall state—

(a) the amount of the penalty referred to in sub-paragraph (1)(a) ("the basic penalty"), and

(b) that the Commissioners propose, in accordance with this paragraph, to recover from the named officer such portion of the basic penalty (which may be the whole of it) as is specified in the notice.

(3) Where a notice is served under this paragraph, the portion of the basic penalty specified in the notice shall be recoverable from the named officer as if he were personally liable under paragraph 98 to a penalty which corresponds to that portion.

(4) Where a notice is served under this paragraph—

(a) the amount which may be assessed under Part IX of this Schedule as the amount due by way of penalty from the body corporate shall be only so much (if any) of the basic penalty as is not assessed on and notified to a named officer; and

(b) the body corporate shall be treated as discharged from liability for so much of the basic penalty as is so assessed and notified.

(5) Subject to the following provisions of this paragraph, the giving of a notice under this paragraph as such shall not be a decision which may be [appealed][2] under paragraph 121.

(6) Where a body corporate is assessed as mentioned in sub-paragraph (4)(a), the decisions of the Commissioners that may be [appealed][2] in accordance with paragraph 121 shall include their decision—

(a) as to the liability of the body corporate to a penalty, and

(b) as to the amount of the basic penalty that is specified in the assessment;

and paragraphs [121A to 123][2] shall apply accordingly.

(7) Where an assessment is made on a named officer by virtue of this paragraph, the decisions which may be [appealed][2] under paragraph 121 at the request of the named officer shall include—

(a) the Commissioners' decisions in the case of the body corporate as to the matters mentioned in sub-paragraph (6)(a) and (b);

(b) their decision that the conduct of the body corporate referred to in sub-paragraph (1)(b) is, in whole or in part, attributable to the dishonesty of the named officer; and

(c) their decision as to the portion of the penalty which the Commissioners propose to recover from him;

and paragraphs [121A to 123][2] shall apply accordingly.

(8) In this paragraph a "managing officer", in relation to a body corporate, means—

(a) any manager, secretary or other similar officer of the body corporate; or

(b) any person purporting to act in any such capacity or as a director.

(9) Where the affairs of a body corporate are managed by its members, this paragraph shall apply in relation to the conduct of a member in connection with his functions of management as if he were a director of the body corporate.[1]

Amendments—[1] Para 99 repealed by FA 2008 s 122, Sch 40 para 21(*h*) with effect from 1 April 2009 (by virtue of SI 2009/571 art 2).

This para repealed only in so far as it relates to conduct involving dishonesty which relates to—

(a) an inaccuracy in a document, or

(b) a failure to notify HMRC of an under-assessment by HMRC (SI 2009/571 art 6).

[2] Insofar as this para continues to apply, word substituted for the word "reviewed" in sub-paras (5), (6), (7); words substituted for the words "122 and 123" in sub-paras (6), (7).

Civil penalties: Misdeclaration or neglect

100—*(1) Subject to sub-paragraphs (3) to (5), where . . .[1]—*

(a) a return [or other notification][1] is made which understates a person's liability to levy or overstates his entitlement to any tax credit or repayment of levy, or

(b) at the end of the period of 30 days beginning on the date of the making of any assessment which understates a person's liability to levy, that person has not taken all such steps as are reasonable to draw the understatement to the attention of the Commissioners,

the person concerned shall be liable to a penalty equal to 5 per cent of the amount of the understatement of liability or (as the case may be) overstatement of entitlement.

(2) Where—

(a) a return for an accounting period—

(i) overstates or understates to any extent a person's liability to levy, or

(ii) understates or overstates to any extent his entitlement to any tax credits or repayments of levy,

and

(b) that return is corrected—

(i) in such circumstances as may be prescribed, and

(ii) in accordance with such conditions as may be prescribed,

by a return for a later accounting period which understates or overstates, to the corresponding extent, any liability or entitlement for the later period, it shall be assumed for the purposes of this paragraph that the statement made by each such return is a correct statement for the accounting period to which the return relates.

(3) Conduct falling within sub-paragraph (1) shall not give rise to liability to a penalty under this paragraph if the person concerned provides the Commissioners with full information with respect to the inaccuracy concerned—

(a) at a time when he has no reason to believe that enquiries are being made by the Commissioners into his affairs, so far as they relate to the levy; and

(b) in such form and manner as may be prescribed by regulations made by the Commissioners or specified by them in accordance with any such regulations.

(4) Conduct falling within sub-paragraph (1) shall not give rise to liability to a penalty under this paragraph if the person concerned satisfies the Commissioners or, on appeal, an appeal tribunal that there is a reasonable excuse for his conduct.

(5) Where, by reason of conduct falling within sub-paragraph (1)—

(a) a person is convicted of an offence (whether under this Act or otherwise), or

(b) a person is assessed to a penalty under paragraph 98,

that person shall not by reason of that conduct be liable also to a penalty under this paragraph.[2]

Amendments—[1] Words "for an accounting period" in sub-para (1) repealed, and words in sub-para (1)(*a*) inserted, by FA 2003 ss 192(1), (8), 216, Sch 43 Pt 4 with effect from 10 July 2003.

[2] Para 100 repealed by FA 2008 s 122, Sch 40 para 21(*h*) with effect from 1 April 2009 (by virtue of SI 2009/571 art 2).

[Civil penalties: incorrect certificates][3]

101—(1) . . . [3]

(2) Where—

(*a*) a person gives, in relation to any supply (or supplies) of a taxable commodity (or taxable commodities) being made to him, to the supplier a certificate that the supply (or supplies) is (or are) to any extent—

(i) for domestic or charity use,

(ii) exempt under any of paragraphs [11,][3] 12, 13, 14, [15, 18 [, 18A][2] and 21][1] [or][4]

(iii) *a half-rate supply (or half-rate supplies)[, or*[4]

(iv) a reduced-rate supply (or reduced-rate supplies),][1] and

(*b*) the certificate is [(or becomes)][3] incorrect,

the person shall be liable to a penalty.

(3) The amount of the penalty to which a person is liable under [this paragraph][3] shall be equal to 105 per cent of the difference between—

(*a*) the amount of levy (which may be nil) that would have been chargeable on the supply (or supplies) if the . . . [3] certificate had been correct, and

(*b*) the amount of levy actually chargeable.

(4) The giving of a [certificate (or not revoking or varying it)][3] shall not give rise to a penalty under this paragraph if [the person concerned][3] satisfies the Commissioners or, on appeal, an appeal tribunal that [the person has a reasonable excuse][3].

(5) Where by reason of giving a [certificate (or not revoking or varying it)][3]—

(*a*) a person is convicted of an offence (whether under this Act or otherwise), or

(*b*) a person is assessed to a penalty under paragraph 98,

that person shall not by reason of [that][3] be liable also to a penalty under this paragraph.

Amendments—[1] Words in sub-para (2)(*a*)(ii) substituted for the words "18 and 21, or", and words in sub-para (2)(*a*) (iii) and (iv) inserted, by FA 2002 s 127 in relation to certificates given in respect of any supplies made after 23 April 2002.

[2] Words in sub-para (2)(*a*)(ii) inserted by FA 2003 s 188(2)(*b*) with effect from 10 July 2003.

[3] Sub-para (1) repealed; words in sub-para (2) inserted; in sub-para (3), words "notification or" repealed; words in sub-paras (3), (4), (5) substituted; and Heading substituted, by FA 2007 ss 23, 114, Sch 2 paras 1, 12, Sch 27 Pt 1(1) with effect from 19 July 2007.

Sub-para (1) previously read as follows—

"Where—

(*a*) a person gives a notification for the purposes of paragraph 11 in relation to any supply (or supplies) of a taxable commodity (or taxable commodities), and

(*b*) the notification is incorrect,

the person shall be liable to a penalty."

Words substituted in sub-para (3) previously read as follows—

"sub-paragraph (1) or (2)".

Words substituted in sub-para (4) previously read as follows—

"notification or certificate", "the person who gave it", and "there is a reasonable excuse for his having given it".

Words substituted in sub-para (5) previously read as follows—

"notification or certificate", and "the giving of the notification or certificate".

Heading previously read as follows—

"Civil penalties: Incorrect notifications etc".

4 In sub-para (2)(*a*)(ii) word inserted, and sub-para (2)(*a*)(iii) repealed, by FA 2006 ss 172(14), 178, Sch 26 Pt 8(1) with effect from 1 November 2007: SI 2007/2901 art 2(1).
These amendments do not apply in relation to a half-rate supply made before 1 April 2006: SI 2007/2901 art 2(2). For this purpose, "half-rate supply" carries the meaning it has in this Schedule before 1 November 2007. FA 2006 s 172(3)–(6) applies for determining when a supply is to be regarded as made: SI 2007/2901 art 2(3).

Interpretation of Part VIII

102—(1) References in this Part of this Schedule to obtaining a tax credit are references to bringing an amount into account as a tax credit for the purposes of levy on the basis that that amount is an amount which may be so brought into account in accordance with tax credit regulations.
(2) References in this Part of this Schedule to obtaining a repayment of levy are references to obtaining either—
(*a*) the payment or repayment of any amount, or
(*b*) the acknowledgement of a right to receive any amount,
on the basis that that amount is the amount of a repayment of levy to which there is an entitlement.

PART IX
CIVIL PENALTIES

Preliminary

103—(1) In this Part of this Schedule "civil penalty" means any penalty liability to which—
(*a*) is imposed by or under this Schedule, and
(*b*) arises otherwise than in consequence of a person's conviction for a criminal offence.
(2) In this Part of this Schedule—
(*a*) references to a person's being liable to a civil penalty include references to his being a person from whom the whole or any part of a civil penalty is recoverable by virtue of paragraph 99; and
(*b*) references, in relation to a person from whom the whole or any part of a civil penalty is so recoverable, to the penalty to which he is liable are references to so much of the penalty as is recoverable from him.
(3) Any notification of an assessment under any provision of this Part of this Schedule to a person's representative shall be treated for the purposes of this Schedule as notification to the person in relation to whom the representative acts.
(4) In this paragraph "representative", in relation to any person, means—
(*a*) any of that person's personal representatives;
(*b*) that person's trustee in bankruptcy or liquidator;
(*c*) any person holding office as a receiver in relation to that person or any of his property;
(*d*) that person's tax representative or any other person for the time being acting in a representative capacity in relation to that person.
(5) In this paragraph "trustee in bankruptcy" includes, as respects Scotland—
(*a*) an interim or permanent trustee (within the meaning of the Bankruptcy (Scotland) Act 1985); and
(*b*) a trustee acting under a trust deed (within the meaning of that Act).

Reduction of penalties

104—(1) Where a person is liable to a civil penalty—
(*a*) the Commissioners or, on appeal, an appeal tribunal may reduce the penalty to such amount (including nil) as they think proper; but
(*b*) on an appeal relating to any penalty reduced by the Commissioners, an appeal tribunal may cancel the whole or any part of the Commissioners' reduction.
(2) In determining whether a civil penalty should be, or should have been, reduced under sub-paragraph (1), no account shall be taken of any of the following matters, that is to say—
(*a*) the insufficiency of the funds available to any person for paying any levy due or for paying the amount of the penalty;
(*b*) the fact that there has, in the case in question or in that case taken with any other cases, been no or no significant loss of levy;
(*c*) the fact that the person liable to the penalty or a person acting on his behalf has acted in good faith.

Matters not amounting to reasonable excuse

105 For the purposes of any provision made by or under this Schedule under which liability to a civil penalty does not arise in respect of conduct for which there is shown to be a reasonable excuse—

(*a*) an insufficiency of funds available for paying any amount is not a reasonable excuse; and

(*b*) where reliance has been placed on any other person to perform any task, neither the fact of that reliance nor any conduct of the person relied upon is a reasonable excuse.

Assessments to penalties etc

106—(1) Where a person is liable to a civil penalty, the Commissioners may assess the amount due by way of penalty and notify it to him accordingly.

(2) If, where an assessment has been notified to any person under sub-paragraph (1) or this sub-paragraph, it appears to the Commissioners that the amount which ought to have been assessed exceeds the amount that has already been assessed, the Commissioners may make a supplementary assessment of the amount of the excess and shall notify that person accordingly.

(3) The fact that any conduct giving rise to a civil penalty may have ceased before an assessment is made under this paragraph shall not affect the power of the Commissioners to make such an assessment.

(4) Where an amount has been assessed and notified to any person under this paragraph, it shall be recoverable as if it were levy due from him.

(5) Sub-paragraph (4)—

(*a*) shall not apply so as to require any interest to be payable on a penalty otherwise than in accordance with this Part of this Schedule; and

(*b*) shall not have effect if, or to the extent that, the assessment in question has been withdrawn or reduced.

(6) Subject to sub-paragraph (7), where a person—

(*a*) is assessed under this paragraph to an amount due by way of a penalty, and

(*b*) is also assessed under any one or more provisions of Part VII of this Schedule for an accounting period to which the conduct attracting the penalty is referable,

the assessments may be combined and notified to him as one assessment.

(7) A notice of a combined assessment under sub-paragraph (6) must separately identify the penalty being assessed.

(8) The power to make an assessment under this paragraph is subject to paragraph 99(4).

Further assessments to daily penalties

107—(1) This paragraph applies where an assessment is made under paragraph 106 to an amount of a civil penalty to which any person is liable—

(*a*) under paragraph 124(3) (failure to provide information); or

(*b*) under paragraph 127(4) (failure to produce a document).

(2) The notice of assessment shall specify a time, not later than the end of the day of the giving of the notice of assessment, to which the amount of any daily penalty is calculated.

(3) For the purposes of sub-paragraph (2) "daily penalty" means—

(*a*) in a case within sub-paragraph (1)(*a*), a penalty imposed by virtue of paragraph 124(3)(*b*); and

(*b*) in a case within sub-paragraph (1)(*b*), a penalty imposed by virtue of paragraph 127(4)(*b*).

(4) If further penalties accrue in respect of a continuing failure after that date to provide the information or, as the case may be, produce the document, a further assessment or further assessments may be made under paragraph 106 in respect of the amounts so accruing.

(5) Where—

(*a*) an assessment to a civil penalty is made specifying a date for the purposes of sub-paragraph (2), and

(*b*) the failure in question is remedied within such period as may for the purposes of this sub-paragraph have been notified by the Commissioners to the person liable for the penalty,

the failure shall be deemed for the purposes of any further liability to civil penalties to have been remedied on the specified date.

Time limits on penalty assessments

108—(1) Subject to sub-paragraphs (2) and (3), an assessment under paragraph 106 to a penalty shall not be made more than [4 years] after the conduct to which the penalty relates.

[(2) An assessment of a person to a penalty in a case involving a loss of levy—

(*a*) brought about deliberately by the person (or by another person acting on that person's behalf), or (*b*) attributable to a failure by the person to comply with an obligation under paragraph 53 or 55,

may be made at any time not more than 20 years after the conduct to which the penalty relates (subject to sub-paragraph (3)).

(2A) In sub-paragraph (2)(*a*) the reference to a loss brought about deliberately by the person includes a loss brought about as a result of a deliberate inaccuracy in a document given to Her Majesty's Revenue and Customs by or on behalf of that person.]

(3) Where, after a person's death, the Commissioners propose to assess an amount of a civil penalty due by reason of some conduct of the deceased—

(*a*) the assessment shall not be made more than [4 years] after the death; *and*

(*b*) if the circumstances are as set out in sub-paragraph (2)—

(i) the modification of sub-paragraph (1) contained in that sub-paragraph shall not apply; but

(ii) any assessment which (applying that modification) could have been made immediately after the death may be made at any time within three years after it.

Amendments—In sub-paras (1), (3)(*a*) words "4 years" substituted for "three years"; sub-paras (2), (2A) substituted for previous sub-para (2), and sub-para (3)(*b*) and preceding word "and" repealed, by FA 2009 s 99, Sch 51 paras 32, 36, with effect from 1 April 2010 (SI 2010/867 art 2(1)). Sub-para (2) previously read as follows:

"(2) Subject to sub-paragraph (3), if levy has been lost—

(*a*) as a result of any conduct for which a person has been convicted of an offence involving fraud,

(*b*) in circumstances giving rise to liability to a penalty under paragraph 55 (failure to notify of registrability etc), or

(*c*) an assessment may be made for any civil penalty relating to that conduct as if, in sub-paragraph (1), for "three years" there were substituted "twenty years"."

The following transitional provisions apply—

- The amendment made to sub-para (1) is disregarded where, for the purposes of sub-para (1), the conduct to which the penalty relates occurred on or before 31 March 2007 (SI 2010/867 art 21).
- The substitution of sub-para (2) is disregarded where, for the purposes of sub-para (2), the conduct to which the penalty relates occurred on or before 31 March 2007. (SI 2010/867 art 22).
- The amendments made to sub-para (3) are disregarded where, for the purposes of sub-para (3), the death was on or before 31 March 2007 (SI 2010/867 art 23).

Penalty interest on unpaid penalties

109—(1) Subject to sub-paragraph (2), where the Commissioners make an assessment under paragraph 106 of any civil penalty to which a person is liable the amount of that penalty shall carry penalty interest for the period which—

(*a*) begins with the day on which the assessment is notified to the person on whom the assessment is made; and

(*b*) ends with the day before the day on which the assessed penalty is paid.

(2) Where—

(*a*) the Commissioners make an assessment under paragraph 106 of an amount of any civil penalty to which any person is liable,

(*b*) they also specify a date for the purposes of this sub-paragraph, and

(*c*) the amount of the penalty assessed is paid on or before that date,

the amount paid before that date shall not carry penalty interest under this paragraph.

(3) Penalty interest under this paragraph shall be compound interest calculated—

(*a*) at the penalty rate, and

(*b*) with monthly rests.

(4) For this purpose the penalty rate is the rate found by—

(*a*) taking the rate applicable under section 197 of the Finance Act 1996 for the purposes of paragraph 81(3); and

(*b*) adding 10 percentage points to that rate.

(5) Where a person is liable under this paragraph to pay any penalty interest, the Commissioners or, on appeal, an appeal tribunal may reduce the amount payable to such amount (including nil) as they think proper.

(6) Subject to sub-paragraph (7), where the person concerned satisfies the Commissioners or, on appeal, an appeal tribunal that there is a reasonable excuse for the conduct giving rise to the liability to pay penalty interest, that is a matter which (among other things) may be taken into account under sub-paragraph (5).

(7) In determining whether there is a reasonable excuse for the purposes of sub-paragraph (6), no account shall be taken of any of the following matters, that is to say—

(*a*) the insufficiency of the funds available to any person for paying any levy or penalty due or for paying the amount of the interest;

(*b*) the fact that there has, in the case in question or in that case taken with any other cases, been no or no significant loss of levy;

(*c*) the fact that the person liable to pay the interest or a person acting on his behalf has acted in good faith.

(8) In the case of interest reduced by the Commissioners under sub-paragraph (5), an appeal tribunal, on an appeal relating to the interest, may cancel the whole or any part of the reduction made by the Commissioners.

Supplemental provisions about interest

110—(1) Interest under paragraph 109 shall be paid without any deduction of income tax.

(2) Sub-paragraph (3) applies where—

(*a*) an amount carries interest under paragraph 109 (or would do so apart from that sub-paragraph); and

(*b*) all or part of the amount turns out not to be due.

(3) In such a case—

(*a*) the amount or part that turns out not to be due shall not carry interest under paragraph 109 and shall be treated as never having done so; and

(*b*) all such adjustments as are reasonable shall be made, including (subject to paragraphs 64 to 76) adjustments by way of repayment.

Assessments to penalty interest on unpaid penalties

111—(1) Where a person is liable for interest under paragraph 109, the Commissioners may assess the amount due by way of interest and notify it to him accordingly.

(2) If, where an assessment has been notified to any person under sub-paragraph (1) or this sub-paragraph, it appears to the Commissioners that the amount which ought to have been assessed exceeds the amount that has already been assessed, the Commissioners may make a supplementary assessment of the amount of the excess and notify that person accordingly.

(3) Where an amount has been assessed and notified to any person under this paragraph, it shall be recoverable as if it were levy due from him.

(4) Sub-paragraph (3)—

(*a*) shall not apply so as to require any interest to be payable on interest (except in so far as it falls to be compounded in accordance with paragraph 109(3)); and

(*b*) shall not have effect if, or to the extent that, the assessment in question has been withdrawn or reduced.

(5) Paragraph 108 shall apply in relation to assessments under this paragraph as if any assessment to interest on a penalty were an assessment under paragraph 106 to the penalty in question.

(6) Subject to sub-paragraph (7), where a person—

(*a*) is assessed under this paragraph to an amount due by way of any interest on a penalty, and

(*b*) is also assessed under any one or more provisions of Part VII of this Schedule for the accounting period to which the conduct attracting the penalty is referable,

the assessments may be combined and notified to him as one assessment.

(7) A notice of a combined assessment under sub-paragraph (6) must separately identify the interest being assessed.

Further assessments to interest on penalties

112—(1) Where an assessment is made under paragraph 111 to an amount of penalty interest under paragraph 109—

(*a*) the notice of assessment shall specify a date, not later than the date of the notice of assessment, to which the amount of interest which is assessed is calculated; and

(*b*) if the interest continues to accrue after that date, a further assessment or further assessments may be made under paragraph 111 in respect of the amounts so accruing.

(2) Where—

(*a*) an assessment to penalty interest is made specifying a date for the purposes of sub-paragraph (1)(*a*), and

(*b*) within such period as may for the purposes of this sub-paragraph have been notified by the Commissioners to the person liable for the interest, the amount on which the interest is payable is paid,

that amount shall be deemed for the purposes of any further liability to interest to have been paid on the specified date.

Up-rating of amounts of penalties

113—(1) If it appears to the Treasury that there has been a change in the value of money since the time when the amount of a civil penalty provided for by this Schedule was fixed, they may by regulations substitute, for the amount for the time being specified as the amount of that penalty, such other sum as appears to them to be justified by the change.

(2) In sub-paragraph (1) the reference to the time when the amount of a civil penalty was fixed is a reference—

(*a*) in the case of a penalty which has not previously been modified under that sub-paragraph, to the time of the passing of this Act; and

(*b*) in any other case, to the time of the making of the regulations under that sub-paragraph that made the most recent modification of the amount of that penalty.

(3) Regulations under sub-paragraph (1) shall not apply to the penalty for any conduct before the coming into force of the regulations.

PART X
NON-RESIDENTS, GROUPS AND OTHER SPECIAL CASES

Non-resident taxpayers: appointment of tax representatives

114—(1) The Commissioners may by regulations make provision for securing that every non-resident taxpayer has a person resident in the United Kingdom to act as his tax representative for the purposes of the levy.

(2) Regulations under this paragraph may, in particular, contain any or all of the following—

(*a*) provision requiring notification to be given to the Commissioners where a person becomes a non-resident taxpayer;

(*b*) provision requiring the appointment of tax representatives by non-resident taxpayers;

(*c*) provision for the appointment of a person as a tax representative to take effect only where the person appointed is approved by the Commissioners;

(*d*) provision authorising the Commissioners to give a direction requiring the replacement of a tax representative;

(*e*) provision authorising the Commissioners to give a direction requiring a person specified in the direction to be treated as the appointed tax representative of a non-resident taxpayer so specified;

(*f*) provision about the circumstances in which a person ceases to be a tax representative and about the withdrawal by the Commissioners of their approval of a tax representative;

(*g*) provision enabling a tax representative to act on behalf of the person for whom he is the tax representative through an agent of the representative;

(*h*) provision for the purposes of any provision made by virtue of paragraphs (*a*) to (*g*) regulating the procedure to be followed in any case and imposing requirements as to the information and other particulars to be provided to the Commissioners;

(*i*) provision as to the time at which things done under or for the purposes of the regulations are to take effect.

(3) Subject to sub-paragraph (4), a person who—

(*a*) becomes subject, in accordance with any regulations under this paragraph, to an obligation to request the Commissioners' approval for any person's appointment as his tax representative, but

(*b*) fails (with or without making the appointment) to make the request as required by the regulations,

shall be liable to a penalty of £10,000.

(4) A failure such as is mentioned in sub-paragraph (3) shall not give rise to liability to a penalty under this paragraph if the person concerned satisfies the Commissioners or, on appeal, an appeal tribunal that there is a reasonable excuse for the failure.

Effect of appointment of tax representatives

115—(1) The tax representative of a non-resident taxpayer shall be entitled to act on the non-resident taxpayer's behalf for the purposes of any provision made by or under this Schedule.

(2) The tax representative of a non-resident taxpayer shall be under a duty, except to such extent as the Commissioners by regulations otherwise provide, to secure the non-resident taxpayer's compliance with, and discharge of, the obligations and liabilities to which the non-resident taxpayer is subject by virtue of any provision made by or under this Schedule (including obligations and liabilities arising or incurred before he became the non-resident taxpayer's tax representative).

(3) A person who is or has been the tax representative of a non-resident taxpayer shall be personally liable—

(*a*) in respect of any failure while he is or was the non-resident taxpayer's tax representative to secure compliance with, or the discharge of, any obligation or liability to which sub-paragraph (2) applies, and

(*b*) in respect of anything done in the course of, or for purposes connected with, acting on the non-resident taxpayer's behalf, as if the obligations and liabilities to which sub-paragraph (2) applies were imposed jointly and severally on the tax representative and the non-resident taxpayer.

(4) A tax representative shall not be liable by virtue of this paragraph to be registered for the purposes of the levy; but the Commissioners may by regulations—

(*a*) require the names of tax representatives to be registered against the names of the non-resident taxpayers of whom they are the representatives;

(*b*) make provision for the deletion of the names so registered of persons who cease to be tax representatives.

(5) A tax representative shall not by virtue of this paragraph be guilty of any offence except in so far as—

(*a*) he has consented to, or connived in, the commission of the offence by the non-resident taxpayer;

(*b*) the commission of the offence by the non-resident taxpayer is attributable to any neglect on the part of the tax representative; or

(*c*) the offence consists in a contravention by the tax representative of an obligation which, by virtue of this paragraph, is imposed both on the tax representative and on the non-resident taxpayer.

Groups of companies etc

116—(1) The Commissioners may make provision by regulations for two or more bodies corporate to be treated as members of a group for the purposes of the Schedule.

(2) Regulations under sub-paragraph (1) may, in particular, make provision for or about—

(*a*) eligibility for group treatment;

(*b*) representative members of groups;

(*c*) applications for, or the variation or ending of, group treatment;

(*d*) the decisions to be made on applications;

(*e*) the variation or ending of group treatment by notice given by the Commissioners otherwise than on an application;

(*f*) treating a member of a group as charged with levy that would otherwise be levy with which another member of the group would be charged;

(*g*) the members of a group liable for levy, or amounts recoverable as levy, due from a member of a group.

(3) The provision mentioned in sub-paragraph (2)(*c*) includes provision—

(*a*) about the time within which applications are to be made,

(*b*) for authorising the Commissioners to extend such time, and

(*c*) for applications that seek group treatment, or its variation or ending, with effect from a time before they are made.

(4) The provision mentioned in sub-paragraph (2)(*e*) includes provision for a notice to have effect from a time before it is given.

(5) Regulations under sub-paragraph (1) may make provision for imposing requirements on a body corporate to notify the Commissioners of prescribed matters relating to group treatment.

(6) A body corporate which fails to comply with any such requirement imposed by such regulations shall be liable to a penalty of £250.

Partnerships and other unincorporated bodies

117—(1) The Commissioners may by regulations make provision for determining by what persons anything required to be done under this Schedule is to be done where, apart from those regulations, that requirement would fall on—

(*a*) persons carrying on business in partnership; or

(*b*) persons carrying on business together as an unincorporated body;

but any regulations under this sub-paragraph must be construed subject to the following provisions of this paragraph.

(2) In determining for the purposes of this Schedule who at any time is the person accountable for any levy in a case where, apart from this sub-paragraph, the persons accountable are persons carrying on any business—

(*a*) in partnership, or

(*b*) as an unincorporated body,

the firm or body shall be treated, for the purposes of that determination (and notwithstanding any changes from time to time in the members of the firm or body), as the same person and as separate from its members.

(3) Without prejudice to section 36 of the Partnership Act 1890 (rights of persons dealing with firm against apparent members of firm), where—

(*a*) persons have been carrying on in partnership any business in the course or furtherance of which there has been done any thing that resulted in the firm becoming liable to account for any levy, and

(*b*) a person ceases to be a member of the firm,

that person shall be regarded for the purposes of this Schedule (including sub-paragraph (7) below) as continuing to be a partner until the date on which the change in the partnership is notified to the Commissioners.

(4) Where a person ceases to be a member of a firm during an accounting period (or is treated as so ceasing by virtue of sub-paragraph (3)) any notice, whether of assessment or otherwise, which—

(*a*) is served on the firm under or for the purposes of any provision made by or under this Schedule, and

(*b*) relates to, or to any matter arising in, that period or any earlier period during the whole or part of which he was a member of the firm,

shall be treated as served also on him.

(5) Without prejudice to section 16 of the Partnership Act 1890 (notice to acting partner to be notice to the firm), any notice, whether of assessment or otherwise, which—

(*a*) is addressed to a firm by the name in which it is registered, and

(*b*) is served in accordance with this Schedule,

shall be treated for the purposes of this Schedule as served on the firm and, accordingly, where sub-paragraph (4) applies, as served also on the former partner.

(6) Subject to sub-paragraph (7), nothing in this paragraph shall affect the extent to which, under section 9 of the Partnership Act 1890 (liability of partners for debts of the firm), a partner is liable for levy owed by the firm.

(7) Where a person is a partner in a firm during part only of an accounting period, his personal liability for levy incurred by the firm in respect of taxable supplies made in that period shall include, but shall not exceed, such proportion of the firm's liability as may be just and reasonable in the circumstances.

Death and incapacity

118—(1) The Commissioners may, in accordance with sub-paragraph (2), by regulations make provision for the purposes of the levy in relation to cases where a person carries on a business of an individual who has died or become incapacitated.

(2) The provisions that may be contained in regulations under this paragraph are—

(*a*) provision requiring the person who is carrying on the business to inform the Commissioners of the fact that he is carrying on the business and of the event that has led to his carrying it on;

(*b*) provision allowing that person to be treated for a limited time as if he and the person who has died or become incapacitated were the same person; and

(*c*) such other provision as the Commissioners think fit for securing continuity in the application of this Schedule where a person is so treated.

Transfer of a business as a going concern

119—(1) The Commissioners may by regulations make provision for securing continuity in the application of this Schedule in cases where any business carried on by a person is transferred to another person as a going concern.

(2) Regulations under this paragraph may, in particular, include any or all of the following—

(*a*) provision requiring the transferor to inform the Commissioners of the transfer;

(*b*) provision for liabilities and duties under this Schedule of the transferor to become, to such extent as may be provided by the regulations, liabilities and duties of the transferee;

(*c*) provision for any right of either of them to a tax credit or repayment of levy to be satisfied by allowing the credit or making the repayment to the other;

(*d*) provision as to the preservation of any records or accounts relating to the business which, by virtue of any regulations under paragraph 125, are required to be preserved for any period after the transfer.

(3) Regulations under this paragraph may provide that no such provision as is mentioned in paragraph (*b*) or (*c*) of sub-paragraph (2) shall have effect in relation to any transferor and transferee unless an application for the purpose has been made by them under the regulations.

Insolvency etc

120—(1) The Commissioners may by regulations make provision in accordance with the following provisions of this paragraph for the application of this Schedule in cases in which an insolvency procedure is applied to a person or to a deceased individual's estate.

In this paragraph "the relevant person" means the person to whom, or the deceased individual to whose estate, the insolvency procedure is applied.

(2) The provision that may be contained in regulations under this paragraph may include any or all of the following—

(*a*) provision requiring any such person as may be prescribed to give notification to the Commissioners, in the prescribed manner, of the prescribed particulars of any relevant matter;

(*b*) provision requiring a person to be treated, to the prescribed extent, as if he were the same person as the relevant person for the purposes of this Schedule or such of its provisions as may be prescribed; and

(*c*) provision for securing continuity in the application of any of the provisions of this Schedule where, by virtue of any regulations under this paragraph, any person is treated as if he were the same person as the relevant person.

(3) In sub-paragraph (2) "relevant matter", in relation to a case in which an insolvency procedure is applied to any person or to any deceased individual's estate, means—

(*a*) the application of that procedure to that person or estate;

(*b*) the appointment of any person for the purposes of the application of that procedure;

(*c*) any other matter relating to—

(i) the application of that procedure to the person to whom, or the estate to which, it is applied;

(ii) the holding of an appointment made for the purposes of that procedure; or

(iii) the exercise or discharge of any powers or duties conferred or imposed on any person by virtue of such an appointment.

(4) Regulations made by virtue of sub-paragraph (2)(*b*) may include provision for a person to cease to be treated as if he were the same person as the relevant person on the occurrence of such an event as may be prescribed.

(5) Regulations under this paragraph prescribing the manner in which any notification is to be given to the Commissioners may require it to be given in such manner and to contain such particulars as may be specified in a general notice published by the Commissioners in accordance with the regulations.

(6) Regulations under this paragraph may provide that the extent to which, and the purposes for which, a person is to be treated under the regulations as if he were the same person as the relevant person may be determined by reference to a notice given in accordance with the regulations to the person so treated.

(7) For the purposes of this paragraph, an insolvency procedure is applied to a person if—

(*a*) a bankruptcy order, winding-up order or administration order is made [or an administrator is appointed][1] in relation to that person or a partnership of which he is a member;

(*b*) an award of sequestration is made on that person's estate or on the estate of a partnership of which he is a member;

(*c*) that person is put into administrative receivership;

(*d*) that person passes a resolution for voluntary winding up;

(*e*) any voluntary arrangement approved in accordance with—

(i) Part I or VIII of the Insolvency Act 1986, or

(ii) Part II or Chapter II of Part VIII of the Insolvency (Northern Ireland) Order 1989,

comes into force in relation to that person or a partnership of which that person is a member;

(*f*) a deed of arrangement registered in accordance with—

(i) the Deeds of Arrangement Act 1914, or

(ii) Chapter I of Part VIII of that Order,

takes effect in relation to that person;

(*g*) a person is appointed as the receiver or manager of some or all of that person's property, or of income arising from some or all of his property;

(*h*) a person is appointed as the interim receiver of some or all of that person's property under section 286 of the Insolvency Act 1986 or Article 259 of the Insolvency (Northern Ireland) Order 1989;

(*i*) a person is appointed as the provisional liquidator in relation to that person under section 135 of that Act or Article 115 of that Order;

(*j*) an interim order is made under Part VIII of that Act, or Chapter II of Part VIII of that Order, in relation to that person; or

(*k*) that person's estate, or the estate of a partnership of which that person is a member, becomes vested in any other person as that person's, or the partnership's, trustee under a trust deed (within the meaning of the Bankruptcy (Scotland) Act 1985).

(8) For the purposes of this paragraph, an insolvency procedure is applied to a deceased individual's estate if—

(*a*) a bankruptcy order, or an order by some other name but corresponding to a bankruptcy order, is made after the individual's death in relation to his estate under provisions of—

(i) the Insolvency Act 1986, or

(ii) the Insolvency (Northern Ireland) Order 1989,

as applied to the administration of the insolvent estates of deceased individuals; or

(*b*) an award of sequestration is made on the individual's estate after the individual's death.

(9) In sub-paragraph (7)—

(*a*) "administration order" means an administration order under [Schedule B1 to][1] the Insolvency Act 1986 or Article 21 of the Insolvency (Northern Ireland) Order 1989;

(*b*) references to a member of a partnership include references to any person who is liable as a partner under section 14 of the Partnership Act 1890 (persons liable by "holding out").

Amendments—[1] Words in sub-para (7)(*a*) inserted, and words in sub-para (9)(*a*) substituted, by the Enterprise Act 2002 (Insolvency) Order, SI 2003/2096 art 4, Schedule paras 31, 33 with effect from 15 September 2003. These amendments do not apply in relation to any case where a petition for an administration order was presented before 15 September 2003: SI 2003/2096 arts 1(1), 6.

PART XI
REVIEW AND APPEAL

[Appeals][1]

121—[(1) Subject to paragraph 122, an appeal shall lie to an appeal tribunal from any person who is or will be affected by any decision of HMRC with respect to any of the following matters—][1]

(*a*) whether or not a person is charged in any case with an amount of levy;

(*b*) the amount of levy charged in any case and the time when the charge is to be taken as having arisen;

(*c*) the registration of any person for the purposes of the levy or the cancellation of any registration;

(*d*) the person liable to pay the levy charged in any case, the amount of a person's liability to levy and the time by which he is required to pay an amount of levy;

(*e*) whether to prepare a special utility scheme for a utility;

(*f*) the imposition of a requirement on any person to give security, or further security, under paragraph 139 and the amount and manner of providing any security required under that paragraph;

(*g*) whether or not liability to a penalty or to interest on any amount arises in any person's case under any provision made by or under this Schedule, and the amount of any such liability;

(*h*) any matter the decision as to which is [appealable][1] under this paragraph of this Part of this Schedule in accordance with paragraph 99(6) or (7);

(*i*) the extent of any person's entitlement to any tax credit or to a repayment in respect of a tax credit and the extent of any liability of the Commissioners under this Schedule to pay interest on any amount;

(*j*) whether or not any person is required to have a tax representative by virtue of any regulations under paragraph 114;

(*k*) the giving, withdrawal or variation, for the purposes of any such regulations, of any approval or direction with respect to the person who is to act as another's tax representative;

(*l*) the giving, withdrawal or variation of a utility direction under paragraph 151(1);

(*m*) whether a body corporate is to be treated, or is to cease to be treated, as a member of a group, the times at which a body corporate is to be so treated and the body corporate which is, in relation to any time, to be the representative member for a group;

(*n*) any matter not falling within the preceding paragraphs the decision with respect to which is contained in—

(i) an assessment under paragraph 78 or 79 in respect of an accounting period in relation to which any return required to be made by virtue of regulations under paragraph 41 has been made, or

(ii) an assessment under any provision of this Schedule other than paragraph 78 or 79.

[*(2) Any person who is or will be affected by any decision to which this paragraph applies may by notice in writing to the Commissioners require them to review the decision.*

(3) The Commissioners shall not be required under this paragraph to review any decision unless the notice requiring the review is given before the end of the period of forty-five days beginning with the day on which written notification of the decision, or of an assessment containing or giving effect to the decision, was first given to the person requiring the review.

(4) For the purposes of sub-paragraph (3) it shall be the duty of the Commissioners to give written notification of any decision to which this paragraph applies to any person who—

(a) requests such a notification;

(b) has not previously been given written notification of that decision; and

(c) if given such a notification, will be entitled to require a review of the decision under this paragraph.

(5) A person shall be entitled to give a notice under this paragraph requiring a decision to be reviewed for a second or subsequent time only if—

(a) the grounds on which he requires the further review are that the Commissioners did not, on any previous review, have the opportunity to consider certain facts or other matters; and

(b) he does not, on the further review, require the Commissioners to consider any facts or matters which were considered on a previous review except in so far as they are relevant to any issue to which the facts or matters not previously considered relate.

(6) Where the Commissioners are required by a notice under this paragraph to review any decision, it shall be their duty to do so.

(7) On a review under this paragraph the Commissioners may (subject to sub-paragraph (9)) withdraw, vary or confirm the decision reviewed.

(8) Where—

(a) it is the duty under this paragraph of the Commissioners to review any decision, and

(b) they do not, within the period of forty-five days beginning with the day on which the review was required, give notice to the person requiring it of their determination on the review,

they shall be deemed to have confirmed the decision.

(9) Where the Commissioners decide, on a review under this paragraph, that a liability to a penalty or to an amount of interest arises, they shall not be entitled to modify the amount payable in respect of that liability except—

(a) in exercise of a power conferred by paragraph 104(1) (penalties) or paragraph 70(6), 86(3) or 109(5) (penalty interest); or

(b) for the purpose of making the amount payable conform to the amount of the liability imposed by this Schedule.][1]

(10) This paragraph has effect subject to paragraph 99(5).

Amendments—[1] Heading substituted for former heading "Review of Commissioners' decisions"; words at the beginning in sub-para (1) substituted for the words "This paragraph applies to a decision of the Commissioners with respect to any of the following matters—"; word in sub-para (1)(*h*) substituted for the word "reviewable"; sub-paras (2)–(9) repealed by the Transfer of Tribunal Functions and Revenue and Customs Appeals Order, SI 2009/56 art 3, Sch 1 para 288 with effect from 1 April 2009, subject to transitional and savings provisions in Sch 3 paras 2, 3.

[Offer of review

121A (1) HMRC must offer a person (P) a review of a decision that has been notified to P if an appeal lies under paragraph 121 in respect of the decision.

(2) The offer of the review must be made by notice given to P at the same time as the decision is notified to P.

(3) This paragraph does not apply to the notification of the conclusions of a review.][1]

Amendment—[1] Paras 121A–121G inserted by the Transfer of Tribunal Functions and Revenue and Customs Appeals Order, SI 2009/56 art 3, Sch 1 para 289 with effect from 1 April 2009.

[Right to require review

121B (1) Any person (other than P) who has the right of appeal under paragraph 121 against a decision may require HMRC to review that decision if that person has not appealed to the appeal tribunal under paragraph 121G.

(2) A notification that such a person requires a review must be made within 30 days of that person becoming aware of the decision.][1]

Amendment—[1] Paras 121A–121G inserted by the Transfer of Tribunal Functions and Revenue and Customs Appeals Order, SI 2009/56 art 3, Sch 1 para 289 with effect from 1 April 2009.

[Review by HMRC

121C (1) HMRC must review a decision if—

(*a*) they have offered a review of the decision under paragraph 121A, and

(*b*) P notifies HMRC accepting the offer within 30 days from the date of the document containing the notification of the offer.

(2) But P may not notify acceptance of the offer if P has already appealed to the appeal tribunal under paragraph 121G.

(3) HMRC must review a decision if a person other than P notifies them under paragraph 121B.

(4) HMRC shall not review a decision if P, or another person, has appealed to the appeal tribunal under paragraph 121G in respect of the decision.][1]

Amendment—[1] Paras 121A–121G inserted by the Transfer of Tribunal Functions and Revenue and Customs Appeals Order, SI 2009/56 art 3, Sch 1 para 289 with effect from 1 April 2009.

[Extensions of time

121D (1) If under paragraph 121A, HMRC have offered P a review of a decision, HMRC may within the relevant period notify P that the relevant period is extended.

(2) If under paragraph 121B another person may require HMRC to review a matter, HMRC may within the relevant period notify the other person that the relevant period is extended.

(3) If notice is given the relevant period is extended to the end of 30 days from—

(*a*) the date of the notice, or

(*b*) any other date set out in the notice or a further notice.

(4) In this paragraph "relevant period" means—

(*a*) the period of 30 days referred to in—

(i) paragraph 121C(1)(*b*) (in a case falling within sub-paragraph (1)), or

(ii) paragraph 121B(2) (in a case falling within sub-paragraph (2)), or

(*b*) if notice has been given under sub-paragraph (1) or (2), that period as extended (or as most recently extended) in accordance with sub-paragraph (3).][1]

Amendment—[1] Paras 121A–121G inserted by the Transfer of Tribunal Functions and Revenue and Customs Appeals Order, SI 2009/56 art 3, Sch 1 para 289 with effect from 1 April 2009.

[Review out of time

121E (1) This paragraph applies if—

(*a*) HMRC have offered a review of a decision under paragraph 121A and P does not accept the offer within the time allowed under paragraph 121C(1)(*b*) or 121D(3); or

(*b*) a person who requires a review under paragraph 121B does not notify HMRC within the time allowed under that paragraph or paragraph 121D(3).

(2) HMRC must review the decision under paragraph 121C if—

(*a*) after the time allowed, P, or the other person, notifies HMRC in writing requesting a review out of time,

(*b*) HMRC are satisfied that P, or the other person, had a reasonable excuse for not accepting the offer or requiring review within the time allowed, and

(*c*) HMRC are satisfied that P, or the other person, made the request without unreasonable delay after the excuse had ceased to apply.

(3) HMRC shall not review a decision if P, or another person, has appealed to the appeal tribunal under paragraph 121G in respect of the decision.][1]

Amendment—[1] Paras 121A–121G inserted by the Transfer of Tribunal Functions and Revenue and Customs Appeals Order, SI 2009/56 art 3, Sch 1 para 289 with effect from 1 April 2009.

[Nature of review etc

121F (1) This paragraph applies if HMRC are required to undertake a review under paragraph 121C or 121E.

(2) The nature and extent of the review are to be such as appear appropriate to HMRC in the circumstances.

(3) For the purpose of sub-paragraph (2), HMRC must, in particular, have regard to steps taken before the beginning of the review—

(*a*) by HMRC in reaching the decision, and

(*b*) by any person in seeking to resolve disagreement about the decision.

(4) The review must take account of any representations made by P, or the other person, at a stage which gives HMRC a reasonable opportunity to consider them.

(5) The review may conclude that the decision is to be—

(*a*) upheld,

(*b*) varied, or

(*c*) cancelled.

(6) HMRC must give P, or the other person, notice of the conclusions of the review and their reasoning within—

(*a*) a period of 45 days beginning with the relevant date, or

(*b*) such other period as HMRC and P, or the other person, may agree.

(7) In sub-paragraph (6) "relevant date" means—

(*a*) the date HMRC received P's notification accepting the offer of a review (in a case falling within paragraph 121A), or

(*b*) the date HMRC received notification from another person requiring review (in a case falling within paragraph 121B), or (*c*) the date on which HMRC decided to undertake the review (in a case falling within paragraph 121E).

(8) Where HMRC are required to undertake a review but do not give notice of the conclusions within the time period specified in sub-paragraph (6), the review is to be treated as having concluded that the decision is upheld.

(9) If sub-paragraph (8) applies, HMRC must notify the appellant of the conclusion which the review is treated as having reached.][1]

Amendment—[1] Paras 121A–121G inserted by the Transfer of Tribunal Functions and Revenue and Customs Appeals Order, SI 2009/56 art 3, Sch 1 para 289 with effect from 1 April 2009.

[Bringing of appeals

121G—(1) An appeal under paragraph 121 is to be made to the appeal tribunal before—

(*a*) the end of the period of 30 days beginning with—

(i) in a case where P is the appellant, the date of the document notifying the decision to which the appeal relates, or

(ii) in a case where a person other than P is the appellant, the date that person becomes aware of the decision, or

(*b*) if later, the end of the relevant period (within the meaning of paragraph 121D).

(2) But that is subject to sub-paragraphs (3) to (5).

(3) In a case where HMRC are required to undertake a review under paragraph 121C—

(*a*) an appeal may not be made until the conclusion date, and

(*b*) any appeal is to be made within the period of 30 days beginning with the conclusion date.

(4) In a case where HMRC are requested to undertake a review by virtue of paragraph 121E—

(*a*) an appeal may not be made—

(i) unless HMRC have decided whether or not to undertake a review, and

(ii) if HMRC decide to undertake a review, until the conclusion date; and

(*b*) any appeal is to be made within the period of 30 days beginning with—

(i) the conclusion date (if HMRC decide to undertake a review), or

(ii) the date on which HMRC decide not to undertake a review.

(5) In a case where paragraph 121F(8) applies, an appeal may be made at any time from the end of the period specified in paragraph 121F(6) to the date 30 days after the conclusion date.

(6) An appeal may be made after the end of the period specified in sub-paragraph (1), (3)(*b*), (4)(*b*) or (5) if the appeal tribunal gives permission to do so.

(7) In this paragraph "conclusion date" means the date of the document notifying the conclusions of the review.][1]

Amendment—[1] Paras 121A–121G inserted by the Transfer of Tribunal Functions and Revenue and Customs Appeals Order, SI 2009/56 art 3, Sch 1 para 289 with effect from 1 April 2009.

[Appeals: further provisions][1]

122—(1) . . .[1]

[(2) Subject to sub-paragraphs (2A) and (2B), where an appeal relates to a decision (whether or not contained in an assessment) that an amount of levy is due from any person, it shall not be entertained unless the amount which HMRC have determined to be due has been paid or deposited with them.][1]

[(2A) In a case where the amount determined to be payable as levy has not been paid or deposited an appeal shall be entertained if—

(*a*) HMRC are satisfied (on the application of the appellant), or

(*b*) the appeal tribunal decides (HMRC not being so satisfied and on the application of the appellant),

that the requirement to pay or deposit the amount determined would cause the appellant to suffer hardship.

(2B) Notwithstanding the provisions of sections 11 and 13 of the Tribunals, Courts and Enforcement Act 2007, the decision of the appeal tribunal as to the issue of hardship is final.][1]

(3) On an appeal under this paragraph relating to a penalty under paragraph 98 (evasion), the burden of proof as to the matters specified in paragraphs (*a*) and (*b*) of sub-paragraph (1) of that paragraph shall lie upon the Commissioners.

Amendments—[1] Heading substituted for former heading "Appeals against reviewed decisions"; sub-para (1) repealed; sub-para (2) substituted; sub-paras (2A), (2B) inserted by the Transfer of Tribunal Functions and Revenue and Customs Appeals Order, SI 2009/56 art 3, Sch 1 para 290 with effect from 1 April 2009, subject to transitional and savings provisions in Sch 3 paras 2, 3. Sub-paras (1), (2) previously read as follows—

"(1) Subject to the following provisions of this paragraph, an appeal shall lie to an appeal tribunal with respect to any of the following decisions—

(*a*) any decision by the Commissioners on a review under paragraph 121 (including a deemed confirmation under paragraph 121(8));

(*b*) any decision by the Commissioners on any such review of a decision referred to in paragraph 121(1) as the Commissioners have agreed to undertake in consequence of a request made after the end of the period mentioned in paragraph 121(3).

(2) Where an appeal under this paragraph relates to a decision (whether or not contained in an assessment) that an amount of levy is due from any person, that appeal shall not be entertained unless—

(*a*) the amount which the Commissioners have determined to be due has been paid or deposited with them; or

(*b*) on being satisfied that the appellant would otherwise suffer hardship—

(i) the Commissioners agree, or

(ii) the appeal tribunal decide,

that it should be entertained notwithstanding that that amount has not been so paid or deposited."

Determinations on appeal

123—(1) Where, on an appeal under paragraph [121][1]—

(*a*) it is found that an assessment of the appellant . . . [1] is an assessment for an amount that is less than it ought to have been, and

(*b*) the appeal tribunal give a direction specifying the correct amount,

the assessment shall have effect as an assessment of the amount specified in the direction and (without prejudice to any power under this Schedule to reduce the amount of interest payable on the amount of an assessment) as if it were an assessment notified to the appellant in that amount at the same time as the original assessment.

(2) On an appeal under paragraph [121][1], the powers of the appeal tribunal in relation to any decision of the Commissioners shall include a power, where the tribunal allow an appeal on the ground that the Commissioners could not reasonably have arrived at the decision, either—

(*a*) to direct that the decision, so far as it remains in force, is to cease to have effect from such time as the tribunal may direct; or

(*b*) to require the Commissioners to conduct, in accordance with the directions of the tribunal, [a review or][1]a further review of the original decision [as appropriate][1].

(3) Where, on an appeal under paragraph [121][1], the appeal tribunal find that a liability to a penalty or to an amount of interest arises, the tribunal shall not give any direction for the modification of the amount payable in respect of that liability except—

(*a*) in exercise of a power conferred on the tribunal by paragraph 104(1) (penalties) or paragraph 70(6) or (9), 86(3) or (6) or 109(5) or (8) (penalty interest); or

(*b*) for the purpose of making the amount payable conform to the amount of the liability imposed by this Schedule.

(4) Where, on an appeal under paragraph [121][1], it is found that the whole or part of any amount paid or deposited in pursuance of paragraph 122(2) is not due, so much of that amount as is found not to be due shall be repaid with interest [at the rate applicable under section 197 of the Finance Act 1996][1].

(5) Where, on an appeal under paragraph [121][1], it is found that the whole or part of any amount due to the appellant by way of any repayment in respect of a tax credit has not been paid, so much of that amount as is found not to have been paid shall be paid with interest [at the rate applicable under section 197 of the Finance Act 1996][1].

(6) Where—

(*a*) an appeal under paragraph [121][1] has been entertained notwithstanding that an amount determined by the Commissioners to be payable as levy has not been paid or deposited, and

(*b*) it is found on the appeal that that amount is due,

[it shall be paid with interest at the rate applicable under section 197 of the Finance Act 1996][1]

[(6A)Interest under sub-paragraph (6) shall be paid without any deduction of income tax.][1]

[(7) Sections 85 and 85B of the Value Added Tax Act 1994 (settling of appeals by agreement and payment of tax where there is a further appeal) shall have effect as if—

(*a*) the references to section 83 of that Act included references to paragraph 121 above, and

(*b*) the references to value added tax included references to climate change levy.][1]

Amendments—[1] The following amendments made by the Transfer of Tribunal Functions and Revenue and Customs Appeals Order, SI 2009/56 art 3, Sch 1 para 291 with effect from 1 April 2009, subject to transitional and savings provisions in Sch 3 paras 2, 3, 9—

- in sub-paras (1)–(5), (6)(*a*), figure substituted for figure "122";
- in sub-para (1)(a) words "made, confirmed or treated as confirmed by the Commissioners on a review under paragraph 121 ("the original assessment")" repealed;
- in sub-para (2)(*b*) words inserted in both places;
- in sub-paras (4), (5), words at the end substituted for the words "at such rate as the appeal tribunal may determine";
- in sub-para (6), words at the end substituted for the words "the appeal tribunal may, if they think fit, direct that that amount shall be paid with interest at such rate as may be specified in the direction.";
- sub-para (6A) inserted;

– sub-para (7) substituted. Text previously read as follows—

"(7) Sections 85 and 87 of the Value Added Tax Act 1994 (settling of appeals by agreement and enforcement of certain decisions of tribunal) shall have effect as if—

(*a*) the references to section 83 of that Act included references to paragraph [121]; and

(*b*) the references to value added tax included references to levy."

PART XII
INFORMATION AND EVIDENCE

Provision of information

124—*(1) Every person involved (in whatever capacity) in making or receiving supplies of taxable commodities, or in any connected activities, shall provide the Commissioners with such information relating to the matters in which he is or has been involved as the Commissioners may reasonably require.*

(2) Information required under sub-paragraph (1) shall be provided to the Commissioners within such period after being required, and in such form, as the Commissioners may reasonably require.

(3) Subject to sub-paragraphs (4) and (5) and to paragraph 107(5) (which relates to supplementary assessments of daily penalties), if a person fails to provide information which he is required to provide under this paragraph, he shall be liable—

(*a*) to a penalty of £250; and

(*b*) to a further penalty of £20 for every day after the last relevant date and before the day after that on which the required information is provided.

(4) Liability to a penalty specified in sub-paragraph (3) shall not arise if the person required to provide the information satisfies the Commissioners or, on appeal, an appeal tribunal—

(*a*) in the case of the penalty under paragraph (*a*) of that sub-paragraph that there is a reasonable excuse—

(*i*) for the initial failure to provide the required information on or before the last relevant date; and

(*ii*) for every subsequent failure to provide it;

and

(*b*) in the case of any penalty under paragraph (*b*) of that sub-paragraph for any day, that there is a reasonable excuse for the failure to provide the information on or before that day.

(5) Where, by reason of any failure by any person to provide information required under this paragraph—

(*a*) that person is convicted of an offence (whether under this Act or otherwise), or

(*b*) that person is assessed to a penalty under paragraph 98 (penalty for evasion) [or to a penalty for a deliberate inaccuracy under Schedule 24 to the Finance Act 2007 (penalties for errors)][1],

that person shall not by reason of that failure be liable also to a penalty under this paragraph.

(6) In this paragraph "the last relevant date" means the last day of the period within which the person in question was required to provide the information.[2]

Amendments—[1] Words in sub-para (5)(*b*) inserted by the Finance Act 2008, Schedule 40 (Appointed Day, Transitional Provisions and Consequential Amendments) Order, SI 2009/571 art 8, Sch 1 para 20(1), (4) with effect from 1 April 2009.

[2] This para repealed by the Finance Act 2009, Section 96 and Schedule 48 (Appointed Day, Savings and Consequential Amendments) Order, SI 2009/3054 art 3, Schedule para 8 with effect from 1 April 2010. Note that sub-paras (3)–(6) continue to have effect on and after 1 April 2010 where HMRC requested information or documents before that date (SI 2009/3054 art 6(*c*)).

Records

125—(1) The Commissioners may by regulations impose obligations to keep records on [persons who—

(*a*) are registered,

(*b*) are required to be registered, or

(*c*) are exempted from the requirement to be registered by regulations under paragraph 53(4).][1]

(2) Regulations under this paragraph may be framed by reference to such records as may be stipulated in any notice published by the Commissioners in pursuance of the regulations and not withdrawn by a further notice.

(3) Regulations under this paragraph may—

(*a*) require any records kept in pursuance of the regulations to be preserved for such period, not exceeding six years, as may be specified in the regulations;

(*b*) authorise the Commissioners to direct that any such records need only be preserved for a shorter period than that specified in the regulations;

(*c*) authorise a direction to be made so as to apply generally or in such cases as the Commissioners may stipulate.

[(4) A duty under regulations under this paragraph to preserve records may be discharged—

(*a*) by preserving them in any form and by any means, or

(*b*) by preserving the information contained in them in any form and by any means, subject to any conditions or exceptions specified in writing by the Commissioners.][3]

(5) . . . [3]

(6) Subject to sub-paragraphs (7) and (8), a person who fails to preserve any record in compliance with—

(*a*) any regulations under this paragraph, or

(*b*) any notice, direction or requirement given or imposed under such regulations,

shall be liable to a penalty of £250.

(7) A failure such as is mentioned in sub-paragraph (6) shall not give rise to any penalty under that sub-paragraph if the person required to preserve the record satisfies the Commissioners or, on appeal, an appeal tribunal that there is a reasonable excuse for the failure.

(8) Where, by reason of any such failure by any person as is mentioned in sub-paragraph (6)—

(*a*) that person is convicted of an offence (whether under this Act or otherwise), or

(*b*) that person is assessed to a penalty under paragraph 98 (penalty for evasion) [or to a penalty for a deliberate inaccuracy under Schedule 24 to the Finance Act 2007 (penalties for errors)][2],

that person shall not by reason of that failure be liable also to a penalty under this paragraph.

(9) The Commissioners may if they think fit at any time modify or withdraw any . . . [3] requirement . . . [3] imposed for the purposes of this paragraph.

Amendments—[1] In sub-para (1), words substituted for the words "persons who are, or are required to be, registered" by FA 2003 s 192(1), (9) with effect from 10 July 2003.

[2] Words in sub-para (8)(*b*) inserted by the Finance Act 2008, Schedule 40 (Appointed Day, Transitional Provisions and Consequential Amendments) Order, SI 2009/571 art 8, Sch 1 para 20(1), (5) with effect from 1 April 2009.

[3] In sub-para (9), words "approval or" and "given or" repealed, and sub-para (4) substituted for previous sub-paras (4) and (5), by FA 2009 s 98, Sch 50 paras 18, 19, with effect from 1 April 2010 (by virtue of SI 2010/815 art 2). Sub-paras (4), (5) previously read as follows—

"(4) Any duty under regulations under this paragraph to preserve records may be discharged by the preservation of the information contained in them by such means as the Commissioners may approve.

(5) The Commissioners may, as a condition of approving under sub-paragraph (4) any means of preserving information contained in any records, impose such reasonable requirements as appear to them necessary for securing that the information will be as readily available to them as if the records themselves had been preserved.".

Evidence of records that are required to be preserved

126—*(1) Subject to the following provisions of this paragraph, where any obligation to preserve records is discharged in accordance with paragraph 125(4), a copy of any document forming part of the records shall be admissible in evidence in any proceedings, whether civil or criminal, to the same extent as the records themselves.*

(2) A statement contained in a document produced by a computer shall not by virtue of this paragraph be admissible in evidence—

(*a*) . . . [1]

(*b*) in civil proceedings in Scotland, except in accordance with sections 5 and 6 of the Civil Evidence (Scotland) Act 1988;

(*c*) in criminal proceedings in Scotland, except in accordance with Schedule 8 to the Criminal Procedure (Scotland) Act 1995;

(*d*) . . . [2, 3]

Amendments[1] Sub-para (2)(*a*) repealed by the Criminal Justice Act 2003 s 332, Sch 37 Pt 6 with effect from 4 April 2005 (by virtue of SI 2005/950).

[2] Sub-para (2)(*d*) repealed by the Criminal Justice (Evidence) (Northern Ireland) Order, SI 2004/1501, s 46(2), Sch 2, with effect from 3 April 2006 (by virtue of 3 April 2006: see the Criminal Justice (Evidence) (Northern Ireland) Order 2004 (Commencement No 3) Order, SR 2006/63, art 2).

[3] Paragraph 126 repealed by FA 2009 s 98, Sch 50 paras 18, 20, with effect from 1 April 2010 (by virtue of SI 2010/815 art 2).

Production of documents

127—*(1) Every person involved (in whatever capacity) in making or receiving supplies of taxable commodities, or in any connected activities, shall upon demand made by an authorised person produce or cause to be produced for inspection by that person any documents relating to the matters in which he is or has been involved.*

(2) Where, by virtue of sub-paragraph (1), an authorised person has power to require the production of any documents from any person—

(*a*) he shall have the like power to require production of the documents concerned from any other person who appears to the authorised person to be in possession of them; and (*b*) the production of any document by that other person in pursuance of a requirement under this sub-paragraph shall be without prejudice to any lien claimed by that other person on that document.

(3) The documents mentioned in sub-paragraphs (1) and (2) shall be produced at such time and place as the authorised person may reasonably require.

(4) Subject to sub-paragraphs (5) and (6) and to paragraph 107(5) (which relates to supplementary assessments of daily penalties), if a person fails to produce any document which he is required to produce under this paragraph, he shall be liable—

(*a*) to a penalty of £250; and

(*b*) to a further penalty of £20 for every day after the last relevant date and before the day after that on which the document is produced.

(5) Liability to a penalty specified in sub-paragraph (4) shall not arise if the person required to produce the document in question satisfies the Commissioners or, on appeal, an appeal tribunal—

(*a*) in the case of the penalty under paragraph (*a*) of that sub-paragraph, that there is a reasonable excuse—

(*i*) for the initial failure to produce the document at the required time; and

(*ii*) for every subsequent failure to produce it;

and

(*b*) in the case of any penalty under paragraph (*b*) of that sub-paragraph for any day, that there is a reasonable excuse for the failure to produce the document on or before that day.

(6) Where, by reason of any failure by any person to provide information required under this paragraph—

(*a*) that person is convicted of an offence (whether under this Act or otherwise), or

(*b*) that person is assessed to a penalty under paragraph 98 (penalty for evasion) [or to a penalty for a deliberate inaccuracy under Schedule 24 to the Finance Act 2007 (penalties for errors)][1],

that person shall not by reason of that failure be liable also to a penalty under this paragraph.

(7) In this paragraph "the last relevant date" means the last day of the period within which the person in question was required to produce the document.[2]

Amendments—[1] Words in sub-para (6)(*b*) inserted by the Finance Act 2008, Schedule 40 (Appointed Day, Transitional Provisions and Consequential Amendments) Order, SI 2009/571 art 8, Sch 1 para 20(1), (6) with effect from 1 April 2009.

[2] This para repealed by the Finance Act 2009, Section 96 and Schedule 48 (Appointed Day, Savings and Consequential Amendments) Order, SI 2009/3054 art 3, Schedule para 8 with effect from 1 April 2010. Note that sub-paras (4)–(7) continue to have effect on and after 1 April 2010 where HMRC requested information or documents before that date (SI 2009/3054 art 6(*c*)).

Powers in relation to documents produced

128—*(1) An authorised person may take copies of, or make extracts from, any document produced under paragraph 127.*

(2) If it appears to him to be necessary to do so, an authorised person may, at a reasonable time and for a reasonable period, remove any document produced under paragraph 127.

(3) An authorised person who removes any document under sub-paragraph (2) shall, if requested to do so, provide a receipt for the document so removed.

(4) Where a lien is claimed on a document produced under paragraph 127(2), the removal of the document under sub-paragraph (2) shall not be regarded as breaking the lien.

(5) Where a document removed by an authorised person under sub-paragraph (2) is reasonably required for any purpose he shall, as soon as practicable, provide a copy of the document, free of charge, to the person by whom it was produced or caused to be produced.

(6) Where any documents removed under the powers conferred by this paragraph are lost or damaged, the Commissioners shall be liable to compensate their owner for any expenses reasonably incurred by him in replacing or repairing the documents.[1]

Amendments—[1] This para repealed by the Finance Act 2009, Section 96 and Schedule 48 (Appointed Day, Savings and Consequential Amendments) Order, SI 2009/3054 art 3, Schedule para 8 with effect from 1 April 2010.

Entry and inspection

129 For the purpose of exercising any powers under this Schedule, an authorised person may at any reasonable time enter and inspect premises used in connection with the carrying on of a business.[1]

Amendments—[1] This para repealed by the Finance Act 2009, Section 96 and Schedule 48 (Appointed Day, Savings and Consequential Amendments) Order, SI 2009/3054 art 3, Schedule para 8 with effect from 1 April 2010.

Entry and search

130—*(1) Where—*

(a) a justice of the peace is satisfied on information on oath that there is reasonable ground for suspecting that a fraud offence which appears to be of a serious nature is being, has been or is about to be committed on any premises or that evidence of the commission of such an offence is to be found there, or

(b) in Scotland a justice (within the meaning of section 307 of the Criminal Procedure (Scotland) Act 1995) is satisfied by evidence on oath as mentioned in paragraph (a),

he may issue a warrant in writing authorising any authorised person to enter those premises, if necessary by force, at any time within one month from the time of the issue of the warrant and to search them.

(2) A person who enters the premises under the authority of the warrant may—

(a) take with him such other persons as appear to him to be necessary;

(b) seize and remove any such documents or other things at all found on the premises as he has reasonable cause to believe may be required as evidence for the purposes of proceedings in respect of a fraud offence which appears to him to be of a serious nature;

(c) search, or cause to be searched, any person found on the premises whom he has reasonable cause to believe to be in possession of any documents or other things which may be so required.

(3) Sub-paragraph (2) shall not authorise any person to be searched by a member of the opposite sex.

(4) The powers conferred by a warrant under this paragraph shall not be exercisable—

(a) by more than such number of authorised persons as may be specified in the warrant;

(b) outside such periods of the day as may be so specified; or

(c) if the warrant so provides, otherwise than in the presence of a constable in uniform.

(5) An authorised person seeking to exercise the powers conferred by a warrant under this paragraph or, if there is more than one such authorised person, such one of them as is in charge of the search shall provide a copy of the warrant endorsed with his name as follows—

(a) if the occupier of the premises concerned is present at the time the search is to begin, the copy shall be supplied to the occupier;

(b) if at that time the occupier is not present but a person who appears to the authorised person to be in charge of the premises is present, the copy shall be supplied to that person;

(c) if neither paragraph (a) nor paragraph (b) applies, the copy shall be left in a prominent place on the premises.

(6) In this paragraph "a fraud offence" means an offence under any of paragraphs 92 to 94.[1]

Cross references—Criminal Justice and Police Act 2001 s 50, Sch 1 Pt 1 (s 50 of that Act which provides additional powers of seizure from premises applies to the power of seizure conferred under sub-para (2) above; for the relevant provisions of the Criminal Justice and Police Act 2001, see the *VAT* section of this publication).

Amendments—[1] This para repealed by FA 2007 ss 84, 114, Sch 22 paras 3, 11(*b*), Sch 27 Pt 5(1) with effect from 1 December 2007 (by virtue of SI 2007/3166 art 3(*a*)).

Order for access to recorded information etc

131—(1) Where, on an application by an authorised person, a justice of the peace or, in Scotland, a justice (within the meaning of section 307 of the Criminal Procedure (Scotland) Act 1995) is satisfied that there are reasonable grounds for believing—

(*a*) that an offence in connection with levy is being, has been or is about to be committed, and

(*b*) that any recorded information (including any document of any nature at all) which may be required as evidence for the purpose of any proceedings in respect of such an offence is in the possession of any person,

he may make an order under this paragraph.

(2) An order under this paragraph is an order that the person who appears to the justice to be in possession of the recorded information to which the application relates shall—

(*a*) give an authorised person access to it, and

(*b*) permit an authorised person to remove and take away any of it which he reasonably considers necessary,

not later than the end of the period of seven days beginning with the date of the order or the end of such longer period as the order may specify.

(3) The reference in sub-paragraph (2)(*a*) to giving an authorised person access to the recorded information to which the application relates includes a reference to permitting the authorised person to take copies of it or to make extracts from it.

(4) Where the recorded information consists of information [stored in any electronic form][1], an order under this paragraph shall have effect as an order to produce the information—

(*a*) in a form in which it is visible and legible [or from which it can readily be produced in a visible and legible form][1]; and

(*b*) if the authorised person wishes to remove it, in a form in which it can be removed.

(5) This paragraph is without prejudice to the preceding paragraphs of this Part of this Schedule.

Amendments—[1] In sub-para (4), words substituted, and words inserted, by the Criminal Justice and Police Act 2001 ss 70, 138, Sch 2 Pt 2 para 13 with effect from 1 April 2003 (by virtue of SI 2003/708); for the relevant provisions of that Act, see the *VAT* section of this publication.

Removal of documents etc

132—(1) An authorised person who removes anything in the exercise of a power conferred by or under paragraph 130 or 131 shall, if so requested by a person showing himself—

(*a*) to be the occupier of premises from which it was removed, or

(*b*) to have had custody or control of it immediately before the removal,

provide that person with a record of what he removed.

(2) The authorised person shall provide the record within a reasonable time from the making of the request for it.

(3) Subject to sub-paragraph (7), if a request for permission to be allowed access to anything which—

(*a*) has been removed by an authorised person, and

(*b*) is retained by the Commissioners for the purposes of investigating an offence,

is made to the officer in overall charge of the investigation by a person who had custody or control of the thing immediately before it was so removed, or by someone acting on behalf of such a person, the officer shall allow the person who made the request access to it under the supervision of an authorised person.

(4) Subject to sub-paragraph (7), if a request for a photograph or copy of any such thing is made to the officer in overall charge of the investigation by a person who had custody or control of the thing immediately before it was so removed, or by someone acting on behalf of such a person, the officer shall—

(*a*) allow the person who made the request access to it under the supervision of an authorised person for the purpose of photographing it or copying it; or

(*b*) photograph or copy it, or cause it to be photographed or copied.

(5) Subject to sub-paragraph (7), where anything is photographed or copied under sub-paragraph (4)(*b*), the officer shall supply the photograph or copy, or cause it to be supplied, to the person who made the request.

(6) The photograph or copy shall be supplied within a reasonable time from the making of the request.

(7) There is no duty under this paragraph to allow access to anything, or to supply a photograph or copy of anything, if the officer in overall charge of the investigation for the purposes of which it was removed has reasonable grounds for believing that to do so would prejudice—

(*a*) that investigation;

(*b*) the investigation of an offence other than the offence for the purposes of the investigation of which the thing was removed; or

(*c*) any criminal proceedings which may be brought as a result of the investigation of which he is in charge or any such investigation as is mentioned in paragraph (*b*).

(8) Any reference in this paragraph to the officer in overall charge of the investigation is a reference to the person whose name and address are endorsed on the warrant concerned as being the officer so in charge.

Enforcement of paragraph 132

133—(1) Where, on an application made as mentioned in sub-paragraph (2), the appropriate judicial authority is satisfied that a person has failed to comply with a requirement imposed by paragraph 132, the authority may order that person to comply with the requirement within such time and in such manner as may be specified in the order.

(2) An application under sub-paragraph (1) shall not be made except—

(*a*) in the case of a failure to comply with any of the requirements imposed by paragraph 132(1) and (2)—

(i) by the occupier of the premises from which the thing in question was removed, or

(ii) by the person who had custody or control of it immediately before it was so removed;

(*b*) in any other case, by the person who had such custody or control.

(3) In this paragraph "the appropriate judicial authority" means—

(*a*) in England and Wales, a magistrates' court;

(*b*) in Scotland, the sheriff;

(*c*) in Northern Ireland, a court of summary jurisdiction, as defined in Article 2(2)(*a*) of the Magistrates' Courts (Northern Ireland) Order 1981.

(4) In England and Wales and Northern Ireland, an application for an order under this paragraph shall be made by way of complaint; and sections 21 and 42(2) of the Interpretation Act (Northern Ireland) 1954 shall apply as if any reference in those provisions to any enactment included a reference to this paragraph.

Power to take samples and examine meters

134—(1) An authorised person, if it appears to him necessary for the protection of the revenue against mistake or fraud, may at any time take, from material which he has reasonable cause to believe is—

(*a*) a taxable commodity which is intended to be, is being or has been the subject of a taxable supply, or

(*b*) a product of the burning of a taxable commodity (other than electricity) which is being or has been the subject of a taxable supply,

such samples as he may require with a view to determining how the material ought to be treated, or to have been treated, for the purposes of the levy.

(2) An authorised person, if it appears to him necessary for the protection of the revenue against mistake or fraud, may at any time examine any meter which he has reasonable cause to believe is intended to be, is being or has been used for ascertaining the quantity of any taxable commodity supplied by a taxable supply.

(3) Any sample taken under sub-paragraph (1) shall be disposed of in such manner as the Commissioners may direct.

Evidence by certificate

135—(1) In any proceedings a certificate of the Commissioners—

(*a*) that a person was or was not at any time registered for the purposes of the levy [or][1],

(*b*) that any return required by regulations made under paragraph 41 has not been made or had not been made at any time,

(*c*) , (*d*) . . . [1]

shall be evidence or, in Scotland, sufficient evidence of that fact.

(2) A photograph of any document provided to the Commissioners for the purposes of this Schedule and certified by them to be such a photograph shall be admissible in any proceedings, whether civil or criminal, to the same extent as the document itself.

(3) In any proceedings any document purporting to be a certificate under sub-paragraph (1) or (2) shall be taken to be such a certificate unless the contrary is shown.

Amendments—[1] Words inserted and repealed by FA 2008 s 138, Sch 44 para 8 with effect from 21 July 2008. Sub-para (1)(*c*), (*d*) previously read as follows—

"(*c*) that any levy shown as due in a return or other notification made in pursuance of regulations made under paragraph 41 has not been paid, or

(*d*) that any amount shown as due in any assessment made under this Schedule has not been paid,".

Inducements to provide information

136—(1) This paragraph applies—

(*a*) to any criminal proceedings against a person in respect of an offence in connection with or in relation to levy; and

(*b*) to any proceedings against a person for the recovery of any sum due from him in connection with or in relation to levy.

(2) Statements made or documents produced or provided by or on behalf of a person shall not be inadmissible in any proceedings to which this paragraph applies by reason only that—

(*a*) a matter falling within sub-paragraph (3) or (4) has been drawn to that person's attention; and

(*b*) he was or may have been induced, as a result, to make the statements or to produce or provide the documents.

(3) The matters falling within this sub-paragraph are—

(*a*) that, in relation to levy, the Commissioners may assess an amount due by way of a civil penalty instead of instituting criminal proceedings;

(*b*) that it is the practice of the Commissioners (without giving any undertaking as to whether they will make such an assessment in any case) to be influenced by whether a person—

(i) has made a full confession of any dishonest conduct to which he has been a party; and

(ii) has otherwise co-operated to the full with any investigation.

(4) The matter falling within this sub-paragraph is the fact that the Commissioners or, on appeal, an appeal tribunal have power under any provision of this Schedule to reduce a penalty.

Disclosure of information

137—(1) Notwithstanding any obligation not to disclose information that would otherwise apply, but subject to sub-paragraph (2), the Commissioners may disclose any information obtained or held by them in or in connection with the carrying out of their functions in relation to the levy to any of the following—

(*a*) any Minister of the Crown;
(*b*) the Scottish Ministers;
(*c*) any Minister, within the meaning of the Northern Ireland Act 1998, or any Northern Ireland department;
(*d*) the National Assembly for Wales;
(*e*) the Environment Agency;
(*f*) the Scottish Environment Protection Agency;
(*g*) the Gas and Electricity Markets Authority;
(*h*) the Director General of Electricity Supply for Northern Ireland;
(*i*) the Director General of Gas for Northern Ireland;
(*j*) an authorised officer of any person mentioned in paragraphs (*a*) to (*i*).

(2) Information shall not be disclosed under sub-paragraph (1) except for the purpose of assisting a person falling within paragraphs (*a*) to (*j*) of that sub-paragraph in the performance of his duties.

(3) Notwithstanding any such obligation as is mentioned in sub-paragraph (1), any person mentioned in sub-paragraph (1)(*a*) to (*j*) may disclose information—

(*a*) to the Commissioners, or
(*b*) to an authorised officer of the Commissioners,

for the purpose of assisting the Commissioners in the performance of duties in relation to the levy.

(4) Information that has been disclosed to a person by virtue of this paragraph shall not be disclosed by him except—

(*a*) to another person to whom (instead of him) disclosure could by virtue of this paragraph have been made; or
(*b*) for the purpose of any proceedings connected with the operation of any provision made by or under any enactment relating to the environment or to levy.

(5) References in the preceding provisions of this paragraph to an authorised officer of any person ("the principal") are to any person who has been designated by the principal as a person to and by whom information may be disclosed by virtue of this paragraph.

(6) Where the principal is a person falling within any of paragraphs (*a*) to (*c*) of sub-paragraph (1), the principal shall notify the Commissioners in writing of the name of any person designated by the principal for the purposes of this paragraph.

(7) No charge may be made for any disclosure made by virtue of this paragraph.

(8) In this paragraph "enactment" includes an enactment contained in an Act of the Scottish Parliament or in any Northern Ireland legislation.

Meaning of "authorised person"

138 In this Part of this Schedule "authorised person" means any person acting under the authority of the Commissioners.

PART XIII
MISCELLANEOUS AND SUPPLEMENTARY

Security for levy

139—(1) Where it appears to the Commissioners necessary to do so for the protection of the revenue they may require any person who is or is required to be registered for the purposes of the levy to give security, or further security, for the payment of any levy which is or may become due from him.

(2) The power of the Commissioners to require any security, or further security, under this paragraph shall be a power to require security, or further security, of such amount and in such manner as they may determine.

(3) A person who is liable to account for the levy on a taxable supply that he makes is guilty of an offence if, at the time the supply is made—

(*a*) he has been required to give security under this paragraph, and
(*b*) he has not complied with that requirement.

(4) A person who is liable to account for the levy on a taxable supply that another person makes to him is guilty of an offence if he makes any arrangements for the making of the supply at a time when—

(*a*) he has been required to give security under this paragraph, and
(*b*) he has not complied with that requirement.

(5) A person guilty of an offence under this paragraph shall be liable, on summary conviction, to a penalty of level 5 on the standard scale.
(6) Sections 145 to 155 of the Customs and Excise Management Act 1979 (proceedings for offences, mitigation of penalties and certain other matters) shall apply in relation to an offence under this paragraph as they apply in relation to offences and penalties under the customs and excise Acts.

Destination of receipts

140

Amendment—Paragraph repealed by the Commissioners for Revenue and Customs Act 2005 ss 50, 52, Sch 4 para 81 and Sch 5 with effect from 18 April 2005 by virtue of the Commissioners for Revenue and Customs Act (Commencement) Order, SI 2005/1126, art 2(2).

Provisional collection of levy

141

Amendment—This paragraph repealed by FA 2001 s 110, Sch 33 Pt 3(3) with effect from 11 May 2001.

[Invoices incorrectly showing levy due

141A—(1) This paragraph applies where—

(*a*) a person issues an invoice showing an amount as levy chargeable on a supply, and

(*b*) no levy is chargeable on the supply, or the amount chargeable is less than the amount shown.

(2) The person shall be liable to a penalty unless he satisfies the Commissioners or, on appeal, a tribunal that there is a reasonable excuse for the inclusion in the invoice of the false information.
(3) The amount of the penalty is £50 or, if more, the following amount—

(*a*) where no levy is chargeable, the amount shown as chargeable;

(*b*) where an amount of levy is chargeable, the difference between that amount and the amount shown as chargeable.

(4) It is irrelevant for the purposes of sub-paragraph (1) whether or not the supply shown on the invoice actually takes place or has taken place.
(5) A reference in this paragraph to an invoice is a reference to any kind of invoice (and not just a climate change levy accounting document).][1]

Amendment—[1] This paragraph inserted by FA 2002 s 128 with effect for invoices issued on or after 24 July 2002.

Adjustment of contracts

142—(1) Sub-paragraph (2) applies in the case of a contract for the supply of a taxable commodity if—

(*a*) the contract is entered into before 1st April 2001 (whether before or after the passing of this Act) or at a time when supplies such as are provided for by the contract are not taxable supplies, but

(*b*) supplies falling to be made under the contract will be, or become or will become, taxable supplies.

(2) The supplier of the commodity may unilaterally vary the contract by adjusting the price chargeable for any supply made under the contract if he does so for the purpose of passing on, to the person liable to pay for the supply, the burden (or any part of the burden) of the levy for which the supplier is liable to account on the supply.
(3) Sub-paragraph (4) applies in the case of a contract for the supply of a taxable commodity if it provides (whether as a result of a variation under sub-paragraph (2) or otherwise) for the passing on, to the person liable to pay for the supply, of the burden (or any part of the burden) of any levy for which the supplier is liable to account on the supply.
(4) The supplier of the commodity may unilaterally vary the contract by adjusting the price chargeable for any supply made under the contract if he does so for the purpose of giving effect (to any extent) to—

(*a*) any change in the rate at which levy is charged on the supply;

(*b*) levy ceasing to be chargeable on the supply.

(5) The powers conferred by this paragraph are in addition to any contractual powers.

Climate change levy accounting documents

143—(1) Provision may be made by regulations requiring registered persons who make taxable supplies—

(*a*) in prescribed cases, or

(*b*) to persons of prescribed descriptions,

to provide the persons supplied with climate change levy accounting documents.

(2) For the purposes of this Schedule a "climate change levy accounting document" for a taxable supply is an invoice—

(*a*) . . . [1]

(*b*) stating the date on which it is issued, and

(*c*) containing the required statements.

(3) For the purposes of sub-paragraph (2)(*c*) "the required statements" means—

(*a*) in the case of a climate change levy accounting document issued under paragraph 27, the statements required by paragraph 27(5);

(*b*) in the case of a climate change levy accounting document whose provision is required by regulations, statements of prescribed particulars of or relating to—

(i) the supply,

(ii) the persons by and to whom the supply is made, and

(iii) the levy chargeable.

(4) Where regulations make provision requiring a climate change levy accounting document to be provided in connection with any description of supply, regulations may make provision for—

(*a*) requiring the accounting document to be provided within a prescribed time after, or at a prescribed time before, the supply is treated as taking place;

(*b*) allowing an accounting document to be provided later than required by the regulations where it is provided in accordance with general or special directions given by the Commissioners.

(5) Regulations may make provision conferring power on the Commissioners to allow the requirements of any regulations as to the statements to be contained in a climate change levy accounting document to be relaxed or dispensed with.

(6) Regulations may make provision for allowing a climate change levy accounting document required to be issued under paragraph 27 to be issued later than the time applicable under paragraph 27(2) where it is issued in accordance with general or special directions given by the Commissioners.

(7) In this paragraph "regulations" means regulations made by the Commissioners.

Amendments—[1] Sub-para (2)(*a*) repealed by FA 2008 s 150 with effect from 21 July 2008. Para (*a*) previously read as follows—

"(*a*) stating that it is a climate change levy accounting document (for which purpose the inclusion of the phrase "climate change levy accounting document" or the phrase "CCL accounting document", whether as shown here or with any of the letters shown here as small letters appearing as capitals, shall be sufficient),".

Service of notices etc

144—(1) Any notice, notification or requirement that is to be or may be served on, given to or imposed on any person for the purposes of any provision made by or under this Schedule may be served, given or imposed by sending it to that person or his tax representative by post in a letter addressed to that person or his representative at the latest or usual residence or place of business of that person or representative.

(2) Any direction required or authorised by or under this Schedule to be given by the Commissioners may be given by sending it by post in a letter addressed to each person affected by it at his latest or usual residence or place of business.

Variation and withdrawal of directions etc

145 Any direction, notice or notification required or authorised by or under this Schedule to be given by the Commissioners may be withdrawn or varied by them by a direction, notice or notification given in the same manner as the one withdrawn or varied.

Regulations and orders

146—(1) Any power under this Schedule to make regulations shall be exercisable by statutory instrument.

(2) A statutory instrument that—

(*a*) contains regulations made under this Schedule, and

(*b*) is not subject to a requirement that a draft of the instrument be laid before Parliament and approved by a resolution of the House of Commons,

shall be subject to annulment in pursuance of a resolution of the House of Commons.

(3) A statutory instrument that contains (whether alone or with other provisions) regulations under paragraph 3(3), 14(3), 15(4)(*a*), 16, 18(2), [18A,][1] 52, 113(1), 148(4), 149 or 151(2) (regulations made by the Treasury) shall not be made unless a draft of the statutory instrument containing the regulations has been laid before Parliament and approved by a resolution of the House of Commons.

(4) Where regulations under this Schedule made by the Commissioners impose a relevant requirement on any person, they may provide that if the person fails to comply with the requirement he shall be liable, subject to sub-paragraph (5), to a penalty of £250.

(5) Where by reason of any conduct—

(*a*) a person is convicted of an offence (whether under this Act or otherwise), or

(*b*) a person is assessed to a penalty under paragraph 98 [or to a penalty for a deliberate inaccuracy under Schedule 24 to the Finance Act 2007 (penalties for errors)][2],

that person shall not by reason of that conduct be liable also to a penalty under any regulations under this Schedule.

(6) In sub-paragraph (4) "relevant requirement" means any requirement other than one the penalty for a contravention of which is specified in paragraph 41(3), 114(3) or 125(6).

(7) A power under this Schedule to make any provision by regulations—

(*a*) may be exercised so as to apply the provision only in such cases as may be described in the regulations;

(*b*) may be exercised so as to make different provision for different cases or descriptions of case; and

(*c*) shall include power by the regulations to make such supplementary, incidental, consequential or transitional provision as the authority making the regulations may think fit.

Amendment—[1] Words in sub-para (3) inserted by FA 2003 s 188(2)(*c*) with effect from 10 July 2003.

[2] Words in sub-para (5)(*b*) inserted by the Finance Act 2008, Schedule 40 (Appointed Day, Transitional Provisions and Consequential Amendments) Order, SI 2009/571 art 8, Sch 1 para 20(1), (7) with effect from 1 April 2009.

PART XIV
INTERPRETATION

General

147 In this Schedule—

"accounting period" means a period which, in pursuance of any regulations under paragraph 41, is an accounting period for the purposes of the levy;

"agreement" includes any arrangement or understanding (whether or not legally enforceable), and cognate expressions shall be construed accordingly;

"appeal tribunal" means a [the First-tier Tribunal or, where determined by or under Tribunal Procedure Rules, the Upper Tribunal;][4];

"auto-generator" has the meaning given by paragraph 152;

"climate change agreement" has the meaning given by paragraph 46;

"climate change levy accounting document" has the meaning given by paragraph 143(2);

"combined heat and power station" has the meaning given by paragraph 148(1);

"the Commissioners" means the Commissioners of Customs and Excise;

"conduct" includes acts and omissions;

"electricity utility" has the meaning given by paragraph 150(2) (but see paragraph 150(4));

"fully exempt combined heat and power station" has the meaning given by paragraph 148(2);

"gas utility" has the meaning given by paragraph 150(3) (but see paragraph 150(4));

["HMRC" means Her Majesty's Revenue and Customs;[4]

"half-rate supply" has the meaning given by paragraph 43(1);[3]

"member", in relation to a group, shall be construed in accordance with regulations under paragraph 116;

"non-resident taxpayer" means a person who—

(*a*) is or is required to be registered for the purposes of the levy, and

(*b*) is not resident in the United Kingdom;

"partly exempt combined heat and power station" has the meaning given by paragraph 148(3);

"prescribed" (except in paragraphs 14(3), 16(3) [, 18A][1] and 148(4)) means prescribed by regulations made by the Commissioners under this Schedule;

"produced"—

(*a*) in relation to electricity, means generated, and

(*b*) in relation to any other commodity, includes extracted;

"reduced-rate supply" has the meaning given by paragraph [44(1)][2] (which, by virtue of paragraph [44(2)][2], has effect subject to [paragraph 44(2A) to (2D) and][5] [paragraphs 45 and 45B][6]);

"registered" means registered in the register maintained under paragraph 53(2);

"representative member", in relation to a group, shall be construed in accordance with regulations under paragraph 116;

"resident in the United Kingdom" has the meaning given by paragraph 156;

"ship" includes hovercraft;

"special utility scheme" has the meaning given by paragraph 29(1);
"subordinate legislation" has the same meaning as in the Interpretation Act 1978;
"supply for charity use" shall be construed in accordance with paragraph 8;
"supply for domestic use" shall be construed in accordance with paragraphs 8 and 9;
"tax credit" means a tax credit for which provision is made by tax credit regulations;
"tax credit regulations" means regulations under paragraph 62;
"tax representative", in relation to any person, means the person who, in accordance with any regulations under paragraph 114, is for the time being that person's tax representative for the purposes of the levy;
"taxable commodity" shall be construed in accordance with paragraph 3;
"taxable supply" shall be construed in accordance with paragraphs 2(2) and 4;
"the United Kingdom" includes the territorial waters adjacent to any part of the United Kingdom;
"utility" has the meaning given by paragraph 150(1).

Amendment—[1] Words in definition of "prescribed" inserted by FA 2003 s 188(2) with effect from 10 July 2003.
[2] In the definition of "reduced-rate supply", figures substituted for "44(3)" and "44(4)" by FA 2007 s 23, Sch 2 paras 1, 10 with effect from 1 November 2007: SI 2007/2902 art 2(1). These amendments only apply in relation to a supply actually made on or after 1 November 2007: SI 2007/2902 art 2(2).
[3] The definition of "half-rate supply" repealed by FA 2006 ss 172(15), 178, Sch 26 Pt 8(1) with effect from 1 November 2007: SI 2007/2901, art 2(1). This amendment does not apply in relation to a half-rate supply made before 1 April 2006.
[4] In definition of "appeal tribunal" words substituted for the words "VAT and duties tribunal"; definition of "HMRC" inserted by the Transfer of Tribunal Functions and Revenue and Customs Appeals Order, SI 2009/56 art 3, Sch 1 para 292 with effect from 1 April 2009.
[5] Words inserted by FA 2009 s 117(1), (3) with effect from 21 July 2009.
[6] Words substituted by FA 2009 s 118, Sch 59 paras 2, 9 with effect where the certification period begins on or after 1 April 2009.

Meaning of "combined heat and power station" etc

148—(1) In this Schedule "combined heat and power station" means a station producing electricity or motive power that is (or may be) operated for purposes including the supply to any premises of—
(*a*) heat produced in association with electricity or motive power, or
(*b*) steam produced from, or air or water heated by, such heat.

(2) In this Schedule "fully exempt combined heat and power station" means a combined heat and power station in respect of which there is in force a certificate (a "full-exemption certificate")—
(*a*) given by the Secretary of State,
(*b*) stating that the station is a fully exempt combined heat and power station for the purposes of the levy, and
(*c*) [complying (so far as applicable) with][1] any provision made by regulations under sub-paragraph (10).

(3) In this Schedule "partly exempt combined heat and power station" means a combined heat and power station in respect of which there is in force a certificate (a "part-exemption certificate")—
(*a*) given by the Secretary of State,
(*b*) stating that the station is a partly exempt combined heat and power station for the purposes of the levy, and
(*c*) [complying (so far as applicable) with][1] any provision made by regulations under sub-paragraph (10).

(4) The Secretary of State shall give a full-exemption certificate in respect of a combined heat and power station where—
(*a*) an application is made for a certificate under this paragraph in respect of the station, and
(*b*) it appears to him that such conditions as may be prescribed are satisfied in relation to the station.

For this purpose "prescribed" means prescribed by regulations made by the Treasury.

(5) The Secretary of State shall give a part-exemption certificate in respect of a combined heat and power station where—
(*a*) an application is made for a certificate under this paragraph in respect of the station, and
(*b*) his decision on the application is to refuse to give a full-exemption certificate.

(6) . . . [1]

(7) In prescribing conditions under sub-paragraph (4), the Treasury must have regard to the object of securing that a combined heat and power station will only be a fully exempt combined heat and power station for the purposes of this Schedule if it is one in which electricity or motive power is produced concurrently with heat in a manner that makes efficient use of the commodities used in their production.

(8) A condition prescribed under sub-paragraph (4) may, in particular, relate to any of the following—

(*a*) a station's outputs;

(*b*) the commodities used in the production of such outputs;

(*c*) the methods of producing such outputs;

(*d*) the efficiency with which such outputs are produced.

(9) For the purposes of sub-paragraph (8), a station's "outputs" are any electricity or motive power produced in the station and any of the following supplied from the station, namely—

(*a*) heat or steam, or

(*b*) air, or water, that has been heated or cooled.

(10) The Secretary of State may by regulations make provision for or about—

(*a*) certificates under this paragraph;

(*b*) applications for such certificates;

(*c*) the information that is to accompany such applications.

(11) The provision that may be made by virtue of sub-paragraph (10)(*a*) includes in particular—

(*a*) provision in respect of the periods for which certificates under this paragraph are to be in force;

(*b*) provision for the (non-retrospective) variation or revocation of such certificates.

Amendments—[1] Words in sub-paras (2)(*c*) and (3)(*c*) substituted, and sub-para (6) repealed, by FA 2003 ss 189(1), (3), 216, Sch 43 Pt 4 with effect for supplies made on or after 22 July 2005 (by virtue of SI 2005/1713).

Determination of efficiency percentages for combined heat and power stations

149—(1) The Treasury may by regulations make provision for determining . . .[1] the efficiency percentage for a combined heat and power station.

(2) Regulations under this paragraph may, in particular, include—

(*a*) provision in respect of methods of calculating efficiency percentages;

(*b*) provision in respect of the measurements and data to be used in calculating such percentages;

(*c*) provision in respect of the procedures for determining such percentages;

(*d*) provision in respect of verifying—

(i) calculations by which such percentages are produced, and

(ii) measurements and data used in such calculations;

(*e*) provision that, so far as framed by reference to any document, is framed by reference to that document as from time to time in force.

(3) In making provision under this paragraph, the Treasury must have regard to the object of securing that the efficiency percentage for a combined heat and power station is (save for any appropriate adjustments) a percentage that reflects a fair assessment of the efficiency with which commodities are transformed in the station into electricity or motive power.

Amendments—[1] Words in sub-para (1) repealed by FA 2003 ss 189(1), (4), 216, Sch 43 Pt 4 with effect for supplies made on or after 22 July 2005 (by virtue of SI 2005/1713).

[Certification of electricity from fully or partly exempt combined heat and power station

149A—(1) The Commissioners may by regulations make provision for the Gas and Electricity Markets Authority, or the Director General of Electricity Supply for Northern Ireland, to certify as respects any quantity of electricity that—

(*a*) the electricity has been produced in a fully exempt combined heat and power station;

(*b*) the electricity has been produced in a partly exempt combined heat and power station and supplied from the station without causing the limit referred to in paragraph 16(2) to be exceeded.

(2) Regulations under this paragraph may provide that for any purposes of this Schedule (or any regulations made under it)—

(*a*) electricity is not to be regarded as having been produced as specified in sub-paragraph (1)(*a*) unless it has been certified under that provision;

(*b*) electricity is not to be regarded as having been produced and supplied as specified in sub-paragraph (1)(*b*) unless it has been certified under that provision.

(3) Regulations under this paragraph may in particular provide that the supply of any electricity does not qualify for the exemption under paragraph 16(2) unless the electricity is certified as specified in sub-paragraph (1)(*b*).

(4) Regulations under this paragraph may also make provision for determining whether electricity is produced and supplied as specified in sub-paragraph (1)(*b*).][1]

Amendment—[1] This paragraph inserted by FA 2002 s 124 with effect from 24 July 2002.

Meaning of "utility"

150—(1) In this Schedule "utility" means an electricity utility or a gas utility.

(2) In this Schedule "electricity utility" means the holder of—

(*a*) a licence under section 6(1)(*d*) of the Electricity Act 1989 (supply licences), or

(*b*) a licence under Article 10(1)(*c*) or (2) of the Electricity Supply (Northern Ireland) Order 1992,

except where the holder is acting otherwise than for purposes connected with the carrying on of activities authorised by the licence.

Until the coming into force of the substitution for section 6 of the Electricity Act 1989 provided for by the Utilities Act 2000, paragraph (*a*) above shall have effect as if the reference to section 6(1)(*d*) were to section 6(1)(*c*) or (2).

(3) In this Schedule "gas utility" means the holder of—

(*a*) a licence under section 7A(1) of the Gas Act 1986 (supply licences), or

(*b*) a licence under Article 8(1)(*c*) of the Gas (Northern Ireland) Order 1996,

except where the holder is acting otherwise than for purposes connected with the carrying on of activities authorised by the licence.

(4) Sub-paragraphs (1) to (3) have effect subject to—

(*a*) any direction under paragraph 151(1), and

(*b*) any regulations under paragraph 151(2).

Person treated as, or as not being, a utility

151—(1) The Commissioners may by direction (a "utility direction") make, in respect of a person (or persons) specified in the direction, provision authorised by sub-paragraph (3).

(2) The Treasury may by regulations ("utility regulations") make, in respect of any person of a description specified in the regulations, provision authorised by sub-paragraph (3).

(3) The provision authorised by this sub-paragraph is provision for—

(*a*) a person who is an unregulated electricity supplier to be treated for levy purposes as being an electricity utility;

(*b*) a person who is an unregulated gas supplier to be treated for levy purposes as being a gas utility;

(*c*) a person who is an electricity utility to be treated for levy purposes as not being an electricity utility;

(*d*) a person who is a gas utility to be treated for levy purposes as not being a gas utility.

(4) References in sub-paragraph (3) to provision for a person to be treated in a particular way for "levy purposes" are to provision for him to be treated in that way for—

(*a*) the purposes of this Schedule, or

(*b*) such of those purposes as are specified in the direction or regulations by which the provision is made.

(5) The power to make any provision by a utility direction or utility regulations may be exercised so that the provision applies in relation to a person only to an extent specified in, or determined under, the direction or regulations.

(6) A utility direction cannot take effect until it has been—

(*a*) given by the Commissioners to each person in respect of whom it makes provision, and

(*b*) published by the Commissioners.

(7) Paragraph 146(7)(*b*) and (*c*) applies to the power to make provision by a utility direction as to a power to make provision by regulations.

(8) In this paragraph—

"unregulated electricity supplier" means a person who—

(*a*) makes supplies of electricity, and

(*b*) is not an electricity utility;

"unregulated gas supplier" means a person who—

(*a*) makes supplies of gas that is in a gaseous state and is of a kind supplied by a gas utility, and

(*b*) is not a gas utility.

Meaning of "auto-generator"

152—(1) In this Schedule "auto-generator" means a person who produces electricity if the electricity that he produces is primarily for his own consumption.

(2) The Commissioners may by regulations specify requirements to be fulfilled before the electricity that a person produces is, for the purposes of sub-paragraph (1), to be taken as produced primarily for his own consumption.

(3) For the purposes of this paragraph, electricity is for a person's own consumption if it is for consumption by him or a person connected with him within the meaning of [section 1122 of the Corporation Tax Act 2010][1].

Amendments—[1] In sub-para (3) words substituted for words "section 839 of the Taxes Act 1988" by CTA 2010 s 1177, Sch 1 para 314(1), (3). CTA 2010 has effect for corporation tax purposes for accounting periods ending on or after 1 April 2010, and for income and capital gains tax purposes for the tax year 2010–11 and subsequent tax years.

Meaning of "levy due for an accounting period"

153 References in this Schedule, in relation to any accounting period, to levy due from any person for that period are references (subject to any regulations made by virtue of paragraph 41(2)(*a*)) to the levy for which that person is required, in accordance with regulations under paragraph 41, to account by reference to that period.

Meaning of "repayment of levy"

154 References in this Schedule to a repayment of levy or of an amount of levy are references to any repayment of an amount to any person by virtue of—

(*a*) any tax credit regulations; or

(*b*) paragraph 63, 87(3) or 110(3).

Interpretation of "in the course or furtherance of a business"

155—(1) Anything done in connection with the termination or intended termination of a business shall, for the purposes of this Schedule, be treated as being done in the course or furtherance of the business.

(2) Where in a disposition of a business as a going concern, or of its assets (whether or not in connection with its reorganisation or winding up), there is a supply of a taxable commodity, that supply shall for the purposes of this Schedule be taken to be made in the course or furtherance of the business.

Meaning of "resident in the United Kingdom"

156 For the purposes of this Schedule a person is resident in the United Kingdom at any time if, at that time—

(*a*) that person has an established place of business in the United Kingdom;

(*b*) that person has a usual place of residence in the United Kingdom; or

(*c*) that person is a firm or unincorporated body which (without having a relevant connection with the United Kingdom by virtue of paragraph (*a*)) has amongst its partners or members at least one individual with a usual place of residence in the United Kingdom.

References to the Gas and Electricity Markets Authority: transitional provision

157—(1) Until such time as a transfer of functions from the Director General of Electricity Supply to the Gas and Electricity Markets Authority ("the Authority") has taken effect, references in paragraph 19 to the Authority shall be taken to be references to the Director General.

(2) Until such time as all the functions of the Director General of Electricity Supply have been transferred in accordance with the Utilities Act 2000 (transfer to the Authority) or abolished, references to the Authority in paragraph 137 shall be taken to include the Director General.

(3) Until such time as all the functions of the Director General of Gas Supply have been transferred in accordance with the Utilities Act 2000 (transfer to the Authority) or abolished, references to the Authority in paragraph 137 shall be taken to include the Director General.

(4) The power conferred by paragraph 146(7) includes, in particular, power for regulations under paragraph 19 to make transitional provision in connection with the transfer of functions from the Director General of Electricity Supply to the Authority."

SCHEDULE 7
CLIMATE CHANGE LEVY: CONSEQUENTIAL AMENDMENTS

Section 30

Provisional Collection of Taxes Act 1968 (c 2)

1 (*amends* PCTA 1968 s 1(1)).

Bankruptcy (Scotland) Act 1985 (c 66)

2 . . . [1]

Insolvency Act 1986 (c 45)

3 . . . [1]

Income and Corporation Taxes Act 1988 (c 1)

4 (*inserts* TA 1988 s 827(1D)).

Insolvency (Northern Ireland) Order 1989 (NI 19)

5 . . . [2]

Finance Act 1996 (c 8)

6 (*inserts* FA 1996 s 197(2)(*g*)).

Finance Act 1997 (c 16)

7—(1) The Finance Act 1997 is amended as follows.
(2), (3) (*amend* FA 1997 ss 51(5), 52(5)).
(4) Sub-paragraph (3) extends only to Scotland.

Amendments—[1] Paras 2, 3: repealed by the Enterprise Act 2002 s 278(2), Sch 26 with effect from 15 September 2003 (by virtue of SI 2003/2093, art 2(1), Sch 1; for transitional provisions see art 4(1), (1A)–(1D), (2), (3), (4)(*b*) thereof (as amended by SI 2003/2332, art 2)).
[2] Para 5 repealed by the Insolvency (Northern Ireland) Order 2005, SI 2005/1455 art 31, Sch 9 with effect from 27 March 2006 (by virtue of the Insolvency (2005 Order) (Commencement No 1) Order (Northern Ireland) 2006, SR 2006/21, art 2; for transitional provisions in relation to preferential status for Crown debts in cases started before that date see the Insolvency (2005 Order) (Transitional Provisions and Savings) Order (Northern Ireland) 2006, SR 2006/22, art 3).

FINANCE ACT 2001

(2001 Chapter 9)

An Act to grant certain duties, to alter other duties, and to amend the law relating to the National Debt and the Public Revenue, and to make further provision in connection with Finance.

[11 May 2001]

PART IV
OTHER TAXES

Value added tax

. . .

99 VAT: re-enactment of reduced-rate provisions

. . .

(6) The consequential amendments in Part II of Schedule 31 to this Act have effect.

. . .

Climate change levy

105 Climate change levy

(1) Schedule 6 to the Finance Act 2000 (climate change levy) is amended as follows.
(2) (*inserts* FA 2000 Sch 6 para 11A).
(3) (*inserts* FA 2000 Sch 6 para 14(2)(*c*)).
(4) (*substitutes* FA 2000 Sch 6 para 14(3)(*c*)).
(5) (*inserts* FA 2000 Sch 6 para 14(3A)).
(6) In paragraph 15(1)(*a*) (exemption for supplies to combined heat and power stations), for "the commodity is to be used by that person" there is substituted "that person intends to cause the commodity to be used".
(7) The amendments made by this section have effect in relation to supplies made on or after 1st April 2001.

PART V
MISCELLANEOUS AND SUPPLEMENTARY PROVISIONS

Supplementary

110 Repeals and revocations

(1) The enactments mentioned in Schedule 33 to this Act (which include provisions that are spent or of no practical utility) are repealed or revoked to the extent specified.
(2) The repeals and revocations specified in that Schedule have effect subject to the commencement provisions and savings contained or referred to in the notes set out in that Schedule.

SCHEDULE 33

REPEALS

Section 110

PART III

OTHER TAXES

Note—The repeals under this Part relating to climate change levy are already in force and have therefore been omitted.

FINANCE ACT 2002

(2002 Chapter 23)

An Act to grant certain duties, to alter other duties, and to amend the law relating to the National Debt and the Public Revenue, and to make further provision in connection with finance.

[24 July 2002]

PART 5

OTHER TAXES

Climate change levy

123 Climate change levy: electricity produced in combined heat and power station

(1) (*inserts* FA 2000 Sch 6 paras 20A, 20B).

(2) Subsection (1) has effect in relation to supplies of electricity made on or after such day as the Treasury may by order made by statutory instrument appoint.

Commentary—*De Voil Indirect Tax Service* **V21.127.**

Orders—FA 2002, section 123, (Appointed Day) Order, SI 2003/603 (the day appointed under sub-s (2) above is 1 April 2003).

124 Climate change levy: certification requirement

(*inserts* FA 2000 Sch 6 para 149A).

125 Climate change levy: exemption for renewable sources

(1) In Schedule 6 to the Finance Act 2000 (c 17) (climate change levy), in paragraph 20(7), (exemption under paragraph 19: liability to account)—

(*a*) for the words from "(2)(*c*)" to "2 years)" substitute "(2)(*g*)",

(*b*) after paragraph (*a*) insert "and", and

(*c*) omit paragraph (*c*) and the preceding "and".

(2) This section has effect in relation to averaging periods under paragraph 20 of that Schedule which end on or after the day on which this Act is passed.

Commentary—*De Voil Indirect Tax Service* **V21.129.**

126 Climate change levy: electricity produced from coal mine methane

(*repealed* by FA 2008 s 149 in relation to electricity generated on or after 1 November 2008).

127 Climate change levy: incorrect certificates

(1) In Schedule 6 to the Finance Act 2000 (climate change levy), in sub-paragraph (2)(*a*) of paragraph 101 (civil penalties: incorrect notifications etc)—

(*a*) in sub-paragraph (ii) for "18 and 21, or" substitute "15, 18 and 21,";

(*b*) (*inserts* FA 2000 Sch 6 para 101(2)(*a*)(iv)).

(2) This section applies in relation to certificates given in respect of any supplies made on or after 24th April 2002.

Commentary—*De Voil Indirect Tax Service* **V21.161.**

128 Climate change levy: invoices incorrectly showing levy due

(1) (*inserts* FA 2000 Sch 6 para 141A).

(2) This section applies only in relation to invoices issued on or after the day on which this Act is passed.

Commentary—*De Voil Indirect Tax Service* **V21.161.**

PART 6

MISCELLANEOUS AND SUPPLEMENTARY PROVISIONS

Supplementary

141 Repeals

(1) The enactments mentioned in Schedule 40 to this Act (which include provisions that are spent or of no practical utility) are repealed to the extent specified.

(2) The repeals specified in that Schedule have effect subject to the commencement provisions and savings contained or referred to in the notes set out in that Schedule.

SCHEDULES

SCHEDULE 40

REPEALS

Section 141

PART 4

OTHER TAXES

(2) CLIMATE CHANGE LEVY

Note—The repeal made under this heading is already in force and has therefore been omitted.

FINANCE ACT 2003

(2003 Chapter 14)

An Act to grant certain duties, to alter other duties, and to amend the law relating to the National Debt and the Public Revenue, and to make further provision in connection with finance.

[10 July 2003]

PART 8

OTHER TAXES

Climate change levy

188 Exemption for fuel used in recycling processes

(1) (*inserts* FA 2000 Sch 6 para 18A)

(2) (*amends* FA 2000 Sch 6 paras 14, 101, 146, 147)

189 CHP exemption to be based on current efficiency

(1) Schedule 6 to the Finance Act 2000 (c 17) (climate change levy) is amended as follows.

(2) In paragraph 15 (exemption for supplies to combined heat and power stations)—

(*a*) (*substitutes* FA 2000 Sch 6 para 15(4)(*b*))

(*b*) omit sub-paragraph (5).

(3) In paragraph 148 (meaning of "combined heat and power station" etc)—

(*a*) (*amends* FA 2000 Sch 6 para 148(2)(*c*) and (3)(*c*))

(*b*) (*repeals* FA 2000 Sch 6 para 148(6))

(4) (*amends* FA 2000 Sch 6 para 149(1))

(5) This section has effect in relation to supplies made on or after such day as the Treasury may by order made by statutory instrument appoint.

190 Supplies not known to be taxable when made, etc

(1) In Schedule 6 to the Finance Act 2000 (c 17) (climate change levy), paragraph 24 (deemed supply: change of circumstances or intentions) is amended as follows.

(2) In the heading, for "*change of circumstances or intentions*" substitute "*change of circumstances etc*".

(3) (*substitutes* FA 2000 Sch 6 para 24(1)–(2))

(4) In sub-paragraph (3), at the beginning insert "Where this paragraph applies,".

(5) (*inserts* FA 2000 Sch 6 para 24(3A))

(6) In sub-paragraph (5) for "sub-paragraph (1)(*c*)" substitute "sub-paragraph (1A)(*c*)".

(7) (*amends* FA 2000 Sch 6 para 34(3))

(8) This section has effect in relation to supplies made on or after such day as the Treasury may by order made by statutory instrument appoint.

191 Deemed supplies

(1) Schedule 6 to the Finance Act 2000 (c 17) (climate change levy) is amended as follows.

(2), (3) (*amend* paras 5(3), 6(3), and *insert* para 6(2A))

(4) Subsection (2) has effect in relation to supplies deemed to be made on or after 31st March 2003, and subsection (3) in relation to supplies deemed to be made on or after the day on which this Act is passed.

192 Amendments about registration, payment etc

(1) Schedule 6 to the Finance Act 2000 (climate change levy) is amended as follows.

(2)–(10) (*amend* paras 41, 53, 62, 78, 91, 93, 100, 125, 135)

Amendments—Sub-s (8) repealed by FA 2008 s 122, Sch 40 para 21(*k*) with effect from 1 April 2009 (by virtue of SI 2009/571 art 2).

193 Electricity from renewable sources etc

(1) Schedule 6 to the Finance Act 2000 (climate change levy) is amended as follows.

(2) (*amends* para 20)

(3) (*amends* para 20B)
(4) The amendment made by subsection (2) has effect where the end of the balancing period referred to in paragraph (*a*) of the sub-paragraph (6) substituted by that subsection falls on or after 31st March 2003.
(5) The amendment made by subsection (3) has effect where the end of the balancing period referred to in paragraph (*a*) of the sub-paragraph (6) substituted by that subsection falls on or after 1st April 2003.

PART 9
MISCELLANEOUS AND SUPPLEMENTARY PROVISIONS
Supplementary

215 Interpretation
In this Act "the Taxes Act 1988" means the Income and Corporation Taxes Act 1988 (c 1).

216 Repeals
(1) The enactments mentioned in Schedule 43 to this Act (which include provisions that are spent or of no practical utility) are repealed to the extent specified.
(2) The repeals specified in that Schedule have effect subject to the commencement provisions and savings contained or referred to in the notes set out in that Schedule.

SCHEDULES

SCHEDULE 43

REPEALS

Section 216

The effect of the repeals set out in this Schedule, so far as relevant to climate change levy, has been noted in the relevant legislation.

FINANCE ACT 2004

(2004 Chapter 12)

An Act to Grant certain duties, to alter other duties, and to amend the law relating to the National Debt and the Public Revenue, and to make further provision in connection with finance.

[22 July 2004]

PART 6
OTHER TAXES

Climate change levy

289 Supplies to producers of commodities
(1) Schedule 6 to the Finance Act 2000 (c 17) (climate change levy) is amended as set out in subsections (2) to (5).
(2) (*inserts* FA 2000 Sch 6 para 13(*b*)(iia)–(iid))
(3) (*amends* FA 2000 Sch 6 para 13(*b*)(iii))
(4) (*amends* FA 2000 Sch 6 para 13, last sentence)
(5) (*inserts* FA 2000 Sch 6 para 13A)
(6) The amendments made by subsections (2) to (4) have effect—
(*a*) as regards biodiesel and bioblend, in relation to supplies made on or after the day on which this Act is passed;
(*b*) as regards bioethanol and bioethanol blend, in relation to supplies made on or after 1st January 2005.

FINANCE ACT 2006

(2006 Chapter 25)

An Act to Grant certain duties, to alter other duties, and to amend the law relating to the National Debt and the Public Revenue, and to make further provision in connection with finance.

[19 July 2006]

PART 9
MISCELLANEOUS PROVISIONS

Climate change levy

171 Climate change levy: rates

(1) (*substitutes* FA 2000 Sch 6 para 42(1) Table)

(2) This section has effect in relation to supplies treated as taking place on or after 1st April 2007.

172 Abolition of half-rate supplies etc

(1) For the purposes of climate change levy, no supply made on or after 1st April 2006 is a half-rate supply.

(2) Subsections (3) to (6) have effect for determining when a supply is to be regarded as made for the purposes of subsection (1).

(3) A supply—

(*a*) of electricity, or

(*b*) of gas that is in a gaseous state and is of a kind supplied by a gas utility,

is to be regarded as made at the time when the electricity or gas is actually supplied.

(4) In the case of a supply of a taxable commodity not falling within subsection (3) by a person who is resident in the United Kingdom—

(*a*) if the commodity is to be removed, the supply is to be regarded as made at the time of the removal,

(*b*) if the commodity is not to be removed, the supply is to be regarded as made when the commodity is made available to the person to whom it is supplied.

This subsection does not apply if subsection (6) (deemed self-supply) applies in the case of the supply.

(5) In the case of a supply of a taxable commodity not falling within subsection (3) by a person who is not resident in the United Kingdom, the supply is to be regarded as made—

(*a*) when the commodity is delivered to the person to whom it is supplied, or

(*b*) if earlier, when it is made available in the United Kingdom to that person.

This subsection does not apply if subsection (6) (deemed self-supply) applies in the case of the supply.

(6) In any case where, by virtue of paragraph 23(3) of Schedule 6 to FA 2000, a person is, for the purposes of that Schedule, deemed to make a supply to himself of a quantity of a taxable commodity—

(*a*) which he has produced, and

(*b*) which does not fall within subsection (3),

the supply is to be regarded as made at the time when he produced that particular quantity of the taxable commodity.

(7) (*amends* FA 2000 Sch 6 para 34(2))

(8) In consequence of subsection (1), Schedule 6 to FA 2000 (climate change levy) is amended as follows.

(9) In paragraph 37 (supplies of electricity or gas spanning change of rate etc) in sub-paragraph (1)(*c*) omit "half-rate supplies or".

(10) In paragraph 38 (other supplies spanning change of rate etc) in sub-paragraph (1)(*c*) omit "half-rate supplies or".

(11) In paragraph 42(1) (amount payable by way of levy)—

(*a*) in paragraph (*a*), for "neither a half-rate supply nor" substitute "not";

(*b*) omit paragraph (*b*);

(*c*) in paragraph (*c*), for "neither a half-rate supply nor" substitute "not";

(*d*) in the Table (and in the Table substituted for it by section 171 of this Act), in the heading to column (2), for "neither a half-rate supply nor" substitute "not".

(12) Paragraph 43 (half-rate for supplies to horticultural producers) shall cease to have effect.

(13) In paragraph 62 (tax credits) in subsection (1)—

(*a*) in paragraph (*c*)—

(i) for "neither a half-rate supply nor" substitute "not";

(ii) omit "half-rate or";

(*b*) omit paragraph (*d*).

(14) In paragraph 101 (civil penalties: incorrect notifications) in sub-paragraph (2)(*a*)—

(*a*) at the end of sub-paragraph (ii) insert "or";

(*b*) omit sub-paragraph (iii).

(15) In paragraph 147 (interpretation: general) omit the definition of "half-rate supply".

(16) Subsections (8) to (15) come into force on such day as the Treasury may by order made by statutory instrument appoint.

(17) The power to make an order under subsection (16)—

(*a*) may be exercised so as to bring a provision into force only in such cases as may be described in the order,

(*b*) may be exercised so as to make different provision for different cases or descriptions of case,

(*c*) includes power to make incidental, consequential, supplemental or transitional provision or savings.

Order—Finance Act 2006 (Climate Change Levy: Amendments and Transitional Savings in Consequence of Abolition of Half-Rate Supplies) (Appointed Day) Order, SI 2007/2901 (1 November 2007 is appointed as the day on which sub-ss (8)–(15) come into force; amendments made by sub-ss (8)–(15) do not apply in relation to half-rate supplies made before 1 April 2006: SI 2007/2901 art 2(2)).

FINANCE ACT 2007

(2007 Chapter 11)

PART 1

CHARGES, RATES, THRESHOLDS ETC

Environment

13 Rates of climate change levy

(1) (*substitutes* Table in FA 2000 Sch 6 para 42(1))

(2) The amendment made by subsection (1) has effect in relation to supplies treated as taking place on or after 1st April 2008.

16 Emissions trading: charges for allocations

(1) The Treasury may impose charges by providing for Community tradeable emissions allowances to be allocated in return for payment.

(2) The Treasury must by regulations make provision for and in connection with allocations of allowances in return for payment.

(3) The regulations must provide for allocations to be overseen by an independent person appointed by the Treasury.

(4) The regulations may make any other provision about allocations which the Treasury consider appropriate, including (in particular)—

(*a*) provision as to the imposition of fees, and as to the making and forfeiting of deposits, in connection with participation in allocations,

(*b*) provision as to the persons by whom allocations are to be conducted,

(*c*) provision for the [creation of criminal offences, or for the imposition and recovery of civil penalties,][1] for failure to comply with the terms of a scheme made under subsection (5),

(*d*) provision for and in connection with the recovery of payments due in respect of allowances allocated (including provision as to the imposition and recovery of interest and penalties), and

(*e*) provision conferring rights of appeal against decisions made in allocations, the forfeiting of deposits and the imposition of penalties (including provision specifying the person, court or tribunal to hear and determine appeals).

(5) The Treasury may make schemes about the conduct and terms of allocations (to have effect subject to any regulations under this section); and schemes may in particular include provision about—

(*a*) who may participate in allocations,

(*b*) the allowances to be allocated, and

(*c*) where and when allocations are to take place.

(6) "Community tradeable emissions allowances" are transferable allowances which—

(*a*) relate to the making of emissions of greenhouse gases, and

(*b*) are allocated as part of a system made for the purpose of implementing any Community obligation of the United Kingdom relating to such emissions;

and "greenhouse gases" means carbon dioxide, methane, nitrous oxide, hydrofluorocarbons, perfluorocarbons and sulphur hexafluoride.

[(6A) Subsection (4)(*c*) does not permit the creation of a criminal offence with maximum penalties in excess of the maximum penalties which an instrument under section 2(2) of the European Communities Act 1972 may provide in respect of an offence created by such an instrument.][1]

(7) Regulations under this section are to be made by statutory instrument.

(8) A statutory instrument containing regulations under this section is subject to annulment in pursuance of a resolution of the House of Commons unless a draft of the regulations has been laid before, and approved by a resolution of, that House.

Amendments—[1] Sub-s (6A) inserted, and in sub-s (4)(*c*) words substituted for words "imposition and recovery of penalties", by FA 2008 s 164 with effect from 21 July 2008.

PART 2

ENVIRONMENT

Other measures

23 Climate change levy: reduced-rate supplies etc

Schedule 2 contains amendments of Schedule 6 to FA 2000 in relation to reduced-rate supplies and other matters.

97 Penalties for errors

Note—Please see *VAT Statutes* ante for the text of this Section.

SCHEDULES

SCHEDULE 2

CLIMATE CHANGE LEVY: REDUCED-RATE SUPPLIES ETC

Section 23

Introductory

1 Schedule 6 to FA 2000 (climate change levy) is amended as follows.

Reduced-rate supplies

2 (*amends* FA 2000 Sch 6 para 4(2)(*b*))

Order—Finance Act 2007 (Climate Change Levy: Reduced-rate Supplies etc) (Appointed Day) Order, SI 2007/2902 (1 November 2007 appointed as the day on which paras 2–10 come into force).

3 (*amends* FA 2000 Sch 6 para 5(3))

Order—Finance Act 2007 (Climate Change Levy: Reduced-rate Supplies etc) (Appointed Day) Order, SI 2007/2902 (1 November 2007 appointed as the day on which paras 2–10 come into force).

4 (*amends* FA 2000 Sch 6 para 6(2A))

Order—Finance Act 2007 (Climate Change Levy: Reduced-rate Supplies etc) (Appointed Day) Order, SI 2007/2902 (1 November 2007 appointed as the day on which paras 2–10 come into force).

5—(1) Paragraph 34 (other commodities: deemed supplies) is amended as follows.

(2) (*amends* FA 2000 Sch 6 para 34(1)(*b*))

(3) (*inserts* FA 2000 Sch 6 para 34(4))

Order—Finance Act 2007 (Climate Change Levy: Reduced-rate Supplies etc) (Appointed Day) Order, SI 2007/2902 (1 November 2007 appointed as the day on which paras 2–10 come into force).

6 (*amends* FA 2000 Sch 6 para 39(1)(*c*))

Order—Finance Act 2007 (Climate Change Levy: Reduced-rate Supplies etc) (Appointed Day) Order, SI 2007/2902 (1 November 2007 appointed as the day on which paras 2–10 come into force).

7 (*substitutes* FA 2000 Sch 6 para 44)

Order—Finance Act 2007 (Climate Change Levy: Reduced-rate Supplies etc) (Appointed Day) Order, SI 2007/2902 (1 November 2007 appointed as the day on which paras 2–10 come into force). The amendments made by this para only apply in relation to a supply actually made on or after 1 November 2007: SI 2007/2902 art 2(2).

8—(1) Paragraph 45 (reduced-rate supplies: variation of notices under paragraph 44) is amended as follows.

(2) (*repeals* FA 2000 Sch 6 para 45(2)–(4))

(3) (*amends* FA 2000 Sch 6 para 45(5))

(4) (*amends* FA 2000 Sch 6 para 45(6))

(5) (*amends* FA 2000 Sch 6 para 45(7))

(6) (*amends* FA 2000 Sch 6 para 45 heading)

Order—Finance Act 2007 (Climate Change Levy: Reduced-rate Supplies etc) (Appointed Day) Order, SI 2007/2902 (1 November 2007 appointed as the day on which paras 2–10 come into force).

9 (*inserts* FA 2000 Sch 6 para 45A)

Order—Finance Act 2007 (Climate Change Levy: Reduced-rate Supplies etc) (Appointed Day) Order, SI 2007/2902 (1 November 2007 appointed as the day on which paras 2–10 come into force). This amendment only applies in relation to a supply actually made on or after 1 November 2007 and on the basis that it is a reduced-rate supply: SI 2007/2902 art 2(3).

10 (*amends* FA 2000 Sch 6 para 147)

Order—Finance Act 2007 (Climate Change Levy: Reduced-rate Supplies etc) (Appointed Day) Order, SI 2007/2902 (1 November 2007 appointed as the day on which paras 2–10 come into force). The amendments made by this para only apply in relation to a supply actually made on or after 1 November 2007: SI 2007/2902 art 2(2).

Notifications and certificates

11 (*amends* FA 2000 Sch 6 para 11(1), (3))

12—(1) Paragraph 101 (civil penalties: incorrect notifications etc) is amended as follows.
(2) (*repeals* FA 2000 Sch 6 para 101(1))
(3) (*amends* FA 2000 Sch 6 para 101(2))
(4) (*amends* FA 2000 Sch 6 para 101(3))
(5) (*amends* FA 2000 Sch 6 para 101(4))
(6) (*amends* FA 2000 Sch 6 para 101(5))
(7) (*amends* FA 2000 Sch 6 para 101 heading)

Commencement

13—(1) Paragraphs 2 to 10 come into force on such day as the Treasury may by order made by statutory instrument appoint.
(2) But any power to make regulations under any provision inserted or amended by any of those paragraphs may be exercised at any time after this Act is passed.
(3) The power to make an order under sub-paragraph (1)—
(*a*) may be exercised so as to bring a provision into force only in such cases as may be described in the order,
(*b*) may be exercised so as to make different provision for different cases or descriptions of case,
(*c*) includes power to make incidental, consequential, supplemental or transitional provision or savings.

SCHEDULE 24

PENALTIES FOR ERRORS

Note—Please see *VAT Statutes* ante for the text of this Schedule.

FINANCE ACT 2008

(2008 Chapter 9)

An Act to Grant certain duties, to alter other duties, and to amend the law relating to the National Debt and the Public Revenue, and to make further provision in connection with finance.

[21 July 2008]

PART 1

CHARGES, RATES, ALLOWANCES, RELIEFS ETC

Environmental taxes and duties

19 Rates of climate change levy

(1) (*amends* FA 2000 Sch 6 para 42(1)).
(2) The amendment made by subsection (1) has effect in relation to supplies treated as taking place on or after 1 April 2009.

21 Carbon reduction trading scheme: charges for allocations

(1) The Treasury may impose charges by providing for carbon reduction trading scheme allowances to be allocated in return for payment.
(2) The charges may only be imposed by regulations.
(3) The regulations may make any other provision about allocations of allowances which the Treasury consider appropriate, including (in particular)—
(*a*) provision as to the imposition of fees, and as to the making and forfeiting of deposits, in connection with participation in the allocations,
(*b*) provision as to the persons by whom allocations are to be conducted,
(*c*) provision for allocations to be overseen by an independent person appointed by the Treasury,
(*d*) provision for the imposition and recovery of penalties for failure to comply with the terms of a scheme made under subsection (4),
(*e*) provision for and in connection with the recovery of payments due in respect of allowances allocated (including provision as to the imposition and recovery of interest and penalties), and
(*f*) provision conferring rights of appeal against decisions made in allocations, the forfeiting of deposits and the imposition of penalties (including provision specifying the person, court or tribunal to hear and determine appeals).

(4) The Treasury may make schemes about the conduct and terms of allocations (to have effect subject to any regulations under this section); and schemes may in particular include provision about—

(*a*) who may participate in allocations,

(*b*) the allowances to be allocated, and

(*c*) where and when allocations are to take place.

(5) In this section—

"carbon reduction trading scheme allowances" means tradeable allowances that—

(*a*) are provided for in a relevant trading scheme, and

(*b*) represent the right to carry on a specified amount of activities that consist of the emission of greenhouse gas or that cause or contribute, directly or indirectly, to such emissions;

"relevant trading scheme" means a trading scheme that—

(*a*) is made under Part 3 of the Climate Change Act 2008,

(*b*) applies to persons by reference to their consumption of electricity (whether or not by reference to other matters as well), and

(*c*) applies only to persons who consume electricity—

(i) for business or charitable purposes, or

(ii) for the performance of functions of a public nature,

(whether or not they also consume electricity for other purposes);

"specified" means specified in the relevant trading scheme.

(6) Regulations under this section are to be made by statutory instrument.

(7) A statutory instrument containing the first regulations under this section may not be made unless a draft of the regulations has been laid before, and approved by a resolution of, the House of Commons.

(8) Any other statutory instrument containing regulations under this section is subject to annulment in pursuance of a resolution of the House of Commons unless a draft of the regulations has been laid before, and approved by a resolution of, that House.

PART 7

ADMINISTRATION

Press releases—HMRC Guidance Note, 18 July 2008 (HMRC set-off across taxes following Finance Bill 2008).

CHAPTER 1

INFORMATION ETC

New information etc powers

114 Computer records etc

Note—Please see *VAT Statutes* ante for the text of this Section.

CHAPTER 3

PENALTIES

122 Penalties for errors

Note—Please see *VAT Statutes* ante for the text of this Section.

123 Penalties for failure to notify etc

Note—Please see *VAT Statutes* ante for the text of this Section.

CHAPTER 4

APPEALS ETC

Reviews and appeals etc: general

124 HMRC decisions etc: reviews and appeals

Note—Please see *VAT Statutes* ante for the text of this Section.

CHAPTER 5

PAYMENT AND ENFORCEMENT

Taking control of goods etc

127 Enforcement by taking control of goods: England and Wales

Note—Please see *VAT Statutes* ante for the text of this Section.

128 Summary warrant: Scotland

Note—Please see *VAT Statutes* ante for the text of this Section.

129 Consequential provision and commencement

Note—Please see *VAT Statutes* ante for the text of this Section.

Set off

130 Set-off: England and Wales and Northern Ireland

Note—Please see *VAT Statutes* ante for the text of this Section.

131 No set-off where insolvency procedure has been applied

Note—Please see *VAT Statutes* ante for the text of this Section.

133 Set-off etc where right to be paid a sum has been transferred

Note—Please see *VAT Statutes* ante for the text of this Section.

Other measures

135 Interest on unpaid tax in case of disaster etc of national significance

Note—Please see *VAT Statutes* ante for the text of this Section.

136 Fee for payment

Note—Please see *VAT Statutes* ante for the text of this Section.

Supplementary

139 Interpretation of Chapter

Note—Please see *VAT Statutes* ante for the text of this Section.

PART 8

MISCELLANEOUS

Climate change levy and landfill tax

149 Climate change levy: coal mine methane no longer to be renewable source

(1) (*repeals* FA 2000 Sch 6 para 19(4A)).

(2) Accordingly, omit—

(*a*) (*repeals* FA 2002 s 126).

(*b*) (*repeals* the CCL (General) Regulations, SI 2001/838 reg 47(2A)).

(3) The repeals and revocation made by this section have effect in relation to electricity generated on or after 1 November 2008.

150 Climate change levy accounting documents: abolition of self-identification

(*repeals* FA 2000 Sch 6 para 143(2)(*a*)).

Other matters

164 EU emissions trading: criminal offences

(1) Section 16 of FA 2007 (EU emissions trading: charges for allocations) is amended as follows.

(2) (*amends* FA 2007 s 16(4)(*c*)).

(3) (*inserts* FA 2007 s 16(6A)).

PART 9

FINAL PROVISIONS

165 Interpretation

166 Short title

Note—Please see *VAT Statutes* ante for the text of these Sections.

SCHEDULES

SCHEDULE 36

INFORMATION AND INSPECTION POWERS

Section 113

Commencement—Finance Act 2008, Schedule 36 (Appointed Day and Savings) Order, SI 2009/404 art 2 (appointed day for the coming into force of Sch 36 is 1 April 2009).

Note—Please see *VAT Statutes* ante for the text of this Section.

SCHEDULE 41

PENALTIES: FAILURE TO NOTIFY AND CERTAIN VAT AND EXCISE WRONGDOING

Section 123

Commencement—Finance Act 2008, Schedule 41 (Appointed Day and Transitional Provisions) Order, SI 2009/511 (appointed day for the coming into force of Sch 41 is 1 April 2010).

Note—Please see *VAT Statutes* ante for the text of this Section.

FINANCE ACT 2009

(2009 Chapter 10)

An Act to Grant certain duties, to alter other duties, and to amend the law relating to the National Debt and the Public Revenue, and to make further provision in connection with finance.

[21 July 2009]

PART 7
ADMINISTRATION

Standards and values

92 HMRC Charter

Note—Please see *VAT Statutes* ante for the text of this Section.

93 Duties of senior accounting officers of qualifying companies

Note—Please see *VAT Statutes* ante for the text of this Section.

94 Publishing details of deliberate tax defaulters

Note—Please see *VAT Statutes* ante for the text of this Section.

Information etc

95 Amendment of information and inspection powers

Note—Please see *VAT Statutes* ante for the text of this Section.

96 Extension of information and inspection powers to further taxes

(1) In paragraph 63(1) of Schedule 36 to FA 2008 (information and inspection powers: meaning of "tax"), for paragraph (*e*) (and the "and" before it) substitute—

"(*e*) insurance premium tax,
(*f*) inheritance tax,
(*g*) stamp duty land tax,
(*h*) stamp duty reserve tax,
(*i*) petroleum revenue tax,
(*j*) aggregates levy,
(*k*) climate change levy,
(*l*) landfill tax, and
(*m*) relevant foreign tax,".

(2) Schedule 48 contains further amendments of that Schedule.

(3) The amendments made by this section and Schedule 48 come into force on such day as the Treasury may by order appoint.

(4) An order under subsection (3) may—

(*a*) appoint different days for different purposes, and
(*b*) contain transitional provision and savings.

(5) The Treasury may by order make any incidental, supplemental, consequential, transitional or transitory provision or saving which appears appropriate in consequence of, or otherwise in connection with, this section and Schedule 48.

(6) An order under subsection (5) may—

(*a*) make different provision for different purposes, and
(*b*) make provision amending, repealing or revoking an enactment or instrument (whenever passed or made).

(7) An order under this section is to be made by statutory instrument.

(8) A statutory instrument containing an order under subsection (5) is subject to annulment in pursuance of a resolution of the House of Commons.

Commencement—Finance Act 2009, Section 96 and Schedule 48 (Appointed Day, Savings and Consequential Amendments) Order, SI 2009/3054 (appointed day for the coming into force of s 96, Sch 48 is 1 April 2010).

97 Powers to obtain contact details for debtors

Note—Please see *VAT Statutes* ante for the text of this Section.

98 Record-keeping

(1) Schedule 50 contains provision about obligations to keep records.

(2) The amendments made by that Schedule come into force on such day as the Treasury may by order made by statutory instrument appoint.

Order—Finance Act 2009, Schedule 50 (Record-keeping) (Appointed Day) Order 2010 (appoints 1 April 2010 as the date for the Sch 50 amendments to come into force).

Assessments, claims etc

99 Time limits for assessments, claims etc

(1) Schedule 51 contains provision about time limits for assessments, claims etc

(2) The amendments made by that Schedule come into force on such day as the Treasury may by order made by statutory instrument appoint.

(3) An order under subsection (2)—

(*a*) may make different provision for different purposes, and

(*b*) may include transitional provision and savings.

Order—Finance Act 2009, Schedule 51 (Time Limits for Assessments, Claims, etc) (Appointed Days and Transitional Provisions) Order 2010 (1 April 2010 is appointed as the date for Sch 51 paras 1–4, 27–43 to come into force).

Interest

101 Late payment interest on sums due to HMRC

Note—Please see *VAT Statutes* ante for the text of this Section.

102 Repayment interest on sums to be paid by HMRC

Note—Please see *VAT Statutes* ante for the text of this Section.

103 Rates of interest

Note—Please see *VAT Statutes* ante for the text of this Section.

104 Supplementary

Note—Please see *VAT Statutes* ante for the text of this Section.

108 Suspension of penalties during currency of agreement for deferred payment

Note—Please see *VAT Statutes* ante for the text of this Section.

109 Miscellaneous amendments

Note—Please see *VAT Statutes* ante for the text of this Section.

PART 8
MISCELLANEOUS

Climate change levy

117 Taxable commodities ineligible for reduced-rate supply

(1) Schedule 6 to FA 2000 (climate change levy) is amended as follows.

(2) (*inserts* FA 2000 Sch 6 para 44(2A)–(2D))

(3) In consequence of subsection (2)—

(*a*) in paragraph 44(2), after "subject to" insert "sub-paragraphs (2A) to (2D) and", and

(*b*) in paragraph 147 (general interpretation), in the definition of "reduced- rate supply", after "subject to" insert "paragraph 44(2A) to (2D) and".

118 Removal of reduced rate where targets not met

(1) Schedule 59 contains provision for removing the reduced rate of climate change levy where the targets set by a climate change agreement have not been met.

(2) The amendments made by that Schedule have effect where the certification period begins on or after 1 April 2009.

SCHEDULES

SCHEDULE 46

DUTIES OF SENIOR ACCOUNTING OFFICERS OF QUALIFYING COMPANIES

Section 93

Note—Please see *VAT Statutes* ante for the text of this Schedule.

SCHEDULE 47

AMENDMENT OF INFORMATION AND INSPECTION POWERS

Section 94

Note—Please see *VAT Statutes* ante for the text of this Schedule.

SCHEDULE 48

EXTENSION OF INFORMATION AND INSPECTION POWERS

Section 95

Note—Please see *VAT Statutes* ante for the text of this Schedule.

SCHEDULE 49

POWERS TO OBTAIN CONTACT DETAILS FOR DEBTORS

Section 97

Note—Please see *VAT Statutes* ante for the text of this Schedule.

SCHEDULE 50

RECORD-KEEPING

Section 98

Order—Finance Act 2009, Schedule 50 (Record-keeping) (Appointed Day) Order, SI 2010/815 (appoints 1 April 2010 as the date for the Sch 50 amendments to come into force).

Climate change levy

18 Schedule 6 to FA 2000 (climate change levy) is amended as follows.

19—(1) Paragraph 125 (records) is amended as follows.
(2) (*substitutes* FA 2000 Sch 6 para 125(4))
(3) In sub-paragraph (9), omit "approval or" and "given or".

20 Omit paragraph 126 (evidence of records that are required to be preserved).

SCHEDULE 51

TIME LIMITS FOR ASSESSMENTS, CLAIMS ETC

Section 99

Order—Finance Act 2009, Schedule 51 (Time Limits for Assessments, Claims, etc) (Appointed Days and Transitional Provisions) Order, SI 2010/867 (1 April 2010 is appointed as the date for Sch 51 paras 1–4, 27–43 to come into force).

Climate change levy

32 Schedule 6 to FA 2000 (climate change levy) is amended as follows.

33 In paragraph 64(1) (repayments of overpaid climate change levy), for "three years" substitute "4 years".

34 In paragraph 66(10) (interest payable by the Commissioners), for "three years" substitute "4 years".

35—(1) Paragraph 80 (time limits for assessments) is amended as follows.
(2) In sub-paragraph (1)(*b*), for "three years" substitute "4 years".
(3) (*substitutes* FA 2000 Sch 6 para 80(3), (3A))
(4) In sub-paragraph (4)—
(*a*) in paragraph (*a*), for "three years" substitute "4 years", and
(*b*) omit paragraph (*b*) (and the "and" before it).

36—(1) Paragraph 108 (time limits on penalty assessments) is amended as follows.
(2) In sub-paragraph (1), for "three years" substitute "4 years".
(3) (*substitutes* FA 2000 Sch 6 para 108(2), (2A))
(4) In sub-paragraph (3)—
(*a*) in paragraph (*a*), for "three years" substitute "4 years", and
(*b*) omit paragraph (*b*) (and the "and" before it).

SCHEDULE 53

LATE PAYMENT INTEREST

Section 101

Note—Please see *VAT Statutes* ante for the text of this Schedule.

SCHEDULE 54

REPAYMENT INTEREST

Section 102

Note—Please see *VAT Statutes* ante for the text of this Schedule.

SCHEDULE 57

AMENDMENTS RELATING TO PENALTIES

Section 109

Note—Please see *VAT Statutes* ante for the text of this Schedule.

SCHEDULE 59

CLIMATE CHANGE LEVY: REMOVAL OF REDUCED RATE

Section 118

PART 1
NEW PROVISION FOR REMOVAL OF REDUCED RATE

1 (*inserts* FA 2000 Sch 6 para 45B)

PART 2
CONSEQUENTIAL AMENDMENTS

2 Schedule 6 to FA 2000 is amended as follows.

3—(1) Paragraph 40 (persons liable to account for levy) is amended as follows.
(2) In sub-paragraph (1), after "sub-paragraph (2)" insert "or (3)".
(3) (*inserts* FA 2000 Sch 6 para 40(3))

4 In paragraph 41(2A) (application of Part 7 where person liable to account otherwise than by reference to accounting period), after "regulations under sub-paragraph (1)(*a*)(ii) above" insert "or by virtue of paragraph 45B(8)".

5 (*inserts* FA 2000 Sch 6 para 42(1A))

6 In paragraph 44(2) (definition of "reduced-rate supply" to have effect subject to paragraph 45), for "paragraph 45" substitute "paragraphs 45 and 45B".

7 (*inserts* FA 2000 Sch 6 para 45A(3))

8—(1) Paragraph 91 (interpretation etc of Part 7 of the Schedule) is amended as follows.
(2) In sub-paragraph (5) (modification of references to accounting periods in case of levy due otherwise than by reference to such periods), after "regulations under paragraph 41(1)(*a*)(ii)" insert "or by virtue of paragraph 45B(8)".

9 In paragraph 147 (interpretation), in the definition of "reduced-rate supply", for "paragraph 45" substitute "paragraphs 45 and 45B".

FINANCE ACT 2010

(2010 Chapter 13)

[8 April 2010]

PART 1
CHARGES, RATES ETC

Other environmental taxes

17 Rates of climate change levy

(1) In Schedule 6 to FA 2000 (climate change levy), for the table in paragraph 42(1) substitute—

"TABLE

Taxable commodity supplied	*Rate at which levy payable if supply is not a reduced-rate supply*
Electricity	£0.00485 per kilowatt hour
Gas supplied by a gas utility or any gas supplied in a gaseous state that is of a kind supplied by a gas utility	£0.00169 per kilowatt hour
Any petroleum gas, or other gaseous hydrocarbon, supplied in a liquid state	£0.01083 per kilogram
Any other taxable commodity	£0.01321 per kilogram".

(2) The amendment made by subsection (1) has effect in relation to supplies treated as taking place on or after 1 April 2011.

18 Climate change levy: reduced-rate supplies

(1) In Schedule 6 to FA 2000 (climate change levy), in paragraph 42(1)(*c*) (reduced-rate supplies), for "20 per cent." substitute "35 per cent.".
(2) The amendment made by subsection (1) has effect in relation to supplies treated as taking place on or after 1 April 2011.

PART 3
OTHER PROVISIONS

Miscellaneous

67 Climate change levy: compatible state aid

In paragraph 42 of Schedule 6 to FA 2000 (amount payable by way of levy), after sub-paragraph (2) insert—

"(3) If a reduced-rate supply is part of an aid scheme within Article 25 of Commission Regulation (EC) No 800/2008, sub-paragraph (4) cites the title and publication reference of that Regulation for the purpose of complying with Article 3(1) of that Regulation.

(4) That citation is Commission Regulation (EC) No 800/2008 of 6 August 2008 declaring certain categories of aid compatible with the common market in application of Articles 87 and 88 of the Treaty (General block exemption Regulation) (OJ 2008 No L214/3) (with the reference to Articles 87 and 88 being read, as a result of the Treaty of Lisbon, as a reference to Articles 107 and 108 of the Treaty on the Functioning of the European Union)."

Climate Change Levy Statutory Instruments

Contents

Chronological list of printed statutory instruments

1997/1431

DISTRESS FOR CUSTOMS AND EXCISE DUTIES AND OTHER INDIRECT TAXES REGULATIONS 1997

Made by the Commissioners of Customs and Excise under FA 1997 ss 51(1)–(3)

Made . . . .*9 June 1997*
Laid before House of Commons . . . .*9 June 1997*
Coming into force . . . .*1 July 1997*

Citation and Commencement

1 These Regulations may be cited as The Distress for Customs and Excise Duties and Other Indirect Taxes Regulations 1997 and shall come into force on 1st July 1997.

Interpretation

2—(1) In these Regulations—

"authorised person" means a person acting under the authority of the Commissioners;

"costs" means any costs, charges, expenses and fees;

"officer" means, subject to section 8(2) of the Customs and Excise Management Act 1979, a person commissioned by the Commissioners pursuant to section 6(3) of that Act;

"person in default" means a person who has refused or neglected to pay any relevant tax due from him;

"relevant tax" means any of the following—

. . .

(*f*) climate change levy;

. . .

"VAT Act" means the Value Added Tax Act 1994;

"walking possession agreement" means an agreement under which, in consideration of any goods and chattels distrained upon being allowed to remain in the custody of the person in default and of the delaying of their sale, that person—

(*a*) acknowledges that the goods and chattels specified in the agreement are under distraint and held in walking possession; and

(*b*) undertakes that, except with the consent of the Commissioners and subject to such conditions as they may impose, he will not remove or allow the removal of any of the specified goods and chattels from the place named in the agreement;

"1994 Act" means Part III of the Finance Act 1994;

"1996 Act" means Part III of the Finance Act 1996;

(2) Any reference in these Regulations to an amount of relevant tax includes a reference to any amount recoverable as if it were an amount of that relevant tax.

Note—Words omitted are not relevant for the purposes of the climate change levy.

Revocations and transitional provisions

3—(1) The Regulations specified in Schedule 3 are hereby revoked to the extent set out there.

(2) Where a warrant is signed before the coming into force of these Regulations, these Regulations shall apply to anything done, after these Regulations come into force, in relation to that warrant or as a consequence of distress being levied.

Levying distress

4—(1) Subject to regulation 5 below, if upon written demand a person neglects or refuses to pay any relevant tax due from him an officer may levy distress on the goods and chattels of that person and by warrant signed by him direct any authorised person to levy such distress.

(2) Where a warrant has been signed, distress shall be levied by or under the direction of, and in the presence of, the authorised person.

(3) Subject to regulation 6 below, distress may be levied on any goods and chattels located at any place whatever including on a public highway.

Restrictions on levying distress

5—(1) Where—

(*a*) an amount of any duty of customs or excise (other than vehicle excise duty) or any agricultural levy of the European Community is due and the Commissioners may be required under section 14 of the 1994 Act to review a decision which, if that decision were varied or withdrawn would cause the amount to be reduced or extinguished;

. . .

no distress shall be levied before expiry of the last day on which the person who is liable to pay the amount concerned is required, by rules made under paragraph 9 of Schedule 12 to the VAT Act, to serve a notice of appeal with respect to that decision. . . .

Note—Words omitted are not relevant for the purposes of the climate change levy.

Goods and chattels not subject to levy

6 No distress shall be levied on any goods and chattels mentioned in Schedule 1 which at the time of levy are located in a place and used for a purpose mentioned in that Schedule.

Times for levying distress

7—(1) Subject to paragraph (2) below, a levy of distress shall commence only during the period between eight o'clock in the morning and eight o'clock at night on any day of the week but it may be continued thereafter outside that period until the levy is completed.

(2) Where a person holds himself out as conducting any profession, trade or business during hours which are partly within and partly outside, or wholly outside the period mentioned in paragraph (1) above, a levy of distress may be commenced at any time during that period or during the hours of any day in which he holds himself out as conducting that profession, trade or business and it may be continued thereafter outside that period or those hours until the levy is completed.

Costs

8—(1) A person in respect of whose goods and chattels a warrant has been signed shall be liable to pay to an officer or authorised person all costs, in connection with anything done under these Regulations described in column 1 of Schedule 2, as determined in accordance with column 2 of that Schedule.

(2) An authorised person may, after deducting and accounting for the amount of relevant tax to the Commissioners, retain costs from any amount received.

Sale

9 If any person upon whose goods and chattels distress has been levied does not pay the amount of relevant tax due together with costs within 5 days of a levy, an officer or authorised person may sell the distress for payment of the amount of relevant tax and costs; and the officer or authorised person, after deducting and retaining the amount of relevant tax and costs shall restore any surplus to the owner of the goods upon which distress was levied.

Disputes as to costs

10—(1) In the case of any dispute as to costs, the amount of those costs shall be taxed by a district judge of the county court of the district where the distress was levied, and he may make such order as he thinks fit as to the costs of the taxation.

(2) In the application of this regulation to Northern Ireland, in the case of any dispute as to costs, the amount of those costs shall be taxed in the same manner as costs in equity suits or proceedings in the county court in Northern Ireland.

SCHEDULE 1

GOODS AND CHATTELS NOT SUBJECT TO LEVY

Regulation 6

1 Any of the following goods and chattels which are located in a dwelling house at which distress is being levied and are reasonably required for the domestic needs of any person residing in that dwelling house—

(*a*) beds and bedding;
(*b*) household linen;
(*c*) chairs and settees;
(*d*) tables;
(*e*) food;
(*f*) lights and light fittings;
(*g*) heating appliances;
(*h*) curtains;
(*i*) floor coverings;
(*j*) furniture, equipment and utensils used for cooking, storing or eating food;
(*k*) refrigerators;
(*l*) articles used for cleaning, mending, or pressing clothes;
(*m*) articles used for cleaning the home;
(*n*) furniture used for storing—

(i) clothing, bedding or household linen;
(ii) articles used for cleaning the home;
(iii) utensils used for cooking or eating food;

(*o*) articles used for safety in the home;

(*p*) toys for the use of any child within the household;

(*q*) medical aids and medical equipment.

2 Any of the following items which are located in premises used for the purposes of any profession, trade or business—

(*a*) fire fighting equipment for use on the premises;

(*b*) medical aids and medical equipment for use on the premises.

SCHEDULE 2

SCALE OF COSTS

Regulation 8(1)

Matter	*Costs*
(1)	*(2)*
1 For attending to levy distress where payment is made of an amount of relevant tax due and distress is not levied:	£12·50.
2 For levying distress—	
(*a*) where an amount of relevant tax demanded and due does not exceed £100:	£12·50.
(*b*) where an amount of relevant tax demanded and due exceeds £100:	12½% on the first £100, 4% on the next £400, 2½% on the next £1,500, 1% on the next £8,000, ¼% on any additional sum.
3 For taking possession of distrained goods—	
(*a*) where a person remains in physical possession of goods at the place where distress was levied (the person to provide his own food and lodgings):	£4·50 per day.
(*b*) where possession is taken under a walking possession agreement:	£7·00.
4 For appraising goods upon which distress has been levied:	Reasonable costs of appraisement.
5 For arranging removal and storage of goods upon which distress has been levied:	Reasonable costs of arrangement.
6 For removing and storing goods upon which distress has been levied:	Reasonable costs of removal and storage.
7 For advertising the sale of goods upon which distress has been levied:	Reasonable costs of advertising.
8 For selling the distress—	
(*a*) where a sale by auction is held at the auctioneer's premises:	15% of the sum realised.
(*b*) where a sale by auction is held elsewhere:	7½% of the sum realised and auctioneer's reasonable costs.
(*c*) where a sale by other means is undertaken:	7½% of the sum realised and reasonable costs.

9 In addition to any amount specified in this scale in respect of the supply of goods or services on which value added tax is chargeable there may be added a sum equivalent to value added tax at the appropriate rate on that amount.

2000/1973

POLLUTION PREVENTION AND CONTROL (ENGLAND AND WALES) REGULATIONS 2000

Revocation—These Regulations revoked by the Environmental Permitting (England and Wales) Regulations, SI 2007/3538 reg 74(1), Sch 22 with effect from 6 April 2008.

2000/3350

FINANCE ACT 2000, SCHEDULE 6 PART V, (APPOINTED DAY) ORDER 2000

Made by the Treasury under the Finance Act 2000 s 30(3)

Made .... *21 December 2000*

1 This Order may be cited as the Finance Act 2000, Schedule 6 Part V, (Appointed Day) Order 2000.

2 The date appointed as the day on which paragraphs 59 and 60 of Part V of Schedule 6 to the Finance Act 2000 come into force is 2 January 2001.

3 The date appointed as the day on which paragraphs 53, 54, 55, 56, 57, 58 and 61 of Part V of Schedule 6 to the Finance Act 2000 come into force is 29 January 2001.

2001/7

CLIMATE CHANGE LEVY (REGISTRATION AND MISCELLANEOUS PROVISIONS) REGULATIONS 2001

Made by the Commissioners of Customs and Excise under FA 2000 s 30, Sch 6 paras 59, 60, 114, 115(4), 116, 117(1), 146(1), 146(4) and 146(7)

Made .... *4 January 2001*
Laid before the House of Commons .... *5 January 2001*
Coming into force .... *29 January 2001*

PART I
PRELIMINARY

Citation and commencement

1 These Regulations may be cited as the Climate Change Levy (Registration and Miscellaneous Provisions) Regulations 2001 and shall come into force on 29th January 2001.

PART II
REGISTRATION

Notification of registrability: form, manner, timing, etc

2—(1) A person who is required to notify the Commissioners under paragraph 55(1) of the Act (notification of registrability for climate change levy) must do so on Form CCL 1.
(2) But a partner so required must do so on Form CCL 1 and Form CCL 2.
(3) Such notification must contain and provide full information and particulars about every matter referred to on Form CCL 1 and, in the case of a partner, Form CCL 2 together with such further details as the Commissioners may require.
(4) A person so required on 29th January 2001 must deliver the notification to the Commissioners no later than 28th February 2001.
(5) A person to whom paragraph (4) does not apply, but who becomes so required after 29th January 2001, must deliver the notification to the Commissioners within 30 days starting from the day after becoming so required.
(6) A person who is required but fails to comply with this regulation remains subject to paragraph 55(1) of the Act.

Changes in particulars

3—(1) A person who has made a notification (the "original notification") to the Commissioners under regulation 2(1), 2(2) or 2(3) at any time must also, as appropriate, notify them about the following items.
(2) The first such item is any inaccuracy or inadequacy in the information, particulars or details contained in or provided with the original notification.

(3) The second such item is any change in circumstances that causes that information or those particulars or details to become inaccurate or inadequate.
(4) The third such item is any change in circumstances relating to that person, that person's business or any other matter with respect to which particulars are contained in the register (or would, were the person registered).
(5) A notification required by this regulation must—
 (*a*) be given in writing,
 (*b*) provide full particulars enabling the register to be kept up to date, and
 (*c*) be delivered to the Commissioners within 30 days.
(6) The first of those 30 days begins, as the case requires, on—
 (*a*) the day after the person discovers that the original notification was inaccurate or is in a position to rectify the inadequacy in that notification (see paragraph (2)), or
 (*b*) the day after the change in circumstances occurred (see paragraphs (3) and (4)).
(7) The full particulars referred to in paragraph (5)(*b*) include (but are not limited to)—
 (*a*) the nature of the relevant inaccuracy, inadequacy or change;
 (*b*) the date on which the inaccuracy in the original notification was discovered or the inadequacy could be rectified;
 (*c*) the date on which the change occurred;
 (*d*) the nature of the inaccuracy, inadequacy or change;
 (*e*) the correct information, particulars or details.
(8) A relevant change of circumstances under paragraph (3) or (4) above includes (but is not limited to)—
 (*a*) the person's name, trading name, address or principal place of business;
 (*b*) the person's status (namely, as sole proprietor, partner, unincorporated body, or body corporate);
 (*c*) the name and address of a partner or a change in the membership of a partnership;
 (*d*) the name and address of a trustee or beneficiary of a trust.
(9) The Commissioners may, on their own initiative or following a notification under this regulation, correct an entry in the register in a case where they are satisfied that it should be corrected or otherwise brought up to date.
(10) Where a person makes a notification under this regulation that itself is or becomes inaccurate, inadequate or misleading, that notification must be treated in the same way as an original notification for the purposes of paragraphs (1) to (9).

Finishing taxable activities

4—(1) This regulation applies to a person who is required to notify the Commissioners that he ceases to intend making, or having made to him, taxable supplies in respect of which he would be the person liable to account for levy (paragraph 57(1) of the Act).
(2) Such a person must make that notification in writing setting out—
 (*a*) the day on which the intention ceased, and
 (*b*) the day on which he made or received the final taxable supply.
(3) This notification must be delivered to the Commissioners within 30 days starting from the day after the intention ceased, or the final taxable supply was made or received, whichever is the later.

PART III
GROUPS

References to groups, etc

5—(1) This Part makes provision about two or more bodies corporate being treated as members of the same group for the purposes of the Act ("group treatment").
(2) For those purposes, or any regulation or direction made by or under the Act—
 (*a*) a body corporate is a member of a group at any time in relation to which it falls to be treated as such a member in accordance with this Part; and
 (*b*) the body corporate which is to be taken to be the representative member for a group at any time is the member of the group which in relation to that time is the representative member under this Part in the case of that group.
(3) A body corporate that is a member of a group shall, under Part V of the Act, be registered in the name of the representative member.

Eligibility for group treatment

6—(1) Subject to the provisions of this Part, two or more bodies corporate are eligible to be treated as members of a group if—
 (*a*) at least one of them is resident in the United Kingdom,
 (*b*) they are all under the same control, and
 (*c*) each of them—

(i) is registered, or is required to notify or has notified the Commissioners under paragraph 55(1) of the Act (notification of registrability), and
(ii) is not a person to whom paragraph 57(1) of the Act applies (loss of registrability).

(2) For the purposes of this regulation, two or more bodies are under the same control if—
(*a*) one of them controls each of the others;
(*b*) one person (whether a body corporate or an individual) controls all of them; or
(*c*) two or more individuals carrying on a business in partnership control all of them.

(3) For the purposes of this regulation, a body corporate shall be taken to control another body corporate only if—
(*a*) it is empowered by statute to control that body's activities, or
(*b*) it is that body's holding company within the meaning of [1159 of and Schedule 6 to][1] the Companies Act [2006][1];

and an individual or individuals shall be taken to control a body corporate only if (were he or they a company) he or they would be that body corporate's holding company within the meaning of [those provisions][1].

(4) A body corporate shall not be the representative member for a group at any time when it does not have an established place of business in the United Kingdom.

Amendments—[1] In para (3), words substituted for words "736 of", "1985" and "that section", by the Companies Act 2006 (Consequential Amendments) (Taxes and National Insurance) Order, SI 2009/1890 art 4(1)(*a*) with effect from 1 October 2009.

Liability for levy due from members of a group

7—(1) Group treatment shall not affect a body corporate being charged with levy in respect of a taxable supply whether to or from another member of the group or otherwise.

(2) However any levy with which a body corporate is charged in respect of a taxable supply treated as made while that body corporate is a member of a group shall be treated for the purposes of the Act as if it were the representative member for that group (instead of that body) which is charged with the levy.

(3) Accordingly the obligation on a member of a group to make a return pursuant to regulations made under paragraph 41 of the Act shall be discharged by the representative member making a return representing the aggregate of what would be the individual returns for the group members were it not for the group treatment.

(4) All bodies corporate who are members of a group when any levy becomes due from the representative member, together with any bodies corporate who become members of the group while any levy remains unpaid, shall be jointly and severally liable for any levy due from the representative member.

(5) References in this regulation to levy being or becoming due from the representative member include references to any amounts being or becoming recoverable as if they were levy due from that member.

Group treatment

8—(1) A body corporate shall be treated as a member of a group only—
(*a*) if a written application by that body corporate for such treatment is approved by the Commissioners, and
(*b*) from a date specified by the Commissioners for such treatment.

(2) A body corporate shall be the representative member for a group only—
(*a*) if a written application by that body corporate for this purpose is approved by the Commissioners, and
(*b*) from a date specified by the Commissioners for this purpose.

(3) The Commissioners need not approve an application by a body corporate to be a member of a group if they are not satisfied that every other proposed member agrees to the body corporate in question being a member of that proposed group.

(4) The Commissioners need not approve an application by a body corporate to be a representative member for a group if they are not satisfied that every proposed member agrees to the body corporate in question being the representative member for that proposed group.

(5) Any application under paragraph (1) or (2) must—
(*a*) be made in writing by the body corporate in question, and
(*b*) include such information and declaration as the Commissioners require.

(6) A body corporate that is a member of a group—
(*a*) shall no longer be a member of that group from the time it ceases to be eligible for group treatment; and
(*b*) shall notify the Commissioners in writing that it will cease or has ceased to be eligible for group treatment.

(7) The notification required by paragraph (6)(*b*) shall be delivered to the Commissioners no later than the earlier of 30 days after the body corporate becomes aware that it will cease to be eligible or 30 days after the body corporate ceases to be eligible.

(8) A body corporate that is the representative member for a group—

(*a*) shall no longer be the representative member for that group from the time it ceases to be eligible to be a representative member; and

(*b*) shall notify the Commissioners in writing that it will cease to be eligible to be a representative member.

(9) The notification required by paragraph (8)(*b*) shall be delivered to the Commissioners no later than the earlier of 30 days after the body corporate becomes aware that it will cease to be eligible or 30 days after the body corporate ceases to be eligible.

(10) The bodies corporate that are treated as members of a group shall take all reasonable steps to ensure that one of their number is the representative member for the group.

(11) If it appears to the Commissioners that there is no representative member for a group they may specify one of the eligible bodies corporate in that group as being the representative member and shall then notify each of the members in writing accordingly.

(12) Any body corporate specified by the Commissioners under paragraph (11), and remaining eligible, shall be taken to be the representative member of the group in question until a lawful substitution takes effect.

(13) A specification made or notice served under paragraph (11) may have effect from a time earlier than when it is made or served.

(14) The first of the 30 days referred to in paragraphs (7) and (9) is the first day after the one on which the body corporate becomes aware that it will cease to be eligible or the day after the one on which the body corporate ceases to be eligible, as the case may require.

Modifications, etc

9—(1) Where—

(*a*) any bodies corporate are treated as members of a group, and

(*b*) a written application for membership from a further eligible body corporate, that includes such information and declaration as they may require, is approved by the Commissioners,

then, from a time specified by the Commissioners, that further body corporate shall be included as a member of that group.

(2) The Commissioners need not approve an application by a body corporate under paragraph (1) if they are not satisfied that every existing member agrees to the further body corporate being a member of the group.

(3) The Commissioners need not specify a time under paragraph (1)(*b*) above that—

(*a*) is sooner than 30 days after the day they receive the relevant application, or

(*b*) is not the first day of an accounting period applying to the group by or under regulations made under paragraph 41 of the Act.

(4) Where any bodies corporate are treated as members of a group and a written application for the purpose, that includes such information and declaration as they may require, is made to the Commissioners, then, from a time specified by the Commissioners—

(*a*) a body corporate shall be excluded from the bodies so treated;

(*b*) one of those bodies corporate shall be substituted for another body corporate as the representative member; or

(*c*) the bodies corporate shall no longer be treated as members of a group.

(5) The Commissioners need not approve an application under paragraph (4) if they are not satisfied that every existing member agrees to the application in question.

(6) The Commissioners need not specify a time under paragraph (4)(*a*), 4(*b*) or 4(*c*) that is

(*a*) sooner than 30 days after the one on which they receive the relevant application, or

(*b*) is not the first day of an accounting period applying to the group by or under regulations made under paragraph 41 of the Act.

(7) Where a body corporate ceases at any time to be treated as a member of a group, and—

(*a*) there is only one other body corporate which was treated as a member of that group immediately before that time, or

(*b*) none of the other bodies corporate which were so treated immediately before that time has an established place of business in the United Kingdom,

the other body corporate or, as the case may be, each of the other bodies corporate shall also cease as from that time to be treated as a member of the group.

Miscellaneous

10—(1) The Commissioners may refuse in full or in part an application under regulation 8(1), 8(2), 9(1) or 9(4) if it appears to them necessary to do so for the protection of the revenue.

(2) A person who has made an application or notification to the Commissioners under this Part must notify them immediately should any information contained in or provided in connection with that application or notification be or become inaccurate.

11—(1) The Commissioners may, by written notice served on each member of a group, exclude a body from group treatment if it appears to them necessary to do so for the protection of the revenue or that the body in question is unable to comply with the requirements of group treatment.
(2) Such exclusion may take effect from a time earlier than when the written notice is served.

PART IV
PARTNERSHIPS AND OTHER SPECIAL CASES

Partnerships

12—(1) This regulation applies for determining by what person anything required to be done by or under the Act is to be done where, apart from this regulation, that requirement would fall on persons carrying on business in partnership.
(2) Any such requirement shall be the joint and several responsibility of every partner.
(3) Subject to paragraphs (4) and (5):
(*a*) compliance with such a requirement by at least one of the partners shall be sufficient compliance by all of them; and
(*b*) in the case of a partnership whose principal place of business is in Scotland, such compliance by a person duly authorised by the partnership shall be sufficient compliance by the partners.
(4) Each partner must comply with the requirement imposed by regulation 2 in relation to the Form CCL 2.
(5) A person joining or leaving a partnership, as the case requires, must comply with the requirements imposed by regulation 3 so far as they apply to any change in the membership of a partnership.

Other unincorporated associations

13—(1) This regulation applies for determining by what persons anything required to be done by or under the Act is to be done where, apart from this regulation, that requirement would fall on persons carrying on business together as an unincorporated body other than a partnership.
(2) Any such requirement shall be the joint and several responsibility of—
(*a*) first, every person holding office in that body as president, chairman, treasurer, secretary or other similar office; or
(*b*) secondly, if there is no such office holder, every person who is a member of a committee by which the affairs of that body are managed; or
(*c*) thirdly, if there is no such office holder or member, every person carrying on that business.
(3) Compliance with such a requirement by one or more of the persons referred to in paragraph (2) shall be sufficient compliance with that requirement by all of them.
(4) But a purported notification under regulation 2(1), 2(2) or 2(3) shall not be treated as complying with any of those regulations unless it is made by a person required to do so under paragraph (2)(*a*), (2)(*b*) or (2)(*c*) of this regulation, as appropriate.

Non resident taxpayers: requirement and provision for tax representatives

14—(1) This regulation applies to a person (a "non-resident taxpayer") who—
(*a*) is or is required to be registered for the purposes of the levy, and
(*b*) is not resident in the United Kingdom.
(2) A person who meets this description must notify the Commissioners in writing of this fact.
(3) Such notification must be delivered to the Commissioners within 30 days starting from the day after the first day on which the person meets the description.
(4) The Commissioners may—
(*a*) require or permit such a taxpayer to appoint some person resident in the United Kingdom to act as his tax representative for the purposes of the levy with effect from a date they specify [(for such residence, see paragraph 156 of the Act)][1], and
(*b*) oblige the taxpayer to request them, no later than such earlier date as they may specify, to approve the appointment of that person as the tax representative.
[In regulations 17(4)(*a*), 18(1)(*e*) and 19(5), "eligible" only refers to a person's being so resident in the United Kingdom.][1]
(5) Any appointment of a person as a tax representative shall take effect only if and from the date approved by the Commissioners.
(6) A request for approval under paragraph (4)(*b*) must be in writing and contain such information and particulars, and corresponding declaration by the taxpayer and the proposed tax representative, as the Commissioners may require.

Amendments—[1] Words in para (4) inserted by the Climate Change Levy (Miscellaneous Amendments) Regulations, SI 2005/1716 reg 8 with effect from 22 July 2005.

15—(1) A non-resident taxpayer may appoint a different tax representative as a replacement for a tax representative whose appointment has taken effect.
(2) Such appointment shall take effect only if and from a date approved by the Commissioners.

(3) A request to the Commissioners for the purposes of paragraph (2) must be in writing and contain such information and particulars, and corresponding declaration by the taxpayer and the proposed replacement tax representative, as the Commissioners may require.

16—(1) The Commissioners may, with effect from a date or dates they specify, for good cause and by way of written notice served on the non-resident taxpayer—
- (*a*) withdraw their approval of any person appointed as a tax representative for that non-resident taxpayer,
- (*b*) require that non-resident taxpayer to replace any tax representative with a different tax representative, and
- (*c*) oblige that non-resident taxpayer to request their approval for a person's appointment as a replacement tax representative.

(2) Regulations 14(5) and (6) shall apply for the purposes of this regulation in corresponding manner as they apply for the purposes of regulation 14(4).

17—(1) This regulation applies in a case where the Commissioners require the appointment of a tax representative under regulation 14(4)(*a*) and the non-resident taxpayer—
- (*a*) becomes liable to a penalty under paragraph 114(3) of the Act (penalty for failing in obligation to request Commissioners' approval of tax representative), or
- (*b*) unreasonably fails to obtain the Commissioners' approval in accordance with regulation 14(4)(*b*) (approval of tax representative).

(2) Where this regulation applies, the Commissioners may give a direction requiring a specified person to be treated as the appointed and approved tax representative of that non-resident taxpayer from a specified date.

(3) Accordingly a person specified in a direction under paragraph (2) shall be treated as the tax representative of the non-resident taxpayer from the specified date until such date as the Commissioners may specify in a further direction.

(4) The Commissioners may only specify a person under paragraph (3) who—
- (*a*) is eligible to act as a tax representative, and
- (*b*) is suitable in all the circumstances to be the tax representative for the relevant non-resident taxpayer.

(5) The Commissioners may give a direction requiring a specified person to be treated as the appointed and approved tax representative of a non-resident taxpayer as a replacement for a person specified in a direction under paragraph (2) of this regulation.

(6) Paragraphs (3) and (4) apply in relation to paragraph (5) in corresponding manner as they apply to paragraph (2).

(7) Regulations 15 and 16 do not apply in relation to a person specified in a direction under this regulation.

18—(1) A person shall cease to be the tax representative for a non-resident taxpayer from when—
- (*a*) the non-resident taxpayer ceases to be registered;
- (*b*) the non-resident taxpayer replaces that person with a different tax representative under regulation 15 or 16;
- (*c*) the Commissioners so direct under regulation 17;
- (*d*) the person dies or becomes incapacitated or subject to an insolvency procedure;
- (*e*) the person ceases to be eligible to be a tax representative;
- (*f*) the person delivers to the Commissioners notification in writing that he withdraws as tax representative for the non-resident taxpayer; or
- (*g*) the non-resident taxpayer delivers to the Commissioners notification in writing that he withdraws an appointment that they permitted but did not require.

(2) A person who is specified in a direction under regulation 17 shall not—
- (*a*) cease to be (or be treated as) the tax representative except in accordance with that regulation; or
- (*b*) be permitted to withdraw under paragraph (1)(*f*) of this regulation.

(3) The name of a tax representative (or a person treated as such) shall be registered against the name of the non-resident taxpayer of whom that person is (or is treated as) the representative (paragraph 53(2) of the Act).

(4) That name shall be deleted from the register if the person ceases to be the tax representative for that non-resident taxable person and the Commissioners consider it appropriate to do so.

19—(1) A tax representative (or a person treated as such) shall notify and provide full particulars to the Commissioners in writing about any of the following matters.

(2) Such notification must be delivered to the Commissioners no later than 30 days starting from the first day after the matter arises.

(3) The first matter is any change in the name, constitution or ownership of the tax representative's business or of any event that may require the register to be varied.

(4) The second matter is the tax representative lawfully ceasing to be the appointed tax representative of the relevant non-resident taxpayer.
(5) The third matter is the tax representative ceasing to be eligible to act as a tax representative.

PART V
PENALTIES

Penalties to be provided for by regulations

20 A person who fails to comply with a requirement imposed on him by or under any of the following regulations shall be liable to a penalty of £250 for each such failure—
(*a*) regulation 2(1), 2(2), 2(3), 2(4) or 2(5) (form, manner, etc of notification about registrability);
(*b*) regulation 3(1), 3(5) or 3(10) (changes in particulars of notification about registrability);
(*c*) regulation 4(2) (notification of ceasing taxable activities);
(*d*) regulation 14(2) or 14(3) (notification by non resident taxpayer);
(*e*) regulation 19(1) or 19(2) (notification by tax representative).

PART VI
INTERPRETATION

Interpretation

21 In these regulations, except where the context requires otherwise—
"the Act" refers to Schedule 6 to the Finance Act 2000 and any reference to a paragraph or Part of the Act refers to the appropriate paragraph or Part of that Schedule;
"Form CCL 1" and "Form CCL 2" refer respectively to the forms numbered 1 and 2 in the Schedule to these Regulations (or to such forms as the Commissioners are satisfied are to like effect);
"levy" refers to climate change levy;
"Part", "regulation" or "regulations" refers to the appropriate Part, regulation or regulations of these Regulations;
"partner" refers to a person carrying on a business in partnership with at least one other person.

SCHEDULE

FORM 1

Climate Change Levy (CCL)
Application for Registration

HM Revenue & Customs

Climate Change Levy (CCL)
Application for Registration

Completing this form

Before you complete this form please make sure that you read *CCL1 Notes* to help you complete your Climate Change Levy (CCL) Application for Registration.

You **do not** need to complete this form if you are not resident in the United Kingdom **and**

- do not make taxable supplies as a gas or electricity utility in the United Kingdom, or
- do not receive or intend to receive taxable supplies of liquefied petroleum gas or solid fuel from a supplier outside the United Kingdom.

Please use capital letters and write clearly in black ink.

When you have completed and signed this form, please send it to:
HM Revenue & Customs
Central Collection Unit (CCL)
Alexander House
Southend-on-Sea
SS99 1AY

1 Please show your Departmental Trader Registration number

☐☐☐ ☐☐☐☐ ☐☐ ☐☐☐☐

2 Please give the name of this business

3 Do you have a trading name?

No ☐ Yes ☐

If yes, please give the trading name of the business

4 What is the legal status of your business?

If your business is a partnership, you must complete and return form *CCL2* as well as this form.

Incorporated Company ☐

Sole Proprietor ☐

Partnership ☐

Public Corporation ☐

Local Authority ☐

Non-profit making body/unincorporated body ☐

Please give, if applicable, the following details from your certificate of incorporation

Company registration number

Date of incorporation *DD MM YYYY*

5 Is your business a Trust?

If your business is a Trust, you must complete and return form *CCL2T* and *CCL2TB* to give details of all Trustees and beneficiaries of the Trust, as well as this form.

No ☐ Yes ☐

6 Give the address of your principal place of business

Postcode

Phone number

Fax number

email address

Website address

7 Please give the anticipated date or actual date of your first taxable supply of an energy product subject to CCL.

- This date must be no earlier than 1 April 2001.
- Please see *CCL1 Notes* for further information on taxable supplies.

Please note: If you are applying as the representative member of a CCL group, please show the date or anticipated date of the first taxable supply to be made by any group member including the representative member.

DD MM YYYY

8 Please indicate your main and subsidiary business activities by inserting the appropriate codes in the boxes.

1 Energy supplier
2 Energy imports
3 Energy exports
4 Self supply of energy

Main

Subsidiary(ies)

Do you use a combined heat and power (CHP) plant to generate energy?

No Yes

If no, go to question 9

If yes, are you participating in the CHP Quality Assurance (CHPQA) Programme?
This programme is run by the Department for Environment, Food and Rural Affairs (DEFRA).

No Yes

If yes, what is your CHPQA certificate number?
If you have more than one CHPQA number please give details in a separate letter.

Has DEFRA issued a certificate confirming that you have a fully exempt CHP plant for CCL purposes?

No Yes

If no, you are registrable in respect of supplies made or supplies you intend to make by any of your partially exempt CHP plants if those supplies exceed the limit advised to you on the DEFRA certificate. Please see the CCL Notice CCL1/2 for more details of the registration requirements for partially exempt CHP plants.

If yes, you are not registrable for CCL in respect of your fully exempt CHP plant(s) for the period covered by the certificate. If the only supplies you are making are from fully exempt CHP plants certified by DEFRA you do not need to complete this form.

If you are applying as the representative member of a CCL group please complete the boxes including CHP plants for all group members.

9 Has your energy supply business been transferred to you as a going concern?

No Yes

Complete the following questions if:

- you are taking over an existing energy supply business from someone else or
- you have changed the legal status of your business.

Please give the Departmental Trader Registration number of the person who transferred the business to you.

Date of transfer *DD MM YYYY*

Do you wish to keep the previous owner's Departmental Trader Registration number?

No Yes

10 Please indicate the preferred stagger for your returns by ticking the appropriate box.
If you intend to apply for non-standard tax periods tick the stagger period most closely matching your non-standard periods.

Stagger 0
Monthly Returns

Stagger 1
Quarters Ending Mar/Jun/Sept/Dec

Stagger 2
Quarters Ending Jan/Apr/Jul/Oct

Stagger 3
Quarters Ending Feb/May/Aug/Nov

11 Do you intend to apply for non-standard tax periods?

No Yes

Do you intend to use the annual return scheme for CCL?

No Yes

Please send me further information about the annual return scheme for CCL

No Yes

12 Please indicate which energy products you supply and where appropriate, those generated from renewable sources. Please also show the number of units supplied each year to business and domestic customers.
If you are applying as the representative member of a CCL group please estimate the energy products supplied for all group companies in the table.

Type	Energy supplied (Y/N)	Renewable source (Y/N/partly)	Business units supplied each year	Domestic or non-business charity units supplied each year
Electricity			kWh	kWh
Gas			kWh	kWh
Liquefied Petroleum Gas (LPG)			kg	kg
Solid and other fuels (coal and lignite, coke and semi-coke of coal and lignite and petroleum coke)			kg	kg

13 Do you want to apply for group registration and register as the representative member of a Climate Change Levy Group?

No ☐ Yes ☐

If yes, you must complete forms *CCL50* and *CCL51*

14 Do you want to apply for divisional registration?

No ☐ Yes ☐

If yes, each division of your company to be registered separately must complete form *CCL1D*

Please note: you cannot apply for both group registration and divisional registration for your company.

15 Have you been involved with any other business registered for CCL or VAT in the last 5 years?

No ☐ Yes ☐

If yes, please give the Departmental Trader Registration number or VAT number.
If you are a partnership or a limited company this means any businesses in which any partners or directors in the business you are seeking to register have been involved in as a sole proprietor, partner or director.
Continue on a separate sheet if necessary.

16 Please give details of your bank or building society account.

If you have a Girobank Account give the sort code and account number for making payments into your account – shown on the front of your cheque book

Sort code

Account number

Girobank Account number

Account title

17 Are you resident in the United Kingdom?

No ☐ Yes ☐

If yes, please go to question 22

18 Do you make taxable supplies as a gas or electricity utility in the United Kingdom?

No ☐ Yes ☐

If yes, you will be liable to register for CCL.
Please go to question 20

19 Do you receive or intend to receive taxable supplies of liquefied petroleum gas or solid fuel from a supplier outside the United Kingdom?

Yes ☐ No ☐

20 Please show your country of residence

☐

21 Do you want to appoint a tax representative?

No ☐ Yes ☐

If yes, form *CCL1TR* must be completed

22 Is your accounts system computerised?

No ☐ Yes ☐

If yes, please give details

Accounting software

☐

Version

☐

Declaration

Please sign and date the declaration below. (For corporate bodies, a director or company secretary must sign the form.) Please tick the appropriate box.

Sole Proprietor ☐

Partner ☐

Company Secretary ☐

Director ☐

Beneficiary of a Trust ☐

Trustee ☐

Authorised Official ☐

I declare that the information given on this form and in any attached sheets is true and complete.

Name

☐

Signature

☐

Date *DD MM YYYY*

☐☐ ☐☐ ☐☐☐☐

For official use

Date of receipt

☐

CCL ID completed/attached

☐

Keyer's initials

☐

Checker's initials

☐

DTRN

☐☐☐ ☐☐☐☐ ☐☐ ☐☐☐

EDR

☐☐☐☐☐☐☐☐

HM Revenue & Customs

Climate Change Levy
Notes for completion of form CCL1

Completing form CCL1

Please read these notes before you fill in the application form *CCL1*. They give you further advice to help you answer the questions correctly.

Please use capital letters and write clearly in black ink. Please make sure that you complete all boxes and include all the information required. We have included a checklist to help you at the end of these notes.

Apply at the correct time. Remember that if you do not apply for registration at the correct time you may be liable to a financial penalty.

Notes to consider

If you are applying to be registered as the representative member of a CCL group please give details of your own company in all questions except for the following: Question 7 should show the date or anticipated date of the first taxable supply to be made by any prospective group member. The information requested for CHP plants in question 8 should be provided for all prospective group members including the representative member. Question 12, details of energy products, should also include details for the prospective representative member and all prospective group members.

If you are applying to be registered as a division the representative of the corporate body should complete form *CCL1* on behalf of the division. Divisional details should be given for questions 8, 12, 16 and 22 but details of the corporate body should be given for other questions. The divisional name should be given at question 3. Please see question 14 of the *CCL1* application form and part *14 Divisional registration* of these notes for more details of divisional registration.

If you are applying for group or divisional registration, you should refer to the CCL Notice CCL1/1 for details of the requirements of group or divisional registration.

When you have completed and signed this form, please send it to:

HM Revenue & Customs
Central Collection Unit (CCL)
Alexander House
Southend-on-Sea
SS99 1AY

General

A person or a business that makes or intends to make taxable supplies, or receives or intends to receive a taxable supply is required to be registered if they are responsible for payment of the CCL to HM Revenue & Customs. This will be so where they make or intend to make supplies of taxable commodities in the United Kingdom (including self supplies), or receive or intend to receive supplies of liquefied petroleum gas or solid fuel products from a supplier resident outside the United Kingdom. A person or unregistered business must notify HM Revenue & Customs if they anticipate becoming, or have become, registrable. Please see part 7 of these notes *Taxable supply of an energy product* for a definition of taxable supplies and the CCL Notice CCL1/1 for further details of the registration requirements.

If you are a utility for gas or electricity supplies because you hold a supply licence, or because you have been made a utility by directions or regulations, then it is likely that you will have to register and charge CCL.

Exceptions

If all the energy supplies you make are excluded from CCL owing to domestic or charity use (or the supplies are deemed to be domestic supplies because of the small quantities involved) you will not be required to register for CCL. You will need to keep records to substantiate the exclusions. Please see the CCLNotice CCL1/3 for more details of excluded supplies.

If you generate electricity primarily for your own use you may be classified as an autogenerator and if so, you will not be required to register for CCL. Likewise if you are an exempt unlicensed electricity supplier you are not required to register.

You will also not be required to register if you only make supplies made from a fully exempt Combined Heat and Power plant (CHP plant) for the period covered by a certificate issued under the CHP Quality Assurance (CHPQA) Programme run by the Department for Environment, Food and Rural Affairs, please see part 8 of these notes *Main and subsidiary business activities* for further details of CHP plants.

Please see the enclosed CCLNotice CCL1/2 for further details of autogenerators, exempt unlicensed electricity suppliers and CHP plants.

Payment methods

Please send your returns to the Central Collection Unit (CCU). We will normally collect the CCL by BACS Direct Debit. Paying by direct debit is easy, quick and you will be protected by the BACS money back guarantee. Please contact the CCU to ask for the direct debit mandate and return it to the CCU at least one month before you send in your first return. If you want to pay by an alternative electronic method, please contact the CCU. Postal payments should be sent direct to the CCU. Please see the front page of these notes for the address of the CCU, their phone number is **01702 366558** or **01702 366364**. For further details of payment methods please see the CCL Notice CCL1/1.

1 Departmental Trader Registration number

If your business is registered with HM Revenue & Customs please enter the Departmental Trader Registration number in the box provided. If you are not sure of this number please enter your VAT number.

2 Name of business

Please show the name of the business in accordance with the notes below:

Incorporated company: If your business is an incorporated company please give the company's name.

Sole proprietor: If you are a sole proprietor give your title (for example, Mr, Mrs, Miss or Ms) followed by your name in full and your surname. Do not use initials.

Partnership: If your business is a partnership the names of the partners must be shown on form *CCL2*.

Divisional registration: For each division you wish to register separately the corporate body should enter the full name of the company and complete form *CCL1* and each division should complete form *CCL1D*. Please see question 14 of the *CCL1* application form and part 14 of these notes *Divisional registration*.

Group registration: If you wish to apply for group registration, the prospective representative member must complete forms *CCL1* and *CCL50*. Form *CCL51* should also be completed by the representative member with the details of the other members. Please see question 13 of the *CCL1* application form and part 13 of these notes *Group registration*.

3 Trading name

If you have a trading name please give the details here. Please give the name of the division if you are applying for divisional registration. Please use the format 'A Division of X Ltd'.

4 Legal status

Show the legal status of your business by entering the appropriate code number in the box. If the business is a company incorporated in the United Kingdom, (limited company) you should also show the company registration number and date shown on your certificate of incorporation.

If you are a non-profit making body registered as an incorporated company please tick 'incorporated company'.

5 Trust

If your business is a Trust, form *CCL2T* should be completed giving details of all Trustees and form *CCL2TB* should be completed giving details of the beneficiaries of the Trust. Form *CCL1* should be completed by a Trustee if the business is run by the Trustees. If the business is run by the beneficiaries all beneficiaries should complete form *CCL1*.

6 Address of business

Give the address of your principal place of business. This is where invoices are issued from, orders are taken, deliveries are made and the day-to-day running of the business is carried out. Please also show phone number, fax number, email address and website address as appropriate.

7 Taxable supply of an energy product

A taxable supply is defined as a supply on or after 1 April 2001 of the following taxable commodities:

- electricity
- gas (any gas in a gaseous state that is of a kind supplied by a gas utility)
- liquefied petroleum gas (LPG) (any petroleum gas or other gaseous hydrocarbon in a liquid state)
- solid and other fuels (coal and lignite, coke and semi-coke of coal or lignite and petroleum coke).

8 Main and subsidiary business activities

Please indicate your main and subsidiary business activities (in relation to CCL) by entering the appropriate codes in the boxes. The codes are defined below:

1 – Energy supplier. You make taxable supplies of energy.
2 – Energy imports. You import energy.
3 – Energy exports. You export energy.
4 – Self supply of energy. This category will include energy suppliers to the National Grid who produce some energy for their own use.

Please see part 7 of these notes *Taxable supply of an energy product* for details of taxable energy supplies.

Special arrangements apply to energy suppliers who use a Combined Heat and Power (CHP) plant to generate energy and who are participating in the CHP Quality Assurance (CHPQA) Programme run by the Department for Environment, Food and Rural Affairs (DEFRA). Electricity from fully exempt CHP plants is not liable to CCL in the period covered by the CHP certificate issued by DEFRA.

FORM 2

Climate Change Levy (CCL)
Partnership Details

HM Customs and Excise

Climate Change Levy (CCL)

Partnership Details

When you have completed and signed this form, please send it together with Form CCL 1 (Application for Registration) using the official envelope provided to:

The Controller
Central Collection Unit (CCL)
HM Customs and Excise
Alexander House
21 Victoria Avenue
Southend-on-Sea
SS99 1AY

Data Protection Act 1998

HM Customs and Excise collects information in order to administer the taxes for which it is responsible (such as VAT, insurance premium tax, excise duties, air passenger duty, landfill tax, climate change levy), and for detecting and preventing crime.

Where the law permits we may also get information about you from third parties, or give information to them, for example in order to check its accuracy, prevent or detect crime or protect public funds in other ways. These third parties may include the police, other government departments and agencies.

Complaints

If you have a complaint, please telephone the National Customs and Excise Advice Service, the telephone number is in the telephone directory.

If you are unhappy with our response you can ask the Adjudicator to look into your complaint. The Adjudicator reviews complaints not settled to your satisfaction by Customs. The recommendations of the Adjudicator are independent and the service is free. The Adjudicator only looks at complaints, not general enquiries. Telephone the Adjudicator on 020 7930 2292.

For official use only

Date of receipt:

DTR No:

These details form part of your application to be registered for Climate Change Levy

Trading name of partnership:

Please make sure that every partner completes and signs one of the sections below. If there is insufficient space to include all partners, please photocopy this form or contact the Central Collection Unit (page 1) for additional copies

Please use BLOCK LETTERS and write clearly in black ink or use typescript.

Full name of partner:

Home Address:

Postcode:

Home Telephone:

Signature: Date:

Full name of partner:

Home Address:

Postcode:

Home Telephone:

Signature: Date:

Full name of partner:

Home Address:

Postcode:

Home Telephone:

Signature: Date:

Full name of partner:

Home Address:

Postcode:

Home Telephone:

Signature: Date:

Full name of partner:

Home Address:

Postcode:

Home Telephone:

Signature: Date:

Full name of partner:

Home Address:

Postcode:

Home Telephone:

Signature: Date:

CCL 2 Page 3 IB(October 2000)

2001/486

CLIMATE CHANGE LEVY (COMBINED HEAT AND POWER STATIONS) EXEMPTION CERTIFICATE REGULATIONS 2001

Made by the Secretary of State for the Environment, Transport and the Regions under FA 2000 Sch 6 para 148(10), (11)

Made . . . .*21 February 2001*

Laid before Parliament . . . .*26 February 2001*

Coming into force . . . .*19 March 2001*

Citation and commencement

1 These Regulations may be cited as the Climate Change Levy (Combined Heat and Power Stations) Exemption Certificate Regulations 2001 and shall come into force on 19th March 2001.

Interpretation

2 In these Regulations,

"CHPQA" means the Combined Heat and Power Quality Assurance Standard, Issue 1, November 2000 published by the Department of the Environment, Transport and the Regions;

"CHPQA certificate" means a certificate issued in respect of a combined heat and power station following assessment of the station against criteria set out in CHPQA, and "CHPQA scheme reference number" means the number stated as the scheme reference number in that certificate;

"efficiency percentage" has the same meaning as in paragraph 15(4)(*b*) of Schedule 6;

"exemption certificate" means a certificate given by the Secretary of State under paragraph 148(4) or (5) of Schedule 6 (full-exemption and part-exemption certificates in respect of combined heat and power stations for the purposes of climate change levy);

"operator" means the person by whom a combined heat and power station is operated;

"prescribed conditions" means any conditions prescribed by regulations made by the Treasury under paragraph 148(4) of Schedule 6;

"Schedule 6" means Schedule 6 to the Finance Act 2000; and

"threshold efficiency percentage" has the same meaning as in paragraph 15(4)(*a*) of Schedule 6.

Applications for, and content of, exemption certificates

3—(1) An application for an exemption certificate in respect of a combined heat and power station shall be made by the operator in writing and shall be accompanied by a copy of the current CHPQA certificate relating to the station.

(2) The operator shall send a copy of the current CHPQA certificate relating to the station to the Secretary of State by 30th June in each year after the year in which an application is made in accordance with paragraph (1).

(3) An exemption certificate shall remain in force until revoked in accordance with regulation 4(2).

(4) An exemption certificate shall state—

(*a*) the date on which it comes into force (which shall not be earlier than the date on which it is issued);

(*b*) the CHPQA scheme reference number of the combined heat and power station to which it relates;

(*c*) whether the station is fully or partly exempt; and

(*d*) (as required by paragraph 148(6) of Schedule 6) its efficiency percentage.

Variation and revocation of exemption certificates

4—(1) If it appears to the Secretary of State that there has been a material change in the circumstances of a combined heat and power station such that—

(*a*) it no longer satisfies the prescribed conditions as being fully exempt; or

(*b*) in the case of a partly exempt station, it now satisfies the prescribed conditions as being fully exempt; or

(*c*) its efficiency percentage has fallen below, or, as the case may be, risen to equal or exceed the threshold efficiency percentage,

he shall vary its exemption certificate by revising the particulars mentioned in regulation 3(4)(c) or (d), as appropriate.

(2) If—

(*a*) a combined heat and power station ceases to operate;

(*b*) the operator fails to comply with regulation 3(2); or

(*c*) the operator makes a written request to that effect to the Secretary of State,

the Secretary of State shall revoke the exemption certificate.

2001/838

CLIMATE CHANGE LEVY (GENERAL) REGULATIONS 2001

Made by the Commissioners of Customs and Excise under FA 2000 s 30 and Sch 6 paras 19(1), 19(3), 21, 22, 23(4), 27(7), 27(8), 29(7), 41(1), 41(2), 43(4), 43(5), 44(5), 62, 63(4), 65, 73, 74, 100(2), 100(3), 118, 119, 120, 125, 146(1), 146(4) and 146(7)

Made . . . .*9 March 2001*

Laid before the House of Commons . . . . *12 March 2001*
Coming into force . . . . *1 April 2001*

PART I
PRELIMINARY

1 These Regulations may be cited as the Climate Change Levy (General) Regulations 2001 and shall come into force on 1st April 2001.

General interpretation

2—(1) In these Regulations and [the Schedules][1], except where the context requires otherwise—
"the Act" refers to Schedule 6 to the Finance Act 2000;
"CCL" refers to climate change levy;
"excluded part", "exempt part" . . . [3] and "reduced-rate part" refer, respectively, to that part of a supply of a taxable commodity that would, by itself, be excluded or exempt from CCL or would be . . . [3] a reduced-rate supply for CCL purposes;
"gas" refers to gas described by paragraph 3(1)(*b*) of the Act;
"Part", "regulation" or "regulations" refers to the appropriate Part, regulation or regulations of these Regulations;
"non-registrable electricity producer" refers to an electricity producer to whom a supply of a taxable commodity is not exempt under paragraph 14(1) of the Act (except in relation to uses of the electricity he produces for which that exemption is retained);
"published notice" refers to a notice published by the Commissioners and not withdrawn by a further notice;
"recipient" refers to the person to whom a supply of a taxable commodity is made;
"registrable person" refers to a person who is registered or required to be registered under Part V of the Act [(including, but for regulations 8 and 9 only (records), a person whom the Commissioners exempt from that requirement under Schedule 1 paragraph 5(9))][2];
. . . [1]
"supplier" refers to a person making a supply of a taxable commodity (but, in the case of regulations 11, 13 and 14, it only refers to the person who is liable to account for the CCL charged on the taxable supply in question (see paragraph 40(1) of the Act—suppliers, and paragraph 40(2) of the Act—supplies made by persons who are neither residents of the United Kingdom nor utilities));
"time of supply" refers to when a supply of a taxable commodity is treated as taking place by or under paragraphs 25 to 39 of the Act;
"working day" excludes Saturday, Sunday and any bank or public holiday.

(2) Where a provision of these Regulations requires the delivery of something to the Commissioners, it must be taken to include a requirement that delivery must be made to any address specified for the purpose in question by the Commissioners in a published notice.

Amendments—[1] In para (1), words substituted, and definition of "Schedule" revoked, by the CCL (General) (Amendment) Regulations, SI 2003/604 regs 2, 3 with effect from 1 April 2003.
[2] Words in definition of "registrable person" inserted by the Climate Change Levy (Miscellaneous Amendments) Regulations, SI 2005/1716 regs 2, 6 with effect from 22 July 2005. However, arrangements initiated or made before 22 July 2005 on the basis of SI 2001/838 Sch 1 para 5(5) or 5(6) as then in force remain subject to the provisions applicable when they were initiated or made (tax credit claims and corrections to over-estimated relief).
[3] In para (1), words ',"half-rate part" ' and 'a half-rate supply or' revoked by the Climate Change Levy (General) (Amendment) Regulations, SI 2007/2903 reg 2, Sch 1 para 1 with effect from 1 November 2007: SI 2007/2903 reg 1. These amendments do not apply in relation to a half-rate supply made before 1 April 2006: SI 2007/2903 reg 2, Sch 1 Note (*a*).

PART II
ACCOUNTING, PAYMENT, RECORDS, TAX CREDITS, REPAYMENTS, SET-OFF, ETC

Accounting periods

3—(1) A registrable person shall be subject to accounting periods.
(2) In the case of a registered person, these shall be each three month period ending on the dates notified to him at any time by the Commissioners for this purpose.
(3) In the case of any other registrable person, these shall be each three month period ending on 31st March, 30th June, 30th September or 31st December.
(4) However, in a particular case, the Commissioners may vary the start, end and length of any accounting period.

Returns

4—(1) A registrable person is obliged to make a return to the Commissioners covering each of his accounting periods.
(2) The registrable person is obliged to make that return no later than the last working day of the month immediately following the end of the period to which it relates.

(3) In the case of an accounting period that does not end on the last day of a month, the registrable person is obliged to make that return no later than the due day directed by the Commissioners.
(4) The Commissioners may allow the registrable person extra time in which to make that return.
(5) The registrable person must make that return in a form that is prescribed by the Commissioners in a published notice ("prescribed form").
(6) The registrable person must make that return by securing that it is delivered either to the address prescribed by the Commissioners in a published notice or to any other address that they may direct or allow.

Content of returns

5—(1) The registrable person must declare in the return the CCL due from him for the relevant accounting period, taking into consideration—

(*a*) the CCL due on taxable supplies—

(i) the time of supply of which is in that accounting period, and

(ii) for which he is liable to account;

and,

(*b*) any authorised or required adjustment or any correction of errors (see regulations 14(2), 17(3), 27 and 28 and, [Schedule 1 paragraph 8(1)(*b*)][1]).

(2) The registrable person must provide in the return accurate information about every matter that the prescribed form requires.
(3) The registrable person must sign, date and declare on the document forming his return that the information provided in it is true and complete.
(4) The registrable person must comply with paragraphs (1), (2) and (3) in the manner prescribed by the Commissioners in a published notice.

Amendments—[1] In para (1), words "in Schedule 1, paragraphs 5(9G) and 8(1)(*b*)" substituted by the Climate Change Levy (General) (Amendment) Regulations, SI 2007/2903 reg 2, Sch 1 para 2 with effect from 1 November 2007: SI 2007/2903 reg 1. This amendment does not apply in relation to a half-rate supply made before 1 April 2006: SI 2007/2903 reg 2, Sch 1 Note (*a*).

Payment

6—(1) A registrable person must pay to the Commissioners the amount of CCL due from him for a given accounting period no later than the due date for the return for that period (see regulations 4(2), 4(3) and 4(4)).
(2) The registrable person must make that payment by securing that it is delivered either to the address or bank account prescribed for this purpose by the Commissioners in a published notice or to any other address or bank account that they may direct or allow.
(3) The Commissioners may allow a registrable person who has made arrangements with them for the payment of any amount of CCL due from him by means of direct debit an extra 7 days in which the payment may be made.
(4) The Commissioners shall only act pursuant to paragraph (3) in accordance with conditions they shall stipulate in a published notice.

[Interpretation of Regulations 6B to 6G

6A In regulations 6B to 6G—

"authorised person" means a person who has been authorised by the Commissioners under regulation 6B(1), and "authorised" and "authorisation" shall be construed accordingly;

"current accounting year" means the period of 12 months commencing on a date indicated by the Commissioners in their notification of authorisation of a person, or while a person remains authorised, the most recent anniversary thereof, and is an accounting period within the meaning of regulation 3;

"the scheme" means the annual accounting scheme established by regulations 6B to 6G;

"transitional accounting period" means the period commencing on the first day of a person's accounting period in which the Commissioners authorise him to use the scheme, and ending on the day immediately preceding the first day of that person's [first current accounting year][2], and is an accounting period within the meaning of regulation 3.][1]

Amendments—[1] Regulation inserted by the CCL (General) (Amendment) Regulations, SI 2002/1152 with effect from 1 June 2002.

[2] Words in definition of "transitional accounting period" substituted by the CCL (General) (Amendment) Regulations, SI 2003/604 regs 2, 5 with effect from 1 April 2003.

[Annual accounting scheme

6B—(1) The Commissioners may, subject to the requirements in paragraph (2) below and in regulations 6C to 6G, authorise a registered person to pay and account for CCL by reference to any transitional accounting period, and any subsequent current accounting year, at such times, and for such amounts, as may be determined in accordance with the scheme.

(2) The Commissioners shall not be required to authorise a person under regulation 6B(1) unless an application is made to the Commissioners in such form and in such manner as the Commissioners may prescribe in a published notice.][1]

Amendments—[1] Regulation inserted by the Climate Change Levy (General) (Amendment) Regulations, SI 2002/1152 with effect from 1 June 2002.

[Admission to the scheme

6C—(1) A person shall be eligible to apply for authorisation if—

(*a*) he has been registered for at least 12 months at the date of his application for authorisation;

(*b*) he has reasonable grounds for believing that the amount of CCL on taxable supplies made or to be made by him in the period of 12 months beginning on the date of his application for authorisation will not exceed £2,000;

(*c*) his registration is not in the name of a representative member of a group of two or more bodies corporate under paragraph 56(2) of Schedule 6 to the Act;

(*d*) his registration is not in the name of a division under paragraph 56(3) of Schedule 6 to the Act; and

(*e*) he has not in the 12 months preceding the date of his application for authorisation ceased to operate the scheme.

(2) The Commissioners may refuse to authorise a person where they consider it necessary to do so for the protection of the revenue.][1]

Amendments—[1] Regulation inserted by the Climate Change Levy (General) (Amendment) Regulations, SI 2002/1152 with effect from 1 June 2002.

[Cessation of authorisation

6D—(1) An authorised person shall continue to account for CCL in accordance with the scheme until he ceases to be authorised.

(2) An authorised person ceases to be authorised when—

(*a*) at the end of any [transitional accounting period][2] or current accounting year the amount of CCL on taxable supplies made by him during that period or year has exceeded £2,000;

(*b*) his authorisation is terminated in accordance with regulation 6E;

(*c*) he—

(i) becomes insolvent and ceases to trade, other than for the purpose of disposing of stocks and assets,

(ii) ceases business or ceases to be registered,

(iii) dies, becomes bankrupt or incapacitated;

(*d*) he ceases to operate the scheme of his own volition.][1]

Amendments—[1] Regulation inserted by the CCL (General) (Amendment) Regulations, SI 2002/1152 with effect from 1 June 2002.

[2] Words in para (2)(*a*) substituted by the CCL (General) (Amendment) Regulations, SI 2003/604 regs 2, 6 with effect from 1 April 2003.

[6E—(1) The Commissioners may terminate an authorisation in any case where—

(*a*) a false statement has been made by or on behalf of an authorised person in relation to his application for authorisation;

(*b*) an authorised person fails to make by the due date a return for his transitional accounting period or current accounting year;

(*c*) an authorised person fails to make by the due date any payment shown as due on any return for his transitional accounting period or current accounting year;

(*d*) the Commissioners receive notification that the amount of CCL on taxable supplies in a transitional [accounting period][3] or current accounting year will exceed £2,000;

(*e*) at any time during an authorised person's [transitional accounting period][2] or current accounting year they have reason to believe that the amount of CCL on taxable supplies during the period or, as the case may be, year will exceed £2,000;

(*f*) it is necessary to do so for the protection of the revenue;

(*g*) an authorised person has not, in relation to a return made by him prior to authorisation, paid to the Commissioners all such sums shown as due thereon; or

(*h*) an authorised person has not, in relation to any assessment made under Schedule 6 to the Act, paid to the Commissioners all such sums due as shown thereon.

(2) Where an authorised person has reason to believe that the amount of CCL on taxable supplies made by him during a transitional accounting period or current accounting year will exceed £2,000, he shall within 30 days notify the Commissioners in writing.][1]

Amendments—[1] Regulation inserted by the Climate Change Levy (General) (Amendment) Regulations, SI 2002/1152 with effect from 1 June 2002.

[2] Words in para (1)(*e*) substituted by the CCL (General) (Amendment) Regulations, SI 2003/604 regs 2, 6 with effect from 1 April 2003.

[3] Words in para (1)(*d*) inserted by the CCL (General) (Amendment) Regulations, SI 2003/604 regs 2, 7 with effect from 1 April 2003.

[6F—(1) The date from which an authorised person ceases to be authorised shall be—

(*a*) where regulation 6D(2)(*a*) applies, the day following the last day of the relevant transitional accounting period or current accounting year;

(*b*) where regulation 6D(2)(*b*) applies, the day on which the Commissioners terminate his authorisation;

(*c*) where regulation 6D(2)(*c*) applies, the day on which any one of the events mentioned in that paragraph occurs; or

(*d*) where regulation 6D(2)(*d*) applies, the date on which the Commissioners are notified in writing of the authorised person's decision to cease using the scheme.

(2) Where an authorised person ceases to be authorised, he or as the case may be, his representative, shall—

(*a*) if his authorisation ceases before the end of his transitional accounting period or current accounting year, make a return within one month of the date specified in paragraph (1)(*b*), (1)(*c*) or (1)(*d*) above, together with any payment due to the Commissioners in respect of his liability for CCL for that part of the period or year arising before the date he ceased to be authorised; or

(*b*) if his authorisation ceases at the end of his transitional accounting period or current accounting year, make a return together with any payment due to the Commissioners in respect of his liability for CCL in accordance with regulations 4, 5 and 6;

and, in either case, from the day following the day on which he ceases to be authorised, account for and pay CCL as provided for otherwise than by the scheme.][1]

Amendments—[1] Regulation inserted by the Climate Change Levy (General) (Amendment) Regulations, SI 2002/1152 with effect from 1 June 2002.

[6G The Commissioners may vary any one of the amounts specified in regulations 6C(1)(*b*), 6D(2)(*a*) and 6E(1)(*d*) and (*e*) and (2) by prescribing a new amount in a published notice.][1]

Amendments—[1] Regulation inserted by the Climate Change Levy (General) (Amendment) Regulations, SI 2002/1152 with effect from 1 June 2002.

Records

7—(1) A registrable person is obliged to keep a record to be known as the "climate change levy account" (periodic summary of CCL due).

(2) A registrable person who makes a claim under regulations 10 and 14(1) (tax credits in respect of bad debts) is obliged to keep a record to be known as the "climate change levy bad debts account".

(3) A registrable person who makes a claim under regulations 11 and 14(1) (other tax credits) is obliged to keep a record to be known as the "climate change levy tax credits account".

(4) A record within this regulation must be kept in the manner stipulated in a published notice.

8 A registrable person is obliged to keep the following records—

(*a*) his business and accounting records;

(*b*) a copy of each CCL accounting document issued by him;

(*c*) each supplier certificate and supporting analysis document received, issued or prepared by or for him to evidence that a taxable supply (or part of such a supply) by or to him was—

(i) excluded or exempt from CCL, or

(ii) a . . . [3] reduced-rate supply;

[(*ca*) any record required by or under Part IV(*a*) (combined heat and power stations);][2]

(*d*) documentary evidence (including any relevant invoice) detailing each taxable supply made by him;

(*e*) documentary evidence (including any relevant invoice) received by him in connection with his receipt of any taxable commodity;

(*f*) documentary evidence regarding the adjustment of an entry concerning the amount of CCL charged for which he is liable to account;

(*g*) documentary evidence regarding any claim by him for a tax credit under regulation 10 (bad debts), regulation 11 (other tax credits) or [Schedule 1][1] (tax credit for recipient) and, in each case, regarding any relevant surrounding circumstances;

(*h*) the documents relevant to any special utility scheme binding him;

(*i*) a record of the information he relies on in making each return pursuant to regulation 5;

(*j*) any other record that may be stipulated in a published notice.

Amendments—[1] Words substituted by the CCL (General) (Amendment) Regulations, SI 2003/604 regs 2, 4 with effect from 1 April 2003.

[2] Para (*ca*) inserted by the CCL (General) (Amendment) Regulations, SI 2003/604 regs 2, 8 with effect from 1 April 2003.

[3] In para (*c*)(ii), words "half-rate or " revoked by the Climate Change Levy (General) (Amendment) Regulations, SI 2007/2903 reg 2, Sch 1 para 3 with effect from 1 November 2007: SI 2007/2903 reg 1. This amendment does not apply in relation to a half-rate supply made before 1 April 2006: SI 2007/2903 reg 2, Sch 1 Note (*a*).

9—(1) A registrable person is required to preserve any record required by regulation 7 or 8 for a period of at least six years.

(2) For the purposes of paragraph (1), a record within regulation 7 need only be preserved in relation to events taking place not more than six years earlier.

(3) For the purposes of paragraph (1), a record within regulation 8(*c*) must be preserved by the registrable person for a period of six years from the time of the final supply to which it relates.

(4) For the purposes of paragraph (1), a record within regulation 8(*d*) or 8(*e*) must be preserved by the registrable person for a period of six years from the relevant time of supply or, if there is no such time, from the time of delivery.

(5) The Commissioners may direct that any such record need only be preserved for such period as they specify shorter than six years.

Bad debts: entitlement to tax credit

10—(1) Paragraph (3) applies where—

(*a*) a person has supplied a taxable commodity and has accounted for and paid the CCL chargeable on the supply,

(*b*) that person and the recipient of the supply are not connected or are not the same person,

(*c*) that person has issued to the recipient a climate change levy accounting document (or, if the issue of such a document is not required by or under the Act, other invoice) relating to the supply showing the CCL chargeable,

(*d*) the whole or any part of the price for the supply has been written off in his accounts as a bad debt, and

(*e*) the period of 6 months referred to in paragraph (8) has elapsed.

(2) Any question whether a person is connected with another for the purposes of paragraph (1) shall be determined in accordance with section 839 of the Income and Corporation Taxes Act 1988.

(3) The person shall be entitled to a tax credit in respect of the amount of CCL chargeable calculated by reference to the outstanding amount (subject to the provisions of this Part including those provisions relating to the making of a relevant claim to the Commissioners).

(4) In this regulation and regulation 16—

"claim" refers to a claim in accordance with regulation 14 or 15, and "claimant" shall be construed accordingly;

"the outstanding amount" refers to—

(*a*) if at the time of the claim no part of the price written off in the claimant's accounts as a bad debt has been received, an amount equal to the amount of the price so written off;

(*b*) if at that time any part of the price so written off has been received, an amount by which that part is exceeded by the amount of the price written off.

(5) In paragraph (4), "received" refers to receipt either by the claimant or by a person to whom has been assigned a right to receive the whole or any part of the price written off.

(6) Accordingly, the tax credit arising under this regulation shall be of an amount equal to such proportion of the CCL charged on the supply as the outstanding amount forms of the total price.

(7) For the purposes of this regulation, where the whole or any part of the price for the supply does not consist of money, the amount in money that shall be taken to represent any non-monetary part of the price shall be so much of the amount made up of—

(*a*) the price excluding the CCL chargeable, and

(*b*) the CCL charged on the supply,

as is attributable to the non-monetary consideration in question.

(8) Neither the whole nor any part of the price for a supply shall be taken to have been written off in accounts as a bad debt until a period of not less than six months has elapsed from the time when such whole or part became due and payable to, or to the order of, the person who made the relevant supply.

(9) Subject to paragraph (8), the whole or any part of the price for a relevant supply shall be taken to have been written off as a bad debt when an entry is made in relation to that supply in the claimant's climate change levy bad debts account (see regulation 7(2)).

(10) Where the claimant owes an amount of money to the recipient of the relevant supply which can be set off, the price written off in the accounts shall be reduced by the amount so owed.

(11) Where the claimant holds in relation to the recipient of the relevant supply an enforceable security, the consideration written off in the account of the claimant shall be reduced by the value of that security.

(12) In paragraphs (8) to (11), "relevant supply" refers to any taxable supply on which a claim is based.

(13) In paragraph (11), "security" refers to—

(*a*) in England, Wales or Northern Ireland, any mortgage, charge, lien or other security;

(*b*) in Scotland, any security (whether heritable or moveable), any floating charge and right of lien or preference and right of retention (other than a right of compensation or set-off).

Other tax credits: entitlement

11—(1) The supplier in each of the following cases is entitled to a tax credit in respect of any relevant amount of CCL charged on the supply in question (subject to the provisions of this Part including those provisions relating to the making of a relevant claim to the Commissioners)—

(*a*) after a taxable supply has been made, there is such a change in circumstances or any person's intentions that, if the changed circumstances or intentions had existed at the time of supply, the supply would not have been a taxable supply;

(*b*) after a supply of a taxable commodity is made on the basis that it is a taxable supply, it is determined that the supply was not (to any extent) a taxable supply;

(*c*) after a taxable supply has been made on the basis that it was . . . [1] a reduced-rate supply, it is determined that the supply was (to any extent) a half-rate or reduced-rate supply;

(*d*) *CCL is accounted for on a half-rate supply as if the supply were neither a half-rate supply nor a reduced-rate supply;*[1]

(*e*) after a charge to CCL has arisen on a supply of a taxable commodity ("the original commodity") to a person who uses the commodity supplied in producing taxable commodities primarily for his own consumption, that person makes supplies of any of the commodities in whose production he has used the original commodity;

(*f*) the making of a taxable supply gives rise to a double charge to CCL within the meaning of paragraph 21 of the Act.

(2) In paragraph (1), "relevant amount of CCL" refers to—

(*a*) in relation to a case described by sub-paragraph (*a*), (*b*), (*c*), ()(*d*)[1] or (*e*) of paragraph (1), the difference between the amount of CCL that ought to have been charged by or under the Act at the time of supply and the amount of CCL that was actually accounted for and paid by the supplier; and

(*b*) in relation to a case described by sub-paragraph (*f*) of paragraph (1), the amount of CCL actually charged and paid on the later supply having regard to the relative times of supply.

Amendments—[1] In para (1)(*c*), words "neither a half-rate supply nor" substituted, para (1)(*d*) and words ", (*d*)" in para (2)(*a*) revoked, by the Climate Change Levy (General) (Amendment) Regulations, SI 2007/2903 reg 2, Sch 1 paras 4–6 with effect from 1 November 2007: SI 2007/2903 reg 1. These amendments do not apply in relation to a half-rate supply made before 1 April 2006: SI 2007/2903 reg 2, Sch 1 Note (*a*).

Tax credits: general

12—(1) The provisions of this Part have effect subject to the requirements of Part III and [Schedule 1][1] (certification scheme for excluded, exempt . . . [2] and reduced-rate supplies).

(2) Accordingly, no tax credit shall arise by virtue of regulation 11 where the circumstances are such that provision is made by [Schedule 1][1] for a tax credit, for the benefit of the recipient, relating to the amount in question.

Amendments—[1] Words substituted by the CCL (General) (Amendment) Regulations, SI 2003/604 regs 2, 4 with effect from 1 April 2003.

[2] In para (1) words ", half-rate" revoked, by the Climate Change Levy (General) (Amendment) Regulations, SI 2007/2903 reg 2, Sch 1 para 7 with effect from 1 November 2007: SI 2007/2903 reg 1. This amendment does not apply in relation to a half-rate supply made before 1 April 2006: SI 2007/2903 reg 2, Sch 1 Note (*a*).

13 A tax credit shall only arise under regulation 10 or 11 if a claim is made by the supplier acting in accordance with regulation 14 or 15, as the case requires.

14—(1) Subject to paragraph (4), the supplier shall claim any such tax credit by bringing it into account when he is accounting for CCL due from him for any accounting period.

(2) Accordingly—

(*a*) the requirements of regulation 5 (content of returns), regulation 6 (payment of CCL) and regulation 7 (CCL accounts) apply subject to paragraph (1); but

(*b*) paragraph (1) applies subject to regulation 27 (corrections) and regulation 28 (corrections not exceeding [£50,000][1]).

(3) A claim subject to paragraphs (1) and (2) shall be regarded as a claim for repayment of CCL for the purposes of paragraph 64 of the Act (supplemental provisions about repayments, etc) (and see paragraph (5)).

(4) Where the total tax credit claimed by a supplier exceeds the total of the CCL due from him for the accounting period in question, the Commissioners shall repay to him an amount equal to the excess (but see regulations 29 and 30).

(5) Given the provision made by paragraph 62(4) of the Act, this regulation has effect subject to paragraph 64 of the Act (application of supplemental provisions about repayments: [4 year time limit][2], unjust enrichment, etc).

Amendments—[1] In para (2)(*b*) figure substituted for figure "£2,000" by the Value Added Tax, etc (Correction of Errors, etc) Regulations, SI 2008/1482 reg 6(1) with effect in relation to under-calculations or over-calculations respectively in the CCL Regulations, SI 2001/838 regs 28(2), (3) which registrable persons first discover in their accounting periods that start on 1 July 2008 or later.

[2] Words in para (5) substituted for "three year time limit" by the Climate Change Levy (General) (Amendment) Regulations, SI 2010/643, regs 2, 3, with effect from 1 April 2010. However, this amendment is to be disregarded for the purpose of FA 2000 Sch 6 para 64(1) where claims made are for the repayment of amounts paid to the Commissioners on or before 31 March 2007.

15—(1) Where the Commissioners have cancelled the registration of a person in accordance with Part V of the Act, and he is not a registrable person, the Commissioners shall repay to him the amount of the tax credit if they are satisfied that he has made a proper claim to them in writing for this purpose.
(2) A claim under paragraph (1) may be combined with a claim under regulation 14(1) if appropriate.
(3) A person making a claim under paragraph (1) must furnish to the Commissioners full particulars in relation to the tax credit claimed including (but not restricted to)—
(*a*) the return in which the relevant CCL was accounted for;
(*b*) the amount of the CCL in question and the date and manner of its payment to the Commissioners;
(*c*) the events by virtue of which the bad debt or entitlement to a tax credit arose; and
(*d*) any supporting documentary or other evidence.
(4) Where the Commissioners are satisfied that a person who has made a claim in accordance with paragraphs (1) and (3) is entitled to a tax credit and that he has not previously had the benefit of that credit, they shall repay to him an amount equal to the credit (but see regulations 29 and 30).
(5) The Commissioners shall not be liable to make any repayment under this regulation unless and until the person has made all the returns which he was required to make (and see regulation 29 and 30).
(6) Given the provision made by paragraph 62(4) of the Act, this regulation has effect subject to paragraph 64 of the Act (application of supplemental provisions about repayments: [4 year time limit][1], unjust enrichment, etc).

Amendments—[1] Words in para (6) substituted for "three year time limit" by the Climate Change Levy (General) (Amendment) Regulations, SI 2010/643, regs 2, 3, with effect from 1 April 2010. However, this amendment is to be disregarded for the purpose of FA 2000 Sch 6 para 64(1) where claims made are for the repayment of amounts paid to the Commissioners on or before 31 March 2007.

Bad debts: supplementary provisions

16—(1) Where—
(*a*) a claimant in relation to regulation 10 has made a taxable supply,
(*b*) there exist one or more other matters in respect of which the claimant is entitled to a debt owed by the recipient (whether or not they involve a taxable supply), and
(*c*) a payment has been received by the claimant from or on behalf of the recipient,
the payment shall be attributed to the taxable supply and the other matters in accordance with the rules set out in paragraphs (3) and (5).
(2) The debts arising in respect of the taxable supply and the other matters are collectively referred to as debts in paragraphs (3) to (5).
(3) The payment shall be attributed to the debt that arose earliest and, if not wholly attributable to that debt, to the other debts in the order of the dates on which they arose.
(4) Attribution under paragraph (3) shall not be made to the extent that the payment was allocated to a debt by the recipient (customer) at the time of payment.
(5) Where—
(*a*) the earliest debt and the other debts to which the whole of the payment could be attributed arose on the same day, or
(*b*) the debts to which the balance of the payment could be attributed in accordance with paragraph (3) arose on the same day,
the payment shall be attributed to each remaining debt according to the proportion that the debt in question contributes to the total remaining debt.

17—(1) Where a supplier—
(*a*) has received the benefit from a tax credit provided for by regulation 10 (bad debts), and
(*b*) a payment—
(i) for the taxable supply in question is subsequently received by him (or by a person to whom has been assigned a right to receive the whole or any part of the price written off), or
(ii) is attributed to that taxable supply by virtue of regulation 16,
that tax credit shall be withdrawn with effect from when sub-paragraph (b)(i) or (b)(ii) is satisfied, as the case requires.
(2) Where a supplier—
(*a*) has received the benefit from a tax credit provided for by regulation 11 (tax credits other than bad debts), and
(*b*) it subsequently transpires that any relevant requirement of this Part is not complied with,

that tax credit shall be withdrawn with effect from when he received that benefit.

(3) Where a tax credit is withdrawn under this regulation—

(*a*) the requirements of regulation 5 (content of returns), regulation 6 (payment of CCL) and regulation 7 (CCL accounts) apply subject to this regulation; but

(*b*) this regulation applies subject to regulation 27 (corrections) and regulation 28 (corrections not exceeding [£50,000][1]).

(4) Paragraph (3) applies subject to paragraph 67 of the Act (assessment for excessive repayment).

Amendments—[1] In para (3)(*b*) figure substituted for figure "£2,000" by the Value Added Tax, etc (Correction of Errors, etc) Regulations, SI 2008/1482 reg 6(1) with effect in relation to under-calculations or over-calculations respectively in the CCL Regulations, SI 2001/838 regs 28(2), (3) which registrable persons first discover in their accounting periods that start on 1 July 2008 or later.

Form and manner of claim for repayment of overpaid CCL if no person entitled to tax credit

18 A claim under paragraph 63 of the Act (claim for repayment of CCL which was not CCL due if no entitlement to tax credit) shall be made in writing to the Commissioners and shall, by reference to such documentary evidence as is in the possession of the claimant, state the amount of the claim and the method by which that amount was calculated.

Tax credits and other repayments: unjust enrichment—reimbursement arrangements to be disregarded

19 In this regulation and in regulations 20 to 25—

"claim" refers to a claim made under regulation 14 or 15 or under paragraph 63 of the Act (claim for repayment of CCL which was not CCL due if no person entitled to tax credit) and "claimed" and "claimant" must be construed accordingly;

"reimbursement arrangements" refers to any arrangements for the purposes of the claim which—

(*a*) are made by the claimant for the purpose of securing that he is not unjustly enriched by the repayment of any amount in pursuance of the claim; and

(*b*) provide for the reimbursement of persons (recipients) who have for practical purposes borne the whole or any part of the cost of the original payment of that amount to the Commissioners;

"relevant amount" refers to that part (which may be the whole) of the amount of the claim which the claimant has reimbursed or intends to reimburse to other persons (recipients).

20 For the purposes of paragraph 64(2) of the Act (defence by the Commissioners that repayment by them of an amount claimed would unjustly enrich the claimant) reimbursement arrangements made by a claimant shall be disregarded except where they—

(*a*) include the provisions described in regulation 21, and

(*b*) are supported by the undertakings described in regulation 25.

21 The provisions referred to in regulation 20(*a*) are that—

(*a*) reimbursement for which the arrangements provide will be completed by no later than 90 days after the repayment to which it relates;

(*b*) no deduction will be made from the relevant amount by way of fee or charge (however expressed or effected);

(*c*) reimbursement will be made only in cash or by cheque;

(*d*) any part of the relevant amount that is not reimbursed by the time mentioned in paragraph (*a*) will be repaid by the claimant to the Commissioners;

(*e*) any interest paid by the Commissioners on any relevant amount repaid by them will also be treated by the claimant in the same way as the relevant amount falls to be treated under paragraphs (*a*) and (*b*); and

(*f*) the records described in regulation 23 will be kept by the claimant and produced by him to the Commissioners in accordance with regulation 24.

22 The claimant shall, without prior demand, make any repayment to the Commissioners that he is required to make by virtue of regulation 21(*d*) or 21(*e*) within 14 days of the expiry of the period of 90 days referred to in regulation 21(*a*).

23 The claimant shall keep records of the following matters—

(*a*) the names and addresses of those persons (recipients) whom he has reimbursed or whom he intends to reimburse;

(*b*) the total amount reimbursed to each such person (recipient);

(*c*) the amount of interest included in each total amount reimbursed to each person (recipient);

(*d*) the date that each reimbursement is made.

24—(1) Where a claimant is given notice in accordance with paragraph (2) he shall, in accordance with such notice, produce to the Commissioners the records that he is required to keep pursuant to regulation 23.
(2) A notice given for the purposes of paragraph (1) shall—
(*a*) be in writing;
(*b*) state the date on which and the place and time at which the records are to be produced; and
(*c*) be signed and dated by the Commissioners.
(3) Such a notice may be given before or after, or before and after, the Commissioners have paid the relevant amount to the claimant.

25—(1) The undertakings referred to in regulation 20(*b*) shall be given to the Commissioners by the claimant no later than the time at which he makes the claim for which the reimbursement arrangements have been made.
(2) The undertakings shall be in writing and shall be signed and dated by the claimant.
(3) The undertakings shall be to the effect that—
(*a*) at the date of the undertakings he is able to identify the names and addresses of those persons (recipients) whom he has reimbursed or whom he intends to reimburse;
(*b*) he will apply the whole of the relevant amount repaid to him (without any deduction by way of fee, charge or otherwise) to the reimbursement in cash or by cheque of such persons (recipients) no later than 90 days after he receives that amount (unless he has properly reimbursed them already);
(*c*) he will apply any interest paid to him on the relevant amount repaid to him wholly to the reimbursement of such persons (recipients) no later than 90 days after he receives that interest;
(*d*) he will repay to the Commissioners without demand the whole or such part of the relevant amount repaid to him or of any interest paid to him as he fails to apply in accordance with the undertakings mentioned in sub-paragraph (*b*) or (*c*);
(*e*) he will keep the records described in regulation 23; and
(*f*) he will comply with any notice given to him in accordance with regulation 24 concerning the production of such records.

Corrections to CCL returns

26 A registrable person—
(*a*) shall only be taken as providing full information in the prescribed or specified form and manner for the purposes of paragraph 100(3) of the Act (disclosure about inaccurate CCL return),
(*b*) with respect to any inaccuracy to which paragraph 100(1)(*a*) of the Act applies (civil penalty for misdeclaration or neglect in relation to inaccurate return),
if he delivers that information in writing to the Commissioners, or acts in accordance with regulation 28, at a time to which paragraph 100(3)(a) of the Act applies (no reason to believe enquiries being made into CCL affairs).

27—(1) A registrable person shall correct any error made by him in accounting for CCL or in connection with his CCL account and, as appropriate, make any adjustment required by regulation (5)(1)(*b*) (adjustments to CCL returns).
(2) That correction or adjustment shall be made within such time and by means of such payment, financial adjustment, entry in accounts or other method as the Commissioners may require.
(3) This regulation has effect subject to, as the case requires—
(*a*) the time limit applying to regulations 14(1), 17(1) and 17(2) (tax credits) (see regulations 14(5) and 17(4)—amounts paid more than [4 years][2] before claim made and assessment subject to time limit in paragraph 69 of Act);
(*b*) the time limit applying to paragraph 8(1) of [Schedule 1][1] (recipient's tax credit) (see paragraph 8(5) of [Schedule 1][1]—amounts paid more than [4 years][2] before claim made);
(*c*) a time limit of [4 years][2] after the end of the accounting period in relation to which the error was made or the adjustment became required; or
(*d*) any time limit for an assessment in relation to the error in question (see paragraphs 78(1), 78(2)(*d*), 79 and 80 of the Act).

Amendments—[1] Words substituted by the CCL (General) (Amendment) Regulations, SI 2003/604 regs 2, 4 with effect from 1 April 2003.
[2] Words in para (3) substituted for "three years" by the Climate Change Levy (General) (Amendment) Regulations, SI 2010/643, regs 2, 4, with effect from 1 April 2010. However, these amendments are to be disregarded for the purpose of FA 2000 Sch 6 para 64(1) where claims made are for the repayment of amounts paid to the Commissioners on or before 31 March 2007.

28—(1) This regulation applies by way of an exception to regulation 27 but only in relation to errors.

(2) Where a registrable person discovers that a return he has previously made is based on an under-calculation he must correct the error by adding an appropriate amount to the CCL due for the accounting period in which the discovery is made under regulation 5(1)(*b*) (CCL due).

(3) Where a registrable person discovers that a return he has previously made is based on an over-calculation he must correct the error by deducting an appropriate amount from the CCL due for the accounting period in which the discovery is made under regulation 5(1)(*b*) (CCL due).

(4) For the purposes of paragraphs (2) and (3)—

"under-calculation" refers to the aggregate, which must not exceed [£50,000][1], of—

(*a*) the CCL due on taxable supplies—

(i) the times of supply of which were in the accounting period to which the previous return related, and

(ii) for which the registrable person in question was liable to account;

(*b*) but which was not properly taken into consideration for that period (see regulation 5(1)) ("understated CCL");

"over-calculation" refers to the aggregate, which must not exceed [£50,000][1], of—

(*a*) amounts that were wrongly taken as CCL due on taxable supplies—

(i) the times of supply of which were in the accounting period to which the previous return related, and

(ii) for which the registrable person in question was liable to account;

(*b*) and which were wrongly taken into consideration for that period (see regulation 5(1)) ("overstated CCL").

[(4A) But if the registrable person's VAT turnover is small, each aggregate in paragraph (4) must not for those purposes exceed 1% of that turnover unless the aggregate is [£10,000 or less][3].

And if that person is not registered for VAT, each aggregate must not for those purposes exceed £10,000.][1]

[The VAT turnover is small only if Box 6 of that person's value added tax return for the prescribed accounting period in which the discovery is made must contain a total less than £5,000,000 (total value of sales and all other outputs excluding any value added tax).][2]

(5) For the purposes of [paragraphs (4) and (4A)][1]—

(*a*) in reckoning the aggregate constituting the under-calculation no allowance shall be made for any overstated CCL; and

(*b*) in reckoning the aggregate constituting the over-calculation no allowance shall be made for any understated CCL.

(6) A registrable person making a correction under paragraph (2) or (3) shall make proper allowance for that correction for the purposes of complying with regulation 7(1) (CCL account) or 7(3) (tax credits account), as appropriate.

(7) Where an error in a return has to any extent been corrected under this regulation—

(*a*) that return shall be regarded as having been corrected to that extent, and

(*b*) the registrable person shall to that extent be taken to have provided full information with respect to the inaccuracy in the prescribed form and manner for the purposes of paragraph 100(3) of the Act (disclosure about inaccurate CCL return).

(8) A person shall not correct an error in a return (where that error is the result of an under-calculation or over-calculation) except in accordance with this regulation.

(9) This regulation has effect subject to, as the case requires—

(*a*) any requirement of the Commissioners under regulation 27(2), and

(*b*) any applicable time limit specified in regulation 27(3).

Amendments—[1] In para (4) figure substituted in each place for figure "£2,000", para (4A) inserted, and words in para (5) substituted for words "paragraph (4)", by the Value Added Tax, etc (Correction of Errors, etc) Regulations, SI 2008/1482 reg 6(1), (2) with effect in relation to under-calculations or over-calculations respectively in the CCL Regulations, SI 2001/838 reg 28(2), (3) which registrable persons first discover in their accounting periods that start on 1 July 2008 or later.

[2] In para (4A), words inserted by the Value Added Tax, etc (Correction of Errors, etc) Regulations, SI 2008/1482 reg 8(1) with effect from 1 July 2008.

[3] In para (4A), words substituted for words "less than £10,000" by the Amusement Machine Licence Duty, etc (Amendments) Regulations, SI 2008/2693 reg 4(1)(*c*) with effect for a discovery first made on 1 November 2008 or later.

Set-off

29—(1) This regulation applies where—

(*a*) a person is under a duty to pay to the Commissioners at any time an amount or amounts in respect of CCL; and

(*b*) the Commissioners are under a duty to pay to that person at the same time an amount or amounts in respect of any CCL (or other tax or duty) under their care and management.

(2) Where the total of the amount or amounts mentioned in paragraph (1)(*a*) exceeds the total of the amount or amounts mentioned in paragraph (1)(*b*), the latter shall be set-off against the former.

(3) Where the total of the amount or amounts mentioned in paragraph (1)(*b*) exceeds the total of the amount or amounts mentioned in paragraph (1)(*a*), the Commissioners may set off the latter in paying the former.
(4) Where the total of the amount or amounts mentioned in paragraph (1)(*a*) is the same as the total of the amount or amounts mentioned in paragraph (1)(*b*), no payment need be made in respect of either.
(5) Where this regulation applies and an amount has been set off in accordance with any of paragraphs (2) to (4), the duty of both the person in question and the Commissioners to pay the amount concerned shall be treated as having been discharged accordingly.

30—(1) This regulation applies where—

(*a*) a person is under a duty to pay to the Commissioners at any time an amount or amounts in respect of any tax or duty (other than CCL) under their care and management; and
(*b*) the Commissioners are under a duty, at the same time, to make a payment or repayment to that person of an amount or amounts of or in respect of CCL.

(2) Where the total of the amount or amounts mentioned in paragraph (1)(*a*) exceeds the total of the amount or amounts mentioned in paragraph (1)(*b*), the latter shall be set-off against the former.
(3) Where the total of the amount or amounts mentioned in paragraph (1)(*b*) exceeds the total of the amount or amounts mentioned in paragraph (1)(*a*), the Commissioners may set off the latter in paying the former.
(4) Where the total of the amount or amounts mentioned in paragraph (1)(*a*) is the same as the total of the amount or amounts mentioned in paragraph (1)(*b*), no payment need be made in respect of either.
(5) Where this regulation applies and an amount has been set off in accordance with any of paragraphs (2) to (4), the duty of both the person in question and the Commissioners to pay the amount concerned shall be treated as having been discharged accordingly.

31—(1) Regulation 29 or 30 shall not require any such amount as is mentioned in paragraph (1)(*b*) of either regulation ("the credit") to be set against any item mentioned in paragraph (1)(*a*) of either regulation ("the debit") where—

(*a*) an insolvency procedure has been applied to the person entitled to the credit;
(*b*) the credit became due after that procedure was applied; and
(*c*) the liability to pay the debt either arose before that procedure was so applied or (having arisen afterwards) relates to, or to matters occurring in the course of, the carrying on of any business relevant for CCL purposes at times before the procedure was so applied.

(2) An insolvency procedure is applied to a person for the purposes of this regulation in the circumstances described by paragraphs 75(2) to 75(5) of the Act (insolvency procedures for purposes of this regulation).

32 A reference in regulation 29 or 30 to an amount in respect of tax or duty includes a reference to an amount of any related penalty, surcharge or interest that may be recovered as if it was an amount of tax or duty.

Special rules for excluded, exempt . . . [2] *and reduced-rate supplies*

33 The provisions of this Part have effect subject to Part III of and [Schedule 1][1] to these Regulations (accounting and payment in the case of excluded, exempt . . . [2] and reduced-rate supplies).

Amendments—[1] Words substituted by the CCL (General) (Amendment) Regulations, SI 2003/604 regs 2, 4 with effect from 1 April 2003.
[2] In para 33 and in preceding heading, words ", half-rate" revoked, by the Climate Change Levy (General) (Amendment) Regulations, SI 2007/2903 reg 2, Sch 1 para 8 with effect from 1 November 2007: SI 2007/2903 reg 1. These amendments do not apply in relation to a half-rate supply made before 1 April 2006: SI 2007/2903 reg 2, Sch 1 Note (*a*).

PART III
EXCLUDED, EXEMPT . . . [1] AND REDUCED-RATE SUPPLIES

Amendments—[1] In heading to Part III, words ", half-rate" revoked, by the Climate Change Levy (General) (Amendment) Regulations, SI 2007/2903 reg 2, Sch 1 para 9 with effect from 1 November 2007: SI 2007/2903 reg 1. This amendment does not apply in relation to a half-rate supply made before 1 April 2006: SI 2007/2903 reg 2, Sch 1 Note (*a*).

Supplier certificates: basic rules

34—(1) Any exclusion or exemption provided for by, under or by virtue of—

(*a*) paragraph 9(2)(*f*) (community heating arrangements), 11 (onward supplies and exports), 12 (transport), 13 (commodity producers), 14 (electricity producers), 15 (combined heat and power stations)[, 18 (non fuel use) or 18A (recycling processes)][2] of the Act, or
(*b*) regulation 41 (or any other relevant regulation made under paragraph 21 of the Act to avoid a double charge to CCL),

shall only be given effect if and to the extent that . . .[3] the recipient [delivers][3] to the supplier a certificate that accords with paragraph (2).

(2) Any such certificate shall—

(*a*) represent that the supply (or a quantified part of the supply) meets the requirements for each such exclusion or exemption,

(*b*) comply, as necessary, with regulations 37(2), 37(3), 37(4) and 38(2), and

(*c*) be supported, if necessary, in accordance with paragraph (3).

(3) Where the certificate represents that a quantified part of the supply meets the requirements for an exclusion or exemption referred to in paragraph (1), the recipient must support that certificate with an analysis document demonstrating that the part is calculated in a manner consistent with regulation 38 and [Schedule 1][1].

Amendments—[1] Words substituted by the CCL (General) (Amendment) Regulations, SI 2003/604 regs 2, 4 with effect from 1 April 2003.

[2] Words in sub-para (1)(*a*) substituted by the Climate Change Levy (Miscellaneous Amendments) Regulations, SI 2005/1716 regs 4, 6 with effect from 22 July 2005. However, arrangements initiated or made before 22 July 2005 on the basis of SI 2001/838 Sch 1 para 5(5) or 5(6) as then in force remain subject to the provisions applicable when they were initiated or made (tax credit claims and corrections to over-estimated relief).

[3] In para (1), words ", before the time of supply," revoked and words substituted for words "has delivered", by the Climate Change Levy (General) (Amendment) Regulations, SI 2007/2903 reg 2, Sch 1 para 10 with effect from 1 November 2007: SI 2007/2903 reg 1. This amendment applies only to a supply that is treated as taking place on or after 1 November 2007: SI 2007/2903 reg 2, Sch 1 Note (*c*).

35—(1) A taxable supply is to be treated as being a [reduced-rate][3] supply only if and to the extent that . . .[3] the recipient [delivers][3] to the supplier a certificate that accords with paragraph (2).

(2) Any such certificate shall—

(*a*) represent that the supply (or a quantified part of the supply) meets the requirements for a [reduced-rate][3] supply in paragraph [44(1)][3] of the Act [(reduced-rate for supplies covered by climate change agreements)][3],

(*b*) comply, as necessary, with regulations 37(2), 37(3), 37(4) and 38(2), and

(*c*) be supported, if necessary, in accordance with paragraph (3).

(3) Where the certificate represents that a quantified part of the supply meets the requirements for a [reduced-rate][3] supply, the recipient must support that certificate with an analysis document demonstrating that the part is calculated in a manner consistent with regulation 38 and [Schedule 1][1].

[(4) This regulation does not apply to a supply made after 31st March 2006.][2]

[(5) Paragraphs (6) to (9) have effect for determining when a supply is to be regarded as made for the purposes of paragraph (4).][2]

[(6) A supply—

(*a*) *of electricity, or*

(*b*) *of gas that is in a gaseous state and is of a kind supplied by a gas utility,*

is to be regarded as made at the time when the electricity or gas is actually supplied.][2]

[(7) In the case of a supply of a taxable commodity not falling within paragraph (6) by a person who is resident in the United Kingdom—

(*a*) *if the commodity is to be removed, the supply is to be regarded as made at the time of the removal,*

(*b*) *if the commodity is not to be removed, the supply is to be regarded as made when the commodity is made available to the person to whom it is supplied.*

This paragraph does not apply if paragraph (9) (deemed self-supply) applies in the case of the supply.][2]

[(8) In the case of a supply of a taxable commodity not falling within paragraph (6) by a person who is not resident in the United Kingdom, the supply is to be regarded as made—

(*a*) *when the commodity is delivered to the person to whom it is supplied, or*

(*b*) *if earlier, when it is made available in the United Kingdom to that person.*

This paragraph does not apply if paragraph (9) (deemed self-supply) applies in the case of the supply.][2]

[(9) In any case where, by virtue of paragraph 23(3) of the Act, a person is, for the purposes of the Act, deemed to make a supply to himself of a quantity of a taxable commodity—

(*a*) *which he has produced, and*

(*b*) *which does not fall within paragraph (6),*

the supply is to be regarded as made at the time when he produced that particular quantity of the taxable commodity.][2,3]

Amendments—[1] Words substituted by the CCL (General) (Amendment) Regulations, SI 2003/604 regs 2, 4 with effect from 1 April 2003.

[2] Paras (4)–(9) inserted by the CCL (General) (Amendment) Regulations, SI 2006/954 regs 1(2), 2 with effect from 1 April 2006.

[3] In para (1), words substituted for words "half-rate" and "has delivered", and words ", before the time of supply," revoked, in para (2) words substituted for words "half-rate", "43", and (horticultural producers), in para (3) words substituted for words

"half-rate", and paras (4)–(9) revoked, by the Climate Change Levy (General) (Amendment) Regulations, SI 2007/2903 reg 2, Sch 1 paras 11–15 with effect from 1 November 2007: SI 2007/2903 reg 1.

The amendments made to paras (1)–(3) do not apply in relation to a half-rate supply made before 1 April 2006: SI 2007/2903 reg 2, Sch 1 Note (*a*).

In relation to a reduced-rate supply or a supply made on that basis, the substitution of words "reduced-rate" for words "half-rate" in para (1), and the amendments made to paras (2), (3), only apply if the supply is made on or after 1 November 2007: SI 2007/2903 reg 2, Sch 1 Note (*b*).

The revocation of words ", before the time of supply", and substitution of words "reduced-rate" for "half-rate" in para (1), only apply to a supply that is treated as taking place on or after 1 November 2007: SI 2007/2903 reg2, Sch 1 Note (*c*).

36—(1) For the purposes of regulation 45(2) (certain supplies to a facility covered by climate change agreement), a taxable commodity shall be regarded for CCL purposes as supplied to a facility that is certified as being covered by a climate change agreement only if and to the extent that . . . [2] the recipient [delivers][2] to the supplier a certificate that accords with paragraph (2).

(2) Any such certificate shall—

(*a*) represent that the supply (or a quantified part of the supply) meets the requirements for a reduced-rate supply in paragraph 44 of the Act (facilities covered by climate change agreements),

(*b*) comply, as necessary, with regulation 37(2), 37(3), 37(4) and 38(2), and

(*c*) be supported, if necessary, in accordance with paragraph (3).

(3) Where the certificate represents that a quantified part of the supply meets the requirements for a reduced-rate supply for the purposes of regulation 45(2), the recipient must support that certificate with an analysis document demonstrating that the part is calculated in a manner consistent with regulation 38 and [Schedule 1][1].

Amendments—[1] Words substituted by the CCL (General) (Amendment) Regulations, SI 2003/604 regs 2, 4 with effect from 1 April 2003.

[2] Words ", before the time of supply," revoked, and words substituted for words "has delivered" by the Climate Change Levy (General) (Amendment) Regulations, SI 2007/2903 reg 2, Sch 1 paras 16 with effect from 1 November 2007: SI 2007/2903 reg 1. This amendment only applies to a supply that is treated as taking place on or after 1 November 2007: SI 2007/2903 reg 2, Sch 1 Note (*c*).

37—(1) A certificate delivered under regulation 34, 35 or 36 (a "supplier certificate") only has effect . . . [1] on or after the certificate's implementation date.

(2) A supplier certificate and an analysis document shall—

(*a*) be in a form prescribed by the Commissioners for this purpose in a published notice, and

(*b*) in the case of the supplier certificate, be signed and dated by a person duly authorised for this purpose by the recipient.

(3) Where regulation 34, 35 or 36 applies to part of a supply and at least one other of them applies to another part of that supply, any supplier certificate the recipient delivers under one of those regulations shall be combined by him with a supplier certificate under any other applicable regulation such that the resulting composite certificate satisfies paragraph (2) of every applicable regulation.

(4) A recipient shall not combine—

(*a*) a supplier certificate relating to the supply of one taxable commodity with a supplier certificate relating to the supply of any other such commodity;

(*b*) a supplier certificate delivered to one supplier with a supplier certificate delivered to another supplier;

(*c*) a supplier certificate relating to a reference number the supplier uses for him with a supplier certificate relating to another reference number the supplier uses for him; or

(*d*) supplier certificates combined contrary to sub-paragraph (*a*) with supplier certificates combined contrary to sub-paragraph (*b*).

(5) A recipient who delivers a supplier certificate to a supplier must deliver a copy to the Commissioners within 30 days of doing so (together with any supporting analysis document).

(6) In this regulation, "implementation date" refers to the earlier of—

(*a*) the fifth working day after the one on which the certificate is delivered to the supplier at any address the supplier designates for this purpose, and

(*b*) the day on which (or any day after which) the certificate is so delivered if, on that day, the supplier first applies the information contained in that certificate to the relevant supplies he makes to the recipient.

(7) To the extent that a person does anything before 1st April 2001 in purported compliance or conformity with or purported pursuit of regulation 34, 35, 36, 38, 43 or this regulation it shall, to that extent, be regarded as having been done on 1st April 2001.

Amendments—[1] In para (1), words "in relation to a supply the time of supply of which is" revoked by the Climate Change Levy (General) (Amendment) Regulations, SI 2007/2903 reg 2, Sch 1 para 17 with effect from 1 November 2007: SI 2007/2903 reg 1. This amendment only applies to a supply that is treated as taking place on or after 1 November 2007: SI 2007/2903 reg 2, Sch 1 Note (*c*).

Supplier certificates: accounting for and payment of CCL

38—(1) [Schedule 1][1] to these Regulations has effect for the purpose of—

(*a*) supplementing the provisions of regulations 34 to 37 (which, accordingly, have effect subject to that Schedule), and

(*b*) determining the manner in which a person who is required to account for CCL does so in the case of a supply of a quantity of a taxable commodity [to which regulation 34, 35 or 36 applies.][2]

(2) A recipient shall include in a supplier certificate the percentage of the supply or supplies on which CCL is not due calculated in accordance with that Schedule (recipient's relief percentage).

(3) This Part and [Schedule 1][1] must be read as one.

Amendments—[1] Words substituted by the CCL (General) (Amendment) Regulations, SI 2003/604 regs 2, 4 with effect from 1 April 2003.

[2] In para (1)(*b*), words substituted for sub-paras (i), (ii) by the Climate Change Levy (General) (Amendment) Regulations, SI 2007/2903 reg 2, Sch 1 para 18 with effect from 1 November 2007: SI 2007/2903 reg 1. In relation to a reduced-rate supply or a supply made on that basis, this amendment only applies if the supply is made on or after 1 November 2007: SI 2007/2903 reg 2, Sch 1 Note (*c*).

Sub-paras (i), (ii) previously read as follows—

"(i) to which regulation 34, 35 or 36 applies, or

(ii) that otherwise includes a reduced-rate part.".

Special cases

39—(1) Regulations 34 to 38 apply, as appropriate, even if the supplier and the recipient are the same person (deemed self-supplies and the case provided for by paragraph (2)).

(2) A recipient who is liable to account for the CCL charged on a taxable supply shall be regarded as the same person as the supplier for the purposes of this Part and [Schedule 1][1] (see paragraph 40(2) of the Act—taxable supplies made by persons who are neither resident in the United Kingdom nor utilities).

Amendments—[1] Words substituted by the CCL (General) (Amendment) Regulations, SI 2003/604 regs 2, 4 with effect from 1 April 2003.

Suppliers to producers of commodities

40—(1) An exemption provided for by paragraph 13 or 14(1) of the Act (supplies to producers of commodities other than electricity and certain supplies to electricity producers) has effect subject to paragraph (2).

(2) The supply of the taxable commodity in question shall be a taxable supply (and not an exempt supply) to the extent that it is to be used by the recipient for the purposes of—

(*a*) headquarters administration facilities;

(*b*) telephone call centres;

(*c*) dedicated visitor centres;

(*d*) any commercial matters (including power for computers and ancillary equipment, and legal, contractual or taxation matters);

(*e*) road tanker deliveries otherwise than at the production site.

(3) This regulation has effect without prejudice to the generality of paragraph 13 or 14(1) of the Act.

Non-registrable electricity producers

41—(1) Paragraph (2) applies if and to the extent that a non-registrable electricity producer produces electricity and makes a supply of it to an electricity utility (or a person treated as such for CCL purposes).

(2) If and to the extent that this paragraph applies, that supply of electricity shall be treated for the purposes of paragraph 14(1) of the Act as a use of that electricity in relation to which the exemption provided for by that paragraph is retained.

42—*(1) A supply of a taxable commodity to a non-registrable electricity producer shall be treated as being a half-rate supply to the extent that he both—*

(a) uses that commodity to produce electricity, and

(b) uses that electricity in making a supply meeting the description of a half-rate supply in paragraph 43(1) of the Act (horticultural producers).

(2) Paragraph (1) has effect subject to regulations 35, 37, 38 and 39.

[(3) This regulation does not apply to a supply made after 31st March 2006.][1]

[(4) Regulations 35(6) to 35(9) (cessation of certification following abolition of half-rate supplies)have effect for determining when a supply is to be regarded as made for the purposes of paragraph (3).][1,2]

Amendments—[1] Paras (3), (4) inserted by the CCL (General) (Amendment) Regulations, SI 2006/954 regs 1(2), 3 with effect from 1 April 2006.

[2] Reg 42 revoked by the Climate Change Levy (General) (Amendment) Regulations, SI 2007/2903 reg 2, Sch 1 para 19 with effect from 1 November 2007: SI 2007/2903 reg 1. This amendment does not apply in relation to a half-rate supply made before 1 April 2006: SI 2007/2903 reg 2, Sch 1 Note (*a*).

43—(1) A non-registrable electricity producer who delivers a supplier certificate that is required to be supported by an analysis document shall annex to that analysis document details of—

(*a*) the quantity of electricity that is attributable to self supplies,

(*b*) the individual quantities of electricity supplied by him to other persons, and

(*c*) the identity and address of each other person to whom he supplies electricity.

(2) This regulation has effect by way of supplement to the requirements of regulations 34(3), 35(3) and 36(3) and, to that extent, is subject to regulation 38.

(3) In this regulation—

"electricity" refers to electricity to which the supplier certificate in question relates;

"self supplies" refers to any supplies of electricity that are deemed by paragraph 23(3) of the Act (use of commodities by producers) to be made to himself by the relevant non-registrable electricity producer (own use).

(4) In these Regulations and [Schedule 1][1] a reference to an analysis document includes a reference to any annexe required by paragraph (1).

Amendments—[1] Words substituted by the CCL (General) (Amendment) Regulations, SI 2003/604 regs 2, 4 with effect from 1 April 2003.

Facilities covered by climate change agreements

44—(1) For the purposes of paragraph 44 of the Act (reduced-rate for supplies covered by climate change agreement), a taxable commodity shall not be regarded as being supplied otherwise than to a facility covered by a climate change agreement solely because it is delivered and stored elsewhere prior to being burned within that facility.

(2) Paragraph (1) does not apply in a case where the taxable commodity in question is electricity or gas.

45—(1) This regulation applies where a taxable commodity is supplied to a non-registrable electricity producer otherwise than at a facility that is certified as being covered by a climate change agreement in accordance with paragraph 44(1) of the Act.

(2) That taxable commodity shall be regarded as supplied to a facility certified as being covered by a climate change agreement to the extent that it is used to produce electricity that is in fact supplied to such a facility by that non-registrable electricity producer.

(3) This regulation has effect subject to regulations 36, 37, 38 and 39.

PART IV
RENEWABLE SOURCE ELECTRICITY

Interpretation of Part IV

46 . . . [1] In this Part—

"exempt renewable supplies" refers to that expression in paragraph 19(2) of the Act;

["MWh" is an abbreviation for megawatt-hour;][1]

["relevant Authority" refers to the Gas and Electricity Markets Authority or, in relation to electricity produced or supplied in Northern Ireland or produced in the Republic of Ireland, the Director General of Electricity Supply for Northern Ireland;][1]

"renewable source contract" refers to the contract mentioned in paragraph 19(1)(*b*) of the Act (contract containing renewable source declaration).

(2)–(4) . . . [1]

Amendments—[1] Para (1) renumbered as regulation 46, and paras (2)–(4) revoked, by the CCL (General) (Amendment) Regulations, SI 2003/604 regs 2, 9, 10 with effect from 1 April 2003.

Generation and certification of renewable source electricity

47—(1) Subject to paragraphs (3) to (15) and regulation 48, electricity is "renewable source electricity" for the purposes of the Act to the extent that it has been generated from renewable sources provided that it is not electricity generated from a large hydro generating station.

(2) In this regulation—

["biomass" means fuel used in a generating station of which at least 98 per cent of the energy content is derived from plant or animal matter, or substances derived directly or indirectly therefrom (whether or not such matter or substances are waste) and includes agricultural, forestry or wood wastes or residues, sewage and energy crops (provided that such plant or animal matter is not or is not derived directly from or indirectly from fossil fuel);][1]

"declared net capacity" means the highest generation of electricity (at the main alternator terminals) which, on the assumption that the source of power is available without interruption, can be maintained indefinitely without causing damage to the plant less so much of that capacity as is consumed by the plant;

"distribution system" and "transmission system" in relation to Great Britain have the meanings given in section 4 of the Electricity Act 1989 as it will have effect once it has been amended by section 28 of the Utilities Act 2000; in relation to Northern Ireland "transmission system" system has the meaning given in article 3 of the Electricity (Northern Ireland) Order 1992;[3]

"fossil fuel" means coal, substances produced directly or indirectly from coal, lignite, natural gas, crude liquid petroleum, or petroleum products (and "natural gas" and "petroleum products" have the same meanings as in the Energy Act 1976);

"generator", except in the definition of "hydro generating station" below, means the operator of a generating station;

"hydro generating station" means a generating station which is wholly or mainly driven by water other than stations driven by tidal flows, waves, ocean currents or geothermal sources and the "station" extends to all structures and works for holding or channelling water for a purpose directly related to the generation of electricity together with any turbines and associated generators directly connected to or fed by such common structures or works;

"large hydro generating station" means a hydro generating station with a declared net capacity of more than 10 megawatts;

"renewable sources" means sources of energy other than [peat,][1] fossil fuel or nuclear fuel and includes—

[(*a*) biomass, and

(*b*)] [1] waste

provided that it is not waste with an energy content 90 per cent. or more of which is derived from fossil fuel;

"waste" has the meaning given in section 75(2) of the Environmental Protection Act 1990 as that subsection will have effect once it has been amended by paragraph 88 of Schedule 22 to the Environment Act 1995, but does not include gas derived from landfill sites or gas produced from the treatment of sewage.

[(2A) For the purposes of this Part and paragraphs 19 and 20 of the Act, coal mine methane shall be regarded as a renewable source and not a fossil fuel (see paragraph 19(4A) of the Act).][2]

(3) In the following paragraphs, except in relation to paragraphs (7), (8) and (12), references to fossil fuel do not include references to any fossil fuel content of [biomass or][1] waste.

(4) Paragraph (11) is to apply where a generating station is fuelled by renewable sources and fossil fuel in order to calculate the respective proportions of electricity generated by that station from renewable sources and from fossil fuel in any period specified by the relevant Authority, but paragraph (11) does not apply to generating stations to which paragraph (10) applies.

(5) Where the renewable sources used to fuel a generating station includes waste (whether or not the generating station is fuelled by waste in combination with other renewable sources or fossil fuel) paragraphs (7), (8) and (9) apply in order to calculate the amount of renewable source electricity which is to be regarded as generated from that waste in any period specified by the relevant Authority.

[(5A) Where the renewable sources used to fuel a generating station includes biomass (whether or not the generating station is fuelled by biomass in combination with other renewable sources or fossil fuel) paragraph (9) applies in order to calculate the amount of renewable source electricity which is to be regarded as generated from that biomass in any period specified by the relevant Authority.][1]

(6) Paragraph 10 applies where fossil fuel is used only for the purposes specified in that paragraph.

(7) Subject to paragraphs (8) and (9), where a generating station is fuelled by waste, the proportion of electricity generated from waste which is to be regarded as renewable source electricity is 50 per cent. of the proportion of electricity which has been generated by that station from waste provided that the relevant Authority determines that the generator has no reasonable grounds to believe that more than 50 per cent. of the energy content of the waste used is derived from fossil fuel.

(8) On request by a generator who considers that more than 50 per cent. of the electricity generated from waste by that station has been generated from waste which is not or has not been derived from fossil fuel, the relevant Authority shall determine in accordance with paragraph (12) the proportion of electricity so generated from such waste and that proportion shall be regarded as renewable source electricity.

(9) Where the relevant Authority determines that a generating station is fuelled by waste at least 98 per cent. of the energy content of which is derived from plant or animal substances (including agricultural, forestry, wood and human wastes or residues), the amount of electricity generated from such waste which is to be regarded as renewable source electricity is 100 per cent. of the electricity which is generated from such [biomass or][1] waste.

(10) Where a generating station uses fossil fuel only for one or more of the following purposes—

(*a*) the ignition of gases of low or variable calorific value;

(*b*) the heating of the combustion system to its normal operating temperature or the maintenance of that temperature;

(*c*) emission control;

provided that the relevant Authority determines that in any year the energy content of the fossil fuel used for the above purposes in the generating station does not exceed 10 per cent. of the energy content of the renewable sources used, that fossil fuel shall be treated as if it were the renewable source used as the remainder of the fuel in the generating station.

(11) Where a generating station is fuelled partly by renewable sources and partly by fossil fuel, (with the exception of generating stations to which paragraph (10) applies) the respective proportions of electricity which have been generated from fossil fuel and any one or more renewable sources shall be determined by the relevant Authority in the manner described in paragraph (12), and the proportion of electricity generated from renewable sources other than waste (to which paragraphs (7), (8) and (9) apply) shall be regarded as renewable source electricity.

(12) In any case where the relevant Authority is required or requires to determine the proportions of electricity generated from either fossil fuel or any one or more renewable sources, it shall do so by reference to the energy content of the relevant fuels.

(13) Where the amount of electricity generated by a hydro generating station has been increased due to the flow rate, height or pressure of water being artificially increased as a result of pumping, the amount of renewable source electricity generated by that station shall be calculated by deducting from the amount of electricity generated by the station any electricity which has not been generated from renewable sources which is used for such pumping.

(14) . . . [1]

(15) Where the relevant Authority is required to make any determination under this regulation it shall only be so required once it has been provided with adequate information on which to base its decision.

Amendments—[1] In para (2), definition of "biomass" inserted, and words in definition of "renewable sources" inserted; words in paras (3), (9) inserted; para (5A) inserted; and para (14) revoked; by the CCL (General) (Amendment) Regulations, SI 2003/604 regs 2, 11–14 with effect from 1 April 2003.

[2] Para (2A) inserted by the Climate Change Levy (General) (Amendment) (No 2) Regulations, SI 2003/2633 with effect from 1 November 2003. Para (2A) revoked by FA 2008 s 149 in relation to electricity generated on or after 1 November 2008.

[3] In para (2) definition of "distribution system and transmission system" revoked by the Climate Change Levy (General) (Amendment) Regulations, SI 2007/2903 reg 2, Sch 1 para 20 with effect from 1 November 2007: SI 2007/2903 reg 1.

48—(1) A quantity of electricity constitutes "renewable source electricity" for the purposes of paragraphs 19 and 20 of the Act only if and to the extent that it complies with regulation 47 and is the subject of a certificate (a "levy exemption certificate") issued by the relevant Authority to confirm that the requirements of regulation 47 are satisfied in relation to that quantity.

[(1A) The relevant Authority must only issue a levy exemption certificate on the basis of the most accurate figures for electricity produced in a generating station that the person who generates that electricity makes known to the Authority.][1]

[(1B) The relevant Authority must disregard any figures that are made known to it or of which it becomes aware after the end of the second month following the end of the month in which the electricity is produced.][1, 3]

(2) Each levy exemption certificate ("[Renewables LEC][2]") shall carry a unique identifying reference ("identifier").

(3) The relevant Authority need not issue a [Renewables LEC][2] in relation to any quantity of electricity under paragraph (1) if—

(*a*) the person who generates that electricity does not provide the relevant Authority with such information, particulars, records and declarations as it may require for the purposes of that paragraph or regulation 47;

(*b*) the person who generates that electricity does not, if so required, provide the relevant Authority with updated readings from any relevant electricity meter;

(*c*) any person authorised by the relevant Authority has not, on request, been granted access at any reasonable time to the premises from where that electricity is generated;

(*d*) any person authorised by the relevant Authority has not, on request and having been granted access to premises in accordance with sub-paragraph (*c*), been permitted—

(i) to inspect or test anything that is on those premises, and

(ii) to inspect any records that are on those premises,

connected with the generation or supply of that electricity;

(*e*) any person authorised by the relevant Authority has not, on request, been granted access to any premises at any reasonable time to take updated readings from any relevant electricity meters;

(*f*) any one or more of sub-paragraphs (*a*) to (*e*) have not been satisfied within such time as the relevant Authority considers reasonable for the purpose in question; or

(*g*) the relevant Authority is for any reason not satisfied that the electricity in question should be regarded as renewable source electricity.

[(4) The relevant Authority need not issue a Renewables LEC as respects a quantity of electricity less than 1 MWh.

However the relevant Authority may aggregate or disaggregate such quantities relating to the same generating station, certifying each complete MWh as appropriate.][1]

[(5) The relevant Authority need not issue a Renewables LEC unless it is satisfied that the Renewables LEC, if issued, would represent electricity consumed or to be consumed in the United Kingdom.

For this purpose, the relevant Authority may have regard in particular to whether any part of that electricity is or may be allocated by the operator of the generating station or a supplier for consumption outside the United Kingdom.][1]

[(6) A Renewables LEC must be regarded for all purposes of this Part as only relating to the actual electricity in relation to which it was issued.][1]

Amendments—[1] Paras (1A), (1B), and paras (4)–(6) inserted by the CCL (General) (Amendment) Regulations, SI 2003/604 regs 2, 15, 16 with effect from 1 April 2003.

[2] Words in paras (2), (3) substituted by the CCL (General) (Amendment) Regulations, SI 2003/604 regs 2, 18 with effect from 1 April 2003.

[3] Para (1B) revoked by the Climate Change Levy (General) (Amendment) Regulations, SI 2007/2903 reg 2, Sch 1 para 21 with effect from 1 November 2007: SI 2007/2903 reg 1. This amendment only applies in relation to figures that have not been disregarded before 1 November 2007 under SI 2001/838 reg 48(1B) or 51B(3): SI 2007/2903 reg 2, Sch 1 Note (*d*).

Conditions for exemption from CCL

49—(1) Any part of a quantity of electricity that is the subject of a [Renewables LEC][2] shall be regarded as never having been renewable source electricity capable of being the subject of exempt renewable supplies for the purposes of paragraph 19 of the Act if one or more of the conditions prescribed in paragraphs (2), (3), (4) and (5) are not fulfilled.

(2) The electricity must not be allocated to a supply to a person who—

(*a*) intends to cause the electricity to be exported from the United Kingdom, and

(*b*) has no intention to cause it to be brought back into the United Kingdom afterwards.

(3) Should the electricity be allocated to some supply pursuant to some renewable source contract, the supplier must inform the relevant Authority of this fact and of the relevant [Renewables LEC][2] identifier.

(4) At any time up to 6 years after the day the electricity is generated—

(*a*) the person who generated it must provide the relevant Authority on request with readily legible records relating to and detailing—

(i) the generation process,

(ii) the supplies made of that electricity and the relevant recipients,

(iii) [any relevant Renewables LEC (and, if different from the relevant recipient, the identity of any person to whom entitlement to that Renewables LEC is transferred)][1], and

(iv) any relevant information, particulars or records referred to in regulation 48(3)(*a*);

and

(*b*) any supplier of that electricity must provide the relevant Authority on request with readily legible records relating to and detailing—

(i) the supplies he received or made of that electricity,

(ii) the relevant recipients of any supplies he made of that electricity, and

(iii) [any relevant Renewables LEC (and, if different from the relevant recipient, the identity of any person to whom entitlement to that Renewables LEC is transferred)][1].

(5) The following time limits apply as part of the conditions described in this regulation—

(*a*) paragraph (3)—the supplier must comply within such reasonable time as the relevant Authority allows for this purpose;

(*b*) paragraph (4)—the generator and the supplier, as appropriate, must comply within such reasonable time as the relevant Authority allows for this purpose.

Amendments—[1] Words in para (4) substituted by the CCL (General) (Amendment) Regulations, SI 2003/604 regs 2, 17 with effect from 1 April 2003.

[2] Words in paras (1), (3) substituted by the CCL (General) (Amendment) Regulations, SI 2003/604 regs 2, 18 with effect from 1 April 2003.

50 Supplies shall not be regarded as exempt renewable supplies for the purposes of paragraph 19 of the Act unless—

(*a*) the supplier provides the recipient with a written notice for the duration of the renewable source contract, updated as necessary, setting out how to identify those supplies of electricity that—

(i) are or will be made under the renewable source contract, and

(ii) are or will be referred to on a climate change levy accounting document (or an invoice) issued in respect of those supplies;

(*b*) the supplier retains a copy of each such notice for 6 years starting from the day after it is provided to the recipient;

(*c*) the supplier supplies a copy of any such notice to the Commissioners no later than the fourteenth day after the Commissioners so request.

51—(1) The exemption provided for by paragraph 19(1) of the Act (exemption: supply of electricity from renewable sources) shall only be given effect if the supplier, and each other person (if any) who is a generator of any renewable source electricity allocated by the supplier to supplies under the renewable source contract in question, has delivered a copy of the relevant notice to the relevant Authority.

(2) In paragraph (1), "relevant notice" refers to the written notice mentioned in paragraph 19(1)(*d*) of the Act relating to the supply of electricity and contract in question (notice to Commissioners agreeing to fulfil conditions of exemption).

[PART IV(A)
COMBINED HEAT AND POWER STATIONS][1]

Amendments—[1] This Part inserted by the CCL (General) (Amendment) Regulations, SI 2003/604 regs 2, 19 with effect from 1 April 2003.

[Interpretation of Part IV(A)

51A—[(1)] [2] For the purposes of this Part and [Schedules 1 and 2][2]—

"authorised person" (except for the purposes of Schedule 2, paragraph 7(*a*)) refers to a person authorised by the relevant Authority;

"CHP declaration contract" refers to the contract mentioned in paragraph 20A(1)(*b*) of the Act;

["CHPQA" refers to the Combined Heat and Power Quality Assurance Standard, Issue 1, November 2000 originally published by the Department for the Environment, Transport and the Regions (including the later of version Final 1.0 or 2.0 of CHPQA Guidance Notes 0 to 4 (including 2(S), 3(S) and 4(S)), 10 to 28 and 30);][2]

"CHP Relief Condition" refers to paragraphs 2 to 7 and paragraph 12 of Schedule 2;

"exemption certificate" refers to a full-exemption certificate or a part-exemption certificate (see paragraphs 148(2) and 148(3) of the Act and the Climate Change Levy (Combined Heat and Power Stations) Exemption Certificate Regulations 2001);

"fully exempt CHP" refers to a fully exempt combined heat and power station (see paragraph 148(2) of the Act);

"indirect supplies" refers to supplies in relation to which provision is made by paragraph 20A(1) of the Act (exemption for supply made by electricity utility of CHP electricity);

"MWh" is an abbreviation for megawatt-hour;

"operator" refers to the person who operates a station or who generates or produces electricity in that station;

"outputs" or "output" refers to the meaning given by paragraph 148(9) of the Act (electricity or motive power produced in a station, and (*a*) heat or steam, or (*b*) air, or water, that has been heated or cooled);

"partly exempt CHP" refers to a partly exempt combined heat and power station (see paragraph 148(3) of the Act);

"QPO" means qualifying power output;

"QPO electricity" refers to electricity that—

(*a*) has been produced in a fully exempt CHP;

(*b*) has been produced in a partly exempt CHP and supplied from it without causing the limit referred to in paragraph 16(2) of the Act to be exceeded;

"station" refers to a fully or partly exempt CHP;

"relevant Authority" refers to the Gas and Electricity Markets Authority or, in relation to electricity produced or supplied in Northern Ireland or produced in the Republic of Ireland, the Director General of Electricity Supply for Northern Ireland.][1]

[(2) In the case of electricity produced in a given station after 21st July 2005, this Part and Schedule 2 (and the related penalties provided for by regulation 60(1)(*ha*) and regulation 60(1)(*hb*)) only apply if at least some of that electricity is supplied otherwise than from that station (indirect supplies, see paragraph 20A(2) of the Act).][2]

Amendments—[1] This regulation inserted by the CCL (General) (Amendment) Regulations, SI 2003/604 regs 2, 19 with effect from 1 April 2003.

[2] Para (1) numbered as such, words therein substituted, definition of "CHPQA" inserted, and para (2) inserted, by the Climate Change Levy (Miscellaneous Amendments) Regulations, SI 2005/1716 regs 6, 7(1), (2) with effect from 22 July 2005. However, arrangements initiated or made before 22 July 2005 on the basis of SI 2001/838 Sch 1 para 5(5) or 5(6) as then in force remain subject to the provisions applicable when they were initiated or made (tax credit claims and corrections to over-estimated relief).

[Certification of electricity produced in a combined heat and power station

51B—[(1) The relevant Authority must certify QPO electricity in accordance with this Part and Schedule 2.][2]

(2) The relevant Authority must only certify on the basis of the most accurate figures for electricity produced in an individual station that the station's operator makes known to the Authority.

(3) The relevant Authority must disregard any figures that are made known to it or of which it becomes aware after the end of the second month following the end of the month in which the electricity is produced.[3]
(4) Paragraph (3)does not apply to regulation 51D, regulation 51E or Schedule 2 paragraph 11 (wrongly certified electricity and periodic reconciliation).[3]
(5) The station's operator must only make known figures for the purposes of paragraph (2) that are made in accordance with the metering requirements of [the CHPQA][2]
[(6) The relevant Authority must only certify for the purposes of paragraphs (1) and (2) on the basis that—

(*a*) each quantity of electricity produced by an individual station is referable to the Annual Operation in which it is produced, and

(*b*) every such quantity in a given Annual Operation comprises the same relative proportions of QPO electricity and non-QPO electricity.

This requirement is subject to the other provisions of this Part and Schedule 2 (non-certification, restricting validity to indirect supplies, reconciliation).
"Annual Operation" has the same meaning as in regulations 2(3), 3(2), 4 and 6(1) of the Climate Change Levy (Combined Heat and Power Stations) Regulations 2005 (namely, 1st January to 31st December).][2]
(7) The relevant Authority must not certify any electricity produced in a station when no exemption certificate is in force for that station.
(8) Where the relevant Authority certifies under paragraph (1), it must issue a levy exemption certificate ("CHP LEC") as respects that electricity.
[The relevant Authority must both certify QPO electricity in accordance with paragraphs (1), (2), *(3)*,[3] (6) and (7) and issue the relevant CHP LEC no later than the end of the third month following the end of the month in which the electricity is produced.
Whilst the relative proportions mentioned in paragraph (6)(*b*) are unknown, the relevant Authority must use a reasonable estimate of what those relative proportions will be.
If the relevant Authority must investigate further whether the electricity in question is "QPO electricity", it must certify the QPO electricity and issue the relevant CHP LEC no later than the end of the month following the month in which that investigation ought reasonably to have been concluded.][2]
(9) A CHP LEC must be regarded for all purposes of this Part and Schedule 2 as only relating to the actual electricity in relation to which it was issued.
(10) Each CHP LEC must carry a unique identifying reference.][1]

Amendments—[1] This regulation inserted by the CCL (General) (Amendment) Regulations, SI 2003/604 regs 2, 19 with effect from 1 April 2003.

[2] Paras (1), (6) and words in para (5) substituted, and words in para (8) inserted, by the Climate Change Levy (Miscellaneous Amendments) Regulations, SI 2005/1716 regs 6, 7(3)–(6) with effect from 22 July 2005. However, arrangements initiated or made before 22 July 2005 on the basis of SI 2001/838 Sch 1 para 5(5) or 5(6) as then in force remain subject to the provisions applicable when they were initiated or made (tax credit claims and corrections to over-estimated relief).

[3] Paras (3), (4), and reference "(3)," in para (8), revoked by the Climate Change Levy (General) (Amendment) Regulations, SI 2007/2903 reg 2, Sch 1 paras 22, 23 with effect from 1 November 2007: SI 2007/2903 reg 1. These amendments only apply in relation to figures that have not been disregarded before 1 November 2007 under SI 2001/838 reg 48(1B) or 51B(3): SI 2007/2903 reg 2, Sch 1 Note (*d*).

[51C—(1) The relevant Authority must neither certify electricity nor issue a CHP LEC as respects any electricity under any of the following circumstances.
(2) The first circumstance is where the quantity of electricity in question is less than 1 MWh.
However the relevant Authority may aggregate or disaggregate such quantities relating to the same station, certifying each complete MWh as appropriate.
(3) The second circumstance is where the relevant Authority is not satisfied that the CHP LEC, if issued, would represent electricity consumed or to be consumed in the United Kingdom.
For this purpose, the relevant Authority may have regard in particular to whether any part of that electricity is or may be allocated by the operator or a supplier for consumption outside the United Kingdom.
(4) The third circumstance is any one or more of the following—

(*a*) the operator not providing the relevant Authority with such information, particulars, records and declarations as the relevant Authority may require for the purposes of this Part or Schedule 2;

(*b*) the operator not providing the relevant Authority with any updated readings the relevant Authority may require from any relevant electricity meter;

(*c*) any authorised person not being granted, on request, access at any reasonable time to the station in question;

(*d*) any authorised person not being permitted, on request and having been granted access to the station—

(i) to inspect or test anything that is at the station and connected with the production or supply of any relevant electricity, and

(ii) to inspect any records that are at that station and so connected;

(*e*) any authorised person not, on request, being granted access to any premises at any reasonable time to take updated readings from any relevant electricity meter;

(*f*) the operator having been notified of an assessment to a civil penalty or to penalty interest in relation to an event subject to this Part or Schedule 2 and, irrespective of any relevant review or appeal, that amount being unrecovered (for assessments, see paragraphs 106 and 111 of the Act; for review and appeal, see Part XI of the Act);

(*g*) any one or more of sub-paragraphs (*a*) to (*e*) not being satisfied within such time as the relevant Authority considers reasonable for the purpose in question;

(*h*) . . . [2]][1]

Amendments—[1] This regulation inserted by the CCL (General) (Amendment) Regulations, SI 2003/604 regs 2, 19 with effect from 1 April 2003.

[2] Para (4)(*h*) revoked by the Climate Change Levy (Miscellaneous Amendments) Regulations, SI 2005/1716 regs 6, 7(7) with effect from 22 July 2005. However, arrangements initiated or made before 22 July 2005 on the basis of SI 2001/838 Sch 1 para 5(5) or 5(6) as then in force remain subject to the provisions applicable when they were initiated or made (tax credit claims and corrections to over-estimated relief).

[51D—(1) If the relevant Authority becomes aware that it has issued a CHP LEC in relation to—

(*a*) production when no exemption certificate was in force for the relevant station, or

(*b*) production in relation to which there is a breach of regulation 51B(5) (metering standards),

it shall as soon as practicable both restrict the validity of that CHP LEC to indirect supplies (see regulations 51I to 51M) and notify that restriction to the person to whom it was issued (see regulation 51B(8)).

(2) A CHP LEC so restricted is referred to in the remainder of this Part and in Schedule 2 as a "restricted CHP LEC" and any other CHP LEC is referred to as an "unrestricted CHP LEC" (but see also Schedule 2 paragraphs 8(3), 11(5) and 13(2)).][1]

Amendments—[1] This regulation inserted by the CCL (General) (Amendment) Regulations, SI 2003/604 regs 2, 19 with effect from 1 April 2003.

[51E—(1) The relevant Authority shall, in carrying out its functions under this Part, have regard to the proper administration of CCL.

(2) The relevant Authority shall in particular, and as appropriate, act in accordance with and have regard to Schedule 2 paragraphs 8, 10 and 11.

(3) The relevant Authority must keep a record of each CHP LEC for 6 years from the date of issue. The record must show the person to whom it was issued, whether the CHP LEC is unrestricted or restricted, and any indirect supply of the electricity to which the CHP LEC is relevant (see regulation 51J(3)).][1]

Amendments—[1] This regulation inserted by the CCL (General) (Amendment) Regulations, SI 2003/604 regs 2, 19 with effect from 1 April 2003.

[CCL treatment dependent on certification

51F Electricity shall not be regarded as QPO electricity for the purposes of regulation 4(1)(*a*) of the Climate Change Levy (Electricity and Gas) Regulations 2001 (direct supplies of electricity by utility from fully exempt CHP) unless it remains the subject of an unrestricted CHP LEC.][1]

Amendments—[1] This regulation inserted by the CCL (General) (Amendment) Regulations, SI 2003/604 regs 2, 19 with effect from 1 April 2003.

[51G—(1) Electricity shall not be regarded as QPO electricity for any of the following purposes unless it remains the subject of an unrestricted CHP LEC—

(*a*) the outputs of a station referred to in paragraph 15(1) of the Act (supplies to CHP exempt if to be used in producing station's outputs);

(*b*) the electricity referred to in paragraphs 16(1)(*a*), 17(3) and 17(4) of the Act (supplies from partly exempt CHP are exempt from CCL if specified limit not exceeded; self-supplies from station exempt if producer not auto-generator).

(2) Each of the following exemptions shall only be given effect subject to the CHP Relief Condition (see regulation 51H(1)) being fulfilled as follows—

(*a*) for paragraph 15(1) of the Act, the Condition must be fulfilled in relation to any QPO electricity that is a relevant output for the purposes of that paragraph (supplies to CHP exempt if for use in producing station's outputs);

(*b*) for paragraph 16(2) of the Act, the Condition must be fulfilled in relation to any QPO electricity referred to in that paragraph (supplies from partly exempt CHP are exempt from CCL if specified limit not exceeded);

(*c*) for paragraph 17(2) of the Act, the Condition must be fulfilled in relation to any QPO electricity that is the subject of the supply referred to in that paragraph (self-supply by auto-generator exempt);

(*d*) for paragraph 17(3) or 17(4) of the Act, the Condition must be fulfilled in relation to any QPO electricity that is electricity for the purposes of that paragraph (self-supplies from fully or partly exempt CHP exempt from CCL if producer not auto-generator).][1]

Amendments—[1] This regulation inserted by the CCL (General) (Amendment) Regulations, SI 2003/604 regs 2, 19 with effect from 1 April 2003.

[51H—(1) Schedule 2 has effect and, accordingly, the CHP Relief Condition binds any person who—

(*a*) represents to a supplier entitlement to the exemption from CCL provided for by paragraph 15(1) of the Act (supplies of taxable commodities to stations, and see also paragraph (4));

(*b*) does not account for CCL on a supply because an exemption is provided for by paragraph 16(2), 17(3) or 17(4) of the Act (supplies from partly exempt CHP and self-supplies from fully or partly exempt CHP);

(*c*) does not account for CCL on a supply because an exemption is provided for by paragraph 17(2) of the Act (self-supply by autogenerator) (but only if the electricity in question is QPO electricity).

(2) Paragraph 1 and regulations 51F and 51G only apply in relation to supplies that are treated as taking place on or after 1 April 2003 (see paragraphs 25 to 39 of the Act, time of supply).

(3) Regulations 51F and 51G apply in addition to regulation 60(1)(*hb*) (penalties relating to CHP Relief Condition)).

(4) Part III and Schedule 1 apply independently of this Part (certification, etc in relation to excluded, exempt . . .[2] and reduced-rate supplies).][1]

Amendments—[1] This regulation inserted by the CCL (General) (Amendment) Regulations, SI 2003/604 regs 2, 19 with effect from 1 April 2003.

[2] In para (4), words ", half-rate" revoked by the Climate Change Levy (General) (Amendment) Regulations, SI 2007/2903 reg 2, Sch 1 para 24 with effect from 1 November 2007: SI 2007/2903 reg 1. This amendment does not apply in relation to a half-rate supply made before 1 April 2006: SI 2007/2903 reg 2, Sch 1 Note (*a*).

[Supplies pursuant to CHP declaration contract

51I Electricity is only "CHP electricity" for the purposes of paragraphs 20A and 20B of the Act (exemption for indirect supplies) if it remains the subject of an unrestricted CHP LEC or a restricted CHP LEC.][1]

Amendments—[1] This regulation inserted by the CCL (General) (Amendment) Regulations, SI 2003/604 regs 2, 19 with effect from 1 April 2003.

[51J—(1) Any electricity that is the subject of a CHP LEC shall be regarded as never having been CHP electricity capable of being the subject of exempt CHP supplies for the purposes of paragraph 20A of the Act (indirect supplies) if one or more of the conditions prescribed in the following paragraphs are not fulfilled.

(2) The electricity must only be allocated to a supply to a person who intends it to be consumed in the United Kingdom.

(3) Should the electricity be allocated to some supply pursuant to some CHP declaration contract, the supplier must inform the relevant Authority of this fact and of the relevant CHP LEC's unique identifying reference (see regulation 51B(10)).

(4) At any time up to 6 years after the day the electricity is produced, any supplier of that electricity must on request and within such time as the relevant Authority considers reasonable provide that Authority with readily legible records relating to and detailing—

(*a*) the supplies that supplier received or made of that electricity,

(*b*) the relevant suppliers or recipients of any supplies that supplier received or made of that electricity,

(*c*) the relevant CHP LECs and, if different from the relevant supplier or recipient, the identity of any person from or to whom entitlement to the CHP LEC was obtained or transferred.][1]

Amendments—[1] This regulation inserted by the CCL (General) (Amendment) Regulations, SI 2003/604 regs 2, 19 with effect from 1 April 2003.

[51K Supplies shall not be regarded as exempt CHP supplies for the purposes of paragraph 20A of the Act unless—

(*a*) the supplier provides the recipient with a written notice for the duration of the CHP declaration contract, updated as necessary, setting out how to identify those supplies of electricity that—

(i) are or will be made under the CHP declaration contract, and

(ii) are or will be referred to on a climate change levy accounting document (or an invoice) issued in respect of those supplies;

(*b*) the supplier retains a copy of each such notice for 6 years starting from the day after it is provided to the recipient;

(*c*) the supplier provides a copy of any such notice to the Commissioners no later than 14 days after the Commissioners request one.][1]

Amendments—[1] This regulation inserted by the CCL (General) (Amendment) Regulations, SI 2003/604 regs 2, 19 with effect from 1 April 2003.

[51L The exemption provided for by paragraph 20A(1) of the Act (indirect supplies) shall only be given effect if the supplier, and each other person (if any) who is an operator in relation to any CHP electricity allocated by the supplier to supplies under the CHP declaration contract in question, has delivered a copy of the notice referred to in paragraph 20A(1)(*d*) of the Act (agreement to fulfil conditions) to the relevant Authority.][1]

Amendments—[1] This regulation inserted by the CCL (General) (Amendment) Regulations, SI 2003/604 regs 2, 19 with effect from 1 April 2003.

[51M—(1) A supply of electricity is exempt from the levy chargeable under paragraph 5(1) of the Act, and electricity is "CHP electricity" for the purposes of paragraphs 20A and 20B of the Act, only if paragraph (2) is satisfied in relation to that electricity.

(2) The electricity must not have been produced when the station that produced it has received State aid exceeding any relevant limit in the "Community guidelines on State aid for environmental protection (2001/C 37/03).][1]

Amendments—[1] This regulation inserted by the CCL (General) (Amendment) Regulations, SI 2003/604 regs 2, 19 with effect from 1 April 2003.

PART V
ELECTRICITY AND GAS

Self-supply of electricity by producer

52—(1) For the purposes of paragraph 23(3)(*b*)(ii) of the Act (self-supply by producer of electricity from taxable commodities), electricity shall be treated as produced from taxable commodities except to the extent that—

(*a*) it is produced from material that is not a taxable commodity for the purposes of the Act (see paragraph 3 of the Act); or

(*b*) it constitutes renewable source electricity as prescribed by regulation 47 (excluding, for this purpose, regulation 48).

(2) Electricity shall not be regarded as falling within paragraph (1)(*a*) to the extent that it is produced by or in—

(*a*) a large hydro generating station within the meaning of regulation 47(2), or

(*b*) a nuclear power station.

(3) Accordingly electricity produced by or in a large hydro station or a nuclear power station shall be treated as produced from taxable commodities for the purposes of paragraph 23(3)(*b*)(ii) of the Act.

Small-scale users of electricity and gas

53—(1) Paragraphs (2) and (4) prescribe the rates for the purposes of paragraph 27(6) of the Act (maximum rates of supply for small-scale electricity and gas users).

(2) In the case of electricity, the prescribed rate—

(*a*) is any rate at which the supplier supplies electricity to a person provided that the supplier issues an invoice or statement of account (however termed or styled) to that person in respect of those supplies no more than once in each period of six weeks, or

(*b*) is the rate at which the supplier supplies electricity to the person in question provided that in any period of one year that includes the Reference Day the maximum demand from that person is less than 100 kilowatts.

(3) The "maximum demand" for the purposes of paragraph (2)(*b*) shall be determined by the supplier as follows—

(*a*) establish the three highest demands for that person in a period of one year including the Reference Day;

(*b*) the mean of those three demands is the relevant "maximum demand";

(*c*) disregard any supplies of electricity made to the person by a different supplier.

(4) In the case of gas, the prescribed rate—

(*a*) is any rate at which the supplier supplies gas to a person provided that the supplier issues an invoice or statement of account (however termed or styled) to that person in respect of those supplies no more than once in each period of six weeks, or

(*b*) in any other case, is 750 megawatt hours in a period of one year.

(5) The rate at which a person must be taken to be supplied with gas for the purposes of paragraph (4)(*b*) shall be determined by the supplier as follows—

(*a*) estimate, for each individual reference number used or to be used by the supplier in question for that person, the quantity of gas to be supplied in the period starting on the Reference Day and ending 1 year later;

(*b*) the relevant gas rate shall be taken to be—

(i) if there is only one such quantity, that quantity; or

(ii) the highest of those individual quantities;

(*c*) disregard—

(i) the aggregate of those individual quantities (if there is more than one);

(ii) any supplies of gas that may be made to the person by a different supplier.

(6) The supplier need not make a further determination under paragraph (3) or (5) if he has reasonable grounds to believe that the further determination would result in the person—

(*a*) remaining a small-scale user; or

(*b*) remaining a person who is not a small-scale user.

(7) In this regulation—

"Reference Day" refers to the day mentioned in paragraph 27(6) of the Act;

"reference number" refers to that expression in paragraph 27(5)(*e*) of the Act;

"estimate" requires the use of any reasonable and accurate method.

Special utility schemes

54—(1) This regulation applies at any time after a special utility scheme has taken effect under paragraphs 29(4) and 29(5) of the Act but before the end of the period specified for which it is to have effect under paragraph 29(3) of the Act.

(2) If the Commissioners are satisfied that there will be no risk to the revenue, they may agree with the utility in question to amend the scheme or terminate it early.

(3) The Commissioners may terminate the scheme early if the utility in question—

(*a*) fails to abide by the scheme despite having elected in writing to be bound by it under paragraph 29(4) of the Act, or

(*b*) becomes, for any reason, incapable of abiding by the scheme.

(4) Termination under paragraph (3) shall take effect from such time as the Commissioners shall state in a written notice served by them for the purposes of that paragraph on the utility in question or on any relevant representative referred to in regulation 57 (representatives: incapacity, insolvency, etc).

(5) The Commissioners shall not state a time in that written notice that is earlier than when it is served under paragraph (4).

(6) Paragraph (5) shall not preclude the Commissioners from recovering by or under the Act any CCL that would have been due at any time up to the time so stated but for the special utility scheme having effect up to that time.

(7) A special utility scheme shall not be either amended or terminated early except in accordance with this regulation.

PART VI
DEATH, INCAPACITY, INSOLVENCY, TRANSFERS

Individuals: death or incapacity

55—(1) The Commissioners may, for CCL purposes and subject to this regulation, treat a person who carries on relevant activities on behalf of an individual who has died or become temporarily incapacitated as if they were the same person.

(2) Such treatment may continue pending someone other than that individual being registered under Part V of the Act in relation to those activities or the incapacity ceasing.

(3) A person who carries on relevant activities in the circumstances described in paragraph (1) must notify the Commissioners of this in writing and that notification must also include the date of death or the date and nature of the incapacity.

(4) This notification must be delivered to the Commissioners within 21 days starting with the day after the person begins carrying on the relevant activities.

(5) In this regulation, "relevant activities" refers to any activities in relation to which the individual in question is or was a registrable person.

Insolvency

56—(1) The Commissioners may, for CCL purposes and subject to this regulation, treat a person who carries on relevant activities of a registrable person to whom an insolvency procedure is applied as if they were the same person.

(2) Such treatment may continue pending someone other than that registrable person being registered under Part V of the Act in relation to those activities or the insolvency procedure no longer being applied.

(3) A person who carries on relevant activities in the circumstances described in paragraph (1) must notify the Commissioners of this in writing and that notification must also include the date the insolvency procedure was first applied.

(4) This notification must be delivered to the Commissioners within 21 days starting with the day after the person begins carrying on the relevant activities.

(5) In this regulation—

"relevant activities" refers to any activities in relation to which the individual in question is or was a registrable person;

"registrable person" may include, as appropriate, the estate of a deceased individual.

(6) An insolvency procedure is applied to a person for the purposes of this regulation in the circumstances described by paragraphs 120(7) to 120(9) of the Act (insolvency procedures for the purposes of this regulation).

Representatives: death, incapacity or insolvency

57—(1) If the Commissioners so require, a representative who controls the assets of a registrable person because of death, incapacity or the application of an insolvency procedure shall, for the purposes of CCL and subject to this regulation, be treated as if he was the registrable person.

(2) Any requirement resulting from paragraph (1) for the representative to pay CCL shall only apply to the extent of the assets he controls.

(3) Any other requirement resulting from paragraph (1) shall apply in the same way as it would have applied to the registrable person but for the death, incapacity or insolvency procedure.

(4) In this regulation—

"relevant activities" refers to any activities in relation to which the registrable person in question is or was registrable;

"registrable person" may include, as appropriate, the estate of a deceased individual.

(5) An insolvency procedure is applied to a person for the purposes of this regulation in the circumstances described by paragraphs 120(7) to 120(9) of the Act (insolvency procedures for the purposes of this regulation).

Insolvency: consumers liable to penalty or interest

58—(1) This regulation applies where, in relation to a person ("the consumer")—

(*a*) the Commissioners assess and notify an amount due by way of penalty from the consumer for conduct falling within paragraph 98 (evasion) or 101 (incorrect notification for exclusion or exemption) of the Act;

(*b*) that amount or any penalty interest it carries remains unpaid; and

(*c*) an insolvency procedure applies to the consumer.

(2) The person appointed for the purposes of the application of the insolvency procedure ("the appointee") must notify the Commissioners of this in writing and that notification must also include the date the insolvency procedure first applied.

(3) This notification must be delivered to the Commissioners within 21 days starting with the day after the appointment takes effect or notice of the penalty or interest reaches the appointee, whichever is the later.

(4) Subject to this regulation, the appointee shall be treated to the extent and for the duration of the appointment as the same person as the consumer for the purposes of Part IX of the Act (civil penalties).

(5) An insolvency procedure is applied to a person for the purposes of this regulation in the circumstances described by paragraphs 120(7) to 120(9) of the Act (insolvency procedures for the purposes of this regulation).

Transfers of going concerns

59—(1) Where—

(*a*) a business carried on by a person who is registered under Part V of the Act is transferred to another person as a going concern,

(*b*) the registration of the transferor has not been cancelled,

(*c*) the transfer requires that the transferor's registration be cancelled and that the transferee either be registered for CCL or notify the Commissioners that he is registrable for CCL, and

(*d*) a written application for this purpose is made to the Commissioners by the transferor and transferee,

the Commissioners may, with effect from the date of the transfer, cancel the registration of the transferor and register the transferee in his place with the registration number previously allocated to the transferor.

(2) Should the Commissioners cancel the registration of the transferor and register the transferee in his place under paragraph (1) then, in order to secure continuity in the application of the Act—

(*a*) any liability of the transferor existing at the date of the transfer to make a return or account for or pay CCL shall become the liability of the transferee;

(*b*) any entitlement of the transferor, whether or not existing at the date of the transfer, to a tax credit or repayment under the Act, Part II of these Regulations or [Schedule 1][1] to these Regulations shall become the entitlement of the transferee;

(*c*) any other provision by or under the Act relating to CCL that applied to the transferor before his registration was cancelled (or any such provision that continues to apply to the transferor after that cancellation) shall apply to the transferee; and (*d*) any circumstances relating to the application of the Act (or any provision made under the Act) to the CCL affairs of the transferor before his registration was cancelled (or any such circumstances that continue to apply to the transferor after that cancellation) shall apply to the transferee.

(3) In addition to the provisions set out in paragraph (2), where—

(*a*) the Commissioners cancel the registration of the transferor and register the transferee in his place under paragraph (1) with effect from a date earlier than the accounting period in which they do so, and

(*b*) either the transferor or the transferee has, in relation to any time on or after that date but before the start of that accounting period—

(i) made a return,

(ii) accounted for CCL, or

(iii) claimed a relevant tax credit,

the matters referred to in sub-paragraphs (b)(i) to (b)(iii) shall be treated as having been done by the transferee.

Amendments—[1] Words substituted by the CCL (General) (Amendment) Regulations, SI 2003/604 regs 2, 4 with effect from 1 April 2003.

PART VII
PENALTIES

60—(1) A person who fails to comply with a requirement imposed on him by or under any of the following provisions of these Regulations shall be liable to a penalty of £250 for each such failure—

(*a*) regulation 5(1), 5(2), 5(3) or 5(4);

(*b*) regulation 6(2);

(*c*) regulation 7(1), 7(2), 7(3) or 7(4);

(*d*) regulation 8;

(*e*) regulation 27(1) or 27(2);

(*f*) regulation 28(6) or 28(8);

(*g*) regulation 37(5);

(*h*) regulation 38 and paragraph 4, 12(3), 14(1), 14(2), 15(*a*) or 15(*b*) of [Schedule 1][1];

[(*ha*) regulation 51B(5);][2]

[(*hb*) regulation 51H(1) and paragraph 2, 3(1), 3(3), 3(4), 3(5), 4, 5, 6, 7, 11(2) or 12(1) of Schedule 2;][2]

(*i*) regulation 55(3) or 55(4);

(*j*) regulation 56(3) or 56(4);

(*k*) regulation 58(2) or 58(3).

(2) A specific act or omission shall attract only one such penalty if the circumstances are such that, but for this paragraph, it would attract more than one penalty.

Amendments—[1] Words substituted by the CCL (General) (Amendment) Regulations, SI 2003/604 regs 2, 4 with effect from 1 April 2003.

[2] Paras (1)(*ha*), (*hb*) inserted by the CCL (General) (Amendment) Regulations, SI 2003/604 regs 2, 20 with effect from 1 April 2003.

PART VIII
CONSEQUENTIAL AMENDMENTS

61 In regulation 2(1) of the Distress for Customs and Excise Duties and Other Indirect Taxes Regulations 1997 under the meaning given for "relevant tax" insert—

"(*f*) climate change levy;"

[SCHEDULE 1][1]

CERTIFICATION AND MANNER OF PAYMENT OF CCL DUE IN THE CASE OF EXCLUDED, EXEMPT . . . [2] OR REDUCED-RATE SUPPLIES

Regulation 38

Amendments—[1] Schedule renumbered by the CCL (General) (Amendment) Regulations, SI 2003/604 regs 2, 21 with effect from 1 April 2003.

[2] Words ", half-rate" revoked by the Climate Change Levy (General) (Amendment) Regulations, SI 2007/2903 reg 2, Sch 1 para 25 with effect from 1 November 2007: SI 2007/2903 reg 1. This amendment does not apply in relation to a half-rate supply made before 1 April 2006: SI 2007/2903 reg 2, Sch 1 Note (*a*).

Paragraphs 1–4	Basic rules.
[Paragraph 5	Compulsory updates, correction and payment of CCL due, exemption from CCL registration.][1]

[Paragraphs 6–11	Tax credit for recipient and reconciliation for input fuel to combined heat and power stations.][1]
Paragraphs 12–15	Miscellaneous: voluntary updates, change of supplier, delivery of information, record keeping.

Amendments—[1] Entries substituted by the Climate Change Levy (Miscellaneous Amendments) Regulations, SI 2005/1716 regs 5(*a*), 6 with effect from 22 July 2005. However, arrangements initiated or made before 22 July 2005 on the basis of SI 2001/838 Sch 1 para 5(5) or 5(6) as then in force remain subject to the provisions applicable when they were initiated or made (tax credit claims and corrections to over-estimated relief).

Basic rules

1 This Schedule applies in relation to a supply to which regulation 34, 35 or 36 applies . . . [1].

Amendments—[1] Words "or that otherwise includes a reduced-rate part" revoked by the Climate Change Levy (General) (Amendment) Regulations, SI 2007/2903 reg 2, Sch 1 para 26 with effect from 1 November 2007: SI 2007/2903 reg 1. In relation to a reduced-rate supply or a supply made on that basis, this amendment only applies if the supply is made on or after 1 November 2007: SI 2007/2903 reg 2, Sch 1 Note (*b*).

2 CCL shall not be due on the percentage of the supply properly determined in accordance with the following formula (the "CCL relief formula"):

$$P = \frac{(C + M \;\; . \; . \; . \;\; + 0.8R)}{Q} \times 100$$

Notes

P = the percentage of the supply on which CCL is not due (the "CCL relief percentage") which must not be less than 0 per cent. nor more than 100 per cent.

Q = the quantity of the taxable commodity supplied.

In the case of electricity:

(*a*) Q includes any of that quantity that falls within the exclusion from CCL provided for by paragraph 9(2)(*f*)—community heating arrangements;

(*b*) Q does not include any of that quantity, apart from as described in (*a*) above, that falls within the exclusion from CCL provided for by paragraph 8—domestic or charity use;

[(*c*) Q does not include any of that quantity that falls within the exemption from CCL provided for by or under paragraph 16, 19 or 20A—electricity supplied exempt directly or indirectly from combined heat and power stations, or electricity supplied from renewable source.][1]

In all cases, Q does not include any quantity referable to exclusions under paragraph 8 (domestic or charity use) but does include any such quantity referable to the exclusion provided for by paragraphs 8 and 9(2)(*f*) (community heating arrangements).

C = the quantity of the taxable commodity referable to the sum of every relevant excluded part (paragraphs 8 and 9(2)(*f*)—community heating arrangements).

M = the quantity of the taxable commodity referable to the sum of every exempt part:

(*a*) paragraph 11—onward supplies and exports;

(*b*) paragraph 12—transport;

(*c*) paragraph 13—commodity producers;

(*d*) paragraph 14—electricity producers;

(*e*) paragraph 15—combined heat and power stations;

(*f*) paragraph 18—non-fuel use;

[(*fa*) paragraph 18A—recycling processes;][1]

(*g*) paragraph 21—regulation 41 of these Regulations (or other relevant regulations made under that paragraph of the Act to avoid double charges to CCL).

. . . [2]

0.8R = 80% of the quantity of the taxable commodity referable to the sum of every reduced-rate part (paragraph 44—climate change agreement).

The paragraph numbers referred to in these notes refer to the relevant paragraphs in Schedule 6 to the Finance Act 2000.

Amendments—[1] Words substituted and inserted by the Climate Change Levy (Miscellaneous Amendments) Regulations, SI 2005/1716 regs 5(*b*), 6 with effect from 22 July 2005. However, arrangements initiated or made before 22 July 2005 on the basis of SI 2001/838 Sch 1 para 5(5) or 5(6) as then in force remain subject to the provisions applicable when they were initiated or made (tax credit claims and corrections to over-estimated relief).

[2] Words "+ 0.5H" in climate change levy relief formula, and words "0.5H = 50% of the quantity of the taxable commodity referable to the sum of every half-rate part (paragraph 43—horticultural producers)." revoked, by the Climate Change Levy

(General) (Amendment) Regulations, SI 2007/2903 reg 2, Sch 1 para 27 with effect from 1 November 2007: SI 2007/2903 reg 1. This amendment does not apply in relation to a half-rate supply made before 1 April 2006: SI 2007/2903 reg 2, Sch 1 Note (*a*).

[2A *(1) For a supply made after 31st March 2006, the CCL relief formula in paragraph 2 is as follows (and the notes there, except the one about "0.5H", apply accordingly).*

$$P = \frac{C+M+0.8R}{Q} \times 100$$

(2) Regulations 35(6) to 35(9) (cessation of certification following abolition of half-rate supplies) have effect for determining when a supply is to be regarded as made for the purposes of sub-paragraph (1).][1,2]

Amendments—[1] Paragraph 2A inserted by the CCL (General) (Amendment) Regulations, SI 2006/954 regs 1(2), 4 with effect from 1 April 2006.

[2] Para 2A revoked, by the Climate Change Levy (General) (Amendment) Regulations, SI 2007/2903 reg 2, Sch 1 para 28 with effect from 1 November 2007: SI 2007/2903 reg 1.

3—(1) Any supplier certificate delivered by the recipient shall represent to the best of the recipient's judgment any information required by regulation 34(2) (exclusions and exemptions), [regulation 35(2) or 36(2) (reduced-rates),][1] or regulation 37(3) (combinations).

(2) A supplier certificate may relate to more than one supply (subject to Part III of these Regulations and the other provisions of this Schedule).

(3) Accordingly, if it relates to more than one supply, a supplier certificate shall provide a recipient's relief percentage based on—

(*a*) the likely number of supplies to which it will relate,

(*b*) the likely quantity of the taxable commodity in question that will be supplied to him by the supplier if those supplies are made, and

(*c*) any other relevant circumstances.

Amendments—[1] In para (1), words substituted for words "regulation 35(2) (half-rates), regulation 36(2) (certain reduced-rates)" by the Climate Change Levy (General) (Amendment) Regulations, SI 2007/2903 reg 2, Sch 1 para 28 with effect from 1 November 2007: SI 2007/2903 reg 1. This amendment does not apply in relation to a half-rate supply made before 1 April 2006: SI 2007/2903 reg 2, Sch 1 Note (a). In relation to a reduced-rate supply or a supply made on that basis, these amendments only apply if the supply is made on or after 1 November 2007: SI 2007/2903 reg 2, Sch 1 Note (b).

4 The supplier shall apply the CCL relief percentage to any supply he makes to which the supplier certificate relates and may, for this purpose, rely on the percentage (the "recipient's relief percentage") provided by the recipient in accordance with regulation 38(2).

[Compulsory updates, corrections and payment of CCL due, exemption from CCL registration][1]

5—(1) The recipient shall review the correctness of the supplier certificate no later than the earlier of—

(*a*) the sixtieth day after the expiry of one year starting from its implementation date, or

(*b*) the sixtieth day after the recipient has burned (or, in the case of electricity, consumed) the last of the taxable commodity supplied to which the supplier certificate relates.

(2) That correctness shall be reviewed in relation to—

(*a*) (if sub-paragraph (1)(*a*) applies), the elapsed period of one year starting with the implementation date (and this period is referred to in sub-paragraph (3) as the "review period"), or

(*b*) (if sub-paragraph (1)(*b*) applies), the CCL relief percentage calculated on the basis of actual events.

(3) If—

(*a*) the review demonstrates that the supplier certificate was correct, and

(*b*) that certificate also relates to supplies made or to be made by the supplier after the end of the review period,

that supplier certificate shall be regarded for the purposes of Part III of these Regulations and this Schedule as having as its implementation date the anniversary of its original implementation date (and sub-paragraphs (1) and (2) shall apply accordingly).

[This sub-paragraph is subject to paragraph 16 (5 year renewal limit).][1]

(4) Sub-paragraphs (5) to (10) apply if the review demonstrates that the supplier certificate was incorrect.

(5) If the supplier certificate was incorrect because the CCL relief percentage applied was too low, the recipient may act in accordance with paragraphs 6 to 10 (provision for tax credits) (subject to paragraph 11).

[(6) For the purposes of sub-paragraph (5), the benefit and extent of any relevant tax credit must be allocated to supplies in reverse chronological order (see paragraphs 6 to 10, tax credits for recipients, etc).

This means that supplies treated as taking place later have priority over supplies treated as taking place earlier.][1]

[(7) Sub-paragraphs (8) to (9F) apply if (*a*) the supplier certificate was incorrect because the CCL relief percentage was too high, and (*b*) paragraphs 24(1B) and 24(3)[, or paragraph 45A,][2] of the Act (Deemed supply: change of circumstances etc [or Reduced-rate supplies: deemed supply][2]) apply accordingly in relation to supplies made on the basis of that certificate in that review period.][1]

[(8) For the purposes of sub-paragraph (7), the extent to which the supplier certificate was incorrect must be allocated to supplies in reverse chronological order (about which see sub-paragraph (6)). Any supplies then deemed to be made under paragraph 24(3) [or 45A(2)][2] of the Act are treated as taking place at the time of the review in question under sub-paragraph (1).][1]

[(9) But the Commissioners may exempt the recipient from any consequential requirement to be registered if the following conditions and requirements are satisfied (for registration, see paragraphs 24(3), 40[, 45A(2)(*a*)][2] and 53(1) of the Act).][1]

[(9A) First, the recipient must not otherwise be a registrable person (for registrable, see regulation 2(1)).][1]

[(9B) Secondly, the recipient must deliver a relevant written application to the Commissioners within 30 days starting from the day after compliance with sub-paragraph (1).][1]

[(9C) That application must include notification of the following—

(*a*) the type and quantity of taxable commodity so deemed to be supplied by the recipient under paragraph 24(3) [or 45A(2)][2] of the Act,

(*b*) the amount of CCL payable by the recipient as a result, and

(*c*) the number of such payments the recipient anticipates having to make annually.][1]

[(9D) Thirdly, the recipient must pay the CCL due on those supplies to the Commissioners no later than the 30th day after the one on which the approval decision is delivered.][1]

[(9E) If the Commissioners do not exempt the recipient but sub-paragraphs (9A), (9B) and (9C) are satisfied, the 30 days for notifying registrability starts on the day the refusal decision is delivered (for notifying registrability, see regulations 2(5) and 20(*a*) of the Climate Change Levy (Registration and Miscellaneous Provisions) Regulations 2001).][1]

[(9F) Exemption from registration under sub-paragraph (9) applies only in relation to the consequential requirement mentioned there in relation to sub-paragraphs (7) and (8). Such exemption may be of limited duration and revoked by the Commissioners at any time.][1]

[(9G) This sub-paragraph applies instead of sub-paragraphs (7) to (9F) to the extent that the supplier certificate was incorrect because the CCL relief percentage was too high in relation to half-rate supplies (see paragraph 43(1) of the Act).

The recipient must pay to the Commissioners, no later than the 30th day after the last one for that person's compliance with sub-paragraph (1), the balance of the CCL due for those supplies.

If the recipient is a registrable person, the error may be corrected by the making of an appropriate adjustment under regulation 5(1)(b) (adjustment in CCL return) in relation to an accounting period ending no later than six months after the last day for that person's compliance with sub-paragraph (1).][1,2]

(10) If the recipient does not review the accuracy of the supplier certificate in accordance with sub-paragraph (1), and the certificate was (or remains) incorrect, paragraph 101 of the Act shall apply accordingly (civil penalty for incorrect certification, etc subject to reasonable excuse).

(11) This paragraph only applies in relation to a supply or supplies to which regulation 34 or 35 applies (supplier certificates for exclusions, exemptions and half-rates).[2]

Amendments—[1] Heading substituted, words inserted in para (3), and paras (6)–(9G) substituted for paras (6)–(9), by the Climate Change Levy (Miscellaneous Amendments) Regulations, SI 2005/1716 regs 5(*c*)–(*e*), 6 with effect from 22 July 2005. However, arrangements initiated or made before 22 July 2005 on the basis of SI 2001/838 Sch 1 para 5(5) or 5(6) as then in force remain subject to the provisions applicable when they were initiated or made (tax credit claims and corrections to over-estimated relief).

[2] In paras (7)–(9), (9C) words inserted, and paras (9G), (11) revoked, by the Climate Change Levy (General) (Amendment) Regulations, SI 2007/2903 reg 2, Sch 1 paras 31–35 with effect from 1 November 2007: SI 2007/2903 reg 1.
The amendment to para (9G) does not apply in relation to a half-rate supply made before 1 April 2006: SI 2007/2903 reg 2, Sch 1 Note (a).
In relation to a reduced-rate supply or a supply made on that basis, the amendments to paras (8), (9), (9C), (11) only apply if the supply is made on or after 1 November 2007: SI 2007/2903 reg 2, Sch 1 Note (b).

[Tax credit for recipient and reconciliation for input fuel to combined heat and power stations][1]

6—(1) The recipient in each of the following cases is entitled to a tax credit in respect of any relevant amount of CCL charged on the supply in question (subject to paragraph 5(5) and the other provisions of this Schedule including those provisions relating to the making of a relevant claim to the Commissioners)—

(*a*) after a taxable supply has been made, there is such a change in circumstances or any person's intentions that, if the changed circumstances or intentions had existed at the time the supply was made, the supply would not have been a taxable supply;

(*b*) after a supply of a taxable commodity is made on the basis that it is a taxable supply, it is determined that the supply was not (to any extent) a taxable supply;

(*c*) after a taxable supply has been made on the basis that it was [not][2] a reduced-rate supply, it is determined that the supply was (to any extent) a . . .[2] reduced-rate supply;

(*d*) *CCL is accounted for on a half-rate supply as if the supply were neither a half-rate supply nor a reduced-rate supply;*[2]

(*e*) after a charge to CCL has arisen on a supply of a taxable commodity ("the original commodity") to a person who uses the commodity supplied in producing taxable commodities primarily for his own consumption, that person makes supplies of any of the commodities in whose production he has used the original commodity.

(2) In sub-paragraph (1), "relevant amount of CCL" refers to the difference between—

(*a*) the amount of CCL that ought to have been charged by or under the Act at the time of supply had the supplier certificate been correct, and

(*b*) the amount of CCL that the supplier accounted for (or ought to have accounted for) on the basis of the incorrect supplier certificate.

Amendments—[1] Heading substituted by the Climate Change Levy (Miscellaneous Amendments) Regulations, SI 2005/1716 regs 5(*f*), 6 with effect from 22 July 2005. However, arrangements initiated or made before 22 July 2005 on the basis of SI 2001/838 Sch 1 para 5(5) or 5(6) as then in force remain subject to the provisions applicable when they were initiated or made (tax credit claims and corrections to over-estimated relief).

[2] In para (1)(*c*) word substituted for words "neither a half-rate supply nor", words "half-rate or" revoked, and para (1)(*d*) revoked, by the Climate Change Levy (General) (Amendment) Regulations, SI 2007/2903 reg 2, Sch 1 paras 36, 37 with effect from 1 November 2007: SI 2007/2903 reg 1. These amendments do not apply in relation to a half-rate supply made before 1 April 2006: SI 2007/2903 reg 2, Sch 1 Note (a).

7 A tax credit shall only arise under paragraph 6 if a claim is made by the recipient acting in accordance with paragraph 8 or 9, as the case requires.

8—(1) Subject to sub-paragraph (4), the recipient shall claim any such tax credit—

(*a*) . . .[1]

(*b*) by bringing it into account when he is accounting for CCL due from him for any accounting period . . .[1].

(2) Accordingly, in the case of a claim under sub-paragraph (1)(*b*)—

(*a*) the requirements of regulation 5 (content of returns), regulation 6 (payment of CCL) and regulation 7 (CCL accounts) apply subject to sub-paragraph (1)(*b*); but

(*b*) sub-paragraph (1)(*b*) applies subject to regulation 27 (corrections) and regulation 28 (corrections not exceeding [£50,000][2]).

(3) A claim subject to sub-paragraphs (1) and (2) shall be regarded as a claim for repayment of CCL for the purposes of paragraph 64 of the Act (supplemental provisions about repayments, etc) (and see sub-paragraph (4)).

(4) Where the total tax credit claimed by a recipient exceeds the total of any CCL due from him for the accounting period . . .[1] the Commissioners shall repay to him an amount equal to the excess (but see regulations 29 and 30).

(5) Given the provision made by paragraph 62(4) of the Act, this paragraph has effect subject to paragraph 64 of the Act (application of supplemental provisions about repayments: [4 year time limit][3], unjust enrichment, etc).

(6) . . .[1]

Amendments—[1] Paras (1)(*a*), (6) and words in paras (1)(*b*), (4) revoked by the Climate Change Levy (Miscellaneous Amendments) Regulations, SI 2005/1716 regs 5(*g*)–(*j*), 6 with effect from 22 July 2005. However, arrangements initiated or made before 22 July 2005 on the basis of SI 2001/838 Sch 1 para 5(5) or 5(6) as then in force remain subject to the provisions applicable when they were initiated or made (tax credit claims and corrections to over-estimated relief).

[2] In para (2)(*b*) figure substituted for figure "£2,000" by the Value Added Tax, etc (Correction of Errors, etc) Regulations, SI 2008/1482 reg 6(1) with effect in relation to under-calculations or over-calculations respectively in the CCL Regulations, SI 2001/838 reg 28(2), (3) which registrable persons first discover in their accounting periods that start on 1 July 2008 or later.

[3] Words in para (5) substituted for "three year time limit" by the Climate Change Levy (General) (Amendment) Regulations, SI 2010/643, regs 2, 3, with effect from 1 April 2010. However, this amendment is to be disregarded for the purpose of FA 2000 Sch 6 para 64(1) where claims made are for the repayment of amounts paid to the Commissioners on or before 31 March 2007.

9—(1) Where the recipient is [not registrable or is exempt from registration (see paragraph 5(9)),][1] the Commissioners shall repay to him the amount of the tax credit if they are satisfied that he has made a proper claim to them in writing for this purpose.

(2) A recipient making a claim under sub-paragraph (1) must furnish to the Commissioners full particulars in relation to the tax credit claimed, including (but not limited to)—

(*a*) any relevant supplier certificate on the basis of which the relevant CCL was accounted for by the supplier;

(*b*) any relevant analysis document supporting any such supplier certificate;

(*c*) the amount of the CCL in question and the date and manner of its payment to the Commissioners whether by the recipient, the supplier or otherwise;

(*d*) the circumstances, events, records and documentary or other evidence by virtue of which the recipient claims that any relevant entitlement to a tax credit arises;

(*e*) the period of time by reference to which the recipient consumed the relevant taxable commodity or was supplied with the relevant taxable commodity by the supplier to whom he delivered the relevant supplier certificate; and

(*f*) any matter, item or particular in any way relevant to the question whether or not a tax credit arises under this Schedule in favour of the recipient.

(3) Where the Commissioners are satisfied that a person who has made a claim in accordance with sub-paragraphs (1) and (2) is entitled to a tax credit and that he has not previously had the benefit of that credit, they shall repay to him an amount equal to the credit (but see regulations 29 and 30).

(4) . . . [1]

(5) Given the provision made by paragraph 62(4) of the Act, this regulation has effect subject to paragraph 64 of the Act (application of supplemental provisions about repayments: three year time limit, unjust enrichment, etc).

(6) . . . [1]

Amendments—[1] Words in para (1) substituted, and paras (4), (6) revoked, by the Climate Change Levy (Miscellaneous Amendments) Regulations, SI 2005/1716 regs 5(*k*), (*l*), 6 with effect from 22 July 2005. However, arrangements initiated or made before 22 July 2005 on the basis of SI 2001/838 Sch 1 para 5(5) or 5(6) as then in force remain subject to the provisions applicable when they were initiated or made (tax credit claims and corrections to over-estimated relief).

[9A Paragraphs 5 to 9 apply subject to the modifications in paragraph 9C, but those modifications are only relevant to the extent that the recipient's relief percentage is determined on the basis of a quantity of taxable commodity referable to paragraph 15 of the Act (supplies to combined heat and power stations).][1]

Amendments—[1] Paragraphs 9A–9C inserted by the Climate Change Levy (Miscellaneous Amendments) Regulations, SI 2005/1716 regs 5(*m*), 6 with effect from 22 July 2005. However, arrangements initiated or made before 22 July 2005 on the basis of SI 2001/838 Sch 1 para 5(5) or 5(6) as then in force remain subject to the provisions applicable when they were initiated or made (tax credit claims and corrections to over-estimated relief).

[9B—(1) For the purposes of the following sub-paragraphs, regard a completed calendar year as one for which 31st December is passed and an incompleted calendar year as one for which 31st December is not passed.

(2) The reconciliation day for a completed calendar year is the earlier of—

(*a*) the first day of the month in the subsequent calendar year in which regulation 3(2) of the Climate Change Levy (Combined Heat and Power Stations) Exemption Certificate Regulations 2001 is met in relation to the station in question (current CHPQA certificate sent to Secretary of State by 30th June);

(*b*) the 60th day after any day in the subsequent calendar year on which the station's exemption certificate is revoked pursuant to regulation 4(2) of those Regulations (station ceases to operate, current CHPQA certificate not sent to Secretary of State by 30th June, or relevant written request to Secretary of State).

The "reconciliation span" relating to this reconciliation day is the completed calendar year.

(3) A reconciliation day for an incompleted calendar year is the 60th day after any day in that incompleted calendar year on which the station's exemption certificate is revoked pursuant to regulation 4(2) of those Regulations.

The "reconciliation span" relating to any such reconciliation day spans 1st January in that calendar year to the day before that reconciliation day, inclusive.][1]

Amendments—[1] Paragraphs 9A–9C inserted by the Climate Change Levy (Miscellaneous Amendments) Regulations, SI 2005/1716 regs 5(*m*), 6 with effect from 22 July 2005. However, arrangements initiated or made before 22 July 2005 on the basis of SI 2001/838 Sch 1 para 5(5) or 5(6) as then in force remain subject to the provisions applicable when they were initiated or made (tax credit claims and corrections to over-estimated relief).

[9C—(1) The recipient must review the correctness of the supplier certificate no later than a reconciliation day in paragraph 9B.

This review is only in relation to that part of the recipient's relief percentage that is determined on the basis mentioned in paragraph 9A (taxable commodities supplied to combined heat and power stations).

(2) That correctness must be reviewed in relation to the efficiency percentage determined for the relevant reconciliation span (for determination of efficiency percentage, see regulations 3(2) and 6(2) of the Climate Change Levy (Combined Heat and Power Stations) Regulations 2005).

In the case of a reconciliation span for an incompleted calendar year, treat the actual efficiency percentage as one determined for the 12 month period preceding the relevant reconciliation day and as if that period was an Annual Operation (for Annual Operation, see regulation 51B(6)), but as zero for any time the exemption certificate stands revoked.

(3) The review must properly take into account—

(*a*) each quantity of taxable commodity supplied on the basis of the supplier certificate or certificates in question and not previously the subject of a review under this paragraph, and

(*b*) the actual efficiency percentage for the station in question at the time or times when that taxable commodity is supplied.

(4) Sub-paragraph (5) or (6) applies if the review demonstrates that the supplier certificate was incorrect as respects the taxable commodity referable to paragraph 15 of the Act (supplies to combined heat and power stations).

(5) If the CCL relief percentage applied was too low, the recipient may act in accordance with paragraphs 6 to 9 (recipient's tax credit for supply incorrectly made on basis of its being a taxable supply) (but only in relation to the taxable commodity referable to paragraph 15 of the Act—supplies to combined heat and power stations).

After 21st July 2005, and irrespective of when the supplies in question were made or other relevant events occurred, paragraph 5(5) does not apply where this paragraph applies.

(6) If the CCL relief percentage applied was too high, paragraphs 5(7) to [5(9F)][2] apply accordingly (deemed taxable self supplies, exemption from registration, payment of CCL due, etc).

(7) This paragraph only applies to supplies made after 31st December 2004, but not to those supplies in relation to which corresponding arrangements have been initiated or made before 22nd July 2005. Corresponding arrangements are only—

(*a*) claims by the recipient for tax credits or similar repayments, or

(*b*) steps taken by the recipient to correct the position following a review demonstrating that a CCL relief percentage was too high (delivery of updated supplier certificate such that error corrected in one year, adjustment in CCL return, payment to Commissioners—see paragraph 5(6) as in force before 22nd July 2005).][1]

Amendments—[1] Paragraphs 9A–9C inserted by the Climate Change Levy (Miscellaneous Amendments) Regulations, SI 2005/1716 regs 5(*m*), 6 with effect from 22 July 2005. However, arrangements initiated or made before 22 July 2005 on the basis of SI 2001/838 Sch 1 para 5(5) or 5(6) as then in force remain subject to the provisions applicable when they were initiated or made (tax credit claims and corrections to over-estimated relief).

[2] In para (6) reference substituted for reference "5(9G)" by the Climate Change Levy (General) (Amendment) Regulations, SI 2007/2903 reg 2, Sch 1 para 38 with effect from 1 November 2007: SI 2007/2903 reg 1. These amendments do not apply in relation to a half-rate supply made before 1 April 2006: SI 2007/2903 reg 2, Sch 1 Note (a).

10 If and to the extent that they may be relevant for the purposes of this Schedule, regulations 19 to 25 (unjust enrichment: reimbursement arrangements to be disregarded) shall apply in relation to a tax credit provided for by this Schedule as if—

(*a*) the reference in regulation 19 to "claim" included a claim made under this Schedule; and

(*b*) the references in those regulations to "(recipient)" or "(recipients)" were not present.

11 No tax credit shall arise under Part II of these Regulations where provision for a tax credit is made in this Schedule.

Miscellaneous

12—(1) The recipient may deliver to the supplier a further certificate updating the information in the original supplier certificate in the light of actual or anticipated [events.][1]

(2) . . .[1]

(3) The supplier shall then apply the CCL relief percentage to any supplies he makes to which the updated supplier certificate relates and may, for this purpose, rely on the relevant recipient's relief percentage as updated.

(4) Paragraphs 5 (compulsory updates) and 6 (recipient's tax credits) have effect subject to any updates made by the recipient under this paragraph.

(5) Any provision of these Regulations, including this Schedule, that applies to or in relation to a supplier certificate shall apply to or in relation to such a supplier certificate as updated under this paragraph.

Amendments—[1] Words in para (1) substituted, and para (2) revoked, by the Climate Change Levy (Miscellaneous Amendments) Regulations, SI 2005/1716 regs 5(*n*), (*o*), 6 with effect from 22 July 2005. However, arrangements initiated or made before 22 July 2005 on the basis of SI 2001/838 Sch 1 para 5(5) or 5(6) as then in force remain subject to the provisions applicable when they were initiated or made (tax credit claims and corrections to over-estimated relief).

13—(1) Where a recipient changes supplier, any supplier certificate delivered to any earlier supplier (and any supporting analysis document) shall not have effect in relation to supplies from the later supplier.

[(1A) Where a supplier changes under paragraph (1) without the recipient's active participation and the supplier certificate and supporting analysis document are transferred to the later supplier—

(*a*) continuity is preserved for all CCL purposes in relation to the change, and

(*b*) the certificate and document are deemed to have been originally given by the recipient to that later supplier.

If there is no such transfer, the supplier certificate and supporting analysis document shall not have effect in relation to supplies from the later supplier.][1]

(2) [In the case of sub-paragraph (1) or if continuity is not preserved in the case of sub-paragraph (1A),][1] paragraphs 5 to 11 shall apply in relation to the combined effect of the supplier certificate the recipient delivered to the earlier supplier and the supplier certificate he delivers to the later supplier.

Amendments—[1] Sub-para (1A) inserted, and words in sub-para (2) substituted, by the Climate Change Levy (Miscellaneous Amendments) Regulations, SI 2005/1716 regs 5(*p*), (*q*), 6 with effect from 22 July 2005. However, arrangements initiated or made before 22 July 2005 on the basis of SI 2001/838 Sch 1 para 5(5) or 5(6) as then in force remain subject to the provisions applicable when they were initiated or made (tax credit claims and corrections to over-estimated relief).

14—(1) A supplier to whom a supplier certificate is delivered shall, within 90 days starting with the day after it is delivered, deliver to the Commissioners in writing a summary of the information contained in that certificate.

(2) The supplier shall include in that summary—

(*a*) such information as is necessary to identify the recipient in question,

(*b*) such information as is necessary to identify each address to which the supplies in question are supplied, and

(*c*) the relevant recipient's relief percentage and, if different, the CCL relief percentage actually applied by the supplier to the supplies in question.

15 A recipient who delivers a supplier certificate shall—

(*a*) retain a copy for a period of six years starting with the time of supply of the final supply to which it relates,

(*b*) retain any relevant analysis document for a period of six years starting with the time of supply of the final supply to which it relates, and

(*c*) make a copy of any such certificate and analysis document available to the Commissioners on request.

[16 A supplier certificate ceases to be valid for the purposes of regulation 34, 35 or 36 on the 5th anniversary of its implementation date (about which, see regulation 37(6)).][1]

Amendments—[1] Paragraph 16 inserted by the Climate Change Levy (Miscellaneous Amendments) Regulations, SI 2005/1716 regs 5(*r*), 6 with effect from 22 July 2005. However, arrangements initiated or made before 22 July 2005 on the basis of SI 2001/838 Sch 1 para 5(5) or 5(6) as then in force remain subject to the provisions applicable when they were initiated or made (tax credit claims and corrections to over-estimated relief).

[SCHEDULE 2

THE CHP RELIEF CONDITION

Regulation 51H(1)]

Amendments—This Schedule inserted by the CCL (General) (Amendment) Regulations, SI 2003/604 regs 2, 22 with effect from 1 April 2003.

[Introduction

1 These obligations are for the purpose of ensuring the correct application of CCL to the outputs of a fully exempt or a partly exempt combined heat and power station.][1]

Amendments—[1] This paragraph inserted by the CCL (General) (Amendment) Regulations, SI 2003/604 regs 2, 22 with effect from 1 April 2003.

[CHP LEC and outputs record

2 A person to whom regulation 51H(1) applies must for the purposes of that regulation keep and maintain a discrete, proper, accurate and true record (the "CHP outputs record") of—

(*a*) any relevant supply of electricity constituting an output of the station in question for the purposes of paragraph 15(1) of the Act (supplies to stations);

(*b*) any relevant supply in relation to which CCL is not accounted for because of an exemption provided for by paragraph 16(2), 17(3) or 17(4) of the Act (supplies from partly exempt CHP and self-supplies);

(*c*) any relevant supply in relation to which CCL is not accounted for because of an exemption provided for by paragraph 17(2) of the Act (self-supply by autogenerator) (but only if the electricity in question is QPO electricity).][1]

Amendments—[1] This paragraph inserted by the CCL (General) (Amendment) Regulations, SI 2003/604 regs 2, 22 with effect from 1 April 2003.

[3—(1) That record must also identify separately, according to the following categories, each MWh of QPO electricity that is an output of the station in question and allocate to each such MWh a CHP LEC issued in respect of QPO electricity.

(2) The categories are—

(*a*) self-supplies of the electricity;

(*b*) supplies made to the person who consumes the electricity;

(*c*) supplies made to a person who makes a supply of the electricity.

(3) A CHP LEC (or any part of it) that remains allocated to a supply must not be allocated to any other supply.

(4) The allocation must be made no later than the [end of the second month following the one in which the CHP LEC is issued][2].

(5) Any restricted CHP LEC must be identified as such in the record no later than the 30th day after the one on which the notification that the relevant Authority has restricted its validity to indirect supplies is received (see regulation 51D and paragraph 11(5)).][1]

Amendments—[1] This paragraph inserted by the CCL (General) (Amendment) Regulations, SI 2003/604 regs 2, 22 with effect from 1 April 2003.

[2] Words in sub-para (4) substituted by the Climate Change Levy (Miscellaneous Amendments) Regulations, SI 2005/1716 regs 6, 7(8) with effect from 22 July 2005. However, arrangements initiated or made before 22 July 2005 on the basis of SI 2001/838 Sch 1 para 5(5) or 5(6) as then in force remain subject to the provisions applicable when they were initiated or made (tax credit claims and corrections to over-estimated relief).

[4 That record must also show the quantity of all electricity that is an output of the station in question but in relation to which no CHP LEC is issued (including for this purpose, and discretely identified, any renewable source electricity (see Part IV) or electricity produced when no exemption certificate is in force for the station).][1]

Amendments—[1] This paragraph inserted by the CCL (General) (Amendment) Regulations, SI 2003/604 regs 2, 22 with effect from 1 April 2003.

[5 That record must show—

(*a*) when each relevant supply of electricity is treated as taking place and the recipient of each such supply;

(*b*) the CHP LEC (if any) relating to that electricity and, if different from the recipient, the identity of any person to whom entitlement to the CHP LEC is transferred;

(*c*) the date (or dates) on which each other event to which it relates occurs;

(*d*) the date on which each entry to the record is made.][1]

Amendments—[1] This paragraph inserted by the CCL (General) (Amendment) Regulations, SI 2003/604 regs 2, 22 with effect from 1 April 2003.

[6 That record must be kept for 6 years starting from each reconciliation day to which it is relevant (see paragraphs 10 and 13(3)).][1]

Amendments—[1] This paragraph inserted by the CCL (General) (Amendment) Regulations, SI 2003/604 regs 2, 22 with effect from 1 April 2003.

[7 Subject to paragraph 6, that record must be made available on request and at any reasonable time to a person authorised by—

(*a*) the Secretary of State, or

(*b*) the relevant Authority.][1]

Amendments—[1] This paragraph inserted by the CCL (General) (Amendment) Regulations, SI 2003/604 regs 2, 22 with effect from 1 April 2003.

[8—[(1) This paragraph only applies whilst the relevant Authority has information on the basis of which it reasonably believes that the person mentioned in paragraph 2 is not fully complying with the CHP outputs record requirements in paragraphs 2 to 7.][2]

(2) The relevant Authority [must][2] refuse to certify or issue any CHP LEC in relation to electricity produced in the station (see regulations 51B(1) and 51B(8)).

(3) The relevant Authority [must][2] also restrict the validity of any relevant and as yet unrestricted CHP LEC to indirect supplies, in which case the relevant Authority must as soon as practicable notify that restriction to the person to whom it was issued (see regulation 51B(8)).

A CHP LEC is relevant for this purpose if it has not been reconciled in accordance with this Schedule (see paragraph 13(1)).][1]

Amendments—[1] This paragraph inserted by the CCL (General) (Amendment) Regulations, SI 2003/604 regs 2, 22 with effect from 1 April 2003.

[2] Sub-para (1) and word in sub-paras (2), (3) substituted by the Climate Change Levy (Miscellaneous Amendments) Regulations, SI 2005/1716 regs 6, 7(9), (10) with effect from 22 July 2005. However, arrangements initiated or made before 22 July 2005 on the basis of SI 2001/838 Sch 1 para 5(5) or 5(6) as then in force remain subject to the provisions applicable when they were initiated or made (tax credit claims and corrections to over-estimated relief).

[Reconciliation of outputs

9 For the purposes of the following paragraphs, regard a completed calendar year as one for which 31 December is passed and an incompleted calendar year as one for which 31 December is not passed.][1]

Amendments—[1] This paragraph inserted by the CCL (General) (Amendment) Regulations, SI 2003/604 regs 2, 22 with effect from 1 April 2003.

[10—(1) The reconciliation day for a completed calendar year is the earlier of—

(*a*) the first day of the month in the subsequent calendar year in which regulation 3(2) of the Climate Change Levy (Combined Heat and Power Stations) Exemption Certificate Regulations 2001 is met in relation to the station (current CHPQA certificate sent to Secretary of State by 30 June);

(*b*) the day in the subsequent calendar year on which revocation of the current exemption certificate takes effect pursuant to regulation 4(2) of those Regulations (station ceases to operate, current CHPQA certificate not sent to Secretary of State by 30 June, or relevant written request to Secretary of State).

The "reconciliation span" relating to this reconciliation day spans 1 January in the completed calendar year to the day before the reconciliation day, inclusive.

(2) A reconciliation day for an incompleted calendar year is any day in that incompleted calendar year on which revocation of the current exemption certificate takes effect pursuant to regulation 4(2) of those Regulations.

The "reconciliation span" relating to any such reconciliation day spans 1 January in that calendar year to the day before that reconciliation day, inclusive.

(3) The relevant Authority shall act in accordance with paragraph 11 no later than the 90th day following a reconciliation day, subject as appropriate to regulations 51C and 51D (relevant Authority neither certifying electricity nor issuing CHP LEC, or relevant Authority dealing with incorrect certification).

(4) A reconciliation day in paragraph (2) may arise irrespective of any overlap between the reconciliation span in that paragraph with the reconciliation span in paragraph (1).][1]

Amendments—[1] This paragraph inserted by the CCL (General) (Amendment) Regulations, SI 2003/604 regs 2, 22 with effect from 1 April 2003.

[11—(1) The relevant Authority shall determine whether insufficient or excessive CHP LECs have been issued and remain unrestricted as respects each reconciliation span, having proper regard to the difference between—

(*a*) the quantity of QPO electricity actually produced in the station during that reconciliation span, and

(*b*) the quantity of QPO electricity represented by the CHP LECs issued as respects electricity produced in the station during that reconciliation span and remaining unrestricted.

(2) If the relevant Authority determines that insufficient CHP LECs have been issued and remain unrestricted as respects a reconciliation span, it must—

(*a*) to the extent of that insufficiency, and

(*b*) as respects that reconciliation span,

issue additional CHP LECs (see regulation 51B(8)) as respects the QPO electricity outputs of the station.

Any such CHP LEC must, within 60 days of issue, be allocated by the person referred to in paragraph 2 to relevant and appropriate supplies identified in the record as taking place in that reconciliation span.

(3) If the relevant Authority determines that excessive CHP LECs have been issued and remain unrestricted as respects a reconciliation span, it must act in accordance with paragraphs (4) and (5), as appropriate.

(4) If the reconciliation day arises because regulation 3(2) of the Climate Change Levy (Combined Heat and Power Stations) Exemption Certificate Regulations 2001 is met (see paragraph 10(1)(*a*)), the relevant Authority must treat the excess CHP LECs as being prospectively referable to figures made known to it by the operator for the purposes of regulation 51B(2) as respects production in the station after the relevant reconciliation day.

(5) If the relevant reconciliation day arises because the exemption certificate is revoked (see paragraph 10(1)(*b*)), the relevant Authority must restrict the validity of any excess CHP LECs to indirect supplies, in which case it must as soon as practicable notify that restriction to the person to whom the CHP LEC in question was issued or to any person appearing to control the station (see regulation 51B(8)).

The relevant Authority must ensure that those CHP LECs remaining unrestricted afterwards (and not yet reconciled, see paragraph 13(1)) collectively represent QPO electricity produced in the station during the reconciliation span.

(6) For the purposes of this paragraph, the relevant Authority must regard calendar year 2003 as beginning on 1 April 2003.

(7) For the purposes of regulation 51B(6) (QPO electricity referable to calendar year), the relevant Authority must not regard electricity referable to before 1 April 2003 as QPO electricity.][1]

[(8) In the case of electricity and a station to which this paragraph applied before 22nd July 2005 but not after 21st July 2005 (see regulation 51A(2)), the relevant Authority must treat 22nd July 2005 as a reconciliation day for an incompleted calendar year running from 1st January to 21st July 2005 inclusive (the "reconciliation span").

The determination in sub-paragraph (1) must be made on the basis that a partly exempt station's annual limit for that incompleted calendar year is the former limit multiplied by the fraction with a numerator of 202 and a denominator of 365.

For these purposes, the "former limit" is the one in force on 1st January 2005 under regulation 5(2) of the Climate Change Levy (Combined Heat and Power Stations) Prescribed Conditions and Efficiency Percentages Regulations 2001.][2]

Amendments—[1] This paragraph inserted by the CCL (General) (Amendment) Regulations, SI 2003/604 regs 2, 22 with effect from 1 April 2003.

[2] Sub-para (8) inserted by the Climate Change Levy (Miscellaneous Amendments) Regulations, SI 2005/1716 regs 6, 7(11) with effect from 22 July 2005. However, arrangements initiated or made before 22 July 2005 on the basis of SI 2001/838 Sch 1 para 5(5) or 5(6) as then in force remain subject to the provisions applicable when they were initiated or made (tax credit claims and corrections to over-estimated relief).

[Monitoring and balancing obligation

12—(1) The CHP outputs record must never show or indicate as respects a reconciliation span—

(*a*) a deficit of unrestricted CHP LECs in relation to the total quantity of QPO electricity identified in the record pursuant to paragraph 3(2)(*a*) and 3(2)(*b*) (self-supplies and supplies to consumers);

(*b*) a deficit of unrestricted plus restricted CHP LECs in relation to the total quantity of QPO electricity identified pursuant to paragraph 3(2)(*a*), 3(2)(*b*) and 3(2)(*c*) (self-supplies, supplies to consumers and supplies to others).

(2) Each deficit representing 1 MWh shall be regarded as a separate breach of this paragraph for the purposes of regulation 60(1)(*hb*) (penalties).

(3) Paragraph (1) has effect subject to paragraphs 3(4), 3(5), 11(2) and 11(5).

(4) Paragraph (1) continues to apply after a CHP LEC is reconciled (see paragraph 13(1)).][1]

Amendments—[1] This paragraph inserted by the CCL (General) (Amendment) Regulations, SI 2003/604 regs 2, 22 with effect from 1 April 2003.

[Interpretation

13—(1) A CHP LEC is "reconciled" for the purposes of this Schedule only if—

(*a*) it is the subject of a reconciliation span in relation to which the relevant Authority has performed its functions under paragraph 10(3), and

(*b*) it is allocated, if required, in accordance with paragraph 11(2).

(2) A CHP LEC the validity of which is restricted under paragraph 8(3) or 11(5) may be regarded as a restricted CHP LEC for the purposes of regulations 51I to 51M.

(3) The CHP outputs record is relevant to a reconciliation day to the extent that it records (or is required to record) events taking place during the reconciliation span relating to that reconciliation day (see paragraphs 6, 10(1) and 10(2)).

(4) See also regulation 51A.][1]

Amendments—[1] This paragraph inserted by the CCL (General) (Amendment) Regulations, SI 2003/604 regs 2, 22 with effect from 1 April 2003.

2001/1136

CLIMATE CHANGE LEVY (ELECTRICITY AND GAS) REGULATIONS 2001

Made by the Treasury and the Commissioners of Customs and Excise under FA 2000 s 30 and Sch 6 paras 14(2), 146(1), 146(7), 151(2) and 152(2)

Made . . . . *22 March 2001*
Coming into force . . . . *1 April 2001*

Citation and commencement

1 These Regulations may be cited as the Climate Change Levy (Electricity and Gas) Regulations 2001 and shall come into force on 1st April 2001.

Interpretation

2 In these Regulations—

"the Act" refers to Schedule 6 to the Finance Act 2000;

"CCL" refers to climate change levy;

"electricity supply licence" refers to a licence mentioned in paragraph 150(2)(*a*) or 150(2)(*b*) of the Act;

"gas" refers to gas described by paragraph 3(1)(*b*) of the Act;

"gas supply licence" refers to a licence mentioned in paragraph 150(3)(*a*) or 150(3)(*b*) of the Act.

Certain supplies by and to unregulated electricity suppliers and electricity utilities

3—(1) An unregulated electricity supplier (within the meaning of paragraph 151(8) of the Act) shall be treated for all CCL purposes as being an electricity utility to the extent of any supplies he makes in relation to which he is in breach of a requirement to hold an electricity supply licence.

(2) A holder of an electricity supply licence, who receives supplies of electricity in the course of acting otherwise than for purposes connected with the carrying on of activities authorised by that licence, shall be treated as being an electricity utility for the purposes of the CCL treatment under paragraph 5 of the Act of the supplies of electricity so received.

(3) In paragraph (1), "unregulated electricity supplier" includes the holder of an electricity supply licence acting otherwise than for the purposes connected with the carrying on of activities authorised by that licence.

Certain supplies of electricity by electricity utilities

4—(1) A person who is an electricity utility shall be treated for the purposes of the CCL chargeable under paragraph 5(1) of the Act (CCL on supplies of electricity) as not being an electricity utility to the extent of any part of a supply he makes of electricity—

(*a*) produced in a fully exempt combined heat and power station, and

(*b*) not supplied to him at any time by another person.

(2) Where an electricity utility makes a supply of electricity on which CCL would be chargeable, but for this paragraph, under both paragraph 5(1) and either paragraph 5(2) or 5(3) of the Act—

(*a*) that electricity utility shall be treated, for the purposes of the CCL chargeable under paragraph 5(1), as not being an electricity utility to the extent of that supply, and

(*b*) CCL shall, accordingly, only be chargeable on that supply under paragraph 5(2) or 5(3).

Supplies to exempt unlicensed electricity suppliers

5—(1) The description of exempt unlicensed electricity supplier prescribed for the purposes of paragraph 14(2) of the Act (exemption: certain supplies to electricity producers) is that given in paragraph (2) of this regulation.

(2) The description referred to in paragraph (1) of this regulation is any exempt unlicensed electricity supplier who—

(*a*) meets the description in paragraph 14(4) of the Act, and

(*b*) is not an auto-generator.

Autogenerators: requirements for electricity produced to be taken as for own consumption

6 Electricity shall only be taken as produced primarily for a person's own consumption for the purposes of paragraph 152(1) of the Act (autogenerators) if it fulfils both of the following requirements at the time it is produced—

(*a*) it must not be produced by an electricity utility or by a person treated as such for the purposes of any supplies of electricity he makes;

(*b*) it must not be produced by a person who has consumed, in the preceding 3 months, less than 75 per cent of the electricity produced by him in that period.

Certain supplies by and to unregulated gas suppliers and gas utilities

7—(1) An unregulated gas supplier (within the meaning of paragraph 151(8) of the Act) shall be treated for all CCL purposes as being a gas utility to the extent of any supplies he makes in relation to which he is in breach of a requirement to hold a gas supply licence.

(2) An unregulated gas supplier (within the meaning of paragraph 151(8) of the Act) shall be treated for all CCL purposes as being a gas utility to the extent that any part of his supplies of gas fall within the exception provided for by paragraph 5 of Schedule 2A to the Gas Act 1986 (exception to prohibition on unlicensed activities for supplies to very large consumers).

(3) A holder of a gas supply licence, who receives supplies of gas in the course of acting otherwise than for purposes connected with the carrying on of activities authorised by that licence, shall be treated as being a gas utility for the purposes of the CCL treatment under paragraph 6 of the Act of the supplies of gas so received.

(4) A holder of a gas supply licence who is not an electricity utility, and who receives supplies of gas and uses that gas to produce electricity, shall be treated as being an electricity utility for the purposes of the CCL treatment under paragraph 5 of the Act of any supplies he makes of the electricity so produced.

(5) In this regulation, "unregulated gas supplier" includes the holder of a gas supply licence acting otherwise than for purposes connected with the carrying on of activities authorised by that licence.

2001/1137

CLIMATE CHANGE LEVY (SOLID FUEL) REGULATIONS 2001

Made by the Treasury under FA 2000 s 30, Sch 6 paras 3(3), 146(1) and 146(7)

Made . . . . *22 March 2001*
Coming into force . . . . *1 April 2001*

Amendment—These regulations are revoked by the Climate Change Levy (Solid Fuel) (Revocation) Regulations, SI 2009/3338, reg 2 with effect from 1 January 2010.

1 *These Regulations may be cited as the Climate Change Levy (Solid Fuel) Regulations 2001 and shall come into force on 1st April 2001.*

2—*(1) Solid fuel is not a taxable commodity for the purposes of Schedule 6 to the Finance Act 2000 if—*

(a) a supply of that solid fuel would otherwise be chargeable with CCL, but

(b) at the time when that supply would be treated as taking place the solid fuel in question has an open market value not exceeding £15 per tonne.

(2) In this regulation—

"CCL" refers to climate change levy;

"solid fuel" refers only to coal and lignite; coke, and semi-coke, of coal or lignite; petroleum coke;

"time when the supply would be treated as taking place" refers to the time of supply determined by or under paragraphs 25 to 39 of Schedule 6 to the Finance Act 2000;

"open market value" refers to the amount that would, by virtue of sections 19(2) and 19(5) of the Value Added Tax Act 1994 and on the basis that no CCL is chargeable, fall to be taken as the value of a supply of that solid fuel for the purposes of value added tax if the supply were for such consideration in money as would be payable by a person standing in no such relationship with any person as would affect that consideration.

2001/1138

CLIMATE CHANGE LEVY (USE AS FUEL) REGULATIONS 2001

Made by the Treasury under FA 2000 s 30 and Sch 6 paras 18(2), 18(3), 146(1) and 146(7) of Schedule 6 to the Finance Act 2000

Amendment—These regulations are revoked by the Climate Change Levy (Fuel Use and Recycling Processes) Regulations, SI 2005/1715 reg 5 with effect from 22 July 2005.

2001/1140

CLIMATE CHANGE LEVY (COMBINED HEAT AND POWER STATIONS) PRESCRIBED CONDITIONS AND EFFICIENCY PERCENTAGES REGULATIONS 2001

Amendment—These regulations revoked by the Climate Change Levy (Combined Heat and Power Stations) Regulations, SI 2005/1714 reg 8 with effect from 22 July 2005.

2005/1714

CLIMATE CHANGE LEVY (COMBINED HEAT AND POWER STATIONS) REGULATIONS 2005

Made by the Treasury under FA 2000 s 30, Sch 6 paras 15(4), 16(2), 16(3), 146(7), 147, 148(4), 148(7), 148(8), 148(9), 149(1), 149(2) and 149(3)

Made . . . .*21 July 2005*
Coming into force in accordance with . . . .*regulation 1*

Preliminary

1 These Regulations may be cited as the Climate Change Levy (Combined Heat and Power Stations) Regulations 2005 and shall come into force on the day after the day on which they are made.

2—(1) In these Regulations—
"the Act" refers to Schedule 6 to the Finance Act 2000;
"CCL" refers to climate change levy;
"CHPQA" refers to the Combined Heat and Power Quality Assurance Standard, Issue 1, November 2000 originally published by the Department for the Environment, Transport and the Regions (the "Standard") (including the later of version Final 1.0 or 2.0 of CHPQA Guidance Notes 0 to 4 (including 2(S), 3(S) and 4(S)), 10 to 28 and 30);
"station" refers to a combined heat and power station or, in appropriate circumstances, to combined heat and power stations forming at least part of a single CHP Scheme.
(2) But, for the purposes of regulation 3(2), "CHPQA" refers to the current issue of that Standard and current versions of those and any subsequent Guidance Notes.
An issue or version is current for these purposes to the extent that it is neither varied, replaced nor revoked by another issue or version.
(3) These Regulations must be applied in a way consistent with the CHPQA and paragraph (2).
But, for the purposes of regulations 3(2) and 4, any reference in the CHPQA to any relevant "registered" quantity (whether or not mentioned in either regulation) must be treated as a reference to the actual quantity of that name for determination and calculation in accordance with the CHPQA.
That determination and calculation must be on the basis of events in relation to the given station during the given Annual Operation (for "Annual Operation", see CHPQA Section 4—1st January to 31st December).

Supplies to combined heat and power stations: exemption for inputs

3—(1) A station's threshold efficiency percentage is set as 20 per cent (see paragraphs 15(2)(*b*), 15(3)(*b*) and 15(4)(*a*) of the Act).
(2) A station's efficiency percentage for a given Annual Operation is its Power Efficiency in relation to that Operation (see paragraphs 15(4)(*b*), 149(1) and 149(2)(*e*) of the Act and Section 5.6 of the Standard).

Supplies from partly exempt combined heat and power stations: exemption for outputs

4 The limit (see paragraph 16(2) of the Act) on the quantity of electricity that may be produced in and supplied from a partly exempt station exempt from CCL for a given Annual Operation is its CHP Qualifying Power Output in relation to that Operation (see Section 5.8 of the Standard).

Fully exempt combined heat and power stations: conditions to be satisfied for full-exemption certificate

5—(1) The condition to be satisfied in relation to a station for the purpose of the Secretary of State giving a full-exemption certificate is as follows (see paragraph 148(4) of the Act).
(2) The station's Quality Index as determined and calculated in accordance with the CHPQA must at least meet the Threshold Quality Index Criterion specified for that station in the CHPQA (see Sections 5.5 and 4 of the Standard).

Transitional provisions: inputs efficiency percentage and outputs partly exempt limit

6—(1) Paragraph (2) applies only if regulations 2(2) and 2(3) result in more than one issue of the Standard or version of a Guidance Note being current during the Annual Operation in question and, if they are treated as separately current for the whole Annual Operation, this yields different efficiency percentages for the purposes of regulation 3(2).
(2) The efficiency percentage in regulation 3(2) is then the weighted mean of those different efficiency percentages.
The weighting must reflect the proportion of fuel input to the station during the period in relation to which the relevant issue or version is current.
That proportion must be calculated relative to the station's actual total fuel input for the Annual Operation in question.

7—(1) Paragraph (2) applies only if regulation 4 results in a limit ("A") for calendar year 2005 that is less than the limit ("B") that would have applied for that year under regulation 5(2) of the Climate Change Levy (Combined Heat and Power Stations) Prescribed Conditions and Efficiency Percentages Regulations 2001.

(2) The limit in regulation 4 for 2005 is then the following sum.

$$\left[\frac{X \times A}{365}\right] + \left[\frac{Y \times B}{365}\right]$$

X = 365 − Y
Y = the number of days elapsed for 2005 up to and including the day these Regulations are made.

Revocations

8 The Climate Change Levy (Combined Heat and Power Stations) Prescribed Conditions and Efficiency Percentages Regulations 2001 and the Climate Change Levy (Combined Heat and Power Stations) Prescribed Conditions and Efficiency Percentages (Amendment) Regulations 2003 are revoked.

2005/1715

CLIMATE CHANGE LEVY (FUEL USE AND RECYCLING PROCESSES) REGULATIONS 2005

Made . . . .*21 July 2005*
Coming into force in accordance with . . . .*regulation 1*

Made by the Treasury under FA 2000 s 30 and Sch 6 paras 18(2), 18(3), 18A(1), 18A(7), 146(7) and 147 to the Finance Act 2000

Citation and commencement

1 These Regulations may be cited as the Climate Change Levy (Fuel Use and Recycling Processes) Regulations 2005 and shall come into force on the day after the day on which they are made.

Interpretation

2 In these Regulations—
"the Act" refers to Schedule 6 to the Finance Act 2000;
"CCL" refers to climate change levy.

Use as fuel or otherwise

3 For the purposes of paragraph 18(1) of the Act (CCL exemption if commodity supplied for non-fuel use)—
(*a*) the uses of a taxable commodity that are specified in Schedule 1 to these Regulations are not to be taken as being uses of that commodity as fuel; and
(*b*) any uses of a taxable commodity that are not specified in Schedule 1 are specified by this paragraph as uses that are to be taken as being uses of that commodity as fuel.

Recycling processes

4 The recycling processes described in Schedule 2 to these Regulations are prescribed for the purposes of paragraph 18A(1) of the Act (CCL exemption if commodity supplied for use in recycling process for which there is a relevant competing process, see paragraph 18A(2) of the Act).

Revocations

5 The Climate Change Levy (Use as Fuel) Regulations 2001 and the Climate Change Levy (Use as Fuel) (Amendment) Regulations 2003 are revoked.

SCHEDULE 1

USES OTHERWISE THAN AS FUEL

Regulation 3(a)

A

WHOLLY NON-FUEL USES

1 Electricity in electrolysis for the production of:
Fluorine
Chloroalkali (chlorine, caustic soda and caustic potash)

Hydrogen peroxide, persulphates, chlorates and peroxyorganic acids by electro-oxidation
Aluminium
Copper
Basic materials directly from an ore or other compound (electrowinning)
Advanced chemicals from other more basic chemicals

2 Electricity in the following types of electrolysis:

Electro-organic synthesis of fine organics and intermediates such as adiponitrile
Gold and silver electrolysis, and the electrolytic dissolution of platinum group metal alloys and alkali earth metals such as sodium, potassium, lithium and calcium
Electrolysis to purify materials (as distinct from electrowinning)
Electrolysis in refining tin or copper from impure metals or ingots
Electrolysis involving sodium chlorate, potassium permanganate, potassium dichromate, managanese dioxide, cuprous oxide, sorbitol, fatty alcohols

3 Electricity in battery formation

4 Natural gas as feedstock to produce hydrogen and for hydrogenation reactions

5 Natural gas in the production of hydrogen and carbon monoxide for the reduction and subsequent purification of nickel

6 Natural gas as a feedstock in producing acetic acid and acetic anhydride by a partial oxidation process

7 Natural gas to provide carbon in producing carbon-carbon composites

8 Natural gas in manufacturing sodium cyanide

9 Natural gas and propane in steam reformers to produce a mixture of hydrogen and carbon monoxide in the production of:

Fertilisers
OXO (Oxonation) chemicals—detergent and plasticiser alcohols
Phosgene
Ammonia
Higher alcohols, synthetic fuels, plastics precursors
Methanol, methyl tertiary butyl ether, formaldehyde, formic acid, acetic acid, methyl amines, single cell proteins

10 Methane as a feedstock in producing higher paraffins and their derivatives

11 Liquefied petroleum gas as a propellant in aerosols

12 Liquefied petroleum gas as feedstock in the cracking process to produce lower olefins

13 Lower olefins as feedstock for conversion by chemical processes

14 Propylene as feedstock in the manufacture of propan-2-ol (iso-propyl alcohol), polypropylene and cumene

15 Petroleum coke in the manufacture of carbon and graphite electrodes

16 Coke as a resistor in electro-thermal furnaces

17 Coke in the manufacture of titanium dioxide by the chloride process

B
MIXED USES

These mixed uses are the only ones that involve relevant commodities being used partly as fuel and partly not, but which are specified as being uses that are not to be taken as being uses of those commodities as fuel (see paragraph 18(3) of the Act).

18 Coal, coke and natural gas as chemical reductants for ironmaking, for example, in blast furnaces

19 Coal, coke and natural gas as chemical reductants in the blast furnace production of zinc and other non-ferrous metals

20 Coal and coke in the recarburising of iron and steel

21 Coke breeze in a sinter plant to assist in the agglomeration of iron ore and its subsequent chemical reduction in blast furnaces

22 Coke injected into electric arc furnaces to control the chemistry of the steel and the steelmaking slag

23 Coke charged to electric arc furnaces to control the oxygen activity of the steel melt

24 Coke as a carburiser in iron casting

25 Coke as a source of carbon dioxide in the Ammonia Soda process for producing soda ash

26 Anthracite as a reductant in the smelting of precious metals

27 Gas for vacuum reduction in metal powder production and to maintain carbon content in metal during the sintering process

28 Gas to maintain or increase the carbon content of metals during heat treatment

29 Natural gas as a reductant in emission control systems, for example, in the reduction of oxides of nitrogen

30 Natural gas in the manufacture of methocrylate monomers and polymers including that natural gas used for emission control which is an integral and essential part of the manufacturing process

31 Natural gas as feedstock in the production of carbon black

32 Natural gas as feedstock in a gas generator supplying a reducing atmosphere for the treatment or annealing of metal products

33 Liquid propane in the production of ethylene where heat is provided either by combustion of the waste products or from another source

34 Commodities in reduction furnaces for the production of lead

35 Commodities in the reduction of chlorine

36 Commodities to form reducing atmospheres, for example, in the refining and manipulation of molten copper to control oxygen levels

37 Commodities in ASARCO (American Smelting and Refining Company) shaft furnaces, the deoxidisation of copper swarf and the annealing of copper and copper alloys to provide a reducing atmosphere

SCHEDULE 2

RECYCLING PROCESSES

Regulation 4

Description

The preparation of scrap metal for recycling.

"Preparation" is only shredding, fragmentation, pre-treatment and melting of scrap.

"Scrap" is only—

(*a*) post–consumer scrap, namely, goods that have performed the function for which they were designed and have been discarded (for example, end of life road vehicles, discarded food cans, steel girders or rods from demolished buildings, worn out battery electrodes, discarded lead roofing);

(*b*) scrap generated from the process of which that preparation forms part or from a different process (for example, off–cuts from metal stampings, unmarketable goods).

"Metal" is only aluminium, lead or steel.

"Melting" is only—

(*a*) the pre-heating and first melting of scrap before casting into intermediates; or

(*b*) the heating of scrap as part of the recycling process before any solidification and re-melting.

It excludes melting of any type of non-scrap metal added to the recycling process to improve the quality or adjust the composition of the recycled metal or intermediates.

"Intermediates" are only items for further processing or re-melting, such as rolling slabs or ingots.

2006/59

CLIMATE CHANGE AGREEMENTS (ENERGY-INTENSIVE INSTALLATIONS) REGULATIONS 2006

Made by the Treasury under FA 2000 s 30 and Sch 6 paras 52(1), 52(2)(a) and 146(7) and approved by a resolution of the House of Commons in accordance with para 146(3) of that Schedule

Made . . . . *18 January 2006*

Coming into force in accordance with . . . . *regulation 1*

1 These Regulations may be cited as the Climate Change Agreements (Energy-intensive Installations) Regulations 2006 and come into force on the third day after the one on which they are made.

2—(1) The energy-intensive installations covered by the Finance Act 2000 Schedule 6 paragraph 51 ("paragraph 51") include any installation falling within any one or more of the descriptions of installation specified in the Schedule to these Regulations.

(2) But paragraph (3) applies where—

(*a*) an installation falls within any one or more of those descriptions, and

(*b*) there is, on the same site as that installation, at least one location at which ancillary activities are carried out.

(3) That installation (taken alone) is not covered by paragraph 51, but the combination of that installation and every such location is to be taken as an installation so covered.

(4) In paragraph (2), "ancillary activities" are only—

(*a*) those that are directly associated with any of the primary activities carried out in the installation,

(*b*) have a technical connection with those primary activities, and

(*c*) could have an effect on environmental pollution.

(5) In paragraph (4)—

"primary activities", in relation to an installation falling within any one or more of the descriptions of installation set out in the Schedule to these Regulations, refers to an activity the carrying out of which at the installation results in the installation falling within one or more of those descriptions;

"environmental pollution" bears the same meaning as in the Pollution Prevention and Control Act 1999.

Commentary—*De Voil Indirect Tax Service* **V21.142**.

SCHEDULE

DESCRIPTIONS OF ENERGY-INTENSIVE INSTALLATIONS INCLUDED AS COVERED BY THE FINANCE ACT 2000 SCHEDULE 6 PARAGRAPH 51

Regulation 2(1)

Each of the following descriptions includes a stipulation that the installation is a stationary technical unit (see the Finance Act 2000 Schedule 6 paragraph 50(6)) that does not fall within any one or more of the descriptions of installation set out in the Table in paragraph 51 of that Schedule.

1 An installation where—

(*a*) nitrogen, oxygen or argon is separated from air, and then compressed or liquefied;

(*b*) nitrogen, oxygen and argon are separated from air, and then made into a compressed or liquefied mixture of at least two of the former.

2 An installation where kaolinitic clay in combination with any of its accessory minerals are extracted and processed.

3 An installation where calcium carbonate based minerals are processed for use as filler or whitener for paper, plastics, pharmaceuticals, ceramics, food, paint or other products.

4 An installation where pre-formed or manufactured metal components are heat-treated to facilitate their efficient formability or to enhance their service performance.

5 An installation where (in controlled, environment-protected structures) horticultural crops are grown, harvested and receive primary preparation for market.

6 An installation where textiles are manufactured.

7 An installation where plastic film is produced using extrusion to convert melted polymer into blown or cast film.

[**8** An installation not otherwise covered by paragraph 51 of Schedule 6 to the Finance Act 2000.][1]

Commentary—*De Voil Indirect Tax Service* **V21.142.**
Amendments—[1] Paragraph 8 inserted by Climate Change Agreements (Miscellaneous Amendments) Regulations, SI 2006/1848 reg 3, with effect from 12 July 2006.

2006/60

CLIMATE CHANGE AGREEMENTS (ELIGIBLE FACILITIES) REGULATIONS 2006

Made . . . .*18 January 2006*
Laid before the House of Commons . . . .*20 January 2006*
Coming into force . . . .*21 January 2006*

The Secretary of State makes the following Regulations in exercise of the powers conferred by paragraphs 50(3), 50(4) and 146(7) of Schedule 6 to the Finance Act 2000—

Citation and Commencement

1 These Regulations may be cited as the Climate Change Agreements (Eligible Facilities) Regulations 2006 and shall come into force on 21st January 2006.

Interpretation

2 In these Regulations—

"eligible process" means a relevant process or activity or a combination of relevant processes or activities as described in the Schedule to these Regulations carried out at an installation or site which, when taken alone or together within the business sector to which the installation or site belongs, meets the energy intensity criteria specified in regulation 3;

"energy costs" means the actual cost of energy, including all taxes except deductible VAT, purchased or generated by the operator of the installation or site or by a business sector;

"import penetration ratio" means the value of imports as a percentage of the value of total sales in the United Kingdom (the latter to include the value of exports);

"installation" means any installation that is covered by paragraph 51 of Schedule 6 to the Finance Act 2000 by virtue of the Climate Change Agreements (Energy-intensive Installations) Regulations 2006;

"production value" means turnover, including subsidies, directly linked to the price of the product, plus or minus the changes in stock of finished products, work in progress and goods and services purchased for resale, minus the purchases of goods and services for resale;

"site" means a site on which there is an installation or part of an installation.

Eligible Facilities

3 (1) This regulation specifies the circumstances in which, for the purposes of determining in connection with concluding or varying a climate change agreement, an installation or site is to be or is to continue to be identified in a climate change agreement as a facility to which the agreement applies.

(2) An installation or a site shall be taken to be a facility for the purposes specified in paragraph (1) only if, at the time of entering into or last varying that climate change agreement—

(*a*) it is an "eligible facility" under the Climate Change Agreements (Eligible Facilities) Regulations 2001, and

(*b*) the installation or site where taxable commodities supplied by taxable supplies are intended to be burned (or in the case of electricity, consumed) over the following 12 month period satisfies the conditions set out in paragraph (3).

(3) The conditions referred to in paragraph (2)(*b*) are that—

(*a*) the installation or site meets the energy intensity criteria, or

(*b*) the installation or site belongs to a business sector that meets the energy intensity criteria, and the taxable commodities referred to in paragraph (2)(b) will be used at the installation or site for the purpose of carrying out an eligible process.

(4) For the purpose of paragraph (3)(*a*) and (*b*) the energy intensity criteria will be met where, for the period referred to in paragraph (2)(*b*), the predicted energy costs—

(*a*) amount to 10% or more of the production value of the installation or site or business sector, or

(*b*) amount to 3% or more but less than 10% of the production value of the installation or site or business sector so long as there is an import penetration ratio of at least 50%.

(5) For the purpose of paragraph (4), the predicted energy costs for the period referred to in paragraph (2)(*b*) shall be determined by the energy costs and production value and import penetration data for the installation or site or business sector during the 12 month period immediately prior to entering into or last varying a climate change agreement.

Commentary—*De Voil Indirect Tax Service* **V21.142**.

[SCHEDULE

LIST OF RELEVANT PROCESSES AND ACTIVITIES

Regulation 2

1 At an installation or site where—

(*a*) nitrogen, oxygen or argon is separated from air, and then compressed or liquefied; or

(*b*) nitrogen, oxygen and argon are separated from air, and then made into a compressed or liquefied mixture of at least two of the former:

separating the above substances from air using one or more of the following air separation technologies: cryogenic distillation, pressure swing adsorption, vacuum swing absorption or membrane separation, compressing and liquefying the separated substances, pumping them (in a compressed or liquefied form) from within the installation for further use within or outside the installation.

2 At an installation or site where kaolinitic clay in combination with any of its accessory minerals is extracted and processed: blasting and crushing, dry mining or hydraulic mining, refining, blending, drying and packaging, classifying, hydrocloning, pumping, centrifuging, grinding, shredding, magnetic separating, bleaching, pressing, pugging, milling, micro-separating.

3 At an installation or site where calcium carbonate based minerals are processed for use as filler or whitener for paper, plastics, pharmaceuticals, ceramics, food, paint or other products: crushing, drying, milling, classifying, screening, packaging.

4 At an installation or site where pre-formed or manufactured metal components are heat-treated to facilitate their efficient formability or to enhance their service performance: all processes and activities involved in the heat treatment of pre-formed or manufactured metal components to facilitate their efficient formability or to enhance their service performance.

5 At an installation or site where (in controlled, environment-protected structures) horticultural crops are grown, harvested and receive primary preparation for market: planting, seeding, heating, lighting, ventilating, irrigating, fertilising, cooling, preparing and sterilising growing media, grading and conveying.

6 At an installation or site where textiles are manufactured: spinning, weaving, knitting, finishing but not printing or dyeing.

7 At an installation or site where plastic film is produced using extrusion to convert melted polymer into blown or cast film: all processes and activities involved in the production of plastic film using extrusion to convert melted polymer into blown or cast film.

8 At an installation or site where geosynthetic materials comprising at least one component made from a synthetic or natural polymer in the form of a sheet, strip or other three-dimensional structure are manufactured for use in geotechnical or civil engineering applications: all processes and activities involved in the manufacture of such materials.

9 At an installation or site where silica sand in combination with any associated minerals is extracted, processed and packaged: blasting, quarrying, crushing, classifying, milling, pumping, grinding, acid leaching, drying and packaging.

10 At an installation or site where potassium chloride is extracted, separated, and purified to produce potash and high-grade soluble potassium chloride: sub-surface mining of sylvinite and other halite minerals, separating potassium chloride from those minerals and purifying it including crushing, grinding, froth flotation, drying, compacting, grading and, where relevant, recrystallising it from supersaturated brine.

11 At an installation or site where glass products or chemicals using glass as a base material are produced from raw materials, pre-formed glass or cullet for use as reflective additives in road markings or as toughened glass for the automotive market: partial melting, fusing, bending, toughening, cutting, grinding, etching, polishing (both mechanical and chemical), surface treating and drying.

12 At an installation (which must be a building where the predominant business activity is commercial temperature controlled storage or product freezing) or site upon which there is such an installation where—

(*a*) products are cooled or frozen for the purposes of—

(i) storing them under controlled temperatures below ambient levels; or

(ii) producing ice; or

(*b*) products are stored under controlled temperatures below ambient levels:

cooling and freezing products and all processes and activities involved in controlling temperatures below ambient levels.][1]

Commentary—*De Voil Indirect Tax Service* **V21.142**.

Amendments—[1] Schedule substituted by the Climate Change Agreements (Eligible Facilities) (Amendment) Regulations, SI 2006/1931 art 2 with effect from 15 August 2006.

[**13** At an installation or site where plastic materials, or plastic products (whether or not these are finished products), are produced by—

(*a*) the application of heat and pressure to; or

(*b*) a chemical reaction involving,

plastics powder, granules, shredded waste or liquid: injection moulding, reaction injection moulding, compression moulding (including hot and cold press moulding), transfer moulding, structural foam moulding, direct screw transfer moulding, rotational moulding (including slush moulding), flexible foam moulding (including dual component processing), blow moulding, casting, expanded polystyrene moulding, expandable materials processing, mixing and compounding, calendering, powder coating (including dip moulding), sintering, thermoforming (including vacuum forming), pultrusion, filament winding, spread coating, hand lay-up and resin transfer moulding.][1]

Amendments—[1] Paras 13–15 inserted by the Climate Change Agreements (Eligible Facilities) (Amendment) Regulations, SI 2009/2458 reg 2 with effect from 1 October 2009.

[**14** At an installation or site where refined salt for use in food products or supplements is prepared or processed from minerals.[1]

Amendments—[1] Paras 13–15 inserted by the Climate Change Agreements (Eligible Facilities) (Amendment) Regulations, SI 2009/2458 reg 2 with effect from 1 October 2009.

[**15** At an installation or site, not being a launderette predominately offering self-service washes or predominately serving the domestic market, where textiles are laundered by washing with water, drying and smoothing save where such laundering is carried out in support of other activities carried out by the business (not being textile rental activities), whether or not such activities are carried out at the installation or site.][1]

Amendments—[1] Paras 13–15 inserted by the Climate Change Agreements (Eligible Facilities) (Amendment) Regulations, SI 2009/2458 reg 2 with effect from 1 October 2009.

2007/2901

FINANCE ACT 2006 (CLIMATE CHANGE LEVY: AMENDMENTS AND TRANSITIONAL SAVINGS IN CONSEQUENCE OF ABOLITION OF HALF-RATE SUPPLIES) (APPOINTED DAY) ORDER 2007

Made by the Treasury under FA 2006 ss 172(16) and 172(17)

Made . . . . *8 October 2007*

1 This Order may be cited as the Finance Act 2006 (Climate Change Levy: Amendments and Transitional Savings in Consequence of Abolition of Half-rate Supplies) (Appointed Day) Order 2007.

2—(1) 1st November 2007 is appointed as the day on which sections 172(8) to 172(15) of the Finance Act 2006 come into force.

(2) The amendments to the Finance Act 2000 Schedule 6 (climate change levy) made by those sections do not apply in relation to a half-rate supply made before 1st April 2006.

(3) In or for the purposes of paragraph (2)—

(*a*) "half-rate supply" carries the meaning it has in that Schedule before 1st November 2007;

(*b*) sections 172(3) to 172(6) of the Finance Act 2006 (abolition of half-rate supplies etc) apply for determining when a supply is to be regarded as made.

(4) Regulations under paragraph 43 or 62 of that Schedule (half-rate for supplies to horticultural producers, and related tax credits) made before 1st November 2007 are unaffected by paragraph (1).

2007/2902

FINANCE ACT 2007 (CLIMATE CHANGE LEVY: REDUCED-RATE SUPPLIES ETC) (APPOINTED DAY) ORDER 2007

Made by the Treasury under FA 2007 Schedule 2 paragraphs 13(1) and 13(3)

Made . . . . *8 October 2007*

1 This Order may be cited as the Finance Act 2007 (Climate Change Levy: Reduced-rate Supplies etc) (Appointed Day) Order 2007.

2—(1) 1st November 2007 is appointed as the day on which Schedule 2 paragraphs 2 to 10 to the Finance Act 2007 come into force (climate change levy: reduced-rate supplies).
(2) The amendments made by paragraphs 7 and 10 of that Schedule only apply in relation to a supply actually made on or after that day.
(3) The amendment made by paragraph 9 of that Schedule only applies in relation to a supply actually made on or after that day and on the basis that it is a reduced-rate supply.
(4) In this article, "supply" and "reduced-rate supply" carry the respective meaning each has in the Finance Act 2000 Schedule 6 (climate change levy) on or after 1st November 2007.

2007/3538

ENVIRONMENTAL PERMITTING (ENGLAND AND WALES) REGULATIONS 2007

Revocation—Relevant parts of these Regulations revoked and replaced by the Environmental Permitting (England and Wales) Regulations, SI 2010/675 reg 108(1), Sch 27 with effect from 6 April 2010 (immediately after the coming into force of the Environmental Permitting (England and Wales) (Amendment) (No 2) Regulations, SI 2009/3381.

Made by the Secretary of State, in relation to England, and the Welsh Ministers, in relation to Wales, under the Pollution Prevention and Control Act 1999 s 2, Sch 1

Made . . . .*13 December 2007*
Coming into force . . . .*6 April 2008*

2010/675

ENVIRONMENTAL PERMITTING (ENGLAND AND WALES) REGULATIONS 2010

Made . . . .*10th March 2010*
Coming into force in accordance with regulation 1(1)(b)

These Regulations are made in exercise of the powers conferred by sections 2 and 7(9) of, and Schedule 1 to, the Pollution Prevention and Control Act 1999.

The Secretary of State, in relation to England, and the Welsh Ministers, in relation to Wales, have in accordance with section 2(4) of that Act consulted—
(a) the Environment Agency;
(b) such bodies or persons appearing to them to be representative of the interests of local government, industry, agriculture and small businesses as they consider appropriate; and
(c) such other bodies or persons as they consider appropriate.

A draft of this instrument has been approved by a resolution of each House of Parliament and by the National Assembly for Wales pursuant to section 2(8) and (9)(d) and (e) of that Act.

The Secretary of State in relation to England, and the Welsh Ministers in relation to Wales, make the following Regulations.

PART 1
GENERAL

1 Citation, commencement, extent and application

(1) These Regulations—
(a) may be cited as the Environmental Permitting (England and Wales) Regulations 2010;
(b) come into force on 6th April 2010, immediately after the coming into force of the Environmental Permitting (England and Wales) (Amendment) (No 2) Regulations 2009; and
(c) extend to England and Wales only.

(2) These Regulations apply to the sea adjacent to England and Wales out as far as the seaward boundary of the territorial sea; and for that purpose—
(a) the sea adjacent to England is so much of the sea adjacent to Great Britain as is not the sea adjacent to Wales or the sea adjacent to Scotland;
(b) the sea adjacent to Wales has the same meaning as it has by virtue of section 158(3) or (4) of the Government of Wales Act 2006; and
(c) the sea adjacent to Scotland has the same meaning as the internal waters and territorial sea of the United Kingdom adjacent to Scotland has by virtue of section 126(2) of the Scotland Act 1998.

2 Interpretation: general

(1) In these Regulations—

"the 1980 Act" means the Highways Act 1980;

"the 1990 Act" means the Environmental Protection Act 1990;

"the 1991 Act" means the Water Resources Act 1991;

"the 1993 Act" means the Radioactive Substances Act 1993;

"the 1995 Act" means the Environment Act 1995;

"the 2007 Regulations" means the Environmental Permitting (England and Wales) Regulations 2007;

"the 2009 Regulations" means the Groundwater (England and Wales) Regulations 2009;

"the Agency" means the Environment Agency;

"agricultural waste" means waste from premises used for agriculture within the meaning of the Agriculture Act 1947;

"the Animal By-Products Regulations" means—

(a) in relation to England, the Animal By-Products Regulations 2005,

(b) in relation to Wales, the Animal By-Products (Wales) Regulations 2006;

"appropriate authority" means—

(a) in relation to England, the Secretary of State, and

(b) in relation to Wales, the Welsh Ministers;

"Category A mining waste facility" means a mining waste facility that is classified as Category A under Article 9 of the Mining Waste Directive;

"class", in relation to a regulated facility, is to be construed in accordance with regulation 8;

"coastal waters" has the meaning given in section 104 of the 1991 Act;

"confidential information" means information that is commercially or industrially confidential in relation to any person;

"date of registration" has the meaning given in paragraph 1 of Schedule 2;

"directly associated activity"—

(a) in relation to a SED activity, has the meaning given in paragraph 2 of Schedule 14,

(b) in relation to any other activity falling within Part 2 of Schedule 1, has the meaning given in paragraph 1 of Part 1 of that Schedule;

"disposal"—

(a) except in relation to a radioactive substances activity, has the meaning given in paragraph 2 of Schedule 9,

(b) in relation to a radioactive substances activity, has the meaning given in paragraph 1 of Part 2 of Schedule 23;

"effluent" has the same meaning as in the 1991 Act;

"emission" means—

(a) in relation to a Part A installation, the direct or indirect release of substances, vibrations, heat or noise from individual or diffuse sources in the installation into the air, water or land,

(b) in relation to a Part B installation, the direct release of substances or heat from individual or diffuse sources in the installation into the air,

(c) in relation to Part A mobile plant, the direct or indirect release of substances, vibrations, heat or noise from the mobile plant into the air, water or land,

(d) in relation to Part B mobile plant, the direct release of substances or heat from the mobile plant into the air,

(e) in relation to a waste operation, the direct or indirect release of substances, vibrations, heat or noise from individual or diffuse sources related to the operation into the air, water or land,

(f) in relation to a mining waste operation, the direct or indirect release of substances, vibrations, heat or noise from individual or diffuse sources related to the operation into the air, water or land, and

(g) in relation to a radioactive substances activity, the direct or indirect release of radioactive material or radioactive waste;

"enforcement notice" means a notice served under regulation 36;

"environmental permit" has the meaning given in regulation 13(1);

"environmental permit condition" means a condition of an environmental permit;

"establishment" has the same meaning as in the Waste Framework Directive;

"excluded waste operation" means any part of a waste operation not carried on at an installation or by means of Part A mobile plant or Part B mobile plant that—

(a) is the subject of a licence under Part 2 of the Food and Environment Protection Act 1985 or does not require such a licence by virtue of an order under section 7 of that Act, or

(b) relates to waste described in regulation 7(1) of the Controlled Waste Regulations 1992;

"exempt facility" has the meaning given in regulation 5;

"exempt groundwater activity" has the meaning given in regulation 5;
"exempt waste operation" has the meaning given in regulation 5;
"exempt water discharge activity" has the meaning given in regulation 5;
"exemption registration authority" has the meaning given in paragraph 2 of Schedule 2;
"existing mining waste facility" means a mining waste facility in operation on 1st May 2008;
"extractive waste" means waste within the meaning of Article 2(1) of the Mining Waste Directive, except where it is excluded from the scope of that Directive by Article 2(2)(a) and (b);
"groundwater" means all water which is below the surface of the ground in the saturation zone and in direct contact with the ground or subsoil;
"groundwater activity" has the meaning given in paragraph 3 of Schedule 22;
"hazardous substance" has the meaning given in paragraph 4 of Schedule 22;
"hazardous waste", except in Section 5.1 of Part 2 of Schedule 1—

(a) in relation to England, has the meaning given in regulation 6 of the Hazardous Waste (England and Wales) Regulations 2005,
(b) in relation to Wales, has the meaning given in regulation 6 of the Hazardous Waste (Wales) Regulations 2005;

"highway drain" means a drain which a highway authority or other person is entitled to keep open by virtue of section 100 of the 1980 Act;
"household waste" has the meaning given in section 75(5) of the 1990 Act;
"inland freshwaters" has the meaning given in section 104 of the 1991 Act;
"installation" has the meaning given in paragraph 1 of Part 1 of Schedule 1;
"lake or pond" and "waters of any lake or pond" have the same meaning as in section 104 of the 1991 Act;
"landfill" has the meaning given in paragraph 2(1)(d) of Schedule 10;
"landfill closure notice" means a closure notice served under paragraph 10 of Schedule 10;
"local authority" has the meaning given in regulation 6;
"mining waste facility" has the meaning given in paragraph 2(1) of Schedule 20;
"mining waste facility closure notice" means a closure notice served under paragraph 10 of Schedule 20;
"mining waste operation" has the meaning given in paragraph 2(1) of Schedule 20;
"mobile plant" means any of the following—

(a) Part A mobile plant,
(b) Part B mobile plant,
(c) waste mobile plant;

"mobile radioactive apparatus" has the meaning given in paragraph 1 of Part 2 of Schedule 23;
"net rated thermal input" has the meaning given in paragraph 1 of Part 1 of Schedule 1;
"non-hazardous waste", except in Section 5.1 of Part 2 of Schedule 1, means waste which is not hazardous waste;
"nuclear site", in relation to a radioactive substances activity, has the meaning given in paragraph 1 of Part 2 of Schedule 23;
"operate a regulated facility" and "operator" have the meaning given in regulation 7;
"Part A activity" and "Part B activity" have the meaning given in paragraph 1 of Part 1 of Schedule 1;
"Part A installation", "Part A(1) installation, "Part A(2) installation" and "Part B installation" have the meaning given in paragraph 1 of Part 1 of Schedule 1;
"Part A mobile plant", "Part A(1) mobile plant", "Part A(2) mobile plant" and "Part B mobile plant" have the meaning given in paragraph 1 of Part 1 of Schedule 1;
"pollutant" means any substance liable to cause pollution;
"pollution", in relation to a water discharge activity or groundwater activity, means the direct or indirect introduction, as a result of human activity, of substances or heat into the air, water or land which may—

(a) be harmful to human health or the quality of aquatic ecosystems or terrestrial ecosystems directly depending on aquatic ecosystems,
(b) result in damage to material property, or
(c) impair or interfere with amenities or other legitimate uses of the environment;

"pollution", other than in relation to a water discharge activity or groundwater activity, means any emission as a result of human activity which may—

(a) be harmful to human health or the quality of the environment,
(b) cause offence to a human sense,
(c) result in damage to material property, or
(d) impair or interfere with amenities or other legitimate uses of the environment;

"prescribed statutory provision" means—

(a) Part 2 of the Food and Environment Protection Act 1985,
(b) section 163 of the 1991 Act,

(c) section 165 of the Water Industry Act 1991, or
(d) any local statutory provision (within the meaning given in section 221 of the 1991 Act) or statutory order which expressly confers power to discharge effluent into water;

"prohibition notice" means a notice served under paragraph 9 of Schedule 22;
"proposed transferee" means the person to whom an operator proposes to transfer an environmental permit in whole or in part;
"public participation provisions" means regulations 26, 29 and 59, and paragraphs 6 and 8 of Part 1 of Schedule 5;
"public register" has the meaning given in regulation 46(1);
"radioactive material" has the meaning given in paragraph 2 of Part 2 of Schedule 23;
"radioactive substances activity" has the meaning given in paragraph 5 of Part 2 of Schedule 23;
"radioactive waste" has the meaning given in paragraph 4 of Part 2 of Schedule 23;
"recovery" has the meaning given in paragraph 2 of Schedule 9;
"register" and "registered", in relation to an exempt facility, have the meaning given in paragraph 1 of Schedule 2;
"regulated facility" has the meaning given in regulation 8;
"regulator" means the authority on whom functions are conferred by regulation 32, or by a direction under regulation 33;
"regulator-initiated variation" means the variation of an environmental permit on the initiative of the regulator under regulation 20(1);
"relevant function" has the meaning given in regulation 9;
"relevant territorial waters" has the meaning given in section 104(1) of the 1991 Act;
"revocation notice" means a notice served under regulation 22(3);
"rule-making authority" means—

(a) in relation to a regulated facility for which a local authority is the regulator, the appropriate authority, and
(b) in relation to any other regulated facility, the Agency;

"SED activity" means an activity falling within Section 7 of Part 2 of Schedule 1;
"SED installation" has the meaning given in Schedule 14;
"sewage effluent" has the meaning given in section 221 of the 1991 Act;
"sewer" has the same meaning as in the 1991 Act;
"standard facility" means a regulated facility described in standard rules published under regulation 26(5);
"stand-alone groundwater activity" means a groundwater activity that is not carried on as part of the operation of a regulated facility of another class;
"stand-alone water discharge activity" means a water discharge activity that is not carried on as part of the operation of a regulated facility of another class;
"statutory order" means any order, byelaw, scheme or award made under any enactment, including an order or scheme confirmed by Parliament or brought into operation in accordance with special parliamentary procedure;
"suspension notice" means a notice served under regulation 37;
"trade effluent" has the meaning given in section 221 of the 1991 Act;
"undertaking", except in relation to a radioactive substances activity, has the same meaning as in the Waste Framework Directive;
"vessel", except in Schedule 1, Part 2, Chapter 2, Section 2.2 and in Schedule 23, Part 2, paragraph 7, has the same meaning as in the 1991 Act;
"waste", except where otherwise defined, means anything that—

(a) is waste for the purposes of the Waste Framework Directive, and
(b) is not excluded from the scope of that Directive by Article 2(1) of that Directive;

"waste battery or accumulator" has the meaning given in Article 3(7) of the Batteries Directive, but does not include any waste which is excluded from the scope of that Directive by Article 2(2);
"waste mobile plant" means plant that is—

(a) designed to move or be moved whether on roads or other land,
(b) used to carry on a waste operation, and
(c) not an installation, Part A mobile plant or Part B mobile plant;

"waste oil" means mineral-based lubricating or industrial oil which has become unfit for the use for which it was originally intended and, in particular, used combustion engine oil, gearbox oil, mineral lubricating oil, oil for turbines and hydraulic oil;
"waste operation" means recovery or disposal of waste;
"water discharge activity" has the meaning given in paragraph 3 of Schedule 21;
"WEEE" has the meaning given in Article 3(b) of the WEEE Directive; and
"working day" means a day other than—

(a) a Saturday or a Sunday,
(b) Good Friday or Christmas Day, or

(c) a day which is a bank holiday under the Banking and Financial Dealings Act 1971.

(2) For the purpose of calculating a period of time from one event to another event, that period—

(a) starts on the day on which the first event occurs; and

(b) ends on the day on which the second event occurs.

(3) In these Regulations, a power to give a direction includes a power to vary or revoke it.

SCHEDULE 1
ACTIVITIES, INSTALLATIONS AND MOBILE PLANT

Regulation 2(1)

PART 2
ACTIVITIES

CHAPTER 1
ENERGY ACTIVITIES

SECTION 1.1
COMBUSTION ACTIVITIES

Interpretation of Section 1.1

1 In this Section "recovered oil" means waste oil which has been processed before being used.

Part A(1)

(a) Burning any fuel in an appliance with a rated thermal input of 50 or more megawatts.

(b) Unless carried on as part of a Part A(2) or Part B activity, burning any—

(i) waste oil;

(ii) recovered oil; or

(iii) fuel manufactured from, or comprising, any other waste,

in an appliance with a rated thermal input of 3 or more megawatts, but less than 50 megawatts.

Interpretation and application of Part A(1)

1 For the purpose of Part A(1)(a) of this Section, where 2 or more appliances with an aggregate rated thermal input of 50 megawatts or more are operated on the same site by the same operator those appliances must be treated as a single appliance with a rated thermal input of 50 megawatts or more.

2 Nothing in this Part of this Section applies to burning fuels in an appliance installed on an offshore platform situated on, above or below those parts of the sea adjacent to England and Wales from the low water mark to the seaward baseline of the United Kingdom territorial sea.

3 In paragraph 2, "offshore platform" means any fixed or floating structure which—

(a) is used for the purposes of or in connection with the production of petroleum; and

(b) in the case of a floating structure, is maintained on a station during the course of production,

but does not include any structure where the principal purpose of the use of the structure is the establishment of the existence of petroleum or the appraisal of its characteristics, quality or quantity or the extent of any reservoir in which it occurs.

4 In paragraph 3, "petroleum" includes any mineral oil or relative hydrocarbon and natural gas existing in its natural condition in strata but does not include coal or bituminous shales or other stratified deposits from which oil can be extracted by destructive distillation.

5 In Part A(1)(b)(iii) of this Section, "fuel" excludes gas produced by biological degradation of waste in a landfill that is not listed in Part 2 of this Schedule.

Part B

Unless falling within Part A(1)(a) of this Section—

(a) Burning any fuel (other than a fuel mentioned in Part A(1)(b)) in—

(i) a boiler;

(ii) a furnace;

(iii) a gas turbine; or

(iv) a compression ignition engine,

with a net rated thermal input of 20 or more megawatts, but a rated thermal input of less than 50 megawatts.

(b) Burning any—

(i) waste oil;

(ii) recovered oil;

(iii) solid fuel which has been manufactured from waste by an activity involving the application of heat,

in an appliance with a rated thermal input of less than 3 megawatts.

(c) Burning fuel manufactured from or including waste (other than a fuel mentioned in paragraph (b)) in an appliance with a net rated thermal input of 0.4 or more megawatts, but a rated thermal input of less than 3 megawatts.

(d) Burning fuel manufactured from or including waste (other than a fuel mentioned in paragraph (b)) in 2 or more appliances which have a combined net rated thermal input of 0.4 or more megawatts, but a rated thermal input of less than 3 megawatts.

Interpretation and application of Part B

1 Part B does not apply to any activity falling within Part A(1) or Part A(2) of Section 5.1.

2 In Part B(c) or (d) of this Section, "fuel" does not include gas produced by biological degradation of waste.

SECTION 1.2
GASIFICATION, LIQUEFACTION AND REFINING ACTIVITIES

Part A(1)

(a) Refining gas where this is likely to involve the use of 1,000 or more tonnes of gas in any 12-month period.

(b) Reforming natural gas.

(c) Operating coke ovens.

(d) Coal or lignite gasification.

(e) Producing gas from oil or other carbonaceous material (or from mixtures of oil or other carbonaceous material), other than from sewage, unless the production is carried on as part of an activity which is a combustion activity (whether or not that combustion activity is described in Section 1.1).

(f) Purifying or refining any product of any of the activities falling within paragraphs (a) to (e) or converting it into a different product.

(g) Refining mineral oils.

(h) The loading, unloading, handling or storage of, or the physical, chemical or thermal treatment of—

(i) crude oil;
(ii) stabilised crude petroleum;
(iii) crude shale oil;
(iv) where related to another activity described in this paragraph, any associated gas or condensate; or
(v) emulsified hydrocarbons intended for use as a fuel.

(i) The further refining, conversion or use (otherwise than as a fuel or solvent) of the product of any activity falling within paragraph (g) or (h) in the manufacture of a chemical.

(j) Activities involving the pyrolysis, carbonisation, distillation, liquefaction, gasification, partial oxidation or other heat treatment of—

(i) coal (other than the drying of coal);
(ii) lignite;
(iii) oil;
(iv) other carbonaceous material; or
(v) mixtures of any of these,

otherwise than with a view to making charcoal.

(k) Odorising natural gas or liquefied petroleum gas where that activity is related to a Part A activity.

Interpretation and application of Part A(1)

1 Part A(1)(j) does not include—

(a) the use of any substance as a fuel;
(b) the incineration of any substance as a waste;
(c) any activity for the treatment of sewage or sewage sludge.

2 In Part A(1)(j), the heat treatment of oil, other than distillation, does not include the heat treatment of waste oil or waste emulsions containing oil in order to recover the oil from aqueous emulsions.

3 In Part A(1), "carbonaceous material" includes such materials as charcoal, coke, peat, rubber and wood, but does not include wood which has not been chemically treated.

Part A(2)

(a) Refining gas where this activity does not fall within Part A(1)(a) of this Section.

Part B

(a) Blending odorant for use with natural gas or liquefied petroleum gas.

(b) The storage of petrol in stationary storage tanks at a terminal, or the loading or unloading at a terminal of petrol into or from road tankers, rail tankers or inland waterway vessels.

(c) The unloading of petrol into stationary storage tanks at a service station, if the total quantity of petrol unloaded into such tanks at the service station in any 12-month period is likely to be 500m3 or more.

(d) Motor vehicle refuelling activities at an existing service station after the prescribed date, if the petrol refuelling throughput at the existing service station in any 12-month period is, or is likely to be, 3500m3 or more.

(e) Motor vehicle refuelling activities at a new service station, if the petrol refuelling throughput at the service station in any 12-month period is likely to be 500m3 or more.

Interpretation of Part B

1 In Part B—

"existing service station" means a service station—

(a) which was put into operation; or

(b) for which planning permission under the Town and Country Planning Act 1990 was granted,

before 31st December 2009;

"inland waterway vessel" means a vessel, other than a sea-going vessel, having a total dead weight of 15 or more tonnes;

"new service station" means a service station which is put into operation on or after 31st December 2009, other than an existing service station;

"petrol" means any petroleum derivative (other than liquefied petroleum gas), with or without additives, having a Reid vapour pressure of 27.6 or more kilopascals, which is intended for use as a fuel for motor vehicles;

"prescribed date" means—

(a) if an application for the grant or variation of an environmental permit was made under the 2007 Regulations on or before 1st January 2010—

(i) if the application was granted, the date of grant,

(ii) if the application was refused and the applicant appeals against the refusal, the date of the appeal determination or the date the appeal is withdrawn, or

(iii) if the application was refused, and the applicant does not appeal against the refusal, the day after the last day on which an appeal could be brought; or

(b) if no such application is made, 1st January 2010;

"service station" means any premises where petrol is dispensed to motor vehicle fuel tanks from stationary storage tanks;

"terminal" means any premises which are used for the storage and loading of petrol into road tankers, rail tankers or inland waterway vessels.

2 Any other expressions used in Part B which are also used in Directive 94/63/EC on the control of volatile organic compound (VOC) emissions resulting from the storage of petrol and its distribution from terminals to service stations have the same meaning as in that Directive.

CHAPTER 2
PRODUCTION AND PROCESSING OF METALS

SECTION 2.1
FERROUS METALS

Interpretation of Section 2.1

1 In this Section, "ferrous alloy" means an alloy of which iron is the largest constituent, or equal to the largest constituent, by weight, whether or not that alloy also has a non-ferrous metal content greater than any percentage specified in Section 2.2.

Part A(1)

(a) Roasting or sintering metal ore, including sulphide ore, or any mixture of iron ore with or without other materials.

(b) Producing, melting or refining iron or steel or any ferrous alloy, including continuous casting, except where the only furnaces used are—

(i) electric arc furnaces with a designed holding capacity of less than 7 tonnes, or

(ii) cupola, crucible, reverbatory, rotary, induction, vacuum, electro-slag or resistance furnaces.

(c) Processing ferrous metals and their alloys by using hot-rolling mills with a production capacity of more than 20 tonnes of crude steel per hour.

(d) Loading, unloading or otherwise handling or storing more than 500,000 tonnes in total in any 12-month period of iron ore, except in the course of mining operations, or burnt pyrites.

Part A(2)

(a) Unless falling within Part A(1)(b) of this Section, producing pig iron or steel, including continuous casting, in a plant with a production capacity of more than 2.5 tonnes per hour.

(b) Operating hammers in a forge, the energy of which is more than 50 kilojoules per hammer, where the calorific power used is more than 20 megawatts.

(c) Applying protective fused metal coatings with an input of more than 2 tonnes of crude steel per hour.

(d) Casting ferrous metal at a foundry with a production capacity of more than 20 tonnes per day.

Part B

(a) Unless falling within Part A(1)(b) of this Section, producing pig iron or steel, including continuous casting, in a plant with a production capacity of 2.5 or less tonnes per hour.

(b) Unless falling within Part A(2)(a) or (d) of this Section, producing, melting or refining iron or steel or any ferrous alloy (other than producing pig iron or steel, including continuous casting) using—

(i) one or more electric arc furnaces, none of which has a designed holding capacity of 7 or more tonnes; or

(ii) a cupola, crucible, reverberatory, rotary, induction, electro-slag or resistance furnace.

(c) Desulphurising iron, steel or any ferrous alloy.

(d) Heating iron, steel or any ferrous alloy (whether in a furnace or other appliance) to remove grease, oil or any other non-metallic contaminant (including such operations as the removal by heat of plastic or rubber covering from scrap cable) unless—

(i) it is carried on in one or more furnaces or other appliances the primary combustion chambers of which have in aggregate a rated thermal input of less than 0.2 megawatts;

(ii) it does not involve the removal by heat of plastic or rubber covering from scrap cable or of any asbestos contaminant; and

(iii) it is not related to any other activity falling within this Part of this Section.

(e) Unless falling within Part A(1) or Part A(2) of this Section, casting iron, steel or any ferrous alloy from deliveries of 50 or more tonnes of molten metal.

SECTION 2.2
NON-FERROUS METALS
Interpretation and application of Section 2.2

1 In this Section "non-ferrous metal alloy" means an alloy which is not a ferrous alloy, as defined in Section 2.1.

2 Part A(1)(c) to (h) and Part B do not apply to hand soldering, flow soldering or wave soldering.

Part A(1)

(a) Unless falling within Part A(2) of this Section, producing non-ferrous metals from ore, concentrates or secondary raw materials by metallurgical, chemical or electrolytic activities.

(b) Melting, including making alloys, of non-ferrous metals, including recovered products (such as refining or foundry casting) where—

(i) the plant has a melting capacity of more than 4 tonnes per day for lead or cadmium or 20 tonnes per day for all other metals; and

(ii) any furnace (other than a vacuum furnace), bath or other holding vessel used in the plant for the melting has a design holding capacity of 5 or more tonnes.

(c) Except where the activity is related to an activity described in Part A(2)(a), or Part B(a), (d) or (e) of this Section, refining any non-ferrous metal or alloy, other than the electrolytic refining of copper.

(d) Producing, melting or recovering by chemical means or by the use of heat, lead or any lead alloy, if—

(i) the activity may result in the release into the air of lead; and

(ii) in the case of lead alloy, the percentage by weight of lead in the alloy in molten form is more than 23 per cent if the alloy contains copper and 2 per cent in other cases.

(e) Recovering any gallium, indium, palladium, tellurium or thallium if the activity may result in their release into the air.

(f) Producing, melting or recovering (whether by chemical means or by electrolysis or by the use of heat) cadmium or mercury or any alloy containing more than 0.05 per cent by weight of either of those metals or both in aggregate.

(g) Mining zinc- or tin-bearing ores where the activity may result in the release into water of cadmium or any compound of cadmium in a concentration which is greater than the background concentration.
(h) Manufacturing or repairing involving the use of beryllium or selenium or an alloy containing one or both of those metals, if the activity may result in the release into the air of any substance in paragraph 6(3) of Part 1 of this Schedule; but an activity does not fall within this paragraph by reason of it involving an alloy that contains beryllium if that alloy in molten form contains less than 0.1 per cent by weight of beryllium and the activity falls within Part B(a) or (d) of this Section.
(i) Pelletising, calcining, roasting or sintering any non-ferrous metal ore or any mixture of such ore and other materials.

Interpretation of Part A(1)

1 In Part A(1)(g), "background concentration" means any concentration of cadmium or any compound of cadmium which would be present in the release irrespective of any effect the activity may have had on the composition of the release and includes such concentration of those substances as is present in—

(a) water supplied to the site where the activity is carried on;
(b) water abstracted for use in the activity; and
(c) precipitation onto the site on which the activity is carried on.

Part A(2)

(a) Melting, including making alloys, of non-ferrous metals, including recovered products (such as refining or foundry casting) where—

(i) the plant has a melting capacity of more than 4 tonnes per day for lead or cadmium or 20 tonnes per day for all other metals, and no furnace (other than a vacuum furnace), bath or other holding vessel used in the plant for the melting has a design holding capacity of 5 or more tonnes; or
(ii) the plant uses a vacuum furnace of any design holding capacity.

Part B

(a) Melting, including making alloys, of non-ferrous metals (other than tin or any alloy which in molten form contains 50 per cent or more by weight of tin), including recovered products (such as refining or foundry casting) in plant with a melting capacity of 4 tonnes or less per day for lead or cadmium or 20 tonnes or less per day for all other metals.
(b) The heating in a furnace or any other appliance of any non-ferrous metal or non-ferrous metal alloy for the purpose of removing grease, oil or any other non-metallic contaminant, including such operations as the removal by heat of plastic or rubber covering from scrap cable, if not related to another activity described in this Part of this Section; but an activity does not fall within this paragraph if—

(i) it involves the use of one or more furnaces or other appliances the primary combustion chambers of which have in aggregate a net rated thermal input of less than 0.2 megawatts; and
(ii) it does not involve the removal by heat of plastic or rubber covering from scrap cable or of any asbestos contaminant.

(c) Melting zinc or a zinc alloy in conjunction with a galvanising activity at a rate of 20 or less tonnes per day.
(d) Melting zinc, aluminium or magnesium or an alloy of one or more of these metals in conjunction with a die-casting activity at a rate of 20 or less tonnes per day.
(e) Unless falling within Part A(1) or Part A(2) of this Section, the separation of copper, aluminium, magnesium or zinc from mixed scrap by differential melting.

Interpretation and application of Part B

1 When determining the extent of an installation carrying on an activity within Part B(e), any location where the associated storage or handling of scrap which is to be heated as part of that activity is carried on, other than a location where scrap is loaded into a furnace, is to be ignored.

SECTION 2.3
SURFACE TREATING METALS AND PLASTIC MATERIALS

Part A(1)

(a) Unless falling within Part A(2) of this Section, surface treating metals and plastic materials using an electrolytic or chemical process where the aggregated volume of the treatment vats is more than 30m3.

Part A(2)

(a) Surface treating metals and plastic materials using an electrolytic or chemical process where the aggregated volume of the treatment vats is more than 30m3 and where the activity is carried on at the same installation as one or more activities falling within—

(i) Part A(2) or Part B of Section 2.1;
(ii) Part A(2) or Part B of Section 2.2; or
(iii) Part A(2) or Part B of Section 6.4.

Part B

(a) Any process for the surface treatment of metal which is likely to result in the release into air of any acid-forming oxide of nitrogen and which does not fall within Part A(1) or Part A(2) of this Section.

CHAPTER 3
MINERAL INDUSTRIES

SECTION 3.1
PRODUCTION OF CEMENT AND LIME

Part A(1)

(a) Producing cement clinker or producing and grinding cement clinker.

(b) Producing lime—
(i) in kilns or other furnaces with a production capacity of more than 50 tonnes per day; or
(ii) if the activity is likely to involve the heating in any 12-month period of 5,000 or more tonnes of calcium carbonate or calcium magnesium carbonate or both in aggregate.

Part A(2)

(a) Unless falling with Part A(1) of this Section, grinding cement clinker.

(b) Unless falling within Part A(1) of Section 2.1 or 2.2, grinding metallurgical slag in plant with a grinding capacity of more than 250,000 tonnes in any 12-month period.

Part B

(a) Storing, loading or unloading cement or cement clinker in bulk prior to further transportation in bulk.

(b) Blending cement in bulk or using cement in bulk other than at a construction site, including the bagging of cement and cement mixtures, the batching of ready-mixed concrete and the manufacture of concrete blocks and other cement products.

(c) Slaking lime for the purpose of making calcium hydroxide or calcium magnesium hydroxide.

(d) Producing lime where the activity is not likely to involve the heating in any 12-month period of 5,000 or more tonnes of calcium carbonate or calcium magnesium carbonate or both in aggregate.

SECTION 3.2
ACTIVITIES INVOLVING ASBESTOS

Interpretation of Section 3.2

1 In this Section "asbestos" means any of the following fibrous silicates: actinolite, amosite, anthophyllite, chrysotile, crocidolite and tremolite.

Part A(1)

(a) Producing asbestos or manufacturing products based on or containing asbestos.

(b) Stripping asbestos from railway vehicles except—
(i) in the course of the repair or maintenance of the vehicle;
(ii) in the course of recovery operations following an accident; or
(iii) where the asbestos is permanently bonded in cement or in any other material (including plastic, rubber or resin).

(c) Destroying a railway vehicle by burning if asbestos has been incorporated in, or sprayed on to, its structure.

Part B

(a) Unless related to an activity falling within Part A(1) of this Section, the industrial finishing of—
(i) asbestos cement;
(ii) asbestos cement products;
(iii) asbestos fillers;
(iv) asbestos filters;
(v) asbestos floor coverings;
(vi) asbestos friction products;
(vii) asbestos insulating board;
(viii) asbestos jointing, packaging or reinforcement material;
(ix) asbestos packing;
(x) asbestos paper or card; or
(xi) asbestos textiles.

SECTION 3.3
MANUFACTURING GLASS AND GLASS FIBRE

Part A(1)

(a) Manufacturing glass fibre.

(b) Manufacturing glass frit or enamel frit and its use in any activity where that activity is related to its manufacture and the aggregate quantity of such substances manufactured in any 12-month period is likely to be 100 or more tonnes.

Part A(2)

(a) Manufacturing glass, unless falling within Part A(1) of this Section, where the melting capacity of the plant is more than 20 tonnes per day.

Part B

Unless falling within Part A(1) or Part A(2) of this Section—

(a) Manufacturing glass at any location with the capacity to make 5,000 or more tonnes of glass in any 12-month period, and any activity involving the use of glass which is carried on at any such location in conjunction with its manufacture.

(b) Manufacturing glass where the use of lead or any lead compound is involved.

(c) Manufacturing any glass product where lead or any lead compound has been used in the manufacture of the glass except—

(i) making products from lead glass blanks; or

(ii) melting, or mixing with another substance, glass manufactured elsewhere to produce articles such as ornaments or road paint.

(d) Polishing or etching glass or glass products in the course of any manufacturing activity if—

(i) hydrofluoric acid is used; or

(ii) hydrogen fluoride may be released into the air.

(e) Manufacturing glass frit or enamel frit and its use in any activity where that activity is related to its manufacture.

SECTION 3.4
PRODUCTION OF OTHER MINERAL FIBRES

Part A(1)

(a) Unless falling within Part A(1) or Part A(2) of Section 3.3, melting mineral substances in plant with a melting capacity of more than 20 tonnes per day.

(b) Unless falling within Part A(1) of Section 3.3, producing any fibre from any mineral.

SECTION 3.5
OTHER MINERAL ACTIVITIES

Part A(2)

(a) Manufacturing cellulose fibre reinforced calcium silicate board using unbleached pulp.

Part B

(a) Unless falling within Part A(1) or Part A(2) of any Section, the crushing, grinding or other size reduction, other than the cutting of stone, or the grading, screening or heating of any designated mineral or mineral product except where the operation of the activity is unlikely to result in the release into the air of particulate matter.

(b) Any of the following activities unless carried on at an exempt location—

(i) crushing, grinding or otherwise breaking up coal, coke or any other coal product;

(ii) screening, grading or mixing coal, coke or any other coal product;

(iii) loading or unloading petroleum coke, coal, coke or any other coal product except unloading on retail sale.

(c) The crushing, grinding or other size reduction, with machinery designed for that purpose, of bricks, tiles or concrete.

(d) Screening the product of any activity described in paragraph (c).

(e) Coating road stone with tar or bitumen.

(f) Loading, unloading or storing pulverised fuel ash in bulk prior to further transportation in bulk.

(g) The fusion of calcined bauxite for the production of artificial corundum.

Interpretation and application of Part B

1 In Part B—

"coal" includes lignite;

"designated mineral or mineral product" means—

(a) clay, sand or any other naturally occurring mineral other than coal;

(b) metallurgical slag;

(c) boiler or furnace ash produced from the burning of coal, coke or any other coal product;

(d) gypsum which is a by-product of any activity;

"exempt location" means—

(a) any premises used for the sale of petroleum coke, coal, coke or any coal product where the throughput of such substances at those premises in any 12-month period is in aggregate likely to be less than 10,000 tonnes; or

(b) any premises to which petroleum coke, coal, coke or any coal product is supplied only for use there;

"retail sale" means sale to the final customer.

2 Part B does not apply to any activity carried on underground.

SECTION 3.6
CERAMIC PRODUCTION

Part A(1)

(a) Manufacturing ceramic products (including roofing tiles, bricks, refractory bricks, tiles, stoneware or porcelain) by firing in kilns, where—

(i) the kiln production capacity is more than 75 tonnes per day; or

(ii) the kiln capacity is more than 4m3 and the setting density is more than 300 kg/m3,

and a reducing atmosphere is used other than for the purposes of colouration.

Part A(2)

(a) Unless falling within Part A(1) of this Section, manufacturing ceramic products (including roofing tiles, bricks, refractory bricks, tiles, stoneware or porcelain) by firing in kilns, where—

(i) the kiln production capacity is more than 75 tonnes per day; or

(ii) the kiln capacity is more than 4m3 and the setting density is more than 300 kg/m3.

Part B

(a) Unless falling within Part A(1) or A(2) of this Section, firing heavy clay goods or refractory materials (other than heavy clay goods) in a kiln.

(b) Vapour glazing earthenware or clay with salts.

Interpretation of Part B

1 In Part B—

"clay" includes a blend of clay with ash, sand or other materials;

"refractory material" means material (such as fireclay, silica, magnesite, chrome-magnesite, sillimanite, sintered alumina, beryllia and boron nitride) which is able to withstand high temperatures and to function as a furnace lining or in other similar high temperature applications.

CHAPTER 4
THE CHEMICAL INDUSTRY

Interpretation of Chapter 4

1 In Part A(1) of the Sections of this Chapter, "producing" means producing in a chemical plant by chemical processing for commercial purposes substances or groups of substances listed in the relevant Sections.

SECTION 4.1
ORGANIC CHEMICALS

Interpretation of Section 4.1

1 In this Section, "pre-formulated resin or pre-formulated gel coat" means any resin or gel coat which has been formulated before being introduced into polymerisation or co-polymerisation activity, whether or not the resin or gel coat contains a colour pigment, activator or catalyst.

Part A(1)

(a) Producing organic chemicals such as—

(i) hydrocarbons (linear or cyclic, saturated or unsaturated, aliphatic or aromatic);

(ii) organic compounds containing oxygen (for example alcohols, aldehydes, ketones, carboxylic acids, esters, ethers, peroxides, phenols, epoxy resins);

(iii) organic compounds containing sulphur (for example sulphides, mercaptans, sulphonic acids, sulphonates, sulphates and sulphones and sulphur heterocyclics);

(iv) organic compounds containing nitrogen (for example amines, amides, nitrous-, nitro- or azo-compounds, nitrates, nitriles, nitrogen heterocyclics, cyanates, isocyanates, di-isocyanates and di-isocyanate prepolymers);

(v) organic compounds containing phosphorus (for example substituted phosphines and phosphate esters);

(vi) organic compounds containing halogens (for example halocarbons, halogenated aromatic compounds and acid halides);

(vii) organometallic compounds (for example lead alkyls, Grignard reagents and lithium alkyls);

(viii) plastic materials (for example polymers, synthetic fibres and cellulose-based fibres);

(ix) synthetic rubbers;

(x) dyes and pigments;

(xi) surface-active agents.

(b) Producing any other organic compounds not described in paragraph (a).

(c) Polymerising or co-polymerising any unsaturated hydrocarbon or vinyl chloride (other than a pre-formulated resin or pre-formulated gel coat which contains any unsaturated hydrocarbon) which is likely to involve, in any 12-month period, the polymerisation or co-polymerisation of 50 or more tonnes of any of those materials, or any combination of those materials in aggregate.

(d) Any activity involving the use in any 12-month period of 1 or more tonnes of toluene di-isocyanate or other di-isocyanate of comparable volatility or, where partly polymerised, the use of partly polymerised di-isocyanates or prepolymers containing 1 or more tonnes of those monomers, if the activity may result in a release into the air which contains such a di-isocyanate monomer.

(e) The flame bonding of polyurethane foams or polyurethane elastomers.

(f) Recovering—

(i) carbon disulphide;

(ii) pyridine or any substituted pyridine.

(g) Recovering or purifying acrylic acid, substituted acrylic acid or any ester of acrylic acid or of substituted acrylic acid.

Part B

(a) Unless falling within Part A(1) of this Section, any activity where the carrying on of the activity by the person concerned at the location in question is likely to involve the use in any 12-month period of 5 tonnes or more of any di-isocyanate or of any partly polymerised di-isocyanate or, in aggregate, of both.

(b) Cutting polyurethane foams or polyurethane elastomers with heated wires.

(c) Any activity for the polymerisation or co-polymerisation of any pre-formulated resin or pre-formulated gel coat which contains any unsaturated hydrocarbon, where the activity is likely to involve, in any 12-month period, the polymerisation or co-polymerisation of 100 or more tonnes of unsaturated hydrocarbon.

(d) Unless falling within Part A(1) of this Section, any activity involving the use of toluene di-isocyanate or partly polymerised di-isocyanate if—

(i) less than 1 tonne of toluene di-isocyanate monomer is likely to be used in any 12-month period; and

(ii) the activity may result in a release into the air which contains toluene di-isocyanate.

SECTION 4.2
INORGANIC CHEMICALS

Part A(1)

(a) Producing inorganic chemicals such as—

(i) gases (for example ammonia, hydrogen chloride, hydrogen fluoride, hydrogen cyanide, hydrogen sulphide, oxides of carbon, sulphur compounds, oxides of nitrogen, hydrogen, oxides of sulphur, phosgene);

(ii) acids (for example chromic acid, hydrofluoric acid, hydrochloric acid, hydrobromic acid, hydroiodic acid, phosphoric acid, nitric acid, sulphuric acid, oleum and chlorosulphonic acid);

(iii) bases (for example ammonium hydroxide, potassium hydroxide, sodium hydroxide);

(iv) salts (for example ammonium chloride, potassium chlorate, potassium carbonate, sodium carbonate, perborate, silver nitrate, cupric acetate, ammonium phosphomolybdate);

(v) non-metals, metal oxides, metal carbonyls or other inorganic compounds (for example calcium carbide, silicon, silicon carbide, titanium dioxide);

(vi) halogens or interhalogen compounds comprising 2 or more of halogens, or any compound comprising one or more of those halogens and oxygen.

(b) Unless falling within any other Section, any manufacturing activity which is likely to result in the release into the air of any hydrogen halide (other than the manufacture of glass or the coating, plating or surface treatment of metal) or which is likely to result in the release into the air or water of any halogen or any of the compounds mentioned in paragraph (a)(vi) (other than the treatment of water).

(c) Unless falling within any other Section, any manufacturing activity involving the use of hydrogen cyanide or hydrogen sulphide.

(d) Unless falling within any other Section, any manufacturing activity (other than the application of a glaze or vitreous enamel) involving the use of, or the use or recovery of, any compound of any of the following elements—

(i) antimony;
(ii) arsenic;
(iii) beryllium;
(iv) gallium;
(v) indium;
(vi) lead;
(vii) palladium;
(viii) platinum;
(ix) selenium;
(x) tellurium;
(xi) thallium,

where the activity may result in the release into the air of any of those elements or compounds or the release into water of any substance listed in paragraph 7 of Part 1 of this Schedule.

(e) Recovering any compound of cadmium or mercury.

(f) Unless falling within any other Section, any manufacturing activity involving the use of mercury or cadmium or any compound of either element or which may result in the release into air of either of those elements or their compounds.

(g) Unless carried on as part of any other activity within this Schedule—

(i) recovering, concentrating or distilling sulphuric acid or oleum;
(ii) recovering nitric acid;
(iii) purifying phosphoric acid.

(h) Unless falling within any other Section, any activity (other than the combustion or incineration of carbonaceous material as defined in the Interpretation of Part A(1) of Section 1.2) which is likely to result in the release into the air of any acid-forming oxide of nitrogen.

(i) Unless carried on as part of any other activity within this Schedule, recovering ammonia.

(j) Extracting any magnesium compound from sea water.

SECTION 4.3
CHEMICAL FERTILISER PRODUCTION

Part A(1)

(a) Producing (including any blending which is related to their production) phosphorus-, nitrogen- or potassium-based fertilisers (simple or compound fertilisers).

(b) Converting chemical fertilisers into granules.

SECTION 4.4
PLANT HEALTH PRODUCTS AND BIOCIDES

Part A(1)

(a) Producing plant health products or biocides.

(b) Formulating such products if this may result in the release into water of any substance listed in paragraph 7 of Part 1 of this Schedule in a quantity which, in any 12-month period, is greater than the background quantity by more than the amount specified in that paragraph for that substance.

SECTION 4.5
PHARMACEUTICAL PRODUCTION

Part A(1)

(a) Producing pharmaceutical products using a chemical or biological process.

(b) Formulating such products if this may result in the release into water of any substance listed in paragraph 7 of Part 1 of this Schedule in a quantity which, in any 12-month period, is greater than the background quantity by more than the amount specified in that paragraph for that substance.

SECTION 4.6
EXPLOSIVES PRODUCTION

Part A(1)

(a) Producing explosives.

SECTION 4.7
MANUFACTURING ACTIVITIES INVOLVING CARBON DISULPHIDE OR AMMONIA

Part A(1)

(a) Unless falling within Part A(2) of Section 6.7, any manufacturing activity which may result in the release of carbon disulphide into the air.

(b) Any activity for the manufacture of a chemical which may result in the release of ammonia into the air other than an activity in which ammonia is only used as a refrigerant.

SECTION 4.8

THE STORAGE OF CHEMICALS IN BULK

Part B

(a) The storage in tanks, other than in tanks for the time being forming part of a powered vehicle, of any of the substances listed below except where the total storage capacity of the tanks installed at the location in question in which the relevant substance may be stored is less than the figure specified below in relation to that substance—

(i) one or more acrylates, 20 tonnes (in aggregate);
(ii) acrylonitrile, 20 tonnes;
(iii) anhydrous ammonia, 100 tonnes;
(iv) anhydrous hydrogen fluoride, 1 tonne;
(v) toluene di-isocyanate, 20 tonnes;
(vi) vinyl chloride monomer, 20 tonnes;
(vii) ethylene, 8,000 tonnes.

CHAPTER 5

WASTE MANAGEMENT

SECTION 5.1

INCINERATION AND CO-INCINERATION OF WASTE

Interpretation of Section 5.1

1 In this Section—

"co-incineration" means the use of wastes as a regular or additional fuel in a co-incineration plant or the thermal treatment of waste for the purpose of disposal in a co-incineration plant;

"co-incineration plant" means any stationary or mobile plant whose main purpose is the generation of energy or production of material products, and—

(a) which uses wastes as a regular or additional fuel; or
(b) in which waste is thermally treated for the purpose of disposal.

If co-incineration takes place in such a way that the main purpose of the plant is not the generation of energy or production of material products but rather the thermal treatment of waste, the plant must be regarded as an incineration plant.

This definition covers the site and the entire plant including all co-incineration lines, waste reception, storage, on site pre-treatment facilities, waste-, fuel- and air-supply systems, boiler, facilities for the treatment of exhaust gases, on-site facilities for treatment or storage of residues and waste water, stack devices and systems for controlling incineration operations, recording and monitoring incineration conditions, but does not cover co-incineration in an excluded plant;

"excluded plant" means—

(a) a plant treating only the following wastes—
  (i) vegetable waste from agriculture and forestry,
  (ii) vegetable waste from the food processing industry, if the heat generated is recovered,
  (iii) fibrous vegetable waste from virgin pulp production and from production of paper from pulp, if it is co-incinerated at the place of production and the heat generated is recovered,
  (iv) wood waste with the exception of wood waste which may contain halogenated organic compounds or heavy metals as a result of treatment with wood-preservatives or coating, and which includes in particular such wood waste originating from construction and demolition waste,
  (v) cork waste,
  (vi) radioactive waste,
  (vii) animal carcasses as regulated by Regulation (EC) No 1774/2002 of the European Parliament and of the Council of 3rd October 2002 laying down health rules concerning animal by-products not intended for human consumption, or
  (viii) waste resulting from the exploration for, and the exploitation of, oil or gas resources from off-shore installations and incinerated on board the installation; or

(b) an experimental plant used for research, development and testing in order to improve the incineration process and which treats less than 50 tonnes of waste per year;

"hazardous waste", in relation to any solid or liquid waste, has the meaning given in regulation 6 of (in relation to England) the Hazardous Waste (England and Wales) Regulations 2005 or (in relation to Wales) regulation 6 of the Hazardous Waste (Wales) Regulations 2005, but does not include—

(a) combustible liquid wastes including waste oils, provided that they meet the following criteria—

(i) the mass content of polychlorinated aromatic hydrocarbons, for example polychlorinated biphenyls or pentachlorinated phenol amounts to concentrations not higher than those set out in the relevant Community legislation,

(ii) these wastes are not rendered hazardous by virtue of containing other constituents listed in Schedule 2 to (in relation to England) the Hazardous Waste (England and Wales) Regulations 2005, or (in relation to Wales) Schedule 2 to the Hazardous Waste (Wales) Regulations 2005 in quantities or in concentrations which are inconsistent with the achievement of the objectives set out in Article 4 of the Waste Framework Directive, and

(iii) the net calorific value amounts to at least 30 MJ per kilogramme;

(b) any combustible liquid wastes which cannot cause, in the flue gas directly resulting from their combustion, emissions other than those from gasoil as defined in Article 1(1) of Council Directive 93/12/EEC relating to the sulphur content of certain liquid fuels or a higher concentration of emissions than those resulting from the combustion of gasoil as so defined;

"incineration plant" means any stationary or mobile technical unit and equipment dedicated to the thermal treatment of wastes with or without recovery of the combustion heat generated, including—

(a) the incineration by oxidation of waste; and

(b) other thermal treatment processes such as pyrolysis, gasification or plasma processes in so far as the substances resulting from the treatment are subsequently incinerated.

This definition covers the site and the entire incineration plant including all incineration lines, waste reception, storage, on site pre-treatment facilities, waste-fuel and air-supply systems, boiler, facilities for the treatment of exhaust gases, on-site facilities for treatment or storage of residues and waste water, stack, devices and systems for controlling incineration operations, recording and monitoring incineration conditions, but does not cover incineration in an excluded plant;

"non-hazardous waste" means waste which is not hazardous waste;

"relevant Community legislation" has the same meaning as in Article 3(2)(a)(i) of the Waste Incineration Directive;

"waste" means any solid or liquid waste as defined in Article 1(1)(a) of the Waste Framework Directive.

Part A(1)

(a) The incineration of hazardous waste in an incineration plant.

(b) Unless carried on as part of any other Part A(1) activity, the incineration of hazardous waste in a co-incineration plant.

(c) The incineration of non-hazardous waste in an incineration plant with a capacity of 1 tonne or more per hour.

(d) Unless carried on as part of any other activity in Part A(1), the incineration of hazardous waste in a plant which is not an incineration plant or a co-incineration plant.

(e) Unless carried on as part of any other activity in Part A(1), the incineration of non-hazardous waste in a plant which is not an incineration plant or a co-incineration plant but which has a capacity of 1 tonne or more per hour.

(f) The incineration, other than incidentally in the course of burning landfill gas or solid or liquid waste, of any gaseous compound containing halogens in a plant which is not an incineration plant or a co-incineration plant.

Part A(2)

(a) The incineration of non-hazardous waste in an incineration plant with a capacity of less than 1 tonne per hour.

(b) Unless carried on as part of any other Part A activity, the incineration of non-hazardous waste in a co-incineration plant.

(c) The incineration of animal carcasses in a plant, which is not an incineration plant or a co-incineration plant, with a capacity of more than 10 tonnes per day but less than 1 tonne per hour.

Part B

(a) The incineration of non-hazardous waste in a plant which is—

(i) not an incineration plant or a co-incineration plant, and

(ii) on premises where there is plant, other than incineration plant or co-incineration plant, which has an aggregate capacity of 50 kilogrammes or more per hour but less than 1 tonne per hour.

(b) The cremation of human remains.

Application of Part B

1 When determining the extent of an installation carrying on an activity within Part B, any location of the following description is to be ignored: any location where the associated storage or handling of wastes and residues which are to be incinerated as part of that activity is carried on, other than a location where the associated storage or handling of animal remains intended for burning in an incinerator used wholly or mainly for the incineration of such remains or residues from the burning of such remains in such an incinerator is carried on.

SECTION 5.2

DISPOSAL OF WASTE BY LANDFILL

Part A(1)

(a) The disposal of waste in a landfill—

(i) receiving more than 10 tonnes of waste in any day, or

(ii) with a total capacity of more than 25,000 tonnes,

but excluding disposals in a landfill taking only inert waste.

SECTION 5.3

DISPOSAL OF WASTE OTHER THAN BY INCINERATION OR LANDFILL

Part A(1)

(a) The disposal of hazardous waste (other than by incineration or landfill) in a facility with a capacity of more than 10 tonnes per day.

(b) The disposal of waste oils (other than by incineration or landfill) in a facility with a capacity of more than 10 tonnes per day.

(c) Disposal of non-hazardous waste in a facility with a capacity of more than 50 tonnes per day by—

(i) biological treatment, not being treatment specified in any paragraph other than paragraph D8 of Annex IIA to the Waste Framework Directive, which results in final compounds or mixtures which are discarded by means of any of the operations numbered D1 to D12 in that Annex (D8), or

(ii) physico-chemical treatment, not being treatment specified in any paragraph other than paragraph D9 in Annex IIA to the Waste Framework Directive, which results in final compounds or mixtures which are discarded by means of any of the operations numbered D1 to D12 in that Annex (for example, evaporation, drying, calcination, etc) (D9).

Interpretation and application of Part A(1)

1 In Part A(1)(b) "disposal" means the processing or destruction of waste oil as well as its storage and tipping above ground.

2 Part A(1) does not apply to the treatment, by means of mobile plant, of—

(a) waste soil; or

(b) contaminated material, substances or products, for the purpose of remedial action with respect to land or controlled waters.

3 The reference to a D paragraph number in brackets at the end of Part A(1)(c)(i) and (ii) is a reference to the number of the corresponding paragraph in Annex IIA to the Waste Framework Directive (disposal operations).

SECTION 5.4

RECOVERY OF WASTE

Part A(1)

(a) Recovering by distillation of any oil or organic solvent.

(b) Cleaning or regenerating carbon, charcoal or ion exchange resins by removing matter which is, or includes, any substance listed in paragraphs 6 to 8 of Part 1 of this Schedule.

(c) Unless carried on as part of any other Part A activity, recovering hazardous waste in a plant with a capacity of more than 10 tonnes per day by means of the following operations—

(i) the use principally as a fuel or other means to generate energy (R1),

(ii) solvent reclamation/regeneration (R2),

(iii) recycling/reclamation of inorganic materials other than metals and metal compounds (R5),

(iv) regeneration of acids or bases (R6),

(v) recovering components used for pollution abatement (R7),

(vi) recovery of components from catalysts (R8),
(vii) oil re-refining or other reuses of oil (R9).

Interpretation and application of Part A(1)

1 Part A(1)(a) and (b) do not apply to any of the following activities, except where the activity involves distilling more than 100 tonnes per day—
(a) distilling oil for the production or cleaning of vacuum pump oil;
(b) an activity which is ancillary to and related to another activity, whether described in this Schedule or not, which involves the production or use of the substance which is recovered, cleaned or regenerated.

2 Part A(1) does not apply to the treatment, by means of mobile plant, of—
(a) waste soil; or
(b) contaminated material, substances or products, for the purpose of remedial action with respect to land or controlled waters.

3 The reference to an R paragraph number in brackets at the end of Part A(1)(c)(i) to (vii) is a reference to the number of the corresponding paragraph in Annex IIB to the Waste Framework Directive (recovery operations).

SECTION 5.5
THE PRODUCTION OF FUEL FROM WASTE

Part A(1)

(a) Making solid fuel (other than charcoal) from waste by any process involving the use of heat.

CHAPTER 6
OTHER ACTIVITIES

SECTION 6.1
PAPER, PULP AND BOARD MANUFACTURING ACTIVITIES

Part A(1)

(a) Producing, in industrial plant, pulp from timber or other fibrous materials.
(b) Producing, in industrial plant, paper and board where the plant has a production capacity of more than 20 tonnes per day.
(c) Any activity associated with making paper pulp or paper, including activities connected with the recycling of paper such as de-inking, if the activity may result in the release into water of any substance in paragraph 7 of Part 1 of this Schedule in a quantity which, in any 12-month period, is greater than the background quantity by more than the amount specified in that paragraph in relation to that substance.

Interpretation of Part A(1)

1 In Part A(1)(c), "paper pulp" includes pulp made from wood, grass, straw or similar materials and references to the making of paper are to the making of any product using paper pulp.

Part A(2)

(a) Manufacturing wood particleboard, oriented strand board, wood fibreboard, plywood, cement-bonded particleboard or any other composite wood-based board.

SECTION 6.2
CARBON ACTIVITIES

Part A(1)

(a) Producing carbon or hard-burnt coal or electro-graphite by means of incineration or graphitisation.

SECTION 6.3
TAR AND BITUMEN ACTIVITIES

Part A(1)

(a) The following activities—
(i) distilling tar or bitumen in connection with any process of manufacture, or
(ii) heating tar for the manufacture of electrodes or carbon-based refractory materials,
where the activity is likely to involve the use in any 12-month period of 5 or more tonnes of tar or of bitumen or both in aggregate.

Part B

(a) Any activity not falling within Part A(1) of this Section or of Section 6.2 involving—
(i) heating, but not distilling, tar or bitumen in connection with any manufacturing activity, or

(ii) oxidising bitumen by blowing air through it, at plant where no other activities described in any Section in this Schedule are carried on,

where the carrying on of the activity is likely to involve the use in any 12-month period of 5 or more tonnes of tar or bitumen or both in aggregate.

Interpretation of Part B

1 In Part B, "tar" and "bitumen" include pitch.

SECTION 6.4

COATING ACTIVITIES, PRINTING AND TEXTILE TREATMENTS

Part A(1)

(a) Applying or removing a coating material containing any tributyltin compound or triphenyltin compound, if carried on at a shipyard or boatyard where vessels of a length of 25 metres or more can be built, maintained or repaired.

(b) Pre-treating (by operations such as washing, bleaching or mercerization) or dyeing fibres or textiles in plant with a treatment capacity of more than 10 tonnes per day.

(c) Treating textiles if the activity may result in the release into water of any substance in paragraph 7 of Part 1 of this Schedule in a quantity which, in any 12-month period, is greater than the background quantity by more than the amount specified in that paragraph in relation to that substance.

Part A(2)

(a) Unless falling within Part A(1) of this Section, surface treating substances, objects or products using organic solvents, in particular for dressing, printing, coating, degreasing, waterproofing, sizing, painting, cleaning or impregnating, in plant with a consumption capacity of more than 150 kg per hour or more than 200 tonnes per year.

Part B

(a) Unless falling within Part A(1) or Part A(2) of this Section or Part A(2)(c) of Section 2.1, any process (other than for the re-painting or re-spraying of or of parts of aircraft or road or railway vehicles) for applying to a substrate, or drying or curing after such application, printing ink or paint or any other coating material as, or in the course of, a manufacturing activity, where the process may result in the release into the air of particulate matter or of any volatile organic compound and is likely to involve the use in any 12-month period of—

(i) 20 or more tonnes of printing ink, paint or other coating material which is applied in solid form,

(ii) 20 or more tonnes of any metal coating which is sprayed on in molten form,

(iii) 25 or more tonnes of organic solvents in respect of any cold set web offset printing activity or any sheet fed offset litho printing activity, or

(iv) 5 or more tonnes of organic solvents in respect of any activity not mentioned in sub-paragraph (iii).

(b) Unless falling within Part A(2) of this Section, re-painting or re-spraying road vehicles or parts of them if the activity may result in the release into the air of particulate matter or of any volatile organic compound and the carrying on of the activity is likely to involve the use of 1 or more tonne of organic solvents in any 12-month period.

(c) Re-painting or re-spraying aircraft or railway vehicles or parts of them if the activity may result in the release into the air of particulate matter or of any volatile organic compound and the carrying on of the activity is likely to involve the use in any 12-month period of—

(i) 20 or more tonnes of any paint or other coating material which is applied in solid form,

(ii) 20 or more tonnes of any metal coatings which are sprayed on in molten form, or

(iii) 5 or more tonnes of organic solvents.

Interpretation and application of Part B

1 In Part B—

"aircraft" includes gliders and missiles;

"coating material" means paint, printing ink, varnish, lacquer, dye, any metal oxide coating, any adhesive coating, any elastomer coating, any metal or plastic coating and any other coating material.

2 The amount of organic solvents used in an activity must be calculated as—

(a) the total input of organic solvents into the process, including both solvents contained in coating materials and solvents used for cleaning or other purposes; less

(b) any organic solvents that are removed from the process for re-use or for recovery for re-use.

3 When determining the extent of an installation carrying on an activity within Part B any location where the associated cleaning of used storage drums prior to painting or their incidental handling in connection with such cleaning is carried on is to be ignored, unless that location forms part of a SED installation.

SECTION 6.5

THE MANUFACTURE OF DYESTUFFS, PRINTING INK AND COATING MATERIALS

Part B

(a) Unless falling within Part A(1) or Part A(2) of any other Section—

- (i) manufacturing or formulating printing ink or any other coating material containing, or involving the use of, an organic solvent, where the carrying on of the activity is likely to involve the use of 100 or more tonnes of organic solvents in any 12-month period,
- (ii) manufacturing any powder for use as a coating material where there is the capacity to produce 200 tonnes or more of such powder in any 12-month period.

Interpretation of Part B

1 In Part B, "coating material" has the same meaning as in Section 6.4.

2 The amount of organic solvents used in an activity must be calculated as—

- (a) the total input of organic solvents into the process, including both solvents contained in coating materials and solvents for cleaning or other purposes; less
- (b) any organic solvents, not contained in coating materials, that are removed from the process for re-use or for recovery for re-use.

SECTION 6.6

TIMBER ACTIVITIES

Part A(1)

(a) Curing, or chemically treating, as part of a manufacturing process, timber or products wholly or mainly made of wood if any substance in paragraph 7 of Part 1 of this Schedule is used.

Part B

(a) Unless falling within Part A(2) of Section 6.1, manufacturing products wholly or mainly of wood at any works if the activity involves a relevant activity and the throughput of the works in any 12-month period is likely to be more than—

- (i) 10,000 cubic metres in the case of works at which wood is only sawed, or wood is sawed and subjected to excluded activities, or
- (ii) 1,000 cubic metres in any other case.

Interpretation of Part B

1 In Part B—

"excluded activity" means any relevant activity (other than sawing) which, ignoring any sawing carried on at the works, would be unlikely to result in the release into the air of any substance in paragraph 6(3) of Part 1 of this Schedule in a quantity capable of causing significant harm;

"relevant activity" means the sawing, drilling, sanding, shaping, turning, planing, curing or chemical treatment of wood;

"throughput" means the amount of wood which is subjected to a relevant activity, but where wood is subject to 2 or more relevant activities at the same works, the second and any subsequent activity is to be ignored;

"wood" includes any product consisting wholly or mainly of wood; and

"works" includes a sawmill or any other premises where relevant activities are carried on.

SECTION 6.7

ACTIVITIES INVOLVING RUBBER

Part A(2)

(a) Manufacturing new tyres (but not remoulds or retreads) if this involves the use in any 12-month period of 50,000 or more tonnes of one or more of the following—

- (i) natural rubber,
- (ii) synthetic organic elastomers,
- (iii) other substances mixed with them.

Part B

(a) Unless falling within Part A(1) or Part A(2) of any Section, the mixing, milling or blending of—

- (i) natural rubber, or
- (ii) synthetic organic elastomers,

if carbon black is used.

(b) Any activity which converts the product of an activity falling within paragraph (a) into a finished product if related to an activity falling within that paragraph.

SECTION 6.8
THE TREATMENT OF ANIMAL AND VEGETABLE MATTER AND FOOD INDUSTRIES

Interpretation of Section 6.8

1 In this Section—

"animal" includes a bird or a fish;

"excluded activity" means—

(a) any activity carried on on a farm or agricultural holding other than—

(i) the manufacture of goods for sale,

(ii) the production of compost for growing mushrooms,

(b) the manufacture or preparation of food or drink for human consumption but excluding—

(i) the extraction, distillation or purification of animal or vegetable oil or fat otherwise than as an activity incidental to the cooking of food for human consumption,

(ii) any activity involving the use of green offal or the boiling of blood except the cooking of food (other than tripe) for human consumption,

(iii) the cooking of tripe for human consumption elsewhere than on premises on which it is to be consumed,

(c) the fleshing, cleaning and drying of pelts of fur-bearing mammals,

(d) any activity carried on in connection with the operation of a collection centre for animal by-products,

(e) any activity for the manufacture of soap not falling within Part A(1) of Section 4.1,

(f) the storage of vegetable matter not falling within any other Section,

(g) the cleaning of shellfish shells,

(h) the manufacture of starch,

(i) the processing of animal or vegetable matter at premises authorised for the feeding of a recognised pack of hounds under the Animal By-Products Regulations,

(j) the salting of hides or skins, unless related to any other activity listed in this Schedule,

(k) any activity for composting animal or vegetable matter or a combination of both, except where that activity is carried on for the purposes of cultivating mushrooms,

(l) any activity for cleaning, and any related activity for drying or dressing, seeds, bulbs, corms or tubers (and "related activity" means an activity being carried on by the same person at the same site),

(m) the drying of grain or pulses,

(n) any activity for the production of cotton yarn from raw cotton or for the conversion of cotton yarn into cloth;

"food" includes—

(a) drink,

(b) articles and substances of no nutritional value which are used for human consumption, and

(c) articles and substances used as ingredients in the preparation of food;

"green offal" means the stomach and intestines of any animal, other than poultry or fish, and their contents.

Part A(1)

(a) Tanning hides and skins at a plant with a treatment capacity of more than 12 tonnes of finished products per day.

(b) Slaughtering animals at a plant with a carcass production capacity of more than 50 tonnes per day.

(c) Disposing of or recycling animal carcasses or animal waste, other than by rendering or by incineration falling within Section 5.1, at a plant with a treatment capacity exceeding 10 tonnes per day of animal carcasses or animal waste or both in aggregate.

(d) Treating and processing materials intended for the production of food products from—

(i) animal raw materials (other than milk) at a plant with a finished product production capacity of more than 75 tonnes per day; or

(ii) vegetable raw materials at a plant with a finished product production capacity of more than 300 tonnes per day (average value on a quarterly basis).

(e) Treating and processing milk, the quantity of milk received being more than 200 tonnes per day (average value on an annual basis).

(f) Processing, storing or drying by the application of heat the whole or part of any dead animal or any vegetable matter (other than the treatment of effluent so as to permit its discharge into controlled waters or into a sewer unless the treatment involves the drying of any material with a view to its use as animal feedstuff) if the processing, storing or drying—

(i) does not fall within any other Section, or Part A(2) of this Section, and is not an excluded activity; and

(ii) may result in the release into water of any substance in paragraph 7 of Part 1 of this Schedule in a quantity which, in any 12-month period, is greater than the background quantity by more than the amount specified in relation to the substance in that paragraph.

Part A(2)

(a) Disposing of or recycling animal carcasses or animal waste by rendering at plant with a treatment capacity exceeding 10 tonnes per day of animal carcasses or animal waste or both in aggregate.

Part B

(a) Processing, storing or drying by the application of heat the whole or part of any dead animal or any vegetable matter (other than the treatment of effluent so as to permit its discharge into controlled waters or into a sewer unless the treatment involves the drying of any material with a view to its use as animal feedstuff) if the processing, storing or drying—

(i) does not fall within another Section, or Part A(1) or Part A(2) of this Section;

(ii) is not an excluded activity; and

(iii) may result in the release into the air of—

(aa) any substance in paragraph 6(3) of Part 1 of this Schedule, or

(bb) any offensive smell noticeable outside the premises on which the activity is carried on.

(b) Breeding maggots in any case where 5 or more kg of animal matter, vegetable matter or both in aggregate, are introduced into the process in any week.

SECTION 6.9
INTENSIVE FARMING

Part A(1)

(a) Rearing poultry or pigs intensively in an installation with more than—

(i) 40,000 places for poultry;

(ii) 2,000 places for production pigs (over 30 kg); or

(iii) 750 places for sows.

SECTION 7
SED ACTIVITIES

Part B

(a) The activities listed in the table below if they are operated above the solvent consumption threshold for the activity.

Activity	*Solvent consumption threshold in tonnes/year*
Heatset web offset printing	15
Publication rotogravure	25
Other rotogravure, flexography, rotary screen printing, laminating or varnishing units	15
Rotary screen printing on textile or cardboard	30
Surface cleaning using substances or preparations which because of their content of volatile organic compounds classified as carcinogens, mutagens or toxic to reproduction under Directive 67/548/EEC on the approximation of laws, regulations and administrative provisions relating to the classification, packaging and labelling of dangerous substances are assigned or need to carry one or more of the risk phrases R45, R46, R49, R60 or R61, or halogenated VOCs which are assigned or need to carry the risk phrase R40	1
Other surface cleaning	2
Vehicle coating and vehicle refinishing	0.5
Coil coating	25
Other coating activities, including metal, plastic, textile (except rotary screen printing on textile), fabric, film and paper coating	5
Winding wire coating	5

Activity	*Solvent consumption threshold in tonnes/year*
Coating activity applied to wooden surfaces	15
Dry cleaning	0
Wood impregnation	25
Coating activity applied to leather	10
Footwear manufacture	5
Wood and plastic lamination	5
Adhesive coating	5
Manufacture of coating preparations, varnishes, inks and adhesives	100
Rubber conversion	15
Vegetable oil and animal fat extraction and vegetable oil refining activities	10
Manufacturing of pharmaceutical products	50

Interpretation and application of Part B

1 For the purposes of Part B—

"adhesive" means any preparation, including all the organic solvents or preparations containing organic solvents necessary for its proper application, which is used to adhere separate parts of a product;

"adhesive coating" means any activity in which an adhesive is applied to a surface, excluding the application of adhesive and laminating associated with printing activities;

"coating" means any preparation, including all the organic solvents or preparations containing organic solvents necessary for its proper application, which is used to provide a decorative, protective or other functional effect on a surface;

"coating activity" means any activity in which a single or a multiple application of a continuous film of a coating is applied (including a step in which the same article is printed using any technique) but does not include the coating of substrate with metals by electrophoretic or chemical spraying techniques;

"coil coating" means any activity where coiled steel, stainless steel, coated steel copper alloys or aluminium strip is coated with either a film forming or laminate coating in a continuous process;

"consumption" means the total input of organic solvents into an installation per calendar year, or any other 12-month period, less any volatile organic compounds that are recovered for reuse;

"dry cleaning" means any industrial or commercial activity using volatile organic compounds to clean garments, furnishing and similar consumer goods excluding the manual removal of stains and spots in the textile and clothing industry;

"flexography" means a printing activity using an image carrier of rubber or elastic photopolymers on which the printing areas are above the non-printing areas, and liquid inks which dry through evaporation;

"footwear manufacture" means any activity of producing complete footwear or parts of footwear;

"heat web offset printing" means a web-fed printing activity using an image carrier in which the printing and non-printing area are in the same plane, where—

(a) the non-printing area is treated to attract water and reject ink,

(b) the printing area is treated to receive and transmit ink to the surface to be printed, and

(c) evaporation takes place in the oven where hot air is used to heat the printed material;

"ink" means a preparation, including all the organic solvents or preparations containing organic solvents necessary for its proper application which is used in a printing activity to impress text or images on to a surface;

"laminating associated to a printing activity" means the adhering together of 2 or more flexible materials to produce laminates;

"manufacturing of coating preparations, varnishes, inks and adhesives" means the manufacture of coating preparations, varnishes, inks and adhesives as final products and where carried on at the same site, the manufacture of intermediates by the mixing of pigments, resins and adhesive materials with organic solvent or other carrier, including—

(a) dispersion and pre-dispersion activities,
(b) viscosity and tint adjustments, and
(c) operations for filling the final product into its container;

"manufacturing of pharmaceutical products" means an activity that involves the—
(a) chemical synthesis,
(b) fermentation,
(c) extraction, or
(d) formulation and finishing,

of pharmaceutical products and, where carried on at the same site, the manufacture of intermediate products;

"the Motor Vehicle Directive" means Council Directive 70/156/EEC on the approximation of the laws of the Member States relating to the type-approval of motor vehicles and their trailers;

"organic compound" means any compound containing at least the element carbon and one or more of hydrogen, halogens, oxygen, sulphur, phosphorus, silicon or nitrogen, with the exception of carbon oxides and inorganic carbonates and bicarbonates;

"organic solvents" means any volatile organic compound which is used alone or in combination with other agents, and without undergoing a chemical change to dissolve raw materials, products or waste materials, as a—
(a) cleaning agent to dissolve contaminants,
(b) dissolver,
(c) dispersion medium,
(d) viscosity adjuster,
(e) surface tension adjuster,
(f) plasticiser, or
(g) preservative;

"other coating activities" means a coating activity applied to—
(a) trailers, defined in categories O1, O2, O3, and O4 in the Motor Vehicle Directive,
(b) metallic and plastic surfaces including surfaces of airplanes, ships, trains, or
(c) textile, fabric, film and paper surfaces;

"printing activity" means any activity (not being a step in a coating activity) for reproducing text and/or images in which, with the use of an image carrier, ink is transferred onto any type of surface, including the use of associated varnishing, coating and laminating techniques;

"publication rotogravure" means a rotogravure printing activity used for printing paper for magazines, brochures, catalogues or similar products, using toluene-based inks;

"reuse" means the use of organic solvents recovered from an installation for any technical or commercial purpose and including use as a fuel but excluding the final disposal of such recovered organic solvent as waste;

"rotary screen printing" means a web-fed printing activity in which liquid ink which dries only through evaporation is passed onto the surface to be printed by forcing it through a porous image carrier, in which the printing area is open and the non-printing area is sealed off;

"rotogravure" means a printing activity, using a cylindrical image carrier in which the printing area is below the non-printing area and liquid inks which dry through evaporation, and in which the recesses are filled with ink and the surplus is cleaned off the non-printing area before the surface to be printed contacts the cylinder and lifts the ink from the recesses;

"rubber conversion" means—
(a) any activity of mixing, milling, blending, calendering, extrusion or vulcanisation of natural or synthetic rubber, or
(b) any ancillary operations for converting natural or synthetic rubber into a finished product;

"surface cleaning" means any activity, except dry cleaning, using organic solvents to remove contamination from the surface of material including degreasing but excluding the cleaning of equipment; and a cleaning activity consisting of more than one step before or after any other activity is to be considered as one surface cleaning activity;

"varnish" means a transparent coating;

"varnishing" means an activity by which varnish or an adhesive coating for the purpose of sealing the packaging material is applied to a flexible material;

"vegetable oil and animal fat extraction and vegetable oil refining activities" means any activity to extract vegetable oil from seeds and other vegetable matter, the processing of dry residues to produce animal feed, the purification of fats and vegetable oils derived from seeds, vegetable matter or animal matter;

"vehicle coating" means a coating activity applied to the following vehicles—

(a) new cars, defined as vehicles of category M1 in the Motor Vehicle Directive, and of category N1 in so far as they are coated at the same installation as M1 vehicles,

(b) truck cabins, defined as the housing for the driver, and all integrated housing for the technical equipment, of vehicles of category N2 or N3 in the Motor Vehicle Directive,

(c) vans and trucks, defined as vehicles of category N1, N2 or N3 in the Motor Vehicle Directive, but not including truck cabins, or

(d) buses, defined as vehicles in category M2 or M3 in the Motor Vehicle Directive;

"vehicle refinishing" means any industrial or commercial coating activity and associated degreasing activities performing—

(a) the original coating of road vehicles as defined in the Motor Vehicle Directive or part of them with refinishing-type materials, where this is carried on away from the original manufacturing line, or

(b) the coating of trailers (including semi-trailers) (category O in the Motor Vehicle Directive);

"volatile organic compound" or "VOC" means—

(a) any organic compound having a vapour pressure of 0.01 or more kPa at 293.15K or having a corresponding volatility under the particular conditions of use, or

(b) the fraction of creosote which exceeds a vapour pressure of 0.01 kPA at 293.15K;

"web-fed" means that the material to be printed is fed to the machine from a reel as distinct from separate sheets;

"winding wire coating" means any coating activity of metallic conductors used for winding the coils in transformers and motors, etc;

"wood and plastic lamination" means any activity to adhere together wood or plastic to produce laminated products;

"wood impregnation" means any activity giving a loading of preservative in timber.

2 An activity is deemed to be operated above the solvent consumption threshold specified for that activity under Part B if the activity is likely to be operated above that threshold in any 12-month period.

3 An activity listed in Part B includes the cleaning of equipment but, except for a surface cleaning activity, not the cleaning of products.

2010/867

FINANCE ACT 2009, SCHEDULE 51 (TIME LIMITS FOR ASSESSMENTS, CLAIMS, ETC) (APPOINTED DAYS AND TRANSITIONAL PROVISIONS) ORDER 2010

Made . . . . *18 March 2010*

The Treasury make the following Order in exercise of the powers conferred by sections 99(2) and 99(3) of the Finance Act 2009.

PART 1
APPOINTED DAYS AND PRELIMINARY PROVISIONS

1 Citation and interpretation

(1) This Order may be cited as the Finance Act 2009, Schedule 51 (Time Limits for Assessments, Claims, etc) (Appointed Days and Transitional Provisions) Order 2010.

(2) In this Order a reference to a paragraph (without more) is a reference to that paragraph of Schedule 51 to the Finance Act 2009.

(3) In this Order—

"The Commissioners" means the Commissioners for Her Majesty's Revenue and Customs;

"FA", followed by a year, means the Finance Act of that year.

"IHTA 1984" means the Inheritance Tax Act 1984;

2 Appointed days

(1) The day appointed as the day on which the amendments made by paragraphs 1 to 4 and 27 to 43 (insurance premium tax, aggregates levy, climate change levy, landfill tax and minor and consequential provision) come into force is 1st April 2010.

(2) The day appointed as the day on which the amendments made by paragraphs 5 to 26 (inheritance tax, stamp duty land tax and petroleum revenue tax) come into force is 1st April 2011.

PART 2
TRANSITIONAL PROVISION

3–15(not relevant to climate change levy)

16 Climate change levy: claims

The amendment made by paragraph 33 is disregarded where, for the purpose of paragraph 64(1) of Schedule 6 to FA 2000 (repayments of overpaid levy), claims made are for the repayment of amounts paid to the Commissioners on or before 31st March 2007.

17 The amendment made by paragraph 34 is disregarded where, for the purpose of paragraph 66 of Schedule 6 to FA 2000 (interest payable by the Commissioners), claims made for the repayment of interest relate to an applicable period which ended on or before 31st March 2007.

18 Climate change levy: assessments

The amendment made by paragraph 35(2) is disregarded where, for the purposes of paragraph 80(1)(*b*) of Schedule 6 to FA 2000 (time limits for assessments), the end of the prescribed accounting period or the date when the levy is due occurred on or before 31st March 2007.

19 The amendments made by paragraph 35(3) are disregarded where, for the purposes of paragraph 80(3) of Schedule 6 to FA 2000 (time limits for assessments), the end of the prescribed accounting period occurred on or before 31st March 2007.

20 The amendments made by paragraph 35(4) are disregarded where, for the purposes of paragraph 80(4) of Schedule 6 to FA 2000 (time limits for assessments), the death occurred on or before 31st March 2007.

21 The amendment made by paragraph 36(2) is disregarded where, for the purposes of paragraph 108(1) of Schedule 6 to FA 2000 (time limits on penalty assessments), the conduct to which the penalty relates occurred on or before 31st March 2007.

22 The amendments made by paragraph 36(3) are disregarded where, for the purposes of paragraph 108(2) of Schedule 6 to FA 2000 (time limits on penalty assessments), the conduct to which the penalty relates occurred on or before 31st March 2007.

23 The amendments made by paragraph 36(4) are disregarded where, for the purposes of paragraph 108(3) of Schedule 6 to FA 2000 (time limits on penalty assessments), the death was on or before 31st March 2007.

24–28(not relevant to climate change levy)

Climate Change Levy Extra-Statutory Concessions

Note—These Concessions are numbered as they appear in VAT Notice 48.

Contents

Extra-Statutory Concessions

7.1 CLIMATE CHANGE LEVY: SALT SECTOR ENTITLEMENT TO A LEVY NEGOTIATED AGREEMENT

Certain provisions for relief from CCL have created the potential for acute distortion of competition within the sector producing refined salt. The sector has now signed with Government an agreement to deliver specific energy-saving targets, and Treasury intend in due course to amend the appropriate Regulations to entitle the sector to the 80 per cent rebate scheme for CCL. Pending such amendment, this ESC allows the discount to the sector with effect from 24 September 2001.

7.2 CLIMATE CHANGE LEVY: EXEMPTION FOR CERTAIN RECYCLING PROCESSES

This concession permits taxable commodities used in certain processes to be treated as being exempt from Climate Change Levy.

Customs reserve the right to refuse to apply the concession, or to withdraw it, if the Commissioners consider it is being used for avoidance of the levy.

THE ARRANGEMENTS

The concession will apply only to taxable commodities used in a recycling process where taxable commodities used in a directly competing primary process are eligible for exemption from CCL under FA 2000 Sch 6 para 18 and the Climate Change Levy (Use as Fuel) Regulations 2001, because they are not used as fuel or treated as not so used (including dual use).

For taxable commodities to be eligible for exemption all of the following criteria must be met—

- the recycling process in which they are used must be less energy intensive than the primary process;
- the recycling process must be liable to a higher CCL charge per tonne of output than the primary process; and
- the objective of the recycling process must be to produce the same output as the primary process.

"Recycling process" means a process by which a substance is manufactured primarily from materials that have been previously used.

"Primary process" means a process by which a substance is manufactured primarily from raw materials.

"Less energy intensive" means using less energy to manufacture an equal quantity of the same output.

The Commissioners must have confirmed that the relevant process is eligible before any claims for relief can be made.

7.4 CLIMATE CHANGE LEVY: SIMPLIFIED BAD DEBT RELIEF ARRANGEMENTS

This concession permits gas and electricity suppliers to enter into arrangements for the administration of Climate Change Levy bad debt relief ("BDR") in a simplified manner.

Customs reserve the right to refuse to apply the concession if the Commissioners consider it is being used to avoidance of the levy.

THE ARRANGEMENTS:

Any gas or electricity supplier who wishes to use these simplified arrangements must notify the Commissioners in writing of their intention prior to making the first claim. The notification must specify the first month in which the arrangements will be utilised, and the billing systems that will be affected.

From that time all subsequent bad debt relief claims originating in the specified billing systems must be included in the arrangements.

(a) *All qualifying criteria within Climate Change Levy legislation must be met before a claim may be made.*

(b) *Each month for commercial accounts only, the supplier must calculate the total values billed to customers and the levy element of these totals. From this, a percentage of levy to total billing will be derived. All supplies liable to levy in a billing system must be included in this calculation; a random sample is not acceptable. Calculations must also be on a system-by-system basis, as combining billing systems may change the result.*

(c) *To make a claim for bad debt relief under these arrangements the supplier will apply to the debt written-off, the percentage calculated in (b) for the most recent six months prior to that in which the claim is actually being made. The percentage to be applied is the percentage that was calculated for the same taxable commodity and from the same energy billing system as that in which the debt arose.*

(d) *Should the application of the above calculations produce an inequitable result in the opinion of either party, then an equitable percentage based on best information should be agreed with Customs and Excise. This agreed percentage would be applied in the accounting period that the inequity is discovered. If an equitable percentage is not agreed with Customs and Excise then the normal bad debt relief rules apply.*

(e) *Suppliers who opt to use these arrangements must pay back the levy element of any payments that are received after levy bad debt relief has been claimed. This must be paid back by applying the same percentage that was used to claim the original relief. Such amounts will be due in the same accounting period in which the payments was received.*

(f) *Should the arrangements prove to be unsatisfactory in that either party considers that it provides an inequitable result, it is a source of dispute or that it proves difficult or time consuming to operate or audit, then the scheme shall be withdrawn at either party's written notification. This notification will not be retrospective without prejudice to the Commissioners' right to refuse to apply the scheme on the grounds of avoidance.*

This concession will be withdrawn on 1 June 2003.

Climate Change Levy
Press releases etc

Contents

Press releases, etc

CLIMATE CHANGE LEVY: AGREEMENTS WITH BUSINESS

13 December 2000. *Commons written answer (Hansard, 13 December 2000, Col 175)*

Mr Clappison: To ask the Chancellor of the Exchequer when he will publish agreements with business, including agreements with individual companies, groups of companies and sectors, relating to the climate change levy. [141467]

Mr Timms: Energy intensive sectors exposed to international competition—as defined by the Pollution Prevention and Control Regulations—will be entitled to 80 per cent rebate on the climate change levy in return for entering into Negotiated Agreements which will deliver demanding reductions in their energy use. These agreements are entered into with the Secretary of State for the Environment, Transport and the Regions.

NEW EXEMPTION FOR CERTAIN RECYCLING PROCESSES

8 July 2002. *Business Brief 18/02*

Customs & Excise have published a new Concession, exempting certain recycling processes from Climate change levy (CCL) [see ESC 7.2 in the *Extra-statutory Concessions* section, ante]. Production processes are exempt from CCL where there is a "dual fuel" or "non-fuel" use of energy, putting recycling processes making the same products at a competitive disadvantage. The new concession exempts those environmentally friendly recycling processes as well.

SCOPE OF THE EXEMPTION

The exemption applies only to recycling processes which produce the same output as processes eligible for exemption from CCL under FA 2000 Sch 6 para 18 and the Climate change levy (Use as Fuel) Regulations 2001, because they are not used as fuel or treated as not so used (including dual uses). The relevant recycling processes must also be less energy intensive and liable to a higher CCL charge per tonne of output than the competing primary process. The full text of the concession is available from the Climate change levy team and has also been published on the Customs & Excise website.

APPLYING FOR THE EXEMPTION

Businesses and trade organisations that consider their processes are eligible for the exemption should apply in writing by means of a pro-forma. This document forms an annex to "CCL technical brief 16", which is available from Customs at the address below and on www.hmce-.gov.uk.

Businesses will not be able to claim the exemption until approval for the particular process has been confirmed by Customs & Excise, but on approval the relief can be backdated to the implementation of the levy on 1 April 2001. As Customs approve particular processes, they will confirm their eligibility on the Department's website and by means of further CCL technical briefs.

If you have any questions about the Climate change levy please contact the National Advice Service on 0845 010 9000. Further technical details about eligibility for the new exemption and a copy of the pro-forma is available from—Climate change levy team, HM Customs & Excise, Ralli Quays, 3 Stanley Street, Manchester, M60 9LA, telephone—0161 827 0924.

NEW EXEMPTIONS FOR CERTAIN NON-FUEL USE OF TAXABLE COMMODITIES

6 February 2003. *Business Brief 2/03*

Customs and Excise have published an extra statutory concession (ESC) exempting further non-fuel uses of taxable commodities from Climate Change Levy (CCL) [see ESC 7.5, ante].

These new exemptions are in addition to those already contained in the Climate Change Levy (Use as Fuel) Regulations 2001 (SI 2001/1138).

The new Regulations necessary will not come into force until later in year. However, from 29 January 2003 Customs and Excise will, by concession, treat those further non-fuel uses (specified below) as if they were already specified under the non-fuel use exemption.

Customs invites applications reclaiming levy already paid in respect of the new exemptions.

NEW EXEMPTIONS

The newly exempt non-fuel uses are—

- Coal, coke and natural gas used as chemical reductants in the blast furnace production of zinc and other non-ferrous metals.
- Liquid propane used in the production of ethylene where heat is provided either by combustion of the waste products or from another source.
- Coal and coke used in the recarburising of iron and steel.
- Natural gas used purely as a feedstock in the production of carbon black.
- Liquefied Petroleum Gas used as feedstock in the cracking process to produce lower olefins.
- Lower olefins used as a feedstock for conversion by chemical processes.
- Coke used in the manufacture of titanium dioxide by the chloride process.

The full text of the concession will be available from the following page on the Customs and Excise website: http://www.hmce.gov.uk/business/othertaxes/ccl.htm

APPLYING FOR A REFUND

Where a supply of a taxable commodity has already been made in respect of one of the newly exempt non-fuel uses, and the levy has been accounted for, a refund of the amount paid by the consumer can be claimed by application to Customs and Excise.

Consumers of taxable commodities can apply for a refund of levy already paid in respect of the new exemptions by completing form CCL 200X, available from the Customs and Excise National Advice Service (0845 010 9000). Claims should be submitted with the supporting evidence required in accordance with the instructions on the application form. Any claim can be backdated to the introduction of the tax on 1 April 2001.

DEADLINE FOR REFUNDS

The ESC will be withdrawn on 30 June 2003. After this date claims for refunds of levy will not be considered.

FURTHER INFORMATION

If you have any questions about the Climate Change Levy please contact the National Advice Service on 0845 010 9000. Further technical detail about the new exemptions is available from the Climate Change Levy Team, HM Customs and Excise, Ralli Quays, 3 Stanley Street, Manchester, M60 9LA. Tel: 0161– 827–0924.

Commentary—*De Voil Indirect Tax Service* **V21.124**.

CCL: PRE-BUDGET REPORT

10 December 2003. *Business Brief 27/03*

There were two announcements relating to climate change levy (CCL) in today's pre-Budget Report.

(I) INTERACTION WITH THE EU EMISSIONS TRADING SCHEME

An EU-wide emissions trading scheme is due to be introduced in 2005. The arrangements for the scheme are set out in the EU Emissions Trading Directive. A UK inter-departmental Government group is considering what changes may be needed to climate change policy instruments such as the CCL and the associated climate change agreements (CCAs), once the

European Union's Emissions Trading Scheme (EU ETS) is introduced. This work is continuing and aims to ensure that the introduction of the EU ETS—

- is consistent with the UK's long-term emissions policy goals expressed in the Energy White Paper published in February 2003;
- is coherent with complementary measures which give equivalent incentives across sectors to reduce emissions;
- is as simple as possible to operate for business. Administration, compliance and transition costs should be kept to a minimum; and
- minimises impacts on international competitiveness and on fuel poverty.

The Government has identified the first change that will be needed to help ensure the successful introduction of the EU ETS. The EU ETS will operate alongside a number of existing climate change policy instruments. One of the main tools of climate change abatement has been the use of CCAs, which tie reductions in the CCL to negotiated agreements, and which have already delivered substantial carbon savings. Taking account of this, the Government has decided to create a level playing field between CCAs and the EU ETS, and will introduce the equivalent CCL discount for those sectors in CCAs who would like their direct emissions to be covered by the EU ETS instead of the CCA, once the scheme is up and running.

(II) CLIMATE CHANGE AGREEMENTS WITH ENERGY INTENSIVE SECTORS

The Government announced in Budget 2003 that it was reviewing the current eligibility criteria for climate change agreements, under which energy-intensive sectors can obtain 80 per cent discounts from the CCL if they agree to increase energy-efficiency or meet targets for emissions reductions. Eligibility to such agreements is currently related to the Pollution Prevention Control Regulations 2000, with the aim of protecting the competitiveness of UK industry, particularly those which are energy intensive. The Government believes that, in keeping with this original principle, there is scope to widen this eligibility while still providing strong incentives to encourage energy efficiency.

Following consultation with industry, the Government has decided that, subject to State aid approval, it will extend the eligibility criteria for CCAs during 2004. Therefore, in addition to the existing criteria, the Government will consider CCAs for sectors which meet a specific energy-intensity threshold, and will look to take account of any competitive distortions in those sectors. Further consultation with industry will take place between Pre-Budget Report 2003 and Budget 2004 on what level the energy intensity threshold should be set, on competition issues and the practicalities (including the administrative burden) of such a system.

FURTHER INFORMATION

Further information on the EU ETS can be found at the Department for Environment Food and Rural Affairs website, at www.defra.gov.uk/environment/climatechange/trading/

Further information on CCAs can be found in Notice CCL1/3 "Reliefs and special treatments for taxable supplies" available on the Customs website at www.hmce.gov.uk/forms/notices/ccl1-3 and from the Customs National Advice Service on 0845 010 9000.

CLIMATE CHANGE AGREEMENTS WITH ENERGY INTENSIVE SECTORS

23 July 2003. *Business Brief 19/04*

The Government has written to trade associations setting out details of the application process for climate change agreements (CCAs) under the new extended eligibility criteria announced in Budget 2004. Having announced in Budget 2004 its intention to extend the criteria, it is now seeking information from sectors to establish which processes will qualify for agreements under the new criteria. Sectors are being invited to submit an application for any processes in their sector they believe to be eligible for a CCA under the extended arrangements.

BACKGROUND

The Government announced in Budget 2003 that it was reviewing the eligibility criteria for CCAs, under which energy-intensive sectors can obtain 80% discounts from the climate change levy if they agree to increase energy-efficiency or meet targets for emissions reductions. Eligibility to such agreements is currently related to the Pollution Prevention Control

Regulations 2000, with the aim of protecting the competitiveness of UK industry, particularly for those sectors which are energy intensive. It was announced in Budget 2004 that, subject to European Commission state aid approval, the Government would extend the eligibility criteria for CCAs. In addition to the existing criteria, the Government will consider CCAs for sectors which meet a specific energy-intensity threshold, and will look to take account of any competitive distortions in those sectors.

DETAIL

To qualify under the new eligibility criteria, businesses will have to be in sectors above a threshold of energy intensity (using the definition of energy intensity set out in the Energy Products Directive relating to purchases of energy products and electricity against production value). All businesses in sectors that meet or exceed a 12% threshold of energy-intensity will be eligible to enter a CCA. Businesses in sectors that meet or exceed a 3% threshold, but are below the 12% threshold, will be eligible to enter an agreement only if they meet or exceed one of the following two international competitiveness tests—

- an import penetration ratio of 50%. This is the percentage ratio of imports to home demand (where home demand is defined as total manufacturers' sales plus imports minus exports); or
- an export to production ratio of 30%. This is the percentage ratio of exports to total manufacturers' sales.

APPLICATION PROCESS

Although any new agreements cannot start until after state aid approval has been given, the Department for Environment, Food and Rural Affairs (DEFRA), who administer CCAs, have now issued instructions and application forms for energy-intensive sectors that believe they should be entitled to eligibility under the new criteria. Sectors that have not been sent details but who wish to consider applying can obtain them from the web at www.defra.gov.uk/environment/ccl/extension.htm.

The application form is in the form of a spreadsheet that automatically makes the calculations needed to determine eligibility. If you have difficulty accessing these forms, please contact James Craig at Future Energy Solutions on 0870 190 6083.

TIMING

It is hoped that agreements made under the new arrangements will be agreed in the autumn and, subject to state aid approval being received in time, come into effect on 1 January 2005 to coincide with the introduction of the EU Emissions Trading Scheme. DEFRA are therefore requesting that applications are returned to them by 31 August 2004 (applications will, of course, be accepted after that date, but a late response will make it more difficult to draw up any agreement in time for the proposed 1 January 2005 start date).

FURTHER INFORMATION

Guidance on the CCA agreement process can be found on the DEFRA website at www.defra.gov.uk/environment/ccl/extension.htm.

Further information on CCAs can be found in Notice "CCL1/3 Reliefs and special treatments for taxable supplies" available on the Customs' website at www.hmce.gov.uk/forms/notices/ccl1-3 and from Customs National Advice Service on 0845 010 9000.

EXTENDED ELIGIBILITY FOR CLIMATE CHANGE AGREEMENTS WITH ENERGY INTENSIVE SECTORS

5 December 2005. *Business Brief 23/05.*

State aid approval has been secured from the European Commission to extend the eligibility criteria that allow sectors to enter into climate change agreements (CCAs) with the Secretary of State for the Department for Environment, Food and Rural Affairs (Defra). Under these agreements, businesses make commitments to reduce their emissions and/or improve their energy efficiency in exchange for an 80% reduction in the rates of climate change levy.

DETAIL

At present, only installations carrying out energy intensive processes in, or similar to those in, Part A of the Pollution Prevention and Control (England and Wales) Regulations, SI 2000/1973 can qualify for CCAs and benefit from the 80% tax reduction.

Providing Parliament approves the regulations needed before the changes can be brought into force, a larger number of energy intensive sectors will be eligible to enter a CCA.

The draft regulations set out the industrial processes that will be eligible for Climate Change Agreements under the new eligibility criteria. To qualify for inclusion in the draft regulations under the new criteria, businesses will have to be in sectors above a threshold of energy intensity (using a definition of energy intensity set out in the EU Taxation of Energy Products Directive which came into force on 1 January 2004). This definition states that—"An energy-intensive business shall mean a business entity . . . where . . . the purchases of energy products and electricity amount to at least 3% of the production value . . . ". There will be a one-off test of energy intensity, based on measuring a four year period of data (the lowest year's data will be discounted). The eligibility thresholds are as follows—

- all businesses in sectors that meet or exceed a 10% threshold of energy intensity; and
- businesses in sectors that meet or exceed a 3% threshold of energy intensity, but fall below the 10% threshold will be eligible to benefit if they meet or exceed the international competitiveness test of having an import penetration ratio of 50% (this is the percentage ratio of imports to home demand, where home demand is defined as total manufacturers' sales plus imports minus exports).

Defra issued instructions and application forms for energy-intensive sectors in summer 2004. The following sectors have so far concluded draft agreements under the extended arrangements, which can be signed formally once the House of Commons has approved the draft regulations and they enter into force—British Calcium Carbonate Federation, covering the production of calcium carbonate based mineral products; Contract Heating Treatment Association, covering the heat treatment of metals; British Compressed Gases Association, covering the production of industrial gases; Kaolin and Ball Clay Association, covering the production or processing of kaolinitic clay. Defra are continuing to negotiate agreements with other sectors.

Those already eligible for CCAs under the current arrangements will continue to benefit and will be unaffected by these changes.

FURTHER INFORMATION

Guidance on the CCA agreement process can be found on the Defra website at http://www.defra.gov.uk/environment/ccl/extension.htm.

Further information on CCAs can be found in Notice 'CCL1/3 Reliefs and special treatments for taxable supplies' available on HM Revenue & Customs' website at www.hmrc.gov.uk and from HM Revenue & Customs' National Advice Service on 0845 010 9000.

Commentary—*De Voil Indirect Tax Service* **V21.141**.

NOTICE OF REQUIREMENT TO GIVE SECURITY FOR ENVIRONMENTAL TAXES

April 2008. *Notice ET1*

Note—See under *IPT* section, ante, for the full text of this notice which is HMRC's Statement of Practice on the circumstances where they may require security for Insurance Premium Tax, Landfill Tax, Aggregates Levy and Climate Change Levy.

Climate Change Levy Index

Defined words and phrases are listed separately at the end.

Words and Phrases

Words in brackets indicate the context in which the word or phrase is used.